1 MONTH OF
FREE
READING

at

www.ForgottenBooks.com

By purchasing this book you are
eligible for one month membership to
ForgottenBooks.com, giving you
unlimited access to our entire
collection of over 1,000,000 titles via
our web site and mobile apps.

To claim your free month visit:

www.forgottenbooks.com/free839106

ISBN 978-0-365-11187-0
PIBN 10839106

This book is a reproduction of an important historical work. Forgotten Books uses
state-of-the-art technology to digitally reconstruct the work, preserving the original format
whilst repairing imperfections present in the aged copy. In rare cases, an imperfection in
the original, such as a blemish or missing page, may be replicated in our edition. We do,
however, repair the vast majority of imperfections successfully; any imperfections that
remain are intentionally left to preserve the state of such historical works.

THE

AMERICANA

A Universal Reference Library

COMPRISING THE ARTS AND SCIENCES,
LITERATURE, HISTORY, BIOGRAPHY,
GEOGRAPHY, COMMERCE, ETC.,
OF THE WORLD

EDITOR-IN-CHIEF

FREDERICK CONVERSE BEACH

EDITOR SCIENTIFIC AMERICAN

MANAGING EDITOR

GEORGE EDWIN RINES

ASSISTED BY MORE THAN TWO THOUSAND OF THE MOST EMINENT
SCHOLARS AND AUTHORITIES IN AMERICA AND EUROPE

Issued under the Editorial Supervision of
The Scientific American

IN SIXTEEN VOLUMES
ILLUSTRATED

SCIENTIFIC AMERICAN COMPILING DEP'T

225 FIFTH AVENUE, NEW YORK

A Few of the Leading Articles in Volume Three

WRITTEN AND SIGNED BY SPECIALISTS

KEY TO PRONUNCIATION.

ä	far, father	ñ	Span. _ñ_, as in _cañon_ (căn'yŏn). _piñon_ (pēn'yŏn)
ā	fate, hate		
a or ă	at, fat	ng	mingle, singing
ã	air, care	nk	bank, ink
ạ	ado, sofa	ō	no, open
à	all, fall	o or ŏ	not, on
		ô	corn, nor
ch	choose, church	ȯ	atom, symbol
		ọ	book, look
ē	eel, we		
e or ĕ	bed, end	oi	oil, soil; also Ger. _eu_, as in _beutel_
ė	her, over: also Fr. _e_, as in _de; eu_, as in _neuf;_ and _oeu_, as in _boeuf, coeur;_ Ger. _ö_ (or _oe_), as in _ökonomie._	ö or oo	fool, rule
		ou or ow	allow, bowsprit
ẹ	befall, elope	s	satisfy, sauce
ē	agent, trident	sh	show, sure
ff	off, trough	th	thick, thin
g	gas, get	ŧh	father, thither
gw	anguish, guava	ū	mute, use
h	hat, hot	u or ŭ	but, us
_h_ or н	Ger. _ch_, as in _nicht, wacht_	ụ	pull, put
hw	what	ü	between u and e, as in Fr. _sur_, Ger. _Müller_
ī	file, ice		
i or ĭ	him, it	v	of, very
i	between e and i, mostly in Oriental final syllables, as, Ferid-ud-din	y	(consonantal) yes, young
j	gem, genius	z	pleasant, rose
kw	quaint, quite	zh	azure, pleasure
ṅ	Fr. nasal _m_ or _n_, as in _embonpoint, Jean, temps_	' (prime). '' (secondary) accents, to indicate syllabic stress	

THE
ENCYCLOPEDIA
AMERICANA

Bournemouth, bŏrn'mŭth, a famous watering-place in the south of England, 30 miles southwest of Southampton, on the English Channel, at the southwest corner of Hampshire, near the boundary of Dorsetshire. It is within the limits of the parliamentary borough of Christchurch, but forms a municipal borough by itself. It is situated on a semicircular bay at the mouth of a small stream, the Bourne, whence it derives its name. ·It has become very popular as a seaside resort for consumptive and other delicate persons. It is to a large extent laid out in villas and detached houses. The Westover Gardens in the centre of the town are a favorite resort; they include a winter garden, where orchestral concerts are regularly given. There are two piers, three arcades, assembly rooms, baths, etc. The buildings include hospitals, a sanatorium, home for consumptives, and some handsome churches, among the latter being the new Bennett Memorial church and St. Peter's church, both beautiful Gothic buildings. In the churchyard of the latter lie buried William Godwin, Mary Wollstonecraft, and their daughter, the wife of Shelley. Pop. (1901) 47,000.

Bourrienne, Louis Antoine Fauvelet de, loo-ę än-twän fō-vę-lä dė boo-ryĕn, French historian and diplomatist: b. Sens, 9 July 1769; d. Caen, 7 Feb. 1834. He was educated with Bonaparte at the school of Brienne, where a close intimacy sprang up between them. On their separation in 1785, when Bonaparte set out to attend the École Militaire in Paris, they vowed an eternal friendship. At the age of 19 he proceeded to one of the German universities, with the view of studying law and languages. He returned to Paris in 1792, and renewed his early friendship with Bonaparte, who employed him in drawing up, along with Gen. Clarke, the text of the Treaty of Campo Formio. From this period Bourrienne's diplomatic career commenced. He accompanied Bonaparte as his private secretary on his expedition to Egypt, and afterward continued in that capacity on his elevation to the consulate. In 1804 he was nominated by the emperor his minister-plenipotentiary at Hamburg. In the end of 1813 he returned to France, where he received the appointment of director of the posts, and in 1814 was made prefect of police. On the abdication of Napoleon he paid his court to Louis XVIII., who, on his restoration, nominated him a minister of state. The revolution of July, 1830, and the loss of his private fortune affected him so much that he lost his reason. He was removed to Normandy, and spent the last two years of his life in a lunatic asylum at Caen, where he died. His 'Mémoires sur Napoléon, le Directoire, le Consulat, l'Empire et la Restauration,' edited by Villemarest (1829–31), contain many interesting particulars of the youth of Napoleon, and also of the history of the directory and consulate, although they are blamed for want of accuracy in many points of detail.

Boursault, Edmé, ĕd-mä boor-sō, French writer: b. 1638; d. Montluçon, 1701. Having gone to Paris and engaged in literature he both gained and lost the favor of royalty, and produced pieces for the stage with permanent success; among others, 'Ésope à la Ville,' and 'Ésope à la Cour,' which still continue on the stage. His two tragedies 'Marie Stuart' and 'Germanicus' are forgotten. Boursault had the misfortune to quarrel with Molière and Boileau. He wrote a severe criticism on the 'Ecole des Femmes' under the title of 'Le Portrait du Peintre.' Molière chastised him in his 'Impromptu de Versailles.' To revenge himself on Boileau, who had ridiculed him in his satires, he wrote a comedy called 'Satyre des Satyres.'

Boussa, boos-sạ. See BUSSANG.

Boussingault, Jean Baptiste Joseph Dieudonné, zhŏn bäp-tēst zhō-zĕf dyė-dŏn-nä boo-săṅ-gō, French chemist: b. Paris, 2 Feb. 1802; .d. there, 12 May 1887. He went to South America in the employment of a mining company, and made extensive travels and valuable scientific researches there. Returning to France he became professor of chemistry at Lyons in 1839, was made a member of the Institute, and then made Paris his chief residence. His works deal chiefly with agricultural chemistry, and include 'Économie Rurale' (translated into English and German); 'Mémoires de Chimie agricole et de Physiologie'; 'Agronomie, Chimie agricole, et Physiologie,' etc.

Boussingaultite, boo-săn-gŏ'-tĭt, a native hydrated sulphate of magnesium and ammonia, having the formula $(NH_4)_2SO_4.MgSO_4 + 6H_2O$. It has a specific gravity of about 1.7. It occurs with boracic acid (q.v.) in the Tuscan lagoons, especially at the fumaroles of Mount Cerboli. Artificial crystals are prisms belonging to the monoclinic system. A related mineral occurs in soft, white, granular masses in Sonoma, Cal.

Boustrophe'don, a kind of writing found on Greek coins, and in inscriptions of the remotest antiquity. The lines do not run in a uniform direction from the left to the right, or from the right to the left; but the first begins at the left and terminates at the right; the second runs in an opposite direction, from the right to the left; the third, again, from the left; and so on alternately. It is called *boustrophedon* (that is, turning back like oxen) because the lines written in this way succeed each other like furrows in a ploughed field. The laws of Solon were cut in tables in this manner.

Boutelle, boo-těl', Charles Addison, American legislator: b. Damariscotta, Me., 9 Feb. 1839; d. 21 May 1901. He served in the navy during the Civil War, entering as an acting master, and being promoted to lieutenant for gallantry in action. In 1870 he became the editor of the Bangor *Whig and Courier*. He was elected to Congress in 1882, and held his seat till December, 1900, when he resigned, and was made a captain on the retired list of the navy. He was chairman of the House Committee on Naval Affairs in the 51st, 54th, and 55th congresses and was author of the bill (1890) authorizing the construction of the first modern battleships of the United States navy.

Bouterwek, Friedrich, frēd'rĭн bow-tèr-věk. German philosopher: b. 15 April, 1766, at Oker, a village not far from Goslar, in North Germany; d. Göttingen, 9 Aug. 1828. He was at first a follower of Kant, but finally attached himself to Jacobi. His 'Ideen zu einer allgemeinen Apodiktik' was the immediate fruit of his intimate acquaintance with the philosophical views of Fr. H. Jacobi. This work was published in two volumes, 1799. It was afterward completed by the 'Manual of Philosophical Knowledge' (1813), and by the 'Religion of Reason' (1824). In this work, as well as in his 'Aesthetik' (1806-1824), he had to contend with many powerful antagonists. Bouterwek has gained a permanent reputation by his 'Geschichte der neuern Poesie und Beredsamkeit' (History of Modern Poetry and Eloquence) (1801-19), a work which, though unequal in some respects, and in parts, especially in the first volume, partial and superficial, is an excellent collection of notices and original observations, and may be considered one of the best works of the kind in German literature. Among his minor productions, a selection of which he published in 1818, are many essays, which are superior to the best of his larger speculative works; for instance, the introduction to the History, in which he gives an account of his literary labors until that period, with great candor and with almost excessive severity against himself. His 'History of Spanish Literature' has been translated into Spanish, French, and English.

Bouto, boo-tō, or Tucuxi, Indian names for the dolphin (*Inia geoffrensis*) of the Amazon.

Bouton, John Bell, American author: b. Concord, N. H., 15 March 1830; d. Cambridge, Mass., 18 Nov. 1902. He edited the Cleveland *Plain Dealer* 1851-5; and was connected with the New York *Journal of Commerce* 1857-89. He contributed for ten years to Appleton's Annual Cyclopedia, and published 'Loved and Lost' (1857); 'Round the Block' (1864); 'Treasury of Travel and Adventure'; 'Round about Moscow' (1887); 'Uncle Sam's Church' (1895); 'Memoirs of General Bell' (1902).

Bouts, Dirk, or Dierick, dèrk or dē-rĭk bowts, Dutch painter: b. Haarlem, about 1410; d. 1475. He was a brilliant colorist and one of the most prominent members of the Flemish school. Among his works are the 'Martyrdom of St. Erasmus' in the Church of St. Peter, Louvain; and the 'Martyrdom of St. Hippolitus' in the cathedral of Bruges.

Bouts Rimés, boo-rẹ-mā (French), words or syllables which rhyme, arranged in a particular order, and given to a poet with a subject, on which he must write verses ending in the same rhymes, disposed in the same order. Ménage gives the following account of the origin of this ridiculous conceit, which may be classed with the eggs and axes, the echoes, acrostics, and other equally ingenious devices of learned triflers. "Dulot (a poet of the 17th century) was one day complaining, in a large company, that 300 sonnets had been stolen from him. One of the company expressing his astonishment at the number. 'Oh,' said he, 'they are blank sonnets, or rhymes (*bouts rimés*) of all the sonnets I may have occasion to write.'" This ludicrous statement produced such an effect that it became a fashionable amusement to compose blank sonnets, and in 1648 a 4to volume of bouts rimés was published. Sarrazin's 'Dulot Vaincu, ou la Défaite des Bouts Rimés,' is an amusing performance.

Boutwell, bowt'well, George Sewell, American statesman: b. Brookline, Mass., 28 Jan. 1818; d. Groton, Mass., 27 Feb. 1905. He was admitted to the bar in 1836; served in the State legislature in 1842-51; governor of Massachusetts 1851-2; was an organizer of the Republican party in 1854, and appointed the first commissioner of the newly established Department of Internal Revenue in 1862. He was representative in Congress 1863-9; one of the managers of the impeachment trial of President Johnson; secretary of the treasury in 1869-73; and a United States senator in 1873-9. Besides numerous speeches he published 'Educational Topics and Institutions' (1859); several works concerning taxation; 'The Constitution of the United States at the End of the First Century' (1896); 'Reminiscences of Sixty Years in Public Affairs' (1902). After 1898 he was especially prominent as a leader of the Anti-Imperialists and vigorous opponent of the Philippine policy of the administration.

Bouvard, Joseph Antoine, zhō-zĕf ăn-twän, French architect: b. Saint-Jean-de-Bournay, 19 Feb. 1840. He was a pupil of Constant Dufeux, whom he assisted in his work connected with the Panthéon, the Law School, and the Palace of the Luxembourg. He was appointed inspector of public works in Paris, and, in 1879, was city architect, making himself famous by his work on the Théâtre Lyrique, the Church of St. Lawrence and the barracks of the Republican Guard. He transformed the old grain market into a Bourse; constructed the railway stations of Sainte Etienne and Marseilles; was architect of the Pavilion of the City of Paris at the exposition of 1878; and created the magnificent central dome of that of 1889. He had charge of the decoration of Paris at the time of the visit of the emperor of Russia, and won great popularity by the magnificence of the festivals which he arranged. In June 1897, he was appointed director of the newly created administrative direction of architecture and promenades. He was made an officer of the Legion of Honor in 1889. He took an important part in the preparation for the Universal Exposition of 1900, being director of architectural services and chief of the management of fetes, under M. Picard.

Bouvardia, boo-vär'dĭ-ạ, a genus of about 25 species of American shrubs or perennial herbs of the natural order *Rubiaceæ*, natives mostly of tropical Mexico, some of Arizona and Texas. Several horticultural varieties are largely cultivated in greenhouses for their terminal cymes of long tubular white, red, or yellow, sometimes perfumed blossoms which are very useful as cut flowers during late fall and early winter. The type species are not cultivated commercially.

Bouvart, or Bouvard, boo-vär, Alexis, Swiss mathematician and astronomer: b. Haute Savoie, 27 June 1767; d. 7 June 1843. He went to Paris about 1785 to study mathematics and astronomy, and in 1793 obtained a position in the Paris Observatory. He is celebrated for his researches in the theory of planetary motions, especially those of Jupiter and Saturn. Later he took up the theory of Uranus, and was the first to suggest that the discrepancies between the old and new observations could only be reconciled by the hypothesis of another undiscovered disturbing planet, an opinion which he retained till his death, three years before the discovery of Neptune. He published 'Nouvelles tables de Jupiter et de Saturne' (1808); 'Mémoire sur les Observations Météorologiques, faites à l'Observatoire de Paris.'

Bouvé, Pauline Carrington, American novelist: b. Little Rock, Ark.; married Thomas Tracy Bouvé in 1898. Besides the historical novel 'Their Shadows Before' (1900) she has published 'La Toison d'Or' from the French of Amedée Achard (1900).

Bouvet, Joachim, French missionary: b. Mans, about 1662; d. Pekin, China, 28 June 1732. Sent by Louis XIV. to China to study the customs and institutions of that country, he was received with favor at the imperial court at Pekin, employed by the emperor in directing various constructions, and allowed to build a church even within the palace. He returned to France in 1697, with permission to take back with him to China as many missionaries as would undertake the voyage. He presented to Louis XIV. 49 works in the Chinese language, and in 1699 departed again for China with 10 associates, among whom was the learned Parennin. He labored for nearly 50 years with indefatigable ardor to promote the progress of the sciences in that empire. He gave an account of the state of China in several treatises and letters, and made a dictionary of the language.

Bouvet, Marie Marguerite, American writer of books for young people: b. New Orleans, 14 Feb. 1865. She has published 'Sweet William' (1890); 'Little Marjorie's Love Story' (1891); 'Prince Tip-Tip' (1892); 'My Lady' (1894); 'A Child of Tuscany' (1895); 'Pierette' (1896); 'A Little House in Pimlico' (1898); 'Tales of an Old Château' (1900).

Bouvier, John, American jurist of French birth: b. Codognan, in the department of Gard, 1787; d. Philadelphia, 18 Nov. 1851. He was of a Quaker family, which emigrated to this country and settled in Philadelphia, when he was in his 15th year. He obtained employment for several years in a book store, became a citizen of the United States in 1812, published a newspaper for a short time at Brownsville, in the western part of Pennsylvania, studied law, and was admitted to the bar in 1818. During his studies he made a complete analysis of Blackstone's 'Commentaries.' In 1822 he began the practice of law in Philadelphia, in which city he resided till his death. He published, in 1839, a 'Law Dictionary, adapted to the Constitution and Laws of the United States of America, and of the several States of the American Union,' the fruit of 10 years' labor. In 1841 he published a new edition of Bacon's 'Abridgement of the Law.' His greatest work, published two months before his death, was the 'Institutes of American Law.'

Bovee, George, American politician: b. Saint James, La., 1840; d. El Paso, Tex., 1903. He was one of the first native whites to join the Republican party. He was elected Secretary of State in 1868, but quarrelled with Gov. Warmoth, the head of the administration, and it was this quarrel and the removal of Bovee by Warmoth which led to the political complications in Louisiana, and the dual State government of 1872 to 1876.

Boves, Jose Tomas, military adventurer in Spanish America; d. 5 Dec. 1814. He was born in Castile, and of the lowest extraction. At the age of 30 he was employed as a naval officer to guard the American coast, but betrayed his trust, and was condemned and imprisoned for bribery and prevarication. After his release, he joined the royal forces, but began to wage war on his own account after the defeat of Cagigal at Maturin. Boves established himself at Calabozo, Venezuela, and with 500 men, many of whom were slaves, defeated Mariño, the dictator of the eastern provinces. He defeated the independents twice, slaughtered all his prisoners, and gained for his army the name of the Infernal Division. He was defeated by Rivas, and a part of his army, being taken captive, were put to death; but he quickly recovered his strength, resumed the offensive, and in 1814 defeated Bolivar and Mariño at La Puerta. The struggle was prolonged with alternate successes and reverses, and with incessant cruelties. Boves advanced toward Valencia, where the independents were fortified, and after a blockade, forced the town to capitulate. To give a more solemn sanction to the terms of capitulation, a mass was celebrated between the two armies, and at the moment of the elevation, the royalist general promised a strict and faithful observance of the treaty; but having entered the town, he ordered the republican officers and a large number of the soldiers to be shot. Boves was again victorious at Anguita, and obliged Bolivar to retreat to Carthagena. He now entered Caracas, and shortly after gained a new victory, and killed or wounded 1,500 of the independents. His last triumph was at Urica; he was struck by a lance, and died upon the field of battle. His funeral was celebrated amid bloody commotion, while his troops were putting to death the men, women, and children whom they had made prisoners.

Bovey, Henry Taylor, Canadian engineer: b. Devonshire, England. He was educated at Cambridge University and took up the profession of civil engineering. He was appointed professor of civil engineering and applied mechanics in McGill University in Montreal in 1887 and has since lived in Canada. He is a member of many professional societies both in England, Canada, and the United States, and is the author of 'Applied Mechanics' (1882); 'Theory of Structures and Strength of Materials' (1893); 'Hydraulics' (1895).

Bovidæ, one of the most extensive and important families of mammals, characterized pre-eminently by the possession of hollow persistent horns in both sexes, and the form of digestive apparatus which involves chewing the cud. The family consists of the large herbivorous animals with cloven hoofs, which are most prominent as game, and which have supplied nearly all our domestic animals, except horses and camels. This family includes all of the ruminants, except the deer, giraffes, and pronghorn, and embraces five sections or sub-families, namely: the antelopes (Antilopinæ); the goats (Caprinæ); the sheep (Ovinæ); the musk-ox (Ovibovinæ); and the oxen (Bovinæ). Although in a general way the members of these sections are easily recognized, all are connected by intermediate examples whose position is assigned with difficulty, so that a general structural likeness covers even such different examples as the delicate antelopes and the heavy cattle. A conspicuous common character is found in the nature of the horns, which gave the name Cavicornia to the group in the early classifications. These horns are always in pairs, and consist of sheaths of horn growing from the skin and covering "cores," which are protuberances of bone from the frontal bones of the skull, varying in form in the different groups, and contain hollow spaces, which are extensions of the frontal sinuses. These horns begin to grow soon after the animal is born, and increase until they attain their full size with the maturity of the individual; with very few exceptions they are worn by both sexes, but those of the males, especially among sheep, are often considerably larger and more effective as weapons than those of the females. No animal outside of this family possesses hollow horns of this character, except the pronghorn, and in this case they are branched, and are annually shed, neither of which conditions ever occurs among the Bovidæ.

The Bovidæ are distributed throughout the whole world, except Australia and South America. They are in the main gregarious, and where the nature of their habitat permits, as on the plains inhabited by most antelopes and certain bison, they gather into enormous herds. The sheep, goats, and some of the antelopes, are confined to mountain ranges; most of the oxen dwell in forests; and the musk-ox is restricted to Arctic lands. Most of these animals, however, show great adaptability to new climates and conditions, have a high degree of variability, and are susceptible of taming and domestication. In consequence they have furnished to mankind the most important of his aids to agriculture, as the cattle, sheep, and goats, which he has been able to take with him to every part of the world, to train to his service, or to develop by careful improvement into the great resources of food and clothing, which they have become. See DOMESTIC ANIMALS, and the names of the various groups and species composing the family.

Bovines, Flanders, a village within a short distance of Lille, celebrated for the memorable victory gained by Philip Augustus of France, over Otho IV. of Germany, and his allies, 27 July 1214. Philip of Valois defeated here, in 1340, 10,000 English troops; and, on 17 and 18 May 1794, the French here defeated the Austrians.

Bovino, Italy, (anciently Bovinum), a fortified town in the province of Foggia, 20 miles south southwest of Foggia, near the Cervaro: the seat of a bishopric, suffragan to Benevento. It has a cathedral, two parish churches, and several convents. The Spaniards were defeated here by the Imperialists in 1734. Pop. 7,613.

Bow, the earliest instrument known, and the most generally diffused, among all savage and barbarous people for the propulsion of missiles in the chase or in war. There are two forms of the bow, the long-bow and the cross-bow, the former of which is the earlier, more general, and by far the more celebrated, as being the weapon of the famous English archers of the Middle Ages, who were popularly said to carry at their belts the lives of four-and-twenty Scots, that being the number of clothyard arrows in their quivers. The long-bow passed out of use as a military weapon with the improvement of firearms; but there were men yet alive in the beginning of this century who remembered that the Highlanders, in the Jacobite rising of 1715, carried bows and arrows: and at the capture of Paris, in 1814, Bashkirs and Circassians, in the service of Russia, were seen in the streets of that city, armed in chain-mail, with bow-cases and quivers. Some of the North American Indians, especially the Comanches and the Apaches were very expert with the bow. Whatever the substance of which the bow is made, whether of wood, horn or steel, its figure is nearly the same in all countries, having generally two inflexions, between which, in the place where the arrow is fixed, is a right line. The Grecian bow was somewhat in the form of the letter Σ: in drawing it, the hand was brought back to the right breast, and not to the ear. The Scythian bow was distinguished for its remarkable curvature, which was nearly semi-circular; that of the modern Tartars is similar to it. The materials of bows have been different in different countries. The Persians and Indians made them of reeds. The Lycian bows were made of

1. Celebes Wild Ox or Anoa.   2. North American Bison or Buffalo.   3. Indian Domestic Buffalo.

the cornel-tree; those of the Ethiopians of the palm-tree. That of Pandarus was made from the horn of a mountain goat, 16 palms in length: the string was an oxhide thong. The horn of the antelope is still used for the same purpose in the East. The long-bow was the favorite national weapon in England. The battles of Crecy (1346), Poitiers (1356), and Agincourt (1415) were won by this weapon. It was made of yew, ash, etc., of the height of the archer. The arrow being usually half the length of the bow, the clothyard was only employed by a man six feet high. The arbalist, or cross-bow, was a popular weapon with the Italians, and was introduced into England in the 13th century. The arrows shot from it were called quarrels.

Of the power of the bow, and the distance to which it will carry, some remarkable anecdotes are related. Xenophon mentions an Arcadian whose head was shot through by a Carduchian archer. Stuart mentions a random shot of a Turk, which he found to be 584 yards; and Mr. Strutt saw the Turkish ambassador shoot 480 yards in the archery ground near Bedford Square. Lord Bacon speaks of a Turkish bow which has been known to pierce a steel target or a piece of brass two inches thick. In the journal of King Edward VI. it is mentioned that 100 archers of the king's guard shot at a one inch board, and that some of the arrows passed through this and into another board behind it, although the wood was extremely solid and firm. It has been the custom of many savage nations to poison their arrows. This practice is mentioned by Homer and the ancient historians; and we have many similar accounts of modern travelers and navigators from almost every part of the world. Some of these stories are of doubtful authority, but others are well authenticated. Some poison obtained by Condamine from South American savages produced instantaneous death in animals inoculated with it. The poisoned arrows used in Guiana are not shot from a bow, but blown through a tube. See AIR-GUN; also ARCHERY.

In music it is the well-known implement by the means of which the tone is produced from viols, violins, and other instruments of that kind. It is made of a thin staff of elastic wood, tapering slightly till it reaches the lower end, to which the hairs (about 80 or 100 horse-hairs) are fastened, and with which the bow is strung. At the upper end is an ornamented piece of wood or ivory called the nut, and fastened with a screw, which serves to regulate the tension of the hairs. It is evident that the size and construction of the bow must correspond with the size of the species of viol-instruments from which the tone is to be produced.

Bow Bells, the peal of bells belonging to the Church of St. Mary-le-Bow, Cheapside, London, and celebrated for centuries. One who is born within the sound of Bow Bells is considered a genuine cockney.

Bow Island, an island in the South Pacific Ocean, near the eastern extremity of the Society Isles, in lat. 18° 6′ S. and lon. 140° 51′ W. It is a low island, of coral formation, about 30 miles in length and 5 miles in breadth. It derives its name from its shape, which is bow-like, the outer edge only being of land, and encircling a great central lagoon. It was discovered by Bougainville in 1768.

Bow Legs, a deformity of the legs in which the knees are far apart and the leg is bowed outward. It is technically known as *genu varum* and is the opposite of knock-knees, or *genu valgum*. Two forms are common, in one the bow is a gradual one, practically the entire leg being bent, in the other the bend takes place quite suddenly just above the ankle. Sometimes the bow is front and back instead of sideways. Bow leg is the commonest of the deformities, making fully 10 per cent of all orthopedic cases. It may be congenital, it is usually due to rickets (q.v.) and perhaps may occur in strong and heavy children who stand too much while very young. In the majority of cases it is outgrown, but in pronounced instances it can be cured only by prolonged correction by means of appropriate braces.

Bow-window, in architecture, properly a window forming a recess or bay in a room, projecting outward, and having for the outline of the plan a segment of a circle. This term is, however, often confounded with bay-window and oriel, which properly designate, the first a similar window with a straight-sided plan, and the second a projecting window not on the ground-floor, and supported on a corbel or other molded base.

Bow-wood. See OSAGE ORANGE.

Bowdich, Thomas Edward, African traveler, one of the victims of the attempts to explore the interior of the Dark Continent: b. Bristol, June 1791; d. 10 Jan. 1824. He was sent to Oxford, but was never regularly matriculated. At an early age he married, and engaged in trade at Bristol. Finding the details of business irksome, he obtained the appointment of writer in the service of the African Company, and set sail for Africa in 1814. In 1816, it being thought desirable to send an embassy to the negro king of Ashantee, Bowdich was chosen to conduct it; and he executed with success the duties of his situation. After remaining some time in Africa he returned home, and soon after published his 'Mission to Ashantee, with a Statistical Account of that Kingdom, and Geographical Notices of other Parts of the Interior of Africa.' Having offended the company in whose service he had been engaged, and having, therefore, no prospect of farther employment, yet wishing ardently to return to Africa for the purpose of visiting its hitherto unexplored regions, Bowdich resolved to make the attempt with such assistance as he could obtain from private individuals. He, however, previously went to Paris to improve his acquaintance with physical and mathematical science. His reception from the French literati was extremely flattering. A public eulogium was pronounced on him at a meeting of the Institute, and an advantageous appointment was offered him by the French government. To obtain funds for the prosecution of his favorite project, Bowdich also published a translation of 'Mollien's Travels to the Sources of the Senegal and Gambia,' and other works; by the sale of which he was enabled, with a little assistance from other persons, to make preparations for his second African expedition. He sailed from Havre in August 1822 and arrived in safety in the river Gambia. A disease, occasioned by fatigue and anxiety of mind, here put an end to his life.

Bowditch, Henry Ingersoll, American physician: b. Salem. Mass., 9 Aug. 1808; d. 14 Jan. 1892. He received his degree at Harvard in 1832; was professor of clinical medicine at Harvard in 1859–67; chairman of the State Board of Health in 1869–79; and president of the American Medical Association in 1877. He announced the law of soil moisture as a cause of consumption in New England; introduced several new features in surgical treatment, and was author of many general and special works in medical science. He was the first to practise chest-puncture in cases of pleurisy.

Bowditch, Henry Pickering, American educator: b. Boston, Mass., 4 April 1840. He was graduated at Harvard in 1861, and subsequently studied chemistry and medicine, and, after the Civil War, in which he reached the rank of major in the Union service, he took a special course in physiology in France and Germany. In 1871–6 he was assistant professor of physiology in the Harvard Medical School, and in 1876 was elected to the full chair but resigned on 9 May 1906. He is a member of the American Academy of Arts and Sciences, as well as of numerous medical societies, and has published many papers on physiological subjects.

Bowditch, bow'dĭch, Nathaniel, American mathematician: b. Salem, Mass., 26 March 1773; d. Boston, 16 March 1838. The son of a cooper he went to school till 10 years of age, when he entered his father's shop. Later he was apprenticed to the ship chandlery business, which he followed till he went to sea. He studied incessantly, during intervals of business and in morning and night hours. Mathematics was the science in which he was most interested, and he mastered algebra and Latin unaided. He had a teacher for French, and in later life he took up Spanish, Italian, and German. He learned navigation and was an omnivorous reader. In 1795 he made his first voyage as clerk, later as supercargo, and in the course of five long voyages rose to be master. Harvard College gave him the degree of M.A. and offered him the professorship of mathematics, which he declined, as he also did a similar offer from the University of Virginia, and the United States Military Academy. Between 1814 and 1817 he translated Laplace's 'Mécanique Céleste,' and appended to it an elaborate commentary. He contributed largely to scientific periodicals, his articles being principally on mathematics and astronomy. He was admitted as a Fellow to the Royal Society of London.

Bowditch's Practical Navigator, a work on navigation of the highest value and utility to seamen, written by Nathaniel Bowditch (q.v.) and published in 1802.

Bowdler, bō'dler, Thomas, English expurgator: b. near Bath, 11 July 1754; d. Rhyddings, South Wales, 24 Feb. 1825. At the age of 16 he went to St. Andrews to study medicine, but graduated M.D. at Edinburgh in 1776, and, after some years of travel, settled in London, devoting himself mainly to charitable work. He lived for 10 years at St. Boniface. Isle of Wight, and for the last 15 years of his life at Rhyddings, near Swansea. In 1818 he published 'The Family Shakespeare,' in 10 volumes; in which nothing is added to the original text; but those words and expressions are omitted which cannot with propriety be read aloud in a family. The work had a large sale, and was long popular, despite the ridicule it brought down upon the head of its over-prudish editor, who had the happiness or unhappiness to add permanently to the English tongue the word "bowlerism" as a synonym for senseless expurgation. The last years of Bowdler's life were given to the task of preparing a purified edition of Gibbon's 'History.'

Bowdlerism. See BOWDLER, THOMAS.

Bowdoin, bō'dŏn, James, American statesman: b. Boston, 8 Aug. 1727; d. there, 6 Nov. 1790. Graduating from Harvard in 1745, he inherited in 1747 a large fortune from his father, a wealthy merchant, and was thus provided with means to gratify his taste for scientific investigation. In 1751 he visited Franklin, who explained to him the results of his electrical researches. A correspondence ensued that lasted many years, and Franklin read Bowdoin's letters before the Royal Society of London. He was a prominent figure in the politics of his State, being elected a member of the General Court 1753–6, and of the Council 1756–69. He presided over the Constitutional Convention in 1779, and to him was due the form of some of the most admired sections of the constitution it drew up. As governor, 1785–6, he quelled Shay's Rebellion. In 1788 he was a delegate to the Federal Constitutional Convention. He was a Fellow of Harvard College from 1779 to 1785 and to it he left a legacy of £400. A founder and first president of the American Academy of Arts and Sciences, he bequeathed it his very valuable library. The degree of Doctor of Laws was conferred upon him by the universities of Yale and Edinburgh. Bowdoin College in Brunswick, Me., was named in his honor. He wrote a poetical paraphrase of Dodsley's 'Economy of Human Life' (1759), and several papers which may be found in the first volume of the American Academy's 'Memoirs.' To the 'Pietas et Gratulatio,' a volume of poems published by Harvard on the accession of George III., he contributed an English poem and two Latin epigrams.

Bowdoin, James, American statesman (son of the preceding): b. Boston, 22 Sept. 1752; d. Naushon Island, Buzzard's Bay, 11 Oct. 1811. He was graduated from Harvard in 1771, studied at the University of Oxford, and traveled in Europe. At the outbreak of the Revolution he returned home and became successively a member of the Assembly, the State Senate, and a delegate to the State Constitutional Convention, 1779. In Jefferson's administration he was appointed minister plenipotentiary at the court of Spain. and associate minister to France. During his residence abroad he accumulated a valuable library, a collection of paintings and drawings by old and modern masters, a cabinet of minerals and fossils. together with models of crystallography, all of which he bequeathed to Bowdoin College, of which he was the earliest patron. During his lifetime he gave it 6,000 acres of land and £1,100, and at his death it became, by will, his residuary legatee. He translated Daubenton's 'Advice to Shepherds.' and was the anonymous author of 'Opinions respecting the Commercial Intercourse Between the United States and Great Britain.'

Bowdoin College, located at Brunswick, Me. It is the oldest institution of higher learning in the State, having been incorporated in 1794, while Maine was a part of Massachusetts. It was named for James Bowdoin, governor of Massachusetts, whose son gave largely to the college. It was not opened to students until 1802. It is under the general patronage of the Congregational Church, but is non-sectarian in government and instruction. In addition to the college proper, the organization includes the Medical School of Maine, founded in 1820. The college confers the degree of A. B. for the completion of the regular four years' course. The work is almost entirely elective after the freshman year. A course in shopwork was added to the curriculum in 1902–3. The campus consists of 40 acres, one mile from the Androscoggin River, about three miles inland from Casco Bay. The buildings include Massachusetts Hall (the original building), King Chapel, Memorial Hall, Mary Francis Searle Science Building, Walker Art Building, Hubbard Hall (the library), Adams Hall, Observatory, and the Sargent Gymnasium. The library, in 1904, contained 76,000 volumes; the students numbered 275, and the faculty 35. A number of Bowdoin graduates have been distinguished in literary and public life; among them are Longfellow and Hawthorne, Thomas B. Reed, and Melville Weston Fuller (chief justice).

Bow'ell, Sir Mackenzie, Canadian statesman: b. Rickinghall, Suffolk, England, 27 Dec. 1823. He went to Canada when 10 years old and learned the printing trade, becoming editor of the Belleville *Intelligencer*. He served in the Canadian militia. After the Confederation he served in the Dominion House of Commons for 25 years. In 1878 he entered the MacDonald Cabinet, and in 1894 formed an administration of his own. He relinquished Cabinet office in 1896, and in 1897 he declared his independence of all party affiliation.

Bowen, bō-en, Francis, American educator and author: b. Charlestown, Mass., 8 Sept. 1811; d. Cambridge, Mass., 21 Jan. 1890. He was graduated from Harvard in 1833, and for a time taught mathematics in Phillips-Exeter Academy. He became instructor in natural philosophy and political economy at Harvard, 1835; studied in Europe, 1839–41, meeting Sismondi and De Gerando. Returning to Cambridge in 1843 he took charge of the 'North American Review,' as editor and proprietor, and conducted it with great ability for nearly 11 years. On account of his having taken the unpopular side in the 'Review' on the Hungarian question, the overseers of Harvard refused to concur with the corporation in appointing him professor of history in 1850. When Dr. Walker became president of Harvard in 1853, Prof. Bowen was elected Alford professor of natural religion, moral philosophy, and civil polity, and held that chair until 1888, when he became professor emeritus. He opposed the doctrines of Darwin and accepted those of Sir William Hamilton. He was a clear, forceful, independent thinker, and possessed a style notable for its energy and precision. As a writer he was most industrious, treating with success widely varying topics. The following is a selected list of his publications: 'Documents of the Constitutions of England and America, from Magna Charta to the Federal Constitution of 1789' (1854); 'The Principles of Metaphysical and Ethical Science applied to the Evidences of Religion' (1855); 'Dugald Stewart's Philosophy of the Human Mind, with Critical Notes' (1854); 'Principles of Political Economy' (1856); 'The Metaphysics of Sir William Hamilton' (1862); 'De Tocqueville's Democracy in America, edited with notes' (1862); 'Logic, or the Laws of Pure Thought' (1864); 'American Political Economy' (1870).

Bowen, Henry Chandler, American editor and publisher: b. Woodstock, Conn., 11 Sept. 1813; d. 24 Feb. 1896. He received a common school education and entered business. In 1848 he helped to found the 'Independent,' in New York, becoming, in 1861, its editor and proprietor, and making the paper famous for its advanced views on public topics.

Bowen, Herbert Wolcott, American diplomatist (son of the preceding): b. Brooklyn, N. Y., 29 Feb. 1856. He was educated at Yale College and at the Columbia Law School. He was appointed United States consul at Barcelona in 1890 by President Harrison, and in 1894 President Cleveland made him consul-general of the same port. At the opening of the Spanish-American war he remained at his post as long as was practicable, and at the conclusion of the war was appointed by President McKinley consul-general at Teheran, and in May 1901 minister plenipotentiary to Persia. He was subsequently appointed minister to Venezuela, and during the hostilities between that country and England and Germany in the opening months of 1903 won general commendation for his skilful diplomacy. He has published 'Verses'; 'Losing Ground'; 'In Divers Tones'; 'De Genere Humano'; 'International Law.'

Bowen, John Wesley Edward, American theologian: b. New Orleans, 3 Dec. 1855. He graduated at Boston University in 1878, and in 1885 received the degree of Ph.D., from the University of New Orleans. He held pastorates in Newark, N. J., Boston, Baltimore, and Washington, 1882–92. Since 1888 he has been professor of the history of theology in Gammon Theological Seminary, Atlanta, Ga. He is a recognized leader in all educational and social movements for the betterment of the colored race, and an example of its possibilities in scholarly attainment. Publications: 'Sermons'; 'Africa and the American Negro'; 'Discussions in Philosophy and Theology'; 'Struggle for Supremacy between the Church and State during the Middle Ages'; 'The Catholic Spirit of Methodism'; 'The Theology and Psychology of the Negro Plantation Melodies'; 'The Psychological Process in the Revelation of Doctrine.'

Bow'er, Archibald, Scottish writer: b. near Dundee, 17 Jan. 1686; d. London, 3 Sept. 1766. He entered the order of Jesuits in 1706. At Macerata, in Italy, according to his own account, he was counselor or judge of the Inquisition. In 1726 he quitted the order of Jesuits and went to Perugia, whence he fled secretly to England and professed himself a convert to the Protestant faith. He obtained respectable patronage, was engaged as a tutor in a nobleman's family, and employed by the booksellers in conducting the 'Historia Literaria,' a monthly review of books, and in writing a part of the 'Universal History,' in 60 vols. 8vo. The money which he gained by these occupations he is believed to have given or lent to the society of the Jesuits, and thus to have purchased his re-admission among them about the year 1744. Subsequently repenting of the engagement he had made with his old associates, he claimed and recovered the property he had advanced. In 1748 he published the first volume of a 'History of the Popes,' which was continued to seven volumes and characterized by the utmost zeal against Roman Catholicism. His money transactions with the Jesuits being at last brought to light, he was generally believed to be a man destitute of moral or religious principle; so that toward the end of his life he had hardly a friend or patron left except Lord Lyttelton. He is said to have died a Protestant.

Bower-birds, a group of birds of the bird-of-paradise family, dwelling in Australia and the neighboring islands, remarkable for the construction of bowers or "play-houses" in addition to their ordinary breeding-nests. All are of moderate size, of dark and plain plumage, having few ornaments of color and none of feather characteristic of other birds-of-paradise, although, like them, they are of aboreal habits, feed mainly upon fruits, and construct rather rude nests for their eggs in branches of trees. In addition to the nest proper, the males of all the bower-birds build upon the ground bowers or shelters of various forms, which serve as places for assembling and holding the series of antics or dances, in rivalry with each other, and as a display of their respective attractions to the females, in which these birds indulge during the season of courtship. These buildings always occupy a little space in the forest which is first carefully cleared of every obstruction, so that they look like small cultivated lawns. A few species are content with such a lawn, but most erect buildings which vary in form according to the species. The satin-bird (*Ptilorynchus violaceus*) of southern Australia forms of twigs, a few inches in length, an oblong, dome-shaped hut, open at each end and floored with twigs. The sides of this hut are formed of slender twigs, planted upright, and leaning inward to form a roof. Its floor, and the ground all about it, are strewn with highly colored feathers and bright objects of all sorts, which the bird brings, day by day, sometimes from a great distance, to add to his store, replacing dull or faded pieces with something better as he finds them. The people of the region are accustomed to search these collections for such lost articles as bits of bright jewelry, which the birds frequently seize and take there. The spotted bower-birds, of the genus *Chlamydera*, form "runs" or avenues about three feet long, formed of a dense platform of sticks fenced in on each side by a hedge of upright twigs, and place near it hundreds of white pebbles, pieces of bleached bone, shells, and bright objects, which they rearrange with incessant activity. One species gathers snail-shells exclusively. Another species make several little huts — a miniature of a village of the black fellows. The most remarkable of these structures, however, is that of a New Guinea species (*Amblyornis inornatus*) which is called "gardener-bird" in the

books. This bird clears a space around the base of a small tree, and then piles up around its base a cone of moss, about 18 inches in height. Outside of this, and at a distance of four or five inches, it plants a circle of twigs, some of which are two feet in length, so that they form a conical hut, covering and enclosing the inner cone. Two doors are left in this outer hut at opposite sides. The twigs of which this "wigwam" is composed are always the thin stems of an epiphytal orchid, which retain their leaves and remain alive and blooming for a long time; and it is believed by Dr. Beccari, who first described this bird, that the orchids are chosen because they will remain alive. He says, however, that this apparent attempt to provide flowers is not restricted to the cabin. Directly in front of the entrance is made a miniature meadow of soft moss, which is kept smooth and clean, and upon which are scattered flowers and fruit of different colors, bright fungi, and brilliantly colored insects, so that the place reminds one of an elegant little garden. Moreover, when these objects have been exposed so long so as to become wilted they are taken away and replaced by others, so that it seems impossible to believe that the birds do not take a real delight in the freshness of their flowers, and the brightness and color of their insects. The activity and curiosity of all these bower-birds are strong characteristics, and they seem to derive great amusement, not only from their architectural arrangements, but in gathering, placing, and rearranging their treasures, and in keeping the premises in the neatest and prettiest condition possible. It is difficult to understand how any other purpose is served by these structures than simply that of providing a convenient place for the lively movements by which they display themselves to the females, as has been alluded to above, and for the duels which frequently take place between rival males, sometimes with fatal results; but to this must be added the gratification of an inherited instinct of acquisitiveness, and a real delight in beautiful things. The species of another genus (*Prionadura*) make similar "bowers" four to six feet high.

Detailed descriptions of these and several other similar birds and their works will be found in the books relating to the ornithology of Australia and New Guinea, and especially in the writings of the Italian naturalists, Beccari and Salvadori. An excellent *résumé* may be read in Lydekker's 'Royal Natural History,' Vol. III. (Lond. 1885). Several species have been brought alive to Europe and may usually be seen, with their curious bowers, in the zoological gardens of London, Paris, and elsewhere; while the museums in New York and Washington contain models of some of their ornamental structures.

Bowers, Elizabeth Crocker, American actress: b. Ridgefield, Conn., 12 March 1830: d. Washington, D. C., 6 Nov. 1895. She made her first appearance on the stage at the Park Theatre, New York, in 1846, and in 1847 married David P. Bowers and appeared in Philadelphia as Donna Victoria in 'A Bold Stroke for a Husband.' She was a stock member of the Arch Street company in Philadelphia until her husband's death in 1857. She remarried in 1860, and in the next year made a professional trip to England with great success. She returned to New York in 1863, and, after fulfilling several engagements, retired from the stage. In 1884 she returned to the stage in 'La Charbonniere,' and in 1886 began a series of performances with her own company at the 14th Street Theatre in New York. She played with Rose Coghlan in 'A Woman of No Importance,' in 1893, and supported Olga Nethersole in her first appearance in the United States in 1894. Her last impersonation was that of Lady Margrave in 'The New Woman' in the early part of 1895.

Bowers, Theodore S., American soldier: b. Pennsylvania, 10 Oct. 1832; d. Garrison's Station, N. Y., 6 March 1866. At the outbreak of the Civil War he was editor of a Democratic paper in Mount Carmel, Ill. After the battle of Bull Run he raised a company for the 48th Illinois Infantry, but declined its captaincy on account of the taunts of former political associates, and went to the front as a private. On 25 Jan. 1862 he was detailed as a clerical assistant at Gen. Grant's headquarters. That officer found him invaluable and kept him near him until the close of the war. He went through the campaigns of Forts Henry and Donelson, and while the army was absent on the Tallahatchie expedition Bowers was left in charge of the department headquarters, having received a regular staff appointment as captain and aide-de-camp. When Van Dorn seized the headquarters at Holly Springs 20 Dec. 1862, Bowers destroyed all the departmental records that would have been of value to the Confederates, refused to give his parole, and made his escape during the night. He was twice brevetted for gallant and meritorious services, and after the war Gen. Grant retained him on his personal staff, having procured his appointment as assistant adjutant-general with rank of major in the United States army, 6 Jan. 1865. He was killed while boarding a moving train.

Bowery, The, a street in New York. It begins at Chatham Square and terminates at Cooper Union. It was long notorious for the resorts located along its length, but its character has undergone improvement.

Bowfin, a fish (*Amia calva*) of the Mississippi Valley. See MUDFISH.

Bowhead, the Greenland or right whale, taking its name from the arched outline of its head. See GREENLAND WHALE.

Bowie, bōʹe, James, American frontiersman: b. Burke County, Ga., about 1790; d. 6 March 1836. He took part in the revolt of Texas against Mexico, and fell in the Alamo massacre. He gave his name to the bowie-knife (q.v.).

Bowie-knife, a long knife shaped like a dagger, but with only one edge, named after Col. James Bowie (q.v.). Its use as a weapon was originally confined to Texas, but is now used in almost all the States of the Union. Col. Bowie is said to have had his sword broken down to within about 20 inches of the hilt in a fight with some Mexicans, but he found that he did such good execution with his broken blade that he equipped all his followers with a similar weapon.

Bowker, Richard Roger, American author: b. Salem, Mass., 1848. He has been prominent in politics as an independent and was the originator of the independent Republican movement of 1879. He has edited the 'Publisher's Weekly,' the 'Library Journal,' and the 'American Catalogue,' and has published 'Work and Wealth'; 'Economics for the People'; 'Copyright: Its Law and Its Literature'; 'Primer for Political Education'; 'Electoral Reform'; 'The Arts of Life'; 'Civil Service Examination.'

Bowles, Francis Tiffany, American naval constructor: b. Springfield, Mass., 7 Oct. 1858. He was graduated at the United States Naval Academy in 1879, and has ever since been prominent in the work of naval construction, with special reference to the rehabilitated United States navy. He has been in charge of construction at the navy yards in Norfolk and Brooklyn, and was made chief constructor of the navy with the rank of rear admiral in 1901.

Bowles, Samuel, American journalist: b. Springfield, Mass., 9 Feb. 1826; d. 16 Jan. 1878. He was editor and proprietor of the Springfield *Republican* and a prominent factor in public affairs. He wrote 'Across the Continent' and 'The Switzerland of America.'

Bowles, William A., Indian agent and chief: b. Frederick County, Md.; d. 23 Dec. 1805. When 13 years of age he ran away from home and joined the British army at Philadelphia. He afterward went among the Creek Indians, married an Indian woman, and was one of the English emissaries to excite them against the Americans. After the war he went to England, and on his return his influence among the Indians was so hostile to the Spaniards that they offered a price of $6,000 for his capture. He was taken in July 1792, sent to Madrid, and afterward to Manila. Having obtained leave to visit Europe, he returned among the Creeks and instigated them to renewed hostilities. He was betrayed again into the hands of the Spaniards in 1804, and died in Morro Castle, Havana. His biography was published in London in 1791.

Bowles, William Lisle, English poet: b. King's Sutton, Northamptonshire, where his father was vicar, 1762; d. Salisbury, 7 April 1850. He was educated at Winchester and Oxford, where he gained high honors. In 1789 he composed a series of sonnets by which the young minds of Coleridge and Wordsworth, then seeking for new and more natural chords of poetry, were powerfully affected to such an extent that Bowles is considered to have created, by his influence, the Lake School of Poetry. In 1806 he issued a critical edition of Pope, which led to a memorable controversy (1809–25), in which Byron and Campbell were his opponents. His other works include: 'The Grave of Howard' (1790); 'Coombe Ellen' (1798); 'The Battle of the Nile' (1799); 'The Spirit of Discovery' (1804), his longest poem; and 'St. John in Patmos' (1832).

Bowling (bōʹlĭng) Green, Ky., a city and county-seat of Warren County, 114 miles southwest of Louisville, of prominence as an educational centre. Here are situated Ogden College, founded in 1877; Potter College for women, opened in 1889; the Southern Normal School; Saint Columbia's Academy: and a business college. The city is surrounded by a fertile agricultural region, has an important trade in hogs and mules, and one of the largest horse markets in the State. It contains two parks, one of 42 acres, and owns and operates its waterworks and electric-lighting establishment. It was incorporated in 1812 and is governed by a mayor elected every four years, and a city council. At the time of the Civil War Bowling Green was of much strategic importance to the Confederate army. Pop. (1900) 8,226.

Bowling Green, Mo., a city and county-seat of Pike County, 90 miles northwest of St. Louis; situated on the Chicago & A. and St. Louis & H. R.R.'s. It was settled in 1820, and incorporated in 1838. Pike College is here located and among the industries of the place are flour and pipe manufacturing. Pop. (1900) 1,902.

Bowling Green, New York City Park, a small open space near the foot of Broadway, originally a village green and an aristocratic centre of the city. Fort Amsterdam, which formerly stood at the south of the green, was removed in 1787 and the governor's residence took its place. The present Green is a very small enclosed park.

Bowling Green, Ohio, a city and county-seat of Wood County; situated on the Cincinnati, H. & D., and the Toledo & O. C. R.R.'s, 22 miles south of Toledo. It carries on a trade in farm produce and is the centre of a region producing oil and natural gas. Among the other industries are iron smelting, canning and glass-cutting. Private companies operate waterworks, gas works, an electric-lighting system, and a hot water heating plant. The city was settled in 1832 and incorporated as a borough 1855 and city in 1900. It is governed by a mayor biennially elected and a board of public service of five members. Pop. (1900) 5,067.

Bowls, Bowling, an American indoor game; also much played in Great Britain, and probably a modification of the English game of skittles (q.v.). It is played in a covered alley of carpenter's work from 65 to 70 feet in length and about 3 feet 6 inches wide. The alley has a gutter on each side, and is slightly convex in the centre, and regularly beveled toward the gutters. At the farther extremity ten pins, generally of ashwood, about 12 inches high, and shaped somewhat like a champagne bottle with a slightly tapering base, are set up in the form of a triangle having its apex toward the bowler; that is, with four pins on the rear or fourth line, three on the third, two on the second, and one on the first line, all being 12 inches apart. The pins are uniform in weight. The balls may never exceed 27 inches in circumference; but smaller sizes are optional. The bowler is entitled to two (formerly three) balls, which he rolls at the pins, the object being to knock down as many pins as possible, the number displaced being registered to the bowler's credit. The first record of a match seems to have been made on 1 Jan. 1840, at the Knickerbocker Alleys, New York; but it was not until 1875 that the bowlers of the principal cities held a convention for the purpose of framing rules for the game, and it was 20 years later when the American Bowling Congress brought the sport into anything like systematic order. The rules of the game in all its varieties are published by the Congress.

Another form of bowls, an ancient English game, is still extremely popular in its own country. It is played on a smooth, level piece of green sward, generally about 40 yards long, and surrounded by a trench or ditch about 6 inches in depth. A small white ball, usually of earthenware, called the jack, is placed at one end of the green, and the object of the players, who range themselves in sides at the other, is so to roll their bowls that they may lie as near as possible to the jack. Each bowl is much larger than the jack, is made of lignum-vitæ or similar wood, and is biased by being made slightly conical, so as to take a curvilinear course; and in making the proper allowance for this bias, and so regulating the cast of the ball, consist the skill and attraction of the game. The side which owns the greatest number of bowls next the jack — each bowl so placed constituting a point — carries off the victory. The game played in Scotland differs in several respects from that of England; and the latter country, unlike the former, has as yet no national bowling association.

Bowman, bō'măn, Alexander Hamilton. American soldier: b. Wilkesbarre, Pa., 15 May 1803; d. there, 11 Nov. 1865. He graduated from the United States Military Academy 1825, and entered the engineer corps. For a time he was assistant professor of geography, history, and ethics at the academy. He acted as assistant engineer in the construction of the defenses, and of the improvement of harbors and rivers on the Gulf of Mexico, 1826–34, and was superintending engineer of the construction of Fort Sumter, 1838–51. Later he was chief engineer of the construction bureau of the United States treasury, and employed in building custom-houses, post-offices, marine hospitals, etc. During the Civil War he was superintendent of the United States Military Academy, and from 20 June 1865 till his death a member of the board of engineers to carry out in detail the modifications of the defenses in the vicinity of Boston, Mass. He attained his lieutenant-colonelcy in the engineer corps, 3 March 1863.

Bowman, Edward Morris, American organist: b. Barnard, Vt., 1848. His musical education was thorough and varied. He studied in New York under Dr. William Mason, in London under Dr. Bridge, in Berlin under Weitzmann and Bendel, and in Paris under Guilmant. He has been conspicuously successful as an organist, choral conductor, and teacher. In 1895 he took charge of the Temple Choir in connection with the Baptist Temple, Brooklyn, N. Y., and succeeded in making popular a high standard of music, both ecclesiastical and secular. In 1891 he succeeded Dr. F. Ritter as professor of music at Vassar College. He was a founder and for eight terms president of the American College of Musicians. His compositions comprise songs, part songs, anthems, and orchestral numbers, and he has published: 'Bowman-Weitzmann Manual of Musical Theory' (1877); 'Harmony: Historic Points and Modern Methods'; 'Formation of Piano Touch'; 'Relation of Musicians to the Public.'

Bowman, Thomas, American Methodist bishop: b. Berwick, Pa., 15 July 1817. He graduated at Dickinson College 1837, and entered the ministry in the Baltimore conference of the Methodist Episcopal Church. In 1848 he organized the Dickinson Seminary at Williamsport, Pa., and was its president for 10 years. In 1858 he was elected president of Indiana Asbury University (now DePauw University), remaining there until May 1872, when he became a bishop. He has visited all the conferences in the United States, Europe, India, China, Japan, and Mexico, and is distinguished for his fine pulpit eloquence.

Bowman, **Sir William,** English anatomist and surgeon: b. Nantwich, 20 July 1816; d. London, 29 March 1892. He was for some time surgeon to King's College Hospital, London, and professor of physiology and anatomy in King's College, and was especially distinguished as an ophthalmic surgeon. He gained the Royal Society's royal medal for physiology in 1842. In 1880 Cambridge, and in the following year Edinburgh, conferred on him the degree of LL.D. He was connected with a large number of scientific societies, both British and foreign, was collaborator with Todd in the great work on the 'Physiological Anatomy and Physiology of Man' (5 vols. 1845-56), and he also wrote 'Lectures on the Eye' (1849); 'Collected Papers' (1892). His baronetcy was conferred on him in 1884.

Bowman's Root, *Gillenia stipulacea,* a hardy perennial herb of the natural order *Rosaceæ,* two to four feet tall, found in rich woods from New York to Georgia, and often planted in shrubberies for their graceful foliage and numerous terminal clusters of white or rose-tinted flowers. The name is also applied to its close relative, *G. trifoliata,* which grows farther south and bears a rather close resemblance to it. Both species are also called Indian physic, American ipecac, Indian hippo, and have been used as tonics and emetics. They are the only species of their genus.

Bowne, bown, Borden Parker, American philosophical writer: b. Leonardville, N. J., 14 Jan. 1847. He was religious editor of the New York 'Independent' 1875-6, becoming professor of philosophy at Boston University in 1876. He has written 'Philosophy of Herbert Spencer' (1874); 'Metaphysics' (1882); 'Principles of Ethics' (1892); 'The Christian Life' (1878); 'The Atonement' (1900), etc.

Bow'ring, Sir John, English statesman and linguist: b. Exeter, 17 Oct. 1792; d. there, 23 Nov. 1872. While still very young he entered a business house in his native town, and in 1811 became clerk to a London firm, on whose business he traveled to Spain. Soon afterward he started on his own account, and made many journeys to the continent. Having extraordinary linguistic ability he made use of his residence in foreign countries to acquire the different languages, and his first publications consisted of translations, especially of the popular poetry of many of the countries he had visited. At the same time he appeared as a supporter of the Radical politics of the time and of the views of Jeremy Bentham, and acted as editor of the 'Westminster Review' from 1824 till 1830. His public life began in 1828, when he was sent to Holland to make a report on the public accounts of that kingdom. He afterward received similar commissions to France, Switzerland, Italy, Egypt, Syria, and Germany, and the Blue-books which appeared from his pen on these separate occasions are considered as models of their kind. He was member of

Parliament for the Kilmarnock burghs from 1835 to 1837, and for Bolton from 1841 to 1849. In the year last mentioned he accepted the lucrative post of consul at Canton, and his services during the four years that he held this post were so appreciated by the ministry that in 1854, the year after his return, he received the honor of knighthood, and was appointed governor of Hong-kong. As governor of Hong-kong he acted with the same energy that he had manifested when consul at Canton; but the step which he took in ordering Canton to be bombarded to punish the Chinese for an insult offered to the British flag, although approved by Lord Palmerston, then at the head of the government, led to his recall, March 1857. The last public commission he received was in 1860, when he was sent to Italy to report on the commercial relations with the new kingdom. He published 'The Kingdom and People of Siam'; and his 'Autobiographical Reminiscences' appeared in 1877. He will, perhaps, be longest remembered as the author of the familiar hymn, 'Watchman, Tell Us of the Night.'

Bow'ser, Edward Albert, American mathematician: b. Sackville, New Brunswick, 18 June 1845. He graduated at Rutgers College in 1868, and since 1871 has been professor of mathematics and engineering there. Since 1875 he has had charge of the United States Coast and Geodetic Survey of New Jersey. He has published 'Analytical Geometry' (1880; 10 ed. 1888); 'Differential and Integral Calculus' (1880; 9 ed. 1887); 'Analytical Mechanics' (1884); 'College Algebra' (1888); 'Academic Algebra' (1888); 'Plane and Solid Geometry' (1890); 'Elements of Trigonometry'; 'Treatise on Trigonometry' (1892); 'Logarithmic Tables' (1895); 'Hydromechanics'; 'Roofs and Bridges.'

Bow'string Hemp, the fibre of the leaves of an East Indian plant, or the plant itself, *Sanseviera zeylanica,* order *Liliaceæ,* so named from being made by the natives into bowstrings. The plant is somewhat like a hyacinth in appearance, and has edible roots. The fibre is fine and silky, but very strong, and may become a valuable article in European manufacture. See HEMP.

Bowyer, bō'yẽr, **Sir George,** English law writer: b. Oxford, 1811; d. London, 7 June 1883. He was called to the bar in 1839. Converted to Catholicism in 1850, he represented Dundalk 1852-68, and the county of Wexford 1874-80, when his Home Rule principles estranged him from the Liberal party, and, in 1876 led to his expulsion from the Reform Club. He succeeded his father as seventh baronet in 1860. He was author of several able works on constitutional law and Catholic subjects.

Bowyer, William, English printer and classical scholar: b. London, 19 Dec. 1699; d. 18 Nov. 1777. He was admitted a sizar of St. John's College, Cambridge, but left the university without a degree in 1722, and became an associate in the printing trade with his father. In 1729 he obtained the office of printer of the votes of the House of Commons, which he held nearly 50 years. He was subsequently appointed printer to the Society for the Encouragement of Learning, the Society of Antiquarians, of which learned body he was admitted a member; and in 1761 Lord Macclesfield procured him the appointment of printer to the Royal Society. In 1767 he was nominated printer of the journals of the House of Lords, and the rolls of the House of Commons. By his will he bequeathed a considerable sum of money, in trust, to the Stationers' Company, for the relief of decayed printers or compositors. His principal literary production was an edition of the New Testament in Greek (1763), with critical notes and emendations. He also published several philological tracts, and added notes and observations to some of the learned works which issued from his press.

Box (*buxus*), a genus of about 20 species of evergreen shrubs or small trees of the natural order *Euphorbiaceæ*, natives of northern Africa, southern Europe, Central America, and similar climates in Asia. The species have small opposite leaves, inconspicuous monoecious flowers in terminal or axillary clusters and nearly globular fruits containing two shining black seeds. Several species are planted for ornament as edgings of borders, as hedges and as individual specimens, especially for topiary work, either in the open air or as glasshouse specimens in tubs, etc., for which uses some of them are particularly adapted since they stand shearing well. They are of slow growth and are not very hardy unless the winters are at all severe. They are propagated by cuttings. *B. sempervirens*, which attains a height of 25 feet or more, has developed several cultivated varieties of which dwarf box, a favorite edging plant, is probably the best known. The very hard, heavy, light yellow wood exported largely from Spain and Portugal is highly valued for turning, carving, and engraving, and for making musical instruments such as flutes, clarionets, etc. The bright yellow wood of *B. balearica*, a larger species than the preceding, native to Turkey and certain islands of the Mediterranean, is largely exported from Constantinople for similar purposes to those of the first mentioned, but is inferior.

Box'berry. See GAULTHERIA.

Box-crab, a large thick-shelled crab (*Calappa flammia*), occurring from North Carolina southward, and not uncommon on the Florida reefs. It is four to five inches across, about an inch and a half deep, with large broad, flat claws, which are folded closely in front. It is admirably adapted to resist the violence of the surf.

Box-elder, or Ash-leaved Maple (*Negundo accroides*), a tree of the natural order *Sapindaceæ*, common from the Atlantic coast to the Rocky Mountains. It attains a height of 70 feet, bears pendulous corymbs of staminate flowers and drooping racemes of pistillate blossoms before the pinnate leaves appear. Its wood is inferior for any purposes except for making wood pulp, bowls, pails, etc. It has become very popular in the western United States for windbreaks, fuel, and shade, for which its rapid growth and hardiness especially adapt it. It is excellent also to protect other trees until they can care for themselves.

Box-turtle, or Tortoise, a turtle of the American family *Cinosternidæ*, having a rather long and narrow shell, in which the under part (plastron) has its front, and usually also its rear lobes hinged to the fixed central part, so that these ends may be lifted up against the carapace, like doors, thus entirely enclosing the animal within the shell. A familiar example is the mud-turtle (*Cinosternum pennsylvanicum*) of the eastern and southern United States, which is four inches long, has a dusky brown shell, and light dots on its head. Eight or 10 other species are known in the southwest, in Central America, and in Guiana. These turtles are mainly aquatic and carnivorous, and lay only a few eggs, which are covered with a glazed shell, thick, but brittle. Another noteworthy species, sometimes placed in a separate genus (*Aromochelys*) because its plastron is only partly movable, is the "musk" or "stinkpot" turtle (*C. odoratum*) of the eastern United States, which emits a musky odor from its inguinal glands. Its dull shell is about 4.50 inches long; it has a long neck, and relatively enormous head marked with two yellow stripes, one above, one below the eye; spends its time mainly in the water; and is disagreeable in odor and disposition. This turtle, however, is kept captive, fattened on swill-milk and eaten in some parts of the country.

Box and Cox, a farce by John M. Morton, the chief characters being the two men from whom the play takes its name. Box and Cox rent from a certain Mrs. Bouncer the same room, but for some time remain ignorant of the fact, as one works by day and the other by night. A holiday discloses the situation, which mutual agreement leaves unaltered.

Box'ers, the name given to the members of a powerful secret society in China. Its avowed object is the driving out from China of all Europeans or other foreigners. The Chinese name for the association is I-ho-ch'uan, which is variously rendered in English. The active efforts of American and European missionaries and the constant encroachments upon Chinese territory by European countries appear to be responsible in great measure for the establishment of the society. The events which precipitated the first demonstrations of the Boxers were the occupation of Kiao-Chau by Germany, the acquisition of Port Arthur by Russia, the taking of Wei-Hai-Wei by England, and the French seizure of Kwang-Chau. Thus the Boxer movement presents itself largely under the aspect of a patriotic uprising against foreign aggression, a fact which goes far to account for the rapidity and thoroughness of its operations in 1900. Early in that year the native population in Shantung were found to be rallying around the standard of the Boxers and adopting its motto, "Uphold the dynasty, drive out the foreigners." The diplomatic corps at Pekin called upon the imperial government to suppress the movement. This the court professed its readiness to do, although there was a suspicion, voiced by the British minister, that the Empress Dowager had fallen under the influence of a native party led by T'ung Fu-hsiang and Yu-hsien, and was temporizing with the Boxers. In May 1900 the Boxers began a concerted movement upon the Chinese capital, which, notwithstanding the protests of the diplomatic corps, remained unchecked by the military forces of the empire. These forces being Manchu troops, their loyalty was open to ques-

BOXING

tion and their sympathies were alleged to be with the Boxer movement. This, at any rate, is the only explanation offered by the Chinese government for its failure to cope with the uprising. The situation had been rendered additionally threatening by the action of the allies in opening fire upon the forts at Taku. On 17 June the warships of the powers were in force at that port; when fired upon by the Chinese they opened a bombardment. The demonstration before Taku had been deprecated by the United States commander, Admiral Kempff, who did not participate in the bombardment. His warning that hostilities would unite the Chinese against the foreigners was justified by events.

In June 1900, Peking was reduced to a state of siege by the Boxers. The position of the foreigners in the capital became precarious. The entire diplomatic corps was cut off from communication with the outside world. In the emergency the · powers hurried military and naval forces to the scene, and an international relief column, under the command of Admiral Seymour of the British navy, moved upon Peking. This force was, however, compelled to retreat, when a short distance beyond Tien-Tsin, with a loss of 300 men. The position of the capital now became desperate. Cut off from communication with the rest of the world, Peking was a scene of turbulence and the centre of wild rumor. It was reported that on 7 July the entire diplomatic corps had fallen a prey to Boxer fury. This rumor was later discredited, the aspect of affairs having been rendered incomprehensible by the receipt of a despatch purporting to emanate from United States Minister Conger, and bearing date 18 July. According to this despatch the diplomatic corps had taken refuge in the British embassy, where they remained in a state of siege by the Boxers, anticipating massacre unless speedily relieved. Meanwhile the allies had concentrated their forces upon Tien-Tsin, capturing the place in the middle of July, but suffering severe loss. The 9th Regiment, United States army, had many casualties, including the loss of its colonel and other officers. The movement had in all directions among the Chinese, who, on 16 July, invaded Siberia. Russia at once proclaimed a state of siege in its Asiatic dominions. The powers did not, as yet, give formal recognition to a state of war, chiefly in consequence of the attitude of the United States, which took the ground that the Chinese government had been overpowered by an insurrectionary movement. On 20 July the powers made a categorical demand to be placed in communication with their diplomatic representatives. The authorities at Peking professed their readiness to comply with the earliest possible moment. The international situation was more clearly defined on 23 July by the appeal of China to the United States for the good offices of the latter in dealing with the powers. See CHINA.

Boxing, as now practised and popularly defined, is a contest of skill, endurance, and pluck between two contestants striking at each other with the closed hand, or fist, covered with a soft leather glove stuffed with horsehair. Contests of this nature, in various forms, are probably coeval with man. The sport was much in

vogue among the Greek and Roman athletes, but in place of the modern tendency to deprive it of its more brutal characteristics, as by the use of gloves, the ancients made the punishment as severe as possible by arming the fists of the combatants with strips of rawhide (the *cestus*), which were often knotted and loaded with lead or iron. In the first half of the 18th century rules were formulated to govern such contests in England, and from that time onward the practice of fighting with the fists for prizes or for championships has been reduced well-nigh to a "science." Methods of striking, ring tactics, etc., have developed until mere brute force has had to give way before intelligence; in other words, the head has defeated the hands.

In 1719 one Figg, an English pugilist, who attained such celebrity as to have his portrait painted by Hogarth, brought about some system in the conduct of the prize-ring. His work was continued by Broughton, himself for many years champion of England and a great upholder of the sport. Regular contests were held, with prizes of money and an emblem of championship, usually a belt, which was held on the condition of meeting all comers, on penalty of surrendering it if declining the trial or beaten by the adversary. The use of a belt as such emblem is of very ancient origin, dating back at least to the time of the siege of Troy. Homer, in describing the games at the funeral of Patroclus, mentions a belt in this connection. There is an unbroken record of championships from the time of Figg down. But since 1860, when the British champion, Tom Sayers, fought the American John C. Heenan, fighting with bare knuckles, which had hitherto been the custom, was suppressed, and in its place the use of gloves was adopted. The laws were, however, frequently evaded by the use of skin-tight gloves. At the present time gloves weighing four ounces are used for championship matches.

With the use of gloves came also the adoption of new rules, named, from their framer's title, the Marquis of Queensberry's rules. Under these wrestling and hugging (which had previously been permitted) were prohibited; the time of each round was limited to three minutes, with intervals of one minute between each round; and the former space of 30 seconds within which a man knocked off his feet might recover himself and be brought back to the fighting-line was reduced to 10 seconds.

Under the new conditions boxing has taken a leading rank as a sport and exercise. In the former aspect legislation has been found necessary to restrict its tendency to degenerate into brutality and to lend its aid to gambling and other vices. As an exercise, however, it holds a high place. It is considered the best system of gymnastics for bringing all the limbs under perfect command: rendering every part of the body pliant, flexible, and firm; acquiring a perfect power of keeping the true centre of gravity in every position, and of extending the body and limbs to the extreme length and recovering again without pause or difficulty; and developing the power of breathing and the "staying" qualities. The practice of boxing also gives to those proficient in it a remarkable power of calmly looking danger in the eye, and preserving both the temper and the courage under trying circumstances unruffled. It is alleged by the defenders of this sport that it encourages individual and therefore national courage; that it leads to a general sense and sentiment of fair play and honor; and that it discourages and renders infamous the use of the knife and other deadly weapons.

Amateur boxers are divided into seven classes considered according to weight — 105 pounds, 115, 125, 135, 145, and 158 pounds, all over the latter weight being classed as "heavy" weights. Among the lighter weights the classes are sometimes termed "bantam" weights, "feather," "light," and "middle" weights. The term "catch weights" implies no restriction as to weight.

The laws governing the practice of the sport vary in different States of the Union and in Great Britain, and cannot be accorded space here. The rules and history may be found in such works as the following: 'Boxiana, or Sketches of Ancient and Modern Pugilism,' by Pierce Egan (London, 4 vols. 1818-24); Michell's 'Boxing' (Badminton Library 1889); 'Cassell's Book of Sports and Pastimes' (New York 1890); Earl's 'Handbook of Boxing' (1893): B. J. Doran's 'Science of Self-Defense' (Toronto 1893); 'Boxing,' in the Oval Series (New York 1896); 'Encyclopædia of Sport' (New York 1902); 'Handbook on Boxing' (New York 1903).

Boxing the Compass, the recital of all the points of the compass in their proper order.

Boxing-day, in England, the day after Christmas, so called from the practice of giving Christmas-boxes or presents on that day. It was made a bank holiday by the act of 1871.

Boxthorn. See LYCIUM.

Boy Bishop, a boy chosen on St. Nicholas' Day, 6 December, by the votes of his fellow-choristers, to act the part of bishop, retaining office until St. Innocent's Day, 28 December. This custom of the mediæval Church, as practised in England, extended to the schools of Winchester and Eton. Dressed in the Episcopal vestments, with mitre, crozier, and ring, the youthful bishop went about attended by a dean and prebendaries and followed by children; went through the forms of blessing and of preaching, more to the entertainment than edification of his hearers. Boy bishops dying during their incumbency, were buried in their Episcopal attire. The custom of electing a boy bishop came to an end in England during the reign of Queen Elizabeth.

Boyaca, bō-yä-kä', United States of Colombia, the most populous department of the republic, lying on the Venezuelan border, southeast of Santander. Mountainous in the west, and consisting of great plains in the east, it produces emeralds, copper, iron, salt, and various cereals. Horses and cattle are raised on the plains. Area, 33,351 square miles; pop. about 720,000. The capital is Tunja.

Boyaca', a town of Colombia, South America, about 60 miles northeast of Bogota. It is inhabited mostly by Indians, contains extensive lime-kilns, and was the scene of a battle, 7 Aug. 1819, between the Spaniards and Gen. Bolivar, which resulted in the defeat of the former, and the establishment of Colombian independence. A college was established here in 1821. Pop. 7,000.

Bo'yar, or Boiar, among the Slavic nations, a free landowner independent of any sovereign. It is synonymous with cech, lech, or bojarin, used by several Slavic tribes, such as the Bohemians and Poles. The word boyar was at first especially used by the Bulgarians, Serbs, and Russians, and then was adopted by the Moldavians and Wallachians. It represented the highest social condition, corresponding in certain respects to that of an English peer. In ancient Russia, the boyars were the next after the princes of the blood, or knezia, who were all originally petty sovereigns. The boyars formed a kind of supreme political body in the state, and acted as the council (duma) of the grand dukes. All the higher offices, civil and military, including the lieutenancies in the provinces, were held by them. While Russia was still divided into several petty sovereignties, the boyars enjoyed the right of choosing for themselves and for their dependents the prince whom they wished to serve, and to leave the service at their pleasure, without any previous notification. When the Grand Dukes of Vladimir and of Moscow stripped these petty princes of their sovereign rights, and transformed them from vassals into subjects, the dignity of boyars was granted to their families. The boyars had their own military retinue and their clients; and their influence on the masses of the people often equalled that of the grand dukes. The sovereign ukases always contained the sacramental words, "ordered by the Grand Duke (subsequently it was 'by the Czar'), and approved by the boyars." Precedence among the boyars was reckoned according to the date of the title, which was hereditary, and the observance of it was carried so far that in the 16th and 17th centuries any boyar of an older creation refused to serve under a younger one. This struggle for rank was ended by the czar, Alexis Michailowitch Romanoff, who destroyed the official records and diplomas of the boyars, but they retained their place among the nobility. Peter the Great wholly abolished their power and official privileges, and the name now remains only as a historical distinction, and a recollection of the past, in families which once possessed the dignity. In Rumania boyars still exist.

Boyce, Henry Harrison, American soldier: b. Ohio 1830; d. New York 1904. He served with distinction in the Civil War, being promoted to captain and then to general. He organized in 1894 the Navy League of the United States and became its secretary. For some years he lived in California where he edited the Los Angeles Tribune, and was chairman of the Republican State Committee.

Boyce, William, English musical composer: b. London, 1710; d. there, 7 Feb. 1779. He was a pupil of Dr. Maurice Greene, organist of St. Paul's. In 1736 he was chosen organist of the church of St. Michael, Cornhill; and was also appointed composer, and afterward (1758) organist to the Chapel Royal. On his setting to music an ode performed at the installation of his patron, the Duke of Newcastle, he was honored with the degree of Doctor of Music; and in 1755 he became master of the king's band. His greatest work is the scholarly 'Cathedral Music' (3 vols. 1760-78), but he will be most generally remembered as the composer of 'Hearts of Oak,' which first occurred in Garrick's pantomime of 'Harlequin's Invasion' (1759). Of his musical compositions a serenata entitled 'Solomon' (1743), is the best.

Boycott. What is popularly known as the boycott is a form of coercion by which a combination of many persons seek to work their will upon a single person, or upon a few persons, by compelling others to abstain from social or beneficial business intercourse with such person or persons. Carried to the extent sometimes practised in aid of a strike it is a cruel weapon of aggression, and its use immoral and anti-social, and the concerted attempt to accomplish it is a conspiracy at common law, and merits and should receive the punishment due to such a crime. It is attempted to defend the boycott by calling the contest between employers and employees a war between capital and labor, and pursuing the analogies of the word to justify thereby the cruelty and illegality of conduct on the part of those conducting a strike. The analogy is not apt, and the argument founded upon it is fallacious. There is only one war-making power recognized by our institutions, and that is the government of the United States and of the States in subordination thereto when repelling invasion or suppressing domestic violence. War between citizens is not to be tolerated, and cannot in the proper sense exist. If attempted it is unlawful, and is to be put down by the sovereign power of the State and nation.

The practices common in a boycott would be outside the pale of civilized war. In civilized warfare women and children and the defenseless are safe from attack, and a code of honor controls the parties to such warfare which cries out against the boycott. Cruel and cowardly are terms not too severe by which to characterize it.

The name was first given to an organized system of social and commercial exclusion employed in Ireland in connection with the Land League and the land agitation of 1880, and subsequently. It took its name from Capt. James Boycott, a Mayo landlord, one of its earliest victims, who as agent for Lord Erne evicted many tenants. A landlord, manufacturer, or other person subjected to boycotting, faces a combination to prevent his buying from or selling to anyone employing labor, etc.; and those refusing to join in a boycott are often threatened with similar interference, loss or injury. Boycotts have been frequently employed in the United States as a means of coercion in labor difficulties. The attitude of courts is not altogether uniform in regard to such combinations. A boycott accompanied by violence is a criminal offense, and such conspiracy is sometimes declared unlawful even when not marked by threats and violence.

Boyd, Andrew Kennedy Hutchison, Scotch clergyman and author: b. Auchinleck, Ayrshire, 3 Nov. 1825; d. London, 2 Nov. 1899. He was educated at King's College, London, and Glasgow University; was ordained in 1851, and was incumbent successively of the parishes of Newton-on-Ayr, Kirkpatrick-Irongray, in Galloway, St. Bernard's, Edinburgh, and at the university city of St. Andrews. He early be-

came known as a contributor to 'Fraser's Magazine,' under the signature "A. K. H. B." Many of these contributions were reprinted in book form under the title, 'Recreations of a Country Parson,' of which three series appeared. In 1890 he was moderator of the General Assembly of the Church of Scotland. He also published 'Graver Thoughts of a Country Parson,' 'Counsel and Comfort Spoken from a City Pulpit,' 'Present-Day Thoughts'; 'Memorials of St. Andrew's Sundays'; 'Toward the Sunset'; 'What Set Him Right'; 'The Best Last'; 'Twenty-Five Years of St. Andrew's'; 'St. Andrew's and Elsewhere'; etc.

Boyd, Belle, Confederate spy: b. Martinsburg, W. Va., 9 May 1846; d. Kilbourn, Wis., 11 June 1900. She rendered invaluable aid to the Southern cause by detecting the Federal plans of campaign and revealing them to the Confederates. Gen. "Stonewall" Jackson sent her a letter of thanks.

Boyd, Ellen Wright, American educator: b. Winsted, Conn., 8 Sept. 1833. She has been principal of Saint Agnes' School, at Albany, N. Y., and has published 'Outlines of Religious Instruction'; 'English Cathedrals'; 'Famous Art Galleries.'

Boyd, James P., American lawyer and author: b. Lancaster County, Pa., 20 Dec. 1836. He was admitted to the bar in 1863 and successively edited several Philadelphia newspapers. His published works comprise: 'Lalecca' (1872); 'Envious Merchant' (1874); 'Building and Ruling the Republic' (1884); 'History of the Crusades' (1890); 'Bible Dictionary' (1896); 'Paris Exposition' (1900); and Lives of Grant, Sherman, Sheridan, Blaine, Harrison, McKinley, Emperor William I.; 'Men and Issues' (1892-1900).

Boyd, John Parker, American soldier: b. Newburyport, Mass., 21 Dec. 1764; d. Boston, 4 Oct. 1830. His father was from Scotland, and his mother a descendant of Tristam Coffin, the first of that family who emigrated to America. He entered the army in 1786 as ensign in the 2d regiment, but peace service did not suit his adventurous spirit and in 1789 he went to India. Under Nizam Ali Khan he was given an important command in Madras and at one time had an army of 10,000 men at his disposal. He remained in India several years, in a sort of guerrilla service, and obtaining much favor. Returning home in 1808 he was appointed colonel of the 4th regiment, United States Army. He took part in the battle of Tippecanoe, November 1811; was made brigadier-general 26 August and held that rank throughout the War of 1812. He was at the capture of Fort George, and in the battle of Chrysler's Field, Canada. In 1816 he went to England to secure indemnity for the loss of a valuable cargo of saltpetre captured by an English cruiser, but procured only a single installment of $30,000. President Jackson appointed him naval officer at Boston in 1830, but his services were almost immediately cut short by his death.

Boyd, Mark Alexander, Scotch writer: b. 1563; d. 1601. He was educated at Glasgow under the superintendence of his uncle, the archbishop of that see, and was equally conspicuous for the alertness of his mind and the turbulence of his disposition. In Paris he reduced himself to distress by gaming, and then, resuming his studies with ardor, went to Bourges to attend the celebrated civilian Cujacius. To this professor he recommended himself by a compliance with his taste in Latin poetry, which gave a preference to Ennius and the elder Latin poets. After leading a wandering life on the Continent for 14 years he returned to Scotland, and died at his father's seat in Ayrshire. He has received much the same eulogium in regard to graces of person, powers of mind, and various accomplishments as the Admirable Crichton. He is popularly known by his 'Epistolæ Heroidum,' and his 'Hymni,' published in the 'Deliciæ Poetarum Scotorum.'

Boyd, **Mary Stuart,** Scottish writer. She was married to Alexander S. Boyd, a well-known illustrator, in 1880, and since 1890 has resided in London. Beside numerous contributions to reviews and other periodicals she has published 'Our Stolen Summer' (1900) ; 'A Versailles Christmastide' (1901) ; 'With Clipped Wings' (1902).

Boyd, **Thomas Duckett,** American educator: b. Wytheville, Va., 20 Jan. 1854. He graduated at Louisiana State University, and has held important posts in the educational institutions of Louisiana. Since 1896 he has been president of Louisiana State University.

Boyd, **Zachary,** Scottish divine: b. Ayrshire, about 1586; d. about 1653. He received the rudiments of his education at Kilmarnock School, and took the academical course in the College of Glasgow. About 1607 he went abroad and studied at the College of Saumur, France. He was appointed a regent in this university in 1611, and is said to have been offered the principalship, which he declined. He spent 16 years in France, during four of which he was a preacher of the gospel. In consequence of the persecution of the Protestants he was obliged to return home in 1621. There he lived successively under the protection of Sir William Scott of Elie and of the Marquis of Hamilton at Kinneil, it being then the fashion for pious persons of quality in Scotland to retain one clergyman at least as a member of their household. In 1623 he was appointed minister of the large district in the suburbs of Glasgow styled the Barony parish, for which the crypts beneath the cathedral church then served as a place of worship. In this charge he continued for the rest of his life. He filled the office of rector of the University of Glasgow 1634-5 and 1645. In 1629 he published his principal prose work, 'The Last Battell of the Soule in Death; whereby are shown the Diverse Skirmishes that are between the Soule of Man on his Deathbed and the Enemies of our Salvation, carefully digested for the Comfort of the Sicke.' This was reprinted at Glasgow in 1831, with a life of the author by Mr. Neil. He published various other works, chiefly devotional, and left a large quantity of manuscript writings, which are preserved in the Glasgow College library. Among the latter is one entitled 'Zion's Flowers,' consisting of poems on select subjects of Scripture history. It is popularly called 'Zachary Boyd's Bible,' and although it abounds in homely and ludicrous passages, it is not without a fine strain of devotional feeling. Boyd left a large legacy to the Glasgow College.

Boy'dell, **John,** English engraver, more distinguished as an encourager of the fine arts than on account of his own productions: *b.* Darrington, Shropshire, 19 Jan. 1719; d. *12* Dec. 1804. He was intended for his father's occupation, which was that of a land-surveyor. Accident having thrown in his way Baddeley's 'Views of Different Country Seats,' he conceived so strong an inclination for engraving that he determined to adopt it as a profession; and accordingly, when above 20, he bound himself apprentice for seven years to Toms, a London engraver. In 1745 he published six small landscapes, and afterward executed as many more views of places in and near London as formed a volume, which he published by subscription. With the profits of this work he established himself as a printseller, and by his liberality to artists in general established a high reputation as a patron of ingenious men. Woollet was employed by him to engrave the celebrated pictures of Niobe and Phaeton, and he furnished other eminent artists with occupation, and was thus enabled to carry on an extensive foreign trade in English prints, which tended greatly to his own emolument and to the credit and advantage of his native country. Having at length established what may be termed an English school of engraving, he next turned his attention to the improvement of the art of painting. With that view he engaged the first artists in the kingdom to furnish the collection of pictures forming the well-known Shakespeare Gallery. The wars arising out of the French revolution having obstructed his continental trade, he was induced in 1804 to solicit an act of Parliament to permit him to dispose of his gallery and paintings by lottery. This he obtained, and lived long enough to see every ticket disposed of, but died before the lottery was drawn.

Boy'den, **Seth,** American inventor: b. Foxboro, Mass., 17 Nov. 1785; d. Middleville, N. J., 31 March 1870. He was brought up on a farm, and attended a district school. Mechanically inclined, he spent much time experimenting in a blacksmith shop. His first invention was a machine for making nails, and in 1809 he undertook to manufacture both nails and files. Soon afterward he invented a machine for splitting leather, and in 1815, he took it to Newark, N. J., where he engaged in the leather business. In 1816 he invented a machine for cutting brads, and, followed this by the invention of patent leather, which he manufactured till 1831, when he began making malleable iron castings, on a system of his own. In 1835 he turned his attention to steam engines; substituted the straight axle for the crank in locomotives; and invented the cut-off now used instead of the throttle valve. In 1849 he went to California, but was unsuccessful, and returned to New Jersey, where he applied himself to farming, and developed a variety of strawberry previously unequaled in size or quality. In 1890, a statue was erected to his memory in Washington Park, Newark, N. J., where he spent the greater part of his life.

Boyè, **Martin Hans,** Danish-American chemist and genealogist: b. Copenhagen, Denmark. 6 Dec. 1812. He was a graduate from the University of Copenhagen in 1832 and from the medical department of the University of

Pennsylvania in 1844. He came to the United States in 1836 and jointly discovered several chemical compounds, as well as perchloric ether in 1841. In 1845 he discovered the first process of refining cotton-seed oil. He was professor of chemistry at the Central High School in Philadelphia, 1845-59, retiring in the year last named. He has published: 'Pneumaties, or the Physics of Gases' (1856) ; 'Chemistry, or the Physics of Atoms' (1857).

Boyer, bwä-yā, Alexis, French surgeon: b. Uzerches, Limousin, 1 March 1757; d. Paris, 25 Nov. 1833. Although in his younger years he had to struggle against poverty and disease, he attended the lectures of Louis and Desault, and after a brilliant career as a student obtained the degree of Master of Surgery in 1787. He became successively surgeon to the Hospital de la Charité and to the Hôtel-Dieu, and was appointed first surgeon to Napoleon, receiving at the same time the title of baron of the empire, with a dotation of 25,000 francs. He became a member of the Institute in 1825, and was consulting surgeon to Louis XVIII., Charles X., and Louis Philippe. His chief works are: 'Traité d'Anatomie' (1797-9) ; 'Traité des Maladies Chirurgicales et des Opérations qui leur Conviennent' (11 vols. 1814-26). He also contributed to the 'Journal de Médecine' and the 'Dictionnaire des Sciences Médicales.'

Boyer, Jean Pierre, zhŏṅ pē-ār, president of the Republic of Hayti: b. Port-au-Prince, 28 Feb. 1776; d. Paris, 9 July 1850. He was a mulatto by birth, but came early to Europe, where he obtained a European education. In 1792 he entered the army, and fought with distinction against the English in San Domingo, but was nevertheless obliged to evacuate the island, to which he did not return till 1802. At first he acted as leader of the mulattoes in the war against the negroes, but afterward effected a union between these in order to prepare the way for the complete independence of the island. When Pétion established a free state in the western part of the island, Boyer undertook the command of the troops which were concentrated in Port-au-Prince. After the death of Pétion, Boyer was elected president in 1818. By his skilful military operations, not less than by his adroit diplomacy, he finally succeeded in uniting the eastern part of the island with the republic, and thus effecting the complete separation of the island from France and Spain in 1825. He also purified the internal administration, raised the financial condition of the republic, and bestowed particular care upon its educational institutions. The contest between mulattoes and negroes, however, still went on, and in the end the latter rose in rebellion against him, and compelled him to leave the island in 1843. He never returned to the place of his birth and of his long-continued activity, but lived for the rest of his life first in Jamaica, and afterward in Paris.

Boyesen, boi'é-sĕn, Hjalmar Hjorth, American novelist: b. Frederiksvärn, Norway, 23 Sept. 1848; d. New York, 4 Oct. 1895. After completing his university studies at Christiania, he came to the United States in 1869 and was editor of a Norwegian journal in Chicago. He returned to Europe in 1872 and studied Germanic philology at Leipsic two years; then,
Vol. 3—2

returning to this country, he was professor of German in Cornell University for six years, and then of Germanic languages and literature in Columbia College till his death. His story of Norwegian life, 'Gunnar,' published in the 'Atlantic Monthly' (1873), and his 'Idyls of Norway and Other Poems' (1883), give proof of his rare imaginative faculty and his deep human sympathies. Besides these, he wrote: 'Tales from Two Hemispheres' (1875) ; 'A Norseman's Pilgrimage' (1876) ; 'Falconberg' (1878) ; 'Goethe and Schiller: Their Lives and Works' (1878) ; 'Ilka on the Hill-Top' (1881, dramatized 1884) ; 'Queen Titania' (1882) ; 'A Daughter of the Philistines' (1883) ; 'Story of Norway' (1886). Some of his works have been translated into German, etc. He was a founder of the New York Authors' Club.

Boyle, Charles (FOURTH EARL OF ORRERY), English physicist: b. Chelsea, 1676; d. 28 Aug. 1731. While a student at Christ Church, Oxford, he published a new edition of the epistles of Phalaris, of which Dr. Bentley questioning the authenticity, he wrote an answer entitled 'Dr. Bentley's Dissertation on the Epistles of Phalaris Examined,' which produced the famous Boyle and Bentley controversy. On leaving the university in 1700 he was chosen member for Huntingdon; and on the death of his brother succeeded to the earldom, and was soon after elected a knight of the Thistle, and received the command of a regiment. He was subsequently raised to the dignity of a British peer, under the title of Lord Boyle. He retired from court soon after the accession of George I., and in 1722 was sent to the Tower on suspicion of being concerned in Layer's plot, but was discharged after six months' imprisonment. He constantly attended the House of Peers as before, but never spoke, though often employed in drawing up protests. Besides the edition of Phalaris, he published a comedy called 'As You Find It'; a copy of verses to Dr. Garth upon his Dispensary; and a Prologue to Southerne's play of the 'Siege of Capua.' His name of Orrery was given to an astronomical instrument invented by Mr. George Graham, whom he patronized.

Boyle, David, Canadian ethnologist: b. Greenock, Renfrewshire, Scotland, 1 May 1842. He went to Canada in 1856, and was first a blacksmith and then a teacher. He later took up geology and discovered the fossils murchisonia boylei, named in his honor. He has, for 15 years, been curator of the Archæological Museum at Toronto. He has written 'Notes on Primitive Man in Ontario' and similar works.

Boyle, John (EARL OF CORK AND ORRERY), son of Charles Boyle: b. 1707; d. 1762. His earliest publication was a translation of two odes of Horace in 1742, which work was followed in 1751 by his 'Translation of the Epistles of Pliny the Younger, with Observations on Each Letter, and an Essay on Pliny's Life.' This translation advanced his reputation as a polite scholar, but has since been eclipsed by the superior version of Melmoth. In 1754 he made the tour of Italy, and employed himself in collecting materials for a history of Tuscany, which he intended to write in a series of letters, 12 only of which have been published since his death. They are written in an agreeable manner, and contain some curious information respecting the Medici family.

Boyle, Richard (EARL OF CORK), English statesman: b. Canterbury, 13 Oct. 1566; d. 15 Sept. 1643 In 1588 he went to Dublin with strong recommendations to persons in power, whose patronage he obtained. The state of Ireland at that time having rendered land very cheap, he took advantage of the circumstance to make some considerable purchases, among which was the estate of Sir Walter Raleigh, consisting of 12,000 acres in the counties of Cork and Waterford, which he obtained on easy terms. He was then appointed clerk of the council under Sir George Carew, the president of Munster, whom he accompanied in various expeditions against the Irish insurgents, in opposition to the English government. On these and other occasions he distinguished himself by his talents and activity, and rapidly augmented his political power and influence. King James I. appointed him privy-councilor for Munster, and afterward for the kingdom of Ireland; in 1616 he was made a peer of that realm by the title of Baron Boyle of Youghall, and in 1620 was created Viscount Dungarvan and Earl of Cork. He was now in the height of his prosperity, living in his castle of Lismore in a style of grandeur more resembling that of a sovereign prince than of a private individual. In 1629 he was made one of the lords justices of Ireland, and in 1631 lord-treasurer of that kingdom. Like most of the English rulers of the sister island, he seems to have employed his power rather for the subjugation than the advantage of the native Irish. He built and fortified towns and castles, and introduced among the people arts and manufactures; but put in force the severe laws of Queen Elizabeth against the Roman Catholics, and transported multitudes of the ancient inhabitants from the fertile province of Leinster to the bogs and deserts of Kerry, supplying their place with English colonists. In 1641 the Earl went to England as a witness against Lord Strafford, then under impeachment, having quarreled with that nobleman during his viceroyalty. Soon after his return home the insurrection of the Irish broke out; on which event he displayed his accustomed activity, enlisting his tenantry under the command of his sons, and taking other measures for the defense of the country. Lord Cork is principally memorable as the founder of a family, several individuals of which have highly distinguished themselves as cultivators of literature, science, and the arts; yet it should not be forgotten that he attained a high degree of contemporary fame, and was designated in the age in which he lived — "The great Earl of Cork."

Boyle, Robert, English philosopher: b. Lismore Castle, Waterford, Ireland, 25 Jan. 1627; d. London, 30 Dec. 1691. He was the seventh son of Richard, the great Earl of Cork. In 1638 he went to Geneva, where he continued to pursue his studies for several years, returning to England in 1644. During this period his father had died, leaving him considerable property. He now went to his estate at Stalbridge, where he devoted himself to the study of physics and chemistry. He was one of the first members of a learned society founded in 1645, which at first went under the name of the Philosophical College. On account of the political disturbances this society retired to Oxford, but was revived after the Restoration under the name of the Royal Society. Boyle occupied himself at Oxford in making improvements in the air-pump. Like Bacon, he esteemed observation the only road to truth. He attributed to matter merely mechanical properties. Every year of his life was marked by new experiments. We are indebted to him, indirectly, for the first certain knowledge of the absorption of air in calcination and combustion, and of the increase of weight which metals gain by oxidation. He studied the chemical phenomena of the atmosphere, and was thus a predecessor of Mayow, Hales, Cavendish, and Priestley. In all his philosophical inquiries he displayed an accurate and methodical mind, relying wholly upon experiments. While endeavoring to settle his faith, he found those defenses of the Christian religion which had been published before his time, unsatisfactory. In order, therefore, to read the original works, which are considered the foundation of Christianity, he studied the Oriental languages, and formed connections with Pococke, Thomas Hyde, Samuel Clarke, Thomas Barlow, etc. The result of his studies was a conviction of its truth, which was manifested not only by his theological writings, but by his benevolence and generous disinterestedness. He instituted public lectures for the defense of Christianity, devoting an annual sum to the payment of a lecturer. Boyle did much for the support of the mission in India, and caused Irish and Gaelic translations of the Bible to be made and printed at his own expense. To his religious principles were united the purest morals, a rare modesty, and an active benevolence. He was interred in Westminster Abbey. Birch published an edition of his works, five volumes, folio, London, 1744.

Boyle, Roger (EARL OF ORRERY), fifth son of the first Earl of Cork, English soldier: b. Waterford, 25 April 1621; d. 16 Oct. 1679. When only seven years old he was created Baron Broghill, by which title he is usually known. He commanded a troop of cavalry raised by his father, was employed in the defense of the castle of Lismore, and displayed his courage and ability on many occasions in the service of Charles I.; on the cessation of whose authority he acted under the parliamentary commissioners in Ireland. When the king was put to death he retired for a while from public life; but being courted by Cromwell, he accepted a commission from him, and assisted him materially in reducing the Irish to subjection. He served his new master with zeal and fidelity, and few persons were more trusted or distinguished by him. Oliver becoming Protector, made Lord Broghill one of his privy-council and a member of his House of Lords. In 1656 he sent him to Scotland, with a commission to govern there, with absolute authority for one year; and his conduct was such as proved satisfactory both to the Scots and the Protector. On the death of Cromwell, becoming aware of the approaching restoration of regal power, he exerted himself with such dexterity and success in promoting it as to obtain much credit for his conduct.

Charles II. rewarded him with the title of Earl of Orrery, and he was appointed one of the lords justices for Ireland.

Boyle, Virginia Frazer, American novelist: b. Chattanooga, Tenn. She was the daughter of Charles Frazer, a Confederate officer, and married Thomas R. Boyle, a lawyer of Memphis. She has published: 'Brokenburne'; 'Devil Tales' (1900); and has written extensively for periodicals.

Boyle Lectures, a series of discourses so named from the founder, Robert Boyle (q.v.), who left a bequest amounting to $250 annually for this purpose, the theme of the lectures to be Christian apologetics. The first series was given in 1692 by Richard Bentley. Among Boyle lecturers whose discourses have been published since 1860 are: J. D. Maurice, C. Merivale, E. H. Plumptre, J. A. Hessey, and H. Wace. The lectures of this course are given annually in a series of eight at the Church of St.-Mary-le-Bow, London.

Boyle's Fuming Liquor, so called from having been invented by Robert Boyle (q.v.), a fetid, yellow liquid, obtained by distilling sal ammoniac with sulphur and lime. It is sometimes used in medicine under the name of *liquor fumans boylii.*

Boyle's Law. See GAS ILLUMINATION.

Boylston, Zabdiel, American physician: b. Brookline, Mass., 1680; d. Boston, 1 March 1766. He studied medicine, settled in Boston, and acquired a prosperous practice. In spite of the almost unanimous opposition of the medical profession and part of the public, he introduced the practice of inoculation for smallpox, having become a firm believer in it. Out of 286 persons inoculated in 1721–2 only six died, and he had the satisfaction of seeing the practice become general in New England long before it became so in England. He visited England in 1725 and was elected a Fellow of the Royal Society. Besides some papers published in the Transactions of that Society he wrote: 'Historical Account of the Smallpox Inoculated in New England. Upon All Sorts of Persons, Whites, Blacks, and of all Ages and Constitutions' (2d ed. 8vo London 1726; reprinted, Boston, 1730).

Boyne, boin, a river of Ireland, which rises in the Bog of Allen, County Kildare, and flows northeast through Meath to Drogheda, below which it enters the Irish Sea. It is navigable for barges up to Navan. The Boyne will ever be memorable in English history for the important victory gained on its banks about three miles above Drogheda, 1 July 1690, by the forces under the command of William III., over those of James II. Though James' personal courage was beyond all question, he, on this occasion, allowed the prudence of the soldier to outweigh the impulses of the soldier. Of his troops 1,500 were killed and wounded, while William lost barely 500 men. In 1736 an obelisk, 150 feet high, was erected at Oldbridge, on the site of the battlefield, in commemoration of this victory. See ORANGE-MEN.

Boynton, Edward Carlisle, American soldier: b. Vermont, about 1825; d. Newburg, N. Y., 13 May 1893. He was graduated from the Military Academy at West Point, N. Y.,

entered the artillery service, and in the war with Mexico was wounded at the battle of Cherubusco. He was professor of chemistry at West Point, 1848–55, and in the University of Mississippi, 1858–61. He wrote a 'History of West Point' (1863); and a 'History of the United States Navy.'

Boynton, Henry Van Ness, American army officer: b. West Stockbridge, Mass., 22 July 1835; d. Atlantic City, N. J., 3 June 1905. He was graduated from Kentucky Military Institute in 1858; and was retained in the faculty of that institution. On the outbreak of the Civil War he resigned his office, and 27 July 1861 was commissioned major in the 35th Ohio Volunteers; was made lieutenant-colonel, 19 July 1863; and commanded the regiment at the engagement of Missionary Ridge, where he was severely wounded. He also commanded at Buzzard's Roost, and was brevetted brigadier-general for gallantry at Chickamauga and Chattanooga. After the war he became a newspaper correspondent. He published 'Sherman's Historical Raid' or 'The Memoirs in the Light of the Record, a Review Based upon Compilations from the Files of the War Office' (1875). He headed the opposition in 1887 to President Cleveland's order for the return of the Confederate battle flags. In 1894 he received a Congressional Medal of Honor for distinguished bravery at Missionary Ridge, and in 1898 was appointed a brigadier-general of volunteers for the war with Spain, and was in command of Camp Thomas, Chickamauga, after 15 August. He became chairman of the Chickamauga and Chattanooga National Military Park Commission and president of the board of education of the District of Columbia.

Boy's Clubs, organizations in which boys constitute the membership. Among clubs formed by boys on their own initiation, those for games and athletics seem to predominate very largely. Clubs for hunting, fighting, etc., are also popular. Sometimes the organizations have a distinctly literary or musical character and sometimes they are chiefly social in their nature. Numbers of clubs are formed for industrial purposes, but judging from statistics secret societies do not meet with as great a degree of favor as would naturally be supposed. These societies for boys are organized by adults; the aims are in general to keep boys from bad surroundings and stimulate them to nobler ideals of life, to refine their taste and encourage them in habits of thrift, industry, and study. Clubs in large cities sometimes have hundreds of members and provide fine buildings, in which opportunity is offered for a variety of activities ranging from manual training and other forms of instruction to social entertainment. The religious interests of the boys are also cared for in various ways. The clubs connected with social settlements are often small, thus affording a better opportunity for reaching the boys personally, an end difficult of achievement in societies with large membership. See Forbush, 'How to Keep Boys' (1900); Forbush, 'The Boy Problem' (1901); Newman, 'The Boys' Club in Theory and Practice' (1900).

Boy'ton, Paul, Irish-American swimmer: b. Dublin, 29 June 1848. He served in the United States navy, 1863–5, and was connected with the United States life-saving service, 1867–9. He invented a rubber life-preserving suit, in which, in 1874, he leaped from a vessel off the coast of Ireland, and, after remaining seven hours in the water, reached land safely. On 28 May 1875 he crossed the English Channel in this suit, swimming across in 24 hours. In 1876 he made the run from the Bayou Goula to New Orleans, La., 100 miles, in 24 hours. In May, the same year, he descended the Danube from Linz to Budapest, 460 miles, in six days. Later he went from Oil City, Pa., to the Gulf of Mexico, 2,342 miles, in 80 days, being exposed at first to great cold and later to extreme heat. In November 1879, he descended the Connecticut River from Canada to Long Island Sound. On 17 Sept. 1881, he started from Cedar Creek, Mont., to swim to St. Louis, Mo., and accomplished the long journey, 3,580 miles, 20 November. In 1888 he made a voyage down the Ohio River. He published an account of his adventures under the title, 'Roughing It' (1886).

Boz, bŏz, a pseudonym used by Charles Dickens in the publication of 'Sketches by Boz.' That the pronunciation of this name now in vogue is not correct is shown by Dickens' explanation of its origin. A younger brother of the author had in childhood received from the latter the nickname Moses, "which being facetiously pronounced through the nose became Bŏses, and being shortened became Bŏz."

Bozeman, bŏz'măn, Mont., a city and county-seat of Gallatin County, on the Northern P. R.R., in the midst of a region of valuable ores, such as gold, silver, coal, and iron. Its industries are breweries, flour and lumber mills, brickyards, stone quarries, and the like, and it contains the State College of Agriculture and Mechanic Arts, opened in 1893. Pop. (1900) 3,419.

Bozen, a town of the Austrian Tyrol, 32 miles northeast of Trent; situated in a hilly region at the junction of the Talfer and Eisak, and on the Brenner Railway. The situation of the town in relation to Germany, Switzerland, and Italy, makes it an important trade centre. There are four annual fairs; the canning of fruit and vegetables is carried on, and manufactures of silk and linen. Among the public buildings are a Gothic church, castle, monastery, and gymnasium. Pop. (1900) 13,632.

Bozman, bŏz'măn, John Leeds, American historian and jurist: b. Talbot County, Md., 25 Aug. 1757; d. there, 23 April 1823. He studied law in London, and afterward practised that profession in his native State, where for several years he acted as deputy attorney-general. His legal reputation, however, rests upon the various law tracts which he published from time to time, as legal questions arose in the courts. He wrote a 'Historical and Philosophical Sketch of the Prime Causes of the Revolutionary War,' in which he praised Washington, and condemned Franklin; but it was suppressed. During the administration of Washington and the elder Adams, he wrote much in the journals of the day, and at a later period in Dennie's 'Portfolio.' In 1822 he published at Washington an essay on the colonization society, in which he discussed the question of the origin of races. His literary reputation

chiefly rests on his 'History of Maryland, from the Earliest Settlement in 1633, to the Restoration in 1660,' a posthumous work, published in 1836, under the auspices of the general assembly of that State.

Boz'rah, bŏz'ra, an ancient city of Palestine, east of the Jordan, and about 80 miles south of Damascus. It was the capital of Og, king of Bashan, and subsequently belonged to the tribe of Manasseh. Early in the Christian era, it became a flourishing place, and was long a great emporium of trade. It is now a scene of ruins.

Bozzaris, Marcos, mär'cŏs bŏ'tsa̤-rĕs, a hero of the Greek war of Independence against the Turks: b. Suli, in .Epirus, about 1790; d. Missolonghi, 1823. He was descended from a Suliote family renowned for its bravery, and after the fall of Suli retired to the Ionian Islands, from whence he made a vain attempt to deliver his native country. He then entered an Albanian regiment in the French service, and in 1813 became a member of the Hetæria, a society formed for national regeneration. In 1820, when the Turks were carrying on war against Ali Pasha, the latter sought aid from the exiled Suliotes, and Marcos Bozzaris returned to Epirus. On the outbreak of the war of independence he at once joined the Greek cause, and distinguished himself as much by his patriotism and disinterestedness as by his military skill and personal bravery. In 1822 he took part in the war which was going on in western Greece, and acquired special renown by his defense of Missolonghi. In the summer of 1823, when he held the command-in-chief of the Greek forces in that port, he was dangerously wounded at a night attack on the camp of the Pasha of Scutari, near Karpenisi, and died soon after. His deeds are still celebrated by the Greeks in many popular songs. Through Halleck's spirited poem, 'Marco Bozaris,' his name and fame have been made familiar to several generations of American school boys.

Brabançonne, bra̤-bäṅ-sŭn, the national song of the Belgians during the revolution of 1830, composed by Jenneval, at that time an actor at the theatre of Brussels, and set to music by Campenhout. Every verse of the song ends with the refrain:

> "La mitraille a brisé l'orange
> Sur l'arbre de la liberté."

Brabançons, bra̤-bäṅ-sôṅ, a class of adventurers and lawless soldiers in the Middle Ages, ready to fight for pay on either side and in any quarter. They derive their name from Brabant, the chief nursery of these troops, and were particularly notorious in France in the 12th century.

Brabant, brä'bănt, or bra̤-bänt', the central district of the lowlands of Holland and Belgium, extending over an area of 4,341 square miles, from the left bank of the Waal to the sources of the Dyle, and from the Meuse and the plains of Limburg to the lower Scheldt. In the Middle Ages it formed a separate independent duchy, called Lower Lorraine. It is divided at present between the kingdoms of Holland and Belgium, into three provinces: (1) Dutch or North Brabant, with an area of 1,980 square miles; (2) the Belgian province of Antwerp, with an area of 1,093 square miles; (3) the Belgian province of South Brabant, with an area of 1,268 square miles. The country is comprehended in a plain, gently sloping to the northwest, occupied in the north by heathy and marshy tracts, and in the south passing into the gentle rising ground which forms the first ascent of the forest of Ardennes. It is copiously watered by the Meuse in the north and the Scheldt in the south, in the former of which the internal transit is furthered by means of canals, among others the South William and the Breda canals, and in the latter by railways, which have their point of union at Mechlin. Under the influence of a northerly, indeed, and moist, but in general healthful and mild climate, the great fertility of the soil renders agriculture and the raising of cattle the principal and most profitable employment of the inhabitants. With this is associated the general diffusion of an active industry, which supports an extensive trade, consisting chiefly of lace, cotton, woolen, and leather goods.

Through Cæsar's campaigns the Romans became acquainted with the inhabitants of Brabant as a mixed race of Germans and Celts. The Menapians, particularly, inhabiting the country between the Rhine, the Meuse, and the Scheldt, made, as the most powerful and warlike among the various tribes, a gallant though ultimately ineffectual resistance to the Roman arms, by whose conquests this portion of Lower Germany was incorporated with the province of Gallia Belgica. In the 5th century the Franks gained possession of Brabant, which in the sixth was, at the partition of the Frank kingdom, assigned to the primitive country of Austrasia; in the 9th century it was united to Lorraine; and on the division of the latter, in 870, became the property of France, from which, however, in the commencement of the 10th century, it was transferred by Henry I. again to Lorraine; in 959 to Lower Lorraine, and thus to Germany. In the beginning of the 11th century it was separated from Lorraine, on Duke Otho, the son of Charles the Fat, who had been invested by the Emperor Otho with Lower Lorraine, dying childless in 1005. After this several Counts of Ardennes and Godfrey of Bouillon possessed it till 1076; the Emperor Henry V. mortgaged it to Godfrey the Bearded, of the family of the Counts of Louvain and Brussels, whose house reigned over Brabant to the middle of the 14th century. As early as 1190 we find the title of Duke of Brabant, in which the former title of Duke of Lower Lorraine or Lothier was gradually absorbed. Under the government of its own dukes Brabant gained rapidly in power and independence, but was engaged in numerous contests with its neighbors, and shifted much in its leanings between Germany and France. Of the six dukes of Brabant, Henry I., II., and III., and John I., II., and III., there are more especially to be mentioned John I., who, by the celebrated battle of Wöringen (1288), united Limburg to Brabant, and is also renowned in Germany as a minnesinger or troubadour, and John III., who, in 1349, received from the Emperor Charles IV. the important privilege of a free judicature, under the name of the Brabantine Golden Bull, in consequence of which his subjects ceased to be amenable to any foreign jurisdiction. With John III. the male heirs of the family of the Counts of Louvain became extinct in 1355, and, by the bequest of his daughter, Joanna, who reigned till 1406, married Wenceslaus of Luxemburg, Brabant came into the possession of the house of Burgundy, and in the first instance to Antony of Burgundy, Joanna's grand-nephew, and second son of Philip the Bold. On Antony's death at the battle of Agincourt, in 1415, and his two successors, his son, John IV., and his brother, Philip, Count of St. Pol, dying childless respectively in 1427 and 1430, Brabant, as the inheritance of Philip the Good, became formally incorporated with the dominions of the house of Burgundy. In this state, however, it did not long continue, and, by the marriage of Mary of Burgundy with the Emperor Maximilian, was transferred to the house of Austria, and subsequently to the Emperor Charles V., who abdicated in favor of his son, Philip II., of Spain. The persecuting edict of the latter, and the Duke of Alva's cruelties, excited a revolt in Brabant, but it was only the northern portion (Hertogenbosch) which succeeded in asserting its independence, and in 1648 was incorporated with the United Provinces under the name of the Generality Territory, while South Brabant remained till 1714 in the possession of the Spaniards. On the extinction of the Spanish-Austrian line in the latter year, Brabant, with the other southern provinces of the Netherlands, reverted to the imperial house of Austria, which, however, was unable long to retain it in peace. On a violent contest breaking out under the Emperor Joseph II., as to the explanation of the provincial privileges which Brabant possessed under the Joyeuse Entrée (q.v.), and the consequent dismissal of the assembly of the states of Brabant and Limburg, the Brabantines assembled of their own authority, and boldly pronounced the separation of Brabant from the supremacy of the house of Austria. Leopold II. settled the dispute after Joseph's death by granting their ancient privileges to the people of Brabant. See BELGIUM.

Bra′bourne, Edward Huggessen Knatch-bull-Huggessen, Lord, English juvenile story writer: b. Mersham Hatch, Kent, 29 April 1829; d. 6 Feb. 1893. His literary fame is due mostly to his stories for children, including: 'Crackers for Christmas' (1870); 'Moonshine' (1871); 'Stories for My Children' (1869); 'Tales at Tea Time' (1872); 'Queer Folk' (1873); 'River Legends' (1874); 'Uncle Joe's Stories' (1878); 'Friends from Fairyland' (1885). He also published 'The Truth About the Transvaal' (1881), and edited the 'Letters of Jane Austen,' his great-aunt (1885).

Braccio da Montone, Andrea, än-drä′-a brä′chō-da-mŏn-tō′nĕ, Italian captain: b. Perugia, of the illustrious family of the Fortebracci, 1368; d. 1424. He early embraced the profession of arms, and entered the service of Ladislas, king of Naples, under the promise that he, if successful, would make him master of Perugia; but when the Perugians, determined to keep out Braccio, offered to open their gates to Ladislas, if he would retain it for himself, he broke faith with Braccio, and accepted their terms. Braccio next served under Florence, afterward attaching himself to

Pope John XXIII., who, on repairing to the council of Constance, where he was deposed, intrusted Braccio with the defense of Bologna. Ladislas being now dead, and the Church without a head, Braccio saw that the moment for which he had waited had arrived; and allowing the Bolognese to redeem their liberty by a money payment, suddenly, in 1416, pounced on Perugia. The Perugians vainly endeavored to resist, and saw themselves, compelled to receive Braccio as their lord. His rule, though firm and occasionally severe, was milder than might have been anticipated; and he soon showed that his wisdom as a statesman was not less than his ability as a captain. Though Braccio had now gained the great object of his life, ambition led him to attempt the conquest of Rome, and he gained several advantages over Sforza, who had long been his rival. Ultimately, however, the new Pope, Martin V., proved more than a match for him, and Braccio, defeated and severely wounded, took the disgrace seriously and would neither take food nor allow his wounds to be examined.

Bracciolini, **Poggio Giovanni Francesco**, pŏdg'ō brä-chō-lē'ē, Italian classical scholar: b. Terra Nuova, near Arezzo, 11 Feb. 1380; d. Florence, 30 Oct. 1459. In 1416 he undertook the laborious task of searching the ancient monasteries for manuscripts; and succeeded in recovering seven orations of Cicero, and a great number of other classical writings. Having impoverished himself in these researches, he accepted an invitation of Cardinal Beaufort to go to England, but, disappointed in his hopes of preferment, and in the literary atmosphere of the country, returned to Italy in 1421, and became apostolic secretary to Martin V. and to several succeeding popes, having served not less than eight popes in the same capacity. On the appearance of the plague at Rome in 1450, he withdrew to Florence, where he was chosen chancellor three years afterward. His 'History of Florence' (translated by his son Jacopo, from Latin into Italian) comprises the period from 1350 to 1455. Among his most finished productions is his 'Dialogue on Nobility.' His writings are on moral, philosophical, and controversial subjects, and comprise many translations, orations, and letters, the latter deriving peculiar interest from their reference to contemporary life. His works have not yet been properly collected, the Basel edition of 1538 being considered imperfect. His biography, by Rev. William Shepherd (1802), was translated into Italian, German, and French.

Brace, **Charles Loring**, American author and philanthropist: b. Litchfield, Conn., 19 June 1826; d. Campier, Switzerland, 11 Aug. 1890. He graduated at Yale in 1846, and studied theology, but held no pastorate. He devoted himself to philanthropy in New York, and lectured, wrote, and worked to enlist aid for the children of the poor. His books include: 'Hungary in 1851' (New York 1852); 'Home Life in Germany' (1853); 'The Norse Folk' (1857); 'Short Sermons to Newsboys' (1861); 'The Dangerous Classes of New York and Twenty Years' Work Among Them' (1872, 3d ed. 1880); 'Free Trade as Promoting Peace and Good Will Among Men' (1879); 'Gesta Christi' (1883), a review of the achievements of Christianity from the earliest days in bettering the moral and social condition of the world; and 'To the Unknown God' (1889).

Brace, **De Witt Bristol**, American physicist: b. Wilson, N. Y., 1859. He graduated at Boston University, 1881; took post-graduate courses at Johns Hopkins, and received his degree of Ph.D., from the University of Berlin, Germany. Since 1887 he has been professor of physics at the University of Nebraska, and has made a special study of radiation and optics. He has written: 'Laws of Radiation and Absorption' (1901).

Brace, **Julia**, American blind deaf-mute: b. Newington, Conn., 13 June, 1806; d. Bloomington, Conn., 12 Aug. 1884. She lost both sight and hearing at the age of four years and five months, and soon forgot the few words she had learned to speak. At the age of 18 she entered the American asylum for the deaf and dumb at Hartford, then under the care of the Rev. Dr. Gallaudet, in which institution she remained for the greater part of her life. Never prepossessing in her appearance, and at her admission, in consequence of over-indulgence, selfish, sullen, and exacting, her case was one of great difficulty. The existence of the triple infirmity under which she labored was hardly known at that time, and she was regarded, consequently, as a psychological curiosity. As compared with some other blind deaf-mutes, whose history has been recorded within a few years past, she did not seem possessed of any extraordinary abilities, and, but for her misfortune, would probably have passed as a very ordinary woman. In all that concerned the outward and physical nature she manifested much intelligence. She sewed very well, threading her needle readily with her fingers and tongue; was very neat and particular in her dress, and exhibited marked habits of order. She possessed great tenacity of memory and nice powers of discrimination. She kept herself apprised of the progress of time, days, weeks, and months, but in her intellectual education never made much progress. Limited as was her knowledge of the alphabet of religion, she was not wanting in manifestations of the moral sense. She appeared to have a perception of right and wrong, and while tenacious of her own rights, did not knowingly invade those of others.

Brace, a beam or bar employed to stiffen a framed structure. In a roof or bridge truss this bar is placed in an inclined position and serves to bind together the principal members. The tool for holding a bit, which carpenters employ in boring, is called a brace, while in nautical phraseology braces are ropes fastened to the yard-arms by means of which sails are shifted horizontally around the masts to catch a particular breeze. In all forms of construction a brace supports by resistance to compression and is thus opposed to a tie or strut which furnishes support by resistance to tension.

Bracebridge Hall, a series of studies of English life by Washington Irving, published in 1822 with the pseudonym 'Geoffrey Crayon. Gent.'

Bracegirdle, **Anne**, English actress: b. about 1663; d. London, 1748. She appeared on the stage as a child in 'The Orphan,' and from 1688 appeared in many popular plays of that time, including several tragic roles, although her forte seems to have been comedy. She was noted for her beauty and numbered adorers by hundreds. She left the stage in 1707. See Russell, 'Representative Actors' (1875); Baker, 'English Actors' (1879).

Bracelet, an ornament usually worn on the wrist, the use of which extends from the most ancient times down to the present, and belongs to all countries, civilized as well as uncivilized. The word has come to us from the French and is ultimately derived from *brachium*, the Latin word for the arm. Bracelets were in use in Egypt at a very remote period. They were of different colors, painted on them in enamel in very bright as well as very delicate shades. They were also then as now frequently made of gold, enchased with various kinds of precious stones. They were not always worn, as with us, on the wrist, but frequently on the upper part of the arm. The ancient Medes and Persians were well known to be extremely fond of this method of adorning themselves; and in the Bible the bracelet is frequently mentioned as an ornament in use among the Jews, both men and women. Among the ancient Greeks, in historical times, bracelets do not appear to have been worn by the men; but, on the other hand, they were worn by the Greek ladies, made of every variety of material, and in every possible form. A preference was generally given to the spiral form, and a bracelet of this kind is described by Homer in the Iliad. Very frequently the spiral bracelets were made to assume the appearance of snakes, which went round the arm twice or thrice, or even a greater number of times. Among the ancient Italian tribes bracelets were also an ornament of the men. The Sabines often wore very heavy ones on the left arm. Among the Romans it was a frequent practice for a general to bestow bracelets on soldiers who had distinguished themselves by their valor. Roman ladies of high rank frequently wore them both on the wrist and on the upper arm. The Arabs and the Orientals generally use them, chiefly as an ornament for women. Among the ancient heathen Germanic tribes they formed the chief and almost only ornament, as is shown by their being so often found in old graves. The men seem to have used them even more than the women, for bracelets have been found in dozens on the arms of the former. The spiral was the favorite form with the ancient Germans as with the ancient Greeks.

Brachial (brā'kĭ-ăl) **Artery.** See ARTERIES.

Brachial Plexus. See NERVES.

Brachiopods, or Brachiopoda, brăk'-ĭ-ō-pŏds, the class of shelled worms, formerly placed among mollusks. The class is named *Brachiopoda* from the feet-like arms, fringed with tentacles, coiled up within the shell, and which correspond to the lophophore of the Polyzoa and the crown of tentacles of the Sabella-like worms. The shell, which lives attached to rocks, is in shape somewhat like an ancient Roman lamp, the ventral and larger valve, being perforated at the base for the passage through it of a peduncle by which the animal is attached to rocks. The shell is secreted by the skin (ectoderm), and is composed of carbonate (Terebratulina) or largely (Lingula) of phosphate of lime.

The body of Brachiopods is divided into two parts, the anterior or thoracic, comprising the main body-cavity in which the arms and viscera are contained, and the caudal portion, that is, the peduncle. The part of the body in which the viscera lodge is rather small in proportion to the entire animal, the interior of the shell being lined with two broad lobes, the free edges of which are thickened and bear setæ, as seen distinctly in Lingula. The body-cavity is closed anteriorly by a membrane which separates it from the space in which the arms are coiled up. The pallial chamber is situated between the two lobes of the mantle (*pallium*) and in front of the membrane forming the anterior wall of the body-cavity. In the middle of this pallial chamber the mouth opens, bounded on each side by the base of the arms. The latter arise from a cartilaginous base, and bear ciliated tentacles, much as in the worm Sabella. In Lingula, Diseina, and Rhynchonella, they are developed, in a closely wound spiral, as in the genuine worms (Amphitrite). In Lingula the arms can be partially unwound, while in Rhynchonella they can not only be unwound but protruded from the pallial chamber. In many recent and fossil forms the arms are supported by loop-like solid processes of the dorsal valve of the shell, but when these processes are present the arms cannot be protruded beyond the shell. The tentacles or cirri on the arms are used to convey to the mouth particles of food, and they also are respiratory in function, there being a rapid circulation of blood in each tentacle, which is hollow, communicating with the blood-sinus or hollow in each arm, the sinus ending in a sac on each side of the mouth.

The digestive system consists of a mouth, œsophagus, stomach, with a liver-mass on each side, and an intestine. The mouth is bordered by two membranous, highly sensitive and movable lips. The stomach is a simple dilatation of the alimentary canal, into which empty the short ducts of the liver, which is composed of masses of cæca. The liver originally arises as two diverticula or offshoots of the stomach. The short intestine ends in a blind sac or in a vent, and is, with the stomach, freely suspended in the perivisceral cavity by delicate membranes springing from the walls of the body.

The nervous system consists of two small ganglia above, and an infracœsophageal pair of larger ganglia, and there are two elongated ganglia behind the arms, from which nerves are given off to the dorsal or anterior lobe of the mantle.

The larva is top-shaped (trochosphere) and is quite active, swimming rapidly about in every direction.

While in their development the *Brachiopoda* recall the larvæ of the true worms; they resemble the adult worms in the general arrangement of the arms and viscera, though they lack the highly developed nervous system of the Annelids, as well as a vascular system, while the body is not jointed. On the other hand they are closely related to the Polyzoa, and it seems probable that the Brachiopods and Polyzoa were derived from common low vermian ancestors, while the true Annelids probably sprang independently from a higher ancestry. They are also a generalized type, having some molluscan features, such as a solid shell, though having nothing homologous with the foot, the shell-gland or odontophore of mollusks.

In accordance with the fact that the Brachiopods are a generalized type of worms, the species have a high antiquity, and the type is remarkably persistent. The Lingula of our shores (*Glottidia pyramidata*) lives buried in the sand, where it forms tubes of sand around the peduncle, just below low-water mark from Chesapeake Bay to Florida. It has remarkable vitality, not only withstanding the changes of temperature and exposure to death from various other causes, but will bear transportation to other countries in sea-water, that has been unchanged. Living lingulæ have been carried from Japan to Boston, Mass., the water in the small glass jar containing the specimens having been changed but twice in four months. The living species of this cosmopolitan genus differ but slightly from those occurring in the lowest fossiliferous strata. Between 80 and 90 living species are known, most of them living, except Lingula, which is tropical, in the temperate or arctic seas, while nearly 2,000 fossil species are known. The type attained its maximum in the Silurian age, and in Palæozoic times a few species, as *Atrypa reticularis*, extended through an entire system of rocks and inhabited the seas of both hemispheres.

Consult Littel-Eastman, 'Text-book of Palæontology' (New York 1900).

Bracht, bräät, Felix Prosper Eugen, German artist, b. Morges, Switzerland, 1842. He is best known as a landscape artist. He studied at Carlsruhe and Düsseldorf, and in 1882 was appointed a professor in the Berlin Academy. Among celebrated paintings by him are 'Stormy Evening on Rügen'; 'Moonlight Night in the Desert'; 'Nightfall on the Dead Sea.' The last named work, now in the National Gallery of Berlin, is considered his best.

Brachvogel, Emil, ä'mĕl braн'fō-gĕl, German novelist and dramatist: b. Breslau, 1824; d. 1878. He is best known by his drama, 'Narcisse' (1857), which attained many editions and was translated into various European tongues. 'Beaumarchais' (1865); 'Benoni' (1860); and 'Glencarty' (1872).

Brachyura, brăk-ĭ-ū'ra, a sub-order of decapodous crustaceans, containing those families in which the abdomen is converted into a short jointed tail folding closely under the breast. The common crab is a familiar example of this group. See CRUSTACEA.

Brack'en (*Pterisaquilina*), a well-known species of polypodiaceous fern, forming the type of the sub-family *Pterideæ.* It has a black, creeping rhizome, from which are sent up large, handsome bipinnate fronds. The sori are arranged along the margins of the pinnules, and are covered by a false indusium formed of the reflexed margin. The bracken or brake is very common in Great Britain where it frequently covers large extents of country. Its root-stock was at one time used for food, but it is neither palatable nor nutritious; that of a New Zealand species (*P. esculenta*) is better suited for this purpose. Various medicinal virtues have been at one time or another ascribed to it, but it is not now used in medicine. The ash produced by burning the fronds has been employed in making soap. Other species are met with in various parts of the world. In verse the word is often loosely employed to indicate ferns in general.

Brack'enbury, Charles Booth, English soldier and military writer: b. Bayswater, Middlesex, 7 Nov. 1831. He served in the Crimean war in 1855; accompanied the Prussian army in the war with Austria (1866), and the Franco-Prussian war (1870-71), and was with the Russian army in the Russo-Turkish war (1877-8). His works include 'European Armaments' (1867); 'The Winter Campaign of Prince Frederick Charles in 1870-71'; 'Reforms of the French Army' (1874), etc.

Brackenbury, Sir Henry, English soldier: b. Bolingbroke, Lincolnshire, September 1837. He entered the Royal Artillery in 1856, served in the central Indian, Ashanti and Zulu campaigns and was made lieutenant-general in 1888, and director-general at the war office in 1899. He has published 'Fanti and Ashanti' (1873); 'Narrative of the Ashanti War' (1874); 'The River Column' (1885).

Brack'enridge, Henry Marie, American author: b. Pittsburg, Pa., 11 May 1786; d. there 18 Jan., 1871. He was educated by his father, H. H. Brackenridge (q.v.) and admitted to the bar 1806. In 1811 he descended the Mississippi River in a "keel-boat" to New Orleans, and was soon appointed deputy attorney-general for the then territory of Orleans, becoming district judge in 1812. In 1817 he was secretary to the commission sent to the South American republics, and in 1821 was appointed U. S. judge for the western district of Florida, holding it until he removed to Pittsburg in 1832. His knowledge of the French and Spanish languages and laws made him of considerable service to the government in all affairs connected with the Louisiana and Florida purchases. He wrote 'Views of Louisiana in 1810' (1812); 'Letter to Mr. Monroe. By an American'; 'Voyage to South America in 1817-18' (1818); 'History of the Late War [1812] between the United States and Great Britain'; 'Recollections of Persons and Places in the West' (1834); 'Essays on Trusts and Trustees' (1842); 'History of the Western Insurrection' (1859), a vindication of his father's share in that affair.

Brackenridge, Hugh Henry, American jurist: b. near Campbelton, Scotland, 1748; d. Carlisle, Pa., 25 June 1816. He came with his father to the United States at the age of five, and was graduated form Princeton in 1771. During the American Revolution he was a chaplain in the army. After being admitted to the bar he removed to Pittsburg, became prominent in his profession, and during the "Whisky Insurrection" (1794) was influential in bringing about a settlement between the government and the malcontents. In 1799 he was appointed to the supreme bench of Pennsylvania. A man of literary tastes, he wrote a number of pieces much thought of in their day. At his graduation he wrote (with Philip Freneau) a poetical dialogue 'The Rising Glory of America.' Other works by him are 'Incidents of the Insurrection in Western Pennsylvania' (1795); 'Law Miscellanies' (1814); 'Modern Chivalry, or the Adventures of Captain Farrago and Teague O'Regan, His Servant,' a political satire and his best work (1st Pt. 1796; 2d, 1806).

Bracket, a short piece or combination of pieces, generally more or less triangular in outline, projecting from a wall or other surface. They may be either of an ornamental order, as when designed to support a statue, a bust, or such like, or plain forms of carpentry, such as support shelves, etc. Brackets may also be used in connection with machinery, being attached to walls, beams, etc., to sustain a line of shafting.

Brack'ett, Anna Callender, American educator: b. Boston, 21 May 1836. She taught in various normal schools, being the first woman principal of such an institution, and was principal of a private school for girls in New York for 20 years. She has published 'Education of American Girls' (1874); 'Philosophy of Education,' from the German (1886); 'Technique of Rest' (1892); 'Woman and the Higher Education' (1893).

Brackett, Frank Parkhurst, American mathematician: b. Provincetown, Mass., 1865. He graduated at Dartmouth College in 1887, and since 1890 has been professor of mathematics and astronomy at Pomona College, Claremont, California. He has written several important mathematical and meteorological papers.

Brackett, Gustavus B., American pomologist: b. Unity, Maine, 24 March 1827. He served in the Civil War, and, at its close, took up the study of horticulture and pomology. He served as an expert at the Paris Exposition (1878) and the Chicago World's Fair (1893), after which he became chief of the Division of Pomology in the United States Department of Agriculture.

Brackett, John Quincy Adams, American lawyer: b. Bradford, N. H., 8 June 1842. After studying law at the Harvard Law School he began the practice of his profession in Boston. He sat for several terms in the Massachusetts legislature (1877–82 and 1884–7), being speaker of the House (1885–7); was lieutenant-governor of the State (1887–90), and governor of Massachusetts (1890–91).

Bracquemond, Joseph Felix, zhō-zĕf fā-lĕks brạk-môṅ, French artist and engraver: b. Paris, 1833. He first exhibited in the Salon of 1852 and his etchings and reproductions of noted masters speedily brought him into notice. His portraits are especially prized and as an etcher he is represented by over 800 plates. He has invented a new method of china decoration and has done much work for the porcelain establishments at Limoges.

Bract, a leaf, from the axil of which a flower or flower-stalk develops, and thus distinguished from the ordinary leaf, from the axil of which the leaf-bud proceeds. Bracts may thus be entirely similar to the ordinary leaves of a plant, in which case they are called leafy bracts; but very commonly they are somewhat changed in form, and although they may be sometimes divided, they are for the most part entire, even when the ordinary leaves are divided. In some cases they are so much changed in form as to be mere scales or threads, and sometimes they are not developed at all, in which case the inflorescence is said to be ebracteate. Owing to the different ways in which the bract appears, it may in some plants be con-

founded with the calyx, in others with the corolla. When the flowers of a plant are sessile, the bracts are often applied closely to the calyx, and are thus apt to be confounded with it; and when the bracts are colored, they are apt to be mistaken for parts of the corolla. When the inflorescence of a plant is branching, subordinate flower-stalks proceeding from one main flower-stalk, bracts are often seen at the base of the former, and these are called bracteoles. A spathe is a kind of large bract.

Brac'teates, thin coins of gold or silver, with irregular figures on them, stamped upon one surface only, so that the impression appears raised on one side, while on the other it appears hollow. They were largely circulated under Otho I., emperor of Germany, and derive their name from *bractea,* signifying leaf of gold or other metal. They are of importance as illustrating history. Bracteated coins, or *bracteati nummi,* is a term used to signify coins or medals covered over with a thin plate of some richer metal. They were usually made of iron, copper, or brass, plated over and edged with gold or silver leaf.

Brac'ton, Henry de, one of the earliest writers on English law, flourished in the 13th century. He studied civil and canon law at Oxford, and about the year 1244, Henry III. made him one of his judges itinerant. Some writers say that he was afterward chief-justice of England; but his fame at present is derived from his legal treatise entitled 'De Legibus et Consuetudinibus Angliæ,' first printed in 1569 (folio). The quarto edition of 1640 was merely a reprint of the first. In 1878–83 Sir Travers Twiss issued a. recension and translation in six volumes. See Scrutton, 'Influence of the Roman Law on the Law of England' (1885).

Brad'bury, William Batchelder, American musician: b. York, Me., 6 Oct. 1816; d. Montclair, N. J., 7 Jan. 1868. In 1840 he began teaching in New York and Brooklyn. In 1847–8 he went to Europe, where he pursued musical studies under Hauptmann and others. He is best known as the composer and publisher of musical collections for schools and choirs, 59 separate works being credited to him. His most important works are 'Young Choir' (1841); 'Flora's Festival' (1845); 'The Golden Chain' (1861); 'Pilgrim Song' (1863); 'The Golden Trio' (1864); 'The Shawm' (1864); 'The Jubilee' (1865); 'Temple Choir'; 'Fresh Laurels' (1867), his last work.

Braddock, Pa., a borough in Allegheny County; on the Monongahela river, and on the Pennsylvania, the Baltimore & O., and the Pittsburg & L. E. R.R.'s; 10 miles above Pittsburg. There are extensive blast furnaces and manufactories of steel rails, steel wire, pig-iron, cement, plaster, etc. The four banks and two trust companies have a combined capitalization of $1,250,000. Braddock has a Carnegie Free Library, a hospital, numerous churches, and public and high schools. The borough was first settled in 1795 on the site of Braddock's defeat and was incorporated in 1867. The government is vested in a burgess and a council of 12 members elected for three years. Pop. (1900) 15,654.

Brad'dock, Edward, British general: b. Perthshire, Scotland, about 1695; d. Great Meadows, Pa., 13 July 1755. Through his father, an officer in the Coldstream Guards, who rose to be a lieutenant-colonel there and major-general of the line, he became in 1710 an ensign in that body, the haughty *élite* of British troops; which had the Duke of Cumberland, captain-general of the whole army, for one of its colonels, men of rank for subalterns, and its very privates chosen by other bodies for commissioned officers. Appointed captain in 1736, he rose to lieutenant-colonel by service on the Continent 1742–5, including Cumberland's battle of Fontenoy in 1745, where the Coldstreams covered themselves with glory; and in 1754 was made major-general of the line, thus paralleling his father. In that year an expedition to destroy the French power in America was resolved on; and on 24 September Braddock was made generalissimo of all the forces there, beyond question as being the officer known to Cumberland who was best able to accomplish the task. But his experience made him overrate formal discipline, and underrate (not only in action but in expert counsel) both foes and allies who lacked it; he could not fully realize new dangers nor appreciate methods of meeting them; he was hot of temper, rough of speech, overbearing in argument, obstinate in opinion; and these, with the martinetism natural enough in an officer of 60 after 43 years of the Coldstreams, and which were not vital in a drilled service, fatally alienated those in the new land on whom he had to depend for safety. Yet he was quick to recognize ability, and warm in acknowledging it; he regarded Washington and Franklin, the former but 22, as the greatest men in the colonies; and when the royal order of 1754 ranking all colonial commissions below all English ones prevented Washington from joining him, he sent a handsome letter asking the latter to be one of his military family, and voluntarily promised to use his influence in securing him a regular English commission. Landing at Hampton Roads, Va., 20 Feb. 1755, he attempted to collect men and stores for his expedition against Fort Duquesne (Pittsburg), but was baffled for many weeks by the sloth, rapacity, and unpatriotic local factions of the colonies, who did their best to justify the contempt with which he heartily if injudiciously visited them. The lack of men, supplies, transportation, and money delayed the expedition to its ruin. He tried to secure a large body of Indians for scouts and allies, but only obtained 40 or 50. He let all but eight of them go through bad judgment, and disgusted those so greatly by his manners that one of them deserted, and the rest warned their friends against coming near. The famous Indian hunter, Capt. Jack, wished to join him, but Braddock refused unless he would conform to military discipline, which the old scout would not do. Finally the expedition started from Fort Cumberland (now Cumberland, Md.) the first week in June, with 2,150 men. The march was most toilsome and slow, involving cutting roads, bridging streams, making causeways, passing through swamps, etc.; and on the 18th, at Little Meadows, 1,200 picked men were chosen to continue the expedition, the rest being left behind under Dunbar. On the night of 4 July he halted two days about 25 miles from his destination, to wait the reports of his Indian scouts and convoy of provisions from Dunbar's camp—to his destruction but not to his blame. Reaching Turtle (now Rush) Creek the road

suddenly ended at a precipice impassable for artillery and wagons, and he decided to quit the ridge, where ambuscade was impossible, and make a double fording across an elbow of the Monongahela. Meantime the French commander, Contrecœur, had decided to withdraw without a blow, but a Capt. Beaujeu asked leave to take a detachment and resist the passage of the second ford, eight miles off. He was given about 200 white troops, and by a brilliant appeal on the morning of the 9th to the Indians, who at first hung back, obtained several hundred of them also. When he came in sight of the English, they had already crossed, and advanced so that both flanks would be exposed for some 200 yards to an enemy who occupied the deep ravines, thick with tangled forest growth and vines, that seamed the river bluff. Braddock's ruinous error was in not beating up ahead on his flanks, as Col. Sir Peter Halket urgently besought him to do the night before; thereby he marched straight into the worst of ambushes. Into these the Indians glided, while the white troops barred the English path in front; and the head of the advancing column went down under a storm of lead. Shaken for a moment, the vanguard moved against the concentric ring; and after another terrible discharge, returned it with a volley that swept away every enemy in sight, and struck Beaujeu and a dozen others dead. The Indians turned to fly; rallied by the other French officers, they returned to cover, and under their unerring fire the English advance broke and retreated; mixing with the rear in the narrow path, both became mingled in a mob which Braddock could not restore to order. Huddled into a 12-foot road, shut in by a forest alive with yells and filled with an invisible foe, they lost all sense or perception, and twice shot down bodies of their own men who had gained slight vantage points, taking their smoke for the enemy's. Fifty Virginians were thus slain at a blow. The regulars refused to charge, though Braddock, with four horses successively shot under him, and the other officers strove to hearten them to invade the wood; the provincials sought to fight Indian fashion behind trees and logs, but Braddock with furious threats and blows drove them back into rank again, where they fell in scores. Washington and Halket begged to have them allowed to leave the ranks, but Braddock still refused. The ammunition began to fail; the baggage was attacked; all Braddock's aides but Washington were shot down; three fourths of the officers, and three fifths of the entire army; and only then would the ill-judging but heroic Braddock give the signal for retreat. Shortly afterward Braddock received a ball through the lungs; not one of the English soldiery would stay to carry him off the field, but one English and two American officers took him from the field to a spot half a mile across the river. Here the dying hero tried to establish a camp for a rallying place, and to care for the wounded and wait for Washington's return from Dunbar; but although the French and Indians had not followed them across, the 100 English soldiers he had induced to stop there stole away again and fled. The officers with their commander marched on till 10 P.M. on the 10th, when they halted and met the convoy from Dunbar, Braddock never ceasing to give calm, skilful, and humane orders; on the 11th he reached

Dunbar's camp, where the news of the rout had set his soldiers also deserting and fleeing in wild panic. Giving up all hope of the expedition in any hands now, he had the stores destroyed to keep them from the enemy, save enough for a flying march; and the remnant of the army proceeded toward Great Meadows, where Braddock expired, leaving his favorite horse and body servant to Washington. Of 1,460 men in the battle, 456 were killed and 421 wounded; 63 out of 89 commissioned officers were killed or injured, and every field officer. The enemy's casualties were about 60. The entire borders were left defenseless and desolated by a fearful Indian war.

Brad'don, Mary Elizabeth (Mrs. Maxwell), English novelist: b. London, 1837, daughter of a solicitor there. She received her education at home, and early showed signs of literary power. After publishing some poems and tales, in 1862 she brought out 'Lady Audley's Secret,' which was almost instantly popular and the first of a long series of clever sensational novels, among which may be mentioned 'Aurora Floyd' (1862); 'John Marchmont's Legacy' (1863); 'Eleanor's Victory' (1863); 'Henry Dunbar' (1864); 'Dead Sea Fruit' (1869); 'Dead Men's Shoes'; 'Rupert Godwin' (1869); 'Hostages to Fortune' (1875); 'Ishmael' (1884); 'The Fatal Three' (1888); 'The Venetians' (1892); 'Thou Art the Man' (1894); 'Sons of Fire' (1895); 'London Pride' (1896); 'Under Love's Rule' (1897); 'In High Places' (1898); 'Rough Justice' (1898); 'His Darling Son' (1899); 'The Infidel' (1900); 'The Conflict' (1903). She conducted the London magazine 'Belgravia' for some time, and some of her stories first appeared there. Her later works do not rely so much on sensational effects for their success as her earlier ones. In all she has published over 60 novels. She is the widow of John Maxwell, a well-known publisher.

Brad'ford, Alden, American historian and journalist: b. Duxbury, Mass., 19 Nov. 1765; d. Boston, 26 Oct. 1843. Originally a Congregational minister he became secretary of State of Massachusetts (1812–24), and editor of the Boston *Gazette* (1826). He wrote 'History of Massachusetts, 1764–1820'; 'History of the Federal Government'; 'Life of Jonathan Mayhew' (1838); 'New England Chronology' (1843).

Bradford, Amory Howe, American clergyman and author: b. Granby, Oswego County, N. Y., 14 April 1846. He was graduated at Hamilton College 1867, Andover Theological Seminary 1870; studied at Oxford University, England, and became pastor of the First Congregational Church, Montclair, N. J., in the year last named. He has written: 'Spirit and Life' (1888); 'Old Wine, New Bottles' (1892); 'The Pilgrim in Old England' (1893); 'Heredity and Christian Problems' (1895); 'The Growing Revelation' (1897); 'Art of Living Alone' (1899); 'The Return to Christ' (1900); 'Age of Faith' (1900); 'Spiritual Lessons From the Brownings' (1900); 'Ascent of the Soul' (1902).

Bradford, Andrew, American printer, son of William Bradford (1663–1752) (q.v.): b. Philadelphia about 1686; d. 23 Nov. 1742. He was the only printer in Pennsylvania from 1712 to 1723. He published the first newspaper in Philadelphia, 22 Dec. 1719, called the *American Weekly Mercury*. It was by him that Benjamin Franklin was first employed, on his arrival in Philadelphia in 1723. In 1732 he was postmaster; in 1735 he kept a book store at the sign of the Bible in Second Street. In 1738 he removed to No. 8 South Front Street, to a house which in 1810 was occupied as a printing house by his descendant, Thomas Bradford, publisher of the 'True American.'

Bradford, Gamaliel, American writer and politician: b. Boston, Mass., 15 Jan. 1831. He has been prominent in politics as an independent, being a strong opponent of the Philippine policy of the administration, and is the author of 'Lesson of Popular Government' (1898); 'Types of American Character.'

Bradford, John, Protestant martyr and theologian: b. Manchester about 1510; d. Smithfield, London, 1 July 1555. He obtained a situation in the commissariat, and having been guilty of some defalcation, known only to himself, was so impressed by a sermon of Latimer on restitution, that he determined not only to sell everything he had in order to make up the defalcation, but to renounce an employment which exposed him to dangerous temptations. He afterward studied at Cambridge, where he received the degree of M.A., and on taking orders was appointed chaplain to the Bishop of London, and Canon of St. Paul's. From this time he devoted himself to the duties of his office with so much zeal and success that he became one of the most popular preachers of his day. In 1552 he was appointed chaplain to Edward VI., but under the reign of Queen Mary became a marked man. On the charge of preaching sedition he was committed to the Tower (occupying the same room with Ridley, Cranmer, and Latimer), and being brought to trial, was condemned to death as an obstinate heretic. His life is said to have been offered to him if he would only promise to refrain from preaching, but even this he had the manliness to refuse, and he was burned at the stake. A complete edition of his works, which include sermons, meditations, various treatises, etc., was published 1848-53.

Bradford, Joseph, American journalist and dramatic author: b. near Nashville, Tenn., 24 Oct. 1843; d. Boston, Mass., 13 April 1886. His real name was William Randolph Hunter. Besides satirical verses he wrote a number of poems which were highly esteemed, especially those on the death of Victor Hugo and of Gen. Grant. His plays, 'Our Bachelors,' and 'One of the Finest,' were very successful and are still popular.

Bradford, Royal Bird, American naval officer: b. Turner, Me., 22 July 1844. He was graduated at the United States Naval Academy in 1865 and received promotion through various grades to the rank of commander. He has made a specialty of equipment, and since 1897 has been chief of the Bureau of Equipment at the Navy Department in Washington.

Bradford, William, American colonial governor and author: b. Austerfield, Yorkshire, England, 1590; d. Plymouth, 9 May 1657. He was one of the signers of the celebrated compact on the Mayflower; and, in 1621, on the death of the first governor, John Carver, was elected to the same office, which he continued to fill (with the exception of a brief period when he declined re-election) until his death. His administration was remarkably efficient and successful, especially in dealing with the Indians. One of his first acts was to adopt measures to confirm the league with the Indian sachem Massasoit. In the beginning of 1622, when the colony was subjected to a distressing famine, a threatening message was received from the sachem of Narragansett in the form of a bundle of arrows bound with the skin of a serpent. The governor sent back the skin filled with powder and ball. This decisive reply finished the correspondence. The Narragansetts were so terrified, that they returned the skin without even inspecting its contents. In return for his kindness and attentions to Massasoit in a dangerous illness, the sachem disclosed to the colony a dangerous conspiracy among the Indians, and it was suppressed. His 'Diary of Occurrences,' covering the first year of the colony, was published in 1622. He left a number of religious compositions in verse; and historical prose writings of great value, the most important being his 'History of the Plymouth Plantation' from the formation of the society in England, in 1602, down to 1647. This disappeared during the American Revolution, but was found in the library of Fulham Palace, England in 1858, and in 1898 was returned to the United States and placed among the archives of Massachusetts. The shorter writings of Bradford will be found in Young's 'Chronicles of the Pilgrims' (1841). See Cotton Mather, 'Magnolia' for life of Bradford; also Tyler, 'History of American Literature' (1898); Walker, 'Ten New England Leaders' (1901).

Bradford, **William**, the first printer in Pennsylvania: b. Leicester, England, 20 May 1663; d. New York, 23 May 1752. Being a Quaker, he emigrated in 1682 or 1683, and landed where Philadelphia was afterward built, before a house was begun. In 1687 he printed an almanac. The writings of George Keith, which he printed, having caused a quarrel among the Quakers, he was arrested in 1692 and imprisoned for libel. On his trial, when the justice charged the jury to find only the fact as to the printing, Bradford maintained that they were to find also whether the paper was really seditious, and that "the jury are judges in law as well as the matter of fact." He was not convicted, but having incurred the displeasure of the dominant party in Philadelphia, he removed to New York in 1693. In that year he printed the laws of the colony. On 16 Oct. 1725, he began the first newspaper in New York, called the *New York Gazette*. In 1728 he established a paper mill at Elizabethtown, N. J. Being temperate and active, he reached a great age without sickness, and walked about on the very day of his death. For more than 50 years he was printer to the government of New York, and for 30 years the only one in the province.

Bradford, **William**, American jurist, attorney-general of the United States: b. Philadelphia, 14 Sept. 1755; d. 23 Aug. 1795. He was graduated at Princeton College in 1772, and commenced the study of the law. In the spring of 1776, upon the breaking out of the war with Great Britain, he joined the militia, in which he attained the rank of lieutenant-colonel. In consequence of ill-health he was obliged to resign at the end of two years, and was admitted to the bar in Philadelphia in 1779. In 1780 he was appointed attorney-general of Pennsylvania. Under the new Constitution he was appointed a judge of the supreme court 22 Aug. 1791. Upon the promotion of Edmund Randolph to the office of secretary of state he received from Washington the appointment of attorney-general of the United States 28 Jan. 1794. In early life he wrote some pastoral poems in imitation of Shenstone; but his principal production was an 'Inquiry how far the Punishment of Death is necessary in Pennsylvania.'

Bradford, **William**, American painter: b. New Bedford, Mass., 1827; d. New York, 25 April 1892. He entered business early in life, but abandoned it for art. His subjects were the ice fields of the North Atlantic, and well known works of his include 'Steamer Panther in Melville Bay under the Light of the Midnight Sun'; 'Crushed by Icebergs'; 'Arctic Wreckers'; 'Land of the Midnight Sun'; and 'Sunset in the North.'

Bradford, English manufacturing city, in the West Riding of Yorkshire, eight miles west of Leeds. It is pleasantly situated on a feeder of the Aire, at the junction of three extensive valleys, and consists of an ancient and a more modern portion, the latter with spacious, well-built streets. The appearance of the town has been almost completely changed since 1861, the corporation having, at a great expenditure of money, effected most extensive street improvements, widening the principal thoroughfares, improving the gradients, and opening up new streets. Spacious covered markets have been erected at a great cost. Among the public buildings are the town-hall (1873), in French Gothic style; St. George's Hall, erected in 1851, and capable of accommodating about 5,000 persons; an exchange, containing a statue of Cobden; a temperance hall; a mechanics' hall, with lecture rooms and library; a technical college, opened in 1882; free library (1872). The schools include the free grammar-school, endowed by Charles II., the girls' grammar-school, and the board schools. In Airedale College young men are trained for the ministry among the Independents. Among the charitable institutions may be noticed the infirmary, the eye and ear hospital, the children's hospital, St. Catharine's Home, an institution for the blind, and alms-houses. There is a fever hospital, to which patients are admitted at moderate charges, and when persons are too poor to pay, the corporation bears the cost. There is also a small-pox hospital. Bradford has several public parks, some of them finely laid out, besides Baildon Moor (600 acres) reserved for recreation purposes. There is an extensive system of waterworks by gravitation, and water, gas, and electric supply undertakings are owned by the municipality. The worsted yarn and stuff trade is the principal industry; there are also alpaca and mohair manufactures (with which Sir Titus Salt's name is connected), manufactures of silk and velvet (the Manningham Mills of Lister & Company), mixed cotton and silk goods; and some cotton factories. In the neighborhood are quarries and iron-works. The town was incorporated in 1847, and its affairs are managed by a mayor, 21 aldermen, and 63 councillors. It was accorded the rank of a city in

1897. The three parliamentary divisions of Central, East, and West Bradford each send one member to Parliament. A United States consulate is established here. Pop. (1901) 279,809.

Bradford, Pa., a city in McKean County, on several railroads; 15 miles northwest of Smethport, the county-seat. It is in an extensive coal, oil, and natural gas region, and is principally engaged in industries connected therewith, besides having machinery, chemical, boiler, and brick and tile works. The city has electric street railroads, daily and weekly newspapers, three national banks, large hospital, several libraries, and is lighted and heated by natural gas. Pop. (1900) 15,029.

Bradford-on-Avon, an ancient market-town of England, in Wiltshire, beautifully situated 28 miles northwest of Salisbury, on both banks of the Lower Avon, here crossed by two bridges — a very old one of nine arches in the centre of the town, and a modern one, Barton Bridge, of four. The town chiefly consists of three regular streets, containing many handsome houses. There is a good parish church of the Holy Trinity, in the Norman and subsequent styles; a town-hall, in Elizabethan style; and some interesting old buildings. Among the latter is the small but unique church of St. Laurence, the only complete specimen of Anglo-Saxon architecture still existing, and of great archæological interest. It was built in the 8th century by Saint Aldhelm, and consists of a chancel, a nave, and a porch on the north side. Woolen cloth is manufactured, but this industry has declined. Bradford was of some note in Anglo-Saxon times, St. Dunstan having been elected Bishop of Worcester at a synod held in it. Pop. (1901) 4,514. See Perkins, 'Abbey Churches of Bath, Malmesbury, and St. Laurence' (1901).

Bradlaugh, Charles, English secularist: b. London, 28 Sept. 1833; d. 30 Jan. 1891. He made himself known by his writings and lectures, and more especially by his efforts to gain admission to Parliament. Being elected for Northampton in 1880, he claimed the right to make affirmation simply, instead of taking the oath which members of Parliament take before they can sit and vote, but being a professed atheist this right was denied him. Though repeatedly re-elected by the same constituency, the majority of the House of Commons continued to declare him disqualified for taking the oath or affirming; and it was only after the election of a new Parliament in 1885 that he was allowed to take his seat without opposition as a representative of Northampton. He was editor of the 'National Reformer.' Not long before his death Parliament erased from its records its resolution prohibiting him from taking the oaths. See the 'Life' (1894) by his daughter and J. M. Robertson.

Bradlee, Nathaniel, American architect: b. Boston, 1829; d. 1888; began the study of architecture in 1846. He achieved marked success, having been the architect of over 500 prominent buildings in the city of Boston. In 1869 he made a national reputation by moving bodily the large brick structure known as the Hotel Pelham to the corner of Tremont and Boylston streets. The work attracted wide attention, both in this country and in Europe. He subsequently superintended the removal of the Boylston Market.

Bradley, Arthur Granville, English author, son of George Granville Bradley (q.v.): b. 11 Nov. 1850. He was educated at Marlborough and Trinity College, Cambridge, and has published 'History of Marlborough College' (1893); 'Life of Wolfe' (1895); 'Sketches from Old Virginia' (1897); 'Highways and Byways of North Wales' (1898); 'The Fight with France for North America' (1900); 'Highways and Byways of the English Lake District' (1901); 'Owen Glyndwyr' (1901).

Bradley, Edward (CUTHBERT BEDE), English author and clergyman: b. Kidderminster, 1827; d. Lenton, 12 Dec. 1889. He was graduated at Durham University, and was rector of Denton, Stretton, and finally Lenton from 1883 until his death. He contributed to 'Punch' and other London periodicals, and published the 'Adventures of Mr. Verdant Green, an Oxford Freshman' (London 1855), a humorous picture of college life. His other works include 'Mr. Verdant Green Married and Done For' (1856); 'The White Wife,' a collection of Scottish legends (1864); 'Little Mr. Bouncer and His Friend, Verdant Green' (1873-4); and several books of travels.

Bradley, George Granville, English clergyman, dean of Westminster Abbey, 1881-1902: b. 11 Dec. 1821; d. London, 12 March 1903. He was educated at Rugby and University College, Oxford, and took orders in the Anglican Church. He was assistant master at Rugby 1846-58; master of Marlborough College 1858-70; master of University College 1870-81. In the last-named year he became dean of Worcester and succeeded Dean Stanley as dean of Westminster. He published 'Recollections of Arthur Penryhn Stanley' (1883); 'Lectures on the Book of Job' (1884); 'Lectures on Ecclesiastes' (1885). He resigned the deanery of Westminster a few months before his death.

Bradley, Henry, English scholar and lexicographer: b. Manchester, England, 3 Dec. 1845. He has twice been president of the Philological Society and has been joint editor of the 'Oxford English Dictionary' from 1889. He has published 'The Story of the Goths' (1888); contributed important articles to the 'Dictionary of National Biography'; etc., and edited the E, F, G, and L portions of the 'Oxford Dictionary'.

Bradley, James, English astronomer: b. Sherborne, Gloucestershire, 1693; d. Chalford, Gloucestershire, 13 July 1762. He was educated at Balliol College, Oxford, and took orders, but his taste for astronomy soon led him in a different direction, and in 1721 he was appointed Savilian professor of astronomy at Oxford. Seven years afterward he made his discovery of the aberration of light. But although this discovery gave a greater degree of accuracy to astronomical observations, yet slight differences remained which he studied during 20 years with the greatest perseverance, and finally discovered that they were fully explained by the supposition of an oscillating motion of the earth's axis, completed during a revolution of the moon's nodes, that is, in about 18 and a half years. He called this phenomenon the "nutation of the earth's axis"; and published his account of it in 1748. By these two discoveries astronomers were, for the first time, enabled to make tables of the motions of the heavenly bodies with the necessary accuracy. Bradley had already, in 1726, explained the method of obtaining the longitude by means of the eclipse of Jupiter's first satellite. In 1742, at the death of Dr. Halley, he received the office of astronomer royal, and removed to the observatory at Greenwich. Here he spent the remainder of his life, entirely devoted to his astronomical studies. His observations in manuscript appeared under the title of 'Astronomical Observations made at the Observatory at Greenwich, 1750–62' (1798, 1805). From this rich mine have been taken thousands of observations, on the sun, moon, and planets, of the highest astronomical value.

Bradley, John Edwin, American educator: b. Lee, Mass. He was graduated from Williams College in 1865, and was successively principal of high schools in Pittsfield, Mass., 1865–8; Albany, N. Y., 1868–86. He was superintendent of schools at Minneapolis 1886–92, and president of Illinois College 1892–1900. He is the author of 'Science and Industry'; 'School Incentives'; 'Healthfulness of Intellectual Pursuits'; 'Work and Play'; 'Talks With Students.'

Bradley, Joseph Philo, American jurist: b. Berne, N. Y., 14 March 1813; d. Washington, D. C., 22 Jan. 1892. He was graduated at Rutgers College in 1836; admitted to the bar in 1839; and became a justice of the United States supreme court in 1870. As a member of the electoral commission he cast the vote which gave the presidency to Gen. Hays, in 1877. He devoted much time to mathematical study.

Bradley, Milton, American manufacturer: b. Vienna, Me., 8 Nov. 1836. He organized the Milton Bradley Company at Springfield, Mass., in 1863, for the manufacture of kindergarten supplies. He has published 'Color in the School Room' (1890); 'Color in the Kindergarten' (1893); 'Elementary Color' (1895); 'Water Colors in the School Room' (1900).

Brad'shaw, John, English judge and regicide: b. Cheshire, England, 1602; d. London, 31 Oct. 1659. He studied law at Gray's Inn, and obtained much chamber practice from the partisans of the Parliament, to which he was zealously devoted. When the trial of the king was determined upon, the resolute character of Bradshaw pointed him out for president, which office, after a slight hesitation, he accepted. His deportment on the trial some describe as lofty and unbending, others as harsh and overbearing. He was subsequently appointed permanent president of the council of state, and received other honors. He rendered himself obnoxious to Cromwell, when the latter seized the protectorate, and was deprived of the chief-justiceship of Chester. On the death of Cromwell in 1658, and the restoration of the Long Parliament, he obtained a seat in the council, and was elected president. He died in 1659, and on his death-bed asserted that, if the king were to be tried and condemned again, he would be the first to agree to it. He was magnificently buried in Westminster Abbey, from which his body was ejected and hanged on a gibbet at Tyburn, with those of Cromwell and Ireton, at the Restoration.

Bradshaw's Railway Guide, a well-known English manual for travelers, first issued by George Bradshaw, a printer and engraver of Manchester, in 1839. It is now published on the first of each month, and contains the latest arrangements of railway and steamboat companies, beside other useful information. There are now many such hand-books in the field, and the idea has since been further developed in the descriptive hand-books of Murray, Bædeker, and others.

Brad'street, Anne, American poet: b. Northampton (probably), England, 1612; d. Andover, Mass., 16 Sept. 1672. She was the daughter of Gov. Thomas Dudley, and married the future governor, Simon Bradstreet, in 1628. She went with him to New England in 1630. She was the first woman of letters in America, her verse being written in the intervals of household cares, and by her contemporaries was styled "The Tenth Muse." Her volume of poems was published in London in 1650. A more complete edition appeared at Boston in 1678, containing, among other additional compositions, her best poem, entitled 'Contemplations.' A third edition was published in 1758. She was the mother of eight children, to whom she makes the following allusion:

I had eight birds hatch't in the nest;
Four cocks there were, and hens the rest;
I nurs't them up with pains and care,
For cost nor labor did I spare;
Till at last they felt their wing,
Mounted the trees and learned to sing.

Her complete works, edited by J. H. Ellis, were reprinted in Boston in 1867, and again in 1897. See Tyler, 'American Literature' (1898).

Bradstreet, John, English soldier in America: b. 1711; d. New York, 21 Oct. 1774. He was, in 1746, lieutenant-governor of St. Johns, Newfoundland. In 1756, when it was considered highly important to keep open the communication with Fort Oswego, on Lake Ontario, he was placed at the head of 40 companies of boatmen, raised for the purpose of supplying it with stores from Schenectady. On his return, 3 July 1756, with 300 of his force he was attacked from an ambuscade, on the Onondaga River, but repulsed and routed the enemy with great loss. In 1758 he commanded a force of 3,000 men in the expedition against Fort Frontenac, which was surrendered 27 August, with all its military stores, provisions, and merchandise, on the second day after he commenced the attack. In 1764 he advanced with a considerable party toward the Indian country, and made a treaty of peace with the various tribes at Presque Isle. He was appointed major-general in 1772.

Bradstreet, Simon, American colonial governor: b. Horbling, Lincolnshire, England, March 1603; d. Salem, Mass., 27 March 1697. Left an orphan at the age of 14, he was brought up under the care of Thomas Dudley (q.v.), whose daughter Anne he married. For a time he was steward to the Earl of Lincoln, and later to the Countess of Warwick. He, with Dudley and Winthrop, determined to emigrate and form a settlement in Massachusetts. Embarking with his wife on the Arbella, 29 March 1630, they anchored off Salem on 12 June. In 1621 Bradstreet was one of those who commenced building at Newtown, now Cambridge, and he resided there for several years. In 1639 he was granted 500 acres of land at Salem. He was also one of the first settlers of Andover, building in 1644 the first mill on the Cochichewick. After the death of his wife in 1672, he seems to have spent his time mainly in Boston and Salem. He was the colony's first secretary, one of the first commissioners of the United Colonies in 1643, and in 1653 vigorously opposed making war on the Dutch in New York, and on the Indians; and it was prevented by his steady and conscientious opposition and the decision of the general court of Massachusetts. He was deputy-governor from 1672 until his election as governor in 1679, in which office he continued until 1686. When Charles II. demanded the colony's charter, Bradstreet thought it better that it should be surrendered than that it should be taken away by judgment. He opposed the arbitrary proceedings of Andros, and when, in 1689, the people put down his authority, they made their former governor their president, and he continued as the head of the administration till May 1692, when Gov. William Phipps arrived, bringing the new charter, in which Bradstreet was named as first assistant. For 62 years he had been in the service of the colony, and he lived to be the "Nestor of New England," for all who came over from England with him, died before him. He was a popular magistrate and official, a man of integrity and piety, and one of the few who stoutly opposed the witchcraft delusion of 1692. See New England Historical and Genealogical Register, Vol. I., pp. 75-6, and Vol. VIII., p. 325, for a reprint of his 'Journal, 1664-83.'

Bradwardine, brăd'wèr-dĭn, or **Bredwardine,** Thomas (DOCTOR PROFUNDUS), English scholar: b. Hartfield, Sussex, about 1290; d. 1349. He was distinguished for his varied learning, and more particularly his treatise, 'De Causa Dei Contra Pelagium,' an extensive work against the Pelagian heresy, for centuries a standard authority. He was chaplain and confessor to Edward III., whom he accompanied to France, being present at Cressy and the capture of Calais. Being appointed archbishop of Canterbury, he hastened to England, but died of the black death on reaching London. Other works by him are: 'De Geometria Speculativa'; 'De Proportionibus'; 'De Quadratura Circuli'; 'De Arithmetica Practica.'

Bradwardine, Baron, a character in Scott's novel of 'Waverley.' He is represented as a rather opinionated retired soldier, living at his seat of Tully Vedlan.

Brady, Anthony Nicholas, American capitalist: b. of Irish parentage, Lille, France, 22 Aug. 1843. He came as an infant with his parents to the United States, and at the age of 13 began to make his own way in life. After engaging successfully in the tea business in Albany, and in that of granite quarrying, he became financially interested in gas companies, railway companies and the like, successfully developing the street railway system of New York and amassing a fortune of many millions. He has also been connected with oil and electric lighting interests.

Brady, Cyrus Townsend, American Episcopal clergyman and author: b. Allegheny, Pa., 20 Dec. 1861. He graduated from the United States Naval Academy, 1883, but resigned, studied theology under Bishop Worthington of Nebraska, and was ordained in 1890. For five years he served as a missionary in Colorado, Missouri, and Kansas; was archdeacon of Pennsylvania, 1895-9, and rector at Overbrook, Philadelphia, from 1899 until his resignation to devote himself exclusively to writing, in which he has attained popularity as a writer of stories and novels of adventure, romance, and history. He has written: 'For Love of Country' (1898); 'For the Freedom of the Sea' (1899); 'Stephen Decatur' (1900); 'Recollections of a Missionary in the Great West' (1900); 'American Fights and Fighters' (1900); 'Commodore Paul Jones' (1900); 'When Blades are Out and Love's Afield' (1901); 'Under Tops'ls and Tents' (1901); 'An Apostle of the Plains' (1901); 'Colonial Fights and Fighters' (1901); 'Under the Ban of the Red Beard' (1901); 'Border Fights and Fighters' (1902); 'Hohenzollern' (1902); 'In the Wasp's Nest' (1902); 'Quiberon Touch' (1901-2); 'Woven With the Ship' (1902); 'The Bishop' (1903); 'Conquest of the Southwest' (1903); 'The Southerners' (1903).

Brady, Henry Bowman, English paleontologist: b. Gateshead, England, 1835; d. 1890. He was prominent as a manufacturing pharmacist and his success in business enabled him to devote much time to scientific research, becoming in time the highest English authority regarding foraminifera. He was the author of several monographs on Mesozoic, Cenozoic, and other foraminifera, and of the more important works: 'Report on the Foraminifera Dredged by H. M S. Challenger, During the Years 1873-6,' and 'Scientific Results of the Challenger Voyage,' Vol. IX. (1888).

Brady, Hugh, American general: b. Northumberland County, Pa., 1768; d. Detroit, 15 April 1851. He entered the United States army as an ensign, 7 March 1792; served with Wayne in his western expedition, after the defeat of St. Clair; was made lieutenant in 1794, and captain in 1799. Having left the military service, he was restored to it in 1808, by President Jefferson, who then began to reform the army. 6 June 1812 he was appointed colonel of the 22d foot, and led his troops in the hard-fought battle of Chippewa. They were almost annihilated, but displayed the greatest courage, Gen. Scott saying in his report, "Old Brady showed himself in a sheet of fire." He displayed equal courage at the battle of Niagara Falls, where he was wounded. He was retained in service, on the reduction of the army, as colonel of the 2d foot, a commission he held until his death. After 1835 he was in command of the department of which Detroit was the headquarters; and while at that place contributed, in no small degree, to the pacification of the frontier, during the Canadian troubles. He was looked on by the army as one of its fathers. He received two brevets, as brigadier-general, 6 July 1822, and as major-general, for long and faithful service, 30 May 1848. Immediately before his death, the chaplain of his corps visited him and sought to speak to him of religious matters. Gen. Brady listened to him, and said, "Sir, that is all right; my knapsack, however, has been packed, and I am ready to march at the tuck of the drum."

Brady, James Topham, American lawyer: b. New York, 9 April 1815; d. there, 9 Feb. 1869. He was educated by his father, an eminent jurist, and admitted to the bar in 1836. His eloquence, skill, and ability at once brought him reputation and a fine practice. Conspicuous for his knowledge in all departments of law, he won verdicts from judges and jurors alike in important patent cases, such as Goodyear *v.* Day; cases involving questions of medical jurisprudence, like the Allaire and Parish will cases, the Huntington forgery case, and Cole homicide case; divorce cases, like that of Mrs. Edwin Forrest, and civil actions of all kinds. He was at his best in criminal cases, where he usually appeared on the side of the defense. At one time he defended successfully in a single week four clients charged with murder. In 1859 he was counsel for Daniel E. Sickles in his trial for the assassination of Philip Barton Key, his opening address for the defense being one of his most notable forensic efforts. Though a States-rights advocate before the War, he supported Lincoln's war measures, making speeches which had considerable influence.

Brady, John, Irish-American ecclesiastic: b. County Cavan, Ireland, 1842. He prepared for the priesthood at All Hallows College in Ireland, was assistant priest in Newburyport, Mass., 1864-8, and since 1868 has been pastor of St. Joseph's Church at Amesbury, Mass. In 1891 he was consecrated auxiliary bishop of Boston and titular bishop of Boston, but still continues his parochial work.

Brady, Nicolas, English prelate: b. Bandon, Ireland, 28 Oct. 1659; d. Richmond, Surrey, 20 May 1726. He was educated at Westminster School, and afterward received the degree of B.A. both at Oxford and at Dublin, and took orders in the Irish Church. Having come to England he obtained several ecclesiastical preferments; among others the rectory of the Church of St. Catharine Cree, London, and that of Richmond, Surrey. This put him in possession of an income which might, but does not seem to have sufficed for his wants, as he thought it necessary to increase it by keeping a school at Richmond. His largest work, a translation of the Æneid, was an absolute failure, but he has made his name a kind of household word, at least in England, by executing, in concert with Nahum Tate, the 'New Versions of the Psalms of David' (1695), which soon came to be commonly used in the Episcopal Church.

Brady, William Maziere, Irish theologian: b. Dublin, 1825. He was for a long period a clergyman in the Established Church of Ireland, but was prominent in the agitation leading to its disestablishment in 1869, and lost several of his preferments by that event. In 1873 he entered the Roman Catholic Church. He has published 'The Episcopal Succession in England, Ireland, and Scotland, 1400–1875' (1876–7); 'Annals of the Catholic Hierarchy in England and Scotland' (1883); 'Anglo-Roman Papers' (1890).

Brady-car'dia, an abnormally slow heart. Brady-cardia occasionally is a family trait, and is then normal. Napoleon is said to have had a heart beat of only 40 to the minute. It may occur during pregnancy, and is often present in the convalescence of fevers, particularly typhoid, acute rheumatism, diphtheria, and pneumonia. It sometimes accompanies disease of the digestive tract; is often present in emphysema, and further present rarely in a number of conditions. Among these may be mentioned fibroid changes in the heart, nephritis, lead, alcohol, tobacco, and digitalis poisoning, in melancholia, general paresis, and in apoplexy. It may mean much or may be insignificant, and its importance is largely measured by its causative factors.

Braekeleer, Ferdinandus dé, fėr-dẹ-nän'doos dė brä'kě-lår, Belgian artist: b. Antwerp, 1792; d. 1883. He was a member of the Antwerp Academy and a director of the Antwerp Museum, and as an instructor was especially successful. Among his works are 'Tobit Burying a Jew by Night' (1817); 'The Baker'; 'Bombardment of Antwerp in 1830'; 'Happy Family'; 'Unhappy Family.'

Braemar, brä-mär', Scotland, a mountainous district in the southwest corner of Aberdeenshire. It contains part of the Grampian range, with the heights of Ben Macdhui, Cairntoul, Lochnagar, etc. The district has some fine scenery, valleys, and hillsides covered with birch and fir, but consists largely of deer-forests. The Balmoral Castle, formerly the residence of the late Queen Victoria, is situated here, on the banks of the Dee, midway between Ballater and Braemar village (Castleton of Braemar).

Brag, a game of cards, played with a full-pack. It is so named because each player endeavors to impose upon his neighbor, by "bragging" about his hand, in an endeavor to make his opponents believe it more valuable than it is. The cards rank as in whist, except the nines and knaves, which take their value from the cards with which they are held. Thus an ace, a nine, and a knave are equivalent to three aces. The hands are shown, not played, the strongest one taking the stakes.

Braga, Theophilo, Portuguese philologist and critic: b. San Miguel, Azores, 24 Feb. 1843. He was educated at the university of Coimbra, and became professor of literature in the Curso Superior de Letras in Lisbon. He is a very voluminous writer and takes important rank as a historian of the literature of the Iberian peninsula. He is also noted as an exponent of the Comtian philosophy. In politics he has been prominent as an active democrat. In addition to other literary activity, he has published several volumes of poems. Among these may be mentioned: 'Stella Matutina' (1863); 'Tempestades Sonoras' (1864); 'Torrentes' (1868), and a collection entitled 'Alma Portugueza' (1893). Of his other works may be noted: 'Historia da Litteratura Portugueza' (1870–81); 'Manual da Litteratura Portugueza' (1875); 'Parnaso Portuguez Moderno' (1877); a volume on Camöens (1880); 'Traços Geraes de Philosophia Positiva' (1877); 'Contos Tradicionaes do Povo Portuguez' (1883); 'Systema de Sociologia' (1884); 'Historia da Universidade de Coimbra' (1892).

Braga, brä'gä, Portugal, a town in the province of Minho, and its capital, situated on a rising ground between the Cavado and D'Este, about 32 miles north-northeast of Oporto. It is surrounded by walls flanked with towers and defended by a castle. The houses are old, the streets broad, but not well laid out. It is the seat of an archbishop who is primate of Portugal, and contains an archiepiscopal palace, a richly ornamented Gothic cathedral of the 13th century, parish churches, monasteries, a college, etc. The manufactures are of some importance. Braga is supposed to have been founded by the Carthaginians, and there exist remains of a Roman temple, amphitheatre, and aqueduct. On a hill some distance east of the town stands the famous pilgrimage church of Bom Jesus do Monte. Pop. (1890) 23,089.

Bragança, brä-gän'sä, the name of two considerable towns in Brazil: (1) A seaport, 100 miles northeast of Para, at the mouth of the Caite, which is here navigable to the town. Pop. of town and district, 6,000. (2) An inland city of about 10,000 inhabitants, 50 miles northeast of Sao Paulo.

Bragança, or **Braganza,** Portugal, the capital of a district (of the same name) in the province of Tras-os-Montes. It was in former times the capital of the province, and is a place of considerable importance. It has the ruins of an ancient castle, one of the finest feudal remains in Portugal. It is the see of a bishop, and there is an extensive manufactory of velveteens, printed calicoes, and woolens. Bragança has given its name to the present royal family of Portugal. Pop. about 5,500.

Bragança, or **Braganza,** House of, the present reigning house of Portugal, derived from Affonso, Duke of Bragança, a natural son of João I., king of Portugal. The constitution of Lamego, 1139, declares that no foreign prince can succeed to the throne; consequently in 1578, on the death of the Portuguese hero Sebastian, in Africa, without issue, his people had recourse to the illegitimate line of Bragança. Philip II. of Spain, however, claimed the throne, and supported his pretensions by an army under the Duke of Alva, who, though in disgrace, was summoned from his retreat for this express purpose. In 1668 the Portuguese shook off the Spanish yoke. In 1801 Napoleon I. declared that the line of the Bragança sovereigns had ceased. John, regent of the kingdom, withdrew to Brazil in 1807, but returned in 1821. At his death in 1826 his son, Dom Pedro, resigned the throne in favor of his daughter, Maria da Gloria, preferring to remain emperor of Brazil, to which office he had been elected by the Brazilians, 18 Nov. 1825.

Bragg, Braxton, American military officer: b. Warren County, N. C., 22 March 1817; d. Galveston, Tex., 27 Sept. 1876. He graduated at West Point in 1837; was appointed second lieutenant in the 3d Artillery; served with distinction under Gen. Taylor in the Mexican war; and retired to private life in 1856. At the outbreak of the Civil War he became a brigadier-general, and was stationed at Pensacola to act against Fort Pickens. In 1862, having been appointed a general of division, with orders to act under Gen. A. S. Johnston, commanding the army of the Mississippi, he took an important part in the two

days' battle of Shiloh. On Johnston's death he was appointed to his command, with the full rank of general, and succeeded Gen. Beauregard as commander of the department in July of the same year. The last command he resigned in December 1863. His chief success was at Chickamauga in September 1863, when he inflicted a defeat on the army of Gen. Rosecrans, but was himself, in turn, defeated by Gen. Grant, which led to his temporary removal from command in January 1864, and he was appointed military adviser to Jefferson Davis. In 1864 he assumed command of the department of North Carolina. After the war he was chief engineer of the State of Alabama, and superintendent of the improvements in Mobile Bay.

Bragg, Edward Stuyvesant, American legislator: b. Unadilla, N. Y., 20 Feb. 1827. He was educated at Geneva (now Hobart) College, and admitted to the bar in New York in 1848. He removed to Fond du Lac, Wis., and was admitted to the Wisconsin bar in 1850, to that of Illinois in 1869, and to that of the United States supreme court in 1877. He served in the Union army during the Civil War, and won his way to the rank of brigadier-general. He was a member of the Union convention at Philadelphia in 1866; representative in Congress in 1877-85; and a delegate to the Democratic National Conventions of 1872, 1884, 1892, and 1896. In the convention of 1884 he seconded the renomination of Grover Cleveland, when he uttered the memorable phrase, "We love him for the enemies he has made." In 1888 he was appointed minister to Mexico; from 15 May to 15 Sept. 1902, was consul-general in Havana and since 15 Sept. 1902 at Hong Kong.

Bragi, brä'jē, the Scandinavian god of poetry. He is represented as an old man with a long flowing beard, like Odin; yet with a serene and unwrinkled brow. His wife was Idunna.

Braham, brä'am, **John,** English tenor singer: b. London (of Jewish extraction), 1774; d. 1856. He made his first appearance as a vocalist at the age of 10. On attaining manhood he proceeded to France and Italy with the view of improving himself in his art, and accomplished this so successfully that on his return after an absence of several years he soon rose to the position of the first English singer of his day. He sung much in opera, but gained his greatest triumphs in national songs, such as 'The Bay of Biscay, O', and 'The Death of Nelson,' and till within a few years of his death he continued to appear in public. His sons, Charles, Augustus. and Hamilton, also adopted the musical profession.

Brahe, Tycho, tī'kō brä, or brä, Swedish astronomer: b. Knudstrup, near Lund, 14 Dec. 1546; d. Prague, Bohemia, 24 Oct. 1601. The district where he was born was then a province of Denmark, but the family was of Swedish origin. He was sent at the age of 13 to the University of Copenhagen with the intention that he should be educated for government service. He evinced great promise as a Latin scholar, but an eclipse of the sun turned his attention to astronomy. His uncle sent him later to Leipsic to study law, but Brahe, while his tutor slept, busied himself nightly with the stars. He succeeded, as early as 1563, in detecting grave errors in the Alphonsine tables and the so-called Prutenic (that is, Prussian) tables, and set about their correction. The death of an uncle, who left him an estate, recalled him to his native place in 1565; but he very soon became disgusted with the ignorance and arrogance of those moving in the same sphere with himself, and went back to Germany. At Wittenberg, where he resided for a short time, he lost part of his nose in a duel with a Danish gentleman; but for the lost organ he ingeniously contrived one of gold, silver, and wax, which fitted admirably. After two years spent in Augsburg, he returned home, where, in 1572, he discovered a new and brilliant star in the constellation Cassiopeia. In 1573 he married a peasant girl. After some time spent in travel, Brahe received from his sovereign, Frederic II., the offer of the small island of Hven or Hoëne, in the sound, 10 miles from Copenhagen, as the site for an observatory, the king also offering to defray the cost of erection, and of the necessary astronomical instruments, as well as to provide him with a suitable salary. Brahe accepted the proposal, and, in 1576, the castle of Uranienburg ("fortress of the heavens") was begun. Here, for a period of 20 years, Brahe prosecuted his observations with the most unwearied industry. Here, also, he was visited by astronomers, mathematicians, philosophers, theologians and princes, among the latter being the future James I. of England, who took a lively interest in the astronomer's work. Asking Brahe what gift he should make in return for the other's courtesy, the scholar replied, "Some of your majesty's own verses." So long as his munificent patron, Frederic II., lived, Brahe's position was all that he could have desired, but on his death in 1588 it was greatly changed. Under Christian IV. Brahe was barely tolerated; but in 1597 his situation had grown so unbearable that he left the country altogether, having been the year before deprived of his observatory and emoluments. After residing a short time at Rostock and at Wandsbeck, near Hamburg, he accepted an invitation of the Emperor Rudolf II.— who conferred on him a pension of 3,000 ducats — to Benatek, a few miles from Prague, where a new Uranienburg was to have been erected for him, but he died shortly after. On his deathbed he solemnly confided his system to his celebrated pupil Kepler, then but 28 years old.

Brahilow, Brailow, brä′ē-low, or **Braila,** brä′ē-la, Rumania, a 'town and port on the left bank of the Danube, about 12 miles above Galatz, and over 120 miles from the Sulina mouth of the river. It is accessible by large sea-going vessels, and carries on a great trade in the export of grain, importing coal, agricultural machinery, etc. Both as regards accommodation for shipping and otherwise it has been much improved in recent years. In the Turkish wars of the latter half of the 18th century Brahilow was several times besieged and taken by the Russians. In 1828 it had to surrender to the Russians after a gallant resistance, but in 1829 the Peace of Adrianople restored it to the Turks. Pop. (1894) 51,116.

Brahma, the first person in the Triad, or Trimurti, of the Hindus, which consists of Brahma the creator; Vishnu the preserver or redeemer; and Siva the destroyer. He is represented with four heads and as many arms,

holding in his four hands a manuscript book containing a portion of the Vedas, a pot for holding water, a rosary, and a sacrificial spoon. The swan is consecrated to him and in the cave temple of Elephanta he is represented as sitting on a lotus, supported by five swans. He is the god of the fates, master of life and death, and, by some, has been represented as the supreme eternal power; but he is himself created and is merely the agent of Brahmă (a neuter noun), the universal power or ground of all existence. He is considered as the author of the Vedas and the lawgiver and teacher of India. The worship of Brahma is regarded as the oldest religious observance in that country. In modern Hindu religion, however, it has been practically superseded by the worship of Vishnu and Siva. The epithets applied to this divinity are very numerous, some of the most usual being Swayambhu, the self-existing; Parameshti, who abides in the most exalted place; Pitamaha, the great father; Prajâpati, the lord of creatures; Lokesa, the ruler of the world. See INDIA; BRAHMANS.

Brahmagupta, Hindu astronomer and mathematician: b. probably toward the close of the 6th century A.D. His 'Brahma-sphuta-siddhanta' (the Improved System of Brahma) is said to be an earlier work recast: portions of it have been translated into English.

Brahman Bull, a bull of the humped cattle, or zebu breed, of India and eastward, regarded with veneration by devout Hindus, and safe from molestation, even when turned loose by temple priests to forage upon the market stalls in city streets. Adorned with trappings and garlands of flowers, these pampered bulls figure largely in religious ceremonials and processions. See also INDIAN HUMPED CATTLE.

Brahmanas, the ancient theological writings appended to the original four Vedas by the Brahmans, or priests, for the purpose of very greatly magnifying their own office as a caste intrusted with the conduct of sacrifices of every kind. There are some 13 of them, with attachments to different parts of the original four Vedas. The Satapatha-Brahmana is the most important and valuable. It is called Satapatha, or "of the hundred paths," because it consists of 100 lectures. It has a very minute and full account of sacrificial ceremonies in Vedic times, and many legends and historical allusions: Nothing could be more wearisome reading; yet the information which can be gleaned in regard to sacrifices, the priestly caste, and many features of the social and mental development of India, is very valuable. A devout belief in the efficacy of invocation and sacrifice appears in the Vedic hymns. This was taken advantage of by the Brahmans to arrange a regular use of these hymns in the two liturgical Vedas, and to establish a proper offering of sacrifices conducted by themselves. The Brahmanas are their endlessly repeated explanations and dictions about sacrifice and prayer.

The third, four, and fifth books of the great work presented in these five volumes deal very particularly with the Soma-sacrifice, the most sacred of all the Vedic sacrificial rites. It concerns the nature and use of "a spirituous liquor extracted from a certain plant, described as growing on the mountains." "The potent juice of the Soma plant, which endowed the feeble mortal with godlike powers and for a time freed him from earthly cares and troubles, seemed a veritable God — bestower of health, long life, and even immortality." The moon was regarded as the celestial Soma, and source of the virtue of the plant. Another branch of the story of sacrifices relates to the worship of Agni, the Fire. It fills 5 out of 14 books, and the ideas reflected in it are very important for knowledge of Brahman theosophy and cosmogony. The ritual of the Fire-altar was brought into close connection with that of the Soma "fiery" liquor.

Brahmans, the first of the four castes of the Hindus. They proceeded from the mouth of Brahma, the seat of wisdom. They form the sacred or sacerdotal caste, whose members have maintained perhaps a more absolute and extensive authority than the priests of any other nation. Their great prerogative is that of being the sole depositaries and interpreters of the Vedas, or sacred books. There are seven subdivisions of the Brahmans, which derive their origin from seven penitents, personages of high antiquity and remarkable purity, who are said to have rebuked the gods themselves for their debaucheries. The great body of the Brahmans pay equal veneration to the three parts of the mysterious trinity, but some attach themselves more particularly to one person of the triple godhead. Thus the Vishnuvites are distinguished by an orange-colored dress, and the mark called nama on their foreheads. The devotees of Siva wear the lingam, and are distinguished from the former by their great abstemiousness. A Brahman should pass through four states. The first begins at about seven, when the duty of the young novice, or Brahmachari, consists in learning to read and write, studying the Vedas, and becoming familiar with the privileges of his caste, and all matters of personal purity. Thus he is taught his right to ask alms, to be exempted from taxes, from capital and even corporal punishment. Earthen vessels belonging to Brahmans, when used by profane persons, or for certain purposes, must be broken. Leather and skins of animals, and most animals themselves, are impure, and must not be touched by them. Flesh and eggs they are not allowed to eat. The Brahman is also taught to entertain a horror of the defilement of the soul by sin; and rules for purification by ablution, penances, and various ceremonies, are prescribed. The second state begins at his marriage, when he is called Grihastha. Marriage is necessary to his respectability. His daily duties become more numerous, and must be more strictly performed. Regular ablutions, fasting, and many minute observances, become requisite. The Brahmans, however, engage in secular employments, political, commercial, etc. The third state is that of the Vana-Prasthas, or inhabitants of the forest, which is now, however, seldom reached. They were honored by kings, and respected even by the gods. Retiring to the forest, green herbs, roots, and fruit were their food: reading the Vedas, bathing morning, noon, and evening, and the practice of the most rigorous penances were prescribed. "Let the Vana-Prastha," says Manu, in the Institutes, "slide backward and forward on the ground, or stand the whole day on tip-toe, or continue rising and sitting down alternately; in the hot season let him sit exposed to five fires; in the rain let

him stand uncovered; in the cold season let him wear wet garments; then, having stored up his holy fires in his mind, let him live without external fire, without a shelter, wholly silent, and feeding on roots and fruit. When he shall have thus become void of fear and sorrow, and shaken off his body, he rises to the divine essence." The fourth state is that of a Sannyasi, in which new and severer penances are to be performed. Suppressing the breath, standing on the head, and other such ceremonies are performed, till the devout patient rises to a participation of the divine nature. It was by the Brahmans that the Sanskrit literature was developed; and they were not only the priests, theologians, and philosophers, but also the poets, men of science, lawgivers, administrators, and statesmen of the Aryans of India. The sanctity and inviolability of a Brahman are maintained, in the eyes of his countrymen, by the most severe penalties. The murder of one of the order, robbing him, etc., are inexpiable sins; the killing of his cow can only be expiated by a painful penance. See Monier-Williams, 'Brahmanism and Hinduism' (1887); Barth, 'Religions of India'; Hopkins, 'Religions of India' (1895).

Brahmaputra, brä'ma-pŏ'tra, a large river of Asia, whose sources, not yet explored, are situated near Lake Manasarovara, in Tibet, near those of the Indus. In Tibet, where it is called the Sanpo, it flows eastward north of the Himalayas, and, after taking a sharp bend and passing through these mountains, it emerges in the northeast of Assam as the Dihong, when the united stream takes the name of Brahmaputra, literally "the son of Brahma." After entering Bengal it joins the Ganges at Goalanda, and farther on the Meghna, and their united waters flow into the Bay of Bengal. The Brahmaputra is navigable by steamers for about 800 miles from the sea, its total length being, perhaps, 1,800 miles. Through the last 60 miles of its course it is from 4 to 5 miles wide, and studded with islands. Its waters are thick and dirty; its banks are mostly covered with marshes and jungles, and are subject to annual inundations. During the season of the overflow, from the middle of June to the middle of September, the level districts of Assam are almost wholly submerged, so that travel is impossible, except on causeways 8 or 10 feet high. The volume of water discharged by the river at such times is immense. Even in the dry season it is equal to 146,188 cubic feet a second, while in the same time, and under the same circumstances, the Ganges discharges only about 80,000.

Brahmo-Somaj, a religious association of India, founded in 1830 by Rammohun Roy, a famous Hindu rajah, who sought to purify Brahmanism from impurities and idolatries, and first styled "The Society of God." The Brahma-Somaj, while accepting what religious truth the Vedas may contain, rejects the idea of their special infallibility, and founds its faith on principles of reason. The members do not in principle recognize the distinction of caste, and have made great efforts to weaken this as well as other prejudices among their countrymen. The foremost exponent of its views was the Babu Keshub Chunder Sen, who with his followers founded the "Brahmo-Somaj of India" in 1858. See Mozoondar, 'Life and Teachings of Keshub Chunder Sen' (1887).

Brahms, Johannes, German composer: b. Hamburg, 7 May 1833; d. Vienna, 3 April 1897. His father was a double-bass player in the Stadt-Theater of his native town, and from him he received his first instruction in musical technique; but his artistic taste was developed under the guidance of the eminent musician, Eduard Marsden of Altona. At the age of 14 years he made his first public appearance as a pianist at Hamburg, playing a set of variations composed by himself. In 1853 he traveled with the noted Hungarian violinist Remenyi on a concert tour of Germany as piano accompanist: this tour was critical for his whole career. In the program of the concert given at Göttingen was Beethoven's Kreutzer Sonata. The piano was a half tone below the true pitch, but Brahms straightway remedied the defect, playing the part from memory and transposing it from A to B flat — a feat which won the admiration of the celebrated violinist Joachim, who was in the audience; and who after the performance made himself known to the young musician; thus commenced a warm friendship which lasted during Joachim's life. He gave the young man commendatory letters to Liszt, then at Weimar, and to Schumann at Düsseldorf, and advised him to give up the concert tour. Brahms acted instantly on this counsel, visited Schumann and showed him some of his compositions, with the result that Schumann recognized in the young artist supreme musical genius, and in his enthusiastic admiration hailed him in an article entitled "Neue Bahnen," published in his 'Neue Zeitung für Musik' as already a master, the great composer of the future, and in the words of John the Baptist (Matt. xi. 3) as rendered in the Latin vulgate, as "he that is to come." Brahms, he declared, had not attained mastership by a gradual development, but had "burst upon us fully equipped as Minerva sprung from the head of Jupiter." Yet at this time the young maestro had produced but very few works' — a string quartet, a scherzo in E flat, and a few songs, among them the dramatic 'Liebestreue.' . His eminent gifts were now generally recognized, and after giving a concert in Leipsic, two music publishers made an engagement with him to publish his compositions; and in 1854 he was appointed music master and choir conductor to the Prince of Lippe-Detmold. From 1858 to 1862 he resided first in Hamburg and then in Zürich, making musical tours and pursuing his musical studies. Going to Vienna in 1862 he was director of the Singakademie there in 1863, but after a few months resigned that office and quitted Vienna, to resume his concert tours throughout Germany. He took up his residence again in the Austrian capital in 1872, and thereafter till his death Vienna was his home, though for some years he made musical tours occasionally; but toward the close of his life he devoted himself almost exclusively to the work of musical composition. In 1877 the English University of Cambridge apprised him of its senate's intention to honor him with the degree of Doctor of Music, but Brahms seems to have ignored the intended courtesy.

By his 'German Requiem,' produced in the Cathedral at Bremen in 1868, at a solemn religious function commemorative of the German soldiers who died in the war with Austria, he fully justified the prophetic utterance of Schumann and won for himself a place in the hearts of the whole German people. He called it the 'German Requiem' to indicate the difference in tone and spirit between it and the traditional requiem, which echoes the doleful strains of the 'Dies Iræ.' In the 'German Requiem' buoyant hope and assurance of God's infinite mercy is the keynote. It is one of a class of sacred compositions, 12 in number, among them the 'Triumphlied' (song of triumph), commemorating the German victories in the war with France in 1871-2, also some choral songs and motets. His other compositions, numbering about 150 pieces, are his secular choral works, among these Schiller's 'Nänie' and the 'Gesang der Parzen' (song of the Parcae); concerted vocal works, among them the 'Liebeslieder' (lays of love); orchestral works, among them four symphonies; chamber music; pianoforte solos; four books of Hungarian dances arranged for pianoforte duet. He never seems to have even attempted to compose an opera, and confessed a distaste for that combination of music and drama. He seldom visited the theatre, and on the rare occasions on which he attended operatic performances he nearly always retired before the completion of the last act.

Brahms is ranked with the classic masters of music, as the peer of Beethoven and Mendelssohn, and inheritor of the traditions of the great school of the German composers. Temperamentally and in his mental habit he is essentially modern, original, and spontaneous; he possesses the warmth of imagination and the quick emotionalism which are assumed to be characteristic of the romantic school, and to these he gives free play. But his creations are cast in the classic molds; or rather they appear to come to the birth naturally in classic forms; hence there is no shadow of incongruity between the matter and the form. See Deiters, translated by Newmarch, 'Brahms: a Biographical Sketch' (1888); Dietrich and Widmann, translated by Heclet, 'Recollections of Johannes Brahms' (1899).

Braid, James, Scotch physician: b. Fife, 1795; d. 25 March 1860. He studied medicine in Edinburgh and settled as a surgeon in Manchester. He is noted for his researches on animal magnetism, which he first called neurohypnotism, and afterward termed hypnotism.

Braid'wood, Thomas, Scotch educator: b. 1715; d. 24 Sept. 1798. He studied at the University of Edinburgh, settled as a schoolmaster in that city, and after 1760 became famous as a teacher of deaf-mutes. In 1783 his school was transferred to Hackney, London.

Braille, Louis, loo-ē brāl, or brä-ē, French educator of the blind: b. Coupvray, 1806; d. 1852. He invented a system of writing with points, used extensively in institutions for the blind. Himself blind almost from birth, at the age of 10 years he was admitted to the Institute for the Blind in Paris, where he soon became proficient in both science and music. In instrumental music he attained a very high rank, becoming one of the most distinguished organists of Paris, and excelling also as a violoncellist. At the age of 20 he had formed the idea of modifying M. Charles Barbier's system of writing with points so as to render it practicable and convenient, and not long afterward it was introduced into the royal institute, although no account of it was published till 10 years later. It was subsequently adopted in most of the continental schools, and a little later in the United States, where it continues, with some modifications, in successful use. The signs of the original system are 43 in number, embracing the entire alphabet, all the diphthongs, and marks of punctuation. Ten fundamental signs form the basis of all the rest. These signs, representing the first 10 letters of the alphabet and the 10 Arabic numerals, are as follows:

A B C D E F G H I J
1 2 3 4 5 6 7 8 9 0

By placing one point under the left side of each fundamental sign, the second series is formed, comprising the next 10 letters. By placing two points under each fundamental sign, the third series, comprising U, V, X, Y, Z, Ç (C soft), É, À, È, Ù, is formed. By placing one point under the right side of the fundamental signs, the fourth series, embracing Â, Ê, Î, Ô, U, Ë, Ï, Ü, Œ, W, is formed. Three supplementary signs represent Ì, Æ, and Ò. The marks of punctuation are the fundamental signs placed two lines below. The system has been applied to musical notation in such a manner as to make the reading and writing of music much easier for the blind than for those who see. The seven notes are represented by the last seven of the fundamental signs, and each of these notes may be written in seven different octaves by merely prefixing a sign peculiar to each octave, and thus the necessity of designating the key of each musical sentence in the ordinary way is avoided. The mode of writing is very simple. The apparatus consists of a board with a surface grooved horizontally and vertically by lines one eighth of an inch apart. Over this board a frame is fitted like that of the common map delineator, and one or more sheets of paper being placed over the board, the points are made with a bodkin, through a slip of perforated tin, ::, which contains all the changes used in the system. As the sheet must be reversed to be read, the writing should be from right to left, that it may be read from left to right. Of course, several copies may be made by one operation. For many years books have been printed in points in various countries. See BLIND.

Brain, that portion of the nervous system contained, for the most part, within the skull. It is usually divided into two parts. The larger mass is termed the cerebrum, the smaller, the cerebellum; from the lower end of the cerebrum the medulla oblongata tapers down into the spinal cord. The brain is, as it were, the great central station of the nervous system. From the surface of the entire body nerve fibres pass into the spinal cord, up the cord and into the brain; these carry impressions of all kinds— touch, taste, sight, hearing, pain, temperature, etc.— from the surface to the brain. Starting in the brain mass itself there is a corresponding series of fibres that run down into the medulla and spinal cord, out into the nerves and end in some muscle or organ of special character. There are literally thousands of incoming fibres, thousands of outgoing fibres and millions of minute cells in direct association with these fibres. Thus it may be seen that the brain is merely a collection of nerve ganglion cells and their associated fibres, both of which have a characteristic appearance as seen by the naked eye; that portion of the brain that preponderates in cells is the "gray matter," and that portion richer in fibres is the "white matter."

Cerebrum.— The larger brain mass, the cerebrum, consists of two symmetrical halves, the hemispheres, separated above by the great longitudinal fissure and held together at the bottom of the fissure by a firm band of fibres, the callosum, and at the base by the cerebral peduncles, which unite below to form part of the pons, and the medulla. All of the fibres passing to and fro go up and down in the peduncles, separating into each hemisphere. The surface of the hemispheres is divided by fissures into several larger areas and a number of smaller ones. Thus in the lower side there is a large fissure, the fissure of Sylvius, below it there are three lobes, the first, second, and third temporal lobes. Running from the great longitudinal fissure, making an angle of about 65° with the Sylvian fissure, the second most marked fissure, that of Rolando, is found. This divides off an anterior region in which the first, second, and third frontal convolutions are to be found. Immediately around the fissure of Rolando are grouped the anterior and posterior parietal lobes, and at the back end of the hemispheres the occipital lobes are situated. All of these lobes are divided into smaller areas by the fissures, the chief end subserved by these fissures being to

---

HUMAN BRAIN.

increase the amount of outside surface of the hemispheres and thus make room for the enormous number of cells that are located in this outermost gray layer, the cortex. A further function seems to be expressed by this division into lobes and convolutions, namely, a localization of function, a concentration of energy as it were, certain types of brain activity being regulated in certain brain areas. Thus it is assumed that the main function of the frontal lobes is largely that of the reasoning faculties and higher intellectual processes. It is very well established that the cells in the cortex that are grouped up and down both sides of the fissure of Rolando are the cells that govern the motor acts of the body; irritate these, and muscular convulsions in certain groups will occur; destroy them by accident or disease, and paralysis, or loss of muscular function, will result. The localization for certain muscle groups, such as those for the head, arm, eyes, leg, etc., are very well known. In the occipital lobes, particularly in certain areas about the angular gyrus, are the centres for sight memories. Their destruction may result in mind blindness (see APHASIA). In much the same manner the memories of sound are located in the temporal convolutions, and there are a large number of areas thus localized. These different areas are all brought into connection, the one with the other, by hosts of fibres, and as already indicated the two hemispheres of the cerebrum are connected by thousands of fibres that are in the callosum. Thus in the adult normal cerebrum all parts of the cortex are brought into close connection with one another and with the other half of the cerebrum; the connections with the cerebellum and with the cord are established as well. The richness of association is an index of the education and intelligence of the individual. These cortical connections are not a helter-skelter. hit-or-miss system; they are all carefully laid down, constituting the human brain one of the most remarkable "switchboards" ever made. Modern anatomy is busy unraveling all the fibres and bundles of fibre tracts, and it will not be many years before the map of the brain will be as well known as that of New York. When that time arrives many unknown problems of nervous and mental disease will be solved and the hideous secrets of the insanities will be laid bare.

In addition to the cortical ganglionic masses of cells, there are a number of similar masses of cells located within the substance of the brain mass. These are subsidiary stations, as it were, for many of the fibre tracts going to and coming from the cortex. These are the caudate and lenticular nuclei, the optic-thalamus, and a number of smaller ones.

Cerebellum.— The cerebellum, or little brain, is situated behind and almost beneath the cerebrum, which partly overlaps it. It is attached to the brain stem by peduncles and its connections with the cerebral centres and those of the cord are many and complex. In minute structure the cerebellum has a number of characteristic features by which it may be recognized under the microscope, but fundamentally the nerve cells are similar, the interstitial connective tissue is the same in kind as in the cerebrum and the blood vessels, veins, and lymphatics have similar properties.

Membranes.— Surrounding the entire brain mass and extending down over the spinal cord there are three coverings. These are an outside strong and thick dura mater, and two inside delicate membranes, the arachnoid and pia mater.

Cavities.— The brain is not a solid organ. It is really a flattened-out expansion of nervous tissue peculiarly grouped about a central cavity. This central cavity at one time was as simple almost as the space occupied by the graphite in a lead pencil, but in the adult brain there are lateral ventricles, third and fourth ventricles, all of which are too complicated to be described here. The ventricles contain a fluid, the cerebrospinal fluid, which also bathes the outside of the brain. The cavities of the brain are continuous with the central cavity of the spinal cord.

This modern conception of the brain as a complicated automatic switchboard may be elaborated to any amount of detail. If one should trace, however, the path of a single impulse from the outside world, be it one of sight, smell, taste, touch, pain, etc., one would trace it, say for pain — first from the point of contact, for instance, of the finger, whence the special nerves of sense would carry it to the spinal cord; here it travels up a definite tract in the cord (for the upward paths of the passages of sensations and the downward ones of messages to act are as definitely known as are the railroads from New York to Chicago); from the cord it passes into the medulla, still in a well-defined path, where only it and its kind travel (about here the fibre tract crosses to the opposite side of the medulla); then through the pons, through the cerebral peduncles, up to the secondary centres, to the cerebellum and the sensory area in the cortex, which is supposed to be situated just behind the motor area. As soon as the sensory impulse reaches the cortex it is felt as pain and referred to the spot in the skin in contact with the irritant. Immediately in the perception of pain, so intimate are the connections of the sensory areas with the motor areas from these motor cells a conscious impulse is flashed down another series of fibres, down the peduncles to the medulla (where the fibres also mostly cross to the opposite side), down the spinal cord, out on a motor nerve to the muscle to cause a muscular act of pulling the hand away from the harmful irritant. This is the long, conscious series. There may also have been a shorter reflex cycle whereby the impulse passed to the spinal cord and an immediate motor connection was made that caused a quick jerking away of the hand, even before the perception of the sensation had taken place. This is the reflex cycle. See REFLEX ACT.

The study of the comparative anatomy and physiology of the nervous system is one of the most enchanting departments of human knowledge. To trace the gradual development of this intricate and marvelously adjusted regulator of the entire body, from its simplest terms of "protoplasm irritability" through the isolated ganglionic masses in such animals as the starfish, the gradual chaining of one mass to another as in the worms and insects, thus bringing a certain relation of one part to another, up to the fusion of different ganglionic masses to form a chief mass, the brain, and secondary masses, the spinal cord — this is a story of so many chapters and volumes that it cannot even be sketched here; but it is

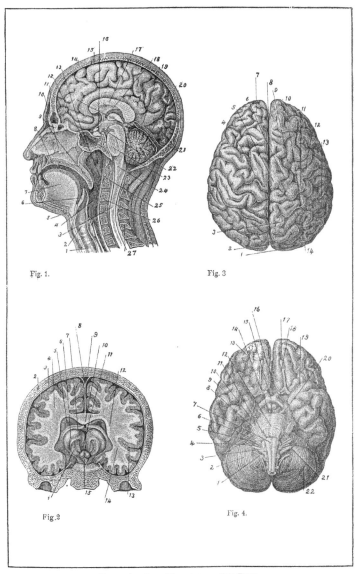

Fig. 1.

Fig. 3

Fig. 2.

Fig. 4.

For explanation of figures, see article Brain.

very certain that the gradual evolution of the nervous system shows the extreme complexity of man's activities. Although throughout the entire series, nerve cells are alike, it is only in the great multiplicity of co-ordinations and connections that man's brain differs from the nervous system of a jellyfish or a worm. It is only in the animal series beginning with *Amphioxus* that a distinct brain mass commences to be seen. But from this point forward the modification in form, size, and complexity is gradual. While man has the most complex brain, he has not the heaviest brain, although in comparison with his size it is the heaviest. The brain of man is usually heavier that that of woman, although at birth and at the age of 14 the female brain is heavier. Taller and heavier persons have usually heavier brains. Weight of brain, however, has no direct relationship with intelligence, as idiots' brains are known that have weighed as much as those of many of the ablest of men. Intellectual capacity, as already said, consists in the great multiplicity of nerve cell connections. In which connection it might also be added that the shape and size of the outside skull bears no constant relation to the shape and size of the inside brain. Cuvier's brain weighed 84 ounces, Gambetta's only 39 ounces. While it is true that a number of celebrated men of recognized brain power have had large brains, there are many more of equal capacity whose brain weights have not been remarkable. Also see MOTOR AREA; MOTOR CO-ORDINATION; NERVOUS SYSTEM; SPEECH CENTRES; TASTE AREAS.

Consult: Barker, 'The Nervous System' (1901); Schäfer, 'Physiology' (1900).

SMITH ELY JELLIFFE,
'Journal of Nervous and Mental Diseases.'

Brain, Diseases of. These are so many and so diverse that a general article cannot readily be written upon them. In general they may be divided into: (1) Developmental defects. These are considered under idiocy, imbecility (qq.v.), etc. (2) Acute infections in which the brain itself or its surrounding membranes are attacked by some form of bacterium, such as the influenza bacillus, the pneumoccus, that ordinarily is the main cause of pneumonia, the typhoid organism, or certain forms of cocci. These diseases are discussed under the heads, encephalitis, meningitis, cerebral abscess, epidemic cerebro-spinal meningitis (qq.v.). (3) Acute and chronic poisoning, including delirium tremens in alcoholism (q.v.), toxic manias (q.v.), etc. (4) Diseases of the blood vessels of the brain. Here is to be classed the general disease apoplexy. This is really three different diseases due to cerebral hemorrhage, cerebral thrombosis, or cerebral embolism. These are discussed here. In all, the symptoms are much alike, as similar areas in the brain may be affected by each. In hemorrhage there is a bursting of one of the cerebral blood vessels, with pouring out of blood into adjacent brain tissue and destruction. A certain blocking of the artery also results. In thrombosis, the walls are diseased and a soft mass collects on the inside of the blood vessel in the brain and blocks it up. This shuts off the circulation in a certain area supplied by the artery and there is degeneration in that area with softening perhaps and cyst formation. In embolism some foreign body from some other part of the arterial system is swept into a blood vessel of the brain and blocks it up. In all three forms of apoplexy the attack may be very slight, if the cause is slight, a temporary loss of consciousness, or a paralysis in one limb, or a hemiplegia that is transitory — these may be all that is noted. But the usual attack of apoplexy is much more severe. The patient is rendered unconscious, the face is purple or congested, there may be voiding of urine and feces, the breathing is slow and snoring in character, the pulse is usually slowed to 50, and often soft and full; nausea and vomiting and lowered temperature may also occur. The pupils may be dilated and the eyes may appear crossed. There is usually noted a difference in the two sides of the face, one side of the body is different from the other, and on lifting the limbs there is a change in their resistance. The patient may remain in this condition and die very soon, or he may have a rising temperature for a week and then die, or he may recover consciousness to find that one entire side of his body is paralyzed, or incapable of being moved by the will. If the right side is involved the patient usually has defects in his speech (aphasia, q.v.). After a few days, this paralysis may pass away, but it usually persists for life in some form or other. Almost invariably the paralyzed limbs improve greatly; at first the leg and later the arm, and the improvement may be very great so that only a slight trace of what was a disabling affliction remains. The shades and variations in symptoms and in the outcome are numberless. The treatment of an attack of apoplexy requires prompt attention. Heat to the extremities, mustard bath to the feet, absolute quiet, removal of constricting bands about the neck, placing the patient on the non-paralyzed side, in many cases blood-letting; these are the generally recognized things to do. The outlook is always serious. Hemorrhage is apt to occur in those over 50, thrombosis in those affected with syphilis, and may occur at any age, embolism usually accompanies some infectious disease, such as pneumonia, rheumatism, scarlet fever, childbirth fever, etc.; and may affect old or young (see DIPLEGIA; HEMIPLEGIA; MONOPLEGIA). (5) Accident or injury to the brain. These may occasion various forms of hemiplegia: diplegia, particularly in the injuries of childbirth; epilepsy, etc. (6) Tumors of the brain (see TUMOR). (7) Organic disease of the brain functions. Here the various insanities may be classed. Softening of the brain is a term denoting either a dementia (q.v.) of old age, or the insanity known as general paresis (q.v.). The insanities in their various forms and phases are treated in their appropriate relations under one inclusive head. See INSANITY.

SMITH ELY JELLIFFE,
Editor 'Journal of Nervous and Mental Diseases.'

Brain Fever. See BRAIN, DISEASES OF.

Brainard, David Legge, American soldier and explorer: b. Norway, N. Y., 1856. Entering the United States army in 1876 he served in Indian campaigns and subsequently accompanied the Greely Arctic expedition 1881-2. He was sergeant in the signal service, served in the Alaskan relief expedition in 1897 and went to the Philippines in 1900 as a major in the subsistence department of the regular army.

Brainard, John Gardiner Calkins, American poet and journalist: b. New London, Conn., 21 Oct. 1796; d. 26 Sept. 1828. After graduation at Yale in 1815 he studied law and practised at Middletown, Conn. In 1822 he went to Hartford and edited the *Connecticut Mirror,* in which many of his early poems appeared. In 1827 he was forced by failing health to resign his editorship. For a time he resided on Long Island, whence he returned to New London to end his days. He issued a volume of poems in 1825, a second and fuller edition of which, under the title of 'Literary Remains,' was published in 1832, with a biographical sketch by John Greenleaf Whittier.

Braine, Daniel Lawrence, American naval officer: b. New York, 18 May 1829; d. 30 Jan. 1898. He entered the United States navy in 1846 and became a rear admiral. He served with distinction through the Mexican and Civil wars. In 1873 he obtained the surrender by Spain of 102 survivors of the Virginius prisoners.

Braine-le-Comte, brăn-lĕ-kôṅt, Belgium, a small and ancient town of the province of Hainaut, about 20 miles southwest of Brussels. It contains a handsome church, founded in the 13th century, and a large well-built château. The Southern Railway branches off from this town, on the west side to Mons and Quiévrain, east to Namur and Charleroi. Among its manufactories are breweries, wire-works, dyeworks, oil,- cotton,- and corn-mills. At one time it manufactured and dealt extensively in tin wares, but this branch of trade is almost if not entirely extinct. Pop. (1899) 8,891.

Brainerd, David, a missionary to the Indians: b. Haddam, Conn., 20 April 1718; d. Northampton, Mass., 9 Oct. 1747. Early impressible by religious influences, he felt himself suddenly converted while taking a walk, 12 July 1739, and the same year entered Yale College to prepare himself for the ministry. Instead of graduating in the regular course he was expelled from the institution in 1742 for having said, in his zeal, of one of the tutors, that he had no more of the grace of God than a chair. He was, however, licensed in July as a preacher, and received an appointment from the society for the propagation of Christian knowledge, as missionary among the Indians near Stockbridge, Mass. He was ordained in 1744, and took up his work among the Indians at the forks of the Delaware in Pennsylvania, making two visits to the Indians of the Susquehanna. He met, however, with but little success, until, after a year, he went to reside among them at Crossweeksung, near Newark, N. J. Here he is said to have produced a great change among the savages, and to have baptized 78, of whom 38 were adults. Having worn out his health by his labors, he set out on a journey to Boston in the spring of 1747, and thence to Northampton, where he died after a short stay in the family of President Edwards, by whom his biography was soon afterward written. His published works are: 'Wonders of God Among the Indians,' and 'Grace Displayed.'

Brainerd, Minn., a city and county-seat of Crow Wing County, 115 miles west of Duluth, situated on the east bank of the Mississippi River and on the Brainerd & N. R.R. It lies in a fertile farming region and trades in grain and other agricultural produce. Lumber and furs are also exported. Here are situated the extensive shops of the Northern P. R.R. There are foundries, flour-mills, a large saw-mill, etc. There is a United States signal service station, a hospital for employees of the Northern P. R.R., and another for lumbermen, a public park, waterworks, electric street railway, electric lighting plant, etc. The city is governed by a mayor, elected biennially, and a city council. Pop. (1900) 7,524.

Brain'stone Coral, a madrepore of the genus *Meandrina,* so named from the general resemblance to the brain of man exhibited in its large rounded mass and numerous winding depressions. When the hemispherical mass is broken, the ridges which bound its furrows (each of which represents the place of a polyp) may be traced inward through its substance.

Brain'tree, Mass., a town in Norfolk County, on the New York, N. H. & H. RR., 10 miles south of Boston. It contains the villages of South and East Braintree; is connected by electric street railroads with the principal neighboring towns and villages, and its industries include granite-quarrying, and the manufacture of rails, tacks, shoes, wool, rubber goods, fans, etc. John Adams, John Quincy Adams, and John Hancock were born in a part of Braintree now within the limits of Quincy. The town was settled about 1629 and was incorporated in 1640. Pop. (1900) 5,981.

Braintree Resolutions, The. There were instructions given by the town of Braintree, Mass., on 24 Sept. 1765, to its representative in the Massachusetts General Court, Ebenezer Thayer, relative to his action in the matter of the Stamp Act. They were drawn by John Adams, one of a committee appointed by the Braintree town meeting for that purpose, accepted unanimously, and published in the Boston *Gazette.* Some 40 Massachusetts towns subsequently adopted them verbatim as their instructions to their own representatives; and John Adams says that Samuel Adams copied several paragraphs into his own draft for the Boston town-meeting. The resolutions declared the tax, even if legal, an unbearable burden and a vexatious interference with the business of a poor and sparsely settled province; that moreover, it was contrary to British common law, and the "foundation principles of the British constitution, that we should be subject to any tax imposed by the British Parliament, because we are not represented in that assembly in any sense, unless it be by a fiction of law"; that to put the cases in the decision of one judge without a jury was "an alarming extension of the power of courts of admiralty," and repugnant to the Great Charter itself, especially as the judges held office only during the pleasure of the Crown, and moreover had a commission on the goods condemned. They enjoin the Braintree representative to "comply with no measures or proposals" for executing the law, but "by all lawful means" obstruct it; to favor entering on the public records "the most clear and explicit assertion of our rights and liberties"; and — most significant of all — "to agree to no steps for the protection of the stamped paper or the stamp officers, because any addition to the laws for preserving the peace would only exasperate the people and endanger public tranquillity."

Braith, Anton, än'tōn brīt, German painter: b. Biberach, Würtemberg, 1836. He was educated at the Stuttgart Art School and the Munich Academy, and soon obtained distinction by his skill in landscape and animal painting. Among his best works are 'A Yoke of Oxen'; 'A Grazing Herd'; 'Going to Drink'; 'Herd Overtaken by a Storm'; 'After the Storm.'

Brake, Bracken, common names for a fern (*Pteris aquilina*) of the family *Polypodiaceæ,* widely distributed in Europe, Asia, and North America, where it often dominates the vegetation of heaths, neglected meadows, etc. It does not fall when the top is killed by frost, and affords excellent cover for small game. From its long, creeping rootstocks, naked stalks, 6 to 20 inches in length, are sent up. Each stalk produces three branches with numerous fern-like pinnate leaves, along the covered edges of which are borne the sori, or spore-producing organs. The rootstock, which is bitter, has been used as a substitute for hops in beer-making, and is still somewhat employed in dressing chamois and kid leather. The tops are often used for bedding animals, and are sometimes mixed with hay as fodder. Although land covered with brake is considered inferior, many such soils, when cultivated, are found to be good. By frequent mowing, or by plowing, the land is readily freed from brake. Several other species of *Pteris* have been called brake and bracken, and some are cultivated as ornamental plants in greenhouses and window-gardens. The rootstocks of a New Zealand species (*P. esculenta*) are often used for food, and are better suited for such use than those of the first-named species, which have served such a purpose only when ordinary food-supply has been scarce.

Brake, a mechanical device for retarding or arresting by means of friction the motion of a wheel or shaft. A wood or metal block, so arranged as to be pressed by levers against the rim of a wheel, constitutes a shoe-brake, the kind used in checking ordinary vehicles, such as wagons. A band passing around a wheel, and which, by tightening, retards its motion, forms a band-brake. The air-brake is the form of mechanism generally used on railroads. See AIR-BRAKE.

Brakelonde, Jocelin de, English chronicler: b. Bury St. Edmunds, in the 12th century. In 1173 he entered the convent of St. Edmunds and began his chronicle which extends over a period of nearly 30 years. The character of the abbot, Samson, described in these annals, influenced Carlyle in the writing of 'Past and Present.'

Bramah, brä'mä, **Joseph,** inventor of the Bramah lock, the Bramah press, etc.: b. Stainborough, Yorkshire, England, 1749; d. 1814. He was first apprenticed to a carpenter and joiner, but finally established himself in business in London as manufacturer of various small articles in metal-work. His subsequent life was distinguished by a long series of inventions, many of which have been found of great utility. Beside those already mentioned, he invented the apparatus used in public houses to bring liquids from the cellar to the bar, and ingenious printing machines. He also made improvements in fire-engines, steam-engines, the manufacture of paper, etc.

Bramante, brä-män'tě, Donato **d'Agnolo,** Italian architect: b. Monte Asdroaldo, near Urbino, about 1444; d. 11 March 1514. He applied himself first to painting, but his passion for architecture soon gained the ascendency, and he shares with Brunelleschi the credit of restoring this art. While yet a young man he went to Milan, where his time was mainly spent at the cathedral. Pope Alexander VI. named him as his architect, and Julius II. made him superintendent of his buildings. At the command of the latter he united the Belvidere with the palace of the Vatican. He persuaded the Pope to order the Church of St. Peter to be torn down, and another to be erected in its place, which should be without an equal in the world. In 1513 the foundation of the present St. Peter's was laid, according to the plan of Bramante. It yet remains the greatest achievement of modern architecture. Bramante did not live to see this work completed. He had begun the edifice with incredible dispatch, but his successors, Raphael, Julius of San Gallo, Peruzzi, and Michael Angelo, altered the original plan, and left nothing of Bramante's workmanship standing except the arches which support the tower of the dome. His writings, in prose and verse, first discovered in 1756, were printed in the same year at Milan.

Bramathe'rium, a genus of antilopidæ, consisting of a gigantic species with four horns. It is allied to sivatherium, which also is four-horned. Both occur in the Upper Miocene, or Lower Pliocene beds of the Sewâlik Hills in India.

Brambach, Kaspar Joseph, kas'par yō'zĕf bräm'baн, German composer: b. Bonn, 14 July 1833. He was a pupil at the Conservatory in Cologne (1851-4), and at Frankfort-on-the-Main he studied under Ferdinand Hiller. In 1859 he became a teacher at the Cologne Conservatory, and in 1861 went to Bonn as state musical director. Giving up that position in 1869, he devoted himself to the work of composing and private teaching. His best works are his cantatas, including 'The Eleusinian Festival'; 'A Hymn to Spring'; 'The Power of Song'; 'Alcestis'; 'Prometheus'; 'Colombus'; and 'Lorelei.' He has also written an opera, 'Ariadne,' and several minor pieces.

Brambanan, bräm-bä'nän, a district of the province of Surakarta, Java, rich in remains of Hindu temples, of which there are six groups, with two apparently monastic buildings. The edifices are composed entirely of hewn stone, and no mortar was used in their construction. The largest is a cruciform temple, surrounded by five concentric squares, formed by rows of detached cells or shrines, embracing an area 500 feet square. In several of these *dagobas* the cross-legged figures of Buddha remain, but the larger figures which must have occupied the central temples have disappeared from all but one.

Bramble, a common, but, in America, little used name for various species of the genus *Rubus,* including blackberry, raspberry, and dewberry. In Europe it is more restricted to *R. fruticosus,* which, from its abundance and its weedy character, has not received the attention of horticulturists.

Brambling, or Mountain Finch, a large migratory finch (*Fringilla montifringilla*), found throughout Europe and in Asia, where it breeds in the northern parts. It is a brightly colored bird, and nearly related to the chaffinch (q.v.).

Bramhall, brăm'hôl, John, Anglican prelate in Ireland: b. Pontefract, Yorkshire, England, 1594; d. 25 June 1663. He was educated at Cambridge, and was on the road to high preferment when he went to Ireland as Wentworth's chaplain in 1633. He soon became archdeacon of Meath, and was consecrated bishop of Derry in 1634. When the civil war broke out, for safety he crossed to England, but the Royalist disasters soon drove him to the Continent. At Paris he disputed with Hobbes on necessity and the freedom of the will. At the Restoration he was given the metropolitan see of Armagh. Bramhall closely imitated Laud in policy, and even resembled him in person, but was far his inferior in intellect. Not strong, but merely obstinate in purpose, the so-called Athanasius of Ireland by his impolitic intolerance sealed the doom of Episcopalian supremacy in Ulster.

Bramley, Frank, English artist: b. near Boston, Lincolnshire, 6 May 1857. He was educated at Lincoln and studied art at Antwerp. Among his works are 'Domino' (1886); 'Old Memories' (1892); 'For of Such is the Kingdom of Heaven' (1891); 'A Mute, Inglorious Milton' (1898); and several notable portraits.

Bran, the husks of ground corn, wheat, rye, or other cereals, separated from the flour. The nutritive value of these husks increases as we proceed from the outside of the grain toward the interior. The outer skin, or coarse bran, is very indigestible, owing to the presence of a layer of silica. The inner skins, called pollards, are more nutritious, containing from 12 to 15 per cent of nitrogenous matter, and from 20 to 30 per cent of starch. Unless ground very finely, however, they are apt to occasion irritation of the bowels and diarrhœa. Though rich in nitrogen, bran appears to possess but little nutritive power. It may be of use to the well fed, who need a laxative, but to the poor who need nourishment it is of very little use. It is, however, of some commercial value, being largely employed in the feeding of horses and cattle, and in brightening goods during the processes of dyeing and calico printing.

Branca, Ascanio, Italian statesman: b. 1840. He studied law at Naples and did journalistic work, and in 1870 was elected to the Italian Chamber of Deputies. He was later made secretary of the ministry of commerce but withdrew from this position in 1885, disapproving of the policy of the ministry. In 1891–2 he was minister of public works in Rudini's cabinet; in 1896–8 minister of finance, and in 1900–2 again minister of public works. He has written 'International Banking and Credit' (1871).

Branch, John, American statesman: b. Halifax County, N. C., 4 Nov. 1782; d. Enfield, N. C., 4 Jan. 1863. He graduated at the University of North Carolina (1801), studied law, became a judge of the superior court, State senator (1811–17). He was governor of his State (1817–20), and a member of the United States Senate (1823–9). He was appointed secretary of the navy by President Jackson, and held this office till the breaking up of the Cabinet in 1831. In 1835 he was a member of the convention to revise the State constitution, and in 1843 was appointed governor of the Territory of Florida, serving until the election of a governor under the State constitution, when he retired to private life. See Lanman: 'Biographical Annals of the Civil Government of the United States.'

Branch, **Mary** Lydia Bolles, American writer of stories for young people: b. New London, Conn., 13 June 1840. She was married to John L. Branch in 1870. Her published works include 'The Kanter Girls' (1893); 'The Old Hempstead House' (1896).

Branch, that portion of a plant produced from a lateral leaf bud on the primary axis or stem. It is looked upon as part of the stem, and not as a distinct organ. A branch generally produces secondary branches, and these give rise to minor ramifications, called branchlets or twigs. The different modes in which branches spring from the stem give rise to the various forms of trees; such as pyramidal, spreading, and weeping. Thus, in the cypress, the branches are erect, forming acute angles with the upper part of the stem; in the oak and cedar, they are spreading, each forming nearly a right angle; in the weeping ash and elm, the angles are oblique; while in the weeping willow and birch, the branches are pendulous, from their flexibility. The comparative length of the upper and under branches also gives rise to great differences in the contour of trees, as seen in the conical form of the spruce, and in the umbrella-like shape of the Italian pine.

Branchial Cysts and Fistulas. In early fetal life the human being possesses a series of four gills or branchi, and five clefts on each side of the head and neck, which in the course of development give rise to the upper and lower jaw and other structures. Should a cleft fail to completely fill in as the body grows it leaves a cavity or branchial cyst, which may at any time become inflamed or develop an abscess. If the opening on the neck persists it is a branchial fistula.

Branchiata, a name applied to all those marine arthropod animals which breathe by gills. The groups include the trilobites, merostomes, and crustacea, but excludes the arachnida. On this account the branchiata is believed by the best authorities to be an artificial group, and the term has therefore been abandoned.

Branchidæ, the name of an hereditary family, the descendants of Branchus; also of a place founded by them. Their original seat was a little south of Miletus in Ionia, where was the famous temple of Apollo Didymeus. After the destruction of the temple, probably toward the close of the 5th century B.C., an attempt was made to rebuild it, but on so colossal a scale that the project was never completed. Its ruins are of great interest to archæologists. Some of the statues, formerly erected along the road leading to the temple, have been removed to the British museum.

Branchiopoda, a division of crustacea of the division Entomostraca. They are for the most part microscopic, and are chiefly distinguished by having the gills attached to the legs, which are generally numerous. The body is sometimes naked, but more frequently is enveloped by a buckler, which in some covers only the head and thorax, and in others the whole body. Some have two or even three eyes, but a greater number have one only. They are all free and continually in motion. Among the *Branchiopoda* are the water-fleas and brine-shrimps, and some also rank the trilobites among them.

Branchiosaurus, an extinct genus of *Amphibia* (q.v.), whose remains have been found very abundantly and very perfectly preserved in the Permian shales of Saxony. It is of especial interest among fossil amphibians because it has been possible to study every stage of its development from embryo to adult. The animal was but a few inches long, proportioned like a salamander, with four limbs and five toes on each foot. Like the modern tadpole, the larva breathed by external gills which were replaced by lungs in the adult.

Branco, Rio, a river of north Brazil, the chief tributary of the Rio Negro. It is 400 miles in length, but 250 miles from its confluence with the Rio Negro navigation is blocked by falls.

Brand, Sir Jan Hendrik, Boer statesman: b. Cape Town, 6 Dec. 1823; d. 15 July 1888. He studied law in Leyden and in 1849 began to practice in the supreme court at Cape Town. In 1853 he became professor of law in the South African College. He early became prominent in public affairs, his sympathies being strongly pro-British. His influence prevented any participation of the Orange Free State in the movement to check British policy in South Africa. In 1863 he was elected president of the Orange Free State and was re-elected every five years until his death. Queen Victoria knighted him in recognition of his aid. Brandford was named in his honor, and Ladybrand was named in honor of his wife.

Brande, William Thomas, English chemist: b. London, 11 Feb. 1788; d. Tunbridge Wells, England, 11 Feb. 1866. He was educated at Westminster School, studied medicine and became an assistant to Sir Humphry Davy, succeeding him in 1813 in the chair of chemistry at the Royal Institution. In 1828 he became a superintendent in the mint. He wrote several standard books on chemistry. His chief works are: 'A Manual of Chemistry,' 'Outlines of Geology,' and an 'Encyclopædia of Literature, Science, and Art' (1842).

Brandeis, Frederick, American organist: b. Vienna, Austria, 1835; d. New York, 1899. At Vienna he studied under Fischof and Czerny. In 1851 he settled in New York, and between 1865–98 filled positions as organist at the Catholic churches of St. John the Evangelist and St. James, and the 44th Street Synagogue, and the Church of Saint Peter and St. Paul in Brooklyn. He composed numerous instrumental and vocal pieces, but is best remembered for his song, "My Love is Like the Red, Red Rose."

Brandenburg, a province of Prussia, surrounded mainly by Mecklenburg and the provinces of Pomerania, Posen, Silesia, and Prussian Saxony. The soil consists in many parts of barren sands, heaths, and moors; yet the province produces much grain, as well as fruits, hemp, flax, tobacco, etc., and supports many sheep. The forests are extensive. The principal streams are the Elbe, the Oder, the Havel, and the Spree. Brandenburg carries on an active trade in manufactured articles, and includes, besides some other districts, the greater part of the former Mark of Brandenburg, which formed the cradle of the Prussian monarchy, and the centre round which the present extensive kingdom has grown up. It is divided into the three administrative divisions of Berlin, Potsdam, and Frankfort, and has a total area of 15,381 square miles. The most of the inhabitants are Lutherans; the rest are chiefly Roman Catholics and Jews. From 1685 to 1688 many French refugees, Walloons, and inhabitants of Lorraine and of the Palatinate, settled in the Mark. At present Brandenburg is the most important of the Prussian provinces, including as it does the capital (Berlin), and the governments of Potsdam and Frankfort. The first people who are known to have inhabited Brandenburg were the Suevi. They were succeeded by the Slavonians, a barbarous people, whom Henry I. conquered and converted to Christianity in the early part of the 10th century. The government was first conferred on a Saxon count, and did not become hereditary till the time of Albert, whose son succeeded to the dignity of elector in 1180. This race becoming extinct, Charles IV. assigned the electorate to his son Sigismund, who became emperor in 1415, and sold the region to Frederick, burgrave of Nuremberg, the ancestor of the present reigning family. Frederick William the Great made various accessions to the territories of his ancestors, and obliged the king of Poland, in 1656, to declare Prussia an independent state. The Old Mark was ceded to Napoleon in 1807, and formed part of the kingdom of Westphalia; but it was restored to Prussia in 1814. The elector of Brandenburg held the seventh rank among the electors of the empire, and had five votes in the Council of Princes. Pop. (1900) 3,107,951. See PRUSSIA.

Brandenburg, a Prussian city, on the Havel, 35 miles west of Berlin, formerly the residence of the reigning family of Prussia. The Havel here expands into a lake, and divides Brandenburg into the Old Town, the New Town, and the Cathedral Island, the last containing a castle and the cathedral. The latter is a late Romanesque building (1170–1318), restored in the 19th century. The industries embrace woolen yarn, silk goods, baskets, leather, etc., and the building of boats is also carried on. Pop. (1900) 49,263.

Brandenburg, Confession of, a confession of faith issued in 1614 by the elector of Brandenburg. It was an attempt to reconcile the religious controversies growing out of the differences in Lutheran and Calvinistic doctrine.

Brandenburg, New. See NEU BRANDENBURG.

Brandes, Georg Morris Cohen, Danish literary critic of Jewish family: b. Copenhagen, 4 Feb. 1842. He graduated at the University of Copenhagen in 1864, and taught there, 1872–7. Several books on æsthetic and philosophic subjects brought on him a charge of skepticism which was not removed by an epoch-making series of lectures, delivered before large audiences, and published under the title, 'The Main Literary Currents of the Nineteenth Century' (1872–82); for his description of the later intellectual position of Europe, as broken away from the orthodoxy and romanticism of the beginning of the century, brought on him the bitter attacks of all the reactionary forces in Denmark. His 'Danske Digtere,' a masterpiece of psychological analysis, appeared in 1877; but the hostility of his enemies induced him in the same year to leave Denmark, and settle in Berlin, where he published, among other works, critical biographies of Lasalle (1877); Esaias Tegnér (1878); and Lord Beaconsfield (1879). Then a lecture tour through Norway and Denmark brought a powerful party to his side, and in 1882 he returned to Copenhagen, his countrymen having guaranteed him an income of $1,000, with the one stipulation that he should deliver public lectures on literature. Among his later works are: 'Den Romantiske Skole i Frankrig' (1882); a biography of Ludvig Holberg (1885); a valuable study of Shakespeare, published in an English translation in 1899; 'Impressions of Russia' (1888); 'Poems' (1899); 'Berlin as an Imperial Court.' Brandes is not only the foremost critic of Denmark, but one of the great literary critics of his age. His works have been translated into German and also into English and French.

Branding, a form of punishment once in use for various crimes, but abolished in England in 1823. It was performed by means of a red-hot iron, and the part which was branded was the cheek, the hand, or some other part of the body. When the practice of arresting judgment in criminal cases by Benefit of Clergy was in force, it was customary to brand on the left thumb any layman who received this benefit, since it was not permitted to a layman to enjoy it more than once. Even after branding had been abolished in all other cases it was for a long time retained in the army as a punishment for desertion, the letter D being marked on the left side of a deserter two inches below the armpit. It was not, however, properly speaking, branded on his side, but marked with ink, gunpowder, or some other substance which would leave a stain that could not be obliterated without destroying the skin at the part. This also has been abolished. In mercantile law the term refers to the stamping of some distinguishing mark upon manufactured articles. (See TRADE MARK.) In cattle-raising districts in the United States, Australia, etc., cattle are branded with the mark of the owner.

Brandis, Christian August, German philologist and historian of ancient philosophy: b. Hildesheim, 13 Feb. 1790; d. Bonn, 24 July 1867. After a course of philological and philosophical studies at Kiel and Göttingen, he graduated from the University of Copenhagen in 1812, and for a short time delivered lectures on philosophy. He was induced by Niebuhr in 1816 to accompany him to Rome as secretary to the Prussian embassy. From 1819 to 1821 he was engaged in conjunction with Immanuel Bekker in collecting materials for a new edition of Aristotle, published in four volumes at Berlin (1831–6). In 1821 he was appointed ordinary professor of philosophy at Bonn, and his professional duties at this university were continued during the rest of his life, being only interrupted by a residence of three or four years in Greece, where he was acting as councilor to King Otho. After his return from Greece he published an interesting and instructive work, for which his residence in that country had furnished him with materials, entitled 'Mittheilungen über Griechenland' (Communications on Greece) (1842), and at

the same time resumed his professorship at Bonn. His two most important works are his 'Handbuch der Geschichte der Griech.-Röm. Philosophie' (1835–60); and 'Geschichte der Entwickelungen der Griech.Philosophie' (1862-4).

Brandon, Canada, a city in Manitoba on the right bank of the Assiniboine River, 132 m. west of Winnipeg, on the Canadian Pacific Railway. The name was given first in 1794 to Brandon House, a trading-post on the Assiniboine, 13 m. east of the present location, and also to the range of hills to the south. Brandon is the railway centre for a fertile farming country and is the second city in size and importance in the province. It stands on the gravelly slopes of the south bank of the river and has excellent sewerage and water systems. Both the business and residence portions are well-built. It has fine churches, schools and public buildings, Brandon College, a Baptist educational institution, and a general hospital. Its manufacturing industries include a large binder-twine factory, machine works, and woolen, flour and saw mills. Across the valley is the Manitoba Experimental Farm of 670 acres; and on the same side of the valley, the Indian Industrial School and one of the Provincial Asylums for the Insane. Pop. (1901) 5,380; (1904 est.) 6,200.

Brandon, Vt., a township of Rutland County, 16 miles northwest of Rutland, on the Central Vt. R.R., near Otter Creek. It contains an academy, two parks, a fine hotel, marble quarries, flour mills, and manufactories of carriages, castings, paint, etc. Pop. (1900) 2,759.

Brandstetter, Hans, Austrian sculptor: b. Hitzendorf, near Graz, 25 Jan. 1854. He first studied wood-carving in Graz and later went to the Academy at Vienna where he was a pupil of Hellmers. His three earliest works won the prize given by the Academy; these are 'Lot's Flight from Sodom,' 'The Flute-player,' and 'Plato.' Among his other works may be mentioned his bronze 'Forest Lily,' 'Prometheus,' 'The Return of the Prodigal Son,' and the busts of Hamerling and Rosegger.

Brandt, Carl Ludwig, kärl lood'vĭg bränt, German-American painter: b. near Hamburg, Germany, 22 Sept. 1831; d. Savannah, Ga., 19 Jan. 1905. He studied art in European art galleries, came to the United States in 1852, and thereafter painted portraits and historical scenes. He became a member of the National Academy in 1872, and was a director of the Telfair Academy of Arts and Sciences at Savannah, Ga.

Brandt, Gerhard, Dutch Arminian clergyman: b. Amsterdam, 1626; d. there, 1685. After completing his studies and making himself a thorough Hebrew and Greek scholar, he became pastor of the Remonstrants, first at Nieukoop and afterward at Amsterdam. His works, almost all written in Dutch, include a 'Life of Admiral Michel Ruyter,' which has been translated into French; a 'Narrative of the Trial of Barneveld, Hoogerbeets, and Grotius'; and a 'History of the Reformation.' The last work, on which his fame chiefly rests, has been translated into English. It is remarkable for the elegance of its style, but written too much in the spirit of partisanship.

Brandt, Hermann Carl George, German-American educator: b. Vilsen, Germany, 15 Dec. 1850. He graduated from Hamilton College,

Clinton, N. Y., in 1872; was instructor there (1874-6), associate professor of German at Johns Hopkins University (1876-82); and since 1883 professor of German at Hamilton. He has published a 'German-English and English-German Dictionary' (1879); 'German Grammar' (1884); a 'German Reader' (1889); and an edition of Lessing's 'Nathan der Weise.'

Brandt, Josef von, Polish painter: b. Szczebrzeszyn, 11 Feb. 1841. He first studied engineering at Paris, then took up painting at Munich as a pupil of Franz Adam and Karl Piloty and opened his own studio. His pictures mostly illustrate the soldier life of the 17th century, though he has painted also some excellent pictures of Polish peasant life. His works include 'Polish Peasants at the Inn,' 'Episode of the Thirty Years' War,' 'The Battle with the Turks near Vienna, 12 Sept. 1683,' 'Cossack Camp,' 'Tartar Battle,' 'Cossacks on the March,' 'Cossacks' Triumphal Song,' and 'Defense of a Farmyard by Polish Cavalry.'

Brandt, Marianne (family name, MARIE BISCHOF), German opera singer: b. Vienna, 12 Sept. 1842. She received her education at the Vienna Conservatory and won her first success on the stage as Recha in 'The Jewess.' She was at Gratz for a short engagement, and in 1868-82 was connected with the Royal Opera in Berlin; in 1876 and 1882 she assisted at the Wagner musical festivals at Bayreuth. After 1882 she made a number of tours and sang at the German Opera in New York for several seasons. She ranks very high both as a singer and an actress, her voice being a contralto.

Brandt, Max August Scipio **von,** German diplomatist: b. Berlin, 8 Oct. 1835. He served for a short time in the army, but was sent on diplomatic business to the East in 1860 and was resident in Japan as German diplomatic representative (1862-75). From 1875 to 1893 he was German minister at Pekin. He has published 'Aus dem Lande des Zopfes' (1894); 'Die Zukunft Ostasiens' (1895); 'Sittenbilder aus China' (1895).

Brandt, Nicholas, German chemist of the 17th century, usually considered the discoverer of phosphorus. Leibnitz mentions him as a chemist of Hamburg, who, during a course of experiments on urine, for the purpose of discovering a solvent which would convert silver into gold, accidentally produced phosphorus, in 1667 or 1669. He communicated or sold his discovery to Kunkel, who showed it to Leibnitz. Boyle, securing a piece of the phosphorus, and knowing from what material it had been obtained, after various experiments succeeded in preparing it, and thus made an independent discovery of the method.

Brandy, the name most commonly applied to the spirit distilled from the juice of the grape, but also given to liquors distilled from other fruits, such as apples, cherries, peaches, etc. All these brandies differ from each other only in the essential oil which they contain, and which gives to each its different flavor and aroma. The alcohol in brandy generally constitutes 50 per cent of the whole, the remaining substances being water, amyl, propyl, and isobutyl, alcohols, glycerol, etc. The aroma is due to œnanthic ether and some volatile oils. A brandy highly esteemed is that of Cognac, exported from southwestern France, and obtained by distilling white wines of the finest quality. An inferior kind of spirit is frequently prepared from the "marc" of grapes and the refuse of wine vats. When first distilled it is as colorless as alcohol, and continues so if kept in bottles or jars. When stored in casks, however, it acquires from the wood a pale amber tint, and in this state is sold as pale brandy. The dark color of brown brandy is produced artificially, to please the public taste, by means of a solution of caramel, and this is frequently added in excess to give a rich appearance to a brandy of low quality. A large proportion of the brandy sold in the United States is simply raw grain spirits flavored and colored. The spirit is imported into France, where it is redistilled and converted into French brandy. Brandy improves in flavor by being kept, but loses in strength. Genuine Cognac brandy has always been both costly and difficult to obtain in this country (the more so on account of the high import tariff collected thereon), the price for the liquor reaching $20 or more per gallon. Of late years the development of viticulture in the western States, particularly in California, has enabled American enterprise to produce a brandy that is everywhere a formidable rival to the French article, and for purity and excellence infinitely preferable to the compounded and doctored spirit for which we have been accustomed to pay so high a price. Genuine brandy consists of alcohol and water, with small quantities of œnanthic ether, acetic ether, and other volatile bodies produced in the process of fermentation. The value of brandy as a medicine depends on the presence of these ethers and other volatile products; when, therefore, it is adulterated with raw grain spirit and water, the amount of these ethers is so reduced that the brandy becomes almost valueless for medical purposes. Imitation brandy is prepared either by flavoring highly rectified spirit with essence of Cognac or by distilling the spirit with bruised prunes, acetic ether, argol, and a little genuine brandy, and adding to the distilled spirit tincture of catechu and spirit coloring. This is said to be greatly improved by keeping. See ALCOHOL; BEVERAGES; DISTILLED LIQUORS.

Brandy Station, Va., a village of Culpeper County, southwest of Alexandria, notable as the scene of several minor battles during the Civil War. The earliest, on 20 Aug. 1862, was distinguished by a fierce cavalry charge on the Federal side; the second, 9 June 1863, resulted in the defeat of the Federal cavalry under Gens. Buford and Pleasanton by the Confederate commander Stuart. See FLEETWOOD. or BRANDY STATION, BATTLE OF. Other battles were fought near here, 13 Sept. 1863; 11 Oct. 1863; and there were also several skirmishes here.

Brandywine Creek, a small river of Pennsylvania and Delaware, formed of two forks, the east and west, which effect a junction in Chester County of the first named State, and, taking a southeasterly course, empties into Christiana Creek two miles below Wilmington. At Chadd's Ford on the Brandywine, 11 Sept. 1777, was fought a severe battle between the British and German troops, 18,000 strong, under Howe, and the Americans, numbering 13,000 men, under Washington, in which the latter were defeated. The consequence of this battle was the occupation of Philadelphia by the British troops.

Branford, Conn., a borough of New Haven County, situated on Long Island Sound, and on the New York, N. H. & H. R.R., about seven miles southeast of New Haven. The harbor admits small vessels. The oyster-beds of Branford form an important industrial feature. Among other occupations are the quarrying of granite, and the manufacture of locks and iron-fittings. The Blackstone Memorial Library, one of the most notable of the smaller American public library buildings, is located here. The place was settled in 1643, and in 1667 a large number of the inhabitants removed to New Jersey, settling at Newark. Branford was named for Brentford, England, and was incorporated in 1893. Pop. (1900) township, 5,706; borough, 2,473.

Brangwaine, the name of the nurse of Yseult in the legend of Tristan. The name appears as Brangäne in Wagner's opera, 'Tristan and Isolde.'

Branicki, Jan Klemens, yän klä′mĕnz bra̧-nĭts′kĕ, Polish statesman: b. 1688; d. 9 Oct. 1771. In his youth he served in the French army. In 1715 he returned to Poland. He rose to the highest dignities, was an opponent of Augustus II., and the zealous champion of the nobility. After the death of Augustus III., he officiated as great constable and first senator of the kingdom, and stood at the head of the Republican party, but defended the privileges of the nobility. He was offered the crown by a great majority of the nobles who constituted the nation. But the party of the Czartoryskis, backed by Russia, was triumphant. Poniatowski was elected, and Branicki was outlawed and escaped to Hungary. As his wife was a sister of the new king, he soon returned and recovered his dignities. He was called by the nation the last patriot, and at his funeral was performed for the last time the mediæval ceremony of the ancient chivalry, that of breaking the coat of arms, and entombing it with the body of the last member of a noble line.

Brank, an instrument formerly in use for the punishment of scolds. It consisted of an iron frame which went over the head of the offender like a common horse-bridle, and had in front an iron plate, which was inserted in the mouth, where it was fixed above the tongue and kept it perfectly quiet. Such instruments are still preserved in the Ashmolean Museum, Oxford, the National Museum of Antiquities at Edinburgh, and in other museums, municipal buildings, and churches in England and Scotland.

Bran′nan, John Milton, American soldier: b. Washington, D. C., 1819; d. New York, 17 Dec. 1892. He graduated at the United States Military Academy in 1841, and entered the 1st Artillery. During the Mexican war he took part in the battles of Cerro Gordo, Contreras, and Churubusco, and in the siege of Vera Cruz and the capture of the city of Mexico, where he was severely wounded. He was brevetted captain for gallant and meritorious conduct at Contreras and Churubusco. He served against the hostile Seminoles in Florida, and at the outbreak of the Civil War commanded the forces engaged in the reduction of the Confederate works on St. John's River, compelling the evacuation of Jacksonville. He commanded a division in the Army of the Cumberland 1863-4, taking part in the advance on Tullahoma, served through the Atlanta campaign and all its operations, and was in the battles of Hoover's Gap, Chickamauga, Missionary Ridge, Kenesaw Mountain, and the siege of Atlanta. On 13 March 1865 he was brevetted major-general of volunteers for gallant and meritorious services during the War. He was stationed at various posts from 1866 until his retirement, 19 April 1882, as colonel of the 4th Artillery.

Bran′ner, John Caspar, American geologist: b. New Market, Tenn., 4 July 1850. He graduated at Cornell University in 1882, and in 1885 took his degree of Ph.D. at the University of Indiana. He was assistant geologist of the Imperial Geological Survey of Brazil 1875-8; special botanist for Thomas A. Edison in South America 1880-1; special agent of the United States Department of Agriculture for investigating cotton and the insects affecting it in Brazil 1882-3; topographical geologist of the Pennsylvania geological survey, anthracite district 1883-5; professor of geology at the University of Indiana 1885-91; State geologist of Arkansas 1887-92. In 1892 he was elected professor of geology at Leland Stanford Jr. University, and since 1899 has been its vice-president. He has written a large number of papers and reports on geology and physical geography, and is associate editor of the 'Journal of Geology.'

Brannon, Henry, American jurist: b. Winchester, Va., 26 Nov. 1837. He studied law and practised his profession in West Virginia 1859-81, becoming circuit judge in 1880, and judge of the State supreme court in 1888. He has published 'Treatise On Rights and Privileges Under 14th Amendment to the Constitution of the United States.'

Brant, Joseph (THAYENDANEGEA), Mohawk chief: b. Ohio, about 1742; d. 24 Nov. 1807. He was sent by Sir William Johnson to a school at Lebanon, Conn., from which grew Dartmouth College. Joining the Episcopal Church he taught religion to the Mohawk Indians, translating into their language parts of the New Testament and the Prayer Book. His services against Pontiac and in the French and Indian war were highly valued. After Sir William Johnson's death, he became, in 1774, secretary to George Johnson, superintendent of Indian affairs, and when the American Revolution began he incited the Indians against the colonies. His presence at the massacre of Wyoming is authoritatively disproved, but he took part in that of Cherry Valley, and in other savage engagements. He was received with great distinction on his tour to England in 1786, and was attached to the military service of Sir Guy Carleton in Canada. He opposed the confederation of the Indians which led to the expedition of Gen. Wayne, and did all he could to prevent peace between the Indians and the United States. He was zealously devoted to the welfare of his own people, a brave warrior, and noted for his ability. In England he collected funds with which he built the first Episcopal Church in Upper Canada. One of his sons, in the War of 1812, was the leader of a body of Canadians and Indians against the United States. The life of Brant has been written by Col. W. L. Stone of New York.

Brant, bränt, or **Brandt, Sebastian,** German poet: b. Strassburg, 1458; d. there, 10 May 1521. He studied law at Basel, took the doctor's degree, and delivered lectures on jurisprudence for many years. In 1501 he was state councilor at Strassburg, and state recorder in 1503. Some of his writings brought him to the notice of Emperor Maximilian, who entrusted him with several important commissions in the interests of the state. He translated Virgil, Terence, and other Latin writers, and wrote a number of law treatises as well as poetry. The work which brought him fame is a poem called 'The Ship of Fools,' first published in Basel 1494, in which he satirizes the vices and follies of his age. This became immediately popular; four editions appeared in one year, and it was translated into Low German, Latin, French, and English. In Germany it was so esteemed that the celebrated preacher Geiler of Kaisersburg delivered public lectures on it from the pulpit at Strassburg. Later editions have been printed, of which the best are by Zarncke (1854), and by Goedecke (1872). The English translations are by Alexander Barclay (1509), and by Henry Watson, the latter reprinted in 1874.

Brant, a small wild goose of the genus *Branta*. The most familiar species, the "common brant" (*Branta bernicla*) is found widely distributed throughout the United States. Its plumage, chin, and cheeks are glossy black, fading into gray at the sides, with its under parts entirely white, and white streaks on the sides of the neck. In its markings it is distinguished from the "black brant" (*Branta nigricans*) of the Pacific coast, which is entirely black underneath. Brants generally travel in flocks, and their comparative sluggishness enables the gunner to procure a larger number in the short time they are present, than of any other sort of goose. They feed on vegetable matter, their chief food consisting of the "eel-grass," for which they dive at low tide. The brant is chiefly a marine bird, rarely seen in the interior of the United States, and breeds in the far North, well within the Arctic Circle. Its nest is made on the ground from grass, mosses, etc., and its four eggs are dirty white in color. The name is sometimes given to other species of goose, as for instance the "snow goose" (q.v.) is sometimes termed "white brant" because of its similarity in size. See GEESE.

Brant-bird, or **Beach-robin**, common names among American gunners for the shorebird (*Strepsilas interpres*), called "turnstone" by British sportsmen and in most books, because of its habit of moving aside pebbles in order to get at the beach-fleas and other small creatures hiding beneath them, upon which it feeds. It also makes a special food upon our shores of the eggs of the "horsefoot," or king crab, which it scratches out of the sand; hence it is known to some as "horsefoot snipe." It stands between the plovers and sandpipers, having a comparatively short bill and legs, and less active manners than most of the latter. It is, perhaps, the most beautiful of the beachbirds, having a highly variegated plumage much alike in both sexes. The bill is black; feet orange; head and sides of neck black and white, with a black band across the breast; throat, lower parts and tail coverts, white; remainder of the plumage chestnut and brown, mottled with black

and set off by a white band on the wing. This is one of the most cosmopolitan of birds, wandering to all parts of the world, yet nowhere, perhaps, numerous.

Brantford, Canada, city, port of entry, and county-seat of Brant County, Ontario; on the Grand River, at the junction of several branches of the Grand Trunk Railway, 70 m. southwest of Toronto and 60 m. east of London. It is named from the Mohawk chief, Joseph Brant (q.v.), to whom a fine monument, a colossal statue, was unveiled in Victoria Square, 13 Oct. 1886. The Grand River is navigable to within about two miles of the city, and is connected therewith by a canal, affording water communication with Lake Erie. A United States consular agent is stationed here. The city is lighted by electricity, and has hand-some churches, schools, and private buildings, a stone courthouse, hospital, house of refuge, etc. It is the seat of the Ontario Institution for the Education of the Blind and of Wickliffe Hall. Brantford is the trade centre of a large and fertile agricultural region; has branches of all the principal banks; and daily and weekly newspapers. The buildings and shops of the Grand Trunk Railway occupy more than 12 acres. The manufactures comprise metal and stoneware, engines, machinery, sash and blinds, agricultural implements, etc. Pop. (1901) 16,619.

Brantôme, Pierre de Bourdeille, pē-ār dé boor-dä-ē brän-tôm, (LORD OF THE ABBEY OF BRANTÔME): b. Périgord, Gascony, about 1540; d. 1614. In his epitaph, composed by himself, he relates in a vaunting manner how he first bore arms under the great Francis of Guise, and afterward served the king, his master. At an early age he received the abbey of Brantôme, but his life was mostly spent in war and gallantry. After the death of Charles IX. he withdrew to his estates and wrote his memoirs, which have a great deal of vanity and self-complacency, mingled with much that is interesting. Brantôme was personally acquainted with the great characters of the time, and an eye-witness of all the important events which then took place, and in some was an actor. He was a courtier, regardless of right or wrong; who does not blame the great, but observes and relates their faults and crimes as ingenuously as if he were uncertain whether they deserve praise or blame; as indifferent about honor and chastity in women as about integrity in men. He places us in the middle of that century when expiring chivalry was contending with the forming and as yet unsettled manners of later times. Brantôme, in the midst of his wandering life, had acquired more learning than most of his fellow soldiers. He has left 'Vies des grands Capitaines Français'; 'Vies des grands Capitaines Étrangers'; 'Vies des Dames Illustres'; and 'Vies des Dames Galantes' (together called 'Recueil des Dames'); besides other works.

Brase'nose, one of the colleges of Oxford University, founded by William Smith, bishop of Lincoln, and Sir Richard Sutton, in 1509. The origin of the name is unknown, farther than that it was transferred to the college from the previously existing Brasenose Hall. Anthony à Wood states that Brasenose Hall had as its sign a nose of brass, being probably a knocker. The college is very rich in endowments, which, however, have suffered owing to the decreased revenue from land.

Brashear (brăsh'ẽr) City. See MORGAN CITY.

Brash'er, Abraham, American army officer: b. New York, 22 Dec. 1734; died in exile during the revolution, in 1782. He was one of the most active associates of the "liberty boys" of his native city. He wrote many of the popular ballads of the revolutionary period, and was a constant contributor to the newspapers of his day. Among his poetical productions were 'Another New Year's Address,' and the 'General's Trips to Morristown,' both of which were favorites in the American camp.

Bras'idas, Spartan general who distinguished himself in the first half of the Peloponnesian war by his courage and his military skill: d. 422 B. C. He first distinguished himself by repelling the attack of the Athenians on the fortress of Methone (431 B.C.). In 429 he was sent to assist Cnemus and participated in the unsuccessful attack on the Piræus; in 427 accompanied the admiral Alcidas to Corcyra; in 425 was severely wounded in the assault on Pylos; and subsequently was elected by his fellow-countrymen to be the leader of an expedition intended to carry the war into Thrace. In 424 he relieved Megara, and passing through Thessaly effected a junction with Perdiccas of Macedon. Within a short time he had gained possession of Arrhibæus, Acanthus, Stagira, Amphipolis, Torone, and Scione. In 423 a truce was agreed upon, and in the same year Mende revolted and Brasidas immediately seized the town. The Athenians had, however, sent a new armament into the field consisting of two armies, and Brasidas, receiving no reinforcements from Sparta, was later forced to surrender the town to one of these armies. Cleon, the leader of the second army, allowed himself to be drawn into a battle at Amphipolis, and was totally defeated, he himself being in the number of the slain. But the Spartan victory was purchased with the loss of their general, who received a fatal wound during the engagement. Brasidas was buried at Amphipolis, within the walls, and long after his death his memory was honored as that of a hero, by the celebration of yearly sacrifices and games. The Greek writers speak highly of Brasidas. Thucydides notices his eloquence, unusual in a Spartan, his justice, liberality, and wisdom, while Plato compares him to Achilles; but circumstances are not wanting to show that he was' endowed with as much Spartan duplicity as Spartan courage.

Brass, Sally, in Dickens' 'Old Curiosity Shop,' an evil and cruel woman who was her brother's law partner and assisted him in carrying out his schemes.

Brass, Sampson, in Dickens' 'Old Curiosity Shop,' an attorney of evil reputation, whom Quilp uses as a tool.

Brass. The quality of brass depends upon the proportions of its two constituents, copper and zinc. The greater the quantity of zinc the lighter the color and the more brittle and springy the alloy; while on the other hand, the greater the quantity of copper, the redder the color and the tougher but softer the alloy. Technically, the term brass is extended to include compounds of copper and tin, as in brass ordnance, the brasses or bearings of machinery, etc.; but such alloys of copper and tin, though styled hard brass, are more strictly varieties of bronze. Brass foil, frequently not more than 1-50,000 of an inch in thickness and known as Dutch leaf, is made by beating out sheets of very thin brass containing a large proportion of copper. Copper and zinc alloys resembling brass are well known in the trade as gilding metal, mannheim gold, pinchbeck, bath metal, Bristol brass, Muntz sheathing metal, spelter solder, and mosaic gold.

In the manufacture of brass, either of two processes may be followed. The direct method is to fuse the zinc in a crucible and gradually add the copper in pieces. But this process is attended with disadvantage, owing to the volatile and oxidizable nature of zinc. The direct method of forming brass is generally followed ; it consists in heating in crucibles or pots a mixture of calamine (carbonate of zinc), charcoal, and thin pieces of scrap or grain copper. For ordinary purposes brass is first cast into plates of about 100 pounds weight ($\frac{1}{4}$ to $\frac{1}{2}$ inch thick) which can be readily broken up, remelted, and cast in a mold of any desirable shape or size.

The following are the usual proportions in the several varieties of brass: Red brass—4 parts copper to 1 part zinc; Yellow brass—2 parts copper to 1 part zinc; Muntz metal—3 parts copper to 2 parts zinc; Spelter solder—1 part copper to 1 part zinc. For brass wire the mixture generally used is five parts copper to three parts zinc, but the proportions vary greatly, according to the purpose for which the wire is to be used. For some purposes, such as the manufacture of pins, where rigidity is of more importance than toughness, and cheapness is essential, it is possible to use Muntz metal; while for drawing into very fine gauges and weaving into the gauze that is used largely in paper-making machinery, much richer grades are employed.

The alloying of copper and spelter is performed in crucibles, generally made 16 inches in depth and 10 inches in diameter at the top tapering to about 9 inches in diameter at the bottom, the thickness of the walls being about 1 inch. These crucibles are heated in "wind furnaces." This furnace is fired with solid fuel and has a natural draft, the height of the chimney stacks varying from 40 feet, where each furnace has its separate stack, to 150 feet where a number of furnaces are connected to one stack. Gas furnaces are also used in combination with generators, in which case producer gas, or sometimes water gas is burned in place of the solid fuel; in these it is usual to heat 10 or 12 crucibles in one furnace or chamber. Reverberatory and tilting furnaces are employed for large castings in sand molds, but for casting ingots in metal molds it is usual to employ a crucible furnace of the "wind furnace" type, the fuel commonly used being coke. Tilting furnaces are largely used in America. The oldest method of making brass, still largely used, is as follows: The metal is cast into long narrow ingots of about 1 cwt. each, and from 3 to 4 inches wide. The molds are generally made of cast iron, cast in halves, which are clamped together with wrought-iron rings. The molds are placed below the surface of the floor of the casting shop, and are supported against the side of the pit at an angle of about 60 degrees. Boards are placed across for the caster to stand upon while pouring the metal from the crucible into the mold. The metal, after careful skimming, is poured into the mold at the top, and when it has set the rings are slipped off the mold and the upper half removed, leaving the casting or ingot exposed. Before the metal is poured into the mold the inside of the mold is well brushed and dressed with resin and cotton-seed oil to prevent adhesion, or carbon in a fine state and whale oil are used, which give the mold an even surface. The ingots are next rolled when cold between ordinary flat rolls until the desired thickness is obtained.

The best process of *slitting* commonly employed in America, for grades of brass which can only be rolled cold, consists of casting the brass in the form of long bars, either square or round, from 1¼ to 1½ inches thick. Each of these bars is rolled down separately in the cold state into a rod about ⅜ inch in diameter, or sometimes less, which is afterward drawn into wire. Pieces weighing from 60 lbs. to 70 lbs. can thus be obtained. The advantage of this process over the old one is that longer lengths are obtained, and labor in the drawing is to some extent saved. A process brought out some years ago in the north of England consisted in casting in a centrifugal mold about 18 inches in diameter, and mounted on a vertical axis revolving at a high speed, so as to produce a casting in the form of a hoop. This was rolled down in open-ended rolls brought together with hydraulic pressure, and working in the same manner as those used for rolling out the tires for locomotives and other railway stock. A large thin hoop about 3 inches wide resulted, which was then cut in circular shears helically, forming a long strip, and this was drawn in the usual way. The great advantage of this method lay in the fact that a heavy piece was obtained, at the same time having a small section ready for drawing. In France a method often employed of making the "slittings" is to roll the metal down into large sheets, which are cut into strips spirally. Another method tried in America consists in casting a solid billet, which is pierced with a suitably constructed mandril to form a cylinder, which is afterwards cut up helically and drawn in the usual way.

In recent years continuous drawing machines have come very much into use. With these machines, instead of winding the wire on to a block, after drawing through one die at a time, the wire is drawn through one die, then wound two or three times round a block, and taken through another die, and so on, the friction on each drum being sufficient to carry the wire forward, and the circumferential speed of the drums being varied to suit the elongation of the wire. Owing, however, to brass being very quickly hardened by drawing, it is not possible to carry on this process *ad infinitum*, unless the wire be annealed periodically. When once it has been annealed it is possible to effect a very large reduction at one draught, the actual amount varying with the composition of the brass, the larger the proportion of copper the

greater the reduction at one draught. (See BRASS AND COPPER INDUSTRY).

The following table shows the weight in pounds of sheet brass of various thicknesses:

Thickness in inches	Weight of sheets per square foot	Thickness in inches	Weight of sheets per square foot
1/64	2.7	17/64	45.95
1/32	5.41	9/32	48.69
3/64	8.12	19/64	51.4
1/16	10.76	5/16	54.18
5/64	13.48	21/64	56.85
3/32	16.25	11/32	59.55
7/64	19.	23/64	62.25
1/8	21.65	3/8	65.
9/64	24.3	25/64	67.75
5/32	27.12	13/32	70.35
11/64	29.77	27/64	73.
3/16	32.46	7/16	75.86
13/64	35.18	29/64	78.55
7/32	37.85	15/32	81.25
15/64	40.55	31/64	84.
1/4	43.29	1/2	86.75

Bras'sarts, or **Brassards,** jointed plates of steel, protecting the upper arm, from the shoulders, which were covered by poldrons, to the elbows, where they were met by the gauntlets. These pieces of armor were not used in the chivalric ages, or in full suits of knightly armor, but in the half armor worn during the wars of Gustavus Adolphus, Wallenstein, and the Low Countries, in the times of Cromwell, when plate armor was going out of use.

Brasses, Monumental or **Sepulchral,** plates of brass, or of a mixed metal resembling brass, called laton, or latten, used as memorials of the dead. They were often made of life size and were cut to the shape of the figure, the details of armor, costume, features, etc., being worked out in incised lines from an eighth to a quarter of an inch in depth. Others, again, are found of much smaller dimensions, and rectangular in form, bearing in miniature the effigies of several figures. Such a plate of the 16th century, in the abbey church of Whalley, Lancashire, England, shows in the middle foreground the effigy of a knight in plate armor, kneeling with his hands clasped as if in prayer, and opposite him, in a similar devotional attitude, that of his wife; while behind the father range the kneeling figures of several sons, distinguished by their costumes as soldiers, priests, etc., and behind the mother a similar row of daughters, the family numbering in all some 20 persons. Underneath is an inscription recording the names of the knight and his wife, with dates, and a statement that he had built the chantry in which the plate was placed. Such brasses are often found affixed to the walls of a church, but it is sometimes uncertain whether they were so placed originally, many plates having been removed in the course of restorations.

The larger outline figures are usually found riveted or leaded into slabs of stone which form part of the church floor, the shallow depressions which hold the plate being cut to the shape. Such an one is the brass of Sir Roger de Trumpington, in Trumpington Church, near Cambridge, England, here shown. It is an excellent and well-preserved delineation of the armor of its day. The date of death is 1289, and this is believed to be the second oldest monumental brass in England; the older example being that of Sir John d'Aubernoun, in the church of Stoke d'Aubernoun, Surrey, bearing date 1277. The earliest brass of which there is any record in England is that of Simon de Beauchamp, of about the beginning of the 13th century; but the figure is no longer in existence. The incised lines were sometimes filled in with a hard enamel, often of varying colors, though in most cases the enamel has disappeared. By the use of these colors it was possible to display the heraldic tinctures of the shield or tabard.

The art of engraving monumental brasses appears to have been introduced into England from the Continent, where it was much practised, and where some very fine specimens are to be found. (The ecclesiastical figure here shown is in a church at Bonn.) There are still a very large number of brasses in English churches, but empty hollows in stones bear witness to-day of the times of the Reformation, the civil wars, and the Puritans, when the hands of fanatics tore away these fine memorials as being "popish,"

Brass of Sir Roger de Trumpington, Trumpington Church, Cambridge.

or those of soldiery reft them from their settings for purposes of gun-founding or revenge.

There are some handsome specimens of brasses mounted on altar-tombs. A fine instance is that of Robert Pursglove, suffragan bishop of Hull, England, in the chancel of St. Mary's Church, Tideswell, Derbyshire. The figure of the bishop is in full vestments, and a quaint inscription records his education by his uncle in Tideswell, and his subsequent career. It is a comparatively modern creation, however, of about the 16th or 17th century. A very handsome altar-tomb in the parish church of Skipton, Yorkshire, was designed by Sir Gilbert Scott,

after the more ancient models. On the top of the tomb are plates depicting a knight and lady of the Clifford family, and at the corners are the symbols of the four Evangelists. A brass fillet around the slab bears an inscription.

Some modern brasses are to be found, incised and enameled in colors with symbolic devices; but they lack the historic value and interest of the mediæval effigies, to which appeal has often been taken for the solution of some question of detail of costume, armor, or heraldry.

Information concerning monumental brasses may be found in Haines' 'Manual of Monumental Brasses'; The Oxford Architectural Society's 'Manual for the Study of Monumental Brasses'; Boutell's 'Monumental Brasses of England'; Waller's 'Series of Monumental Brasses from the 13th to the 16th Century'; Belcher's 'Kentish Brasses'; Creeney's 'Monumental Brasses on the Continent'; Gough's 'Sepulchral Monuments'; Cotman's 'Suffolk Brasses'; Dugdale's 'Monasticon Anglicanum';

Brass of an Ecclesiastic, Bonn, Germany.

English county histories; and the publications of the Royal Societies of Antiquaries and of Archæologists.

Brasseur de Bourbourg, Charles Etienne, shärl ä-tē-ĕn brạ-sér dẽ boor-boor, French writer on American history, archæology, and ethnology: b. 1814; d. 1874. He entered the priesthood, was sent to North America by the Propaganda, and lived and traveled here and in Central America for a number of years, partly in the performance of ecclesiastical functions. Among his works are 'Histoire du Canada'; 'Histoire des Nations civilisées du Mexique et de l'Amérique Centrale'; 'Gramatica de la Lengua Quiche'; 'Monuments anciens du Mexique'; 'Études sur le Système graphique et la Langue des Mayas.'

Bras'sey, Lady Anne, English descriptive writer: b. London, about 1840; d. 14 Sept. 1887. After her marriage she spent half of her life at sea on Lord Brassey's yacht, the Sunbeam. Her travels are interesting, popular, and have passed through many editions. They are 'Natural History of a Voyage on the Sunbeam'; 'Sunshine and Storm in the East'; 'Tahiti'; 'In the Trades, the Tropics, and the Roaring Forties,' and 'Three Voyages in the Sunbeam.'

Brassey, Thomas, English engineer and railroad contractor: b. Baerton, Cheshire, 7 Nov. 1805; d. Hastings, 8 Dec. 1870. After receiving an ordinary education he was, at the age of 16 years, apprenticed to a surveyor, whom he succeeded in business. After building parts of the Grand Junction and the London and Southampton railways, he contracted, in 1840, in partnership with another, to build the railway from Paris to Rouen. In a few years he held under contract, in England and France, some 10 railways, involving a capital of $180,000,000, and employing 75,000 men. In partnership with Betts and Peto he undertook the Grand Trunk of Canada, 1,100 miles in length, including the great bridge at Montreal. His army of men were employed in nearly every part of Europe, South America, Australia, India, etc. He amassed great wealth, but continued to be generous to the needy, and modest and simple in his tastes and manners. Sir Arthur Helps wrote his 'Life' (1872).

Brassey, Sir Thomas, English politician, first Baron Brassey, son of Thomas Brassey (q.v.): b. Stafford, 11 Feb. 1836. He was educated at Rugby and University College, Oxford, and entered Parliament for Devonshire in 1865, subsequently sitting for Hastings 1868-86. He served as civil lord of the admiralty 1880-4, and was secretary to the admiralty in 1884-5. In 1886 he was elevated to the peerage as Baron Brassey. From 1895 to 1900 he was governor of Victoria. He has published 'Work and Wages' (1872); 'The British Navy' (1882-3); 'Lectures on the Labor Question' (1878).

Brattleboro, brăt't'l-bŭr-ō, Vt., a town in Windham County on the Connecticut River in the southeastern part of the State, on the Boston & M., and Central Vermont R.R.'s. The town was first settled in 1724 at Fort Dummer by a garrison from Massachusetts. The settlement at Fort Dummer was the first permanent civilized settlement in Vermont. The town was chartered in 1753 and incorporated as a village in 1832. Its present form of government is by a board of three selectmen elected annually in March and five village bailiffs elected annually in May. The town is situated in a picturesque rich farming region, is the trade centre of south-east Vermont and contains the State Asylum for the Insane, Brooks Public Library and has many fine churches, Brattleboro Academy and an excellent system of high and graded schools. The city has 4 banks, 2 national with a capital of $550,000; deposits $1,500,000; 2 savings, deposit $4,500,000, surplus $450,000. Brattleboro has many manufactures, chief of which is the factory of the Estey Organ Company. Pop. (1903) 6,000.

O. L. FRENCH,
Editor 'Vermont Phœnix.'

Braun, August Emil, ow'goost ā'měl brown, German archæologist and writer on art: b. Gotha, 19 Aug. 1809; d. 12 Sept. 1856. He received his early education at his native town, and continued his studies at Göttingen. From 1832 to 1833 he resided at Dresden, whence he went to Rome in company with Gerhard, with whom he had formed a close intimacy. In the same year he was appointed first librarian and then assistant secretary to the Archæological Institute, and in 1834 became editor of the 'Bulletino,' and in 1837 of the 'Annali' of that institution. His chief works are: 'The Judgment of Paris'; 'The Artistic Representations of the Winged Bacchus'; 'Ancient Works in Marble' 1st and 2d decades; 'The Greek Doctrine of the Gods'; 'The School of Art Mythology,' with 100 copperplate engravings, translated into English by Grant; 'The Ruins and Museums of Rome,' constituting an excellent guide-book for artists and antiquaries.

Braun, Kaspar, German wood-engraver: b. Aschaffenburg, 1807; d. Munich, 29 Oct. 1877. He studied engraving in Munich and in Paris under Prévière. In Munich he founded, with Dessauer, a xylographic institute, which later became a school of engraving. In 1843 he, in association with Friedrich Schneider, founded the 'Fliegende Blätter.' The chief works which Braun has illustrated are 'Die Nibelungenlied'; the 'Volkskalender'; 'Götz von Berlichingen'; and 'Münchner Bilderbogen.'

Braun, Ludwig, German painter: b. Schwäbisch Hall, 23 Sept. 1836. He was educated at Munich and Paris, and a number of water colors of the Schleswig-Holstein war were the means of obtaining him a contract to paint a cycle of pictures illustrating the history of the family of the Count of Hunolstein. His favorite subjects are battle scenes, and he accompanied the Austrian army in the Danish war and the Germans in the Franco-Prussian war. Among his works are 'The Capitulation of Sedan'; 'The Entry of the German Army Into Paris'; and 'The Germans in Versailles.' He has also painted several very successful panoramas, including 'The Battle of Sedan'; 'The Battle of Mars-la-Tour'; and the 'Battle of Lützen.'

Braunsberg, browns'běrk, Prussia, a town in the province of eastern Prussia, and government of Königsberg, on the Passarge, about four miles from its junction with the Frische Haff. It is the residence of the bishop of Ermeland, and has a Roman Catholic Lyceum, a gymnasium, a seminary for priests, a normal school; and manufactures of linen, woolens, and leather; and a good trade. Pop. (1904) 13,000.

Brauro'nia, (1) a name sometimes given to the Greek goddess, Artemis, from her shrine at Brauron, Attica; (2) a Greek festival in honor of Artemis held every four years at Brauron, in which every Attic woman must take part before she could marry. The rites were performed by girls from 5 to 10 years old, and a part of the ceremony consisted in their imitation of the actions of bears.

Brauwer, brow'ér, or **Brouwer, Adrian,** Dutch painter: b. Haarlem, or Oudenarde in East Flanders, 1608; d. Antwerp, 1640. He made designs of flowers and birds, which were stitched upon caps and bonnets sold by his mother, a poor woman, to the peasants. Francis Hals, a distinguished painter of Haarlem, happening to see some of these, was so struck by the talent which they evinced that he invited the young artist to receive instructions at his house, where he kept him hard at work in a garret, and appropriated to himself the proceeds of his pictures. Here Brauwer remained for many months, ignorant of the estimation in which his talent was held abroad, until by the assistance of his fellow pupil, Adrian van Ostade, he was enabled to escape to Amsterdam. The discovery of the reputation he had acquired seems to have crushed rather than incited his ambition. Perceiving the prices which his pictures commanded, and his own facility in executing them, he yielded to a natural taste for gross pleasures, and painted only when it was necessary to procure money to indulge in dissipations. During the wars with Spain he started on a journey to Antwerp, but being unprovided, with a passport he was imprisoned on suspicion of being a spy. The Duke d'Aremberg, a fellow prisoner, recognizing his talent, induced him to paint something. The subject was a group of soldiers playing at cards, which the artist sketched from his prison window, and the picture being shown to Rubens he at once pronounced it a work of Brauwer, whose release he immediately procured, and whom, from admiration of his genius, he received as an inmate into his house. Brauwer's longing for his old life, however, soon induced him to leave his protector, and after a brief career of reckless dissipation he died in the public hospital of Antwerp.

Bravi, brä've, the name formerly given in Italy, and particularly in Venice, to those who were ready to hire themselves out to perform any desperate undertaking. The word had the same signification in Spain, and both the word and the persons designated by it were found in France in the reign of Louis XIII. and during the minority of Louis XIV. At the end of the 15th century they are described as being armed to the teeth, with an arquebuse in their hands, a cutlass at their side, masked by a bushy beard and enormous moustaches, and wearing a long and thick forelock called a *ciuffo,* which they used to bring down over their face when they wished to conceal it entirely.

Bravo, Leonàrdo, lä-ō-när'dō brä'vō, Mexican revolutionary patriot: b. near San Luis de Potosi, 1766; enlisted in the revolutionary cause, and died of prison fever, in the hands of the Spaniards, in the city of Mexico, in 1812. The Spanish commander had repeatedly offered him his liberty on condition of taking service in the royal army, but, though the fever caused by confinement in a filthy dungeon was wearing out his life, he steadily refused to save it on such conditions.

Bravo, brä'vō, **Nicholas,** Mexican statesman, son of Leonardo Bravo: b. Chilpanzingo, 1790; d. 22 April 1854. He participated in the revolution against Spain (1810–17), and later aided Iturbide in establishing a republic, and supported him until 18 May 1822, when Iturbide proclaimed himself emperor. To this step Bravo was opposed, and he contributed in no small degree to Iturbide's deposition. He again became a member of the provisional government which remained from 1 April 1822 till 10 Oct. 1824, when the federal constitution took effect, under which he was elected to be vice-president until 1 April 1829, Guadalupe Vittoria being president. The politics of Mexico had now become involved in a controversy in which the order of freemasons, divided into two parties, one known as the *Escoses* and the other as *York-inos,* contended at once for the Scotch and ancient York rituals, and the one for a centralized, and the other for a federal, form of government. Bravo was grand master of the Scotch division, and when the federal system prevailed he became a leader of the opposition. Notwithstanding this, he had been elected vice-president; but when, on 23 Dec. 1827, the standard of revolt was raised at Otaviba, he became the head of the movement. The purpose of the *pronunciamiento* was to replace the actual members of the executive government with men of the *Escoses,* and to dismiss Mr. Poinsett, then United States minister in Mexico, who was charged with too actively favoring the other party. Bravo was defeated and expelled, but was recalled in 1830 by President Bustamente, and sent by him against the insurgent Guerrero, who was taken in arms and executed by Bravo's orders, 14 Feb. 1833. After this Bravo remained in retirement until July 1839, when, as president of the council, he was charged with the supreme administration of the government during an interim of a week. Again from 26 Oct. 1842, till March 1843, he was substituted as president by Santa Anna, during his absence as dictator at the head of the army. For the last time he held executive power as temporary president from 29 July to 4 Aug. 1846, when he was deposed by a revolution. On the commencement of the war between Mexico and the United States, he took up arms in behalf of his country, and participated in the battle of Cerro Gordo. In the autumn of 1853 he was accused by the ministers of Santa Anna of having secretly joined Juan Alvarez in the insurrection he had set on foot; but he at once denied the accusation and declared that he had retired from public life forever.

Bra'vo, The, a novel by James Fenimore Cooper, is a tale of Venice in the 16th century, full of mystery and intrigue, and the high-sounding language which years ago was thought the natural utterance of romance. Don Camillo Monforte, a Paduan noble, has a right by inheritance to a place in the Venetian Senate. He becomes obnoxious to the Council, and a bravo is set on his track to kill him. He has fallen in love with Violetta, a young orphan heiress designed for the son of an important senator; and she consents to elope with him. A priest marries them, but by a trick she is separated from him and carried off. The Bravo, sick of his horrible trade, has refused to take a hand in the kidnaping of Violetta; and confesses to Don Camillo all he knows of it, promising to help him recover his bride. Jacopo, the Bravo, finds her in prison and contrives her escape to her husband; but is himself denounced to the Council of Three, and pays for his treachery to them with his head. The romance is of an antiquated fashion; and has not the genuineness and personal force of Cooper's sea stories and 'Leatherstocking Tales,' which grew out of an honest love for his subjects.

Bravo-Murillo, Don **Juan**, dōn hoo-än' brä'vō-moo-rē'lyō, Spanish statesman: b. Badajoz, June 1803; d. Madrid, 11 Jan. 1873. In 1825, he entered the College of Advocates at Seville, and showed great devotion to the monarchy. When the Progressistas came into power he went to Madrid, and founded a law magazine, the 'Boletin de Jurisprudencia.' In 1836, he became secretary of the Department of Justice under Señor Isturiz. In 1847 he became minister of Trade and Public Instruction, and, in 1849–50, of Finance. In 1851 he formed a cabinet, with himself as premier, but, in 1853, it was superseded by that of Gen. Lersundi. The oppressive measures adopted by Bravo-Murillo and his successors led to the revolution of 1854, and the attainment to power of Marshals Espartero and O'Donnell.

Bravura (bra-voo'rä) Air, an air so composed as to enable the singer to show her skill in execution by the addition of embellishments, striking cadences, etc. It is sometimes used for the style of execution.

Brax'ton, Carter, signer of the Declaration of Independence: b. Newington, King and Queen County, Virginia, 10 Sept. 1736; d. 10 Oct. 1797. He inherited several plantations, and passed the early part of his life in the enjoyment of his fortune in his native State, and in England, where he resided some years. In 1765 he took an active part in the eventful session of the house of burgesses of Virginia, in which the resolutions of Patrick Henry were adopted, and in the subsequent assemblies which were dissolved by the governor. He was next a member of the conventions which were the first step toward the substitution of popular for the royal government; and on 15 Dec. 1775, was elected delegate to the continental congress, as successor of Peyton Randolph, and as such affixed his name to the Declaration of Independence. He did not remain long in Congress, but served in the legislature of Virginia until 1786, when he became one of the executive council. The close of his life was embittered by pecuniary embarrassments, and the entire wreck of his fortune.

Brax'y, or Dysentery in Sheep, inflammation of the coats of the intestines. It is often preceded by diarrhœa, and attended by fever and constitutional disturbances. A sudden change of pasturage, more particularly from a succulent to a high and dry pasture, is one of the most frequent causes, and to this may be added exposure to wet and cold after traveling. It is a much more serious disease than simple diarrhœa, and often becomes fatal in the course of a few days. The name is also applied to a blood disease resulting from plethora, which is considered by some to be the true braxy. In this case also a sudden change of pasturage is the most frequent cause of the disease, but the change which generally produces it is the reverse of that which produces the former, namely, a change from a low diet to rich and nourishing food. This disease is even more fatal than the former, and runs its course in a few hours. As there is no means of saving an animal which is once attacked, the only course is to avoid the causes which lead to the disease.

Bray, Anna Eliza, English woman of letters: b. London, 25 Dec. 1790; d. there, 21 Jan. 1883. Her maiden name was Kempe; she studied for the stage, but in 1818 was married to Charles A. Stothard, son of the famous artist, and, after his death, became the wife of the Rev. Edward A. Bray, vicar of Tavistock. From 1826 to 1874 she wrote a series of novels, one of which, 'The Talba, or the Moor of Portugal,' brought her the acquaintance of Southey. In 1884 they were collected in a 12-volume edition. She wrote the 'Life of Thomas Stothard' (1856), and many books of travels. Her letters addressed to Southey, on the superstitions and scenery of Tavistock, entitled 'The Borders of the Tamar and the Tavy' (1836; new ed. 1879), and 'A Peep at the Pixies; or, Legends of the West' (1854), are much esteemed. Mrs. Bray's 'Autobiography' appeared in 1884.

Bray, Sir Reginald, English architect: d. 1503. He was the second son of Sir Richard Bray, one of Henry VI.'s privy councilors, and stood high in the favor of Henry VII., for whom he is understood to have designed, if he did not actually execute, the beautiful chapel at Westminster which bears that monarch's name. Another of his works, and now his final resting-place, is the almost equally beautiful chapel of Saint George's at Windsor.

Bray, Thomas, English clergyman: b. Marton, Shropshire, 1656; d. London, 15 Feb. 1730. Having entered the ministry of the Established Church he founded in 1698 the Society for Promoting Christian Knowledge and in 1700 organized the Anglican Church in Maryland. In the following year he secured a charter for the Society for the Propagation of the Gospel in Foreign Parts. He was rector of Saint Botolph's, Aldgate, London, from 1706. He devised a system of lending libraries for parish purposes and in 1723 established the still existing society of Associates of Dr. Bray, which carries on his benevolent undertakings. He published a 'Directorium Missionarium' (1726); 'An Essay Toward Promoting All Necessary and Useful Knowledge' (1697), and several lesser works.

Bray, The Vicar of (SIMON ALEYN), incumbent of a small English parish near Maidenhead, Berkshire, from 1540 to 1588, during the reigns of Henry VIII., Edward VI., Mary, and Elizabeth. He kept his vicarage by changing his faith according to that of the state for the time being, becoming a Protestant with Henry, Catholic again in the reign of Mary, and Protestant again on the accession of Elizabeth. His principle was to live and die Vicar of Bray, and to it he adhered. The modern ballad, 'In Good King Charles' Golden Days,' makes the versatile vicar live in the reigns of Charles II., James II., William III., Anne, and George I. The parish is 23 miles west of London and has a population of 5,750.

Bray, a maritime town of Ireland, partly in county Dublin and partly in Wicklow, though mainly in the latter, picturesquely situated on both banks of the Bray, which here forms the boundaries of these two counties, 12 miles southeast of Dublin. The town, which has been popularly designated "the Irish Brighton," has been much improved in recent years, new houses being built, and a broad esplanade formed. Pop. (1901) 7,000.

Brayera, also known as Cusso or Kousso, a handsome ornamental tree, of Abyssinia belonging to the rose family. Its scientific name is *Hagenia Abyssinica*. The leaflets number 6 to 12 to each leaf, and its stamens are in separate flowers from its pistils. The bunches of pistillate flowers, made into an infusion, are used in medicine for the expulsion of worms, especially the tape worm. The taste is bitter and unpleasant. The active principle is kosin, which is sometimes given by itself.

Brayman, Mason, American soldier and lawyer: b. Buffalo, N. Y., 1813; d. 1895. He learned the printer's trade in early life, but took up the study of law and was admitted to the bar in 1836. Removing to Illinois he was employed by that State to settle the difficulties with the Mormons of Nauvoo, and secured their removal in 1844. He served in the Federal army during the Civil War, and at its close was brevetted major-general. He was territorial governor of Idaho 1876–81, and after the last named date practised his profession at Ripon, Wis., until his death.

Brazen Sea, the copper basin or vase which King Solomon placed in the priest's court for the uses of the servitors. It was 5 cubits high and 30 in circumference, and was supported on 12 oxen facing outward. It seems probable that its original purpose was symbolical rather than practical. King Ahaz removed it to a stone pedestal and it was finally destroyed by the Chaldæans, who carried off the copper to Babylon.

Brazen Serpent, a bronze or copper figure which Moses is said to have made and set up before the Israelites for the healing of all who had been bitten by venomous serpents. As this was subsequently superstitiously applied by the Israelites it was destroyed by King Hezekiah. Among the Phœnicians the serpent was regarded as the symbol of the god of healing.

Brazil (The United States of Brazil), a republic bordering upon all of the South American countries except Chile, shares to a greater or less extent the natural resources and physical characteristics of each. But even more than its neighbors it requires, for the development of these resources on an adequate scale throughout its length (2,500 miles), and breadth (4,000 miles), both immigration and new industrial enterprises. The central fact concerning the vast Amazon region, stretching across the continent from a few degrees north to about 16° south of the equator, is that its rank vegetation defies the efforts of casual settlers, and nothing less than a teeming population could properly subdue it to human uses. The total area of Brazil, according to the most recent computation, is 3,218,130 square miles; and this includes the largest compact body of fertile and habitable territory that yet remains unimproved, and even, in part, unexplored. Nearly the entire population of the republic is still found on a com-

paratively narrow strip of land extending southward along the Atlantic coast from Pará, below the mouth of the Amazon, to the line of Uruguay. In other words, the white people have clung to the fringe of the continent which their ancestors took possession of in the 16th century in the fashion we shall presently describe; and no civilizing conquest and occupation of the interior, such as occurred in North America, have been effectively undertaken. Except along or comparatively near the coast, the Brazilian states have less than one inhabitant per square mile. The number of inhabitants in the entire country was estimated at 21,565,000 in 1900, distributed as follows among the 20 states of the republic, and including 750,000 for the federal district:

State	Population	State	Population
Minas Geraes....	4,277,000	Para	652,000
Bahia ....,.......	3,335,000	Parahyba	596,000
San Paulo.......	2,520,000	Sergipe	450,000
Pernambuco	2,089,000	Piauhy	425,000
Rio Grande do Sul	1,350,000	Rio Grande Norte Santa Catharina..	407,000 405,000
Rio de Janeiro..	1,300,000	Parana	380,000
Ceara	1,000,000	GoYaz	340,000
Alagoas	781,000	Amazonas	240,000
Maranhao	660,000	Espirito Santo...	201,000
		Matto Grosso....	157,000

There were 2,705,000 foreigners in Brazil, namely, Italians, 1,300,000; Portuguese, 800,000; Germans, 300,000; Spanish, 100,000; Poles, 80,000; French, 10,000; English, 5,000; North Americans, 500; other nationalities, 110,000.

Comparing the above figures with those given a decade earlier, we conclude that the estimate for 1900 is probably too high. The total population in 1890, including 600,000 uncivilized Indians, was stated to be only 14,333,915.

History.— Brazil was discovered in 1500 by a companion of Columbus, Vicente Pinzon, who made no settlement, and, indeed, would not have been justified in doing so. The bull of Pope Alexander VI. (4 May 1493) had bestowed upon Portugal the lands which should be found east of the line of demarcation, and commissioners of Spain and Portugal had agreed, on 7 June 1494, that the position of the line of demarcation should be changed so that it should pass, north and south, 370 leagues west of the Cape Verde Islands, instead of at a distance of only 100 leagues west of those islands, where the Pope had established it. Accordingly Spain was precluded by her own act from claiming the eastern portion of the continent of South America. A Portuguese commander, Pedro Alvarez Cabral, when on his way around the Cape of Good Hope to the Far East, in 1500, encountered severe storms which drove his vessels from their course; and through this mischance he reached the Brazilian coast in April. Mass was celebrated there on Easter Day; the country was declared a dependency of Portugal, and a stone cross was erected. There Cabral himself embarked for India, but first sent a vessel to Lisbon with a report of this important discovery. As soon as practicable after receiving the account of his new possession, Dom Manuel placed three vessels under the command of Amerigo Vespucci, instructing this Florentine to make good Portugal's claim to the land which a Spaniard had discovered. Thus, from the beginning, Brazil was marked out as a field for international competition. Vespucci's first voyage being unsuccessful, a second was undertaken with better results. He remained for five months at a point he named "All Saints," and when it became necessary to return left 12 men as a garrison in a small fort. The impression created by the experiences of the early adventurers was not highly favorable. Poor and unattractive, indeed, did this land seem in comparison with India and Africa. During the years that followed Portuguese merchants dispatched vessels to trade for Brazil-wood, and the Portuguese government jealously resisted French and Spanish attempts to gain a foothold or carry on commerce eastward of the line of demarcation; but the court at Lisbon continued to prefer the profits to be won along the course that Vasco da Gama had opened up. The first settlements, therefore, were not made by the government, but by grantees whom the government induced to colonize by assigning to each leader a splendid possession, or "captaincy" — no less than 50 leagues of coast, with feudal powers and the privilege of extending his domain as far inland as he desired. Thus the province of San Paulo was settled by an expedition under Piratininga; next Affonso de Sousa explored the coast from Rio de Janeiro (so called because it was discovered 1 Jan. 1531) to the Rio de la Plata. Lopes de Sousa received two allotments of 25 leagues each, one being near Pernambuco and Paraiba. Fernandez Coutinho and Pedro da Campo Tourinho established themselves near the spot where Cabral landed. Francisco Pereiro Coutinho received a grant of a captaincy, extending from Rio San Francisco to Bahia. The captaincy of Pernambuco was given to Duarte Coelho Pereira; and so the most attractive portions of the coast were distributed. Cattle and sugar-cane being introduced from Madeira, the systematic cultivation of the latter began; though some authorities maintain that both sugar-cane and coffee are indigenous to Brazilian soil. Enormous difficulties were encountered from the first by proprietors and planters. Only men of large means (including some of those adventurers who had amassed fortunes in India), were able to equip and maintain such a considerable force as was necessary if these undertakings were to be successful. The natives were, as a rule, extremely mistrustful, besides being the most savage of their kind, as Southey has shown in his elaborate description of them. ('History of Brazil,' by Robert Southey, 1810). Cannibalism was universally practised. In general, the nature of these Indians appears to have been far more debased, and their practices more revolting than the nature and customs of the Red Men of North America; the task of civilizing them seemed more utterly hopeless. Yet one striking exception to the general experience may be noted. The first settler in Bahia was Diogo Alvarez, a young man of noble family, who was wrecked on the shoals near that port. "Part of the crew," says Southey, "were lost, others were eaten by the natives." Diogo secured the favor of the Indians by recovering things from the wreck. Afterward he led them in battle, using his musket to such good effect that he became their sovereign, and took daughters of the chiefs of the savages to be his wives. "The best families in Bahia," we are told, "trace their origin to him."

By the middle of the 16th century the captaincies of those men whose names have been mentioned, and still other adventurers, were scattered along the coast from the mouth of the Amazon to the mouth of the Rio de la Plata. The great mineral wealth of the country had not been discovered at that time, and the settlements were chiefly devoted to the cultivation of sugar. What with savages surrounding these widely separated posts; Spaniards threatening them from the rear (the Spanish troops then holding the regions afterward to be known as Paraguay and Argentina); and the French from time to time attempting to establish themselves on the coast; it was found necessary to provide for the common defense by concentrating the Portuguese power in the hands of a governor-general. The feudatories had to submit to the revocation of some of their privileges, though they remained on the soil which they owned.

The first governor-general was Trome da Sousa, and his capital was Bahia. In 1549 he was reinforced by a fleet of six vessels with 320 soldiers and officials, 400 convicts, 300 free colonists, and 6 Jesuits. At different times wards of the Crown, female orphans of good family, were sent out, provided with portions from the royal estates, and given to the provincial officers in marriage. The establishment of the College of San Paulo in Piratininga followed hard upon the arrival of the first bishop of Brazil in 1552, and of a number of Jesuits in 1553. Avowed friends and protectors of the natives, these members of the Society of Jesus took upon themselves the pioneers' task, and their college became a centre of influence. Intrusive French settlers at Rio de Janeiro were driven out by the governor, and a Portuguese colony was founded there in 1567. But the progress of Brazil, in so far as it was dependent upon the aid of the mother country, was checked, if not entirely arrested, during a period of 60 years. Philip II. of Spain acquired the crown of Portugal in 1578-80, and the union of the two countries — or rather, the subordination of the weaker nation — continued until 1640. Brazil received little attention during all these years, in part because she was identified with Portugal, but still more for the reason that her inferiority to the Spanish possessions in mineral wealth was taken for granted. The transfer of allegiance invited attack by English fleets. In 1586 Witherington sacked Bahia; Cavendish, in 1591, burned San Vicente; Lancaster, in 1595, captured Olinda. A futile attempt to found a permanent colony was made by the French (1612-18), and the Dutch dispatched a fleet against Bahia in 1624.

The Dutch in Brazil.— Most important were the efforts made at this time by an association of Dutch merchants, the famous Dutch West India Co., which commissioned Count Maurice of Nassau to promote the interests of his countrymen in South America. The enormous power of this corporate company, which, as Bancroft says, was "given leave to appropriate continents," and, when "invested with a boundless liberty of choice, culled the rich territories of Guiana, Brazil, and New Netherland," was exerted in a large part of the region lying between Maranhão and Bahia. After the revolution of 1640, Brazil was, indeed, no longer Spanish, but the new Portuguese executive of the house of Bragança was too poor and weak to adopt such vigorous measures as were required. Accordingly a suggestion offered by a native of Madeira named Vieyra was welcomed, inasmuch as this plan relieved the government of the obligation to fight the Dutch West India Co. Vieyra proposed the establishment of a commercial company at Lisbon similar to that which had its headquarters at Amsterdam. The Brazil Co. of Portugal was organized, and in 1649 sent out its first fleet. After five years of severe fighting, the Portuguese merchants overcame the Dutch merchants.

For half a century Brazil was permitted to remain at peace. In 1710, however, a French squadron under Duclerc attacked Rio de Janeiro and suffered defeat. On 12 September of the following year Admiral Duguay Trouin arrived off Rio with a new fleet and 6,000 men. The governor was compelled to capitulate and to pay a large sum of money. A great change in the industrial conditions of the southern districts was produced by the discovery of diamonds at this time (1710-30), and by the rush to the gold regions opened up by the enterprise of the colonists of San Paulo — a hardy race, doubtless with a large admixture of Indian blood, much addicted to adventurous raids into the interior. Their explorations extended westward into Paraguay and northward into Minas, Goyaz, and Cuyabá in the state of Matto Grosso. Gold was discovered in the regions last mentioned; by the beginning of the 18th century there were five towns of considerable importance in Minas Geraes; and that state is now, as we have seen, the most populous of the republic. Laborers were withdrawn from the sugar industry by the superior attractions of mining, and Brazil lost her leading position as a sugar-producing country. The conspiracy of Minas in 1789 was the first sympathetic movement in Brazil occasioned by the Revolutionary War in North America. Inspired by the success of the English colonies in achieving independence, the inhabitants of Minas formed a project to throw off the Portuguese yoke, but the plot failed, the leader was hanged, and the conspirators were banished to Africa, from which continent slaves were being imported in large numbers. It was an unprofitable exchange for America. The French Revolution, among its extraordinary consequences, promoted Brazil from the humble position of a colony to be the seat of government of the Portuguese power, and the only American monarchy. In 1807 the threat of the invasion of Portugal by Napoleon sent the prince regent, afterward King John or Dom João VI., across the ocean (29 November). With him went the queen, the royal family, the great officers of state, and members of the nobility. He created many new offices, and otherwise made the machinery of government in Brazil much more elaborate than it had ever been; and, to meet the increased expenses that these changes involved, at first imposed new taxes, and afterward, by debasing the money standard, inaugurated the long period of financial error that has impeded the advancement of the country. On the other hand, Brazilian ports were declared open to the commerce of all nations at peace with Portugal. Thus John favored industrial development and injured it at the same time. Numbers of artisans and manufacturers from England, Germany, France, and Sweden came to take advantage of the new opportunity. In 1816 the School of Fine Arts was founded by French painters and sculptors. The occupation of Portugal by French troops was offset in the new world by the incorporation of French Guiana with Brazil (1809); but the treaty of Vienna in 1815 restored Guiana to France. On 16 Jan 1815, the title of kingdom was conferred upon Brazil; and an important extension of the domain of this unique American monarchy was effected six years afterward, when Uruguay was united with it under the title of the Cisplatine State. But this union, like the occupation of French Guiana, was destined to be temporary, owing to the policy adopted by Argentina. See ARGENTINA.

Independence Proclaimed.— The general movement in favor of independence that transformed the Spanish colonies north, south, and west of Brazil into republics, produced conspiracies and plots in Bahia and Pernambuco. Troops were brought out from Portugal to restrain every violent manifestation of the republican spirit; meanwhile, however, in Portugal itself the revolution of 1820 had led to a modification of the old autocratic system, and the forces from that country, openly sympathizing with the aspirations of the Brazilian people, compelled King John to yield. The latter withdrew from America soon afterward (26 April 1821), leaving his son, Dom Pedro, to work out the problem in Brazil as best he might. The attitude of the Cortes of Portugal in this crisis was exceedingly unwise: instead of offering concessions, it directed the dissolution of the central government, and ordered Dom Pedro to return to Portugal. Assured of the support of the people of Rio de Janeiro and San Paulo, who requested him to disobey this command, Dom Pedro proclaimed the independence of Brazil, 7 Sept. 1822. He became constitutional emperor the following month. In the hostilities which ensued the Brazilians were so successful that independence was assured before the end of 1823. The constitution of the empire was adopted on 25 March 1824. But a peculiar situation in the ruling family remained to be disposed of. Since October 1822, Dom Pedro had been emperor of Brazil, while his father was king of Portugal. The dramatic climax occurred 25 Aug. 1825, when a treaty was signed in London by virtue of which King John first assumed the title of emperor of Brazil and then immediately abdicated in favor of his son. As the popularity of Dom Pedro I. was due to the disposition he showed at first to accede to the wishes of the liberals, so it is necessary to ascribe his loss of popularity in the years 1826-31 to his unwillingness to trust the people more and more, as their demand for participation in the government steadily increased. The statement found in some recent histories, to the effect that Pedro I. was a brutal tyrant, whose reign ended in public disgrace, is positively incorrect, and inculcates false views of this entire period. It was his tact that saved the monarchy in 1821; but the growth of republicanism in the next decade was much more rapid among the people than at his court, and finally the breach became so wide that no course was left to him but to surrender his crown before the succession of his son, the second Pedro, should be disputed, and to take ship for Lisbon, where it had become a duty to defend the claim of his daughter, Maria II., to the throne of Portugal. At any time after 1810 outrageous tyranny on the part of Portuguese rulers would have thrown Brazil into the advancing column of revolutionary states. The significant facts are, that Pedro I. was able to postpone the inevitable change for 10 years, and that Pedro II. (whose majority was proclaimed 23 July 1840) succeeded in maintaining the monarchical form in America until 15 Nov. 1889. The regency by which the affairs of Brazil were administered (1831-40) was much like a republican government, especially after 1834. Probably it would have been impossible to revert to a monarchy if the weakness and misconduct of the regents had not brought discredit upon everything savoring of democracy; certainly the rôle of emperor in the largest American country could not have been sustained so long except by a sincere advocate of progress, and an enlightened patron of every humanitarian and scientific enterprise. Such was Pedro II. The suppression of the revolution of 1848; the discontinuance of the importation of slaves, in 1853; and the creditable part taken by Brazil in thwarting the ambitious designs of the Argentine dictator, Rosas (See ARGENTINA)— these are the chief events before 1855. In that year a Brazilian squadron was sent to settle a dispute with Paraguay as to the right of way for Brazilian vessels on the Paraná River, which, rising in Brazil, flowing through Paraguay, and finally through the territory of Argentina, should be open to the commerce of all three nations equally. (The warships failed to accomplish the desired result, and for a decade vexatious restrictions were placed upon the vessels of Brazil, Argentina, and the United States. In 1864 an outrage by Señor Lopez, the dictator of Paraguay, brought on a war in which Brazil, Argentina, and Uruguay were allied against the offending country. (See PARAGUAY). This bitter struggle, protracted until 1870, cost Brazil the lives of many thousands of her citizens, and in money about $300,000,000. In the year following the restoration of peace a law was enacted for the abolition of the institution of slavery, the growth of which had been checked, as we have seen, in 1853. It was provided that thenceforth every child born of slave parents should be free.

Brazil a Republic.—A bloodless revolution terminated the reign of Dom Pedro II., and the Federal republic was proclaimed, 15 Nov. 1889. A provisional government, instituted for this purpose, published (24 Feb. 1891) the constitution of "The United States of Brazil," resembling that of the United States of America in nearly every respect, though Brazilian senators serve for nine years, like those of Argentina, while the president's term of office is but four years. Marshal Deodoro da Fonseca, head of the provisional government, was confirmed in the presidency by the constitutional congress, and Gen. Floriano Peixotto was elected vice-president. The next president (15 Nov. 1894) was Prudente de Moraes Barros. The third president, Dr. Manoel Ferraz de Campos Salles, was elected for the term beginning 15 Nov. 1898. His successor, Señor Francisco de Paula Rodrigues Alves, inaugurated 15 Nov. 1902, made a statement of the national policy in his inaugural address which should receive general attention. It may be summarized as follows: A good financial condition in the republic is of prime importance; but scarcely less essential are reforms in the laws applicable to civil suits and elections. Agricultural and commercial conditions must be improved, and endeavors made to

attract immigration and capital. Modern systems of sanitation must be installed at the ports, including Rio de Janeiro. The augmentation of the army and navy may be undertaken when the condition of the treasury warrants such expenditures.

It will be readily understood that the circumstances to which reference has been made in this sketch — such as the issuance of large amounts of paper currency, which it was formerly the fashion to call irredeemable; the change from the basis of slave to free labor; the overthrow of the monarchy; foreign wars, and rebellions in one state after another — have combined to depress Brazilian credit and retard industrial development. To these unfavorable influences must be added the decline in the prices of coffee, Brazil's staple product, and of sugar, her chief reliance in times past. On the other hand there is observable a tendency toward greater stability in the national policy; a large amount of paper money has been called in and destroyed; and at least a moderate interest has been shown recently in efforts to develop the enormous natural resources of the country.

The complete statistics of the import and export trade of Brazil for the year 1901 (the latest which can be satisfactorily analyzed), show the following results: Imports were valued at £19,702,758, exclusive of bullion; exports were £40,621,993. The imports from Great Britain formed 31.389 per cent of the entire import trade; exports to the same country and its possessions, 12.951 per cent of total export trade. Imports from the United States amounted to £2,463,938; exports to the United States, £17,462,650, being 43.116 per cent of the whole merchandise exported from Brazil. Imports from Germany were £1,868,751; exports to Germany, £6,014,812. France imported Brazilian goods to the value of £4,761,907. Argentina exported to Brazil merchandise of the value of £2,651,287. The balance of trade in favor of Brazil is seen to depend chiefly upon the exchange of products with the United States. An estimate for the year 1900 shows imports from the United States, $11,516,681; exports to the United States, $64,914,507. In 1902, the imports from the United States appear to be somewhat less than in 1900, while the exports to the United States show a considerable increase. During the 30 years preceding 1902, the United States has purchased from Brazil goods to the amount of $1,762,622,527, and sold to her goods to the amount of only $303,813,166 — the balance of trade in favor of Brazil for that period being $1,458,809,361, contributed by the United States alone. Keeping these figures in mind, we now examine the last message of President Campos Salles (3 May 1902), which shows the improvement in the financial situation by comparison of the year 1898 with 1902. In the former year, he says, gold payments were suspended; the paper money in circulation amounted to 788,364 centos; the rate of exchange average 7 3-16; amount required for the redemption of the funding loan was 115,997 centos; Brazilian bonds were at 50 per cent discount; the amount due on the 1897 loan was £1,122,083; treasury notes to the amount of 20,350 centos of reis were in circulation; the treasury owed 11,000 centos of reis to the Banco da Republica; £274,694 were due for war material. To meet these various debts there were in the treasury 5,500 centos, and £81,713 in the agency at London. In 1902 gold payments had been resumed; the paper money in circulation was reduced by 107,000 centos of reis; the rate of exchange was 12d.; the paper money in circulation, which formerly was worth only £23,500,000, had increased in value to £34,000,000; Brazilian bonds abroad were quoted 35 per cent higher; the rest of the 1897 loan had been paid; not a single treasury bill was in circulation. There were £2,000,000 in cash in London, besides 1,000,000 in consols, and 12,000 centos deposited in the Banco da Republica. "Finally, the era of deficits has been banished, and that of surpluses has been instituted." The enormous advantage of Brazil in her trade with the United States makes such results possible, and places much more ambitious financial achievements easily within her reach. The total debt of the republic, expressed in gold of the United States, was stated to be $440,701,893 in 1901.

Army and Navy.—The Brazilian navy in 1901 comprised: 2 battleships of the old style; 2 coast-defense vessels, comparatively modern; 2 old monitors; 7 small cruisers, of which number 3 were unarmored; 6 gunboats, armored, and 18 unarmored; 24 torpedo-boats of all classes; 4 torpedo-cruisers; 2 submarine boats. To man these vessels there were 4,000 seamen, 1,000 stokers, and 450 marine infantry. The army included 484 staff officers; 1,573 officers and 9,035 men in the infantry, and, in the cavalry and engineers, 606 officers and 3,179 men, and 1,400 cadets. The only serious war-cloud at the beginning of 1903 arose out of a dispute with Bolivia over Acré. See ACRE RIVER.

Climate.— The rainy season begins for the hot lowlands of the north in December or January and continues until May or June, the remaining half of the year being dry. In the highlands of the southern and central regions the four seasons of the year are well defined. Throughout the Amazon basin the seasonal variation of temperature is small — from 75° to 90°; and the prevailing winds, the "trades" from the east, mitigate the equatorial conditions. In the high plains of the states of Rio Grande do Sul and San Paulo the mercury sometimes falls to the freezing point. Except in the neighborhood of swamps, marshy or undrained districts, etc., the climate is moderately healthful, and the mortality in the best of the towns does not compare unfavorably with that of cities in the United States.

Resources.— In 1902 the exports of coffee to the United States amounted to 764,658,963 pounds, valued at $47,004,453. The total exports of rubber from the Amazon valley (lower, upper, and Iquitos districts) in 1901 were 46,-992 tons. Tobacco, cotton, cacao, Brazil nuts, rice, sugar — these are some of the vegetable products. There is practically no limit to the number of agricultural enterprises that can be successfully carried on in the table-lands, the broad, open valleys, and the lowlands forming the basin of the Amazon. In the higher regions and mountains the mineral wealth of the republic is being developed. During the first seven months of 1901, 2,435,866 grams of gold, 37,915 tons of manganese, and precious stones to the value of 464 centos, were exported from the state of Minas Geraes. The iron-ore regions are situated within a zone of about 3,200 square miles, from 3,000 to 5,000 feet above the level of the sea, and about 310 miles from Rio de Janeiro, which is the nearest port. The output

of diamonds and carbons in the state of Bahia is of special interest. Prior to the discovery of the South African mines this was the greatest diamond-producing centre, and the Paranguacu district is the only place in the world where carbons are found of marketable size. An excellent statement is made by Señor Fontoura Xavier, consul-general of Brazil in New York, who enumerates the gems found in Goyaz, Matto Grosso, Paraná, Rio Grande do Sul, and San Paulo, as well as in the states mentioned above. Black diamonds, emeralds, sapphires, rubies, beryls, amethysts, garnets, opals, chalcedonies, sapphirines, agates, and cornelians are found, some of them in great abundance. "One of the carboniferous basins of Brazil is in the state of Santa Catarina. In the state of Rio Grande do Sul there have been discovered four large outcrops of coal. Bitumen exists in nearly all of the states." Native sulphur, nitrate, salt, sulphate of magnesia are also mentioned. The average annual value of the gold and diamonds exported is said to be about $7,400,00. In Rio Grande do Sul are copper mines, in Paraná quicksilver mines; galena and lead mines in widely separated regions.

Finances.— The revenues of Brazil for the fiscal year 1903 were estimated at 40,967,942 *milreis*, gold, and 248,018,000 *milreis*, paper. The various sources of the receipts and their amounts in *milreis* were as follows:

	Gold	Paper
Revenues from imports............	31,420,000	122,722,000
Internal revenue..................	1,337,666	36,743,000
Consumption taxes................	....	32,660,000
Extraordinary revenues...........	180,276	6,755,000
Paper-money redemption fund......	....	2,150,000
Paper-money guaranty fund.......	7,870,000	....
Lease of Goverment railways......	160,000	1,658,000
Amortization of internal debt.....	....	5,200,000
Port-improvement fund	....	2,530,000
Total........................	40,967,942	248,018,000

The expenditures for the same period were estimated at 41,399,062 *milreis*, gold, and 244,462,545 *milreis*, paper, and distributed as follows:

	Gold	Paper
Department of Justice and Internal Affairs................	....	16,424,481
Department of Foreign Relations	905,500	631,020
Navy Department..................	....	26,700,664
War Department...................	....	47,569,437
Department of Industry, Communications, and Public Works......................	3,783,315	68,030,477
Department of Finance	36,710,247	85,105,565
Total........................	41,399,062	244,462,845

Education.— See EDUCATION IN LATIN-AMERICA.

Bibliography.—Agassiz, 'A Journey in Brazil' (1868); Bureau of Am. Republics, Washington, D. C., Handbook of Brazil (geographical sketch); Burton, 'Explorations of Highlands of Brazil' (1869); Cardim, 'Narrativa epistolar de una viagem' (Lisboa 1847); 'Collecção das leis e decretos' (1827); Debidour 'Le Brésil avant le XIX° siècle' (Nontran 1878); Dundonald (Earl of) 'Narrative' (1859); 'Empire of Brazil at Exhibition of 1876' (Rio de Janeiro 1876); Fletcher, 'Brazil and the Brazilians' (1868); Graham, 'Journal of a Voyage to Brazil' (1824); Handelmann, 'Geschichte von Brasilien' (1860); Hartt, 'Thayer Expedition . . . Geology and Physical Geography of Brazil' (1870); Henderson, 'A History of Brazil' (1821); Heriate, 'Descripcão do estado Maranhão, etc.' (Vienna 1874); Herndon and Gibbon, 'Exploration of the Valley of the Amazon' (Washington, Public print., 1853–54); U. S. 32 Cong.-Senate, Exec. doc. No. 36; Homem de Mello 'Integração da nacionaledade Brazilaira' (Rio de Janeiro 1895); Kidder and Fletcher, 'Brazil and the Brazilians' (1857); Koster, 'Travels in Brazil' (1817); La Grasserie, 'Lois civiles du Brésil (1897); Lery, 'Reise in Brasilien' (Münster 1794); Lopes de Sousa, 'Diario da navegação' (Lisboa 1839); Magalhaes de Gandova 'Histoire de la Province de Sancta-Cruz.' In Ternaux-Compans' 'Voyages, etc.' (1837–41); Moreira, 'Agricultural Instructions for Those Who May Emigrate to Brazil' (1876); 'Negociaciones entre la repub. orient. de Uruguay y el imp. de Brasil' (Rio de Janeiro 1858); Southey, 'History of Brazil' (1810–19); Stade, 'Captivity Among the Wild Tribes of Eastern Brazil' (Hakluyt Soc. 1874); 'Statement submitted to the President of U. S. as arbitrator' (New York 1894); Todd, 'Report on Voyage of U. S. S. Wilmington up the Amazon River' (Washington, Gov't Print., 1899); Varnhogen, 'Examen de quelques points de l'histoire geographique' (1858); 'Historia geral do Brazil' (Rio de Janeiro 1876); 'Historia das lutas com os Hollendezes' (Lisbon 1872); Warren, 'Para; or Scenes and Adventures on Banks of Amazon' (1851); Wied-Neuwied (Prince), 'Travels in Brazil' (1820); Zeballos, 'Argument for the Argentine Rep. Upon the Question With Brazil in Regard to Territory of Misiones' (Washington 1894).

MARRION WILCOX,
Authority on Latin-America.

Brazil', Ind., a city and county capital of Clay County, 16 miles northeast of Terre Haute. It is an important railroad centre and in its vicinity are rich mines of block coal. Inexhaustible deposits of clay and shales are also found here and the city contains manufactures of pumps, tiles, machinery, etc. Brazil was incorporated in 1873, is governed by a mayor, elected quadrennially, and a city council; has a public library and controls its own waterworks. Pop. (1900) 7,786.

Brazil-cabbage, or Chow Caraibe (*Caladium sagittifolium* or *Xanthosoma sagittifolium*), a West Indian plant of the natural order *Araceæ*, widely cultivated in the tropics for its starchy edible tubers, which are used like potatoes, and its succulent leaves, which are cooked like spinach. The plant almost entirely lacks the acrid principle which characterizes other members of the order.

Brazil-nut, Castanea, Cream Nut, Niggertoe, Para Nut, the seeds of two species of Brazilian trees, the only ones of their genus, of the natural order *Myrtaceæ*. The better known species, *Bertholletia excelsa*, is a tree which often attains a height of 150 feet and a diameter of four feet. It has bright green, leathery leaves, two feet long and six inches wide, and cream-colored flowers followed by very hard-shelled

fruits about six inches in diameter, containing about 20, three-sided, wrinkled seeds which are largely exported from Para and from ports of French Guiana. They are used for dessert and confectionery and for the manufacture of an expressed oil used in oil painting, lubricating, and lighting. Though of stately dimensions, the tree is of little decorative use. It covers extensive tracts in northern Brazil, and is especially abundant along the Amazon and Orinoco rivers. The seeds of the monkey-pot tree, known as sapucaia nuts (q.v.), are considered superior to Brazil-nuts, but are not yet commercially important, owing to the distance they must be transported from the interior country.

Brazil Tea, a drink prepared from the leaves of *Ilex paraguensis.*

Brazil-wood. A dark-red or brown dyewood exported from the West Indies, Brazil, and other South American countries. Various grades appear in the market under diverse names, such as Pernambuco wood (*Cæsalpinia echinata*), St. Martha wood, and All Saints' wood, which are most valued. Except in a few cases botanists have not definitely determined the species which furnish the different grades, but large quantities are derived from *C. brasiliensis*, a small tree, bipinnate leaves, and flowers in panicles. It is indigenous in rocky ground, especially in the West Indies. The valuable part is the heart-wood, of which there is but little when compared with the thick, valueless sap-wood. This useful part is at first light colored, but becomes dark when exposed to light, air, moisture, etc. Formerly it was largely used in dyeing, but coal-tar dyes and other manufactured dyes have generally supplanted it. It is still used in ink-making. The name is said to be derived from Braxilis, not Brazil, since sappan wood, which is believed to be identical, was used prior to the discovery of America.

Brazilian Grass, an incorrect name popularly applied to a substance used in the manufacture of a very cheap kind of hats, known as Brazilian grass hats, and also as chip hats. It consists of strips of the leaves of a palm. *Chamærops argentea*, which are imported for this manufacture, and chiefly from Cuba.

Brazilian Pebble, a colorless and transparent variety of quartz, used for high-grade lenses.

Braz'ing, or Brass-soldering, the process of uniting two pieces of brass, two pieces of copper, or one of each by means of a hard solder, that is, a solder which fuses at a comparatively high temperature. The solder is applied in the form of a coarse powder, and is always mixed with borax, to prevent the oxidation of the metals soldered together. It is usual to moisten this mixture with water before spreading it over the surfaces to be joined. When the solder has been applied in this state, the pieces of metal are slowly heated, by which the water is made to evaporate, leaving a crust of the solder on the parts where it is required. The pieces are then exposed to a stronger heat, until the borax melts and fluxes the solder, which suddenly flushes the joints of the pieces of metal, and thus unites the two surfaces, making them into one piece. The whole is now allowed to cool, and is afterward dressed with a file. Pieces of metal united in this way are held together as firmly as if they were only one piece.

Brazos, brä'zŏs, formerly called **Brazos-de-Dios,** a large river in Texas, rising in the elevated region of northwestern Texas, once known as the Staked Plain, between the parallels of 33° and 34°. It flows southeastward between the Colorado and Trinity, and after a course of about 900 miles falls into the Gulf of Mexico, between Quintana and Velasco, 40 miles west-southwest of Galveston. It is navigable by steamers during the wet season for about 300 miles. Among the towns on its banks the chief is Waco, about halfway from its mouth, now an important railway centre. The cotton plantations on the Brazos are highly productive.

Brazos de Santiago, da sän-te-ä'gō, Texas, a village 30 miles east of Brownsville, on the northern bank of the Rio Grande, in Cameron County. The battles of Palo Alto and Resaca de la Palma, in 1846, were fought about half way between Brazos and Matamoras. It carries on much coasting and foreign trade, although a shifting sand bar is a serious obstacle to its commerce.

Brazza, brät'sȧ (ancient B R A C H I A), an island of Austria, in the Adriatic Sea, belonging to Dalmatia, of which it constitutes a separate administrative district; lat. 43° 16' N.; lon. 16° 37' E. It is 24 miles long, and from five to seven broad; contains 20 villages, and is separated from the mainland by a channel 12 miles broad, which affords excellent anchorage for shipping. The island is mountainous and well wooded; and in the valleys vines are grown, from which are made the best wines in Dalmatia. It produces also good oil, almonds, and saffron, and grain in small quantity. Much attention is paid to the cultivation of bees and silk-worms. The chief town, St. Pietro di Brazza, has a small port, defended by a mole. Pop. (1900) 24,465.

Brazza-Savorgnan, Pierre Paul François Camille, pē-âr pōl frȧṅ-swä kä-mēl brät-sa-sä-vôr-nyäṅ, French explorer: b. on board ship, off Rio de Janeiro, Brazil, 26 Jan. 1852; d. Dakar, French West Africa, 15 Sept. 1905. He entered the French navy in 1875, after becoming a naturalized French citizen, and during 1876–8 explored the Ogowe and Congo regions of Africa, and made treaties between France and the natives, founding Franceville and several other villages. In 1886 he was made governor of the French Congo and Gaboon colonies, which he had thus secured. Brazzaville on the Congo River is named after him. After a sojourn in France, he returned to Africa in 1890 as commissioner-general of the whole of French Congo. The next six years were spent in explorations and securing of French authority in central Africa, after which, in 1897, he returned to France.

Brazzaville, brät'sȧ-vēl, a town on the French side of the Congo at the lower end of Stanley Pool. It stands nearly opposite Leopoldville, in the Congo Free State. See BRAZZA-SAVORGNAN.

Breach, the aperture or passage made in the wall of any fortified place, by the ordnance of the besiegers, for the purpose of entering the fortress. They should be made where there is the least defense, that is, in the front or face of the bastions. In order to divide the resistance of the besieged, breaches are commonly made at once in the faces of the attacked bastions and in the ravelin. This is effected by battering, and at such places as the cannon do not reach, by the aid of mines. The breach is called practicable if it is large enough to afford some hope of success in case of an assault. This is generally considered to be the case if it allows a passage to 14 men abreast. Frequently, however, a breach of much less extent, even of half that width, may be entered.

Breach, any violation of law or obligation. A continuing breach is one where the condition of things constituting a breach continues during a period of time, or where the acts constituting a breach are repeated at brief intervals. In pleading, breach is that part of the complaint in which the violation of the defendant's contract is stated. It is usual in assumpsit, where the common-law rules of pleading are still in force, to introduce the statement of the particular breach, with the allegation that the defendant, contriving and fraudulently intending craftily and subtilely to deceive and defraud the plaintiff, neglected and refused to perform, or performed the particular act, contrary to the previous stipulation. In debt, the breach or cause of action complained of must proceed only for the non-payment of money previously alleged to be payable; and such breach is very similar whether the action be in debt on simple contract, specialty, record, or statute.

Breach of Promise of Marriage.— An action lies for this on the part of either man or woman, though, as a rule, only the latter is believed to be substantially injured or deserve damages. There must be a legal and valid consideration, but as there are always mutual promises they are a sufficient consideration for each other. The minds of the parties must meet; that is, there must be a request or proposition on the one side and an assent on the other. If the communications between the parties are verbal, the only questions which usually arise relate to evidence and proof. The exact words or time or manner of the promise need not be proved, but it may be inferred from the conduct of the parties and from the circumstances which usually attend a promise to marry. (15 Mass. 1; 2 Penn. St. 80.) When the parties are at a distance from each other, and the offer is made by letter, it will be presumed to continue for a reasonable time for the consideration of the party addressed, and if accepted within a reasonable time, and before it is expressly revoked, the contract is then complete.

A promise of marriage is not within the third clause of the fourth section of the statute of frauds, relating to agreements made upon consideration of marriage; but if not to be performed within one year it is within the fifth clause, and must therefore be in writing in order to be binding. If no time be fixed and agreed upon for the performance of the contract, it is in contemplation of law a contract to marry within a reasonable period after request, and either party may call upon the other to fulfill the engagement, and in case of default may bring an action for damages. If both parties lie by for an unreasonable period, and do not treat the contract as continuing, it will be deemed to be abandoned by mutual consent. The defenses which may be made to an action for breach of promise of marriage are, of course, various; but it is only necessary to notice in this place such as are in some degree peculiar. Thus, if either party has been convicted of an infamous crime, or has sustained a bad character generally, and the other was ignorant of it at the time of the engagement; or if the woman has committed fornication, and this was unknown at the time to the man who promised to marry her; or if the woman is deeply involved in debt at the time of the engagement, and the fact is kept secret from her intended husband; or if false representations are made by the woman, or by her friends in collusion with her, as to her circumstances and situation in life and the amount of her fortune and marriage portion,— any of these facts, if properly pleaded, will constitute a good defense. If after the engagement either party is guilty of gross misconduct, inconsistent with the character which he or she was fairly presumed to possess, the other party will be released. If the woman insists upon having her property settled to her own personal use, it is said that this will justify the man in breaking off the engagement. So, if the situation and position of either of the parties as regards his or her fitness for the marriage relation is materially and permanently altered for the worse (whether with or without the fault of such party) after the engagement, this will release the other party.

Breach of Warranty.— In sales of personal property an express warranty is one by which the warrantor covenants or undertakes to insure that the thing which is the subject of the contract is, or is not, as there mentioned; as that a horse is sound, that he is not five years old, etc.

An implied warranty is one which, not being expressly made, the law implies by the fact of the sale. For example, the seller is understood to warrant the title of goods he sells, when they are in his possession at the time of the sale. ¹1 Ld. Raym. 593.¹ In general there is no implied warranty of the quality of the goods sold. The rule of the civil law was that a fair price implied a warranty of quality. This rule has been adopted in Louisiana and South Carolina. There may be an implied warranty as to character, and even as to quality, from statements of the seller, or a purchase for a specified purpose. Any substantial failure, in the article supplied to the buyer in pursuance of the contract of sale, to come up to the quality warranted, amounts to a breach of the warranty, and proof of it establishes the buyer's right to an action therefor. This rule applies to all cases where the remedy sought is by an action on the warranty for damages, or by way of set-off in a suit for the purchase-money; in such cases the buyer is bound to prove the breach and the damages suffered by him in consequence of it, and can recover only to the extent of the damage so proved. A warranty of soundness does not extend to a visible defect. A vendor of personal property is not liable for latent defects, known to him, but unknown to the purchaser, unless he has used some artifice to deceive the purchaser in regard to such defects or has warranted the article. Where an article is warranted as fit for a certain purpose, the seller is liable for an injury sustained by the vendee in consequence of its unfitness. Under an executory contract to sell goods *in transitu,* the vendor is obliged to tender a merchantable article. On a sale of an article known to be intended for food there is an implied warranty that it is sound, wholesome,

and fit to be used as an article of food, (15 Hun, 504.) The authority of an agent to warrant goods sold will be implied where it is usual in the market to give a warranty on the sale of such goods; such authority, however, will be implied only as to goods sold at the time of the warranty, which will not extend to subsequent sales in the absence of express warranty.

Breach of Duty.—The non-performance of a duty, or the performance of it in such a manner that injury is done to one's employer, through want of integrity or due diligence and skill. It is assumed that there is an implied contract between an employer and the person that he employs, according to which the latter agrees to perform the duties entrusted to him in such a manner that the interests of his employer shall not suffer. In case of breach of duty, what is called an action of assumpsit — that is, an action for the recovery of damages for the non-performance of a promise, which, though not under seal, is yet founded on proper consideration — may be brought by the one who has sustained an injury, against the persons by whom the breach has been committed.

Breach of Peace.— The taking part in any riot, affray, or tumult, which is destructive to the public tranquillity, or the causing others to do anything to injure the public tranquillity. The former are actual, the latter constructive breaches. In both cases the breach of the peace may be either felonious or not felonious. The felonious breaches of the peace are three in number: (1) The riotous assembling of 12 or more persons, and not dispersing upon proclamation; (2) the riotous demolishing of churches, houses, buildings, or machinery; (3) maliciously sending, delivering, or uttering, or directly or indirectly causing to be received, knowing the contents thereof, any letter or writing threatening to kill or murder any person. The remaining offenses are not felonious, and include: (1) affrays; (2) riots, routs, and unlawful assemblies, which must have at least three persons to constitute them; (3) tumultuously petitioning; (4) forcible entry or detainer, which is committed by violently taking or keeping possession of lands or tenements with menaces, force, and arms, and without the authority of the law; (5) riding, or going armed, with dangerous or unusual weapons, terrifying the good people of the land; (6) spreading false news; (7) false and pretended prophecies, with intent to disturb the peace. Finally, there are two constructive breaches of the peace, namely, challenging another to fight, or bearing such a challenge, and the making public by either printing, writing, signs, or pictures. malicious defamations of any person, especially a magistrate, in order to provoke him to wrath or expose him to public hatred, contempt, and ridicule.

Breach of Trust.— A violation of duty by a trustee, executor, or any other person in a fiduciary position. A trustee is not permitted to manage an estate entrusted to him, in such a manner as to derive any advantage to himself, and at the same time he is bound to manage it in such a manner that the person for whom he has it in trust shall reap from it the greatest possible advantage. Accordingly money held in trust by a trustee must be invested by him in government stock, or in certain other special securities, for the behoof of him for whom he has the money in trust; and if he has not done so he is, as a general rule, liable for interest on the trust funds. Formerly it was the duty of the trustee to invest money in government securities alone, but under certain acts (unless the trust deed expressly forbids) a number of other sound investments are allowed. A trustee who has grossly mismanaged his trust may have to repay money lost, with interest, and sometimes compound interest. (See TRUSTEE.) The court of chancery has adopted two rules to guide the decisions with respect to the liability consequent upon a breach of trust. The purport of the first is, that with a view not to strike terror into persons acting for the benefit of others, the court will deal leniently with trustees who have endeavored fairly to discharge their duty, and in case of any misapplication of the trust money the court will not hold the trustees liable on slight grounds. The second rule is, that care must be had to guard against any abuse of their trust on the part of the trustees. A fraudulent misuse of trust funds is punishable as a misdemeanor with fine and imprisonment.

Bread and Bread Making. Bread is the product obtained by baking a mixture made of wheat flour or the meal from any cereal and water alone, milk, or milk and water, shortening and yeast, or baking powder. Unleavened bread is that made without yeast or other leavening agent. Ordinarily, the term bread is applied to the product made from wheat flour, but other cereals either alone or mixed with wheat are used for bread-making purposes, as rye, corn, and, to a limited extent, barley. Wheat and rye, however, are the only cereals which yield a gluten specially adapted to retaining gas and producing a light, porous dough and bread.

Bread making is an ancient art. In prehistoric times there is abundant evidence of the baking and use of cereals as food. The earliest historians speak of bread and bread making. Bread is frequently mentioned in the Bible, particularly unleavened bread, suggesting that leavened bread was known at that time. It was in Egypt that bread making first reached any degree of perfection. The art of bread making has kept pace with the advance of civilization; the more perfect the system of bread making, the higher the grade of civilization. From Egypt, bread making was introduced into Greece and from there into Italy, and later it followed with the advance of Roman civilization. Among the more civilized American Indian nations, particularly the Aztecs and cliff-dwellers, bread making reached a comparatively high grade.

Methods of bread making vary considerably among different nations, although the underlying principles with all are essentially the same. The main differences are in the way in which the yeast or ferment material is employed, and the method of manipulation. During recent years, study of the yeast plant has resulted in improved methods of bread making. The purity of the yeast and the quality of the flour are the two most essential features for the production of bread of good quality.

Yeast is a unicellular plant which readily reproduces itself by the process of "budding" when added to a batter containing small amounts of saccharine, mineral, and nitrogenous matter. Flour contains all of the food required for the propagation of the yeast plant, which secretes a number of chemical compounds called enzymes which are active agents in bring-

ing about the chemical changes that take place in bread making. Pasteur in his work on fermentation states: "In introducing a quantity of yeast into a saccharine wort, it must be borne in mind that we are sowing a multitude of minute living cells, representing so many centres of life, capable of vegetating with extraordinary rapidity in a medium adapted to their nutrition. This phenomenon can occur at any temperature between zero and 55° C. (131° F.), although a temperature between 15° C. and 30° C. (59° F. and 86° F.) is the most favorable to its occurrence." The individuality of the yeast plant, the nature and amount of its food supply and the conditions under which it develops determine the value of the yeast. When compelled to work in the presence of or to contend with other ferment bodies, the yeast is contaminated and is of lessened value for bread-making purposes. Yeast, like plants of higher orders, is often poorly nourished. Yeast used for brewing purposes is developed from healthy, vigorous, well-nourished yeast plants, and is called high yeast. See BREWING.

The different forms in which yeast is used, as dry cakes, sour dough, compressed soft cakes, brewers' yeast, etc., are simply different ways for preserving and introducing the yeast into the dough so as to leaven the entire mass. The different kinds of yeast vary with the individuality and character of the yeast plants.

Air takes an important part in bread making; its action upon yeast is briefly summarized by Pasteur as follows: "Fermentation by means of yeast appears, therefore, to be essentially connected with the property possessed by this minute cellular plant of performing its respiratory functions, somehow or other, with oxygen existing combined in sugar. Its fermentative power varies considerably between two limits, fixed by the greatest and least possible access to free oxygen which the plant has in the process of nutrition. If we supply it with a sufficient quantity of free oxygen for the necessities of life, nutrition, and respiratory combustions; in other words, if we cause it to live after the manner of a mold, properly so called, it ceases to be a ferment; that is, the ratio between the weight of the plant developed and that of the sugar decomposed, which forms its principal food, is similar in amount to that in the case of fungi. On the other hand, if we deprive the yeast of air entirely, or cause it to develop in a saccharine medium deprived of free oxygen, it will multiply just as if air were present, although with less activity, and under these circumstances its fermentative character will be most marked: under these circumstances, moreover, we shall find the greatest disproportion, all other conditions being the same, between the weight of yeast formed and the weight of sugar decomposed. Lastly, if free oxygen occur in varying quantities, the ferment power of the yeast may pass through all the degrees comprehended between the two extreme limits of which we have spoken."

According to Brown, "yeast cells can use oxygen in the manner of ordinary aerobic fungi, and probably require it for the full completion of their life-history; but the exhibition of their fermentative functions is independent of their environment with regard to free oxygen."

From the investigations of Pasteur, Brown, and others, it would appear that during kneading and aeration, the fermentation process is changed from anaerobic to aerobic form, which appears necessary in order that the full development and complete workings of the yeast cells can take place.

The principal chemical changes which take place in bread making are: (1) production of carbon dioxide and alcohol; (2) change of insoluble carbohydrates to soluble form; (3) production of lactic and other acids; (4) formation of volatile hydrocarbon derivatives; (5) change of solubility and molecular structure of the proteid compounds; (6) formation of amide and ammonium compounds from proteids; and (7) partial oxidation of the fat. The agents which bring about these chemical changes are ferments and heat. The yeast plant, as previously stated, secretes a number of enzymes or chemical products which are active agents in producing chemical changes. Diastase and invertase act upon the carbohydrates forming dextrose sugars which undergo alcoholic fermentation. This results in the production of about one per cent each of carbon dioxide and alcohol. During the process of baking, nearly all of the alcohol is expelled, as only traces of alcohol have been obtained in fresh bread. The joint action of the yeast and heat upon the starch granules results in changing about 6 per cent of the starch to soluble forms as dextrin and dextrose sugars. Some of the starch grains are ruptured, others are partially disintegrated by the ferment action, while many appear to be unaltered. These physical changes of the starch granules render bread more susceptible to the action of the digestive fluids.

Lactic, acetic, and occasionally butyric and other acids are formed during bread making, particularly if the alcoholic ferment becomes inactive and sour dough is formed. From .3 to .4 per cent of acid, calculated as lactic acid, is formed and unites with the gluten proteids during the baking process. The amount of volatile hydrocarbon derivatives formed during bread making is small, less than .10 of a per cent. These compounds give the characteristic aroma to freshly baked bread.

The wheat proteids undergo a number of chemical changes during bread making. (See WHEAT; WHEAT FLOUR.) While the proteids of wheat are mainly in the form of insoluble glutens, small amounts are present as albumin and globulin. Wheat gluten is composed of two substances: gliadin, a glue-like body, and glutenin, a gray powder to which the bands of gliadin adhere. Gliadin constitutes the binding material of the flour, and enables the dough to retain the carbon dioxid gas formed during fermentation and this leavens the bread. An excessive amount of gliadin produces a soft sticky dough, while an excess of glutenin reduces the power of expansion of the dough. In hard wheat flours, the gluten is composed of about 35 per cent glutenin and 65 per cent gliadin. The ratio of gliadin to glutenin determines very largely the quality of the bread. The removal of the gliadin proteid from flour results in a loss of bread-making properties, as the dough fails to expand. Any interference with the gliadin-glutenin ratio in flour affects its bread-making qualities.

Yeast is employed in bread making, not only to produce gas and expand the dough, but also to produce other chemical changes as formation of acid bodies that combine with the proteids to form acid proteids which frequently favorably affect the gliadin-glutenin ratio. Because of the difference in the amounts of gliadin and glutenin in flours, the methods of bread making must be varied to meet the requirements of different kinds of flour.

In average bread making, from 1½ to 2 per cent of dry matter is lost by fermentation and the formation of volatile products as carbon dioxid, alcohol, volatile hydrocarbons, and ammonium products. The losses fall alike upon both the carbohydrates and proteids. With prolonged fermentation, the losses of dry matter may amount to 5 per cent or more.

Bread varies in chemical composition according to the quality of the flour from which it is made. Some flours contain 12 per cent and more of proteids, while others contain 8 per cent and less, according to the composition of the wheat from which the flour has been milled. (See WHEAT.) Flours of high protein content contain proportionally less starch than low protein flours. The starch and protein content of flour and bread vary inversely.

COMPOSITION OF BREAD.

Bread made from white straight grade flour of:	Water Per cent	Protein Per cent	Starch and Carbohydrates Per cent	Ash Per cent	Fat Per cent
(1) High protein content	36.97	10.12	51.70	.45	.76
(2) Average protein content	32.90	9.57	55.44	.81	1.28
(3) Low protein content	32.10	7.21	59.29	.52	.88

When either whole or skim milk is used, the bread contains more protein. The use of milk in bread making is desirable because of its increasing the nutritive value of the bread product. The amount of fat in bread varies with the amount of lard, butter, or other form of shortening used in the making. Occasionally a large amount of lard is used to prevent the bread from drying out too rapidly.

The composition of bread is influenced also by the method of milling the wheat. The outer and aleurone layers of the wheat kernel contain more nitrogen, fat, and ash than the floury portion, hence their addition, as in graham and entire-wheat flours causes the bread to be richer in these compounds. When milled from the same lot of wheat, graham, entire-wheat, and white flours have the following composition:

	Protein Per cent	Fat Per cent	Carbohydrates Per cent	Ash Per cent
Straight (white flour)..	11.99	1.61	75.36	.50
Entire-wheat flour.....	12.26	2.24	73.67	1.02
Graham flour..........	12.65	2.44	74.58	1.72

Digestion experiments have shown that the finer grades of white flour are more digestible than either graham or entire-wheat flour; the comparative digestibility of the three kinds of flour being as follows:

	Per Cent Digested		
	Protein	Carbo-hydrates	Calories
White bread.........	85.3	97.5	90.1
Entire-wheat bread...	80.4	94.1	85.5
Graham bread.......	77.6	88.4	80.7

The higher degree of digestibility of the white bread results in its furnishing a larger amount of available nutrients to the body than is supplied by either graham or entire-wheat. The available nutrients in the three kinds of flour milled from the same lot of wheat are as follows:

	Protein Per Cent	Carbo-hydrates Per Cent	Calories Per gram
White flour.........	10.2	73.5	3.650
Entire-wheat	9.9	69.3	3.445
Graham	9.8	66.3	3.350

White bread when properly made from a glutinous flour has a high degree of digestibility, and with the exception of some of the oat preparations supplies the body with more available nutrients than is secured from any other cereal.

Bread is not generally subject to adulteration, although various forms of sophistication have been practised. The most common form of adulteration is the use of a small amount of alum with damaged and inferior grades of flour. Occasionally rye bread is in part prepared from wheat flour. Wheat bread also has been prepared from flour of mixed cereals, as corn and wheat. During recent years this practice has practically ceased in the United States owing to national laws regulating the taxing and branding of wheat flours when mixed with other cereals or materials.

During the process of baking, the temperature of the oven may range from 225° to 260° C.; the interior of the loaf, however, does not reach 100° C. Various forms of ovens, heated in different ways and with different kinds of fuel are in use. Modern bake ovens are usually so constructed as to secure the highest efficiency from the fuel consumed and to prevent unnecessary losses of heat by radiation. Some ovens are provided with self-registering thermometers and thermostats for the regulation of the temperature, also devices as trucks, racks, and trays for receiving the bread. The bake-ovens in use in different countries vary widely in form and method of heating. Before stoves were used, bread was baked in special ovens usually adjacent to open fireplaces. In some localities, brick bake-ovens were built out of doors. A fire was made in the oven and when the bricks were sufficiently heated. the coals were removed and the unbaked bread was placed in the hot oven, where it readily baked. This plan of heating ovens is even now in use in some European countries. For home bread-making purposes in the United States stoves provided with bake-ovens are used almost exclusively.

Bread, as offered in the market, is made in loaves of various forms, which usually weigh about one pound. In some countries laws regulating the weight of the bread are rigidly enforced, and bakeries are subject to sanitary inspection. During the process of doughing flour will absorb from 40 to 60 per cent of water. During the baking process a part of this water is expelled as steam. On account of the additional water absorbed, a pound loaf of bread can be made from .65 to .75 pounds of flour. A barrel of flour weighing 196 pounds will make from 275 to 300 pound loaves of bread, which will contain about 170 pounds of dry material. Since bread readily loses water, allowance is usually made in baking for subsequent shrinkage in weight. Because of greater power for absorption of water, some flours are more valuable for bread-making purposes than others. The larger the amount of gluten which a flour contains, the greater is the power to absorb water and to produce a large number of loaves per barrel. A low gluten content influences the moisture content of bread more than it does the size of the loaf. Flour which contains a well-balanced gluten can have 10 or even 20 per cent of starch or other material added without influencing the size of the loaf, and on the other hand, the addition of moist gluten to dough does not materially increase the power of expansion or the size of the loaf. Flours which possess poor qualities of expansion are often improved by blending with those of different character. In many larger bakeries, special machinery has been devised for the blending of different qualities of flour. In some bakeries, one kind of flour is used for making the sponge which is then mixed with another kind in making the dough. Some of the more expensive and higher grades of flour are often used in this way to impart quality to the bread product. Comparative baking trials are made when flours are tested for technical purposes, the same weight of flour, yeast, water, and other materials being used. From the tests the physical properties of the bread are determined, as color, size of loaf, weight, odor, and taste.

Special trade names are given to different kinds of bread. In some bakeries, a bread known as home-made or domestic bread is made. Different kinds of bread are usually due to differences in manipulation, as extent of fermentation, kneading, lightness of dough, etc. For domestic purposes, a moist loaf of good quality is usually preferred to one that is extremely porous and readily dries. Different names are applied to various bread products, as Vienna bread, a high-grade white bread made with yeast, milk, shortening, salt, and in some instances a small amount of sugar. Various other ingredients are sometimes used in bread making, as potatoes, potato starch, potato water, barley water, buttermilk, molasses, etc. These materials take only a secondary part in the process, influencing the taste and flavor more than the composition, unless used in large amounts. The flavor of bread is due to the small amount of ethereal products formed during fermentation by the action of the ferments in the yeast and the soluble ferments or enzymes in the flour. Undesirable as well as the desirable flavoring products are developed during the process of fermentation in case the yeast is of poor quality or the flour is unsound.

There are many different kinds of bread made from the different cereals, as pumpernickel, which is made from the graham of rye, flat bread made in large flat cakes without yeast from wheat flour, and baked on the top of a hot stove. This bread is extensively used in the Scandinavian countries. Black bread is used by the peasantry in many European countries.

Aerated bread is made by forcing carbon dioxide through the dough instead of securing a like result by fermentation with yeast, etc., as in the ordinary method of bread making.

For home bread making, Miss Shepperd in her 'Hand-Book of Household Science,' gives the following directions: "Bread with Home-Made Yeast.— One cup of good home-made yeast, one cup of milk and water (one half cup of each) and two level teaspoonfuls of salt. Have the temperature of liquid and flour 75° F. and make into a dough stiff enough to handle without flour, let rise three hours, or until double in size, keeping always at 75° F., and when risen, mold into loaves, let stand one hour and bake." The home-made yeast is made as follows: "Stir one half pint of flour to a smooth batter with one half pint of cold water. Over this pour one quart of boiling water, pouring slowly and stirring rapidly. Place over the fire, and cook four or five minutes. Add two level tablespoonfuls of sugar and one of salt. When cooled to 75° F., add one ounce of compressed yeast, or one pint of home-made yeast. Keep as nearly 75° F. as possible for 24 hours, stirring down once in four or five hours. Keep in a glass jar in a cool place. The jar must be thoroughly washed and scalded before putting fresh yeast into it."

"Compressed Yeast Bread.—To make bread with compressed yeast, break a one-half ounce cake of compressed yeast into small pieces in a cup, and cover with cold water. Place in a bowl one pint of liquid — one half milk and one half water. Make the temperature of the mixture 75° F. Into this liquid put two level teaspoonfuls of salt, stir in a cup of sifted flour; stir the yeast and water in the cup, and pour into this; put in another cup of flour and beat it well. Continue to stir in flour, keeping sides of bowl clean, and kneading with the spoon until nearly stiff enough. Then bathe the hands, wipe them dry, flour the board, and knead the dough until it ceases to adhere to the hands or board, when no flour is used. Grease the bowl with some nice-flavored fat and treat the top of dough after putting into the bowl in the same way. Cover the bowl with a white cloth and allow the dough to rise. See that the air is not cooler or warmer than 75° F. Let the dough rise three hours, or until it is double its original size, knead well and mold into loaves, put in greased pans, grease over the top, let rise one hour, when it will again double its size if properly manipulated, then bake."

These methods of making bread are partienlarly adaptable to hard wheat flours. For soft wheat flours, other methods in which more salt is used, a longer time allowed for fermentation, and a stiffer dough is made, will be found to give better results. Because of differences in the composition of the various kinds of flour, no directions can be given which are alike applicable to all. The method of bread making which is suited to one flour does not necessarily give the best results with other flours. In fact,

it is necessary to vary the conditions of preparation according to the kind of flour used.

HARRY SNYDER,
Chemist, University of Minnesota.

Bread-fruit (*Artocarpus incisa*), a tree of the natural order *Urticaceæ*, native of the Indian Archipelago and of the southern Pacific Islands. It attains a height of 30 or 40 feet; is often limbless for half its height, bears leathery, glossy dark green, three- to nine-lobed leaves, one to three feet long; has compact, club-shaped, yellow catkins of male flowers, 9 to 15 inches long, and sub-globular heads of female flowers with spongy receptacles; and usually seedless, spheroidal fruits, at first green, later brown, and lastly yellow, six inches or more in diameter, hanging by short thick stalks singly or in clusters of two or three from the smaller branches. The rough rind is irregularly marked in squares and other figures with raised centres. The unripe fruit contains a milky juice, and when in the edible stage it resembles fresh bread, being white and mealy. It is then slightly tart. Later it becomes yellow, juicy, and tastes of decay. In tropical countries where it has been introduced and particularly in its original home, the fruit is highly valued as a nutritious food, being prepared for use in various ways. When baked it resembles plantain rather than wheaten bread, being sweetish, slightly astringent, but otherwise almost tasteless. When fresh fruits cannot be procured, it is sometimes slightly fermented, beaten to a pasty mass, and so used. Another common way of preparing it is to beat it to a paste with cocoanut milk and to serve it mixed with bananas, plantains, etc. Since the trees produce two or three crops annually, and since the bearing seasons of different varieties overlap more or less, the fruit may be obtained during the greater part of the year. Not alone for the fruit is the tree valuable; in the South Sea Islands its fibrous inner bark is woven into cloth resembling, but inferior in softness and whiteness, to that made from the paper mulberry which is similarly employed in those islands; the gummy exudation from the bark, boiled with cocoanut oil is used for caulking canoes, pails, etc.; the beautiful yellow wood is light and soft, but when exposed to the air becomes dark like mahogany, and is used for canoes, furniture, and the interior work in houses. The tree has been cultivated to a slight extent in southern Florida, but the fruits rarely appear even in the most southern markets of the United States, because they do not bear shipment well, and unless used very soon after being gathered become hard and disagreeable in taste. For an account of the introduction of the bread-fruit tree into the West Indies in the last decade of the 18th century, when such feats were more difficult and less common than a century later, see Curtis, 'Botanical Magazine' (pp. 2869-71). A near relative of the bread-fruit tree is the jack (q.v.).

Bread Making. See BREAD.

Bread-nut (*Brosimum alicastrum*), a tree of the natural order *Urticaceæ*, a native of the West Indies and closely related to the bread-fruit. The tree, which is very large, bears shining lance-shaped leaves; globose catkins of male and female flowers on different trees; and yields a gummy, milky juice from its bark. The round, yellow fruits (drupes), which are about three inches in circumference, contain each a single seed. When roasted or boiled they are used like bread, and, having a flavor which resembles hazel nuts, form a pleasant food. In the United States the tree has not been cultivated.

Bread Riot in New York, The, a riotous demonstration in New York, 13 Feb. 1837. The financial policy of President Jackson had created an era of wild-cat banks, currency inflation, extravagant speculation, and high prices which bore cruelly on the poor, flour being $12 a barrel, partly owing to a short crop the year before, and other prices in proportion. In New York the general distress was intensified by the great fire of 15–16 Dec. 1835, which destroyed nearly 700 business and other buildings, covering some 13 acres in the heart of the city and occasioning a loss of $20,000,000. For some time the Jacksonian press had been denouncing the grain dealers as the cause of the famine prices, mentioning especially Eli Hart, the leading commission merchant, and the houses of Meech and Herrick, although as they were commission dealers their stocks were obviously not private hoards. On 13 Feb. 1837, just before Jackson's term expired, these papers announced a public meeting in City Hall Park at 4 P.M., the call being headed "Bread, Meat, Rent, Fuel! Their prices must come down!" The call was signed by eight men, two of whom — Moses Jacques and Alexander Ming, Jr. — were well-known and very violent demagogues. Jacques was made chairman, and with Ming, and others, made furious speeches inflaming the passions of the crowd. Some one at length indicated Hart's store, on Washington Street, between Dey and Cortlandt, as a vast hoard of provisions to relieve their distress, and the crowd surged toward it. The police were swept away and beaten, and although two of the three iron doors held, the centre one was battered in, and the crowd began throwing flour barrels and sacks of grain into the street, staving in and tearing open such as did not burst by their own fall, and as one of the papers remarked, "lowering prices by leaving less on the market." A fresh onslaught by the police was repelled; and it was not till well into the evening that a body of militia dispersed the mob, which by this time had thrown into the street about 500 barrels of flour and 1,000 bushels of wheat, the most of it relieving no one. Herrick's stock was somewhat damaged also, and Meech's store attacked. The disturbance was attributed to the foreigners, but although the two ringleaders were foreign, four of the eight names signed to the call were American, and the natives certainly looked on at the mob without trying to assist the officers.

Bread-root (*Psoralea esculenta*), a leguminous plant with edible, farinaceous tubers. It is the *Pomme blanche* or *Pomme de terre* of the French pioneers. It is common on the higher prairies from Texas through Iowa to Wisconsin.

Bread-winners, The, a brief novel, appeared anonymously in 1883. The kindly interest shown by Alfred Farnham, a retired army officer, in Maud Matchin, the handsome but vulgar daughter of a master carpenter in a western city, turns her head, and she confesses her love to him, which is not reciprocated. Maud's rejected lover, Sam Sleeny, journeyman in Matchin's employ, is jealous of Farnham. Dominated by Offitt, a demagogue, he joins a labor organization. Farnham loves Alice Belding, who refuses him, but still returns his love. During a strike Farnham organizes patrolmen. The mob attacks his house, and Sleeny assaults Farnham, but fails to kill him. Offitt, who now pays his addresses to Maud, enters Farnham's home, assaults and robs him, and Alice and Mrs. Belding come and nurse him. Offitt turns suspicion to Sleeny, hastens to Maud, and urges her to fly with him. Suspecting, she refuses, gets and reveals his secret. Sleeny, who has been arrested, breaks jail, and at Maud's home meets Offitt and kills him. Sleeny is tried for killing Offitt, and acquitted upon the ground of temporary insanity. The book is a brilliant presentation of the conditions of "labor" at that period. Its authorship was acknowledged in 1902 by John Hay.

Breadalbane, brĕd-äl'băn, a district in the western part of Perthshire, in the centre of the Grampians, which here cover a large tract of the county in length and breadth. This district is a complete mixture of high and low hills, yielding pasture for large flocks of sheep and shelter for game, with intermediate valleys, some of which are susceptible of cultivation, while others are merely areas of peat and heath. Loch Tay lies in the centre of the district. Kenmore and Killin are the largest villages.

Breadth, a term in art, used to denote means or effects whereby an artist becomes distinguished for largeness and mastery of treatment. Breadth of style in art is shown in work which gives the impression of these qualities, manifested in simplicity, comprehensiveness, and due subordination of detail. In a work of art possessing the true characteristics of breadth, the eye, passing from one feature to another, takes in, as it were, the whole subject and meaning at a single glance.

Break-Circuit Chronometer, the name applied to a box-chronometer to which a device has been attached for breaking an electric circuit at stated intervals, usually once in two seconds.

Break'er. See COAL MINING.

Breakespere, brāk'spèr. See ADRIAN IV.

Breaking Bulk, the act of breaking open of a bundle, parcel, etc., and taking the contents, so as to constitute in law a conversion or the like.

Breakwater, an obstruction of any kind raised to oppose the action of the waves, and make safe harbors and roadsteads. The outer mole of the harbor of Civita Vecchia was built by the Emperor Trajan for this purpose; and the piers of ancient Piræus and of Rhodes are of the same class of structures. Herod, it is stated by Josephus, in order to form a port between Dora and Joppa, ordered mighty stones to be cast into the sea in 20 fathoms water, to prepare a foundation; the greater number of them 50 feet in length, 9 feet deep, and 10 feet wide, and some were even larger than these. In the use of such immense blocks of stone, the true principles of constructing a permanent barrier to the waves, appear to have been better understood than they were 17 centuries afterward. Breakwaters are generally solid and made of stone, but there are also floating breakwaters which serve the same purpose. These are built of strong open woodwork, divided into several sections, and secured by chains attached to fixed bodies. The breakers pass between the beams of such a structure as if through a sieve, and in the passage nearly all their force is destroyed. It is estimated that a breakwater of this description will last for 25 years. Stone breakwaters are usually constructed by sinking loads of unwrought stone along the line where they are to be laid, and allowing them to find their angle of repose under the action of the waves. When the mass rises to the surface, or near it, it is surmounted with a pile of masonry, sloped outward in such a manner as will best enable it to resist the action of the waves, or it is covered, as at Plymouth, England, with large blocks of stone, which do not rise high above the surface of the water. Sometimes the breakwater has to be constructed of solid masonry from its foundation. The breakwater at Dover, England, is built in this way, there being no stone in the neighborhood to form a base of the kind described. The most gigantic breakwater ever constructed is that which was erected by French engineers to protect the harbor of Cherbourg. The history of the building of this

base, and 339 feet at the top, the angle of the slope being 60°. This was strengthened by an interior concentric cone, 5 feet 10 inches within the outer one. The frame of each was made of 80 large upright timbers 24 feet long and 1 foot square. On these were erected 80 more of 14 feet in length, making, for the 2 exterior and 2 interior portions, 320 of these uprights. The machine was then planked, hooped, and firmly bolted together. The first cone was built and floated at Havre, then taken to pieces, transported to Cherbourg, and floated off and sunk on 6 June 1784; and the second on 7 July following, in the presence of 10,000 spectators; but before the cavity of this one could be filled with stones, its upper part was demolished in a storm of five days' continuance in August, and the stones it contained were spread over the bottom, interfering with the placing of the next cone. The original plan was to set 90 of these cones, of 150 feet diameter at base, 60 at top, and 65 feet high, in succession, and fill them with loose stones or masonry, and the spaces between them with a network of iron chains, to break the force of the waves. Several modifications of the plan were attempted, the net

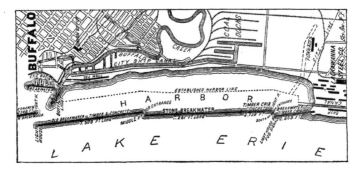

breakwater affords an amusing and instructive example of the folly of ignoring experience and the laws of nature. When Louis XVI. appointed commissioners to report upon the best locality for establishing, opposite the English coast, a port and naval arsenal, they recommended the construction of a dike over two miles in length, in water 70 feet deep, in front of the harbor of Cherbourg, by sinking a vast number of ships filled with masonry as a basis, and covering these with heavy stones to within 18 feet of the surface. And when at last four of the ablest naval officers and engineers of France were appointed to execute the work, which was regarded as one of the most stupendous operations, certainly the greatest piece of hydraulic architecture ever undertaken by man, the plan they adopted was one which proved impracticable after having been prosecuted from the year 1784 to 1789, at enormous expense. This plan was the construction of huge truncated cones of timber, which, of the reduced size at which they were actually built, measured 36 feet in height, with a circumference of 472 feet at the

result, after years of labor and an expense of upward of $6,000,000, being a number of isolated mounds of stone, extending in a crescent for about 2½ miles. In 1830 the work was again taken up, and completed in its present form about 1856. For a full account of this stupendous work, consult Cresy's 'Encyclopædia of Civil Engineering.'

There are many important breakwaters in the United States, and each decade finds an increasing number of them as the demands of trade, and the liberality of the government demands and permits their construction. The latest of these (1903) is the great breakwater at Buffalo, N. Y., built to form a harbor for the immense lake traffic centring at that city. This structure forms the most important section of a long line of breakwaters that extend for 4½ miles along the water-front. At the time that the present work was undertaken there existed the north breakwater, which is built of concrete and extends for 2,200 feet, with a light at its southerly end. Opposite this light and to the westward of it is the northerly end of what is known as the old breakwater, a timber and concrete structure 7,608 feet long. There is a light at the northerly end of the old breakwater, with a harbor entrance between it and the southerly light of the north breakwater. To the south of the old breakwater is the new structure now being considered. It consists of a stone breakwater 7,261 feet in length, which connects with a timber and concrete structure extending south for another 2,739 feet, with a light at its southerly extremity. Parallel with the previous structure, and slightly to the westward of it, is a timber crib breakwater, 2,803 feet long, which runs northerly from Stony Point. It has a light on its northern extremity, and the opening between this and the last named breakwater forms the south harbor entrance, the opening between the stone breakwater and the old breakwater being known as the middle harbor entrance. The 7,261-foot stretch of the new breakwater is of the rubble mound type, stone-topped, while the southerly end of it, 2,739 feet, is of timber crib construction, to enable vessels to moor alongside of it inside of the harbor.

The new breakwater is built in the open waters of Lake Erie, parallel with the shore, 1,500 feet out from the pierhead line of the harbor, and in 30 feet of water. The first operation was to deposit two parallel ridges of small rubble on the lake bottom, one on the lake side and one on the shore side of the proposed breakwater, the intervening space being filled in with gravel. Another five feet of rubble ridges were added and again filled in with gravel, the mound thus formed being raised to within 10 feet of the surface of the water. The breakwater was then built up for the remaining 10 feet to the surface of the lake by dumping upon it large rubble stones. The slopes of the structure were covered with a revetment of large stones, lowered into place in close touch with each other, so as to completely cover the rubble mound, the object of these heavy quarried stones being to prevent displacement of the rubble by the action of the water. Then came the important work of covering the mound with large capping stones, quarried to prescribed dimensions, many of the stones measuring as much as six feet in thickness. These stones were carried out by five large floating derricks, each with a lifting power of 20 tons. The capping stones were laid snugly together, the finished top and side of the breakwater presenting a fairly even and true appearance. The illustration shows very clearly the way in which the top of the breakwater is finished, the heavy top angle stones serving by their weight and friction to prevent the heavy seas from taking hold of the rubble mound, loosening it and washing it away. A cross section of the breakwater as thus constructed shows it to be normally about 140 feet wide at the bottom and 14 feet wide at the top.

While the masonry breakwater was being constructed, the work of building the timber-crib structure was also going on apace. As compared with the rubble-mound type, the timber and concrete form has the advantage of being cheaper in construction. In building it the first step was to prepare a foundation and for this purpose a powerful clam-shell dredge built especially for the work was used to dredge a trench along the line of the breakwater in the bottom of the lake 95 feet in width, and 50 feet in depth through the clay. Then through the centre of this trench another excavation was dredged out which was 50 feet in width and extended everywhere to solid rock. The next task was to fill in the trench thus formed with gravel which was brought to the spot in scows and dumped in, a bed of gravel 30 to 40 feet in depth being formed in this way. Upon this was placed an embankment of rubble stone eight feet high, which formed a foundation for the timber cribs. These cribs were built of sawn timber and were 36 feet wide, 22 feet high, and from 60 to 180 feet long. They were towed to position over the foundation and sunk by loading with stone. The superstructure was built in 3 benches, the first 6 feet, the second 10 feet, and the third 12 feet above the mean water level of the lake. Each bench was 12 feet wide. As shown in the illustrations, a certain portion of the crib breakwater, as finished, is of this construction; but the larger portion of it has been capped with concrete. This was done to strengthen the structure, the heavy gales of 12 Sept. and 21 Nov. 1900, in the latter of which the wind reached a velocity of 80 miles an hour, having loosened up and broken the above-water timber coping and finish. In repairing the ravages of the storm, the damaged superstructure was removed and the cribs cut down to an elevation of two feet below the mean lake level. Upon this, concrete blocks, forming longitudinal and cross walls, were placed, and the pockets thus formed filled in with rubble stone, and roofed in with heavy concrete work, which was carried up to the level of the original breakwater. In place of the three benches of the crib superstructure, the reconstructed portion shows a parapet and a banquette. The parapet which is exposed to the lake side covers a width of 27 feet and its crest is 12 feet above mean lake level. The banquette is 8 feet wide and is uniformly 4 feet above the lake level. The new breakwaters have taken some six or seven years to construct, and the cost has been $2,200,000. Consult: 'Reports of the Chief of Engineers U. S. A.'; Spon, 'Dict. of Engineering'; Stevenson, 'The Construction of Harbors'; De Cordemoy, 'Les portes modernes.'

Bream, a sluggish fresh-water fish (*Abramis brama*) of the carp family, common in European lakes and rivers, and especially numerous in the English fens, where it finds all the conditions most favorable, and reaches a weight of seven or eight pounds. It is edible, but too lethargic to afford sport. Another species (*A. blicca*), is smaller, silvery white, and a favorite with those who enjoy quiet angling. In the United States the term "bream" is given rather indefinitely to several minnows and sunfish; and to various marine fishes, better known as sea-breams (q.v.).

Brearley, William Henry, American journalist and author: b. Plymouth, Mich., 18 July 1846. He served in the Michigan infantry during the Civil War, was connected with several Detroit papers 1870–92; founded the Detroit Museum of Art 1883. He has published 'Recollections of the East Tennessee Campaign'; 'Wanted, a Copyist'; 'Leading Events of the American Revolution.'

Breast, in female animals, a glandular structure, containing vessels for the secretion of milk, and excretory ducts, which open by small orifices in the nipple, and discharge the secreted fluid for the nourishment of the child. At the centre of each breast there is a small projection, the nipple, and this is surrounded by a dark ring termed the areola. The nipple is the part which the infant seizes in its mouth, and through the passage of which the milk flows into the mouth of the child in the act of suction. The glandular structure of the breast is covered by fat, except at the forepart of the nipple and the integument. The breast is liable to many diseases, from irritation during nursing, bruises of the part, undue pressure from tight clothes, and from constitutional causes. Inflammation of the breast is very common during nursing, or from a superabundant secretion of milk. After delivery, the nourishment of the infant being from the breast, there is an increased determination of blood to that part to enable it to perform the necessary function, and thus, when there is any cause of irritation, there is a tendency to increased action in that part, which frequently terminates in inflammation. Lacteal swelling is another troublesome disease of the breast. It is confined to the nipple, and consists of a large collection of milk in one of the lactiferous tubes, the orifice of which has been closed from inflammation. See MAMMARY GLANDS.

Breast-wheel. See WATER-WHEEL.

Breasted, James Henry, American Egyptologist: b. Rockford, Ill., 27 Aug. 1865. He studied at Yale and Berlin, and has been a professor of Egyptology and Semitic languages at the University of Chicago from 1894. He has published 'An English Edition of Erman's Egyptian Grammar' (1898): 'De Hymnis in Solem sub Rege Amenophide IV. Conceptis' (1894); 'A New Chapter in the Life of Thutmose III.' (1900).

Breastplate, a piece of defensive armor covering the breast, originally made of thongs, cords, leather, etc. (hence lorica, cuirass), but afterward of brass, iron, or other metals. It may be considered as an improvement of the shield or buckler, which was borne on the left arm, and moved so as to protect successively all parts of the body. It being perceived that the free use of both hands in the employment of offensive weapons was important, the defensive armor was attached to the body, and received different names from its position, use, etc., as for instance, breastplate, cuisses, greaves. These different species of defensive armor are of little use against firearms, and have therefore generally fallen into disuse in modern war. (See CUIRASS.) Breastplate, in Jewish antiquity, was a folded piece of rich, embroidered stuff worn by the high-priest. It was set with 12 precious stones bearing the names of the tribes. It was also called the breastplate of judgment, because it contained the Urim and Thummim.

Breastwork, in the military art, every elevation made for protection against the shot of the enemy. Wood and stone are not suitable for breastworks, on account of their liability to splinter. The best are made of earth; in some circumstances, of fascines, dung, gabions, bags of sand, and of wool. The thickness of the work must be in proportion to the artillery of the enemy. In general it ought not to be less than 10, nor more than 18, or at most 24 feet thick. The rule of Cugnot is, that the breastwork should be so high that nothing but the sky and the tops of trees can be seen within cannon-shot from the interior of the intrenchments. If this rule cannot be followed on account of the height of neighboring mountains, the interior of the fortification ought to be secured by traverses.

Breath (A.S. _braed_, odor, breath). The ordinary breath has a slight odor, and contains nitrogen, oxygen, carbon dioxide, ammonia, water, and organic impurities. In quiet breathing it probably never carries microbes. In diseases of the mouth, and teeth, nose, throat, lungs and stomach, in constipation, and in fevers the breath may become offensive. Should a simple antiseptic mouthwash or a laxative fail to remove the trouble an underlying disease must be sought out and treated. A suitable mouthwash is Dobell's solution or listerine. Deodorizers, like coffee, cardamon, cloves, etc., may be resorted to for temporary sweetening of the breath, but they have little effect in permanently removing the condition.

Breathing and Health. Essential to continuance of physical being are food, water, and air, and the most important is air. The supply of food may be cut off for days or weeks and life remain in the body. The quality may be poor and amount reduced, and, while it affects health and perhaps reduces strength, life will not go out for a long time. Cut off the supply of air completely for 14 minutes and life becomes extinct. Change from purity of air to that which is only slightly contaminated and in an hour vitality lessens. Headache and nausea appear, and unless there is return to fresh and pure air, disintegration of tissue and physical break-down follow. These facts are patent to all, and are referred to as a starting point to consider how breathing may be used for the establishment and continuance of perfect health. The diseases most dreaded by the medical fraternity are those of a pulmonary nature. They are, in many cases, the result of insufficient air supply and inefficient means of securing it. Diseases affecting digestion follow close upon those relating to the lungs, and these, too, can be regulated by and through breathing. Nervous disorders, likewise, succumb very readily when breathing is properly ordered.

The act of breathing is, then, so important that it should have the attention of every individual. To use it to its best advantage every one must know something of its action and of the parts directly affected by it. There is instinctive breathing and mentally directed breathing. Every one breathes. Instinctive breathing begins at birth and continues through life. If we could always be in fresh air and have little to do we would need no more knowledge of the operation than has any animal. Even for great physical activity instinctive breathing would be sufficient, because every physical exertion would increase the rapidity and breadth of the instinctive act. But we are thinking animals, and we live in conditions requiring more than ordinary physical action. Excitement, nervous movements, high living, and attributes of mind cause us to throw off poisons and gases which the breathing apparatus must take care of. To dispose of these we must go beyond instinctive breathing and adopt mentally directed action.

. Breath is air taken through the nose and mouth into the lungs, which are elastic sacks made of microscopic vessels suspended on the bronchial tubes in the chest. They expand and collapse as they are acted upon by organs made of muscle. When they expand they draw air into the body; when they collapse they expel air. The muscles which operate them are those of the chest. The chief one is the floor of the chest, called the diaphragm. Those next in importance are the costal muscles, located in the ribs. The next, the dorsal muscles, located in the back. Last, the pectoral muscles in the upper chest in front. The muscles already noted are those which dilate the lungs and draw air into the body. Their action produces inspiration of breath, and that action expands the chest. Their return to normal position permits the collapse of the air-cells of the lungs. Such return is, however, insufficient to cause complete collapse of air-cells and the expulsion of all air. Return is assisted, and expulsion made complete, by calling into use the abdominal muscles and those in the ribs below the diaphragm. It becomes, then, very important to know the location of the diaphragm. This organ is attached in front to the end of the breast bone. One should find this location by pressing with his fingers. Men find it easily because the ribs spread quickly where they leave the breast bone. Women find it less easily as the ribs are close together. But follow up to the point where the very end of the breast bone is located. The diaphragm attaches at the sides to the ribs. One can tell where by placing the hand flat on the side and inhaling a deep breath; that which pushes first against the hand from within is the diaphragm, which is from one to two inches lower than the level of the end of the breast bone. It attaches to the sides all around and into the small of the back, where it is a little lower than at the sides. One should study the location of the diaphragm day after day, until it is definitely fixed in mind. Many who have supposed they knew how and where to take breath by using the diaphragm will find their conception has been that it is lower than it is. The real reason for having the correct location clearly in mind is to avoid careless and, possibly, harmful practice. The reason for repeating the examination of location so many times is that the mind may go instantly to it in order to direct voluntary inspiration and expiration. Another common error is to suppose the lungs to be located in the upper chest. Ask one if his lungs are sound and he will pound high in front. The largest portion of the lungs is in the sides and back. He pounds over the space occupied by the heart. This common error leads many who practise voluntary breathing into misdirected effort, which is liable to be harmful.

. Breathing divides into inspiration and expiration. Inspiration (breath taking) is instinctive and involuntary. The latter is like the former, but it is greatly amplified and extended. Our attention now goes to voluntary inspiration. Its primary physical act is expansion of the diaphragm. Evidence of that is discovered wherever that organ connects with outer parts of the chest, in the generous expansion of those parts, and by quite a little expansion of parts of the body

below the diaphragm. The latter action is caused by the pressure of the centre of the diaphragm (quite in the middle of the body) downward upon the abdominal viscera. Deep breathing, or taking large draughts of air, is always accompanied by generous spread of the body at the level of the diaphragm, and considerable spread of the portion just below that level. Few adults will do this upon the first attempt at mental direction of inhalation, because they have lost the natural habit. If they will study for a few minutes quiet instinctive (not directed) breathing, they will find they really do breathe as described above. But this is not enough for "breathing for health." It must be amplified through mental direction; on the line of instinctive breathing, only much more extensively.

The custom of taking deep breath can be developed into habit in a short time, and it should be used daily. Direct the thought during inhalation to generous expansion of the body in the neighborhood of the diaphragm, and after such expansion has begun, enlarge the sides and back above the diaphragm. Fill the lungs fully, retain the air a few seconds and exhale completely. Such complete exhalation implies that breath shall be forced out by drawing in the abdomen. After repeating the act of inspiration and expiration four or five times, which, by the way, should never be done violently, one can feel the more active rush of blood through the body. This demonstrates that the cleansing process of the circulatory system is accomplishing its work. When a good glow is established refrain from further exercise for the time, but resume it when quietness is again restored. Five or ten minutes given to this practice every morning and evening will, in a month, establish physical strength. Followed through a term of years it will rebuild the body and make it almost invulnerable against the attack of disease. Persons with weak lungs or sluggish circulation can, by this means, become rugged and very active. So far-reaching is the result that great physical strength is acquired. Even the usually expected elements of decay, as manifested in carious teeth and falling hair, are arrested or prevented. The success of all physical treatment lies in the regularity and persistence with which it is followed. In a few weeks or even in one week, the benefit will be observed, but the rebuilding of a body requires persistent practice for a year at least.

Practice of the above nature increases the lung space. Probably no new air-cells can be created, although some authorities claim that there are. The expanding power of existing air-cells is enlarged, and the muscles which cause the expansion greatly increase their power. Such expansion can be measured. It is well to take the bust measure, passing the tape-measure around the body just below the arm pits, and take measurement on the first day of each month thereafter. Comparison with previous measure will show constant increase for a full year. How great an increase to expect depends upon the person. From two to five inches in a year is usual. A more perfect measure of development is given by the spirometer which, as its name implies, is a breath-measure. It records the vital capacity of the lungs. Test measurements in over 500 students proved that every one gained in size of lungs, and many made marvelous changes in their physical condition. The spirometer records the cubic inches of air space in the lungs. Such capacity varies in accordance with the height, and is greater in men than in women. Tall people have largest lungs, ordinarily, and those who are slim, rather than stout, increase most through practice. Records show that the increase in air capacity in one year averages from 25 to 33 per cent. All this has direct bearing on health. In the lungs the air-cells are surrounded by minute blood vessels. All the blood, after its course through the body, passes to the lungs to discharge its gatherings and to receive the supply of oxygen necessary for life. It is evident that if the air supply is increased 25 per cent, cleansing and oxygenation take place more quickly and more thoroughly. It is recognized among physicians that the purity of the blood is the most important element in keeping well. Meeting the attack of bacilli is the triumph of medical science. The germ of disease is found in the blood, and in modern science inoculation for destroying such germ is the keynote. In the practice of breathing every individual has nature's method of doing what medical science does. It goes beyond that, in that breathing provides prevention as well as cure. The ounce of prevention is the most valuable. Disease germs can hardly find lodgment, and they certainly cannot propagate, in a body which is perfectly well. A feeling of lassitude and "run down" is the admonition which shows that germs are at work. Your doctor tells you to take long walks in the open air. He says in other words that oxygen must be supplied to the lungs. Much surer are we to respond to health-laws if such training as all can have has made the taking of large draughts of air possible.

Above we have described inhalation and exhalation. While we have not sought to formulate a complete system of training, we have given enough to show what may be done. At first, daily practice will be gentle. This will bring into correct use all physical organs which govern breathing. When one realizes ease in action he should make the dual act of inspiration and expiration more generous. Expiration should now be made more complete. That is, make exhalation forceful by drawing in the abdominal muscles and lower ribs greatly. This will also cause broader inspiration. Thus the two sets of muscles will be powerfully increased, and the expanding power of the lungs will be enlarged.

When breath is imbibed in large quantities it should be retained a little time that it may purify the blood. Three or four seconds are long enough at first, but the time may be increased gradually until one can hold it 30 or more seconds. The physical act of holding the breath consists of arresting the inspiratory muscles when they have drawn breath in and refusing to allow them to return to their relaxed position. The very act of thus commanding adds to their strength. It is one of the contributing factors toward strengthening the whole body. The tendency of modern life to greater physical activity accentuates the need of symmetrical development of the lungs and their controlling forces.

FRANK HERBERT TUBBS,
Editor 'Music Life.'

Brébeuf, Jean de, zhŏṅ dĕ brā-bĕf, Jesuit missionary: b. Bayeux, France, 25 March 1593; d. 16 March 1649. He set sail in 1625 with Champlain, arrived at Quebec when but a single house was seen there, and fixed his residence among the Hurons. He learned their language, and gained their confidence. In 1649 they were suddenly attacked by the Iroquois, and Brébeuf fell into the hands of the latter, by whom he was put to death with frightful tortures. His 'Catechism Translated into the Language of the Hurons' was published at Paris in 1652.

Breccia, brĕ'chạ, a conglomerate composed of angular pieces of the same or of different rocks, united by a cement or matrix, which, according to its nature, forms the several varieties of calcareous, silicious, etc. The conglomerate known by the name of pudding-stone differs from that of breccia only in having the composing fragments rounded. Calcareous breccia is often found in the form of fine marble, apparently composed of fragments produced by some disrupting force, and then united by the infiltration of carbonate of lime among them. The angular form of the fragments seems to indicate that they have never been exposed to much friction, and have therefore probably originated at no great distance from their present site. In some cases a kind of spurious breccia has been formed by the breaking up of calcareous beds, and their subsequent union by means of infiltration, without any change of their original position. Marble breccia thus formed is remarkable for the size of its fragments. In the calcareous districts of many countries caverns and extensive fissures are seen filled with a reddish mass, composed of lime, sand, and oxide of iron, enclosing angular fragments of different rocks, and a great number of bones more or less broken. To such masses the name of osseous breccia has been given. They are most frequently met with on the shores of the Mediterranean.

Brèche de Roland, brĕsh dĕ rō-läṅ, "the breach of Roland," a defile in the Pyrenees, between France and Spain, which, according to a well-known legend, was opened up by Roland, one of the paladins of Charlemagne, with one blow of his sword Durandal, in order to afford a passage to his army. It is an immense gap between the walls of a mountain barrier rising to the height of 9,500 feet above the level of the sea, and from 300 to 600 feet above the bottom of the defile. The defile itself varies in width from 200 to 300 feet. It lies about 43 miles north of Huesca, from which it can at times be seen.

Brechin, brĕн'n, a parliamentary and municipal burgh of Scotland, in Forfarshire, is romantically situated on the left bank of the South Esk, 12½ miles northeast of Forfar, and eight west of Montrose. It is a very ancient royal burgh, and was formerly walled. The chief industry is the manufacture of linens, and the neighborhood exports a considerable quantity of grain. In ancient times there was an abbey of Culdees in this place, and in 1150, when Brechin was constituted an episcopal see by David I., it is supposed that the site of this establishment was that chosen for the foundation of the cathedral. The cathedral church of St. Ninians, which now forms the parish church, is situated on the north edge of a precipitous ravine, which separates the burgh-lands from those of Brechin Castle. The ancient round tower, which is the leading architectural feature of the town, stands at the southwest angle of the church. Such towers are common in Ireland, but are seldom seen in Scotland. The Mechanics' Institution is a handsome building, with a beautiful hall, and there is a valuable public library. Pop. (1901) 8,941.

Breck, James Lloyd, American clergyman: b. Philadelphia, 27 June 1818; d. Benicia, Cal., 30 March 1876. He graduated at the University of Pennsylvania in 1838, and at the General Theological Seminary, New York, in 1841. The same year he went to Wisconsin, and aided in the formation of the diocese there in 1847. He was one of the founders of the Nashotah Theological Seminary, remaining as instructor there until 1850, when he went to St. Paul, Minn., as a missionary. There he established an associate mission, and assisted in supplying mission stations for 80 miles around. From 1852 to 1857 he was engaged in missionary work among the Chippewa Indians. In 1858 he established church services at Faribault, Minn., and founded the Seabury Divinity School. He prepared the way for building church institutions there, and was the forerunner of Bishop Whipple. In 1867 Dr. Breck went to Benicia, Cal., where he established church enterprises similar to those at Nashotah and Faribault.

Breck, Samuel, American soldier: b. Middleborough, Mass., 25 Feb. 1834. He is descended from Edward Breck, who came to Dorchester, Mass., from Ashton, England, about 1630. He graduated at West Point 1855, and took part in the Seminole war of 1855-6. During the Civil War he was assistant adjutant-general of McDowell's division, and afterward of the 1st Army Corps, being engaged in the occupation of Fredericksburg and in the Shenandoah Valley expedition, to intercept the retreat of the Confederate forces under Gen. Jackson in 1862. From July 1862 to 1870 he was assistant in the adjutant-general's office at Washington, in charge of rolls, returns, books, blanks and business pertaining to the enlisted men of the regular and volunteer forces, and engaged in the preparation and publication of the 'Volunteer Army Register.' He became brigadier-general and adjutant-general in 1897, and was retired by operation of law, 25 Feb. 1898.

Breck'enridge, Hugh Henry, American artist: b. Leesbury, Pa., 1870. In 1892 he was awarded the European scholarship of the Pennsylvania Academy of the Fine Arts, and studied in Paris under Bouguereau, Ferrier, and Doucet Since 1894 he has been an instructor, and became secretary of the faculty in the Pennsylvania Academy of the Fine Arts, and in 1898 organized the Darby School of Painting. His work was awarded a medal at Atlanta in 1895, and received honorable mention at the Paris Exposition of 1900.

Breckenridge, Minn., a village and county-seat of Wilkin County, on the Red River of the North, about 50 miles south of Fargo, North Dakota. It is reached by the Northern Pacific and Great Northern railroads and is the centre of a very fertile region. It contains flour mills, grain elevators, etc., and steamboats ply between it and the Red River towns in Manitoba. Pop. (1900) 1,282.

Breck'inridge, Clifton R., American legislator and diplomatist: b. Lexington, Ky., 25 Nov. 1846. He is a son of John Cabell Breckinridge (q.v.), and received a public school education and served in the Confederate army and navy. After the war he attended Washington College (now Washington and Lee University) for three years, and engaged in mercantile business in Pine Bluff, Ark. He was elected to Congress in 1882 as representative-at-large, as a Democrat; was re-elected in 1884, 1886, 1889, 1890, 1892 and 1894, and served on the Committee on Ways and Means during the greater part of his congressional life. He was United States Minister to Russia 1894-7.

Breckinridge, or Breckenridge, John, American statesman: b. Augusta County, Va., 2 Dec. 1760; d. Lexington, Ky., 14 Dec. 1806. In 1795 he was made attorney-general of the new State of Kentucky, and he served in its legislature from 1797 to 1800. He entered the United States Senate in 1801, becoming four years later attorney-general in Jefferson's cabinet, in which office he died.

Breckinridge, John, American clergyman: b. Cabell's Dale, Ky., 1797; d. 1841. He entered the Presbyterian ministry, and was chaplain of the National House of Representatives, 1819-21. He was pastor at Lexington, Ky., 1823-6, and in Baltimore 1826-31. He was subsequently professor of theology at Princeton Theological Seminary, and was chosen president of Oglethorpe University, Georgia, just prior to his death. He is remembered for a famous theological debate held with Rev. John Hughes, subsequently archbishop of New York, published under the title 'Roman Catholic Controversy' (1836).

Breckinridge, John Cabell, Vice-President of the United States, grandson of John Breckinridge (1760-1806, q.v.): b. near Lexington, Ky., 21 Jan. 1821; d. Lexington, Ky., 17 May 1875. He practised law in Lexington until 1847, when he was chosen major of a volunteer regiment for the Mexican war. He sat in Congress in 1851-5, and in 1856 was elected Vice-President, with James Buchanan as President. In 1860 he was the pro-slavery candidate for the presidency, but was defeated by Abraham Lincoln. A United States senator from March to December 1861, he then entered the Confederate army, was appointed a major-general in 1862, and held some important commands during the Civil War. He was secretary of war in Jefferson Davis' cabinet, at the close of the struggle, and escaped to Europe, whence he returned in 1868, and resumed his law practice.

Breckinridge, Joseph Cabell, American military officer, nephew of John Cabell Breckinridge (q.v.): b. Baltimore, Md., 14 Jan. 1842. He practised law in Danville, Ky., till the beginning of the Civil War, when he joined the Union army. He was made a first lieutenant in the regular army 1863, captain in 1874, brigadier and inspector-general in 1889, and major-general of volunteers, 4 May 1898. He served in the Santiago campaign and had a horse shot from under him.

Breckinridge, Robert Jefferson, Presbyterian clergyman and theological writer, brother of John Breckinridge (1797-1841, q.v.): b. Cabell's Dale, Ky., 8 March 1800; d. 27 Dec. 1871. He was originally a lawyer. He was president of Jefferson College in 1845-47; from 1847 he was pastor at Lexington, Ky. He was an old-school leader in the division of the Presbyterian

Church in 1837 into Old and New schools. He was a strong supporter of the Union during the Civil War. His chief works were 'Knowledge of God, Objectively Considered' (1857): 'Knowledge of God, Subjectively Considered' (1859).

Brec'on, or Brecknockshire, a county of South Wales, with an area of 719 square miles; pop. (1901) 59,906. It is one of the most mountainous counties of the principality, and presents much bold and magnificent scenery. Near its centre rises the mountain called the Van or Beacon, belonging to the Black Mountains, which traverse its southern portion. It has a height of 2,901 feet, and is the culminating point of South Wales. The river Wye forms a natural boundary between t' is county and Radnor, and the Usk, rising in the Black Mountains, crosses the county and flows through a fine valley toward the town of Brecon. About two miles east from the latter is Brecknock Mere, one of the largest lakes in South Wales, abounding in otters, pike, tench, perch, and eels. A considerable quantity of agricultural produce is sent to the markets in the neighboring English counties. The chief manufactures are coarse woolens, stockings, and other worsted stuffs; there are also extensive ironworks. Chief towns, Brecon, Builth, Crickhowell, Hay, and Llanelly.

Brecon, or Brecknock, Scotland, the capital of Brecknockshire, stands in an open valley at the confluence of the Honddu and Usk, and consists chiefly of three principal and several minor streets. Three bridges span the Honddu and one the Usk. The principal edifices are the county jail, barracks, Christ's College (an important educational institution on the model of the large public schools), the Independent Theological College, and several of the places of worship. St. John's Church is a fine old building, cruciform, with a massive tower, partly early English, partly in later style. At Brecon the celebrated actress, Mrs. Siddons, was born. Pop. (1901) 5,875.

Breda, Jan van, yǎn vǎn brä-dä', Flemish painter: b. Antwerp, 1683; d. 1750. He studied at first under his father, who had acquired some reputation, but afterward became a close imitator of Breughel de Velours and Wouvermans, of whose works he made copies, which the most practised eye is scarcely able to distinguish from the originals. He resided several years in England, where he enjoyed a high name, and was much employed by the king and the nobility. On his return in 1725 he was appointed director of the Academy of Antwerp, and was so highly valued by his townsmen that his paintings were often the objects of keen competition.

Breda, Holland, a town in the province of North Brabant, 24 miles southwest of Bois-le-duc, on the Merk, being a strong frontier fortress, it was formerly of the greatest importance to Holland, as the chief point of the line of fortresses in front of the Meuse. The fortifications consisted of 15 bastions, as many ravelins, and five horn-works, besides the citadel. These being removed, the chief strength of the place now lies in its marshy environs, which may easily be laid under water. Breda received city rights in 1534; and since that time has often been a subject of contention between the Dutch, Spaniards, and French. It was delivered by treachery into the hands of the Duke of Parma

in 1581, but was retaken by Maurice of Orange in 1590. The latter capture was accomplished by means of a boat loaded with turf, in which 70 Dutch soldiers were concealed. Spinola took Breda in 1625, after a siege of 10 months, but it was retaken by the Dutch under Frederick Henry of Orange, in 1637. During the French Revolutionary War Dumouriez made himself master of the city and fortress in February 1793, and would thereby have prepared the way for the conquest of Holland had he not been forced, by the loss of a battle at Neerwinden, to evacuate the city and fortress, 4 April. In September 1794 Breda was attacked by the army of Pichegru, but did not s irrender till all Holland was conquered, in the winter of 1794. On the approach of the Russian vanguard, under Gen. Benkendorf, in December 1813, the French garrison made a sally, and the patriotic citizens, profiting by the occasion, rose en masse, shut the gates, and prevented the French from returning into the town. A peace was concluded at Breda between England and Holland in 1667. Pop. (1899) 26,097.

Breda, Declaration of, a proclamation of amnesty issued by Charles II. of England, 4 April 1660.

Bredahl, brä-däl', Christian Hviid, Danish poet: b. Hellestrup, 1784; d. 1860. He was educated at the gymnasium and the university of Slagelse. Owing to his love for an out-door life, he turned his attention to agriculture and in 1824 he bought a small piece of land near Sorö, which he cultivated himself. His great work is 'Dramatic Scenes,' which was published in six volumes, the first volume appearing in 1819. He also published several polemical works, directed against the Danish romanticism and the realistic writings of the time. In all his works, he shows a love for nature and the natural conditions of life, and a dislike for modern culture; his 'Dramatic Scenes' attacks both the nobility and the priesthood.

Breden, brä-děn, Christine (ADA CHRISTEN), Austrian poet: b. Vienna, 6 March 1844. She was at first an actress, but in 1864 settled in Vienna and began her literary career. In 1873 she married Adalmar Breden, but still used her pseudonym. Her first publication was a collection of poems entitled 'Lieder einer Verlorenen' (1868); her other works include 'Treasures'; 'Our Neighbors'; 'The Virgin Mother, a Story of the Vienna Suburbs' (1892); a novel, 'Ella' (1873); and a drama, 'Faustina' (1871).

Brederode, brä'de - rŏ - de, Hendrick (COUNT), Dutch patriot: b. 1531; d. 1568. He joined with Counts Egmont and Horn in opposing the tyranny of Cardinal Granvella, the Spanish governor of the Netherlands. In 1566, he presented to Margaret of Parma, who had succeeded Granvella, the famous 'Request,' which gave rise to the insurrection of the Gueux, or "Beggars." Under the grinding oppression of the Duke of Alva's administration in the Low Countries, he was obliged to retire to Germany.

Brederoo, Gerbrant Adriaenszoon, gär'-bränt ä'drě-än-zōn brä-dä'rō, Dutch dramatist and poet: b. Amsterdam, 16 March 1585; d. there, 8 July 1618. His best poems are 'The Meditative Song Book' and 'The Great Fountain of Love,' collections of grave and gay pieces, all of which have been very popular, and since his time often reprinted. His lyrics are admired for their musical verse and their tender sensibility; but his masterpiece is unquestionably the 'Jerolimo' ('Spaansche Brabander Jerolimo'), a comedy based upon a French version of one of Mendoza's plays. Another comedy, 'Moortje,' is an adaptation from Terence. See Ten Brink, 'Gerbrand Adriaenszoon Brederoo' (1859).

Bredow, Gabriel Gottfried, gä'brĭ-ĕl gŏt'-frĕd brä'dō, German historian: b. Berlin, 14 Dec. 1773; d. Breslau, 5 Sept. 1814. He was for a time professor at Eutin, and a·colleague of the celebrated Voss; afterward professor at Helmstädt, and still later at Frankfort-on-the-Oder, whence he went to Breslau on the removal of the university to that place. He was distinguished for his patriotism and his literary works. His 'Handbuch der alten Geschichte' (Manual of Ancient History) passed through five editions, the fifth of which appeared in 1825. He was the author of 'Chronik des Neunzehnten Jahrhunderts' (Chronicle of the 19th Century); 'Epistolæ Parisienses'; 'Untersuchungen über Geschichte, Geographie, und Chronologie' (Researches in History, Geography, and Chronology); and of the very useful 'Historische Tabellen' (Historical Tables), which were translated into English.

Brée, brä, Matthæus Ignatius van, Belgian painter: b. Antwerp, 1773; d. there, 1839. He chiefly excelled in historical painting, for which he gained a prize in 1797. His characteristics are said to have been originality and vigor of conception and patience in execution, yet he worked with great rapidity, as he presented to Napoleon in a few hours a tableau of the manœuvres of the fleet on the Scheldt before Antwerp. His first work which attracted attention was the 'Death of Cato.' Among his principal works are 'Rubens Dictating his Dying Testament'; 'The Tomb of Nero at Rome, with a group of Itinerant Musicians and Lazzaroni'; 'Death of Count Egmont'; 'Van der Werff Addressing the Famished Populace During the Siege of Leyden in 1576'— the burgomaster is represented as saying, "Take my body and divide it amongst you." Van Brée had the title of painter to the Empress Josephine, and represented many scenes connected with the French occupation of Belgium. He replaced Herreyns as director of the Academy of Fine Arts at Antwerp, and gained a high reputation by his teaching. He also evinced a capacity to excel in sculpture and lithography.

Breech and Breech-loader. The breech of a gun is that portion of a gun immediately behind the bore, and which in modern smallarms and artillery is removed to enable the process of loading to be effected. The chief advantages of this method, over muzzle-loading, are that it greatly increases the quick-firing capacity of the weapon, and adds to the length of range and accuracy of aim, while affording much facility for cleaning. Though it has only been successfully adopted in quite modern times, the breech-loading principle is nothing new, as some of the earliest cannon were so constructed. The first weapon of this description utilized as a regular military arm was the needle-gun adopted by the Prussian government so long ago as 1841, though its efficacy and superiority for warlike purposes was not demonstrated till the success-

ful campaigns of Prussia against Denmark and Austria in 1864 and 1866. Other nations also speedily armed their troops with breech-loading rifles, the French having adopted the Chassepôt breech-loader in 1866, and in Britain the old Enfield rifle having been converted into a breech-loading weapon and supplied to the troops the same year. In 1871 the Snider or converted Enfield began to be superseded by the Martini-Henry rifle, and this again has been superseded in the British army by the Lee-Metford magazine rifle. Other European nations have also adopted different forms of breechloading rifles. The principle of breech-loading has also been applied to artillery, the names of Armstrong and Krupp being associated with some of the first modern guns of this type. See ARTILLERY; MUSKET; RIFLE; SMALL ARMS.

Breeches, a garment for the legs, especially, as distinguished from trousers, for covering the upper portions of the legs. In England breeches were formerly called hose. Breeches or hose were in use even among the ancient Babylonians, and with them were made so as to cover the foot and supply the place of stockings. In Europe we find hose first used among the Gauls, hence the Romans called a part of Gaul breeched Gaul (Gallia braccata). In the 5th century they had become fashionable in Rome. In the time of Queen Elizabeth and James I. the breeches had assumed enormous dimensions, being stuffed out with various materials, as wool, hair, etc. King James' partiality for such breeches is well known, and we find him represented in an old engraving with wide stuffed breeches tapering to the knee, slashed and adorned with lace. In the reign of Charles I. they took the form of short trousers, loose at the knee, and ornamented with ribbons, lace, etc. In the time of William III. the tight knee-breeches came in, and have been supplanted by trousers only in the 19th century.

Breeches Bible, a name given to a Bible printed in 1579; and so called from the reading of Gen. iii. 7: "They sowed figge tree leaves together and made themselves breeches." As a matter of fact this Bible has no more distinctive right to the name than Wyclif's version, in which the same words are also found.

Breeches Buoy. See LIFE SAVING SERVICE.

Breeching, a rope used to secure the cannon of a ship of war, and prevent them from recoiling too much in the time of battle. It is of sufficient length to allow the muzzle of the cannon to come within the ship's side to be charged.

Breede, brä'dĕ, a river in Cape Colony; which rises in the Warm-Bokkeveld, and flows chiefly in a southeasterly direction through the district of Zwellendam, entering the Indian Ocean at St. Sebastian's Bay, about 60 miles northeast of Cape Agulhas, the most southerly point of Africa. It is navigable for vessels drawing not more than 10 feet of water to a distance of 40 miles, and drains a very fertile district.

Breeding, the process of procreation as applied to any or all classes of organisms. In this article the term is largely used to describe the breeding of domesticated animals. Originally the different variations of types or breeds had their origin in the accident of circumstance and the natural tendency of all animal life toward variation; but since man began to exercise control, and to appropriate various breeds or types to his own use, reproduction has been almost entirely along the lines of natural and artificial selection. Thus we may very properly limit the definition of breeding as discussed in this article to the art by which domestic breeds are obtained. Probably the best-known as well as the most ancient maxim of "breeding," and one which has been expressed in one form or another by every ancient writer on husbandry and agriculture of which there is any record, is the familiar aphorism that "like produces like." A natural result of this was the practice of breeding from the best type-specimens. There does not seem at first to have been any consistent system of selection, and as the standard of excellence varied with the passing periods there was no real progress in breed-development, as we understand it to-day. About the middle of the 18th century Robert Bakewell, an Englishman, originated a system of breeding live stock based upon the idea that the principle of "like begetting like" went much farther than the general similarity of the offspring to the parents, and extended to the minutest details of the organization. He made a special study of the form and proportions of animals, and formulated a definite standard of excellence representing the form and internal qualities that he desired to obtain. This standard governed his actions when making selections for breeding purposes. He succeeded so far in molding the plastic forms of the cattle upon which he experimented as to arouse the interest of other breeders, with the result that to-day there are many varieties of improved breeds, all of them of remarkable excellence, but each differing from the others in the characteristics that have been bred into them, to adapt them to special purposes or conditions of environment.

Heredity in Breeding.— There is good reason to believe that not only the external characteristics of the parents are reproduced in the offspring, but that internal structure and functional activity, and in fact every peculiarity of the organization of the parents are also transmitted. Innumerable illustrations from every department of organic life confirm this theory, and if further proof be needed, the hereditary transmission or predisposition to disease will supply it. For instance, it sometimes happens that mares affected with such diseases as ringbone, navicular disease, etc., in consequence of which they are unfitted for work but are kept as breeders, have colts in which are combined all the good qualities of the parents, but which at the age of five or six years develop diseases similar to those of the disabled parents. Not only are the hereditary characteristics of conformation, temperament, and disease transmitted, but frequently also, the habits and characteristics which have been developed by special conditions of environment, or because of some particular training they have received from man. Illustrations of this may be found in the tendency of well-bred short-horns to mature early and acquire fat rapidly; and the ability of Jerseys and other dairy breeds to secrete a large supply of milk. With the horse, the English thoroughbred racer and the American trotter furnish the most convincing illustrations of what breeders consider the transmission of acquired characters. It is the various breeds of dogs, however, that form the best examples. It is a common experience of the hunter to discover a setter, pointer, or retriever that has never been "shot over" before, but which "works" with as much skill and steadiness as the most experienced sporting dog. The transmission of *abnormal characteristics of structural conformation* is another fruitful source of the variation of types, as for instance the Dorking fowls, whose characteristic of a fifth toe has been inherited, it is claimed, from a five-toed fowl brought to Britain by the Romans. Similar instances of the working of this law may be found in abundance in every branch of organic life. It does not follow, however, that the immediate offspring of a parent marked by some abnormalism will develop the same characteristic; but that it will make its reappearance in some subsequent generation is an indisputable fact. This phenomenon is technically known as "atavism" (q.v.), but it is more generally described as "throwing-back," "breeding-back," etc. Instances of characteristics that have been extinct for half a century, but which reappear with all the peculiarities of the original breed are in the experience of every breeder. In brief, an offspring may unite in itself the prominent characteristic of one or both parents, or it may resemble a grandparent, or even a remote ancestor; but it is equally the offspring of all its ancestors and, within its own organization in a latent condition are the characteristics of all preceding generations, any one of which may be duplicated in its own offspring. It is at this point that the "law of co-relation" asserts itself, which Miles in his 'Stock Breeding' defines as "any peenliarity in the development of one organ or set of organs, usually accompanied by a corresponding modification or suppression of organs belonging to some other part of the system." With regard to domestic animals, whose flexibility or plasticity of organization is perhaps greater than other animals, we find that the principal causes of animal variation are climate, food, and habit, and that the distinguishing characteristics of the different breeds have been the result of the modifying influences of the environment to which they have been subjected. Thus the small breeds of sheep and cattle in mountainous countries are in decided contrast to those of the same species obtaining their food-supply in the lowlands or fertile valleys. Indeed the relation of the size of animals to their food-supply has been commented upon by writers from the earliest times.

The function of reproduction in the animal organization is also affected by the conditions above mentioned. The procreative ability of many wild species becomes weak or extinct if the animals are subjected to confinement; yet in direct contrast to this we find domesticated varieties more prolific than the wild species — for example, tame ducks deposit more eggs than wild ones; and the same fact is true of dogs, swine, rabbits, pigeons, etc. All authorities are agreed that this greater fecundity is due to the better food-supply and the security generally of domestic conditions. It has been observed that throughout the entire animal kingdom smaller species of animals are more prolific than the larger ones, and certain it is that they breed at an earlier age, at shorter intervals, and have a greater number of young at each birth.

Breeding from close affinities is known as "in-and-in breeding," the best definition of which is that of Randall, 'Practical Shepherd,' "breeding between relatives, without reference to degree of consanguinity." Possibly no other practice in breeding has been fought over so much as that of "in-and-in" breeding. The opponents of the practice assert that the offspring of closely related parents are born with a predisposition to disease, and that in any event they will suffer from a lack of fecundity. Before going farther into this question, it will be well to state that while high-breeding implies the breeding from animals within the family limits, yet all high-bred animals are not necessarily "in-and-in" bred, although they must be closely bred to a greater or less extent. When a breeder wished to secure a type representing the highest standard of excellence, he has found it necessary to select animals for breeding-stock that possessed the characters he wished to reproduce in the offspring. It followed, therefore, seeing that it is only animals descended from a common ancestor, and having the same hereditary tendencies that possess the desired variations, he was usually compelled to breed together animals that were more or less closely related. No matter how right or how wrong the practice of "in-and-in" breeding may be, it is an indisputable fact that all the successful breeders have practised it more or less in order to retain and fix in their animals the desired tendencies and characters. The most cursory examination of herd-books and breeding-registers will show how closely related all the most valuable animals have been to each other. What may be considered to be the opposite of "in-and-in" breeding, is the practice of pairing together animals belonging to distinct breeds. This is known technically as "cross-breeding." It frequently happens that the offspring of a first-cross between distinct species possess very desirable qualities, but their sterility prevents the formation of a new or intermediate race, so that the cross has to be repeated to secure another such offspring. The mule is the most familiar example of such a cross. Cross-bred cattle while not sterile as is the case with mules, are yet incapable of transmitting their good qualities to their offspring.

The period of gestation in all mammals is determined by causes yet unknown. That it would seem to have some relation to the size of the animal may be gathered from the following examples: Elephant, 20 to 23 months; giraffe, 14 months; dromedary, 12 months; the different varieties of buffalo, from 10 to 12 months; ass, 12 months; mare, 11 months; cow, 285 days; bear, 6 months; reindeer, 8 months; monkey, 7 months; sheep and goat, 5 months; sow, 4 months; beaver, 4 months; lion, 108 days; dog, fox, and wolf, 62 days; cat, 50 days; rabbits, 30 days; squirrel and rat, 28 days; guinea pig, 21 days. The same rule may be traced in the periods of incubation in birds.

To sum up, the art of breeding consists in the exercise of judgment and skill in the matter of selection. The parents must be chosen in accordance with some well-defined purpose and for the conditions under which they will be placed. High-bred males have been found to impress their own good points upon their offspring, more than do high-bred females. In the opinion of many successful breeders, the dangers of "in-and-in" breeding are considerably lessened when a high-bred sire, rather than an inferior animal, is employed. Miles, 'Stock-Breeding,' lays down the rule that "in the improvement of grades as well as pure-bred animals, the selection of breeding-stock must go hand in hand with a judicious system of feeding and management, as the artificial characters which are impressed by the male upon his offspring can only be retained through the influence of essentially the same conditions that originally produced them."

Breeding, Plant. The fundamental principles of plant breeding are simple and may be stated in few words; the practical application of these principles demands the highest and most refined efforts of which the mind of man is capable, and no line of mental effort promises more for the elevation, advancement, prosperity, and happiness of the whole human race. Every plant, animal, and planet occupies its place in the order of nature by the action of two forces —the inherent constitutional life force with all its acquired habits, the sum of which is hereditary; and the numerous complicated external forces or environment. To guide the interaction of these two forces, both of which are only different expressions of the one eternal force, is, and must be, the sole object of the breeder, whether of pants or animals. When we look about us on the plants inhabiting the earth with ourselves and watch any species day by day, we are unable to see any change in some of them. During a lifetime, and in some cases perhaps including the full breadth of human history, no remarkable change seems to have occurred. And yet there is not to-day one plant species which has not undergone great and to a certain extent constant change. The life forces of the plant in endeavoring to harmonize and adapt the action of its acquired tendencies to its surroundings may, through many generations, slowly adapt themselves to the necessities of existence; yet these accrued forces may also produce sudden and, to one not acquainted with its past history, most surprising and unaccountable changes of character. The very existence of the higher orders of plants now inhabiting the earth has been secured to them only by their power of adaptation to crossings, for through the variations produced by the combination of numerous tendencies, individuals are produced which are better endowed to meet the prevailing conditions of life. Thus, to nature's persistence in crossing we owe all that earth now produces in man, animals, or plants; and this magnificently stupendous fact may also be safely carried into the domains of chemistry as well, for what is common air and water but nature's earlier efforts in that line, and our nourishing foods but the result of myriad complex chemical affinities of later date.

Natural and artificial crossing and hybridizing are among the principal remote causes of nearly all otherwise perplexing or unaccountable sports and strange modifications, and also of many of the now well-established species. Variations without immediate antecedent crossing occur always and everywhere from a combination of past crossings, and environments for potential adaptations often exist through generations without becoming actual, and when we fully grasp these facts there is nothing mysterious in the sudden appearance of sports; but still further intelligent crossings produce more immediate results and of great value, not to the plant in its struggle with natural forces, but to man, by conserving and guiding its life forces to supply him with food, clothing and innumerable other luxuries and necessities. Plant life is so common that one rarely stops to think how utterly dependent we are upon the quiet but magnificently powerful work which plants are constantly performing for us. It was once thought that plants varied within the so-called species but very little, and that true species never varied. We have more lately discovered that no two plants are exactly alike, each one having its own individuality, and that new varieties having endowments of priceless value and even distinct new species can be produced by the plant breeder with the same precision that machinery for locomotion and other useful purposes is produced by the mechanic. The evolution and all the variations of plants are simply the means which they employ in adjusting themselves to external conditions; each plant strives to adapt itself to environment with as little demand upon its forces as possible and still keep up in the race. The best endowed species and individuals win the prize, and by variation as well as persistence. The constantly varying external forces to which all life is everywhere subjected demand that the inherent internal force shall always be ready to adapt itself or perish. The combination and interaction of these innumerable forces embraced in heredity and environment have given us all our bewildering species, none of which ever did or ever will remain constant, for the inherent life force must be pliable or outside forces will sooner or later extinguish it. Thus, adaptability as well as perseverance is one of the prime virtues in plant as in human life. Plant breeding is the intelligent application of the forces of the human mind in guiding the inherent life forces into useful directions by crossing to make perturbations or variations of these forces and by radically changing environments, both of which produce somewhat similar results, thus giving a broader field for selection, which, again, is simply the persistent application of mental force to guide and fix the perturbed forces in the desired channels. Plant breeding is in its earliest infancy. Its possibilities, and even its fundamental principles, are understood but by few. In the past it has been mostly dabbling with tremendous forces which have been only partially appreciated, and has yet to approach the precision which we expect in the handling of steam or electricity; and notwithstanding the occasional sneers of the ignorant, these silent forces embodied in plant life have yet a part to play in the regeneration of the race which, by comparison, will dwarf into insignificance the services which steam and electricity have so far given. Even unconscious or half conscious plant breeding has been one of the greatest forces in the elevation of the race. The chemist and the mechanic have, so to speak, domesticated some of the forces of nature, but the plant breeder is now learning to guide even the creative forces into new and useful channels. This knowledge is a most priceless legacy, making clear the way for some of the greatest benefits which man has ever received from any source by the study of nature. A general knowledge of the relations

and affinities of plants will not be a sufficient equipment for the successful plant breeder. He must be a skilful botanist and biologist, and, having a definite plan, must be able to correctly estimate the action of the two fundamental forces — inherent and external — which he would guide.

The main object of crossing genera, species or varieties is to combine various individual tendencies, thus producing a state of perturbation or partial antagonism by which these tendencies are, in later generations, dissociated and recombined in new proportions, which gives the breeder a wider field for selection. But this opens a much more difficult one,— the selection and fixing of the desired new types from the mass of heterogeneous tendencies produced,— for by crossing, bad traits, as well as good, are always brought forth. The results now secured by the breeder will be in proportion to the accuracy and intensity of selection and the length of time they are applied. By these means the best grains, fruits, nuts, and flowers are capable of still further improvement in ways which to the thoughtless, often seem unnecessary, irrelevant or impossible. When we capture and domesticate the various plants, the life forces are relieved from many of the hardships of an unprotected wild condition, and have more leisure, so to speak, or, in other words, more surplus force to be guided by the hand of man under the new environments into all the useful and beautiful new forms which are constantly appearing under cultivation, crossing and selection. Some plants are very much more pliable than others, as the breeder soon learns. Plants having numerous representatives in various parts of the earth generally possess this adaptability in a much higher degree than the monotypic species, for, having been subjected to great variations of soil, climate and other influences, their continued existence has been secured only by the inherited habits which adaptation demanded; while the monotypic species, not being able to fit themselves for their surroundings without a too radical expensive change, have only continued to exist under certain special conditions. Thus, two important advantages are secured to the breeder who selects from the genera having numerous species — the advantage of naturally acquired pliability, and in the numerous species to work upon by combination for still further variations. The plant breeder, before making combinations, should with great care select the individual plants which seem best adapted to his purpose, as by this course many years of experiment and much needless expense will be avoided. The difference in the individuals which the plant breeder has to work upon are sometimes extremely slight. The ordinary unpractised person cannot, by any possibility, discover the exceedingly minute variations in form, size, color, fragrance, precocity and a thousand other characters which the practised breeder perceives by a lightning-like glance. The work is not easy, requiring an exceedingly keen perception of minute differences, great practice and extreme care in treating the organisms operated upon; and even with all the naturally acquired variations added to those secured by crossing and numerous other means, the careful accumulation of slight individual differences through many generations is imperative, after which several generations are often but not always necessary to thoroughly "fix" the desired type for all practical purposes.

The above applies to annuals or those plants generally reproduced by seed. The breeder of plants which can be reproduced by division has great advantage, for any individual variation can be multiplied to any extent desired without the extreme care necessary in fixing by lineal breeding the one which must be reproduced by seed. But even in breeding perennials the first deviations from the original form are often almost unappreciable to the perception, but by accumulating the most minute differences through many generations the deviation from the original form is often astounding. Thus, by careful and intelligent breeding any peculiarity may be made permanent, and valid new species are at times produced by the art of the breeder, and there is no known limit to the improvement of plants by education, breeding, and selection.

The plant breeder is an explorer into the infinite. He will have "no time to make money," and his castle,— the brain,— must be clear and alert in throwing aside fossil ideas and rapidly replacing them with living, throbbing thought, followed by action. Then, and not until then, shall he create marvels of beauty and value in new expressions of materialized force, for everything of value must be produced by the intelligent application of the forces of nature which are always awaiting our commands. The vast possibilities of plant breeding can hardly be estimated. It would not be difficult for one man to breed a new rye, wheat, barley, oats, or rice which would produce one grain more to each head, or a corn which would produce an extra kernel to each ear, another potato to each plant, or an apple, plum, orange, or nut to each tree. What would be the result! In five staples only in the United States alone the inexhaustible forces of nature would produce annually without effort and without cost:

15,000,000 extra bushels of wheat,
5,200,000 extra bushels of corn,
20,000,000 extra bushels of oats,
1,500,000 extra bushels of barley,
21,000,000 extra bushels of potatoes,

But these vast possibilities are not alone for one year, or for our own time or race, but are beneficent legacies for every man, woman, or child who shall ever inhabit the earth. And who can estimate the elevating and refining influences and moral value of flowers with all their graceful forms and bewitching shades and combinations for color and exquisitely varied perfumes? These silent influences are unconsciously felt even by those who do not appreciate them consciously, and thus with better and still better fruits, nuts, grains, and flowers will the earth be transformed and man's thoughts turned from the base destructive forces into the nobler productive ones, which will lift him to higher planes of action toward that happy day when man shall offer his brother man not bullets and bayonets, but richer grains, better fruits, and fairer flowers. Cultivation and care may help plants to do better work temporarily, but by breeding plants may be brought into existence which will do better work always, in all places and for all time. Plants are to be produced which will perform their appointed work better, quicker, and with the utmost precision. Science sees better grains, nuts, fruits,

and vegetables all in new forms, sizes, colors, and flavors, with more nutrients and less waste, and with every injurious and poisonous quality eliminated, and with power to resist sun, wind, rain, frost, and destructive fungus, and insect pests; fruits without stones, seeds or spines; better fibre, coffee, tea, spices, rubber, oil, paper and timber trees, and sugar, starch, color, and perfume plants. Every one of these and ten thousand more are within the reach of the most ordinary skill in plant breeding. Man is slowly learning that he, too, may guide the same forces which have been through all the ages performing this beneficent work which he sees everywhere, above, beneath, and around him in the vast teeming animal and plant life of the world.

LUTHER BURBANK,
American Pomological Society.

Breed's Hill, Mass., a slight elevation in the Charlestown district of Boston, about 700 yards from Bunker Hill. Although the famous engagement of 17 June 1775 is known 'as the Battle of Bunker Hill, the fighting was done on Breed's Hill. Here was located the American redoubt, against which the British made their three historic charges, and here Warren fell. Bunker Hill monument stands on Breed's Hill.

Breese, Kidder Randolph, American naval officer: b. Philadelphia, 14 April 1831. He entered the navy in 1846 and served in the Civil War. In 1861 he commanded the third division of Porter's mortar flotilla in the attacks on New Orleans and Vicksburg; in 1863 and 1864 he was lieutenant commander on the Mississippi and took part in the most important engagements; in 1865 he was fleet-captain at the attack on Fort Fisher. He was made captain in 1874.

Breeze-fly. See BOT-FLY.

Brefeld, Oskar, ōs'kär brā'fĕlt, German botanist: b. Telgte, Westphalia, 19 Aug. 1839. He was educated at Halle, Munich, and Würzburg. In 1875 he was a lecturer at Berlin; in 1878 he became professor at Eberswald, in 1884 at Münster, and in 1898 at Breslau. His investigations have been chiefly in mycology and he introduced a number of new methods in the study of this science, particularly the use of "gelatine cultures." He has written 'Researches in the Field of Mycology.'

Bregenz, brā-gĕnts' (Latin, *Brigantium*), a town of Austria-Hungary, in Vorarlberg, 77 miles west by north of Innsbruck. It occupies a beautiful site on a slope which rises from the Lake of Constance and terminates on Mount Gebhard, where the ruins of the ancient stronghold of the Counts of Montfort are still seen. It consists of an old town, very poorly built, and a modern, which is more attractive. Among its edifices are three churches and two monasteries, a town hall, and a museum of Roman antiquities, found in the vicinity. Its chief manufacture is framework and other wooden fittings for houses, and it trades in corn, fruit, wine, butter, and cattle. There are saltpetre works, blast furnaces, and coal mines in the vicinity. Pop. (1900) 7,600.

Bregma. In the infant, a little behind the forehead in the middle line of the skull there is a diamond-shaped opening where the bones have not yet closed together. This situation is known as "bregma," and is taken as a landmark in medical and anthropological measurements.

Bre'hon (Irish, *breitheamh*, a judge), an ancient magistrate among the Irish. These magistrates seem to have been hereditary, and before the introduction of Christianity probably combined the offices of judge and priest. They administered justice to their respective tribes — each tribe had one brehon — seated in the open air upon some sods placed on a hill or eminence. The poet Spencer, in his 'View of the State of Ireland.' refers to the Brehon law as an unwritten code handed down by tradition. He was, however, mistaken in regarding it as an unwritten code. Patriarchal as was the administration of the Brehon law, its transmission was not left to tradition. In the earliest manuscripts extant it is said to have been revised by St. Patrick and other learned men, who expunged from it the traces of heathenism, and formed it into a code called the Senchus Mor, about 440, and it is implied that a previous written code existed. The Brehon law was exclusively in force in Ireland until 1170. Various ineffectual attempts were made by the English government to suppress it, and it was finally abolished by James I. in 1605. The Brehon laws, like other laws passed at the same period of European history, contained, with some rude principles of justice, many barbarous institutions. The state of society indicated in them seems to be a sort of transition from the communal ownership and periodical repartition of the land, found among several Teutonic nations, to a manorial organization. Several distinct social ranks are indicated, ranging from the nobles to the serfs. They had regular courts, with the right of appeal from lower to higher ones. Most offenses, even including murder, could be commuted by fines, which were fixed with minute precision; but the fines were paid in kind, since coined money was unknown. The laws also carefully provide for and regulate the raising of the children of the upper classes by members of the subordinate classes. The marriage laws were of a very loose character, and the law of inheritance is obscure and complicated. Until recently these laws have been involved in great obscurity. A commission was appointed in 1852 to superintend the publication and translation of the ancient laws of Ireland; and between 1865 and 1885 an edition of the Senchus Mor was published in five volumes. See Maine, 'Early History of Institutions' (1875).

Breisach, brī-zäн, or Alt Breisach, a town of Baden. on an isolated basalt hill (804 feet) on the right side of the Rhine. 14 miles west of Freiburg. The Mons Brisiacus of Cæsar, it was taken by Ariovistus when he invaded Gaul; being regarded as the key to western Germany, it figured prominently in the wars of the 17th and 18th centuries. The minster is a 13th century structure. It carries on an active trade in lumber and cattle, and manufactures beer, wall paper, wine, etc. Pop. (1900) 3,500.

Breitbach, brīt'bäн, Karl, German painter: b. Berlin, 14 May 1833. He was educated at the Berlin Academy and in Paris under Couture. He first devoted himself to landscape painting. but later became both a genre and a portrait painter. Among his works are: 'Mill of St. Ouen near Paris'; 'The Trianon Park'; 'Sunrise in the Bavarian Highlands'; 'Kirmess — Joy'; 'Kirmess — Sorrow'; 'Village Children Bathing'; 'At the Fortune Teller's'; and portraits of Weber and others. He has also painted interior decorations.

Breitenfeld, brī'tĕn-fĕlt, a village of Saxony, four miles north of Leipsic. Here two battles were gained by the Swedes during the Thirty Years' War. In the first, fought on 7 Sept. 1631, Gustavus Adolphus, joined by the Saxons, defeated Tilly and Pappenheim; in the second, on 2 Nov. 1642, Torstenson, who had succeeded on the death of Baner to the command of the Swedish army in Germany, again defeated the Imperialists under the Archduke Leopold and Piccolomini, who had advanced to the relief of Leipsic, invested by the Swedes. Leipsic surrendered after the battle. Breitenfeld was also the scene of a portion of the battle of Leipsic, won by the allies against Napoleon, 16–19 Oct. 1813.

Breitkopf, Johann Gottlob Immanuel, yō'hän gŏt'lŏb ĭm-män'oo-ĕl brīt'kŏpf, German printer and publisher: b. Leipsic, 1719; d. 1794. He was educated in the university of his native city, and following out a scientific study of printing, he evolved improvements in musical notation and in German text. To him is probably due the present form of modern printed music. In 1764 he established in Leipsic the publishing house known as Breitkopf and Härtel from 1795. He was the author of 'Ueber die Geschichte der Erfindung der Buchdruckerkunst' (1779); 'Ueber den Druck der Geographischen Karten' (1777–9).

Breitman, Hans, hänts brīt'mạn. See LELAND, CHARLES GODFREY.

Brekelenkam, brä-kĕ-lĕn'käm, Quirin, Dutch painter: b. Zwammerdam, near Leyden, about 1620; d. Leyden, 1668. He was to some extent an imitator of Dou, and perhaps his pupil. His subjects are from the life of the people, and his treatment marked by fidelity to nature and breadth of style. Among his most characteristic paintings are: 'The Fireside'; 'Monk Writing'; 'Interior'; 'The Sandwich'; 'Game of Cards'; and 'A Brazier.'

Bremen, brä'mĕn, Germany, a port and free city, and an independent member of the empire, one of the three Hanse towns, is situated on the Weser, about 50 miles from its mouth, in its own small territory of 98 square miles, besides which it possesses the town and port of Bremerhaven at the mouth of the river. The town is divided into the old town (Altstadt), on the right bank of the river: the new town (Neustadt), on the left bank of the river, and the extensive suburbs (Vorstädte). The first is separated from the suburban quarters adjoining by the ramparts of the city. now converted into walks and pleasure-grounds, and forms a sort of semicircle on the right bank of the river. The new town lies on the left bank of the river opposite the old. with which it is connected by three bridges, two of them crossing the main stream, and the third crossing an arm of it called the Little Weser, besides a railway bridge. Extensive suburbs lie on this side also. The streets of the old town are generally narrow and crooked, and lined with antique houses in the style of the Middle Ages. This is the business quarter of the city, and contains the chief public buildings. including the cathedral. the old Gothic council-house, with the famous wine

cellar below it, the modern town-hall, the Schüt-
ting or merchants'-house, the old and the new
exchange, etc. The new town has straight, well-
built streets, lined mostly with dwelling-houses
and shops. The suburbs also consist chiefly of
dwelling-houses, and as these often have gardens
in front, the streets have a very pleasant aspect.
The chief ecclesiastical building is the cathedral, a Romanesque edifice, founded in 1044,
subsequently added to at various times, and in
1888–93 provided with two new western towers.
There are several other old and interesting
churches, as those of St. Ansgar, St. Stephen,
and St. John. Among buildings of recent erection are the court-house, savings bank, and railway station. There are several squares and
open spaces, and besides the pleasure-grounds
formed from the ramparts, a large public park
has been laid out on the north side of the town.
Bremen is well supplied with schools and other
educational institutions, and possesses a museum,
a library (120,000 volumes), an observatory, etc.
The manufacturing establishments include
tobacco and cigar factories, sugar-refineries, rice-
mills, iron-foundries, and machine works, rope
and sail works, and ship-building yards. It is
from its commerce, however, that Bremen
derives its importance. Its situation renders it
the emporium of Hanover, Brunswick, Hesse,
and other countries traversed by the Weser, and
next to Hamburg it is the principal seat of the
export and import trade of Germany. The
Weser has been deepened so that sea-going ships
drawing 17 feet of water can now ascend to the
Bremen docks, but the great bulk of the shipping
trade centres in Bremerhaven and Geestemünde.
Bremerhaven is now a place of over 18,000
inhabitants, and is provided with excellent docks
capable of receiving the largest vessels; it is connected by railway with Bremen, where the chief
trading companies, merchants, and brokers have
their offices. The greater portion of the German
trade with the United States passes through
Bremen. and it is the chief port of emigration
on the Continent. The chief imports are tobacco,
raw cotton, and cotton manufactures, wool and
woolen manufactures, rice, coffee, grain, petroleum, etc., which are of course chiefly re-export-
ed to other parts of Germany and the Continent. Next to Liverpool, Bremen is to-day the
leading European cotton market. Before the organization of the cotton exchange in 1872, the
German merchants had been getting their product chiefly from Havre and Liverpool, very little
being imported direct. To become independent
of British ports, it was necessary to get the pat-
rouage of the inland spinners. This proved no
easy task. Not until a decade had passed did
the Bremen exchange cease to be a local institution and acquire a standing of national importance; but ever since the development has been
phenomenal. While the importation of cotton in
the year 1870 amounted to only 157,689 bales,
it ran up to 397,998 bales in the year 1880. Ten
years later there were 812,538 bales and the year
1900 showed the enormous figure of 1,567,045
bales. The new cotton exchange opened in 1902
is said to be not only the most imposing structure of this nature in the world, but also the
most complete in the appointments necessary
for carrying on the business of buying and selling cotton and supplying the leading merchants
and brokers with office and sample rooms.

Bremen first rose into note about 788, when
it was made the seat of a bishopric by Charlemagne. It was afterward raised to the dignity
of an archbishopric, and by the end of the 14th
century it had become virtually a free imperial
city. At the Treaty of Westphalia in 1648 the
archbishopric was secularized, and became a
duchy under the supremacy of Sweden. In 1731,
when the elector of Brunswick gained possession of the duchy, the privileges of Bremen as
a free city were confirmed. From 1810 to 1813
it formed part of the French empire. The constitution is in most respects republican. The
legislative authority is shared by the senate, a
body of 18 (12 of whom must be lawyers, and
5 merchants) elected for life, and presided over
by two of their own number alternately, who
have the title of burgomaster; and by an assembly of 150 citizens elected for six years. The
executive power is intrusted to the senate and
senatorial committees. Pop. of the total territory (including Bremerhaven) (1902) 224,700.

Bremer, brä'mér, Fredrika, Swedish novelist: b. Tuorla, Finland, 17 Aug. 1801; d. Arsta,
31 Dec. 1865. At 17 she was taken on a tour
through Germany, Switzerland, and France. In
1828 appeared the first volume of her 'Sketches
of Everyday Life,' but the second volume, 'The
H. Family' (1833; English translation, 1844),
first revealed her power. From this time she
devoted herself to writing stories that quickly
became popular in translations far beyond the
bounds of Sweden, and she varied her literary
labor by long journeys in Italy, England, the
United States, Greece, Palestine, which supplied
the materials for her 'Homes of the New
World' (1853), and 'Life in the Old World'
(1862), full of fine descriptions of scenery and
vivid pictures of social life, with sound views
on political and moral questions. The admirable
translations of Mary Howitt had preceded her
in the United States as well as England, and
insured her an equally warm welcome on both
sides of the Atlantic. On her return to Sweden
she gave herself up to philanthropy, but more
particularly to the education and emancipation of
women, and the consequent propagandist character of her later novels, 'Bertha,' and 'Father
and Daughter' (1859), was detrimental in no
small degree to their literary value. Her religions views she set forth in her 'Morning
Watches' (1842). She has been called the Jane
Austen of Sweden. Of her stories perhaps the
most perfect is 'The Neighbors' (1837). 'The
Diary,' 'The President's Daughters,' 'Brothers and Sisters,' and 'Strife and Peace, or
Scenes in Dalecarlia,' are only less known.

Bremerhaven, brä'mér-hä-fĕn, the port of
Bremen, Germany, on the east shore of the
Weser estuary, nearly 10 miles from the open
sea, and 39 north-northwest of Bremen. It was
founded by Bremen, in 1827, on ground acquired
from Hanover, and rapidly became a thriving
place. A second dock was opened in 1866, a
third in 1874. and in 1888 a great port, with
docks, was undertaken at Nordenham, on the
opposite bank. Bremerhaven was the scene, in
1875, of a dynamite explosion on board a mail
steamship, by which 60 persons were killed. The
Geeste separated Bremerhaven from Geestemünde. Pop. (1900) 20,300.

Brend'amour, brän-dạ-moor, Franz Robert,
German engraver: b. Aix-la-Chapelle, 16 Oct.

1831. He was educated in his art at Cologne under Stephan. In 1856 he went to Düsseldorf and established a xylographic studio, which rapidly became well known and one of the leading institutions of its kind. He later set up similar studios in Berlin, Leipsic, Brunswick, Stuttgart, and Munich, to conducting which he devoted most of his time. Among his best works are a collection, 112 engravings, after drawings by Rudolf Elster; illustrations for several works, including Immermann's 'Der Oberhof,' and Count Waldersee's 'Der Jäger'; 'The Odyssey,' after drawings by Preller, and eight frescoes in the Rathhaus at Aix-la-Chapelle.

Bren'dan, or Brenainn, Saint, of Clonfert: b. 484 at what is now Tralee in Kerry; d. 577. He was educated under his relative, Bishop Erc, and St. Jarlath of Tuam, and was ordained by the former. Shortly afterward he went on a seven years' voyage in search of "the mysterious land far from human ken"; but without success. Later he visited and lived in Brittany for a time, and after his return he again set out to seek the distant paradise, which he ultimately found. When he again reached Ireland he founded the monastery of Cluain Fearta (Clonfert), and he seems to have visited Scotland at this time. His two voyages form the basis of the celebrated mediæval legend of the 'Navigation of St. Brendan'; but in the legend they are united into one and combined with other stories. Where Brendan's voyages really led him we do not know. The Book of Lismore contains a life of St. Brendan.

Another Irish saint of the same name was born about 490 and died in 573. He was a friend of Columba, and founded a monastery at Birr (Parsonstown) in King's County.

Brendel, Heinrich Albert, hīn'rīH äl'bĕrt brĕn'dĕl, German painter: b. Berlin, 7 June 1827; d. 1895. He studied at the Berlin Art Academy under Krause, and in Paris as a pupil of Couture and Palizzi. After traveling in Italy and Sicily, he lived in Paris, 1854–64; he then returned to Germany and lived in Berlin and Weimar, becoming director of the Art School at the latter place. He devoted himself almost entirely to animal painting, and his pictures of sheep are considered especially fine. His works include: 'Peasant's Farm,' 'Interior of Sheep Stable,' 'Sheep Leaving Stable.'

Bren'eman, Abram Adam, American chemist: b. Lancaster, Pa., 28 April 1847. He graduated at Pennsylvania State College in 1866, and after service as an instructor, was full professor of chemistry 1869–72. From 1875 to 1882 he was assistant, lecturer, and professor of industrial chemistry at Cornell. Since then he has resided in New York, engaged in professional work as a writer, analyst, and chemical expert. He is the inventor of the Breneman process of rendering iron non-corrosive, and has made a special study of water and its contaminations. He has written: 'Manual of Introductory Laboratory Practice' (1875); 'Report on the Fixation of Atmospheric Nitrogen' (1890); and numerous contributions to chemical and other journals.

Brenham, brĕn'ăm, Texas, a city and county-seat of Washington County, on the Gulf, C. & S. F. and the Houston & T. C. R.R.'s, west of Houston. It is the centre of an agricultural

Vol. 3—6.

and cotton region, and has two cotton compresses, a cotton factory, and a cottonseed-oil mill, as well as other manufacturing interests. It is the seat of the Blim Memorial and Evangelical Lutheran colleges, has a library, two parks, and fair grounds. Pop. (1900) 5,968.

Bren'nan, Thomas Francis, Irish Catholic prelate: b. Tipperary, 1853. He was educated at Allegheny College, Pa., at Rouen, and Innsbruck. He was engaged in missionary work in Pennsylvania and was later made bishop of Dallas, Texas. In 1893 he went to Labrador, and in 1894–5 was auxiliary bishop of Newfoundland; since then he has been acting auxiliary bishop of Albano and Frascati, Italy.

Bren'ner, Mount, a mountain in the Tyrol, situated between Innsbruck and Sterzing, and between the rivers Inn, Aicha, and Adige, forming part of the Tyrolese Alps, 6,777 feet high. The road from Germany to Italy traverses this mountain. It reaches the elevation of 4,658 feet, and is about 12 miles long. This is one of the lowest roads practicable for carriages over the main chain of the Alps, and also one of the most ancient, having been used by the Romans. In 1867 a railway over the Brenner Pass was opened, so that Italy and Germany were connected by an unbroken line of rails.

Bren'nus, the name or title of several princes of the ancient Gauls, supposed to be derived from the Kymrian brenhin, a king. A leader of the Senones, a Gallic nation in the upper part of Italy, the most famous personage who is mentioned under this name, made an invasion into the Roman territory about the year 390 B.C. A battle was fought near the river Allia, the Romans were totally defeated, and Brennus took possession of the city, which had been previously abandoned by the inhabitants. The capitol only was provided with a garrison, but several aged citizens of rank, amounting in the whole to about 80, had resolved to remain in the city and devote themselves to the infernal deities. Attired in their sacerdotal, consular, and triumphal robes, they seated themselves in their chairs of office in the middle of the forum, awaiting death. When Brennus arrived at the forum, he was struck with astonishment at their venerable aspect. The Gauls looked upon them as so many statues of deities, and feared to go near them, but ultimately they were all massacred. Rome was sacked, and all the inhabitants who yet remained in their houses were slain. Brennus then assaulted the capitol, and being repelled with considerable loss, he set fire to the city and leveled it with the ground. While the garrison of the capitol was in great distress Brennus attempted a surprise by night, in which he would have succeeded had not the cackling of the geese, sacred to Juno, alarmed the garrison, in consequence of which the Gauls were repulsed. After six months Brennus offered to raise the siege and leave the Roman territory for 1,000 pounds of gold. When the gold was weighed, Brennus threw his sword into the scale beside the weights and cried out, "Woe to the vanquished!" According to Polybius the Gauls returned home in safety with their booty. According to the Roman legend followed by Livy, Brennus was defeated, and his army entirely destroyed by Camillus, a distinguished

Roman exile who had retired to the city of Ardea, and who arrived with succor in time to save the capitol.

Another Brennus in 279 B.C. advanced into Greece with an enormous force, said to have amounted to 150,000 foot and 61,000 horse. After ravaging Macedonia he entered Thessaly and marched toward Thermopylæ, where an army of 20,000 Greeks was assembled, supported by an Athenian fleet on the coast. The Gauls were repulsed in a sanguinary battle, but, in order to separate the Greeks, they dispersed themselves to plunder the country. Brennus himself attacked the temple of Delphi, which was defended by only 4,000 men, but was again repulsed, and carried out of the battle fainting with his wounds. Unwilling to survive his defeat, he put an end to his life by copious draughts of wine. The Greeks attributed their victory to the assistance of Apollo.

Brent, Charles Henry, American clergyman: b. Newcastle, Ontario, Canada, 1862. He was graduated at the University of Trinity College in 1884, ordained deacon in the Protestant Episcopal Church in 1886, priest in 1887, and consecrated the first bishop of the Protestant Episcopal Church for the Philippine Islands in December 1901. He served in the ministry of St. Paul's Pro-Cathedral, Buffalo, 1887–8; removed to Boston in the latter year, where he had charge of the parish of St. John the Evangelist, and later of that of St. Stephen's Church, devoting himself entirely to the missionary work of the latter parish. He has performed considerable literary work; was on the editorial staff of the New York *Churchman* for some time, and is the author of 'With God in the World,' and other books.

Brent Goose. See BRANT.

Bren'ta (ancient MEDOACUS MAJOR), a river in north Italy. Its source is Lake Caldonazzo in the Tyrol, eight miles southeast of Trent, whence it flows southeast, with a winding course of 112 miles, and falls into the Adriatic through the canal of Brenta-nova or Brentono, at Brondolo. Formerly its embouchure was at Fusina, opposite Venice. The old course has been formed into a canal, and is the chief means of communication between Padua and Venice, the new channel being comparatively little used.

Brentano, brěn-tä'nō, **Clemens,** German poet: b. Frankfort-on-the-Main, 8 Sept. 1778; d. Aschaffenburg, 28 July 1842. He studied at Jena, and resided by turns there and at Frankfort, Heidelberg, Vienna, and Berlin. In 1818 he retired to the convent of Dülmen, in Münster, and the latter years of his life were spent at Ratisbon, Munich, and Frankfort-on-the-Main. These frequent changes were due to a restless disposition, combined with morbid and misanthropic views, which gave a peculiar character to his writings. With a powerful imagination, his genius was tinged with mysticism, eccentricity, and a strong tendency to sarcasm. He was the brother of Elizabeth von Arnim, Goethe's "Bettina." Among his principal works are 'Satires and Poetical Fancies' (1800) ; 'The Mother's Statue' (1801), an ultra-romantic production, which he himself calls a very wild romance; 'The Joyous Musicians' (1803) ; 'Ponce de Leon' (1804) ; 'The Founding of Prague' (1816), said to be his most successful drama; 'Gokel, Hinkel, und Gakeleia' (1838),

a satire on the times; 'History of the Brave Caspar and the Beautiful Annerl' (2d ed. 1851), which is considered a masterpiece as a novelette.

Brentano, Franz, German philosopher: b. Marienberg, 16 Jan. 1838. He was professor of philosophy at Würzburg, but in 1873 resigned his position on account of the doctrine of the infallibility of the Pope; and was professor at Vienna, 1874–80. He has written 'Psychology of Aristotle,' 'New Riddles,' and 'Psychology from an Empirical Standpoint' (in agreement with Lotze and the English empirical psychologists).

Brentano, Lorenz, German American politician: b. Mannheim, 4 Nov. 1813; d. Chicago, 18 Sept. 1891. He studied law at Heidelberg, represented Mannheim in the Lower House of Baden, and was a member of the National Assembly in 1848. He withdrew from this body with the majority of the radical party in 1849. He was placed at the head of the revolutionary government of Baden, but suspected of treachery to his party, was forced to flee to Switzerland. In 1850 he came to the United States, lived for a time on a farm in Michigan, and then went to Chicago. Here he practised law and established the Illinois *Staatszeitung,* which he made one of the most influential papers in the northwest in the interest of the Federal government. He was a member of the Illinois legislature in 1862; United States consul at Dresden 1872–6, and member of Congress from Illinois in 1876.

Brentano, Lujo, loo'yō, German political economist: b. Aschaffenburg, Bavaria, 18 Dec. 1844. He studied at Dublin and at four German universities; and, after attaining a post in the Royal Statistical Seminary in Berlin, went to England to study the condition of the working classes, and especially trades' associations and unions. The outcome of this was his work, 'On the History and Development of English Guilds' (1870) ; 'Die Arbeitergilden der Gegenwart' (1871–2). He has been professor at Breslau (1873), Strasburg, Vienna, Leipsic, Munich (1891). He supports the "Socialists of the Chair" (*Kathedersozialisten*) against the German free-trade school, and has written works on 'Wages' (1877) ; 'Labor in Relation to Land' (1877), and 'Compulsory Insurance for Workmen' (1881), on the English Chartists, on the Christian Socialist movement in England, and numerous polemical pamphlets.

Brent'ford, the county town of Middlesex, England, seven miles west of London. It has a weekly market and two annual fairs. Here Edmund Ironside defeated the Danes, under Canute, in 1016; and Prince Rupert a part of the parliamentary forces, under Col. Hollis, in 1642. Sion House, the magnificent edifice of the Duke of Somerset, where Lady Jane Grey resided, now belonging to the Duke of Northumberland, was built here on the site of a suppressed nunnery. Brentford has a considerable retail trade, a soap manufactory, and extensive sawing and planing mills. Pop. (1891) 13,738; (1901) 15,171.

Brenton, William, colonial governor: b. England, early in the 17th century; d. Newport, R. I., 1674. His family came to Rhode Island from Hammersmith, England, where they were of good social standing. Between 1635 and 1669 Brenton was the colony's representative at

Boston, lieutenant-governor, president of the colony, and governor under the Charles II. charter 1666–9. He was one of the nine original proprietaries of Rhode Island; he selected and surveyed the site of Newport, and built a large brick residence where Fort Adams now stands. Brenton's Point and Brenton's Reef in Narragansett Bay preserve his name. See 'Rhode Island Colonial Records,' Vols. I. and II., *passim.*

Brenz, Johann, yŏ'hän brĕnts, German reformer: b. 1499; d. 1570. He was one of the authors of the *Syngramma Suevicum,* bearing upon the controversy with Zwingli and Œcolampadins, on the subject of the Lord's Supper. He was the most resolute among the opponents of the interdict of Charles V., escaping death only by resorting to flight.

Brereton, Austin, English journalist: b. Liverpool, England, 13 July 1862. He went to London in 1881, has been dramatic critic of 'The Sphere' from 1901, and prior to that date was connected with 'The Stage'; 'The Theatre'; Sydney (N. S. W.) *Morning Herald;* and the 'Illustrated American,' New York. He has published Henry Irving's 'A Biographical Sketch' (1883); 'Some Famous Hamlets' (1884); 'Dramatic Notes' (1886); 'Shakespearean Scenes and Characters' (1886); 'Romeo and Juliet on the Stage' (1890); 'Sarah Bernhardt' (1891); 'Gallery of Players' (1894); 'Short History of the Strand Theatre' (1899); 'Cheltenham' (1899); 'By the Silent Highway' (1901); 'Peg Woffington, On and Off the Stage' (1901); 'The Well of St. Anne' (1901); 'A Ramble in Bath' (1901).

Brescia, brĕ'sha (Latin, *Brixia*), an episcopal city of Lombardy, Italy. It is situated at the foot of the Alps, 40 miles northwest of Verona, on a fertile and beautiful plain on the banks of the rivers Mella and Garza. It is the capital of the province of the same name, and is a handsome and flourishing city, of a square form, about four miles in circuit, and surrounded by walls. Its streets are spacious, and its public buildings numerous, particularly its churches, which are further remarkable for the number and value of the paintings with which they are enriched. A few of them only, however, have much pretension to architectural beauty; among those that have are the cathedral, a handsome structure of white marble, and the Church of San Domenico. But, however plain in exterior appearance most of the Brescian churches may be, they are all richly decorated within with the most beautiful frescoes, and other creations of taste and art. The other buildings most worthy of notice are the Palazzo della Logia, and the Broletto. The first was intended for the palace of the municipality, or city hall. It is composed of the richest marbles, and was worked upon by the first architects of the 15th and 16th centuries successively. The Broletto, the ancient palace of the republic, combines the characters of fortress and city hall, and is surmounted by a great tower, whose deeply cleft Italian battlements produce a singularly grand effect. The whole is in a colossal style, and marked by the peculiar characteristics of the age in which it rose — supposed to be about the end of the 12th, and beginning of the 13th century. The city contains also a lyceum, two gymnasia, an athenæum, a college, with a museum of antiquities,

and a botanic garden; a public library, with 30,000 volumes; a theological seminary, a handsome theatre, a corn exchange, an extensive hospital, and other educational and charitable establishments. There are 72 public fountains in the streets and squares, besides some hundreds of private ones. Outside the town is a cemetery, begun in 1815, designed by Vantini.

Brescia is a place of considerable trade and manufacturing industry. Near it are large iron-works, and its firearms are esteemed the best that are made in Italy. It has also silk, linen, and paper factories, tan-yards, and oil-mills, and is an important mart for raw silk. But it derives its greatest interest from its fine Roman remains, having been at one time the seat of a Roman colony. These first attracted attention in the 17th century; although, so far as regards inscriptions, they had been objects of especial care to the citizens of Brescia for two centuries before this period, but it was not till 1820 that any very earnest efforts were made to bring the buried remains of entire buildings to light. Since that period some remarkable discoveries have been made, embracing besides numerous statues and inscriptions the beautiful marble temple of Vespasian, and a number of noble and magnificent Corinthian columns, with many fragments of moldings and ornaments, some gilt, and all of great elegance. Brescia was the seat of a school of painting of great merit, to which many eminent artists belonged, including Alessandro Bonvicino, commonly called "Il Moretto," who flourished in the 16th century, and was remarkable for the deep devotional feeling which he threw into his sacred subjects, as well as for his excellence as a portrait painter. The city is of great antiquity, having been the chief town of the Cenomani, a Gallic tribe, who were conquered by the Romans. It became the seat of a Roman colony under Augustus about 15 B.C., and afterward a municipium. In the year 412 it was burned by the Goths; and was soon afterward destroyed by Attila; but was rebuilt about the year 452. It was taken by Charlemagne in 774. In 936 Otho I. of Saxony declared it a free city, and it so remained for nearly three centuries, taking an active part in the feuds of the Guelphs and Ghibellines, and ultimately put itself under the protection of Venice in 1426. In 1796 it was taken by the French, and was assigned to Austria by the general treaty signed at Vienna 9 June 1815. In 1849 it was involved in the commotions of continental Europe; its streets were barricaded, but the city was eventually captured by the Austrians under Gen. Haynau. It was ceded to Sardinia by the Treaty of Zürich in 1859. Pop. (1896) 67,500; (1901) 70,618.

Breslau, brĕs'low, a city of Germany, the second in size in the Prussian dominions, being exceeded in population only by the capital, Berlin; the capital of the province of Silesia. It is situated in a spacious plain at the confluence of the Ohlau and the Oder, the latter dividing in into two main portions (the largest on the left bank), which, with islands in the river, are connected by a large number of bridges. The streets of the older quarters are narrow, those of the newer broad. There are electric and other tramways. The public squares and buildings are handsome. The fortifications which surrounded the old or inner city have been converted into promenades, and the ditch into an ornamental sheet of water. The cathedral, built in 1148–1680, and restored in 1875, the Protestant churches of St. Elizabeth and St. Mary Magdalene, the Rathhaus or city-hall, a Gothic structure of the 14th and 15th centuries, the municipal buildings, the government buildings, the building for the provincial diet, the royal residence, court-houses, exchange, and university buildings are among the most remarkable buildings. The university was founded in 1702 as a Roman Catholic institution, with which was combined the Protestant university at Frankfort-on-the-Oder, transferred hither in 1811. The university has attached to it a museum of natural history, a cabinet of antiquities, a library of 320,000 volumes, including many old works and manuscripts, an observatory, a picture gallery, a botanic garden, etc. The number of students is about 1,500. There are numerous other educational institutions, as well as hospitals and asylums. Breslau carries on an extensive trade in the products and manufactures of Silesia, principally in corn, wool, metals, glass, coal, and timber. The Oder is navigable and there is a connection with Berlin by the Oder-Spree Canal. The industries comprise iron-founding, bell-founding, the manufacture of machinery, railway carriages, organs, and other musical instruments, cigars, oil, spirits, etc., brewing, and glass-painting. There are two annual wool-fairs, which are largely attended. Breslau was the seat of a bishopric by the year 1000; an independent duchy from 1163 to 1335; was ceded to Austria, after many wars and calamities, in 1527. It was conquered by Frederick II. of Prussia in 1741. It was from this time the scene of frequent warfare, being successively attacked by Austrians, French, Russians, and Prussians. It was twice occupied by the French, in 1807 and 1813. Its fortifications were destroyed by Napoleon in 1807, but it finally remained in the hands of Prussia. Pop. (1895) 405,041; (1900) 422,738; (1903) 433,350.

Bressani, Francesco Giuseppe, frän-chĕs'kō joo-sĕp'pĕ brĕs-sä'nẹ, Italian missionary: b. Rome 1612; d. Florence 9 Sept. 1672. He labored during nine years among the Huron Indians of Canada, was captured and ill treated by the Iroquois, and afterward sold to the Dutch and kept in bondage until 1644, when he was ransomed. On his return to Italy, he published a book on the Jesuit missionaries in Canada.

Bressay, brĕs'sā, one of the Shetland Islands, lying east of the mainland, and separated from it by Bressay Sound, about six miles long and one to three in breadth. Its line of coast is rocky and deeply indented; the interior is hilly, rising in the Wart of Bressay to 742 feet, and is to a great extent covered with peat-moss. There are a number of small streams and small lakes. On the south there are three bold headlands, the Ord, the Bard, and the Hammar. The inhabitants are mostly crofters, sailors in the merchant service, or fishermen. Hosiery is the only manufacture. Bressay Sound forms a safe harbor (Lerwick Harbor), one mile or more in breadth, having Lerwick on its west side. Pop. (1891) 802; (1901) 1,686.

Brest, a fortified seaport and naval station of France, in the department of Finistère, in the former province of Brittany, situated at the mouth of the Penfeld, 320 miles south by west from Paris. It has one of the best harbors in France, and a safe roadstead, capable of containing 500 men-of-war in 8, 10, and 15 fathoms at low water, and it is the chief station of the French marine. The coast on both sides is well fortified. The entrance to the roads, known as Le Goulet, is narrow and difficult, with covered rocks that make it dangerous to those not well acquainted with it. There are immense magazines, workshops, barracks, roperies, etc., and the dockyard employs from 8,000 to 9,000 men. Several docks are cut in the solid rock. Brest, which in the Middle Ages was of so much importance that it was said, "He is not Duke of Brittany who is not lord of Brest," had sunk by the beginning of the reign of Louis XIII. to little more than a village. Richelieu resolved to make it the seat of a vast naval arsenal, but little was done till the beginning of the reign of Louis XIV., when Duquesne came to superintend the works. Vauban followed him, and fortified it. In 1694 the combined fleets of England and Holland disembarked a force which attempted to take Brest, but was repulsed with great loss. On 1 June 1794 the French fleet was beaten off Brest by the British, under Howe, who took from them six ships of the line, and sunk a seventh. The manufacturing industry of Brest is inconsiderable, but its commerce is extensive. Its chief exports are cereals; its principal imports colonial produce and naval stores. Pop. (1896) 74,538.

Brest-Litovski, brĕst-le-tŏfs'kĕ, a fortified town of Russia, in the government of Grodno, on the Bug, 120 miles east of Warsaw. Brest-Litovski was a possession of Poland till 1795, and is one of the oldest Slav towns. The place is an important railroad centre and of considerable commercial importance because of its situation, and has a large trade in cloths, leather, and soap. It is a fortress of the first rank, with vast magazines and military stores. Pop. (1897) 46,542.

Bretagne. See BRITTANY.

Bretèche, a name common to several wooden, crenellated, and roofed erections, used in the Middle Ages in sieges by the assailants to afford protection while they were undermining the walls, and by the besieged to form defenses behind breaches. Later, the name was given to a sort of roofed wooden balcony or cage, crenellated and machicolated, attached by corbels, sometimes immediately over a gateway.

Breteuil, Louis Charles **Auguste** le Tonnelier, loo-ē ô-goost lẹ tŏn-nĕl-yä brĕ-tẹ-y' (BARON DE), French diplomatist: b. 1730; d. 2 Nov. 1807. After a period of military service he became in 1758 minister plenipotentiary at Copenhagen, and afterward occupied similar posts in Sweden, Austria, Naples, and again in Vienna. His embassy to Vienna explains his attachment to the Queen Marie Antoinette. As minister and secretary of state after Necker's dismissal in 1789, he was a zealous defender of the monarchy; he was therefore considered as one of the greatest enemies of the Revolution. After the capture of the Bastile, he escaped by a hasty flight. In 1790 Louis XVI. entrusted him with secret negotiations for his restoration to the throne, at the principal northern courts. The convention issued a decree against him. In 1802 he returned, with the permission of the government, to France.

Brethren, Bohemian, a Christian sect of Bohemia, formed from the remains of the stricter sort of Hussites in the latter half of the 15th century. They took the Scriptures as the ground of their doctrines throughout. Being persecuted, they fled into Poland and Prussia. See BOHEMIAN BRETHREN; MORAVIAN CHURCH; UNITED BRETHREN.

Brethren of the Christian Schools, an order established at Rheims by the Saint Jean Baptiste de La Salle (q.v.). The object of the order was to provide instruction for the poorer classes of the population, and hence the name. The members take upon themselves the vows of chastity, poverty, and obedience. Their costume is a coarse black cassock, and a small collar or band around the neck, for the house, and a hooded cloak and a wide hat for outdoor purposes. Their teaching is mainly rudimentary, although in some of their schools Latin and the higher mathematics form part of the course. They have modified their instruction from time to time to make it meet the wants of the classes whom they teach. Thus, in 1831 they opened evening schools for adults, wherein they received and taught mechanics and other poor laborers who had no time to devote to learning in the day. The Brethren of the Christian Schools are sometimes improperly called the "Christian Brothers." The latter have nearly the same rule and object, but form an independent order. See BROTHERS OF THE CHRISTIAN SCHOOLS; ORDERS, RELIGIOUS.

Brethren of the Free Spirit, a sect which sprang up on the upper Rhine near the beginning of the 13th century. They are frequently confounded with the Lollards, Beguards, or Beguins. They held that the universe was a divine emanation; that man, so far as he gave himself to the contemplative life, was a Christ, and as such, free from law, human or divine (Romans viii. 2, 14). Many edicts were published against this sect, but it continued to exist under various names, such as Picards and Adamites, till about the first quarter of the 15th century.

Brethren of the Holy Trinity, a religious society, founded in France near the close of the 12th century, whose members pledged themselves to give a third part of their revenues to procuring the redemption of Christians who had fallen captive to the infidels, and were in Mohammedan slavery. It was established by John of Matha, a Parisian theologian, and Felix de Valois.

Brethren of the Lord, The. Great controversy has existed concerning the expressions in the New Testament relating to the "brethren of Jesus," and theologians have been divided on the question of the perpetual virginity of Mary the mother of Jesus. The term "brethren of the Lord" occurs but once in the New Testament (1 Cor. ix. 5), but there are several other passages that refer apparently to actual brothers of Jesus (Gal. i. 19; Matt. xii. 46-50, etc.). Some have claimed that the brethren referred to were later sons of Mary by Joseph, the reputed father of Jesus; others have contended that they were sons of Joseph by a former marriage, and others again have sought to prove that these brethren were sons of Alphæus, the husband of a sister of Mary, and therefore the cousins of Jesus.

Brethren of the Strict Observance, the stricter Franciscans, or Regular Observatines.

Bretigny, brĕ-tēn-yē, a village of France in the department of Eure-et-Loire, six miles southeast of Chârtres, on the Paris & O. R.R. By the treaty of Bretigny, concluded on 8 May 1360, between Edward III. of England and John II. of France, the latter, who had been taken prisoner at the battle of Poitiers, recovered his liberty on a ransom of 3,000,000 crowns, to be paid in six years. Edward renounced his claim to the crown of France, and relinquished a portion of his conquests and possessions in that country, including Anjou and Maine, and the greater part of Normandy; receiving the cession in independent sovereignty of the duchy of Aquitaine, with all its dependencies; Gascony, Poitou, Saintonge, Aunis, Agenois, Périgord, Limousin, Quercy, Rouergue, Angoumois, together with Calais, the counties of Ponthieu and Guines, and the viscounty of Montreuil.

Breton, Jean Baptiste Joseph, zhŏṅ bäp-tĕst zhō-zĕf brĕ-tôṅ, French journalist: b. Paris 16 Nov. 1777; d. 6 Jan. 1852. His public career as journalist and stenographer was nearly parallel with representative government in France. He was present as stenographer at the session of 10 Aug. 1792, when the power passed from the hands of an individual to those of an assembly; and of 2 Dec. 1851, when it passed from the hands of an assembly to those of an individual. His services were also in constant requisition at the courts as an interpreter for English, German, Italian, Spanish, Dutch, and Flemish suitors. He was a frequent contributor to the 'Dictionnaire de la Conversation,' and among other papers wrote the article on stenography.

Breton, Jules Adolphe, zhül ä-dôlf, French painter: b. Courrieres 1 May 1827; d. Paris 5 July 1906. He was educated at St. Omer and at Douai, and studied under Félix Devigne and at Drölling's atelier in Paris. The subjects of his earlier pictures, such as 'Misère de Désespoir' (1849), were taken from the French revolutionary period; but he soon turned to the scenes from peasant life which he has treated in a most poetic and suggestive manner, with an admirable union of style with realism. In 1853 he exhibited 'La Retour des Moissonneurs' and in 1855 his celebrated 'Les Glaneuses.' He is represented in the Luxembourg by 'La Bénédiction des Blés' (1857), admirable for its rendering of sunlight; 'Le Rappel des Glaneuses' (1859); and 'Le Soir' (1861). His later works were simpler in their component parts and larger in the scale of their figures, and of these 'La Fontaine' is a typical example. Breton was also known as a poet.

Breton, de los Herreros, brä-tôn' dā lōs ā-rā'rōs, Don Manuel, Spanish dramatist: b. Quel, province of Logroño 19 Dec. 1800; d. Madrid 13 Nov. 1873. He was the most notable Spanish poet of the first half of the 19th century. He gave to the Spanish stage 150 plays, some of them original, others derived from ancient Spanish sources, or translated from French or Italian. In him the old French comedy finds not so much an imitator as its last true representative. Among his best original comedies are: 'I'm Going Back to Madrid,' 'Here I am in Madrid,' 'This World is All a Farce,' 'Die Once and You'll See.' He was less successful in the historic drama than in comedy.

Bret'on Literature. See CELTIC LANGUAGE AND LITERATURE.

Brets, Brettys, or **Brits,** Britons, the name given to the Welsh or ancient Britons in general; also to those of Strathclyde, as distinguished from the Scots and Picts.

Bretschneider, brĕt'shnī-dėr, **Heinrich Gottfried von,** German writer: b. Gera, 6 May 1739; d. 1 Nov. 1810. He was educated at the institute of Herrnhuters at Ebersdorf, entered the army as a cornet in the regiment of Count Brühl, was present at the battle of Kolin, and afterward became captain of a Prussian freecorps, and was made prisoner by the French. During his forced stay in France he acquainted himself with the language, and with the spirit of the people. On his return he was appointed governor of Usingen in Nassau. This government being shortly suppressed, he traveled in England and France, and became associated with Count Vergennes, who employed him in diplomatic missions. He returned to Germany in 1772, and was shortly afterward engaged in the service of Austria, where he was first named vice-governor of the banat of Temesvar. This banat having been incorporated in Hungary in 1778, he obtained the appointment of librarian to the University of Buda. Here his hostility to the monks, and especially to the Jesuits, led him into trouble; although the Emperor Joseph II., who held the same views, declared himself his protector. He was obliged to retire from Buda, and was appointed librarian at Lemberg, and also counselor to the government. In 1809 he retired with the title of aulic counselor. His views were liberal and somewhat sceptical, and with his active opposition to the monastic orders, gained him many enemies. His principal works are: 'Reise nach London und Paris' (1817); 'Almanach der Heiligen' (for the year 1788); 'Wallers Leben und Sitten' (1793).

Bretschneider, Karl Gottlieb, German theologian: b. Gersdorf, Saxony, 11 Feb. 1776; d. Gotha, 22 Jan. 1848. He studied theology at Leipsic, was appointed pastor at Schneeberg in 1807, general superintendent at Gotha in 1816, and afterward councilor of the Upper Consistory there. Bretschneider established a reputation as a sound and judicious thinker of rationalistic bias, and his theological writings are admitted to have a permanent value. In 1820 appeared his 'Probabilia de Evangelii et Epistolarum Johannis Apostoli Indole et Origine,' an attack upon the Johannine authorship from internal evidence, and in 1824 his 'Lexicon Manuale Græco-Latinum in Libros Novi Testamenti.' Another work of importance is his 'Handbuch der Dogmatik' (4th ed. 1838). Bretschneider also wrote on many other theological questions and controversies.

Bret'ten, a town of Baden, Germany, the birthplace of Melanchthon, 16 miles eastnortheast of Carlsruhe by rail. The house in which Melanchthon was born belongs now to a foundation bearing his name for the support of poor students, established in 1861. A monument was erected in 1867. Pop. (1900) 4,800.

Bretts and Scots, Laws of, the name given in the 13th century to a code of laws in use among the Celtic tribes in Scotland, the Scots being the Celts north of the Forth and Clyde, and the Bretts being the remains of the British inhabitants of the kingdom of Cambria, Cumbria, or Strathclyde, and Reged. Edward I. issued in 1305 an ordinance abolishing the usages of the Scots and Bretts. Only a fragment of them has been preserved.

Bretwalda, brĕt'väl-da, a title applied to one of the Anglo-Saxon tribal chiefs or kings, who, it is supposed, was from time to time chosen by the other chiefs, nobility, and caldormen to be a sort of dictator in their wars with the Britons. The following are mentioned by Bede, but Hallam and other historians doubt whether any sovereign in those early times possessed such authority: 492 A.D., Ella, king of Sussex; 571, Ceawlin, king of Wessex; 594, Ethelbert, king of Kent; 615, Redwald, king of the West Angles; 623, Edwin, king of Deira; 634, Oswald, king of Bernicia; 643, Oswy, king of Bernicia.

Breughel, brĕ-Hĕl', the name of a celebrated Dutch family of painters, the first of whom adopted this name from a village not far from Breda. This was Pieter Breughel, also called, from the character and subject of most of his representations, the "Droll" or the "Peasants' Breughel." He was born in 1510 (according to Mechel, in 1530), was a pupil of Peter Koeck van Aelst, traveled in Italy and France copying the beauties of nature, and after his return fixed his residence at Antwerp, where he was received into the Academy of Painters in that place. He subsequently married the daughter of his instructor, Koeck, and removed to Brussels, where he died in 1570 (according to some in 1590). In his rural weddings, his rustic feasts and dances, he strikingly represents the gaiety of the villagers, as he himself had frequently observed them, in disguise, in his youth. He also etched, but many of his pictures have been engraved by others. He left two sons — Pieter and Jan. The former (called the Younger Breughel), preferring subjects affording striking contrasts, painted many scenes in which devils, witches, or robbers are the principal figures. This particular turn of genius procured him the name of "Hell Breughel." Among his pieces are: 'Orpheus Playing on his Lyre Before the Infernal Deities,' and also 'The Temptation of St. Anthony.' The former picture hangs in the gallery of Florence. The second brother, Jan, was distinguished by his landscapes and small figures. From his usual dress he received the title of "Velvet Breughel." He also painted for other masters landscapes as backgrounds to their pieces, and sometimes little figures in them. He was a very prolific artist. In connection with Rubens he represented Adam and Eve in Paradise. The figures in this picture are painted by Rubens. This piece, his 'Four Elements,' also 'Vertumnus and Pomona,' which were all executed jointly with Rubens, are among his principal performanecs. He is said to have been born in 1568; other authorities say 1569, 1575, or 1589. He visited Italy, and enriched his imagination with beautiful scenery. He is said to have died in 1642, or by other authorities 1625. Other members of this family, belonging to a later period, are Ambrose, who was director of the Antwerp Academy of Painting between 1635 and 1670; and Abraham, who for a time resided in Italy, and died in 1690; the brother of the latter, John Baptist, who died in Rome; and Abraham's son, Caspar Breughel, known as a painter of flowers and fruits.

Breve, brĕv, a note of the third degree of length, and formerly of a square figure, as ⊟; but now made of an oval shape, with a line perpendicular to the stave on each of its sides: 𝄺. The breve, in its simple state, that is, without a dot after it, is equal in duration to one quarter of a large, or to two semibreves, and is then called imperfect; but, when dotted, it is equal to three eighths of a large, or to three semibreves, which being the greatest length it can assume, it is then called perfect. It is now chiefly used at the close of passages or compositions.

Brevet', a term borrowed from the French, and applied in the United States and Great Britain to rank in the army conferred upon officers on account of special and long service, and higher than that for which regimental pay is received. Thus a brevet-major serves as captain in his regiment, and draws pay as such.

Breviarium of Eutropius, the only existing work by Eutropius. It is a treatise in 10 brief books or chapters, recounting the history of Rome from the foundation of the city to the time of Valens, 364 A.D. Its style is notably good and the work has been much drawn upon by later writers. The best critical edition of 'The Breviarium' is that by Droysen.

Breviary (from the Latin *breviarium*), a summary or abridgment of prayers. The breviary is the book containing the daily offices which all who are in orders, or enjoy any Catholic benefice, are obliged to read. It is an abridgment of similar offices previously in use. The breviary contains prayers or offices to be used at the seven canonical hours of matins and lauds, prime, tierce, sext, nones, vespers, and compline. It is not known at what time the use of the breviary was first enjoined. In the Acts of the Apostles we find the third, sixth, and ninth hours especially mentioned. From Clement of Alexandria, Tertullian, Cyprian, and others, we learn that the observance of these hours was general among Christians. St. Basil, St. Jerome, and St. Ambrose speak of the seven hours called canonical. The services in use in the convents and monasteries in the early ages were very exhaustive from their great length. A council held at Tours in 567 enjoined that matins and vespers should never have less than 12 psalms each, and that the former should have 30 in Lent. It was under Pope Gregory VII. (1073-85) that the abridgment of the offices began to be considered necessary. In 1241 a breviary revised by Haymon obtained the approbation of Gregory IX., and was introduced in all the churches of Rome under Nicholas III. In 1568 Pius V. published a breviary which has remained, with few modifications, to the present day. The Roman breviary, however, was never fully accepted by the Gallican Church, which persisted in maintaining its own offices. The Ultramontane party there had long struggled in vain for the introduction of the Roman breviary, but from 1840 to 1864, by a final and vigorous effort, the opposition of the Gal-

lican party was overcome, and the uniformity of usage generally established, though to the dissatisfaction of a large number of French Catholics.

The Psalms occupy a large place in the breviary, the order of the reading being so arranged that in general 100 psalms shall be recited in a week. Passages from the Old and New Testament and from the fathers have the next place. All the services are in Latin, and their arrangement, which is adapted to the various seasons and festivals of the Church, is very complex. The English Book of Common Prayer is based on the Roman breviary. There is a translation of the breviary into English by the Marquis of Bute (1880).

Breviary of Alaric, a compendium of Roman law dated from the first decade of the 6th century and compiled at the command of Alaric II., king of the Visigoths. It consisted of abridgements of the code and novels of Theodosius, the institutes of Gaius, etc., and contained a detailed commentary styled the 'Interpretatio.' It was intended for the Roman subjects of the Visigothic ruler, and must not be confused with the 'Forum Judicum' or 'Judicum Liber,' which Alaric put forth for his barbarian vassals. See Lee, 'Historical Jurisprudence' (1900).

Brevipen'nes, a family or subdivision of birds, but occupying a different position in different systems. Cuvier makes it a family of the order *Grallæ* or waders. In more modern systems it corresponds to the order of Cursorial birds or *Ratitæ*. It includes at least two genera, the ostrich and the cassowary. The Dodo and Apteryx are also referred to it. The Brevipennes have a resemblance in several of their distinctive characteristics to the *Gallinacea*. Their pectoral muscles are reduced to extreme tenuity, and the sternum has no ridge, while the muscles of the thighs are of great strength and thickness. They are thus fitted for walking or running, rather than for flying. As their name implies their wings are short.

Brevoort', James Renwick, American artist: b. Westchester County, N. Y., 20 July 1832. His art studies were made chiefly in Europe, where he spent several years sketching scenes in England, Holland, and Italy. In 1861 he was elected an associate of the National Academy, and in 1863 a full member. Since 1872 he has been its professor of perspective. His specialty as a painter is landscape work, and the following pictures of his are well known: 'Lake of Como' (1878); 'Storm on English Moor' (1882); 'New England Scene'; 'Morning in Early Winter' (1884); 'The Wild November Comes at Last'; 'Windy Day on a Moor' (1886).

Brewer, David Josiah, American jurist: b. Smyrna, Asia Minor, 20 June 1837. He graduated at Yale College 1856, at Albany Law School 1858. He studied law in the office of his uncle, David Dudley Field, and was admitted to the bar in New York in 1858. Removing to Kansas, he became prominent in his profession. He was judge of the supreme court of Kansas 1870-81, and was appointed United States judge for the 8th circuit in 1884. He rendered a memorable decision on the Kansas Prohibition Law, affirming the right of liquor manufacturers to compensation, for which he was severely criticised by the Prohibitionists. President Harrison elevated him to the supreme court of the United States in 1889. He was made a member of the Venezuelan commission by President Cleveland in 1896, and was chosen its chairman.

Brewer, John Hyatt, American musician: b. Brooklyn, N. Y., 1856. He studied piano, organ, and theory under local teachers, particularly Dudley Buck. He has filled the position of organist at the Church of the Messiah and the Clinton Avenue Congregational Church, Brooklyn, and since 1881 at the Lafayette Avenue Presbyterian Church in that borough, where he is also professor of vocal music at Adelphi College. His compositions include church music, vocal music, and works for the piano, organ, and orchestra.

Brewer, Leigh Richmond, American Protestant Episcopal bishop: b. Berkshire, Vt., 20 Jan. 1839. He was ordained in 1867, and after serving as rector of Grace Church, Carthage, N. Y., 1866-72, and Trinity Church, Watertown, N. Y., 1872-80, was consecrated missionary bishop of Montana in the year last named.

Brewer, Thomas Mayo, American ornithologist: b. Boston, Mass., 21 Nov. 1814; d. 23 Jan. 1880. He was graduated at Harvard College in 1835, and was editor of the Boston *Atlas* in 1840. He edited Wilson's 'Ornithology' and 'Birds of North America,' and, in conjunction with Baird and Ridgeway, wrote 'A History of North American Birds.'

Brewer, William Henry, American agricultural scientist: b. Poughkeepsie, N. Y., 14 Sept. 1828. He was graduated from the Sheffield Scientific School, New Haven, in 1852, and has been professor of agriculture there from 1864. He has been a member of the National Academy of Sciences from 1880, of the Connecticut State board of health from 1892, and of the State board of agriculture for a long period. He has been one of the most prominent American leaders in agricultural research and is a valued authority on all related topics. Besides contributing to the 'Report on Cereal Production' in the United States Tenth Census (1883), he has edited the 'Botany of California' (1886).

Brew'erton, Henry, American soldier: b. New York, 1801; d. Washington, D. C., 17 April 1879. He was graduated with the class of 1819 at West Point. Commissioned second lieutenant in the corps of engineers, he first served as assistant in determining the 45th degree of north latitude at Rouse's Point, N. Y. He was assistant and professor of engineering at West Point (1819-21). Thereafter he was almost continuously engaged in such important engineering works as repairing the fortifications in New York harbor, construction of Fort Jackson, La., of Fort Adams, Newport, R. I., of the defenses of Charleston harbor, S. C., of the fortifications and improvements of Baltimore harbor (1861-4), and of Forts Monroe and Wool, for the defense of Hampton Roads, Va. He was brevetted brigadier-general in the United States army, 13 March 1865, for long, faithful, and meritorious services, and was retired from active service 7 March 1867, "having been borne on the Army Register more than 45 years." Dickinson College conferred the degree of LL.D. upon him, 8 July 1847.

Brewing and Malting. Brewing is the process of making fermented drinks, such as ale, beer, cider, etc. See BEER.

MALTING.— Malting is the preparing of cereals by germination or growth for the process of mashing. Barley is the grain commonly used for making malt for lager beer, ale, stout, vinegar and yeast-makers' or distillers' mash, etc., while wheat malt is used to a large extent in the production of weiss beer.

The barley is first cleaned in order to remove foreign seeds, straw, broken kernels, etc., by means of sieves and blower fans. As the character of the beer depends largely upon that of the malt, and as the latter's character can be determined during malting, it follows that there are various methods of details in malting. The following are the general manipulations employed:

Steeping.— Malting is in reality an artificial or forced growth of a seed, the changes taking place being similar to those when the seed is planted in the soil. The first requisite is moisture. This is given to the grain by placing it in steep tanks containing water of a certain temperature. Steep tanks are cylindrical iron vessels having conical bottoms so that all the grain will drop out when tank is emptied. They are generally placed on the top floor of the malthouse. The grain remains in the steep tank until it has absorbed the desired amount of water, the time differing for different kinds and quality of grain or the process of the maltster. For barley the duration of steeping is generally from 36 to 60 hours, averaging about 48 hours.

Growing or Germinating Floors.— The malthouse usually consists of several floors. The water in the steep tank is drained off and the

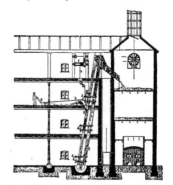

Floor Malt House with Power Shovel, and Bucket Elevator for Green Malt.

wet barley dropped upon these floors below. The barley is now spread in heaps of about 12 to 14 inches high (occupying rather more than one third and less than one half of the floor space). The barley now dries out somewhat and begins to sprout or grow and small hair-like fibres, called rootlets, begin to show. As heat is generated during growth, which is undesirable above a certain temperature, and as further proper growth requires pure air, it is necessary to aerate the growing barley (now called green-malt). This is done by what is called "turning the heap," which consists of reshoveling the green malt in such a manner that the lower kernels of the old heap will be at the top in the new heap. (During turning, the green malt is thrown through the air in a thin sheet or stream, whereby it is aerated and cooled. The new heap now occupies a larger floor space, is consequently of less height on the floor.) This turning is repeated at regular intervals so that at the end of the growing period the heap covers the entire floor to a height of from five to six inches. This growth usually takes about five days, during which time water is sprinkled upon the heap whenever it becomes too dry.

Kilning or Drying.— After the green malt shows the desired degree of sprouting, it is necessary to quickly check further growth. This is done by drying it upon the kiln. The green malt is shoveled by means of a power shovel to one end of the floor where it drops through an opening into a bucket elevator and is conveyed to the kiln. The kiln usually has two floors placed one above the other made of strips of wire or perforated sheet metal and heated by means of an open fire from below. Above the upper floor, in the dome, drafts are placed to carry off the vapors, but in modern constructions suction fans are used to promote drying. The green malt is spread evenly upon the upper kiln floor about 18 inches high, where it remains for 24 hours, during which time it is only partially dried. It is now dumped or dropped upon the lower floor (commonly by mechanical dumping floors which turn open in sections on an axis or bearing like the grate in a furnace). The malt on this lower kiln is again spread evenly and then subjected to a higher temperature until the desired degree of dryness is obtained, which usually takes from 20 to 24 hours.

Malt Cleaning.— The malt as it comes from the lower kiln is not yet suitable for brewing as it contains the rootlets and some kernels that were crushed or injured on the floors or during conveying. The malt now passes through cleaning machines consisting of sieves and blowers which remove the rootlets, dust and small and broken kernels.

Mechanical Malting.—As floor malting is restricted to only the cooler months of the year and possesses other disadvantages as to cost of labor and buildings, mechanical systems are coming more and more into use. The steeping of the grain as well as the kiln drying, however, remain generally the same as in the floor system.

Pneumatic Floor Malting.— This system employs box-shaped compartments to hold the grain during the growing period. Through this receptacle air that has been purified and given the proper degree of moisture, as well as cooled or warmed to the proper temperature, is circulated. The conditions of temperature and humidity can thus be made the same all the year round no matter what the conditions of weather may be outside. The green malt in this system is not turned by hand, but by a series of screws or propellers driven by power, traveling through it at regular intervals.

Drum Malting.— The advantages here are similar to those stated above. The drums consist of two concentric cylinders having the same ends. In the space between the cylinders the steeped grain is placed, this space not being filled quite full. The cylinders are perforated with small holes so that moistened or heated or cooled air can be forced through the grain from the centres or sucked through from the outside. By revolving the drum the grain is constantly tumbling, that is, the kernels nearest the inside cylinder fall against the outside cylinder, and this in connection with the air current passing through gives the same turning and aeration to the grain as in turning a heap in floor malting, and requires no labor. There are several systems of malting drums, differing principally in the manner in which the air is warmed and moistened and the direction in which it is forced through the drum.

BREWING.— *Brewing Materials.*— The materials used in the United States are principally the following: Barley malt is the most important and generally used. It gives to the beer not only its substances, but also to a great extent its character. Malt also supplies peptase and diastase, two substances that change the nature of certain other constituents during mashing. Peptase changes the insoluble albuminoids of the malt into soluble or desirable ones. Diastase changes the unfermentable starch contained in the malt and other materials into fermentable sugars and dextrins.

Caramel and black malt, consisting of ordinary malt that has been treated differently during malting, are used to impart color to the wort in order to produce darker beers, also to impart to the beer a more pronounced malt aroma or flavor. Only a small amount, proportionately, of these are used mixed with other materials.

Malt adjuncts or other starch containing materials, and brewing sugars are used for the triple purpose: of producing more durable beers, since these adjuncts contain very little albumen; of producing paler beers than could be made with malt alone; and for reducing the cost of production. These are rice and corn products, such as corn grits, corn meal, corn starch, corn flakes, and brewing sugars, glucose, etc. Flakes are made by steaming corn grits and passing them through hot steel rollers in order to change them so as to dissolve better during mashing. Flakes and sugars, such as grape sugar, glucose, etc., are sometimes used, instead of corn grits or rice (which require cooking) when a cooker is not installed. Flakes are added directly to the mash in the mash tub, and sugars to the wort in the kettle. Brewing sugars are used to a moderate extent only as a brewing material for lager beers, finding more extended use in the production of English beers such as ale, stout, etc.

Hops are added to the boiling wort for the purpose of imparting (1) tannin, which aids in the elimination of undesirable albuminoids in the wort; (2) hop oil, which gives the beer its hop aroma, and (3) hop resin, which gives the beer its bitter taste and furthermore tends to preserve it. Water acts as a solvent for substances contained in the beer. Its composition has considerable influence on the character of the beer produced. It must contain certain mineral substances. See Hops.

Brewing Operations.— Modern breweries are usually divided into three departments, namely:

the elevator or mill house where the materials are prepared and weighed; the brew house, where the wort is produced, and the cellars

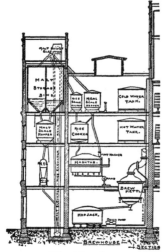

Mill and Brew House.

where the wort is fermented and treated to produce the finished beer. The arrangement is on the gravity plan, that is, in each department the material of wort or beer is elevated or

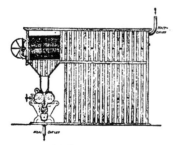

Malt Mill and Screening Reel.

pumped only once to the top and from there descends through the different stages of manufacture by gravity.

Elevator or Mill House.— Here the malt is cleaned and stored. The desired amount of malt for the beer is weighed out in a scale hopper, and from thence passes through the malt mill where it is crushed so as to loosen the starch in the kernels. The crushed malt is then trans-

ferred to the storage hoppers in the brew house ready for use. Rice and corn goods are either stored in the mill house, weighed in bulk and elevated to a storage hopper in the brew house, or dumped (usually in smaller breweries) directly from the sacks into the cooker.

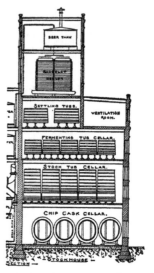

Gravity or Tower Brewery Cellars.

Brew House.— The brew house generally contains the following vessels: hot and cold water tanks; malt and cereal (rice or corn) hoppers; the cereal cooker, mash tub, kettle, and hop jack and cooler.

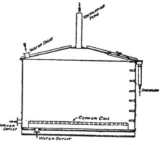

Hot Water Tank, Sectional View.

Mashing in Cereal Cookers.— Cookers are of two kinds; open ones or, as they are usually called, rice tubs, and closed or pressure cookers.

In these vessels rice or corn (grits or meal) is boiled for a certain length of time in order to loosen up or soften the hard flinty condition of their starch so as to render it able to be more completely dissolved or acted upon in the mash tub. Crushed malt to the amount of about one quarter the weight of corn goods is added in the open cookers. The mashing method in the

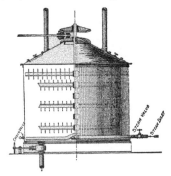

Cooker, showing Stirrer and Steam Connection.

open cooker varies somewhat among different brewers, the following being about the average method: The materials are mixed with water so as to have a temperature of 30° R. (100° F.). The mash is held at this temperature for about 15 minutes then run up to 56° R. (158° F.), and held for 30 minutes, then heated quickly to boiling and boiled from 45–75 minutes for corn goods depending on the fineness of the material, and 30 minutes for rice. The cereal mash is then run down to the mash tub where the mash is finished. Pressure cookers are used to some

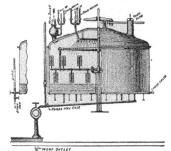

Mash Tub with Foremasher, Liquid Gauge, Attemperating Device and Three-way Cock.

extent, but not generally, in American breweries. They differ from the open cookers in that, being closed the mash can be boiled under pressure and consequently, at a higher temperature

than in open cookers. Hereby a more complete softening or dissolving of the starch is obtained and consequently a better yield or extraction of the materials.

Mashing in Mash Tubs.— The mash tub, like the open cooker, has a stirrer, and a heating coil, but is further supplied with a strainer or perforated false bottom for clarifying the wort, and a sprinkling device or sparger for washing out the grains. In the mash tub the mash is started and, when the mash from the cooker has been added, the combined mash is finished. The mashing method here varies considerably depending upon the character of the beer that is to be produced, and is consequently one of the most important of the brewing operations.

The method of mashing for the production of a beer of average character is approximately as follows: The crushed malt and water are mixed so as to have a temperature of 30° R. (100° F.) and the mash allowed to rest at this temperature

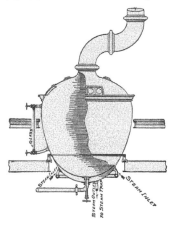

Brew Kettle, showing Liquid Gauge, Steam Jacket, and Steam Connections.

for one hour. The temperature of the mash is now raised to 54° R. (153° F.) to 55° R. (156° F.), in about 15 to 20 minutes, by running in the boiling corn or rice mash from the cooker (with the addition of steam should same be necessary). This temperature is held for 10 to 15 minutes, during which time the stirrer is operated continuously. It is at this stage that the diastase in the malt inverts or changes both the starch contained in the malt as well as that in the corn or rice into unfermentable dextrin and fermentable sugars.

The mash is now heated with steam and hot water, in 15 to 20 minutes, to 59° R. (165° F.) and the stirrer stopped. The mash is now allowed to rest from 30 minutes to one hour in order to allow the hulls of the malt to settle so as to act as a filtering material for the wort, after which the wort is run into the kettle.

After the wort has run off, the solid substances remaining in the mash tub, called grains, are washed out or sparged with water in order to recover as much of the wort contained in them as possible. The grains are then thrown out of the mash tub and sold as cattle feed.

Boiling the Wort in Kettle.— The kettle consists of a pear-shaped copper vessel having a double or jacketed bottom for heating the wort,

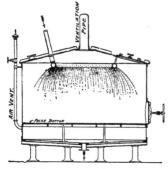

Hop Jack, Sectional View.

and a vent pipe to roof for conducting off the vapors generated during boiling. The steam outlet of the coil or jacketed bottom is connected to a steam trap which automatically discharges the water condensed in the coil or jacket without materially reducing the pressure of the steam. The wort as soon as it runs clear from the mash tub is collected in the kettle. Steam is turned on in the kettle as soon as the jacketed bottom is covered with wort. This wort, and that continuously running in is then heated to and kept at about 70° R. (190° F.) in order to destroy the action of the diastase and prevent further saccharification in the wort taking place. When the kettle is full or nearly so, steam is further turned on and the wort brought to boiling and boiled for one hour when it should show a good "break." During this boiling the undesirable albuminoids are precipitated in finely divided form, rendering the wort turbid. Upon continued heating these albuminoids unite or lump together and leave the wort between these lumps clear and transparent. This clarification is called the "breaking" of the wort.

Hops are now added, usually about two fifths of the total amount used, after which addition the wort again becomes turbid due to the further precipitation of albuminoids by the tannic acid contained in the hops. After about 40 minutes further boiling the wort should again clarify or show its second break when another two fifths of the hops are added and the wort boiled about 20 minutes. The remaining one fifth of the hops are added and the wort run out of kettle into hop jack immediately. This last quantity of hops is usually of a better quality and is not boiled with the wort as its addition is for the purpose of imparting the hop aroma to the wort. This aroma is due to the hop oil of the hops which is volatile at boiling

temperature and would escape, and be rendered useless, if the wort were boiled for any considerable time. All or part of this last hop addition is sometimes placed in the hop jack and the boiling wort run upon it.

Wort in Hop Jack.— The hop jack consists of a round or square iron tank, having a perforated false bottom or strainer and a sparger or sprinkler similar to that of the mash tub. The wort, with the hops, is run into the hop jack and allowed to rest until the hops have settled so as to form a filtering material for the clarification of the wort. As soon as this takes place the wort is pumped to the surface cooler or beer tank located at the top of the cellars. After the wort has all been removed the hops are washed out or sparged with hot water in order to recover as much of the absorbed wort as possible.

Surface Cooler and Beer Tank.— The surface cooler consists of a shallow iron pan of a length and width very large in proportion to its depth so as to give the wort as much surface as possible. Hereby the wort is cooled quite rapidly and aerated.

The beer tank, an iron cylindrical vessel closed at the top, is rapidly supplanting this cooler, since the latter, by the large surface it presents, endangers the wort to infections by impurities or germs always more or less present in the air. As soon as the wort on the surface cooler or in the beer tank cools to about 50° R. (145° F.) the danger of its infection by impurities, bacteria, etc., begins. From this stage until the beer is finally marketed, months later, it requires the daily, almost hourly vigilance of the brewer to keep it pure and free from contamination.

Baudelot Cooler.— This consists of a series of pipes or tubes arranged in vertical tiers, over the outside of which the wort flows, while through them the cooling medium is circulated.

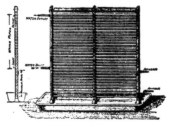

Baudelot Cooler.

It is usually made in two sections, the upper being of copper tubes, containing cold water, and the lower of steel containing ammonia.

The Cellars.— The wort after cooling enters the cellars, where it is fermented, stored kraeusened bunged, fined, filtered, and racked ready for the market.

Fermentation of Wort.— The wort as it comes from the cooler is run into fermenting tubs in which the yeast has previously been placed. Sometimes the yeast is added after the tubs are filled with wort. The yeast, from one to one and a half pounds to the barrel of wort, is usually given, not in its natural state, but first mixed with an equal quantity of wort and thoroughly aerated.

The fermentation now begins. Within 15 to 24 hours white bubbles appear on the surface around the sides of the tub. The wort at this time is covered with a head of thick, lumpy consistency composed largely of albuminoid matter. The whole surface now soon becomes covered with a fine white froth, which soon changes to a frizzled appearance called "kraeusen" stage. The froth head then moves toward the centre, the fermentation becomes more active, the froth head rises higher and becomes darker and the fermentation now passes into the "high kraeusen" stage, generally after about 70 to 80 hours. This stage is maintained for about 48 to 72 hours when the head begins to collapse and deepens in color to the end of the fermentation. The temperature is then gradually reduced by means of cooling attemperators to 3° R. (39° F.) in the next 3 or 4 days. Total duration of fermentation, 10 to 11 days.

Storage of Beer.—After the wort is fermented the beer is filled into storage vats (closed at the top) where it is stored at a temperature near the freezing point for about two or three months. During this storage period there is a slight progress of secondary or after fermentation and the yeast settles, and, what is most important in bottle beer that is to be pasteurized, there is a further precipitation of albuminoids.

Chip Cask Treatment.—When sufficiently matured in storage the beer is run or pumped into the chip casks, so called because in them wooden chips are placed to retain the sediment produced by the finings. In the chip cask, two properties must be imparted to the beer that it did not possess during storage, namely, life or proper amount of carbonic acid gas contents, and brilliancy. Life is given the beer by addition of 8 to 10 per cent of kraeusen, (that is, young beer in the first, or kraeusen stage of fermentation). This when added to the old "flat" storage beer continues to ferment, and, as the casks are closed the gas generated gives life to the whole amount of beer contained.

For bottle beer, kraeusen made from grape sugar is used, as grape sugar contains no albuminoids as does the kraeusen from regular fermenting worts.

Brilliancy is given to the beer by removing the yeast and other particles in suspension by means of finings made from isinglass. After bunging the cask, a certain pressure only (4½-5 pounds) is desired and any excess pressure generated above this is automatically removed by an automatic blow-off device called the bunging apparatus.

Filtration of Beer.—Although beers will generally become clear in the chip cask if they are left there long enough, they are now almost universally filtered after they have become moderately fine (clear) in the chip cask. Thereby much time is saved, also a large part of the finings and chips. Furthermore, filtration furnishes a more brilliant beer than can generally be obtained by chip cask treatment only. Modern beer filters differ considerably in construction, but are all alike in that they contain several or many compartments or cells filled with filter mass or pulp (a substance similar to blotting paper) through which the beer is forced. The filter mass or pulp can be used again and again, being washed after each use to remove the beer and sediments it collects during filtration. The operation of filtration is as follows: The bunging apparatus is disconnected and air pressure (15 to 20 pounds) is put on the chip cask and the beer thereby forced through the filter.

Racking of Beer.—From the filter the beer passes to the racking bench, which must be placed at a higher level in order to cause a back pressure upon the filter and prevent foaming. The racking device consists of two or more faucets of which one is always open so as to give a steady flow of beer.

Carbonating.—Beer is often carbonated. This is the mechanical forcing of carbonic acid gas into the beer by which time, labor, space, and cost of chip casks are saved, besides obtaining a more durable beer.

Pitching and Varnishing.—In order to prevent the beer in wooden vessels from soaking into the wood, they are coated on their insides with an inert or insoluble substance. This is shellac varnish for the large brewery vessels, and pitch for the trade packages.

Bibliography.— *Relating to American Beers and Malting, and Americanized Methods of Producing English Beers:* Robert Wahl and Max Henius, 'The American Handy-Book of the Brewing, Malting and Auxiliary Trades' (Chicago, 2d ed. 1902) ; *in German,* Hantke, 'Handbuch für den amerikanischen Brauer u. Malzer' (Milw. 1897).

English Beers and Malting as Practised in England and English Colonies: Walter J. Sykes, 'Principles and Practice of Brewing (Lond. 1902) ; Frank Faulkner, 'Theory and Practice of Modern Brewing' (Lond. 1888) ; Herbert E. Wright, 'A Handy Book for Brewers' (Lond. 1897) ; E. R. Southby, 'Practical Brewing' (Lond. 1889) ; Frank Thatcher, 'Brewing and Malting' (Lond. 1898) ; Lawrence F. Briant, 'Laboratory Textbook for Brewers' (Lond. 1898) ; Moritz and Morris, 'Textbook of the Science of Brewing' (Lond. 1896).

In German Language on German Brewing and Malting: Julius E. Thausing, 'Die Theorie und Praxis der Malzbereitung und Bierfabrikation' (5th ed., Leipsic 1898) ; Eugen Prior, 'Chemie und Physiologie des Malzes und Bieres' (Leipsic 1896) ; W. Windisch, 'Das Chemische Laboratorium des Brauers' (Ber. 1902) ; Franz Fasbender, 'Mechanische Technologie der Bierbrauerei und Malzfabrikation' (Vien. 1881-90).

English Translations: Julius E. Thausing, 'Theory and Practice of the Preparation of Malt and the Fabrication of Beer' (Translated from the German by William T. Brannt, revised with addition of American methods by A. Schwarz and H. A. Bauer) (Phila. 1882) ; Alfred Jörgensen, 'Micro-organisms and Fermentation' (translated from the Danish by Alex. K. Miller and A. E. Lennholm) (Lond. 1900) ; Emil Chr. Hansen, 'Practical Studies in Fermentation' (translated from the Danish by Alex. K. Miller) (N. Y. 1896). ROBERT WAHL.

Wahl-Henius Institute of Fermentology.

COMPOSITION OF VARIOUS BEERS AS PER ANALYSIS MADE BY THE WAHL-HENIUS INSTITUTE OF FERMENTOLOGY, CHICAGO, ILL. (FIGURES DENOTE PER CENT.)

American Lager Beers	Time of Analysis	Extract in Beer (apparent)	Extract in original Wort	Alcohol by Weight	Real Extract	Albuminoids	Sugar	Lactic Acid	Ash	Phosphoric Acid	Obtained In
Average of 15 samples	1887	4.53	13.73	3.77	6.46	0.51	2.00	0.16	0.194	0.072	Different States
Average of 88 samples	1889	4.85	13.30	3.64	6.21	0.50	1.99	0.11	0.20	.....	" "
Average of 210 samples	1890	3.93	13.45	4.01	5.70	0.56	1.20	0.10	0.18	.....	" "
Average of 176 samples	1893	3.66	12.53	3.64	5.50	0.390	1.62	....	....	.....	" "
Beers from 10 different cities. A..	1895	3.30	12.35	3.72	4.91	0.41	1.29	0.09		0.066	" "
B..	1895	4.04	13.04	3.45	6.15	0.39	1.62	0.120		0.058	" "
C..	1895	4.09	14.23	4.16	5.92	0.44	1.83	0.103		0.060	" "
D..	1895	2.88	13.62	4.41	4.80	0.45	1.39	0.102		0.069	" "
E..	1895	3.82	12.46	3.53	5.46	0.37	1.45	0.135		0.075	" "
F..	1895	2.91	12.18	3.81	4.56	0.33	1.50	0.069		0.063	" "
G..	1895	4.00	11.93	3.26	5.41	0.48	1.97	0.085		0.068	" "
H..	1895	4.97	14.57	3.82	6.73	0.46	3.36	0.126		0.075	" "
I..	1895	3.12	13.45	4.25	4.95	0.33	1.50	0.073		0.060	" "
J..	1895	3.37	13.10	4.00	5.10	0.35	1.25	0.054		0.060	" "
Average of 247 samples	1890	3.60	12.93	3.82	5.29	0.46	1.62	0.101		0.068	" "
Canadian lager	1900	3.15	12.1	3.77	4.88	0.01	1.13	0.072		0.003	" "
Mexican lager	1900	3.37	12.51	3.77	4.97	....	1.01	....	....	....	" "
Mexican lager	....		13.27	4.01	5.25	0.5	1.114	0.124	0.203	0.089	" "
Some typical American tonics. A..	1895	7.82	17.27	3.88	9.51	0.63	3.87	0.208		0.105	" "
B..	1896	13.74	18.74	2.06	14.62	0.85	9.84	0.113		0.140	" "
C..	1896	7.41	20.78	5.50	9.78	0.64	4.94	0.180		0.107	" "
D..	1896	5.23	17.01	4.87	7.27	0.51	2.00	0.090		0.085	" "
E..	1896	5.47	16.86	4.69	7.48	0.88	2.87	0.212		0.129	" "
F..	1896	7.58	17.46	4.06	9.54	0.77	0.96	0.288		0.155	" "
G..	1896	8.20	21.70	5.60	10.72	1.26	3.58	0.212		0.144	" "
Some typical Am. temperance beers. A..	....	2.15	6.66	1.88	3.05	0.18	0.85	0.063		0.03	" "
B..	....	5.50	8.31	1.22	6.07	0.09	2.55	0.036		0.02	" "
C..	....	3.27	6.66	1.44	3.90	0.19	2.55	0.025		0.025	" "
D..	....	1.95	6.55	1.94	2.80	....	....				" "

Ales, Porters, Stouts and American Weiss Beers	Time of Analysis	Extract in Beer (apparent)	Extract in original Wort	Alcohol by Weight	Real Extract	Albuminoids	Sugar	Lactic Acid	Ash	Phosphoric Acid	Obtained In
Allsopp's India Pale Ale, Red Hand	1901	2.23	15.14	5.44	4.70	0.44	0.66	0.144		0.045	Chicago.
McEwen's Sparkling Ale	1901	3.35	21.62	7.80	6.65	0.85	2.67	0.378		0.0765	"
Wm. Younger & Co.'s Sparkling Ale, Monk Brand	1901	1.87	18.03	6.84	4.90	0.64	0.80	0.153		0.067	"
Olde English Ale, Dog's Head bottling	1901	3.92	24.39	8.75	7.59	0.91	1.60	0.162		0.0855	"
American Stock Ales, average of 9 samples	1896	3.21	16.73	5.55	5.64	0.46	1.81	0.256		0.061	"
American Cream Ale	1901	2.25	13.60	4.75	4.45	0.37	1.06	0.144		0.04	"
American Sparkling Ale	1899	3.98	13.98	4.08	5.82	0.40	1.52	0.135		0.06	"
American Sparkling Ale	1901	2.15	13.80	4.90	4.40	0.38	0.91	0.135		0.04	"
American Pale Ale	1900	3.56	13.05	4.01	5.35	0.37	1.34	.....		.....	"
Canadian Stock Ale	1900	3.20	14.45	4.75	5.30	0.51	1.36				"
Stouts.											
Guinness' Extra Bottled Foreign Stout, white label	1901	3.40	18.22	6.29	6.15	0.75	0.97	0.243		0.108	"
American Brown Stout	1900	5.45	18.15	5.37	7.83	0.56	2.06	....		.....	"
Porters.											
American Porter	1899	2.95	13.25	4.19	4.87	0.40	1.49	0.135		0.061	"
Canadian Porter	1900	4.00	14.30	4.37	5.91	0.53	1.31	0.102		.....	"
American Weiss Beers.											
American Weiss Beer	1900	2.52	9.29	2.85	3.82	0.57	1.00	....		....	"
Weiss Beer	1901	2.24	9.28	2.97	3.58	0.42	0.91	0.342		0.036	"

German, Austrian and Bohemian Export Beers	Time of Analysis	Extract in Beer (apparent)	Extract in original Wort	Alcohol by Weight	Real Extract	Albuminoids	Sugar	Lactic Acid	Ash	Phosphoric Acid	Obtained In
Pilsener, Bürgerliches Bräuhaus	1901	3.43	12.83	3.95	5.25	0.42	1.29	0.099		0.063	Chicago.
Pilsener, Genossenschafts-Brauerei.	1901	4.61	14.20	4.07	6.48	0.52	2.15	0.108		0.0855	"
Pilsener, Anton Dreher	1901	2.42	10.80	3.52	4.05	0.34	1.00	0.072		0.050	"
Thüringer	1895	3.45	12.59	3.76	5.07	0.41	1.67	0.09		0.08	"
Nürnberger, Tucher	1895	5.15	.....	4.31	7.07	0.51	2.06	0.135		0.095	"
Brauhaus Würzburg Export Beer.	1901	5.35	15.03	4.07	7.22	0.47	2.13	0.099		0.0075	"
Kulmbacher	1887	4.50	15.30	4.48	6.80	0.44	1.77	0.04	0.29	0.08	"
Muenchener, Löwen Bräuhaus	1901	4.13	13.53	3.95	5.95	0.44	1.57	0.090		0.060	"
Muenchener, Pschorr	1895	6.12	.....	3.47	7.61	0.46	2.69	0.108		0.08	"
Muenchener, Pschorr Bräu	1901	4.40	13.26	3.72	6.12	0.41	1.72	0.072		0.054	"

Brewing Industry in America. To narrate the history of the art of beermaking is to tell a story that is as old as the human race. To trace the art of brewing from its early days down to the present time it is necessary that one should pass through all the ages of antiquity, for the art that was practiced so crudely by the prehistoric peoples was followed with less primitive methods by both the Egyptians and the Assyrians. Later, the Greeks and Romans made their brews, while, from the earliest recorded times, the Teutonic races have pursued this art so successfully that praise of their skill has long taken the form of poem and prose, in song and story, while the tributes of esteem that are everywhere paid to Gambrinus, the acknowledged patron saint of brewing, is but another method by which the lovers of beer strive to testify their appreciation of the beverage for which his name stands synonymous.

As far as America is concerned the history of the brewing industry may be traced to 1620, for when the Pilgrim Fathers landed on Plymouth Rock they brought with them considerable knowledge as to the best methods of making their favorite beverages, the fiery potions which even they loved to drink, "and not a man afraid," as well as the lighter, but still sturdy brews with which every true Englishman sometimes made "merrie." Homebrewed as this beer was in the beginning, the natural growth of the colonies soon suggested that it be put to a more practical use, and it was thus that their knowledge of the brewing craft finally resulted in the establishment of the industry of beermaking.

In the New England colonies, where people were more addicted to the use of stronger spirits than beer, the colonial lawmakers adopted a statute by which they granted immunity from taxes and an additional prize in money to any brewer who should be sufficiently energetic to manufacture more than 500 barrels of "honest beer" in a single year, for they held that beer was a beverage which not only added to the prosperity of the country by giving the farmer a profitable market for the grain he might be able to raise, but which supplied the people with a drink of such mild form that, instead of leading to intoxication, it actually contributed to the spread of that temperate spirit upon which the "good order" of the colony so much depended. It was thus that the infant brewing industry was established and fostered by the colonial officials of Massachusetts, and, though the growth of the industry was slow compared to what one would imagine it should have been, it had expanded sufficiently by 1795 to produce nearly 2,000,000 gallons of beer per annum.

The great adversary against which the brewing industry has been obliged to contend has almost invariably been the result of matters of legislation. Ever since the days of the Egyptians the growth or decline in the art of beermaking may be traced directly to this cause. Under liberal laws, intelligently administered, the industry has prospered, while the legislative enactments inspired by ignorance or fanaticism have hampered the expansion of the trade more seriously than it could have been retarded by any other influence. Thus, while we have no reason to believe that any laws directly adverse to the brewing craft were passed prior to 1795, the fact that the legislation that was enacted was more favorable to the cheap distribution of distilled liquors had a tendency to give an advantage to the manufacturers and dealers in strong beverages against which the makers of the milder beers found it difficult to contend. It is true that some of the greatest minds in the country recognized the value of the brewing industry as an aid to the promotion of national temperance, and sought to aid it in every way in their power, but they were opposed by strong influences from several quarters, from the few who were opposed to the drinking of even such a mildly alcoholic beverage as beer, to the strong clique which represented the interests of the manufacturers of and dealers in the more potent liquors. During the Washington administration, Congress, in its consideration of the first federal revenue law, recognized the importance of fostering the brewing industry as an aid to public morality; again, in 1789 Madison publicly expressed the hope that the industry of brewing would extend its influence into every State of the Union, while Thomas Jefferson's firm stand in regard to the liquor question will never be forgotten. "No nation is sober," he said, "where the dearness of fermented drinks substitutes ardent spirits as a common beverage."

Prior to the middle of the 19th century, the term "beer" in the United States generally implied that beverage that is now more commonly known to us as "ale." In 1810, when the production of malt liquors in this country amounted to less than 6,000,000 gallons per annum, the 129 breweries which were manufacturing this product made practically nothing but ale and porter, and it was not until about 1846, when the increasing German immigration created the demand for the favorite beverage of these people, lager beer, that any brewer found it necessary to manufacture such a drink. With them, of course, the Germans had brought a practical knowledge of the art of lager beermaking, and as they were not satisfied with the native brews of the Americans, it was not long before lager beer breweries began to spring into existence in every community in which the German population was sufficiently numerous to support such an enterprise. In the beginning, of course, the Americans were inclined to be suspicious of this new beverage. It was milder than their brews, and, at first, they did not take kindly to it, but, gradually, as time passed, their prejudices were overcome, and, to-day, beer, or in other words, lager beer, has become so thoroughly the national beverage of the American people that the production of ale and porter in the United States does not now exceed 1,000,000 barrels per annum.

It was the outbreak of the Civil War that brought about the financial exigencies which resulted in the adoption of excise measures more favorable to the production of the lighter beverages. To raise a revenue sufficient to save the Government from the disasters which threatened required heroic measures. It was no time for the display of fanaticism; it was no time for race prejudices to come to the front. What was required was money, and, as the result, the internal revenue laws were created. As these threw burdens of taxation chiefly upon the manufacturers of ardent spirits, the industry of brewing took a new lease of life, and the effect of the passage of these laws, in July, 1862, may be seen in the development of the industry even up to the present day.

It was in 1862, at the moment when it was seen that there was to be an opportunity for the advancement of the brewing industry, that the Brewers' Association was formed. While this organization owed its existence partly to selfish interests, to the desire for self-protection and the better advancement of the trade, its fundamental purpose was a more patriotic one, its members binding themselves together to aid the Government in the perfection of the revenue laws so far as they applied to the manufacture of malt liquors, and to assist by their influence in the collection of such revenues, as well as to secure themselves against the possibility of unjust discrimination. Thus, from the beginning of its history, the Brewers' Association has remained true to its traditions, and, when the throes of the great struggle for national unity had ended, it still continued to co-operate with the Government in all matters relating to the internal revenue. When we remember the meagre 2,000,000 gallons of malt liquors that were produced in the United States in 1795, the following table of statistics indicate the steady development of this industry during the past century more eloquently than any words of mine could picture it:

PRODUCTION OF BEER, 1863—1904.

YEAR	Number of barrels	YEAR	Number of barrels
1863	2,006,625	1884	18,998,619
1864	3,141,181	1885	19,185,953
1865	3,657,181	1886	20,710,033
1866	5,115,140	1887	21,121,526
1867	6,207,408	1888	21,680,219
1868	6,146,663	1889	25,110,853
1869	6,342,055	1890	27,561,944
1870	6,574,617	1891	30,477,162
1871	7,740,260	1892	31,815,836
1872	8,659,427	1893	34,554,317
1873	9,063,123	1894	33,314,783
1874	9,600,907	1895	33,561,411
1875	9,152,697	1896	35,826,048
1876	9,702,352	1897	34,112,091
1877	9,810,060	1898	37,103,396
1878	10,241,471	1899	36,581,114
1879	11,103,084	1900	39,330,849
1880	13,347,111	1901	40,614,158
1881	14,311,028	1902	44,540,127
1882	16,152,085	1903	47,700,179
1883	17,737,872	1904	48,708,133

Whereas, in 1810, there were but 129 breweries in the United States there are now more than 2,250 such establishments, ranging in size from the little breweries which have been established by enterprising proprietors of German gardens to the enormous beer manufactories with an individual output of more than 1,000,000 barrels per annum. Some few of the breweries make ale, or porter, but the greater number make nothing but the favorite drink of the Germans, the lager beer which must now be considered as one of the great commercial factors in the United States. Moreover, while the American brewers formerly catered exclusively to a restricted local market, within the past 30 years the art of beermaking has attained such a point of perfection that this product can now be shipped, both in barrels and in bottles, from one end of the country to the other, while a further idea of the immense importance of this trade may be gathered from the facts that while the capital invested in this country in the beer industry is not less than $415,284,468, according to the figures reported by the 1900 census, the annual output of the country shows an aggregate value of more than $237,000,000. More than 50,000 men are directly engaged in the interests of brewing, and its contributions to the support of the United States, in internal revenue taxes alone, amount to more than $33,000,000 per annum. That the bottling branch of the industry has also assumed proportions which entitle it to serious consideration is shown by the fact that the product of one brewery alone now amounts to more than 42,000,000 bottles per annum.

While such figures are valuable in the sense that they are reliable manifestations of the growth of the brewing industry, there is a deeper and broader side to the question of its development that is a matter of far greater importance, for the modern brewer, while he is proud of the fact that his craft has grown to be one of the great industries of this great nation, still takes even greater pride in the knowledge that the science of brewing has made more marked scientific advancement during the past 35 years of its history than it had made in all the years that had previously elapsed since those days of "merrie England" when Falstaff and his coterie of jolly fellows joked together over their generous tankards of some foaming brew.

For example, we may say that it has been only within the past 35 years that anything approaching scientific principles have ever been applied to the art of brewing. Since 1870, however, the establishment of brewers' schools to teach the higher knowledge of the craft have brought theory and practice into such close association that a field of competition has been opened that had never existed prior to that time. Thus, during the sixties the principles governing the production of beer were practically the same as those which had been followed by our forefathers in their breweries in 1905, for while every branch of applicable science, including chemistry, botany and mechanics had experienced marvelous development, these changes meant nothing to the art of brewing, except in the general sense that they were preparing the foundation upon which the more scientific art might be constructed.

The first great improvement in the art of brewing, and especially that portion of it to which the physiology of fermentation may be applied, was the result of the labors of Pasteur in Paris, and Hansen at Copenhagen. From the earliest days beer has been known to be a perishable product, but the character of the causes which made it spoil was a problem that nobody had been able to solve. By his discoveries of the physiology of the organisms of fermentation, Pasteur not only proved that these diseases of beer might rationally be traced to a sort of bacteria, but indicated the manner in which such diseases might be avoided through the application of a process of wort cooling and fermentation, while Hansen went a step farther by not only finding another cause for such diseases in the brewers' yeast, which might easily become, by contact, under certain circumstances, with similar organisms closely resembling it, far more injurious than any bacteria, but brought his labors to a most logical conclusion by developing a process of cultivating yeast in large quantities and in such absolute purity from a single germ that he prevented the introduction of wild yeast into the brew. The immediate adoption of these innovations by the leading brewers of the United States resulted in some very material changes in the practical operations of the breweries. Thus, the discovery of the principle of preventing infection brought about the substitution of suitably closed apparatus in place of the old-fashioned open cooler, but this improvement was simply one step in the efforts of the manufacturers to meet the requirements of the new scientific methods of brewing. It was followed by more ingeniously constructed machinery, all tending toward a cleaner and better product. There were processes for the production of filtered air; there were other processes for the sterilization of water, for everything that now entered into the product must be germ-proof, absolute protection against infection being the keynote of the new science. Under the present methods, therefore, from the very moment that the beer leaves the brew-kettle, to pass over the coolers, and through the process of fermenting and lagering, and even up to the very moment that it is served as a refreshing and revivifying beverage, no effort is spared to protect it from infection. See BREWING and MALTING.

Physiology and theoretical chemistry have also exerted their influence to bring about the present wonderful development in the science of brewing. During the past few decades the most complicated processes in the malting of barley, in mashing and in fermentation have been so thoroughly explored that the knowledge derived from these researches has created a magnificent foundation upon which the malster and the brewer have been able to build more solidly than ever before in the history

of the craft. In this connection, moreover, reference must be made to an invention which has effected more radical changes in the brewing industry than almost any one single factor, for without it many of the innovations and improvements which are regarded as of such vital importance to-day could never have been made. This invention is the ice machine, without which artificial refrigeration upon any extraordinarily extensive scale, such as exist in many of the big brewing plants at this time, would have been entirely impracticable. It was since 1870 that the imperfect ice-making machine which was shown by the French inventor, Carre, was regarded as so great a curiosity that persons who were interested in such things traveled long distances to inspect it. To-day, however, conditions have changed so materially that it is only the very insignificant brewing establishments that are not equipped with model ice machines.

One of the distinctly American innovations which have tended so greatly to improve the science of brewing during the past few decades is the new method of collecting and utilizing in its purity all the carbonic-acid gas formed during the process of fermentation. By the discovery of this purely American method it has become possible to abandon the old-fashioned "kraeusen" process of carbonating, which was formerly the only method in general use. In other words, the finished product of the brewery may now be charged with the best and purest natural carbonic-acid gas that it is possible to obtain, and as this method of collecting this by-product of fermentation produces such a superabundance of the carbonic-acid gas that it may readily be liquefied, there is no reason why every other product of that kind should not eventually be crowded out of the market.

As this is not the only occasion upon which the American ingenuity has solved problems relating to the science of brewing over which some of the greatest European authorities have experimented vainly for many years, it is not strange that the brewers of the United States should be able to produce some of the best, and, at the same time, some of the most durable beer in the world. Not only have the latest and most scientific methods in brewing that can be credited to the European investigators been in use in the country, almost from the very moment of their discovery, but several of the processes which have actually originated in this country have since been accepted by foreign scientists as the most rational methods known. In 1893, Prof. Delbrueck of Berlin, and Prof. Schwackhoefer or Vienna, were sent to America by their respective governments to make a detailed inquiry into American brewing methods. Naturally every facility was offered them, and in their special report, they gave the brewers of the United States much of the credit which they deserve for having developed the primitive craft to such a high standard of perfection.   JOHN A. MANZ,

Graduate of the Royal Brewing Academy, Weihenstephan, Bavaria; Atlantic City Brewing Co.

Brew'ster, Benjamin Harris, American lawyer: b. Salem County, N. J., 13 Oct. 1816; d. Philadelphia, 4 April 1888. He graduated at Princeton in 1834, was admitted to the Philadelphia bar (1838), and for nearly half a century practised with ardor and success the profession he loved. In 1846 he was one of a commission to adjudicate the claims of the Cherokee Indians against the United States; in 1867 he became attorney-general of Pennsylvania, and in December 1881 President Arthur made him attorney-general of the United States. Shortly after the death of President Garfield, Attorney-General Wayne MacVeagh retained Brewster to assist in the prosecution of the "Star Route" conspirators. In boyhood he was severely injured by burns received while bravely attempting to rescue his sister from a fire into which she had fallen. He was an impressive orator, and possessed scholarly attainments of a high order. Both Princeton and Dickinson colleges conferred the degree of LL.D. upon him.

Brewster, Chauncey Bunce, American bishop: b. Windham, Conn., 5 Sept. 1848. He is a direct descendant of Elder Brewster of Plymouth Colony fame. He graduated at Yale in 1868, Berkeley Divinity School, 1872, and was ordained priest, 1873. He was rector of Christ Church, Rye, N. Y., 1873–81; Christ Church, Detroit, 1881–5; Grace Church, Baltimore, 1885–8; Grace Church, Brooklyn, N. Y., 1888–97. On 8 June 1897 he was elected coadjutor-bishop of Connecticut, and consecrated in New Haven, 28 Oct. 1897. Upon the death of Bishop Williams, in 1899, Bishop Brewster became diocesan of Connecticut. Beside sermons and pastoral charges, he has written 'The Key of Life' (1885); 'Good Friday Addresses' (1894): 'Aspects of Revelation' (1901), being the Baldwin lectures before the University of Michigan. Yale and Trinity colleges, have conferred the degree of D.D. upon him.

Brewster, Sir David, Scottish natural philosopher: b. Jedburgh, 11 Dec. 1781; d. Allerly, near Melrose, 10 Feb. 1868. He entered the University of Edinburgh, where the lectures of Robison and Playfair attracted him to scientific pursuits. His first investigations were on the subject of the polarization of light, upon which he communicated some important observations to the 'Transactions of the Royal Society of Edinburgh.' In 1808 he became editor of the Edinburgh 'Encyclopedia,' to which he contributed a number of valuable articles. In 1816, while repeating the experiments of Biot on the action of fluids on light, he made those observations which resulted in the invention of the kaleidoscope. In 1819, in conjunction with Jameson, he founded the Edinburgh 'Philosophical Journal,' of which he was sole editor (1824–32). Brewster was one of the founders of the British Association, whose first meeting was held at York in 1831, and he presided over it on the occasion of its 20th meeting, held at Edinburgh in 1850. In 1832 he received the honor of knighthood along with a pension from the government. Both before and after this time his services to science obtained from many quarters the most honorable recognition. The French Institute, of which he had been a corresponding member since 1825, appointed him one of its eight foreign associates, 4 Jan. 1849,

and he was also among the members of the academies of St. Petersburg, Berlin, Vienna, Stockholm, and Copenhagen. From Prussia he received the Order of Merit in 1847, and in 1855 the cross of an officer of the Legion of Honor was bestowed on him by Napoleon III. From 1838 to 1859 he was principal of the united colleges of St. Leonard's and St. Salvador at St. Andrews, and in the latter year he was unanimously chosen principal of the University of Edinburgh — an office which he continued to hold till his death. His chief works are: 'Treatise on the Kaleidoscope'; 'Letters and Life of Euler'; 'Letters on Natural Magic'; 'Treatise on Optics'; 'Martyrs of Science'; 'More Worlds than One'; 'Memoirs of the Life, Writings, and Discoveries of Sir Isaac Newton' (1855); besides numerous communications to the Royal Societies of London and Edinburgh, contributions to the 'Encyclopedia Britannica,' the Edinburgh and North British 'Reviews,' and other periodicals.

Brewster, Frederick Carroll, American lawyer: b. Philadelphia, Pa., 15 May 1825; d. Charlotte, N. C., 30 Dec. 1898. He graduated at the University of Pennsylvania, read law with his father, and was admitted to the Philadelphia bar, 1844, of which he became a leader and one of its brightest ornaments. He was elected city solicitor (1862); judge of the court of common pleas (1866–9); attorney-general of the State (1869–70). He was successful as counsel in the famous Stephen Girard will case, and secured the decision in the Chestnut Street bridge case, wherein a decree was entered in the United States supreme court allowing the city of Philadelphia to cross the Schuylkill River by bridge. He published 'Reports of Equity, Election, and other Cases in the Courts of the County of Philadelphia' (1869); 'Digest of Pennsylvania Supreme Court Cases' (1869); 'Brewster's Blackstone, with Annotations of Decisions on the Rule in Shelly's Case' (1887); 'A Treatise on Practise in the Pennsylvania Courts' (1887–8).

Brewster, William, elder of the Plymouth pilgrims: b. Scrooby, England, 1560; d. Plymouth, Mass., 16 April 1644. He was educated at Cambridge, and entered the service of William Davison, ambassador in Holland, but presently retired to Scrooby manor house in Nottinghamshire, where his attention was chiefly occupied by the interests of religion. He was one of the company who with William Bradford attempted to find an escape to Holland, and were thrown into prison at Boston. Having obtained his liberty, he first assisted the poor of the society in their embarkation, and then followed them to Holland. Here he opened a school at Leyden, for instruction in English, and also set up a printing press. He was chosen a ruling elder in the Church at Leyden, and came to New England in 1620 with the first company of the Pilgrims. Until 1629 the principal care of the Church at Plymouth devolved upon him, though, as he was not a regular minister, he could never be persuaded to administer the sacraments. See Steele, 'Chief of the Pilgrims'; 'Life of William Brewster' (1857).

Brewster's Law. See LIGHT.

Brialmont, Henri Alexis, ŏṅ-rē ä-lĕk-sē brē-al-môṅ, Belgian military writer: b. Venlò, 25 May 1821. He entered the army in 1843 as lieutenant of engineers, and in 1877 became lieutenant-general. Among his works are 'Considérations Politiques et Militaires sur la Belgique' (1851–2); 'Précis d'Art Militaire' (1850); 'Histoire du Duc de Wellington' (1856), translated into English by Gleig; 'Etudes sur la Défense des Etats et sur la Fortification' (1863); and many works on fortification. He has fortified Namur, Bucharest, Liège, and other places.

Bri'an (surnamed BOROIMHÉ or BORU): b. 926; d. 23 April 1014. He figures in early Irish annals as a celebrated chieftain, and son of Kennedy, king of Munster. He succeeded to both Munsters, nearly identical with counties Tipperary and Clare, in 978. Having defeated the Danes of Limerick and Waterford, he turned his arms against O'Maclachaghlin, or Malachi, who had a nominal supremacy over the whole island, and became king in his stead, levying tribute, or boroimhé, from which circumstance he derived his surname from the rulers of all the different provinces. He distinguished himself as much in peace as in war, contributed greatly to the progress of civilization, and made many internal improvements. He fell at Clontarf, after gaining a signal victory over the Danes, who had leagued with a revolted chief called Maelmora.

Brianchon, Charles Julien, shärl zhü-lē-än̄ brẹ-än̄-shón̄, French mathematician: b. Sèvres, 1785; d. 1865. Besides some important papers contributed to French mathematical journals, he has left small treatises on lines of the second order (1817), and the application of the theory of transversals (1818). He is best known by a theorem, the correlative of Pascal's which he published in 1806. The theorem is: If a hexagon is circumscribed to a conic, the straight lines joining the three pairs of opposite vertices are concurrent.

Briançon, brẹ-än̄-són̄, a town in France, in the department of Hautes-Alpes, on the right bank of the Durance, 35 miles northeast from Gap, and near the Italian frontier. It is a fortress of the first class, occupying an eminence at the foot of the Col de Genèvre, 4,284 feet above the level of the sea, and has sometimes been called the Gibraltar of the Alps, forming, as it does, a central point from which troops can be marched to all their most important passes. Briançon is a town of great antiquity. According to Pliny it was founded by the Greeks. Pop. (1896) 7,177.

Briansk, bryänsk, a town in Russia, in the government of, and 70 miles west-northwest from Orel, on the right bank of the Desna. It is surrounded with an earthen rampart, contains 16 churches, a monastery, with a seminary, and two poorhouses. It has a considerable trade in grain, hemp, hemp-oil (sent to St. Petersburg and Riga), honey, and wax; and in linen, cables, and cordage, rowware, bark, mats. lime, and tar, which are sent to Kherson, Odessa, and other parts of the Black Sea. It contains imperial building-yards, for which the oak forests in the neighborhood supply material. Near it are a cannon-foundry and a manufactory of small arms. Pop. (1897) 23,520.

Briare, brẹ-är, a town of France, in the department of Loiret, on the Loire, 25 miles south of Montargis. The canal, to which the town is indebted for its importance, is the oldest work of the kind in France, having been begun in the reign of Henry IV., though it was not finished till 1740. It establishes, by means of its junction with the canal of Loing at Montargis, a communication between the Loire and the Seine, and conveys the various products of the province, watered by the former, to Paris.

Briareus, brī-ā'rẹ-ŭs (also called ÆGÆON), a giant with 100 arms and 50 heads, the son of Uranus and Gæa. His two brothers, Cottus and Gyes, were formed in a similar manner, and their formidable appearance struck their father with such terror that he imprisoned them at their birth in the bowels of the earth. In the war with the Titans Jupiter (Zeus) set them free, and by their assistance gained the victory. When Juno, Neptune, and Minerva conspired to bind the sovereign of the gods, Thetis brought Briareus from the depths of the sea (how he came there is not known) to the relief of the trembling Jove. Virgil places Briareus in the vestibule of hell. He was employed with his hundred-handed brothers in watching the Titans in Tartarus. Various other fables are told of these gods, who are supposed to be personifications of the extraordinary phenomena of nature manifested in volcanoes, earthquakes, and other commotions.

Bribe, a reward given to a public officer or functionary, to induce him to violate his official duty for the benefit or in compliance with the wishes of the party by whom or on whose behalf the bribe is given or promised. Bribery, at common law, is the receiving or offering any undue reward by or to any person whomsoever, whose ordinary profession or business relates to the administration of public justice in order to influence his behavior in office and to incline him to act contrary to his duty and the known rules of honesty and integrity. Certain writers limit bribery at common law to persons concerned in the administration of justice. The offense is much broader than this according to the weight of authority. It is said by Bishop to be the voluntary receiving or giving of any thing of value in payment for an official act done or to be done, and that it is not confined to judicial officers or other persons concerned in the administration of justice, but that it extends to all officers connected with the administration of the government, executive, legislative, and judicial. and under the appropriate circumstances, military. In nearly all of the States of the American Union, however, the offense is now defined by statute, so that a resort to common law is not often necessary, except for general principles. Bribery may be committed with respect to officers *de facto* as well as officers *de jure.* The offense of the giver and of the receiver of the bribe has the same name. For the sake of distinction, that of the former — that is, the briber — might be called active bribery; while that of the latter — that is, the person bribed — might be called passive bribery. The thing offered or accepted need not be money, but may be property, services or anything else of value. It must be of some value, but as the essence of the offense is its tendency to prevent justice in any of the departments of government, executive, legislative, or judicial, the degree of value of the bribe is not essential. It has been held, however, in Indiana, under a statute prohibiting the giving or receiving anything of value, that an officer who received a note could not be convicted, because the note, not being enforceable, was of no value.

At common law and under the statutes, in order to constitute bribery there must be a corrupt intent to influence the officer or other person, or on his part, to be influenced, in the discharge of his official duties. It is not essential, however, unless specially required by a statute, that the act induced, or sought to be induced, shall favor, aid, or benefit the person giving the bribe himself. The act which is induced or sought to be induced by the bribe must be an act in discharge of a legal duty. It is not bribery if the act is in discharge of a mere moral duty. Bribery is regarded in the United States as being of such a serious nature that it is made a felony in nearly all of the States, and the punishment for the various species of bribery may be, in New York, and many other States, imprisonment for a period not exceeding 10 years. «Bribery at common law, in a judge in relation to a cause pending before him, was regarded as an offense of so grave a nature that it was sometimes punished as high treason before the 25 Edw. III., and at this day is certainly a very high offense, and punishable not only with forfeiture of the offender's office of justice, but also with fine and imprisonment,» etc. Bribery in England is punished in inferior officers with fine and imprisonment, but in judges, especially the superior ones, it has always been looked upon as a heinous offense. In the United States in many jurisdictions bribery at elections, either effected or attempted, is a disqualification for office, and an election procured by bribery is void. An attempt to bribe, though unsuccessful, has been held to be criminal, and is punished in many States as severely as the substantive offense. The reason for the law is plain. The offer is a great temptation to the weak or the depraved. It tends to corrupt, and as the law abhors the least tendency to corruption, it punishes the act which is calculated to debase, and which may affect, viciously, the morals of the community.

Brice, Arthur John Montefiore, English barrister and traveler: b. 27 June 1859. He founded and for some time edited the 'Educational Review,' and has traveled extensively in Europe, Asia, the Arctic regions, and North and South America. He has published 'Stanley, the African Explorer' (1888); 'Florida and the English' (1888); 'David Livingstone' (1889); 'Leaders into Unknown Lands' (1891); 'Geographical Methods' (1895); 'The Great Frozen Land' (edited 1895).

Brice, Calvin Stewart, American capitalist: b. Denmark, Ohio, 17 Sept. 1845; d. New York, 15 Dec. 1898. He practised law in Cincinnati from 1866 to 1880, when he became interested in railroad and various other financial undertakings. He was presidential elector on the Tilden ticket in 1876 and the Cleveland ticket in 1884 and chairman of the Democratic National Committee in 1888. In 1890 he was elected United States Senator from Ohio, and served on the Appropriations, Pensions, Pacific Railroad, and Public Buildings and Grounds committees. Shortly before his death he formed a syndicate which secured vast railroad and mining concessions in China.

Brice, Saint, French prelate: b. Tours; d. there, 13 Nov. 444. He is commemorated on 13 November. On the death of Saint Martin he was made Bishop of Tours. St. Brice's Day, 1002, is memorable in old English history for a great massacre of the Danes. It was believed that it was a concerted attempt to exterminate all the Danes in England; but, failing of its bloody purpose, it led to reprisals by the Danish King Sweyn.

Brice, Jefferson, a figure in Dickens' 'Martin Chuzzlewit,' intended as a caricature of an American journalist of 60 years ago.

Brick, a rectangular mass of clay, dried in the sun or baked in a kiln, and used for building purposes. To mold wet clay into cubes for the erection of walls and houses was one of the first efforts of man at architecture. There still exist in perfect preservation sun-dried bricks made by the Babylonians and Egyptians over 4,000 years ago. On some of these are valuable inscriptions relating to the cause of their making, family history, etc. In many cases straw was mingled with the clay in order to give it greater coherence. The story of the Egyptian taskmasters and the brick-making Israelites told in Exodus i. 14; v. 4-19, is too well known for further reference here. Scarcely less ancient than these Babylonian and Egyptian bricks are the «adobe» bricks of Yucatan and Mexico. There still exist in Colorado, Arizona, New Mexico, Texas, and California hundreds of these 'dobe houses, some of them more than 300 years old and still inhabited. The Aztecs and other American aborigines were adepts at using this material, and constructed wonderful architecture out of it. The present Indian town of Laguna, in New Mexico, illustrates the decadence of this art, which the Spanish found so perfect in Old Mexico.

The modern methods of building-construction in America, by which towering skeletons of steel are used as a framework, compel the use of vast quantities of brick as «filler.» Not even the manufacturers can give an accurate estimate of the number of bricks made in the United States annually, but a conservative figure would be 25,000,000,000. Of this enormous output about $1,000,000 worth is exported. At Peterborough, England, 800,000,000 brick are made annually.

Varieties.— There are about 100 different varieties of brick now made in the United States, so marvelously has this industry grown of late. One can now order bricks of almost any conceivable size, shape, or hardness. The material varies. Common brick for rough wall work and filling comes from the soft sand clays along the Hudson and in New England, Kansas, and the Far West. Fine face-brick for the fronts of buildings is usually made from the better clays of Staten Island, New Jersey, and Pennsylvania. Powerful machinery now grinds up shale, fire-clay, quartz, spar, calcine, lime, ochre, and like hard materials to form the imperishable fire-brick and vitrified brick. The former is used between the beams and joists of the modern «sky-scraper,» to make the building impervious to fire, as this brick has been already so heated that further heat, even in a mighty conflagration, affects it little. Vitrified brick is used mostly for street pavements; some cities, like

New Haven, Conn., being paved almost entirely with it. This material wears for years, and is probably the most economical paving known. Terra-cotta tiling and pipe for drains are also included as part of their output by many brick manufacturers, as well as the beautiful colored and glazed bricks used for mantels and ornamental work. Probably 80 per cent of all the brick made is the rough and semi-rough for wall work. Some of the largest American cities have stringent fire laws which compel all buildings in the corporate limits to be built of brick, stone, or iron. Denver, Col., and other western cities are in this class, a majority of their houses being of brick.

Manufacture.— Scattered over almost every part of the United States and Canada are brickyards. There are about 12,000 manufacturers of brick in the United States, 8,000 of whom are large concerns using more or less machinery. Some of these latter have yards in which 10 machines are working, each machine capable of turning out 100,000 finished bricks per day. This means 1,000,000 bricks a day for one yard. As the average period of work per year is eight months, such a yard can (and usually does) produce 200,000,000 bricks each season. Scarcely any of the larger firms but has at least one of these machines. One enormous plant just established at Dover Point, Mass., covers a vast area, and has huge traveling cranes which move 20-ton loads of brick with gentleness and precision. Electric lights and power thus enable a few men to do the work of a hundred by the old methods.

Brick-clay consists largely of hydrated silicate of alumina, with iron in varying quantities, and sand, or free silica. It varies greatly in adhesiveness, hardness, and value. The hand method of working the clay into brick is still used by about 4,000 small yards in the United States. By it one or two men can mold and kiln about 50,000 rough bricks in a season, though under favorable conditions they may make considerably more. The clay is usually dug in the autumn and allowed to freeze and thaw until spring, thus disintegrating the mass thoroughly through the action of frost. It is then either spaded until all lumps are removed, or put into a horse-power pug-mill, where it is ground up more thoroughly. The mold is simply a box, open at both ends, the size of the brick desired. The protruding clay is planed off with a straight-edge, and the cube of wet clay is then allowed to dry in sheds for some hours before it is placed in a kiln for firing. This latter process usually takes from 10 to 15 days, and must be carefully attended to, so that the brick shall not become cooled until the operation is finished. After cooling, stacking, and counting, the bricks are ready for the market.

Of the 8,000 concerns in the United States who may properly be termed manufacturers, about 50 per cent use what is known as the "stiff plastic" process of making brick, which is now recognized as the best and most economical of all. It saves from 20 per cent to 40 per cent in labor and makes a perfectly homogeneous brick. If the material to be worked is of a hard or flinty nature (shale), it is first ground in a "dry-pan," after which it is raised by means of a cup elevator and passed through a screen to the pug-mill, or mixer, the tailings from the screens being returned to the dry-pan. If the material is sufficiently open, as

good brick-clay should be, it can be run direct to the pug-mill with little disintegration or grinding. The pug-mill is usually 10 or 12 feet long and contains a series of mixing knives, by which the clay and water are mixed to a proper consistency. From this mixer the clay passes into the brick machine, where it is compressed by a heavy auger into a solid and continuous column, being forced on to the cutting-table through a die of proper size to form the length and width of the brick. The cutting is done by fine steel piano-wires on a revolving wheel, working automatically. One of these machines is capable of turning out an average of 100,000 bricks per day. A belt traveling a little faster than the column is moving, separates the severed cubes and carries them to the re-press. This latter squares their corners and edges, gives them a smooth, polished surface, and imprints upon them any lettering or design desired. The cubes are not put through the re-press unless intended for front- or face-brick. The common, rough brick go immediately from the cutting-table to the dryer, which consists of a series of tunnels built of brick 4 feet wide and 5 feet high by 120 feet long. These tunnels are heated by a furnace underneath, by steam pipes, or (in large plants) by a blower which conveys the waste heat from the cooling kiln. The cubes are loaded on little cars and run into these tunnels, where they remain till drawn out at the end of 24 hours thoroughly dried. Each tunnel holds about 5,000 bricks. The bricks are then ready for the kilns, which are of various designs. The down-draft is a favorite modern method of construction. This requires small structures, round, 10 or 12 feet high and 30 feet in diameter, held in place by heavy iron bands to prevent warping from the intense heat. The floors are made of perforated blocks. Superheated air from the furnaces is forced from the top down through the brick piled within, through the floor, and either out through a chimney or into other kilns or dryers. The interior of these kilns under fire is a solid sheet of twisting flame and heat, turning the brick a cherry red, if of common clay, and white, if of harder material. This is kept up for from six to ten days, when the fires are drawn and the mass allowed to cool. The continuous kiln of from 16 to 22 chambers has been tried considerably of late, and has produced some exceptionally economical results. This stiff plastic method enables the handling of the clay cubes as they leave the cutter without preliminary drying. This and its simplicity make it very popular, and it is rapidly superseding all other methods. The machine is being made for export to Spain and other countries, and is in use in most of the larger yards in America.

About 40 per cent of the 8,000 manufacturers mentioned above are compelled by the nature of their material to use the "soft-mud process." Clays of a short, sandy nature, or those with a disposition to excessive lamination, are readily treated by this system, and beautiful sand-faced brick results. As a rule the Hudson River yards use this system, as well as many in New England and the Middle West. The clay passes first through the separator to free it of lumps, whence it is elevated to the pug-mill compartment of the brick machine. In the pug-chamber it is thoroughly mixed, and water added to make it of the proper consistency to mold easily. The machine presses it into wooden molds, which are sanded inside to prevent adhesion of the clay to the mold, and are removed automatically. They are then placed on a revolving dumping-table, where they are dumped on to pallets, the empty mold being again sanded and passed to the machine for use again. Then the brick goes to the dryer and afterward to the kiln. It takes much longer to make brick by this mold method, but a very fine brick is produced, with a perfectly homogeneous body to it.

Not more than 10 per cent of the manufacturers can or do use the expensive "dry press" method, which takes the finer clays and presses them with a force of 20,000 pounds to the square inch into steel molds. The clay is nearly dry when this is done, so that the cakes can be handled with ease at once. The objection urged by some against this method is that the brick resulting is too porous and apt to absorb moisture, and "sweat" or disintegrate. Still, for the finer clays this method possesses advantages which will cause it to be used for a long time, and it may never be abandoned. The beautiful clays of Staten Island and in portions of New Jersey and Pennsylvania are nearly white, very fine, and smooth in texture. These work up into most artistic front- or face-brick for the exterior of fine buildings, or for decorative mantel and chimney work in the interiors. It is the most costly brick known to the trade. The machinery used in this process is simple, consisting of presses, dies, and molds. It naturally requires less time to dry and kiln these bricks, but the process is not a rapid one.

Fire-brick, paving-brick, fire-proof lathing, and other forms of excessively hard brick are made from shale, quartz, and difficult material generally. This has to be ground up by ponderous dry-pans before it can be cast into shape. The mold system is of necessity most used in making this class of goods, though some excellent work is turned out by the stiff plastic method above described. The lathing contains a proportion of sawdust to enable nails to be driven into it. In this category should come the terra-cotta brick for roofing, etc. Enormous quantities of fire-proof brick are now being made for the huge new buildings of our modern cities. Its manufacture is a distinct trade in itself. Modern American-made brick, of whatever design or quality, is 10 times harder and more durable than that of most other countries, though produced at a fraction of the cost. But for the great weight of brick our exports would be enormous. Each year American ingenuity perfects additional machinery enabling better and cheaper brick to be made. The brick of to-day will outwear five of those made even 10 years ago, as a rule. For further information regarding the uses of brick, see BUILDING MATERIALS; BRICK-MAKING MACHINERY; CLAY-WORKING MACHINERY; etc.

Brick-laying and Brick-work. See MASONRY AND BUILDING.

Brick-making Machinery, machines and structures employed to prepare, mold, and dry, plastic clay into rectangular blocks of various sizes which, after being hardened by baking in ovens or kilns, are commercially known as bricks, and are extensively used for building purposes.

For information relative to the sizes, composition, qualities, and various uses of bricks, and the general history of brick-manufacture, see BRICK.

The different types of brick-making machines are exceedingly numerous, but they may be conveniently divided into three classes: soft-clay molding machines, die-working machines, and dry-clay working machines. In the soft-clay molding machines, which are also known as sand-molding machines, clay taken directly from the bank is mixed with water and tempered in the machine, and then pressed into sanded molds which are fed in automatically beneath the press-box. The molds thus filled under pressure are then moved forward to a delivery table, where they are emptied and then returned for refilling. This process makes bricks of a fine homogeneous quality, but is slow, and the machines are as a rule used by the smaller manufacturers.

Die-working machines are of two types: those in which the clay is moved out continuously by means of a rotating auger, and those in which the clay is pressed out in bars of specific lengths by the reciprocating motion of a plunger.

These machines are employed in what is commonly known as the stiff-tempered process of brick-making, the product of which is, perhaps, that most generally approved by brickmakers, builders, engineers, and architects. In both types, the bar of clay is cut up into bricks of the desired size by wires which, according to the mechanical contrivances adopted to operate them, give to these machines the additional designations — end-cut and side-cut.

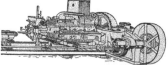

FIG. 1.—Auger Brick Machine.

Fig. 1 shows a modern auger machine. It consists essentially of a hopper (a) entering the tempering case (b) which contains the tempering shaft (c) carrying the tempering knives (d) on its side, and the expressing screw (f) on its end opposite to the forming die (g). The hopper is square, but larger at the bottom than at the top, in order to prevent jamming, and being provided with rounded corners, prevents the clay from sticking in them. It opens into the tempering case at one side of its centre line, so that the clay fed into the machine is forced into contact with the revolving tempering knives on the upward part of their motion. This tends to agitate the clay in the hopper, thus preventing clogging and an irregular supply of clay to the tempering device. Additional clogging of clay in the hopper is obviated by the use of an irregular faced cast-iron roller situated at the bottom of the hopper immediately above the line of tempering knives, and on the side towards which the knives revolve. The tempering knives force the clay against the roller to which it adheres, thus enabling them to cut through the solid mass of fine clay and lumps, but, as this roller revolves about once every minute, the adhering clay is brought within the path of the knives which carries it off and tempers it, and also effectually cleans the throat of the hopper of the most sticky and tenacious clays.

The tempering part of the machine consists of a strong cast-iron, cone-shaped case within which the tempering device revolves. This device consists of a horizontal shaft into which are set radially and spirally, strong tempering knives of wrought-iron or steel. The revolution of the shaft forces the knives through the clay, which being free from much water, and therefore quite stiff, does not slip before the knives, but is cut by them through and through and thus thoroughly tempered, the air escaping back through the untempered clay. The spiral position of the knives also forces the clay forwards so that by the time it reaches the smaller end of the tempering case it is ready to be formed into bricks.

At this point the clay is taken up by the expressing screw, and is slid forward within the steam-heated screw-case and delivered as a solid round column to the forming-die from which it issues in the form of a continuous bar of clay of the required dimensions.

Since, in accordance with the laws governing the movement of fluids under pressure, the clay as it moves through the die is retarded by friction at the corners, and moves more freely at the centre, a peculiar shaped "former" is employed to facilitate the flow of the clay to the corners, and retard it opposite to the long sides of the die, thus re-enforcing the angles of the bar of clay and ensuring square and well defined corners to the bricks. This former is secured to the screw-case by a hinge and swinging-bolt which enables it to be quickly opened for the removal of stones, and like the screw-case,

Fig. 2.—Automatic Wire Cutter for End-cut Bricks.

being heated by steam, facilitates the sliding and the forming of the clay. As the bar of clay emerges from the forming-die, it passes through a small chamber called the "sander," filled with fine dry sand which adheres to the surface of the bar, and renders the bricks when green, much nicer to handle and prevents them from sticking together on the barrows, in the hacking, or on the drying cars, and improves their color when burnt.

Of the various devices employed to cut the clay bar thus formed, into bricks, the automatic end-cut wire cutter is probably the best. (See Fig. 2.) It consists of a regulating frame or table on to which the bar of clay is carried from the sander and by which the cut-off is controlled. The belt carrying the bar of clay runs around a measuring wheel which determines the exact lengths to be cut according to the desired size of bricks. The cut-off wires are strained on

steel bows or springs to a tension, which while sufficient to cut, yet yields readily to obstructions such as stones, either cutting around them, or springing over them and operate hour in and hour out automatically and without any trouble. A broken wire may be replaced at once without stopping the machine. The wires are carried by their springs on a sprocket-wheel over and through the bar of clay, and are guided so as to make a square cut, by a cam encased in an oil-tight case. The partly severed brick is supported and held against the unsevered bar until completely cut off, when it is dropped on to the off-bearing belt which immediately carries it off, the cutting wire returning above the bar between the brick and the uncut end of the bar.

Off-bearing belts are of the endless type and may be arranged to carry the bricks cut off from the continuous clay bar, to distances as great as two hundred feet across the yard, from which they may be wheeled to convenient points for hacking (the stacking up of green bricks on platform cars for artificial drying), or loaded directly upon the dryer cars as may be required.

An auger end-cut machine of this type is capable of an average daily product of 75,000 bricks. Its weight complete is about 20,000 pounds, and it is equipped with a friction-clutch driving-pulley 48 inches diameter, by 12 inches face. Its length from outer edge of driving-pulley to end of 16-feet length off-bearing frame is about 52 feet, and the rear end of the machine occupies a floor space of 8 feet. (See Fig. 2.)

Of side-cut devices, the rotary cutter is perhaps the most simple in construction, and the most reliable in operation. Its action is entirely automatic and extremely sensitive to regulation. It produces bricks of uniform thickness and smooth angles. Being independent of reciprocating action, the cutter may be run at any desired speed, and as the wires always move downwards and forwards, making an angle with the top surface and outer edge of the bar, all obstructions are pushed from the surface into the body of the bar, thus preventing the ruffled edges common to many side-cut bricks.

In the machine shown in Fig. 3, the pair of bevel gears (a) are encased in a dirt tight case when the machine is in operation. These gears together with the measuring wheel situated immediately under the bar of clay, forms the con-

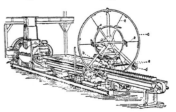

Fig. 3.—Automatic Side-cut Brick Machine.

nection between the cutting reel and the origin of motion of the moving bar of clay, and enables the revolving cutter to instantly and auto.

matically adapt itself to any changes of speed in the movement of the clay bar. The bar of clay is supported on the bottom face and at one side thus ensuring a smooth sharp cut. The slit through which the wire passes is just wide enough to accommodate the thickness of the wire used. The two vertical side-plates (b) are hinged so that they will open outward if a stone or other hard substance is pushed against them by the cutting wire, and after expelling the same return instantly to the normal position of support. The measuring wheel is of a given diameter for each thickness of brick, thus requiring a change of the wheel if a change in the size of the brick is desired. Such a change is generally accomplished in about half an hour. Recent improvements have developed cutters that enable manufacturers of paving bricks, to make "builders" and "pavers" simultaneously. For example, two bricks out of every six cut at each revolution of the cutter may be 2 inches thick, and the other four 4 inches thick, or any other combination that may be desired. The adjustable variations in thickness are by graduations of sixteenths of an inch, and the scope of the cutter runs from bricks 2 inches thick to blocks 5 inches in thickness. The large ring (c) is turned with a 2-inch V groove in its outer edge, and is supported by the two smaller wheels (d) engaging in the groove so that the weight of the larger wheel is entirely supported by them, thus relieving the cutting wires from all strains other than that due to the cutting of the bricks. The looped wires (e) are about 12 inches long, and are attached to tempered steel springs which while keeping the wires taut, yet permit a necessary amount of flexibility. A wiper, not shown in the illustration, automatically cleans the wires between each cut. The slow motion of seventeen turns per minute of the cutting reel, cuts one hundred bricks per minute, and may be operated to cut twice that number with perfect safety.

An auger machine equipped with the side-cut device of the type described has a capacity of about 50,000 bricks per day.

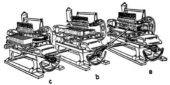

FIG. 4.— Board Delivery Cutting Table.

Of the various forms of cutting devices, the delivery cutting table may be described as a general third type. (See Fig. 4.) This table cuts 12 bricks at a time, automatically drawing a smooth board under the bricks as they are cut. The upper portion of the table travels forwards upon a track while the wires are being drawn through the bar of clay, thus compensating for its forward motion, while a slight pressure upon the lever during its return stroke brings the table to its original position and places the board loaded with bricks ready for removal.

The apparatus weighs about 900 pounds, and measures about 9 feet in length, including hand lever in operating position. Modifications of this table are employed for cutting chimney blocks and hollow ware of large section. Diagrams (a), (b), (c) of Fig. 4, illustrate in the order given, the operation of the device — (a) beginning of cut, (b) end of cut, (c) delivery of the bricks.

Automatic indenting cutters are employed to produce round edged bricks or blocks for street paving purposes. It appears to be a matter of some controversy as to whether any advantage other than the rounding of corners or edges is gained by the practice of repressing bricks for paving purposes. It is the general opinion that repressing breaks the original bond formed between the particles in molding the material into shape in the brick machine and fails to establish a new bond equally as good. The automatic indenting cutter is calculated to do away with the repress in this particular class of bricks.

To facilitate the handling of bricks in their green condition and to prepare them for the drying and burning processes, various appliances are employed which ensure more or less economy in time and labor. The brick-edger is an attachment, 5 feet 8 inches long, which may be placed on end-cut brick machines to automatically turn the bricks on edge as they are being transferred to the off-bearing belt. Such an attachment will save the labor of one man on an output of 30,000 bricks per day.

The pallet carrier is from 16 to 32 feet in length, and is employed to facilitate the transfer of the bricks from the off-bearing belt to pallets of either wood or metal. If the clay worked is somewhat soft, so that the resulting bricks will not bear piling up on each other without defacement, pallets, each holding about eight bricks on edge may be used, and the bricks dried in this position in cars or in racks under the drying sheds.

The head-sander and brusher is a device, which in connection with a regular brick machine, is employed to produce head-sanded stretcher or stock-bricks. It consists of a continually moving belt carrying a series of angle-iron supporting pieces, corresponding in length to the bricks. The operator stands at the head of the head-sander and close to the automatic cut-off, and transfers to the supporting pieces on the belt only those bricks which are free from stone or other disfigurement. The bricks thus guided and supported, are carried by the belt between two pairs of revolving circular brushes. Dry sand in a box is kept constantly against the faces of these brushes, so that when they revolve against the horizontal motion of the bricks, the sand is brushed into both heads of each brick, thus producing a stiff-tempered end-cut brick with sanded faces and heads, so that the heads burn the same color as the faces. The capacity of the machine is about twenty-five bricks per minute, and it may also be used to sand bricks that are intended for repressing.

Repressing is a process employed to produce bricks suitable for fronts of buildings, ornamental tablets and corner pieces with designs in relief, or intaglio, and other shapes of any desired design. The great many varieties of machines used for this purpose are called presses, and are operated either by steam or hand power.

The hand press shown in Fig. 5, is equipped with a very powerful lever, and has a steel-lined box with a top-plate and plunger faced with

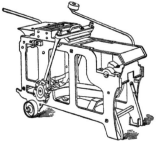

FIG. 5.— Hand-brick Repress.

steel, conveniently arranged for refitting whenever necessary. It weighs about 900 pounds; occupies floor space 20 inches by 3 feet 6 inches, exclusive of the lever, and may be readily moved upon the rollers under the forward end, from place to place about the works.

Power represses are made with one or two sets of plungers or pressure shafts, and are built with a capacity to exert pressures up to 45,000 pounds. A machine with two sets of plungers working against the mold-box, has a repressing capacity of 15,000 fine front bricks, or 20,000 street pavers per day.

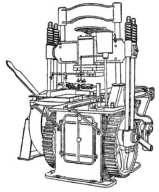

FIG. 6.— Power Repress.

Fig. 6 shows a repress in which a single plunger acts against the molding die, the pressure of the brick being taken on a solid base instead of a moving cam or plunger. It is capable of being readily adjusted to any thickness of brick, and the pressure can be regulated by the hand-wheel on the top of the plunger or shaft. Various kinds of dies can be used, and these changed with very little loss of time. Roman, Norman, or Pompeiian brick can be pressed upon it as well as the smaller sizes, also a great variety of ornamental brick, shape brick, and tiles. It has an estimated weight of about 7,000 pounds; is equipped with a friction-clutch pulley 36 inches diameter, 8-inch face, which in operation runs at the rate of about 80 revolutions per minute, and is capable of turning out about 28,000 standard size bricks per day.

The dimensions adopted by the National Brick Manufacturers' Association in the United States, for standard hard-burnt common building brick, are 8¼ x 4 x 2¼ inches, and for a pressed front brick, 8⅜ x 4 x 2⅜ inches. All modern brick machines are capable of producing bricks of these sizes. See BRICK; CLAY-WORKING MACHINERY; KILNS; PIPE, MANUFACTURE OF.

W. MOREY, JR.,
Consulting Engineer, New York.

Bricks Without Straw, a novel by Albion W. Tourgée, containing a modern application of the Biblical phrase. The words are an allusion to the darkest days of the Hebrew bondage in Egypt, when the toilers were ordered to furnish their own straw without diminishing the number of bricks produced in a given time.

Bridal Wreath. See SPIRÆA.

Bride, Saint. See BRIDGET.

Bride and Bridegroom, words of Anglo-Saxon origin applied from very early times to a newly married wife and husband, the more common form at present being bride and groom. It has been usual from the earliest period of antiquity to pay especial honors to a bride and groom, and in every age and among every people, the wedding-day has been devoted to joyous and solemn ceremonies. It was celebrated among the Athenians by offerings made in the morning to particular divinities, to Zeus and Hera, and especially to Artemis, who was thought to look with disfavor upon marriages. At nightfall she was conducted to the bridegroom's house, in a chariot drawn by a pair of mules, and furnished with a kind of couch, on which she sat between her husband and one of his nearest friends. The bridal procession moved on, greeted and accompanied by friends bearing nuptial torches and singing songs. Then followed the marriage feast, to which, contrary to the usual Greek practice, women as well as men were invited; and at its close the bride was conducted by the bridegroom to her apartment, where a law of Solon required that they should eat a quince together. On the day after the marriage, presents were made to the newly married couple by their friends. Among the Romans the same custom prevailed, in memory of the rape of the Sabines. The wedding day was fixed, at least in early times, by consulting the auspices. The Roman marriage was usually, though not always, unattended by religious rites. The bride was conducted to the house of the bridegroom by a procession and bore in her own hands the emblems of diligence, a distaff and a spindle with wool. The bridegroom received her within with fire and water, a symbol, perhaps, of purification, and the ceremonies of the day were concluded by a repast given to friends and relatives. The bridal apartment, to which she was conducted by matrons who had not had more than one husband, was magnificently decked with flowers, and minstrels and friends sang without during the night.

In the days of our ancestors various ceremonies, often "more honored in the breach than the observance," were followed. The bride was undressed and put to bed by the bridemaids, and the bridegroom submitted to the same operation, at the hands of the groomsmen. Then the posset, a drink made of milk, wine, yolks of eggs, sugar, cinnamon, and nutmeg, had to be served. Then there was sometimes another dilatory proceeding in the sewing of the bride in a sheet. The arraying of the bride in white, the wedding feast, and the giving of presents are ancient customs. As early as the time of James I., the presents received by the bride of Sir Philip Herbert amounted in value to $12,500, a notable expenditure of the kind for those days, but frequently surpassed at the present time by the value of a single bridal gift. The bridal kiss is of unknown antiquity. The old missals, which date long before the "common prayer book," enjoined it as an essential part of the marriage ceremony. Moreover, it was always done in church. The priest, too, at one time, enjoyed the privilege of kissing the bride. Groomsmen claimed and took it for a long period. The ordinary accessories of the weddings of our days may mostly be traced to ancient times. The marriage ring probably encircled the finger of the wife of the first Pharaoh, and was certainly used in the Roman ceremonies under the emperors. Its heathen origin nearly led to its abolition by the Puritans of Cromwell's time. The wedding ring is always put and worn on the fourth finger of the left hand, because it was supposed in ancient times that an artery ran from this part directly to the heart. The bridecake is no less sanctified by antiquity than the ring. It is a symbol of plenty, and is intended to express the hope that the newly married pair may be always supplied with an abundance of the good things of this life. In ancient days wheat was sprinkled upon the head of the bride with the same intent. At present this custom is superseded by the scattering of rice upon the bride and groom as they leave the house after the reception. The throwing of an old shoe after the couple shows traces of an old superstition. Passing bits of the cake through the wedding ring nine times, and putting them under the pillow to dream upon, was a practice in vogue long before our great-grandmothers lived and loved. Putting up the slices in white paper boxes is an innovation of later times. Wine was an invariable accompaniment of all marriages, long before the marriage feast at Cana. In times past it was customary to drink it in the church, the priest having first blessed the cup, however, to suit it to the holiness of the place. The Jews universally hold to the custom of wine-drinking on the occasion of a marriage. After the bride and groom have drunk from the glass it is broken to remind them of mortality.

Modern custom lengthens out the privileges of bride and bridegroom beyond the wedding day. In former times, when the religious ceremony and the attendant festivities were over, all bridal honors ceased. These are now prolonged by the bridal tour. The term honeymoon, formerly applied to the first month of married life, is now more vaguely used and is sometimes given to the entire period of the bridal tour, even when that is extended over many weeks.

Bride of Abydos, The, a poem by Lord Byron, published in 1813. From this a melodrama was adapted a few years later by Dimond.

Bride of Lammermoor, The, by Sir Walter Scott, one of the group of 'Waverley Novels' called 'Tales of my Landlord.' The scene is laid on the east coast of Scotland, in the year 1700. The hero is Edgar, Master of Ravenswood, a young man of noble family, penniless and proud. He has vowed vengeance against the present owner of the Ravenswood estates, Sir William Ashton, lord keeper, whom he considers guilty of fraud; but foregoes his plans on falling in love with Lucy, Sir William's daughter. There is a secret betrothal; the ambitious Lady Ashton endeavors to force her daughter to marry another suitor; and in the struggle Lucy goes mad, and Ravenswood, thinking himself rejected, comes to an untimely end. The most famous character in the book is the amusing Caleb Balderstone, the devoted old steward of Ravenswood, who endeavors constantly to save the family honor and to conceal his master's poverty by ingenious devices and lies, and whose name has become the symbol of "the constant service of the antique world." Though sombre and depressing, the 'Bride of Lammermoor' is very popular, and the plot has been used by Donizetti in the opera 'Lucia di Lammermoor.'

Bride of Messina, The, a tragedy by Schiller, based on Sophocles' 'Œdipus Tyrannus.' It was brought out in 1803.

Bride of the Sea, a poetical name given to the city of Venice in allusion to the custom of wedding the Adriatic Sea with a ring. This picturesque ceremony was annually observed by the doges.

Bride'well, formerly a famous house of correction in Blackfriars, London. The name originally belonged to a well dedicated to St. Bride. Henry VIII. built on this site, in 1522, a palace for the accommodation of the Emperor Charles V., which became a residence of Wolsey, and under Edward VI. was, in 1553, converted into a workhouse for the poor, and a house of correction for the idle and vicious. Prisoners here were made to work during their confinement, as in most other houses of correction. From this, as one of the earliest houses of correction, there originated the generic term, "a bridewell" — a house of correction. It was governed by a keeper who was independent of the sheriff of London.

Bridge, Horatio, American naval officer: b. Augusta, Me., 8 April 1806; d. Athens, Pa., 18 March 1893. He graduated at Bowdoin College in the famous class of 1825, which included Longfellow, Hawthorne, J. S. C. Abbott, and G. B. Cheever. He was admitted to the bar in 1828, and for 10 years was in practice at Skowhegan and Augusta, Me. In 1838 he entered the United States navy as paymaster; made a cruise in the Cyane (1838-41); in the Saratoga upon the coast of Africa (1843-4), some account of which was published in 1845 under the title 'Journal of an African Cruiser,' edited by his friend, Hawthorne. From 1854-69 he was chief of the bureau of provisions and clothing. In 1873 he was retired as pay-director with the relative rank of commodore. He wrote 'Personal Recollections of Nathaniel Hawthorne' (1893).

Bridge, **Sir John Frederick**, English organist and composer: b. Oldbury, Worcestershire, 5 Dec. 1844. He was organist of Trinity Church, Windsor, Manchester Cathedral, and in 1875 became full organist of Westminster Abbey. He was also made professor of harmony at Owens College, Manchester, and afterward professor of harmony and counterpoint at the Royal College of Music. Among his works are the oratorio, 'Mount Moriah'; the cantata, 'Boadicea'; the cantata, 'Callirhoë'; the oratorio, 'The Repentance of Nineveh'; etc. He has set many hymns to music, notably Gladstone's Latin version of 'Rock of Ages.'

Bridge, a game of cards. It is played with one pack of cards, and the four players are styled the dealer, the leader, the dummy, and the pone. Bridge is allied to whist, and like that game is played in more than one way. See De La Rue, 'The Laws of Bridge' (1889); Foster, 'Bridge' (1901); Dunn, 'Bridge, and How to Play It' (1901); Steele, 'Simple Rules for Bridge' (1902).

Bridge. In its broadest sense, the term signifies any kind of a connecting structure. Specifically, it defines a structure erected for the purpose of continuing a roadway over a stream, valley, or any other natural or artificial obstruction.

The origin of the term is difficult to trace, and the art of bridge-building itself is so ancient, that its beginning lies in the efforts of primitive man who felled trees, or swung jungle vines across the streams to facilitate his movements on his hunting trips, or when engaged in trade from village to village.

The construction of a bridge, however, as an engineering structure, although quite elemental in its engineering features, may be traced back more or less accurately to the Chinese who appear to have been the first people to employ the masonry arch for the purpose of continuing roadways across streams.

The art of bridge-building, however, as developed in the various countries was not evolved from the earlier Chinese practice, but independent practice characterizes its development in each country, and by the very nature of the structures built in the past, the present-day investigator is enabled to formulate very clear and accurate ideas as to the character, customs, and importance of the peoples who built them.

The Egyptians seem to have had but little use for bridges, and none have survived among the structures of their ancient civilization. Similar conditions appear to have obtained among the Balylonians and the Assyrians, and the earliest examples that remain, other than those of the Chinese, appear to belong to the "Hittite" and "Pelasgic" tribes, who inhabited the shores of the Mediterranean Sea during a pre-historic period antedating that of the building of Troy. Their engineering methods appear to have been imitated by the Cretans, whose cities in Asia Minor, Greece, and Italy, and in the countries bordering on the Mediterranean, were connected by macadamized roads which required bridges that were constructed by a high order of engineering skill. They were somewhat similar to the one built at a later period across the Euripus in Euboea, a province of Greece, and consisted of massive abutments and piers of masonry with a connecting superstructure of planks. The typical Greek method is shown by the bridge at Assos, in which parallel stone lintels doweled together are employed to connect the piers and abutments.

On the other hand, the engineering genius of the "Pelasgic" tribes was inherited and developed by the Etruscans and the Romans in the application of the basic principles of the arch.

The bridges at Vulci, Bieda, and Cora, in Italy, in which true round arches are employed to connect the piers, are a class of structures which were probably unknown to the Greeks. These were built during the seventh and sixth centuries B. C., and the Roman bridge-building methods were carried through stages of greater and greater perfection until the fourth century B. C., when the Roman policy of constructing great military roads to bind their possessions together, permitted the highest development of their engineering skill, in structures of this kind.

The brilliant and unrivalled career of bridge and viaduct construction thus inaugurated by the building of the famous Via Appia, and culminating in the erection of the eight great bridges of Rome, has furnished models for all the succeeding centuries, and are applicable to-day to the construction of stone structures.

Some of the bridges of the Republican period still remain. Of these, the Ponto Lupo, and the viaduct for the Anio Vetus Aqueduct was built about 143 B. C., and consists of great stone arches of tufa and travertine; while the viaduct near Gabii, built about 122 B. C., consisting of seven arches about 292 feet long, is still in use. Within Rome itself, the Æmilian bridge, built in 179-142 B. C. across the Tiber, is supposed to have been the first stone bridge to span that stream, all the others having been constructed of wood, a material which continued in use until quite a late period for bridges across wide rivers. Another, the Sublician bridge built by Ancus Martius across the Tiber between the Janiculum and the Aventine Mountain was famous for its defense by Horatius Cocles against the great army under Lars Porsena. The only one of the urban bridges of Rome that remains intact, is the Fabrician Bridge, or "Ponte Fabricio," built in 62 B. C., but the greater part of the most magnificent of them all, the Ælian Bridge, or "Ponte Sant' Angelo," built by Hadrian in 136 A. D., also remains. The former consists of two round Roman arches of peperino and tufa, faced with massive blocks of travertine; the latter consist of eight arches, arranged to give an upward grade toward the center of the structure, thus adding greatly to its architectural effect.

Of the important bridges built on the great military roads of the Empire — the Appia, the Aurelia, the Flaminia, the Via Salaria or Pont Salaro, the Cassia, the Valeria, the Latina, and the Æmilia, those built during the Augustan period were the most remarkable. The Flaminia commenced at the Mulvian Bridge and ended at the Ariminium (Rimini) Bridge. The latter, which consists of five great arches with a total length of 236 feet, is the best preserved of them all; but vestiges of a great many others still remain, the most important being those near Narni and Borghetto, the great one at Vincenza, rebuilt at Verona, and those near Aosti and Calzi.

With the expansion of the Empire many bridges were built upon the fine macadamized roads which connected the various provinces with the Eternal City, by the Roman legions under the direction of their skillful military engineers. Of these, the greatest was the bridge across the Danube, built in 103 A. D., by the engineer Apollodorus, to enable the Emperor Trajan to conquer Dacia. It consisted of massive stone piers connected together by a superstructure of wood with a total length of 4,770 feet. It was subsequently destroyed by Hadrian, but the great piers are still standing.

Prior to its construction, intervals of such enormous length had been spanned by temporary bridges of boats, a practice handed down from a period reaching farther back than that of Xerxes, Darius, Hytarpus, or Cyrus — in the sixth century B. C., and illustrates effectively the consummate daring of the Roman engineer. It is interesting to note in this connection, however, that the most celebrated bridges built by the Romans were not generally distinguished for the great span of their arches, their great total length, or the peculiar lightness of their piers, but for their excellence of construction, and durability. The span of their arches seldom exceeded 70 or 80 feet, and their height was nearly half the span, thus giving them a semi-circular form, or what constituted a segment of that form.

In all the countries which formed the provinces of the Roman Empire, with the exception of the Spanish Peninsula, most of the bridges built by the Romans were allowed to fall to pieces during the Dark Ages, so that very few of them have survived. The ruins and foundations of some still exist near Vairon, and Chateau Neuf, in France, but are not of sufficient size to convey much of an idea of the special characteristics of the structures. In Spain, however, the high culture of the Moors insured the preservation of these superb examples of Roman engineering. Of these, the best examples are the bridges at Cuenca, Evora, Martorell, Merida, Chavas, Alconetar, Orense, Olloniego, Almazan, Ona, and Salamanca. The greater number of them were built by Trajan, and that of Salamanca is the most magnificent of all. Many of these structures were adorned by triumphal and memorial arches at each end, or in the center, which, while adding greatly to their architectural effectiveness, also served the purpose of a toll gate, or a fortification. Interesting examples of these are the bridges at Saint Chamas, in France, and the Ponte Salaro at Rome.

The Moors not only preserved the Roman structures, but imitated them and built many bridges fully their equals in size and elaborateness of design. The bridge at Cordova, across the Guadalquivir, is one of the most notable examples of their work, and also that of Alcantara, across the Tagus, built by Lacer during the reign of Trajan. It consists of six granite arches of a total length of 600 feet, with a

width of 26 feet, which carries the roadway at a height of 45 feet above the level of the river.

The early history of Oriental bridge-building appears to extend back to the days and works of Semiramis, who is credited by Diodorus Siculus, with the construction of a bridge across the Euphrates at Babylon about 776 B. C., and is described by him as a movable drawbridge, 30 feet wide, supported by stone piers.

The earliest existing examples of Oriental work, however, appear to be the bridges at Dizfel and Shuster, in Persia, which were probably built during the rule of the later Achæminid Kings over Iran, about 350 B. C. Their design embodies the wide pointed arch characteristics of later Mohammedan architecture, and are still in a fair state of preservation.

It is noteworthy, that, while the culture and continuity of the Byzantine and Mohammedan civilizations maintained in good condition the bridges already built, and created new ones of equal usefulness and magnitude, the science and art of bridge-building was practically lost in the European countries during the six centuries which comprised the Dark Ages. In the 12th century, however, the architectural and engineering sciences felt the awakening impulses which culminated in the magnificent structural creations of the Renaissance. The revival was first experienced in Italy and France. Bridges were built not only by the governing authorities but also by the churches — the building of a bridge being considered in the nature of a pious undertaking. Bridges were built at Tours, Orleans and Vienna, and many other large cities, and the Rhone was spanned at Lyons and Avignon by two fine bridges, the last-named being about 3,000 feet in length. It was built during the years 1178-88, by Benezet, a shepherd mason, who subsequently founded an association of bridge-builders which was known as the Frères Pontiers, or "Brethren of the Bridge". It is remarkable on account of the elliptical curvature of the arches, the radius of which is shorter at the crown than at the haunch, and, therefore, conforms more nearly to the linear equilibrated arch, than the modern elliptical arch which has the longer radius at the crown. It consisted of 19 arches. The span of the largest arch was 110 feet 9 inches, with a height of 45 feet 10 inches. Four of the arches still remain.

The bridges built in southern France were particularly fine. The Saint Esprit, the Beziers, the 'Montauban and the Pont Valentré; at Cahors, are some of the best examples of those built during the period covered by the later part of the 13th and the earlier part of the 14th centuries. The application of the system of end and central towers for purposes of fortifications, received the highest development at this time. This was especially true in France where the mediæval social conditions made such fortifications an absolute necessity. In this respect, Germany and Spain were far behind France, although the monumental bridge across the Danube at Ratisbon, built by the Germans in 1135, and the bridge across the Elbe at Dresden, were very fine examples of this kind. Also, the Spanish bridges at Zomora, Tudela, Lograno, and Palencia, built during the period 1135 to 1192. These bridges are of the pointed arch

BRIDGES.

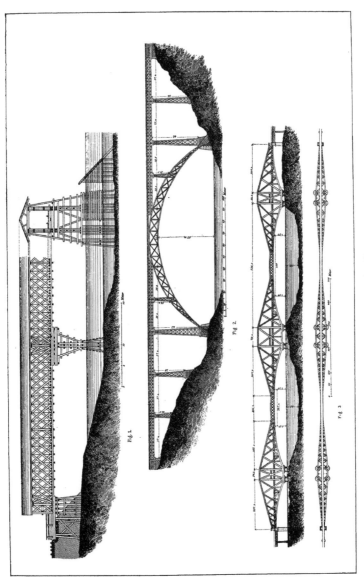

Fig. 1.

Fig. 2.

Fig. 3

1. Roofed wooden-truss or lattice bridge.
2. Railway bridge over the Douro at Oporto, Portugal.
3. Frith of Forth bridge, Scotland.

TYPES OF BRIDGES.

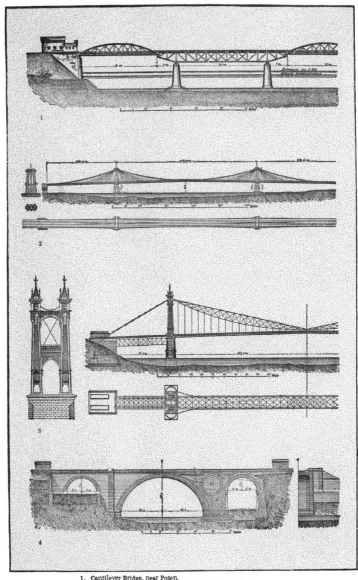

1. Cantilever Bridge, near Posen.
2. Cable Suspension Bridge, over the East River, New York.
3. Chain Suspension Bridge, over the Monongahela River, at Pittsburg.
4. Stone Arch Bridge, near Berne.

type, some of them consisting of as many as 20 arches.

Of the Italian bridges built during this period, the best examples are the Ponte Vecchio in Florence, built in 1362, the bridge at Mantua, and the Rialto Bridge over the Grand Canal in Venice, built in 1588. These bridges were of the covered type, that is, they had a covered gallery which was flanked by a double line of booths and small shops in which all kinds of merchandise were exposed for sale. In Italy, the use of wood as a material of construction was generally adhered to until the 13th century, although in France, and in the other countries of northern Europe it had been generally supplanted by masonry. Yet, at the close of the 15th century, Italy had some fine stone structures — the bridges at Mossa and Signa in Tuscany, and the Ponte del Diavolo near Lucca; while France had many large wooden bridges at several important points.

The engineers of the Renaissance returned to the round arch typical of the Roman bridges, but they showed great boldness in their designs, by increasing the span of the arches. The bridge across the Adda at Trezzo, built under the orders of Bernabo Visconti, Duke of Milan, during the latter part of the 14th century, consisted of a single arch of granite with a span of 251 feet; while the bridge over the Ticino at Pavia, consisted of seven pointed arches of brick work, each 70 feet in span, and 64 feet in height.

Of the smaller Italian bridges, the most famous is the Bridge of Sighs at Venice, built during the latter part of the 16th century, to connect the Ducal Palace with the prison.

In England, the use of stone as a material of construction may be traced back to the middle of the 10th century, by records which authorized the building of a triangular pointed arch stone bridge at Croyland, Lincolnshire, in 943. The present structure, known as the Croyland Bridge, however, although one of the oldest stone bridges in England, appears to have been built about the latter part of the 14th century. It is also triangular in form, and consists of three pointed arches which span the waters of the Welland, the Nyne, and the Catwater drain. On account of its steep grade it can be used only by foot passengers.

The work of the "Brethren of the Bridge" order, carried the art of bridge-building up to the 17th century, and a great many fine structures were built in all parts of Europe. In France, the most important were the Trilpot, Tours, Gignac, Neuilly, and Blois Bridges, and in England, the Blackfriars, Westminster, Winston and Kelso. The date of the building of the first London bridge across the Thames is quite uncertain; but, there is very little doubt that it was built of timber and had to be frequently reconstructed. The so-called great London Bridge was built of stone, between the years 1176 and 1209, by an architect sent from France for that purpose. It had a covered gallery which was lined on both sides by shops, like a regular street. It consisted of nine pointed arches, each 60 feet in span, and had a total length of about 700 feet. It was supplanted by the structure now known as "Old London Bridge," in 1831. This structure consists of five elliptical arches, of which the center arch has a span of 152 feet, with a height of 29½

feet above high water mark. The other arches are 140 feet in span, with a height of 27½ feet. The total length of the structure is 1005 feet, and it carries a roadway 53 feet wide between the parapets. The Blackfriars Bridge across the Thames was built between the years 1760 and 1770. It consists of nine elliptical arches. The central arch has a span of 100 feet, and the others decrease gradually from 98 feet in those next to the center, to 70 feet in those at the ends. The Westminster Bridge was built between the years 1738 and 1750. It consists of 15 arches, of which the center arch is 76 feet in span, and the span of the others decreases at the rate of four feet for each succeeding arch, except the two shore arches, each of which have a span of 25 feet. Other notable English stone bridges built during the 18th century, are the Winston Bridge over the River Tees, and the Kelso Bridge over the Tweed. The former has a superb arch 109 feet in span, while the latter consists of five arches, each of which are 72 feet in span. Perhaps the most notable stone arch bridge built in any country during the 18th century, is the Pont-y-tu-prydd, across the River Taff in Wales. It was built by William Edwards, an ordinary stone mason, in 1750, after two failures due to excessive weight of the haunches, which in the third and successful attempt were lightened by the introduction of pierced spandrils. It consists of a segmented arch 140 feet in span, with a height of 35 feet, and its most curious feature is the gradual increase of its width from 14½ feet at the crown of the arch to 16 feet at the abutments.

The most remarkable bridges constructed in France during the 18th century, were the work of the famous Department of Ponts et Chaussees. The best examples of their work are the Blois Bridge over the Loire, the construction of which was commenced in 1720, and which consists of 11 elliptical arches, ranging from about 55 feet to 86 feet in span; the bridge over the Loire at Tours, the construction of which was commenced in 1755, and which consists of 15 elliptical arches, each 80 feet in span, and separated by piers 16 feet thick; the Trilport Bridge over the Maine, built in 1760, consisting of three skew arches, the middle arch of which has a span of 81 feet, and the side arches, spans of about 77 feet; the Neuilly Bridge across the Seine, built between the years 1768 and 1774, and which consists of five elliptical arches, each 128 feet in span; and the Gignac Bridge over the Herault, built in 1793, and which consists of an elliptical center arch about 107 feet in span, flanked by two semi-circular arches, each of which have a span of 83 feet.

Although the masonry and stone arch bridges of the 19th century cannot be considered as showing much, if any, structural improvement over those of preceding times, it is a fact that the engineers of the 19th century have used their better knowledge of the theory of those structures, obtained from the progress of the science of statics, to increase the spans of the arches far beyond the limits set by the earlier practice.

Of these later productions, the largest stone arch in the world is that of the Luxemburg Bridge, completed in 1901; it is 277 feet in span, and rises to a height of about 138 feet above the level of the water. Other modern stone arches of magnitude are the Grosvenor Bridge over the River Dee at Chester, England, consisting of a single arch with a span of 200 feet, and the Cabin John Bridge near Washington, D. C., built in 1853–1859, to carry the Washington aqueduct, which consists of a single arch with a span of 220 feet.

This brief enumeration of the notable 19th century stone arch bridges may be terminated very appropriately with the mentioning of the Waterloo Bridge across the Thames. It consists of nine elliptical arches of Aberdeen granite, of 120 feet span each, with a rise of 32 feet. The total length of the structure, including the approaches, is 2456 feet, and it carries a horizontal roadway 41½ feet wide between the parapets.

About the beginning of the 19th century, metal began to be extensively introduced as a material of construction, and although the masonry arch was superior in beauty and durability, the metal bridge gave greater strength in proportion to the weight of the structure; was capable of being built more quickly and cheaply, and therefore, being better adapted to keep pace with the tremendous activity of modern railway construction, it soon almost completely supplanted the stone structures.

The first structure in which the new material was used appears to be the bridge across the Severn near the town of Ironbridge, Shropshire, England. It was built by Abraham Darby, the owner of the iron-works of Coalbrookdale, in 1779, and consists of a single arch 100 feet in span, with a rise of 45 feet. The arch is composed of five cast-iron ribs which form the segment of a circle. The successful construction of such a structure being thus clearly demonstrated, several others, of bolder design, were built during the last quarter of the 18th century, of which the Wearmouth Bridge, over the Wear at Sunderland, completed in 1796, is the most elegant example of the type. As originally constructed, it consisted of a single arch 236 feet in span, with a rise of 34 feet above the springing lines, which were 95 feet above the level of the river.

From these beginnings, the evolution of various types of metal arch structures was rapid. A larger percentage of wrought iron was employed in the material of construction, affording greater flexibility in the methods of construction and design, and the capability of spanning greater intervals with single spans. The most notable of the structures built about this time (the early part of the 19th century) was the Southwark Bridge across the Thames, erected in 1819. It consists of three arches, of which the central arch is 240 feet in span, and the side arches 210 feet each. They are composed of massive cast-iron arch ribs, which being set without any provisions to counteract the effects of expansion, and being much heavier than is necessary to sustain the loads to which they are subjected, gives a structure which is merely the imitation of one stone, with the additional fault of a great wastefulness of the material of construction. Its construction, however, served a valuable purpose in the development of metal arch engineering. It suggested the principle of hinged arches, which was subsequently taken under consideration by the mathematicians of

Europe in 1841, and developed into a perfect theory, which made the metal arch a statically determinate structure on absolutely immovable foundations, and one that was provided against distortion and rupture under conditions of varying temperature.

Although the fine cast-iron bridges such as the Westminster and the Blackfriars, built across the Thames during the period covered by 1860 to 1870, consisted of arches with spans as great as 185 feet, the metal hinged-arch bridges built since 1873, have surpassed them greatly, not only in the length of the spans, but in the economy of the material of construction.

An exception to this statement, however, must be noted in the case of the bridge across the Mississippi, at St. Louis, Missouri, which was completed in 1874. It consists of three unhinged structures the center arch being 520 feet in span. Of the hinged-arch bridges the following are the most notable. The Alexander III. Bridge across the Seine at Paris, built in 1899, consisting of a single arch with a span of 362½ feet, composed of arch-ribs made up of wedge-shaped cast-steel sections bolted together; the steel-arch railway bridge across the Niagara River, built in 1897, consisting of a single arch with a span of 550 feet; and the highway and foot-bridge completed in 1899 across the Niagara Gorge, just below the Falls, consisting of a single steel arch with a span of 840 feet, which makes it the largest single span steel-arch bridge in the world, and is approximated to in size only by the steel-arch of the Viaur Viaduct in France, which is 762 feet in span.

Some of the other handsome and important structures of the metal hinged-arch type well worthy of mention are the following: The Washington Bridge over the Harlem River, at New York, completed in 1889, which consists of two magnificent arches, each 510 feet in span, flanked by four masonry arches at one end, and three at the other, each 50 feet in span; the German steel-arch bridges across the Rhine at Bonn and Düsseldorf, the former with a central arch of 614 feet span, and two side arches each 307 feet in span, and the latter with two arches each 595 feet in span; the Pia Mia Bridge over the Douro at Oporto, Portugal, consisting of a main steel arch, 525 feet in span with a rise of 123 feet; and the steel arch on Garabit Viaduct over the Truzere, in central France, which has a span of 540 feet with a rise of 170 feet.

As the tensile strength of wrought iron and steel was greatly increased by improved processes of manufacture, greater feats of bridge-construction were dared by the bridge engineers, and various types of suspension and cantilever bridges, especially suitable for very long spans, were designed and successfully erected. Even the more important wire cable and chain structures of the early 19th century, such as the Schuylkill River Bridge, at Philadelphia, built in 1816, with a span of 408 feet; the bridge across the Menai Strait, between the Island of Anglesey and Carnarvonshire, in Wales, completed in 1826, with a span of 580 feet, and Fribourg Bridge, in Switzerland, built in 1834, with a span of 870 feet, were completely overshadowed by the works of the American engineers during the period dating from 1848 up to the present time. Of these magnificent struc-

BRIDGES.

Fig. 1 Forth Bridge, from North Queensferry, (from a photograph by J. Patrick & Son, Edinburgh). ² The Bridge, from perth end. ³ Britannia Tubular Bridge (Figs. ³ and ⁴ from photographs by Valentine & Sons, Limited, Dundee). ⁴ Conishe Viaduct (Figs. ⁴ and ⁵ from photographs by Lockwood and Stephens, Newport, Mon.).

world; but, they are entirely outclassed in magnitude by the almost marvelous creations of American engineering genius already described.

Bridges built on the cantilever or balanced span principle, rank with those of the suspension and girder-and-arch type, for the purpose of spanning great intervals.

In order to trace the evolution of the cantilever-bridge from the girder, and to understand its relation to the truss, a brief mention of the tubular bridges which were originated by Robert Stevenson, engineer of the Chester and Holyhead Railway, England, to carry that railway across the Menai Strait is necessary.

A series of experiments conducted by Stevenson in conjunction with Fairbairn, demonstrated that a rectangular tube with a cellular top and bottom, gave a girder in which the greatest strength was derived from the least amount of material. The result was the construction of the Conway and Britannia Bridges, the former across the Conway River and the latter across the Menai Strait, in 1846 and 1847, respectively. The Conway tube consisted of a single span of 400 feet, and the Britannia of four spans, two of 460 feet each, and two of 230 feet each in the clear. The example set by Stevenson was followed in a few other cases, the most important of which was the Victoria Bridge across the St. Lawrence, near Montreal, Canada, built in 1854. It consisted of 24 spans ranging in length from 242 to 247 feet each, and one span of 330 feet. It had a total length of 9144 feet, or nearly one and three-quarter miles, and required about 9000 tons of iron for the construction of the tubes. It was replaced in 1898-99, by a pin-connected truss bridge of 24 spans of 254 feet each, and one span of 348 feet, which represented a total weight of 20,000 tons of steel, but which was capable of sustaining a load five times greater. The Victoria Bridge was the last important structure of this type. It simply disappeared from engineering practice when the special conditions which developed it ceased to exist; but, it led the way to the plate girder bridges. It taught the engineer to cut away all the useless material in his structures and retain only the effective working skeleton, and thus inaugurated a truly scientific method of metal construction, by which the weight of the structure was greatly reduced, and consequently the cost of construction.

In the meantime, the principle of the truss, first enunciated by Palladio, the famous Italian architect, about 1560, and subsequently developed still further, and without doubt independently, by such genius' as Ulric Grubermann, Timothy Palmer, Lewis Wernway, Theodore Burr, William Howe, Wendall Bollman, and others of equal merit, during the period extending from 1754 to 1854, was diverted from its application to wooden bridges, and used in the construction of metal structures. The combining of the truss and the girder was the next logical step in the evolutionary process, and to Roebling belongs the credit of demonstrating the practicability of building long span braced girder or truss bridges with iron and steel as the material of construction. As the cantilever bridges are a class of structures actually composed of hinged continuous braced girders, their intimate relation to the girder and truss bridges is quite obvious. They were, however, not much used until the last quarter of the 19th century. The construction of the Kentucky Viaduct in 1876, and the Niagara Cantilever in 1883, demonstrated the ease with which they could be built without the use of costly false work, and soon afterwards many bridges were built both in Europe and America. The most important of these are the following. The bridge across the Hudson at Poughkeepsie, New York, built in 1889, which consists of five river spans ranging from 546 to 548 feet in length, and a total length of 6767 feet; the Red Rock Cantilever Bridge across the Red River in California, built in 1890 with a center span of 660 feet, and a total length of 990 feet; the Memphis Bridge across the Mississippi River at Memphis, Tennessee, built in 1892, with a truss span of 621 feet, and two cantilever spans of 700 feet each, which are the longest of the kind in the United States; the St. John River Cantilever in New Brunswick, built in 1895, with a main span of 477 feet, and a total length of 813 feet; the great Forth Bridge across the Frith of Forth, in Scotland, which was completed in 1890, and consists of two shore spans of 680 feet each, and two main spans of 1710 feet each, which were the longest cantilever spans in the world until the building of the Quebec Cantilever across the St. Lawrence River, the construction of which began in 1900, and which has a clear span of 1800 feet.

All bridge structures, regardless of the materials of construction, may be divided into three classes — " Beam Bridges," " Suspension Bridges," and " Arch Bridges," which in turn may be subdivided into several other classes according to their modern uses,— such as Railway Bridges, Highway Bridges, Movable Bridges, Pontoon Bridges and Military Bridges.

Modern railway bridges are almost exclusively constructed of steel, and consist of trusses or plate girders designed to sustain uniform loads ranging from 3000 to 4800 pounds per linear foot of track, according to the length of span and the service required.

Highway bridges include all bridges used for roadway purposes alone. They may be constructed of wood, metal, masonry, or concrete, and are usually designed to sustain uniform loads ranging from 1000 to 1800 pounds per linear feet of track, according to the length of span and the service required.

Movable bridges or drawbridges include the various types of structures over rivers, that can be moved in order to allow a clear passageway for vessels.

The modern structures of this type may be divided into the following classes: (1) Swing Bridges; (2) Rolling Bridges; and (3) Lift Bridges; of which the first are the most commouly used.

A swing bridge consists of a wooden or metal truss supported at the center by a pier located in the middle of the stream, so that when the bridge is closed, the ends of the truss rest upon abutments on the shores on either side. It is operated by a turntable, upon which it rests, which is revolved by a rack and pinion arrangement worked by hand power, steam, or electricity.

A rolling bridge consists of a single truss mounted on rollers, and which is pushed out

from one side across the span, or of two trusses, on each side of the span which are pushed out and connected at the center of the span where the water ends are locked together when the bridge is closed. It is operated by the rope and drum method, and is not used to any great extent.

Lift bridges are of various kinds — the " vertical lift," the " hinged lift," and the " rolling lift " bridges. The simplest is the vertical lift bridge consisting of a truss which is raised vertically to the desired height, both ends rising in guides arranged on towers. The hinged lift bridge is raised by being revolved in a vertical plane around hinges at one end. The rolling lift bridge is also lifted in a vertical plane, but has in addition a limited rolling motion. All lift bridges usually have a counter-weight to assist the lifting effort, and are generally designed to move quickly — one minute being frequently specified as the time of opening or closing at points where land and water traffic is heavy.

The longest swing bridges ever constructed are the Interstate Bridge at Omaha, Nebraska, which has a total length of 520 feet; the Thames River Drawbridge at New London, Connecticut, which has a length of 503 feet; and the Arthur Kill Drawbridge between Staten Island, New York, and New Jersey, which has a swing span of 496 feet.

The most notable of the hinged or pivot-bascule bridges are the Tower Bridge across the Thames, near the Tower of London, England, which consists of a suspension and drawbridge combined with a central bascule span of 200 feet, formed by two leaves or trusses, hinged at the opposite towers; and the bridges at Chicago, Milwaukee, Buffalo, and Boston, in the United States.

The modern pontoon bridges are a development of the ancient bridge-of-boats principle. The most notable example of the type is the pontoon bridge across the Hooghly River, at Calcutta, India, which briefly described will serve to convey a very satisfactory idea of such structures. It is 1530 feet in length between the abutments on each bank of the river, and consists of a superstructure carried on 14 pairs of pontoons in the form of rectangular iron boxes with rounded bilges and wedge-shaped ends, which are held in position across the river by means of chain cables laid across, and anchors laid up and down the stream. The superstructure consists of trestle-work, which carries a plank roadway and foot-path platform having a total width of 62 feet at a height of 27 feet above the surface of the river. This height is sufficient to allow ordinary boat navigation, for the passage of large vessels is provided for by arrangements which permit the opening of a span 200 feet wide, by the temporary removal of four of the pontoons and the superstructure carried by them, twice a week.

Military bridges are temporary structures erected to facilitate the movements of troops, their supplies, and their armament, during the course of extensive field operations. The proper equipment of a modern army includes the material required for the construction of pontoon bridges of a limited length. This material consists of the necessary cables, and pontoons of canvas, the metal or wooden frames of which

BRIDGE OVER THE RHINE AT BONN, PRUSSIA (Upper).
BRIDGE OVER THE AARE AT BERN, SWITZERLAND (Lower).

are capable of being "knocked down" and packed for transportation. Spar bridges are usually made with round timbers cut near the location of the bridge. The most efficient and useful are those built in the form of trestles consisting of timber frames on which the stringers carrying the roadway are placed. The most notable examples of military bridge construction in the United States are the pontoon bridge built across the Potomac at Harper's Ferry, under the direction of General Banks, in February, 1862, which was composed of 60 boats, and the trestle 80 feet high and 400 feet long, built at another period of the Civil War across the Potomac Creek, Virginia, for railroad purposes.

For further information see articles entitled BRIDGE CONSTRUCTION, AMERICAN; BRIDGE CONSTRUCTION, MODERN METHODS OF; FOUNDATION; etc. WILLIAM MOREY, JR.
Consulting Civil and Mechanical Engineer.

Bridge-Building Brotherhood, a fraternal religious order formed in the 12th century in southern France. Its object was the building of bridges and the keeping of ferries. Tradition connects its origin with St. Bénezét, through whose efforts a bridge across the Rhone at Avignon was begun in 1117. After the completion of this bridge in 1185 the order received the sanction of Clement III. The order was dissolved by Pius II.

Bridge Construction, American. The application of scientific principles to the construction of bridges is more complete to-day than ever before. This statement applies to the specified requirements which the finished structure must fulfill, the design of every detail to carry the stresses due to the various loads imposed, the manufacture of the material composing the bridge, the construction of every member in it, and finally the erection of the bridge in the place where it is to do its duty as an instrument of transportation.

A close study of the economic problems of transportation in the United States and the experimental application of its results led the railroad managers to the definite conviction that, in order to increase the net earnings while the freight rates were slowly but steadily moving downward, it was necessary to change the method of loading by using larger cars drawn by heavier locomotives, so as to reduce the cost of transportation per train mile. While these studies had been in progress for a number of years and there was a gradual increase in the weight of locomotives, it is only within the past five years that the test was made, under favorable conditions and on an adequate scale, to demonstrate the value of a decided advance in the capacity of freight cars and in the weight of locomotives for the transportation of through freight. The test was made on the Pittsburg, B. & L. E. R. R., which was built and equipped for the transportation of iron ore from Lake Erie to Pittsburg, and of coal in the opposite direction.

When the economic proposition was fairly established, it was wonderful to see how railroad managers and capitalists met the situation, by investing additional capital for the newer type of equipment, and for the changes in road bed and location necessarily involved by that in the rolling stock. Curves were taken out or diminished, grades were reduced, heavier rails were laid, and new bridges built, so that practically some lines were almost rebuilt. The process is still going on and money by the hundred millions is involved in the transformation and equipment of the railroads. Some impression of the magnitude of the change in equipment may be gained from the single fact, that one of the leading railroads has within a few years expended more than $20,000,000 for new freight cars alone, all of which have a capacity of 100,000 pounds.

The form of loading for bridges almost universally specified by the railroads of this country consists of two consolidation locomotives followed by a uniform train load. These loads are frequently chosen somewhat larger than those that are likely to be actually used for some years in advance, but sometimes the heaviest type of locomotives in use is adopted as the standard loading. The extent to which the specified loadings have changed in eight years may be seen from the following statement based on statistics compiled by Ward Baldwin and published in the 'Railroad Gazette' for 2 May 1902.

Of the railroads whose lengths exceed 100 miles, located in the United States, Canada, and Mexico, only 2 out of 77 specified uniform train loads exceeding 4,000 pounds per linear foot of tracks in 1893, while in 1901, only 13 out of 103 railroads specified similar loads less than 4,000 pounds. In 1893, 37 railroads specified loads of 3,000 pounds and 29 of 4,000 pounds, while in 1901, 4,000 pounds was specified by 50, 4,500 pounds by 14, and 5,000 pounds by 17 railroads. The maximum uniform load rose from 4,200 in 1893 to 7,000 pounds in 1902.

In a similar manner in 1893 only 1 railroad in 75 specified a load on each driving wheel axle exceeding 40,000 pounds, while in 1901 only 13 railroads out of 92 specified less than this load. In 1893 only 21 of the 77 railroads specified similar loads exceeding 30,000 pounds. The maximum load on each driving wheel axle rose from 44,000 pounds in 1893 to 60,000 pounds in 1901.

The unusual amount of new bridge construction required caused a general revision of the standard specifications for bridges, the effect of which was to include the results of recent studies and experiment, and to eliminate some of the minor and unessential items formerly prescribed.

Meanwhile another movement was in progress. Experience having shown the great advantage of more uniformity in various details and standards relating to the manufacture of bridges both in reducing the cost and the time required for the shop work, an effort was begun to secure more uniformity in the requirements for the production and tests of steel, which is the metal now exclusively employed in bridges.

With greater uniformity in the physical, chemical and other requirements for steel, as determined by standard tests, the unit stresses to be prescribed for the design of bridges will naturally approach to a corresponding uniformity. To what extent this is desirable may be inferred from the fact that the application of several of the leading specifications to the design of a railroad bridge under a given live road yields results which may vary by an amount ranging from zero to 25 per cent of the total weight.

In the revision of specifications a decided tendency is observed to simplify the design by making an allowance for impact, vibration, etc., by adding certain percentages to the live load according to some well-defined system. It needs but relatively little experience in making comparative designs of bridges under the same loading, to show the advantage of this method over that in which the allowance is made in the unit stresses according to any of the systems usually adopted in such a case. Not only are the necessary computations greatly simplified, but the same degree of security is obtained in every detail of the connections as in the principal members which compose the structure.

Experiments on a large scale are very much needed to determine the proper percentage of the live load to be allowed for the effect of impact, so as to secure the necessary strength with the least sacrifice of true economy. An investigation might also be advantageously made to determine the proper ratio of the thickness of cover plates in chord members which are subject to compression, to the transverse distance between the connecting lines of rivets. The same need exists in regard to the stiffening of the webs of plate girders, concerning which there is a wide variation in the requirements of different specifications.

A movement which has done much good during the past decade and promises more for the future is that of the organization of bridge departments by the railroad companies. The great economy of making one design rather than to ask a number of bridge companies to make an equal number of designs, of which all but one are wasted, is the first advantage; but another of even greater significance in the development of bridge construction is that which arises from the designs being made by those who observe the bridges in the conditions of service and who will naturally devote closer study to every detail than is possible under the former usual conditions. The larger number of responsible designers also leads to the introduction of more new details to be submitted to the test of service, which will indicate those worthy of adoption in later designs. In order to save time and labor and secure greater uniformity in the design of the smaller bridges, some of the railroads prepare standard plans for spans varying by small distances. For the most important structures consulting bridge engineers are more frequently employed than formerly, when so much dependence was placed upon competitive designs made by the bridge companies.

An investigation was made by a committee of the Railway Engineering and Maintenance of Way Association in regard to the present practice respecting the degree of completeness of the plans and specifications furnished by the railroads. It was found that of the 72 railroads replying definitely to the inquiry, 33 per cent prepare "plans of more or less detail, but sufficiently full and precise to allow the bidder to figure the weight correctly and if awarded the contract to at once list the mill orders for material"; 18 per cent prepare "general outline drawings showing the composition of members, but no details of joints and connections"; while 49 per cent prepare "full specifications with survey plan only, leaving the bidder to submit a design with his bid." If, however, the comparison be made on the basis of mileage represented by these 72 railroads, the corresponding percentages are 48, 24, and 28 respectively. The total mileage represented was 117,245 miles. A large majority of the engineers and bridge companies that responded were in favor of making detail plans.

The shop drawings, which show the form of the bridge, the character and relations of all its parts, give the section and length of every member, and the size and position of every detail whether it be a reinforcing plate, a pin, a bolt, a rivet, or a lacing bar. All dimensions on the drawings are checked independently so as to avoid any chance for errors. The systematic manner in which the drawings are made and checked, and the thorough organization of every department of the shops, make it possible to manufacture the largest bridge, to ship the pieces to a distant site, and find on erecting the structure in place that all the parts fit together, although they had not been assembled at the works.

The constant improvement in the equipment of the bridge shops, and the increasing experience of the manufacturers who devote their entire time and attention to the study of better methods of transforming plates, bars, shapes, rivets, and pins into bridges, constitute important factors in the development of bridge construction.

As the length of span for the different classes of bridges gives a general indication of the progress in the science and art of bridge building, the following references are made to the longest existing span for each class, together with the increase in span which has been effected approximately during the past decade.

In plate girder bridges the girders, as their name implies, have solid webs composed of steel plates. A dozen years ago but few plate girders were built whose span exceeded 100 feet, the maximum span being but a few feet longer than this. To-day such large girders are very frequently constructed. The longest plate girder span was erected on the Mahoning division of the Erie R.R. in 1902 and measures 128 feet 4 inches between centres of bearings. The longest ones in a highway bridge are those of the viaduct on the Riverside Drive in New York, erected in 1900, the span being 126 feet. The heaviest plate girder is the middle one of a four-track bridge on the New York C. R.R. erected in 1901 near Lyons, N. Y. Its weight is 103 tons, its span 107 feet 8 inches and its depth out to out 12 feet 2 inches.

The large amount of new construction and the corresponding increase in the weight of rolling stock have combined to secure a more extensive adoption of plate girders and the designs of many new details for them. These affect chiefly the composition of the flanges, the web splices, the expansion bearings and the solid floor system. Although solid metal floors built up of special shapes were first introduced into this country 15 years ago, their general adoption has taken place largely within the past decade on account of their special adaptation to the requirements of the elevation of tracks in cities. Solid floors may not only be made much shallower than the ordinary open type, thereby reducing the total cost of the track elevation, but they also permit the ordinary track con-

THE BROOKLYN BRIDGE AND SUSPENSION BRIDGE, NO. 3, ON WHICH WORK HAS JUST
COMMENCED. EAST RIVER, NEW YORK.
BIRD'S EYE VIEW OF NEW YORK, SHOWING THE BRIDGES BUILT AND BUILDING
ACROSS THE EAST RIVER.

struction with cross-ties in ballast to be extended across the bridge, thus avoiding the jar which otherwise results as the train enters and leaves the bridge, unless the track is maintained with extraordinary care.

The necessity for bridges of greater stiffness under the increased live loads has also led to the use of riveted bridges for considerably longer spans than were in use six or seven years ago. The use of pin-connected trusses for spans less than about 150 feet is undesirable for railroad bridges, on account of the excessive vibration due to the large ratio of the moving load to the dead load or weight of the bridge itself.

While riveted bridges are now quite generally used for spans from 100 to 150 feet, they have been employed to some extent up to $181\frac{1}{2}$ feet. The recent forms of riveted trusses do not, however, conform to the general character of European designs, but embody the distinctively American feature of concentrating the material into fewer members of substantial construction. With but rare exceptions the trusses are of the Warren, Pratt, and Baltimore types with single systems of webbing. At a distance where the riveted connections cannot be distinguished, the larger trusses have the same general appearance as the corresponding pin bridges.

The recent examples of viaduct construction with their stiff bracing of built-up members and riveted connections exhibit a marked contrast to the older and lighter structures with their adjustable bracing composed of slender rods. The viaduct which carries the Chicago & N. W. R.R. across the valley of the Des Moines River, at a height of 185 feet above the surface of the river is 2,658 feet long. It was built in 1901, is the longest double-track viaduct in the world, provided those located in cities be excluded, and is an admirable type of the best modern construction. The tower spans are 45 feet long and the other spans are 75 feet long. Four lines of plate girders support the two tracks. Along with this viaduct should be mentioned the Viaduct Terminal of the Chesapeake & O. R.R. at Richmond, Va., whose length, including the depot branch, is 3.13 miles. A large part of this is not very much higher than an elevated railroad in cities. The excellent details and clean lines of this substantial structure give it a character which is surpassed neither in this country nor abroad. It may be added that the highest viaduct in this country, and which was rebuilt in 1900, is located 17 miles from Bradford, Pa., where the Erie R.R. crosses the Kinzua Creek at a height of 301 feet. It has a length of 2,053 feet.

While the elevated railroads which have been built recently also embody many of the characteristics of the best viaduct construction, special study has been given to improve their æsthetic effect. The use of curved brackets, of connecting plates whose edges are trimmed into curves so as to reduce the number of sharp angles, and of rounded corners of posts, constitute some of the means employed. The results are seen in the structures of the Boston Elevated R.R. and in some of the latest construction in Chicago.

The longest span of any simple truss in America is that of the bridge over the Ohio River at Louisville, erected in 1893. Its span

centre to centre of end pins is $546\frac{1}{2}$ feet. Since that time several other bridges of this kind have been built which are considerably heavier, although their spans are somewhat shorter. The most noteworthy of these are the Delaware River bridge on the Pennsylvania R.R. near Philadelphia, and the Monongahela River bridge of the Union R.R. at Rankin, Pa., both of which are double-track bridges. The Delaware River bridge was erected in 1896, each one of its fixed spans having a length of 533 feet and containing 2,094 tons of steel. The Rankin bridge was erected in 1900. Its longer span has a length of 495 feet $8\frac{7}{8}$ inches between centres of end pins and contains about 2,800 tons of steel. It may also be added that the locomotive and train load for which this bridge was designed is the heaviest that has yet been specified. The heaviest simple span in this country is the channel span of the double deck bridge over the Allegheny River at Pittsburg, Pa., on the Pennsylvania lines west of Pittsburg, erected in 1902. It has four trusses and weighs about 3,000 tons.

The recent changes in the details of pin-connected truss bridges have been mainly the result of efforts to eliminate ambiguity in the stresses of the trusses, to reduce the effect of secondary stresses, and to secure increased stiffness as well as strength in the structure. Double systems of webbing have been practically abandoned so far as new construction is concerned. The simplicity of truss action thus secured permits the stresses to be computed with greater accuracy and thereby tends to economy. Before the last decade very few through bridges and those only of large span were designed with end floor beams in order to make the superstructure as complete as possible in itself and independent of the masonry supports. Now this improved feature is being extended to bridges of small spans. Similarly dropping the ends of all floor beams in through bridges so as to clear the lower chord and to enable the lower lateral system to be connected without producing an excessive bending movement in the posts has likewise been extended to the smaller spans of pin bridges and is now the standard practice. The expansion bearings have been made more effective by the use of large rollers and of bed plates so designed as to properly distribute the large loads upon the masonry. In the larger spans of through bridges the top chord is curved more uniformly, thereby improving the æsthetic appearance. These chords are also given full pin bearings, thus reducing the secondary stresses.

The stiffness of truss bridges has been secured by adopting stiff bracing in the lateral systems and sway bracing, instead of the light adjustable rods formerly used. At the same time adjustable counter ties in the trusses are being replaced in recent years by stiff ones, while in some cases the counters are omitted and the main diagonals designed to take both tension and compression.

Some of the same influences referred to above have led to much simpler designs for the portal bracings by using a few members of adequate strength and stiffness in general character to those of the trusses.

Such steady progress in the design and construction of railroad bridges of moderate span has, unfortunately, no adequate counterpart in highway bridges. The conditions under which highway bridges are purchased by township and county commissioners are decidedly unfavorable to material improvements in the character of their details. It is a comparatively rare occurrence that the commissioners employ a bridge engineer to look after the interests of the taxpayers by providing suitable specifications, making the design, inspecting the material, and examining the construction of the bridge to see that it conforms to all the imposed requirements. These provisions are only made in some of the cities, and accordingly, one must examine the new bridges in cities to learn what progress is making in highway bridge building.

The lack of proper supervision in the rural districts and many of the smaller cities results in the continued use of short trusses with slender members built up of thin plates and shapes, whose comparatively light weight causes excessive vibration and consequent wear, as well as deterioration from rust. Under better administration plate girders would be substituted for such light trusses, making both a stiffer structure and one more easily protected by paint. The general lack of inspection and the consequent failure to protect highway bridges by regular repainting will materially shorten their life and thereby increase the financial burden to replace them by new structures. Some progress has been made by adopting riveted trusses for the shorter spans for which pin-connected trusses were formerly used, but the extent of this change is by no means as extensive as it should be, nor equal to the corresponding advance in railroad bridges.

The channel span of the cantilever bridge over the Mississippi River at Memphis, Tenn., was for some years the longest one of any bridge of this class in America. It measures 790½ feet between centers of supports. This bridge was finished in 1892, or only two years after the close of the seven-year period of construction and erection of the mammoth cantilever bridge over the Firth of Forth in Scotland. See BRIDGE (*Cantilever Bridges*). The cantilever bridge erected in 1903 over the Monongahela River in Pittsburg has a span a little longer than that of the Memphis bridge. It is on the new extension of the Wabash R.R. system, and the distance between pier centres is 812 feet. There is another one being built which will not only have a longer span than any other cantilever bridge in this country, but longer than that of any other bridge in the world. It is located near Quebec, Canada, and its channel span over the St. Lawrence River is to have the unprecedented length of 1,800 feet, or nearly 100 feet longer than that of the Forth cantilever bridge and 200 feet longer than the Brooklyn suspension bridge. The towers will have a height of 360 feet above high tide. It will accommodate a double-track railroad, besides two electric railway tracks and highways. In the piers the courses of masonry are four feet high and individual stones weigh about 15 tons each. The character of its design and the simplicity of its details will permit its construction with unusual rapidity and economy for a bridge of this magnitude.

The Brooklyn bridge, completed in 1883, is still the largest suspension bridge in the world, its span being 1,595½ feet. More people cross this bridge than any other in any country. The Williamsburg Bridge (q.v.), completed in 1904, has a span of 1,600 feet, and its capacity will be very much greater than that of the Brooklyn Bridge. Each of its four cables has a safe strength of over 10,000,000 pounds in tension. See BRIDGE (*Suspension Bridges*).

One of the most interesting developments relating to the subject under consideration is the construction of a considerable number of metallic arch bridges in recent years and the promise of their still greater use in the future. On account of their form they constitute one of the handsomest classes of bridges.

The first important steel bridge in the world was completed in 1874. It is the arch bridge which in three spans crosses the Mississippi River at St. Louis. Its arches are without hinges and their ends are firmly fixed to the piers. This is one of the most famous bridges in existence. For a long time after its construction no metallic arches were erected in this country, although many were built in Europe. In 1888, however, the highway bridge across the Mississippi River at Minneapolis was erected, consisting of two spans of 456 feet each and which still remains the longest span of any three-hinged arch. The following year the Washington bridge over the Harlem River in New York was completed. It consists of two spans of 510 feet in the clear and has the largest two-hinged arch ribs with solid web plates. See BRIDGE.

These were followed by a number of arches of various types, the most noted of which are the two arch bridges over the Niagara River. The first one is a spandrel-braced, two-hinged arch with a span of 550 feet, and replaced the Roebling suspension bridge in 1897. It accommodates the two tracks of the Grand Trunk R.R. on the upper deck and a highway on the lower deck. The other bridge has arched trusses with parallel chords and two hinges. It replaced the Niagara and Clifton highway suspension bridge in 1898, and as its span is 840 feet, it is the largest arch of any type in the world. The manner in which this arch was erected furnishes an illustration of the effort which is made by engineers to conform the actual conditions so far as possible to the theoretic ones involved in the computation of the stresses. Since the stresses in an arch having less than three hinges are statically indeterminate, stresses of considerable magnitude may be introduced into the trusses if the workmanship be imperfect, the supports not located with sufficient precision, and the arch closed without the proper means and care.

The Niagara and Clifton arch was first closed as a three-hinged arch and then transformed into a two-hinged arch by inserting the final member under the sum of the computed stress due to the weight of the truss, and that due to the difference between the temperature at which the closure was made and that assumed as standard in the stress computations. This stress was secured in the member by inserting it when the hydraulic jack which forced apart the adjacent ends of the shortened chords registered the required amount of pressure. The arch had been erected as a pair of cantilevers from each side extending 420 feet out beyond the supports, and when the closure was made the two arms came together

Copyright by the Scientific American.

ROLLING LIFT BRIDGES.

within a quarter of an inch of the computed value. Such a result involving the "accuracy of the calculation and design of the entire steel work, the exactness with which the bearing shoes or skewbacks were placed, and the perfection of the shopwork" has been truly characterized as phenomenal. In order to reduce secondary stresses to a minimum the members were bolted up during the cantilever erection and the bolts replaced by rivets after the closure of the arch rib.

The past decade witnessed the introduction and extensive development of arches of concrete and of concrete-steel construction. In the latter kind a small amount of steel is embedded in the concrete in order to resist any tensile stresses that may be developed. During this period more than 150 concrete-steel bridges have been built in this country. In the same year in which the largest metallic arch was completed, the five concrete-steel arches of the bridge at Topeka, Kansas, were finished. The largest one has a span of 125 feet and still remains the largest span of this type in America, although it has been exceeded in Europe. Considerably larger spans are included in the accepted design for the proposed Memorial bridge at Washington.

It is the smaller steel structures which are destined more and more to be replaced by arches of this material. The steel bridges require repainting at frequent intervals, constant inspection, occasional repairs, and finally replacing by a new structure after a relatively short life, on account of rust and wear, unless it is required even sooner on account of a considerable increase in the live load. The concrete arch requires practically no attention except at very long intervals.

The safety of operating the traffic makes it desirable to have as few breaks as possible in the regular track construction of a railroad, and this constitutes an additional reason why concrete or stone arches are being substituted for the smaller openings. The decreasing cost of concrete tends to an extension of this practice to openings of increasing size. In 1901, however, a bridge was completed which marks a decided departure from previous practice. The Pennsylvania R.R. built a stone bridge, consisting of 48 segmental arches of 70 feet span, at the crossing of the Susquehanna River at Rockville, Pa. It is 52 feet wide, accommodates four tracks and cost $1,000,000. This bridge has not only the advantage of almost entirely eliminating the cost of maintenance, but it also has sufficient mass to withstand the floods which occasionally wreck the other bridges on that river. In 1903 the same railroad built a similar bridge over the Raritan River at New Brunswick, N. J.

Of movable bridges the largest swing span existing was erected in 1893 at Omaha over the Missouri River. Two years later a four-track railroad swing bridge was built by the New York C. R.R. over the Harlem River in New York, which is only 389 feet long between centres of end pins, but which weighs about 2,500 tons, and is accordingly the heaviest drawbridge of any class in the world.

During the past decade a remarkable development was made in drawbridge construction by the modification and improvement of some of the older types of lift bridges and the design of several new types. At South Halstead Street a direct-lift bridge was built in 1893 over the Chicago River, in which a simple span 130 feet long and 50 feet wide is lifted vertically 142½ feet by means of cables to which counterweights are attached. Formerly, only very small bridges of this kind were used, as those, for instance, over the Erie Canal.

In 1895 a rolling-lift bridge over the Chicago River was completed. In this new design each leaf of the bridge rotates to a vertical position it rolls backward at one end. When closed the two leaves are locked at the centre, but they are supported as cantilevers. This form has been found to have so many advantages for the crossings of relatively narrow streams, where an unobstructed waterway is required and the adjacent shores are needed for dock room, that a score of important structures of this class have been built in different cities. The largest span that has been designed is 275 feet between centres of supports, while the widest one is to accommodate eight railroad tracks crossing the Chicago Main Drainage Canal.

About the same time and under similar conditions another type of bascule bridge was built at Sixteenth Street, Milwaukee, in which, as each leaf moves toward the shore, one end rises and the other falls, so that its centre of gravity moves horizontally, thus requiring a very small expenditure of power to operate the bridge.

Several improved forms of hinged-lift bridges have also been designed and built in Chicago and elsewhere. In a small bridge erected in 1896 on the Erie R.R. in the Hackensack meadows there is only a single leaf hinged at one end and lifted by a cable attached to the other end. The counterweight rolls on a curved track so designed as to make the counterbalance equally effective in all stages of opening and closing the bridge.

A novel bridge was built in 1902 over the ship canal at Duluth which is different from any other type in this country. The general scheme is similar to that of a design made by a French engineer who built three of the structures in different countries. It consists of a simple truss bridge 393 feet 9 inches long, supported on towers at a clear height of 135 feet above high water. Instead of supporting the usual floor of a highway bridge it supports the track of a suspended car which is properly stiffened against wind pressure and lateral vibration, the floor of the car being on a level with the docks. This ferry is operated by electricity. The loaded car, its hangers, trucks, and machinery weigh 120 tons. In the French design a suspension bridge was used instead of the simple truss bridge.

A bridge across the Charles River between Boston and Cambridge deserves especial mention and marks a decided advance in the growing recognition on the part of municipal authorities of the importance of æsthetic considerations in the design of public works. It consists of 11 spans of steel arches whose lengths range from 101½ to 188½ feet. Its width is 105 feet between railings. It is claimed that this bridge "will be not only one of the finest structures of its kind in this country, but will be a rival of any in the Old World." Its length between abutments is 1.767½ feet, and it is estimated to cost about $2,500,000.

BRIDGE CONSTRUCTION

The problems incident to the replacing and strengthening of old bridges frequently tax the resources of the engineer and demonstrate his ability to overcome difficulties. Only a few examples may be cited to indicate the character of this work. In 1900 the Niagara cantilever bridge had its capacity increased about 75 per cent by the insertion of a middle truss without interfering with traffic. In 1897 the entire floor of the Cincinnati and Covington suspension bridge was raised four feet while the traffic was using it. It may be of interest to state that the two new cables, 10½ inches in diameter, which were added to increase the capacity of the bridge, have just about three times the strength of the two old ones, 12⅓ inches in diameter, and which were made a little over 30 years before. In the same year the old tubular bridge across the St. Lawrence River was replaced by simple truss spans without the use of false works under the bridge and without interfering with traffic. On 25 May 1902 the Pennsylvania R.R. bridge over the Raritan River and canal at New Brunswick, N. J., was moved sidewise a distance of 14½ feet. Five simple spans 150 feet long and a drawbridge of the same length, weighing in all 2,057 tons, were moved to the new position and aligned in 2 minutes and 50 seconds. The actual times that the two tracks were out of service were respectively 15 and 28 minutes. On 17 October 1897, on the same railroad near Girard Avenue, Philadelphia, an old span was moved away, and a new one, 235 feet 7 inches long, put in exactly the same place in 2 minutes and 28 seconds. No train was delayed in either case.   HENRY S. JACOBY, *College of Civil Engineering, Cornell.*

Bridge Construction, Modern Methods of: An instructive exposition of these methods requires a brief consideration of the principles of design and the controlling factors therein.

All framed structures may be divided into two classes — those designed to sustain only a permanent or "dead load," which acts with unvarying forces, and those which sustain not only the dead load consisting of their own weight, but also the action of a "live load" applied by the movement of railway trains, ordinary vehicles and horses, men, etc., over them.

Roof trusses, cranes, cantilevers, etc., are of the first class, while bridges belong to the second.

All bridge structures may be conveniently divided into three classes — (1) "beam bridges," (2) "suspension bridges," (3) "arch bridges." The first exert only vertical pressures upon the supporting piers and abutments; the second exert a horizontal pull on the towers and anchorages; while the third exert a horizontal push in addition to the vertical pressures.

"Beam bridges" are of a great variety of forms, including those commonly known as simple bridges, drawbridges, continuous bridges, and cantilever bridges. Over 90 per cent of the modern bridges are simple bridges, of which there are two classes — truss bridges and girder bridges. In the former the floor is supported by two or more frame structures, called trusses: in the latter the floor is supported by solid built-up beams. Girder bridges are generally used for short spans, seldom exceeding 100 feet; but the truss bridges are used for larger spans, and also for spans as short as 50 feet.

A simple framed structure or truss is one composed of straight "members" or parts joined together by pins or rivets, so as to form a rigid framework. The most rigid form is that of a triangle, as it is the only figure the shape of which cannot be altered without changing the length of its sides. It is, therefore, the "truss element," and all framed structures, no matter how complicated in construction, may be treated as a combination of triangles when no superfluous members are present.

The forces such structures are designed to resist are those of tension, compression, and shearing. These forces when external are called "strains," while the corresponding internal forces developed in the several members of the structure to resist the strains, are called stresses.

Owing to the frequent confused and indiscriminate use of the terms strain and stress by some authors, a great deal of popular misunderstanding exists as to their exact designations. According to the best authorities, however, a strain is the distortion of a body under the action of one or more external forces, and it is the immediate cause of the stress developed in the body to resist that distortion. Under certain conditions, however, a stress may by reaction and transmission act as an external force, as in the case of the stresses in the masonry supports of a bridge which react upon the superstructure and are in effect external forces and have to be treated as such. In solid bodies, within certain limits, the intensity of the stress is equal to the amount of the strain, and as enunciated by Hookes' Law, equal increments of one develop equal increments of the other; but, it is evident that stresses cannot thus continue to increase indefinitely in proportion to the strains, and a point is necessarily reached when a greater increment of distortion is required to develop a given increment of stress. This point is known as the "elastic limit." Below this point, a distorted body returns to its original form and size when the straining force ceases to act; but, beyond the limit, the strain increases more rapidly than the stress, or than the straining force which is always the equal of the stress, and the body does not return to its original dimensions, since a portion of the distortion remains as a "permanent set."

In the designing of a truss, the members are guarded against "taking a set," by keeping the working stresses well within the elastic limit of the material of construction.

A bridge truss is designed to act as a beam and it is, therefore, usually subjected to longitudinal strains of tension or compression only, and develops in its members corresponding tensile or compressive stresses. Fig. 1 shows a

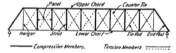

FIG. 1.— Simple Truss.

simple bridge truss with its several members designated as struts, ties or tie-rods, etc., according to the character of the stresses developed in them by the combined action of the dead and live loads.

In the "struts" the stresses are compressive; in the "ties" tensile. The upper and lower "chords" are placed in compression or tension according to the direction of action of the external forces applied to the structure. In a truss supported at the ends and bearing a downward acting load, the upper chord is always in compression, and the lower chord always in tension. "Counterbraces" are designed to resist both

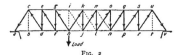

FIG. 2.

tensile and compressive strains alternately, as they may be applied by the changing positions of the load. No truss-member can act simultaneously in full tension and compression, but may do so partially, since the stress developed in any member by the strains of two or more external forces is equal to and of the same sign as the algebraic sum of all those forces. Thus a tie may resist a compressive strain without becoming a counterbrace, or a strut may resist a tensile strain without becoming a tie, so long as the contrary strains are smaller than those for which the member is designed, and which continue to act at the same time.

Fig. 2 shows the action of a truss. As already stated, a truss acts as a beam, and a load applied at (h) will be carried to the abutments at (a) and (v) along the several members as indicated by the arrows, leaving the post (hi), the ties (ij) (kl) (mn), and the hanger (cb) and (tw) idle, and they may be removed without weakening the truss under that particular loading, since it would still remain a combination of triangles properly joined. Fig. 3 shows the conditions with the load applied at (j), with the ties (ij) and (jm) under stress, and the ties (hk) and (kl) idle. Fig. 4 shows

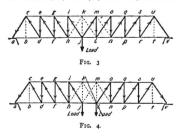

FIG. 3.

FIG. 4.

two equal loads applied at the middle points (j) and (l). Since the part of the load at (j) going to (v) is just balanced by the part of the load at (l) going to (a), there is no stress in (jk) (lm) (jm) and (kl), nor in the counter ties (hk) and (mn).

From an inspection of these conditions it is obvious that a truss is not weakened on account of a lack of symmetry in the arrangement of its individual members, or as a whole

structure, provided all the members are properly designed to carry their respective loads.

The economy and the efficiency of the truss lies in the panel or quadrilateral system. Fig. 5 shows its development from the triangular

FIG. 5.

king-post truss by the addition of the side panels. It appears that this system was first introduced by Palladio about 1570, but was little used until the close of the 18th century, when it was re-discovered by Burr, and came into extensive use in the United States and is the progenitor of nearly all the forms of bridge trusses now in use in this country, its most valuable feature — a constant angle for the inclined members and its panel system being transmitted to the "Long," "Pratt," "Howe," and to many other later forms of trusses.

The "Bollman," "Warren," and "Fink" trusses, embodying the pure triangular types

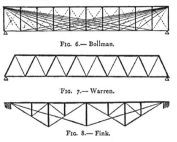

FIG. 6.— Bollman.

FIG. 7.— Warren.

FIG. 8.— Fink.

(see Figs. 6, 7, and 8), preceded those of the quadrilateral system. They were, however, unstable under the action of a live load which subjected their members to different strains alternately, with a consequential deterioration of the material and a shortening of the life of the

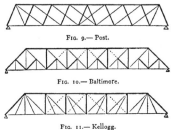

FIG. 9.— Post.

FIG. 10.— Baltimore.

FIG. 11.— Kellogg.

structure. These considerations led to the development of the quadrilateral type in which each member is required to resist a strain of only one particular character. Of these, the more important other than those already mentioned, are the "Post," "Baltimore," "Kellogg," and "Whipple-Murphy," shown by Figs. 9, 10, 11, 12, respectively. The "Whipple-Murphy" was the first to approach to the modern iron truss-bridges. The first bridge of this type, a span of 146 feet, was built by Whipple in 1852, near Troy, N. Y., on the Rensselaer and Saratoga Railway.

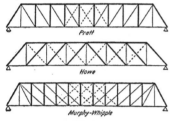

Pratt

Howe

Murphy-Whipple

FIG. 12.

In 1861, Linville introduced wide forged eyebars and wrought iron posts in the web system, while two years later, Murphy substituted wrought iron for all of the compression members, and established in this country the distinctive practice of eye-bars and pin connections, which is still applied to long span steel truss-bridges. The credit of originating the correct theory of truss action, however, belongs to Whipple.

In Europe, the prevailing method of construction is the riveted system, which in this country is limited to plate girders and lattice

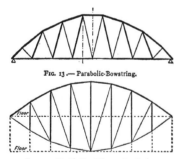

FIG. 13.— Parabolic-Bowstring.

FIG. 14.— Double-Bowstring or Lenticular.

FIG. 15.— Pegram.

trusses of less than 200 feet span. In this system the chords are formed of angles or channel and plates riveted together with splice

joints, thus making them continuous from one end to the other. The web members are riveted to the chords directly, or by means of special plates, which are riveted to both.

Other forms of bridge trusses than those already described, which have many claims to economy and excellence of design, are the "parabolic bowstring," the "double bowstring" or "lenticular," the "Pegram," and the "Petit" trusses, shown by Figs. 13, 14, 15, and 16.

FIG. 16.— Petit.

A plate girder bridge consists of two or more girders connected by systems of lateral and transverse bracings. In its simplest form a plate girder is composed of a vertical web plate to the top and bottom of which are riveted pairs of horizontal angle irons, forming the flanges, and to the ends, vertical angles which transmit the load to the support. The structural forms of girders are modified in many ways to adapt them for different purposes. Increase in the ratio of the depth of the web to its thickness necessitates the addition of "stiffeners." These are vertical angles riveted on to the web in pairs on opposite sides at intervals along the span. As the span increases, two or more web plates are used, spliced end to end. In long spans the flanges also require splicing. See Fig. 17.

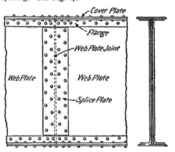

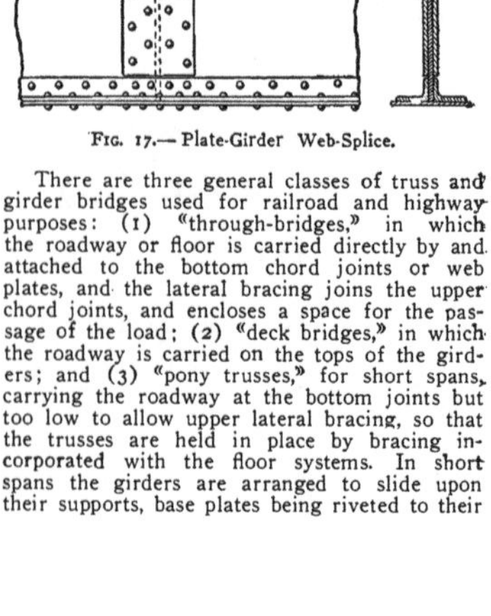

FIG. 17.— Plate-Girder Web-Splice.

There are three general classes of truss and girder bridges used for railroad and highway purposes: (1) "through-bridges," in which the roadway or floor is carried directly by and attached to the bottom chord joints or web plates, and the lateral bracing joins the upper chord joints, and encloses a space for the passage of the load; (2) "deck bridges," in which the roadway is carried on the tops of the girders; and (3) "pony trusses," for short spans, carrying the roadway at the bottom joints but too low to allow upper lateral bracing, so that the trusses are held in place by bracing incorporated with the floor systems. In short spans the girders are arranged to slide upon their supports, base plates being riveted to their bottoms and bed-plates to the supports. In spans 75 feet or less, expansion and contraction due to changes in temperature are provided for by the use of hinged bolsters, while for longer spans rollers are introduced between the base and bed-plates. The thickness of the webs and the composition of the flanges of plate girders, relative to the increased stresses developed by greater loads and longer spans, is accurately fixed by experience. In railroad bridges, the web plates ought not to be less than three eighths of an inch in thickness, while those in highway bridges ought not to be less than five sixteenths of an inch; but, in the general design of plate girders, it is well to exceed these values.

In the composition of the flanges, each pair of angles ought to be riveted to the web plate, with their backs projecting a little beyond it, to counteract any lack of straightness in the edge of the web plate, thereby allowing anything to rest upon the flange fairly. When required, additional flange area is obtained by riveting one or more cover plates to the horizontal limbs

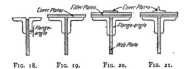

FIG. 18. FIG. 19. FIG. 20. FIG. 21.

of the angles; their number, however, ought to be so limited that the length of the rivets used are not more than five times their diameter. Since the stress in the web plate is transmitted to the covers through the angles, the sectional area of the angles ought to be equal to or greater than that of the cover plates. In a girder, the bending moment requires cover plates of different lengths. This necessitates the notching of the cross-ties unequally. This is obviated by various modifications of the flange — by using a narrow outer cover extending the whole length of the girder and placing filler plates under it, or by the use of two small angles, the cross-ties being notched to fit the vertical legs of the angles. See Figs. 18, 19, 20, 21.

Other methods are illustrated by Figs. 22 and

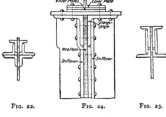

FIG. 22. FIG. 24. FIG. 23.

23, while Fig. 24 shows the section of a flange at the end of a girder.

The functions of intermediate web stiffeners are in a rather undetermined condition, and the

practice in their use varies considerably. It may be broadly stated, however, that the general practice is to use stiffeners $3\frac{1}{2}'' \times 3\frac{1}{2}'' \times \frac{3}{8}''$ angles for spans below 50 feet; $5'' \times 3\frac{1}{2}'' \times \frac{3}{8}''$, angles for spans from 50 to 100 feet, and $6'' \times 4'' \times \frac{3}{8}''$ angles for spans over 100 feet.

The size and weight of web plates are limited by the processes of manufacture and available equipment. Therefore, large girders require several web splices. In their simplest form they consist of plates equal in length to the clear distance between the flange angles, and are riveted to each of the two abutting web plates by two or more rows of rivets, with a pair of stiffener angles attached.

For spans less than 60 feet, splices in the flanges may usually be avoided, as angles and cover plates of sufficient length can be readily obtained. In any case it is more economical to reduce the number of splices to a minimum, even at the additional cost of the extra length angles and cover plates. Flange angles are usually spliced with cover-angles with rounded roots which fit into the fillets of the other angles, while the outer cover splices are so arranged that the outer cover near the splices may be extended so as to form the splice plate. Fig. 25 shows a very efficient splice, designed in accordance with the best specifications so as to develop the full strength of the net section of the web. The main splice plates extend from flange to flange, and two flats are riveted over the vertical legs of the flange angle, thereby reaching parts of the web not reached directly by the other plates, and adding greatly to the strength of the whole splice. Since the efficiency of a rivet to resist bending strains at a joint is proportional to the square of its distance from the neutral surface, therefore, in a splice of this type, with a web 7/16 inch thick and 84 inches deep, and the unit stress in the outer fibre 17,000 pounds per square inch, the resisting moment of the gross section of the lower half of the web is equal to 4,373,000 pound-inches, and that of the net section 3,538,200 pound-inches.

The upper and lower flanges of the two or more girders constituting a bridge are held in line by a series of braces, each of which is composed of one or two angles. These braces and the flanges form horizontal trusses, which are called the upper and lower lateral systems. The Warren type, in which the panel points of the upper system are directly above the middle points between the panel points of the lower system, is the one most frequently employed.

Rigid cross frames, each consisting of two struts and two diagonals connected with a stiffener on each end girder, are placed at the ends of the girders and at intermediate points and constitute what is known as transverse bracing.

The floors of "through" railroad plate-girder bridges may be constructed by a system of floor beams and stringers, or made solid. The former method is the one most extensively employed. The floor beams are simply plate-girders of short spans, and are usually placed from 12 to 18 feet apart, and riveted to the main girders, the web splice plates of which are extended to reinforce the web plate of the floor beams. From each end of the floor beams a triangular gusset plate riveted to the girder extends to the top flange. The outer edge of the gusset plate is stiffened by a pair of angles, which are bent over at the upper ends and riveted to both the flange and stiffener angles.

Either I beams or short plate girders may be used for stringers. In the latter case no cover plates are used and the web plates are allowed to project above the flange angles, the cross-ties being carried upon the top flanges. The arrangement of a floor system, in which the ties rest upon horizontal shelf angles, riveted to the web near the lower flange, or one in which the cross-ties rest on the bottom flanges, which are weakened and the lateral bracing loosened by the spring of the floor, is very objectionable. According to the best practice the cross-ties in deck bridges rest directly upon the top flanges of the two girders supporting each track.

Solid floor construction includes many different types. In some, continuous metal floors support the rails on ordinary cross-ties in bal-

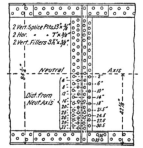

FIG. 25.

last, while in others the ballast is omitted and the cross-ties rest on the metal floor, or the rails rest directly on the metal floor. Solid floors were built as early as 1874, the track rails being laid close together on top of the girders and overspread with the ballast. This gave a

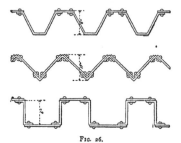

FIG. 26.

continuous track practically free from the objections applicable to the crossing of wooden bridge floors supported on stringers. Floors

consisting of metal troughs were introduced in 1887. They were constructed by riveting together alternately inverted trough plates, as shown in Fig. 26, with the cross-ties laid directly in the troughs or imbedded in ballast. In 1888, the New York Central & Hudson River Railroad adopted this system as a standard for through bridges, and have retained it as such up to the present time for bridges of a limited depth of floor. The necessity for very shallow floors for elevated tracks in large cities, and for plate girders at street crossings, have led to the production of several designs employing I beams and continuous cover plates. The solid floors of highway bridges usually consisted of either a continuous metal floor or one in which the metal was used in combination with concrete or some other material for the permanent foundation upon which the street and sidewalk paving was laid. The latest development in this line is the extensive use of reinforced concrete for both highway and railroad bridges.

Examples of bridges with reinforced concrete floors are quite numerous, and the application of the system is being widely and rapidly extended both in the United States and Europe. Fig. 27 shows the section of a bridge floor constructed of Monier arched plates, and Fig. 28 the floor of a foot-bridge in Lincoln Park, Chicago. The floor beams are placed at the panel points, 18 feet apart, with two beams placed close together, with expansion joints between them, at the centre of the span. From these beams a series of two groups of quadruple steel

FIG. 27.

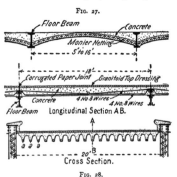

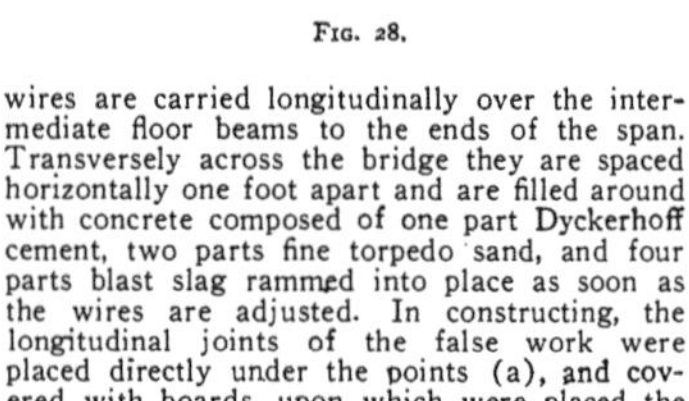

FIG. 28.

wires are carried longitudinally over the intermediate floor beams to the ends of the span. Transversely across the bridge they are spaced horizontally one foot apart and are filled around with concrete composed of one part Dyckerhoff cement, two parts fine torpedo sand, and four parts blast slag rammed into place as soon as the wires are adjusted. In constructing, the longitudinal joints of the false work were placed directly under the points (a), and covered with boards, upon which were placed the forms for making the corrugation. The wires were then stretched under a tension of 60 pounds and secured in the proper position by hook bolts attached to the bottoms of the joints.

These bolts were removed when the concrete filling was firmly set.

The use of reinforced concrete is not limited to the construction of solid bridge floors. Many concrete-steel arch bridges have been built in the United States, and a much greater number of girder bridges in Europe. The usual girder construction is monolithic, and consists of a slab stiffened with ribs or girders on the under side. Unstiffened slabs are used only for very short spans, such as ordinary box culvert work; while rib-stiffened slabs are applied to spans ranging from 25 to 50 feet. For spans exceeding 50 feet the arch type is almost universally employed, and many concrete-steel arches exceeding 150 feet have already been built, and much larger spans are now being planned. The reinforced concrete arch bridge occupies a medium position between the metal and the stone arch bridges, being almost as light as the former and very nearly as durable as the latter. It is particularly suitable for the foot and highway bridges across railway tracks and small streams and canals, where the requirements of light weight, freedom from corrosion, and low cost are important factors. In the earlier methods of construction only the arch ring was reinforced, but now the reinforcement is applied to the spandrel and parapet walls also; being practically steel skeletons imbedded in concrete. In the earlier bridges the arch was built plain, but the present practice in the United States is in the direction of ribbed arch construction, while in Europe hinged arches are also being used, and the Monier method of construction appears to be the one most extensively used. (a)-Fig. 29 shows a Monier arch at Nymphemburg, Bavaria. It has a span of 87 feet, a total width of 33 feet, and carries a roadway 21 feet

In the Wünsch form of construction the reinforcement consists of a series of forms of double T-shaped members, of which the extradosal are placed horizontally, with the flanges upward, and the intradosal conforming to the curve of the arch and placed with the flanges downward. Their webs overlap at the crown of the arch and are riveted together, while the ends are connected by vertical tie rods which extend downward into the pier or masonry abutment, and is anchored to a transverse girder

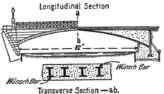

Longitudinal Section

Transverse Section —ab.

FIG. 30.

extending along the bridge. These frames are placed parallel to each other longitudinally across the arch, at intervals ranging from 18 to 24 inches apart, the ratio of the reinforcement cross-section to that of the concrete at the crown being about 2 to 100. Fig. 30 shows the Emperor Bridge at Sarajevo, Bosnia — a Wünsch arch of about 82 feet span, with a width of 23 feet, one of the longest spans of its kind, and all of the details of construction.

In the Hennebique ribbed arch system, the reinforcement consists of longitudinal arched ribs which carry a floor slab stiffened by trans-

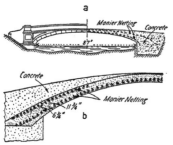

FIG. 29.

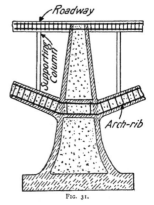

FIG. 31.

wide, paved with wood blocks, which rest directly on the arch ring at the crown and on the concrete filling over the haunches. The structure is designed to sustain wagon loads of 26 tons. The reinforcement consists of continuous steel nets at both the extrados and the intrados of the arch ring. This is known as the "double reinforcement" type, but it is not used so extensively as that shown by (b)-Fig. 29, in which the intradosal is continuous, but the extradosal extends up the haunches only to a limited distance from the skewback.

verse joints between the ribs. In short spans up to 60 feet the arched ribs are placed from 5 to 10 feet apart, and form the sole reinforcement of the slab. In spans exceeding 60 feet, the arch ring is stiffened intradosally as shown by Fig. 31. The longest span reinforced conerete bridge up to date was built under this system across the Vienne at Chatellerault, France, in 1899. It has a centre span of 164 feet, and two side spans of 131 feet each, making a total length of 443 feet. The arch rings are about 19½ feet wide and carry a roadway platform 26¼ feet in width. It cost about $35,000.

The "Melan" system employs a series of arched steel ribs placed parallel to each other, at intervals ranging from 2½ to 3½ feet apart. Their shape corresponds closely to that of the depth and profile of the arch ring, which is usually the only portion of the structure reinforced. In short spans the ribs are simply rolled I beams bent to the curve of the arch ring, but in the larger spans they are in the form of lattice steel arches. Perhaps the finest example of foot-bridge construction by this system is the bridge from Laurel Hill to the Ice

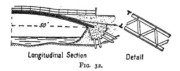

Longitudinal Section   Detail

FIG. 32.

Glen, at Stockbridge, Mass., shown in Fig. 32. It has a span of 100 feet, is 7½ feet wide, and is reinforced with four parallel I beams bent to the curves of the arch, with their ends bolted to transverse angles in the abutments. Over 125 bridges, with spans ranging from 12 to 136 feet, have been built in the United States since the introduction of the system by Emperger in 1884. The credit for the most successful introduction of reinforced concrete bridges in the United States, however, belongs to Edwin Thacher, who was the first American engineer to design them according to the elastic theory or the law of flexure in solid arches. His system employes a series of flat steel bars in pairs, placed parallel to each other at proper distances apart. The top and bottom of each pair conform to the curve of the extrados and intrados respectively, and extend for some distance into the abutments or piers. The bars of each pair are not connected with each other, but are provided with rivet head projections spaced at close intervals, which are designed to increase the adhesion of the concrete to the steel. They act in a manner similar to the flanges of an imbedded beam and serve to assist the concrete to resist the thrusts and bending moments applied to the arch. A greater number of concrete steel bridges are built by the Thacher system in the

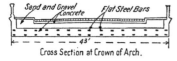

Sand and Gravel Concrete   Flat Steel Bars

Cross Section at Crown of Arch.

FIG. 33.

United States than by any of the others described. The most notable example is the Thacher Y bridge at Zanesville, Ohio, completed in 1901. It is built at the confluence of

the Muskingum and Licking rivers and has three branches which radiate from the triangular central pier to the three opposite banks. Two of the branches have three spans and the other, two spans, having a total length of 828 feet. The thickness of the arch ring at the crown varies from 18 inches for the short spans of 81 feet to 30 inches for the longer spans of 122 feet, with a width of 43 feet over the arches, and 42 feet between the walls of the parapets. See Fig. 33.

Other important examples are the Jacaguas bridge in Porto Rico and the Green and Goat Island bridges at Niagara Falls, N. Y. The former carries the military road from San Juan to Ponce, across the Jacaguas River at Juana Diaz. It has three spans — a central span of 120 feet and two side spans of 100 feet each, with a width of 20 feet. The Green and Goat Island bridges were constructed in 1900 — one from the mainland to Green Island and the other from Green Island to Goat Island. The former, which is the larger of the two, consists of three spans, having a total length of 371 feet, and an over-all width of 44 feet, reinforced by 12 pairs of Thacher bars in each arch ring. It cost a little over $102,000.

One of the latest systems of reinforcement employs a top and bottom row of corrugated steel bars, ranging from ½ to 1½ inches square placed longitudinally of the arch, and following the curves of the extrados and intrados respectively, with the corresponding bars of the two layers in the same vertical plane.

Increased reinforcement when necessary is obtained by doubling the number of extradosal bars, or by the introduction of transverse bars in each layer of longitudinal bars, so as to form a square-mesh network. The longitudinal bars are usually spaced from 5 to 8 inches apart, and the transverse bars 24 inches apart. In the Seeley Street bridge over Prospect Avenue, in the borough of Brooklyn, New York city — a fine example of the method — additional reinforcement is obtained by stirrups of vertical tie bars, which are located at the intersections of the longitudinal and transverse bars, and connect the longitudinal bars of the extradosal and intradosal layers.

The use of reinforced concrete in the construction of bridges has proved so satisfactory that concrete steel spans of much greater length than those already built have been designed by several well-known engineers, of which perhaps the most interesting and instructive is one by William H. Burr, professor of civil engineering, Columbia University, for a memorial bridge across the Potomac at Washington, D. C. The design was submitted in competition with others at the request of the chief of engineers of the United States army and was awarded the first prize. It calls for a bridge proper composed of a centre-draw span of steel, 159 feet long, flanked on each side by three segmental arches of concrete steel, 192 feet long, with a rise of 29 feet. They are of the ribbed type, with exterior ribs of granite masonry, and interior ribs of concrete steel 30 inches deep at the crown, and 7 feet 3 inches deep at the springing lines.

The great value of reinforced concrete has not only been satisfactorily demonstrated in its application to bridge work, but also as a material for many other forms of structures usually built of iron or steel and steel and masonry combined. It is well known that the average life of iron or steel railroad bridges is about 20 years at the most, while a great many deteriorate rapidly under the influence of heavy traffic, atmospheric conditions, and the effects from gases from the locomotives, and have to be replaced in a much shorter time; but, although they cannot compete in durability with masonry structures, the cheapness of iron and steel ren-

In designing any one of these forms of trusses the calculations may be grouped according to their application, to the web system composed of the upper and lower chords, the vertical and end posts, the suspenders and the main and counter diagonals; to the floor systems; and to the lateral bracing and sway bracing. It is not practicable to give in this article detailed descriptions of the various members composing those systems, but Fig. 34 is introduced to show the complete details of a 100 foot

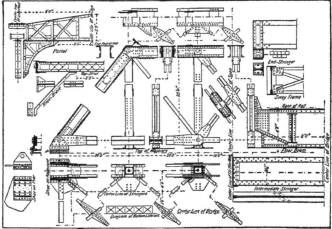

FIG. 34.

ders them more economical, while for bridges of long spans no other material is available. Many roads, however, are replacing their short span iron or steel bridges with arches of masonry or reinforced concrete, which is also applied extensively to the construction of culverts. For further information on the use of reinforced concrete for other purposes than that of bridges and culvert work, see articles on BUILDINGS, CONDUITS, DAMS, FOUNDATIONS, RESERVOIRS, and SEWERS.

According to the best specifications for standard American railroad bridges, the forms of metallic trusses most suitable for various spans may be generalized as follows: Plate-girders for spans ranging from 15 to 75 feet; riveted trusses for spans ranging from 75 to 120 feet; and pin-connected trusses for spans from 120 to 200 feet and over. Riveted trusses are usually of the Warren type, but for spans under 180 feet the pin-connected Pratt truss with inclined end posts is the most economical. As the span increases from 180 to 250 feet it is modified by curving the upper chord and takes the form of a single intersection truss. For longer spans ranging from 250 to 450 feet the newer simple truss bridges employ the Petit or the Baltimore trusses.

span pin-connected truss for a single track through bridge, and will serve to convey a very accurate idea of the design of such a structure.

"Draw bridges" may be classified as "swing bridges," "rolling bridges," and "lift bridges." Swing bridges are of the simple or double type and may be constructed of trusses or girders, so as to be wholly or partially continuous. The earlier forms had a tower over the central pier from which chains extended to the ends of the truss, or the platform. These ends rested freely upon the abutments so that a live load on one

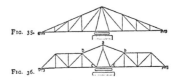

FIG. 35.

FIG. 36.

end lifted the other, and the arrangement was entirely bad, approximating to that of the triangular truss shown in Fig. 35, and is now obsolete, while the modern swing bridges are of the type shown in Fig. 36. In this design, when the bridge is fully loaded the position of the members (a b) is such that the members (b c) carry the greater part of the load to the turntable, and insure a better distribution of the load thereon. They are generally known as "centre-bearing" or "rim-bearing," according to the method of supporting the turn-table on the centre pier. Fig. 37 shows the centre-bearing method where the entire weight is carried on the central pivot. It is applicable to short spans. Fig. 38 shows the rim-bearing method where the entire load is carried on a circular drum which moves upon a series of wheels or rollers arranged around the circumference of the turn-

it is quite exceptional to find one properly equipped for that purpose when it is closed. A truss acts as a beam, and to be able to determine its reactions by the application of the equations of the "Theorem of Three Moments," it is necessary that it should be supported rigidly at three points. It is obvious that this is not the case if the ends are not raised in the closed position, and entails the greatest difficulty in the determination of the stresses under varying temperatures, so much so that the ends may be thrown out of line to an extent sufficient to derail a train moving on to the bridge, and to

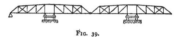

Fɪɢ. 39.

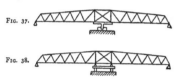

Fɪɢ. 37.

Fɪɢ. 38.

table. As a general rule plate-girder swing bridges have a centre-bearing and truss bridges a rim-bearing, but the style of bearing is usually determined by the available vertical height under the bridge, or the distance from the base of the rail to the top of the pier. There is one serious objection, however, to a purely rim-bearing bridge, which has led to a great deal of thought relative to the proper distribution of the load upon the turn-table. In a purely rim-bearing turn-table no load is carried by the centre pin, and as the rollers, instead of moving in the proper circle get out of line constantly, the centre pin is subjected to more or less lateral displacement. This is partially obviated in the latest designs by so distributing the weight that a portion of it is carried by the centre pin, which not only relieves the weight on the rim, but assists in keeping the rollers in their proper place. Plate-girder swing bridges are the most suitable up to a length of 200 feet. They are stiffer under moving loads, simpler in construction, and more economical than lattice girders or pin-connected trusses.

The machinery employed for operating swing bridges consists of devices for raising and lowering the ends and for turning the bridge. The motive power may be supplied by steam or gas engines, or by electricity, but it is usually in the form of hand power. This power is expended in lifting the ends, in overcoming the inertia of the structure or putting it in motion, and in turning the bridge out of and into position. The simplest way to apply the power to turn a swing-bridge is to exert a pull on its ends by means of an attached rope, and it is a good auxiliary method to be kept for use at any time when the regular driving machinery happens to fail; but in the design of a bridge the operating machinery and the kind of motive power to be employed need to be considered only in connection with the space allowance necessary to house the motor and the attachments to the motor shaft. In general practice these conditions are very well satisfied; but, in the American swing-bridges, the end lifting arrangements are far from being satisfactory, and

make the bridge dangerous at all times. The practice of lifting the ends by wedges as soon as the bridge is closed is objectionable on account of the resulting reactions under a dead load, and the only satisfactory arrangement appears to be the method of locking the ends by bolts or pins, so that no reactions are produced when the bridge is unloaded, or by the construction of double swing bridges as shown in Fig. 39.

"Cantilever bridges" were developed through the decisions resulting from the discussion of the merits and demerits of the continuous bridges built in Europe prior to 1870. It was noted that in a continuous bridge a slight variation in the height of one of the supports produced great changes in the strains and stresses, and that if the chords were cut near the inflection points for full loads those for partial loads would occur at those points also and thus render the reactions statically determinate. In 1860 Ritter proposed to avoid the disadvantages of continuity by cutting or hinging one chord of a three-span truss at its four inflection points, as shown by Fig. 40. His proposition involved

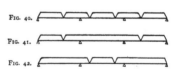

Fɪɢ. 40.

Fɪɢ. 41.

Fɪɢ. 42.

the fundamental principle of the modern cantilever, but the proposed truss was defective owing to its being cut at too many places. A three-span truss has four supports and consequently four reactions under a load. To determine these reactions four conditions are necessary. The principle of statics gives two — that the sum of the vertical forces is zero, and that the sum of their moments about any centre is zero. The other two conditions may be established by hinging the chord in two places since the moment of each of the hinges is zero, so that the forms shown by Figs. 41 and 42 are made statically determinate relative to strains and stresses, and not subject to change by a slight change in one support. Furthermore, since their shear and moment diagrams, and that of a continuous truss are the same, they preserve the advantages of continuity relative to the distribution of the strain possessed by the continuous truss system, while they eliminate its greatest disadvantages.

The practicability of building out long-span cantilever beams from the opposite banks of a stream until they connected at the middle point was first considered in connection with the principle of the suspension system, in which the truss is supported by cables and stays. Trowbridge proposed to do away with the cables and depend altogether upon the stays for support; but, as it was impracticable to extend the stays conveniently and effectively to the middle of the centre span, he arranged to bridge the interval between the water ends of the anchor spans with a simple truss, as shown in Fig. 43.

FIG. 43.

In the practical application of the principle to the modern cantilever bridges the towers are supplanted by balanced anchor spans, the ends of which are connected by a simple truss. In the simplest form they consist of three spans, as shown in Fig. 44, with the anchor trusses supported at the piers on a single point; but

FIG. 44.

a better condition of reactions is obtained by supporting the trusses on the pier at two points, as shown in Fig. 45. The disadvantages of a continuous structure are thus avoided, and by omitting the diagonals in the panel over the pier the reactions at the points a and bc are ren-

FIG. 45.

dered positive for all loads on the cantilever arm.

The cantilever system is best adapted to long spans where the ratio of dead to live load is great, and is not economical for short spans where that ratio is small. For spans ranging from 500 to 1,500 feet it is as economical as the arch and the suspension bridges; but, for spans

the construction of the piers and the erection of the trusses lead to the conclusion that its selection was practically a mistake. In comparison with continuous structures, the cantilever system has the same advantages possessed by the former over a series of simple trusses of equal spans; that is, in the preservation of the uniform distribution of the moments, and the susceptibility of being erected, panel by panel, where false work is impracticable.

"Suspension bridges" are the type of structures best adapted for long spans. They were very economical when the ultimate strength of steel wire was 160,000 pounds per square inch, and the structures were dimensioned for a working load of 40,000 pounds per square inch, but now, since high grade steel wire having an ultimate tensile strength of 225,000 pounds per square inch is available for suspension cables, the economy and practicable spans of suspension bridges has been greatly increased, and several large structures rivaling those already constructed — notably the Brooklyn bridge, completed in 1883, which has a central span of 1,595 feet, and the Manhattan bridge, the second across the East River, completed in 1904, which has a central span of 1,600 feet, are in the course of erection, or being definitely planned, their economy and other superlative advantages for spans exceeding 1,500 feet, where false work cannot be used, being very clearly recognized. The most notable of the structures now being built or proposed are the third bridge across the East River, between the Brooklyn and Manhattan bridges, the tower foundations of which are already established, and a proposed bridge with a span of 3,200 feet across the Hudson River, to connect New York city with the Jersey shore. The modern improvements in the methods of construction are such that although the last named bridge will be more than twice the size of the Brooklyn bridge, which consumed 13 years of labor in its construction, it is estimated that the proposed structure could be built in about six years. Up to date only three suspension bridges have been completed and used for railroad traffic — the Niagara, the Brooklyn, and the Manhattan. The Niagara bridge, built in 1854, sustained the wear and tear of heavy railroad traffic for 43 years, its only fault being its large deflection which required slow speed in crossing. The others have proved entirely satisfactory for all the purposes for which they were designed. In the construction of a suspension bridge, see Fig. 46, the anchorages and towers are erected first, then the cables are swung between the towers over which they pass from the anchorages, then the vertical hanger rods are attached to the cables, and finally the stiffening truss which actually car-

FIG. 46.

exceeding 1,500 feet, it cannot be built as economically as the latter, notwithstanding the fact that the Forth bridge in Scotland, one of the most important of its kind, has spans of 1,700 feet, since many considerations relative to

ries the floor of the bridge is built out, panel by panel, from each tower and secured to the hangers. It is common practice to use a system of secondary cables called "stays," which extend from the top of the towers, and are attached at intervals to the bottom of the stiffening span, at which point their inclination is tangential to the main cables at the tops of the towers. These stays are superfluous members, as the stiffening trusses can be properly designed to sustain safely all the moments and shears to which they may be subjected, without the aid of the stays, and it is probable that they will be omitted in the structures of the future. As commonly employed, their purpose is to prevent oscillations in the truss under the effects of wind strain or unsymmetrical loads. The use of the stiffening truss may be briefly explained as follows: A suspended cable sustaining only its own weight assumes the curve known as the elastic catenary. In the case of a bridge the weight of the roadway and the live load is much greater than the weight of the cables and produces stresses and elongations which cause them to deflect from the theoretical curve, while additional deflections are produced by the sag of the cables, which increases or decreases with the rising or falling of temperature, and which together with the oscillations caused by wind and the application of unsymmetrical loads make the structures unstable to the point of actual destruction due to a lack of rigidity. It is the office of the stiffening truss to supply this rigidity, and to distribute the effects of partial loads uniformly over the cables. The stiffening truss is necessary only between the towers. In some bridges it extends from tower to tower without breaks in the chords, while in others the upper chord is cut at the middle of the span, or the chords are fitted with sliding joints at that point to allow for the effects of live loads and changes of temperature. Additional rigidity in the structure is obtained by giving the stiffening truss an upward camber in the form of a parabolic curve, the sustaining hangers being provided with sleeve nuts at their their lower ends permitting them to be adjusted in length so that the tension upon them is equal under an uniform load. These hangers are all equal in size and are dimensioned to resist a tension equal to the maximum floor load applied to them. They are provided with eye-loops at the upper end, by which they are connected with a bolt to bands that encircle the cables. These cables, instead of hanging in vertical planes, as might be supposed, are "cradled"; that is, they are drawn together at the middle of the span, so that the distance between them at that point is less than at the towers, resulting in slightly decreasing the sag and giving an additional stiffness to the bridge against lateral oscillations, at the expense of only a very small percentage of increase in the stresses of the cable. On the tops of the towers the cables rest freely in movable saddles through which the strains due to loads on the main span are transmitted to the anchorages upon the slightest motion of the saddles on their rollers. See Fig. 47. As this motion cannot occur until the friction of the rollers has been overcome, the strain on the parts of the cables between the towers and the land is less than the strain on the parts between the towers themselves, when the main span only, is covered with a live load. The effect of the difference of the horizontal components of these strains on the tops of the towers is to pull them over toward each other.

To transmit these strains to the anchorages, see Fig. 48, the wires of the cables are passed around pins or terminated in sockets at (a), which are attached to a series of eye-bars, connected with the anchor plate (b), imbedded in the masonry of the anchorages. These eye-bars vary in their inclination until they become vertical at the plate, and are provided with special blocks of iron and stone at the connecting pins at the points of change in direction to resist the strains due to the angular deviation. The

FIG. 47.   FIG. 48.

stresses in the anchor bars decrease with the decrease of the inclination from the vertical, therefore the upward pull on the anchor plate is much less than the strain on the cables. The exact amount of this upward pull is difficult to determine, since the anchor bars are closely surrounded with masonry and concrete, so as to secure the greatest degree of stability and to protect them from corrosion, and are therefore unreachable; but it is supposed that the variation in stress is similar to that occurring in a belt passing around a portion of a pulley. Relative to methods of cable connections, it has been proposed to connect the cables directly to terminal sockets on the water sides of the towers and to connect the back stays in a similar manner to their land sides. The special advantages of the method, however, have never been practically determined.

Many novel methods have also been suggested for stiffening the cables. A system of trussing by which the cables are connected with the roadway has been used to some extent in short span bridges. In such cases, however, it has been found more practicable to make the cables of links or eye-bars, therefore the structures cannot be considered true suspension bridges. Another method provides for a main span hinged at several points, thus converting it into a two-hinged arch if hinged at (a) and (b); into a three-hinged arch if hinged at (a), (c), and (b), and into a cantilever bridge if the system of hinges is applied to the land spans also. See Fig. 49. Two other methods may

FIG. 49.

be mentioned, although in both cases the structures are inverted arches. Fig. 50 shows a cable trussed on its upper side by bracing which connects it with two straight chords extending from the tops of the towers to the middle of the span. Fig. 51 shows two parallel cables or wire link chains, connected by a system of bracing. This method has been embodied in a plan for the bridge across the Hudson River, which has already been mentioned as one of the great proposed suspension bridges to be built in the near future. It is an open question as to whether the braced cable or the unstiffened cable system is the more advantageous for long span bridges. Trussing the cables undoubtedly possesses the advantages due to an increase in the stiffness of the structure under a live load, and the reduction in weight of the roadway trusses; but, since they are actually inverted arches, they possess such elements of uncertainty and complexity due to temperature conditions and live load that they do not appear to be a step in the right direction in the construction of long span bridges.

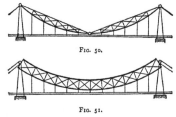

FIG. 50.

FIG. 51.

"Metallic arch bridges" may be grouped into three principal classes, according to their mode of support or the number of hinges in each truss. (1) Two-hinged arches, with a hinge at each abutment, and continuous throughout; (2) three-hinged arches, with a hinge at each abutment and one at the crown; and (3) continuous arches with the ends fixed rigidly to the abutments. One-hinged arches with the hinge at the crown have been built, but are obsolete on account of their theoretic disadvantages. The simplest and most efficient type is the three-hinged arch, usually composed of a horizontal upper chord, which is united to a curved or broken lower chord by vertical and diagonal bracing, and when thus connected it is designated as "spandrel-braced," and the hinge at the crown is placed in the lower chord, and the floor system is supported directly by the upper chord at the panel points. See Fig. 52. The arch ribs are either metallic built-up girders

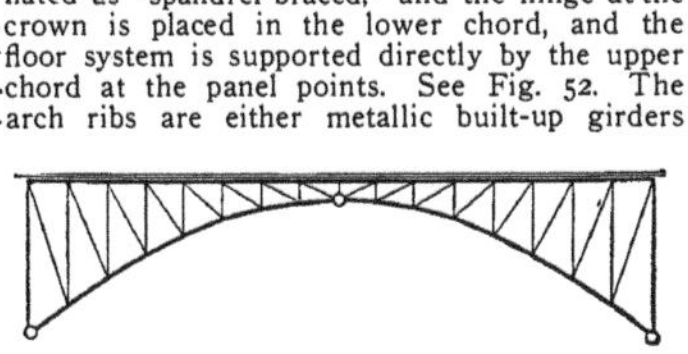

FIG. 52.

with solid webs, or with diagonal bracing connecting the flanges. The relative merits of the three types may be briefly stated as follows, together with a reference to one or more of the most notable structures of each type:

In the two-hinged arches the strains and stresses cannot be determined except by taking into account the deformation of the material which is always supposed to occur within the elastic limit; therefore they possess all the disadvantages of continuous structures, and although they require the most careful work in their construction, it is impossible to predict their degree of security under the action of loads that may develop stresses exceeding the

elastic limit of the material. On the other hand, they have a reduced deflection at the crown; their deformation due to temperature is less, and being stiffer than the three-hinged arch, are better adapted than the latter for long spans designed to sustain heavy railroad traffic. The largest two-hinged arches with solid webs ever built are those of the Washington bridge over the Harlem River at New York city, completed in 1889. They have a clear span of 510 feet and a clear rise of 92 feet. The largest steel trussed two-hinged arch in this country is that of the structure which replaced the Niagara Falls and Clifton suspension bridge in 1898. It has a clear span of 840 feet, and a clear rise of 150 feet. The largest arch of this type abroad is that of the Garabit viaduct in France, which has a span of 541 feet and a rise of 213 feet.

Practically all of the remarks applied to the two-hinged arches also apply to arches with fixed ends. The finest example of this type is the Saint Louis bridge, over the Mississippi River, completed in 1874. Its central arch has a clear span of 520 feet and a rise of 47 feet, while the adjacent arches have a span of 520 feet and a rise of 44 feet.

The three-hinged arches are statically determinate structures, in which the reactions and stresses due to any loading can be found without any assumption derived from the theory of elasticity, as exactly as those of a simple beam or truss. Subject to more deflection and deformation, and therefore not as stiff as are the other types, it is unsuitable for heavy railroad traffic, but is eminently satisfactory for highway bridges, and the roofs of train sheds and exposition buildings, where the span is too great for the economical employment of simple roof trusses. The largest arches of this type ever constructed were those of the Liberal Arts Building, at the Columbian Exposition at Chicago, in 1893.

The latest important addition to the list of metallic arch bridges is the structure just completed across the Zambesi, in central Africa, on the line of the proposed Cape to Cairo railroad. It is situated at a short distance below the famous Victoria Falls, and consists of a combination girder and arch, three-span structure, of a total length of 650 feet, the central arch of which has a span of 500 feet, and carries the roadway at a height of 420 feet above the level of the water. All the material was shipped from England and the structure was built in a year.

Bibliography.— For further technical and detailed information consult: Berg, 'American Railway Bridges and Buildings' (Chicago 1898); Burr, 'Stresses in Bridges and Roof Trusses' (New York 1886); Cooper, 'American Railroad Bridges' (New York 1890); Foster, 'Treatise on Wooden Trestle Bridges' (New York 1891); Waddell, 'Pocket-Book for Bridge Engineers' (New York 1898); Warren, 'Engineering Construction in Iron, Steel, and Timber' (New York 1894); Wright and Wing, 'A Manual of Bridge Draughting' (Stanford University 1896). Also consult the 'Transactions of the American Society of Civil Engineers,' and the various engineering magazines and periodicals. WILLIAM MOREY, JR., C.E., *Consulting Civil and Mechanical Engineer, New York.*

Bridge Designs, Railway. Bridges have been in use from prehistoric times. Even the scientific forms, now looked upon as most modern, were developed in a crude way by the ancients, timber cantilever structures being built by the Chinese in the time of Confucius.

Bridge design, of necessity, continued in an elementary stage as long as timber and masonry were the only materials in use, and long spans were impracticable with such materials, though the "Towne" lattice spans, built entirely of plank connected with hard wood pins, were as nearly perfect as was possible without the use of iron, and some of these spans are still doing effective duty after 80 years of continued use.

The earliest use of iron in bridges began with the use of cast-iron posts and cast-iron arches, but this material was not found entirely satisfactory for long-span bridges. The first real development began with the use of wrought-iron, which was first used in this country in vertical tension members in the "Howe" truss about 1840, and in inclined tension members in the "Pratt" truss about 1845. The use of wrought-iron tension members with wood and cast-iron compression members continued until about 1860, when Howard Carroll, an Irish engineer, assistant to Chief Engineer Gray, of the New York Central, introduced the riveted lattice bridge, built entirely of wrought-iron, which was developed by his successors on that road, and used until very recent years. Wrought-iron plate girders were also first built about 1860.

J. H. Linville, between 1850 and 1860, introduced on the Pennsylvania Railroad a type of truss with flat diagonals and hexagonal rolled-iron posts, and about this same time Bollman and Fink introduced on the Baltimore & Ohio their multiple suspension types of trusses with flat diagonals and vertical iron posts. John W. Murphy adopted Whipple's ideas and developed a truss on Whipple's lines with cast-iron posts and square bar tension members with loop eyes.

A long step in the evolution of properly designed compression members was made by David Reeves about 1864, when he began the use of the rolled iron, round segmental "Phœnix" column, and about that date he also developed the hydraulic upset-end on tension members, which were made by the Phœnix Iron Company, first on round rods and afterwards developed into eyes on flat bars, and these two features were combined in the "Phœnix" bridge, which was far in advance of any bridge construction at that date, and quickly came into very general use. While it still preserved the use of cast-iron for connections, it permanently did away with any further use of cast-iron for compression members, and its simplicity and ease of erection made it by far the best type developed up to that time. Many of these bridges are still in use, and those that have been replaced have generally been removed on account of the great increase of rolling loads to be carried, and not on account of inherent defects in the design.

With the use of "eye bars" the pin-connected type of truss came into practically universal use in this country, since it had great advantages over riveted bridges in many respects; but owing to its ease of erection, it was in many cases carried to ridiculous extremes, and spans as small as 25 and 30 feet were constructed with individual members so light and insignificant that the structure had no rigidity. In recent years there has been a very general disuse of this type of construction for spans under 150 feet, and the best engineering practice now calls for riveted structures for small spans, though American engineers still use the pin-connected type for long spans almost universally.

The general principles of railroad bridge construction have not undergone much change in the last 20 years, as practically all spans are built on the general lines of the "Pratt" truss, with vertical compression members and inclined tension members, or on the lines of the "Warren" truss, with all main web members inclined, but the constantly increasing weight of the locomotives in use has tended to the use of heavier and more rigid structures with long panels and as few members as possible, more substantial details, solid floors, stiff lateral and vibration bracing, and other features of present engineering practice, which reduce vibration and add to the rigidity of the structure.

The rapidly increasing capacity of American bridge building shops and their ability to fabricate and handle single members of sizes impossible to obtain a few years ago, has enabled the American engineer to design bridges with practically no shop limitations, and he has thus been free to make designs solely with the idea of producing a structure with the maximum strength and rigidity and the minimum weight of material.

The rapid advance thus brought about would have been impossible had not the ingenuity of the erecting engineer kept pace with that of the designing engineer, but this specialty of erection has reached such an advanced stage that spans of 1,800 feet, with single members weighing 120 tons, are now erected as rapidly as any smaller span.

One of the recent tendencies of American practice has been to substitute plate girder spans for all short bridges, in place of the various types of lattice girders and pin-connected spans heretofore in general use, and very few engineers use any type of steel structure except a plate girder for spans under 90 or 100 feet. Some engineers prefer this type for spans as long as 125 feet. To summarize general practice, it can be said that this type of span is used for spans from 26 to 100 feet, spans under 20 feet being either arches or rolled beams, and spans over 100 feet running into riveted trusses. Plate girders are frequently built with solid floors, with the ties bedded in ballast, and the latest floors of this kind are built of reinforced concrete slabs or arches, as the older trough floors and buckle plate floors have been found unsatisfactory, owing to the impossibility of preventing rapid deterioration from rust. Plate girder spans over 70 feet long generally rest on pin bearings at each end, to allow for deflection, and have cast-steel end shoes.

The usual present practice is to build all spans between 100 feet and 175 feet with riveted trusses, and the old style, multiple-intersection, riveted span has entirely given way to the riveted, single-intersection truss with long panels. For deck spans, the old practice of supporting the ties directly on the upper

1. 812-foot Cantilever Bridge over Monongahela River at Pittsburgh, Pa.
2. 415-foot Draw Span over Harlem River at Seventh Avenue, New York City.
3. 135-foot Through Span with solid floor, W. P. T. Ry. Co., Pittsburgh, Pa.
4. 820-foot Proposed Arch for Henry Hudson Bridge over Harlem River, New York City.

chord has largely disappeared, and either a solid ballasted floor is used, or a regular floor system is laid, consisting of cross floor beams resting on the upper chords, and longitudinal stringers framed between floor beams.

For through spans the ordinary practice is to use a floor system with cross floor beams riveted in between the vertical posts and longitudinal stringers riveted between the floor beams, but in many cases a solid ballasted floor is used, in which case the lower chords are reinforced against bending by supporting them at their middle points from a sub-panel in the truss, or by making deep lower chords capable of withstanding the bending in addition to the direct stress. Fig. 3 shows a 135-foot double track through span with solid floor built with deep lower chord sections.

Spans over 175 feet are usually built with pin connections and, where the span is long, the upper chord is generally curved so as to give a maximum depth at the centre, and truss depths are proportioned so as to give a practically uniform upper chord section throughout. Upper and lower laterals and transverse bracing are now universally built of riveted members, and the older form of tension rods used for purposes of wind and vibration bracing has entirely disappeared. Simple truss spans of this character have been built to a maximum length of 550 feet, which is the length of the channel span over the Ohio River at Louisville, Ky., this being the longest span of its kind in the world, though the 675-foot suspended span of the Quebec cantilever bridge, now under construction, will largely exceed this.

Such spans could and would be built of much greater length if it were not for the fact that in navigable rivers of a magnitude requiring such spans, the government will not allow the waterway to be even temporarily obstructed with falsework, so that for long spans it is more economical to use a cantilever or some other type of structure that can be erected without placing any obstruction in the main channel.

In draw spans, the recent changes in practice have been in the same direction as for through spans, as far as the trusses, floor and bracing are concerned. The practice of counter-bracing the trusses by means of diagonal counter rods has been abandoned, and stiff riveted diagonals are used, capable of carrying either tension or compression where reverse stresses occur. For draw spans of short span or in cities or other situations where there is not plenty of room for a swing bridge, the "rolling lift" bridge has been adopted and has proved most efficient. For long draw spans, the centre pier revolving span is still the type in common use, and for spans up to 400 feet a central pivot bearing is generally used. For spans over 400 feet a rim-bearing turntable drum rolling on a circle of conical, cast-steel wheels has been found most satisfactory, and for very heavy spans two concentric drums and circles of wheels are used.

The use of steam as an operating power for swing bridges has almost disappeared, being replaced by electric motors, which are more economical and do away with many difficulties encountered in the use of steam engines and their boilers.

Fig. 2 shows the 415-foot draw span of the Central Bridge, carrying Seventh Avenue over the Harlem River in New York City, together with the lattice girder approach spans thereto.

The metal arch bridge is a type of structure developed almost wholly in recent years, and there are various modifications of this type, some being built as spandrel arches, in which the web members connect a horizontal top chord with an arched lower chord, having the floor system supported on the top chord or framed in between vertical posts at the top chord level, while others are built as braced ribs, having both chords arched and connected together with the web members, and the floor supported on vertical posts resting on the braced rib at panel points. Each of these types of arch spans is further varied by being built by some engineers with two pin bearings at the two supports, and by others with the addition of a third pin bearing at the crown. It is contended by the advocates of two hinges that the omission of the centre hinge adds considerably to the rigidity of the span, but it has not yet been conclusively demonstrated that the third hinge adds appreciably to the vibration, and this third hinge disposes of the great uncertainty of temperature stresses, and allows the exact calculation of the true stresses and sections by static methods, so that it has considerable advantage and is more in use than the two-hinged type. Many long spans have been built of this type, the longest span being the upper span over the Niagara River, which is a braced rib arch of 840 feet span.

Fig. 4 shows the proposed Henry Hudson Memorial Bridge over the Harlem River in New York City, with a steel arch span of 820 feet.

Suspension bridge design has not been changed as much as other types in recent years, owing perhaps to the fact that this type has not been adopted to any extent for railroad bridges on account of its flexibility, for while a flexible cable can be made sufficiently stiff for comparatively light highway loads, it would require so much material in the stiffening trusses to satisfactorily provide for heavy railroad moving loads that some other type of structure would prove more economical. However, in the few spans of this type which have been recently built, there have been some radical improvements over older designs. The stiffening trusses have been greatly increased in depth and strength, and rocking steel towers with the cables made fast to the top have taken the place of rigid towers with the cables supported on rolling shoes over the top. The three large suspension bridges over the East River between New York and Brooklyn are excellent types of the evolution of this form of structure, and, while the Williamsburg Bridge is the longest span of its kind in existence, having a span of 1,600 feet, the Manhattan Bridge, now being built, is the most modern span.

The cantilever bridge has come into very general use in recent years, not because of the economy in metal required, as this type weighs more than a simple truss or an arch of equal span, but because of the great advantage that it can be erected without putting falsework in the main channel. Since the government now prohibits even temporary interference with navigation, it has made this type practically mandatory for long spans, as, if any other type is adopted, the span must be erected with additional material, causing it to act temporarily as a cantilever, and this additional material overbalances the saving of any type adopted. When the erection is considered, therefore, it has been found that the cantilever is the most economical of all types for long spans, and while some engineers claim that a suspension bridge is cheaper for very long spans, it is certain that equal rigidity cannot be obtained for equal cost by using a suspension bridge on a span of less than 1,500 feet, and even considerably above this span the cantilever will in all probability prove the most economical. For this reason the cantilever has practically become the standard type for all long spans, and several very notable bridges of this kind have recently been completed and are now under construction. The cantilever over the Saint Lawrence River at Quebec, having a span of 1,800 feet, is the longest span of any kind in the world.

Cantilever bridges are comparatively new, but even in the few years in which they have been in use they have been greatly improved in their general arrangement, details, and erection devices. The capacity of the bridge shops to manufacture eye bars as large as 16 inches $\times$ 2 inches and 83 feet long, centre to centre of eyes, with pin holes 13 inches in diameter, and heads as large as 36 inches in diameter, as well as to build and ship single compression members weighing 100 tons, together with the ability of the erecting gangs to put these huge pieces in place with moving travelers, has given the designing engineer practically unlimited opportunities, and has brought about the construction of several very large spans of this type in the last two years, notably the 1,800-foot span at Quebec, the 1,182-foot span at Blackwell's Island, N. Y., and the 812-foot span over the Monongahela River at Pittsburgh, Pa. The first two bridges are not yet completed, but the Pittsburgh cantilever is shown in Fig. 1.

Stone arch bridges are an excellent type for short spans, where the owners can afford the first cost, as the repairs are practically nothing, but this type has not changed in recent years, though in the modified form of the reinforced concrete arch it is being introduced quite generally for ornamental bridges in parks and cities where the æsthetic requirements are more important than economy, and it is an excellent type for this use, but cannot be economically used for long spans carrying heavy loads.

The many wide navigable rivers in this country have given the American bridge engineer unequalled opportunities to show his ability in the design, construction and erection of long spans, and that he has made good use of these opportunities is proved by the fact that the longest span of every type of bridge has been, or is being, constructed by American bridge engineers. In all probability the maximum length of spans has not yet been reached, as it has been proved to be practical to build spans up to 1,800-feet, and there is nothing to prevent the construction of much longer spans, if they are found to be paying investments.

The following is a partial list of the largest spans of various types of steel bridges now built or building:

TRUSS SPANS.

675 feet — Suspended span of the Cantilever over the St. Lawrence River at Quebec, Can.
630 feet — Fixed span of the Blackwells Island Cantilever, New York City.
621 feet — Fixed span of the Cantilever over the Mississippi River at Memphis, Tenn.
550 feet — Span over the Ohio River at Louisville, Ky.
548 feet — Span over the Ohio River at Cincinnati, Ohio.
535 feet — Span over the Delaware River near Philadelphia, Pa.

DRAW SPANS.

520 feet — Draw over the Missouri River at Omaha, Neb.
503 feet — Draw over the Thames River at New London, Conn.
491 feet — Draw over the St. Louis River at Duluth, Minn.
415 feet — Draw over the Harlem River, New York.

ARCHES.

840 feet — Arch over Niagara River at Niagara Falls, N. Y.
721 feet — Arch over Viaur River, France.
614 feet — Arch over Rhine at Bonn, Germany.
595 feet — Arch over Rhine at Dusseldorf, Germany.
591 feet — Arch Kaiser Wilhelm Eridge over Wuppur River, Mungsten, Germany.
550 feet — Arch over Niagara River at Niagara Falls.
541 feet — Arch Garabit Viaduct over Truyere River, France.

CANTILEVERS.

1800 feet — Cantilever over St. Lawrence River at Quebec, Can.
1710 feet — Cantilever over Firth of Fourth, Scotland.
1182 feet — Cantilever over Blackwells Island Channel, New York City.
820 feet — Cantilever, Lansdown Bridge, India.
812 feet — Cantilever over Monongahela River, Pittsburgh, Pa.
790 feet — Cantilever over Mississippi River at Memphis, Tenn.

SUSPENSION BRIDGES.

1600 feet — Span of Williamsburg Bridge, New York City.
1595 feet — Span of Brooklyn Bridge, New York City.
1470 feet — Span of Manhattan Bridge, New York City.

The three first mentioned truss spans are parts of large cantilever structures, so that the longest independent truss span is the 550-foot span over the Ohio river at Louisville.

The Viaur Arch in France is not a true arch, as it is a combination of an arch over the central opening, counterbalanced by two semi-arches extending back over each of the shores.

The Arch spans over the Rhine at Bonn and Dusseldorf, are through spans with the floor suspended from the arch ribs, while all the other arches are deck structures with the floor above the crown of the arch.

This list might be indefinitely extended and many structures might be added which are notable for particular features, such as the extremely flat arch of the Alexander III bridge in Paris, having a span of 362 feet with a rise of less than 19 feet. Many viaducts might also be added, which are notable not from any great length of spans, but from the extreme heights above the gorges they cross. The greatest of these is the Gokteik Viaduct in Burmah, where the track is 825 feet above bottom of gorge.

HENRY W. HODGE,
Consulting Engineer, New York.

Bridge Foundations. See FOUNDATIONS.

Bridge Shops and Shop Practice. The working plant of a bridge company is composed of several shops and departments so arranged in their relation to each other, that the movement of the material handled by them is continuous and in one direction — the rough material entering at one end of the plant and passing out as a finished product at the other. This arrangement insures the reduction to a minimum the time lost in handling, and also the greatest possible economy in the cost of production.

Each of these shops is under the immediate charge of a foreman or superintendent who reports daily to the general superintendent or manager of the plant, who makes out the programme of work, and prescribes the dates upon which the different pieces of work are expected to be completed, the desideratum being to keep the various shops continually working, and to complete the various parts of the bridges in the order in which they are required at the place of erection.

The buildings of the various shops are usually of fireproof construction and conform to the requirements of larger size, good lighting, heating, and ventilation. They are connected by narrow-gauge railway tracks, which run lengthwise through them so as to facilitate the transportation of the material from one part of the works to another with the least amount of handling. Ample yard-room is provided at the ends of the buildings and also around them for the storage of partially completed material awaiting their turn for the finishing touches before shipment. These yards are usually laid out so that the carrying distance is as short as possible, and the work of carrying is accomplished by overhead traveling cranes.

These shops may be designated and described as follows:

(1) "Power Plant," consisting of large batteries of boilers for generating steam, and engines for driving the dynamos through which power and light are furnished to all parts of the works, and other engines for operating the air-compressors which furnish the power for the portable pneumatic drills, riveters, hammers, and reamers, and also the compressed air used for the draft of rivet furnaces, and blacksmith forges; for the cleaning of finished material, and for painting them by means of spraying devices.

In some cases, the hydraulic pumps and accumulators which supply the water to the hydraulic presses and riveters are also located in the buildings of the power plant, all the machinery of which is installed in duplicate so that in case of an accident it would not necessitate the shutting down of the entire plant during the time consumed in making repairs.

Although the first cost of a centralized power plant is comparatively high, its advantages over that of a scattered system may be briefly summed up as follows: Cheap grades of fuel may be used under the boilers, and mechanical stokers may be employed and thus reduce the number of firemen required by the several boilers of the scattered plants. The number of engine attendants is also greatly reduced, their places being filled by a few electricians to keep the wiring and motors in working condition. The power may be transmitted to every part of the plant with the smallest amount of loss.

(2) "Receiving Yard," where the material for each bridge is properly selected, classified, and stored.

(3) "Straightening Department," where the irregularities in the material, due to the shortcomings of the rolling mill processes, are corrected by more accurate methods. The buckles in the plates, and the deviations from true alignment in the plates are eradicated by passing them through a series of rolls usually consisting of six sets. These rolls are so arranged that the vertical distance between them can be made less at one end than at the other, so that by passing a plate through them several times, it can be stretched unequally and any imperfections in the alignment of its edges thus corrected. Beams, channels, Z-bars, and other odd shapes are best straightened by the application of local pressure to the parts out of line either by screw presses, or by the action of a plunger operated by a power-driven cam. Badly sprung shapes and plates may be straightened by being hammered cold, or after being heated; it is, however, very destructive to the material and should be employed only as a last resort.

(4) "Templet and Pattern Shop," in which the templets for striking the positions of the rivet and pin holes, and the mold patterns for iron and steel castings are made.

A templet is a board or framework of boards, one side of which is an exact representation of one of the sides of the metal shape or piece required to be made. On it, the positions for all the rivet holes, pin holes, bevels and notches are accurately marked, and these are subsequently transferred to the metal piece by punching, scratching or other means, preparatory to the final operations of punching, boring, drilling, reaming, shearing, etc. Templets are usually made of soft white pine boards ⅞ inch in thickness. When very accurate fitting is required, they are laid out full size on the floor of the shop; but, for small and general work, they are made in separate pieces from the detail drawings. As a rule, as many parts as possible of a structure are designed to be in duplicate so that the number of templets required will be as small as possible, and the final fitting and assembling of the work facilitated and simplified.

(5) "Laying-out Shop," where each individual metal shape, plate, and piece is accurately marked in accordance with the templets.

(6) "Punch and Shear Shop," where the various plates, shapes and pieces are sheared or cut to the required length and bevel, and the holes marked from the templets are punched by suitable machines. See article under title METAL WORKING MACHINERY in this encyclopedia.

When the thickness of the pieces is greater than the diameter of the punch, punching will unduly strain the material, and the holes will not be straight and smooth. The holes in such plates and shapes are usually drilled, although the process is much slower and more expensive. Single and gang drills are used for this purpose.

Wrought iron and soft and medium steel when of the proper thickness may be easily punched; but, hard steel must always be drilled as it cannot be punched without cracking.

Since the diameters of the edges of a

punched hole correspond to the diameters of the punch and die respectively, and gives the hole a tapering instead of a cylindrical form, the usual practice is to require all holes, and especially those in the tension members to be reamed to a diameter ⅛ inch larger than that of the punch, so as to remove all of the material injured by the process of punching.

After passing through this shop, all the material is completely ready to be fitted together and riveted to form the final bridge members for which they were designed to form a part. Each piece when completed is marked with a number or letter designating its proper position in the finished member, and all the pieces belonging to the same structure are marked by a job number so that they may be easily identified in the assembling shop.

(7) "The Assembling Shop." This is usually arranged so that all the heavy work is handled on one side, and the small work on the other. All the different pieces which make up the various members are assembled, fitted and bolted together, and then turned over to the

(8) "Riveting Shop" where the riveting is accomplished by various forms of compressed-air, steam and hydraulic riveters.

When the member exceeds ten tons in weight, it is more economical to use portable riveters than stationary riveting machines. As a rule, hydraulic riveters are the most efficient. They do not get out of order easily, and always exert their full pressure upon the rivets; but, in their portable form they are very cumbersome, and therefore, the pneumatic portable riveters are found to be the most convenient in such cases.

Rivets are made of soft steel, and their lengths ought to be such that when put into the holes they will project enough to furnish a sufficient amount of metal to fill the holes completely when they are compressed. Before insertion they are heated to a cherry red, great care being taken, however, not to burn the metal in the heating, and thereby render them hard and brittle. On the other hand, if driven when they are too cold they will not fill the holes completely, and although apparently all right will be weak in the head. All rivet heads ought to be smooth and free from cracks, and concentric with their holes.

(9) "The Machine Shop" is equipped with an endless variety of metal working machines such as planes, borers and turning machines, etc., which are employed to finish the bearing surfaces of the riveted members, and other parts which are used in their construction such as pins, rollers, beds and sole plates, anchor bolts and the various bearing parts of turntables.

The material for the pins and rollers as usually received from the mills has a diameter ⅛ inch greater than that of the finished pins, and has to be turned down to the required size and the threads cut on the ends for the pin nuts. The planers are employed to smooth off the faces of the bed and sole plates of the expansion joints.

(10) "The Forge Shop" is equipped to turn out three classes of work — the manufacture of rivets, the general smith work required in a steel structure, and the forging of eye-bars.

The soft-steel bars of which the rivets are made are first heated and then passed into the rivet making machine where they are upset, headed and cut into the required length at one operation. The rivets most generally employed in structural work range from ¾ to ⅞ inch in diameter.

The operations designated as general smith work consist of the bending of plates, shapes and angles in accordance with the requirements of the drawings, the upsetting of the ends of adjustable tension members, the making of clevices and loop eye-rods, and all forgings such as punches, drift pins, and riveting cups that may be needed by the plant.

All the large tension members of pin-connected structures are made in this shop. The steel flats from which these eye-bars are made are handled as follows: About four feet of one end of the bar is heated to a cherry red in the forge and then placed in the up-setting machine which forms a solid head very nearly the size of the finished head. It is then reheated and placed in the die of the steam hammer and hammered out to the proper size and thickness, and a hole punched in the centre of the head to facilitate the finish boring. A careful watch is kept for flaws, and all of those discovered are cut out since they prevent a perfect weld, and are, no matter how small, a source of weakness in the bar. The head on the other end of the bar is formed in a similar manner. A number of bars are then placed in the annealing furnace and brought gradually to a cherry red temperature, after which they are allowed to cool gradually so as to remove local stresses that might have been induced by the processes employed in upsetting and forging the head. The exactitude required in this work is indicated by Cooper's Specifications, 1901, according to which, Chord pins are required to fit the pin holes within $\frac{1}{50}$ of an inch for pins less than 4½ inches diameter; while for larger pins, the clearance may be $\frac{1}{32}$ of an inch. It is also required that the bars must be bored to lengths within $\frac{1}{32}$ of an inch for each 25 feet of the total length.

(11) "The Painting and Shipping Department" consists of sheds and yards where the material after being inspected and stamped is painted and prepared for shipment.

There are many different kinds of paint employed for this purpose consisting of compounds with mineral, asphaltum, and graphite bases; but, the shop painting required by the usual specifications is one coat of boiled linseed oil which after drying makes a first class base for the final painting in the field after erection. The best method of applying the paint is by the hand with a brush. Spray painting by means of compressed-air has the advantage of greater rapidity, but it is quite wasteful, and unless very carefully done, will not distribute the paint evenly.

After leaving the shops, and before shipment, the material is carefully examined in detail to see that it conforms in every particular to the drawings and specifications, by the inspectors of both the bridge company and the purchaser. A large percentage of this work is done by inspection companies. These companies employ a large number of inspectors who are sent from one place to another to examine the work on hand. The inspection companies bid for the inspection work at so much per ton of material. Although these companies usually keep a permanent inspector at the works of a large bridge concern, and are therefore able to greatly reduce the cost of inspection to the purchaser, the system is subject to many objections, the principal one being the fact that the actual inspector is personally unknown to the purchaser. The exceedingly satisfactory services rendered by these companies, however, is clearly demonstrated by the large amount of work handled by them, and their high professional reputation.

The general method of inspection may be briefly stated as follows: When the inspector of the purchaser arrives at the works of the bridge company, he is furnished with a set of the plans and drawings of the bridges to be inspected, and starts in at once to familiarize himself with the shops and working methods of that particular plant. He then ascertains the rolling mills from which the rough material for the structures will be obtained, and begins the work of actual inspection at that point. All the material is carefully examined for flaws and surface defects, and tested for strength, and when found satisfactory is stamped by him with a hammer, and then forwarded to the works of the bridge company. Subsequently, he keeps a general oversight of the material as it passes through the various shops and departments of the bridge works until it has passed out of them and is ready for the final examination.

For methods of testing see article under title TESTING MACHINE in this encyclopedia.

WILLIAM MOREY, JR., C. E.,
*Consulting Civil and Mechanical Engineer,
New York.*

Bridge of Allan, a town of Scotland, in Stirlingshire, on the border of Perthshire, on the banks of the Allan, about three miles north of Stirling, with which it is connected by the Caledonian Railway. and a line of tramway cars. Owing to the mildness of its climate and the beauty of its situation, Bridge of Allan is a favorite spring and summer resort for invalids. It is built partly on a plateau of considerable height and partly on low ground on the banks of the river, and is finely laid out with trees and public walks. It is frequented partly on account of its mineral wells.

Bridge of Sighs, a bridge in Venice, dating back to 1597. It spans the Rio della Paglia, connects the ducal palace with the prisons, and forms a graceful structure 32 feet above the water, enclosed at the sides and arched overhead. It contains two passages, through which prisoners were led for trial, judgment, or punishment.

Bridgeport, Conn., a city, port of entry, and county-seat of Fairfield County, on Long Island Sound, and on the New York, N. H. & H. R.R.; 18 miles southwest of New Haven, and 58 miles northeast of New York. It is the third city in the State. The city and town are conterminous, and about 15 square miles in area. Pop. (1900) 70,996.

Bridgeport harbor is the estuary of a small tidal river, the Pequonnock, and a tidal inlet called Pembroke Lake, with a peninsula between them on which East Bridgeport, the chief manufacturing section, is built. Below the junction the harbor is about two miles long to the Sound,

and a mile wide. The main city lies along the west side to its mouth, the business centre opposite the peninsula; the shore is a plain, rising on the west to an elevation of about 70 feet called Golden Hill, the finest residence section, and commanding a beautiful view of the Sound and city. Down the Sound about three miles is the suburb of Black Rock, a favorite summer resort, with its island-guarded harbor, a great yachting rendezvous. There are three handsome parks, about 250 acres in all: Beardsley, left in great measure to its wild state, and the more charming therefor; Washington, and Seaside, of some 75 acres, on the shore west of the harbor, with a sea-wall and a two-mile drive, and monuments to the soldiers and sailors of the War, and to Elias Howe and P. T. Barnum, the sewing-machine of the one and the business enterprise of the other having largely developed the city. Of the cemeteries, the finest is Mountain Grove, of some 75 acres, near the western boundary; others are Lakeview, in east Bridgeport, and Park, in North Bridgeport. There are also two Roman Catholic cemeteries. The most notable public buildings are the government building, with the post-office and customhouse; the county court-house; the Barnum Memorial Institute, bequeathed to the Historical Society and the Scientific Society in common; the Young Men's Christian Association and the Burroughs Library buildings. Very interesting is the Barnum & Bailey circus in its winter home.

Bridgeport, like all the cities of western Connecticut, is primarily an immense gathering of the manufacturing departments of New York salesrooms; but many of them started as local Bridgeport institutions, and have remained identified with the city. These establishments are multiplying with great rapidity. By the census of 1900, there were 832, employing 20.462 workmen and supervisors, using $33,066,890 capital, paying $10,622,558 in wages and salaries, $9,133,-236 for materials, and turning out $37,883,721 in products. Of these, no figures are given for the two most noted products, sewing-machines and ammunition, from their being concentrated in two or three establishments, mainly the Wheeler & Wilson Company with its 10 acres of works, and the Union Metallic Cartridge Company; but $4,147,452 was brass castings, $3.224.198 corsets, $2,412,796 foundry and machine-shop products, $1,007,244 hardware, cutlery and edge tools, $633,577 rubber goods, $366,585 carriages and wagons. Other products are steel bridges, ordnance and firearms, monumental bronze, bicycles, wire, velvet and plush, silk, belting, undertakers' goods, ice, fur goods, lamps, leather goods, musical instruments and graphophones, britannia, pottery, sporting goods, typewriters, carriages, and many more. The city's transportation facilities aid this growth. The railroad trackage is ample; a new station is to be built and the tracks raised, at an expense of some $3,000,000. The harbor is safe and admits quite large vessels; there are daily steamer lines to New York, and much barge and coasting business. The river, creeks, and Pembroke Lake are spanned by two or three dozen strong bridges. Electric railway service is thoroughly developed, continuous lines running to New Haven and New York.

Education, Churches, Charities, etc. — The public school system has 22 grammar schools and a high school; in 1900 the attendance was 10,255. There is a free public library, organized in 1881, with about 40,000 volumes; four daily and several weekly newspapers. The city has the extraordinary number of 57 churches, the chief denominations being the Methodist (11), Congregationalist (10), Roman Catholic (9, with three convents), Baptist and Episcopal (6 each), and Lutheran (4), with a Jewish synagogue, a Russian Orthodox Greek and a Hungarian Orthodox Greek Catholic. Of many charitable organizations and institutions, the chief are the Young Men's Christian Association and Young Women's Christian Association, the Bridgeport Hospital, the United States Marine Hospital, and the Widows' Home. Secret societies are in great number. The oldest Masonic lodge, St. John's, dates from 1762.

Government and Finance.— The mayor is elected for two years. The city has a council and administrative boards, with a single commissioner of public works, all appointed by the mayor excepting the popularly elected school board. The city's assessed valuation is about $64,000,000, its debt $1,275,000, and its tax rate $13 per $1,000. The annual outlay is about $1,000,000, the largest item being $170,000 for schools. There are five national banks.

Population.— 1810, 1,089; 1820, 1,500; 1830, 2,800; 1840, 3,294; 1850, 7,560; 1860, 13,209; 1870, 18,969; 1880, 27,643; 1890, 48,866; 1900, 70,996, of whom 22,281 were foreign-born.

History.— The first settlement was made in 1639, on lands bought from the Paugusset Indians, who in 1659 were relegated to a reservation on Golden Hill. It was called Pughquannock or Pequonnock, and formed a parish in the towns of Fairfield and Stratford, where the inhabitants went to church till they built their own first one in 1695. In 1694 they petitioned to have it renamed Fairford; the legislature chose Fairfield Village instead; they rejected it and the next year fixed on Stratfield, which, however, was not legalized till 1701. In 1703 the first school building was erected, previous teaching having been in the church on week-days. In 1707 the first services of the Episcopalians were held; in 1748 their first church was built. In 1775 a company from here joined Arnold's expedition to Quebec; and there was much privateering from this place in the Revolution. In 1795 the first newspaper, the *American Telegraphe,* was issued. In 1800 the borough of Bridgeport was incorporated, including the village of Newfield, which had grown up at the water-side, the old settlement being along the Boston and New York turnpike, or "Old Stage Road," now in part North Avenue. In 1806 the first bank, Bridgeport Bank, was organized. In 1821 the town of Bridgeport was set off, having then 1,700 inhabitants, 218 dwellings, 73 stores and warehouses, and an assessed valuation of $24,701. On 28 Sept. 1824, the first steamer ran from Derby past Bridgeport to New York; 16 April 1832, the first Bridgeport steamer, the Citizen, began regular trips. The Housatonic Railroad was opened to New Milford in February 1840; the New York, N. H. & H. began running to Fairfield, 2 Sept. 1848, to New York, 1 Jan. 1849. This ushered in the period of real city development, 1850-60. Gas was introduced December 1861; water, 1854-5; P. T. Barnum bought large tracts of land in East Bridgeport and opened it

up after 1850; in 1856 the Wheeler & Wilson Company removed here from Watertown and greatly enlarged their plant; the Howe Company came in 1863, and the Union Metallic Cartridge Company in 1865. In 1870 the city annexed a part of Fairfield; in 1899 Summerfield, and West Stratford across Pembroke Lake. (See Orcutt's 'History of Stratford and Bridgeport,' 1886.)

FRANK STAPLES,
Treasurer Board of Trade.

Bridg'er's Pass, a Rocky Mountain defile in southern Wyoming, several miles in length and having a high elevation. Its walls, almost perpendicular, rise from 1,000 to 2,500 feet. Before the opening of the Pacific Railroad it was an important feature of the overland stage route.

Bridges, Fidelia, American artist: b. Salem, Mass., 19 May 1835. She studied art under William T. Richards in Philadelphia; has been associate member of the National Academy of Design from 1869, and of the American Water Color Society from 1870. She has done much landscape work, her earlier paintings being mainly executed in oil, while her later ones are usually in water colors.

Bridges, Robert, American iron-worker. Extremely little is known of him personally. He settled at Lynn, Mass., and in 1643 organized a company to work the deposits of "bog iron-ore" in that vicinity. He went to London, and organized a "Company of Undertakers for the Iron Works," comprised of wealthy Englishmen, who advanced £1,000 for the work. Foundrymen were brought from England and Scotland, a plant was established on the Saugus River, and for several years furnished most of the iron used in this country, though ultimately the undertaking failed, owing to the scarcity of money and difficulty of making collections. In 1645 Bridges was a commissioner to confer with the governors of the French provinces in Canada. The Colonial records show him to have been a member of the general court, and its speaker in 1646.

Bridges, Robert, English poet: b. 23 Oct. 1844. Educated at Eton and Corpus Christi College, Oxford, he afterward studied medicine and held several hospital appointments, retiring from the active exercise of his profession in 1882. He is one of the most scholarly of modern English poets and has published, usually privately, eight plays and several collections of poems. Among his works are 'Prometheus'; 'Achilles in Scyros'; 'Eros and Psyche'; 'Shorter Poems'; 'Milton's Prosody.'

Bridges, Robert, American author: b. Shippensburg, Pa., 13 July 1858. After graduating at Princeton he joined the staff of the New York *Evening Post,* and later became assistant editor of 'Scribner's Magazine.' For many years he wrote the keen and witty book reviews in *Life* under the signature of DROCH. His work in book form has appeared as follows: 'Humours of the Court, a Comedy, and Other Poems' (1893); 'Overheard in Arcady' (1894); 'Suppressed Chapters and Other Bookishness' (1895); 'Bramble Brae' (1902), a volume of poems.

Brid'get, the name of two saints in the Roman Catholic Church.

1. SAINT BRIGET, or SAINT BRIDE, b. Fochard, Armagh, Ireland, about the beginning of the 6th

century. She was exceedingly beautiful, and to avoid the offers of marriage and other temptations to which this worldly advantage exposed her, implored God to render her ugly. The prayer was granted, and, retiring from the world, Bridget built herself a cell under a large oak, hence the name Kill-dara or Kildare, the cell of the oak. Hither she was followed by numerous other virgins, and an order of nuns was established which spread into different countries and flourished for centuries. Saint Bride is one of the chief Irish saints, and was held in great reverence in Scotland.

2. SAINT BRIDGET, BIRGIT, or BRIGITTE, daughter of a Swedish prince: b. about 1302; d. Rome, 1373. At the age of 16 she married Ulf Gudmarssen, afterward seneschal of Nericia, by whom she had eight children. Her husband and she then made a vow of mutual continence. On her husband's death she founded the convent of Wadstena, in East Gothland, under the rules of Saint Augustine. She made a pilgrimage to Palestine, and died on her return. She was canonized in 1391. She had left, under the title 'Revelations,' a series of mystic writings, which, after due examination by the proper authorities, were pronounced inspired by Gregory XI. and Urban VI. These writings have been translated into Latin and French. The order of St. Bridget, called also sometimes that of St. Salvator, or the Holy Saviour, continued in Sweden till the Reformation, and still includes some religious houses in Italy, Portugal, and other countries. Her youngest daughter, Catherine, was also canonized, and became the patron saint of Sweden.

Bridgeton, a city, port of entry, and county-seat of Cumberland County, N. J., on the Cohansey River, and on the New Jersey C. and the West Jersey & S. R.R.'s, 38 miles south of Philadelphia. It is a very old settlement, having been a place of considerable importance before the Revolutionary War. Its surroundings are agricultural, and it has manufactures of glass, gas-pipe, nails, machinery, flour, oil-cloth, woolen goods, shoes, and shirts, and also large fruit and vegetable canning interests. It has a public park, Tumbling Dam, which contains a picturesque lake and a fine field for athletics. The city contains the South Jersey Institute, the West Jersey Academy, Ivy Hall Seminary, Seven Gables Seminary, a public high school, two national banks, good water and sewerage systems, and electric lights and street railroads. Its excellent climate and scenic attractions have made the city a popular resort for summer tourists and residents. Pop. (1900) 13,913.

Bridgetown, the capital of the island of Barbados, in the West Indies. It extends along the shore of Carlisle Bay, on the southwest coast of the island, and is nearly two miles long, and about a half mile broad. On entering the port, its appearance is very pleasing, the houses being embosomed in trees, while hills of moderate height rise behind, studded with elegant villas. Many of the houses have balconies, painted in gay colors, which give them a lively and cheerful appearance. The town contains a handsome square, called Trafalgar Square, in which there is a bronze statue of Lord Nelson, placed there with great ceremony in 1813. The principal buildings include the Church of St. Michael, now the cathedral of the diocese; the Church of St.

Mary; the Jewish Synagogue; the Central School; Harrison's Free School; a handsome market-place; the barracks at the south extremity of the city; and the military hospitals. Bridgetown has been at several periods much damaged by fire. The last calamity of that kind occurred in 1845, when a large portion of the town was destroyed. Pop. over 21,000.

Bridgewater, Francis Egerton (THIRD DUKE OF), British nobleman: b. 1736; d. 8 March 1803. He was the youngest son of Scroop, fourth Earl and first Duke of Bridgewater, and succeeded his elder brother, the second Duke, in 1748. His estate of Worsley contained valuable coal mines, and with the view of establishing communication between these and Manchester, seven miles distant, he conceived the idea of a navigable canal. Having accidentally made the acquaintance of James Brindley, and perceived his great engineering talents, he employed him in the construction of this work, which, after encountering much opposition and ridicule, was at last triumphantly carried through. To the execution of this scheme the Duke devoted all his energies and fortune, restricting his expenditure for many years to £400 per annum.

Bridge'water, Francis Henry Egerton (EIGHTH EARL OF), English clergyman: b. London, 11 Nov. 1756; d. Paris, 11 Feb. 1829. He held several preferments in the English church, but his later years were spent in Paris, where he lived with a family of cats and dogs dressed as men and women, who accompanied him upon his drives. By his will he left $40,000 to be invested in the public funds to be awarded to the author of the best treatise 'On the Power, Wisdom, and Goodness of God as Manifested in the Creation.' The selection of the author was left to Davies Gilbert, then president of the Royal Society, who decided to divide the sum among eight persons for as many treatises on various aspects of the theme. The Earl was the author of several scientific, historical, and other works, and bequeathed all his manuscripts to the British Museum with $60,000 to keep up and extend the collection. See BRIDGEWATER TREATISES.

Bridgewater, or Bridgwater, a municipal borough and port, in the county of Somerset, England, on the Parret. Although the town is about 10 miles from the sea, vessels drawing 19 feet of water can come up to the quay at spring-tides; but great inconvenience is sometimes caused by the bore. The river divides the town into two parts, which are connected by an elegant iron bridge of one arch. The houses are generally well built, and chiefly of red brick. Among the chief buildings are the parish church (St. Mary Magdalene's), a handsome ancient structure, with a tower and spire; St. John's Church; the town hall, a handsome building in the Venetian style; corn exchange; borough jail; market-house; and custom-house. There is a free grammar school, an infirmary, and almshouses. A considerable shipping trade is carried on, chiefly coastwise. The tonnage entered and cleared annually is usually about 180,000 tons. The imports are timber, grain, coal, tallow, wine, esparto, linseed, etc.; exports, timber, bricks, etc. The chief manufacturing industry is that of bath-bricks which are made here (and indeed nowhere else) in great quantities. Ordinary bricks are also largely made, and there are engineering establishments, breweries, tanneries, foundries, oil-mills, etc. Bridgewater obtained its name, Burgh-Walter, from its having belonged to Walter de Douay, one of William the Conqueror's followers. In the civil war the inhabitants embraced the cause of Charles I., and defended the town resolutely against the Parliamentarians, but surrendered (1645) to Fairfax. In the castle built by King John, the Duke of Monmouth lodged, and was here proclaimed king in 1685, before the battle of Sedgemoor, which was fought about three miles from the town. Bridgewater then became the theatre of Feversham's and Jeffreys' barbarity. Up till 1870, when it was disfranchised for bribery, Bridgewater returned two members to Parliament. Pop. (1901) 15,209.

Bridgewater, a town in Plymouth County, Mass., on the New York, N. H. & H. R.R., 27 miles south of Boston. It contains five villages and has a State normal school, the State Farm, State Almshouse, a public library, a savings bank, and manufactures of iron, nails, tacks, boots, shoes, and brick. Pop. (1900) 5,806.

Bridgewater Treatises, The, works which grew out of a singular contest in compliance with the terms of the will of the last Earl of Bridgewater, who died in 1829. He left $40,000 to be paid to the author of the best treatise 'On the Power, Wisdom, and Goodness of God, as Manifested in the Creation.' The judges decided to divide the money among the authors of the eight following treatises: 'The Adaptation of External Nature to the Moral and Intellectual Constitution of Man,' by Dr. Thomas Chalmers (1833); 'Chemistry, Meteorology, and the Function of Digestion,' by William Prout (1834); 'History, Habits, and Instincts of Animals,' by William Kirby (1835); 'Geology and Mineralogy,' by Dean (William) Buckland (1836); 'The Hand . . . as Evincing Design,' by Sir Charles Bell (1833); 'The Adaptation of External Nature to the Physical Condition of Man,' by John Kidd, M.D. (1833); 'Astronomy and General Physics,' by William Whewell (1833); 'Animal and Vegetable Physiology,' by Peter Mark Roget (1834). All these essays were published as Tracts for the Times, and have had a great circulation and influence.

Bridge Whist. See WHIST.

Bridgman, Elijah Coleman, American missionary: b. Massachusetts, 1801; d. Shanghai, China, 1861. He graduated at Amherst College, 1826, and at Andover Theological Seminary, 1829, and immediately joined Dr. Morrison at Canton. He soon atttained a wonderful mastery of the Chinese language, becoming in 1839 official interpreter to Imperial Commissioner Lin, and in 1844 interpreter and secretary to the United States Minister, Caleb Cushing. He founded 'The Chinese Repository,' a magazine of the greatest value and interest for all subjects relating to the Flowery Kingdom. He compiled a Chinese 'Chrestomathy' in the Canton dialect, a quarto volume of 734 pages, and the first practical manual of that dialect prepared in China.

Bridgman, Frederick Arthur, American artist: b. Tuskegee, Ala., 10 Nov. 1847. He studied at the Brooklyn Art School, and at the National Academy of Design, New York, and was a pupil of J. L. Gérôme, and at the Ecole des Beaux Arts, in Paris. In 1872 he went to Africa and began to paint subjects belonging to that part of the world, somewhat in the manner of Gérôme, but with a greater mastery in color. He has long resided in Paris, where he has exhibited his works with great success. He is noted for figure pieces and Oriental and archæological pictures. Among his paintings are: 'An American Circus in Normandy'; 'L'Arabe'; 'Pharo'; and 'Burial of a Mummy,' which was awarded a prize at the Paris Exposition of 1878. He is a member of the National Academy of Design, New York, and a Chevalier of the Legion of Honor.

Bridgman, Herbert Lawrence, American journalist and explorer: b. Amherst, Mass., 1844. Graduating at Amherst College in 1866, he entered journalism and became associate editor of the Brooklyn *Standard Union.* In 1894 he accompanied and wrote an account of the Peary auxiliary expedition; in 1897 he was with Prof. Libbey of Princeton when the latter scaled the "Enchanted Mesa" of New Mexico; and in 1899 he comanded the Peary auxiliary expedition on the steamship Diana.

Bridgman, Laura Dewey, American blind deaf-mute: b. Hanover, N. H., 21 Dec. 1829; d. 24 May 1889. She was a bright, intelligent child, but at two years of age her sight, hearing, and smell were entirely destroyed by fever. Yet she learned to find her way about the house and neighborhood, and even to sew and to knit a little. In 1839 Dr. Samuel G. Howe, of Boston, undertook her care and education at the Perkins Institution. The first attempt was to give her a knowledge of arbitrary signs, by which she could interchange thoughts with others. Then she learned to read embossed letters by touch; next, embossed words were attached to different articles, and she learned to associate each word with its corresponding object. The next step was to procure her a set of metal types, with the letters cast at the ends, and a board with square holes for their insertion, so that they could be read by the finger. In six months she could write the names of most common objects, and in two years had made great bodily and mental improvement. Her touch grew in accuracy as its power increased; she learned to know people almost instantly by touch alone. In a year or two more she was able to receive lessons in geography, algebra, and history. She received and answered letters from all parts of the world, and was always employed, and, therefore, always happy. She learned to write a fair, legible hand, to read with great dexterity, to think and reason well, and at last became a teacher to others afflicted like herself. See her biography by Mary S. Lamson (1878).

Bridle, the headstall, bit, and reins, by which a horse is governed. It is an instrument of high antiquity. Pliny ascribes the invention of the bridle to Pelethronius, king of the Lapithæ. The first horsemen guided their horses with a rope or stick, and the sound of the voice. A cord drawn through the nose is sometimes used for other animals. The ancient Thessalian coins often represent a horse with a long rein trailing on the ground. The Romans were trained to fight without bridles, as an exercise in the manege. On Trajan's Column soldiers are thus represented at full speed. The parts of a modern bridle are the snaffle or bit; the headstall, or leathers from the top of the head to the rings of the bit; the fillet, over the forehead and under the foretop; the throat-band, which buttons under the throat; the reins; the noseband, buckled under the cheeks; the trench, the cavesan, the martingal, and the chaff-halter.

Brid'lington, or **Burlington,** a town of Yorkshire, England, incorporated in 1899. It is situated on a beautiful bay, 37 miles northeast from York, on the Hull and S. R.R., and consisting of one principal and several smaller streets. It is a favorite watering-place, with a fine harbor. The parish church forms part of an ancient priory of elegant architecture, but now much defaced. There are several Dissenting chapels and a free grammar school. A considerable trade is carried on in corn. Pop. (1901) 12,473.

Brid'port, a seaport and municipal borough, in Dorsetshire, England, lying between the rivers Bride, or Brit, and Asker, in a fertile valley surrounded by hills, 15 miles west from Dorchester and about 1½ miles from the sea. The Bride and Asker unite a little below the town, the united stream being called the Brit, and form a safe and commodious harbor for vessels not over 250 tons. Bridport consists mainly of three spacious streets, containing many well-built modern houses, chiefly of brick. In the centre of the town is the town hall and market-house, a handsome building in the Grecian style. The parish church of St. Mary's is a beautiful structure, cruciform, with a central tower, and contains a fine organ. At the northern entrance to the town is the more recent and less attractive St. Andrew's Church. There are, besides, several Dissenting chapels, schools, a library and scientific institute; and extensive manufactures of shoe-thread, ropes, cordage, sail-cloth, fishing-nets, etc. Bridport was a parliamentary borough from the reign of Edward I. to the passing of the Redistribution Act of 1885, when it was disfranchised. Pop. (1901) 5,710.

Brie, brē, a former province of France, lying between the Seine and the Marne, and now contained in the departments of Aisne, Marne, and Seine-et-Marne. It was divided into Brie Française, which belonged to the government of Ile de France, and Brie Champenoise, which was divided into upper and lower Brie, and comprised in the government of Champagne. A third division once existed, called Brie Poilleuse; this was afterward incorporated with Brie Champenoise. The latter was the largest of the divisions, and had for its capital Meaux, the most important town in the whole province. Its chief wealth was in vineyards and pastures; and its butter and cheese acquired and still retain a wide celebrity. Brie Française produced grain in great abundance, and was likewise a good grazing country. In ancient times this province was partly covered by a vast forest, portions of which are still to be seen. It was subjugated by the Franks, who annexed it to the kingdom of Neustria. In the ninth century it was ruled by its own counts. One of these, having obtained the earldom of Troyes or Champagne, in 968, united the two provinces, which thenceforth shared the same fortunes. Both passed into the possession of the Crown in 1361.

Brief (from the Latin *brevis,* short), a brief or short statement or summary, particularly the summary of a client's case which the solicitor draws up for the instruction of counsel. In American practice a brief is an abridged statement of a party's case. It should give the names of the parties to the action, their residence and occupation, and tell the character in which they sue and are sued, and wherefore they prosecute or resist the action. It should contain an abridgement of all the pleadings; a chronological and methodical statement of the facts, in language easily understood; a summary of the questions in issue, and of the evidence which is to support each of the issues; the names of the witnesses by whom the facts are to be proved, or if there be written evidence, an abstract of that evidence; a description of the personal character of the witnesses, whether morally good or bad, whether they are naturally timid or overzealous, firm or wavering, and the like. It should contain also a summary of the evidence of the opposite party, if known, and such facts as are adapted to oppose, confute, or repel it. The object of the brief is to inform the person who tries the case of the facts important for him to know. In some of the State courts and in the supreme court of the United States it is customary or requisite to prepare briefs of cases for the perusal of the court. These are usually printed. Briefs vary according to the purposes for which they are to be used. The points in a brief intended for the court should be printed in a bold, heavy-faced letter, although subordinate matter may be put in capitals, italics, and common type, according to its importance. A brief intended for the court must be in decorous language, and respectful to a judge from whose decision an appeal has been taken, and to the opposite party and counsel and all other persons named therein.

Brief, Papal, a pastoral letter in which the Pope gives his decision on some matter that concerns the party to whom it is addressed. The brief is an official document, but of less public character than the bull. It usually deals with matters comparatively private and subordinate, not, as the bull, with matters affecting the Church at large, or an entire nation. It is not signed by the Pope himself, but by an officer called "Il Segretario de' Brevi," and is sealed on red wax with the Pope's private seal, the fisherman's ring. Briefs are of two kinds: apostolical, those which issue from the Pope himself; and penitentiary, issuing from the office which bears that name.

Briel, brēl, or **Brielle,** brē-ĕl', sometimes The Brill, a fortified seaport town on the north side of the Island of Voorne, near the mouth of the Meuse, in the province of South Holland, Netherlands. It contains a government arsenal and military magazines, and possesses a good harbor. The tower of St. Peter's Church serves as a lighthouse. Its male inhabitants are chiefly engaged as pilots and fishermen. Briel may be considered as the nucleus of the Dutch republic, having been taken from the Spaniards by William de la Marck in 1572. This event was the first act of open hostility to Philip II., and paved the way to the complete liberation of the country from a foreign yoke. The celebrated admirals De Witt and Van Tromp were natives of Briel. Pop. about 4,500.

Brienne, brē-ĕn, **John of,** celebrated crusader: b. 1148; d. 1237. He was the son of Erard II., Count of Brienne; was present at the siege of Constantinople in 1204, and afterward, in 1209, married the granddaughter and heiress of Amaury, king of Jerusalem. Brienne thus obtained an empty title, and having been crowned at Tyre in 1210, defended himself, though with a very inferior force, against the attacks of the Saracens. The Emperor Frederick II., having engaged to join the crusade, provided the sovereignty of the Holy Land were ceded to him, Brienne abdicated in his favor, and gave him his eldest daughter, Yolande, in marriage. He afterward, in 1222, married Berengaria, sister of Ferdinand of Castile, as his second wife, and retired from the East; but the state of affairs there again brought him on the stage. He was crowned Emperor of the East in 1231, and continued to defend his dominions against all aggressors. more especially against the united forces of Vataces, emperor of Nicæa, and Azan, king of Bithynia.

Brienne, brē-ĕn, or **Brienne-le-Château,** lē-shạ-tō, or **Brienne-Napoléon,** nạ-pō-lē-ôn, a small town of France, department of Aube (Upper Champagne), about 23 miles northeast of Troyes, was the seat of the military academy at which Napoleon received his first instruction in the military art. Brienne-le-Château was afterward celebrated as the scene of a portion of the final struggle in 1814, in which the empire was overthrown, Napoleon being here defeated by the allies under Blücher.

Brienz, brē-ĕnts, a town of Switzerland, in the canton of Bern, beautifully situated on a narrow ledge at the foot of the Bernese Alps, and on the northeast shore of the Lake of Brienz. Its church, built in 1215, together with some old ruins and a handsome school, is finely situated on a height. Brienz is noted for its cheese, and as the centre of the Oberland wood-carving industry. The Lake of Brienz, one of the most picturesque in Switzerland, is formed by the river Aare, and discharges its water through the valley of Interlaken into Lake Thun, lying 24 feet below it. The lake has daily steamboat service between Brienz and Interlaken, and by this route many tourists visit the famous Giessbach Fall.

Bri′er Creek, a small stream rising in Warren County, Ga., flowing southeast for about 100 miles, and entering the Savannah River a few miles east of Jacksonborough. It is noted for a battle during the Revolutionary War. After the American victory on Kettle Creek, in February 1779, Gen. Ashe was sent by Lincoln at the head of about 1,500 troops to drive the British from Augusta. The British, under command of Gen. Campbell, evacuated the city, retreated to Brier Creek, and after crossing destroyed the bridge. Ashe pursued them, arrived at the creek 27 February, and there, 3 March, he was surprised by 1,800 British under Gen. Prevost. The American troops were hastily called to arms, and as the British advanced opened upon them a heavy fire, but an unfortunate movement in their line gave the enemy an advantage which decided the fortune of the day. The Americans were put to flight, many were drowned in trying to swim the Savannah, or were lost in the swamps. Their total loss was about 200 killed and wounded, and as many

others taken prisoners. The British had only 5 killed and 11 wounded.

Bri′erley Hill, a market-town of Staffordshire, England, on the Stour, nine miles west of Birmingham. It has several churches, a town hall, and a free library. The district abounds in coal, ironstone, and clay. The inhabitants are mostly employed in the iron rolling-mills and boiler-works, and in the making of bricks, nails, chains, anchors, spades, glass, pottery, etc. Pop. (1901) 12,040.

Bri′erly, Bob, the 'Ticket-of-Leave-Man,' in Tom Taylor's play of that name.

Brieuc, brē-ė, **Saint** (*Briocum*), France, a town in the department of Côtes du Nord, about a mile above the mouth of the Gouët, in the Bay of Saint Brieuc. It is very poorly built, but contains an ancient cathedral, a diocesan seminary, a school of hydrography, and a library of over 20,000 volumes. Its port, in the village of Légué, at the mouth of the river, admits vessels of 300 to 400 tons, and the town is engaged to some extent in the Newfoundland cod-fishery. On a height near it are the remains of the Tower of Cesson, which is visible 15 miles at sea. Pop. over 16,000.

Brig, a square-rigged vessel with two masts. The term is sometimes used as equivalent to brigantine, but modern American usage makes a difference. See BRIGANTINE.

Brigade, in general, an indeterminate number of regiments or squadrons. In the British army a brigade of infantry is generally composed of three regiments; a brigade of horse, of from 8 to 12 squadrons; and one of artillery, of five guns and a howitzer. A number of brigades form a division, and several divisions an army corps. A brigade-major is the chief of the brigade-staff. A brigadier-general commands a brigade. In the United States army three regiments of infantry or cavalry usually constitute a brigade, but there may be two regiments only, or more than three. The American brigade, like the British, is commanded by a brigadier-general. The brigade combination was introduced by Gustavus Adolphus, whose example was followed by Turenne, who formed brigades of 3,000 to 4,000 men. The use of the term in the French service is somewhat equivocal. In the gendarmerie, as formerly in the cavalry, a brigade is the small fraction of an army under the command of a subaltern officer. In the regular army a brigade now contains two or three regiments of infantry or cavalry, or else a mixed body.

Brigadier-General, a military officer of intermediate rank between a major-general and a colonel; the officer in the army of the United States who commands a brigade.

Brig′andine, a piece of mediæval armor, consisting of thin jointed scales of plate, generally sewed upon linen or leather, the whole forming a coat or tunic.

Brigands, a name first given during the imprisonment of King John in Paris (1358) to the mercenaries who held the city, and whose misbehavior rendered them obnoxious. Froissart applied it to a kind of irregular foot soldiery, from whom it was transferred to simple robbers. It is now used especially of such of these as live in bands in secret mountain or forest retreats. In this sense the pest has been common to most countries, by whatever name the robbers may have been known — whether the escaped slaves and gladiators of Rome, the pre-Islamite brigands of Arabia, English outlaws and highwaymen. German robber nobles, the later banditti of Mediterranean countries and of Mexico, American stage-coach robbers, Australian bushrangers, or the dacoits and hill robbers of Asia. It has ever flourished under weak or corrupt governments, and patriotism at times has swelled its ranks, always largely recruited from those disposed readily to join in any political movement, and has transformed them into guerrilla companies, who have carried on a bitter warfare against the invader. Such Spanish bands harassed the French during the Peninsular war; in Italy the Austrian troops were frequently engaged in expeditions against the banditti led by the daring Bellino ("*Il Passatore*"), and in Greece the Klephts rendered brave and worthy service in the war of independence. In Cuba, in 1888, political discontent was made the excuse for the brigandage then rampant in the island, where four provinces were on this account declared in a state of siege. Religious persecution also has encouraged brigandage; in Bosnia, which has always produced the most perfect specimens of bandits, it was formerly very common, the unhappy Christians, who were reduced by the Turks to the condition of serfs, frequently taking to the mountains in despair, and then wreaking vengeance on their oppressors. Generally speaking, in countries with a notably scanty population, which is yet in many districts as notably overcrowded, brigandage will be found still in existence. Vigorous steps have been taken during the last 50 years to repress the practice, and in some countries with signal success. In Greece, organized companies of brigands, as distinguished from bands of highway robbers, fortuitously collected, have disappeared; and, in Italy, the chiefs with whom princes made treaties are found only in history. Nevertheless, brigandage is by no means obsolete. In Hungary, where it has flourished from time immemorial, and where even the free towns in the 15th century enrolled companies for organized rapine, and thus raised it to the height of an institution, it has found a stronghold in the shades of the Bakony Forest, whose swineherds are said to be in league with the bétyars, and even to do an occasional stroke of business on their own account. In Sicily it is to be feared that this is still the only trade which really prospers in the island (see Mafia); and the bands that infest the Turkish frontier are notoriously dangerous to the wayfaring merchant and the defenseless tourist. In 1887 special attention was attracted by the boldness of brigands in the Pyrenees, Tuscany, Servia, Macedonia, Asia Minor, and Mexico.

Brigantes, brĭ-găn'tēz, the name of the most powerful of the old British tribes, inhabiting the country between the Humber and the Roman wall.

Brig'antine, a sailing-vessel with two masts, the foremast rigged like a brig's, the mainmast rigged like a schooner's; also called "hermaphrodite brig." The term is applied to different kinds of vessels by mariners of different countries. The term "brigantine" was formerly applied to a light, flat, open vessel, with 10 or 15 oars on a side, furnished also with

sails, and able to carry upward of 100 men. The rowers, being also soldiers, had their muskets lying ready under the benches. Brigantines, being very fast sailers, were frequently made use of, especially in the Mediterranean, for the purpose of piracy, from which fact they derived their name.

Briggs, Charles Augustus, American clergyman and author: b. New York, 15 Jan. 1841. For a number of years he was pastor of the Presbyterian church at Roselle, N. J. In 1874 he was appointed professor of Hebrew in Union Theological Seminary, New York. He was tried for heresy in 1892, and was acquitted. In 1897 he formally severed his connection with the New York Presbytery and became a clergyman of the Protestant Episcopal Church. He is one of the foremost Biblical scholars in the world, and the Episcopal Church in this country might be searched in vain to find his equal as a teacher of Hebrew and the cognate languages and as an authority in that department of learning, or even one who is entitled to be put in the same class with him. Among his works are: 'American Presbyterianism' (1885); 'The Bible, the Church, and the Reason' (1892); 'The Higher Criticism of the Hexateuch' (1893); 'The Messiah of the Gospels' (1894); 'The Messiah of the Apostles' (1895).

Briggs, Charles Frederick, American author and journalist: b. Nantucket, Mass., 1804; d. Brooklyn, N. Y., 20 June 1877. Throughout his life he was engaged in journalism in New York, and under the pseudonym of Harry Franco was widely known. In 1844 he founded the 'Broadway Journal,' and for a time Edgar Allen Poe was his associate editor. He was connected with 'Putnam's Magazine' (1853–6); the New York *Times*, the *Evening Mirror*, the Brooklyn *Union*, 1870–4, and the 'Independent.' Publications: 'Harry Franco; a Tale of the Great Panic' (1837); 'The Haunted Merchant' (1843); 'Working a Passage' (1844); 'Trippings of Tom Pepper' (1847); 'Seaweeds from the Shores of Nantucket' (1853); and in collaboration with Augustus Maverick, 'The Story of the Telegraph, and a History of the Great Atlantic Cable' (1858).

Briggs, George Nixon, American politician: b. Adams, Mass., 13 April 1796; d. Pittsfield, Mass., 12 Sept. 1861. He was governor of Massachusetts from 1844 to 1851, and one of the founders in that State of the Republican party. He spent one year at an academy, studied law, was admitted to the bar in 1818, and soon established a reputation as one of the best criminal lawyers in the State. From 1831–43 he was a representative in Congress, serving through one Congress as chairman of the Post-Office Committee. During his term as governor extraordinary efforts were made to induce him to pardon Prof. Webster, the murderer of Dr. Parkman, but he refused to interpose. For 16 years he was a trustee of Williams College, and at all times a noted advocate of temperance. His death was the result of an accident received from a gun. His life has been written by W. C. Richards under the title of 'Great in Goodness.' (1866).

Briggs, Henry, English mathematician: b. Warley Wood, Yorkshire, 1561; d. Oxford, 26 Jan. 1631. He entered St. John's College, Cambridge, and distinguished himself by his acquirements in mathematics. In 1596 he was appointed first lecturer on geometry in the newly elected establishment of Gresham House or College, London, and in 1619 became in like manner first Savilian professor of geometry at Oxford. This professorship he held till his death. Briggs' great works are his 'Logarithmorum Chilias Prima' (1617); 'Arithmetica Logarithmica' (1624); 'Trigonometria Britannica' (1633).

Briggs, Le Baron Russell, American educator: b. Salem, Mass., 11 Dec. 1855. He was graduated from Harvard University in 1875, was assistant professor of English there, 1885-90, and professor from 1890. Since 1891 he has been dean of the university. He has written 'Old Fashioned Views of Modern Education'; 'Original Charades'; 'School, College, and Character.'

Brigham, brĭg'ăm, **Amariah, American** physician: b. New Marlborough, Mass., 26 Dec. 1798; d. Utica, N. Y., 8 Sept. 1849. He began practice at Enfield, Mass., about 1821, but soon removed to Greenfield, where he became widely known for his skill as a surgeon. In 1828 he went to Europe and spent a year studying in the hospitals. In 1831 he settled in Hartford, Conn., and in 1840 was appointed superintendent of the retreat for the insane there. Two years later he accepted a similar position at the State Lunatic Asylum, Utica, N. Y., where he remained till his death. He was a skilful business man, an able physician, and was frequently called to act as an expert in the courts. Publications: 'Treatise on Epidemic Cholera' (1832); 'Influence of Mental Cultivation on the Health' (1833); 'Influence of Religion upon the Health and Physical Welfare of Mankind' ·(1835); 'Inquiry Concerning the Diseases and functions of the Brain, the Spinal Cord, and Nerves' (1840); 'The Asylum Souvenir' (1849); 'Mental Exertion in Relation to Health' (1866). See C. E. Goodrich, 'Sermon on the Death of Amariah Brigham' (1850).

Brigham, Sarah J. (LATHBURY), American illustrator and writer for young people: b. Manchester, N. Y., 1835. She was married to J. R. Brigham in 1854. She has written: 'Under Blue Skies' (1886); 'Leopold and His Wheel' (1896); 'The Pleasant Land of Play' (1898); 'The Bond of Honor.'

Brigham, William Tufts, American ethnologist: b. Boston, Mass., 24 May 1841. He was admitted to the Massachusetts bar in 1867, was for a year botanical instructor at Harvard and served for a time on the Boston school board. He removed to Honolulu in 1888, and has since been in charge of the Bishop Museum of Ethnology there. He has published: 'Cast Catalogue of Antique Sculpture'; 'Guatemala, the Land of the Quetzal'; 'Volcanic Manifestations in New England.'

Bright, Charles, English civil engineer: b. London, 25 Dec. 1863. He is the youngest son of Sir Charles Tilston Bright, who laid the first Atlantic cable, and has been himself employed in cable-laying in many parts of the world, as well as on various surveying expeditions. He has published 'Science and Engineering During the Victorian Era'; 'Submarine Telegraphs'; 'Underground Cables'; 'Ancient Methods of Signalling'; 'The Evolution of the Electric Telegraph, 1837-97'; 'The Life of Sir Charles Bright'; 'Imperial Free Trade'; 'Imperial Telegraphy.'

Bright, James Franck, English historical writer: b. London, 29 May 1832. He was educated at Rugby, and University College, Oxford, and was master at Marlborough College and head of the modern department there for 16 years. Since 1874 he has been dean of University College, and honorary Fellow of Baliol from 1878. He has written 'History of England to 1880'; 'Joseph II.' (1897); 'Maria Theresa' (1897).

Bright, Jesse D., American politician: b. Norwich, N. Y., 18 Dec. 1812; d. Baltimore, Md., 20 May 1875. He received an academic education, was admitted to the Indiana bar (1831), and became a circuit judge, State senator, and lieutenant-governor. From 1845 to 1857 he was a United States senator and president of the Senate during several sessions. Re-elected in 1857, he was expelled for alleged disloyalty, 5 Feb. 1862, the chief evidence against him being a letter addressed to "His Excellency, Jefferson Davis, President of the Confederation of States," recommending a friend who had an improvement in firearms to dispose of. Bright maintained that at the date of the letter (March 1861) he had no idea that there would be war, and wrote it to get rid of the inventor. Subsequently, he settled in Kentucky, and in 1866 was elected to the State Senate.

Bright, John, English statesman and orator: b. Greenbank, Rochdale, Lancashire, 16 Nov. 1811; d. 27 March 1889. His father, Jacob Bright, who belonged to a Quaker family originally connected with Wiltshire, migrated to Rochdale early in the century, and there established himself as a successful cotton-spinner and manufacturer. John Bright, who was the second of 10 children, was educated at Rochdale, Ackworth, York, and finally at Newton, near Clitheroe. At the age of 15 he entered the cotton-spinning business of his father, where, even at that early age, he showed much shrewdness and practical energy. Not satisfied, however, with merely mercantile affairs, he took an enthusiastic interest in such public questions as the abolition of slavery and the Reform Bill of 1831-2, while he diligently educated himself in public speaking at the debates of the Rochdale Literary and Philosophical Society. In 1835 he traveled in Greece, Egypt, and Palestine, and gave an account of the journey in a series of lectures delivered in his native town; but his career as a notable public speaker began with the free-trade movement. To relieve the pressure upon the working population of England occasioned by commercial depression and a bad harvest, it was proposed to cheapen bread by the repeal of the corn duty, and in an association formed for this purpose at Manchester in 1838 Mr. Bright was made a member of committee. In the following year this association, at a meeting in London, was widened into the famous Anti-Corn Law League, with Richard Cobden and John Bright as its two most prominent members. Yet it was not until after the death of his first wife, in 1841, that the latter put all his strength into the repeal campaign. In the autumn and winter of that year he organized branches of the League and addressed meetings in nearly all the large towns of England. It was inevitable that such a prominent politician should find a place in Parliament, and accordingly, in 1843, he was elected as representative of the city of Durham. Having entered Parliament, he made his maiden speech in August of the same year on a motion in favor of carrying out the recommendations of the Import Duties Commission of 1840. Thereafter he seized every opportunity to press this question of repeal. The opposition from both of the great parties in the house was dogged, and the controversy might have lasted long but for the widespread sympathy occasioned by the Irish famine. In January 1846 Parliament was summoned, and Sir Robert Peel announced that his government was prepared to reduce and almost abolish the corn duties. This resolution was carried, but on the question of Irish coercion the government was defeated, and at the general election which followed (1847), John Bright was elected for Manchester. The corn duty question having been satisfactorily settled, he now turned his attention to such subjects as a reform in the affairs of Ireland and India, an extension of the suffrage, the adoption of voting by ballot, and the establishment of a national system of education. At the dissolution of Parliament in 1852 he was re-elected for Manchester, but by his strenuous denunciation of the Crimean war (1854), and his equally decided disapproval of the Chinese war (1856), he was rejected by his constituency at the general election of 1857. This result was made known to him at Florence, where he had retired to recruit after a serious illness, but the disappointment which it caused him was mitigated by his election by his election for Birmingham, and in 1858 he returned to public life after an absence of two years. During the American Civil War he sturdily advocated the abolition of slavery, and gave his passionate adherence to the cause of the North, although as a Lancashire cotton-spinner his business suffered severely from a continuance of the struggle. About this time, also, his name became closely identified with reform in the electoral representation, and he had the satisfaction of seeing the principles for which he had contended embodied in the Reform Bill (1867) passed by Mr. Disraeli. He had no desire for office, but his presence in the cabinet councils of the Liberal party had now become so necessary that he was constrained to accept the presidency of the Board of Trade in Mr. Gladstone's government (1868), and in this position he gave powerful assistance in passing the act for the disestablishment of the Irish Church, the Irish Land Act, and the Elementary Education Act. Owing to ill health he retired from office in 1870, but re-entered the ministry as chancellor of the duchy of Lancaster in 1873. When the Liberal party returned to power in 1880 he again accepted this position, but two years later he found it necessary to resign because he disagreed with his colleagues on their Egyptian policy and the bombardment of Alexandria. At this time and for some years previously he had not appeared often upon public platforms, but in 1883 he delivered a notable speech when installed as lord rector of Glasgow University, and another in Birmingham in the same year when celebrating the 25th anniversary of his connection with that city. In 1886 he opposed the Home Rule Bill introduced by Mr. Gladstone, and until his death he strongly identified himself with the Unionist party in its efforts to defeat the Home Rule policy. This

opposition was weighted with the same characteristics which had secured his success in previous movements — a transparent sincerity of purpose which found its fearless exposition by pen and speech in direct, racy, idiomatic English. As an orator his platform manner was remarkable for its ease and unstudied simplicity; the richness and lucidity of his diction, abounding in happy epithets, often edged with irony or glancing with humor; a spirit of outspoken truthfulness breathing through all his utterances; while he was possessed of a voice which laid a spell upon his audience by its clear, round, sonorous fullness. Perhaps the most splendid expression of his sympathetic nature is found in the speeches in which he pleaded for justice to the oppressed populations whether in Ireland or India, while the same broad humanity, even more than the doctrines which were his Quaker birthright, animated his denunciations of war. He was a member of the Society of Friends, and was married first to a Miss Priestman, who died in 1841, and again to a Miss Leatham, who died suddenly in 1878. His life and speeches in two volumes were published in 1881 by G. Barnett Smith, and his public letters by H. J. Leech in 1885.

Bright, Richard, English physician: b. Bristol, 28 Sept. 1789; d. 16 Dec. 1858. He studied at Edinburgh, Berlin, and Vienna. His name is associated with Bright's disease (q.v.), he being the first who investigated its character.

Brightly, Frederick Charles, American lawyer: b. Bungay, England, 26 Aug. 1812; d. Germantown, Pa., 24 Jan. 1888. He came to the United States in 1831, and was admitted to the Philadelphia bar (1839). In 1870 he retired to devote himself to legal writing and compilation, for which he had pre-eminent gifts. His private law library of 5,000 volumes was one of the best collections in America. Publications: 'Law of Costs in Pennsylvania' (1847); 'Reports of Cases Decided by the Judges of the Supreme Court of Pennsylvania' (1851); 'Equitable Jurisdiction of the Courts of Pennsylvania' (1855); 'Analytical Digest of the Laws of the United States, 1789-1869' (1865-9); 'Digest of the Decisions of the Federal Courts' (1868-73); 'Bankrupt Law of the United States' (1871); 'Leading Cases on the Law of Elections' (1871); 'Digest of the Laws of Pennsylvania, 1700-1883' (1883); and other works.

Brighton (formerly BRIGHTHELMSTONE), a maritime town and favorite watering-place in England, county of Sussex, 50½ miles south of London. It is situated on a gentle slope, and is a clean and well-built town, with handsome streets, terraces, squares, etc., and a massive sea-wall, with a promenade and drive over three miles in length, one of the finest in Europe. The buildings of note are entirely modern, and not numerous. The most remarkable is the Pavilion, built by George IV. (then Prince of Wales), between 1787 and 1825. It cost upward of $5,000,000. It is a building in the Oriental style of architecture, with a handsome stone front 300 feet in length, and a large Oriental dome 84 feet high in the centre. The Pavilion was discontinued as a royal residence by Queen Victoria in 1841, and was purchased of the Crown by the town of Brighton in 1850. Pop. (1901) 123,478.

Bright's Disease. See KIDNEY.

Brigittines, or **Order of Our Saviour,** a branch of the Augustinians, founded about the year 1344 by Saint Bridget of Sweden, and approved by Urban V. in 1370. It owes its origin to the monastery built by Bridget at Wastein, near Linköping, in Sweden. It embraces both monks and nuns, who occupy contiguous buildings. The prioress is superior in temporal concerns, but spiritual matters are managed by the monks. All the houses of the order are subject to the bishop of the diocese, and no new one can be founded without express permission of the Pope. The number of male religious in each monastery was fixed by the rule at 25, and that of females at 60; but this regulation has ceased to be strictly enforced. Indeed, there are few establishments for both sexes now existing, though some are yet maintained in Germany, Flanders, and other countries; most of them, including the parent house at Wastein, were destroyed at the Reformation. There are two rich convents of Brigittines at Genoa, into one of which only ladies of high family are admitted. The only house of the order in England was the rich institution known as Sion house, founded by Henry V. on the Thames, 10 miles from London. It was one of the first suppressed by Henry VIII. After passing through the hands of the dukes of Somerset and Northumberland, it was restored to the religious by Queen Mary, and again dissolved under Elizabeth. The nuns then left England, and after various troubles established themselves in Portugal.

Bril, the name of two Dutch painters, (brothers), who distinguished themselves as landscape artists. (1) MATTHEW, b. Antwerp, 1550; d. 1584. When a very young man he went to Rome, and was so much esteemed by Gregory III. that he was employed on the galleries and salons of the Vatican. (2) PAUL, b. about 1556; d. about 1626. He was much superior to Matthew, and hearing of his success at Rome joined him there. The two brothers appear for some time to have worked together on the same pieces; but after Matthew's early death Paul was employed by Sixtus V., and executed six large paintings in his summer palace.

Brilliant. See DIAMOND.

Brimstone. See SULPHUR.

Brindisi, bren'dē-sē, (ancient BRUNDUSIUM), a seaport and fortified town in the province of Leece in southern Italy, 45 miles east-northeast of Taranto. In ancient times Brundusium was one of the most important cities of Calabria. It was one of the chief cities of the Sallentines, and the excellence of its port and commanding situation in the Adriatic were among the chief inducements to the Romans to attack them. The Romans made it a naval station, and it was the scene of important operations in the war between Cæsar and Pompey. Virgil died here 19 B.C. On the fall of the western empire it declined in importance. In the 11th century it fell into the possession of the Normans, and became one of the chief ports of embarkation for the Crusades. Its importance as a seaport was subsequently completely lost, and its harbor blocked. In 1870 the Peninsular & Oriental Steam Navigation Company put on a weekly line of steamers between Brindisi and Alexandria, and Brindisi is now an important station for passengers and mails to and from India and the East. There is also a trade with British, Austrian, and other ports. Latterly, the harbor accommodation has been considerably improved. The chief exports are wine, olive-oil, and figs; the chief import, coal. Pop. (1901) 25,317.

Brindley, James, English engineer: b. Thornsett, Derbyshire, 1716; d. Turnhurst, Staffordshire, 30 Sept. 1772. At 17 he became apprentice to a millwright, and on the expiration of his indentures began business as an engineer, and in 1752 displayed great talent in contriving a water-engine for draining a coal-mine. Several important inventions introduced him to the patronage of the Duke of Bridgewater, then occupied in planning a communication between his estate at Worsley and the towns of Manchester and Liverpool by water. This immense work, ridiculed by scientific men of the period as impracticable, Brindley undertook and carried out by means of aqueducts over valleys, rivers, etc. The first portion of the Bridgewater Canal (to Manchester) was opened in 1661, the whole system being complete in the end of 1772. See Smiles, 'Lives of the Engineers' (1861–2).

Brine Shrimp, the only animal, except a species of fly (*Ephydra*), which lives in the Great Salt Lake of Utah. It is a phyllopod crustacean, with stalked eyes, a delicate, slender body, which is provided with 11 pairs of broad, paddle-like or leaf-like feet. It is about one quarter of an inch long. Similar forms live in brine vats in various parts of the world. *Artemia fertilis* abounds in Great Salt Lake. It may often be seen swimming about in pairs and has a nauplius young like that of the brine shrimp of Europe. It produces young by budding (parthenogenesis), as well as from eggs. A species observed near Odessa produced females alone in warm weather; and only in water of medium strength were males produced. The eggs of *A. fertilis* have been sent in moist mud from Utah to Munich, Germany, and specimens raised from the eggs by Siebold, proving the great vitality of the eggs of these Phyllopods, a fact paralleled by the similar vitality of the eggs of the king-crab. *A. gracilis* of Verrill has thus far only been found in tubs of concentrated salt water on railroad bridges in New England.

Brinjaree, brĭn'ja-rē. **Dog,** the East Indian greyhound.

Brin'ton, Daniel Garrison, American surgeon, archæologist and ethnologist: b. Thornbury, Pa., 13 May 1837; d. Atlantic City, N. J., 31 July 1899. During the Civil War he was a surgeon in the Union army, and from 1867 to 1887 was editor of the 'Medical and Surgical Reporter.' In 1884 he was appointed professor of ethnology at the Academy of Natural Sciences in Philadelphia; and, in 1886, professor of American linguistics and archæology in the University of Pennsylvania. Among his many works are notes on the 'Floridian Peninsula' (1859); 'The Myths of the New World' (1868); 'American Hero Myths' (1882); 'Aboriginal American Anthology'; 'Primer of Mayan Hieroglyphics' (1896); 'Religions of Primitive Peoples' (1897); etc. He edited 'The Library of Aboriginal American Literature' in eight volumes (1882–5), and was a high authority on all American archæological topics.

Brinton, John Hill, American surgeon: b. Philadelphia, 1832. He graduated at the University of Pennsylvania (1850), and at the Jefferson Medical College (1852), serving through the Civil War as a surgeon. In 1882 he was appointed professor of the practice of surgery and clinical surgery at Jefferson Medical College. He has written 'Consolidated Statement of Gunshot Wounds' (1863); with J. H. Porter, 'History of the Organization of the Medical Department of the United States Army' (1864), a MS. in the surgeon-general's library at Washington; 'Description of a Valve at the Termination of the Right Spermatic Vein in the Vena Cava' (1856); 'Operative Surgery in General' (1881); 'The March of Surgery' (1882).

Brinvilliers, Marie Madeleine Marguerite **d'Aubray,** mä-rē mäd-lēn mär-gä-rēt dō-brā brăn-vẹ-yä (MARQUISE DE), French poisoner: b. Paris, about 1630; executed 16 July 1676. She was the daughter of a civil-lieutenant of Paris, and married in 1651 the Marquis of Brinvilliers. About 1659 the Marquis introduced to his house a young cavalry officer, named Godin de Sainte-Croix, for whom his wife conceived a violent passion. The Marquis, occupied with his own pleasures, seemed indifferent, but her brothers remonstrated, and her father, scandalized at her misconduct, had Sainte-Croix openly arrested in her carriage and taken to the Bastile in 1665. Sainte-Croix remained in prison about a year, and made there the acquaintance of an Italian, who taught him the art of preparing poisons. On his liberation he imparted his discoveries to Madame de Brinvilliers, who had in the meantime assumed an air of piety, visiting the hospitals, and ministering to the sick, and had thus reconciled herself to her family; but the affront offered her by her father remained in her mind, and she had resolved to revenge it. Sainte-Croix, apparently from cupidity, seconded her design. He supplied her with poisons, with which she experimented first on the patients in the hospital. She occupied eight months in administering poison to her father, and at last killed him suddenly without being suspected. By the aid of Lachaussée, an old domestic of Sainte-Croix, whom she caused to enter their service, she also succeeded in poisoning her brothers. She is said to have attempted her husband, with a view to marry Sainte-Croix, but did not succeed. Sainte-Croix died suddenly, it is said from the falling off of a mask of glass which he used to protect himself in preparing a subtle poison. A packet addressed to Madame Brinvilliers, containing poisons labelled with descriptions of their effects, revealed their conspiracy. Among a number of letters there was one containing a promise of $6,000, which Sainte-Croix had exacted as the price of his assistance. Madame Brinvilliers fled to Liége, and took refuge in a convent. Her extradition being obtained, she was inveigled from the convent by a pretended lover, brought to Paris, and on the evidence of Lachaussée, together with her own confession, condemned to be beheaded and afterward burned. See Pirot, 'La Marquise de Brinvilliers' (1883).

Brion, Friederike Elizabeth, frē-dēr-ē'kē ä-lē'zä-bĕt brẹ-ôñ, German lady: b. Niederrödern, Alsace, 1752; d. 1813. To her Goethe dedicated several lyrics and she is the supposed original of Maria, in 'Götz von Berlichingen,' as well as of other Goethean heroines. She figures in a well-known episode in Goethe's 'Dichtung und Wahrheit,' and is often styled from her place of residence, FRIEDERIKE VON SESENHEIM.

Brion, Gustave, French artist: b. Rothau, Alsace, 24 Oct. 1824; d. Paris, 4 Nov. 1877. He is noted for his Alsatian scenes and many of his works are to be found in American collections. Among them are: 'A Marriage in Alsace' and 'The Sixth Day of Creation.' He illustrated Hugo's 'Les Misérables' and 'Notre Dame de Paris.'

Brion, Luis, loo-ēs' brẹ-ōn', Colombian admiral: b. Curaçao, 6 July 1782; d. 20 Sept. 1821. He was sent at an early age to Holland to receive his education, his father being a native of that country, and there entered the Dutch army. He was offered a commission in 1799, but being recalled by his parents, returned to Curaçao. Receiving permission from his parents, he visited the United States, where he studied navigation. Upon the death of his father, who bequeathed him a large fortune, he bought a vessel and made several voyages; entering into speculation on his own account, he was very successful, and returned to Curaçao in 1804, where he established a mercantile house. The political events in Venezuela of 1808-10 brought Brion rapidly into notice; he volunteered his services to the republic of Caracas, and in 1811 was appointed captain of a frigate. He now devoted all his resources and his energies to the patriotic cause. At his own expense he fitted out a fleet of vessels, and attacked the Spanish forces at the island of Marguerite, where he gained a signal victory. Brion distinguished himself at the conquest of Guiana, and also at Santa Marta and Cartagena. During a residence at Savanilla he reduced the custom house duties; this coming to the ear of Bolivar, he directly countermanded the order, which so preyed upon the mind of Brion, that he became ill, and leaving the squadron returned to Curaçao, and soon died in poverty.

Briosco, Andrea, än-drä'ạ brẹ-ŏs'kō, Italian sculptor and architect: b. 1470; d. 1532. He designed the Church of Santa Giustina at Padua as well as a celebrated candelabrum in the Church of San Antonio there; and the Delle Torre tombs in San Ferno at Verona.

Brioude, brē-ood, a French town in the department of Haute Loire, capital of the arrondissement of the same name, situated near the left bank of the river Allier, on the site of the ancient town of Brivas. The old bridge at La Vieille Brioude, long celebrated as being the widest in span of any known, fell down in 1822. In the 16th century, many of the inhabitants of Brioude rose in favor of Lutheranism, but were afterward subdued by the Roman Catholic party. To Americans the town is of interest as the birthplace of Lafayette. A considerable traffic in grain, hemp, and wine is carried on here. Pop. (1891) 4,928.

Briquette, brē-kĕt', the name, originally French ("small brick"), given to a comparatively new form of fuel, made mostly from waste coal dust, and used, not merely for household purposes, but in various industries.

A briquette is simply an admixture of coal dust with pitch, molded under pressure and heat, the pitch or some similar substance being introduced to form the cementing material.

Brisach. See BREISACH, ALT.

Brisbane, brĭz'băn, **Sir Thomas Mac-Dougall,** Scottish general and astronomer: b. Brisbane, near Largs, the seat of his family, 23 July 1773; d. there, 27 Jan. 1860. He entered the army and in 1793 took part in all the engagements of the campaign in Flanders. In 1796 he was sent to the West Indies, and in 1812 commanded a brigade under the Duke of Wellington in Spain. He took part in the battles of Vittoria, Orthes, and Toulouse, and received the thanks of Parliament for conspicuous bravery at the battle of the Nive. On the abdication of Napoleon he was sent to America. In 1821 he was appointed governor of New South Wales, which post he continued to occupy for four years. His administration was active and intelligent, and tended greatly to promote the prosperity of the colony. He introduced at his own expense a good breed of horses, and promoted the cultivation of the vine, as well as of sugar, cotton, and tobacco. At the same time he devoted himself with great diligence to the study of astronomy. He had an observatory erected at his residence of Paramatta, and catalogued 7,385 stars, until then scarcely known to astronomers. For this great work, known as the 'Brisbane Catalogue of Stars,' he received the Copley medal of the Royal Society. On his return to Scotland he devoted himself entirely to science. He had an astronomical, and later a magnetic observatory established at his residence at Makerstoun. The observations which he made there, with the aid of able assistants, fill three large volumes of the published 'Transactions' of the Royal Society of Edinburgh, of which he was president from the death of Sir Walter Scott. He founded two gold medals for scientific merit, one in the gift of the Royal Society, the other in that of the Society of Arts.

Brisbane, the capital of the colony of Queensland, Australia, on the Brisbane River, about 25 miles by water from its mouth in Moreton Bay, and about 500 miles north of Sydney. It was named in honor of Sir Thomas Brisbane (q.v.). Of the four parts into which the town is divided, North Brisbane is situated in the heart of the city, on the north bank of the river, and South Brisbane faces it on the south. Fortitude Valley is a large division on the north bank, to the east and northeast of North Brisbane, mostly situated on a peninsula formed by the winding of the river. The fourth division, Kangaroo Point, is on the south bank, comprising a point of land projecting between North Brisbane and the above peninsula. The streets are laid out as regularly as the tortuous course of the river will permit. The chief buildings are situated in North Brisbane, among them being Parliament House, where the legislature sits; Government House, in the Botanic Gardens; the government offices; the supreme court; the post-office; the technical college; the treasury buildings, a large structure of great architectural beauty; the old and the new town-hall; and the customs-house. Many of the banks have fine edifices, particularly the Queens-land National Bank. The chief educational institutions are the Normal School, the boys' and girls' grammar schools, and the school of the Christian Brothers. Other buildings and institutions are the masonic and temperance halls; the School of Arts, with a good library; the museum; the Queensland Club; the large general hospital, and several special hospitals; an orphanage and a large jail in South Brisbane; the Opera House, one of the best theatres in Australia. The Victoria Bridge connects South with North Brisbane. It cost upward of $555,000, and replaces an older one destroyed by a flood in 1893. It consists of six steel spans supported on five cast-iron cylinders filled with concrete, the abutments being of masonry and concrete; and the total length is about 1,041 feet. Much of the cross-river traffic is carried on by the ferries. The leading parks and gardens are the Botanic Gardens, with the Queen's Park, in North Brisbane, at the river-side, finely laid out; Victoria Park, to the north of North Brisbane; Albert Park, Mount Coot-tha, Bowen Park, and the gardens of the Acclimatization Society in Fortitude Valley; and Musgrave, Dutton, and Woolloongabba parks in South Brisbane. There is extensive wharf accommodation, and South Brisbane has a dry-dock. There is regular steamer connection with Sydney, London, and elsewhere, and adequate railway communication with Sydney and other chief towns in Australia. The crimate is dry and healthy, but the temperature is often very high during the summer. Among the industrial establishments are a sugar-refinery, tobacco factories, flour-mills, etc. The trade is important, among the exports being gold, wool, sugar, etc. Originally founded as a penal settlement in 1825, Brisbane was incorporated in 1859. A United States consul is stationed here. Pop. (1896) estimated at 100,913.

Briscoe, Margaret Sutton. See HOPKINS, MARGARET SUTTON BRISCOE.

Brise'is, a girl of Lyrnessus, called also HIPPODAMIA. When her country was taken by the Greeks, she fell to the share of Achilles in the division of the spoils. Agamemnon afterward took possession of her, and Achilles thereupon made a vow to absent himself from the field of battle at Troy. This incident Homer makes one of the chief features of his 'Iliad.'

Brisgau, brēz'gow, or **Breisgau,** a district of the grand-duchy of Baden, between the Rhine and the Black Forest, which, with the district of Ortenau, formerly constituted a landgraviate in the southwestern part of Germany. Though chiefly in possession of Austria since the 15th century, it was governed by its own laws. At the Peace of Lunéville (1801) Austria ceded Brisgau, one of the oldest possessions of the House of Hapsburg, to the Duke of Modena, after whose death it fell to his son-in-law, the Archduke Ferdinand of Austria, as Duke of Brisgau. By the Peace of Presburg (1805) it was assigned to Baden, with the exception of a small part, and still belongs to the grand-duchy.

Brissac, brē-säc, **Count de.** See COSSÉ, CHARLES DE.

Brisson, Barnabé, bar-na-bä brē-sôn, French jurist: b. 1531; d. 15 Nov. 1591. Henry III. commissioned him to collect and edit the ordinances of his predecessors and his own, which appeared under the title 'Code de Henri III.' In 1589, he was made first president of the parliament, and after Henri's death, in August of the same year, proclaimed the Duke de Mayenne, the Chief of the League, lieutenant-general of the kingdom. Brisson soon after became suspected by the faction of the «Sixteen,» who ruled in Paris, and who thought that he was favorable to Henri IV. He was accordingly arrested and summarily hanged. Among his works of importance are: 'De Verborum Ouæ ad Jus Pertinent Significatione. etc.' (1557); 'Observationum Divini et Humani Juris Liber' (1564); 'De Formalis et Solemnibus Populi Romani Verbis, etc.' (1583), still in use; 'Opera Minora' (1606).

Brisson, Eugène Henri, è-zhän ôn-rē, French politician and journalist: b. Bourges, 31 July 1835. He entered the chamber of deputies in 1871, and won much attention by urging amnesty for the Communists and other political offenders. Since then he has been one of the foremost members of the Radical party. He was elected president of the chamber in 1881, and retained that office until the overthrow of the Ferry ministry, in 1885, when he accepted the premiership. He was re-elected to the presidency of the chamber in 1894, and, in 1895, he retired from the ministry and was a conspicuous candidate for the presidency of France. In 1898 he again accepted the premiership, but his cabinet was soon otherthrown. On 8 June 1906 he was elected president of the House.

Brisson, Mathurin Jacques, ma-too-răn zhäk, French savant: b. Fontenay-le-Comte, 30 April 1723; d. Versailles, 23 June 1806. He was instructor to the children of the royal family of France in physics and natural history. He was also censor royal, member of the Academy of Sciences, and of the Institute, and succeeded Nollet in the chair of natural philosophy at the College of Navarre. He translated Priestley's work on 'Electricity,' although he opposed his theories, and still more those of Franklin. The most able of his writings are on specific gravity and on ornithology. Buffon quotes frequently from Brisson's 'Ornithologia' (1760). He published in 1800 a 'Dictionnaire raisonné de physique.'

Brissot de Warville, Félix Saturnin, fä-lĕks sä-toor-năn brē-sŏ dė vär-vĕl, French animal painter: b. Sens, 1818. His paintings are renowned for their truthful representations of nature, their scenes being laid chiefly in Touraine and Normandy, or in the forests of Fontainebleau and Compiègne. Among them are: 'The Thicket' (1881); 'Return of the Flock' (1885); 'A Corner of the Sheepfold' (1888).

Brissot de Warville, Jean Pierre, zhŏn pė-är brē-sŏ dė vär-vĕl, French political writer, and one of the leaders of the Girondists: b. Ouarville, near Chartres, 14 Jan. 1754; executed, Paris, 30 Oct. 1793. He took the name D'Ouarville, which he afterward anglicized into De Warville, from the village of Ouarville, where he was born. He was designed for the law, and placed with a procurator in Paris; but early turned his attention to public affairs, associating himself with such men as Pétion, Robespierre, Marat, etc. In 1780 he published his 'Théorie des Lois Criminelles,' and two years afterward an important collection called the 'Bibliothèque des Lois Criminelles.' During this period he edited for a time, at Boulogne-sur-Mer, the 'Courier de l'Europe', a translation from an English journal. He also visited England, where he endeavored to found a lyceum and establish a journal in connection with it. Failing in this enterprise, he returned to Paris, where his works had already classed him among the philanthropic theorists of the day. He was suspected of the authorship of an anonymous pamphlet, and thrown into the Bastile. On his liberation he engaged with Clavières and Mirabeau in some works on finance, which appeared under the name of the latter. Threatened with a new arrest, he escaped to England, and being there introduced to the Society for the Abolition of Negro Slavery, resolved to form a similar society in Paris. This society, which numbered many distinguished names among its members, and ultimately accomplished its object, he founded along with Clavières, Mirabeau, and others, and undertook a voyage to the United States to study on its behalf the problem of emancipation. On his return the Revolution was about to break out, and Brissot embraced it with ardor. He was not a member of the States-general, but was elected to the National Assembly for Paris and to the Convention for the department of the Eure et Loir. As leader of the Girondist party, his history belongs henceforward to the history of France. He voted, out of policy, for the death of Louis XVI., subject to confirmation by the vote of the people; and he caused war to be declared against Holland and England in February 1793. This was his last political act. Until the close of his career he was engaged in defending himself against the Montagnards. Brissot was inferior to Vergniaud as an orator, but his writings exercised a powerful influence on the Revolution. In the early part of his career his opinions were very extreme. In a passage, afterward used against him, he carried his advocacy of individual rights so far as to justify not only theft, but cannibalism. Proudhon was accused of having borrowed from him the maxim, «La propriété c'est le vol.» His 'Mémoires pour servir à l'histoire de la Révolution' appeared in 1830.

Brissotins, brē-sŏ-tăn. See GIRONDISTS.

Bris'ted, Charles Astor, American author: b. New York, 1820; d. Washington, D. C., 15 Jan. 1874. He was the son of the Rev. John Bristed, and grandson of John Jacob Astor, founder of the Astor Library. He graduated with high honors at Yale in 1839, and then spent five years at Trinity College, Cambridge, England, where he took a number of prizes and became a foundation scholar. He traveled extensively, and contributed many papers on light social topics and ephemeral subjects to the magazines of England and America. His wide culture and exact scholarship made his work attractive to all cultivated readers. He wrote 'Selections from Catullus' (1849); 'Letter to Horace Mann' (1850), a reply to certain attacks on Stephen Girard and J. J. Astor; 'The Upper Ten Thousand' (1852); 'Five Years in an English University' (1852), his most important book; 'Pieces of a Broken-Down Critic' (1857); 'Letter to Dr. Henry Halford Jones (that is, Dr. J. G. Holland), editor of the Wintertown Democrat (that is, Springfield Republican), concerning his habit of giving Advice to Everybody and His Qualifications for the Task' (1864); 'The Interference Theory of Government' (1867). Most of his work was published, under the pseudonym of CARL BENSON.

Bristle-tails, wingless insects of the order *Thysanura.* These agile creatures have a long flattened body, with metallic scales, in form somewhat like those of butterflies. The antennæ are very long, setiform, many-jointed; the mouth-parts are free, with long palpi; the maxillary palpi being seven-jointed and the labial palpi · four-jointed. The mandibles are stout, sunken in the head, and armed with teeth for gnawing. The prothorax is very large, and all the rings of the body are of much the same size, so that the insect bears a general resemblance to the myriapods. The anal stylets are long and large, which, with the smaller ones inserted on the subterminal rings of the.abdomen, aid greatly in locomotion, though these insects run with great rapidity and do not leap like the *Poduridæ,* and thus remind us, as well as in their general appearance, of certain wingless cockroaches. Like cockroaches in one of its habits also is *Thermobia domestica,* which abounds in the chinks and crannies of the rouges of houses, and comes out at night, shunning the light. The «silver witch» (*Lepisma saccharina*) is not uncommon in old, damp houses, where it has the habits of the cockroach, eating cloths, tapestry, etc. In general form, *Lepisma* may be compared to the larva of *Perla,* a net-veined neuropterous insect. The body is long and narrow, covered with rather coarse scales, and ends in three many-jointed anal stylets, or bristles, which closely resemble the many-jointed antennæ, which are remarkably long and slender. They undergo no metamorphosis. Consult: Packard, 'Our Common Insects' (1873); Sharp, 'Insects' (1899).

Bristles, the stiff hairs which grow upon the back of the hog, and are used to a great extent in the manufacture of brushes. They are of several varieties of color and quality, distinguished as black, gray, yellow, white, and lilies. The last is the soft, silvery quality used for shaving-brushes. Russia and Germany are the chief sources of supply, but they are also obtained from France and Belgium, and large quantities of inferior quality have recently been received from China. The quality of bristles depends on the length, stiffness, color, and straightness—white being the most valuable. The best bristles are produced by hogs that inhabit cold countries.

Bris'tol, Augusta Cooper, American writer and lecturer: b. Croydon, N. H., 17 April 1835. She was State lecturer to the Patrons of Husbandry of New Jersey (1881-4), and is the author of 'Poems' (1868); 'The Relation of the Maternal Function to the Woman Intellect' (1876); 'The Philosophy of Art' (1880); 'The Present Phase of Woman's Advancement' (1880); 'Science as the Basis of Morality'; 'The Web of Life,' a collection of poems, (1895).

Bristol, Conn., a town in Hartford County, on the New England R.R., 17 miles west of Hartford. It has a public library, electric light and street railroad plants; national and savings banks; manufactures of clocks, brass goods, table ware, tools, bells, woolen and knit goods. It was incorporated as a borough in 1893. Pop. (1900) 6,268.

Bristol, a city of England, situated partly in Gloucestershire, partly in Somerset, but forming a county in itself. It stands on the confluence of the rivers Avon and Frome, whence the Avon pursues a course of nearly seven miles to the Severn. The Avon is a navigable river and the tide rises in it to a great height. Bristol is 118 miles due west from London, or two hours by rail. It stands partly on a number of eminences, partly on the lower ground at their foot. The manufacturing and business parts are on the lower levels, while the hills are now almost wholly covered with private houses. The districts of Clifton, Redland, and Cotham, situated within the limits of the borough and in the midst of charming scenery, are studded with mansions and villas, the attractions of these portions of the city being greatly increased by the Clifton and Durdham Downs. The bed of the river Avon is situated about 315 feet below the summit of Clifton Down, from which a handsome suspension bridge is thrown across the river, uniting the two counties. Its length from the centres of the piers is 703 feet, its height above high water mark 245 feet.

Area.—By the.Boundaries Extension Bill of 1904 the city covered an area of 17,004 acres, and contained an estimated population of 364,000 with a ratable value of £1,820,683. As compared with the period of the Municipal Corporations Reform Act of 1835 when the area was increased from 755 to 4,461 acres, it will be seen that the size of the city has increased nearly fourfold in less than three-quarters of a century.

Geology.—The geological features of Bristol are of varied interest. Within a radius of five miles a complete series of rocks from the upper part of the old red sandstone to the top of the coal measures, and from the new red sandstone to the inferior oolite, is directly accessible to study in numerous quarries, and the fine cliffs of the Avon Gorge. The geology of Bristol may be studied in the 'Memoirs of the Geological Survey for 1876' in Sanders's Geological Map of Bristol, and in the Geological Survey Maps.

Churches, Hospitals, Etc.—Bristol is rich in ancient architecture, both ecclesiastical and domestic. The Cathedral, founded in 1142, was originally an abbey church. It exhibits various styles of architecture, the chapter house and its vestibule being Norman; the Lady chapel early English; the chancel and choir, the Berkeley and Newton chapels decorated; the groining of the transcepts, the central tower, and cloisters perpendicular. The nave, its aisles, and western towers are modern additions, having been erected at intervals since 1865. There are several fine old churches, but they are all excelled by Saint Mary Redcliffe, perhaps the finest parish church in the kingdom. It is commonly said to have been founded by Simon de Burton, about 1293, but part of it is considerably older than this, and is believed to be as old as 1200. It is cruciform, with western tower and spire. The western door is the principal entrance, but there are also porches on the northern and southern sides. The south porch, the south transcept, the tower, and much of the lower part of the church belong to the decorated style, and the north porch is an excellent specimen of it, the interior in particular being very beautiful. The remainder of the church, including the Clerestory, is of the Perpendicular Period. William Canynge, five times Mayor of Bristol, whose name is so prominent in the Chatterton controversy, is said to have restored this church about 1445-7. Other churches worthy of mention are Temple Church, with its leaning tower; Saint Stephen's, All-Saints', Saint Mary-le-Port, Saint Philip's, Saint James, and Saint John. Under the tower of this last church was one of the entrances to the ancient City of Bristol, and the gateway still exists. The Independents, Baptists, and Wesleyans have some noteworthy chapels. The Roman Catholics have a pro-Cathedral in Clifton, and several chapels and convents; altogether between 200 and 300 separate buildings in the city are dedicated to the cause of christianity.

Saint Peter's Hospital adjacent to the church of Saint Peter, the seat of the poor law administration, is a very fine example of early domestic architecture. The buildings of various banks, and insurance offices in Corn street and Clare street are worthy of notice from a modern architectural point of view.

Libraries.—The most modern public building is the Bristol Central Library adjoining the Bristol Cathedral, completed in 1906, from designs by Mr. Percy Adams, F. R. I. B. A. A public library existed in Bristol early in the 15th century, and as no other record can be found of any such library prior to this in any part of the kingdom must belong to Bristol. The Library was that of the Kalendars, a brotherhood of clergy and laity who were attached to the Church of All-Hallows or All-Saints', still standing in Corn street. In 1613 the existing City Library was founded. Dr. Tobias Mathew, Archbishop of York at this time gave a number of books, to which he added subsequently a considerable portion of his library «for the free use of merchants and shopkeepers of the city.» In 1740 the building still standing in King street was erected, minus the wing. In 1874 the Public Libraries Act was adopted and two years later the building was opened under the Act as the Bristol Central Library. The year 1906 saw the opening of the New Central Libraries in Cottage Green, a palatial building erected by the munificent bequest of a wealthy citizen, Mr. Vincent Stuckey Lean. The salient features of the historic King Street Library are preserved in this building in the «Bristol Library,» an apartment exactly reproducing the original room in King street with the self-same old oak presses and wonderfully carved chimney piece of Grinling Gibbons. Here are shelved books dealing with the history of the city; the books of Archbishop Mathew, and other notable gifts of books by Bristol citizens, amongst them being the Collectanea of Proverbs, Folk lore, etc., collected by Mr. Vincent Stuckey Lean and presented to the city by

his executors. This collection is made accessible by means of an exhaustive catalogue compiled under the direction of the City Librarian of Bristol, Mr. E. R. Norris Mathews, F. R. Hist. S. F. R. S. L.; the early printed books and illuminated MSS. being separately catalogued. The public library movement in Bristol has advanced with rapid strides from small beginnings. The system is extended by means of commodious branches to all parts of the city, nine branches serving respective wards and circulating 750,672 volumes in the course of a year, whilst the various newsrooms and reading rooms are visited annually by a number of persons exceeding 2,500,000.

Art Galleries.—The Bristol Art Gallery was presented to the city by Sir William Henry Wills, now Lord Winterstoke. The building adjoins and communicates with the museum and was opened to the public in February, 1905. Internally a large and lofty top lighted central hall is surrounded by rooms on the ground floor devoted to the display of antiquities, a spacious marble staircase leads to picture galleries which form a splendid suite of communicating apartments.

Museum.—The Bristol Museum, originally a private proprietary institution, became the property of the citizens of Bristol in 1893. It is especially rich in objects illustrative of mineralogy, geology and palæontology; no less than 200 «types» and figured fossils are preserved here, described by such men as Agassiz, Riley, Stutchbury, Fitton, Huxley, Owen, and many others. The zoological collections are likewise of importance.

Electric Lighting.—The Bristol Corporation is responsible for the electric lighting of the city. The first instalment of public street lighting in 1893 consisted of 96 lamps, the total number now is 677 arc lamps. For private lighting purposes the demand has reached the total of 185,897 lamps. The use made of electricity for power purposes is increasing rapidly. The electric tramways of Bristol are controlled by a private company. The overhead trolley system is in use, and a service of motor cars has recently been instituted to connect the sections, and to open up outlying districts.

Industries, Etc.—Bristol has long been famous for its glass works, potteries, soap works, tanneries, tobacco factories, chocolate factories, and chemical works, as well as for ship building and machinery yards. Coal is found and worked extensively within the limits of the borough. Bristol carries on an export and import trade with all parts of the world. Cereals and flour are the most important imports, others being cheese, butter, bacon, cattle, sugar, timber, petroleum, hides. The total value of imports and exports in 1905 was $14,776,044. The total tonnage entered and cleared at Bristol in 1905 was 2,084,503. The present dock system comprises a dock of 19 acres at Avonmouth on the Gloucestershire bank of the Avon, and of 12 acres (deep water area) at Portishead on the Somerset bank of the river, two miles below Avonmouth; and a floating harbor of 70 acres in the heart of the city. The latest enterprise in dock construction is that of the Royal Edward Dock at Avonmouth which covers an area of 30 acres, and provides accommodation for vessels much larger than any afloat. The first sod was cut on 5 March 1902; it was opened in 1908. The depth of water on the inner sill is at mean spring tides 40 feet and at mean neap tides 30 feet. The length of the dock is 1,120 feet and the width 1,000 feet. The entrance lock is 875 feet long, and 100 feet wide. On each side are piers at which steamers land mails and passengers, who reach London over an almost straight line in 2½ hours. Bristol traders colonized Newfoundland and established commerce with the West Indies and the American colonies. The city has long been known for its ship building interests, and the Great Western, the first steamship to cross the Atlantic, was built at Bristol in 1838. A United States Consul is stationed here.

Education.—The principal institution for the higher education is the University College, opened in 1876, and having a medical school attached to it. A movement is on foot to make it the central seat of learning for the West and South of England with the power of conferring degrees. The university claims the honor of being the first to open its door to women students.

The Grammar School dates from pre-Reformation days. In 1532 it was endowed by Robert and Nicholas Thorne. The Cathedral School likewise dates back to the Reformation, it being part of the Cathedral Corporation established by Henry VIII. in 1538. The City School, or Queen Elizabeth's Hospital for boys, was founded in 1586, and owes its existence to John Carr, a wealthy Bristol citizen. The Red Maids School for girls is the foundation of Alderman Whitson by bequest in 1627. The Clifton College, opened in 1862, has for many years ranked high as an English Public School. The College buildings and grounds occupy a large area East of Clifton Downs. The Merchant Venturers' Technical College was originally a trade school. In 1875 the endowed schools commissioners appointed the Society of Merchant Venturers as trustees. The building —a monument to the liberality of that society— was almost totally destroyed by fire in October 1906, and is now in course of re-erection. Other educational establishments are: The Clifton, and the Redland High Schools for girls; Clergy Daughters' School; about 45 Council schools directed by the education committee of the Bristol Corporation, inclusive of three higher grade and science schools; a day industrial school; a school for cookery; truant school; and an institution for the deaf and dumb. The Congregationalists erected in 1906 a commodious college building at Cotham for the training of students for the ministry.

Charity.—The charitable institutions of Bristol are so numerous and of such importance that adequate mention of them here is impossible. The invested funds devoted to charitable work yield a revenue exceeding $300,000 per annum, which sum supports almshouses, asylums, homes, and schools, and provides for pensions and gifts of all descriptions. The name most familiar in a long list of benefactors is that of Edward Colston, whose name is handed down to successive generations by three great commemorative societies instituted to perpetuate his grand philanthropy. These societies are instrumental in raising funds by voluntary subscriptions amounting to upwards of $15,000 per annum. The charities, formerly regulated by the Corporation, are now by decree of the Charity Commissioners, administered by trustees. The Merchant Venturers' Society, which, as early as the 7th year of Edward IV., claimed to be an ancient guild, has endowed and supports others, whilst denominational bodies are mainly responsible for the remainder, one of the most remarkable being the Ashley Down Orphanages, founded in 1836 by the Rev. George Müller.

Government.—The city is governed by a Council consisting of 22 aldermen, and 66 councillors, the former being elected for a term of six years, and the latter for a term of three years, agreeably with the provisions of the Municipal Corporations Act. The Mayoral list of Bristol extends in unbroken sequence from the year 1216, when «the King (Henry III.) with his counsellors and tutors came to Bristol as to a safe place, at which time he permitted the town to choose a Mayor after the manner of London.» In June, 1899, or more than 600 years after the institution of the office, Queen Victoria was graciously pleased to direct that the Mayor of the City of Bristol should in future bear the style and title of Lord Mayor.

History.—The celtic name of Bristol was Caer Oder, or the City of the Chasm (namely, through which the Avon flows). The name Bristol is derived from the Anglo-Saxon bricg, a bridge, and stow, a place. Between 1239 and 1247 a new channel was dug from the Frome in order to provide better accommodation for shipping. In the reign of Edward II. Bristol rebelled against the royal authority and was held by the citizens against the sovereign for four years. In 1373 it was constituted a county of itself, by Edward III. It was made the seat of a bishopric by Henry VIII. in 1542. During the Civil War between Charles I. and the Parliament it declared in favor of the latter, but was stormed and taken by the Royalists under Prince Rupert. After the battle of Naseby it was taken by Fairfax, and its formidable castle was razed to the ground. In 1831 the Reform agitation gave origin to riots that lasted for several days. The rioters destroyed various public and private buildings, among which was the bishop's palace, and a number of them lost their lives. Bristol was united as a bishop's see to Gloucester in 1837. The first bishop of Bristol and Gloucester united was James Henry Monk, created in 1837. By the Bristol Bishopric Act Bristol was again separated from Gloucester, and Dr. Forrest Browne was enthroned, 28 Oct. 1897. Sabastian Cabot, Chatterton, and Southey were natives of Bristol. The city returns four members to Parliament.

Bibliography.—Latimer, 'Annals of Bristol,' 17th, 18th and 19th centuries, 1887-1900; Nicholls and Taylor, 'Bristol Past and Present' (1881-2, 3 vols.); Manchee, 'Report of the Charity Commissioners' (2 vols., 1831); Arrowsmith, 'Dictionary of Bristol' (new ed., 1906); Reports of the Bristol Chamber of Commerce; 'British Association Hand Book' (Bristol 1898).

E. R. NORRIS MATHEWS,
L. ACKLAND TAYLOR.

Bristol, N. H., a town in Grafton County, 32 miles north from Concord. It is at the junction of the Pemigewasset and New Found rivers; is the terminus of the Bristol branch of the Boston & M. RR., and has become a place of summer resort. It has a public library, and flannel, wooden ware, and paper manufactories. Pop. (1900) 1,600.

Bristol, Pa., a borough in Bucks County; on the Delaware River, the Pennsylvania RR., and the Pennsylvania Canal; 21 miles northeast of Philadelphia. It has a national bank, high school, electric light and street railroad plants, a noted mineral spring, and manufactories of carpets, hosiery, and foundry products. It is in a rich fruit and truck farming region, and is the centre of considerable trade. It was originally called Buckingham, and was settled in 1681. A ferry connects it with the town of Burlington on the New Jersey side of the Delaware. Pop. (1900) 7,104.

Bristol, R. I., a town and county-seat of Bristol County, on Narraganset Bay, and the New York, N. H. & H. R.R., 15 miles southeast of Providence. It has an excellent harbor, facilitating a large daily passenger and freight service for Fall River and Providence. It is the seat of the widely known Herreshoff shipbuilding works, where a number of noteworthy sailing and steam yachts and torpedo boats have been constructed; and also of the Saunders & West yacht-building yards. The town has a handsome brown stone library building containing some 15,000 volumes, eight churches, 17 public schools, large market gardening and coast trade interests, and manufactories of rubber, woolen, and cotton goods. Bristol is the site of the residence of King Philip, the great Narraganset chief. Pop. (1900) 6,901.

Bristol, Tenn. and Va. (post-office, Bristol, Tenn. or Va.), a city in Sullivan County, Tenn., and Washington County, Va., adjoin and to all intents and purposes are one place, the centre of State street being the boundary line between the two States, running due east and west. Bristol is the centre of several railroads and is contiguous to the great coal, iron, and timber regions of Southwest Virginia, East Tennessee, Western North Carolina, and Eastern Kentucky, and is the seat of King College (Presbyterian), for males; Sullins College (Southern Methodist), and Virginia Institute (Baptist), for girls; Bristol Normal College for colored people (Presbyterian), and six public schools, three on each side of the town, four white and two colored. Bristol is principally engaged in the manufacture of furniture, leather, flour, lumber, iron, staves, wood pulp, barytes, bark extract, and patent medicines, with a number of smaller industries. Bristol is situated in a beautiful valley surrounded by lofty mountains, is 1,760 feet above the sea level, and is the headquarters for two railroads, V. I. C. & C. Co., three daily newspapers, thirteen wholesale houses, and has a Government building. The present city charter provides for two city councils, one for each State, and a mayor, elected biennially. Pop. (1900) 9,850.

A. C. SMITH,
Editor 'Bristol News.'

Bristol Bay, an arm of Bering Sea, lying immediately to the north of the peninsula of Alaska. It receives the waters of two large lakes, by which communication with the interior is opened up for a considerable distance.

Bristol Brick, or Bath Brick, a kind of brick used for cleaning steel, manufactured for some years exclusively in Bridgewater and Bristol, England. A small vein of the sand required for this purpose was found near Liverpool, but was soon exhausted. One of the owners or operatives, who had been concerned in the works at Bristol, visited the United States in 1820, where by accident he discovered that the same kind of sand which was used for the Bristol bricks might be procured at South Hampton, N. H. Since that period, bricks fully equal to the imported article have been manufactured in this country.

Bristol Channel, an arm of the Irish Sea, extending between the southern shores of Wales and the western peninsula of England, and terminating in the estuary of the Severn. It is about 90 miles long, and from 15 to 50 miles wide. It is remarkable for its high tides and the rapidity with which they rise. At Chepstow spring-tides rise as high as 60 feet. On its coast are situated the towns of Cardiff, Swansea, Ilfracombe, Tenby, etc. It receives the waters of the Usk, Severn, Wye, Avon, Parrott, Taw, and Torridge rivers. At the entrance of the channel is Lundy Island.

Bristow, Benjamin Helm, American lawyer: b. Elkton, Ky., 20 June 1832; d. 22 June 1896. He was admitted to the bar in Kentucky in 1853. He served with distinction in the Civil War, and at its close was appointed United States district attorney of Kentucky. In 1874 he became secretary of the treasury, and made his name memorable by the exposure and prosecution of a notorious whiskey ring. He removed to New York in 1876, and had an extensive legal practice there.

Bristow, George Frederick, American musician: b. Brooklyn, N. Y., 1825; d. New York, 1898. From 1851 to 1862 he was the conductor of the New York Philharmonic Society, and later of the Mendelssohn Union. The greater part of his life was spent as an organist in the churches, and as a teacher in the public schools of New York. He wrote 'Rip Van Winkle,' an opera produced in New York 1855; 'Daniel,' an oratorio (1867); 'Arcadian Symphony' (1874); and 'The Great Republic,' a cantata (1880).

Bristow, Joseph L., American politician: b. Flemingsburg, Ky., 1859. He was educated for the ministry, but became editor of the Salina, Kan., Republican, and soon after entered politics. He was secretary of the Republican State Committee in 1896, and in 1898 was appointed fourth assistant postmaster-general. In 1900 he became active in exposing frauds in the postoffice department.

Bris'tow Station, now Bristoe, Va., a village in Prince William County, four miles southwest of Manassas Junction. On 27 Aug. 1862 a drawn battle took place near the Federal army under Gen. Hooker, and a Confederate one under Gen. Early, and on 14 Oct. 1863, the Federal troops under Gen. Warren repulsed with severe loss a Confederate attack under Gen. A. P. Hill.

Britain. See GREAT BRITAIN.

Britain, Ecclesiastical History of, by the Venerable Bede, or Bæda (673-735). Bede was by far the most learned Englishman of his time; one of the greatest writers known to English literature; in a very high sense "the Father of English History"; an extensive compiler for English use from the writings of the Fathers of the Church; an author of treatises representing the existing knowledge of science; and a famous English translator of Scripture. A recent authority calls him "the greatest name in the ancient literature of England"; and Green's 'History' says of him: "First among English scholars, first among English theologians, first among English historians, it is in the monk of Jarrow that English literature strikes its roots. In the 600 scholars who gathered round him for instruction, he is the father of our national education." It was in point of view and name only that Bede's great work was an ecclesiastical history. It covered all the facts drawn from Roman writers, from native chronicles and biographies, from records and public documents, and from oral and written accounts by his contemporaries. It was written in Latin; first printed at Strasburg about 1473; King Alfred translated it into Anglo-Saxon; and it has had several editions and English versions in recent times.

Britain, New. See NEW BRITAIN.

Britan'nia, the ancient name of Britain. Under the name of Britannia, Great Britain is personified as a helmeted woman seated on a globe or an insulated rock, leaning with one arm on a shield, and the other grasping a spear or trident.

Britannia Metal, an alloy that has come into very general use in modern times, many domestic utensils, such as spoons and teapots, being made of it. Such articles are commonly electro-plated, and made to resemble real silver. It consists chiefly of tin and antimony, but often contains also a small quantity of copper, zinc, and bismuth. A common proportion is 140 parts of tin, three of copper, and nine of antimony; but the best alloy is composed of 90 parts of tin and 10 of antimony. The copper is used mainly to impart color to the combination. The manufacture of the metal was introduced into England about 1770. Queen's metal is one of the varieties of Britannia metal.

Britannia Tubular Bridge, an iron tubular bridge across Menai Strait, which separates Anglesea from Wales, about one mile from the Menai suspension bridge. It has two principal spans of 460 feet each over the water, and two smaller ones of 230 feet each over the land; constructed 1846-50. See BRIDGE.

Britan'nicus, the son of the Roman emperor, Claudius, by Messalina: b. about 42 A.D.; poisoned 55 A.D. He was passed over by his father for the son of his new wife Agrippina. This son became the Emperor Nero, whose fears that he might be displaced by the natural successor of the late emperor caused him to murder Britannicus.

British America, the general name for the whole northern part of the North American continent beyond the territory of the United States. It extends from lat. 41° to 78° N., and from lon. 52° to 141° W. The frontier line between British America and the United States was determined by the conventions of 1839 and 1846. It is bounded east by the Atlantic Ocean, Davis Strait, and Baffin Bay; north by the Arctic Ocean; northwest by Alaska; west by the Pacific Ocean; and south by the United States. In its broadest sense British America includes Upper and Lower Canada, the Hudson Bay, and Northwestern territories, Nova Scotia, Newfoundland, Cape Breton, Prince Edward Island, and New Brunswick, with Vancouver Island in the Pacific, but all British possessions on or near the American continent. Each of these will be treated under its own title.

British Association for the Advancement of Science, a society first organized in 1831, mainly through the exertions of Sir David Brewster. Its first meeting was held at York, 27 Sept. 1831. Its objects are thus described in the preamble to the rules of the association: "To give a stronger impulse and a more systematic direction to scientific inquiry; to promote the intercourse of those who cultivate science in different parts of the British empire with one another and with foreign philosophers; to obtain a more general attention to the objects of science and a removal of any disadvantages of a public kind which impede its progress." The second meeting took place at Oxford in 1832, under the presidency of Dr. Buckland, and since then a meeting has been held every year up to the present. All the principal towns of the United Kingdom have on one or more occasions formed the place of rendezvous, a different locality being chosen every year. In 1884 the meeting took place at Montreal, in 1897 at Toronto, and in 1902, the 72d annual meeting was held in Belfast, Ireland. The meeting for 1903 will be held at Southport and that for 1904 at Cambridge. The sittings extend generally over about a week. The society is divided into sections, which, after the president's address, meet separately during the sittings for the reading of papers and conference. Soirees, conversaziones, lectures, and other general meetings are usually held each evening during the meeting of the association. The sections are: A. Mathematics and Physics; B. Chemistry; C. Geology; D. Zoology; E. Geography; F. Economic Science and Statistics; G. Mechanical Science; H. Anthropology; I. Physiology; K. Botany; and L. Educational Science. Local committees are formed to arrange for meetings, etc. The important national benefits conferred by the labors of various members of the association have long been duly recognized. Among these may be mentioned more especially the experiments on electricity and magnetism which have achieved such important consequences in the establishment of the electric telegraph and a more thorough knowledge of the laws which govern the weather and other meteorological phenomena. In mechanical science the labors of members of the British Association have been productive of the most important results. As the funds which the society collects at each meeting are more than sufficient to cover its expenses, it is enabled each year to make direct grants for the pursuit of particular scientific inquiries, which otherwise could not be conducted so efficiently, if at all; but besides this direct encouragement, its indirect influence on the promotion of science is undoubtedly great in many ways. Among the presidents of the association have been many distinguished men, including Dr. Whewell (1841), the Earl of Rosse (1843), Sir John Herschel (1845), Sir R. Murchison (1846), Sir

David Brewster (1850), Sir George Airy (1851), Sir Richard Owen (1858), Prince Consort (1859), Lord Armstrong (1863), Sir Charles Lyell (1864), Sir J. D. Hooker (1868), T. H. Huxley (1870), Lord Kelvin (1871), J. Tyndall (1874), Sir John Lubbock (1881), Lord Rayleigh (1884), Lord Playfair (1885), Sir William Huggins (1891), Sir A. Geikie (1892), and Sir W. Crookes (1898).

British Central Africa Protectorate, The, a portion of British Central Africa, lying around the shores of Lake Nyassa, and extending to the banks of the Zambezi. It includes all British Nyassaland, as well as the Shire Highlands, and the greater part of the basin of the river Shire. The expenses of administering the Protectorate are partly met out of revenue locally raised, and further by an annual grant from the Imperial government. The administration is in the hands of a commissioner acting under the foreign office. The port of British Central Africa is Chinde, at the mouth of the Zambesi, where a small concession has been granted by the Portuguese government. The area of the Protectorate is about 40,000 square miles; the European inhabitants number about 500, and the native inhabitants are about 850,000.

The principal occupation of the European settlers is planting; and many thriving plantations of coffee, sugar, cinchona, and tobacco have been established. The chief towns, Blantyre, Zomba, Fort Johnston (the principal port on Lake Nyassa, and naval depot), Karonga (north end of Lake Nyassa, the starting point for Tanganyika, and Kotakota (west coast of Lake Nyassa). The Protectorate is divided into 12 districts, managed by a number of collectors and assistant collectors, judicial officers, etc. There is at least one judicial officer, and in some cases two or three, in each district. Almost the entire trade of British Central Africa is with the United Kingdom. There is telegraphic connection through Umtali with the South African system.

Bibliography.— Scott Keltie, 'The Partition of Africa' (1895); Deele, 'Three Years in Savage Africa' (1897); Johnson, 'British Central Africa' (1897).

British Columbia, the most westerly province of the Dominion of Canada, lies on the Pacific Ocean, and has a series of coast-line fiords or passages unexcelled on any shore in the world. The province extends from south to north from lat. 49° N. to lat. 60° N. Its eastern boundary follows the crest of the Rocky Mountains as far as 55° N. and then follows lon. 120° W. up to lon. 60° N. British Columbia has an area of some 383,000 square miles, being thus more than three times the extent of the British Isles.

Climate. — The climate of British Columbia is as varied as the terrane. The Japan current on the Pacific Ocean acts in the same way as the Gulf Stream on the Atlantic, and makes a mild, though at certain seasons a very wet, climate. The writer has seen roses blooming in the garden at Christmas in Victoria. But the damp breezes from the Pacific Ocean having deposited their moisture on the west slope of the Coast Range pass over eastward as dry Chinook winds, so that 150 miles from the coast regions are found the Okanagan and Thompson River valleys where irrigation is required. As water is plentiful on the mountain slopes, fruit growing is carried on successfully in this irrigated region. Every variety of climate is thus obtainable in British Columbia, from the humid flats of the Pacific islands to the dry plains of the interior, and then to the icy cold and perpetual snow of the Rocky Mountain slopes. The valleys thus grow cereals in some parts, on the lower lands luxuriant grasses, and fruit of every kind in many places. The climate of Victoria, on Vancouver Island, has the balmy and delightful sweetness of the Lotus-Eaters' land.

Physical Geography and Mining. — The greater part of British Columbia is made up of mountains, including the Rockies and Selkirks on the east and the Coast and Island ranges on the west, with an average height of about 8,000 feet. To the west of the great ranges there is a wide and elevated plateau in which is to be found chief agricultural areas. From and through these great mountains run a variety of large rivers — the Columbia, the Fraser, the Skeena, the Stikine, the Liard and the Peace. Naturally the initial resources and development of such a region would be minerals, timber, fish and similar products. The total mineral products of the province up to and including 1904 has been $226,201,851. The first gold production was in the placer-mining period from 1862 onwards, when the banks of the "golden" Fraser and other creeks or rivers yielded some $50,000,000. Then commenced (about 1895) the serious lode mining which is now running into the five millions yearly. The total production of placer and lode gold up to the end of 1904 was $98,255,359; that of silver $21,716,870; of lead $12,559,139; of copper $21,381,791; of coal and coke $68,274,893; of other minerals $4,013,799. The total production of the mines in 1895 was $1,266,954; in 1900 it was $4,732,105; in 1904 it was $5,747,000.

The country is divided into districts. Kootenay has an area of 15,000,000 acres and contains a large amount of agricultural land requiring, however, irrigation. The name is synonymous with the idea of mineral wealth and its mountains are rich in gold, silver, coal, lead and copper. In the last few years a number of towns have grown up around and in connection with these mines — Revelstoke, Nelson, Kaslo, Rossland, Traill, New Denver, Sandon, Slocan City, Fernie, etc. Yale has about the same area and includes the rich valleys of the Okanagan, the Nicola, the Similkameen and the Kettle River country. It has large cattle ranges and fruit farms as well as the Boundary mineral region. Lillooet contains some 10,000,000 acres, is bisected by the Fraser River, and well adapted for cattle raising and dairying. Big game is common and there is still some placer mining. Westminster is about half the size of Lillooet and includes the Fraser River valley, which has the second largest compact area of agricultural land in the province. Lumbering is an important industry and salmon-canning its best known business. Cariboo has about 93,000,000 acres and was the centre of the great placer mining excitement of the sixties, when so much gold was taken out of its creeks. Hydraulic enterprises are in process of development and some-half a dozen companies are now operating upon a large scale. Cassiar has 105,000,000 acres and is largely unexplored. There have been gold discoveries, however, in Omenica, in the vicinity of Dease Lake and recently in the Atlin country. Comox includes the northern part of Vancouver Island and contains the chief logging camps of the province. It is rich in timbers, fish, minerals and agricultural land, though, as yet, very sparsely populated. This latter description, outside of Victoria and its vicinity, will apply to the whole of Vancouver Island. The gross output of its collieries in 1904 was 1,023,013 tons.

Lumber and Fishing. — The timber resources of British Columbia are enormous and include birch, hemlock, cedar, maple, oak, spruce and pine. The trees are large in size and the Douglas pine is, in particular, an important native product. Up to 1871 the lumber cut of the province was estimated at 250,000,000 feet and from 1871 to 1888 at 595,000,000 feet. In the latter year there were 25 saw-mills with an area under lease of 135,063 acres and a lumber cut of 31,868,884 feet; in 1898 there were 45 saw-mills with a leased area of 1,576,000 acres and a cut of 124,546,658 feet; in 1902 there were 105 mills, an area under lease of 453,251 acres, and a product of 281,945,866 feet, with a net revenue to the province of $215,275. The shipments abroad in 1902 were 57,121,435 feet, while, in 1904 the two great milling concerns — the Hastings and the Chemainus saw-mills — shipped a total of 43,033,782 feet, worth $535,545. The chief subject of complaint for some years past in connection with the lumber industry has been the United States duty of $2.00 per 1,000 feet which Canadian concerns have to face while their own markets are free to American dealers.

The fisheries of the province are also extensive and resourceful. In 1902 the salmon pack of the Fraser River was 327,095 cases; of the Skeena River, 154,875 cases, of other rivers and inlets 144,012 cases — a total of 625,982 cases. For various reasons, however, the industry has not been a growing one of late years. In 1896 the yield was 601,570 cases, in 1897 it reached the point of 1,015,477 cases; in 1901 the production was 1,236,156 cases; in 1904 it was only 465,849 cases. But the waters of British Columbia teem with many other kinds of fish, including halibut, black-cod, the oolachan, cod and bass, sturgeon, shad, oil-fish, white fish and trout. The total value of the yield of its fisheries between 1876–1903 was $75,000,000; the yield in 1903 alone was valued at $4,748,365. In this connection the sealing industry has a greater place in international discussion than it holds in local production. From 1871 to 1903 the total result of Canadian pelagic sealing was 798,109 seal skins. The number of seals killed in 1883 was 9,195; in 1893, 70,592; in 1903, 20,496.

Miscellaneous Affairs of the Province. — The imports of the province in 1903 were $11,141,-068, and in 1905 $12,565,019. The exports were, respectively, $15,604,896 and $16,677,882. The revenues of British Columbia in 1902–3 were $2,044,630 and the net expenditure $3,393,182. In 1903–4 they were, respectively, $2,638,260 and $3,030,237. Between 1892 and 1903 the total revenues were $16,121,785 and the expenditures

$24,743,377. The provincial liabilities on 30 June 1904 were $11,382,786, incurred largely in the development period of a country whose riches had not been made easily accessible by nature. The area of British Columbia is, in acres, 236,922,177, the number of houses, according to the census of 1901, was 36,938, the families, 38,445, the male population 114,160, and the females 64,497. As to origin 104,589 were English, Irish or Scotch, 25,488 were Indian and 19,482 Chinese or Japanese. There were 10,088 persons classed as "Americans" in the province and 17,164 who had been born in the United States. The Church of England had 40,689 adherents, there were 25,047 Methodists, 34,081 Presbyterians, 33,639 Roman Catholics and 10,027 Buddhists. The rural population was 87,825 and the urban 89,447. The chief railway is, of course, the Canadian Pacific Railway, with various branch lines, but the Grand Trunk Pacific will enter the province within a few years, the Great Northern of the United States has already reached Vancouver, and the Canadian Northern expects to cross the mountains before many years. Other and small lines are under construction or being actively promoted. The annual income of the province is placed at $51,-801,119 divided as follows: Fisheries, $4,546,-377; animals, $14,987,174; forest and furs, $2,835,555; farm dairy products, $1,240,226; field crops, $3,100,577; fruits and vegetables, $453,938; wool, $8,288; eggs, $426,629; manufactures, $24,202,355.

Early History and the Hudson's Bay Company. — When Sir Francis Drake sailed up and down the Pacific coast of North America in 1578–9 and took possession of what is now the State of California, in the name of Queen Elizabeth, he is said to have sailed as far north as the entrance of the Strait of Juan de Fuca. In 1592 the Spaniard whose name is borne by those straits entered them and sailed a good distance up the Strait of Georgia, between Vancouver Island and the mainland of British Columbia. Juan Perez, another Spaniard, in 1774 and Behring, the Danish navigator, in 1748, touched at points of this territory. But it remained for Captain Cook in 1778, under instructions from the British government, to really explore its coasts and give names to places since well known to history.

Other explorers followed — Hanna, Meares, Portlock, Dixon, Haro, Duncan and Barkley — until in 1792 Captain George Vancouver came with instructions to carry out a thorough survey of the intricate coast lines of the future province. After this period, for many years, Great Britain ceased to show any interest in the country. To the aggressive, enterprising traders of the Hudson's Bay Company was due the fact that the British flag was kept flying at all and that it was not eventually replaced by that of the United States, as in Oregon and Washington. In this connection the arrival of the company's steamer *Beaver* by way of Cape Horn, in 1835, marked an important era in the history of the province. Of the overland explorers the chief were Sir Alexander Mackenzie, 1793, Lewis and Clark, 1804–6, Thompson in 1807, Simon Fraser in 1808, the Astor expedition of 1810–11. From this time until the middle of the 19th century the history of what was

BRITISH COLUMBIA AND
MANITOBA AND
NORTHERN TERRITORIES

After much discussion of the subject throughout the province, the passing of resolutions by
the provincial legislature and prolonged consideration at Ottawa the terms of union agreed
upon included six members in the House of
Commons and three in the Senate; construction,
to be commenced by the Dominion within two
years, of a railway connecting eastern Canada
with the Pacific coast; a land grant from the
province to the Dominion government through
the entire extent of British Columbia for the
railway and not to exceed 20 miles on either side
of the line; payment in return of $100,000 per
annum to the province for the use of these lands;
assumption by the Dominion of the charge of the
Indians and their lands; complete responsible
government and an entirely elective assembly
to be established in the province whenever desired by the people. In November 1870 a provincial election was held and the terms of union
approved. The new legislature met on 5 Jan.
1871, the proposals were unanimously ratified
and, on 20 Jan. 1872, British Columbia entered
confederation. The constitution was then reorganized upon a popular basis and in 1871, the
elections under the new system took place.

Later Political Events. — Hon. J. W. Trutch
was appointed the first lieutenant-governor and
Hon. J. F. McCreight the first premier. Succeeding prime ministers were Amor de Cosmos,
G. A. Walkem, A. C. Elliott, J. Walkem, Robert Beaven, Wm. Smithe, A. E. B. Davie, John
Robson, Theodore Davie, J. H. Turner, C. A.
Semlin, Joseph Martin, James Dunsmuir, E. G.
Prior and Richard McBride. Following the
entry into confederation came prolonged and
at one time acute differences with the Ottawa
government over the non-completion of the
Canadian Pacific Railway. For some eight
years, while that great undertaking was in the
struggling stages of inception and preliminary
construction, the discontent in the province was
very great. There were even threats of secession and talk of annexation to the United
States. Meantime, however, construction went
on slowly and surveys continuously. The imperial authorities were complained to and missions came from Eastern Canada and others
went to London. Finally, Lord Carnarvon, as
colonial secretary, suggested terms of settlement which were agreed to by both parties and
which involved the construction and completion
of the Canadian Pacific Railway by 1 Jan. 1891.
It was completed in 1885. A visit of Lord Dufferin, as governor-general, to the coast in 1876
had, meantime, done much to smooth asperities
and promote the settlement of this vexed and
vital question.

Government. — British Columbia has a lieutenant-governor appointed by the Dominion
government. The supreme court has a chief
justice and four judges. There are six county
court judges. The province is represented in
the Dominion Parliament by three senators and
seven members of the House of Commons. The
local legislature consists of one chamber of 42
members. Victoria is the capital of the province. Its government building is among the
finest in Canada.

J. CASTELL HOPKINS,
*Author of 'Canadian Annual Review of Public
Affairs.'*

British **East** Africa, a name defining a vast district lying between German East Africa and the Italian protectorate of Somaliland. Its area is vaguely estimated to be over 1,000,000 square miles. The territory contains the valley of the Upper Nile and the mountainous region of equatorial Africa. The inhabitants comprise Bantu tribes, among which are the Waganda and Wangoro, Musai, and Galla tribes, Swahili on the coast, and negroes on the Nile. Ivory, gum, India rubber, sesame seeds, cocoanuts, copra, coir maize, rice, and hides are exported. The government is principally vested in the British East African Protectorate, but in 1894, Uganda (q.v.), north of Victoria Nyanza, was made a separate British protectorate and received a separate administration. The government is rapidly opening up the country, constructing roads and telegraphs, and taking steps to suppress slavery and the slave trade. The coast is unhealthy for Europeans, but most of the interior plateaus are salubrious. The British East African Protectorate extends for about 400 miles along the north coast from Umba at the mouth of the Umba River and has a total area of about 300,000 square miles. See EAST AFRICA, BRITISH; EAST AFRICA PROTECTORATE.

British Economic Association, a society established in London in 1890 with the design of advancing economic investigations through the medium of a quarterly styled 'The Economic Journal.' This periodical is the most valuable one of its class and is open to the expression of very diverse views upon economic questions. Viscount Goschen has been the president of the association from its founding. It gives an annual dinner in London, but holds no regular scientific meetings.

British Empire, the aggregation of states, dependencies, and controls which is subject in the last resort to the British Parliament. Officially it was not entitled to the name till 1876, when Queen Victoria assumed the title Empress of India; but the term was in current use long before. It is the largest body of land and of people under any one jurisdiction on the globe, comprising about one fourth of the earth's surface, and of its inhabitants: over 11,500,000 square miles, exclusive of Egypt and Egyptian Sudan, or 12,500,000 with them, and 400,000,000 population. Extensive portions of it lie in each of the five grand divisions of the globe: about 121,000 square miles in Europe, 3,700,000 in America, 1,865,000 in Asia, 2,700,000 in Africa, 3,175,000 in Australasia. Its organization is entirely different from that of any other "empire" in history. The control of the central government over the outlying sections varies from its autocracy to their virtual independence; the most valuable parts are the least controlled, and have become the most valuable largely by that freedom. None of them pay any taxes into the imperial treasury, and the mother country derives her profit from them solely through trade relations, and as furnishing employment for the overflow of British youth. Indeed, movements for independence are forestalled by the concession of whatever privileges are claimed by the self-governing dependencies, even to the imposition of discriminating duties on British goods; and it is a postulate of British politics that no

forcible resistance shall be offered if any of these wishes to withdraw altogether.

The nucleus of the empire is the United Kingdom of Great Britain and Ireland, ruled nominally by a hereditary sovereign; actually by a parliament with one chamber popularly elected and the other composed of hereditary peers. Even the latter in practice always yields to the popular house when that body is firmly set on a given policy.

The subordinate portions fall under six classes: (1) Wholly self-governing communities: their sole ties to the mother country being an ornamental governor whose real functions are social and argumentative, the right of appeal from their supreme courts to the English Privy Council (even that curtailed in Australia), and the home government's nominal right of vetoing their laws, which, in fact, is never exercised. Canada, Australia, and Cape Colony are the chief exemplars. (2) Those where the home government appoints part of the legislative body as well as the governor. This is entirely composed of the Channel Islands, Malta, Cyprus, Ceylon, Mauritius, Jamaica, the Leeward Islands, British Guiana, and Rhodesia. (3) "Crown colonies," where the ruling body, an executive and council (sometimes two councils, executive and legislative), are wholly appointed by the home government, without local representation, and are directly responsible to the colonial secretary, except with India, the greatest of this type, which is under a special secretary of state and home council. Of the others, the chief are the new conquests of the Boer states (this form of government being avowedly provisional for them); the British settlements on the west coast of Africa — Sierra Leone, Nigeria, the Gold Coast, Gambia, and Lagos; the Straits Settlements, and Hong Kong; in America, British Honduras, Trinidad, the Windward and Falkland islands; in Australasia, Fiji. The titles of these imperial rulers are various: governor, commissioner, high commissioner, resident, etc. (4) Those administered by a single official under the colonial secretary, without a council. Such are Gibraltar and Aden, Ascension (under the control of the admiralty); in Africa, Basutoland, Bechuanaland, and the protectorates of British Central and Eastern Africa, and British Somaliland — administered respectively by the consul-general at Zanzibar, a resident commissioner, and a consul-general at Berbera. (5) Government by a trading corporation, licensed and supervised by the home government, formerly the chief colonial system in Europe, and the only intelligible object of colonization. Great Britain has now but one dependency of this type: British North Borneo, where the company's governor must be confirmed by the colonial secretary. (6) Mere control of a native government by a resident commissioner, or power to interfere if judged advisable, or sometimes scarcely more than the marking out of a "sphere of influence" within which other nations are debarred from meddling. The chief types of this class are 50 or 60 native states of India, Zanzibar, Uganda, and the native states of the Malay peninsula. A seventh type is so peculiar that its *locus* is not usually classed as part of the British empire at all, although in fact one of the most firmly held and decisively administered:

1. City of Victoria from Parliament Buildings   2. House of Parliament

Egypt, where the province is nominally part of Turkey, the official position of Lord Cromer is consul-general and minister plenipotentiary, and the title of Great Britain to possession is that of surviving partner of an international financial control.

In detail, the components of the empire, the dates and method of acquirement, and the title by which they are held, are as follows:

Europe.— 1. The United Kingdom. England in its modern sense, though much restricted toward the north, first owned a common overlord in 827; broken up by the Danes, it became a wholly Danish kingdom in 1013, again an English one in 1042, part of an Anglo-French system in 1066, and was practically restored to itself in 1214, with its northern limits as now. Wales was finally subjugated by Edward I., after a long war with Llewellyn ap Jorwerth, in 1284. Scotland, a kingdom owning overlordship to England, received a king by English arbitration in 1291, revolted and was conquered, revolted again and won its independence in 1314; with the accession of its king, James I., to the English throne in 1603 the two crowns were united, and in 1707 the Scotch parliament was abolished and Scotland incorporated with England. The Isle of Man, a Scandinavian lordship, was ceded to Scotland in 1266 and to England in 1290. The Orkneys and Shetlands were pledged by Denmark to James III. of Scotland in 1468, as security for his wife's dowry, and never redeemed. Ireland was invaded by Strongbow in 1169, nominally annexed to England by right of conquest in 1172; but only a small cantle of it, "the Pale," was effectively occupied till the time of Elizabeth, and the island as a whole was first effectively subjugated by Cromwell. It was governed by its own parliament till 1800, when the Act of Union incorporated it with Great Britain. 2. The Channel Islands (Guernsey, Jersey, etc.), in the bay of Avranches off the French coast, are the sole remnants of the French possessions of the Angevin house. 3. The fortress rock of Gibraltar, and the small plain at its foot on which the town is built, were taken from Spain in 1704, during the war of the Spanish succession. 4. Malta, with Gozo, etc., islands south of Sicily, were taken from France in 1800, during the Napoleonic wars. Malta is the chief British naval station in the central Mediterranean.

Asia.— 1. India, with Burma. For the component parts of this mighty possession, three fifths the size of the United States without Alaska, and for its government, see its name. Its nuclei were three factories of the East India Company: Fort St. George, now Madras, built 1639; Bombay, received from Portugal in 1662 as part of the dowry of Catharine of Braganza, queen of Charles II.; and Fort William, now Calcutta, founded by Job Charnock in 1686. The attempt of the French to build a colonial dominion on the ruins of the Mogul empire, in the 18th century, forced the company's local officers to act in self-defense; with the result that northeastern India fell into their hands, the decisive event being the battle of Plassey (1757). Wars, cessions, annexations, protectorates, residencies, etc., have gradually brought all the rest of the peninsula under English control. The company ceded its rights to the English government in 1858. 2. Ceylon, the tip of the Indian peninsula, is independently governed. It was taken by England from the Dutch in 1796, during the

French wars, but not ceded to her till the Peace of Amiens in 1802. 3. Cyprus, an island south of Asia Minor: was ceded by Turkey in 1878, as a result of the Russo-Turkish war, in return for a treaty by which Great Britain agreed to defend Turkey against further territorial demands from Russia. 4. Aden, on the south coast of Arabia: was taken by the British in 1839 as a coaling station, in compensation for the maltreatment of shipwrecked British sailors by the natives. The island of Socotra to the east, off the mainland of Africa, was annexed in 1888; and the two — with Perim Island at the mouth of the Gulf of Aden, and the Kuria-Murias on the east coast of Arabia — form one administration, a dependency of the Bombay presidency. 5. The Straits Settlements: This group, comprising the end of the Malacca peninsula, was transferred in 1867 from the control of the Indian government to that of the colonial secretary. It consists of (1) Penang, formerly called Pulo Penang and later Prince of Wales Island, originally received by a British adventurer as dowry with a native chief's daughter, then turned over to the East India Company in 1786; (2) Malacca, occupied by the British in 1795, but not formally ceded to them by the sultan of Johore till 1824, along with (3) the island of Singapore, the capital of the whole. Some of the native Malaccan states are also under British protection. 6. Hong Kong, China, was occupied by the British in 1841, as a result of the opium war, and ceded to them in 1843. 7. Labuan, an island off Borneo, of which Great Britain obtained the cession in 1846, with great hopes of its coal mines and harbor not borne out by experience; it has also been a convict settlement. 8. British North Borneo, ceded to a commercial company by native sultans in 1877, but taken under British protectorate in 1888. 9. Brunei and Sarawak, southwest of the above, are governed by native rulers, but under British protection.

Africa.— 1. Sierra Leone, on the west coast: was started as a settlement of freed negro slaves in 1787; transferred to the Crown in 1807. 2. The Gold Coast: settlement of 1672 by the Royal African Company, made a dependency of Sierra Leone on the dissolution of that company in 1822, formally ceded by the Dutch in exchange for trade privileges in 1872, and made a Crown colony in 1874. 3. Gambia: settlement united with Sierra Leone in 1822, like the Gold Coast; made a separate colony 1843, reunited to Sierra Leone 1868, then included in the British West African Settlements colony till 1888, when it was again made a separate colony. 4. Lagos, West Africa: the town was an old slave mart destroyed by the British in 1851; the colony was ceded to them by the native rulers in 1861. 5. Nigeria: the Niger coast protectorate was constituted in 1884, old trading rights having been previously exercised for generations; the present protectorate of Nigeria was set up 1 Jan. 1901. 6. Cape Colony: taken possession of as a derelict in 1796, the settlement having thrown off Dutch rule; administered for seven years, then returned to the Dutch; again captured in 1806, Holland having become part of Napoleon's empire; retained till the general peace of 1815, then bought from Holland for $30,000,000. 7. Natal and Zululand: taken from the Dutch settlers and annexed 1843. 8. Basutoland: annexed to Cape Colony 1871, as the result of an appeal by the Basutos from the claims of the Orange Free State; separated as a special protectorate 1884. 9, 10. The Transvaal and the Orange River Colony: conquered 1900. 11. Zanzibar and Pemba. Pemba was ceded to the British East African Company in 1888 by the sultan of Zanzibar. The latter island was given over to a German protectorate in 1886 by an Anglo-German convention; in 1890 transferred to England in exchange for the island of Heligoland off the German coast, possessed by England and a thorn in the German flesh. 12. East Africa protectorate: recognized by Germany and France in 1890, with that of Zanzibar, for considerations as above and trading rights, and the recognition of the French protectorate over Madagascar. 13. Central Africa protectorate: organized 1891 from the territories of the British South Africa Company. 14. Bechuanaland, constituted a protectorate over native South African tribes in 1895. 15. Rhodesia: the territories of the Royal South Africa Company, chartered in 1889, were brought under the colonial office in 1898, with Matabeleland and Mashonaland. 16. British Somaliland, completing the circle around Africa up to Socotra and Aden; protectorate under the East India Company 1884, constituted a Crown colony 1898.

North America.— 1. The Dominion of Canada is the chief. Its nucleus was the territory which fell under British sway by the French and Indian War 1755–60, definitely ceded in 1763. This was divided in 1791 into Upper Canada and Lower Canada, the latter as a real settlement founded by loyalist refugees from the United States, who also founded New Brunswick. England also held north of the United States: (1) Nova Scotia, conquered from the French in 1713, after a previous occupancy 1654–67; (2) Cape Breton, conquered 1748, and restored to France, conquered again in 1758 and ceded by France in 1763, when it was annexed to Nova Scotia; again separated 1784, again united 1820; (3) Prince Edward's Island, till 1799 called Isle St. Jean or St. John Island, then changed in honor of the Duke of Kent; captured from the French 1745, restored, again taken and held in 1758, ceded 1763 and annexed to Nova Scotia, in 1773 again separated. (4) Newfoundland, an old fishing station, ceded by France in 1713. In 1841 Upper and Lower Canada were united. In 1867 the united province was joined with Nova Scotia and New Brunswick into the Dominion of Canada. In 1871 this was joined by British Columbia, formed 1866 out of the older British Columbia and Vancouver Island, the former organized 1858 from the old Hudson Bay territory of New Caledonia; the latter a Hudson Bay territory made a Crown colony in 1849. In 1873 Prince Edward's Island also came into the dominion. Meantime, in 1869, it had acquired the Northwest Territories, and in 1870 set off Manitoba and at once admitted it into the dominion; Keewatin district was created in 1876; Assiniboia, Alberta, Saskatchewan, and Athabasca in 1882. 2. Newfoundland, which still refuses to join the dominion: its history is outlined above. Labrador forms a part of Newfoundland for administrative purposes. 3. The Bermuda Islands: settled 1609. 4. The Bahama Islands: ceded by Spain 1783, after alternate conquest and reconquest. 5, 6. The Windward Islands and the Leeward Islands: taken by the English in the general agreement with France for partitioning

the West Indies in 1660. 7. Jamaica, with Turk's Island and Caicos Island: taken from the Spaniards in 1655. 8. Barbados: colonized 1625, made a Crown colony in 1663. 9. Trinidad, with Tobago: captured in 1797 during the French wars. 10. British Honduras: settled early in the 18th century, but not ceded to Great Britain by treaty from Spain till 1783, formerly known as Balize or Belize. 11. British Guiana: partitioned off from the other Guianas in 1803, and formerly ceded by treaty in 1814.

South America.— The Falkland Islands, east of the southern tip of the continent: fought for by British, French, and Spanish for many years; then nominally controlled by Argentina till 1833, when the British took possession of them for a finality, and established a colony in 1851; it includes also South Georgia to the eastward.

The South Atlantic.— In the No-Man's Land between South America and Africa, and unrelated to either, the British hold three islands. 1. St. Helena: definitively secured from the Dutch by the East India Company in 1673, transferred to the home government in 1834. 2. Ascension: 700 miles northwest of St. Helena, settled in 1815 after Napoleon's deportation. 3. Tristan d'Acunha: a triad of little islands about half-way from the Cape of Good Hope to South America, garrisoned by the British in 1816 while Napoleon was at St. Helena.

Australasia.— 1. The Confederation of Australia, formed 1901. The first colony in Australia was the convict settlement of New South Wales, made a self-governing colony in 1841. Western Australia was founded in 1829, South Australia in 1836. Victoria, settled in 1835 as Port Philip, was set off from New South Wales in 1851. Queensland was settled from Moreton Bay in 1825. Tasmania was a convict settlement of the island of Van Diemen's Land from 1803 on, but in 1852 the convict deportation there was stopped, and the colony made self-governing as Tasmania. 2. New Zealand was colonized in 1845. 3. The Fiji Islands came under British sway in 1874 by voluntary cession from Thakombau, the leader of the native chiefs. 4. British New Guinea was delimited and formally annexed in 1884. 5. There are a considerable number of islands in the western Pacific which have come into British hands at various periods, by occupation. The largest are: the Tongas, part of the New Hebrides and the Solomons, Ellice, Gilbert, Union, Cook, and Monahiki.

British Guiana, gē-ǎn'a̤. See GUIANA.

British Gum. See DEXTRIN.

British Honduras. See HONDURAS.

British India. See INDIA.

British Legion, The, a corps raised in Great Britain in 1835, numbering 10,000 men, under the command of Gen. De Lacy Evans, to assist Queen Isabella of Spain in the war with Don Carlos. They rendered much assistance to the queen, defeating her Carlist rivals in several battles, notably at Ayetta, during the two years of their campaign. Gen. Evans was himself defeated at Hernani in 1837, but subsequently captured that place and also several others. He acted in conjunction with a naval force under Lord John Hay.

British Museum, a national depository of science, literature, and art, which owes its origin to the will of Sir Hans Sloane, an eminent physician and naturalist, who, dying in 1753, bequeathed to the nation his collection of medals and coins, antiquities, seals, cameos, drawings, and pictures, and his library, consisting of 50,000 volumes and manuscripts, on the condition of the payment of $100,000 to his heirs. This offer was agreed to by Parliament, which authorized a lottery of $500,000 to implement the bargain, as well as to purchase other collections. Montague House, which was bought for the purpose, was appropriated for the museum, which was first opened on 15 Jan. 1759. The original edifice having become inadequate, a new building was resolved on in 1823, the architect being Sir R. Smirke, whose building was not completed till 1847. It forms a hollow square, facing the cardinal points. The south, or Russell Street front, is the principal one, having an imposing columnar façade of the Ionic order. This, as well as the other three, looks into the central square court, which measures about 320 feet by 240. There are two stories of galleries and rooms round the greater part of the building. Smirke's designs were no sooner completed than it was found that additional accommodation was needed in various departments, and several new rooms were provided; but the library accommodation being wholly inadequate for the accommodation of the readers, as well as for the reception of new books, a grant was obtained from Parliament for a new library building in 1854, and it was completed and opened in 1857, at a cost of $750,000. It was erected in the interior quadrangle, and contains a circular reading-room 140 feet in diameter, with a dome 106 feet high. The whole arrangements have been completed with the utmost economy in regard to space, and besides ample accommodation for books, the reading-room now contains accommodation for 300 readers comfortably seated at separate desks, which are provided with all necessary conveniences. More recently, the accommodation having become again inadequate, it was resolved to separate the objects belonging to the natural history department from the rest, and to lodge them in a building by themselves. Accordingly a large natural history museum has been erected at South Kensington, and the specimens pertaining to natural history (including geology and mineralogy) have been transferred thither, but they still form part of the British Museum. Externally this building is somewhat heavy in character, but the interior has been treated in a most artistic manner. The British Museum is under the management of 48 trustees, among the chief being the Archbishop of Canterbury, the lord-chancellor, and the speaker of the House of Commons. In all the staff of the institution numbers over 320 persons. The museum is open daily, free of charge. Admission to the reading-room as a regular reader is by ticket, procurable on application to the chief librarian, there being certain simple conditions attached. In 1900 there were 198,566 persons using the reading-room, and 689,249 visitors in addition. The institution contains something like 2,000,000 volumes in the department of printed books. A copy of every book, pamphlet, newspaper, piece of music, etc., published anywhere in British territory, must be conveyed free of charge to the British Museum. There are various catalogues and hand-books prepared by the officers of the museum, and containing classified descriptions of the con-

tents of the different departments. Of these there are eight, namely, the department of (1) printed books, maps, charts, plans, etc.; (2) of manuscripts; (3) of natural history; (4) of Oriental antiquities; (5) of Greek and Roman antiquities; (6) of coins and medals; (7) of British and mediæval antiquities and ethnography; (8) of prints and drawings.

British North America, the Dominion of Canada and the island of Newfoundland, with the portion of Labrador belonging to the latter. The Bermudas may also be included.

British Somaliland, a territory on the west coast of Africa under the protection of Great Britain, lying along the Gulf of Aden from about lon. 43° to 49° E., and extending from about lat. 11° to 8° N. On the east and southeast it is bounded by Italian Somaliland, on the south and west by Abyssinia, and on the northwest by French Somaliland. It has an area estimated at nearly 70,000 square miles, lacking in fertility largely on account of a lack of natural irrigation. The surface is in great part mountainous. The climate is more healthful in the interior than along the coast where there is more dampness. Among the chief products are sheep, cattle, skins, ostrich feathers, myrrh, and incense. The principal ports are Bulhor, Zeyla, and Berbera. The latter, which is the capital, has a good harbor and is in winter the scene of considerable commercial activity. The combined imports and exports are valued at about $2,500,000. The protectorate, created in 1884, is administered by a consul-general under control of the Crown. In 1894 the boundary between this protectorate and Italian Somaliland was defined. In the spring of 1903 an agitation in this region in favor of the Mad Mullah (q.v.), led to a considerable loss among the British troops and their withdrawal in April. The inhabitants are related to the Abyssinians and Gallas, and on account of their nomadic habits there are no accurate statistics of population. See Peel, 'Somaliland' (1899); Swayne, 'Seventeen Trips Through Somaliland' (1900); Hendebert, 'Au pays des Somalis et des Comoriens' (1901).

British South Africa Company, a corporation established in 1889, with a royal charter, by Cecil Rhodes and others, for the purpose of controlling, settling, administering and opening up by railways and telegraphs, etc., certain districts in Central South Africa. Mashonaland was first settled, and, in 1893, Matabeleland was annexed and settled after the defeat of King Lobengula. In 1895, North Zambesia, in British Central Africa, was added, as well as a strip of territory in the Bechuanaland Protectorate. This territory has been called Rhodesia, or British Zambesia; area, about 500,000 square miles. In consequence of the filibustering raid of Dr. Jameson, an officer of the company, near the close of 1895, Rhodes resigned his connection with the company in 1896, and a joint administrator of the territory was appointed by the British crown. See RHODESIA.

British West Indies. See WEST INDIES.

Britomar'tis, a nymph of Cretan mythology, fabled to have been raised by Artemis into a deity, on the occasion of drowning herself to escape from the pursuit of Minos. She was presented as patroness of hunters and fishermen.

The name was chosen by Spenser to represent in the 'Faerie Queene' the personification of chastity, and thus contained an allusion to the Virgin Queen, Elizabeth.

Brit'tany, or Bretagne, formerly one of the largest provinces of France, being a peninsula washed by the Atlantic on all sides except the east, where it joined Poitou, Anjou, Maine, and Normandy. It now forms five departments, Finistère, Côtes-du-Nord, Morbihan, Ille-et-Vilaine, Loire-Inférieure, containing, in 1896, 3,175,961 inhabitants on 13,130 square miles. It is supposed to have received its name from those Britons who were expelled from England and took refuge here at various periods between the 5th and 7th century. Before that time it bore the name of Armorica. It formed one of the duchies of France, and was held by sovereigns nearly independent and often at war with the French monarchs till it was united to the crown by the marriage of Louis XII. with Anne of Brittany, the widow of Charles VIII., in 1499. It was given by Louis XII. to Claude, Countess of Angoulême, who married Francis I., and was reunited to the crown in 1532. The province was divided into Upper and Lower Brittany. Agriculture in this territory is very backward, and it is estimated that about one half of the surface lies waste. Corn and wine are produced in small quantities. Flax and hemp, apples, and pears are abundant and of good quality. Cider is the principal drink. Salt is made on the coast, and coal, lead, and iron are found in various parts. There are manufactures of hemp, flax, and iron. The fisheries also employ many of the inhabitants. The people of Brittany still retain their ancient language, which is closely allied to Welsh, and is exclusively used by the peasantry in the western part of the province. Many Celtic remains are found throughout the country.

Brittle Star, also called **Snake Star,** and **Sand Star,** a member of the order of *Ophiurida,* class *Asteroidea,* of the phylum *Echinodermata* (q.v.). It is characterized by the body forming a flattened disk, with cylindrical arms, the stomach not extending into the arms, and there is no intestine or anal opening. The ambulacral furrow is covered by the ventral shields of the tegument, so that the ambulacral feet project from the sides of the arm. It moves faster than the true star-fish, the arms being more slender and flexible. An ophiuran which has accidentally lost an arm can reproduce it by budding. In species of *Ophiothela* and *Ophiactis* the body divides in two spontaneously, having three arms on one side and two on the other, while the disk looks as if it had been cut in two by a knife, and three new arms had then grown out from the cut side.

The ophiurans in most cases undergo a decided metamorphosis like that of the star-fish. The larva, called a "pluteus," is free-swimming, though in some species the young, in a modified larval condition, reside in a pouch situated above the mouth of the parent, finally escaping and swimming freely about.

Our most common brittle star is *Ophiopholis aculeata,* which may be found at low-water mark, and especially among the roots of *Laminaria* thrown upon the beach. It is variable in color, but beautifully spotted with pale and brown, its general hue being a brick-red. Ophiurans are widely distributed, and live at depths between low-water mark and 2,000 fathoms. Fossil ophiurans do not occur in formations older than the Upper Silurian, where they are represented by the genera *Protaster, Palæodiscus, Acroura,* and *Eucladia;* generic forms closely like those now living appear in the mushcelkalk beds of Europe (Middle Trias).

Brit'ton, John, English archæologist: b. 7 July 1771; d. London, 1 Jan. 1857. In 1787 he came to London, and was employed for six years as cellarman in the Jerusalem Tavern, Clerkenwell, and afterward served in the same capacity in the London Tavern. He next entered the employment of a hop merchant in Southwark, and then an attorney's office in Gray's Inn. During all this period he had sedulously cultivated his taste for reading during his leisure hours, and took part in the proceedings of several debating societies. In 1799 he accepted an engagement from a Mr. Chapman to write, sing, and recite for him at a theatre in Panton Street, Haymarket, at a salary of three guineas per week. From this period his literary career may be said to have commenced, developing itself at first in the form of pamphlets, song-books, and similar minor subjects. He soon advanced, however, to a higher grade, and in 1801 appeared the first two volumes of the 'Beauties of Wiltshire,' by J. Britton and E. W. Brayley. These collaborateurs, with others, subsequently completed a similar work for all the other counties of England (1801–16, 18 vols.; 1825, 26 vols.). In 1805–14 Britton published his 'Architectural Antiquities of Great Britain' in four volumes, supplemented in 1818–26 by another entitled 'Chronological History and Graphic Illustrations of Christian Architecture in England.' These were followed by his 'Cathedral Antiquities,' in 14 volumes (1814–35); and the 'Dictionary of the Architecture and Archæology of the Middle Ages' (1832–8).

Britton, Nathaniel Lord, American scientist: b. New Dorp, Staten Island, N. Y., 15 Jan. 1859. He was professor of botany in Columbia School of Mines in 1888–96, and later director of the New York Botanical Garden. He has written 'Geology of Staten Island' (1880); 'Catalogue of the Flora of New Jersey' (1882); and collaborated in preparing 'An Illustrated Flora of the Northern United States, Canada.'

Brit'zka, a Russian traveling carriage, the head of which is always a movable calash, having a place in front for the driver, and a seat behind for servants. The body is so arranged that the traveler can sleep therein at night.

Brives-la-Gaillarde, brēv-lạ-yärd (ancient BRIVA CURRETIA), a town in France, department of Corrèze, situated amidst vineyards and orchards, on left bank of the Corrèze, surrounded by a fine avenue of elms. The houses are substantially built of stone, but the streets are narrow, and the public squares indifferent. It contains a church of St. Martin dating from the 12th century, some ancient houses in the Gothic style, and a library. Its industries include the manufacture of leather, cotton goods, pottery, wax candles, etc., and it also carries on an active trade in truffles, wool, wine, and nuts. Pop. (1896) 18,111.

Brix'ham, an English town in Devonshire, situated on the English Channel, 23 miles south of Exeter. It covers the sides of two hills, and is divided into Upper and Lower Brixham. The parish church is a large ancient structure, in the Perpendicular style. The trade of Brixham is chiefly in fish, and is of considerable extent, London, Bath, and Bristol receiving supplies from this place. The port possesses also a number of vessels engaged in the coasting and foreign trade; those in the latter plying chiefly to the Mediterranean. Ship-building and the manufacture of sails, ropes, paint, etc., are among the other industries. Brixham is celebrated in history as the place where the Prince of Orange, afterward William III., landed, 4 Nov. 1688. In 1858 a cave was discovered on Windmill Hill, containing the bones of extinct mammals, some flint implements, etc. Pop. (1901) 8,090.

Bri'za, a genus of grasses, commonly called quaking-grass, maiden's-hair, or lady's-tresses. There are about 30 species, chiefly found in South America. *B. media* is a native of the United States, and is found occasionally in pastures in the eastern States.

Broach, or Baroach, India, a seaport town in Guzerat, Bombay, situated on the Nerbudda, about 30 miles from its mouth. The river here is crossed by a railway bridge, and for about a mile in front of the town is lined with a massive stone wall. Broach is surrounded with ruinous walls, and has narrow streets, with houses mostly of two stories and built of brick. There are no buildings of interest. It is an ancient place, and one of the oldest seaports of western India, and was formerly famous for its cotton manufactures. The town was taken by storm by the British in 1772, and, with the district, ceded to them by treaty with Scindiah in 1803. Formerly it had a great export of cotton, and it still carries on a trade in cotton, grain, and seeds with Bombay and Surat. Pop. (1901) 42,300 (including many Parsees). The district of Broach lies on the east side of the Gulf of Cambay. Broach cotton holds the highest place in the Bombay market. Area, 1,453 square miles; pop. about 350,000.

Broad Arrow, a government mark placed on British stores, guns, etc., to distinguish them as public or Crown property. It was the cogni-

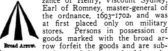

Broad Arrow.

zance of Henry, Viscount Sydney, Earl of Romney, master-general of the ordnance, 1693-1702, and was at first placed only on military stores. Persons in possession of goods marked with the broad arrow forfeit the goods and are subject to a penalty, and it is made felony by statute to obliterate or deface it. The mark is also used in the Ordnance Survey maps to denote points from which measurements have been made.

Broad Church, a name given originally to a party in the Church of England, regarded as being midway between the Low Church or Evangelical section and the High Church or Ritualistic; now widely applied to the more tolerant and liberal section of any denomination.

Broad-headed Snake. See DEATH-ADDER.

Broad Mountain, an elevation in the anthracite coal region of Pennsylvania; a plateau of conglomerate rock, about three miles wide and 2,000 feet above the sea, undulating just enough to contain three shallow coal-basins intermediate between the Pottsville and Mine Hill on the south, and the Mahoning and Shamokin coal-fields on the north.

Broad Piece, a term applied to some English gold pieces broader than a guinea, particularly Caroluses and Jacobuses.

Broad River, a stream of North and South Carolina, rising at the foot of the Blue Ridge, in the western part of the former State, and entering York district in South Carolina. It then takes a southerly course through a rich and highly productive tract of country covered with fields of maize and cotton, and finally unites with the Saluda to form the Congaree River. The city of Columbia is at their junction. The river is about 225 miles in length, and is navigable for shallow-draft boats for upward of 140 miles.

Broad Seal War, 1838-9, a disputed-election case in New Jersey and in Congress; turning in New Jersey on the power of a county official, in collusion with the State executive, to nullify the result of a State vote; in Congress on the right of the clerk to base official action on information not before Congress. New Jersey then elected her six congressmen on general ticket, and in 1838 that of the Democrats carried the State by an average of about 100; but the Whig county clerk of Middlesex County threw out the vote of South Amboy, with 252 Democratic majority, for lack of the election-clerk's signature, and for other irregularities, giving the Whigs five of the six seats. The Democrats claimed that such technicalities had been repeatedly waived, and were countervailed by like ones in Whig towns; and, even so, that by law the governor and council, as a canvassing board, must send at once for any missing return and pass on its validity. Those officials were Whigs, however, and they decided that they could not go behind the clerk's certificate, and issued credentials to the Whig candidates under the "broad seal" of the State. This would have made only the usual party broil, but that the national House stood 119 Democrats to 118 Whigs without the New Jersey members, so that the decision carried with it control of the organization of Congress. The Democratic clerk of the House. H. A. Garland, of Virginia, on its meeting 2 Dec. 1839, omitted the New Jersey members in his roll-call, on the ostensible ground that their seats were to be contested and he must leave the decision to Congress; really because excluding them gave his party the speaker and the committees, and incidentally secured himself the clerkship however the contest was decided. This was utterly illegal, as there could be no contest till a congress was organized to bring a contest before; but he doubtless felt it as legitimate as the trick by which the Whig members were sent there, and that party could hardly complain of unfairness. For three days there was helpless rage and anarchy in the House, the clerk refusing to put the question upon any of the motions to bring order out of the chaos. Finally on the 5th the leaders of both parties called in John Quincy Adams (q.v.), the one member who had no party or affiliations of any sort, and who was respected as at once immutably just, unshrinkingly courageous, and of the highest parliamentary knowledge. He called upon the meeting to organize itself, offered a resolution ordering the clerk to call the names of the New Jersey members with credentials, and on the clerk's refusal announced that he would put the question himself. He was at once elected speaker *pro tem.*, and for six days more the fight went on to choose a permanent speaker, with both New Jersey delegations voting. On the 11th a motion was carried that neither delegation had a right to vote till the contest was decided; on the 16th a compromise was made by which R. M. T. Hunter, of Virginia, a Whig who favored the Democratic sub-treasury scheme, was chosen speaker. On 10 March 1840 the Democratic contestants were seated; on 16 July the majority report of the committee on the case, declaring them duly elected, was accepted by a vote in which all but 22 Whigs refused to take part, on the ground that the report and testimony were too long to examine. The political prize at stake had caused the parties to exchange principles, as they did earlier on the Louisiana Purchase and later on the Electoral Commission; the Democrats, though strict-constructionists, disregarded State certificates and insisted on going behind the returns; the Whigs, though upholding equity against forms, clung to the sanctity of a State certificate however obtained.

Broad-top Mountain, a trapezoidal plateau of semi-bituminous coal measures, in Huntingdon and Bedford counties, Pennsylvania. The highest point is about 2,600 feet above the sea. It is surrounded by a red shale valley, and an outside ring of Devonian rocks, called Terrace, Harmer, and Sidelong mountains. Through gaps in this ring flows the Raystown branch of the Juniata. The mountain contains two principal coal basins. It contains in its deepest troughs about 900 feet of coal measures, and takes in the Pittsburg coal bed, with one of the limestones above it. Coal was mined here for blacksmithing nearly 100 years ago. The coal is a semi-bituminous steam coal, containing from 12 to 18 per cent of volatile matter, and of the same qualities as Cumberland coal.

Broad'bent, Sir William Henry, English physician: b. Yorkshire, 23 Jan. 1835; d. London, 10 July 1907. He was educated at the Royal School of Medicine in Manchester and at Paris. He was at first appointed physician to the Western General Dispensary; then physician to the London Fever Hospital and the Saint Mary's Hospital successively. He was physician extraordinary to Queen Victoria, 1898–1901; and in the latter year was appointed physician-in-ordinary to King Edward VII. He was a member of the Medical Society of London and was censor of the Royal College of Physicians, 1888–9. and 1895–6. He wrote 'The Pulse' and 'The Heart.'

Broad'casting, a mode of sowing grain by which the seed is cast or dispersed upon the ground with the hand, or with a machine devised for sowing in this manner; opposed to planting in drills or rows.

Broad'head, Garland Carr, American geologist: b. Albemarle County, Va., 30 Oct. 1827. He studied at the University of Missouri and

was long the State expert in geology. He was professor of geology at the University of Missouri, 1887–97, and he is considered an authority on the Missouri coal measures. His writings include 'Geological Survey of Missouri Iron Ores and Coal Fields'; 'Geological Survey of Missouri'; and 'Illinois Geological Survey Report.'

Broad'hurst, Henry, English politician and labor organizer: b. Oxfordshire, 13 April 1840. As a boy he worked in a blacksmith's shop; then as a stone mason till 1872. He has been prominent in the labor movement; in 1875 he was secretary of the Labor Representative League and of the parliamentary committee of the Trades Union Congress. He has been a member of Parliament for Stoke-upon-Trent, 1880–5; for Bordesley, 1885–6; for Nottingham, 1886–92. He was under-secretary in the Home Department in 1886, and has served on several royal commissions for the investigation of the condition of the laboring class. He wrote 'Handy Book on Leasehold Enfranchisement' (with Sir R. T. Reid).

Broad'mouth, or Broad'bill, one of about a dozen species of small lethargic, songless birds of the family *Eurylæmidæ,* having a notable breadth of beak. Flocks of these birds are distributed through the woods from the Himalayas to the Philippines. The broadmouths are brilliant in plumage, and mainly fruit-eaters, with the exception of two species of the genus *Calyptomena,* which are insectivorous.

Broads, The Norfolk, England, a series of lakes, usually said to be formed by the widening or broadening out of the rivers. The broads *par excellence* are those of the Bure or North River (which empties into the sea at Yarmouth), and its tributaries, the Ant and the Thurne. The broads have grown greatly in favor with holiday-makers in recent years.

Broad'side, in a naval engagement, the whole discharge of the artillery on one side of a ship of war, above and below. The fighting power of a ship was formerly estimated by the weight of her broadside. The term is also applied to any large page printed on one side of a sheet of paper, and, strictly, not divided into columns. In this sense it is sometimes called a broadsheet.

Broad'stairs, England, a watering-place in the Isle of Thanet, Kent, two miles northeast of Ramsgate. It is said that the name is derived from the width of the passage leading down to the sea. Pop. (1901) 6,460.

Broad'sword, a sword with a broad blade, designed chiefly for cutting, formerly used by some regiments of cavalry and Highland infantry in the British service. The claymore or broadsword was formerly the national weapon of the Highlanders.

Broad'way, the chief thoroughfare, and the principal business street of New York. Starting from Bowling Green at the lower extremity of the island, it runs nearly due north to 14th Street, whence it takes a westerly diagonal course to 78th Street, at which point it again runs due north to 103d Street. Taking the westerly trend again to 108th Street, it thence runs north again, and, following the course of the old post road, is continued under the name of Broadway as far as Albany. Its continuous

LOOKING DOWN LOWER BROADWAY, NEW YORK.

course is interrupted by two public squares; Union Square at 14th Street, and Madison Square at 23d Street. Below Madison Square it is devoted mainly to office buildings and wholesale establishments. Above Madison Square (where it intersects Fifth Avenue and 23d Street) are theatres and the chief hotels. Its length below 59th Street is about five miles, and is traversed by an electric railway. A portion of the subway is excavated under the part of Broadway which is above 42d Street, and also that part below Park Place.

Broad'wood, John, English pianoforte manufacturer: b. Cockburnspath, Scotland, 1732; d. 1812. Going to London, he entered into partnership with a Swiss maker of harpsichords, named Burkhardt Tschudi, the firm being known as Tschudi & Broadwood. In 1769 his partner retired, and on his death four years later his son became a partner with Broadwood; but from 1783 till 1795, when Broadwood's son entered into partnership with him, he had the sole control of the business. The firm has long been known as John Broadwood & Sons. By the skill of Broadwood and those associated with him many improvements were introduced in the construction of the pianoforte, and for a long time the history of the firm was practically the story of the progressive development of that instrument.

Brobdingnag, an imaginary country described by Dean Swift in 'Gulliver's Travels.' The inhabitants are represented as being of enormous size and the details of their environment in proportion; whence has arisen the adjective "brobdingnagian."

Broca, Pierre Paul, pē-är pōl brŏ-kä, French surgeon and anthropologist: b. Sainte-Foy-la-Grande, department of the Gironde, 28 June 1824; d. Paris, 9 July 1880. In 1841 he began the study of medicine at Paris, became hospital surgeon in 1844, anatomical assistant in the Faculty of Medicine in 1846, preparator in anatomy in 1848, and professor in 1867. Between 1861 and 1865 he carried out his famous researches on the localization of cerebral functions. He gained great distinction in anthropology, and in 1859 founded the Paris anthropological society. During the Franco-German war he engaged in hospital work at La Pitié, but when peace was concluded he resumed his teaching. In 1872 he founded the 'Revue d' Anthropologie,' and four years later he established the Ecole d'Anthropologie, which formed the nucleus of the later Institut Anthropologique. His writings are numerous and important.

Brocade', a fabric having a pattern of raised figures; often a stuff of silk, enriched with a raised pattern of flowers, foliage, and other ornaments. Formerly it signified a stuff woven all of gold or silver threads, or in which silk was mixed with such threads; at present all stuffs are so called if they are worked with raised flowers or other figures, and especially when the figures are in more than one color. Brocade is in silk what damask is in wool. Brocatelle, in which cotton and wool are used instead of silk, is an imitation of brocade.

Brocatelle'. See BROCADE.

Brocchi, Giovanni Battista, jŏ-vän'nē bät-tēs'tä brŏk'kē, Italian mineralogist and geologist: b. Bassano, 18 Feb. 1772; d. Khartum,

25 Sept. 1826. In 1808 his valuable researches upon iron mines and metalliferous mountains procured him the office of inspector of mines in the newly established kingdom of Italy. In 1814 he published a work on the structure of the Apennine range, with an account of the fossils of its strata. He corrected the erroneous view of Brieslak, who supposed Rome to occupy the site of an extinct volcano, to which he ascribed the tufa and other volcanic materials found on the seven hills. Brocchi, on the other hand, satisfactorily showed that they are derived either from Mont Albano or Monte Cimino. Both of these are extinct volcanoes, the first 12 miles, the other still farther, to the north of the city. In 1823 Brocchi sailed for Egypt with the view of exploring the mineral resources of that country. He received a commission from Mehemet Ali to examine his recent conquest of Sennaar, but the climate proved too much for his constitution.

Broc'coli, a variety of the cauliflower, hardier and with more color in the flower and leaves. The chief varieties are green, purple, and dwarf broccoli. It is inferior in flavor to cauliflower, but serves as a substitute for it when the latter cannot be obtained. See CAULIFLOWER.

Brochantite, brŏ'shŏn-tīt (from BROCHANT DE VILLIERS, a French mineralogist), an orthorhombic transparent or translucent mineral, with hardness 3.5-4; specific gravity, about 3.90; lustre vitreous, pearly on one cleavage face. It is a basic copper sulphate having the formula $Cu\ SO_4.\ 3\ Cu\ (OH)_2$. It much resembles atacamite, like which it occurs in many copper mines, notably in the Urals, in Cornwall. England, and in Chili. In the United States its most important localities are in Utah and Arizona.

Brochs, brŏʜs, class of edifices peculiar to Scotland, particularly in the northern counties, including Orkney, Shetland, and the Western Isles, more than 300 in all being known. A broch is a hollow circular tower of dry-built masonry, rarely more than 70 or less than 40 feet in total diameter, occasionally at least 50 feet high, and enclosing a circular court or area from 25 to 45 feet in diameter. The wall, which may be from 9 to 20 feet thick, is carried up solid for about 10 feet, except where pierced by the narrow passage giving entrance to the interior court, or where chambers are hollowed within its thickness and opening off the court. Above this height there are horizontal galleries in the wall, each about 6 feet high and 3 feet wide, running completely round the tower, except where crossed by the stair giving access to them, and having windows placed above each other, and all looking into the central area. The only external opening is a doorway about 5 or 6 feet high, and rarely more than 3 feet wide. The passage varies from 9 to 18 feet in length. and about 4 feet from its outer entrance is the door. Many of the brochs are found in naturally strong positions. such as a precipitous eminence or a promontory projecting into a loch, and further defenses are afforded by ditches and embankments, earthen ramparts, and dry stone walls. Hence it is clear that they were intended to serve as places of shelter and defense, for which purpose they are admirably contrived, as they form a series of strongholds that could be reduced only by a regular siege, the inmates being safe against missiles and even against fire, from the height and strength of the walls. Provided with a sufficiency of food, and obtaining water from a well inside the enclosure, the people thus sheltered could hold out for an indefinite time. The relics found in the brochs, like the structures themselves, are Celtic in character, and belong to post-Roman times. The Brochs were probably built as places of refuge from the Scandinavian vikings that for centuries were a scourge to many of the European coasts, but little or nothing of their history is known. The relics include swords, spears, knives, axes, and chisels of iron, with rings, bracelets, pins, and other articles of bronze or of brass. Numerous articles made of bone and horn are also found, with stone implements, as querns, mortars, pestles, bowls and cups, lamps, etc. Pottery of various kinds is also found. Spinning and weaving were evidently practised by the broch-builders. Agriculture, hunting, and fishing furnished subsistence; and animal food was furnished by the stag, roe, reindeer, ox, sheep, goat, and pig, as well as by the whale, porpoise, cod, haddock, and other denizens of the sea.

Brock, Sir Isaac, English soldier: b. Guernsey, 6 Oct. 1769; d. Queenston, Canada, 13 Oct. 1812. He was educated at Southampton and Rotterdam, and entered the army as ensign in the 8th Regiment in 1785. In 1791 he transferred to the 49th Infantry, and saw service in the West Indies. In 1802 he went to Canada at the head of that regiment, returning three years afterward; but in 1806 he was again in North America. He became major-general in 1811, and in the following year compelled the surrender of the American general Hall at Detroit. For this service he received knighthood in the Order of the Bath, but he did not live long to enjoy the honor; for during an attack on Queenston by another American force, only three days after he was knighted, he was mortally wounded. The sum of £1,575 was voted by the House of Commons for a monument to Brock, which now stands in the south transept of St. Paul's Cathedral, London. There is another monument to him at Queenston, erected at public cost in 1842.

Brock, Thomas, English sculptor: b. 1847. He studied under J. H. Foley and finished after the latter's death a number of his works. Among his productions is the Longfellow bust in Westminster Abbey. He is a member of the Royal Academy.

Brockedon, brŏk'dĕn, **William,** English artist and inventor: b. Devonshire, 1787; d. London, 1854. He was the discoverer of a method by which plumbago and its dust (previously thrown away as valueless) could be freed from impurities and re-solidified, so as to make a superior description of lead pencils, of various degrees of hardness, well adapted for artists' use. Mr. Brockedon was a painter, and author of 'The Passes of the Alps,' with over 100 folio engravings from drawings by himself. He also produced 'Italy, Classical and Picturesque' (1842-3); and 'Egypt and Nubia' (3 vols. 1846-9).

Brock'en, a mountain in Germany, popularly known as Blocksberg, the highest summit of the Harz Mountains (about 3,745 feet), in the Prussian government of Magdeburg. It was known to the Romans as Mons Bructerus. The bare, treeless summit is covered with snow from November to June; and on it are a hotel and an observatory. Under certain atmospheric conditions the visitor may see a gigantic figure of himself reflected on the clouds (the "Spectre of the Brocken"). According to a popular legend the German witches used to assemble here on Walpurgis Night (q.v.) for an annual orgy. Two driving-roads and a railway lead up the mountain. Many tourists visit the Brocken during the summer, and in clear weather an extensive view may be obtained.

Brocket (Fr. *broche,* a "spit" or "tine"), a book-name given to Brazilian deer of the sub-genus *Coassus,* because of their spike-like antlers. There are three species, varying in height from 19 to 27 inches, namely: (1) Guazuviva (*Coassus nemorivagus*), or Brazilian deer; (2) Pita (*Coassus rufus*); (3) A similar form, the pudu (*Pudua humilis*) of the Chilean Andes, the smallest of all deer, having spike horns only about two inches long.

Brockett, Linus Pierpont, American author: b. Canton, Conn., 16 Oct. 1820; d. Brooklyn, 13 Jan. 1893. He graduated at the Yale Medical School in 1843, and practised medicine for a few years. Later he devoted himself to editorial and other literary work. He wrote a 'History of Education'; 'Men of Our Day'; 'The Year of Battles'; 'Epidemic and Contagious Diseases'; 'The Great Metropolis'; etc.

Brockhaus, Friedrich Arnold, frēd'rĭH är'nŏld brŏk'hows, German publisher, founder of the publishing firm of Brockhaus in Leipsic: b. Dortmund, 4 May 1772; d. Leipsic, 20 Aug. 1823. He was educated at the gymnasium of his native town, and in 1793 went to Leipsic, where he devoted two years to the acquisition of scientific knowledge and the principal modern languages of Europe. In 1795 he established at Dortmund a mercantile house for the sale of English manufactures, which he removed to Arnheim, in the Netherlands, in 1801, and to Amsterdam in 1802. Although he managed his business with success, he abandoned it out of distaste for mercantile pursuits in 1804, and entered into the book trade at Amsterdam. After the annexation of Holland to the French empire (1810), Brockhaus returned to Germany, and he re-opened his establishment in Altenburg (1811). In 1813 the firm received the title of F. A. Brockhaus. In 1808 Brockhaus had purchased the copyright of the German 'Conversations-Lexicon,' which had been begun in 1796. In 1809-10 he completed the first edition by the publication of two supplementary volumes. In 1812 he began to publish the second edition of this work, which was finished under his own editorship. It was favorably received and had an extensive sale. The business now rapidly extended, and was removed to Leipsic in 1817. It still is carried on by the grandsons of the founder, and there are now chief branches in Berlin and Vienna. Among the literary undertakings of the house have been several important critical periodicals and some large historical and bibliographical works. The 'Conversations-Lexikon,' distinctively associated with the name of Brockhaus, has now reached a 14th edition.

Brockhaus, Hermann, German Orientalist: b. Amsterdam, 28 Jan. 1806; d. Leipsic, 5 Jan. 1877. He was educated at Amsterdam and at Göttingen and Bonn, where he devoted himself to Oriental languages. He lived for a long time in France and England and then settled in Dresden. In 1839 he went as professor to Jena, and in 1841 to Leipsic, where he became professor of Sanskrit, a position he held until his death. He published many works on Oriental literature, and edited the great 'Allgemeine Encyklopädie' of Ersch and Gruber.

Brockton, Mass., a city in Plymouth County, situated on the N. Y., N. H. & H. R.R.; 20 miles south of Boston. It is one of the largest boot- and shoe-manufacturing places in the country, and beside these articles has extensive manufactures of rubber goods, shoe machinery and supplies, tools, and bicycles. It contains the villages of Campello, Montello, Marshall's Corner, Brockton Heights, Clifton Heights, and Salisbury Square. It was settled in 1700, was incorporated as a town in 1821, and chartered as a city in 1881. There are two national and two savings banks, a public library, with over 26,000 volumes; public school property valued at over $500,000; and a property valuation exceeding $26,000,000. Pop. (1900) 40,063.

Brockville, Canada, port of entry, and the chief town of the united counties of Leeds and Grenville, Ontario, on the Saint Lawrence River below the Thousand Islands and on the Grand Trunk Railway. It is 125 miles by rail south of Montreal and 40 miles by water below Kingston and is a terminus of the Canadian Pacific Railway, and of the Brockville, Western & Sault Ste. Marie Railway. It is a port for the Saint Lawrence steamers and is connected by ferry with Morristown, New York State. Brockville is lighted by gas and electricity and has excellent sewerage systems. It has numerous churches and public buildings, a collegiate institute, 4 public schools, 1 separate school, a manual training school, and an art school. The manufactures comprise stoves, carriages, agricultural implements, hats, cigars, chemicals, lumber, flour, gloves, tools, machinery, and foundry products. It is named after General Sir Isaac Brock (q.v.). Pop. (1904) 9,044.

Brockway, Zebulon Reed, American penologist: b. Lyme, Conn., 28 April 1827. His connection with prison administration began at the Connecticut State Prison. He was connected successively with the penitentiaries of Albany and Monroe counties, N. Y., and with the House of Correction, Detroit, Mich. He is best known in connection with the penal-reform methods introduced during his superintendency of the New York State Reformatory at Elmira, a position which he filled from 1876-1900. He has written numerous papers and magazine articles on penology.

Broderick, brŏd'rĭck, David Colbreth, American legislator: b. Washington, D. C., 4 Feb. 1820; d. Lake Merced, Cal., 16 Sept. 1859. He was defeated for Congress in New York in 1846; went to California, and was elected a member of the Constitutional Convention of 1849; served as speaker of the Senate; and was elected to the United States Senate in 1856, where he opposed the admission of Kansas.

Broderip, brŏd'rĭp, William John, English naturalist: b. Bristol, 21 Nov. 1789; d. London 27 Feb. 1859. He graduated from Oriel College, Oxford, in 1812; studied law, and was called to the bar in 1817; and subsequently occupied several legal posts. In 1851 he became treasurer of Gray's Inn, with which office was combined that of librarian. He was an enthusiastic naturalist, and made many fine collections, his conchological cabinet being purchased for the British Museum. In 1847 he published 'Zoological Recreations,' and five years later appeared 'Leaves from the Note-Book of a Naturalist.'

Brod'head, John Romeyn, American historian: b. Philadelphia, 2 Jan. 1814; d. New York, 6 May 1873. He graduated at Rutgers College in 1831. He was author of a 'History of the State of New York,' and he made in Europe a valuable collection of documents bearing upon American history, that was published by the State of New York.

Brodiæa, brō-dī-ē'a, a small genus of western American corm-rooted plants of the natural order *Liliaceæ,* which are popular as garden flowers. The species are of low growth, and have several purple, red, white, or yellow funnel-shaped flowers on a scape. According to some authors several related genera are grouped in this, and cultural methods vary in consequence. For list of species and cultural directions consult: Bailey and Miller, 'Cyclopedia of American Horticulture' (N. Y. 1900-02).

Bro'die, Sir Benjamin Collins, English surgeon: b. Winterslow, Wiltshire, 9 June 1783; d. Broome Park, Surrey, 21 Oct. 1862. His father superintended his education till he was 18, after which he went to the Hunterian School of Anatomy. In 1803 he became a pupil of Sir Everard Home at St. George's Hospital, and in 1805 was appointed assistant to Mr. Wilson, demonstrator of anatomy. In 1809 he became a lecturer of the school and assistant surgeon of the hospital. In 1810 he was elected Croonian lecturer to the Royal Society, and the excellence of his papers caused him to be elected a Fellow, and in the following year he received the Copley medal. His reputation as a distinguished surgeon was now established, and his professional career became one of uniform success. From 1819 to 1823 he was professor of anatomy at the Royal College of Surgeons. In 1822 he was elected a full surgeon at St. George's. He continued giving clinical lectures there till 1830, when the increasing demands of his profession compelled him to discontinue them. In 1832 he succeeded Sir Everard Home as sergeant-surgeon to William IV., and was made a baronet by patent in 1834. Queen Victoria continued him in the same appointment. From 1835 to 1846 he was a member of the Court of Examiners of the College of Surgeons, and in 1844 he was president of the court. In 1858 he was elected president of the Royal Society, which honor he held till 1861. For some years before his death his sight failed, and for about two years he was almost totally blind. As a professional practitioner his gains exceeded those of almost any man of like profession in his time. In 1851 he republished a selection of his earlier essays, entitled 'Physiological Researches.' His work on 'Pathological and Surgical Observations on Diseases of the Joints' (1818) was esteemed of great value both in Great Britain and on the Continent, and went through many editions. In 1854 he published a work in a colloquial form entitled 'Psychological Inquiries.' The dialogue is not controversial, and the work contains the mature opinions of the author on various speculative subjects.

Brod'rick, George Charles, English educator: b. Castle Rising, Norfolk, England, 5 May 1831. He was educated at Eton and Balliol College, Oxford, and University of London. He was called to the bar in 1859. From 1877–9 he was a member of the London School Board. In 1881 he became warden of Merton College. Among his works are: 'Political Studies'; 'English Land and English Landlords'; 'Memorials of Merton College'; 'Short History of Oxford University'; and 'Memories and Impressions.'

Brodrick, William St. John Freemantle, English statesman: b. 14 Dec. 1856. He was educated at Eton and at Balliol College, Oxford. From 1880–5 he was member of Parliament for West Surrey; 1886–92, financial secretary to the war office; 1895–8, under-secretary of state for war; 1898-1900 under-secretary of state for foreign affairs; afterward becoming secretary for war.

Brod'sky, Adolf, Russian violinist: b. Taganrog, South Russia, 21 Feb. 1851. He first played in public at the age of nine, and later went to Vienna to pursue his musical studies. In 1879 he became director of the symphony concerts in Kieff, and later held a professorship in the Leipsic Conservatory. As a soloist he appeared in concerts in several of the leading cities of Europe. He came to the United States and taught for a time in Scharwenka's Conservatory, New York, but returned to Leipsic. In 1895 he was made director of the Royal College of Music, Manchester, England.

Bro'dy, Austria, a town in Galicia, near the Russian frontier, 58 miles east-northeast of Lemberg, on a swampy plain. It has broad streets, houses mostly built of stone, an old castle, three churches, Jewish synagogue, etc. About two thirds of its inhabitants are Jews, who have a hospital for themselves and a college for the instruction of artists and mechanics. The commerce, carried on principally by Jews, is important, the town being favorably situated for the interchange of goods between Austria and Russia, and Turkey. Pop. about 20,000.

Broglie, brō-lē, a family distinguished in the annals of French wars and diplomacy, which derives its origin from Piedmont. Among its members are:

1. FRANÇOIS MARIE, DUC DE, French soldier: b. Paris, 11 Jan. 1671; d. Ferrières, 22 May 1745. From 1689 he fought with distinction in the Netherlands, Germany, and Italy. He was also employed in diplomatic affairs, and concluded a treaty between France, England, and Prussia in 1725. He rose by degrees till in 1734 he became marshal of France. In the war of the Austrian succession he had the chief command of the armies in Bavaria and Bohemia.

2. VICTOR FRANÇOIS, DUC DE, French soldier: b. (the eldest son of the preceding), 19 Oct. 1718; d. Münster, 1804. He commenced his career under his father in the battles of Guastalla and Parma (1734); was engaged in all the wars of France, and was created marshal in 1759.

Jomini considered him the only French general who had shown constant ability during the Seven Years' war. He was engaged in the battles of Hastenbeck, Rossbach, Sondershausen, and Lützelberg, and, being appointed to the chief command, defeated the Prussians and Hessians at Bergen in 1759, for which Francis I. of Austria created him a prince of the empire. In 1760 he gained another victory at Corbach, but was defeated, together with the Prince of Soubise, at Willingshausen, in the following year. In consequence of this and the favor of Soubise at court he was exiled. He was recalled in 1764, and in 1789, when the Revolution broke out, Louis XVI. appointed him minister of war; at the same time he received the command of the troops that were to keep Paris in check. The desertion of the National Guard rendered all his efforts vain, and Broglie left France. In the campaign of 1792 he commanded a division of the *émigrés* without success. After its close he withdrew entirely from public life.

3. VICTOR CLAUDE, PRINCE DE BROGLIE, French soldier: b. (third son of the preceding), 1757; d. Paris, 27 June 1794. He entered at first into the views of the revolutionary party. He was deputy of the nobility of Colmar to the States-General in 1789. After the dissolution of the Constituent Assembly he was appointed field-marshal in the army of the Rhine, but upon his refusal to acknowledge the decree of 10 August, suspending the royal authority, was deprived of his command, summoned before the revolutionary tribunal, and led to the guillotine.

4. ACHILLE CHARLES LÉONCE VICTOR, DUC DE, French statesman: b. Paris (son of the preceding), 1 Dec. 1785; d. Paris, 25 Jan. 1870. In 1816 he married a daughter of Madame de Staël and was made a member of the chamber of peers. After the Revolution of 1830 the Duc de Broglie and Guizot were the heads of the party known as *doctrinaires*. He was minister of public instruction for a short time in 1830, and minister of foreign affairs from October 1832 to April 1834. In 1849 he was a conservative member of the Legislative Assembly, and after the *coup d'état* he continued a bitter enemy of the imperial régime. His later years were devoted to philosophical and literary pursuits.

5. JACQUES VICTOR ALBERT, DUC DE: b. Paris (son of the preceding), 13 June 1821; d. 1901. In 1846 he became secretary to the embassy at Madrid, whence he was transferred to that at Rome, but the revolution of 1848 caused him to give up public life. From that time he became known as an able writer in political reviews. In 1856 he published 'L'Histoire de l'Eglise et de l'Empire,' in six volumes, a work which gained him a chair in the Academy. In 1871 he was elected to the National Assembly for the department of Eure, and in the same year became ambassador at London. He led the opposition to Thiers during 1872–3, and finally succeeded in defeating him. In the latter year he became minister of foreign affairs and president of the council, but in 1874 he suffered defeat. In 1885 he again gave up political life and devoted himself to his historical studies. Among his works are 'Le Secret du Roi Louis XV.' (1878); 'Frédéric II. et Marie-Thérèse' (1883); 'Maurice de Saxe et le Marquis d'Argenson' (1891); 'La Paix d'Aix-la-Chapelle' (1892); 'Le Père Lacordaire' (1895); 'Malherbe' (1897); etc.

Brogny, Jean **Allarmet**, zhŏṅ ăl-lär-mä bı̆ŏṅ-yĕ, Italian cardinal: b. Brogny, near Annecy, Savoy, 1342; d. Rome, 16 Feb. 1426. Although a swineherd in his youth, he attained, by his learning and virtues, a position of great influence and eminence in the Church. He was successively made bishop of Viviers, of Ostia, archbishop of Arles, and bishop of Geneva, and finally cardinal and chancellor of the Church of Rome. During the great schism which divided the Church for more than 40 years Brogny devoted himself to the work of conciliation. The Council of Constance being called for that purpose by John XXIII. and the Emperor Sigismund, the former was deposed at the sixth session, after which Brogny presided as senior cardinal until the 41st, when Cardinal Colonna was elected Pope, 14 Nov. 1417, chiefly through Brogny's influence, under the name of Martin V., and the holy see was once more established at Rome. As president of the Council of Constance he had to pronounce the sentence of death upon Huss, to whom he had shown great kindness during the trial, having visited him several times in his prison and exhorted him, but in vain, to save his life by recanting his creed. The cardinal was the founder of the hospital of Annecy, and of the College of St. Nicolas at Avignon.

Brogue, brŏg (Ir. and Gael. *brog*), a coarse and light kind of shoe made of raw or half-tanned leather, of one entire piece, and gathered round the foot by a thong, formerly worn in Ireland and the Highlands of Scotland. The term is also used of the mode of pronunciation peculiar to the Irish, but whether the word in this sense is the same as in the other is doubtful.

Broiling, the cooking of meat or fish on a gridiron above a fire, or by laying it directly on the coals, a very wholesome method of cookery. See COOKERY.

Broke, **Sir Philip Bowes Vere**, British admiral: b. Ipswich, 9 Sept. 1776; d. 2 Jan. 1841. He entered the navy in 1792, and, after he had seen much active service, distinguished himself in 1813 as commander of the frigate Shannon, in the memorable action which that vessel, in answer to a regular challenge, fought with the Chesapeake off the American coast. The Shannon, carrying 38 guns and 330 men, in an engagement of only 15 minutes boarded and captured the Chesapeake, carrying 49 guns and 440 men. Sir Philip, who was severely wounded in the action, was immediately made a baronet, and in 1815 Knight Commander of the Bath. He became rear-admiral in 1830.

Broken Hill, Australia, a mining town in the western part of New South Wales, south of Stanley Range, about 925 miles west of Sydney. It stands in a district which contains many silver mines; and asbestos, lead, gold, copper, etc., are also found here. One of the silver mines, the Proprietary, is the most productive in the world. It is connected with Silverton and Adelaide by rail. Pop. about 20,000.

Bro**ken-wi**nd, a disease in horses, often accompanied with an enlargement of the lungs and heart, which disables them for bearing fatigue. In this disease the expiration of the air from the lungs occupies double the time that the inspiration of it does; it requires also two efforts rapidly succeeding each other, attended by a slight spasmodic action, in order fully to accomplish it. The disease is caused by rupture of the air-cells, and there is no known cure for it. See HEAVES.

Broker (Lat. *abrocator*, perhaps from the Saxon *abroccan*, to break up, from which is derived "abbroachment," the breaking up of goods or selling at retail). The early use of this term designated a retailer of goods, generally supposed to belong to another person, and thence applied to any one making a bargain as the agent of another for the sale or purchase of goods. The distinctive character of a broker was that he acted in behalf of another and in his name; at least, when the contract came to be consummated, the name of the principal was in the ordinary course disclosed. It was a further incident of a broker's employment that he did not have possession of the goods sold, or receive possession of the goods purchased, in which respect he differed from a factor. And these principles still apply. But the office of broker has been vastly extended by the increasing exigencies of commercial business.

The most important kinds of brokers are here enumerated. Bill and note brokers negotiate the purchase and sale of bills of exchange and promissory notes. They are paid a commission by the seller, and it is not their custom to disclose the names of their principals. There is an implied warranty that what they sell is what they represent it to be, and should a bill or note sold by them turn out to be a forgery, they are held to be responsible; but it would appear that by showing a payment over to their principals, or other special circumstances attending the transaction proving that it would be inequitable to hold them responsible, they will be discharged. (Edwards, Bills, 291; 4 Duer, 79). The authorities, however, are not in harmony upon this question. (See 3 Allen 258; 1 Hill 287; 21 E. C. L. 379.) Exchange brokers negotiate bills of exchange drawn on foreign countries, or on other places in this country. It is sometimes part of the business of exchange brokers to buy and sell uncurrent bank notes and gold and silver coins, as well as drafts and checks drawn or payable in other cities; although, as they do this at their own risk and for their own profit, it is difficult to see the reason for calling them brokers. Insurance brokers procure insurance, and negotiate between insurers and insured. Merchandise brokers negotiate the sale of merchandise without having the possession or control of it, as factors have. Pawnbrokers lend money in small sums, on the security of personal property, at usurious rates of interest. They are licensed by the authorities, and excepted from the operation of the usury laws. Real estate brokers are those who negotiate the sale or purchase of real property. They are a numerous class, and, in addition to the above duty, sometimes procure loans on mortgage security, collect rents, and attend to the letting and leasing of houses and lands. Ship brokers negotiate the purchase and sale of ships and the business of freighting vessels. Like other brokers they receive a commission from the seller only. Stock brokers are those employed to buy and sell stock in incorporated companies. The stock brokers are associated together in the larger cities under the name of the Board of Brokers.

(See STOCK EXCHANGE.) This board is an association, admission to membership in which is guarded with jealous care. Membership is forfeited for default in carrying out contracts, and rules are prescribed for the conduct of the business, which are enforced on all members. The purchases and sales are made at sessions of the board, and are all officially recorded and published by an officer of the association. Stock brokers charge commission to both buyers and sellers of stocks.

Bro'mal Hydrate is prepared by adding bromine to iced alcohol, distilling and combining with water. Its crystals resemble those of chloral hydrate in appearance and chemical properties, and are soluble in water. The drug has a sedative action tending to produce sleep, and is employed in nervous conditions and to diminish the attacks in epilepsy. It has little effect on pain, and should not be used when the heart is weak or the stomach upset.

Bro'mamide, a volatile crystalline substance without odor or taste and containing bromine. It is insoluble in water and is employed as a sedative in acute and chronic rheumatism and neuralgia.

Bromberg, brŏm-bārH, Prussia, a town in the province of Posen, 69 miles northeast of the city of that name; situated on the Brahe six miles west of its confluence with the Vistula. It is well built, has two Protestant and two Roman Catholic churches, a synagogue, asylum for the blind, a gymnasium, and a real-gymnasium. Pop. (1895) 46,417.

Brome, Alexander, English poet and dramatist: b. 1620; d. 1666. He seems to have been a lawyer by profession, and at one time attorney to the court. He is best known as the author of many royalist songs and epigrams. He published 'The Cunning Lovers,' a comedy (1654); 'Fancy's Festivals' (1657); 'Songs and Poems' (1661); 'Translation of Horace' (1666).

Brome, Richard, English dramatist: d. about 1652. He was at first the servant and afterward the friend of Ben Jonson, who encouraged him in his literary work, and on whose style his plays are modeled. The best and most popular of his dramas, some of them comedies dealing with the everyday life of his time and others of a more romantic character are: 'The Court Beggar' (acted 1632); 'The Love-sick Court' (published 1659); 'The Queen and Concubine' (published 1659); 'The Northern Lass' (printed 1632); 'The Sparagus Garden' (acted 1635); 'The Antipodes' (acted 1638), and 'A Jovial Crew' (acted 1641).

Brome-grass, the common name of the genus Bromus. Nearly 200 species have been described, occurring in both the Old and the New World. They are known by having their spikelets many-flowered, two awnless glumes to each floret, two paleæ or valves, the lowermost of which has a rough, straight, rigid awn proceeding from below the tip of the valve. These grasses have great power of resisting drought, and have proved themselves valuable forage plants on the high, dry plains of the western United States. Some species are cultivated for hay in the eastern States, but are not much relished by cattle. The giant brome-grass is known as cheat or chess, and is found in wheat-fields. This has been introduced from Europe.

Bromelia, a genus of about 25 species of monocotyledonous, stemless herbs of the natural order Bromeliaceæ, natives of tropical America, introduced into other warm climates for the sake of the fibre obtained from their leaves, and cultivated in greenhouses to some extent for ornament. The species have stiff leaves like the pineapple, and flowers in panicles. B. pinguin, the wild pineapple or pinguin, a native of the West Indies, is perhaps best known because of its use as a tropical hedge-plant, for which its numerous sword-shaped, spiny, rigid leaves, three to six feet long, and two inches wide, specially adapt it. The leaves are also ornamental, being bright green at first and turning red with age. The reddish pubescent flowers in compact panicles are followed by edible fruits as large as plums. These fruits are used to make a pleasant cooling drink. B. sylvestris, which has smaller leaves, furnishes a fibre said to be superior to the preceding species. Other species also yield a fibre of greater or less value.

Bro'mic Acid ($HBrO_3$), a monobasic acid, forming salts called bromates. When bromine is dissolved in caustic potash a mixture of bromide and bromate of potassium is obtained, which can be separated by crystallization, $3Br_2 + 6KHO = 5KBr + KBrO_3 + 3H_2O$. Free bromic acid can be prepared by passing chlorine into bromine water, $2Br + 10Cl + 6H_2O = 2HBrO_3 + 10HCl$. The acid is best obtained by decomposing potassium bromate by argentic nitrate, and acting on the resulting argentic bromate by bromine, $5AgBrO_3 + 3Br_2 + 3H_2O = 5AgBr + 6HBrO_3$. Bromic acid is a strongly acid liquid, reddening and then bleaching litmus paper. On concentration at 100° it decomposes into bromine and oxygen. It is decomposed by sulphur dioxide (SO_2), by sulphide of hydrogen (H_2S), and by hydro-bromic acid (HBr). Bromates are with difficulty soluble in water, and are decomposed on heating into oxygen and bromides.

Bromide, brō'mīd, a combination of bromine with a metal or a radical. Bromides are soluble in water, except silver and mercurous bromides; lead bromide is very slightly soluble. They are detected in analysis by the following reactions: Argentic nitrate gives a yellowish precipitate of AgBr, insoluble in dilute nitric acid, and soluble in strong ammonia. Chlorine liberates bromine, and, if the liquid is shaken up with ether, a yellow ethereal solution floats on the liquid. Heated with sulphuric acid and MnO_2, bromides yield vapors of Br, which turns starch yellow.

Bromidro'sis (bromos, a bad odor + hidros, sweat), malodorous or stinking perspiration, usually excessive in quantity and due mostly to bacterial decomposition of the sweat. The parts most affected are the arm-pits and the feet, but the latter are not attacked in persons who go barefoot. The victims are mostly anæmic, nervous persons. Very hot water, formaldehyde, salicylic acid, and boric acid are the most used applications, the latter being dusted in shoes and stockings. The sweat also sometimes smells of certain odoriferous substances, not necessarily offensive, which have been taken; for example: asafœtida, copaiba, denzoic acid, musk, onion, or garlic. It also may develop a peculiar odor in cholera, smallpox or typhoid fever, and smell of urine in uremia. Rarely it gives a pleasant odor of violet or pineapple. The sweat in some colored races has a distinctive, unpleasant smell.

Bro'mine, a non-metallic element. Symbol Br; atomic weight, 79.4 for $H = 1$, or 80.0 for $o = 16$. Bromine was discovered in 1826 by Balard, in the salts obtained by the evaporation of sea water. Bromine is liberated from the sodium and magnesium salts by the action of free chlorine, and is separated by ether, which dissolves the bromine. This red-colored solution is removed, saturated with potash, evaporated, and heated to redness, and the bromide of potassium is heated with manganese dioxide and sulphuric acid. The bromine is liberated in the form of a deep red vapor, which condenses into a dark, reddish-black liquid. Specific gravity, 2.97. It boils at 63°, and its vapor density is 5.54 times that of air. It has an irritating smell, and when inhaled is poisonous. It dissolves in 30 parts of water, and the solution has weak bleaching properties. Bromine and hydrogen do not unite in the sunlight, but do when they are passed through a red-hot porcelain tube, forming hydrobromic acid (HBr), which is also obtained by the action of phosphorus and water on bromine. It is a colorless, fuming gas, which liquefies at 73°, very soluble in water. The concentrated solution contains 47.8 per cent of HBr; it boils at 126°, and has powerful acid properties; it neutralizes bases, forming bromides and water. Hypobromous acid, HBrO, is only known in solutions; it has bleaching properties. Bromine can displace chlorine from its compounds with oxygen, while chlorine can liberate bromine from its compounds with hydrogen. Free bromine turns starch yellow.

Bromine has been applied externally as a caustic but rarely. Its chief officinal preparations are bromide of ammonium, useful in whooping-cough, infantile convulsions, and nervous diseases generally; and bromide of potassium, now very extensively used, especially in epilepsy, hysteria, delirium tremens, diseases of the throat and larynx, bronchocele, enlarged spleen, hypertrophy of liver, fibroid tumors, etc. Also, as an antaphrodisiac, for sleeplessness, glandular swellings, and skin diseases. The alterative properties of bromide of potassium are similar to, but less marked than, those of the iodides. Its preparation is the same as iodide of potassium, substituting an equivalent quantity of bromine for iodine — $6KHO + Br_6 = 5KBr + KBrO_3 + 3H_2O$. It has a pungent saline taste, no odor, and occurs in colorless cubic crystals, closely resembling the iodide. As a hypnotic its usefulness is much increased by combining it with morphia or chloral hydrate.

Bro'mipin, a yellow, bland liquid of simple oily taste, and composed of oil of sesame with 10 per cent of bromine. It is easily borne by the stomach and does not readily produce bromism, therefore in some cases it is substituted for the bromides which it resembles in its action on the nervous system.

Bro'mism, a condition which results from the accumulation of bromides in the system, owing to the ingestion of greater quantities than the body can get rid of. The breath is fetid, the skin breaks out in an acne eruption, the throat is insensitive to touch so that it may be tickled with a feather, and there is loss of memory,

heaviness of intellect, great sleepiness, and depression of spirits. If the drug is still continued there may be paralysis, loss of sight and hearing, inability to speak above a whisper, and various symptoms of mental derangement. The symptoms usually quickly subside on stopping the drug.

Bromley, England, a town of Kent, 10 miles south-southeast of London. It has a market square with a large market-house, and has rapidly increased by the erection, in its vicinity, of large groups of houses occupied by London merchants. The most notable place of worship is the modern church of St. Peter and St. Paul. Pop. (1901) 27,358.

Bro'moform, a clear, heavy, volatile liquid of ethereal odor and sweetish taste, soluble in alcohol or ether though not in water. It is analogous to iodoform and chloroform, and is made like the latter from alcohol or acetone. It is somewhat anesthetic and has been used like chloroform, but its special use is in "whooping-cough," in which a few drops are given in solution or mixture several times a day.

Bro'mol, the precipitate formed when bromine water is added to a solution of carbolic acid. It occurs in crystals, is antiseptic, and may be taken internally for diarrhœa or cholera morbus, or applied to wounds or ulcers in the form of a salve.

Brompton, England, a suburban district of London, in Kensington, associated with the names of Burke, Canning, and other eminent men.

Bromus. See BROME GRASS.

Bromvogel, the South African name for the hornbill (q.v.).

Bronchi, brŏng'kī, the two branches into which the trachea or windpipe divides in the chest, one going to the right lung, the other to the left, and ramifying into innumerable smaller tubes — the bronchial tubes. See LUNGS.

Bronchitis (Gk. bronchia, the bronchial tubes + itis, a suffix denoting inflammation), inflammation of the bronchi. Acute bronchitis is a "cold in the chest," and may be simple or may accompany typhoid fever, malaria, influenza, whooping-cough, or tuberculosis. It is very common in young children, in the aged, and in those whose work involves the inhalation of fumes or dust. Sedentary indoor occupations and overheated rooms are predisposing conditions. In some people the bronchi are very susceptible, and "catching cold" means an attack of bronchitis. The mucous membrane of the bronchi is red, swollen, and inflamed, and after the first day or two exudes large quantities of mucus which must be coughed up. There may be a sudden onset with pains in the back and limbs, a feeling of languor and restlessness, tightness or pain in the chest, and fever. The cough is at first dry, but soon is accompanied by much sputum. Often the symptoms are very slight, lasting only a day or two, but the usual duration is one or two weeks. Complete return to health may be much delayed. In infants and old people pneumonia frequently supervenes. At the onset a hot foot-bath, hot lemonade to produce free sweating, a mustard plaster to the chest, and a cathartic may cut short an attack. Later ipecac, senega, squills, ammonia, etc., are given to loosen the mucus and relieve the congestion. Codeine will allay the cough. Chronic bronchitis occurs most frequently in middle life or old age, and commonly accompanies disease of the heart, liver or kidneys, and gout. Cold and changeable weather brings on the symptoms year after year, so that a person will "take cold every time the weather changes." The mucous membrane is atrophied, or in places thickened, and the tubes are irregularly dilated. There may be shortness of breath on exertion, asthmatic attacks, spells of coughing, profuse expectoration, and occasionally spitting of blood. Fever is rare. The general health is not impaired to the extent that it is in tuberculosis, but a change to a dry, bracing climate may be advisable. Turkish baths, creosote, ipecac, and potassium iodide are among the favorite remedies. A form of acute or chronic bronchitis, in which membranous casts of the bronchial tubes are formed and coughed up, is known as fibrinous bronchitis. Consult Allbutt's 'System of Medicine'; and Osler's 'Principles and Practice of Medicine.'

Bronchocele, brŏng'kō-sēl, an indolent tumor on the forepart of the neck, caused by enlargement of the thyroid gland, and attended by protrusion of the eyeballs, anæmia, and palpitation.

Bronchotomy, brŏng-kŏt'ō-mĭ, in surgery, an incision into the windpipe or larynx, between the rings, to afford a passage for the air into and out of the lungs when any disease prevents respiration in the usual way, or to extract foreign bodies which have got into the trachea, or in cases of suffocation, drowning, etc. It is known as tracheotomy or laryngotomy, according as the windpipe or the larynx is operated on.

Bronco, or **Broncho,** the small horse of the plains in western United States and in Mexico. In Texas it is called "Mustang." It is descended from the horses of Arabian stock, brought to America by the early Spaniards, and exhibits still certain Arabian features due to this ancestry. Many of the Spanish horses were captured by the Indians, and some escaped from their owners. Of the former, great numbers deserted their Indian captors, and roamed with their free companions over the plains of the Southwest, where they multiplied rapidly, and adapted themselves to the local conditions of climate and vegetation. Thus they returned to a wild state in this country, which has been considered as the original habitat of the horse family, but which presents nowhere, unless on the pampas of South America, an aboriginal type of horse. These wild horses have more recently been captured, and bred in captivity; and have been modified by admixture of blood with horses from the eastern United States. They are famous for their endurance, despite their rather weak hind quarters. Their heads are proportionately very large, and not handsome, but the little animals are extremely intelligent and serviceable.

Brondel', John B., American clergyman: b. Bruges, Belgium, 1842. He studied in the American College of the University of Louvain and was ordained to the Catholic priesthood in 1864. He came to America and from 1867–77

was rector at Steilacoom, Wash., and at Walla Walla, 1877–8. In 1879 he became bishop of Vancouver Island, and was appointed, in 1883, administrator apostolic of Montana, becoming later bishop of Helena. Bishop Brondel is especially known for his labors among the Indians.

Brongniart, Adolphe Théophile, ä-dŏlf tä-ō-fēl brō-nyär, French botanist, son of Alexandre Brongniart: b. Paris, 14 Jan. 1801; d. there, 19 Feb. 1846. He first studied medicine, and received his diploma of doctor of medicine in 1826; but afterward turned his attention to the physiology of plants and antediluvian phytology. In 1834 he was elected a member of the Academy of Sciences, as successor to Desfontaines; and in 1839 professor of botany at the Museum of Natural History in Paris. His researches were various, and among his numerous works are 'Histoire des végétaux fossiles' (1828–47); 'Essai d'une classification naturelle des champignons' (1825); 'Mémoire sur la structure et les fonctions des fenilles' (1871).

Brongniart, Alexandre, ä-lĕks-ändr, naturalist and mineralogist: b. Paris, 5 Feb. 1770; d. there, 7 Oct. 1847. He turned his attention at a very early age to the study of the ceramic art; and after having served for some time in the army on the medical staff, was appointed, in 1800, director of the porcelain manufactory at Sèvres, where he revived the art of painting on glass. In 1807 appeared his 'Traité Elémentaire de Minéralogie'; and about the same time his labors in the department of natural history brought him into contact with Cuvier, whom he aided materially in classifying the newly discovered fossils of Montmartre. Along with Cuvier he engaged in the composition of the 'Essai sur la Géographie Minéralogique des Environs de Paris,' first published in 1811, and afterward in 1822, much enlarged, under the title of 'Description Géologique des Environs de Paris.' In 1844 appeared his 'Traité des Arts Céramiques.' He succeeded Haüy as professor of mineralogy in the Museum of Natural History in 1822.

Broni, brō'nē, a town of northern Italy, with mineral springs, 11 miles southeast of Pavia. Near by is the castle of Broni, where Prince Eugène obtained a victory over the French in 1703.

Bronn, Heinrich Georg, hīn-rīн gä-ōrн brŏn, German naturalist: b. Ziegelhausen, 1800; d. 1862. He was educated at the University of Heidelberg, where he was nominated professor in 1833, and appointed lecturer on zoology in succession to Leonhard. Among his various scientific works may be named 'A System of Antediluvian Zoöphytes' (1827); 'Lethæa Geognostica,' an important geological work (1837); 'History of Nature' (1841–9); and 'Universal Zoölogy' (1850).

Bronsart, Hans von, hänts fŏn brŏn-sär (properly SCHELLENDORFF, HANS VON BRONSART), German musician: b. Berlin, 1830. He studied in Berlin and Weimar, becoming a pupil of Liszt. After tours to European cities he directed concerts in Berlin. From 1867–87 he was intendant of the Royal Theatre in Hanover, and from 1887–95 filled a similar position in Weimar. His compositions for the piano are among the best known of his works. He wrote also the orchestral pieces, 'Christnacht' and 'Frühlingsphantasie.'

A PITCHING BRONCHO.

Bronte, brŏn'tā, Anne (Acton Bell). See BRONTE, CHARLOTTE, EMILY AND ANNE.

Bronte, Charlotte, Emily, and Anne, English novelists. Their father, Patrick Brontë (1777-1861), belonged to a family of Irish protestants named Prunty or Brunty. He was born in the village of Emdale, in County Down, Ireland. By schoolmastering he earned money enough to take him to the University of Cambridge, where he graduated B.A., at Saint John's College, in 1806. Ordained the same year to a curacy in Essex, he subsequently migrated to Yorkshire, and in 1811, obtained the living of Hartshead-cum-Clifton, to the cast of Halifax. There he met his future wife, Maria Branwell of Penzance, then on a visit to her friends in the north. They were married on 29 Dec., 1812. Both husband and wife, it is interesting to note, had a zest for writing. A little manuscript in Mrs. Brontë's hand is still extant; and Mr. Brontë published between 1811 and 1818 two volumes of meditative verse and two didactic stories, one of which follows the lines of Richardson's 'Pamela.' In 1815 Hartshead was exchanged for Thornton, another small parish near Bradford, in a bleak and lonely district. To this new home the Brontës brought with them two children, Maria and Elizabeth. At Thornton were born Charlotte (21 April 1816), Patrick Branwell (26 June 1817), Emily Jane (30 July 1818), and Anne (17 Jan. 1820).

A month after the birth of their last child, the Brontës moved to Haworth, near Keighley, a village that then consisted mainly of a street of gray stone houses running irregularly up a hillside by the church and the graves to the parsonage near the summit. As perpetual curate of the parish, the elder Brontë there passed his life; and there the children all grew up within sight of the broad and sweeping moors, wild and bleak in winter but grand and glorious in summer. Mrs. Brontë, a frail woman like her daughters, died in September, 1821, worn out by the birth and care of six children; and the next year, Miss Branwell, an unmarried sister, came to Haworth to manage the household with the aid of the faithful old servant "Tabby." After the death of his wife, Mr. Brontë, always eccentric and austere, grew morose; and Miss Branwell seems to have been rather prim and reserved. Wherefore the children were left much to themselves. In 1824 the daughters were placed in a school at Cowan Bridge, a hamlet on the road between Leeds and Kendal, where they remained for about a year to their great discomfort. Just after leaving school Maria and Elizabeth died of consumption, brought on, Charlotte thought, by bad food and brutal treatment.

Soon after this, Charlotte, Emily, and Branwell—for so they always called their brother—began to write "original compositions" in a curious microscopic hand, which they stitched into booklets and covered with brown paper. The specimens of Charlotte's stories, such as 'The Adventures of Ernest Alembert,' which have been printed as literary curiosities, show a facile pen and a remarkable command of vague and ornate phrases. She, and no doubt Emily and Branwell, had been reading Scott and the Gothic romances. In January, 1831,

Charlotte was sent to a school kept by Margaret Wooler at Roehead, between Leeds and Huddersfield. Though she remained there but a year, she formed a strong attachment for Miss Wooler and several of the girls, especially for Ellen Nussey, with whom she kept up a life-long correspondence. In 1835, she returned to Roehead as a teacher, in company with Emily as a pupil. After three months Emily became homesick and her place was taken by Anne. Charlotte stayed on with Anne till Christmas, when both returned to Haworth. Charlotte was completely worn out by the work for which she was ill adapted. During the next years Emily remained at home, while Anne and Charlotte went out as governesses. Charlotte had a hard time of it in her first position, but received better treatment on a second trial in 1841. In the meantime, she rejected two offers of marriage. With a view to setting up a school of their own, Charlotte and Emily went over to Brussels in 1842 to prepare themselves, especially in French and German, at the Pension Héger, a large school under the management of M. Paul Héger and his wife. They advanced rapidly in their studies, receiving high praise from their master. Called home within a year by the death of Miss Branwell, Emily remained with her father, but Charlotte returned for a year as teacher of English. Homesickness and anxiety for her father, whose eyesight was failing, brought Charlotte back to the parsonage. Brief as was the sojourn abroad, it was of the greatest value to the sisters. Without that experience, neither of them would likely have written novels that are still read.

In 1846, Charlotte, Emily, and Anne published jointly a volume of 'Poems' under the names of Currer, Ellis, and Acton Bell. The little volume was hardly noticed, though it contained Emily's fine stanzas on the 'Old Stoic.' At this time each of the sisters was getting ready a novel. After travelling from publisher to publisher, Emily's 'Wuthering Heights,' and Anne's 'Agnes Grey' were accepted, and published together in December, 1847, under the authors' pseudonyms, and "on terms somewhat impoverishing." Fifty pounds was advanced to Newby, the publisher, on account and never returned. Charlotte's 'Professor,' which became detached from the other two novels in the long journey, was everywhere rejected; but Smith and Elder intimated to her that they were willing to consider "a novel of a more striking and exciting character." 'Jane Eyre,' by Currer Bell, already completed, was at once accepted and published in October, 1847, two months before her sisters' novels came out. In January, 1848, it went into a second edition with a dedication to Thackeray. Charlotte Brontë at once took her place among the great novelists of the period.

The next year appeared Anne's second novel, the 'Tenant of Wildfell Hall.' By this time sorrow and death were settling over the Yorkshire parsonage. Branwell, who had started out in life with the intention of becoming a portrait painter, fell into evil ways and slowly degenerated through long years under the eyes of his sisters. After several attacks of delirium tremens, the end came in September, 1848. When he felt the approach of death, he rose to his feet and died standing in order to prove that as long as there is life there is strength of will to do as one chooses. Emily drooped and died on 19 December, refusing to see a physician till just before the end. Among the poems she left unpublished were the memorable 'Last Lines,' and several other stanzas which Matthew Arnold justly placed by the side of Byron's poems for vehemence, passion, and pain. Anne, long in declining health, was taken over to Scarborough where she died of consumption on 28 May 1849, within sight and sound of the sea she passionately loved. She lies buried in the Scarborough churchyard. Like Emily, she also left behind "last verses" in a noble but more subdued key. Charlotte lived on with her father in great loneliness, publishing 'Shirley' in 1849 and 'Villette' in 1853. She visited London several times, and on two occasions she met Thackeray, with whom she was greatly puzzled. To Mrs. Elizabeth Gaskell the novelist, who made her acquaintance among the lakes of Westmoreland in 1850, she seemed like one from whom suffering had taken "every spark of merriment" and "to be shy and silent from the habit of extreme, intense solitude." After a courtship of some years, broken off by her father, she married on 19 June 1854, the Rev. Arthur Bell Nicholls, who had served as curate at Haworth. Her married life, which promised much happiness, was brief. She passed a few months on her husband's estates in Ireland and then returned to Haworth to die on 31 March 1855. She was buried in the church by the side of Emily and Branwell. Two years after her death, the 'Professor,' nine times rejected, was published with a note by Mr. Nicholls. The fragment of a story called "Emma,' which had been begun in 1854, appeared in *Cornhill Magazine* for April 1860, along with Thackeray's beautiful tribute under the title of the 'Last Sketch.' Settling permanently in Ireland, Mr. Nicholls died there in 1906.

A glamour rests over these children of an Irish clergyman who had strayed to the Yorkshire moors. What Charlotte said of Emily and Anne may be said of herself also: "For strangers they were nothing; for superficial observers less than nothing; but for those who had known them all their lives * * * they were genuinely good and truly great." In them all, except perhaps Charlotte, lurked consumption; and they all died young. Two were endowed with unusual talents and two were geniuses. Much, no doubt, that has been reported of Branwell is legendary, but he certainly possessed the Brontë taste for art and letters. A beautiful reproduction of his portrait of Emily was engraved from a photograph for the Haworth edition of 'Wuthering Heights' (1900). At one time he aspired to win a name in literature. A letter of his to Wordsworth, inclosing a few stanzas of verse and asking for the poet's opinion of them, is as pathetic as remarkable in tone and style. "From the day of my birth," he said, "to this the nineteenth year of my life I have lived among secluded hills, where I could neither know what I was or what I could do. I read for the same reason that I ate or drank, because it was a real craving of nature. I wrote on the same principle as I spoke—out of the impulse and feelings of the mind; nor could I help it, for what came, came out, and there was the end of it."

That pressure of utterance which opium and alcohol brought to naught in this case, was characteristic of the sisters. They wrote because they could not help it. Anne possessed less of the Brontë fire. Fragile and gentle like her mother, she was "the prettiest * * * with light brown hair, violet eyes, and pencilled eyebrows." Without the outlook that came to Emily and Charlotte from their stay abroad, she moved in the narrowest circle of experience easily imaginable. Her novels, in consequence, suffer much by comparison. They are, however, storehouses of biographical incident relating to the family, and for themselves they are interesting, notwithstanding their crudeness, as transcripts of Yorkshire ways and manners at a time when the daughters of clergymen were forced to become governesses.

Emily's genius towered far above the rest. Of the poems the sisters published together, only hers cling to the memory. Under more favorable surroundings she should have become a poet ranking with Christina Rossetti and Mrs. Browning. One may pick flaws enough in 'Wuthering Heights.' It is ill put together and perhaps the author has not fully realized her aim. It is no doubt brutal where it was intended not to be. But it displays the same intense power of utterance as the poems. It is one of the great things in English fiction, not much like any romance before or since its time. Over it hangs the mystery of the moors and their solitary wanderer.

'Wuthering Heights,' however, has never gained the popularity of Charlotte's novels. To many it is nightmarish and repellent. It is not softened by the humanity of Charlotte who mingled more with the world. 'Jane Eyre' is based upon Charlotte's experiences as schoolgirl and governess. As a picture of the life of the times in the north, it came as a startling revelation. Its characters were drawn on hard and unconventional lines totally unlike the run of novels women were then writing. Against the author was brought the charge of coarseness and brutality, though no mind was ever cleaner than hers. The novel was really the wail of a human soul compelled to haunt the Yorkshire moors. 'Shirley' was quieter in tone; but it caused a stir in the north, for the characters were easily recognized portraits, among which was a superb study of Emily as Shirley Keeldar of quivering lip, dilating nostrils, and wild, fascinating eyes, when moved to passion or strange, Titanic visions. 'Villette,' which is the 'Professor' worked over, was founded on Charlotte's life in Brussels. Though it suffers somewhat from its foreign setting, it is perhaps her masterpiece. Lucy Snowe and Paul Emanuel are her most elaborate characters, and nowhere else has Charlotte Brontë so subtly analyzed states of mind verging into madness.

Bibliography.—'The Life of Charlotte Brontë' by Mrs. Elizabeth Gaskell (London 1857, afterwards revised and frequently reissued) is among the finest biographies in the English language. It should be supplemented, however,

From the drawing by Richmond

CHARLOTTE BRONTË

by C. K. Shorter, 'Charlotte Brontë and her Circle' (London 1896) and 'Charlotte Brontë and her Sisters' (New York 1905). Interesting but less valuable biographies of Charlotte Brontë have been written by T. W. Reid (London 1877), and A. Birrell (London 1887). Consult also 'Emily Brontë' by A. Mary F. Robinson in the 'Eminent Women Series' (Boston 1883); Swinburne's 'A Note on Charlotte Brontë' (London 1877); F. A. Leyland's 'The Brontë Family' (London 1886); Wright's 'The Brontës in Ireland' (New York 1893); and the 'Publications' of the Brontë Society. The 'Life and Works of the Sisters Brontë' with a preface by Mrs. Ward, and introduction and notes to Mrs. Gaskell's 'Life' by C. K. Shorter (7 vols. London and New York 1899-1900) is the best complete edition yet published. Charlotte Brontë's 'Adventures of Ernest Alembert' is included in Nicholl and Wise, 'Literary Anecdotes of the Nineteenth Century' (Vol. II. London 1896).

WILBUR L. CROSS,
Professor of English, Yale University.

Brontothe′rium, or Titanotherium, a genus of the extinct mammals first found in the Bad Lands of South Dakota, and later in Nebraska and Colorado. The formation is Miocene and the genus is but one of an extinct family of herbivorous mammals. It had the following features: The skull was long and depressed, with a large pair of horn cores, placed transversely on the maxillary bones, in front of the orbits; the nasal bones, which were greatly developed and firmly co-ossified, protruded over the narial orifice; the brain cavity was small and did not extend over the cerebral hemispheres or the cerebellum, and but little over the olfactory lobes; the neck was of medium length and stout; axis was large and extended transversely, being massive, with odontoid process stout and conical; lumbars were slender and not as large as the dorsals, and there were four sacral vertebræ; a long and slender tail, indicated by the caudals: limbs somewhat shorter than the elephant's; radius separated from the ulna; carpal bones short and supporting four toes; tibia separated from the fibula; three toes of almost equal size on the hind foot.

Bronze, an alloy consisting of proportions of copper and tin, varying according to the purpose desired, to which lead, zinc, and silver also, are sometimes added for the purpose of giving greater brilliancy to the compound, or rendering it more fusible, the zinc being introduced in the form of brass. In some of the modern bronzes, brass is used instead of tin; these are then nothing more than brass, consisting of very large proportions of copper. Bronze was used by the ancient Assyrians and Egyptians. Layard brought many ornaments and other articles of this metal from Assyria. It is more fusible, as well as harder than copper, and has also a fine-grained metal, taking a smooth and polished surface; hence its universal use, both in ancient and modern times, in making casts of all kinds, medals, bas-reliefs, statues, etc. Its color is a reddish-yellow, and is darkened by exposure to the atmosphere. It has been found, on examination, that the bronze weapons of the Greeks and Romans were of the best composition for securing the greatest density in the alloy, and

the cutting edges were brought to the highest point of tenacity by hammering. Gun-metal consists of about 90 parts of copper to 9 or 10 of tin. Old cannon are frequently used for casting statues, for which the proportions are similar. Bell-metal consists of 78 of copper and 22 of tin. For edge-tools — copper, 100 parts; tin, 14. For medals — copper, 89; tin, 8; zinc, 3, are used. For ornamental articles, zinc and lead are frequently added. These four metals are usually contained in the bronzes of France. There is some difficulty in making bronze, from the liability to the loss of tin, zinc, etc., by oxidization. A greenish color is imparted to ancient bronzes by oxidization, which is imitated in modern bronzes by chemical appliances. An alloy called phosphor-bronze, consisting of about 90 per cent of copper, 9 of tin, and from .5 to .75 of phosphorus has been found to have peculiar advantages for certain purposes. The addition of phosphorus increases the homogeneousness of the compound, and by varying the proportion of the constituents, the hardness, tenacity, and elasticity of the alloy may be modified at pleasure. Great hardness and tenacity with little elasticity can be conferred on it for the making of ordnance, and hardness and tenacity combined with permanent elasticity can be given to it for the making of parts of machines, etc. In the elastic condition it is peculiarly well adapted for the bearings of machinery, since it produces very little friction. The addition of phosphorus has another important effect. When the proportion exceeds .5 per cent it gives a warmer color to the bronze, making it resemble gold largely alloyed with copper. This form of the alloy is therefore largely used for works of art. The name of steel-bronze is given to bronze condensed and hardened artificially, as in the making of cannon the bore of which is enlarged by forcing in several strong steel cylinders of different sizes in succession. Aluminum-bronze is a gold-colored alloy of copper and aluminum, manganese-bronze, a bronze containing manganese and iron, possessing valuable properties. See BRONZES.

Bronze Age, the period represented by archæologists as intervening between the Stone Age and the Iron Age. The demarcations of these periods, however, are far from being clearly defined, and overlap to some extent. The use of stone for weapons, utensils, etc., naturally preceded the use of metals by primitive man, and the order in which the different metals would come into service would depend upon several factors. The nearness of the metallic deposits to the surface of the earth, the relative degree of purity in which they are usually found, and ease in smelting and working, would all affect the sequence of their introduction. The study of the traces of the Bronze Age in Europe apparently leads to the conclusion that throughout that continent the introduction of copper and its alloys was nearly synchronous, but the transition to the Iron Age took place more or less slowly in different regions, the new metal being introduced from the south and superseding bronze soonest where the paths of early commerce were most numerous or most frequently trodden. In Great Britain and Scandinavia the Bronze Age lingered much longer, according to certain archæologists, than in Italy, France, and Spain. In Greece, the use of bronze distinguishes the Mycenæan period, especially in its earlier days. In the New World, especially in Peru, the existence of the Bronze Age is indicated. The chronology of the three ages presents marked difficulties, and the periods should be regarded as stages of evolution in civilization still exemplified among races of slow development. The Bronze Age in Europe may be approximately placed between 2000 B.C. and 1800 B.C.

Bronze **Wing, Bronzewing Pigeon,** or Bronze **Pigeon,** any of several different species of the genus *Phaps,* found in Australia, Tasmania, and New South Wales. These are birds of beautiful plumage, obtaining their name from the lustrous bronze color with which the wings are variously marked. The most familiar species is the "common bronzewing" (*Phaps chalcoptera*), a plump, deliciously edible bird, weighing about a pound, and distributed throughout Australia. It nests on low branches on trees near swamps. The "brush bronzewing" (*P. elegans*) of southern Australia and Tasmania, is a groundkeeping bird and resembles a partridge in its habits. Another species is the "harlequin bronzewing" (*P. histrionica*), found in great flocks in the northwestern part of New South Wales. Sometimes the ground-pigeons of the genus *Geophaps* are called "bronzewings."

Bronzes, in archæology, works of art cast in bronze. Egyptian idols of bronze are contained in the British Museum. The most celebrated antique bronze statues are, the 'Sleeping Satyr'; the two youthful athletes; the colossal equestrian statue of Marcus Aurelius, at Rome; the Hercules of the capitol; the colossal head of Commodus; the statue of Septimius Severus in the Barberini Palace. Bas-reliefs, vaults, and doors of public edifices were ornamented with decorations of the same metal. Urban VIII. took from the Pantheon alone 450,000 pounds of bronze, which he used for the ornaments of St. Peter's, and for the cannon of the castle of St. Angelo. One of these was composed wholly of bronze nails taken from the portico, and bore the inscription, *Ex clavis trabalibus porticus Agrippæ.* Bronze was considered by the ancients as sacred to the gods; and the Roman emperors who struck gold and silver coins could not strike them of bronze without the permission of the Senate; hence the inscription S. C. (*Senatus consulto*). The words *moneta sacra* are found only on bronze medals. All the instruments of sacrifice and sacred vessels of the ancients were of bronze. (For the method of casting in bronze among the ancients, see Winckelmann's 'History of Art,' book ii.) The moderns have also made much use of bronze, particularly for statues exposed to accidents or the influence of the atmosphere, and for casts of celebrated antiques. The molds are made on the pattern, of plaster and brick-dust. The parts are then covered on the inside with a coating of clay as thick as the bronze is intended to be. The mold is now closed and filled on its inside with a nucleus or core of plaster and brick-dust, mixed with water. When this is done the mold is opened, and the clay carefully removed. The mould, with its core, is then thoroughly dried, and the core secured in its position by bars of bronze, which pass into

it through the external part of the mold. The whole is then bound with iron hoops, and the melted bronze being poured in through an aperture left for the purpose fills the cavity previously occupied by the clay, and forms a metallic covering to the core. It is afterward made smooth by mechanical means.

Bronzing. Bronze of a good quality acquires by oxidization a fine green tint, called *patina antiqua*, or, by the Romans, *ærugo*. Sal-ammoniac and salt of sorrel dissolved in vinegar, and applied with a soft rag or brush, will produce this result. The process must be repeated several times to have its full effect. The proportions given by Dr. Ure are three fourths of an ounce of sal-ammoniac and a drachm and a half of salt of sorrel to a quart of vinegar. Bronzing is also the process by which a body of plaster, wood, or metal is made to receive a bronze-like surface. Brass castings are bronzed by the application, after cleaning and brightening them, of vinegar and sal-ammoniac. A variety of liquid solutions are prepared for bronzing copper and other metals, in which verdigris, sal-ammoniac, salt of sorrel, cinnabar, alum, and common salt are employed. To bronze wood and other articles, waste gold-leaf, ground in with honey and washed, or mosaic gold ground with bone ashes, is applied, with size or oil varnish. Gypsum casts are bronzed with black-lead.

Bronzino, Agnolo, or **Angilo,** än'yō-lō, or än'jē-lō brōn-zē'nō, Italian painter of the Florentine school: b. Monticelli, near Florence, 1502; d. 1572. He was a pupil of Jacopo da Pontormo, and an admirer and imitator of Michael Angelo. One of his best paintings is a Christ in the church of Santa Croce, at Florence.

Brooch, an ornament worn on the dress, to which it is attached by a pin stuck through the fabric. Brooches are of great antiquity, and were formerly worn by men as well as women. They were used by both sexes among the Greeks and Romans, and also in the Middle Ages. Among the Highlanders of Scotland there are preserved, in several families, ancient brooches of rich workmanship and highly ornamented. Some of them are inscribed with characters to which particular virtues were attributed, and seem to have been used as a sort of amulet or talisman.

Brook Farm, a community organized in 1841 near West Roxbury, Mass. Under the leadership of George Ripley and his wife an association was formed with a few stockholders; and a farm of 200 acres was purchased. Among the members of this association were Nathaniel Hawthorne, Charles A. Dana, John S. Dwight, and George P. Bradford; other prominent people connected with Brook Farm were Ralph W. Emerson, Amos B. Alcott, Theodore Parker, George W. Curtis, and Margaret Fuller. The ideal of the association was to promote the re-organization of society in accordance with the principles of co-operation. The life of the community was very simple; every one had some share of the work to do, the rate of pay being practically the same for all kinds of work; and all had a share in the educational advantages and the social enjoyments. There were a number of industrial employments besides the tilling of the farm, and the surplus product was

sold to outsiders. The school was also an important feature, furnishing instruction in all grades, including college subjects; pupils outside the community were received on the payment of a small fee. In 1843 the association, coming under the influence of Albert Brisbane, adopted the organization of the phalanx according to the plan of Fourier, and established the three "primary departments" of agriculture, domestic industry, and mechanic arts; it became also a centre of the Fourierist propaganda. After this change the prosperity of Brook Farm declined rapidly; on 3 March 1846 the new building, the Phalanstery, was burned, and the association finally dissolved in October 1847.

Bibliography.— Codman, 'Brook Farm, Historic and Personal Memoirs'; Frothingham, 'Life of George Ripley'; Noyes, 'History of American Socialisms'; Swift, Lindsay, 'Brook Farm, Its Members, Scholars, and Visitors.'

Brooke, Francis Key, American Protestant Episcopal bishop: b. Gambier, Ohio, 2 Nov. 1852. He was graduated from Kenyon College in his native town in 1874, and entering the Episcopal ministry was successively rector in the Ohio towns of College Hill, Portsmouth, Piqua, and Sandusky; and in St. Louis, Mo.; and Atchison, Kan. In 1893 he was consecrated bishop of Oklahoma and Indian Territory.

Brooke, Henry, Irish dramatist and novelist: b. Rantavan, Ireland, about 1703; d. Burrator, Devonshire, 10 Oct. 1783. He was educated at Dublin University, and began to practice at the bar; but his taste was decided for poetry and general literature, and he came forward as an author by publishing a tragedy called 'Gustavus Vasa,' which was remarkably popular at the time, and was translated into French, though it is now almost forgotten. He wrote several other tragedies, and also several novels, one of which, the 'Fool of Quality,' possesses considerable merit, and was re-published with a preface by Rev. Charles Kingsley. The death of his wife, and the loss of a favorite child, completely broke his spirit, and he lived for a short time in a state of second childhood.

Brooke, Sir James, English rajah, celebrated as the Rajah of Sarawak: b. Bengal, 1803; d. Burrator, Devonshire, 11 June 1868. He was brought at an early age to England, and having completed his education there obtained a cadetship in the Indian army. He distinguished himself in the Burmese war (1826), and subsequently sailed to China. On this voyage there rose in his mind the idea of ridding the Eastern Archipelago from the scourge of piracy, and ameliorating the condition of the inhabitants. Having come into the possession of a large fortune by the death of his father, he bought one of the royal yachts, and set sail for the East (October 1838). Having directed his course to the island of Borneo, he found Muda Hassim, uncle of the king of Borneo, and Rajah of Sarawak, a district on the northwest coast of the island, engaged in suppressing a revolt. The rajah being hard pressed, agreed to make him his successor in return for his assistance. The offer was accepted. Brooke took command of the rajah's army, and speedily reduced the rebels to submission. Being now established in the government, and recognized as Rajah of Sarawak by the sultan of Borneo (1841), he endeavored to induce the Dyak na-

tives to abandon their irregular and piratical mode of life, and to turn themselves to agriculture and commerce. For this end he published a code of laws, establishing free trade and personal equality, and declaring piracy a crime punishable with death. His efforts were wonderfully successful. In conjunction with the British naval commanders he carried on war against the pirates with great vigor. A sum of money was paid by government for the head of each pirate, and under this system the Malay rovers were soon almost extirpated. On his return in 1847, Mr. Brooke was received with general favor, his position was recognized by the government, he received the honor of Knight Commander of the Bath, and was made governor of Labuan, an island near Sarawak which had been acquired by the British. After his return to Borneo he continued to labor as before for the extension of British influence. In 1850 he went as ambassador to Siam, and not long after gave up his post as governor of Labuan. On the outbreak of the war with China in 1857, his residence was suddenly attacked by about 4,000 Chinese, and he himself only escaped by swimming across the river. His adherents soon rallied, however, and at the head of a large body of Malays and Dyaks he drove the Chinese from Sarawak with the loss of half their number. In 1863 he finally returned to England, leaving the government in the hands of his nephew, Charles Brooke. Whatever may be thought of the policy of Sir James Brooke, there can be no doubt as to the benefits derived from it by the people of Sarawak. He established civilization and opened up a trade where previously they had scarcely any existence. Under his administration Sarawak increased from a village of 1,000 inhabitants to a town of 16,000, while the trade increased in the same proportion.

Brooke, John Rutter, American military officer: b. Pottsville, Pa., 21 July 1838. He entered the army as captain in a volunteer regiment on the breaking out of the Civil War in 1861, and resigned in February 1866, with the rank of brevet major-general. He became colonel in March 1879; brigadier-general, 6 April 1888, and major-general, 22 May 1897. After the declaration of war against Spain, he was placed in command of the 1st Provisional Army Corps, and subsequently distinguished himself in the campaign in Porto Rico, and was made a member of the joint military commission to arrange the cession of the island to the United States. On 13 Dec. 1898, he was appointed military and civil governor of Cuba, a post which he held till April 1900, when he was succeeded by Gen. Leonard Wood. On 10 May following, he succeeded Maj.-Gen. Wesley Merritt as commander of the Military Department of the East, with headquarters in New York.

Brooke, Stopford Augustus, English clergyman and author: b. Letterkenny, Donegal, Ireland, 14 Nov. 1832. After a brilliant course at Trinity College, Dublin, he was ordained in the Anglican Church in 1857. From that year till 1859 he officiated as curate of St. Matthew's, Marylebone (London); and in 1876, after having held various other clerical appointments, he became minister of Bedford Chapel, Bloomsbury, where he officiated till his retirement from regular ministerial work in 1894. In 1872 he was appointed one of the chaplains-in-ordinary to the queen. Having become a Unitarian in his views, he left the Church of England in 1880, but till 1894 still continued to occupy the same pulpit, Bedford Chapel being private property. He has gained a high reputation as a preacher and writer on religious subjects, and also as a poet, but more especially as a literary critic and historian of English literature. His chief works are 'Life and Letters of the Late Frederick W. Robertson of Brighton' (1865); 'Christ in Modern Life' (1872); 'Theology in the English Poets' (1874); 'Primer of English Literature' (1876), an admirable little work; 'Riquet of the Tuft' (1880), a love drama; 'The Early Life of Jesus' (1888); 'Poems' (1888); 'History of Early English Literature: from Its Beginning to the Accession of Alfred' (1892), the only work in English treating adequately its special subject; 'Tennyson: His Art and Relations to Modern Life' (1894); 'The English Poets from Blake to Tennyson' (1894); 'Jesus and Modern Thought' (1894); 'The Old Testament and Modern Life' (1896); 'The Gospel of Joy' (1898); besides several volumes of sermons. His son, Stopford Wentworth Brooke, was pastor of the First (Unitarian) Church in Boston, Mass, 1886-98.

Brookhaven, Miss., a city and county-seat of Lincoln County; on the Illinois C. R.R.; 56 miles south of Jackson, the State capital. It is the seat of Whitworth Female College (Methodist), one of the most popular educational institutions in the South, and St. Francis School (Roman Catholic), and is the trade centre for a large farming, cotton, and yellow pine lumbering region. An electric light and power plant is owned by the city. Pop. (1904) 4,000.

Brookings, S. D., a city and county-seat of Brookings County; on the Chicago & N. R.R.; 60 miles north of Sioux Falls. It is chiefly a dairying place; has electric lights, waterworks, and several mills; and is the seat of the South Dakota Agricultural College and of the United States Experiment Station. Pop. (1900) 2,346.

Brook'ite, a mineral only known in the form of orthorhombic crystals. It is an oxide of titanium, having the formula TiO_2. It is found in a variety of colors, red, yellow, black, and brown. It has a hardness of 5.5 to 6.0, and a specific gravity of 3.9 or 4.0. It occurs in Switzerland, in the Tyrol, and in Wales. In the United States it is found (in stout black crystals known as "arkansite") at Magnet Cove, Ark.; also at Paris, Maine, in Ulster County, N. Y., and in North Carolina. The mineral was named for the English mineralogist, H. J. Brooke.

Brooklime (Veronica Beccabunga, and V. americana), two species of speedwell, perennial plants of the natural order Scrophulariaceæ common in ditches and wet places in Europe and America respectively, and attractive for their axillary racemes of bluish flowers, for which they are grown in damp places for ornamental purposes.

Brookline, Mass., a town in Norfolk County, on the Charles River, and the Boston & A. R.R.; three miles west of Boston, with which it is connected by electric railroad. It contains the villages of Cottage Farm, Longwood, and Reservoir Station; has a granite town house,

public library (64,000 volumes), and manufactories of electric motors, and philosophical instruments, but is chiefly a place of suburban residence, being the most beautiful and wealthy suburban town in the country. It was first settled in 1634, and was known as "the hamlet of Muddy River" until its incorporation as Brookline in 1705. Consult Bolton. 'Brooklyn: the History of a Favored Town' (1897). Pop. (1904) 23,500.

Brooklyn, N. Y., the second largest of the five boroughs of New York city. It includes the entire area of the county of Kings and was, until 1898, when it was consolidated with New York, the fourth largest city in point of population in the United States. It covers the western extremity of Long Island, is situated in lat. 40° 41' 50" N., lon. 73° 59' 50" W., and has an area of 77.52 square miles, extending from the East River, an arm of the sea which separates it from the borough of Manhattan, the old city of New York, to the Atlantic Ocean and to Newtown Creek and Queens County on the east. Its extreme length from Newtown Creek to Brighton Beach, on the Atlantic shore, is 11 miles, and its average width is over 7 miles. It appears to have been formed by nature to be the site of a great city, for so many natural advantages are rarely to be found within a similar area fo the building up of a great industrial and commercial community. The island of Manhattan is the centre of the business activity of the American metropolis, and it may retain that primacy for all time, but its restricted area limits its capacity and forbids its expansion. The tendency has been for some years to expand skyward and to utilize to the utmost the ground area of the island by the erection of lofty buildings, many of them exceeding 20 stories in height, but there is a limit to expansion in this direction, and there seems no possibility of adding to the amount of Manhattan waterfront available for purposes of commerce, while the high price of land caused by the imperious demands of trade compels those engaged in business in Manhattan to seek their homes elsewhere. Brooklyn has profited during the greater part of its history from this compulsion, and its population has increased at a constantly accelerated ratio as the demands of business have made property more valuable in the older portion of the city. Since 1860 Brooklyn has advanced in population more rapidly than any other American city, although the period of its most rapid growth dates from the opening of the first bridge across the East River in 1883. Brooklyn's large territorial area, much of which is still devoted to market gardening, must, for many years to come, keep the cost of a home within the resources of people of moderate means, especially as regards the outlying sections, which are thoroughly covered by electric railways. The character of the soil and the freedom from any rocky hills makes nearly every foot of ground admirably suited to building purposes. The greater part of the borough is situated at a considerable elevation above tide-water. A low range of sand-hills, from 50 to 200 feet high, runs north and east through its centre, which slopes gently down on both sides to the East River and the Atlantic Ocean.

The natural configuration of the site simplifies drainage and other similar municipal problems to a material extent, while the loca-

WATER TOWER AND ENTRANCE TO PROSPECT PARK.   MEMORIAL ARCH, PLAZA ENTRANCE TO PROSPECT PARK.

tion of the borough, between ocean, river, and bay, mitigates the extremes of winter cold and summer heat, and makes it a desirable place of residence throughout the year.

Its advantages as a centre of commerce and industry are no less than those which made it famous as a city of homes before its consolidation with the metropolis. Its water-front available for shipping comprises two miles on Newtown Creek, including its basins, and nearly 10 miles on the East River and New York Bay. The construction of large docks, such as those of the Atlantic and Erie basins — the latter being the chief point of entry of the canal barges that bring great cargoes of grain from the distributing centre at Buffalo to the Brooklyn grain-elevators — have largely increased the wharfage facilities of the borough.

Most large cities grow by the absorption of outlying suburbs and adjacent villages, and in this respect the experience of Brooklyn has been striking. The name of Brooklyn, which was derived from the town of Breucklen, in Holland, the home from which came most of the earliest settlers, was first attached to a small trading-village that grew up on the shores of the East River near what is now the Fulton ferry to Manhattan. There were several other villages in the county which for a long time retained their individuality and developed along their own lines. Across the Wallabout swamp, to the eastward — "Wallabout" being derived from a settlement of Walloons — a village was laid out in 1827 which was incorporated under the name of Williamsburg and in 1851 became incorporated as a city. Then Williamsburg swallowed up the older and adjacent villages of Bushwick and Greenpoint, just as Brooklyn had already swallowed up Bedford and Gowanus. In 1854 Brooklyn and Williamsburg were consolidated. The town of New Lots, including the village of East New York, came next, and the work of absorption, as far as Brooklyn was concerned, was completed in 1894, when the towns of Flatbush, New Utrecht, Gravesend, and Flatlands were made part of the city, the corporate limits of which then included all of Kings County. It was a natural process, but usually, when a large city is surrounded by suburbs that are destined to absorption, the lines of development of the suburbs are indicated and set in accordance with their inevitable destiny, and annexation entails no confusion. It was different with Brooklyn. Williamsburg, Flatbush, Canarsie, Bushwick, and East New York — more than 20 villages and hamlets all told, that are now a part of the borough of Brooklyn — had each its own plan and its own system of nomenclature. The result has been hopeless and to a large extent irremediable confusion. Duplication of street names may be corrected by the substitution of new names for the old, and much has already been done in that direction, but the confusion resulting from the multiplicity of independent plans on which the various parts of the borough were originally laid out have never been wholly corrected, and Brooklyn will continue to be a puzzle to strangers and even to old residents.

It is as a city of homes — of middle-class homes — that Brooklyn has gained its distinctive character among American cities. The
Vol. 3—12.

very wealthy can afford to live in Manhattan, and the very poor have no alternative but to crowd into its hive-like tenements, but it may he said that, as a rule, the palace and the tenement — using the latter word in its ordinary, not its technical sense — are alike unknown in Brooklyn. No place of like population is freer from those congregations and nurseries of crime and disease known as "slums," and in no city is a larger proportion of the population housed under decent and sanitary conditions. It is for this reason, and because the growth of Brooklyn has kept pace in other respects with its growth in numbers, that the population increased from 279,122 in 1860 to 599,495 in 1880; 1,166,582 in 1900, and 1,291,597 in 1903.

The earliest settlement of the Dutch in Kings County was made in 1619, but it was not until more than a century later that Brooklyn had any organized existence. It was the scene of Washington's first battle and defeat during the American Revolution. That battle was fought only about six weeks after the American Congress in Philadelphia had adopted the Declaration of Independence. Washington's army, as yet raw and totally unused to warfare, was massed among Brooklyn's hills, while Gen. Howe, with 30,000 seasoned fighting men, occupied Staten Island. The British crossed to Long Island, landing on the plains of New Utrecht, and on the morning of 27 Aug. 1776, a general advance was made on the American lines. The attack was made at three points. One division advanced through the marshes of Gowanus, and, despite a gallant resistance, drove back the Maryland regiment to the main body of American troops. A second point of attack was through what is now known as Battle Pass, in Prospect Park, where the Americans were forced back on the entrenched position at Fort Green, but the heaviest blow was struck through the advance of a strong flanking party. It had early that morning passed along the northern base of the ridge of hills in what is now the Twenty-fourth ward, stopping at the Howard House, a tavern in East New York, and impressing its owner as a guide. It then advanced upon Washington's forces from the east. A misty night fell, with no general engagement, and by morning Washington had withdrawn his troops, under cover of fog, across the East River. The British retained possession of Brooklyn until the evacuation of New York at the close of the war. Brooklyn's most memorable association with Revolutionary history, however, lies in the fact that the British prison ships — the Jersey and its consorts — were moored in Wallabout Bay, and the bones of 11,000 victims of British severity who died in those floating slaughter-pens are buried at Fort Green, where a worthy monument to their patriotic devotion is soon to be erected.

Brooklyn was incorporated as a village in 1801, and at about that time the federal government made its first purchase of land at the Wallabout for navy-yard purposes. The Brooklyn navy yard is now the best equipped in the possession of the U. S. government. It covers an area of over 100 acres, with a capacious drydock, and a mechanical plant capable of shipbuilding on the most extensive scale. Some of the finest ships in the United States navy have been constructed here, and its great repair shops are kept constantly at work. A splendidly equipped naval hospital occupies a fine site in connection with the yard.

Brooklyn village was incorporated as a city in 1834, with George Hall as its first mayor. In 1854 came consolidation with Williamsburg, and thereafter the growth of the city was steady and rapid. Street railway enterprises opened highways through outlying farm districts, and these speedily became transformed into great thoroughfares, and Brooklyn has now 713 miles of streets, of which the principal ones are paved with asphalt.

The surface and elevated railroad lines, all operated by electricity, have ·549.7 miles of tracks, and in 1902 carried 324,898,322 passengers. The growth of Brooklyn, so largely accelerated by the bridge opened in 1883, seems likely to be further stimulated by the early completion of the two additional bridges now in course of construction. The tunneling of the East River, under direction of the New York Rapid Transit Commission, will also tend materially toward Brooklyn's further growth.

It has been generally assumed that Brooklyn is merely "the sleeping-place of Manhattan." It is undoubtedly true that many thousands of those who are engaged in business in Manhattan find their homes in Brooklyn,— the number has been estimated at between 65,000 and 100,000; but the fact remains that Brooklyn itself is one of the greatest manufacturing centres of the United States. In many important branches of industry it leads all its competitors. Its most important industry, at the time of the last census, was foundry and machine-shop produets, in which there was $13,725,518 invested, and wages to the amount of $5,641,132 were paid to 7,753 workmen. Brooklyn's sugar-refining industry is by far the most important in the United States, nine tenths of the sugar consumed in the country being refined here. In this and · in the closely allied coffee-roasting industry, the amount of capital invested is nearly $20,000,000, the annual value of the finished product being, sugar, $16,629,982; coffee, $12,247,162. The manufacture of chemicals is another industry in which much capital is invested, and in which 2,984 people find employment. Some of the leading publishers of the United States have located their printing and bookbinding establishments in Brooklyn. It is also the seat of jute manufacture, glass and porcelain factories cordage works, and other important industries.

Brooklyn's public-school system, up to the date of consolidation with New York, held a high place in the esteem of public educators. In 1897 it was merged in the public-school system of the greater city, but it still possesses many of the characteristics that formerly distinguished it, and few if any cities in the world have a better equipped galaxy of public schools. It has six high schools, of which one is devoted to manual and technical instruction, while another is wholly given over to commercial instruction. Its 133 grammar schools are crowded almost beyond their capacity every day in the school year. Many of the schools in the poorer neighborhoods are kept open during the summer months as recreation schools for the benefit of children who remain in the borough during the ordinary school vacation, and who

are taught many things outside of the ordinary school curriculum.

Brooklyn has no university, but it has many excellent private schools and academies, some of which, such as the Polytechnic Institute, Adelphi Academy, and St. John's College, hold collegiate rank and may grant degrees. The parochial schools also hold high rank, while the Pratt Institute affords thorough technical training to hundreds of pupils.

The Brooklyn Public Library, with which the excellent Brooklyn Library has recently been incorporated, maintains an extensive system of branch libraries throughout the borough; and when this is supplemented by the system of libraries recently presented by Mr. Andrew Carnegie, no community in the United States will be better equipped in this direction.

One of the most notable of the educational institutions in Brooklyn is the Brooklyn Institute of Arts and Sciences. This valuable and practically unendowed institution is, as regards its present buildings, situated upon high ground adjacent to Prospect Park, on what is known as the East Side Park lands, of which 11$\frac{7}{10}$ acres have been leased to the trustees for 100 years. It is the development of a school of arts and sciences founded during the middle of the 19th century by Augustus Graham, a philanthropist of English extraction. It has expanded under the direction of Prof. Franklin W. Hooper and a public-spirited board of trustees into what is likely to prove the nucleus of a great national academy. It already has a well-furnished museum, which is especially rich in prehistoric American relics, and departments of archæology, architecture, astronomy, botany, chemistry, domestic science, electricity, engineering, entomology, geography, geology, law, mathematics, microscopy, mineralogy, music, painting, pedagogy, philology, philosophy, photography, physics, political science, and psychology, each of which is presided over by an expert in the science. Only the first section of the museum building has as yet been erected, but when completed the entire structure will cover a large area, with four interior courts to provide light for the central portions of the building. It will contain on the first floor rooms for collections illustrating the general history of the arts and architecture; on the second floor rooms for the illustration of the practical arts and sciences; and on the third floor galleries for the illustration of the history of painting, engraving, etching, and decorative art. It is expected that before long the splendid library of the Long Island Historical Society will find accommodations within the museum building.

Brooklyn's public park system has been developed on a scale altogether commensurate with the character of the borough, and full advantage has been taken of the cheapness of land to make provision for the needs of the future in the matter of breathing places and pleasure grounds. The oldest and best known, although not the largest of these, is Prospect Park, which includes 516 acres of rolling land, with picturesque lakes and an unrivaled growth of old forest trees. Prospect Park is beautifully laid out, special care having been taken during the 40 years of its existence as a park to preserve its natural characteristics. Its statuary includes figures of J. S. T. Stranahan, one of the pioneers in the matter of providing public parks; John Howard Payne, Thomas Moore, Washington Irving, Beethoven, and Mozart. There is also, at the foot of Lookout Hill, a memorial shaft in honor of the Maryland soldiers who fell in the battle of Long Island.

Another notable pleasure ground is Brooklyn Forest, which includes 536 acres on the crown of the ridge of hills on the Queens County border. Except for the laying out of walks and paths it has been left in its natural state. It affords splendid views of the Atlantic Ocean and Jamaica Bay, Sunset Park, a reserve of 14 acres on the shores of New York Bay, and the Coney Island Concourse, which runs along the Atlantic shore and contains 70 acres, are unique in their location. In addition there are nearly 40 small parks and recreation grounds in the borough. The system of parkways and boulevards under the care of the park department covers 42 miles of well-paved roadways, to which additions are constantly being made.

W. C. BRYANT,
Editor Brooklyn Times.

Brooks, Charles William Shirley, English journalist, editor of 'Punch': b. London, 29 April 1816; d. there, 23 Feb. 1874. He settled in London, wrote dramas, contributed to the leading periodicals and journals, and for five sessions wrote the 'Parliamentary Summary' for the *Morning Chronicle.* By its proprietors he was sent, in 1853, on a mission to report on the condition of labor and the poor in Russia, Syria, and Egypt, and a result of his observations appeared in 'The Russians of the South' (1856). He wrote political articles, attracted attention by several dramas and burlesques, and in 1854 joined the staff of the London 'Punch.' In 1870 he succeeded Mark Lemon as its editor. His novels, which include 'Aspen Court' (1855); 'The Gordian Knot' (1860); 'The Silver Cord' (1861); 'Sooner or Later,' with illustrations by Du Maurier (1866-8); 'The Naggeltons' (1875), show keen observation. He also wrote 'Amusing Poetry' (1857). His son, REGINALD SHIRLEY, collected Brook's 'Wit and Humor from Punch' (1875).

Brooks, Elbridge Gerry, American Universalist clergyman: b. Dover, N. H., 29 July 1816; d. Philadelphia, Pa., 8 April 1878. His first pastorate was at West Amesbury, Mass., in 1837, and he was subsequently in charge of churches at East Cambridge, Mass., Lowell, Mass., Lynn, Mass., New York, and Philadelphia.

Brooks, Elbridge Streeter, American author, son of Elbridge Gerry Brooks (q.v.): b. Lowell, Mass., 14 April 1846; d. Somerville, Mass., 7 Jan. 1902. He was the author of more than 40 books for young people, intended to familiarize them with American history, among which are 'Historic Boys'; 'Chivalric Days'; 'The Story of the American Indian'; 'The Story of New York'; 'Heroic Happenings' (1893); The True Story of George Washington' (1895); 'The Century Book of Famous Americans' (1896); 'Stories of the Old Bay State' (1899); 'A Godson of Lafayette' (1900); 'Under the Allied Flags' (1901). He edited the 'Wide Awake Magazine' for several years, and was the literary adviser of the Boston publishing house of D. Lathrop Company from 1895 until his death.

Brooks, James Gordon, American poet: b. Claverack, N. Y., 3 Sept. 1801; d. Albany, 20 Feb. 1841. He studied law, and removed in 1823 to New York, where he became editor of the 'Minerva,' a literary journal, and afterward of the 'Literary Gazette,' the 'Athenæum,' and the *Morning Courier,* continuing in all these papers the publication of his verses. In 1828 he married Mary Elizabeth Aikin, who had written under the signature of Norma, and the next year appeared the 'Rivals of Este, and Other Poems, by James G. and Mary E. Brooks.'

Brooks, John, American soldier, and governor of Massachusetts: b. Medford, 1752; d. 1 March 1825. While pursuing the study of medicine he displayed a love for military exercises, and having settled as a medical practitioner at Reading undertook the drilling of a company of minute men, with whom, on the news of the expedition to Lexington, he marched in time to see the retreat of the British. Promoted soon after to the rank of major in the Continental service, he assisted in throwing up the fortifications on Breed's Hill, and was especially serviceable to the army as a tactician. He was made lieutenant-colonel in 1777, and in the battle of Saratoga stormed the intrenchments of the German troops. He was a faithful adherent of the commander-in-chief during the conspiracy at Newburg. Washington requesting him to keep his officers within quarters, that they might not attend the insurgent meeting, his reply was: "Sir, I have anticipated your wishes, and my orders are given." Washington took him by the hand, and said: "Col. Brooks, this is just what I expected from you." After the peace he resumed the practice of the medical profession in Medford, and was for many years major-general of the militia of his county. In the War of 1812 he was adjutant-general of Massachusetts, and in 1816 was elected governor of that State, an office to which he was re-elected annually till 1823, when he declined being again a candidate.

Brooks, John Graham, American lecturer on economics: b. Acworth, N. H., 19 July 1846. He was graduated from the Harvard Divinity School in 1875, and subsequently studied in the universities of Berlin, Jena, and Freiburg. He was for a time in the work of the Unitarian ministry, and was for several years a lecturer in the extension department of the University of Chicago. For two years he served as an expert in the department of labor at Washington, making a report in 1893 upon workingmen's insurance in Germany. He has published 'Charity and the Unemployed'; 'The Pope and the Encyclical on Labor'; 'The Social Unrest' (1903).

Brooks, Maria Gowan, (MARIA DEL OCCIDENTE). American poet: b. Medford, Mass., about 1795; d. Matanzas, Cuba, 11 Nov. 1845. She spent her youth in Charlestown, Mass., and the rest of her life in London, New York, and Cuba. Her chief poem is 'Zophiel, or the Bride of Seven,' the first canto of which appeared in Boston in 1825, and the rest was finished under Southey's supervision in 1833. 'Idomen, or the Vale of Yumuri,' is an autobiography (1843).

Brooks, Noah, American journalist and author: b. Castine, Maine, 30 Oct. 1830; d. Los Angeles, Cal., 16 Aug. 1903. From 1850 he was connected with newspapers in Massachusetts, California, Washington, and New York.

He published many popular books for boys, among which are 'The Fairport Nine' (1880); 'Our Baseball Club' (1884); 'How the Republic is Governed'; 'American Statesmen' (1893); 'Short Stories in American Party Politics' (1896); 'The Boys of Fairport'; 'The Mediterranean Trip.'

· Brooks, **Peter Chardon,** American merchant: b. Medford, Mass., 6 Jan. 1767; d. Boston, 1 Jan. 1849. He began his business career as secretary in a marine insurance office in Boston, and presently became its principal. He rapidly acquired a fortune, retiring in 1803, and for the remainder of his life took an active interest in municipal and philanthropic affairs. He was the president of several benevolent associations, a member of the first city council of Boston, and sat in both houses of the State legislature. He was one of the most prominent opponents of the lottery schemes then countenanced by many respectable persons. One of his daughters married Rev. H. L. Frothingham (q.v.), and several prominent Boston families of to-day claim him as an ancestor. See Everett, 'Life of Peter C. Brooks.'

Brooks, **Phillips,** American Protestant Episcopal bishop: b. Boston, Mass., 13 Dec. 1835; d. there, 23 Jan. 1893. He inherited the best traditions of New England history, being on the paternal side the direct descendant of John Cotton, and his mother's name, Phillips, standing for high learning and distinction in the Congregational Church. Born at a time when the orthodox faith was fighting its bitterest battle with Unitarianism, his parents accepted the dogmas of the new theology, and had him baptized by a Unitarian clergyman. But while refusing certain dogmas of the orthodox Church they were the more thrown back for spiritual support upon the internal evidences of evangelical Christianity. Transition to the Episcopal Church was easy; the mother became an Episcopalian, and the future bishop received all his early training in that communion. But heredity had its influence, and in after life he declared that the Episcopal Church could reap the fruits of the long and bitter controversy which divided the New England Church only as it discerned the spiritual worth of Puritanism, and the value of its contributions to the history of religious thought and character. Such were the early surroundings of the man, and the subsequent influences of his life tended to foster this liberal spirit. When he entered Harvard, he came into an atmosphere of intense intellectual activity. James Walker was the president of the college, and Lowell, Holmes, Agassiz, and Longfellow were among the professors. He graduated with honor in 1855, and soon after entered the Episcopal Theological Seminary at Alexandria, Va. The transition from Harvard to this college was an abrupt one. The standards of the North and South were radically different. The theology of the Church in Virginia, while tolerant to that of other denominations, was uncompromisingly hostile to what it regarded as heterodox.

When the Civil War was declared he threw himself passionately into the cause of the Union. Yet his affection for his Southern classmates, men from whom he so widely differed, broadened that charity that was one of his finest characteristics, a charity that respected conviction wher-

ever found. No man, in truth, ever did so much to remove prejudice against a Church that had never been popular in New England. To the old Puritan dislike of Episcopacy and distrust of the English Church as that of the oppressors of the colony, was added a sense of resentment toward its sacerdotal claims and its assumption of ecclesiastical supremacy. But he nevertheless protested against the claim by his own communion to the title of «The American Church,» he preached occasionally in other pulpits, he even had among his audiences clergymen of other denominations, and he was able to reconcile men of different creeds into concord on what is essential in all. The breadth and depth of his teaching attracted so large a following that he increased the strength of the Episcopal Church in America far more than he could have done by carrying on an active propaganda in its behalf. His first charge was the Church of the Advent, in Philadelphia; in two years he became rector of Holy Trinity Church in the same city. In 1869 he was called to Trinity Church, Boston, of which he was rector until his election as bishop of Massachusetts in 1891.

It is impossible to give an idea of Phillips Brooks without a word about his personality, which was almost contradictory. His commanding figure, his wit, the charm of his conversation, and a certain boyish gayety and naturalness, drew people to him as to a powerful magnet. He was one of the best-known men in America; people pointed him out to strangers in his own city as they pointed out the Common and the Bunker Hill monument. When he went to England, where he preached before the queen, men and women of all classes greeted him as a friend. They thronged the churches where he preached, not only to hear him but to see him. It was said of him that as soon as he entered a pulpit he was absolutely impersonal. There was no trace of individual experience or theological conflict by which he might be labeled. He was simply a messenger of the truth as he held it, a mouthpiece of the Gospel as he believed it had been delivered to him. Although in his seminary days his sermons were described as vague and unpractical, he was as great a preacher when under 30 years of age as at any later time. His early sermons, delivered to his first charge in Philadelphia, displayed the same individuality, the same force and completeness and clearness of construction, the same deep, strong undertone of religious thought, as his great discourses preached in Westminster Abbey six months before his death. His sentences are sonorous; his style was characterized by a noble simplicity, impressive, but without a touch that dramatic effect was strained for. He passionately loved nature in all her aspects, and traveled, always in search of the picturesque; but used his experience with reserve, and his illustrations are used to explain human life. His treatment of Bible narratives is not a translation into the modern manner, nor is it an adaptation, but a poetical rendering, in which the flavor of the original is not lost though the lesson is made contemporary. He used figures of speech and drew freely on history and art for illustrations, but not so much to elucidate his subject as to ornament it. As might be expected of one who, in the world's best sense, was so thoroughly a man, he had great influence with young men and was one of the most popular of Harvard preachers. It was his custom for 30 alternate years to go abroad in the summer, and there, as in America, he was regarded as a great pulpit orator. He took a large view of social questions, and was in sympathy with all great popular movements. His advancement to the episcopate was warmly welcomed by all parties, except one branch of his own church with which his principles were at variance, and every denomination delighted in his elevation as if he were the peculiar property of each. His works include 'Lectures on Preaching' (1877); 'Sermons' (1878-81); 'Bohlen Lectures' (1879); 'Baptism and Confirmation' (1880); 'Sermons Preached in English Churches' (1883); 'The Oldest Schools in America' (Bos. 1885); 'Twenty Sermons' (N. Y. 1886); 'Tolerance' (1887); 'The Light of the World, and Other Sermons' (1890); and 'Essays and Addresses' (1894). His 'Letters of Travel' show him to have been an accurate observer, with a large fund of spontaneous humor. See Allen, 'Life and Letters of Phillips Brooks'; Howe, 'Phillips Brooks' (1902).

Brooks, Preston Smith, American politician and legislator: b. Edgefield, S. C., 4 Aug. 1819; d. Washington, D. C., 27 Jan. 1857. He was graduated at South Carolina College in 1839; elected to the legislature of his native State in 1844; raised a company for the Mexican war and led it as captain in the famous Palmetto regiment. He was sent to Congress in 1853, made his first speech in February 1854, on the subject of the Nebraska bill; speaking also in June of the same year on the Pacific railroad bill. On 22 May 1856, Senator Sumner, of Massachusetts, having employed in a speech in the Senate various expressions which had greatly incensed the members of Congress from South Carolina, Brooks entered the Senate chamber, after the Senate had adjourned, while Sumner was seated at his desk engaged in writing, and with blows on the head from a gutta-percha cane struck the Senator to the floor, where he left him insensible. On 2 June a committee of the House of Representatives reported in favor of Mr. Brooks' expulsion. In the final action upon the report there were 121 votes in favor of and 95 opposed to it, which, being less than the requisite two thirds vote, prevented the House from agreeing to the resolution. Mr. Brooks, however, resigned his seat, and, 8 July, pleaded guilty before the court at Washington upon an indictment for assault, and was sentenced to a fine of $300. Having addressed his constituents on the subject of the assault, he was re-elected to Congress by a unanimous vote, and made, on 7 Jan. 1857, a second speech on the Nebraska bill.

Brooks, Shirley. See BROOKS, CHARLES WILLIAM SHIRLEY.

Brooks, William Keith, American zoologist: b. Cleveland, Ohio, 25 March 1848. He has been a professor of zoology in Johns Hopkins University from 1876. Among his published books are 'Handbook of Invertebrate Zoology' (1882); 'Heredity' (1884); 'The Development and Protection of the Oyster in Maryland' (1884); 'A Monograph of the Genus Salpa' (1893); 'Foundation of Zoology' (1898).

Brooks, William Robert, American astronomer: b. Maidstone, Kent, England, 11 June 1844. He was educated in the United States, and in 1874 founded the Red House Observatory at Phelps, N. Y., where he discovered 11 comets. Since 1888 he has been in charge of the Smith Observatory at Geneva, N. Y., where he has discovered 12 more comets. In 1887 he was elected a Fellow of the Royal Astronomical Society of Great Britain.

Brooks of Sheffield, a fictitious personage alluded to in Dickens' 'David Copperfield.'

Brooks's, a noted London Club founded in 1764. It was originally a sporting establishment, managed by Almack, and its second proprietor was named Brooks, the club subsequently taking its name from him. It is situated at No. 60 Saint James Street, and is political in character.

Broom, various shrubs of the closely allied genera *Genista, Cytisus,* and *Spartium,* of the natural order *Leguminosæ,* natives mostly of the warm and temperate parts of the Old World. The name is not applied to species which do not have the long, slender twigs, but is restricted to those characterized by these slender branches and numerous axillary flowers. *Genista monosperma (Spartium monospermum* of some botanists), a Spanish and north African species, attains a height of 10 feet; has almost leafless, grayish branches; small, simple, linear, silky leaves; fragrant white flowers in short lateral racemes; and one-seeded pods. It is planted in shrubberies and is grown in greenhouses in preferably loose, dry soil. *G. tinctoria,* dyer's greenweed, a native of Europe and western Asia, is an erect shrub about three feet tall with somewhat pubescent branches and many flowered axillary racemes which are terminally panicled. Its branches, leaves, and blossoms are used to dye wool yellow, or, when mixed with wood, green. *Cytisus scoparius,* Scotch or common broom, a native of middle and southern Europe, attains a height of 20 feet, but usually much less, has erect, slender branches, short petioled leaves, generally large, solitary, long-stalked, drooping yellow flowers and brownish black pods. It has been largely introduced into the United States for ornament, and is hardy almost as far north as Washington. It succeeds on dry soils, and produces an abundance of bloom in late spring and early summer. The stems and leaves, which are very bitter and nauseous tasting and smelling, have been used in dyeing and tanning, and the fibre of the former used to make cloth and paper. The wood of large specimens is highly valued for turning and cabinetmaking. *C. albus,* white or Portugal broom, a native of the Mediterranean region, which attains a height of three feet, sometimes even 20 feet, has fascicles of axillary flowers, for which it is frequently planted in shrubberies. Many other species are valued for ornamental planting, for pasturage, and since their flowers yield abundant nectar, for bee forage. *Spartium junceum,* Spanish broom, a native of southern Europe, is an upright shrub, 10 feet tall, with slender, green branches, fragrant yellow flowers which appear continuously during summer, and in California where the plant has been introduced, almost throughout the year. It grows on dry soils and in rocky places. Its fibre is used to some extent in Spain, Italy, and France for rope- and cloth-making, and even for making some kinds of lace. See CYTISUS; GENISTA; SPARTIUM.

Broom-corn, (1) (*Sorghum vulgare*, millet or Guinea-corn), a plant of the order of grasses, with a jointed stem, rising to the height of 8 or 10 feet, extensively cultivated in North America, where the branched panicles are made into carpet-brooms and clothes-brushes. The seed is used for feeding poultry, cattle, etc. (2) *Sorghum saccharata*, from which a kind of syrup or molasses is made.

Broom Rape (*Orobanche ramosa*), an annual parasitic plant of the natural order *Orobanchaceæ*, a native of Europe but established in America, especially in tobacco and hemp fields, where it often does great damage by sucking the juices of the plants which it eventually kills. Its slender, brownish or straw-colored stems attain a height of 6 to 15 inches, bear small scales instead of leaves, and light blue sessile flowers, followed by an abundance of minute seeds which rapidly spread the pest. Clean seed, clean cultivation and change of crops upon the land for several years are the only safeguards and remedies.

Broom-sedge. See ANDROPOGON.

Brooms and Brushes, Manufacture of, in the United States. Europeans use to this day a broom made from hickory withes for rough sweeping, and it was not until about 1850 that Americans discovered the valuable properties of a variety of the indigenous Indian maize for broom making. The industry was for a time carried on in a desultory way, but the first factory established for the manufacture of brooms from corn was opened in 1859, by Ebenezer Howard, at Fort Hunter, Montgomery County, N. Y. Factories were also soon started in Fort Hunter by John D. Blood, who formed the firm of Blood & Herrick, and by Ebenezer Howard, who formed that of Howard & Bronson. All of the broom factories established at Fort Hunter have since become absorbed by the American Broom and Brush Company, and all are in operation to-day. The broom and whisk-broom industry is now carried on in the Eastern States almost entirely by the American Broom and Brush Company, which, besides the factories named, also have works at Buffalo, N. Y., Dallas, Pa., Baltimore, Md., and Richmond, Va. The business in the Western States is in the hands of the Cupples Woodenware Company, of Saint Louis, and Roseboom & Company, of Chicago. In 1880 there were in the United States 980 establishments for the manufacture of brooms and brushes, with a capital of $4,186,-897, and a product valued at $10,560,855. In 1900 there were reported 1,526 establishments, with a capital of $9,616,780, and a product valued at $18,490,847. Many brooms are made by hand in various penitentiaries throughout the country. There are also many brooms made in blind asylums, as the work is found especially adapted to blind men.

Broom Tops, the fresh and dried tops of *Cytisus scoparius* (common broom). There are two official preparations; the decoction (*decoctum scoparii*), consisting of a pint of distilled water to an ounce of the dried tops, and the juice (*succus scoparii*), made of three ounces of the fresh expressed juice to a pint of rectified spirits. They are valuable diuretics, especially in cardiac dropsies. Scoparine and sparteia are the two active principles; the action of sparteia is analogous to that of conia.

Brose (Gaelic *brothas*), a dish sometimes used in Scotland, made by pouring boiling water, milk, or the liquor in which meat has been boiled, on oatmeal, and mixing the ingredients by immediate stirring. Butter may be added, and sweet milk when the brose is made with water. It is kail brose, water brose, or beef brose, according to the liquid used. Athole brose, a famous Highland cordial, is a compound of honey and whiskey.

Brother Jonathan, a name of personification applied to the people of the United States, as "John Bull" is to the people of England. The most widely accepted explanation of its origin rests on the tradition that Washington, on assuming command of the New England Revolutionary forces, being in great straits for arms and war material, and having a high regard for the judgment of his friend the governor of Connecticut, Jonathan Trumbull, said in that emergency, "We must consult Brother Jonathan." This expression, being repeated on other difficult occasions, came into common use, and at last was extended to the entire people of the country. See NATIONAL NICKNAMES.

Brotherhood of Andrew and Philip, a religious order founded in 1888, and which has spread among the churches of 19 denominations and is represented in a large proportion of the States. Its official organ is 'The Brotherhood Star.' The pledge of service is similar to that of the Brotherhood of Saint Andrew (q.v.). The name of the society contains an allusion to the fact that Andrew, the first of the 12 disciples to become a follower of Christ, immediately after entering upon his discipleship sought out his brother Philip and brought him to the Master.

Brotherhood of Saint Andrew, a religious organization of the Protestant Episcopal Church, founded in 1883 in St. James' Parish, Chicago. It has more than 1,200 active chapters, exclusive of the junior department. The society has extended to Canada, England, Scotland, Australia, the West Indies, and South America. The official organ of the brotherhood is 'St. Andrew's Cross,' published monthly. There are two rules, one of prayer and one of service. The pledge of service binds every member to make an earnest effort to bring at least one young man each week within the hearing of the gospel.

Brotherhood of Saint Paul, a fraternity of the Methodist Episcopal Church, founded in 1895, for the spiritual and social benefit of its members. Of the three orders into which it is divided — the Order of Jerusalem, the Order of Damascus, and the Order of Rome — the first is for new members and those who are not professing Christians; the second for members of the Methodist Episcopal Church, and the third for advanced Christians. The brotherhood has a ritual and a regalia.

Brothers of the Christian Schools, commonly called Christian Brothers. This is a Society of men belonging to the Roman Catholic Church who devote themselves exclusively to the education of youth. The Society was founded in 1680 by Jean Baptiste de la Salle, Canon of the Metropolitan Church of Rheims, who, in the year 1900, was canonized by Pope Leo XIII.

The Society spread rapidly in France, partly because the Brothers made French the language of the schools instead of Latin, and partly because they did away with the individual system of teaching by grouping the pupils together into distinct classes. They abandoned the lecturing style in all their instructions for the Socratic method, introduced object-lessons and added museums to the equipment of the school.

These bold innovations in education met with popular favor and official recognition, and did more than anything else to bring about a general system of primary instruction in France. In consequence of these reforms in the traditional methods of teaching, the Christian Brothers have come to be considered the founders of primary education in Europe. In due time, the Society spread to Italy, Belgium, Germany, Austria, England, and Ireland; and also to Canada, the United States, South America, India, and South Africa.

The general methods of teaching followed by the Brothers, are explained in the 'Government of the Christian Schools,' while the qualities which they should possess as teachers are expounded in the 'Twelve Virtues of a Good Master.' Besides these two manuals, the Society has published for the benefit of its members numerous works on education and pedagogy together with a series of text-books on all subjects taught in the schools, including logic, ethics, literature, philosophy, methodology, mathematics, physics, etc.

The Christian Brothers established a College for the training of teachers in 1684, which was the first of its kind in Europe. They opened Sunday Schools in 1699, also the first of their kind, in which secular as well as religious instruction was given in the afternoon. They have novitiates in every "province" of the Society for the religious formation, and scholasticates for the pedagogical training of their members. They direct schools of all grades from the primary to the college; they have agricultural and technical schools as well as Normal Colleges, orphanages and "protectories." In the United States, they have 6 colleges and 90 other institutions taught by 980 Brothers. Altogether, the Society had in September 1904, 1,570 schools with 15,500 Brothers and 321,000 pupils.

The Society was suppressed in 1792 at the beginning of the French Revolution, was restored in 1803 by order of Napoleon I., and incorporated with the University of France in 1808. It was again officially suppressed in France in 1904 during the war against religious Congregations waged by Premier Combes, but continued to live and flourish in other countries.

The Christian Brothers wear a distinctive religious habit and take the three vows of religion. As they do not take "orders," they are free to devote themselves entirely to the work of education.

BROTHER POTAMIAN,
Professor of Physics in Manhattan College.

Brothers of the Sacred Heart, a Roman Catholic congregation established in Lyons, France, in 1820 by Père André Coindre, of the Society of Missionaries. In 1847 five Brothers came from France to this country to take charge of parish schools and asylums. They have establishments in the diocese of New Orleans, Natchez, Mobile, Natchitoches, Savannah, Trenton, Indianapolis, Manchester, Providence, Boston, Indian Territory, and over 30 places in Canada. In September 1900 at a general Chapter of the Congregation held in France, two provinces were formed, one for the United States and the other for Canada. The object of the Brothers is the Christian education of youth in schools, asylums and colleges. A novitiate for the province of the United States was opened in Metuchen, N. J., June 1901.

Brothers of Our Lady of Lourdes. This congregation was founded by Very Rev. S. M. Gloriux in 1830. Its object is the Christian education of youth, especially the poor, the care of orphan asylums, and the nursing of the sick and old people in hospitals. Pope Leo XIII. approved the congregation and its rule 18 July 1892. The Brothers conduct a House of Studies and a boarding and day school at South Park, Wash., and a protectory for Homeless Boys at Pittsburg and New Derry, Pa.

Brothers of Charity, a congregation founded for the purpose of securing the sanctification of its members by the practice of the three simple vows aand the observance of its constitution. Its special object is the ministry of charity in maintaining and ministering to the aged, the sick and the insane, in sheltering the poor, in educating poor children and performing any other work of charity to which they may be called. The congregation was founded in Belgium about 1809 by Rev. I. Triest, Canon of Saint Bavon, Ghent.

Brothers of the Christian Instruction, a Roman Catholic Institute founded at Saint Brieuc, France, by the Abbé John Mary De la Mennais, and approved by the Holy See in 1891. The Order was established in Canada in 1886 and has 12 establishments in the archdiocese of Montreal; one in the archdiocese of Ottawa, one in the diocese of Saint Hyacinth, two in the diocese of Three Rivers, and one in the diocese of Valleyfield. The object of the Order is the Christian education and instruction of youth. General motherhouse at Ploermel, France; Provincial House and Novitiate at Laprairie, near Montreal.

Brotherhoods, Religious. See ORDERS, RELIGIOUS.

Brothers and Clerks of the Common Life, an institute founded by Gerhard Groot, a deacon of Deventer in 1384 for the purpose of providing a home for men who desired to live an austere Christian life without taking perpetual vows. See COMMON LIFE, BROTHERS OF THE.

Brotherton, Alice (WILLIAMS), American author and lecturer: b. Cambridge, Ind. She married William Ernst Brotherton, 18 Oct. 1876. She has lectured on Shakespeare and other subjects in English literature, contributed to magazines, and published the volumes: 'Beyond the Veil' (1886); 'The Sailing of King Olaf' (1887); and 'What the Wind Told the Tree-tops' (1888).

Brough, John, American statesman: b. Marietta, Ohio, 17 Sept. 1811; d. Cleveland 29

Aug. 1865. In his youth he was a printer's apprentice. He studied at the Ohio University and later entered journalism. As a Democratic orator he became well-known. In 1846 he entered the legal profession. In 1864 the Republican Union party nominated him for governor and he was elected by a joint vote of all electors advocating war. He has been called the "war governor" of his State.

Brougham, Henry (BARON BROUGHAM AND VAUX), British statesman and jurist: b. Edinburgh, 19 Sept. 1778; d. Cannes, 7 May 1868. His father, Henry Brougham, belonged to an old Westmoreland family, and his mother, Eleonora Syme, was a niece of Robertson the historian. He was educated at the High School and the University of Edinburgh, entering the latter at the age of 16. At the age of 18 he wrote an essay, 'Observations on the Phenomena of Light,' which, being sent to the Royal Society, was printed in its 'Transactions' for 1796. He also contributed a paper to each of the next two volumes of the Royal Society's 'Transactions.' On leaving college he devoted himself to the study of law at Edinburgh, and was admitted a member of the Society of Advocates in 1800. As a member of the Speculative Club he was brought into contact with Jeffrey, Horner, and others afterward famous; and along with the above-mentioned writers and Sydney Smith bore a chief part in the starting of the 'Edinburgh Review' in 1802, to which he contributed a great number of articles. In 1803 appeared his 'Inquiry into the Colonial Policy of the European Powers,' a work which showed a wide extent of knowledge in the author, and drew upon him considerable attention. In it he expressed his decided hostility to the slave-trade. Finding too circumscribed a field for his abilities in Edinburgh, he removed to London, and in 1808 was called to the English bar. One of the first occasions on which he distinguished himself in his professional capacity was in 1810, when he spoke before the House of Lords in behalf of some Liverpool merchants who wished the repeal of the orders in council prohibiting trade with the states subject to France. The same year he entered Parliament as member for the rotten borough of Camelford, joined the Whig party, which was in opposition, and soon after obtained the passing of a measure making the slave-trade felony. He also succeeded, before the dissolution of Parliament, in getting the orders in council repealed. At the general election in 1812 he endeavored to get himself elected as one of the members for Liverpool, but was defeated by Canning, and remained without a seat till 1816, when he was returned for Winchelsea. He represented this borough up to 1830. On his return to Parliament he began his life-long efforts in the cause of education by obtaining the appointment of a committee to inquire into the state of education among the poor of the metropolis. In 1819 he and his friends established a model school for the children of the poorer classes in London. In 1823 he was instrumental in founding the first mechanics' institute. In 1825 he published his 'Practical Observations upon the Education of the People,' which ran through 20 editions. The same year he was elected lord rector of Glasgow University; and also introduced a bill into Parliament for the incorporation of the

London University, of which he may be considered one of the chief founders. He also bore an active part in establishing the Society for the Diffusion of Useful Knowledge in 1827, the first publication of which was his 'Discourse on the Objects, Pleasures, and Advantages of Science.' Meantime his reputation as a brilliant speaker and able advocate had been gradually increasing, and his fearless and successful defense of Queen Caroline in 1820-1 placed him on the pinnacle of popular favor. Two of the speeches spoken by him in this course are looked upon as classic specimens of English eloquence. But the part he took in the defense of the queen brought him into disfavor with the king, and delayed his promotion for some years, so that it was not till 1827 that he was made a king's counsel. In Parliament he continued to speak against negro slavery, and in favor of what may be considered the most valuable of the reforms that we owe to him; namely, the amendment of the common law and of the judicial administration. On this subject he delivered a famous speech of six hours' duration, on 7 Feb. 1828. At the general election of 1830 he was returned for the large and important county of York, an honor which he attributed chiefly to a celebrated speech delivered by him shortly before on the slave-trade. In the ministry of Earl Grey he accepted the post of lord chancellor, and 22 Nov. 1830, was raised to the peerage, with the title of Baron Brougham and Vaux. The Reform Bill of 1832 received his warmest support in the House of Lords. In 1834, when the Whig ministry were dismissed, Lord Brougham of course lost the chancellorship, and this proved the end of his official life, as he was never afterward a member of any ministry. Henceforth he devoted himself chiefly to legal and social reforms, maintaining his hostile attitude toward slavery, and continuing his labors in the cause of popular education. He was a zealous opponent of the corn laws. In connection with the acts of his later years, we may mention his presidency of the Law Amendment Society, and of the Social Science Association. He latterly resided much at Cannes, in the south of France. He married, in 1819, Mary Anne Eden, and had two daughters, one of whom died in infancy in 1820, the other in 1839, at the age of 17. Lord Brougham accomplished a large amount of literary work, contributing to newspapers, reviews, and encyclopedias, besides writing several independent works; and he had no mean reputation in mathematics and physical science. His works, collected by himself, and published in 10 volumes (Edin. 1855-7), include: 'Lives of Men of Science, Time of George III.'; 'Lives of Men of Letters, Time of George III.'; 'Eminent Statesmen'; 'Natural Theology'; 'Rhetorical and Literary Dissertations and Addresses,' 'Rhetorical and Political Dissertations'; and 'Speeches on Social and Political Subjects.' He also, along with Sir Charles Bell, brought out an edition of Paley's 'Natural Theology'; translated the oration of Demosthenes 'On the Crown'; and in 1855, conjointly with Mr. E. J. Routh, published an 'Analytical View of Sir Isaac Newton's Principia.' He was president of University College, London, chancellor of Edinburgh University, D.C.L. of Oxford, and a member of the Institute of France. Lord Brougham must be looked upon as one of the most remarkable men of his century. His energy and industry were enormous, his versatility surprising. He was a mathematician, a historian, a biographer, an essayist, a moral and political philosopher, a lawyer, an orator, and a statesman. As an orator and parliamentary debater he was inferior to Canning alone.

Brougham, John, Irish actor and playwright: b. Dublin, 9 May 1810; d. New York, 7 June 1880. He was at first a student of surgery, but when thrown on his own resources he adopted the stage as a profession. After a short experience as actor, playwright, and manager, he came to America in 1842. Eighteen years later he returned to England, but in 1865 he again came to the United States, and remained here till his death. He wrote about 100 plays, including 'The Game of Love'; 'Romance and Reality'; 'Love's Livery'; 'The Duke's Motto,' etc., and contributed largely to periodicals.

Brougham, a close four-wheeled carriage with a single inside seat for two persons, or a four-wheeled close carriage with two seats, accommodating four persons. Each type is glazed in front and has a raised seat for the driver. Named after Lord Brougham.

Broughton, Hugh, English Biblical scholar: b. Owlbury, Shropshire, 1549; d. London, 4 Aug. 1612. He was educated at Cambridge, and early became distinguished for his familiarity with the learned tongues. He entered the Church, but his views coming under ecclesiastical disapproval, he went to the Continent for a time. For several years he preached to an English congregation in one of the cities of Holland. He wrote: 'A Concert of Scripture'; and an 'Explication of the Article of Christ's Descent into Hell.' Ben Jonson in two of his plays holds up to ridicule this Puritan preacher.

Broughton, brow'tôn, Lord (JOHN CAM HOBHOUSE), Baron, English statesman and writer: b. Bristol, 27 June 1786; d. London, 3 June 1869. He was educated at Westminster School and Trinity College, Cambridge, where he graduated B.A. in 1808, and M.A. in 1811. He was an intimate friend of Lord Byron, and accompanied him in his travels to Greece and Turkey in 1809. In 1812 appeared his 'Journey Through Albania and Other Provinces of Turkey.' In the years 1813 and 1814 he accompanied the allied armies in Germany, and was present at the battle of Dresden. He also accompanied Byron to Italy in 1816-17, and visited Rome and Venice with him. He suggested an extension of the fourth canto of 'Childe Harold,' which Byron dedicated to him, and by arrangement with the poet he undertook to write for it a series of notes, for which his observations during their journey furnished materials. These notes were written at Venice, and ultimately formed a separate work, 'Historical Illustrations of the Fourth Canto of Childe Harold,' published by Murray in 1818. Hobhouse was an advanced liberal in politics, and on his return took an active part in the advocacy of reforms. In 1816 he published anonymously the 'Hundred Days in Paris,' which from its hostility to the Bourbon cause, gave great offense to the governments of France and England, and a French translator and the publisher of it were fined

and imprisoned for writing an anonymous pamphlet, the 'Trifling Mistake.' Broughton was committed to Newgate, and there lay for almost three months. That year he was returned for Westminster, and became a supporter of liberal measures, as the Reform Bill of 1832, the repeal of the Test and Corporation acts, the removal of Catholic disabilities, etc. In February 1832, he entered Lord Melbourne's ministry as secretary of war, and became a privy councilor. In 1833 he was made chief secretary for Ireland, but lost his seat in seeking re-election. In 1834, he was made chief commissioner for woods and forests, and the following year became president of the board of control. He lost his seat for Nottingham in 1847, but a seat was found for him at Harwich, which he continued to occupy till he was raised to the peerage in 1851. He had succeeded his father as baronet in 1831. As he left no male issue, the title became extinct, the baronetcy passing to his nephew.

Broughton, Rhoda, English novelist: b. North Wales, 29 Nov. 1840. Much of her life has been passed at Oxford. Her novels, especially the earlier ones, show great cleverness, and are very popular. They include 'Cometh Up as a Flower' (1867); 'Not Wisely but Too Well' (1867); 'Red as a Rose Is She' (1870); 'Goodbye, Sweetheart, Goodbye' (1872); 'Nancy' (1873); 'Belinda' (1883); 'Doctor Cupid' (1886); 'Alas!' (1890); 'A Beginner' (1894); 'Scylla or Charybdis?' (1895).

Brouncker, or Brounker, William, British mathematician: b. 1620; d. 1684. He became Viscount Brouncker of Castle-Lyons, in Ireland, inheriting the title from his father. He was strongly attached to the royal cause, and in 1660 was one of the first to sign the declaration which hailed Monk as the restorer of the laws and privileges of the nation. At the Restoration he was appointed to several lucrative offices, and on the formation and incorporation of the Royal Society became its first president. This honorable office he continued to hold for 15 years. His mathematical attainments must have been of a high order, as he is admitted to have been the discoverer of continued fractions, and of an important theorem relating to the quadrature of the equilateral hyperbola. He also published experiments on the recoiling of guns, and a translation of Descartes' 'Musicæ Compendium,' with notes.

Broussa, brö'sa. See BRUSSA.

Broussais, François Joseph Victor, French physician: b. Saint Malo, 17 Dec. 1772; d. 17 Nov. 1838. Educated at the college of Dinan, he entered the army and soon attained the rank of sergeant; but a severe illness caused him to give up a military career and devote himself to medicine. He studied at Brest and Paris, and in 1820 obtained a professorship at Val-de-Grâce, a chair which he exchanged in 1831 for that of general pathology in the faculty of medicine at Paris. His first important work was his 'Recherches sur la Fièvre Hectique' (1803), which was followed by the more celebrated 'Histoire des Phlegmasies ou Inflammations Chroniques' (1808), and 'Examen de la Doctrine Médicale Généralement Adoptée' (1816). In these works he propounded what is known as the physiological system of medicine. According to him irritation or excitation is the fundamental property of all living animal tissues, and diseases are produced by an undue increase or diminution of that property. Broussais also taught and wrote on phrenology.

Brousson, Claude, French martyr: b. Nismes, 1647; d. Montpellier, 4 Nov. 1698. He was educated for the law, and practised as an advocate first at Castres and Castelnaudary, and afterward in the Parliament of Toulouse, where the Protestants, to whom he belonged, were often indebted to him for the zeal and ability with which he defended their cause. In 1683, when the government had resolved on recalling the edict of Nantes, and trying the effect of persecution as a means of suppressing the Reformation, it was at Brousson's house the deputies from all the churches assembled, and resolved that, even were their churches destroyed they would still hold their meetings, though it should be under the canopy of heaven. His part in this and other important movements marked him out as one of the first objects of attack; and on receiving warning of an intention to arrest him, he sought an asylum at Lausanne, where he published several works, exposing the persecutions to which the Protestants of France were subjected, and awakening the sympathy of their brethren in all other parts of Europe. Nor was he satisfied merely to aid the cause with his pen. At the hazard of his life he returned to France, and continued for four years among the recesses of the Cevennes, preaching the gospel. In 1693 he repaired to Holland, where a pension was given him by the States-General; but the sufferings of his persecuted countrymen were ever uppermost in his mind, and he visited many courts of Europe to plead their cause, and more than once went to France for their instruction and encouragement. He was on a mission to France when, a price having been set on his head, he was arrested at Oleron, tried at Montpellier, condemned to be broken on the wheel, and executed accordingly.

Broussonet, Pierre Marie Auguste, French naturalist: b. Montpellier, 28 Feb. 1761; d. there, 27 July 1807. In Paris he studied natural history; went to England and pursued ichthyology, and after three years' residence there returned and was assistant in the College of France. At this period he communicated a number of valuable papers to the Academy of Sciences, of which he became a member. In 1785 he was appointed secretary to the Paris Agricultural Society. Merino sheep and the Angora goat are said to have been first introduced by him into France. The Revolution breaking out, he became connected with the Girondists. On the downfall of that party he was arrested at Montpellier, but having escaped, crossed the Pyrenees under the pretext of botanizing, and arrived in Spain destitute. Later he went to Africa and resumed his botanical studies, making some important collections. Returning to France, after executing various missions he was appointed, in 1805, to the chair of botany at Montpellier. In the same year he became a member of the Corps Législatif. He died from the effects of a fall by which the brain had been seriously injured. Besides his 'Ichthyologiæ Decas Prima' (1872), his publications include important memoirs of ichthyology and botany.

Broussonetia, a genus of trees. See MULBERRY.

Brouwer, or **Brauwer, Adrian.** See BRAUWER, ADRIAN.

Brower, Daniel Roberts, American physician: b. Philadelphia, Pa., 1839. In 1864 he was appointed assistant surgeon of the United States volunteers and has since been medical superintendent of the Eastern Lunatic Hospital of Virginia, 1868-75, and professor of nervous diseases in the Rush Medical College of Chicago, and in the Woman's Medical College of the Northwest University at Evanston, Ill. He has published a 'Manual of Insanity.'

Brower, Jacob Vradenburg, American explorer and archæologist: b. York, Mich., 21 Jan. 1844; d. 1905. He served in the cavalry and the navy during the Civil War, was a member of the Minnesota legislature, 1867-73, and discovered numerous prehistoric mounds at Mille Lac and other points in Minnesota. He published 'The Mississippi River and Its Source' (1893); 'Prehistoric Man at the Head Waters of the Mississippi' (1895); 'The Missouri River and Its Utmost Source' (1896); 'Quivira' (1898); 'Harahey' (1899); 'Mille Lac' (1899).

Brown, Aaron Venable, American politician: b. Brunswick County, Va., 15 Aug. 1795; d. 1859. He studied law, and commenced practice in Nashville, Tenn. He was partner in business with President Polk, until the latter entered upon his congressional career; served in almost all the sessions of the legislature of Tennessee between 1821 and 1832; was a member of the House of Representatives in Congress from 1839 to 1845; and was in that year elected governor of Tennessee. He was a delegate to the southern convention held at Nashville in 1850, and submitted a report to that body known as the Tennessee platform. He was also a member of the convention of the democratic party at Baltimore in 1852, to which he reported the platform adopted by them. In 1857 he became a member of President Buchanan's cabinet, in which he held the office of postmaster-general.

Brown, Abbie Farwell, American writer for young people: b. Boston, about 1875. She has published 'The Book of Saints and Friendly Beasts' (1900); 'In Days of Giants' (1902); 'The Lonesomest Doll' (1901); 'Star Jewels' (1905).

Brown, Abram English, American historical writer: b. Bedford, Mass., 21 Jan. 1849, and has ever since resided there. He is the author of 'Beneath Old Roof Trees' (1896); 'Beside Old Hearthstones' (1897); 'History of Bedford' (1892); 'Glimpses of New England' (1894); 'Flag of the Minute Men' (1894); 'Faneuil Hall and Market'; 'John Hancock.'

Brown, Alexander, American historian: b. Glenmore, Nelson County, Va., 5 Sept. 1843; d. 29 Aug. 1906. He served in the Confederate army during the Civil War and from 1880 devoted himself to literature. He wrote 'New Views of Early Virginia History' (1886); 'The Genesis of the United States' (1890); 'The Cabells and Their Kin' (1895); 'The First Republic in America' (1898); 'The History of Our Earliest History' (1898); 'English Politics in Early Virginia' (1901).

Brown, Alice, American novelist and writer of short stories descriptive of phases of New England life: b. Hampton Falls, N. H., 5

Dec. 1857. She taught school for several years, but has given herself entirely to literary pursuits for some years. Her work is most careful and conscientious in character, displaying equal literary skill and sympathetic insight into character. She has published: 'Fools of Nature'; 'Meadow Grass' (1895); 'By Oak and Thorn,' a volume of English travels (1896); 'The Road to Castaly,' a work of verse (1896); 'The Day of His Youth' (1896); 'Tiverton Tales' (1899); 'King's End'; 'Margaret Warrener'; 'Mercy Otis Warren,' a biography; 'The Mannering'; 'High Noon.'

Brown, Benjamin Gratz, American politician: b. Lexington, Ky., 28 May 1826; d. St. Louis 13 Dec. 1885. He practiced law in Missouri, and was a member of the State legislature in 1852-8. In the Civil War he served in the Union army, recruiting a regiment, and becoming a brigadier-general of volunteers. In 1863-7 he was United States Senator from Missouri, and in 1871 was elected governor of his State. He was the candidate for the vice-presidency of the United States on the ticket with Horace Greeley in 1872.

Brown, Caroline Virginia (KROUT), American novelist: b. Crawfordville, Ind. She has published 'Knights in Fustian' (1900); Bold Robin and His Forest Rangers' (1905); 'On the We-A Trail' (1905).

Brown, Charles Brockden, American novelist: b. Philadelphia 17 Jan. 1771; d. 22 Feb. 1810. He descended from a family of Quakers, was remarkable in his childhood for his attachment to books, and at the age of 16, after having received a liberal education, had already formed plans of extensive literary works. The delicacy of his constitution incapacitated him for the bustle of business and all athletic amusements. During frequent visits to New York he became intimate with a literary club, who fostered his devotion to letters, and increased his eagerness to be conspicuous as a writer. He kept minute journals, indited essays and dissertations, and cultivated, with unremitting assiduity, the arts of composition. The first novel which he wrote was entitled 'Sky Walk,' subsequently incorporated in 'Edgar Huntley.' 'Wieland,' his first published novel, appeared in 1798. It soon acquired the reputation of a powerful and original romance. The next was 'Ormond, or the Secret Witness' (1799), which had neither the success nor the merit of the other, but still exhibits uncommon powers of invention and description. At this time Brown had begun no less than five novels, two of which — 'Arthur Mervyn' and 'Edgar Huntley,' — were completed and sent forth almost immediately. In the former the ravages of the yellow fever, which the author had witnessed in New York and Philadelphia, are painted with terrific realism. All these works abound in both excellencies and faults, and are strikingly original. In 1801 he published another novel,— 'Clara Howard,'— less open to exception, but also less deserving of praise. Its form is different from that of the others, being epistolary. The last of his novels was 'Jane Talbot' (1804). It is deficient in interest, and indeed in all respects inferior to its predecessors. In April 1799, Brown published the first number of the 'Monthly Magazine and American Review.' This work he continued until the end of the

year 1800, writing abundantly for it. Circumstances compelled him to relinquish it; but in 1805 he commenced another journal, with the title of the 'Literary Magazine and American Register,' and in this undertaking persevered for five years. In 1806 he entered upon a new work, a semi-annual 'American Register,' five volumes of which he lived to complete and publish. It is now and must long be consulted as a valuable body of annals. In 1809 it was discovered that his lungs were seriously affected, and he then consented to travel for the recovery of his health. The remedy, however, was applied too late. In November of that year he betook himself to his chamber, as he thought, for a few days; but his confinement lasted until February, and ended only with his life. His writings are characterized by rich diction, variety of incident, and vivid representation, but he deals too much in the extravagant and the horrible.

Brown, Charles Rufus, American clergyman and Hebrew scholar: b. East Kingston, N. H., 22 Feb. 1849. He was graduated at the United States Naval Academy in 1869, at Harvard in 1877, and at Union Theological Seminary in 1879. He was ordained a Baptist minister in 1881 and held pastorates at Salem and Worcester, Mass. He has been professor of Hebrew at Newton Theological Institute since 1886, and has written 'An Aramaic Method' (1884-1893) and text-books in the Oriental languages.

Brown, Elmer Ellsworth, American educator: b. Kiantone, N. Y., 28 Aug. 1861. After holding several professional posts he became professor in the University of California in 1893, was professor of the theory and practice of education there from 1898 and in 1906 became U. S. Commissioner of Education. He wrote 'Democracy in the Universities' (1891); 'The Making of Our Middle Schools' (1903); 'Origin of American State Universities' (1905); etc.

Brown, Emma Elizabeth, American author and artist: b. Concord, N. H., 18 Oct. 1847. She was educated in the Concord common schools. She has written lives of Washington, Grant, Garfield, Holmes, and Lowell; 'From Night to Light,' 'Child Toilers,' and much verse, besides contributing papers to leading magazines.

Brown, Ernest William, American mathematician: b. Hull, England, 29 Nov. 1866. He was educated at Christ's College, Cambridge, England, and was a professor of mathematics at Haverford College, Pa., 1891-1906, and since 1906 at Harvard University. He is a fellow of the Royal Society of England, and the author of 'Treatise on the Lunar Theory.'

Brown, Ford Madox, English painter, grandson of Dr. John Brown of Edinburgh, the author of the Brunonian system of medicine: b. Calais, France, 16 April 1821; d. London 6 Oct. 1893. He studied at Bruges, Ghent, and Antwerp, and after a three years' residence in Paris he went to England about 1845. In 1844 and 1845 he contributed (unsuccessfully) cartoons of the 'Finding of the Body of Harold,' 'Justice,' and other subjects to the competitive exhibition for the frescoes of the Houses of Parliament. In 1865 he opened in London an exhibition of many of his pictures, including 'The Last of England' (1852); 'The Autumn Afternoon'; and 'Work' (1865); the last named having occupied him for several years. Only a month before his death he completed the last of the 12 Manchester town-hall frescoes, on which he had been engaged for a long time. Among his other works are 'Lear and Cordelia' (1849) ; 'Pretty Baa-Lambs' (1851) ; 'Chaucer at the Court of Edward III.' (1851) ; and 'Cordelia's Portion.' He is generally rated as a pre-Raphaelite, but though a close intimacy existed between him and the brotherhood, he never actually joined them. See Hueffer, 'Ford Madox Brown: a Record of His Life and Work'. (1896).

Brown, Francis, American scholar: b. Hanover, N. H., 26 Dec. 1849. He was graduated from Dartmouth College in 1870, and the Union Theological Seminary, New York, in 1877. He was instructor in biblical philology in the latter institution 1879-81, and associate professor of the same 1881-90. Since the year last named he has been professor of Hebrew there. He is the author of 'Assyriology: Its Use and Abuse in Old Testament Study' (1885) ; 'The Teaching of the Twelve Apostles' with Hitchcock; 'Hebrew and an English Lexicon of the Old Testament' with Driver and Briggs (1891-1901).

Brown, SIR George, English military officer: b. near Elgin, Scotland, 1790; d. 1865. He served in the Peninsular war, and in the American campaign of 1814, being wounded at the battle of Bladensburg. He became lieutenant-general in 1851; and distinguished himself in the Crimean war at Alma, Inkermann, and Sebastopol. He was made K. C. B. in 1855.

Brown, George, Canadian statesman: b. Edinburgh, Scotland, 19 Nov. 1818; d. 9 May 1880; educated at the high school there. He emigrated to the United States with his father, and assisted in the management of a newspaper at New York; but in 1843 removed to Toronto, Canada, where he founded a newspaper, *The Globe*, which was very successful. In 1852 he was returned to Parliament, and rapidly rose to the first rank as a debater and advocate of reforms. In 1858 he was called to the office of premier, and formed an administration which, however, owing to an adverse vote of the Assembly, lasted only three days. In 1864 he joined the coalition government as leader of the reform section, and took an active part in the conferences held at Charlottetown and Quebec on the subject of the federation of the North American colonies; but resigned his office as minister in December 1865. He was called to the Senate in 1873, and the year after went to Washington along with Sir Edward Thornton to negotiate a commercial treaty with the United States. He died of a gunshot wound inflicted by a discharged employee. See Mackenzie, 'Life and Speeches of the Hon. George Brown' (1882).

Brown, George, American rear-admiral: b. Indiana, 19 June 1835. He entered the navy in 1849 and served with distinction in the Federal navy during the Civil War. He was in command of the Norfolk navy yard, 1866-97, being appointed a rear-admiral in 1893.

Brown, George Douglas, Scottish novelist: b. Ochiltree, Ayrshire, Scotland, 1869; d. London, 28 Aug. 1902. He was educated at the universities of Glasgow and Oxford and was successively reporter for a London journal and literary adviser to a publishing house. His novel of Scottish life, 'The House with the Green Shutters,' published in 1902, attracted great attention in England and the United States. See 'Life' (1903).

Brown, George Loring, American landscape artist: b. Boston, 2 Feb. 1814; d. 25 June 1889. He went abroad at 16 and on his return, two years later, was a pupil of Washington Allston. In 1840 he went to Paris to study under Isabey. Among noted pictures by him are 'Doge's Palace and Grand Canal' ; 'Bay of Naples' ; 'Moonlight Scene' ; 'The Crown of New England' ; and 'The Bay of New York,' the two latter acquired by Edward VII. when visiting the United States as Prince of Wales.

Brown, George William, American jurist: b. Baltimore, Md., 1812; d. 1890. After studying law he was admitted to the bar and in 1860 was elected mayor of his native city. At the time of the passage of troops through Baltimore, 19 April 1861, he placed himself at the head of the 6th Massachusetts regiment then on its way to Washington, and did everything in his power to suppress the riot which the appearance of the soldiers had occasioned. He was chief justice of the Maryland supreme court, 1873-88, and with two others compiled the first 'Digest of the Decisions of the Maryland Court of Appeals' (1847).

Brown, Glenn, American architect: b. Fanquier County, Va., 13 Sept. 1854. He has practised his profession in Washington, D. C., since 1878. He is the author of 'Water Closets: a Historical, Mechanical and Sanitary Treatise' (1884) ; 'Healthy Foundations for Houses' (1885) ; 'Trap Syphonage' (1886) ; 'History of the United States Capitol' (1900).

Brown, Goold, American grammarian: b. Providence, R. I., 7 March 1791; d. Lynn, Mass., 31 March 1857. He is known as the author of 'Brown's Grammar,' a school text-book widely used for some generations, and still in circulation. He published 'First Lines of English Grammar' (1823) ; 'Grammar of English Grammars' (1850-1) ; etc. He taught an academy in New York for 20 years.

Brown, Harvey, American army officer: b. Rahway, N. J., 1795; d. Clifton, Staten Island, 31 March 1874. He graduated at West Point in 1818 and was in constant service for more than 45 years. In the Black Hawk expedition, the Seminole Indian campaigns, in the Army of Occupation in Mexico, and to the time of the Civil War, he did gallant duty, for which he received several brevets. In 1862 he was brevetted a brigadier-general in the regular army and promoted colonel, and in 1863 was promoted to major-general, and retired.

Brown, Helen Dawes, American novelist and lecturer upon English literature: b. Concord, Mass., 1857. She has published 'Two College Girls' (1886) ; 'The Petrie Estate' (1893) ; 'Little Miss Phœbe Gay' (1895) ; 'Phœbe Gay in Her Sixteenth Year' ; 'A Civilian Attache.'

Brown, Henry Billings, American jurist: b. Lee, Mass., 2 March 1836. After studying law in the Yale and Harvard law schools he went to Detroit and was there admitted to the bar in 1860. In 1875 he was appointed United States district judge for eastern Michigan, retaining this post till 1890, when he became an associate justice of the supreme court of the United States. He retired in 1906. He has compiled a volume of admiralty reports.

Brown, Henry Kirke, American sculptor: b. Leyden, Mass., 24 Feb. 1814; d. Newburg, N. Y., 10 July 1886. He made the equestrian statue of Washington in Union Square, New York, the altar piece for the Church of the Annunciation in the same city, portrait busts of William Cullen Bryant, Dr. Willard Parker, Erastus Corning and other New York men, and the statue of De Witt Clinton in Greenwood cemetery. The last named was the first bronze statue cast in the United States. Mr. Brown brought skilled workmen from Europe and did the first work in bronze casting attempted in this country. Some of his other well-known works are a statue of Lincoln in Prospect Park, Brooklyn, and equestrian statues of Gen. Scott and Nathanael Greene for the national government.

Brown, J. Appleton, American artist: b. Newburyport, Mass., 24 July 1844; d. 1902. He studied art in Boston and Paris, and after having a studio in Boston for some years removed to New York in 1890 and became a member of the Society of American Artists. Noted works by him are 'Old Road near Paris'; 'On the Merrimac at Newburyport'; 'The Grain Field' (1902).

Brown, Jacob, American general: b. Bucks County, Pa., 9 May 1775; d. Washington, 24 Feb. 1828. He was descended from members of the Society of Friends; supported himself in early life by teaching school; was also employed for some time as a surveyor of public lands in Ohio; and settling in Jefferson County, N. Y., in 1799, became one of the pioneers in that part of the country. He next joined the militia service as a militia general in 1812; was soon after appointed brigadier-general in the regular army, and in 1814, major-general; assisted in the defense of Sackett's Harbor in 1813; exhibited much bravery in the battle of Chippewa, in that of Niagara Falls, and at the siege of Fort Erie; received the thanks of Congress and a gold medal, «emblematical of his triumphs»; and finally, at the termination of the war, continued in the army as major-general, and in 1821 succeeded to the supreme command.

Brown, James, American book-publisher: b. Acton, Mass., 19 May 1800; d. 10 March 1855. He began life as a servant in the family of Prof. Hedge, of Cambridge, who gave him instructions in the classics and in mathematics. He next entered, as shop boy, the service of William Hilliard, and in due time was taken into the Boston publishing firm of Hilliard, Gray & Company. Upon its dissolution, by the death of some of the partners, he became one of the firm now known as Little, Brown & Company, and remained in this connection until his death. The special province of the firm was the publication of law books and importation of foreign editions in the general trade, in which departments his scholarly accomplishments and taste were conspicuous and of good service in improving the style of book-making in America.

Brown, John, Scotch covenanting martyr: b. about 1627. He is said to have fought against the government at Bothwell Bridge in 1679, and to have been on intimate terms with the leaders of the persecuted party. He was shot by Claverhouse and a party of his dragoons at Priestfield, or Priesthill, in the upland parish of Buirkirk, Ayrshire, where he cultivated a small piece of ground and acted as a carrier, in 1685.

Brown, John, Scottish biblical scholar: b. Carpow, Perthshire, 1722; d. 19 June 1787. By his own intense application to study he became acquainted with the French, Italian, German, Arabic, Persian, Syriac, and Ethiopic languages, as well as the Greek and Hebrew. He became pastor at Haddington, Scotland, in 1751, and remained in that relation till his death, though called to a pastorate in the Dutch Reformed Church in New York in 1784. In general he preached three sermons every Sabbath day. He was appointed professor of theology to the Associate Synod in 1768. His most important works are: 'The Self-interpreting Bible'; 'Dictionary of the Bible'; 'Explication of the Assembly's Catechism'; 'The Christian Journal'; 'Explication of Scripture Metaphors'; 'System of Divinity'; 'General History of the Church'; 'Particular History of the Churches of England, Scotland, and Ireland;' and 'Harmony of Scripture Prophecies.' His 'Dictionary of the Bible,' and 'Self-Interpreting Bible,' so called from the copious marginal references to other passages of Scripture by which it is distinguished, have gone through many editions.

Brown, John, Scottish physician, founder of the Brunonian system in medicine: b. Bunele, Berwickshire, 1735; d. London, 17 Oct. 1788. His parents were in a very humble sphere in life, his father being merely a day laborer. Like the children of other Scottish cottars, however, he received the advantage of being educated at the parish school, where he was very soon distinguished for his abilities, and the rapid progress he made in his studies. His father having died, his mother married a weaver, and young Brown was bound an apprentice to that business; but the distaste he evinced for it was so great as to induce his stepfather to cancel his indentures, and remove him to the grammar school of Dunse, where he was looked upon as a prodigy — reading all the Latin authors with the greatest facility, and soon making considerable progress in Greek. In 1755 he went to Edinburgh, with the intention of studying divinity and entering the Church, but soon abandoned his theological studies. Having been employed by a medical student to translate his thesis into Latin, he succeeded so well that the elegance and purity of the language attracted the notice and encomiums of the professors and led to his commencing the study of medicine. In the year 1765 he married, and opened a boarding house for the accommodation of medical students; but being irregular and intemperate in his habits was soon reduced to bankruptcy. Having taken the degree of doctor in medicine at St. Andrew's, he commenced practice in Edinburgh, and produced his celebrated work, entitled the 'Elements of Medicine.' He then commenced lecturing on the practice of physic, and made use of this work as his text-book. He divided all diseases into two classes, those resulting from a deficiency, and those resulting from an excess of excitement; the one class to be treated with stimulants, the other with debilitating medicines. Becoming involved in pecuniary embarrassments he removed to London in 1786. The system of physic which he taught, though no longer accepted as a system, had a distinct influence on subsequent practice.

Brown, John, American merchant: **b.** Providence, R. I., 27 Jan. 1736; d. there, 20 Sept. 1803. A man of energy and enterprise, he developed the industry and extended the trade of his native city in a notable degree, being, it is said, the first merchant in Rhode Island to carry trade to China and the East Indies. Though having large interests at stake in the existing order of things, he was a leader in the cause of the American Revolution, and headed the party which destroyed the Gaspée in Narragansett Bay, 17 June 1772. He was chosen a delegate to the Continental Congress in 1784, but did not take his seat in that body. When Rhode Island refused to adopt the national Constitution, he did more than any other man toward securing the final reversal of that opposition. From 1799 to 1802 he was a representative in Congress. He at all times fostered the interests of the Baptist Church, contributed largely to the endowment of the present Brown University, laid the cornerstone of its original hall, and was its treasurer from 1775 to 1796.

Brown, John, American soldier: b. Sandisfield, Mass., 19 Oct. 1744; d. Stone Arabia, N. Y., 19 Oct. 1780. He graduated at Yale 1771, studied law in Providence, R. I., and in 1773 settled in Pittsfield, Mass., where he identified himself actively with the patriot cause. In 1775 he was a delegate to the provincial Congress, and was with Ethan Allen at the capture of Ticonderoga. In the same year he assisted in the capture of Fort Chambly, planned the attack on Montreal which resulted disastrously, and was at the storming of Quebec. Congress commissioned him a lieutenant-colonel in 1776, and in 1777 he conducted an expedition against Ticonderoga and the posts in its vicinity, releasing one hundred American prisoners and capturing large quantities of stores and provisions. Soon after this he retired from the service on account of his detestation of Arnold. At Albany in the winter of 1776-7 he published a handbill denouncing Arnold, predicting that he would become a traitor, and closing with the remarkably prophetic words, "Money is this man's God, and to get enough of it he would sacrifice his country." Brown was afterward employed in the Massachusetts service, and in the autumn of 1780, with the Berkshire militia, marched up the Mohawk valley for the relief of Schuyler and to act as circumstances might require. He ·was killed in ambush with 45 of his men at Stone Arabia, in Palatine, on his birthday.

Brown, John, Scottish clergyman: **b.** Whitburn, Linlithgowshire, 12 July 1784; d. Edinburgh, 13 Oct. 1858. He was ordained pastor of the burgher congregation at Biggar in 1806. In 1821 he removed to the care of the United Secession Church, Edinburgh, and afterward that of the Broughton-place Church. The burgher and anti-burgher seceders having come together in 1820, under the name of the united associate synod, he was chosen one of their professors of divinity in 1835. He took the part of the parent society on the division in the British and Foreign Bible Society, concerning the circulation of the Apocrypha, and the voluntary side on the question of church establishments. Having, by residence within the royalty of the

city of Edinburgh, become liable to the payment of an annuity tax, which was levied upon him, for the support of the city ministers, he refused to pay, and suffered his goods to be distrained; and in reply to the proceedings of the civil authorities, he preached and published two sermons on the "Law of Christ Respecting Civil Obedience, Especially in the Payment of Tribute," which, with notes and additions, became finally an octavo volume. In 1847 he and his congregation entered the United Presbyterian Church. Other works of his are: 'The Resurrection of Life' (1852); 'Expository Discourses on the Epistle of Saint Peter' (1848); 'Discourses and Sayings of Christ' (1850).

Brown, John, American abolitionist leader: b. Torrington, Conn., 9 May 1800; d. 2 Dec. 1859. His paternal ancestry was of Mayflower stock, his grandmother of Welsh, his mother of Dutch. His grandfather was a captain in the Revolution. His father, who drew his abhorrence of slavery from Jonathan Edwards, an anti-slavery champion, shared in the forcible rescue of fugitive slaves in 1798. The son found his warrant against slavery in the Bible, where its defenders found their warrant for it. From the age of five he grew up in Ohio. He was an exceedingly active and adventurous boy, who loved play-fights, but not real ones, disapproved of war, and in manhood paid annual fines rather than perform militia duty. His detestation of slavery was confirmed by witnessing the abuse of a slave boy; he swore in his own words, "eternal war against slavery" and throughout his career he never lost sight of this life-work. His 12 children who grew to maturity (out of 20 he had by two wives) were ingrained with his spirit, pledged themselves to him in prayer to spend their lives making it operative, and bore great privations to furnish him the means of so doing. He became a farmer and leather-dresser, surveyor, shepherd, and wool dealer; unfixed, unprosperous, and esteemed "shiftless." This was certainly not due to indolence or lack of honor; his immense family and want of money-getting faculty were partly responsible, his absorption in a fixed idea and lack of interest in money-getting still more. By 1834, then in Pennsylvania, he had devised an association of abolitionist families to educate colored youth, believing that it would force the South into speedy emancipation. Seeking co-operation in this plan, he removed to Ohio in 1835, and to Massachusetts in 1846; in 1840 he made surveys of Oberlin College lands in Virginia, and projected a negro colony there. In 1846 Gerrit Smith (q.v.) offered 100,000 acres of northern New York lands in small farms to colored families who would clear them; and in 1848, to work among them, Brown bought a farm in North Elba, where his family lived till his death, working with and for him. History can hardly parallel so large a family's unanimity of self-sacrifice for a social ideal, in whose behalf they stinted themselves ungrudgingly: a testimony to the father's commanding nobility of soul. From thence, by grace of contributions from abolitionists who had come to know and respect him, he traveled often on errands of organizing resistance to slavery. In 1850, after the passage of the Fugitive slave law, he visited Springfield, Mass., his former residence, and formed a "League of Gileadites," sworn to stand by each other in the rescue of fugitive slaves.

In 1854 Kansas had become, in the eyes of both South and North, the decisive battle ground of the two systems, and five of Brown's sons living in Ohio set out thither to swell the free-soil ranks; they settled a few miles from Ossawatomie, and Brown joined them in October 1855, against his intention. The family were among the most stalwart defenders of the Territory for the next two years against the fraud and terrorism by which the Border Ruffians plunged it into anarchy and bloodshed. John Brown's career there brought him into national prominence from the conspicuousness of the stage rather than the magnitude of the actions. Its most dramatic incidents were the retaliatory murder of five pro-slavery men at Pottawatomie, 24 May 1856, the capture of Capt. Pate at Black Jack, 2 June, and the magnificent defense of Ossawatomie against a crushing force of Missourians in August. It has never been narrated, even by Northerners without sympathy for the slavery cause, except with strong partisan bias pro or con, and from its very nature, it probably never can be. The judgment passed on it depends not merely on the view taken of his cause (of which an impartial estimate is not impossible), but on the questions whether that cause would have succeeded in any event, and whether he helped or harmed it. No proof of either is possible, and favor or disfavor toward fanatical enthusiasts is one of the deepest lines of cleavage among human spirits. As the victory for freedom was won, it is the fashion to assume that it never was in doubt; that active warfare was needless; that the influx of free settlers would soon have caused the pro-slavery invaders to desist in despair; that Brown acted as a lawless ruffian who justified the other party, and that he only discredited and hampered his own side. But it is still quite rational to maintain the older view, of which the premises are certainly correct, whatever the deduction may be. The pro-slavery party had no such illusions; from the first they openly proclaimed the struggle for Kansas a war for life or death, and carried it on by the machinery of war. They constituted a government by open fraud and maintained it by open violence; sacked towns, burnt houses, assassinated some of their opponents, and illegally imprisoned others; while the United States courts dispersed their foes by legal anathema, and the United States troops acted as their army. If no resistance had been offered, it is not apparent why these methods should have been less employed or less successful in 1858 than in 1856; the prize would not have been less and the incentive would have grown greater. It is certain that such peaceful submission of the free-soilers would have been hailed by the Pierce and Buchanan parties as proof incontestable that the Republican charges of illegality and outrage were mere libels. It is therefore at least arguable that it was Brown, Montgomery, Lane, and the other fighters, by their stubborn and «lawless» defiance to sheer foreign conquest, plunging Kansas into open and bloody anarchy, who shamed the government into withdrawing its help to the invaders, and convinced the slavery party that force was no longer available. Incidentally, they gave the non-combatants a free community in which to decry their champions.

Whatever may be the judgment now, the Eastern abolition leaders at that time had no thought of suppressing him: they furnished him some moneys and supplies for whatever plan he privately deemed best, feeling sure at least of some bold heartening stroke for the cause. For many years he had entertained the project of establishing, in the Maryland or Virginia mountains, a stronghold for fugitive slaves, where they could withstand attacks and if necessary reach Pennsylvania. He thought the knowledge of this refuge might stimulate the slaves into a dash for freedom, and the insecurity of slave property might drive the South into emancipation. That he could suppose the United States would allow such a guerrilla fortress and firebrand within its jurisdiction for a day, seems scarcely compatible with sanity, but Brown was insane only as all religious, intense idealists tend to become so. At the last, his plan developed into one for a stroke that should startle the country into action, draw recruits to him, and leave no chance for compromise or delay. Characteristically, he seems not to have doubted that the country would stand by him. He chose to assault the United States arsenal at Harper's Ferry, thus not only securing arms for his presumed fugitives, but making the country ring; without reflecting that this was open war against the nation, and that even the abolitionists could not uphold him. In 1857 he began drilling a small band of adherents at Tabor and Springfield, Iowa, but his trusted drillmaster, Forbes, gave the alarm, and the scheme was postponed. At length, in June 1859, he and some of his men hired a farm near Harper's Ferry, and two of his women came to keep house there; he gradually collected the remainder, 22 men besides himself, with some arms; and late Sunday evening, 16 October, with 18 men, seized the armory and took possession of the village. He made hostages of some leading citizens, and had a few neighboring planters and their slaves brought in. But the remaining citizens armed themselves, assailed and shot several of Brown's men, and surrounded the rest, and on Monday evening Col. Robert E. Lee came from Washington with a company of marines, and cooped Brown and his six remaining men into the engine-house. Brown fought there till the two sons with him were killed, and himself supposed to be mortally wounded, before he would surrender. Why he had not retreated to the mountains on capturing the arsenal was never explained, even by himself. He was tried before a Virginia court, but defended by Massachusetts counsel, sentenced as was inevitable and just, and hanged at Charlestown, W. Va. His testimony on the trial, and his demeanor and language all through, produced an ineffaceable impression on the North, revealing a character of heroic simplicity, purity, and grandeur; if his action was mad, he himself was not; and even his adversary, Gov. Wise, of Virginia, admired his "clear head, courage, fortitude, and simple ingenuousness," and felt him to be wholly truthful. The actual importance of the Harper's Ferry raid, in determining or hastening secession, has always been exaggerated, by his friends as praise and by his foes as detraction: to suppose that secession would not have come after Lincoln's election, had there been no such raid, is to ignore all American history for many years previous. But the revolt of the slave power seemed to justify his prevision and action; he became the popular incarnation of the spirit of liberty, its great pioneer and martyr; and the slogan of the North was: "John Brown's body lies a-mouldering in the grave, but his soul goes marching on!" His nature had something of the sublime; and great natures have their function and service as well as great intellects. No community could exist with such men for statesmen; perhaps none can be great without some such men for prophets.

Brown, John, Scottish physician and essayist, son of John Brown (1784-1858 q.v.): b. Biggar, 22 Sept. 1810; d. Edinburgh, 11 May 1882. He graduated in 1833 and began practice as a physician. His leisure hours were devoted to literature, many of his contributions appearing in the 'North British Review,' 'Good Words,' and other periodicals. His collected writings, published under the title of 'Horæ Subsecrivæ,' (leisure hours) (1858-82), embrace papers bearing on medicine, art, poetry, and human life generally. Several of his sketches, such as 'Rab and His Friends,' 'Our Dogs,' 'Pet Marjory,' 'Jeems the Doorkeeper,' on which his fame chiefly rests, have been published separately. Humor, tenderness, and pathos are his chief characteristics. See Peddie, 'Recollections of Dr. John Brown' (1893).

Brown, John George, Anglo-American painter: b. Durham, England, 11 Nov. 1831. He was educated in the common schools in Newcastle-on-Tyne, and came to the United States in 1853. He studied in the schools of the National Academy of Design; was elected an academieian in 1863; received honorable mention at the Paris Exposition in 1899; and in 1900 was president of the American Water Color Society. He is best known for his pictures of bootblacks and street urchins. Among his famous pictures are: 'A Merry Air with a Sad Heart'; 'The Stump Speech'; 'The Passing Show'; 'Be Mine'; and 'Training the Dogs.'

Brown, John Hamilton, American inventor: b. Liberty, Maine, 28 July 1837. At the age of 18 he was apprenticed to a gunsmith and in 1857 entered business in Haverhill, Mass. He served in the Civil War as a sharpshooter, and in 1882 was a member of the American Rifle Team at Wimbledon. He began in 1883 to perfect the invention of a weapon for military use later known as the Brown segmental wire-wound gun, which, after numerous government tests, was pronounced a success.

Brown, John Howard, American editor: b. Rhinebeck, N. Y., 8 Nov. 1840. After studying law in New York and engaging in journalism in Washington, D. C., and Augusta, Ga., he became a publisher in New York. In 1896 he removed to Boston to become editor-in-chief of 'Lamb's Biographical Dictionary of the United States.' He is the author of 'American Naval Heroes' (1898), and of numerous contributions to periodical literature.

Brown, John Lewis, French artist: b. Bordeaux, 16 Aug. 1829; d. 1892. He studied under Belloc and Roqueplan and was famous as an impressionist painter of military and hunting scenes, as well as of studies of horses and dogs. Among his numerous works are: 'Steeple Chase' (1861); 'At the Outposts' (1865); 'Relay of Omnibus Horses' (1884); 'Hohenlinden' (1887).

Brown, John Newton, American Baptist clergyman: b. New London, Conn., 29 June 1803; d. 1868. He studied at what is now Colgate University, Hamilton, N. Y., and filled successive pastorates at Buffalo, N. Y.; Providence, R. I.; Malden, Mass.; and Exeter, N. H. While at Exeter he commenced his literary labors by editing the 'Encyclopædia of Religious Knowledge' (1835). In 1838 he became a professor of exegetical theology and ecclesiastical history in the New Hampton theological institution, N. H., where he remained till 1845. He edited 'The Christian Chronicle and National Baptist' (1849-68), and was the author of 'The New Hampshire Confession' (1852).

Brown, John W., American author: b. Schenectady, N. Y., 21 Aug. 1814; d. Malta, 9 April, 1849. He graduated at Union College in 1832, and was settled as an Episcopal minister at Astoria, N. Y. In 1845 he became editor of the 'Protestant Churchman.' He was the author of 'Christmas Bells, a Tale of Holy Tide, and Other Poems,' and of several prose tales of a religious character.

Brown, John Young, American lawyer: b. Claysville, Hardin County, Ky., 28 June 1835; d. Henderson, Ky., 11 Jan. 1904. He graduated at Center College, Danville, 1855, studied law, and was admitted to the bar. In 1859 he was elected to Congress, but not having attained the constitutional age, could not take his seat. He was again elected to Congress in 1868, but his seat was refused him by the House because of political disabilities. Finally he served in Congress (1873-7). He retired to the practice of law and during 1891-5 he was Democratic governor of Kentucky.

Brown, Joseph Emerson, American statesman: b. Pickens County, S. C., 15 April 1821; d. Atlanta, Ga., 30 Nov. 1894. He was educated at Calhoun Academy, and graduated at Yale in 1846. He settled in Canton, Ga.; served in the State legislature, and was elected governor in 1857; serving three terms. As war governor he opposed Jefferson Davis in the matter of the conscription laws and raised 10,000 recruits to oppose Sherman's march to the sea; but would not allow them to leave the State. After the war he gave hearty support to the reconstruction measures, and supported Gen. Grant for the presidency. He was Chief-Justice of Georgia in 1868, and United States Senator in 1880-91.

Brown, Lancelot, English landscape gardener, sometimes called "Capability Brown": b. at Kirkharle, 1715; d. 1773. He commenced life as a kitchen gardener, but by his industry and genius, rose rapidly in public estimation till he came to be regarded as a kind of oracle in taste in regard to all rural improvements, agricultural, horticultural, and even architectural. His extensive employment enabled him to realize a handsome independence, and he adorned the station to which he had worked his way with more graces and virtues than are often displayed by those who have been born to it. He obtained the dignity of high sheriff of Huntingdon in 1770. He avoided the stiff formality of the older landscape gardens, but is charged with having often sinned against good taste by endeavoring to reform natural scenery, and force it, under all circumstances, to assume the form of clumps, belts, and serpentine canals. His architectural performances are remarkable for their interiors.

Brown, **Moses**, American naval officer: b. Salisbury, Mass., 1742; d. at sea 1804. He was a sailor in early life, and commanded the United States privateer *General Arnold*. He was the first commander of the sloop of war *Merrimac*, having the rank of captain U. S. N. He was retired by Thomas Jefferson and re-entered the merchant service.

Brown, **Nicholas**, American merchant and philanthropist: b. Providence, R. I., 4 April 1769; d. there, 27 Oct. 1841. He graduated at Brown University, 1786. Through the death of his father in 1791, he inherited a handsome fortune, formed a partnership with his brother-in-law, Thomas P. Ives, and became one of the most successful and best-known merchants of America. He was a nephew of John Brown (1736-1803, q.v.). In 1792 he gave $500 to Brown University with which to purchase law books. This was the beginning of a long series of endowments and benefactions to that institution, which took its present name in honor of him in 1804, when he endowed a professorship of oratory and *belles-lettres*. In 1822 he built Hope College, at an expense of $20,000; Manning Hall in 1834, at a cost of $18,500; and a president's house in 1840, costing $7,000. The total of his various gifts amounted to $160,000. He was a trustee from 1791 to 1825; a fellow, 1825-41, and a most efficient treasurer from 1796 to 1825. He was also a generous donor to the Providence Athenæum and Butler Hospital for the Insane. He served several terms in the State legislature, and in 1840 was a presidential elector.

Brown, **Oliver Madox**, English artist, son of Ford Madox Brown (q.v.): b. 1855; d. 1874. From early boyhood he showed remarkable capacity both in painting and literature, especially prose fiction and poetry. His two most promising pictures were 'The Tempest — Prospero and the Infant Miranda' (exhibited in 1871 at the International Exhibition, South Kensington), and 'A Scene from Silas Marner' (1872). 'Gabriel Denver' (1873), and some other unfinished novels, besides sonnets and other poems, show wonderful literary power in one so young. His 'Literary Remains' were published in 1876.

Brown, or **Browne**, **Robert**, English clergyman, the founder of a religious sect first called "Brownists," and afterward "Independents": b. Tolethorpe, Rutlandshire, about 1550; d. Northampton, about 1633. He studied at Cambridge, from whence, in 1572, he removed to London. Here he supported himself by teaching; but soon returned to Cambridge and began openly to attack the government and liturgy of the Church of England as anti-Christian. He first ascended the pulpit at Norwich in 1581, where he succeeded in converting a number of Dutch, who had a congregation there, to his opinions. He then went to Middleburg, in Holland, with his followers, and wrote a book called 'A Treatise of Reformation without Tarrying for any Man.' In 1586 he returned to England, and, as he still labored to gain converts, was excommunicated by the Bishop of Peterborough. This censure, joined perhaps

with the evaporation of his zeal, induced him to submit, and in 1586 he became master of Stamford Grammar School, a post which he occupied till 1590, when he was presented to the living of Acworth, in Northamptonshire. He died in Northampton jail, where he had been sent for assaulting a constable. The sect of Brownists, far from expiring with their founder, soon spread so as to become a subject of great alarm; and a bill was brought into Parliament which inflicted on them very severe pains and penalties. In process of time, however, the name Brownists was merged in that of Congregationalists, or Independents, under the latter of which titles they formed a powerful party in the commonwealth.

Brown, **Robert**, Scottish botanist: b. Montrose, 21 Dec. 1773; d. London, 10 June 1858. He finished his education in 1795, when he became ensign and assistant surgeon in a Fifeshire fencible regiment, which he accompanied to Ireland, remaining there till 1800. He was then, through the influence of Sir Joseph Banks, appointed naturalist to Capt. Flinders' surveying expedition to Australia or New Holland. The whole continent of Australia was circumnavigated, the coast at various points examined, and Brown remained in the colony, visiting various parts of New South Wales and Van Diemen's Land, till 1805. He returned with nearly 4,000 species of plants, and was shortly after appointed librarian to the Linnæan Society, and was now able to devote himself to the systematic study of his plants. He continued to make the result of his investigations known in communications to the Linnæan and Royal societies. One of his earliest papers was on a group of the family of plants named by Jussieu *Apocyneæ*, which he succeeded in establishing as a separate family under the title already given them by Jussieu of *Asclepiadeæ*. In 1810 he published the first volume of the great work he had been preparing on the plants of Australia and Tasmania, entitling it 'Prodromus Floræ Novæ Hollandiæ et Insulæ Van Diemen.' No second volume of it ever appeared. He was the first English writer on botany who adopted the natural system of classification which has since entirely superseded that of Linnæus. In 1814 he published a botanical appendix to Capt. Flinders' account of his voyage, entitled 'General Remarks, Geographical and Systematical, on the Botany of Terra Australis.' In 1828 he published a brief 'Account of Microscopical Observations on the Particles Contained in the Pollen of Plants, and on the General Existence of Active Molecules in Organic and Inorganic Bodies.' He was the first to call attention to the presence of these active molecules. The movement of the granules of the fovilla (or semi-fluid matter contained in the pollen grains) which he believed to be purely physical, or non-organic, has on the Continent acquired the name of the Brownian or Brunonian movement. He also wrote botanical appendices for the voyages of Ross and Parry, the African exploration of Denham and Clapperton and others, and described, with Dr. Bennet, the plants collected by Dr. Horsfield in Java. In 1810 he received the charge of the collections and library of Sir Joseph Banks, which were afterward bequeathed to him for life. He transferred them in 1827 to the British Museum, and was appointed keeper of botany in that institution. He became a Fellow of the Royal Society in 1811, D.C.L. of Oxford in 1832, a foreign associate of the French Academy of Sciences in 1833. He had the Copley medal in 1839, and was appointed president of the Linnæan Society in 1849. He also received the decoration of the highest Prussian order of civil merit, presided over by Baron Humboldt, who called him *Botanicorum facile princeps*. As a botanist Brown occupied the very highest rank. He made the microscope and the study of development the basis of his classification; and by his skill in the application of ascertained facts to the elucidation of obscure and the explanation of doubtful phenomena, greatly advanced our scientific knowledge of the vegetable kingdom. His works, contained chiefly in the 'Transactions' of learned societies and other inaccessible forms, are not of a nature to be popular.

Brown, Robert, Scottish scientist: b. Campster, Caithness-shire, 1842; d. 1896. He explored the coast of Spitzbergen, Greenland, and the western shore of Baffin Bay in 1861, made charts of the interior of Vancouver, and with Whymper, in 1867, made discoveries as to the inland ice of Greenland, since borne out by those of Peary. He traveled extensively in the Barbary States, lectured on scientific themes in Glasgow and Edinburgh, and was a member of learned societies in Europe and America. He published 'Manual of Botany' (1874); 'Peoples of the World' (1882–5); 'Science for All' (1877–82).

Brown, SIR Samuel, English engineer: b. London, 1776; d. Blackheath, Kent, 15 March 1852. After serving with honor in the English navy he was made a retired captain in 1842. He is remembered for his system of making iron chain cables, and as the designer and builder of the earliest iron suspension bridge in England, at Berwick-on-Tweed. The famous chain pier was designed by him. He was knighted in 1838.

Brown, Samuel, Scottish chemist and poet: b. Haddington, 23 Feb. 1817; d. Edinburgh, 20 Sept. 1856. He graduated from the University of Edinburgh with extraordinary attainments, began his public career by delivering, in 1840, in association with his intimate friend, Edward Forbes, a course of lectures on the philosophy of the sciences, and having established among his auditors, as he had before among his teachers, the conviction that he was destined to great achievement, renounced all else that he might have won, to devote himself to the slow experimental realization of a great scientific conception. In 1849 he delivered in Edinburgh a series of lectures on the history of chemistry, tracing its progress from its playful childhood among the Greeks, through the Oriental and Mediæval alchemists, with most fascinating sketches of Roger Bacon and Paracelsus; passing thence through the epoch of Stahl and Priestley, till the young and unfortunate Lavoisier changed the whole form of chemical science, opening a new path to all succeeding philosophers. In 1850 he published the 'Tragedy of Galileo.' Many of his lectures and essays have been collected since his death, under the title of 'Lectures on the Atomic Theory, and Essays Scientific and Literary.'

Brown, Samuel Robbins, D.D. (1810–80), American scholar, educator and missionary: b. East Windsor, Conn., 16 June 1810; d. Munson, Mass., June 1880. He established the first Christian Protestant school in China, brought the first Chinese students to America for education, and was the chief instrument in establishing (at Elmira, N. Y.) the first woman's college in America, chartered as such, and translated the New Testament into Japanese 13 days after the formation of the American Board of Commissioners for Foreign Missions. His mother was Phœbe Hinsdale, one of the first and best known of American hymnologists. Educated at Munson Academy, Yale College and the Theological Seminary at Columbia, S. C., he supported himself most of the time by teaching music, one of his pupils being Miss Bulloch, who became the mother of President Theodore Roosevelt. He sailed with his young bride in 1838 to China and at Macao organized and taught in the school of the Morrison Education Society, which was later removed to Hong Kong, where Dr. Brown was wounded by pirates. He returned to America in 1847, bringing with him Yung Wing (who afterward brought 120 Chinese students to America) and Wong, who became a famous physician. Most of Dr. Brown's Chinese pupils rose to positions in the Imperial Customs and other Government services, which required a knowledge of English. Remaining in America until 1859, as pastor and teacher at Owasco Lake, N. Y., he went out to Japan to found the mission of the Reformed Church in America. He trained up a native ministry and many Japanese pupils who have since become editors, statesmen, scholars, presidents of colleges, or otherwise active in the remaking of the Japanese Empire. He wrote the first Grammar of Colloquial Japanese and other works for the mastery of the language, and made scholarly translations besides the whole of the New Testament. See his life, 'A Maker of the New Orient' (1902), by William Elliot Griffis.

Brown, Sanger, American physician: b. Bloomfield, Ontario, 17 Feb. 1852. He was graduated from the Bellevue Hospital Medical College, New York, 1880, and has since held several important professional posts, becoming professor of neurology in the Post Graduate Medical School of Chicago in 1890. He was the earliest to demonstrate that the occipital lobe is the centre of vision in monkeys.

Brown, Thomas, Scotch metaphysician: b. Kirkmabreck, Kirkcudbright, 9 Jan. 1778; d. London, 2 April 1820. He was educated at the University of Edinburgh, where he obtained the professorship of moral philosophy. He distinguished himself, at a very early age, by an acute review of the medical and physiological theories of Dr. Darwin, in a work entitled 'Observations on Darwin's Zoonomia.' But he chiefly deserves notice on account of his metaphysical speculations, his chief work being 'Lectures on the Philosophy of the Human Mind' (1822). His system reduces the intellectual faculties to three great classes — perception, simple suggestion, and relative suggestion, employing the term suggestion as nearly synonymous with association. His development of the theory of cause and effect was first suggested by Hume.

Brown, Thomas Edward, English poet: b. Isle of Man, 1830; d. Clifton, England, 29 Oct. 1897. After a brilliant career at Christ Church College, Oxford, he became assistant master at Clifton College, Bristol, in 1862, resigning in 1892. His work, though strong and remarkably original, failed to attract general attention during his lifetime, but when collected in 1900, contemporaneously with two volumes of his 'Letters,' they drew forth extended notices from leading critical reviews and journals in England and the United States. His poems, which are written in Anglo-Manx dialect for the most part, are chiefly narrative, and include 'Betsy Lee' (1873); 'Fo'c's'le Yarns, including Betsy Lee' (1881); 'The Doctor and Other Poems' (1887); 'The Manx Witch and Other Poems' (1889); 'Old John and Other Poems' (1893).

Brown, Sir William, English merchant and philanthropist: b. Ballymena, Ireland, 1784; d. 1864. In 1800 he removed with his parents to Baltimore, Md., and became the partner of his father in the linen trade there. In 1809 he set up a branch of the business in Liverpool and subsequently founded the famous mercantile house of Brown, Shipley & Company. He sat in Parliament four years from 1846, advocated free trade and decimal coinage, gave $200,000, in 1857, to establish a free public library in Liverpool, and built the original library building and museum there.

Brown, William Garrott, American writer: b. Marion, Ala., 24 April 1868. He graduated at Harvard in 1891, taking highest honors in history, and became assistant in the Harvard Library. In 1892 he took an active part in the Presidential campaign, serving on various committees and stumping Massachusetts in behalf of Cleveland. He has made a special study of Southern history, and since 1900 has devoted himself to writing and lecturing on this topic, contributing chiefly to the 'Atlantic Monthly.' His writings in book form are: 'Andrew Jackson' (1900); 'History of Alabama' (1901); 'The Lower South in American History' (1902); 'Stephen A. Douglas' (1902); 'Golf' (1902); 'History of the United States Since the Civil War' (1903); 'A Gentleman of the South' (1903).

Brown, William Montgomery, American Protestant Episcopal bishop: b. Orrville, Ohio, 6 Nov. 1855. He entered the Episcopal ministry, became archdeacon of Ohio in 1891, and in 1898 was consecrated coadjutor bishop of Arkansas, becoming bishop of that diocese in the year following.

Brown-Séquard, Charles Edouard, shärl ä-dd-är brown-sä-kär, Franco-American physiologist and physician: b. Mauritius, 1818; d. Paris, 1 April 1894. His father was a sea captain from Philadelphia, who married on the island a lady named Séquard. The son studied in Paris and graduated M.D. in 1846. He devoted himself mainly to physiological research, and received numerous prizes, French and British, for the results of valuable experiments on blood, muscular irritability, animal heat, the spinal cord, and the nervous system. In 1864 he became professor of physiology at Harvard, but in 1869 returned to Paris as professor of pathology in the School of Medicine. In 1873 he became a medical practitioner in New York, treating especially diseases of the nervous system; and in 1878 succeeded Claude Bernard as professor of experimental medicine at the Collège de France. He repeatedly lectured in England. His publications include lectures on 'Physiology and Pathology of the Nervous System' (1860); on 'Paralysis of the Lower Extremities' (1860); and on 'Nervous Affections' (1873).

Brown, the color produced when certain substances — wood or paper, for example — are scorched or partially burned. Brown is not one of the primary colors in a spectrum. It is composed of red and yellow, with black, the negation of color. It is also the name of a genus of colors, of which the typical species is ordinary brown, tinged with grayish or blackish. The other species are chestnut brown, deep brown, bright brown, rusty, cinnamon, red brown, rufous, glandaceous, liver-colored, sooty, and lurid.

Brown Bear. See BEAR, BROWN.

Brown Coal, a variety of bituminous coal, and formed like it of vegetable remains, but more woody or fibrous in its formation. It usually belongs to later formations than the common coal, and on this account has been called modern coal. Brown coal is at first hardly to be distinguished from common coal, but it has a brown streak when scratched, and when exposed to the air rapidly deteriorates, falling to powder in a few months, while the kind called lignite tears and splits. Brown coal contains much more water than common coal, and is thus less valuable as fuel. Where better fuel is scarce, however, it is largely used. See LIGNITE.

Brown Spar, a name given to the brown varieties of dolomite whose color is due to the presence of iron carbonate.

Brown Thrush, or Thrasher. See THRASHER.

Brown University, an educational institution in Providence, R. I. Its charter was granted by the General Assembly of the State in 1764 and the institution was opened in Warren in 1765 as Rhode Island College. Its founding was due to the wish of the Baptists to have a college under their own control and it has ever since been affiliated with the Baptist Church, although remaining unsectarian. The college was removed to Providence in 1770 and in 1804 its name was changed to Brown University in honor of Nicholas Brown (q.v.), whose various gifts to the college were not far from $160,000 in amount. Under its fourth president, Francis Wayland (q.v.), 1827-55, the university was practically reorganized. Under President Elisha Benjamin Andrews (q.v.), 1889-98, the number of students increased from 268 to 860. In 1891 the Woman's College was founded, and in 1897 this was accepted by the corporation as the Woman's College in Brown University. Since the presidency of the Rev. W. H. P. Faunce began in 1899, the institution has grown very rapidly; a $2,000,000 endowment has been secured; and several large and important buildings have been erected, including the John Carter Brown Library, the Administration Building, the Engineering Building, Caswell Hall, and Rockefeller Hall.

At the end of 1906 there were 86 professors and instructors, 935 students and about 6,100 graduates; in 1905 the productive funds were $2,988,866, income, $671,918, and there were 150,000 volumes in the library. F. T. GUILD, *Registrar and Secretary of Faculty.*

Browne, Charles Farrar ("ARTEMUS WARD"), American humorist: b. Waterford, Me., 26 April 1834; d. Southampton, England, 6 March 1867. He learned the printer's trade, and while working on the *Carpet Bag*, a Boston comic weekly, began his career as one of the most widely popular of American writers and lecturers. 'Artemus Ward's Sayings,' written for the Cleveland *Plain Dealer*, extended his fame as a clever and witty writer. His humorous lectures, especially those on Mormonism, proved most successful in this country and in England. He died of consumption while on a lecture tour in the latter country. Browne's humor had a quality of its own, and was essentially democratic and American. His winning personality never failed to put an audience in a receptive mood. His works in book form are: 'Artemus Ward: His Book' (1865); 'Artemus Ward: His Travels Among the Mormons' (1865); 'Artemus Ward: His Book of Goaks' (1865); 'On the Rampage' (1865); 'Artemus Ward Among the Fenians' (1865); 'Artemus Ward in London' (1867); 'Artemus Ward's Lecture at Egyptian Hall' (1869). While in England he made several contributions to 'Punch,' beginning with the number for 1 Sept. 1866. Compare M. D. Landon's biographical sketch, prefixed to 'Artemus Ward, His Works Complete' (1875).

Browne, Charles Francis, American artist: b. Natick, Mass., 21 May 1859. He studied at the Boston Art Museum, the Philadelphia Academy of Fine Arts, and the Paris Ecole des Beaux Arts. He has been for some years lecturer and instructor in the history of art in the Chicago Art Institute, and has exhibited both in this country and Europe.

Browne, Edward Granville, English Orientalist: b. Uley, England, 7 Feb. 1862. He was educated at Eton and Pembroke College, Cambridge. He traveled in Persia (1887-8), becoming lecturer in Persian at Cambridge in the year last named. He has published 'A Traveler's Narrative, Written to Illustrate the Episode of the Báb,' Persian text and English translation with notes (1891); 'The New History of Mirzá and Ali Muhammad the Báb' (1893); 'A Year Amongst the Persians' (1893).

Browne, Edward Harold, English prelate: b. Aylesbury, Buckinghamshire, 6 March 1811; d. Winchester, Hampshire, 19 Dec. 1891. He was educated at Emmanuel College, Cambridge, took orders in the Anglican Church in 1836, and was consecrated Bishop of Ely in 1864. In 1873, he was transferred to Winchester, resigning this bishopric in 1891. He was a prominent advocate of the old Catholic movement in Germany and one of the Old Testament company of revision of the King James version of the Bible. He published 'An Exposition of the XXXIX. Articles' (1850-3); 'Sermons on the Atonement and Other Subjects' (1859); 'The Messiah Foretold and Expected' (1862); 'The Pentateuch and the Elohistic Psalms in Reply to Bishop Colenso' (1863); 'The Stripe, the Victory, and the Kingdom' (1872); 'Position

and Parties of the English Church' (1875); 'Commentary on Genesis' in the 'Speaker's Commentary.'

Browne, Frances, Irish poet: b. Stranorlar, Donegal, Ireland, 16 June 1818. When she was 18 months old she lost her sight from smallpox. From her brothers and sisters attending the village school she obtained as much information as they were acquiring, and listened to such books as they would read to her. 'Robinson Crusoe' and 'Mungo Park's African Adventures' were among these works. The prose writings of Sir Walter Scott, with which she became familiar from their being read to her, deeply influenced her mind. In 1841 she commenced contributing verse to the 'Athenæum,' edited at that time by Mr. T. K. Hervey. He became interested in her story, related it with considerable effect in the 'Athenæum,' paid her for her writings, and introduced her to other publications, from which she also derived pecuniary benefits. In 1844 the 'Star of Atteghei' and other poems appeared in a small volume, which was well received. Among the advantages accruing to the poet from it, was her being placed on the pension list for £20 a year by Sir Robert Peel, prime minister.

Browne, Francis Fisher, American editor and author: b. South Halifax, Vt., 1 Dec. 1843. During the Civil War he served in the 46th Massachusetts Volunteers. He edited the 'Lakeside Monthly,' 1869-74, and in 1880 became editor of 'The Dial,' Chicago, which under his direction has come to be one of the two or three American literary journals worthy of being ranked with the best English periodicals of similar scope. Publications: 'Every-day Life of Abraham Lincoln' (1886); 'Volunteer Grain' (1896), poems. He has edited 'Golden Poems by British and American Authors' (1881); 'Golden Treasury of Poetry and Prose' (1883); 'Bugle Echoes: a Collection of Poems of the Civil War' (1886).

Browne, George Forrest, English bishop: b. York, England, 1833. He was educated at St. Catharine's College, Cambridge, and ordained 1858. He was appointed theological tutor and bell lecturer in ecclesiastical history in the Episcopal Church of Scotland, 1862; fellow and lecturer at St. Catharine's, 1863-5; secretary and chief organizer of the Cambridge local examinations. He was rector of Ashley, 1869-75; Disney professor of archæology, 1887-92; canon of St. Paul's, 1891-7; bishop of Stepney, 1895-7; whence he was transferred to the see of Bristol. He is the author of 'Ice Caves of France and Switzerland' (1865); 'The Venerable Bede' (1879); 'University Sermons' (1878-80); 'The Ilam Crosses' (1889); 'Early English Church History' (1893); 'The Church at Home Before Augustine' (1894); 'Augustine and His Companions' (1895); 'Conversion of the Heptarchy' (1896); 'Theodore and Wilfrid' (1897); 'History of St. Catharine's College' (1902); 'Life and Works of St. Aldhelm,' and various publications of the Church History Society (1894-7).

Browne, George Waldo, American author: b. Deerfield, N. H., 8 Oct. 1851. For five years he edited 'American Young Folks,' and is a well-known writer for young people. He has written over 100 serials and several hundred short stories and articles for the leading juvenile periodicals. Of his books the best known are: 'The Woodranger' (1899); 'Two American Boys in Hawaii' (1899); 'Pearl of the Orient' (1900); 'Legends of the Hills' (1901). His most recent juveniles include 'For Home and Honor' (1902); 'From Switch to Lever' (1902); 'Zip the Acrobat' (1902); Comrades Under Castro' (1903); 'With Roger's Rangers' (1905).

Browne, **Hablot Knight**, English caricaturist, better known by his pseudonym of PHIZ: b. London, 15 June 1815; d. Hove, Brighton, 8 July 1882. He was educated at a private school, and at an early age began to draw caricatures with great spirit. In 1835 he succeeded Seymour as the illustrator of Dickens' 'Pickwick,' and so happy and successful was his pencil that he was engaged to illustrate 'Nicholas Nickleby'; 'Dombey and Son'; 'Martin Chuzzlewit'; 'David Copperfield,' and other works of that great novelist. He subsequently contributed many graphic illustrations to the novels of Lever, Ainsworth, Scott (the Abbotsford edition of the Waverley Novels), and to an illustrated edition of Byron, besides sending many comic sketches to the illustrated serials of the time. See Thompson, 'Life and Labors of H. K. Browne' (1884).

Browne, **Isaac Hawkins**, English poet: b. Burton-on-Trent, Staffordshire, 1706; d. 1760. He was educated at Trinity College, Cambridge, and called to the bar, but he did not practise. He wrote 'Design and Beauty'; 'The Pipe of Tobacco' (in which he imitates Pope, Young, Swift, and others); and a Latin poem, 'De Animi Immortalitate,' modeled on Lucretius and Virgil. The last-named received high commendation from the scholars of his time, and has been several times translated into English. Browne had a great reputation as a wit and conversationalist.

Browne, **John Ross**, American author and traveler: b. Ireland, 1817; d. Oakland, Cal., 9 Dec. 1875. He came to America when a child, his father settling in Kentucky. At the age of 18, having learned stenography, he went to Washington, and for several years was employed as shorthand reporter in the Senate. His desire for travel led him to take a whaling cruise, in the course of which he visited the greater part of the world. In 1849 he was a government commissioner in California, and reported the State Constitutional Convention proceedings. In 1851, and again in 1861, he traveled extensively in Europe and the Holy Land, visiting Iceland, Russia, Poland, and other countries. Commissioned by the government to study the mineral resources west of the Rocky Mountains, he presented an elaborate report, reviewing the mines, climate, topography, agriculture, commerce, etc., of that region. His books of travel were illustrated with humorous drawings of his own. He was United States minister to China in 1868-9. Publications: 'Etchings of a Whaling Cruise' (1846); 'Yusef: a Crusade in the East' (1853); 'Adventures in the Apache Country' (1869); 'The Land of Thor' (1866); 'Adventures of an American Family in Germany' (1867); 'Crusoe's Island, with Sketches of Adventures in California and Washoe' (1864); 'Resources of the Pacific Slope' (1869).

Browne, **Junius Henri**, American journalist: b. Seneca Falls, N. Y., 14 Oct. 1833; d. New York, 2 April 1902. He was a graduate of Saint Xavier College, Cincinnati. In 1861 he became war correspondent for the New York *Tribune*, was wounded at Fort Donelson, and taken prisoner while engaged in an abortive expedition to run the Vicksburg batteries. After an imprisonment of 20 months in seven different prisons, he eluded his guard at Salisbury, N. C., traveled 400 miles through a hostile country, and reached the Union lines 14 Jan. 1865. His list of Union soldiers who died at Salisbury, published in the *Tribune*, is the only authentic account of their fate. After the War he served as correspondent of the New York *Tribune*, *Times*, and other journals, and contributed many articles to leading periodicals. His best-known works are: 'Four Years in Secessia' (1865); 'The Great Metropolis: A Mirror of New York' (1869); 'Sights and Sensations in Europe' (1872). A series of articles on women, which he wrote for the 'Galaxy,' created a sensation in literary circles. His 'Four Years in Secessia' was hastily prepared and lacked much grace and elegance in its literary form, but its descriptions of various incidents of the war and particularly its information concerning the conditions of the Southern prisons and the Northern soldier confined in them, render the book especially valuable.

Browne, SIR **Thomas**, English prosaist, scholar, and physician: b. 19 Oct. 1605, London, parish of Saint Michael, Cheapside; d. Norwich, 19 Oct. 1682. His father, who had been a mercer at Upton, in Cheshire, and came of an ancient and honorable family, died early; and Browne's mother soon married Sir Thomas Dutton. Browne received his early education at Winchester College, and in 1623 was sent as a fellow-commoner to Broadgate Hall (now Pembroke College) Oxford. Here he graduated B.A., 21 June 1626, and M.A., 11 June 1629. Early becoming interested in the natural sciences, he devoted most of his time at Oxford to the study of medicine, and for some time after graduation practised medicine in Oxfordshire. Later on, he accompanied his step-father to Ireland on a tour of inspection of its forts and castles. After this, Browne continued his travels through France and Italy, spending some time at the celebrated schools of physic at Montpellier and Padua, and doubtless acquiring some of the "six languages" which, "besides the jargon and patois of several provinces," he later stated that he understood. On his way back to England he traveled through Holland, where in 1633 the University of Leyden conferred upon him the degree of Doctor of Medicine. After his return, he established himself as a physician at Shipden Hall, near Halifax. He was much "resorted to for his skill in physic," and spent his leisure hours in study and contemplation.

At Shipden Hall, 1635-36, Browne composed the beautiful contemplative soliloquy known as the 'Religio Medici.' It was written for his "private exercise and satisfaction," and was not intended for publication. It was, however, widely circulated in manuscript among his literary friends, and was at last surreptitiously published in 1642 by Andrew Cooke. Browne, in self-defense, published a correct edition in 1643: and almost simultaneously appeared a series of

"Observations" on the work, penned in 24 hours by the eminent Sir Kenelm Digby. The book at once became immensely popular, both at home and abroad. In 1664, John Merryweather published a Latin version of it; and Dutch, French, and German translations appeared in 1665, 1668, and 1680 respectively. Because of the "daring skepticism" which it combined with "implicit faith in revelation," it was placed in the Index Expurgatorius of the Catholic Church. Between 1642 and 1881, the treatise ran through 33 English editions.

In 1637 Browne moved to Norwich, where he practised medicine and pursued his literary studies till his death. On 10 July 1637, he was incorporated Doctor of Physic at Oxford. He married, 1641, Dorothy, fourth daughter of Edward Mileham, of Burlingham St. Peter. She bore him 12 children, and survived him three years. Throughout the civil wars he remained at heart a Royalist, and ever regretted what he called "the horrid murther of King Charles I." But his calm spirit "quietly rested under the drums and tramplings" of the revolution, and he took no active part in the upheaval of the times.

Browne's reputation for learning and research was greatly increased in 1646 by the publication of his elaborate work, "Pseudodoxia Epidemica; or, Enquiries into very many received tenets and commonly presumed truths, which examined prove but Vulgar and Common Errors." This treatise is encyclopedic in scope, and must have grown to its final extent through many years of slow accretion. It was soon translated into Dutch, German, and French; and attracted no little attention among scholars by the vast and recondite learning it displayed. Browne's advice and assistance soon became sought by scholars engaged in scientific and antiquarian pursuits. Among the best known men of the time who sought his acquaintance was John Evelyn, with whom in 1658 he began a correspondence which lasted through his life. In October 1671, Evelyn journeyed to Norwich to visit Browne; and wrote, in his diary, an account of Browne's surroundings. The house and garden were "a paradise and cabinet of rarities, and that of the best collecions, especially medals, books, plants, and natural things." Evelyn noticed particularly Browne's extensive collection of birds' eggs.

In 1658 Browne composed the solemn 'Hydriotaphia, Urn-Burial; or, A Discourse of the Sepulchral Urns lately Found in Norfolk.' At the same time he published the most fantastic of his writings, 'The Garden of Cyrus; or, The Quincuncial, Lozenge, or Network Plantations of the Ancients, Artificially, Naturally, Mystically Considered.' In December 1664, he was created socius honorarius of the College of Physicians, and received the diploma of the institution on 6 July 1665. On 28 Sept. 1671, he was knighted by Charles II., on the occasion of a royal visit to Norwich. Although Browne's literary activity continued unabated until his death, he published nothing after 1658. He died on his 77th birthday, and was buried in the church of St. Peter Mancroft, Norwich. In 1840, some workmen who were making a new grave accidentally fractured the lid of Browne's coffin with a pickaxe. The skeleton was thus exposed, and the sexton took possession of the skull. It is now on exhibition in the Norfolk and Norwich Hospital.

Many of Browne's manuscript writings were published posthumously. In 1684 his friend Archbishop Tenison brought out a collection of 'Miscellany Tracts' on subjects ranging from the ancient monuments of Norwich to the plants mentioned in the Bible and the fishes eaten by our Saviour with his disciples after his resurrection from the dead. In 1690 his son, Dr. Edward Browne, published his beautiful 'Letter to a Friend, upon occasion of the death of his intimate friend,' which forms a sort of prelude to the careful dissertation on 'Christian Morals'—intended perhaps as a continuation of the 'Religio Medici' —which was first published in 1716 by Archdeacon Jeffrey. A collection of the 'Posthumous Works of the learned Sir Thomas Browne, Knt., M.D., late of Norwich,' was published by an unknown editor in 1712. It contains, among other tracts, a striking fragment of an essay on "Dreams."

Browne belongs to the class of mystical soliloquists who love to discourse to themselves about fantastic subtleties too fine to excite the curiosity of vulgar minds, but who yet are not too self-engrossed to allow the friendly reader to overhear their musings. He loves to "turn the world round" not only for his own, but also for his reader's "recreation," and to lead the reader with him through a labyrinth of fancy until both "lose themselves in a mystery." His works are lacking in design, uneven, whimsical, and capricious; but they reveal a personalty serene, altruistic, tolerant, mystical, reverent, and friendly. Furthermore, he commands a style that for lordly eloquence and orchestral harmony remains unrivaled in the entire history of English prose.

Browne's greatest work is the 'Religio Medici.' In this treatise, which combines the meditations of many leisure hours, he has revealed all of the emotional affluence of his soul. It is a mystical acceptance of the creed of the Anglican Church, leavened with a touching tolerance of other beliefs. Paradoxically it combines an imaginative scepticism with a naive credulity. Browne believed in witches, for example; and refused to accept the Copernican system of astronomy because it contradicted the literal statements of the Hebrew Scriptures. But there is no narrowness in Browne's most characteristic mood. He rises on the wings of exaltation until he soars into the presence of Infinitude and glows with a religious ecstasy known of all nations and of all times.

The 'Pseudodoxia' is a less worthy work. It is a vast chaos of recondite lore, bewildering by the very extent of its voluminous observation. It opens with an inquiry into the sources of error not a little resembling Bacon's famous arraignment of "Idols"; But Browne had no true sense of natural law, as Bacon understood it, and often fallacies pursue him in his pursuit of fallacy.

'The Garden of Cyrus' is a fanciful dissertation on the quincunx, that geometrical arrangement of five points familiar in the five of a domino. As Coleridge said, Browne finds "quincunxes in heaven above, quincunxes in earth below, quincunxes in the mind of man, quincunxes in tones, in optic nerves, in roots of trees, in leaves, in everything.»

The grandeur of Browne's style is displayed most fully in 'Hydriotaphia.' Some Roman sepulchral urns accidentally unearthed in Norfolk furnished him with the suggestion for this eloquent monody, which, beginning with an historical discussion of ancient modes of burial, soon develops into a solemn homily on death and the vicissitudes of worldly fame. The style shows an eloquent spontaneity rather than a conscious mastery of art. It would not be a serviceable model for a modern writer; it is hyper-latinised and capricious; but it is incomparable for pompous rhythm and resonant harmony.

Bibliography.— The standard edition of Browne's works is that edited by Simon Wilkin (4 vols. 1835-6) which has been called the best edited book in the language; it contains a life by Dr. Johnson. The posthumous works (ed. 1712) contain also a life and Whitefoot's minutes. Consult: S. T. Coleridge, 'Literary Remains'; Edward Dowden, 'Puritan and Anglican Studies'; Edmund Gosse, 'Sir Thomas Browne'; W. A. Greenhill, introductions (to separate vols. of Browne) 'Golden Treasury Series'; Walter Pater, 'Appreciations'; Sir Leslie Stephen, 'Hours in a Library' (vol. I); J. A. Symonds, introduction, 'Camelot Series.'

CLAYTON HAMILTON,
Sometime Tutor in English, Columbia University.

Browne, Thomas Alexander (ROLF BOLD-REWOOD), Australian romancer: b. London, England, 6 Aug. 1826. He is a son of Capt. Sylvester Browne, a founder of Melbourne, Australia. He was educated in Sidney College, and has written 'Ups and Downs: a Story of Australian Life' (1879); 'Robbery Under Arms: Life and Adventures in the Bush' (1888); 'A Squatter's Dream Story' (1890); 'The Miner's Right' (1890); 'A Colonial Reformer' (1890); 'A Sydney Side Saxon' (1891); 'A Modern Buccaneer' (1894); 'The Crooked Stick' (1895); 'The Sphinx of Eaglehawk' (1895); 'The Sealskin Cloak' (1896); 'My Run Home' (1897); 'Plain Living' (1898); 'A Canvas Town Romance' (1898); 'The Babes in the Bush' (1900); 'In Bad Company' (1901); 'Ghost Camp' (1902).

Browne, Ulysses Maximilian (COUNT VON), Austrian military officer: b. Basel, 23 Oct. 1705, of an Irish Jacobite family; d. 26 June 1757. He entered the Austrian service at the age of 12, and became one of the foremost field marshals in the army of Maria Theresa. As governor of Silesia (1739-42), he had to face the first of Frederick the Great's attacks, and in the Seven Years' War he commanded the Austrians at Lobositz (1756). He was mortally wounded at the battle of Prague.

Browne, William, English poet: b. Tavistock, Devonshire, 1591; d. Ottery Saint Mary, Devonshire, about 1643. He was educated at Oxford, and spent a quiet, tranquil life. His poetry is graceful and fanciful, and abounds in beautiful pictures of English scenery. Browne has always been much admired by the poets.

His chief work is 'Britannia's Pastorals' (1613-16). 'The Shepherd's Pipe' (1614) is a collection of eclogues, and 'The Inner Temple Masque' (1614-15) tells the story of Ulysses and Circe. His minor poems are very fine. The best modern editions are by Hazlitt for the Roxburghe Club, and by Gordon Goodwin, 'The Muse's Library.'

Browne, William George, English traveler: b. London, 25 July 1768; d. northern Persia, 1813. In several expeditions he traveled through Egypt and some parts of the interior of Africa, and through Asia Minor and Armenia. In 1812 he proposed a more extensive journey through central Asia. He had already, in 1813, arrived at Tabreez, on his way to Tartary, when his party was attacked by banditti and himself murdered. He was the author of 'Travels' in Africa, Egypt and Syria (1800).

Browne, William Hand, American author: b. Baltimore, 31 Dec. 1828. He studied medicine and graduated M.D. at the University of Maryland, but soon turned his attention to English literature, in certain departments of which he came to be an authority. He edited the 'Southern Review' (1867-8), and the 'Southern Magazine' (1870-5); he was librarian at Johns Hopkins University from 1879 to 1891, when he became professor of English literature. He has translated F. Spielhagen's 'Hammer and Anvil' (1870); Turgenieff's 'Spring Floods' (1874); and Falke's 'Greece and Rome' (1882). In collaboration with R. M. Johnston he wrote 'Historical Sketch of English Literature' (1872); and a 'Life of Alexander H. Stephens' (1878); with J. T. Scharf, 'History of Maryland' (1878); and with S. S. Haldeman he compiled 'Clarendon Dictionary: Concise Hand-Book of the English Language' (1882). He has also written 'George Calvert and Cecilius Calvert, Barons Baltimore'; 'Maryland: the History of a Palatinate' (1884); and has edited 'Archives of Maryland: Proceedings and Acts of the General Assembly, 1637-44' (1883); and 'Selections from the Early Scottish Poets.'

Browne, William Hardcastle, American lawyer and author: b. Philadelphia, 14 Nov. 1840. In 1865 he was admitted to the Philadelphia bar, where he has since practised, but he is best known for his legal and literary compilations, chief of which are: 'Digest of the Law of Divorce and Alimony in the United States' (1890); abridged editions of Blackstone's 'Commentaries' (1894); and Kent's 'Commentaries' (1895); 'Law of Negligence in Pennsylvania' (1896); 'Law on Decedents' Estates in Pennsylvania' (1897); 'Witty Sayings by Witty People' (1898); 'Odd Derivations of Words and Phrases' (1900); 'Waverley Novels,' abridged (6 vols. 1901), and others.

Brownell, Clarence Ludlow, American journalist and author: b. Hartford, Conn., 6 June 1864. He studied at Harvard University and Stevens Institute of Technology, and for five years was English instructor in government and private schools in Japan. For some years he has been a constant contributor of articles on Japanese life, etc., to American magazines and newspapers, and is steadily at work on a history of Japan and Buddhism in that country. He has written: 'Tales from Tokio' (1900).

Brownell, Franklin P., Canadian artist: b. New Bedford, Mass. He makes specialties of portraits and figure-painting. For some years he has been principal of the Ottawa Art School. His canvas, 'The Photographer,' is in the National Gallery at Ottawa.

Brownell, George Griffin, American educator: b. Fairfield, N. Y., 2 July 1898. He graduated at Syracuse University, 1893, and studied at the Sorbonne, Paris, 1893–4, and at Johns Hopkins University, 1894–8, when he was appointed professor of Romance languages at the University of Alabama. He wrote for *Harper's Weekly* 'The Lone Star Republic' (1894), and 'The Vale of Andorra' (1895); he has edited for college use the Spanish texts 'El Capitán Veneno' (1901), and 'El Pájaro Verde' (1901); and has contributed frequently to 'Modern Language Notes' on subjects relating to the Romance languages and literatures.

Brownell, Henry Howard, American poet and historian: b. Providence, R. I., 6 Feb. 1820; d. East Hartford, Conn., 31 Oct. 1872. His first essay in poetry was a spirited versification of Farragut's 'General Orders' to the fleet below New Orleans. Afterward he was appointed to an honorary place on the Hartford, flagship, and had opportunity to observe actual naval warfare. In 'The Bay Fight' he describes, with truth and force, the battle of Mobile Bay. He collected and published his many occasional verses in 'Lyrics of a Day; or, Newspaper Poetry by a Volunteer in the United States Service' (1864).

Brownell, Thomas Church, American Protestant Episcopal bishop: b. Westport, Mass., 19 Oct. 1779; d. Hartford, Conn., 13 Jan. 1865. He was graduated from Union College, Schenectady, N. Y., in 1804. The next year he accepted the post of tutor in Latin and Greek in that institution; in 1807 was appointed to the chair of belles-lettres and moral philosophy; and in 1809 was chosen the first professor of chemistry and mineralogy. He entered the Episcopal ministry in 1816, and in connection with his professional duties gave himself to the work of a missionary in Schenectady. In 1818 he became an assistant minister in Trinity Church, New York. He was consecrated Bishop of Connecticut, 27 Oct. 1819, and removed at once to his new field of labor. During his long episcopate of 45 years, Bishop Brownell was actively and efficiently engaged in the duties of his station. Washington (now Trinity) College, at Hartford, Conn., took its rise under his auspices in 1824; and he became its first president, resigning in 1831. In 1852 he became presiding bishop in the American Episcopal Church. He published 'The Family Prayer Book' (1823); 'Religion of the Heart and Life' (1839–40); 'Consolation for the Afflicted'; 'The Christian's Walk and Conversation'; etc. A bronze statue of Bishop Brownell has been placed on the campus of Trinity College.

Brownell, William Crary, American essayist and critic: b. New York, 30 Aug. 1851. Having graduated from Amherst, he devoted himself to critical and editorial work in New York city. He became an editor of 'Scribner's Magazine', and among his writings are: 'French Traits: an Essay on Comparative Criticism' (1889); 'French Art' (1892); 'Newport' (1896); and other works.

Brownie, a spirit of goblin, in old popular superstitions of Scotland, supposed to haunt old houses, especially those attached to farms. He might be called the Robin Goodfellow of Scotland. In the night he helped the family, and particularly the servants, by doing many pieces of drudgery, performing domestic labors while the inmates of the household slept. If offered food or any other recompense for his services, he decamped and was seen no more.

Browning, Elizabeth Barrett, English poet: b. Durham, 6 March 1806; d. Florence, Italy, 29 June 1861. Her father, Edward Moulton, or Moulton-Barrett, as soon after her birth he began to write his name, was a country gentleman who resided at the foot of the Malvern Hills, and in this beautiful retreat Elizabeth's girlhood was passed. She early began to commit her thoughts to writing, and in 1826 appeared her volume entitled 'An Essay on Mind and Other Poems,' anonymously published. Viewed as the production of a young lady of 20, this book is indeed a remarkable one; but in after years its author was so dissatisfied with it that she omitted it in the collected editions of her poems. In 1833 appeared a translation by her of the 'Prometheus Bound,' of Æschylus. A collection entitled 'The Seraphim and Other Poems' was produced in 1838, the principal piece being a lyric drama shadowing forth the feelings and emotions which may be supposed to have been excited in an angelic being by the spectacle of the crucifixion. Both in this and in a subsequent work, 'The Drama of Exile' (1840), she chose for her theme the fall and redemption of man, subjects on which Milton had already employed his genius, and in the treatment of which, though exhibiting much grandeur and sublimity, Mrs. Browning can scarcely be said to have approached him. Always feeble in health, she was now nearly brought to the verge of the grave by the rupture of a blood vessel, and having been taken to Devonshire to promote her recovery, received there a severe shock from the drowning of a favorite brother. For several years she was confined to a darkened chamber, and saw only a few of her most intimate friends, but nevertheless continued to busy herself with study and composition. Her health was at length partially restored, and in 1846 she was married to Mr. Robert Browning, a gentleman already well known in the literary world as a poet and dramatist. After their union they went to Italy, and continued subsequently to reside for the most part in Florence. In 1850 a collected edition of Mrs. Browning's works appeared in two volumes, including several new poems, and among others 'Lady Geraldine's Courtship,' one of the finest of her productions, and remarkable, it is said, as having been composed in the incredibly short space of 12 hours. Her 'Sonnets from the Portuguese,' included in this volume, were written after her engagement, and first privately printed. They have no parallel for excellence in their peculiar kind in our literature. 'Casa Guidi Windows,' a poem on the struggles of the Italians for liberty in 1848–9, appeared in 1851. The longest and most finished of all her works, 'Aurora Leigh,' a romantic narrative and didactic poem in blank verse, was published in 1856. Her last volume, 'Poems Before Congress,' appeared in 1860, and cannot be said to have added greatly to her reputation.

Several detached pieces of hers appeared from time to time in the 'Cornhill Magazine,' up to the period of her death. 'Last Poems,' by Mrs. Browning, published by Robert Browning in 1862, and 'Greek Christian Poets and the English Poets,' translations and essays of hers published by Mr. Browning in 1863, were followed in 1866 by his publication of 'Selections from the Poems of Elizabeth Barrett Browning' (2d series 1880). The 'Letters of E. B. Browning,' edited by Frederick G. Kenyon (1897), are a definitive presentation of her character and career in a selection from a very large mass of correspondence collected by Mr. Browning himself. It is a chronicle, and practically a life, by reason of the character of the letters and the addition of connecting links of narrative. The letters give an unusually full and interesting revelation of the course of her life. The poetry of Mrs. Browning is characterized by much pathos and depth of feeling, combined with great vividness and powers of description. It partakes eminently of the modern English school, as represented by Tennyson and others, at times obscure and transcendental, but animated throughout by the most noble and exalted sentiments, and illuminated from time to time by flashes which, in their bearings on the unseen world of mind and spirit, seem almost supernatural. In their married life she and Robert Browning found mutual happiness and help, the good influences of which are reciprocally manifested in their writings.

Browning, Orville Hickman, American politician: b. Harrison County, Ky., 1810; d. Quincy, Ill., 10 Aug. 1881. While performing the duties of clerk in the office of the county and circuit clerk of Bracken County, he pursued a course of classical studies at Augusta College. Admitted to the bar in 1831, he settled in practice at Quincy, Ill., where he subsequently resided. In 1832 he served through the Black Hawk war, and became a member of the Illinois legislature, 1836-43. In conjunction with Abraham Lincoln he organized the Republican party in Illinois at the Bloomington convention. When the Civil War broke out he warmly supported the government, and in 1861 was appointed to the United States Senate to fill the vacancy caused by the resignation of Stephen A. Douglas. President Johnson made him secretary of the interior in 1866, and for one year from March 1868 he also acted as attorney-general. In 1869 he was elected to the State Constitutional Convention, and after that he retired to the practice of his profession.

Browning, Oscar, English author: b. London, 17 Jan. 1837. He was educated at Eton and at King's College, Cambridge, where he was graduated with classical honors in 1860. From 1860 to 1875 he was a master at Eton, and since 1876 has been lecturer in history and political science at Cambridge. He has also served as principal of the University Training College for teachers, and in other educational capacities. Twice he has been an unsuccessful candidate of the Liberal party for Parliament. He is a voluminous writer on subjects of education, history, biography, etc., and among his works are: 'Cornelius Nepos' (1868); 'Netherlands in the 16th Century' (1869); 'Thirty Years' War' (1870); 'Modern England' (1879); 'Modern France' (1880); 'History of Educational Theories' (1881); 'History of England' (1890); 'Life of George Eliot' (1890); 'Goethe: Life and Works' (1891); 'The Citizen: His Rights and Responsibilities' (1893); 'Life of Peter the Great' (1898); 'Wars of the 19th Century' (1899); 'History of Europe, 1814-43' (1901); 'Letters from India' (1902).

Browning, Robert, English poet: b. Camberwell, a suburb of London, 7 May 1812; d. Venice, 12 Dec. 1889. His father, Robert, who was a clerk in the Bank of England, and was himself a lover of books, a classical scholar and ready at versifying, had the boy educated in a school at Peckham, after which he attended lectures at University College. His father's family being dissenters, his mind was trained and his character formed under influences less peculiarly English than those to which youths are exposed in the great public schools and the two leading universities of that country. At the age of 20 he traveled on the Continent and resided for some time in Italy, where he made diligent study of the mediæval history of that country, so fruitful in themes for poetry such as his genius was to produce. In 1833 he published anonymously his first book, 'Pauline'; spent some months in Russia, in 1834; and in the following year issued 'Paracelsus,' a dramatic poem in five parts. In 1837, at the suggestion of Macready, he wrote the tragedy of 'Strafford,' which was produced at Covent Garden in May of the same year, with no marked success. His next poem, 'Sordello,' was printed in 1840, and the obscurity of its introspective subtleties injured the poet's reputation with the critics. Notwithstanding this, he published (1841-6) the 'Bells and Pomegranates' series, in which were included the three plays, 'Pippa Passes,' 'King Victor and King Charles,' and 'Colombe's Birthday'; the four tragedies, 'The Return of the Druses,' 'A Blot in the 'Scutcheon' (produced by Macready at Drury Lane in 1843), 'Luria,' and 'A Soul's Tragedy'; while among the lyrics were 'The Pied Piper of Hamelin,' 'How They Brought the Good News from Ghent to Aix,' and 'The Lost Leader.' In 1846 he married Elizabeth Barrett (q.v.), and settled with her in Florence, where they remained for nearly 15 years. During his residence there he published 'Christmas Eve and Easter Day' (1850), and 'Men and Women' (1855), the latter containing such characteristic poems as 'Andrea del Sarto,' 'Fra Lippo,' 'Childe Roland,' 'Evelyn Hope,' 'One Word More,' and 'Up at a Villa.' When the poet's wife died in 1861 he returned to London, and entered upon his richest literary period by publishing 'Dramatis Personæ' (1864). These dramatic monologues, of which there were 17, include 'Rabbi Ben Ezra,' 'Abt Vogler,' 'Prospice,' 'Caliban upon Setebos,' and 'A Death in the Desert.' Recognition of his literary fame, which came slowly, was made in 1867, when he was elected an honorary Fellow of Balliol, an M.A. of Oxford, and later an LL.D. of Cambridge. It was not, however, until 1869, that 'The Ring and the Book' was published, and this poem, which accentuates every characteristic of the poet, still remains his central achievement. The poem, which is epical in length if not in method, is the story of a murder told 10 times over in wide variety of intention by various persons connected with the tragedy. His next publication was the short poem of 'Hervé Riel,' the proceeds from which were devoted to the relief of Paris after the siege in 1871. Following this came 'Balaustion's Adventure' (1871), including a translation of Euripides' 'Alcestis'; 'Prince Hohenstiel-Schwangau, Saviour of Society' (1871), an imaginary conception of how Louis Napoleon might justify his policy; 'Fifine at the Fair' (1872), in which the relations of the sexes are discussed; 'Red-Cotton Night-Cap Country' (1873), a story of love, penitence, and suicide, the scene of which is laid in Normandy; 'Aristophanes' Apology' (1875); 'The Inn Album' (1875), a story of a woman's wrongs; 'Pacchiarotto and Other Poems' (1876), in which 'Pacchiarotto, and How He Worked in Distemper' conveys an implication of Browning's own method in the poetic art; 'The Agamemnon of Æschylus' (1877); and 'La Saisiaz' (1878), in which immortality is discussed. As a kind of new departure he published a first set of 'Dramatic Idylls' (1879), and a second series (1880), of which the more important are 'Martin Relph,' 'Pheidippides,' and 'Ivan Ivanovitch.' The volumes which have followed are 'Jocoseria' (1883); 'Ferishtah's Fancies' (1884); 'Parleyings with Certain People of Importance in Their Day' (1887), and 'Asolando' (1889). The latter volume was published when the author was on his death-bed, and an account of its favorable reception was almost the last information he received. His body was brought from Venice to England, where, in national recognition of his genius, it was buried in Westminster Abbey between Cowley and Chaucer. In such fashion, and in ungrudged completeness, was his poetic greatness acknowledged at the last. Its too tardy recognition by the popular voice was largely due to the prevailing belief that poetry is for the mental dalliance of a lazy hour, and also to the persistency with which Browning had mocked at this belief in the athletic hardiness of mind which he required in his readers. Moreover he seemed always inclined, to the dismay of the public, to press forward into service the superficial defects of his solid interior qualities. Thus, at times, his wide scholarship strayed off into pedantry; his secure skill in verse dropped ever and again into grotesque Bohemian robustness of phrase and rhyme; his swift intuitive glance into the problems of life seemed to create in him an artistic impatience of detail which, in the structure of his verse, became a thrifty brusqueness of expression tending toward cipher; and, above all, his most notable gift of analysis, his power to track the most hidden motive to its last retreat, seemed ever tending to lapse into an introspective subtlety akin to the cob-webberies of the schoolmen. Yet, aside from these occasional shortcomings, there remain his learning, his humor, his mastery of artistic expression, his immense range of sympathy, his spiritual insight, and the height and strength of his ideals to make him one of the greatest of modern poets.

Brownism. See BROWN, ROBERT.

Brownists, a name given during the latter part of the 16th century to those who were afterward known in England and Holland under the denomination of Independents, called Brownists from Robert Brown (q.v.). See also INDEPENDENTS.

Brownlee, William Craig, American clergyman: b. Torfoot, Lanarkshire, Scotland, 1784; d. New York, 10 Feb. 1860. His paternal ancestors for many generations were the "Lairds of Torfoot." He graduated M.A. at the University of Glasgow, was licensed to preach, and came to America in 1808. For a time he taught Latin and Greek in Rutgers College, but in 1826 was installed as one of the ministers of the Collegiate Reformed Dutch Church in New York city. He was a vigorous controversialist, earnestly opposing the Quakers and Roman Catholics. His writings include: 'Inquiry into the Principles of the Quakers' (1824); 'The Roman Catholic Controversy' (1834); 'Treatise on Popery' (1847); 'Lights and Shadows of Christian Life' (1847); 'Deity of Christ'; 'History of the Western Apostolic Church'; and some minor religious tracts and pamphlets.

Brownlow, William Gannaway, American clergyman, journalist, and politician: b. Wythe County, Va., 29 Aug. 1805; d. Knoxville, Tenn., 29 April 1877. Early left an orphan and penniless, he earned enough as a carpenter to give himself a fair education, and in 1826 became an itinerant Methodist preacher. He began his career as a political agitator in 1828 by advocating in Tennessee the re-election of President John Quincy Adams, and in Calhoun's own district in South Carolina he publicly opposed nullification. From 1838 until its suppression by the Confederates in 1861, he published and edited at Knoxville a paper called *The Whig*, his fiery editorials causing him to become known as "the fighting parson." He upheld slavery but opposed secession, a course which subjected him to much persecution. He refused to take the Confederate oath of allegiance, and in consequence was imprisoned on a charge of treason, but finally released and sent into the Union lines, 3 March 1862. On the reconstruction of Tennessee in 1865 he was elected governor and served two terms. He advocated the removal of the negroes to a separate territory and opposed giving them the ballot. In 1869 he was elected to the United States Senate and served until 1875, during which time he was a member of the committees on pensions and revolutionary claims. He wrote: 'The Great Iron Wheel Examined' (1858), a defense of Methodism; 'Sketches of the Rise, Progress, and Decline of Secession: With a Narrative of Personal Adventures Among the Rebels' (1862); and, with Prynne, 'Ought American Slavery to be Perpetuated? A Debate at Philadelphia, September 1858,' in which Brownlow took the affirmative side (1858).

Brownson, Henry Francis, American lawyer and author: b. Canton, Mass., 7 Aug. 1835. He graduated at Holy Cross College, Worcester, Mass., and was admitted to the bar September 1856, after having studied for some years in Paris and Munich. From June 1861 to January 1871 he served in the United States army, chiefly in the artillery, and attained the rank of brevet-major. He wrote various articles for 'Brownson's Quarterly Review' (1853-61), but has chiefly devoted himself to editing the works of his father, Orestes A. Brownson; namely, 'Works of O. A. Brownson' (1883-7); 'Literary, Scientific, and Political Views of O. A. Brownson' (1893). He has also written 'Religion of Ancient Craft Masonry' (1890);

'Faith and Science' (1895); 'Equality and Democracy' (1897); 'Early, Middle, and Latter Life of O. A. Brownson' (1898–1900).

Brownson, Orestes A., American publicist: b. Stockbridge, Vt., 1803; d. 1876. His writings embrace philosophical, political, sociological and theological subjects. As a child he displayed deep religious feeling and a keen intellectual interest in all theological questions. He was brought up without any strictly defined creed, but at the age of 19 formally joined the Presbyterian Church. This move was the beginning of a long series of religious variations, which terminated in his reception into the Catholic Church in 1843. Soon becoming dissatisfied with Presbyterianism he sought refuge in Universalism, abandoning, as he himself says, Supernaturalism for Rationalism. After leaving Presbyterianism, in 1825, he applied for and received a letter of fellowship as a preacher from the General Convention of Universalists. It was shortly after this that he fell in with the socialistic theories of Robert Owen, who had come to this country to establish his communistic colony at New Harmony, Indiana. Under the influence of Owen's ideas, Brownson co-operated in founding and establishing the Workingman's Party to advance Socialism in the sphere of practical politics. Through Owen Dr. Brownson also came in contact with Frances Wright, who lectured throughout the United States in the interest of the Socialist propaganda. But Brownson's enthusiasm in the political side of the question was short-lived and he soon abandoned the political movement, and returned to his pulpit, but as an independent preacher, responsible to no church, sect or denomination. In 1832 he came under the influence of Dr. Channing, to whom he pays a grateful but discriminating tribute in his work 'The Convert,' written after his conversion to the Catholic Church. In 1836 he went to Boston to preach to the laboring classes, and becoming convinced of "the necessity of a new religious organization of mankind," established for that purpose "The Society for Christian Union Progress," whose object was the union and progress of mankind on broad humanitarian lines. The "new doctrine" inculcated and preached during this period by Dr. Brownson was a mixture, in part drawn from the Eclecticism of Cousin and from the Communism of the Saint-Simonians, a philosophico-religious sect then recently sprung up in France. Brownson's attitude was at this time ultra-radical; he utterly denied the Church and the Priesthood in the religious order, and the distinction of classes in the social order, and would have made all government but the instrument to level men and their institutions to the lowest terms of the socialistic idea. But by 1840 he began to retrace his steps, and after much study and reflection, and after having read for the first time, as he himself tells us in 'The Convert,' Aristotle on Politics, "came to see that the condition of liberty is order, and that in this world we must seek not equality, but justice." Up to this point in his career Dr. Brownson had followed negative lines in his religious and intellectual life from a belief in a supernatural Christianity, as represented by Presbyterianism, to the broadest Socialism which denied the supernatural life of man altogether. He

now began an advance forward to a positive and supernatural conception of the world. "I had now settled in my mind," he says, "that the progress of man and society is effected only by supernatural assistance, and that this assistance is rendered by Almighty God, in perfect accordance with nature and reason, through providential men." With this conception as his premise, after some four years of struggle and study, he arrived at the conclusion that he must logically accept the Catholic Church as the divinely established institution for the supernatural guidance and direction of mankind. After receiving instruction from Bishop Fitzpatrick, of Boston, Dr. Brownson was baptized a Catholic in 1844, and died in the Catholic communion. After his entrance into the Catholic Church he became its ardent and vigorous champion, though sometimes in the advocacy of his views he came into conflict with ecclesiastical authority. He was a vigorous and trenchant writer, bold and uncompromising in his views, when he believed them logical, and often in controversy unsparing in his method against an adversary. His temperament was polemical and fearless, his interest keen, and his advocacy enthusiastic of whatsoever cause he might be pleading. He was a sincere lover of truth and unflinching in pursuing his conclusions. He was perhaps the greatest publicist whom America has produced. His writings are voluminous, covering a vast variety of subjects, and have been published in 20 volumes (1882–87) by his son, Henry F. Brownson. A 'Life' in 3 volumes by the latter appeared in 1900.   CONDÉ B. PALLEN,

Editorial Staff, 'Encyclopedia Americana.'

Brownstone, the reddish-brown sandstone of the Triassic Age, so named originally in the Eastern United States, where it occurs in New Jersey and Connecticut. The name is now generally used for any brown sandstone adapted for building purposes, but the most important stones included under this name are those just mentioned, which are quarried at Portland and Middletown, Conn., and the Cambrian or Pre-Cambrian sandstones that are worked near Marquette, Mich. The use of brownstone has greatly diminished in recent years, granite and limestone having largely superseded it in public favor.

Brownsville, Texas, a city, port of entry, and county-seat of Cameron County, situated on the Rio Grande River, and the Rio G. R.R., opposite Matamoras, Mexico. It contains the cathedral of the Immaculate Conception, the Convent and Academy of the Incarnate Word, a United States government building, and a national bank, and has a large trade with Mexico. In the suburbs is Fort Brown, a garrisoned United States post. In May 1846 Brownsville was occupied and fortified by a small body of United States troops, who maintained their position in the face of a heavy bombardment that lasted for 160 hours, and in November 1863 it was taken from the Confederates by a Federal army under Gen. Banks. Pop. (1900) 6,305.

Brownwood, Texas, a city and county-seat of Brown County, situated on the Gulf, C. & S. F., and the Fort Worth & R. G. R.R.'s, 140 miles northwest from Austin. It was settled in 1866 and incorporated in 1878. It trades in wheat, hay, cotton, cattle, hides, and pecan nuts.

There are flour mills, cottonseed-oil mills, and manufactories of wire-fencing, saddle and harness, ice, etc. Here are located the Daniel Baker College, under Presbyterian auspices, and the Howard Payne College, controlled by the Baptists. The city owns its waterworks. Pop. (1900) 3,965.

Broz′ik, Vaczlav, Bohemian artist: b. near Pilsen, 1852; d. 1901. He was a pupil at the Prague Academy, and also of Piloty. Most of his subjects were taken from the history of Bohemia, and as a historical painter he won high rank. Among his works may be mentioned the 'Embassy of Ladislas of Bohemia to Charles VII. of France'; 'The Execution on the White Mountain'; 'The Ballad Singer'; and 'The Imperial Councilors Thrown Out of the Window at Prague.' His 'Columbus at the Court of Ferdinand and Isabella' is in the Metropolitan Museum, New York.

Bruce, a noble family of Scotland, two members of which occupied the throne after one had pretended to it in vain. Distinguished members were:

1. ROBERT, seventh lord of Annandale: b. 1210; d. 1 April 1295. He was one of the 13 claimants of the crown in 1290, when, by the demise of Margaret, the "maiden of Norway," the posterity of the last three kings of Scotland had become extinct, and the succession reverted to the posterity of David, Earl of Huntington, and younger brother of King William, the Lion. The question of succession speedily resolved itself into a simple alternative between two competitors, John Baliol, the great-grandson of David by his eldest daughter, Margaret, and Robert Bruce, the grandson of David by his second daughter, Isabel. The contest was, by mutual consent, referred for decision to King Edward I. of England, who pronounced, in accordance with principles that would not now be disputed, that "in all indivisible heritages the more remote in degree of the first line of descent is preferable to the nearer in degree of the second," and thus gave the kingdom to Baliol, from whom he required homage and fealty. Bruce now retired to England, took service in the English army, and fought against Baliol in the war which resulted in the subjugation of Scotland to England. He returned to his English estates soon after the resignation of Baliol, and died about 1296.

2. ROBERT, son of the preceding, Earl of Carrick and Annandale: d. 1304. He constantly followed the fortunes of Edward, and fought bravely against Wallace and the patriot party of Scotland. After having assisted in defeating Wallace at Falkirk, he is said to have slackened his zeal for England, but did so little for the national cause that he was able to make his peace with Edward, when, a little later, after the capitulation at Irvine, Wallace was driven with his adherents into the northern mountains.

3. ROBERT, son of the preceding, Earl of Carrick, and afterward king of Scotland: b. 21 March 1274; d. 9 July 1329. He acted at first as Edward's liegeman, but vacillated between the two parties, taking no very active part in the struggle between Wallace and England, but inclining to the national cause when a gleam of success enlivened the hopes of the patriots, and, at the approach of Edward, making his peace with the conqueror. He was one of those con-

sulted by the king in the settlement of Scotland as an English province, and was permitted to retain the extensive lands of his ancestors unalienated. In 1306, Comyn, the son of Baliol's sister, a nobleman distinguished by his efforts to recover the independence of his country, arrived in Dumfries about the same time with Bruce. By appointment he met Bruce alone in the church of the Minorites, who there stabbed him with his dagger; whether by premeditated treachery or in a sudden fit of passion cannot now be ascertained. Bruce now assumed the title of king, summoned the Scots to his standard, and was crowned, without any opposition, at Scone. Edward immediately sent Aymar de Valence, Earl of Pembroke, with a great army to chastise the rebels. The force of Bruce was almost immediately destroyed, six of his best knights made prisoners, and he himself, thrown from his horse, was rescued only by the devotion of Seaton. For two months, with his brothers and the ladies of his household, he wandered to and fro in the Grampian Hills, till, his party being discovered, defeated, and forced to separate, he buried himself for concealment in the island of Rathlin, on the north of Ireland. His three brothers, and others, were captured; and the brothers were soon after hanged at Carlisle. In the spring of 1307 Bruce returned from his retreat, surprised his own castle of Carrick, defeated small parties of English in many skirmishes, and was enabled to maintain himself among the hills and forests until Edward called out an army and marched toward the borders, but died on his way, leaving to his son a charge not to bury his bones till he had borne them in triumph from Berwick bounds to the utmost highlands. For three years Edward II. paid no attention to his father's advice or the Scottish war, but in the autumn of 1310 he marched into Scotland as far as the Forth without encountering an enemy, for Bruce wisely declined to give him battle. In the next year he sent his favorite Gaveston to renew the war, who penetrated beyond the Forth, but still gained no advantage, Bruce constantly retreating before him, keeping the hills, where he could not be assailed, and harassing the English by constant petty skirmishes in which he mostly worsted them. The following years were passed by Edward in ignoble contentions with his Parliament, and by Bruce in gradually but surely recovering all that he had lost in Scotland, until, in 1314, the strong hill fortress of Stirling alone held out for the English, and even that the governor, Mowbray, had been forced to consent to surrender if it should not be relieved before the feast of St. John the Baptist. This at length aroused Edward, who, at the head of a large army, encamped in the neighborhood of the beleaguered fortress, and was there met by Bruce at the head of 30,000 picked men, on the eve of the festival fixed for its surrender. The battle of Bannockburn, which succeeded, was the bloodiest defeat which the English ever suffered at the hands of their Scottish neighbors. It fixed the crown securely on the head of Bruce, and at once enabled him to exchange his prisoners, who were of the highest rank in England, against his wife, his sister, and his other relatives, who had long languished in captivity. After this success the Scottish people assumed the offensive and invaded Ireland, where they at first gained considerable successes, and of which island Edward

Bruce was crowned king. While the dissensions lasted between Edward II. and his barons, Robert Bruce repeatedly devastated the borders and all the north of Yorkshire, even to the walls of York, into which he on one occasion chased the English king in disgrace, narrowly failing to make him prisoner. In 1323 this bloody war, which had raged, with few pauses, for 23 years, was brought to a close by a truce concluded between the two kingdoms for 13 years, to remain in force even in the event of the death of one or both of the contracting parties. Four years after this Edward II. was compelled to abdicate in favor of his son, Edward III., and Bruce, seeing his occasion in the distracted state of England, renewed the war, with the avowed intention of forcing Edward to renounce his claim of sovereignty over the crown of Scotland. In 1328 this renunciation was made; Scotland was declared sovereign and independent; Jane of England, the sister of Edward, was affianced to David, prince of Scotland; and Robert Bruce paid £20,000 sterling to defray the expenses of the war. He died the next year, having, after a life of incessant toil and warfare, secured the independence of his country, and won the crown, which he left undisputed to his son.

4. EDWARD: d. 1318. He was a brother of Robert I., of Scotland, who, after distinguishing himself in the Scottish war of independence, crossed in 1315 to Ireland to aid the native septs against the English. After many successes he was crowned king of Ireland at Carrickfergus, but fell in battle near Dundalk.

5. DAVID, son of the preceding, king of Scotland: b. about 1320; d. 22 Feb. 1371. Shortly after his accession, at the age of nine years, his kingdom was invaded, and his crown wrested from him by Edward Baliol, son of that John Baliol whom Edward I. had compelled to resign the crown. In support of his claim Edward III. maintained a fierce strife on the borders, in active though undeclared hostilities to the Scots. David, with his young queen, Jane of England, escaped to France, where he resided till 1341, when, the nobles Murray, Douglas, and Stuart having expelled Baliol from the throne into the northern counties of England, he ventured to return. In 1346, while Edward III., with the flower of his army, was absent in France, David suddenly invaded England at the head of 33,000 men. He was met at Neville's Cross, Durham, by a force of 11,200 irregular troops under Queen Philippa. The Scottish troops were totally defeated, leaving 15,000 men dead on the field of battle and their king a prisoner. From this time until 1357 David was detained a prisoner in the Tower of London, when he was liberated after the battle of Poitiers, on agreeing to pay 100,000 marks in 20 half-yearly instalments.

Bruce, Blanche Kelso, American colored politician: b. Prince Edward County, Va., 1841; d. 1898. Born in slavery but educated with the son of his master, and subsequently a student at Oberlin College, he became a planter in Mississippi in 1869. Entering politics he became a United States senator from Mississippi in 1875, the first negro member of the National Senate. He was appointed register of the United States Treasury in 1881, holding office till 1885, and was reappointed to the same office by President McKinley in 1897.

Bruce, Catherine Wolfe, American patron of science: b. New York; d. there 13 March 1900. She was a cousin of Catherine Lorillard Wolfe, from whom she inherited a fortune, which she used in furthering astronomical study. She gave $50,000 to the Harvard Observatory in 1888. The Bruce Memorial Telescope at Arequipa, Peru, was her gift. In 1897 she established a gold medal fund for the Astronomical Society of the Pacific.

Bruce, James, Scottish traveler: b. Kinnaird House, Stirlingshire, 14 Dec. 1730; d. there 27 April 1794. He became a wine merchant in 1754, but on the death of his wife he took up the study of languages, and availed himself of the opportunities of his trade to visit Spain, Portugal, and the Netherlands. In 1758 he inherited his father's estate, and he consequently relinquished the wine trade in 1761. Lord Halifax, appreciating Bruce's character, proposed to him a tour of discovery, in which he promised him his protection and support. He pointed specially to the exploration of the coast of Barbary, in completion of the labors of Shaw, and hinted also at the discovery of the sources of the Nile. In the meantime Halifax offered him the consulship of Algiers, which was accepted. His consulship lasted for two years, and on its expiration in 1765 he visited successively Tunis, Tripoli, Rhodes, Cyprus, Syria, and several parts of Asia Minor, where, accompanied by an able Italian draughtsman, he made drawings of the ruins of Palmyra, Baalbec, and other remains of antiquity. Having now formed his plan for visiting Abyssinia, he set out for Cairo in June 1768, after about a year spent in Syria, navigated the Nile to Syene, crossed the desert to the Red Sea, passed some months in Arabia Felix, and reached Gondar, the capital of Abyssinia, in February 1770. On 14 Nov. 1770, he succeeded in reaching the sources of the Abai, then considered the main stream of the Nile. His 'Travels to Discover the Source of the Nile' appeared in 1790 in five large quarto volumes. The authority of the work, in regard to facts of natural history and human manners, was questioned on its first appearance; but the truth of his descriptions, however, has been amply confirmed by travelers who have visited the same regions. This enterprising traveler lost his life in consequence of an accidental fall down stairs.

Bruch, brooH, Max, German composer: b. Cologne 6 Jan. 1838. He studied at Bonn under Breidenstein, and at Cologne as a special pupil of Hiller, in 1853-7. During this period he completed several of his musical compositions. In 1865 he was director of the musical institute of Coblentz; and from 1870 to 1880 lived in Berlin and Bonn. In 1880 he went to Liverpool to become director of the Philharmonic Society; in 1883 he came to the United States and conducted his own oratorio 'Arminius' in Boston; in 1887 he was made a member of the Berlin Academy; and in 1890 obtained the title of royal professor. Bruch ranks among the foremost of the modern composers. His best works include: 'The Flight of the Holy Family'; 'Ulysses'; 'Arminius'; 'Lied von der Glocke' (words by Schiller); 'Achilles'; 'Scenes from the Frithjof's Saga'; 'Roman Triumph Song'; 'Salamis,' etc.

Bruchési, broo-kā'zē, Napoléon Paul, Canadian Roman Catholic prelate: b. Montreal,

20 Oct. 1855. He pursued his theological studies at Paris and Rome, being ordained priest in 1878. In 1887 he was made a canon at the cathedral in Montreal. He was successively vicar at St. Bridget's and St. Joseph's churches in Montreal, and in 1897 was appointed archbishop of Montreal to succeed the late Monsignor Fabre.

Bruchsal, brooh'säl, a town of Baden, on both sides of the Salzbach, 12 miles from Carlsruhe, now an important railway centre. It is an ancient town, was a common residence of the prince-bishops of Spires from the 12th century, and the residence formerly occupied by them is still standing. This is a building in the rococo style, erected in 1720–70, and in connection with it is a fine garden with fountains. In the Church of St. Peter the prince-bishops were buried. Soap, paper, cigars, etc., are made. Pop. (1900) 13,567.

Bru'chus, a genus of beetles belonging to the section tetramera, and the family *Rhyncophora* or *Curculionidæ*. The antennæ are 14-jointed, and are filiform, serrate, or pectinated, not geniculated as in the more normal *Curculionidæ*. It contains small beetles which deposit their larvæ in the germs of leguminous plants, and, when hatched, devour their seed. *B. pisi* is destructive to the garden pea.

Brucine, broo'sïn (from Brucea), an alkaloid discovered in 1819, and obtained in the preparation of strychnine, from which it is separated by boiling alcohol. It crystallizes in white and transparent prisms, with a rhomhoidal base. It has a very bitter taste, but no smell, and is less poisonous than strychnine. It is insoluble in ether, and dissolves in a mixture of 850 parts of cold and 500 parts of boiling water. Nitric acid gives it a scarlet, and sulphuric acid a rosy tint, but both turn gradually to yellow. A solution of copper turns it to violet. These reactions distinguish brucine both from strychnine and morphine. The salts of brucine are tolerably numerous, and are prepared by double decomposition, or by direct combination of the brucine with the acid. They are for the most part crystallizable, and like the base have a bitter taste. They are not used in medicine. Symbol $C_{23}H_{26}N_2O_4 + 4H_2O$.

Brucioli, or Bruccioli, Antonio, än-tō'nē-ō broo-chē-ō'lē, Italian reformer and scholar: b. Florence, about 1500; d. after 1554. In 1522, having become implicated in a conspiracy against Giuglio di Medici, who then governed Florence in the name of Leo X., he took refuge in France, where he became acquainted with the doctrines of the reformers, and probably embraced them. On the expulsion of the Medici in 1527 he returned to Florence, but, by his free declamation against monks and clergy, brought his orthodoxy in question, and was imprisoned on several charges, among which that of heresy was included. He would have been executed but for the interference of powerful friends, who obtained a commutation of his sentence into banishment. He retired to Venice with two brothers, who were printers, and availed himself of their press to publish a great number of works, of which the most celebrated is a translation of the Bible into Tuscan. The boldness of his annotations caused it to be ranked as a heretical work. Brucioli was living in 1554, but the exact date of his death is not known. The

number of his volumes is said to have exceeded that of his years. Among his works are Italian translations of Pliny, Aristotle, and Cicero, and annotated editions of Petrarca and Boccaccio.

Bru'cite, a native hydrate of magnesia, having the formula $Mg(OH)_2$. It has a hardness of 2.5 and a specific gravity of about 2.4. Its color is white, often tinted blue or green. At Texas, Pa., it crystallizes in hexagonal (rhombohedral), tabular plates whose bases show pearly lustre while the edges are vitreous to waxy. A fibrous, pearly variety occurs at Hoboken, N. J. Delicate blue and green crystals were found at Tilly Foster, N. Y. Brucite was named for Dr. A. Bruce, an American mineralogist who first described it as a species.

Bruck, Karl Ludwig, kärl lood'-vĭg brook (BARON), Austrian statesman: b. Elberfeld, 8 Oct. 1798; d. Vienna, 23 April, 1860. In 1821 he went to Trieste in order to take part in the war for Grecian independence, and remaining there several years, founded the Trieste Lloyd (later the Austrian Lloyd), a combination of insurance societies. In 1848 he was a member of the German National Assembly; after the Vienna revolution of October 1848 he became minister of commerce and public works. In this office he introduced a number of reforms in the industrial policy of the government, established important telegraph lines, built a number of highways and railroads, and founded the Austro-German postal union. In 1849 the emperor gave him the rank of baron, but in 1851 he was compelled to resign his ministry. In 1855 he became minister of finance; he was not able to introduce the reforms he wished, and when a period of general financial disaster resulted from the Italian war, Bruck was personally blamed. He accordingly obtained his dismissal from the emperor and the next day committed suicide. He was officially declared innocent one month after his death.

Brucker, Johann Jakob, yō'hän yä-kŏb brook'ẽr, German historian: b. Augsburg, Bavaria, 22 Jan. 1696; d. there, 26 Nov. 1770. He was educated at Jena, and in 1744 became pastor at Augsburg. His most important work is a 'Critical History of Philosophy' (1741-4), in Latin, which was the first complete history of the different philosophical schools. In contains biographical matter of great value.

Bruckner, Anton, än'tŏn brook'nẽr, Austrian organist and composer: b. Ansfelden, 4 Sept. 1824; d. 11 Oct. 1896. He was mostly self-educated, but after serving as organist in the cathedral at Linz he studied for a time in Vienna under Simon Sechter, whom he succeeded as court organist. He later became professor of music at the Vienna conservatory and lecturer on music at the University. Bruckner is to some extent an imitator of Wagner; his best known compositions are his symphonies; he has written also some religious music, including a Te Deum and several masses.

Brueis, or Bruys d'Aigaïlliers, François Paul, French admiral: b. Uzès, 11 Feb. 1753; d. 1 Aug. 1798. He entered the navy at an early age, and gradually rose in the service. In 1798 he was employed to convey Bonaparte and his army, which were to effect the conquest of Egypt and the East, and having managed to elude the vigilance of Nelson, who had been long watching for him, reached the Bay of Abukir, and disembarked the troops in safety. Brueis moored his fleet in a position naturally so strong that he deemed it impregnable; but by the heroic daring of Nelson, he found the precautions which he had taken turned to his disadvantage. In the battle which ensued, he fell fighting boldly, a little before his ship, the Orient, of 100 guns, blew up. See ABUKIR.

Bruges (Flemish, *Brugge*), a city of Belgium, capital of West Flanders, situated about 60 miles northwest of Brussels, about 8 miles from the sea, surrounded and intersected by canals which connect it with Ostend and other places. By these canals fairly large vessels can reach Bruges; and a ship canal to connect it with the sea at Zeebrugge, a port on the North Sea, 7½ miles distant, was begun 25 Feb. 1900. This will allow ships of 25 feet draft to reach the wharves of the city. Bruges has over 50 bridges, all opening in the middle for the passage of vessels. The Halles (containing cloth and other markets) is a fine old building, with a famous belfry or tower 350 feet high, in which is a fine carillon of 48 bells. Bruges has also a beautiful town hall dating from the 14th century; a palace of justice, noted for a magnificently adorned fireplace; an academy of painting, sculpture, and architecture; a public library, etc., and many valuable specimens of architecture and sculpture. In the Church of Notre Dame, which has a spire 290 feet high, are the splendid tombs of Charles the Bold and of Mary of Burgundy, his daughter, constructed in 1550, besides many other artistic treasures. The cathedral of Saint Sauveur dates from the 13th and 14th centuries, and is unattractive externally, but has a fine interior, and there are other notable churches. Philip the Good here founded the order of the Golden Fleece in 1430; and the celebrated Jan Van Eyck, or John of Bruges, the supposed inventor of painting in oil, was born here. From the 7th century Bruges was rapidly acquiring importance. It was fortified by Count Baldwin in 837, walled first in 1053, and again in 1270. During the government of the rich and powerful counts of Flanders, who resided there from the 9th to the 15th centuries, its woolen manufactures grew and flourished to an amazing extent. The wealth of the citizens was enormous; a single merchant gave security for the ransom of Jean sans Peur, the last count of Flanders, to the amount of 400,000 crowns of gold. Under the Austrian dynasty, at the close of the 15th century, the rebellious conduct of the inhabitants of Bruges called upon it such destructive vengeance that henceforth its greatness died away, its trade was transferred to Antwerp, and the religious persecution and ferocity of the Spanish under Philip II. and the Duke of Alva completed the process of its ruin. The remains of ancient buildings, abandoned monasteries, and streets half deserted from the diminished population of the modern city, give Bruges an antiquated and venerable appearance. Many of the houses are very old, but in a state of excellent preservation. Bruges is still, by means of its canals, an entrepôt of Belgian commerce. The chief articles manufactured here are lace, linen, damasks, light woolen goods, cottons, mixed stuffs, beer, etc. It exports agricultural produce and manufactured goods, and imports wine, oil, colonial produce, etc. Pop. (1900) 52,867. See Gilliat-Smith, 'Bruges' in 'Mediæval Towns Series' (1901).

Brugg, a town in the Swiss canton of Aargau, on the right bank of the Aar, and near the mouth of the Reuss, 36 miles east-southeast of Basel by rail. Near it is the site of Vindonissa, the chief Roman station in Helvetia; and it was also the cradle of the house of Hapsburg, whose ruined castle, founded in 1020, crowns a wooded height two miles distant. Nearer is the abbey of Königsfelden (1310; converted in 1872 into an asylum), in the vaults beneath which are interred many of the members of the Austrian royal family. Zimmerman, the philosopher, was born here in 1728. Pop. (1900) 2,629.

Brugmann, Friedrich Karl, frēd′-rĭu kärl broog-man, German philologist: b. Wiesbaden, 16 March 1849. He was educated at Halle and Leipsic; was instructor in the gymnasium at Wiesbaden and at Leipsic; and in 1872–7 was assistant at the Russian institute of classical philology at the latter place. In 1877 he was lecturer at the University of Leipsic, and in 1882 became professor of comparative philology there; in 1884 he took the same position at the University of Freiburg, but returned to Leipsic in 1887 as successor to Curtius. He is one of the chief representatives of the new school of philologists and his researches have done much to revolutionize the study of philology. As joint editor with Curtius of 'The Studies in Greek and Latin Grammar,' he wrote an article for this work on 'Nasilis Sonans,' in which he defended theories so radical that Curtius afterward disclaimed them. His conclusions are now generally accepted. His most important work, summarizing his conclusions, is 'Outline of the Comparative Grammar of the Indo-Germanic Languages' (translated into English); he also wrote 'Morphological Researches in the Indo-Germanic Languages' (with Osthoff); 'A Problem of Homeric Textual Criticism' (1870); 'Lithuanian Folk Songs and Tales' (1882); 'The Present Position of Philology'; 'Greek Grammar'; and 'Short Comparative Grammar' (1902). Brugmann was knighted by the king of Saxony, and in 1896 received the degree of LL.D. from Princeton University.

Brugsch, Heinrich Karl, German Egyptologist; b. Berlin, 18 Feb. 1827; d. Charlottenburg, 9 Sept. 1894. A work entitled 'Scriptura Ægyptiorum Demotica,' published in 1848, gained him the favor of Alexander von Humboldt and Frederick William IV., the latter of whom enabled him to complete his studies by visiting the museums of Paris, London, Turin, and Leyden. In 1853 he made his first visit to Egypt and assisted Mariette in his researches, being appointed on his return in the following year assistant in the Berlin Egyptian Museum. He accompanied the Prussian embassy to Persia in 1860, and four years later became consul at Cairo. Returning in 1868, he was appointed to the chair of Egyptology at Göttingen, but soon resigned in order to take charge of the Cairo School of Egyptology. He was soon raised to the rank of bey, and some time afterward to that of pasha. In 1876 he came to the United States as Egyptian commissioner to the Centennial Exposition at Philadelphia. In 1883 he traveled in Egypt, Syria, Greece, and Italy, with Prince Frederick Charles of Prussia, and in 1885-6 he twice visited Persia, partly on official business. He was again in Egypt in 1891, and in the following year he made a journey to the Libyan desert. Brugsch's chief work is the Hieroglyphisch-demotisches Wörterbuch' (1867-82). His other writings include 'Reiseberichte aus Ägypten' (1855); 'Grammaire Démotique' (1855); 'Monuments de l'Egypte' (1857); 'Geographische Inschriften altägyptischer Denkmäler' (1857-60); 'Histoire d'Egypte' (1859); 'Recueil des Monuments Egyptiens' (1862-85); 'Reise der königlich Preussischer Gesandtschaft nach Persien' (1862-3); 'Hieroglyphische Grammatik' (1872); 'Geschichte Ägyptens unter den Pharaonen' (1877); Dictionnaire Géographique de l'ancienne Egypte' (1877-80); 'Religion und Mythologie der alten Ägypter, nach den Denkmälern' (1888); 'Thesaurus Inscriptionum Ægyptiacarum' (1883-91); 'Die Ägyptologie' (1890); 'Aus dem Morgenlande, Altes und Neues' (1893); etc. His 'History of Egypt from the Monuments' has appeared in English. In 1894 his autobiography appeared under the title 'Mein Leben und Wandern.'

Brühl, Heinrich (COUNT VON), Saxon politician: b. Weissenfels, Prussia, 13 Aug. 1700; d. Dresden, 28 Oct. 1763. As a page he gained the favor of Frederick Augustus I. of Poland, and on the death of the king in 1733, the crown of Poland with the other regalia being, through the good fortune of Brühl, intrusted to him, he carried them immediately to the new elector, Augustus III., and showed the greatest activity in promoting his election. He had cunning and skill sufficient to govern his master and get rid of his rivals and succeeded in keeping everybody at a distance from the king. No servant entered his service without the consent of Brühl, and even when he went to the chapel all approach to him was prevented. Brühl kept 200 domestics; his guards were better paid than those of the king himself, and his table more sumptuous. Frederick H. says of him, "Brühl had more garments, watches, laces, boots, shoes, and slippers, than any man of the age. Cæsar would have counted him among those curled and perfumed heads which he did not fear"; but Augustus III. was no Cæsar. When this idle prince loitered about smoking, and asked, without looking at his favorite, "Brühl, have I any money?" "Yes, sire," was the continual answer; and to satisfy the king's demands he exhausted the state, plunged the country into debts, and greatly reduced the army. At the beginning of the Seven Years' War it comprised but 17,000 men, and these were compelled to surrender at Pirna from want of the necessary supplies. Brühl fled with the king, the pictures, and the china, to Poland; but the archives of the state were left to the victor. He was no less avaricious of titles and money than of power. An examination after his death showed that he owed his immense fortune to the prodigality of the king rather than to unlawful means of accumulation. His own profusion was often beneficial to the arts and sciences.

Bruhns, bröns, Karl Christian, German astronomer: b. Plön, Holstein, 22 Nov. 1830; d. Leipsic, 25 July 1881. He was the son of a locksmith, going in 1851 as locksmith and mechanic to Borsig, and then to Berlin with Sie-

mens and Halske, he attracted the attention of Encke by his remarkable powers as a computer, and was appointed in 1852 as assistant, and in 1854 as observer, in the Berlin Observatory, and in 1859 as instructor in the university. In 1860 he was called to Leipsic as professor of astronomy and director of the new observatory to be constructed there, which, under his skilful direction, grew into one of the finest structures of its kind in Europe. He is known as the discoverer of five comets, an able computer of cometary and planetary orbits, and for his important work in geodesy in connection with the European triangulation.

Bruise, or **Contusion,** an injury caused by a blow or sudden pressure, in which the skin is not wounded, and no bone broken or dislocated. Both terms, but more particularly the latter, are employed in surgery to include all such injuries from a black eye to a thoroughly crushed mass of muscle. In the slighter forms of this injury, as in ordinary simple bruises, there is no tearing, but only a concussion of the textures, the utmost damage done being the rupture of a few small blood vessels, occasioning the discoloration always observed in these cases. In more severe contusions, the subjacent structures — muscles, connective tissue, vessels, etc.— are more or less ruptured, and in extreme cases are thoroughly crushed and usually become gangrenous. The quantity of blood extravasated depends chiefly upon the size and number of the ruptured blood vessels, but partly also on the nature of the textures of the injured part. Thus, a lax tissue, as that of the eyelids, favors the escape of blood into the surrounding parts. Simple and not very severe bruises require little treatment other than the rest necessary for the avoidance of pain; but the removal of the swelling and discoloration may be hastened by the application of various local stimulants, which seem to act by accelerating the circulation through the bruised part, and promoting the absorption of the effused fluid. Friar's balsam, compound soap liniment, or poultices made with the roots of black bryony beaten to a pulp, are popular remedies of this class. Tincture of arnica has a great reputation; but experiments have made it very doubtful whether it is any more efficacious than simple spirit of the same strength. A solution of sulphurous acid, and hazeline and other preparations of the American witch-hazel are of more value. They should be kept constantly applied to the bruised part on lint or cotton wool. Pugilists, who are probably better acquainted with ordinary bruises than any other class of men, are in the habit of removing the swelling of the eyelids that often naturally occurs during a prize fight to such an extent as to close the eyes, by at once puncturing the eyelids at several points with a lancet; and their favorite remedy for a black eye or other bruise on the face is a fresh beefsteak applied locally as a poultice. Bruises of a more severe nature, as when there is much breaking or crushing of the tissues, must, of course, at once be referred to the care of a surgeon.

Brüll, Ignaz, Austrian pianist and composer: b. Prossnitz, 7 Nov. 1846. He was educated at Vienna under Epstein and Dessoff and played at concerts there and in London. His first composition appeared in 1861 and since then he has been instructor at a school of music in Vienna and has won distinction as a composer. His works include several numbers for the piano; orchestral pieces and operas, among them, 'The Beggar of Samarkand'; 'The Golden Cross'; 'Bianca'; 'Queen Marietta'; 'The Heart of Stone'; and 'The Hussar.'

Brumaire, brü-mār', the second month of the year in the French revolutionary calendar. It commenced on 23 October and ended on 21 November, thus comprising 30 days. It received its name from the fogs that usually prevail about this time. The 18th of Brumaire, VIII. year (9 Nov. 1799), is celebrated for the overthrow of the directory and the establishment of the sway of Napoleon. See CALENDAR.

Brumidi, broo-mē'dē, **Constantine,** Italian painter: b. Rome, 20 June 1805; d. Washington, D. C., 29 Feb. 1880. After study in his native city he was given many important commissions, and some of his best works are found in the Vatican and the more modern Roman palaces. The occupation of Rome by the French caused him to emigrate to America, and in 1852 he became a citizen of the United States. After settling in this country he executed much of the decoration of the national capitol, and began work on a series of historical paintings, forming a belt about the base of interior of the dome, the first frescoes in America.

Brummagen, Joe. See CHAMBERLAIN JOSEPH.

Brummel, George Bryan ("BEAU BRUMMEL"), English dandy: b. London, 1778; d. Caen, 29 March 1840. He was educated at Eton and Oxford, at both of which places he acquired great distinction by his taste in dress, which afterward made him the autocrat in the world of fashion. At the age of 16 he casually made the acquaintance of the Prince of Wales, afterward George IV., who conceived a wonderful fancy for him and made him a cornet in his own regiment, the 10th Hussars. Brummel was now introduced into the most aristocratic society in England, and through the favor of the prince had rapid promotion in the army, though his carelessness was such that he often did not know his own troop. The death of his father in 1794 put him in possession of a fortune of £30,000, which he expended in a course of sumptuous living, extending over a period of 21 years, during which his dicta on matters of etiquette and dress were received in the *beau monde* as indisputable. He kept a magnificent bachelor establishment, gave splendid dinners, and basked in all the sunshine that youth, money, and princely favor could bestow. But the fickle temper of the prince regent at last tired of Brummel, and an estrangement took place. The beau's creditors now began to be clamorous, and in 1814 he crossed the channel to Calais, where he resided for many years, partly supported by the remains of his own fortune and partly by remittances from friends in England. In 1824, when George IV. passed through Calais on his way to Hanover, Brummel ventured again to address himself to him, but was unceremoniously repulsed. Subsequently to this he was appointed consul at Caen, but after holding this office for a few years it was abolished as unnecessary, and he was reduced to absolute poverty. His mind, too, gave way, and he died in a lunatic asylum.

Brun, or **Brunn, Malte-Conrad** (generally known as MALTE-BRUN), Danish geographer: b. Thisted, Jutland, 12 Aug. 1775; d. 14 Dec. 1826. While yet very young he produced some poems which gave great promise of his rising to eminence as a poet, though his father had destined him for the Church. About this time the French Revolution called forth a host of ardent champions of the cause of progress throughout Europe, and the young poet embraced it with enthusiasm. He abandoned the Church for the bar, and subsequently became editor successively of two journals, in which his advocacy of liberal principles provoked a state prosecution that compelled him to take refuge in the Swedish island of Hven, once the residence of Tycho Brahe. From this he shortly afterward received permission to return to Copenhagen; but some fresh attacks on the government again made him an exile, and he retired first to Sweden and then to Hamburg, where a wealthy merchant entrusted him with the education of his children. Not long after, his admiration of Napoleon Bonaparte, then rapidly advancing to the head of affairs, prompted him to take up his abode in France; but the elevation of his idol to the post of consul for life opened Brun's eyes to his ambitious designs. He had the courage openly to blame the weakness of the senate in yielding to them, and for the time withdrew from the pursuit of politics. He now directed his attention to the science of geography. In 1803 he published, along with Mentelle and Herbin, the commencement of 'Géographie Mathématique, Physique, et Politique de toutes les Parties du Monde,' a work which was completed in 16 volumes in 1807, and in the composition of which Brun's share amounted to about a third. Before the completion of this work his reputation as a writer had been firmly established, and in 1806 he received an appointment on the staff of the *Journal des Débats,* for which he continued to write articles on foreign politics until his death. In 1808 appeared his 'Tableau de la Pologne,' and the same year he joined M. Eyriès in starting the 'Annales des Voyages, de la Géographie, et de l'Histoire,' which proved the introduction into France of regular periodical geographical literature. In 1810 was published the first volume of his 'Précis de la Géographie Universelle,' completed in eight volumes in 1829, and reissued in 12 volumes in 1831. During the Hundred Days Brun adhered to the legitimist cause, and published an 'Apologie de Louis XVIII.' Toward the end of 1821 he lent powerful assistance in establishing the Société de Géographie. Besides the works already mentioned, he was the author of various geographical and political treatises too numerous to particularize.

Brunaï, broo-nä'ē, **Bruneï,** broo-nä'ē, or **Bruni,** broo'nē, **Borneo,** a territory on the northwest part of the island, situated between Sarawak and British North Borneo, under the protection of Great Britain. It has an area of about 18,000 square miles. It exports sago, gutta-percha, rubber, etc. Until 1888 it was nominally an independent Mohammedan territory, whose sultan was formerly overlord of the whole island. Its population is variously estimated at from 50,000 to 125,000, divided into trade castes. The capital, Brunai, on a river of the same name, about 14 miles from its mouth, is a miserable, dirty town, built on piles, with some 30,000 inhabitants, who trade with Singapore.

Brunanburgh, broo-năn-bur′ŏ, Scotland, the scene of a battle in which Athelstan and the Anglo-Saxons defeated a force of Scots, Danes, etc., in 937; locality very doubtful. The battle forms the subject of one of the oldest Anglo-Saxon poems.

Brunck, Richard Francois Philippe, rɪʜ′ärt fräntz fē-lĕp broonk, French critic: b. Strasburg, 30 Dec. 1729; d. same place, 12 June 1803. He made rapid progress in learning when he studied with the Jesuits in Paris, but neglected study as soon as he entered into active life. While in winter quarters at Giessen, as commissary of war during the French campaigns, he resided with a professor who, by his advice and example, revived his love of letters and led him to the study of the classics. When Brunck returned to Strasburg he devoted all his leisure time to Greek, and at the age of 30, and while holding public office, attended the lectures of the Greek professor of the university. The zeal which had encouraged him to undertake this laborious study was increased by the pleasure of overcoming difficulties, and he became fixed in the conviction that all the instances of apparently careless writing in the Greek poets were only errors of the transcribers. Entertaining this opinion, he altered whatever displeased him, overthrew the order of the verses, and permitted himself liberties which criticism must needs reject. To this rage of altering he gave himself up, particularly in the marginal comments of his books, and in the numerous copies which he made of the Greek poets, more for his own pleasure than for use. This arbitrary process is so visible, even in the editions he has published, that much caution is required in using them. Brunck has nevertheless been of essential service to Greek literature, and since the revival of letters few scholars have so effectually promoted it. He published a valuable edition of Virgil. Of his Greek editions mention may be made of those of the 'Analecta,' 'Apollonius Rhodius,' 'Aristophanes,' 'The Gnomic Poets,' and his masterpiece, 'Sophocles,' for which the king allowed him a pension of 2,000 francs. At this time the French Revolution interrupted his studies. He adopted the new ideas with enthusiasm, but without deviating from the principles of moderation. He was arrested at Besançon during the Reign of Terror, and did not obtain his liberty until after the death of Robespierre. In 1791 and again in 1801 economical reasons obliged him to sell part of his library. As he was passionately fond of his books, and his former fortune had enabled him to collect an excellent library, this was a severe privation. From this time Greek became his aversion; but he prepared an edition of Terence, and had Plautus ready for publication when he died in 1803. Many of his papers are in the library at Paris.

Brundu′sium, or **Brundis′ium,** now BRINDISI, brĭn-dē′sē, Italy, a city of Calabria, on the shores of the Adriatic. It was taken by the Romans 267 B.C., and became a colony of the republic 244 B.C. During the Illyrian war, 229 B.C., it was the naval and military station for the

Roman fleet and army, and its fine harbor rendered it on many subsequent occasions the centre of warlike operations. Vergil died here 19 B.C.

Brune, Guillaume Marie Anne, gē-yŏm mä-rē än broon, French soldier: b. Brives la Gaillarde, 13 March 1763; d. 2 Aug. 1815. While young he went to Paris to study law. At the breaking out of the Revolution he was a printer and had made himself known by some small pieces of his own composition. He now devoted himself ardently to politics, was connected with Danton, and played an active part in the tempests of that period. Till 10 Aug. 1792 he was engaged in publishing a daily newspaper. Afterward he went as civil commissary to Belgium. In 1793 he entered the military service in the revolutionary army in the Gironde. He aided Barras to put down the Jacobins, who had assaulted the camp of Grenelle, 10 Oct. 1795. Afterward he distinguished himself as general of brigade in the Italian army, in the battle of Arcola and in the attack on Verona. When the directory of Switzerland declared war Brune received the chief command of an army, entered the country without much opposition in January 1798, and effected a new organization of the government. In 1799 he received the chief command in Holland, defeated the British, 19 September, near Bergen, and compelled the Duke of York to agree to the treaty of Alkmaar, 18 October, by which the British and Russians were to evacuate the north of Holland. In January 1800, he was made a councilor of state, and was placed at the head of the Army of the West, in occupation of La Vendée, and contributed greatly to the re-establishment of tranquility in the revolted province. He was appointed commander-in-chief of the Italian army 13 August. Toward the end of December he led his troops over the Mincio, conquered the Austrians, passed the Adige 8 Jan. 1801, took possession of Vicenza and Roveredo, and concluded an armistice, 16 January at Treviso, with the Austrian general Bellegarde, by which several fortified places in Italy were surrendered to the French troops. When peace recalled him to the council of state toward the end of November 1802, he laid before the legislative body for confirmation the Treaty of Peace with the court of Naples. Next year he went as ambassador to Constantinople. He prevailed there at first over the British party, and received from the Turkish ministry the highest marks. of honor; but when new dissensions arose between the two powers he left Turkey. During his absence, 19 May 1804, he was appointed marshal of the empire. At the end of 1806 Napoleon appointed him governor-general of the Hanseatic towns, and soon after commander of the troops in Swedish Pomerania against the king of Sweden. This monarch invited the marshal to a personal interview, in which he endeavored to convert him to the cause of Louis XVIII. Brune refused every proposal. After the revolution of 1814 he acknowledged Louis XVIII., and received the cross of Louis, but no appointment. This was the cause of his declaring himself for Napoleon immediately upon his return. He received the chief command of an important army in the south of France and was made a peer. When circumstances changed again he delayed a long time before he gave up Toulon, which was in his possession in 1815, to the troops of

Louis XVIII., and sent in his resignation to the king. This circumstance, the severities exercised by his command, and a report that he was the murderer of the Princess Lamballe, excited popular feeling against him. While retiring from Toulon to Paris he was recognized at Avignon by a royalist mob, which broke into his hotel and shot him. His body was exposed to the most shameful insults, and then thrown into the river Rhone.

Brunei, or Bruni. See BRUNAI.

Brunel, broo-nĕl', **Isambard,** ĭ'sam-bärd, Kingdom, English engineer: b. Portsmouth, (son of Sir Mark Isambard Brunel, q.v.), 9 April 1806; d. 15 Sept. 1859. He was educated at the Henri IV. College at Caen, France. The bent of his genius was toward mechanical pursuits, and at the age of 20 he commenced practical engineering under his father at the Thames Tunnel, for which he acted as resident engineer. During the progress of the works he was more than once in imminent danger of his life by the breaking in of the river, and only saved himself by swimming. His attention was mainly directed to steam navigation and railway engineering, and of his works in these departments may be mentioned, among others, the Great Western, Great Britain, and Great Eastern steamships; the entire works on the Great Western Railway, to which he was appointed engineer in 1833; and the railway viaduct over the Tamar at Saltash. He was also the engineer of the Hungerford suspension bridge. The genius of the younger Brunel was undoubted, but in carrying through his operations he was like his father, too apt to regard merely the attainment of a grand and brilliant result without taking into consideration the losses and expense which might thereby be occasioned to those who had invested their capital in the undertaking. This was more especially the case with the Great Western Railway. It was remarked, in contrasting him with George Stephenson, that the works of the former never paid, while those of the latter always did. While on board the Great Eastern — his last work — the day before she quitted the Thames on her first disastrous cruise, Mr. Brunel was suddenly seized with paralysis and had to be carried home. In a week afterward he expired. He became a Fellow of the Royal Society in 1830, and D.C.L. of Oxford in 1857.

Brunel, SIR Mark **Isambard,** English engineer: b. Hacqueville, near Rouen, 25 April 1769; d. 12 Dec. 1849. He was the son of a Normandy farmer, and educated at the seminary of St. Nicaise, Rouen. From early boyhood he displayed a decided turn for scientific and mechanical pursuits, amusing himself with the construction of ships, musical instruments, and machines of different sorts. At the age of 15 he went to Rouen, where he took a course of lessons in drawing, perspective, and hydrography. In 1786 he entered the French naval service and made several voyages to the West Indies, in which he distinguished himself both by his inventive mechanical genius and the attention and ability with which he discharged the duties of a seaman. In 1793 he returned to France, and, having paid a visit to Paris, and taken part in the proceedings at one of the political clubs, he narrowly escaped proscription by venturing to oppose the ferocious doctrines then

current, and was obliged to make his escape to America. Shortly after his arrival there he joined a party of Frenchmen in an expedition to explore the regions around Lake Ontario, and in 1794 he was appointed one of the surveyors of the canal now connecting Lake Champlain and the river Hudson. He was afterward employed, both as engineer and architect, on various undertakings in the city of New York, including the erection of forts for its defense and the establishment of an arsenal and foundry. In 1799 he went to England and settled at Plymouth, where he married Miss Sophia Kingdom, whom he had formerly known at Rouen. His first work in this country was the construction of a copying-machine; and he soon established his reputation as a mechanician by the invention of a machine for making the block-pulleys for the rigging of ships, which effected an immense saving in labor and expense and is still in full operation in English naval dockyards. Of Brunel's subsequent achievements may be mentioned more especially the erection of the steam saw-mill in Chatham dockyard; a machine for making seamless shoes for the army; machines for making nails and wooden boxes, for ruling paper and twisting cotton into hanks; and lastly, a machine for producing locomotion by means of carbonic acid gas, which, however, though partially successful, was ultimately abandoned. But the great work by which his name will be transmitted to posterity was the Thames tunnel, which, though almost a complete failure as a commercial speculation, was nevertheless a wondrous monument of engineering skill and enterprise. It was commenced in March 1825, and opened to the public in 1843, after a multitude of disasters and obstacles had been endured and surmounted. He was elected a Fellow of the Royal Society in 1814, and vice-president from 1832-3. In 1841 the honor of knighthood was conferred on him.

Brunelleschi, Filippo di Ser Lappi, fê-lêp' pô dē sār lăp'pĕ broo-nĕl-lĕsh'ē, Italian architect: b. Florence, 1377; d. same place, 15 April 1446. He first studied painting and sculpture, and brought the art of perspective to perfection; but as an architect he gained most distinction, having, according to his countrymen, revived the Doric, Ionic, and Corinthian orders. He invented various ingenious mechanical contrivances. He applied himself particularly, however, to architecture; and learned the art of drawing to make his architectural plans; statuary, to adorn them; and mechanics, that he might be able to raise the materials. He was also profoundly versed in mathematics and geometry. He is said to have drawn views of the finest monuments in Florence in perspective — an art which then excited much astonishment. This varied knowledge prepared him for bold and difficult undertakings, and he gained the name of the restorer of architecture. As a statuary he was much indebted to his intimate connection with Donatello, who was then very young but very able. Both went to Rome. Here Brunelleschi conceived the idea of restoring architecture to the principles of the Greeks and Romans in the hope of making the revived classic forms supersede the Gothic then in vogue. When the architects assembled in 1407 at Florence to consult on the building of the dome of the Cathedral of Santa Maria, the plan which

Brunelleschi proposed received but little attention, and he went back to Rome.

It was necessary, however, to have recourse to him, as the undertaking far surpassed the powers of the other architects. He engaged to erect a dome which, by its own weight and by the strong connection of its parts, should hang suspended. This proposal seemed so wonderful that the author was regarded as insane. As all other plans, however, failed to answer the expectations of the magistrates, Brunelleschi was again recalled, and ordered to explain the mode in which he intended to execute his plan. This he refused to do, but built two small chapels according to his new system. On this the charge of erecting the dome was committed to him. Aided only by his own genius he accomplished the work, which remains one of the boldest creations of the human mind. But the ingenious lantern, which formed the upper part of the dome, was not finished when he died in 1444. It was completed, however, according to his first design. Few monuments of architecture are so noble as this wonderful building. Only the dome of St. Peter's in Rome, which was built since, excels it in height, but is inferior to it in lightness and grandeur of style. Michael Angelo said it was difficult to imitate Brunelleschi and impossible to excel him. Brunelleschi was the author of a great number of other masterpieces of architecture.

Brunet, Jacques Charles, zhäk shärl broonä, French bibliographer: b. Paris, 2 Nov. 1780; d. same place, 14 Nov. 1867. He began his bibliographical career by the preparation of several auction catalogues, of which the most interesting is that of the Count d'Ourches (Paris 1811), and of a supplementary volume to Cailleau's and Duclos' 'Dictionnaire Bibliographique' (Paris 1802). In 1810 was published the first edition of his 'Manuel du Libraire et du l'Amateur de Livres,' in three volumes, which gained such universal applause that in 1814 a second, and in 1820 a third edition, of four volumes each, were demanded. This work showed him the worthy successor of the meritorious Debure. A sixth edition of his great work appeared between 1860 and 1865 in six volumes, the last containing a Table Méthodique, or classified catalogue, in which the works are arranged in classes according to their subjects.

Brunetière, Ferdinand, French critic: b. Toulon 19 July 1849; d. Paris 9 Dec. 1906. He was editor of the *Revue des Deux Mondes* and became a member of the French Academy in 1893. In criticism he inclined to the idealist as opposed to the naturalist school, and was a severe critic of literary fads. His principal works are: 'History and Literature' (1884); 'The Naturalist Romance' (1883); 'Essays on Contemporary Literature' (1892); 'Epochs of the French Theatre' (1892). In 1897 he delivered a series of lectures in Harvard, Johns Hopkins, and Columbia universities.

Brunhilda, broon-hĭl'dạ, the name of (1) a legendary, (2) a historical person.

1. In the 'Nibelungenlied,' the young and stalwart queen of Iceland, wife of Gunther, the Burgundian king. She passionately hated Kriemhild and her husband, Siegfried, who had once been her own lover; and she caused his murder by the hands of Hagen. Originally she was identical with the Norse Walkyrie Bryn-

hildr, who, for a fault, was stripped of her divinity by Odin and sank into a charmed sleep, from which she was awakened by Sigurd (Siegfried).

2. The daughter of the Visigothic king Athanagild, who married King Sigbert of Austrasia in 567, and afterward, as regent of her two grandsons, Theodebert II., king of Austrasia, and Theodoric II., king of Burgundy, divided the government of the whole Frankish world with her rival Fredegunda, who governed Neustria for the youthful Clotaire II. On the death of Fredegunda in 598, she seized on Neustria, and for a while united under her rule the whole Merovingian dominions, but was overthrown in 613 by a combination in their own interests of the Austrasian nobles under the nominal leadership of Clotaire II., and put to death by being dragged at the heels of a wild horse.

Bruni, broo'nē, Bru'no, or **Bru'nus, Leonardo,** lā-o-när'do ("ARETINO," from his birthplace), Italian humanist: b. Arezzo, 1370; d. Florence, 9 March 1444. He studied law and philosophy at Florence, but under the influence of the Greek scholar Chrysoloras finally took up the study of the classics. In 1405 he obtained a position as papal secretary, an office which he held under four Popes, Innocent VII., Gregory XII., Alexander V., and John XXIII. He went with the latter to the council of Constance in 1414, but in 1415 he moved to Florence, where he devoted himself to literary work. Here he wrote his history of Florence in 12 volumes, for which service he obtained the right of citizenship and was made state secretary there in 1427. He translated the works of Aristotle, Plato, Plutarch, Demosthenes, and Æschines. He wrote also 'Commentarius Rerum Suo Tempore Gestarum'; 'De Origine Urbis Mantuæ'; 'De Romæ Origine'; and 'Epistolæ Familiares.'

Bruni, broo'nē, **Island,** Australasia, an island off the southern part of the east coast of Tasmania, from which it is separated by D'Entrecasteaux Channel. It has a length of 32 miles, a varying breadth of 1 to 11 miles, and an area of 160 square miles. Coal is mined.

Bru'nings, Christian, Dutch engineer: b. Neckerau, 1736; d. 1805. In 1769 the states of Holland appointed him general inspector of rivers. This introduced him to a share in several important commissions; for instance, that for the improvement of the dike system in 1796; that for draining the tracts between Nieuwskogs and Zevenhoven in 1797, etc. His most important works were his improvements in the diking of the lake of Haarlem, the improved diking and deepening of the Oberwasser, which at high tides often inundated vast extents of country, together with the change in the course of the Waal and the canal of Pannerde, by which the beds of the Rhine, the Waal, and the Leck were improved.

Brunn, Heinrich von, hĭn'rĭн brun, German archæologist: b. Wörlitz, Anhalt, 23 Jan. 1822; d. Munich, 23 July 1894. He was professor of archæology at Munich, and published several works of high repute among scholars.

Brünn, Austria, the capital of Moravia, and of a circle of the same name, situated on the railway from Vienna to Prague, 70 miles north-by-east of Vienna, and nearly encircled by the rivers Schwarza and Zwittawa. It consists of an older portion in the centre, surrounded by fine promenades and pleasure-grounds that have taken the place of the old walls and ramparts, and of extensive newer quarters and suburbs surrounding this. It contains a cathedral and other handsome churches; a landhaus, where the provincial Diet meets; several splendid palaces, a gymnasium, polytechnic institute, museum, botanic garden, etc. It has extensive manufactures of woolens, which have procured for it the name of the Austrian Leeds, and in some 70 works employs about 12,000 hands. Other industries embrace cotton, linen, jute, machinery, hardware, chemicals, soap, and candles; beer and spirits. It is the centre of the Moravian commerce, a great part of which is carried on by fairs held at Brünn every three months. Near it is the fortress of Spielberg, on a hill about 940 feet high, in which Baron Trenck and Silvio Pellico were confined, and which now serves only as a prison. It is surrounded with finely laid-out grounds. Brünn was formerly a free imperial city, an important fortress, and the residence of the margraves of Moravia. It was unsuccessfully besieged by the Taborites in 1428; by Torstenson in 1645; by the Prussians in 1742. It was occupied by the French in 1805, and Napoleon made it his headquarters after the battle of Austerlitz. It was taken again by a division of the French army in 1809, when it suffered severely. In 1866 it was occupied by the Prussians. Pop. (1900) 109,000.

Brunne, brün, Robert of, the name by which ROBERT MANNING, a monk of the order founded by St. Gilbert of Sempringham, is usually designated. His monastery was in Lincolnshire, near the modern town of Bourn, and he lived in the reigns of Edward II. and Edward III. His chief work is his 'Handlynge Synne,' a free and amplified translation into English verse of William of Waddington's 'Manuel des Pechiez,' with such judicious omissions and excellent additions as made his version much more entertaining than the original. The purpose of the book was to convey religious instruction to the people in the agreeable form of moral anecdotes. It is of great importance from the linguistic point of view, as one of our best landmarks in the transition from the early to the later Middle English. He also made a new version in octosyllabic rhyme of Wace's 'Brut d'Angleterre,' and added to it a popular translation of the French rhyming chronicle of Peter Langtoft of Bridlington. Robert deliberately wrote in English instead of French, in order to reach the common people, to give them the means "for to haf solace and gamen, in felauschip when tha sit samen (together)."

Brunnow, broo'nöff, Philipp (COUNT VON), Russian diplomatist: b. Dresden, 31 Aug. 1797; d. Darmstadt, 12 April 1875. He entered the Russian service in 1818. He was present in a civil capacity in the campaigns of 1828 and 1829 against the Turks, and in 1839 was sent on a special mission to London, where, in the following spring, he was accredited as permanent ambassador. In this capacity he soon acquired distinction as a diplomatist. After retiring from London on the outbreak of the Crimean war, in 1854, he represented Russia in Frankfort, and, together with Count Orloff, was sent to the Conference of Paris in 1856. He was afterward appointed to the court of Prussia; but in 1858 he returned to his old place in London, where he represented Russia at the conferences in 1864 and 1871. He was raised to the rank of count in 1871, and in 1874 retired to Darmstadt.

Bru'no, St., the name of two saints of the Roman Catholic Church.

1. The apostle of Prussia: b. about 970; d. 1008. He entered the order of St. Benedict and accompanied St. Adalbert on his mission to Prussia. He was appointed chaplain to the emperor, Henry II., and was a zealous missionary in Poland, Russia, and Hungary. Having been taken by the pagans of Lithuania, he had his hands and feet cut off, and was afterward beheaded.

2. The founder of the Carthusian order: b. Cologne about 1030; d. Della Torre, Calabria, 1101. He was educated in the school of the collegiate church of St. Cunibert, in which he afterward received a canonship, and then studied at Rheims, where he so distinguished himself that Bishop Gervais appointed him to superintend all the schools of the district. He attracted many distinguished scholars, and among others Odo, afterward Pope Urban II. Subsequently he was offered the bishopric of Rheims, but the immorality of his times induced him to go into solitude. In 1084 or 1086 he repaired with six friends of a like disposition to a narrow, bleak valley, called Chartreuse, about 15 miles from Grenoble, where they built an oratory and separate cells, and founded one of the severest orders of monks, named from their location Carthusians. In the meantime Urban II. became Pope, and in 1089 invited his former instructor to his court. Bruno reluctantly obeyed, but refused every spiritual dignity, and in 1094 received permission to found a second Carthusian establishment in the solitude of Della Torre, in Calabria, where he died. Leo X., by whom he was beatified, in 1514, permitted the Carthusians to celebrate a mass in honor of him; and Gregory XV., who ordered the process of his canonization, in 1623 extended it to the whole Roman Catholic Church.

Bruno, Giordano, jôr-dä'nō broo'nō, Italian philosopher: b. Nola, Naples, about 1550; d. Rome, 16 Feb. 1600. He entered the order of Dominicans and became distinguished for the originality and poetical boldness of his speculations. In 1580, probably on account of the persecutions which he drew upon himself by his religious doubts and his satires on the monks he was forced to take refuge at Geneva. Here, however, he was soon persecuted by the Calvinists for his paradoxes and his violence. In 1583 he stood forth at Paris as the antagonist of the Aristotelian philosophy, and as teacher of the ars Lulliana. His disputes with the Aristotelians caused him to leave Paris, and he then went to London, where he published several of his works, and to Oxford, where he taught for a short time. In 1585 he went by way of Paris and Marburg to Wittenberg, and from 1586 to 1588 taught his philosophy there. He then went to Helmstadt, where, protected by Duke Julius of Wolfenbüttel, he remained till 1589. He was then engaged at Frankfort-on-the-Main with the publication of some works, particularly 'De Monade, Numero, et Figura,' but left this city in 1592, and returned to Italy. He remained peacefully in Padua until 1598, when the inquisition of Venice arrested him and transferred him to Rome. After an imprisonment of two years, that he might have opportunity to retract his doctrines, he was burned for apostasy, heresy, and violation of his monastic vows. This death, which he might have averted eight days before by a recantation, he suffered with fortitude. While his violent attacks on the prevailing doctrines of the Aristotelian philosophy, and on the narrow-minded Aristotelians themselves, everywhere created him enemies, his rashness and pride threw him into the hands of his executioners. His philosophical writings, which have become very rare, display a classical cultivation of mind, a deep insight into the spirit of ancient philosophy, wit, and satire, as well as a profound knowledge of mathematics and natural philosophy. In 1585 appeared at Paris his famous 'Spaccio della Bestia Trionfante' (a moral allegory,' with many satirical strokes on his own times) ; also his work 'Della Causa, Principio ed Uno' (Venice and London 1584) ; besides 'Del Infinito, Universo, e Mondi.' The former contains the foundation, the latter the application of metaphysics to the natural world. The doctrine is a pure Pantheism, connected with very peculiar notions of God — *Deus est monadum monas, nempe entium entitas* — a more complete Pantheistical system than had been previously exhibited, and which, since his time, Spinoza only — who, like Descartes, borrowed his ideas — has reduced to a more systematic form. The notion that God is the soul of the universe, and the world endowed with organization and life, might have been forgiven by his contemporaries; but his inference that the world is infinite and immeasurable, and his doctrine of the plurality of worlds, at the moment when the new system of Copernicus was attacked from all quarters, could not but be looked upon as a crime. His writings are mostly in the form of dialogues, without any methodical order. His language is a strange mixture of Italian and Latin. His style is violent and fiery. The originality and loftiness of his ideas take a powerful hold on those who can understand him. His logical writings, in which he boldly and skilfully applies Raymond Lully's art of topical memory, are more obscure and less interesting. His belief in magic and astrology, notwithstanding his enlightened views of the nature of things, is to be attributed to the spirit of his age. He also wrote poems, among others, 'Degli Eroici Furori,' and a satirical comedy, 'Il Candelajo.' A collection of his Italian works by Wagner appeared at Leipsic in 1830. A biography by Domenico Berti (Florence 1868), is of special interest and importance on account of the new papers it brings to light regarding the official examination of Bruno before the Inquisition of Venice.

Bruno the Great, German ecclesiastic: b. 925; d. Rheims, 11 Oct. 965. He was the Archbishop of Cologne, third son of Henry the Fowler, and brother of the Emperor Otho I. He had a great share in the events of his time, and surpassed all the contemporary bishops in talents and knowledge. He was made Archbishop of Cologne in 953, and Duke of Lorraine in 954, and had much trouble in bringing into due subjection his unruly subjects. A numerous train of learned men from all countries, even from Greece, continually followed him, and his excellent example was imitated by many prelates. Commentaries on the five books of Moses, and the biographies of some saints, are ascribed to him.

Brunonian Theory, an hypothesis framed by Dr. John Brown, 1735–88 (q.v.), according to which the living system was regarded as an organized machine endowed with excitability, kept up by a variety of external or internal stimuli, that excitability constituting life. Diseases were divided into sthenic or asthenic, the former from accumulated and the latter from exhausted excitability. Darwin, author of the 'Zoonomia,' adopted the theory with enthusiasm, and Rasori introduced it into Italy, where it flourished for a time, and then had to be abandoned, as it ultimately was everywhere.

Brunswick, Ferdinand, Duke of, German soldier: b. Wolfenbüttel, 11 Jan. 1721 ; d. Brunswick, 3 July 1792. He was the fourth son of Duke Ferdinand Albert, and was educated for the military profession. In 1739 he entered the Prussian service, was engaged in the Silesian wars, and became one of the most eminent generals in the Seven Years' War (q.v.). He commanded the allied army in Westphalia, where, always opposed to superior forces, he displayed superior talents. He drove the French from Lower Saxony, Hesse, and Westphalia, and was victorious in the two great battles of Crefeld and Minden. After the peace he resigned his commission on account of a misunderstanding with the king. From that time he lived at Brunswick, the patron of art and literature.

Brunswick, Friedrich Wilhelm, Duke of, German soldier: b. 9. Oct. 1771 ; d. Quatre Bras, 16 June 1815. He was the fourth and youngest son of Duke Karl Wilhelm Ferdinand of Brunswick (q.v.). He was educated for the army, and in 1786 was appointed by the king of Prussia successor of his uncle, Frederick Augustus, Duke of Oels and Bernstadt. He then went to Lausanne, remained two years in Switzerland, and upon his return was made captain in a Prussian regiment of foot. During the war against France in 1792 and the following year he fought in the Prussian armies and was twice wounded. In 1806 he took part in the war against France with all the fire which the oppression of Germany and his father's unhappy fate had kindled in him. He finally joined the corps of Blücher, and was made prisoner with him at Lübeck. On the death of his eldest brother he would have succeeded to the dukedom, as his other brothers were incapacitated by disease, but Napoleon prohibited his succession. He raised a free corps in Bohemia to operate against the French, but though he gained a victory over 4,000 Westphalians he was unable to make an effectual stand on the Continent. He embarked his troops for England, landed in 1809, and was received with enthusiasm. His corps immediately entered the British service, and was afterward employed in Portugal and Spain. The Parliament granted him a pension of £6.000 until he returned to his hereditary dominions, 22 Dec. 1813. The events of 1815 called him again to arms, and he fell at Quatre Bras.

Brunswick, House of, a royal German house, the true founder of which was Albert Azo II., Marquis of Reggio and Modena, a descendant, by the female line, of Charlemagne, who had also extensive domains in Lombardy, and in 1047 married Cunigunda, heiress of the Counts of Altorf, and thus united the two houses of Este and Guelph. The previous history of the Este family is uncertain. Guelph, the son of Azo, was created Duke of Bavaria, in 1071. He married Judith of Flanders, who was descended from Alfred the Great of England. The most powerful of this line was Henry the Proud, who succeeded in 1125, and by his marriage with the daughter of Lotharius II. acquired Brunswick and Saxony. Brunswick ultimately fell to a younger branch of the family, and Otho, the great-grandson of Henry by this branch, was the first who bore the title of Duke of Brunswick (1235). John, eldest son of Otho, founded the house of Lüneburg. Albert the Great, a younger son of Otho, conquered Wolfenbüttel, and on his death (1278) his three sons divided his dominions. Henry founded the house of Grubenhagen, Albert became Duke of Brunswick, and William Duke of Brunswick-Wolfenbüttel. Henry Julius, of this last branch, inherited Grubenhagen (1596). Ernest of Zell, of the second branch, who succeeded (1532), conquered the territories of Wolfenbüttel, and left two sons, by whom the family was divided into the two branches of Brunswick-Wolfenbüttel (IL) or Brunswick-Lüneburg, and Brunswick-Hanover from the latter of which comes the present royal family of Great Britain. The former was the German family in possession of the duchy of Brunswick down to 1884, when this line became extinct on the death of the last duke, Wilhelm I., who ascended the throne of the duchy in 1831. Ernest Augustus, of the Brunswick-Hanover House, was created Elector of Hanover in 1692. He married Sophia, daughter of Elizabeth, the daughter of James I. of England. Their son George succeeded his father as Elector of Hanover in 1698, and was called to the throne of Great Britain as George I. in 1714, under the Act of Settlement of 1701, which invested the succession in the heirs of the Princess Sophia, being Protestants. The British sovereigns continued to rule Hanover till the accession of Victoria, when the Duke of Cumberland succeeded. The present Duke of Cumberland, titular Duke of Brunswick and king of Hanover, would have become ruler of Brunswick but for the events which transferred Hanover to Prussia; and Prince Albert of Prussia was elected regent of Brunswick instead.

Brunswick-Lüneburg, Karl Wilhelm Ferdinand (DUKE OF), German soldier: b. (eldest son of the reigning duke, Charles of Brunswick, and of a sister of Frederick the Great) 9 Oct. 1735; d. Ottensen, near Altona, 10 Nov. 1806. He was carefully educated, and his military ambition was early kindled by the achievements of Frederick II. He commanded the Brunswick troops in the allied army in the Seven Years' war, and in the fatal battle at Hastenbeck, 28 July 1757, he recaptured a battery that had been taken by the French; calling forth from Frederick a statement that "he showed him for a hero." He was instrumental in deciding the victory of Crefeld. He took the most active part in all the enterprises of his uncle Ferdinand; and Frederick's esteem for him continued to increase. In 1764 he married the Princess Augusta of England. He practised the greatest economy, living mostly retired from public business, and devoted to

the arts and sciences. In 1773 he entered the Prussian service and became general of infantry, but had no opportunity of displaying his military talents. After the death of his father (1780) he entered upon the government with zeal and activity. Anxious for the improvement of the finances, he diminished his household, discharged the debts of the state, encouraged agriculture, extended the liberty of commerce, undertook or assisted in the erection of considerable buildings, and by causing Italian operas, masquerades, etc., to be exhibited gratis, provided also for the amusement of the public. Yet, with the best intentions, he was often unsuccessful. This was the case with his plans for the improvement of public education. He invited men of learning into the country at great expense, but the projected reformation having met with innumerable obstacles, they became a burden to the state. In 1787 he commanded a Prussian army for the support of the stadtholder of Holland. When the wars of the French Revolution broke out, he received the chief command of the Austrian and Prussian army, and issued at Coblenz, 15 July 1792, a manifesto, drawn up in a very haughty style, which did more injury to the allied forces than a hostile army could have done. The duke designed to press forward from Lorraine to Paris to cut off its supplies, and thus force it to surrender by famine. Longwy was taken, 23 August, and Verdun, 2 Sept. 1792. But in Champagne, a country of itself unproductive, the transport of provisions for the army from the frontiers was rendered difficult by mountains and forests. Dumouriez was encamped in the vicinity of St. Menehould, and skirmishes took place daily; but the skilful dispositions of Dumouriez culminated in the defeat of the Germans by Kellermann at Valmy, 20 Sept. 1792, and Brunswick-Lüneburg was obliged to conclude an armistice and evacuate Champagne. Custines took Worms and Spires during this retreat, and captured the fortress of Mainz, 21 October, and soon afterward Frankfort, which latter city, however, was retaken by the Prussians and Hessians, 2 December. The endeavors of the Germans, therefore, were principally directed to the recapture of those places. To this end the Duke, in conjunction with the Austrians, opened the campaign on the upper Rhine, in 1793, took the fortress of Königstein 7 March, conquered Mainz 22 July, and prepared to attack the strong fortress of Landau, then in the power of the French. The French, on the other hand, 14 September, made a general attack on the Duke and Wurmser, from Strasburg to Saarbruck. On that day the Duke had a sanguinary engagement with Moreau in the vicinity of Pirmasens, a town belonging to the landgraviate of Hesse-Darmstadt. The French were driven from their camp near the village of Hornbach as far as the Saar. A month later the Duke, having formed a union with Wurmser, succeeded, 13 October, in his attack on the lines of Weissenburg and his attempt to draw nearer to Landau. In order to gain another strong point of support he ventured, on the night of 16 November to make an assault upon the mountain-fortress of Bitche, which is the key of the Vosges, as the roads from Landau, Pirmasens, Weissenburg, and Strasburg unite at that place. This attempt miscarried. Between the 28th and the 30th of November, however, he defeated a division of the army of the Moselle at Lautern, which was pressing through the mountains, under the command of Hoche, with the intention of relieving Landau. But the daily attacks of Hoche and Pichegru, without regard to the sacrifice of men, and the successful attempt of the latter to break the Austrian lines near Fraschweiler, 22 December, forced the Austrians to retreat beyond the Rhine, and occasioned the retreat of the Duke also. As some difficulties had already risen between Austria and Prussia, he laid down the chief command of the army in the beginning of the year 1794. The Duke continued to labor for the welfare of his country until 1806. Although now of such an age that he might have retired without reproach from public life, yet he assumed burdens beyond his powers. At the beginning of the year 1806, commissioned by the king of Prussia, he made a journey to St. Petersburg relative to the war that soon broke out with France. He was then placed at the head of the Prussian army. But his physical strength was not equal to his moral energy, as was proved by the battles of Jena and Auerstädt, in the latter of which he was mortally wounded.

Brunswick, Ga., a city and county-seat of Glynn County, situated on St. Simon's Sound, eight miles from the Atlantic Ocean; on the Plant System and the Southern R.R.'s; 80 miles south-southwest of Savannah. Its settlement dates back more than 100 years, and its importance as a commercial port has been developed since the close of the Civil War. It has an admirable and spacious harbor, provided with a brick lighthouse; is connected with New York, Fernandina, and Savannah by regular steamship lines; and exports large quantities of cotton, phosphates, tar, turpentine, and pine lumber. The city is the seat of a U. S. marine hospital and is a popular summer and winter resort, with fine hotels. Pop. (1900) 9,081.

Brunswick (Ger., BRAUNSCHWEIG), Germany, a duchy and sovereign state in the northwest part of the Germanic empire, comprising an area of 1,425 square miles. It is divided into eight districts—three larger and five smaller, detached from each other and surrounded by foreign possessions. About one half of the land is arable. Of the cultivated area of Brunswick 75 per cent belongs to private persons, 14 per cent to corporations, and 11 per cent to the state. The minerals are of some importance, including iron, lead, copper, some gold and silver, salt, asphalt, peat; besides marble, granite, sandstone, and other kinds of stone. The forests cover a considerable area, and over 72 per cent of this is in the hands of the state. The most important cultivated crops are grain, flax, hops, tobacco, potatoes, the sugar-beet, and fruits. A good deal of attention has been given in recent times to the improvement of the breeds of cattle, sheep, and horses. The industrial occupations are varied if not individually important, and embrace beet-root sugar, tobacco and cigars, paper, glass, flax, jute, and woolen goods, hats, wooden wares, chemicals, porcelain, sewing and other machines, lacquered wares, salammoniac, chicory, and madder. The lacquered wares and porcelain of Brunswick are famous even in foreign countries. Brunswick, the capital, is the centre of trade. In 1806 the duchy was annexed by Napoleon to the kingdom of Westphalia, but its native prince, Frederick William, was restored in 1813. In the German Confederation Brunswick held the 13th rank, with two votes in the Assembly and one along with Nassau in the Diet. It was afterward a member of the North German Union, formed after the dissolution of the old confederation by the victories of Prussia in the short campaign of 1866. As a state of the German empire it now sends two members to the Bundesrath and three deputies to the Reichstag. In its internal government Brunswick is a constitutional monarchy. The Representative Assembly consists of 21 deputies of the principal taxpayers, 10 of towns, 12 of communes, and 3 of the clergy. The estimated revenue and expenditure for 1898-9 were respectively $3,686,250 and $3,610,000; the debt $15,571,600. The prevailing religion is the Lutheran. Pop. (1895) 434,213.

Brunswick, Germany, capital of the duchy of the same name (q.v.), situated on the Ocker, and on the railway from Hanover to Berlin. It was formerly one of the free cities of Germany, but it is now subject to the duke, and has been the ducal residence since 1754. The principal buildings are the new ducal palace, the mint, the house in which the Diet assembles, the town-house, the arsenal, the cathedral, museum, and picture gallery, and the public wine cellars. The ramparts of the old fortifications have been levelled and formed into a promenade. The older streets are narrow and tortuous, and antiquated in appearance. The Collegium Carolinum was founded in 1745, and intended as a medium between the common schools and the universities. It has enjoyed a high reputation even in foreign countries, particularly in England and Russia. The principal manufactures are wool, yarn, linen, porcelain, pasteboard, paper-hangings, and chemical preparations. There is a large commerce in grain, woolens, and manufactured articles. The traffic in home produce, and the carrying trade, have been much increased by the system of railways. The Brunswick fairs, though now declining, were formerly of great importance. Pop. (1895) 115,938.

Brunswick, Me., a town in Cumberland County, situated on the right bank of the Androscoggin, 26 miles northeast of Portland; pop. of township in 1891, 6,012. The falls of the Androscoggin afford excellent seats for several mills and manufactories. Bowdoin College (q.v.) is located here, and connected with it is the Medical School of Maine, established in 1820. Pop. (1900) 6,800.

Brun'swick Black, a quick-drying varnish, made of turpentine, asphaltum, and linseed oil. It is used as a lacquer for roughly coating finished iron work, and also in the preparation of microscopic slides.

Brun'swick Green, a green pigment, prepared by exposing copper turnings to the action of hydrochloric acid in the open air. It is a pale bluish-green, insoluble, cupric oxychloride, $CuCl_2.3CuO.4H_2O$. It derives its name from Brunswick, Germany, where it was first made by Gravenhorst.

Brun'ton, Mary (BALFOUR), Scotch novelist: b. Burra Island, in the Orkneys, 1778; d. 1818. In her 20th year she married Dr. Alexander Brunton, minister at Bolton, near Haddington; afterward at Edinburgh. She wrote 'Discipline' and 'Self-Control,' two novels which met with favor. At her death she left 'Emmeline,' a tale, and other pieces, which were published by Dr. Brunton, with a biographical sketch.

Brush, Charles Francis, American scientist: b. Euclid, Ohio, 17 March 1849. He graduated at the University of Michigan in 1869. He invented the modern arc system of electric lighting and founded the Brush Electric Company. He was decorated by the French government in 1881 for his achievements in electrical science. In 1891 he won a long contest in the Federal courts over the rights to the manufacture and sale of storage batteries; and in 1900 he was awarded the Rumford medal by the American Academy of Arts and Sciences.

Brush, Edward N., American physician: b. Glenwood, Erie County, N. Y., 23 April 1852. He was educated at the University of Buffalo, edited the 'Buffalo Medical Journal' (1874–89), and was assistant in the State Lunatic Asylum at Utica, 1878–84, and in the Pennsylvania Hospital for the Insane at Philadelphia, 1884–91. In the year last named he became physician-in-chief of the Shepard and Enoch Pratt Hospital, Baltimore. He has written much upon the subject of insanity and was associate editor of the 'American Journal of Insanity' 1878–84, and also from 1897.

Brush, George De Forest, American artist: b. Shelbyville, Tenn., 28 Sept. 1855. He studied under Gérôme in Paris and first attracted attention by his pictures of Indian life. His later work is almost entirely figure composition. He exhibited 'The Artist,' and 'Mother and Child,' at the Paris Exhibition of 1900, and received its gold medal. He is a member of the Society of American Artists and an associate of the National Academy of Design.

Brush, George Jarvis, American mineralogist: b. Brooklyn, N. Y., 15 Dec. 1831. He received a public school education and graduated at Yale, where he studied science in 1852. He subsequently studied in Germany. Since 1855 he has held professorships at Yale — that of metallurgy down to 1864, and that of mineralogy since that date. He has been a leading official of the Sheffield Scientific School since 1864. His writings on mineralogy are authoritative.

Brush, an instrument used for painting, or for removing dirt by light rubbing, from floors, furniture, etc. They are generally made of hair, bristles, whalebone, or of various vegetable fibres, and are divided into two classes — simple and compound. Simple brushes are composed of a single tuft, and compound brushes consist of several tufts inserted in a handle. Painters' brushes are examples of the former, and ordinary hair brushes of the latter.

Brush-bird. The scrub-bird (q.v.) of Australia.

Brush-grass (*Andropogon gryllus*), a grass of South Europe, with stiff wiry roots which are used for making brushes.

Brush-turkey, a mound-building gamebird of Australia, *Catheturus lathami.* See MEGAPODES.

Brus'sa, or **Brous'sa,** Asia Minor, a Turkish city, and capital of the vilayet of Khodavendikyar, situated in a fertile and finely wooded plain, which is enclosed by the ridges of Olympus, and abounds in hot, sulphurous and chalybeate springs, which are much frequented. A railway runs between Brussa and Mudania, its port, on the Sea of Marmora. The inhabitants are Turks, Greeks, Armenians, and Jews, engaged in commerce, in the culture of the vine, and in the manufacture of carpets, gauze, etc. A considerable number of persons are employed in mulberry culture, the reeling of silk, and silk manufacture, Brussa silks being in great demand throughout the Orient, though much raw silk is sent to Lyons to be manufactured. Caravans passing from Aleppo and Smyrna to Constantinople promote the commerce of the town. Before the earthquake of 1855 it contained close upon 150 mosques, and was adorned with an immense number of fountains; but from the earthquake and a terrible conflagration the former splendor of the town suffered greatly. It is a picturesque and interesting place, however, gardens, groves, and streams of running water being interspersed among the buildings. The castle, which is about a mile in circumference, is supposed to represent the Prusa of the ancients. Brussa was long the capital of Bithynia, and one of the most flourishing towns in the Greek empire of Constantinople. In 1326 it was taken by Orkhan, son of Othman, founder of the Ottoman dynasties; and from that epoch it was the residence of the Turkish sovereigns until the seat of empire was transferred to Adrianople. Pop. about 76,000.

Brussels (Flem. BRUSSEL; Fr. BRUXELLES), of the province of South Brabant, Belgium, a city of which it is the capital, and also the capital of the country. It is situated on the small river Senne, about 50 miles southeast of the German Ocean; lat. 50° 51′ N.; lon. 4° 22′ E. Brussels is built partly on the acclivity of a hill, partly on the plain, in a country agreeably diversified by sloping heights. Like many other Continental towns whose political situation has changed, its old fortifications have been transformed into boulevards. These surround the older portion of the city, extending for nearly five miles; they are planted with elms and linden trees in four rows, and form a wide and agreeable promenade commanding an extensive view of the surrounding country. The numerous gates, most of which bear the names of the principal high roads or railways which traverse the kingdom, are nearly all modern, but the Porte de Hal, built in 1379, is a remnant of the ancient fortifications, a large military tower of remarkable construction, which in later days was long used as a prison. The city now extends far beyond the boulevards. The Senne enters it by two branches, great part of one of these being now covered over. The stream is not navigable, but Brussels possesses water communication by means of canals with Charleroi, Mechlin, Antwerp, and the ocean. In many quarters within the boulevards Brussels still presents a congeries of twisted streets. That part of the upper or new town inside the boulevards, which contains the royal palace, is the principal exception. The suburbs, outside the boulevards, especially in the upper town, are large, and have recently greatly increased. The principal are the

Quartier Leopold and the Quartier Louise, which are regularly and elegantly built. The principal buildings of the new town are the king's palace, the palace of the chambers, the palace of justice (a magnificent new building of colossal proportions in the classical style), the palace of the fine arts, the public library and museum, etc. The upper town is ornamented with a fine park of 17 acres, with fountains and statues, around which most of the principal buildings are situated. The lower town is rich in ancient architecture. The hôtel de ville (built 1401-55), one of the finest municipal buildings in Belgium, is an imposing Gothic structure with a spire 364 feet high. The square in front of it is perhaps the most interesting of all the public places of Brussels. The cathedral of St. Gudule is the finest of many fine churches, richly adorned with sculptures and paintings. It was founded in 1010, and its reconstruction, commenced in 1226, was carried on till the 17th century. The churches of Notre-Dame-de-la-Chapelle and Notre-Dame-des-Victoires are also edifices of great beauty. The monuments of Brussels, and the specimens of painting and sculpture with which its public buildings are adorned, are too numerous to mention.

The manufactures and trade of Brussels are greatly promoted both by its canal communications and by the network of Belgian railways. Printing, type-founding, and all the other departments of bookmaking give employment to a large section of the population. Until 1852 the reprinting of French contemporary works was extensively carried on, but in that year a treaty with France gave protection to works of literature and art. Lace was an ancient manufacture, and is still of some importance; the printing of cotton and woolen fabrics, muslins, etc., and many minor manufactures are carried on. Brussels carpets are chiefly made at Tournai, but some are manufactured in the city. There are breweries, distilleries, sugar refineries, foundries of iron and brass, steam engine factories, etc. The trade carried on by the canals and railways is that of a capital city and manufacturing town, for the supply of internal wants and the distribution of its own products. The languages spoken in Brussels are French, and Flemish or Dutch, the former principally spoken in the new town, the latter chiefly in the old. English is also a good deal spoken, owing to the number of English residents and visitors.

The scientific, literary, artistic, and benevolent institutions of Brussels comprise a free university, founded in 1834, a proprietary institution, with about 60 professors and assistants, comprising four faculties, mathematical and physical sciences, belles-lettres, law, and medicine; a school of geography, founded in 1830, with an extensive museum, embracing geology, chemistry, and natural history; one of the finest observatories in Europe, the Belgian Royal Academy of Sciences, Letters, and Fine Arts, and the Royal Academy of Fine Arts; the public library, containing 350,000 volumes and 30,000 valuable manuscripts; the picture gallery, with the finest specimens of Flemish art; the Royal School of Medicine; many institutions for elementary education; societies of horticulture and other natural sciences; several hospitals; an infirmary; a philanthropic society, etc.

During the Middle Ages Brussels did not attain the extent or importance of several other cities of the Low Countries. The Emperor Otho dated a decree from Brussels in 976. It was walled by Baldric, Count of Louvain, in 1044. It was more completely fortified in 1380, the wall then following nearly the line of the present boulevard. During the 15th century it was twice burned and once ravaged by the plague. It was the scene, in 1568, of the execution of Counts Egmont and Horn. It was bombarded and burned by the French in 1695, and was the headquarters of Marlborough after the battle of Ramilies. It was taken by the French in 1794, and retained till 1814, when it became the chief town of the department of the Dyle. From 1815 to 1830 it was one of the capitals of the kingdom of the Netherlands, and in 1830 it was the chief centre of the revolt which separated Belgium from Holland. Since then it has been the capital of the Belgian kingdom, and one of the centres of European civilization, being especially distinguished, far beyond its relative importance, for the cultivation and patronage of art. The population of Brussels, including the suburbs, 1 Dec. 1897, was 551,011. The foreign element is prominent, especially the French.

Brussels Conference, the current name of two abortive international conferences: one on the usages of war, July-August 1874; the second on bimetallism, in the autumn of 1892.

1. The harsh treatment of prisoners and noncombatants in the Franco-German war aroused a humane feeling in protest. At the Congress of Universal Alliance in Paris, June 1872, a Society for the Improvement of the Condition of Prisoners of War was formed, which sent a circular to the chief European powers asking them to appoint delegates to a congress on this subject at Paris. England and France declined, because the request came from no official source; but Russia substituted a project of her own, and Gortchakoff invited the powers to a conference at Brussels, ostensibly to lay before them a proposal for "a code to determine the laws and usages of warfare, and to limit the consequences and diminish the calamities consequent upon war, as far as it may be possible or desirable." England, however, sent but one delegate, the United States none, and the South American states were refused any share. To the dismay of the promoters, the meeting was at once turned into an engine for the exact reverse of their intentions. The dominating force throughout was that of Germany and Russia, whose views and purposes were identical; and it soon became clear that the real object of the call was to strengthen their hands as militant states by throwing overboard the entire fabric of international law on the obligations of humanity, and substituting the baldest assertion of the naked rights of irresponsible force. The original topic of prisoners of war, when brought up, was refused discussion by the Russian delegate, Jomini, on the ground that the governments did not wish to hamper themselves. The question of revising the articles of the Geneva Convention (q.v.) on the treatment of the sick and wounded, and the neutrality of clergymen, physicians, etc., attending them, was also thrown out by him, on the ground that for military reasons it was necessary to revise the whole convention, and that the states "most apt in the

initiative of war" should have the right to "insist on their necessities." The question of what constitutes "effective occupation" was still more vital. The obvious interest of aggressive states was to insist, as did Germany, that it "need not manifest itself by visible signs," so that a town once occupied should still be considered so even if the troops were removed, and any rising of the inhabitants be punishable as treason; and that it was sufficiently established by "flying columns," or as defined by a satiric German, "three Uhlans and a trumpet." This denial of all rights of self-defense against invasion was almost unanimously rejected by the other delegates, however; and the principle substituted that there must be actual occupation by adequate force, and lines of communication kept open; that it "exists only when the territory is placed actually under authority of the hostile army, extends only to the territory where such authority is established, and exists only so long as the belligerent is able to exercise it." The right of *levee en masse*, or armed insurrection of the body of a people, is linked with this; and naturally the states itching for conquest wished to confine belligerent rights to regularly enrolled armies, and oblige the rest of the people to submit when these are defeated. Of course no such rule adopted by the belligerents themselves would ever bind a people who wanted to rise, but it would form a plea for much political murder before it was repealed. Jomini said that war had so changed its nature in modern times that it was necessary to "regulate the inspirations of patriotism," for fear they might be "more disastrous to the country itself than to the oppressor"; and that "those grand explosions of patriotism which took place in the beginning of the century cannot continue to occur in our day, at least not in the same form." On this head it was proposed that any inhabitant of a country under occupation who should give information to the "enemy" (his own people) should be handed over to "justice." But this philanthropic repression of self-defense in its own interest, and outlawry of the means by which Prussia gained her own independence, was not agreed to. All these assaults on natural right were opposed by the British delegate. An attempt was made to discuss reprisals or retaliation, but it was refused. Restriction of bombardment of the interior of towns without harming the fortifications was sought, but flatly refused by Germany and Russia, on the ground that "experience had shown it (the bombardment) to be one of the most efficient means of securing the objects of a war," which is true of sack, massacre, and other things banned by civilization. Finally a proposal was made that, at the option of the belligerent, neutrals should be obliged to receive and care for (at the belligerent's expense) the wounded; in other words, that a strong power could make its neutral neighbors depots to keep its armies in condition.

2. The change in relations between gold and silver, which has produced so much financial and political demoralization in the last quarter century, was the subject of three international conferences within that time: at Paris, August 1878 and April 1881, and at Brussels, November 1892. The last named was called by President Harrison for both business and political reasons. The accumulation of silver under the Sherman

Act of 1890 was threatening the country with a fall to the single silver standard, only averted by the bond sales of 1893 and the repeal of the act; and the free-coinage movement which convulsed the country in 1896 was making headway, had been approved by the platform on which Harrison was elected, and demanded some recognition. Abroad, the recent adoption of the gold standard by state after state was raising gold to a premium, and arousing the fear that it was too scarce for the sole money of ultimate payment; the fall in silver was causing much loss and dislocation of trade, and many believed that its demonetization was the sole cause of this, and of the low price of commodities (which they called the high price of gold), and that its restoration by common agreement would raise its price again and restore equilibrium of commerce. The call was accepted by all the European states and Mexico, 20 with the United States; and all the 50 delegates were present, but those of Germany, Austria, and Russia were forbidden to debate or vote. The president was Montefiore Levi, of Belgium; vice-president Edwin H. Terrell, United States minister to Belgium. The United States delegation drew up the order of business, and offered a resolution that "it is desirable that some means should be found for increasing the use of silver in the currency systems of the nations," and, while stating their own belief in general bimetallism, suggested two plans short of this, to which Mr. Alfred Rothschild, of the British delegation, added a third. The resolution was favored by most of the delegations, who indeed would not otherwise have been sent there; but was too general to be of any service, and was laid on the table and not taken up. A special committee reported on the three schemes before it: (1) That of A. Soetbeer, too involved for international agreement; (2) Rothschild's, as altered in committee, essentially, that all Europe should buy 30,000,000 ounces of silver yearly, the United States to keep on buying 54,000,000; unlimited free coinage to be established in British India and Mexico; the agreement to run for five years unless silver rose to an agreed price before that; (3) Moritz Levy's, laid before the conference of 1881, to withdraw from circulation all gold coin and notes under 20 francs. The British delegation refused to support this unless joined with something like the Rothschild plan of maintaining the gold price of silver; the Latin Union members would not have this because it involved fresh purchases of silver; nor the United States, because of its unfairness to us; and Rothschild withdrew his plan. Thereupon the conference began discussing bimetallism till they adjourned, 15 December, for the holidays, to reconvene the following May if the governments thought it advisable; but the election of President Cleveland meantime had taken it out of the immediate political field as an adjunct, and it did not meet again. See INTERNATIONAL LAW; U. S., DIPLOMACY OF THE.

Brussels Lace. See LACE.

Brussels Sprouts, a garden vegetable (*Brassica oleracea* var. *gemmifera*), derived from the same species as cabbage and cauliflower, like which it is cultivated as an autumn crop more widely in Europe than in America.

Brut, Roman de, a poem in eight-syllable verse, composed by Robert Wace, but indirectly modeled upon a legendary chronicle of Brittany, entitled 'Brut y Brenhined' (Brutus of Brittany), discovered in Armorica by Walter, archdeacon of Oxford, and translated into Latin by Geoffrey of Monmouth. Wace presented his poem to Eleonore of Guyenne in 1155, and it was translated into Anglo-Saxon by Layamon.

The poem relates that after the capture of Troy by the Greeks, Æneas came to Italy with his son, Ascanius, and espoused Lavinia, daughter of King Latinus; she duly presented a son to him. This son, as well as Ascanius, succeeded to the throne, which devolved at last upon Silvins, son of Ascanius, who became the father of Brutus, from whom the 'Roman' takes its name. Brutus slew his father with a misdirected arrow, and fled. First he went to Greece, where he delivered the Trojan captives; next he conquered the Armorican Isles, to which he gave the name of Britain. Afterward he made war upon the king of Poitou and founded the city of Tours, which he named in honor of his son. From Poitou he returned to the Armorican Isles, overcoming the giants in possession, and renamed it Britain. He founded the city of London and reigned long and gloriously there. The narrative now concerns itself with the descendants of Brutus. The adventures of Lear, of Belin, of Brennus who voyaged to Italy, of Cassivellaunus who so bravely resisted Cæsar, of all the bellicose chiefs who opposed the dominion of the Roman emperors, are minutely related. King Arthur, however, is the real hero of the 'Roman de Brut.' Arthur performs prodigies of valor, is the ideal knight of his order of the Round Table, and finally departs for some unknown region, where it is implied he becomes immortal, and never desists from the performance of deeds of valor. In this portion of the narrative figure the enchanter Merlin; the Holy Grail, or chalice in which were caught the last drops of the Saviour's blood as he was taken from the cross; Lancelot of the Lake; Tristan and his unhallowed love; Perceval and his quest of the Holy Grail. The 'Roman' became unprecedentedly popular, and it was publicly read at the court of the Norman kings.

Brütt, Ferdinand, German painter: b. Hamburg, 13 July 1849. He was educated at the Weimar art school and settled in Düsseldorf in 1876; was professor at the art school there in 1893; and in 1900 went to Cronberg. The subjects of his earlier pictures were from the life of the modern peasants or from the history of the 18th century, but in later years he has painted scenes from the life of the city. His works include: 'Peasant Delegation'; 'The Prince on the Promenade'; 'At the Exchange'; 'In the Art Gallery.'

Bruttii, an ancient people of Italy, living in the southwestern peninsula, now Calabria. The Greeks had several flourishing colonies on the coast and had to some extent conquered the inhabitants of the interior; the Lucanians also made themselves masters of some portions of the interior. But about 350 the people revolted, and, assisted by the Lucanians, gained their independence and captured several Greek cities. At this time they were called by the Greeks Bruttii (rebels). They remained independent till they united with Pyrrhus against Rome and were subdued by the Romans in 272 B.C. In the second Punic war they sided with Hannibal, and after his expulsion from Italy were heavily punished by the Romans, robbed of considerable of their territory, entirely deprived of their independence, and not allowed to bear arms.

Brutus, or Brute, in the fabulous history of Britain, the first king of the island, according to Geoffrey of Monmouth. He is said to have been the son of Silvius, and grandson of Ascanius, the son of Æneas, and to have been born in Italy. He landed at Totness, in Devonshire, destroyed the giants who then inhabited Albion, and called the island from his own name. At his death the island was divided among his three sons: Locrine had England, Cumber Wales, and Albanact Scotland.

Brutus, Decimus Junius, Roman soldier: d. 43 B.C. He served under Cæsar in the Gallic war, and in the civil war he commanded the fleet destined to besiege Massilia. Cæsar afterward appointed him to the government of further Gaul. Nevertheless he joined the conspiracy against Cæsar, and volunteered, on the memorable Ides of March, to conduct his friend and benefactor to the place of slaughter. When the tragedy was consummated, Decimus Brutus retired to Cisalpine Gaul, and there maintained himself for some time, but was ultimately deserted by his troops, betrayed to Antony, and put to death by order of that general.

Brutus, Lucius Junius, a Roman patriot, sometimes called the Elder, to distinguish him from Marcus Junius, the slayer of Cæsar, lived about 500 B.C. According to the legend, he was the son of Marcus Junius and the elder daughter of Tarquin the Proud, the last king of Rome, and is represented as having saved his life from the cruelty of that prince by feigning idiocy, whence he received the surname of Brutus (Stupid). Yet the king associated him with his own sons, Aruns and Titus, in a mission which he sent to Delphi to inquire into the meaning of a portent, which had caused much alarm at Rome. After receiving the reply to the question they were charged to propound, the young men enquired of the oracle which of the three should be king in Rome, no one of them being, it is observable, heir to that dignity. To this the reply was, "Whichever shall first kiss his mother." So, on their return to Italy, Titus and Aruns ran to kiss the queen mother; but Lucius Junius, as he landed from the galley, pretending to slip, fell prostrate and kissed the soil of Rome, in the belief that by "mother" the oracle had meant mother earth. When Lucretia, the wife of Collatinus, plunged a dagger into her bosom that she might not outlive the insult which she had suffered from Sextus, the son of Tarquin, Brutus is said to have drawn the dagger from the wound, and to have sworn vengeance against the Tarquins whose banishment he then demanded and procured. Then (about 509 B.C.) he is said to have been chosen one of the two first consuls. According to the legend, a conspiracy to restore the monarchy having been supported by the two sons of Brutus, he, after the crime had been proved, ordered the lictors to execute the law, and did not leave the assembly till after the execution. At length Tarquin marched against Rome. The consuls advanced to meet him. Brutus led the cavalry; Aruns, son of Tarquin, commanded the body opposed to him. They pierced each other with their spears at the same moment, and both fell. The Romans conquered, and Brutus was buried with great splendor. The details of the story of Brutus, which may be regarded as a poetical legend, have been shown by Niebuhr to be irreconcilable with history.

Brutus, Marcus Junius, Roman republican: b. 85 B.C.; d. 42 B.C. He was the son of that Marcus Junius Brutus whom Pompey caused to be murdered, and of Servilia, the half sister of Cato. He lost his father when he was only eight years old, but his mother and uncles carefully directed his education. On the outbreak of the civil war he followed the example of Cato, and joined the Pompeians, notwithstanding his aversion to their leader. After the unfortunate battle of Pharsalia, he surrendered himself to Cæsar, who received him generously, allowed him to withdraw from the war, made him in the following year governor of Cisalpine Gaul, and afterward conferred on him the government of Macedonia. Notwithstanding these benefits, Brutus allowed himself to be drawn by Cassius and others into the conspiracy against Cæsar, who had now made himself master of the supreme power in the state. Cæsar was assassinated in the senate house. In public speeches Brutus explained the reasons of this deed, but he could not appease the dissatisfaction of the people, and retired with his party to the capitol. Antony succeeded in exciting the popular indignation against the murderers of Cæsar, and they were compelled to flee from Rome. Brutus went to Athens, raised a large force, and also gained over the troops in Macedonia. Thus, master of all Greece and Macedonia, he stood at the head of a powerful army. He went to Asia and joined Cassius, whose forces were also strong. At Philippi they fought the army of Antony and Octavius. Cassius was beaten by Antony, and caused himself to be killed. Brutus repulsed Octavius, by whom, however, he was soon afterward totally defeated. Seeing his cause ruined, he ended his life by falling upon his sword. Brutus was a man of little independent judgment, a mere student, liable to be swayed by others, and he was in no sense a martyr to a genuine patriotism. He was the author of philosophical and historical treatises, orations, etc., none of which now survive.

Bruyas, Jacques, zhäk brü-yą, French Jesuit: b. 1637; d. 1712. In 1666 on coming to Canada he went as a missionary to the Iroquois, and later established one of the earliest missions among the Mohawk Indians. He was a student of their language, and wrote in Latin a valuable work on the 'Mohawk Radicals.'

Bruyère, Jean de la, zhŏṅ dė lą brü yâr. See LA BRUYÈRE.

Bruyn, Barthel, bär'tĕl broin, German painter: b. Cologne, 1493; d. about 1556. His earlier works show the influence of some of the German masters, but later he imitated Michael Angelo and other Italian painters. His masterpiece is the altarpiece for the Church of St. Victor at Xanten. His numerous works are mostly in Cologne and Munich; among them are: 'Martyrdom of St. Ursula'; 'Adoration of the Magi'; 'Corpus Christi'; 'Saint Catherine'; and a number of portraits.

Bryan, Mary Edwards, American author: b. Jefferson County, Florida, 1844. She began writing at an early age, and before the war was a regular contributor to the 'Southern Field and Fireside,' and other journals. Her published books are: 'Manch' (1879); 'Wild Work' (1881), a story of Louisiana reconstruction; 'The Bayou Bride'; 'Kildee' (1886); 'Uncle Ned's White Child'; 'Ruth, an Outcast'; 'His Legal Wife'; 'The Girl He Bought'; 'My Own Sin'; 'His Wife's Friend.'

Bryan, William Jennings, American political leader: b. Salem, Ill., 19 March 1860. He was graduated at Illinois College, Jacksonville, in 1881, and at the Union College of Law, Chicago, in 1883. He practised law at Jacksonville from 1883 to 1887, when he removed to Lincoln, Neb. He was elected to Congress in 1890, and again in 1892. From 1894 to 1896 he was editor of the Omaha *World-Herald*. In 1896 he was nominated for President by the Democratic National Convention at Chicago, and also by the People's party and Free Silver Republicans, on a platform demanding the free and unlimited coinage of silver by the United States at a ratio of 16 to 1, regardless of the action of other nations, a financial policy which he had for some time advocated with much earnestness and eloquence of both tongue and pen. He was defeated at the polls by McKinley. During the war with Spain, he was colonel of a Nebraska regiment of volunteers, but saw no field service. In 1900 he was a presidential candidate, of the Democrats, Populists, and Free-Silver Republicans, upon an anti-imperialistic and anti-trust platform, with a reiterated demand for free-silver. He was again defeated by William McKinley. Soon after the election he established The Commoner, a political weekly. He wrote 'The First Battle: a Story of the Campaign of 1896' (1896), which contains some of his speeches and a biographical sketch by his wife; besides he published numerous articles in periodicals.

Bryant, Edwin Eustace, American lawyer and author: b. Milton, Vt., 10 Jan. 1835; d. Toronto, Can., 1903; educated at the New Hampton Institute; removed to Wisconsin 1858. He served in the Civil War and from 1868-72 was private and executive secretary to the governor of Wisconsin. In 1878 he was elected to the legislature of the State; in 1882 was adjutant-general of Wisconsin, and from 1885-89, assistant United States attorney-general for the post-office. He was the author of several well-known law books.

Bryant, Henry Grier, American explorer and geographer: b. Allegheny City, Pa., 7 Nov. 1859. He graduated at Princeton. 1883, and from the law department of the University of Pennsylvania, 1886. He has contributed literary articles to various magazines and encyclopædias. In 1891 he organized and conducted an exploring expedition to the Grand Falls of Labrador, was second in command of the Peary Relief Expedition in 1892, and in 1897 led an exploring expedition to the Mount Saint Elias region of Alaska. In 1895 and 1897 he was a delegate to international geographical congresses in London and Berlin.

Bryant, Jacob, English philologist and antiquary: b. Plymouth, 1715; d. 1804. He studied at Eton and King's College, Cambridge, became afterward tutor of the sons of the famous Duke of Marlborough, the eldest of whom he also accompanied to the Continent as his secretary. After his return he received, by the influence of his patron, a lucrative post in the ordnance, which gave him leisure for his researches into Biblical, Roman, and Grecian antiquities. His most important work is the 'New System of Ancient Mythology' (1774-6). He was engaged in a famous dispute on the veracity of Homer and the existence of Troy, in which he endeavored to show that there never was such a city as Troy, and that the whole expedition of the Greeks was a mere fiction of Homer. The object of one of his earlier treatises, which appeared in 1767, is to show that the island Melita, on which Saint Paul was wrecked, was not Malta, but situated in the Adriatic. He endeavored to illustrate the Scriptures by explanations drawn from Josephus, from Philo the Jew, and from Justin Martyr; but in this, as in all his writings, his learning and his ingenuity are misled by his love of controversy and paradox.

Bryant, John Howard, American poet: b. Cummington, Mass., 22 July 1807; d. Princeton, Ill., 14 Jan. 1902. He was a brother of William Cullen Bryant (q.v.). He studied at the Rensselaer Polytechnic Institute, Troy, N. Y., removed to Illinois in 1831, and from 1832 until his death lived on his farm at Princeton, performing the greater part of its work with his own hands. He held numerous local offices, served in the State legislature in 1842, and 1858; was a Free-soil candidate for Congress in 1854; and a delegate to the convention which organized the Republican party in 1856. He was an intimate friend of Abraham Lincoln, who appointed him collector of internal revenue for the Fifth Illinois district, 1862-6. The poems which were the product of his leisure hours show him as a lover of nature, which he described minutely and effectively, and a man of refined tastes and kindly feelings. His first printed poem, 'My Native Village,' appeared in the 'United States Review and Literary Gazette' in 1826, his brother William then being editor of that journal. His collected work may be found in 'Poems' (1855), and 'Poems Written from Youth to Old Age, 1824-84,' privately printed at Princeton, Ill., in 1885.

Bryant, Neil, American actor and minstrel performer: b. Keesville, N. Y., 1835; d. Brooklyn, N. Y., 6 March 1902. He was the youngest of three brothers, long prominent in the negro minstrel entertainment business. He made his first appearance on the minstrel stage in 1845, and soon became the champion American flute-player. With his brothers he opened a theatre at 472 Broadway, New York, in 1857, which they retained for 10 years. The oldest brother having died in 1867, the others continued in the same business in other locations in New York, but after the death of the second brother in 1875, Neil became unsuccessful and lost the most of what he had acquired. He retired from the stage in 1883 and was subsequently employed in the coast survey.

Bryant, William Cullen, American poet and journalist: b. Cummington, Mass., 3 Nov. 1794; d. New York, 12 June 1878. His father, Dr. Peter Bryant, a physician, was a man of much literary culture, as well as large experience in public affairs. He prepared, when he was but 14, a collection of poems, which were published in Boston in 1809. In that volume appeared 'The Embargo,' the only poem dealing with the politics of the day he ever wrote. In the following year Bryant entered Williams College as a student of law, but left without taking a degree in 1815, when he was admitted to the bar. In that year he became a contributor to the 'North American Review,' in which appeared the following year his 'Thanatopsis,' a poem in blank verse, which from the first has commanded profound admiration. Six years later he published a second collection of poems, which brought him into a wide fame. The principal piece, 'The Ages,' is a didactic poem, in which he sketches the past progress of the world, concluding with a glowing picture of America, and its occupation by the new race. He definitely abandoned law for literature in 1825, and went to New York, where he founded the 'New York Review,' and a year after became the editor of the Evening Post, an old established paper with which he was connected till his death. In 1832 he issued another collection of poems, which was republished in Great Britain with a preface by Washington Irving. In the summer of 1834, accompanied by his family, he went to Europe, and traveled through England, France, Germany, and Italy, remaining in the latter country for a considerable time. In 1845 he again visited Europe, and still again in 1849, when he extended his journey to Egypt and the Holy Land. The incidents of these and subsequent travels, both in Europe and America, were described in letters written to the Evening Post, which were reprinted in separate volumes, entitled 'Letters of a Traveler,' and 'Letters from Spain and Other Countries.' A complete edition of his poems up to 1855 was published in that year, and in 1863 appeared a small volume entitled 'Thirty Poems.' His last works of importance are his translations of the 'Iliad' (1870) and the 'Odyssey' (1872), translations which many American critics rank above any that had hitherto appeared in the English language. Early in 1878 appeared 'The Flood of Years,' his last poem of any great length, in which the poet, in strains that remind the reader of 'Thanatopsis,' reviews the life of man as the ridge of a wave ever hurrying on to oblivion the forms that appear on its surface but for a moment, concluding, however, with the expression of a confident hope in the future of mankind, even though the present is most dark and drear. At the time of his death he was engaged, in conjunction with Sydney Howard Gay, on a popular history of the United States, the first volume of which appeared in 1876.

Bryaxis, Greek sculptor: flourished in the 4th century B.C. He cast a statue in bronze of Seleucus, king of Syria, and assisted in adorning the mausoleum with bas-reliefs. He also executed five gigantic statues at Rhodes, a statue of Pasiphaæ, and other works. According to Clemens Alexandrinus, two of his statues were attributed by some to the celebrated Phidias.

Bryce, George, Canadian clergyman and educator: b. Mount Pleasant, Ontario, 22 April 1844. He was graduated at the University of

WILLIAM CULLEN BRYANT.

Toronto in 1867, and was ordained to the Presbyterian ministry in 1871. His great work was the foundation of Manitoba College and in assisting the foundation of Manitoba University. He has written: 'Manitoba, Its Infancy, Growth, and Present Condition' (1882) ; 'A Short History of the Canadian People' (1886) ; and 'Canada and the Northwest' (1887).

Bryce, James, British historian and politician: b. Belfast, 10 May 1838. His father, James Bryce, LL.D., was a Scotchman, well known as a distinguished teacher and geologist, and a master in the high school of Glasgow from 1846 to 1874. He received his early education at the high school and University of Glasgow, and latterly at Trinity College, Oxford, where he graduated B.A. with a double first-class in 1862, being in the same year elected a Fellow of Oriel College. In 1867 he became a barrister of Lincoln's Inn. From 1870 till his resignation in 1893, he was regius professor of civil law at Oxford. He entered Parliament in 1880 as member for the Tower Hamlets division of London, and since 1885 he has represented South Aberdeen as a Liberal and Home Ruler. He was chancellor of the duchy of Lancaster and a member of the cabinet in the Liberal ministry of 1892, and two years later he became president of the Board of Trade, a post which he held till the change of government ensuing upon the general election of 1895. In 1905 he became Chief Secretary for Ireland and in December 1906 ambassador to the United States. He is D.C.L. of Oxford, LL.D. of Edinburgh and Glasgow; in 1894 he was elected a Fellow of the Royal Society, and many foreign honors have been conferred on him. His two most important works are: 'The Holy Roman Empire' (1864, afterward enlarged and republished) and 'The American Commonwealth' (1888), a very full exposition of the American Constitution, system of government, and administration, political machinery, etc. He has also written: 'Transcaucasia and Ararat' (1877); 'Impressions of South Africa' (1897); and 'Studies in History and Jurisprudence' (1901).

Bryce, Lloyd, American editor and novelist: b. Long Island, N. Y., 1852. From 1889 to 1896 he was editor of the 'North American Review.' His works include: 'Paradise'; 'A Dream of Conquest'; 'The Romance of An Alter Ego'; 'Friends in Exile.'

Bryden, Henry Anderson, English author: b. 3 May 1854. He was educated at Cheltenham College, and later studied for the bar. In early life he won a national reputation as an athlete, especially as runner. His travels in South Africa have been extensive. Among his books are: 'Kloof and Karroo: Sport, Legend, and Natural History in Cape Colony'; 'Gun and Camera in Southern Africa'; 'Tales of South Africa'; 'The Victorian Era in South Africa'; 'Nature and Sport in South Africa' : 'An Exiled Scot' (1899) ; 'Animals of Africa' (1900) ; 'From Veldt Camp Fires' (1900).

Brymner, Douglas, Canadian archivist: b. Greenock, Scotland, 1823. Trained for a mercantile career, he was engaged in business until 1856, when ill health compelled his retirement. He emigrated to Canada in 1857, and engaged in journalism, becoming editor of the Presbyterian and associate editor of the Montreal *Herald.*

In 1872 he was appointed historical archivist of Canada, and for 30 years labored tirelessly in collecting and arranging the historical records and documents of the Dominion. His series of annual reports, each entitled 'Report on the Canadian Archives,' constitute a rich treasury of original documents for every phase of Dominion history.

Bryn Mawr College, an educational institution for women, at Bryn Mawr, Pa.; founded in 1880 by Joseph Taylor. Its standard of admission is very high; its system of undergraduate studies combines required courses and varied elective groups. At the end of 1902 it reported: Professors and instructors, 38; students, 339; volumes in the library, 32,000; productive funds, $1,000,000; income, $131,000; benefactions, $25,000.

Bry'ony (*Bryonia*), a genus of seven climbing perennial herbs of the natural order *Cucurbitaceæ*, natives of Europe and Asia. Common bryony (*B. dioica*), which attains a height of from 6 to 12 feet, has long, white, branching, ill-smelling, fleshy roots, one half inch thick; five-lobed roundish leaves; racemes of staminate flowers and axillary, greenish-white, pistillate, short-stemmed flowers in corymbs, followed by red berries as large as peas. Probably because of its repulsive odor the plant has been reputed as poisonous, but is used to some extent medicinally. The young shoots of this and the following species are often used like spinach. Common bryony is frequently planted for ornament in Europe, but like its relatives has not become very popular in the United States for this purpose. White bryony (*B. alba*) attains a height of from 6 to 12 feet, has thick, yellowish tuberculate roots, long-stemmed leaves and long-stemmed pistillate flowers in racemose corymbs. Abyssinian bryony (*B. abyssiniana*), which by some botanists is considered a species of the genus *Coccinia*, yields edible roots. Black bryony (*Tamus communis*), belongs to the natural order *Dioscoreaceæ*.

Bryophyl'lum, a small genus of succulent herbs of the natural order *Crassulariaceæ*, natives of warm climates. *B. calycinum*, the only species cultivated in greenhouses, is a native of the Maluccas and Mexico. It is two to four feet high with reddish stems, fleshy leaves, and compound panicles of pendulous flowers. Both calyx and corolla are reddish green and cylindrical, the former about an inch long, the latter two inches or more. The plant is specially interesting since the leaves when laid on damp sand or moss or placed in moist air, produce new plants from the notches in their margins. In Bermuda, where they are called "floppers," in some of the West Indian islands, and parts of the southern United States, the plant is a weed in fence rows, upon stone walls, etc., and sometimes a pest in fields. Its leaves are said to be tart in the morning, tasteless at noon, and bitterest in the evening, from the absorption of oxygen at night and its release in daylight.

Bryozo'a, the name given by Ehrenberg to a class of molluscoid animals, the peculiarities of which had been previously observed by J. V. Thompson, who had called them polyzoa. See POLYZOA.

Brzesc Litewski, b-zĕteh lĭ-tĕff'skĭ, or **Brest Litovsky,** Russia, a fortified town in the government of Grodno, on the right bank of the river Bug, about 110 miles south of Grodno. It was formerly the capital of a Lithuanian palatinate, and contains an old castle, a high school, three churches, and a synagogue, and has a considerable transit trade. It is at the junction of railroads from Odessa to Königsberg and Moscow to Warsaw, and two fairs are held here annually. In 1794 Suwaroff gained here a victory over the Poles. Pop. (1897) 46,500.

Bua, boo'a, a small island in the Adriatic, belonging to the Dalmatian district of Spalatro, Austro-Hungary; is connected with the town of Trau by a bridge. During the latter period of the Roman empire many political offenders and heretics were confined here. It contains six villages, of which Santa Croce, or Bua, is the principal. The productions of the island comprise dates, wine, olives, and particularly asphaltum, of which there is a remarkable well.

Buache, Philippe, fē-lēp bü-äsh, French geographer: b. Paris, 7 Feb. 1700; d.' 24 Jan. 1773. He spent seven years in arranging a new repository of maps and charts. In 1729 he became chief geographer to the king, and in the following year a member of the academy of sciences, in which he had been the means of instituting a professorship of geography. His notions of geography were in some respects peculiar. He asserted that there was a vast continent about the South Pole, traversed by lofty mountains and gigantic rivers. The suggestion, that at Bering Strait a connection between Asia and America might be traced, came from him. He published 'Considerations géographiques et Physiques sur les Nouvelles Découvertes au nord de la Grande Mer' (1753); 'Atlas Physique' (1754).

Buansuah, boo-an-soo', a wild dog (Cyon primævus), found throughout India, especially in the forests along the foothills of the Himalayan Mountains. It is smaller than a wolf, but similar in habits, and reddish in color. It hunts in companies, and a pack of these dogs is able to overcome any of the wild beasts in the jungle, except the elephant and rhinoceros, but they are very shy of mankind. It is generally known in the south as the dhole. See DOG.

Bubach. See INSECT POWDER.

Bu'balis or Bubale, a North African antelope (Alcelaphus bubalinus), thought to be the bubalus of the ancients. It is one of the hartbeests (q.v.), and equals a large stag in size, with an ox-like head and muzzle, and lyrate horn, heavily ringed. It is bay in color, with a black tuft on the end of the tail.

Bubas'tis, or Bubastus, a city of ancient Egypt, now in ruins; mentioned in the Old Testament as Pi-Beseth, now known as Tel-Basta; situated in the delta of the Nile, southwest of Tanis; was built in honor of the goddess Pasht, called by the Greeks Bubastis. This goddess was represented by the figure of a cat, and many mummied cats have been found in the tombs of Bubastis. On the north side of the city began the canal between the Nile and the Red Sea, constructed by Pharaoh Neco. Bubastis was taken by the Persians 352 B.C., and its walls dismantled. Among the ruins of this city have been found remains of costly and magnificent temples. Here were celebrated solemn feasts to the goddess .Pasht.

attended by people from all parts of Egypt, even to the number of 700,000 at one time, as is stated by Herodotus.

Bubble Shell, the thin, inflated bubble-like shell of a gastropod mollusk (Bulla), the shell usually without a spire. On each side of the head is a large swimming flap (epipodium), and one species flits about in shallow pools on mud flats. Our eastern Atlantic coast species are Bulla occidentalis and Haminea solitaria, the latter found in Vineyard Sound. They mostly live in rather deep water, at least below low-tide mark.

Bubna und Littitz, boob'na, lĭt-tĭtz', Ferdinand (COUNT OF), Austrian field marshal: b. Zamersk, Bohemia, 1768; d. Milan, 6 June 1825. He was early in life, the chamberlain of the emperor of Austria, afterward entered the military service, and after distinguishing himself on various occasions, at Manheim, in the defense of Bohemia (1800), and at Austerlitz, gained at Wagram, in 1809, the rank of field-marshal-lieutenant. In the war of 1813 he commanded an Austrian division with much honor, was present at the battles of Lützen, Bautzen, Dresden, and Leipsic, and in 1814 received the chief command of the Austrian army which was to pass through Geneva to the south of France. He advanced upon Lyons, but was unsuccessful, till the corps of Bianchi and Hessen-Homburg came to his assistance. Bubna remained at Lyons till the return of the allied forces, and then retired to Vienna. After the landing of Napoleon in 1815, he again led a corps against Lyons, and in Savoy opposed Marshal Suchet, till Paris was conquered, and the marshal retreated beyond Lyons. He then took possession of Lyons without opposition, established a court-martial to punish the disturbers of public order, and proceeded with greater severity than on his former campaign. In September he marched back to Austria, and received for his services valuable estates in Bohemia from the emperor. In the insurrection of Piedmont, 1821, the Count de Bubna received the chief command of the Austrian troops destined to restore the ancient government. After the accomplishment of this commission, he was appointed general commandant of Lombardy.

Bu'bo, a genus of birds belonging to the family Strigidæ, or owls. They have a small ear aperture, two large feathered tufts like horns on the sides of the head, and the legs feathered to the toes. B. maximus is the eagle owl, or great owl. It is a native of Europe. The corresponding American species is B. virginianus.

Bubo, a hardening and enlargement of lymphatic glands, generally the inguinal, as in the Oriental or Levantine plague, syphiloid gonorrhœa, etc., always, unless dissipated by medical interference, followed by suppuration. In cases of true infecting syphilis a suppurating bubo is a rare complication, although induration of the glands in the later forms of the disease is almost invariably present. See BUBONIC PLAGUE.

Bubon'ic Plague, a disease supposed to be identical with the plague known as the Black Death, which had its origin in China, and made its first appearance in Europe 543 A.D., at Constantinople. It derives its modern name from the fact that it attacks the lymphatic glands in the neck, armpits, groins, and other parts of the body. The swollen parts are extremely sensitive to the touch, the patient suffers from headache, vertigo, high fever, vomiting, and great prostration. Another feature is the appearance of purple spots and a mottling of the skin. In severe cases death generally ensues in 48 hours, and, at best, recovery is slow. It is now generally agreed that this plague is a germ disease. The bacillus has been identified by Indian bacteriologists as well as by European and American investigators. It is found without trouble in the blood of the patient, and cultures are made in beef tea or glycerine preparations. The bacilli resemble those of chicken pox, and are said not to survive more than four days of dessications. At the Hoagland laboratory in Brooklyn, N. Y., extensive experiments have been made, both in the culture of the germs and in an anti-toxin, by means of which immunity from this scourge may be obtained. The disease has been called "the poor's plague," from the fact that it first attacked the half-starved masses who congregate in the slums of the cities. This was the case in Bombay, where so fatal were its ravages that a panic ensued and more than 450,000 people, one half the population, left the city. Pure air, wholesome food, the free external use of cold water, and proper sanitary regulations modify to some extent the attacks of the plague, and, more than anything else, have been the cause of the comparative exemption of Europeans from it. It has, however, visited some of the cities of Europe.

History.—The first authentic description of the bubonic plague is contained in the writings of Rufus of Ephesus, who described the disease as having existed in northern Africa during the 3d or 4th century B.C. He presented the testimony of physicians of that period to corroborate his arguments. Since that time the disease has been variously described by writers under the name of Levantine, Oriental, and Bubonic Plague, and the black plague, or black death. These designations are more or less open to criticism and lack scientific foundation. In the reign of Justinian, 542 A.D., the disease appeared in Egypt, and within a year extended to Constantinople, where it is said to have caused the death of 10,000 persons in one day. In 1352 the plague spread through the whole of Europe and nearly one fourth of the population died. It is estimated by Hecker that during this reign of terror, out of 2,000,000 inhabitants of Norway, but 300,000 survived. It was estimated by Pope Clement VI. that the mortality from black death for the entire world was 40,000,000. This outbreak lasted about 20 years. During the great plague of London, in 1665, there were 63,596 deaths out of a population of 460,000. It was believed the infection was introduced by bales of merchandise from the Levant. The sanitary condition of London, at the time, was notoriously bad. It is a significant fact that those who lived out of town and on barges and ships on the Thames did not contract the disease.

Characteristics.—The bacillus of the bubonic plague was discovered and studied by Kitasato and Yersin, working independently, and at about the same time, in 1894, during the epidemic of the plague at Hong Kong. It is found in large numbers in the pus, in the lymphatic glands, and occasionally in the internal organs. It is apparently present in the blood only in the acute

hemorrhagic types of the disease, and shortly before death. An anti-plague serum injected into a young Chinaman at the Catholic mission at Canton in June 1896, who was attacked with a severe type of the disease, was effective. It is believed the plague is transmitted solely through infection from previous cases. What part, if any, the soil plays in propagating the disease has not been settled. The natives of Eastern countries are strongly impressed with the belief that the germ is contained in the ground. Exactly what influence the climate and temperature have in the propagation of the plague is not known. It is apparent, however, that hot, dry air is fatal to the disease, and that moist, warm air is favorable to it. It even may be very active in cold weather. This was shown by the outbreak that occurred on the Volga River, in Russia, in the severe winter of 1878. Like typhus fever, the plague is unknown in the tropics, and, like typhus, again, usually selects its victims from the lowest class, and thrives on filth and famine. The usual period of incubation is from three to six days. In the usual or severe forms, the earlier symptoms are similar to those that usher in typhus fever. The invasion is abrupt, associated with chills, great depression, blunted condition of the intellect, pains in the bones and high fever. Death frequently occurs within 48 hours, and even earlier. When life is prolonged for five or six days the prognosis is more favorable. The germ can be carried in rags, general merchandise and clothing. Rigid quarantine with disinfection of all articles should be strictly enforced when it appears in any country.

Remedies.—The chief causes of the plague are famine and filth. Serums seem to be unavailable against these obstacles, as is even the use of antipyretics or stimulants. As a preventive serum, that of Prof. Haffkins has proven the most effectual. See SERUM THERAPY. The compulsory evacuation of infected cities and districts has accomplished much. Indeed, this was the most available remedy during the epidemic in the Punjab district in 1896-7, and is the first preventive of a spread in case of an outbreak. The cities of India lie close to the river, the same being sacred, and the population multiplying upon their banks. As the river bottoms prevent proper drainage this militates largely in favor of the disease. The miserable "chawli," or huts, of the natives, squat low on the alluvial soil, which absorbs all drainage and gives out pestilential gases. The Hindu has little or no vitality to battle with the disease. His state of demoralization makes a livelihood impossible, and famine fosters the plague. The Mohammedans, unlike the Hindus, do not burn their dead bodies; nor like the Parsees, place them in the Towers of Silence, on Malabar Hill, to be eaten by the vultures. By burying in shallow graves, they aid the spread of the disease, contaminating all underground supplies of water.

Animals also spread the plague. Mice, rats, cats, and monkeys have been known to infect a ship and bring the scourge from a foreign port. Excessive precautions are taken at all ports leading from Asia, that of the Suez Canal being the most dangerous and carefully guarded highway into Europe. Every ship and, indeed, every passenger and piece of baggage is scrutinized, with a view to discovering the first symptoms of the plague in the victim or suspicious article of merchandise that may lead to infection. Precautions, however, are quite impossible in the incipient stages of the disease, as the evidences may not appear in the victim till he or she is already marked for death. Fever, swelling of the lymphatic glands, and utter prostration are soon superseded by the appearance of the bubos in groin, neck, and face, when death occurs in 90 cases out of a possible 100, within a period varying from five hours to as many weeks, depending upon the constitution of the victim. The white races are more immune than any other. The mode of life in civilized countries is conducive to successful battle with the plague. As it is rather sporadic than epidemic, even in the East, there should be little fear of its securing a foothold on western soil. Two cases of the disease were brought into New York harbor, 18 Nov. 1899, from Santos, Brazil, on the British steamship J. W. Taylor. The infected vessel was refused a landing, but was placed in quarantine and steps instantly taken to make sure and complete the isolation of the disease. Health Officer Doty, of New York, announced that the chances of the bubonic plague reaching this country through the ports of New York were extremely remote. Active measures were also taken in the summer of 1900 to disinfect the Chinese quarter of San Francisco in which the plague had appeared. In Honolulu heroic measures were adopted to stamp out the infection.

Bucaramanga, boo-ka-rạ-män′gạ, the capital of the department of Santander, in Colombia, South America, 185 miles north-northeast of Bogota. It is an important coffee centre, and in the neighborhood are mines of gold, copper, and iron. A United States consul is resident here. Pop. 16,000.

Bucareli y Urzua, Antonio Maria, än-tō′-nē-ō mä-rē′ạ boo-cä-rā′lē ē ŭrt-zoo′ä, Spanish soldier and administrator: b. Seville, 24 Jan. 1717; d. Mexico City, 9 April 1779. He was governor of Cuba in 1760–71, and viceroy of New Spain (Mexico) from 1771 till his death.

Buccaneer, The, a narrative poem by Richard Henry Dana. It was first published in 1827, and the scene of a portion of the work is laid in Block Island, Rhode Island.

Buccaneers′, a name applied to various bands of English and French freebooters in America, whose exploits form a remarkable part of the history of the 17th century. The origin of these associations of buccaneers seems to have been the arrogant pretensions of the Spaniards to the dominion of the whole of America. The English and French settlers combining against them for mutual defense, acquired from their precarious life in the vicinity of the Spanish settlements, adventurous and lawless habits, and became ultimately, in some of the islands of the Caribbean Sea, little better than pirates. The earliest association of this kind began about 1525, but they afterward assumed greater magnitude. After the assassination of Henry IV. in France in 1610, several Frenchmen sought a residence on the island of St. Christopher, one of the Antilles. Driven thence in 1630, some of them fled to the western coast of San Domingo, others to the small island of Tortugas, in the vicinity. Several Englishmen, led by a similar disposition, associated themselves with the latter. The fugitives at San Domingo employed themselves especially in the chase of wild cattle, of which there were large herds on the island. They sold the hides to the mariners who landed on the coast, and as they cured the flesh by smoking it before the fire, like the American savages, they were called buccaneers, from the Caribee *boucan,* a place for smoke-drying meat. These hunters lived in the rudest state of nature, enjoying in common all that they had taken in the chase or acquired by robbery. The Spaniards, who could not conquer them, determined to extirpate all the cattle on the island, and thus obliged the buccaneers either to cultivate the land as husbandmen, or to join the other freebooters on the island of Tortugas. These bold adventurers attacked, in small numbers and with small means, but with an intrepidity which bade defiance to danger, not only single merchant vessels, but several of them together, and sometimes armed ships. Their common mode of attack was by boarding. They directed their efforts especially against the Spanish ships which sailed for Europe laden with the treasures of America. By the repeated losses which they suffered, the Spaniards were at last so discouraged that they seldom offered a serious resistance. It happened once that a ship of the buccaneers fell in with two Spanish galleons, each of which had 60 cannon, and 1,500 men on board. To escape was impossible, and the pirates could not think of surrender. Their captain, Laurent, made a short speech to them, sent one of his men to the powder room with orders to set fire to it upon the first sign which he should give him, and then placed his men in order of battle on each side. "We must sail between the enemy's ships," cried he to his crew, "and fire upon them to the right and left." This manœuvre was executed with extraordinary rapidity. The fire of the pirate killed so many people on board both ships that the Spaniards were struck with a panic, and let him escape. The Spanish commander was afterward put to death on account of the disgrace which he had brought upon his nation. Their frequent losses greatly reduced the trade of the Spaniards with America. The buccaneers now began to land on the coast, and to plunder the cities. Their manner of dividing the booty was remarkable. Every one who had a share in the expedition swore that he had reserved nothing of the plunder. A false oath was of extremely rare occurrence, and was punished by banishment to an uninhabited island. The wounded first received their share, which was greater according to the severity of their wounds. The remainder was divided into equal parts, and distributed by lot. The leader received more than the others only when he had particularly distinguished himself. Those who had perished in the expedition were not forgotten. Their part was given to their relations or friends, and in default of them, to the poor and to the Church. Religion was strangely blended with their vices, and they began their enterprises with a prayer. The wealth acquired was spent in gambling and debauchery, for it was the principle of these adventurers to enjoy the present and not care for the future. The climate and their mode of life gradually diminished their number, and the vigorous measures of the British and French governments at last put an end to their outrages, which had, perhaps, been purposely tolerated. From this band of pirates arose the French settlements on the western half of San Domingo. In the beginning of the 18th century the piracies of the buccaneers had entirely ceased. See Raynal, 'History of the Two Indies'; Burney, 'History of the Buccaneers'; Stockton, 'Buccaneers and Pirates of Our Coasts' (1898).

Buccari, book'ka-rē, or Bakar, an Austro-Hungarian free port on the Gulf of Quarnerno, a few miles east of Fiume. It stands on the slope of a hill with a castle at the top, and its harbor, though small, is safe. Fishing, shipbuilding, and linen manufacturing are carried on here, the tunny fisheries being of the greatest importance. The wine of the district is also exported. Pop. (1890) 1,950.

Buc'cinator, the trumpeter's muscle, one of the maxillary group of muscles of the cheek. They are the active agents in mastication. The buccinator circumscribes the cavity of the mouth and, aided by the tongue, keeps the food under the pressure of the teeth; it also helps to shorten the pharynx from before backward, and thus assists in deglutition.

Buccin'idæ, a family of mollusks belonging to the order *Prosobranchiata,* and the section *Siphonostomata.* They constitute part of Cuvier's *buccinoida.* They have the shell notched in front, or with the canal abruptly reflected so as to produce a varix on the front of the shell. The leading genera are *buccinum terebra, eburna, nassa, purpura, cassis, dolium, harpa,* and *oliva.* These shellfish are much valued as the source of the dye commonly called royal purple.

Buccinum, the typical genus of the family *Buccinidæ.* In English they are called whelks, which are not to be confounded with the periwinkle, also sometimes called whelk. *B. undatum* is the common whelk. Species of the genus exist in the cretaceous rocks, but it is essentially Tertiary and recent.

Buccleugh, bŭk-klü', the title (now a dukedom) of one of the oldest families in Scotland, tracing descent from Sir Richard le Scott in the reign of Alexander III. (latter half of the 13th century), and first becoming conspicuous in the person of the border chieftain Sir Walter Scott, of Branxholm and Buccleugh — the latter an estate in Selkirkshire. The son of Sir Walter, bearing the same name, was raised to the peerage, in 1606, as Lord Scott of Buccleugh, and his successor was made an Earl in 1619. In 1663 the titles and estates devolved upon Anne, daughter of the second Earl, who married the Duke of Monmouth, illegitimate son of Charles II., the pair, in 1673, being created Duke and Duchess of Buccleugh, etc. Subsequently the dukedom of Queensberry passed, by marriage, into the family. The sixth Duke of Buccleugh, William Henry Walter Montagu Douglas-Scott, succeeded to the title in 1884.

Bucen'taur, a mythological being, half man and half ox or ass. The splendid galley in which the Doge of Venice annually sailed over the Adriatic on Ascension Day also bore this name. Dropping a ring into the sea, he espoused it in the name of the republic, with the words, "Desponsamus te. mare, in signum veri perpetuique dominii." The custom originated in 1176, when the doge, having refused to deliver up the Pope, who had taken refuge in Ven-

ice, to the emperor, encountered and defeated the imperial fleet which was sent to reduce the Venetians.

Buceph'alus, the horse of Alexander the Great, which he bought for 13 talents (about $5,000). Philonicus, a Thessalian, offered to sell him to King Philip; but Philip, who considered the price too great, commanded the unmanageable steed to be led away, when the young Alexander offered to mount him. He mounted accordingly, and to the astonishment of all, the horse obeyed him, and willingly submitted to his guidance, though he had never before obeyed a rider. Alexander, from this circumstance, conceived such an affection for him that he never rode upon any other horse; and Bucephalus also, when caparisoned for battle, suffered no other rider. He died of a wound, and Alexander caused him to be buried near the Hydaspes, and built over his grave a city, which he called Bucephala.

Bucer, bū'sėr, or Butzer, **Martin,** German Protestant theologian: b. Schelestadt, Alsace, 11 Nov. 1491; d. Cambridge, 28 Feb. 1551. He entered the Dominican order in 1506, but in 1521 left the order, and became a convert to Lutheranism. He was at first preacher at the court of Frederick, the elector of the Palatinate, afterward in Strasburg, and at the same time professor in the university there for 20 years. He took part in the conference of Marburg with the hope of reconciling Luther and Zwinglius. In 1548 King Edward VI. of England, at the suggestion of Archbishop Cranmer, invited him to Cambridge, where he was professor of theology. In 1557 Queen Mary caused his bones to be burned. The Cardinal Contarini called him the most learned divine among the heretics. He wrote a commentary on the Psalms under the name of Aretius Filinus, and many other works. See Baurn, 'Capito and Butzer' (1860); Tollin, 'Servet und Butzer' (1880); Mentz and Erichsen, 'Zur 400-jährigen Geburtsfeier Martin Butzer' (1891).

Buch, Leopold **von,** lā'ō-pŏld fŏn booн, German geologist: b. Stolpe, Prussia, 26 April 1774; d. Berlin, 4 March 1853. He studied under the celebrated Werner in the mining school of Freiberg in Saxony, where Alexander von Humboldt was his fellow-student, and early began to distinguish himself by his geological writings. His first works were Descriptions of the Mineralogy of Landeck, and of the Geognosy of Silesia. Up to 1798 he had adopted the Neptunian theory of Werner, with some modifications; but now saw cause to abandon it, and to recognize the volcanic origin of the basalts. He saw Vesuvius for the first time in 1799; but afterward, in 1805, had an opportunity, along with Humboldt and Gay Lussac, of witnessing its actual eruption. In 1802 he examined the extinct volcanoes of Auvergne in the south of France. The results of all these geological travels were given to the world in a work entitled 'Observations During Travels in Germany and Italy' (1802-9). Indefatigable as an observer, Von Buch turned his steps from the south of France in 1806, and proceeding to Scandinavia spent two years in examining its physical constitution. This furnished the materials for his well-known work entitled 'Travels in Norway and Lapland.' In 1815 he visited the Canary Isles. These volcanic isles furnished the starting point from which Von Buch commenced a regular course of study on the production and activity of volcanoes. This is attested by his standard work on the subject, entitled 'Physical Description of the Canary Isles' (1825). On his return from the Canaries he visited the basaltic group of the Hebrides and the coasts of Scotland and Ireland. His geological excursions, even in countries which he had repeatedly visited before, continued without interruption at a very advanced age, till within a few months of his death. Alexander von Humboldt, who had known him intimately for a period of more than 60 years, called him the greatest geologist of our period. He was unmarried, and lived aloof from the world, entirely devoted to scientific pursuits. Besides the works already mentioned he was the author of many important tracts on paleontology, as, 'On the Ammonites' (1832); 'On the Terebratulæ' (1834); 'On the Ceratities' (1841); and 'On the Cystidæ' (1845). Another of his works not to be omitted is his 'Geological Map of Germany.'

Buchan, bŭk'ăn, **Alexander,** Scottish meteorologist: b. Kinnesswood, Kinross-shire, Scotland, 11 April 1829. He was a teacher in Edinburgh, 1848-60, becoming in the latter year secretary to the Scottish Meteorological Society and in 1878 curator of the library and museum of the Royal Society of Edinburgh. He has published 'A Handy Book of Meteorology' (1867); 'Introductory Text-Book of Meteorology' (1871). He contributed to the Encyclopædia Britannica, 9th edition, the article on 'Meteorology.'

Buchan, David, English voyager and explorer: b. 1780; d. about 1837. He obtained a lieutenant's commission in the navy in 1806, and in 1810 his admiral, Sir John Duckworth, dispatched him to the river Exploits, for the purpost of exploring the interior and opening a communication with the natives. He reached the mouth of the river in January 1811, and with 34 men and 3 guides penetrated through the greatest difficulties 130 miles into the country. Buchan afterward became high sheriff of Newfoundland. On a subsequent expedition he was lost with his ship Upton Castle. In 1818 Buchan was appointed to the command of an Arctic expedition. The admiralty fitted out two expeditions that year — one to discover the northwest passage, the other to reach the North Pole. The Dorothea and Trent were the vessels selected for the second expedition, under Capt. Buchan and Lieut. (afterward Sir John) Franklin. Latitude 80° 34' N. was the most northerly point gained by this expedition.

Buchan, John, Scottish novelist: b. Perth, Scotland, 26 Aug. 1875. He was educated at Glasgow University and Brasenose College, Oxford. His published books include 'Sir Quixote' (1895); 'Musa Piscatrix' (1896); 'Scholar Gipsies' (1896); 'Sir Walter Raleigh' (1897); 'John Burnet of Barns' (1898); 'A History of Brasenose College' (1898); 'Grey Weather' (1899); 'A Lost Lady of Old Years' (1899); 'The Half-hearted' (1900); 'The Watcher by the Threshold' (1902).

Buchan, Elspeth (Simpson), Scottish religious enthusiast, founder of a sect: b. near Banff, 1738; d. near Dumfries, 1791. She was educated in the Scottish Episcopal Church, but on her marriage to Robert Buchan, in Glasgow, became, like him, a burgher seceder. In 1779, or thereabout, she broached dogmas of her own, soon deserted her husband and moved to Irvine, where she made a number of converts, among them Mr. Hugh Whyte, a relief clergyman. In 1784, the people assaulted Mr. Whyte's house, which the Buchanites had made their tabernacle. They then, 46 persons in all, set up a sort of community at a farm-house 13 miles from Dumfries, waiting for the millennium or the day of judgment, fasting for weeks in the expectation that they would be fed like the young ravens that cry, and adjuring all fleshly vanities. A few left, accusing Mrs. Buchan of tyranny and dishonesty, but the majority of her votaries were faithful to her to the last. She called her disciples around her death-bed and communicated to them, as a secret, that she was the Virgin Mary, who had been wandering through the world since the Saviour's death, and that she was only going to sleep now, and would soon conduct them to the new Jerusalem. Her disciples, in the expectation of her re-appearance, refused to bury her until ordered by a justice of the peace. The sect became extinct in 1848. See Buchanites.

Buchan, William, Scottish physician: b. Ancrum, Roxburghshire, 1729; d. 1805. He commenced practice at Edinburgh, and having for a considerable time directed his attention to a digest of popular medical knowledge, published in 1769 his work entitled 'Domestic Medicine; or, the Family Physician,' an attempt to render the medical art more generally useful by showing people what is in their own power, both with respect to the prevention and cure of diseases. It is constructed on a plan similar to that adopted by Tissot in his 'Avis au Peuple.' It appealed to the wants and wishes of so large a class of the community, that, considering it to have been the first work of the kind published in Britain, there is no wonder that it should have attained success. Before the death of the author 19 large editions had been sold. Duplanil of Paris, physician to the Count d'Artois (Charles X.), published a translation in five volumes, with notes, which rendered the work so popular on the Continent that in a short time no language in Christendom wanted its translation. It would almost appear that the work met with more undivided applause on the Continent than in Britain. While many English and Scottish physicians conceived that it was as apt to generate as to cure or prevent diseases, by inspiring the minds of readers with hypochondriacal notions, those of other countries entertained no such suspicions. Among the testimonies of approbation which Dr. Buchan received from abroad was a huge gold medallion, sent by the Empress Catherine of Russia, with a complimentary letter. The work became more popular in America and the West Indies than in the older hemisphere. Buchan published two other works: 'A Treatise on Gonorrhœa'; 'An Advice to Mothers on the Subject of their own Health, and on the Means of Promoting the Health, Strength, and Beauty of Their Offspring.' He was buried in Westminster Abbey.

Buchanan, bū-kăn'ăn, **Andrews Hays,** American educator: b. Washington County, Ark., 28 June 1828. He was graduated at Cumberland University in 1853; and took a special course in civil engineering and mathematics in Lincoln University; taught civil engineering in 1854-61; was military topographical engineer in the Confederate army during the Civil War; and became professor of mathematics and civil engineering in Cumberland University in 1869. He was employed by the superintendent of the United States Coast and Geodetic Survey to take charge of the triangulation of Tennessee, on which work he was engaged for four months in every year from 1876 to 1896. He was the author of 'Plane and Spherical Trigonometry'; etc.

Buchanan, Claudius, Scottish missionary clergyman: b. Cambuslang. Scotland, 1766; d. 1815. He took orders in the Church of England. and was appointed chaplain to the East India Company in 1795. From this time the remainder of his life was occupied in missionary labors in India, and in forwarding the translation of the Bible into the Indian languages. In 1800 he was appointed professor of Greek, Latin, and English in the College of Fort William. He returned to Europe in 1808, afterward visited the Holy Land, and was engaged at his death in a translation of the New Testament into Syriac. He published 'Christian Researches in Asia, with a Notice of the Translation of the Scriptures into the Oriental Languages' (1811), and several other works.

Buchanan, Francis, Scottish traveler: b. Stirlingshire, 15 Feb. 1762; d. 1829. He traveled extensively in the East Indies, making collections illustrative of the botany, zoology, etc., of the countries which he visited, and published 'A Journey from Madras Through the Countries of the Mysore, Canara, and Malabar, Performed Under the Orders of the Marquis Wellesley for the Purpose of Investigating the State of Agriculture, Arts, and Commerce, etc., in the Dominions of the Rajah of Mysore' (1807). He contributed largely to the scientific journals of the day, and in 1819 published a 'History of the Kingdom of Nepal,' and in the same year a 'Genealogy of the Hindu Gods,' which he had drawn up some years before with the assistance of an intelligent Brahmin. In 1822 appeared his 'Account of the Fishes of the Ganges,' with plates.

Buchanan, Franklin, American naval officer: b. Baltimore, 17 Sept. 1800; d. Talbot County, Md., 11 May 1874. At an early age he entered the navy, becoming lieutenant in 1825 and master-commandant in 1841. The organization of the United States Naval Academy was committed to him in 1845 and he was made the first superintendent. During the Mexican war he took part in the siege of Vera Cruz. In Commodore Perry's expedition to Japan he had command of the flagship. In 1855 he was raised to the rank of captain, and in 1861 resigned from the United States navy, intending to follow his State in secession, but later asked to be restored. Upon the refusal of his request. he entered the Confederate navy. In command of the Merrimac in Hampton Roads, he sank the Congress and the Cumberland, being severely wounded during the engagement. In 1863 he commanded the naval defenses at Mobile, Ala., there constructing the ram Tennessee. After promotion to the rank of admiral in the Confederate navy

he was for some time senior officer in the Confederate navy and commanded at the battle of Mobile Bay, where he was defeated by Farragut, lost a leg. and was made prisoner. At the close of the War he became president of the Agricultural College of Maryland.

Buchanan, George, the chief representative of humanism in Scotland: b. near Killearn, Stirlingshire, February 1506; d. Edinburgh, 28 September 1582. He came of Celtic stock, and his family though poor was of honorable descent, tracing connection, some five generations back, with the great houses of Albany and Lennox. His father died while George was a child, and the family of five sons and three daughters was brought up by his mother, born Agnes Heriot of Trabroun in Haddingtonshire. His early education was gained at the common schools, tradition naming those of Killearn and Dumbarton; and at the age of 14 he was sent by his maternal uncle to the University of Paris, then in the throes of the struggle between humanism and Lutheranism on the one hand, and scholasticism and Catholicism on the other. He remained here for two years, his principal academic occupation being the writing of Latin verse. At the end of these two years, the death of his uncle and his own serious illness compelled his return to Scotland. In the autumn of 1523 he took part in an abortive expedition against England, led by the Regent Albany. In the spring of 1525 he went to Saint Andrews, where he graduated in October of the same year, the fee for his Bachelor's certificate being remitted on account of poverty. He returned to Paris in 1526, and, after two years as a bursar of the Scots College there, he took his Master's degree. Beginning in 1529, he taught for three years as "regent" in the College of Ste. Barbe, one of the most fully equipped and most liberal in the University, receiving food and lodging from the College and fees from the students. Here he was already known as a writer of stinging epigrams. He resigned his regentship to become tutor to the young Earl of Cassillis, a post he occupied for five years. living at first in Paris, but returning to Scotland with his pupil in 1535. It was during the latter part of this engagement that he first roused the antagonism of the Franciscan order by his 'Somnium,' a Latin poem paraphrasing the well-known Scots satire 'How Dunbar was desyrit to be ane Fryer.' At the conclusion of his period with Cassillis, he was appointed tutor to one of the natural sons of James V., and through this came into close relations with the court. At the instance of the King he produced two more short satires against the Franciscans, and began his 'Franciscanus', a brilliant and elaborate piece of invective, finished much later. The wrath roused by these attacks forced Buchanan to flee from Scotland to save his life; and after a short sojourn in England. where he addressed poems to Henry VIII. and Cromwell. he returned to Paris. There he found Cardinal Beatoun, who had been the chief agent in driving him out of Scotland, and for safety he was glad to accept a position in the Collège de Guyenne at Bordeaux. under André de Gouvéa, formerly his colleague at Ste. Barbe. He remained here three years, counting among his pupils the celebrated Montaigne, and among his acquaintances, J. C. Scaliger. While at Bordeaux Buchanan translated into Latin the 'Medea' and the 'Alcestis' of Euripides, and composed his two original dramas, 'Jephthes' and 'Baptistes.' Leaving Bordeaux in 1542 or 1543, he seems to have returned to Paris, where he may have taught till about 1545 in the Collège du Cardinal Lemoine; but the record of these years is obscure, and for the next three we are altogether without evidence as to his residence or occupation. In 1547 we find him in Portugal, again under André de Gouvéa, teaching in the College of Arts of the University of Coimbra. On Gouvéa's death, the College fell into the hands of the Jesuits, who proceeded to accuse Buchanan of heresy. After a persecution of a year and a half, he was shut up for some months in a monastery to be instructed in the true faith by the monks. There he made most of his famous Latin translations of the Psalms, and during the same period produced his poems to Leonora. On his liberation in 1552, he spent a short time in England, then returned to France, where for a while he held once more the office of regent, this time in the Collège Boncourt. In 1555 his patron, Charles du Cossé, Comte de Brissac, appointed him tutor to his son Timoleon, whom he instructed from the age of 12 to that of 17, living sometimes in France, sometimes in Italy. During these years Buchanan seems to have given closer attention than formerly to the religious controversies of the day; and when he returned to Scotland about 1561, he took the side of the reformed Church of Scotland. In spite of this decision for Protestantism, we find him soon after his return acting as tutor to Queen Mary, and writing court masques and complimentary poems. He received an annual pension of 250 pounds Scots, a sum apparently inadequate to his needs. In 1564 the Queen bestowed on him a pension of 500 pounds Scots from the income of the Abbey of Crossraguel, but this he seems to have had difficulty in collecting. His friendly relations with Mary continued till the murder of Darnley in 1567, which turned him into her open enemy. He wrote the virulent 'Detectio Mariæ Reginæ Scotorum,' the work which was the chief means of spreading throughout Europe a belief in the guilt of the Queen. Meantime Buchanan had become an important figure in the Scottish Church, and in 1567 he was Moderator of the General Assembly which demanded Mary's abdication in favor of her son. About this time he produced his two most important vernacular writings, the 'Admonition to the Trew Lordis', a pamphlet in support of the party of the young King James and against the house of Hamilton; and the 'Chamæleon,' an attack on Maitland of Lethington.

In 1566 Buchanan was appointed Principal of Saint Leonard's College of Saint Andrews University; but he resigned his Principalship in 1570 to take charge of the education of the young King, James VI., then four years old; and he continued to superintend his instruction for about eight years. During this period he was for a short time Director of Chancery, and later Keeper of the Privy Seal. In spite of these appointments, he does not seem to have held, or to have sought, a leading position

in politics. The most important writings of his later years were a dialogue, 'De Jure Regni apud Scotos,' a defence of Scotland's treatment of Mary; and his 'Rerum Scoticarum Historia,' published in 1582. In September of that year he died, and was buried in Grayfriars Churchyard in Edinburgh.

The comparative obscurity into which Buchanan's name and writings have sunk today is in striking contrast to the splendor of his contemporary reputation. Throughout the latter part of the sixteenth century he was regarded by men of letters in Europe as easily the most distinguished representative of humanism in Britain, and this reputation continued for more than a century after his death. The contrast is explained by the medium in which he wrote. Like most of his learned contemporaries, he had no doubt that Latin was to be the universal language of the future, and almost all his writings are in that language. His mastery of Latin remains the admiration of scholars, but for the world in general his works are dead.

By genius and temperament he was a poet, and his Latin verses represent his best work. These belong to the conventional types of his age. Of his satires, the most notable are those already mentioned, against the Franciscans. To modern taste they pass the bounds of decency; but in brilliance and point they stand in the first rank of post-classical productions. His epigrams are entitled to the same blame and the same praise. He wrote complimentary poems to most of the persons of distinction with whom he came in contact, and an epithalamium on the marriage of Mary and the Dauphin, containing a famous passage in praise of the Scots. More genuinely poetical is his piece on 'The First of May.' His love-poetry need not be taken as having any relation whatever to his experience. Such poems as those to Leonora and Neæra are merely academic exercises in the fashion of the Renaissance on the model of Catullus and Tibullus. Of his dramatic efforts, the most artistic is 'Jephthes,' a play which still holds a place among the best of the attempts to revive the drama of antiquity. 'Baptistes,' under the guise of the story of John the Baptist, is a thinly-veiled parable expressing Buchanan's views on kingship. His most ambitious poem is the 'De Sphæra,' an elaborate exposition of the Ptolemaic system of astronomy; and his most popular production is his Latin translation of the Psalms into a variety of classical metres. The last continued to be used as a schoolbook in his native country into the nineteenth century.

Of his prose works, his 'De Jure Regni' sets forth explicitly and with special reference to Scotland the same doctrine of the sovereignty of the people which was shadowed in 'Baptistes.' Both this work and his history earned the distinction of being later suppressed by the government. The 'Historia' covered the history of Scotland from the earliest times till 1580; and while far from being a critical work in the modern sense, is much more discriminating than most of the chronicles that preceded it. Its chief value is for the period of his own life, and here his authority is that of the honest partisan.

The general impression left by his work is

JAMES BUCHANAN,
FIFTEENTH PRESIDENT OF THE UNITED STATES.

that of an acute, vigorous, and independent mind, poetical rather than practical or philosophical; of a temperament capable of strong emotion; of a character showing some of the defects common to most men of his age, but on the whole straightforward and robust. And if the use of Latin has caused his writings to cease to be read to-day, it is to be remembered that for the Europe of his own time he was the foremost man of letters in Britain, and in the opinion of such judges as the Scaligers and Montaigne, the first Latin poet in Europe.

Bibliography.—Buchanan's complete works were collected by T. Ruddiman (re-edited by Peter Burman, 2 vols., Lugduni Batavorum, 1725). The vernacular writings have been issued by the Scottish Text Society, with life and notes by P. Hume Brown (Edin. 1892). The 'Lives' by Irving and Chalmers are now superseded by P. Hume Brown's 'George Buchanan' (Edin. 1890). Shorter sketches are those of D. Macmillan (Edin. 1906), and of Robert Wallace, 'Famous Scots Series' (Edin. 1900). His portraits are discussed in Drummond's 'Portraits of Knox and Buchanan' (1875). Bibliographies are given by Ruddiman and Irving.

WILLIAM A. NEILSON,
Professor of English, Harvard University.

Buchanan, George, Scottish surgeon: b. Glasgow, 1827. He became surgeon of the Western Infirmary of Glasgow and later served as civil surgeon with the British army in the Crimean war. In 1888 he was elected president of the surgical section of the British Medical Association, and in 1900 was appointed professor of clinical surgery in the Glasgow University. He was the author of 'Camp Life in the Crimea'; 'On Lithotrity, with Cases'; 'Clinical Surgery'; 'Radical Cure of Inquinal Hernia in Children'; 'Talipes Varus'; 'Faure's Storage Battery and Electricity in Surgery'; and 'Anæsthesia Jubilee, a Retrospect.' He was one of the editors of the 'Glasgow Medical Journal,' and also edited the 10th edition of the 'Anatomist's Vade Mecum.'

Buchanan, James, fifteenth President of the United States: b. Stony Batter, Franklin County, Pa., 22 April 1791; d. Lancaster, Pa., 1 June 1868. His father was by birth an Irishman, who had quitted Europe in 1783, and established himself on a farm at Stony Batter. The son was educated at Dickinson College, Carlisle, where he graduated. He subsequently entered the office of James Hopkins of Lancaster to study law, and was admitted to the bar in 1812. Although holding Federalist opinions at this time he supported the War of 1812. In 1814 he was elected to the legislature of Pennsylvania, and in 1820 was sent to Congress, of which he continued a member till 1831, being re-elected four times. He then entered upon a career of diplomacy, being charged by President Jackson with a special mission to Russia for the conclusion of a commercial treaty. On his return, in 1833, he was elected to the Senate. About this time the anti-slavery agitation began to assume importance. Buchanan wished to prevent the agitation reaching Congress, by declaring its incompetency to deal with it. He held that constitutionally it was a question for the individual States, and that it was better for all parties, even for the slaves themselves, that

it should remain so. Under the presidency of Polk, 1845–9, Buchanan was intrusted with the functions of secretary of state. The annexation of Texas and the war with Mexico were the chief events of his administration. During the presidency of Gen. Taylor he retired from public life. In 1853 Gen. Pierce, on being elected President, named him ambassador of the United States at London. He held this appointment till 1856. The Central American boundary and the project of the annexation of Cuba were the principal subjects discussed during his embassy. With Mason and Soulé he signed the Ostend manifesto which recommended the acquisition of Cuba. While maintaining with ability the views of his own country, he gained the esteem of that to which he was deputed by the prudence and moderate tone of his diplomacy. He returned to America in 1856, being chosen as candidate for the presidency by the Democratic party. He was elected by a large majority over Fremont, the Republican candidate, and inaugurated in March 1857. His foreign policy inclined to the aggressive views he had always advocated, but the questions of slavery and State-rights were at this period approaching a crisis which made home administration of much greater importance. As President he deferred constantly to pro-slavery leaders and was unduly influenced by their threats of secession. His character for statesmanship suffered greatly from his vacillation in dealing with the first measures of the seceders; but it must be considered that the position of a ruler holding office as the *locum tenens* of his successor is not favorable to a vigorous administration in a difficult crisis. He took up the position that while the States had no right to secede, the nation had no power to prevent their doing so. He supported the administration of Lincoln, and lent his influence to the vigorous prosecution of the War, declaring that the North would sustain the administration almost to a man, and that it ought to be sustained at all hazards. Consult his own defense of his course, 'Mr. Buchanan's Administration on the Eve of the Rebellion' (1866): Curtis, 'Life of James Buchanan' (1883).

Buchanan, Robert Christie, American soldier: b. Baltimore, about 1811; d. Washington, 29 Nov. 1878. He graduated at the United States Military Academy in 1830, and served in the Black Hawk war in the rank of second lieutenant. From 1837–8 he served in the Seminole war, and from 1845–6 in the military occupation of Texas. During the Mexican war he was promoted for gallantry. In 1856 he was placed in command of the military district of Oregon and northern California. Early in the Civil War he was promoted lieutenant-colonel. He fought in the Peninsular campaign, and on the Rappahannock, winning at Gaines Mills the rank of brevet-colonel, and at Malvern Hill that of brevet-brigadier-general. He was in the battles of Antietam and Fredericksburg, and was promoted brevet-major-general. In 1864 he was assistant provost-marshal for New York. In 1870 he retired from active service.

Buchanan, Robert Williams, English poet and novelist: b. Caverswall, Staffordshire, 18 Aug. 1841; d. London, 10 June 1901. He received his education in Glasgow, and while young went to London to engage in literature.

His attack upon Dante Gabriel Rossetti, 'The Fleshly School of Poetry,' drew a famous letter from that poet on 'The Stealthy School of Criticism,' and a scathing pamphlet from Swinburne, 'Under the Microscope' (1872). It should be added that in later life he regretted his course in this matter. His poems include 'Undertones' (1863); 'Idylls and Legends of Inverburn' (1865); 'London Poems,' his best effort (1866); 'North Coast Poems' (1867); 'Book of Orm, the Celt' (1868); 'St. Abe and His Seven Wives' (1871); 'Napoleon Fallen: a Lyrical Drama' (1871); 'The Drama of Kings' (1871); 'Ballads of Love, Life and Humor' (1882); 'The City of Dreams' (1888); 'White Rose and Red'; 'The Wandering Jew' (1893). His best novels are 'The Shadow of the Sword' (1876); 'A Child of Nature' (1879); 'God and the Man' (1881); 'The Martyrdom of Madeline' (1882); and 'Foxglove Manor' (1884).

Buchanan, William Insco, American diplomat: b. near Covington, Ohio, 10 Sept. 1852. Educated in country schools, living on a farm in early life; removed to Sioux City, Iowa, 1882. In 1894 he was appointed United States minister to the Argentine Republic; in 1903 was appointed United States minister to the Republic of Panama.

Buchana'nia, a genus of *anacardiaceæ*, named after Dr. Buchanan Hamilton, a well-known Indian botanist. *B. latifolia* is a large Indian tree, the kernel of the nut of which is much used in native confectionery.

Buchanites, bŭk'ăn-īts, a sect of enthusiasts who sprung up at Irvine, in the west of Scotland, about 1783. Rev. Hugh White, the minister of a congregation of the Relief Church in that town, having been invited to preach in the neighborhood of Glasgow, Elizabeth Buchan, the wife of a painter, was captivated with his eloquence, and writing to him, announced that he was the first who had spoken to her heart, and requested permission to pay him a visit at Irvine, that the work of her conversion might be perfected. On her arrival she was joyfully received by the members of the congregation, engaged without intermission in religions exercises, went from house to house, conducted family worship, answered questions, resolved doubts, explained the Scriptures, and testified that the end of the world was at hand, and that it was the duty of every Christian to abandon the concerns of time and prepare for the reception of Christ. White was complained of to the presbytery, by which he was deposed from his ministry. Thus a distinct party was formed, the meetings of which were commonly held at night, and on these occasions the new prophetess indulged in her reveries, styling herself the Woman of the Twelfth of Revelations, and White her first-born. Such gross outrage on the common sense of the inhabitants occasioned a popular tumult, to save her from the fury of which the magistrate sent her under escort to some distance; after which, with her clerical friend, and about 40 deluded followers, she wandered up and down the country, singing, and avowing that they were travelers for the New Jerusalem, and the expectants of the immediate coming of Christ. They had a common fund, and did not consider it necessary to work, as they believed God would not suffer them to want. See BUCHAN, ELSPETH.

Bucharest, boo-ka̤-rĕst', or **Bukarest** (Rumanian, *Bucuresci,* that is, "city of joy"), formerly the chief city of Walachia, now the capital of the kingdom of Rumania, on the Dimbovitza, 37 miles from its mouth. It is the most populous city of southeastern Europe after Constantinople and Budapest, and is spoken of by the Rumanians as the Paris of the East. Besides being the seat of government, Bucharest is the residence of a Greek archbishop. The houses are mostly of one story, built of brick, pointed externally, and have metal roofs. The streets are mostly narrow and crooked, the most important being the Boulevard, running from east to west, the Calea Victoriei, the Lipscani, and the Karlsstrasse. There are statues to Joan Heliade-Radulescu, the father of Rumanian literature; George Lazar; and others. Twelve bridges, five of iron, and seven of stone, cross the Dimbovitza, a small, muddy stream that formerly caused a good deal of damage by inundations. From 1885 till 1896 extensive fortifications were erected, there being now 18 forts in the circle of defense. The inhabitants nearly all belong to the Greek Church. The churches are very numerous, but few of them are architecturally noteworthy; the chief being the metropolitan cathedral, built in 1656, restored in 1834, and standing on a hill, and the Roman Catholic cathedral, built in 1875-84, one of the chief ornaments of the city. Bucharest has a university, and connected with it a public library and a museum of natural history and antiquities. There are four lyceums, two gymnasia, some technical and military schools, a conservatory of music, girls' schools, and other educational institutions. There are a few fine public buildings, of which the most conspicuous is the royal palace, recently rebuilt; among the others being the new Palace of Justice, the National Theatre, the athenæum, the post-office, and several fine hotels. What chiefly distinguishes Bucharest is the magnificence of the public gardens. There is a mixture in the population of eastern habits, with European civilization among the upper classes. The manufactures comprise iron goods, earthenware, leather, linen, soap, paper, beer, etc., but they are of no great importance. There is an active trade, Bucharest being an entrepôt both for the kingdom of Rumania and for adjacent countries. It imports manufactured goods, and exports grain, wool, honey, wax, tallow, and cattle, the produce of the country. In 1698, when it became the capital of Walachia, it was only a village. It was pillaged by the Servians in 1716; taken by the Russians in 1769 and 1806; occupied by them again in 1828-9 and 1853-4; by the Austrians in 1774. 1789, and 1854; was partly destroyed by fire in 1847; and became the capital of Rumania in 1862. Peace congresses were held here, 1772-3, and in 1812, and in 1886 peace was concluded here between Servia and Bulgaria. Pop. (1899) 282,071. See BUCHAREST, PEACE OF; BUCHAREST, UNIVERSITY OF.

Bucharest, Peace of, a treaty signed 28 May 1812, between Russia and the Porte. In November 1806 the Emperor Alexander took up arms for the protection of Moldavia and Walachia, and on account of the violation of the free navigation of the Bosphorus. He occupied Moldavia, upon which the Porte declared war against Russia, 7 Jan. 1807. An armistice, however, was agreed upon at Slobosia, 24 Aug. 1807, and after the expiration of the truce in April 1808, it was tacitly continued; but in April 1809 the war was renewed. The Russians advanced to Bulgaria, and after two fierce campaigns remained masters of the Danube. The Porte now offered terms of peace. A congress was opened at Bucharest in December 1811. Napoleon did all in his power to induce the Porte to continue the war; but the interposition of Great Britain and Sweden, as well as the concessions of Russia, and the distrust of the Porte toward Napoleon, brought to a conclusion the Peace of Bucharest. The Porte gave up to Russia all Bessarabia and a third of Moldavia, with the fortresses of Choczim, Bender, Ismail, and Kilia, so that the Pruth, as far as its confluence with the Danube, became the boundary between the two powers, and from thence the left bank of the Danube as far as Kilia, and even to its entrance into the Black Sea. The Russians gave back the rest of their conquests. In Asia the boundaries were established as before the war. The boundary then settled between Russia and Turkey was modified in favor of the Porte at the Peace of Paris, 30 March 1856.

Bucharest, University of, a university in the city of Bucharest, under the control of the state government of Rumania. It was founded in 1864. In addition to the usual academic, scientific, and professional departments, with courses followed by about 4,300 students, there is a school of pharmacy. There are museums and laboratories connected with the university.

Bücheler, Franz, fränts bük'ē-lėr, German philologist: b. Rheinberg, 3 June 1837. He studied at Bonn and has been professor there from 1870. His specialty has been in the field of ancient Italian dialects. He has published 'Grundriss der lateinischen Deklination' (1866), and other important works, and since 1878 has been an associate editor of the 'Rheinisches Museum für Philologie.'

Bucher, Anton von, än'tōn fōn booн'ėr, German polemical writer: b. Munich, 8 Jan. 1746; d. 1817. He was educated in the Latin schools of the Jesuits, studied at Ingoldstadt, and was consecrated priest in 1768. In his different offices as a public teacher he did a great deal in his day to instruct and enlighten his country. He incurred the enmity of the Jesuits by his satirical attacks upon them. His contributions to the history of the Jesuits in Bavaria (Beiträge zur Geschichte der Jesuiten in Baiern) are of great historical value. His collected works appeared in 1819-20.

Buchez, Philippe Joseph Benjamin, fē-lēp zhō-zėf bŏn-zha-mȧн' bü-shä, French philosopher: b. Matange-la-Petite (now in Belgium), 31 March 1796; d. Rodez, France, 12 Aug. 1865. He gave himself up to the study of the natural sciences, and in particular to medicine, receiving his doctor's degree in 1825. He was bitterly hostile to the government of the Restoration, and was one of those who, in 1821, founded the French Society of Carbonari. He became chief editor of the 'Journal des Progrès des Sciences et Institutions Medicales,' and in 1826 assisted in editing the 'Producteur,' a weekly paper which advocated the doctrines of Saint-Simonism. In 1831 he founded a journal of moral and political science, called 'L'Européen,' in which he expounded those doctrines which owe

their origin chiefly to himself, and have been collectively denominated 'Buchezism.' The fundamental idea of his system is that of the progress and development of the human race. But progress presupposes an aim, and this aim must be pointed out beforehand, or *revealed*. Thus the idea of progress leads him to the orthodox belief in revelation. This theory is worked out in his 'Introduction à la Science de l'Histoire' (1833); and his 'Essai d'un Traité Complet de Philosophie au Point de Vue du Catholicisme et du Progrès' (1839). Along with his predilections for the Catholic Church he still retained his strong democratic and republican opinions, and with M. Roux-Lavergne published 'Histoire Parlementaire de la Révolution Française, ou Journal des Assemblées Nationales, depuis 1789 jusqu'en 1815' (40 vols. 1833-8). After the revolution of 1848 he was elected to the constituent National Assembly, of which he was soon appointed president. Thenceforth he held aloof from public life, prosecuting his studies and writing several works, among which is the 'Histoire de la Formation de la Nationalité Française' (1859).

Buchhalz (booн'hälts) **Family,** a series of sketches by Julius Stinde, representing life among the middle-classes of the German capital. The books are entertainingly written, and are very popular in Germany.

Büchner, Friedrich Karl Christian Ludwig, frēd-riн kärl krēs'tī-än lood-vȳg büн'nėr, German physician and materialist philosopher: b. Darmstadt, 29 March 1824; d. Darmstadt, 1 May 1899. He studied at Giessen, Strasburg, Würzburg, and Vienna; became a lecturer at Tübingen University; and, in 1855, published 'Kraft und Stoff' (14th ed. 1876; English translation, 'Force and Matter' 1870), in which he attempted scientifically to establish a materialistic view of the universe. A violent controversy was raised; and Büchner saw himself compelled to resign his university post, and begin medical practice in Darmstadt. He wrote numerous contributions to periodicals on physiological and pathological subjects, as also in support of his atomistic philosophy; published in the latter department 'Natur und Geist' (1857); 'Aus Natur und Wissenschaft' (1862-84); as well as works on Darwinism, the idea of God, the intelligence of animals, etc.; and has translated Lyell's 'Antiquity of Man' (1864).

Büchner, Georg, gā'órg, German poet, brother of F. K. C. L. Büchner (q.v.): b. Goddleau, near Darmstadt, 17 Oct. 1813; d. Zurich, Switzerland, 19 Feb. 1837. In 1834 he entered the political arena with a manifesto entitled 'The Rural Messenger,' and bearing the motto: "Peace to the cabin; war to the palace." To escape arrest he fled to Strasburg, where he studied the philosophies of Descartes and Spinoza. He wrote a drama in 1834 on 'The Death of Danton,' the work of a genuine but undisciplined poet. His 'Complete Works,' with biography, was published in 1879.

Buchner, Hans, hänts booн'nėr, German scientist: b. Munich, 1850. After studying at the universities of Strasburg and Giessen, he became lecturer on hygiene at Munich in 1880 and professor in 1892. He has made many important researches in bacteriology.

Büchner, Luise, loo-ēz bü<small>H</small>'nėr, German poet and novelist, sister of Georg Büchner: b. 12 June 1821; d. Darmstadt, 28 Nov. 1877. Her first publication, 'Women and Their Calling' (1855), was followed by many others on the "woman's rights question"; it commanded much attention, and reached a fifth edition (1883). She wrote a volume of tales, 'From Life' (1861); 'Poet-Voices of Home and Foreign Lands'; several original poems; 'Woman's Heart'; some 'Christmas Stories'; etc.

Büchner, Max, German traveler and scientist: b. Hamburg, 25 April 1846. After serving as surgeon in the German army and navy, he traveled around the earth (1875), and spent some time in New Zealand. In 1878 he bore presents from the emperor to Muatiamvo, in the kingdom of Lunda, in equatorial Africa. After several vain attempts to break through toward the north, he returned to the coast. In 1884 he accompanied Nachtigal in founding the colonies of Togo and Kamerun, in western Africa, where he acted temporarily as representative of the German empire, fought the natives, and concluded treaties with chiefs in the interior. In 1888, as conservator of the Ethnographical Museum of Münich, he traveled in Australia, Guinea, and East Asia. He wrote 'A Trip Through the Pacific Ocean' (1878); and 'Kamerun' (1888).

Buchon, Jean Alexandre, zhôn ä-lĕks-ändr bü-shôn, French historical writer: b. Ménetou-Salon, 21 May 1791; d. 30 April 1846. Having gone to Paris, he became collaborateur on several liberal journals, and early took part in the opposition to the restoration. He was in consequence several times prosecuted by the government, and his writings, such as his 'Vie de Tasse' (1817), were interdicted. In 1821 he gave a course of lectures in the Athenæum on the history of dramatic art in England; and in the following years he traveled over the greater part of Europe for the purpose of collecting documents to illustrate the history of France during the Middle Ages. After his return he published his 'Collection des Chroniques Nationales Françaises, écrites en Langue Vulgaire du XIIIme au XVIme Siècle' (47 vols. 1824-9), which he began with the 'Chroniques de Froissart' (15 vols. 1824-6). He was appointed inspector of the archives and libraries of France in 1828, and in 1829 inspector-general of the departmental and communal archives; but soon lost his office through a change of ministry. In addition to the works of this indefatigable writer already mentioned, may be named his 'Histoire Populaire des Français' (1832); 'La Grèce Continentale et la Morée' (1843); 'Histoire des Conquêtes et de l'Etablissement des Français dans les Etats de l'ancienne Grèce sous les Ville-Hardouin' (1846); besides his editions of Brantôme, etc.; and his articles in cyclopedias and magazines.

Buchtel, book'tĕl, **Henry Augustus,** American clergyman and educator: b. Akron, Ohio, 30 Sept. 1847. He was educated at Asbury (now De Pauw) University, entered the Methodist ministry, and held pastorates in various parts of Indiana, New York, New Jersey, and Colorado. Since 1900 he has been chancellor of the University of Denver. In 1906 he was elected governor of Colorado.

Buchtel College, a co-educational institution in Akron, Ohio, founded in 1871, under the auspices of the Universalist Church, and named for John R. Buchtel, who gave it $500,000. In 1905 its productive funds were $190,000, and income $49,206 and the value of the buildings and grounds about $300,000. It had 17 professors, and 243 students, and some 9,000 volumes in its library.

Buchu, bū'kū, a South African name for several species of *barosma*, especially *B. crenata, crenulata*, and *serratifolia*. They belong to the order *Rutaceæ*, and the section *Endiosmeæ*. They have a powerful and usually offensive odor, and have been recommended as antispasmodics and diuretics.

Buck, Carl Darling, American philologist: b. Bucksport, Me., 2 Oct. 1866. He graduated from Yale in 1886; took the degree of Ph.D. there in 1889; and was a member of the American School of Classical Studies at Athens in 1887-9. In 1892, he became professor of Sanskrit and comparative philology at the University of Chicago. He has written 'Vocalismus der Oskischen Sprache'; 'Discoveries in the Attic Deme of Ikaria' (in 'Papers of the American School of Classical Study, Athens,' Vol. V.); 'The Oscan-Umbrian Verb System'; 'Latin Grammar' (with W. G. Hale); and several papers in the 'American Journal of Philology.'

Buck, Dudley, American organist and composer: b. Hartford, Conn., 10 March 1839. After musical study at home and in Leipsic, whence he returned in 1862, he became organist at Park Church, Hartford, and successively at St. James' Church, Chicago, Music Hall, Boston, and St. Ann's Church, Church of the Holy Trinity, and Plymouth Church, Brooklyn, retiring in 1903. He has written several books: 'A Dictionary of Musical Terms'; a work on 'The Influence of the Organ in History' (1882), etc. The 'Centennial Cantata,' for the opening of the Exposition of 1876, by appointment of the U. S. Centennial Commission, the 'Forty-sixth Psalm' the 'Legend of Don Munio,' the 'Golden Legend,' and the 'Marmion' symphonic overture, are among his larger works with orchestra. He has also composited chamber music, songs, and male-voice pieces. Among his later works may likewise be mentioned 'The Voyage of Columbus,' 'The Light of Asia,' 'The Christian Year,' and 'Deseret,' a comic opera.

Buck, Jirah Dewey, American physician and theosophist: b. Fredonia, N. Y., 1838. He graduated in 1864 from the Cleveland Homœopathic College, became professor in that institution and later settled in practice in Cincinnati. He was afterward made professor of therapeutics in the Pulte Medical College. He is well-known for his theosophical studies and has been elected president of the Theosophical Society in America. Among his works are 'The Nature and Aims of Theosophy'; 'A Study of Man and the Way to Health'; 'Mystic Masonry'; 'Browning's Paracelsus and Other Essays'; 'Why I Am a Theosophist.'

Buck, a name sometimes distinctively appropriated to the adult male of the fallow deer, the female of which is a doe. The term is often also applied to the male of other species of deer, as of the roebuck, although never to that of the red deer, which, when mature, is a stag or a hart.

Buck-bean, Bog-bean, or **Marsh-trefoil** (*Menyanthes trifoliata*), a beautiful plant belonging to the *Menyantheæ*, a subdivision of the natural order of the *Gentianaceæ*. It is common in spongy, boggy soils, throughout the northern temperate lands, and flowers about the latter end of May and early June. It has a procumbent stem rising to a height of 6 to 12 inches, and covered by the sheaths of the leaves, and a creeping jointed root. The leaves are trifoliate (like those of clover), with obtuse, ovate leaflets. The flower-stalk terminates in a thyrse of white flowers, rose-colored outwardly. The calyx is five-parted, the corolla funnel-shaped, spreading, and clothed on the inner surface with a coating of dense fleshy hairs. The fruit consists of a one-celled, two-valved capsule containing numerous seeds. The whole plant, the root especially, has an intensely bitter taste, and an extract of it ranks as a valuable tonic quite equal in its effects to gentian. It is not so frequently employed now, however, as it used to be. It is said to be beneficial in intermittent fevers, gout, liver complaints, dropsy, scurvy, etc. In the north of Europe it is sometimes used instead of hops to give bitterness to beer; and in Lapland an unpalatable kind of bread is made from the powdered roots.

Buck'board, a four-wheeled vehicle having the seat mounted on an elastic board instead of springs. Buckboards were intended originally for rough and hilly roads and were rather primitive in construction, but became so popular that the styles at present employed are greatly improved in form and finish.

Buckets, in water-wheels, are a series of cavities into which the water is delivered, on the circumference of the wheel to be set in motion. By the revolution of the wheel the buckets will be alternately erected so as to receive water and inverted so as to discharge it; the loaded side will descend, and present the empty buckets in succession to the current, and thus keep up a constant revolution of the wheel. Buckets made of wood and of various metals, are also used for many other mechanical purposes, as in grain-elevators, dredges, etc.

Buckeye. The name in the central and southern United States for native species of trees of the horse-chestnut genus, especially the sweet buckeye (*Æsculus octandra*), abundant in Ohio and southward. See HORSE-CHESTNUT.

Buckeye State, a nickname applied to the State of Ohio.

Buck'ham, Matthew Henry, American educator: b. Leicestershire, England, 1832. He came to the United States in infancy. In 1851 he graduated from the University of Vermont and later became principal of the academy of Lenox, Mass. After studying and traveling in Europe, he became professor of Greek in the University of Vermont, and in 1871, president. He has written numerous sermons, addresses, and reviews.

Buckhound. See DEERHOUND.

Buckingham, bŭk'ĭng-ăm, **George Villiers, Duke of,** British courtier: b. Brooksby, Leicestershire, 20 Aug. 1592; d. Portsmouth, 24 Aug. 1628. He was the unworthy favorite of James I. and Charles I. His family went to England from Normandy in the time of William the Conqueror. His father was George Villiers, Knight; his mother was descended from the ancient family of Beaumont. His father died when he was 13, and at 18 he was sent to France. where he resided three years, and acquired great skill in all bodily exercises. This, together with his beauty of person and graceful manners, made so great an impression on James I., who gave him the familiar name of Steenie, that in less than two years he was made a knight, a gentleman of the bed-chamber, baron, viscount, Marquis of Buckingham, lord high admiral, lord warden of the Cinque Ports, etc., and at last dispenser of all the honors, offices, favors, and revenues of the three kingdoms, according to the dictates of his ambition, his cupidity, and his caprice. The nation was indignant at seeing merit undervalued, the people trampled upon, the nobility humbled, the crown impoverished and degraded, to elevate and enrich a weak and insolent favorite. Such rapid and undeserved promotion likewise caused many private jealousies. In 1623 he engaged in a romantic adventure with Charles, Prince of Wales, in connection with which traitorous views have been attributed to him. The Earl of Bristol was negotiating a marriage for the prince with the Infanta of Spain. Buckingham persuaded the prince to go to Madrid, and carry on his suit in person. They set out incognito, passed through various adventures, and saw on their way the Princess Henrietta Maria of France, whom Charles afterward married. The result of this journey is well known. The marriage was broken off, war declared with Spain, and Bristol was impeached. Buckingham was created a duke during his absence, and whatever misconduct may have been associated with the design or execution of his mission, his favor with the king and prince remained unimpaired. James died in March 1625, and in May of the same year Buckingham was sent to France as proxy for Charles I., to marry the Princess Henrietta Maria. In the following year the unpopularity of the war with Spain, and the failure of the expedition to Cadiz, caused his impeachment, from the consequences of which he was saved by his favor with the king. His intrigues soon after brought on war with France, and he was intrusted with an expedition to succor the Rochellese, but they refused his aid, and he carried his forces to the Isle of Rhé, where, after three months spent in unskilful operations, he suffered a defeat in re-embarking which cost 2,000 men. Notwithstanding this proof of incapacity, a large force was again intrusted to him to renew the attempt on Rochelle. He went to Portsmouth to superintend the preparation, and there was assassinated by John Felton, a lieutenant who had withdrawn from the army in consequence of being disappointed in promotion.

Buckingham, George Villiers, Duke **of,** son of the preceding: b. Westminster, 30 Jan. 1628; d. Kirkby Moorside, Yorkshire. 16 April 1687. After studying at Trinity College, Cambridge, he traveled abroad, and on his return home. after the commencement of the civil war, he was presented to the king at Oxford. He served in the royal army, under Prince Rupert and Lord Gerard. His estate was seized by the Parliament; but having obtained the restoration of it, he traveled with his brother into France and Italy. In 1648 he returned to England, and was with Charles II. in Scotland, and at the battle of Worcester. He followed that prince abroad, and served as a volunteer in the French army in Flanders. He afterward returned to England, and in 1657 married the daughter of Lord Fairfax, by which means he repaired the ruin of his fortune in the royal cause. He, however, preserved the favor of Charles II., and at the Restoration was made master of the horse. He also became one of the king's confidential ministers, who were designated by the appellation of the "Cabal" (1667–73). His political conduct was, like his general behavior, characterized by unprincipled levity and imprudence. In 1666 he engaged in a conspiracy to effect a change of the government; notwithstanding which, he recovered the favor of King Charles, which he repeatedly abused. The profligacy of his private life was notorious. He seduced the Countess of Shrewsbury, and killed her husband in a duel; and he was more than suspected of having been the instigator of the infamous Col. Blood to his brutal outrage against the Duke of Ormond, whom he attempted, with the assistance of other ruffians, to carry to Tyburn and hang on the common gallows. In 1677 he was, together with the Earls of Shaftesbury and Salisbury and Lord Wharton, committed to the Tower for a contempt, by order of the House of Lords, but on petitioning the king, they were released. He plotted against the government with the Dissenters, and made himself an object of contempt to all parties. Pope ('Moral Essays,' epistle 3d) has more strikingly than accurately described his death. His abilities were far superior to those of his father; and among his literary compositions the comedy, or rather the witty burlesque, of 'The Rehearsal' may be mentioned as a work which displays no common powers, and which greatly contributed to the correction of a corrupted public taste.

Buckingham, James Silk, English traveler and editor: b. Flushing, Cornwall, 25 Aug. 1786; d. London, 30 June 1855. He made three voyages to Lisbon while yet a mere boy. In 1815 he went to Bombay, and in the following year, after many vicissitudes, to Calcutta, where he established the Calcutta *Journal*, but the censorship of the press was then in full force in India, and Buckingham, having offended government, his printing presses were seized, and he himself compelled to quit the presidency of Bengal and return to England, where he began to deliver lectures in London in favor of free trade to the East, and the extinction of the East India Company's monopoly. He also established in London, 1824, the *Oriental Herald*, and four years later the *Athenæum*, now one of the foremost English weeklies, and prepared for the press the manuscript journals of his travels. In 1822 appeared 'Travels in Palestine'; in 1825, 'Travels in Arabia'; in 1827, 'Travels in Mesopotamia'; and in 1830, 'Travels in Assyria and Media.' In 1832 he was chosen member of Parliament for Sheffield, and retained his seat till 1837. Subsequently to this he made a tour of three years in America, resulting in the publication of eight volumes on the United States, and one on British North America. In 1843 he became secretary to

the British and Foreign Institute — a literary club which he had mainly contributed to form; but in this capacity he unfortunately drew upon himself the animadversions of 'Punch,' which at last fairly extinguished the society. In the later years of his life he delivered lectures in various parts of the country. He was a zealous promoter of the temperance cause, and president of the London Temperance League. In 1849 appeared his 'National Evils and Practical Remedies.' He also published two volumes on Belgium, the Rhine, and Switzerland, and two on France and Piedmont, the result of tours on the Continent. His last work was his 'Autobiography,' two volumes of which appeared in 1855, but its completion was prevented by the author's death. A few years before this the East India Company had granted him a pension, which was afterward continued to his widow, and he had also a pension of £200 a year from the civil list.

Buckingham, Joseph Tinker, American journalist: b. Windham, Conn., 21 Dec. 1779; d. Cambridge, Mass., 11 April 1861. His father exhausted his whole property in supporting the American army during the Revolution, and died leaving a family without means of support. At Worthington, Mass., Joseph was apprenticed to a farmer, with whom he remained for several years, during which he made himself acquainted with the rudiments of an English education. At 16 he entered a printing-office and became acquainted with the elements of the profession in which he was afterward to gain distinction. In Boston, 1806, he began life for himself by the publication of 'The Polyanthus,' a monthly magazine, which, after one year, was discontinued and not resumed until 1812. In 1809 he published for six months the 'Ordeal,' a weekly. In 1817 he began the publication of 'The New England Galaxy and Masonic Magazine,' which he continued until 1828. From 1831 to 1834 he published 'The New England Magazine.' In 1824 he published the first number of the Boston *Courier*, which he continued to edit until 1848. Mr. Buckingham was several times elected to the legislature, serving in both Houses. Among his publications deserving mention are: 'Specimens of Newspaper Literature, with Personal Memoirs, Anecdotes and Reminiscences' (1850); and 'Personal Memoirs and Recollections of Editorial Life' (1852).

Buckingham, William Alfred, American politician: b. Lebanon, Conn., 28 May 1804; d. Norwich, 3 Feb. 1875. He was educated in the common schools; worked on his father's farm; was also a school-teacher, and at Norwich, 1825, began business in dry-goods, becoming later a manufacturer and something of a capitalist. In 1849 he was elected mayor of Norwich, to which office he was repeatedly chosen. For nine years (1858–66) he was governor of Connecticut, and as one of the most efficient of the "war governors" achieved a national fame. He served as United States senator from 1869 till his death. He was active in the temperance cause, and a liberal giver to Yale College and to many benevolent objects.

Buckingham, or Bucks, an inland county, England, bounded north and northwest by Northampton; northeast and east by Bedford and Hertford; southeast by Middlesex; southwest by Berks, and west by Oxford. Its length,

BUCKINGHAM PALACE, LONDON, ENGLAND.

HAMPTON COURT, LONDON.

north to south, is about 45 miles; greatest breadth, east to west, 23 miles; area, 746 square miles. The vale of Aylesbury, stretching through the centre of the county, and celebrated for its fertility, furnishes rich pasturage for vast numbers of cattle and sheep. The total area under all kinds of crops, bare fallow, and grass is somewhat more than 400,000 acres, of which considerably more than half is in permanent pasture. The chief cereal crops are wheat, barley, and oats, each occupying annually from about 22,000 to 30,000 acres. Between 4,000,000 and 5,000,000 pounds, or about 1,900 tons of butter, are annually made in this county. The breeding and fattening of cattle are largely carried on, Herefords and short-horns being favorite breeds. The manufactures of Buckinghamshire are unimportant. Among them are straw-plaiting and the making of thread lace, wooden articles, such as beechen chairs, turnery, etc. There are also paper-mills, silk-mills, and other manufactures. The mineral productions of this county are of no great importance. The county is watered by the Ouse, the Thame, the Thames, and other streams, and is intersected by the Great Western and Northwestern R.R.'s. Buckingham is nominally the county town, but Aylesbury is the assize town. Buckinghamshire used to contain three parliamentary boroughs, namely, Aylesbury, Buckingham, and High or Chipping Wycombe, which now give name to corresponding parliamentary divisions. The county thus returns three members to the House of Commons. It gives the title of earl to the family of Hobart Hampden. Pop. (1901) 195,234.

Buckingham, a municipal and formerly a parliamentary borough of England, capital of the county of its own name, 50 miles northwest of London, situated on a peninsula formed by the Ouse, which is here crossed by three stone bridges. The town hall and jail are large and commodious buildings. The parish church, erected in 1781, is a spacious structure, with a square tower, surmounted by an elegant spire, and there are also several other places of worship, and a free grammar-school, founded by Edward VI. Malting and tanning are carried on to some extent; and a good deal of business is done in wool and hops. In the vicinity are several limestone quarries, and one of marble. Pop. about 3,500.

Buckingham Palace, a royal palace in London, facing St. James's Park. It is the town residence of the king.

Buck'land, Cyrus, American inventor: b. Manchester, Conn., 10 Aug. 1799; d. 26 Feb. 1891. After learning the trade of a machinist, he assisted in building the machinery for the first cotton-mills erected at Chicopee Falls, and became, in 1828, patternmaker in the United States armory, Springfield, where he remained for 28 years, becoming master mechanic. He designed machinery and tools for the manufacture of firearms; remodeled old weapons and designed new ones; perfected a lathe for turning out gun-stocks; invented machines to bore and turn gun-barrels and for rifling muskets, and many other novelties in the manufacture of firearms and ordnance. Much of his machinery was adopted by foreign governments. As he received nothing for his labor at the armory, excepting his salary, Congress voted him

$10,000 when ill-health compelled him to resign. In all he received from Congress for his inventions $70,000.

Buckland, Francis Trevelyan, English naturalist: b. Oxford, 17 Dec. 1826; d. London, 19 Dec. 1880. He was the son of William Buckland (q.v.); graduated at Christ Church, Oxford, and having studied medicine in Paris and London, he was for some time house surgeon to St. George's Hospital, when he joined the 2d Life Guards as assistant surgeon, a post which he held for nine years. His strong passion for natural history soon absorbed all his thoughts, and he became a constant contributor to 'Field' and other periodicals. Latterly he devoted himself with enthusiasm to pisciculture, a subject on which he was long the leading authority. His advice on the subject was sought by several foreign governments, and he was the means of introducing salmon and trout into the Australian and New Zealand waters. He was appointed inspector of salmon fisheries in 1867, and his reports as commissioner led to the passing of several useful acts of Parliament. Besides a great quantity of pleasant gossipy articles contributed to various periodicals, he published 'Curiosities of Natural History' (1857–72); the 'Logbook of a Fisherman and Zoologist' (1876); a 'Natural History of British Fishes' (1881); and other works.

Buckland, William, English geologist: b. Axminster, Devon, 12 March 1784; d. 15 Aug. 1856. He was educated first at Winchester, afterward at Corpus Christi College, Oxford, took his degree of B.A. in 1803, and obtained a fellowship in 1808. From early childhood he had been familiar with the ammonites and other fossils in the lias quarries near his native town, and with advancing years the bent of his mind to geological pursuits was developed and confirmed. In 1813 he was appointed reader in mineralogy at Oxford, and in 1818 a readership of geology was instituted for him. In 1825 he was presented by his college to the living of Stoke Charity, near Whitchurch, Hants, and the same year he became one of the canons in the Christchurch Cathedral, Oxford. He was one of the eight selected to write the celebrated 'Bridgewater Treatises,' and in 1836 his essay was published, under the title of 'Geology and Mineralogy Considered with Reference to Natural Theology.' In 1845, he was made dean of Westminster, and in 1847 one of the trustees of the British Museum. His papers contributed to various societies and periodicals were very numerous. He was a fellow and twice president of the Geological Society of London, and of the Royal Society from 1818.

Bucklan'dia, a handsome evergreen Javanese and East Indian tree (*B. populnea*), of the natural order *Hamamelidaceæ*, the only species of its genus. It is said to attain considerable height, often more than 30 feet without branches, and occasionally a circumference of more than 20 feet at the height of a man's chest from the ground. Its timber is widely used in the East.

Bucklandite, the name of two minerals: (1) Bucklandite of Hermann, a variety of epidote; (2) Bucklandite of Levy, a variety of allanite distinguished by being anhydrous. It occurs in small black crystals having the form and physical properties of allanite in an iron mine near Arendal, Norway.

Buckle, **Henry Thomas,** English historian: b. Lee, Kent, 24 Nov. 1822; d. Damascus, 29 May 1862. He was the son of a wealthy merchant, and received his education partly at home, and partly at Dr. Halloway's School, Gordon House, Kentish Town. His delicate health prevented his remaining long at school, but his love of learning and indefatigable industry as a student supplied any deficiencies in his training, and he was to a great extent self-educated. At an early age he entered his father's counting-house, but he displayed no aptitude for business; and when at the age of 18 his father's death left him an ample fortune, he devoted himself entirely to study. The only thing he allowed to distract him from his more serious pursuits was his favorite game of chess, in which he attained such excellence as to be recognized as one of the first English masters of the game; but even this he gave up when he found it encroached too much on his time. He had formed a plan, to which he dedicated his life, of writing the 'History of Civilization in England' in conformity with certain philosophical principles, and with an exhaustive treatment in regard to details which he deemed indispensable to historical accuracy, which made the work he had undertaken one of almost incalculable magnitude. He only succeeded in finishing two volumes. The first, published in 1858, stated with copious illustrations the plan of the work; the second, issued in 1861, contained a digression on the histories of Scotland and Spain, intended further to illustrate his design, and demonstrate the principles on which it was based. These works gave rise to much controversy, but it has been generally agreed that they exhibit great boldness and originality of design, with profound and accurate scholarship, and possibly also with a good deal of what was the object of the historian's strongest aversion in others, dogmatism. His death occurred when he was on a voyage undertaken for the restoration of his health.

Buckle, a metal instrument consisting of a rim and tongue, forming a clasp, used for fastening straps or bands in dress, harness, etc. In making buckles, both brass and iron are used, and the chief kinds are called tongue, roller, brace, and gear buckles. The use of buckles, instead of shoe-strings, was introduced into England during the reign of Charles II. They soon became very fashionable, attained an enormous size (the largest being called Artois buckles, after the Comte d'Artois, brother of the king of France), and were usually made of silver, set with diamonds and other precious stones. In the latter half of the 18th century the manufacture of buckles was carried on most extensively in Birmingham, there being at one time not less than 4,000 people directly employed in that city and its vicinity, who turned out 2,500,000 pairs of buckles annually. When the trade was at its height, however, fashion changed, and in 1791 buckle-makers petitioned the Prince of Wales for sympathy, on the ground that, owing to the introduction of shoe-strings, their trade was almost ruined. The prince promised to assist them as far as he could by wearing buckles himself, and enjoining his household to do the same; but fashion

was too strong even for him, and before the close of the century, a great staple trade of Birmingham had become extinct, though shoe-buckles are still by no means unknown.

Buckler, a kind of small shield formerly worn on the left arm, a piece of armor varying in form and material, among the latter being wickerwork, wood covered with leather, a combination of wood and metal, etc.

Buck'ley, **James Monroe,** American clergyman and editor: b. Rahway, N. J., 16 Dec. 1836. He was educated at Pennington Seminary and Wesleyan University, and studied theology at Exeter, N. H., and in 1858 entered the ministry of the Methodist Episcopal Church. He has had charges at several places, including Detroit, New York, and Brooklyn, the last of which he retained from 1866 to 1880. Since 1880 he has been editor of the New York *Christian Advocate*. He has published 'Two Weeks in the Yosemite and Vicinity' (1873); 'Christians and the Theatre' (1876); 'Oats or Wild Oats' (1885); 'Travels in Three Continents' (1895); 'Extemporaneous Oratory' (1899); and other works.

Buckley, **Samuel Botsford,** American botanist and geologist: b. Torrey, Yates County, N. Y., 9 May 1809; d. Austin, Texas, 18 Feb. 1884. He graduated from Wesleyan University in 1836. During his travels in the Southern States he investigated the botany, choncology, etc., of those regions, discovering many new species of plants and shells. Among the flora was the new genus *Buckleya*, which was named in his honor. He determined the height of Mount Buckley, North Carolina, and of several other summits. From 1860-1 he was connected with the State survey of Texas and from 1866-7 was State geologist of Texas. He wrote many papers of a scientific nature and a work on the trees and shrubs of the United States.

Buck'minster, **Joseph Stevens,** American clergyman: b. Portsmouth, N. H., 26 May 1784; d. 9 June 1812. His father, Joseph Buckminster, a scholarly and eloquent preacher, sent the son to Harvard, where he was graduated in 1800, afterward becoming a teacher in Phillips Exeter Academy, among his pupils being Daniel Webster. In 1804 he entered upon the work of the ministry as pastor of the Brattle Street Church, Boston, and at once took his place as a writer and preacher of the finest gifts, to grow in power and public esteem until the day of his premature death. He was a member of the Anthology Club of Boston, and a contributor to the 'Monthly Anthology.' His pulpit influence aided to develop a more literary style of sermon, while his oratorical ability was equal to his skill in composition. He was a representative of the Liberal Congregationalism, which, soon after his death, became Unitarian in belief. His works, in two volumes, were published in 1839. See also his 'Memoirs,' by his sister (1851).

Buck'nell **University,** a co-educational institution in Lewisburg, Pa.; organized in 1846, under the auspices of the Baptist Church; reported in 1901: Professors and instructors, 31; students, 500; volumes in the library, over 19,000; grounds and buildings valued at more than $350,000; endowment, $425,000; president, John H. Harris, LL.D.

Buck'ner, Simon Bolivar, American soldier and politician: b. Kentucky, 1 April 1823. He was graduated at West Point in 1844, taught there, as assistant professor, during the next two years, and served in the Mexican war, 1846-8, under Gens. Taylor and Scott. He was brevetted first lieutenant, and also captain, for gallantry at the battles of Churubusco and Molino del Rey. From 1848 to 1850 he served at West Point as assistant instructor in infantry tactics. In 1855 he resigned from the army and engaged in various occupations, civil and military, in Illinois and Kentucky. When the Civil War began he joined the Confederate army as a brigadier-general. Afterward he rose to distinction, attaining the rank of lieutenant-general, and taking a prominent part in several important events of the war, notably in the defense and surrender of Fort Donelson, 16 Feb. 1862. He was one of the pall-bearers at Gen. Grant's funeral in 1885, by the personal selection of the great soldier himself, who had been warmly attached to him for many years. In 1896 he was nominated for vice-president by the National (Gold) Democrats, having previously served a term as governor of Kentucky.

Buckram, a coarse fabric, linen or cotton, sized with glue. It is used in making garments to give them, by stiffening, the form intended, and as a cover in bookbinding.

Buck'shot, a leaden shot larger than swanshot. About 160 or 170 of them weigh a pound. They are especially designed to be used in hunting deer and other large game.

Buckshot War, 1838, a disputed-election case in Pennsylvania, of national importance as bearing on the nature of the "domestic violence," from which the Constitution requires the Federal government to protect the States. As usual, fraud under legal forms was met by retaliation in defiance of them. The legislature that year had to elect a United States senator; and the return of Democratic candidates in Philadelphia gave that party a majority on joint ballot, though the Senate was 22 Whig (Anti-Masonic) to 11 Democratic. But the Democratic congressional candidate in one of the city districts was defeated; his party charged it to frauds in the Northern Liberties district (now in Philadelphia), and the 10 Democratic election judges threw out its entire vote of some 5,000, giving him the certificate of election. At once the seven Whig judges met and gave the certificate not only to their candidate, but to their legislative candidates who were not elected even with the Northern Liberties vote: obviously to fight till their congressman was restored. The secretary of State was chairman of the Whig State committee, received the Whig certificate first (professedly at least), refused to acknowledge any others, and publicly advised his party to claim the election and hold it out. Armed crowds of both parties collected at Harrisburg "to see fair play" when the legislature met, 4 December; and for some days the sessions were held with a roaring mob outside. The Whig returns alone were handed in by the secretary of State; the Whig senate organized, and then adjourned on account of the mob; one member is alleged to have threatened them with "ball and buckshot," whence the name. In the Representatives' hall both parties organized and chose speakers, the Whigs, T. S. Cunningham,

and the Democrats, William Hopkins; the former then adjourned, whereupon the latter held the hall with a guard and the Whigs had to meet outside. The Whig governor, Joseph Ritner, called on the State militia to be ready to rescue the capital from a "lawless mob," and appealed to the commandant, at Carlisle, and next to President Van Buren, for help against "domestic violence," which was refused on the ground that this phrase referred only to insurrection against lawful authorities, whereas this was only a political struggle to determine who the lawful authorities were, in which the government could not decently interfere. (The same excuse was afterward made for leaving Kansas at the mercy of the Border Ruffians, though the Federal court put the United States soldiery into their hands.) About 1,000 militia were brought to Harrisburg; but after a fortnight's stay departed, as the city was entirely quiet, and the rival houses holding regular sessions. The cooler Whigs, however, saw that the secretary of State could not justify his assumption of power; enough Cunningham members joined the Hopkins House to give it a majority, and on the 25th the senate acknowledged it as the true one, whereupon the other broke up and its members gradually drifted in — all but Thaddeus Stevens (q.v.), who would not take his seat during the session. The legislature elected as senator Daniel Sturgeon, then State treasurer, who as such refused to honor Ritner's bill for the employment of the militia. See U. S., DISPUTED ELECTIONS IN THE.

Buck'skin, a soft leather of a yellowish or grayish color, made originally from deerskin, but now usually from sheepskin. The softness which is its chief characteristic is imparted by using oil or brains in dressing it. The name is also given to a kind of twilled woolen cloth without a pile or "face."

Buck'stone, John Baldwin, English actor and playwright: b. London, 14 Sept. 1802; d. 31 Oct. 1879. From 1823 to 1853 he was a well-known London comedian. He became manager of the Haymarket Theatre, and produced nearly 200 plays, which were all successful, largely owing to his knowledge of stage effect and humor. He made a visit to the United States in 1840. Among the best of his pieces are: 'The Wreck Ashore'; 'Victorine'; 'Green Bushes'; 'The Flowers of the Forest'; 'Married Life'; 'Leap Year'; 'Second Thoughts'; and 'Nicholas Flam.'

Buckstone, Lucy Isabella, English actress (daughter of John Baldwin Buckstone): b. 1858; d. London, 17 March 1893. After acting for a time in the provinces, she appeared on the London stage in 1875 in the play of 'David Garrick.' Among her best known roles were those of Annette in 'The Bells' and Lucy Ormond in 'Peril.'

Buck'tails, the New York State Democrats opposed to De Witt Clinton, 1812-28; originally the members of the Tammany Society in New York, from the buck's tail worn in their hats as a badge. Their factional opposition to Clinton, under Martin Van Buren and other important local leaders, extended to his advocacy of the Erie Canal, authorized 15 April 1817; the Tammany men were fiercest in opposition to it, and the name "Bucktails" was given to all the anti-Canal Democrats. Clinton was an ungracious and tactless politician, and in 1824 the Bucktails carried the State and ousted him from the office of canal commissioner; which primitive bit of "spoils," in a community not then hardened to it, created a reaction that gave him two terms more in the governorship. His death in 1828 dissolved his party, and the "Bucktails," under Van Buren and the other members of the "Albany Regency" (q.v.), became the Democratic party in the State.

Buck'thorn (*Rhamnus catharticus*), a shrub, native of Great Britain, naturalized in the United States, where it is cultivated for hedgerows in the Mississippi valley and westward. It is not very common in the States east of the Alleghanies. The stem is covered with a dark-brown bark, and divides into numerous branches with strong spines. It grows to seven or eight feet. The leaves are elliptical and serrated. The male and female flowers are on different plants. The calyx is of a greenish yellow. There is no corolla. The fruit is a round black berry, containing four seeds. It flowers in May, and the seeds ripen in September. The berries are medicinal. They form a powerful purgative, but, being harsh in action, are seldom used in modern practice. The juice of the ripe berries, mixed with alum, forms the sap-green of artists. The bark yields a beautiful yellow dye.

Buck'wheat (*Polygonum fagopyrum*, Linn.), a species of grain supposed to be a native of Asia, and called *blé Sarrasin*, or Saracen wheat, by the French, after the Saracens or Moors, who are believed to have introduced it into Spain. It thrives on poor soils, comes rapidly to maturity, and is most frequently planted in tracts that are not rich enough to support other crops. It is extremely sensitive to cold, being destroyed by the least frost, but it may be planted so late and reaped so early as to incur no danger from that source. Its flowering season continues for a long time, so that it is impossible for all the seeds to be in perfection when it is reaped, and the farmer must decide by careful observation at what period there is the greatest quantity of ripe seeds. Buckwheat does not exhaust the soil, and by its rapid growth and its shade it stifles weeds, prevents their going to seed, and leaves the field clean for the next year. As a grain, buckwheat has been principally cultivated for oxen, swine, and poultry; and although some farmers state that a single bushel of it is equal in quality to two bushels of oats, others assert that it is a very unprofitable food. Mixed with bran, chaff, or grain, it is sometimes given to horses. The flour of buckwheat is occasionally used for bread, but more frequently for cakes fried in a pan. In Germany it serves as an ingredient in pottage, puddings, and other food. In the United States it is very extensively used throughout the winter in griddle-cakes. Beer may be brewed from it, and by distillation it yields an excellent spirit. It is used in Danzig in the preparation of cordial waters. Buckwheat is much cultivated by the preservers of game as a food for pheasants. If left standing it affords both food and shelter to the birds during winter. With some farmers it is the practice to sow buckwheat for the purpose only of plowing it into the ground as a manure for the land. The best time for plowing it in is when it is in full blossom, allowing the land to rest till it

decomposes. While green it serves as food for sheep and oxen, and mixed with other provender it may also be given with advantage to horses. If sown in April two green crops may be procured during the season. The blossoms may be used for dyeing a brown color. It is frequently cultivated in this country in the Middle States, and also in Brabant, as food for bees, to whose honey it imparts a flavor by no means unpleasant. The principal advantage of buckwheat is that it is capable of being cultivated upon land which will produce scarcely anything else, and that its culture, compared with that of other grain, is attended with little expense.

Buckwheat-tree, an evergreen shrub of the genus *Cliftonia*, natural order *Cyrillaceæ*; also called titi. It is a native of the southern United States, where it is found in the neighborhood of water. It bears fragrant white flowers, followed by drooping fruits, which suggest the name.

Bucol'ic, a term derived from a Greek word meaning "herdsman." It is equivalent to the word pastoral, derived from the Latin, and is applied to pastoral poetry of the kind especially descriptive of rural life as led by cowherds and mountain shepherds. Of this class of poetry Theocritus and Vergil left the highest examples. See PASTORAL POETRY.

Bu'crane, an ornamental design carved in relief on the altars of Greece and Rome. It represented an ox skull with garlands depending. This decoration is sometimes seen as an architectural detail with other animals' heads introduced in place of the original ox-head.

Bucy'rus, Ohio, city and county-seat of Crawford County, situated on the Sandusky River and on the Pennsylvania, the Ohio C., and Sandusky division of the Pa. R.R.'s. Stockraising and farming are carried on in the surrounding region and the city is actively engaged in manufacture. Among the products of the mills and shops are machinery, ventilating apparatus, plows, vehicles, and furniture. There are school and county buildings, a reservoir, and waterworks. There is a park in the city, and numerous mineral springs in the surrounding region. Bucyrus was settled in 1818 and incorporated in 1829. Pop. (1900) 6,560.

Bud, a modified shoot in which, owing to the non-development of the axis, the lateral organs become crowded together. It contains the rudiments of future organs, as stems, branches, leaves, and organs of fructification. The usual form of a bud is an elongated ovoid, and according to their position they are described as terminal, that is, formed at the end of a branch, or axillary, that is, produced in the axils of a leaf. Besides the rudimentary organs found in the interior, buds are in cold or temperate climates often covered externally with a viscous and resinous coating, and furnished internally with a downy tissue, destined to defend the enclosed organs from the rigor of winter. No envelopes of this kind are observed on the buds of the greater number of tropical plants. Buds on exogenous plants are in their commencement cellular prolongations from the medullary rays, which force their way through the bark. The cellular portion is surrounded by spiral vessels, and covered with rudimentary leaves. When the vascular part of the bud develops the central cellular portion remains as pith, enclosed in a medullary sheath, which isolates it from the parent stem. Thus it remains till the second year. The bud here described, which contains the rudiments of future leaves, branches, etc., is called a leaf-bud. Sometimes more than one bud is found in or near the axil of a single leaf, in which case all but the proper axillary bud are called accessory buds. The buds begin to show themselves as soon as the leaves have taken their full development. They are then very small, as the developed leaves absorb the nutritive juices of the plant. leaving them little nourishment. On the fall of the leaf they enlarge, and take the form they are to retain during winter, in which season they are stationary. On the return of spring they begin to swell, and burst the scales which form their external covering, and the young shoots which these have served to protect now make their appearance. The external scales of the bud are usually deciduous, that is, they fall off when the young shoot appears; sometimes, however, they are persistent. These scales sometimes represent leaf-blades, as in lilac; sometimes stipules, as in the beech; or petioles, as in the horse-chestnut. Flower-buds are produced in the axil of leaves called floral leaves or bracts. They are not capable of extension by the development of the central cellular portion, and instead of the conservative organs of plants. leaves, and branches, they produce the reproductive organs, flowers, and fruit. Perennial herbaceous plants spring from a subterranean bud called the turio, which is developed annually, and from which the new stem is produced. The bulb is a species of bud of this kind. The arrangement of the leaves in a leaf-bud is called its vernation; of the petals and sepals in a flower-bud, its æstivation.

Bud Moth. An apple pest. See APPLE.

Budæ'us. See BUDE, GUILLAUME.

Budapest, boo'dạ-pĕst, the united towns of Buda or Ofen, and Pest or Pesth, the one on the right, the other on the left of the Danube, forming the capital of Hungary, the seat of the Hungarian parliament and supreme courts, about 135 miles southeast from Vienna. Buda, which is the smaller of the two, and lies on the west bank of the river (here flowing south), consists of the fortified Upper Town on a hill, the Lower Town or Water Town at the foot of the hill, and several other quarters, including Old Buda farther up the river. Among the chief buildings are the royal castle and several palaces, the arsenal, town hall, government offices, etc.; the Church of St. Matthew, dating from the 13th century, during the Turkish occupatiou a mosque for 150 years, and recently rebuilt; and the finest Jewish synagogue in the empire. Pest, or the portion of Budapest on the left or east bank of the river, consists of the inner town of Old Pest on the Danube. and a semicircle of districts — Leopoldstadt, Theresienstadt, Elizabethstadt, etc. — which have grown up around it. The river is at this point somewhat wider than the Thames at London, and the broad quays of Pest extend along it for from two to three miles. It is spanned by fine suspension and other bridges. Pest retains, on the whole, fewer signs of antiquity than

many less venerable towns. Its fine frontage on the Danube is modern, and includes the new houses of parliament, opened in 1896. the academy of science, with a library of 180,000 volumes, exchange, custom house, and other important buildings. The oldest church dates from 1500; the largest building is a huge pile used as barracks and arsenal. Other buildings include the old and the new town house, national museum, National theatre, university buildings, various palaces, the Royal Opera House, etc.

Budapest contains the most important of the three universities of Hungary, attended by about 4,500 students, and having over 220 professors, lecturers, etc. Another important educational institution is the technical high schools, with 60 teachers and 1,100 to 1,200 students, and a library of 60,000 volumes. In commerce and industry Budapest ranks next to Vienna in the empire. Its chief manufactures are machinery, gold, silver, copper, and iron wares, chemicals, textile goods, leather, tobacco, etc. A large trade is done in grain, wine, wool, cattle, etc. At Budapest are the largest electrical works in all Europe. Engineers employed there have brought to perfection the science of applying electricity to motors. They constructed there the first successful underground trolley lines. The city contains the important parks of the Stadtwäldchen, about 1,000 acres in extent, and Margaret Island. It is divided into 10 municipal districts, three on the Buda side of the river, and seven on the Pest side. The Elizabeth suspension bridge over the Danube River was completed and formally opened for traffic 10 Oct. 1903. It was named in commemoration of the late Queen Elizabeth of Hungary. The bridge was originally planned in 1893 by the Budapest Board of Trade. It has two piers, one on each side of the river, built on substantial ground. Its clear span over the river Danube is 951½ feet. There are land approaches on each side of the river, each having a length of 40 meters. thus giving the entire bridge a total length of fully 3,014 feet. The two piers have a total height of 212 feet each over the zero level of the water. Both of them are made of steel and rest upon granite foundations. The highest point at the centre of the bridge is 59 feet from the zero level of the river. The bridge has a total width of 59 feet, 36 feet of which is carriageway, and 11½ feet for each of two footways. Budapest is strongly Magyar in character and sentiment, and as a factor in the national life may almost be regarded as equivalent to the rest of Hungary. Old Buda was founded by the Romans about 150 A.D., and was known as Aquincum. Pest is of much later origin, first being heard of in the 13th century. The citadel of Buda was captured by the Turks after Mohacs in 1526. From 1541 to 1686 Buda was the seat of a Turkish pasha, the Turks being then driven out. The towns were united as one municipality in 1873. It was not until 1799 that the population of Pest began to outdistance that of Buda; but from that date its growth was very rapid and out of all proportion to the increase of Buda. In 1799 the joint population of the two towns was little more than 50,000; in 1890 it was 506,384; in 1900, 732,322.

Buddha, bood'ạ, or bŭd'ạ (to know, intelligence), the generic name for a deified teacher of the Buddhists. These hold that innumerable Buddhas have appeared to save the world, among them one in the present period, also known as Sākyamuni, or Saint Sākya, who is believed by some to have been the ninth incarnation of Vishnu; by others the son of the moon, and regent of the planet Mercury. He was a reformer of Brahminism, introducing a simple creed, and substituting a mild and humane code of morality for its cruel laws and usages. His personal name was Siddhartha, and his family name Gautama; and he is often called also Sakya-muni (from Sakya, the name of his tribe, and muni, a Sanskrit word meaning solitary). His father was king of Kapila-vastu, a few days' journey north of Benares. Siddhartha was early filled with a deep compassion for the degeneracy and misery of the human race, and a deep feeling of the vanity of earthly things. His melancholy thoughts would not be stifled in the enjoyments of his father's court: he must find peace for his own soul and bestow it on others. To this end he left his father's court and after having attended the schools of the Brahmans without profit and lived for years a life of solitude and asceticism, he at last, by dint of profound meditation, acquired clear notions on the life of man and his relations to the universe, and found out the true path which was to lead his fellow-creatures to the goal of life. It was then that he became the Buddha, and began to teach his new faith in opposition to the prevailing Brahmanism. The first place at which he taught, or, in the mystic phrase of Buddhism, "turned the wheel of the law," was Benares. He soon made many converts, especially among the lowly and oppressed, for his teaching was addressed to all alike, without distinction of person or caste. Many of the Brahmans also joined him, wearied with the severe and oppressive observances of their own religion, which contrasted so unfavorably with the simplicity of the new faith. Among his earliest converts were the monarchs of Magadha and Kosala, in whose kingdoms he chiefly passed the latter portion of his life, respected, honored, and protected.

The theory of the "four sublime verities" lies at the foundation of the doctrines of the Buddhists. The first verity is that pain is inseparable from existence, inasmuch as existence brings old age, sickness, and death; the second, that pain is the offspring of desire, and of faults which desire has made us commit in previous states of existence (for Sakya-muni adopted fully the prevailing doctrine of Brahmanism with regard to the transmigration of souls) or in the present; the third verity tells us that existence, and therefore pain, can only cease through Nirvana; the fourth, that in order to attain Nirvana our desires and passions must be suppressed, every obstacle to the extinction of desire must be set aside, the most extreme self-renunciation must be practised, and we must, in short, forget our own personality so far as possible. The last verity is the most important in its practical application, as pointing out the way to salvation and providing a rule of conduct. The way to salvation consists of eight parts or conditions that a man must fulfil. The first is in Buddhistic language right view; the second is right judgment; the third is right language; the fourth is right purpose; the fifth is right profession; the sixth is right application; the seventh is right memory; the eighth is right meditation. The five fundamental precepts of the Buddhist moral code are not to kill, not to steal, not to commit adultery, not to lie, and not to give way to drunkenness. To these there are added five others of less importance, and binding more particularly on the religious class, such as to abstain from repasts taken out of season, from theatrical representations, etc. There are six fundamental virtues to be practised by all men alike, namely, charity, purity, patience, courage, contemplation, and knowledge. These are the virtues that are said to "conduct a man to the other shore." The devotee who strictly practises them has not yet attained Nirvana, but is on the road to it. The Buddhist virtue of charity is universal in its application, extending to all creatures, and demanding sometimes the greatest self-denial and sacrifice. There is a legend that the Buddha in one of his stages of existence (for he had passed through innumerable transmigrations before becoming "the enlightened") gave himself up to be devoured by a famishing lioness which was unable to suckle her young ones.

There are other virtues, less important, indeed, than the six cardinal ones, but still binding on believers. Thus not only is lying forbidden, but evil speaking, coarseness of language, and even vain and frivolous talk, must be avoided. Buddhist metaphysics are comprised in three theories — the theory of transmigration (borrowed from Brahmanism), the theory of the mutual connection of causes, and the theory of Nirvana. The first requires no explanation. According to the second, life is the result of 12 conditions, which are by turns causes and effects. Thus there would be no death were it not for birth; it is therefore the effect of which birth is the cause. Again, there would be no birth were there not a continuation of existence. Existence has for its cause our attachment to things, which again has its origin in desire; and so on through sensation, contact, the organs of sensation and the heart, name, and form, ideas, etc., up to ignorance. This ignorance, however, is not ordinary ignorance, but the fundamental error which causes us to attribute permanence and reality to things. This, then, is the primary origin of existence and all its attendant evils. Nirvana is eternal salvation from the evils of existence, and the end which every Buddhist is supposed to seek. It is not so easy to determine exactly what this Nirvana means, however; but the best authorities (Burnouf, Turnour, Spence Hardy, Barthélemy Saint-Hilaire, etc.) affirm that it means the complete annihilation of the thinking principle. Sakya-muni did not leave his doctrines in writing; he declared them orally, and they were carefully treasured by his disciples.

THE ELIZABETH SUSPENSION BRIDGE AT BUDAPEST.

and written down after his death. The determination of the canon of the Buddhist scriptures as we now possess them was the work of three successive councils, and was finished two centuries at least before Christ. The religion soon spread through Hindustan, though it was afterward (probably through persecution) entirely banished from it. Many rock temples, inscriptions, etc., testify to its former prevalence in this region. From Hindustan it spread in all directions — to Ceylon, Java,· Cochin-China, Laos, Burma, Pegu, Nepal, Tibet, Mongolia, Tartary, China (where Buddha is called Fo), and Japan, in which countries it still prevails. At present it is professed by perhaps a third of the human race.

Bibliography.— Koeppen, 'Die Religion des Buddha' (1857–9); Max-Müller, 'Buddhist Nihilism' (1869); Wurm, 'Der Buddha' (1880); Oldenberg, 'Buddha: Sein Leben, Seine Lehre' (1881); Arnold, 'The Light of Asia' (1882); Eitel, 'Buddhism: Its Historical, Theoretical, and Popular Aspects' (1884); Monier-Williams, 'Buddhism in Its Connection with Brahmanism' (1888); Jennings, 'The Indian Religions' (1890); Rhys-Davids, 'History and Literature of Buddhism' (1895); La Vallée-Poussin, 'Bouddhism: études et Matériaux' (1898); Warren, 'Buddhism in Translations' (1896).

Buddhism, Esoteric. See THEOSOPHY.

Buddhis'tic Architecture. See INDIAN ART.

Bud'ding, in gardening, the art of multiplying plants by causing the leaf-bud of one species (or, more commonly, variety) to grow upon the branch of another. The operation consists in shaving off a leaf-bud, with a portion of the wood beneath it, which portion is afterward removed by a sudden jerk of the operator's finger and thumb, aided by the budding-knife. An incision in the bark of the stock is then made in the form of a **T** ; the two side lips are pushed aside, the bud is thrust between the bark and the wood, the upper end of its bark is cut to a level with the cross arm of the **T**, and the whole is bound up with netting or worsted, the point of the bud alone being left exposed. In performing the operation, a knife with a thin flat handle, and a blade with a peculiar edge is required. The following conditions are essential to the success of the operation: First, the bud must be "ripe," that is, fully formed — which is known by its plumpness and hardness. If too young, it will not succeed, because it has not acquired vitality enough to depend upon its own resources, until that new growth has taken place which attaches it to the stock. If too old, "sprung," or beginning to grow, it is also unfit for use, because the new organs belonging to the young growth need an instant and uninterrupted supply of food, which in the beginning the bud cannot obtain from the branch. Secondly, the bark of the stock must "run freely," that is, must separate readily from the wood below it. This separation is necessary in order that the bud may be inserted beneath the bark; and is always attended by the presence of a large quantity of the viscid

matter called cambium, which is in fact a mixture of young tissue in the act of organizing and of organizable matter. The bud coming in contact with this substance, young and full of vitality, readily forms an adhesion with it, and thus the operation is complete. On this account young branches should always be chosen, since the bark never runs so freely, that is, there is never so great a collection of cambium under it in old branches. Those of the year in which the operation is performed are the best, provided they are advanced toward maturity. Shoots far advanced in a second year's growth are, however, often used, and with success. With regard to the time of performing the operation, autumn is preferred in this country, but it may be practised also in spring. Buds take better in autumn, because the stock has at that period ceased growing, and is chiefly occupied in storing up the organizable material required for the nutrition of the young organs, of which the bud, by the act of insertion, has become one. It ought to be borne in mind that the nearer the constitution of the stock approaches that of the bud, the greater is the success that attends this operation. If they are in any considerable degree dissimilar, the operation becomes precarious; if very different, it is impracticable.

In animals, a form of reproduction, as of the hydra, the sea-anemones, the coral polyps, ascidians, etc. The nature of the process, due to rapid cell-division developed locally, is best seen in the hydra (q.v.), where young hydras arise from protusions, well called "buds," from the side of the parent stock, and later are constricted off and become free individuals. In the corals, as a result of throwing out lateral buds from the base, arises a colony, or compound coral like most of the reef-building forms, such as the brain-coral (Meandrina). In the hydra and other animals the new individual arising by budding becomes free from the parent.

Buddleia, bŭd-lē'ya, or **Buddlea,** a genus of about 70 species of shrubs or trees of the natural order *Loganiaceæ*, natives of the tropics and warmer temperate regions of the world. A few of the hardiest species, none of which are quite hardy in the northern United States, are cultivated as ornamental plants, for which purpose they are specially fitted by their attractive, usually deciduous, but sometimes almost persistent wooly foliage and panicles and their cluster or racemes of tubular or bell-shaped flowers produced abundantly during the summer. The flowers, which in some species are fragrant, range in color from yellow to red, white to purple, and in some cases have more than one color in individual flowers. They may be propagated from seed or cuttings and are found to thrive in well-drained soil in sunny situations. They are popular in the southern United States and the West Indies.

Budé, Guillaume, gĕ-yōm bü-dā, French scholar, more generally known under the Latin form Budœus: b. Paris, 1467; d. 1540. He was royal librarian and master of *requêtes*. From his 24th year he devoted himself to study with the greatest zeal, in particular to belles-lettres, to mathematics, and to Greek. Among his philosophical, philological, and juridical works, his treatise 'De Asse et Partibus ejus,' and his commentaries on the Greek language, are of the greatest importance. By his influence the Collège Royal de France was founded. He enjoyed, not only as a scholar, but also as a man and citizen, the greatest esteem. His works appeared at Basel (1557). See E. de Budé, 'Vie de Guillaume Budé' (1884).

Bude (būd) Light, an exceedingly brilliant light, produced by directing a current of oxygen gas into the interior of the flame of an argand-lamp or gas-burner, by which intense combustion is established and a dazzling light obtained. This plan of lighting was adopted in the House of Commons in 1840 and continued till 1852, when another system of lighting was introduced. It was invented by Mr. Gurney of Bude, in Cornwall, and hence the name.

Budg'ell, Eustace, English miscellaneous writer: b. Exeter, 19 Aug. 1686; d. London, 4 May 1736. He was educated at Trinity College, Oxford, went to London, and entered the Inner Temple. He was a relative of Addison, who in 1717, when principal secretary of state in England, procured for Budgell the place of accountant and comptroller-general of the revenue in Ireland. He lost these places when the Duke of Bolton was appointed lord-lieutenant, in 1718, apparently through some dispute. He then returned to England, where, in 1720, he lost $100.000 by the South Sea bubble. In 1733 he commenced a weekly paper, called 'The Bee,' which was very popular. On the death of Tindal, the author of 'Christianity as Old as the Creation,' a will was produced by which $10,000 was left to Budgell. This sum was so disproportionate to the testator's circumstances (his whole estate did not amount to so much), and the legacy so contrary to his known intentions, that suspicions arose respecting the authenticity of the testament; and Budgell's reputation was completely blasted. Ruined in fortune and character, he ended his life by drowning himself in the Thames. He wrote 37 papers in the 'Spectator' signed X.; also others in the 'Guardian,' etc.

Budgerigar', the dealer's name for the Australian grass-parakeet (q.v.). This small parrot has become a common cage-bird in all parts of the world, and goes by a great variety of names, among which "zebra," "shell," and "warbling grass-parakeet" are perhaps the most common.

Budg'et, the annual statement relative to the finances of a country, made by the proper financial functionary, in which is presented a balance sheet of the actual income and expenditure of the past year, and an estimate of the income and expenditure for the coming year, together with a statement of the mode of taxation proposed to meet such expenditure. In the United States the budget is in effect made up in the House of Representatives, to which, at the opening of each congressional session, the secretary of the treasury submits a list of estimates of expenditures for the coming year. Upon these the appropriation bills are based by separate committees. The term "budget," however, is not commonly employed in this country. In England the chancellor of the exchequer sub-

mits to Parliament a yearly statement of necessary governmental expenditures.

Budweis, bood'vĭs (Czech Budejovice), a town of Bohemia, on the navigable Moldau, 133 miles northwest of Vienna by rail. It has a cathedral with a detached belfry dating from about 1550, manufactures of stoneware, porcelain, machines, lead pencils, saltpetre, etc., besides a brisk trade in grain, wood, coal, and salt. In its many educational institutions, including two gymnasia, high, agricultural, trade, industrial, and other schools, instruction is given in both German and Bohemian. In the neighborhood is Schloss Frauenberg (1840-7), the seat of Prince Schwarzenberg. Pop. (1900) 39,400.

Buel, Clarence Clough, American editor and author: b. Laona, Chautauqua County, N. Y., 29 July 1850. He was connected with the New York *Tribune* from 1875 to 1881, when he joined the staff of the 'Century Magazine'; and, in 1883, in conjunction with Robert Underwood Johnson, began the editing of the celebrated 'Century War Articles,' which were afterward expanded into the notable 'Battles and Leaders of the Civil War' (1887).

Bu'el, Samuel, American clergyman: b. Troy, N. Y., 11 June 1815; d. New York, 1 Feb. 1891. He was graduated from Williams College in 1833, and from the General Theological Seminary, New York, in 1837. He was rector successively in Marshall, Mich., Schuylkill Haven, Pa., Cumberland, Md., Poughkeepsie, N. Y., and New York until 1866. From 1866 to 1869 he was professor of ecclesiastical history in the Seabury Divinity School, Faribault, Minn., and professor of divinity there, 1869-71, when he was elected to the chair of systematic divinity and dogmatic theology in the General Theological Seminary, a position which he held until his retirement as professor emeritus in 1888. He wrote 'The Apostolical System of the Church Defended, in a Reply to Dr. Whately on the Kingdom of Christ' (1844); 'Eucharistic Presence, Sacrifice, and Adoration' (1874); 'A Treatise of Dogmatic Theology' (1890); and translated F. H. Reusch's 'Conference at Bonn: Proceedings, August 1875, Between Old Catholics, Orientals, Members of the Anglican and American Churches, from Europe and America' (1876).

Buell, Don Carlos, American military officer: b. Lowell, Ohio, 23 March 1818; d. near Rockport, Ky., 19 Nov. 1898. He was graduated at West Point in 1841, and served in the Mexican war. When the Civil War broke out he was adjutant-general of the regular army, and was made a brigadier-general of volunteers and attached to the Army of the Potomac. In November 1861 he succeeded Gen. W. T. Sherman in command of the department of the Ohio. He resigned from the volunteer service on 23 May 1864, and on 1 June following, also resigned his commission in the regular army. He was president of the Green River (Ky.) Iron Works from 1865 to 1870, when he engaged in coal mining. From 1885 to 1890 he served as United States pension agent at Louisville.

Bu'ell, Marcus Darius, American Methodist clergyman: b. Wayland, N. Y., 1 Jan. 1851. He was graduated at New York University, 1872; studied theology at Boston University, and at the universities of Cambridge, England, and Berlin, Germany, being admitted to the New York East Conference of the Methodist Church, 1875. He was pastor at Portchester, N. Y., Brooklyn, N. Y., and Hartford, Conn., from 1875 to 1884, when he was appointed professor of New Testament Greek and exegesis in Boston University. Since 1889 he has been dean of the theological faculty there. He has written 'Studies in the Greek Text of the Gospel of St. Mark' (1890).

Buen Ayre, hwän i'rä, or Bonaire, a small island off the coast of Venezuela, belonging to the Dutch. It is 50 miles in circumference, and inhabited chiefly by Indians, with a small mixture of Europeans; mountainous; producing a few cattle, goats, large quantities of poultry, and a considerable quantity of salt. It has springs of fresh water. On the southwestern side is a good harbor. Pop. 4,926.

Buena Vista, bwä'na vēs'tä, a village of Mexico, seven miles south of Saltillo, where, on 22-23 Feb. 1847, some 5,000 United States troops, under Taylor, defeated 20,000 Mexicans under Santa Anna. The American army engaged at Buena Vista consisted in large part of volunteers, most of whom had no military experience; and on account of the unequal daring and composure displayed by them at different times the battle would have been lost again and again but for the heroic conduct of the regular artillery. The Americans had taken a strong position on the 21st and were attacked on the 22d, though the main battle did not begin till the 23d, continuing with only slight intermission throughout the day. Santa Anna's attacks were successfully repulsed and on the 24th he was compelled to retreat. The American losses were 746 killed and wounded and the Mexican about 2,000. This battle practically closed the campaign in the north. See MEXICAN WAR. Consult Carleton, 'The Battle of Buena Vista' (1848), Howard, 'Gen. Taylor' (1892).

Buenaventura, bwä-na-vĕn-tū'ra, a seaport of Colombia, on the Bay of Choco, on a small island at the mouth of the Dagua, 200 miles southwest of Santa Fé de Bogota. It is the port of Santa Fé de Bogota, Popayan, and Cali.

Buendia, Juan, hoo-än' bwän'dę-ä, Peruvian general: b. Lima, 1814. He was put in command of the Army of the South in the Chilean war in 1879, and attacked 10,000 Chileans on the heights of San Francisco, 8 November, where he was defeated with terrible loss. He was court-martialed, but freed from blame and afterward served in the defense of Lima.

Buenos Ayres, bwä'nōs i'räs, one of the provinces of Argentina, lying west of the La Plata and Atlantic Ocean, and separated from Patagonia by the Rio Negro. The chief rivers are the Paraná, with its tributary, the Plata River, and the Rio Salado. The province presents nearly throughout level or slightly undulating plains, known as the pampas of Buenos Ayres. They are covered with tall, waving grass, which affords pasture to vast numbers of sheep, cattle, and horses. These constitute the chief wealth of the inhabitants; and their products, along with wheat, are the chief exports. The climate is generally healthy. For judicial purposes the province is divided into four dis-

tricts, and for administrative ones into 100. The capital is La Plata. The executive power resides in a governor and vice-governor, indirectly elected for three years, and the legislative power in a Congress, composed of a Chamber of Deputies of 100 members, biennially elected, and a Senate of 50, elected biennially. The Congress sits from 1 May to 31 August. Pop. about 1,500,000.

Buenos Ayres. Federal capital and principal port of importation and exportation of the Argentine Republic, and the largest of all the cities of the southern hemisphere. From its population (over one million inhabitants in 1906) it occupies the second place among the Latin cities of the world, coming directly after Paris. It is situated 34° 36′ 21″ 4 latitude south, which in the northern hemisphere corresponds to the latitudes of Los Angeles (California) and Yokohama (Japan); its longitude is 58° 21′ 33″ 3, west from Greenwich: it is situated 20 metres above the level of the sea, upon the right bank of the La Plata River, which is at this point about 30 miles wide, and distant 172 miles from its mouth where it empties into the Atlantic Ocean. It is the metropolis, commercially, politically, and socially, of the extreme south of the continent. Distant 5,220 miles from London and 4,370 miles from New York, it is the terminal port for 10 transatlantic lines of steamships which unite it with European ports, and it is also the centre from which radiate 6,600 miles of railroads, which end in Patagonia in the south, and in the west and north connect it with the frontiers of Chile and Bolivia. It is also the principal port for all the river traffic for a distance of 3,400 kilometres (2,250 navigable miles), extending the whole length of the rivers La Plata, Uruguay, Paraná, and tributaries, connecting it with Montevideo, capital of the eastern Republic of Uruguay, and with Ascuncion, capital of Paraguay. Its climate is one of the most changeable in the world, though its annual average temperature corresponds to those of Genoa (Italy); San Francisco (California); Tokyo (Japan); Sydney (New South Wales).

General Topography.—The city is spread out upon a plain on the right bank of the Rio de la Plata. 125 miles west of the city of Montevideo, which lies on the north margin of the estuary. Buenos Ayres extends 11¼ miles from north to south, and 15½ miles from east to west, with a circumference of more than 38 miles.

The plan of the city is quadrangular, similar to a chess-board. In the central part the streets are 32 feet wide and the blocks are 429 feet in length. By municipal regulations the height of the front of the buildings cannot exceed one and one-third times the width of the street. In 1892 the Avenue de Mayo was completed and opened. This avenue is 100 feet wide and a mile and a half long, and divides from east to west the oldest and most densely populated part of the city. It is well paved with asphalt and has in the centre three safety islands, with double electric light posts, facing each block, and a row of plane trees extending the entire length. The buildings along this avenue vary in materials and in the number of stories. At the extreme eastern end it opens upon the Plaza de Mayo with an area of more than four acres, beautified with trees and flanked with public buildings;—the "Casa Rosada" ("Pink House") or Executive Palace, the old House of Congress, the Commercial Exchange, the Cathedral, the municipal buildings, the "Bank of the Nation," and other establishments of importance. At the extreme western end is the recently inaugurated Palace of Congress, of monumental proportions, which cost $6,000,000.

The district of the Boca (about 100,000 inhabitants) in the city of Buenos Ayres, upon the left bank of the Riachuelo, and the district of Avellaneda (12,000 inhabitants) in front of Barracas to the south, upon the right bank, in the jurisdiction of the Province of Buenos Ayres, are united by a draw-bridge and other similar devices, and the people living there are for the most part occupied in the traffic of the harbor, and represent a business capital of $150,000,000 invested in this traffic. Moreover, the railroads to the west and to the south, which assist in this traffic, represent a capital of $201,-500,000.

Harbors, Wharves, Markets, etc.—The location of the city, owing to the shallowness of the river, demanded the construction of an extensive harbor. Its facilities are as follows:—inner harbor, comprising the north and south basins and docks and the Boca del Riachuelo; outer harbor, comprising the outer roads and channels through which shipping enters; the south channel, 11 miles long, having a depth of 17 to 22 feet; and the north channel, with a depth of from 20 to 23 feet. Both channels are 350 feet wide at entrance and marked by buoys. This harbor was built in 11 years (from 1886 to 1897) and cost $35,000,000 gold. It covers a superficial area of 165 acres and consists of two canals (about 21 feet deep), one from the entrance and the other from the outlet (both provided with luminous buoys), which nevertheless do not satisfy the demands of traffic; two shipyards, four docks, and two dry docks; 24 warehouses with a capacity, roughly estimated, of 20,000,000 cubic feet, which can hold 2,400,-000 tons of merchandise, and which extend for 1½ miles fronting the wharves, the latter having a length of 6 miles (the same length as the harbor of Antwerp). It has grain elevators whose capacity amounts to 200,000 tons. Within the circumference of the harbor are 3½ miles of railroad. The wharf for animals on foot has room for 40,000 sheep and more than 1,500 beeves.

The Boca del Riachuelo has a depth of 18 feet and is bordered by wharves for 3 miles, and has a movement of 1,200,000 tons of merchandise per annum.

Facing these wharves on the right bank is the "Central Fruit Market," the largest warehouse in the world; it occupies an area equal to nine square blocks in New York. The cost of its construction was $4,155,000. In the year 1904 it stored 188,930 tons of wool, hides, and other products of the cattle industry. It is the principal exchange for all business pertaining to the exportation of the fruits of the country.

The southern railroad has its own dock, on the right bank of the Boca del Riachuelo, 23 feet deep, with 1½ miles of wharves, for the exportation of agricultural and cattle products from the southern part of the Province of Buenos Ayres.

Commerce.—Compared with the principal harbors of the world, the harbor of Buenos Ayres stands in eleventh place, and is second after New York in foreign commerce in all America. In 1905 there entered and cleared 27,279 steamships and sailing vessels, with a total register of 10,771,947 tons. At the time of its greatest activity, the port harbors as many as 1,400 steamships and sailing vessels moving in and out. In 1904 the general movement of passengers was 142,525 outgoing, and 241,971 arriving, making an increase from immigration of 100,000 persons (exactly 99,446). The harbor of Buenos Ayres receives 84 per cent. of the importations for the entire country, and sends away 51 per cent. of the national exports. About $17,000,000 are to be spent in enlarging and widening this harbor to enable it to meet the expected development of commerce of the city and of the industries of the country.

Parks.—Buenos Ayres has 79 parks and squares, with an area of 2,320 acres, one of the finest park systems in the world; the Zoo is one of the largest and the best kept in the whole continent; the Botanical Garden is only second to Rio Janeiro's; squares, with profusion of flowers and handsome trees, are beautified with monuments to heroes of the Independence.

Schools, Libraries, etc.—As in many other cities the school buildings do not have the needed space for games and outdoor activities such as school gardening, etc. Already it is a thought that the school buildings to be erected in the future should be located in the centre of the parks and public gardens, as in Japan. The school buildings in Buenos Ayres, with much ornamented façades, are quite unfitted for their purpose, having not the proper accommodations in the interior; Italian architects imported the scheme of treating the façade as a mere screen, disregarding modern hygienic exigencies for educational plants. In 1904 there were 238 public schools in which 117,483 scholars were enrolled. There were 2,973 teachers (2,050 women) in the elementary grades. The number of pupils from 6 to 14 years of age was 188,271, there now being only 15 per cent. illiterate against 20 per cent. in 1895. In the secondary institutions of instruction (except the normal) 2,638 pupils were enrolled. The number of attendants in the seven normal schools of the city was 2,282, and a business college counted 668 pupils. The university has 2,380 students. The public libraries were consulted by 35,358 persons and possessed 48,876 books.

Press.—More than 200 newspapers are published in the city of Buenos Ayres,—most of them in Spanish: but some are in Italian, English, French, Scandinavian, Russian, Hebrew, and Arabic. "La Nacion" and "La Prensa" have a daily circulation of over 100,000 copies and have the most extensive telegraph services in the world. "La Prensa" is a kind of institutional newspaper. The beautiful building, one of the handsomest in the city, is endowed to social services, and contains library, free evening schools for commerce and for music, offices for free medical assistance, free legal aid, free chemical laboratory, etc. "La Nacion" is entering the same line.

Sanitation.—The sanitary system (running water and sewers) is excellent and has cost the city $46,875,180. When in 1875 these works were proposed, there had been few years that

1. Plaza de Mayo (May Square). Showing City Hall and Catholic Cathedral.
2. Plaza de Mayo (May Square). Showing Government House.

the city had not suffered through terrible epidemics, cholera morbus in 1865 and 1873, and yellow fever in 1871. Since 1885, thanks to the extension of these works of sanitation, to the efforts of the Board of Health in the inspection of foods, and the struggle against tuberculosis and other contagious diseases, the mortality has been reduced from 44 per 1,000 in 1875 to 22.7 in 1894 and to 14.2 in 1906. There has likewise been a considerable reduction in the death rate of infants under one year of age, which in 1889 was 195 for each 1,000 born, and dropped to 141 in 1894, to 102 in 1899, and to 83 in 1904. In the same year the proportion in Christiania was 100, 111 in Paris, 146 in London, 162 in New York, 166 in Hamburg, and 202 in Berlin. The birth rate in Buenos Ayres is 33.5 per cent. and has diminished rapidly from 35 per cent. in 1903, 37 per cent. in 1902, 39.5 per cent. in 1901, 41 per cent. in 1899, 44.5 per cent. in 1893 and 46 per cent. in 1891.

The sewage of the city is handled by the circulating or dynamic sewage system. Drainage works costing over $35,000,000 discharge into the estuary of La Plata near Quilmes, 15.5 miles southeast of Buenos Ayres.

Another question which occupies the Argentine hygienists is to find a type of sanitary dwelling which will correspond to the change of customs and to the increase of population. Buenos Ayres is the only city in the world with buildings suited to a mild climate which suddenly had to face modern conditions demanding a congested population and the rapid distribution of a heavy traffic, resulting from its being an important seaport. As they are now, the city blocks are not adapted to meet these demands. They have an area of more than four acres and there is no provision for an empty space in the centre. Therefore, the city lots are too long, the houses receiving light and air from a court or *patio*, which in the case of a many-story building does not provide for either. Besides, long houses do not afford privacy or comfort and are heated with difficulty—a serious detriment in a city where the temperature falls as low as 28° F., together with great moisture in the air.

Public Utilities.—The principal streets are lighted with electric lights, are well paved with asphalt, blocks of wood and granite, and are kept in good repair, cleaned, and sprinkled. The internal business of the city is very considerable. In 1904 there were 315 miles of street car lines, of which 166 miles were electric and 149 miles were horse-car lines; the latter power is gradually being exchanged for electric traction. During the year 1905 there were constructed 111½ kilometres of electric roads. In 1905 the street railroads carried 171,243,538 passengers, 22,262,849 more than during the previous year. In 1905 there were 19,248 carts, 5,126 carriages, of which 2,300 were for hire, and 300 automobiles. 125 more than in 1904. In 1904 the five railroad stations handled 13,-734,238 passengers and 3,566,998 tons of merchandise. The post-office handled 83,104,000 letters and 76,062,000 packages and pamphlets.

Water required for general purposes is drawn from the estuary five miles above the city. The water works consist of two tunnels, subfluvial and subterranean, 18,702 feet in length, with two pumps capable of raising 6,073,320 cubic feet of water to a height of 49.2 feet every 24 hours. The filtered water is carried to a central reservoir at the highest point in the city. This distributing reservoir is provided with forcing pumps having three distinct flows: there are 12 tanks, elevated in groups one above another at 39.3, 55.7, and 72.1 feet respectively. It is the most noticeable iron construction in the city; 16,000 tons of iron were used in building it. The exterior is of pressed brick and vitrified tiles and presents a very handsome architectural appearance. The annual consumption of water is 11,000,000 gallons or a daily average of 33.5 gallons per capita.

The telephone service is very deficient. In 1903 it had 6,500 subscribers and had connections with the cities of La Plata (38 miles), Rosario (186 miles), and by cable with Montevideo (125 miles).

Industries.—Buenos Ayres is not especially industrial. There are not more than 90,000 workmen in its factories and workshops, where they work hides, wood, metals, clay for bricks, chemical products, constructive materials, manufactures pertaining to lights, furniture, carpets and hangings, clothes, preserved foods, etc.; and this production is stimulated by the protection of the custom-house, in spite of which Buenos Ayres is well supplied with articles made in Europe and America. According to the last industrial census taken in 1904 in the city of Buenos Ayres, there were 8,877 industrial establishments as follows:

Industries	Capital	Value of Output	Employees		Motors—H. P.
			Men	Women	
Food	$8,000,000	$16,000,000	6,184	234	3,713
Building........	3,900,000	7,500,000	7,873	..	2,643
Clothing and toilette........	8,000,000	14,500,000	10,711	4,739	1,640
Wood, furniture, etc.....	3,750,000	6,000,000	6,035	280	1,064
Metals..........	6,350,000	5,000,000	7,936	96	1,976
Arts and ornaments........	1,700,000	2,000,000	1,722	151	383
Graphic arts...	3,300,000	3,500,000	3,684	259	882
Textiles and leather	7,200,000	15,000,000	5,393	5,084	4,315
Chemicals......	1,600,000	3,000,000	1,644	849	787
Various	5,500,000	18,500,000	4,253	1,383	2,555
Total........	$49,300,000	$91,000,000	55,435	13,077	19,858

Banking, Finance, etc.—Buenos Ayres supports 16 banks of discount with a joint capital of $80,000,000. Of those 10 are foreign and represent all the principal places of the world except New York, notwithstanding that in 1905 the business transacted with the United States amounted to $44,637,901, having increased 110 per cent. during the last 5 years; all of this business had to be done through London banks. In 1904 the Bolsa de Comercio (Chamber of Commerce) transacted business to the amount of $174,061,251, and the Clearing House passed through $2,875,924,788.35. The municipal taxes amounted to $7,500,000. 41 per cent. of which is devoted to loans for new undertakings, 29 per cent. for direct taxes, and 11½ per cent. for indirect taxes.

In 1904 landed property was sold to the value of $42,500,000, against $26,000,000 in 1903 and

$19,800,000 in 1902. The value of buildings constructed in 1904 amounted to $12,000,000. In 1904 there were transfers of real estate amounting to $42,240,000. There were 133 fires with a loss of $366,000. The insurance paid was $1,100,000. During the first semester of 1906 the Minister of Justice recognized the authorized agents of 55 miscellaneous societies, with a joint capital of $44,000,000.

Population, Social Conditions, etc.—The census of 1869 gave the population of Buenos Ayres as 187,346 inhabitants, and prophesied 900,000 for 1919; in 1895 it had 663,854 and in December 1906 had reached 1,111,000. The increase has been at the rate of 40 per cent. in a decade (inferior alone to Chicago). Buenos Ayres has more than 440,000 foreign residents, of whom 230,000 are Italians, 105,000 Spanish, 28.000 French, 6,000 English, and 6,000 German. The greater part of the landowners of the Province of Buenos Ayres and the Pampas prefer to live in the city of Buenos Ayres, enjoying the rent of their land or hoping that the improvements on their neighbors' lands will increase the value of their own. In this respect, that province and this territory are to the city of Buenos Ayres what Ireland has been to London. Because of this and because the city is the seat of the national government. also because of the many commercial establishments engaged in foreign trade, Buenos Ayres is a centre, where the light and splendor of a great capital never die out. It has 20 theatres where in the single season of 1905 appeared Saint-Saëns, Puccini, Sara Bernhardt, Coquelin, Rejane, Tina di Lorenzo, Jeanne Hading, Novelli, Caruso, etc. Nevertheless, this wealth, which is the result of the absenteeism above referred to, retards the progress of the country districts and gives birth to a close, feudal plutocracy. Such a social condition is not best fitted to call forth a truly democratic public spirit. However, the spirit of association commences to enjoy a broader outlook, there being a constant increase in the number of educational and civic associations whose object is to make all classes participate in social well-being. The charitable institutions are disposed more and more to abandon their cut-and-dried methods, and instead of lessening the effects of poverty, they endeavor to prevent its causes through a collective social crusade, hoping that before long a law against child-labor will be passed and that model reformatories and juvenile courts will be established to better the condition of children.

In 1904 there were 5,110 persons in the asylums. The free municipal lodging house gave lodging and board to 41,578 persons. the Salvation Army to 40,305. the French Charity Association to 5,046. The criminals arrested in 1904 for each 1,000 inhabitants from 15 to 70 years of age, were divided as to nationality as follows:—German 4.23; Argentine, 8.70; Spanish, 8.26; French, 3.40; English, 4.93; Italians, 6.61; Uraguayan, 8.65. The criminals of the decade 1895-1904 are divided according to ages thus: less than 16 years, 8 per cent.; from 16 to 20 years, 17 per cent.; from 21 to 25, 22.5 per cent.; from 26 to 30, 18.7 per cent.; from 31 to 35, 12.9 per cent.; from 36 to 40, 9.1 per cent.; from 41 to 45, 5.2 per cent.; from 46 to 50, 3.2 per cent.; from 51 to 60, 2.4 per cent.; over 60, 0.8 per cent. The number of suicides was 239, the causes being as follows;—family quarrels, 18.5 per cent.; tired of life, 13.4 per cent.; physical suffering, 12.5 per cent.; crossed in love, 5.4 per cent.

In 1895 there were 929 births for each 10,-000 foreign women. In 1895 for each 10,000 foreign women from 15 to 50 years of age were born 929 children of a foreign mother; and for each 10,000 Argentine women were born 1,926 children, or it may be a share of 1,605 for each 10,000 women of the entire birth rate. In 1904 these figures decreased to 850, 1,300, and 1,403 respectively. In 1904 there were 74 marriages and 146 deaths for each 10,000 inhabitants.

Government.—The communal government of the city is a kind of government by commission, composed of an Intendente and a deliberating council appointed by the national executive authority. The amount of expenditures for the year 1905 was $8,126,660.

As is evident, it can hardly be said that Buenos Ayres enjoys self-government, strictly speaking. Nevertheless the government possesses considerable prestige, resembling in this respect an aristocratic city. For this reason the public employees seek for the reward of public opinion, and it has been said that there is not a city in the world where so much is accomplished for the same amount of money. On the other hand, as a consequence of paternal government, apathy is to be found in furthering official action. The *Asistencia Publica*, or Board of Health. can truly be called the best in the world. The 18 hospitals are well kept, many in very appropriate buildings. The sale of food in the 35 markets of the city is scrupulously controlled.

JUAN A. SENILLOSA,
Former Argentine Consul General to Canada.

Buenos Ayres, University of (Universidad Nacional de Buenos Aires), the national university of Argentina and the largest institution of learning in South America. Its students number nearly 2,380, and its courses cover law and government, mathematics, science, and philosophy.

Buff, a mixed color, something between pale pink and pale yellow. It was adopted by the English Whig party, in combination with blue, as their distinctive color; and, possibly in consequence of that circumstance, the Whig party having been opposed throughout to all the measures of government which led to the American Revolution, was chosen as the national uniform of the Americans at the opening of the Revolutionary War.

Buff Leather, a leather prepared by saturating the hides with some aluminous substance, and afterward with oil. Leather prepared in this way is softer and more flexible than any other kind, and on that account it is much used for soldiers' cross-belts, gloves, and other military accoutrements. Its color is naturally light yellow, but it is in some cases bleached before being used. The buff leather used in former times to make the jerkins, worn under coats of mail to deaden the pressure of the metal on the body, and to prevent any contusion from a blow, was made from the hide of the urus, or wild bull of central Europe, the common name of which was buffe, whence the name of the leather was derived.

THE HARBOR OF RIO.

MAY AVENUE, BUENOS AIRES.

The Government House is in the distance. The street's pavement is of Trinidad asphalt laid by an American Company

Buffalmacco, boo-fal-mäk'kŏ (assumed name of BUONAMICO CHRISTOFANI), Italian painter who flourished according to Vasari during the first half of the 14th century. The same authority attributes to him the frescoes depicting the Passion in the hall of the Campo Santo in Pisa, and states that he worked in Arezzo, Florence, Bologna, and Cortona. He is mentioned by Boccaccio in the 'Decameron.'

Buffalo Bill. See CODY, WILLIAM F.

Buffalo, N. Y., county-seat of Erie County, the second city in the State and eighth in the United States; situated at the eastern end of Lake Erie and on its outlet the Niagara River. Its centre is 24 miles south of Niagara Falls, and its important suburbs, the Tonawandas, are half-way between. It lies due west 297 miles by rail from Albany and 499 from Boston; northwest 425 miles from New York, and 417 from Philadelphia; about 410 southwest of Montreal; and 540 east of Chicago. It is, therefore, about a midway point from the East to Chicago. It extends about 10 miles along the lake and river front, and half as far east; area, 42 square miles.

Buffalo, which began at the mouth of Buffalo Creek, has spread mainly north and east up a gradual rise, to a great plateau some 80 feet above the lake and 620 above sea-level. It is laid out in wide rectangular streets, beautifully shaded and decorated with shrubbery, and more completely than any other city in the world: No less than 335 miles of its over 700 miles of streets are asphalted, 105 are stone-paved, and many more are macadamized. The chief business streets are Main, running north and northeast from the lake to the city limits; Delaware Avenue, parallel with it; Niagara, north and northwest along the lake and river front to Tonawanda; and Broadway, which with Genesee and Sycamore widen spoke-like from the heart of the business district around Lafayette and Niagara Squares. Each of these is several miles long. The finest residence streets are Delaware Avenue and North Street, crossing it at right angles a mile north of the centre; they are set with large separate mansions, with great lawns, gardens, and shrubberies, a fashion followed in the new residence streets to the north.

Municipal Service and Improvements.— The street cleaning and sprinkling services, costing $180,000 a year, and the garbage collection, costing $110,000, are notably efficient; the sewage collected through over 420 miles of mains is emptied into Niagara River and carried swiftly away; the first public bath house erected in New York State under the law of 1895 was opened here in 1897. All these things, with the cool summer climate which attracts many visitors, enable Buffalo to claim the distinction of being the cleanest and healthiest city in the United States, its death rate in 1900 being 14.8 and in 1901 12.25. The waterworks, built in 1888, are supplied from the lake; they cost $9,100,000, and are owned by the city; the reservoirs have a storage capacity of 200,000,000 gallons a day, the average consumption is about 100,000,000, and there are over 500 miles of mains; the service costs $650,000 a year. Electric lighting is almost universal in business houses and the finer residences, from the cheap power furnished by Niagara Falls. The police department numbers 785 men, with 13 stations

and a harbor patrol steamer, and costs nearly $800,000 a year. The fire department has 26 steam fire engines, 6 chemical engines, and 23 hose companies, with three fire boats, the latest systems of storage and signal boxes, and 498 men; the cost is $675,000 a year. An important municipal improvement has been the transfer of telegraph and telephone, police, and fire-alarm wires, from overhead poles to subways. The street-car service of Buffalo was the first in the United States to equip itself with electricity, and to give free transfers; it has seven companies, and covers over 200 miles of line, extending to all the suburbs, down the river to Niagara Falls, and across it to Canada. More than 50 miles of the track is in the city, which has also a steam belt line of the N. Y. C. along the lake and river front, and west and north to above Delaware Park.

Public Parks and Cemeteries.— The park system includes six large parks of 1,149 acres in all, connected by a magnificent system of boulevards, parkways, speedways, and approaches, covering 224 acres, and 74 acres of minor places and squares. Much the largest is Delaware Park, on the north side, of 362 acres, with a lake ("Gala Water") of 46½ acres in the western part; here and in the adjacent grounds the Pan-American Exposition of 1901 was held. It is continued by Forest Lawn Cemetery of 239 acres on the south —by far the greatest of the 26 cemeteries of the city, and containing the monuments to the Indian chief Red Jacket and to President Fillmore — and by the fine grounds of the State Insane Hospital, with 203 acres, on the west. On the southeast is Humboldt Park of 56 acres. Overlooking the lake at the river entrance is "The Front," a bold bluff 60 feet high, and the site of Fort Porter, where several companies of United States soldiery are stationed. The Parade Ground here has 48 acres, and is a favorite promenade from its superb view. On the south side of the creek are South Park, 155 acres, Cazenovia Park, 106 acres, Riverside Park, 22 acres, and Stony Point Park, 22½ acres, on the lake front. There are several attractive parks and squares in the centre of the city, among them Lafayette, Niagara, Franklin, Washington, and Delaware. Lafayette contains the Soldiers 'and Sailors' Monument, costing $50,000.

Chief Buildings.— Among the many fine structures in the city, the first place must be given to Ellicott Square, the largest and most magnificently equipped fireproof office building in the world; it occupies an entire block, and contains over 400,000 feet of floor space, or over nine acres, with 16 elevators. Of the others, besides churches, cathedrals, and institutional buildings mentioned elsewhere, the most notable are the two handsome buildings preserved from the Exposition — the Albright Art Gallery, and the New York State Building, housing the Buffalo Historical Society; the new Federal Building, containing the post-office and the custom-house, a large freestone structure which cost $2,000,000; the city and county hall on Franklin Street, of granite, in the shape of a Latin cross, with a tower 245 feet high, completed in 1880 at a cost of about $1,400,000; the Music Hall and the Board of Trade building, both noble edifices; the State Arsenal; the Old and New Armories; the Masonic Temple and Y. M. C. A. building; the Grosvenor Library; the

Normal School and the three High Schools; the Erie County and Buffalo Savings Banks; the Erie County Penitentiary; and the mammoth grain elevators.

Trade and Commerce.— Buffalo's position as the eastern terminal of the commerce of the Great Lakes, and the distributing point from the East to its ports, has made it the greatest city built up on them except Chicago and Cleveland, and one of the great world-ports in the volume and variety of produce trans-shipped, although ice-bound for one third of the year. In 1902, 4,781 vessels arrived at this port, with a gross tonnage of over 6,000,000; and the customs receipts were over $900,000. Naturally, its foremost handlings are of western produce, grain, flour, provisions, and live stock; its average annual receipts of grain, though varying with the crop, are about 150,000,000 bushels, of ·flour 14,000,000 barrels. Next to this is its live-stock business; it handles more horses and sheep than any other American port, and ranks among the first in cattle and swine. It receives some 15,000,000 pounds of fish yearly, largely from Georgian Bay off Lake Huron, and sends it to ·inland parts not only East, but as far west as the Rocky Mountains. Lumber is another immense interest, its receipts amounting from 150,000,000 to 250,000,000 feet a year; and it receives some 1,500,000 tons of iron ore. Of these last two a large part goes to Tonawanda, whose business, however, is really part of Buffalo's. The coal traffic is also enormous: some 10,000,000 tons are received yearly by rail, two thirds anthracite, of which about 3,000,000, nearly all anthracite, is shipped westward by water. About 100,000 tons of salt are among its exports, and nearly $10,000,000 worth of packed meat. The total export trade is now over $16,000,000 a year.

This immense development has been made possible by a vast co-operation of United States, State, and municipality in facilities for handling the business — breakwaters, stone piers, basins, canals, railroads, etc. Originally, as with all the lake ports, the harborage was only the shallow mouth of a small river, Buffalo Creek, navigable now for two miles inward. But the government has built a great series of stone and cement breakwaters, four miles long, costing over $2,000,000, and forming an inner and an outer harbor, the best on the lakes; this is extended to Stony Point, four miles above the mouth of the creek. The State has built Erie Basin, with a breakwater and stone docks, at the end of Erie Canal just below the mouth of the creek; and the city has deepened the creek and built a ship canal two miles long between it and the lake, one of two such, at the end of which are the Lehigh coal docks. No less than 16 steamship and steamboat lines run from Buffalo to different points on the lakes, besides summer excursion routes. The Welland Canal about 20 miles west, across the neck of land between Erie and Ontario, connects it with the latter and the St. Lawrence. The Erie Canal makes a waterway through the heart of the State to the Hudson River. As to railroads, it is the terminal of the main line or some spur of every trunk road from Philadelphia to Quebec: from the east, in the United States, the New York Central, main line and West Shore; Erie; Lehigh Valley; Delaware, Lackawanna & Western; Pennsylvania; Buffalo, Rochester & Pittsburg;

Buffalo & Susquehanna; from the west, the Lake Shore & Michigan Southern; Michigan Central; New York, Chicago & St. Louis; Wabash; from Canada, Canadian Pacific; Grand Trunk; Canada Southern. There are 250 passenger trains a day; 700 miles of railroad track within the city limits, and six of the city's square miles are owned by the railroads. To the Canada side at Fort Erie and Bridgeburg there are several ferry lines, and the great International Bridge from Squaw Island to Bridgeburg, completed in 1873 at a cost of $1,500,000. The internal conveniences for carrying on this traffic are correspondent. There are nearly 50 grain elevators, fixed and floating and transfer towers, with a storage capacity of 28,000,000 bushels, and able to take care of 5,000,000 bushels a day. Some of these are among the largest in the world; the chief one, the Great Northern, with a capacity of 3,000,000 bushels. The first elevator in the world was built here in 1843. The largest coal pocket in the world is that of the D., L. & W. here, 5,000 feet long; the coal docks can handle 29,000 tons a day; the railroad coal-stocking trestles are in the east part. Their stock yards, 75 acres in extent, are in East Buffalo.

Manufactures.— Two great advantages of Buffalo in manufacturing are natural gas, for which the city has laid mains; and the electric power furnished from Niagara, whose tunnels are within 20 miles. At present, about 50,000 persons are employed in manufacturing industries in the city, in 4,000 establishments. By the census of 1900, the figures were: Establishments, 3,962; capital, $103,939,655; employees, 476,902; wages paid, $19,915,817; cost of materials, $73,359,466; value of products, $122,230,061. The principal industries apart from food, mason, and carpenter work, tinsmithing and jobbing, etc., were — wholesale slaughtering and meat packing, $9,631,187; foundry and machine-shop products, $6,816,057, — but to this should be added iron and steel, architectural and ornamental iron work, and hardware, $3,685,063, making a total of $10,501,120, for iron products altogether, or the most important single branch; the Lackawanna Steel Company, capitalized at $40,000,000, has the largest and most capacious individual plant in the world, with a separate breakwater a mile long and a capacious private harbor — linseed oil, $6,271,170, partly used in its $753,519 of paint making; malt and malt liquors, $6,229,940; railroad cars, $4,553,333; soap and candles, $3,818,571; flour and grist-mill products, $3,263,697; planing-mill products, $3,095,760; factory-made clothing, $3,067,723; chemicals, $1,939,378; patent medicines and compounds, $1,855,808; leather and leather goods, $1,756,084; factory-made furniture, $1,644,671; besides over $1,000,000 each of carriages and confectionery, and large quantities of jewelry, saddlery and harness, tobacco products, and other articles, embracing some 200 different industries in all. Notice should be taken of fine printing, lithographing, and engraving, in which Buffalo ranks high artistically.

Finances and Banking.— The assessed valuation of the city has increased in 30 years from about $38,000,000 to over $250,000,000, nearly all real estate, with a tax rate of 17.12. The bonded debt is some $16,000,000, with an annual interest charge of about $650,000; but there is a sinking fund of about $1,250,000, and the city owns property valued at about $21,000,000. Also,

MAP OF
BUFFALO

of this debt $3,754,382 is for water bonds, on which an income is earned. The city expenses are some $6,000,000 a year. The post-office receipts are over $1,000,000 yearly, and the internal-revenue receipts about $2,000,000. There are nine banks of discount (five national), with about $8,000,000 capital and surplus and $45,000,000 deposits; two trust companies, with $1,400,000 capital and surplus; and four savings banks, with over $35,000,000 deposits and $6,000,000 surplus.

Churches.— Buffalo is the seat of a Roman Catholic and of an Episcopal bishop, and has two handsome and impressive cathedrals; the Catholic cathedral being a Gothic structure of blue stone trimmed with white, and has a set of 42 chimes. Besides these there are 37 Catholic churches, 13 chapels, and 12 convents; and 171 Protestant, besides 16 missions and chapels, the most numerous being the Methodist Episcopal (24 English, 3 German), Baptist (25 churches and 5 missions), Lutheran (13 German, 5 English, 3 Scandinavian), Presbyterian (18), Protestant Episcopal (16, with 11 missions), and German United Evangelical (15). There are also nine synagogues. Of the church buildings, besides the cathedrals, the most notable are Trinity (Episcopal) and the First Presbyterian.

Charities.— There are 12 children's refuges in Buffalo, and 9 homes and refuges for adults; besides a S. P. C. C. and S. P. C. A., and many religious associations for relieving distress; 18 hospitals, besides the United States Marine Hospital; the Erie County almshouse; lodging and supply stations for the temporary relief of the indigent; a city physician, a district nursing association, and diet kitchens; a German Y. M. A. and the Y. M. C. A.; and a Women's Educational and Industrial Union. Of the children's institutions, the most notable is the free Fitch Institute for poor children, a combined orphanage, crèche — day nursery for children of poor working mothers — training school for nursemaids, etc.; all managed by the Charity Organization Society (organized 1877, the first in the United States), with its home in the building. Of the other institutions, special note may be made of the Buffalo Orphan Asylum, St. John's Orphan Home, the Home for the Friendless, St. Vincent's and St. Joseph's orphanages (Roman Catholic), St. Mary's Asylum for Widows and Foundlings and St. Mary's Institution for Deaf Mutes, the Church Home for Aged Women, and the Ingleside Home for Erring Women.

Education and Intellectual Associations.— The city in 1903 had 67 grammar schools, with about 100 school buildings, some 1,300 teachers, and an average attendance of about 60,000; a truant school; 33 Catholic parochial schools, with an estimated attendance of some 20,000; two high schools, third one building — the Central with two annexes, and the Masten Park — with attendance of some 2,400; 25 private schools and academies; and some 20 free kindergartens (partly in connection with the schools), orphan-asylum schools, etc. Of the higher institutions, the chief is Buffalo University, organized in 1845, with affiliated law, medical, and dentistry schools, and a cancer laboratory, 80 professors, and 700 students; others are Niagara University, Canisius' (1870) and St. Joseph's Colleges, the Academy of the Sacred Heart and Holy Angels' Academy (the last four Catholic), the German Martin Luther Seminary (Evangelical Lutheran, 1854), and the Buffalo College of Pharmacy. All the hospitals have training schools for nurses. The Fine Arts Academy (1862) is located in the public library building; the Buffalo Historical Society (1862), with interesting relics and a large library, in the former New York State Building of the Exposition of 1901, now belonging to the society; the Buffalo Society of Natural Science (1861), with a valuable museum of natural history, in the Buffalo Library building. There are many other art and literary associations; 8 dramatic and 13 musical clubs, besides 23 social clubs; and 8 theatres.

Libraries.— The two chief ones are the Buffalo Public Library, installed in a handsome new building in 1897, with about 175,000 books and 16,000 pamphlets; and the Grosvenor, for reference only, with 65,000 books and 4,000 pamphlets. Besides these, there are many institutional, private, and special libraries: the chief being that of the Historical Society, with 12,000 volumes and 23,000 pamphlets; others are the Lord Library of 5,000 volumes in the same building; the State Law Library, with about 15,000 volumes; the Catholic Institute, with over 11,500 volumes and 500 pamphlets; the Medical Library of the University, with 6,000 volumes; the Lutheran and the German Y. M. A., the Polish and the Adam Mickiewicz, the North Buffalo Catholic Association and the St. Michael's Y. M. Sodality, the Erie Railway Employees' Association, the Harugari, etc.

Newspapers.— In 1903 there were published in Buffalo 88 regular periodicals: 11 dailies, 31 weeklies, 6 Sunday, 2 fortnightly, 35 monthly, and 3 quarterly.

Government.— A four-years' mayor; an alderman from each of the 25 wards, and nine councilmen at large; a city clerk appointed by the council, and health, fire, park, police, and civil-service boards appointed by the mayor; the remaining officials elected by the people.

Population.—In steadiness of rapid growth, Buffalo ranks among the foremost of American cities. It first appears in the census in 1820, with 2,095; 1830, 8,668; 1840, 18,213; 1850, 42,261; 1860, 81,129; 1870, 117,714; 1880, 155,134; 1890, 255,664; 1900, 352,387; 1903, about 385,000. It will be noticed that the last 20 years have brought a great increase instead of decrease in its rate of development, and there are no signs of falling off. In 1890 it was eleventh, in 1900 eighth, among our cities; and as it was twin with New York for third in rate of growth among cities of 300,000 and over, it may rise higher yet. The foreign-born population numbered 104,252, or 29.6 per cent; the native-born of foreign parents, 155,716; and only 90,860 of its people, or little over one fourth, were native whites of native parentage. Of the foreign-born, about 50,000, or nearly half, were German, 13,000 being Polish-German Jews; 11,000 were Irish; but 23,400 were Englishmen from England or Canada, which should be added to the citizenship of English blood. In 1878, of all children born in the city, 1,975 were of German descent, against 2,056 of all other descents.

History.— The site of Buffalo was originally a basswood forest, amid which an Indian tribe, the Kahkwas, between the Neutrals and the Eries, hunted and fished along the creek; it was exterminated by the Iroquois before 1651, and not a single Indian lived there again for more than a century and a quarter. In 1679 La Salle passed the spot in his 60-ton sloop the Griffin, the first sailing vessel ever on Lake Erie, built at Cayuga Creek below. In 1687 the Baron La Houtan recommended it to the French government as the proper site for a fort to command the fur trade down the Niagara, and marked a "fort supposé" on his map; but no attention was paid to him. In 1764 Col. Bradstreet built Fort Erie across the river on his Indian campaign. In 1780 the Senecas, driven from their old haunts by Sullivan's campaign, settled along the creek inland; the next winter an English family captive among them heard them call the creek by a name they translated "Buffalo," — whether rightly or not is disputed, but probably enough the herds had sought the salt-licks to the east. Their narrative was published in 1784, and in the treaty of Fort Stanwix that year between the English and the Iroquois, the name was used as familiar to the latter. The Indian settlement soon became known as "the village on the Buffalo," currently shortened to "Buffalo village," and presently to "Buffalo," without any official sanction. The land had formed part of the grant of James I. to the Plymouth Company in 1625, and that of Charles II. to the Duke of York in 1664. The consequent dispute between Massachusetts and New York was compromised in 1786, and ultimately the Holland Company of aliens became patentees in trust in 1792, and by legislative permission owners in fee in 1798. Meantime a few settlers had straggled in; a trader named Cornelius Winne in 1789; two families in 1794 and 1796; and in 1797, when there were half a dozen houses, the first white child was born, a girl. A number of others took up residence there by 1803. In that year, by the advice of their surveyor, Joseph Ellicott, the founder of Buffalo, who had assisted his brother Andrew in laying out the city of Washington, and was convinced that here was the site of another great city, the company had him plot a village, and in 1804 sold the first lots. He called it New Amsterdam, and named the streets after the members of the company, but the settlers disregarded all his names and his oxbow line for Main Street, where his own mansion was to be. In 1810 the town of Buffalo was incorporated, including several now separate townships. In 1811 the first newspaper, the Buffalo Gazette, was established. In 1813 Buffalo village was incorporated, and received a new charter in 1822. In the War of 1812, after the storming of Fort Niagara by the British in December, a force of British and Indians under Gen. Riall was detailed to destroy Black Rock and Buffalo; on the 29th captured the latter, and the next day burned all but seven or eight houses, coming back 1 January and burning all but three of the rest. The settlers re-occupied their homes to some extent on the 6th, but it was not generally rebuilt till 1815; on 10 April 1814 Gen. Scott put it under military rule. In 1818 the first steamer, Walk-in-the-Water, was launched. For many years, however, supremacy was balanced between it and Black Rock down the river, now the northern part of the city, where at that time was the ferry across the Niagara to the Canada side; but in 1825, after a fierce struggle, the former secured the terminal of the Erie Canal, and in five years

its 2,412 inhabitants had grown to over 8,000, and its future was assured. Long after, however, able capitalists invested heavily in Dunkirk, 48 miles south, in faith that it and not Buffalo was the coming lake port. In 1832, it became a city, and the next year it annexed Black Rock. Buffalo has given two Presidents to the United States, Millard Fillmore and Grover Cleveland, the latter its mayor in 1882. From 1 May to 1 Nov. 1901, the Pan-American Exposition was held here, and on 6 September President McKinley was shot while attending it.

See publications of the Buffalo Historical Society; Smith, 'History of the City of Buffalo and Erie County' (1884); Ketchum, 'History of Buffalo' (1864-5); Powell, 'Historic Towns of the Middle States' (1899).

EDWARD H. BUTLER,
Editor Buffalo Evening News.

Buffalo, a name frequently misapplied to the American bison, but more properly designating a type of heavy oxen, of the tropics of the Old World, long domesticated in the Orient. Buffalo are characterized by their long, angulated horns, broad and flat at the base, so as to form in some cases a shield over the forehead; and by their broad, splay feet, particularly adapted to wading in muddy waters, where they mainly feed on aquatic grasses and other plants. There are three distinct species.

The largest and fiercest buffalo is the black "cape," or South African species (*Bos caffer*) found throughout the entire south of Africa, northward to Abyssinia. It reaches a length of six feet, and in old bulls the relatively short horns join at their bases, so as to form a helmet-like mass, which makes the head almost invulnerable. The horns curve "outward, downward, and backward, and then forward, upward, and inward." This buffalo is bluish-black, and nearly hairless. Its chief enemies are the lion and man, whose combined efforts have greatly decreased its numbers. The buffalo are warned of the approach of danger by the buffalo-birds (q.v.), which constantly hover near them. Another species (*B. pumilus*) is widely scattered throughout the west, and central parts of Africa. It is smaller than the more southern species, and is chestnut in color. The most widely domesticated of the buffalo is that of India (*B. bubalus*), called "arni" (feminine "arna") by the Hindu. It differs greatly in appearance from the African species, having a cow-shaped head, and long, much flattened, triangular horns, covered with transverse wrinkles, which curve regularly outwards and backwards towards the shoulder, and do not form a buckler over the forehead. The bull is ashy-black in color, frequently with white feet, and is smaller than the African buffalo, never exceeding 16 hands at the withers. It is in the wild state an animal of tremendous power and ferocity, and is regarded by sportsmen as one of the most dangerous beasts of the jungle. It has long been employed in the rice-fields of the Orient, as far east as Japan; the ordinary "water-buffalo" or "carabao" of the Philippines is a small variety. It was long ago introduced into Egypt for service in the boggy lowlands of the Delta, and is now extending up the Nile to the lake regions of central Africa. A variety exists in the Niger valley, and another, called "sanga," and distinguished by its very long horns, is do-

BUFFALO BREAKWATER.

ORIGINAL CRIB SUPERSTRUCTURE IN FOREGROUND; CONCRETE RECONSTRUCTION IN DISTANCE.

STONE BREAKWATER, SHOWING TOP ANGLE STONES.

THE COMPLETED CONCRETE BREAKWATER.

mesticated in Abyssinia. The Indian buffalo is also employed in marshy farming districts in Turkey, Hungary, Italy, and Spain, where it is able to work in ground too wet and soft for the other cattle, and to pasture upon coarse, marsh grasses. Its hide makes good leather, and its milk is excellent, and is greatly used in India for the making of the semi-fluid butter called "ghee."

Buffalo-berry (*Shepherdia argentea*), an American shrub of the natural order *Elæagnaceæ*, cultivated in the Western plains region for its edible berries, and planted for hedges, wind-breaks, and ornament to some extent elsewhere. The plant, which is sometimes tree-form, attains a height of about 18 feet, has thorny stems, small, silvery foliage, yellowish densely fascicled diœcious flowers at the nodes, and globular, one-seeded, yellow or red tart fruits, about the size of currants. Though introduced into cultivation before the blackberry, this plant gained slowly in popularity until the plains region became settled, where, being perfectly hardy, it took the place of tender fruits in the cold and dry West. The fruits make acceptable jellies and preserves, but seem not to be needed where other bush-fruits can be raised. The plants are readily propagated by means of seeds, cuttings, and occasional suckers. They succeed in any good garden soil.

Buffalo-bird, any of several birds which remain about cattle, and feed upon their parasites. Most of them are starlings (q.v.) of plain dark plumage, with the habit of gathering into noisy flocks. Those of South Africa, almost always seen in company with buffaloes and rhinoceroses, belong to the genus *Buphaga*, and are commonly termed "ox-peckers," "beef-eaters," or "rhinoceros-birds." They cluster upon the backs of these animals while they rest or slowly feed, and pick from them ticks and similar pests; and they also serve as watchmen for their hosts, arousing them by their cries whenever anything suspicious happens. The wild and tame buffaloes of the Orient are similarly attended by the starlings of the genus *Eulabes*. These wait about the villages until the cattle come in from pasture at sunset, when the birds throng about them, and relieve them of troublesome insects, to the manifest comfort of the resting cattle. In Africa the larger mammals are frequently served in the same way by certain small, white herons, also called "buffalo-birds" by the colonists.

Buffalo Bug. See CARPET BEETLE.

Buffalo-fish, a large, coarse, fresh-water fish of which there are four varieties; three inhabiting the waters of the Mississippi valley, and one the river Usumacinto in Mexico. The formation of the head suggests the name, for from the nose to the top of the shoulders it has the high, humpy pitch of the bison. In Louisiana they are known as "gourdheads." The common big-mouthed buffalo-fish (*Ictiobus cyprinella*) reaches a length of three feet and a weight of 50 pounds. In the spring freshets of the Mississippi valley, at spawning time, it swims in great shoals on to the flooded marshes, where the receding waters make it an easy victim to the farmers, who kill great numbers of them for fertilizers. In body they are stout and of a dull, brownish-olive hue, not silvery, with dusky fins. The black, or mon-grel, buffalo-fish (*I. urus*) has a smaller, more oblique mouth, and a much darker color; the fins being almost black. The small-mouthed or white, buffalo-fish (*I. bubalus*) is the most abundant. It does not run so large as the common buffalo, 35 pounds being its limit. In color it is pale, almost silvery. See Jordan and Evermann, 'American Food and Game Fishes.'

Buffalo-gnat, a fly allied to the black-fly (q.v.), *Simulium pecuarum*, of the family *Simuliidæ*, order *Diptera*, a larger and more formidable species than the black-fly of the northern and subarctic regions. It attacks in the lower Ohio and the Mississippi valley various domestic cattle, horses, sheep, poultry, dogs, and cats, and is especially hurtful to mules and horses, killing many. Hogs show at first the effeets of the bite but very little; yet large numbers die soon after the attack, while others die about six weeks after the disappearance of the buffalo-gnats; they usually perish from large ulcerating sores, which cause blood-poisoning. Animals bitten by many buffalo-gnats show all the symptoms of colic, and many people believe that these bites bring on that disease. The animal attacked first becomes frantic, but within a very short time ceases to show symptoms of pain, submits passively to the affliction, rolls over and dies; sometimes all within the space of three or four hours. Animals of various kinds become gradually accustomed to these bites, and during a long-continued invasion but few are killed toward the end of it. The larvæ are found more particularly attached to submerged logs, wholly or partly submerged stumps, brush, bushes, and other like objects in the larger creeks and bayous of the region to which they are common. They cluster together, and fastened by the posterior protuberance or by a minute thread, they wander and sway about, but do not venture above the water. When fully grown the larvæ descend to near the bottom of the stream, sometimes 8 or 10 feet, to make their cocoons. The adult fly, on emergence from the pupa, rises quickly to the surface, runs a few inches over the water, and the wings expanding almost instantly it darts away. The time of appearance of the swarms is regulated by the earliness or lateness of the spring, and consequently it is much earlier in the southern parts of the Mississippi valley. As a rule, they can be expected soon after the first continuous warm weather in early spring. In 1885 the first swarms were observed in Louisiana, 11 March, in Mississippi and Tennessee, 1 May, and in Indiana and Illinois, 12 May. Their presence is at once indicated by the actions of the various animals in the field. Horses and mules snort, switch their tails, stamp the ground, and show great restlessness and symptoms of fear. If not harnessed to plow and wagon they will try to escape by running away. Cattle rush wildly about in search of relief. Consult: Osborn, 'Insects Affecting Domestic Animals' (Bulletin 5 n. ser. United States Department of Agriculture, Division of Entomology, 1896).

Buffalo Grass, a strong-growing North American grass (*Tripsacum dactyloides*), so called from forming a large part of the food of the buffalo, and said to have excellent fattening properties; called also gama grass.

Buffalo Historical Society, Buffalo, N. Y. Foremost among institutions of its kind west of New England and the older Atlantic seaboard cities is the Historical Society of Buffalo, N. Y. Founded in the spring of 1862, Millard Fillmore was its first president; and it was at his suggestion that 50 citizens of Buffalo agreed to pay $20 each per year for five years, thus founding the first maintenance fund of the institution. In President Fillmore's inaugural address, 2 July 1862, the principal objects of the society were stated to be to "discover, procure and preserve whatever may relate to the history of Western New York in general, and of the City of Buffalo in particular." For many years the society occupied various leased quarters with its small museum and library, and its progress was slow; but throughout its more than forty years of existence it has always included among its members the most substantial and representative families of Buffalo. From 1887 to 1902 the society occupied rooms in the Buffalo Public Library building. The need of a building of its own had long been apparent. The nucleus of a building fund had been formed by a gift of $5,000 from the Hon. James M. Smith, and various building projects had been under consideration, when, in 1900, legislation incident to the construction at Buffalo of a building for New York State at the Pan-American Exposition, opened the way for securing a permanent and worthy home for the society. Through the efforts of Senator Henry W. Hill, aided by Wilson S. Bissell, Andrew Langdon and others, a bill was enacted which enabled the State to expend $100,000, out of its exposition appropriation of $300,000, toward the erection of a permanent building, and also providing for adding thereto $25,000 from the City of Buffalo, and funds from the Historical Society; said building to be placed on park lands, and at the close of the exposition to become the property of the Historical Society, the city being bound to make an annual appropriation toward its maintenance. Under this agreement a building was erected in Delaware Park, at a cost of some $200,000. The only permanent building connected with the Pan-American Exposition, it has the added interest of being the scene of President McKinley's last public reception, 5 Sept. 1901, prior to that held the next day in the Temple of Music at which he received the wound from which he died, 14 September.

The Historical Society building stands in a beautiful and easily accessible site in Delaware Park, the principal park of Buffalo. It is 130 by 80 feet in dimensions, 50 feet high, perhaps the most notable example in America of the pure Doric order of architecture. It is of white marble, the northern facade faced with three-quarter columns, the south side having a portico 61 by 17 feet, embellished by 10 Doric columns and approached by marble steps 40 feet in width. The columns are of the same proportion as those of the Parthenon, 3 ft. 6 in. in diameter at the base. Within, the chief structural material is black marble. Situated on sloping ground, the edifice has three available floors, the basement being for the most part but little below the ground level. In the middle of the main floor is the grand hall, two stories high, and lighted, as is the upper floor, by side windows and skylights. The library, lecture hall and administrative offices are on the main floor, the museums and portrait galleries above. A notable feature of the building is the massive bronze doors, presented by Andrew Langdon; the design by J. Woodley Gosling, the sculptural work by R. Hinton Perry; the principal panels bear female figures typifying "History" and "Ethnology," the bronze transom containing a group showing "Science" and "Art." In the Central Hall is a bronze statue of Lincoln, Charles H. Niehaus, sculptor, a gift to the Society from the Lincoln Birthday Association of Buffalo, now affiliated with it.

Notable features in the museum include the Dr. James coin collection, valued at $15,000; the Dr. Jos. C. Greene collection of Egyptian and Oriental articles, casts, etc.; the Cottier, Scoville and other Indian collections, the Atkins Alaska collection; the Civil War and Lincoln collection of Julius E. Francis, founder of the Lincoln Birthday Association; and many relics of the pioneer days in Western New York, and on the Great Lakes. Many articles formerly belonging to President Millard Fillmore are here shown, as are relics of Lincoln, Grant, other Presidents and famous men.

The Historical Society library (13,000 volumes, 8,000 pamphlets) is a free reference library. It includes the special collection known as the Dr. John C. Lord library, owned by the City of Buffalo but cared for by the Historical Society; and the private library of Mrs. Millard Fillmore. The Society is also rich in manuscript material, which is being drawn on for its annual volume of publications. (Vol. V., 8vo. pp. 546, 1902). Besides its meetings, lectures and receptions for members, the Society makes its possessions and facilities available free to the public, by means of popular lectures in its own lecture hall on Sunday afternoons, talks and various exercises for clubs and school classes, etc., the aim of the management being to make it as useful as possible to the community. It has a membership of upwards of 700, of which 410 are resident, paying $5 per year, 140 life members, fee $100, the rest honorary and corresponding.

ANDREW LANGDON,
President Buffalo Historical Society.

Buf'fer, any apparatus for deadening the concussion between a moving body and the one on which it strikes. In the United States the buffers used on passenger cars are composed of a head, bar and stem and are placed at the centre of each end of the car. On English railways they are placed in pairs at each end, and are fastened by rods to springs under the framework to deaden the concussions caused when the velocity of part of the train is checked.

Buffet, bŭf-fā', anciently a little apartment, separated from the rest of the room, for the disposing of china, glass, etc. It is now a piece of furniture in the dining-room, called also a sideboard, for the reception of the plate, glass, etc. In France many mansions have a detached room called *buffet*, decorated with pitchers, vases, fountains, etc. The word is very commonly applied to the space set apart for refreshments in public places.

Buffet, bu̇-fā', Louis Joseph, French politician: b. Mirecourt, Vosges, 26 Oct. 1818; d. 1898. In 1848 he was elected to the Chamber of Deputies from the Vosges, and held the po-

BUILDING OF THE BUFFALO HISTORICAL SOCIETY.

sitiou of minister of commerce and agriculture under the presidency of Louis Napoleon. He then took a prominent part in the "Tiers Parti," which sought to join liberal reforms to loyalty to the government, later becoming its leader. He became a member of M. Emile Ollivier's cabinet in January, 1870, occupying the portfolio of minister of finance, but after only three months' service resigned. In 1871 he was again elected to the National Assembly, of which he was elected president to succeed M. Jules Grévy, 4 April 1873. In 1875 he formed a new cabinet, becoming himself vice-president of the council and minister of the interior, but owing to his having made himself unpopular with the members of his own party, he failed of re-election to the Assembly, and resigned his seat in the Cabinet in 1876. He was, however, in June of the same year elected a life member of the Senate.

Buf'fington, Adelbert Rinaldo, American military officer: b. Wheeling, W. Va., 22 Nov. 1837. He was graduated at the United States Military Academy in 1861; entered the ordnance department; was promoted colonel in 1889, and became chief of ordnance with the rank of brigadier-general, 5 April 1899. He had command of the National Armory in 1881-92; is the inventor of a magazine firearm, carriages for light and heavy guns, and parts of models of 1884 Springfield rifles: introduced gas forging furnaces and improved methods in the Springfield armory; and originated the nitre and manganese method in use there for bluing iron and steel surfaces of small arms.

Buf'flehead, a small plump duck of American inland waters (*Charionetta albeola*), remarkable for its beauty of coloring. It is about 13 inches in length, and the plumage of the drake is black and white, with the crested head, shaped like a puff-ball, rich, silky, changing green. The female is smaller, and more protectively colored in a dull-brown plumage, with white markings. Its food consists of larvæ, shells, seeds, etc., and it frequents gravelly shores and wooded ponds, breeding in holes of trees and burrows, from the great lakes northward to the Arctic Circle. It lays about 12 large, dark-colored eggs. It is of small value to the sportsman, and requires little skill in shooting, except when on the wing, at which time it is remarkable for the speed with which it flies, and the peculiar whistling sound of its wings. It is sometimes called "butterball," because of its roundness, and "spiritduck," a name derived from the Indians, owing to its faculty for vanishing and reappearing from the surface of the water with amazing skill.

Buffon, George Louis Leclerc, zhôrzh iloo-ê le-klâr bü-fôn (COMTE DE), French naturalist of distinction: b. Montbard, Burgundy, 7 Sept. 1707; d. Paris, 16 April 1788. He received from his father, Benjamin Leclerc, counselor to the parliament of his province, a careful education. Chance connected him at Dijon with the young Duke of Kingston, whose tutor, a man of learning, inspired him with a taste for the sciences. They traveled together through France and Italy, and Buffon afterward visited England. In order to perfect himself in the language without neglecting the sciences, he translated Newton's 'Fluxions,' and Hales' 'Vegetable Statics.' After some time he pub-

lished some works of his own, in which he treated of geometry, natural philosophy, and rural economy. He laid his researches on these subjects before the Academy of Sciences, of which he became a member in 1733. The most important were on the construction of mirrors for setting bodies on fire at a great distance, as Archimedes is said to have done, and experiments on the strength of different kinds of wood, and the means of increasing it, partienlarly by removing the bark of the trees some time before felling them. Buffon, in his earlier years, was animated only by an undefined love of learning and fame, but his appointment as superintendent of the Royal Garden (now the Jardin des Plantes), in 1739, gave his mind a decided turn toward that science in which he has immortalized himself. Considering natural history in its whole extent, he found no works in this department but spiritless compilations and dry lists of names. There were excellent observations indeed on single objects, but no comprehensive work. Of such a one he now formed the plan, and to aid him in this, by examining the numerous and often minute objects embraced in his plan, he associated himself with Daubenton, and, after an assiduous labor of 10 years, the two friends published the three first volumes of the 'Natural History'; and, between 1749 and 1767, twelve others, which comprehend the theory of the earth, the nature of animals, and the history of man and the viviparous quadrupeds. The most brilliant parts of them, the general theories, the descriptions of the characters of animals, and of the great natural phenomena, are by Buffon. Daubenton limited himself to the description of the forms and the anatomy of the animals. The nine following volumes, which appeared from 1770 to 1783, contain the history of birds, from which Daubenton withdrew his assistance. Buffon published alone the five volumes on minerals, from 1783 to 1788. Of the seven supplementary volumes, of which the last did not appear until after his death in 1789, the fifth formed an independent whole, the most celebrated of all his works. It contains his 'Epochs of Nature,' in which the author, in a style truly sublime, and with the triumphant power of genius, gives a second theory of the earth, very different from that which he had traced in the first volumes, though he assumes at the commencement the air of merely defending and developing the former. This great labor, with which Buffon was occupied during 50 years, is, however, but a part of the vast plan which he had sketched, and which has been continued by Lacépède in his history of the different species of cetaceous animals, reptiles, and fishes, but has remained unexecuted as far as regards the invertebrate animals and the plants. There is but one opinion of Buffon as an author. For the elevation of his views, for powerful and profound ideas, for the majesty of his images, for noble and dignified expression, for the lofty harmony of his style in treating of important subjects, he is perhaps unrivaled. His pictures of the sublime scenes of nature are strikingly true, and are stamped with originality. The fame of his work was soon universal. It excited a general taste for natural history, and gained for this science the favor and protection of nobles and princes. Louis XV. raised the author to the dignity of a count, and D'Argivilliers, in the reign of Louis XVI., caused his statue to be erected, during his life, at the entry of the Royal Cabinet of Natural Curiosities, with the inscription "Majestati naturæ par ingenium." The opinions entertained of Buffon as a natural philosopher and an observer have been more divided. Voltaire, D'Alembert, Condorcet, have severely criticised his hypotheses and his vague manner of philosophizing from general views. But although the views of Buffon on the theory of the earth can no longer be defended in detail, he will always have the merit of having made it generally felt, that the present state of the earth is the result of a series of changes which it is possible to trace, and of having pointed out the phenomena which indicate the course of these changes. His theory of generation has been refuted by Haller and Spallanzani, and his hypothesis of a certain inexplicable mechanism to account for animal instinct is not supported by facts; but his eloquent description of the physical and moral development of man, as well as his ideas on the influence which the delicacy and development of each organ exert on the character of different species of animals, are still of the highest interest. His views of the degeneracy of animals, and of the limits prescribed to each species by climates, mountains, and seas, are real discoveries which receive daily confirmation, and furnish to travelers a basis for their observations, which have entirely wanting before. The most perfect part of his work is the 'History of Quadrupeds'; the weakest, the 'History of Minerals.' Buffon was of a noble figure, and of great dignity of manners. His conversation was remarkable for a simplicity which strikingly contrasted with the style of his writings. The best edition of his 'Natural History' is that published from 1749 to 1789, in 36 volumes.

Buffoon (Italian Buffone), a comic singer in the opera buffa, or the Italian intermezzo. The Italians, however, distinguish the buffo cantante, which requires good singing, from the buffo comico, in which there is more acting. Buffoonery is the name given to the jokes which the buffoon introduces. The word is no doubt borrowed from the Low Latin, in which the name buffo (cheeked) was given to those who appeared on the theatre, with their cheeks puffed up, to receive blows on them, and to excite the laughter of the spectators. Afterward the name came to signify a mimic, a jester in general.

Bufo, bū'fō, a genus of batrachians, the type of the family Bufonidæ. The body is inflated, the skin warty, the hind feet of moderate length, the jaws without teeth, the nose rounded. At least 20 species are known.

Bu'fonite, literally, toad-stone; a name given to the fossil teeth and palatal bones of fishes belonging to the family of Pycnodonts (thick teeth), whose remains occur abundantly in the Oölitic and Chalk formations. The term bufonite, like those of serpents' eyes, batrachites, and crapaudines, by which they are also known, refers to the vulgar notion that those organisms were originally formed in the heads of serpents, frogs, and toads.

Bu'ford, John, American soldier: b. Kentucky, 1825; d. Washington, D. C., 16 Dec. 1863. He was graduated at West Point in 1848; was appointed to the 1st Dragoons, and served in the Sioux expedition, 1855, in the Kansas disturbances of 1856–7, and in the Utah expedition, 1857–8. On 12 Nov. 1861 he was appointed major in the inspector-general's corps, attached to Gen. Pope's staff, 26 June 1862, made a brigadier on 27 July, and commanded a cavalry brigade under Hooker in the northern Virginia campaign. He was chief of cavalry in the Maryland campaign, and succeeded Gen. Stoneman on McClellan's staff. He took part in the engagement at South Mountain, Antietam, Fredericksburg, and Beverly Ford; and at Gettysburg began the attack before Reynold's arrival on 1 July, and rendered important services at Wolf's Hill and Round Top. After the engagement at Culpeper he pursued the enemy across the Rapidan, and cut his way to rejoin the army north of the Rappahannock. His coolness, fine judgment, and splendid courage were notable, and in a few months he acquired an influence over men as remarkable as it was useful. His military sagacity was far-reaching and accurate, and made him one of the most trusted and respected officers in the service, and his death, caused by disease contracted during months of active service and constant exposure, was widely lamented in the army. A major-general's commission reached him the day he died, and a monument to his memory was placed on the Gettysburg battlefield in 1895.

Buford, Napoleon Bonaparte, American soldier: b. Woodford County, Ky., 13 Jan. 1807; d. 28 March 1883. He was graduated at West Point, 1827, did garrison duty in Virginia and Maine as second lieutenant in the 3d Artillery, and was assistant professor of natural and experimental philosophy at the military academy, 1834–5, when he resigned his commission, became an engineer in the service of the State of Kentucky, 1835–42, and a merchant and iron founder at Rock Island, Ill., 1843–61, being president of the Rock Island & P. Ry, 1857–61. He entered the Civil War as colonel of the 27th Illinois Volunteers, took part in the battle of Belmont, 7 Nov. 1861, the attack on Island No. 10 in the Mississippi River, March–April 1862, captured Union City, Ky., 31 March 1862, took part in the expedition to Fort Pillow, the siege and battle of Corinth, and the siege of Vicksburg, February 1863. On 24 Aug. 1865, he was mustered out of service with the rank of brevet-major-general of volunteers, conferred for gallant and meritorious services during the Rebellion. He was special commissioner of Indian affairs during 1868, and for inspecting the Union Pacific Railroad, 1867–9. During the negotiations after the battle of Belmont the Confederate Gen. Leonidas Polk wrote of Buford, whom he had known at West Point: "He is as good a fellow as ever lived and most devotedly my friend — a true Christian, a true soldier, and a gentleman every inch of him."

Bug, an insect of the order Hemiptera. Bugs are characterized by the beak-like sucking mouth-parts, composed of the mandibles and maxillæ, which are ensheathed by the large expanded labium; by the free, large prothorax, the usually angular short body, and the irregularly veined wings, the veins being but few in number, while the fore wings are often half coriaceous and thick. The metamorphosis is incomplete. There are many wingless parasitic forms, and many aquatic species.

The triangular head is nearly always sunken into the prothorax, and is small in proportion to the rest of the body; the eyes are small, nearly globular, and very prominent, and the three ocelli are set far back, while the short, bristle-like, or filiform antennæ, with from 5 to 13 or more joints, are inserted below and far in advance of the eyes, so that the front is broad and flat. The parts of the mouth form a four-jointed, solid, hard beak. The mandibles and maxillæ are long and style-like, the latter with out palpi; they are ensheathed at their base by the canaliculate labium, which has obsolete palpi. The labium is well developed, being generally acutely triangular. The thorax is like that of beetles, the prothorax being broad above, and the wings, when folded, concealing the rest of the body. The legs are situated close together, with coxæ and trochanters very similar to those of the *Coleoptera*. The body is usually very flat above, or, in the more or less cylindrical species, somewhat broad and flat. The body is less concentrated headwards than in the *Coleoptera*, though much more so than in the *Orthoptera*, and in this respect, as well as in other essential characters, the group is intermediate between these two orders. Both pairs of wings are very equal in size and alike in shape, except in the higher families, where they are very unequal, the hinder pair being very small.

The legs are slender, and often very long, owing to the great length of the femora and tibiæ, while the tarsi, like those of the lowest *Coleoptera*, are two- or three-jointed. The abdomen has six to nine segments apparent, though the typical number is 11. The stigmata are very distinct, being often raised on a tubercle. On the basal ring of the abdomen are two cavities in which are sometimes seated vocal organs, as in the male cicada, and in the metathorax of some species are glands for secreting a foul odorous fluid. In the *Cicadidæ* and *Phytocoris* the ovipositor is perfect and much as in the saw-flies and wasps.

The active nymphs of the *Hemiptera*, like those of the locusts, resemble closely the imago, differing mainly in possessing the rudiments of wings, which are acquired after the second molting. After two changes of skin (four in all) they assume the pupa state, which differs mainly from that of the larva in having larger wing-pads. While the development of the imago ordinarily occupies the summer months, in the *Aphides* it takes but a comparatively few days, but in the 17-year cicada as many years as its name indicates. An exception to this mode of development is seen in the nymph of the male coccus, which, somewhat as in the higher orders, spins a silken cocoon, and changes into an inactive pupa. Apterous individuals, especially females, sometimes occur, especially in the aquatic *Hydrometra*, *Velia*, and *Limnobates*, and in many other genera the hind pair of wings are often absent. There are about 50,000 species living and fossil. Some species are of great size, especially the *Hydrocores*, a division containing the aquatic genera, *Velia*, *Nepa*, *Belostoma*, and *Notonecta*, and which first appeared in the Jurassic formation. But the oldest known fossil insect (*Protocimex silurica*) was apparently a bug; traces of one wing having been found in the Upper Ordovi-

cian beds of Sweden. Consult: Packard, 'Guide to Study of Insects' (1889); 'Entomology for Beginners' (1899); Comstock, 'A Manual for the Study of Insects' (1895); Sharp, 'Insects' (1899).

Bug, two rivers in European Russia. One rises near the confines of Volhynia, in the northwest of government Podolsk, and proceeds first east and then southeast to Oliviopol, where it enters government Kherson, which it traverses almost centrally from north to south, and falls into the estuary of the Dnieper, near Kherson. Its chief affuents are the Ingul, Balta, Tchertal, and Solonicha. It has a course of 500 miles, but its navigation is greatly obstructed by rocks and sandbanks. The second river rises in Galicia and joins the Vistula at the fortress of Novogeorgieosk, about 20 miles north-northwest of Warsaw. It is navigable for nearly 300 miles.

Bugason, boo-ga-sŏn′, Philippines, a town on the island of Panay. Pop. (1900) about 15,000.

Bug′bane, a genus of herbs (*Cimicifuga*), of the natural order *Ranunculaceæ*, tall, perennial plants, of which some 10 species are natives of the northern temperate regions, and are often planted, in spite of their disagreeable odor, for ornamental purposes in hardy borders in exposed places or in partial shade. The species have large decompound leaves, and racemes of white flowers, which appear during summer and early autumn. In some species the fruits are attractive in appearance. One species, black cohosh, or black snakeroot (*C. racemosa*) is used in domestic and rural medicine as an infusion for various ailments.

Bugeaud de la Piconnerie, Thomas Robert, tō-mä rō-bâr bü-zho-dė-la̧-pē-kŏn-ė-rē (Duc d'Isly), marshal of France: b. Limoges, 15 Oct. 1784; d. Paris, 10 June 1849. He belonged to an Irish family which had settled in France with James II. on his abdication. He entered the army in 1804 as a grenadier, was corporal at Austerlitz, made the campaigns of Prussia and Poland, and was wounded at Pultusk in 1806. He afterward went into Spain as lieutenant adjutant-major, gained new promotion, and remained with the army of Aragon till 1814. During these long wars he repeatedly distinguished himself, and received honorable mention from Suchet, his commander-in-chief. On the restoration of the Bourbons he gave in his adhesion to them; but on the landing of Bonaparte, followed the general example by deserting to his old master. After the revolution of 1830 he was appointed *maréchal de camp*, and in 1831 obtained a seat in the Chamber of Deputies, where he often displayed great good sense, though in a style of oratory so blunt and rustic as occasionally to excite the risibility of his opponents. He was afterward sent to Algeria, where he gained many advantages over the Arabs, and showed himself possessed of the kind of talents necessary to cope successfully with them and their celebrated leader, Abd-el-Kader. On the revolution of 1848, it is said that, if permitted, he would have effectually put down the insurgents and secured the throne to Louis Philippe. He gave in his adhesion to the republic, but remained unemployed. He was better received by President Louis N_{apoleon}, who appointed him commander-in-chief of the army of the Alps.

Bugenhagen, Johann, called POMERANUS, yō'hän po-mèr-än'ŭs boo-gĕn-hä'gĕn, or DOCTOR POMMER, German reformer: b. Stettin, 1485; d. Wittenberg, 20 April 1558. He fled from his Catholic superiors to Wittenberg in 1521, where he was made, in 1522, professor of theology. Luther derived assistance from his profound exegetical learning in preparing his translation of the Bible. In 1525 he gave occasion for the controversies about the sacrament, by a work against Zwinglius on the communion. He acquired more reputation by his 'Interpretatio in Librum Psalmorum' (1523). He effected the union of the Protestant free cities with the Saxons, and introduced into Brunswick, Hamburg, Lübeck, Pomerania, Denmark, and many other places, the Lutheran service and church discipline. For the Lower Saxons he translated the Bible into Low German (1533). He was a faithful friend to Luther, and delivered his eulogy. Together with Melanchthon, he composed the 'Interim of Leipsic.' He wrote also a 'History of Pomerania.'

Bugg, Lelia Hardin, American author: b. Ironton, Miss. She graduated from the Ursuline Academy, Arcadia, Mo., and continued her studies at Trinity College, Washington. She has written: 'The Correct Thing for Catholics' (1893) ; 'A Lady' (1894) ; 'Correct English' (1895) ; 'Orchids: a Novel' (1896) ; 'The Prodigal's Daughter' (1898) ; 'The People of Our Parish' (1899).

Bugge, bŭg-gĕ, Elseus Sophus, Norwegian philologist: b. Laurvig, 1833; d. Christiania, 8 July 1907. After obtaining an education at the Universities of Christiania, Copenhagen, and Berlin he was made professor of comparative philology and Old Norse, at Christiania. He was an eminent authority on northern languages and among his works are an edition of the songs of the Edda, 'Norrœen Fornkvœdi' (1867) ; 'Gamle norske Folkeviser' (1858) ; 'Norrœne Skrifter of sagnhistorik Indhold' (1864–73) ; and a notable edition of the Volsunga and Hervarar sagas.

Bugge, Thomas, Danish astronomer: b. Copenhagen, 12 Oct. 1740; d. 15 June 1815. After Tycho Brahe, he was the greatest astronomer of Denmark. First officiating as professor, he afterward spent most of his time in traveling abroad, and was sent to Paris in 1798 to confer with the commission of the French institute on the subject of the introduction of uniform weights and measures, on which occasion he was made a member of that learned body.

Buggy, a name given to several species of carriages or gigs: In the United States, a light one-horse four-wheeled vehicle with or without a hood or top; in India, a gig with a large hood to screen those who travel in it from the sun's rays; in England, a light one-horse two-wheeled vehicle without a hood.

Bugiardini, Giuliano, joo-lē-ä'nō boo-jär-dē'nĕ, Italian painter (also known under the Latinized form of his name, as JULIANUS FLOR-ENTINUS) : b. Florence, 29 Jan. 1475; d. 16 Feb. 1554. He studied under Ghirlandajo and Albertinelli, and collaborated with Michael Angelo.

Among his best works are: 'The Martyrdom of St. Catherine' ; 'Betrothal of St. Catherine' ; 'John the Baptist' ; 'Virgin with Saints' ; 'Virgin with John the Baptist.'

Bugis, boo'jēz, a people of the Indian archipelago, chiefly inhabiting Macassar and Boni, in the island of Celebes. They are muscular, middle-sized, and of a light-brown color, some being even fair. Their dress consists of a piece of red or blue striped cotton, which they wrap about their loins, and pass between their legs. They bind their jet-black hair very tastefully, in a red or blue cotton handkerchief. They pluck out the hair of their beards, and ornament their arms and legs with brass wire above the wrists and ankles, and to these the children attach bells. They are, to a notable degree, proud, passionate, revengeful, and crafty; yet they are regarded as the most civilized of the natives of Celebes, and are the chief trading people in the Malay archipelago. Their fondness for commerce has led to their settling in many places out of Celebes, and a "Bugis quarter" is to be found in most of the large towns of the different islands. They build ships of 50 or 60 tons burden, and their voyages extend from Sumatra to New Guinea. From Macassar the voyage begins with the east monsoon, the prahus trading as they proceed west until they reach Rhio, and even Malacca and Acheen, when they are prepared to return with the change of the season. They take with them native cotton cloths, gold-dust, nutmegs, silver dollars, birds'-nests, camphor, benzoin or frankincense, and tortoise shell; and return with European broadcloths and cottons, opium, unwrought iron, and tobacco, which they partly sell at the intermediate ports as they sail homeward. This is their most important voyage, but they make many subordinate ones for collecting birds'-nests, feathers, tortoise shell, trepang, and other articles of commerce.

Bu'gle, a genus of hardy herbs (*Ajuga*), of the natural order *Labiatæ*, mostly natives of the cooler parts of Europe and Asia, but cultivated for ornament in many temperate countries. The species, which attain heights ranging from 5 to more than 10 feet, have many whorls, usually of blue, purple, pink, or white flowers, and are useful for planting in the rear of borders. They are readily propagated by seeds or division. Some of the species have escaped, and may be found growing wild on moist land and in the borders of woods.

Bugle, a treble instrument of brass or copper, differing from the trumpet in having a shorter and more conical tube, with a less expanded bell. It is played with a cupped mouthpie;e. In the original form it is the signal horn for the infantry, as the trumpet is for the cavalry.

Bugle, a shining, elongated glass bead, usually black, used in decorating women's apparel and also in trafficking with savage tribes.

Bu'gloss, a popular name for various species of the genera *Anchusa, Lycopsis,* and *Echium,* of the natural order *Boraginaccæ.*

Several species of *Anchusa*, which is also known as alkanet, are cultivated for ornament. They are hardy, have blue or purple blossoms in panicled racemes, which are used as cut flowers. The plants are easily raised from seed and thrive well in sunny places. The species of *Lycopsis*, to which some botanists restrict the name bugloss, are not cultivated in America, but in some parts of Europe certain ones, especially *L. arvensis*, are considered weeds. Several species of *Echium*, popularly known as viper's bugloss, are cultivated under glass in Europe and America, especially in California, where three species are grown out of doors. They are coarse herbs or shrubs which bear beautiful spikes of very numerous white, blue, red or violet flowers with prominent stamens. They are particularly useful where the soil is too poor for many other garden plants, because they produce more numerous and more highly colored blossoms upon such soils than upon rich soil. Indeed, upon rich soil they may fail to blossom altogether.

Bu'gong Moth, a species of owlet-moth *Agrotis spina* of the family *Noctuidæ*. It occurs in millions in certain localities in Victoria, Australia. It hibernates as a moth, and in this stage was formerly an important article of food with the native tribes.

Bugo'nia Myth, also Bugonia lore, "Bugonia craze," and "Bugonia superstition." For more than 2,000 years a superstition has prevailed among the masses that besides the usual production of honey-bees in hives, they originated by spontaneous generations from the carcasses of dead animals, and chiefly from those of oxen. Thus, says Osten Sacken, arose in Greece the term Bugonia (from Βοῦς ox; and γονή progeny) as well as the Latin names Bugenes melissae or Taurigenæ apes, "oxen-born bees." Greeks, Carthaginians and Romans spoke of the Bugonia as an every-day occurrence. The poet Archelans calls them the "factitious progeny of a decaying ox." This superstition has also prevailed in northern Africa and some parts of Asia; it continued to exist through the Middle Ages, and survived till the 16th and 17th centuries, being mentioned by Redi, Aldrovaldi (1602), while Melanchthon regarded it as a divine provision. The original cause of this delusion, which has been finally exploded by Osten-Sacken, lies in the fact that a fly which mimics the honey-bee in shape and its hairy clothing (*Eristalis tenax*, of the order *Diptera*), and which breeds in the carcasses of animals, has always been mistaken for the honey-bee. It is a true fly, with only one pair of wings and no sting, and is a little stouter and larger than a honey-bee. Its larva is the "rat-tailed maggot," that lives in open cess-pools, sewers, etc., and decaying carcasses on which the corrupt liquid forms during the secondary stage of putrescence. The Bugonia myth is, as shown by Osten-Sacken, the foundation of Samson's riddle; the supposed honey-bee issuing from the lion's carcass was evidently the Eristalis fly. This insect is now distributed over a greater part of the world, and is abundant in the United States. It was first detected at Cambridge, Mass., in 1875 by Osten-Sacken himself. Consult Osten-Sacken on the Oxenborn Bees of the Ancient (Bugonia) and their relation to *Eristalis tenax*.

Bu'hach, a preparation for destroying insects made by grinding the flower-heads of certain species of chrysanthemums. See IN-SECT POWDER.

Buhl- (bool) work, a description of inlaid work, consisting at first of inserting a brass scroll or pattern in a ground of dark-colored tortoise-shell or wood; but at a later period the use of wood of a different color, instead of metal, was introduced by Reisner, and to his process the modern practice of buhl-work is chiefly confined. It consists in cutting out a pattern from two veneers of different colored woods, which are glued together with a piece of paper laid between them; the pieces are then separated by running a thin knife through the paper, the patterns are carefully taken out, and the figure removed from the one veneer is inserted into the cavity of the other, the dust of the wood being rubbed in to fill the interstices. A little glue is then rubbed in, and the work laid aside to dry, after which it is ready to be glued to the box or piece of furniture which it is wished to ornament. The cutting of the pattern is effected by the use of a very fine saw, of the kind known as a key-saw, which can readily be made to run around the sinuosities of the patterns. The suitable designs for this work are continuous figures like a running vine, or the honeysuckle, the saw completing these without the necessity of discontinuing the work to commence anew. Two pieces of buhl-work are thus produced; but three are frequently obtained by gluing together three pieces of wood, and cutting out in the same manner. It is not, however, found expedient to combine a greater number of pieces. The French term for buhl-work and all sorts of inlaid work, is marqueterie. The name buhl is derived from a French cabinet-maker, André Charles Boulle or Boule, formerly miscalled Buhl, b. 1642, d. 1732. He raised cabinet-making to an art industry, and Reisner, above mentioned, was a German contemporary of Boulle's.

Bühler, Johonn Georg, yŏ'hän gā'örg bü'lër, German Orientalist: b. Berstel, Hanover, 19 July 1837; d. April 1896. He pursued his studies in Göttingen, Paris, and London, and in 1863 accepted the chair of Oriental languages in Elphinstone College, Bombay. Among his other labors while in India, he undertook tours into various provinces in search of ancient manuscripts, portions of his collections going to enrich the libraries of European universities. Returning from India in 1880, he became professor of Sanskrit and Indology in the University of Vienna. The breadth and accuracy of his knowledge in various departments of Oriental learning made him an ultimate authority. He collaborated in 1868 in the establishment of the Bombay Sanskrit Series, in 1867–84 in the production of a 'Digest of Hindu Law'; and in 1887 in the founding of the 'Wiener Zeitschrift für die Kunde des Morgenlandes.' His work upon the 'Grundriss der Indo-Arischen Philologie und Alterthumskunde' was interrupted by his death from drowning in Lake Constance.

Buhrstone (ber), or **Burrtone**, a variety of quartz containing many small, empty cells, which give it a peculiar roughness of surface. They are used principally as mill-stones. The best kinds are creamy white, with a granular and somewhat cellular texture, and are obtained in the Tertiary formation of the Paris basin, and chiefly at La-Ferté-sous-Jouarre. They are cut into wedge-shaped parallelopipeds, called panes, which are bound together with iron hoops to form large mill-stones. Numerous substitutes for the French buhr stone have been found in the United States, the most important being furnished by the buhrstone rock of the bituminous coal measures of northwestern Pennsylvania and eastern Ohio; but they cannot compete in the great markets with the French rock.

Building. The remarkable physical development of the United States in the last 20 years, with its attendant increase of wealth, is most strongly evidenced in the number of buildings of every character constructed during that period throughout the country. As an incentive to artistic improvement, and an example of co-operated effort and grouping of buildings, the World's Fair at Chicago, re-echoed in varying forms at the expositions of Atlanta, Nashville, Buffalo, and St. Louis, though temporary in character, has exerted a strong influence. Many new schemes of magnitude have been projected along lines which will require years for their completion, but the start has been made intelligently and with a view to the final result. It is only necessary to cite the proposed buildings of the University of California, at San Francisco, and of Washington University, at St. Louis, to suggest the power of this influence. The business and residential sections of the larger cities — and it might almost be added the outlying suburban districts — have undergone in many instances a complete transformation. The improvement and expansion of the steel, cement, brick, and terra-cotta industries (qq.v.) have done more to facilitate this transformation within the cities proper than any other causes. Fortunately the allied mechanical and decorative arts have kept pace with them, and in spite of the popular feeling that our cities are for the most part unsightly, they are more cosmopolitan, convenient, and interesting as to their buildings than ever before.

For the large majority of new buildings the systems of construction hitherto in vogue have been used without great change, and probably will continue to be so used. We must therefore look for signs of structural development, rather to the constructions commonly designated slow-burning, steel-skeleton, and fireproof.

In point of materials, and possibilities of decorative effect, the architect's palette has been extended to an incredible degree. Facilities of transportation make it possible to use granites, marbles, all kinds of stone, brick, and woods, ornamental bronze and iron, the most approved systems of plumbing, heating, lighting, and elevators, without approaching the domain of extravagance, and even without overstepping the limits of true economy. There has been a steady tendency toward more stable, permanent, and beautiful construction,— the outgrowth of public sentiment, which in its turn has been stimulated by the results attained. It would have been quite impossible 20 years ago, even had individual fortunes at that time been large enough to create the demand, to build the palatial residences, churches, hotels, and office buildings which we now look upon as commonplace, for in many trades skilled artisans were not to be had, and the difficulties of securing proper materials were too great.

Steel structural building of the commercial type has advanced to such an extent, and involves such colossal operations, that vast corporations have been formed for this especial purpose. These corporations are affiliated with financial institutions seeking investments, with owners of real estate desiring to make improvements, and with large manufacturing concerns furnishing materials of construction, so that the necessary conditions for undertakings of importance are kept constantly related. The Fuller Construction Company, The Norcross Brothers Company, The Wells Brothers Company, and others of a similar nature, carry on a business chiefly made up of steel structural buildings, aggregating many millions of dollars per annum, and widely scattered throughout the United States. These companies employ armies of men, covering every building trade and involving details of office management, methods of erection and finishing, transportation and storage of materials, and the harmonizing of the various and often conflicting elements entering into such undertakings, which are almost incredible, and can be appreciated only after the most minute investigation. It may be said in general that these constitute the great movements in building which distinguish the opening years of the 20th century.

Slow-burning Construction.— In buildings requiring special provisions against the spread of fire, and where the artistic effect is not of prime importance, a frequent mode of construction is that known as "slow-burning" or "mill" construction. This has been brought about in a great measure through the efforts of the mutual fire-insurance companies in New England. The system consists usually in building outside walls (generally of brick) of concentrated piers or buttresses, connected by a thin curtain wall; the girders, beams, and interior columns are made of large timbers, and the floors of plank of a suitable thickness. It is essential to avoid concealed hollow spaces, such as furring, where dirt would accumulate. The underlying theory of slow-burning construction is that whereas small timbers, such as the three-inch joists and studs, and the one-inch flooring of ordinary construction, readily burn through and are destroyed, large timbers, under the influence of severe heat, char but do not burn through readily, as the charred surface forms a non-conductor and protects the interior. If, however, for any reason they should burn to destruction, all connections are so made that the timbers can fall out of their places without disintegrating the masonry or columns on which they rest.

Beams are spaced every 8 or 10 feet between centres, and should not be painted for several years after completion of the building, in order to avoid dry-rot. The ends of timbers in masonry bear on iron plates with anchors, or rest in cast-iron boxes, with air spaces in the sides, which permit a circulation of air, and

STEEL SKELETON CONSTRUCTION.

reduce the risk of dry-rot. Floor planks are not less than three inches in thickness, and for spans of 12 feet usually four inches. The larger spans are less desirable than the smaller. These planks should not be over nine inches wide. They should be planed on both sides, and grooved on the edges, the grooves being filled with hard-wood splines.

Top floors are made of 1¼-inch boards of southern pine, maple, or other hard wood. It is desirable to lay top floors over a three-quarter-inch bed of mortar, or two thicknesses of heavy sheathing paper.

For rooms where there is unusual risk of fire, such as hot-air drying, it is well to protect the ceilings with plastering on metal lath, filling in solid so as to avoid any cavities. Wooden posts should be covered with asbestos paper and tin.

Roofs are best when flat, and are constructed in the same way as the floors. They should be covered with tin, gravel, or duck. Where the roof is pitched, it should be covered with shingles or slate, laid over a three-quarter-inch bed of mortar.

Superposed columns are connected by iron caps, bases, and pintles, arranged to give a proper bearing for the girders.

Partitions, if used, should be two-inch tongued-and-grooved plank set on end, and plastered both sides, on metal lath.

Doors and shutters are built of two or more thicknesses of inch boards, covered on all sides with asbestos paper and tin, lock jointed.

The underwriters' associations have formulated in detail the best practice in mill construction, and are willing to advise on all questionable points.

Steel-skeleton Construction.— The closing years of the 19th century witnessed a development in the structural use of steel for buildings which is wholly without precedent. While columns and floor beams of iron or steel had been in use for many years as interior supporting members, it was not until conditions demanded buildings of extraordinary heights that the metal framework was extended to the exterior as well as the interior structure. Exterior walls constructed entirely of masonry must be made too thick for economy of space and materials if the building which they enclose is more than six or seven stories high.

The first step was made by introducing iron columns in the masonry of the outside walls, with the sole purpose of supporting the adjacent floors, the masonry of the walls carrying itself on its own independent foundations. This system was found also to lack economy after the possible height of buildings had been increased a few stories. The culmination of the system was reached when the exterior frame was designed to carry not only the floors and their various loads, but also the exterior walls. Each story now has its enclosing wall independent of the story above and below it, so that, as is frequently the case, the outer facing or curtain wall of the high building is started at several levels at the same time at intervals of two or three stories.

There would seem to be no limit constructively to which this kind of building can be carried, provided the area of the building at the base is sufficiently large.

Vibration and deflection under the pressure of the wind must be provided against by stiffening braces or ties in the floors or partitions, more particularly where the height of the structure is relatively great.

Where streets are narrow, the crowding together of a number of such buildings darkens the streets and often produces disagreeable and even dangerous currents of air. The trend of legislation in large cities is toward restriction of height, Boston having already fixed a limit of 125 feet from the sidewalk level to the top of the cornice line.

There are three elements which enter into the construction of the steel-skeleton building, — foundations, columns, and floors. Of these three elements the column is the most important: for while foundations may settle, deranging the floor levels and causing the building to lean out of plumb; and while floors may bend or break without serious danger to any parts of the structure other than themselves,— columns, if they fail, may entail the collapse of the entire structure. For this reason, in the best work, columns are made of the softer, less brittle grades of steel, while floor beams are permitted of "medium" steel, a harder and consequently more brittle grade.

Many sections of columns have been devised, each having its own particular advantages, but columns in which all the surfaces, except those between riveted plates, are accessible, are generally to be preferred. These columns usually consist of a single web or plate, with one or more flange plates connected to the web by riveted angles. Other sections have been devised, made of Z bars or of channels connected by lattice plates, and a very ingenious column is that known as the Gray column, made up of angles in pairs connected by ties. The choice of any one form depends upon the stability of its section, the ease of procuring the parts of which it is composed, and the facility of connections. It is sometimes necessary to use the box column, but it is not to be recommended by reason of the inaccessibility of the interior surfaces. Water and steam pipes are sometimes run inside the fireproofing of columns next to the steel, but this is to be avoided if possible.

Columns are usually made in two- or three-story lengths. The bearing parts are carefully ground normal to their axis, and the connections are made by riveted cover plates. The extraordinary weights which these columns are called upon to carry, demand on ordinary soils a very extended footing. If this were attempted by the old method of brick or stone piers, the foundations would have to be carried to such depths that the system would not be economical. The customary method is that known as the grillage-beam system, in which the column starts from an iron or steel shoe which bears upon steel beams extending on opposite sides of the shoe, and bearing in turn upon one or more layers of beams bolted together and completely imbedded in concrete; under all is a layer of concrete whose area depends upon the compressive resistance of the soil. In rare cases the foundation is of solid rock, and the area may then be reduced to a minimum.

A peculiar type of grillage foundations is required for columns on or near party lines, beyond which the foundations may not extend. A cantilever construction is then used, whereby the wall column foundation is united by beams to the nearest interior column foundation, so that the two act together and in a measure counterbalance each other. Where foundations occupy an interior corner of a property, and must be maintained inside two intersecting party lines, it is often necessary to combine four grillages in the same fashion. Where the soil is of a very compressible nature, as is frequently the case in many parts of Chicago, the entire area of the building may have to be covered by a distributing foundation of concrete and beams, forming a pan upon which the building floats. This has been followed in some cases by settlements due to the leakage of the underlying soil, a result which might easily develop from the construction of other buildings in the immediate neighborhood. Where possible, it is preferable to penetrate through soft soils to a firm bed. In the lower part of Manhattan Island bed-rock has been reached by pneumatic caissons. These caissons are made of steel plates riveted together. The excavation is made under or in the caisson under air pressure sufficient to hold back any water-bearing material which may underlie the foundations of adjoining buildings. After the caisson has been sunk to its proper depth it is filled with concrete or such other masonry as has been designed to form the foundation. Hydraulic caissons have also been used for the same purpose. Where excavations adjoin high buildings on sandy soil, and are carried to a greater depth than the grillages, as in the case of the work on the subway in lower Broadway, New York, an artificial freezing process is sometimes resorted to. A network of tiny pipes is inserted into the sand foundation, winding in and out among each other, so as to reach every part of the foundation soil. A cold salt solution is sent through the pipes, causing the sand foundation to freeze solid. This is a very expensive process and not to be employed unless other means fail. See FOUNDATION.

The floors used in steel-skeleton construction may be of any of the ordinary fireproof types, but in designing the floors it is necessary to connect the columns by steel beams or girders, which act best for the stability of the building if arranged in continuous straight lines. The voids between the girders are spanned by beams, whose spacing is dependent upon the style of floor to be used, varying from 5 to 12 feet, the spaces between being filled by brick arches or porous terra-cotta tiles, or by concrete slabs. The amount of material in the beams must be exactly sufficient for the work — no more or less. This is essential, not only for economy, but also to reduce the dead loads on the joints, columns, and foundations. There are many varieties of each of these systems, nearly all requiring the use of steel ties, plates, or rods. For spans over 12 feet the monolithic concrete floor reinforced by steel bars or metal lath has been used, but there is a great tendency to deflection. The long-span systems are still in their infancy.

The girders of the exterior walls, commonly known as spandrel girders, are used at or near the level of each floor, and should be connected to the columns by knee or angle braces.

While the exterior walls of the building are carried in part on the spandrel girders, it is customary to rivet additional angles or channels on the outer face of the columns for the support of the outer four or more inches of the wall.

All projecting parts of the exterior, such as belt courses, cornices, and balconies, must be supported by special framings. The ornamental finish of cornices having any great projection is often secured to the frame by iron hangers.

All parts of steel framework, except those buried in concrete, such as grillage beams, should be painted with the greatest care, as their preservation depends almost entirely on the quality of paint used and the way in which it is applied. All surfaces should be first thoroughly cleaned of scale and rust. It has been found that concrete adheres to a clean steel surface, and is a sufficient protection. All remaining parts should be given a coat of oil at the shops; they should then be painted with a coat of red lead or graphite paint upon arrival at the building, followed by a second coat after they are assembled. Sometimes a third coat is given, but it is scarcely necessary if the two previous coats have been properly applied.

Fireproofing. — While the steel-skeleton building is economical from the constructive standpoint, its usefulness and safety are greatly impaired if it is left unprotected against the ravages of fire. Many systems of fireproofing have been devised, all of which, however, consist in enclosing the parts with a non-combustible substance, — usually a clay product, or concrete or plaster, — applied in blocks or molded forms, set in mortar. For the outside of exterior columns and girders it is considered sufficient to lay the outer facing of the wall, if of brick or terra-cotta, directly against the metal. Granite, by reason of its friability under the combined action of heat and water, should be kept sufficiently far away from the structural parts to allow of the insertion of a layer of concrete. For all other parts of the skeleton the usual protections consist of two inches of porous terra-cotta block, plaster block, or cinder concrete. Columns and beams are sometimes enveloped with a sheet of wire cloth or expanded metal, and plastered.

None of these systems may be considered absolutely perfect, since they have all shown serious signs of deterioration under the continued action of a fierce fire, but it is a conceded fact that concrete, as a fire-resisting material, is unequaled.

In connection with fireproofing it is essential that interior partitions be built of non-combustible materials. Those most frequently employed are of the same nature as the fireproofing just described. Porous terra-cotta blocks and plaster blocks, three or four inches in thickness, dependent upon the height of the story in which they occur, have certain advantages by reason of the rapidity with which they can be set up, and the ease with which they can be removed where alterations are desired. Partitions are often made of small T or angle irons, over which is spread expanded metal or wire cloth in one or two thicknesses, to which the plastering is directly applied. Double thickness partitions of this sort are more sound-proof than those first mentioned.

In many so-called fireproof buildings wood finishes are desired, which with the contents are a menace; but experience has shown that fire can usually be confined to the room in which it originates, and can be checked in a few minutes. Methods of fireproofing wood have been devised, and consist of injecting a fireproofing solution into the pores, either under pressure or by capillarity. Its use is not frequent, however, being largely limited to war-ships.

Exterior Finishes.— The artistic effect of a building depends more upon its color than upon its form either in general lines or detail. This is due to the fact that a good color sense is commoner than an appreciation of line and form. So true is this that many excellent designs have been utterly ruined by execution in unpleasing materials, and many meretricious designs receive public commendation entirely due to their satisfactory color effect. The search for novel and beautiful, as well as durable effects, has led to a great multiplication and improvement of materials.

Of all exterior materials the granites easily hold first place for buildings requiring dignity and durability. The finer granites come from New England, and range from various tones of white, through the deepening grays, into the dark reds, greens, and blacks. Many of the granites present beautiful surfaces when polished, and in general combine well in color scheme with almost any other material. The southern granites, so called, are not truly granites in the geological sense. They lack warmth and brilliancy of color, and by reason of their softness stain easily in a harsh climate or smoky atmosphere.

Sandstones, such as those from Ohio, Maryland, Pennsylvania, and Massachusetts, are reliable materials, the particles being well cemented together. They vary in color from the whites to the browns, and have practically superseded the Connecticut brown-stone used extensively in the 'sixties and 'seventies, but whose loose stratification resulted in early deterioration upon exposure.

Of the limestones, that from Indiana has had great popularity by reason of its softness for cutting when fresh, the large sizes in which it is obtainable, and, in the buff varieties, its beautiful color. The stone hardens upon exposure to the air, but its color changes, improving for a year or two, to become almost black after a period of 7 to 10 years.

The white marbles of Vermont, New Hampshire, and Georgia are thoroughly reliable, but discolor without assuming the soft warm tones of the old marble structures of Greece and Italy.

Gneisses abound throughout the Eastern States, some of them approaching very closely in texture to the true granites.

For durability and permanency of color, combined with economy, no exterior facing can surpass natural red brick. The appreciation of red brick has fortunately developed beyond the point where the smooth Philadelphia pressed variety is considered the only brick desirable for the finest work, so that we now have reds toning into the browns and purples, and combined often with dark headers, from which it is possible to lay up a simple surface full of artistic interest. Outside the plain red, there is a wide variety of brick within certain limits; whites, buffs, browns, or grays are easily obtainable both in the plain colors and mottled, and made by either the wet or the dry process. Color, width, and style of mortar joints, if used knowingly, can be made to intensify or soften the natural color of the brick. American enameled brick holds its own with the English, and is invaluable for light-shafts and damp places.

Nearly all makes, however, craze or chip in time.

Architectural terra-cotta, as an exterior finish, easily claims first rank in point of development. Many steel structures are covered entirely with it, excepting perhaps parts near the ground, subject to abrasion. It can be made in almost any color by means of "slips" or "glazes," and it lends itself readily to decoration. The use of terra-cotta is of advantage to the architect, in that he can see the models for every part of the work as they are in process, and vary them to his satisfaction before they are finally cast. Economy in the use of terra-cotta comes chiefly from minimizing the number of molds; but this must be guarded against, for, if pushed to excess, monotony is likely to result.

Ornamental bronze, copper, and iron work, through improved processes of manipulation, have added greatly to the possible richness of exterior effect.

Outside enclosures of sheet metal, such as iron or aluminum, are rarely æsthetic. Corrugated sheet iron has been used extensively for freight sheds, wharf enclosures, and similar ordinary constructions, where no effort for good looks has been made. The enclosure of steel-skeleton buildings with metal is not to be counted upon where such buildings are tenanted, as it is too great a conductor of heat.

Rough-cast and plaster work are most admirable and sympathetic as exterior wall finishes, where the extremes of temperature from winter to summer are not too great. Even adobe structures are possible in the South and West, but their use is most limited. Rough-cast or pebble-dash is applied to both masonry walls and lath; it is more durable on masonry, as the expansion and shrinkage of lath tend to disintegrate the mortar. Rough-cast is combined frequently with timber work in imitation of the old English half-timber constructions, and is specially adapted to domestic buildings of the freer country sort.

Concrete walls, where of the right texture and color, such as that made from coquina in Florida, have a pleasing effect.

Roof coverings comprise tin, copper, slag, tiles, slate, and shingles, each having its own appropriateness. Copper is the only permanent one of those mentioned, and slag is the next best. Tiles and slate require constant repairs, and shingles rarely last more than 20 years. Shingles lend themselves admirably to staining, and are deservedly popular. Thatch is attempted where picturesqueness is demanded.

A roof interesting from the constructive standpoint is that commonly used on the steel-skeleton building. It is known as actinolite, and consists of a number of thicknesses of heavy felts bedded upon a smooth Portland-cement surface, and covered with a roofing cement on which are laid vitrified tiles with the joints thoroughly filled, practically forming a pavement.

Interior Finishes.— For ordinary buildings the interior finish of floors, walls, and ceilings must necessarily be simple, consisting of cement or wood for the floors, and plaster for the walls and ceilings, except that in the case of mill construction walls are usually made of hard red brick, pointed inside the same as outside, and ceilings consist of the dressed undersurface of the floor planking white-washed, painted, or varnished.

Cement floors are the most permanent, particularly where they are subjected to moisture, although the hard pine and maple flooring commonly used is less tiresome to walk on and is sufficiently durable.

The so-called patent plasters have come largely into use by reason of their hardness and quick-setting quality. They are mixed by machine in fixed proportions, and are therefore more dependable in quality than the ordinary lime mortar. If applied to lath, the patent plasters require that the lath, if of wood, shall be wet before application, or, if of metal, that the metal be of heavy threads, as the finer wire cloth is sometimes eaten away by the ingredients of the plaster.

Tiles, whether of marble, ceramic, or glass, form excellent interior finishes, except that small tiles for floors are likely to loosen, and frequent joints in tiling become unsightly through discoloration. The glass tile known as "opalite" produces a finish similar to enameled brick, and has been shown in some cases to be more lasting. Interlocking rubber tiles are desirable in cases where there is risk of slipping, such as for elevator floors. They are also good deadeners of sound.

Beautiful effects of mosaic, both of marble and of glass, are easily obtainable — a great variety of color and design is largely in their favor. All of these applied finishes require a solid base, preferably of masonry or concrete.

The variety of woods for interior finish is almost without limit, and has been greatly increased by staining and by methods of finish.

In no department of interior ornamentation has greater progress been made than in plaster work — a system which can be pushed to almost any point of elaboration, and which lends itself perfectly to painted decoration. In fact, there are few materials that cannot be simulated in plaster if the decoration is clever.

The field of interior decoration was never wider, and the knowledge of the application of leathers, stamped, modeled, and woven fabrics, and the thousand and one other forms of wall applications, never better understood.

In marble for interior use America is not particularly fortunate. Granite and limestone produce satisfactory results, but most of the American marbles are cold and lacking in richness of texture. Among the best marbles are the Knoxville Gray, and a few of the whites. For the more beautiful effects recourse must be had to the imported marbles, such as Sienna, Numidian, Pavonnezza, Alps Green, and others.

EDGAR V. SEELER,
Architect.

Building and Loan Associations, co-operative organizations, originally designed to aid their members in procuring homes, at the lowest cost, and on the easiest terms. Later developments gave them some of the functions of a bank for savings. The associations are a development, dating from about 1835, when a few experimental ones existed in the United States, the movement beginning in Pennsylvania. The original associations proving successful, plans were gradually improved, until by 1850 they became an established part of American institu-

tions. They have been operated under various titles, besides the above, as mutual loan associations, home assistance associations, co-operative savings and loan associations, and co-operative banks, the latter title being popular in New England.

The basic plan of these associations is the issuing of stock, which is paid for in monthly instalments, and the loaning of the money thus raised to shareholders, borrowers paying twice as much per month as lenders. It has been common to give the shares a maturing value of $200 each, on which the holders pay $1 per month as long as they are lenders or investors, and $2 per month, as soon as they become borrowers on their stock. In addition to the $2, the borrower is also liable to have to pay a premium to secure his loan, when there are more shareholders seeking loans than there is money to loan.

Under such an arrangement an association received an average of $1.50 per month per share, and in the course of a little more than 11 years this was theoretically sufficient to bring the shares to par value. In practice, the shares would sometimes run out in 10 years, if premiums on loans ran high, and sometimes 12 or more years were required for shares to reach the $200 value, if the association had passed through hard times. When the shares reached the $200, or other maturing value, the lenders received their money back, and the borrowers had their loans canceled. Under the early plans, the maturing of the shares wound up the association. This was a hardship to many, and as a result the issuing of shares in annual series has become common. This enables outsiders to come in and take shares any time a new series is opened, or to purchase the most recent series, by paying the dues for the number of months such series has run.

The legislatures of the various States have made laws rendering easy the forming of these associations, because they have proven to be a good means of enabling wage workers to build and own their own homes. The parties interested manage their own affairs, and as the money is loaned out as fast as it comes in, there is seldom any loss by speculation. To illustrate how these associations assist a man of small means to build and pay for a home, let us follow the system from his point of view. Suppose he has a lot of land, for which he has paid $400. He can subscribe for five shares of an association, of the par value of $200 each, paying therefor $5 per month. Every month, or every few months, there will be money to be loaned, and he attends the meetings, and when he thinks the premiums are low, he bids in a $1,000 loan. If he has bid 10 cents premium on this, he must pay $2.10 each month on his shares, from the time he receives the use of the money. As a matter of fact he does not handle the money, but having bid successfully, and the directors having passed upon his lot and proposed house as a safe loan, he sets a builder to work, and his house is put up, the association taking a mortgage on it for $1,000, and the builder collecting his $1,000 from the association. Every month he pays his $10.50 into the association, just as if he were paying rent, and in 10 or 11 years the shares mature, and the home is paid for.

The plan appeals to the wage worker, because of the easy payments. It appeals to small lenders, because it affords them a sort of savings-bank, and encourages systematic savings. Small tradesmen and merchants are almost as apt to becomes interested in such associations as are those who work for a weekly wage, and the economical methods by which a large amount of money is borrowed and loaned safely have attracted many to the associations as being a safe depository, and sure to pay 6 per cent dividends.

Originally, these associations were usually confined to a town or locality, no loans being made beyond the territory where most of the members lived and knew the value of the property. But within recent years both State and national associations have been organized, which do business anywhere within the limits of their larger territory.

The management of an association is usually lodged in a board of directors elected annually from the shareholders, and whose members serve without pay. They pass upon the loans, and having investments of their own to protect, closely guard the association treasury. The secretary is customarily the only salaried officer, and is often paid for doing the detail work by a system of small fees. Sometimes the fines levied on delinquents are his sole compensation.

Each association. makes minor laws of its own, and many vary the plan as above given in numerous details; but the general principles here outlined are the same with all. In 1905 there were 5,265 of these associations, having a membership of 1,631,046, and total assets of $600,342,586.

Building Lease, a lease of land for a long term of years, usually 99 years, at a rent called a ground-rent, the lessee covenanting to erect certain edifices thereon, and to maintain the same during the term. At the expiration of the lease the houses built become the absolute property of the landlord, unless otherwise provided in the contract. See LEASE.

Building Materials. The materials used for structural engineering and architectural purposes may be conveniently divided into two general classes—"Materials of Construction," such as the woods, stone, metals, cements, etc., and "Materials of Consumption," such as coal, water, oil, etc., which are consumed or transformed while being used.

In this article, the materials of construction will be briefly considered according to their physical and chemical properties, and their adaptability for various purposes, leaving the consideration of the materials of consumption to the sphere of chemistry and physics where they properly belong.

Apart from their chemical composition, the principal properties of building materials important to the engineer are the "density" or specific gravity of the substance; its "resistance" or capacity to withstand strains and stresses; the "hardness" or power to oppose penetration; its "toughness" or capacity to elongate under tension without rupturing; its "brittleness," which is the opposite of toughness; and, its behavior under conditions of varying temperature, or when worked in the many ways required by structural operations.

Timber or Wood.—The following general facts relative to the physical properties of wood have been determined by experiments: (1) Bleeding has not much effect on the strength

of wood, but increases its flexibility slightly, and it is probable that bled timber will stand exposure to the weather fully as well as the unbled. (2) In general, moisture absorbed in the form of sap, or in the form of water after seasoning, reduces the strength of wood. Well-seasoned wood or that which contains not more than 12 per cent. of moisture is from 75 to 100 per cent. tronger than green timber. (3) In artificially-dried timber any remaining moisture exists in a uniform percentage throughout the mass, a condition which requires months, and sometimes years to attain in heavy air-dried timber. (4) The strength per square inch of section of large timbers is in every way equal to that of small timbers. provided they are equally sound and contain the same percentage of moisture. (5) In general, the strength of woods of uniform structure increases with their specific gravity, that is, the heaviest wood is generally the strongest. Oak, however, appears to be an exception to this rule. (6) Seasoned wood will increase in weight to the extent of 5 to 15 per cent. if exposed to the weather. This excess of weight can be easily reduced by keeping the timber in a warm dry place for a week or ten days.

The opposite table gives the physical properties of some of the woods suitable for structural, interior finishing, decorative and other similar purposes. The "elastic limit" given in the table is a relative quantity, as there is no definite "elastic limit" in woods similar to that in metals.

In selecting and preparing timber or wood for structural purposes, a careful consideration of the following facts in addition to those already stated is quite important: (1) That timber grown in moist soils decays more quickly than that grown in dry, sandy soil, and that, usually, the best timber is that grown in a dark soil intermixed with gravel, with the exception of the various kinds, such as poplar, cypress, willow and all others that naturally grow best in a wet soil. (2) That the wood of trees grown upon the plains, or in the centre of forests is less dense than that of those grown upon the edge of a forest or upon the side of a hill. (3) In temperate latitudes, as in the United States, standing timber should be selected in the latter part of July or the first part of August, when the sound and healthy trees are indicated by fresh green leaves, in contrast to the unsound and unhealthy trees, the leaves of which begin to turn yellow at that season of the year. Decaying branches, a scarcity of leaves, and the tendency of the bark to become rough and to separate from the wood, are positive indications that the physical properties of the wood are impaired.

The trees selected should be those that have most nearly attained their full maturity, a period which varies greatly with the different species. As a rule, the age and the rate of growth of a tree may be ascertained from the number and the width of the rings of annual increase which are exhibited in a cross-section of the wood. (4) Timber should be felled or cut either in midsummer or in midwinter. In midsummer, the most suitable time is in the month ot July. A tree should be cut as near to the ground as possible, as the lower part of the trunk furnishes the best timber. (5) As soon as a tree is felled it should be "dressed" by having its bark stripped off, then raised from the ground and the sap-wood removed, and finally squared or reduced to the required dimensions. (6) In the inspection of timber the quality of the wood may be ascertained by observing that its color, as exhibited by a cross-section, is practically uniform in the heart. It may be a little deeper in color at the centre than near the white-colored sap-wood next to the bark, but the gradation should be uniform and free from sudden transitions of color, or white spots, which are infallible signs of decay; that it is free from "wind-shakes" or circular cracks which separate the concentric layers of wood from each other, and which constitute a very serious defect; that it is free from "splits," "checks," and "cracks," which extend very deeply toward the centre; and that it is free from large or decayed knots, which tend to materially affect its strength.

acter. Other serious defects are indicated by the presence of many knots, which, although the timber may be sound, stamps it as being of stunted growth, and is commonly known as "knotty timber," and a spirally winding grain characteristic of "twisted wood" which is unfit for long pieces. Dry-rot is indicated by yellow stains; elm and beech are very quickly affected by it if left with the bark on after felling.

The proper seasoning and preserving of timber is of the utmost importance in connection with its use as a material of construction. Freshly cut timber contains from 35 to 50 per cent. of moisture, which may be reduced to 17 or 25 per cent., by exposure to the air in seasoning one year, and to below 12 per cent., by artificial drying in a comparatively short time.

There are various processes of seasoning. Natural seasoning requires a period ranging from 2 to 8 years, according to the size and physical properties of the wood. Timber of large dimensions is not only improved in strength, but is rendered less liable to warp and crack when becoming seasoned, by being previously immersed in water for several

PHYSICAL PROPERTIES OF TIMBER OR WOOD.

(As determined by tests of seasoned timber, containing 12 per cent. or less of moisture.)

The stresses are given in pounds per square inch

NAME OF WOOD.	ULTIMATE RESISTANCE TO —					Elastic limit	MODULUS OF—			ORDINARY WORKING STRESS			Weight per cubic foot (pounds)
	Tension	Compression (length)	Compression (cross)	Shearing (length)	Shearing (cross)		Elasticity	Ultimate bending	Elastic bending	Tension	Compression	Transverse	
Ash (American).	17,000	7,200	1,900	1,100	6,820	7,900	1,640,000	10,800	7,900	2,000	1,000	1,200	39
Birch	15,000	8,000	......	....	5,600	......	1,645,000	11,700	......	2,000	1,000	1,200	33
Cedar (American red)...........	10,600	6,000	600	400	1,300	5,600	900,000	7,000	5,600	1,300	700	900	24
Chestnut	11,100	5,300	....	....	1,500	......	1,130,000	8,000	......	1,400	600	900	41
Fir	13,000	......	......	1,300	......	......	1,500,000	......	......	......	......	......	.....
Gum..	......	7,000	1,400	800	5,800	7,800	1,700,000	9,600	7,600	1,200	900	900	37
Hemlock........	8,700	5,700	......	400	2,700	......	....	7,000	......	......	......	750	25
Hickory (American aver.).....	19,500	9,500	2,500	1,000	6,200	11,200	2,400,000	17,000	12,000	2,000	1,200	1,800	50
Lignum-vitæ ...	11,800	9,800	....	....	....	......	11,000	......	......	1,500	1,100	1,500	83
Maple	11,000	7,000	1,800	550	6,000	......	10,000	......	......	......	......	......	49
Oregon pine....	13,000	5,700	800	500	......	6,400	1,600,000	7,800	6,400	1,400	700	1,000	32
Oak (black).....	10,000	7,300	1,900	1,100	......	8,100	1,740,000	10,800	8,100	1,400	900	1,200	45
Oak (white)....	13,600	8,500	2,200	1,000	4,400	9,600	2,090,000	13,000	9,600	1,700	1,000	1,500	50
Pine (Southern yellow).....	13,000	8,000	1,200	835	5,600	10,000	2,070,000	12,600	9,500	1,600	1,000	1,500	38
Pine (Cuban)...	13,000	8,700	1,200	770	5,000	11,000	2,300,000	13,600	10,600	......	......	......	....
Pine (loblolly) ..	13,000	7,400	1,150	800	......	9,200	2,050,000	11,300	9,400	2,100	900	1,200	33
Pine (white)....	10,000	5,400	700	420	2,500	6,400	1,590,000	7,000	6,400	1,200	700	900	24
Poplar..........	7,000	5,000	......	....	......	......	......	6,500	......	900	600	750	....
Spruce (Northern)...........	11,000	6,000	800	400	3,250	......	1,400,000	8,000	......	1,200	700	900	26
Spruce (Southern)...........	1,200	7,300	1,200	800	......	8,400	1,640,000	10,000	8,400	1,200	700	900	30
Walnut (black) .	10,500	7,500	2,500	....	4,700	5,700	1,300,000	8,000	......	1,000	1,000	900	38

Furthermore, the condition known as "brash-wood," is generally consequent to the decay of the tree on account of age, and is characterized by a reddish color of the wood which becomes porous, and breaks off short without splintering; while "belted" timber is that which has been killed, or which has died from some unavoidable cause, before being felled, and is of a highly objectionable char-

weeks. When the seasoning is accomplished naturally by exposure to the air, the timber should be piled under a shed and kept dry, with a free circulation of air about it, but without being exposed to strong currents of the same. The bottom pieces should be placed upon skids raised about two feet from the ground, and a space of at least an inch should be allowed between the horizontal layers.

Slats or piling strips should be placed between the layers at each end of the pile, and also at short intervals between the ends so as to prevent the timber from "winding." It is important that these strips should be placed directly one over the other and that they should not be less than one inch in thickness. Care should be taken to pile the heavy timbers upon the ground floor of the shelter, and the light stuff upon the upper portion, with a clearance of at least two and one-half feet between the piles. The timber should be repiled from time to time, and all pieces showing any indications of decay should be removed, so as to prevent their affecting that which remains sound and healthy. The gradual method of seasoning is undoubtedly the most suitable for preserving the strength and durability of the timber; but, as already stated in the preceding paragraphs, it has been very definitely ascertained by tests that the results of artificial methods properly applied do not indicate that those qualities are materially affected by such processes, while other important advantages, such as the reduction in the time required for seasoning, and the uniformity of the percentage of moisture contained in the seasoned product, are unquestionably obtained. The hastening of seasoning by steaming the timber has been successfully accomplished, and the saturation of timber with a solution of corrosive sublimate, to secure it against dry-rot, and to protect it from the attacks of worms, has proved very satisfactory. Kiln-drying, however, is applicable only for boards and other pieces of small dimensions, and has a tendency to crack the wood and impair the strength in various ways, unless it is accomplished very slowly. Timber ought not to be seasoned by either charring, or smoking, and should not be painted unless it has been thoroughly seasoned, as such methods and applications effectually prevent the drying of the wood in the interior of the piece, so that fermentation sets in and decay soon takes place.

The principal processes of impregnation are the following: "Kyanizing," introduced by Kyan in 1832, consists of saturating the wood with a solution containing 1 pound of chloride of mercury to 4 gallons of water under a pressure of 15 pounds per square inch; "Burnettizing," introduced by Burnett in 1838, by which the wood is impregnated with a solution of 1 pound of chloride of zinc to 10 gallons of water, under an endwise pressure of 150 pounds to the square inch; the process introduced by Boucheri, by which the wood is impregnated with a solution of 1 pound of sulphate of copper to 12½ gallons of water, under a pressure of 15 pounds per square inch; "Creosoting," introduced by Bethel, by which the wood is impregnated with the oil of creosote mixed with bituminous matter under an endwise pressure of 150 to 400 pounds per square inch. The Kyanizing and the Boucheri processes are applied to standing timber, that is, while the tree is still growing, the head is cut off and the top of the stem is hollowed into the form of a bowl and filled with the solution which, being replenished from time to time, soaks down into the tree, killing it as it goes down, but thoroughly saturating the wood and imparting to it a remarkable degree of durability. Timber may be creosoted by simply steeping it in the oil of creosote, but the "creosoting" and "burnettizing" of timber of large dimensions is accomplished with the aid of special apparatus that gives the requisite pressures. Creosoting is the most satisfactory method of preserving timber used as piles for wharves against the attacks of the "Teredo" or ship-worm, but it is not an infallible remedy.

The presence of vegetable albumen in timber appears to be the primary cause for its deterioration. The most necessary element in the healthy growing tree, it is the most pernicious of all in that which is dead. The sapwood contains a large proportion of it and other fermentable elements, the putrefactions of which cause dry-rot or sap-rot, and produce various forms of injurious fungi, therefore, in order to correct these evils, the most effective method to preserve timber is to expel or exhaust its fluids, solidify its albumen, and introduce an antiseptic liquid. This appears to be accomplished in the most satisfactory manner by the process introduced by Robbins in 1865, by which the liquids are dissipated and the albumen solidified by heating the wood in a chamber raised to a temperature of $212°$ Fahr., and then submitting it to the vapor of coal-tar, resin or bituminous oils, which being at a temperature of not less than $325°$ Fahr., readily takes the place of the vapor expelled by the lower temperature.

Stone.— To be suitable for building purposes, it is essential that a stone should possess the qualities of durability, permanency of color, strength and toughness, and should be susceptible of being inexpensively quarried, and easily worked. The greater number of such stones belongs to some one of the following classes of rocks: (1) The crystalline silicious; (2) the calcareous; and (3) the fragmentary rocks, including the sandstones and slates.

Of the crystalline silicious rocks, the best known and the most suitable are the granites and the syenites, which possess an average crushing strength ranging from 12,000 to 16,000 pounds per square inch. Some authorities credit them with an ultimate crushing strength ranging from 25,000 to 30,000 pounds per square inch, but the results of the latest tests are indicative of the smaller values, which are, however, all sufficient for any kind of building purposes. These stones, varying greatly in their physical composition and color are found in large quantities in all parts of the world. They are very proof against the action of frost, and are commonly quite permanent in color, which ranges in the modern varieties, from a sparkling whitish gray to dark gray, and from a delicate pink to a dark red. Until recently, on account of their great hardness, granite was only employed for massive masonry in which roughly dressed stones could be appropriately used, or where the magnitude of the structures permitted the great expense involved by dressing and polishing; but, the development of improved forms of stone-cutting and dressing machinery during the last few years permits of its being turned and carved into columns, pilasters, and other forms, and polished perfectly, at a comparatively small' expense, so that it is being used more and more extensively, and is becoming one of the·most popular of all building stones.

Although quarried in practically every eastern State embracing the Appalachian Mountain system, from Maine to North Carolina, and in the States of California, Montana, Wyoming, Colorado, Minnesota, Wisconsin and Missouri, the greatest supply of granite in the United States is furnished by Maine and Massachusetts. The Maine granites, principally derived from the Hurricane Island quarries, are mostly of the light gray variety, although a limited amount of the pink and red varieties are also quarried and are found to be commercially available. The Massachusetts granites are of a rich dark blue-gray color, and are extensively quarried in the vicinity of Quincy, while other fine granites of similar qualities are quarried at Concord, New Hampshire, and Westerly, Rhode Island.

While the United States is one of the largest producers of granite, it is also one of the largest importers of the stone. Red granites from the quarries at Peterhead, Scotland, and the gray granites from Aberdeen are quite largely imported into this country for monumental work. They take a very high polish, and are of great durability, especially the coarse red variety. This is also the case with the red and gray Canadian granites, which are extensively quarried in Quebec, New Brunswick, Nova Scotia, Ontario and near Victoria, in British Columbia. In the United States, besides granite and syenite, the other crystalline silicious rocks available to some extent for building purposes are porphyry, gneiss and trap. Porphyry, although a very handsome building stone, with large crystalline structure, and colors ranging through shades of white, gray, pink, red and black, is used only to a limited extent in rough construction on account of its great hardness, and the consequent difficulty of cutting and polishing it within a reasonable limit of expense. Gneiss is more extensively used; it resembles granite in composition, but unlike granite, it has a well-defined cleavage, which allows it to be split into thick slabs. Trap is a sombre-hued rock, which is very difficult to work, and is seldom used as a material of construction, except in the form of paving blocks, or as crushed stone for making concrete or road material.

Of the calcareous rocks, the most suitable for structural purposes are the limestones and the marbles. These consist of carbonate of lime, and differ in quality rather than in composition, the marble having a crystalline structure capable of taking a high polish. The olitic limestones, possessing great strength, their resistance to compression ranging from 12,000 to 17,000 pounds per square inch, are of a very fine and even texture. The most widely known in the United States are those quarried in Indiana and Kentucky, and commouly known as "Bedford Stone;" they are handsome in color and are very easily worked. The colors of limestones range through broken shades of pink, red, yellow, green and blue, imparted to the structure by various impurities. Dolomitic limestone, commonly known as dolomite, contains magnesia in addition .to the carbonate of lime; is somewhat coarse in quality, and is quarried in nearly every State of the Union, to supply an apparently permanent local demand. The most favorably known of the foreign varieties is that obtained from the quarries of the Isle of Portland, England, and the French stones quarried near Caen, Normandy. The latter is a soft, fine grained stone of a light color very suitable for carved work, but entirely unfitted for exposed structures in cold climates, on account of its highly absorbent quality.

The marbles are much softer than the limestones, and have a crushing strength ranging from 7,000 to 8,000 pounds per square inch. They are the most showy and ornamental of all building stones, and have been very popular since the earliest times. A great many beautiful varieties are quarried in various parts of the United States, but about 60 per cent. of the total amount is quarried in the State of Vermont, the principal centres of the industry being at Dorset, West Rutland, Middlebury, Wallingford, Brandon and Pittsford. These marbles are of all varieties of texture, and range in color from pure white to dark green, and dark blue, the white stones often being veined and mottled with the darker colors. Very beautiful marbles are also quarried in Tennessee. They are particularly noticeable on account of their variegated colors, which include many shades of chocolate and red, and lemon yellow, olive and green, which form an endless variety of color combinations of striking effect. The distribution of these Appalachian marbles extends from Vermont to Georgia, and are extensively quarried in all of the States bordering that mountain system. On the other hand, although very fine marble deposits exist in many of the States in the Rocky Mountain region, they have not been worked to any great extent, up to the present time.

The most notable of the foreign marbles are those of Italy, the French Pyrenees and Belgium, although Germany, Austria, Spain, Portugal and Ireland, also furnish many varieties of fine texture and color. Among the most beautiful of these European productions are the "Brocatelle" marbles, having a light yellow body marked with veins and blotches of dull red, and the Languedoc, having a brilliant scarlet body color blotched with white, both of which are obtained from the Pyrenees; the "Black and Gold," a black limestone veined with yellow; the pure white stone of Carrara, and the "Giallo Antico," a yellow marble, all three of which are obtained from Italy; and the Saint Anne marble having a deep blue-black body color marked with white veins, and the pure black marble known as "Belgian Black," which are obtained from Belgium.

Of the fragmentary rocks, a great variety of sandstones are used for facing, lintels, and general , structural purposes, while slate is used for roofing, for floor tiles, flagging and mantels. Sandstones are composed of rounded and angular grains of sand, bound together by such cementing materials as silica, oxide of iron and carbonate of lime, into the form of solid rocks. The presence of silica gives a white colored stone of durable quality, but very difficult to work. Cementation by oxide of iron gives a reddish or brownish stone of medium durability, fairly easy to work. Carbonate of lime cement gives a gray-colored stone much softer than the other two varieties, and much easier to work, but much less durable. Sandstones vary in texture from those having a very fine grain to those composed of pebbles. The latter are divided into two classes — the "conglomerates" composed of rounded pebbles, and "breccias" composed of angular pebbles. Some sandstones have a clayey cement which makes them unfit for building purposes, while others, although they do not contain hardly any cement, and owe their tenacity to the pressure under which they were consolidated, make good building stone. As a general rule, sandstones are softer when first quarried, than after a period of seasoning by exposure to the air. They vary in color from light gray, buff, drab and blue, through shades of brown, pink and red. Their resistance to compression ranges from 9,000 pounds per square inch in the Ohio sandstone, to 12,000 pounds in the New Jersey stone; while the "Medina" stone and the bluestone of New York have a crushing strength of 14,000 pounds per square inch. Other well-known and extensively quarried varieties are the "Berea" stone of Ohio, and the "Portland" stone of Massachusetts and Connecticut.

Slate consists of an indurated clay which may be easily split into sheets of various sizes and considerable thinness. The principal quarries in this country are located in Maine, Vermont, Pennsylvania and New York, while those of Ardennes in France, and of Wales in England, are the greatest producers in Europe.

The methods employed in quarrying building-stone vary with the character of the stone, but the ultimate object of all of them is to obtain large and well-shaped blocks free from incipient fractures. Therefore, explosives are used as little as possible for that purpose, and the work of dressing is very largely done by hand. A great deal of machinery, however, is employed for the purposes of sawing, planing and polishing, and for splitting slate.

The durability of a building stone is one of the most important factors in its value as a material of construction. Durability is the ability of a stone to withstand the deterioration induced by its exposure, to the action of changing weather and temperature conditions, to the chemical agencies in the moisture of the atmosphere, and to the disintegrating action of growing organisms. The normal strengths of the softest building stones are much greater than is necessary for structural purposes, but under the action of the natural elements and agencies just stated, they disintegrate more or less rapidly according to their structure and the materials of which they are composed. Granites suffer disintegration chiefly from changes of temperature, and are affected but little by the expansion and contraction due to the absorption of water and its subsequent freezing in cold climates; and are almost entirely unaffected by the chemicals ordinarily held in the atmosphere, or carried by rain. Limestones suffer even less by expansion and contraction, but deteriorate much more quickly under the action of the chemicals in the air and rain; while the sandstones, on account of their porous structure, suffer chiefly from the effects of expansion and contraction and disintegrate so rapidly from the effects of frost that they are unsuitable for building purposes in countries with cold climates.

As the durability or "life in years" of a given variety of building stone would, therefore, vary greatly under different climatic conditions, it is obvious that the engineer and architect cannot be too careful in selecting the stones best suited to the climatic and other conditions of the localities in which his structure is to be built. In order to make the selection intelligently, it is necessary for him to know the special qualities of the various stones, according to their structural constituents, and the natural causes by which those constituents were formed into rocks. The porosity, or the capacity to absorb moisture, of the various classes of stone available for building purposes, varies from $\frac{1}{2}$ to 2 per cent. in the granites; 2 to 4 per cent. in the limestones, and 2 to 8 per cent. in the sandstones, and their hardness or resistance depends on the firmness with which the particles of which they consist are bound together. In the igneous or metamorphic rocks, the bond is the result of crystallization, and in the sedimentary rocks it is due to cementation by depositions of silica, etc., between the individual grains as already described. The resistance of a stone to frost action may be conveniently and accurately tested by soaking it in water and then freezing it; the process being repeated a number of times and the amount of disintegration noted.

Artificial Stones.— These are represented by a great variety of artificial compositions of which the basis is hydraulic cement. The best known varieties are the "Béton-Coignet," a French production composed of Portland cement, silicious hydraulic cement and clean sharp sand. These constituents when mixed together with a small amount of cold water make a plastic compound which is hardened in molds to the consistency of a stone, very suitable for various building purposes; the "Ransome stone," which consists of a mixture of sand and silicate of soda, moulded into blocks and slabs, are hardened under pressure in a hot solution of chloride of calcium; "Portland stone," consisting of a mixture of Portland cement and sand, or sand and gravel, rammed while wet and plastic into molds to harden; "McMurtrie stone," consisting of the Portland stone mixture to which a certain amount of alum and potash soap is added so as to deposit compounds of alumina in the pores of the stone and thus reduce its porosity; the "Sorel stone," another French product, made by adding a solution of chloride of magnesium to the oxide of magnesium; and various kinds of "sand bricks" made by mixing sand and lime into a moist paste, which after molding into blocks of various sizes, are hardened by heat in suitable furnaces. The Portland stone, under various trade names, is very extensively used in the United States; the Ransome stone in England, and the French products mostly in the country in which they were originated. All of them possess considerable merit for building purposes, except the Sorel stone, which is mainly used for making emery wheels.

Cement is applied in various ways for structural purposes other than simply as a bonding material. The several varieties of cements consisting of common lime, hydraulic lime, and those classified as "natural," "Portland" and puzzolanic cements, when combined with sand, and broken stone or gravel, or other hard material in fragments, afford several varieties of concrete which are extensively used for foundations in damp and soft or yielding soils; for breakwaters and for sea walls; for sidewalks, pavements and sustaining walls, and for subterranean and submarine masonry, under almost every combination of circumstances occurring in practice.

Combined with structural iron and steel, and now generally known as "re-inforced concrete," its sphere of application has been greatly extended, especially as a structural material for bridges, and in the construction of fireproof buildings. It has been demonstrated by actual test, that in these lines its general durability and fire-resisting qualities are not only superior to any other material, but that by its use the cost of large structures, such as office buildings, etc., may be reduced at least 20 per cent., as compared with the estimated cost of the steel and tile of ordinary fireproof construction.

The use of various kinds of brick and tile, and of iron, steel and other metals for building purposes, is too familiar to note, however, that during the last decade, the tensile strength of structural iron and steel have been more than doubled by improved processes of manufacture, and they have almost entirely supplanted wood and stone in those portions of large structures which are subjected to the greatest strains, and also where economy of space is of vital importance.

For further detailed information relative to the production and strength of various kinds of building materials, and the specific purposes for which they are most suitable, see articles entitled ARCHITECTURE; BRICK; BUILDING; BUILDING STONE; CEMENT; CONCRETE; REINFORCED CONCRETE; IRON; LUMBER INDUSTRY IN THE UNITED STATES; STEEL, MANUFACTURE OF; TIMBER LANDS; WOOD; AND SPECIAL ARTICLES ON GRANITE; LIMESTONE; MARBLE; SANDSTONE; MASONRY, STRENGTH OF MATERIALS, in this Encyclopædia.

Bibliography.—Also consult: Hall, 'Treatise on the Building and Ornamental Stones of Great Britain' (London, 1872); Johnson, 'The Materials of Construction' (New York, 1899); and Merrill, 'Stones for Building and Decoration' (New York, 1891).

WILLIAM MOREY, JR., C. E.,
Consulting Civil and Mechanical Engineer.

Buisson, Ferdinand Edouard, fär-dē-nŏṅ ä-door-är bwē-sŏṅ, French educational administrator: b. Paris, 20 Dec. 1841. After completing his studies at Paris he went to Neuchatel, Switzerland, where he taught from 1866 to 1870. His appointment by Jules Simon in 1871 as inspector of elementary schools aroused much agitation on account of his advocacy of the secularization of the schools. The opposition of the Church party led to his resignation. In 1873 he was sent to the exposition in Vienna, to represent French educational interests; in 1876 he came to Philadelphia on a similar mission, and in 1878 was in charge of the educational section of the Paris Exposition. In 1879 he was made director of elementary instruction and became prominent for the reforms introduced during his administration. After resigning from this post in 1896 he accepted the professorship of pedagogy in the *Faculté des Lettres.* His strong stand on the Dreyfus question attracted much attention. He is the author of an authoritative 'Dictionary of Pedagogy' (1882–4), and has also written 'Liberal Christianity'; 'Orthodoxy and the Gospel in the Reformed Church'; 'The Teaching of Sacred History in Primary Schools'; 'Duties of American Scholars'; 'Pedagogical Lectures and Talks'; and a life of Sébastian Castellion.

Bukowina, boo-kō-vē'nä ("beech land"), Austria-Hungary, a province in the extreme east of the empire, surrounded by Galicia, Russia, Moldavia, and Hungary. Area, 4,035 square miles. It is traversed by offsets of the Carpathians, culminating at 6,077 feet; gives rise to many rivers flowing toward the Black Sea; and abounds in wood, along with considerable mineral riches. Pop. (1900) 729,921.

Bul-tso ("borax lake"), Thibet, a lake situated 100 miles northwest of Lassa. It has an area of 24 square miles.

Bulacan, boo-lä-kan', Philippines, a town in Luzon, about 22 miles northwest of Manila, with which it is connected by railway. The town is composed mainly of native huts, although there are factories in which silk matting is made. Sugar-boiling is also an industry of importance. The place has strategic advantages, which caused it to become a theatre of military operations after the Spanish-American war. It was fully pacified in 1900, and made a military post by the United States authorities. Pop. about 14,000.

Bulama, boo-lä'ma, an island on the west coast of Africa, one of the Bissagos. It is 18 miles long and 9 broad, and is situated about two miles from the mouth of the Rio Grande. It is very fertile, but not easy of access. It is now occupied by the Portuguese. See BISSAGOS.

Bulan, boo-län, Philippines, a town of the province of Albay, situated in the southeastern part of the island of Luzon. Pop. about 11,000.

Bulau, boo'low, or Tikus, ti'koos, an animal of the mole family (*Talpidæ*) and genus *Gymnura* (*G. rafflesii*), a native of Sumatra and Malacca, bearing a considerable resemblance to the opossum. The muzzle is much prolonged, the fur pierced by a number of long hairs or bristles, and the tail naked. It is possessed of glands which secrete a kind of musk.

Bulawayo, boo-lä-wä'yō, Rhodesia, the principal town and chief commercial centre of Matabeleland, South Africa, 490 miles northeast of Mafeking, 1,360 miles from Cape Town, with which it is connected by railroad. It has several hotels, good business blocks and residences, banks, and telephone service, and is rapidly growing in size and importance. A few years ago it was the chief town of the Matabele tribe, though only a collection of rude huts, in an enclosure of wattles, whose inhabitants were savages of the lowest type. The royal kraal is now replaced by the government house, which communicates by an avenue a mile and a half long with the town proper. Pop. (white) about 5,000.

Bulb, the name given to a leaf bud belonging to certain perennial herbaceous plants, and particularly to the monocotyledons. It is always underground, and is supported by a kind of solid and horizontal plate lying between it and the true root. To this flattened portion the fleshy scales of which the bulb is externally formed are fixed by their base. The interior contains the rudiments of the flower-stalks and leaves. The outermost scales are thin and dry like paper, but they become more fleshy and succulent in the interior. Sometimes the scales are of one piece, a single scale embracing the whole circumference of the bulb, as in the onion and the hyacinth. They are then named "coated" or "tunicated bulbs." At other times the scales are smaller and free at the sides, and cover one another only in the manner of tiles on a roof, as in the white lily. Lastly, the coats are sometimes so close as to be confounded together, so that the bulb seems as if formed of a solid and homogeneous substance. Such bulbs are called "solid," and they are exemplified in the common saffron. Bulbs again are either "simple," as in the tulip or squill, or they are "multiple," or formed of several small bulbs collected under the same envelope, as in garlic. Bulbs are reproduced every year, but differently in different species, the new bulbs sometimes being formed in the centre, sometimes at the side, sometimes above, sometimes below the old bulbs.

Bulbul, bŭl'bŭl, a small, brilliantly plumaged thrush-like bird of the family *Pycnonotidæ*, species of which are found in Asia, Persia, India, and South Africa. The South African one (*Pycnonotus tricolor*) is remarkable for becoming intoxicated by syringa berries and similar fruits, at which time it is easily captured and caged. The common Indian bulbul (*P. hæmorrhous*) is a familiar and favorite bird of European residents, and often builds its nest in their gardens and on the verandas. The pugnacity of the males is utilized by the natives for their amusement, the birds being caught and trained to fight for small prizes. The name "bulbul" was applied to the little Persian nightingale (q.v.), and first introduced into English poetry by Lord Byron, after which its praises were much sung by the poets of the day.

Bulfinch, Charles, American architect: b. Boston, 8 Aug. 1763; d. there, 15 April 1844. He was graduated from Harvard in 1781, for several years traveled in Europe, studying architecture, which he adopted as a profession upon his return in 1786. In 1793 he built the first theatre in Boston. In the course of his career he designed more than 40 churches and public buildings in New England. Among them were: the State house, Suffolk county courthouse, Massachusetts General Hospital, and remodeled Faneuil Hall in Boston; the State prison and MacLean Asylum, at Charlestown; the county jail and University Hall in Cambridge; and the State house in Augusta, Me. From 1817 until its completion in 1830 he was the architect of the national capitol at Washington. Consult: Ellen Bulfinch, 'Life and Letters of Charles Bulfinch, Architect' (1896).

Bulfinch, Thomas, American author: b. Boston, Mass., 15 July 1796; d. there, 27 May 1867. He graduated at Harvard University in 1814. Although engaged in business he managed to devote considerable time to literature. Among his best-known works are 'The Age of Fable' (1855); 'The Age of Chivalry' (1858); 'Legends of Charlemagne' (1864); 'Oregon and Eldorado' (1866).

Bulgaria, bŭl-gār'ĕą, or bool-gä'rĕą, a principality in Europe, bounded north by the Danube and Rumania; east by the Black Sea; south by Turkey; and west by Servia; capital. Sofia. It has an area of 38,080 square miles. Its surface is a gradually sloping plain, broken by occasional mountains, which give rise to many rapid tributaries to the Danube. There is little mining, although the mountains are rich in minerals. The soil is excellent and the slopes of the mountains are richly wooded. The inhabitants, though not skilled in agriculture, export a considerable quantity of grain, chiefly wheat. Fruit and vegetables are raised in abundance. Roses are largely cultivated for the production of the attar: 80,000 gallons of wine are made annually; silk worms are bred in some regions; and tobacco forms an important crop. Domestic industries are chiefly carpets, cloths, hosiery, and ribbons. The roads are very bad, and there is but a single line of railroad, about 500 miles, on the route between Vienna and Constantinople. All traffic is carried on by the rivers, and the export trade by the Black Sea. The government is Christian. There is a national militia, and military service is compulsory. The Bulgarians were originally a Tartar nation, which in the 4th century was settled on the Volga. The ruins of their former capital may still be seen in the neighborhood of Kazan. Their kingdom, which occupied a part of the Asiatic Sarmatia of the Greeks, was called Great Bulgaria, and is now comprehended in the Russian government of Orenburg. They afterward removed to the countries between the Bog and the Danube, and called their territories Second Bulgaria. The first Bulgarian kingdom south of the Danube was founded in the latter half of the 7th century, but the Bulgarians who established it were comparatively few in number, and after their adoption of Christianity in the 9th century they became completely mixed up with the Slavonic inhabitants, though the whole became known as Bulgarians. The greatest ruler of this kingdom was Symeon (888–927), who subjugated the greater part of the peninsula, and raised the Archbishop of Bulgaria to a position independent of the Patriarch of Constantinople. Under the son of Symeon this empire fell to pieces. The western half broke off and formed a separate kingdom, with Ochrida in Macedonia for its capital; and the eastern portion was subdued by the Byzantine emperor, John Zimisces, who reincorporated it with the empire. The western Bulgarian kingdom existed only till about 1018, when it also was subdued by Basil II., «the slayer of the Bulgarians.» Toward the end of the 12th century, however, the Bulgarians revolted and managed to establish a third kingdom between the Balkan range and the Danube, which, sometimes weak and sometimes powerful, continued to exist till the advent of the Turks. The last ruler of this kingdom was conquered by Bajazet I. about 1390, and for nearly 500 years the Turks ruled supreme. In 1876, on account of the atrocities of the Turkish soldiers, an insurrection broke out. Russia took the part of Bulgaria against Turkey, and the war of 1877–8 followed. (See BATAK.) By the first article of the Treaty of Berlin, 13 July 1878, the principality of Bulgaria was constituted, made tributary to Turkey, and placed under the suzerainty of the Sultan. In 1879, Alexander of Battenberg, a German prince, was chosen sovereign of part of Bulgaria, the rest being made a separate province called East Rumelia, to prevent Bulgaria from becoming a strong state. In 1885 there was a revolution in East Rumelia, which annexed itself to Bulgaria. Servia intervened, and Alexander was forced to abdicate. Against Russia's will, Ferdinand of Saxe-Coburg accepted the vacant throne in 1887. The government is that of a hereditary prince as chief executive, with responsible ministers and Legislative Assembly (one for every 10,000), elected directly by the people for three years; it pays annual tribute to the Sultan. Pop. (1900) 3,733,189: about 74 per cent Bulgarians, 19 per cent Turks, the rest Spanish Jews, with a sprinkling of Greeks; 77 per cent are of the faith of the Orthodox Greek Church; only 2½ per cent Moslems.

Bulgarian Language and Literature. Bulgaria and the adjacent provinces of Macedonia are considered to have been the cradle of the old Slavic languages. The ancient Bulgarian language was the richest of them all, and was the scriptural language of the Greek-Slavic Church, and the great medium of ecclesiastical literature in the ancient Slavic lands. The Russian language is said to have been molded by missionaries of the Greek Church sent from Bulgaria about the 11th century, while the future empire was still in a state of semi-barbarism. The Russian tongue has preserved many inflections which the Bulgarian has lost. After the overthrow of the Bulgarian kingdom at the close of the 14th century, the grammatical structure and purity of the language became impaired by mixture with the Wallachian, Alba-

nian, Rumanian, Turco-Tartar, and perhaps Greek vernaculars; and the modern Bulgarian language has only the nominative and vocative of the seven Slavic cases, all the rest being supplied by prepositions. It has an article, which is put after the word it qualifies, like that of the Albanians and Wallachians. Among the ancient Bulgarian ecclesiastical literature must be mentioned the translations of the Bible by Cyril and Methodius, and the writings of John of Bulgry in the 10th century. Grammars of the Bulgarian language have been published by Neofyt in 1835, and by Christiaki in the following year. Venelin, a young Russian scholar, sent to Bulgaria by the Russian archæographical commission, published in 1837 a grammar and two volumes of a history of the Bulgarians, but died while he was engaged in preparing a third volume. A new grammar was given to the public by Bogojev in 1845, and finally in 1849, by the Rev. E. Riggs, an American missionary stationed at Smyrna, who also sent a Bulgarian translation of Gallaudet's 'Child's Book on the Soul' to New York. Dictionaries of the Bulgarian language have been compiled by Neofyt and Stojanowicz. A Bulgarian version of the New Testament was printed at Smyrna in 1840 for the British and Foreign Bible Society. The Bulgarian national songs are numerous, and are similar to those of the Servians. Czelakowsky's collection of Slavic songs contains a number of Bulgarian songs. Bogojev has published several historical poems. Among more recent writers may be mentioned the poet Christo Boteff, and the poet-novelist Ivan Vazoff, while a publication on the subject of education has appeared from the pen of Neofyt.

Bulgarin, Faddéï Venediktovich, fä-dä'ē vä-nä-dĭk'tō-vĭch bool'gär-ĭn, Russian author: b. Minsk, 1789; d. 13 Sept. 1859. He served in the Russian army, but, finding himself neglected, in 1810 joined Napoleon. In 1819 he returned to St. Petersburg, where his writings soon attracted notice by their intense satire and servility. In 1825 he started the *Ssevernaja Ptchelá* (*Northern Bee*), a daily paper, which for long was alone permitted to discuss political questions. A zealous supporter of reaction and of absolutism, he enjoyed, through relations with the secret police, an unlimited power. He was a witty and versatile writer, and published travels, histories, novels, and statistical works.

Bulgaris, bool-gä'rēs, Demetrius, Greek statesman: b. Hydra, 1803; d. Athens, 11 Jan. 1878. While a young man he held office in his native city and took a prominent part in the Grecian war for independence. In 1831, after the downfall of Cape d'Istria, he had charge of the administration of the Department of Marine; but on the accession of King Otho he retired from office. After the revolution of 1843 he was a member of the Senate, and from 1848 to 1849 was minister of finance in the Cabinet of Canaris. During the Crimean war he was at the head of the Cabinet and as minister of the interior put an end to internal disorder and conciliated the powers. In 1857 he resigned and entered the Senate as a leader of the opposition. At the outbreak of the revolution of 1862 he was made regent, and chose Canaris and Rufos as his colleagues, but was deposed by the former. In 1865, 1872, and 1874–5 he was again at the head of the Cabinet.

Bulga'rus, Italian jurist: b. Bologna in the 11th century; d. 1166. He was one of the famous group of writers known as the "Four Doctors" of Bologna, and his most noted work is a legal commentary, 'De Regulis Juris.'

Bulim'ia, a disease characterized by insatiable hunger. Persons suffering from this disorder are never satisfied. When the stomach is surfeited they throw off the food they have taken, half-digested, and with violent pain. It frequently occurs in the insane, in cases of paresis, etc., and usually appears as a concomitant of other diseases, as certain intermittent fevers, and diseases of the stomach and bowels, particularly such as are produced by the tapeworm.

Buli'mus, a genus of land-snails of the family *Helicidæ*, the species of which are mainly restricted to South America, especially Peru, Ecuador, and Bolivia. Some of the species are very large, as are also their eggs, those of *B. oblongus* being about the size of a sparrow's. There is an egg of another species in the British Museum which measures exactly one and three fourths inches in length.

Bulkeley, Morgan Gardner, American politician: b. East Haddam, Conn., 26 Dec. 1837. At the age of 15 he entered a mercantile house in Brooklyn, N. Y., and in a few years became a partner in it. When the Civil War broke out he went to the front as a private in the 13th New York regiment, and served during the McClellan-Peninsula campaign under Gen. Mansfield at Suffolk, Va. In 1872, he came to Hartford, organized and became president of the United States Bank in that city, and later was elected president of the Aetna Life Insurance Company, a position he still holds (1903). For 30 years he has been a prominent figure in local and state politics. He was four times elected mayor of Hartford, 1880–8, and in 1889 was elected governor. At the State election in November 1890 the first gubernatorial election under the new secret ballot law, the Democratic ticket received a considerable plurality over the Republican ticket; but a majority being necessary to elect, there was some doubt whether there had been a choice by the people for governor or treasurer. Accordingly the matter went before the General Assembly, which met in January 1891, and in which the Republicans had a majority of four on joint ballot, the Senate being Democratic. A long contest ensued between the two Houses, the Senate claiming the election of the recent Democratic candidates, and refusing to recognize in any manner Governor Bulkeley and those hold-over Republican officials. The matter was finally settled on 5 Jan. 1892, when the State supreme court, in the *quo warranto* suit brought against Governor Bulkeley by the Democratic candidate for governor, found "Morgan G. Bulkeley to be governor, both *de facto* and *de jure*," and his right to hold over till both houses of the General Assembly should unite in declaring the election of his successor was affirmed. As the two houses could not agree the governor remained in office for another full term. In November 1892 the Democratic ticket swept the State. Governor Bulkeley has since, as chairman of the Connecticut highway and bridge commission, interested himself earnestly in trying to procure a fine stone bridge across the Connecticut at Hartford.

Vol. 3—18.

Bulkeley, Peter, American colonist and clergyman: b. Bedfordshire, England, 31 Jan. 1583; d. Concord, Mass., 9 March 1659. He was educated at Cambridge, and for 21 years was rector of a Bedfordshire parish. Being removed from this by Archbishop Laud, for non-conformity to certain ceremonies of the Church, he left England and became the first minister at Concord, in the colony of Massachusetts, of which famous town he was the chief founder. He was the author of some Latin poems, which are contained in Cotton Mather's 'History of New England'; also of some English verse, and of a theological treatise, 'The Gospel Covenant Opened,' published in London in 1646. He was as remarkable for his benevolence and kind dealings as for the strictness of his virtues.

Bulk'head, the name given to a variety of forms of partition. In its nautical sense a bulkhead is a wall or partition extending across the ship for the purpose of dividing the hold into compartments, for separating classes of merchandise, for strengthening the vessel, or more especially for confining water which may leak in, to the compartment in which the breach occurred. In large vessels longitudinal bulkheads are employed, as well as those running athwartships, and communications between the compartments are maintained by means of doors which can be instantly closed in case of accident and for the purpose of maintaining forced draught. One of the most important bulkheads in a ship is the one farthest forward, which is built with great strength, being designed to withstand the shock of ramming another vessel, an iceberg, etc., and confining the damage to a small portion of the vessel. It is hence known as the collision bulkhead. Another form of bulkhead is a strong framework used in the construction of tunnels, to prevent the irruption of water, quicksand, etc., into the workings. The term is also applied to the facing (generally of timber) that supports the seawall of a harbor, and somewhat illogically to the sloping flap doors often used to cover the entrance of a dwelling-house cellar.

Bull, Charles Stedman, American physician. He was graduated from Columbia College in 1864, and at the College of Physicians and Surgeons in 1868. He is surgeon to the New York Eye and Ear Infirmary, consulting ophthalmic surgeon to St. Luke's and Presbyterian hospitals, and St. Mary's Hospital for Children. He is professor of ophthalmology in Cornell University. He has written: 'Eye Defeets Which May Cause Apparent Mental Dulness and Deficiency in Children' (1901); 'Tuberculosis of the Eye' (1900); both in the 'Transactions' of the New York Academy of Medicine; 'Vascular Tumors of the Orbit' (1900), and other articles on his specialty in the 'Transactions' of the American Ophthalmological Society, the 'Medical News' and 'Medical Record.'

Bull, George, English bishop: b. Wells, Somersetshire, 25 March 1634; d. 17 Feb. 1710. Having graduated with distinction at Oxford, he was ordained at the early age of 21, and soon became rector of St. George's, near Bristol. Here he made himself beloved by all, and kept his parish in peace during those troublesome times. In 1658 he became rector of Suddington St. Mary's in Gloucester, and in 1662, of Suddington St. Peter's. In 1669 he published in the Latin tongue his most important work, called 'Harmonia Apostolica,' an attempt to reconcile the apparent contradictions between St. James and St. Paul on the doctrine of justification. This publication extended his fame to foreign countries, and his reputation procured him a stall in the cathedral of Gloucester. In 1705 he was promoted to the bishopric of St. David's. See edition of his works, with a life, etc., Clarendon Press, Oxford (1827).

Bull, George Joseph, Canadian ophthalmic surgeon: b. Hamilton, Ontario, 16 Feb. 1848. He was graduated at McGill University in 1869, studied in Paris, and began the practice of medicine in Montreal, devoting himself especially to diseases of the eye. He made his residence in Paris in 1886, and has won celebrity as an expert in ophthalmic subjects. He has written 'Ophthalmia and Optometry,' and many similar works.

Bull, John, English musician: b. Somersetshire, about 1563; d. Antwerp, 12 March 1628. He was appointed organist in the Queen's Chapel in 1591; first music lecturer at Gresham College in 1596; and organist to James I. in 1607. A Catholic, he fled beyond the seas in 1613, and at Brussels entered the archduke's service. In 1617 he became organist at Antwerp cathedral. Little of his music has been printed. The claim advanced for his authorship of 'God Save the King,' is unfounded.

Bull, John, the popular name of personification for the English nation. Its origin is obscure. Its first literary use appears to have been in Arbuthnot's famous 'History of John Bull,' written in ridicule of the Duke of Marlborough. The name is also used for an Englishman.

Bull, Ole Bornemann, ō-le bôr'ne-män bul, Norwegian violinist: b. Bergen, 5 Feb. 1810; d. near there, 17 Aug. 1880. He secured great triumphs both throughout Europe and in America by his remarkable playing, which won for him a distinct and unique position in the musical world as a virtuoso of extraordinary talent and mastery of the violin. He conquered serious discouragements in preparing for his career, throughout which public interest and admiration were no less awakened by his manliness and grace of bearing than by his skill as a musician. At his début (Paris 1833) he was honored by the presence of Paganini, and that master was witness to the young aspirant's triumph. Bull afterward studied and turned to good account the method of Paganini. In business life he met with various successes and reverses. He lost all his money in ·a scheme to found a colony of his countrymen in Pennsylvania, and had to take to his violin to repair his broken fortunes. He afterward making in this country, settled at Cambridge, Mass., and retained a summer residence in Norway. Consult: 'Ole Bull: A Memoir' by Sara C. Bull (Boston 1883).

Bull, Papal, an authoritative letter issued by the Roman pontiff acting in his official capacity as head of the Church. A Papal Brief is also an official letter of the pontiff of a less formal and weighty character, and differs in

sundry particulars from the Bull, especially in its seal. The seal of the Bull, from which comes the name of the instrument is a *bulla* or globular mass of lead on which is impressed the name of the reigning Pope, also those of Saints Peter and Paul, abbreviated, S. Pe, S. Pa. The material of the Bull is parchment, but of the Brief, white paper; and the seal of the Brief is of red wax, stamped with the Fisherman's Ring, which gives the impress of St. Peter in a boat fishing. There are other peculiarities in matter and manner distinguishing the Bull from the Brief, but it suffices to note the foregoing. Of Papal Bulls that have played a signal part in history ecclesiastical or civil especially worthy of mention are the Bull *Clericis laicos* (1296) of Boniface VIII. by which the French clergy were forbidden to pay taxes to King Philip the Fair unless these were approved by the Pope; the Bull *Exsurge Domine* of Leo X. against Martin Luther (1520); the Bull *In Coena Domini* against heretics and fautors of heresy, dating from the 15th century, but re-enforced by Pius V. in 1571 and ordered to be publicly read in all parish churches yearly on Holy Thursday; the Bull *Unigenitus* (1713) against quietism and Jansenism; the Bull *Dominus ac Redemptor,* of Clement XIV., abolishing the Jesuit order (1773), and the Bull *Pastor æternus* (1870), which defined papal infallibility.

Bull, a ludicrous speech in which the ideas combined are totally incongruous or contradictory. A good example is Artemus Ward's saying of Jefferson Davis that "It would have been money in Jefferson Davis's pocket if he had never been born."

Bull and Cow, the names given by English-speaking races from time immemorial to the male and female respectively of bovine cattle. The words are probably imitative, the root-idea of "bull" being a suggestion of its bellowing; while "cow"— which in early English, as yet in Scotch and some provincial dialects, is pronounced *coo* — is imitative of the lowing call to the calf. Since these animals have become domesticated, and most of the males been castrated, the term has come to mean more particularly an unmutilated ox. On the other hand, the large size and robust qualities of the bull have led to a transference of the term to the males of various other animals having no zoological resemblance, or very little, to the cattle. Thus we speak of "bull and cow" elephants, moose, wapiti, seals, whales, and even alligators; while various animals, as the bull-snake take the name as expressive of some bull-like quality, as a habit of snorting, or because of horn-like appendages (for example, bullhead catfish).

Bull-baiting, the sport of setting dogs on a bull, which was tied to a stake and torn to death for the amusement of the spectators. In this case the dogs, which were set upon the bull singly, were trained to seize the bull by the muzzle, technically, "to pin" the bull; but they were very frequently tossed on the horns of the animal. Sometimes also the bull was allowed to run loose in the arena, and then several dogs were set upon him at once. Bull-baiting was a favorite sport in England till about the time of George IV.

Bull-dog, a dog of moderate size, derived previous to the 13th century, from a cross between the old British mastiff and the large pug of extreme southeast Asia. Both its ancestors still exist as separate breeds. An average mature specimen will weigh 40 to 50 pounds. They are squat and muscular in build, with short legs, rather higher behind than in the front, especially if the front legs are very much bowed. Their chests and heads are abnormally broad for their size. The lower jaw overlaps the upper and is of extraordinary strength. The teeth are large. especially the two canines, and very strongly fixed in the jawbone, giving the dog a holding power beyond that of any other breed. The coat is close and short. The most variable feature is the color, which ranges from all black to all white among dogs bred for show purposes, but a brindle is more natural. For many centuries this dog was used for "baiting," or biting at, the bull, as a popular recreation; and up to more recent times men of brutal disposition used it for public dog-fights. It was through these exhibitions that the bull-dog got his bad name for temper, but now he is mainly kept as a watch-dog. In that capacity he is invaluable, and so gentle is his disposition that he is the safest canine companion for children. About the year 1900 a small variety of the bull-dog was evolved in the neighborhood of Brussels, but as it was first shown in Paris it has always been known as the "French" bull-dog. It is in the main a miniature of the English bull-dog. The most notable difference, other than that of size, being that the ears are shaped like those of a bat, and are carried erect, or "pricked," giving the animal a very alert, sharp look.

Bull-fight, a contest between men and bulls, conducted as a public spectacle. Once popular in Greece and Rome, this form of entertainment was introduced by the Moors into Spain, and universally adopted in the cities of the kingdom, where, as well as in Mexico and some other parts of the world, it is still much in favor. The bull-fight is held in an arena of greater or less magnificence, called in Spanish the *plaza de toros.* The bulls are turned out, one by one, with many forms of pomp and solemn ceremonial, into the open space, where they are assailed, first by horsemen, called *picadores,* who attack them with the lance; then, when one or more horses have been wounded, and one or more men have met with injury or perilous mishap — in which case a crowd of active footmen, called *chulos,* provided with crimson banners, take off the attention of the bull — the *banderilleros,* armed with sharp-barbed darts with fireworks and flags attached to them, worry the bull until he is covered with shafts, bleeding and scorched, his glossy hide black and crisp from the explosion of the fireworks. Then comes the last act of the tragedy, when the skilful *matador* enters the arena slowly and alone, clothed in plain black, and armed with a long, straight sword and a stick, called a *muleta,* with a piece of red silk fastened to it. With his sword he seldom fails to give the *coup de grace* to the tortured bull, sheathing the blade, with one sure thrust, up to the hilt in his body just at the juncture of the neck and spine. Mules drag out the slaughtered carcass, amid the sound of trumpets and acclamations of the spectators; the dead or dying horses are removed; the arena is strewed with fresh sawdust; another bull is introduced; and so goes on the combat, until perhaps a score of bulls and a larger number of horses have been slaughtered to delight the spectators. The Spanish settlers of Mexico and South America introduced bull-fighting into the New World.

Bull-frog, a widely distributed, edible North American frog (*Rana catesbyana*) found in sluggish waters throughout the eastern half of the United States and Canada, and so called because of its loud, bass voice. It is from five to eight inches long, and of various shades of green, with the legs spotted. It lays its eggs in strings and the tadpole does not reach maturity until two years old. The same name is given by English-speaking people in various parts of the world to other large bellowing frogs, as the "bull-frog" of Siam and Malaya (*Callula pulchra*). See FROG.

Bull, Golden. See GOLDEN BULL.

Bull Run, First Battle of. The first great battle of the Civil War occurred Sunday, 21 July 1861, in the vicinity of Manassas, Va. The Union forces were commanded by Brig.-Gen. Irvin McDowell, the Confederates by Gen. Joseph E. Johnston, who had arrived from Winchester at noon of the 20th with nine regiments of his army, and assumed command. The battlefield was west of Bull Run, and near the crossing of that stream by the turnpike running nearly west from Alexandria to Warrenton. Bull Run is known as a narrow, winding stream with rugged and misty precipitous banks, but with numerous fords, flowing southeastwardly, being about 25 miles west of Alexandria, and from three to five miles east of Manassas.

McDowell marched from his camps in front of Arlington and Alexandria on the afternoon 16th July, with five divisions, commanded respectively, by Brig.-Gen. Daniel Tyler, four brigades; Col. David Hunter, two brigades; Col. S. P. Heintzelman, four brigades; Brig.-Gen. Theodore Runyon, two brigades; and Col. Dixon S. Miles, three brigades. The Fourth Division was left as a reserve in the region of Fairfax, guarding the lines of communication. The advance division, Tyler's, reached Centreville the morning of the 18th and sent a brigade to Blackburn's Ford in reconnoissance. After a sharp skirmish in which both sides lost about 60 men, it withdrew toward Centreville, to which point McDowell, hearing of the operations at Blackburn's Ford, directed the concentration of four divisions.

The Confederate "Army of the Potomac" had been concentrated at Manassas under Gen. Beauregard. In expectation of a Union advance it occupied the south bank of Bull Run for eight miles from Union Mills Ford, at the crossing of the railroad to Alexandria, to the Stone Bridge at the Warrenton turnpike, three brigades being thrown forward of that position, one of them to Fairfax Court House. These brigades fell back before the Union advance, skirmishing slightly. Ewell's brigade, the right of the line, was at Union Mills, with Holmes in support; Jones' brigade at McLean's Ford; Longstreet's at Blackburn's Ford; Bonham's between Mitchell's and Ball's fords; Cocke's at Lewis' Ford; and Evans' demi-brigade at the Stone Bridge forming the Confederate left. Of Johnston's Army of the Shenandoah, Jackson's brigade was in support of Bonham, and Bee and Bartow in support of Cocke.

From each of these fords fair roads led to Centreville. Gen. Beauregard had planned an attack upon Centreville which involved an advance of his whole force upon that point. This was officially approved by Gen. Johnston before daylight of the 21st, but at sunrise it was rendered impossible by McDowell's initiative. The

bridge, discovering the movement, withdrew 11 companies and formed them on a ridge half a mile north of the road as the head of Hunter's column entered the open fields which extended a mile north of the Warrenton road. Evans made stubborn resistance, and was soon supported by Bee's brigade, and Imboden's battery. While the position was hotly contested the Confederates were pressed back down the hill, across the valley of Young's branch, a tributary of Bull Run, to the plateau south of it upon which were the Robinson and Henry houses. Two of Tyler's brigades crossed above the Stone Bridge

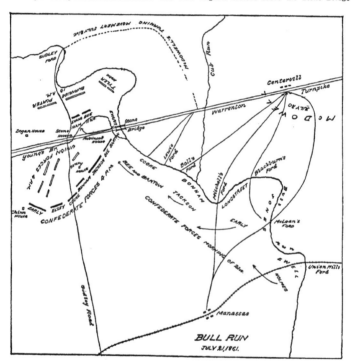

plan was then changed to an attack on the Union left from Blackburn's Ford. This also was abandoned from the same cause.

McDowell, who had first intended to attack the enemy's right, after the affair at Blackburn's Ford, finding the ford at Sudley Spring two miles beyond the Confederate left, decided to attack from that direction. While Tyler feinted before the Stone Bridge, Hunter and Heintzelman, by a long detour, crossed at Sudley Spring and moved south toward the Warrenton turnpike in the enemy's rear. Evans, at the

and joined Hunter and Heintzelman in their advance. The fighting continued desperate until noon, and for new troops was, for both sides, most remarkable, but the Confederate line, though stubbornly contesting the ground, began to disintegrate, and the road to Manassas was crowded with retiring soldiers.

Gen. Johnston describes the Confederate situation at two o'clock as "critical"; Gen. Beauregard terms it a "pressing exigency," and speaks of the retirement of "our shattered battalions," and of the fighting line as having "lost its cohesion." Dr. Jones, Jackson's distinguished biographer, records that "the retreat became every moment more disordered," that Bee's quick eye "now told him that all was lost," and that "he could not reform his line."

At that hour a Union victory seemed assured. Johnston and Beauregard reached the position together. The troops on the line of Bull Run that had been held there by the demonstrations of two Union brigades designed to mask McDowell's turning movement, were ordered in haste to the new line which was at right angles to the first. Jackson soon arrived with five regiments and two batteries. Hampton's Legion joined him, and the Union advance was checked. Other arrivals strengthened the line. Kirby Smith's brigade of Johnston's army appeared about three o'clock, having just arrived on the field from Manassas, and pushed its three regiments toward the right of the Union line. Early's brigade of Beauregard's force, from the extreme right of his line, hastened beyond Smith's brigade, now commanded by Col. Elzey, and supported by Stuart's cavalry, appeared directly on the Union right flank. Two regiments from Bonham, and two from Cocke, also arrived upon the Union right. These also were of Beauregard's army. This turned the check which that portion of the Union line had received, first into retreat, and then into a disorganized withdrawal, except that the rear guards maintained fair order till the columns were well off the field, the right retracing its long detour by Sudley Spring. At Cub Run, half-way to Centreville, the batteries of a pursuing column broke up the wagons and batteries on the bridge, compelling the abandonment of 13 guns. From this point the movement to the rear was still farther disorganized, to which condition the vehicles of many visitors, congressmen, correspondents and officials largely contributed. The attempt to rally the troops at Centreville failed, though Gen. Johnston reported that the "apparent firmness" of the Union reserves at that point checked the pursuit. The army, in great part disorganized, streamed on to Washington.

After the severe stress in which the Confederate leaders found themselves from 11 o'clock until about 3, the sudden change on the Union side, first from assaulting to cessation of fighting; next, to a general retreat, and, later, to widespread panic, was as much a surprise to the enemy as to the Union commanders. It was not until the second day after the battle that the Confederates ascertained the full extent of the Union stampede. Upon this point President Davis wrote Gen. Beauregard: "You will not fail to remember that, so far from knowing that the enemy was routed, a large part of our forces was moved by you in the night of the 21st to repel a supposed attack upon our right, and the next day's operations did not fully reveal what has since been reported of the enemy's panic."

McDowell's strength at Centreville appears to have been about 28,000 men and 49 guns. His report says he crossed Bull Run with 18,000 men. A very careful estimate made from official records in 1884, by Gen. James B. Fry, McDowell's adjutant-general at the battle, gives the number actually engaged as 17,676.

Gen. Beauregard reported his strength on the field when the battle opened at 27,833 and 49 guns; and after Johnston's delayed troops and Holmes' brigade had arrived in the afternoon as

31,972 and 57 guns. A very careful estimate by Gen. Thomas Jordan, his adjutant-general, fixed the number actually engaged at 18,053, thus showing the two sides to have been about equal on the firing line.

The Union loss as reported was: Killed, 460; wounded, 1,124; missing, 1,312; total, 2,896. Union guns captured or abandoned, 29. The Confederate loss reported was: Killed, 387; wounded, 1,582; missing, 13; total, 1,982.

H. V. BOYNTON.

Bull Run, Second Battle of, 30 Aug. 1862. When McClellan on the peninsula had reached the vicinity of Richmond, Lee, to prevent McDowell's corps at Fredericksburg from re-inforcing McClellan, ordered Jackson in the Shenandoah to make a demonstration that should detain all available troops for the defense of Washington. Jackson advanced, and in a brilliant campaign drove Banks out of the valley, and forced him across the Potomac. By a masterly retreat, he regained the upper valley in spite of McDowell and Fremont, and soon after appeared on McClellan's flank at Mechanicsville and participated in the seven days' battles.

On 27 June the Union authorities united the three corps of McDowell, Fremont, and Banks into the Army of Virginia under the command of Maj.-Gen. John Pope. He had concentrated his forces between Sperryville and Warrenton, and began to operate with his cavalry against Lee's railroad lines about Gordonsville. His mission also was to prevent Lee from concentrating upon McClellan, when he should withdraw from the peninsula. Lee promptly sent Jackson's Division, followed by Ewell's and A. P. Hill's, to Gordonsville. On 7 August these moved from Gordonsville toward Pope's position at Culpeper, and 9 August encountered Banks at Cedar or Slaughter Mountain. Banks attacked, instead of holding his position as Pope's plan contemplated, and while at first brilliantly successful, he was at last defeated. Jackson, however, retreated on the 11th across the Rapidan.

On the 13th Lee ordered Longstreet, with his own and Hood's divisions, to Gordonsville. R. H. Anderson's division was ordered to follow. Upon their arrival Pope was largely outnumbered. Lee planned a move for the 18th against Pope's left, but this officer learned of the plan through the capture of Stuart's adjutant-general, re-crossed the Rappahannock, and took position behind it on the 20th. Lee next arranged to cross at Sulphur Springs, turn Pope's right, and move upon his communications. This failed. Pope, at the same time, had planned to cross the river and attack Lee's right and rear, but a sudden flood prevented the movement. Lee then sent Jackson's corps far beyond Pope's right by way of Salem and Thoroughfare Gap to cut Pope's railroad line at Manassas. Jackson succeeded, passing around Pope's right, capturing Bristoe Station and Manassas with its immense supplies on the night of 26 August. Pope moved to attack him at Manassas. On the night of the 27th and early on the 28th, Jackson's three divisions withdrew by different roads, and soon after noon of the 28th assembled on the battlefield of the first Bull Run.

On the night of the 25th Pope's headquarters were at Warrenton Junction. Reynolds' Division had joined him on the 23d. On the 25th the advance of Heintzelman's corps arrived from the Army of the Potomac, Hooker's and Kearny's divisions, and Fitz-John Porter, with the divisions of Sykes and Morell of his corps. These two corps with Reynolds' Division were the only re-inforcements that Pope received from the Army of the Potomac until after the battle of Manassas.

On the night of the 27th Pope, supposing Jackson at Manassas, ordered general concentration in that direction. Porter's failure to move promptly under this order constituted one

Jackson was just north of it on the first Bull Run field. The Union approach led Jackson to attack, thus revealing his position, which Pope had been vainly seeking. This was the battle of Gainesville, being a very bitter fight between Taliaferro's Division and two brigades of Ewell, and King of McDowell's advance.

After the close of the fight, in the absence of McDowell, his two divisions retreated, Rickett's to Bristoe Station, and King's to Manassas. At daylight of the 29th the Union forces were again put in motion to pursue Jackson. His line was

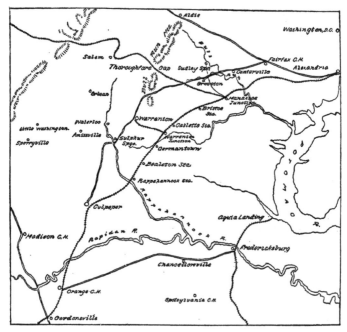

THEATRE OF
SECOND BULL RUN CAMPAIGN

of the charges under which he was subsequently court-martialed and cashiered. Rickett's Division, the rear of McDowell's corps, upon the information from the cavalry that Longstreet's forces were entering Thoroughfare Gap, moved to the gap and held Longstreet back during the day, and into the evening of the 28th. In the afternoon of the 28th Pope, supposing Jackson east of Bull Run, ordered his army to Centreville, Heintzelman and Reno by the fords of Bull Run, McDowell, Sigel, and Reynolds by the Warrenton turnpike. The advance along the turnpike was begun without the knowledge that

mainly along an unfinished railroad, the left near Sudley Spring, and his right on high ground north of the Warrenton road overlooking Groveton. The Union forces attacked throughout the day, with brief intermissions. The contest was desperate, and Jackson's line, though hard pressed at various points, maintained its organization. Porter's failure to here attack the Confederate right was another of the charges under which he was tried. Subsequently, however, he was exonerated by the findings of an army board, and restored to his rank by act of Congress. McDowell arrived late, with King's Division.

As it moved into action it encountered the head of Longstreet's column, which had achieved its junction with Jackson. In less than an hour, in a bloody contest, Hood's Division of Longstreet's force had ended the battle of Groveton. Snch were the preliminaries of the Second Bull Run.

The battle of Manassas, the Second Bull Run, was fought 30 August, the day following the action at Groveton. The movement covered the ground of McDowell's and Johnston's battle of the year before. Jackson's line occupied the position from Sudley Spring to the heights overlooking Groveton. Lee, whose forces were now all up, formed Longstreet's line across the Warrenton turnpike on high ground about a mile west of Groveton. On this ridge he established a number of batteries under Stephen D. Lee and Walton. The line then turned east south of the turnpike, and extended toward the Sudley Spring road. The Confederate position south of the Warrenton road seemed not to be suspected by Pope. The fact that after the action of the afternoon before Jackson's troops had retired to their morning position Lee had withdrawn Longstreet's advance to. form on better ground, misled Pope and caused him to insist that the enemy was retreating. At noon, after reconnoissances north of the road, he therefore ordered vigorous pursuit. Porter was to push west on the Warrenton pike followed by King's Division on his right and Reynolds' on his left. Ricketts' Division, followed by Heintzelman's corps, was to pursue on the Haymarket road. Sigel's and Reno's corps were the reserves.

About four o'clock Porter advanced with his own corps and King's Division pushed in on Jackson's line with great vigor, and assault followed assault, each made with great pertinacity. Lee seemed willing to let them continue in order to exhaust his opponents. At length Jackson sent for help, and Longstreet was ordered to his assistance. This officer had, however, posted his batteries so as to enfilade Jackson's front, and instead of sending troops, opened with a terrific flanking fire of artillery. The Union lines were repulsed with great loss. Nearly all of Pope's forces had been put in north of the turnpike and had been seriously repulsed. All Union support was now directed to defend the position against Longstreet's forces south of the Warrenton pike. The whole of Longstreet's line went forward toward the road with a rush. There were five divisions — Wilcox on the left, then Evans (Hood), Anderson, Kemper, and Jones. As soon as Jackson, north of the road, saw the advance of Longstreet he ordered his own line forward. The corps of Heintzelman and Reno resisted this attack, but were gradually forced back. The supreme struggle of the Union forces was to hold two elevated positions near the Henry and Chinn houses. The latter, known as Bald Hill, was carried by the Confederates. after persistent and sanguinary fighting. The Henry house hill was held against repeated assaults. The Union army was in retreat across Bull Run, and the possession of the hill was necessary to maintain an orderly retreat.

The Union troops remained in possession until eight o'clock, when the last of Pope's army moved unmolested toward the Stone Bridge, crossing Bull Run about midnight. The bridge was then destroyed and the Union army concentrated at Centreville. It was a Union defeat, but not a rout. While there was much straggling, the main army had retreated in good order, and Lee did not pursue. In the management of the battle Lee had displayed his eminent generalship in a striking manner. Pope's chief error had been in persisting, before his attack was delivered, that the enemy was in retreat.

Pope was re-inforced at Centreville by the strong corps of Sumner and Franklin from the Army of the Potomac. Here also he found supplies. His army had fought for two days almost entirely without food or forage. Lee began pursuit the afternoon of the day after the battle. Jackson leading from Sudley Ford, and marching by a circuitous route toward Fairfax Court House, seven miles in rear of Centreville. Passing Chantilly, he turned toward the Warrenton turnpike and formed in front of Ox Hill, his right extending toward the pike. He was far in advance of Longstreet, and wholly without support. He was attacked by the two divisions of Reno under Stevens, and later by Kearny. Stevens and Kearny were killed, and Jackson was repulsed.

Longstreet came up at night, and at noon the next day (2 September) Pope's army was ordered by the authorities at Washington to withdraw within the defenses of the city. Pope's losses throughout the campaign from 16 August to 2 September were: Army of Virginia, killed and wounded 5,318, missing 2,787; Army of the Potomac. killed and wounded 3,613, missing 1,115; 9th Army Corps, killed and wounded 1,204, missing 319; Kanawha division, killed and wounded 64, missing 42; total killed and wounded 10,199; captured or missing 4,263. The Confederate losses are not fully reported, but the best estimates placed them at about 8,500. There are no official returns which enable a presentation of the exact strength of either army during the campaign up to 30 August, but the best estimate places the Union forces at about 65,000 to 70,000, and the Confederate at 54,000.

References: 'Official Record of the War of the Rebellion,' Vol. II.; George H. Gordon, 'History of the Campaign of the Army of Virginia'; John G. Nicolay, 'Outbreak of the Rebellion'; John C. Ropes, 'The Army Under Pope'; The Century Co., 'Battles and Leaders of the Civil War'; A. L. Long, 'Memoirs of Robert E. Lee'; J. E. Cooke, 'Stonewall Jackson'; Fitzhugh Lee, 'Life of Gen. Robert E. Lee'; Joseph E. Johnston, 'Johnston's Narrative'; William Allen, 'The Army of Northern Virginia in 1862'; G. F. R. Henderson, 'Stonewall Jackson and the American Civil War'; Alfred Roman, 'The Military Operations of General Beauregard in the War Between the States'; the Count of Paris, 'History of the Civil War in America.' H. V. BOYNTON.

Bull-snake. See PINE SNAKE.

Bull-terrier. See TERRIER.

Bull-trout. (1) A salmon-like trout of North America. See SALMON-TROUT. (2) The Dolly Varden trout (q.v.)

Bulla, a genus of mollusks called, from the thinness of their shells, bubble-shells. The shell is oval, ventricose, convoluted externally, or only partially invested by the animal. The animal has a large cephalic disk bilobed behind; the lateral lobe is much developed. It occurs in temperate and tropical seas from 25 to 30 fathoms. Over 50 recent species are known and 70 fossil, the latter from the Oölite onward.

Bullace, a small tree or shrub allied to the prunes. It is akin to the variety *Spinosa* (the sloe), but differs in having the peduncles and under side of the leaves pubescent and the branches slightly spinous, whereas the *Spinosa* has the peduncles glabrous, the leaves ultimately so also, and the branches decidedly spinous. It stands midway between the plum and the sloe. In England its fruit is used for making jam. The tree is seldom found in America.

Bullæ, miniature blisters, or blebs. They are larger than vesicles, with a large portion of cuticle detached from the skin and a watery transparent fluid between. The skin beneath is red and inflamed.

Bullant, Jean, zhŏn bú-län, French architect: b. probably in Ecouen about 1515; d. Paris, 10 Oct. 1578. He studied at Rome and after his return to France became supervisor of the royal buildings. He was connected with the erection of the Tuileries and built the pavilion named for him. He was also the architect of the Hôtel de Soissons for Catherine de Medici. In 1570 he succeeded Primaticcio at Fontainbleau.

Bullbat, a name in the Southern States for the nighthawk (q.v.), a bird which flies in the dusk like a bat, and makes a booming sound.

Bulle, bûl-lĕ, **Konstantin,** German historian: b. Minden, 30 March 1844. He studied philosophy and history at Jena and Bonn, taught in the high school at Bonn and became director of the gymnasium there in 1879. In 1887-90 he was a member of the Reichstag. After some philosophical studies he devoted himself to historical work and wrote: 'History of Recent Times 1815-71'; 'History of the Years 1871-7' and 'History of the Second Empire and the Italian Kingdom.' The first two were combined and published as 'History of Recent Times' in 1886.

Bullen, bûl'lĕn, **Frank Thomas,** English author and lecturer: b. Paddington, London, 5 April 1857. He received but scanty schooling, and after a few years' experience as errand boy, etc., went to sea as ordinary seaman in 1869, becoming chief mate after several years. He left the sea in 1883 and was junior clerk in the English meteorological office, 1883-99. His contributions to nautical literature have attracted widespread attention. The earliest of these, 'The Cruise of the Cachelot' (1898) being the most noted. His other books include: 'Idylls of the Sea'; 'The Log of a Sea Waif' (1899); 'The Men of the Merchant Service'; 'With Christ at Sea'; 'A Sack of Shakings' (1901); 'The Apostles of the Southeast'; 'Deep Sea Plunderings' (1901); 'A Whaleman's Wife' (1902).

Buller, bûl'lĕr, **Sir Redvers Henry,** English general: b. Devonshire, 1839. He joined the 60th Rifles as ensign in 1858; in 1862 was promoted to the rank of lieutenant, and eight years later to that of captain. He was a major in 1874, lieutenant-colonel in 1878, colonel in 1879, and major-general in 1884. He served with his regiment in the Chinese campaign of 1860, and on the Red River expedition in 1870. During the Ashantee war he acted as quartermaster-

general and head of the intelligence department, and gained special mention for his behavior in several engagements. He also served with distinction during the Kaffir war of 1878, and the Victoria Cross was conferred on him in 1879 for his gallant conduct in saving the lives of two officers and a trooper of the Frontier Light Horse during the retreat at Inhlobane in the Zulu campaign. He was chief of the staff to Sir Evelyn Wood in the war against the Boers in 1881, and in Egypt in the following year, gaining special distinction for his services at Kassassin, Tel-el-Kebir, and elsewhere. In the Sudan campaign of 1884-5 he was chief of the staff to Lord Wolseley, and was in command at the battle of Abu-klea when Sir Herbert Stewart had been wounded. From 1887 till 1890 he held the post of quartermaster-general of the army, and from 1890 till 1897 he acted as adjutant-general to the forces. In 1886-7 he was under-secretary to the lord-lieutenant of Ireland, and in 1891 was promoted to the rank of lieutenant-general. He was created K.C.M.G. in 1882, K.C.B. in 1885, and G.C.B. in 1894. In 1899 he went to Natal as commander in the war with the Boer republics, and succeeded in relieving Ladysmith after it had been besieged 118 days. His various reverses prior to this event caused him to be superseded by Gen. Roberts, and on his return to England he was placed on the retired list in consequence of an unwise speech of his. The publication of official documents, still later, practically destroyed his reputation as a commander, it being shown by these he had advised Gen. White, the defender of Ladysmith, to give up the defense and surrender to the Boers.

Bullers of Buchan, a large oval cavity in the rocks on the east coast of Aberdeenshire, about six miles to the south of Peterhead, forming a sort of pot or caldron about 150 feet deep, open to the sky above and communicating with the sea below by a natural arch or horizontal passage, into which the waves often rush with a tremendous noise.

Bullet, the projectile used for small-arms, either spherical or of an elongated form. The elongated bullet is now in general use for rifles, and there has also been introduced some means of dilating the bullet at the moment of explosion, so that it is forced into the grooves of the rifle and exactly fits the barrel. In some cases there is merely a cavity left at the base of the bullet into which the gases formed on the explosion of the gunpowder are forced, so that these have the effect of dilating the bullet in the manner required. In other cases a plug is inserted in the cavity, which is driven forward by the explosion of the gunpowder, and has the same effect. Spherical bullets remained in use long after the invention of the rifle, though several kinds of elongated bullets were suggested by various inventors of the 17th and 18th centuries. In 1837 the French adopted an elongated bullet invented by Delvigne, but this was superseded by the Minié bullet about 1846. A similar form, but with a wooden plug instead of an iron cup to cause the expansion, was introduced into the English army with the Enfield rifles of 1855. Previous to this, in 1841, the Prussians had adopted the celebrated needle breech-loading rifle, with an egg-shaped bullet resting on a thick wad which alone took the grooves of the rifle. In 1864 the three-grooved Enfield barrel was combined with the Snider breech-action in the rifles of the English army. The bullet supplied with this arm had a plug of baked clay and a hollow head, the lubrication being effected by bees'-wax placed in four cannelures running round its base. In 1866 the Chassepôt rifle was adopted by the French authorities, the bullet having shoulders serving the same end as the wad in the needle-gun bullet. The temporarily introduced Snider-Enfield rifles were replaced in 1874 by the much better Martini-Henry type, whose bullet, though longer and of smaller diameter, has the cylindrical form with domed end found in the French Chassepôt. The lubrication in this case was effected by a covering of wax-paper and a bees'-wax wad. The diminution in the diameter of the bullet was carried still further in the Enfield-Martini rifle of 1886, the bullets then supplied measuring only about two fifths of an inch in diameter; and in several subsequent types of rifle they are of still smaller diameter. This decrease in calibre has been accompanied by an increase in length in order to preserve the weight of the bullet, and it has also been found necessary to cover the lead of the bullet with a thin coating of some such metal as steel, copper, nickel, or German silver. These changes are all embodied in the bullets of the Lee-Metford magazine rifle, and the necessity for lubricators is thus done away with. The Lee-Metford bullet has a length of 3·05 inches, and the diameter of ·312 inch. There is considerable variation in the weight of bullets. The old Brunswick bullets weighed 557, the Minié, 680 grains. The Enfield bullet had a weight of 535 grains; the Snider and Martini-Henry, 480; the Enfield-Martini, 384, while the Lee-Metford bullet weighs only 216 grains. The French Lebel magazine rifle has a bullet with a weight of 215 grains, and in a later French form, the Berthier, the weight is 205 grains. The Lebel bullet is flattened at the point in order to lessen the risk of explosion in the magazine. The German Mauser and Mannlicher magazine rifles have bullets of the same weight as the Lee-Metford. The slenderness of modern rifle bullets has necessitated the construction of rifles of very small bore, and this in turn has compelled the substitution of pellets of compressed powder for the older loose powder. In recent years a peculiar kind of bullet known as the Dum-Dum has been employed by English troops in warfare with uncivilized races, as the frontier tribes of India. In this the lead core is inserted from the top, not from the base, as in other bullets, and the lead being unprotected at the point, has to sustain the shock of the impact. The consequence is that it expands in the wound, and thus, even though it should pass right through a person's body, its effects are very severe, and likely to stop the onrush of the foe.

Bullet-tree, or Bully-tree (*Mimusops Balata* or *Sapota Mulleri*), a forest tree of Guiana and neighboring regions, order *Sapotaceæ*, yielding an excellent gum known as balata, having properties giving it in some respects an intermediate position between gutta-percha and india-rubber, and making it for certain industrial purposes more useful than either. The timber of the tree also is valuable.

Bullfinch, an European finch (*Pyrrhula europæa*), frequently kept as a cage bird, mainly because of its ability to learn to whistle tunes, the most capable birds, trained in Germany, acquiring as many as six. The training of "piping bullfinches" is a special art, and various domestic varieties are bred, some of which bring high prices. Its natural song is not remarkable. The bullfinch is a large bird of its kind, with a big inflated beak, and soft dense plumage. It is pearl-gray above and dull red on the under parts; the crown of the head, the beak, and the tail and wing quills are black, the latter crossed by a broad white bar. The colors of the female are duller than those of the male. Several similar species are known elsewhere, one (*P. cassini*) inhabiting Alaska. See CAGE BIRDS.

Bullheads, or "horned-pouts," are small, dark-colored catfish, abundant everywhere east of the plains, and, by introduction, in California and Oregon. They are mud-loving fishes, remaining on the bottom and feeling for food with the barbels, one on each side of the mouth and two under the chin. The "common bullhead" (*Ameiurus nebulosis*) varies in length, at full age, from 18 to 24 inches, and occasionally weighs 5 pounds. It is brownish-black in color, with a fine, scaleless, rubber-like skin, a big head, and a long upper jaw. It is a gluttonous biter, gorging the bait, so that the book must often be cut out of its interior. A smaller species, the black bullhead (*A. melas*) may be distinguished by the smaller anal fin and its nearly white rays. The southern "flat-headed cat" (*A. platycephalus*) has an eel-like form and a greenish brown hue, and is almost entirely herbivorous. Several of the large "catfish" (q.v.) of the western lakes belong to this genus.

Bulliard, Pierre, pē-ār bül-yär, French botanist: b. Aubepierre en Barrois, about 1742; d. Paris 1793. He was educated at the College of Langres, where he showed a decided taste for natural history, proceeded to Paris to pursue his medical studies, and employed his leisure in collecting the materials of a 'Flora Parisiensis,' which he afterward published in six volumes, with colored plates. Among his other works are a 'Herbier de la France,' and a 'Dictionnaire Élémentaire de Botanique,' which has been repeatedly printed.

Bullinger, Heinrich, hĭn'rĬH bül'ling-ĕr, Swiss reformer: b. Bremgarten, 18 Aug. 1504; d. Zürich, 17 Sept. 1575. He studied first at Emmerich, in the duchy of Cleves, and afterward at Cologne. His intention was to become a Carthusian monk, but after perusing the writings of Melanchthon and other reformers he changed his views, formed a close connection with Zuinglius, became one of the most strenuous supporters of his views, and ultimately succeeded him in his charge of Zürich. He was one of the authors of the first Helvetic Confession, drew up in concert with Calvin the formulary of 1549, by which the differences between the churches of Zürich and Geneva on the subject of the Lord's Supper were happily terminated, and kept up a close correspondence with the lately published by the Parker Society, conprincipal English reformers. The Zürich Letters, tains part of this correspondence, and among others, letters addressed to him by Lady Jane Grey. The most important of his many writings is a 'History of the Reformation.' See lives by Hess (1828-9); Vestalozzi (1858); also Heinrich, 'Bullinger und seine Gattin' (1875); Zimmermann, 'Die Züricher Kirche und ihre Antistes' (1877).

Bullion, bŭl-yón, uncoined gold or silver, in bars, plate, or other masses. United States standard bullion contains 900 parts of pure gold or pure silver, and 100 parts of copper alloy. The coining value of an ounce of pure gold is $20.67183, and the coining value of an ounce of standard gold is $18.60465. The coining value in standard silver dollars of an ounce of pure silver is $1.2929, and the coining value of an ounce of standard silver is $1.1636. The word bullion was of frequent use in the proceedings respecting the Bank of England from 1797, when the order of council was issued that the bank should discontinue the redemption of its notes by the payment of specie to 1823, when specie payments were resumed; for, by a previous law, the bank was authorized to pay its notes in uncoined silver or gold, according to its weight and fineness. The investigations of the bullion committees, and the various speenlations on the subject of bullion, related to the supply of gold and silver, whether coined or not, as the basis of the circulating medium. The discovery of the mines in America did not at first add materially to the stock of bullion in Europe. The total addition for the first 54 years was about $85,000,000; not quite so great an amount of value (in gold at least) as Russia has obtained from the Ural mines in less than half the time. The average annual supply from all the American sources during the 54 years from 1546 to the end of the 16th century, was rather more than $10,000,000. During the 17th century the annual average was about $16,250,000; in the next half century it was $27,500,000; and in the years 1750 to 1803 it was $38,000,000.

Bul'lock, Alexander Hamilton, American politician: b. Royalston, Mass., 1816; d. 1882. He was educated at Amherst College and the Harvard Law School and was admitted to the bar in 1841. After practising law in Worcester, Mass., he was elected to the Massachusetts House of Representatives in 1845 and re-elected in 1861, when he became speaker. In 1849 he became a member of the State Senate. He held many judicial offices, was mayor of Worcester in 1859, and from 1866-8 was governor of his State.

Bullock, Charles, English clergyman, editor and author: b. 24 Feb. 1829. He entered the Anglican ministry in 1855, was curate of Ripley, Yorkshire, 1857-9; of Luton, Bedfordshire, 1859-60; rector of St. Nicholas', Worcester, 1860-74. He has edited 'The Fireside Magazine,' 'Home Words,' and other periodicals, and among his published works are 'The Way Home'; 'The Royal Year'; 'England's Royal Home'; 'Shakespeare's Debt to the Bible'; 'Popular Recreation'; 'The Poet of Home Life'; 'Biography of Frances Ridley Havergal'; 'Crowned to Serve.'

Bullock, Charles Jesse, American economist: b. Boston, 21 May 1869. He graduated at the Boston University in 1889, devoted himself to special studies, and was appointed to the chair of economics in Williams College. He is the author of 'The Finances of the United States, 1775-89' (1895); 'Introduction to the Study of Economics' (1900); 'Essays on the Monetary History of the United States' (1900); and has edited 'Currencies of the British Plantations in North America.'

Bullock, Rufus Brown, American politician: b. Bethlehem, N. Y., 28 March 1834; d. 27 April 1907. He was educated at Albion Academy and early in life went to Georgia in connection with a business enterprise. During the Civil War he was connected with the quartermaster's department in the Confederate army. In 1867 he became a member of the State Constitutional Convention of Georgia and in the following year was elected governor. His championship of the negro members expelled from the legislature brought him such violent opposition that he resigned from office. He was actively engaged in the promotion of the railroad and industrial interests of his own State and was government director of the Union P. R.R.

Bullock, Shan F., Irish novelist: b. Crom, Fermanagh, Ireland, 17 May 1865. He has written a number of popular works. Among them are: 'The Awkward Squads' (1893); 'By Thrasna River' (1895); 'Ring o' Rushes' (1896); 'The Charmer' (1897); 'The Barrys' (1899); and 'Irish Pastorals' (1901). His work is remarkably individual and his studies of life in the north of Ireland are faithful reflections of Irish life and character.

Bullock, William A., American inventor: b. Greenville, Greene County, N. Y., 1813; d. Philadelphia, 14 April 1867. He learned the trade of machinist, and having started a periodical, 'The Banner of the Union,' he invented a printing-press in connection with that enterprise. He removed to New York and devoted himself to the construction and gradual development of a "planetary press," finally producing the Web perfecting press that delivers 30,000 papers per hour, printed, cut and folded. While handling one of his presses he met with an injury that proved fatal.

Bulls and Bears, a popular phrase used in connection with the stock market. The term "bulls" is applied to the operators attempting to force up prices, and the term "bears" to those seeking to lower them.

Bull's Horn Coraline (so named because the shape of the cells is like a bull's horn), a zoophyte of the family *Cellariadæ*. It is the *Eucratia loricata*. It is branched subalternate, and has the cells conical, with a raised orifice, beneath which is a spinous process.

Bulnes, Manuel, mä-noo-el' bool-nãs, Chilean soldier and statesman: b. Concepcion, 25 Dec. 1799; d. Santiago, 18 Oct. 1866. He served in most of the battles of the Chilean revolution. In 1838 he commanded the Chilean army of 5,000 men against Santa Cruz, in Peru, and was finally instrumental in driving Santa Cruz from the country and breaking up the Peru-Bolivian confederation. In 1841 he was elected president of Chile and served for four years. He was afterward senator and councilor of state.

Bülow, Bernhard, bĕrn'härt bü'lō, **Count von,** German statesman: b. Klein-Flottbeck, Holstein, in the spring of 1849. He came of a distinguished family, and was, on the mother's side, of Danish ancestry. He was educated at Lausanne, Leipsic and Berlin, studied law and served in the Franco-German war, where he rose to the grade of lieutenant. After filling the posts of secretary of legation at Rome, St. Petersburg, and Vienna, he became chargé d'affaires at Athens during the Russo-Turkish war, and later was secretary of the Berlin Congress. In 1888 he was appointed minister to Rumania, and in 1893 ambassador to Italy. He was called home to become minister of foreign affairs. His skilful treatment of the Samoan difficulty won him popular favor in his own country. During the Chinese complications in 1900 he fully supported the emperor's foreign policy. When Prince Hohenlohe resigned, 16 Oct. 1900, Von Bülow was called to succeed him as chancellor of the empire.

Bülow, Bertha von, bär'ta fōn, German story writer: b. Warmbrunn, Silesia, 30 Sept. 1850. Among her stories which enjoy great popularity are 'Merry Tales' (1891); and 'Once in May and Other Stories' (1892). She has also written some good comedies, namely, 'Theory and Practice' (1890), and 'Two Peaceful Ones' (1892).

Bülow, Friedrich Wilhelm (COUNT VON DENNEWITZ), frēd-rĭH vĭl'helm, Prussian general: b. Falkenberg, 16 Feb. 1755; d. Königsberg, 25 Feb. 1816. In his 14th year he entered the Prussian army. In the war of 1806 he was a lieutenant-colonel at the siege of Thorn, and distinguished himself in various battles. In 1808 he was made major-general and general of brigade. When the war against France broke out in 1813 he fought the first successful battle at Möckern, 5 April; 2 May took Halle, and protected Berlin from the danger which threatened it, by his victory at Luckau 4 June. He saved Berlin a second time by the memorable victory of Grosbeeren, 23 August, and relieved the same city a third time by the great victory at Dennewitz. For this service the king made him one of the few grand knights of the Iron Cross, and after the end of the campaign bestowed on him the title Count Bülow of Dennewitz, and made the same hereditary in his family. At the storming of Leipsic, 19 October, he took an important part. At the opening of the campaign of 1815 he received the chief command of the fourth division of the army, with which he contributed so essentially to the victory of Waterloo, that the king gave him the command of the 15th regiment of the line, which was to bear in future the name of the Regiment of Bülow von Dennewitz.

Bülow, Hans Guido von, hänts gwē'dō fōn, German pianist and composer: b. Dresden, 8 Jan. 1830; d. Cairo, Egypt, 12 Feb. 1894. He studied the piano under Liszt, and made his first public appearance in 1852. In 1855 he became leading professor in the Conservatory at Berlin; in 1858 was appointed court pianist; and in 1867 he became musical director to the king of Bavaria. His compositions include overture and music to 'Julius Cæsar,' 'The Minstrel's Curse,' and 'Nirvana'; songs, choruses, and pianoforte pieces. He was considered one of the first of pianists and orchestral conductors. In 1875–6 he gave a series of concerts in the principal cities of the United States. His Letters appeared 1895–7.

Bülow, Heinrich (hīn'rĭH) **von,** German military writer: b. Falkenberg, in Altmark, about 1757; d. Riga, Russia, 1807. He studied in the military academy at Berlin, and afterward entered the Prussian service. But he soon retired, and occupied himself with the study of Polybius, Tacitus, and J. J. Rousseau, and then served for a short period in the Netherlands. He afterward undertook to establish a theatre, but immediately abandoned his project, and visited the United States, whence he returned poor in purse but rich in experience, and became an author. His first work was on the 'Art of War,' in which he displayed uncommon talents. He wrote a book on 'Money,' translated the 'Travels of Mungo Park,' and published in 1801, his 'History of the Campaign of 1800.' In 1804 he wrote 'Lehrsätze des neuern Krieges' (Theory of Modern Warfare) and several other military works, among which is his 'Tactics of the Moderns as They Should Be.' In the former he points out the distinction between strategy and tactics, and makes the triangle the basis of all military operations. This principle of his was opposed by Jomini, and other French writers. His history of the war of 1805 occasioned his imprisonment in Prussia, at the request of the Russian and Austrian courts. He died in the prison of Riga. He was a follower of Swedenborg.

Bülow, Karl Eduard von, kärl ĕd-wärd fōn, German author: b. Berg vor Eilenburg, Saxony, 17 Nov. 1803; d. Öttishausen, 16 Sept. 1853. His literary fame rests mainly on his 'Book of Tales,' after ancient Italian, Spanish, French, English, Latin, and German originals (4 vols. 1834–6), which was followed by a supplementary volume. Of his own original compositions, the 'Springtide Wandering Among the Hartz Mountains' is one of the best. He wrote also the very interesting story of 'The Youth of a Poor Man of Toggenburg,' founded on the autobiography of Ulrich Bräker, a Swiss weaver. He published the original later.

Bülow, Margarete von, mar-ga-rä'ta fōn, German novelist: b. Berlin 1860; d. near there, 2 Jan. 1885. She wrote four volumes of stories, namely, 'Stories' (1885); 'Jonas Briccius' (1886); 'Chronicle of the Riffelshausen Folks' (1887); 'New Stories' (1890). She delineated character with great precision, and displayed true insight into the human heart. She lost her life in an attempt to rescue a boy from drowning.

Buloz, François, frän-swä bü-lō, French publicist: b. Bubbens, Savoy. 20 Sept. 1803; d. Paris, 12 Jan. 1877. In 1831 he became editor of the 'Revue des Deux Mondes,' the celebrated French fortnightly literary magazine. From 1835–45 he also edited the 'Revue de Paris.' For 10 years (1838–48) he was director of the Comédie Française.

Bulrampur, bool-rŭm-poor', a town of India, in the Fyzabad division of Oudh, the residence of the Maharaja of Bulrampur. It has a trade in rice, etc., besides manufactures of cotton and other articles. Pop. (1891) 14,849.

Bulrush, a popular name for tall, reed-like plants which grow in marshy places, and which for the most part belong to the genus *Scirpus*. The common bulrush is frequent in clear waters and about the borders of rivers throughout Europe, as well as in North America and New

South Wales. The roots are thick and stout, creeping under water in the deep mud; the stems are of a dark-green color, and four or five feet or more in height, and are naked, smooth, round, tough, pliant, and spongy within. Their base is covered with several sheathing scales, partly ending in leafy points. They are useful for packing and thatching, and especially for plaiting into the bottom of chairs.

Bulthaupt, Heinrich Alfred, hīn'rĭн äl-frĕd boolt'houpt, German poet and dramatist: b. Bremen, 26 Oct. 1849. On quitting the university he was for a while a private tutor; then traveled in the East, Greece, and in Italy. He was a lawyer in his native town for some years, and in 1879 became custodian of the city library. Of his dramatic compositions the list is very long, comprising tragedies, 'Saul'; 'A Corsican Tragedy'; plays dealing with the questions of the time, 'The Workman'; comedies, comic operas, etc. He has also written 'Dramaturgy of the Theatre'; 'Dramaturgie der Klassiker,' a work of exceeding value; and 'Dramaturgie des Schauspiels'; also 'Dramaturgy of the Opera' (2 vols.).

Buluwayo. See BULAWAYO.

Bulwer, John, English physician. He flourished in the 17th century and appears to be entitled to the honor of having first pointed out a method of instructing the deaf and dumb. His works include 'Philocophus, or the Deafe and Dumbe Man's Friend' (1648); 'Chironomia, or the Art of Manual Rhetoric'; 'Chirologia, or the Natural Language of the Hand,' and 'Anthropometamorphosis.'

Bulwer, William Henry Lytton Earle (BARON DALLING AND BULWER), English author and diplomatist, brother of Sir Edward Bulwer-Lytton (q.v.): b. London, 13 Feb. 1801; d. Naples, 23 May 1872. He was minister to Madrid in 1843; in 1849 had a diplomatic mission to Washington, and was one of the negotiators of the Bulwer-Clayton Treaty (q.v.); was ambassador to Turkey in 1858-65. He was created Baron Dalling and Bulwer in 1871. His works include 'An Autumn in Greece' (1826); 'France, Social, Literary, and Political' (1834-6) 'Life of Byron' (1835); 'Historical Characters' (1868-70); 'Life of Palmerston' (1870-4).

Bulwer-Clayton Treaty, a treaty negotiated at Washington, D. C., in April 1850, by John M. Clayton, secretary of state under President Taylor, and Sir Henry Bulwer, British minister to the United States. It provided that neither the United States nor Great Britain should attempt to control a proposed canal across Nicaragua. The treaty provided further for the neutrality of the canal and it guaranteed encouragement to all lines of interoceanic communication. The terms of the treaty were afterward much disputed. In 1882 the United States government intimated to Great Britain that the canal having become impracticable because of reasons for which Great Britain alone was responsible, the United States considered the treaty as no longer binding, but Great Britain continued to hold it as in force. On 3 March 1899, Congress passed a bill providing for the construction of a canal on the Nicaragua route, which also authorized the President to open negotiations with Great Britain for the abroga-

tion of the Bulwer-Clayton Treaty, and under the last clause a convention between the two countries, abrogating the portions of the treaty that were deemed to be against the interests of the United States was signed in Washington, 5 Feb. 1900. See TREATIES.

Bulwer-Lytton, Edward George Earle (first LORD LYTTON), English politician and novelist: b. London 25 May 1803; d. Torquay, Devonshire 18 Jan. 1873. The Bulwers, long descent from the Normans and Vikings, perhaps as a ready explanation of their bold and turbulent spirit. The novelist's father, William Earle Bulwer, was colonel of the 106th regiment or Norfolk rangers. His mother, Elizabeth Barbara, was the only daughter of Richard Warburton Lytton of Knebworth in Hertfordshire, the family seat since the time of Henry VII. From her and her father, who was a learned scholar, Bulwer claimed to have derived his love for letters. As a boy he lived much among his grandfather's books and read through three circulating libraries. He wrote volumes of Byronic verse, some of which was published at the age of seventeen. Prepared for the university at various private schools, he entered Trinity College, Cambridge, at Easter in 1822; but soon migrated to Trinity Hall, where it was not necessary to attend lectures. At Cambridge he was a conspicuous member of the Union; he won the Chancellor's medal in 1825, and sketched two novels. At this time he also read enormously in history and began the practice of keeping those huge commonplace books which afterwards became useful in preparing his historical novels. Before receiving his bachelor's degree in 1826, he published more Byronic verse, fell desperately in love, made a tour of Scotland and the English lakes, and passed a season in Paris, where he was received into the most brilliant *salons*. Returning to London "a finished dandy," he married on 29 Aug., 1827, Rosina Doyle Wheeler, a beautiful Irish girl of some accomplishments. The marriage led to an estrangement from his mother and the young man was consequently thrown upon his own resources. He settled with his wife at Woodcot House in Berkshire, where he attempted to live in style from what he could earn with his pen. The marriage proving uncomfortable, a legal separation was obtained in 1836 after years of a life apart. On the death of his mother in 1843 he inherited Knebworth and assumed the surname of Lytton.

To pass by Bulwer's numerous contributions to annuals and periodicals, he published in 1827, 'Falkland,' a sentimental novel in imitation of Rousseau's 'Nouvelle Héloise.' After a quick passage through the sentimental stage, he came out with 'Pelham' in 1828, a brilliant novel founded upon what he had seen of high life in London and Paris. It was likewise Bulwer's first excursion into politics and crime. Late in the same year followed 'The Disowned,' a curious novel which the author called "metaphysical" inasmuch as the characters are intended to stand for "certain dispositions influential upon conduct." After 'Devereux' (1829), an experiment in historical romance, Bulwer took up the criminal novel, publishing 'Paul Clifford' (1830) and 'Eugene Aram'

(1832), which are among his most characteristic books. By this time a popular novelist,
he displayed during the coming years extraordinary versatility. With 'The Pilgrims of the
Rhine' (1834) he began a series of fantastic
tales which he called ideal and poetic, announcing that they should be judged "by the rules
rather of poetry than prose." The chapter entitled "The Life of Dreams" elaborates a
clever system of dreaming, evidently made use
of in our day by Du Maurier in 'Peter Ibbet-
son' and by Kipling in 'The Brushwood Boy.'
Occult philosophy was cleverly employed in
'Zanoni' (1842) and speculation about the
future age of electricity in 'The Coming Race'
(1871). A series of ghost stories culminated
in 'The Haunted and the Haunters' (1861)
hardly surpassed in its kind. Historical romance. resumed in 'The Last Days of Pompeii'
(1834), was continued in 'Rienzi' (1835), 'The
Last of the Barons' (1843), 'Harold' (1848),
and the incomplete 'Pausanias' (posthumous,
1876). The best of these novels stand for an
attempt to get near to the facts of history.
In the midst of this work was planned a comprehensive history of 'Athens, its Rise and Fall,'
of which two volumes appeared in 1837. Another
idealization of the criminal in 'Lucretia' (1847)
provoked considerable criticism, to which he replied with 'A Word to the Public' (1846). To
test his popularity, Bulwer now published
anonymously in Blackwood's Magazine three
experiments in 18th century humor. The series
comprises 'The Caxtons' (1849), 'My Novel'
(1853), and 'What Will He Do With It'
(1858). Though a little too obviously in the
manner of Sterne, the novels are among Bulwer's best work. They were, curiously enough,
as well received by the public as if they had
borne the author's name. Somewhat like them
is 'Kenelm Chillingly' (1873), interesting besides for its infusion of autobiography.

Throughout his career, Bulwer never ceased
to cultivate his muse. From the Byronic influence that marked his poems down to 1830, he
worked into satire, addressing himself "to the
humors rather than to the passions of men."
The 'Siamese Twins' (1831) a poem of four
books in the metre of 'Hudibras' appeared in
a volume of miscellaneous poems, of which the
longest is one on Milton. 'The New Timon;
A Poetical Romance of London' (1846), a
satire on men then prominent in politics and
literature, is memorable for the reference to
Tennyson as "Schoolmiss Alfred," and for
Tennyson's caustic stanzas in a reply contributed to Punch, 28 Feb. 1846. Among Bulwer's
other collections of verse are 'Poems and Ballads,' translated from Schiller (1844); an epic
in two volumes on 'King Arthur' (1848-9);
'The Lost Tales of Miletus' (1866); and a
translation of the 'Odes and Epodes of Horace'
(1869). If Bulwer did not gain much fame as
a poet, he exactly hit popular taste in three
plays—'The Lady of Lyons' (1838), 'Richelieu' (1838) and 'Money' (1840)—which still
keep the stage.

Bulwer's rôle in letters has obscured for
later times the part he played in politics. From
1831 to 1841 he sat in parliament as a liberal
member for St. Ives. Huntingdonshire. and
then for Lincoln. After making his maiden
speech in support of the Reform Bill, he devoted his energies largely in favor of copyright
on original works, cheap postage on newspapers, and the laws affecting dramatic literature
and the stage. His early speeches on these subjects are still worth reading. In 1834, he
issued a spirited pamphlet on the 'Present
Crisis,' which went through 20 editions and
influenced greatly the election that brought
Lord Melbourne back to power. The new
premier offered him a lordship in the admiralty
but the post was declined. In 1841, Bulwer
lost his seat owing to his willingness to accept
a slight tax on corn. Ten years later he advocated protection to this extent in 'Letters to
John Bull, Esq.'; and in 1852 he returned to
parliament as a conservative member for Hertfordshire. His numerous speeches of this
period relate to the excise duties, the Crimean
War, China, and the East India Company. On
the formation of the Derby Ministry in 1848, he
became secretary to the colonies. While holding this office he organized the new colony of
British Columbia. He spoke in support of
Disraeli's reform bill of 1859 but against the
measures introduced by Lord Russell and Gladstone in 1860 and 1866. As a reward for his
services, he was elevated to the peerage in 1866,
as Baron Lytton of Knebworth. Before this
he received the degree LL.D. from both of the
great English Universities. In 1854 he was installed honorary president of the associated
societies of Edinburgh University, and he was
twice elected lord rector of the University of
Glasgow. To the last he kept up his literary
work. 'The Parisians' was running in Blackwood's Magazine when the end came at Torquay on 18 Jan. 1873.

As a novelist Bulwer was subjected to fierce
assaults from the critics throughout his career.
Thackeray, for example, in a review of 'Ernest
Maltravers' ridiculed and scorned his bad art,
affected style, "his eternal whine * * *
about the good and the beautiful" and "the
dulness of his moral sense." Still there is the
other side. In various prefaces to his novels
and especially in two papers contributed to the
Monthly Chronicle for 1838, Bulwer carefully
elaborated his views on the art of fiction, drawing clear distinctions between the novel and the
drama as he understood and practiced them.
He never aimed at the dramatic novel wherein
each incident and conversation must contribute
to the working out of a logical plot. "It is
often desirable," he said with reference to the
novel, "to go back instead of forward,—to
wind, to vary, to shift the interest from person
to person" that the reader may not become
fatigued. In that aim he succeeded. However
much his novels may fail in technical details,
they have never failed to find an audience.

Bibliography.—Unfortunately there is no adequate life of Bulwer or critical edition of his
novels, indicating the many important changes
he made in the text from time to time. Uncritical editions of the novels are numerous. To
his 'Speeches' (two vols., Edinburgh 1874),
his son, the Earl of Lytton, prefixed a memoir
dealing with his political career. The period
of his life from 1803 to 1832 is covered by a
most interesting autobiography, half fact and
half fiction. and several supplementary chapters
by his son. published together under the title
'Life, Letters, and Literary Remains' (2 vols.,

London 1883). After the death of Lady Lytton, her executrix, Louisâ Devey, published in vindication of her memory 'Letters of the Late Edward Bulwer, Lord Lytton to his Wife' (New York 1889).   WILBUR L. CROSS, *Professor of English, Yale University.*

Bulwer-Lytton, Edward Robert. See LYTTON, EDWARD ROBERT BULWER.

Bum-boat (perhaps originally "boom-boat," from the boom rigged out from the side or a man-of-war at anchor, to which boats may make fast), employed by hucksters to visit ships lying at anchor, with supplies of provisions, trinkets, clothing, etc., for sale to the sailors.

Bumblebee, a wild bee of some species of the genus *Bombus,* of which upward of 50 species inhabit North America. Few occur in the southern hemisphere or tropical regions, and none in Africa south of the Sahara or in Australia, while they are the only bees inhabiting Arctic and Alpine regions. The bumble, or humble, bee is recognized by its large, thick, hairy body and long bass hum. The colonies of bumblebees are not numerous compared with those of wasps, or the stingless or the honey bee. A populous colony in England and America may number from 300 to 400 individuals. The proportion of sexes and castes of *Bombus muscorum* in England were found by Smith to be, in a colony of 120, 25 females, 36 males, and 59 workers. The roundish oval cells differ in size and have no exact arrangement. Besides the cells containing the young, the old discarded ones are made to serve as honey tubs or pollen tubs, and there are also the cells of the guest or Psithyrus bees (q.v.). In good weather and when flowers are plentiful the bees collect and store honey in abundance, and when the empty pupa-cells are full they form special cells made entirely of wax, and these are filled with honey, and left open for the benefit of the community (Sharp). Hofer states that special tubs for the storing of pollen are sometimes constructed. Putnam says that the larvæ make their own cells of silk, which are finally strengthened with wax by the old bees. Bumblebees have been seen working in warm moonlight nights. About two centuries ago Godart stated that a trumpeter bee is kept in some nests to rouse the colony to work by three or four o'clock in the morning, and this has been recently confirmed by Hofer, who observed the fact in his laboratory. If the trumpeter was removed its place was filled the next morning.

There is a great deal of variation in our bumblebees, and, besides the local and climatic varieties, polymorphism is apparently marked, as Packard has (in *Bombus fervidus*) detected two sets of males and females, the large and the small; but whether there are two sizes of workers has not yet been ascertained.

The queen bees lay their eggs in masses of bee-bread attached to the top or sides of the old cells, in little enclosures formed by thin partitions set up by the bee after the eggs have been deposited. Thus placed, says Packard, in a mass of food, the young larvæ, on hatching, begin, by eating the food, gradually to construct their cells in the manner described by Putnam, who gives the following account of the economy of the bumblebee colony:

The queen awakens in early spring from her winter's sleep beneath the leaves or moss, or in deserted nests, and selects a nesting-place, generally in an abandoned nest of a field-mouse, or beneath a stump or sod, and immediately collects a small amount of pollen mixed with honey, and in this deposits from seven to fourteen eggs, gradually adding to the pollen mass until the first brood is hatched. She does not wait, however, for one brood to be hatched before laying the eggs of another; but, as soon as food enough has been collected, she lays the eggs for the second.

As soon as the larvæ are capable of motion, and commence feeding, they eat the pollen by which they are surrounded, and gradually separating, push their way in various directions. Eating as they move, and increasing in size quite rapidly, they soon make large cavities in the pollen mass. When they have attained their full size, they spin a silken wall about them, which is strengthened by the old bees covering it with a thin layer of wax, which soon becomes hard and tough, thus forming a cell. The larvæ now gradually attain the pupa stage, and remain inactive until their full development. They then cut their way out, and are ready to assume their duties as workers, small females, males, or queens.

It is apparent that the irregular disposition of the cells is due to their being constructed so peculiarly by the larvæ. After the first brood, composed of workers, has come forth, the queen bee devotes her time principally to her duties at home, the workers supplying the colony with honey and pollen. As the queen continues prolific, more workers are added, and the nest is rapidly enlarged. About the middle of summer eggs are deposited which produce both small females and males. All eggs laid after the last of July produce the large females or queens; and, the males being still in the nest, it is presumed that the queens are impregnated at this time, as, on the approach of cold weather, all except the queens, of which there are several in each nest, die.

Consult Putnam, 'Notes on the Habits of Some Species of Humblebees'; and Packard, 'The Humblebees of New England and Their Parasites' (Proceedings Essex Institute, IV.); Sharp, 'Insects,' Part II.

Bum'blefoot, a corn or abscess on the feet of domestic fowls, thought to arise from roosting on narrow perches or walking on sharp pebbles. The disease is sometimes incurable, but in other cases yields to the daily application of lunar caustic.

Bumblepuppy, a coined word used to describe the attempts of unskilful persons to play whist; opposed to scientific whist and "the rigor of the game."

Bummalo'ti, a fish (*Harpodon nehereus*), related to the salmon, but marine, which is caught in large quantities on the western coast of India, dried, salted, and exported all over the East. A trade-name is "Bombay duck."

Bump'ing Posts, constructions at the ends of railroad tracks in shifting yards, intended to prevent cars from running off the track. They are usually strong wooden frames with buffers placed at such a height as to receive the blow of the platform or coupler of the car. Banks of earth or cinders are sometimes utilized for this purpose and portable metal posts known as shipblocks are frequently employed as bumping posts.

Bumpo, Natty. See LEATHERSTOCKING.

Bump'us, Herman Carey, American educator: b. Buckfield. Maine, 5 May 1862. He was graduated from Brown University in 1884, was professor of biology at Olivet College, Mich, 1886–9; professor of zoology in Clark University, Worcester, Mass., 1890–1; and professor of comparative anatomy in Brown University from 1892. In 1898 he was appointed director of the biological laboratory of the United States Fish Commission at Wood's Hole, Mass. He is the author of 'A Laboratory Course in Invertebrate Zoology' (1893).

Bunce, Francis Marvin, American naval officer: b. Hartford, Conn., 25 Dec. 1836; d. there, 19 Oct. 1901. He entered the naval service in 1851, and was graduated from the naval academy in 1857. In 1862 as executive officer of the Penobscot he took part in the engagement with the rebel batteries at Yorktown, Va. Assigned to temporary duty with the army, he had charge of the disembarkation of the heavy artillery and mortars for use in the investment of Yorktown by Gen. McClellan, April 1862. He commanded a successful expedition up Little River, between North and South Carolina, destroying several schooners and large quantities of cotton, turpentine, and resin, together with extensive salt works. With the monitor Patapsco in 1863 he took part in all the actions in which she was engaged during the siege of Charleston, and was wounded by the premature explosion of ·a cartridge. Later he was chief of scouts on the staff of Admiral Dahlgren. On 5 Sept. 1865 he was placed in command of the monitor Monadnock, and took that vessel from Philadelphia to San Francisco, the first extended sea voyage ever made by a monitor. On 1 March 1895 he was selected to command the North Atlantic squadron, with the rank of active rear-admiral. On 1 May 1897 he went to the Brooklyn navy yard and there superintended the conversion of many fast ships and yachts for war service. It is said that the government's policy of furnishing the navy with abundant ammunition for target practice and giving prizes for the best shots, a policy which produced such admirable results in the Spanish-American war, was due to the efforts of Admiral Bunce. He was commissioned rear-admiral 6 Feb. 1898, and retired from active service 25 Dec. 1898.

Bunce, Oliver Bell, American author: b. New York, 8 Feb. 1828; d. there, 15 May 1890. After spending several years as clerk in a stationery store, and bookseller and publisher on his own account, he became manager of the publishing house of James G. Gregory, which he conducted very successfully for many years. It was at his instigation that the fine edition of Cooper's works, with steel and wood engravings by F. O. C. Darley, was planned and published. For a short time he was a reader for Harper & Bros., but in 1869 he formed a connection with D. Appleton & Company, that ended only with his death. He edited 'Appleton's Journal,' and largely planned and carried through for the firm some of their most famous illustrated publications. such as 'Picturesque America,' 'Picturesque Europe,' 'Picturesque

Palestine.' In addition to office business his literary aptitudes and ambitions kept him at work in spite of chronic invalidism. He wrote among other works, 'Romance of the Revolution' (1852) ; 'A Bachelor's Story' (1859) ; 'Life Before Him' (1860) ; 'Bachelor Bluff, His Opinions, etc.' (1881) ; 'Don't: A Manual of Mistakes and Improprieties' (1883), of which over 100,000 copies have been sold ; 'My House: An Ideal' (1884), a graphic study of a country home; and 'The Adventures of Timias Terrystone: a Novel' (1885). As a very young man he wrote three plays which were accepted and produced on the stage with success: 'Fate, or the Prophecy,' a tragedy; 'Love in '76,' a comedy; 'Marco Bozzaris,' an heroic tragedy. The second of these was played by Laura Keene, the other two by James W. Wallack.

Bun'co, a familiar term applied to the practices of a certain class of swindlers. The trickster trades upon the credulity of an apparently well-to-do stranger in the city, under pretense of some connection with the latter's friends or native place, or by similar expedients. After confidence is secured, counterfeit money is imposed upon him, he is induced to cash "bogus" checks, etc., or even becomes the victim of more direct robbery.

Buncombe, swollen political oratory not directed to the point in hand or the audience present. but to the achievement of a charlatanic reputation outside. "Twisting the tail of the British lion," and other like feats of windy chauvinism, are specimens of buncombe; the object of the speaker being, not primarily to impress the hearers, but to make the general populace admire his swaggering patriotism. The reputed origin of the story is an anecdote of a member of the North Carolina legislature, from Buncombe County in that State, who told the thin remnants of a house he had nearly emptied by his dull and pointless remarks, that they might go, too, as he was only "speaking for Buncombe." Wheeler, 'History of North Carolina.'

Bundelcund, bŭn-dĕl-kŭnd', or Bandalkhand, bŭn-dĕl-känd', India, a tract, consisting partly of certain British districts connected with the Northwest Provinces, and partly of a number of small native states subordinate to the central India agency. Its surface is considerably diversified. and there are several ranges of hills, some of which reach the height of 2,000 feet. It has soil of every variety, which yields almost every grain and plant of India. Its waters are carried by different streams to the Jamna, and so to the Ganges. The total area is 20,559 square miles, of which the British districts occupy 10.332. Population of the latter (1901) about 1,400,000.

Bundesrath, boon'dĕz-rät, the German federal council which represents the individual states of the empire, as the Reichstag represents the German nation. It consists (1900) of 58 members, and its functions are mainly those of a confirming body, although it has the privilege of rejecting measures passed by the Reichstag.

Bundi, boon'de, India, a principality in Rajputana. under British protection; area, 2,300 square miles. Although small, Boondee is important as the medium of communication between the north and south. Pop. 295,675. Bundi, the capital, is picturesquely situated, and its antiquity, numerous temples, and magnificent fountains give it a very interesting appearance. Pop. 22,544.

Bun′galow, an East Indian term for a kind of country house with a thatched or tiled roof. Bungalows are generally of one story, though sometimes of two, and have verandas running round them to afford shelter from the sun. Public bungalows for travelers (daks) are maintained by government on the main highways.

Bun′gay, England, a market town in Suffolk, on the right bank of the Waveney, 30 miles northeast of Ipswich. It is well built; the streets, spacious and well paved, diverging from a moderate-sized area in the centre of the town, forming a market-place, in which is a handsome cross. It has two fine churches. The principal trade is in corn, coal, flour, lime, and malt, in which a considerable amount of business is done. There is also an extensive printing-office and stereotype foundry. Adjoining the town is a very spacious common. Pop. about 4,000.

Bunge, boon′ge, **Alexander,** Russian botanist: b. Kiev, 24 Sept. 1803; d. 1890. He was educated at Dorpat, and after taking the degree of M.D. in 1825 he traveled in Siberia and the eastern part of the Altai Mountains, and then joined the mission of the Academy of St. Petersburg to Pekin, where he remained eight months and procured an extensive herbarium. In 1833, by invitation of the Academy of St. Petersburg, he made a second Asiatic journey, and in 1836 settled as professor of botany at Dorpat. His principal publications are catalognes of the plants which he collected in China and near the Altai Mountains.

Bunge, Frederic George, Russian jurist: b. Kiev (brother of the preceding), 1 March 1802; d. 1897. He was educated at Dorpat, and for many years was professor of law there. His writings, principally upon the history of law and rights in the countries around the Baltic Sea, are numerous and valuable.

Bungert, August, ow′goost boon′gārt, German composer: b. Mülheim, Prussia, 14 March 1846. He studied under Kufferath at Mülheim, at Cologne, and Paris. He held a position as musical director at Kreuznach, then went to Berlin, where he continued his studies under Kiel, and later moved to Genoa. His compositions include an opera cycle, 'The Homeric World,' consisting of two main parts, 'The Iliad,' and 'The Odyssey'; 'Tasso'; 'The Students of Salamanca,' a comic opera; 'On the Wartburg'; and a number of songs. The songs are considered his most successful productions.

Bu′nias, a small genus of plants of the natural order *Cruciferæ*, mostly natives of southeastern Europe and adjacent Asia. Some of the species, especially *B. orientalis,* called hill-mustard, have been cultivated for forage, and have become weeds where they have escaped from cultivation. Since they are not very leafy and are not relished by stock, they have not become popular.

Bunion, a small, hard, painful tumor, formed in any part of the foot, but especially in the metatarsal joints. It consists in a swelling of the bones themselves, which fact distin-

guishes bunions from corns. It appears to be caused by the pressure of a boot or shoe which is too tight, especially when the feet are a little deformed. The best means to relieve the pain is to remove the causes of the tumor as soon as possible, to give rest to the foot, and to apply lotions and emollient poultices.

Bunker·Hill, Mass., an eminence, 110 feet high, in the Charlestown district of Boston, connected by a ridge with another elevation, 75 feet high, named Breed's Hill. These heights are memorable as being the scene of a battle, 17 June 1775, commonly known as the battle of Bunker Hill. The city of Boston was occupied by the British under Gen. Gage, who had resolved to begin offensive operations against the rebels. This design becoming known in the American camp, it was determined to seize and fortify the heights of Charlestown on the night of 16 June. The execution of this perilous mission was confided to Cols. Prescott and Pepperell at the head of a brigade of 1,000 men; and at dawn of day a strong redoubt was already completed on Breed's Hill. About 1,500 Americans advanced successively to the relief of Prescott, and Gen. Warren entered the redoubt as a volunteer, refusing the command which was tendered to him. At about two thirty o'clock, two columns of the British advanced to a simultaneous assault; they were received with a terrific fire, and were twice repulsed in disorder. When the Americans had exhausted all their ammunition, Prescott gave the order for retreat. They received a destructive volley as they left the redoubt, and Warren fell, shot through the head with a bullet. The retreat was harassed by a raking fire from the British ships and batteries, but there was no pursuit beyond Charlestown Neck. The British loss was 226 officers and men killed, and 828 wounded; that of the Americans 145 killed or missing, and 304 wounded. Although a defeat, the moral result of this action was great. The Americans had seen superior numbers of the disciplined soldiers of England retreat before their fire, and had given the proof that they were able to defend their liberties. On Breed's Hill, and near the spot where Warren fell, stands the Bunker Hill Monument, the corner-stone of which was laid by the Marquis de Lafayette, 17 June 1825. This monument was inaugurated 17 June 1843. It consists of a plain granite shaft, 220 feet high, 31 feet square at the base, and 15 at the top. The monument affords a magnificent panoramic view of the surrounding country.

Bunner, Henry Cuyler, American author: b. Oswego, N. Y., 3 Aug. 1855; d. Nutley, N. J., 11 May 1896. He became a journalist in 1873, and was editor of 'Puck' from shortly after its start till his death. He was author of 'A Woman of Honor' (1883); 'Airs from Arcady and Elsewhere' (1884); 'The Midge' (1886); 'The Story of a New York House' (1887); 'Zadoc Pine and Other Stories' (1891); 'Short Sixes' (1891); 'The Runaway Browns' (1892); 'Jersey Street and Jersey Lane' (1896).

Bun′ning, Herbert, English composer: b. London, 2 May 1863. He graduated from Brasenose College, Oxford, and was for a time lieutenant in the 4th Hussars, but resigned his commission to study music in France and Italy. He remained abroad four years (1886–90), and after his return to England was musical director in the Lyric Theatre, 1892–3, and in the Prince of Wales Theatre, 1895-6. Among his musical compositions are 'Shepherd's Call'; 'Village Suite'; and 'La Princesse Osra,' an opera produced at the Royal Opera, Covent Garden, in July 1902.

Bun'odont, a term applied to animals in which the crowns of the molar teeth are composed of a number of low rounded cones or cusps. The pig is one of the best examples among living animals; the teeth of monkeys and other omnivorous or frugivorous animals, including man, are also of this type. It is probable that the molars of many if not all modern mammals have been evolved from bunodont teeth, for the ancestors of many races of the modern hoofed animals, carnivora, and some other groups, show a series of stages in the evolution of the teeth leading from the omnivorous bunodont type into the specialized grinding or cutting teeth (selenodont) of the modern animals. See TEETH.

Bun'sen, Christian Karl Josias (CHEVA-LIER), German statesman and philosopher: b. Korbach, Waldeck, 25 Aug. 1791; d. Bonn, 28 Nov. 1860. He studied philology under Heyne at Göttingen, and subsequently went to Holland and Denmark, to acquire a critical knowledge of the Danish and Dutch languages. In 1815 he made the acquaintance at Berlin of the celebrated Niebuhr, and in 1816 proceeded to Paris, where he studied Persian and Arabic under Sylvestre de Sacy. The same year he visited Rome, where he married, and renewed his intimacy with Niebuhr, then Prussian ambassador at the papal court. Niebuhr procured him the appointment of secretary to the Prussian legation, and in 1823 Bunsen assumed Niebuhr's duties, being later, and in 1827, formally accredited as resident Prussian minister. In this capacity he continued till 1838, and conducted several important negotiations with the papal see, the result of one of which was the brief of Leo XII. relative to mixed marriages. His next mission was to Berne, as ambassador to the Swiss Federation. During his residence at Rome Bunsen had industriously pursued his philosophical and historical studies, including more especially that of the Platonic philosophy, and investigations into the religious and ecclesiastical history of mankind. The liturgies of the Church received his especial attention, and a service of his own framing, introduced by him into the chapel of the Prussian embassy at Rome, was printed by order of the king of Prussia, who wrote a preface to it. This work was published without the author's name at Hamburg in 1846, under the title of 'Allgemeines Evang. Gesang-und Gebetbuch' ('General Hymn and Prayer Book of the Evangelical Lutheran Church'), and may be regarded as a new edition of the 'Versuch Eines Allgemeinen Evang. Gesang-und Gebetbuchs,' published at Hamburg in 1833. In 1841 Bunsen was summoned to Berlin from Switzerland to proceed to England in charge of a mission for the establishment, in conjunction with that country, of a bishopric at Jerusalem. Shortly afterward he was nominated Prussian ambassador to England. In 1844 he was consulted on the subject of granting a constitution to Prussia, and is said to have drawn

up and submitted to government the form of one which bore a very close resemblance to that of Great Britain. In the Schleswig-Holstein affair he strenuously supported the claims of Prussia and the German Confederation in opposition to those of Denmark. From the opposite views taken by him to those of his government in relation to the Russian war he was recalled from London in 1854, and, abandoning politics, retired to Heidelberg to devote himself exclusively to literary pursuits. The results of these have established his reputation as one of the most profound and original critics in the department of biblical and ecclesiastical history. Among these are 'Die Verfassung der Kirche der Zukunft' ('The Constitution of the Church of the Future') (1845); 'Ægyptens Stelle in der Weltgeschichte' ('Egypt's Place in the World's History') (1845); 'Hippolytus und Seine Zeit' ('Hippolytus and His Time') (1851); and lastly, his greatest work, 'Bibelwerk für die Gemeinde' ('Bible Commentary for the Community'), the first part of which was published in 1858, and was intended to be completed in 1862. It had occupied his attention for nearly 30 years, and, as he informs us, was regarded as the grand centre-point to which all his literary and intellectual energies were to be devoted. Death interposed to prevent him completing his undertaking. Ill health caused him to spend the winters of 1858–9 and 1859–60 at Cannes, in the south of France, returning thence in the spring of 1860 to Bonn (whither he had recently transferred his abode from Heidelberg), where he died. Three volumes of his 'Bibelwerk' had been published at his death (the first, second, and fifth), and this great work was completed in his spirit and by the aid of his manuscripts under the editorship of Holtzmann and Kamphausen, in nine volumes (1858–70).

Bunsen, Robert Wilhelm Eberard, German chemist: b. Göttingen, 31 March 1811; d. 16 Aug. 1899. He studied at Göttingen University, and at Paris, Berlin, and Vienna; was appointed professor at the Polytechnic Institute of Cassel 1836; extraordinary professor at the University of Marburg 1838, and ordinary professor there 1841; professor at Breslau 1851; and finally professor of experimental chemistry at Heidelberg 1852. Among his many discoveries and inventions are the production of magnesium in quantities, magnesium light, spectrum analysis, and the electric pile and the burner which bear his name (see below). Among his works are 'Chemische Analyse durch Spektralbeobachtungen' (with Kirchhoff, 1861: new ed. 1895); 'Gasometrische Methoden' (1857; English by Roscoe); and 'Anleitung zur Analyse der Aschen und Mineralwasser' (1874). He retired from active teaching in 1889.

Bunsen Battery, a modification of the Grove battery, plates or bars of gas coke being used instead of platinum. The electromotive force is slightly less than that of the Grove battery.

Bunsen Burner, a form of gas-burner especially adapted for heating, consisting of a tube in which, by means of holes in the side, the gas becomes mixed with air before consumption, so that it gives a non-illuminating, smokeless flame. Burners of this nature are part of the indispensable outfit of a chemical laboratory.

Bunt, sometimes called **Smut Ball, Pepper Brand,** and **Brand Bladders,** the most formidable disease, perhaps, to which wheat is subject, but one which may in most instances be greatly modified, and which seldom in the present day does material injury, except where there is careless cultivation. Like many other of the diseases to which the cereal plants are subject, it arises from the attack of a parasitic fungus (*Uredo caries*). It is generated in the ovary of wheat and a few other *Gramineæ,* and very rarely on the stem. It is formed at an early stage of growth, before the ear is free from the sheath; and indeed the plants which are affected by the parasite may be readily recognized by their unusual luxuriance, being generally several inches higher than plants not affected, larger in bulk, and often producing a greater number of stems from the same root. The bunted grains are shorter and blunter than the sound, of a dark-green when young, but when old of a pale brown, or sometimes nearly black. The contents of the ovary are reduced to a uniform black powder or paste, which has an offensive smell like that of decayed fish. Various substances have been used by cultivators to prevent the growth of bunt, such as salt, quicklime, arsenic, corrosive sublimate, etc. Careful washing and a selection of good seed will alone prevent much mischief, but it is advisable to take some more stringent measures with a view to destroy the vitality of the bunt spores. For this purpose Dombasle's method is the most successful. It consists in thoroughly wetting the grain with a solution of sulphate of soda (Glauber's salts), then drying the wheat with quicklime, which combines with the water to make sulphate of lime (gypsum), which acts as a manure, while the caustic soda destroys the vegetative powers of the bunt spores.

Bunter Sandstone, one of the three great divisions of Triassic formation. It is the lowest, that is, the oldest, of the series. It corresponds to the *grès bigarré* (variegated freestone or grit) of the French. In the Hartz it is more than 1,000 feet thick; in Cheshire and Lancashire, England, about 600. The footprints formerly known as those of chirotherium, now known to be labyrinthodont, are found in the bunter; the plants are chiefly ferns, cycads, and conifers.

Bunting, Jabez, English clergyman: b. Monyash, Derbyshire, 1778; d. London, 16 June 1858. His parents were members of the Wesleyan Church and removed to Manchester when he was a child. While at school he attracted the attention of Dr. Percival, who employed him as his amanuensis, and at his death made him one of his executors. He early joined the Church; became a traveling preacher in 1799; joined the Conference after the death of Mr. Wesley, and was appointed to the Oldham circuit. After traveling four years he was sent to London, where he gained great popularity as a pulpit and platform orator. After remaining two years in London he was removed to Manchester, where he distinguished himself as an advocate of ecclesiastical order and discipline in a controversy with some disaffected Methodists. In this controversy he gave such evidence of a knowledge of the polity of Wesleyan Methodism as secured for him the favor of the entire body to which he belonged. He was four times president of the Methodist Conference; 17 years missionary secretary; and three years as editor. In 1835 he was chosen president of the theological school, and was looked upon as the acknowledged leader of the Methodists, superintending the interests of the body at home and abroad, while, at the same time, his influence was felt in other evangelical denominations, and also in the political world, statesmen frequently resorting to him for advice. Yet he derived only the ordinary emoluments of a Methodist minister — a yearly salary of £150, with house-rent and taxes. During all the distractions connected with the secessions that have taken place in the Wesleyan body, Dr. Bunting remained a firm, unwavering adherent and advocate of the doctrines and discipline of the Church as they came from the hands of John Wesley, and to his influence and indefatigable zeal are largely to be ascribed the permanency and prosperity of the Wesleyan connection.

Bunting, one of a group of cone-billed birds, forming the genus *Emberiza,* represented in Europe by several large, brown-streaked, or yellowish finches, of which the corn-bunting, reed-bunting, and cirl-bunting (qq.v.) are well known in Great Britain. The corn-bunting, which is considerably larger than a house sparrow, is brown in color with darker streaks on the upper parts or whitish brown with dark brown spots and lines on the under parts, and has a slightly forked tail. The reed-bunting has a black head and throat and the nape and sides of the neck are white. The head of the cirl-bunting is olive-green, with bright yellow patches on the cheek and over the eyes. The term is used in the United States for two or three similar birds, such as the dick-cissel, and snow-bunting (qq.v.). All the buntings are good singers, and the term is applied by dealers in cage birds not only to the true European buntings, but to many other seed-eaters, such as the ortolan and our indigo-bird.

Bunting, a thin woolen stuff, of which flags are usually made; hence, flags, collectively.

Bun'ya-bun'ya, the native Australian name of the *Araucaria bidwillii,* a fine Queensland tree with cones larger than a man's head, containing seeds that are eagerly eaten by the natives.

Bunyan, John, English preacher and author: b. Elstow, near Bedford, Bedfordshire, England, 1628; d. Swan Hill, London, 31 Aug. 1688. The Bunyan's were an old family in Bedfordshire but Bunyan's immediate ancestors for several generations had been obscure, and Bunyan's own father, Thomas Bunyan, was a tinker. Of his mother, Margaret Bentley, little is known. In spite of their lowliness, however, these parents trained Bunyan with some care and sent him to the Bedford schools. Then he took up the trade of tinker, at which, until he became an established preacher, he worked industriously. In the latter part of 1645 and the early months of the following year he fought in the Civil War, but on which side is uncertain. Froude maintains that he was in the Royalist army, whereas Macaulay and Brown, to whom the weight of authority must be given, state that the evidence goes to show that Bunyan was with the Parliamentarians. In 1646, he returned to his trade in Elstow, and at about

1. Lapland Longspur Bunting.
2. Chaffinch.
3. Wild Canary.
4. Meadow Bunting.
5. Cardinal.
6. Rose-breasted Grosbeak (Male).
7. Reed Bunting (Male and Female).

the age of twenty married a wife, whose goodness of character is the accepted proof that
Bunyan was better than he represented himself.

Of far more importance in giving character
to Bunyan's career was his spiritual life. Besides being brought up religiously and at a time
of peculiarly strong belief in the literal truth
of hell and heaven, of damnation and atonement, of devils and evil spirits, Bunyan's boyhood and early manhood were not only a continual struggle between the inclinations of an
active, pleasure-loving youth and the terror lest
he be doomed to eternal perdition, but also
a spiritual anguish heightened by one of the
most imaginative of minds of which there is
record. "He was," says William James ('The
Varieties of Religious Experience'), "a typical
case of the psychopathic temperament, sensitive of conscience to a diseased degree, beset by
doubts, fears, and insistent ideas, and a victim
of verbal automatisms, both motor and sensory. These were usually texts of Scripture
which, sometimes damnatory and sometimes
favorable, would come in a half-hallucinatory
form as if they were voices, and fasten on his
mind and buffet it between them like a shuttle-
cock." Though in most ways a wholly respectable character, he speaks of himself, in his autobiography, 'Grace Abounding,' as a most
blasphemous youth, in return for which he was
warned and tormented by visions to which he
gave little heed. When the visions left him
he tells us that he became worse, nor were some
narrow escapes from death sufficient to make
him repent. His marriage had a good effect on
him; he went to church regularly and was reverent, though, he says, in a formal way. He
still liked his sports and was in the habit of
playing cat on the village green Sunday afternoons. The effect of a peculiarly vivid vision
of a warning voice from heaven while he was in
the act of striking the cat, was to make him
despair of ever being redeemed from his wicked
courses. Yet he began to mend his ways, first
giving up his profanity, then his love of bell-
ringing, and lastly his dancing, though it took
him "nearly a full year before he could quite
leave that." He became esteemed as a godly
man, but he feared that he had no depth of repentance. Overhearing some poor old women
talking of the new birth and of the ways of
resisting the devil, he became convinced that he
"wanted the true tokens of a truly godly man."
Though he meditated much on their sayings,
though he gave up all his evil companions, and
once or twice had visions of the way to salvation, two questions obtruded themselves,
"Whether he was elected?" and "How if the
day of grace should now be past and gone?"
After much questioning, distress of mind, and
manifold temptations that Satan put in his
way, he gained some comfort from the Scriptures. The preaching and talk of Gifford, the
Bedford minister, made him feel worse and
worse; he seemed to himself to be utterly base
and corrupt. Temporary comfort came in the
Song of Solomon, but about "a month after, a
very great storm came down upon me, which
handled me twenty times worst than all I had
met with before." Satan was continually with
him; he feared that he had blasphemed against
the Holy Ghost. This temptation lasted about

a year, but partly from texts in the Bible, and
partly from the ministrations of Gifford and
Luther's 'Comment on the Galatians,' he received some comfort. Even so, he was subject to another temptation, which endured a
year, "to sell and part with the most blessed
Christ." He feared that he had committed the
unpardonable sin, and he was so torn between
despair and hope that, after another conflict of
three-quarters of a year, he fell into sickness.
Even then he was tempted, but his mind and
body grew whole together, and from this time
on, about 1655, he seems to have felt himself
redeemed.

In 1653 Bunyan joined the Bedford church,
and two years later, "after I had been about
five or six years awakened," he began preaching
at the suggestion of "some of the most able
of the saints." He was at first appalled by the
gravity of his mission, but finding that he gave
comfort to many he grew more confident. The
secret of his success lay in the fact that "I
preached what I felt, what I smartingly did
feel; even that under which my poor soul did
groan and tremble to astonishment." So great
was the sincerity and success of his mission that
he raised for himself much opposition among
the Anglican divines, and was much slandered.
Almost simultaneously, he began his very prolific career as author with a book of controversy
directed against the Quakers, 'Some Gospel
Truths Opened' (1656).

On 12 Nov. 1660, shortly after the return of
Charles II., Bunyan was arrested for preaching.
Refusing to flee or to agree not to preach, he
was lodged in the Bedford county jail. Failing
to get his case heard, he remained here for
twelve years, except for a few weeks of liberty
in 1666. During his unjust imprisonment, Bunyan had some access to the outside world, frequently visiting his church and once going as
far as London. In the sense that he had much
leisure to write, his confinement was of advantage to him. He composed and had published
many books of which the most famous was
'Grace Abounding to the Chief of Sinners'
(1666). On his release, in 1672, from jail, in
accordance with the Declaration of Indulgence
of Charles II., he became minister of the Bedford church. In 1675-76, Bunyan was again
imprisoned, this time for six months in the
small jail on Bedford bridge. The fact is important because it is probable that there he
wrote, among other books, at least two-thirds of
the first part of 'Pilgrim's Progress.' This
part was first published in 1678, and a second
edition with some additions, as the character of
Mr. Worldly Wiseman, appeared the same year.
The third came out early in 1679 and since then
editions have been numberless. The second
part appeared in January 1685. In the interval
between the two were published the other books
for which Bunyan is best known next to 'Pilgrim's Progress' and 'Grace Abounding'—
'The Life and Death of Mr. Badman' (1680)
and 'The Holy War' (1682). Aside from the
imprisonment of 1685 and some persecution
Bunyan's last years were quiet. His influence
from his preaching and his writing was very
widely diffused, and he was, in these respects,
second to scarcely any man in England. He
met his death in doing a characteristic act of

charity: having successfully reconciled a father and son at Reading, he was, while continuing his journey to London, overtaken by a rain storm and died from the effects of the exposure, in his sixtieth year.

Bunyan ranks among the most popular of English authors: his 'Pilgrim's Progress' is said to be read more widely than any other book in the language, except the Bible. It has been translated into over 70 foreign tongues. The reasons for its extraordinary vogue lie in the simplicity of the style, the fervor of the imagination, the universality of its spiritual appeal; no book is more widely intelligible or freer from sectarian dogmas. In all his books he appears as an unsurpassed master of a simple, direct, vernacular style.

Bibliography.— Editions of Bunyan's four more important works are numerous, and there are several of his collected works. Altogether he wrote about 60 books. Among the many lives that of the Rev. John Brown, 'John Bunyan, His Life, Times, and Work' (1885), is the most complete and authoritative. Froude's life in the 'English Men of Letters' (1880) and that by Canon Venables in the 'Great Writers Series' are also good; to the latter a full bibliography is added. Consult also Dowden, 'Puritan and Anglican Studies' (1901) and James *op. cit.* (1902).

WILLIAM T. BREWSTER,
Professor of English, Columbia University.

Bunzlau, boontz'low, the name of several European towns:

1. A town of Prussia, in the province of Silesia, near the Bober, 25 miles west of Liegnitz. It was formerly surrounded by fortifications, but handsome promenades now cover most of the area once occupied by them. In the market-place is an iron obelisk to the Russian general, Kutusov, who died here in 1819. Earthenware, glass, iron, etc., are manufactured. Pop. (1895) 13,870.

2. JUNG BUNZLAU, a town of Bohemia, 31 miles northeast of Prague, the capital of the circle of Bunzlau. It stands on the left bank of the Iser, is well built, and has an old castle, an old and a new town-house, and other interesting buildings. Its inhabitants are chiefly engaged in manufacturing cottons, woolens, starch, sugar, spirits, beer, etc. Pop. (1890) 11,518.

3. ALT BUNZLAU, a small town of Bohemia, situated on the Elbe.

Buol-Schauenstein, bwäl-show'en-stĭn, **Karl Ferdinand** (COUNT), Austrian statesman: b. 17 May 1797; d. Vienna, 28 Oct. 1865. He was minister in succession at Carlsruhe, Stuttgart, Turin, and St. Petersburg. He was second Austrian plenipotentiary at the Dresden Conference (1850), after which he was minister at London until the death of Schwarzenberg recalled him to Vienna to hold the portfolio of foreign affairs. He presided at the Vienna Conference in 1855, and represented Austria at the Congress of Paris.

Buonaparte, bwŏ-nä-pär'tĕ. See BONA-PARTE.

Buonarotti, bwŏ-när-rŏt'tĕ, **Filippo:** b. Pisa, 11 Nov. 1761; d. Paris, 15 Sept. 1837. He received an excellent education under the auspices of the Grand Duke Leopold, but forfeiting the friendship of that prince on account of his sympathies with the French revolutionists, he resorted to Corsica, where he commenced a journal of so inflammatory a character that he became involved in difficulties with the government. After having spent some time in Sardinia, where he was invited to draw up a liberal constitution for the people, he went to Paris to urge the desire of the people of the Corsican island of St. Pierre for annexation to France. French citizenship was conferred upon him; he was employed in important missions in Corsica and Oneglia, and became an ardent partisan of the Terrorists. Having been detained for some time in prison after the fall of Robespierre, he founded the Pantheon Association, and when this was dissolved by the government he joined the conspiracy of Babeuf and was sentenced to transportation, but was finally permitted to retire to Geneva, and afterward went to Brussels, where in 1828, he published his 'Conspiration de Babeuf.' Returning to Paris after the revolution of 1830, he spent the rest of his life in poverty and obscurity.

Buonarroti, Michael Angelo. See MICHEL-ANGELO.

Buononcini, Giovanni Battista, jŏ-vän'nē bät-tēs'tä bwŏ-nŏn-chē'nĕ, Italian composer: b. Modena, 1672. In 1697 he went to Vienna and soon after to Berlin, where his opera 'Polifemo' had great success. After living a while at Rome, he went, in 1720, to London, and became there one of the most powerful rivals of Handel. Everything in England at that time was made to bear upon party politics, and Buononcini became the favorite of the Whigs, while Handel was supported by the Tories. But upon a trial of skill, in an opera of their joint composition, the talent and taste of Buononcini proved an unequal match for the genius of his rival.

Buontalenti, Bernardo, bĕr-när'do bwŏn-tä-lĕn'tĕ (DELLE GIRANDOLE), Italian painter, sculptor, and architect: b. Florence, 1536; d. 6 June 1608. When 11 years of age an inundation of the Arno broke into the quarter of Florence where his family resided, and carried off every member of it except himself. Cosmo de Medici, on learning the disaster, received him into his palace, and improved the taste which he had displayed for drawing by placing him in the schools of Salviati, Bronzino, and Vasari. He displayed great versatility of mind, and excelled not only in the kindred arts of painting, sculpture, and architecture, but distinguished himself as a mathematician, a military engineer, and an inventor of machines.

Buoy, boo'ĭ, any floating body employed to point out the particular situation of anything under water, as of a ship's anchor, a shoal, etc. They are of various shapes and constructions. The can buoy is of a conical form and is used for pointing out shoals, sand-banks, etc. Channel buoys are usually painted red on the starboard hand coming in from sea, and black on the port hand. They are also numbered in order from seaward, with even numbers on the starboard and odd numbers on the port hand. The cask buoy is in the form of a cask; the larger are employed for mooring, and are called mooring buoys. Spar buoys are wooden poles weighted at the thick end, by which they are moored. They are used in inland waters and in situations where, by reason of ice, iron buoys would be damaged in winter. Whistling buoys are provided with apparatus, operated by the waves, which compresses air and discharges it through a whistle. A bell buoy is a large fixed buoy to which is attached a bell which is sounded by the heaving of the sea, serving as a signal in foggy weather. The life or safety buoy is intended to keep a person afloat till he can be taken from the water. Its most usual form is a ring of cork covered with painted canvas and having beckets at its circumference. Life buoys are sometimes equipped with a port-fire or signal light which is kindled by pulling a lanyard at the moment of heaving overboard. Gas buoys are charged with compressed gas and provided with a suitable burner. The gas being lighted, and burning continuously, such buoys serve as a guide at night. Electric buoys are illuminated by connection with power on shore by means of a cable.

Bupalus, bū'pa-lŭs, Greek sculptor: fl. at Chios about 500 B.C. He and his brother Athenis are best known for their satirical conflict with the poet Hipponax. Augustus adorned many of the Roman temples with works of the two brothers, who used the pure white marble of Paros. Pausanias represents Bupalus as being an elegant architect as well as a sculptor.

Buphaga, bū-fa-ga, a genus of birds of the starling family (*Sturnidæ*), whose species are found in various parts of Africa, where they are of great use from their habit of feeding on the parasites infesting cattle. They are popularly known as beef-eaters or ox-peckers, and are distinguished from the true starlings by a stouter beak, bare nostrils, more curved claws, and some other characters. The South African ox-pecker (*B. africana*) inhabits Natal, while farther north the genus is represented by a red-billed species (*B. erythrorhyncha*). A third species is found still farther no.th and also in the Transvaal.

Buphagus, in ancient mythology, a son of Japetus and Thornax, who was killed by Diana for an attempt upon her chastity. A river of Arcadia was named after him. Buphagus was also one of the surnames of Hercules, which was given to him on account of his gluttony.

Buphonia, bū-fō'nyạ (Gr. βουφόνος ox-killer), an ancient Athenian festival in honor of Zeus, celebrated every year on the 14th of Scirophorion, on the Acropolis. Barley and wheat were placed on the altar, and the ox destined for the sacrifice was permitted to go and eat the grain, when a priest armed with an axe sprang forward and slew the ox, and then secreted himself. The other priests, as if not knowing the author of the deed, made inquiry, and, failing to ascertain anything, for lack of a better victim arraigned the axe, found it guilty, and condemned it. The Buphonia were also called Diipolia.

Buphthalmum, in botany, a genus of the *Syngenesia Polygamia Superflua;* natural order, *Compositæ Oppositifoliæ; Corymbiferæ, Jussieu.* Essential character: stigma of the hermaphrodite floscules undivided; seeds have the sides, especially in the ray, edged; receptacle chaffy. There are 12 species, of which *B. frutescens,* shrubby ox-eye, rises with several woody stems from the root, and grows to the height of 8 or 10 feet, furnished with leaves very unequal in size, some of which are narrow and long, others broad and obtuse. The foot-stalks of the larger leaves have, on their upper side, near their base, two sharp teeth standing upward, and a little higher there are generally two or three more growing on the edge of the leaves. The flowers are produced at the ends of the branches, single; these are of a pale yellow color, and have scaly calyxes. It grows naturally in America. *B. arborescens,* tree ox-eye, seldom grows higher than three feet, sending out many stalks from the root, which are succulent; it has spear-shaped leaves, placed opposite; the flowers are produced upon foot-stalks, which are two inches long; the flowers are larger than those of the *B. frutescens,* and of a bright yellow color. They appear in July, August, and September. Some of the *Buphthalmum* plants are shrubs, but most of them are herbs. The flowers are commonly terminating, and mostly of a yellow color. See OX-EYE.

Buprasium, a town of ancient Greece, in Elis, often mentioned by Homer as one of the chief cities of the Epians. It had ceased to exist in the time of Strabo, but the name was still attached to a district situated on the left bank of the Larissus, and on the road leading from Dyme to Elis. The region is now identified with the plain of Bakouma.

Buprestidæ, bu-prĕs'tĭ-dē, a family of coleopterous insects (beetles), many of which are remarkable for the splendor of their appearance. This family is included in the pentamerous section of *Coleoptera,* which was formed by Latreille, and so named because the members of it have five joints in the tarsi. The characters of the *Buprestidæ* are: body ovate, elongated, somewhat broad and obtuse in front, but pointed behind; eyes oval, with the antennæ inserted between them; jaws powerful. They walk slowly, but fly with great rapidity, especially in warm weather. They are very fond of sunning themselves on bushes or the branches of trees. When one attempts to seize them, sometimes even when one approaches them, they allow themselves to fall suddenly to the earth, or fly rapidly away. There are several hundred species belonging to this family, most of which are found within the tropics, and the tropical species are those which are chiefly distinguished by the brilliancy of their colors. The prevailing color appears to be green, but species are often found of a blue, red, golden, or other color. The *B. gigas* of Linnæus, which is about two inches in length, and one of the largest of the family, has bright golden elytra, or wing-cases, which are often used as ornaments by the inhabitants of South America, of which continent it is a native.

Bura, in ancient mythology, a daughter of Jupiter, or, according to some authorities, the offspring of Ion and Helice, from whom Bura, or Buris, once a flourishing city of ancient Greece, on the Bay of Corinth, received its name.

Bura, in ancient Greece, one of the 12 original Achæan cities, which stood formerly close to the sea, on the Bay of Corinth, but, having been destroyed, with the neighboring town of Helice, by a terrible earthquake, the surviving inhabitants rebuilt it afterward about 40 stadia from the coast, and near the small river

Buraicus. Bura was situated on a hill, and contained temples of Ceres, Venus, Bacchus, and Lucina, the statues of which were sculptured by Euclidas of Athens. On the banks of the river Buraicus was a cave consecrated to Hercules, and an oracle usually consulted by the throwing of dice. The ruins of Bura are close to the road from Megastelia to Vostitza, and the cave of Hercules Buraicus is visited by tourists.

Bur-marigold, a large genus of annual and perennial herbs (*Bidens*) of the natural order *Compositæ*, mostly natives of North America, but widely distributed in other countries, chiefly as weeds, but some as garden plants. The best known ornamental species is *B. grandiflora,* a native of South America; and the most common North American species is *B. frondosa,* which is popularly and variously known as devil's bootjack, stick-tight, beggar-tick, Spanish-needle, etc., and is especially troublesome in wool and on clothing, to which the seeds stick like burs.

Burbank, Luther, American plant breeder: b. Lancaster, Worcester county, Mass., 7 March 1849; of English-Scotch ancestry; educated in common schools and local academy; worked as a boy in a plow factory, showing some inventive capacity, but soon began market-gardening and seed-raising in a small way, and developed the Burbank potato in 1873; removed to Santa Rosa, Cal., 1 Oct. 1875, where he has since resided and carried on his work. His many and important "new creations" of fruits, flowers and vegetables have made him the best-known plant-breeder in America, and probably in the world. The characteristics which are the special factors in the success of his work are, the large extent of his experiments, his keenness of preception of slight variations in plant-qualities, and the rapidity with which he develops new qualities, this rapidity being due to a combination of multiple hybridizing, selection, and grafting of seedling plants on mature stocks, so that immediate results as to flowers and fruits are got from seedling stems. But the final and most important factor in Burbank's success is the inherent genius of the man, whose innate sympathy with Nature, aided by the practical education in plant biology derived from thirty years of constant study and experiment, enable him to perceive correlations and outcomes of plant growth which seem to have been visible to no other man. As the history of Burbank's life is the history of his work, the remainder of this biographical sketch may advantageously be devoted to a brief consideration of the character and method of creation of some of his principal new plant varieties.

Burbank has originated and introduced a remarkable series of plums and prunes. No less than twenty varieties are included in his list of offerings, and some of them, notably the Gold, Wickson, Apple, October Purple, Chalco, American and Climax plums and the Splendor and Sugar prunes are among the best known and most successful kinds now grown. In addition he is now perfecting a stoneless plum, and has created the interesting plum-cot by hybridizing the Japanese plum and the apricot. The plum-cot, however, has not yet become a fixed variety and may never be, as it tends to revert to the plum. The stoneless and seedless plum is being produced by selection from the descendants of the crossing of a single fruit in a small wild plum with only part of a stone with the French prune; the percentage of stoneless fruits is gradually increasing with succeeding generations. The sugar prune, which promises to supplant the French prune in California, is a selected product of a second or third generation variety of the *Petite d'Agen,* a very variable French prune. The Bartlett plum, cross of the bitter Chinese *simoni* and the Delaware, a Burbank hybrid, has the exact fragrance and flavor of the Bartlett pear. The Climax is a cross of the *simoni* and the Japanese *triflora.* The Chinese *simoni* produces almost no pollen, but few grains of it ever having been obtained, but these few grains have enabled Burbank to revolutionize the whole plum shipping industry. Most of Burbank's plums and prunes are the result of multiple crossings, in which the Japanese Satsuma has played an important part. Hundreds of thousands of seedlings have been grown and carefully worked over in the twenty years' experimenting with plums, and single trees have been made to carry as many as 600 varying seedling grafts.

Burbank has originated and introduced the Van Deman, Santa Rosa, Alpha, Pineapple, "No. 80," the flowering Dazzle, and other quinces; the Opulent peach, cross-bred from the Muir and Wager; the Winterstein apple, a seedling variety of the Gravenstein; and has made interesting, although not profitable, crosses of the peach and nectarine, peach and almond, and plum and almond.

Next in extent, probably, to his work with plums is his long and successful experimentation with berries. This work has extended through twenty-five years of constant attention, has involved the use of forty different species of *Rubus,* and has resulted in the origination and introduction of a score of new commercial varieties mostly obtained through various hybridizations of dewberries, blackberries, and raspberries. Among these may especially be mentioned the Primus, a hybrid of the Western dewberry (*R. ursinus*) and the Siberian raspberry (*R. cratægifolius*), fixed in the first generation, which ripens its main crop before most of the standard, well-known varieties of raspberries and blackberries commence to *bloom;* the Iceberg, a cross-bred white blackberry derived from a hybridization of the Crystal White (pistillate parent) with the Lawton (staminate parent), and with beautiful snow-white berries so nearly transparent that the small seeds may be seen in them; the Japanese Golden Mayberry, a cross of the Japanese *R. palmatus* (with small, tasteless, dingy yellow worthless berries) and the Cuthbert, the hybrid growing into tree-like bushes six to eight feet high and bearing great, oval, golden, semi-translucent berries which ripen before strawberries; and Paradox, an oval, light-red berry obtained in the fourth generation from a cross of Crystal White Blackberry and Shaffer's Colossal Raspberry. While most of the plants from this cross are partly or wholly barren, this particular outcome is an unusually prolific fruit producer. An interesting feature of Mr. Burbank's brief account, in his "New Creations" catalogue of 1894, of the berry experimentation, is a reproduction of a photograph showing "a sample pile of brush twelve feet wide, fourteen feet high and twenty-two feet long, containing 65,000 two and three-year-old seedling berry bushes (40,000 Blackberry X Raspberry hybrids and 25,000 Shaffer X Gregg hybrids) all dug up with their crop of ripening berries." The photograph is introduced to give the reader some idea of the work necessary to produce a satisfactory new race of berries. "Of the 40,000 Blackberry-Raspberry hybrids of this kind 'Paradox' is the only one now in existence. From the other 25,000 hybrids two dozen bushes were reserved for further trial."

Leaving Burbank's other fruit and berry creations unreferred to, we may refer to his curious cross-bred walnut results, the most astonishing of which is a hybrid between *Juglans californica* ('staminate parent) and J. *nigra* (pistillate parent), which grows with an amazing vigor and rapidity, the trees increasing in size at least twice as fast as the combined growth of both parents, and the clean-cut, glossy, bright-green leaves, from two to three feet long, having a sweet odor like that of apples. This hybrid produces no nuts, but curiously enough the result of the reverse hybridization (*i. e.*, pollen from *nigra* on pistils of *californica*) produces in abundance large nuts of a quality superior to that possessed by either parent.

Of new vegetables Burbank has introduced, besides the Burbank and several other new potatoes, new tomatoes, squashes, asparagus, etc. Perhaps the most interesting of his experiments in this field is his attempt, apparently destined to be successful, to produce a spineless and spicule-less cactus (the spicules are the minute spines, much more dangerous and harder to get rid of than the conspicuous long, thorn-like spines), edible, for stock, and indeed for man. This work is chiefly one of pure selection, for the cross-bred forms seem to tend strongly to revert to the ancestral spiny condition.

Among the many new flower varieties originated by Burbank may be mentioned the Peachblow, Burbank, Coquito, and Santa Rosa roses, the Splendor, Fragrance (a fragrant form) and Dwarf Snowflake callas, the enormous Shasta and Alaska daisies, the Ostrich plume, Waverly, Snowdrift and Double clematises, the Hybrid Wax myrtle, the extraordinary Nicotunia, a hybrid between a large, flowering Nicotiana and a petunia, several hybrid Nicotianas, a dozen new gladioli, an ampelopsis, several amaryllids, various dahlias, the Fire poppy (a brilliant flame colored variety obtained from a cross of two white forms) striped and carnelian poppies, a blue Shirley (obtained by selection from the Crimson field poppy of Europe), the Silver Line poppy (obtained by selection from an individual of *Papaver umbrosium* showing a streak of silver inside), with silver interior and crimson exterior, and a crimson California poppy (*Escholtzia*) obtained by selection from the familiar golden form. Perhaps his most extensive experimenting with flowers has been done in the hybridizing of lilies, a field in which many plant breeders have found great difficulties. Using over half a hundred varieties as basis of his work, Burbank has produced a great variety of new forms. "Can my thoughts be imagined," he says, in his "New Creations" of 1893, "after so many years of patient care and labor [he had been working over sixteen years], as, walking among them [his new lilies] on a dewy morning, I look upon these new forms of beauty, on which other eyes have never gazed? Here a plant six feet high, with

yellow flowers, beside it one only six inches high with dark red flowers, and further on one of pale straw, or snowy white, or with curious dots and shadings: some deliciously fragrant, others faintly so; some with upright, others with nodding flowers: some with dark green, woolly leaves in whorls, or with polished light green, lance-like, scattered leaves."

So far no special reference has been made to the more strictly scientific aspects of Burbank's work. Burbank has been primarily intent on the production of new and improved fruits, flowers, vegetables and trees for the immediate benefit of mankind. But where biological experimentation is being carried on so extensively it is obvious that there must be a large accumulation of data of much scientific value in its relation to the great problems of heredity, variation, and species-forming. Burbank's experimental gardens may be looked on from the point of view of the biologist and evolutionist as a great laboratory in which, at present, masses of valuable data are, for lack of time and means, being let go unrecorded. The Carnegie Institution has therefore made a grant of $100,000 to Burbank, payable $10,000 annually, beginning with 1905, to enable him to note, collect and collate the scientific data which his extensive experimentation is constantly affording. Of Burbank's own particular scientific beliefs touching the "grand problems" of heredity we have space to record but two: first, he is a thorough believer in the inheritance of acquired characters, a condition disbelieved in by the Weismann school of evolutionists; second, he believes in the constant mutability of species, and the strong individuality of each plant organism, holding that the apparent fixity of characteristics is a phenomenon wholly dependent, for its degree of reality, on the length of time this characteristic has been ontogenetically repeated in the phylogeny of the race.

For other accounts of Burbank and his work, see articles in the illustrated magazines of 1903 and 1904, and "New Creations in Plant Life," by W. S. Harwood. Burbank has written but little himself, namely, only a few essays to be read at horticultural and other meetings, the article on Plant-breeding in this Encyclopedia, Vol. III, and his short series of catalogues, 1893-1901, called "New Creations."

VERNON L. KELLOGG,
Professor of Entomology, Leland Stanford Jr. University.

Bur'bot, a fresh-water fish (*Lota lota*) of the cod family, inhabiting northern Europe and America. It is numerous in the inland waters of the northern States and Canada, where it displays the nocturnal voracity of its race. It ordinarily weighs about five pounds, but has little market value. It is more often called cusk, ling, or loche among us, than burbot, which is the British designation.

Burbridge, Stephen Gano, American soldier: b. Scott County, Ky., 19 Aug. 1831; d. 1894. He organized the famous 26th Kentucky Regiment, which he led for the Union at Shiloh, where he was promoted to the rank of brigadier-general of volunteers. He was engaged in the Vicksburg expedition under Gen. Grant; led the charge at Arkansas Post and at Port Gibson, being the first to enter each of these places; was retired with the brevet of major-general in 1865,

Burchard, Samuel Dickinson, American clergyman: b. Steuben, N. Y., 6 Sept. 1812; d. Saratoga, N. Y., 25 Sept. 1891. He was for many years a Presbyterian pastor in New York. During the presidential campaign of 1884 a company of clergymen, about 600 in number, called on James G. Blaine, the Republican candidate, at the Fifth Avenue Hotel, New York. Dr. Burchard made an address, in which he affirmed that the antecedents of the Democracy were "rum, Romanism, and rebellion," and this denunciatory speech on the very eve of the election created intense excitement throughout the United States and alienated from Blaine many Democratic votes upon which he had reckoned. It is generally conceded that Burchard was thus largely instrumental in electing Grover Cleveland.

Bur'chell, William John, English explorer: b. Fulham, about 1782; d. 1863. He was in the service of the East India Company on the island of St. Helena, 1805-10, and then went to South Africa. Here he spent several years in exploring and making a large natural-history collection. In 1825 he made a tour in South America. On all his expeditions he was generally entirely alone. A large part of his collections are now in the British Museum.

Burchiello, Domenico, dō-mā-nĕ'kŏ boor-kē-ĕl'lŏ, Italian poet: fl. 15th century, at Florence, where he was probably born. He was the son of a barber named Giovanni, and was called originally only Domenico. He assumed the name of Burchiello afterward for reasons that cannot be assigned. His fame began about 1425. He was first registered as a barber in 1432. Some writers have reproached him for shameful vices, and represented him as a low buffoon who did everything for money. Others have defended him. His shop was so famous that learned and unlearned, high and low, assembled there every day, and Cosmo the Great caused a picture of it to be painted on one of the arches of his gallery. It appears here divided into two portions; in one Burchiello is acting the part of a barber; in the other that of a musician and poet. The portrait of Burchiello himself is painted over his shop. It is extremely difficult to decide upon the absolute value of his satires, as the local and personal allusions in them are obscure. They were composed for his contemporaries, with a studied obscurity and extravagance of expression. His style is, nevertheless, pure and elegant. His burlesque sonnets are enigmas, of which we have no intelligible explanation, nothwithstanding what Doni has done. The narrative and descriptive parts are very easy to be understood; but the wit they contain is, for the most part, so coarse, that the satire fails of producing its effeet. They are, on the whole, lively, but licentious. The best editions of his sonnets are those of Florence, 1568, and of London, 1757.

Burckhardt, boork'hart, **Johann,** yō'hän, **Karl,** German astronomer: b. Leipsic, 30 April 1773; d. 22 June 1825. He acquired a fondness for astronomy from the study of the works of Lalande, and made himself master, at the same time, of nearly all the European languages. He wrote a Latin treatise 'On the Combinatory Analytic Method' (Leipsic 1794). He then studied practical astronomy with Baron von Zach at the latter's observatory on the See-berg, near Gotha, and assisted his patron, from 1795-7, in observing the right ascension of the stars. Von Zach recommended him to Lalande, at Paris, who received him at his house 15 Dec. 1797. Here he distinguished himself by the calculation of the orbits of comets; participated in all the labors of Lalande and those of his nephew Lefrançois Lalande; took an active part in the observatory of the École Militaire; and translated the first two volumes of Laplace's 'Mécanique Céleste' into German (Berlin 1800-2). Being appointed adjunct astronomer by the board of longitude, he received letters of naturalization as a French citizen 20 Dec. 1799. His important treatise on the comet of 1770, which had not been visible for nearly 30 years, although, according to the calculations of its orbit, it should have returned every five or six, was rewarded with a gold medal by the Institute in 1800. This treatise, which proposed some improvements in Dr. Olbers' mode of calculation, is contained in the 'Memoires de l'Institut' for 1806. During this year he was made a member of the department of physical and mathematical sciences in the Academy; in 1818 was made a member of the board of longitude; and, after Lalande's death, astronomer in the observatory of the École Militaire. In 1814 and 1816 he published in French, at Paris, 'Tables to Assist in Astronomical Calculations.' He also wrote some treatises in Von Zach's 'Geographical Ephemerides.' His labors in the board of longitude were particularly valuable.

Burckhardt, Johann Ludwig, yō'hän lood'-vig boork-härt, Swiss explorer: b. Lausanne, 24 Nov. 1784; d. Cairo, 17 Oct. 1817. He studied at Leipsic, Göttingen, and London, giving special attention to Arabic. In 1809 he started on an expedition to Africa for the African Association at London; assuming the disguise of an Oriental at Malta he went to Aleppo and remained there over a year and a half studying Arabic and the history of Mohammedanism. Then he visited Damascus and traveled through Palestine to Cairo, arriving there in September 1812; here he joined a caravan going through the Nubian Desert by a route never before traveled by Europeans, and reached the Red Sea in July 1814. He then crossed over to Asia Minor and went to Mecca, where he became a Moslem and joined a body of pilgrims going to Mount Ararat. In 1815 he returned to Cairo and from there traveled through the rigion of Mount Sinai, climbing the mountain. Shortly after his return from this trip he died of the fever just as he was about to start on another expedition. He was the author of 'Travels in Nubia' (1819); 'Travels in Syria and the Holy Land' (1822); 'Travels in Arabia' (1829); 'Notes on the Bedouins and Wahabys' (1830); 'Arabic Proverbs' (1830).

Bur'dekin, a river of the northeast of Queensland, with a course of about 350 miles. With its affluents it waters a large extent of country, but it is useless for navigation.

Burden, Henry, American inventor: b. Dumblane, Scotland, 20 April 1791; d. Troy, N. Y., 19 Jan. 1871. He was brought up on a farm, and at an early age showed his inventive genius by making a variety of labor-saving machinery, including a threshing-machine. He came to the United States in 1819 and engaged in the manufacture of agricultural implements.

He invented an improved plow; the first cultivator made in this country; machines for making horse-shoes and hook-headed spikes used on railroads; a self-acting machine for rolling iron into bars; and a new machine for making horse-shoes, which received a rod of iron and turned out completed shoes at the rate of 60 a minute.

Burden of Proof, in legal procedure, the obligation to establish by evidence certain disputed facts. As a general rule this burden lies on the party asserting the affirmative of the issue to be tried or question in dispute, or on the party who would fail if no evidence were adduced on either side. Burden of proof is to be distinguished from *prima facie* evidence or a *prima facie* case. Generally, when the latter is shown, the duty imposed upon the party having the burden will be satisfied; but it is not necessarily so. In criminal cases, on the two-fold ground that a prosecutor must prove every fact necessary to substantiate his charge against a prisoner, and that the law will presume innocence in the absence of convincing evidence to the contrary, the burden of proof, unless shifted by legislative interference, will, in criminal proceedings, be on the prosecuting party, though in order to convict he must necessarily have recourse to negative evidence. The burden of proof throughout is on the government. This subject is treated by all writers on Evidence, as Taylor, Roscoe, and Powell in England; Dickson in Scotland; and Greenleaf in the United States. Consult also Bentham's 'Rationale of Judicial Evidence.'

Burdett', SIR Francis, English politician: b. 25 Jan. 1770; d. 23 Jan. 1844. He was educated at Westminster, and after two years at Oxford made a Continental tour. In 1796 he obtained a seat in Parliament through the patronage of the Duke of Newcastle; but he soon abandoned the Tory party and made himself conspicuous by his advocacy of liberal measures. In 1802 he stood for Middlesex, but though at first elected he finally lost his seat in 1806, after much costly litigation. He was more successful in 1807 at Westminster, where his election at the head of the poll was hailed as a great popular triumph. In 1810 he published a letter in Cobbett's 'Political Register,' denying the right of the House of Commons to imprison for libel, as they had recently done in the case of John Gale Jones. This letter, having been brought under the notice of the House, was declared a gross breach of its privileges, and a warrant was issued by the speaker for the committal of Sir Francis to the Tower. He denied the legality of the warrant, and declared his determination to surrender only to force. The public mind was strongly agitated; but prorogation of Parliament relieved him from his imprisonment in the Tower, and he became perhaps the most popular man in the kingdom. In attaining this popularity he was greatly aided by the graces of his appearance and the talents which he undoubtedly possessed. Ultimately, however, his fervor cooled, and he owed his last seat in Parliament to the Conservatives of Wiltshire.

Burdett, SIR Henry, English publicist and statistician: b. 1847. He served in an administrative capacity in the Queen's Hospital, Birmingham, and the Seaman's Hospital, Greenwich, and was secretary of a department of the London Stock Exchange. He was founder and editor of 'The Hospital.' His works are numerous, and cover a wide range. Among them are 'Official Intelligence of British, American, and Foreign Securities' (17 vols.); 'The National Debt'; 'National Debts of the World'; 'Local Taxation in England and Wales'; 'Colonial Loans, Finance, and Development'; 'Seventeen Years of Securities'; 'The Admiralty and the Country'; 'Hospitals and Asylums of the World'; 'Hospitals and Charities, a Year-book of Philanthropy'; 'Hospitals and the State'; 'Architects, Hospitals, and Asylums'; 'A Practical Scheme for Old Age Pensions'; 'The Nursing Profession'; 'Housing of the Poor'; and 'Official Nursing Directory.'

Burdett-Coutts, RIGHT HON. Angela Georgina (BARONESS), English philanthropist: b. 21 April 1814; d. London 30 Dec. 1906. In 1837 she inherited much of the property of her grandfather, Thomas Coutts, the banker, on the death of his widow, the Duchess of St. Albans (formerly the actress, Miss Mellon). Besides spending large sums of money in building and endowing churches and schools, she endowed the three colonial bishoprics of Cape Town, Adelaide, and British Columbia. She founded an establishment in South Australia for the improvement of the aborigines, and established a fishery school at the Irish village of Baltimore (1887). To the city of London she presented, besides several handsome fountains, the Columbia Market, Bethnal Green (1870), for the supply of fish in a poor district. She also built Columbia Square, consisting of model dwellings at low rents, for about 300 families. The home established by her at Shepherd's Bush has rendered great assistance to many unfortunate women, and the People's Palace owes much to her generosity. In 1871 she was created a peeress in her own right as Baroness Burdett-Coutts. In 1877 she organized the Turkish Compassionate Fund, to relieve the sufferings of the peasants in Turkey, and in recognition of her services the Sultan conferred upon her the Order of the Medjidie. In 1881 she was married to William Ashmead-Bartlett, who in 1882 obtained the royal license to assume her name.

Burdette', Robert Jones, American humorist: b. Greensboro, Pa., 30 July 1844. He served in the Union army during the Civil War. He is famous for humorous newspaper skits, of rare variety, charm, and unrepetitious freshness; begun in the Burlington (Iowa) *Hawkeye,* of which he became associate editor in 1874. Among his works are : 'The Rise and Fall of the Moustache,' a lecture (1877) ; 'Hawkeyes,' collected articles (1880) ; 'Life of William Penn' (1882) ; 'Sons of Asaph'; 'Chimes from a Jester's Bells' ; etc. He was licensed as a Baptist clergyman in 1887.

Bur'dick, Francis Marion, American jurist: b. De Ruyter, N. Y., 1 Aug. 1845. He was graduated at Hamilton College in 1869, and at its law school in 1872. He practised law in Utica, N. Y., from 1872 to 1883, and was later professor of law at Hamilton College, and at Cornell. Since 1891 he has been professor of law at Columbia. He has written 'Law of Sales'; 'Law of Partnership'; and other legal textbooks.

Burdock, a small genus (*Arctium*) of coarse perennial or biennial herbs of the natural order *Compositæ*, natives of temperate Asia and Europe, but widely distributed as weeds throughout the world. Common burdock (*A. lappa*), which often attains a height of four feet, is sometimes planted in flower-borders for its foliage, which makes a good screen; and in Japan, where it has been improved by cultivation, for its enlarged parsnip-like roots, which are eaten as a boiled vegetable. Formerly the roots were used in medicine, but they seem to be generally classed with many other domestic remedies of doubtful value. The plant is best known as a weed in waste land, but usually on good soil. Its globular burs become attached to the wool of sheep and to clothing. Their presence injures the price of wool.

Burdwan, bŭrd-wän, or Bardwan, bärd-wan', India, a town and capital of a division of the same name in the lower provinces of Bengal, on the left bank of the Damoda, 68 miles northwest of Calcutta, with which it is connected by railway. There is a titular rajah of Burdwan, who resides here in a spacious palace, with gardens, etc.; and there are also a large collection of temples and a shrine of Pirba-haram. Pop. 34,477. The division has an area of 13,956 square miles, and a population of about 8,250,000, and is divided into the districts of Burdwan, Bankura, Birbhum, Hugli, Midnapur, and Howrah. The chief crops are sugar, indigo, tobacco, cotton, and the usual cereals. Mulberry-trees are cultivated, and coal is raised.

Bureau, bū'rō, or bū-rō', the chamber or official apartments of an officer of government, and the body of subordinate officials who labor under the direction of a chief. The term «bureau system,» or «bureaucracy,» is applied to those systems of government in which the business of administration is carried on in departments, each under the control of a chief; and is opposed to those in which the officers of government have a co-ordinate authority. Sometimes a mixture of the two systems is found. Thus the business of the executive branch of government may be carried on by bureaus, while the administration of justice is in the hands of co-ordinate judges. In the United States, bureau is the universal word for a chest of drawers.

Burette, bū-ret', a graduated glass tube occasionally used for dividing a given portion of any liquid into small quantities of a definite amount.

Burg, Adriaan (ä'drē-än) van der, Dutch painter: b. Dordrecht, 1693; d. 1733. He studied under Arnold Houbraken, distinguished himself by his portraits, and acquired a reputation which would soon have procured him an independence. But intemperate habits rendered his talents of no avail, and hurried him to a premature grave. His freedom of touch and fine coloring are his distinguishing excellences. His best-known pieces are two large pictures at Dordrecht, one of which gives on a single canvas portraits of the managers of the orphan hospital, and the other portraits of the officers of the Mint.

Burg, Johann (yō'hän) Tobias, Austrian astronomer: b. Vienna, 1766; d. 1834. He attracted the notice of Van Swieten, who was then at the head of the commission appointed to reform the scholastic establishments of Austria, and through his patronage obtained the means of prosecuting the study of mathematics, and more especially of astronomy, for which he showed a decided inclination. In 1791 he became professor of physics at Klagenfurt, and in 1792 was appointed colleague of Trisnecker at the Observatory of Vienna. In 1798, the French Institute having proposed a prize for the determination, by at least 500 observations, of the mean place of the apogee and ascending node of the moon, Burg sent in a memoir in which the determination was made by a most accurate and ingenious method, not from 500 but 3,232 observations. The tables contained in it were afterward published by the Institute, and constitute the chief foundation of his fame. In 1813 he became almost entirely deaf and retired from public life to Wiesenau, Carinthia.

Burg, Prussia, a town in the province of Saxony, 12 miles northeast of Magdeburg, on the Ihle, where it joins a canal uniting the Havel with the Elbe. It has four churches, a hospital, a gymnasium, and a well-endowed institution for the bringing up of orphan children, and is the seat of civil and judicial administration for the circle. Its manufactures are extensive, especially of woolens, for which it was a centre as early as the 12th century. Cloths for army purposes are largely made. There are also spinning mills, dye works, machine works, tanneries, oil works, etc. Pop. (1895) 19,397.

Bur'gage Tenure, in England, a tenure in socage, whereby burgesses, citizens, or townsmen hold their lands or tenements of the king or other lord for a certain yearly rent. In Scotland that tenure by which the property in royal burghs is held under the Crown, proprietors being liable to the (nominal) service of watching and warding, or, as it is commonly termed, "service of burgh, used and wont."

Burgas, boor-gäs', or Bourgas, Turkey, a seaport of the province of eastern Rumelia, situated on the Black Sea. The bay on which it stands is of sufficient depth for large vessels, and the exports are grain, iron, butter, wine, and also woolen goods for Constantinople. The principal source of the prosperity of the town is the manufacture of pottery, pipe-bowls, cups, etc., for which a superior clay is found in the neighborhood. Pop. about 12,000.

Burgdorf, boorg'dôrf, Switzerland, a town in the canton of Bern, situated on the Emmen. It is the entrepôt for the linen goods and cheeses of the Emmenthal. The castle which stands here was formerly a place of great strength. Pestalozzi resided from 1798 to 1804 in the château of Burgdorf, and converted it into an educational institution. In the vicinity are the baths of Sommerhaus. Pop. 8,400.

Bur'geo Islands, Newfoundland, a group of islands on the southern coast, much visited by summer tourists and artists from the eastern States and Canada. The population is chiefly engaged in fishing. Burgeo, the principal town, has a population of less than 1,000.

Bür'ger, Gottfried August, gŏt'frēd ow'-goost, German poet: b. 1 Jan. 1748, at Wolmerswende, near Halberstadt; d. Göttingen, 8 June 1794. He showed an early predilection for solitary and gloomy places and the making of verses, for which he had no other model than hymn-books. He learned Latin with difficulty. In 1764 he studied theology at the University of Halle, and in 1768 he went to Göttingen, in order to exchange theology for law, but soon formed connections here equally disadvantageous to his studies and his morals, so that his grandfather, who had hitherto maintained him, withdrew his support. The friendship of several distinguished young men at the university was now of great service to him. He studied the ancient classics and the best works in French, Italian, Spanish, and English, particularly Shakespeare, and the old English and Scottish ballads. Percy's 'Reliques' was his constant companion. His poems soon attracted attention. In 1772 he obtained the office of baillie in Alten-Gleichen, but throughout his life he was involved in pecuniary difficulties. In 1774 he married the daughter of a neighboring baillie, named Leonhart, but his marriage was unfortunate. He conceived a violent passion for the sister of his wife, and married her, in 1784, soon after his first wife's death. She also, his celebrated «Molly,» died in the first year of their marriage. At the same time he was obliged, by intrigues, to resign his place. He was made professor extraordinary in Göttingen, but received no salary, and this favorite poet of the nation was obliged to gain his living by poorly rewarded translations for booksellers. A third marriage in 1790, with a young lady of Swabia, who had publicly offered him her hand in a poem. completed his misfortunes; he procured a divorce from her two years afterward. The government of Hanover afforded him some assistance shortly before his death. His songs, odes, elegies, ballads, narrative poems, and epigrams hold a very high place in German literature. Schlegel especially commending his work, though Schiller criticised him very severely. The first collection of his poems appeared in Göttingen in 1778. His complete works were first published by Reinhard at Göttingen in four volumes in 1796-8. and this edition has been repeatedly published since. Other editions of his works and letters have also been published, and his life has been written by Döring, Pröhle ('G. A. Bürger: Sein Leben und Seine Dichtungen,' Leipsic, 1865), and others.

Burger, Ludwig, lood'vǐg boor'gèr, German painter and illustrator: b. Cracow, 19 Sept. 1825. He studied at the Berlin Art Academy, at the same time working at book-illustrating, he was also a pupil of Couture at Paris. Among his best drawings are the illustrations for the works of La Fontaine and a collection of 20 plates known as 'Die Kanone.' Since 1869 he has done considerable work in interior decoration, particularly at the Berlin city hall.

Burgers, boor'gèrs, Thomas Francis, Transvaal statesman: b. Cape Colony, 1834; d. 1881. He was educated for the ministry at Utrecht and was pastor of the Dutch Reformed Church of Hanover. Cape Colony. Some of the rationalistic views he expressed led to his trial for heresy, but he was acquitted. He was elected president of the Transvaal republic in 1872 and held the office until 1877, when the republic was annexed by Great Britain.

Burges, bèr'jěs, Tristam, American statesman and orator: b. Rochester, Mass., 26 Feb. 1770: d. Providence, R. I., 13 Oct. 1853. When 15 years old he attended a school in the vicinity for six weeks, and again the next year for six weeks more. This was all the instruction he received from others until he reached the age of 21. In September 1793, he entered Rhode Island College, now Brown University, graduated three years later with the first honors of his class, and was admitted to the bar in 1799. He became a leader of the Federal party, and in 1811 was elected to a seat in the State legislature. In 1815 he was made chief justice of Rhode Island, and afterward became professor of oratory and belles-lettres in Brown University. In 1825 he was elected to Congress, and almost immediately achieved a national reputation by his speech on the judiciary. He continued in Congress until 1835. Many of his most brilliant efforts were in defense of the American tariff system, and his logic and sarcasm won for him an unrivaled reputation as a debater. See Bowen, 'Memoirs of Tristam Burges.'

Bur'gess, Alexander, American Protestant Episcopal bishop: b. Providence, R. I., 31 Oct. 1819; d. St. Albans, Vt., 8 Oct. 1901. He was a younger brother of George Burgess, first bishop of Maine. He was graduated from Brown University in 1838, and from the General Theological Seminary in 1841. He was successively rector at East Haddam, Conn., 1842-3; St. Mark's, Augusta, Me., 1843-54; St. Luke's, Portland, Me., 1854-67; St. John's, Brooklyn, N. Y., 1867-9; and Christ Church, Springfield, Mass., 1869-78. In 1878 he was consecrated first bishop of the diocese of Quincy, Ill. He wrote a popular religious text-book, 'Questions for Bible-Classes and Sunday-schools' (1855), and a 'Memoir of the Life of George Burgess, First Bishop of Maine' (1869).

Bur'gess, Edward, American naval architect: b. West Sandwich, Mass., 30 June 1848; d. Boston, 12 July 1891. He was educated at Harvard, where he graduated in 1871, and became secretary of the Boston Society of Natural History. He was instructor of entomology at Harvard from 1879 to 1883. He then became a designer of sailing-yachts. In 1884 he designed the Puritan, the winner of the America's cup in 1885; and a year later the Mayflower, the winner in 1886. He was also the designer of the Volunteer, which won the cup in 1887.

Burgess, Frank Gellett, American humorous writer and illustrator: b. Boston, 30 Jan. 1866. He was graduated from the Massachusetts Institute of Technology in 1887; was a draughtsman with the Southern P. Ry. 1887-90. and instructor in topographical drawing in the University of California, 1891-4. In 1895-7 he came prominently before the reading public as a publisher and writer of eccentric and humorous literature, such as his journal called 'The Lark,' and poem, 'The Purple Cow' (1897). In 1898 he removed to London. but returned to America in 1900. He edited 'Petit Journal des Refusées' (1897), and has written 'The Lark Almanac' (1898); 'Vivette' (1898); 'The Nonsense Almanac' (1898); 'The Lively City o' Ligg' (1898); 'Goops and How to be Them' (1900); 'A Joyous Journey Round the Year' (1901); 'Romance of the Commonplace' (1902); 'A Gage of Youth' (1901).

Burgess, George, bishop of Maine: b. Providence, R. I., 31 Oct. 1809; d. Haiti, 23 April 1866. After graduating at Brown University, and holding a tutorship in that college, he traveled in Europe, and studied for two years in the universities of Göttingen, Bonn, and Berlin. He was rector of Christ Church in Hartford from 1834 to 1847, when he was consecrated first bishop of the diocese of Maine, and became, at the same time, rector of Christ Church in Gardiner. Both offices he filled with great ability. He published two academic poems, a metrical version of a portion of the Psalms, 'Pages from the Ecclesiastical History of New England' (1847); 'The Last Enemy Conquering and Conquered' (1850), and various sermons.

Burgess, James, Scottish archæologist: b. Kirkmahoe, Dumfriesshire, 14 Aug. 1832. He went to India in 1855, and there entered upon educational work in Calcuttta and Bombay. In 1886 he was made director-general of the archæological surveys of India, retiring under age limit in 1889. From 1872 to 1884 he published the 'Indian Antiquary.' His works include: 'The Temples of Shatrunjaya' (1869); 'The Rock Temples of Elephanta' (1871); 'Scenery and Architecture in Gujarat and Rajputana' (1873); and other books; also many writings in the 'Epigraphia Indica,' 'Archæological Reports' (1874-87), etc.

Burgess, John William, American educator: b. Cornersville, Tenn., 26 Aug. 1844. He was educated at Cumberland University, Lebanon, Tenn., and at Amherst College, Mass., graduating there in 1867; studied law, and began to practise in 1869. During this year he was appointed professor of English literature and political economy at Knox College, Galesburg, Ill. Two years later he studied in Göttingen, Leipsic, and Berlin. On his return, he became professor of history and political science at Amherst, in 1870 professor of history, political science, and international law in Columbia College, and in 1880 professor of constitutional and international history and law. In 1906 he became Roosevelt Professor of American history and institutions at Berlin University. He has published 'Political Science and Comparative Constitutional Law' (1890); 'The Middle Period of United States History' (1897); 'The Civil War and the Constitution' (1901); 'Reconstruction and the Constitution' (1902); etc.

Burgess, Neil, American actor: b. Boston, 1846. Not long after entering the theatrical profession, he undertook in a stage emergency to fill the place of an actress, and his success in the humorous female role assumed led to his entering that line permanently. He acted in 'Josiah Allen's Wife' and in 'Widow Bedott.' The latter was very popular, as was also 'Vim,' produced in 1883. 'The Country Fair,' a play which he brought out in 1889, ran for more than two years. Mr. Burgess has lately undertaken vaudeville acting.

Burgess, a word used in somewhat varying senses, but generally meaning a freeholder, or a person invested with all the privileges of a citizen in a borough or corporate town. Those entered on the burgess roll of English boroughs are householders who have resided and paid rates for 12 months prior to July in any year. In the United States the uses of the word have undergone some specific changes, and in States having boroughs as political divisions,

as Connecticut, New Jersey, and Pennsylvania, it carries an implication of magisterial authority. See BOROUGH; BURGH.

Burgh, bẽrg, the same as borough. The spelling borough is the common one in England and the United States, while burgh is that which chiefly prevails in Scotland, as Scarborough, Edinburgh. A burgh of barony, in Scotland, is a certain tract of land created in a barony by the feudal superior, and placed under the authority of magistrates. A royal burgh in Scotland is a corporate body created by a charter from the Crown. There is a convention of royal burghs. In the United States the termination -borough was for generations added to the names of places, as in England; but, under a decision of the United States Board on Geographic Names, the form is now -boro, as Brattleboro.

Burgher, bẽrg'ẽr, the name applied to a former subdivision of the Scottish Secession Church. The Secession, which originated through the withdrawal of Ebenezer Erskine and some other ministers from the Scottish establishment in 1732, split in two in 1747, part having felt free to take, while others refused, what they deemed an ensnaring burgess oath. They reunited in 1820 under the name of the Associate Synod, and, joining with the «Relief» in 1847, formed the United Presbyterian Church.

Burgin, George B., English novelist and journalist: b. Croydon, Surrey, England, 15 Jan. 1856. He became private secretary to Baker Pasha and accompanied him to Asia Minor as secretary of the Reform Commission in Armenia. In 1885 he returned to England and was for a time sub-editor of 'The Idler.' Among his works are: 'The Dance at the Four Corners'; 'Tuxter's Little Maid'; 'The Judge of the Four Corners'; 'Tomalyn's Quest'; 'Fortune's Footballs'; 'The Cattle Man'; 'The Hermits of Gray's Inn'; 'The Bread of Tears'; 'The Tiger's Claw'; 'A Son of Mammon'; 'A Wilful Woman'; 'The Shutters of Silence.'

Burgkmair, Hans, hänts boork'mẽr, German painter and engraver: b. Augsburg, 1473; d. about 1531. He is supposed to have been a pupil of Albert Dürer. Several of his frescoes and paintings in oil upon wood are still preserved in his native town; but though possessed of considerable merit, they have contributed far less to his fame than his woodcuts, in which he at least equaled Dürer, and has scarcely been surpassed by Holbein. Among his most famous works are the 'Triumph of the Emperor Maximilian I.,' embracing 135 cuts, with a text written by that emperor; and a series, 'The Wise King,' including 237 cuts, in which the deeds of the same ruler are represented.

Burglary, at common law, the breaking and entering the house of another in the nighttime, with intent to commit a felony therein, whether the felony be actually committed or not. Burglary at common law, and in its first degree in the statutes of the various States, must, in general, be committed in a mansion-house actually occupied as a dwelling, but if it be kept by the owner *animo revertendi,* though no person resides in it in his absence, it is still his mansion. But at common law burglary may be committed in a church. In New York (Penal Code

§ 496), and in some other States in which the New York statute has been adopted, burglary at common law, or in the first degree, must be committed in the night, but in New York and in some other States burglary in the second and third degrees may be committed in the daytime, and it is burglary in the third degree in New York feloniously to enter a building, whether inhabited or not, either in the daytime or night. Before the offense is complete there must be both a breaking and an entry or an exit. An actual breaking takes place when the burglar breaks or removes any part of the house, or the fastenings provided for it, with violence. Constructive breakings occur when the burglar gains an entry by fraud, conspiracy, or threats. The least entry, with the whole or any part of the body, hand or foot, or with any instrument or weapon, introduced for the purpose of committing a felony, will be sufficient to constitute the offense. Burglary is a felony in all of the States, and in North Carolina it may be punished with death or imprisonment. In New York it is punishable as follows: Burglary in the first degree, imprisonment for not less than 10 years; second degree, not exceeding 10 years; third degree, not exceeding 5 years.

Bürglen, a village of Switzerland, in the canton of Uri, about a mile from Altorf, is the traditional birthplace of William Tell. The supposed site of the patriot's house is now occupied by a chapel, erected in 1522, upon the walls of which are represented certain well-known scenes from his history.

Bur'gomaster, the title of the chief magistrate of a city or a large town in Germany and the Netherlands, practically equivalent to mayor.

Burgomaster, a sailor's name for certain large domineering gulls of the genus *Larus.*

Burgos, Francisco Javier de, frän-thēs'kō hä'vēr dè boor'gōs, Spanish statesman and poet: b. Motril, Granada, 1778; d. 1845. In his dramatic compositions he sought to restore the classical Spanish comedy. Among them are: 'The Three Equals'; 'The Masked Ball'; and 'The Optimist and the Pessimist.' He wrote a celebrated 'Ode to Reason.'

Burgos, a city of northern Spain, the capital of the province of Burgos, and formerly of Old Castile, and once the residence of its kings. It stands on the declivity of a hill, on the right bank of the Arlanzon. The streets are narrow and dark, the finest in every respect being that called the Huerto del Rey. Places of promenade are numerous; the one most frequented, and justly forming the boast of the town, being the Espolon. The most remarkable structure is the cathedral, one of the finest buildings of the kind in Europe. It was begun in 1221, but was not finished for several centuries. It is built of white marble in the form of a Latin cross, and is about 300 feet long by 200 broad, and its size is such that service can be performed in eight chapels at once without confusion. Its interior, as well as its exterior, is of great magnificence, is adorned with fine carvings and paintings, and contains numerous monuments, in particular the tombs of Don Fernando and the Cid, both natives of Burgos, and celebrated throughout Spain for their heroic achievements in the wars with the Moors. There are several other fine churches, but the rest of the public buildings are not deserving of notice. The wool of Old Castile passes principally through Burgos, and it has some woolen manufactures. Burgos is the see of an archbishop, and at one time contained a university. Pop. (1900) 31,413. The province of Burgos is bounded on the north by Santander, east by Alava, Logroño, and Soria; south by Segovia, and west by Palencia and Valladolid. The area is 5,650 square miles. Pop. (1897) 340,001.

Burgoyne, bèr-goin', **John,** English general and dramatist: b. 24 Feb. 1723; d. London, 4 Aug. 1792. He was the son of Capt. John Burgoyne, and grandson of Sir John Burgoyne of Bedfordshire, although reputed to be a natural son of Lord Bingley. Educated at Westminster, he entered the army at an early age, and while a subaltern eloped with Lady Charlotte Stanley, daughter of the Earl of Derby. By this alliance his military advancement was secured. After an election to Parliament in 1761, he served with distinction in Portugal, and was sent to America in 1775. He joined Gen. Gage at Boston, with large reinforcements, and witnessed the battle of Bunker Hill, of which he has left an animated description. After proceeding to Canada as governor, he returned to England, but in 1777 was despatched to take command of that expedition from Canada against the United States, the failure of which so largely contributed to the establishment of American freedom. Indeed, few battles have led in their ultimate influence to results so great as did the surrender of Burgoyne with 5,791 fighting men, well provided with artillery, at Saratoga, to the army of Gen. Gates. On his return home, he was received by the king with marked disfavor. Burgoyne did not possess the genius of a great general, and was in many respects utterly inadequate to the tasks imposed upon him, yet no one can read his work written in his own defense, 'State of the Expedition from Canada' (London 1780), without acknowledging his courage, and detecting qualities, which, in a less exalted station, might have been of much service to his country. Disgusted with his treatment by the government, he retired to private life, and devoted his leisure to the production of dramas, some of which, as 'The Maid of the Oaks,' 'The Lord of the Manor,' etc., were highly popular in their day. His best play, 'The Heiress,' has been successful not only in its original tongue, but also in several foreign versions. He was made commander-in-chief in Ireland in 1782, and in 1787 was one of the managers of the impeachment of Warren Hastings, whose trial lasted through several years after Burgoyne's death. See SARATOGA, BATTLES OF.

Burgoyne, Sir John Fox, English officer of engineers: b. 24 July 1782; d. 7 Oct. 1871. He was the son of Gen. John Burgoyne; was educated at Eton and at the Royal Military Academy at Woolwich; entered the Royal Engineers in 1798; served at Malta in 1800, in Sicily with Gen. Stewart in 1806, in Egypt in 1807, and in the Peninsula with Sir John Moore and Wellington from 1809 to 1814. He shared in the celebrated retreat on Corunna, and was present at all the sieges, generally as first or second in command of the engineers, and at most of the battles of the Peninsular war, in which he was twice wounded. During the War of 1812, he assisted as lieutenant-colonel and chief engineer in the attack on New Orleans. In 1826 he accompanied the army of Gen. Clinton to Portugal in the same capacity. He was appointed chairman of the Board of Public Works in Ireland in 1830 and in 1845 became inspector-general of fortifications in England. He was made a lieutenant-general in 1851, and on the outbreak of the Crimean war was sent to Turkey to provide for the defense of Constantinople. After returning to England he was again sent out to Sebastopol, where he was chief of the engineering department till recalled in 1855. He received the order of the Medjidie from the Sultan of Turkey, was made a general in 1855, the following year was created a baronet, in 1868 a field-marshal, and for some years, up to his death, held the appointment of constable of the Tower of London. In 1859 a work was published in London under the title of 'Military Opinions of Gen. Sir J. F. Burgoyne,' in which many of his official writings were collected.

Burgrass. See SANDBUR.

Bur'grave, a count who in the Middle Ages had command of a castle or burg. Burgraves were appointed to their office by the emperor or by the bishops; and belonged to the nobility by virtue of their office. Their powers differed in different places, but as a rule they were entrusted with keeping the public peace, the oversight of trade and the market, and the command of the troops and the police in their districts. As the free cities grew in power they were separated from the jurisdiction of the burgrave. The office lost its significance in the course of the 13th century, but the title is retained by some princely families to the present time, as, for instance, by the kings of Prussia who have the title of Burgrave of Nuremberg.

Bur'gundy, Louis (DUKE OF), Dauphin of France: b. Versailles, 6 Aug. 1682; d. 18 Feb. 1712. He was grandson of Louis XIV. and father of Louis XV. A boy of ungovernable passions and temper, great haughtiness of bearing, and sensuality of life, he is said to have been much corrected in character and conduct by the influence of his preceptor, the saintly Fénelon. At the age of about 15 he married Princess Adelaide of Savoy; was made generalissimo of the army in 1701; and on the death of his father became heir-apparent to the throne. He was called the Grand Dauphin, and from his relationship to two of the greatest sovereigns of France his figure gains a historical importance out of all proportion to that of his own personality and career.

Bur'gundy, a region of western Europe, so called from the Burgundians, a Teutonic people originally from the country between the Oder and the Vistula. They migrated to the region of the Upper Rhine, and in the beginning of the 5th century they passed over into Gaul, and after a long struggle obtained possession of the southeastern part of this country. Here they founded a kingdom, which had as its seat of government sometimes Lyons and sometimes Geneva; but having become engaged in a war with the Franks, they were at last wholly subdued in 534. More than one kingdom of Burgundy, so called, subsequently arose, as well

as the important county of Burgundy (Upper Burgundy, Franche-Comté); but the most important state of this name was the duchy of Burgundy (Lower Burgundy), consisting principally of the French province Bourgogne (Burgundy, properly so called). The long line of ancient Dukes of Burgundy became extinct in 1361 with the death of Duke Philip, and Burgundy was immediately united by King John of France with the French crown. The dignity of Duke of Burgundy was restored in 1363 by his grant of the dukedom to his youngest and favorite son, Philip the Bold (q.v.). In 1368 he married Margaret, the widow of the last Duke Philip of the old line, only daughter and heiress of Louis III., Count of Flanders, and thereby greatly augmented his possessions, which now included Flanders, Mechlin, Antwerp, and Franche-Comté. In 1402 he was made regent of France, an appointment which gained him the hatred of the king's brother Louis, Duke of Orleans, and led to the struggle between the Orleanist and the Burgundian factions. In 1404 Philip died, and was succeeded by his son, John the Fearless, who was stabbed by the companions of the dauphin in 1419. His son and successor, Philip the Good (q.v.) gained great accessions of territory, including Hainault, Holland, Zealand, Namur, and in 1431 Brabant and Limburg, which reverted to him from a younger branch of his family. In 1441 he also obtained possession of Luxemburg. On his marriage with his third wife, Isabella, daughter of King John of Portugal, he founded the order of the Golden Fleece. His son, Charles the Bold (q.v.), who succeeded him in 1467, became the inveterate enemy of Louis XI. of France, and one of the most powerful princes in Europe. He acquired Gueldres in 1475, but perished in the fatal battle of Nancy in 1477, leaving behind him a daughter, Maria, the sole heiress of his states. She married Maximilian of Austria, who thus obtained the Netherlands and Upper Burgundy. The king of France received the dukedom of Burgundy, which he assumed as a male fief. Henceforth the territories that had belonged to Charles shared the fortunes either of France or of the empire. In the empire what was called the circle of Burgundy for a time embraced Franche-Comté and the Netherlands. In the Peace of Madrid, in 1526, Francis I. was obliged to agree to the cession of the duchy of Burgundy to Charles V. of Germany, but the cession was never carried out, and in the Peace of Cambray, in 1529, Charles renounced his claim to it. Franche-Comté was conquered by Louis XIV., and retained by him at the Peace of Nimeguen in 1678. After this time the name Burgundy is best known as designating one of the provinces or governments of France.

Burgundy (called also Burgundy Proper, or Lower Burgundy), formerly a province in the east of France, lying on the west of Franche-Comté, and on the south of Champagne. It now forms the four departments of Yonne, Côte-d'Or, Saône-et-Loire, and Ain. It is one of the most productive regions in France. The principal product is wine. See BURGUNDY WINES.

Burgundy Pitch, the resinous exudation of the stem of the spruce fir (*Abies excelsa* or *Pinus abies*), melted and strained. It is obtained from Switzerland, but is seldom genuine. It is hard and brittle, opaque, of a dull reddish-brown color, empyreumatic odor, and aromatic taste. It gives off no water when heated, is not bitter, and is free from vesicles. It consists chiefly of resin and a little volatile oil, whence its odor. The resin resembles that of turpentine. Pitch plaster acts externally as a slight stimulant to the skin. Burgundy pitch enters also into the composition of the iron plaster. It takes its name from Burgundy in France, where it was first prepared.

Burgundy Wines, famous French wines, deriving their name from the ancient province of Burgundy. They have a reputation superior to their present popularity. They are nevertheless wines of delicious flavor and bouquet. It has been supposed that they would not well bear a sea-voyage, but it is now settled that when transported to America and back, their quality is greatly improved. The most renowned red wines of Burgundy are Romané-Conti, Clos-Vougeöt, Chambertin, and Richebourg. Chambertin was the favorite wine of Louis XVI. and Napoleon. Chablis, a white wine, has many admirers, but is inferior to the best growths of the Garonne and the Rhone.

Burhánpur, boor-han-poor', a town of the Nimar district, Central Provinces, British India, formerly the capital of Khandesh, is situated on the Tapti River, about 300 miles northeast of Bombay. It is situated on high ground, and is well planned and built. It has a mosque and other buildings worthy of note, and was once famous for its manufactures of gold and silver brocade, muslin, and silks, which still exist to some extent, though the town has long been declining.

Burhel. See BAHRAL.

Buri, boo'rē, the grandfather of Odin, in Norwegian mythology. According to the legends 12 streams flowed from the spring Hvergelmir in Niflheim (the region of shadows), and later in their course were frozen, thus surrounding the region of elemental fire (Muspelheim) with blocks of ice. From this ice came the giant Ymir and the cow Audhumla; from the cow's udder came four streams of milk with which the giant was fed. Audhumla was nourished by licking the salt ice-blocks, and as she licked them a man's hair appeared on the first day; a man's head on the second day and the whole man on the third day; this was Buri. He was of giant size and strength; he had a son Bor through whom he was the grandfather of Odin, Vili, and Ve.

Bur'ial, the ordinary method of disposing of the dead, a practice which varies among different peoples. Among savage races, and even among some civilized peoples of the East, exposure to wild animals or birds of prey is not uncommon. The careful embalming of the dead by the ancient Egyptians may be regarded as a special form of burial. But by far the most common forms of disposing of the dead have been burning and interring. Among the Greeks and Romans both forms were practised, though among the latter burning became common only in the later times of the republic. In this form of burial the corpse, after being borne in procession through the streets, was

placed upon a pyre built of wood, and profusely sprinkled with oils and perfumes. Fire was set to the wood, and after the process of cremation was complete the bones and ashes were carefully gathered together by the relatives and placed in an urn. With the introduction of the Christian religion, consecrated places were appropriated for the purpose of general burial, and the Roman custom of providing the sepulchre with a stone and inscription was continued by the Christians. The practice of cremation now declined and finally disappeared, but has recently to some extent been revived. See BURYING-PLACES; CREMATION; FUNERAL RITES; MOUND BUILDERS; MUMMY; etc.

Buriats, boo-rē-äts', a Mongol people, forming a branch of the Kalmucks, and who submitted to the Russians in 1644. They inhabit the southern part of the government of Irkutsk and Transbaikalia, and number more than 200,000. They support themselves by their flocks, by hunting, and the mechanical arts, particularly the forging of iron. Their dress consists partly of leather. Their religion is partly Lamaism and partly Shamanism; and their idols are sometimes painted on cloth, and sometimes made of wood, metal, felt, and sheepskin.

Buridan, Jean, zhŏn bü-rē-däṅ, French scholastic philosopher: b. Béthune, Artois, about 1300; d. after 1358. He studied at Paris, where he attached himself as a disciple of Occam to the party of the Nominalists, and at a later time became himself a teacher. In the end he was forced by his opponents to flee from Paris, when he betook himself to Vienna, where he is said to have been influential in bringing about the establishment of the university. Here also he wrote some logical and ethical treatises, in which he appears as a zealous adherent of the Aristotelian philosophy. Buridan was a supporter of the doctrine of Determinism (q.v.), and he is now chiefly known through having his name attached to an illustration that he is said to have used in support of his views, and known as "Buridan's Ass." He is said to have supposed the case of a hungry ass placed at an equal distance from two equally attractive bundles of hay, and to have asserted that in the supposed case the ass must inevitably perish from hunger, there being nothing to determine him to prefer the one bundle to the other. This illustration, however, is not found in any of his works, and from its nature it would appear more likely to have been used by the assailants of the doctrine of Determinism. He wrote 'Compendium Logicae' (1489), and other works.

Bu'rin, or Graver, the principal instrument used in copper engraving, is made of tempered steel, and is of prismatic form, the graving end being ground off obliquely to a sharp point. The distinctive style of a master is frequently described by such expressions as a soft burin, a graphic burin, a brilliant burin, etc.

Buriti (bu-rī-tē') Palm, a lofty, fan-leaved palm (*Mauritia vinifera*), common in swamps in northern Brazil. It bears abundant crops of scaly nuts about two inches long, from the reddish oily pulp of which a confection is made by boiling with sugar. The nuts also yield an oil which is emulsified to make a popular drink. After the tree is felled numerous cuplike holes are made in the prostrate trunk.

These become filled with a reddish fluid, which is used as a beverage. Its taste resembles some sweet wines.

Burke, Edmund, political philosopher and orator: b. Dublin 12 Jan. (probably) 1729; d. Beaconsfield, England, 9 July 1797. He was the son of a solicitor in good practice. His mother was a Roman Catholic, but he and his two brothers adopted the religion of their Protestant father. Always, however, he was tolerant of Catholicism. At the age of 14 he entered Trinity College, Dublin, where he took his bachelor's degree in 1748. In this period, as his letters show, he had fits of enthusiasm over various studies— a *furor mathematicus*, succeeded by a *furor logicus*, a *furor historicus*, and a *furor poeticus*. The 17 years between 1748 and 1765, when his career was finally determined by his election to Parliament, he spent in different employments. Going to London with the intention of taking up law, he succumbed to the attractions of literature and philosophy. He travelled in England and on the Continent, frequented debating clubs and theatres, and did more or less hack work for publishers. He printed nothing, however, with which his name is connected till the two books of 1756: 'A Vindication of Natural Society' and 'A Philosophical Inquiry into the Origin of Our Ideas on the Sublime and Beautiful.' In the first he attempted to refute Bolingbroke's arguments against revealed religion by showing that they might be urged with equal force against the organization of society. In the second he took up a subject much discussed at the time; and though his speculations have been superseded, he has the credit of stimulating Lessing to the production of 'Laokoon.' Burke also wrote or helped to write an 'Account of the European Settlements in America' (1757), and an 'Abridgment of the History of England' (1758). In 1759 he began to edit the *Annual Register*, with which he was connected for 30 years. In 1761 he went to Ireland, attached in some indefinite way to William Gerard Hamilton—"Single-speech" Hamilton—who was secretary to the lord-lieutenant. After two years in Dublin he returned to England; there he joined the famous Literary Club, with which are associated the names of Johnson, Goldsmith, Sir Joshua Reynolds, and Garrick.

In recognition of his abilities and of the knowledge of politics which he had shown in the *Annual Register*, he was offered the post of private secretary to Lord Rockingham when the latter became prime minister in 1765. In the same year he was elected member of Parliament from Wendover. Within a week or two he made a strong impression with two speeches for the repeal of the Stamp Act. Upon the fall of the Rockingham ministry, Burke, who might have had a place with the new administration, remained with his friends. Turning to their account his literary powers, he began his series of great political tracts. In 1769 he put forth 'Observations on the Present State of the Nation,' a reply to a pamphlet by George Grenville. In this controversy Burke showed himself a master of the details of revenue and finance. At this time he took part in some transactions which afforded his enemies a handle against him. Though he had been living almost from hand to mouth till he entered

Parliament, he bought in 1768 an estate worth upwards of $100,000. The underlying facts have never been determined with complete satisfaction. This much, however is clear: Burke lived on terms of intimacy with his brother Richard and a distant kinsman, William Burke. Richard and William, together with Lord Verney, a political patron of Edmund, speculated in stock of the East India Company, and later Richard was engaged in questionable dealings in West Indian lands. That these ventures were shared by Burke has been charged but never proved. On the other hand it can be shown that most of the money for the purchase of his estate he borrowed from Lord Rockingham. After getting the place, he had to borrow right and left to maintain it. Probably his faults were neither dishonesty in speculation nor venality in Parliament, but undue ambition to live as he thought became his position, carelessness and improvidence, and an adherence to eighteenth century standards of propriety, which in such matters were lower than ours.

Whatever his shortcomings in managing his private affairs, his services to the public were very great. He was on the side of the people in the long contest over John Wilkes. Since his sentiments on this subject were in general those of the 'Letters' of Junius, he was suspected of being Junius. This accusation he denied; and his 'Thoughts on the Cause of the Present Discontents' (1770) showed so many differences on minor points that—were no other evidence available—it must be concluded that Burke was not Junius. In the 'Thoughts' Burke argued that the king and a small knot of advisers were building up power for themselves; that powers of government are held in trust for the people; and that popular impatience must therefore be indulged. But, true to his conservative instincts, he would not accept the radical reforms commonly proposed—universal suffrage and the disfranchisement of "rotten boroughs." He would have changes more gradual. During the years immediately following 1770 Burke devoted his energies to keeping the Rockingham Whigs united against the efforts of the king to win them over. Without Burke, says John Morley, "the Rockingham connection would undoubtedly have fallen to ruin, and with it the most upright, consistent, and disinterested body of men then in public life."

From his political activity Burke withdrew for a time in 1773 for a trip to France. There he observed two things which he strongly dreaded: atheism and an eager questioning of the "allowed opinions which contribute so much to the public tranquillity." This atheism and speculation, he perceived—and he was one of the few who were so clear-sighted—were working toward revolution. His fear of these tendencies he expressed in Parliament not long after his return.

By this time Burke had won a substantial reputation throughout the United Kingdom. Indeed, as early as 1766 at least one Irish municipality had voted him the freedom of the city; and in succeeding years English mercantile organizations passed resolutions commending his labors in behalf of commerce. Finally in 1774, when troubles with America were thickening, Bristol, the trading centre of the west of England, a city which had everything to lose and nothing to gain from a war with the colonies, elected him to Parliament. At the conclusion of the poll his colleagues had promised obedience to the instructions of his constituents. Burke, however, declared his independence: "Your representative owes you, not his industry only but his judgment; and he betrays you instead of serving you if he sacrifices it to your opinion." To this declaration he adhered when in 1778 a bill was proposed relaxing restrictions upon Irish commerce. The English merchants, including those of Bristol, protested; but Burke replied, "England and Ireland may flourish together. The world is large enough for us both. Let it be our care not to make ourselves too little for it." ('Two Letters to Gentlemen in Bristol.') For this liberality Burke was never forgiven, and in the election of 1780 he was forced to seek a new constituency.

It was during his six years as member for Bristol that, in the contest over America, he rose to his full height as a statesman. He was almost alone among the speech-makers of that time in always going below the superficial considerations of the moment to the fundamental fact that in the long run restraint and violence defeat themselves. In addition to many minor speeches scattered through the 'Parliamentary History' he made three great contributions to the subject: 'Speech on American Taxation,' 19 April 1774; 'Speech on Conciliation,' 22 March 1775; and 'Letter to the Sheriffs of Bristol,' 3 April 1777. In the first he argued that the tea duty was of no use to England for revenue; that it served only to irritate the Americans; and that by winning the loyalty of the colonists England would get more than she could ever take by force. In the second speech Burke maintained that England must conciliate, and that the only way was by yielding. In the 'Letter' he reviewed the struggle and in the light of events justified his own position. Of the three pieces that on 'Conciliation' is the best. Not even when dealing with India does Burke excel in grasp of details, in lucid presentation of a large mass of facts, and in ripened political wisdom. Then, too, he saw what so many failed to observe, that the real cause of the contest lay deeper than the casual orders of a governor or the retaliation of a mob; and that America, in resisting the encroachments of royal prerogative, was fighting a battle for the liberties of Englishmen at home.

Though Burke could not win over Parliament to his views on America, he had better success with his 'Speech on the Plan for Economical Reform' (1780). People were staggering under the debt from the American war and agitating for a general reform of Parliament. Burke opposed such radical changes; he proposed to abolish some offices, consolidate others, and reduce salaries. One of the offices which he reformed, that of paymaster of the forces, he himself occupied in 1782. At that time the North ministry yielded to the Whigs, who were temporarily united under Lord Rockingham, Charles James Fox, and Lord Shelburne. Burke, owing in part to infirmities of his temper and the suspicions against him, got only this third-rate position, instead of a place in the cabinet. The Whigs were scarcely in their seats when Lord Rockingham died and Lord Shelburne became head of the administration. At

once Fox and Burke refused to work with him, and by joining their old enemy Lord North, in what is known as the Coalition, they broke up the Whig party. Burke is accused of deserting his principles for purely personal motives. His conduct is hard to defend; for he attacked Shelburne with asperity, and under the Coalition resumed for a few months the office of paymaster.

Against this dubious course we may set his strenuous advocacy of reform in India. That country was victim of the corrupt and cruel system of the East India Company. Burke was familiar with the subject, for he had been a member of select committees on Indian affairs and had drawn two important reports. He is also supposed to have framed the East India bill commonly known as Fox's. At any rate he defended it (1 Dec. 1783) in one of his best speeches. The bill, however, was defeated, and the Coalition, which supported it, driven from office. Early in 1785 Burke renewed the attack in his 'Speech on the Nabob of Arcot's Debts'— a preliminary to the proceedings against Warren Hastings. In 1786 Burke drew the articles against Hastings. The trial dragged on till 1795; and though the verdict at last was for acquittal, Burke had none the less succeeded in reforming the government of India; for he had trumpeted the wrongs of that "emptied and emboweled" land till public sentiment would no longer tolerate them.

Before the trial of Hastings had closed, the French Revolution had broken out. Burke looked upon it, not as the emancipation of oppressed masses, but as an effort of atheists and political theorists to uproot the settled order. Since his views were hostile to those of the more radical Whigs, he began to draw away from the men with whom he had been allied against the encroachments of the crown in England and America. In 1790 he widened the breach still further by aggressive proclamation of his opinions in 'Reflections on the Revolution in France.' The book had for that day an enormous sale and divided Great Britain into two parties: one composed of Burke and an uncongenial company of Tories; the other of liberals, many of whom had been Burke's lifelong associates. Burke himself violently quarreled with his old friend Fox. The seeming contradiction between his early position and his later is accounted for in part by the fact that he grew more conservative with age, in part by his desire to preserve the balance between monarch and subject. In England the crown had been the aggressor; in France, he thought, the people. Moreover, he had always insisted that liberty is "inseparable from order"; and in France he saw nothing but disorder. As the Revolution progressed, Burke became more and more wrought up, so that in each of his succeeding utterances —'Letter to a Member of the National Assembly' (1791), 'Appeal from the New to the Old Whigs' (1791), 'Thoughts on French Affairs' (1791), 'Remarks on the Policy of the Allies' (1793), 'Observations on the Conduct of the Minority' (1793), and 'Letters on a Regicide Peace' (1796)—the reasoning grew feebler, the scolding shriller.

During the same period, when Burke was dealing with a subject on which he was more thoroughly informed, Ireland, he showed his old qualities of statesmanship. He had always been a champion of his down-trodden native land. When Ireland caught the contagion of the French Revolution, and when the war between England and France made Ireland still more restless, Burke urged for Ireland the same policy of conciliation that he had urged for America. In letter and pamphlet he unceasingly advocated relieving the Catholics of their political disabilities.

In 1794 he retired from Parliament. He was to have received a peerage with the title Lord Beaconsfield; but since the death of his son left him without direct male heir, he accepted instead a pension. This was the occasion of a fresh attack upon him by his enemies. He replied effectively in the 'Letter to a Noble Lord' (1796).

His zeal in behalf of the wretched and the oppressed was not a mere vague sentiment; it was a motive in his daily conduct. When the poet Crabbe was obscure and penniless Burke took him into the family, found a printer for his verses, and finally obtained for him a living in the Church. At the time of the Revolution Burke also kept open house for French refugees and established a school for their children. Burke's principles of statesmanship, when briefly set down, seem very bald and simple. The basis of his system is explained in a sentence from one of his letters: "The principles of politics are those of morality enlarged." The first of the moral laws upon which he rested great weight was justice; the second, generosity. Knowing that perfect justice could never be obtained, that human institutions are at best compromises, he was not a theorist, he did not fall into the fallacy that the machinery of government may be constructed as if men were uniform, passive units. These phases of his bent for the practical are in the last analysis a trust in experience. A man who clings so tenaciously to experience is likely to be an uncompromising conservative; and Burke was for his generation and all generations since, the "great pleader for conservatism." As an orator he frequently produced no immediate effect. His gestures were clumsy, and when he spoke in public his voice was somewhat harsh, he dropped into a strong Irish brogue, and at times a hurried articulation. But, above all, he overestimated the capacity of his hearers. Not content with a concise presentation of leading points, he insisted on applying profound philosophic principles. Yet some of his speeches, notably at the trial of Warren Hastings, produced a profound effect. This effect was largely due to the vigor of his style as a writer. He was virile, vivid in description, and unsurpassed in lucid and logical arrangement of material.

In the winter of 1756-1757 he married Jane Nugent, daughter of a physician. Her capacity for management lifted many burdens from his shoulders. His only child, a son, Richard, died in 1794.

Among his important writings or speeches not already mentioned are 'Address to the King' (1777), 'Letter to Sir Hercules Langrishe' (1792), 'Thoughts and Details on Scarcity' (1795).

Bibliography.—There are in the market three or four editions of Burke's writings and speeches, substantially complete. The best short life is in the 'Dictionary of National Biography.'

John Morley's Life of Burke (1879) in the English 'Men of Letters' is excellent; also his 'Burke, a Historical Study' (1867). Of the earlier lives James Prior's (2d. ed. 1826) is the best. Of course Burke bulks large in the standard histories and memoirs of England in the 18th century.

HAMMOND LAMONT,
Editor New York Nation; Editor 'Burke's Speech on Conciliation with America.'

Burke, Jane, better known as CALAMITY JANE; American army scout and mail carrier: b. Princeton, Mo., 1852; d. Deadwood, S. D., 1 Aug. 1903. She was reared on the plains and early became an Indian scout, and was an aide to Gen. Custer and Gen. Miles in numerous campaigns. For several years she was the government mail carrier between Deadwood, S. D., and Custer, Mont.

Burke, John, Irish genealogist: b. near Parsonstown, Ireland, 1786; d. Aix-la-Chapelle, 27 March 1848. His life was devoted to genealogical research. In 1826 he began to publish a 'Genealogical and Heraldic Dictionary of the Peerage and Baronetage of the British Empire' and subsequent works by him were: 'A Genealogical and Heraldic History of the Commoners of Great Britain and Ireland' (1833-8), which in subsequent editions appeared as 'A Dictionary of the Landed Gentry.'

Burke, SIR John Bernard, English herald and genealogist; son of John Burke (q.v.): b. London, 1815; d. Dublin, 13 Dec. 1892. He was educated at Caen in Normandy, was trained as a lawyer and called to the bar in 1839. Besides editing the successive issues of the 'Peerage' founded by his father (49th ed. 1887), he published other works on the 'Landed Gentry' (1846); 'Extinct Peerages' (1846); 'Anecdotes of the Aristocracy' (1849); 'Family Romance' (1853); 'The Vicissitudes of Great Families' (1859); 'The Rise of Great Families' (1873); 'The Book of Precedence' (1881); and 'Reminiscences' (1882).

Burke, Maurice Francis, American clergyman: b. Ireland, 5 May 1845. He came to the United States in childhood and was educated in Chicago and Notre Dame, Ind., and in the American College, Rome, where he was ordained to the Roman Catholic priesthood in 1875. Returning to the United States, he took charge of a parish in Joliet, Ill. In 1887 he was consecrated bishop of Cheyenne, Wyo., and in 1893 was transferred to the see of St. Joseph, Mo. Bishop Burke is known as a fine linguist.

Burke, Robert O'Hara, Australian explorer: b. county Galway, Ireland, 1820; d. Australia, 28 June 1861. After serving in the Austrian army he went to Australia, and after seven years' service as inspector of police was appointed commander of an expedition to cross the continent of Australia from south to north. He and his associate, Wills, reached the tidal waters of the Flinders River, but both perished of starvation on the return journey. They were among the very first white men to cross the Australian continent from south to north.

Burke, Thomas Martin Aloysius, American clergyman: b. Ireland, 10 Jan. 1840. He came in childhood to Utica, N. Y., and was educated in Toronto and Baltimore and was ordained to the Roman Catholic priesthood in

1864. He was appointed to labor in Albany and became successively vicar-general and administrator. In 1894 he was consecrated bishop of Albany.

Burke, Thomas Nicholas, Irish clergyman and orator: b. Galway, 1830; d. 1883. He was educated in Italy, where he entered the Order of St. Dominic. Going to England, he preached in that country and later in Ireland, gaining a high reputation as an orator and becoming familiarly known as "Father Tom." In 1872 he made a visit to the United States and lectured in reply to Froude, his addresses appearing in print under the title of 'English Misrule in Ireland.'

Burke and Hare, two miscreants, of whom William Burke, a native of Ireland, was detected, tried, and executed at Edinburgh, in 1829, for the murder of numerous individuals, his accomplice, Hare, escaping the hangman by turning king's evidence. At this time the "resurrectionists" were busy at their nefarious trade, but the vigilance with which the burying-grounds throughout the country were watched rendered a supply of subjects for anatomical schools almost impracticable, and the demand for dead bodies consequently became great. This led Burke and Hare to murder, by suffocation, many poor waifs who were decoyed into Hare's lodging-house, and whose bodies they sold to Dr. Robert Knox, proprietor of an anatomical theatre in Edinburgh. The case of Burke and Hare brought home to the public mind more clearly than ever how necessary it is that schools of anatomy should receive a regular supply of subjects for dissection, and in 1832 an act was passed for supplying the anatomical schools throughout the kingdom from the unclaimed dead in the hospitals.

Bürkel, Heinrich, hĭn'rĭH bür'kĕl, German painter: b. Pirmasens, 30 March 1813; d. Munich, 10 June 1869. He was educated at Munich and in Italy; he is chiefly a genre painter; his scenes from the Bavarian and Tyrolean Alps were among the first of their kind, and his village and tavern scenes rank among the best in modern art. Among his paintings are 'Scenes in an Inn' and 'Winter Scenes in the Tyrol.'

Bur'kitt, Francis Crawford, English Biblical scholar: b. London, 3 Sept. 1864. He was graduated at Trinity College, Cambridge. He has published 'Early Christianity Outside the Roman Empire' (1899); 'Fragments of Aquila' (1897); 'The Rules of Tyconius' (1894); 'Two Lectures on the Gospels' (1900); etc.

Burleigh, bër'lĭ, George Shepard, American writer, brother of William H. Burleigh (q.v.): b. Plainfield, Conn., 26 March 1821; d. Providence, R. I., July 21, 1903. He has published 'The Maniac and Other Poems'; 'Signal Fires on the Trail of the Pathfinder.'

Burleigh, William Cecil (LORD), English statesman: b. Bourn, Lincolnshire, 13 Sept. 1520; d. London, 4 Aug. 1598. He was secretary of state under Edward VI. and Elizabeth, and prime minister of England for 40 years. In 1588 Parliament was assembled, and, by his advice, a plan of religious reform was laid before it. In this he had a considerable share; and he also took the leading part in the establishment of the Thirty-nine Articles of faith, which form the basis of the reformed religion

of the State. To him is also due the regulation of the coinage, which had been altered since Henry VIII.'s time. He was created Baron Burleigh in 1571, and, in 1588, concluded an advantageous treaty with the Netherlands. His policy was both cautious and comprehensive and he was entirely unaffected by personal prejudices in his management of public affairs. Consult: Nares, 'Memoirs of Lord Burghley' (1828-31); Charlton, 'Life' (1847); Hume, 'Great Lord Burleigh' (1898).

Burleigh, William Henry, American poet: b. Woodstock, Conn., 2 Feb. 1812; d. Brooklyn, N. Y., 18 March 1871. Bred on a farm, at 16 he became apprentice to a clothier, then to a village printer, and continued to labor in various places as journeyman printer, and finally as editor. In the latter capacity he had charge of the 'Literary Journal' at Schenectady, the *Christian Witness*, at Pittsburg, and the *Washington Banner*, in which papers, and in others, he published many short poems. A collection of them was published in 1840.

Burlesque, the comic effect arising from a ludicrous mixture of things high and low. High thoughts, for instance, are clothed in low expressions, or noble subjects described in a familiar manner, or *vice versa*.

Burlingame, Anson, American diplomatist: b. New Berlin, N. Y., 14 Nov. 1822; d. St. Petersburg, Russia, 23 Feb. 1870. After graduating from the Harvard Law School in 1847 he practiced law in Boston, and entering politics was active as a Free Soil advocate in 1848, and in 1854 was sent to Congress as a representative of the American Party. His vigorous denunciation of the assault upon Senator Sumner by Preston Brooks brought him a challenge from the latter, which was accepted, but Brooks declined to travel to the rendezvous in Canada. In 1861 he was sent as minister to Austria but was not received by the Austrian government on account of his advocacy of Hungarian independence. He was minister to China 1861-67, and in the last-named year was appointed ambassador from China to the United States and various European governments. On 4 July 1868 he concluded the noted 'Burlingame Treaty' which gave reciprocal privileges to China and the United States. After concluding treaties between China and Denmark, Sweden, Holland and Prussia, he died while arranging a treaty between China and Russia.

Burlingame, Edward Livermore, an American editor, son of Anson Burlingame (q.v.): b. Boston, 30 May 1848. He studied at Harvard and acted as private secretary to his father, who was United States minister. Since 1879 he has been associated with the publishing house of Charles Scribner's Sons, and in 1886 became editor of 'Scribner's Magazine.'

Burlington, England. See BRIDLINGTON.

Bur'lington, Iowa, a city and county-seat of Des Moines County, on the west bank of the Mississippi River at the intersection of the Chicago, Burlington, and Quincy, and several other lines of railroad. Its industries include the manufacture of machinery, furniture, agricultural tools, flour, linseed oil, soap, and many other articles, and extensive railroad shops are situated here. The city contains among its

The city was settled in 1677, by Friends, under the name of New Beverly. The name was subsequently changed to Bridlington, in honor of the Yorkshire town of that name on the North Sea, commonly called Burlington, and the spelling was presently made to accord with the pronunciation. The city was for many years the seat of government of West Jersey; and was the residence of the last colonial governor, William Franklin. It was bombarded by the British in 1776. Pop. (1900) 7,394.

Burlington, Vt., a city, port of entry and county-seat of Chittenden County, on Lake Champlain and the Central V. and Rutland R.R.'s; 40 miles northwest of Montpelier. It has a very large lake commerce and manufactories of lumber, cotton, and woolen goods, and iron. The environment is agricultural. The city is the seat of the State University of Vermont and of the State Agricultural and Medical colleges; Bishop Hopkins Hall; the Roman Catholic Cathedral; the Fletcher, Billings, and Burlington Law libraries; a county court-house; United States government building, and a Young Men's Christian Association Hall. Burlington is noted for its benevolent and educational institutions, which include the Mary Fletcher Hospital, Home for Aged Women, Home for Friendless Women, Home for Destitute Children, Adams Mission House, Louisa Howard Mission, Providence Orphan Asylum, Cancer Relief Association, Lake View Retreat, several sanitariums, the Vermont Episcopal Institute, St. Joseph's and St. Mary's academies (Roman Catholic), and high and graded schools. The city was settled in 1773; was a garrisoned post during the War of 1812; and was incorporated in 1865. Its material development has been largely due to its great lumbering industries. The famous Col. Ethan Allen is buried beneath a handsome monument in Greenmount Cemetery. Pop. (1900) 18,640.

Burlington Limestone, a limestone of sub-Carboniferous age, named for its occurrence near Burlington, Iowa. It is also found in other parts of the Mississippi valley. This limestone is of light color and fine-crystalline, resembling lithographic stone. It has important industrial value.

Bur'ma, the largest province of British India. It is on the east side of the Bay of Bengal, and at one time formed the greater portion of a

varies from less than 60 inches in some places to 190 or more in others. About half the soil is believed to be cultivatable, but a comparatively small portion is as yet under cultivation, though agriculture is extending year by year. Since the occupation of the country by the British it has rapidly increased in prosperity, and the revenue is generally greater than the expenditure. The imports and exports together exceed $50,000,000, the bulk of the trade being with Great Britain. The capital and principal port is Rangoon. Other towns are Moulmein, Akyab, and Bassein. Upper Burma has an area of 83,473 square miles, and is on the whole similar in character to Lower Burma, but less productive, and has generally a smaller rainfall. It is rich in minerals, including gold, silver, precious stones, marble, iron, lead, tin, antimony, arsenic, sulphur, and petroleum. Only a few of these are worked. The chief precious stones are the ruby and the sapphire; amber and jade are also found. All precious stones used to be sent to the royal treasury and strangers were prohibited from approaching the places where they were found. These districts are still the subject of special regulation under the British rule. The whole country is intersected by numerous streams, which, following the direction of the chief mountain chains, flow generally south to the Indian Ocean. The chief of these are the Irrawadi, the Salween, and the Chindwin, which joins the Irrawadi, the combined stream being of great volume. The Irrawadi is of great value as a highway of communication and traffic, being navigable beyond Bhamo, near the Chinese frontier. In their upper courses the rivers flow through narrow valleys; in their lower courses they traverse low-lying districts, and in the rainy season often overflow their banks. Among the wild animals of the country are the elephant, rhinoceros, tiger, leopard, deer of various kinds, and the wild hog. The rivers abound with fish. Of domestic animals we may mention the ox, buffalo, horse, elephant, and cat. In the southern districts, owing to the numerous rivers, the soil is most productive. Here grow rice, sugar cane, tobacco, cotton, indigo, and all the tropical fruits. Tea is cultivated in many of the more elevated parts. The forests produce timber of many sorts, including teak. A great part of the trade of the country is carried on by means of the Irrawadi River. From Bhamo

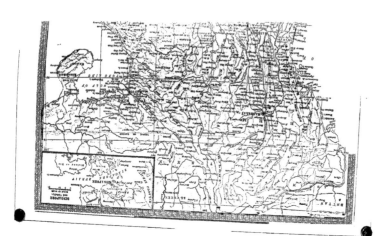

goods are conveyed to China, and this branch of trade is believed to be capable of great development. Rice is the great crop (occupying about 80 per cent of the cultivated area), and this grain forms the chief export, others being teak, cotton, and silk stuffs, petroleum, saltpetre, paper, and lacquer ware. Railways have been introduced, and the number of miles open is now about 1,000. From Rangoon two lines proceed north, one along the left bank of the Irrawadi to Prome and Meaday, the other through the Sittaung valley to Mandalay, and from that on the other side of the Irrawadi to Bhamo and Mogaung.

The Burmese have many skilful weavers, smiths, sculptors, workers in gold and silver, joiners, etc. Among industrial establishments are rice-mills, saw-mills, a few works for iron goods, ship-building yards, cutch works, etc. Other industries include boat-building, weaving, pottery, lacquerwork, and brasswork. The weaving of cotton and silk goods is carried on by the women everywhere. The pottery of the country is strong and durable, if not especially artistic; and the gold and silver work finds numerous purchasers outside the country. Wood-carving is extensively practised for the adornment of houses, boats, etc. The native vessels plying on the Irrawadi and other rivers are often of 100 to 150 tons burden, while thousands of small craft are engaged in trade or fishing. Large numbers of good cigars are made by women, and are partly used in the country, partly exported. The buildings among the Burmese are very slight, as the government used to require them to be chiefly of wood or bamboo, and prohibited the use of stone or brick except for pagodas, and other important structures.

People.— The Burmese are divided into several tribes, and belong to the common Indo-Chinese stock. Among the tribes other than the Burmese proper are the Karens, Kakhyens, Shams, etc. The Burmese proper are of a brown color, with lank, black hair, and vigorous, well-proportioned frames. No Burmese can have more than one wife; but he may have as many mistresses as he will. The latter live in the same house with the wife, and are her servants. The Burmese women enjoy a good deal of freedom; are not shut up as in some parts of the East, and can even engage in a lawsuit in their own name. The chief amusement of the Burmese is their theatre, where declamation, dancing, and music are given by turns. The new year (which begins in April) is celebrated with what is known as the "water feast," when young men and women throw water on each other and the passers-by. The Burmese usually write on palm leaves with an iron style or on black tablets with a pencil; the rich have libraries, with books, the leaves of some of which are thin pieces of ivory, with gilt edges. Their materia medica is chiefly confined to herbs, spices, and mercury; with vaccination they have long been acquainted. The language is monosyllabic, like Chinese, and written with an alphabet (derived from India), the characters of which are more or less circular. Among the common people the principal part of the male dress consists of a double piece of cloth about five yards long, loosely wrapped about the body. Over this a frock is worn, with sleeves open in front, and reaching below the knees. The lower classes of women wear only a single garment, resembling a sheet, wrapped round the body and fastened under the arms. Men of rank wear a long robe of flowered velvet or satin, with open sleeves and collar, a mantle or scarf being thrown over this. On the head is worn a high velvet or silk cap, plain or embroidered, according to rank. The men wear earrings, often of large size. Women of the higher classes generally wear a shift which reaches only to the pit of the stomach, where it is drawn tight and fastened by strings. This is covered by a loose jacket, with tight sleeves. A piece of silk or cloth encircles the waist and descends to the feet. When a woman wishes to be particularly fine she stains her nails and palms a red color, and tinges her teeth and the edges of her eyelids with black. Both sexes wear the hair long; the men tying it in a knot on the crown of the head, the women on the back. Sandals are often worn, but neither boots, shoes, nor stockings; every man, woman, and child, however, carries an umbrella. The chewing of betel and smoking of tobacco are universal. The Kakhyens or Singfo are a courageous people inhabiting the upper basin of the Irrawadi above Bhamo. They practise a sort of nature worship, and are active as traders, though at present rather lawless. Their villages are ruled by hereditary chiefs. The Chinese from Yunnan have of late years settled in considerable numbers as traders and agriculturists in the Kakhyen country; and in Lower Burma they are now a highly important element in the population as traders and otherwise. In the hilly districts of Tenasserim and Pegu we find the Karens, a somewhat secluded people, less intelligent and more ignorant than the Burmese, and not so purely Mongolian in physical character. The Talaings or Mons of the Irrawadi delta resemble the Burmese, but speak a distinct language. The Shans are a numerous people closely allied to the Siamese, and inhabiting eastern and northeastern Burma, together with portions of the neighboring countries.

The native government was an absolute monarchy, the king having unlimited power over life and property. The seat of government, after oscillating between Ava and Amarapura, was latterly fixed in Mandalay, a new town founded in 1857, and situated in a dusty plain a little over two miles from the left bank of the Irrawadi, and about 28 miles northwest from Amarapura. The king was assisted in governing by a council of state known as the *Hloot-daw,* to which belonged at once the functions of a legislature, a cabinet, and a supreme court of justice. It was composed of officials of 14 grades, the president being the king himself, some other member of the royal family, or the prime minister. The king had power to punish at his pleasure anyone, including even the great officers of state. The public revenue was derived from taxes levied in a very irregular and capricious manner, and as the officials received no fixed salary corruption and oppression were extremely prevalent. The criminal laws were barbarously severe. Capital punishment was commonly inflicted by decapitation, but crucifixion and disemboweling were also practised. Torture might be applied to principals or witnesses; and trial by ordeal was not unknown. The standing army was small. Levies were made, in case of war, by way of conscription; and a specified number of houses was required to furnish a soldier or pay a fine. The religion of the country is that of Buddha, which is said to exist here in great purity. The tutelary divinities worshipped in various Buddhist countries are unknown, and the vows of poverty and chastity taken by the monks are said to be less frequently broken here than elsewhere. The Burmese possess a complete system of education, so far as male children are concerned. All boys are required to reside in a religious house for three years, and there they act as servants to the priests, who instruct them in reading, writing, and arithmetic, as well as the doctrines of their religion. The census of 1901 returned a population of 9,184,121, of whom 88.6 per cent were Buddhists, the density per square mile being 55, against 184 for India. Upward of 90 per cent of the population dwell in rural areas, and no tendency toward gravitation to the towns is observed. Although population has been steadily increasing in Burma the fact that an enormous tract of country not previously enumerated was now included in the census operations renders any comparison with the figures of 1891 misleading. Within Burma proper, however, an increase of over 19 per cent is found to have occurred, and a birth-rate of over 38 per mile compares not unfavorably with average European standards. Notwithstanding the fact that the social position of women is so assured in Burma and that there is no suspicion of the existence of female infanticide, women number only 962 in 1,000, against 1,006 and 1,022 in Bengal and Madras. But the explanation probably lies in the preponderance of the male element among the numerous immigrants into the province. Marriage in Burma is a purely secular ceremony, and elementary education is far more widely dispersed than in India, one individual in five being able to read and write.

History.— The Burmese empire is of little note in ancient or general history. Buddhism and civilization are said to have been introduced from India. The last native dynasty was founded by a Burmese called Alompra, a man of obscure birth, who defeated the Peguans, and in 1753 obtained possession of Ava. Having made himself master of Burma, he invaded Siam; but, during this invasion he died suddenly in 1760. Alompra ruled well and wisely, and Namdogee, his eldest son and successor, who died in 1764, inheriting his father's spirit, introduced various reforms and useful measures. Shembuan (Tshen-bo-yen), the emperor's brother, became regent as guardian for his nephew Momien; but he usurped the throne himself and conquered Siam. In 1771, however, Siam recovered its independence, while the principal part of the Burmese forces were engaged in a war with China. In this war they were victorious, and compelled the Chinese whom they took prisoners to intermarry with Burmese females, and to remain in their territory. In 1776 Shembuan left his empire, much enlarged, to his son, Chenguza. This prince lived in the unrestrained indulgence of every appetite till in 1782 he was dethroned and put to death. In consequence of the revolution, Mentaragyi, the fourth son of Alompra,

ascended the throne. He ordered his nephew, Momien, who was a state prisoner, to be drowned, and in 1783 subdued the kingdom of Arracan. He then engaged in a war with Siam, which continued till 1793, when peace was made on certain conditions. About this period, it happened that some robbers fled from the Burmese empire, and took refuge in the territory of the East India Company. The Burmese demanded that they should be delivered up, and on their demands not being immediately complied with, marched with a strong force into the offending country. At the same time they carried on a friendly negotiation with the government in Calcutta, which resulted in the surrender of the criminals, and the conclusion of a treaty of amity and commerce between the two governments, negotiated by Capt. Symes. The last victory of the Burmese was in 1822 over the province of Assam. The party driven from Assam, together with the Burmese rebels, fled to the British territories, whence they intended to invade Burma. The British government disarmed the insurgents, but refused to deliver them up or to drive them from the island of Shapuri, which they had occupied. At length the Burmese sovereign demanded of the government at Calcutta the cession of northern Bengal as being a part of Ava, and in January 1824 his forces marched into Cachar, which was under British protection. Lord Amherst, as governor-general of the British East Indies, now declared war against Burma, and Gen. Archibald Campbell prosecuted it so successfully that after the victory at Prome (1–3 Dec. 1825), he obliged the monarch to conclude a peace at Palanagh in 1825. As the treaty was not ratified on the part of the Burmese emperor by the time specified (18 Jan. 1826), Campbell renewed the war and stormed the fortress of Munnum. On 24 February the peace was ratified, and the war concluded with the cession of Arracan, Mergui, Tavoy, etc. In 1852 a second war broke out at the conclusion of which Rangoon and the whole of Pegu fell into the hands of the British. About 1860 the new city Mandalay supplanted Amarapura as the capital. In 1867 British steamers were permitted by treaty to navigate Burmese rivers, and not long after traffic was carried on up the Irrawadi as far as Bhamo. In 1885 the outrageous proceedings of King Theebaw provoked another war, and a British force proceeded from Rangoon up the Irrawadi River, took Mandalay, and sent King Theebaw a prisoner to Rangoon. On 1 Jan. 1886, Theebaw's dominions were annexed to the British empire by proclamation of the viceroy of India (the Earl of Dufferin). After the annexation there was a considerable amount of scattered fighting with dacoits and others, but the country is now comparatively quiet, is being opened up to commerce, and is rapidly advancing in prosperity. In 1897 Burma was constituted a province, and placed under a lieutenant-governor instead of a chief-commissioner.

Bibliography.— Spearman, 'British-Burma Gazetteer' (1880); Mason, 'Burma: Its People and Productions' (1882–3); Phayre, 'History of Burma' (1883); Geary, 'Burma After the Conquest' (1886); Smeaton, 'The Loyal Karen of Burma' (1886); Yoe, 'The Burman, His Life and Notions' (2d ed. 1896); Bird, 'Wanderings in Burma' (1897); Hart, 'Pic-

turesque Burma, Past and Present' (1897);
Ferrar, 'Burma' (1898); Harmer, 'The Story
of Burma' (1901).

Burmeister, Hermann, hĕr'män boor'mĭs-
tĕr, German scientific writer: b. Stralsund,
15 Jan. 1807; d. Buenos Ayres, Argentina, 2
May 1892. He distinguished himself as a geologist and zoologist in his native country, and
settled permanently in Argentina, where he con-
tinned his investigations. 'Manual of Entomol-
·ogy'; 'History of Creation' (1843); and 'The
Fossils of Horses Found Among the South
American Pampas' (1875), are among his
books.

Burmeister, Richard, German-American
musical composer: b. Hamburg, Germany, 7
Dec. 1860. He received an academical educa-
·tion in Hamburg; studied with Franz Liszt, and
in Rome, Budapest, and Weimar; made concert
tours in Europe in 1883–5 and in the winter of
1893; was at the head of the piano department
of Peabody Institute, Baltimore, Md., 1885–97;
·and settled in New York in the latter year. He
made concert tours all over the United States
and was director of the Scharwenka Conservatory, New York, in 1897-9. He has composed
'The Sisters' (a dramatic tone poem), numerous songs, and piano, violin, and orchestra
pieces; and arranged Liszt's 'Concerto Pathét-
ique,' originally for two pianos, for the piano
·and orchestra.

Bur'naby, Frederick Gustavus, English
·soldier and traveler: b. Bedford, England, 3
March 1842; d. 17 Jan. 1885. He was educated
·at Bedford and Harrow, and entered the Royal
Horse Guards in his 18th year as cornet. In
1861 he became lieutenant, in 1866 captain, major
in 1879, lieutenant-colonel in 1880 and finally,
in 1881, was appointed colonel, a rank which he
held till his death. In 1875 he made his famous
ride to Khiva — a journey that presented great
difficulties. During the ride, which he undertook partly because he had learned that the Russian government kept Europeans out of central Asia, he suffered severely from the intense
cold prevailing at the time when he crossed the
steppes. In 1876 he rode through Asiatic Turkey and Persia. Of both these journeys he published narratives, namely, 'Ride to Khiva'
(1876, 11th ed. 1877, new ed. 1884), and 'On
Horseback Through Asia Minor' (1877).
While serving as lieutenant-colonel of the Royal
Horse Guards in the Egyptian campaign, he
was killed at the battle of Abu-Klea.

Burnand', Sir Francis Cowley, English
author: b. 29 Nov. 1837. He was educated at
Eton and Trinity College, Cambridge, and at
first studied with a view to entering the Church
of England, but when in 1858 he became a Roman Catholic he devoted himself to legal
studies, and was called to the bar in 1862.
By that year he had already achieved some
success as a writer, and in consequence he seldom practised. After about a year's connection with 'Fun' he joined the staff of 'Punch'
in 1863, becoming editor in 1880. He resigned
this position 14 Feb. 1906. His book, 'Happy
Thoughts,' republished from 'Punch,' went
through several editions, and was followed by
'More Happy Thoughts' (1871); 'Happy
Thought Hall' (1872); 'Quito at Home'
(1890). Other successful productions of his

are the extravaganzas, 'New Light on Darkest
Africa,' and 'Ride to Khiva' (making fun out
of H. M. Stanley and Col. Burnaby respectively), the parody on Ouida's novel, 'Strath-
more,' which he published under the title of
'Strapmore,' and 'The Modern Sandford and
Merton.' Numerous plays have come from his
pen, mostly of the nature of burlesques and
light comedies, such as the plays 'Black-eyed
Susan' (a burlesque of Douglas Jerrold's
drama), and 'The Colonel.' In 1879 he issued
a history of the Amateur Dramatic Club, which
he had founded at Cambridge University. He
collaborated with Sir A. Sullivan in the light
operas 'The Chieftain,' produced in 1894, and
'Contrabandista.'

Burnap, George Washington, American
Unitarian clergyman: b. Merrimack, N. H.,
1802; d. 1859. He was graduated at Harvard
College in 1824, and in 1827 he was ordained
pastor of the First Independent Church in Baltimore, where he remained until his death. He
was a voluminous writer, his publications being
chiefly of a theological and controversial character. They include a doctrinal work on the
'Controversy Between Unitarians and Other
Denominations of Christians' (1835); 'Lectures
to Young Men'; 'Lectures on the Sphere and
Duties of Woman'; 'Lectures on the History
of Christianity'; 'Expository Lectures on the
Principal Texts of the Bible Which Relate to
the Doctrine of the Trinity'; and various other
works of theology, as well as numerous occa-
sioual addresses.

Burne-Jones, Sir Edward, English painter:
b. Birmingham, 28 Aug. 1833; d. London, 17
June, 1898. In 1852 he went to Exeter College,
Oxford, where he was a fellow student of William Morris, and afterward became acquainted
with A. C. Swinburne (who dedicated his
'Poems and Ballads' to him). His first intention was to enter the Church of England, and
it was not till he had reached his 22d year that
he seriously devoted himself to art studies;
but, going to London in 1855, he came under
the influence of D. G. Rossetti and the Pre-
Raphaelite movement, and soon attained consid-
crable success in various departments of artistic
work. In 1859 he set out on a journey through
Italy in order to see the productions of the early
Italian painters and sculptors, and on his return to England he gave in his stained-glass
designs and his pictures splendid promise of
his subsequent triumphs. In 1865 he began a
series of illustrations to Morris' 'Earthly Paradise,' and he also executed some 70 designs
for the 'Story of Cupid and Psyche,' besides
pictures dealing with the same subject. He was
elected a member of the Old Society of Painters
in Water Colors in 1864, but withdrew from it
in 1870, and from this year till 1877 scarcely
ever exhibited in London. In the Grosvenor
Gallery exhibition of the latter year, however,
his works formed the chief attraction. He received the Cross of the Legion of Honor in
1880, was elected in 1885 Associate of the Royal
Academy, a position which he resigned in 1893
(having only exhibited one picture at the Academy, 'The Depths of the Sea'), and he was
created a baronet in 1894. His most important
pictures are 'Day, Night'; 'Spring, Summer,
Autumn, Winter' (1867-8); 'The Wine of
Circe' (1869); 'Chant d'Amour' (1873); 'Be-

guiling of Merlin' (1877), an illustration of Tennyson's 'Merlin and Vivien'; 'Six Days of Creation' (1877); 'The Golden Stairs' (1880); 'The Wheel of Fortune' (1883); 'Wood Nymph'; 'King Cophetua' (1884); 'Laus Veneris'; 'The Depths of the Sea' (1886); and 'The Briar Rose' series (1890). He holds a specially high place as a designer for stained-glass windows, and in many other departments of decorative art. His leading characteristics as a painter are his fertile imagination and fine poetic feeling, qualities which no painter of the century has possessed in anything like the same degree. The Old-World dreaminess of his work is finely aided by his wonderful power as a colorist. In common with his friends, Morris and Rossetti, he exercised a most potent influence on Victorian art. See Bell, 'Edward Burne-Jones' (1902).

Burnes, SIR Alexander, Scottish soldier and traveler: b. Montrose, 1805; d. Cabul, 2 Nov. 1841. Having obtained a cadetship, he joined the Bombay native infantry in 1821. Here his proficiency in Hindustani and Persian procured him two regimental appointments as interpreter, and contributed greatly to his future promotion. In 1830 he was appointed to proceed to Lahore, ostensibly for the purpose of delivering a present of horses from the king of England to Runjeet Singh, but really for the purpose of acquainting himself with the lower Indus, with the view of opening it up to commercial enterprise. On returning from this mission, which he successfully accomplished, he proposed a mission into central Asia, and having obtained the sanction of the government, set out in January 1832, descended the Sutlej to Lahore, and proceeded thereafter to Peshawur, Cabul, and Bokhara. He afterward traveled with a caravan across the desert of Merv, visited the shah of Persia in his capital of Teheran, traveled southward to the Persian Gulf, and reached Bombay after a year's absence. He published an account of this journey in 1834, under the title of 'Travels into Bokhara.' He was afterward sent to England as the bearer of his own despatches, received the special thanks of the court of directors, and was presented with the gold medal of the Royal and the silver medal of the French Geographical Society. He returned to India in 1835, and in the following year was sent on a commercial mission to Cabul. While there he discovered that Russia was intriguing to detach the emir, Dost Mohammed, from the British alliance, and on finding the emir disposed to be friendly to Great Britain, he urged Lord Auckland to come to terms with him. His advice was, however, rejected, and a force was dispatched in 1839 to reinstate Shah Sujah on the throne. Burnes accompanied the force as second political officer, and received the honor of knighthood. On the breaking out of an insurrection in Cabul, he was murdered with his brother and several other Europeans.

Bur'net, Gilbert, British prelate and historian: b. Edinburgh, 18 Sept. 1643; d. London, 15 March 1715. Having graduated at Marischal College, Aberdeen, he zealously devoted himself to the study of law and divinity. In 1661 he qualified as a probationer in the Church, and traveled into Holland in 1664. On his return he was made Fellow of the Royal Society in London, and ordained to the living of Sal-

toun, Haddingtonshire, in 1665. In 1669 he was made a professor of divinity at Glasgow, where he published his 'Modest and Free Conference Between a Conformist and a Nonconformist,' and wrote his 'Memoirs of the Dukes of Hamilton' (1676); and was offered a Scottish bishopric, which he refused. His 'Vindication of the Authority, Constitution, and Laws of the Church and State of Scotland,' in which he maintains the cause of Episcopacy, was much approved of at court, and several bishoprics were successively offered him and refused. In 1673 he was made chaplain in ordinary to the king, and was in high credit both with Charles and the Duke of York. Removing to London he received the appointment of chaplain to the Rolls Chapel in 1675, and shortly afterward the lectureship at St. Clement's. The nation being alarmed on account of the progress of Catholicism, Burnet undertook a 'History of the Reformation in England.' He gave a first volume to the public in 1679, when the affair of the popish plot was in agitation. It procured for the author the unprecedented honor of thanks from both houses of Parliament. The second appeared in 1681; the third, which was supplementary, in 1714. The high character of Burnet as a divine caused him to be sent for by the witty and profligate Earl of Rochester, when, exhausted by a course of libertinism, he was sinking into the grave. The result of his conferences with the dying nobleman he gave to the world in his celebrated 'Account of the Life and Death of the Earl of Rochester.' About this time he wrote a letter to the king censuring his public misgovernment and private vices. His connection with the opposition party was now very intimate, and he attended Lord William Russell to the scaffold, when executed for his share in the Rye House plot. He published during this period several works in favor of liberty and Protestantism, and wrote the lives of Bishop Bedell and Sir Matthew Hale (1682); and in 1683 made his translation of More's 'Utopia.' On the accession of James he made a tour in France and Italy, and in 1687 he published an account of his travels in a series of letters to Robert Boyle. When at Utrecht he was invited to The Hague by the Prince and Princess of Orange, and had a great share in the councils relative to Britain. James caused a prosecution for high treason to be commenced against him in Scotland, and demanded his person from the states, who refused to deliver him up. In the revolution he took an active part, accompanying the Prince of Orange to England as chaplain, and was rewarded for his services by the bishopric of Salisbury. On taking his seat in the House of Lords, he displayed his usual moderation in regard to the non-juring clergy and dissenters. As a prelate, Bishop Burnet distinguished himself by fervor, assiduity, tolerance, and charity. In 1699 he published his 'Exposition of the Thirty-nine Articles.' The scheme for the augmentation of poor livings out of the first-fruits and tenths due to the Crown, known as Queen Anne's Bounty, originated with Burnet. He left behind him in manuscript his well-known 'History of His Own Times' (1723-34), upon which the best judgment to-day is that nothing could be more admirable than his general candor, his accuracy as to facts, the fullness of his information, and the

BURNE-JONES.

The Prioress's Tale.

justice of his judgments both of those whom he vehemently opposed and of those whom he greatly admired. The value of the work, says a recent authority, "as a candid narrative and an invaluable work of reference, has continually risen as investigations into original materials have proceeded."

Burnet, Jacob, American jurist: b. Newark, N. J., 22 Feb. 1770; d. Cincinnati, Ohio, 10 May 1853. Admitted to the bar in 1796, he removed to Cincinnati, then a village with about 500 inhabitants, and was a member of the territorial government from 1799 till the establishment of a State government in 1803. In 1821 he was appointed judge of the supreme court of Ohio, and was elected United States senator in 1828. Burnet was elected a member of the French Academy of Sciences upon the recommendation of Lafayette, and published in 1847 a volume of 'Notes on the Northwestern Territory.' He was prominent in civic enterprises in Cincinnati for over half a century, assisting to establish the Lancastrian Academy; helping to found the Cincinnati College, whose first president he was; besides being president of the Ohio Medical College, and the Cincinnati Colonization Society.

Burnet, John, Scottish engraver, painter and art-critic: b. Fisher-row, near Edinburgh, 20 March 1784; d. 1868. He learned etching and engraving, and with Sir William Allan and Sir David Wilkie, was a student in drawing and painting at the Trustees' Academy, Edinburgh. In 1806 he went to London, where he engraved Wilkie's 'Jew's Harp'; 'Blind Fiddler'; 'Rent Day'; 'Rabbit on the Wall'; 'Chelsea Pensioners Reading the Gazette of the Battle of Waterloo' (his largest and most elaborate work); 'Letter of Introduction'; 'Death of Tippoo Saib'; and 'Village School.' He also engraved plates from several recent painters, from the Rembrandts in the National Gallery, and from several of his own paintings. He published 'Practical Treatise on Painting' (1827); 'Rembrandt and His Works' (1849); 'Life and Works of J. W. M. Turner,' with Cunningham (1852).

Burnet, Thomas, English divine and philosopher: b. Croft, Yorkshire, about 1635; d. London, 27 Sept. 1715. He was educated under Dr. Ralph Cudworth at Cambridge, and afterward traveled as tutor to several young noblemen. In 1681 he made himself known by his 'Telluris Theoria Sacra,' which he subsequently translated into English. In 1685 he became master of the Charter-house, and after the revolution of 1688 was appointed chaplain in ordinary and clerk of the closet to King William. In 1692 he published 'Archæologia Philosophica, sive Doctrina antiqua de Rerum Originibus,' but the freedom of opinion displayed in this work led to the removal of the author from the clerkship of the royal closet. Two posthumous works of this author appeared in 1727 — the treatises 'De Fide et Officiis Christianorum'; 'De Statu Mortuorum et Resurgentium.' All the works of Burnet exhibit him as an ingenious speculator, rather than as a patient and sober inquirer concerning the moral and natural phenomena of which he treats. His great work, the 'Theory of the Earth,' is one of the many systems of cosmogony in which Christian philosophers have attempted to reconcile the Mo-

saic account of the creation, paradise, and the deluge, with the traditions of the ancients and the principles of modern science. His speculations are recommended by sublimity of description and eloquence of style. In his 'Archæologia Philosophica' he has combated the literal interpretation of the history of the fall of man; and to expose its improbability he has introduced an imaginary dialogue between Eve and the serpent, which, as coming from the pen of a divine, is singular enough. It is only to be found in the first edition of the work.

Burnet, William, American colonial governor: b. The Hague, Holland, 1688; d. 1729. He was a son of Gilbert Burnet (q.v.) and was appointed governor of New York and New Jersey in 1720. Two years later he founded at Oswego the earliest English trading post on the Great Lakes as the first step in his able Indian policy in New York which accomplished very much for the interests of the mother country and the colonies. In 1728 he was transferred to the governorship of Massachusetts and New Hampshire and was speedily involved in disputes with the Assembly of the former colony over the question of salary.

Burnet, the popular name of two genera of plants, both of which belong to the natural order Rosaceæ. (1) Garden Burnet (Poterium sanguisorba), a perennial plant which grows to the height of about two feet; leaves smooth, alternate, imparipinnate, composed of serrate leaflets; flowers arranged in rounded heads of a purplish color, with the female flowers above and the male flowers below. It is found wild in sunny places among rocks and in open fields, from New York to Maryland. It is cultivated in kitchen gardens for its aromatic leaves, which are used to season salads. It is also an excellent food for cattle. (2) Canadian Burnet (P. canadense) is also a perennial plant; calyx in four divisions; stamens, four; its stem is straight, from three to six feet in height; leaflets ovate, smooth. This plant grows chiefly in bogs and wet places from Newfoundland to Georgia, and west to Michigan.

Burnet Moth, the name for the genus of hawkmoths, called Anthrocera, or, by some Zygæna. Anthrocera filipendulæ is the six-spot burnet moth. The six spots, which are on the superior wings, are red, while the rest of the wings are green. Its caterpillar, which feeds on the plantain, trefoil, dandelion, etc., is yellow, spotted with black. A. loti is the five-spot burnet moth. It is less common. The caterpillar feeds on honeysuckle, bird's foot, trefoil, etc.

Burnett', Frances Eliza Hodgson, Anglo-American novelist: b. Manchester, England, 24 Nov. 1849. In 1865 she went to Tennessee with her parents, and there married in 1873 Dr. S. M. Burnett. Divorced from him in 1898 she married in 1900 Stephen Townsend, an English writer. Her first conspicuous literary success was 'That Lass o' Lowrie's,' a story of collier life in her native county, which appeared originally in 'Scribner's Magazine,' and in book form in 1877. Her other works, which usually appeared first in serial form, include 'Theo, a Love Story' (1877); 'Kathleen Mavourneen' (1879); 'Haworth's, a Novel' (1879); 'Louisiana' (1880); 'A Fair Barbarian' (1881); 'Esmeralda,' a play (1881); 'Through One Administration' (1883); 'Little Lord Fauntleroy,' a story of child-life, which has had very great success both as novel and as drama (1886); 'Sara Crewe' (1888); 'Little Saint Elizabeth' (1889); 'Two Little Pilgrims' Progress' (1895); 'A Lady of Quality' (1896); 'His Grace of Ormonde' (1897); 'The Captain's Youngest' (1898); 'In Connection with the De Willoughby Claim' (1899); 'The Making of a Marchioness' (1901); 'The Little Unfairy Princess' (1903). Mrs. Burnett's work shows great versatility in the creation of character, and has but little of the sensational element.

Bur'nett, James (LORD MONBODDO), Scottish judge: b. at the family seat of Monboddo, in Kincardineshire, 1714; d. Edinburgh, 26 May 1799. After studying at Aberdeen and Edinburgh he went to the University of Groningen, whence he returned in 1737, and commenced practice as an advocate at the Scottish bar. In 1767 he was raised to the bench on the decease of his relative, Lord Milton. He distinguished himself by his writings as a metaphysician, having published a work on the 'Origin and Progress of Language' (1773–92), and 'Ancient Metaphysics' (1779–99, six volumes). Lord Monboddo was an enthusiastic admirer of ancient literature, and especially of the works of Plato and other Grecian philosophers. His works contain many interesting observations, but also exhibit some strange and paradoxical opinions. Thus he seriously advocates the existence of satyrs and mermaids, and has advanced some whimsical speculations relative to the affinity between the human race and the monkey tribe, which exposed him to a good deal of ridicule on the first publication of his theories. Both his official and his private character were extremely respectable; and he was, notwithstanding some eccentricities, a man of learning and ability.

Burnett, Peter Hardeman, American pioneer and writer: b. Tennessee, 1807; d. 1895. In early life he removed to Missouri and thence to Oregon, where he assisted in establishing a territorial government and sat for two terms in the legislature. He was one of the first of the gold hunters in California in 1848, and actively advocated organization of civil government without delaying for action of Congress. When the new constitution was adopted he was elected governor, resigning in 1851. He was judge of the supreme court, 1857–8, and president of the Pacific Bank of San Francisco, 1863–80. He published 'The Path Which Led a Protestant Lawyer to the Catholic Church' (1860); 'The American Theory of Government Considered with Reference to the Present Crisis' (1861); 'Recollections of an Old Pioneer' (1878); 'Reasons Why We Should Believe in God, Love God, and Obey God' (1884).

Burnett Prizes, two prizes established by John Burnett, merchant of Aberdeen, on his death in 1784. He left a fund from which were to be given every 40 years two theological prizes (not less than $6,000 and $2,000) for the best two essays in favor of the evidence that there is an all-powerful, wise, and good Being, and this independent of all revelation. The first competition was in 1815, when Dr. Brown, principal of Aberdeen University, gained the first prize, and Dr. John Bird Sumner, afterward archbishop of Canterbury, the second. In 1855 the first prize was adjudged to the Rev. R. A. Thompson, Lincolnshire, and the second prize to the Rev. Dr. John Tulloch, afterward principal of St. Mary's College, St. Andrews. The destination of the fund was applied by Parliament in 1883 to the establishment of a lectureship on natural theology in the University of Aberdeen.

Bur'ney, Charles, English composer and writer on music: b. Shrewsbury, 12 April 1726; d. Chelsea, London, 12 April 1814. He studied music under the organist of Chester Cathedral there, and at Shrewsbury, under the direction of his half-brother, an organist, and afterward in London between 1744 and 1747, under Dr. Arne. In 1751 he obtained the place of organist at Saint Margaret's Church, Lynn Regis, in Norfolk. Here he commenced his 'General History of Music.' In 1760 he returned to London, where his compositions and the musical skill of his eldest daughter, then eight years of age, excited admiration. In 1769 he took the degree of doctor of music at Oxford. In 1770 he visited France and Italy, and two years afterward, the Netherlands and Germany, for the sake of his great work. He published accounts of both tours. After his second return he became a Fellow of the Royal Society. In 1776 appeared the first volume of his 'General History of Music from the Earliest Ages to the Present Period' (4to), the second in 1782, and the third and fourth in 1789. He was the author of several other valuable works, among which are the 'Memoir of Handel,' and a 'Life of Metastasio.' He died in the office of organist at Chelsea Hospital, and in receipt of a pension of $1,500. He wrote most of the musical articles in Rees' Cyclopedia. His second daughter, Frances or Fanny (Madame d'Arblay, q.v.), well known as an authoress, published a memoir of her father.

Burney, Charles, English classical scholar and critic, son of Charles Burney (1726–1814, q.v.): b. Lynn, Norfolk, 4 Dec. 1757; d. 28 Dec. 1817. He received his education at the Charter-house School, at Caius College, Cambridge, and King's College, Aberdeen, where he took the degree of M.A. He carried on a private school, distinguished himself as a writer in the 'Monthly Review' and the 'London Magazine,' to which he contributed many articles on classical literature; subsequently entered into holy orders, and obtained some preferment in the Church. His valuable collection of books, many of them enriched with manuscript notes, was purchased by Parliament for the British Museum.

Burney, Frances. See D'ARBLAY, MADAME.

Burn'ham, Clara Louise (ROOT), American novelist: b. Newton, Mass., 25 May 1854. She is the daughter of George F. Root (q.v.), and has lived in Chicago since childhood. Her novels include 'No Gentleman' (1881); 'A Sane Lunatic' (1882); 'Dearly Bought' (1884); 'Next Door' (1886); 'Young Maids and Old' (1888); 'The Mistress of Beech Knoll' (1890); 'Miss Bagg's Secretary' (1892); 'Dr. Latimer' (1893); 'Sweet Clover, a Romance of the White City' (1894); 'The Wise Woman' (1895); 'Miss Archer Archer'

(1897); 'A Great Love' (1898); 'A West Point Wooing' (1899); 'A Right Princess' (1902). She has also written libretti for her father's cantatas.

Burnham, Daniel Hudson, American architect: b. Henderson, N. Y., 4 Sept. 1846. He studied architecture in Chicago and designed notable structures there, including the Rookery, Calumet Club, the Temple, Masonic Temple, and the great Northern Hotel, as well as Ellicott Square, Buffalo, and large buildings in other cities. He was director of works at the Chicago World's Fair.

Burnham, Sherburne Wesley, American astronomer: b. Thetford, Vt., 1838. He started in life as a stenographer, and became a clerk in the United States Circuit Court, northern district of Illinois. He took up astronomy as an amateur, and, in 1876, became connected with the Chicago Observatory, and later with the Lick Observatory, receiving also an appointment as professor of practical astronomy at the University of Chicago. He has made notable discoveries of double stars, having catalogued 1,274 new ones. In 1874 he was made a Fellow of the Royal Astronomical Society of England, receiving its gold medal in 1894 for his discovery and measurement of double stars.

Burnham Beeches, the fragment of an ancient forest in Buckinghamshire. It is situated some 25 miles northwest of London, and is famous for its enormous beech trees. Since 1883 the Burnham Beeches tract of 374 acres has been open to the public as a park by the Corporation of London.

Burning-bush, or **Waahoo,** a tall shrub (*Euonymus atropurpureus*) of the natural order *Celastraceæ* with oval-oblong leaves, and purple flowers occurring in fours. It is common throughout the middle west from New York to Wisconsin and Nebraska, and southward. It is sometimes cultivated for the ornamental effect of its long drooping peduncles of crimson fruit.

Burning-glass, a lens which readily brings the rays of light that fall upon it to a focus so as to cause them to kindle any combustible matter on which they are directed. The lenses commonly used as burning-glasses are convex on both sides. If a second lens, of a smaller focal distance, is placed between the first and its focus, so as to intercept the rays which pass through the first, the effect is greatly augmented. Glasses of this kind have been made with a diameter of two or three feet. Several accidents in modern times have shown that conflagrations may be caused by convex water-bottles, etc., which have the form of burning-glasses, if the rays of the sun are concentrated by them upon combustible substances lying within their reach. Burning mirrors or reflectors with a smoothly polished surface which reflects the rays of the sun and brings them to a focus may be used like burning-glasses. Spherical mirrors of this kind are the most common, but parabolic ones are the most suitable. The ancients were acquainted with such mirrors, and, as is well known, Archimedes, during the siege of Syracuse by Marcellus, is said to have set on fire the fleet of the latter by means of mirrors. Buffon in 1747, by means of a compound mirror formed of a combination of plane mirrors, set on fire, almost instantaneously, a piece of beech wood covered with tar, at the distance of 66 feet; and with a stronger combination he afterward burned wood at the distance of 200 feet, melted tin at the distance of 150, lead at the distance of 130, and silver at the distance of 60 feet.

Bur'nisher, a blunt, smooth tool, used for smoothing and polishing a rough surface by pressure, and not by removing any part of the body. Other processes of polishing detach the little asperities. Agates, tempered steel, and dogs' teeth are used for burnishing. It is one of the most expeditious methods of polishing, and one which gives the highest lustre. The burnishers used by engravers are formed to burnish with one end and to erase blemishes with the other.

Burn'ley, England, a parliamentary county, and municipal borough in Lancashire, about 22 miles north of Manchester, situated on the small river Brun, near its confluence with the Calder. The town presents a modern appearance, and is, generally speaking, well built, mostly of stone. The town-hall is a large, handsome building, erected in 1887; there is also a commodious exchange, and a convenient market hall. Among the churches the chief place is due to St. Peter's, an ancient building modernized. The churches of St. James, St. Paul, and St. Andrew are all very modern structures; and there are numerous other places of worship. There are board and other schools; an ancient grammar school with modern scientific departments; mechanics' institute and technical school; public baths; and a Victoria Hospital. Burnley owns its gas, water, and electric works, public markets, and abattoirs, deriving considerable income from each. The manufactures and commerce of Burnley have rapidly increased in recent years. The staple manufacture is cotton goods, and there are large cotton-mills, worsted-mills, and several extensive foundries and machine-shops, with collieries, quarries, and other works in the vicinity. Burnley is situated on the Leeds and Liverpool Canal, has a good water supply, and has five railway stations. It seems to have been a Roman station, and various Roman remains have been dug up in and around it. Burnley was made a parliamentary borough with one member in 1867. Pop. (1901) 97,000.

Burnoose, bér-noos', a large kind of mantle in use among the Bedouin Arabs and the Berbers of northern Africa, commonly made of white or undyed wool, but sometimes also of red, blue, green, or some other color, and having a hood which may be drawn over the head in case of rain. In Spain also a similar garment is worn which bears the similar name of albornoz, and the name has also been applied to different kinds of upper garments worn by women of other European countries.

Burnouf, Emil Louis, á-mĕl loo-ē búr-noof, French Orientalist, cousin of Eugène Burnouf (q.v.): b. Valognes, Manche, 25 Aug. 1821. After a normal-school training, he became professor of ancient literature in the faculty of Nancy, and in 1867 director of the French School in Athens. Among his works are: 'Essay on the Veda' (1863); 'Sanskrit-French Dictionary'; 'History of Greek Literature'; 'Science of Religions'; 'The Athenian Legend'; 'The Mythology of the Japanese'; 'The City and the Acropolis of Athens'; and

'Contemporary Catholicism' (1879). He also edited the letters of his cousin, Eugène Burnouf.

Burnouf, Eugène, ė-zhăn, French Orientalist: b. Paris, 12 Aug. 1801; d. there, 28 May 1852. He commenced his studies at the College of Louis-le-Grand, became a pupil in the École des Chartes in 1822, passed as a lawyer in 1824, and soon after devoted himself to the study of Oriental languages. In 1826 he attracted the attention of men of learning throughout Europe by publishing, in conjunction with his friend, Lassen, an 'Essay on the Pali,' or the sacred language of the Buddhists in Ceylon and the Eastern Peninsula, and in 1827 by furnishing an explanatory text to the series of lithographic plates prepared by Geringer and Chabrelle to illustrate the religion, manners, customs, etc., of the Hindu nations inhabiting the French possessions in India. This work was not completed till 1835. In 1832 he was admitted into the Academy of Inscriptions, and in the same year was appointed to the professorship of Sanskrit in the Collége de France, an office which he held till his death. His fame is chiefly due to his having, so to speak, restored to life an entire language, the Zend or old Persian language in which the Zoroastrian writings were composed. Anquetil-Duperron had obtained the text of the extant works of this sacred language of the Persians. It is the glory of Burnouf to have interpreted those works with the aid of the Sanskrit. To this part of his labors belong his 'Extrait d'un Commentaire et d'une Traduction nouvelle du Vendidad-Sadé (1830); 'Observations sur la Grammaire de M. Bopp' (1833); 'Commentaire sur le Yaçna' (1833–5). Burnouf also distinguished himself by his labors on Buddhism. On this subject he published the text accompanied by a translation of the 'Bhâgavata Purâna' (1840–7); 'Introduction à l'Histoire du Bouddhisme Indien' (1st vol. 1844), etc. A fortnight before his death the Academy of Inscriptions elected him secretary for life.

Burns, Alexander, Canadian educator: b. Castlewellan, Ireland, 12 Aug. 1834; d. 22 May 1900. He went to Canada in 1847, and was graduated at Victoria College, Toronto, in 1861, joining the Methodist Church. From 1868 to 1878 he was president of Wesleyan Ladies' College, Hamilton, Ontario. He was tried for heresy by the Ontario Methodist Conference in 1882, but acquitted.

Burns, Anthony, American fugitive slave: b. Virgina, about 1830; d. Saint Catherine's, Ontario, 27 July 1862. Escaping from slavery he worked in Boston during the winter of 1853–4; but on 24 May 1854 — the day after the repeal of the Missouri Compromise and the passing of the Kansas-Nebraska Bill had inflamed the North against the slave power — was arrested on warrant of Charles F. Suttle through his agent Brent. The next day he was taken before United States Commissioner Edward G. Loring for examination; but Wendell Phillips and Theodore Parker secured an adjournment for two days. Burns, meanwhile, was confined in the court-house under a strong guard, and on the evening of the 26th a great mass meeting in protest was held at Faneuil Hall. T. W. Higginson and others had planned to stampede the meeting into storming the court-house and rescuing Burns, and at the appointed time battered in a door and attempted the rescue themselves, relying upon assistance in their undertaking. The size of the meeting, however, prevented the signals from working well and the leaders from emerging, and after a scuffle in which a deputy was fatally stabbed and several assailants wounded, the latter retired. The next day Loring, an ardent upholder of the Fugitive Slave law, delivered Burns to his claimant on evidence entirely illegal and worthless even under that law. Escorted by a strong military guard Burns was taken to a government cutter, through streets draped in mourning and crowds ready to stone the soldiers. A riot at the wharf was only prevented by the action of Rev. Daniel Foster upon his saying "Let us pray!" The crowd uncovered and stood quiet while Burns was taken on board. Indictments were drawn against his would-be rescuers, but quashed for want of evidence. Burns afterward gained his liberty, studied theology at Oberlin College, and was eventually settled over a Baptist colored church in Saint Catherines, Ontario, where he died. Consult: Stevens, 'Anthony Burns: a History' (1856); Adams, 'Richard Henry Dana: a Biography' (1891); Higginson, 'Cheerful Yesterdays' (1898).

Burns, John, English labor organizer and Socialist leader: b. London, October 1858. He was of humble birth and became a factory employee at the age of 10. He was an omnivorous reader and imbibed his socialistic views from a French fellow laborer. By working a year as engineer on the Niger River, he earned enough for a six months' tour of Europe. He constantly addressed audiences of workingmen, and was a persistent labor agitator. He was one of the leaders in the West End riot in London, February 1887, and was imprisoned the same year for maintaining the right of public meeting in Trafalgar Square. He has been thrice elected to the London county council and has sat in the House of Commons as member of Battersea since 1892. In 1905 he became President of the Local Government Board.

Burns, Robert, Scottish poet: b. near Ayr, Scotland, 25 January 1759; d., Dumfries, 21 July 1796. His father, William Burnes or Burness, a native of Kincardineshire, had been a gardener; but at the time of the poet's birth was a nurseryman on a small piece of land on the banks of the Doon in Ayrshire. He was a man of strong intelligence and deep piety, but unsuccessful in his struggle with poverty. His mother was Agnes Brown, a woman of ability, and, though of meagre book education, well-versed in folk-song and legend. Robert, the eldest of seven children, went to school for three years, 1765-68, under John Murdoch in the neighboring village of Alloway. Later he was in attendance for a few months each at Dalrymple parish school in 1772, at Ayr Academy in 1773, and at Kirkoswald about 1776; but the more important part of his education he received from his father and his own reading. In 1766 William Burness had borrowed money to rent the farm of Mount Oliphant; and the future poet by the time he was sixteen was doing a man's work, overstraining his immature physique in performing his share in the vain effort of the family to keep its head above water. The scene of the struggle was moved

ROBERT BURNS

in 1777 to Lochlea, about ten miles distant, where in 1784 his father died. During the Lochlea period, Burns, ambitious to improve his position, went to the neighboring town of Irvine to learn flax-dressing. Nothing came of this move; but while resident there he formed that acquaintance with a dissipated sailor to which he himself ascribed the beginning of his licentious adventures. On his father's death, Robert and his brother Gilbert rented the farm of Mossgiel, but this experiment was no more successful than those previously made. While here he contracted an intimacy with Jean Armour, which brought upon him the censure of the Kirk-session. Finally the poet, disheartened by successive bad harvests and irritated by the attempts of his father-in-law to cancel his irregular marriage with Jean and to hand him over to the law, determined to emigrate. For ten years he had been composing verses. some of which had brought him considerable local fame, and these he collected and published in order to raise money for the voyage; but the unexpected success of this volume (Kilmarnock 1786) roused his literary ambition, gave him fresh courage, and led him to change his plans. Instead of sailing for the West Indies, he went to Edinburgh in November 1786, and during that winter was the literary lion of the season. Here he met such celebrities as Dugald Stewart. the philosopher; Blair, the rhetorician; Henry Mackenzie. the author of 'The Man of Feeling'; Lord Glencairn; the Duchess of Gordon; and Creech, the publisher. The last-named undertook an enlarged edition of his poems (Edinburgh 1787); and while waiting for the profits of this volume, Burns made several tours through the country, traces of which are to be found in a number of occasional poems. Creech finally paid him enough to enable him to give substantial help to his brother in Mossgiel, and to rent and stock the farm of Ellisland in Dumfriesshire. Hither in 1788 he brought Jean Armour, to whom he was now regularly married, his success and fame having reconciled her parents to the match; and for three years he tried farming. But failure still dogged him, and in 1791 he moved to Dumfries. where he lived on a position in the excise service which he had obtained while still at Ellisland through the influence of some of the powerful acquaintances he had made in Edinburgh. He had, however, lost heart; and after a few years of drudgery, varied with the drinking bouts to which he was constantly tempted both by habit and by the invitation of foolish admirers, he died at Dumfries in his 38th year.

Biographies of Burns have frequently been crowded with attempts to disentangle or to explain away the facts of his numerous amours. There is much controversy over the identity of the semi-mythical Mary Campbell. the "Highland Mary" of the songs; much curiosity over the precise degree of Platonism in his feeling for Mrs. McLehose, the "Clarinda" of his letters, and the inspirer of a number of lyrics; much difference of opinion as to whether and how long he was in love with his wife. Into these details we do not enter. It is clear enough that Burns was a man of exceptionally powerful passions, that the extreme and depressing hardships of his youth. and, indeed, of the greater part of his life, along with his natural tenden-

cies to conviviality, drove him to excesses or self-indulgence; and that while he strove often and painfully after better things, his striving was many times without avail. "The sport," he calls himself, "the miserable victim of rebellious pride, hypochondriac imagination, agonizing sensibility and bedlam passions." These phrases are true enough, though they do not imply the further explanation of his pitiful career that is found in the habits of his class and time, and the untoward nature of his environment.

Something of his education has already been indicated. His schooling left him with a good grammatical knowledge of English, and a reading knowledge of French. His father's care and his own eagerness gave him no slight knowledge of literature; and among other authors we know that he read. of older literature, the Bible, Shakespeare, Spenser, Jonson, Bunyan, Dryden, Locke, Molière, Wycherley; of his own century, Addison, Steele, and Pope; Ramsay, Fergusson, Thomson, and Beattie; Fielding, Smollett, Sterne. and Mackenzie; Shenstone, Gray. and Goldsmith; Hume, Robertson, and Adam Smith; and a number of philosophical and theological works. This list is by no means complete, but it is sufficient to correct the impression that Burns's was an "untutored Muse."

The literary influences apparent in the work of Burns are of two main classes: English and Scottish. So far as he fell under the former of these he was an inferior poet of the school of Pope, an ardent admirer and imitator of such minor master as Shenstone. In this field his critical judgment was never more than commonplace, and his imitations never first-rate. Almost all his greatest work was done in his native dialect, and here he is the heir, as well as the last great representative, of an ancient national tradition. Previous to the 17th century there existed a Scottish literature of considerable variety and distinction, produced in part under the patronage of the court. But the Reformation and the Union of the Crowns of England and Scotland resulted in the disuse of the vernacular for dignified and courtly writing, and it rapidly lost social prestige. until as a literary medium it survived only in the songs of the peasantry and in an occasional piece of satire. The 18th century, however, saw a revival of interest in purely Scottish letters, and the publication of such compilations as Watson's 'Choice Collection of Comic and Serious Scots Poems' (1706-9-11), and Allan Ramsay's 'Evergreen' (1724) and 'Tea-Table Miscellany' (1724-27) was the result of an impulse that showed itself also in renewed attempts to compose in dialect. Among the most important leaders in this movement were William Hamilton of Gilbertfield (who modernized the 15th century poem on Wallace), Allan Ramsay, and Robert Fergusson; and each of these had a share in inspiring Burns to work in that field in which he achieved his greatest triumphs. Their influence was both general and particular. They showed him by their own success what could be done in the native idiom; and they gave him models of which he was not slow to avail himself. Many of Burns's best known poems are all but imitations of productions. usually inferior, by Ramsay and Fergusson, and to them and their poetical ancestors he was indebted not only for suggestions as to theme and method of treatment, but also for his most characteristic verse-forms. This readiness on the part of Burns to accept from his predecessors all that they had to give, and to seek to maintain loyally a national tradition rather than to strive after mere novelty, has much to do with his success in carrying that tradition to its highest pitch, and in becoming, in a sense almost unique, the poet of his people.

The first kind of poetry which Burns thoroughly mastered was satire; and the most important of his successful efforts in this form, 'The Twa Herds, or The Holy Tulzie,' 'Holy Willie's Prayer,' The 'Address to the Unco Guid.' 'The Holy Fair,' and the 'Address to the Deil,' were all written within less than a year (1785-6). Whatever Burns's feelings may have been about what he suffered in his own person from the discipline of the Kirk, it is clear that the impulse that gave these poems their fire and their influence was something much larger than mere personal grudge. Against the narrow dogma and tyrannical conduct of the so-called "Auld Licht" party in the Scottish Church, there had sprung up the "New Lichts," demanding some relaxation of Calvinistic bonds and preaching charity and tolerance. Though not a member of this or any ecclesiastical faction, Burns sympathized strongly with their protest; and the shafts of his satire were directed against both the doctrines of the orthodox party and their local leaders. For some time after the Reformation the Scottish people seem to have submitted willingly to the rigorous domination of the Presbyterian ministers; but, after the struggle against Rome and the persecutions of the Covenanting times had alike become matters of history, there began to appear a more critical attitude towards their spiritual leaders. The revolt against authority that spread throughout Europe in the latter part of the 18th century manifested itself in Scotland in a growing disposition to demand greater individual liberty in matters of conduct and belief. It was this disposition that Burns voiced in his satires, local conditions determining the precise direction of his attack. The substantial justice of his cause, the sharpness of his wit, the vigor of his invective, and the imaginative fervor of his verse, all combined to bring the matter home to his countrymen; and he is here to be reckoned a great liberating force.

Several of the satires were published in the Kilmarnock volume, and along with them a variety of other kinds of poetry. In the words of his Preface, "he sings the sentiments and manners he felt and saw in himself and his rustic compeers around him." Some of these are descriptive of sides of humble Scots life with which he himself was in the closest contact. 'The Twa Dogs' gives a democratic peasant's view of the lives of lairds and farmers; and the sketch of the factor in this poem has been taken as a reminiscence of what his father had to endure from the arrogance of such an agent. 'The Cotter's Saturday Night' describes with affectionate reverence the order of his father's house; 'Puir Mailie,' 'The Auld Mare Maggie,' 'To a Mouse,' and others, reveal the kindliness of the poet's heart in his relation to animals; 'Hallowe'en' gives a vivid picture of rustic

mirth and manners, and preserves a mass of folk-lore. Of the additional poems that appeared in the Edinburgh editions the most notable was 'Tam o' Shanter,' Burns's best sustained piece of narrative, a poem that indicates that, had he worked this vein farther, he might have ranked with Chaucer as a teller of tales in verse.

A large quantity of Burns's poetry remained in MS. at the time of his death. Of this, much the most remarkable is 'The Jolly Beggars,' in the opinion of many his most brilliant production. This cantata carries to its highest point the far-descended literature of the rogue and the beggar, and its superb spirit and abandon show how heartily the poet could sympathize with the very dregs of society. It is to be noted that, alone among pieces that reach his highest level, it is chiefly in English. Burns wrote besides a large number of Epistles, Epigrams, Epitaphs, and other personal and occasional verse, the quality and interest of which vary much, but throughout which one constantly finds phrases and stanzas of superb quality. He came to write verse with great ease; but the result of the training he gave himself in artistic discrimination was to check mere fluency, and to lead him to discard much that was of inferior value in his improvisations. Thus the proportion of his work possessed of real poetic distinction is very high.

But the national importance of Burns, though increased by his influence upon the liberalizing movements of his time, and by his vital descriptions and characterizations of the peasant life of the Scotland of his time, is based chiefly on his songs. The period of Presbyterian despotism already referred to had forced the lyric Muse of Scotland into low company, and as a result Burns found Scottish song still pure and fine in melody, but hopelessly degraded in point of both poetry and decency. From youth he had been interested in collecting the sordid fragments he heard sung in cottage and tavern, or found printed in broadsides and chap-books; and the resuscitation of this all-but-lost national heritage came to be regarded by him in the light of a vocation. Two points are especially to be noted about his song-making: first, that almost all sprang from real emotional experiences; second, that almost all were composed to a previously existing melody. He had begun the composing of love-songs while still almost a boy, and he continued it to the end. During his visit to Edinburgh in 1786-7, he formed a connection with the editor of Johnson's 'Musical Museum,' and for this publication he undertook to supply material. Few of the traditional songs were such as could appear in a reputable volume, and Burns's task was to make them over into presentable form. Sometimes he retained a stanza or two, sometimes only a line or refrain, sometimes merely the name of the melody: the rest was his own. His method was to familiarize himself with the traditional air, to catch a suggestion from some stanza or phrase of the old song, to fix upon an idea or situation for the new poem; then, humming or whistling the melody about the fields or the farmyard, as imagination and emotion warmed within him, he worked out the new verses, coming into the house to write them down when the inspiration began to flag. Careful consideration of this process, for the reality of which we have his own authority as well as the evidence of the raw material and the finished product, will explain much of the precise quality and function of Burns as a song-writer. In George Thomson's collection of 'Scottish Airs' he had a share similar to that in Johnson's undertaking, his work for these two publications constituting the greater part of his poetical activity during the last eight or nine years of his life. It was characteristic that, in spite of his financial stringency during these years, he refused to accept any recompense, pre-ferring to regard this as a patriotic service. And a patriotic service it was of no small magnitude. By birth and temperament he was singularly fitted for just such a task, and his fitness is proved not only by the impossibility of separat-ing, by a mere examination of the finished songs, the new from the old, but by the unique extent to which his productions were accepted by his countrymen, and have passed into the life and feeling of his race.

Bibliography.—The early collected editions of the works of Burns are now superseded, and the material first published by Currie, Allan Cun-ningham, Hogg, and Motherwell. has been in-corporated in more modern editions. In the 'Life and Work,' ed. by R. Chambers and rev. by W. Wallace (4 vols., Lond. and N. Y. 1896), the writings are incorporated in the life in chronological order, and Wallace has made many additions and corrections. 'The Cen-tenary Burns,' ed. by W. E. Henley and T. F. Henderson (4 vols., Edin. and Bost. 1896-97, also cheaper, on small paper, 1901), contains a mass of bibliographical and textual matter, and is essential for a study of the text and sources. Other good editions are those of W. Scott Doug-las (6 vols., Edin. 1877-79; and 3 vols., Edin. 1893) which have good notes; "Globe" edition, ed. Alex. Smith, containing poems, songs, and letters in one volume; of the poems and songs only, the third "Aldine," ed. by Sir Harris Nicholas, rev. by G. A. Aitken (3 vols., Lond. 1893); the "Cambridge" (Bost. 1897) containing the text, introductory essay, and some of the notes of the "Centenary" ed. by A. H. Lang and W. A. Craigie (1 vol., N. Y. 1896). The main source for the life is the letters and poems. To the letters contained in the larger editions already named should be added the cor-respondence between 'Robert Burns and Mrs. F. A. Dunlop,' ed. by W. Wallace (Lond. 1898). The most authoritative life is that in the Cham-bers-Wallace edition; that in French by Aug. Angellier (2 vols., Paris 1893) is scholarly and sympathetic; that by J. G. Lockhart (rev. by W. S. Douglas, Lond. 1882) called forth Carlyle's famous review; that by J. C. Sharp (E. M. L. series, Lond. 1879) was the occasion of a notable essay by R. L. Stevenson, but is itself narrow and limited in sympathy; that by J. S. Blackie (Great Writers series. Lond. 1888) has a good bibliography by J. P. Anderson.

WILLIAM A. NEILSON,
Professor of English, Harvard University.

Burns, William Wallace, American soldier: b. Coshocton, Ohio. 3 Sept. 1825; d. Beaufort, S. C., 19 April 1892. He was graduated from West Point in 1847. He served in the war with Mexico. and also in the Union army dur-ing the Civil War, becoming major-general of

volunteers. In 1865 he was brevetted briga-dier-general and was for many years afterward in the Commissary Department at Washington.

Burns and Scalds, injuries produced by the application of excessive heat to the human body. They are generally dangerous in pro-portion to the extent of surface they cover, and a widespread scald may cause serious consequences on account of the nervous shock. Congestion of the brain, pneumonia, inflamma-tion of the bowels, or lock-jaw may result from an extensive burn. Hence the treatment re-quires to be both local and constitutional. If there is shivering or exhaustion, hot brandy and water may be given with good effect, and if there is much pain, a sedative solution of opium. The local treatment consists in dredging the burn with fine flour and then wrapping it up in cotton-wool. An application of equal quan-tities of olive oil and lime water, called carron oil, is much recommended by some, the part being afterward covered with cotton. The main thing is to keep the air from the injured part, and therefore, when a blister forms. although it may be pricked, the loose skin should not be removed.

Burnside, Ambrose Everett, American soldier: b. Liberty, Ind., 23 May 1824; d. Bris-tol, R. I., 13 Sept. 1881. He served an appren-ticeship to a tailor, but received a nomination to West Point, where he graduated in 1847. After serving some years in garrison duty he left the army as first lieutenant in 1852 and from 1853 until 1858 was engaged in the manufacture of firearms at Bristol, R. I., during this period, in 1856, inventing the Burnside breech-loading rifle. Upon the outbreak of the Civil War (q.v.) in 1861 he returned to the army as colonel of volunteers, serving from May to August of that year as Colonel of the Rhode Island volunteers, and as such taking part in the first battle of Bull Run (q.v.). On 6 August he was promoted brigadier-general of volunteers and from October 1861 to January 1862 supervised the organization of the "Coast Division" of the Army of the Potomac. From January to July 1862 he commanded the De-partment of North Carolina; in February captured Roanoke Island, occupied Newbern, N. C., and took Fort Macon, Beaufort. He was raised to the rank of Major-general of volun-teers on 18 March 1862 and placed in command of the troops that subsequently constituted the Ninth Army Corps. In July 1862 and again after the second battle of Bull Run (q.v.) he was offered the command of the Army of Vir-ginia which. after the battle of Bull Run, had been merged into the Army of the Potomac, but each time declined the offer and served with the Ninth Army Corps under McClellan. In this capacity he participated in the Maryland cam-paign (q.v.) against Lee, rendering important services in the battles of South Mountain and Antietam (qq.v.), in the latter action on 17 September commanding the left wing. On 10. November of that year he superseded Gen. McClellan in command of the Army of the Potomac. On 13 December he crossed the Rap-pahannock and attacked Gen. Lee near Freder-icksburg, but was repulsed with a loss of over 10,000 men, and was soon after trans-ferred to the department of Ohio. In November 1863 he successfully held Knoxville against a superior force, and in 1864 he led a corps, under Gen. Grant, through the battles of the Wilderness and Cold Harbor. Resigning in April 1865 he was elected governor of Rhode Island (1866-8), and United States senator in 1875 and 1881.

Burnside, Helen Marion, English artist and poet: b. Bromley Hall, 1844. She published a book of poems in 1864, which made her widely known. From 1880 to 1889 she was designer to the Royal School of Art Needlework. She has published 'The Lost Letter,' 'Tales for Children,' and many occasional contributions in prose and verse to leading magazines.

Burnt Ear, a disease in grain caused by a fungus (*Uredo carbo*), which covers the seed coat with a black dust, while leaving the interior apparently uninjured, but abortive.

Burnt Offering, one of the sacrifices enjoined on the Hebrew Church and nation. It is called, in their language, *olah*, from the root *alah*, to ascend, because, being wholly consumed, all but the refuse ashes was regarded as ascending in the smoke to God. In the New Testament it is called *holokautōma*, meaning a whole burnt offering, an offering wholly burnt. In the Vulgate it is called *holocaustum*, which has the same meaning. Stated burnt offerings were presented daily, every Sabbath, at the new moon, at the three great festivals, on the day of atonement, and at the feast of trumpets. Private ones might be presented at any time.

Burnt Sienna, an ochreous earth known as sienna earth (*terra di Sienna*) submitted to the action of fire, by which it is converted into a fine orange brown pigment used in both oil and water-color painting.

Burnt Umber, a pigment of reddish-brown color obtained by burning umber, a soft earthy mixture of the peroxides of iron and manganese, deriving its name from Umbria in Italy.

·**Burnt Wood Work.** See PYROGRAPHY.

Burntisland, bŭrnt-ī′land, Scotland, a royal burgh and seaport of Fife, on the north shore of the estuary of the Forth, 7½ miles north by west of Edinburgh. It is a favorite summer residence and bathing-place as well as a busy port. It has four churches (Established, Free, United Presbyterian, and Episcopal), a town-hall, music-hall, mechanics' library, a large board school, etc. The harbor is capacious, of great depth, and of easy access. A dock with an area of five and a half acres was completed in 1876, and extensions have since been made. A second wet dock is being constructed with a depth of 28 feet on the sill, and provided with coal-shipping machinery of the most modern type. Vegetable oil and oil-cake are made, and there are railway repairing works and a distillery. Burntisland is a steamboat ferry station on the North British Railway, and is also connected with the Forth Bridge. It unites with Kinghorn, Dysart, and Kirkcaldy in sending a member to Parliament. Pop. about 5,000.

Burr, Aaron, American clergyman: b. Fairfield, Conn., 4 Jan. 1716; d. Princeton, N. J., 24 Sept. 1757. He graduated at Yale and was settled as pastor of the Presbyterian church of Newark, N. J. In 1748 he became president of the College of New Jersey, now Princeton University, succeeding the first president, Dickinson, who held office only a few months. He married a daughter of Jonathan Edwards, and was the father of Aaron Burr (q.v.), third Vice-President of the United States. He published a Latin grammar, known as the 'Newark Grammar,' and 'The Supreme Divinity of Our Lord Jesus Christ.'

Burr, Aaron, American statesman: b. Newark, N. J. (son of the preceding), 6 Feb. 1756; d. Port Richmond, Staten Island, 14 Sept. 1836. Before he was three years old his parents died, leaving him a considerable estate. He entered the sophomore class of Princeton College in 1769, and graduated in 1772. At the outbreak of the Revolution Burr enlisted as a private, and joined the force before Boston. He volunteered for the expedition against Canada and took part in the attack upon Quebec. For this service· he was raised to the rank of major. As aide-de-camp to Gen. Putnam, Burr was engaged in the defense of New York, and shortly after (1777) was promoted lieutenant-colonel with the command of his regiment, the colonel being a civilian. He was at Valley Forge, and distinguished himself at the battle of Monmouth, where he commanded a brigade in Lord Stirling's division. During the winter of 1778 he was stationed in Westchester County, N. Y., but early in the following spring he resigned his commission, partly on account of ill health, and partly through disappointment at not being more rapidly promoted. Burr belonged to the Lee and Gates faction; he always affected to despise the military talents of Gen. Washington; and it is not improbable that these circumstances interfered with his professional career. In 1782 he was admitted to the bar in Albany, and in July of the same year he married Mrs. Provost, the widow of a British officer who had died in the West Indies. In 1783 he began to practise in New York, and soon obtained a lucrative business. In politics his success was rapid and brilliant. In 1784 he was elected to the State legislature; he was appointed attorney-general of New York in 1789, and United States senator in 1791. While in the Senate, several influential members of Congress recommended him for the mission to France, but Washington, with marked emphasis, refused to appoint him. He left the Senate in 1797, and the following year was returned to the State legislature. Some aspersions upon his conduct while in that body, which were thrown out by John B. Church, led to a duel between Burr and that gentleman, in which, however, neither party was injured. Burr was very efficient in the presidential canvass of 1800. To his efforts may be attributed the success of the Republicans in New York, upon the action of which State the result in the Union depended. On account of the prominence he thus obtained, the friends of Jefferson brought him forward for the Vice-Presidency. An equal number of votes having been thrown for Jefferson and Burr in the Electoral College, the election of a president devolved upon the House of Representatives. Most of the federal members, taking advantatge of the singular turn in affairs, supported Burr. The contest lasted several days. Upon the 36th ballot Jefferson was chosen President, and, in accordance with the provisions of the Constitution at that time, Burr became Vice-President. His conduct in permitting himself to be used by his political opponents in order to defeat the candidate of his party, whom he himself had supported, dissolved his connection with the Republicans and destroyed his political influence. The Federalists nominated him for governor of New York in 1804. Some of the leading men of that party refused to support him, and he was defeated. The contest was bitter, and led to a duel between Burr and Alexander Hamilton (q.v.), 11 July 1804, in which the latter was killed. Burr was compelled to give up his residence in New York. After his retirement from the Vice-Presidency in April 1805, he made a journey to the southwest. His conduct gave rise to the suspicion that he was organizing an expedition to invade Mexico, with the purpose of establishing an empire there which should embrace some of the southwestern States of the Union. He was arrested in Mississippi, and taken to Richmond, Va., for trial, upon an indictment for treason. After a protracted investigation before Chief Justice Marshall the prosecution was abandoned, and Burr was acquitted in September 1807. In 1808 he went to Europe, expecting to get means to carry out his Mexican design. He was disappointed; and after living abroad four years, part of the time in extreme poverty, he returned to America in 1812. He resumed his profession in New York, but never regained his former position at the bar. In 1833 he married Mme. Jumel, a wealthy widow, but they soon separated. Mr. Burr had but one child, the accomplished Theodosia Allston. (See Burr, Theodosia.) In person he was below the medium height, but his manners and presence were very attractive. He was an adroit, persevering, but not a great lawyer. He cannot be said to have been an orator, yet he was an effective and ready speaker. It has been usual to regard Burr as a brilliant, and even a great man, who was led astray by moral obliquity. In regard to the looseness of his principles, there can be no doubt; but there is a growing tendency to relieve his name of much of the odium that formerly attached to it. Consult Davis, 'Memoirs of Aaron Burr' (1836); Parton, 'Life of Aaron Burr' (1858); Tompkins, 'Burr Bibliography' (1892); Todd, 'The True Aaron Burr' (1902); McCaleb, 'The Aaron Burr Conspiracy' (1903).

Burr, Edward, American soldier: b. Booneville, Mo., 19 May 1859. He studied at Washington University 1874-8, and at the United States Military Academy 1878-82, and on graduation at the latter was assigned to the corps of engineers with the rank of second lieutenant. He was promoted first lieutenant in 1883, and captain in 1894; and as lieutenant-colonel of volunteers commanded the battalion of engineers in the campaign against Santiago de Cuba in June-July 1898. He is a member of the American Society of Civil Engineers.

Burr, Enoch Fitch, American mathematician and clergyman: b. Green's Farms, Fairfield County, Conn., 21 Oct. 1818. He graduated at Yale in 1839, and became pastor of the Congregational Church in Lyme, Conn., in 1850. Since 1868 he has been a lecturer at Amherst College. Among his works are: 'A Treatise on the Application of the Calculus to the Theory of Neptune' (1848); 'A Song of the Sea' (1873); 'Aleph, the Chaldean' (1891).

Burr, George Lincoln, American historian: b. Oramel, N. Y., 30 Jan. 1857. He graduated at Cornell in 1881 and entered its faculty in 1888, becoming professor of ancient and mediæval history there. He has written 'The Literature of Witchcraft,' and works on superstition and persecution. He was expert in history to the Venezuelan Boundary Commission (1896-7).

Burr, Theodosia (Mrs. Joseph Allston), daughter of Aaron Burr (1756-1836): b. New York, 1783; d. 1813. She was carefully educated and became very accomplished, showing particular linguistic talent. After the death of Mrs. Burr she presided over her father's household until her marriage in 1801 to Governor Allston of South Carolina. Her correspondence with her father after her removal to the South is of great interest and shows continued devotion to his interests. Her beauty, brilliant personality, and relationship to the famous statesman drew public attention to her, especially during her father's trial, and had the effect of enlisting the public sympathy on his behalf. In 1812 she sailed from Charleston in the Patriot for New York, but the vessel was never heard from and was believed to have been lost in the storm or sunk by pirates.

Burr, William Hubert, American educator: b. Waterloo, Conn., 14 July 1851. He graduated at Rensselaer Polytechnic Institute 1872; was employed by the Wrought Iron Bridge Company of New York, and later on the water supply and sewerage system of Newark, N. J. He was assistant professor, and later professor of rational and technical mechanics at Rensselaer Polytechnic Institute 1876-84; became assistant engineer of the Phœnix Bridge Company 1884, and subsequently its general manager; was professor of engineering in the Lawrence Scientific School of Harvard University 1892-3; consulting engineer to the New York city department of public works 1893-5; of parks and of docks 1895-7; and later of bridges. Since 1893 he has been professor of civil engineering at Columbia, and in 1904 became a member of the Isthmian Canal Commission. He is author of 'The Stresses in Bridge and Roof Trusses'; 'Arched Ribs and Suspension Bridges'; 'Elasticity of the Materials of Engineering'; 'The Theory of Masonry Arches,' etc.

Burrage, Henry Sweetzer, American clergyman: b. Fitchburg, Mass., 7 Jan. 1827. He was graduated from Brown University, 1861, and entering the 36th Massachusetts as a private, rose to the rank of captain, and brevet-major of volunteers. After the war he resumed his studies, graduated at Newton Theological Seminary, 1867, was at the University of Halle, Germany, 1868-9, and became a Baptist clergyman in 1869. He was pastor at Waterville, Maine, 1869-73; editor of Zion's Advocate, 1873-; recording secretary of the American Baptist Union, 1876-. He has edited: 'Brown University in the Civil War' (1868); 'Henry W. Longfellow's 75th Birthday' (1882); 'History of the 36th Regiment of Massachusetts Volunteers' (1884); and has written 'The Act of Baptism in the History of the Christian Church' (1879); 'History of the Anabaptists in Switzerland' (1882); 'Baptist Writers and their Hymns' (1888); 'History of the Baptists in New England' (1894). 'The First Mention of Pemaquid in History' (1894); 'The St. Croix Commission' (1895).

Bur'rard In'let, an inlet of British Columbia, forming a fine harbor, and having Vancouver, the terminus of the Canadian Pacific Railway, on its southern shore.

Burrill, Thomas Jonathan, American naturalist: b. Pittsfield, Mass., 25 April 1839. He graduated at the Illinois State Normal University in 1865, and in 1867 was botanist of Powell's first Rocky Mountain Expedition. Since 1868 he has been a member of the faculty of the University of Illinois and has held the following offices in the University: Professor of botany and horticulture since 1868; dean of the College of Science, 1877–84; vice-president since 1879; acting president, 1889–90, 1891–94 and 1904; dean of the Graduate School since 1894. The degree of LL.D. was conferred upon him in 1893 by the Northwestern University. He is a member of several American and foreign scientific societies, and is well known from his writings under more than 100 titles mostly upon the parasitic diseases of plants, bacteriology, microscopy, fruit growing, forestry, landscape gardening, and modern education.

Bur'ritt, Elihu, ē-lī'hū ("THE LEARNED BLACKSMITH"), American reformer: b. New Britain, Conn., 8 Dec. 1811; d. 7 March 1879. The son of a shoemaker, he was educated in the common schools of his native village, and at the age of 16 was apprenticed to a blacksmith. An early conceived project of reading the Scriptures in their original languages led him to philological studies in the intervals of labor, and by diligence and a remarkable facility he was soon able to understand works in several languages. He removed to Worcester to take advantage of the library of the Antiquarian Society there, and while still plying his trade became acquainted with the principal ancient and modern languages. In 1846 he went to England, where he formed the "League of Universal Brotherhood," whose object was "to employ all legitimate means for the abolition of war throughout the world." He was constantly engaged in writing and lecturing, and took a prominent part in all the European peace congresses. He returned to America in 1853. He was consular agent at Birmingham, 1865–8. The promotion of temperance, cheap ocean postage, and the abolition of American slavery were leading objects of his continued exertions. His principal publications are: 'Sparks from the Anvil' (1848); 'Thoughts and Things at Home and Abroad' (1854); 'Chips from Many Blocks,' etc.

Burritt College, a co-educational institution, in Spencer, Tenn.; organized in 1848 under the auspices of the Christian Church; reported at the end of 1905: Professors and instructors, 10; students, 214; volumes in the library, 3,854; grounds and buildings valued at $20,000; income, $4,000; number of graduates, 284.

Burro. See DONKEY.

Burrough, or Borough, Stephen, English navigator: b. Devonshire, 25 Sept. 1525. Being employed to search for a northeast passage to the Indies, he set out in 1556, and after doubling the North Cape sailed along the north coast of Russia, touched at Nova Zembla and the Isle of Waigatz, and reached lat. 70° 30′ N. The account of his voyage, contained in Hakluyt's collection, proves him to have been an active and intelligent sailor.

Burroughs, George, American clergyman: d. Salem, Mass., 19 Aug. 1692. He was graduated at Harvard College in 1670, was a preacher at Falmouth, now Portland, Me., in 1676, and at Salem in 1680. In consequence of some dispute with his people he returned to Portland in 1683, but, when that town was destroyed by the Indians in 1690, came back to Salem. Though a person of unblemished character, he became one of the victims of accusation by the confessing witches. It was testified that two of his wives had appeared to the witnesses, saying that he was the cause of their death, and threatening, if he denied it, to appear in court. He was also accused of performing feats of extraordinary strength by diabolical assistance, such as carrying a barrel of molasses, holding out a gun by a finger placed in the muzzle, and of having "tortured, afflicted, pined, consumed, wasted, and tormented" one Mary Wolcott. Although he asserted his innocence so as to draw tears from the spectators, and recited the Lord's Prayer, which it was supposed no witch could repeat without mistake, he was condemned and executed.

Burroughs, George Stockton, American educator: b. Waterloo, N. Y., 6 Jan. 1855; d. 1901. He graduated at Princeton College, 1873, and at its Theological Seminary, 1877. He removed to New England in 1880, and served in the ministry of the Presbyterian Church in Fairfield and New Britain, Conn. He was professor of biblical literature at Amherst College, 1886–92; president of Wabash College, Crawfordsville, Ind., 1892–9; and became professor of Old Testament language and literature in Oberlin Theological Seminary in 1899.

Burroughs, John, American essayist and naturalist: b. Roxbury, N. Y., 3 April 1837. He taught school for about eight years, was for a time a journalist, and then became a clerk in the Treasury Department and subsequently a national bank examiner. He settled on a farm in New York State and has since devoted himself to fruit-culture, nature-study, and literature. Many of his papers were written in his barkcovered study (to which he has given the name "Riverby") on the banks of the Hudson. The personal element is very marked in his writings, and the charm of his easy familiar style has done much to popularize the study of nature. His books on rural themes include: 'Wake Robin' (1871); 'Winter Sunshine' (1875); 'Birds and Poets' (1877); 'Locusts and Wild Honey' (1879); 'Pepacton; Notes of a Walker' (1881); 'Fresh Fields' (1884); 'Signs and Seasons' (1886); and 'Sharp Eyes' (1888); 'Indoor Papers.' He has also written 'Notes on Walt Whitman' (1867); 'Whitman: a Study' (1897); 'The Light of Day'; and 'Squirrels and Other Fur-Bearers.' In 1903 he accompanied President Roosevelt on a trip through the West, including a lengthy sojourn in the Yellowstone National Park in close communion with the wild life of that magnificent game preserve.

JOHN BURROUGHS.

AUTHOR AND NATURALIST.

Burroughs, Marie (LILLIE ARRINGTON), American actress: b. San Francisco, 1866. At the age of 18 she went to New York and made her début as Gladys in 'The Rajah,' assuming the stage name of Marie Burroughs. She appeared as Mary Bleakern in 'The Middleman,' Vashti in 'Judah,' etc. In 1894 she was the star in 'The Profligate.' In 1899 she acted with Stuart Robson in 'The Meddler' and in 1900 filled the role of Guida Landresse in 'The Battle of the Strong.'

Burroughs, Stephen, American adventurer: b. Hanover, N. H., 1765; d. Three Rivers, Canada, 28 Jan. 1840. The son of a Congregational clergyman, his vicious jokes and propensity to trick people into misadventures made him early reputed the worst boy in town. At the age of 14 he ran away from home to join the army, which he later deserted. After studying under a clergyman in Connecticut, he entered Dartmouth College, where he continued his mischievous career. He left the college clandestinely before graduating, and was successively privateersman, ship's physician, and schoolmaster. At length he determined to go where he was unknown and preach. Under the name of Davis he had excellent success as pastor of a Congregational church in Pelham, Mass., until after nearly six months his character was revealed by persons who had formerly known him. Having entered into relations with a gang of counterfeiters, though still occasionally preaching, he was arrested in Springfield for passing counterfeit money, and convicted. He was imprisoned at Northampton, and for his numerous attempts to escape was loaded with chains. He sought to end his sufferings by firing the jail and was afterward removed to Castle Island in Boston Harbor, whence he affected his escape with seven other prisoners, but was retaken. When he was released he went to Canada, where for many years he was at the head of an association of counterfeiters. In the latter part of his life he thoroughly changed his conduct, joined the Roman Catholic Church, and passed his last years in receiving and educating at his residence the sons of wealthy Canadian gentlemen. He was beloved by his pupils, had an extensive library of choice books, and was noted for his happy faculty of communicating his great stores of knowledge. Few men have possessed equal capacity, and even during the worst part of his career his charitable deeds were hardly less remarkable than his iniquities. He described his early life in two autobiographical volumes, written with great naturalness and force.

Burrowing Owl, a small owl (*Speotyto cunicularia*) common on the open plains of both North and South America, where it makes its nest in burrows. It is mottled gray in color, has very long legs, scantily feathered, and stands erect upon them in a manner different from that of owls generally. It is gregarious, and is especially prevalent on the North American plains in the « towns » of the prairie dogs; and in South America it lives with the vizcachas, and cavies, and is thought to warn them by its excited notes whenever an enemy approaches. Among the many unowl-like traits of this curious little exile from the woods is its cry, which has no resemblance to the ordinary hoot of an owl, but more nearly resembles the chattering

of a cuckoo. This owl makes its home wherever it can in some abandoned burrow of a ground-squirrel or other animal, but, failing this, it digs a little cave-like hole of its own, which it furnishes with a bed of soft materials, whereon are laid about eight globular white eggs. The food of these owls consists almost entirely of insects and mice. Consult Coues, 'Birds of the Northwest' (Washington 1874); Sclater and Hudson, 'Argentine Ornithology' (London 1888).

Burrowing Perch. See CULPER.

Burrows, William, American naval officer: b. near Philadelphia, Pa., 6 Oct. 1785; d. at sea, 5 Sept. 1813. He served in the war with Tripoli and commanded the sloop Enterprise in its successful action with the British brig Boxer off the coast of Maine. Both Burrows and the British commander were killed in the fight, and they were buried side by side at Portland. Congress struck a medal in honor of the victory and its hero.

Bursar, or Bursary, an endowment in one of the Scotch universities, corresponding to an exhibition in an English university, and intended for the support of a student during his ordinary course, and before he has taken a degree in the faculty in which he holds the bursary. Each of the four universities of Scotland has a greater or smaller number of bursaries. As yet the University of Aberdeen is better provided than any of the others with this class of endowments. Bursaries are in the gift sometimes of the Senatus Academicus of the university to which they belong, sometimes of the town-council of the city in which the university is situated, and sometimes of private individuals. With regard to the manner in which they are bestowed, some are obtained after competitive examination, and others are given by the patrons for special reasons. As the former method of bestowing them is found to be the more beneficial in its results, it is gradually becoming the prevailing one, as at Aberdeen it has always been. Bursaries which are in the gift of the Senatus Academicus are all bestowed in this way.

Burschenschaft, boor'-shĕn-shäft, an association of students in Germany, formed in 1815, which had for its object the political regeneration of Germany.

Burs'lem, England, a market town and municipal borough in Staffordshire, within the parliamentary borough of Hanley, in « The Potteries.» It is well built, chiefly of brick; has electric tramways, a fine town-hall, covered market, public baths, hospital, and the Wedgwood Institute, comprising a free library, a museum, and a school of art, erected in honor of Josiah Wedgwood, who was born at Burslem in 1730. The building is an excellent exemplification of the structural application of ceramics. Burslem has four Established churches, and places of worship for Independents, Baptists, Methodists, and Roman Catholics. It has extensive manufactures of china and earthenware, and carries on coal mining. Pop. (1901) 38,766.

Burt, Mary Elizabeth, American educator: b. Lake Geneva, Wis. She studied at Oberlin College and entered the teaching profession. For three years she was a member of the Chicago board of education. Later she undertook editorial work and lecturing. She edited 'Little Nature Studies for Little People'; 'Seed Thoughts from Robert Browning,' etc.; has contributed frequently to periodical literature and is the author of: 'Browning's Women'; 'Literary Landmarks'; 'The World's Literature'; 'German Iliad (Siegfried)'; 'Stories from Plato and other Classic Writers'; and collaborated in writing 'The Literary Primer,' and 'The Boy General.'

Burt, Thomas, English labor leader: b. Northumberland, 12 Nov. 1837. He began work in the coal-mines at 10 years of age. In 1865 he began to take an interest in the labor movement and soon became prominent as a trades-unionist. He was president of the Trades Union Congress in 1891. Since 1874 he has had a seat in Parliament as a Liberal.

Burt, William A., American surveyor: b. Worcester, Mass., 13 June 1792; d. 18 Aug. 1858. After acting as a surveyor in New York State he removed to Michigan in 1824. Between 1840 and 1847 he surveyed a great part of northern Michigan. He introduced improved methods of surveying and invented the solar compass. He was judge of the Michigan circuit court and member of the legislature, and one of the projectors of the Sault Ste. Marie canal.

Bur'ton, Ernest De Witt, American Biblical scholar: b. Granville, Ohio, 4 Feb. 1856. He graduated at Denison University in 1876 at Rochester Theological Seminary in 1882, and went to Europe for further study in Leipsic and Berlin. From 1882–3 he taught in the Rochester Theological Seminary; and from 1883–92, in the Newton Theological Institution, first as associate professor and later as professor of New Testament Interpretation. In 1892 he was appointed head professor of New Testament Interpretation in the University of Chicago. Among his works are: 'Syntax of the Moods and Tenses in New Testament Greek'; 'Harmony of the Gospels for Historical Study' and 'Handbook of the Life of Christ' (in collaboration with W. A. Stevens); 'Records and Letters of the Apostolic Age'; 'Handbook of the Life of Paul'; 'Constructive Studies in the Life of Christ' (in collaboration with Shailer Mathews). In 1892 he became associate editor of the 'Biblical World,' and in 1897 of the 'American Journal of Theology.'

Burton, Sir Frederick William, Irish artist: b. Limerick, 1816; d. London, 15 March 1900. He received his education in Dublin. He was elected to the Royal Hibernian Academy in 1837, and in 1842 exhibited at the London Royal Academy. He is best known for his work as director of the National Gallery in London, to which post he was chosen in 1874, and which he held for 20 years.

Burton, John Hill, Scottish historian: b. Aberdeen, 22 Aug. 1809; d. 10 Aug. 1881. He was educated at the grammar school and Marischal College in that city. He studied law and was admitted to the bar in 1831. He never succeeded in gaining much practice, and soon turned his attention to literature, contributing to the 'Westminster,' the 'Edinburgh' and 'North British' reviews, as well as being a member of the staff of the *Scotsman*. With Sir John Bowring he edited Bentham's works, as well as an

illustrative 'Benthamiana,' with the aim of making more widely known the opinions of the great apostle of utilitarianism and radicalism. His first original work of importance, was the 'Life and Correspondence of David Hume' (1846), followed next year by the 'Lives' of Lord Lovat and Duncan Forbes of Culloden. In 1849 he published his 'Political and Social Economy'; in 1852 he compiled 'Narratives from Criminal Trials in Scotland.' He commenced in 1853 the publication of his chief work, the 'History of Scotland,' with two volumes covering the period from the Revolution of 1688 to the extinction of the last Jacobite rebellion in 1746. This was afterward completed by seven volumes commencing with Agricola's invasion and ending with the Revolution of 1688. A second edition of the complete history was published in eight volumes in 1873. A series of literary and historical sketches contributed to 'Blackwood's Magazine' formed the basis of two of his best-known books, 'The Scot Abroad' and 'The Bookhunter.' His last important historical work was the 'History of the Reign of Queen Anne' (1880). In 1854 Mr. Burton was appointed secretary to the Scottish Prison Board, and he continued his connection with this department as a commissioner of prisons until his death. The success of his 'History of Scotland' brought him the appointment of historiographer royal for Scotland, the degree of LL.D. from Edinburgh University, and that of D.C.L. from Oxford.

Burton, Lewis William, American clergyman: b. Cleveland, 9 Nov. 1852. He was educated at Kenyon College and the Philadelphia Divinity School; took orders in the Protestant Episcopal Church in 1878, and was successively in charge of parishes in Cleveland, Richmond, and Louisville. In 1896 he became bishop of Lexington, Ky.

Burton, Richard, American poet and journalist: b. Hartford, Conn., 14 March 1859. He graduated from Trinity College, Hartford, and took a degree at Johns Hopkins University. His published poems are 'Dumb in June' (1895), and 'Memorial Day' (1897).

Burton, Sir Richard Francis, English traveler, linguist, and author: b. Barham House, Herfordshire, 19 March 1821; d. Trieste, Austria, 20 Oct. 1890. He was educated at Oxford, with the intention of entering the Church; but in deference to his own urgent request, his father obtained a commission for him in the East India Company's service. He joined the army in 1842, served for some years in Sind, under Sir C. Napier, explored the Neilgherry Hills, published an important work on Sind, and acquired a complete knowledge of the Persian, Afghan, Hindustanee, and Arabic languages. Returning to England in 1851, he soon afterward set out to explore Arabia, disguised as an Afghan pilgrim, and published on his return a 'Personal Narrative of a Pilgrimage to El-Medinah and Mecca' (1855), as the result of this daring adventure. His next expedition was into the Somali country in East Africa, from whence he proceeded to the Crimea, where he was chief of the staff of Gen. Beatson, and organized the irregular cavalry. After peace was proclaimed, Burton set out in 1856 along with Capt. Speke to explore the lake region of Central Africa. The expedition was absent three years, and during that time the great Lake Tanganyika was discovered by Burton. Subsequently he made a journey in the western states of North America, and published an account of the Mormon settlement at Utah, in his 'City of the Saints.' In 1861 he married, and he received the same year an appointment as consul at Fernando Po. While fulfilling his duties here he explored the Bight of Biafra, visited the Kamerun Mountains, and conducted a dangerous mission to the king of Dahomey. Afterward he was transferred to the consulate of Santos in Brazil, and here he explored his own province, visited the Argentine Republic, crossed the continent to Chile and Peru, returned home after exploring the Pacific coast, and published his 'Explorations of the Highlands of Brazil.' He was now (1871) made consul of Damascus, but was soon recalled, and in the following year, after a journey to Iceland, an account of which he wrote, he was appointed consul at Trieste. While occupying this position he led two expeditions into Midian (1876-8); and in company with Commander Cameron he conducted an expedition into the gold-producing country behind the Gold Coast. He remained English consul at Trieste until his death. In his latter years his services to geographical science were acknowledged by the gold medals of the French and English geographical societies, while in 1886 his services to his country were tardily recognized by the honor of knighthood. Besides the books of travel already mentioned, he was the author of many others, such as: 'Sind, or the Unhappy Valley' (1851); 'Goa and the Blue Mountains' (1851); 'Falconry in the Valley of the Indus' (1852); 'First Footsteps in East Africa' (1856); 'The Lake Region of Central Africa' (1860); 'Abeokuta, or an Exploration of the Kamerun Mountains' (1863); 'Narrative of a Mission to the King of Dahomey' (1864); 'The Nile Basin' (1864); 'Vikram and the Vampire' (1869); 'Zanzibar' (1872); 'Two Trips to Gorilla Land' (1875); 'Ultima Thule, or a Summer in Iceland' (1875); 'Etruscan Bologna' (1876); 'Sind Revisited' (1877); and 'The Gold Mines of Midian' (1878). In 1885-8, he published a remarkable literal translation of the 'Arabian Nights' entitled 'The Thousand Nights and a Night.' His manuscript translation with notes, from the Arabic of 'The Scented Garden,' of great value to scholars, was burned by his widow, who deemed it an immoral work. Consult lives by Hitchman (1887); Lady Burton (1893); Stisted (1897).

Burton, Robert, English clergyman and author: b. Lindley, Leicestershire, 1576; d. 1640. He was educated at Oxford, took orders, and became rector of Seagrave in Leicestershire. His learning, which was various and extensive, is copiously displayed in the 'Anatomy of Melancholy, by Democritus Junior', first published in 1621, and repeatedly reprinted. He was a man of integrity and benevolence, but subject to strange fits of hypochondriac melancholy which rendered his conduct flighty and inconsistent. He is reputed to have undertaken the composition of his 'Anatomy of Melancholy' with a view to the dissipation of his morbid feelings. Among those who have been most deeply indebted to Burton is Sterne, as may be seen in his 'Tristram Shandy.'

Burton, William Evans, English comedian and author: b. London, 24 Sept. 1804; d. New York, 10 Feb. 1860. He received a classical education, intending to adopt the ministry as a profession. In 1822 he took charge of a printing establishment and edited a magazine. His first appearance on the stage was at the Haymarket in 1832. He was very successful both in Great Britain and the United States; and built the National Theatre in Philadelphia, and owned another in New York. He compiled a 'Cyclopædia of Wit and Humor.'

Burton-upon-Trent, England, a municipal and county borough, in Staffordshire, on the north bank of the Trent, in a low, level situation. It is substantially built. Malting and iron-founding are carried on to a considerable extent, but it is chiefly celebrated for its excellent ale, of which vast quantities are made for both home consumption and exportation. There are about 20 breweries at work, giving employment in the various departments of the trade to about 10,000 men and boys. The largest brewing establishments are those of Messrs. Bass & Co., and Messrs. Allsopp, the former of which covers considerably more than 100 acres of ground. These two companies alone are said to pay to government £800,000 annually as duty on the ale brewed by them. Contrary to common usage, the brewers employ hard water obtained from wells instead of soft water. There are in all about 50 places of worship in the town, which also possesses a grammar school, girls' high school, numerous board and other elementary schools, four blocks of alms-houses, a dispensary and infirmary, a public library and reading-rooms, school of science and art, handsome public baths, etc. Pop. (1901) 50,400.

Burt'sell, Richard Lalor, American clergyman: b. New York, 14 April 1840. He studied in Rome and was ordained to the priesthood in 1862. After returning to the United States and having charge of parishes in New York he was appointed "defender of the marriage tie" being the first to fill this office, which in 1884 was instituted in the Catholic Church in the United States. Having become connected with the movement headed by Rev. Dr. McGlynn, he was retired from his parish to one of less prominence in 1890. In 1904 he was elevated to the dignity of Domestic Prelate by Pope Pius X. and is now (1905) rector of Saint Mary's Church, Kingston, N.Y.

Buru, boo-roo', or **Boeroe,** Malaysia, an island of the archipelago, in the residency of Amboyna, from which it lies about 40 miles to the west. Area, with the small island of Amblau, 3,360 square miles; population variously estimated at from 10,000 to 50,000. The marshy coast lands are notoriously unhealthful, but lofty mountains rise in the interior, one peak (Tomahoe) attaining an altitude of 10,320 feet. A dense natural forest covers most of the country, and only a very small portion has been brought under cultivation. The soil is rich, and vegetation everywhere luxuriant.

Burwash, Nathanael, Canadian educator: b. Argenteuil, near Saint Andrews, Quebec, 25 July 1839, of a loyalist family, who left Vermont during the American Revolution. He was educated at Victoria College, Cobourg, and Yale University, and entered the Methodist ministry in 1860. He was professor in Victoria College, 1867-73; dean of faculty of theology in 1873, and has been president and chancellor of Victoria University, Toronto, from 1887. He was secretary of education for the Methodist Church in Canada, 1874-86, and has devoted much time toward bringing about university federation in the province of Ontario. He has published 'Memorials of Edward and Lydia Jackson' (1874); 'Wesley's Doctrinal Standards' (1881); 'Handbook on the Epistle to the Romans' (1887); 'Inductive Studies in Theology' (1896); 'Manual of Christian Theology' (1900); 'Life and Times of Egerton Ryerson' (1902).

Bury, bĕr'ĭ, John B., Irish scholar: b. 16 Oct. 1861. He was graduated from Trinity College, Dublin, of which he is a Fellow; in 1893 became professor of modern history in Dublin University, and professor of Greek there in 1898. He has written 'History of the Later Roman Empire from Arcadius to Irene' (1889); 'Student's History of the Roman Empire from Augustus to Marcus Aurelius' (1893); 'History of Greece to Death of Alexander the Great' (1902); and has edited Pindar's 'Isthmian Odes'; and 'Nemean Odes'; Freeman's 'History of Federal Government in Greece and Italy'; and Gibbon's 'Decline and Fall of the Roman Empire.'

Bury, Richard de, or **Richard Aungerville,** English clergyman and author: b. 1281; d. 1345. He was made bishop of Durham in 1333. His principal work, 'Philobiblon,' was intended to serve as a handbook to the library which he founded in connection with Durham College at Oxford (afterward suppressed). It gives an interesting account of how he collected his library, describes the state of learning in England and France, and closes with an explanation of the rules for the management of his library, which were founded on those adopted for the library of the Sorbonne.

Bury, bĕr'ĭ, England, a municipal and parliamentary borough, in Lancashire, eight miles north-northwest of Manchester. It is well situated on a rising ground between the Irwell and the Roche, and, being much improved in recent times, now presents the appearance of a clean and well-built town. It has a handsome town hall, an athenæum, a technical school and art gallery, a savings bank, the Bury Bank, Trevelyan Club, and Philips Hall, grammar school, public baths, railway station, etc. Among the churches, St. Mary's (the parish church) and St. Thomas' are perhaps the finest, being highly ornate Gothic buildings with tower and spire. There is also a handsome chapel belonging to the United Methodist Free Church, a fine Presbyterian church, and a Roman Catholic chapel. The staple manufacture is that of cotton, and there are also large woolen factories, bleaching and printing works, dyeworks, foundries, etc. The late Sir Robert Peel was born at Chamber Hall in the vicinity in 1788; and a bronze statue of him adorns the town. Bury was made a parliamentary borough, returning one member in 1832. Pop. about 60,000.

Bury St. Edmund's, England, a parliamentary and municipal borough in Suffolk, situated on the Lark, 26 miles from Ipswich. It contains four churches, two of them being fine old Gothic edifices. These are places of worship belonging to the Independents, Methodists, Baptists, and others; and among other buildings a shire-hall, a guild-hall, a corn exchange, athenæum, with library, etc. Agricultural implements are manufactured, and there is a large trade in agricultural produce. Of many benevolent institutions the principal is a free grammar school founded by Edward VI. Bury St. Edmund's sends one member to Parliament. It is an ancient place, and derived its name from St. Edmund, a king of the East Angles, who was buried here. The barons in John's reign met here, and swore to obtain the ratification of Magna Charta. Bury St. Edmund's contains the remains of an abbey, once the most wealthy and magnificent in Great Britain. Pop. about 17,000.

Burying-beetles, coleopterous insects of the family *Silphidæ.* The carrion or sexton beetles are useful in burying decaying bodies of birds, mice, etc., in which they lay their eggs. The larvæ are crustaceous, flattened, with the sides of the body often serrated, black and of a fetid odor. They undergo their transformations in an oval earthen cocoon. In *Necrophorus* the antennæ have 10 apparent joints, and the rounded club is four-jointed. The genus *Silpha,* of which *S. lapponica* is a common species, differs in the third joint of the antenna being no longer than the second but shorter than the first. In *Necrophilus* the third joint is as long as the first. *N. surinamensis* has a yellow thorax with a central irregular black spot. *Catops* and its allies live in fungi, carrion, and ants' nests, and are small, black, oval insects. There are between 800 and 900 species of the family, many of which are small and live in caves (see CAVE-DWELLING ANIMALS) or in nests of ants.

Burying-places, localities of sepulture of the dead. The custom of burying the dead in public places prevailed among the most ancient nations, including the Romans, who afterward, in the flourishing periods of the republic, burned their dead and kept the ashes in tombs, collected in urns. The ancient Germans buried their dead in groves consecrated by their priests. With the introduction of the Christian religion consecrated places were appropriated for the purpose of general burial; and it was regarded as ignominious not to be buried in consecrated earth. The deprivation of the rites of burial was therefore part of the punishment of excommunication. The Romans provided their gravestones, upon which were inscribed the name of the deceased, and the wish, *Sit illi terra levis* ("May the earth rest lightly upon him"). This custom was preserved by the Christians. The Egyptians, Greeks, and Romans erected over the graves of men of rank, or persons otherwise remarkable, pyramids, mausoleums, or temples. After the introduction of Christianity little churches, called chapels, were erected over the dead. Early Christian martyrs were often buried in caverns, which by degrees were enlarged to spacious subterranean vaults. Subsequently others considered themselves happy if their bones were allowed to repose near the ashes of a martyr. As early as the 4th century the Christians built churches over the sepulchres of the holy martyrs; and in the belief that a place was sanctified by their ashes they anxiously sought out, on the erection of new churches in cities, or the transformation of heathen temples into

Christian churches, the remains (relics) of the martyrs, and buried them under the altar of the new church to communicate to it a character of greater sanctity. The Emperor Constantine, who died in 337, is supposed to have been the first person who ordered his tomb to be erected in a church. This was done in the Church of the Apostles at Constantinople, of which he was the founder, and therefore probably considered himself as peculiarly entitled to this privilege. He was soon imitated by the bishops, and later all those who had enriched the Church were distinguished by this honor. The Emperors Theodosius and Justinian, indeed, forbade the erection of sepulchres in churches, but in vain. Leo the Philosopher again permitted them to everybody. At present interment in churches is almost everywhere suppressed, or at least permitted only under certain restrictions. Even in Naples and Rome the general practice of erecting sepulchres in churches was forbidden in 1809, and the foundation of burial places without the city was provided for. The custom introduced by the communities of Moravian Brothers, who form their burial places into gardens, is now becoming general; and cemeteries, instead of exhibiting merely dull ranges of tombstones, are adorned with flower plots and ornamental shrubbery. The celebrated burying-place of Père la Chaise, near Paris, is one of the most beautiful and interesting spots in the world. See also CATACOMBS.

Busaco, boo-sä'kō, a hamlet in the province of Beira, on the north side of the river Mondego. It is memorable for the battle, 27 Sept. 1810, between Wellington and Masséna. Wellington, with about 40,000 men on a retreat before Masséna, with a force of 65,000, availed himself of the favorable position of the sierra or ridge here for checking the pursuit.

Busbecq, or **Busbequius**, Ogier Ghislain de, ō'jĭ-ĕr gĕz-lăn dĕ bŭs-bĕk, Flemish diplomatist and author: b. Comines, 1522; d. 1592. After having studied in the most celebrated universities of Flanders, France, and Italy, he entered the service of Ferdinand, king of the Romans, who in 1555 sent him as ambassador to Constantinople. After seven years he returned home, and next was sent to accompany the Archduchess Elizabeth (who was to be married to Charles IX.) on her journey to France. Busbecq remained there as steward to Elizabeth, and when she left France, after the death of her husband, he remained as ambassador of Rudolph II. Two important works of his survive, 'Legationis Turcicæ Epistolæ Quatuor,' in which the policy, the power, and the weakness of the Porte are so profoundly and clearly explained that even at present information may be drawn from them; and 'Epistolæ ad Rudolphum II.,' a very important work for the history of those times. His style is pure, elegant, and simple. During his stay in Turkey he collected Greek inscriptions and manuscripts.

Busby, bŭz'bĭ, Richard, English schoolmaster: b. Lutton or Sutton, Lincolnshire, 22 Sept. 1606; d. 6 April 1695. He was educated at Westminster School and at Oxford, where he entered Christ Church in 1624, and graduated B.A. four years later, and M.A. in 1631. He became a tutor of his college, and at the age of 33 was appointed prebendary and rector of Cudworth, in Somersetshire. In 1638 he was provisionally appointed headmaster of Westminster School, and two years later was confirmed in this appointment, which he held continuously till his death. He was strict in discipline and a successful teacher, and among his pupils were many of the greatest men of his time, Dryden, Locke, Atterbury, South, Henry, Hooper, and others. His published works were mainly school books, now long out of date. He was buried in Westminster Abbey.

Busby, a military headdress worn by hussars, artillerymen, and engineers, consisting of a fur hat, with a bag of the same color as the facings of the regiment hanging from the top over the right side. The bag appears to be a relic of a Hungarian headdress, from which a long padded bag hung over, and was attached to the right shoulder as a defense against sword cuts.

Busch, Moritz, German publicist: b. Dresden, 13 Feb. 1821; d. 1899. He was educated at Leipsic, and in 1847 began his literary work by translating a number of the novels of Dickens and Thackeray. As a member of the Radical party he was disappointed by the failure of the revolutionary movement of 1848, and came to the United States in 1851, but returned to Germany in 1852. He also traveled in the Orient in behalf of the Austrian Lloyds. In 1856 he became editor of the *Grenzboten*, and in this paper defended the policy of Bismarck. In April 1870 he was appointed to a position in the Foreign Office, and accompanied Bismarck to France at the time of the Franco-Prussian war. In 1873 he gave up his official position to become the editor of the Hannoverschen *Kuriers*, but continued to be a confidant of Bismarck and strongly advocated the chancellor's policy in his articles for the press. After his visit to the United States he wrote 'Journeys from the Hudson to the Mississippi,' and 'The Mormons.' Other works of his are: 'American Humorists' (translations of selections from Mark Twain, Bret Harte, etc.); 'The History of the International'; 'The Humor of the German People'; 'Count Bismarck and His People During the War with France'; 'Our Chancellor' (a life of Bismarck); and 'Bismarck; Some Secret Pages of His History' (translated into English).

Busch, Wilhelm, German cartoonist: b. Wiedensahl, Hanover, 15 April 1832. He first studied engineering at the Polytechnic School at Hanover, but later studied art at the academies of Düsseldorf, Antwerp, and Munich. In 1859 he drew his first cartoons for the 'Fliegende Blätter.' His work is marked by keen satire and his later productions are far behind his earlier in form. He published a series of his sketches with explanatory text, including 'Saint Antonio of Padua'; 'The Pious Helena'; 'Father Filucius'; 'Max and Moritz'; and 'Hans Huckebein.'

Busching, Anton Friedrich, än-tōn frēd'rĭн bü'shing, German geographer: b. Stadthagen, Schaumburg-Lippe, 27 Sept. 1724; d. Berlin, 28 May 1793. He studied theology in Halle from 1744, and was for a time minister of a Protestant church in St. Petersburg. When acting as a traveling tutor he became convinced of the defects of existing geographical treatises, and resolved to write a new one, which he began on his return to Germany in 1752, by publishing a short description of Schleswig and Holstein as a specimen. In 1754 he was made professor of philosophy in Göttingen. In 1766 he was made director of the united gymnasiums of Berlin and the suburb Kölln. Before his great 'Erdbeschreibung,' which he began to publish in 1754 in separate volumes, and which, though not entirely completed by the author, passed through eight editions during his life, neither the Germans nor any other nation had a thoroughly scientific geographical work. Another of his important writings is the 'Magazin für Historiographie und Geographie' (1767-93).

Busenbaum, Hermann, hĕr'män boo'zĕnbowm, German Jesuit: b. Notteln, 1600; d. Münster, 31 Jan. 1668. He taught moral philosophy at Cologne, and was rector of the Jesuit College at Münster. He is best known through his casuistical work, 'Medulla Theologiæ Moralis, Facili ac Perspicua Methodo Resolvens Casus Conscientiæ,' in which he treats of the principles of the Jesuit morals in a detailed and systematic manner. This book passed through 45 editions between 1645 and 1670, and has been reprinted in modern times. After Damiens' attempt to assassinate Louis XV. of France, the charge was made that it had taught the Jesuits' approval of murder and regicide; it was therefore publicly condemned by the order, and burned by the Parliament of Toulouse.

Busento, boo-sĕn'tō, a river of southern Italy, joining the Crati at Cosenza. The Goths, it is said, dug Alaric a secret grave in the bed of this stream, which they temporarily diverted from its course.

Bush, George, American biblical scholar: b. Norwich, Vt., 12 June 1796; d. Rochester, N. Y., 19 Sept. 1859. He graduated at Dartmouth College in 1818, and studied theology at Princeton, N J., from 1820 to 1822. In 1831 he became professor of Hebrew and Oriental literature in the University of the City of New York. Embracing the doctrines of Swedenborg in 1847, he became a minister of the New Church and editor of the 'New Church Repository.' Among his works are a 'Life of Mohammed' (1832); a 'Hebrew Grammar' (1835); 'Bible Commentaries' (1840).

Bush-Brown, Henry Kirke, American sculptor: b. Ogdensburg, N. Y., 21 April 1857. He studied art in Paris and Italy, and has a studio in New York. His most important works are equestrian statues of Gens. Meade and Reynolds, at Gettysburg; the statue of Justinian, Appellate Court, New York; Indian Buffalo Hunt; Chicago World's Fair; statues for Hall of Records, New York.

Bush Creepers, the English name of the *Uncotillinæ*, a subfamily of the *Sylviidæ*. These birds have sharply conical bills and long, pointed wings. They are usually diminutive in size, active in habits, have a twittering note, and build their nests in thickets, solitary bushes, or trees. They are found in the warmer parts of both hemispheres, some of them, however, being migratory.

Bush-dog, a small wild dog (*Icticyon venaticus*), resembling a fox in appearance, found in Guiana and Brazil. It is distinguished by its one molar tooth in the upper jaw, has close hair, and a short, stubby tail. Compare Fox-dog.

Bush-hog. See River-hog.

Bush-quail, the Anglo-Indian name for the button-quail (q.v.).

Bushbuck, any of several African antelopes, frequenting thickets and bushy regions. The name applies especially to the diminutive antelopes of the genus *Cephalolophus*, which the Dutch of South Africa called "duykers" (q.v.). These include the smallest members of their race, some of them standing only 13 inches high at the shoulders. They haunt the rocky hillsides, leaping with extraordinary agility from stone to stone, and diving into the thickets at the first alarm. They feed upon berries, leaves, buds, and similar food, rather than upon grass, and their flesh has a delicate flavor. The name "bushbuck" is also given, especially in South Africa, to the larger antelopes of the genus *Tragelaphus*, more distinctively known as "harnessed" antelopes, because their hides, often richly colored, are conspicuously marked with whitish stripes, suggesting a harness thrown over the back. The largest of these handsome antelopes is the west African bongo (*T. euryceros*), of the forests of the Gaboon region, which stands nearly four feet high, and has horns 30 inches long. On the opposite side of the continent the nyala (*T. angasi*) frequents the fever-stricken swamps of the east African coast. Another well-known species of the swamps of southern and eastern Africa is Spekes antelope (*T. spekei*), native names for which are "nakong" and "sititunga." It differs from its fellows in having a uniform grayish-brown silky coat, without any "harness," but the young are faintly striped and spotted. This species is one of the best known of African antelopes, wherever rivers or swamps occur, and still survives in considerable numbers. That species most often called "bushbuck" is the "guib" (*T. scriptus*), still to be found in the jungles along the African rivers from Abyssinia to the Cape. It is remarkable for its inferior size, which is about that of a goat; and for the variability of its markings, which has led to much confusion in describing it. The variety most common in Cape Colony is uniformly dark brown, with no stripes whatever, and only a few spots on the haunches. This genus of antelopes is closely allied to that of the koodoos (q.v.), and resembles them in that the females are hornless, and usually differ in color from the males.

Bushel, a dry measure containing eight gallons or four pecks. The standard bushel in the United States (originally known as the Winchester bushel) contains 2150.42 cubic inches and holds 77.627 pounds of pure water at a temperature of 39.8° F., and 30 inches atmospheric pressure. The English standard, the imperial bushel, has a capacity of 2218.20 cubic inches and holds 80 pounds of pure water at 62° F. See Weights and Measures.

Bushido, boo-shē'dō ("the way of the warrior"), the ethical code of the Samurai, the Japanese order of knighthood. It is in some ways like the code of the knights of the Middle Ages, demanding courage, honor, and loyalty to country and rulers; it also enjoins the duty of suicide by hari-kari (q.v.) to avoid loss of honor. Although the formal code was given up when feudalism was abolished in Japan, its ideals still have great influence on the people, and many of the most prominent of the nation were educated according to its principles. It has given woman a remarkable position in Japan and even yet instils in the young loftier ideals. See SAMURAI.

Bushmaster, a large pit-viper (*Lachesis mutus*) of the rattlesnake family, numerous in northeastern South America, and called by the natives "surucucu." It is the largest and most venomous snake known, sometimes reaching a length of nine feet. Its ground color is pale yellow, darker on the back, and marked with a chain of jagged brown spots, and lighter on the belly. It has no rattle, but its tail terminates in a horny spur, which when the tail is vibrated, strikes against the ground, producing a rattling noise, which can be heard several feet. It is similar to the rattlesnake in its habits, dwells wholly upon the ground, and its poisonous apparatus is greatly developed, making it a very deadly serpent, and one much feared.

Bushman, or **Bosjesmans,** a dwarf African race inhabiting the Kalahari desert and some of the more northerly portions of Cape Colony. Their average height seems to be rather less than five feet, but the Bushmen of the Cape are more stunted than those living farther north. The skin is of a dirty yellowish color, and they have repulsive countenances, with a somewhat prominent forehead, thick lips, large ears, and small, deep-set, restless eyes. They are essentially a nomadic people, neither tilling the soil nor rearing domestic animals, but subsisting on the flesh of various wild animals, and on wild bulbs, roots, fruits, etc. They live in rocky caves or in rude nest-like structures in a bush.

Bushnell, Asa Smith, American politician: b. Rome, N. Y., 16 Sept. 1834; d. Columbus, O., 15 Jan. 1904. He began a business career, removed to Ohio in 1851 where he was a manufacturer of mowers and reapers. He served in the Civil War, commanding the 152d Ohio Volunteers. In 1895 he was elected governor of Ohio, and was re-elected in 1897.

Bushnell, Horace, American theologian: b. Litchfield, Conn., 14 April 1802; d. Hartford, 17 Feb. 1876. He graduated at Yale in 1827, engaged in journalistic and educational work, then studied law and theology at Yale, where for a time he was a tutor, and in 1833 he began his brilliant pastorate of the North Congregational Church in Hartford, from which he retired owing to failing health in 1853. His writings on theological subjects were as remarkable for the interest and discussion which they aroused among religious scholars and thinkers as for their originality and independence of thought and vigor of utterance. Both as writer and preacher he was a commanding figure, and his influence was far-reaching. His works include: 'Principles of National Greatness; Christian Nurture' (1847); 'God in Christ' (1849); 'Christian Theology' (1851); 'Sermons for the New Life' (1858); 'Nature and the Supernatural' (1858); 'Character of Jesus' (1861); 'The Vicarious Sacrifice' (1865); 'Women's Suffrage, the Reform Against Nature' (1869); 'Forgiveness and Law' (1874). See Mary B. Cheney, 'Life and Letters of Horace Bushnell' (1880); T. T. Munger, 'Horace Bushnell, Preacher and Theologian' (1899). The public services of Dr. Bushnell as a citizen were such as to make him long remembered for his civic pride and devotion to the interests of the city

where his lifework was performed. Bushnell Park, Hartford, named in his honor, is a monument to his initiative and persistent efforts, whereby mainly the city came into possession of one of its chief adornments.

Bushrangers, the name for desperadoes in Australia who, taking to the bush, supported themselves by levying contributions on the property of all and sundry within their reach. Considerable gangs of these lawless characters have sometimes collected, a body of 50 holding part of New South Wales in terror about 1830. A gang of four fell victims to justice in 1880, after having robbed a bank and committed other outrages. Since then little has been heard of outrages of this class.

Bushtit, a very small titmouse of the genus *Psaltriparus*, two species of which inhabit the western United States. One, the least bushtit (*P. minimus*), is found in summer from the Rocky Mountains to the Pacific coast, and is noted for its nest, which is formed of moss, down, lint of plants, and similar materials, and is shaped like an old-fashioned purse, 8 or 10 inches in length, suspended from the branch of a bush, and entered by a small hole near the top. The lining is of feathers and downy materials, and the eggs are 8 to 10 in number, and pure white. A southern variety of this is the lead-colored bushtit. A Mexican species (*P. melanotis*) is distinguished by black patches on each side of the head. The resemblance in the nesting habits of these birds to those of the European titmouse will be noted. See TIT-MOUSE.

Bushwhacker, a term applied during the Civil War to men living in the States where military operations were carried on, who professed to be neutrals and to be solely occupied in their ordinary vocations, but who seized opportunities to harass or attack individual soldiers or small bodies off their guard.

Busi'ris, a mythical Egyptian king mentioned by Apollodorus. Egypt had been for nine years subject to famine when Phrasius, a soothsayer of Cyprus, arrived to inform the king that the scarcity would not cease unless a foreigner were sacrificed each year to Zeus. Busiris made Phrasius the first victim, and established the custom of immolating a foreigner every year, Hercules was one year seized and bound to the altar, ready to be offered up, when he burst his chains and put Busiris to death.

Busk, George, English scientist: b. St. Petersburg, 1807; d. 1886. In the early part of his career he served as surgeon in the British navy, retiring in 1855. Later he devoted himself to the study of geology, paleontology, and kindred sciences, and became an authority in certain departments of zoology. He was a Fellow of the Royal Society and of the Geological Society of London.

Buskin (Latin *cothurnus*), a kind of high-soled shoe or half-boot, worn upon the stage by the ancient actors of tragedy, in order to give them a more heroic appearance. The Greek word *kothornos* denoted a sort of closed boot, fitting either foot, worn by women; the tragic boot being the *embates* or *embas*. The word is figuratively employed by the Latin authors for tragedy itself, or for a lofty and elevated style.

Bussang, boo'săng, or Boussa, a town of central Africa in lat. 10° 14′ N.; lon. 4° 11′ E. It is walled, and being surrounded by rocks is a place of considerable strength. The houses are irregularly placed, and thus cover a space of ground disproportioned to the number of inhabitants. The soil of the country is fertile, producing corn, yams, cotton, rice, and timber trees in great abundance. Among the wild animals are elephants, hippopotami, lions, etc. It has obtained a melancholy notoriety from the place where Mungo Park met his death in 1805. Pop. estimated at 12,000 to 18,000.

Bus'sey, Benjamin, American merchant: b. Canton, Mass., 1 March 1757; d. Roxbury, 13 Jan. 1842. He was a soldier in the Revolutionary War, became a silversmith in Dedham, afterward a merchant in Boston, where he acquired a large property, from which he bequeathed about $350,000 to Harvard College, one half for founding the Bussey Institute, a school of agriculture and horticulture, and one half for the support of the law and divinity schools of the college.

Bussi D'Amboise, Louis de Clermont D'Amboise, loo-ē dĕ klēr-mŏṅ däṅ-bwä bü-sē däṅ-bwä (Sieur de): b. 1549; d. 19 Aug. 1579. He acquired an infamous notoriety by the prominent part he took in the massacre of St. Bartholomew. He afterward attached himself to the Duke of Anjou, and obtaining the command of the castle of Anjou, made himself universally odious by his pride and oppression. He had the meanness to pander to the low passions of the Duke, and undertook to seduce the wife of the Count of Montsoreau. The intrigue cost him his life. Montsoreau having come to the knowledge of it, obliged his wife to write Bussi, giving him a rendezvous at the castle of Constancières. Bussi arrived with a single confidant, and was immediately met by Montsoreau, who killed him.

Busson, Charles, shär̃l bü-sŏṅ, French painter: b. Montoire, Loir-et-Cher, 15 July 1822. He studied under Rémond and François and devoted himself to landscape painting. His style was not marked by the characteristics of the "open air school," but recalled the canvases of earlier masters in his chosen branch of art. Among his paintings are 'Les Ruines du Château de Lavardin' and 'La Chasse au Marais.'

Bussu (bús-soo) **Palm,** a plant (*Manicaria succifera*), common in the swamps of northern Brazil. Though it rarely exceeds 15 feet in height, it has huge leaves, said to be the largest undivided leaves produced by any palm, even reaching 30 feet in length by 4 or 5 feet in width. After splitting the midrib from end to end the leaves are laid obliquely upon rafters to form thatch for houses. This position makes the spaces between the veins act as gutters to carry off water. The spathes are used by the Indians for caps and bags and for cloth-making. The large, hard, three-seeded, olive-green fruits do not seem to be used commercially.

Bussy-Rabutin, bü-sē-ra-bü-tăṅ, or **Roger de Rabutin,** Comte de Bussy: b. Epiry, Nivernois, 1618; d. Autun, 1693. He entered the army at the age of 13, and made several campaigns. Turenne, in a letter to the king, describes him as the best officer in his army, as far as songs were concerned. His scandalous chronicle,

entitled 'Histoire Amoureuse des Gaules,' cost him the loss of his official appointment and a year's imprisonment in the Bastile. He was a correspondent of Madame de Sévigné, and is often mentioned in her letters. He had the vanity to suppose that he excelled her in her peculiar art, and his letters were afterward published in seven volumes.

Bust (French *buste,* Italian *busto,* of uncertain origin), in sculpture, the representation of that portion of the human figure which comprises the head and the upper part of the body. The bust did not become common among the Greeks until the time of Alexander, nor among the Romans till the time of the empire. Among the Greeks, the portrait busts of the learned formed an important branch of art. The artists in these works exhibited a singular power of expressing character, and in this way we possess what are probably faithful likenesses of Socrates, Plato, and other distinguished persons. The first Roman bust that can be depended upon as giving a correct likeness is that of Scipio Africanus the elder. The number of busts of the time of the Roman empire is very considerable, but those of the Roman poets and men of letters have not been preserved in so large numbers as those of the Greeks. A collection of drawings of antique busts was made by Fulvius Ursinus, and published with the title, 'Virum Illustrium Imagines' (Rome 1569; Antwerp 1606); subsequently a similar collection was published in the 'Iconographie Grecque' of Visconti (Paris 1811), which was followed by his 'Iconographie Romaine' in 1817.

Bustamante, boo-stạ-män'tä, **Anastasio,** Mexican statesman and revolutionist: b. Tiquilpan, Michoacan, 27 July 1780; d. San Miguel Allende, 6 Feb. 1853. In 1808 he joined the Spanish army, and for a time fought against the party of the revolutionists, but in 1821 he acted with Iturbide. He was made vice-president and commander of the army, in the administration of Guerrero, 1829. He afterward revolted and led the Centralist party, and in 1830 became acting president of Mexico. In 1832 Santa Anna opposed him at the head of an army, and he was conquered and banished 1833. When the Centralist party returned to power he was recalled, and in 1837 was elected president of Mexico. In 1842 he was obliged to retire from the presidency, and was succeeded by Santa Anna. He served in the Mexican army in the war with the United States, retiring from military service in 1848.

Bustamante, Carlos Maria, cär'lōs mä-rē'ạ, Mexican historian: b. Oajaca, 4 Nov. 1774; d. 21 Sept. 1848. He studied law and in 1801 began its practice. In 1805 he became editor of the *Diario de Méjico.* He held a command under Morelos in 1812, and was captured at Vera Cruz. He was released, and became a member of Congress and held other public offices. His works treat of various periods of Mexican history, and are of special value, as he was an eye-witness of much that he describes. He published a history of the Mexican Revolution (1823–32), and histories of the times of Iturbide and of Santa Anna.

Bustard Quail, the name given by Anglo-Indians to the button-quail (q.v.).

1. Little Bustard.　　　2. Great Bustard.

Bustards, a family of game birds (*Otididæ*) of the Old World, which, however, are not gallinaceous, but are related in structure on the one hand to the cranes, and on the other to the plovers. They are inland birds, haunting dry, grassy, and sandy plains, and in the more settled districts resorting to stubble-fields and pasture-land. They have strong legs and feet, as well as good wing-power, and spend more of their time on the ground than in flight. Most of them are birds of handsome plumage, the upper parts being mottled with brown and reddish tints, set off with white and black. Ornamental plumes are characteristic of the group, and often form crests, or ruffs, about the head, neck, and breast. Bustards are known in the Mediterranean regions, and throughout southern Asia to China and Japan. They also abound all over Africa, and one species (*Eupodotis australis*) inhabits Australia, where it is called "native turkey." Those of North Africa and western Asia are known as "houbaras," and form the favorite game-birds of that semi-desert region. Certain small species of India, favorites with sportsmen, are called "floricans." The typical, and best-known bustard, however, is *Otis tarda*, now extinct in Great Britain, but numerous throughout the Mediterranean countries. · It has somewhat the size and form of an American turkey, and is the largest and one of the most valuable of European game-birds. A remarkable feature of this species is the fact that a great pouch, opening under the tongue, is developed in the throat of the male of some examples during the breeding season. This phenomenon is restricted to adult birds, and the pouch disappears at other times of the year. Its utility is unknown. A much smaller but otherwise similar species, the little bustard (*Otis tetrax*), is another favorite with European sportsmen. The term is sometimes erroneously applied to other large birds, such as the Magellanic goose of Argentina. Consult: Aflalo, 'Sport in Europe' (London 1901); Seebohm, 'Birds of Asia' (London 1901); Bryden, 'Nature and Sport in South Africa' (London 1897).

Busybody, The, a pen name under which Benjamin Franklin wrote a series of papers, modeled on 'The Spectator' of Addison; also a comedy by Mrs. Centlivre, 1709.

Bu'tades. See DIBUTADES.

Butch'er, Samuel Henry, Irish classical scholar: b. Dublin, 16 April 1850. He was educated at Marlborough College, and Trinity College, Cambridge, and was a lecturer at University College, Oxford, 1876-82. In the last mentioned year he succeeded John Stuart Blackie as professor of Greek in the University of Edinburgh. He has published a 'Prose Translation of the Odyssey (with A. Lang q.v.) (1879); 'Demosthenes' (1881); 'Some Aspects of the Greek Genius' (1891); 'Aristotle's Theory of Poetry and the Fine Arts, with a Critical Text and Translation of the Poetics' (1895).

Butcher. See ABATTOIR.

Butcher-bird, a shrike of the family *Laniidæ*, representatives of which range throughout the northern hemisphere. They are birds of moderate size, and gray and white in color, with black markings upon the head, wings, and tail, which are properly included among the insect-eating birds, but have developed certain falcon-like traits. They are of powerful build, with hooked beaks, and strong claws, and in winter, when insect prey is not easily obtained, they are accustomed to strike down small birds, and to seize mice, shrews, etc. These they carry off in their claws to some thorn-tree, or to a fence with spikes, and impale them one by one upon the thorns, or other sharp points, in order to fix them firmly while they feed upon their flesh. It often happens, however, that their love of the chase exceeds their appetite, so that they will catch and store away several victims, whose frozen bodies remain hanging upon the thorns, like meat in a butcher's shop; the Germans have a popular belief that nine victims are thus stored at a time, and call the birds "nine-killers." These shrikes make rude nests in trees and lay four or five brownish spotted eggs. They feed their young upon insects, and these form the larger part of their own fare, especially grasshoppers. A typical species, common all over northern North America is the great northern shrike (*Lanius borealis*), which is rarely seen in the United States, except in winter. Another species, the loggerhead (*L. ludovicianus*), dwells in the southern States and is somewhat smaller in size. Consult: Ingersoll, 'Wild Life of Orchard and Field' (1902). See SHRIKE.

Bute, bũt, John Patrick Crichton-Stuart, (3d MARQUIS OF): b. Mountstuart, 12 Sept. 1847; d. 9 Oct. 1900. He was educated at Harrow and Oxford. In 1872 he married a daughter of Lord Howard. He was mayor of Cardiff in 1891-2, and after the latter year was lord-lieutenant of Buteshire. From 1892 to 1898 he was lord rector of St. Andrew's University. He was the author of 'Early Days of Sir William Wallace'; 'The Burning of the Barns of Ayr'; and 'Altus of St. Columba.' He owned some 117,000 acres of landed property. In 1868 he joined the Roman Catholic Church and some years later published a translation of the Roman 'Breviary.'

Bute, John Stuart (3d EARL OF), British statesman: b. Edinburgh, 25 May 1713; d. 10 March 1792. His grandfather was created a peer in 1703, and the family was connected with the royal Stuart line. In 1737 he entered Parliament. In consequence of his opposition to the measures of the ministry was left out when a new Parliament was convened in 1741. Offended by this neglect, Bute retired to his estates, and lived there, wholly secluded, till the landing of the Pretender in Scotland in 1745 induced him to go to London, and offer his services to the government. He had attracted the notice of the Prince of Wales. He soon gained influence, and succeeded in making himself indispensable to the prince. At his death, in 1751, he was appointed, by the widowed princess, chamberlain to her son, and was intrusted by her with his education. Bute never lost sight of his pupil, and possessed so much more influence with the Princess of Wales than her son's particular tutors, the Earl of Harcourt and the Bishop of Norwich, that they resigned their offices. George II. died 25 Oct. 1760, and two days after Bute was appointed member of the privy council. In March 1761 the Parliament was dissolved, and Bute was made secretary of state. Pitt, who saw his resolution in the new council justified, gave in his resignation the same year. This event made an unfavorable impression on the nation; but Bute, possessing the unbounded confidence of his king, stood at the head of the state. After a severe contest in Parliament, he concluded a peace with France. The terms for England were perhaps not disproportionate to the successes obtained during the war; but Bute was obliged to bear the most bitter reproaches. He, however, succeeded in winning the popular favor, and everything seemed to promise the power of the minister a long continuance. The influence of Bute seemed unbounded, when it was made known, contrary to expectation, that he had resigned his office as prime minister, and was in future to live as a private man. In 1766 Bute declared in the House of Lords that he had wholly withdrawn from public business, and no longer saw the king; still it was not doubted that his great influence continued. On the death of the Princess of Wales, 1772, he seems first to have given up all participation in the affairs of government. He spent his last years on his estate. A costly botanical garden, a library of 30,000 volumes, excellent astronomical, philosophical, and mathematical instruments, afforded him occupation. His favorite study was botany, with which he was intimately acquainted. For the queen of England he wrote the 'Botanical Register,' which contained all the different kinds of plants in Great Britain (9 vols. 4to). This work is remarkable, both for its splendor, in which it excels all former botanical works, and for its rarity. Only 12 copies were printed, at an expense of more than $50,000.

Bute, an island of Scotland, in the estuary of the Clyde, with an area of 30,000 acres, belonging principally to the Marquis of Bute. It is about 15 miles long, and the average breadth is 3½ miles. Agriculture is in an advanced state, and there are about 20,000 acres under cultivation. The herring fishery is also a source of considerable profit. The only town is Rothesay, whose ancient castle is one of the interesting antiquities of the island. The climate of Bute is milder than that of almost any part of Scotland. The county of Bute comprises the islands of Bute, Arran, Great Cumbræ, Little Cumbræ, Inchmarnock, and Pladda, with a total area of 143,997 acres, but only a small part is under cultivation. Arran is about double the size of Bute, but the other islands belonging to the county are small. Pop. (1901) 18,800.

Bu'tea, a small genus of trees or woody vines of the natural order *Leguminosæ*, natives of China and India, noted for their racemes of large rich usually scarlet papilionaceous flowers, for which they are cultivated in warm countries and to a small extent in warm greenhouses. The best-known species (*B. frondosa*) is called the dhak or pulas tree in India, and is grown out of doors in California. It is a leafy tree, attains a height of 50 feet, and bears very showy orange-crimson flowers, which are used in the East under the name keesoo or teesoo for dyeing yellow or orange. Its fibrous roots and bark are used for caulking boats, making rope, etc. Its red, resinous gum, with which the twigs are frequently covered, is said to be very rich in tannin, and is found in the markets of India.

Butin, Ulysse Louis Auguste, ü-lês loo-ê ō-goost bü-tăṅ, French painter: b. St. Quentin, 1838; d. Paris, 9 Dec. 1883. He was a pupil of Picot and Pils. His subjects are mostly from the life of the French fishermen, and his work shows remarkable truthfulness to nature. Among his best paintings are 'The Departure'; 'Fishing'; and 'Burial of a Sailor at Villerville.'

Butler, Amos William, American ornithologist: b. Brookville, Ind., 1 Oct. 1860. He received his education at the University of Indiana and in 1895 was elected president of the Indiana Academy of Science. He has been general secretary of the American Association for the Advancement of Science from 1891 and has published 'The Birds of Indiana' and lesser works.

But'ler, Andrew Pickens, American politician: b. Edgefield District, S. C., 7 Nov. 1796; d. near Edgefield Court-house, 5 May 1857. He was admitted to the bar in 1819, and in 1824 was elected to the legislature as the representative of his native district. In 1831, a period marked by the apprehended collision of South Carolina with the Federal government, on the nullification issue, he was elected colonel of a regiment of cavalry. In 1833, still a member of the legislature, he was made a judge of the courts of general sessions and common pleas. Subsequently, when a change was made in the judiciary system, he was transferred to the supreme bench of the State, where he continued until 1846, when he was elected a senator in Congress. Soon after taking his seat in this body, he was appointed chairman of the Judiciary Committee. One of his earliest speeches was against making Col Benton lieutenant-general of the army. The Kansas question, the action of the naval retiring board, the abolition question, and all others affecting the peculiar interests of South Carolina, and the general welfare of the South, engaged him in frequent debate, in which he always took a conspicuous part. His last speech was in reply to Mr. Sumner, and in defense of South Carolina.

Butler, Benjamin Franklin, American lawyer: b. Kinderhook Landing, N. Y., 17 Dec. 1795; d. Paris, France, 8 Nov. 1858. He was a lineal descendant of Oliver Cromwell. He studied law under Martin Van Buren, whose partner he subsequently became. From 1821 to 1825 he was district attorney of Albany County. He was elected to the Assembly in 1828, and from 1834 to 1838 was United States attorney-general. He was also acting secretary of war during part of Jackson's administration. He organized the law department of the College of the City of New York and for many years was one of the foremost members of the New York bar.

Butler, Benjamin Franklin, American lawyer and soldier: b. Deerfield, N. H., 5 Nov. 1818; d. Washington, D. C., 11 Jan. 1893. He studied law, was admitted to the bar in 1841, and beginning practice at Lowell, Mass., became distinguished as a criminal lawyer and politician. He was a member of the State legislature in 1853, of the State Senate in 1859-60, and a delegate to the Democratic National Convention of 1860, which met at Charleston and adjourned to Baltimore. He supported the nomination of John C. Breckenridge, which rendered him so unpopular in the North that he was defeated for governor of Massachusetts in that year. Butler had risen to the rank of brigadier-general of militia; and at the outbreak of the Civil War, he marched with the 8th Massachusetts Regiment, and, after a check at Big Bethel, was appointed to the command of Baltimore and of eastern Virginia, with his headquarters at Fort Monroe. In February 1862 he commanded the military forces sent from Boston to Ship Island, near the mouth of the Mississippi; and, after New Orleans had surrendered to the naval forces under Farragut, he held military possession of the city. Relieved of his command, he acted under Gen. Grant in his operations against Petersburg and Richmond in 1864. Returning to Massachusetts at the end of the war, he took an active part in politics as an extreme radical, advocated the impeachment of President Johnson, and in 1866–75 was a member of Congress. In 1877 and 1879 he was defeated as candidate for governor of Massachusetts, but in 1882 was elected by a large majority. In 1884 he ran for the presidency as the candidate of the Greenback and Anti-Monopolist parties, but was defeated, carrying no State. He published 'The Autobiography and Personal Reminiscences of Maj.-Gen. Benjamin F. Butler' (1892). Consult: Parton, 'Butler in New Orleans' (1863); Bland, 'Life of Benjamin F. Butler' (1879).

Butler, Charles, English Roman Catholic historian: b. London, 15 Aug. 1750; d. there, 2 June 1832. He was nephew of the Rev. Alban Butler (q.v.) He was called to the bar in 1791, and was the first Roman Catholic who was admitted, after the passing of the relief bill of that year. He wrote 'Horæ Biblicæ,' giving a history of the original text, early versions, and printed editions of the Old and New Testaments, and also of the 'Koran,' 'Zend-Avesta,' and the 'Edda.' This first appeared in 1797, and was followed by 'Horæ Juridicæ Subsecivæ,' a connected series of notes respecting the geography, chronology, and literary history of the principal codes and original documents of the Grecian, Roman, feudal, and canon law. He continued and completed Hargrave's 'Coke Upon Littleton'; supervised the sixth edition of Fearne's 'Essay on Contingent Remainders'; wrote a history of the geographical and political revolutions of Germany, and a 'Historical and Literary Account of the Formularies, Confessions of Faith, or Symbolic Books of Roman Catholic, Greek, and Principal Protestant Churches.' During the last 25 years of his career he principally devoted his pen to the vindication of the Roman Catholic Church. He published numerous biographies of eminent Roman Catholic divines and authors; continued his uncle's 'Lives of the Saints,' and produced 'Historical Memoirs of the English, Irish, and Scottish Catholics.' When Southey's ultra-Protestant 'Book of the Church' appeared, it was replied to in Butler's 'Book of the Roman Catholic Church,' which gave rise to six answers on the Protestant side, two of which were responded to by Butler. His 'Reminiscences' appeared 1822–7. As a constitutional lawyer his reputation was very high.

Butler, Charles, American lawyer: b. Kinderhook Landing, N. Y., 15 Feb. 1802; d. New York, 13 Dec. 1897. He was admitted to the bar in 1824 and subsequently as agent of the New York Life Insurance and Trust Company did much to help forward the development of the western part of the State. He was one of the founders of the Union Theological Seminary in 1835 and was for many years president of the council of New York University.

Butler, Clement Moore, American Episcopal clergyman: b. Troy, N. Y., 16 Oct. 1810; d. Philadelphia, Pa., 5 March 1890. He was a graduate from Trinity College, Hartford, in 1833, and from the General Theological Seminary in 1836. He was successively rector of churches in Boston and Washington, D. C., and of Grace Church in Rome, Italy, and from 1864 to 1884 professor of ecclesiastical history in the Episcopal Theological School in Philadelphia. He was the author of 'The Book of Common Prayer Interpreted by Its History' (1846); 'Old Truths and New Errors' (1850); 'Saint Paul in Rome' (1865); 'Inner Rome' (1866); 'Manual of Ecclesiastical History' (1868–72).

Butler, Lady Elizabeth Southerden Thompson: b. Lausanne, Switzerland, about 1844; married, 1877, Sir William Francis Butler (q.v.). She received her education in Italy, came to England in 1870, and first exhibited at the Royal Academy in 1873. Her 'Roll-Call' (1874) gained her a great reputation, and was purchased by Queen Victoria. Among her other pictures, which deal almost exclusively with military subjects, are: 'Missing' (1873); '28th Regiment at Quatre Bras' (1875); 'Balaclava' (1876); 'Inkerman' (1877); 'Defense of Rorke's Drift' (1881); 'Scotland Forever' (1881); 'Floreat Etona' (1882); 'The Charge of the Scots Greys at Waterloo' (1882); 'Evicted' (1890); 'Camel Corps' (1891); 'Halt in a Forced March' (1892); 'Dawn of Waterloo' (1895); 'Steady the Drums and Fifes' (1897); 'Tent Pegging in India' (1902). She is a sister of Mrs. Alice Meynell, the writer (q.v.).

Butler, Howard Russell, American landscape artist: b. New York, 3 March 1856. He graduated from Yale in 1876 and the Columbia Law School in 1881, and studied art in New York and Paris. He organized the American Fine Arts Society and was its first president.

Butler, James (DUKE OF ORMOND). English statesman: b. London, 19 Oct. 1610; d. Kingston Hall, Dorsetshire, 21 July 1688. When Strafford became lord-lieutenant of Ireland, Butler was made commander of the army, but as it consisted of only 3,000 men, he could do little more than keep the enemy in check, and was obliged to agree to a cessation of hostilities; after which, having been created a marquis, he was appointed lord-lieutenant. On the ruin of the royal cause he retired to France. After the execution of Charles he returned to Ireland with a view of raising the people; but on the landing of Cromwell returned to France. While abroad he exerted himself to further the restoration of Charles; and when that event was brought about by Monk, returned with the king. Before the coronation he was created Duke, and assisted at that ceremony as lord high-steward of England. In 1662 he was again appointed lord-lieutenant of Ireland, which country he restored to comparative tranquillity, and was an active benefactor to it by encouraging various improvements, particularly the growth of flax and manufacture of linen. On the exile of Lord Clarendon, his attachment to that nobleman involved Butler in much of the odium attached to him, and although, on his recall from Ireland, nothing, on the most rigorous inquiry, could be proved against him, he was removed by the machinations of Buckingham. For six years he was deprived of court favor, but at length was again appointed lord-lieutenant of Ireland, which place he held during the remainder of the reign of Charles, but soon after resigned, his principles not suiting the policy of James. He died at his seat in Dorsetshire, leaving behind him the character of a man who united the courtier and the man of honor and integrity better than any nobleman of the time.

Butler, John, American royalist leader in the American Revolution: b. Connecticut; d. Niagara, 1794. He became a leading resident of Tryon County, N. Y.; commanded the Indians in the Niagara campaign (1759) and in the Montreal expedition (1760). At the outbreak of the Revolution he sided with the Tories and became deputy superintendent of Indian affairs. In 1776 he organized a band of marauders, chiefly Indians, and fought the battle of Oriskany (1777); in July 1778, he commanded at the brutal Wyoming massacre. In 1780 he took part in Sir John Johnson's raid on the Mohawk settlements. At the end of the war he fled to Canada, and was appointed Indian agent.

Butler, Joseph, English prelate and theologian: b. Wantage, Berkshire, 18 May 1692; d. Bath, 16 June 1752. After some previous education at a grammar school he was sent to an academy at Tewkesbury, with a view to ordination as a minister among the Dissenters. While occupied by his studies he gave a proof of his talents by some acute and ingenious remarks on Dr. Samuel Clarke's 'Demonstration of the Being and Attributes of God,' in private letters addressed to the author. He likewise paid particular attention to the points of controversy between the members of the Established Church and the Dissenters, the result of which was a determination to be no longer a Nonconformist; he therefore removed to Oxford in 1714. Having taken orders, he was in 1718 appointed preacher at the Rolls Chapel, and the sermons which he preached while holding this office, especially the first three, 'On Human Nature,' occupy an important place in the history of ethical science. In 1736 he was appointed clerk of the closet to the queen. The same year he published his celebrated work, the 'Analogy of Religion, Natural and Revealed, to the Constitution and Course of Nature.' In 1738 Butler was promoted to the bishopric of Bristol on the recommendation of Queen Caroline; and in 1750 obtained his highest preferment — the bishopric of Durham. He was interred in Bristol Cathedral. His other published works include: 'Fifteen Sermons Preached at the Rolls Chapel' (1726); 'Six Sermons Preached Upon Public Occasions'; etc. The first collected edition of his works was published in 1804 at Edinburgh. An excellent edition of his famous 'Analogy' is that of Fitzgerald (1860). Mr. Gladstone brought out an edition of his works in two volumes (1896), and also published a volume of 'Subsidiary Studies on Butler.'

Butler, Josephine Grey, English philanthropist: b. Milfield, Gloucestershire, about 1828; d. 30 Dec. 1906. Married George Butler, afterward Canon Winchester, 1852. She was prominent in efforts for the higher education of women, and for moral reform, and published:

'Life of John Grey of Dilston'; 'Life of Catherine of Sierra'; 'Recollections of George Butler'; 'The Lady of Shunem'; 'Personal Reminiscences of a Great Crusade'; 'Prophets and Prophetesses'; 'Nature Races and the War'; 'Silent Victories'; 'The Hour Before the Dawn'; 'Government by Police'; 'The Constitution Violated'; 'Women's Work and Women's Culture'; Life of Oberlin'; 'A Voice in the Wilderness.'

Butler, Matthew Calbraith, American army officer: b. near Greenville, S. C., 8 March 1836. He studied law at Stonelands, near Edgefield Court-house, and was admitted to the bar in December 1857. He was elected to the legislature of South Carolina in 1860; entered the Confederate service as captain of cavalry in the Hampton Legion in June 1861, and became a major-general through the regular grades; lost his right leg at the battle of Brandy Station on 9 June 1863. He was elected to the legislature of South Carolina in 1866; was United States senator in 1877–95; commissioned a major-general of volunteers for the war with Spain, 28 May 1898; and was appointed one of the American commissioners to arrange and supervise the evacuation of Cuba.

Butler, Nicholas Murray, American educator: b. Elizabeth, N. J., 2 April 1862. He was graduated at Columbia University in 1882; took a special course in Berlin and Paris in 1884–5; and was then called to Columbia University, where he was an assistant in philosophy, 1885–6; tutor, 1886–9; and adjunct professor, 1889–90; and dean of the faculty of philosophy, 1890–2. He was a founder and the first president (1886–91) of the New York College for the Training of Teachers, now a part of Columbia University, and as member of the New Jersey State Board of Education (1887–95) introduced manual training into the public school system of that State. On 6 Jan. 1902 he was unanimously elected president of Columbia University to succeed Seth Low, then mayor-elect of New York. He has edited 'The Educational Review'; 'The Teachers' Professional Library'; 'The Great Educators Series'; 'The Columbia University Contributions to Philosophy and Education'; and the 'Monographs on Education in the United States,' which formed a part of the exhibit of the United States bureau of education at the Paris Exposition of 1900, and published a volume of miscellaneous essays, addresses, etc., entitled 'The Meaning of Education' (1898).

Butler, Samuel, English satirical poet: b. Strensham, Worcestershire, 12 Feb. 1612; d. London, 25 Sept. 1680. He passed some time in his youth at Cambridge, but never matriculated at the university. He was afterward clerk or steward to several country gentlemen, and latterly lived in London. He resided some time with Sir Samuel Luke, a commander under Cromwell. In this situation Butler acquired the materials for his 'Hudibras' by a study of those around him, and particularly of Sir Samuel himself, a caricature of whom constituted the celebrated knight Hudibras. The first edition of 'Hudibras' was published in 1663 and was brought under the notice of the court by the well-known Earl of Dorset. It immediately became highly popular with the prevailing party in Church and state, and served as a general

NICHOLAS MURRAY BUTLER,
PRESIDENT OF COLUMBIA UNIVERSITY.

source of quotation; the king himself perpetually answering his courtiers out of 'Hudibras.' Celebrated as it rendered its author, it did nothing toward extricating him from indigence. He was buried in St. Paul's Church, Covent Garden, at the expense of his friend, Mr. Longueville, of the Temple, and a monument was, 40 years after, erected to his memory, in Westminster Abbey, by Alderman Barber, the printer. 'Hudibras,' both in its style and matter, is one of the most original and witty works that were ever written. As a work intended to ridicule the Puritans its attraction was great but temporary, but as applicable to classes of character found in all ages, its satire will always be relished. Butler's 'Remains in Verse and Prose' appeared in 1759.

Butler, Samuel, English author and composer: b. Langar, 4 Dec. 1835; d. London, 19 June 1902. He was educated at Shrewsbury School and Cambridge University, and with Henry Festing Jones composed many gavottes, figures, etc., and the cantata of 'Narcissus.' He was also an artist of merit, and for several years exhibited at the Royal Academy. He is best known, however, as a brilliant, original writer in more than one field, and as a master of irony had few equals and still fewer superiors among his contemporaries, in this particular more nearly approaching Swift than anyone else. His published books include 'A First Year in Canterbury Settlement' (1863); 'Erewhon, or Over the Range,' his most remarkable work, with the exception of 'Erewhon Revisited'; 'Fair Haven,' an ironical defense of Christianity' (1873); 'Life and Habit' (1877); 'Evolution, Old and New' (1879); 'Unconscious Memory' (1880); 'Alps and Sanctuaries of Piedmont and the Canton Ticino' (1881); 'Luck or Cunning as the Means of Organic Modification' (1886); 'Ex Veto' (1888); 'Life of Dr. Samuel Butler of Shrewsbury and Bishop of Lichfield' (1896); 'The Authoress of the Odyssey' (1897); 'The Iliad of Homer, Rendered into English Prose' (1900); 'Erewhon Revisited' (1901).

Butler, William, American army officer: b. Prince William County, Va., 1759; d. Columbia, S. C., 15 Nov. 1821. He served in the Revolution in Pulaski's corps; afterward, under Pickens, Lee, and Greene; won fame as commander of the Mounted Rangers; and, after the war, became (1796) major-general of militia. He was a member of the Convention which adopted the Federal Constitution; helped frame the South Carolina constitution; was a member of Congress (1801–11); and commanded the South Carolina troops in 1812.

Butler, William Allen, American lawyer and man of letters: b. Albany, N. Y., 20 Feb. 1825; d. Yonkers, N. Y., 9 Sept. 1902. He was a son of Benjamin F. Butler (1795–1858, q.v.), and was graduated at the New York University in 1843 and began the practice of law. He wrote in 1857 'Nothing to Wear,' a satirical poem, which became famous almost immediately and was not only reprinted in England but translated into French and German. His other publications include a volume of his collective poems (1871); 'Mrs. Limber's Raffle (1876); 'Oberammergau'; 'Domesticus' (1886).

Butler, Sir William Francis, British general: b. Tipperary County, Ireland, 31 Oct. 1838. He was educated at Dublin, and joined the army in 1858 as ensign in the 69th Regiment. In 1863 he became lieutenant, and in 1874 was promoted to the rank of major. He served on the Red River expedition of 1870–1, and about the same time was sent on a special mission to the Saskatchewan territories. He accompanied the Ashantee expedition in 1874, and in 1879 acted as staff officer in Natal. He also served in Egypt in 1882, and held important commands under Lord Wolseley in the Sudan campaign of 1884–5. From 1890 till 1893 he was in command at Alexandria, and in 1892 was raised to the rank of major-general. He has since had command of the 2d Infantry Brigade at Aldershot, of the southeastern district at Dover, 1896–8; in Cape Colony, 1898–9; and of the Western District since 1899, and concurrently at Aldershot, 1900–1. He has published 'The Great Lone Land: A Narrative of Travel and Adventure in the Northwest of America' (1872); 'The Wild North Land' (1872), the story of a winter journey across northern North America; 'Akim-Foo' (1875), a story of the Ashantee war; 'Far Out' (1880); 'Red Cloud, the Solitary Sioux' (1882); 'The Campaign of the Cataracts' (1887); 'Charles George Gordon' (1889); 'Sir Charles Napier' (1891); and 'Sir George Colley' (1899). He was made K.C.B. in 1886 and in 1900 was appointed Lieutenant-General.

Butler, William Morris, American physician: b. Maine, 1850. He was educated at Hamilton College and the New York College of Physicians and Surgeons; has been professionally connected with several homœopathic hospitals, and has been professor of nervous diseases at the Metropolitan Postgraduate School of Medicine, New York. He has published 'Home Care for the Insane.'

Butler, William Orlando, American general: b. Jessamine County, Ky., 1791; d. Carrollton, Ky., 6 Aug. 1880. He was about devoting himself to the legal profession when the War of 1812 broke out. Enlisting as a private soldier in Capt. Hart's company of Kentucky volunteers he gained distinction in the battles at Frenchtown and the river Raisin. Subsequently he took a conspicuous part in the battles of Pensacola and New Orleans, was brevetted major, 23 Dec. 1814, acted as aide-de-camp to Gen. Jackson from 17 June 1816 to 31 May 1817, when he tendered his resignation, resuming for the next 25 years the profession of the law. From 1839 to 1843 he served as a representative in Congress from that district, in the interests of the Democratic party. Nominated as a candidate for governor of Kentucky in 1844, he was defeated by the influence of Clay. Created major-general, 29 June 1846, he led with great spirit the daring charge at Monterey, and although wounded on that occasion, still remained for several months with the army. On 18 Feb. 1848, he succeeded Gen. Scott in command of the army in Mexico. The most important operation during his tenure of this office was the defeat of Padre Jarauta and his guerrilla forces by Gen. Lane. His military administration in Mexico was brought to a close on 29 May 1848, when he announced the ratification of the treaty of peace. After his return to the United States he was nominated in 1848 by the Democratic party as candidate for the vice-presidency. He was the author of 'The Boatman's Horn and Other Poems.'

Butler, Zebulon, American military officer: b. Lyme, Conn., in 1731; d. Wilkesbarre, 28 July 1795. He served in the French and Indian war, and in the Revolutionary War also. He commanded the garrison at Wyoming Valley at the time of the massacre of 3 July 1778.

Butler, Pa., a borough and county-seat of Butler County, situated on the Conequessing Creek, and on the Pennsylvania, the Pittsburg & W., the Buffalo, R. & P., and the Bessemer & L. E. R.R.'s. It is the centre of a region having oil and natural gas. The chief industry is glass manufacture, and there are also flouring mills, a large planing mill, and several oil-well supply manufactories. Pop. (1900) 10,853.

Butler University, a co-educational (non-sectarian) institution in Irvington, a suburb of Indianapolis, Ind.; organized in 1855 as Northwestern Christian University. In 1903 it had 25 professors and instructors, and 306 students.

Bu'to, an Egyptian goddess whom the Greeks identified with Leto or Latona. She was represented under the guise of a serpent, and the city of Buto, which took its name from her, is supposed to have occupied a site on an island in the modern Lake Burlos in the Delta of the Nile.

Buton, boo'tòn, Boeton, or Butung, an East Indian island, southeast of Celebes, belonging to Holland. Its area is about 1,700 square miles. It is fertile and densely wooded, and is governed by a native chief, subject to the Dutch government. The population, mainly Malays, is about 100,000. The chief town is Buton at the southwestern end of the island.

Bütschli, büt-shlē, Otto, German zoologist: b. Frankfort-on-the-Main, 1848. Since 1878 he has been professor of zoology in the University of Heidelberg. He was one of the first to establish knowledge of nucleus and cell division, and his writings upon protoplasm and bacteria have been widely read and discussed. He has published 'Protozoen'; 'Untersuchungen über mikroskopische Schäume und das Protoplasma' (1892); 'Untersuchungen über die Mikrostructur künstlicher und natürlicher Kieselsäuregallerten' (1900).

Butt, Clara, English contralto singer of note: b. Southwick, Sussex, 1 Feb. 1873. She was educated at the Royal College of Music, and made her début at Lyceum Theatre, London, on 5 Dec. 1892, in the opera 'Orfeo.' She has taken part in three Handel festivals, and ranks among the very first of contralto singers. She was married to Mr. Kennerly Rumford in June 1900.

Butt, Isaac, Irish politician: the first to make political use of the phrase "Home Rule"; was the son of a Protestant rector: b. County Donegal, 16 Sept. 1813; d. 5 May 1879. Educated at Raphoe and at Trinity College, Dublin, he gained a brilliant reputation for his accomplished scholarship. In 1852 he was elected to Parliament as a Liberal Conservative for Youghal, for which constituency he sat until 1865. He defended Smith O'Brien and others in the state trials of 1848, and, with equal fearless-

ness and self-devotion, all the Fenian prisoners between the years 1865 and 1869. In 1871 he was elected for the city of Limerick to lead the Home Rule party. He published 'History of Italy' (1860); and 'The Problem of Irish Education' (1875).

Butte, būt, Mont., a city and county-seat of Silverbow County, on the Great N., the Northern P., and the Union P. Railways. It is on the high plateau between the Rocky Mountains and the Bitter Root mountains, 5,800 feet above the sea level. The city is well-built, the more imposing buildings being the city hall, courthouse and jail, opera-house, the federal building, and a fine public high school, completed at a cost of $125,000. The Montana State School of Mines is located here. The public school system is excellent, and there is a public library of more than 35,000 volumes.

Mining, Manufacturing, etc. — Butte is the largest mining town in the world, employing thousands of persons in this industry alone. Copper is the chief production, although there are valuable deposits of gold and silver. The Great Anaconda Copper mine is here, and many other valuable mining properties are within a radius of a few miles of the city. The copper production alone is about one-half that of the United States, and the total annual mineral output is estimated at more than $40,000,000. Probably no city of equal size in the country is so exclusively given over to a single industry.

Butte is the trade and jobbing centre for southern and western Montana; has an extensive trolley system; gas and electric lights; national and other banks; and several daily and weekly newspapers.

Government, etc. — Butte is governed by a mayor, elected biennially, and a city council. It spends annually about $200,000 for schools, and about $50,000 each for the fire, police, and street-cleaning departments. Butte was settled as a gold-placer camp in 1863, laid out as a town in 1866, and grew rapidly after the successful opening up of quartz mining in 1875. It was incorporated by the Territorial Legislature in 1879, and reincorporated in 1888. In 1881 it was made the county-seat of Silverbow County. Pop. in 1870 about 300; (1880) 3,363; (1890) 10,723; (1900) 30,470; (1904, including suburbs) 60,000.

Butter, a product of milk, consisting largely of butter-fat and usually obtained by churning cream or milk, and working the product to remove water and other constituents.

Butter has been in use from early historic days. It is first mentioned in the Bible in Gen. xviii. 8. It was used as food and medicine, as an ointment, and for burning in lamps. The Greeks probably learned of it from the Scythians or Thracians, and the Romans from the Germans. It was made from the milk of sheep and goats, and later of cows, the method of making being to churn it in skin bags or pouches. Formerly butter was prepared by direct churning of the milk; this was both laborious and wasteful of butter-fat. To reduce labor and loss the system of setting the milk and skimming off the cream was evolved; since 1877 this method has given way to the use of centrifugal force for the separation of the cream and milk.

To-day the process of making is divided into the operations of creaming, churning, working,

.and finishing. The fat exists in the form of small globules in the milk, in suspension. In the setting system the milk was placed in shallow pans about four inches high, or in deep ones of about 18 inches, and advantage was taken of the fact that the fat globules, being lighter than water and other constituents of the milk, would rise to the surface by the force of gravity. Large fat globules will rise more rapidly than small ones, and the size of the globules varies with different breeds of cattle. In the shallow-pan system the milk is set as soon as possible after it is drawn, and the cream is skimmed off in 24 or 36 hours. This system is wasteful in that the skim milk often contains 0.5 to 1.5 per cent of fat. The deep-setting system is less wasteful, the fat in the skim- milk being often reduced to 0.2 per cent. The new-drawn, warm milk is placed in cans surrounded or submerged in water at about 40° F., and the rapid reduction in temperature causes the globules to rise quickly. The cream is removed by dipping it off, or the skim-milk is drawn off from the bottom of the can. The fat left in the skim-milk consists of the small fat globules.

The introduction of the separator and use of centrifugal force has resulted in a more perfect and rapid separation. This force exceeds that of gravity a thousand-fold. The system of separation is continuous, a constant, uniform flow of milk being conducted into a bowl or drum revolving at from 5,000 to 9,000 or more revolutions per minute. The inlet tube is in the centre of the bowl and reaches almost to the bottom; here the constituents in the milk separate, the heavier serum gravitating to the circumference of the bowl, the fat — the lightest portion — remaining in the centre. These are forced upward by the incoming milk, and the separated milk escapes through a side tube, while the cream passes through a small outlet in the centre. This last outlet can be closed or opened in some machines, thus regulating the percentage of fat in the cream. The machines are of various sizes, from those worked by hand power and doing 200 to 500 pounds of milk per hour, to power machines of 2,000 pounds and over per hour capacity. Some makes have appliances within the bowl to increase the efficiency. A good separator, well run, will not leave more than from 0.05 to 0.1 per cent of fat in the separated milk.

The cream may be churned at once if sweet cream butter is desired, or "ripened" or soured. The aim in ripening is to develop certain flavors in the butter, and a certain degree of acidity which aids in churning and influences the texture. In this latter case cream should be cooled as it leaves the separator; if it is to be churned next day the temperature of cooling should be 65° to 70° F. If the second day, 55° to 60° F.; and if four days or more, 40° F. It should then be held at such temperature that it will reach the desired degree of acidity by the time it is desired to churn. The degree of acidity may be determined by various tests. Ripening may be effected by adding to the cream a "starter" of sour cream, sour milk, buttermilk, or a commercial preparation of the desired organisms or bacteria. In any case only desirable organisms should be permitted in the ripening room, as undesirable ones rapidly affect flavor. In some cases it is considered advisable to pasteurize the milk or cream,

the milk being heated to kill all germs, then the sample may be inoculated with desirable ones. During ripening the cream is usually held constant at a temperature between 60° and 70° F. until ready to churn.

In churning, the fat globules receive such agitation that they unite into masses. This is usually done in a churn (q.v.) and at a temperature ranging from 50° to 65° F. It is wise to churn at as low a temperature as possible, the best results being obtained at such a degree that the particles of fat unite readily, and, when united, form firm granules of butter. Churning should stop when the particles are the size of wheat. The buttermilk may be drawn off and the butter washed; it is then worked, either by hand or by the butter-worker (q.v.), to remove buttermilk, water, etc., salted, and packed as required.

Scrupulous cleanliness and attention to detail, from the feeding of the cows to the placing of the product in the hands of the consumer, are imperative. See CREAMERIES; DAIRYING.

The composition of butter varies, but is approximately: Fat, 85 per cent; protein, 1 per cent; ash (salt), 3 per cent; water, 11 per cent. The percentage of fat should not fall below 80 per cent, nor the water rise above 15 per cent. The percentage of fat in butter of good quality often rises to 86 or 88 per cent. The water content is the most variable, running up to 25 per cent, and in some cases higher. The fats of butter are glycerides of fatty acids. About 15 per cent of the fats are volatile, and at least in some cases aid in giving flavor and odor. Oleine, palmitine, and myristine are the three leading fats present; the former, being fluid at ordinary temperatures and variable in amount, influences the hardness of the butter. The quality of butter is judged by its flavor, texture, color, amount of salt, and general appearance. Flavor counts about 45 per cent of the points, and varies with the market. Some markets require a mild, delicate butter; for the supply of such the cream is often pasteurized: others require a high flavor, almost verging on rancidity. Whatever is desired, that flavor should be pronounced, with an absence of rancidity or other flavors. Texture carries 25 per cent of the points and depends upon the granular condition of the fats. The more distinctly the granules show up when the butter is broken the better the texture. The right color depends upon the market requirements; usually a bright golden yellow, as naturally yielded when cows are on grass, is considered ideal. It should be uniform. To ensure this, it is sometimes necessary to use some butter-color: formerly the main one used was arnotto; now the coal-tar colors, aniline yellow, and butter yellow, are used, although turmeric, saffron, carrot-juice, or marigold leaves would do. The coloring matter is usually dissolved in some oil, and the preparations are of standard strengths. Some South American countries require the butter to be a deep orange or red color. A small quantity of salt is often added to improve the palatability; it has little influence on the keeping qualities. The amount varies with trade requirements. Unsalted or slightly salted butter is largely used in Europe and the United Kingdom. The finish and packing of the butter should be attractive and neat. The styles are numerous, but attempts are being made to standardize. The American butter-tub is largely used here. It holds from 50 to 70 pounds. In Canada and Australia a box holding 56 pounds is used for the export trade. The Danes ship their butter in firkins containing 112 pounds. For local trade the standard rectangular pound print is 4⅝ × 2½ × 2⅜ inches. These are wrapped in parchment paper and packed in specially made boxes.

Oleomargarine is the most common adulterant, and its detection, especially when present in only small amounts, is difficult. Cottonseed and other oils have been added to increase the water-holding capacity of the butter, and in butters for South America glucose has been added as a preservative. The various preservatives, as borax, boracic acid, etc., sold under their own and other names, are now recognized as adulterants.

Renovated or process butter is generally low-grade butter which has been melted and put through a process to remove the disagreeable odors and taste; sometimes it is then mixed with soured separated or whole milk or cream, and granulated. If the primary article is not too inferior, the resulting product can be sold as good creamery butter; generally its keeping qualities are impaired. In some States and in the United Kingdom all butter so treated must be distinctly branded "Renovated."

During the year 1850 the amount of butter made on farms in the United States was 313,345,306 pounds. In 1899 that made on farms and in factories was 1,491,871,673 pounds. Over two thirds of the butter is made on the farms, but the factory system is increasing. The average value of that made on farms was 16.7 cents per pound, and that made in creameries and factories 20 cents. The cost of transporting the milk to factories is about 1.5 cents per pound of butter. Denmark is at present the leading butter-exporting country of the world, with a record in 1898 of 160,143,255 pounds, valued at $34,575,634, the average price being the highest on the market.

The coefficient of digestibility of butter-fat is 98 per cent or over. It is well assimilated, and, like other fats, is a source of heat and energy. Its value as a food and methods of usage are well known. Butter containing 82.4 per cent butter-fat has a fuel value per pound of 3,475 calories, and in a number of dietary studies butter furnished 1.9 per cent of the total food, and 19.7 per cent of the total fat of the daily food. Further information is given in Prof. Atwater's reports on dietary studies. Fresh and salt butter are equally valuable. Clarified butter is used in cooking. It is ordinary butter freed from casein and water by heating.

Bibliography.— Fleischmann, 'Book of the Dairy'; Gurler, 'American Dairying'; Oliver, 'Milk, Cheese, and Butter'; United States Department of Agriculture, 'Butter Making on the Farm'; 'Farmers' Bulletin No. 57'; Wing, 'Milk and Its Products'; Woll, 'Grotenfelt's Modern Dairy Practice.'
S. Fraser,
Instructor in Farm Practice, Cornell University.

Butter, Artificial. See Oleomargarine.

Butter and Eggs, a troublesome weed. See Toad-Flax.

Butter-bur (*Petasites vulgaris*), a composite plant, with large rhubarb-like leaves and purplish flowers, growing by the side of streams, allied to colt's-foot. The flowers appear before the leaves.

Butter-color, a preparation employed to color butter and its imitations. Annatto was formerly largely used for this purpose, but is now superseded by coal-tar colors and other coloring substances. Owing to the small quantities used in coloring butter they are quite harmless.

Butter-fishes. The two best known butter-fishes in American waters are denizens of the Atlantic. One (*Poronotus triacanthus*) is the butter-fish or dollar-fish of the coast of Massachusetts and New York, the harvest-fish of New Jersey, the dollar-fish of Maine, the sheepshead of Cape Cod, the pumpkinseed of Connecticut, and the star-fish of Norfolk. It swims mostly in company with large jellyfish, whose streamers, while often protecting it from other depredators, are frequently the cause of its death from their stings. The body is ovate and flat, the dorsal and anal fins are each very pointed, and the tail is long and widely forked.

The harvest-fish (*Peprilus paru*) is another "butter-fish" found from Cape Cod southward to Brazil, but it is most abundant about the mouth of Chesapeake Bay, where it is locally called "whiting." It has the habit of swimming beneath the Portuguese man-of-war. It is a delicious little pan-fish, about six inches long. On the Pacific coast there are three species, one of which (*P. simillima*) is the Californian "pompano," abundant during summer about Santa Cruz, where it is highly prized for its rich and delicate quality, and reaches 10 inches in length. Consult: Jordan and Evermann, 'American Food and Game Fishes' (1902).

Butter Making. See Butter.

Butter Rock, an obsolete name for certain alums.

Butter-tree, various tropical or subtropical trees of different genera and even families. Their seeds yield fixed oils which resemble butter and are similarly used or are employed for lighting. The leading group is perhaps the genus *Bassia* of the natural order *Sapotaceæ.* Of this genus the best-known species are *B. longifolia*, the Indian oil-tree, whose wood resembles teak, and is in use in the East; *B. butyracea*, the Indian butter-tree, whose light wood is of no commercial importance; and *B. latifolia*, the East Indian Mahowa, Mahwa, or Madhuca. Beside the oil obtained from each of these trees, *B. butyracea* yields an edible fruit, and the corollas of *B. latifolia* are either eaten raw or are used for making a liquor or for distilling their essential oil. *Butyrospermum Parkii*, formerly referred to the genus *Bassia*, is the butter-tree of central Africa. It yields the galam or shea butter, obtained by boiling the seeds, which is locally an important article of commerce. The oil is obtained by boiling the kernels of the sun or kiln-dried seeds in water. It possesses long-keeping qualities. Various species of the genus *Caryocar* (q.v.), natives of South America, are known as butter-trees.

Butter-worker, a machine designed to unite the small particles of butter, remove the buttermilk and water, and incorporate the salt,

1. AMBLYPODIA AMANTES. 3. MORPHO CYPRIS.

1. MULBERRY SILKWORM, Caterpillar
   AND Adult.

2. SOUTH AMERICAN SILK MOTH
3. CHINESE SILK MOTH
4. AILANTHUS MOTH.

giving the product a uniform appearance. Hand and power machines are made, the large power workers being also used for blending butters to make them uniform. The makes are variable and numerous; some being combined with a churn, the butter not being removed until it is finished. The former method of working by the hands injured the texture of the product and was too slow. With the present machinery the butter is untouched by hand, can be held at a temperature of 45° to 55° F. during working, and is handled expeditiously. They are a necessity in all creameries and dairies where butter is made in large quantities. See also BUTTER; CREAMERIES; DAIRYING.

Buttercup, the popular name of two or three species of the *Ranunculus* (q.v.).

But'terfield, Daniel, American soldier: b. Utica, N. Y., 18 Oct. 1831; d. Cold Spring, N. Y., 17 July 1901. At the outbreak of the Civil War he was colonel of the 12th New York Militia. He served in the Peninsular campaign, and under Pope and McClellan in 1862. At Fredericksburg he commanded the 5th Corps, and at Chancellorsville and Gettysburg was chief of staff. He served as chief of staff to Hooker at Lookout Mountain, and Ringgold, and Pea Vine Creek, and commanded a division at Buzzard's Roost, Resaca, Dallas, New Hope Church, Kenesaw, Lost Mountain, and other battles. He was brevetted major-general in the regular army. He resigned in 1869, and became chief of the United States sub-treasury in New York. He was author of 'Camp and Outpost Duty' (1862). He is buried in the West Point military cemetery, an elaborate and costly marble tomb marking the spot.

Butterfield, William, English architect: b. 7 Sept. 1814; d. London, 25 Feb. 1900. He first attained distinction by the introduction of color into ecclesiastical buildings with the aid of bricks and mosaic. Among the notable structures designed by him are St. Augustine's College at Canterbury; Keble College, Oxford; All Saints' Church, Margaret Street, London; and the cathedral at Melbourne.

Butterfly, one of the day-flying or diurnal *Lepidoptera* (often called *Rhopalocera*). This group is at once distinguished from the moths by their knobbed antennæ, which are never hairy or pectinated. The body is small, but there is a greater equality in the size of the three regions than in the moths, the abdomen being much shorter and smaller, as a general rule, than in the lower families of *Lepidoptera.* The ocelli are usually wanting; the spiral tongue or maxillæ are long and well developed; and the large, broad wings are carried erect when in repose, and are not held together during flight by a bristle and socket as in most of the moths.

The larvæ or caterpillars vary greatly in shape and in their style of ornamentation, but they uniformly have, besides the thoracic legs, five pairs of abdominal legs. The pupa is called a "chrysalis" or "aurelian," from the bright golden hues which adorn those of many species. They disappear as the wet tissues beneath the pupa-skin harden, just before the fly appears. The pupa is usually angulated on the sides of the thorax and along the upper side of the abdomen. A few species, such as those of *Vanessa,* hibernate, while several species, such as *V. antiopa,* are social as young larvæ. Butterflies also occasionally swarm while in the perfect state, such as species of *Colias, Cynthia,* and *Danais,* multitudes of which are sometimes seen passing overhead in long columns. They are truly tropical insects, since Wallace mentions that three times as many species (600) occur at a single point (Para, Brazil) as in all Germany, where scarcely 200 species live. There are about 13,000 species known; about 1,000 inhabit North America, and probably the number will be increased to 1,200, while about 130 species have been found in New England and its immediate border.

The butterflies are divided into six families, beginning with the more primitive and ending with the most specialized, they are: (1) *Hesperiidæ*; (2) *Papilionidæ*; (3) *Pieridæ*; (4) *Lycænidæ*; (5) *Erycinidæ*; and (6) *Rymphalidæ.* In the last three families, which comprise the majority of butterflies, the first pair of legs are more or less modified, differing from the two hinder pairs, especially in the male *Nymphalidæ,* in the more or less aborted tarsi, or toe-joints. Butterflies are especially liable to local variation, and to seasonal and dimorphic changes; all these varieties, subspecies, and temperature-forms, are becoming better known from year to year. Sharp anticipates that eventually the number of species of butterflies may amount to from 30,000 to 40,000 forms. South America is the metropolis of butterflies, as it is of other groups of *Lepidoptera,* being the richest in species of any other continent.

Certain *Nymphalidæ (Danais,* etc.) have glands at the end of the body secreting a repulsive fluid (see MIMICRY); in others there are remarkable differences between the sexes (*Ithomiides*); in certain butterflies some of the scales are battledore shaped, and secrete a special odor (*Androconia*). The species of *Ageronia,* a South American genus, make a clicking noise when flying. While caterpillars are plant-eaters, those of several *Lycænidæ* are known to be carnivorous, feeding on plant-lice and scale insects.

Bibliography.— Harris, 'A Treatise on Some of the Insects Injurious to Vegetation (3d ed. 1862); Scudder, 'Butterflies, Their Structure, Changes, and Life-histories' (1881); 'Butterflies of the Eastern United States and Canada' (1887-9); French, 'The Butterflies of the Eastern United States' (1886); Edwards, 'Butterflies of North America' (1868-88); Strecker, 'Butterflies and Moths of North America Diurnes' (1878); Kirby, 'A Synonomic Catalogue of Diurnal Lepidoptera' (1871-7); Holland, 'The Butterfly Book' (1898); also the European works of Haebner, Herrick-Schaeffer, Boisduval, Doubleday and Hewitson, Staudinger, Eimer, Aurivillius, Moore, Niceville, Romanoff, Oberthür, Godman and Salvin, 'Biologia Centrali Americana.'

Butterfly-fish, or Coral-fish. These beautiful fish, representing the large family *Chætodontidæ* and its allies of the scaly-finned group (*Squamipinnes*) of marine fishes, obtain their English names from their oval form, brilliancy, and their quickness of movement, and the fact that their principal habitat is in and around the tropical coral-reefs. They are so compressed as to resemble the "pumpkin-seed" sunfishes of the ponds, and are aided in keeping their balance by a very high, arched dorsal fin, and an anal fin extended beyond the tail. Their colors are always gay, usually rich orange-yellow, as a ground tint, set off by broad, black bars and fin ornaments in great variety, besides blue and red touches. The type-genus *Chætodon* is represented by several species in the West Indies, and southward, some of which occasionally drift northward in the path of the Gulf Stream. More numerous in American waters is the "black-angel" (*Pomacanthus arcuatus*), common around Porto Rico and at Key West, where it is caught in traps, or sometimes speared. The "blue-angel" (*Holacanthus ciliaris*) represents a genus containing several West Indian species, of which the most important is the "rock beauty" (*H. tricolor*), often exceeding a foot long, and good food, as well as most beautiful. The name "angel-fish" is also given in Bermuda to several similar fishes of the genus *Angelichthys*, called in Spanish "isabellitas." All these fishes are carnivorous, and Jordan remarks that their excessive quickness of sense and motion enable them to maintain themselves in the struggle for existence in the close competition of the coral reefs, notwithstanding that they are made so conspicuous to their enemies by their bright colors. Consult: Jordan and Evermann, 'Food and Game Fishes of America' (1902).

Butterfly Orchid, a common book name for two varieties of orchids, namely: (1) *Habenaria chlorantha;* (2) *H. bifolia.*

Butterfly Plant, an orchid (*Oncidium papilio*) brought from Trinidad. It is so called because its large yellow and red blossoms, poised on slender footstalks and vibrating with every breath of wind that blows, resemble butterflies hovering on the wing. It is also applied to the Indian butterfly plant, *Phalænopsis amabilis,* of Lindley, not of Blume, which is another orchid. It is a very beautiful epiphyte.

Butterfly Shell, one of the separated plates of a large species of chiton (*Cryptochiton stelleri*), about six inches long. These separate white valves are cast ashore on the beaches of California, where they are gathered as curiosities.

Butterfly-weed, PLEURISY-ROOT, a handsome American perennial herb (*Asclepias tuberosa*) of the natural order *Asclepiadaceæ*, common in dry ground almost throughout the United States and southern Canada. The large, irregular, yellowish-brown tubercular roots have a nauseous, bitter taste, and are reputed useful in lung and throat troubles, rheumatism, etc., but seem to be less popularly used than formerly. The hairy stems, which rise to a height of two or three feet, bear alternate oblong lanceolate leaves, and several umbels of short-peduncled, bright orange-yellow flowers followed by erect pubescent pods. Unlike other members of the genus, this plant has not a milky sap.

But'erick, Ebenezer, American pattern maker: b. Sterling, Mass. 1825; d. Brooklyn, N. Y., 31 March 1903. In early life he was a tailor's apprentice, and in 1859 set up in business for himself in Fitchburg, Mass., and shortly after began experiments in pattern-making, the result of which was the invention of the tissue paper dress-pattern. He removed to New York in 1864, and founded subsequently the Butterick Company, retiring from business in 1881.

But'terine, a substance prepared in imitation of butter, from animal or vegetable fats. The fat is first freed from all impurities, and by heat converted into oleine. The oleine is then transferred to a churn containing a small quantity of milk and churned into butterine. Lastly, it is colored in imitation of butter. Freshly prepared, it is sweet and palatable, and when spread on bread or cold toast is but slightly inferior to a fair quality of butter. The process has attained such perfection in the matter of manufacture in the United States that it takes an expert to distinguish it from genuine butter, and laws have been passed compelling tradesmen to label each package containing it so that no one may be deceived. See OLEOMARGARINE.

But'termere, a small but beautiful sheet of water in the famous Lake district of England, six miles southeast of Derwentwater.

Buttermilk, the fluid left behind after churning milk for butter. It possesses a specific gravity, somewhat higher than ordinary milk, owing to the removal of the fat, and varying between 1.032 and 1.035 per cent at 59° F. It may be fresh or sour, according to the method of churning. It should not contain more than 0.5 to 0.6 per cent of butter-fat. Its composition is variable, an average of 85 analyses being: Water, 90.1 per cent; fat, 1.1; protein, 4.0; milk sugar and lactic acid, 4.0; ash, 0.7 per cent. Its dry matter is practically all digestible, and it is a healthy and nutritious beverage, much relished by many people. Its fuel value per pound is 165 calories. It has about the same value as skimmilk for pig-feeding, and is used in conjunction with corn meal or some other grain, excellent pork being produced. It is also used for calf-feeding, although failures are reported in the undertaking. In fattening poultry it is highly esteemed. See also BUTTER.

Butternut (WHITE WALNUT), a large spreading tree (*Juglans cinerea*) of the natural order *Juglandaceæ*, native of America, where it ranges from New Brunswick to Georgia and westward to Dakota and Arkansas. It sometimes attains a height of 100 feet, but usually varies from 50 to 80. It has smooth, gray bark, large compound pubescent leaves, small flowers, followed by oblong, pointed, ribbed green nuts covered with viscid hairs. The ripe nuts when dried have very hard shells and are highly prized, for dessert in regions where the trees grow; and the green nuts are used for making pickles. The bark of the stems has been used in dyeing and that of the root in medicine. The wood is used to some extent for cabinet work and interior finish of houses, but is less popular than black walnut. An inferior sugar can be made from the sap. The tree is not quite so attractive as the walnut and is less densely covered with foliage, but is less attacked by insects.

But'terwort, a genus of about 30 species of small succulent plants (*Pinguicula*) of the natural order *Lentibulariaceæ*, widely distributed throughout the world in bogs and other wet ground. The species have rosettes or tufts of leaves, from among which single-flowered scapes arise to about a foot. The short, thick, sticky-haired leaves attract small insects which are covered by the in-rolling leaf-margins and digested. The leaves of certain species, especially of the common butterwort (*P. vulgaris*) are used like rennet to coagulate milk, and thus form a favorite food in Lapland and the Alps. The milk (reindeer milk in Lapland) is poured upon the leaves, strained, allowed to stand 48 hours, or until creamy and somewhat acid, when it is ready for use as food or for impregnating other milk for the same purpose. This property is said by some authorities to account for the English name, but others attribute the name to the buttery feeling of the leaves. Several species are cultivated for their dainty flowers, and as curiosities on account of their carnivorous habits, but they are rather difficult to manage unless conditions are naturally right. They are less popular in America as greenhouse plants than in Europe. Several species are natives of the United States.

Butterworth, Hezekiah, American story writer and poet: b. Warreu, R. I., 22 Dec. 1839; d. there, 5 Sept. 1905. He was editor of the Youth's Companion, 1871-4. He published many popular juvenile stories and travels, including 'Zig-Zag Journeys' (1876-1890); 'Songs of History: Poems and Ballads upon Important Episodes in American History' (1887); 'The Wampum Belt, or the Fairest Page of History' (1896); 'A Knight of Liberty'; 'The Patriot Schoolmaster'; 'Poems for Christmas, Easter, and New Year'; 'The Boyhood of Lincoln'; 'Boys of Greenway Court'; 'In Old New England'; 'Traveler Tales of China'; 'Over the Andes'; 'Great Composers'; 'South America'; and many others.

Buttmann, but'man, Philip Karl, German philologist: b. Frankfort-on-the-Main, 5 Dec. 1764; d. Berlin, 21 June 1829. He spent most of his life at Berlin, where he taught in the Joachimsthal University. His best-known works are his 'Greek Grammar' (1792); 'Lexilogus for Homer and Hesiod' (1818).

Button, Sir Thomas, English navigator in the early part of the 17th century, the successor of Hudson in exploring the northeastern coast of North America. He sailed in 1612 with two vessels, the Resolution, and the Discovery, passed through Hudson Strait, and was the first to reach land on the western coast of the bay. The point which he touched was in lat. 62°, and was named by him Carey's Swan's Nest. Being obliged to winter in this region, he selected a position near the mouth of a river, first named by him Nelson's, after the master of his ship. Every precaution was taken against cold and icebergs, yet the severity of the climate occasioned much suffering to his crew, and was fatal to a few of them. During the next summer he explored and named several places on the coast of Hudson Bay, and advancing to lat. 65°, became convinced of the possibility of the Northwest Passage.

Button, a small circular disk or knob of mother of pearl, horn, metal, or other material, with a shank or perforations through its centre for attachment to an object, and made to fit into a hole formed in another one for its reception, the two fastening the objects together. Its chief use is to unite portions of a dress together. The ancient method of fastening dresses was by means of pins, brooches, buckles and tie-strings. Buttons of brass are found on dresses of the 16th century. Gilt buttons were first made in 1768, and those of papier-mâché in 1778. Buttons of vegetable ivory are now all but universally used for tweed coats and vests. The palm fruit which yields it is called corozo nut. It is not unlike true ivory but softer, and is easily turned and dyed. These buttons are often mottled with some stain to suit the common patterns of tweed stuffs. Mother of pearl buttons are formed of the beautiful substance of which the large flat shell of the pearl oyster consists, and this has long been a favorite material for buttons. Small cylinders are first cut out of the shells with a tubular saw. These are then split into disks, which are shaped by a steel tool, drilled with holes, and finally polished with rotten stone and soft soap, or by a more recent method with ground charcoal and turpentine. Shirt studs as well as flat and globular buttons with metal shanks are also made of this substance.

Among other animal substances used for buttons are ivory, bone, horn, and hoof. From this last so-called horn buttons were some years ago made in enormous numbers by pressing them in heated dies in which the design was cut. There are many kinds of composition buttons. Glass buttons are made in great variety. For pinched buttons small rods of colored glass are heated at the ends, and pressed into shape by means of a pair of rather long hand pliers, on the ends of which are a die and its counterpart, likewise kept hot. Other kinds are cut out of colored sheet glass, which is coated on the back with tin amalgam like a mirror. With other varieties, some beautiful glass buttons are made in Bohemia, either partly or wholly of aventurine glass; and of this gold-spangled material artistically inwrought with other colors, studs and solitaires still more remarkable for their beauty and minute patterns are made at Venice. Porcelain buttons were a few years ago nearly all of French manufacture, but are now made principally at Prague. The plastic clay is pressed into molds of plaster of Paris in the same way as small objects are usually produced in earthenware. Some are plain and others are painted or printed with patterns. More or less expensive buttons are made of ornamental stone, such as agate, jasper, and marble. Occasionally they are formed of amber, jade, or of still more costly materials, as pearls and gems. In recent years, improved methods and machines have been introduced for the shaping as well as for the polishing and finishing of bone, corozo, and wood buttons. In England, Birmingham is the seat of the button trade, which, however, is much more largely developed in France. Brass buttons were made in Philadelphia in 1750, and hard-wood buttons were made there soon after. The button factory in Waterbury, Conn., now the seat of the metal button manufacture, was established about 1800. Horn buttons were made in the United States as early as 1812, and the production of buttons covered by machinery was begun at Easthampton, Mass., by Samuel Williston in 1827. The making of composition buttons was begun at Newark, N. J., in 1862. Up to 1900 there had been 1,355 patents for buttons issued by the patent office of the United States. In 1850 there were in the United States 59 establishments for the manufacture of buttons, with an output whose value was placed at $964,359. In 1900, according to the returns of the Twelfth Census, there were 238 establishments, with a capital of $4,212,568, and an output valued, including custom-work and repairing, at $7,695,910,. The value of imported buttons was stated in 1900 at only $600,982, as against $2,176,046 in 1891. For a valuable detailed account of the button industry in the United States, consult Bulletin 172 of the Twelfth Census.

Button-quail, a small quail-like bird of the genus *Turnix*, of which there are some 20 species in various parts of the Old World, some of which are termed bustard-quail, bush-quail, ortygan, and hemipode. They frequent wooded places, and afford good sport for the gunner. The females, as well as the males, are brightly colored. They are one of the smallest game birds known, inhabit woody places, and feed generally on berries and insects.

Buttonwood, a name often given to the North American plane (*Platanus occidentalis*). See PLANE.

Buttress, in architecture, a structure of masonry used to resist the thrust of an arch or vault. It takes the form of a great proportionate thickening of the walls at the point where the thrust affects the wall, the thickness sometimes increasing until the mass of masonry is set across the general direction of the wall. Thus in the developed Gothic style it nearly replaces the wall, because all the space between buttress and buttress is occupied by a great window. In the case of an archway in a single wall it often happens that the two sides or outer edges of the wall are carried up in such a way that they are spread wider toward the base and approach one another at the top, by means of certain offsets or steps, and these extensions of the wall are called buttresses, although they are mere widenings of the wall. In like manner some English Gothic church towers have curious diagonal spurs projecting on the four corners, in the form of short pieces of wall built on a prolongation of a diagonal of the square plan, and these are considered as buttresses, although they have very rarely any thrust to resist, because the tower is not often occupied by vaulted chambers, and because the meeting of the two walls would provide sufficient masonry for the practical purpose. It is a use that style that these considerations are lost sight of.

Historically, the real buttress begins to show itself in Romanesque work along the walls of the aisles, and is at first a slight projecting pilaster-like thickening of the wall, or a rounded projection like an engaged shaft of a column. These are called by special names, as buttress-pier, pilaster-strip, etc. They were very inadequate for their purpose (see ROMANESQUE) and their presence shows the uneasiness of the early builders in trying to dispense with the precautions taken by their masters, the Romans of the Empire, and their hesitation in building what alone would do the work. As the vaulting within became concentrated on certain points, when groined vaults superseded barrel-vaults for the aisles, the need of the buttress became more evident, and in some Romanesque churches they have been built up afterward, the walls being stayed up with great cost and trouble after they had begun to spread under the thrust of the vault. It is not until the ribbed vault came in and the Gothic style came into being that the buttress took its permanent shape of a piece

of wall, thin in comparison to its projection; that is to say, having much its greatest dimension in the direction of the thrust of the vault and therefore at right angles with the wall of the church. See FLYING BUTTRESS.

RUSSELL STURGIS.

Buttz, Henry Anson, American educator: b. Middle Smithfield, Pa., 18 April 1835. He was graduated at Princeton in 1858, and entered the Methodist ministry the same year. He has been president of Drew Theological Seminary since 1880, and has written much on polemics, exegetics and hermeneutics.

Buty'ric Acid, an acid obtained from butter; it also occurs in perspiration, in cod liver oil, and other fats, and in meat juice. When obtained, as it may be from butter and from sugar, it is in the form of a clear, oily, volatile fluid. It combines with bases, and forms crystalline salts, which possess no taste. Butyric acid is a colorless liquid, having a smell like that of rancid butter; its taste is acrid and biting, with a sweetish after-flavor. Formula, $C_3H_7.Co.oH$.

Buxar, buks'är, or **Baxar,** a town of British India, in the district of Shahabad, presidency of Bengal, situated on the south bank of the Ganges, about 60 miles below Benares. It is celebrated for a victory which confirmed the British in the possession of Bengal and Bahar, 23 Oct. 1764. Pop. (1891) 15,506.

Buxton, Jedediah, English mathematical prodigy: b. Elmton, Derbyshire, England, 20 March 1705; d. there 1772. Although the son of a school master and one of the most remarkable of mathematical calculators, he never advanced above the station of a farm laborer, owing to his incapacity to acquire any education outside of mental arithmetic.

Buxton, Sydney Charles, English publicist: b. Oehlen 1853. He was educated at Clifton College and Trinity College, Cambridge, and has sat in Parliament as member for Poplar since 1886. He was under-secretary for the colonies 1892–5, Postmaster-General in the Liberal Cabinet, 1905, and has published 'Handbook to Political Questions,' which has reached a ninth edition; 'Political Manual'; 'Finance and Politics: An Historical Study, 1873–85'; 'Handbook to Death Duties'; 'Mr. Gladstone as Chancellor of the Exchequer: a Study' (1901); 'Fishing and Shooting' (1901).

Buxton, SIR Thomas Fowell, English philanthropist: b. Earl's Colne, Essex, 1 April 1786; d. 19 Feb. 1845. He was educated at Trinity College, Dublin, and in 1811 joined the firm of the celebrated brewers, Truman, Hanbury & Company, and took an active share in carrying on the business. In 1816, on the occasion of the Spitalfields distress, he made his first public effort in a speech at the Mansion House, and afterward succeeded in organizing an extensive system of relief. He next proceeded, in concert with his sister-in-law, the celebrated Mrs. Elizabeth Fry (q.v.) to examine into the state of prisons; and as the result of his inquiries produced a work entitled 'An Inquiry Whether Crime and Misery are Produced or Prevented by Our Present System of Prison Discipline,' which attracted great attention, and led to the formation of the Prison

Discipline Society. In 1818 he was elected member of Parliament for Weymouth, and continued to sit for it in successive Parliaments till 1837. He distinguished himself by his enlightened zeal in the cause of humanity, and was long the right-hand man of Wilberforce, who, on retiring from public life selected Buxton as the person best qualified to carry out those of his benevolent schemes which remained uncompleted. In 1823 he moved, and with a slight modification, carried a resolution to the effect that slavery, being repugnant to the Christian religion and the British Constitution, ought to be abolished. Subsequently in 1831 he made such an impression on the house and country by an admirable speech that the government were glad to take the matter into their own hands and give full effect to emancipation. After his retirement from Parliament the slave trade occupied much of his thoughts, and he published a work entitled 'The Slave-trade and Its Remedy.' In 1840 he was created a baronet. See 'Memoirs of Sir T. F. Buxton, Bart' (1872).

Buxton, a town in Derbyshire, England, 37 miles northwest of Derby, and 25 southsoutheast of Manchester. Buxton has long been famous for its calcareous springs, the waters being taken for indigestion, gout, rheumatism, and nervous and cutaneous diseases. The locality was known to the Romans, who had baths here. The season extends from May to October, some 15,000 persons visiting the springs annually. The town is 900 feet above sea-level and is situated in a deep valley. Much of the splendor of Buxton is due to the Dukes of Devonshire, one of whom, in 1780, at the cost of $600,000, erected an immense three-storied pile of buildings, called the Crescent. Near Buxton is the Diamond Hill, famous for its crystals; and Poole's Hole, a gas-lit stalactite cavern 770 yards long. Mary, Queen of Scots, was at Buxton when in the custody of the Earl of Shrewsbury. Pop. (1901) 10,181.

Buxtorf, Johann, yŏ'hän bŭks'tôrf (THE ELDER), German Orientalist: b. Kamen, Westphalia, 25 Dec. 1564; d. Basel, 13 Sept. 1629. Being very learned in Hebrew and Chaldaic, in the acquirement of which he obtained the assistance of many learned Jews, he was engaged by the magistrates of Basel to become professor of those languages, which he taught with great success. His chief works are: 'Lexicon Chaldaicum Talmudicum et Rabbinicum'; 'Thesaurus Linguæ Hebraicæ'; 'Biblica Hebraica Rabbinica'; 'Synagoga Judaica hoc est Schola Judæorum'; 'Institutio Epistolaris Hebraica'; 'Concordantiæ Bibliorum Hebraicorum.'

Buxtorf, Johann (THE YOUNGER), German Hebraist: b. Basel, 13 Aug. 1599; d. there, 16 Aug. 1664; son of the preceding. He succeeded his father in the chair of Hebrew at Basel, and occupied it for 34 years, until his death. The same chair was filled by his son and his nephew successively during 68 years longer, making a combined occupancy of this professional chair by the Buxtorf family for an unbroken period of 140 years. He completed and published two of his father's principal works, the most important publication of his own being the 'Lexicon Chaldaicum et Syriacum.'

Bux'us, the genus name of a number of shrubs or small trees. See Box.

Buys-Ballot, bois-bạ-lō, **Christophorus Henricus Didericus,** Dutch meteorologist: b. Kloetinge, Zeeland, 10 Oct. 1817; d. Utrecht, 2 Feb. 1890. He studied at the University of Utrecht, where he became professor of mathematics in 1847, and professor of experimental physics in 1870. In 1854 he received the appointment of director of the Royal Meteorological Institute at Utrecht. He was one of the initiators of the new system, under which, by daily synoptical weather reports, and simultaneous observations by land and sea, materials are collected for forecasting changes. His own observations have resulted in the determination of a general law of storms, known as the Buys-Ballot law. The inventor of a system of weather signals, he was largely instrumental in bringing about an international uniformity in meteorological observations. His works include 'Changements Périodiques de la Température' (1847); and, in English, 'Suggestions on a Uniform System of Meteorological Observations' (1872-3).

Buyukdereh, bĭ-yook'dĕ-rä, a little town on the western side of the Bosporus, situated in the midst of a large, deep-bosomed valley. It is the summer residence of the Christian embassies at Constantinople, and its gardens and palaces, not less than its natural beauty and coolness, make it a favorite promenade ground. A group of plane-trees, the most splendid on the Bosporus, the Russian palace, distinguished by the regularity of its architecture, and the extensive gardens of Baron Hübsch, are particularly mentioned. The tradition that Godfrey of Bouillon encamped here with his army is not alluded to in the original records of the crusades.

Buzfuz, Sargeant, a character introduced by Dickens in the 'Pickwick Papers.' He is the barrister who becomes counsel for the plaintiff in Mrs. Bardell's breach of promise suit against Mr. Pickwick, and is remarkable for the ingenuity he displays in drawing incriminating inferences from ordinary and inconsequential occurrences.

Buz'zard, a term given in America to two distinct groups of birds — buzzard-hawks of the genus *Buteo* and its allies, also familiar to Europeans, and the turkey-buzzard — a vulture. The buzzard-hawks are closely related to the eagles, from which they are distinguished by the smaller size in the majority of cases, the smaller and rounder head, and a slow and heavy manner of flight. They feed chiefly upon the smaller mammals and reptiles, seldom catching or disturbing poultry, although popularly accused of it and styled "hen-hawks." Important North American species of the genus *Buteo* are the red-tailed, red-shouldered, Swainson's, and broad-winged hawks, all of which are elsewhere described under their names. The most important of the genus *Archibuteo* is the rough-legged hawk (q.v.), and the handsomest one, the squirrel hawk (q.v.) of California. In the southern United States the name usually refers to the common black vulture (*Cathartes aura*). See TURKEY BUZZARD.

Buzzard's Bay, on the southeast coast of Massachusetts, is about 30 miles long, and has a mean breadth of 7 miles. It is sheltered from the ocean and separated from Vineyard

Sound by the Elizabeth Islands. Its chief harbors are those of New Bedford, Fairhaven, Wareham, and Mattapoisett.

Buz'zing, the sounds produced by many insects, other than by mechanical means, that is, by friction. How the buzzing of bees, flies, etc., is produced has been a disputed question. Two distinct sounds may be distinguished — one, a deep noise, is due to the vibration of the wings, and is produced whenever a certain rapidity is attained; the other is an acute sound, and is said to be produced by the vibrations of the walls of the thorax, to which muscles are attached; this sound is specially evident in *Diptera* and *Hymenoptera,* because the integument is of the right consistence for vibration. In both of these, observers agree that the spiracles are not concerned in the matter. Laudois tells us that the wing-tone of the honey bee is A′; its voice, however, is an octave higher, and often goes to B″ and C″. The sounds produced by the wings are constant in each species, except where, as in *Bombus,* there are individuals of different sizes; in these the larger ones generally give a higher note. Thus, the comparatively small male of *B. terrestris* hums on A′, while the large female hums an entire octave higher. Consult Sharp, 'Insects' (New York 1899); Packard, 'Textbook of Entomology' (New York 1898).

By-Law, a particular or private law, as the local or subordinate law of a city, town, private corporation or other organization. The power to make by-laws is usually conferred by express terms of the charter creating the corporation; though, when not expressly granted, it is given by implication, and it is incidental to the very existence of a corporation. The Constitution of the United States and acts of Congress made in conformity to it, the Constitution of the State in which a corporation is located, and all acts of the legislature constitutionally made, together with the common law as there accepted, are of superior force to any by-law; and any by-law, when contrary to either of them, is void, whether the charter authorizes the making of such by-law or not; because no legislature can grant power larger than it possesses.

Byblos, bĭb'lŏs, an ancient maritime city of Phœnicia, now called Jebail, a little north of Beyrout. It was the chief seat of the worship of Adonis or Thammuz.

Byerly, William Elwood, American mathematician: b. Philadelphia, 13 Dec. 1849. He graduated at Harvard College in 1871; was assistant professor of mathematics at Cornell University from 1873-6 and at Harvard from 1876-81, when he became professor. Among his works are: 'Elements of Differential Calculus'; 'Elements of Integral Calculus'; 'Problems in Differential Calculus'; and a 'Treatise on Fourier's Series and Spherical, Cylindrical and Ellipsoidal Harmonics.'

By'ers, Samuel Hawkins Marshall, American historical writer: b. 23 July 1838. During the Civil War he served in the Union army, was taken prisoner, and while in prison at Columbia, S. C., wrote the famous song 'Sherman's March to the Sea.' He was consul at Zürich, Switzerland, from 1869 to 1884, and consul-general to Italy in 1885. Among his works are: 'Iowa in War Times'; 'Switzerland and the Swiss'; 'Twenty Years in Europe'; and many poems.

Byford, William Heath, American physician: b. Eaton, Ohio, 20 March 1817; d. 1890. He graduated at the Ohio Medical College and a few years later became professor in the Evansville Medical College. He established a practice in Chicago; in 1857 became professor of obstetrics and diseases of women and children, in the Rush Medical College of that city, and in 1880, professor of gynecology in the same institution. For many years he was president and professor of clinical surgery in the Women's Hospital Medical College, and was twice president of the American Medical Association. Among his works are: 'Practice of Medicine and Surgery Applied to Diseases and Accidents Peculiar to Women'; 'Philosophy of Domestic Life'; and 'Theory and Practice of Obstetrics.'

By'ington, Ezra Hoyt, American author: b. Hinesburgh, Vt., 3 Sept. 1828; d. Newton, Mass., 16 May 1901. He was educated at the University of Vermont and Andover Theological Seminary; entered the Congregational ministry and filled several pastorates. Among his works are: 'The Puritan in England and New England'; 'The Puritan as Colonist and Reformer'; 'The Christ of Yesterday, To-day, and Forever'; and histories of a number of local churches.

Byles, Mather, American clergyman: b. Boston, 26 March 1706; d. there, 5 July 1788. He was ordained over the church in Hollis Street, in Boston, in the year 1733, and obtained a distinguished position among the contemporary clergy. He was learned after the manner of those times, and was more addicted to literary recreations, and had a keener relish of the later humanities, than was then common among the members of his profession. As a proof of his recognized excellence in polite letters, we may accept the fact that he was the correspondent of some of the chief poets and authors of England. He was himself a votary of the muses in a small way, and a volume of his miscellaneous poems was published in 1744. He gave an early expression, too, to the loyalty which distinguished his character through life, in a poem on the death of George I. and the succession of his son, in 1727, when he was but 21 years of age. He also tempered the bereavement which Gov. Belcher had suffered in the loss of his wife in 1734, by such consolation as an elegiac epistle could convey. It is not likely, however, that his name would have been preserved to this time had his reputation depended on the merits of his poetical effusions. The cheerful flow of his spirits and frank gaiety of his conversation seem to have been something out of the common way, and to have left an enduring mark on the memories of that generation. His piety was tinctured with no asceticism, and the lively sallies of his sprightly imagination, always kept within the limits of decorum, were restrained by no fear of injuring his personal or clerical dignity. He was an ardent Royalist and in 1777 was sentenced to banishment, but was allowed to remain under guard in his own house. This severity was soon relaxed for a while, and afterward renewed. One of the stories told of him is, that wishing to have an errand done at a distance, he asked the sentry to undertake it. The man objected on the ground that he could not leave the door unguarded; on which the doctor volunteered to be his substitute, and, accordingly was seen by some one in authority, in powdered wig and cocked hat, with a musket on his shoulder, walking up and down before his house, keeping guard over himself. His release from custody soon followed, on which occasion, alluding to these changes of treatment, he said that he had been "guarded, regarded, and disregarded."

Byllynge, Edward, English provincial governor: d. 1687. He became joint purchaser with John Fenwick of a large tract of land in what is now the State of New Jersey. Upon the occasion of a dispute between the two proprietors, nine tenths remained, by Penn's decision, with Byllynge and was long known as "the Byllynge Tenths." He was governor of the province of West Jersey in 1677.

Byng, bĭng, George Viscount Torrington, English admiral: b. Wrotham, Kent, 27 Jan. 1663; d. 17 Jan. 1733. He entered the navy at the age of 15. In 1688 he recommended himself to William of Orange, and for his gallant conduct at the sea-fight of Malaga was knighted by Queen Anne. In 1718 he commanded the English fleet sent to Sicily for the protection of the neutrality of Italy, and on 31 July utterly destroyed the Spanish fleet off Messina. He was created Viscount Torrington in 1721.

Byng, John, English admiral: b. 1704; d. 14 March 1757. He was the son of Viscount Torrington, and by his own merits, as well as the influence of his name, was raised to the rank of admiral. His attempts to relieve Fort St. Philip, in Minorca, when blockaded by a French fleet under La Galissonière, proved abortive, and his hesitation in engaging the enemy, when a bold attack might have perhaps gained him the victory, excited the clamor of the nation against him. The ministry, who wished to avert the public odium from their unsuccessful measures, beheld with seeming satisfaction the unpopularity of Byng, and when he was condemned by a court-martial they suffered him, though recommended to mercy, to be sacrificed to the general indignation, and he was shot at Portsmouth.

Bynkershoek, bĭn'kĕrs-hook, Cornelius van, Dutch jurist: b. Middleburg, Zealand, 29 May 1673; d. 16 April 1743. He studied at the University of Franeker, and after praetising as a barrister at The Hague, became professor of law at Leyden, and president of the supreme council of Holland. He was one of the most learned among modern civilians. His books are in Latin, and his treatise 'De Foro Legatorum Competente' was translated by Barbeyrac into French under the title of 'Du Juge Compétent des Ambassadeurs' (1728). His most important writings are the 'Observationes Juris Romani'; 'De Dominio Maris'; 'Quæstiones Juris Publici'; and a digest entitled 'Corpus Juris Hollandici et Zelandici.' A complete edition of his works was published at Geneva in 1761, and at Leyden in 1766.

Byn'ner, Edwin Lassetter, American novelist: b. Brooklyn, N. Y., 1842; d. Boston, 1893. He was librarian of the Boston Law Library, and author of short stories and of several novels, including 'Tritons' (1878);

'Agnes Surriage' (1886); 'Penelope's Suitors' (1887).

Byr, bŭr, Robert, pseudonym of KARL ROBERT EMMERICH BAYER (q.v.).

Byrd, bĕrd, William, American lawyer and author: b. Westover, Va. 1674; d. there, 26 Aug. 1744. He received a liberal education in England, possessed one of the largest libraries in the colonies, and, having a large property, lived in a splendid style, unrivaled in Virginia. He was a member and at last president of the King's Council. To French Protestants fleeing to Virginia from persecution in France, he extended the most generous assistance. The towns of Richmond and Petersburg were laid out by him, and he was one of the commissioners for establishing the boundary line between Virginia and North Carolina. He was a member of the Royal Society, and as a patron of literature and art deserves remembrance. His own writings include the 'Westover Manuscripts,' embracing 'The History of the Dividing Line'; 'A Journey to the Land of Eden'; and 'A Progress to the Mines.' In 'The Virginia Magazine of History and Biography' (1902) appeared his letters, revealing much of interest concerning his personality and career.

Byrd, William, composer. See BIRD, WILLIAM.

Byrgius, bĕr'jĭ-ŭs, Justus (properly JOBET BÜRGI), Swiss mathematician: b. Lichtensteig, Canton of St. Gall, Switzerland, 28 Feb. 1552; d. Cassel, Germany, 31 Jan. 1632. He was invited to Cassel by the landgrave of Hesse to superintend the observatory which he had there erected, and constructed a number of astronomical instruments, some curious clocks, and other machines. A discovery involving that of the logarithms, and another exhibiting an application of the pendulum to clocks, have been attributed to him. He is eulogized by Kepler for his talents, but censured for his indolence and undue reserve, which kept back his discoveries from the public.

Byrne, Thomas Sebastian, American clergyman: b. Hamilton, Ohio, 29 July 1842. In youth he was an expert machinist, but deciding to enter the priesthood of the Roman Catholic Church he went, after preparatory training, to the American College in Rome. In 1869 he was ordained in Cincinnati. He devoted himself to literature and teaching in Mt. St. Mary's Seminary; for a time had charge of the Cincinnati Cathedral and again became connected with the seminary, acting as rector until 1894. He wrote 'Man from a Catholic Point of View.'

By'rom, John, English poet and stenographer: b. near Manchester, 29 Feb. 1692; d. 26 Sept. 1763. He was educated at Merchant Taylor's School and Trinity College, Cambridge, and for some time studied medicine, but his chief means of livelihood for many years, till he inherited the family estates in 1740, was teaching shorthand on a system invented by himself. He was on friendly terms with many of the eminent men of his time. His earliest writings were a few papers to the 'Spectator'; his poems (collected in 1773) were chiefly humorous and satirical, and show remarkable facility in rhyming.

Byron, **George Gordon,** sixth lord, English poet: b. London, 22 Jan. 1788; d. Missolonghi, Greece, 19 April 1824. He was the son of "Mad Jack Byron," a good-looking, profligate soldier, who married the divorced Marchioness of Carmarthen, and had by her a daughter Augusta, later Mrs. Leigh. Captain Byron became a widower in 1784, and, a little more than a year later, married a Scotch heiress, Catherine Gordon of Gight.. Their only child, the poet, was born at No. 16 Holles street, Cavendish Square, and was lame from birth, his right foot being so contracted that he hobbled with difficulty. The influences surrounding the child were deplorable. John Byron, to escape his creditors, had to flee to France, where he died in 1791. Mrs. Byron, with a much reduced income, resided in Aberdeen and proved to be a most indiscreet mother, now fondly petting her child, now reviling him. She was actually guilty of reproaching him for his lameness. The boy himself was capable of great affection for his nurse and for a cousin, Mary Duff, and his schoolmates seem to have regarded him as warmhearted. His education was not neglected during his early years, but tutors and schools could not make up for his lack of training at home. He learned, however, to love nature amid the Scotch hills.

In 1794 the grandson of the then Lord Byron died, and the six-year old boy became heir to the peerage, which he inherited in 1798. Then 1's mother obtained a pension and left Scotland, Byron being made a ward in chancery and Lord Carlisle being appointed his guardian, though his mother's lawyer, John Hanson, really looked after his welfare. A quack tortured his foot, and schoolmasters tried to make him studious, his main mental nutriment consisting, apparently, of the Bible and poetry. He wrote love verses to a young cousin, endured his mother's caprices, and was doubtless glad to be entered at Harrow in 1801, where, however, he was at first discontented and not liked. He could not make a scholar of himself, though, as Mr. Coleridge has shown, his classical attainments have been much underrated; but he was a good declaimer and through his pluck in fighting and in athletics, despite his deformity, he became a leader in the school. He was romantically devoted to his friends, and once offered to take half the thrashing a bully was giving to the boy who later was known as Sir Robert Peel. Impulsiveness characterized both his insubordinate attitude toward the school authorities, and his love affair with his cousin and senior, Mary Anne Chaworth, who soon married and left him disconsolate. His affection for her seems never to have been entirely effaced. Altogether, his childhood and youth were well adapted to produce a wayward man.

In October 1805 he went into residence as a nobleman at Trinity College, Cambridge. He took full advantage of his privileges, ran into debt, though he had an allowance of £500 a year, gambled, consorted with pugilists, won fame as a swimmer, travelled about in style, and, last but not least, after stormy quarrels with his mother, successfully asserted his claim to be his own master. He formed some warm friendships with promising students, notably with John Cam Hobhouse, afterward Lord Brough-

ton (q. v.), he dabbled in literature and wrote verses, and he received his M. A. "by special privilege as a peer," in July 1808. Nearly two years previously he had printed 'Fugitive Pieces,' a volume of poetry, but had destroyed all save two or three copies because a clergyman fr'end had objected to one poem as too free. A small edition of what was practically the same book, 'Poems on Various Occasions,' appeared early in 1807. A few months later this was reissued with considerable alterations as 'Hours of Idleness,' which was again altered in a second edition of March 1808, two months after the now famous slashing review from the pen of Brougham had appeared in the 'Edinburgh.'

Byron's youthful volume certainly gave little indication of the genius he was soon to display, but it called for no severe chastisement. Hence, the editor of the "Edinburgh," Jeffrey, got only what he deserved when Byron pilloried him in 'English Bards and Scotch Reviewers,' which appeared anonymously about the middle of March 1809, and was at once successful. It is still decidedly readable in parts and ranks with the best satires of its kind. It went through five editions in two years, the last being suppressed by its author, because he had become the friend of many of his victims.

Meanwhile, Byron had settled—if such a word may be used of his riotous occupation of his domain—at Newstead Abbey, and had repaired it on borrowed money. In March 1809 he took his seat in the House of Lords. Then he prepared himself for a tour of the Continent, which was begun with Hobhouse and three servants in July. That Byron was to any marked extent as dissipated and misanthropical as his own Harold does not seem likely.

The travellers sailed to Lisbon and saw something of Portugal, Spain, Malta, Albania, and Greece. At Athens Byron finished the first canto of 'Childe Harold' and celebrated the charms of his landlady's daughter, Theresa Macri, the 'Maid of Athens.' Then the friends visited Asia Minor and reached Constantinople shortly after Byron's famous swim from Sestos to Abydos (3 May 1810). About two months later Hobhouse returned to England and Byron to Athens, where, after a tour of the Morea, he spent the winter of 1810-11, apparently studying and writing and making excursions. He reached England, by way of Malta, about 20 July 1811.

Throughout his travels he had been in severe financial straits, which his mother had shared. Immediately on his return she was taken ill, and before he could reach her side she died. He mourned for her in a passionate way, and the practically simultaneous deaths of three friends also afflicted him and gave him an excuse for writing melancholy verses. He had brought to England with him the first two cantos of 'Childe Harold' and his paraphrase of the 'Ars Poetica,' the 'Hints from Horace.' The latter, which he is said to have preferred, was immediately accepted by a publisher, but for some reason it did not appear during Byron's life. 'Childe Harold,' after some delay, was the means of uniting its author with his famous publisher, John Murray. It appeared in March 1812, after Byron had made a successful speech in the House of Lords. As all the world knows he awoke one morning and found himself famous as a poet; it is no wonder that he put a parliamentary career, in which he might have done great good, forever behind him.

It has been for some years fashionable to sneer at the first two cantos of 'Childe Harold;' but they are at least effective poetry, and their novel theme and romantic tone fitted them for the early readers who went wild over them. Melancholy and cynicism in a youth were more likely to attract than to shock men and women who were subjects of the Regent and contemporaries of Napoleon. Byron, who had previously made a fast friend of his would-be adversary, Thomas Moore (q. v.), became the social lion of the day. He was young and reckless, and unfortunately gave occasion for scandal through his relations with the notorious Lady Caroline Lamb (q. v.), and the equally frail Lady Oxford. People could also gossip about his handsome face, and his drinking, and his strange diet for the reduction of his disfiguring obesity. His pecuniary difficulties, too, and his folly in presenting the money from his copyrights to his connection Dallas doubtless caused tongues to wag. He enjoyed his vogue, but not to such an extent as to grow idle. After the failure of the anonymous 'Waltz,' he gave the world 'The Giaour' in May 1813, 'The Bride of Abydos,' in December of the same year, and 'The Corsair,' two months later. All were dashed off, all were very popular, all deepened the atmosphere of mystery about him. Scott's supremacy as a romantic poet passed to the newcomer, and although the lines on the Princess Charlotte caused some hard feeling and he threatened to quit poetry, Byron continued for two years to have his fling both as a poet and as a gay man of the world. 'Lara' appeared in August 1814; 'Hebrew Melodies' in January 1815; 'The Siege of Corinth' and 'Parisina' in January and February 1816. The sums paid by Murray for these poems — Byron, harassed by debt, at last began to be businesslike — show plainly how well he continued to hold his public. Except for such lyrics as 'She walks in beauty like the night,' the work of this period has failed to hold later generations. This is due no doubt to an unwholesome desire on the part of a puritanical race "to take it out" upon Byron's far from impeccable character and career, as well as to a natural change of taste toward greater polish and refinement, and to the effect of such a story as that he wrote the first sketch of 'The Bride of Abydos' in four nights after coming home from balls. That latter-day criticism has been altogether wrong in correcting the excessive praise given by Byron's contemporaries to this facile group of poems cannot be maintained; but it is well to remember that copious power is a good sign of genius, that Byron managed to put into 'The Giaour' not a little narrative vigor and into the whole group of Oriental tales much of the color and the spirit of the East, and that English literature would have been deprived of many beautiful lyric and descriptive passages if he had allowed society completely to turn him from writing verse.

Meanwhile Byron had seen much of Moore and Rogers and had met, after many years, his half-sister, Mrs. Leigh, the 'Augusta' of some of his best poems, and the being of all others to whom his heart went out most fondly. In after years his memory and hers were to be clouded by a dark suspicion which, whether true or false, would probably never have soiled the ears of the world but for the jealousy of another woman — his wife. Whether the scandal which Mrs. Stowe (q. v.) spread and which Byron's own grandson, Lord Lovelace, unaccountably revived will ever be substantiated or laid completely to rest is a matter upon which the data for a decision are not forthcoming. In the interim generous minds and hearts will prefer to believe in the purity of the 'Epistle to Augusta.'

The story of Byron's courtship and marriage, while less mysterious than that of Milton, is not a clear one. In 1812 he seems to have been rejected by an heiress, Miss Anna Isabella Millbanke, four years his junior and a connection of his flame, Lady Lamb. The young woman appears to have been fond of mathematics and theology, to have written poems, to have been somewhat priggish and prudish, and very self-centred. Some correspondence was kept up between the pair and, as a marriage seemed likely to steady his habits and better his fortunes, Byron proposed again by letter in September 1814. This time he was accepted. Miss Milbanke was apparently proud of her catch and Byron of his. They were married on 2 Jan. 1815 and they seem to have got on well at first, though each later made reports to the contrary. The young wife soon inherited money and promised him a child, she behaved himself well on the surface, took an interest in the management of Drury Lane, saw something of Sir Walter Scott (always his defender), and helped Coleridge to publish 'Christabel.' But the pair were evidently incompatible, and after the birth of their only child, Augusta Ada, on 10 Dec. 1815, a separation was arranged for, Lady Byron believing that her husband was insane — a notion obviously stupid, but possibly charitable from her own point of view. The doctor, the lawyer, and the father-in-law she let loose upon Byron may have irritated him into conduct that did not allay her suspicions. It is all a tangle; perhaps the easiest way out is to censure Byron and resolutely refrain from admiring his wife.

The separation was followed by an astonishing public clamor against Byron, whose friends seem to have thought his life in danger. Sir Leslie Stephen has contended that the public indignation was not unnatural. Perhaps it was not, in the sense that it represented some of the worst elements of human nature. For a society that tolerated the Regent and his boon associates to fawn upon a man and then to condemn him unheard on the score of practically unspecified charges was simply to put an indelible blot upon Englishmen of the upper and middle classes — a blot the blackness of which may be somewhat gauged from the depth of the vindictiveness with which Byron's fame has been since attacked by many of his countrymen. It by no means follows, however, that Byron was at all justified in writing and publishing his numerous poems and passages relating to the separation — though literature would do ill without 'Fare Thee Well,' and would like to have had a chance to see his destroyed novel on the 'Marriage of Belphegor' — or that he can be excused for much of his conduct during the exile that began at the end of April 1816 and lasted for the rest of his spectacular life. One can, however, pardon his constant desire to shock the British public; and, taking account of his temperament, one can understand his varying moods of conciliatory tenderness and defiant scorn toward his implacable wife.

Byron first visited Belgium, traveling luxuriously. Then he went, by the Rhine, to Geneva, where he met the Shelleys and Claire Clairmont, who had made up her mind in London to be his mistress. She bore him in January 1817 a daughter, Allegra, with whom he charged himself and whose death in 1822 grieved him deeply. The intercourse with the Shelleys at Geneva was more beneficial to Byron than to Shelley. 'The Prisoner of Chillon,' the most popular of his poems of the type, the third canto of 'Childe Harold' which, thanks to Shelley, showed the influence of Wordsworth, the stanzas 'To Augusta,' and other poems are memorials of the period and proofs that his experiences had ripened Byron's poetic powers. After the Shelleys returned to England, Byron, with Hobhouse, crossed into Italy.

He was in Milan in October 1816 and then went for the winter to Venice, where he practically remained for three years. His excesses in the Palazzo Macenigo are unfortunately but too well known; yet, although his health and his character suffered from them, to say nothing of his reputation, he did not a little studying, and his poetical genius continued active. The fourth canto of 'Childe Harold' and 'Manfred,' which date, in part at least, from 1817 and reveal the effects of a visit to Rome, show his genius almost at its zenith, and 'Beppo,' suggested by Frere's 'Whistlecraft,' preluded the greatest of his works — perhaps the greatest of modern English poems — the incomparable medley 'Don Juan,' the first canto of which was finished in September 1818. The first two cantos, between which he wrote 'Mazeppa,' were published, without indication of either author or publisher, in July 1819.

Meanwhile Byron had met the Countess Teresa Guiccioli, the young, beautiful, and accomplished daughter of Count Gamba of Ravenna. They became passionately attached to one another, and, aided by the customs of the country, were constantly together at Ravenna and other places, Venetian society finally giving them up when she resided under his roof. After some extraordinary business negotiations with the lady's elderly husband, it looked as if the temporarily weary lover might regain his freedom; but finally the affection of the Countess prevailed, and Byron, yielding to an influence higher and better than any he had known of late, established himself near her at Ravenna at the end of 1819. Here for a time, at her request, he gave up 'Don Juan,' and, after some translating from the Italian poets, began to write dramas.

His first play was 'Marino Faliero,' in writing which Byron departed from English models and made a diligent study of authorities. It was finished in the summer of 1820 and played unsuccessfully at Drury Lane the next spring. The year 1821 saw the writing of the more effective 'Sardanapalus,' 'The Two Foscari,' the powerful, though not stylistically adequate 'Cain: a Mystery,' 'Heaven and Earth,' another 'Mystery,' and the inception of 'Werner,' his best

acting play, taken largely from Harriet Lee's (q. v.) story 'Kruitzner.' That Byron had little dramatic genius is generally admitted; the literary power which he could not avoid putting into any composition is not, in the case of these experiments, sufficiently recognized.

While writing his dramas, Byron had more trouble with Count Guiccioli, who was finally separated from his wife, and he was led by the Gambas to take a deep interest in the Carbonari conspiracies. He had already in his poetry given evidence of liberal political sentiments; now he subscribed for the patriotic cause, headed a section of the conspirators, and, but for his birth and fame, would have got into trouble with the Austrian authorities. The Gambas and the Countess were exiled from Ravenna, and Byron, after some lingering, joined them at Pisa in November 1821. Here he saw much of Shelley, Medwin, Trelawny, and other Englishmen, and here, sometime in 1822, he wrote an ineffective drama, 'The Deformed Transformed.' The same year he made with Shelley and Leigh Hunt (q. v.) the unfortunate arrangements which induced the latter to come to Italy and begin the publication of the quarterly journal, 'The Liberal.' The details of this affair are too complicated to be entered upon without ample space. Shelley was imprudent, Byron rather brutal, Hunt exasperating. Shelley's death complicated matters still further, and 'The Liberal' expired after four numbers. Its most memorable item was Byron's masterly satire upon Southey, 'A Vision of Judgment,' written in 1821. This Murray had been chary of publishing after the trouble he had had with the orthodox on account of 'Cain' — an episode which had a good deal to do with Byron's willingness to establish a journal the chief expense of which he knew would fall on himself.

Meanwhile 'Don Juan' had been taken up once more, in a deeper vein, and the Gambas had been ordered to leave Tuscany. Byron, whose health and spirits were impaired, followed them to Genoa in the autumn of 1822. Here he wrote his satire 'The Age of Bronze,' upon the political reaction of the time, as well as his poor narrative poem 'The Island,' and the later cantos of 'Don Juan.' He was growing restless and feared that he was losing his powers; but, fortunately, for his fame at least, a new outlet for his energies was at hand. A Whig and Liberal committee was formed in London to aid the Greek revolutionists and at Trelawny's suggestion Byron was made a member. He proposed to go in person to the Levant, and by midsummer of 1823 he completed his elaborate preparations for the expedition. Sailing from Genoa, with rising spirits, he reached Cephalonia early in August. Here he remained four months writing excellent letters of advice and sensibly waiting for a clear opportunity for action, not, in all likelihood, for an offer of the Greek crown. At the end of December 1823 he accepted the invitation of Prince Alexander Mavrocordatos to co-operate in the organization of Western Greece and sailed for Missolonghi, where he was cordially welcomed. He appears to have shown great tact in harmonizing opposing factions and considerable practical genius as an organizer. He had no chance to do any fighting with the wild troops over whom he was placed as commander-in-chief, but he did hold out successfully against a mutiny, awing by his courage the Suliotes that broke into his tent while he was ill. He recovered somewhat, but exposure to fatigue and the constant rains told heavily upon him, and he took no care of himself. At last he was prostrated with ague and received only the crudest medical attention. After much delirium he passed into a long slumber, which ended in his death at six o'clock in the evening of 19 April 1824. The news was a shock to the world. His body was sent to England and was buried, not in Westminster Abbey, but at Hucknall Torkard, near Newstead Abbey. The Greeks would have liked, more appropriately, to bury him at Athens, and, fortunately, they did secure his heart for interment at Missolonghi. There is no incongruity, however, in thinking of him as reposing, after his stormy life, in company with his passionate mother and his long line of wild ancestors.

Byron's position in English literature is a much disputed matter. Foreigners, influenced by the spell cast by his genius upon the romantic writers of their own countries as well as by his devotion to freedom and by the fact that his work in translation does not offend by its slipshod features, almost unanimously — whether they be Frenchmen, or Germans, or Italians, or Spaniards, or Russians,— place him only below Shakespeare. The English-speaking world knows the work of Chaucer, Spenser, and Milton too well to admit such a high estimate of his genius; but it seems to have gone farther astray in depreciation than foreigners have in appreciation of his extraordinary gifts and achievements. With a few honorable exceptions like Matthew Arnold, English critics have magnified Byron's plain moral and artistic delinquencies and have minimized his powerful intelligence, his great range of work — he is one of the best of letter writers and the most brilliant of satirists, as well as the arch-romantic and revolutionary poet, and a notable descriptive and lyric one — his copious creative power, and his great "sincerity and strength." They have judged him as somewhat finicky connoisseurs of verse instead of as impartial appraisers of literature. They have underestimated the hold he has kept upon youth and the attraction which his later work, especially 'Don Juan,' so frequently exercises upon intelligent men of mature years. Whether he will ever receive his due from the more cultured of his countrymen is problematical; but there have been indications of late that a less banal attitude is being taken toward both him and his works. He may not be the greatest English poet of modern times, but he is certainly the most effective of all the enemies of cant.

Bibliography.— The bibliography of Byron is naturally immense. His memoirs, given to Moore, were burned, after many family complications, in 1824. Moore's 'Life, Letters, and Journals of Lord Byron' (1830) is the standard biography. It was included in Murray's edition of the collected 'Life and Works' (1832-5; 17 vols. 1837). The number of separate editions of the poems and of translations is enormous, all previous editions being superseded by Murray's edition of the works in 13 volumes (6 of

prose, edited by R. E. Prothero, 1898-1901; 7 of verse, edited by E. H. Coleridge, 1898-1904). The best 1-vol. edition of the poems is that by Coleridge (1905); the [American] Cambridge edition by P. E. More (1905) is also good. The large list of memoirs and books of biographical value may be represented here by Karl Elze's 'Lord Byron' (1870), J. C. Jeaffreson's 'The Real Lord Byron' (1883), and John Nichol's 'Byron' in the 'English Men of Letters' (1880). Reminiscences by Lady Blessington, Medwin, the Countess Guiccioli, E. J. Trelawny, Hobhouse, Leigh Hunt, and many others should also be consulted. Of critical essays, favorable and unfavorable, those by Matthew Arnold, Charles Kingsley, Macaulay, John Morley, J. A. Symonds, and Swinburne may be mentioned. The mass of continental criticism is very large and is steadily increasing.

WILLIAM P. TRENT,
Professor of English Literature, Columbia University.

Byron, Harriett, a character in Richardson's novel, 'Sir Charles Grandison.' She was attached to the hero and was the writer of the greater part of the letters comprising the novel.

Byron, Henry James, English dramatist and actor: b. Manchester, January 1834; d. London, 11 April 1884. He studied at first for the medical profession, and afterward for the bar, but his passion for the stage caused him to abandon them. He was the first editor of 'Fun,' and also started another paper entitled the 'Comic Times,' which soon ceased to appear. Many of his chief plays were produced at various theatres with which he was connected as manager, but they were not financially successful. He wrote an imense number of pieces, including a great many farces, burlesques, and extravaganzas, besides comedies or domestic dramas, such as 'Fra Diavolo' (1858); 'Cyril's Success,' probably his best work; 'Dearer than Life'; 'Blow for Blow'; 'Old Sailors' (1874); 'The Lady of Lyons'; 'Uncle Dick's Darling'; 'The Promoter's Box'; 'Partner's for Life'; and 'Our Boys' (1878). which had a run of four years and three months, the longest on record. He also wrote the novel 'Paid in Full' (3 vols., 1865).

Byron, John, English naval officer: b. Newstead, 8 Nov. 1723; d. 10 April 1786. At the age of 17 he sailed with Lord Anson on a voyage round the world, but was wrecked on the coast of the Pacific, north of the Straits of Magellan. Byron, with some of his unfortunate companions, was conducted by the Indians to Chile and remained there till 1744, when he embarked on board a ship of St. Malo and in 1745 returned to Europe. At a subsequent period he published a narrative of his adventures, which is extremely interesting. In 1758 he commanded three ships of the line and distinguished himself in the war against France. George III., who wished to explore the part of the Atlantic Ocean between the Cape of Good Hope and the southern part of America, gave Byron command of a frigate, with which he set sail in June 1764. After having circumnavigated the globe he returned at the end of two years to England, where he arrived in May 1766. Although Byron's voyage was not fruitful in discoveries, it still deserves an honorable place in the history of voyages round the world, since he was the first of those renowned circumnavigators of the globe, including Wallis, Carteret, and Cook, whose enterprises were not merely mercantile, but were directed to scientific objects. In 1769 Commodore Byron was appointed to the government of Newfoundland, which he held till 1775. He was raised to the rank of vice-admiral of the white in 1779, and died in 1786. Such was his general ill fortune at sea, that he was called by the sailors «Foul-Weather Jack.»

Byron Bay, a bay on the northeastern coast of Labrador, situated about lat. 55° N., and lon. 58° W., and north of Hamilton Inlet. The width of the bay is about 50 miles.

Byron Island, Micronesia, a small island of the Gilbert group, in the Pacific Ocean, about 12 miles in length, abounding in cocoanuts. It was discovered by Commodore Byron in 1765, and belongs to Great Britain.

Byssus, bĭs′sŭs, a kind of fine flax, and the linen made from it, used in India and Egypt at a very early date. In the latter country it was used in embalming, and mummies are still found wrapped in it. As an article of dress it was worn only by the rich. Dives, in Christ's parable (Luke xvi. 19), was clothed in byssus, and it is mentioned among the riches of fallen Babylon (Rev. xviii. 12). Byssus was formerly erroneously considered as a fine kind of cotton. The fine stuff manufactured from the byssus is called more particularly «sindon.» Foster derives the word byssus from the Coptic. Byssus was also used by the ancients, and is still used, to signify the hairlike or threadlike substance (also called the beard), with which different kinds of sea-mussels fasten themselves to rocks. Pinna marina, particularly, is distinguished by the length and silky fineness of its beard, from which very durable cloths, gloves, and stockings are still manufactured (mainly as curiosities) in Sicily and Calabria.

Byström, Johan Niklas, Swedish sculptor: b. Filipstad, Wermland, Sweden, 18 Dec. 1783; d. Rome, 11 March 1848. He studied art in Stockholm, and in 1810 went to Rome. In 1815 he returned, and winning the favor of the crown prince by his statue of the latter, received several important commissions. Several years before his death he again took up his residence in Rome. Among his more important works are: 'Drunken Bacchante'; 'Nymph Going into the Bath'; 'Reclining Juno'; 'Hygieia'; 'Dancing Girl'; a statue of Linnæus and colossal statues of several of the kings of Sweden.

Byttneriaceæ, bŭt-nĕ-rĭ-ā′sē-ē (or more properly BÜTTNERIACEÆ), (after the botanist Büttner), a natural order of exogenous plants, with the following characteristics. Its members are trees or shrubs, with simple alternate leaves and opposite stipules; flowers disposed in clusters, which are axillar or opposite to the leaves; calyx and corolla with five divisions, but the latter sometimes wanting; stamens of the same number as the petals, or double or multiple, in general monadelphous; anthers always two-celled; carpels, from three to five in number, more or less completely united, each cell with two or three ascending ovules or a greater num-

ber; styles free, or more or less united; fruit generally a globular capsule dehiscent or indehiscent. This order is distinguished from the *Malvaceæ* by its two-celled anthers and by the fact that its seeds are generally furnished with a fleshy endosperm. The order is divided into six sub-orders, one of which takes its name from the genus *Byttneria*, which gives its name to the whole order. The chief genus of this sub-order is *Theobroma cacao*, from the seeds of which cocoa is prepared. The genus *Guazuma*, a native of Brazil, belonging to the same sub-order, is cultivated for the sake of its fruit, which is edible and filled with a sweet and pleasant mucilage. Another genus of this sub-order, *Abroma*, is valuable on account of its fibre, from which strong cordage is manufactured. The genus *Astropæa* is said to contain the most beautiful plants; all the species are remarkable for the mucilage they contain. ·

Byzantine Empire, called also the Roman empire of the East, the Eastern empire, and the Greek empire.

History.— On the death of Theodosius the Great, 395 A.D., the division of the great Roman empire into East and West became permanent. The eastern portion, with Constantinople, the ancient Byzantium, for its capital, was bequeathed to the elder son Arcadius, with whom the line of Byzantine emperors properly commences. During his minority Rufinus was his guardian and minister, between whom and Stilicho, the minister of the Western empire, a fierce rivalry existed. The Goths laid waste Greece. Eutropius, the successor, and Gainas, the murderer of Rufinus, were ruined by their own crimes. The latter lost his life in a civil war excited by him (400). Arcadius and his empire were now ruled by his proud and covetous wife Eudoxia, till her death (404). The Isaurians and the Huns wasted the provinces of Asia and the country along the Danube. Theodosius the Younger succeeded his father (408), under the guardianship of his sister Pulcheria. Naturally of an inferior mind, his education had made him entirely imbecile and unfit for self-command. Pulcheria, who bore the title of Augusta, administered the kingdom ably. Of the Western empire, which had been ceded to Valentinian, Theodosius seized upon West Illyria (423). The Greeks fought with success against the king of the Persians, Varanes. The kingdom of Armenia, thrown into confusion by internal dissensions, and claimed at the same time by the Romans and the Persians, became now a bone of contention between the two nations (440). Attila laid waste the dominions of Theodosius, and obliged him to pay tribute (447). After the death of her brother Pulcheria was acknowledged empress (450). She was the first female who attained this dignity, and giving her hand to the senator Marcian, raised him to the throne. His wisdom and valor averted the attacks of the Huns from the frontiers, but he did not support the Western empire in its wars against the Huns and the Vandals with sufficient energy, and afforded shelter to a part of the Germans and Sarmatians who were driven to the Roman frontiers by the incursions of the Huns. Pulcheria died before him in 453. Leo I. (457), a prince praised by contemporary authors, was chosen successor of Marcian. His expeditions

PALATINE CHAPEL AT PALERMO

against the Vandals (467) were unsuccessful. His grandson Leo II. succeeded, but survived only a few months, when Zeno, the father of Leo, who had previously been appointed his colleague, became sole emperor (474). The government of this weak emperor, who was hated by his subjects, was disturbed by rebellions and internal disorders of the empire. The Goths depopulated the provinces till their king Theodoric turned his arms against Italy (489). Ariadne, widow of Zeno, raised the minister Anastasius, whom she married, to the throne (491). The nation, once excited to discontents and tumults, could not be entirely appeased by the alleviation of their burdens and by wise decrees. The forces of the empire, being thus weakened, could not offer an effectual resistance to the Persians and the Bulgarians along the Danube. To prevent their incursions into the peninsula of Constantinople, Anastasius built the long wall, as it is called. After the death of Anastasius the soldiers proclaimed Justin emperor (518). Notwithstanding his low birth he maintained possession of the throne. Religious persecutions, undertaken at the instigation of the clergy, and various crimes, into which he was seduced by his nephew Justinian, disgrace his reign. He was renowned as a legislator, and his reign was distinguished by the victories of his general Belisarius; but how unable he was to revive the strength of his empire was proved by its rapid decay after his death. Justin II., his successor (565), was an avaricious, cruel, weak prince, governed by his wife. The Longobardi (Lombards) tore from him part of Italy (568). His war with Persia, for the possession of Armenia (570), was unsuccessful; the Avari plundered the provinces on the Danube, and the violence of his grief at these misfortunes deprived him of reason. Tiberius, his minister, a man of merit, was declared Cæsar, and the general, Justinian, conducted the war against Persia with success. The Greeks now allied themselves, for the first time, with the Turks. Against his successor, Tiberius II. (578), the Empress Sophia and the general Justinian conspired in vain. From the Avari the emperor purchased peace; from the Persians it was extorted by his general, Mauritius or Maurice (582), who, after the death of Tiberius in the same year, was declared his successor. Mauritius, under other circumstances, would have made an excellent monarch, but, for the times, wanted prudence and resolution. He was indebted for the tranquillity of the eastern frontiers to the gratitude of King Chosroes II., whom, in 591, he restored to the throne, from which he had been deposed by his subjects. Nevertheless, the war against the Avari was unsuccessful, through the errors of Commentiolus. The army was discontented, and was irritated now by untimely severity and parsimony, and now by timid indulgence. They finally proclaimed Phocas, one of their officers, emperor. Mauritius was taken in his flight and put to death (602). The vices of Phocas and his incapacity for government produced the greatest disorder in the empire. Heraclius, son of the governor of Africa, took up arms, conquered Constantinople, and caused Phocas to be executed (610). He distinguished himself only in the short period of the Persian war. During the first 12 years of his reign the Avari

and other nations of the Danube, plundered the European provinces, and the Persians conquered the coasts of Syria and Egypt. Having finally succeeded in pacifying the Avari, he marched against the Persians (622), and defeated them; but during this time the Avari, who had renewed the war, made an unsuccessful attack on Constantinople in 626. Taking advantage of an insurrection of the subjects of Chosroes, he penetrated into the centre of Persia. By the peace concluded with Sirocs (628), he recovered the lost provinces and the holy cross. But the Arabians, who now became powerful under Mohammed and the caliphs, conquered Phœnicia, the countries on the Euphrates. Judea, Syria, and all Egypt (635–641). Among his descendants there was not one able prince. He was succeeded by his son Constantine III., probably in conjunction with his stepbrother Heracleonas (641). The former soon died, and the latter lost his crown in a rebellion, and was mutilated. After him Constans, son of Constantine, obtained the throne (642). His sanguinary spirit of persecution, and the murder of his brother Theodosius (650), made him odious to the nation. The Arabians, pursuing their conquests, took from him part of Africa, Cyprus, and Rhodes, and defeated him even at sea (653). Internal disturbances obliged him to make peace. After this he left Constantinople, and in 663 began an unsuccessful war against the Lombards in Italy. He died at Syracuse in 668. Constantine IV., Pogonatus, of Constans, vanquished his Syracusan competitor Mezentius, and, in the beginning of his reign, shared the government with his brothers Tiberius and Heraclius. During the early part of his reign the Arabians inundated all Africa and Sicily, penetrated through Asia Minor into Thrace, and attacked Constantinople, for several successive years, by sea. Nevertheless, he made peace with them on favorable terms. But on the other hand, the Bulgarians obliged him to pay a tribute (680). Justinian II., his son, who succeeded him in 685, weakened the power of the Maronites, but fought without success against the Bulgarians and against the Arabians. Leontius dethroned this cruel prince, and after mutilating, banished him to the Tauric Chersonese (695). Leontius was dethroned by Apsimar, or Tiberius III. (698), who was dethroned by Trebelius, king of the Bulgarians, who restored Justinian (705): but Philippicus Bardanes rebelled anew. With Justinian II. the race of Heraclius was extinguished. The only care of Philippicus was the spreading of Monothelism, while the Arabians wasted Asia Minor and Thrace. Philippicus reigned from 711 to 713, when he was deposed by Anastasius, who at the end of three years retired to a monastery, the army sent out against the Arabians having revolted against him, and proclaimed their leader, Theodosius, emperor. This prince, known as Theodosius III., after a reign of only 14 months, was compelled in his turn to yield the throne to Leo the Isaurian, general of the army of the East, who refused to recognize him, and marched against Constantinople (May 717). Leo repelled the Arabians from Constantinople, which they had attacked for almost two years, and suppressed the rebellion excited by Basilius and the former emperor Anastasius. From 726 the abolition of the worship of images absorbed his attention, and the Italian provinces were allowed to become a prey to the Lombards, who thus put an end to the exarchate of Ravenna (728), while the Arabians plundered the eastern provinces. After his death (741), his son Constantine V. ascended the throne — a courageous, active, and noble prince. He vanquished his rebellious brother-in-law Artabasdes, wrested from the Arabians part of Syria and Armenia, and overcame at last the Bulgarians, against whom he had been long unsuccessful. He died (775), and was succeeded by his son Leo IV., who fought successfully against the Arabians, and this latter by his son Constantine VI. (780), whose imperious mother, Irene, his guardian and associate in the government, raised a powerful party by the restoration of the worship of images. He endeavored, in vain, to free himself from the dependence on her and her favorite, Stauratius, and died in 797, after having had his eyes put out. The war against the Arabians and Bulgarians was long continued; against the first it was unsuccessful. The design of the empress to marry Charlemagne excited the discontent of the patricians, who placed one of their own order, Nicephorus, upon the throne (802). Irene died in a monastery. Nicephorus became tributary to the Arabians, and fell in the war against the Bulgarians (811). Stauratius, his son, was deprived of the crown by Michael I., and he, in turn, by Leo V. (813). Leo was dethroned and put to death by Michael II. (820). During the reign of the latter the Arabians conquered Sicily, Lower Italy, Crete, and other countries. He prohibited the worship of images, as did also his son Theophilus (829-42). Theodora, widow of Theophilus and guardian of his son Michael III., put a stop to the dispute about images (842). During a cruel persecution of the Paulicians, considered to be an offshoot of the Manichæans, the Arabians devastated the Asiatic provinces. The dissolute and extravagant Michael confined his mother in a monastery. The government was administered in his name by Bardas, his uncle, and after the death of Bardas by Basil, by whom Michael was put to death (867). Basil I., who came to the throne in 867, was not altogether a contemptible monarch. He died 886. The reign of his learned son, Leo VI. (the Philosopher), was not very happy. He died 911. His son, Constantine VII. Porphyrogenitus (that is, "born in the purple"), a minor when he succeeded his father, was placed under the guardianship of his colleague, Alexander, and after Alexander's death, in 912, under that of his mother Zoe. Romanus Lacapenus, his general, obliged him, in 919, to share the throne with him and his children, Constantine VIII. and Stephanus. Constantine subsequently took sole possession of it again, and reigned mildly, but weakly. His son, Romanus II., succeeded him in 959, and fought successfully against the Arabians. To him succeeded, in 963, his general Nicephorus II. (Phocas), who was put to death by his own general, John Zimisces (969), who carried on a successful war against the Russians. Basil II., son of Romanus, succeeded this good prince in 976. He vanquished the Bulgarians and the Arabians. His brother, Constantine IX. (1025), was not equal to him. Romanus III. became emperor (1028) by marriage with Zoe, daughter of Constantine. This dissolute but able princess caused her husband to be executed, and successively raised to the throne

Michael IV. (1034), Michael V. (1041), and Constantine X. (1042). Russians and Arabians meanwhile devastated the empire. Her sister Theodora succeeded her on the throne (1054). Her successor, Michael VI. (1056), was dethroned by Isaac Comnenus in 1057, who became a monk (1059). His successor, Constantine XI., Ducas, fought successfully against the Uzes. Eudocia his wife, guardian of his sons, Michael, Andronicus, and Constantine, was intrusted with the administration (1067), married Romanus IV., and brought him the crown. He carried on an unsuccessful war against the Turks, who kept him for some time prisoner. Michael VII., son of Constantine, deprived him of the throne (1071). Michael was dethroned by Nicephorus III. (1078), and the latter by Alexius I., Comnenus (1081). Under his reign the Crusades commenced. His son, John II., came to the throne (1118), and fought with great success against the Turks and other barbarians. The reign of his son, Manuel I., who succeeded him (1143), was also not unfortunate. His son, Alexius II., succeeded (1180), and was dethroned by his guardian, Andronicus (1183), as was the latter by Isaac (1185). After a reign disturbed from without and within, Isaac was dethroned by his brother Alexius III. (1195). The Crusaders restored him and his son, Alexius IV.; but the seditious Constantinopolitans proclaimed Alexius V., Ducas Murzuphlus, emperor, who put Alexius IV. to death. At the same time Isaac II. died. During the last reigns the kings of Sicily had made many conquests on the coasts of the Adriatic. The Latins now forced their way to Constantinople (1204), conquered the city, and retained it, together with most of the European territories of the empire. Baldwin, Count of Flanders, was made emperor; Boniface, Marquis of Montferrat, obtained Thessalonica as a kingdom, and the Venetians acquired a large extent of territory. In Attalia, Rhodes, Philadelphia, Corinth, and Epirus, independent sovereigns arose. Theodore Lascaris seized on the Asiatic provinces, in 1206 made Nice (Nicæa) the capital of the empire, and was at first more powerful than Baldwin. In 1204 a descendant of the Comneni, named Alexius, established a principality at Trebizond, in which his great-grandson John took the title of emperor. Neither Baldwin nor his successors were able to secure the tottering throne. He himself died in captivity among the Bulgarians (1206). He was followed first by Henry, his brother, then by Peter, brother-in-law of Henry (1217), and then by Robert of Courtenay, son of Peter, who succeeded in 1219, but was not crowned till 1221. With the exception of Constantinople, all the remaining Byzantine territory, including Thessalonica, was conquered by John, emperor of Nice. Baldwin II., brother of Robert, succeeded and reigned under the guardianship of his colleague, John of Brienne, king of Jerusalem, till 1237, after which he was sole ruler till 1261. In that year Michael Palæologus, king of Nice, conquered Constantinople, and Baldwin died in the West, a private person. The sovereigns of Nice, up to this period were Theodore Lascaris (1206); John Ducas Vatatges, a good monarch and successful warrior (1222); Theodore II., his son (1254); John Lascaris (1259), who was deprived of the crown by Michael Palæologus in December

1259, who himself received the crown 1 Jan. 1260. In 1261 Michael took Constantinople from the Latins. He labored to unite himself with the Latin Church, but his son, Andronicus II. (1282), renounced the connection. Internal disturbances and foreign wars, particularly with the Turks, threw the exhausted empire into confusion. Andronicus III., his grandson, obliged him to divide the throne, and at length wrested it entirely from him (1328). He waged war unsuccessfully against the Turks, and died in 1341. His son, John Palæologus, was obliged to share the throne with his guardian, John Cantacuzene, during the first years of his reign. The son of the latter, Matthew, was also made emperor. But John Cantacuzene resigned the crown, and Matthew was compelled to abdicate (1355), when John Palæologus, the son of Andronicus III., became sole emperor. Under his reign the Turks first obtained a firm footing in Europe, and conquered Gallipoli (1357). The family of Palæologus from this time were gradually deprived of their European territories, partly by revolt, partly by the Turks. The Sultan Amurah took Adrianople (1361). Bajazet conquered almost all the European provinces except Constantinople, and obliged John to pay him tribute. The latter was, some time after, driven out by his own son, Andronicus, who was succeeded by his second son, Manuel (1391). Bajazet besieged Constantinople, defeated an army of western warriors under Sigismund, king of Hungary, near Nicopolis (1396), and Manuel was obliged to place John, son of Andronicus, on the throne. Timur's invasion of the Turkish provinces saved Constantinople for this time (1402). Manuel then recovered his throne, and regained some of the lost provinces from the contending sons of Bajazet. To him succeeded his son John, Palæologus II. (1425), whom Amurath II. stripped of all his territories except Constantinople, and laid under tribute (1444). To the Emperor John succeeded his brother Constantine Palæologus. With the assistance of his general, Justinian, a Genoese, he withstood the superior forces of the enemy with fruitless courage, and fell in the defense of Constantinople, by the conquest of which (29 May 1453) Mohammed II. put an end to the Greek or Byzantine empire. In 1461 David Comnenus, emperor of Trebizond, submitted to him, and at a subsequent period was put to death. See Gibbon, 'Decline and Fall of the Roman Empire'; Pears, 'Fall of Constantinople' (1885); Bury, 'The Later Roman Empire' (1889); Oman, 'Byzantine Empire' (1892); Harrison, 'Byzantine History in the Early Middle Ages' (1900).

Byzantine Literature.— The Greek literature of the period of the Byzantine empire is almost entirely destitute of originality, and derives importance almost entirely from the mass of valuable historical material embodied in it. Among the historians proper the more notable are Procopius of Cæsarea; Agathias, who wrote an account of Justinian's reign; Nicephorus Gregoras; Anna Comnena, daughter of the Emperor Alexius I., author of a highly laudatory life of her father; Pachymerus; George Codinus; Constantine VII., Porphyrogenitus, from whom we have many works on history, law, politics, and science; John Cantacuzenus, emperor and historian; and at the very end of the period, Michael Ducas. Poetry, in the proper sense of the word. can scarcely be said to have existed at all. Theodorus Prodromus, who flourished in the later 12th century, is the chief of the versifiers, among his works being a long romance having Rhodanthe and Dosikles as its heroine and hero, some dramas, historical poems, epistles, etc. Georgius of Pisidia, in the early 7th century, wrote war poems; Nicetas Eugenianus, a contemporary of Prodromus, wrote a work in imitation of the latter's romance; and among other writers of verse were Theodosius, of the latter half of the 10th century, Tzetzes and Joannes Pediasimus, the latter two being better known as annotators of the Greek classical writers. Manuel Philes of Ephesus (about 1280-1330) has left many dramas; and we have hymns from Germanus, a patriarch of Constantinople; Theodorus Studites; Porphyrogenitus; Cosmas, an 8th-century writer; Joannes Damascenus (John of Damascus); and Theophanes Ho Graptos. Among writers of grammatical and similar works the most notable are Tzetzes (about 1180), who annotated Homer, Hesiod, Æschylus, and especially Aristophanes; Eustathius, archbishop of Myra in Lycia in 1174, best known for his commentary on Homer; Manuel Moschopulus, a 13th-century scholiast; Joannes Pediasimus, of the latter part of the 14th century, chiefly known for his scholia on Hesiod's poems; and Demetrius Triclinius, a scholiast contemporary with Pediasimus. Their work is less valuable in itself than as a link with the more reliable work of their predecessors, or as containing much that would, but for them, have been lost to us. Of the lexicographers Suidas, who lived during the 10th century, is much the most important; but the works of Photius in this department are also of value. Joannes Doxopater, of the later 11th century, wrote on rhetoric; and in the department of philosophy we find the names of Michael Bellus the younger (about 1018-1105), who also wrote historical and other works, and Joannes Italus. The theologians include Joannes Damascenus, already mentioned, author of Sacra Parallela, a collection of passages from the fathers; and Nicephorus Callistus, a 14th-century writer on ecclesiastical history.

Byzantine Art.— The style which prevailed in the Byzantine or Eastern Roman Empire, as long as it existed (395-1453) and which has prevailed since in Greece, in the Balkan Peninsula as far as allowed by the Turkish conquerors (as for instance, in convents), and in neighboring lands, such as Moldavia and the Russian lands north of it, and Armenia with other parts of Asia Minor. Byzantine architecture may be said to have assumed its distinctive features in the church of St. Sophia, built by Justinian in the 6th century, and still existing as the chief mosque in Constantinople. It is more especially the style associated with the Greek Church as distinguished from the Roman. The leading forms of the Byzantine style are the round arch, the circle, and in particular the dome. The last is the most conspicuous and characteristic object in Byzantine buildings, and the free and full employment of it was arrived at when by the use of pendentives the architects were enabled to place it on a square apartment instead of a circular or polygonal. In this style of building incrustation, the masking or covering of brick surfaces with more precious materials, was largely in use. It depended much on color and surface ornament for its effect, and with this intent mosaics wrought on grounds of gold or of positive color are profusely introduced, while colored marbles and stones of various kinds are made much use of. The capitals are of peculiar and original design, the most characteristic being square and tapering downward, and they are very varied in their decorations. Byzantine architecture may be divided into an older and a newer (Neo-Byzantine) style. The most distinctive feature of the latter is that the dome is raised on a perpendicular circular or polygonal piece of masonry (technically the drum) containing windows for lighting the interior, while in the older style the light was admitted by openings in the dome itself. The Byzantine style had a great influence on the architecture of western Europe, especially in Italy, where Saint Mark's in Venice is a magnificent example, as also in Sicily.

Our knowledge of the earliest decorations other than mosaic is very slight. It is gathered from painted manuscripts, book bindings often of metal and ornamented with precious stones, a few enamels, and some glass ware, and a very few paintings on wood, forming parts of the iconostasis or choir screen of this or that church of the Greek form of Christianity. The mosaics are the most important decorations of the earlier art, so far as we have any knowledge of it, and these are more familiar to Europe as found in the churches of Ravenna than in any building farther East. The fact that Moslem rule requires the covering up as with whitewash of these representations when a church is taken over for a mosque, makes it probable that at some future time many fine early mosaics will be uncovered.

The characteristic of Byzantine art is rich decorative effects almost to the exclusion of accurate drawing or modeling of the human figure or faithful representation of nature in any form. Early or late, the attitudes of personages represented are formal and conventional, but the robes are splendid, the backgrounds are rich and the effect is that of a splendid colored pattern with but slight representative or expressional meaning. Sculpture has never risen to excellence; it is almost limited to decorative carvings, of book covers and sacred objects, reliefs in ivory and casting of small figures in bronze. The earlier statues of emperors and the like are chiefly remarkable for the lingering Roman traditions.

The art sometimes called Neo-Byzantine is of the 10th and following centuries, and has a surprising vigor and individuality. One of the typical churches is that of Saint Elias at Salonica. This has a plan like that of a northern Romanesque church, the three apses, east, north, and south, radiating from the sanctuary, which is covered by a cupola having a high, twelve-sided drum with vertical walls pierced with windows forming a continuous arcade, and a very low-pitched roof which covers the shallow, dome-shaped ceiling. That type of cupola is the one which has been used all through the provinces which are now included in European Russia, and in the lands on the Black Sea which still belong to Turkey, as well as in Greece proper. Paintings often replace mosaics in these more recent churches.

Byzantium, bĭ-zăn'shĭ-ŭm, the name of the city of Constantinople before its name was changed by Constantine the Great. It was founded by a colony of Greeks from Megara, who, under a leader named Byzas, settled on what seemed a favorable spot at the entrance to the Thracian Bosporus, in 658 B.C. The city which was built by the first colonists was named after their leader. Other colonists followed from different quarters, especially from Miletus, and Byzantium was already a flourishing town when it was taken and sacked by the Persians, in the reign of Darius, the son of Hystaspes. After the retreat of the Persians (479 B.C.) Byzantium soon recovered itself. During the Peloponnesian war it acknowledged for some time the supremacy of the Athenians, but afterward fell away. Alcibiades recovered it for Athens (409), but it was taken by Lysander in 405. At a later period the Byzantines received support from Athens in their resistance against Philip of Macedon. The barbarian Thracians, who occupied the neighboring territory, and the Celts (Galatians), in their migrations to the East, often appeared to threaten the safety of the town; but in spite of this, chiefly owing to its favorable position for commerce, it continued to prosper, and survived the decay of most of the other Greek cities; and even under the Romans it was left free to manage its own affairs, and was allowed to demand dues from all ships passing through the Bosporus, only part of these being claimed by the Romans. At the end of the 2d century of the Christian era Byzantium, unfortunately for itself, sided with Pescennius Niger against Septimius Severus. By the latter it was besieged for three years, and when at last it was forced to surrender Severus ordered its walls to be razed to the ground, deprived the city of its privileges, and placed it under the jurisdiction of the Perinthians. For a time the prosperity of the city was annihilated, until a new and more brilliant era began for it under Constantine the Great. (See CONSTANTINE; CONSTANTINOPLE.) Its early form of government was that of an aristocracy, which passed into an oligarchy. In the year 390 B.C. it received from Thrasybulus a democratical constitution, closely resembling that of the Athenians. Byzantium was the great entrepôt for the grain trade between the countries bordering on the Black Sea and those bordering on the Ægean.

Bzovius, Abraham (Pol. *Bzowski*), Polish scholar and divine: b. Proszowice, near Miechow, 1567; d. Rome, 31 Jan. 1637. At the request of Pope Paul V., he spent several years of the latter part of his life in the Vatican, as librarian of the *Virginio dei Ursini*, and actively engaged in literary pursuits. He was a member of the order of the Dominicans, one of the most voluminous writers of his age, gained for himself a high reputation as professor of philosophy and theology at Milan and Bologna, and crowned the labors of his life by continuing the celebrated ecclesiastical annals of Cæsar Baronius, who had left them off at the year 1198, and completed only 12 volumes. Bzovius carried them to the year 1532, in 9 volumes.

C

C the third character of the English alphabet and of all the alphabets derived from the Latin. In its form it is a modification of the primitive Greek *gamma*. That primitive form was ⟨, an angle with vertex pointing to the left; it is the reverse of the ancient Phœnician 7, which points to the right, and of the Old Hebrew *gimel*, 7. The Latin **C** (used also by the Greeks to some extent) is the ancient Greek ⟨ rounded, just as the later Greek *gamma* symbol, Γ, is the angular symbol erected. The Russian alphabet retains the Greek symbol Γ, but its place is fourth, because in that alphabet the sign for the denti-labial V holds the third place. The Greek *gamma* (⟨, Γ,) seems to have always represented the same sonant guttural as the English *g* in "go." To express the corresponding mute guttural the Greeks attached the ⟨ to an upright line, |, making Κ. In the Latin alphabet of the Romans, as represented in their earliest inscriptions, the C stood for the same sonant guttural as in the Greek, *g* hard; for example, *lecio*, later written *legio; macistratus*, later *magistratus;* yet at the same time the C represented also the surd guttural K, as it still does in English except before the vowels *e* and *i* and the diphthongs *æ* and *œ* in words from the Latin. Thus the early Latin alphabet was without the symbol K. There is in this use of the character C in ancient Roman epigraphy ground for the inference that the early Romans confounded the two gutturals *k* and *g* hard, as in some localities or in some classes of people the termination *ing* becomes *ink*, and "something" becomes "somethink." But at a later period the distinction between *g* hard and *k* was recognized, and then for the designation of the mute guttural the *kappa* (K) of the Greek alphabet came into use in Latin writing. But the *k* was afterward rejected, and its only use in Latin was in writing the word *kalendæ* (abbreviated to *kal.* or *k.*) and as an abbreviation of *Carthago* (Carthage) and of the personal name *Cæso.* No doubt the persistence of *k* in *kalendæ* was due to the adherence of the Pontifices to the antique forms of the official calendars; and the K standing for the forename Cæso was retained as a means of abbreviating that name and distinguishing it from the abbreviation of the name Caius : C. Julius Cæsar is Gaius, but K. Fabius Ambustus is Cæso. But the *k* having been discarded from the Latin alphabet, its function was assigned to the symbol C, while for representation of the sonant guttural a modified form of C was adopted, namely, the G with the value of *g* in "go." The soft *g*, equal to *j*, was probably unknown to the Romans before the general debasement of the Latin language. After the symbol *k* had been discarded and been superseded by C, the symbol C, with the power of *gamma*, was retained as an initial abbreviation of Gaius, name for a man, and of Gaia (with C reversed Ɔ), name of a woman. C was also retained in the formula Cn. as an abbreviation of Gnæus. This use of the initial C as representing *g* hard (sonant guttural) recalls the primitive equivalence for the Romans of the two gutturals *k* and *g* hard; but the modern Latinists, unacquainted with such use of C, have usually pronounced Gaius "Kains" and Cnæus "Knæus," instead of "Gæus" and "Guæus." In the Anglo-Saxon, its alphabet having been derived from the Latin, the C had everywhere the value of K, and the same is to be said of the Gælic; that fact gives presumptive proof that at the first contact of the Gælic and Germanic races with men of Latin speech the C in all situations was equivalent to *k* in Latin; and the German word Kaiser is proof that when the Germans first heard of Julius and the Cæsars who succeeded him the head of the Roman state was "*Kaisar*," not "*Cæsar*." The change in the pronunciation of C from *k* to *s*, as in French and English; to *ch* as in Italian, to *ts* as in German, appears to have come about long after the fall of the Roman empire.

Ça Ira, sä ē-rạ, a popular song of the great French Revolution. The origin and date of this song are both uncertain, and there are various versions of the words claiming to be original. In all probability it dates from May or June 1790. French writers say that Benjamin Franklin, in speaking of the American Revolution, frequently used the expression "Ça ira" ("it will succeed"). The French republicans caught up the phrase, and "consecrated" it to their own revolution in a popular hymn. The air to which it was adapted was a popular *carillon*, a favorite one with Marie Antoinette. The refrain or chorus of one of the versions runs thus :—

> "Ah ! ça ira, ça ira, ça ira,
> En dépit d' l'aristocrat' et d' la pluie,
> Ah ! ça ira, etc.
> Nous nous mouillerons, mais ça finira,"

referring to the rain which fell during the taking of the Bastile.

Caaba, kä'bạ, or kä'ạ-bạ, or Kaaba, properly a quadrangular structure, applied partienlarly to a celebrated temple at Mecca. According to Mussulman tradition, the first Caaba was built by the angels on the model of the pavilion which surrounds the throne of the Most High; the second was built by Adam, with whom it was removed to the skies, where it still exists in a right line above the Caaba of Mecca; the third was built by Seth, but perished in the deluge; the fourth, which now exists, was built by Abraham and Ishmael. The name is specially given to a small cubical oratory in the temple in the centre of a large space surrounded by galleries. This is the point toward which the prayers of all Mussulmans are directed. On one of its sides is inwrought the famous oval black stone, believed to be one of the precious stones of paradise, and to have been brought by the angel Gabriel to Abraham, when he was constructing the Caaba. At first, according to one version, of a dazzling whiteness, the Moslems say that it grieved and wept so long for the sins of the human race that it became gradually opaque, and at length absolutely black; or, in another version, that it has been blackened by the tears of pilgrims, shed for sin. It is an object of profound veneration to the pilgrims who resort to the sacred city. This inner Caaba is surrounded with a veil of black silk, and is opened but two or three times a year, and none but the faithful are permitted to approach it. The temple of the Caaba is older than the time of Mohammed, previous to whom it was the Arab pantheon, containing the nation's idols.

Caaing-whale, kä-ing hwäl, one of several species of porpoise-like cetaceans of the Killer family (*Orcidæ*), characterized by its globose head; properly *Globiocephalus melas,* of the North Atlantic Ocean. It is from 16 to 24 feet long, 10 feet in diameter at its thickest part, and weighs between 5,000 and 6,000 pounds. Its pectoral fins are about 5 feet long and 18 inches broad, and its dorsal fin is very low. With the exception of a white streak, which begins in the form of a heart under the throat and gradually narrows to the vent, the whole of the body is of a glossy black color, and hence the fish is frequently known as the blackfish (q.v.) or black dolphin. The teeth are arranged at considerable distances in the upper and under jaw in such a manner that those of the upper jaw fit into the spaces left in the lower jaw, and conversely. Their number is very variable. They are conical in shape, strong, rather long, and end in a point which is a little curved backward and inward. The caaing-whale is very abundant and very widely distributed. It is found in the whole of the Arctic Ocean, and also in the German, Atlantic, and Pacific oceans, and even in the Mediterranean Sea. It is remarkable for its gregarious habits, being often found in schools numbering several hundreds, which are led by an old and experienced male whom, it is said, they never abandon. On this account its pursuers always endeavor to force the leader on shore, and when this is accomplished all the rest follow him and are likewise stranded—hence the Scotch name "caaing," equivalent to "driving." In the stomachs of these animals are usually found the remains of cod-fishes and various species of cuttle-fish, as well as of herrings, ling, and other fishes. The caaing whale is pursued chiefly on account of its oil. See WHALE.

Caama, kä'mạ. See HARTBEEST.

Cab, a carriage with two or four wheels, usually drawn by one horse, and plying for hire; a hackney-carriage. One well-known two-wheeled variety is the hansom, named after the inventor. Public cabriolets — hooded chaises carrying one person besides the driver — were introduced in London in 1823, and the name was soon after shortened to cab. See COACH; HACKNEY-CARRIAGE.

Cabal', an English ministry under Charles II. (1667-73), composed of Clifford, Ashley, Buckingham, Arlington, and Lauderdale, the initials of whose names form this word, whence perhaps its use as a designation. But the use of this word to signify a body of intriguers was not originally derived from this circumstance, as sometimes supposed, for the word cabale, derived from cabala (q.v.), was used in that sense in French before this time.

Cab'ala, or **Cabbala** (reception), is used by the Jews to denote sometimes the traditions of their ancestors regarding the interpretation of the Scriptures; sometimes, and most commonly, their mystical philosophy. The opinions of scholars respecting the origin of the Cabalistic philosophy are very various. The Jews derive the Cabala from the most ancient times of their nation, nay, even from Adam himself. But Cabalistic doctrines in reality seem to have had their origin about 200 years before Christ, and were derived from the mingling of Oriental ideas with those belonging to the Mosaic religion that was the result of the captivity. It was long before the Cabala reached its full development, however, the chief landmarks in its history being the writings of Philo Judæus and the appearance of the books called the Sefer Jezirah, 'Book of Creation,' and the Sefer Zohar, 'Book of Light.' The age of both is doubtful. The earliest probable date for the Sefer Jezirah is the beginning of our era. The earliest mention of the Sefer Zohar is in 1290, and the author is not supposed to have lived much before 1000. The Cabala is divided into the symbolical and the real. The symbolical portion treats principally of letters, to which it gives mystical significations. The real, which is opposed to the symbolical, and comprehends doctrines, is divided into the theoretical and the practical. The aim of the theoretical is to explain the Scriptures according to the secret traditions, and to form therefrom a philosophical system of metaphysics, physics, and pneumatology. The practical portion, on the other hand, pretends to teach the art of performing miracles, and that merely by an artificial application of the divine names and sentences in the Scriptures. After the revival of science many scholars studied the Cabala. The most famous modern Cabalists are Henry More and Christian Knorr, the latter of whom published a compilation of the Cabalistic writings in Latin (1677). See JUDAISM — THE CABALA.

Caballero, Fernan, fĕr-nän' kä-bạ-lyä'rō, pseudonym of CECELIA BÖHL VON FABER, Spanish novelist, daughter of a German settled in Spain and married to a Spanish lady: b. Morges, near Lausanne, Switzerland, 25 Dec. 1796; d. Seville, 7 April 1877. Brought up in Germany, she went to Cadiz with her father in 1813. Her first novel, 'La Gaviota,' appeared in 1849, and was followed by 'Elia,' 'Clemencia,' 'La Familia de Alvareda,' etc., as well as by many shorter stories. In 1859 she published a collection of folk-tales under the title, 'Cuentas y Poesias Populares Andaluces.' Some of her works have appeared in English translations, including 'La Gaviota' (translated as 'The Sea-Gull,' 1867); 'Elia: or Spain Fifty Years Ago' (1868); 'Air-Built Castles'; and 'The Bird of Truth' (1881). The chief charm of her writings lies in her descriptions of life and nature in Andalusia. She was three times left a widow; her last hus•

PILGRIMS AROUND THE CAABA.

band was a lawyer named De Arrom. She forms the subject of one of the 'Six Life Studies' (1880) of M. B. Edwards.

Cabanel, Alexandre, ä-lĕks-ändr kä-bạ-nĕl, French artist: b. Montpellier, 28 Sept. 1823; d. Paris, 23 Jan. 1889. He studied with Picot, and after 1860 gave himself mainly to portrait painting. He was for many years a professor of the Académie des Beaux Arts and was especially popular with American patrons. Among his many portraits of Americans is that of Miss Catherine Wolfe, now in the Metropolitan Museum, New York, which contains also his 'Queen Vashti and King Ahasuerus,' and 'Birth of Venus.' See Stranahan, 'A History of French Painting' (1899).

Cabanis, Jean Louis, zhŏn loo-e kä-bạ-nĕs, German ornithologist: b. Berlin, 1816. He made an ornithological tour through North and South Carolina, 1839-41, and in 1849 became custodian of the ornithological department of the Berlin Zoological Museum. His investigations were largely instrumental in establishing a natural classification, and were published in Wiegmann's 'Archiv für Naturgeschichte' (1847), and in the 'Museum Heineum' (1850–63). Cabanis founded the 'Journal für Ornithologie' in 1853.

Cabanis, Pierre Jean Georges, pē-är zhŏn zhŏrzh, French physician and philosopher: b. Cosnac, department of Charente-Inférieure, 5 June 1757; d. Rueil, near Paris, 5 May 1808. In his 16th year he went to Warsaw as secretary of a Polish lord, where the proceedings of the stormy Diet of 1773 filled him with melancholy and contempt of mankind. He began at Paris a complete translation of the 'Iliad'; became acquainted with Madame Helvetius, and through her with Holbach, Franklin, and Jefferson, and became the friend of Condillac, Turgot, and Thomas. In his 'Serment d'un Médecin' he formally took leave of the belles-lettres. He professed the principles of the Revolution, and was intimately connected with Mirabeau, who made use of his ideas, and obtained from him the work on public education which Cabanis published himself in 1791, after the death of Mirabeau. He lived in still closer intimacy with Condorcet. At the time of his death he was a member of the Senate. His 'Rapports du Physique et du Moral de l'Homme' (1882), improved, is his most important work. It displays considerable power of analysis, and advocates the most extreme materialistic doctrines.

Cabat, Nicolas Louis, nĭk-ō-lä loo-e kä-ba, French artist: b. Paris, 1812; d. 1893. He studied with Flers and became prominent among painters of the landscape realistic school. Among his works are 'Pond at Ville d'Avray' (1834); 'A Spring in the Wood' (1864); and 'A Morning in the Park of Magnet' (1877).

Cab'bage, a biennial plant, too well known to need description, and constituting one of the most valuable classes of vegetables. The *Brassica oleracea,* the original species from which the numerous varieties of cultivated cabbages are derived, although in a wild state very remote in appearance from the full, round head which our plants present, is scarcely more so than the kale, cauliflower, broccoli, etc., all of which belong to the same family. The principal varieties are known to have existed at least as far back as the 16th century, but minor varieties are being constantly produced by selection and intercrossing. The parent stock is of highly vegetable character, as its habitat and habit alike show; and placed in more favorable conditions its growth becomes luxuriant. More normally it is carried back into the stem, and this may accordingly become swollen and turnip-like, in which case we have the kohl-rabi, of which an extreme subterranean and almost turnip-like variety has also arisen, or may be, as in the Jersey cabbage, largely applied to the purpose of the growth of the stem, which may reach a height of 8 to 10 feet, and furnish not only walking-sticks, but even spars for small thatched roofs, etc. The vegetative overplus may, however, also be applied to the formation of buds, which accordingly develop with peculiar exuberance, giving us Brussels sprouts. The most evolved and final variety is the cauliflower, in which the vegetative surplus becomes poured into the flowering head, of which the flowering is more or less checked; the inflorescence becoming a dense corymb instead of an open panicle, and the majority of the flowers aborting, so as to become incapable of producing seed. Let a specially vegetative cabbage repeat the excessive development of its leaf parenchyma, and we have the wrinkled and blistered savoy. Again a specially vegetative cauliflower gives us an easily grown and hardy winter variety, broccoli, from which, and not from the ordinary cauliflower, a sprouting variety arises in turn.

The common cabbage is by far the most valuable to both man and beast. It is also the most productive; for it is believed that an acre of ground will yield a greater weight of green vegetable matter (and thus be more profitable to the farmer) in the shape of cabbage than in that of any other vegetable whatever. It is very abundantly produced by clay soils which are unfit for turnips, and the farmers who cultivate such soils will find it a vegetable worthy of much attention. The cabbage furnishes green fodder for cows and sheep, which is at least as good as turnips or carrots, fattening the animals equally fast, and rendering their milk, butter, etc., to the full as sweet; and is so far preferable, as it keeps later in the spring, and thus supplies green food when no other can be procured. It is eaten by men in three forms, all of which have their admirers, but which vary much in respect to their wholesomeness and digestibility. These forms are sliced raw, plain-boiled, and salted cabbage or sauerkraut (q.v.), the favorite dish of the German nation. Raw cabbage, sliced fine and eaten with vinegar, either cold, or hot enough merely to wilt the vegetable, is one of the lightest and most wholesome articles of vegetable food, and in this shape will supply a green summer vegetable through the whole of the winter. Its use cannot be too highly recommended. Boiled cabbage takes longer to digest and is more trying to a weak stomach.

Cultivation.— The cabbage being biennial, the main crop must be sown the autumn previous to that in which it is to be reaped. Field cabbages and the drum-head varieties that are used in gardens, being late in character, may be sown in July, or from the third week of that month to the second week of August. But the smaller and early sorts used in gardens should not be sown before the first week of August, nor later than the second week of that month. If the plants are reared earlier, they are apt to run to seed the following spring; and if, on the other hand, they are reared later, they will not acquire strength enough to withstand the cold of winter before it comes upon them. For successive crops to be used in the shape of young summer cabbages, one or two sowings may be made from the beginning of March to the beginning of April. Autumn-sown plants may be planted out in rows permanently as soon as they are strong enough. Additional plantations from the same sowing may be made in spring, to be followed by others, made at intervals, up till July, from spring-sown plants. Thus a close succession of usable cabbage may be obtained the year round. In the northern parts of the United States cabbages for the early summer market are sown about September, kept under glass or frames during winter, and planted out in spring. For later markets the seed is sown in beds as early as possible in spring (about March), and transplanted later. Cabbages are sometimes preserved for winter by inverting them and burying them in the ground. Cabbage coleworts may be obtained from any good early variety of cabbage. They are simply cabbages which are not permitted to form hearts, but are used while the leaves are yet green and the hearts more or less made. Three sowings should be made for the rearing of these: the first about the middle of June, the second about the same time in July, and the third about the last week of the latter month, or the first week of August. These sowings will provide crops of green cabbages from October till March or April, if the winter is not destructive, after which they begin to run to seed.

Cabbage-bark. See ANDIRA.

Cabbage-bug. See CABBAGE-INSECTS.

Cabbage-butterfly, a name given to several species of butterfly, hence called *Brassicariæ*, which deposit their eggs on cabbage-leaves; for example, *Pieris brassicæ*.

Cabbage-fly, a species of insect (*Anthomyia brassicæ*) of the same order (*Diptera*) as the house-fly, the larvæ of which prey upon the roots of cabbages. The *Anthomyiæ* deposit their eggs in the earth, and the different species receive different names according to the particular roots upon which the larvæ feed. Thus we have the potato-fly, the turnip-fly, etc.

Cabbage-insects, certain insects injurious to the cabbage, some of which also prey on the radish. The harlequin cabbage-bug (*Murgantia histrionica*) destroys in the southern States, by its punctures, cabbages, turnips, radishes, mustard, etc. It is a black-and-orange-colored bug. The newly hatched insect is pale green marked with black, but with successive molts takes on certain orange markings. The eggs hatch on the third or fourth day after laying, and the young bugs go through all their molts and are ready for reproduction in about two weeks. There are many generations in the course of the summer; and on the advent of winter the adult insects crawl under rubbish to hibernate. The earliest specimens in the spring congregate upon mustard and early radishes, flying later to cabbages. The very young, as well as the old, combine to destroy the plant, which wilts as if poisoned. The insect is very difficult to kill, so that destruction of the over-wintering individual is the important point to be striven for. Diluted kerosene emulsion must be applied, not too strong to ruin cabbages. The caterpillar of the cabbage-moth (*Pieris brassicæ*) preys on cabbage and turnip leaves. Cabbages are more or less injured by the web-moth (*Plutella xylostella*), the zebra caterpillar (*Mamestra picta*), the cabbage aphis, the cabbage-weevil (*Otiorhynchus picipes*), etc. All these can best be destroyed by the use of pyrethrum, or dilute kerosene emulsion.

Cabbage-moth. See CABBAGE-INSECTS.

Cabbage-palm, a name given to various species of palm-tree, from the circumstance that the terminal bud, which is of great size, is edible and resembles cabbage, as the *Areca oleracea,* a native of the West Indies, the simple unbranched stem of which grows to a height of 150 or even 200 feet. It is crowned by a head of large pinnated leaves. The flowers are placed on a branching spadix and protected by a double spathe. The unopened bud of young leaves is much prized as a vegetable, but the removal of it completely destroys the tree, as it is unable to produce lateral buds. *Ptychosperma* (*Seaforthia*) *elegans* is the cabbage-palm of New South Wales. The name is also given to the *Euterpe montana* and the *Chamærops palmetto*.

Cabbage-rose, a species of rose (*Rosa centifolia*) of many varieties, supposed to have been cultivated from ancient times, and eminently fitted, from its fragrance, for the manufacture of rose-water and attar. It has a large, rounded, and compact flower. It is called also Provence (or more correctly Provins) rose, from a town in the French department of Seine-et-Marne, where it is much cultivated.

Cabbage-tree, a name given to the cabbage-palm, and also to a tree of the genus *Andira* (q.v.).

Cab'bala. See CABALA.

Cabeiri, kă-bī'rī, or **Cabiri,** heroes or divinities, venerated by the ancients in Samothrace, Lemnos, and in different parts of the coasts of Greece, Phœnicia, and Asia Minor, as the authors of religion and the founders of the human race. The multiplicity of names applied to the same character, the interchange of the names of the divinities themselves with those of their priests, the oracular law which enjoined the preservation of ancient barbaric names, and thus led to a double nomenclature, sacred and profane, together with the profound secrecy of the rites, have involved the subject in great obscurity. Some have thought that the Eastern mythology and the Druidism of western Europe contain traces of the Cabeiri. Some say there were six, three male and three female, children of Vulcan and Cabira, daughter of Proteus. Others make two, sons of Jupiter or Bacchus. In Samothrace four were venerated. The mysteries celebrated there, in the obscurity of night, were the most famous.

Ca'bell, James Lawrence, American sanitarian: b. Nelson County, Va., 26 Aug. 1813; d. Overton, Va., 13 Aug. 1889. He was graduated at the University of Virginia in 1833, where he later filled the chair of anatomy. During the Civil War he had charge of military hospitals for the Confederate government. He devised measures to check the yellow fever epidemic at Memphis and was president of the National Board of Health from 1879 till his death.

Cabell, William, American statesman: b. Licking Hole, Va., 13 March 1730; d. Union Hill, Va., 23 March 1798. He was a member of the House of Burgesses of Virginia upon the outbreak of the Revolution; took an active part in the affairs of the new nation, and before the adoption of the Federal Constitution was presiding magistrate for the United States in Virginia.

Cabell, William Lewis, American soldier and lawyer: b. Danville, Va., 1 Jan. 1827. He graduated at West Point 1850, and served in the 7th Infantry 1858. In 1858 he was attached to Gen. Harney's staff in the Utah expedition. Between 1859-69 he was chiefly engaged in constructing forts in the country occupied by the Comanches, Kiowas, and other savage tribes. Resigning in 1861 he entered the Confederate service and rose to the rank of brigadier-general. While on a raid into Kansas in 1864 he was captured and held prisoner of war until 28 April 1865. Since 1872 he has practised law at Dallas, Texas, being four times mayor of the city. He was a United States marshal, 1885–9.

Cabello. See PORTO CABELLO.

Ca'ber, the undressed stem of a tree, 20 or more feet long, used for trial of strength in Scottish athletic games. It is held upright against the chest, by the smaller end, and tossed so as to strike the ground with the heavier end and turn over. The contestant making the farthest toss with the straightest fall is winner.

Cabes, kä'bĕs, or **Gabes,** Africa, a town and port of the French protectorate of Tunis. It stands at the foot of the Jebel Hamarra, on the right bank of the Wad-er-rif, near the head of the Gulf of Cabes, and may be said to consist of several villages. It has some export trade in dates, henna, etc. The Gulf of Cabes (Syrtis Minor) has at its entrance the islands of Kerkenna and Jerba. Its chief seaport is Sfax. Pop. of Cabes, 13,000.

Cabet, Etienne, ä-tě-ĕn kä-bä, French communist: b. Dijon, 2 Jan. 1788; d. St. Louis, Mo., 9 Nov. 1856. He was brought up for the bar, and was appointed attorney-general of Corsica, from which office, however, he was soon dismissed. He was sent to the chamber of deputies in July 1831, and there made himself so obnoxious to the government by his violent speeches, and at the same time by his inflammatory pamphlets and a journal entitled 'La Populaire,' that he was indicted for treason, and rather than subject himself to the imprisonment to which he was sentenced, withdrew for five years to England. While there he published the 'Voyages en Icarie,' in which he elaborated his scheme of communism, which from 1842 to 1848 passed through five editions. On 2 Feb. 1848, a band of Icarians left France

for the Red River in Texas, where Cabet had secured a tract of 400,000 acres of land, the free use of which was open to the settlers, under condition that before their departure they should deposit all their funds in the hands of Cabet, who assumed the financial and general control of the expedition. But the expedition turned out badly, and lawsuits were instituted against Cabet; and on 30 Sept. 1849, after he had left France for Texas, he was found guilty by default of swindling his disciples, and sentenced to two years' imprisonment. Meanwhile, with his colony of Icarians much reduced in number, he took up his abode at Nauvoo, on the Mississippi, in May 1850, and soon after returned to Paris. There, after a protracted trial, his innocence was fully established. 26 July 1851, by the court of appeal, and the judgment against him cancelled. He returned to Nauvoo, where he continued to preside over his colony; but many disappointments and cares embittered his life and accelerated his death. In justice to Cabet it should be said that the highest moral tone prevailed in Nauvoo, and whatever may be the politico-economical objections to his system, the colony presented, as far as the conduct of the settlers was concerned, a model of purity and industry.

Cabeza de Vaca, Alvar Nuñez, äl'bär noon'yĕth kä-bā'tha dä bä'kạ, Spanish explorer: b. 1507 (?); d. about 1564. He was second in command in the ill-fated expedition of Pánfilo de Narvaez to Florida in 1528. After the loss of their commander, Cabeza de Vaca, with a few survivors, landed west of the mouth of the Mississippi, and after eight years of wandering and captivity among the Indians, reached a Spanish colony on the Pacific. He returned to Spain, and in 1540 was appointed Governor of La Plata. He explored Paraguay, but became unpopular with the colonists, and after a defeat by the Indians was arrested on the charge of one of his subordinates, returned to Spain (1544), found guilty, and banished to Africa. Eight years later he was pardoned and made judge of the Supreme Court at Seville. He has left an account of his travels and explorations in 'Shipwrecks of Alvar Nuñez' and 'Commentaries.'

Cabezon, a name applied to three or four distinct fishes.

1. *Larimus breviceps,* occurring in seas from the West Indies to Brazil, and belonging to the family of croakers, or *Sciænidæ.* It reaches a length of 10 inches.

2. *Scorpænichthys marmoratus,* a member of the *Cottidæ,* or sculpins. It is found from Puget Sound to San Diego, reaches a length of 30 inches, and is a common food-fish, but its flesh is coarse and tough.

3. The smooth cabezon (*Leptocottus armatus*), also a sculpin of the Pacific coast.

4. *Porichthys notatus,* a member of the *Batrachoidiæ,* found from Puget Sound to Lower California, which reaches a length of 15 inches, and is sometimes called "singing-fish."

Cabillonum. See CHÂLON-SUR-SAÔNE.

Cabinda, kạ-bĕn'dạ, or **Kabinda,** Africa, Portuguese seaport and territory, north of the mouth of the Congo. The territory is bounded by the Atlantic on the west, the Congo Free State on the south, and French Congo on the north. The inhabitants are governed by numerous petty chiefs. The town, situated about 40 miles north of the Congo estuary, carries on a considerable trade and has shown marked growth since the introduction of a high tariff in the Congo State. Its people are noted for their ship-building and other handicrafts. Pop. 10,000.

Cabinet, a collective name popularly given to the leading officers of state in a number of constitutional governments, acting as a body of advisers to the head of the state, and in some as the chief executive council and controller of legislation as well. The uniform name, however, implies a uniformity of nature which does not exist. The status and functions of different cabinets are widely divergent. The earliest one, that of England, is of a type exactly opposite to the next oldest, that of the United States; and all others are based on one of these two forms. Those of other constitutional monarchies in Europe, that of Japan, and that of the republic of France, are of the English type; those of Switzerland and the Latin-American republics are of ours. The English cabinet is to all intents and purposes a committee of the legislative body, in which its members have seats, before which they expound and defend the legislative measures they prepare, and to which they are directly responsible. They confine business mainly to measures of their own drafting, dictate its order, and carry on all the executive work of the State besides; they are, in fact, "the government," in current phrase. They act as a body, each minister supporting the proposals agreed on by the majority, or else retiring, and all resigning in a body if their proposals are voted down. They have even gained the immense power of being able to dissolve their own head body, the Parliament, and ordering a new election to test the sense of the people; a result due to their being the agents of the new sovereign, the Parliament, as they were of the older one, the monarch. When the power of proroguing Parliament was taken from the monarch, it was naturally given, not to Parliament itself, but to its deputies. This system was called by Walter Bagehot "Cabinet Government" specifically, as opposed to presidential government of fixed tenure; and his classification has been universally accepted. The American group is not, properly speaking, a cabinet at all, in the sense of a unified body. It does not act as a unit, and has no responsibility as a unit. Cabinet here is merely a popular name for the group of heads of the chief departments, whom the President consults by individuals or collectively at will, or not at all. Their functions are advisory only, and the President is under no obligation to take their advice; they are responsible only to him, and can be dismissed by him at any time. They have nothing to do with legislation, and by law are prohibited from being members of the legislative body. Obviously, their position resembles much more that of the advisers of an autocrat than of an all-powerful entity like the English government; but the former are never styled a Cabinet. The resemblances of the types are mainly confined to two: the ministers who form the Cabinet are selected by the actual head of the state, whose assistants they are to be, whether he is prime minister or president; and they are all of one political party. Even here, however, the difference between the systems is strongly marked. The premier in a "Cabinet government" has very little liberty of selection. His ministers must be able debaters first and able men of affairs next, and successful politicians besides. If they cannot defend their policy effectively on the floor in Parliament, the government may be turned out; and practical incapacity may render all defense of no avail. But men of such varied powers and success are never very plentiful, and the premier can do little more than allot offices among a small group whom he finds to his hand. On the contrary, the United States Cabinet official need not speak in public, and even if he is a practical failure the President can dismiss him or allow him to resign without affecting his own tenure of office. The President, therefore, may fill such a post with a totally unknown man, in reliance on his unproved ability, without serious risk, and some such appointments have been eminently successful. As to party, the premier's action is equally compulsory, since his majority would vote down a party opponent's measure at once; while the President, having no legislation to carry through, and secure his place, can exercise a somewhat wider independence, though personal feeling and party urgency usually keep the selections within the limits.

The British cabinet, a shortened name for "cabinet council"— that is, a council held in the king's cabinet, or private room—gained its name under Charles I., about 1630-40, when it was merely a committee of the privy council to expedite business; and all through that and the next century it was steadily drawing power to itself. But the kings did not give up their control over the power of appointing the great officers of state without a long and bitter struggle; and it was not till George III.'s insanity loosened his hand that it can be said to have won the final victory. Even then, and during the early 19th century, its unity had by no means become so rigid as now; during the latter there were many instances of members of the cabinet opposing the measures of the majority, and even of the premier, and still retaining their places in it. But by the 'thirties it had pretty much settled into its present constitution and rules. An important change was made in 1782, just after the American Revolution, when its honorary members were dropped, and the membership confined to "efficient" members,— officers of state so important that they cannot be excluded from it, or personalities so powerful that vanished offices are kept constructively alive to make place for them. There is no absolute limit to the number of members, but custom dictates not less than 11, and the necessity of coming to some agreement and transacting business prohibits its being much in excess of 15. The premier assigns the offices, and almost invariably takes for himself the control of finances or foreign relations — that is, first lord of the treasury or secretary of state for foreign affairs. There are also the four other chief secretaries of state — for war, for home affairs, for the colonies, and for India; the chancellor of the exchequer, the first lord of the admiralty, the lord privy seal, the lord president of the privy council, and the lord chancellor; the chief secretary for Ireland, the postmaster-general, the president of the board of trade, and the chancellor of the Duchy of Lancaster (one of the defunct posts used to give an able man a place in the cabinet). Other officers can be called in if desired. The prime minister presides, but has no added authority; if he is a strong man, however, no member would remain in the cabinet if steadily opposed to his general policy. All the cabinet's deliberations are secret; no minutes are taken, and it would be a gross breach of faith to reveal the struggles of opinion within it which result in an agreement on a line of policy.

The American Cabinet, or "President's Cabinet," has, of course, grown with the growth of the departments. There were but four Cabinet officers at the outset, the secretaries of state, of war, and of the treasury, with the attorney-general. Of these, following the English tradition, in which from necessity, foreign affairs had held the highest place, the secretaryship of state was regarded as the most important and honorable, and its incumbent was considered to be in the line of succession for the presidency, as for several administrations proved to be the case. John Quincy Adams was the last of these, and he appointed his chief rival, Henry Clay, secretary of state with the presidential succession in view. The same notion has lingered to our own day, and caused the secretary of state to be termed the "premier" of an administration; in itself an absurd and meaningless term, but with color given to it by the preference for this post among some of the ablest party leaders ambitious of the presidency. The next officer added was the secretary of the navy, whose office was created in 1798. In 1829 the postmaster-general was raised to the Cabinet, though the office had existed 35 years, in 1849 the secretaryship of the interior was created and made of Cabinet rank; in 1889 was added the secretary of agriculture, and in 1903 the secretary of commerce and labor. In accordance with Congressional action in 1886 the Cabinet officers rank in order of succession to the presidency, as follows: Secretary of state, secretary of war, secretary of the treasury, attorney-general, postmaster-general, secretary of the navy, secretary of the interior, secretary of agriculture, and secretary of commerce and labor. It will be noted that after the original four the others are named in order of the creation of their departments, not of their elevation to Cabinet rank. The term "cabinet" is sometimes used of the heads of our State departments advisory to the governor; but this is even less defensible than our national term, as the officers are elected by the people on the same ticket with the governor, and he has no power of appointment or dismissal. The municipal officers accessory to a mayor are sometimes so called; which has justification in the fact that some of them are appointed by him. See U. S.— CABINET OFFICERS, etc.

Cabinet Organ, a small portable reed organ or harmonium, designed for domestic use or for very small churches or schools.

Cabi'ri. See CABEIRI.

Cable, George Washington, American novelist and miscellaneous writer: b. New Orleans, La., 12 Oct. 1844. His father died when he was 14 years of age, and he had to leave school and seek employment as a clerk in order to support his mother and sisters. In 1863 he joined the Confederate army as soldier in a cavalry regiment, and served till the conclusion of the Civil War, when he returned to New Orleans and again took to commercial life. But in 1879, being by this time a practised writer, and having had considerable success with his literary ventures, he decided to devote himself entirely to authorship. In 1884 he took up his residence in Massachusetts, where he has originated a system of "home culture clubs." His first important book, 'Old Creole Days' (1879), appeared originally in 'Scribner's Magazine'; and since its publication he has written 'The Grandissimes' (1880); 'Madame Delphine' (1881); 'The Creoles of Louisiana' (1884), a history; 'Dr. Sevier' (1884); 'The Silent South' (1885), a plea for the negro; 'Bonaventure' (1888); 'The Negro Question' (1888); 'Strange True Stories of Louisiana' (1889); 'John March' (1894); 'Strong Hearts'; 'The Cavalier' (1901); 'Bylow Hill' (1902). For most readers the chief interest of Mr. Cable's novels lies in their excellent descriptions of Creole life, a subject which he may be said to have introduced into literature. His pictures of negro life are equally effective, and he handles dialect in a masterly manner.

Cable, Ransom R., American railroad manager: b. Athens, Ohio, 1834. He had almost no educational advantages, and early in life removed to Rock Island, Ill., where he was at first in the coal, flour, and lumber business, but later came to be wholly identified with Illinois railroads, and particularly the Chicago, R. I. & P. Ry. He was elected a director in 1877, and was successively vice-president, general manager, and in 1898, chairman of the board of directors.

Cable, a large rope or iron chain. The term cable is most frequently used in its nautical sense to describe the means by which a ship is connected with her anchor. The large ropes used for towing, or for making a vessel fast to a buoy or pier, are commonly known as hawsers. The term cable is also applied to the large suspensory ropes (usually of twisted or parallel wire) from which suspension bridges are hung, and to the endless ropes used to operate the kind of street cars commonly called cable cars or grip cars. Rope cables are made of hemp, manila, or other fibre, or of wire, twisted into a line of great compactness and strength. The circumference of hemp rope varies from about 3 to 26 inches. A certain number of yarns are laid up left-handed to form a strand; three strands laid up right-handed make a hawser; and three hawsers laid up left-handed make a cable. The strength of a hemp cable of 18 inches circumference is about 60 tons, and for other dimensions the strength is taken to vary according to the cube of the diameter. Wire rope has within recent years largely taken the place of hemp for towlines and hawsers on board ship. These usually consist of six strands, laid or spun around a hempen core, each strand consisting of six wires laid the contrary way around a smaller hempen core. The wires are galvanized or coated with a preservative composition. Wire ropes are usually housed on board ship by winding them round a special reel or drum. Hemp cables, moreover, have for long been almost wholly superseded by chain cables; the introduction of steam on board ship having brought in its train the powerful steam windlass wherewith to manipulate the heaviest chains and anchors required.

Chain cables are made in links, the length of each being generally about 6 diameters of the iron of which it is made, and the breadth about 3½ diameters. There are two distinct kinds of chain cables — the stud-like chain, which has a tie or stud welded from side to side, and the short-link or unstudded chain. The cables for use in the mercantile service are made in 15-fathom lengths, but in government contracts chain cables are required to be made in 12½-fathom lengths, with one swivel in the middle of every alternate length, and one joining-shackle in each length. Besides the ordinary links and joining-shackles, there are end-links, splicing-tails, mooring-swivels, and bending-swivels. The sizes of chain cables are denoted by the thickness of rod iron selected for the links. The following table gives certain ascertained quantities concerning the cables in ordinary use:

Thickness of Iron	Weight of Stay-pin	Weight per Fathom	Breaking Strain
½ in.	½ oz.	13½ lbs.	6 tons
1 "	3½ "	54 "	24 "
1½ "	12 "	121 "	60 "
2 "	28 "	215 "	99 "
2¼ "	40 "	272 "	120 "

Compared with the strength of hempen cable, a chain cable of one inch diameter of rod is equivalent to a hemp cable 10½ inches in circumference; 1¼ inches, to 13½ inches; 1½ inches, to 16 inches; 1¾ inches, to 18 inches; and 2 inches, to 24 inches. In navigation a cable's length is a nautical measure of distance equaling 120 fathoms, or 720 feet, by which the distances of ships in a fleet are frequently estimated. This term is often misunderstood. In all marine charts a cable is deemed 607.56 feet, or one tenth of a sea mile. In rope-making the cable varies from 100 to 115 fathoms; cablet, 120 fathoms; hawser-laid, 130 fathoms, as determined by the British admiralty in 1830. According to Ure a cable's length is 100 to 140 fathoms in the merchant service. The wire rope used for submarine telegraphy is also called a cable. See CABLES, SUBMARINE.

Cables, Submarine, specially constructed ropes of wire, hemp, and gutta-percha, or other water-proofing and protecting materials, laid on ocean or river beds for the purpose of providing means of electrical communication across large bodies of water.

Until the discovery of gutta-percha such communication was impossible, as water is so good a conductor of electricity that the submersion of current-carrying wires was dependent upon complete insulation. In this gum, however, such a perfect insulator was found that submarine communication all over the world became merely a question of time, experience, and necessity. In 1843 Prof. S. F. B. Morse suggested electrical communication between the United States and Great Britain, but it was not until more than 20 years had passed

that practical telegraphy across the Atlantic Ocean was established.

Early Cables. — The first under-water cables were short ones laid across rivers; later the English Channel was electrically "bridged" in this manner. In 1852 Dover and Ostend were connected by a cable 75 miles long and containing six wires. In 1854 Sweden and Denmark, Italy and Corsica, and Corsica and Sardinia were linked. In the same year the New York, Newfoundland, and London Telegraph Company was incorporated, mainly through the efforts of Cyrus W. Field and Peter Cooper, of New York, for the purpose of laying a cable between Newfoundland and Ireland, a distance of about 2,000 miles. It received a charter from the Newfoundland legislature, with an exclusive right for 50 years to establish a telegraph between the American continent and Europe via Newfoundland. In 1856 Cape Ray and Cape Breton were united, as well as Prince Edward's Island and New Brunswick. The same year Mr. Field organized the Atlantic Telegraph Company. It was supported by both the United States and British governments, but the results of its efforts were discouraging for several years. In August 1857 an attempt was made to lay a cable by the American frigate Niagara and the British ship-of-war Agamemnon, but about 300 miles from the Irish coast the cable parted, owing to a strain caused by a sudden dip of the sea-bottom. In 1858 the same two ships, each with half the cable on board, steamed to a point in the Atlantic midway between Valentia, Ireland, and Heart's Content, Trinity Bay, Newfoundland, spliced the cable, and, steering in opposite directions, safely landed the ends at their destinations on 5 August. The cable was 2,500 miles in length, weighed about one ton per mile, and cost $1,256,250. It was composed of seven copper wires encased in gutta-percha, which in turn was surrounded by a covering of hemp saturated with oil, pitch, and beeswax; the whole being protected by an outer sheath composed of 18 strands of seven iron wires each. Despite the success in laying, however, the cable was practically useless. The current was so weak that a message of 90 words from Queen Victoria to President Buchanan took 67 minutes to transmit, and after a few more messages the cable ceased to transmit signals. Two more cables were laid in this year to connect Great Britain with the Continent,— one to Holland and the other to Hanover; and 1859 saw, among other cable connections, the joining of England with Denmark and France, and of Malta with Sicily. In 1860 a cable was laid between France and Algiers, and in 1861 Malta was connected with Alexandria, and Batavia with Singapore. Failures were met with in attempts to lay cables through the Red Sea and from Falmouth to Gibraltar, and these, with the ill-success of the Atlantic cable, caused great disappointment to the promoters of the latter enterprise. Capital seemed to have made up its mind that a successful cable across the Atlantic was impossible. In 1865, however, another cable of 2,300 miles, and weighing 4,000 tons, was shipped on the Great Eastern, and was successfully paid out for 1,065 miles from Valentia, when it broke, and was abandoned after vain attempts to grapple the lost end. The following year the Great Eastern sailed with a lighter but stronger cable of 2,370 miles and laid it successfully. She then grappled the lost cable of the year before, recovering it from a depth of two miles, spliced it, and completed the task by landing the end at Heart's Content.

Advance in Cable-Laying.— With two cables now linking America and Great Britain, confidence was restored, and the manufacture and successful laying of submarine cables went on at a rapid rate. In 1869 a line was laid from Brest, France, to St. Pierre, Newfoundland (a distance of 3,100 miles), by a French company. In 1873 a cable joined the cities of Lisbon and Pernambuco, and in 1874 and 1875 two more cables were laid between Valentia and Heart's Content. The latter weighed less than 900 pounds per mile. Another line from Penzance, Cornwall, to St. Pierre, 2,920 miles, was laid in 1879, and one from England to Panama in 1882.

Meanwhile an incident had occurred which greatly influenced the expansion of submarine cable systems. In 1870 the British government purchased the entire land telegraph system of the British Isles, and the capital thus liberated, about $50,000,000, was largely reinvested in submarine cable ventures. In 1872 a number of small competing companies with lines through the Mediterranean were consolidated into the Eastern Telegraph Company, and in the following year the Eastern Extension, Australasian, and China Telegraph Company was formed by the amalgamation of companies owning cables farther east. Since then the Eastern, Eastern Extension, and Associated Cable companies have become practically one immense organization.

In 1884 John W. Mackey and James Gordon Bennett organized a cable system across the Atlantic from Valentia to Torbay, N. S., in the interests of the Commercial Cable Company and the New York *Herald*. Consolidation of competing companies followed as a matter of course, and now there are practically, besides the French lines, but two competing cable companies in the north Atlantic field — the Anglo-American and the Commercial Cable companies. There are now 15 cables between North America and Europe, some of which run into New York harbor. The cables of 1858, 1865, and 1866 are "dead," and three others have but a brief tenure of life. Nine are "alive" and active.

Recently another great cable-laying boom has set in. France proposes to connect its colonies by a system under its own control. A German cable has been laid from Emden, Germany, to New York, via the Azores, which works in conjunction with the Commercial Cable Company. That company has recently laid its fourth cable connecting New York and London, via Canso, the Azores, and Waterville in Ireland.

Pacific Cables.— In the Pacific Ocean the Commercial Company has constructed a cable 6,912 miles long, and costing $12,000,000, laid from San Francisco, via Honolulu, the Midway Islands, and Guam, to Manila, in the Philippines, with an ultimate extension to Shanghai or Hong Kong. The first section, from San Francisco to Honolulu, 2,413 miles, was opened 1 Jan. 1903. This section is the most hazardous on the route, depres-

sions of 5,160 and 5,269 fathoms having been encountered, and the profile displaying mountains of immense elevation and valleys of corresponding depth. A level plain, with an average depth of 2,700 fathoms, extends throughout the second section, from Honolulu to the Midway Islands; the bottom being of soft mud and extremely favorable for cable-laying. Thence toward Guam an average of 3,200 fathoms is found, and favorable conditions are maintained throughout. The last section is similar in its profile to the first, though the depth averages less, being from 1,400 to 2,700 fathoms. The sea-bed is extremely irregular in outline, with many reefs and depressions.

The cable is built around a core formed of copper wire insulated by gutta-percha, around which layers of jute yarn are wound. This, in turn, is sheathed in small cables, each formed of several strands of steel wires. An outer covering of jute yarn, the whole saturated with a bituminous compound, binds together the conducting and protecting wires in one solid mass. The landing of the shore end of the cable at San Francisco was effected thus: A section of 6½ miles was cut from the main cable on board the cable-steamer Silvertown, and loaded on a tender, which steamed toward the shore. On approaching the line of breakers, which were heavy, the shore end was floated on balloon buoys placed every 10 fathoms, and a team of 12 horses dragged it ashore, where it was spliced to the permanent shore connection, and the tender returned to the Silvertown, on board which the shore section was respliced to the main cable. The cable-ship then started for Honolulu in the evening of 14 Dec. 1902.

The Silvertown was specially built for cable-laying purposes. On this trip she carried 2,413 nautical miles of cable, weighing 4,807 tons. She arrived off Honolulu on 25 December and landed the shore end by buoying the cable; but she employed no tender or horses. Two spider-sheaves were sent ashore, and fixed by sand anchors about 60 yards apart. A hauling-line was paid out from the ship, reeved through the sheaves, and brought on board again. One end of this line being attached to the cable, and the other to the picking-up gear, the engines were started and the cable was dragged toward the shore.

Another Pacific cable is being constructed jointly by the governments of Great Britain, Canada, and Australia across the Pacific from Vancouver to Fanning Island, Fiji Islands, Norfolk Island, and thence to New Zealand and Australia. It will be about 8,000 miles long, and the 3,600 mile stretch from Vancouver to Fanning Island will be the longest single section in the world. This new cable brings the Australasian colonies 10,000 miles nearer to Canada than they were before, and there is now completed a British telegraph girdle of the world which touches foreign territory only at Madeira and St. Vincent, in the Cape Verde Islands, both belonging to Britain's old ally, Portugal.

Mention has already been made of the consolidation of competing lines in the Mediterranean and the East into the Eastern Telegraph Company. To this huge organization belongs a marvelous network of submarine cables — practically all the cables from Land's End, in England, through the Mediterranean to Suez, on through the Red Sea to Aden, across the Indian Ocean to Bombay, thence linking into the system Madras, Singapore, Hong Kong, Manila, Australia, and New Zealand. In addition, practically all the cables which now surround Africa, and many of those which cross the ocean and follow the coast-line of South America are in its control. To such an organization the laying of 15,000 miles of cable from England to Australia, via the Cape of Good Hope, at a cost of over $15,000,000, was comparatively easy. Yet this great line may be traced from Land's End in England to Adelaide in South Australia, a distance which a modern Atlantic liner would take six weeks to steam over. The length of cable is more than half way round the globe, and about eight times longer than the first Atlantic cable.

Cable Statistics.— In all there are now about 252,400 miles of submarine cables, enough to go about eight times around the globe. They have cost about $200,000,000, but their market value is considerably higher, as deep-sea cables are solid and profitable investments. Of the total mileage, the Eastern and its associated companies control practically half, or, to be precise, 99,262 nautical miles of cables, with 161 stations and 11 cable steamers. All told there are 42 cable steamers in the world, including those owned by the cable-construction companies and governments, with gross tonnage of about 65,000 tons. There are about 1,700 submarine cables ranging from a quarter of a mile to 15,000 miles. Nearly all the short lines belong to governments, but although only about 420 cables belong to private companies, these include at present all the deep-sea cables and about 90 per cent of the total length of cables in the world.

The life of a deep-sea cable, aside from injuries by ships' anchors, rocks, sharks, sawfish, and swordfish has been variously estimated at from 30 to 40 years. Sharks occasionally bite cables and leave some of their teeth embedded, and sawfish and swordfish attack them, especially in tropical waters, but on the level plains of ooze two miles or more below the surface cables seem to be almost imperishable. In shallow water they are more exposed to damage. Deep-sea cables generally weigh from one to one and a half tons per mile, but the portions lying in shallow water are so heavily armored as to weigh from 10 to 30 tons per mile. Yet last year the ocean cables of the Commercial Company were severed by ships' anchors five times. In the Firth of Forth in Scotland no less than 13 ship's anchors were once found entangled in a length of four miles of cable.

Cable Tariffs and Codes.—In the early days the Atlantic Telegraph Company started with a minimum tariff of $100 for 20 words, and $5 for each additional word. Later this was reduced to $25 for ten words. It was not till 1872 that a rate of $1 a word was introduced. This word-rate system proved so popular that it was soon adopted universally, and since 1888 the cable rate across the Atlantic has been down to 25 cents a word. Rates now range from the 25-cent tariff across the Atlantic to about $5 a word between England and Peru. The average for the whole world is roughly $1 a word. This the Commercial Company proposes to charge from America to the Philippines, as compared with the present rate of $2.35 by the circuitous route across the Atlantic, through the Mediterranean, the Red Sea, across the Indian Ocean, and on to Manila via Hong Kong. Even from New York to far-away New Zealand the rate is now only about $1.50 per word. The cost of cabling, however, is greatly influenced by "coding," a system by which business men use secret words for commercial messages, and which has developed to an extraordinary degree of perfection. One code word will frequently stand for 10 or 15 words, and there are instances where one word has been used to represent over 100 words. Practically all commercial cablegrams are coded, and nearly all departments of commercial and industrial life nowadays have their special codes.

Speed of Transmission.— The cost of deep-sea cables makes it vitally important to get as much work out of them as possible. In the first place the transmission time of messages has been greatly reduced. Formerly from many parts of the world it took 5 or 10 hours to deliver a cablegram where it now takes from 30 to 60 minutes, and across the Atlantic the companies, for stock-exchange purposes at any rate, send a cablegram and get a reply in two or three minutes. In the second place, where traffic is heavy, speed of transmission of the signals has been greatly increased. Across the Atlantic and on three or four of the busy lines of the Eastern Company the art of cable telegraphy has been highly developed.

On the first Atlantic cables the speed was about seven words a minute in one direction only. The speed of recent Atlantic cables is as high as from 40 to 45 words a minute in both directions — that is, from 80 to 90 words a minute. Thus, compared with the early days, the speed and therefore the value of the best cables has been multiplied more than ten times over by means of some of the most ingenious and delicate machinery in modern industry. On the first Atlantic cable it was found that, using land telegraph methods of signaling, the speed was only one or two words a minute. The first great forward step was to send exceedingly feeble currents and to use extremely sensitive receiving instruments. Lord Kelvin's mirror galvanometer supplied the instrument needed. By this means the speed of the early Atlantic cables was raised to seven or eight words a minute. Subsequently, when heavier cables were laid, the speed was increased to as much as 20 words a minute.

The Siphon Recorder.— In 1870 Lord Kelvin perfected his siphon recorder for working long cables, and it at once supplanted the mirror instrument, as it worked just as well with feeble currents, gave a written record of signals received, and enabled one man to do the work of two. An exceedingly light coil of fine wire (in shape and size like the long, narrow O which would be obtained by winding several hundred turns of fine silk thread around the palm of the open hand) is delicately suspended between the two poles of a powerful magnet. As the electric signals from the cable flow through the coil of wire, it swings round under the influence of the magnet, back or forward according as the current is positive or negative. The motions of the coil are transmitted by silken fibres to a little glass siphon about as thick as a needle and three or four inches long, suspended so as to swing with perfect freedom. One end

Photographed by F. B. Foy.

CABLE STEAMER "ANGLIA" LAYING SHORE END OF THE NEW CAPE-OF-GOOD HOPE CABLE AT ST. VINCENT.

Cape Verde Islands, 10th February, 1900. This is the second section of the 15,000-mile cable line to Australia.

of the siphon dips into a pot of ink, and the other end hangs close above a moving strip of paper. The signals are so feeble that if the end of the glass siphon rested on the paper it would not move at all, but by causing the siphon to vibrate continuously against the paper the free motion of the siphon is not interfered with, and the ink is spluttered upon the paper so that the siphon traces a line of very fine dots and thus records the signals transmitted through the cable. This instrument, though crude at first, has gradually been perfected. It is now the most important part of modern cable apparatus.

The Duplex System.— The next improvement, undoubtedly the greatest ever made for increasing speed, was the invention of a successful system of "duplexing" cables by Dr. Alexander Muirhead and Herbert Taylor in 1875. This invention rendered it possible simultaneously to send messages both ways through a long ocean cable. In 1878 the Direct United States cable across the Atlantic was successfully duplexed, and a speed of 16 words a minute obtained each way at the same time. Duplexing cables has now become such a fine art, chiefly through the labors of Dr. Muirhead, that the capacity of cables, and therefore their commercial value, has been practically doubled. Since 1875 about 80,000 miles of ocean cables have been duplexed almost entirely on the Muirhead system.

The increasing traffic across the Atlantic and the pressure of competition led next to an increase in the size of the copper "core" which conducts the electric signals. The resistance of a wire delays the electric current and therefore the speed. By doubling the size of the copper core the resistance is halved and the speed greatly increased. The copper wires used for telegraphy on land weigh about 200 pounds per mile. In 1894 two cables were laid across the Atlantic, one for the Commercial Cable Company and the other for the Anglo-American Company. The copper core of the former weighed 500 pounds per mile, while the latter weighed no less than 650 pounds per mile. or as much as three ordinary land wires. The result was that the speed obtained with these two cables was as high as 40 to 50 words a minute, or, working duplex, from 80 to 90 words a minute. On previous Atlantic cables 25 to 28 words a minute was the maximum each way. Owing to the reduction of rates the benefit of this tenfold increase of speed since the early days has gone almost entirely to the general public.

Automatic Transmission.— The increase in speed brought up another difficulty. No human operator can send so fast. The key used for signaling through cables by hand is practically the same as the ordinary Morse key used for land telegraphy, except that two keys are used side by side, one to send positive signals and the other negative signals, the letters of the alphabet being indicated by various arrangements of the two kinds of signals. First-class cable operators can send as many as 30 words a minute for a few minutes, but a sustained speed of 20 words a minute, when working by the hour, is regarded as very good. To take full advantage of the speed of a modern Atlantic cable therefore, it is necessary to have some automatic method of transmitting. The advantages of automatic transmission are higher speed, greater

uniformity of signals, more legibility, and fewer mistakes.

The method adopted is simple and beautiful, — a modification of the Wheatstone system. The message is first punched as a series of holes in a paper tape. This perforated tape is then run through an automatic transmitter, and by means of a system of small levers the required signals are transmitted at any desired speed. The operator has a wooden stick in each hand with which he strikes one or other of the three keys of the small perforator directly in front of him. One key punches a right-hand hole, another key a left-hand hole, and the middle key makes a space. In this way the cablegram before him is transmitted at the rate of about 20 words a minute into a perforated tape. From the perforator the tape runs into an automatic transmitter, or "auto." There is a row of small central holes in the tape, and on each side is a row of larger holes. The latter represent the message. A small star wheel in the "auto" engages with the central line of holes and feeds the tape along at a uniform rate. A couple of small steel rods about the size of a knitting-needle, one for each of the two rows of message holes, continually vibrate against the paper. When either of them enters a perforation in the paper, a lever connected with it moves and makes an electric contact, sending a short, sharp signal into the cable.

Cable Relays.— Recently several still more wonderful inventions have been perfected. There is good reason to believe that it is now possible to work a typewriter in New York by playing on a typewriter keyboard in London, and *vice versa.*

The little tape perforator in the first machine of the series has three keys. These have to be struck on the average four times for each letter, and much practice is required to become skilful in using it. Several tape-perforators with ordinary typewriter keyboards have been invented. The success of a machine of this kind will mean that cable messages will be transmitted by simply playing on a typewriter keyboard, the striking of the keys perforating the transmitting tape, which then runs through the "auto," which sends signals through the cable to the other end, where they are written in ink by the siphon recorder. It is at this latter point that has lain the great difficulty that has baffled cable inventors for years. By the time that an electric signal has passed through a long section, say 1,000 miles, of ocean cable, it has become so feeble that it can be recorded only by the extremely delicate mechanism of the siphon recorder. It has not been possible, until recently, to retransmit automatically into another section. On land, relays are used. For instance, messages from New York to Chicago are automatically repeated at Buffalo and Meadville, and by automatic repeating every 600 or 800 miles it is an every-day occurrence to telegraph direct between New York and San Francisco. A relay capable of performing similar work for cables has been a dream of cable engineers and inventors for years, and in default of such an instrument "human relays" have been employed; that is, at the end of one section of a cable an operator takes the paper record of a cablegram as it comes from the siphon recorder and retransmits it.

But the cable relay is now an accomplished fact. The only hope of constructing such an instrument was to utilize the siphon recorder. One difficulty has been that the movements of the siphon, as shown by the paper records, have till recently been most irregular. There has been what photographers would describe as "lack of definition" about the signals, rendering it hopeless to attempt to relay them automatically by machinery. The first thing to do was, therefore, to straighten and sharpen up the signals a bit, and a very able group of cable engineers, including H. A. C. Saunders, electrician-in-chief of the Eastern and its associate cable companies, his assistant, Walter Judd, with Dr. Muirhead, inventor of the cable duplex, and Messrs. Brown and Dearlove, succeeded in sharpening them. They secured very regular signals, usually described as "square signals." This result was obtained by means too technical to be described here, but the chief device used is known as an "inductive shunt." Having squared the signals, it was now possible, though by no means easy, to construct a cable relay. Two have recently been perfected. One is known as the Brown & Dearlove relay, the principal inventor of it being S. G. Brown. The other has been invented by Dr. Muirhead. In both a fine wire terminating in a platinum contact-point takes the place of the ink in the siphon of a recorder. The contact-point, instead of resting on the paper tape, rests on a rapidly moving metallic surface divided into two parts. In the Brown & Dearlove relay this contact-surface consists of a constantly revolving metallic drum or wheel. The siphon, with its wire and contact-point, "skates," as the inventor describes it, with the utmost freedom on the periphery of this wheel. The drum looks like a phonograph cylinder. As the siphon skates upon the right or left half of this drum it makes a positive or a negative electric contact and automatically transmits a corresponding signal with renewed energy into the next section of cable. In the Muirhead relay the moving metallic surface consists of a small plate vibrating rapidly. The result is the same. Able in this way to make definite electrical contacts through a long ocean cable, an operator can easily work, by means of these contacts, local apparatus moved by more powerful currents. In this way both Mr. Brown and Dr. Muirhead have devised perforators which reproduce at the receiving station perforated tape identical with that used for transmitting the message at the sending station. This tape is available for retransmission through an "auto," this plan having the advantage that the signals are retransmitted in as perfect form as the original signals; and, theoretically at any rate, the process may be repeated indefinitely, so that it would be possible to send a cable message automatically through a dozen stations from England to Australia. This will no doubt be done in time, but it is a very slow process getting such complicated and delicate inventions into commercial use. It is a question of time and growth. The Brown & Dearlove relay has been adopted by the Eastern Company, and has been in commercial use for some months at Mediterranean stations. Dr. Muirhead's relay has also proved very successful in several long-distance tests.

From this description of cable relays it will be seen that an operator, by playing on a typewriter keyboard in London, can now produce a perforated tape in New York. A machine invented by the writer of this article is so arranged that by simply turning a handle it works a typewriter automatically under the control of a perforated paper tape, something after the fashion of a mechanical piano, at a speed of 90 words a minute. In order that this machine may print messages from a perforated tape produced by the cable relays it is necessary that all the letters shall be of equal length, and the writer has devised a new cable alphabet that not only fulfills this condition, but is also about 12 per cent shorter than the cable alphabet at present in use.

Hence, it is now possible, at any rate theoretically, automatically to typewrite a cable message across the Atlantic in page form at a speed 12 per cent faster than the cables can at present be operated. More than this, by the same mechanism it is feasible to operate a linotype or typesetting machine automatically, so that the fantastic possibility presents itself of playing on a typewriter keyboard in London and setting type automatically in New York.

DONALD MURRAY.

Cabool. See KABUL.

Caboose, că-boos', the cook-room or kitchen of a ship. In smaller vessels, the name is given not to a room but to an enclosed fire-place, hearth, or stove, for cooking on the main deck. The cook-room is also known as the "galley." The name caboose is also given to a railroad car on freight or construction trains, used for carrying brakemen, or workmen, tools, etc.

Cab'ot, George, American statesman: b. Salem, Mass., 3 Dec. 1751; d. Boston, 18 April 1823. He was educated at Harvard College. In 1791 he became United States senator for Massachusetts, and proved a steadfast friend of the Washington administration. He yielded essential aid to Hamilton in perfecting his financial system. In 1814 he was chosen a delegate to the memorable Hartford Convention, and was elected president of that assembly. See Lodge, 'Life and Letters of George Cabot' (1877).

Cabot, James Elliott, American biographer: b. Boston, Mass., 18 June 1821; d. 16 Jan. 1903. He was the friend and literary executor of Emerson and in 1887 published 'A Memoir of Ralph Waldo Emerson,' a work undertaken at the request of the Emerson family.

Cabot, John, or **Giovanni Cabota** (in the Venetian dialect, ZUAN CABOTA), an Italian navigator in English employ; the discoverer of the continent of North America. On 5 March 1496, he was given by Henry VII. of England letters patent authorizing him to take possession of any countries he might discover. Under this charter, in May 1497, he embarked in a single vessel, accompanied by his son Sebastian, and sailed west, as he said, 700 leagues, when, on 24 June 1497, he came upon land which he reported to have been a part of a continent, and which he assumed to be in the dominions of the Grand Cham. A letter of that year represents him as having sailed along the coast for 300 leagues; he landed, but saw no person, though he believed the country not uninhabited. He planted on the soil the banners of England and of Venice. On his return he discerned two islands to the starboard, but for want of provisions, did not stop to examine them. He reached Bristol in August. His discovery attracted the favor of the English king, who on 3 Feb. 1498, granted him special authority to impress six English ships at no higher charges than were paid for ships taken for the king's service, to enlist companies of volunteers, "and theym convey and lede to the londe and iles of late founde by the seid John." This license has been erroneously called a second charter; it was not so; the charter of 1496 was still valid and sufficient. This license is the last record that has been found of the career of John Cabot. He himself made no voyage under it, whether from illness or death, or other reason, can only be conjectured. Neither the time nor the place of his death, nor his age, is known. Neither is it known what country gave him birth. He was a Venetian only by denization. As he is found residing at Bristol the conjecture would arise that he was born an Englishman; but the license granted him in February 1498 calls him "Kabotto, Venician," a phrase which in our day, and still more in those days of stricter feudal rule, clearly implies that he was not a natural-born subject of the king of England. Had he been so, he would have been claimed as an Englishman. Consult: Harrisse, 'Cabot, John, The Discoverer of North America, and Sebastian, His Son: a Chapter of the Maritime History of England under the Tudors (1496-1557)' (1895).

Cabot, Sebastian, English navigator: b. Bristol, about 1474; other authorities say 1477; d. London 1557. He was the son of John Cabot (q.v.). Sebastian was early instructed in the mathematical knowledge required by a seaman, and at the age of 17 had made several voyages. In 1496 John Cabot obtained from Henry VII. letters patent empowering him and his three sons, Lewis, Sebastian, and Sanctius, to discover unknown lands, and conquer and settle them. In consequence of this permission the king supplied one ship, and the merchants of London and Bristol a few smaller ones, and John and Sebastian sailed to the northwest. In 1497 the coast of Newfoundland, or, as some think, of Labrador, was reached. The accounts of this voyage are attended with much obscurity; but a second patent was granted to John Cabot in 1498, and it seems that, in a subsequent voyage, the father and son sailed as far as Cape Florida, and were actually the first who saw the mainland of America. Little, however, is known of the proceedings of Sebastian Cabot for the ensuing 20 years; but it seems that, in the reign of Henry VIII., by the patronage of Sir Thomas Peart, vice-admiral of England, he procured another ship to make discoveries, and attempted a southern passage to the East Indies, in which he failed. This disappointment is supposed to have induced him to quit England and visit Spain, on the invitation of Ferdinand. The death of the king lost him his patron, and in a few years he returned to England, and was employed by Henry VIII. to find out the northwest passage. After this expedition he again entered the Spanish service, and in 1526 began a voyage which resulted in his reaching the river La Plata, where he discovered St. Salvador,

and erected a fort there. He returned to England toward the latter end of the reign of Henry VIII. At the beginning of the reign of Edward VI. he was introduced by the protector Somerset to the young king, who settled a pension on him as grand pilot of England. From this time he was consulted on all questions relating to trade and navigation; and in 1552, being governor of the company of merchant adventurers, he drew up instructions, and procured a license for an expedition to discover a passage to the East Indies by the north. He was also governor of the Russian company, and was very active in their affairs. He was the first who noticed the variations of the compass; and he published a large map of the world, as also a work under the title of 'Navigazione nelle parti Septentrionali, per Sebastiano Cabota' (1583). See Nicholls, 'Remarkable Life of Sebastian Cabot' (1869); Winship, 'Cabot Bibliography' (1900).

Cabra, kä'brạ, Spain a town in the province and 29 miles south-southeast of Cordova, in a valley almost environed by mountains. It has wide streets; a large irregular, but imposing looking square; two large and handsome parish churches; a richly endowed college, etc. Pop. (1902) 13,000.

Cabral, or **Cabrera,** Pedro Alvarez, pä'drõ äl'bạ-rĕth kạ-brāl', Portuguese navigator: b. about 1460; d. about 1526. In 1500 he received command of a fleet bound for the East Indies, and sailed from Lisbon, but having taken a course too far to the west he was carried by the South American current to the coast of Brazil, of which he took possession about 24 April 1500, in the name of Portugal. Continuing his voyage he lost several ships and men in a storm, but with the remainder he visited Mozambique, and at last reached India, where he made important commercial treaties with native princes, and then returned to Europe. Consult: Fiske, 'Discovery of America,' Vol. II. (1892) ; Capistrano de Abreu, 'Descobrimento do Brasil' (1883).

Cabrera Bobadilla Cerda y Mendoza, Luis **Gerónymo** Fernandez de, loo-ēs hā-rõn'ē-mõ fĕr-nän'dĕth dä kạ-brā'rạ bõ-bạ-dĕl'ya thär'da ē mĕn-dõ'thạ, Spanish colonial governor: b. Madrid, about 1590; d. near there, 1647. He was viceroy of Peru 1629-39, during which period the useful properties of cinchona bark were discovered and the third ascent of the Amazon made. The cruelty of the Spaniards caused a revolt among the Urn Indians near Lake Titicaca, which Cabrera had great difficulty in suppressing.

Cabrera, Ramon, rä'mon kạ-brā'rạ, Carlist general: b. Tortosa, Catalonia, 31 Aug. 1810; d. Wentworth, England, 24 May 1877. He was brought up for the clerical profession, for which, however, he was unfitted by his love of pleasure and dissipation. When civil war broke out between the partisans of Don Carlos and those of the queen Isabel II., the priests became the most zealous champions of Don Carlos, and their enthusiasm acted so powerfully upon the impetuous spirit of young Cabrera, that he joined in 1833 a small band of guerrillas. He fought with singular ferocity, which rose to fury, when, 16 Feb. 1836, upon the order of the queen and of Mina, Gen. Nogueras put to death Cabrera's aged mother and his three helpless sisters. Cabrera took vengeance upon all the Christinists who fell into his hands. His enemies treated him like a wild animal, and hunted him, after he had laid waste Aragon, Valencia, and Andalusia, from one place to another. After a temporary defeat at Torre Blanca he eventually took Morella. Hence in 1838 Don Carlos created him Count de Morella, and at the same time lieutenant-general, and in this capacity Cabrera continued to fight for the cause of the pretender, and for what he considered the cause of the priesthood and the Church, until 1840, when he was compelled to flee to Paris. By order of Louis Philippe he was arrested and consigned to the fortress of Ham, but was soon set free. In 1848 the French revolution filled Cabrera with the most sanguine expectations; which, however, were doomed to disappointment, as on his arrival in Catalonia he was but indifferently received, and on 27 Jan. 1849, he was severely wounded at Pasteral, although he succeeded in making good his escape to France. In August of the same year he took up his abode in London, where he married a rich English woman. When Alphonso XII. was proclaimed king of Spain in 1875 Cabrera advised the Carlists to submit to him.

Cabrera, kä-brä'ra, a small Spanish island, one of the Balearic Isles, about 10 miles from Majorca. It is about three miles in length and breadth and the coast is irregular. The chief industry of the island is fishing and the permanent population is very small. During the war in the Peninsula Spain used it as a place for receiving convicts.

Cabrilla, or **Hind,** one of the sea-basses (*Epinephelus maculosus*) found in the Atlantic from Charleston to Brazil. It attains a length of 18 inches and is highly esteemed as food. Another sea-bass (*Paralabrax maculatofasciatus*) living along the coast of lower California and highly regarded as a food-fish; is called the spotted cabrilla. See SEA-BASS.

Cabul, Cabool, or **Kabul.** See KABUL.

Cacao, ka-kä'ō, or **Cocoa.** The term "cocoa," a corruption of cacao, is almost universally used in English-speaking countries to designate the seeds of the small tropical tree known to botanists as *Theobroma cacao*, from which a great variety of preparations under the name of cocoa and chocolate for eating and drinking are made. The name "chocolate" is nearly the same in most European languages, and is taken from the Mexican name of the drink, "chocolatl" or "cacahuatl." The Spaniards found chocolate in common use among the Mexicans at the time of the invasion under Cortez, in 1519, and it was introduced into Spain immediately after. The Mexicans not only used chocolate as a staple article of food, but they used the seeds of the cacao tree as a medium of exchange.

The manner of preparing it for drinking was long kept a secret by the Spaniards, who sold it at a high price to the wealthy classes. The first notice of its use in England appears in the 'Public Advertiser' of 16 June 1657, which stated that "In Bishopsgate Street, in Queen's Head Alley, at a Frenchman's house, is an excellent West India drink, called chocolate, to be sold, where you may have it ready at any time; and

also unmade, at reasonable rates." In the time of Charles II., the price of chocolate was 6s. 8d. a pound — equivalent to $6.00 or more in our currency. Had it not been for the monopoly Spain long possessed, which kept the price at a point where only the rich could afford to use it, cocoa would probably have come into as general use as tea and coffee did later.

Cocoa and chocolate were first made in this country in Dorchester, Mass., in 1765; and it is an interesting fact that the manufacture has been continued in the same place ever since and that it now represents one of the largest industries in the country.

The botanical characters of the genus to which the cacao tree belongs are given as follows:

Order *Sterculiaceæ.*—Tribe *Buettnerieæ;* calyx, 5-partite, colored; petals, 5; limb cuculate, with a terminal, spatulate appendage; column, 10-fid; fertile lobes, bi-antheriferous; anthers, bilocular; style, 5-fid; fruit, baccate, 5-celled; cells pulpy, polyspermous; embryo exalbuminous; cotyledons, fleshy, corrugate; trees, leaves entire; pedicels fascicled or solitary, lateral. (Grisebach's 'Flora of the British West Indies,' p. 91.)

The cacao tree can be cultivated in suitable situations within the 25th parallels of latitude. It flourishes best, however, within the 15th parallels, at elevations varying from near the sealevel up to about 2,000 feet in height.

An estimate of the world's production of crude cocoa in 1903 was 126,795,074 kilograms, or 279,532,420 pounds. The estimated consumption of crude cocoa in Europe and the United States in 1903 was 127,452,366 kilograms, or 280,981,486 pounds. The consumption in the United States in 1860 was only about three fifths of an ounce for each inhabitant. In 1903 the consumption was over 12 ounces for each inhabitant. In 1903 the countries from which the main supplies of crude cocoa were drawn took rank as follows: Ecuador, San Thomé, Brazil, Trinidad, Venezuela, San Domingo.

The countries consuming the largest amount of cocoa in 1903 took rank as follows: The United States, Germany, France, Great Britain, Holland, Spain. In 1893 the United States stood fifth in the list of consumers, and France had the first place.

The various kinds of cocoa may be placed in about the following order of merit: Finest Caracas (called Chaon) of Venezuela; the finest Maracaibo (of which very little, if any, is produced of late years); the finest Magdalena, of New Granada, of which the production is small and rarely exported; Soconusco, from the state of that name in Mexico; Java, from the island of that name; the finest Guayaquils from Ecuador. The cocoas from Trinidad, Surinam, Grenada, Para, Bahia and Africa, are classed as "good ordinaries."

In Ecuador, the country from which the largest supply of crude cocoa is drawn, the trees grow to a height of from 20 to 30 feet and the base of the trunk is from 8 to 10 inches in thickness. They are raised from fresh seeds which are planted in rows about five yards apart. They begin to bear in the sixth or seventh year and in the tenth year reach full maturity. The blossom is very small, pinkish white, and waxlike in appearance. It grows directly out of the main trunk and branches. If it fructifies, the petals fall off, and from the stamens, in the course of from fifty to seventy days, an oblong pod is developed. This pod is of golden color, and contains some twenty to thirty-five grains of cacao, enveloped in a gummy liquid, which coagulates on exposure to air. The outer rind of this pod is dark or golden yellow in color and very hard, a sharp instrument being necessary to cut it open. Its size varies, according to the kind of cacao, from 8 to 15 inches long by from 2 to 6 inches thick. The outer rind is marked by longitudinal furrows, more or less pronounced, which indicate the interior arrangement of the seeds.

The average yield of the trees varies in the different countries in which they grow. In Ecuador the average is said to be from one to two pounds of dry cocoa to a tree. In Surinam the average is about two and one third pounds. The fully ripened pods are detached from the tree with a long pole armed with two prongs, or a knife at its extremity. The pods are left in a heap on the ground for about twenty-four hours; they are then cut open and the seeds are taken out and carried in baskets to the place where they undergo the operation of sweating or curing. There the acid juice which accompanies the seeds is first drained off, after which they are placed in a sweating box, in which they are enclosed and allowed to ferment for some time, great care being taken to keep the temperature from rising too high. The fermenting process is, in some cases, effected by throwing the seeds into holes or trenches in the ground, and covering them with earth or clay. The seeds in this process, which is called "claying," are occasionally stirred to keep the fermentation from proceeding too violently.

The cocoa is brought into the market in its crude state, as almond-shaped seeds which differ in color and somewhat in texture. They are first cleaned and then roasted, great care being taken to secure a uniform effect. By the roasting the shell becomes more readily detachable, and its complete removal is the next step. The crushing of the seeds into small fragments is easily accomplished; and this is followed by a thorough winnowing, by which the lighter shells are carried away by themselves, leaving the clean fragments of the roasted seeds ready for further manipulation.

The result of many analyses of the roasted seeds shows the following averages: Moisture, 6.51; fat, 49.24; theobromine, .43; starch, 10.43; cellulose, 3.1; other carbohydrates, glucosides, etc., 7.78; protein matters, 18.33; ash, 3.92.

The clean shells are used for the preparation of a wholesome and very low priced drink. The cracked cocoa or coarsely ground product of the roasted seeds is called "cocoa nibs" or cracked cocoa; the finely pulverized product of the roasted seeds from which a portion of the fat has been removed in order to make it more digestible and prevent it from caking, is called "breakfast cocoa" or "powdered cocoa." In the preparation of chocolate, the fragments are ground by a complicated mechanism until they attain the highest degree of fineness, and constitute a perfectly homogeneous mass or paste without removing any of the fat. The pure product of seeds prepared in this way, to which nothing is added and from which nothing is

taken away, is known as plain chocolate or bitter chocolate. Sweet chocolate is made by working into the mass a certain percentage of sugar. For flavoring, vanilla is generally used.

The fat or "cocoa butter," so called, constituting an average of about 50 per cent of the seeds, is, when pure and freshly extracted, of a pale, yellow color. Its consistency is about that of tallow. It is insoluble in water; completely soluble in sulphuric ether and the essential oil of turpentine. It is used very extensively in the manufacture of confections, and by pharmacists as the basis of pomades and ointments. Considered as a food and as a medicinal substance, it possesses the same fundamental property as other fat.   JAMES M. BUGBEE.

Ca'capon, or **Great Capon,** a river in West Virginia. It flows nearly northwest through Hampshire and Morgan counties, and enters the Potomac about five miles from Berkeley Springs. Its length is about 140 miles.

Caccianiga, Antonio, Italian writer: b. Treviso, 1823. He founded a satirical magazine called 'Lo Spirito Folletto' at Milan in 1848; being exiled after the revolution of 1848 was for six years a journalist in Paris. He has been mayor of Treviso subsequently, and is the author of 'Il proscritta' (1853); 'Bozzetti morali ed economici' (1869); 'La Vita Campestre'; 'Villa Ortensia' (1876).

Caccini, kä-chē'nē, **Giulio,** Italian composer: b. Rome about 1546; d. Florence, 1618. He was styled the father of a new music, having been the first to write an opera for performance in a public theatre. His works include 'Daphne,' and 'Apollo's Battle with the Serpent.'

Caceres, Andres **Avelino,** Peruvian military officer and statesman: b. Ayacucho, in southern Peru, 11 Nov. 1838. While still young he was actively engaged in political strife, serving as an officer under Castilla and Prado, and when the latter was overthrown, was imprisoned for a year. He distinguished himself at the taking of Arequipa. In 1857 he became military attaché to the legation of the Peruvian government at Paris, and was stationed at that post until 1860. In the Chilean war (1879-83) he served in nearly all of the battles, being rapidly promoted from colonel to the rank of general, and, after the taking of Lima, was made second vice-president in the provisional government of Calderon (June 1883). The imprisonment of Calderon, the president, and the absence of the first vice-president made him acting president of Peru. In his refusal to acknowledge Iglesias, whom the Chileans had placed at the head of the government at Lima, as president, Caceres was supported by the interior provinces, and he at once planned to depose him. In his first attempt to take Lima, in August 1884, he was repulsed in a bloody street fight, but after raising a larger force he appeared before the city, 1 Dec. 1885, and peaceably persuaded Iglesias to submit the office of president to a general election. This resulted in the election of Caceres, and on 3 June 1886 he was inaugurated president of Peru. The country prospered greatly under his administration, gradually recovering from the ill effects of the war; a private company absorbed the state railroads and guano beds and took over a portion of the national debt. In 1890 he was defeated for the presidency by Bermudez, but was soon afterward, in 1891, appointed by him Peruvian minister to France and Spain. In 1894, upon the death of President Bermudez, the party of Caceres seized the reins of government, Caceres was proclaimed dictator, and the Congress forced to elect him president. The ex-dictator, Piérola, however, disputed his right to the office and besieged the city, on 18 March 1895, after a bloody conflict, taking it. A treaty of peace was signed between the two parties, in which Caceres was obliged to resign the presidency. He soon afterward fled and Piérola was elected president 10 July 1895.

Caceres, kä'thä-rĕs, Spain, a town in Estremadura, capital of the province of the same name, 24 miles west by north of Truxillo. It consists of an old and a new town, the former crowning the top of a hill, and surrounded by a strong wall flanked with towers, and the latter built round it on the lower slopes. The houses are tolerably well built, but the streets are mostly narrow and steep. Among the objects worthy of notice are four churches, several old feudal mansions, and the bull-ring. Pop. (1902) about 16,000. The province of Caceres is the second largest of Spain, in the north of Estremadura, owned chiefly by large proprietors, and mostly devoted to cattle-raising; the north half is a good wine country. The area is over 8,000 square miles, and the population about 400,000.

Cáceres Nueva. See Nueva Cáceres.

Cachalot. See Sperm Whale.

Cachar, kä-chär', a district of Assam, India, bounded east by Manipur and the Naga Hills, south by the Lushai Hills, west by Sylhet and the Jaintia Hills, and north by Nowgong district. It comprises a series of fertile valleys diversified by low hills and almost surrounded by mountain ranges. The Barak River flows through the district, its course here being about 130 miles. Lignite and petroleum have been found. Salt is manufactured in small quantities. The forests are of great extent, and constitute the chief natural wealth of the district. Rice and tea are extensively cultivated. Area, 2,472 square miles; pop. (1902) 467,300. The chief town is Silchar.

Cache, the name of (1) a river in Arkansas, flowing northwest about 150 miles into the White River, near Clarendon, Monroe County; (2) a peak of the Rocky Mountains in Idaho, height 10,451 feet; (3) a fertile valley in the Wasatch Mountains in Utah and Idaho. It is 60 miles long and from 10 to 20 miles wide, and has and has several villages, of which Logan is the largest.

Cache, käsh, a hole in the ground for hiding and preserving provisions which it is inconvenient to carry; used by settlers or travelers in unpeopled parts of North America, and by Arctic explorers.

Cachet, Lettres de, lĕtr dĕ kä-shä, a term formerly applied especially to letters proceeding from and signed by the kings of France, and countersigned by a secretary of state. They were at first made use of occasionally as a means of delaying the course of justice, and appear to have been rarely employed before the 17th century as arbitrary warrant for the detention of private citizens, and for depriving them of their personal liberty. During the reign of Louis XIV. their use became frightfully common, and by means of them persons were imprisoned for long periods, or for life, on the most frivolous pretexts. Sometimes, however, such arrests were favors on the part of the king, as they withdrew the accused from the severer punishment to which they would have been liable upon trial before the courts. *Lettres de cachet* were abolished at the Revolution.

Cachexy, ka̤-kĕk'sĭ, or **Cachexia,** ka̤-kĕk-sĭ-a̤, (Gr., "evil habit of body"), a morbid state of the bodily system, in which there is great weakness, with or without the local manifestation of some constitutional disease. It is not a disease of itself, but the result of diseases such as gout, cancer, lead-poisoning, tuberculosis, syphilis, intermittent fever, excessive use of alcohol, etc. Thus scrofulous cachexia means the condition of body due to scrofula, shown by slender form, narrow or deformed chest, pallor, diseased glands, large prominent joints, etc.

Cachexia Strumipriva. See Thyroid Gland, *Diseases of.*

Cachoeira, ka̤-shwä'e̤-ra̤, Brazil, a town in the state and 62 miles northwest of Bahia. It stands on the Paraguassu, which divides it into two unequal parts and has often injured it by inundations, and is the entrepôt for the traffic of a large extent of surrounding country. The chief exports are coffee, cotton, and tobacco. Pop. 15,000.

Cacholong, a mineral of the quartz family, a variety of opal, often called pearl-opal. It is usually milk-white, sometimes grayish or yellowish white, opaque or slightly translucent at the edges. It often envelops common chalcedony, the two minerals being united by insensible shades. It also associates with flint and semi-opal.

Cachou, kä-shoo', an aromatic sweetmeat in the form of a silvered pill, used for giving an agreeable odor to the breath.

Cachucha, kä-choo'cha̤, an Andalusian dance, resembling the *bolero*, performed to a graceful air in 3–4 time and with a strongly marked accent.

Cacique, kä-sēk', or **Cazique,** a title borne by, or a designation given to, the chiefs of Indian tribes in Central and South America, Cuba, Haiti, etc. The term was formed by the Spaniards from a native Haitian word.

Caçique, one of several South American icterine birds, forming the genus *Cassicus,* and closely related to the Baltimore oriole (q.v.). They are sometimes uniform black, sometimes black relieved by chestnut, yellow, green, or scarlet; the bill is frequently white instead of the usual black or brown. The caçiques are noted for their intricately woven, pouch-like nests, composed of thin bark and grasses, several of which, sometimes a yard in length, hang from the outer twigs of a single branch of some large tree, usually overhanging the water, as an extra precaution of safety against monkeys and snakes.

Cac'odyle, or Cac'odyl, kăk'ō-dĭl, -dĭl (Gr., «having a bad smell»), in chemistry, a monad radical having the formula $As(CH_3)_2$, and of special interest to the chemist because it was the first radical known in which a metal or a metalloid is combined with an organic base. The compound $As_2(CH_3)_4$, which was discovered by Bunsen in 1837, and which can exist in the free state, is often called cacodyle, but it is more correctly known as dicacodyle since its molecule consists of two cacodyle radicals. Dicacodyle is obtained in the pure state by heating cacodyle chloride with zinc in an atmosphere of carbon dioxide, but a mixture of cacodyle oxide and dicacodyle (known formerly as Cadet's fuming liquid) may be obtained by distilling potassium acetate with an equal weight of arsenic trioxide. Mercuric oxide (HgO) converts both of the constituents of Cadet's liquid into cacodylic acid, $(CH_3)_2AsO-(OH)$; and this, in turn, is converted into cacodyle chloride, $As(CH_3)_2Cl$, by the action of corrosive sublimate and fuming hydrochloric acid. Cacodyle oxide (known also as alkarsin) may be obtained in the pure state by distilling the chloride with an aqueous solution of caustic potash in an atmosphere of carbon dioxide. Dicacodyle is a colorless liquid, heavier than water, boiling at 338° F., and characterized by an intensely disagreeable smell suggestive of garlic. Dicacodyle is known to the chemist as tetra-methyl di-arsenid.

Cacomistle, kăk-ō-mĭs-ĕl, a small Mexican animal (*Bassariscus astutus*), closely related to the raccoon, and similar in its haunts and habits. It is slender, about 10 inches long, with a sharp, fox-like face, large bright eyes surrounded with light patches, and erect ears. The long, soft fur is light brown above, darker along the back; the under parts are white, and the bushy tail has six broad white rings running around it.

Cacongo, kä-kŏng'gō, or **Kakongo,** a former district of Guinea, Africa, extending along the South Atlantic Ocean, in lat. 5° S., just north of the mouth of the Congo. The Cacongo River enters the sea in lat. 5° 12′ S. This territory was claimed by the Portuguese, and Cabinda is the northern part of it; the south and east to the Congo have been absorbed in the Congo Free State.

Cactaceæ. See CACTUS.

Cactus, the common name for all members of the family *Cactaceæ*, an order of calycifloral dicotyledons, found in luxuriance in the arid sections of the United States and South America. Both the Greeks and Latins were perfectly familiar with this curious monstrosity of nature, the word being κάκτος in Greek and *cacti* in Latin. Linnæus included all these species under the one generic term cactus, of which there were about 1,000 species. One of these is a native of Ceylon, with which the ancients were familiar. But the true home of the cactus is in America. Like the watermelon, it has the faculty of absorbing into itself a vast bulk of water, making its stem most succulent. The most common kind, met with in southern Mexico, is the *Opuntia coccinellifera*, which grows as a succession of small, oblong, thick leaves and is not very spiny.

The economic uses of the cacti are many, especially among primitive peoples. One or two species of the genus *Anhalonium* yield alkaloids which are used in medicine and which were known and used to produce intoxication by the Indians before the advent of the whites. The peculiar reticulations of the vascular or wood systems of many species render them very useful in the manufacture of art goods, otherwise known as curios in many sections. The various species are of most importance as articles of food for man and beast. In the semi-tropical and tropical regions of America a large group of the plants belonging to the genus *Cereus* and its allies furnish edible fruits known to the Spanish-American as *pitellas* (*petia*). These grow for the most part on tall, branching, and columnar plants, similar to the familiar giant cactus (*Cereus giganteus*) of the Arizona desert. These fruits vary in size from three-fourths of an inch to two inches in diameter, depending upon the species. Along the Texas frontier forms grow which are known as Mexican strawberries to the English speaking peoples.

By far the greater part of the fruit produced by this family of plants comes from the flat-jointed prickly pears belonging to the genus *Opuntia*, the fruits of which are known in Spanish-America as *tunas*. Some of these are extensively cultivated throughout the highland region of Mexico and the Mediterranean region of Europe, Asia, and Africa especially. Prickly pears, although natives of the American continent and its continental islands, are now cultivated or have become naturalized throughout the tropical and subtropical regions of the world. The fruits are eaten raw, dried and in the form of preserves. Their juices are also expressed and fermented into a drink called colonche. It is less common now than formerly to find a distilled drink made from the tuna on account of the deleterious effects of tuna alcohol.

On account of their ability to absorb and retain large quantities of water, the cacti, especially the prickly pears, often become important to the stockmen in portions of our southwestern states. They remain green and succulent long after other fruits have dried up and become worthless. The rancher then resorts to this rough feed to save his stock. He may singe the horns off with a brush or, if his herds are large, he may singe them with a modified plumber's torch, or he may even chop the plants into small pieces and feed them in this way.

It is a common practice in southwestern Texas to feed prickly pear and cottonseed meal to stock during the winter. In the vicinity of San Antonio dairymen for a number of years have fed prickly pear to their dairy cows along with a liberal supply of grain and hay. Prickly pears furnish the succulence so essential in milk production and so difficult to obtain in a semi-arid region.

When driven to extremity travelers in the desert have been known to resort to these plants for water supply. The pulpy tissues, preferably of such forms as the barrel cactus (*Echinocatus*) are macreated to set the juices free. A rather unpalatable and somewhat purgative drink is thus obtained which relieves thirst to a measure.

The flowers and stems of the night-booming cereus (*Cereus grandiflorus*) have been used in medicine, in the form of a fluid extract, as a cardiac stimulant. Its action resembles that of digitalis, but is less uniform.

Cactus Wren, a small wren (*Campylorhynchus brunneicapillus*) inhabiting the arid and desolate regions of the Mexican border. It is grayish brown above, darker on the head, nearly pure white beneath, with a spotted breast, and a white line over the eye. It makes a large flask-shaped nest of grasses and twigs, lined with feathers, and laid in the crotch of a cactus. This nest is entered by a covered way or neck several inches in length. It is a very sprightly bird with a clear, ringing song.

Ca'cus, in Roman legend, a huge giant, in some accounts a son of Vulcan, who lived in a cave on Mount Aventine. Having stolen and dragged into his cave some of the cattle which Hercules had carried away from Geryon in Spain, he was killed by that hero, who discovered his place of hiding by the lowing of the oxen within, in response to the lowing of the remainder of the flock as they were passing the entrance of the cave.

Cada Mosto, kä'dạ mō'stō, or **Ca da Mosto, Alois da,** Italian navigator: b. Venice about 1432; d. 1464. In 1455 he departed from Lagos, sailed into the river Senegal, which had been discovered five years before, and after trading in slaves and gold he steered for Cape Verd, where he joined two other discovery ships, and visited, in company with them, the mouths of the Gambia, the riches of which had been greatly extolled. In 1456 Cada Mosto, in company with two other ships, made a second voyage to the Gambia. On the way thither they discovered the Cape Verde Islands. The description of his first voyage, 'Il Libro de la prima Navigazione per l'Oceano alle Terre de' Negri della Bassa Etiopia, di Luigi Cada Mosto' (Vicenza 1507, and Milan 1519), the oldest of the voyages of the moderns, is a masterpiece. The arrangement is admirable, the narrative interesting, the descriptions clear and accurate.

Cadamba, kä-dăm'bạ, or **Kudumba,** the wood of several species of *Nauclea,* an Indian genus of *Cinchonaceæ. N. (Uncaria) gambir* is the source of gambier.

Cadas'tral Survey (F. *cadastre,* from It. *catastro,* from low Lat. *capitastrum,* "a register for a poll-tax"; Lat. *caput,* "the head"), a territorial survey in which objects are represented in their relative positions and magnitudes. A cadastral survey differs from a topographical one, in not magnifying the principal objects. It requires consequently to be made on a larger scale than the topographical survey, so as to admit of a proportionally accurate representation of towns, houses, roads, rivers, etc. The scale on which the map of the United Kingdom is being prepared $\frac{1}{2500}$ of the linear measure of the surface surveyed, is an example of the scale of a cadastral survey. This scale nearly corresponds with 25 inches to the mile. See SURVEYING.

Caddis-fly, the common name of any of the order *Trichoptera,* a group of aquatic insects, related to and by many supposed to be the ancestors of the moths and butterflies (*Lepidoptera*). They resemble the lower moths, but the wings are not scaled, except in a very rudimentary way. They differ from moths in having no true "tongue" or well-developed maxilla adapted for sucking the nectar of flowers, but as in moths the mandibles are either absent or obsolete. About 150 species are thus far known to live in North America. The larvæ are called "caddis-worms," "case-worms," or "cad-bait." They are more or less cylindrical, with well-developed thoracic feet, and a pair of feet on the end of the abdomen, varying in length. The head is small, and like that of a tortricid larva, which the caddis-worm greatly resembles, not only in form, but in its habit of rolling up submerged leaves. They also construct cases of bits of sticks, sawdust, or grains of sand, which they drag over the bottom of quiet pools, retreating within when disturbed. They live on vegetable matter and on water-fleas (*Entomostraca*) and small aquatic larvæ. When about to pupate they close up the mouth of the case with a grating, or, as in the case of *Helicopsyche,* which is coiled like a snail-shell, by a dense silken lid with a single slit, and in some instances spin a slight, thin, silken cocoon, within which the pupa state is passed. The pupa is much like that of the smaller moths, except that the mandibles are present, and wings and limbs are free from the body. After leaving its case it makes its way over the surface of the water to the shore, sometimes going a long distance. The female deposits her eggs in a double gelatinous, greenish moss, which is attached to the surface of some aquatic plant. Consult: McLachlan, 'Monograph of the Trichoptera of the European Fauna'; Banks, 'A List, Synopsis, Catalogue, and Bibliography of the Neuropteroid Insects of Temperate North America'; 'Transactions of the American Entomological Society,' Vol. XIX; also a paper by Newham and Betten in 'Bulletin of the New York State Museum,' 47.

Caddoan (kä'dō-an) **Indians,** a family of North American Indians, comprising the Arikari tribe in North Dakota; the four Pawnee villages, Grand, Tapage, Republican, and Skidi, in the Indian Territory; and the Caddo, Kichai, Wichita, and other tribes, formerly in Louisiana, Texas, and Arkansas. The present number of these Indians is about 2,130, of which 416 are in North Dakota, the rest in the Indian Territory.

Cade, John (the Jack Cade of Shakespeare), Irish rebel: d. 11 July 1450. Early obliged to flee from Ireland, he took refuge in France. In 1450 he passed over to England at the moment of great popular dissatisfaction with the ministers of Henry VI. He at once pretended to be a relative of the Duke of York, assumed the name of Mortimer, raised the standard of rebellion in Kent, 8 May, and very soon found himself at the head of 20,000 men. He advanced to Blackheath, and interchanged notes with King Henry, to whom he made known the griefs of his companions. He defeated the royal troops which were sent against him, and entering London, 1 July, immediately caused the execution of two of the offensive ministers. At first he kept his army under rigorous discipline, but after a few days' residence in the capital their propensity to plunder could no longer be restrained, and they pillaged some of the finest houses. This aroused the citizens against them, and on the night of 5

1. Leaf-cactus (Phyllocactus anguliger). 2. Stapelia (simulating a cactus). 3. A Cereus (Cereus dasycanthus). 4. Globe-cactus (Echinocactus horizonthalonius). 5. Wart-cactus (Mammilaria pectinata). 6. Hairy Opuntia (Opuntia filipendula)—a. the blossom, enlarged. 7. Melon-cactus (Melocactus communis). 8. Giant Cactus (Cereus giganteus)—a, blossom, enlarged; b fruit, enlarged. 9. Mexican Opuntia (Opuntia coccinellifera)—a, the fruit ("prickly pear"), enlarged.

CACTUS.

Flower of the Hedgehog Cactus.

July Cade met with his first defeat. A promise of pardon now dispersed most of his followers, and finding his force no longer sufficient for resistance he took to flight, but was overtaken and killed.

Cade, Oil of, a thick oily liquid obtained in France, Spain, and northern Africa by the dry distillation of the wood of *Juniperus oxycedrus,* of the pine family (*Coniferæ*). It has a not unpleasant tarry odor, and is largely employed in the treatment of skin diseases, especially certain forms of eczema.

Cadell', Francis, Scottish explorer in Australia: b. Cockenzie, Scotland, 1822; d. 1879. Becoming assured of the navigability of the Murray River in Australia he made an extended exploration of that stream in 1850. Subsequently forming a navigation company he reached by steamboat a point 300 miles from the river's mouth, and in 1858 explored the Murrumbridgee River, and in 1858 the Darling River as far as Mount Murchison. While in command of a vessel sailing from Amboyna he was murdered by his crew.

Cadenabbia, kä-dě-näb'bē-ạ, a health resort, beautifully situated among orange and citron groves, on the western shore of Lake Como, Italy. Its famous Villa Carlotta contains works by Canova and Thorwaldsen.

Cadence, the concluding notes of a musical composition or of any well-defined section of it. A cadence is perfect, full, or authentic when the last chord is the tonic preceded by the dominant; it is imperfect when the chord of the tonic precedes that of the dominant; it is plagal when the closing tonic chord is preceded by that of the subdominant; and it is interrupted, false, or deceptive when the bass rises a second, instead of falling a fifth.

Cadency, in heraldry, a system of marks intended to show the descent of a younger branch of a family from the main stock.

Caden'za, in music, a flourish of indefinite form introduced upon a bass note immediately preceding a close.

Cad'er Id'ris, a mountain in Merionethshire, Wales, the beginning of a chain running northeasterly. The ridge is nearly 10 miles long, and with its breadth of from one to three miles makes an elevation of great massiveness. Its greatest height is 2,925 feet.

Cadet-Gassicourt, Louis Claude, loo-e klōd kä-dä-gäs-ī-koor, French scientist: b. 1731; d. 1799. He filled several important offices, such as apothecary to the Hôtel des Invalides, inspector of French hospitals in Germany, and chemical director to the Sèvres Porcelain Works. He published a variety of researches in pure and applied chemistry, but is best known by the fuming liquor still called by his name, and the subject of an elaborate research by Bunsen.

Cadet de Vaux, Antoine Alexis, äṅ-twän ä-läks-īs kä-dä-dė-vō, French chemist: b. Paris, 1743; d. 1828. He was at first an apothecary, but for many years devoted himself to agriculture, writing on the effect which the destruction of mountain forests has in diminishing the copiousness of the springs in the valleys, the improvement of vineyards, the cultivation of foreign plants, and the providing of substitutes for the usual articles of food in times of scarcity. He was one of the principal editors of the 'Journal d'Economie rurale et domestique,' and of the 'Cours complet d'Agriculture pratique.'

Cadet, kạ-dĕt', a word having several significations.

1. A younger son of a family; that is, one junior to the eldest or heir by primogeniture.

2. In the former French military service, a gentleman who served in the ranks without pay, for the purpose of learning the art of war.

3. In the United States and Great Britain a pupil of a military or naval academy or training-ship, as of the United States Military Academy at West Point; the United States Naval Academy at Annapolis; the Royal Military Academy at Woolwich; or the Royal Military College at Sandhurst.

Cadet's Fuming Liquid. See CACODYLE.

Cadi, kä'dē, or **Kadi,** in Arabic, a judge or jurist. Among the Turks cadi signifies an inferior judge, in distinction from the mollah, or superior judge. They belong to the higher priesthood, as the Turks derive their law from their prophet.

Cadillac, Antoine de la Mothe, äṅ-twän dė lạ mōt kạ-dē-yäk, French military commander: b. Gascony, France, about 1660; d. France, 1720. He came of good family, and having entered the army was for some time captain in Acadia. In 1694 Frontenac placed him in command of Michilimackinac, where he remained until 1697. Cadillac then brought to the attention of Louis XIV. a well-considered scheme for a permanent settlement and trading post in the Northwest. On receiving the monarch's approval he founded Detroit in 1701, establishing 50 soldiers and 50 settlers at that point. From 1712 to 1717 he was governor of Louisiana, returning to France in the year last named. The town of Cadillac, Mich., was named in his honor. Consult: Burton, 'Cadillac's Village, a History of the Settlement, 1701–10' (1896); Parkman, 'A Half Century of Conflict' (1892).

Cadiz, kä'dĕth or kä-dīz (anciently GADES), a seaport, and one of the handsomest cities in Spain, is situated at the extremity of a long tongue of land projecting from the Isla de Leon, off the southwestern coast of Andalusia. The narrowness of the land communication prevents its capture by a military force while the garrison is master of the sea. It is walled, with trenches and bastions on the land side; the houses are high, and the streets narrow. The chief buildings are the great hospital, the custom-house, the old and new cathedrals, two theatres, the bull-ring, capable of accommodating 12,000 spectators, and the light-house of St. Sebastian. From the harbor the town has a fine appearance. The Bay of Cadiz is a very fine one. It is a large basin enclosed by the mainland on one side, and the projecting tongue of land on the other. It is from 10 to 12 leagues in circumference, with good anchorage and protected by the neighboring hills. It has four forts, two of which form the defense of the grand arsenal, La Caracca, in which are 3 basins and 12 docks. Cadiz has long been the principal Spanish naval station. It was the centre of the Spanish-American trade, and the commerce of the port was very extensive before the separation of the colonies. The preparation of salt from pits belonging to the government was formerly an important branch of industry, but is now of comparatively little consequence. The manufactures of Cadiz are of comparatively little importance, but in regard to the extent and value of its commerce it ranks as one of the first ports in Spain. Its imports consist of all kinds of foreign and colonial produce, coal, cotton, and woolen manufactures, etc.; its exports of wines, fruits, oils, and other products of Spain. The town of Santa Maria, opposite Cadiz, is the principal depot of the wines of Xeres. Notwithstanding the political agitations of recent years, the commerce of Cadiz has continued comparatively prosperous. Cadiz was founded by the Phœnicians about 1100 B.C., and subsequently belonged in succession to the Carthaginians and the Romans. It was taken by the Earl of Essex in 1596, and from its bay Villeneuve sailed previous to the battle of Trafalgar in 1805. In 1809 it became the seat of the central junta, and afterward of the Cortes. It sustained a long blockade from the French (1810-12), which was not raised till after the battle of Salamanca. In 1823 the French entered it after a short siege. An insurrection occurred in Cadiz in 1868, and the town was declared in a state of siege in December, but in the following January the siege was raised. Pop. (1897) 70,177.

Cadiz, Ohio, a village and county-seat of Harrison County, about 25 miles northwest of Wheeling, W. Va., and 120 miles east northeast of Columbus. Cadiz has commercial interests of some importance, and is the commercial center of a great wool-growing district. It is also noted as a banking centre. Cadiz was the home of Edwin M. Stanton (q.v.). Pop. (1900) 1,755.

Cadmea, the name given to the acropolis of Thebes, Bœotia, because it was said to have been founded by Cadmus. Only fragments of its walls remain.

Cadmia, a name used by early writers (1) for the mineral calamine (q.v.); and (2) for the sublimate of zinc oxide that often collects on the walls of furnaces used in the reduction of metallic ores, when those ores happen to contain zinc.

Cad′mium, a metallic element resembling zinc in its chemical properties, and discovered by Stromeyer in 1817, in a specimen of zinc carbonate. Cadmium often occurs in ores of zinc to a small extent, blende sometimes containing as much as 3 per cent of cadmium sulphide. The commercial supply of the element is obtained as a by-product in the smelting of zinc, chiefly in Belgium and Silesia. Cadmium sulphide also occurs native as the mineral greenockite (q.v.), otherwise known as "cadmium blende." In the distillation of zinc ores the cadmium, being more volatile, passes over first; and advantage is taken of this fact for the isolation of the metal in the arts. In Silesia, where the zinc ores often contain considerable quantities of cadmium, the first portion of the distillate is likely to contain as much as from 3 to 10 per cent of cadmium. This is mixed with coal or charcoal and redistilled at a low, red heat. Cadmium, mixed with a little zinc,

passes over; and by one more distillation the metal is obtained in a fairly pure form. To eliminate the last traces of zinc, the crude metal is dissolved in hydrochloric acid, and its sulphide is then dissolved in concentrated hydro-a current of sulphuretted hydrogen. The sulphide is then dissolved in concentrated hydrochloric acid, and the subsequent addition of carbonate of soda precipitates the carbonate of cadmium, which is reduced to the oxide upon ignition. The pure oxide thus obtained may then be reduced to the metallic form by distillation with charcoal.

Metallic cadmium is lustrous and resembles tin in appearance, though it has a bluish tinge. It is stronger than tin, but, like that metal, it emits a peculiar crackling sound, or "cry," when bent. At ordinary temperatures it is quite ductile and malleable, and may be drawn into thin wire, rolled into thin sheets, or hammered into foil. At about 175° F. it becomes brittle, however, so that it can be pulverized in a mortar. Cadmium has the chemical symbol Cd. Its specific gravity is about 8.65. It melts at 600° F., and boils at about 1,500° F., yielding a yellow vapor. Its atomic weight is 112.4 if $O = 16$, or 111.6 if $H = 1$. Its specific heat is about 0.055, and its linear coefficient of expansion is about 0.0000185 per Fahrenheit degree. Metallic cadmium is used to a limited extent in the preparation of alloys, its general effect being to reduce the melting-point of the alloy to which it is added. The total production of the metal per annum is probably about two tons.

In its chemical relations, cadmium, like zinc, is a dyad. Metallic cadmium undergoes a slow, superficial oxidation upon exposure to the air; and when sufficiently heated in the presence of air it oxidizes rapidly and may even take fire. The resulting oxide, CdO, is brown in color and readily dissolves in acids, with the production of the corresponding cadmium salts. One of the best known of these salts is the iodide, CdI_2, which is used in photography and in medicine, and may be obtained by the action of hydriodic acid, HI, upon cadmium carbonate, or metallic cadmium. The bright yellow sulphide, CdS, is formed when the stream of sulphuretted hydrogen gas is passed through a slightly acid solution of a cadmium salt; and this fact is used in the detection and isolation of cadmium in qualitative analysis. The sulphide is used as a pigment, under the name of "cadmium yellow"; it is brilliant in color, and does not change upon exposure to air or light.

Cad′mus, in Greek mythology the son of Agenor and grandson of Poseidon. With his brothers he was sent by his father to seek for his sister, Europa, who had been carried away by Zeus, and he was not to return without her. After several adventures, the oracle at Delphi commanded him to desist from further search, to intrust himself to the guidance of a heifer, and where he should stop to build a city. He accordingly went to Bœotia, where he wished to sacrifice the cow to Athena. But his companions, attempting to bring water from the fountain of Ares for the purpose of the sacrifice, were slain by the dragon that guarded it. Cadmus killed the dragon, and, at the command of Athena, sowed its teeth in the earth; armed men immediately sprang up, whom he called Sparti (the sowed), but who perished in a contest with each other, excepting five. With the remainder he built the city of Cadmea or Thebes (see THEBES). He became by his marriage with Harmonia the father of Antinoe, Ino, Semele, Agave, and Polydorus. After ruling for a time the city which he had built, and the state which he had founded, he proceeded, at the command of Bacchus, with Harmonia to the Enchelæ, conquered their enemies, the Illyrians, became their king, and begat another son, Illyrius. Tradition states that Cadmus came to Bœotia from Phœnicia, 1550 B.C., conquered the inhabitants who opposed him, and, in conjunction with them, founded the above-mentioned city. To promote the improvement of his subjects he taught them the Phœnician alphabet, the employment of music at the festivals of the gods, besides the use of copper, etc. Another Cadmus, of Miletus, a son of Pandion, was regarded among the Greeks as the first who wrote in prose. He lived about 600 B.C.

Cado'gan, George Henry (5TH EARL), English statesman: b. Durham, 12 May 1840. He was educated at Christ College, Oxford, and entered Parliament as member for Bath in 1873, becoming under-secretary for war in 1875, and under-secretary for the colonies, 1878–80. He was lord privy seal, 1886–95, and lord-lieutenant of Ireland, 1895–1902.

Cadol, Victor Edouard, věk-tōr ĕd-oo-ärd ką-dōl, French dramatist: b. Paris 1831; d. 1898. He was long prominent as a journalist, being on the staff of 'Le Temps' and one of the founders of 'L' Esprit Francais.' Among his very numerous works, many of which were written in collaboration, are 'Les ambitions of de M. Fauvel' (1867); 'Thérèse Gervais' (1893); 'L'archduchesse' (1897). A corrected edition of his dramas appeared in 1897 entitled 'Théâtre inédit.'

Cadoo'bergia Wood. See EBONY.

Cadore, kä-dō'rä, or Pieve di Cadore, a town of Italy, in the province and 22 miles north-northeast of the town of Belluno, on the Piave, derives its chief interest from being the birthplace of Titian.

Cadorna, Raffaele, räf-fä-ěl' kä-dór-na, Italian general: b. Milan 1815; d. Turin 6 Feb. 1897. He served in the Crimean war, and in 1860 was made war minister in Tuscany's provisional government, and military commandant of Sicily in 1866. He suppressed the Bourbon insurrection in Palermo in the latter year, and in 1870 captured Rome and was its military governor for a time. In 1871 he entered the Italian Senate. He was the author of 'La liberazione di Roma nel 1870' (1889).

Cadoudal, Georges, zhŏrzh kä-doo-dal, French Chouan chief: b. Brittany, 1 Jan. 1769; d. Paris, 25 June 1804. In the protracted and sanguinary contests between the Royalists and Republicans during the French Revolution, the Chouans and Vendéans were the most resolute supporters of the Royal cause; and the energy and ability of Cadoudal soon raised him to an influential place among the adherents of the house of Bourbon. At this time attempts were made by Napoleon to gain over Cadoudal to the cause of the republic, and a lieutenant-generalship in the army was offered as the price of his submission; but he firmly declined all these overtures. He afterward engaged, in con-

cert with Gen. Pichegru and others, in a conspiracy having for its object the overthrow of the consular government and the restoration of the monarchy; which being discovered, Cadoudal was arrested, and executed. See CHOUANS.

Caduceus, ką-dū'sę-ŭs, the staff considered as a symbol and attribute of the Greek god Hermes and the Roman god Mercury. It is generally represented as having two serpents twined around it in opposite directions, their heads confronting one another. It is probable that the staves carried by heralds and public criers gave rise to this fable, the fluttering ribbons or fillets tied to the end of the staff, or the green wreaths or boughs which were tied around it, giving the suggestion of the presence of living serpents. Several different fables were invented by late Greek writers to account for the serpents in a miraculous way. The fable tells that Apollo gave his staff to Mercury in consideration of his resigning to him the honor of inventing the lyre. As Mercury entered Arcadia with this wand in his hand he saw two serpents fighting together; he threw the staff between them, and they immediately wound themselves around it in friendly union. The caduceus is Mercury's peculiar mark of distinction. With this he conducted the shades to the lower world, and from it received the name of **Caducifer;** yet we find it on ancient coins in the hands of Bacchus, Hercules, Ceres, Venus, and Anubis. Among the moderns it serves principally as an emblem of commerce.

Cadwalader, kăd-wŏl'ä-děr, George, American lawyer and soldier: b. Philadelphia, 1804; d. there, 3 Feb. 1879. He practised law till 1846; was made brigadier-general of volunteers; and won distinction at Chapultepec. He resumed his law practice till 1861; became major-general of State volunteers; was placed in command at Baltimore; accompanied Patterson's expedition to Winchester (1861); and, as one of a military board, directed the United States army operations.

Cadwalader, John, American soldier: b. Philadelphia, 10 Jan. 1742; d. Shrewsbury, Pa., 10 Feb. 1786. At the outbreak of the Revolution he was placed in command of a battalion and soon became brigadier-general. He fought at Trenton, Brandywine, Germantown, and Monmouth. In 1777 he organized the militia of eastern Maryland. In 1778 he challenged and wounded Thomas Conway for plotting against Washington. His daughter became, in 1800, the wife of Lord Erskine.

Cæcilian, sē-sĭl'ĭ-ąn, a member of a family of batrachians, the *Cæciliidæ,* regarded as forming an order, called Apoda, or Gymnophiona. They are long, worm-like animals, lacking all traces of limbs, and having only a rudiment of a tail. There may be as many as 250 vertebræ. The hinder end is blunt and hardly to be distinguished from the head. The body is covered with a soft, moist skin, and the jaws are armed with rather feeble teeth. These animals are found in the tropical parts of America, Africa, and Asia, where they burrow like earthworms, which they resemble. They are often found in the nests of ants, which they devour. They also feed on worms. The breeding habits of these creatures are very interesting, but are not well understood. The eggs are laid either in the water or near it. One species found in Ceylon lays a mass of eggs which are connected by a cord, thus resembling a string of beads. They are deposited in a burrow near the water, and are incubated by the mother until the escape of the young. About 30 species of these animals are known.

Cæcilius Statius, sĕ-cĭl'-ĭ-ŭs stä'shĭ-ŭs, Roman comic poet: b. Milan, about 200 B.C.; d. 168 B.C. His contemporaries ranked him with Plautus and Terence. He wrote over 30 comedies of which fragments remain.

Cæculus, sĕk'ū-lŭs, in mythology, a son of Vulcan, and a great robber, who lived in Italy, and built Præneste.

Cæcum, sē'kŭm, a blind process or sac in the alimentary canal of various animals. In fishes the cæca are often numerous and long; and birds have generally two near the termination of the intestines. Mammals have commouly only one. In man the "blind-gut" is small and situated at the beginning of the colon. See INTESTINE.

Cædmon, kăd'mŏn, the first Anglo-Saxon poet: d. 680. According to Bede's 'Ecclesiastical History' Cædmon was a swine-herd to the monks of Whitby, and never gave evidence of any poetical talent until one night a vision appeared to him, and commanded him to sing. When he awoke, he found the words of a poem in praise of the Creator of the world impressed upon his memory. This manifestation of talent obtained for him admission into the monastery at Whitby, where he continued to compose devotional poems. An edition of his paraphrase of parts of the Scriptures was printed at Amsterdam in 1655, edited by Junius. Thorpe published an edition of it (London 1832) for the Society of Antiquaries. It has been assumed by some that Milton took some ideas of 'Paradise Lost' from the poems of Cædmon. It is certain that they were very popular among the English and the Saxon part of the Scottish nation, and furnished plentiful materials to the makers of mysteries and miracle plays. In the Bodleian Library at Oxford is a manuscript the contents of which are ascribed to Cædmon, but the best authorities do not consider it to be his. Consult: Ten Brink, 'Early English Literature'; Morley, 'English Writers,' Vol. II. (1888).

Cælius Aurelianus, sē'lĭ-ŭs ô-rē-lĭ-ā'nŭs, Latin physician, generally supposed to have been a native of Numidia, and to have flourished in the 2d century of the Christian era. He was a member of the sect of the Methodici, and the author of a medical work still extant. In this work, 'De Morbis Chronicis et De Morbis Acutis,' Cælius divides diseases into two great classes, the acute and the chronic.

Cælius Mons, sē'lĭ-ŭs mŏns, one of the seven hills on which Rome was built. It is said to have received its name from Cælius Vibenna, an Etruscan, to whom it was assigned. The palace of Tullus Hostilius was on this mount. It is at present covered with ruins.

Caen, kän, France, a town in the department Calvados, and the ancient capital of Normandy, 125 miles northwest of Paris, and about nine miles from the mouth of the Orne, which is here navigable and crossed by several bridges. There is a dock connected with the sea by both river and canal. Caen is the centre of

an important domestic trade, the market of a rich agricultural district, and carries on extensive manufactures. The streets are broad, regular, and clean, the houses well-built of white freestone, and it possesses various ancient and remarkable edifices. The public promenades and recreation grounds are beautiful, and there are various extensive squares and "places." The church of La Trinité, a fine edifice in the Norman-Romanesque style, restored in modern times, was formerly the church of the Abbaye-aux-dames, founded in 1066 by Matilda, wife of William the Conqueror. The church of St. Stephen was founded at the same time by William the Conqueror, as the church of the Abbaye-aux-hommes, and though considerably modified since is a noble and impressive edifice. It has two fine western towers 295 feet high. The Abbaye-aux-hommes, built by the Conqueror, who was buried in it, is now used as a college, having been rebuilt in the 18th century. One of the finest churches in Caen is that of St. Pierre, whose tower (255 feet), terminated by a spire, is exceedingly elegant. Among other public buildings are the Hôtel de Ville, the prefecture, and the palace of justice. Caen possesses a university faculty or college, a public library with some 100,000 volumes, a gallery of paintings with valuable works of old masters, a natural history museum, an antiquarian museum, etc. The hospital of the Abbaye-aux-dames is one of the best regulated in France. The hospital of the Bon-Sauveur is another admirable institution. The city was formerly fortified, and there are remains of a castle begun by William the Conqueror and finished by Henry I., but since much altered and now used as barracks. Caen first rose into importance in the time of William the Conqueror. In 1346 it was taken by Edward III., at which time it was said to be larger than any city in England except London. Henry VI. of England founded a university here in 1431, Caen having been in the possession of the English from 1417 to 1450. It suffered much in the religious wars between the Protestants and Roman Catholics of France. Admiral de Coligny captured it for the Protestants in 1562. Caen carries on ship-building, and its manufactures embrace linen, woolen, and cotton goods, lace, ropes, metal goods, and various other articles. It carries on a considerable trade in timber and other articles, including agricultural produce exported to England, to which also is still exported the Caen building stone famous for many centuries. Malherbe, Laplace, Elie de Beaumont, and Auber were born in this city or in its vicinity, and are commemorated by statues. Pop. (1901) 44,524.

Caen-stone, a cream-colored oolitic limestone from Caen in Normandy, identical with the Bath oolite of England. It is easily carved and has long been highly esteemed as a building stone. Westminster Abbey, Canterbury Cathedral, and other English churches are built of it.

Cænopus, sē'nō-pŭs, a genus of fossil rhinoceroses of the Oligocene Epoch in North America. This animal was hornless, smaller and less heavily porportioned than any living species, the Sumatran rhinoceros coming nearest to it in this respect.

Cænotherium, sē-nō-thē'rĭ-ŭm, an extinct primitive ruminant, characteristic of the Oligocene formations of Europe. It was no larger than the modern chevrotain of Java and had many archaic characters, the four-toed feet, short skull, and complete series of 44 teeth being the most remarkable. See RUMINANTS, FOSSIL.

Caernarvon, kär-när′vŏn. See CARNARVON.

Cærula′rius, Michael, Greek ecclesiastic, the Patriarch of Constantinople, 1043-9. By dispensing with the Latin ritual in many churches of Bulgaria and protesting against the use of unleavened bread by the Latins in the Eucharist, he completed the division between the Latin and the Greek communions. He was formally excommunicated by Pope Leo IX.

Cæsalpinieæ, sĕs-ăl-pĭn′i-ĕ, a subdivision of the natural order of plants *Leguminosæ*, containing several genera. The botanical characteristics of the sub-order are: calyx in five divisions, joined together at different points, or often cleft to the base, with prefloration imbricated or valvular: petals equal or fewer in number; stamens often not symmetrical to the other parts of the flower, or very irregular, sometimes very numerous, sometimes partly abortive, rarely regular; very often free, or lightly joined together at the base only; ovaries raised on a free support, or joined in part to the calyx and becoming legumes, which sometimes contain only one single or double ovule, and of which the pericarp may have a fleshy consistence; seeds without perisperm; embryo often straight; stalk arborescent or fruticose, sometimes creeping; leaves simple, or more frequently compound; in the latter case frequently bipinnate. The typical genus is *Cæsalpinia,* to which belong the Brazil-wood, Sapan-wood, Nicaragua-wood, etc.

Cæsalpinus, Andreas, än′drā-as sĕs-al-pī′-nŭs, or Andrea **Cesalpino,** Italian physiologist: b. Arezzo, Italy, 1519; d. 23 Feb. 1603. He is first mentioned in public life as a professor of botany in the University of Pisa. He was subsequently made chief physician to Clement VII., and lived during the remainder of his life at Rome. He published works upon botany, mineralogy, medicine, and the highest questions of philosophy. In his first publication, entitled 'Speculum Artis Medicæ Hypocraticum,' his knowledge of the system of the circulation of the blood is stated in the clearest manner. The following passage is taken from the second chapter of its first book: "For in animals we see that the nutriment is carried through the veins to the heart as to a laboratory, and its last perfection being there attained, it is driven by the spirit which is begotten in the heart through the arteries and distributed to the whole body." The system accepted since the time of Harvey could hardly be more definitely or accurately stated. His philosophical speculations are contained mainly in his 'Quæstiones Peripateticæ.' The philosophy of Cæsalpinus was scholastic Aristotelianism, with a leaning toward some of the methods and doctrines of the later transcendental or absolute systems. He reduces the world to the simplicity of two only substances, God and matter, and he makes all finite intelligences, all human, angelic, and demoniac souls, to belong to the latter element. Two things are remarkable about his system: (1) the boldness of speculation, unparalleled in his age, with which he seeks a purely scientific view of the universe; and (2) its entirely materialistic character. But

more important than either his anticipation of Harvey's discovery, or his speculative opinions, were his botanical labors. He was styled by Linnæus the first orthodox or systematic botanist, and his work on plants was a hand-book to Linnæus in all his classifications. Botany in the time of Cæsalpinus was the popular witchcraft: as a science, it consisted in a mass of erudition about the imaginary but marvelous virtues of plants. Cæsalpinus sought successfully to transfer it from the realm of magic to that of science. He proposed the basis of classification upon which the whole system of Linnæus rests, namely, the distinction of plants in their parts of fructification. He lived quietly to an old age at Rome, submitting all his speculations to the supremacy of the Church, and presenting in his life an example of every virtue.

Cæsar, the name of a patrician family of the Julian gens, tracing its origin to Julius, the son of Æneas. The first member of the family who occurs in history with the surname of Cæsar was Sextus Julius Cæsar, prætor, 208 B.C. Cæsar was the family name of the first five Roman emperors. With Nero the imperial family became extinct (68 A.D.), and Cæsar became merely a title of dignity. The emperor, who bore the title of Augustus, appointed his successor, with the title of Cæsar. On medals and monuments we find the title Cæsar preceding the name of the emperor, as "Imp. Cæsar Nerva Trajanus Augustus," and following that of the designated successor, as "Marc. Aurel. Antonin. Cæsar." In the lower Greek empire, a new dignity of Sebastocrator was conferred, and that of Cæsar became the third rank in the state. From Cæsar are derived the German "kaiser" and the Russian "czar."

Cæsar, Gaius Julius, the greatest representative of the genius of Rome, a man of consummate ability alike as a general, a constructive statesman, and a writer. He was born, according to all the ancient authorities, 12 July 100 B.C., but Mommsen, in his 'History of Rome,' has made it probable that the year should be given as 102. Of purest patrician ancestry, and with a family tradition intimately associated with the rule of the senatorial oligarchy, he was yet, from early youth, a champion of the popular party. His aunt Julia had married Marius, and when, upon the latter's death in 86, Cinna became the leader of the Populares, Cæsar entered into intimate relations with him and in 83 married his daughter Cornelia. But the following year Sulla returned from the East and overwhelmed the foes of the senate. A reign of terror for the Marian party followed. With characteristic boldness, Cæsar refused to divorce his wife at the order of the dictator, and lost, in consequence, his property, his position as priest of Jupiter, and almost his life. The famous story that Sulla pardoned him with the remark that "he would one day be the ruin of the aristocracy, for in him there was many a Marius," though vouched for by both Suetonius and Plutarch, seems strikingly inconsistent with Sulla's usual remorseless logic. Partly to avoid further trouble, and partly to gain that military experience which was at Rome deemed a prerequisite to an official career, he now went to Asia, and, as a staff officer, served with distinguished bravery at the siege of Mytilene, and afterward against the pirates in Cilicia, but returned home upon receiving news of Sulla's death in 78. As pleading in the courts was the natural avenue to popular favor, we presently find him acting as prosecutor in two cases involving extortion in provincial administration. But the culprits, Dolabella and Antonius, belonged to the senatorial order, and his eloquence, though it won applause, failed to move juries composed of senators. He determined to perfect himself in oratory by studying under the most famous teacher of the age, Apollonius Molo of Rhodes. On the way thither he fell into the hands of pirates near Miletus, and was held for a ransom of 50 talents (over $55,000). During a stay of almost 40 days he won the admiration of his captors by his coolness and wit, and laughingly promised to crucify them all as soon as he should obtain his freedom, a threat which he promptly carried out to the letter. He studied under Molo only a short time, however, for the renewal of hostilities by Mithridates against the Roman province of Asia brought him into the field with some hastily levied troops, and, after brief but effective service, he returned to Rome in the winter of 74–73. He had been elected pontifex in his absence, and now took part, with the utmost energy, in the attempts that were being made to overthrow the Sullan constitution. This was accomplished in the year 70, though in a totally unexpected manner, by the legislation of Pompey and Crassus, both of whom had, previous to that time, been supporters of senatorial prerogative. Meanwhile Cæsar, by his unfailing courtesy and good will, and a lavish generosity that soon plunged him deep into debt, had been winning all hearts. In 69 he was elected quæstor, and was assigned to the province of Further Spain. But before his departure he lost his aunt Julia and his wife Cornelia. At the former's funeral he caused busts of Marius to be carried in the procession, to the great delight of the populace, and in the two memorial addresses which he delivered in the forum he eulogized the aims and leaders of the people's party. In Spain he must have noted with appreciation the work of the great Marian general, Sertorius, the first man who tried to Romanize the provincials. Upon his return, in 67, he entered into friendly relations with Pompey, and supported the Gabinian and Manilian laws, by which the latter was to receive the supreme command against the pirates and Mithridates, with powers unprecedented in the history of the republic. In 65 he was ædile, and met the demands of his office with unheard-of magnificence in buildings and games. In particular, he stirred the people to frantic enthusiasm by secretly erecting in the capitol new trophies of Marius, to replace those which Sulla had destroyed. In 63 he was chosen pontifex maximus, an office of great prestige and prominence in a state in which religion and politics had always been closely associated. That he had knowledge of the Catilinarian conspiracy of this year is by no means unlikely. But he took no part in it, and the aristocracy was unable to persuade Cicero to include him in the list of the conspirators. In 62 he was prætor, and in the following year went as governor to Further Spain, where for the first time he commanded an army and became conscious of his military genius. Toward the end of 61 Pompey returned to Rome, a victor over the entire East,

but was coldly received by the distrustful senate, which refused to ratify his acts in Asia and to make the assignments of lands promised to his veterans. Cæsar, returning from Spain, seized his opportunity, and about the time of his election to the consulship, reconciled Pompey and Crassus, whose enormous wealth made him indispensable, and formed with them the so-called First Triumvirate. The alliance was strengthened by the marriage of Pompey with Cæsar's daughter Julia. During his consulship in 59 Cæsar carried, among other measures, a popular agrarian bill, the ratification of Pompey's acts, and a stringent law against extortion in the provinces, while he won to his support the whole equestrian order, to which the collectors of the public revenues belonged, by modifying the terms of their last contract with the state. His popularity enabled him to secure the assignment to himself for five years (subsequently increased to 10) of the provinces of Cisalpine Gaul, Illyricum, and Transalpine Gaul, together with four legions. The following eight years (58–51) witnessed those brilliant campaigns which ended in the complete subjugation of Gaul, and its acceptance of the laws, language, and civilization of Rome. The first three years of war brought all Gaul to his feet, but the love of liberty was still too strong in this brave people, and dangerous revolts broke out year after year. In 55 he crossed the Rhine on the famous bridge, and later made his first expedition to Britain, which he invaded again the following year. Finally, in the winter of 53–52, Vercingetorix, Gaul's greatest hero, and a born leader of men, organized a general uprising of all the tribes. The flame of insurrection swept over the whole country. The campaign culminated in the siege of Alesia (Alise in Burgundy), an almost impregnable fortress into which the Gallic chieftain had thrown himself with 80,000 men. Cæsar invested the place with less than 60,000, and was presently himself invested by an enormous army of relief, estimated at over 240,000 men. But he completely routed this vast host, and Vercingetorix, worn out by hunger, surrendered. By the end of the following year Cæsar was at last able to address himself to the peaceful organization of the new territory.

At Rome, however, a crisis was imminent. The ties between Cæsar and Pompey were being rapidly dissolved. The death, in 54, of Julia, Pompey's wife and Cæsar's daughter, was followed in 53 by the defeat and death of Crassus in the Parthian war. Pompey became more and more jealous of his rival's military glory, and the senate, resolved to crush Cæsar at any cost, and itself unable even to keep order in the streets of Rome, made friendly overtures to Pompey, and in 52 made him sole consul, with practically the powers of a dictator. Cæsar's term of office would expire on 1 March 49. It was essential to his safety that he should retain his provinces and his army until after he should be elected consul for 48. But the aristocracy was plainly determined that there should be an interval during which he would be a mere private citizen, defenseless against the attacks of his enemies. It is certain that Cæsar acted with great moderation, even sending to Italy two of his legions which the senate declared were needed for the war in the East, but which, as he had foreseen, were instead placed in camp at Capua. At length, in January 49, the decisive step was taken. The senate ordered Cæsar to lay down his command on pain of being proclaimed a public enemy. The tribunes of the people, Antony and Quintus Cassius, who had in vain interposed their veto, fled to him for protection in their inviolable office, Cæsar with a single legion crossed the Rubicon, the frontier stream of Italy, and war was begun.

In the ensuing five years, all that remained for him of life, the amazing energy and resourcefulness of this extraordinary man are most impressively displayed. In three months, without striking a blow, he was master of Italy, and Pompey, with a small force, barely escaped from Brundisium across the Adriatic. Cæsar had no ships on which to follow him, and, besides, the veteran Pompeian forces in Spain must be crushed before they could join their commander. Accordingly, after first securing, through his lieutenants, Sicily and Sardinia, he crossed the Pyrenees into Spain, and, in a brief campaign of 40 days, perhaps the most brilliant in all his career, extricated himself from apparently certain destruction, and forced the surrender of the entire opposing army. All Spain now declared for him. On his way back he received the submission of Massilia (Marseilles), which had been besieged by Decimus Brutus and Trebonius. Eleven days were spent in Rome in administrative work, and early in January 48 he crossed the Adriatic and proceeded to invest Pompey, near Dyrrachium, now Durazzo. But his force was quite insufficient, and, to deprive his foe of the advantage of the sea, he retreated into Thessaly, whither Pompey followed him, and the decisive battle was fought on the plain of Pharsalus, 9 Aug. 48. Pompey had 47,000 infantry and 7,000 cavalry; Cæsar only 22,000 infantry and 1,000 cavalry. But the latter's army was composed of veterans, and numbers did not avail. Pompey fled to Egypt, where he was brutally murdered. Cæsar, who had followed him with all speed, was nearly trapped in Alexandria by the forces of the young king Ptolemy, but ultimately, upon the arrival of reinforcements, defeated them, and set Cleopatra upon the throne. He then passed through Syria and Asia Minor, putting affairs on a permanent basis, and incidentally defeating Pharnaces, a son of the great Mithridates. The victory was announced in the famous despatch, "*Veni, vidi, vici*" ("I came, I saw, I conquered"). Upon his return he announced his intention of pardoning all who had fought against him. In December he left Rome for Africa, where the campaign against the Pompeians, commanded by Scipio and Cato, ended in a sweeping victory at Thapsus, 6 April 46. Cato, unable to defend Utica, committed suicide. Cæsar returned to Rome in June, and, after celebrating his victories over the Gauls, Egyptians, Pharnaces, and Juba, king of Numidia, who had fought against him at Thapsus, by four magnificent triumphs, flung himself into the work of legislation. Among his reforms was the placing of the calendar, for the first time, upon a scientific basis. But these labors were interrupted by a dangerous revolt in Spain, headed by Pompey's sons, and the campaign against them, ending in the hard-fought battle of Munda, 17 March, and the final settlement of affairs in Spain, necessitated his absence from Rome from the end of 46 to September 45. The senate welcomed him upon his return with the most servile flattery. He was already tribune for life; he was now made, for life, dictator and *præfectus morum*, a new term for the censorship, his head was stamped on the coinage, the month of Quintilis was renamed Julius, and he was given divine honors. With absolute power thus lodged in his hands, he set about the permanent reconstruction of the government and the social fabric. He made the senate a much larger and more representative body, increased the number of magistrates, reduced by one half the recipients of the donation of grain, passed several laws in the interest of the debtor class and of Italian agriculture, prohibited farming by slave labor exclusively, inaugurated a far-reaching plan to colonize in the provinces the unemployed population of Rome and Italy, and laid a legal foundation for the principle of limited local self-government of all Roman communities, wherever they might be. He had in mind, but did not live to carry out, the codification of the laws, the building of public libraries, the draining of the Pontine marshes, the making of a canal through the Isthmus of Corinth, and the taking of a general census which should form a just basis for the imposition of taxes throughout the empire.

But he had risen too high to escape hatred. The plot to assassinate him probably originated in the personal spite of Gaius Cassius, but many of the conspirators, in particular Marcus Brutus, were foolish enough to believe that by the death of the dictator the republic could be restored. On 15 March 44 B.C., at a meeting of the senate held in the hall attached to Pompey's theatre, he fell at the feet of his great rival's statue, pierced by 23 wounds.

In studying Cæsar's life, one is especially struck by three points: his sane perception of the concrete fact, his indomitable energy, and his many-sidedness. More clearly than any other man of that time, he saw that the senatorial oligarchy had been proven wholly incompetent to govern a great empire, and that the problem could be solved only by the concentration of all power in the hands of a single man. Augustus cautiously veiled the change to monarchy; Julius bluntly called things by their real names and paid the penalty with his life. He was an able orator, but of his speeches, warmly praised by Cicero and Quintilian, none has come down to us. A treatise on grammar and one on astronomy have also perished. But his enduring fame as a writer rests upon the seven books of 'Commentaries on the Gallic War' (the eighth book is by Aulus Hirtius) and the three books of 'Commentaries on the Civil War.' The former, essentially a political document, published in 51 B.C., is unsurpassed in its succinct simplicity and strength.

Bibliography.—The principal ancient authorities are the biographies of Plutarch and Suetonius, Cicero's 'Letters,' Sallust's 'Catiline,' Cæsar's own 'Commentaries,' and the Roman histories of Velleius Paterculus, Appian, and Dion Cassius. Mommsen's account in his 'History of Rome' is brilliant but over-enthusiastic. The following books may be recommended: Fowler, 'Julius Cæsar and the Foundation of the Roman Imperial System' (New York 1899); Dodge, 'Cæsar' (Boston 1892); Froude, 'Cæsar' (New York 1884); Napoleon III. 'Histoire de Jules César' (English translation

New York 1865); continued by Stoffel, 'Histoire de Jules César; la guerre civile' (Paris 1887); Holmes, 'Cæsar's Conquest of Gaul' (London 1899). NELSON G. McCREA, *Professor of Latin Literature, Columbia University.*

Cæsarea, ses-ä-rē'ạ, the ancient name of many cities: (1) CÆSAREA PHILIPPI, or PANEAS, named after Philip, tetrarch of Galilee, son of Herod the Great, who founded it in 3–2 B.C., near the source of the Jordan. It is mentioned twice in the Gospels. On its site is the small modern village of Banias. (2) CÆSAREA PALESTINÆ or STRATONIS, on the shores of the Mediterranean, about 55 miles northwest from Jerusalem. It was built with great magnificence by Herod the Great, and became the metropolis of Palestine, and the seat of the Roman proconsul, as well as a busy seaport. It was the place where Herod Agrippa was smitten by the angel (Acts xii: 20–23), where Cornelius the centurian resided (x.), and St. Paul was imprisoned two years (xxiii.–xxv.). It was a place of some importance during the Crusades, but is now a scene of ruin and of utter desolation. Eusebius was bishop of Cæsarea. (3) The ancient capital of Cappadocia in Asia Minor, originally called Mazaca, and now Kaisarieh. It is situated in the southeast of the vilayet of Angora, at the foot of the Erjish Dagh, about 160 miles to the southeast of the town of Angora. It was once supposed to contain 400,000 inhabitants. It has now about 70,000 inhabitants, and its position makes it a place of considerable trade. The manufacture of carpets, though of quite recent introduction, is of some importance. Foreign goods are received by way of the railway from Angora to Constantinople. The name Cæsarea dates from the time of Tiberius, and under Valerian the city was captured by Sapor, when a large number of its inhabitants were slain.

Cæsarean Operation, a surgical operation, which consists in delivering a child by means of an incision made through the walls of the abdomen and womb. There are three cases in which this may be necessary: first, when the child is alive and the mother dead, either in labor or in the last two months of pregnancy; second, when the child is dead, but cannot be delivered in the usual way on account of the deformity of the mother or the disproportionate size of the child; and third, when both mother and child are living, but delivery cannot take place from the same causes as in the second case. In many instances both mother and child have survived this critical operation; and cases are known in which it has been successfully performed by the mother herself. The etymology of the name is doubtless from the Latin verb *cædere,* to cut; though a popular myth attributes it to Julius Cæsar, who, according to Pliny, was brought into the world in this manner. The operation appears to have been known from ancient times. See SURGERY.

Cæsa'rion, the son of Julius Cæsar and Cleopatra, put to death by order of Augustus.

Cæsa'rius, Saint, of Arles, French prelate of the 6th century, consecrated Bishop of Arles in 502. Before the general adoption by monastic orders of the Rule of Saint Benedict his *Regulæ Duæ* formed a standard of discipline much esteemed by the founders of orders.

Cæsarius of Nazian'zus, Christian scholar of the 4th century. From Alexandria, where his education was received, he went to Constantinople and rose to distinction as a mathematician and physicist. In the Latin editions of Saint Gregory are four dialogues ascribed to him, and he is also credited with a work styled 'Contra Gentes.'

Cæsar's Commentaries. This great work contains the narrative of Cæsar's military operations in Gaul, Germany, and Britain. It was given to the world in the year 51 B.C. Every victory won by Cæsar had only served to increase the alarm and hostility of his enemies at Rome, and doubt and suspicion were beginning to spread among the plebeians, on whom he chiefly relied for help in carrying out his designs. When public opinion was evidently taking the side of the Gauls and Germans the time had come for Cæsar to act on public opinion. Hence the 'Commentaries,' a hasty compilation made from notes jotted down in his tent or during a journey. As to its truthfulness we cannot decide absolutely, the Gauls not having written *their* commentaries. But if Cæsar sinned in this respect, it was probably by omission, not by commission. Things the Romans might not like he does not mention: the sole aim of the book is to gain their suffrages. There is no allusion to the enormous fortune Cæsar acquired by plunder. On the other hand, he speaks of his cruelties — for instance, the killing in cold blood of 20,000 or 100,000 prisoners — with a calmness that to us is horrible, but which the Romans would deem natural and proper.

Cæsars, The Era of, also known as the Spanish Era, a period of time reckoned from 1 Jan. 38 B.C., being the year following the conquest of Spain by Augustus. It was much used in Africa, Spain, and the south of France; but by a synod held in 1180 its use was abolished in all the churches dependent on Barcelona. Pedro IV. of Aragon abolished the use of it in his dominions in 1350. John of Castile did the same in 1383. It was used in Portugal till 1415, if not till 1422. The months and days of this era are identical with the Julian calendar, and to turn the time into that of our era, subtract 38 from the year; but if before the Christian era, subtract 39.

Cæsium, sē'zĭ-ŭm, a metallic element discovered in 1860 by Bunsen and Kirchhoff, in the form of the chloride, in a mineral spring at Dürkheim, Bavaria. The metal is widely disseminated, but is seldom found in any considerable quantity. It never occurs in the metallic state, but usually as the chloride or oxide, and commonly associated with the rare element rubidium. Its most important source is the mineral pollucite (q.v.), or pollux, which is found on the island of Elba and in the vicinity of Hebron, Me., and which contains as much as 36 per cent of cæsium oxide, with no rubidium. Cæsium forms stable salts, and strongly resembles potassium in its chemical properties. It may be separated from this metal, however, by taking advantage of the fact that cæsium platinochloride is much less soluble in water than the corresponding potassium compound. Metallic cæsium cannot be obtained by reducing the oxide with carbon, but is best prepared by the electrolysis of a fused mixture of the cyanïdes of cæsium and barium, using aluminum electrodes. It is a silvery white metal, quite soft and ductile, and oxidizing rapidly upon exposure to the air. It also decomposes water with the production of sufficient heat to ignite the liberated hydrogen. Cæsium has a specific gravity of 1.88, and melts at about 80° F. Its chemical symbol is Cs, and its atomic weight is 133 (O = 16). Its oxalate and nitrate are used to a limited extent in medicine. The spectrum of cæsium is characterized by two blue lines, from which circumstance the element takes its name (cæsius, bluish-gray). It is readily recognized by the spectroscope, and was the first element discovered by that instrument.

Cæstus. See CESTUS.

Cæsura, se-zū'ra (Lat., literally a cutting), in verse, the separation of the last syllable of any word from those which precede it, and the carrying it forward into another foot. The term originally belongs to classical verse, in which the cæsura renders the syllable on which it falls long (if not otherwise so), and is accompanied by a slight pause, hence called the cæsural pause, as in the following line:

Ille la*tus* niveum molli fultus hyacintho.

See RHYTHM, VERSE.

Caf, käf, or Kaf, a fabled mountain of the Mohammedans which encircles the whole earth. It is the home of giants and fairies, and rests upon the sacred stone Sakhral, one grain of which gives miraculous powers to its possessor. This stone is of an emerald color, and its reflected light is the cause of the tints of the sky.

Café, kä-fā, a coffee-house, enlarged by American usage to include restaurants of all descriptions.

Caffarelli, François Marie Auguste, fräṅswä mä-rē ō-güst käf-fa-rēl'lē, French general: b. Falga, Haute-Garonne, 7 Oct. 1766; d. 23 Jan. 1849. At the beginning of the revolution he was employed in the Sardinian army, but joined the army of the republic as a simple dragoon. In 1804 he was charged with the mission to Rome to induce the Pope to come to Paris to perform the ceremony of Napoleon's coronation, and on his return was made governor of the Tuileries. He was wounded at Austerlitz, accompanied Prince Eugene in Italy, and took part in the war in Spain. In 1814 he was chosen by Napoleon to conduct the empress and their son from Paris to Vienna. He retired from public life after the battle of Waterloo.

Caffarelli, Gaetano Majorano, gä-ā-tä'nō mä-yō-rä'nō, Italian vocalist: b. Province of Bari, Italy, 16 April 1703; d. Naples, 30 April 1783. As a boy he was considered the finest soprano of his time, his only possible rival in later years being the famous Farinelli.

Caffarelli du Falga, Louis Marie Joseph, loo-ē mä-rē zhō-zēf käf-fa-rēl-lē dü fäl-gä, French general: b. Falga, 13 Feb. 1756; d. Syria, 27 April 1799. He protested against the right of the national assembly to dethrone the king, and was dismissed from the army and imprisoued. Being released and reinstated, he distinguished himself in the army of the Rhine, under Jourdan. He accompanied the expedition of Napoleon to Egypt.

Caffeine, käf'fē-ĭn, an alkaloid occurring in the coffee bean, and having the formula $C_8H_{10}N_4O_2$. It is believed to be identical with the alkaloid theine, which occurs in tea, and also with guaranine (the alkaloid of guarana); and it is present in small amounts in cocoa. It may be prepared by adding basic acetate of lead to a strong decoction of coffee or tea until the tannin that is present has all been precipitated, removing excess of lead by a stream of sulphuretted hydrogen, and then evaporating the filtrate until the caffeine crystallizes out. When prepared in this manner caffeine consists of a mass of silky needles which contain more or less water. It is but slightly soluble in water, alcohol, or ether. It has a bitter taste, and although it acts as a weak base its salts are decomposed by water. See also COFFEE.

Caf'fery, Donelson, American lawyer: b. Saint Mary Parish, La., 10 Sept. 1835; d. 30 Dec. 1906. He was educated at Saint Mary's College, Md., studied law and was admitted to the bar. He served in the Confederate army. 1861-5, was State senator in 1892, and United States senator, 1893-1901. From 1896 his political affiliations were with the Gold Democrats.

Caffi, Ippolito, ĭp-pō-lē'tō käf'fē, Italian artist: b. Bulluno, 1814; d. near Lissa, 20 July 1866. He studied in Venice and excelled in matters of perspective and effects of light. Among his chief works are 'Isthmus of Suez'; and 'Carnival Scene on the Piazetta, Venice' (1855). He was killed on the Italian battleship Re d'Italia in a naval battle off Lissa, being present on that occasion with the design of painting a picture of the engagement. He also painted the 'Panorama of Rome.'

Caf'fyn, Kathleen Mannington (HUNT) ("IOTA"), English novelist: b. Waterloo House, County Tipperary, Ireland. She was trained as a hospital nurse, was married to Mannington Caffyn, a surgeon and author, and after his death began novel writing under the pseudonym of "Iota." Her first book, 'A Yellow Aster' (1894), attracted much attention. It is a "problem novel" and has been followed by 'Children of Circumstances' (1895); 'A Comedy in Spasms'; 'A Quaker Grandmother' (1896); 'Poor Max' (1898); 'Anne Mauleverer' (1899); 'The Minx' (1900); 'The Happiness of Jill' (1901).

Caftan, käf'tän, the national garment of the Turks, in the form of a loose gown, generally white, with pale-yellow flowers. It is made of woolen or silk stuff, and sometimes lined with costly fur.

Cagayan, kä-gä-yän', an island of the Philippine group; the largest of six small islets, known as the Cagayan-Sulu group. It is five miles wide and eight miles long. Pop. (1900) 3,500. There are mountains attaining a height of 1,100 feet. The chief products are tobacco and sugar. There are pearl and shell fisheries. Cagayan was sold by Spain to the United States with Cibitu, in 1900, upon payment of $100,000, having been inadvertently excluded from the terms of the treaty of peace.

Cage-birds, birds kept in cages for the benefit or enjoyment afforded by their powers of song, beauty of plumage, ability to talk, or companionship. They have been so kept by human beings ever since prehistoric times. The first essential for the maintenance of birds in captivity is a cage as large as possible, and as nearly like the bird's original habitat as circumstances permit. Cleanliness is a prime necessity, and the bird should be given a constant fresh supply of water for bathing and drinking purposes, and as much fresh air and light as possible, always, however, avoiding draughts and the sun's direct rays. The food and necessary attention bestowed on the bird vary according to the species.

Birds are captured by means of birdlime or a falling net, but many are taken from their nests when young, and so tamed, or are bred solely for market purposes. An important trade throughout Europe is the rearing of cage-birds, especially German canaries. The best-known songster, and probably the most popular cagebird, is the common canary (q.v.), originally a native of the Canary Islands. It is typical of captive birds generally, in the marked change produced by captivity and selective breeding, in coloring and size, from that in its original wild state. Other widely known and popular cagebirds are the nightingale, goldfinch, cardinal, mocking-bird, bullfinch, the Indian bulbul, several European thrushes, and others, all of which are fine singers. Among the birds kept because of their beauty are the parrakeets, love-birds, cockatoos, macaws, the whydah-bird, the painted finches, and others. Those imitating human speech are not so plentiful, consisting chiefly of the parrot, of which there are several species, and the starlings, especially the English species, and the Indian mina-bird (qq.v.). Owing to the change of climate, and especially the cold, nine tenths of the African parrots transported to Europe or North America die before learning to speak. It is advisable, therefore, to purchase such birds in the spring, thus giving them a chance to become gradually acclimated.

In the case of all cage-birds most particular attention should be paid to their food, and overfeeding must be especially guarded against. Frequently ailments can be greatly benefited by a fresh supply of food given in smaller quantities. Insectivorous birds are most troublesome to care for in regard to food, as their diet is less easily obtained. In case of inability to procure the accustomed food, finely chopped meat should be substituted, and a reasonable quantity of spiders is always beneficial. The universal and most acceptable food to nearly all birds, however, is canary-seed, with which hemp, rape, or oats may frequently be mixed to advantage. Seed-eating birds should be given such fresh vegetable matter as soft green leaves, chickweed, or lettuce, at regular intervals. Sugar in small quantities is also beneficial, but acid fruits of all kinds should be avoided. A prime necessity in the rearing of cage-birds is something on which the bird may sharpen its bill. This is most easily supplied in the form of sandpaper, or, better, cuttle-fish bone, which is essential to the health of breeding birds. A bird's nails are apt to grow so long as to become troublesome to it, but in clipping them care should be taken to use a sharp pair of scissors, avoiding a possible injury to the foot by twisting. In case of illness due to overfeeding, a drop of castor oil may prove beneficial, especially if it is accompanied by a change of surroundings, quiet, and a simpler diet for a time.

Consult: Bechstein, 'Cage and Chamber Birds'; and Greene, 'Notes on Cage Birds.'

Cagliari, Paolo, pä'ō-lạ, käl-yä'rē. See VERONESE, PAOLO.

Cagliari, käl-yä'rē, Sardinia, the capital of the island situated on a hill slope near the south coast. It consists of four parts: (1) the Castle or old town; (2) the Marina; (3) Estempache; (4) the Villa Nuova or new town. It is fortified, and is the residence of the viceroy and of an archbishop, and the seat of a university founded in 1596, and revived and remodeled in 1765. Cagliari has some manufactures, and is the chief emporium of the Sardinian trade. There are dockyards and a spacious and safe harbor. The "Castle" contains some important buildings, including palaces of the nobility. The cathedral, partly faced with marble, was completed in 1312, but afterward modernized. There are some interesting remains of Roman times, including an amphitheatre and ancient dwelling-houses. Cagliari was the residence of the kings of Sardinia from 1798 to 1814. It is connected by railway with the most important Sardinian towns. Pop. (1902) 55,300.

Cagliostro, Alessandro, äl-lĕs-än'drō käl-yōs'trō (COUNT OF) (real name *Giuseppe Balsamo*), Italian charlatan: b. Palermo, 8 June 1743; d. St. Leon, Italy, 26 Aug. 1795. He entered the order of the Brothers of Mercy, where he found an opportunity to cultivate his talents for medical science, by which he afterward distinguished himself. But as he showed at the same time a great love of dissipation, he was compelled to separate from the order. He returned to Palermo, where, among other tricks, he deceived some credulous persons by his pretended skill in magic and the finding of hidden treasures. He also showed himself adroit in counterfeiting handwriting, and attempted to get possession of a contested estate by means of a forged document, but was discovered and was obliged to flee. He now determined to go to Rome, and in his journey through Calabria became acquainted with Lorenza Feliciani, daughter of a belt-maker, who appeared to him intended by fortune to assist his designs. He formed an intimacy with her, and they began their travels, in which he assumed the character of a man of rank, first appearing under the name of the Marquis Pellegrini, and finally under that of the Count Cagliostro. He traveled through many countries of Europe, stopped in the capital cities, and by his chemical mixtures, his tricks, and by the amours of his companion, gained considerable sums. He knew how to cheat with great ingenuity, and was always fortunate enough to preserve himself by an early flight, if men's eyes began to be opened, or waking justice threatened him with imprisonment. The discovery of the philosopher's stone, the preparation of a precious elixir vitæ, etc., were the pretenses by means of which he extracted considerable sums from credulous people. Many had recourse to his assistance, not indeed to be initiated into the mysteries of magic, but to purchase at a high rate different kinds of medicine, one of which was the water of beauty. This profitable business employed him many years; but his trade in medicine began to grow less lucrative, and he determined to seek his fortune as the founder of a new and secret sect. In pursuance of this plan he passed himself off during his second residence in London for a freemason, and played the part of a magician and worker of miracles, in which character he drew upon himself the eyes of all the enthusiasts in Europe. The Countess Cagliostro, on her part, did not remain idle. She was the first and most perfect scholar of her husband, and ably played the part of a priestess to this new order. His plan for reviving an old Egyptian order, the founders of which he declared to be Enoch and Elias, contained a mass of absurdities, but his pretensions to supernatural power, the mystery with which his doctrines were enveloped, his pretended ability to work miracles, his healing the sick without pay, with the greatest appearance of generosity, and the belief that, as the Great Kophta (this name he had taken as the restorer of Egyptian masonry), he could reveal the secrets of futurity, gained him many friends and supporters. Cagliostro again traveled through Europe, and attracted great attention in Mittan, Strasburg, Lyons, and Paris. While in this last city (1785) he has the misfortune to be implicated in the scandalous affair of the necklace, and was banished the country as a confidant of Cardinal Rohan. He now returned to London, and sent many epistles to his followers, wherein he bitterly complained of the injury he had received in France, and painted the French court in the blackest colors. From London, where he could not long remain, he went to Basel and other cities in that quarter. But at length, listening to the repeated entreaties of his wife and other friends, he returned (1789) to Rome. Here he busied himself about freemasonry; but being discovered and committed to the Castle of St. Angelo, he was condemned by a decree of the Pope to imprisonment for life as a freemason, an arch heretic, and a very dangerous foe to religion.

Cagnacci, kän-yä'chē. See CANLASSI.

Cagnola, Luigi, loo-ē'jē kän-yō'lạ, MARCHESE, an Italian architect: b. Milan, 9 June 1762; d. Inveriga, 14 Aug. 1833. He was a member of the State Council, and was much engaged in political affairs. His most celebrated works are the Arco della Pace, «Arch of Peace,» commenced in 1807 and finished in 1837; the Porta di Marengo, subsequently called Porta di Ticino (both built by order of Napoleon), at Milan; the Campanile, at Urgnano, completed in 1829, and the Mausoleum for the Metternich family.

Cagnoli, kän-yō'lē, **Antonio,** Italian astronomer: b. Zante, Ionian Islands, 1743; d. Verona, Italy, 1816. He was attached in his youth to the Venetian embassy at Paris, where, after the year 1776, he showed more love for astronomy than for diplomacy. Having settled in Verona in 1786 he constructed an observatory in his own house, by his observations in which he enriched the science of astronomy with many discoveries. After the destruction of his observatory by the French (1798), who, however, compensated him for his loss, his instruments were transferred to the observatory of Brera in Milan, and he was appointed professor of astronomy in the military school at Modena. His best works are 'Notizie Astronomiche adat. all' Uso comune' (1802); 'Trigonometria Piana e Sferica' (second edition, Bologna, 1804).

Cagots, kạ-gō', a race or caste of men, living in the south of France in the region of the Pyrenees, regarded as pariahs or social outcasts. In former ages they were shut out from society as lepers, cursed as heretics, and abhorred as cannibals; their feet were bored with an iron, and they were forced to wear a piece of red cloth in the shape of a duck's foot on their clothes by way of distinction. The only trade they were allowed to follow was that of sawyers or carpenters. They had to enter the church by a special door, and had a special corner set apart for them with a holy-water vessel for themselves. Opinions are divided with regard to the origin of the Cagots, of whom there are now comparatively few. They have been considered by some to be remains of the Saracens conquered by Charles Martel. The most plausible conjecture is that which derives them from the Visigoths who established themselves in the south of France and in Spain in the 5th century. The origin of the name has been the subject of equal controversy. Among numerous derivations, is that from *canis* and *gothus,* «dogs of Goths.» Others derive the name from a word simply meaning leper, and believe that the Cagots were originally lepers, who as such were expelled from the society of and intercourse with their fellowmen. Until the French Revolution the Cagots were not considered as citizens. Some remains of them, or of corresponding outcasts, are to be found under various names in different parts of France. Similar remains are also found among the mountains of North Spain. Consult Michel, 'Histoire des Races Maudites de la France et de l'Espagne.'

Cahan, kä'hạn, Abraham, Russo-American journalist and novelist: b. Vilna, Russia, 7 July 1860. He came to the United States in 1882 and has edited several Yiddish periodicals in New York. He has written 'Yekl, a Tale of the New York Ghetto'; 'Raphael Narizokh,' in Yiddish; 'The Chasm'; 'The Imported Bridegroom and Other Stories'; 'The White Terror and the Red' (1904).

Cahawba, kạ-hô'bạ, a river of Alabama, rises in Jefferson County, and after passing through a rich coal region, joins the Alabama at Cahawba, in Dallas County. It is navigable by small boats for 100 miles.

Cahens'lyism, a popular name given to a movement in the United States in 1891, among Roman Catholics speaking other languages than English, to have bishops or priests of their respective nationalities appointed over them. It took its name from Herr Cahensly, a layman, secretary of St. Raphael's Society for the protection of German Catholic immigrants to this country, on the supposition that he was the chief inspirer of the movement. On a visit to the United States in 1893 Herr Cahensly denied his connection with the scheme. It was vigorously opposed by most of the English-speaking prelates of the Roman Catholic Church in this country. It received no official sanction by the Vatican authorities, and, after considerable agitation in the Catholic and secular press, died out. As a matter of fact, owing to the large immigration of Roman Catholics speaking foreign tongues, priests of their respective nationalities are often appointed to administer to their spiritual needs. This is especially notable in the instance of the Italians. To meet this necessity in the archdiocese of New York, the study of Italian is now made compulsory in its diocesan seminary for all candidates for the priesthood.

Cahors, ka̤-ōr, France, (ancient CADUR-CUM), capital of the department of Lot, and on the river of that name, 60 miles north of Toulouse. It is nearly surrounded by the river, and communicates with the opposite shore by three bridges, one of which is ancient. Before the conquest of Gaul by Cæsar it was the capital of the Cadurci, and under the Romans, who gave it the name of Divona, it was adorned with a temple, theatre, baths, an immense aqueduct, and forum. Several Roman roads can still be traced in its vicinity. Among the principal edifices are the cathedral, an irregular structure, supposed to be partly Roman; an episcopal palace, now converted into the prefecture; three old churches; barracks; a theatre; and a lyceum or college. Cahors had formerly a university, which was united with that of Toulouse in 1751. It was founded in 1322 by Pope John XXII, a native of the town. The celebrated jurist Cujas was a professor, and Fénelon a student in it. To the latter an obelisk has been erected. The manufactures are insignificant; but a considerable trade is carried on in the red wine of the district, and in brandy. Coal is worked in the vicinity. Clément Marot, the poet, was born here. Cahors was given up to the English by the Treaty of Brétigny in 1360. It revolted, and returned to France in 1428. Pop. (1902) about 15,000.

Caiaphas, ka'ya̤-fa̤s, the high-priest of the Jews at the time when the crucifixion took place. Previously, when the resurrection of Lazarus had spread dismay among the Jewish functionaries, it was Caiaphas who suggested the expediency of putting the Saviour to death, and when he was arrested in Gethsemane he was carried first to Annas, and then to Caiaphas, from whom he was transferred to the hands of the civil authority. Caiaphas was deposed, 35 A.D., and Jonathan, son of Annas, appointed in his stead.

Caibarien, kī-bä-re̤-än', Cuba, a town of the province of Santa Clara, situated on the northern seacoast; it has sponge fisheries and some trade. Pop. about 8,000.

Caicos, kī'kōs, **Cayos,** or **The Keys** (from the Spanish *cayo*, a rock, shoal, or islet), one of the island groups comprehended under the general name of the Bahamas, belonging to Great Britain, consisting of six islands besides some uninhabited rocks; between lat. 21° and 22° N. and lon. 71° and 73° W. The largest, called the Great Key, is about 30 miles long. They are wooded and tolerably fertile, and at one time produced cotton, but at present the inhabitants are few in number, and mostly engaged in fishing and the preparation of salt. In 1873 the Turks Islands and the Caicos were united into a commissionership under the governor of Jamaica. Pop. 1,784.

Cailletet, Louis Paul, loo-ē̆ pōl ka̤-yĕ-tä, French chemist: b. Châtillon-sur-Seine, 1832. He studied at the School of Mines in Chatillon and subsequently gave especial attention to original research. He was able to liquefy both oxygen and nitrogen in 1877 and was at once elected corresponding member of the Académie des Sciences, becoming a full member in 1884. He was made an officer of the Legion of Honor in 1889.

Cailliaud, Frédéric, frä-dĕ-rĭk ka̤-yō, French traveler: b. Nantes, France, 9 June 1787; d. there, 1 May 1869. In examining the mineral resources of Egypt, he rediscovered the ancient emerald mines of Jebel Zobara, near the Red Sea; and his report of a journey to Siwah, led to its annexation by Egypt in 1820. In 1821-2 he accompanied Ibrahim Pasha's expedition to the White Nile, and his 'Journey to Meroe' (1826-7), contained the first reliable information of that district. He also published 'Voyage à Oasis de Thebes' (1821). In 1827 he settled as conservator of the Natural History Museum at Nantes, where he died.

Caillie, René, rĕ-nä ka̤-yä, French traveler: b. Mauzé, Poitou, France, 19 Sept. 1799; d. Paris, 8 May 1838. He became an African traveler early in his career, obtaining his living by trading with the Moors, who taught him Arabic. On his travels he dressed in Arabic style and passed as an Egyptian. Having gone to Senegal he learned that the Geographical Society of Paris had offered a premium of 10,000 francs to the first traveler who should reach Timbuctoo. On 13 June 1827 he reached for the first time the shores of the Niger, which he crossed. He then traveled about 200 miles eastwardly over territories never visited before, arriving at Timé 3 August. Here he was detained by illness until 9 Jan. 1828, when he struck on a new road previously unknown to geographers, and reached Jenne on 11 March. Here he embarked for Timbuctoo, where he arrived about 11 April, after one month's sail on the Niger. After a short stay of a fortnight, and after a tedious and painful return passage through the desert, he reached Fez, 12 August, and from there returned to France. On his arrival at Toulon he was received with the utmost enthusiasm. He was the first European who ever returned from Timbuctoo, and who had achieved success, while expeditions supported by government had resulted in failure. A special prize of 10,000 francs was awarded to him by the Geographical Society, with the annual prize of 1,000 francs for the most important discovery. The order of the Legion of Honor was conferred upon him by the king, and he became, at the same time, the recipient of a salary in connection with an office, to which he was appointed in the Senegal service. Furthermore, a pension from the fund set apart for eminent literary and scientific men was decreed to him by the minister of the interior, and his 'Journal d'un voyage à Timbouktou et Jenné, dans l'Afrique centrale, etc.,' with geographical data added by Jomard, was published at the expense of government, and appeared at the beginning of 1830 in three volumes.

Caiman. See CAYMAN.

Cain, the eldest son of Adam and Eve; the first murderer, who slew his brother Abel. For the biblical account of Cain and his descendants see Gen iv.-vii. Modern biblical scholars assume that Genesis iv. is a composite of stories relating to several Cains. The posterity of Cain became extinct at the flood. Cain founded the first city, and his descendants were the first inventors and promoters of the useful and agreeable arts. Josephus relates that he became the leader of a band of robbers, committed all sorts of licentiousness, corrupted the simplicity of primitive manners by his luxury, established the right of property by setting up landmarks, and was the inventor of weights and measures. A Gnostic sect of the second century were called "Cainites." See RELIGIOUS SECTS.

Cain, Auguste Nicolas, ŏ-güst nĭk-ō-lä kạ-ăṅ, French sculptor: b. Paris, 4 Nov. 1822; d. there, 7 Aug. 1894. He was in early life a carpenter, but subsequently studied under Guionnet and Rude, and devoted his attention chiefly to groups of animals. He received the bronze medal in the Great Exhibition of 1851, another medal in 1864, and a third at the Universal Exposition in 1867. Among noted works by him are 'Eagle Defending its Quarry' (1852); 'Combat Between Two Tigers' (1878); 'Rhinoceros Attacked by Tigers.'

Cain, Richard Harvey, American clergyman: b. Greenbrier County, Va., 12 April 1825; d. Washington, D. C., 18 Jan. 1887. He entered the ministry at an early age; was elected to the South Carolina constitutional convention in 1867, and to the State Senate in 1868; was a member of Congress 1876–1880. He was made bishop in the African Methodist Episcopal Church and placed in charge of the churches in Louisiana and Texas, and later was transferred to the first Episcopal district of that church. While in Texas he organized Paul Quinn College in Waco.

Cain, William, American civil engineer: b. Hillsboro, N. C., 14 May 1847. He was graduated from the North Carolina Military Institute and has since been professor of mathematics and civil engineering in the University of North Carolina. He has published 'Theory of Voussoir, Solid and Braced Arches' (1874); 'Maximum Stresses in Framed Bridges' (1878); 'Solid and Braced Elastic Arches' (1879); 'Symbolic Algebra' (1884); 'Practical Designing of Retaining Walls' (1888).

Caine, Thomas Henry Hall, English novelist and dramatist: b. Runcorn, Cheshire, 14 May 1853. He received his education in the Isle of Man and at Liverpool, and qualified as an architect, but abandoned architecture in order to become a journalist. He lived in London with Dante Gabriel Rossetti from 1881 till the latter's death in 1882, and in that year appeared his 'Recollections of Rossetti.' He had previously published 'Richard III. and Macbeth' (1877), a critical work, and 'Sonnets of Three Centuries' (1882). In 1883 appeared his 'Cobwebs of Criticism,' a review of the contemporary critiques of Wordsworth, Shelley, Byron, Keats, and other poets; and in 1887 he contributed to the Great Writers series a 'Life of Coleridge.' His first novel was 'The Shadow of a Crime' (1885), followed by 'A Son of Hagar'; but 'The Deemster' (1887) (dramatised as 'Ben-ma-Chree'), first brought him fame. His subsequent novels include 'The Bondman' (1890); 'The Scapegoat' (1891); 'The Prophet' (1892); 'The Manxman' (1894); 'The Christian' (1897); 'The Eternal City' (1901); 'The Prodigal Son' (1904). Of 'The Christian' nearly 100,000 copies were sold in England, and as many more in the United States, within the first year after publication.

On both continents it provoked great discussion, the verdict in England being generally unfavorable to the motive of the book, while in the United States it was generally favorable. It was immediately translated into most of the languages of Europe, and provoked the same divided opinion everywhere. He has traveled in Morocco, Iceland, Russia, and North America, and acted in Canada as representative of the Society of Authors in negotiations concerning Canadian copyright. His most successful novels deal with Manx life, in the description of which he reveals intimate knowledge of his subject and considerable literary power.

Caique, kä'ĕk, a light boat or skiff much used in the Levant, and particularly in the Bosphorus.

Caird, kärd, Edward, Scottish philosopher: b. Greenock, 22 March 1835. He was educated in his native town and at the universities of Glasgow and Oxford; was a Fellow and tutor of Merton College, and was professor of moral philosophy at Glasgow from 1866 till 1893, the year of his appointment as master of Balliol College, Oxford, in which post he succeeded Prof. Jowett. He is author of 'Account of the Philosophy of Kant' (1878); 'Social Philosophy and Religion of Comte' (1885); 'Hegel' in Blackwood's Series of Philosophical Classics (1883); 'Critical Philosophy of Immanuel Kant' (1889); 'Essays on Literature and Philosophy' (1892); and 'The Evolution of Religion' (1893). He is a brother of John Caird (q.v.).

Caird, John, Scottish clergyman: b. Greenock, 15 Dec. 1820; d. London, 30 July 1898. He was educated at the Grammar School of Greenock, and at Glasgow University, where he took a high place both in arts and divinity. Having entered the ministry of the Church of Scotland, in 1845 he became minister of Newton-upon-Ayr, and two years later was transferred to Lady Yester's parish church, Edinburgh. Between that date and 1862, when he became professor of divinity in Glasgow University, he was minister of Errol, Perthshire (1849–57), and of Park Church, Glasgow (1857–62). In 1873 he was elected principal of his university, a position which he held till his resignation in 1898. He died before his resignation had taken effect. He published sermons (his sermon 'Religion in Common Life,' preached before the queen, had an immense circulation, and was described by Dean Stanley as the greatest sermon of the century); 'Introduction to the Philosophy of Religion' (1880); and 'Spinoza' (1888) in Blackwood's Philosophical Classics. In 1899 appeared 'The Fundamental Ideas of Christianity,' under the editorship of his brother, being the Gifford Lectures delivered in 1891–2 and 1895–6, accompanied by a memoir of the author.

Cairn, kärn (Gaelic carn), a name given to heaps of stones, common in Great Britain, particularly in Scotland and Wales, generally of a conical form. Some are evidently sepulchral, containing urns, stone chests, bones, etc. Others were erected to commemorate some remarkable event, and others appear to have been intended for religious rites. See TUMULUS.

Cairnes, kärnz, John Elliot, British political economist: b. Castle Bellingham, County Louth, 26 Dec. 1823; d. London, 8 July 1875.

After an education at Kingstown and Chester he was for a time employed in his father's brewery at Grogheda, but ultimately went to Trinity College, Dublin. He was graduated in 1854, and two years afterward was appointed Whately professor of political economy at Dublin. His first series of lectures was published in 1857, under the title 'The Character and Logical Method of Political Economy.' In 1859 he was elected professor of political economy and jurisprudence in Queen's College, Galway, and seven years later was appointed to the corresponding chair in University College, London; but in 1872 the state of his health compelled him to give up active teaching. He had been called to the Irish bar in 1857, but he hardly ever practised. During the later years of his life he suffered much from the effects of an accident to his knee, which befell him while hunting in 1860, and for some time before his death was completely crippled. In 1862 he issued a work in defense of the northern States of America, entitled 'The Slave Power,' which had a very large circulation. The most important of his others works are 'Essays on Political Economy, Theoretical and Applied' (1873); and 'Some Leading Principles of Political Economy newly Expounded' (1874). He takes rank as one of the leading economists of the 19th century.

Cairnes, William Elliott, English army officer: d. London, 19 April 1902. He obtained a lieutenant's commission in 1884, and became a captain in 1890. He published 'The Absent-Minded War'; 'The Army from Within'; 'The Coming Waterloo'; and 'Lord Roberts as a Soldier in Peace and War.'

Cairngorm, kärn-görm' (that is, "blue cairn"), a mountain of Scotland belonging to the Grampian Hills, on the border of Banffshire and Inverness-shire, three miles north of Ben Macdhui in Aberdeenshire. Its summit is 4,084 feet above the level of the sea, and its sides are clothed with pine forests. The group of mountains to which it belongs is known as the Cairngorm Mountains. It is particularly celebrated for the regular, brownish yellow crystals of quartz found on it and known as cairngorms. These are also found in many other places, and are much used for seals, brooches, etc. Specimens weighing a good many pounds are sometimes found.

Cairns, kärnz, **Hugh MacCalmont** (EARL), Irish lawyer and parliamentary debater: b. County Down, Ireland, 1819; d. Bournemouth, England, 2 April 1885. He was called to the bar at the Middle Temple in 1844, and was returned to Parliament for Belfast in 1852, and quickly made his mark in the House by his fluency and readiness in debate. He became Queen's Counsel in 1856, in 1858 solicitor-general, and in 1866 attorney-general under Lord Derby. Later in the same year he was a judge of appeal, and in 1867 was created Baron Cairns. Under Disraeli's premiership he became Lord Chancellor in 1868, and again in 1874, and was created Viscount Garmoyle and Earl Cairns in 1878. For some years he led the Conservatives in the House of Lords with equal dexterity and vigor, and is ranked among the finest parliamentary orators of recent years.

Cairns, John, English theologian: b. Berwickshire, 23 Aug. 1818; d. Edinburgh, 14 March 1892. He was ordained at Berwick in 1845, where he remained till 1876, becoming also in 1867 professor of theology in the United Presbyterian Church, and principal in 1879. He was an eminent preacher and the author of the article 'Kant' in the 'Encyclopædia Britannica' (8th ed.); contributed to the new edition of Herzog's 'Real-encyklopädie'; and published the 'Life of John Brown, D.D.' (1860); and 'Unbelief in the 18th Century' (1881). See Cairns, 'Principal Cairns' (1903).

Cairo, kī'rō (Arabic, *El Kâhira,* "The Victorious," or *Masr el Kâhira*), Egypt, capital of the country and largest town of Africa, situated on the right bank of the Nile, about seven miles above the point where it divides to form the two main branches of its delta. The town is built between the river-bank and the northwestern end of the hills known as Jebel Mokattam, on whose most advanced spur stands the citadel in a commanding position well above the rest of the city. During the last 40 years the town has lost much of its Oriental character, but the Arab quarters still present a maze of very narrow streets lined by curious buildings in endless variety of style. The houses are mostly built of yellow limestone, with flat roofs; and many of them have small gardens behind. In the more modern parts of the city the streets are broader, and many of them are lined by trees and lighted by gas. The European quarter, known as Ismailiyeh, forms the western part of modern Cairo, and its centre is the octagonal Ezbekiyeh Garden (20½ acres), with plants from many regions and with an artificial pond. Here, too, are many cafés, concert-halls, and other similar buildings. Among the more notable buildings of the European quarter are the consulates, the opera-house, open in winter, the Italian summer theatre, English and German churches, the ministerial offices, and the barracks. The chief business street of Cairo, known as Muski, runs east-southeastward from the neighborhood of the Ezbekiyeh, and the Boulevard Mehemet Ali extends from about the same place southeastward to the citadel. Cairo has more than 500 mosques, but many of them are wholly or partly in ruins. The finest of all is the Sultan Hasan Mosque, a truly noble building with a lofty minaret. Others worthy of mention are: that built in the 9th century by Ahmed ibn Tulûn in imitation of the one at Mecca; the Hakim Mosque, dating from the beginning of the 11th century; the Hosen Mosque of the son of Ali, Mohammed's son-in-law; the Sitti-Zeynab Mosque, named after a grandchild of the prophet; the Azhar Mosque, famous for its schools of theology, which are attended by Mohammedans from all parts of the world; and the Alabaster Mosque of the citadel, with the tomb of Mehemet Ali, the finest of the modern mosques. The tombs in the burying-grounds outside the city, many of them in the form of mosques, also deserve mention, especially those known as the tombs of the caliphs. The most important gate of the city is the Bab-en-Nasr, through which large numbers of pilgrims pass every year on their way to Mecca. The mosques contain valuable libraries, but the chief library of the city is the viceregal one, founded in 1870, and now con-

TOMBS OF THE MAMELUKES, CAIRO.

taining about 60,000 volumes, largely in manuscript. The trade of Cairo is large and the bazaars and markets are numerous, there being special bazaars for gold and silver smiths, tapestry merchants, saddlers, armourers, shoemakers, etc. Beside the numerous Mohammedan places of worship Cairo contains English, French, German, Coptic, and other churches and Jewish synagogues, and there are European schools and hospitals. The Egyptian Institute, founded at Alexandria in 1859, is now located in Cairo.

The suburb of Bulak, in the northwest of the town, opposite the island of Bulak, forms the port of Cairo, and its narrow streets present a busy scene of Oriental life. The island of Bulak and the left bank of the Nile are reached by a great iron bridge, and there is also a railway and general traffic bridge below the island. To the southwest of the modern town and also on the Nile bank stands the suburb of Old Cairo or Masr el-Atika. On the left bank of the river, almost directly opposite Old Cairo, is the suburb of Gizeh. It has government buildings, a zoological garden, etc., but its chief attraction is the great Egyptological Museum formerly in Bulak, but removed here in 1889. From Gizeh a road and a tramway lead southwestward to the famous group of pyramids called the pyramids of Gizeh. On the island of Roda, between Gizeh and Old Cairo, the celebrated Nilometer still stands. Cairo enjoys a very mild climate, and is in consequence visited in winter by many Europeans suffering from chest and lung ailments. Many of these stay at Helwan, a small place about 14 miles south-southeast of the town. Cairo is in railway communication with Alexandria, Damietta, Suez, etc., and with Upper Egypt, and the Fresh-water Canal connects it with Ismailia and Suez. In 1896 electric tramways were introduced in the most important streets. Cairo is the residence of the Khedive, the seat of a Coptic and a Greek Orthodox patriarch, and it contains all the highest public offices of the country. El-Fostat, "The Tent," now Old Cairo, was founded by Amru, lieutenant of Caliph Omar, in 640 A.D. In 969, when the Fatimite dynasty gained possession of the country, the new city to the north was founded. Saladin surrounded it with walls of stone and built the citadel. He also constructed a wooden aqueduct from the Nile to the citadel, a work afterward replaced by the still existing aqueduct of stone. Cairo was taken by the French in 1798, and was occupied by the British in 1882, after the battle of Tel-el-Kebir. Pop. (1897) 570,062, including Fellahin, Copts, Turks, Arabs, and other Orientals, beside about 25,000 foreigners from the chief European countries, especially Italy, Greece, France, Austria, England, and Germany.

Cairo, Ill., city, port of entry and county-seat of Alexander County, situated at the junction of the Mississippi and other rivers, 150 miles southeast of Saint Louis on the Illinois Central, Cleveland, C., C. & St. L. and other railroads. The city was first settled in 1838 by William Bird and was incorporated as a city in 1857. Cairo is governed by a mayor and a council of 14 members elected for two years, who select the other administrative officers. It has a large transit trade in agriculture and lumber, and affords a good market for the produce and trade of the Mississippi Valley. The industries include a sewing-machine factory, box factories, handle factory, flour mills, wagon works, foundries, etc. The city has five banks with a combined capital of $400,000 and a surplus of $350,000. A United States custom house is located in Cairo and it has a free public library, court-house, United States Marine Hospital and Saint Mary's Infirmary. The Federal Government during the Civil War used the town as a depot for military supplies. For many years, until levees were built, the city suffered from frequent floods which greatly impeded its progress, but it is now growing in wealth and population, has many fine churches and an excellent system of education. Pop. (1904) 16,235.

E. E. ELLIS,
Editor Cairo Daily Telegram.

Caisson, a water-tight chest or casing, used in the construction of bridges, quays, etc., large enough to contain an entire pier, which is built in it, the caisson being sunk to the bed of the river. (See FOUNDATION.) The pneumatic caisson has an air-chamber in which men may work at the bottom of the water, air being forced in to keep the water out, and the air-space being entered by what is called an air-lock. This form of caisson is used where the water is too deep to permit of the construction of a coffer-dam. The name is also applied to an air-tight structure which is sunk below a vessel by the admission of water, and raises the vessel when the water is pumped out; and to the boat-shaped gate used to close the entrance to a dry dock. (See DOCK.) In military language, the ammunition carriage attached to a battery of artillery. In architecture caisson signifies a panel left in a vaulted ceiling, or more rarely in a flat ceiling or a wall. They are sometimes square or of other forms, but the most common arrangement is a series of sunken octagons with much smaller sunken squares set diagonally between. The caisson was decorated with mouldings and ornaments of stucco painted and gilded.

Caisson Disease, or **Compressed Air Disease,** a disorder occurring among workers in compressed air, as in bridge-caissons. After working in an atmosphere of compressed air the return to normal pressure is brought about gradually in an anteroom, which is called an "air-lock." If this transfer takes place rapidly the symptoms may appear quite suddenly. The usual factors are high pressure, poor ventilation, and prolonged exposure. Old people, those addicted to alcohol, and those with organic disease are most susceptible. Slight transient symptoms, such as ringing of the ears and giddiness, are not uncommon; more severe symptoms are rare. When the disease is well marked we may have rupture of the ear-drum, nose-bleed, spitting of blood, pain in the stomach, vomiting, various neuralgic pains, paralysis — especially of the legs and bladder, incoherent speech, prostration, and loss of consciousness. The disease lasts from a few hours to several days, but the paralysis may persist for months. The fatal cases show congestion of the internal organs, especially the brain. Death may be sudden or occur in three or four days. When the symptoms come on suddenly the patient should be at once returned to the compressed air and given oxygen to breathe.

Caités, or **Caetés,** kä-e-tåz', an extinct tribe of Brazilian Indians which, up to the close of the 16th century, inhabited a large portion of the eastern coast region north of the Sao Francisco. Of the Tupi race, they were more warlike than other branches of that family, and, while they exhibited traits that indicated at least a crude sort of civilization, such as life in fixed villages and the practice of agriculture, they were the most cannibalistic of all the Brazilian tribes. In 1554 they murdered the bishop of Bahia and his companions, who were shipwrecked on that coast, and their ravages upon the settlements of the colonists aroused an enmity that finally resulted in their complete extinction.

Caithness, kåth'nĕs, Scotland, most northern county of the mainland; area, 686 square miles. The surface is generally level or undulating, and there are few hills of any height, except on the Sutherland border. Much of the surface is deep moss or peaty moor, but there is a fair proportion of fertile land in the eastern part. About one quarter of the whole surface is under crops and rotation grasses, or in permanent pasture. Of corn crops oats is by far the most important. Only a very small portion of the county is wooded. The coast is prevailingly bold and rocky, the chief headlands being Dunnet Head on the north coast, Duncansby Head at the northeast corner, Noss Head and the Ord on the east coast. The largest bays are Dunnet Bay on the north and Sinclair's Bay on the east, but Thurso Bay and Wick Bay are also noteworthy. There are many lakes, some of them very attractive. The largest is Loch Watten, near the centre of the county. Of the rivers only the Thurso, the Forss, and the Wick need be mentioned. Caithness is poor in metallic minerals, but excellent flagstones have been quarried for many years and form one of the chief exports of the county. Many of the inhabitants are engaged in fishing, and Wick is one of the chief centres of the Scottish herring-fishery. The manufactures are mainly subsidiary to its other industries. Wick, the county town, is a royal burgh, and Thurso is the only other town. The antiquities of Caithness are numerous, and include old castles, so-called Picts' houses, monoliths, etc. The county returns one member to Parliament, and Wick joins with Kirkwall, Tain, and other places in sending another representative. Pop. (1901) 33,850.

Caius, kä'yŭs. See GAIUS.

Caius Cestius, kä'yŭs ses'ti-us, **Pyramid of,** a sepulchral monument, a pyramid of the time of Augustus, standing at Rome. Built of brick and stone and incrusted with white marble, it is more than 114 feet in height, while each side of the base measures 90 feet. This contains a small burial chamber, which is painted with arabesque.

Caius, kĕz, **John,** English physician, the founder of Caius College, Cambridge University: b. Norwich 6 Oct. 1510; d. Cambridge 29 July 1573. His name was Kaye or Key, which he Latinized into Caius. He took his degrees at Gonville Hall, Cambridge, and was chosen Fellow of his college. While at Cambridge he distinguished himself by various translations from the classics. He spent some time in travel-ing on the Continent, studied medicine at Padua, under Montanus and Vesalius, and took his doctor's degree at Bologna (1541). In 1542 he lectured at Padua on the Greek text of Aristotle, and in the following year made a tour through Italy, visiting the principal libraries, in order to compare the manuscripts of Galen and Celsus. He returned to his native country in 1544, and practised, first at Cambridge, then at Shrewsbury, and afterward at Norwich. He was appointed by Henry VIII. lecturer on anatomy to the company of surgeons, London. In 1547 he became Fellow of the college of physicians, and was appointed court physician to the young king Edward VI., which appointment he retained under Queens Mary and Elizabeth. In the reign of the latter, an exciting controversy arose between the surgeons and physicians of London, as to the right of the former to administer internal remedies for the sciatica. Caius argued the negative so ably on behalf of the physicians that the decision was against the right of the surgeons to continue the practice of administering medicines. He was elected president of the college of physicians for seven years in succession. There is extant a book of the college annals from 1555 to 1572 written by him in Latin, the earliest account we have of the transactions of that college. He was dismissed from the royal service in 1568 on suspicion of favoring the Catholic party. He obtained permission to endow and raise Gonville Hall into a college, which still bears his name (Gonville and Caius College), and accepted the mastership thereof. The last days of his life were passed in the seclusion of his college. His works are numerous, on various subjects; many of them have been reprinted in modern times.

Caius (kĕz) **College.** See GONVILLE AND CAIUS COLLEGE.

Caix, kä-ĕks, **Napoleone,** Italian philologist: b. Bozzolo, near Mantua, 1845. His education was obtained at Cremona and Pisa, and in 1869 he was called to the chair of ancient languages in the Lyceum of Parma, becoming professor of Romanic languages and comparative philology in the Institute of Higher Studies in Florence in 1873. He has been a prolific writer and among his many works are 'Saggio sulla storia della lingua e dei dialetti d' Italia' (1872); 'Sulla lingua del Contrasto' (1876); 'Le origini della lingua Poetica Italiana' (1880).

Cajabamba, kä-hạ-bäm-bä', Ecuador, capital of the province of Chimborazo, 102 miles south of Quito, on the arid plateau of Topi, at an elevation of 9,480 feet. The former town of Riobamba, founded on this site in 1533, was in 1797 overwhelmed by an earthquake in which 30,000 lives were lost. Pop. 16,000.

Cajamarca, kä-hạ-mär-cä', or **Caxamarca,** Peru, the name of a department and city in the valley of the upper Marañon, or Amazon. The department lies in a very mountainous region. Pop. 213,391. The city stands on the eastern declivity of the Andes in a rich silver mining district, 75 miles from Trujillo. It contains several handsome churches, and flourishing manufactories of woolens and cutlery. The inhabitants are considered the best workmen in silver and iron in Peru. An extensive trade between the inland provinces and Lambeyeque and Truxillo is carried on through this town. Woolen fabrics form the chief exports, and European manufactures, sugar, brandy, wine, iron, steel, and other articles are imported in return. In the vicinity are the baths of the Incas, and a volcanic lake, into which, according to tradition, were cast the throne and regalia of the Peruvian monarchs, the last of whom, Atahuallpa, perished here by the hands of Pizarro. Pop. 12,000.

Cajeput, kăj'e-pŭt, or **Cajuput Oil,** the volatile oil obtained from the leaves of the cajeput-tree (*Melaleuca cajuputi* or *minor*), belonging to the order *Myrtaceæ.* This tree has lanceolate, aromatic leaves and spikes of odorless flowers, and is common in many islands of the Malay Archipelago. Booro, one of the Moluccas, yields the bulk of the oil exported. It is mostly sent to Singapore, whence it is reexported to other countries. The oil is of a pale-green color, very liquid, lighter than water, of a strong smell, resembling camphor, and of a strong pungent taste. It is often adulterated with other essential oils. The color of the oil depends on the presence of a little copper, which must be removed before the oil is fit for use in medicine, in which it has many applications, being used as a carminative, an antispasmodic, a rubefacient, and a sudorific. *Kayuputi,* the native name of the tree, means "white wood," and refers to the color of the bark.

Cajetan, kăj'ĕ-tan, or **Cajetanus,** Tommaso de **Vio,** Italian cardinal: b. Gaeta, 25 July 1470; d. Rome, 9 Aug. 1534. He entered the order of Dominican friars, graduated as a doctor, and was elected general of his order in 1508. When Pope Julius II. was summoned to appear before the council of cardinals assembled at Pisa and afterward at Milan, in the interest of King Louis XII. of France, Cajetan undertook its defense, asserting that to the Pope alone belonged the power of convening a council. He was appointed cardinal in 1517 by Leo X., and sent as a legate in Germany to bring the emperor Maximilian and the king of Denmark into the league formed against the Turks. His efforts to make Luther recant his doctrines proved in vain. In 1519 he was present, as Roman legate, at the assembly of the electors of the empire, and sided with the partisans of Don Carlos of Spain, who was elected emperor under the name of Charles V. Then he returned to Rome, but was soon ordered by Adrian VI. to Hungary, which was invaded by the Turks. In 1524 he was recalled to Rome by Clement VII. On the capture of Rome in 1527, being taken prisoner by the imperial troops, under the command of the constable of Bourbon, he had to pay 5,000 crowns as a ransom for his liberty. See Schilbach, 'De Vita ac Scriptis de Vio Cajetani' (1881).

Cajigal de la Vega, Francisco Antonio, frän-thĕs'kō än-tō'nĕ-ō kä-hē-gäl dä la vä'gạ, Spanish colonial governor: b. Santander, 5 Feb. 1695; d. there, 30 April 1777. He held the post of governor of Santiago, Cuba, 1738–47, and in 1742 during the course of the war between Spain and England, repelled an attack by Admiral Vernon. He was governor-general of Cuba 1747–60, and while in office established an arsenal and a navy yard at Havana. During a part

of 1760 and the year following he was viceroy of Mexico.

Cajori, cä-jō'rē, Florian, Swiss-American mathematician: b. Saint Aignan, Switzerland, 28 Feb. 1859. He came to the United States in 1875 and studied at the University of Wisconsin. He has been professor of mathematics in Colorado College from 1898, besides holding similar positions prior to that date. He has published 'The Teaching and History of Mathematics in the United States' (1890); 'A History of Mathematics' (1894); 'A History of Elementary Mathematics' (1896); 'A History of Physics' (1899).

Cakchiquel, käk-chē-kăl', a tribe of Mayan stock occupying northern and central Guatemala. They are probably an off-shoot of the Quichés, as they resemble that tribe closely in customs and language. They were conquered by Alvarado in 1524, and at that time had a well-developed civilzation, as is shown by their architectural ruins and their system of hieroglyphic writings.

Cake-urchin, Sand-cake, or **Sand-dollar,** a flat, round sea-urchin (*Echinarachnius parma*) which lives buried in the sand in the shallow portions of the North Atlantic, from low-water mark to 40 fathoms. It is occasionally thrown ashore on beaches. The body is protected by limestone plates, and the "ambulacra," or delicate suckers, are arranged in a rosette on the upper side of the animal, the mouth being on the under side. See also SEA-URCHIN.

Cal'aba-oil, an excellent illuminating oil obtained from calaba-nuts, the seeds of *Calophyllum calaba*, a tree of the order *Guttiferæ* that flourishes in Brazil and the West Indies, and yields useful timber.

Calabar, kä-lä-bär', or **kal-ạ-bär',** Africa, the former name of a district on the west coast, extending eastward from the Niger delta, and now included in the Niger Territories. The name is now applied to two towns and two rivers in that region. Old Calabar is a port in southern Nigeria, situated on the east bank of the estuary of the Cross River at the point where it receives the waters of the Old Calabar River. It contains, among other buildings, a Presbyterian Mission Institute for natives, a large prison, good hospitals, and marine workshops. Its climate, like that of all coast settlements in this part of the continent, is very unhealthy. The rainfall is very great, tornadoes are frequent, and the temperature is very high. The value of its exports, consisting chiefly of palm-oil, palm kernels, and rubber, exceeds $1,000,000, and its imports are valued at rather more. New Calabar is situated farther west on one of the mouths of the Niger known by the same name. Its trade is less than that of Old Calabar, but is nevertheless of considerable value.

Calabar Bean, or **Ordeal Bean,** the brown or reddish-brown kidney-shaped seed of *Physostigma venenosum*, a climbing, woody, west African vine of the pea family (*Leguminosæ*). The flowers are purple, resembling the sweet-pea, and each pod contains two or three seeds, which are about one inch long with a blackish groove along the convex edge; and in the interior an air-cavity which enables the heavy seeds to float on water. This bean is very poisonous, and has been much used in paste or in infusion in the trial by ordeal of west African medicine-men. If the person accused of witchcraft or crime vomited the mixture, he was declared innocent; if he did not vomit, death ensued. At one time 70 children in Liverpool ate some of the beans; one who ate four seeds did not vomit and died; all the rest vomited and recovered. In poisoning with this bean vomiting should be encouraged, the stomach washed out, and atropine, the antidote, administered.

Cal'abash Gourd, Bottle Gourd, White Pumpkin, *Lagenaria vulgaris,* the only cultivated or common wild species of its genus which belongs to the natural order *Cucurbitaceæ,* distinguished from the species of the closely related genus *Cucurbita* by having white instead of yellow flowers; separated instead of united anthers, and seeds with distended edges. It is a climbing annual vine, 30 to 40 feet long, with a musky odor and sticky feeling. It is a native of tropical Asia and Africa, and is grown in warm countries for its very variable smooth, hard-shelled fruit, which, while young and soft, is used by some races as food; but much more generally the ripe fruits are used for making utensils such as dippers, cups, and pitchers. Some of the largest fruits are used in India and other Eastern countries in raft-construction and for buoys. These fruits range in size from a few inches to five feet or even more, and from their resemblance to various objects are called Hercules' club, dipper, bottle, snake, sugar trough, etc. The plant is often cultivated in the southern United States, but is less freuently seen in the north. where the season is usually too short for the fruits to fully mature. A sunny exposure in warm, quick soil, and cultivation similar to that given squashes and melons will suit the plant well.

Calabash Nutmeg, a tree (*Monodora muristica*) of the order *Anonaceæ,* introduced into Jamaica probably from west Africa. The fruit resembles small calabashes; hence the name. It is called also American nutmeg, or Jamaica nutmeg.

Calabash-tree, a tree (*Crescentia cujete*) of the West Indies and the continent of America, of the order *Bignoniaceæ,* about the height and dimensions of an apple-tree, with crooked, horizontal branches, wedge-shaped leaves, pale-white flowers on the trunk and branches, and a roundish fruit, from two inches to a foot in diameter. The greenish-yellow skin of the fruit encloses a thin, hard, and almost woody shell, which is used for the same purposes as water-cans, goblets, cups, etc. So hard and close-grained are these shells that when they contain fluid they may even be put several times on the fire as kettles, without any injury. When intended for ornamental vessels, they are sometimes highly polished, and have figures engraven upon them, which are variously tinged with indigo and other colors. The calabash contains a pale-yellow juicy pulp of an unpleasant taste, which is esteemed a valuable remedy in several disorders, both external and internal.

Calabazar, kä-lạ-bạ-thär', Cuba, a city of the province of Santa Clara, situated 20 miles north of the city of Santa Clara. It has a fine municipal building. Pop. 1,575.

Calabozo, kä-lạ-bŏ-thŏ', Venezuela, a town in the state of Miranda (Guzman Blanco), 120 miles south-southwest of Caracas, on the left bank of the river Guarico, in the midst of the Llanos. It was founded in 1730, is tolerably well built, and has rather a pleasing appearance. Its church, though not very handsome, is commodious. The principal wealth of the inhabitants consists of cattle. The neighboring ponds abound in electrical eels. Pop. 6,000.

Calabrese (käl-ạ-brä'zĕ) Il, Italian painter whose real name was MATTIA PRETI (q.v.): b. Calabria, 1613; d. Malta, 1699. He was chiefly celebrated for his frescoes. He worked for a considerable time in Malta, being employed in executing pictures on the walls of the cathedral.

Cala'bria, Italy, division of the kingdom, comprising the southwest peninsula or toe of Italy, from about 40° N. lat. to the Strait of Messina; area estimated at 6,663 square miles. It was formerly divided into three provinces — Calabria Citra, the most northerly; Calabria Ultra I., the most southerly; and Calabria Ultra II., between the two former; but these have been renamed respectively Cosenza, Reggio, and Catanzaro. The central region is occupied by the great Apennine ridge, wild and bleak, to which, however, whole colonies with their cattle migrate in the summer. The flats near the coast are marshy and unhealthy, and inhabited by herds of buffaloes; but the valleys at the foot of the mountains are well watered and produce most luxuriant vegetation. The vine, the orange and lemon trees, the fig, the olive, and all the fruits of southern climes, grow there to perfection. The climate was reckoned salubrious in ancient times; but in some places the accumulation of stagnant water produces disease in the hot season. Corn, rice, saffron, anise, licorice, madder, flax, hemp, olives, almonds, cotton, and sugar-cane are raised in abundance. Sheep, horned cattle, and horses are numerous. Near Reggio a kind of mussel is found, called *Pinna marina,* from whose silky byssus or beard a beautiful fabric is manufactured, remarkable for its extreme lightness and warmth. Coral is also obtained. The quarries and pits afford alabaster, marble, gypsum, alum, chalk, rock-salt, lapis lazuli, and the fine copper renowned in ancient times.

Calabria corresponds with the ancient Bruttium and part of Lucania, while the ancient Calabria corresponds to the heel of Italy. It early received numerous Greek colonies, and formed part of Magna Græcia. In 268 B.C. it was conquered by the Romans. The Saracens had occupied the greater part of it when it was conquered by the Normans in the 11th century. Since then it has constantly followed the fate of the kingdom of the Two Sicilies, with which it was united to the kingdom of Italy in 1860. It was visited by continuous earthquakes from 1783–87. The greater part of the inhabitants are poor. Formerly the country was much infested by brigands and brigandage is not yet entirely extinct. The language of the people is a corruption of the Italian. Pop. (1900) 1,366,982.

Caladium, kạ-lä'dĭ-ŭm, a genus of succulent perennial herbs of the natural order *Aroideæ.* There are about a dozen species, natives of tropical America. Several are largely planted for ornament, for which their long petioled, often brilliantly marked, large, arrow-shaped leaves specially commend them. They give a rich subtropical effect in outdoor or greenhouse planting, and, being of rather easy culture, are very popular. The perennial rhizome is planted in rich, moist soil in the greenhouse, and transplanted in the garden after danger of frost has passed. Plenty of water is essential. In autumn the rootstock is dug before frost touches it, and stored in a cool, dry cellar.

Calah, kā'lạ, an ancient city mentioned in Genesis x. 12 as one of those built by Asur. It is the city called Kalchu in the Assyrian inscriptions, which say that it was founded by Shalmaneser I. about 1250 B.C. It was rebuilt by Asurnazirpal about 880 B.C., who erected a wall on the northern side and a large palace. His successors also built palaces in the city. It is now known as Nimrud, where a number of important ruins and inscriptions have been found. among them the so-called "black obelisk" which tells of the tribute paid by Jehu, king of Israel, to Shalmaneser II.

Calahorra, kä-lạ-ōr'rạ, Spain, a town of Old Castile, near the south side of the Ebro, in the province of Logroño, and 40 miles east-southeast of the city of Logroño. It is a bishop's see, and contains three parish churches and three convents. In 78 B.C. this town, then called Calagurris, siding wth Sertorius, was besieged by Afranius, one of Pompey's generals, and the inhabitants reduced to such extremity that they fed on their wives and children; whence the Romans were wont to call any grievous famine *fames Calagurritana.* Quintilian was born here. Pop. 8,821.

Calais, kạ-lā, France, a seaport town, and fortified place of the first class, in the department of Pas-de-Calais, 20 miles northeast from Boulogne, on the Strait of Dover, and about 23½ miles southeast of the port of Dover. It is situated at the junction of several canals, and by railway is directly connected with Paris, from which it is distant 185 miles. The town consists of two portions, almost entirely separated by basins or water areas connected with the harbor accommodation. These are Calais proper or the old town farther to the north, and St. Pierre or the new town lying to the south, and incorporated with the other portion only in 1885. The whole is enclosed by a new line of circumvallation, and is also defended by a citadel and detached forts and batteries. On the land side the country is flat and marshy, and can be laid under water to strengthen the defenses. The streets are broad and well paved, the houses substantially built of brick, and the hotels in general excellent. The chief square is the Place d'Armes, where the Hôtel de Ville, built in 1740 (restored in 1867), is situated. The principal church, Notre Dame, contains a fine altar-piece in Genoa marble. Other noteworthy objects are the Hôtel de Guise, originally founded by Edward III. of England; the column erected to commemorate the landing of Louis XVIII. in 1814; theatre; barracks; and the Hôtel Dessin. Calais is the seat of a commercial court and chamber of commerce, and has a college, a commercial school, school of design, school of hydrography, etc.

The harbor is accessible at all states of the tide, and is entered between two long piers. The works include a dry or graving dock 426 feet long at bottom, and having a depth of water on the sill of 28 feet 8 inches (at spring tides). There is also a wet-dock 27 acres in extent, with a depth of 25 feet. Calais is one of the principal ports for the debarkation of travelers from England (who are landed at the new railway station), there being day and night communication with Dover by steamboat. The number of travelers arriving and departing by sea is considerably over 200,000 per annum. There is a submarine cable to England from this port. The manufactures of the town are important. The silk and cotton tulle or bobbinet trade employs about 15,000 artisans. Various other industries are also carried on, such as flax-spinning, engineering, net-making, brewing, etc. Vessels are built here, and fitted out for the cod, mackerel, and herring fisheries. A considerable trade is carried on in grain, wool, wine, sugar, timber, coal, etc., and not less than 55,000,000 of eggs are annually exported to England. Calais is a town of considerable antiquity. In 1347 it was taken by Edward III. of England, after a siege of 11 months. The famous incident of the six burgesses having their lives saved at the intercession of Queen Philippa belongs to this siege. In 1558 it was retaken by the Duke of Guise, being then the last relic of the French dominions of the Plantagenets, which at one time comprehended the half of France. Pop. (1901) 59,793.

Calais, kăl'ĭs, Me., city, port of entry, and county-seat of Washington County, situated on the St. Croix River, opposite St. Stephen, N. B., and on the St. Croix & P. and the Canadian P. R.R.'s, 120 miles east of Bangor. It is the extreme northeast seaport of the United States and is connected by steamship lines with Boston, Portland, and St. John, N. B. It has a large lumber trade and numerous foundries, machine shops, shipyards, and other extensive mechanical industries; a national bank, several newspapers, high and grammar schools, electric lights, a public library, and an assessed property valuation of $2,500,000. Pop. (1900) 7,665.

Calais, Pas de. See PAS-DE-CALAIS.

Cal'aite. See TURQUOISE.

Calaman'co, a woolen stuff made in the Netherlands, the warp of which is sometimes mixed with silk or goats' hair. It has a fine gloss, and is checkered in the warp, so that the checks are seen on one side only. It was fashionable in Addison's time.

Cal'amander Wood, a hard wood of Ceylon, obtained from a species of ebony-tree. See EBONY.

Cal'amary. See CEPHALOPODA, SQUID.

Calamatta, Luigi, Italian engraver: 1. Civita Vecchia, Italy, 12 July 1802; d. Milan, 8 March 1869. He was educated in Rome, but was much in Paris, and is sometimes spoken of as French. He founded a school of engravers in Brussels under government direction, and in his latest years was professor of drawing in the Academy of Milan. He is well known by his engraving of the head of Napoleon.

Calamba, ka-läm'bạ, Philippines, a town of the province of Laguna, situated in the southern part of the island of Luzon, about 30 miles southeast of Manila. It is connected with several important towns by highways, and has a telegraph station. Pop (1898) 11,480.

Calambac, aloes-wood, the product of a tree *(agila)* growing in China and some of the Indian islands. It is of a very light, spongy texture, and contains a soft, fragrant resin, which is chewed by the natives.

Calambuco, kä-lam-boo'kō, a very durable tree, found in the island of Luzon, Philippines. It is indestructible by ants, and is used for shipbuilding, making farming implements, etc.

Calame, Alexandre, ä-lĕks-ändr ka-läm, Swiss landscape artist: b. Vevey, Switzerland, 28 May 1810; d. Mentone, France, 17 March 1864. His life was passed mainly in Geneva, where a monument was erected to him in 1880. He was ranked among the best landscape painters of his day and he excelled the most, if not all, of his contemporaries in portraying Alpine scenery. Among works by him are: 'Bernese Oberland'; 'Wetterhorn'; 'Lake of Lucerne'; 'Shreckhorn'; 'Lake of the Four Cantons.'

Calamianes, kä-la-mē-ä'nĕs, a cluster of islands in the Philippine Archipelago, Busuanga, Calamian, and Linacapan are the most important; Busuanga is 36 miles long and 17 miles broad. They lie between lat. 11° 25′ and 12° 20′ N. and about lon. 120° E. The islands are mountainous and well timbered. They produce rice, cacao and great quantities of wax and honey. The climate is unhealthful. Pop. 14,291.

Cal'amine, a native basic silicate of zinc, having the formula $(ZnOH)_2SiO_3$. The mineral, now known as smithsonite, was formerly included here, but James Smithson, in 1803, showed that the two species are distinct. Calamine occurs in hemimorphic, rhombohedral crystals, usually white, with a vitreous lustre, a hardness of from 4.5 to 5, and a specific gravity of between 3.4 and 3.5. It also occurs in massive forms, sometimes mammillary in shape, and often cellular. In the United States calamine is found in New Jersey, Pennsylvania, Virginia, Missouri, Utah, and Montana. In localities where it occurs pure and in quantity, it constitutes a valuable ore of zinc.

Cal'amint, any plant of the genus *Calamintha,* belonging to the natural order *Labiatæ.* The plants are herbs or shrubs with usually entire leaves, and dense whorls of purple-white or yellow flowers, with a two-lipped corolla and didynamous stamens not projecting from the corolla. Five species are British. They all contain a volatile oil, and a pectoral medicine is obtained from them. In the United States several species are also found.

Cal'amis, Greek sculptor, statuary and embosser of Athens, a contemporary of Phidias, who flourished between 467 and 429 B.C. Pliny bestows the highest praises upon his horses. Among his most celebrated works were a statue in metal of Apollo Alexicacos, in Athens, in 429 B.C., and which has erroneously been supposed to be the Apollo Belvedere; a colossal statue of Apollo in bronze, 30 cubits in height, which was taken to Rome by Lucullus; and a Jupiter Ammon consecrated by Pindar at Thebes.

Cal'amite, a genus of fossil plants very characteristic of the coal measures. They occur in the Devonian rocks, and in other formations up to the Jurassic, in which one species is found. Their classification is not finally determined, but they are generally regarded as closely related to the *Equisetaceæ* or horsetails. The stalks are striated lengthwise, and interrupted with rings marking a regular articulation.

Calamity Jane. See BURKE, JANE.

Cal'amus, a remarkable genus of palms, the plants of which belong to the eastern countries, and are very different from most other palms, having slender, many-jointed, reed-like stems, often stretching to a length of several hundred feet. Some have the stems erect, others climb and trail among other trees on which they support themselves, hanging on by the hooked prickles that terminate their leaves. Some have leaves at intervals along the stem, others only at the extremity. The stems are hard, smooth, and siliceous on the surface, and from their toughness and pliancy they are much used in the countries where they grow for matting, strong ropes, plaited work, etc. Bridges over streams are frequently made of ropes formed by twisting up their stems, and the native vessels of the Eastern seas often carry cables of the same kind.

Calamus, a popular name for the sweet flag *(Acorus calamus),* of the natural order *Aroideæ.* This plant is found in wet land from Nova Scotia to Florida, and westward to Kansas and Minnesota. The pungent bitterish acrid root-stocks have been used in medicine, especially among the colored people of the southern United States. It is sometimes cultivated as an ornamental plant in wet places, and is attractive for its erect, sword-shaped leaves, which in one variety are striped with yellow.

Cal'amy, Edmund, Puritan clergyman: b. London, England, February 1600; d. there, 29 Oct. 1666. He studied at Pembroke Hall, Cambridge (1616-19), where he attached himself to the Calvinistic party, and in 1639 was chosen minister of St. Mary's, Aldermanbury, London. He entered warmly into the controversies of the time, and became noted as a leading man on the side of the Presbyterians. He had a principal share in the composition of 'Smectymnuus,' a work intended as a reply to Bishop Hall's 'Divine Right of Episcopacy,' and one of the most able and popular polemics of the day. Like the mass of the Presbyterian clergy, he was monarchical and not republican in his political opinions. He disapproved, therefore, of the execution of Charles, and of Cromwell's protectorate, and did not hesitate to avow his attachment to the Royalist cause. He was ejected for nonconformity in 1662.

Calamy, Edmund, English clergyman, grandson of the preceding: b. London, 5 April 1671; d. there, 3 June 1732. He was pastor of a congregation in Westminster and published an abridgement of Baxter's 'History of His Life and Times,' with a continuation; 'Inspiration of the Scriptures'; 'Life of Increase Mather'; 'Historical Account of My Own Life'; and also carried on through the press controversies with Bishop Hoadly and others.

Calancha, Antonio de la, Peruvian chronicler: b. Chuquisaca, 1584; d. Lima, 1 March 1654. He belonged to the Augustinian order, and was rector of the College of San Ildefonso in Lima. He wrote 'Crónica moralizada del Orden de S. Agustin en Peru,' first printed at Barcelona in 1638 in folio, which is an important source for early Peruvian history. It was continued in a second volume, never completed, however, by Fray Diego de Cordova (Lima 1653). The first volume was translated into French as 'Histoire de l' Eglise du Perou aux Antipodes' (Toulouse 1653), and Brulius' 'Historia Peruana' (Antwerp 1651) is called a translation. The Spanish bibliographer Antonio credits Calancha with another work. 'De immaculatæ Virginis Mariæ conceptionis certitudine' (Lima 1629), but had not seen a copy. Brunet merely quotes Antonio on this point.

Cal'anus, Indian philosopher, much esteemed by Alexander the Great. At the age of 73, 323 B.C., being seized with illness at Persepolis, he caused a funeral pile to be erected, which he ascended with a composed countenance, and expired in the flames, saying, that having lost his health and seen Alexander, life had no more charms for him.

Calas, Jean, zhŏñ kä-lạs, or kä-lạ, French judicial martyr: b. Languedoc, 1698; d. Toulouse, 9 March 1762. Brought up in the Protestant religion, he had established himself as a merchant in Toulouse. He had four sons and two daughters whom he educated himself, and was held in general esteem, when he was suddenly accused of the crime of murdering one of his sons. In 1761 his eldest son, Marc Antoine, a young man of irregular habits and a gloomy disposition, was found strangled in his father's house. It was reported that the unfortunate youth had been put to death by his father because he wished to become a Catholic. Jean Calas and his whole family were arrested, and a prosecution instituted against him, in support of which numerous witnesses came forward. The parliament of Toulouse condemned him, by eight voices against five, to be tortured and then broken on the wheel; and on 9 March 1762, the sentence was executed. He suffered the torture with firmness, and protested his innocence to the last. The youngest son was banished forever, but the mother and servant were acquitted. The family of the unhappy man retired to Geneva. Voltaire, then at Ferney, became acquainted with them, and for three years exerted himself to defend the memory of Calas, and to direct attention to the defects of the criminal law. The widow and children of Calas also solicited a revision of the trial. Fifty judges once more examined the circumstances, and declared Calas altogether innocent, 9 March 1765. The king by his liberality sought to recompense the family for their undeserved losses, and people of the first rank emulated each other in endeavoring to relieve them. See Coquerel, 'Jean Calas et sa Famille' (1858).

Calasiao, kạ-lä-se-ä'ō, Philippines, a town of the province of Pangasinan, situated in the western part of the island of Luzon, a few miles from the coast of the Gulf of Lingayen. Pop. (1898) 13,750.

Calatafimi, kä-lạ-tä-fē'mē, Sicily, town in the western part of the island, in the district of Trapani, and 21 miles east-southeast of the city of Trapani. It is situated in a mountainous district, near the river Gaggera, is badly built, and has a ruinous castle on the summit of a neigh-

boring hill, now used as a prison. The environs are well cultivated and extremely fertile. In 1860 a battle took place here between Garibaldi's forces and Landi's Neapolitan troops, in which the latter were defeated. Pop. 10,964.

Calatagirone, käl-ta-je-rō'nä, or **Caltagirone** (ancient CALATA HIERONIS), Sicily, town in the province of, and 34 miles southwest of Catania. It stands on two hills, and consists generally of spacious, clean, and well-built streets. There is a fine promenade and market-place, beside which stands the old castle. It is the see of a bishop, and has several churches and a college. Its inhabitants are said to be the best workmen in the island. It has a considerable commerce, and is celebrated for the manufacture of terra-cotta ware. It was fortified by the Saracens, and wrested from them by the Genoese. Roger Guiscard gave it important privileges. Pop. about 34,000.

Calatayud, kạ-lä-tạ-yood', Spain, the second city of Aragon, 45 miles southwest of Saragossa. It stands on the Jalon, near its confluence with the Jiloca, at the foot of two rocky heights crowned with the ruins of Moorish forts. The upper or Moorish town is a very wretched place; but the modern town below is well built, and contains many remarkable edifices, among which the most conspicuous are the Church of Santa Maria, once a mosque, and surmounted by an octagonal tower; and that of St. Sepolcro, a Doric structure containing many curious relics. Red wines are produced in the neighborhood, and about 10 miles from the town there are sulphurous baths. The poet Martial was born at Bilbilis, a former town on the site of the present Bambola, two miles east of Calatayud. Pop. 11,055.

Calatrava, kä-lạ-trä'vạ, **Order of,** a Spanish order of chivalry, originated during the Moorish wars. Calatrava la Vieja, taken from the Moors in the 12th century by the king of Castile, was committed to the Templars, who guarded it till 1158. At this time, a powerful army advancing to besiege it, they despaired of being able to defend it, and restored it to the king, who offered it in absolute property to whosoever would defend it. Two monks of the abbey of Citeaux (Cistercians), in France, presented themselves and were accepted. They preached a crusade, and offered a pardon of sins, and being supplied with money and arms, were able to repel the invaders. Thereupon, having received the investiture of the town and other donations, they instituted the same year (1158) an order into which all the nobility of Castile and Navarre were emulous to enter. In 1164 the chevaliers of this order, by sanction of Pope Alexander III., separated themselves from the monks, and the order became purely military. They still followed the rule of the Cistercians, until Paul III. dispensed them from the vow of chastity. The almost uniform success of the Knights of Calatrava against the Moors gave rise to rashness, and in 1197 they were defeated and nearly exterminated, the survivors transferring the seat to the castle of Salvatierra. In 1523 the grandmastership was transferred to the crown by a papal bull, the knights being permitted to marry once by way of compensation for their loss of independence. Since 1808 the body has been continued as an order of merit.

Calatrava la Viega, kä-la-trä'vạ lạ vē-ä'hạ, a ruined city of Spain, situated on the Guadiana, about 12 miles northeast of Ciudad Real. Its defense against the Moors, undertaken by Raymond, abbot of Fitero, and Diego Velasquez in 1158, after it had been abandoned by the Templars, is famous on account of its having originated the Order of Calatrava (q.v.) in 1158.

Calaveras, käl-a-vä'rạs, a river of California, rises among the hills at the foot of the Sierra Nevada, in Calaveras County, and after a westerly and southwesterly course joins the San Joaquin River, a few miles below Stockton.

Calaveras Grove, the most northern of the California groves of big trees, containing about 100 of these trees. The tallest one standing is known as the "Keystone State," and is 325 feet in height and 45 feet in girth; the "Mother of the Forest" is another feet of notable size, being 315 feet high and 61 feet in circumference. The grove is a State reservation.

Calaverite, a native gold telluride, AuTe₂. It was originally described by Genth as a very rare massive gold (and silver) telluride from Boulder County, Col. It is now the commonest of the gold ores of Cripple Creek and occurs there in beautiful triclinic crystals. It is often confused with "sylvanite" by the miners. It has a brilliant metallic lustre, pale bronze-yellow color, a hardness of 3, and a specific gravity of about 9.

Calc-tufa, a variety of calcite essentially travertine. It is formed in small streams by the deposit of calcium carbonate in a cellular form. It often contains fossil twigs, moss, leaves, seeds, etc.

Calcaire, Grossier, käl-cär grō-sē-ä, a chief type of the Eocene Tertiary series of the Paris and London basins. Its limestone strata furnish building material for the city of Paris The fossils of the Calcaire Grossier are remarkable for number, and for the variety of forms, rising up to the mammalia.

Calcar, or Kalkar, Jan Stephanus van, yän stē-fän'ŭs vän käl'kär, Dutch painter: b. Calcar in Cleves, 1499; d. Naples, 1546. He studied so thoroughly the works of Titian, that their pictures cannot always be distinguished. The 'Mater Dolorosa,' in the Boisserée collection in Stuttgart, a perfect work of art, is by him. Another small picture of his, the 'Infant Christ with the Shepherds,' was a favorite with Rubens. In this piece the light is represented as proceeding from the child. He designed almost all the portraits in Vasari's Lives, and the figures for the anatomical work of Vesalius.

Calca'reous, a term applied to substances partaking of the nature of lime, or containing quantities of lime. Thus, we speak of calcareous waters, calcareous rocks, calcareous soils. Calcareous spar is calcite (q.v.). See also CALC-TUFA.

Calcasieu, käl'kạ-shū, a river of Louisiana, rising in the western part of the State. It flows through the parish of the same name, and after a southerly course of about 200 miles enters the Gulf of Mexico through Lake Calcasieu.

Calcasieu Lake, situated in Calcasieu Parish, about five miles from the Gulf of Mexico, is little more than an expansion of the river of the same name. Length, about 18 miles; greatest breadth, five or six miles.

Calceola'ria (Latin, *calceolus*, a little shoe, alluding to the form of the corolla), a genus of plants of the natural order *Scrophulariaceæ*, natives of South America, especially of Chile and Peru. They are characterized by having a corolla with a very short tube, with two lips, concave or shaped like a hood, the upper one very small, the under one greatly inflated. They are common as greenhouse or outdoor plants. These are upward of 60 species, of which about 20 are cultivated in the gardens of Europe, and their varieties are very numerous. The flowers of the indigenous species are white, yellow, and purple. They are greatly excelled in beauty by the cultivated varieties, which acquire numerous tints in these colors, and have besides on the lower part of the corolla, the part which bears the strictest resemblance to a shoe, large spots, or innumerable small points of a different color, which have a very graceful effect. They grow best in a rich, open, sandy garden mold, and are propagated by seeds or cuttings, the herbaceous kinds mostly by the former method.

Calchaqui, kạl-chä'kē, a South American tribe formerly living, in the northwestern part of Argentina. They were conquered by the Incas in the 15th century, and the ruins of their buildings and tombs indicate quite an advanced stage of civilization. They were visited by the Jesuit missionaries, but strongly opposed the inroads of the Spaniards. The tribe is now extinct and all record of their language is lost.

Calchas, käl'käs, a legendary priest and prophet of the Greeks at the time of the Trojan war, who foretold that Troy would not be subdued by them till the 10th year of the siege. He himself accompanied the Greek army to Troy. During the siege, the Greeks were attacked by a plague, and Calchas declared that it was the effect of Apollo's anger, because they had deprived his priest of his daughter Chryseis, whom Agamemnon had selected as his mistress. He counseled the Greeks to appease Apollo by restoring the damsel; and it was by his advice that they afterward built the wooden horse. There are various legends relating to his death.

Calciferous, a geologic term applied to the sandy limestones found in Pennsylvania, extending across New Jersey and New York to Canada, and known as the Beekmantown beds. An equivalent formation is found in the magnesium limestones of Iowa and Missouri.

Cal'cimine, a mixture of zinc-white, glue, water, and pigments, used to finish the plaster walls of buildings. See WHITEWASH.

Calcination, a term now used as practically equivalent to roasting or oxidation. It is derived from the Latin word *calx*, meaning quicklime, and received its present signification by extension from its original meaning of obtaining lime from limestone by the application of great heat. By calcination many substances are reduced to a friable condition, and freed from constituents capable of passing off in the form of gas or vapor. Thus various salts may be deprived of water of crystallization, and rendered amorphous in this way; the hydrated carbonate of magnesium is reduced to the pure oxide, known as calcined magnesia; limestone is converted into quicklime, etc. Calcination is usually the first process in the extraction of metals from their ores. The oxides of metals

Photograph by J. Horace McFarland Co.

CALCEOLARIA (FISHERMAN'S BASKET).

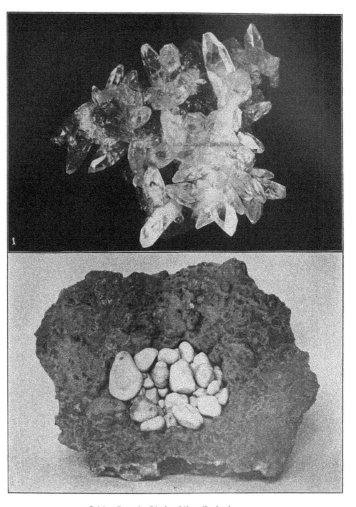

1. Calcite Crystals, Bigrigg Mine, England.
2. Calcite "Bird's Nest," Reichelsdorf, Hesse, Germany.

produced by this process were formerly known as calxes, but this term is now disused. It depends on circumstances which oxide is obtained, if the metal, like lead, can form more than one. The weight of the total calx is equal of course to that of the metal and the oxygen with which it has combined, but the calx itself is specifically lighter than the metal. Platinum, gold, silver, and some other metals, are not affected in this way, and on this account they are called the noble metals. See COMBUSTION.

Cal'cite, -sĭt, a native carbonate of calcium, crystallizing in the rhombohedral system, and exhibiting hundreds of distinct crystals of general forms or "habits." The mineral also occurs massive, fibrous, granular, lameller, compact, earthy, stalactitic, nodular. Its typical crystals exhibit a very perfect cleavage, commonly splitting up, from a blow, into many small rhombohedrons. Pure crystals have a specific gravity of about 2.72, and a hardness of about 3, though the latter varies somewhat with the face of the crystal. Calcite may be transparent, translucent, or opaque, and in color may vary from white, or colorless, to black, also brown, violet, blue, green, yellow, and red. It exhibits the phenomenon of double refraction powerfully, and transparent crystals of it (called "Iceland spar" because first obtained from Iceland) are used in the manufacture of polarizing prisms. (See LIGHT.) Limestone, marble, and chalk are commonly classed as massive or cryptocrystalline varieties of calcite. Oolite (q.v.) is a granular limestone composed of innumerable minute rounded concretions. Pisolite is a similar variety in which the spheres are as large as peas. The stalactites and stalagmites of many caves (q.v.) are calcite. Mexican onyx, travertine, and calc-tufa (q.v.) are a few of the many other varieties of calcite. Varieties containing other metallic carbonates are known as baricalcite, strontianocalcite, ferrocalcite, etc. Calcite effervesces briskly even in cold acid. It occurs abundantly all over the world; especially choice specimens come from Germany, England, Mexico; Rossie, N. Y.; Joplin, Mo., and Lake Superior.

Calcite Group, in mineralogy, an important series of rhombohedral carbonates including calcite, dolomite, ankerite, magnesite, mesitite, siderite, rhodochrosite, smithsonite, and sphærocobaltite.

Cal'cium, a metallic element first obtained in the free state by Sir Humphry Davy in 1808. Its compounds are exceedingly abundant and are widely distributed. Calcium carbonate, $CaCO_3$, is familiar in the various forms of marble, chalk, limestone, and calcite. The sulphate, $CaSO_4$, is also very common, and is perhaps best known in the form of gypsum, which contains two molecules of water, and therefore has the formula, $CaSO_4 + 2H_2O$. Calcium phosphate also occurs in nature in considerable quantities, both in the form of fossilized bones and as apatite (q.v.), and its various modifications. Metallic calcium may be obtained by the electrolysis of the fused chloride (which melts at a red heat), or by decomposing the iodide with metallic sodium. It has a light yellow color, has a hardness about equal to that of gold, and (according to most authorities) is very malleable and ductile. Its chemical symbol is Ca, its specific gravity is about 1.58, and its atomic weight is 40.0 if $O = 16$, or 39.7 if $H = 1$. Perfectly dry air does not affect it at ordinary temperatures, but in moist air it becomes rapidly coated with the hydrate, $Ca(OH)_2$. When strongly heated in air it burns with a yellow flame, taking up oxygen to form the oxide, CaO. It decomposes water rapidly, passing into the form of the hydrate, with evolution of hydrogen. It melts at a red heat, has a specific heat of about 0.169, and has an electrical resistance only about one twelfth of that of mercury.

In its chemical relations calcium is a dyad. It combines with almost every known acid, and yields a vast number of compounds, many of which are of great industrial value. Of these the best known are the carbonate, oxide, hydrate, chloride, sulphate, fluoride, carbide, and bisulphide, and the indefinite mixture of the chloride and hypochlorite known as bleaching-powder (q.v.).

The carbonate occurs native in large quantities, as already noted. It is also commonly present in ground water as obtained from wells and springs. It is almost insoluble in pure water, but dissolves to a considerable extent when the water contains free carbon dioxide in solution. It is this compound that gives to water what is known as "temporary hardness." Upon boiling, the free carbon dioxide held in solution is expelled, and the lime carbonate is therefore precipitated also, so that the water loses that part of its hardness which is due to the presence of the carbonate. This effect is well illustrated, in regions where the soil is rich in limestone, by the crust of lime carbonate that is deposited upon the interior of household kettles that are used for heating water. Calcium carbonate also gives rise, in steam boilers, to troublesome deposits that keep the water out of contact with the metal plates, which often become overheated and seriously impaired in consequence. To prevent this action chemists often recommend the addition to the water in the boiler of a certain amount of ammonium chloride (sal ammoniac). This compound combines with the lime carbonate to form calcium chloride, which is exceedingly soluble, and ammonium carbonate, which is volatile, and therefore passes away with the steam. Beautiful as this process is in theory, it cannot be recommended for adoption in practice, because if the sal ammoniac is present in any excess it induces rapid corrosion of the boiler-plates. For a further discussion of boiler-scale, see SCALE.

When calcium carbonate (more familiarly known as carbonate of lime) is strongly heated in a current of air, it loses its carbon dioxide and becomes converted into a substance known to the chemist as calcium oxide CaO, and in the arts as quicklime, burnt lime, or simply lime. Pure calcium oxide (or lime) is a white, amorphous substance, extremely infusible, glowing with a dazzling white light when strongly heated, possessing caustic properties, and acting as a powerful chemical base. When treated with about one third of its own weight of water, lime passes into the form of the hydrate or hydroxide, $Ca(OH)_2$, with the evolution of much heat. The process of converting it into the hydrate by the addition of water is called slaking, and the resulting hydrate is known in the arts as slaked lime. Mortar is composed of a mixture of slaked lime and sand, the silica (or sand) slowly combining with the lime to form a silicate after the mortar has been applied. Slaked lime, or calcium hydrate, is somewhat soluble in water, its solution being known as lime water.

Calcium chloride is formed when calcium carbonate is dissolved in hydrochloric acid. It is exceedingly soluble, but upon evaporation of its solution it separates in white, needle-like crystals having the formula $CaCl_2 + 6H_2O$. When these are heated to about 400° F. they lose two thirds of their water of crystallization and become converted into $CaCl_2 + 2H_2O$, in which form the chloride is commonly used. Thus prepared, calcium chloride is a white, porous solid, which absorbs moisture with great avidity, and hence is exceedingly valuable to the chemist and physicist for drying air and other gaseous bodies. It forms crystalline compounds with ethyl and methyl alcohols, which are again resolved, by the addition of water, into calcium chloride and the free alcohol. On account of this property it has been used for the preparation of these alcohols in the pure state.

Calcium sulphate occurs native in the anhydrous form, as the mineral anhydrite; and, combined with two molecules of water, it also occurs abundantly as gypsum. It is soluble in 400 parts of water, and, like the carbonate, it occurs quite generally in the waters of wells and springs. Like the carbonate, too, it makes the water in which it occurs hard; but the hardness due to the presence of the sulphate cannot be removed by boiling, and it is therefore said to be "permanent." Calcium sulphate produces deposits in steam boilers that are far more troublesome and injurious than those due to the carbonate, since the sulphate is deposited in a hard, compact, stony form, and can be removed only with difficulty. See SCALE.

When gypsum is moderately heated it loses its water of crystallization and becomes converted into a substance that is commercially known as plaster of Paris, from the fact that the gypsum from which it is prepared (and which is also called plaster of Paris, though rarely), occurs abundantly in the Tertiary formations of the Paris basin. Plaster of Paris, when moistened by the addition of the proper quantity of water, takes up two molecules of water again, and rapidly sets into a hard, solid mass which expands somewhat at the instant of solidification. It is greatly used in making casts and molds. These are harder and better when the plaster is wetted with a solution of alum than they are when pure water is used for this purpose. If equal weights of the anhydrous sulphates of calcium and of potassium are wetted with about four parts of water, the mixture sets like plaster of Paris, with the formation of a double sulphate of calcium and potassium, having the formula, $CaSO_4.K_2SO_4.H_2O$. The casts so obtained exhibit polished surfaces, superior to those obtained with the pure plaster.

Calcium fluoride, CaF_2, occurs native as fluor spar, or fluorite, and is used to some extent as a flux in metallurgical operations, to which circumstance it owes its name (Latin *fluor*, a flux). It is also used in the manufacture of vases and other ornamental articles and as a source of hydrofluoric acid, which is set free when the fluoride is treated with warm sulphuric acid.

Calcium carbide, CaC_2, has long been known, and was prepared by Wöhler in 1862 by melting an alloy of zinc and calcium in the presence of

carbon. Its commercial importance, however, dates from the discovery made by Mr. T. L. Willson in 1892, that it can be formed by the direct combination of lime and carbon at the temperature of the electric furnace. Large quantities of it are now made by this process at Niagara Falls, at Spray, N. C., and elsewhere. Calcium carbide in its commercial form is a dark-gray substance, often almost black. It is hard, infusible, and incombustible, with a specific gravity of about 2.24. Its value in the arts depends upon the remarkable fact that when it is thrown into water a double decomposition occurs, by which acetylene gas is formed, in accordance with the equation $CaC_2 + 2H_2O = C_2H_2 + Ca(OH)_2$. See ACETYLENE; CARBIDE.

Calcium sulphite, $CaSO_3$, is formed and precipitated as a white powder when a solution of a calcium salt is added to a solution of an alkaline sulphite. The sulphite so formed requires 800 parts of pure water to effect its solution. It is far more soluble in sulphurous acid, however, and it is believed that the sulphurous acid acts upon it to produce a new but comparatively unstable compound, $CaSO_3.SO_2$, to which hypothetical substance the name calcium bisulphite, or bisulphite of lime, has been given. Upon exposure to air the bisulphite solution gradually deposits crystals of the monosulphite, having the composition, $CaSO_3.2H_2O$. On the commercial scale the bisulphite solution is prepared by passing sulphur dioxide gas (SO_2) through "milk of lime" (that is, water containing slaked lime in suspension). The monosulphite of lime is first formed, and by the continued action of the sulphur dioxide this passes into solution in the form of the bisulphite. The usefulness of bisulphite of lime in the arts depends upon its power of dissolving the gums and resins by which the fibres of wood are cemented together. Thus, in the sulphite process of manufacturing wood pulp, chips of wood are submerged in a solution of the bisulphite and heated for some hours in closed digesters, by the action of steam. By this means the chips are disintegrated, the gummy connective materials being entirely dissolved away, and the wood being thereby reduced to a mass of separate fibres, which after simple washing and bleaching, are ready for use in the manufacture of paper.

Calcium Carbide. See ACETYLENE; CALCIUM; CARBIDE.

Calcium Light, a brilliant light produced by directing the flame of an oxy-hydrogen blowpipe against a block of compressed quicklime. It had long been known that lime emits a light of extraordinary brilliance and whiteness when strongly heated in this manner, but the first practical application of the principle was made by Capt. Thomas Drummond in 1825, in connection with the trigonometrical survey of Ireland. The calcium light is now constantly employed in the production of theatrical effects, and for the projection of photographic pictures upon a screen. It is also called Drummond light, lime-light, and oxy-hydrogen light.

Calculating-machines. The simplest form of calculating mechanism in common use is the slide-rule, which consists usually of three strips, bearing graduations, the centre strip sliding between the others. The scales being graduated to logarithms, and one function of a number being on a stationary strip, and another function on the sliding strip, movements of the strip afford a sight reading of a variety of calculations. A mechanism identical in principle with the slide-rule is the calculating-circle, in which graduated rings are substituted for the strips or slides.

The counter used in street cars to register fares, the cyclometer, odometer, and cash-register are all simple forms of calculating machines, based on the principle common to nearly all these machines, namely, the use of a disk or wheel bearing figures from 0 to 9 inclusive. A very simple form is shown in the illustration. When the disk at the right has completed one revolution it advances the centre disk one step; and so on successively at each revolution of the right-hand disk until after 10 revolutions the centre disk has likewise completed a full revolution, when it in turn advances the left-hand disk one step and thus registers 100. The train of disks may be extended to register any number desired. Apertures in the casing of the train enable the figures to be read.

During recent years the keyboard type of calculating machine has come into extended use in banks, business houses, and other concerns where numerous and tedious calculations have to be made. There are a number of these machines, but that of Dorr E. Felt of Chicago is

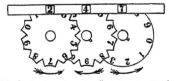

Wheels of a form of counter, illustrating the principle common to nearly all calculating machines.

perhaps the best known. This was introduced in 1889, and has been improved several times, the different styles being known as the comptograph and comptometer. The comptograph is the more complete machine of the two, and prints the record of its work as performed. The comptometer is very similar, but does not print its record, and hence cannot be used for listing. Either machine performs any of the four arithmetical operations of adding, subtracting, multiplying, and dividing, besides extracting the square root. In the comptograph the totals are recorded in front of the operator, and, if, by accident, wrong keys have been struck, they can be instantly released by touching a release key, after which the correct keys can be struck.

The keys resemble those of a typewriter. They are arranged in columns, the first column on the right representing units (1, 2, 3, etc.), the next column tens (10, 20, 30, etc.), the next hundreds, and so on. Two figures (a large and a small one) appear on the top of each key. In addition and multiplication the keys are struck with reference to the large figures, while in subtraction, division, and square root, the small figures (which are red) guide the operator. Addition is performed by touching the large figure keys of the proper numbers to be added, and standing in their proper columns, all the columns being added at one time, the carrying being done automatically by the machine, with

no attention from the operator. In multiplication the operator begins at the right of the row of keys indicated by the first figure of the multiplier, and strikes each successive row in the same row toward the left as many times as indicated by the corresponding figure in the multiplicand, and then proceeds with each of the other figures of the multiplier as with the first, beginning always in the column of keys in which the figure of the multiplier stands. To multiply such a sum as 198 by 377, it is only necessary to strike three keys, but these must be selected according to their positions in the columns.

In dividing, the number to be divided is first struck on the keys, precisely as in addition, and then the divisor is struck with respect to the smaller figures on the keys, the operator striking the proper keys continually (never more than nine times) until the figures in the complementary place agree with the number of strokes on the keys, and the answer then shows on the register.

In 1900 Felt patented a machine to compute in pounds, shillings, and pence, and this is now being introduced in Great Britain. James Mallmann, of Sheboygan, Wis., has recently produced a machine of the keyboard type that has attracted some attention. So has D. J. T. Hiett, of St. Louis. Somewhat less pretentious among new machines is the arithmachine of Henry Goldman, of Chicago, and the machine of James B. Moore, of New York, operating with registering tape and slides.

Among foreign machines that have attracted comment are the Thomas machine, used in France; the Tate, an improved Thomas, employed in Great Britain; the Odhner, used in Poland; and Babbage's differential machine, which cost $100,000, and calculates logarithms besides performing operations in trigonometry.

The Hollerith electric tabulating mechanism used by the United States Census Bureau is prominent among the remarkable calculating machines that have been developed in America. Three separate machines constitute the outfit. The first one punches holes in cards, in any one or more of 240 places; the second tabulates the cards, while the third sorts them. Machine No. 1 has a keyboard of 240 keys, this being the number of answers called for in the census blanks of the bureau. The operator takes a return blank, representing the report of some individual, and, as he reads it, strikes the appropriate keys, which results in the punching of a card, that becomes a mechanical counterpart of the original return. As the average number of questions answered on each return is but 15, the work is not so tedious as might be inferred from the statement as to 240 questions.

When the cards of a State have been punched, they are brought to the tabulating machine, which is the real calculator. This machine reads the holes of the cards that are fed into it, and makes an electrical record of each hole, according to its position, adding up the totals for each hole, and showing them on dials. When the cards are all fed through, the total of each of the 240 replies is enumerated. The third machine is a sorting box, which serves to secure answers to cross-questions. For instance, if it is desired to know how many white persons are among the total number convicted of crime, the sorting box will locate all cards having the holes corresponding to these two statements, and give the total. In this way a great variety of statistics are made available which it would be too expensive to gather or compute in any other way. For other information on this subject, see CASH REGISTER. C. H. COCHRANE.

Calculus. As used in medicine the term calculus (*Lat. calculus,* a pebble or small stone) is applied to certain concretions occurring in the cavities or tissues of the body, usually as the result of the deposition of solids from some natural secretion. Calculi may be of many different sorts, and vary greatly in consistency, some being merely crumbly masses that can be crushed between the fingers, while others are extremely hard. Calculi occurring in the lachrymal or tear passages are called dacryoliths, while salivary calculi are formed in the salivary glands or their ducts, and amygdoliths in the tonsils. So-called rhinoliths are concretions which sometimes develop in the nasal cavities, usually as the result of the presence of some foreign body. The tartar on the teeth is sometimes spoken of as dental calculus. Pneumoliths occur in the lung, and broncholiths in the bronchi; pancreatic calculi are found in the pancreas. The breast and prostrate gland also occasionally harbor calcareous concretions, which in the former case are called lacteal calculi. The deposits of chalk about the joints in gouty persons are sometimes referred to as arthritic calculi. Intestinal calculi or enteroliths may give rise to serious disturbances, and if they happen to occur in the vermiform appendix often simulate date or other fruit stones in appearance. Before appendicitis was well understood their true nature often passed unrecognized and when they were discovered in cases of the disease the malady was mistakenly attributed to the swallowing of such foreign bodies. The two most important types of calculi, however, are the biliary calculi or gallstones, and urinary calculi.

Gall-stones are very common and fortunately usually do not give rise to symptoms. It is estimated that in Europe 10 per cent of the entire population have gall-stones, while in this country their frequency is held to be about 7 per cent. As their formation is probably encouraged by sedentary life and conditions favoring stagnation of the bile such as tight lacing, lack of exercise, and constipation, they are three times commoner in women than in men. They rarely give symptoms in younger persons, and about half of the patients are over 40 years of age. Pregnancy is said to be of importance in favoring their formation. Biliary calculi may be extremely small or may attain considerable size, stones as large as an English walnut not being at all uncommon. They also vary greatly in number and the smaller ones may be present in hundreds. They are composed principally of cholesterin (q.v.), with varying but much smaller amounts of bile pigment. lime and magnesium salts, fatty acids, and bile acids. It is now generally assumed that an inflammatory or catarrhal condition of the mucous membrane of the gall-bladder (q.v.), usually induced by microorganisms, furnishes the starting point of gall-stone formation. As already stated gall-stones may remain in the gall-bladder for years without causing symptoms, or their presence may be accompanied by inflammatory changes in the organ. or they may enter the gall-ducts and give rise to disturbances of various sorts, of which pain, local tenderness, persistent or remittent jaundice, clay-colored stools, and chills and fever are conspicuous features. While a rational and hygienic mode of life will do much to prevent the formation of gall-stones, if they are present and give rise to symptoms that are at all severe surgical intervention is usually necessary to effect a cure.

Urinary calculi may be found either in the kidney, ureter, or bladder, and are accordingly called renal, ureteral, or vesical calculi. Kidney stones of small size often pass into the ureter and during their journey downward to the bladder give rise to seizures of renal colic which in the agony and general prostration they cause are very similar to those of biliary colic. The pain is felt lower down in the abdomen and also in the back; frequently also radiating along the inner surface of the thigh. Aside from the attacks of colic renal stones may cause pain in the back, chills, fever, and bloody or turbid urine containing pus. "Coral calculi" are large stones which gradually fill the pelvis of the kidney, and in the conformation reproduce with great fidelity the irregularities and recesses of this cavity. Very small concretions pass into the bladder without difficulty and are evacuated in the urine as "gravel." Stone in the bladder is rare in women and in the male sex is seen oftenest in infancy and after the fiftieth year. The symptoms include pain increased by jolting or bodily motion, frequent urination, pain at the end of urination — and sometimes sudden stoppage of the stream owing to the fact that the stone rolls into the neck of the bladder shutting off the flow — and usually bloody and turbid urine. Stone is especially common in old persons on account of the cystitis (q.v.) often present. Urinary calculi may be composed of various materials, of which uric acid and urates, calcium oxalate ("mulberry calculus"), calcium phosphate and ammonio-magnesium phosphate are the commonest, singly or in combination. Rarer forms are made up of calcium carbonate, cystin, or xanthin. The cut section usually shows a laminated structure and a nucleus or starting point, which may be a blood clot, a shred of tissue, a bit of mucous, a small renal calculus, a mass of urates or a foreign body. Any conditions encouraging excessive deposition of the urinary constituents predispose to urinary calculi. Among such causes are lack of exercise, digestive disorders, defect oxidation. excesses in eating or drinking, catarrhal conditions of the urinary tract, etc. The tendency to stone formation is particularly pronounced in those having what is called the gouty or lithemic diathesis. The diagnosis of renal calculi is facilitated by the use of the *x*-ray, while for the detection of bladder stones a special form of steel sound termed a "stone searcher" is introduced into the bladder. The cystoscope is also of great service in this field. Individuals predisposed to stone should keep the urine abundant by the free use of water — preferably distilled — and milk, should take much open air exercise, and avoid the consumption of large amounts of meat, fats, sugar, or alcohol. Green vegetables, salads, bread, poultry, fish, eggs, and fruit should form the main articles of diet. Despite the claims of nostrum venders, when a stone is once formed there is little chance of its being dissolved by any plan of internal medication. If the condition causes decided symptoms surgical removal of the offending body is indicated. See LITHOTOMY; LITHOTRITY.

KARL M. VOGEL, M. D.,
New York City.

Calculus, The Infinitesimal.—The Infinitesimal, or Differential and Integral, Calculus is not so much a branch of mathematics as a method or instrument of mathematical investigation, of indefinite applicability. The masters now seldom try to treat it in less than a thousand large pages; here we may hope no more than to expose its basic principles, to illustrate its characteristic processes, and to exhibit some of its nearer-lying applications, with their results. Even so little will require utmost condensation and self-explaining abbreviations.

We might define the Calculus as the Theory and Application of Limits, so central and dominant is this latter concept. We must, then, clear the ground for its full presentment. Successive addition of the unit 1, continued without end, gives rise to the *Assemblage* of positive integers, in which all additions, multiplications, and involutions are possible. This assemblage is *ordered: i.e.* of two different elements, a and b, either $a < b$ or $a > b$; and if $a < b$ and $b < c$, then $a < c$. To make all subtractions (inverses of addition) possible, we annex the symmetric assemblage of *negative* integers, any negative integer, as a' (or $-a$), being *defined* by the equation $a + a' = 0$, this o itself being defined by $a - a = 0$. To make all divisions (inverses of multiplication) possible, we annex the assemblage of *Fractions*, quotients of integers by integers. This total assemblage of integers and their quotients, both $+$ and $-$, we may call the *domain* or assemblage of *rational real* numbers, wherein all direct operations (of addition and multiplication) and also the inverses (subtraction and division) are possible.

The operation of involution is direct, a special case of multiplication, but is not commutative like addition and multiplication: thus $a + b = b + a$, $ab = ba$, but in general $a^b \neq b^a$. Hence the direct operation a^b, yielding c, has two inverses: Given b and c, to find a, and given a and c, to find b. The former gives rise to roots or surds, the latter to logarithms. But neither of these can in general be found in the universe of rationals; to make such inversions always possible, we must still further enlarge the domain of number by annexing *Irrationals*. These demand exact definition. Divide the assemblage of rationals into two classes, A and B, any member a of the first being $<$ any member b of the second. Three possibilities present themselves:

1. A may contain and be closed by a number $\alpha >$ any other a but $< $ any b.

2. B may contain and be closed by a number $\beta <$ any other b but $>$ any α.

3. Neither A may contain a largest a, nor B a smallest b. Thus we may form (1) A of 2 and all rationals < 2; or (2) B of 2 and all rationals > 2, —in either case 2 is a *border* (frontière) number; or (3) A of all negatives and all positive rationals whose squares are < 2 and B of all positive rationals whose squares are > 2. Here there is *no border* number among rationals. But a border does exist, *defined* as $>$ any a but $<$ any b. We name it *second root* of 2 and denote it by

$\sqrt{2}$ or $2^{\frac{1}{2}}$. All such common borders are called *Irrationals*. The assemblage of irrationals is determined by all possible such partitions of rationals (A, B). The assemblage of all rationals and all such irrationals is the assemblage of Reals. It remains and is possible to extend the operations of arithmetic to all reals. In 'particular,' the assemblage of rationals is *dense; i.e.* between every two there is an infinity of others; in the same sense the assemblage of reals also has density. Again, always on dividing all reals into A and B, each member of $A <$ each member of B, there will be a border γ, the greatest in A or the least in B, all less numbers being in A, all greater in B. Hence, and in this sense, the assemblage of reals is named *continuous*.

In this continuum, admitting no further introductions, suppose a magnitude to assume successively an infinity of values: $v_1, v_2, \ldots v_n, \ldots v_{n+k}, \ldots$; it is then called a *variable*, V, and its values in order form a *sequence*, S. It often happens that V will approach some *constant L*, so that by enlarging n we may make and keep the modulus or absolute worth (*i.e.*, regardless of sign) of the difference $V - L <$ *any preassigned positive magnitude*, ϵ, for all following values of V; in symbols, $|V_{n+k} - L| < \epsilon$ for every positive k. Then L is called the *Limit* of V: $L = Lim. V$. Plainly, V cannot have two limits as thus defined. It is easily seen that V will have a limit when and only when $|V_{n+k} - V_n| < \epsilon n$. If V changes always in the same sense, by increase or decrease, it has a limit when and only when $|V| <$ always than some fixed number n. When V increases (positively or negatively) beyond any assignable n, it is often said to have ∞ as limit.

A perfect *geometric illustration* is found in the sequences I and C of inscribed and circumscribed regular polygons of the circle. Here every C is $>$ every I; also $C_n - I_n < \epsilon$; also $C_{n+k} - C_n < \epsilon$, $I_{n+k} - I_n < \epsilon$, $C_n - A < \epsilon$, $A - I_n < \epsilon$ (A being the circle-area): hence A is the common *limit* both of C_n and of I_n, for n increasing *without limit* ($n \doteq \infty$).

Algebraically, if $c_1, c_3, c_5 \ldots c_{2n+1} \ldots$ be the sequence (O) of odd convergents, and $c_2, c_4, \ldots c_{2n}, \ldots$ the sequence (E) of even convergents in an interminate continued fraction as $\frac{1}{1+1} \frac{1}{+1} \frac{1}{+1} \frac{1}{+6+1} \frac{1}{+} - \ldots$, then every $C_{2n+1} > C_{2n}$, also $C_{2n+1} - C_{2(n+k)+1} < \epsilon$, $C_{2n} - C_{2(n+k)} < \epsilon$; and $C_{2n+1} - (\sqrt{13} - 3) < \epsilon$, $(\sqrt{13} - 3) - C_{2n} < \epsilon$. The odd convergents from above and the even convergents from below close down endlessly upon their *common limit*, $\sqrt{13} - 3$,—as quadrants of an hyperbola and its conjugate close down upon their common asymptote.

The difference $|V - L|$ is a *variable small at will* and is called *Infinitesimal* (σ); its *limit* is o. The quotient of two σ's will generally be a variable; if it has a finite limit L, the σ's are named *of the same order;* if the limit of the quotient is o (or ∞), then the numerator (or denominator) is of *higher* order. If any σ be chosen as standard, it is called *principal* infinitesimal; any other whose pth root is of the same order as the principal σ is itself said to be of pth order.

Easy theorems are now proved as to the limits of the sum, difference, product, quotient of variables. In general: If $R(u, v, w, \ldots)$ be a rational function of simultaneous variables,

$u, v, w, \ldots$, and if $u, v, w \ldots$ have limits $l, m,$ $n \ldots,$—then $R(u, v, w \ldots)$ has a limit $R(l, m, n \ldots)$— always provided that this latter does not involve a division by o, which has no sense.

If two V's differ at most by a σ, and one has a limit, the other has the same limit. Herewith there becomes possible a Calculus of the *Limits* of Variables instead of the Variables themselves. These limits are often far the more important, as we shall soon see.

A variable V (or sequence $v_1, v_2 \ldots$) is *bounded above* when we may assign a value M that it cannot exceed; then there is a certain smallest number, its *upper limit*, which it cannot exceed. Similarly, it is *bounded below* when we may assign an m below which it cannot sink; then there is a certain greatest number, its *lower limit*, under which it cannot descend. If V may assume either of these limits as one of its values, then that limit is *attainable* and is a *Maximum* or a *Minimum*; otherwise it is *unattainable*. If V be a proper fraction, its limits, o and 1, are not attainable. When V may assume every value between its *attainable* limits, a and b, it is said to vary *continuously* in the interval $[a, b]$. But if a, or b, or both, be unattainable, we shall write $\{a+o, b\}$ or $[a, b-o]$, or $[a+o, b-o]$.

When to values of one magnitude correspond values of another, the magnitudes are called *Functions* of each other (Leibnitz). The one to which arbitrary values may be supposed given is called the *argument* or *independent variable;* the other, whose corresponding values may be reckoned or observed (or which at least exist), is called *the function*. Such are a number and its logarithm or sine; the radius of a sphere and its surface or volume; the elasticity of a medium and the velocity of an undulation through it; etc.... The general functional connection of x and y is expressed by $F(x, y) = o$. If this F be an entire polynomial in x and also in y, then F is *algebraic*, otherwise *transcendental*. If F be solved as to y, thus $y = f(x)$, then y is an *explicit* function of x; otherwise, an *implicit* function. If $f(x)$ be the quotient of two entire polynomials in x, then $f(x)$ is a *rational* function of x; otherwise, *irrational*. If to any one value of x there corresponds only one value of y, then y is a *one-valued* or *unique* function of x; if x be also a unique function of y, then there exists between x and y a *one-to-one correspondence*.

If $y = f(x)$ and $x = \phi(y)$ express the same correspondence between x and y, then f and ϕ denote *inverse* functions. A function may reduce to a *constant*; as $x^n = 1$, for every finite x when $n = o$.

As x ranges in $[a, b]$, $f(x)$ will also range. Similarly $f(x)$ may have an upper limit M and a lower limit m; then $f(x)$ is *bounded* in $[a, b]$, $[m, M]$ is its *interval* and $M - m$ its *oscillation*. If either m or M be absent (or ∞), this *oscillation* is ∞. If we cut $[a, b]$ into n sub-intervals (a_k, b_k) $(k = 1, \ldots n)$, then plainly the upper limit of $f(x)$ will be M in *at least one* $[a_k, b_k]$ and $> M$ in none; the *oscillation* will not be $> M - m$ in any $[a_k, b_k]$.

If as x approaches c, no matter how, $f(x)$ approaches $f(c)$ as its limit, then $f(x)$ *is continuous at c* (i.e. for $x = c$). Or, if $f(x)$ be bounded in $[c - \sigma, c + \sigma]$ and if the limit of its oscillation be o for σ vanishing, then $f(x)$ *is continuous at c*. That is, we must be able to make and *keep* the oscillation of $f(x)$ *small as will* by making and keeping the fluctuation in x *small at will*.

It may be that limit $f(c + \sigma) = f(c)$ only for $+\sigma$, then $f(x)$ is named continuous *right of c*; or that Lim. $f(c + \sigma) = f(c)$ only for $-\sigma$, then $f(x)$ is named continuous *left of c*. Only when $f(x)$ is continuous both right *and* left of c [$f(c)$ being the same], is $f(x)$ *continuous at c*.

If $f(x)$ be continuous at all points (values of x) right of a and left of b, it is named *continuous in $[a, b]$*.

The infinitesimal $[c - \sigma, c + \sigma]$ is called the (immediate) *vicinity* (or neighborhood) of c.

A change in the value of a v is conveniently denoted by Δv, read difference-v or Delta-v; hence Δx and Δy will denote corresponding (simultaneous) differences or changes in x and y.

If now $y = f(x)$ be continuous in $[a, b]$, we may cut this latter up into finite sub-intervals, Δx, each so small that the *oscillation* of y in each shall be $< \epsilon$. Hence Heine calls y *uniformly* (equably, *gleichmässig*) continuous in $[a, b]$. This corresponds to *uniform convergence*, as of a power-series, $y = \overset{n=\infty}{\underset{n=0}{\Sigma}} C_n x^n$, as opposed to non-uniform or *infinitely slow convergence* (Seidel, 1850). Finer discriminations must here be omitted.

Continuity is the supreme functional property with which the Calculus is concerned. Sine and cosine are everywhere continuous, but $\tan x$ is discontinuous for $x = (2n \pm 1)\pi/_2$, where $\tan x$ drops from $+\infty$ to $-\infty$. Similarly $\dfrac{1}{x-a}$ at $x = a$, an extremely important discontinuity.

So $y = \left(e^{\frac{1}{x}} - 1\right) \Big/ \left(e^{\frac{1}{x}} + 1\right)$ is discontinuous at $x = o$, leaping from -1 to 1, the *discontinuity* is 2. It is generally assumed that Continuity holds throughout the Processes of Nature.

Again, $y = \sin \dfrac{1}{x}$ is *not defined* for $x = o$, but whatever value be assigned it there, it remains *discontinuous*, since $\sin \dfrac{1}{x}$ vibrates infinitely fast between $+1$ and -1 for $x \doteq o$.—Again, $f(c \pm \sigma)$ may approach a limit for σ vanishing, yet not approach $f(c)$. Thus, let $f(x) = x^2 + \dfrac{x^2}{1+x^2} + \ldots$, a decreasing geometrical series, ratio $(1 + x^2)^{-1}$, hence Lim. $f(x) = 1 + x^2$. Then as $x \doteq o$, $f(x) \doteq 1$, Lim. $f(\pm o) = 1$; but for $x = o$, $f(x) = f(o) = o$.—There are many immediate consequences of continuity, which we have no space to discuss here, such as: A function continuous in $[a, b]$ *attains* its upper and lower limits (its maximum and minimum); it also assumes at least once every value between $f(a)$ and $f(b)$,—a property, however, not peculiar to continuous functions (Darboux).

The notion of *function* is at once extended to *several variables*, $u = f(x, y, \ldots)$, one- or many-valued, algebraic or transcendental, etc., as before. Here each variable, as x, has its range or interval $[a, b]$; so y its $[b, b']$, etc. All possible sets of values $(x, y \ldots)$ form an assemblage or the Domain (D) of variation. Any set (or point) for which any variable has an extreme or border value, as a or a', b or b', is a *border* point; the assemblage of all such is the *border* or *contour* of D. A simple geometric depiction of D in rectangular coördinates for only two variables, x and y, would be a rectangle with sides $x = a$, $x = a'$, $y = b$, $y = b'$; of three variables, x, y, z, it would be a cuboid bounded by the planes $x = a$, $x = a'$, $y = b$, $y = b'$, $z = c$, $z = c'$; etc. The point (x, y) or (x, y, z) may be anywhere *in* or *on* the rectangle or cuboid. Such a D may be thought cut up into *elements*, infinitesimal rectangles or cuboids. Suppose any point $(a_1, b_1, \ldots)$ within an element. If now $f(x, y, \ldots)$ approaches $f(a_1, b_1, \ldots)$ as limit, as point $(x, y, \ldots)$ approaches point $(a_1, b_1, \ldots)$, *no matter how*, then $f(x, y, \ldots)$ is called *continuous at* $(a_1, b_1, \ldots)$. This amounts to saying that the *oscillation* of f shrinks towards zero as the element contracts, *no matter how*, about the point; that is, infinitesimal function-changes correspond to any and all infinitesimal argument-changes in the immediate vicinity of the point.

Any $f(x, y, \ldots)$ is called *continuous* within D when continuous at every point in D, *border included*; but *on* this border, as x, y, $\ldots$ approach a_1, b_1, $\ldots$ the point must not get without D. An f is continuous in the *(immediate) vicinity* of a point, when continuous within an infinitesimal D including that point. In general, theorems holding for functions of one variable may be extended, with proper modifications, to functions of several variables.

Derivatives.—In the study of functional dependence, the main subject of scientific inquiry, it is of first importance to know how corresponding changes in the magnitudes are related. To discover this, we form the quotient of corresponding differences, $\frac{\Delta y}{\Delta x}$, called *Difference-Quotient* (DQ). In general, it is very complex, but breaks up into two parts, one *independent* of Δx, the other *vanishing with* Δx. The first is the important part and is named *Derivative* (D) or Differential Coefficient (DC). More formally, if $y = f(x)$ be a unique continuous function of x in $[a, b]$, and x be any point therein, and if $\frac{\Delta y}{\Delta x} = \frac{f(x \pm \Delta x) - f(x)}{\pm \Delta x}$ approaches a limit as Δx approaches o *no matter how*, then that limit is called *Derivative* (D) of $f(x)$, as to x, at the point x. If $f(x)$ has a D at every point of $[a, b]$, the assemblage of them forms a new function, the Derivative of $f(x)$ for $[a, b]$, which we may write $f'(x)$ with Lagrange, or $Df(x)$ with Cauchy. Hence

$$\frac{\Delta f(x)}{\Delta x} = f'(x) + \sigma.$$

Geometric Interpretation.—The Differential Calculus originated in the Problem of *Tangents*. Let P be any point of a curve referred to rectangular axes X, Y, and let P be between Q and Q'. Draw secants PQ, PQ', sloped θ and θ' to X, and ϕ to each other; draw ordinates through P, Q, Q'; through P and Q' draw parallels to X, meeting ordinates through Q and P at D and D'. Then $PD = \Delta x$, $D'Q' = \Delta'x$, $DQ = \Delta y$, $PD' = \Delta'y$.

Also $\frac{\Delta y}{\Delta x} = \tan\theta$, $\frac{\Delta'y}{\Delta'x} = \tan\theta'$, $\tan(\theta' - \theta) = \tan\phi$. If now by approaching Q and Q' to P we can *make* and *keep* ϕ, and therefore $\tan\phi$, small at will, then the secants settle

down into a common position called *tangent* to the curve at P (sloped r to X) and the common limit of $\frac{\Delta y}{\Delta x}$ and $\frac{\Delta'y}{\Delta'x}$ is tan τ; or $f'(x) = \tan$ r. But if P were an *angular point*, then PQ and PQ' would *not* tend together, $\frac{\Delta y}{\Delta x}$ would tend to one limit, the *progressive* differential coefficient, and $\frac{\Delta'y}{\Delta'x}$ to another limit, the *regressive* differential coefficient; only when these two *coalesce* is there a *Derivative* proper. Thus in $y = x\left(e^{\frac{1}{x}} - 1\right) \Big/ \left(e^{\frac{1}{x}} + 1\right)$, at the Origin, Lim. $\frac{\Delta y}{\Delta x} = \left(e^{\frac{1}{x}} - 1\right) \Big/ \left(e^{\frac{1}{x}} + 1\right)$, the *progressive* $DC = 1$, the *regressive* $DC = -1$, the two limiting positions of the secants are perpendicular.

How thickly may such *salients* be strewn along a curve? To have a D, i.e. to be *differentiable*, plainly the function must be continuous; it was long thought that this *necessary* condition was *sufficient*, that the continuous function possessed in general a D, save at certain special points. It was *Riemann* who first suggested (at least as early as 1861) the astonishing possibility that such an $f(x)$ as $\sum\limits_{n=1}^{n=\infty} \frac{\sin(n^2 x)}{n^2}$, though everywhere continuous, was nowhere differentiable; but as he left no proof, it was generally thought he meant that it was possible to find such salients in every infinitesimal $[x, x + \Delta x]$, which was easy to show; but *Weierstrass* thought he meant strictly that the D did not exist for any value of x. In any case Weierstrass himself produced (July 18, 1872) an example of such a function, $y = \sum\limits_{n=0}^{n=\infty} b^n \cos(a^n x \pi)$,—where a is an odd integer, b a positive < 1, and $ab > 1 + \frac{3}{2}\pi$,—which, though everywhere continuous, has nowhere a D, since the *progressive* and *regressive* Difference-Quotients are everywhere opposite in sign and increase oppositely toward ∞ as they pass over into Differential Coefficients ('Math. Werke von K. Weierstrass, II,' p. 71-4). *Geometrically*, in the graph of the differentiable function, the polygon formed by n consecutive chords tends towards the curve for $n = \infty$, PQ and PQ' tend to coalesce as Q and Q' both approach P, the triangle PQQ' becomes flatter and flatter (we may suppose the arc QPQ' steadily enlarged under a microscope to its original length as Q and Q' close down on P), the curve we may say is *elementally straight* at P. But with Weierstrass's function the polygon remains always reëntrant, a zigzag, and consecutive chords, PQ and PQ', tend to *separate* at a straight angle. Such discontinuities may yet present themselves to the future student of nature.

If $y = x^2$ $\Delta y = 2x\Delta x + \overline{\Delta x}^2$, $\frac{\Delta y}{\Delta x} = 2x + \Delta x$, whence $D_x y \equiv \frac{dy}{dx} \equiv y_x = 2x$. Here y is the area of a square whose side is x, and $2x$ is the border of the square perpendicular to which the D square expands, the D is *the front of variation*.

Similarly, if $y = \pi x^2$, $D_x y = 2\pi x$, the circumference, the front of variation perpendicular to which x varies. If $y = x^3$, $D_x y = 3x^2 =$ the front of variation perpendicular to which x varies. If $y = \frac{4}{3}\pi x^3$, $D_x y = 4\pi x^2 =$ the sphere-surface, the front of variation perpendicular to x. For $y = x^4$, $D_x y = 4x^3 =$ again the whole front of variation, though here our powers of envisagement fail us. Thus we are conducted to the Derivation of *Assemblages*, for which the reader must be referred to this latter subject.

Kinematic Illustration.—Let $s =$ length of path of a moving point P, described in time t; Δs and $\Delta t =$ corresponding changes in s and t; then $\frac{\Delta s}{\Delta t} = \bar{v} = average\ speed$ during Δt;

Lim. $\frac{\Delta s}{\Delta t} = D_t s = instantaneous\ speed$ at $t = speed\ at\ the\ instant\ t$ (*i.e.* end of t and beginning of Δt). There is no motion *at* the instant of time, nor *at* the point of path, but only *during* the time and space immediately about the point and instant. *Instantaneous speed* is a technical term for *limit of average speed* in the immediate vicinity of the point and instant. This instantaneous speed generally varies with t, and its D as to t is named *acceleration* and is written $\frac{dv}{dt}$. The product of this acceleration by the *mass* of the moving P yields the all-important notion of *force*. The D of this acceleration might be called *second acceleration*, but the notion has not yet proved useful in *Mechanics* (q.v.).

The *notation* for D may be this or that. Newton used the dot, thus $\dot{s}$, to denote derivative as to t, as still do the British; Lagrange, the accent, $F'(x)$, still common; Cauchy, the *operator* D, with or without subscribed argument x; others subscripts, as y_x, y_1, etc.; most common, most expressive, but possibly misleading is the Leibnitzian $\frac{dy}{dx}$, *not* a fraction (thus far at least), not the quotient of dy divided by dx, but the limit of the fraction $\frac{\Delta y}{\Delta x}$ for Δx vanishing, no matter how. Sometimes we write $\frac{d}{dx}$ for D_x, thus: $y_x = D_x y = \frac{d}{dx} y = \frac{dy}{dx}$, etc.

Lagrange ('Théorie des Fonctions,' I) attains the notion of *Derived Functions* (or *Ds*) by substituting $x + \xi$ for x in $F(x) = a_0 + a_1 x + a_2 x^2 + \ldots a_n x^n$, whence $F(x + \xi) = F(x) + F'(x) \cdot \xi + \frac{F''(x)}{\underline{2}} \cdot \xi^2 + \ldots + \frac{F^{(n)}(x)}{\underline{n}} \cdot \xi^n$, where each F turns out to be formed from the preceding in the same way; they are the *Derived Functions* of F. A near-lying Generalization considers $f(x) = \sum\limits_{n=0}^{n=\infty} a_n(x-a)^n$, supposed absolutely convergent for all values of $|x - a| < R$, *i.e.* for x within $[a - R,\ a + R]$. Then in the same $[\ ]$ all the ∞ series

$$\sum_{n=m}^{n=\infty} \frac{\underline{n}}{\underline{n-m}} a_n(x-a)^{n-m} \quad (m = 1, 2, 3, \ldots)$$

will also converge absolutely. Denote them in turn by $f'(x)$, $f''(x)$, ... Choose ξ so that $|x - a| + |\xi| < R$; then the series $\sum\limits_{m=0}^{m=\infty} \frac{f^{(m)}(x)}{\underline{m}} \cdot \xi^m$ will also converge absolutely in the same $[\ ]$ and will equal $f(x + \xi)$. These Sums $f'(x)$, $f''(x)$, ... are called 1st and 2d, ... *Derived Functions* of $f(x)$, which may be called its own oth Derived Function. If instead of the inconvenient Lagrangian accents we put Cauchy's D's with proper exponents, we perceive that these latter, denoting order of differentiation, obey the same laws as ordinary exponents:

$$D^{m+n} = D^m \cdot D^n = D^n \cdot D^m,\ \text{etc.}$$

It is usual, though not quite satisfactory, to denote the value of any derived function at any point $(x = a)$ by writing a for x, thus: $f^{(n)}(a)$. At this stage the D-notation is not so convenient. These special values are seen to be $f^{(n)}(a) = \underline{n} \cdot a_n$. On finding hence the a's and substituting in the definition of $f(x)$ we get $f(x) = f(a) + \sum\limits_{n=1}^{n=\infty} \frac{f^{(n)}(a)}{\underline{n}} (x-a)^n = \sum\limits_{n=0}^{n=\infty} \frac{f^{(n)}(a)}{\underline{n}} (x-a)^n$.

Such is the ordinary *Taylor's Series*, or Maclaurin's (more justly Stirling's) in case $a = 0$.

Lagrange supposed (amazingly, Picard) *any* arbitrary $f(x)$ expansible in positive integral powers of $(x - a)$, except for special values of a. However, presupposed only uniqueness and continuity in a definite interval, there may be *no* value of a in the interval for which such expansion is possible. Thus, $f(x) = (-x)^p$ for $x < 0$ and $= x^p$ for $x \geq 0$ cannot be developed in positive integral powers of x for x positive and p not integral. Hence this Lagrangian notion of derived function, while in general agreeing with the notion of D as limit of difference-quotient, is not yet so universal.

The notion of *Differential*, though unnecessary at this stage, is commonly introduced thus: From $\frac{\Delta y}{\Delta x} = \frac{\Delta f(x)}{\Delta x} = f'(x) + \sigma$, $\Delta y = \Delta f(x) = f'(x) \Delta x + \sigma \Delta x$. This first part of $\Delta f(x)$, namely, $f'(x) \Delta x$, proportional to Δx and of the same order of infinitesimality, may be defined as the *Differential* of $f(x)$ and may be denoted by $df(x)$, which is thus a *finite variable* for $\Delta x \lessgtr 0$. For $f(x) = x$, we have $dx = \Delta x$, which is therefore *differential* of x. Hence $\frac{dy}{dx} = \frac{df(x)}{dx} = f'(x)$, *i.e.* the D of $f(x)$ as to $x =$ the *quotient* of the differentials of $f(x)$ and x (Leibnitz). Here $\frac{dy}{dx}$ is strictly a *fraction* whose terms are by no means " ghosts of departed quantities " (Berkeley). *Geometrically*, dy is the Δy (or DQ) prolonged *up* to the tangent at P, $=$ change of the ordinate of the tangent when abscissa changes by dx; Lim. $\frac{\Delta y}{\Delta y} = 1$. This notion of differential, though useful in geometry, mechanics, and elsewhere, rather embarrasses theoretical development of the subject. Hence the terms *Differentiation* ($=$ Derivation), to *differentiate*, and hence the names Differential Calculus, Differential Coefficient.

On these bases the structure of the DIFFEREN-TIAL CALCULUS may now be safely erected. Primary formulæ, easily established, are as follows (D meaning always *Derivative as to x, u, v*, etc., being *simultaneous* functions of x):

$$D(u+v-w) = Du + Dv - Dw;$$

$$D(uv) = Du \cdot v + u \cdot Dv = uv\left(\frac{Du}{u} + \frac{Dv}{v}\right);$$

$$D\left(\frac{u}{v}\right) = \left(\frac{u}{v}\right)' = \frac{u' \cdot v - u \cdot v'}{v^2};$$

$$(u \pm c)' = u'; \quad (cu)' = c \cdot u'.$$

Very important is *Mediate Derivation*, when y is function of a function of x, as $y = \phi(u)$, $u = f(x)$, hence $y = \phi\{f(x)\} = F(x)$. *If then ϕ and f have definite D's, $\phi'(u)$ and $f'(x)$*, we have $\frac{dy}{dx} = \frac{dy}{du} \cdot \frac{du}{dx}$, hence $y_x = y_u \cdot u_x = \phi'(u) \cdot f'(x)$. But y_x may exist even when the supposition fails, and this rule with it.

In particular, if $y = f(x)$ and inversely $x = \phi(y)$, and if either variable has a $D \neq 0$, so has the other. For if $f'(x) = \text{Lim.} \frac{dy}{dx} \neq 0$, then $\frac{dx}{dy} = 1 \Big/ \frac{dy}{dx}$; hence $\text{Lim.} \frac{dx}{dy} = \frac{1}{f'(x)}$, or $\phi'(y) = \frac{1}{f'(x)}$, *i.e.*, in general, the D's of x as to y and of y as to x are *reciprocals of each other:* $y_x \cdot x_y = 1$.

If $y' = f'(x)$ be $+$, then x and y increase (or decrease) together, $f(x)$ is called *increasing* at x. But if y' be $-$, then x and y change oppositely, $f(x)$ is *decreasing* at x.

Hence if $f'(c) \neq 0$, $f(x)$ must be $> f(c)$ on one side of the point c, and $< f(c)$ on the other. Hence *Rolle's Theorem:* If $f(x)$ vanishes at a and b and has a D at every point *within* $[a, b]$, then this D, $f'(x)$, vanishes at some point within $[a, b]$.

Now, $f(x) \equiv (b - a)\{\phi(x) - \phi(a)\} - (x - a)\{\phi(b) - \phi(a)\}$ is such an $f(x)$, made to order, ϕ being differentiable within $[a, b]$. Hence $f'(x) = (b - a)\phi'(x) - \{\phi(b) - \phi(a)\}$ must $= 0$ for some $\bar{x}$ in $[a, b]$. Hence $\phi(b) - \phi(a) = (b - a)\phi'(\bar{x})$. Commonly we write a for x and $x + h$ for b; then $\bar{x} = x + \theta h$, where θ is in $[0, 1]$, so that $\phi(x + h) - \phi(x) = h\phi'(x + \theta h)$, the extremely important formula for *finite increments*. Hence we see at once that if the D is everywhere 0 within an interval, the function is constant in that interval; and hence that two functions whose D's are equal in an interval can themselves differ only by a constant in that interval —a Theorem at the base of the Integral Calculus.

Passing now to D's, we first attempt $y = e^x$. Hence

$$y + dy = e^{x + dx} = e^x \cdot e^{dx} = e^x\{1 + dx + (dx^2)\}.$$

Hence

$$\frac{dy}{dx} = e^x\left(\frac{e^{-1}}{dx}\right) = e^x\left[1 + \frac{dx}{2} + \frac{dx^2}{\underline{3}} + \dots\right].$$

This [ ] is term by term, except the first, less than e^{dx}, whose limit is 1; hence Lim. [ ] is 1: hence $\text{Lim.} \frac{dy}{dx} = e^x$, or $De^x = e^x$. *The exponential e^x is unchanged by Derivation as to its*

exponent. Hence $De^u = e^u \cdot u_x$. Hence, if $y = \log x$, $e^y = x$, $e^y \cdot y_x = 1$, $y_x = e^{-y} = \frac{1}{x}$; or

$D \log x = \frac{1}{x}$. Hence $D \log u = \frac{u_x}{u}$. Hence, if $y = x^m$, $\log y = m \log x$; $Dy = Dx^m = mx^{m-1}$. For $y = \sin x$,

$$2 dy = \sin(x + 2dx) - \sin x = 2 \cos(x + dx) \sin dx;$$

$$\frac{dy}{dx} = \cos(x + dx) \frac{\sin dx}{dx}; \text{ hence}$$

$$y_x = D \sin x = \cos x = \sin\left(x + \frac{\pi}{2}\right); \text{ hence}$$

$D \sin u = \cos u \cdot u_x$. Hence $D \cos x = -\sin x = \cos\left(x + \frac{\pi}{2}\right)$. Hence derivation of sine and cosine as to the angle merely adds $\frac{\pi}{2}$ to the angle. Also, $D \tan x = 1 + \overline{\tan x^2} = \overline{\sec x^2}$. If $y = \sin^{-1}x$, $\sin y = x$, $y_x \cdot \cos y = 1$, $y_x = \frac{1}{\sqrt{1 - x^2}}$; hence $D \sin^{-1}u = \frac{u_x}{\sqrt{1 - u^2}}$. Similarly for $\cos^{-1}$. If $y = \tan^{-1}x$, similarly $D \tan^{-1}x = \frac{1}{1 + x^2}$. Specially, $D \sin^{-1}\frac{x}{a} = \frac{1}{\sqrt{a^2 - x^2}}$, $D \tan^{-1}\frac{x}{a} = \frac{a}{a^2 + x^2}$. Similarly we treat the hyperbolic sine and cosine and tangent (*hsx, hcx, htx*), and their inverses $hs^{-1}x$, $hc^{-1}x$, $ht^{-1}x$, with the important results: $Dhsx = hcx$, $Dhcx = hsx$, $Dhtx = 1 - \overline{htx^2}$,

$$Dhs^{-1}x = \frac{1}{\sqrt{x^2 + 1}}, \quad Dhc^{-1}x = \frac{1}{\sqrt{x^2 - 1}},$$

$$Dht^{-1}x = \frac{1}{1 - x^2},$$

with easy generalization for u and $\frac{x}{a}$,--formulæ especially important in Integration. By Derivation the anti-transcendentals are thus reduced to algebraic forms, while the exponentials and goniometries return into themselves; hence the inverse of Derivation, whatever it may be, applied to algebraic forms, may give rise to transcendentals. So much for ordinary *algebraic* and simply *periodic* functions.

The *Infinite Series* cannot always be differentiated by differentiating term by term, but only under certain conditions of *equable convergence*. If each term $f_n(x)$ of $f(x) = L \sum_{n=0}^{n=\infty} f_n(x)$ be unique and continuous *and if Σ converge*, for every x in $[a, a+d]$, and if $\text{Lim.} f(x) = f(a)$,—for such a series the Theorem holds: *If each term has a finite progressive DC, $f_n'(a)$, and if the series of DC's, $\sum_{n=0}^{n=\infty} \frac{f_n(a + dx) - f_n(a)}{dx}$, converges equably for every $dx > 0$ and $< d$, then* $\sum_{n=0}^{n=\infty} f_n'(a)$ *also converges and*

$$= L \sum_{n=0}^{n=\infty} \frac{f_n(a + dx) - f_n(a)}{dx}, \text{ for } dx = +0.$$

In general, this narrower Theorem will answer: *If*, for every x in $[a, a+d]$, each $f_n(x)$ is unique, continuous, and has a D (and for $x = a$ at least a progressive DC), and if both $\sum\limits_{n=0}^{n=\infty} f_n(x)$ and $\sum\limits_{n=0}^{n=\infty} f'_n(x)$ converge, the latter equably, *then* $Lf(x) = f(a)$, *and* $f(x)$ *has a progressive DC at* a, *which is* $\sum\limits_{n=0}^{n=\infty} f_n'(a)$; *i.e.* we form the D of the infinite series by summing (to ∞) the D's of the terms (for details see *Real Variable, Theory of Functions of the.*

For D of $f(z)$ as to z, where $z = x + iy$, see *Complex Variable, Theory of Functions of.*[*]

A D of a first D is called a *second D*, written variously $f''(x)$, D_{x^2}, $\dfrac{d^2}{dx^2}$, and so on for the 3d, 4th, ... nth D's. We see at once,

$$D^n x^m = \frac{\lfloor m}{\lfloor m-n}x^{m-n}, \quad D^n \frac{\sin}{\cos} x = \frac{\sin}{\cos}\left(x + n\frac{\pi}{2}\right),$$

$$D^n \frac{a}{(x+b)^m} = (-1)^n \frac{a\lfloor m+n-1}{\lfloor m-1(x+b)^{m+n}}.$$

A rational fraction must first be decomposed into *such* fractions. The exponential e^x repeats itself steadily, $D^n e^{ax} = a^n e^{ax}$; hence $\phi(D)e^{ax} = \phi(a)e^{ax}$, ϕ being algebraic and rational. The log x is at once reduced to a fraction by $D \log x = \dfrac{1}{x}$. For a product uv we have *Leibnitz's Theorem*:

$$D^n(uv) = u_n v + n u_{n-1} v_1 + \frac{n(n-1)}{1\cdot 2} u_{n-2} v_2 + \dots,$$

---

[*] The simultaneous Variation o. x and y is vividly depicted by the graph of $f(x, y) = 0$. But we may image it otherwise, thus: Let P and Q depict the Variables x and y, one moving on X, the other on Y, and let the elastic rod PQ connect them. As P moves uniformly along X, Q will slide up and down along Y, obeying $f = 0$. The assemblage of x-values is strewn evenly along X, the assemblage of y-values is not strewn evenly along Y, but is stretched, compressed, folded, crumpled in countless ways. The study of y_x becomes the study of the *intimate texture* of this Y-axis bearing the assemblage of y-Values.

If now $z = x + iy$, $w = u + iv$ be complex *variables*, and $w = f(z)$, then w is indeed compounded of x and y, not however in just any combination, as $x^2 \pm y^2$, $x \pm 2iy$, but only in the one combination, as $x + iy$. The domain of z is the XY-plane, of w the UV-plane, as which two we may take the floor and a wall or the ceiling. Not having a 4th dimension at command, we cannot envisage $w = f(z)$ as a surface, as we did $y = f(x)$ as a curve. We must again think of two points P and Q, in XY and UV, connected by an elastic rod, PQ: as P moves about in XY, Q moves about in UV, obeying $w = f(z)$. We may think of the texture of XY as uniform, then the texture of UV will not be uniform, but stretched, compressed, folded, and crumpled in countless ways. The study of w_z now becomes the study of this intimate *texture of UV*. As in $y = f(x)$ the derivative y_x is the part of the $\frac{dy}{dx}$ that is entirely independent of dx, so w_z must be independent of dz; but $dz = +o$ or $= -o$, so in general w_z is the same no matter how $dz \doteq o$, along whatever path of Value. *Geometrically* this signifies that if p, p' be two intersecting paths of z, and q, q' the corresponding intersecting paths of w, then p and p', q and q', *intersect under the same angle*. Hence the angles of the curvilinear triangle (q, q', q'') = the angles of the corresponding curvilinear triangle (p, p', p''); hence the two corresponding infinitesimal rectilinear triangles of the chords (or tangents) will be similar, the *ratio of similitude* being w_z, which of course varies from point to point; the one plane is a *map* of the other and the textures are *similar in the smallest parts*. Such is the geometric interpretation of the Derivative of *Functions of a Complex Variable* (q. v.). It would seem that such interpretations might be indefinitely extended.

---

precisely as in the Binomial Theorem, the subscripts denoting the D's. For a quotient $y = \dfrac{u}{v}$, we write $u = vy$, $u_1 = v_1 y + v y_1$, $u_2 = v_2 y + 2v_1 y_1 + v y_2, \dots, u_n = v_n y + n v_{n-1} y_1 + \dots + v y_n$. From these $(n+1)$ simultaneous equations we form the *eliminant* of the n unknowns, y, y_1, $y_2, \dots y_{n-1}$; this eliminant is linear in y_n and yields

$$y_n = \frac{(-1)^n \lfloor n}{v^{n+1}}\begin{vmatrix} u & v & 0 & 0 & 0 & \dots \\ u_1 & v_1 & v & 0 & 0 & \dots \\ \frac{u_2}{\lfloor 2} & \frac{v_2}{\lfloor 2} & v_1 & v & 0 & \dots \\ & & & & & \\ \frac{u_n}{\lfloor n} & & \dots & v_1 & v \end{vmatrix}$$

Applications.—1. Let P be any ordinary point of a curve, S the foot of the ordinate y, T and N the feet (on X) of tangent and normal at P. Since $y_x = \tan\tau$, $SN = y \cdot y_x$, $ST = y \cdot x_y$, and we easily express PN, PT, etc. Also, if ϕ = angle of intersection of $y = f(x)$ and $Y = F(x)$, then $\tan\phi = \dfrac{y_x - Y_x}{1 + y_x Y_x}$. If the curves touch, the numerator = o; if they are perpendicular, the denominator = o.

2. *Envelopes.*—Let $F(x, y; \ p) = o \qquad (1)$ be a system of curves distinguished by varying values of the parameter p. For any special value of p, $F(x, y; \ p) = o$ will be one curve and

$$F(x, y; \ p + \Delta p) = o \qquad (2)$$

a neighboring curve. Where do they meet? What relation connects x and y of the intersection, I, of any such pair? We must combine (1) and (2) and eliminate p. If in the result we pass to the limit for $\Delta p \doteq o$, we shall find the *locus of the intersection of consecutives* (or the *Envelope*) of the system. For (2) we may put (1)−(2), or still better

$$\frac{F(x, y; \ p + \Delta p) - F(x, y; \ p)}{\Delta p} = o. \qquad (3)$$

It will be equivalent to invert the procedure, to pass to the limit and then eliminate p. So we get

$$F_p(x, y; \ p) = o, \qquad (4)$$

between which and (1) we now eliminate p. This eliminant connects x and y for every intersection of two consecutives of the system, every *instantaneous pivot* about which the curve starts to turn into a neighboring position. *But this is not all.* It connects the x and y of all other points where meet two curves (branches) corresponding to the same p, as may thus be seen. Assign any pair of values to x and y, *i.e.*, take any point in the plane, and ask what members of $F = o$ pass through it, *i.e.* what are the corresponding values of p? There are n such, if F be of nth degree in p. When only two of these p-roots be equal. Only when the p-discriminant of $F = o$ vanishes; *i.e.*, when the eliminant of p between $F = o$ and $F_p = o$ vanishes, as we know from *Algebra*: Hence this eliminant connects x and y for all points where meet two curves corresponding to the same or equal p's. This will include all *cusps* and *nodes* as well as *instantaneous pivots*; hence the p-eliminant = o will be the equation of all *cusp-loci* and *node-loci* as well as of *envelope proper*.

Illustration.—Find the envelope of a straight line AB on which the intercept between X and Y is a constant c. The equation of AB is

$$\frac{x}{a}+\frac{y}{\sqrt{c^2-a^2}}-1=0=F(x,\ y;\ a).$$

Another $A'B'$ of the system is

$$\frac{x}{a'}+\frac{v}{\sqrt{c^2-a'^2}}-1=0 \quad (a'=a+\varDelta a),$$

and another $A''B''$ is

$$\frac{x}{a''}+\frac{v}{\sqrt{c^2-a''^2}}-1=0 \quad (a''=a-\varDelta a).$$

The Intersections I' and I'' of these two with AB are definite. As A' and A'' close down upon and coalesce in A, I' and I'', always definite, close down upon and coalesce in their common limit I, the *instantaneous pivot* about which AB starts to turn. Differentiating and eliminating a we find the 4-cusped Hypocycloid, $x^{\frac{2}{3}}+y^{\frac{2}{3}}=c^{\frac{2}{3}}$, as the envelope, or path of the *instantaneous pivot* I.

Hence Plücker's double conception of a curve as *path* of a point gliding along a straight line that turns about the point, and *envelope* of a straight line that turns about a point that glides on the straight line. The relation connecting the corresponding magnitudes, arc-length s (of the path) and angle α (through which the straight line turns), is the *intrinsic equation* of the curve. The $\frac{DQ}{ds}$, is named *average curvature* of $\varDelta s$; its limit $\frac{d\alpha}{ds}$ is named *instantaneous curvature* (κ) at P. Plainly $\varDelta\alpha=\varDelta\tau$; hence

$$\kappa=\frac{d\tau}{ds}=\frac{d\tau}{d\tan\tau}\cdot\frac{d\tan\tau}{dx}\cdot\frac{dx}{ds}=\frac{y''}{(1+y'^2)^{\frac{3}{2}}}.$$

(N.B. *The Differential Triangle PDQ* formed by $\varDelta x$, $\varDelta y$, $\varDelta s$, yields at once

$$s_t^2=x_t^2+y_t^2,\quad \frac{dx}{ds}=\frac{1}{\sqrt{1+y_x^2}},\quad \frac{dy}{ds}=\frac{v_x}{\sqrt{1+y_x^2}}$$

In the circle κ is the constant $\frac{1}{r}$, hence the curvature of the circle is the *reciprocal of the radius*. For any point of any curve the reciprocal of this curvature is called the *radius of curvature*, ρ; hence this ρ at any point is the *radius of a circle of equal curvature*, hence called *circle of curvature*.

To illustrate.—Draw PT and PN, tangent and normal to the curve; about K' and K'' on PN, with radii $\rho'>\rho$ and $\rho''<\rho$, through P draw two circles, one less, the other greater than the circle of curvature. Let ρ' and ρ'' approach and coalesce in ρ; then K' and K'' approach and coalesce in K, the *center of curvature*, and the $\odot$ about K is the *osculatory circle*.

Otherwise, through P, and Q' and Q'' on opposite sides of P, draw a circle. Let mid-normals to PQ', PQ'' meet PN at S', S'', and each other at S'''; as Q' and Q'' approach and coalesce in P, S', S'', S''' all approach and coalesce in their common limit, S (or K). Hence the osculatory circle = circle *through three consecutive points* of a curve, and *center of curvature = intersection of two consecutive normals*.

The coordinates (u and v) of K are given by $u=x-\frac{y''}{y'}(1+y'^2), v=y+\frac{1}{y'}(1+y'^2)$. Eliminating x and y between these equations and the equation of the curve, we get the equation connecting u and v for every K, *i.e.* the *equation of the Evolute*, or locus of the centers *of curvature* of the original curve (the *Involute*). Since $v_u \cdot y_x+1=0$, the tangents at corresponding P and K are perpendicular, *the normal to the involute* is *tangent to the evolute*. Also, it is easy to prove that the arc-length in *Evolute* can differ only by a constant from the *radius of curvature* (ρ) in *Involute*. Hence a point of a cord held tight while being unwound from the *evolute* must trace an *involute*; hence the former name. To any involute there is only one evolute, but to any evolute there are infinitely many (so-called parallel) involutes,—an excellent illustration of a one-valued determination with many-valued inverse, and also of the definiteness of differentiation as compared with the indefiniteness of its inverse, Integration (see below). Some curves reproduce themselves in their evolutes, notably Cycloid and Logarithmic Spiral, which latter inspired the engraving and epitaph on the tomb of Jacob Bernoulli (1654-1705): *Eadem mutata resurgo*. The general theory of the Contact of curves, Asymptotes, etc., beautifully exemplifies this Calculus, but cannot be treated here (see *Curves, Higher Plane*).

Indeterminates.—If for $x=a$ both terms of a fraction $y=\frac{\phi(x)}{\psi(x)}$ vanish, then y loses definiteness, taking the unmeaning form, $y'=\frac{\phi(a)}{\psi(a)}=\frac{0}{0}$. (Cf. *Algebra.*)

The fundamental example is $y=\frac{x^m-a^m}{x-a}$, for $x=a$. However, we may still seek Lim. $\frac{\phi(x)}{\psi(x)}$ for $x=a\ne 0$, though it would be arbitrary to assume this limit as the *value* of $\frac{\phi(a)}{\psi(a)}$ (Darboux). If $x-a$ be removable from both terms, we may cancel it for $x\ne a$, and then seek the limit for $x=a$. Thus $\frac{x^3-a^3}{x-a}=x^2+ax+a^2$ for $x\ne a$; this last $=3a^2$ for $x=a$; hence $\underset{x=a}{\text{Lim.}}\frac{x^3-a^3}{x-a}=3a^2$, but not $\frac{x^3-a^3}{x-a}=3a^2$ for $x=a$, unless arbitrarily. Now $\underset{x=a}{\text{Lim.}}\frac{\phi(x)}{\psi(x)}=\underset{x=a}{\text{Lim.}}\frac{\phi'(a)}{\psi'(a)}$ for $\phi(a)=0=\psi(a)$ (L'Hospital).

Hence the ordinary rule: Take the limit of the quotient of the D's of the terms at the critical value. Or, expand the terms in the neighborhood of a, simplify, cancel the vanishing common factor, and evaluate for $x=a$. Similarly, with proper modification, we treat $\frac{\infty}{\infty}$; and $\infty-\infty$, reduced to $\frac{0}{0}$. Indeterminate exponentials like 1^∞, 0^∞, etc., are first reduced to $\frac{0}{0}$ by passing to Logarithms.

Maxima, Minima, are already defined, and

accordingly at such points the D must change sign; hence must pass through o, if *continuous*. This passage is from $+$ to $-$ for a maximum, from $-$ to $+$ for a minimum. Hence the ordinary rule: To maximize or minimize $f(x)$, put $f'(x) = o$; the x-roots will yield maximal or minimal values of $f(x)$ according as they make $f''(x)$ negative or positive. For $f''(x) = o$, treat 3d and 4th D's precisely as the 1st and 2d D's. The same rules result from expanding $f(x)$, as by Taylor's Theorem. Special cases (as of D discontinuous) call for special treatment, often geometrical or mechanical preferably.

The geometric depiction of a *function of two independent variables*, $z = f(x, y)$ or $F(x, y, z) = o$, is of course a *surface* (S): at any point (x, y) in the plane erect the corresponding value of z; the ends of these z's form S. We may pass on S from P to P' in ∞ of ways; *e.g.*, parallel to ZX; then x and z would change, but not y. Hence there would be simultaneous $\varDelta x$ and $\varDelta z$, but $\varDelta y = o$. Then $L\dfrac{\varDelta z}{\varDelta x}$ is written $\dfrac{\partial z}{\partial x}$ (Jacobi), and is read *partial D of z as to x*. Similarly, for a path of P parallel to YZ, there are simultaneous $\varDelta y$ and $\varDelta z$, but $\varDelta x = o$; $L\dfrac{\varDelta z}{\varDelta y} = \dfrac{\partial z}{\partial y} = $ *partial D of z as to y*.

For $u = f(x, y, z)$ intuition fails, but we think each P in $[x, y, z]$ as *weighted* with the proper u instead of erecting this u perpendicular to $[x, y, z]$. As P moves, the weight u changes. For motion parallel to X both $\varDelta y$ and $\varDelta z$ are o and $L\dfrac{\varDelta u}{\varDelta x} = \dfrac{\partial u}{\partial x}$, etc. Of course, the foregoing presumes that z and u actually admit of the Derivations in question.

Differentials, Partial and Total.—By Definition, $d_x u = \dfrac{\partial u}{\partial x} \cdot \varDelta x = partial Differential$ of u as to x, etc. $du = \dfrac{\partial u}{\partial x} \varDelta x + \ldots = \dfrac{\partial u}{\partial x} \cdot dx + \ldots = $ *total Differential* of u. $\varDelta u = \dfrac{\partial u}{\partial x} \cdot \varDelta x + \ldots + \varepsilon \varDelta x + \ldots = $ *total Difference* $= u$.

Geometrically, on $z = f(x, y)$, the path of x-change is parallel to ZX, hence $\dfrac{\partial z}{\partial x} = \tan \tau$, as before. Similarly $\dfrac{\partial z}{\partial y} = \tan v$. The plane through the tangents to these paths (at P) is in general the plane tangent at $P(x, y, z)$ to S. Clearly its equation is $w - z = (u - x)\dfrac{\partial z}{\partial x} + (v - y)\dfrac{\partial z}{\partial y}$ (u, v, w, the current coördinates for the plane). This equation assumes the symmetric form $(u - x)F_x + (v - y)F_y + (w - z)F_z = o$, since $\dfrac{\partial z}{\partial x} = -\dfrac{F_x}{F_z}$, etc. Hence the equations of the normal are $\dfrac{u - x}{F_x} = \dfrac{v - y}{F_y} = \dfrac{w - z}{F_z}$.

As to *existence*, the tangent plane is conditioned like the tangent line. Through $P(x, y, z)$ and two neighbor points, Q and R (as $x + \varDelta x$, y, $z + \varDelta_x z$, and x, $y + \varDelta y$, $z + \varDelta_y z$), pass a secant plane $\varPi$. Let R and Q descend any wise upon P. If the tiltings of $\varPi$ approach o, if $\varPi$ settles down toward the same fixed position, no matter how $\varDelta x$ and $\varDelta y$ approach o, *i.e.* independently of $\dfrac{\varDelta y}{\varDelta x}$ and y_x, then the limiting position of $\varPi$ is the tangent plane at P. But at the vertex P of a cone $(x^2 + y^2 = m^2 z^2)$, $\varPi$ rolls forever round the cone as Q and R circle round P. Here, at (o, o, o), $\dfrac{\partial z}{\partial x} = \dfrac{x}{m^2 z}$ and $\dfrac{\partial z}{\partial y} = \dfrac{y}{m_2 z}$ lose all meaning, as do tangent plane and normal.

In general there is no such notion as Total Derivative of $z = f(x, y)$, x and y independent; but if both be functions of an arbitrary t, we have the *Total D* of z as to this t:
$$\frac{dz}{dt} = \frac{df}{dt} = \frac{\partial f}{\partial x} \cdot \frac{dx}{dt} + \frac{\partial f}{\partial y} \cdot \frac{dy}{dt},$$
an extension of mediate derivation. Of course, the possibility and definiteness of the operations are implied. Hence again
$$dz = df = \frac{\partial f}{\partial x} \cdot dx + \frac{\partial f}{\partial y} \cdot dy,$$
or the *Total Differential* $=$ the sum of the *Partial Differentials*. For $t = x$, $\dfrac{dz}{dx} = f_x + f_y \cdot y_x$, or $dz = f_x \cdot dx + f_y \cdot dy$, a fundamental theorem holding when at (x, y) the DQ
$$\frac{f(x + \varDelta x, y + \varDelta y) - f(x, y + \varDelta y)}{\varDelta x}$$
is an *equably continuous function* of y and $\varDelta x$.

Higher D's are *pure* when the same *Independent Variable* is retained, *mixed* when it is changed. So $\dfrac{\partial^2 z}{\partial x^2}$, $\dfrac{\partial^3 z}{\partial y^3}$ are pure, but $\dfrac{\partial^2 z}{\partial x \partial y}$ is mixed. In mixed D's the question arises: Is the *order of Derivation indifferent?* The answer is, Yes, $\dfrac{\partial^2 z}{\partial x \partial y} = \dfrac{\partial^2 z}{\partial y \partial x}$, but only under conditions. For a power-series the case is clear, but the general investigation is subtle, and the result is involved and tedious. The theorem holds: When, for x in $[a - h, a + h]$ and y in $[b - k, b + k]$, $f(x, y)$ is uniquely defined, *and* the $\frac{1}{2}(n - 1)(n + 2)$ DC's
$$\frac{\partial^m f}{\partial x^{m - r} \partial y^r} \begin{pmatrix} r = o, 1, \ldots m \\ 1 \leq m \leq n - 1 \end{pmatrix}$$
exist and are finite, *and* all the mixed ones are continuous as to both x and y, *then* everywhere in the same rectangle $(2h, 2k)$ all the other mixed DC's below the nth order exist, and the order of derivation is indifferent. Also, if, *besides*, everywhere in the rectangle the $(n - 1)$ mixed DC's of nth order, $\dfrac{\partial^n f(x, y)}{\partial x^{n - 1} \partial y}$, $\dfrac{\partial^n f(x, y)}{\partial x^{n - 2} \partial y^2}, \ldots \dfrac{\partial^n f(x, y)}{\partial x \partial y^{n - 1}}$, exist finite, *and* at $[a, b]$ are continuous as to both x and y, *then* all other mixed DC's exist at $[a, b]$, the order of derivation being indifferent. Space is wanting for the proofs.

The Taylorian Series or *Law of the Mean* may now be extended, under proper conditions, to develop $f(x, y)$ near (x, y), thus:
$$f(x + h, y + k) = f(x, y) + \left\{ h \frac{\partial f}{\partial x} + k \frac{\partial f}{\partial y} \right\}$$
$$+ \frac{1}{2} \left\{ h^2 \frac{\partial^2 f}{\partial x^2} + 2hk \frac{\partial^2 f}{\partial x \partial y} + k^2 \frac{\partial^2 f}{\partial y^2} \right\} \cdots$$
$$+ \frac{1}{\lfloor n} \sum_{p = 0}^{p = n} {}_n p \frac{h^{n - p} \cdot p \partial^n f(x + \theta h, y + \eta y)}{\partial x^{n - p} \partial y^p}.$$

Symbolically,

$$f(x+h, y+k) = \Sigma e^{h\frac{\partial}{\partial x} + h\frac{\partial}{\partial y}} f(x, y).$$

The last term is the remainder R_n, which must converge upon o, for $n \doteq \infty$, to be neglected. A sufficient condition therefore is that the partial D's of f remain finite near (x, y) for $n \doteq \infty$. This is not a necessary condition, however, to find which is not easy nor attempted here.

Geometrically, take the tangent plane at P as XY, the normal as Z. Develop $z = f(x, y)$ near $P(o. o, o)$ so that $\Delta x = h = x$, $\Delta y = k = y$, $\Delta z = z$. We have

$$z = f(x, y) = \left\{ x\frac{\partial}{\partial x} + y\frac{\partial}{\partial y} \right\} f(o, o) +$$

$$\frac{1}{|2} \left\{ x^2\frac{\partial^2}{\partial x^2} + 2xy\frac{\partial^2}{\partial x \partial y} + y^2\frac{\partial^2}{\partial y^2} \right\} f(o, o) + \{x^3, y^3\}.$$

Since x, y, z are all infinitesimal and $\frac{\partial f}{\partial x} = o = \frac{\partial f}{\partial y}$ at (o, o, o), z is infinitesimal of 2d order. Call the 2d D's in order A, B, C and put $x = r \cos \theta$, $y = r \sin \theta$, where θ is the angle with ZX of a normal plane, making a *normal section*, through Z. Hence $\frac{2z}{r^2} = A\overline{\cos\theta}^2 + 2B\cos\theta\sin\theta + C\overline{\sin\theta}^2$

$+ \{r\}$, hence Lim. $\frac{2z}{r^2} = A\overline{\cos}\,\theta^2 + 2B\cos\theta\sin\theta + C\overline{\sin\theta}^2$, which is easily seen to be the curvature, $\kappa = \frac{1}{\rho}$, of this normal section. For a perpendicular normal section, $\theta' = \theta + \pi/2$,

$\kappa' = \frac{1}{\rho'} = A\overline{\sin\theta}^2 - 2B\sin\theta\cos\theta + C\overline{\cos\theta}^2$;

hence $\frac{1}{\rho} + \frac{1}{\rho'} = A + B$, a *constant* for all pairs of perpendicular normal sections (Euler), important in Physics and formerly taken as measure of the curvature at $P(o, o, o)$.

Consider the surface $2z = Ax^2 + 2Bxy + Cy^2$. It is a *Paraboloid* (Pd); it fits on S only at $P(o, o, o)$, elsewhere departs from S. The sections of S and Pd are not the same for $z = c$, but close down on each other for $c \doteq o$. The Pd-section is an ellipse, an hyperbola, or a parabola, according as $B^2 - AC < o$, $> o$, or $= o$. Suppose it enlarged under the microscope to a constant size as $c \doteq o$; then the S-section steadily closes down on it as limit.

Hence Pd and S agree *elementally* at $P(o, o, o)$; also they agree in curvature (of their own normal sections), hence Pd is called the *osculating paraboloid* of S at (o, o, o). All these parallel sections, for changing c, are similar, hence $Ax^2 + 2Bxy + Cy^2 = 1$ is taken as type and called *Indicatrix* (Dupin). This indicatrix is an ellipse for $B^2 - AC < o$, the S is cup-shaped or synclastic; it is an hyperbola for $B^2 - AC > o$, the S is saddle-shaped (anti-clastic), like a mountain-pass. The indicatrix has two Axes, tangents to sections of greatest and least curvature both of Pd and S at P (any point of S) which are mutually perpendicular and named *principal sections*. Now let P start to move on S facing along either (say the least) axis or principal section. This axis starts to turn about P. Let P continue to move on S facing always along the turning axis. The tangent to its path will give the direction of this axis at every point of its path, which path

is called a *Line of Curvature* (LC). Plainly through every point of S there pass in general two and only two LC's (Monge), each the envelope on S of a system of principal tangents to S. These LC's cut up S into elementary curvilinear rectangles and yield an excellent system of coordinates (u, v). If the indicatrix be a circle, then all its axes are principal, through the point P there pass an ∞ of LC's, every normal section is principal, the point P is an *umbilic* or *cyclic* point. If the indicatrix be a parabola, then S is edged or ridged (cylindric) at P.

The notion of *surface-curvature* is generated and defined quite like that of line-curvature. Draw the normal N to S at every point of the border B of ΔS, forming a ruled surface, R. Draw parallel to each N a radius of a unit-sphere, forming a cone C cutting out $\Delta S'$, on the sphere-surface, which subtends a (so-called) solid angle $\Delta \alpha$ at the center. This we also define as the solid angle of the N's, and further define the *average curvature of* ΔS as the ratio $\frac{\Delta \alpha}{\Delta S}$. (Think of a cord passed round the gorge of R and then tightened, compressing R into C without changing the solid angle.) If the unit solid angle or stereradian (Halsted) be subtended by r^2, then the whole solid angle about center $= 4\pi$; then the metric numbers of $\Delta \alpha$ and $\Delta S'$ are equal, hence the curvature of $\Delta S = \frac{\Delta S'}{\Delta S}$, and Lim. $\frac{\Delta S'}{\Delta S} = S_s' = \alpha_s =$ instantaneous curvature at P (in ΔS) $= K$.

If R, R' be the principal radii of curvature at any P on S, then $K = \frac{1}{RR'}$; moreover, this K is *not affected* by bending S in any way without stretching or tearing—a beautiful Gaussian theorem of profound philosophic import. In this sense, an S that may be flattened out into a plane (a Developable) has o-curvature; for such, RR' must become ∞; hence either $R = \infty$ or $R' = \infty$. But $RR' = (1 + p^2 + q^2)/(rt - s^2)$, where $p = z_x$, $q = z_y$, $r = z_{xx}$, $s = z_{xy}$, $t = z_{yy}$ (Euler). Hence $rt - s^2 = o$ is the equation of *Developables*. For *Applicables* and further illustrations, see SURFACES, THEORY OF.

The difficulty in dealing with *Implicit functions* (defined by unsolved equations) lie in the *Existence-theorems*, which can only be stated. I. Let $F(x, y) = o$ at (x_0, y_0), and have 1st partial D's finite and continuous about (x_0, y_0), and $F_y \neq o$ at (x_0, y_0): then there *is* a $y = \phi(x)$ that becomes y_0 for $x = x_0$, and satisfies identically $F(x, y) = o$ in the vicinity, and is unique, and has a D, $y_x = \phi'(x) = -F_x/F_y$. II. Quite similarly for $F(x, y, z) = o$, $z = \phi(x, y)$, the last statement being: *has two partial D's*.

$z_x = -\dfrac{F_x}{F_z}$, $z_y = -\dfrac{F_y}{F_z}$; and so on for n variables.

Most generally (III) let $F_1, \ldots, F_n$ be n functions of m variables $x, y, \ldots$, and n variables $u, v, \ldots$, all the F's vanishing at $(x_0, y_0, \ldots, u_0, v_0, \ldots)$, all admitting partial D's in that vicinity, and $J(F_1, \ldots, F_n; u, v, \ldots) \neq o$ (p. 13), at $(x_0, y_0, \ldots, u_0, v_0, \ldots)$: then there *is* a system of functions of m independents $x, y, \ldots$ that become $u_0, v_0, \ldots$ at $(x_0, y_0, \ldots)$, that satisfy identically all the F's in that vicinity, and that have partial D's.

Hence we have as ordinary rule for finding y_x from $F(x, y) = o$: Differentiate F as to x

regarding y as a function of x, as in mediate derivation, and solve the result as to y_x.

To find now *maximum* or *minimum* y in $F(x, y) = 0$, we have $y_x = 0$, $\therefore F_x = 0$; also, therefore, $F_{xx} + F_y \cdot y_{xx} = 0$. If $F_y \neq 0$, there is maximum for F_{xx} and F_y *like-signed*, minimum for F_{xx} and F_y *unlike-signed*, and no determination for $F_{xx} = 0$.*

Often we seek (so-called) *relative maximum* and *minimum* of $z = f(x, y)$ when $F(x, y) = 0$. The former equation is a surface S, the latter an intersecting surface determining a path over S,—we seek the peak and valley points in this path. Differentiating we find as the prime condition, $f_x \cdot F_y - f_y \cdot F_x = 0 = J(f, F; x, y)$, from which and $F = 0$ we find the x and y that maximize or minimize f.

More generally we seek *maximum* or *minimum* of a function of $(m+n)$ variables, $f(x, y, \ldots u, v, \ldots)$, under n conditions $F_1(x, y, \ldots u, v, \ldots) = 0, \ldots F_n(x, y, \ldots u, v, \ldots) = 0$. Theoretically we might eliminate n variables $u, v, \ldots$ leaving the other m independent; better to let them remain considered as functions of the m independents, $x, y, \ldots$ Hence, on putting each partial $D = 0$, we get m equations which, with the n $F = 0, \ldots F_n = 0$, form $(m+n)$ equations for finding $(m+n)$ unknowns $x, y, \ldots u, v, w, \ldots$ To discriminate between maximum and minimum by the sign of d^2f will now be tedious, but often geometrically or mechanically unnecessary.

Swifter and simpler is Lagrange's 'Method of Multipliers.' We form a new function, $\phi(x, y, \ldots u, v, \ldots) = f(x, y, \ldots u, v, \ldots) - \Sigma \lambda F(x, y, \ldots u, v, \ldots)$. Only so long as each $F = 0$ will $\phi = f$ identically for all values (under consideration) of the variables. We now determine these λ's so as to make vanish simultaneously all the partial D's of ϕ as to $x, y, \ldots u, v, \ldots$ The n conditions are rolled off from the $u, v, \ldots$ upon the n λ's. We may proceed similarly in dealing with *Envelopes*, where $(n+1)$ parameters are connected by n conditions.

Transformation of Variables is often necessary, like transformation of Coördinates, the formulæ, simple at first, soon become highly complicated and we are led into the *Theory of Substitutions, Invariants, Reciprocants* and the like, which cannot be treated here.

Integration.—As the Differential Calculus is the doctrine of Limits of Quotients of Simultaneous Infinitesimal Differences, so the INTEGRAL CALCULUS is the doctrine of Limits of the Sums of Infinitesimal Products that increase in number while decreasing in size, both indefinitely. The type is the quadrature of an area (A) bounded by X, a curve $y = f(x)$, and two end-ordinates, $x = a$ and $x = b$. Cut it into n strips, ΔA, standing each on a Δx; their sum is A; plainly $Y \Delta x > \Delta A > y \Delta x$, Y being the greatest, y the least, ordinate standing on its own particular base Δx. Then $\Sigma \Delta x = b - a$, if $y = f(x)$ be continuous, finite, one-valued throughout $[a, b]$, each $Y - y$ is an ε, hence $\Sigma(Y - y)\Delta x < \varepsilon \Sigma \Delta x$, or $< (b-a)\varepsilon$; hence Lim. $\Sigma(Y - y)\Delta x = 0$. Hence A is the common limit of every $\Sigma y \Delta x$, written $\int_a^b y\,dx$, named

* From foregoing sections it is seen that, to max- resp. minimize z a function of independent x and y, we must have, as first condition, $z_x = 0 = z_y$; and similarly for any number of independents. The secondary conditions are too complicate for discussion here.

Definite Integral (DI) of $f(x)$ (the *Integrand*) as to x, between the *extremes* (end-values) a and b. The total sign of Integration is

$$\int \ldots dx \text{ or } \int_x, \quad \int \text{ being an extended } S, \text{ meaning}$$

Limit of Sum.

Plainly, exchanging extremes (a and b) merely reverses the integral by reversing Δx, $\int_b^a = -\int_a^b$. Also $\int_a^b = \int_a^c + \int_c^a$, $f(x)$ being supposed integrable throughout, from a to b, and to c. Also $\int c\phi x\,dx = c \int \phi(x)\,dx$. Also $\int_a^b f(x)\,dx = \int_{a\pm c}^{b\pm c} f(x\pm c)\,d(x\pm c)$,—a mere change of origin. Also $\int[\phi(x) \pm \psi(x)]\,dx = \int \phi(x)\,dx \pm \int \psi(x)\,dx$. We easily prove the almost obvious *Theorem of the Mean:* If $f(x) = \phi(x) \cdot \psi(x)$, each factor integrable, and $\psi(x)$ always of same sign, in $[a, b]$, then $\int_a^b \phi(x)\psi(x)\,dx = \phi(\bar{x}) \int_a^b \psi(x)\,dx$, $\bar{x} = a + \theta(b-a)$. Hence $I_b = f(b)$, $I_a = -f(a)$, where the D is again the *front of variation* of the Integral I or Area A. Hence we readily reckon many integrals as:

$$\int_a^b x^n dx = \frac{b^{n+1}}{n+1} - \frac{a^{n+1}}{n+1} = \left\{\frac{x^{n+1}}{n+1}\right\}_a^b, \; n \text{ a pos. int.;}$$

$$\int \cos x \, dx = \left\{\sin x\right\}_a^b, \; \int_a^b \sin x \, dx = \left\{-\cos x\right\}_a^b;$$

$$\int_a^b \sqrt{r^2 - x^2}\,dx = \frac{1}{2}\left\{x\sqrt{r^2-x^2} + r^2 \sin^{-1}\frac{x}{r}\right\}_a^b,$$

this seen at once from the figure (circle-quadrant), as also

$$\int_a^b \sqrt{r^2 + x^2}\,dx = \frac{1}{2}\left\{x\sqrt{r^2+x^2} + r^2 hs^{-1}\frac{x}{r}\right\}_a^b,$$

seen from $y^2 - x^2 = r^2$. We perceive that the $f(x)$ is always the D of the so-called *Indefinite Integral*, the expression to be evaluated at b and a. This is easily proved variously to be always the case. Thus, if $f(x) = \phi'(x)$ for x in $[a, b]$, then $\{I - \phi(b)\}_b = f(b) - \phi'(b) = 0$, for every value of b in the range of Integrability. Hence $I - \phi(b) = C$. For $b = a$, C is found to be $= -\phi(a)$; hence

$$I = \int_a^b \phi'(x)\,dx = \phi(b) - \phi(a),$$

Hence, to calculate the integral of any integrand from a to b, find the function of which the integrand is the D, and take the difference of its values at b and a. The D of the integral is the integrand, *so far as form* goes, but the *value* depends on the extremes. Since b may be any x in the range of integrability, it is common to write it x, using x in double sense, not necessarily confusing. So long as a is unassigned, C is undetermined; hence it is common to omit a and write $\int^x f(x)\,dx = \phi(x) + C$, where under $\int$ we may put z or any other symbol for x. The integral depends for its *form* solely on f; for its *value*, on a and b also.

Hence *integration* and *derivation* or *differentiation* are *inverse operations* and $\int = D^{-1}$, $D = \int^{-1}$. The direct D yields a definite result, the inverse $\int$ yields a result definite only as to *form*, up to an *additive constant, C.* (Cf. Evolute and Involute, above). Derivation simplifies, reducing even transcendents to algebraics; Integration complicates, lifting algebraics and even rationals up into transcendents $\left(\text{as } \sqrt{a^2-x^2} \text{ and } \dfrac{1}{x}\right)$. Derivation is deductive and can create no new forms. Integration is inductive and creates an ∞ of new forms, all defined as integrals.

Operating directly on $y = f(x)$ by a series of differentiations as to x, say $\psi(D)$, we get some function of x, as X, or $\psi(D)y = X$. If we know X and ψ, we may seek that $y \equiv f(x)$ that will yield X on being subjected to the train of operations $\psi(D)$; *i.e.* we seek to *invert* at once the totality of operations $\psi(D)$, so that $y = \dfrac{X}{\psi(D)} = \psi^{-1}(D)X$. This inversion is solving the *Differential Equation* $\psi(D)y = X$, and is perhaps the most profound of mathematical operations, of immense and even unconquerable difficulty, overcome as yet only in special cases. Thus $x^2\dfrac{d^2y}{dx^2} - 3x\dfrac{dy}{dx} + 4y = 2x^2$, where $\psi(D) \equiv x^2D^2 - 3xD + 4$, yields, as result of the inverse $\phi^{-1}(D)$ or $\dfrac{1}{\psi(D)}$,

$$y = x^2(A + B\log x + \overline{\log x}^2),$$

where A and B are arbitrary constants. Other forms of $\psi(D)$, quite as simple, yield far higher transcendents.

Inverting a table of elementary D's we get a table of *elementary Integrals.* The art is to *reduce* other forms, if possible, to these elementary forms; when impossible, we must introduce transcendents *defined by integrals.*

Change of Variable is the most fruitful method of Reduction. By mediate derivation, $D_x\phi(u) = \phi'(u) \cdot u_x$; also $D_u\phi(u) = \phi'(u)$; hence $\int \phi'(u)du = \phi(u) = \int \phi'(u) \cdot u_x \cdot dx$. In this 2d $\int$, all is supposed expressed through x.

Hence, to pass from an *old* to a *new* variable of integration, multiply by the D of the *old* as to the *new*, or divide by the D of the *new* as to the *old*; *i.e.* under the $\int$ sign,

$$du = u_x \cdot dx, \quad dx = \frac{du}{u_x}.$$

Of course, the extremes must be properly adjusted.

Integration by parts is also a powerful reductive process. From $(uv)_x = u_xv + uv_x$ we have

$$uv = \int u_xv\,dx + \int uv_x\,dx, \text{ or} \int uv_x\,dx = uv - \int u_xv\,dx.$$

This latter $\int$ may be simpler, or may return into the first, or other advantages may accrue. Thus $\int \cos x \cdot \cos x \cdot dx = \sin x \cdot \cos x + \int \overline{\sin x}^2 \cdot dx$

$$= \sin x \cdot \cos x + x - \int \overline{\cos x}^2 dx;$$ whence

$2\int \overline{\cos x}^2 \cdot dx = x + \sin x \cos x.$ Similarly for any integral power of sine or cosine except $(\sin x)^{-1}$, $(\cos x)^{-1}$, which are reduced by passing to the half-angle, $\dfrac{x}{2}$.

What is the range of such reductions? *What functions can we thus integrate in terms of known functions?* Few enough. Of *Algebraics,*

I. *Rational functions,* $\dfrac{\phi(x)}{\psi(x)}$, by decomposition into part-fractions.

II. *Rational functions* of x and $\left(\dfrac{ax+b}{cx+d}\right)^{a/\beta}$, $\left(\dfrac{ax+b}{cx+d}\right)^{a'/\beta'}$, ... Put $\dfrac{ax+b}{cx+d} = u^m$, m being L.C.M. of β, β', ... Herewith the $\int$ becomes rational in u.

III. *Rational functions* of x and $\sqrt{ax^2 + 2bx + c}$.

If we think of $y^2 = ax^2 + 2bx + c$ as a conic, and $y - \beta = u(x - \alpha)$ as a secant through a point (α, β) of the conic, then we may express both x and y rationally through u, which reduces this case to I; (α, β) may be taken variously. Generally we bring y^2 to the form of sum or difference of two squares by putting $x = z + h$.

IV. *Rational functions* of x and y, these being coördinates of a *unicursal* $F(x, y) = 0$. We shall then have $x = \phi(u)$, $y = \psi(u)$, where ϕ and ψ are rational, whereby these Abelian Integrals reduce to I.

The binomial $x^n(a + bx^n)^p$ can be reduced to II, and hence integrated, not generally, but in these important cases, by putting $u = x^n$:

1. p integral; if $\dfrac{m+1}{n} = \dfrac{r}{s}$ (r and s integers), put $\sqrt[s]{u} = z$.

2. $\dfrac{m+1}{n}$ integral; if $p = \dfrac{r}{s}$ (r and s integers), put $\sqrt[s]{a+bu} = z$.

3. $\dfrac{m+1}{n} + p$ integral; if $p = \dfrac{r}{s}$ (r and s integers), put $a + bu = uz^s$.

If $f(x)$ be rational in x, $\sqrt{ax+b}$, $\sqrt{cx+d}$, put $ax + b = v^2$, which reduces it to 3.

Of Transcendentals.—1. *Rational functions* of $\sin x$ and $\cos x$. Put $u = \tan\dfrac{x}{2}$, a very important substitution.

2. *Rational functions* of e^{ax}. Put $u = e^{ax}$.

3. *Rational Integral functions* of x, e^{ax}, e^{bx}, ... $\sin mx$, $\sin nx$, ..., $\cos mx$, $\cos nx$, ... Express the sines and cosines through imaginary exponentials. In the result express the imaginaries through sines and cosines. Here

are included rational functions of the *hyper-sine* and *-cosine*.

4. *Rational Integral functions* of x and $\log x$, or x and $\sin^{-1}x$. Put $x = e^u$, or $x = \sin u$.

If $f(x) = R(x, \sqrt{T})$, T of 3d or 4th degree in x, we cannot rationalize but must introduce *Higher Transcendents*. Let

$$u = \int_x^\infty \frac{dx}{\sqrt{T}} = \int_x^\infty \frac{dx}{\sqrt{4(x-e_1)(x-e_2)(x-e_3)}}.$$

Here x and u are functions of each other and it seems natural to take u as function, x as argument; but in $I = \int \frac{dx}{\sqrt{1-x^2}} = \sin^{-1}x$, $x = \sin I$ is a much simpler (periodic) function of I than I is of x; hence we may suspect that x above is a simpler (periodic?) function of u than u of x. Hence Abel thought the theory might be simplified by inverting the dependence before him assumed—one of the greatest divinations in mathematical history. We write

$$x = \wp(u) \text{ (Weierstrass)}, \quad u = \int_{\wp(u)}^\infty \frac{dx}{\sqrt{T}} = \wp^{-1}(x).$$

Hence $u_\wp = -\dfrac{1}{\sqrt{T[\wp(u)]}}$, and so on. Now just as sine and cosine have *one* period 2π, so $\wp$ has *two* periods, 2ω and $2\omega'$, it is an *Elliptic* or *Doubly periodic* function. The Theory of such Functions, one of the most august creations of the last century, is conspicuous in Analysis. Of Hyper-elliptic Integrals there is no space to speak.

The integral of an Infinite Series may be found by integrating term by term *only when* the series converges uniformly within an interval comprising the extremes of the integration.

It is seen that the integrable forms are absolutely many, relatively few, the integration generally giving rise to a *new function*.

Thus far we have raised no question as to *Integrability*, the Integrand being supposed unique, continuous, finite, and therefore integrable, in $[a, b]$. But when, if ever, may we let one or more of these conditions fall? As to continuity, Riemann has discussed profoundly, *In what cases is a function integrable, and in what not ?* and still further precision has been attained by Du Bois Reymond and Weierstrass.[*] It is of particular interest to know whether $\Sigma y dx$ will vary finitely with varying modes of divisions of $[a, b]$. Riemann calls the sub-intervals $\delta_1, \delta_2, \ldots \delta_n$; the greatest fluctuation of function-value in each δ_k he calls D_k; then must $\Sigma \delta_k D_k$ be *infinitesimal*. Thence follows that when, as each δ_k sinks indefinitely small, the sum of sub-intervals, in which D is $> o$, itself is infinitesimal, *then* the Sum Σ has a definite limit, the same however $[a, b]$ be subdivided. Hence the integral

$$I = \mathop{L}_{\substack{\delta_k \doteq 0 \\ k=0}}^{\substack{k=n \doteq \infty}} \Sigma f(x_k)\delta_k = \int_a^b f(x)dx \text{ exists when } f(x)$$

is finite and unique in $[a, b]$, and when for every infinitesimal positive ϵ there is also a positive δ such that $|\Sigma - I| < \epsilon$ when each $\delta_k < \delta$. Plainly such is the case (1) for $f(x)$ *continuous throughout* $[a, b]$; but also (2) when $f(x)$ is finitely discontinuous at a finite number of

points in $[a, b]$, and when $f(x)$ has an ∞ of maxima and minima, or is quite undetermined (though finite) at a finite number of points in $[a, b]$, as $\sin \dfrac{1}{(x-1)(x-2)}$ at 1 and 2; (3) even when $f(x)$ is *discontinuous* or finitely *indeterminate* at an ∞ of points and has an ∞ of maxima and minima in the vicinity of an ∞ of points, provided only all these points of finite function-fluctuation form *not* a *linear* but only a *discrete mass of points* (Punktmenge) —the function is then said to be only *pointwise* (punktirt) *discontinuous* (Hankel).—A *discrete mass* or manifold of points is an ∞ of points in a finite interval $[a-h, a+h]$, so distributed in subintervals that the *sum* of these subintervals may be made small at will by enlarging at will the number of subintervals. Otherwise, the mass is *linear*. Functions *linearly discontinuous* are *not* integrable. (For Cantor's more comprehensive theory of Derived Masses ('Math. Ann.,' XVII, 358f), see *Assemblages*.

Du Bois Reymond has shown ('Jour. f. d. r. u. d. a. Math.,' 79, 21f) that the *product* of two such integrable functions is itself integrable.

Thus far the integrand has been *finite*. But the *DI* $\int_0^1 \dfrac{dx}{\sqrt{1-x^2}} = \pi/2$, although the integrand $= \infty$ at 1. In general, if $f(x)$ be ∞, or discontinuous, or oscillatory at $x = c$ in $[a, b]$, then $\int_a^b f(x)dx$ loses meaning; but if the sum

$$\int_a^{c-a} f(x)dx + \int_{c+\beta}^b f(x)dx \text{ nears a definite limit}$$

no matter how α and β approach 0 indefinitely, then this limit is named *value of* $\int_a^b f(x)dx$. Such is the case only when $\int_{c-a'}^{c-a} f(x)dx$ and $\int_{+\beta}^{c+\beta'} f(x)dx$ converge *each* toward 0, as α, α', β, β', all close down on 0, $\alpha' < \alpha$, $\beta' < \beta$; *i.e.* the immediate neighborhood of c must contribute infinitesimally to the integral. Similarly for any number of points not forming a *linear mass*.

So, too, we may let either *extreme*, as b, increase towards ∞, if only the total contribution of the infinitely remote region be infinitesimal, *i.e.* if $\int_{b'}^b f(x)dx < \sigma$ for b however large, b' being *first* taken sufficiently large.

Double Integrals. $\int\int f(x, y)dx\,dy$.—Think of a finite region R in XY, at each point of which is erected a perpendicular z, all forming a cylindric volume (V) bounded by XY, the surface $z = f(x, y)$, and the cylindric surface standing on the border (B) of R. To find V we may cut up R into elements (ΔR), as by parallels to X and Y, and V into elementary cylinders (ΔV) on these elementary bases. Plainly $V = L \Sigma f(x, y) \Delta R = \int f(x, y) dR$. Here we assign no extremes to R, the integration stretches over all of R, so that B corresponds to the extremes of simple integration. It is and

---

[*] For yet greater refinement and generalization, see *Lebesgue*. Annali di Matematica, 1902, 259f.

must be indifferent in what order the elements $\varDelta R$ are taken; hence we may sum first along a strip parallel to X, and then sum all such strips along Y. This double summing is expressed by a *Double Integral* (*II*) thus:

$$L \, \varSigma [\varSigma f(x, y) \varDelta x] \varDelta y = \int_a^{a'} \int_b^{\beta} f(x, y) dx \, dy.$$

Here for any value of x the values of y are determined by the equation of B. Hence b and β are functions of x; but a and α depend on the extreme parallels to Y tangent to B, hence are absolute constants.

It is geometrically clear that *II* is perfectly *definite*, but we must ask in default of Geometry, when does $\varSigma$ approach the *same* limit independently of the function-value chosen for each $\varDelta R$ and of the way in which each $\varDelta R \doteq o$, as their number $\doteq \infty$? Answer: When $\varSigma D_k \cdot \varDelta R_k \doteq o$ as each $\varDelta R_k \doteq o$, D_k being the greatest fluctuation in function-value in $\varDelta R_k$. When is this the the case? Answer: (1) When $f(x, y)$ is continuous throughout R; (2) when f at single points or on single lines (at ∞^1 points) becomes finitely discontinuous or indeterminate or oscillatory; (3) when f becomes thus finitely discontinuous or indeterminate or oscillatory along an ∞ of lines (at ∞^2 points), *if only* the sum of the elements ($\varDelta R$'s), where $D > o$, is itself $< \varepsilon$ (infinitesimal); *i.e.* when the linear masses do *not* form an areal (or planar) mass, *i.e.* when their initial elements form not a linear but only a discrete mass.

May $f(x, y)$ attain ∞ and *II* retain sense? Answer: If f attains a definite ∞, but only at definite points, or along a curve and of order < 1, then the *II* remains definite and finite; also the order of integration remains indifferent. Here the contribution, to the *II*, $\doteq o$ as the element of area (in XY) shrinks toward o along the curve; *i.e.* the volume V shoots up to ∞ only along an infinitely sharp edge.

So, too, the *region* R may stretch out any way towards ∞, if f shrinks faster than R spreads; *e.g.*, R may spread over all the plane, if in all remote regions f becomes o of higher than 2d order. Minuter discussion must be foregone.

Extremely important is the *change of variables* in *II*. In simple integration $du = u_x dx$ under the $\int$, whereby we pass from x to u as variable of integration. In passing from x, y to u, v, under the $\int\int$, $du \, dv = M dx \, dy$, but what is M? It is $\dfrac{\partial u}{\partial x} \cdot \dfrac{\partial v}{\partial y} - \dfrac{\partial u}{\partial y} \cdot \dfrac{\partial v}{\partial x} = \begin{vmatrix} u_x & v_x \\ u_y & v_y \end{vmatrix} = \dfrac{\partial(u, v.)}{\partial(x, y)} = J(u, v; x, y)$. This remarkable expression, introduced by Jacobi and named by him *Functional Determinant*, is called *Jacobian* (Salmon). As already exemplified, it plays the rôle of *derivative of the system* $\{u, v\}$ *as to* $\{x, y\}$. In fact, $\dfrac{\partial(u, v)}{\partial(x, y)} \cdot \dfrac{\partial(x, y)}{\partial(u, v)} = 1$ —just as $\dfrac{du}{dx} \cdot \dfrac{dx}{du} = 1$. Also $\dfrac{\partial(u, v)}{\partial(x, y)} = \dfrac{\partial(u, v)}{\partial(w, z)} \cdot \dfrac{\partial(w, z)}{\partial(x, y)}$, as $y_x = y_u \cdot u_x$. Again, if $\dfrac{du}{dx} = o$, then $u = c$; so, if $\dfrac{\partial(u, v)}{\partial(x, y)} = o$, then $F(u, v) = c$, and so on.

From *DI* we readily pass to the *triple I*, $\int_a^{a'} \int_b^{b'} \int_c^{c'} f(x, y, z) dx \, dy \, dz$, and hence to *multiple I's* in general. The higher Jacobian maintains its rôle: $du \, dv \, dw = J \, dx \, d_y \, dz$, $J = \dfrac{\partial(u, v, w)}{\partial(x, y, z)} = \begin{vmatrix} u_x & u_y & u_z \\ v_x & v_y & v_z \\ w_x & w_y & w_z \end{vmatrix}$; and so on in general.

Thus, to pass from rectangular to polar coördinates, $x = \rho \cos \vartheta$, $y = \rho \sin \vartheta$; $J(x, y; \rho, \vartheta) = \rho$; under $\int\int$, $dx \, dy = \rho d\rho d\vartheta$—this latter is in fact the elementary curvilinear rectangle.—To pass from rectangular to spherical coördinates, $x = \rho \cos \vartheta \sin \phi$, $y = \rho \sin \vartheta \sin \phi$, $z = \rho \cos \phi$, whence $J(x, y, z; \rho, \vartheta, \phi) = \rho^2 \sin \phi$, and $\rho^2 \sin \phi d\rho d\vartheta d\phi$ is in fact the rectangular curvilinear volumetric element under $\int\int\int$. Analogy readily extends these forms to n-fold spaces. Thus the Jacobian appears geometrically as a real *derivative*, the limit of the ratio of two simultaneous changes.

The single $\int_a^b f(x) dx = F(b) - F(a)$, where $f = F'$ expresses the sum-value of f, integrated along the length $b-a$, through the *end-values* of some F at b and at a; can the double $\int\int f(x, y) dx \, dy$ integrated over the region R also be expressed through the *end-values* of some $F(x, y)$ along the contour of R? This query is much harder to answer, but is answered similarly: If $f(x, y)$ is integrable in R, then in general $\int^x f(x, y) dx$ is for every included value of y a continuous function of x, $F(x, y)$, and for every included value of x an integrable function of y. Then the *DI* $\int\int f(x, y) dx \, dy = \int F(x, y) \sin \nu ds$, where s is the contour of R and $\nu =$ slope of the normal (drawn inwards at any point of s) to the $+Y$-axis. This latter is a curvilinear $\int$, geometrically depicted as a wall built up (*resp.* down) along the contour s of R.—Similarly a $\int\int\int$ of f extended throughout a volume (or three-wayed spread) may be expressed through the end-values of a certain F integrated over the entire surface (S) of the volume, whereby a space-integral is turned into a surface-integral; and conversely:

$$\int\int\int \left(\frac{\partial \phi}{\partial x} + \frac{\partial \psi}{\partial y} + \frac{\partial x}{\partial z} \right) dx \, dy \, dz =$$

$$\int\int \left(\phi \frac{\partial n}{\partial x} + \psi \frac{\partial n}{\partial y} + \chi \frac{\partial n}{\partial z} \right) dS,$$

where $\varDelta n$ along the normal to S corresponds to $\varDelta x$ on X, etc. These conversions (of Green and Riemann) are equally important to pure and to applied mathematics.

The nearest-lying geometric problem of integration is *Quadrature*, already discussed. *Rectification* is finding a straight-length = an arc-length. This latter must be *defined* as the *common limit* of the length of inscribed and circumscribed polygons of which each side $\doteq$ o.

Since $s_t = \sqrt{(x_t)^2 + (y_t)^2}$, $s = \int \sqrt{(x_t)^2 + (y_t)^2} dt$.

If now $x = \phi(t)$, $y = \psi(t)$, be continuous functions of t, with finite limits of value, then this integration is possible, the curve is *rectifiable*. Such is *not* the case in Weierstrass's curve; there the oscillations (maxima and minima) are infinitely many in every neighborhood however small, nor is the variation finite in any such neighborhood—the arc is infinite between any two points.

Volume is given by triple Integration,

$$\int\int\int dx\,dy\,dz,$$ extremes defined by the bounding surface. Often the area of a section perpendicular (or possibly oblique) to an axis, as X, is a function of x, $_xS = f(x)$; then $V = \int _xS\,dx$.

In the important case of *Revolutes* (of an area bounded by X, the curve, and two y-ordinates), $_xS = \pi y^2$, $V = \pi \int y^2 dx$.

Quadrature of a curved surface is sometimes called *Complanation*.

Here again the area must be defined as the common limit of the surface area of polyhedra inscribed and circumscribed, no matter how. The surface element dS or $(\varDelta S)$ about P may be viewed as projected into the element $dx\,dy$ in XY and as having a limiting ratio $_1$ with the corresponding element $\varDelta \varPi$ in the plane tangent at P. The slope of this plane to $XY = \gamma = $ slope of normal to Z; hence Lim. $\dfrac{\varDelta S}{\varDelta x \varDelta y} = $ Lim. $\dfrac{\varDelta S}{\varDelta \varPi} \cdot \dfrac{\varDelta \varPi}{\varDelta x \varDelta y} = L \dfrac{\varDelta \varPi}{\varDelta x \varDelta y}$ sec $\gamma = \{F_x^2 + F_y^2 + F_z^2\}^{\frac{1}{2}}/F_z$; hence $S = \int\int\{ \quad \}^{\frac{1}{2}}/F_z dx\,dy$, the region of integration in XY being the projection thereon of S, under obvious conditions. Often the surface is given *parametrically*, i.e., x, y, and z as functions of the independents, u and v. Then we write off the rectangular array $\begin{Vmatrix} x_u & y_u & z_u \\ x_v & y_v & z_v \end{Vmatrix}$, and form therefrom the three Jacobians, by deleting the columns in order, commonly written A, B, C. Hence, by easy substitution for F_x, F_y, F_z, $S = \int\int \sqrt{A^2 + B^2 + C^2}\, du\,dv.$*

To every point (x, y, z) of S there is coordinated a point (uv) of a plane.

For Revolutes, $S = 2\pi \int y\,ds$.

Differentiatio de Curva in Curvam.—We have found the D of an $\int$ as to either extreme, but the integrand may contain a *parameter*, thus $\int f(x;\ p)dx$. The $\int$, being then a function of f, is also a function of p and may be differentiated as to p, giving rise to *Parametric Derivation*. Thus, $I = \int_a^b epx\,dx = \left\{ \frac{1}{p}epx \right\}_a^b$; hence $I_p = \left\{ \frac{bv-1}{p^2}epx \right\}_a^b$. If now we differentiate

---
* Also $S = \int\int \sqrt{EG - F^2}\, du\,dv$, $E = x_u^2 + \cdot_u^2 + z_u^2$, $G = x_v^2 + \cdot v^2 + z_v^2$, $F = x_u \cdot x_v + y_u \cdot y_v + z_u \cdot z_v$ (Lagrange).

the integrand first, and then integrate, we obtain the same result. Hence the order Integr.$_x$ Der.$_p$ is equivalent to Der.$_p$ Integr$_x$. This holds generally, if for a definite interval $[p,\ p+\varDelta p]$, and for $[a, b]$, $\dfrac{\partial f(x,\ p)}{\partial p}$ is in general (with possible exception of only discrete masses of points) a continuous function of both x and p; then $\dfrac{\partial}{\partial p}\int_a^b f(x,\ p)dx = \int \dfrac{\partial f(x,\ p)}{\partial p} dx$.

If p appears in either a or b or both, then $\dfrac{\partial}{\partial p}\int_a^b f(x,\ p)dx$

$$= f(b,\ p)\dfrac{db}{dp} - f(a,\ p)\dfrac{da}{dp} + \int_a^b \dfrac{\partial f(x,\ p)}{\partial p} dx.$$

If the $\int_a^b$ be an integrable function of p, $F(p)$, in $[\alpha,\ \beta]$, integrating as to p we get $\int_\alpha^\beta \left\{ \int_a^b f(x, p)dx \right\} dp = \int_\alpha^\beta F(p)dp$, and the order of integration is indifferent while f is a continuous function of both x and p.

Thus the $\int_a^b$ may be treated as function of any parameter in f, when the extremes are constant, as o, 1, $\pm \infty$, and this gives rise to an important set of concepts and to the *Theory of Definite Integrals*. Thus, for $0 < a < 1$, $\int_0^\infty \dfrac{x^{a-1}}{x+1}dx = \dfrac{\pi}{\sin a\pi}$, and is a function of a. Among such the *Eulerians* are conspicuous, especially that of 2d species (Legendre), $\int_0^\infty x^{a-1}e^{-x}dx$, denoted by $\Gamma(a)$, or better by the Gaussian $\varPi(a - 1)$, through which countless others are expressible. This Γ- or $\varPi$-function has remarkable properties:

1. $\Gamma(a+1) = a\Gamma(a)$, or $\varPi(a) = a\varPi(a-1)$,—the factorial property, $\lfloor n = n \lfloor n-1$. But the factorial loses its meaning for n not a positive integer, while Γ and $\varPi$ retain theirs: thus, $\Gamma(\frac{1}{2}) = \sqrt{\pi}$, $\Gamma(\frac{3}{2}) = \frac{1}{2} \cdot \frac{1}{2}\sqrt{\pi}$.

2. $\Gamma(a)\,\Gamma(1 - a) = \dfrac{\pi}{\sin a\pi}$, Euler's beautiful discovery. Hereby arguments complemental to 1 are set in mutual relation, as $\sin(\pi - \alpha) = \sin \alpha$, $\tan \alpha \cdot \tan\left(\dfrac{\pi}{2} - \alpha\right) = 1$, so that for $\Gamma(\frac{1}{2})$ we may reckon $\Gamma(\frac{1}{2})$. Hence we need reckon $\Gamma(a)$ only for a in $[0, \frac{1}{2}]$, as $\sin a$ only for a in $[0, \pi/2]$.

$\Gamma(a)$ and particularly $\log \Gamma(a)$ may now be differentiated with highly interesting results, as $\dfrac{d^2 \log \Gamma(a)}{da^2} = \sum_{n=0}^{n=\infty} \dfrac{1}{(a+n)^2}$. This $\varSigma$ is uniformly convergent for $a > 0$; hence we may integrate term-wise from 1 to a and get, $\dfrac{d \log \Gamma(a)}{da} = (a-1) \sum_{n=0}^{n=\infty} \dfrac{1}{(1+n)(a+n)} + C$, where C is the Eulerian or Mascheronian Constant $= \dfrac{\Gamma(1)'}{\Gamma(1)} = -\Gamma(1)' = .5772156649 \ldots$ calculated by Euler to 15 and by Legendre to 19 decimals.

Hence, by a 2d Integration,

$$\log \Gamma(a) = \sum_{m=1}^{m=\infty} \log \frac{m\left(\dfrac{m+1}{m}\right)^{a-1}}{a+m-1},$$

$$\Gamma(a) = \prod_{m=1}^{m=\infty} m^{a-1} \frac{\left(\dfrac{m+1}{m}\right)^{a-1}}{a+m-1}$$

$$= \frac{m(m+1)^{a-1}}{a(1+a)\left(1+\dfrac{a}{2}\right)\cdots\left(1+\dfrac{a}{m-1}\right)}$$

$$= \frac{(m+1)^a}{a(1+a)\left(1+\dfrac{a}{2}\right)\cdots\left(1+\dfrac{a}{m-1}\right)}, \quad (m \doteq \infty).$$

Such is Gauss's *Definition of* $\Gamma(a)$ for every finite a for which no factor in the denominator vanishes. Herewith we are brought to the expression of functions not through infinite series but through infinite *products*, as already exemplified in Wallis's formula:

$$\frac{\pi}{2} = \frac{2}{1} \cdot \frac{2}{3} \cdot \frac{4}{3} \cdot \frac{4}{5} \cdot \frac{6}{5} \cdot \frac{6}{7} \cdots$$

This subject, of infinite range, cannot be pursued here—"hills peep o'er hills, and Alps on Alps arise." The fundamental theorems were rigorously proved first by Weierstrass (Jour. f. d. r. u. d. a. Math., LI). It may be added that the 1st Eulerian, $\displaystyle\int_0^\infty \frac{x^{a-1}}{(1+x)^{a+b}}dx$, is denoted by $B(a, b)$ (Binet) and is connected with the 2d by $B(a, b)\Gamma(a+b) = \Gamma(a)\cdot\Gamma b$, and being expressible thus simply through F has not so much independent significance.

The central notion of the *Integral Calculus*, the LIMIT of a SUM, is more obvious than that of the *Differential Calculus*, the LIMIT of a QUOTIENT. The foundations of the one are also seen to be much broader than those of the other, so that the former is *not merely* the inverse of the latter. The twain seize upon the two great aspects of History, the Dynamical and the Statical, Process and Result. While the Integral Calculus borrows its speed and directness from the Differential Calculus, its own reaction upon this latter is instant and powerful. Thus, from integration by parts we have

$$\int \phi'(y)dy = y\phi'(y) - \int \phi''(y)dy; \quad -\int \phi''(y)dy$$

$$= -\frac{1}{2}y^2\phi'(y) + \frac{1}{2}\int \phi'''(y)y^2dy; \quad \text{and so on.}$$

Evaluating between the extremes o and h we get Bernoulli's Series (with Remainder);

$$\phi(h) = \phi(o) + h\phi'(h) - \frac{h^2}{\lfloor 2}\phi''(h) + \frac{h^3}{\lfloor 3}\phi'''(h) - \cdots$$

$$\pm \frac{1}{\lfloor n}\int_o^h y^n\phi^{(n+1)}(y)dy.$$ To avoid the alternation in sign we take $\int \phi(a-u)du$ and proceed as before: then on putting $a = x_0 + h$,

$$\phi(x_0+h) = \phi(x_0) + h\phi'(x_0) + \frac{h^2}{\lfloor 2}\phi''(x_0) + \cdots$$

$$+ \frac{1}{\lfloor n}\int u^n\phi^{n+1}(x+h-u)du, \quad o < h < R.$$

Such is the swiftest, directest, nearest-lying deduction of the fundamental *Taylor's Series*, by which the value of ϕ at (x_0+h) is built up out of the value of ϕ and its D's at x_0. The R_n is here yielded as a definite integral, from which form the other forms, as Lagrange's,

Cauchy's, Schlömilch's, come at once on applying the Maximum-Minimum Theorem. This development holds under the two necessary and sufficient conditions (Pringsheim):

1. That $\phi(x)$ possess everywhere in $[x_0, x_0+R]$ definite finite differential coefficients of every finite order;

2. That $\text{Lim.} \dfrac{1}{\lfloor n}\phi^{(n)}(x_0+h)\cdot k^n$ converge uniformly on o (for $n = \infty$) for all pairs (h, k) for which $o \leq h \leq h+k < R$.

The Infinitesimal Analysis or Method of Limits is very highly developed and is applicable to almost every subject of exact thought, often asserting itself in the most surprising fashion, as in the *Theories of Numbers* and of *Knots*, to which it might seem wholly alien, suddenly unlocking and laying wide open secret passages utterly unsuspected. In particular the Integral Calculus shows itself amazingly and unendingly fertile in the generation of new notions. As other and still other fields are exposed to investigative thought, the Calculus will receive more and more applications, and there seems to be no limit to the subtlety and refinement of its processes, to the keenness and penetration that may be given to this two-edged sword of the spirit, the strongest, sharpest, and most flexible ever fashioned or wielded by the mind of man.

Historical Sketch.—Passing by anticipations, especially of Integration, that reach back at least to Archimedes (287-212 B.C.), we come to Barrow's 'Lectiones opticæ et geometricæ' (1669-70), on which *Newton* collaborated, how much no one knows. Barrow used the Differential Triangle even in 1664 (indefinite parvum, . . . ob indefinitam curvæ parvitudinem), ca:ling Δy a and Δx e (as Fermat used A and E, 1638). Newton was busied with Series at Cambridge, 1665-6 (eo tempore pestis ingruens coegit me hinc fugere—in his famous letter, filling thirty pages in the *Opuscula*, to Oldenburg, Secretary of the Royal Society, 24th October, 1676). His MS. 'De analysi per æquationes numero terminorum infinitas' (partially published first in Wallis's Works, vol. II, 1693) was shown to Barrow, Collins, Lord Brouncker in 1669, wherein he used o for a magnitude ultimately vanishing, as had James Gregory already in his 'Geometriæ pars universalis' (1667, Venice). He treated Rectification, Cubature, and Mass-Center determinations as reducible to Quadrature and to be solved by introducing the notion of 'Momentum' = instantaneous change, thus going beyond Barrow. Newton's 'Methodus Fluxionum et Serierum infinitarum' was ready for the press before 1672, but not printed till 1736. In it he proposes, (1) to find the velocity at any instant from the space traversed up to each instant, (2) to find the latter (space) from the former (velocity)—the two problems of Derivation and Integration conceived kinematically. The equicrescent magnitude x, as a space, is called *fluens* (Cavalieri *fluens*, 1639, Napier *fluxus*, 1614, Clavius *fluere*, 1574); the velocity he writes $\dot{x}$ and calls *fluxio*—our Derivative (as to the time t). *Momentum* varies as fluxion, is written $\dot{x}o$, and corresponds to our Differential x (incrementa indefinite parva). This treatise seems to have been revised after 1673, hence does not clearly attest Newton's knowledge in 1671. *Leibnitz* wrote, 26 Oct., 1675 (following Cavalieri), *Omnia w*, etc.; but 29 Oct., 1675,

Utile erit scribi $\int$ pro omn. ut $\int l$ pro omn. l

id est summa ipsorum l; again, the same day,

nempe ut $\int$ augebit, ita d minuet dimensiones.

$\int$ autem significat summam, d differentiam.

There and then was born the «Algorithm of the Differential» and Integral «Calculus.» Under date of 11 Nov., 1673, Leibnitz wrote $\int ydy = \frac{y^2}{2}$, but the 3 was originally 5. His «Characteristic Triangle», equivalent to Differential Triangle, he took not from Barrow but from Pascal. All attempts to show any real dependence of Leibnitz on Newton have failed. The germs of the new Method were abroad in the air.

Bibliography.—Leibnitz and his school, especially the Bernoullis, poured forth memoirs abundantly. Leibnitz' first, 'Nova Methodus pro maximis et minimis, itemque tangentibus, etc.,' appeared in the Leipzig *Acta Eruditorum*, 1684. Newton gave his method of prime and ultimate ratios in geometric form in his 'Philosophiæ Naturalis Principia Mathematica', 1687. Johann Bernoulli's 'Lectiones Mathematicæ' was the first text-book of the Integral Calculus, composed at Paris 1691-2, published 1742; Taylor, 'Methodus incrementorum directa et inversa' (1715); D'Alembert, 'Mémoire sur le calcul intégral' (1739); Maclaurin, 'A Treatise on Fluxions' (1742); Euler, 'Introductio in Analysin Infinitorum' (1748)—resuming and expanding all knowledge on the subject, «one of the most contentful, beautiful, and fruitful works that ever left the press,»—'Institutiones Calculi Integralis' (1768-70); Cramer, 'Introduction à l'analyse des lignes courbes algébriques' (1750); Lacroix, 'Traité du calcul dif. et du cal. int.' (1797); Lagrange, 'Théorie des fonctions analytiques' (1797); Cauchy, 'Cours d'analyse' (1821), 'Leçons sur le calcul différentiel' (1829); Duhamel, 'Cours d'analyse' (1840), 3d ed., by Bertrand (1874-5); De Morgan, 'Diff. and Int. Calculus' (1842); Todhunter, 'Diff. and Int. Calculus' (1852); Price, 'Infinitesimal Calculus' (1854); Gerhardt, 'Die Entdeckung der höheren Analysis' (1855); Bertrand, 'Traité du Cal. Diff. et du Cal. Int.' (1864-70); Hermite, 'Cours d'Analyse' (1873); Williamson 'Dif. and Int. Calculus' (1872-74); Meyer, 'Theorie der bestimmten Integrale'—nach Lejeune-Dirichlet (1875); Lipschitz, 'Lehrbuch der Analysis' (1877-80); Houël, 'Cours de Calcul Infinitésimal' (1878-9); Dini, 'Analisi Infinitesimale' (1877-8), 'Fondamenti per la teorica delle funzioni di variabili reali' (1878); Harnack, 'Die Elemente der Dif.- und Int. rechnung' (1881); Stolz, 'Allgemeine Arithmetik' (1885-6), 'Grundzüge der Differential- und Integralrechnung' (1893-6-9); Tannery, 'Introduction à la théorie des fonctions d'une variable' (1886); Laurent, 'Traité d'Analyse' (1885-92); Picard, 'Traité d'analyse' (1891-1903); Genocchi-Peano, 'Calcolo differenziale e principii di calcolo integrale' (1884, German translation 1898-9); Cantor, 'Geschichte der Mathematik' (1880-1900/1);

Jordan, 'Cours d'Analyse' (1893-4-6); Serret, 'Cours de Calcul dif. et int.' (1868, Harnack's German transl., 2d ed., by Bohlmann and Zermelo, 1899-1904-5); de la Vallée Poussin, 'Cours d'Analyse Infinitésimale' (1903); Goursat, 'Cours d'Analyse mathématique (1902-4); Humbert, 'Cours d'Analyse' (1903-4); Borel, 'Leçons sur les fonctions de Variables réelles (1905); Kiepert-Stegemann, 'Grundriss der Differential- u. Integral-rechnung' (1905). American works are omitted as familiar.

WILLIAM BENJAMIN SMITH,
Professor of Mathematics, The Tulane University of Louisiana.

Calculus of Variations, The. The *Calculus of Variations* is a natural outgrowth of the *Infinitesimal Calculus* (q.v.)—in particular of the *Integral Calculus* (q.v.) and of *Differential Equations* (q.v.). In the Integral Calculus, properly speaking, only integrals of the type $\int f(x, \alpha_1, \alpha_2, \ldots) dx$ are considered, where $f(x, \alpha_1, \alpha_2, \ldots)$ is a function of the variable of integration x and of several parameters $\alpha_1, \alpha_2, \ldots$ which are independent of x. In solving differential equations of the type $dy/dx = f(x, y)$ we are in one sense dealing with a new type of integral, $\int f(x, y) dx$. Such integrals, in which y is to be replaced by a certain function of x, are called *line integrals* (q.v.).

The integrals considered in the Calculus of Variations are essentially of this kind, but we shall see that the more interesting problems are those in which still another element is introduced. The integral

$$(1) \qquad I = \int_{x_0}^{x_1} f(x, y, y') dx ,$$

where $y' = dy/dx$, can be evaluated whenever y is known as a function of x. For if $y = \phi(x)$ be the known value of y in terms of x, and if $\phi(x)$ and $\phi'(x) = d\phi(x)/dx$ be substituted for y and y' respectively under the integral sign, the integrand becomes a function of x alone, and the integral itself has a definite numerical value, at least under certain very general restrictions which need not be stated here. Thus to every function of x which can be substituted for y there corresponds a definite number—the value of I calculated as above for that function. The relation $y = \phi(x)$ defines a curve C in the plane of x and y. We shall denote the value of I which corresponds to the function $\phi(x)$ by the symbol I_ϕ.

The central problem of the Calculus of Variations is the determination of a curve $K[y = \phi(x)]$, for which the value of I, I_κ, is less than [greater than] the value of I for any other curve C $[y = \phi(x)]$, which satisfies the conditions of the particular example.

In most of the simpler examples it is specified or implied by the conditions of the problem that the curves C considered shall all pass through each of two given fixed points $P_0 (x_0, y_0)$ and $P_1 (x_1, y_1)$, whose abscissæ are respectively x_0 and x_1, the limits of integration of the integral I. Hence only those functions of x, $\phi(x)$ are to be considered for which $\phi(x_0) = y_0$ and $\phi(x_1) = y_1$.

In order to clarify the general problem, let

us consider the example

$$L = \int_{x_0}^{x_1} \sqrt{1 + y'^2} \, dx \; .$$

This is a familiar integral; it is the formula for the length of any curve $y = \phi(x)$ between any two of its points. With respect to this integral the statement of the simplest problem of the Calculus of Variations is as follows: Given two fixed points P_0 (x_0, y_0) and P_1 (x_1, y_1) in the xy plane; to determine that curve $y = \phi(x)$ joining P_0 and P_1 for which the value of the integral L (i.e., the length of the arc P_0P_1) is at a minimum. Accepting the Euclidean postulate that the shortest distance between two points is measured along the straight line joining them, it is evident a priori that the solution of this example is the straight line P_0P_1, or

$$y = y_0 + (x - x_0)(y_1 - y_0)/(x_1 - x_0) \; .$$

It is at least plausible that any conditions which we may discover must, in this particular example, be satisfied by this function.

It is easy to see how this simple problem may be generalized. For we might inquire what is the shortest path between a fixed point and a fixed curve, or between two fixed curves. Again, obstacles may be placed in the plane, and the shortest path then sought. This latter idea leads to an important application of the general theory: the determination of the shortest path between any two fixed points of a given surface, the surface being thought of as an obstacle placed in the plane. The most general problem of the kind mentioned above may be thought of as the determination of a certain shortest path.

An entirely distinct generalization of the preceding problem is that in which the integrand involves derivatives of higher order than the first, i.e., of the type: $\int f(x, y, y', y'', \ldots y^{(n)}) dx$. Another is that in which the integral involves several dependent variables:

$\int f(x, y, z, \ldots, y', z', \ldots) dx$. Finally, the integral considered may involve two (or more) independent variables and require two integrations: $\int \int f(x, y, z, p, q) \, dx \, dy$, where p and q denote $\partial z/\partial x$ and $\partial z/\partial y$, respectively, and where the function to be determined is a function of x and y which is to be substituted for z. Further generalizations are evident and would tend only to confuse if stated here. We shall return briefly to these generalized problems, but we shall state theorems principally for the simple integral I in one dependent and one independent variable. Many of these theorems can be generalized without essential difficulty to the other cases which have been mentioned.

Returning to the integral (1), let us consider the history of the problem very briefly. Although a previous problem had been considered by Newton in 1687 ('Phil. nat. prin. Math.,' II, Sec. 7, Prop. 34), the first problem which gave rise to any general theory and encouraged investigation was the so-called problem of the brachistochrone—or curve of quickest descent —which we shall discuss as a particular example. This problem was stated by Johann Bernoulli in 1698, solved by him in the following year, by his brother Jacob in 1701 in an

important memoir dealing with more general problems, and by Euler in 1744 in an important treatise 'Methodus inveniendi lineas curvas . . . '. It has remained of interest down to the present day, probably the last paper concerning it being that by Bolza, 'Bull. Amer. Math. Soc., 1904, No. 1,' in which a final solution is given. In the paper mentioned Euler first gave the first necessary condition (known as «Euler's condition,» or less properly as «Lagrange's condition») in its general form, and developed the theory in several directions, solving incidentally many problems from the formal standpoint. Following Euler, Lagrange introduced many simplifications and generalizations in a series of important papers (cf. his 'Works,' and his books 'Théorie des fonctions' and 'Calcul des fonctions'). In particular the Method of Multipliers for the treatment of problems of relative extrema, which we shall discuss briefly, is due to Lagrange. The other prominent names in the early history are Legendre, for whom the second condition is named; Gauss, who first studied double integrals with variable limits; Jacobi, who discovered the condition which bears his name; and Du Bois-Reymond, who initiated the very modern critical development of the theory. We shall restrict ourselves to a reference to Todhunter, 'A History of . . . the Calculus of Variations . . . ' (Cambridge, 1861); and Pascal, 'Calcolo delle variazioni' (Milan, 1897, German translation by Schepp, 1899); and Kneser, 'Variationsrechnung' and 'Ency. der Math. Wiss., II A 8, 1900'; and Bolza, 'Lectures on the Calculus of Variations' (Chicago, 1905). In these books exact and complete references to the literature of the subject and notes concerning its history up to the dates of publication may be found. It should be noted that only the latter of these books contains references to the important developments published since 1900.

Precise Statement of the Problem.—It is evident upon examination that the naive conception of the problem does not permit of exact mathematical treatment. For definiteness, let us suppose that the function $f(x, y, y')$ in (1) is an analytic function of its three arguments inside of a certain three-dimensional region R, which may be finite or infinite, but which expressly does not include any points at infinity. Let us also restrict ourselves to curves of the type $y = \phi(x)$, where $\phi(x)$, together with its first derivative $\phi'(x)$, is a continuous, single-valued function of x in the interval $x_0 \leq x \leq x_1$, and where $\phi(x_0)$ and $\phi(x_1)$ are equal, respectively, to the ordinates y_0 and y_1 of the fixed points P_0 and P_1. We shall call these «curves of the class B.» If there is a single one of these curves $y = \psi(x)$, or K, for which I_ϵ is less than [greater than] I_ϵ for any other curve C $[y = \phi(x)]$ of the class B, that curve K is said to render the given integral I an absolute minimum [maximum]. It is evident that this will rarely occur, as is also the case in extrema of functions of a single variable. If we no.

$$(2) \quad \phi(x) = \psi(x) + \eta(x) \, , \qquad \eta(x) = \phi(x) - \psi(x) \, ,$$

and if there exists a positive number δ such that I_ϵ is less than [greater than] I_ϵ whenever the condition

$$(3) \quad |\eta(x)| < \delta \, , \quad |\eta'(x)| < \delta \, , \quad x_0 \leq x \leq x_1 \, ,$$

then K is said to render the integral I a weak

minimum [maximum] among the curves of the class B. If instead of (3) we merely require the condition

(4) $\qquad |\eta(x)| < \delta , \quad x_0 < x \leq x_1 ,$

the curve K is said to render a *strong minimum* [maximum]. If in addition to (3) [or (4)] we also require that

$$\eta(x_i) = 0 ,$$

(5) $\quad x_0 + (i-2)\cdot\delta \leq x_i \leq x_0 + (i-1)\cdot\delta \leq x_1 ,$

$$i = 2, 3, \ldots (n+1) ,$$

where $n \cdot \delta = x_1 - x_0$, the curve K is said to render I a *limited weak* [*strong*] *minimum* [*maximum*].

Geometrically these conditions mean that the curves compared to K must lie, in the case of a strong extremum (*i.e.*, maximum or minimum), close to the curve K; in the case of the weak extremum, they must lie close to K and vary only a little from K in direction; in the case of a limited extremum, they must cut K at least once in every vertical strip of width δ.

It is easy to show that if K is to render I an extremum (of any sort), $\psi(x)$ must satisfy the equation

(6) $\qquad \dfrac{d}{dx}\left(\dfrac{\partial f}{\partial y'}\right) - \dfrac{\partial f}{\partial y} = 0 ,$

or

$$\frac{\partial^2 f}{\partial y'^2} y'' + \frac{\partial^2 f}{\partial y \, \partial y'} y' + \frac{\partial^2 f}{\partial x \, \partial y'} - \frac{\partial f}{\partial y} = 0 ,$$

which is known as *Euler's* (or less properly as *Lagrange's*) *equation*. For we have

(7) $\quad I_e = \displaystyle\int_{x_0}^{x_1} f\{x, \; \psi(x) + \eta(x), \; \psi(x) + \eta'(x)\} dx ,$

which must be a minimum [maximum] for $\eta(x) = 0$. Replacing $\eta(x)$ by $\epsilon \cdot \lambda(x)$, where $\lambda(x)$ is a certain function and ϵ is a variable parameter, I_e will evidently be a function of the parameter ϵ alone:

(8) $\quad I_e = F(\epsilon) = \displaystyle\int_{x_0}^{x_1} f(x, \; \psi + \epsilon\cdot\lambda, \; \psi' + \epsilon\cdot\lambda') dx .$

It is easy to show that the ordinary rule applies and that we can have an extremum only if

(9) $\; dI_e/d\epsilon = F'(\epsilon) = \displaystyle\int_{x_0}^{x_1} \{f_y(x, \psi + \epsilon\cdot\lambda, \psi' + \epsilon\cdot\lambda')\lambda$

$$+ f_{y'}(x, \; \psi + \epsilon\lambda, \; \psi' + \epsilon\lambda')\cdot\lambda'\} dx = 0 ,$$

when $\epsilon = 0$, or $F'(0) = \displaystyle\int_{x_0}^{x_1}(f_y\cdot\lambda + f_{y'}\lambda') dx = 0$,

where $f_y = \partial f/\partial y$, etc. Integrating the second term by parts, we get

(10) $\; F'(0) = 0 = \left[\lambda(x) f_{y'}(x, \; \psi, \; \psi')\right]_{x_0}^{x_1}$

$$+ \int_{x_0}^{x_1}\lambda(x)\left\{f_y(x, \; \psi, \; \psi') - \frac{d}{dx}f_{y'}(x, \; \psi, \; \psi')\right\} dx,$$

or since $\lambda(x)$ evidently vanishes for $x = x_0$ and for $x = x_1$,

(11) $\displaystyle\int_{x_0}^{x_1}\lambda(x)\left\{f_y(x, \psi, \psi') - \frac{d}{dx}f_{y'}(x, \psi, \psi')\right\} dx = 0.$

But $\lambda(x)$ was itself any permissible function of x, and it is easy to show that the integral of such a product, of which one factor is arbitrary, can vanish only if the other factor vanishes. This gives precisely the equation (6). Certain further considerations are necessary to show

that this proof, which implicitly assumes the existence of the second derivative of $\psi(x)$, does not involve any restrictions. (Cf. Bolza, 'Lectures,' chap. i).

Assuming the further details without proof, it becomes evident that any curve K, $y = \psi(x)$ which is to render I a minimum (of any sort) must satisfy. the differential equation (6). Since f and its derivatives are known functions, (6) is an ordinary differential equation of the second order, linear in $d^2y/dx^2(=y'')$. The coefficient of y'' is $d^2f/dy'^2(=f_{y'y'})$. If this coefficient $f_{y'y'}$ does not vanish, one and only one solution of (6) passes through a given point in a given direction. The general solution of (6) contains two arbitrary constants:

(12) $\qquad y = f(x, \alpha, \beta) .$

Any one of these solutions, *i.e.*, any solution whatever of (6) is called an *extremal*. Hence the required curve K, if it exists, must be an extremal, and it is necessary to search for it only among the extremals. But K was to connect P_0 and P_1. Usually, however, there is only one of the extremals (12) which passes through two given points, for the equations,

(13) $\quad y_0 = f(x_0, \alpha, \beta) , \quad y_1 = f(x_1, \alpha, \beta) ,$

usually determine α and β, and hence also determine a single extremal joining P_0 and P_1. If this is actually the case, either that extremal is the required solution K, or else there is no solution of the problem.

A large number of special cases lead to differential equations which can be solved directly.

For example, if $I = \displaystyle\int_0^{x_1}\sqrt{1 + y'^2} dx$, we shall have

$f(x, y, y') = \sqrt{1 + y'^2}$, whence $f_x = f_y = f_{xy'} = f_{yy'}$ $= f_{xy} = 0$, $f_{y'} = y'/(1 + y'^2)^{\frac{1}{2}}$, $f_{y'y'} = 1/(1 + y'^2)^{\frac{3}{2}}$, and the equation (6) takes the form $y'' = 0$. The only solutions of this differential equation are the straight lines $y = ax + b$. It follows that if there is any curve of the class B in the plane along which the distance between two given fixed points is at a minimum, that curve is the straight line joining the two points. This result is independent of the Euclidean postulate, and depends only upon the definition of length by means of the preceding integral.

The problem of the brachistocrone, mentioned above, is to find the curve along which a particle with initial velocity v_0 will descend most quickly from a given initial point P_0 to another given point P_1. It is easy to show that the time of descent is given by the formula

$$t = \int_{x_0}^{x_1}\frac{\sqrt{1 + y'^2}}{\sqrt{v_0^2 - 2g(x - x_0)}} dx ,$$

hence Euler's equation (6) is

$$\frac{d}{dx}\left(\frac{\partial f}{\partial y}\right) - \frac{d}{dx}\left(\frac{y'}{\sqrt{1 + y'^2}\sqrt{v_0 - 2g(x - x_0)}}\right) = 0 ,$$

which gives at once $y'^2 = c^2(1 + y'^2)(v_0 + 2g(x_0 - x))$. It is easy to solve this equation in parameter form, and we find:

$$x - A = -\frac{A + B}{2}(1 - \cos\omega) ,$$

$$y - C = -\frac{A + B}{2}(\omega - \sin\omega) ,$$

where
$$A = \frac{v_0}{2g} + x_0 ,$$
$$B = \frac{c^2 - v_0^2}{2g} - x_0 .$$

These extremals are cycloids on horizontal bases, the radius of the generating circle being $(A + B)/2$, and one cusp being at the point (A, C). Further investigation is necessary to decide just when a given pair of points can be connected by such a cycloid (cf. Bolza, 'Lectures,' p. 236). If such a cycloid can be drawn, we can infer that it is the solution if there is any solution. If no such cycloid can be drawn, we can infer that there is no solution in the region R.

The problem of finding the geodetic lines on a given surface is that of minimizing the integral,

$$I = \int_{x_0}^{x} (E + 2Fy' + Gy'^2)^{\frac{1}{2}} dx ,$$

where $z = \phi(x, y)$ is the surface and where $E = 1 + z_x^2$, $F = z_x z_y$, $G = 1 + z_y^2$. Euler's equation therefore coincides with the usual equation for the geodetic lines:

$$\frac{d}{dx} \left(\frac{Gy' + F}{\sqrt{E + 2Fy' + Gy'^2}} \right) = \frac{E_y + 2F_y y' + G_y y'^2}{2\sqrt{E + 2Fy' + Gy'^2}} ,$$

and the geodetic lines are the extremals of this problem, *i.e.*, no line not a geodetic can be a shortest line on a surface.

Though the proof of the necessity of Euler's condition was satisfactory, even in a cruder form, to the originators of the subject, a desire to formulate sufficient conditions arose. Thus Legendre showed that a *second necessary condition* for a minimum [maximum] is that the condition

$$f_{y'y'}(x, \psi(x), \psi'(x)) > 0 [< 0] \quad \text{for} \quad x_0 \leqq x \leqq x_1$$

be satisfied along the supposed solution $y = \psi(x)$ between the end points. We shall prove this, and we shall see that the same condition is actually a sufficient condition for a weak limited minimum if the sign $=$ be removed.

Jacobi then showed, by means of the second variation of the given integral, that a *third necessary condition* for a minimum [maximum] is that the quantity

$$\Delta(x, x_0) = \eta_1(x) \eta_2(x_0) - \eta_2(x) \eta_1(x_0)$$

should not vanish for any value of x in the interval $x_0 < x < x_1$, where $\Delta(x, x_0)$ is a solution of the equation

$$f_{y'y'} \eta'' + \frac{df_{y'y'}}{dx} \eta' + \left(\frac{df_{yy'}}{dx} - f_{yy} \right) \eta = 0 ,$$

which vanishes for $x = x_0$. The proof, which is omitted, can be found in Bolza, 'Lectures,' chap. ii. A beautiful geometrical interpretation of this condition exists: if we consider the one parameter family of extremals through (x_0, y_0), and call their envelope E, the extremal which joins x_0 to any point beyond its point of tangency with E cannot possibly render the integral a minimum [maximum] between those two points, *i.e.*, the envelope of the extremals through (x_0, y_0) *bounds* all the points which can possibly be reached by a minimizing extremal from x.

It was long believed that Jacobi's condition, together with the previous two, was a sufficient condition. That such is not the case was first
Vol. 3—27.

pointed out by Weierstrass, who also showed that *Jacobi's condition*, while not sufficient for a minimum in general, *is sufficient for a weak minimum* (if the point (x_1, y_1) lies *inside* the envelope of the extremals through (x_0, y_0). (Cf. Bolza, 'Lectures,' chap. iii.)

That the preceding conditions are not sufficient is most readily seen by giving an actual example in which the extremals, though all the above conditions are satisfied, do not minimize the integral. Such is the example (see Bolza 'Lectures,' p. 73),

$$f(x, y, y') = y'^2(y' + 1)^2 .$$

Here the extremals are straight lines, but it is easy to join two points for which all the preceding conditions are satisfied by a simple broken line for which the value of the integral is less than that along the straight line extremal. Of course, the comparison line used varies considerably from the straight line extremal in direction, though not in position.

Weierstrass, in 1879, gave a fourth necessary condition. He defines a new function,

$$E(x, y, y', p) = f(x, y, y') - f(x, y, p) \\ - (y' - p) f_p(x, y, p) .$$

Then *Weierstrass's (fourth) necessary condition* for a minimum [maximum] is

$$E(x, y, y', p) \geqq 0 \quad [\leqq 0] \quad x_0 \leqq x \leqq x_1 ,$$

where x, y, p are the values of x, y, dy/dx along the extremal between the end points, and where y' is any finite number whatever. (Cf. Bolza, 'Lectures,' chap. iii.) Since we have

$$\text{Limit}_{y' = p} \left[\frac{E(x, y, y', p)}{(y' - p)^2} \right] = \frac{\partial^2 f}{\partial y'^2} \bigg|_{y' = p} ,$$

it follows that it is also necessary that $f_{y'y'} \geqq 0$, which is precisely *the second (Legendre's) necessary condition* mentioned above. It is easy to show that if (a) the end points can be joined by an extremal K, (b) a one parameter family of extremals $[y = \psi(x, \alpha)]$ can be found, one of which is K itself, and one and only one of which passes through each point of the plane near K, so that $y' = p(x, y)$ can be found, *i.e.*, a function which gives the slope of the extremal of the family at any point (x, y) near K, then the integral

$$J = \int_{x_0}^{x_1} [f(x, y, p) + (y' - p) f_p(x, y, p)] dx$$

is independent of the path of integration inside the field just constructed near K, and we have

$$I_c - I_x = \int_{x_0}^{x_1} E(x, y, y', p) dx \bigg]_{\text{along } C} ,$$

where C is any curve of the class B in the field about K, since $I_x = J_x = J_c$. It follows that the condition

$$E(x, y, y', p) \geqq 0 , \quad x_0 \leqq x \leqq x_1 ,$$

for all x and y near K and for the function $p(x, y)$ just mentioned and for any finite value of y' whatever, is a *sufficient condition for a strong minimum*, if the sign of equality holds only for $p = y'$. (Cf. Osgood, 'Annals of Mathematics,' II, 3; Bolza, 'Lectures,' chap. iii.)

It is possible to show (cf. Hedrick, 'Bull. A. M. S.,' IX, 1) that *for a limited minimum* the conditions remain the same except that *Jacobi's condition may be omitted*. The conditions in the various cases may be summarized in the following scheme:

	Limited Variations.		Unlimited Variations.	
	Weak.	Strong.	Weak.	Strong.
Necessary.	Euler's, Legendre's necessary.	Euler's, Legendre's necessary, Weierstrass's necessary.	Euler's, Legendre's necessary, Jacobi's necessary.	Euler's, Legendre's necessary, Jacobi's necessary, Weierstrass's necessary.
Sufficient.	Euler's, Legendre's sufficient.	Euler's, Legendre's sufficient, Weierstrass's sufficient.	Euler's, Legendre's sufficient, Jacobi's necessary.	Euler's Legendre's sufficient, Jacobi's necessary, Weierstrass's sufficinet.

It is seen on glancing at the table that from the simple conditions (Euler's and Legendre's) for limited weak variation we proceed to any other case by adding Weierstrass's conditions in the case of a strong minimum, and Jacobi's in case of an unlimited minimum, only. The above table represents *substantially* the present known conditions.

In special problems the irksomeness of these conditions can sometimes be circumvented. For instance, *given a problem in which* $\frac{\partial^2 f}{\partial y'^2} > 0$ *for all values of* x, y, y', *then the necessary and sufficient condition for a limited strong minimum is the possibility of finding a solution of Euler's equation joining the two given end points.* Such is the case in the geodetic problem and also in the integral which leads to Hamilton's principle; and in each of these cases, fortunately, a limited strong minimum is all that is desired. Similar simplification occurs in every case when $\frac{\partial^2 f}{\partial y'^2} > 0$ for *all* x, y, y'. For then Legendre's and Weierstrass's conditions are always satisfied, and may be abstracted from the above table. For this reason Hilbert has called a problem in which $\frac{\partial^2 f}{\partial y'^2} > 0$ for all x, y, y' contained in a singly connected region R, in which the given end points lie, a *"regular"* problem of the Calculus of Variations.

Considering the example $\int_{x_0}^{x_1} \sqrt{1 + y'^2}\, dx$, we see that $f_{y'y'} > 0$ for all finite values of x, y, and y' whatever. Since

$$E(x, y, y', p) = \frac{(y' - p)^2}{2} f_{y'y'}(x, y, \xi), \quad y' \gtrless \xi \gtrless p,$$

it follows that such an example surely satisfies Weierstrass's sufficient condition, provided that a field exist in the manner specified above. But in this case, since the extremals are all straight lines in the plane, it is obvious that all other conditions are satisfied. Hence the straight line joining any two points actually minimizes the given integral, *i.e.*, the straight line is the "shortest" line between any two of its points if the preceding integral be the definition of length.

In the problem of the brachistochrone, mentioned above, it is shown that the extremals found (cycloids) actually render the integral of the problem a minimum provided no cusp lies between the end points (cf. Bolza, 'Lectures,' chap. iv., pp. 126, 136, 146).

Returning to the integral which defines length, it is evident that some other integral might as well have been selected as the definition of length, if we are not to assume an intuitive knowledge of it. The variety of choice is limited only by the selection of those properties which we desire to have hold. This leads very naturally to The Inverse Problem of the Calculus of Variations: Given a set of curves which form a two-parameter family. What is the condition that they be the extremals of a problem of the Calculus of Variations? What are the conditions that they actually render the integral · thus discovered a minimum? Let $y = F(x, a, b)$ be the given family. Then (cf. Bolza, 'Lectures,' p. 31) the integrand of any integral for which these are extremals must satisfy the equation

$$\frac{\partial f}{\partial y} - \frac{\partial^2 f}{\partial y' \partial x} - \frac{\partial^2 f}{\partial y' \partial y} y' = G(x, y, y') \cdot \frac{\partial^2 f}{\partial y' \partial y'},$$

where $y'' = G(x, y, y')$ is the differential equation of the given family. This equation for $f(x, y, y')$ always has an infinite number of solutions, of which only those are actually solutions of the given inverse problem which satisfy the relation $f_{y'y'} > 0$, and these are solutions in any region free from envelopes of one-parameter families of the given extremals. Some interesting conclusions for particular forms are to be found in a paper by Stromquist, 'Transactions of American Mathematical Society' (1905).

Another interesting class of problems are the so-called isoperimetric problems. These are problems in which a further restriction is placed upon the solution by requiring that it shall give a second (given) integral a given value. Such is, for example, the problem of finding the curve of maximum area with a given perimeter. The problem is treated by means of the so-called method of multipliers, which is too long for presentation here. (See Bolza, 'Lectures,' chap. vi.)

This article is too short to give any account of the details of the work for double integrals. Suffice it to say that the known methods follow closely those given above for simple integrals. In the other possible problems mentioned above the same holds true. An interesting application of these other problems occurs in the well-known *Problem of Dirichlet*, which is fundamental in mathematical work. Another is the important problem of *Minimum Surfaces*. Another is the well-known theory of mechanics based upon *Hamilton's Principle* or one of the analogous mechanical principles. The modern methods have made these theories more rigorous.

Bibliography.—The following is a list of the more important works and articles published in America concerning the Calculus of Variations: Carll, 'Calculus of Variations' (New York, 1885); Osgood, 'Annals of Mathematics' (II, 3, and Trans. A. M. S., II); Whittemore, 'Annals of Mathematics' (II, 3); Hancock, 'Various papers in Annals of Mathematics and Calculus of Variations' (Cincinnati, 1894); Bliss, 'Thesis' (Chicago, 1901); and various papers, 'Annals of Mathematics' and 'Transactions American Mathematical Society'; Hedrick, 'Bulletin American Mathematical Society,' IX (1901-5); Bolza, various papers, 'Bulletin American Mathematical Society,' 'Transactions American Mathematical Society,' etc. (1901-5); 'Brochures published in the Chicago Decennial Publications, including the Lectures on the Calculus of Variations mentioned above (Chicago, 1904).

The foreign literature is well collected for reference in the foot-notes to Bolza's 'Lectures,' and in the following books and articles: Todhunter, 'History of the Calculus of Variations' (Cambridge, 1861); Moigno-Lindeloff, 'Calcul des Variations' (Paris, 1861); Pascal, 'Calcolo delle variazioni' (Milan, 1897, German Trans., Leipzig, 1899); Kneser, 'Variationsrechnung' (Braunschweig, 1900); Kneser, 'Ency. der Math. Wiss., II, A 8' (Leipzig, 1904); Zermelo u. Hahn, 'Ency. der Math. Wiss., II, A 8a' (Leipzig, 1904).

The literature is altogether extremely extensive, covering, as it does, a period of over two hundred years. It is evident that the more important papers for present use are those of recent date.

An important phase of the subject which has necessarily been overlooked is the general proof by Hilbert (1900) that at least an *improper* minimum always exists. (See Bolza, 'Lectures,' chap. vii.)

EARLE RAYMOND HEDRICK,
Professor of Mathematics, University of Missouri.

Calcut'ta ("the ghaut or landing-place of Kâli" from a famous shrine of this goddess), India, the capital of British India, and of the presidency and province of Bengal, is situated on the left bank of the Hooghly (Húghli), a branch of the Ganges, about 80 miles from the Bay of Bengal. The Hooghly is navigable up to the city for vessels of 4,000 tons or drawing 26 feet; the navigation, however, on account of sand-banks which are continually changing their size and position, is dangerous. The river opposite the city varies in breadth from rather more than a quarter to three quarters of a mile. The city may be said to occupy an area extending along the river for about five miles from north to south, and stretching eastward to a distance of nearly two miles in the south, narrowing in the north to about half a mile. The eastern boundary is nominally formed by what is known as the Circular Road, the Lower Circular Road forming part of the southern boundary. Another eastern boundary on the north is the Circular Canal, which runs for some distance parallel to the Circular Road. The southwestern portion of the area thus spoken of is formed by the Maidan, a great park stretching along the river bank for about one and three quarter miles, with a breadth in the south of one and a half miles. This grassy and tree-studded area is one of the ornaments of Calcutta; it is intersected by fine drives, and is partly occupied by public gardens, a cricket ground, race-course, etc., and partly by Fort William, which rises from the river bank. It was built in 1757–73, being begun by Clive after the battle of Plassey, and is said to have cost about $10,000,000. Along the river bank there is a promenade, and drive known as the Strand Road, which has for the most part been reclaimed from the river by successive embankments. Along the east side of the Maidan runs Chauringhi Road, which is lined with magnificent residences, and forms the front of European fashionable residential quarter. Along the north side of the Maidan runs a road or street known as the Esplanade, on the north side of which are Government House and other public buildings. The European commercial quarter lies north of the Esplanade, between it and another street called Canning Street, having the river on the west. The centre of this area is occupied by Dalhousie Square (enclosing a large tank or reservoir), and here there are a number of public buildings, including the post-office, telegraph office, custom house, Bengal secretariat, etc. The European retail trade quarter occupies a small area to the east of the quarter occupies a small area to the east of above area. Everywhere outside of the European quarters Calcutta is interspersed with *bastís*, or native hamlets of mud huts, which form great outlying suburbs. "The growth of the European quarters, and the municipal clearings demanded by improved sanitation, are pushing these mud hamlets outward in all directions, but especially toward the east. . . . They have given rise to the reproach that Calcutta, while a city of palaces in front, is one of pigstyes in the rear." First among the public buildings is the Government House, the viceregal residence, situated, as already mentioned, on the Esplanade. It was built in 1799–1804, and with its grounds occupies six acres. Four wings extend toward the four points of the compass from a central mass which is crowned with a dome and approached from the north by a splendid flight of steps. Besides accommodating the viceroy and his staff it contains the council chamber in which the supreme legislature holds its sittings. The high court, the town hall, the bank of Bengal, the currency office, post-office, etc., are among the other public buildings in this locality, while further to the north stands the mint, near the bank of the Hooghly. The chief of the Anglican churches in Calcutta is the cathedral of St. Paul's, at the southeastern corner of the Maidan, a building in the "Indo-Gothic" style, with a tower and spire 201 feet high, consecrated in 1847. St. John's Church, or the old cathedral, is another important church, in the graveyard surrounding which is the tomb of Job Charnock, founder of Calcutta. The chief Presbyterian church is St. Andrew's or the Scotch Kirk, a handsome Grecian building with a spire. The Roman Catholics have a cathedral and several other churches; there are also places of worship for Greeks, Parsees, and Hebrews. Hindu temples are numerous, but uninteresting; among the Mohammedan mosques the only one of note is that which was built and endowed by Prince Ghulam Mohammed, son of Tippoo Sultan. The religions, educational, and benevolent institutions are numerous. Various missionary and other religious bodies, British, European, and American, are well represented. There are four government colleges—the Presidency College, the Sanskrit College, the Mohammedan College, and the Bethune Girls' School. There are five colleges mainly supported by missionary efforts; besides several others, some of them under native management. Other educational institutions include Calcutta Medical College, a government school of art, Campbell Vernacular Medical School, and a school of engineering at Howrah, on the western side of the river. Besides these there is the Calcutta University, an examining and degree-conferring institution. Among the hospitals are the Medical College Hospital, the General Hospital, the Mayo Hospital (for natives), and the Eden Hospital for women and children. The Martinière (so named from its founder, Gen. Martin, a Frenchman in the Company's service) is an important institution for the board and education of indigent Christian children. Elementary and other schools are increasing in numbers. In this connection we may mention the Asiatic Society, founded by Sir W. Jones in 1784, for the study of the languages, literature, antiquities, etc., of Asia; and the Botanic Garden, which occupies a large area on the right bank of the river. Calcutta possesses a number of public monuments, most of them in or about the Maidan. Several governors-general are thus commemorated, as also Sir David Ochterlony and Sir James Outram, «the Bayard of the East,» of whom there is an admirable equestrian statue by Foley. The city is lighted partly by gas, partly by electricity. There is an extensive system of tramways. The sanitation of Calcutta, though vastly improved in recent years, is still defective, more especially in the suburban districts, where the *bastís* or native huts are so common. One difficulty in the way is the site of the city itself, which is practically a dead level. An act which came into force in 1889 brought a large additional area under the municipal authorities, and since then much has been done in the way of drainage, opening up of arterial streets, alignment of roads, etc. The water supply has also been greatly increased, and filtered water from the Hooghly (there is a pumping station at Palta, 16 miles above Calcutta) is now available at the daily rate of 36 gallons per head in the city, and over 15 in the suburbs, besides a supply of unfiltered water for washing and other purposes. The mortality over the entire municipality in 1893 was 29.5 per 1,000, a great improvement on former times. The death-rate is far higher among the natives than among the Europeans, and in the native quarters cholera is said to be seldom entirely absent. The healthiest months are July and August, which form part of the season of rains; the unhealthiest are November, December, and January. The mean temperature is about 79°, the average rainfall a little over 66 inches. The port of Calcutta extends for about 10 miles along the river, and is under the management of a body of commissioners. Opposite the city it is crossed by a great pontoon bridge, which gives communication with Howrah for vehicles and foot passengers, and can be opened at one point to let vessels pass up or down. It cost $1,100,000. Besides the accommodation for shipping furnished by the river, there are also several docks. The trade is very large, Calcutta being the commercial centre of India. There is a very extensive inland trade by the Ganges and its connections, as also by railways (the chief of which start from Howrah), while almost the whole foreign trade of this part of India is monopolized by Calcutta. In 1897–8 the gross tonnage of the shipping inward and outward was over 5,000,000 tons; while the total of exports and imports was 71,994,608 tens of rupees, the exports being largely in excess of imports. The chief exports are opium, jute, and jute goods, tea, grain and pulse, oilseeds, raw cotton, indigo, hides and skins, silk and silk goods, etc. The most important import is cotton goods. The jute manufacture is extensively carried on, also that of cottons.

The first factory in Bengal of the East India Company, which was incorporated by royal charter in the year 1600, was established at Hooghly, 28 miles farther up the river, in 1644. Job Charnock, the company's agent, was driven out of this settlement in 1686, and the English then occupied part of the present site of Calcutta, which in 1689–90 became the headquarters of the commercial establishments of the company in Bengal. In 1700 the company acquired from Prince Azim, son of the Emperor Aurengzebe, the three villages of Sutánati, Kalikata (Calcutta), and Govindpore, for an annual rent of 1,195 rupees, and these formed the nucleus of the present city. The original Fort William, named after William III., was built in 1696, on a site considerably to the north of the present fort. Calcutta was taken and plundered by Suraj-ud-Dowlah in 1756, and retaken by Lord Clive in 1757. To the capture by Suraj-ud-Dowlah belongs the episode of the «Black Hole» (q.v.) of Calcutta. When the British recovered possession, much of the town was in ruins and had to be rebuilt, so that it may be said to date only from 1757. Clive built the new Fort William on the site of Govindpore, between 1757 and 1773. In 1773 Calcutta became the seat of British government for the whole of India. Since then the history of Calcutta has been a record of progress and prosperity. Pop. (1901) 1,121,664.

Caldara, Polidoro. See CARAVAGGIO.

Calderon, Francisco Garcia, Peruvian statesman: b. Arequipa, 1834; d. Lima, Perú, 21 Sept. 1905. At the age of 21 he was a professor of Jurisprudence, a member of the Peruvian Congress 1867, and minister of the treasury 1868. After the occupation of Lima by the Chilean army, during the war between Chile, Peru, and Bolivia, 1879–81, he was made president of a provisional government formed under the protection of the Chilean authorities, February 1881. He pledged himself to conduct his government upon principles not opposed to the fundamental conditions demanded by Chile for the final arrangement of peace, but failing to do this, he was arrested, 6 Nov. 1881, by order of Gen. Patrick Lynch, rear-admiral and general-in-chief of the Chileans, and sent as a prisoner to Valparaiso. Upon his return to Lima in 1886 he was elected president of the senate. His principal work is a 'Dictionary of Peruvian Legislation.'

Calderon, Manuel Alvarez, mä'noo-ĕl äl'bä rĕth, Peruvian lawyer and diplomatist: b. Lima, Peru, 2 June 1852. He was graduated from the University of San Marcos, Lima. He is a member of the Illustrious College of Lawyers at Lima, has been professor of the science of finance at this university, and from 14 July 1900 has been minister plenipotentiary from Peru to the United States.

Calderon, kăl'dèr-ŏn, **Philip Hermogenes,** English painter, of Spanish parentage: b. Poitiers, 3 May 1833; d. London, 30 April 1898. He was the son of Juan Calderon, at one time professor of Spanish literature in King's College, London. Coming to England about 1845, he became shortly afterward the pupil of a civil engineer; but his artistic ability was so pronounced that his father allowed him to devote himself to the study of art at the British Museum and the National Gallery. In 1853 he went to study under Picot at the Ecole des Beaux Arts in Paris. He first exhibited at the

Academy in 1853, his picture being named 'By the Waters of Babylon.' Among the many pictures he subsequently produced are: 'Broken Vows' (1857); 'Far Away' (1858); 'The Gaoler's Daughter' (1858); 'Never More' (1860); 'Liberating Prisoners on the Young Heir's Birthday' (1861); 'After the Battle' (1862), one of his most successful works; 'The English Embassy in Paris on the Day of the Massacre of St. Bartholomew' (1863); 'Her Most High, Noble, and Puissant Grace' (1865), the last two being probably his finest works; 'Whither?' (1867 — his diploma picture); 'Sighing His Soul Out in His Lady's Face' (1869); 'Spring Driving Away Winter' (1870); 'On Her Way to the Throne' (1871), a sequel to his masterpiece of 1865; 'Victory' (1873); 'Half-hours with the Best Authors'; 'La Gloire de Dijon' (1878); 'Home They Brought Her Warrior Dead'; 'Aphrodite'; 'The Answer' (1897); and 'Ruth' (1897). Elected A.R.A. in 1864, he became, three years later, a full academician. He gained in 1867 the first French gold medal awarded to an English artist.

Calderon, Serafin Estebanez, sĕr-ä-fēn' ĕs-tā'nĕth käl-dā-rōn', Spanish writer: b. Malaga, Spain, 27 Dec. 1801; d. Madrid, 7 Feb. 1867. He was professor of poetry and rhetoric at Granada, 1822-30, but resigned and went to Madrid. There he collected a library of old Spanish literature, especially of ballads, whether manuscript or in print: the collection is in the National Library at Madrid. He wrote a volume of poems, 'Poesias del Solitario' (1833); a novel, 'Christians and Moriscos' (1838), and a very valuable study of 'The Literature of the Moriscos.' He also wrote 'The Conquest and the Loss of Portugal,' and a charming volume of 'Andalusian Scenes.'

Calderon de la Barca, kăl'dèr ŏn dŭ lạ bär'kạ, Frances Erskine (INGLIS), Scottish-American writer: b. Scotland about 1810. Her father, Mr. Inglis, was a grandson of Col. Gardiner who fell at Preston-Pans. She resided in her youth for several years in Normandy, and then emigrated with her mother to the United States, where they established a school at Boston, in which the daughter officiated as teacher for six years. In 1838 she married the Spanish minister at Washington, Don Calderon de la Barca, and afterward accompanied her husband to Mexico. In 1843 she published 'Life in Mexico,' which gained for her considerable literary reputation.

Calderon de la Barca, Pedro, pā'drō käl-dā-rōn' dä la bär'kạ, Spanish dramatist: b. Madrid, 17 Jan. 1600; d. 25 May 1681. He received his early education in the Jesuits' college of his native city, and studied at Salamanca, where he devoted himself chiefly to history, philosophy, and jurisprudence. His poetical genius early discovered itself. Before his 14th year he had written his third play, 'El Carro del Cielo.' His talent for this species of poetry, which has brought his name down to posterity, and perhaps his powers of invention in the preparation of entertainments for festivals, soon gained him friends and patrons. When he left Salamanca in 1625, to seek employment at the court of Madrid, many noblemen interested themselves in bringing forward the young poet. But having an inclination for the military profession, he entered the service in 1625, and bore arms with distinction for 10 years in Milan and the Netherlands. From these countries, it has been observed, he usually drew his heroes of comedy. In 1636 he was recalled by Philip IV., who gave him the direction of the court entertainments, and, in particular, the preparation of plays for the court theatre. The next year he was made knight of the order of Santiago, and he served in 1640 in the campaign in Catalonia. The unexpected termination of the war restored him again to his peaceful occupation. The king now conferred on him a monthly pension of 30 escudos de oro; but he still employed his talents with unintermitted industry in composing for the theatre and the Church. The king spared no cost in the representation of his theatrical pieces. Ten years after, in 1651, he procured permission from the order of Santiago to enter the clerical profession, and in 1653 obtained a chaplain's office in the archiepiscopal church at Toledo, without quitting, however, his former occupation. But as this situation removed him too far from court, he received, in 1663, another at the king's court chapel (being still allowed to hold the former); and at the some time a pension was assigned him from the Sicilian revenue. His fame greatly increased his income, as he was solicited by the principal cities of Spain to compose their autos sacramentales, for which he was liberally paid. He bestowed particular pains on the composition of these pieces, and in fact, eclipsed all that the Spanish literature, so rich in this department of fancy, had hitherto produced. These subjects were particularly suited to his religious turn of mind; and he set a peculiar value on his performances of this kind, so as even to disparage his other works, which deserve no mean reputation. Religion is the ruling idea, the central point, of his poems. Whatever subject he handles he exhibits true poetical genius. Even allowing that he is inferior in richness of invention to Lope de Vega, he certainly excels him in fineness of execution, elevation of feeling, and aptness of expression. If we find in him much that is foreign to our modes of thinking and feeling, to our accustomed views and manner of expression, we shall have occasion much oftener to admire his unrivaled genius. The Spanish nation esteem Calderon among the greatest poetical geniuses. Among his dramatic works are many pieces of intrigue, full of complicated plots and rich in interesting incidents. There are, besides, heroic comedies and historical plays, some of which merit the name of tragedies. To this class belongs the 'Constant Prince,' which deserves an honorable place among romantic tragedies of the first rank. Besides these, Calderon has left 95 autos sacramentales, 200 loas (preludes), and 100 saynetes (farces). He wrote his last play in the 80th year of his age. The smaller poems of Calderon, his songs, sonnets, ballads, etc., notwithstanding the applause which they received from his contemporaries, are now forgotten; but his plays have maintained their place on the stage, even more than those of Lope de Vega. The number of his collected plays amounts to 128. He wrote, however, many more, some of which were never published. The most complete edition of his works is that published by D. Juan de Vera Tassis y Villarroel (Madrid 1685, 9 vols.). 'The Constant Prince' shows, perhaps, in the highest degree, Calderon's tragic powers. It turns on one of the most perplexing of all subjects, that is, the idea of destiny, managed in a truly poetical way, in a tragedy terminating happily. The great fertility of Calderon's invention has heaped up an abundance of materials from which foreign theatres might be much enriched. It is to be regretted that his works have not been chronologically arranged. We might then have traced the growth of mysticism in his mind, and seen it striking root more deeply as he advanced in life. At the age of 62 he was admitted into the fraternity of San Pedro. Before his death he was elected their *capellan mayor*. He left them all his property, for which they erected a splendid monument to his memory. Among his imitators, Tirso de Molina is worthy of mention, as the author of the 'Inflexible Stranger,' which has been often imitated. He also found imitators among his rivals in other countries. Corneille and Molière are believed to have built some of their renowned productions upon the foundations he had provided. See Schmidt, 'Die Schauspiele Calderons' (1857); Trench, 'Essay on the Life and Genius of Calderon' (1880); Menendez y Pelayo, 'Calderon y su teatro' (1881); Günther, 'Calderon und seine Werke' (1888).

Calderon y Beltran, ē bĕl-trän', Fernando, Mexican dramatist and poet: b. Guadaljara, 20 July 1809; d. Ojocaliente, 18 Jan. 1845. Throughout Spanish America his plays, such as 'The Journey,' 'Anne Boleyn,' and 'The Return of the Crusader,' have been extremely popular, and as a lyrist he is much admired by the Mexican public.

Calderwood, kôl'dèr-wùd, David, Scottish clergyman and ecclesiastical historian: b. Dalkeith, 1575; d. Jedbury, 29 Oct. 1650. In 1604 he was settled as a minister of Crailing, in Roxburghshire, where he distinguished himself by his opposition to episcopal authority. In 1617 he was banished from the realm for his contumacy, and went to Holland, where, in 1623, he published his famous work entitled 'Altare Damascenum.' Some time afterward he returned to Scotland, and became minister of the church of Pencaitland, near Edinburgh. He then engaged in writing the history of the Church of Scotland, in continuation of that of Knox, a work which was published from his manuscript in 1842-9 in eight volumes.

Calderwood, Henry, Scottish philosopher: b. Peebles, 10 May 1830; d. Edinburgh, 19 Nov. 1897. He received his early education at the Edinburgh Institution and High School. He afterward attended the university of that city, and while a student published his 'Philosophy of the Infinite' (1854), an attempt to controvert the views of Sir William Hamilton. He became minister of Greyfriars United Presbyterian Church, Glasgow, in 1856, and in 1868 was elected professor of moral philosophy in Edinburgh University, a chair which he occupied for the rest of his life. His chief works are his 'Handbook of Moral Philosophy' (1872); 'Relations of Mind and Brain' (1881); and 'Evolution and Man's Place in Nature' (1893).

Caldicott, kôl'dĭ kŏt, Alfred James, English musician and composer: b. Worcester, England, 1842; d. 24 Oct. 1897. After studying at Leipsic under Richter and Moscheles he was organist of Saint Stephen's Church in his native town for a time, becoming professor in the Royal College of Music in 1882. Among his works, beside many songs, glees, etc., are the cantatas 'The Widow of Nain' (1881); and 'A Rhine Legend' (1883); and the operettas, 'A Moss Rose Pent' (1883); and 'Old Knockles' (1884).

Caldwell, Alexander, American banker: b. Drake's Ferry, Huntington County, Pa., 1 March 1830. He attended public and private schools until 16 years of age. In 1847 he enlisted as a soldier in the Mexican war, entering the company of his father, who was killed at one of the gates of the city of Mexico. In 1848 he returned to Columbia, Pa., where he entered a bank, and later took up business. In 1861 he removed to Kansas, where he engaged in the transportation of military supplies to the various posts on the plains, and became largely interested in railroad and bridge building. He was elected to the United States Senate as a Republican, took his seat 4 March 1871, and served until 24 March 1873, when he resigned.

Caldwell, kôld'wĕl, Charles, American physician: b. Caswell County, N. C., 14 May 1772; d. Louisville, Ky., 9 July 1853. He studied medicine at Philadelphia, and in 1795 translated from the Latin, Blumenbach's 'Elements of Physiology.' He published also a 'Life of General Greene' (1819), a work on mesmerism, and other volumes. In 1819 he became professor of the institutes of medicine in Transylvania University, Lexington, Ky. He subsequently founded a medical school in Louisville.

Caldwell, Charles Henry Bromedge, American naval officer: b. Hingham, Mass., 11 June 1828; d. Boston, 30 Nov. 1877. He did a notable service in an expedition against a tribe of cannibals inhabiting one of the Fiji Islands, defeating them in a pitched battle and destroying their town. In the Civil War he commanded the Itasca, taking part in the bombardment of forts Jackson and St. Philip and the Chalmette batteries, and in the capture of New Orleans. He was promoted commodore in 1874.

Caldwell, Howard Walter, American historian: b. Bryan, Ohio, 26 Aug. 1858. He was graduated from the University of Nebraska in 1880 and is professor of American history and jurisprudence there. He has written 'History of the United States, 1815-1861' (1896); 'Studies in History' (1897); 'A Survey of American History' (1898); 'Some Great American Legislators' (1899); 'Life of Henry Clay' (1899); 'Expansion of the United States' (1900).

Caldwell, James, American clergyman: b. Charlotte County, Va., April 1734; d. 24 Nov. 1781. After graduating at the College of New Jersey, now Princeton University, he became Presbyterian pastor at Elizabethtown. During the growing antagonism between the colonies and Great Britain, he warmly took the side of the former, and when hostilities began, became chaplain to the New Jersey brigade, and took an active share in its campaigns, fighting "with the sword in one hand and the Bible in the other." Irritated at the unexpected and obstinate resistance made by the Jersey troops and yeomanry, the English began to burn the houses and pillage the property of the villagers at Connecticut Farms. In one of the houses was the family of Mr. Caldwell, whose wife had retired to a back room with her two youngest children — one an infant in her arms — where she was engaged in prayer, when a musket was discharged through the window. Two balls struck her in the breast, and she fell dead upon the floor. On 23 June Gen. Knyphausen made a second incursion with about 5,000 troops. On this occasion he passed over the same route to Springfield, where a battle was fought. Among the most active in the fight was the chaplain Caldwell. There is a tradition, well authenticated, that in the hottest period of the action the wadding of a portion of the Jersey infantry gave out, which fact being communicated to Caldwell, he rode to the Presbyterian Church, and hastily collecting the psalm and hymn books which were in the building, he distributed them to the soldiers with the exhortation, "Now put Watts into them, boys!" The British were finally compelled to retrace their steps, which they did with all possible rapidity. He was shot and killed by an American sentinel in the course of a dispute over a package the latter desired to examine. Sixty-four years after Caldwell's death a monument was raised to his memory in Elizabeth.

Caldwell, Merritt, American educator: b. Helron, Me., 29 Nov. 1806; d. Portland, Me., 6 June 1848. He was graduated from Bowdoin College in 1828 and was subsequently professor of mathematics and English literature in Dickinson College, Pa. He published 'Manual of Elocution' (1846); 'Philosophy of Christian Perfection' (1847); 'Christianity Tested by Eminent Men;' 'The Doctrine of the English Verb.'

Caldwell, Samuel Lunt, American Baptist clergyman: b. Newburyport, Mass., 13 Nov. 1820; d. Providence, R. I., 26 Sept. 1889. After studying at the Newton (Mass.) Theological Institution he entered the ministry and was successively pastor at Bangor, Me., 1846–58; and of the First Baptist Church in Providence 1858–73; professor of Church history in the Newton Theological Institution 1873–8; and president of Vassar College 1878–85.

Caldwell, William, Scottish-American educator: b. Edinburgh, Scotland, 10 Nov. 1863. He was graduated from the university of his native city and was assistant professor of logic and metaphysics in that institution 1887-8. In 1891 he was called to the Sage School of Philosophy, Cornell University, N. Y.; in 1892 to the University of Chicago, and since 1894 has been professor of moral and social philosophy in the Northwestern University at Evanston, Ill. He has published 'Schopenhauer's System in Its Philosophical Significance.'

Ca'leb, son of Jephunneh, a descendant of the tribe of Judah, or according to some authorities a foreigner of Kenezite origin incorporated with that tribe, according to Ussher born 1530 B.C. was sent with Joshua and 10 others to examine the land of Canaan. When Joshua had conquered the country, Caleb reminded the Jews of the promise which had been made by God, that they should enjoy this country. He obtained the city of Hebron for his share of the spoil, besieged and captured it, and drove out three giants, or Anakim. He then marched against Kirjath-sepher, and offered his daughter Achsah to the first who should enter it. Othniel, his nephew, was the successful aspirant for the fair Jewess.

Caleb Williams, a novel by William Godwin (1794), a curious, rambling, half sensational and half psychological story. It met with immediate popularity, and furnished the suggestion of the well-known play 'The Iron Chest.'

Caledo'nia, the name by which the northern portion of Scotland first became known to the Romans. The year 80 of the Christian era is the period when Scotland first becomes known to history. The invasion of Cæsar did not immediately lead to the permanent occupation of southern Britain. It was only in the year 43 that the annexation of this portion of the island to the Roman empire began. It was completed superficially about 78, and two years were occupied in reconciling the natives to the Roman yoke. Agricola then moved northward, invading Scotland by the eastern route, and occupying the country up to the line of the Friths of Clyde and Forth. Agricola ran defensive works across this line, and hearing, in the third year of his occupation, rumors of an organized invasion in preparation by the Caledonians, a name applied to the dwellers north of the boundary, he resolved to anticipate them, and again advanced northward. The Roman army marched in three divisions. The weakest, consisting of the ninth legion, was attacked by the barbarians, who fought their way to the Roman camp. Agricola came to the rescue, and the Romans were victorious. The Roman army now advanced to Mons Grampius, where they found the enemy, 30,000 strong, under a chief named Galgacus. Agricola had to stretch his line as far as he deemed prudent to prevent being outflanked. The auxiliaries and Romanized Britons were in the centre and front, the legions in the rear. The Caledonians are described as riding furiously about in chariots between the two camps. Each chief (Roman and Caledonian) made a set speech to his followers; that of Galgacus was peculiarly eloquent. The Caledonians were armed with small shields, arrows, and large pointless swords. Their chariots routed the Roman cavalry, but afterward became embarrassed in the broken ground; and when the Roman auxiliaries charged the masses of the enemy with the gladius, they gave way before a method of fighting to which they were unaccustomed. Some further manœuvres occurred, but the victory of the Romans was complete. It does not appear, however, to have been productive of great effects, as next morning the enemy had entirely disappeared. Such is the account given by Tacitus of the only one of the numerous battles between the Romans and the Caledonians, of which we have a detailed description. The site of the battle remains undetermined, and the origin of the name Caledonian remains in equal obscurity. Various derivations are given of the word, but whether it was a native term, and to what exact people it applied, cannot with certainty be determined. The name Caledonian is first used by Pliny, who, as well as Tacitus, is supposed to have derived it from Agricola. The name is applied by Ptolemy to one of the numerous populations of North Britain. The use of the name by Tacitus gave it immediate popularity with the Romans, and to the same source its subsequent popularity in Britain is to be traced. Its historical importance is therefore exclusively limited to this first mention of it. See Dr. Smith, 'Dictionary of Greek and Roman Geography,' and Burton, 'History of Scotland.'

Caledo′nian Canal, in Scotland, counties of Inverness and Argyle, connects the North with the Irish Sea, extending from Murray Frith through Lochs Ness, Oich, and Lochy, in the great glen of Caledonia, to Loch Eil. The total length is 60½ miles, of which the lochs compose 37½. The canal was begun in 1803, and opened for navigation about the close of 1823.

Calef, Robert, American merchant of Boston: b. about 1648; d. Roxbury, Mass., 13 April 1719. His fourth son, also named Robert, died in 1722 or 1723, aged about 41. One or the other of these men was the author of a remarkable book on the witchcraft delusion in New England. The best authorities, notably James Savage and Wm. F. Poole, ascribe it to the younger, who was about 23 when it appeared. The book was entitled 'More Wonders of the Invisible World' (Lond. 1700), the title being suggested by Cotton Mather's 'Wonders of the Invisible World.' The substance of it had been circulated in manuscript several years previous to its publication and its malicious attacks on Cotton and Increase Mather caused a bitter and life-long quarrel between the former and the author. The book abounds in malicious innuendos, directly charges the Mathers with inciting and being in full sympathy with the Salem tragedies, and accuses the Boston ministers, in their advice of 15 June 1692, of endorsing the Salem methods. When the book was printed and came back to Boston it was denounced and hated because it was an untruthful and atrocious libel on the public sentiment of Boston, and on the conduct of its ministers. It is said that Increase Mather publicly burned it in the Harvard College yard. The animus of the book has been greatly misunderstood, and the popular idea that Calef was a stalwart agent in putting an end to Salem witchcraft is both a myth and a delusion. Its historical value and the author's character have been greatly overrated. His personal history is a blank which the most assiduous investigation has never been able to fill, or even to supply with the most common details. It is not known where or when he was born, when he died, or where he was buried, although he lived in Boston and his will is on file in the Suffolk records. His book has now become very rare and copies bring high prices in the book auctions. It was reprinted at Salem in 1796, 1823, and 1861, and at Boston in 1828 and 1865.

W. N. CARLTON,
Trinity College, Hartford.

Calendar, a system of dividing time into years, months, weeks, and days for use in civil life, or a register of these or similar divisions. Among the old Romans, for want of such a register, it was the custom of the Pontifex Maximus, on the first day of the month, which began with the new moon, to proclaim (*calare*) the month, with the festivals occurring in it. Hence, *calendæ* (the first of the month) and

calendar. The periodical occurrence of certain natural phenomena gave rise to the first division of time. The apparent daily revolution of the sun about the earth occasioned the division into days. The time at which a day begins and ends has been differently fixed, the reckoning being from sunrise to sunrise, from sunset to sunset, from noon to noon, or from midnight to midnight. The changes of the moon, which were observed to recur every 29 or 30 days, suggested the division into months, but the month now used, though nearly equal to a lunation, is really an arbitrary unit; and, as a still longer measure of time was found necessary for many purposes, it was supplied by the apparent yearly revolution of the sun round the earth, producing the changing seasons. The time of this revolution is now known to be 365 days, 5 hours, 48 minutes, and 46 seconds, but as it has at various times been reckoned differently, this has given rise to corresponding changes in the calendar. This unit of time is called a solar year. The division into weeks, which has been almost universally adopted, is not founded on any natural phenomenon, and, as it originated in the East, has been attributed to the divine command to Moses in regard to the observation of the seventh day as a day of rest. By other authorities it has been ascribed to the number of the principal planets, a theory supported by the names given to the days. It was not used by the Greeks, nor by the Romans, till the time of Theodosius. The great influence of the sun's course upon the seasons naturally attracted the attention of men at all periods to this phenomenon; accordingly all nations in any degree civilized have adopted the year as the longest unit of time. The year of the ancient Egyptians was based on the changes of the seasons alone, without reference to the lunar month, and contained 365 days, which were divided into 12 months of 30 days each, with five supplementary days at the end of each year. The Jewish year consisted of lunar months, of which they reckoned 12 in the year, intercalating a 13th when necessary to maintain the correspondence of the particular months with the regular recurrence of the seasons. The Greeks in the earliest period also reckoned by lunar and intercalary months. They divided the month into three decades, a system also adopted long afterward at the time of the French Revolution. It possesses the advantage of making the smaller division an exact measure of the larger, and under it the number of a day in the 10-day period readily suggests its number in the month. The Greeks in the time of Solon had a year of 12 months, alternately of 29 and 30 days, the total number of days being 354, and the year being very nearly equal to a lunar one. Soon afterward a month of 30 days began to be intercalated every other year in order to reconcile their year with that founded on the sun's movement, but as the error was still very large the intercalary month was afterward omitted once in four times. The Jewish and also the Greek year thus both varied in duration according as the intercalary month was introduced or omitted. This, with the uncertainty as to the exact duration of the year, was a constant source of confusion.

Various plans for the reformation of the calendar were proposed from time to time; but all proved insufficient till Meton and Euctemon finally succeeded in bringing it to a much greater degree of accuracy by fixing on the period of 19 years, in which time the new moons return upon the same days of the year as before (as 19 solar years are very nearly equal to 235 lunations). (See CYCLE.) This mode of computation, first adopted by the Greeks about 432 B.C., was so much approved of that it was engraven with golden letters on a tablet at Athens. Hence the number showing what year of the moon's cycle any given year is is called the golden number. This period of 19 years was found, however, to be about six hours too long. This defect Calippus, about 102 years later, endeavored to remedy, but still failed to make the beginning of the seasons return on the same fixed day of the year.

The Romans first divided the year into 10 months, but they early adopted the Greek method of lunar and intercalary months, making the lunar year consist of 354, and afterward of 355 days, leaving 10 or 11 days and a fraction to be supplied by the intercalary division. This arrangement, which was placed under the charge of the pontiffs, continued until the time of Cæsar. The first day of the month was called the calends. In March, May, July, and October, the 15th, in other months the 13th, was called the ides. The ninth day before the ides (reckoning inclusive) was called the nones. The other days of the months they reckoned forward to the next calends, nones, or ides, whether in the same or the succeeding month, always including both days in the reckoning. Thus the 3d of March, according to the Roman reckoning, would be the fifth day before the nones, which in that month fall on the 7th. The 8th of January, in which month the nones happen on the 5th, and the ides on the 13th, was called the 6th before the ides of January. Finally, to express any of the days after the ides, they reckon in a similar manner from the calends of the following month. From the inaccuracy of the Roman method of reckoning it appears that in Cicero's time the calendar brought the vernal equinox almost two months later than it ought to be. To check this irregularity Julius Cæsar invited the Greek astronomer Sosigenes to Rome, who, with the assistance of Marcus Fabius, invented that mode of reckoning which, after him who introduced it into use, has been called the Julian calendar. The chief improvement consisted in restoring the equinox to its proper place in March. For this purpose two months were inserted between November and December, so that the year 707 (46 B.C.), called from this circumstance the year of confusion, contained 14 months. In the number of days the Greek computation was adopted, which made it 365¼. The number and names of the months were kept unaltered with the exception of Quintilis, which was henceforth called, in honor of the author of the improvement, Julius. To dispose of the quarter of a day it was determined to intercalate a day every fourth year between the 23rd and 24th of February. This was called an intercalary day, and the year in which it took place was called an intercalary year, or, as we term it, a leap year.

This calendar continued in use among the Romans until the fall of the empire, and throughout Christendom till 1582. The festivals of the Christian Church were determined by it. With regard to Easter, however, it was necessary to have reference to the course of the moon. The Jews celebrated Easter (that is, the Passover) on the 14th of the month Nisan (or March); the Christians in the same month, but always on a Sunday. Now, as the Easter of the Christians sometimes coincided with the Passover of the Jews, and it was thought unchristian to celebrate so important a festival at the same time as the Jews did, it was resolved at the council of Nice, 325 A.D., that from that time Easter should be solemnized on the Sunday following the first full moon after the vernal equinox, which was then supposed to take place on 21 March. As the course of the moon was thus made the foundation for determining the time of Easter, the lunar Cycle of Meton was taken for this purpose; according to which the year contains 365¼ days, and the new moons, after a period of 19 years, return on the same day as before. The inaccuracy of this combination of the Julian year and the lunar cycle must have soon discovered itself on a comparison with the true time of the commencement of the equinoxes, since the received length of 365¼ days exceeds the true by about 11 minutes; so that for every such Julian year the equinox receded 11 minutes, or a day in about 130 years. In consequence of this, in the 16th century, the vernal equinox had changed its place in the calendar from the 21st to the 10th; that is, it really took place on the 10th instead of the 21st, on which it was placed in the calendar. Luigi Lilio Ghiraldi, frequently called Aloysius Lilius, a physician of Verona, projected a plan for amending the calendar, which, after his death, was presented by his brother to Pope Gregory XIII. To carry it into execution, the Pope assembled a number of prelates and learned men. In 1577 the proposed change was adopted by all the Catholic princes; and in 1582 Gregory issued a brief abolishing the Julian calendar in all Catholic countries, and introducing in its stead the one now in use, under the name of the Gregorian or reformed calendar, or the new style, as the other was now called the old style. The amendment ordered was this: 10 days were to be dropped after 4 Oct. 1582, and the 15th was reckoned immediately after the 4th. Every 100th year, which by the old style was a leap year, was now to be a common year, the fourth century divisible by 4 excepted; that is, 1600 was to remain a leap year, but 1700, 1800, 1900 of the common length, and 2,000 a leap year again. In this calendar the length of the solar year is taken to be 365 days, 5 hours, 49 minutes, and 12 seconds, the difference between which and the true length is immaterial. In Spain, Portugal, and the greater part of Italy, the amendment was introduced according to the Pope's instructions. In France the 10 days were dropped in December, the 10th being called the 20th. In Catholic Switzerland, Germany, and the Netherlands the change was introduced in the following year, in Poland in 1586, in Hungary 1587. Protestant Germany, Holland, and Denmark accepted it in 1700, and Switzerland in 1701. In the German empire a difference still remained for a considerable time as to the period for observing Easter. In England the Gregorian calendar was adopted in 1752, in accordance with an act of Parliament passed the previous year, the day after 2d September becoming the 14th. Sweden followed in 1753.

The change adopted in the English calendar in 1752 embraced another point. There had been previous to this time various periods fixed for the commencement of the year in various countries of Europe. In France, from the time of Charles IX., the year was reckoned to begin from 1 January; this was also the popular reckoning in England, but the legal and ecclesiastical year began on 25 March. The 1st of January was now adopted as the beginning of the legal year, and it was customary for some time to give two dates for the period intervening between 1 January and 25 March, that of the old and that of the new year, as January 1752-3. Russia alone retains the old style, which now differs 13 days from the new; but has it in contemplation to adopt the Gregorian calendar at an early date.

In France, during the Revolutionary epoch, a new calendar was introduced by a decree of the National Convention, 24 Nov. 1793. The new reckoning was to begin with 22 Sept. 1792, the day on which the first decree of the new republic had been promulgated. The year was made to consist of 12 months of 30 days each, and, to complete the full number, five *fête* days (in leap year six) were added at the end of the year. Instead of weeks, each month was divided into three parts, called decades, consisting of 10 days each; the other divisions being also accommodated to the decimal system. The names of the months were so chosen as to indicate, by their etymology, the time of year to which they belonged. They were as follows:

Autumn (September 22 to December 22):
Vendémiaire (vintage month), October
Brumaire (foggy month), November
Frimaire (sleet month), December
Winter (December 22 to March 22):
Nivôse (snowy month), January
Pluviôse (rainy month), February
Ventôse (windy month), March
Spring (March 22 to June 22):
Germinal (bud month), April
Floréal (flower month), May
Prairial (meadow month), June
Summer (June 22 to September 22):
Messidor (harvest month), July
Thermidor (hot month), August
Fructidor (fruit month), September

The 10 days of each decade were called:

1 Primod.	4 Quartidi	7 Septidi
2 Duodi	5 Quintidi	8 Octidi
3 Tridi	6 Sextidi	9 Nonidi
	10 Decadi, the Sabbath	

This calendar was abolished at the command of Napoleon, by a decree of the senate, 9 Sept. 1805, and the common or Gregorian calendar was re-established on 1 January of the following year. See also Chronology; Cycle; Epoch.

Calendar, French Revolutionary. See Calendar.

Calgary, Canada, city in the Province of Alberta, situated at the confluence of the Bow and Elboe rivers; on the Western Division of the Canadian Pacific Railway; 640 miles west of Winnipeg, 420 miles east of Vancouver, and 2,260 miles northwest of Montreal. It is the junction place for Edmonton and northern points, for Macleod and southern points, and for Donald, B. C., and western points.

Industries and Business Interests.— It is probably the chief distributing point of the two new Provinces, and there are 63 eastern manufacturers established locally with large houses or agencies. It is the centre of the trade of a great ranching country and the chief source of supply for the mining districts in the mountains beyond. Lumber is largely made from logs floated down the Bow River. Amongst the chief industries are one soap factory valued at $50,000, two flour mills and elevators valued at $200,000, one abattoir valued at $200,000, two sash and door factories, a sawmill, a brewery and an artificial gas company. There is also a company recently established for boring for natural gas, and the Alberta Portland Cement Company has just started operations with a capital to be expended on plant of about $500,000. Calgary has also a considerable and growing live-stock trade and is the seat of eight bank branches.

Public Works, Buildings, etc.—The value of the buildings erected in 1904 was $1,250,000, and in 1905, $1,300,000; there are 25 miles of plank side-walks, 11 miles of sewer lines, 17½ miles of water mains and three miles of concrete; the value of the water-works plant is $250,000, and there are in the city two electric light plants — one owned by the municipality at a cost of $65,000 and the other by the Calgary Water-Power Company at a cost of $90,000. There are five churches and three large public school buildings which cost $175,000. The Western Canada College is located here. There are also three hospitals, a sanitarium, an opera house, railway shops, municipal buildings and four parks.

Irrigation Interests in the Vicinity.— Some 14 miles east of Calgary is a great tract of fertile but hitherto arid country upon which the Canadian Pacific Railway is spending millions for irrigation purposes. Its works consist of a great ditch through clay, embankments piled by steam shovels and a narrow gauge railway, cuts in which hundreds of men and horses are sometimes supplementing the work of the steam shovel, and sometimes preparing ground for it. About two miles from Calgary is the intake, a set of sluice gates, prepared for lifting by steam winches, and for admitting the water of the Bow River into a big ditch or canal. The river flows on a ridge which must be cut through, in order that the ditch may convey water northward and eastward. This meandering cutting, some 16 miles long, constitutes the main canal, and is very heavy. It terminates in a reservoir planned to cover about 800 acres, some 9 miles eastward of Calgary. Thence secondary canals having a total length of 250 miles in the western irrigation district will convey the water through 500 miles of distributing ditches.

Population.— Incorporated in 1894, its growth in population has, of late years, been very great. In 1904 it was stated to have 6,500 people; official estimate (1906) place its population at 15,000. J. Castell Hopkins, *Editor of 'The Canadian Annual Review of Public Affairs.'*

Calhoun, kăl-hoon', **John Caldwell**, American statesman: b. Ableville District, S. C., 18 March 1782; d. Washington, D. C., 31 March 1850. He was graduated with distinction at Yale College in 1804, and was admitted to the South Carolina bar in 1807. After serving for two sessions in the legislature of his native

State, he was elected to Congress in 1811. From that time until his death, a period of nearly 40 years, he was seldom absent from Washington, being nearly the whole time in the public service, either in Congress or in the Cabinet. When he first entered Congress the disputes with England were fast approaching actual hostilities, and he immediately took part with that portion of the dominant party whose object was to drive the still reluctant Administration into a declaration of war. They succeeded, and, as a member of the Committee on Foreign Relations, he reported a bill for declaring war, which was passed in June 1812. When Monroe formed his administration in 1817, Calhoun became secretary of war, a post which he filled with great ability for seven years, reducing the affairs of the department from a state of great confusion to simplicity and order.

In 1824 he was chosen Vice-President of the United States under John Q. Adams, and again in 1828 under Gen. Jackson.

In 1828, a protective tariff was enacted which bore very heavily on the agriculturists of the South and hence was known throughout that section as "The Tariff of Abominations." Mr. Calhoun prepared a paper declaring that the "United States is not a union of the people, but a league or compact between sovereign states, any of which has the right to judge when the compact is broken and to pronounce any law to be null and void which violates its conditions." This paper was issued by the legislature of South Carolina and was known as the "The South Carolina Exposition." This view of the United States Constitution as a compact between the States had been many years before strongly expressed in the Virginia and Kentucky resolutions, the former being drawn up by James Madison, often styled the "Father of the Constitution," and the latter by Thomas Jefferson. The Kentucky resolutions had suggested nullification as a remedy. Alexander Hamilton in "The Federalist" frequently spoke of the United States as a "Confederate Republic" and a "Confederacy" and called the Constitution a "compact." Washington frequently referred to the Constitution as a "compact," and spoke of the Union as a "Confederated Republic." At the time of the Louisiana Purchase Hon. Timothy Pickering of Massachusetts advocated the right and advisability of secession and Hon. Josiah Quincy of the same State in 1811 expressed similar views. Hence John C. Calhoun propounded no new or strange doctrine, but one which had found advocates before, and in the North as well as in the South.

In 1828, the friendly relations between Mr. Calhoun and President Jackson were broken off, when the latter ascertained that Calhoun had sought to have him called to account for his acts in the Seminole War. This breach was still further enlarged when Calhoun refused to co-operate with President Jackson in the effort to reinstate Mrs. Eaton in Washington society.

When Mr. Calhoun found that the repeal of the tariff of 1828 could not be secured through President Jackson, he resigned the Vice-Presidency and entered the Senate from South Carolina. On 26 July 1831 he published a paper favoring free trade and declaring that the

"great conservative principle of Union is nullification." The tariff question was settled by a compromise in 1832.

Mr. Calhoun feared that the slavery quarrel would some day disrupt the Union and therefore endeavored to check all discussion of this issue. He opposed Jackson's removal of the funds from the National Bank and also assailed the "spoils system." He supported Van Buren's "sub-treasury system," favored his re-election and secured for him the electoral vote of South Carolina. He defended Tyler for vetoing the recharter of the United States Bank and as Secretary of State under that President was largely instrumental in bringing about the annexation of Texas. He regretted the division of the Union into sections, but, recognizing a fact which already existed, he advocated a dual executive, one from the North, the other from the South, each having the power to veto an act approved by the other; thus preventing the passage of any law offensive to either section. His motive in this was the preservation of the Union, which he dearly loved.

He died 31 March 1850, having spent the last few months of his life in writing his "Disquisition on Government" and his "Discussion on the Constitution and Government of the United States" which has been pronounced the most remarkable discussion of the rights of minorities ever written.

Mr. Calhoun was of attractive personality and of irreproachable character, to which Daniel Webster testified in his grand eulogy on the great South Carolinian.

His 'Collected Works' appeared 1853-4, and his correspondence, edited by Jameson, in 1900. See lives by Jenkins (1851); Von Holst (1882); Benton, 'Thirty Years' View' (1854).

J. T. DERRY,
Author History of Georgia.

Calico-printing, the art of producing on calico or cotton cloth varigated patterns by the process of printing; the object, as a rule, being to have the colors composing the designs as fast as possible to washing and other influences. It is similar to the art of dyeing, but differs from it in so far that the coloring matters are fixed on certain parts of the fabric only, to form a pattern. Linen, wool, and silk fabrics are printed in a similar manner, but less extensively. The origin of the art of printing is probably coeval with that of dyeing (q.v.). India is generally regarded as the birthplace of calico-printing, and the word calico is derived from the name of the Indian town Calicut, where it was at one time extensively manufactured and printed. Calico-printing, as an Egyptian art, was first described by Pliny in the 1st century. Indian printed chintz calicoes were introduced into Europe by the Dutch East India Company, and the first attempts at imitating them in Europe are said to have been made in Holland, but at what exact date is uncertain. The art, however, soon spread to Germany and England, where it is said to have been introduced about 1676, two of the earliest works being situated at Richmond, on the Thames, and at Bromley Hall, Essex. In 1738 calico print-works were established in Scotland in the neighborhood of Glasgow, and in 1764 at Bamber Bridge, near Preston, in Lancashire. At the present time the chief seats of the calico-printing trade in Great Britain are still in the neighborhood of Glasgow and Manchester. The chief European seat of calico-printing is Mülhausen, in Germany, and it is practised in various towns in France, Austria, Russia, Switzerland, Holland, and the United States.

Calico-printing is of a highly complex character, and enlists not only the co-operation of the arts of designing, engraving, bleaching, and dyeing, but also an important element of success, the science of chemistry.

The first operation to which the gray calico is submitted, as it comes from the loom, is that of singeing. This consists in burning off the loose downy fibres from the surface by passing the pieces rapidly, in an open and stretched condition, over red-hot plates or a row of smokeless Bunsen gas flames. The object of singeing is to obtain a smooth printing surface on the calico, thus ensuring the production of clear, sharp impressions during the printing process. The next operation is that of bleaching, which consists in boiling the fabric with weak alkaline solutions, followed by a treatment with cold dilute solutions of bleaching-powder and acid, interspersed with frequent washings with water. By these means the natural impurities of the cotton are removed, and the calico ultimately presents a snow-white appearance. A number of pieces are now stitched together, wrapped on a wooden roller, and passed through a so-called shearing machine, in which, by means of a spiral cutter similar to that in a lawn-mower, any projecting knots, loose fibres, or down are finally removed. In this condition the calico is ready for the printer.

The printing of the patterns upon the cloth may be carried out in various ways, the earliest method being by means of wooden blocks, on which the figures of the patterns stood out in relief. Where several colors were employed in one pattern, a block for each color was necessary. In a set of blocks for one pattern, each block, although at first having the same design drawn upon it, was cut in such a manner that it ultimately transferred only a single color, which appeared in different parts of the pattern. When all the blocks had been applied, the various colors printed completed the original design. To ensure accurate juxtaposition of the colors, each block was furnished with brass points at the corners, in order to guide the workman. The printer first furnished the face of the block with the requisite color by pressing it several times on a piece of woolen cloth suitably stretched and supported on a so-called color-sieve, and which had been previously brushed over with color by a boy attendant. The printer then applied the block to the surface of the calico, which was stretched on a long table covered with felt, striking the back of the block with his hand or with a small mallet. The operation of block printing was slow and tedious and though many improvements have been introduced, and it can even be effected by mechanical power, as in the so-called Perrotine machine, it is now only employed to a very limited extent for certain special kinds of work. Another mode of printing, introduced about 1760, is by means of engraved copperplates, but its employment is also similarly restricted.

The modern method of printing, which dates from 1785, is effected by means of engraved copper cylinders, and this method has now practically superseded all others.

The method of engraving employed varies according to the kind of pattern to be put on the roller. In the case of very large patterns the figures are engraved by hand on the cylinders themselves with the use of the ordinary tools of the copper-plate engraver. For smaller designs, however, which are often repeated, it is usual in the first instance to engrave the pattern by hand on a very small cylinder of soft steel in intaglio, just as it will ultimately appear on the copper. This steel cylinder, which is called a die, is then tempered to a high degree of hardness, and by means of machinery is pressed against another cylinder of soft steel, on which the pattern is thus made to appear in relief. This last cylinder, called the mill, is then hardened, and, being pressed against the copper cylinder, the figures are indented and the roller is ready for use. In the first instance the original pattern of the designer has always to be reduced or enlarged, so as to repeat an exact number of times over the roller to be engraved. In order to reduce the amount of skilled labor one repeat only of the pattern is engraved on the die; the mill, which is of larger diameter, has two, three, or four repeats; while the number of repeats on the circumference of the copper cylinder is still greater. A third method of engraving, which has now largely superseded the foregoing, is that of etching, in conjunction with the pantograph system of transferring the design to the copper roller. The roller, being coated uniformly with a bituminous varnish, has the pattern traced on the varnish in the pentagraph machine by a set of diamond points, and it is then submitted for a very brief period to the action of nitric acid. In the parts where the pattern has been traced the varnish is removed, there the copper is speedily attacked by the acid, and the pattern is thus etched upon it. After removing the varnish the roller is ready for printing.

The cylinder printing machine consists of a large central iron drum, around which are arranged one or more engraved copper rollers, according to the number of colors to be printed simultaneously. Each roller is provided with the means of making several adjustments, in order to determine the exact position of the color which it prints. The central drum is wrapped with cloth, and it is further provided with an endless blanket and back-cloth, so as to present a yielding surface to the printing rollers. The cloth to be printed passes from a roll behind the machine, round the central drum, in a tightly stretched condition, while the several printing rollers press forcibly against it. Each roller, as it revolves, is fed with color from a small trough below, the superfluous color being scraped off the plain surface of the roller by means of a sharp-edged steel blade, or "doctor," thus leaving the color only in the engraved portions. As the rollers thus charged with color press against the cloth, the latter absorbs or withdraws the color from the engraving, and the pattern is thus transferred to the calico. By this machine as much work can be performed in three minutes as could be done by block-printing in six hours. After the cloth has received the impression from the rollers it passes over a series of steam-heated flat iron chests, or cylinders, and is thus dried.

In close connection with the printing-machine department is the so-called color-house or color-shop, where the solutions of coloring matters are suitably thickened and made ready for the printer. The color-house is provided with numerous steam-heated copper pans, so arranged on supports that they can be readily turned over for emptying or cleaning. The color mixtures are stirred with wooden blades by hand, or by mechanical agitators, and carefully strained through cloth before use. The thickening of the color solutions with starch, flour, gum, dextrine, albumen, etc., is necessary to prevent the spreading of the color by capillary attraction beyond the printed parts, and thus ensure sharp and neat impressions. Near the color-house is a chemical laboratory, and a drug-room containing the store of coloring matters, dyewood, extracts, thickenings, chemicals, etc.

The various classes or styles of calico-prints are usually arranged either according to the chief dyestuffs employed or their mode of application. Each of these primary styles may be further separated into subdivisions, of which the most important are the discharge and resist styles, which refer to the manner in which the pattern is produced. The following include the chief styles of calico-prints at present in vogue:

Madder Style.—This is so named because the chief dyestuff formerly employed in it was madder. This dyestuff belongs to the class of so-called mordant-colors. Such dyestuffs are worthless if employed alone by the calico-printer, and only furnish useful colors if applied in conjunction with certain metallic salts or mordants, of which the chief ones here employed are the acetates of aluminum and iron. At first the pattern is printed on the white calico with these or similar mordants alone, and only after they have been suitably fixed is the madder or other similar coloring matter applied in the dye-bath, where for the first time the desired colored pattern appears. The aluminum mordant yields red and pink, iron yields purple or black, a mixture of iron and aluminum yields chocolate, etc. The fixing of the mordant after printing and drying is effected by passing the printed calico through the so-called ageing-machine, a large chamber suitably heated and charged with moisture, where the acetic acid of the printed mordants is driven off, leaving the aluminum salt in an insoluble form on the calico. A more complete fixing of the mordant is subsequently effected by passing the fabric through solutions containing silicate or arseniate of soda, and a final washing completes its preparation for dyeing. The dyeing operation consists in boiling the fabric in a solution or decoction of the requisite dyestuff. After dyeing, the stained unprinted portions are cleaned and purified, while the printed colors are rendered more brilliant by washing, soaping, coloring, etc. Variety of effect is produced by printing the same fabric two or three times (print, cover, pad) with various designs before proceeding to the ageing, etc. If in the first instance a portion of the pattern is printed with lime-juice (citric acid), it resists or prevents the fixing of the mordants applied over it in the second and third printings, and the part remains undyed and appears as a so-called resist white. In a similar manner stannous chloride, mixed with aluminum acetate before printing, resists the fixing

of iron mordants printed over the aluminum mordant, and a resist red pattern under a purple cover is obtained, presuming madder to be the dyestuff employed. Alizarin now replaces the madder formerly used, and similar variegated effects are obtained if other mordant dyestuffs are employed, for example, cochineal, quercitron bark, etc. Formerly a preparation of madder, termed garancine, was largely employed, and gave rise to the garancine style, in which the colors were fuller and darker, the prevailing hues being browns, chocolates, drabs, etc. Since the range of colors yielded in the madder style is limited, additional colors, as green, blue, or yellow, may be printed in by block after dyeing, etc., and are fixed by steaming. If the whole fabric is evenly impregnated with mordant by means of a "padding-machine" and dried, and then a pattern is printed over the mordant with lime-juice, the mordant is removed or discharged in the printed parts, and remains white in the subsequent dyeing. Such a print would be termed a padded style with discharge white.

Steam Style.— Many coloring matters, differing from each other widely in character, are fixed by the operation of steaming instead of by dyeing, so that this style is somewhat varied in character. Ordinary steam-colors consist of a thickened mixture of dyewood extract and mordant, with the addition of assistant metallic salts and acids. The mixture is printed upon the white calico, which, after drying, is exposed from a half to one hour in closed chambers to the action of steam. This steaming operation effects the combination of the coloring matter and mordant, and the color is thus developed and at the same time fixed upon the calico. Black is produced with logwood extract and chromium acetate, scarlet is produced with cochineal extract and stannous chloride. The prints are washed and dried after steaming, the colors being usually bright, but not very fast. Steam-colors, fast to light and soap, are obtained in a similar manner by printing mixtures of alizarin and allied coloring matters with mordants, and then steaming. These are used in the so-called madder extract or steam alizarin style, in which red, pink, purple, etc., appear. In the pigment style use is made of pigments, or insoluble colored mineral powders, as ultramarine-blue, chrome yellow, Guignet's green, etc. These are mixed with a solution of egg or blood albumen, printed, and steamed. The albumen, coagulates on steaming, and thus adheres firmly to the cloth, at the same time enclosing the pigments within the coagulum. Such colors are fast to light and soap, and may therefore be printed simultaneously with the steam alizarin colors for the production of variegated fast prints. Another class of colors are the so-called basic colors, as magenta, aniline blue, etc. Their solutions may also be thickened with albumen, printed, and steamed, to give fast steam-colors. It is more usual, however, to print a mixture of the thickened color solution and tannic acid, and to pass the steamed print through a boiling solution of tartar emetic. By this means an insoluble color-lake (tannate of antimony and color-base) is fixed on the calico, which is fast to soaping, but not to light. Basic colors applied in this manner are now usually printed along with the steam alizarin colors, instead of pigments, thickened with albumen, and variegated fast prints are thus obtained. Loose pigment colors are basic colors thickened with starch or gum tragacanth only, and then steamed. Such prints do not even stand washing with cold water.

Turkey-red Style.— In this style use is made of the fact that turkey red is at once bleached by the action of chlorine. Plain dyed turkey-red calico is printed with tartaric acid, dried, and passed through a solution of bleaching-powder. In the printed parts chlorine gas is evolved, the red is destroyed, and a white discharge pattern is produced. A blue pattern results if Prussian blue is added to the printing mixture; yellow is obtained if a lead salt is added, and the fabric is afterward passed through bichromate of potash solution, whereby yellow chromate of lead is produced; green results from a mixture of the blue and yellow; black is printed direct. These and other discharge colors may also be obtained by other methods.

Indigo Style.— Of the numerous indigo styles in use it is only possible to refer to one or two of the most important. Indigo blue patterns on a white ground are obtained by printing a thickened solution of finely-ground indigo and caustic soda on white calico, previously impregnated with glucose. A subsequent steaming reduces the indigo to indigo white, and causes it to penetrate the fibre, while a final washing oxidizes, regenerates, and fixes the color. A resist white pattern on a blue ground is obtained by first printing upon white calico a resist paste composed of gum or flour, China clay, sulphate of copper, etc. When the printed calico is dyed in the indigo vat the paste resists the entrance of the color, partly in a mechanical and partly in a chemical manner, hence the blue is only fixed in those parts which are unprotected by the paste, after the removal of which by washing, the white pattern appears. Various resist colors, as yellow, green, etc., are obtained by the addition of different chemicals to the paste and altering the after-processes. A discharge white pattern on a blue ground is obtained by printing on plain indigo-blue-dyed calico a solution of bichromate of potash thickened with gum, and then passing the fabric through a solution containing sulphuric and oxalic acids. During this passage there is liberated, in the printed parts only, chromic acid, which at once oxidizes and destroys the blue, producing the desired white pattern. Colored discharge patterns are produced similarly by employing albumen thickening instead of gum thickening, and adding to the printing mixture such pigments as are not affected by acids, for example, vermilion, chrome yellow, Guignet's green, etc.

Bronze Style.— Manganese brown or bronze is decolorized by reducing agents; hence white discharge patterns on a bronze ground are obtained by printing plain manganese-brown-dyed calico with a mixture of stannous chloride and oxalic acid, and then steaming. Colored discharge patterns are obtained if coloring matters are added to the printing mixture which are not affected by reducing-agents, or which even require stannous chloride as a mordant to develop the color, as Prussian blue, chrome yellow, Persian-berry yellow, Brazil-wood pink, safranine, acridine orange, etc.

Aniline Black Style.— Aniline black being a product of the oxidation of aniline, patterns in this color on a white ground are obtained by printing a thickened solution of aniline hydrochloride containing the oxidizing agent, sodium chlorate, and a salt of copper or vanadium. When the printed fabric is slightly steamed or exposed to a moist, warm atmosphere, the impression, which is at first devoid of color, gradually becomes dark green, and this by a final treatment with an alkaline solution, soap, etc., changes at once to a rich black. The color is extremely fast to light, alkalis, acids, etc., and it is largely employed by the printer, both alone and in conjunction with dyed or steam colors. The development of the black during the ageing or oxidizing process occurs only in the presence of a mineral acid, hence resist whites are obtained by first printing the design on the white calico with thickened solutions of substances of an alkaline or reducing character, or salts of organic acids, as acetate of soda, and then printing or padding over all with the aniline black mixture, ageing, steaming, etc. Where the design is printed the alkalinity entirely prevents the development of the black. Pigment colors thickened with albumen, also certain benzidine colors, containing an admixture of chalk, acetate of soda, etc., are largely employed in this manner. These resist colors may also be printed immediately after the application of the aniline black mixture, before the development of the color by ageing.

Azo Color Style.— The so-called insoluble azo colors result from the interaction of an azo compound and a phenol. Two methods of printing based upon this principle are employed. One method is to print the design with a thickened solution of β-naphthol on the white calico, and then pass the fabric through a very cold solution of the azo compound (developing-bath), when the design at once appears in a color corresponding to the azo compound employed. Another method is to print the design with a thickened solution of the azo compound upon calico which has been previously impregnated with a solution of sodium-naphthol and dried; in this case the color of the design is developed in the moment of impression. The necessary azo compounds are obtained by the action of nitrous acid, on salts of amido substances for example, paranitraniline, naphthylamine nitrotoluidine, dianisidine, etc., each of which yields a distinct color, bright red, claret red, orange, blue, etc. The naphthol-prepared cloth and also the azo compounds are somewhat unstable, so that this style is not successfully printed without considerable care. The insoluble azo colors, also the direct or benzidine colors, are capable of furnishing discharge patterns, since, in common with the azo colors generally, they are readily decomposed and destroyed by reducing-agents. It suffices to print calico dyed with these colors, as benzopurpurine, chrysophenine, benzoazurine, Mikado brown, etc., with a mixture containing stannous acetate, zinc powder, or other similar reducing-agent, and then steam the printed fabric, to obtain white discharge patterns. If there be added to the printing mixture such mordants and coloring matters as are not affected by reducing-agents, for example, safranine, auramine, etc., a variety of colored discharges are obtained, exactly as in the bronze style. Many of the benzidine colors may also be printed direct on white calico to furnish color designs, but such prints are not particularly fast to washing.

Cal'icut, India, a seaport in the presidency of Madras, on the Malabar coast, six miles north ot Beypur, in the midst of extensive palm groves. It is an important place, with various public offices and institutions, including court-house, customs-house, lunatic asylum, Anglican, Lutheran, and Roman Catholic missions, municipal and other schools, barracks, lighthouse, etc. The town dates from the 13th century, and was the first port in India visited by Europeans. It was from the name of this place that the word calico was derived. Vasco da Gama visited it in 1498, and in 1510 Albuquerque wrecked the town. In 1766 Calicut was taken by Hyder Ali, and in 1790 it fell into the hands of the British. Cardamoms, teak, sandal-wood, pepper, and wax are the principal exports. Pop. (1901) 75,510.

California, principal Pacific coast State of United States (No. 31 in order of admission), bounded north by Oregon, south by Mexico (Lower California), east by Nevada and Arizona, west by Pacific Ocean. Extreme length about 800 miles, coast line 1,097 miles, greatest width about 270 miles. Area (No. 2 in United States) 158,360 square miles (2,380 water). Pop. (1900) (No. 21 in United States) 1,485,053 or 9.5 to square mile (No. 37 in density). Whites, 1,402,727.

Topography and Climate.— Its peculiar shape, determined no more by political than by natural delimitations, gives California a character unique among the States, climatically and economically. It has a climate all its own, and its boundaries include all that climate in North America. It is longest of the States; and, in proportion to its length, narrowest. It corresponds with an area which upon the Atlantic seaboard should run as far inland as does North Carolina, and as long coastwise as from Charleston to Boston. This in itself gives large range of climate by latitudes; but its topography and its colimitations greatly increase this range. Its peculiar projection or "leaning out" upon the Pacific; its enormous coast line (somewhat less than one fifth total coastline of the United States); and particularly its "exposure" to the west and south upon this great equalizer; its contact on the east with the "Great American Desert"; its huge mountain systems; and its orographic protection against the north, are all vital factors in determining its atmospheric temperament. While the Atlantic seaboard is made humid by the warm Gulf Stream, and is open to the north (its mountains being scattered, low, and well inland), California is screened from the Arctic air-currents by a vast Alpine range, almost unbroken in its whole length and with its lowest passes 50 per cent higher than the highest peak east of Colorado. The State has 120 peaks exceeding 8,000 feet; 41 exceeding 10,000 feet; and 11 exceeding 13,000 feet. From its northern boundary down to Point Concepcion, California is washed by the cold Kuro Siwo, or Japan current, swinging back from the Arctic; and the exposure is largely westerly. From this point southward, the exposure is more southerly, the Japan current is deflected far offshore, and the coast is sheltered by a long line ot islands. Tempered on one side by an equable

ocean, on the other by 1,000 miles of arid lands, the climate of California is still further differentiated by its mountain systems. Roughly speaking, it is all "under wall." Two huge cordilleras, inosculating at the north and south, form an almost complete circumvallation of the great agricultural region; while to the south, though the ranges are much broken down, there is something like a repetition of this pattern, on a much smaller scale; the whole forming something like an inverted figure 8. In their major loop, these ranges enclose one great central valley, practically level, of 18,000 square miles,— or about the aggregate area of Massachusetts, New Jersey, and Delaware,— screening it from the Arctic, and filtering the winds from sea and desert. This great rampart is broken down only at the Golden Gate, through which, in a mile-wide passage, the drainage of this enormous watershed reaches the sea. In their imperfect minor loop, there is a broken congeries of valleys aggregating an almost equal area, sheltered from the desert, but as a rule partially open toward the sea. To the east of the main wall lies a large but almost uninhabited area, strictly desert, and part of the great interior wastes. The inclination of State to the west, and its consequent southern exposure, is indicated by the fact that despite its narrowness the extremes are three fourths as far apart in longitude as in latitude. The corner of San Bernardino County is nearly 500 miles more easterly than False Cape; while from Oregon to the Mexican line the north and south distance is about 655 miles.

The Coast Range, altitude 2,000 to 8,000 feet, rather closely follows the coast line from Oregon to Point Concepcion; south of which topographic hinge it so breaks down as to be relatively unimportant. The Sierra Nevada, proximately following the east line of the State, at an average distance of 50 to 100 miles therefrom, is "the largest and most interesting chain of mountains in the United States" (J. D. Whitney). Really part of the gigantic spine which extends from Lower California to Alaska, this range in California is 600 miles long and 75 to 100 miles wide — its base covering four times the area of Massachusetts. The snow-line averages about 30 miles wide. Its surpassing peak (Mt. Whitney, highest in the United States) is 14,522 feet (Langley). Its passes average 11,000 feet, the lowest being 9,000 feet, and the most used (Kearsarge) 12,000 feet. The western slope is gradual, averaging about 100 feet to the mile; its eastern slope 10 times as rapid, being by far the steepest general gradient in North America. At many points the fall is 10,000 feet in 10 miles; and from the highest peak in the United States one looks down nearly 15,000 feet into Death Valley, some 200 feet below sea-level. This vast granitic range is the most remarkable register of glacial action on the continent. Decapitated by "perhaps a vertical mile" (Muir) it is still the most Alpine cordillera in North America. It holds 1,500 glacial lakes — the lake line being at about 8,000 feet. Of small residual glaciers, Muir has counted 65 between 36° 30′ and 39°. Its yosemites (including the famous one so-called, the Hetch-Hetchy, and minor ones) are famous among geologists as well as travelers,— well-like valleys gouged deep in the granite by glaciers, and of scenery nowhere surpassed. The highest water-fall in the world (the Pioneer, 3,270 feet) is in this region. Upon the huge moraines left by that continental incubus of ice grow the noblest coniferous forests in the world — greatest in variety of species, in density of merchantable lumber and in size, age, and beauty of trees. These forests cover 44,700 square miles (a larger area than the entire States of New Hampshire, Vermont, Massachusetts, Connecticut, Rhode Island, Delaware, and Maryland together). California takes fifth in area of forests and second in stand of lumber (200,000,000,000 feet, exceeded only by Oregon with 225,000,000,000. Cut, 1900, 864,000 M.). Seven national forest reserves in the State cover 8,511,794 acres. The Big Tree (*Sequoia Gigantea*) is the largest and oldest of growing things on earth; averaging 275 feet high and 20 feet diameter. The largest reach over 325 feet high and 38 feet diameter, with an age of 5,000 years. Muir "never saw a Big Tree that had died a natural death." The other Sequoia (*Sempervirens*), or California redwood, covers an area of about 2,000 square miles. It is second only to the Big Tree in size, reaching 18 feet diameter; and like it is found nowhere else. It belongs to the Coast Range, as the Big Tree to the Sierra. It is almost exclusively used in California for sheathing. The immunity of a city like San Francisco from great fires, though windy, hill-built, and of "frame," is largely due to the non-inflammability of this redwood lumber. The sugar pine, the noblest pine yet discovered, reaches 245 feet high and 18 feet diameter; the yellow pine 220 feet high and 8 feet diameter; the Douglas spruce, king of spruces. 200 feet high, 6 feet diameter; the Libocedrus, or incense cedar, 150 feet high and 7 feet diameter; the white silver fir 200 feet high, 6 feet diameter; the "magnificent" silver fir 250 feet high and 5 feet diameter. The nut pine, or piñon, is a small and shabby tree, but of great economic importance in feeding the Indians; in a good year its crop of excellent nuts is enormous. These are often fed to horses instead of barley. There are many varieties of oaks (which reach great size); also maples, yews, birches, alders, sycamores, cottonwoods, aspens, madroños, etc. A California palm (*Washingtonia*) is native in mountain cañons along the southerly desert, and is now largely used for street ornamentation. Specimens planted by the Franciscans have reached a height of 80 feet. The flora of the State includes about 2,500 species, and is of great interest. In the great central valley in February or March one can travel 400 miles, treading flowers at every step; and as much is true in other parts of the State.

No other State contains a moiety of the vast number of exotic trees now in California. Fruit, ornamental, and shade trees from every country in the world have been acclimated here. Nearly 9,000,000 tropical fruit trees were bearing in 1900. Millions of "pepper-trees" (*Molle*) from Peru are used on streets, etc.; and of Australian eucalyptus, (introd. 1858), there are now over 10,000,000, including about 100 varieties for fuel and ornament. Setting 2,000,000 acres to orchard and other trees within a gencration has partially balanced the deforestation by lumbermen.

The most striking meteorological feature of California is perhaps the ordering of its seasons, of which it has practically but two, the wet and dry. The winter, or "rainy season," is approximately from late October to late April, with 15 to 25 rainy days, an annual precipitation ranging from 23.53 inches for San Francisco (and far greater in the extreme north) to 14.56 inches for Los Angeles, and 10 for San Diego. For six months after 1 May, rain is practically unknown, except showers in the high mountain regions. In the high Sierra the winter precipitation takes form of snow, with an annual fall of 30 to 50 feet, thus supplying the natural reservoirs which feed the streams, upon irrigation from which agriculture largely depends. But in Oregon, which bounds California on the north, we have the familiar eastern seasons; and again in Arizona and Nevada, abutting upon the east, winter snow and summer rains characterize the meteorology. Thus, climatically, California differs altogether from all its neighbors, and has well been called an "Island on Land." Within its own limits, also, it has extraordinary range of climates, as it were in strata, following the topographic contours. Thus in the vicinity of Los Angeles it is possible at times to take a sleigh-ride within 12 miles of the city on one side (and looking down upon blossoming orange groves not five miles distant), and by an hour's ride to bathe in the Pacific, which has here a winter temperature of 60°. Within a short journey from almost any given point one may find almost any variety of climate, from below sea-level to nearly 15,000 feet above it; from the extreme but arid and non-prostrating heat of the desert to eternal snow; from palms and perennial roses to the primeval coniferous forests, or to the desolation of alkaline Saharas. Although all California shares the seasonal peculiarity of "California climate," the northern and southern parts of the State — roughly dividing at Point Concepcion and the Tehachepi Range — are very unlike meteorologically. The upper portion is relatively humid, with more than twice the average rainfall, with far larger streams and vastly richer forestation. At Crescent City, on the far north coast, precipitation often reaches 80 inches per year. The trend of the coast is here northerly, and the region shares something of the extraordinary humidity of Oregon. The smallest precipitation is in the desert southeast corner, averaging only three inches annually at Yuma. The seven counties habitually termed "Southern California" — though the geographic southern half of the State would include 13 counties — have an average rainfall of but about 15 inches. This precipitation is insufficient to insure crops, except cereals (which are not irrigated but depend on the rains). This broad difference between the two sections in rainfall has been chief factor in an extraordinary difference of development within the last 15 years. Compelled by aridity to resort to irrigation; compelled by the magnitude of this task to associative effort, the southern communities have suddenly developed a generic type of agriculture and of life quite unlike anything else in the Union. The paragraph on population shows something of the disproportionate settling-up of the southern end of the State — an entire reversal of the balance which obtained for nearly 40 years, during which the population was overwhelmingly about the Bay, and San Francisco

CALIFORNIA

was practically California, socially, politically, and financially..

About San Francisco there is a steady and brisk wind movement, flowing in through the narrow gap of the Golden Gate. In Southern California, while there is daily ebb and flow of air-currents (in the morning from off the sea, and at night down from the mountains), a real wind is very rare. Hurricanes and cyclones are absolutely unknown in the State. Despite the great heat of the deserts, and high mercury sometimes recorded in the valleys, the dryness of the atmosphere renders it harmless, and sunstroke is unknown. Seasonal diseases, typhoids, malarias, and pernicious fevers, summer diseases of children, gastric or hepatic diseases, are rare. Mean summer temperature San Francisco 60°; winter mean 51°; greatest daily range temperature Los Angeles 29°, as against 69° for Boston. The modern migration to California has been largely attracted by this unique and hospitable climate, free from the dangerous heats of summer and the bitter winter cold of the regions east of the Rocky Mountains. In the inhabited portions of this State, extreme cold is unknown; while owing to rapid radiation, the summer nights are always so cool as to call for blankets.

The fauna of California is peculiarly interesting, and includes considerably over 100 species of mammals, though the larger game varieties have in a half century been nearly exterminated. At the American occupation, elk were seen in droves of thousands. Great numbers were killed from the deck of steamers plying to Sacramento. Occupation of the State by Indians immemorially, and by Spaniards for nearly a century, had not appreciably diminished the wild animals; but the same wanton spirit which in a score of years exterminated tens of millions of the American bison on the great plains has in California made the great mammals nearly extinct. The grizzly bear, once in great abundance in all parts of the State, is now very scarce; the black, cinnamon, and brown bear are more common. Sea lions of a ton weight are still numerous along the coast, and their populous rookeries a few hundred feet from the cliff House in San Francisco are an object of interest to travelers. The California lion, mountain lion, or puma, is still not infrequent, and wildcats abound in the mountains. The coyote is common, and of utility in decimating the hordes of rabbits; though an ill-judged bounty on coyote scalps has of late years much reduced the numbers of this small wolf. The beaver, once in vast numbers here, is now confined to the remotest mountain streams; and the valuable sea otter is almost extinct. Black-tailed and mule deer are still reasonably frequent; but the antelope, which once roamed the northern and southern valleys in great bands, have hardly a representative left. The same is true of the mountain sheep (*Ovis Ammon*), once common in all the higher ranges. Spermophiles, or ground squirrels, and five species of gopher, are numerous and a great pest to the farmer. Jack rabbits and "cotton-tails" are abundant in all parts of the State, despite community "drives" in which sometimes tens of thousands are killed in a day. The birds of California number above 350 species. The largest winged creature in North America is the California condor. Quail of two species are in vast abundance throughout the State.

While the Pacific coast of North and South America in general is peculiarly liable to seismic disturbances, California had never experienced an earthquake of the first magnitude, nor anything approaching that of Charleston, S. C., in 1886; nor that of New Madrid, Mo., until those of April 1906, when San Francisco was devastated and a large portion of the city subsequently burned, with a property loss of over $200,000,000 and numerous lives and the surrounding cities and towns suffered severely. The severest shocks previous to this were in 1812, when 30 people were killed by the fall of a church tower in Capistrano; and that of 1872, when about a score perished in Owen's Valley.

River Systems.— As in most arid States, the drainage of California is simple. For some 300 miles on its southeastern edge the State is bounded by the Colorado River, which rises in the Rocky Mountains in Colorado and flows 1,360 miles to the Gulf of California. It has no tributaries whatever from California, all eastbound streams from the Sierra Nevada being lost in the desert. On the western coast, though a few rivers reach the sea (like the Klamath, Mad, Eel, and Salinas) they are relatively unimportant and incidental. The real drainage system of the State has outlet through San Francisco Bay and the Golden Gate, by the two chief inland rivers which join about 60 miles northeast of San Francisco. Both rise in Sierra Nevada, the Sacramento (370 miles long) to the north, the San Joaquin (350 miles long) to the south. Their main course averages along nearly the median line north and south, through nearly two thirds the length of the State. They have no tributaries worthy of the name from the great westerly mountain wall, the Coast Range; their waters being fed almost exclusively from the vast Alpine chain which is in effect, though not politically, the eastern boundary of California down to latitude 35° 30″. Their important feeders from the Sierra are the Feather, Yuba, Cosumnes, American, Mokelumne, Kern, Kings, etc. All these are fine mountain torrents, beloved of sportsmen, and flowing through magnificent scenery, but not of rank as waterways. The most important is the Feather, which has a large drainage area. Several streams in Southern California, like the Los Angeles, San Gabriel, and Santa Ana, reach the sea, but all are practically exhausted by irrigation uses, except during winter flood-water. The many streams from the abrupt eastern slopes of the Sierra Nevada all disappear in alkaline "sinks," — like Pyramid Lake, Owen's Lake, Mono Lake, and Death Valley,— and never even in flood reach the ocean by their great natural conduit, the Colorado River. The lakes of California are not important as to navigation. Tulare Lake, receiving the drainage of the Kern, Kaweah, and Kings rivers, is 700 square miles in area, but only 40 feet deep. In very high water its overflow reaches the San Joaquin; but ordinarily its income of waters is cared for by evaporation. Lake Tahoe in the extreme north, at an elevation of 6,200 feet, is 20 miles long and 1,500 feet deep, and famous for the purity of its waters, the beauty of its scenery, and its trout. It is the largest of the glacial lakes, of which there are a great number in the Sierra, mostly at altitudes exceeding the highest mountain summits east of Colorado. The lower-lying lakes of the State are mostly without outlet, and of various degrees of brackishness, culminating in the "sink" of the Amargosa River nearly 200 feet below sea-level on the eastern side of the range; where evaporation has left vast alkaline deposits, now of great commercial value.

Geology.— The main axis of the Sierra Nevada is of granite throughout. To the north there are some metamorphic peaks, and many summits are capped with volcanic materials. Mt. Shasta in the far north is an extinct Volcano (14,470 feet). So also is Lassen's Peak (10,577 feet). This granite core is flanked by a very heavy mass of slaty metamorphic rocks,— mostly argillaceous, chloritic, and talcose slates,— constituting the great auriferous belt of the Sierra. The Coast Range is made up almost entirely of cretaceous and tertiary marines, chiefly sandstones and bituminous shales. It is in this belt that the great recent development of petroleum has been made.

Besides the vast reaches of alluvial soils in the lower valleys, which were first attacked for agriculture, an enormous area of disintegrated granite gravels along the foothills and first acclivities has been found the most productive soil in the State, particularly with reference to valuable crops. These great gravel beds, which seem to the farmer from the black "bottoms" of Ohio the most unpromising of soils, are in reality rich in all the elements of plant food. The vast majority of the valuable orchards, particularly of Southern California, are planted upon this granitic detritus; and without exception the finest oranges and other citrus fruits come from this soil. The relative aridity of California, long supposed to be a curse, is now known to be a two-fold blessing. Exhaustive analyses, comparative with every portion of the Union, show these gravels to average much richer in chemical constituents than soils leached out by excessive rainfall. Furthermore, the fact that precipitation is not invariably sufficient to insure crops has compelled irrigation, which does insure them; so that farmers in the arid lands have much greater crop-certainty than those of regions with most abundant rainfall.

Agriculture.— In no item of its history has California been more unlike other States than in development and sequences of agriculture. The first (and for 60 years commercially chief) industry was cattle — derived from herds introduced from Mexico by Viceroy Galvez, 1769, and chief wealth of the Mission establishments and Spanish colonists. It was a generation after the American occupation before agriculture was seriously undertaken; and for another term of years it was chiefly a gigantic seasonal "gamble with the weather" in dry-farming of cereals. The characteristic features of agriculture up to about 1870 were enormous holdings,— reckoned at least by tens of thousands of acres,— with the single crop (almost exclusively wheat and barley) and purchase of every other article of necessity or luxury. On areas of hundreds of square miles apiece there were an individual or corporate owner, a single crop, a few hundred hirelings at the height of the season, and their temporary quarters. A few of these enormous ranchos still survive; and Miller and Lux still farm about 1,000,000

acres, with 20,000 acres in a single field. But within a generation the typical character of agriculture in California has radically changed. The greatest recorded drouth (1864) which not only destroyed grain but hundreds of thousands of cattle (60,000 head being sold that year in Santa Barbara at 37½c. per head), exclusion of the Chinese, who had been the chief reliance for labor on the great ranchos, the fall in wheat, and other factors, led to the breaking up of these gigantic domains. A slight idea of the change may be had from the census fact that in 1850 the average size of all California farms was 4,456.6 acres; and in 1900, 397.4 acres. Along with this great dry-farm gambling — for such it was — sheep became a leading industry in the State, particularly in Southern California.

Within about 15 years — that is, since 1885, — the general character of California farming has changed to small holdings, occupied not by tenants but by American owners, with families, with diversified crops, and obliged to purchase only the luxuries of life; with intensive methods and certainty (by irrigation) of crops. California has now more than one fourth of all the irrigators in the United States. The average size of irrigated farms is in Southern California 21¼ acres; in rest of State about 82 acres. The typical California farm under the modern régime is perhaps 10 acres; irrigated either by its own pumping plant or from a community ditch, and yielding an annual income of not less than $200 per acre.

Perhaps the greatest single factor in bringing about this structural change was the orange. In 1862 there were 25,000 orange trees in the State, all seedlings, and deriving from Mexico, where the fruit was introduced by the Spaniards nearly three and a half centuries earlier. In 1873 two seedless orange trees from Brazil were sent from the Department of Agriculture in Washington to Riverside, California. From these two parent trees has sprung the modern orange industry of California — and practically of the United States; as Florida, the only other orange State in the Union, yielded in 1900 273,000 boxes of oranges to California's 5,882,000. Millions of trees from their buds are now bearing or growing in this State, and the hereditary fruit, seedless and delicious, leads the American market. This crop, highly remunerative, and practically continuous (shipments being made every month in the year) has been for these reasons, and æsthetic ones, a large attraction to high-class immigration, and an important factor in shaping agricultural methods. For development of the industry, see statistics below.

In deciduous fruits, total production, shipments fresh, canning and drying, California has within a generation come to lead the Union; as it leads in all tropical fruits.

California is first successful grower of sugar beets, and has by far the largest factories. In 1900 it had 37.4 per cent of acreage and 44.9 per cent of beet sugar product of the entire Union. The sensational achievements of Luther Burbank in hybridizing fruits — for instance, the creation of a large plum without any pit whatever — are already world-famous. Almost as remarkable results have been reached in floriculture. Seeds and bulbs are raised on

CALIFORNIA.

1. Mt. Shasta, from Sisson's.   2. Mt. Tamalpais, near San Francisco.

a great scale; carnations, calla lilies, and other flowers being grown outdoors by the 10-acre field.

Total area of California farms is now over 45,000 square miles; considerably exceeding entire area of States of Massachusetts, New Hampshire, Vermont, Connecticut, Rhode Island, and Maryland. The State is eleventh in the Union in per capita value of farm products ($88) and fifth in value products per farm ($1,816 as compared with Ohio, $929).

California has (1900) 72,542 farms; total value of farm property, $796,527,955; total value farm products 1899, $131,690,606. Total acreage in farms, 28,828,951 acres, of which 11,958,837 acres are improved. The area farmed has increased 34.5 per cent since 1890. In 1850 there were 872 farms; in 1860, 18,716. The development of farming is briefly indicated as follows:

Year	Farms	Acres	Val. farm Property	Value Products
1900.....	72,542	28,828,951	$796,527,955	$131,690,606
1890.....	52,894	21,427,293	772,065,570	87,033,290
1880.....	35,934	16,593,742	305,099,443	59,721,425
1870.....	23,724	11,427,105	147,617,176	39,884,820

The largest number of farms is in Los Angeles County (6,577); three other counties have over 3,000 farms each; Santa Clara, 3,995; Sonoma, 3,676; and Fresno, 3,290. Of all farms, 70,935 are farmed by whites; 658 by Indians; 777 by Chinese; 135 by negroes; 37 by Japanese.

Dairy cows have increased more than seventy-fold since 1850, now numbering 307,245. Of other neat cattle there are 1,137,379; horses, 421,293; mules, 87,000; sheep, 1,724,968; swine, 598,336. Total animal products 1899, $36,324,894 — including milk, butter, and cheese, $12,128,471; animals sold and slaughtered, $15,754,985; poultry and eggs, $6,356,746; wool, $1,707,088. Sheep and wool have decreased steadily since 1879, with the great increase in value of lands for farming. The principal crops in 1899 were: Wheat, $20,179,044; hay and forage, $19,436,398; orchard fruits, $14,526,786; tropical fruits, $7,219,082; grapes and small fruits, $6,534,236; barley, $10,645,723; corn, oats, and rye, $2,652,777; hops (nearly one fourth of total United States output), $925,319; sugar beets (nearly half total United States output, $1,550,346; potatoes and sweet potatoes, $2,773,140; dry beans (one fourth total output of United States), $1,022,586; other vegetables, $2,929,465. The total value of farm crops in 1899 was $95,365,712.

From 1850 to 1900 the population has increased sixteen-fold; number of farms over eighty-fold. California is one of the few States that in the last 30 years has added more to its agricultural than to its other population.

Irrigation and Horticulture.— Development of the new and characteristic agricultural era in California is outlined by these statistics (1900):

	No. Irrigators	Acres Irrigated	Value Irrigated Crop
United States .	102,819	7,263,273	$84,433,438
California	25,611	1,445,872	32,975,361

Of the 72,542 farms in the State, 25,675 or 35.4 per cent are irrigated, an increase of 44 per cent in 10 years; the number of irrigators

has increased in the same term 87 per cent. Total cost of construction of all irrigating systems, $19,181,610; so the irrigated crop of 1899 alone paid nearly $14,000,000 in excess of total cost of works. Los Angeles County leads by far in number of irrigators (4,066); only Fresno (2,459) having one half as many. In number of acres Fresno County is far in the lead, with 283,737 acres; Kern next with 112,533, and Merced, 111,330.

Of the total 1,445,872 acres irrigated, 1,293,608 are irrigated from streams; the balance from wells, 6,894 farms being irrigated from wells. More than half of all the flowing artesian wells in the United States are in California; and besides these a large number of farms are served by power pumps from phreatic wells. There are 1,913 main canals and ditches, aggregating 5,106 miles. In many places tunnels driven into the foothills supply streams for irrigation.

Of deciduous orchard trees there are in the State 28,138,471; including (in that order) plums and prunes, peaches, apricots, apples, pears, and cherries. The value of their product is $14,526,786. In 1900 the number of plum and prune trees is greater than total number of all deciduous orchard trees in 1890. The number of apricot trees has more than doubled in the decade.

Total number of semi-tropical fruit trees has increased from 1,809,161 in 1890 to 8,996,459 in 1900. Of the latter number, 62.8 per cent are orange trees; 17 per cent olives; 16.6 per cent lemons; 2.1 per cent figs. Other trees included are guavas, kaki, limes, pineapples, pomelos, etc. The counties of San Bernardino, Los Angeles, Riverside, and Orange contain more than four fifths of the orange trees. The number for the State is nearly five times as great as in 1890. Orange and lemon shipments, 1890, 2,400 carloads; 1900, 18,000 carloads. San Diego and Los Angeles counties contain more than half the lemon trees of the State, the number being more than 18 times as great as in 1890. There are 5,648,714 orange; 1,493,113 lemon; 1,530,164 olive trees in the State.

Strawberries, blackberries, raspberries, and other small fruits produced in 1899, $911,411. Fifty-two of the 57 counties raise grapes. California is the principal wine-producer of the Union, yielding more than one half the total product. The yield for 1899 was 5,492,216 gallons of wine and 3,403,368 centals of raisin grapes. California is the only raisin State; its annual product is about 40,000 tons.

Mining.— So early as 1690, Loyola Casallo mentions seeing placer gold in California; large nuggets were described (by Antonio Alcedo, 1786) in the 18th century. Not later than 1841, gold was found on San Francisquito Creek, Ventura County, about 45 miles from Los Angeles, and was "washed" there by Mexicans on a modest scale. On 19 Jan. 1848, James W. Marshall, an American from New Jersey, employed by the Swiss pioneer, John Sutter, in building a saw-mill near Coloma, on the north fork of the American, picked up yellow metallic flakes in the mill-race; the news spread in spite of efforts to suppress it, and in a few months the gold rush was on. Up to 1848 the whole United States had produced less than $12,000,000 in gold since the discovery of Amer-

CALIFORNIA

ica; in five years following California alone
yielded over $258,000,000. The annual gold
product of the State, from the discovery to 1859
inclusive, was in million dollars, 5, 10, 45, 75,
85, 65, 65½, 65, 57, 50, and 50. Not until 1865
did annual gold output of California fall below
$30,000,000. Up to 1 Jan. 1900, the gold pro-
duct of California was $1,409,849,068. Since
that time the annual output has been between
$15,000,000 and $16,000,000. No other State or
country in the world has approximated this
aggregate yield, though in the last few years
Colorado has led California in annual production of gold. This first bonanza in United
States history had a profound economic, socio-
logic, and political effect. "Sound money" was
as yet unknown in this country; silver and gold
together in the whole Union up to 1848 had not
reached $25,000,000 in total output; and the
instability of the currency prior to the California gold discovery is familiar to students. The
California gold-find not only precipitated such
a shifting of population as had not before been
dreamed of on this continent; it not only
brought about the admission to the Union of
a State distant 2,000 miles from any other
State,— California was the first State in the
geographic western half of the United States,
and sixth west of the Mississippi River,— it
furnished the finances for the great civil cleavage nominally most concerned with slavery, and
gave the free States a majority in the United
States Senate. It is probably not fanciful to
hold that this "irrepressible conflict" could not
so soon have opened had the nation been so
short of bullion and of credit as it was prior
to the gold discovery of 1848. Furthermore,
in 1859, almost exclusively with California capital, labor, enterprise, and machinery, the great
silver bonanzas of Nevada (just across the
Sierra) began the remarkable record of 21
years, in which they produced over $306,000,000
in bullion.

The first mining in California by Americans
was crude, as it had been in Mexican days —
"washing out" the auriferous gravels in the
"gold pan." The first step in advance was the
"rocker," employing two men, and foreshadow-
ing a certain associative effort. Next came the
"Long Tom," which made also for stability,
since it could not be carried. Then came the
sluice-box, a small wooden flume with wooden
riffles on the bottom, behind which the gold
sank and was saved, while the lighter sand and
gravel were swept on by the swift current. In
1852, E. E. Matteson, a Connecticut Yankee,
invented hydraulic mining, the greatest advance
ever made in the placers. Water under high
pressure, served through a nozzle called the
"monitor," thrown 200 or 300 feet with such
nozzle force that a crowbar could not be thrust
into the jet, ate away whole hillsides almost as
hot water disintegrates sugar; the detritus passing through long, riffled sluice-boxes. While
this invention was the most essential yet made
in mining, it was long disastrous to ultimate
development of the State, agriculturally. In
1880 it was proved by engineers' measurements
that on the Yuba River alone more than
100,000,000 cubic yards of gravel had been
washed by hydraulics into the bed of the stream,
raising it 70 feet; and burying 15,000 acres of
farm lands under the débris. After a long and
bitter fight, the "anti-Slickens" campaign ended

in 1884 in favor of the agricultural interests,
and hydraulic mining in California has never
since been on a large scale.

"Quartz mining" — that is, deep mining on
the original veins from whose waste the placers
derive — began in 1851, but did not take chief
rank for many years. Now it is the principal
form of gold mining in this State; and as it
requires large capital, experience, and time, gold
mining no longer attracts the multitude, though
the State annually produces three times as much
gold as set all the East in a fever half a century
ago. California is the only ante-bellum State in
the Union which has never had "soft money"
or a depreciation of currency. The largest mint
in the world is located in San Francisco.

In the 'sixties, extensive experiments were
made by Thomas Scott of the Pennsylvania
Railroad to develop petroleum in California,
even shipping around the Horn barrels for the
expected product. For various reasons, chiefly
administrative, the experiment failed. The
enormous seepages in many parts of the Coast
Range tempted further prospecting, and finally
producing wells began to be struck in the
Puente, in Ventura County, and in Los Angeles
city. In 1893 there were about 100 wells in
California, producing in the year 400,000 barrels. By 1897 the annual product had increased
to 1,903,411 barrels; and by 1900 to 4,324,484
barrels. In the latter year there were 1,590
producing wells and 470 drilling. Since then
the increase has been rapid. During 1901, 1,116
wells were completed, and 526 drilling, besides
259 dry holes; and the product was 8,786,330
barrels. Total production in California up to
and including 1901, 27,850,205 barrels; output
for 1902, about 12,000,000 barrels. The oil fields
embrace 17 counties, in a line over 600 miles
long; chief producers, Kern, Los Angeles, and
Ventura counties. Wells are from 700 to 2,000
feet deep. In the Summerland district most of
the production is from wells put down in the
ocean from piers. Extensive pipe lines now
under construction will deliver at tide water the
oil from Kern River and other districts.

California is the first State in the Union in
total production of gold, and second in present
annual output; second in present output of
copper; eighth or ninth in output of silver; first
in borax and soda; fourth in petroleum; fifth
in salt; first in asphaltum, quicksilver (with
two fifths of the total production of the world),
and soda.

Total value of mineral products for California in 1901 was $34,355,981, in 46 items.
Principal products, with yield and value:

Gold.............	....	$16,989,044
Copper...........	34,931,785 lbs.	5,501,782
Petroleum........	7,710,315 bbls.	2,961,102
Quicksilver.......	26,720 flasks	1,285,014
Silver............	....	1,229,356
Borax............	22,221 tons	982,380

Other interesting items are asphalt and bituminous rock, $378,573; lime, $334,688; mineral
waters, $559,057; salt, 126,000 tons, $366,376;
soda, $400,000. There is also considerable pro-
duction of turquoise, tourmaline, antimony, asbestos, fuller's earth, graphite, manganese, magnesite, platinum, etc.; 54 of the 57 counties
produce minerals.

Manufactures.— Between its first census
(1850) and that of 1900, California gained 1,500
per cent in population and 2,196 per cent in aver-

SOUTHERN CALIFORNIA PALMS.

CALIFORNIA ROSE GARDEN.

age number of wage-earners engaged in manufacturing. Although chiefly an agricultural and mining State, it had in 1900 140,330 persons engaged in manufacturing. In the last decade there has been great increase in number of establishments, capital, wage-earners, and value of products. This has been due to discovery and development of a cheap fuel, namely, petroleum. Though length of transcontinental haul (2,000 to 3,000 miles) from the great factory centres acted as a "high protective tariff," and many raw materials were abundant here, imported fuel-coal at $8 to $10 per ton was a heavy handicap to manufacturing. Within a decade, petroleum has become, from practically nothing, the third mineral product of California, reaching over 12,000,000 barrels in 1902. This is equivalent to coal at about $3 per ton, and has enormously stimulated manufacturing. Twenty-five years ago, Prof. J. D. Whitney, dean of American geologists, was doubtful of any future for petroleum in California, and stated that certainly this State would never have flowing wells. There are now many "gushers" in California, and the petroleum industry is one of the most important. The locomotives of California railroads chiefly burn crude petroleum. Steam roadbeds and country highways are "sprinkled" with petroleum for thousands of miles. An overwhelming majority of manufacturers in the State now use it for fuel; and as local development of oil is only in its infancy, increase of manufacturing may be expected to take even longer strides. In the decade the per cent increase has been 58.8 in number of manufacturing establishments; 39.9 in capital; 41.9 in value of products; and in part of the State these figures have been nearly doubled. The leading manufactures are: Refining sugar and molasses, $15,909,998; slaughtering and meat-packing, $15,717,712; lumber and timber products, $13,764,647; flouring and grist-mill products, $13,100,944; canning fruits and vegetables, $13,081,829; foundry and machine shop products, $12,047,149; wines and liquors, $9,261,600; car construction, $7,553,626; tanning and finishing leather, $7,405,981; printing and publishing, $6,858,192; explosives, $4,283,818.

Manufacturing statistics, 1900: Number of establishments, 12,582; capital, $205,395,025; average number of wage-earners, 91,047; value of products, $302,874,761. In per capita value of manufactured products California is twelfth State, with $203.95 per capita; United States average, $170.90 per capita. It is also twelfth in number of manufacturing establishments, and first in wages. It is eleventh in dairy products; fifth in capital in lumber; first in canning fruits and vegetables; first in all dried fruits; sixth in canning fish; eighth in number of establishments, and twelfth in value of product, in piano-making; third in ship-building; fifteenth in flour. The canning of fruits and vegetables has reached its highest development in California; and in output this State easily leads the Union,— being about three times in excess of the 6 New England States, 10 Southern States, 6 Western States, and Washington and Oregon, all together. Its product, 1900, was $13,081,829. More than one half all canned peaches; more than two thirds all canned pears; nearly one half all canned cherries; nearly four fifths all canned plums; more than one half all canned beans; more than one half all dried

fruits, produced by the whole United States are from California. The increase in all items of manufacturing has been by far largest in the city of Los Angeles, where, for instance, the per cent gain in a decade has been in number of establishments, 88.7; number of wage-earners, 107.7; value of products, 115.3. The 1900 census specifies 181 manufacturing industries in California. Another new, but highly important industrial advance is long-distance transmission of electric power from mountain streams. In this California has for years led the world. When a 33,000-volt, 82-mile line from San Bernardino Mountains to Los Angeles was installed (1900), it far exceeded any other line in the world in length and voltage. Then 40,000 volts were brought 140 miles from Yuba River to Oakland — with cable crossing Carquinez Straits by suspension span of 4,400 feet, 300 feet in air. The longest power transmission in the world is (1903) from Colgate to San Francisco, 211¼ miles. Plants are now building to transmit 28,000 horse-power from Kern River, 116 miles, to Los Angeles; and 120,000 horse-power from San Joaquin River, 180 miles to San Francisco; and 218 miles to Los Angeles. One electric company expended $250,000 per month throughout 1902, in electric development in and around Los Angeles; and is expending even larger sums in 1903. Two other companies in northern part of State are developing 169,000 horse-power for long-distance transmission.

Within the decade, ship-building has had great impetus, and California is now third State in the Union in this industry. The Oregon, Olympia, Ohio, and other United States war vessels were built in San Francisco.

Commerce, Navigation, etc.— The position of California (commanding, from the best seaport in 5,000 miles of Pacific coast, the shortest routes to the Orient); its great coast-line,— two thirds of total United States frontage upon the Pacific,— and its relation as outlet for an enormous inland territory, give great importance to its commerce. San Francisco, though ninth city of the Union in population, is third in commerce. Its exports for 1902 were $47,601,422; imports, $36,078,270. Operations in the Philippines, and development of the Oriental trade are bringing about for California the realization of Seward's prophecy that "the Pacific is to be the chief theatre of the world's activities." The bay of San Francisco, with a shore-line of 300 miles, open to the ocean only by the mile-wide Golden Gate, and receiving through the two great central rivers the drainage of the vast interior valley, is reckoned next to Sydney among the world's best harbors. San Diego at the extreme south has a well-sheltered natural harbor, entrance to which is now being improved by the government. At San Pedro an enormous breakwater is being constructed by the government, which will enclose an excellent artificial harbor. At the roadstead of Santa Monica, a wharf 4,700 feet long serves rapidly growing commerce. There are several minor ports scattered along the coast. California has seven lines of oceanic steamers — plying to China, the Philippines, Sandwich Islands, Alaska, Mexico, Panama, and Chile, and coastwise. There are six lines of river steamers, five concerned with San Francisco and its river system. The Sacramento is navigable to the capital city of that name,

90 miles from San Francisco; the San Joaquin to Stockton, about an equal distance. The Colorado, on the desert east boundary of the State, is sixth or seventh among the great rivers of North America; and though a sandy, shifting, and impetuous stream is navigable for small steamers for over 300 miles above its mouth in the California Gulf (in Mexico). In 1902 exports by sea from San Francisco included treasure, $14,851,789; flour and wheat, $14,458,321. During the same year exports from San Francisco to China were $15,819,922; to Japan, $6,858,942.

Fisheries.— San Francisco is now leading whaling port in the world; and despite great decay of this once noted industry there are still about 25 vessels engaged. Product (1902) 10,976 barrels oil; 110,662 pounds whalebone; 15,566 pounds ivory. In 1855 there were engaged in whale fisheries in the Pacific 650 vessels, manned by 15,000 men. In fish canning, California is sixth State in the Union. This is principally salmon pack. Fisheries for local markets employ many hundred people, but statistics are not available. In marine and fresh-water fishes the State is probably richest in the Union. Salmon, sturgeon, rock-fish, smelt, halibut, soles, tom-cod, mackerel, Spanish mackerel, and a great variety of other sea fish are abundant. The barracouda (*Sphyrœna argentea*), pompano (*Trachynotus*), sand-dab, red-snapper, and "small fry" are characteristic and famous food fishes; while soles and flounders, differing from those of the Atlantic seaboard, are a noted delicacy. These marine fish are in market the whole year. The leaping tuna of Southern California disputes with the Florida tarpon place as gamiest of sea fish. At Catalina Island there are great annual tournaments for capture of this fish with light rod, reel, and 21-strand line. Tuna of 251 pounds, and black sea-bass, or Jew fish, of 380 pounds, are the record with this frail tackle. The coast is extraordinarily rich in shell-fish. Crabs of extraordinary size, but very delicate; shrimps, crawfish closely resembling the eastern lobster, but without mandibles, are very abundant. The native oyster is small, but flavorsome, and eastern oysters transplanted to the coast propagate well and are of excellent flavor. Mussels, clams, razor-shells, cockles, and other edible mollusks are abundant and good. The Rocky Mountain trout is indigenous here, and grows to large size. Within the last 25 years all the eastern varieties of trout have been successfully introduced into this State. Taken altogether, California exceeds any other State in variety, size, and abundance of trout. Black bass, shad, cat-fish, and carp have also been colonized here on a large scale. Game fishes in the streams, as well as game birds and animals, are carefully protected by "close seasons."

Railroads and Street Railways.— Mileage of railroads in the State (1900) 5,500; chiefly pertaining to the two great transcontinental lines, the Southern P., and the Atchison, T. & S. F. R.R.'s. So rapid is the development of electric lines, urban and suburban, that statistics are constantly changing. San Francisco and vicinity have about 400 miles (mostly cable roads in the city and electrics outside). In Los Angeles there are (1903) 170 miles electric roads, with 500 miles of suburban lines in active construction. In 1870, railroad mileage of California

was 525; and there were no urban lines whatever. San Francisco invented in 1873 the first successful urban rapid transit in the world, and its cable system is still probably without rival. A new transcontinental railroad is now building from Salt Lake City to Los Angeles, about 800 miles.

State Finances.— Total assessed valuation, 1902, $1,290,750,465; in 1890, $584,578,036. State tax, .382c. Bonded debt nominally, $2,500,000; but the State owns the bonds. Total county indebtedness, $3,175,942.

Banks.— In 1900 there were 37 national banks, capital $10,975,000, total resources $62,135,611; 178 commercial banks, capital $26,981,972, total resources $146,495,782; 53 savings banks, capital $7,655,705, total resources $173,872,499; 19 private banks, capital $890,142, total resources $2,798,391; grand total, 287 banks; capital, $46,502,820; total resources, $385,302,285. In 1902 there were 321 banks, and their net gain in deposits over 1901 was $55,405,951.

California far exceeds any other State of the Union in average amount deposited in banks to each depositor, with $764.52 per capita, against the United States average of $408.30. One in every seven of entire population is a depositor. In clearing-house business, San Francisco stands about sixth city in the Union. Its clearances, 1901, were $1,134,499,932. Clearances, Los Angeles, 1901, $145,170,809.

Education.— California leads the Union in enrollment of college students, having 1 to every 419 of total population, and surpasses New England in pro rata of pupils in secondary schools. There are (1900) 5 State Normal Schools, 120 high schools, 7,119 kindergarten, primary, and grammar schools; with grand total of 7,706 teachers, 372,352 scholars; $19,135,722 value of school property. Annual expenditures for secondary public schools is over $6,000,000. California is the only State in the Union with two great free universities. The State University at Berkeley ranks second among American universities in number of undergraduates and in total number of students, being exceeded only by Harvard. Total enrollment, 2,470 (1,026 women). It is fourteenth in size among the universities of the world. Resources, $7,260,000; supported by State tax of 2 cents on every $100 valuation. Mrs. Phœbe A. Hearst, widow of United States Senator Hearst, has contributed great sums to the university, and has secured in a competition open to all the world (won by M. Bénard of Paris), a complete architectural plan whose buildings will cost at least $10,000,000. Leland Stanford Jr. University was founded 1891 by Gov. and United States Senator Leland Stanford and wife. The widow has recently turned over to the university the complete endowment they designed, amounting to nearly $30,000,000. A harmonious architectural plan, of symmetry and beauty unrivaled at present by any university in the world, has already been carried far enough to accommodate the 1,200 students (of whom one third are women) and has cost several millions. University affairs in California are in the hands of noted educators from the East; standards are high, and friendly rivalry has done much to promote educational affairs throughout the State; while the two universities have together about five times the enrollment that the one

A DRY SALT SEA IN THE COLORADO DESERT, CAL.

The Indian laborers have washed the salt and stacked it into cones ready for the mill.

had 12 years ago. David Starr Jordan is president of Stanford, and Benjamin Ide Wheeler of the State University. The accrediting system has been developed to high efficiency. Co-education in both universities is not an experiment, but acknowledged success. There is a large number of colleges, private schools, seminaries, academies, and other educational institutions, besides those under State supervision; also medical, law, and other schools. Educationally, California ranks very high in the Union. A large number of distinguished teachers have been attracted by climatic and other considerations. It pays its teachers in public schools the highest average salaries in the Union ($943, as compared with $620 for Ohio).

Public libraries are very numerous, and are to be found even in the smallest cities. With its free public library of 80,000 volumes, San Francisco has four other libraries aggregating 200,000 volumes — besides the great Sutro library of 500,000 titles, not yet available to the public. Los Angeles has a library of about 70,000 volumes. In circulation, California libraries are much more active than those of the East. Average number of books distributed per capita: Chicago, .96; Philadelphia, 1.40; Boston, 2.13; Los Angeles, 3.45. Circulation per volume: Boston, 1.76; Los Angeles, 7.40.

Of philanthropic and temperance organizations; of literary, social, fraternal, and other societies, California has an extraordinary number; due to the cosmopolitan character and average education of its immigrants. Women's clubs, the Young Men's Christian Association, the Women's Christian Temperance Union, and other federated bodies are here much stronger than in most States. In proportion to population California has twice as many newspapers as New England. In San Francisco alone are 242 periodicals in 13 languages. The first kindergarten in America was established in San Francisco.

Churches.— No recent statistics available. In 1890 there were 1,505 church buildings, seating capacity, 422,609; value church property, $12,000,000; number of communicants, 280,619. Of these, 156,846 were Roman Catholics*, about 37,000 Methodists; 19,000 Presbyterians; 11,000 to 12,000 each Baptists and Congregationalists. With increase of 22.9 per cent in population in the decade, these totals have been greatly changed; but probably not the order — nor extensively, the proportions. In 1900 Los Angeles city had one church to every 662 of population, as compared to New York with one church to every 6,424 of population.

Charitable and Penal Institutions.— California has two State prisons, two industrial reform schools, five asylums for insane, one for deaf, dumb, and blind, and a great number of public and private hospitals, asylums, orphanages, etc.

State Government.— State officers elected for four years, except assemblymen for two; no bar to re-election; governor's salary, $6,000; two thirds vote in each house passes bill over governor's veto. If he does not act on any bill within 10 days, it becomes law, unless adjournment of legislature prevents return of bill, in

* Roman Catholic figures include entire family; other denominations only communicants.

which case it becomes operative if within 10 days after such adjournment, the governor approves it. Legislature limited to 40 members in Senate, 80 in House; meets biennially, in January of odd-numbered years. Sessions not limited, but pay allowed members only for 60 days —$8 per day, with traveling expenses and mileage 10 cents per mile. No bill can be introduced after 50th day of session. State constitution is notable for numerous restrictions on legislative action; provision for three fourths' majority verdict of juries in civil cases; and prohibition of Chinese suffrage and of employment of Chinese on State works or by corporations.

United States Representatives.— Two senators, eight congressmen (prior to apportionment of 1901, seven congressmen). Electoral vote, nine.

Population.— The settlement of California, steadily progressive for 55 years, has been marked by two of the most remarkable shiftings of population anywhere recorded. Everything considered, the "Gold Rush" of 1848-9 has no parallel. In first 12 months after the discovery of a small flake of gold at Sutter's Mill, 42,000 Americans from the far eastern States made their way across the unbroken plains with wagons. This great migration continued uninterruptedly for years. Its demands brought about the first large development of steam navigation; and the finest clipper ships that had ever been built were constructed for the California trade. In 1845 the white population of California was about 5,000; 4,000 of whom were Spanish Californians, 360 Americans, 300 English, Scotch, and Irish, and the remainder "scattering." By 1850 this number had increased to 92,597; by 1860 to 379,994. That is, in 12 years over 370,000 persons reached California by an overland journey of 2,000 miles; or by a voyage of 19,000 miles around the Horn in sailing ships; or by the 5,000-mile voyage by way of Panama, with its difficult passage of the isthmus. For the first decade this precipitate migration was overwhelmingly of men; and this preponderance of males, with dearth of families and of women, colored in almost every social, political, and economic aspect the early fortunes of the State. The scarcity of home life, and profligate abundance of money, brought about an era of luxury in private and public expenditures on such a scale as was then hardly dreamed of in the eastern States. San Francisco had less than 150,000 people when it began to build the largest hotel in the world — covering two and a half acres and costing $7,000,000. The State had a population of less than half a million during the Civil War, but it contributed more than one third as much to the expenses of the United States Sanitary Commission as all the rest of the "loyal States" together, with their population of 18,500,000. Its cash contribution to this cause was over $1,200,000. Everything was in this proportion. Enormous subscriptions were sent to relieve great catastrophes of fire, pestilence, or war, in all parts of the world. Huge gifts were made to education and other public utilities, on a scale never yet surpassed and at that time elsewhere unheard of. For a generation San Francisco was a proverb the world over of princely living and princely giving. This large population of young men, vigorous, adventurous, mostly unattached, far from home and the conventions, and under excitation of sudden wealth, shaped and established such an epoch, social and financial, as no other American State has ever comparably known.

It was only after the first decline in the "diggings" — after the pursuit of gold became less a fortuitous scramble for surface nuggets, and mining had come to demand skill, patience, and business methods — that attention began to be paid to the soil. Though for 80 years, already the Franciscan missionaries had proved, in little oases about their missions, the wonderful fertility of California, the aridity of climate and the "look" of the land, so unlike in color and texture to soils recognized as fertile at home, led the adventurers to believe for years that California was worthless except for mining and stock-raising. It was only when the real fecundity of the soil began to be understood that character of population underwent essential change. Immigration in the first decade was almost purely of male fortune-hunters, with no thought of permanent residence. They came to get rich and go home. But when the slow comprehension dawned that in agricultural possibilities the State was inconceivably richer than in mineral resources, and that here was not only the most hospitable of climates, but the most generous land for home-building, an entirely different type of migration began — the migration of families. This stream, small at first, has continued steadily since about 1870. In 1886 the completion of a competing railroad into southern California — to which its first transcontinental line had brought but slow increase of population or development — precipitated another migration numerically greater than the Gold Rush, almost as rapid, far longer continued, and of entirely different category. It was characteristically of well-to-do and educated families, without the heroic qualities of the pioneers, but of much higher average in the civic and financial scale. They came not to tame a wilderness, but to enjoy such a land as travelers seek along the Mediterranean. They came by Pullman cars instead of "prairie schooner"; instead of felling forests they planted groves of tropical fruits; instead of building frontier cabins, they erected a class of homes such as probably cannot be found among an equal population. It is only by reference to the peculiar character of this migration that the development and progress of California in all social, educational, and material lines during the last 15 years seems at all credible.

In 1880 the population was 864,694; in 1890, 1,208,130; in 1900, 1,485,053; the latter figure being more than 16 times as large as the population of 1850. The recent great increase in population, however, has been disproportionately in the seven southern counties of the State. Much more than half of the State gain for 20 years has been in eight counties, including in the northern half of the State only the city and county of San Francisco. Since 1880, Los Angeles has outstripped in population 99 other American cities then numerically larger. In 1900 it was thirty-sixth city in the Union in population, and only 13 cities in the Union had gained as many people in the decade. There are 57 counties, with 116 incorporated cities and towns; 19 places exceeding 5,000 population;

10 exceeding 10,000; and 4 exceeding 25,000. Of the total population of 1,485,053, whites are 1,402,727; colored, 11,045; Chinese, 45,753; Japanese, 10,151; Indians, 15,377. The total males are 820,531; females, 664,522. While in most of the far eastern States the excess of females to males is increasing, in California the growth is toward a balance; the number of women to every 100,000 men having risen from 72,657 in 1890, to 80,987 in 1900. Of the total population, 1,117,813 are native born, and 367,240 foreign.

The 15,377 Indians in California, comprising at least 14 different linguistic stocks, live principally on three reservations in the north; 1 at Yuma, and 32 mission reservations, all on the edge of the desert in the south. They are mostly self-supporting, peaceful, and fairly industrious farmers, with government day schools everywhere among them; besides which, 2,934 Indian children are in public schools. Their chief art is basket-making, in which some tribes lead the world for beauty and value of product. The record price for a basket is $2,000; but prices average from $5 to $50. The government is now encouraging this industry by teaching it in Indian schools.

Chief Cities.— San Francisco, largest city west of Saint Louis (about 2,000 miles by rail) and largest on entire Pacific coast of North and South America; has population (1900), 342,782, a gain of 43,785 in the decade. It is ninth city in the Union in population and twentieth in increase in the decade. The population was 2,000 in February 1849; 5,000 in July; 20,000 in December of same year. In 1850 it was about 25,000 (United States census figures destroyed by fire). In 1860 it was 56,802; in 1870, 149,473; in 1880, 233,959. Los Angeles was, in 1880, 135th city in the Union in population; in 1890, 57th; in 1900, 36th, having gained in the last decade 52,089, which makes it 14th city in gross increase. In 1850 it had 1,610 inhabitants; in 1860, 4,385; in 1870, 5,728; in 1880, 11,183; in 1890, 50,395; in 1900, 102,479. In 1902 it was fifth city in Union in number of new buildings erected, and eighth in value of new buildings; first in expenditure per capita for new buildings. It has the largest proportionate telephone service in the world, with 1 telephone to every 8 persons; San Francisco coming next with 1 to every 12 persons; then Detroit with 1 to every 24,— as compared with Boston 1 to every 31, New York 1 to every 41, Chicago 1 to every 44. Oakland, across the bay from San Francisco, has grown from 48,682 in 1890 to 66,960 in 1900; Sacramento, State capital, has 29,282 population. Other cities are San José, 21,500; San Diego, 17,700; Stockton, 17,506; Alameda, 16,464; Berkeley (seat of State university, and Asylum for Deaf, Dumb, and Blind), 13,214; Fresno, 12,470; Pasadena, 9,117; Riverside, 7,973; Vallejo, 7,965; Eureka, 7,327; Santa Rosa, 6,673; Santa Barbara, 6,587; San Bernardino, 6,150; Santa Cruz, 5,659; Pomona, 5,526. No other place exceeded 5,000 in 1900.

History.— The name California, for which so many preposterous derivations have been urged, is taken from a Spanish romance, called 'Sergas de Esplandian' ('Exploits of Esplandian') by Ordoñez de Montalvo (translator of Amadis de Gaul), printed about 1510, and often mentioned in old sources. It was a mythi-

CORONADO BEACH, CALIFORNIA.

cal island "on the right hand of the Indies, very near the Terrestrial Paradise," peopled with Amazons and Griffins. The name was first applied to the peninsula (discovered by Jimenez 1533) and is first recorded thus in Preciado's diary of Ulloa's coastwise voyage in 1539. In time it came to be used indefinitely for the whole Pacific coast from the peninsula practically to Nootka; and later "the Californias," differentiated into Baja (or Lower) California and Alta (Upper) California, the former including about what is now the Mexican Peninsular Territory. The first European to touch the present State was Alarcon, who went up the Colorado River some hundreds of miles in 1540. The first seaboard exploration was by Cabrillo 1542; and the next important coast explorations were by Sir Francis Drake 1579, and Vizcaino 1602. The first colonization of Upper California was by the Franciscan missionaries under Junipero Serra, with a small escort of Spanish troops. These pioneer missionaries had by 1800 founded 18 missions, whose total population, mostly Indian neophytes, was 13,000. Three other missions were established by 1823. The mission period lasted about 65 years; converted over 80,000 Indians; erected in the wilderness at least $1,000,000 worth of buildings, and had developed stock-raising and wheat on a scale which astonished Humboldt. In 1834 the Mexican government "disestablished" the missions and confiscated their property. The Indians were scattered, and perished in great numbers. The buildings were plundered and left to decay. At present the Landmarks Club (incorporated) is preserving the mission edifices. The State passed from Spanish rule to that of the Mexican republic, 1821; was seized, practically without resistance, by the United States in 1845, and ceded by Mexico at close of Mexican war; admitted to the Union, 9 Sept. 1850. The American discovery of gold caused an unprecedented transcontinental migration (see *Population*). Aside from the great impetus given steam and clipper ships, the migration had other unique features — like the Merchant's Express, which employed 5,000 men, 2,000 wagons, and 20,000 yoke of oxen in freighting across the continent; and the Pony Express, which carried mail (letters only) at $5 per half ounce, 1,950 miles horseback from Independence, Mo., to San Francisco, in 10 days; and the Butterfield stages, 8 times a month between St. Louis and San Francisco, via Texas and New Mexico; quickest time, 21 days from New York to San Francisco. Extraordinary records were made in this overland traffic. Robert H. Haslam, ("Pony Bob") made one continuous ride of 380 miles; and William F. Cody ("Buffalo Bill") one of 384, without stopping except for meals and to change horses — both as riders of the Pony Express. Quickest time made by this route (1,950 miles), 7 days, 17 hours. The growth of this overland traffic led California capitalists, heavily subsidized by government, to build a transcontinental railroad. Ground was broken at Sacramento for the Central P. R.R., 8 Jan. 1863. The road was completed by driving of a spike of pure California gold by Gov. Stanford in presence of distinguished company at Promontory, Utah, 10 May 1869. In 1877 the Southern P. R.R. from Texas tidewater to San Francisco was completed. In 1885 the Atchison, T. & S. F. R.R. reached Los Angeles from St. Louis; and within the last two years has been extended to San Francisco. The latter and the Southern P. R.R. are the longest railroad systems in the world, each with a mileage much over 7,000. The modern development of California dates from competition of these two lines during the decade beginning 1886.

The swift creation of an American commonwealth by the sudden horde of adventurous pioneers upon whom that duty at once devolved, is perhaps the most remarkable monument to the genius of the American people for self-government. Ninety thousand wanderers, homeless, wifeless, and chaotic in the wilderness, fevered by enormous and sudden gains, without cities or laws or communication with the outside world, within a year installed soberly and firmly all essential machineries of an American State. The desperadoes who flocked in from all parts of the world — including a large contingent of Australian convicts — were firmly suppressed, though not at once. Between 1849 and 1856 there were in San Francisco alone 1,000 homicides and 7 executions. In 1856 the second vigilance committee, composed of the best citizens, judicially, after full and formal trial, publicly hanged half a dozen worst desperadoes, and banished scores of others on pain of death. Since that time life and property have been quite as safe in California as in the eastern States. Chinese exclusion, though finally a national measure, was brought about by California, which then contained a majority of all Chinese in this country. In 1879 California voted exclusion by 154,638 to 883. The number of Chinese in the State has decreased from 75,132 in 1880 and 72,472 in 1890 to 45,753 in 1900. The bitterness aroused by the exclusion struggle has passed, and Chinese are well treated.

California entered the Union as a free State, thus giving balance of power to the North. In State elections since the war it has been peculiarly independent, having gone Democratic in 1867, 1875, 1882, 1886 (Democratic governor and Republican lieutenant-governor, who became governor by his superior's death) and 1894; Republican in 1871, 1879, 1890, 1898, and 1902.

Next to the gold excitement (see *Mining* and *Population*) the most sensational era in California history was the great bonanza silver period from 1859 to 1880. The mines were in Nevada, but were owned in San Francisco, and an era of stock-gambling theretofore unheard of in history, and probably not yet surpassed, sprang from their sensational yield. Stocks on the San Francisco board rose $1,000,000 a day for many months, and sales in one year were $120,000,000. Everybody gambled in stock, from bankers to scrub-women. In 1875, with less than 200,000 population, San Francisco had 100 millionaires. The "Consolidated Virginia" mines paid $1,000,000 per month dividends for nearly two years. One lode was valued at nearly $400,000,000; $250,000,000 was spent in "developing" a small group of hills. The decadence of these great bonanzas, following the subsidence of gold mining to sober methods, at last turned more general attention to agriculture, the real wealth of the State (see *Agriculture*). In 1880 California was first in the Union only in gold, sheep, and quicksilver; all other industries being far down the list. It is now second in gold; ninth in sheep; first in diversity of crops; first in wines, total fruits, canned fruits, dried fruits, barley; first in number of irrigated farms; first in average wages in manufacturing establishments; first in borax, asphalt, quicksilver, platinum; second in copper; third in wheat; second in beet sugar; second in hops; first in oranges, lemons, olives, and all semi-tropic fruits, honey, prunes, walnuts, almonds, beans, grapes, pears, peaches, cherries, apricots, etc.; first in electric power transmission; third in ship-building; fourth in petroleum; fifth in total value products per farm; eleventh in value farm products per capita; twelfth in total value manufactured products.

The highest California gold product in any one year was $85,000,000. The total agricultural products for 1899 were $131,000,000; and total value of manufactured products (1900) $302,000,000.

A South Sea bubble as wild as the Comstock silver stock-craze was the great "Land Boom" of southern California, 1886-7; a period of land-gambling never quite equaled in any other part of America. An area as large as New England was involved, with varying intensity; but the chief focus of excitement was in Los Angeles, San Bernardino, and San Diego counties. Scores of thousands of city lots were staked out far from towns, hundreds of miles of cement sidewalks and curbs were laid; scores of big hotels and other buildings erected as baits, and great quantities of lands (purchased at from $10 to $30 per acre) were sold in town lots at $1,000 to $10,000 per acre. In Los Angeles County alone, with a population then not over 50,000, real estate transfers recorded in 1887 were over $100,000,000. Excursion auction sales of new "towns" sometimes realized $250,000 in a day; and $100 was often paid for place in the line waiting for a sale to open. The collapse of this gigantic bubble, early in 1888, was as extraordinary in its freedom from disaster as it had been in its inflation. Not a bank failed, nor a business house of respectable standing; and while desert town lots reverted to acreage and acreage values, all really desirable real estate, rural and urban, has constantly advanced in value every year — thanks to the uninterrupted continuance of large and wealthy immigration. Building of homes and setting out of orchards continue on an extraordinary scale. During 1902, besides other buildings, more than 4,000 new residences were erected in the city of Los Angeles. "Local option" is in force; and nearly all towns of southern California are "prohibition."

BIBLIOGRAPHY.— *Outline Reference and Reading List.*— General History: T. H. Hittell, 'History of California' (4 vols. 1897, exhaustively indexed and by one author); H. H. Bancroft, 'History of California' (7 vols. 1890, by anonymous staff, and inadequately indexed); J. S. Hittell, 'History of San Francisco' (1876, concise and reliable, to its date). Mission Period: A. Duhaut-Cilly, 'Voyage autour du Monde, 1826-9' (2 vols. 1835); Alex. Forbes, 'History Upper and Lower California' (1839); Helen Hunt Jackson ("H. H."), 'Glimpses of Three Coasts' (1886), reprinted in 'Glimpses of California and the Missions' (1902). The vast bulk of sources on this

period is in Spanish, and inaccessible to English students.

Contemporary writers on Pioneer period American occupation: Rev. Walter Colton, 'Three Years in California' (1850); J. Q. Thornton, 'Oregon and California in 1848' (2 vols. 1849); Edwin Bryant, 'What I Saw in California' (1849); Lieut. J. W. Revere, 'Tour of Duty in California' (1849); F. Soulé, 'Annals of San Francisco' (1855); Bayard Taylor, 'California and Mexico' (1850), and 'Home and Abroad' (1862, 2d series); A. M. Majors (manager "Merchants' Express"), 'Seventy Years on the Frontier' (1893).

Mining: C. H. Shinn, 'Mining Camps' (1885), and 'Story of the Mine' (1896); also both Hittells, *sup.*

Physiography, Mountains and Forests: John Muir, 'The Mountains of California' (1894), and 'Our National Parks' (1901).

Climate, Modern Development, and General: Chas. Dudley Warner, 'Our Italy' (1892); Chas. Nordhoff, 'California for Health, Pleasure, and Residence' (1882), and 'Northern California' (1874); T. S. Van Dyke, 'Southern California' (1886), and 'Millionaires of a Day' (1892) (Land-Boom); Lindley and Widney, 'California of the South' (1896); "H. H." as above; Wm. E. Smythe, 'Conquest of Arid America' (1900); Chas. F. Lummis, 'The Right Hand of the Continent' (1903).

Statistical: 'Twelfth Census United States' (1900), Bulletins 10, 136, 164, 237, etc.; McCarthy's 'Statistician and Economist' (San Francisco), v. d. Reports, United States Department Agriculture, etc.

CHARLES FLETCHER LUMMIS,
Editor of 'Out West Magazine.'

California, Gulf of, or Sea of Cortez, an arm of the Pacific Ocean, separating lower California from the Mexican mainland. It is 700 miles in length and varies in width from 40 to 100 miles. There is but little navigation carried on there. On the western coast are pearl fisheries. The gulf was discovered by Cortez, and for some time was called after him. The river Colorado empties into the northern extremity.

California, Lower or Old, a territory of the Republic of Mexico, forming a peninsula in the Pacific Ocean, united on the north to the continent, from which it is separated on the east, throughout its entire length, by the Gulf of California. It is about 750 miles in length, and in different places 30, 60, 90, and 150 miles wide. The coast forms many capes, bays, and havens, and is fringed by numerous islands. A chain of mountains extends throughout, of which the greatest height is from 4,500 to 4,900 feet above the sea, the latter being the height attained by its culminating point, Cerro de la Giganta. The chain is almost destitute of vegetation, having only here and there a few stunted trees or shrubs. It has a single volcano, and possesses distinct traces of volcanic origin. The foot of the range is covered with cactuses of remarkable size. Some of the hollows, where the soil is formed of decomposed lava, are tolerably fertile. On the plains the soil is often of the richest quality, and when the advantage of irrigation can be obtained, raises the most abundant crops; but this advantage often fails, owing to the great deficiency of water. Rain seldom

THE CAMPUS OF THE UNIVERSITY OF CALIFORNIA.

falls in summer, and the streams are very insignificant. The climate varies much according to locality. On the coast of the Pacific the temperature ranges in summer from 58° to 71°; the sky is peculiarly clear and perfectly cloudless, except toward sunset, the tints of which are remarkable for variety and beauty. At a distance from the coast, where the sea breeze is not enjoyed, the summer heat is excessive. The principal vegetable products are maize, manioc, wheat, grapes, oranges, lemons, pineapples, and many other varieties of the finest fruits. In the valleys horses, sheep, and cattle are raised successfully. The fish on the coast are very abundant, and a pearl-fishery was long very successfully carried on. Gold mining is also carried on with considerable success. La Paz, in the south, is the capital; Ensenada, in the north, is a rising port. California was explored by order of Cortez in 1532–3. The region was visited by Drake as early as 1579. In 1697 the Jesuits formed establishments in the territory, built villages and missions, and in some measure civilized the natives. On their expulsion in 1767, the missions were carried on by the Dominicans. Pop. (1895) 42,245, of whom probably about half are Indians.

California, University of, a university which is a part of the State educational system in California, but supported as well by the income from endowments and by national aid.

In 1869 the College of California, which had been incorporated in 1855 and which had carried on collegiate instruction since 1860, closed its work of instruction and transferred its property, on terms which were mutually agreed upon, to the University of California.

The university was instituted by a law which received the approval of the governor, 23 March 1868. Instruction was begun in Oakland in the autumn of 1869. The commencement exercises of 1873 were held at Berkeley, 16 July, when the university was formally transferred to its permanent home. Instruction began at Berkeley in the autumn of 1873. The new constitution of 1879 made the existing organization of the university perpetual.

The professional schools were contemplated in the original plan, but not organized till later. The governing body, the board of regents, consists of the governor and lieutenant-governor of the State, the speaker of the Assembly, the State superintendent of public instruction, the presidents of the State Agricultural Society and the Mechanics' Institute of San Francisco, and the president of the university (all regents ex officio), and 16 others appointed by the governor for a 16-year term with the advice and consent of the Senate. The university is divided into the following departments: (1) The four colleges of general culture, including letters (degree of bachelor of arts), social sciences (bachelor of letters), natural sciences (bachelor of science), and commerce (bachelor of science); (2) the five colleges of applied science, agriculture, mining, mechanics, chemistry, and civil engineering (leading to the degree of bachelor of science); (3) the Mark Hopkins Institute of Art; (4) the Hastings College of the Law; (5) the college of medicine; (6) the postgraduate medical department; (7) the college of dentistry; (8) the California College of Pharmacy. The nine colleges first mentioned are situated at Berkeley; the others are in San Francisco; the Lick Observatory on Mount Hamilton was established as a part of the university in 1888.

In 1896 Mrs. Phœbe Apperson Hearst informed the regents that she proposed to erect a building, but wished first a worthy general plan for the Berkeley campus, and that she would bear the expense of an international competition to obtain such a plan. In 1898 an international jury assembled at Antwerp and voted upon more than one hundred plans submitted, awarding prizes to eleven competitors, who were invited to visit the university and to prepare revised plans for a second competition. In September, 1899, the jury met again in San Francisco and gave the first prize ($10,000) to M. Emile Bénard of Paris. After a long stay in Berkeley and many conferences with the university authorities, M. Bénard undertook a revision of his drawings to fit the plans to the actual necessities of the site and the prospective needs of the university. In December, 1900, he submitted a design which the regents adopted as the permanent plan. To Mr. John Galen Howard has been entrusted the development of the plan, as supervising architect. In realization of the Hearst plan, three buildings are (1905) approaching completion; the Hearst Memorial Mining Building, given by Mrs. Hearst for the College of Mining of the university and as a memorial to the late Senator George Hearst; California Hall, for which an appropriation of $250,000 was made by the California legislature, and the president's house. A fourth building has been erected — the beautiful Greek Theatre, an open-air auditorium, seating 8,000, patterned after the classic theatres of Greece and the Greek colonies, and given to the university by Mr. William Randolph Hearst. The fifth of the new buildings will be the library, for which generous provision was made by Mr. Charles F. Doe of San Francisco, who bequeathed $700,000 for this purpose.

At Berkeley there are 175 officers of instruction distributed among 36 departments, 2,700 students, a library of 130,000 volumes, an art gallery, museums and laboratories, also the agricultural experiment grounds and stations, which are invaluable adjuncts of the farming, orchard, and vineyard interests of the State. In San Francisco there are 150 officers of instruction, besides demonstrators and other assistants, and 600 students. Tuition in the colleges at Berkeley, during regular sessions, is free to residents of California; non-residents pay a fee of $10 each half year. In the professional colleges, in San Francisco, except that of law, tuition fees are charged. The instruction in all the colleges is open to all qualified persons, without distinction of sex. The constitution of the State provides for the perpetuation of the university with all its departments.

In 1904 there were 4,175 students in all the departments, of whom about 40 per cent were women: it is also to be noted that a comparatively large proportion of students are in the general or academic courses, as distinguished from the technical and professional courses.

JAMES SUTTON,
Recorder of the Faculties.

Calig'ula, Gaius Cæsar Augustus Germani-cus, Roman emperor, a son of Germanicus and Agrippina: b. 31 Aug. 12 A.D., in the camp at Antium, and brought up among the legions; d. 24 Jan. 41 A.D. He received from the soldiers the surname of Caligula, on account of his wearing the *caligæ*, the boots commonly used by the soldiers. He understood so well how to insinuate himself into the good graces of Tiberius that he not only escaped the cruel fate of his parents, and brothers, and sisters, but was even loaded with honors. Whether, as some writers inform us, he removed Tiberius out of the way by slow poison is uncertain. When the latter was about to die he appointed, according to Suetonius, Caligula and the son of Drusus, Tiberius Nero, heirs of the empire. But Caligula, universally beloved for the sake of his father Germanicus, was able without difficulty to obtain sole possession of the throne. Rome received him joyfully, and the distant provinces echoed his welcome. His first actions were just and noble. He interred, in the most honorable manner, the remains of his mother and of his brother Nero, set free all state prisoners, recalled the banished, and forbade all prosecutions for treason. He conferred on the magistrates free and independent power. Although the will of Tiberius had been declared by the senate to be null and void, he fulfilled every article of it, with the exception only of that above-mentioned. When he was chosen consul he took his uncle, Claudius, as his colleague. Thus he distinguished the first eight months of his reign by many magnanimous actions, when he fell sick. After his recovery, by a most unexpected alteration, which has given good grounds to suspect his sanity, he suddenly showed himself the most cruel and unnatural of tyrants. The most exquisite tortures served him for enjoyments. During his meals he caused criminals, and even innocent persons, to be stretched on the rack and beheaded: the most respectable persons were daily executed. In the madness of his arrogance he even considered himself a god, and caused the honors to be paid to him which were paid to Apollo, to Mars, and even to Jupiter. He also showed himself in public with the attributes of Venus and of other goddesses. He built a temple to his own divinity. At one time he wished that the whole Roman people had but one head, that he might be able to cut it off at one blow. He frequently repeated the words of an old poet, *Oderint dum metuant* — "let them hate so long as they fear." He squandered the public money with almost incredible prodigality. One of his greatest follies was the building of a bridge between Baiæ and Puteoli (Puzzuoli), in order that he might be able to boast of marching over the sea on dry land. He had it covered with earth, and houses built on it, and then rode over it in triumph. He gave a banquet in the middle of the bridge, and to celebrate this great achievement ordered numbers of the spectators whom he had invited, to be thrown into the sea. On his return, he entered Rome in triumph, because, as he said, he had conquered nature herself. After this, he made preparations for an expedition against the Germans, passed with more than 200,000 men over the Rhine, but returned after he had traveled a few miles, and that without having seen an enemy. Such was his terror, that, when he came to the river, and found the bridge obstructed by the crowd upon it, he caused himself to be passed over the heads of the soldiers. He then went to Gaul, which he plundered with unexampled rapacity. Not content with the considerable booty thus obtained, he sold all the property of both his sisters, Agrippina and Livilla, whom he banished. He also sold the furniture of the old court, the clothes of Marcus Antoninus, of Augustus, Agrippina, etc. Before he left Gaul, he declared his intention of going to Britain. He collected his army on the coast, embarked in a magnificent galley, but returned when he had hardly left the land, drew up his forces, ordered the signal for battle to be sounded, and commanded the soldiers to fill their pockets and helmets with shells, while he cried out, "This booty, ravished from the sea, is fit for my palace and the capitol!" When he returned to Rome, he was desirous of a triumph on account of his achievements, but contented himself with an ovation. Discontented with the senate, he resolved to destroy the greater part of the members, and the most distinguished men of Rome. This is proved by two books which were found after his death, wherein the names of the proscribed were noted down, and of which one was entitled *Gladius* (Sword), and the other *Pugillus* (Dagger). He became reconciled to the senate again when he found it worthy of him. Caligula's morals were, from his youth upward, corrupt. After he had married and repudiated several wives, Cæsonia retained a permanent hold on his affections. A number of conspirators, at the head of whom were Chærea and Cornelius Sabinus, both tribunes of the prætorian cohorts, murdered him in the 29th year of his age, and the fourth of his tyrannical reign, which thus lasted from 37 to 41 A.D.

Ca'liph (successor, successor and representative) is the name assumed by the successors of Mohammed in the government of the faithful and in the high-priesthood. Caliphate is therefore the name given by historians to the empire of these princes which the Arabs founded in Asia, and impelled by religious enthusiasm, enlarged, within a few centuries, to a dominion superior in extent to the Roman empire. The title is still borne by the Sultan of Turkey. Mohammed, in the character of the prophet of God, made himself the spiritual and temporal ruler of his people. In the following account the dates both of the Hegira and the Christian year are often given. The difference in the mode of computing the Mohammedan year has caused considerable divergencies among authorities in regard to the exact dates of the particular events of Mohammedan history.

After the death of the Prophet the election of a successor occasioned considerable excitement, Mohammed having left no son and nominated no successor. Abdallah Ebn Abu Koafas, called Abubekr, that is, father of the virgin (because his daughter Ayesha was the only one of the wives of Mohammed whom he had married as a virgin), obtained the victory over Ali, the cousin and son-in-law of Mohammed, and became the first caliph, 632 A.D. (year of the Hegira 11). Victorious over enemies at home by the aid of his general Khaled, "the Sword of God," he proceeded, as the Koran directs, to spread the doctrines of Mohammed by arms among the neighboring nations. With the watchword conversion or tribute, a numerous army, consisting entirely of volunteers inspired with zeal for the holy war, penetrated into Syria and Mesopotamia, but before much could be done, Abubekr died after he had filled the place of the Prophet two years and four months.

Omar, another father-in-law of the Prophet, now became second caliph, and under him the war was continued. The Moslems having once acquired a strong footing in Syria by the treacherous surrender of Bosra, they undertook, under Khaled, the siege of Damascus, and having repulsed two large armies, sent by the Emperor Heraclius to the relief of the city, they obtained possession of it by a capitulation (635 A. D.), the terms of which were perfidiously broken, Khaled pursuing and slaughtering the retreating Christians. By him and other generals, though not without a brave resistance on the part of the Greeks, the subjugation of Syria was completed (638 A.D., of the Hegira 17). Jerusalem having been compelled to surrender (636 A.D., Heg. 15), Omar proceeded thither in person to fix the terms of capitulation, which subsequently served as a model in settling the relations of the Moslems to the subject Christians. These terms were carefully observed by the conscientious caliph. The new Persian empire of the Sassanidæ was also overthrown, and Mesopotamia and other extensive regions overrun. Equally successful was the Mohammedan general, Amru, in Egypt, which was subjected to the caliphate in two years (641). Omar was the first who bore the appellation of Emir al Moumenin ("Prince of the Faithful")—a title inherited by all succeeding caliphs. Many of these conquests were over Christian populations who readily changed their creed and adapted themselves to the new rule.

After the murder of Omar by a revengeful slave (644 A.D., Heg. 23), a council, appointed by him on his death-bed, chose Osman, or Othman, son-in-law of the Prophet, passing over Ali. Under him the empire of the Arabs continued to expand. From Egypt the tide of conquest advanced westward along the northern coast of Africa, as far as Ceuta. Cyprus too (647 A.D.), and Rhodes (654 A.D.) were conquered; but the former was lost again two years after. An agitation against Othman now arose, partly owing to the fact that he favored and aggrandized his own family connections in every way, and intrusted the provinces, not to the most capable, but to his favorites. To many also the claims of Ali to the caliphate were deemed superior to those of Othman. The dissatisfaction thus excited occasioned a general insurrection in the year 656 (Heg. 34), which terminated in Othman's death.

Ali, the son-in-law of the Prophet by Fatima, became the fourth caliph, by the choice of the people of Medina, and is regarded as the first legitimate possessor of the dignity by a numerous sect of Mohammedans, which gives him and his son, Hassan, almost equal honor with the Prophet. This belief prevails among the Persians, and others who belong to the Shiite sect as opposed to the Sunnites or orthodox. Instead of being able to continue the conquests of his predecessors, Ali always had to contend with domestic enemies. Among these was Ayesha, the widow of the Prophet, called the mother of the faithful; also Tellah, Zobeir, and especially the powerful Moawiyah, governor of Syria, who all laid claim to the government. These were able to create suspicion, and spread the report that Ali had instigated the murder of Othman. In vain did he endeavor to repress the machinations of his enemies by intrusting the government of the provinces to his friends. Nowhere were the new governors received. The discontented collected an army, and made themselves masters of Bassora. Ali defeated it, and Tellah and Zobeir fell; but he could not prevent Moawiyah and his friend Amru from extending their party and maintaining themselves in Syria, Egypt, and even in a part of Arabia. Three men of the sect of the Kharejites proposed to restore concord among the faithful, by slaying each one of the three heads of the parties, Ali, Moawiyah, and Amru; but Ali only fell (661 A.D., Heg. 40). He was a man of a cultivated mind, and was the author of a collection of sentences or moral maxims, etc. His son, the mild, peaceful Hassan, had no desire to defend the caliphate against the indefatigable Moawiyah; a treaty was concluded between the two, by which Hassan solemnly abdicated the government (661). Some years later he perished by poison, said to have been administered by one of his wives at the instigation of Moawiyah.

Moawiyah I. transferred the seat of the caliphate from the city of the Prophet, Medina, where it had hitherto always been, to Damascus, in the province of which he had formerly been governor (673 A.D., Heg. 54). With him began the series of the caliphs called Ommiades (or Ommayads), which name this family bore from Moawiyah's progenitor, Ommiyah. Not long after his accession he was obliged to quell an insurrection of the Kharejites by a campaign, and a rebellion at Bassora by severe punishments. He then seriously meditated the entire subversion of the Byzantine empire (q.v.). Rhodes was attacked, and the famous colossus was broken in pieces. His son Jezid marched through Asia Minor, meeting but little resistance; then crossed the Hellespont and laid siege to Constantinople, but was obliged to raise it (669 A.D., Heg. 49). Other generals were more successful against the Turks in Khorasan, and the regions extending to the borders of India.

The next caliph, Jezid (or Yazid), was not altogether a worthy successor of his father, the politic Moawiyah (680 A.D., Heg. 60). At first he was not acknowledged by the two holy cities, Mecca and Medina, which, as long as the caliphs had resided in the latter city, had enjoyed a principal voice in their election, but which had not been consulted when Moawiyah, according to the custom of the caliphs, appointed his successor in his lifetime. The discontented espoused the cause, either of Houssain, the famous son of Ali, or of Abdallah, Zobeir's son, both of whom had laid claim to the caliphate. A rebellion of the inhabitants of Irak, in favor of Houssain, led by Moslim, Houssain's cousin, was suppressed by the prudence and decision of Obeidallah, governor of Cufa; and Houssain, who had accepted the invitation of the conspirators, was killed (680 A.D., Heg. 61), to the great grief and rage of all those who took part with Ali's family—a feeling still cherished by the Shiites. Abdallah

Ebn Zobeir was recognized as caliph in Medina, where Jezid was detested for his voluptuousness and scepticism. On this account Medina was invested, stormed, and sacked; and Mecca, in which Abdallah took shelter, was besieged, but during the siege Jezid died.

After Jezid's death (683 A.D., Heg. 64) his son, Moawiyah II., a weak but pious youth, became caliph, but after a reign of 40 days he died when he was meditating abdication. By this time Abdallah Ebn Zobeir had caused himself to be proclaimed as Prince of the True Believers, and he had a powerful following. For a period anarchy prevailed. Irak, Hejaz, Yemen, and Egypt acknowledged Abdallah Ebn Zobeir as caliph. In Syria, Dehac, regent to Abdallah, was at first chosen caliph; but the people of Damascus appointed Merwan I., of the race of the Ommiades, caliph, who made himself master of all Syria and Egypt. Khorasan separated from the caliphate, and submitted to a prince of its own choosing — the noble Salem. In the following year (684 A.D., Heg. 65) Soliman Ebn Sarad excited a great rebellion of the discontented in Syria and Arabia, and pronounced both caliphs deposed, but was defeated by the experienced soldier Obeidallah. Merwan (who died in 685) had been compelled to promise on oath to leave the caliphate to Khaled, the son of Jezid, yet he nominated his son Abdalmelek as his successor. Under him (685 A.D., Heg. 65) Mokthar, a new rebel against both caliphs, was subdued by one of them, Abdallah (686 A.D., Heg. 67); but this only made Abdallah more formidable to Abdalmelek, who, in order to be able to direct all his forces against him, concluded a peace with the Greek emperor, Justinian II., in which, reversing the order of the Koran, he conceded to the Christians a yearly tribute of 50,000 pieces of gold. He then marched against Abdallah, defeated him twice, and took Mecca by assault. In this last conflict Abdallah fell. Thus Abdalmelek united under his dominion all the Mussulmans; but the resistance of governors and wars with the Greeks kept him constantly occupied. He was the first caliph that caused money to be coined. He died 705 A.D. (Heg. 86). Under Walid I., his son, the Arabs conquered in the east Charasm and Turkestan (707 A.D., Heg. 88); in the north Galatia (710 A.D.); and in the west Spain (711 A.D.). (See SPAIN.) He died in 716 (Heg. 97). His brother and successor Soliman besieged Constantinople, but his fleet was destroyed by Greek fire, and his army suffered severely from famine. He died while on his way to take part in the siege in 717 (Heg. 99). Omar II., his successor by Soliman's last will, was equally unsuccessful in the conduct of the war. Having incurred the displeasure of the Ommiades by his indulgence toward the sect of Ali, he was poisoned by them (721 A.D., Heg. 102). Jezid II., his successor also by the disposition of Soliman, died of grief for the loss of a female favorite, of whose death he was the author (723 A.D., Heg. 104). His successor was Hisham, who reigned till 743. He had to suppress several revolts, the chief being that of Zaid (739-40). About this time the Abbassides, descendants of Abbas, son of Abdalmotaleb, uncle of the Prophet, began to be formidable. Under Hisham an end was put to the progress of the Saracens in the west by the energy of Charles Martel, who annihilated their armies at Tours in 732, and at Narbonne in 736. Walid II. was murdered after a reign of one year (744 A.D., Heg. 124).

After the still briefer reigns of Jezid III. and of his brother Ibrahim, Merwan II. followed, with the surname (respectable among the Arabs) of the Ass (Al Hemar). Ibrahim, the Abbasside leader, being imprisoned and put to death by this prince, his brother, Abul Abbas, took up the cause of the Abbassides and assumed the title of caliph. In the resulting war Merwan was twice defeated, and fell (750 A.D., Heg. 133). With him terminates the series of caliphs of the race of Ommiyah. The furious Abdallah, uncle of Ibrahim and Abul Abbas, treacherously destroyed almost all the Ommiades by a horrible massacre at a meeting to which they had been inveigled. One of the family, Abderrahman, grandson of Hisham, having taken refuge in Spain, escaped the massacre and founded the independent caliphate of Cordova. See SPAIN.

Abul Abbas, first of the Abbasside caliphs, died young in 754 A.D. (Heg. 136). His brother, Abu Giafar, called Al Mansur ("the Victorious"), was obliged to contend with a rival in his uncle, Abdallah, whom he, however, overcame. He acquired his surname by his victories in Armenia, Cilicia, and Cappadocia. Spain was lost by him, however, as well as Africa. In the year 764 he founded the city of Bagdad on the Tigris, and transferred thither the seat of the caliphate (768 A.D., Heg. 149). He died on a pilgrimage to Mecca, leaving immense treasures (775 A.D., Heg. 158). Mohammed Mahdi, his son and successor, a man of a noble character, had to contend with the turbulent inhabitants of Khorasan under the pretended prophet, Hakem, and died 785 A.D.; and Musa or Hadi, his grandson, met with the same opposition from the Ali party under Houssain. Hadi's mother was a strong-minded, ambitious woman, who wished to rule her son, and with him the state, and this led him to try to poison her. She, however, caused him to be smothered before he could effect his purpose.

Hadi was followed, not by his son, but by his brother Harun (786 A.D.), who was denominated Al Rashid ("The Upright") on account of his justice, and is famous for promoting the arts and sciences. He concluded a truce (an actual peace could never be made with Christians) with the Greek empress, Irene (788 A.D.), who consented to pay him tribute. Yahya, a member of the house of Ali, disputed with him the possession of the throne, but subsequently submitted. Harun, however, tarnished his reputation by the murder of Yahya, and still more by the murder of his sister, and her favorite the Barmecide Giafar, and by the expulsion and persecution of the whole family of the Barmecides, whose services to the state and himself had been of very great value. Harun divided the empire among his three sons. Al Amin, as sole caliph, was to reign over Irak, Arabia, Syria, Egypt, and the rest of Africa: under him Al Mamun was to govern Persia; Turkestan, Khorasan, and the whole East; and Motassem was to rule Asia Minor, Armenia, and all the countries on the Black Sea. The younger brothers were to succeed Amin in the caliphate. At Thus, in Khorasan, through which Harun was passing, in order to quell a rebellion that had broken out in Samarcand, he was arrested by death, of which he had been forewarned by extraordinary dreams (809 A.D., Heg. 190).

Al Amin the faithful (his proper name was Mohammed) was undeserving of this name. Untrue to his obligations as a ruler, and addicted to all kinds of sensuality, he left the discharge of his duties to his vizier Fadhel. The vizier, from hatred of Mamun, persuaded the caliph to appoint his son his successor, and deprive Motassem of his portion of territory. A war arose between the brothers. Mamun's general, Thaher, defeated the armies of the caliph, took Bagdad, and caused Amin to be put to death (813 A.D., Heg. 194).

Mamun was recognized as caliph. Nobler in his inclinations than Amin, he cherished the arts and sciences; but, like his brother, he left the government and armies to his ministers. His measures to secure the caliphate to the Alides in order to please Riza, his favorite, excited the powerful Abbassides to an insurrection. They declared Mamun to have forfeited the throne, and proclaimed Ibrahim caliph, but submitted again, after the death of Riza, when the caliph had changed his sentiments. The vast empire of the Arabs, embracing numberless provinces in two quarters of the globe, could hardly be held under his sceptre. There is but one step, and that an easy one, under a weak sovereign, from a viceroyalty to a kingdom. The wisdom of the former Abbassides could only retard this evil; the faults of the latter precipitated it. Even under Harun Al Raschid the Agladides had founded an independent empire in Tunis (800 A.D., Heg. 181), as had likewise the Edrisides in Fez. Thaher, having been appointed governor of Khorasan, made himself independent. From him the Thaherides derived their origin. Mamun sent Thomas, a Greek exile, with an army against the Greek emperor, Michael II. the Stammerer. Thomas depopulated Asia Minor, and laid siege to Constantinople; but a storm destroyed his fleet (823 A.D., Heg. 207). A second attack on the imperial city was repelled by the aid of the Bulgarians. Thomas was taken prisoner, and executed. Toward the many religious sects into which the Mussulmans were then divided Mamun acted with toleration. He died 833 A.D. (Heg. 218). During his government (about 830 A.D., Heg. 215), the African Arabs conquered Sicily and Sardinia, where they maintained themselves about 200 years, till the latter island was torn from them by the Pisans in 1016-17, and the former island by the Normans between 1061 and 1090.

Motassem, at first named Billah (by the grace of God), Harun's third son, built a new city, Samara, 56 miles from Bagdad, and transferred thither his residence. In his wars against the Greeks and rebellious Persians he first used Turkish soldiers. From grief at the death of his private physician, Motassem became insane, and died 842 A.D. (Heg. 227).

Vatheb Billah, his son, member of the Motazelite sect, exerted himself to promote the advancement of science; but he was an enervated voluptuary, and died of nervous weakness (846 A.D., Heg. 232). A contest for the succession, between his brother Motawackel and his son Mothadi, was decided by the already powerful and arrogant Turkish bodyguard in favor of the former, the more unworthy competitor.

Under Motawackel it became more and more customary to carry on all wars by means of Turkish mercenaries. Thus the Arabs were rendered unwarlike and effeminate, as must necessarily be the case in a hot climate with those who do not live in constant activity. Motawackel manifested a blind hatred of the Alides, who were sparing even the memory of the deceased. He moreover evinced a malignant spirit, and a proneness to sensuality and cruelty. His own son, Montasser, trained to early indulgence in both these vices, and often barbarously treated by him, conspired against him with the Turkish bodyguards, and effected his murder (861 A.D., Heg. 247).

The Turks, who now arrogated the right of electing the caliphs, called the murderer to the throne of the faithful, and compelled his brothers, who were innocent of the atrocious act, and whose revenge they feared, to renounce the succession which had been designed for them by Motawackel. Montasser died soon after of a fever, caused by the goadings of remorse (862 A.D., Heg. 248). The Turks then elected Mostain Billah, a grandson of the caliph Motassem. Two of the Alides became competitors with him for the caliphate. One of them, at Cufa, was defeated and put to death; but the other founded an independent empire in Tabristan, which subsisted half a century. The discord of the Turkish soldiers completed the dismemberment of the empire. One party raised to the throne Motaz, second son of Motawackel, and compelled Mostain to abdicate. Motaz Billah soon found means to get rid of him as well as of his own brother Muwiad. He then meditated the removal of the Turkish soldiers; but before he found courage to execute his projects they rebelled on account of their pay being in arrear, and forced him to resign the government. He soon after died (869 A.D., Heg. 255). They conferred the caliphate on Mohadi Billah, son of the caliph Vathek, but deposed this excellent prince 11 months after, because he attempted to improve their military discipline.

Under Motawackel's third son, the sensual Motamed Billah, whom they next called to the caliphate, Muaffek his brother succeeded, by his prudence and courage, in overcoming the dangerous preponderance of these Turks. Motamed transferred the seat of the caliphate from Samara back to Bagdad in the year 873 (Heg. 259), where it afterward continued. In the same year, owing to a revolution in the independent government of Khorasan, the dynasty of the Thaherides gave place to that of the Soffarides, who eventually extended their dominion over Tabristan and Segestan. The governor of Egypt and Syria, Achmet Ben Tulun, also made himself independent (877 A.D., Heg. 263), from whom are descended the Tulunides. The brave Muaffek annihilated, indeed, the empire of the Zinghians, in Cufa and Bassora, 10 years after its formation (881 A.D., Heg. 268); but he was unable to save the caliphate from the ruin to which it was continually hastening.

Motamed died soon after him (892 A.D., Heg. 279), and was succeeded by Muaffek's son, Mothadad Billah. He contended unsuccessfully with a new sect that had arisen in Irak — the Carmathians (899 A.D., Heg. 286) — against whom his son, Moktaphi Billah (902 A.D., Heg. 289), was more fortunate. He was still more successful in a war against the Tulunides, as he again reduced Egypt and Syria in 905 (Heg. 292). Under his brother, Moktadar Billah, who succeeded him at the age of 13 years (909 A.D., Heg. 296), rebellions and bloody quarrels about the sovereignty disturbed the government of the empire. He was several times deposed and reinstated, and finally murdered (931 A.D., Heg. 319). During his reign Abu Mohammed Obeidallah rose in Africa, who, pretending to be descended from Fatima, daughter of the Prophet (therefore from Ali), overthrew the dynasty of the Aglades in Tunis, and founded that of the Fatimites (910 A.D., Heg. 298). Not satisfied with reigning independent of the caliph, this party, as descendants of the Prophet, asserted themselves to be the only lawful caliphs.

Shortly afterward the dynasty of the Bouides, in Persia, rose to authority and power (925 A.D., Heg. 315). Khorasan was still independent. The only change was that the Samanides had taken the place of the Soffarides. In a part of Arabia the heretic Carmathians ruled; in Mesopotamia, the Hamadamites. In Egypt, which had just been recovered, Akschid, from a governor, was called to be a sovereign. From him descended the Akschidites. Kaher Billah, Mothadad's third son, merited his fate, on account of his malice and cruelty. The Turkish soldiers having recovered their power drove him from the throne into exile (934 A.D., Heg. 322), in which he perished five years afterward. Rhadi Billah, his brother, bore the dignity of an emir al omra ("captain of the captains"), with which the exercise of absolute power, in the name of the caliph, was united; and thus the caliph was more and more thrown into the back-ground. The first who was invested with this dignity was Raik; but it was soon torn from him by the Turk Jakan, by force of arms, in the year 939 (Heg. 327). Jakan extended the power of the office to such a degree as to leave the caliph nothing, but the name of his temporal sway, and even assumed the right of determining the succession to the throne. Raik was indemnified by receiving Cufa, Bassora, and Irak Arabi as an independent government.

The next caliph, Motaki Billah, Moktader's son, made an effort to regain his independence by the murder of Jakun; but he was soon compelled by the Turkish soldiers to appoint Tozun, another of their countrymen, emir, who made this office hereditary. He formally devised it to a certain Schirzad, but it soon came into the possession of the Persian royal house of the Bouides, whose aid the succeeding caliph, Mostaki Billah, solicited against the tyranny of Schirzad. The first Bouide emir, Moezeddulat, left it as an inheritance to his posterity. Not the caliph but the emir now reigned in Bagdad, though over only a small territory. In every remote province there were independent princes.

To continue the catalogue of the names of those who were henceforward caliphs would be superfluous, for these Mussulman popes had not by any means the power of the Christian. It would be too tedious to trace the branches into which the history of the caliphate is now divided; but we must briefly show the great changes which the different states and their dynasties have undergone, and which gave rise to the dominion of the Ottoman Porte.

During the minority of the Akschidite Ali, the Fatimite Morz Ledinillah, at that time caliph in Tunis, subjugated Egypt in 969 (Heg. 358),

and founded Cairo, which he made the seat of his caliphate. There were, consequently, at this time three caliphs,— at Bagdad, Cairo, and Cordova,— each of which declared the others heretics. But the Fatimites as well as the Abbassides fell under the power of their viziers, and, like them, the Ommiades in Cordova were deprived of all power by the division of Spain into many small sovereignties, till they were entirely subverted by the Morabethun.

Ilkan, king of Turkestan, having conquered Khorasan, and overthrown the Samanides, was expelled again by Mahmud, prince of Gazna, who founded there the dominion of the Gaznevides, in 998 (Heg. 388), who were soon, however, overthrown in turn by the Seljuk Turks under Togrul Beg, in 1030 (Heg. 421). This leader conquered also Charasm, Georgia, and the Persian Irak. Called to the assistance of the Caliph Kajem Bemeillah, at Bagdad, against the tyranny of the Bouide emirs, he proceeded to Bagdad, and became emir himself in 1055 (Heg. 448), by which means the dominion of the Turks was firmly established over all the Mussulmans. To his nephew, Alp Arslan (who defeated and took prisoner the Greek emperor Romanus Diogenes), he left this dignity, with so great power that these Turkish emirs al omra were frequently called the sultans of Bagdad. Turkish princes, who aspired to be sovereigns in the other provinces, were at first satisfied with the title of atabek (father, teacher), such as the atabeks of Irak and Syria, of Azerbijan, Farsistan (Persia), and Laristan. It was the atabeks of Syria and Irak with whom the Crusaders had principally to contend. The first was called Omadeddin Zenghi; by the Franks, Sanguin. They were afterward termed sultans. The Caliph of Bagdad was recognized by all as the spiritual sovereign of all Mussulmans; his temporal authority did not extend beyond the walls of Bagdad. Noureddin, Zenghi's son, being requested by the Fatimite caliph Adhed to protect Bagdad against his vizier, sent to Cairo, in succession, Shirkuh and Salaheddin or Saladin; but the latter overthrew the Fatimites (as schismatic anti-popes), and usurped the authority of Sultan of Egypt in 1170 (Heg. 556), with which he united Syria, after Noureddin's death. This is the great Salaheddin (Saladin), the formidable enemy of the Christians, the conqueror of Jerusalem. The dynasty which commenced with him was called, from his father, Ayoub, the Ayoubites. They reigned over Egypt till expelled by the Mamelukes in 1250. The Seljuk sultans of Irak were overthrown in 1194 (Heg. 590) by the Charasmians; and as those of Khorasan were extinct, there remained of the Seljuk dominions nothing but the empire of Iconium or Roum, in Asia Minor, from which the present Turkish empire derives its origin. See OTTOMAN EMPIRE.

The Charasmian sultans extended their conquests far into Asia, until their territories were invaded by the Tartars under Genghis Khan, in 1220 (Heg. 617). They were finally totally destroyed by his son Octai. Bagdad, also, the remains of the possessions of the caliphs, became the easy prey of a Mongol horde under Holagu, in 1258 (Heg. 636), by the treachery of the vizier Al Kami, and a slave, Amram, under the 56th caliph Motazem. The nephew of the cruelly murdered Motazem fled to Egypt, where he continued to be called caliph under the protection of the Mamelukes, and bequeathed the Mohammedan popedom to his posterity. When the Turks conquered Egypt, in 1517, the last of these nominal caliphs was carried to Constantinople and died, after returning to Egypt in 1538. The Turkish sultans subsequently assumed the title of caliph, and have retained it to the present day, with the claim of spiritual supremacy over all Mussulmans, though this claim is little regarded out of his own dominions, and strongly disputed by the Persians.

Calip'pus, a Greek astronomer, who was the first to discover the inaccuracy of the golden number or period invented by Meton, and attempted to remedy it by the invention of a new cycle of 76 years, being only six hours less than the quadruple of Meton's period. It commenced 331 B.C., and being adopted particularly by astronomers in giving the date of their observations, is frequently mentioned by Ptolemy. Though more perfect than Meton's period, it was shown to be inaccurate by Hipparchus, who substituted for it a cycle of 345 years.

Calisa'ya Bark, the yellowish bark of *Cinchona Calisaya* (q.v.).

Calisthen'ics, or **Callisthenics,** the art of promoting gracefulness, strength, and health by means of the lighter forms of gymnastic exercise. See GYMNASTICS.

Cal'iver, an early form of hand-gun, musket, or arquebuse, lighter and shorter than the original musket, fired without a rest and much more rapidly. It seems to have gone out of fashion about 1630.

Calixtines, kạ-lĭks'tĭnz, or **Utraquists,** a sect of the Hussites in Bohemia, who differed from the Roman Catholics principally in giving the cup in the Lord's Supper to laymen, from which circumstance they got their name, derived from the Latin *calix*, "a cup." For their tenets see HUSS, JOHN.

Calix'tus, the name of several popes. 1. The first was a Roman bishop from 217 to 224, when he suffered martyrdom. 2. GUIDO, son of Count William of Burgundy, archbishop of Vienne, and papal legate in France, was elected in 1119, in the monastery of Clugny, successor of the expelled Pope, Gelasius II., who had been driven from Italy by the Emperor Henry V., and had died in this monastery. In the same year he held councils at Toulouse and at Rheims, the latter of which was intended to settle the protracted dispute respecting the right of investiture. As the Emperor Henry V. would not confirm an agreement which he had already made on this subject, Calixtus repeated anew the excommunication which he had already pronounced against him when legate in 1112. He excommunicated also the anti-pope, Gregory VIII., and renewed former decrees respecting simony, lay investiture, and the marriage of priests. Successful in his contest with the emperor on the subject of investiture by means of his alliance with the rebels in Germany, in particular with the Saxons, he made his entrance into Italy in 1120, and with great pomp into Rome itself; took Gregory VIII. prisoner in 1121, and banished him to a monastery. He availed himself of the troubles of the emperor to force him, in 1122, to agree to the Concordat of Worms. After an energetic pontificate he died in 1124. 3. CALIXTUS III., chosen in 1168

Vol. 3—29.

in Rome as anti-pope to Paschal III., and confirmed by the Emperor Frederick I. in 1178, was obliged to submit to Pope Alexander III. As he was not counted among the legal popes, a subsequent Pope was called Calixtus III. This was a Spanish nobleman, Alfonso Borgia, counselor of Alfonso, king of Aragon and the Sicilies. He was made Pope in 1455. He was at this time far advanced in life, but equaled in policy and energy the most enterprising rulers of the Church. He appointed an ecclesiastical commission to reconsider the case against Jeanne d'Arc, and its decision was that she died a martyr to her faith, her king, and her country. In order to appease the displeasure of the princes and nations occasioned by the proceedings of the councils of Constance and Basel, he instigated them to a crusade against the Turks. His intention was counteracted in Germany by the discontent of the states of the empire with the Concordat of Vienna, and in France by the appeals of the universities of Paris and Toulouse against the tithe for the Turkish war. King Alfonso, moreover, was indignant at the refusal of the Pope to acknowledge his natural son Ferdinand as king of Naples.

Calixtus (properly CALLISEN) **Georg, gä'-õrg,** German clergyman, the most able and enlightened theologian of the Lutheran Church in the 17th century: b. Medelbye, Schleswig, 14 Dec. 1586; d. 19 March 1656. In 1609 he visited the universities of the south of Germany; in 1612 those of Holland, Britain, and France, where his intercourse with the different religious parties and the greatest scholars of his time developed that independence and liberality of opinion for which he was distinguished. In 1614 he was made professor of theology at Helmstedt, and he held this post till his death. His treatises on the authority of the Holy Scriptures, transubstantiation, celibacy, supremacy of the Pope, and the Lord's Supper belong, even according to the judgment of learned Roman Catholics, to the most profound and acute writings against Roman Catholicism. But his genius and the depths of his exegetic and historical knowledge exposed him to the persecutions of the zealots of his time. His assertion that the points of difference between Calvinists and Lutherans were of less importance than the doctrines in which they were agreed, and that the doctrine of the Trinity was less distinctly expressed in the Old Testament than in the New, and his recommendation of good works, drew upon him the reproach of heresy. He made Christian morality a distinct branch of science, and, by reviving the study of the Christian fathers and of the history of the Church, prepared the way for Spener, Thomasius, and Semler.

Calking, kôk'ĭng, the process of driving tarred oakum into the seams between the planks of ships, in order to render the joints watertight. A wisp of the oakum is drawn out and rolled together between the hands, and, being laid over the seam, is driven by a wedge-shaped instrument called a calking iron. The work is afterward gone over with a more powerful instrument of the same kind, which is held by one man and struck with a beetle held by another. When all the oakum is forced in that is practicable, the seams are payed over with melted pitch, and where they are to be covered with copper, a thread of spunyarn is laid in to make them flush with the planks.

Calkins, kô-kĭns, **Franklin Welles**, American writer: b. Iowa County, Wisconsin, 5 June 1855. He has traveled extensively in the Rocky Mountains, 1870–86; and is the author of 'Frontier Sketches' (1893); 'Indian Tales' (1893); 'Hunting Stores' (1893); 'The Cougar Tamer' (1899).

Calkins, Gary Nathan, American scientist: b. Valparaiso, Ind., 18 Jan. 1869. He was graduated at the Massachusetts Institute of Technology in 1890; had charge of scientific expeditions to Alaska in 1896 and 1897; and in 1900 was instructor in Zoology at Columbia University.

Call, Wilkinson, American senator: b. Russellville, Ky., 9 Jan. 1834. He went to Florida as a boy, adopted the legal profession; served as adjutant-general in the Confederate army, and was presidential elector for the State-at-large in 1872 and 1876, and the same year was a delegate to the Democratic National Convention. He was chosen senator by the Florida legislature under the provisional government established by President Johnson, but was denied admission. In 1879 he was elected senator and took his seat on 18 March. He was re-elected in 1885 and 1891, serving until 3 March 1897.

Cal'la, a genus of plants of the natural order *Araceæ*, consisting of herbaceous marsh plants with creeping or floating stems, cordate leaves, and spadices of small flowers enveloped in large leafy spathes. The flowers are succeeded by red berries. *C. palustris* occurs in cold bogs, from New Jersey to Nova Scotia, and west to Michigan in America, and in the north of Europe. It has a creeping root-stock extremely acrid in taste, but which, when deprived of its acridity by maceration and boiling, is made by the Laplanders into bread. The Trumpet Lily, or Lily of the Nile (*Richardia æthiopica*), is sometimes referred to this genus.

Cal'lahan, James Morton, American publicist: b. Bedford, Ind., 4 Nov. 1864. He was graduated at the University of Indiana in 1894, lecturer on American diplomatic history at Johns Hopkins University 1898–1902, and since 1902 professor of history and political science, West Virginia University. He has written 'Neutrality of the American Lakes' (1898); 'Cuba and International Relations' (1899) ; 'American Relations in the Pacific and the Far East' (1901); 'The American Expansion Policy.'

Callao, käl yä'ō or käl lä'ō, Peru, the port of Lima, and the starting point of the Callao, L. & Oroya R.R. It is situated in lat. 12° 4' S., lon. 77° 8' W. The railway connects the seaboard with a point near the head of navigation on the Amazon River, and the line of the inter-continental railway, according to surveys tentatively approved in 1902, will pass through Oroya. Thus Callao, as a crossroads port, is favorably situated for sharing in the future commercial development of South America, though it has not a very good harbor. After the defeat of the combined forces of Peru and Bolivia by Chile in 1880, Callao was bombarded by a Chilean fleet. (See CHILE.) In 1867 it had a similar experience at the hands of Spain. For early history see PERU. On 28 Oct. 1746, a great wave destroyed the town, the frigate San Firmin was carried far inland, 19 vessels were stranded, and 4,600 people killed (see LIMA). The famous castle of Callao, planned by the French mathematician Godin, was the last point on the Pacific coast to be surrendered by the Spaniards. Pop. (including province, of which area is 14 square miles) 48,118.

Callaway, Morgan, American educator: b. Cuthbert, Ga., 3 Nov. 1862. He was educated at Emory College, Ga., and at Johns Hopkins University, and has been professor of English in the University of Texas from 1890. He has published 'The Absolute Participle in Anglo-Saxon' (1889); 'The Appositive Participle in Anglo-Saxon' (1901).

Callaway, Samuel Roger, American railroad president: b. Toronto, Canada, 24 Dec. 1850; d. New York, 1 June 1904. At the age of 14 he entered the employ of the Grand T. Ry., and later was in the service of the Canadian Express Company, and Great W. Ry. His rapid progress thereafter may be summarized as follows: in 1875 he became superintendent of the Detroit & M. R.R.; in 1880, manager of the Chicago & G. T.; in 1884, vice-president of the Union P. and allied lines of nearly 6,000 miles; president of the Toledo, St. L. & K. C. R.R., 1887–95; president of the Lake Shore & M. S., 1897–8; president of the New York C. & H. R. R.R., 1898–1901. He was regarded as one of the ablest railway managers in the United States. From 1901 he was president of the American Locomotive Company.

Callcott, kôl'kŏt, SIR **Augustus Wall,** English painter: b. Kensington, 20 Feb. 1779; d. there, 25 Nov. 1844. He studied portrait-painting under Hoppner, but soon discovered that his genius lay in another department of art, and was so successful in his delineation of landscape, that in 1807 he was elected an associate of the Royal Academy. In 1837 he was knighted, and in 1843 was appointed keeper of the royal collections of pictures. He suffered much from ill health for many years before his death. Callcott excelled in the delineation of coast scenes, and like Turner, has been called the "Modern Claude."

Callcott, John Wall, English composer, brother of Augustus Wall (q.v.) : b. Kensington, 20 Nov. 1766; d. near Bristol, 15 May 1821. He at first intended to become a surgeon, but abandoned the intention, and devoted himself to music. In 1785 he competed for the prizes of the Catch Club, and gained three out of four gold medals. In the following decade the same club awarded him 20 medals. In 1790, when Haydn arrived in England, he studied under him, and the same year obtained from Oxford the degree of musical doctor. In 1805 he published his 'Musical Grammar'; and in 1806 was preparing to deliver lectures on music at the Royal Institution when his mind gave way. He never completely recovered, although his insanity left him on one occasion for three years. He ranks among the most eminent of English composers.

Called Back, a sensational tale by "Hugh Conway" (FREDERICK JOHN FARGUS), published in 1883. Extremely sensational in character, and with little literary merit, the graphic force of this story, the rapidity of its movement, its directness, and its skilful suspension of interest, gave it for a season so extraordinary a vogue that it outsold every other work of fiction of its year.

Calleja del Rey, käl-yä'ha dĕl rä, **Felix Maria,** Spanish general: b. Medina del Campo, 1750; d. Cadiz, 1820. He distinguished himself in Mexico by quelling the insurrection instigated in 1810 by Hidalgo, who was on the point of seizing the city of Mexico, when Calleja was charged by the viceroy Venegas to oppose his progress. After encounters, in which both parties strove to surpass each other in a display of cruelty and brutality, Calleja succeeded in defeating Hidalgo's army, and on 2 Jan. 1812, he took possession of the principal fortress Zitaquaro, and massacred the inhabitants. Hidalgo, who fell near Guadalajara, was succeeded by the priest, Morelos, who defended Cuautla Amilpas against the attack of Calleja with great bravery until 2 May 1812, when famine forced him to surrender. Calleja again signalized his victory by acts of barbarism, and was rewarded for his zeal, 4 March 1813, by the appointment of viceroy, in which capacity he continued to alienate the feelings of the Mexicans by his relentless rigor. The priest, Morelos, fell into his hands and was shot, 22 Dec. 1815. Subsequently he promulgated an amnesty, but as he was unable to restore peace to the distracted country, he was recalled. On his return to Spain he was created Conde de Calderon, and in January 1820, while preparing to sail from Cadiz against the revolutionists of Paraguay, his troops having mutinied, he was captured and remained prisoner in the fortress of the Isla de Leon until the insurrection was quelled by Ferdinand VII., when he died, soon after having recovered his liberty.

Cal'lender, James Thomas, American publicist: b. England; d. 1803. He was exiled for his pamphlet 'The Political Progress of Great Britain.' He wrote: 'Sketches of the History of America'; 'The Prospect Before Us.'

Callender, John, American historian: b. Boston, Mass., 1706; d. Newport, R. I., 26 Jan. 1748. He collected many valuable papers relating to the Baptists in America; and published 'A Centennial Discourse on the Civil and Religious Affairs of the Colony of Rhode Island' (1739), which was the only history of that State for more than a century. The State Historical Society reprinted it, with notes by Rev. Romeo Elton (1838), and a memoir of the author.

Cal'lernish, Scotland, a village and district in the island of Lewis, on Loch Roag, 16 miles west of Stornoway, famous for its circles of standing-stones. The main circle is 40 feet in diameter, formed of 12 unhewn blocks of gneiss from 10 to 13 feet high, with a larger block in the centre. From this circle rows of stones project to the east, west, and south. There are upward of 40 blocks altogether.

Callet, Antoine François, än twän frän swä ka-lō, French historical painter: b. Paris, 1741; d. 1823. He obtained his earliest prize in 1764 for a painting entitled 'Biton and Cleobis' and became a member of the Academy in 1780. He painted portraits of Louis XVI., Louis XVIII. and the Comte d'Artois, and several other works now in the Louvre.

Callet, Jean François, zhŏṅ frän-swä, French mathematician: b. Versailles, 1744; d. 1798. He completed his studies at Paris in 1768, and in 1779 gained the prize which the Academy of Arts at Geneva had proposed for escapements in watches. In 1788 he was appointed professor of hydrography at Vannes, and shortly after obtained the same appointment at Dunkirk. He was afterward professor of the geographical engineers at the Depôt de la Guerre, Paris. He is best known by his 'Tables of Logarithms.'

Calilchthys, käl-ĭk'thĭs, a genus of fishes belonging to the abdominal malacopterygians, and family *Siluridæ* or sheat-fishes. They are natives of hot climates, and are said to make their way over land in search of water during dry seasons.

Callic'rates, Greek architect of the 5th century B.C. He was a contemporary of Ictinus and with him erected the Parthenon at Athens.

Callicrat'idas, a Spartan, succeeded Lysander in the command of the Lacedæmonian fleet against the Athenians, in 406 B.C. He defeated Conon at Mitylene, and was afterward himself defeated by the Athenians at Arginusæ, where he was drowned.

Calligo'num, a genus of shrubs belonging to the *Polygonaceæ.* They are leafless plants, with small flowers, branches jointed, dichotomous, and the fruit a large, four-cornered nut. The root of *C. Pallasia,* a leafless shrub found in the sandy steppes of Siberia, furnishes from its roots, when pounded and boiled, a gummy, nutritious substance like tragacanth, on which the Calmucks feed in times of scarcity, at the same time chewing the acid branches and fruit to allay their thirst.

Callimachus, Greek poet and grammarian: b. Cyrene, about 310 B.C.; d. about 240. He opened in Alexandria a school of grammar, that is, of the belles-lettres and liberal sciences, and could boast of several scholars of distinguished attainments, such as Eratosthenes, Apollonius Rhodius, Aristophanes of Byzantium, and others. Ptolemy Philadelphus presented him with a place in the museum, and gave him a salary, as he did other men of learning. After the death of Philadelphus, he stood in equal favor with Ptolemy Euergetes. Under these circumstances he wrote most of his works, the number of which was very considerable. With the exception of some fragments, we have of these only 64 epigrams and 6 hymns. His poem on Berenice has been preserved in the Latin adaptation of Catullus ('De coma Berenices'). Callimachus' poems bear the stamp of their age, which sought to supply the want of natural genius by a great ostentation of learning. Instead of noble simple grandeur, they exhibit an overcharged style, a false pathos, and a straining after the singular, the antiquated, the learned. His elegies are mentioned by the ancients with great praise. and served Propertius as models. The best edition of the hymns and epigrams is that of Meineke (Berlin 1861).

Callim'achus, Greek artist, supposed to have lived about the end of the 5th century. His work is celebrated by some of the ancient writers, and he is said to have been the inventor of the Corinthian capital.

Callinger, kăl-lĭn-jär', or **Kalinjar,** India, a hill fort in the northwest provinces, division of Allahabad, and district of Banda, 90 miles southwest of the town of Allahabad. The summit of the hill on which it stands is about 1,200 feet above the plains below. At the southeastern base of the hill is a decaying village, which was formerly a place of considerable importance and the capital of a rajahship. The whole summit of the hill, comprehending a plain five miles in circuit, is encompassed by an immense rampart of Mohammedan construction. It was surrendered to the British in 1812. There are a number of interesting caves, tombs, temples, and statues here.

Calli'nus of Ephesus, the earliest Greek elegiac poet, flourished probably about 700 B.C. Only one elegy and a few fragments are extant; these have been edited by several scholars, among them Bergk, in the 'Poetæ Lyrici Græci.'

Callion'ymus, a genus of fishes (the dragonets) belonging to the family *Gobüdæ*. They are distinguished by having the eyes very near together, teeth on the jawbone but none on the roof of the mouth, six gill-rays, and the first dorsal fin long, usually much elevated and, in many species, brightly colored.

Calliope, kăl lī'ō pē. 1. In Greek mythology, one of the Muses (q.v.). She presided over eloquence and epic poetry. She is said to have been the mother of Orpheus by Apollo. She was represented with an epic poem in one hand and a trumpet in the other, and generally crowned with laurel.

2. An asteroid (No. 22). It was discovered by Hind, on 16 Nov. 1852.

3. A musical instrument, consisting of a series of steam whistles, pitched to produce the notes of the scale, and grouped together and operated by a keyboard.

Calli'ope Humming-bird. See HUMMING-BIRD.

Cal'lisen, Henry, Danish physician and surgeon: b. Pentz, Holstein, 1740; d. Copenhagen, 5 Feb. 1824. He educated himself by his own exertions, and was made, in 1771, chief surgeon in the Danish fleet, and in 1773 professor of surgery at the University of Copenhagen. He wrote in 1777 his 'Institut. Chirurgiæ Hodiernæ,' which was received with applause by all Europe.

Callisthenes, Greek historian: b. Olynthus, about 365 B.C.; d. 328. He was a nephew and pupil of Aristotle, and was appointed to attend Alexander the Great in his expedition against Persia. His republican sentiments rendered him unfit for a courtier, but his unpardonable crime was his opposition to the assumption of divine honors by the conqueror. On a charge of treason, he was put to death, by what method historians are not agreed. Of several historical works written by him only fragments remain.

Cal'listhenics. See GYMNASTICS.

Callis'to, in Greek mythology, a nymph of Artemis, daughter of Lycaon, king of Arcadia. According to the most prevalent story of this maiden, Zeus loved her, and her son Arcas was hid in the woods, and preserved, while she was changed by the jealousy of Hera into a bear. Zeus placed her, with her son, among the stars, as the constellation of the Great Bear.

Callistratus, kăl-lĭs'trạ-tŭs, Athenian orator: b. about 400 B.C.; d. 361. His eloquence is said to have fired the imagination of the youthful Demosthenes. For his Spartan sympathies he was condemned to death by the Athenians, and on his return from exile in Macedonia was actually executed.

Callot, Jacques, French engraver: b. Nancy, 1592; d. there 1635. He overcame many obstacles in his study of art, twice running away from his parents. He went to Italy, learned drawing in Rome, soon gave himself up entirely to his love for engraving, and became famous for his etchings. In the space of 20 years he designed and executed about 1,600 pieces, most of them, except sacred subjects, representations of battles, sieges, dances, festive processions, etc. The 'Misères et Malheurs de la Guerre,' in 18 pieces, may be mentioned as a remarkable series. He executed works of this kind for Cosmo II. of Florence, Louis XIII. of France, and the Duke of Lorraine. His 'Fair' and his 'Beggars' are called his best pieces. He was the first who used in his etchings the hard varnish — the *vernice grosso dei lignaiuoli* of the Italians. He was distinguished for his piety, magnanimity, and regularity of life.

Cal'low, William, English water color artist: b. Greenwich, 28 July 1812. He studied in Paris and was for seven years professor of water color painting to the family of Louis Philippe. He has received many medals and is the senior member of the Royal Society of Painters in Water Colors. He still continues to exhibit and is the author of 'Illustrated Book of Versailles'; 'Work Illustrative of Deep Sea Fishing,' etc.

Calluna. See HEATH.

Callus, an abnormal hard growth, either carneous or osseous. The new growth of bony substance between the extremities of fractured bones, by which they are united, is an instance of the latter. External friction or pressure produces the former, as in the hands of laborers and the feet of persons who wear ill-fitting shoes. See CORN.

Calmar, kăl'mär. See KALMAR.

Calmet, Augustin, ô-güst-ăṅ kạl-mā, French exegetical and historical author: b. Mesnil-la-Horgne, near Toul, France, 26 Feb. 1672; d. Paris, 25 Oct. 1757. He entered the order of St. Benedict in 1688, and became the head of several abbeys in succession. In 1698 he became teacher of philosophy and theology in the abbey of Moyen-Moutier. He was an industrious compiler of voluminous works. Among them are: 'Commentary on the Old and New Testaments' (Paris 1707–16); 'Historical and Critical Dictionary of the Bible'; and 'Ecclesiastical and Civil History of Lorraine.'

Calmon, Marc Antoine, märk ăṅ-twäṅ kȧl-môṅ, French political economist: b. Tamnies, Dordogne, 3 March 1815; d. Paris, 13 Oct. 1890. He entered the National Assembly as life member in 1875, but will be longest remembered for his writings on political economy, which include 'Les impôts avant 1789' (1865); 'William Pitt, étude financière et parliamentaire'

(1865); 'Histoire parlementaire des finances de la Restauration' (1868–70); 'Etude des finances de l'Angleterre depuis la réforme de Robert Peel, jusqu 'en 1869' (1870).

Calmon du Pin e Almeida, Miguel, Brazilian statesman: b. Santa Amara, Bahia, 22 Dec. 1796; d. Rio de Janeiro, 5 Oct. 1865. He entered the Constituent Assembly in 1822, was senator in 1840, prime minister in 1840 and again in 1843 and resided in Europe as special envoy 1844–7. He was created viscount in 1849 and Marquis of Abrantes in 1854.

Calms, Region of, tracts in the Atlantic and Pacific oceans, on the confines of the trade-winds, where calms of long duration prevail. This region is not the same all the year through, but follows the course of the sun, and lies farther north or farther south according to the hemisphere in which the sun happens to be. About the winter solstice its average northern limit is in lat. 5° N., and in the months about the summer solstice its average northern limit is about 12° N. lat. The southern limit lies nearly always to the north of the equator, varying between lat. 1° and 3° N.; but it is sometimes, though rarely, so far south as lat. 1° or 2° S. During the months following the winter solstice its average breadth is four degrees, while in the months following the summer solstice it is about six degrees. The calms prevail especially on the northern margin of this region, but even there there is an occasional light breeze, but not sufficient to fill the sails. The climate of this region is extremely unpleasant, for the atmosphere is moist and foggy, and the sky generally overcast and gloomy. Almost every day there occurs a violent storm of thunder and lightning, accompanied by sudden blasts of wind, and by rain which falls in regular streams for hours together. On this account the region is dangerous to navigators. To increase these dangers there is between lat. 4° and 10° N., and lon. 18° and 23° W., a tract of considerable extent, which seamen call the "rainy sea," and which, with only rare intervals of calm, is visited by almost constant storms of thunder and lightning, and violent falls of rain, from which it is very difficult for a sailing vessel to make its escape.

Cal'mucks. See KALMUCKS.

Calomarde, or **Calomarda, Francisco Tadeo,** frän-thĕs'kō tä-dä'ō kä-lō-mär'dạ (COUNT OF ALMEIDA), Spanish statesman: b. Villel, Aragon, 1775; d. Toulouse, France, 1842. He studied law, entered political life and sustained the national cause in resistance to Napoleon. In 1814 on the return of Ferdinand VII., Calomarde was made chief secretary of the department of Indian affairs. Here he was convicted of bribery and banished to Toledo and afterward to Pamplona. In 1823 he received the appointment of secretary to the regency, and subsequently an important office in the royal household, and he was appointed minister of justice. He organized the corps of royalist volunteers, recalled the Jesuits, reopened the convents, and closed the universities. In 1832, when Ferdinand's death was supposed to have taken place, Calomarde was the first to bend his knee before Don Carlos. The king recovered physically, but lingered in a semi-idiotic condition: of this Calomarde took advantage, by extorting from him his signature to the act

of 31 Dec. 1832, in which Ferdinand abdicated in favor of Don Carlos. When Ferdinand revealed this fraudulent proceeding, Calomarde was banished to Aragon, and later avoided imprisonment by escaping to France in disguise. Here he passed the rest of his days in obscurity.

Cal'omel, the sub-chloride, or "mild" chloride of mercury, HgCl (or Hg$_2$Cl$_2$); known to chemists as "mercurous chloride," to distinguish it from corrosive sublimate, HgCl$_2$, which is known as "mercuric chloride." (For its preparation see MERCURY.) In the use of calomel as a medicine, particular attention should be given to its liability to generate corrosive sublimate by decomposition. This effect may be produced by bitter almonds or cherry-laurel water, or any other substance containing hydrocyanic acid, being administered simultaneously with it. Nitro-muriatic acid produces the same effects, as also, to some degree, the chlorides of potassium, sodium, and ammonium. It is rendered ineffectual by the alkalies and alkaline earths. Calomel is regarded as the most valuable of the mercurial preparations, though some medical innovators reject it. It is employed as a purgative, operating chiefly upon the liver by stimulating its secretory functions. Being slow in its action, and liable to salivate if too long retained, it is usually administered with some saline cathartic. It is also given as a remedy for worms, and as an alterative in derangement of the liver.

Calomel occurs native in Spain, Bohemia, Servia, Mexico, and elsewhere, in the form of tetragonal crystals white in color (or nearly so) with a hardness of from 1 to 2, and a specific gravity of 6.48.

Calonne, Charles Alexandre de, shärl ä-lĕks-ăndr dĕ kä-lŏn, French statesman: b. Douai, 20 Jan. 1734; d. Paris, 30 Oct. 1802. He succeeded Necker in 1783 as comptroller-general of the finances, and found not a single crown in the treasury. In this office he continued till 1787. During this period he maintained the public credit by a punctuality till then unknown in the payments of the royal treasury, though he found it drained to the lowest ebb. He labored with unwearied assiduity to restore the equipoise between the annual income and expenditure, and to provide a supply for the emergencies of the state, without increasing the burdens of the people. For this purpose he advised the king to revive the ancient usage of convening the national assemblies of the "notables," to whom he proposed the bold project of suppressing the pecuniary privileges and exemptions of the nobility, clergy, and magistracy. This measure alarmed those powerful bodies, and Calonne found it necessary to retire to England, where he wrote two defenses of himself — his 'Petition to the King,' and 'Reply to Necker.' On the breaking out of the Revolution he supported the Royalist party with much zeal, both by his pen and his journeys to various countries of Europe on their account.

Calophyllum, a genus of trees belonging to the natural order *Guttiferæ,* and natives of warm climates. They have large shining leaves, with numerous transverse parallel veins. Some of the species yield excellent timber. *C. inophyllum* affords a medical resin, the tacamahac of the East Indies. The seeds yield an oil which is used for burning, for making ointment, etc. *C. calaba* is a West Indian species whose oil is used for illuminating purposes.

Calores'cence, the phenomenon of the transmutation of heat rays into light rays; a peculiar transmutation of the invisible calorific rays, observable beyond the red rays of the spectrum of solar and electric light, into visible luminous rays, by passing them through a solution of iodine in bisulphide of carbon, which intercepts the luminous rays and transmits the calorific. The latter, when brought to a focus, produce a heat strong enough to ignite combustible substances, and to heat up metals to incandescence; the less refrangible calorific rays being converted into rays of higher refrangibility, whereby they become luminous.

Calor'ic (Latin, *calor*, "heat"), a name formerly given to a hypothetical, imponderable fluid, whose existence was postulated in order to explain the observed phenomena of heat. It is known that no such fluid exists, and the word is now practically obsolete, except as an adjective in such expressions as "caloric effect," "caloric engine," etc., where it stands for the words "thermal," or "heat," though sometimes in a special sense. (For a statement of the principles of the old caloric theory, consult Preston, 'Theory of Heat,' p. 34.) See also HEAT; THERMODYNAMICS.

Caloric Engine, a name originally given by Ericsson to a form of hot-air engine invented by him, in order to distinguish it from other engines whose operation depends upon the same general principles; but now commonly applied to every form of hot-air engine in which the source of the motive power is a furnace external to the working cylinder, but associated with it. In these engines air is admitted to the working cylinder, where it is heated by contact with the hot cylinder wall. Its pressure at once rises, and it is then allowed to expand, pushing a piston before it. A new supply of air is next admitted, and the process is repeated indefinitely. Hot-air engines are useful for pumping and other small work, especially because they do not need a skilled engineer. They have also been thoroughly tried upon a large scale, but without lasting success. Doubtless the inventors who have striven to overcome the immense practical difficulties that appear to be inherent in the hot-air engine have been stimulated by the knowledge that in the steam-engine an enormous quantity of heat is required merely to evaporate the water that is used, before a single pound of pressure can be exerted upon the piston of the engine. The heat so expended appears to be largely wasted, and hence it might be hoped that some form of air-engine can be devised that will avoid this apparent source of loss, and be correspondingly more efficient. (See THERMODYNAMICS.) It does not appear that this hope is likely to be fulfilled by the hot-air engine; and the gas-engine (q.v.) must be regarded as a far more promising subject for the exercise of inventive genius, and a far more formidable rival of the steam-engine. (For more detailed accounts of the hot-air engines now in use, consult Hutton, 'Heat and Heat Engines,' and Carpenter, 'Text-Book of Experimental Engineering.' The latter volume contains useful directions for testing such engines. For the general theory of the hot-air engine, see

Wood, 'Thermodynamics,' and Rankine, 'The Steam-Engine and Other Prime Movers.'

Cal'orie, or **Cal'ory,** the unit of heat; the amount of heat necessary to raise the temperature of a kilogram of water one degree Centigrade, or from 0° to 1° C. It is used as a standard of heat by physicists as the term "foot-pound" is employed as the unit of energy. It is also known as the "greater calorie," to distinguish it from the "small calorie," in which the unit of mass is the gram instead of the kilogram. See CALORIMETRY.

Calorimeter, Respiration. The respiration calorimeter is an instrument which has proved of great value for studying the fundamental laws of nutrition, as well as more practical problems. It takes its name from the fact that it is used to measure and study the products of respiration and to measure energy in the form of heat. The apparatus was devised (1896-1903) by Professors W. O. Atwater and E. B. Rosa, under the auspices of the United States Department of Agriculture, co-operating with the Storrs (Connecticut) Experiment Station and the Wesleyan University, some of the features being suggested by the respiration apparatus elaborated a number of years ago by Pettenkofer of Munich.

The apparatus includes a copper walled chamber about seven feet long, four feet wide, and six and one-half feet high, in which the man who served as subject of the experiment lives one or more days and nights, usually at least four. An opening in the front of the apparatus, sealed during an experiment, serves as both door and window. A smaller opening in the side, called the food aperture, having tightly-fitting caps on both ends, is used for passing food, drink, excreta, and other materials into and out of the chamber. There is a telephone by which the subject may communicate with those outside. The chamber is furnished with a folding chair, table and bed. Air is kept in circulation through the chamber at the rate of not far from two and one-half cubic feet a minute. Thus, while the dimensions of the chamber are rather small, the subject finds nothing particularly disagreeable or uncomfortable in his sojourn within it, save for the restricted space and the monotony of the prescribed daily routine.

The circulation of air is effected by a special pump, which measures the volume of the ventilating current and at regular intervals draws measured samples of the outgoing air for analysis. At the same time samples of the incoming air are also taken for analysis. From these determinations the amounts of respiratory products — carbon dioxid and water — given off by the subject may be computed.

The diet during an experiment is uniform from day to day. All food and drink, and all solid and liquid excreta are carefully weighed, sampled and analyzed. By comparing the chemical elements and compounds received by the body in food, drink and inhaled air with those given off in the solid, liquid and gaseous excretions, it is possible to strike a balance between the total income and total outgo of matter in the body and to determine whether it has increased or diminished its store of material. In this way a gain or loss of even a small

CALORIMETER

fraction of an ounce of body fat or protein during a period of one or several days can be detected and measured.

At the same time it is desirable to study the metabolism of energy. This is done likewise by determining the balance of income and outgo. The measurements made in these investigations are in terms of heat, since other forms of energy may be transformed into it. To this end it is necessary to know how much energy is taken into the body in food and drink, how much is given off unused in the solid and liquid excreta, and how much is transformed in the body and given off in the forms of heat and external muscular work.

burned outside the body, that is by their heats of combustion, as learned by burning samples of them with oxygen in an apparatus called the bomb calorimeter.

As regards the outgo of energy it must be remembered that heat is constantly given off within the chamber of the man's body, whether he is at work or at rest. When he is at rest, *i. e.*, doing no external muscular work, there is nevertheless a great deal of muscular work going on within his body. Even when he is asleep the organs of respiration, circulation and digestion are active. The energy of the internal work is transformed into heat in the body and leaves the body as heat. In rest ex-

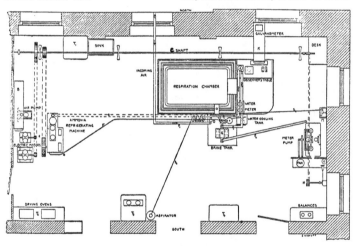

FIG. A. GROUND PLAN OF RESPIRATION CALORIMETER LABORATORY.

A. Device for regulating temperature of ingoing current.
B. Tank for compressed air used to drive valves of meter pump and operate brine pump of freezing apparatus.
C. Shaft for driving meter pump and other mechanism.
F. Feed pump bringing ammonia to freezing apparatus.
R. Return pipe conveying ammonia from freezing apparatus.
O. Food aperture.
P_1. Pipe bringing air to freezing tank.
P_2. Pipe conveying air from freezing tank to respiration chamber.
D. Freezer used to remove moisture from ingoing air.

P_3. Pipe conveying air from respiration chamber to freezer.
P_4. Pipe conveying air from freezer to meter pump.
G. Freezer used to remove moisture from outgoing air.
S_1. Pipe conveying air for analysis from chamber to aspirator.
S_2. Pipe conveying sample of ingoing air for analysis to meter.
M. Small meter used to measure samples of ingoing air.
H. Secondary shaft connecting main power shaft with meter pump.
K. Box where galvanometer is read.
T_1, T_2, T_3, and T_4. Balances, drying oven, sink, and tables used for analytical operations.

So far as we know the only energy received by the body is the potential energy of the food, and the only forms in which it leaves the body are (1) partly in the potential energy of the unoxidized residues of food and body material which are eliminated in the solid and liquid excreta, but (2) chiefly in the kinetic energy resulting from the oxidation of material in the body, and leaving the body, so far as is known, only as heat and external muscular work.

The potential energy of the food and excretory products is measured by the amount of heat generated when these substances are

periments, practically all the kinetic energy leaves the body as heat. In work experiments part is put forth as muscular power applied to the pedals of a bicycle-dynamo, which transforms this external muscular energy into heat and as an ergometer, measures its amount. The problem is to measure the whole heat including that which left the body as heat and that which resulted from the transformation of the muscular work. The method consists in collecting this heat, for measurement, and at the same time providing that there shall be no gain or loss in the amount.

The chamber of the calorimeter is enclosed by double metal walls, which are surrounded on all sides by walls of wood with air spaces between, so that the temperature within the chamber is not greatly affected by changes in the temperature of the room outside. Very delicate thermo-electric elements arranged in series and connected with a galvanometer, show changes in the temperature of the metal walls; and devices for heating and cooling the walls are arranged so that their temperature may be kept as near that of the interior of the chamber as desired and the very small amounts of heat that may pass through them into or out of the calorimeter may be made to counterbalance each other. The temperature of the ventilating air current is also regulated so that neither more nor less heat is taken in than is brought out. Accordingly there is no gain or loss of heat either through the walls of the chamber or by the ventilating air current.

The heat produced within the chamber is that from the energy of the material oxidized in the man's body. The only way this heat can escape is by the proper agencies for carrying it out and measuring it, two in number. A small portion of the heat generated within the chamber is carried out by water vapor in the ventilating air current. The excess of vapor in the air leaving the chamber over that in the air entering it represents the amount given off as vapor from the body of the subject, and has required heat to vaporize it. The amount of this heat is computed by factor from the amount of water vapor and the temperature at which it leaves the chamber.

The larger part of the heat generated within the chamber is absorbed and carried out of it by a current of cold water, flowing through a copper pipe around the interior. The cooling surface of the pipe is increased by thin disks of copper fastened at close intervals along the coil. The water enters the chamber at a low temperature, passes through the copper coil, absorbs heat from the chamber and passes out at a higher temperature. The quantity of water and the difference between the temperatures at which it enters and leaves the coil are carefully determined and show how much heat was thus brought out of the chamber. Adding the heat brought out by the water vapor in the ventilating air current to this heat we have the whole heat produced.

By regulating the temperature and rate of flow of the water current, the heat is absorbed and carried out of the chamber as fast as generated, at the same time keeping the temperature within the chamber at a point agreeable to the subject and almost absolutely constant. So delicate are the measurements of temperature of the air within the chamber, and of the metal walls, that the observer sitting outside the apparatus and noting the changes every two or four minutes, immediately detects a rise or fall of even one one-hundredth of a degree. The accuracy of the respiration calorimeter is shown by the fact that in check experiments in which large quantities of alcohol were burned in a lamp in the chamber 99.8 per cent of the theoretical amount of carbon-dioxid, 100.1 per cent of the theoretical water, and 99.9 per cent of the energy were measured. In the average of 32 experiments with man, covering 107 days,

the energy measured was 99.9 per cent of the theoretical amount, and the value for carbon and hydrogen was equally satisfactory. Fig. A. shows the general plan of the apparatus and accessories.

The data for the matabolism of matter and of energy, obtained as heretofore explained, taken in connection with what is known of the physiological processes that go on in the body, give more accurate information than can be otherwise obtained regarding the ways in which food is used in the body, the quantities of different food ingredients that are needed to supply the demands of the body, the different conditions of rest and work, and the comparative nutritive value of different food materials. A respiration calorimeter, like that described, has been built, under government auspices, at Bonn, Germany, and a form adapted for experiments with steers has just been completed at the Pennsylvania Experiment Station, in cooperation with the United States Department of Agriculture.

C. F. Langworthy,
U. S. Agricultural Dept., Washington, D. C.

Calorim'etry, ("heat measurement"), the art of measuring the quantity of heat that a body absorbs or emits when it passes from one temperature to another, or when it undergoes some definite change of state. In order to execute such measurements it is first necessary to adopt some convenient and accurate unit, in terms of which the quantities of heat that are to be measured can be expressed. Several such units have been proposed, but none has yet met with universal favor among physicists. One of the simplest that has been suggested (at least so far as the principles involved are concerned) is the quantity of heat that is required to melt a kilogram or a pound of ice. Evidently it will require precisely 10 times as much heat to melt 10 pounds of ice as to melt one pound, and hence, if the quantity of heat required to melt one pound of ice is taken as the unit of heat, the measurement of any given quantity of heat becomes reduced to the simple operation of observing how many pounds of ice the proposed quantity of heat can melt. The earliest form of heat-measuring device (or "calorimeter") based upon this idea is that invented by Dr. Joseph Black about the year 1760. It consists simply of a block of clear ice, in which a cavity is made, the cavity being closed by a slab of ice laid upon the main block. To make the use of this device plain, let us suppose that it is desired to determine the quantity of heat that is given out by a certain fragment of platinum in cooling from 100° F. to the freezing-point. The chamber in the block of ice is first carefully wiped dry, and the platinum, heated accurately to 100°, is quickly introduced, and the covering lid of ice is laid in place. The platinum gives up its heat to the ice about it, with the result that a certain weight of the ice is melted, and a corresponding weight of water collects within the chamber. When it is certain that the platinum has attained the temperature of the ice, the slab covering the excavation in the main block is lifted off, and the water that has collected about the platinum is removed and weighed. The quantity of heat given out by the platinum is then known at once, if the accepted unit of heat is the quantity required to melt one pound of ice. Lavoisier and Laplace improved Black's calorimeter in certain respects, while retaining its main features. Their instrument consists essentially of three distinct concentric chambers. The object upon which the experiment is to be performed is placed in the inner chamber, and the ice whose melting is to serve as a measure of the heat given out is placed, in the form of broken lumps, in the intermediate chamber, surrounding the object to be investigated. In the outer chamber, which encloses the other two as completely as possible, broken ice is also introduced, to prevent the conduction of heat into the apparatus from the outside. The quantity of ice melted is determined by observing the amount of water that is formed in the middle chamber, this being drawn off by a conveniently situated tube and tap. This apparatus has been described as an improvement upon that of Black; but the only way in which it can be said to be an improvement is in the respect that it does not call for large blocks of pure, clear ice. In other particulars it is somewhat inferior to the simpler apparatus of Black. The quantity of water that is produced, for example, cannot be determined with the same degree of accuracy in Lavoisier and Laplace's instrument. The ice calorimeter of Bunsen was a far greater advance. This ingenious apparatus consists of an inner chamber, for the reception of the object to be studied, and an outer enveloping one, which is entirely filled with a mixture of ice and water, and from which a graduated capillary tube is led away. The whole instrument is surrounded by broken ice, as in Lavoisier and Laplace's form, in order to protect the interior parts from the effect of external thermal influences. When the apparatus is in perfect working order, the mixture of ice and water in the intermediate chamber should be neither melting nor freezing, but should be in exact equilibrium in this respect. Upon the introduction of the object to be studied into the central chamber, the ice in the intermediate chamber begins to melt, just as in the types of calorimeter already considered; but the essential peculiarity of Bunsen's instrument consists in deducing the quantity of ice that is melted by observing the change of volume of the contents of the intermediate chamber, as shown by the motion of the water in the graduated capillary tube that leads away from that chamber; advantage being taken, for this purpose, of the known fact that ice diminishes in volume upon melting, so that when the exact diminution in the volume of the contents of the intermediate chamber is known, we can calculate with a considerable degree of precision the quantity of ice that has been melted. Bunsen's calorimeter is an admirable instrument, capable of giving results of great accuracy when intelligently handled.

Another unit of heat that suggests itself quite naturally is the quantity of heat given out by a pound of steam when it condenses into a pound of water at the same temperature. A calorimeter based upon this idea was also used by Bunsen, but the steam calorimeter was brought to its present excellent form largely through the labors of Dr. J. Joly. In his type of the instrument the object to be studied is suspended from one arm of a delicate balance. After being accurately counterpoised, the object

is bathed in an atmosphere of steam, with the result that it absorbs a certain amount of heat as its temperature rises to that of the steam. But the heat thus absorbed by the body under examination can be obtained only from the steam itself; and, since saturated steam cannot part with heat in this way without condensing, it follows that there is deposited upon the body a weight of condensed moisture that corresponds precisely to the quantity of heat that has been absorbed. The amount of this moisture is determined by careful weighing; and it is evident that the quantity of heat absorbed by the experimental body in passing from its original temperature to the temperature of the steam is then immediately known, if we take, as the unit of heat, the quantity of heat that is given out by a pound of steam in condensing into a pound of water at the same temperature. In practice, numerous corrections are of course necessary, as with all other instruments of precision. It may be added that although the ice and the steam calorimeters are primarily intended to determine the heat emitted or absorbed by a body in passing from any given temperature to some one particular temperature that is always the same (that is, the freezing-point in the one case and the boiling-point in the other), yet it is always possible to determine the quantity of heat emitted or absorbed by the body between any two temperatures, by performing two experiments in succession, the body having these respective temperatures as its initial temperatures in the respective experiments. It is plain that the quantity of heat emitted or absorbed between the proposed initial and terminal temperatures can then be obtained by simply subtracting one of these results from the other.

Another and more familiar unit of heat is the quantity of heat required to warm a given weight of water by one degree on a given thermometric scale. (See Caloric.) Thus in general engineering practice in the United States and in England, it is customary to define a heat unit as the quantity of heat that is required in order to raise the temperature of a pound of water one degree on the Fahrenheit scale. This definition is good enough for rough purposes, because it conveniently happens that there is no great difference between the quantity of heat required to warm a pound of water from 32° to 33° and the quantity required (for example) to warm it from 99° to 100°. This, however, we can only regard as a fortunate accident; and for accurate scientific purposes we must recognize that the equality is only approximate, and we must adopt some particular temperature range as a part of our definition. Thus it is common to define the British heat unit, when great accuracy is desired, as the quantity of heat required to raise the temperature of a pound of water from 59° to 60°; although some authorities, apparently without sufficient reason, make the temperature range from 32° to 33°, and others have chosen other positions on the temperature scale for the defining degree. It is unfortunate that no general agreement has yet been reached on this point. In accurate scientific work the unit of heat is usually taken as the quantity of heat required to warm a kilogram of water from 15° C. to 16° C., or (which is practically the same thing) from 14.5° to 15.5° C. It would appear that several very good reasons could be assigned for selecting 40° C.

as the standard temperature to be used in defining the heat unit. For example, the specific heat of water has its minimum value not far from that point; or, in other words, any small uncertainty in the actual realization of the temperature contained in the definition would have little or no effect if that temperature were 40° C. Again, 40° C. is the temperature at or near which the differences between the various thermometric scales that are in practical use reach their maximum; and this means that at or near this temperature a slight error in the standardization of the thermometer that is used would have the least effect upon the verification of the heat unit. Moreover, 40° C. (104° F.) is a temperature that is likely to be always greater than the general temperature of the laboratory in which work is being carried out; and it is well known to be easier to realize a temperature that is higher than that of the surrounding air, than it is to realize one that is lower. From every point of view, therefore, 40° C. (or thereabouts) would appear to be the best temperature to assume in establishing the definition of the heat unit; a unit of heat being then defined as the quantity of heat required to raise the temperature of a kilogram of water from (say) 39° C. to 40° C. Yet, cogent as these reasons would appear, no authority has yet suggested this particular temperature as the standard.

In measuring the quantity of heat emitted by a body by observing the change of temperature produced in a given mass of water when the water absorbs the heat so emitted, a great variety of forms of apparatus may be used. In some cases the heated body may be plunged into the water directly, the water being kept well stirred, and its temperature taken at the beginning and end of the experiment. In other cases, and especially when the body under examination cannot be allowed to come in contact with the water, it is necessary to adopt some more elaborate method, such as enclosing the experimental body in a water-tight envelope of some kind, and afterward making due allowance for the heat capacity of the envelope. In cases, for example, in which the heat generated by the combustion of fuel is to be measured, the fuel must be enclosed in an air-tight crucible, to which oxygen is admitted by one tube, and from which the products of combustion are drawn off by another. The crucible is surrounded by a mass of water that is disposed in such a way as to intercept and absorb as much of the heat that is produced as possible. A direct observation of the temperature of the water in the calorimeter is made before and after the combustion, and the change of temperature so obtained gives a first approximation to the amount of heat that has been liberated. This result has to be corrected, however, for the thermal capacity of each part of the calorimeter that has been warmed during the experiment, and for that of the gases admitted and drawn off, and also for any loss of heat that may have occurred through radiation. The precise details of the corrections will vary, however, with the design of the calorimeter, and with the mode of conducting the experiments.

For a discussion of the relations of the different units of heat that have been mentioned above, and for an account of the experiments that have been made for determining the differences in the heat capacities of water at different temperatures, see HEAT. A very good account of the subject of calorimetry in general will be found in Preston's 'Theory of Heat,' which also contains valuable references to original papers. The various forms of calorimeter that are used in practical engineering are explained and illustrated in Carpenter's 'Text-Book of Experimental Engineering.'

Calotropis, a genus of asclepiads forming shrubs or small trees, natives of the tropics of Asia and Africa. There are three species, and their flowers have a somewhat bell-shaped corolla, expanding into five divisions. *C. gigantea,* the largest of the genus, forms a branching shrub or small tree about 15 feet high, with a short trunk four or five inches in diameter. Its flowers are of a pretty rose-purple color. Cloth and paper have been made from the silky down of the seeds. The bark of the roots of several of the species furnishes the substance called mudar, which is used in India as a diaphoretic. The juice has been found very efficacious in the cure of elephantiasis, in syphilis, and anasarca. From the bark of the plant is made a substance called mudarine. The bark of the young branches also yields a valuable fibre. The leaves warmed and moistened with oil are applied as a dry fomentation in pains of the stomach; they are a valuable rubefacient. The root, reduced to powder, is given in India to horses. An intoxicating liquor, called bar, is made from the mudar by the hillmen about Mahabuleshwar, in the western Ghauts.

Calot'tists (French, *Calottistes,* kä-lō-tēst'), or the RÉGIMENT DE LA CALOTTE, a society which sprang up at Paris in the last years of the reign of Louis XIV., and took their name from the word *calotte,* a flat cap formerly worn by the priests, which was the symbol of the society. All were admitted whose odd behavior or character, foolish opinions, etc., had exposed them to public criticism. Every one who made himself particularly ridiculous received letters-patent, authorizing him to wear the calotte. They had a singular coat of arms, on which was the sceptre of Momus, with bells, apes, rattles, etc. On their principal standard were the words, *Favet Momus, luna influit.* On the death of Torsac, the colonel of the Calottists, the *éloge* (a spirited satire on the academical style), which the Calottists pronounced on this occasion, was suppressed. Aimon, colonel of the guards, hastened to Marshal Villars with their complaints, and concluded with the words, "My lord, since the death of Alexander and Cæsar, the Calottists have not had any protector besides you," and the order was retracted. They became, however, too bold, attacked the ministers and even the king himself; and the regiment was in consequence dissolved. After the restoration the epithet *Régime de la Calotte,* was applied to the clerical influence in politics.

Cal'otype, a photographic process invented by Talbot. Paper saturated with iodide of silver is exposed to the action of light, the latent image being subsequently developed and fixed by hyposulphite of soda.

Calo'vius (Latinized form of original German name, KALAU), **Abraham,** German polemic: b. Mohrungen, Prussia, 16 April 1612; d. 25 Feb. 1686. He was the chief representative of controversial Lutheran orthodoxy in the 17th century, and waged war incessantly on Arminian, Socinian, Reformed, and Roman Catholic doctrines, and with the greatest bitterness against Calixtus. He was six times married, the last time in his 72d year. His chief writings are: 'System of Theological Locations'; 'History of Syncretism'.

Caloy'ers, (καλός, "beautiful," "good"; and γέρων, "an old man"), Greek monks belonging with a few exceptions to the order of St. Basil, who led a very austere life, eating no meat and observing the fasts of the Greek Church very rigidly. They do not even eat bread unless they have earned it. During their seven weeks of Lent they pass the greatest part of the night in weeping and lamentations for their own sins and for those of others. The caloyers of the Greek Church occupy a position of much greater importance than the members of the religious fraternities of the Church of Rome, inasmuch as all the higher Church dignitaries — bishops, archbishops, and patriarchs are chosen from their number. They are, indeed, the only individuals in the Greek Church who are instructed in theology, and even among them the amount of theological learning is very limited. They are commonly educated at the monasteries on Mount Athos, and on the Isle of Patmos, but besides these there are many monasteries dispersed over the archipelago and the Morea, and a few elsewhere belonging to this class of monks. Their most celebrated monastery in Asia is at Mount Sinai. They do not all agree as to their mode of life. Some of them are cenobites; that is, they live in common. Others are anchorites, living alone, or with only one or two companions; and others again are recluses, who live in grottoes or caverns in the greatest retirement, and are supported by alms supplied to them by the monasteries. There are also convents of female caloyers. The Turks sometimes call their dervishes by this name.

Calpe, kăl'pē, the ancient name of the rock of Gibraltar (q.v.), at the southern extremity of Spain, the northern of the two hills called by the ancients the "Pillars of Hercules." Across the straits of Gibraltar, on the African coast, was Abyla, the southern pillar.

Calpee. See KALPI.

Calprenède, Gautier de Costes de la, French romance writer: b. Tolgou, Gascony, 1610; d. Paris, 1663. He was an officer of the guards and royal chamberlain, and one of the authors who in the 17th century brought into fashion a new kind of voluminous and long-spun romances of chivalry. He wrote: 'Cassandra'; 'Cleopatra'; and 'Pharamond,' besides some tragedies. His romances were highly celebrated, and are the best of their kind.

Calpur'nia, the fourth wife of Julius Cæsar, married to him 59 B.C. She was a daughter of L. Calpurnius Piso Cæsonius, who was consul 58 B.C. Shakespeare introduces her into his tragedy, 'Julius Cæsar.'

Calpurnius, Titus, surnamed **Siculus,** Latin poet: b. about 30 A.D.; d. about 80. Seven eclogues composed by him are extant, but nothing whatever is known with certainty about his life, and even his name is doubtful. The poems attributed to him are evidently modeled on Vergil's more famous eclogues. They are

smooth, flowing, and melodious, but lacking in simplicity and naturalness. See NEMESIANUS.

Caltanissetta, käl-tạ-nē-sĕt'tạ, Sicily, capital of the province of the same name, on the right bank of the Salso, 62 miles southeast of Palermo. It is fortified, and has a citadel and cathedral, broad streets, and well-built houses. In the vicinity, at Terra Pilata, are springs of petroleum and of hydrogen gas, a mud-volcano, and important sulphur mines, producing annually about 5,500 tons. Caltanissetta owes its origin to the Saracens, by whom it was called *Kalat al Nisa* ("the lady's castle"). Pop. (1901) 44,600. The province of the same name has an area of 1,445 square miles. Pop. 330,972.

Caltha, the genus of ranunculaceous plants to which the marsh-marigold (*C. palustris*) belongs. See COWSLIP.

Cal'throp, Samuel Robert, American Unitarian clergyman: b. Swineshead Abbey, Lincolnshire, England, 7 Oct. 1829. He was educated at Cambridge University and came to the United States in 1853. He entered the Unitarian ministry in 1860 and has been pastor of a church in Syracuse, N. Y., for several years. He has published 'Essay on Religion and Science'; 'The Rights of the Body'; 'The Primitive Gospel and Its Life of Jesus.'

Calton Hill, a hill in the city of Edinburgh at the eastern end of Princes Street. It is rocky, and has a broad, grassy summit, which commands a view of the Forth and the surrounding country. On the hill are monuments in memory of Dugald Stewart and Lord Nelson, and one in commemoration of the victory at Waterloo.

Caltonica, Sicily, a town in the province of Girgenti, situated 15 miles northwest of the town of Girgenti. The sulphur works in the neighborhood produce annually upward of 1,000 tons of sulphur. Salt is also manufactured in the district. Pop. 7,000.

Caltrop, a kind of thistle growing in southern Europe. It is armed with prickles, which, if trodden on by men or animals, are capable of wounding. Hence in the military art the name of caltrop is given to an instrument with four iron points disposed in a triangular form, three of them being turned to the ground, and the other pointing upward. They are used to impede the progress of cavalry.

Calumba, or **Colombo,** the root of the *Cocculus palmatus,* a herbaceous plant, belonging to the natural order *Menispermaceæ,* which grows in Ceylon in the neighborhood of Colombo, whence it is said to derive its name. It is imported in the form of round slices or cut pieces, the interior of which is of a greenish-yellow color, while its thick and furrowed skin is greenish-brown; its odor is slightly aromatic, but somewhat nauseous; its taste extremely bitter. Calumba is often administered as a tonic, and is considered an excellent stomachic. It is regarded as of great value in chronic diarrhœa and dysentery; but it is necessary that all symptoms of inflammation should have disappeared before it can be used. It is usually given as a decoction, less commonly in the form of pills or powders. The root of a gentian, the *Frasera Walteri,* is sometimes substituted for the true calumba, and is hence frequently called the false calumba. It is not very bitter, and is almost without smell; it has no very marked effects.

Calumet, Mich., a township in Houghton County, at the terminus of the Mineral Range R.R., 42 miles north of L'Anse. It is the seat of the famous Calumet and Hecla copper mine, the richest in the world, producing nearly 50,000 tons a year. It is the trade and supply centre of the Superior mining district, and has a national bank, several weekly newspapers, manufactories, and an assessed property valuation of over $26,000,000. Pop. (1900) 25,991.

Calumet, the pipe of peace, a tobacco-pipe used by the North American Indians. On ceremonial occasions, as when Indian chiefs and warriors meet in peace, or at the close of a war with those of another nation, in their talks and treaties with the whites, or even when a single person of distinction comes among them, the calumet is handed round with ceremonies peculiar to each tribe, and each member of the company draws a few whiffs. To accept the calumet is to agree to the terms proposed; to refuse it is to reject them. Some symbols of amity are found among all nations; the white flag or flag of truce of the moderns, and the olive branch of the ancients are similar in character to the Indian calumet. There is also, it appears, a calumet used in the ceremonial declaration of war, and differently made from that of peace. Tobacco is smoked in the calumet, and the leaves of various other kinds of plants. The bowl of this pipe is made of different kinds of soft stone, especially a kind of red soapstone, and the stem of a reed, or of some light kind of wood which is easily perforated. This stem is adorned in various ways; sometimes it is marked with the figures of animals and hieroglyphical delineations, and almost universally has beautiful feathers attached to it, disposed according to the taste of the individual, or of the tribe to which he belongs.

Calumpit, Philippines, a town of the province of Bulacan, situated in the southwestern part of the island of Luzon on the Pampanga River. It is about 27 miles northwest of Manila, with which it is connected by rail. Pop. about 15,000.

Calvados, käl-vä-dös, France, a department in Normandy, bounded on the north by the English Channel, east by the department Eure, south by Orne and La Manche, and west by La Manche. Area, 2,145 square miles. It comprises the ancient Auge, Bessin, and part of Lieuvin. The region is undulating and picturesque, and possesses rich pastures. The principal rivers are the Touques, Dives, Orne, and Vire, which are navigable for small vessels. Agriculture is in a more advanced state than in many other parts of France. Dairies are numerous and well managed, and large herds of cattle are brought in from the departments of Finisterre, Côtes-du-Nord, etc., to be fattened on the pastures for the markets of Paris, Rouen, and Caen. Horses of the Norman breed are extensively reared and held in high estimation. The principal manufactures are linen and lace. The latter, near Caen and Bayeux, employs about 50,000 hands. About 25,000,000 of oysters, procured in the roads of

Cancale, are annually laid down in beds at the mouth of the Seulles. The department is divided into six arrondissements, containing 37 cantons. Chief town, Caen. Pop. (1901) 407,639.

Calvados, a dangerous ridge of rocks on the northern coast of Normandy in lat. 49° 22' N., and extending to the west of Orne for the space of 10 or 12 miles. It is so called from a vessel belonging to the Spanish Armada which was wrecked on it, and gives its name to the department.

Calvaert, käl'värt, **Dionys** (called in Italy DIONISIO FLAMMINGO), Flemish painter: b. Antwerp, 1555; d. Bologna, Italy, 17 March 1619. He went very young to Italy as a landscape painter, where, in order to learn how to draw figures, he entered the school of Fontana and Sabbatini, in Bologna, with the latter of whom he visited Rome. After having passed some time in copying the paintings of Raphael, he opened a school at Bologna, from which proceeded 137 masters, and among these Albano, Guido, and Domenichino. The Bolognese regarded him as one of the restorers of their school, particularly in respect to coloring. Calvaert understood perspective, anatomy, and architecture; but the attitudes of his figures are sometimes mean and exaggerated. His best paintings are to be seen at Bologna.

Calvary, the English name for the eminence which was the scene of the crucifixion of Jesus Christ. It lay beyond but near Jerusalem, and by some is identified with the old House of Stoning, or place of public execution, according to the law of Moses, on the top of the remarkable knoll outside the Damascus gate, on the north side of Jerusalem. It was from this cliff that the criminal used to be flung before being stoned (according to the Talmud), and on it his body was afterward crucified; for the spot commands a view all over the city, and from the slopes round it the whole population might easily witness the execution.

Calvé, käl'vä, **Emma,** French opera singer: b. Madrid, Spain, 1864. Her real name is Emma de Roquer. She was born of a French mother and Spanish father, and was educated in a convent school in the south of France. She made her début at Brussels in Gounod's 'Faust.' She has made successful tours of the United States in leading roles, her first appearance in New York being on 29 Nov. 1893.

Calverley, käl'vėr lĭ, **Charles,** American sculptor: b. Albany, N. Y., 1 Nov. 1833. He has won distinction with groups and figures and portrait busts of Greeley, Cooper, Howe, etc. He was elected to the National Academy of Design in 1875.

Calverley, Charles Stuart, English poet, son of the Rev. Henry Blayds: b. Martley, Worcestershire, 22 Dec. 1831; d. London, 17 Feb. 1884. In 1852 his father dropped the name of Blayds and resumed that of Calverley, formerly borne by his family. He was educated at Christ's College, Cambridge, and during his college career showed great skill in Latin and Greek composition, and in 1856 was second in the classical tripos. As a writer of humorous English verse he also made himself famous.

He afterward studied for the bar, and was called in 1865, but his promising legal career was cut short by a serious accident which befell him on the ice in the winter of 1866-7. The effects of this misfortune clouded the whole of the remainder of his life. As a parodist and writer of light verses Calverley is perhaps unequaled, but his published volumes are not numerous. The earliest of them appeared in 1862 under the title of 'Verses and Translations'; and the others are 'Translations into English and Latin' (1866); 'Theocritus Translated into English Verse' (1869); and 'Fly Leaves' (1872). A 'Memoir and Literary Remains' were published in 1885 by Sendall.

Cal'vert, George. See BALTIMORE FAMILY.

Calvert, George Henry, American writer: b. Baltimore, Md., 2 Jan. 1803; d. Newport, R. I., 24 May 1889. He was a great-grandson of Lord Baltimore. After graduating at Harvard in 1823, he studied in Germany; then returning to Baltimore, became editor of the 'American' and a contributor to various periodicals. His published books include 'Poems' (1847); 'Joan of Arc' (1860); 'Goethe, his Life and Works' (1872); 'Brief Essays and Brevities' (1874), and 'Wordsworth: a Biographic Æsthetic Study' (1875); 'Three Score and Other Poems' (1883).

Calvert, Leonard. See BALTIMORE FAMILY.

Calvi, Lazzaro and **Pantaleone,** lätz-ä'rō and pän-tä-lā-ō'nē käl'vē, Genoese painters, sons of Agostino Calvi: the former b. 1502; d. 1606; the latter died 1595. They painted in concert many pictures in Genoa, Monaco, and Naples. In particular, the façade of the Palazzo Doria (now Spinola), a spirited composition crowded with figures, is highly extolled. Lazzaro was the more inventive genius of the two, his brother generally working out the details of their joint productions.

Calvin (Modified from the French form Cauvin or Caulvin), **John.** Swiss reformer of the 16th century. B. Noyon, Picardie, 10 July, 1509; d. Geneva, Switzerland, 27 May, 1564. Though born in humble condition, his father, by virtue of certain official relations that he sustained to the ecclesiastical court and diocese of Noyon was able by personal influence to further the interests of his family. Calvin's mother was distinguished alike by personal beauty and piety. Even as a lad Calvin was deficient in physical vigor, but gave early tokens of more than ordinary intellectual powers, a circumstance that attracted to him the regards of a noble family at Noyon who received him under their care and gave to him the same opportunities of schooling as were enjoyed by their own children (1523). It was his father's original intention to fit him for the priesthood and in pursuance of that object he was sent to the Collége de la Marche at Paris; then to the Collége Montaigu where he was trained in logic by a learned Spaniard who afterward directed the education of Ignatius Loyola while a student at the same school. He easily stood in the front rank of his fellow-students but was little disposed to affiliate with them and from a certain unsocial severity of bearing acquired among them the nickname of the "Accusative Case."

He was already 18 and had done some preaching when from motives of ambition his father changed his plans with reference to him and determined to have him prepared for the profession of the law, putting him for that purpose under instruction at Orléans (1528) and Bourges (1530), where he applied himself to his studies with the same assiduity evinced at Paris, and attained immediate distinction though at the expense of impaired health. Without confining himself strictly to the curriculum of the school he devoted himself at the same time to the study of Greek under the German Professor Wolmar, whose Protestant views strengthened the bias toward the new faith already existing in his pupil's mind, for his attention had previously been drawn to the careful study of the Scriptures by his kinsman Olivetan, the first Protestant translator of the Bible into French. When Calvin was 22 his father died, whereupon the young man gave up his law studies and returned to Paris and theology, issuing soon after his first publication, an annotated edition of Seneca's "De Clementia."

Up to this point it is safe to presume that his interests and ambitions were purely those of a humanist, and whatever thought he may have had in regard to the need of reform in the matters of church doctrine and discipline, he doubtless felt with Erasmus and Reuchlin that all the reforms that might be required would come about as the result of completer knowledge.

It was not long after this that he experienced what he calls his "sudden conversion." He writes: "After my heart had long been prepared by the most earnest self-examination, on a sudden the full knowledge of the truth, like a bright light, disclosed to me the abyss of errors in which I was weltering, the sin and shame with which I was defiled." His experience is near of kin to that of Luther, and we are set thinking also of the "great light" that shone upon Saul as he was nearing Damascus. Yet with all the profound disclosure thus made to him, he still felt no special call to the work of preaching the reformed doctrine, and sought only for the undisturbed retirement that would permit him farther prosecution of his studies.

His friend Nicholas Cop had been elected to the rectorship of the University of Paris and at his request Calvin prepared for him an inaugural address which was substantially a defence of the reformed doctrine (1533). To the Sorbonnists this was intolerable, and Calvin was obliged to escape to Basel, where in 1536, at the age of 26, he published his "Institutes." This remarkable work was intended to be a vindication of the Protestant doctrine, and its dedication to the reigning King, Francis I, sought to create royal sympathy for the cause and for its persecuted adherents. It has been claimed that no other work, written at so early an age, has produced such a marked influence upon the opinions and practices both of contemporaries and posterity. Although the book as then composed was but the germ of what it was subsequently developed into, yet the line initially laid down in it Calvin never swerved from. By his Catholic opponents his work was styled the "Koran of the heretics."

From Basel he made a secret visit to his old home in Picardie, returning by way of Geneva, where he arrived on the 5th of August, 1536. Here it had been his intention to remain but a single night. The situation, political and religious, which he there confronted, however, vetoed his plans and really determined his entire subsequent career. That situation briefly outlined is as follows: The Duke of Savoy, unable to secure the submission of Geneva, had by the aid of Pope Leo X forced upon the city the reluctant acceptance of John, the Bastard of Savoy, as bishop, it being stipulated that the civil administration of the city should be vested in the Duke. The Genevese revolted under the lead of Berthelier and Bonnivard, but were defeated, Berthelier was executed and Bonnivard became the 'Prisoner of Chillon' (1530–1536). Defeat did not however extinguish the spirit of revolt. Of the two parties into which the Genevese were divided the Confederates ("Eidgenossen," a word from which perhaps comes the word Huguenot) looked for relief to the Swiss and the Mamelukes favored supporting the Duke. The Confederates prevailed, the Duke was worsted and all power both military and civil passed into the hands of the people. This was in 1533.

To this civil overturning succeeded an ecclesiastical revolution. Protestant tendencies had established themselves in Bern, and from there had extended themselves to Geneva. The struggle in the latter place was a severe one, but Protestantism gained ground till under the leadership of Farel and with the assistance of Bern an ecclesiastical reconstruction was effected, the Bishop driven out, Protestantism established, and Geneva left independent. This meant not only a new form of doctrine and mode of worship, but a reformed system of morals, and thereby a strain put upon the large profligate element of the population that soon worked a reaction strenuously encouraged by the Savoyards and the Catholic priests. The entire city was in this way wrought into a condition of tumultous faction, and it was just in the midst of this warring of civil, moral and ecclesiastical elements that Calvin arrived at Geneva as already stated, and took lodgings for the night with the distinct intention of going on to Basel the next day. Farel who was in charge of the Protestant movement accidentally learned of Calvin's presence in the city, got into communication with him, and in an interview graphically described by Calvin in the preface to his "Commentary on the Psalms" (a work especially rich in autobiographical references), entreated him to remain and help work out the problem of Protestantism in Geneva, denouncing upon him the curse of God if he refused. Calvin was awe-stricken by what seemed to him the prophetic deliverance of Farel and yielded to his Elijah-like expostulation, so that the dictum is well justified that "Farel gave Geneva to the reformation and Calvin to Geneva."

He prefaced his work in Geneva by introducing and setting in operation a system of stringent regulations relative to doctrine, discipline and daily conduct. Amusements like dancing and card-playing were punishable offences, not because in his judgment inherently wrong, but because so abused that the only safe course was to prohibit them altogether. The stringency of

this policy excited a revolt led by the Libertines, so styled, and participated in even by many of the same "Eidgenossen" that had helped wrest Geneva from the grasp of the Duke. The opposition culminated in an act of Council expelling Calvin and Farel from the city (1538), the latter going to Neufchâtel, and Calvin to Strasburg, where, with a sense of relief, he thought to find himself free to gratify his tastes and resume his studies. Here again, however, as at Geneva, he was stirred by an intimidating call and applied himself to the work of ministering to the French refugees there gathered. It was during his stay in Strasburg that he married a lady of admirable character, with whom he lived in relations of tender attachment till her death nine years later, their only child, a son, dying in early infancy.

In Geneva, in the meantime, matters had been going from bad to worse, till by the united voice of government and people Calvin was recalled. Crime and vice had become rampant. Catholics were scheming for the restoration of the old faith. Cardinal Sordelet had addressed to the people a flattering and cajoling letter calculated to win them back to the Catholic Church. To that letter Calvin while still in Strasburg had published a reply both sagacious and masterly. Bern was suspected of having ambitious political designs on the city. The local government was too weak to maintain itself amid such a storm of conflicting elements and so after three years the people turned again helplessly to the man they had exiled. He fought against the overtures tendered him but was overborne by their earnestness and unanimity and came back to Geneva to make there his life-long home (1541).

Calvin entered at once upon his office of administrative head of the city considered in both its ecclesiastical and civic character. Though combining the two in his own person he was no Erastian, and Church and State stood to him as theoretically distinct, and yet contributing, each, to the interests of the other, the Church infusing its spirit into the State and the State in turn furnishing authoritative support to the Church. Civil authority which had previously been widely distributed he made more oligarchic and vested it primarily in what was known as the Little Council of twenty-five. The code devised for the city bears everywhere the marks of Calvin's authorship. For this his legal training especially qualified him. Larger and smaller matters alike came under his purview. Like the English Alfred the Genevese legislator braced his system of enactments by a liberal infusion of the Mosaic letter and spirit. Ecclesiastical discipline was delegated to the Consistory composed at first of 18 members, 6 clerical and 12 lay, with Calvin as its president. The city was divided into districts or parishes and a system of vigilance so thoroughly organized that every family was at least once a year visited by responsible parties for purposes of censure, counsel or relief.

Although introducing his administration with a measure of moderation its animus soon evinced itself in a way that made evident to the lawless and vicious classes what it was they had to contend with, and a wide-reaching opposition began immediately to organize itself. This opposition included the Libertines and the "Patriots," which latter class bitterly opposed the close aristocratic lines with which the previous popular government had been replaced, and regarded with jealousy the foreigners that in great numbers were coming to make their home at Geneva. The enmity toward him and his administration was still farther fomented by the irrational and merciless severity shown in the punishment of small offences, such as the beheading of a child for striking its mother, the committal of heretics to the flames, the eliciting of testimony by torture. His rule was one of terror and he was both feared and hated. Mobs attempted to intimidate him. Dogs in the street were named after him. To antagonize Calvin was a crime, as Castellio found to his cost, and to speak disrespectfully of predestination, as did Bolsee, a felony. But cases like these two are quite eclipsed by the instance of Servetus.

Servetus was a Spaniard, a scholar of independent thought, who convinced himself of the groundlessness of papal claims, but without cordially accepting the theology of Protestantism. In 1531 he published a book entitled «The Errors of the Trinity.» Irritated by Calvin's treatment of him and his speculations he retorted upon him and the reformed doctrine flatly and acrimoniously. Though out of sympathy with the Roman Catholic Church Servetus continued for twenty years in outward conformity with its doctrine and discipline and then wrote another volume under the title «The Restoration of Christianity.» This was issued by him during his residence at Vienne and resulted in his arrest at the instance of the Archbishop. A copy of the work came under Calvin's eye, who declared that if Servetus were to come to Geneva he should not get away alive if his authority was sufficient to prevent it. Having escaped from Vienne Servetus did come to Geneva, where his presence soon reached the knowledge of Calvin, who ordered his arrest. Thirty-eight heretical propositions were alleged against him, among others the rejection of the Trinity and speculations leaning toward pantheism: and, although he conducted his defence with vigor and with a degree of acuteness, he was condemned and, to the disgrace of the Protestant cause, was burned a little way out from Geneva on the 27th of October 1553. It is claimed in behalf of Calvin that he tried to mitigate the severity of the penalty. However that may be, he was set on pursuing Servetus to the death, and it is on record that he wrote as follows to Farel two months before the execution,— «I hope the sentence will be capital but desire the atrocity of the punishment to be mitigated.» It has to be remembered however that all of this was in keeping with the barbarism of the age and that so gracious-spirited a man as Melancthon gave to it his assent.

During the entire course of his conflict with heresy and the Libertines, Calvin was actively engaged in preaching and lecturing. He had crowds of hearers from all parts of Europe. Protestant refugees were in attendance upon his lectures and discourses and went back carrying with them the impression made upon them by his doctrines and personality. Thus was he able to stamp himself ineffaceably upon the religious thought of his own and aftertimes, and to cause Geneva to sustain to the Latin nations in particular a relation similar to that subsisting between Wittenberg and the Germanic. The weight and permanence of the influence he exerted was due partly to his own idiosyncrasies. Both his mode of thinking and his policy of action were measurably determined by his natural temperament and his physical debility. He was composed principally of will and brain, with too little of the tenderer sensibilities to sweeten the action of the one or to rectify the aberrations of the other. Naturally enough then he made the doctrine of God's sovereignty the key-stone of his system, and could conceive of heresy as being none other than the unpardonable sin. The same combination of volitional and intellectual genius made him also a born organizer enabling him to compact and mature the reform tendencies of the times into a corporate whole where before everything had been incipient and sporadic.

Calvinism is Augustinianism in its developed and protestant form, the two theologians coinciding in their views of predestination, sin, and grace, though differing in the matter of justification and other less important matters. The keynote of Calvinism is not predestination, as is sometimes claimed, but divine sovereignty, out of which, understood as Augustine and Calvin understood it, predestination issues as a necessary corollary. Predestination so derived carries with it perforce the notion that those who are elected to be saved are so elected by the arbitrary action of the divine will; — «He hath mercy on whom he will have mercy, and whom he will he hardeneth.» The motive therefore leading to God's exercise of grace in specific cases has its inexplicable grounds in the mind of God, and is nowise referable to any condition existent in the sinner. 'Infralapsarianism,' 'Permissive Decree,' etc., are merely philosophical attempts to relieve divine arbitrariness from the charge of immorality.

For a detailed history of the life of Calvin see Merle d'Aubigné's 'History of the Reformation in Europe in the Time of Calvin.' For a briefer outline of the same consult G. P. Fisher, 'The Reformation.' See also under 'Calvin' and 'Calvinism' in Schaff-Herzog Encyclopædia of Religious Knowledge. A very complete Bibliography is given in Schaff's 'Creeds of Christendom.'

CHARLES H. PARKHURST,
Madison Square Presbyterian Church, N. Y.

Calvin, Samuel, Scottish-American scientist: b. Wigtonshire, Scotland. 2 Feb. 1840. He came to the United States when a youth and served in the Civil War. He studied geology as a life pursuit, and since 1874 has been professor of geology at the University of Iowa, and State geologist of Iowa since 1892.

Calvinism. See CALVIN, JOHN.

Calvinistic Methodists, a section of the Methodists in Great Britain, distinguished by their Calvinistic sentiments from the ordinary Wesleyans, who are Arminian. Wesley and Whitefield, the colleagues in the great evangelistic movement in the 18th century, differed with regard to the doctrines of grace, Wesley being Arminian, and Whitefield Calvinistic. Whitefield may be regarded as the founder of Calvinistic Methodism. Other names, and especially that of Howell Harries, of Trevecca, should be mentioned in connection with it. In its distinctive form it dates from 1725, but did not completely sever its connection with the English Church till 1810. In government it is now Presbyterian. Its great seat is Wales. The Calvinistic Methodists exist in three divisions: the Whitefield Connection, 1741; Countess of Huntingdon's Connection (Huntingdonians), 1748; Welsh Methodists, 1750.

Calvo, kä̇l′vō, Carlos, Argentine jurist and author: b. Buenos Ayres, 26 Feb. 1824; d. Paris, 4 May 1893. On 25 June 1860 he was accredited to the courts of Paris and London as minister plenipotentiary, and resigned after having fulfilled his special mission. In 1885 he became Argentine minister at Berlin. In 1869 he was elected a corresponding member of the Paris Academy of Moral and Political Sciences, and later received the decoration of an officer of the Legion of Honor. He wrote numerous works, mostly in French, the most important of which are: 'Complete Collection of Treaties, Conventions, and Other Diplomatic Acts of All the Latin-American States' (11 vols., 1862–9); 'Historical Annals of the Revolution in Latin America' (15 vols. 1864, and later dates); 'International Law in Theory and Practice' (2 vols. 1870–2; 3d ed. 5 vols. 1881–8), a work considered by jurists as one of the most remarkable on its subject; 'Study on Emigration and Colonization' (1875); 'Dictionary of Public and Private International Law' (2 vols. 1885); 'Manual of Public and Private International Law' (3d ed. 1892).

Cal′vus, Gai′us Licin′ius Ma′cer, Roman orator and poet, a son of the annalist and orator of the same name: b. 82 B.C.; d. about 47. He left 21 orations, but few fragments survive. One of these, against Vatinius, whose counsel Cicero was, produced so powerful an effect that the accused interrupted the orator and exclaimed, "Judges, am I to be condemned because my accuser is eloquent?" His poems were ranked with those of Catullus.

Calx, properly lime or calk (hence "calcareous earth"); but the term is more generally applied to the residuum of a metal or mineral which has been subjected to violent heat, burning, or calcination, solution by acids, or detonation by nitre, and which is or may be reduced to a fine powder.

Calycanthus, kăl-ĭ-kăn′thus, a genus of plants of the natural order *Calycanthaceæ.* About a dozen species of American and Japanese fragrant shrubs often grown for ornament. *C. floridus,* and *C. glaucus* are found in the Alleghany Mountains from Pennsylvania southward; *C. occidentalis,* in California. They are popularly known as sweet-scented shrub and Carolina or American allspice. The leaves are green and rather large, and the flowers usually some shade of chocolate or purple. Both are sweet-scented. In the northern United States the species are scarcely hardy, though some thrive in the vicinity of New York city upon well-drained, rather rich soil in somewhat sheltered situations.

Calycifloræ, a subclass of exogenous or dicotyledonous plants, characterized by having both calyx and corolla, petals separate and stamens attached to the calyx.

Cal′ydon, an ancient city of Ætolia, celebrated in the stories of King Œneus, the Calydonian boar, and Dejanira and Hercules.

Calydon, Forest of, a large forest mentioned in the Arthurian legends; it is supposed to have been in the northern part of England, or it may have been the wooded portion of the midland counties, which include also the "Sherwood" of Robin Hood.

Calydo′nian Boar, in Greek mythology, a boar sent to lay waste the fields of Œneus, king of Calydon, the ancient capital of Ætolia, when he omitted a sacrifice to Artemis. The goddess sent the boar when Œneus was absent on the Argonautic expedition. No one dared to face the monster, until Meleager, the son of Œneus, with a band of heroes, pursued and slew him. The Curetes laid claim to the head and hide, but were driven off by Meleager. Later accounts make Meleager summon to the hunt heroes from all parts of Greece, among them the maiden Atalanta, who gave the monster the first wound.

Calymene, a genus belonging to the fossil order of the trilobites, characteristic of the Upper Silurian formations of Europe. In this genus the head is almost semicircular, and deeply divided by longitudinal furrows. The eyes are situated on the lateral lobes. The rings of the thorax and abdomen are difficult to distinguish from each other. The thoracic segments are from 10 to 14 in number. The abdominal rings are distinct and never attached to each other. The genus includes about 20 species, of which the *Calymene Blumenbachii* may be taken as the type. The members of this genus have the power of rolling themselves up like a ball.

Calypso, in Greek mythology, a daughter of Atlas (some say of Nereus and Doris, or of Oceanus and Thetis). She inhabited the woody island Ogygia, situated deep in the ocean, and lived remote from all intercourse with gods and men.

Calyptra, the hood of the theca or capsule of mosses. The same name is given to any hoodlike body connected with the organs of fructification in flowering plants.

Calyptræa, a genus of gasteropod mollusks belonging to the family of the *Calyptræidæ,* resembling limpets in certain characteristics, but differing from them in structure. This genus consists of small marine shellfish, conical in form, but sometimes very flat; they are fragile, and are distinguished by a conical scale or testaceous process attached to the bottom of the cavity of the shell. The branchiæ of this mollusk are composed of long and thing hairlike filaments. It is sometimes found as a fossil.

Calyx, in botany, the exterior covering of a flower; that is, the outermost floral envelope, consisting of a circle or whorl of leaves external to the corolla, which it encloses and supports. The parts or leaves which belong to it are called sepals; they may be united by their margins, or distinct, and are usually of a green color and of less delicate texture than the corolla. In many flowers, however (especially monocotyledons), there is little or no difference in character between calyx and corolla, in which case the whole gets the name of perianth.

Cam, Auguste Nicolas, ô-güst nĭk-ô-lä kän, French sculptor: b. Paris, 1822. He was a pupil of Rude; his first works represent small animals, but he later chose the large beasts and birds of prey for his subjects. Among his best-known works are 'Linnets Defending Their Nest Against Rats'; 'Tiger in Conflict with a Crocodile'; and 'Eagle and Vulture Wrangling over the Carcass of a Bear.'

Cam, kän, or **Caõ,** kän, Diogo, Portuguese explorer of the 15th century, who followed up the course of Prince Henry of Portugal, and in 1484 discovered the mouth of the Congo, near whose bank an inscribed stone erected by him as a memorial was found in 1887. He afterward examined the coast as far as lat. 22° S.

Cam, kăm, an English river formed by the junction of two streams, one of which (the Granta) rises in Essex and flows northwest, while the other (the Rhee) rises in the north of Hertfordshire, and flows northeast. The united stream flows sluggishly northward through Cambridgeshire, and falls into the Ouse some four miles south of Ely after a course of about 40 miles. The university town of Cambridge is situated on its banks a few miles below the confluence of the head-streams. It is navigable to Cambridge.

Cam, in machinery, a simple contrivance for converting a uniform rotary motion into a varied rectilinear motion, usually a projecting part of a wheel or other revolving piece so placed as to give an alternating or varying motion to another piece that comes in contact with it and is free to move only in a certain direction.

Cam and Isis, a familiar couplet by which the sister universities of Cambridge and Oxford are often mentioned. The allusion is to the rivers on which they are situated.

> " May you, my Cam and Isis, preach it long;
> The right divine of kings to govern wrong."
> Pope, " The Dunciad."

> " The drooping Muses, (Sir Industry,)
> Brought to another Castalie,
> Where Isis many a famous nursling breeds
> Or where old Cam soft passes o'er the lea,
> In pensive mood."
> Thomson, " Castle of Indolence."

Camaieu, ka̱-mî'ū, or **Camayeu,** a painting wherein there is only one color, and where the lights and shades are of gold, wrought on a golden or azure ground. When the ground is yellow the French call it *cirage;* when gray, *grisaille.* This kind of work is chiefly used to represent bas-reliefs. The Greeks called pieces of this sort μονοχρώματα. The word is also applied to a painting in two or three different colors, which, however, do not represent the natural colors of the objects depicted.

Camajuani, kä-ma̱-hwä'nĕ, Cuba, an inland city in the province of Santa Clara. It has rail connection with the capital and other northern cities. Pop. about 5,000.

Camal'dolites, Camaldulians, or **Camaldunians,** a religious order established in 1012, by St. Romuald, a Benedictine of Ravenna, in the valley of Camaldoli, near Arezzo, in the Apennines, and confirmed afterward by Pope Alexander II. They were originally hermits living in separate cells, but as their wealth increased the greater part of them associated in

convents. They existed in Italy, France, Germany, and Poland. In the 18th century there were five independent fraternities of them, which are here mentioned in the order of their foundation: (1) at Camaldoli; (2) at Murano in the Venetian territory; (3) on Monte Corona, near Perugia; (4) at Turin; (5) the French fraternity, the first establishment of which was that of Notre Dame de la Consolation. They all had in common white garments, and the austere rules of the Benedictines. The hermits wore beards, and had still more severe rules than the monks in regard to fasting, silence, and penauces. Their life was devoted to contemplation rather than to active work. A small branch of the order, consisting of nuns, was founded in 1086. There is in the vicinity of Naples a mountain which takes its name from a convent of the Camaldoli situated on its top, from which the traveler enjoys a prospect of remarkable grandeur and beauty. It is one of the most charming of all the beautiful views around Naples; yet the spot is not much visited by travelers.

Camalig, kä-ma̱-lĕg', Philippines, a town in the southeast part of the island of Luzon, situated within a few miles of the city of Albay. Pop. 14,868.

Cámara y Livermore, Manuel de la, mä'-noo-ĕl dä lä kä'ma̱-rä ē lĭv'er-mōr, Spanish naval officer: b. in Malaga in 1836, his father being a Spaniard of the middle class, his mother an English woman. In 1903 he was in command of the *Escuadron de instruccion,* or training ships for cadets. During the Spanish-American war his name was associated with plans for the relief of the provincial capitals of the Spanish West and East Indies. First, in May 1898, it was suggested that a squadron, commanded by him as vice-admiral, might be sent from Spain for the relief of Havana. Second, a month later, he actually started to go to Manila, where Capt.-Gen. Augustin was shut in by Admiral Dewey and the insurgents. On 16 and 17 June the Cadiz reserve squadron under Admiral Cámara left port and sailed eastward through the Mediterranean. His fleet included troopships convoyed by the Pelayo and the best of the men-of-war, except those with Cervera in the West Indies. The United States consul at Port Said protested against permitting the Spanish fleet to refill its bunkers with coal there; nevertheless Cámara received orders to proceed through the Suez Canal. At this juncture an official bulletin of the navy department at Washington announced that Commodore Watson would "take under his command an armored squadron with cruisers and proceed at once to the Spanish coast." That was on 27 June. As though to emphasize the threat, came Cervera's defeat on 3 July. On 6 July Cámara's squadron was recalled to protect the Spanish coast; and so Watson's fleet, which had scarcely begun to exist, had yet completely fulfilled its destiny. Admiral Cámara's advancement to the grade he held in 1898 was very honorably won by service in Mexico, South America, Cuba (during the Ten Years' war), and the Philippines.

Camarasaurus, kăm-a̱-ra-sôr'ŭs, a genus of amphibious dinosaurs (see DINOSAURIA), resembling the brontosaurus (q.v.), but of more massive proportions, with heavier fore limbs and shorter tail. An incomplete skeleton found in the Jurassic strata near Cañon City, Col., was the first of these gigantic animals discovered in America. It was deposited in the American Museum of Natural History, New York. The length of this animal was estimated by Prof. Cope at 75 feet; its name was suggested by the hollow-chambered vertebræ of the back and neck. The atlantosaurus, of which the femur is over six feet long and two feet across at the head, was probably the same animal.

Camargue, La, lạ kạ-märg', France, an island in the department of Bouches-du-Rhône, formed at the mouth of the river by its two principal branches. It has an area of about 300 square miles. It is protected from the inundations of the river by dykes, and is mostly an unhealthy tract of pools and marshes, only a small portion of its being culivated. Horses and cattle are raised on the island.

Camarilla, a word first used in Spain, but now in other countries also, to express the influence of certain persons in obstructing the operation of the official organs of government. When Ferdinand VII., in 1814, returned to Spain, he was surrounded by flatterers, who prevailed upon him to violate his promise of giving the people a constitution. They were called *camarilla* either from the room where they remained in waiting, or in allusion to the Council of Castille (*Camara de Castilla*). Until the revolution of 1820 the camarilla consisted mostly of men without talent, but passionately opposed to everything new; but when the king recovered his power in 1823 they became more influential and have since repeatedly interfered with the ministers. The thing itself is old enough; priests, favorites, and women have often formed camarillas in monarchies and other governments.

Camarina, kä-mạ-rē'nạ, Sicily, an ancient town on the southern coast of the island, founded by a colony from Syracuse, about 600 B.C. Its first overthrow, which occurred 553 B.C., was the result of a revolt from the parent city. On its reduction it was razed to the ground, but was afterward rebuilt. It was in an exposed position in the Roman and Carthaginian wars, and was several times taken, retaken, and destroyed. Scarcely any vestiges of the ancient town remain.

Cam'arines, North and **South,** Philippines, two provinces in the southeastern part of the island of Luzon. The name is also applied more vaguely to the whole of the southeastern peninsula of the island. The Camarines provinces are bounded north by the province of Tayabas; south by the province of Albay, which forms the southern extremity of the peninsula; east by the Pacific Ocean; and west by the great Bay of Albay. The formation of the peninsula is volcanic; the Caravallos range of mountains extends its whole length, from north to south, and seven of its peaks are active volcanoes. One of them, which is continually emitting smoke and flame, is well known to mariners coming from the east, and forms a kind of natural lighthouse. The most important product is rice. The soil of the two provinces possesses the same remarkable fertility which accompanies all the volcanic formations throughout the archipelago. Tobacco, sugar, coffee, cocoa, and indigo, are largely produced for ex-

portation; but the chief occupation of the inhabitants of the Camarines is the culture of the pineapple, and the manufacture of pina cloth (q.v.). The women of the Camarines are esteemed the most skilful embroiderers in Luzon of the delicate pina. The skill of the women of these provinces is also singularly displayed in the working of gold and silver filigree. All the artificers in precious metals are women; and some articles of jewelry, especially their neck chains, are very beautiful. The agriculture of the Camarines indicates in some respects a degree of progress beyond that of the other provinces of the island. The ox, and occasionally the horse, are used in plowing, instead of the slow, unwieldy buffalo, so generally preferred by the native East Indian farmer. The Camarinians have also discarded the primitive plow, formed from a single piece of crooked timber, with a point hardened by fire; and have substituted in its place a more modern style of implement. The provinces have well-constructed roads; and many of the rivers are traversed by substantial stone bridges. The Naga River, which drains the lakes Bato, Baao, Buhi, and Iryga, and empties into the Bay of San Miguel, is navigable about 40 miles for vessels drawing not more than 13 feet of water. The industrial development of these provinces has been accompanied by a notable increase in population; and this being composed, with but small exception, of the brown race of the Philippines, which has yielded so readily to the influences of Christian civilization. The Camarines have not had their progress retarted, like other provinces of Luzon, by the troublesome presence of the wild negrito race.

Camass-rat, kạ-mǎs-rǎt, a pocket-rat of the northwestern United States, similar to the gopher (q.v.). Its chief food is the camass (*Camasia esculenta*).

Cambacérès, Jean Jacques Régis, zhŏṅ zhǎk rā-zhē käṅ-bạ-sā-rǎs, Duke of Parma, French statesman: b. Montpellier, 18 Oct. 1753; d. Paris, 8 March 1824. His zeal and talents soon obtained him distinction, and the office of a counselor at the *cour des comptes* at Montpellier. At the beginning of the Revolution he received several public offices, became in September 1792 a member of the Convention, labored in the committees, particularly in the committee of legislation. On 12 Dec. 1792 he was commissioned to inquire of Louis XVI. whom he desired for his counsel, and it was on his motion that the counsel was allowed to communicate freely with the king. In January 1793 he declared Louis guilty, but disputed the right of the Convention to judge him, and voted for his provisory arrest, and in case of a hostile invasion, death. On 24 January he was chosen secretary of the Convention. As a member of the Committee of Public Safety he reported, in the session of 26 March, the treason of Dumouriez. In August and October 1793 he presented his first plan for a civil code, in which his democratical notions were displayed. He was a member of the Council of the Five Hundred, where he presented a new plan for a code civil. This *Projet de Code Civil*, 1796, became subsequently the foundation of the Code Napoléon. On 20 May 1797 he left his seat in the council. A year afterward he appeared among the electors of Paris;

and after the revolution of the 30th Prairial, VII. (19 June 1799), was made minister of justice. On the 18th of Brumaire he was chosen second consul, and in that office made the administration of justice the chief object of his attention. After Napoleon had ascended the throne, Cambacérès was appointed arch-chancellor of the empire, and after obtaining many high distinctions, became in 1808 Duke of Parma. During the campaign against the allied powers in 1813, Cambacérès was made president of the council of regency. At the approach of the allies in 1814 he followed the government to Blois, and from that place sent his consent to the abdication of the emperor. When Napoleon returned in 1815 Cambacérès was again made arch-chancellor and minister of justice, and subsequently president of the Chamber of Peers. After the second fall of Napoleon he was banished, as a regicide, but in 1818 was permitted to return.

Cambaluc, käm-bạ-look', the name by which the city we now know as Pekin became known to Europe during the Middle Ages. It was the form given by Marco Polo (q.v.) to the Tartar word, *Khambalu.*

Cambay, kăm-bā', British India, a seaport of Hindustan, Bombay presidency, the chief town of a native state of the same name, at the head of the Gulf of Cambay, 82 miles north-northwest of Surat. It was once a place of importance, but owing to the silting-up of the harbor, has greatly declined. The tides rush in with violence, and rising from 30 to 40 feet, enable the largest vessels to approach the shore; but again, at ebb, leave them dry. Among the buildings are several mosques and Hindu temples, and many religious structures of the Jains. The natives are expert jewelers and goldsmiths, and agate, carnelian, and onyx ornaments are exported. The trade is chiefly in cotton, ivory, and grain; the latter product being shipped to Bombay. Pop. 31,390. The state has an area of 350 square miles, and a population of 89,722.

Cambert, Robert, rō-bār kän-bär, French musician: b. Paris, about 1628; d. London, 1677. He founded the Royal Academy of Music, now the Paris Grand Opera. He was the first French opera composer, his works including 'La Pastorale' (1659), the first French opera; 'Pomone' (1671); 'Ariadne'; and 'Adonis.' For 22 years he was associated with the Abbe Perrin in the conduct of French opera, and going to England subsequently became "Master of the Music" to Charles II.

Cam'berwell, England, a parliamentary and municipal borough of London, on the south of the Thames, in Surrey, between Lambeth and Deptford. Its three divisions, North Camberwell, Peckham, and Dulwich, each return one member to Parliament. Pop. (1901) 259,258. See LONDON.

Camberwell Beauty, the common English name of the *Vanessa antiopa,* a large and beautiful butterfly found in Great Britain, but much more common on the continent of Europe and in North America, where it is called Mourning Cloak (q.v.). It measures three inches or more between the extremities of its extended wings, which are of a dark-brown color, with a broad light-yellow border, and a row of blue spots near the edge. The caterpillar feeds on the leaves of the birch, willow, and poplar. When fully grown the caterpillar is black, with bright-red spots along the back, and small spines over the whole body.

Cambiaso, käm-bē-ä'sō, **Luca** (called LUCHETTO DA GENOVA), Italian painter: b. Moneglia, 1527; d. Madrid, 1585. His best works are the 'Martyrdom of St. George'; and the 'Rape of the Sabines.' Late in life, at the invitation of Philip II., he visited Madrid, and executed a fine composition, representing the 'Assemblage of the Blessed,' on the ceiling of the Escurial.

Cambier, kän-bē-ā, **Ernest,** Belgian explorer: b. Ath, 1844. He entered the army, serving as adjutant on the general's staff, and in 1877 went as geographer on the first expedition of the International African Association, under the leadership of Crespel. The latter died in Zanzibar in 1878, and Cambier became leader. Accompanied by Wauters and Dutrieux, he started for the interior from Bagamoyo, and after a difficult journey reached Unyamwezi; after the death of Wauters and Dutrieux's return to Europe, he went on to Karema on Lake Tanganyika. Here, in September 1879, he established the first post and scientific station of the association, and remained there till 1882. He published 'Rapports sur les Marches de la première Expédition de l'Association internationale.'

Cam'bium, in botany, the layer of delicate thin-walled cells separating the wood from the bast in a great many stems and in a cross section appearing as a ring. The growth of the stem takes place by the deposition on the outside of the wood, of new wood-layers formed from the cambium, and on the inside of the bast, of new layers of bast formed from the outer cells of the cambium layer. In conifers and dicotyledonous woody perennials the primary bundles are arranged in a circle, and their cambium layers are thus made to form a more or less continuous ring of cambium in the stem. By the deposition of new layers of wood and bast regularly taking place, especially in spring, at the inner and outer surfaces of this cambium-ring, the stem is caused to increase in thickness.

Cambles, a gluttonous king of Lydia, who is said to have eaten his own wife, and afterward killed himself for the act.

Cambo'dia, or **Camboja,** Indo-China, nominally a state under a French protectorate, but practically a French dependency, situated on the lower course of the Mekong, 220 miles from northeast to southwest, and 150 miles broad, comprising an area of 40,530 square miles. It is bounded on the southeast and south by French Cochin-China; on the southwest by the Gulf of Siam; on the north by Siam; on the east, toward Anam, where the frontier traversing imperfectly explored territories is vague, by the territories of independent Mois tribes. The coast, 156 miles long, indented about the middle by the Bay of Kompong-Som, offers but one port, Kampot. Among the numerous islands along the coast are Kong, Rong, Hon-Nan-Trung, etc., most of them inhabited. The principal river, the Mekong (in Cambodian, Tonlé-Tom, "Great River"), flows through Cambodia from north to south, as far as Chen-Tel-Pho, and thence southwest till, at the town of Pnom-Penh, it divides into two arms, the Han-Giang, or Bassac, and the Tien-Giang, or Anterior River, both flowing south. Above Pnom-Penh is a north-northwest outlet for the surcharge of the Tonlé-Tom, the Tonlé-Sap ("Sweet Water River"), expanding into the Great Lake, 100 miles by 25 miles in area, with a depth of 65 feet at its maximum magnitude. The greater part of the country is low and well watered and heavily timbered. The climate presents a dry and a wet season (June to November) and is fairly healthy. The soil is very fertile, producing large quantities of rice, besides maize, sugarcane, cotton, betel, tobacco, indigo, coffee, etc. Timber is abundant. Gold and precious stones are found, besides iron, tin, and limestone. Cattle are exceedingly numerous. Among wild animals are the elephant, wild buffalo, deer, and tiger. The Cambodians were formerly a highly cultured and civilized race. Various architectural remains, witnessing to former greatness, are found throughout the country. The present population is very mixed. The religion is Buddhism. In early times Cambodia was a powerful state to which even the kings of Siam paid tribute, but it gradually fell into decay, until about the close of the 18th century the Siamese annexed part of Cambodia to their own land, and reduced the rest of the country to a state of dependency. France, on 11 Aug. 1863, concluded a treaty with the king of Cambodia, Nerodom, placing Cambodia under a French protectorate. This treaty was superseded by that of 17 June 1884, under which the king of Cambodia accepted all the reforms, administrative, judiciary, financial, and commercial, which the government of France might institute. The chief imports are salt, sugar, wine, and various manufactured goods, such as textiles, and arms; the exports include salt-fish, spices, cotton, tobacco, and rice. The capital is Pnom-Penh. Pop. 1,500,000.

Cambodia, or **Mekong,** a large river of southeastern Asia, which rises in Tibet, passes through Yunnan, a province of China, Laos, Anam, Cambodia, and French Cochin-China, and falls into the Chinese Sea by several mouths, after a course of about 2,600 miles. Its navigation is much interrupted by sand-banks, rapids, etc., at various points of its middle and upper course. The Tonle-Sap ("Great Lake"), is connected with the Mekong.

Cambon, Jules Martin, zhül mär-tăň kăň bôň, French diplomatist: b. Paris, 5 April, 1845. He studied for the law and fought in the Franco-Prussian war, reaching the grade of captain. Entering the civil service, he became prefect of Constantine in 1878, prefect of the Department du Nord in 1882, prefect of the Rhone in 1887, governor-general of Algeria in 1891, and ambassador to the United States in 1897. He represented Spain in drawing up the Spanish-American protocol in 1898.

Cambon, Pierre Joseph, pě är zhŏ-zěf, French statesman: b. Montpellier, 17 June 1754; d. Brussels, 15 Feb. 1820. Engaged in commercial pursuits, he became interested in the Revolution, and on hearing of the flight of Louis XVI. he caused the republican government to be proclaimed in his native town. He was sent to the legislative assembly, and while supporting the cause of democracy, gave particular attention to financial matters. Most of the great measures which enabled the government to get through the revolutionary period were suggested or controlled by him; and to him the honor is due of having laid the foundation of the modern financial system of France. He promoted the confiscation of the estates of the émigrés in 1792, and made, after 10 August, a report in which he argued that Louis XVI., having held a secret correspondence with the enemies of France, was guilty of high treason. He presided over the last sittings of the legislative assembly, and afterward took his seat as a member of the Convention. Here he opposed with equal energy the partisans of monarchy and of terrorism. When Louis XVI. was arraigned before the Convention, he voted for his immediate death, and against the appeal to the people. He opposed the creation of the revolutionary tribunal, and insisted upon trial by jury. At the opening of the Convention, he had been appointed member of the Committee on Finances; 7 April 1793 he entered the Committee of Public Safety. On 2 June, when the Girondists were threatened by the infuriated mob calling for their proscription, he boldly took his place among them, hoping to be able, through his name of the Committee on Public Safety, to save them from violence and arrest. The next year he made another report on the administration of finances, which is considered a masterpiece of financial ability, and gives a full sketch of the plan which was afterward adopted for the regular registration of public debt. In the conflict which brought on the revolution of the 9th Thermidor, Cambon took part against Robespierre and his adherents; but though he had been instrumental in their defeat, he was charged with having been their accomplice, and a warrant was issued against him. He succeeded in baffling the search for him, and on the amnesty proclaimed by the Convention on its adjournment, he retired to an estate in the vicinity of Montpellier, where he devoted himself to agriculture. In 1815 he was elected a member of the Chamber of Deputies. On the second return of the Bourbons, he was exiled as a regicide.

Cambon, Pierre Paul, pě är pŏl, French diplomatist: b. Paris, 20 Jan. 1843. He was graduated at the Ecole Polytechnique in 1863, and, after serving as secretary to Jules Ferry, became secretary of prefecture for the Alpes-Maritimes, prefect of the Aube, and French resident-general in Tunis. He was appointed ambassador to Spain in 1886, was transferred to Constantinople in 1890, and to London in 1898.

Cam'borne, England, a market town of Cornwall, 11 miles northwest of Falmouth, situated on the slope of a gently rising hill. There is a granite church in the Perpendicular style, restored in 1862, and several other places of worship. It also contains a market-hall, a mining-school, a working-man's institute, and a museum of mineralogy. Near it are tin and copper mines. Pop. (1901) 14,726.

Cambrai, kăň-brä, or **Cambray,** France (Flemish, KAMBRYK), a fortified city on the Scheldt, in the department Nord, 45 miles south of Lille. From this place the linen cloth known by the name of cambric got its name. Cambrai is the seat of an archbishop. The Revolution stripped it of all its principal ornaments. The beautiful cathedral and the tomb of its archbishop, the celebrated Fénelon, were razed to the ground. There is a new monument to the memory of Fénelon in the present cathedral, a modern building of indifferent architecture. There is a large and handsome modern Hôtel de Ville, and an ancient belfry tower. Cambrai is the seat of a diocesan seminary, communal college, etc. It has a public library with 40,000 volumes and 1,400 MSS. Cambric and other linen goods, cotton, lace thread, leather goods, sugar, soap, beer, etc., are manufactured; and there is a trade in grain, oil-seed, hemp, etc. Cambrai is the Camaracum of the Romans. In 1508 the league against Venice was concluded at Cambrai between the Emperor Maximilian, Louis XII., the Pope, and Ferdinand of Aragon; in 1529 the peace with Charles V. Louis XIV. took Cambrai from the Spaniards in 1677, and it was finally confirmed to France by the Treaty of Nijmegen in 1678. Pop. 25,250.

Cam'bria, the Latin name of Wales, derived from Cymri, the name of the branch of the Celts to which the Welsh belong, and the name which they always give to themselves.

Cambrian Period, the name proposed by American geologists for the first or earliest time period of the Paleozoic era; in it were deposited the rocks of the Cambrian series. In Cambrian time animal life on the earth was already highly differentiated. All the great types of vertebrates were present then and definitely characterized. The principal types, so far as the fossil evidence goes, were Brachiopods and Trilobites, but many others existed, such as mollusks, marine worms, siliceous sponges, graptolites, and jellyfish, and by the end of the period starfish and crinoids. It is probable that plants, such as seaweeds, existed, but the evidence is very obscure. The climate during the Cambrian period was probably warm, even up to the Arctic Circle, but not torrid. This evenness of temperature may have been due to a much larger part of the earth's surface being covered by water than in later time, or to a difference in the composition of the atmosphere, more carbon dioxide being present.

At the beginning of Cambrian time the North American continent had already begun to take shape. A great land mass, which may have had lofty mountain ranges, extended from Labrador westward and northward, probably reaching as far south as St. Louis, and as far west as the Pacific coast. Its northern boundary is unknown, but probably was north of the Arctic Circle. To the south long narrow strips of land and narrow sounds occupied parts of Newfoundland, Nova Scotia, New Brunswick, and New England. A large Appalachian island, its west shore marked by what is now the Blue Ridge, extended from Vermont to Alabama; its eastern boundary is unknown, but was east of the present Atlantic coast-line. This Appalachian island was separated from the continental land mass to the west by a narrow sound. Southwest of the continent another long but narrow land mass, now the Sierra Nevada, extended from Puget Sound to Mexico, and another large island reached from the Kootenai district of British Columbia southward to Colorado. There were besides smaller islands in

Missouri and Texas. During Cambrian time the continental land mass slowly sank, and by the end of the Cambrian a great interior sea covered the whole Mississippi valley.

Cambrian System (from "Cambria," an ancient name for Wales), a term first used by Murchison and Sedgwick in describing the great series of slates and grits on the boundary between England and Wales, about 1835. Murchison, however, included the rocks in his Lower Silurian system, and the Cambrian was not generally recognized as a separate system until over 20 years later. The Cambrian system is fairly well defined at its base, since the rocks are deposited upon the upturned, eroded edges of Algonkian and Silurian strata, indicating a great time break. The top of the Cambrian grades into the Silurian. In North America the rocks of the Cambrian system are divided into three series, as follows: (1) the Lower Cambrian, or Georgian, containing *Olenellus* fossils; (2) the Middle Cambrian, or Acadian, with *Paradoxides* fauna; and (3) the Upper Cambrian, or Potsdam, with *Olenus* fauna. The Cambrian rocks were laid down along the shores of the great Algonkian continent that extended from Labrador to the Pacific Ocean, and as far south as St. Louis, in the narrow sounds that covered parts of Newfoundland, Nova Scotia, New Brunswick, and New England, and around the shores of the Appalachian and the Sierra Nevada uplifts. The rocks indicate generally a period of tranquil change, the ocean slowly advancing over the sinking continent and islands, just as one may see it to-day along great stretches of coast. The rocks are chiefly shallow water formations, including conglomerates, sandstones, and shales, though limestones, indicating deep water, are found in western Vermont, Nevada, and British Columbia. In a few places, as at South Mountain, Pa., there are rocks representing lava and volcanic ash interstratified with detrital sediments.

The Cambrian rocks undoubtedly cover a great area in North America, but are, over long stretches of country, buried beneath later sediments. The total thickness so far as known is not over 12,000 feet as a maximum, unless part of the underlying Algonkian be included. The Rhode Island Cambrian is 1,000 feet thick, the New Brunswick 2,500 feet, the Arizona 5,000 feet. The rocks are classified by Wolcott into these geographic provinces: (1) the Atlantic or eastern border, including the Nova Scotia basin, and the basin extending from southeast Newfoundland, across New Brunswick and Maine, into Massachusetts; (2) the Appalachian or eastern border province; (3) the Rocky Mountain or western border province; (4) the interior or continental province, including the region of the central and upper Mississippi and Missouri valleys, the Adirondacks of New York and Canada, and the deposits found in Dakota, Wyoming, Arizona, and Texas.

In Europe the Cambrian rocks are developed more fully than in North America; thus the conglomerate sandstones, shales, slates, and quartzites of the Welsh Cambrian are fully 20,000 feet thick. They are rocks indicating shallow-water conditions, and show three divisions. They extend from Wales, along Sweden, Norway, and Lapland into Russia, having in Sweden a thickness of 2,000 feet. To the east the Cambrian formations thin out, and in central Russia die out altogether, the Ordovician resting directly on the Archæan. There are considerable areas of Cambrian in Germany, Bohemia, France, Portugal, and Spain; also in northeast China, in the Salt Range in India, in Australia, and in Argentina. See CAMBRIAN PERIOD.

'Report of the British Association' (Sedgwick 1835); Dana's 'Manual of Geology'; Geikie's 'Text-Book of Geology'; 'Bulletin 81 of the United States Geological Survey.'

Cambric, kăm-brĭk, a fine, thin kind of linen cloth manufactured originally, it is said, at Cambrai (q.v.) in French Flanders, whence the name. Cambric is manufactured in the north of Ireland, in England, Switzerland, and France, and is now chiefly used for handkerchiefs. The name is also applied to a cotton fabric which is in reality a kind of muslin.

Cambridge, kăm brĭdj, **Ada,** the pseudonym of **Mrs.** George Frederick Cross, English novelist: b. Saint Germains, Norfolk, England, 21 Nov. 1844. She was married in 1870 to Rev. G. F. Cross and went with him to Victoria in that year, since 1893 living near Melbourne. She is the author of 'My Guardian' (1877); 'In Two Years' Time' (1879); 'A Mere Chance' (1882); 'A Marked Man' (1891); 'The Three Miss Kings' (1891); 'Not All in Vain' (1892); 'A Little Minx' (1893); 'A Marriage Ceremony' (1894); 'Fidelis' (1895); 'A Humble Enterprise' (1896); 'At Midnight' (1897); 'Materfamilias' (1898); 'Path and Goal' (1900); 'The Devastators' (1901); 'Thirty Years in Australia' (1903); 'Sisters' (1904); etc. She has also written several notable poems.

Cambridge, Adolphus Frederick (1ST DUKE OF): b. London, 25 Feb. 1774; d. 8 July 1850. He was the youngest son of George III., and the uncle of Queen Victoria. There entered the British army as ensign when 16 years of age, and completed his education at the German university of Göttingen. He leaned at first to the side of the opposition on the question of the French war, but afterward sided with the government. ·He took part in the campaign in the Netherlands (1793), and fell into the hands of the French at the battle of Hondschoote, but was soon afterward exchanged. In 1801-3 he was employed in Hanover, vainly endeavoring to preserve it from occupation by foreign powers. In 1816 he was again sent to Hanover by the British prince regent, in the capacity of governor-general, and in 1831 was appointed viceroy of Hanover. In 1837, on the separation of Hanover from the British crown, he returned to England again. From that period until his death he was best known to the public as the president of charitable societies, and the chairman at the anniversary dinners of public associations.

Cambridge, George William Frederick Charles (2D DUKE OF), English general, son of the preceding: b. Hanover, 26 March 1819; d. 17 March 1904. He became colonel in the army in 1837, and major-general in 1845. In 1850 he succeeded his father as Duke of Cambridge, in 1854 was advanced to lieutenant-general, and in 1856 to that of general. He commanded the two brigades of Highlanders which formed the first division of the army sent to the Crimea. He led these troops into action at the battle of Alma, and at Inkerman had a horse shot under him. Directed by his physician to withdraw for a time from camp life, he retired first to Pera, and soon after to England. On the resignation of Viscount Hardinge in 1856, he was appointed commander-in-chief of the British army. He retired in 1895.

Cambridge, England, an inland county bounded on the north by the county of Lincoln; on the west by Northampton, Huntingdon, and Bedford; on the south by Hertfordshire and Essex; and on the east by Suffolk and Norfolk. A great part of northern half of the county belongs to the fen district and is very flat, farther south it is undulating, and in the southeast some heights occur. The principal rivers are the Cam or Granta, and the Ouse, with the Nen in the north. An important portion of the county, including the Isle of Ely, belongs to the great artificially drained tract known as the Bedford Level (q.v.). About nine tenths of the total acreage of the county is now productive, and a greater proportion of land is under corn crops than in any other county in the kingdom. Potatoes, turnips, and mangold are the chief green crops. The southern portion of the county abounds in dairy farms, celebrated for the production of excellent butter and cheese. The part of the county extending from Gogmagog Hills to Newmarket is chiefly appropriated to sheep-walks. The chief mineral productions are the phosphatic nodules known as coprolites, lime, and clay for brick and tiles; and peat is cut for fuel. For parliamentary purposes the ancient county is divided into three divisions — Wisbech, Chesterton, and Newmarket, and embraces also the parliamentary borough of Cambridge, each returning one member to parliament. Administratively the ancient county embraces the two counties of Cambridge and the Isle of Ely. There are two municipal boroughs, Cambridge and Wisbech. The educational institutions include a day training college for schoolmasters, and the new Homerton undenominational training college for women at Cambridge, and a theological college founded in 1876 at Ely; there are also more than 225 elementary schools in the county. See also CAMBRIDGE, UNIVERSITY OF.

Cambridge, England, capital of the county of Cambridge, is situated on the Cam, about 56 miles n.e. by rail from London. It is a municipal and parliamentary borough, the seat of a celebrated university (see CAMBRIDGE, UNIVERSITY OF), and has a large agricultural market.

Geology.— The geological formation of Cambridge and the surrounding district consists chiefly of clay. The following strata are to be found,— Chalk Marl, Cambridge Greensand, Gault, Kimeridge Clay, Oxford Clay, Ampthill Clay, Cherryhinton Chalk, and some recent alluvium which borders the rivers and tributaries, consisting of peat, sandy loam, etc. The town is made up of three main thoroughfares, two running north and south and the other east and west, connected by a number of short streets.

Public Buildings, Libraries, etc.— The city possesses a Guildhall, including municipal buildings, law courts, and public free library. There is also a spacious corn exchange, attended weekly by buyers from all parts of the United Kingdom, and a cattle market. Addenbrooke's Hospital is a noted institution, connected as it

CAMBRIDGE

is with the Cambridge University Medical School. Cambridge was one of the first towns to establish a public free library, which now comprises a central library and three branches with a collection of upwards of 50,000 volumes.

Churches.— In its early history Cambridge was fortunate in the number of its churches, two of which are worthy of mention. The church of Saint Benedict's is the oldest, being of pre-conquest date. It possesses a tower in Saxon architecture. That of the Holy Sepulchre or "Round Church" is one of four round churches in England and was probably in existence about the year 1130. The largest parish church is that of Saint Mary the Great (the University church), built in the perpendicular style. Other churches of interest are The Abbey (Early English. 13th century), Saint Edward (rebuilt in the 14th century with the exception of the tower which is a work of the 12th century), Saint Michael (13th century), Trinity (about 1274), Saint Mary the Less (1340), Saint Botolph (14th century) and Saint Peter, which has examples of 12th century architecture. The history of nonconformity in Cambridge dates from the year 1457, and it is now well represented by its churches. The Roman Catholics have a fine church built in the early decorated style. It was commenced in 1887, through a donation from Yolande Marie Louise Lyne-Stephens. Of theologians Cambridge was the birthplace of Jeremy Taylor; it was at Cambridge the Rev. Charles Simeon founded the evangelical school of the Church of England, and at the same period Robert Hall, the great Baptist preacher, attracted large congregations. Johnny Stittle, the hedger, occupied a unique position at the end of the 18th and beginning of the 19th century, drawing a large congregation from both town and University. Thomas Hobson was famous as a carrier. He is said to have been the first to let out horses for hire, and the originator of the proverb "Hobson's Choice." His fame must have extended far beyond the limits of the University, as in 1617 a quarto tract appeared under the title of 'Hobson's Horse Load of Letters, or Precedents for Epistles of Business.'

Education.— Cambridge has 20 public elementary schools, including higher grade schools, among which we may note the Perse grammar schools, founded by Dr. Stephen Perse in 1615. The Wesleyans are represented in education by the Leys school, the Roman Catholics by Saint Edmund's House, the Presbyterians by Westminster College, and more recently the Congregationalists have removed from Cheshunt, Herts, to Cambridge, preliminary to the erection of a new college. Homerton College has about 150 female students in training for educational duties.

Railroads.— The railway companies which have connections at Cambridge are the Great Eastern, the Great Northern, the Midland, and the London North Western.

Public Works.— The redrainage of the whole borough was carried out a few years ago, and sewage works were constructed at a total cost of about £170,000. Two other recent undertakings were the building of a new police station at a cost of about £20,000, and the purchasing and setting out of land for a new cemetery, covering 25 acres, at a cost of about £16,000.

Recreation Grounds.—Cambridge is fortunate in its number of common lands and recreation grounds, numbering in all and having a total area of 300 acres. Of the recreation grounds Parker's Piece is a noted cricket and football ground, where all the University matches were played, until they purchased their own grounds.

Government.— The corporation of Cambridge, under the "Municipal Reform Act," consists of a mayor, 10 aldermen and 30 councillors. The University also returns its quota of two aldermen and six councillors. The town returns one member to Parliament.

History.— There is every proof that in its early days Cambridge was an important trading centre. Its situation on the Cam made it easily accessible from the surrounding district for miles around, and provender, fuel, and merchandise was conveyed by water to all parts of East Anglia. It was the seat of Stourbridge Fair, one of the largest fairs in Europe. That the Romans occupied the town is evident from the fact that numerous Roman remains have been found at various periods. Miles of ancient earthworks, said to be of British origin, surround Cambridge, and in the town itself there is a large mound called "Castle Hill," probably of Saxon origin and raised as a defence against the incursions of the Danes. In the years 870 and 1010 the town was destroyed by the Danes. William the Conqueror built a castle here in 1068. The year 1110 is alleged to be the date of the origin of the university, at which time we read that learned monks visited Cambridge to teach their philosophy and other primitive sciences. Richard II. held a Parliament at Cambridge in 1388. The town was frequently visited by the plague ("Black Death"), and in 1630 the mortality was terrible. At the time of the Civil War Oliver Cromwell (formerly a student of Sidney Sussex College) represented Cambridge in Parliament, and the town supplied a large number of men for the Parliamentary army. William Dowsing did considerable damage both to the colleges and to the parish churches in 1643. Queen Victoria and her consort visited Cambridge in 1845 and again in 1847, and as chancellor of the university, the influence for good, exercised by the Prince Consort, was predominant. The King and Queen visited Cambridge on 1 March 1904 to open the new university museums. The second meeting of the British association was held at Cambridge in 1833, and subsequent meetings were held in 1845, 1862, and 1904. Apart from the University, Cambridge would lose much of its importance. The colleges with their various styles of architecture, surrounded by gardens and "college walks," are a constant source of delight. The river Cam winds its course through the college grounds for a distance of about three quarters of a mile. Nine bridges connect the colleges and grounds where nature and art combine. Below the town, the river is the scene of the well-known college boatraces which occasion the visit of thousands of people from far and near.

Area and population.— The town covers an area of 3,278 acres. Much house property has been destroyed to make room for the continuous additions to colleges and university buildings, with the result that residents have migrated to adjacent districts. Pop. (1901) 38,379.

Bibliography.— Atkinson and Clark, 'History of Cambridge' (1897); Carter, 'History of Cambridgeshire' (1819); Clark, 'Historical and

Descriptive Notes on Cambridge'; Conybeare, 'History of Cambridgeshire' (1897) ; Cooper, 'Annals of Cambridge, 695–1853' (5 vols.), and 'Memorials of Cambridge' (3 vols., 1866) ; Dean Stubbs, 'Cambridge and Its Story' (1903). Consult also Cambridge Guides, dating from 1811 to present day. J. PINK,
Chief Librarian of the Public Library.
W. A. FENTON,
Senior Assistant of the Public Library.

Cambridge, Mass., city and one of the county-seats of Middlesex County, situated on the Charles River and the Fitchburg railroad; opposite to and connected with Boston by nine bridges. It was founded in 1630–31, under the name of "Newe-Towne," or "Newtown," and did not receive its present name until several years later. In 1636 the General Court appropriated $2,000 to locate a school in Old Cambridge, which later became Harvard College, now Harvard University. In 1631 Cambridge was 35 miles long and only one mile wide, including the townships now incorporated as Billerica, Bedford, Lexington, Arlington, Brighton, and Newton, all these having been gradually separated from it. The city was formerly divided into villages called Old Cambridge, Cambridgeport, East Cambridge, and North Cambridge, names which are still used to designate certain districts. It has grown into a populous manufacturing centre, where glass, furniture, organs, steam-engines, etc., are made, the value of which amounts annually to over $35,000,000. Here also is located the massive stone courthouse of Middlesex County. The first printing office in the United States was located in Cambridge, and the 'Bay Psalm-Book,' published by Stephen Day and printed in 1640, was the first book from this press. Cambridge has now extensive printing establishments, including the Riverside Press; the Athenæum Press, and the University Press. For historical and literary associations, Cambridge is one of the most famous cities in the United States. The venerable Washington elm, under which Washington took command of the American army, 3 July 1775, stands at the corner of Mason and Garden streets. "Craigie House," built by Col. John Vassall in 1759, was Washington's headquarters in 1775–6, and afterward became the home of the poet Henry W. Longfellow until his death. On Elm Avenue is "Elmwood," the birthplace and home of James Russell Lowell, who lived here 1819–91. A part of this place has been bought by public subscription, to be preserved as a public park. This city has been the home of such distinguished men as Oliver Wendell Holmes, William Henry Channing, Margaret Fuller Ossoli, Col. Thomas Wentworth Higginson, Louis Agassiz, John Fiske, and Charles Eliot Norton. The fine city hall and land for a park was the gift of a former citizen, Frederick H. Rindge, who also presented the city with a public library, an institution now called the Rindge Manual Training School, and other benefactions which amounted to more than $1,000,000. The beautiful Mount Auburn cemetery is partly in Cambridge and partly in Watertown. Among important buildings are those of Harvard University; Radcliffe College; Cambridge Hospital; Manual Training School; the Latin and High Schools; Public Library; and Middlesex County Court-house. In recent years much has been accomplished toward developing a system of parks which will eventually include nearly the entire river front. Pop. (1900) 91,886. Consult: Paige, 'History of Cambridge' (1877) ; Powell, 'Historic Towns of New England' (1898). See HARVARD UNIVERSITY.

Cambridge, Ill., the county-seat of Henry County, a village on the Rock Island and Peoria R.R., about 28 miles southeast of Rock Island. Surrounded by a productive agricultural district, it has a thriving domestic and export trade in farm produce, grain and cattle, etc. Pop. (1904) 2,000.

Cambridge, Md., a city and county-seat of Dorchester County, about 58 miles southeast of Baltimore. on the Choptank River, and on the Seaford & Cambridge R.R. Cambridge was settled in 1684 and was incorporated as a city in 1900. It is governed by a mayor who is elected every two years by the city council, which consists of five members, the mayor and four aldermen. The aldermen are chosen by the different wards in the city. Cambridge has important manufactures of underwear and lumber and as the centre of a fertile agricultural district has an active trade in farm produce and live stock. The oyster canning industry is also carried on to a considerable extent. Pop. (1903) 6,100.

Cambridge, N. Y., a village in Washington County, situated on the Delaware & Hudson R.R., about 28 miles northeast of Albany. The Cambridge Valley Agricultural and Stockbreeders' Association is located in the valley. Pop. (1903) 2,000.

Cambridge, Ohio, city and county-seat of Guernsey County, on the Baltimore & O. and the Pennsylvania R.R.'s, 55 miles north of Marietta. It is situated in a coal and iron region which has also deposits of pottery clay ; and the industries are chiefly mining and manufactures connected with these resources. There is also natural gas used for heating. The city owns and operates its waterworks. The city has five banks, court-house, children's home, and Carnegie Library. It was settled in 1804 and was incorporated as a city in 1887. Pop. (1900) 8,241.

Cambridge Manuscript, the Codex Cantabrigiensis or Bezæ, the most famous of the uncial MSS. in the University Library, Cambridge, England, consisting of a copy of the four Gospels and the Acts of the Apostles. It was presented in 1581 to the University of Cambridge by Theodore Beza (q.v.) the celebrated Calvinistic divine. The Codex Bezæ and the Codex Laudianus at Oxford, differ widely in text from all those of other codices. Scrivener, the editor and other critics look upon these divergences as interpolations of which the Codex Bezæ is said to contain no less than six hundred. Scrivener, nevertheless, believes that the Codex Bezæ which originated probably in the south of France in the 6th century, is derived from an original of not later than the 3d century. Bornemann on the other hand contends that the Codex Bezæ contains the original text and that other versions are mutilated. Scrivener's criticism is interesting. "While the general course of the history and the spirit of the work remain the same as in our commonly received text, we perpetually encounter long passages in Codex Bezæ which resemble that text only as a loose and explanatory paraphrase recalls the original form from which it sprung. Save that there is no difference in the language in this instance, it is hardly an exaggeration of the facts to assert that Codex D (that is Codex Bezæ) reproduces the *textus receptus* of the Acts much in the same way that one of the best Chaldee Targums does the Hebrew of the Old Testament, so wide are the variations in the diction, so constant and inveterate the practice of expanding the narrative by means of interpolations.³ See BIBLE — Codex Bezæ D.

Cambridge Platform, a system of church order and polity agreed on by a synod of New England churches, held at Cambridge, Mass., in 1648. It was a resolution rather than a decree, the platform itself denying the synod's authority to pronounce the latter. Its chief positions were: The one true and immutable form of church government has been prescribed in God's word. Christ is the supreme head of his Church, which, since his advent, consists of distinct, equal, and self-governing bodies under him, not too large to meet conveniently in one place nor too small to carry on church work effectively. They are therefore monarchies as to him, democracies in themselves, and aristocracies as to each other; but obligated to mutual communion of care, counsel, monition, worship, succor, and transfer of members. Synods are useful, but not permanent, nor with authority for censure or discipline; but when their decisions accord with God's word they should be submitted to. Christ has deputed extraordinary but temporary power to his apostles, ordinary and permanent power to the churches. Officers are advantageous, but not indispensable, and each church may appoint and remove its own, but should consult its neighbor churches when feasible. These officers consist of bishops, pastors or elders (synonymous in function), and deacons who can act officially only in temporal matters. Ordination is the solemn installation of a church head into his place, following his election. The relation of civil magistrates to church affairs is also expounded.

Cambridge Platonists, the name given to a school of theological and philosophical thinkers of the English Church who were connected with Cambridge University, and who exercised an important influence during the latter half of the 17th century. The most important members of this school were Benjamin Whichcote, John Smith, Ralph Cudworth, Henry More, Nathaniel Culverwel, John Worthington, and George Rust. Joseph Glanvil and John Norris were both Oxford men and much younger than the Cambridge thinkers, though representing the same general intellectual tendency. Sir Thomas Browne, author of 'Religio Medici' and 'Christian Morals,' is also a representative of the Platonic type of thought, but his work as an author belongs to a somewhat earlier period.

In theology, the influence of these men was in favor of toleration and liberality of view. They maintain that dogmatic uniformity is unattainable, and that the welfare of both church and state demands toleration and latitude of religious opinion. Hence they were frequently termed latitudinarians (q.v.). This position was the result of a faith in reason and a conviction that free inquiry and discussion could not be prejudicial to theological truth, and that rigid uniformity of doctrine is neither possible nor desirable. At the same time they distinguish between dogma and true religion. The former is external and necessarily changes from time to time. Religion is the spiritual life springing up in the soul, the union with the divine, which manifests itself through the moral life. The spiritual life is no mere subjective fancy, but is the true reality, more real and abiding than the world of sense and matter.

In philosophy, the Cambridge Platonists were idealists, emphasizing the reality of the ideal essences of things and the higher truth and reality that these possess, both in the intellectual and moral sphere, as opposed to what is material and sensuous. Cudworth, who was the most learned and, in many respects, the most important representative of the school, names his two chief works, 'The True Intellectual System of the Universe,' and 'The Eternal and Immutable Principles of Morality.' From these titles the general standpoint of the whole movement appears. Cudworth was acquainted with the writings of Descartes, and corresponded with him on philosophical subjects, but the real inspiration of the school came from Plato and Neo-Platonists like Plotinus, Proclus, Hierocles, all of whom are abundantly quoted in uncritical fashion. Negatively, too, their thought and activity were influenced greatly by Hobbes (q.v.), who stands for materialism and for relativity and a naturalistic system of ethics. Indeed the work of Cudworth and Henry More, the two most prominent writers of the school, may be said to be explicit attempts to refute Hobbes. Cudworth's work is the more ponderous and learned, abounding in quotations drawn from many sources. In More we find a more mystical tendency, with perhaps deeper speculative insight.

Bibliography.— J. Tulloch, 'Rational Theology and Christian Philosophy in England in the Seventeenth Century' (Vol. II., 2d edition, 1874); H. Hallam, 'Introduction to the Literature of Europe'; H. Sidgwick, 'An Outline History of Ethics'; Erdmann, 'History of Philosophy.' In addition, many of the writings of representatives of the school are accessible in English form.

J. E. CREIGHTON,
Professor of Philosophy, Cornell University.

Cambridge, University of. Situated at Cambridge, England. Its origin is very obscure, and of its early history, before the 12th century, there are only very scanty records. It is clear that a university existed long before the foundation of the oldest college, and that it was powerful enough to claim and to obtain from the town very important privileges, such as immunity from taxation, the right to test weights and measures, and to prescribe what amusements should be allowed or forbidden. From the bitter feeling aroused by the possession of these and other privileges frequent serious outbreaks of hostilities arose between the town and the university, resulting in the wanton destruction of valuable records, which has left little or no material for a connected history. It is probable that the university owed its origin to the schools in connection with the Priory of St. Frideswyde and the conventual church at Ely. The earliest recognition of Cambridge as a university is contained in a writ of the second year of Henry III., 1217, ordering all clerks who had been excommunicated for their adherence to Louis, son of the King of France, to depart the realm. The number of students was increased in the same reign by a migration of students from Paris in 1229, and further by a like migration from Oxford in 1240. In the early part of the 13th century students lived where they pleased. but in time they inaugurated a system of hostels or lodging houses, in which a number had to live under the supervision of a superior; and out of this system of hostels sprang the collegiate system. The oldest of the colleges, Peterhouse, was founded in 1284 by Hugh de Balshan, Bishop of Ely; it was followed by Clare College, founded in 1326 by Lady Elizabeth, granddaughter of Edward I.; Pembroke Hall, in 1347, by Marie de St. Paul; Gonville Hall, afterwards Gonville and Caius College, in 1348, by Edmund Gonville; Trinity Hall, in 1350, by William Bateman, Bishop of Norwich; Corpus Christi College, in 1352, by the joint efforts of two Cambridge communities, the Guild of Corpus Christi, and the Guild of the Blessed Virgin; King's College, in 1441, by King Henry VI.; Queen's College, in 1448, by Margaret of Anjou, though it was not till 1475 that it received its code of statutes from Elizabeth Woodville, the consort of Edward IV.; St. Catherine's Hall, in 1452, by Robert Wodelarke, Provost of King's College; Jesus College, in 1497, by John Alcock, Bishop of Ely; Christ's College, in 1505, by the Lady Margaret, Countess of Richmond, mother of Henry VII.; St. John's College, in 1511, also by Lady Margaret; Magdalene College, in 1542, by Sir Thomas Audley; Trinity College, formed by the union of the earlier foundations of Michaelhouse, 1324, and of King's Hall, 1337, and founded in 1546 by Henry VIII.; Emmanuel College, in 1584, by Sir Walter Mildmay, a college dear to all Americans as that in which John Harvard, founder of Harvard College, was educated; Sidney Sussex College, in 1596, by the Lady Frances Sidney, Countess of Sussex; Downing College, in 1800, by Sir George Downing; Selwyn College Public Hostel, founded in 1882 in memory of George Augustus Selwyn, late Bishop of Lichfield, formerly Bishop of New Zealand. Each of these colleges is a separate corporation governed by its own statutes and practically independent of the university, though the connection between the two is necessarily very close, as every member of the university is a member of some one of the colleges, as a non-collegiate student. The head of a college is styled the Master, except in the case of King's College, where he is styled the Provost, and of Queen's College, which is ruled by the President. Other college officers are the Tutor, who stands in *loco parentis* to the undergraduates, and the Dean, who is responsible for the services in the College Chapel, and for college discipline.

A code of statutes was given to the university by Queen Elizabeth, and this code remained in force till 1858, when a new code was framed by a Royal Commission; this latter code was again revised in 1882, when they took their present form. In 1874 all religious tests were finally abolished except for Degrees in Divinity; and in 1894 the university surrendered the last of its privileges over the town which it had retained since the 13th century, and then only put an end to the bitter feeling which had existed for centuries between the town and the university, and which had led to frequent outbreaks of hostilities between the two bodies.

The university was incorporated in the reign of Elizabeth, by the name of "The Chancellor, Masters and Scholars of the University of Cambridge." The executive authority of the university rests in theory with the Chancellor, who is elected for life; but as he is non-resident, it is practically in the hands of the Vice-Chancellor, who is elected annually from among the heads of colleges. The ultimate decision of all questions touching academic policy rests with the Senate, a body composed of all those members of the university who have proceeded to the M.A. or some higher degree, and whose names are on the Register of Members of the Senate. All legislative proposals so far as they are consistent with the statutes, which can only be altered by act of Parliament, are framed by the Vice-Chancellor in conjunction with the Council of the Senate, a body elected by the resident members of the Senate and consisting of the Chancellor, the Vice-Chancellor, four Heads of Colleges, four professors, and eight other members of the Senate. These proposals, having received the sanction of the Council, are offered to the Senate in the form of Graces or resolutions, and must pass the Senate before they can take effect. Of the other officers of the university the most important are the two Proctors, whose duty it is to attend to the discipline of all persons *in statu pupillari* and to read the Graces in the Senate House; the Registrar, who keeps the archives of the university; the Public Orator, who is the voice of the university on all important occasions, who writes letters in the name of the university, and who presents all honorary degrees in a Latin speech; the Librarian, who has charge of the University Library. A General Board of Studies supervises the system of teaching as a whole, and each department of study is controlled by a professor and a syndicate or board. The teaching of the undergraduates is undertaken partly by the university and partly by the colleges. It takes mainly the form of lectures, delivered either by the university professors or readers, and open to all members of the university; or by college lectures to members of particular colleges or groups of colleges.

The academical year is divided into three terms: the Michaelmas Term, lasting from 1 Oct. to 14 Dec.; the Lent Term from 8 Jan. to within a few days of Easter; the Easter Term from three weeks after Easter to 24 June. The undergraduates reside either in rooms belonging to the several colleges or in rooms in the town licensed for the purpose. They dine together in the College Hall, but all other meals are taken in their own rooms. Academical dress, a gown and square college cap. must be worn in the College Hall and Chapel. Before proceeding to any examination for a degree they must have resided for the greater part of each of nine terms; and must have passed the previous examination, commonly called the "Little Go," a somewhat elementary examination in Classics, Mathematics, and Divinity. Exemption from this examination can be obtained by passing various non-university examinations. The student can then, if he wishes to proceed to an "Honors" degree, devote the rest of his time to his special subject, and having kept his terms, is qualified to become a Candidate for Honor in a tripos, as honor examinations are called. If he wishes merely to obtain a pass degree he must first pass the general examination of somewhat similar nature to the previous, but more advanced, and can then proceed to one of the special examinations, as they are called. These examinations are in the same subjects as the tripos examinations, but the questions set are of a much less advanced nature. A student who passes a tripos is called an honorman; one who passes in a special examination is called a Passman (commonly "Pollman," from οἱ πολλοι). The names of successful candidates are arranged in three classes, called in the case of the mathematical tripos, Wranglers, Senior Optimes, and Junior Optimes; in the case of the examinations merely first, second, and third class. To the rule that every student before proceeding to a degree must have "kept" residence at least nine terms, there are some important exceptions. Graduates of other universities, British and foreign, who can produce evidence of special qualifications, can qualify for the B.A. degree by passing a tripos examination, or by submitting for approval a dissertation on some subject connected with the special branch of study. Students from various educational institutions for adults both at home and in the colonies, which are said to be "affiliated" to the University, are allowed practically the same privileges. Further, diplomas in Sanitary Science, Tropical Medicine, Agriculture, Geography, Mining Engineering, and Forestry are granted, after examination, to persons who are not members of the university. Having obtained the B.A. degree the student can then, after the lapse of three years, proceed to the M.A. degree, and thereby, for the first time, he obtains a voice in the government of the university. He can exercise a vote in the Senate, and can "non-placet" or oppose the Graces offered to the Senate by the Council. Of the degrees above that of B.A., the M.A. is the only one that is conferred without further examination or exercise. The degree of Doctor in the various faculties can only be obtained by examination or by a dissertation. Degrees other than these already mentioned which are conferred by the university, are the degrees of Doctor in Divinity, Law, Medicine, Music, Letters, and Science; Master in Law and Surgery, Bachelor of Divinity, Law, Music, Medicine, and Surgery. The university has power to confer honorary degrees, without residence or examination, on distinguished persons, noblemen, bishops, deans, and heads of colleges. Before 1850 the only avenue to an honor's degree was by way of the mathematical tripos, or by the mathematical and classical tripos combined. The last half century has witnessed a remarkable development. New triposes have been established in Moral Sciences, Theology, Natural Sciences, Law, History, Economics, Mediæval and Modern Languages, Oriental Languages, and Mechanical Sciences; while new professorships

have been founded in Archæology, Fine Arts, Latin, Anglo-Saxon, Experimental Physics, Mechanism and Applied Science, Surgery, Agriculture, Sanscrit, and Chinese. This last was founded by Sir Thomas Wade, who was the first professor and who bequeathed to the university the first Chinese library outside China. The number of students attending the school of medicine number about 400. Provision is also made for the teaching of Hindustani, Tamil, Burmese, Persian, Russian, etc.

Of the university buildings the most important is the University Library, containing over 700,000 volumes, and over 8,000 manuscripts, including the famous Codex Bezæ. This library is entitled by the Copyright Act to a copy of every book published in the United Kingdom, and a large sum is expended every year in the purchase of foreign books and periodicals. The Fitzwilliam Museum contains a valuable collection of paintings, ancient marbles, and coins. The Observatory stands about a mile from Cambridge, and is splendidly equipped with instruments large and small. The Museums and Laboratories of Science cover a large space of ground in the centre of the university and include laboratories, lecture rooms, and workshops for all departments of science and medicine. These museums have been erected at great cost during the last few years, and were formally opened by King Edward in 1905. The Engineering Laboratory, probably one of the best equipped of its kind in existence, provides adequate instruction for the profession of engineer. The Cavendish Laboratory of Experimental Physics was the gift of the seventh Duke of Devonshire, late Chancellor of the University. The Sedgwick Museum of Geology was built as a memorial to the late Adam Sedgwick, Professor of Geology. Other museums are those of Classical Archæology, Botany, Mineralogy, etc. The Botanic Garden occupies over 20 acres, and contains an extensive range of plant houses, a large arboretum, etc.

Two colleges, Girton and Newnham, have been established just outside Cambridge for the education of women. The students at these colleges are admitted to university and college lectures and to the various examinations for honors. The names of those who pass are placed in the published lists, and certificates are granted to them. Many of them have obtained the highest honors, but the university confers no degrees upon them.

Two movements of the last half century have served to bring the university "into closer connection with education generally throughout the country." By the Local Examinations, established in 1858, the standard of instruction in so-called Middle Schools has been raised to and maintained at a high standard of excellence; and the movement has spread beyond all expectations. In 1878 the number of candidates offering themselves for examination was 6,396; in 1906 it was 16,257. Examinations are held at centres all over the Kingdom as well as in the Colonies. The other movement, known as the University Extension Movement, has had an equally remarkable success. It originated in a course of lectures delivered in one or two of the large towns in the north of England in 1867. During 1886 lectures were delivered at about 50 centres, and were attended by 8,000 students. In 1906 the number of centres was nearly 90 and the number of students 13.900. The scheme is "an attempt to solve the problem of how much of what the universities do for their non-students can be done by university lectures for persons unable to go to a university." The method of teaching "has four characteristic features—the lecture, the class, the weekly paper work, and the examination."

The members of the university whose names are on the Board in 1906 numbered 13,819, of whom 7,192 were members of the Senate, and 3.207 undergraduates. The annual income of the university is about £64,000; that of the colleges about £310,000. The university sends two Members to Parliament elected by the Senate. The polling is continued for two or more days and the university is exempt from the provisions of the School Act.

Bibliography. — Cooper, 'Annals of Cambridge'; Mullinger, 'History of the University of Cambridge'; 'Statutes and Ordinances of the University'; 'Student's Handbook to the University and Colleges of Cambridge'; 'Quarterly Review' (April 1906).

Cambridgeshire, England, an inland agricultural county situated in the western part of England; greatest length about 50 miles; breadth 30 miles; area 820 square miles. Arable land, meadow, and pasture constitute about three-fourths of the county, the rest being flat. The surface is marshy, flat, and thinly wooded, except in the southern portion, which is somewhat elevated and on the chalk formation. The northern section forms part of the Bedford Level. The principal watercourses are the Lark River, the Nene, which borders the county on the north, and the Ouse, which crosses the middle of the county from west to east, with its tributary, the Cam. All of these are navigable for some distance. For parliamentary purposes the county is divided into three sections (northern, or Wisbech, western, or Chesterton, and eastern, or Newmarket) and embraces also, the parliamentary borough of Cambridge. each of which returns one member. Cambridge University also returns two members. There are a day training college for schoolmasters and the New Homerton training college for women at Cambridge, a theological college at Ely, and about 230 elementary schools (see CAMBRIDGE). In the higher sections beans and wheat are produced; the black spongy soil of the fens, when drained and burned, in dry years, produces large crops of wheat, oats, barley, potatoes, cole-seed, hemp, hay, and flax; fine. butter and cream-cheese are produced on the meadows of the Cam; and the Isle of Ely, a part of the fen-tract and within the Bedford Level, is noted for its garden vegetables. Cattle and sheep are reared on the thin chalky soils, and horses, cattle, sheep, and pigeons on the fens. The manufactures are mostly confined to articles used in the agricultural industry; there are paper and parchment mills and coarse earthenware and needles are manufactured. Cambridgeshire was anciently the seat of a powerful tribe, the Iceni. Prop. 190,687.

Cambronne, Pierre Jacques Étienne, pē-âr zhäk ä-tē-ĕn kän-brŏn (COUNT OF), French general: b. Saint-Sebastian, near Nantes, 26 Dec. 1770; d. 5 March 1842. He served on the national guard in the Vendée in 1792; distinguished himself by the capture of a Russian battery at Zurich in 1799; and took part in the campaigns of 1806-13. He went to Elba with Napoleon, and returned with him in 1815. Napoleon made him general and gave him the rank of count. At the battle of Waterloo he commanded a division of the Old Guard, and is credited with having made the famous reply to the demand for surrender, La guarde meurt et ne se rend pas ("The guard dies, but never surrenders"). It is now certain, however, that he did not say this, but gave himself up as a prisoner to Gen. Halkett, and was taken to England. At the time of the restoration of the Bourbons he was on the list of proscriptions, but was exonerated by two court-martials, and in 1820 appointed commandant of Lille by Louis XVIII.

Cambuscan', a prince of Cambaluc (Peking), whose name is a corruption of Genghis Khan, while the description applies apparently to his grandson, Kublai Khan. This was Milton's form of the Cambynskan of Chaucer's fragment of a metrical romance, 'The Squieres Tale.' Spenser continues and finishes the tale in his 'Faerie Queene' (IV., ii. and iii.); and John Lane, a friend of Milton's father, also wrote a continuation. Some of the romantic elements in it are widespread in Oriental story, occurring in the 'Arabian Nights,' the 'Panchatantra,' and elsewhere.

Cambyses (kăm-bi'sēz) **I.,** Persian king. His historical character is involved in great doubt, but he is commonly identified as the son and successor of Teispes, and father of Cyrus the Great (q.v.).

Cambyses II., king of the Medes and Persians: d. 522 B.C. He was the son of Cyrus the Great, and grandson of Cambyses I., and became, after the death of his father, king of the Medes and Persians, 529 B.C. In the fifth year of his reign he invaded Egypt, killed King Psammenitus, plundered Memphis, and conquered the whole kingdom within six months. He now wished to send a fleet against Carthage, to conquer Ethiopia, and to obtain possession of the temple of Jupiter Ammon. The first of these expeditions, however, did not take place, because the fleet, which was manned with Phœnicians, refused obedience to him. The army which was sent against the Ammonites perished in the desert; and the troops, at whose head he himself had set out against the Ethiopians, were compelled by hunger to retreat. From this time he gave himself up to the greatest cruelties.. On his entrance into Memphis, seeing the Egyptians engaged in the celebration of a feast in honor of their god Apis, whom they had found, he believed that they were rejoicing at his misfortunes. He caused the holy bull to be brought before him, slew him with his own sword, and caused the priest to be scourged with rods. To drown his remorse he indulged in wine. No relation was held sacred by him when intoxicated. He caused his brother Smerdis, a dream concerning whom had disturbed him, to be murdered. His sister and wife Atossa, who lamented the death of Smerdis, he killed with a blow of his foot. These and other acts, almost indicating insanity, had irritated his subjects. A magian availed himself of this discontent, and obtained possession of the throne under the name of Smerdis, whose death had been concealed. Cambyses had resolved to go to Susa, in order to punish him, when, according to the account of Herodotus, as he was mounting his horse, he received a wound in the hip from his sword, in consequence of which, he soon died, at Eebatana, Syria, leaving no children. Somewhat different accounts are given by Ctesias and others.

Cam'den, Charles Pratt (1st Earl of), English statesman: b. 1713; d. London, 18 April 1794. After studying at Eton and King's College, Cambridge, he entered as a student at Lincoln's Inn, and in due time was called to the bar. In 1754 he was chosen member of Parliament for the borough of Downton. After acquiring great reputation as an advocate, he was, in 1757, appointed attorney-general, having the same year been elected recorder of the city of Bath. While he held the office of chief justice of the common pleas Wilkes was arrested on a general warrant as the author of the 'North Briton.' He was committed to the tower as a state prisoner; and being brought, in obedience to a writ of habeas corpus, before the court of common pleas, Chief Justice Pratt discharged him from his confinement on 6 May 1763. The behavior of the judge on this occasion, and in the consequent judicial proceedings between the printers of the 'North Briton' and the messengers of the House of Commons, and other agents of the ministry, was so acceptable to the metropolis that the city of London presented him with the freedom of the corporation, in a gold box, and requested to have his picture. In July 1765 he was raised to the peerage, by the title of Baron Camden; and about a year after made lord chancellor. In this capacity he presided at the decision of a suit against the messengers who arrested Mr. Wilkes, when he made a speech, in which he stated that "it was the unanimous opinion of the court, that general warrants, except in cases of high treason, were illegal, oppressive, and unwarrantable." On his opposing the taxation of American colonies, he was deprived of the seals in 1770. He came into office again as president of the council, under the administration of the Marquis of Rockingham, in March 1782; on whose death, he resigned the following year. He soon after, however, resumed his place under Mr. Pitt, and, in 1786 was made Earl Camden. His popularity was very great in the American colonies, as is shown by the many counties, towns, and villages named in his honor.

Camden, William, English antiquary and historian: b. London, 2 May 1551; d. Chiselhurst, Kent, 9 Nov. 1623. He received part of his education at Christ's Hospital and St. Paul's School, after which he studied at Oxford, and in 1575 was appointed second master of Westminster School. He devoted himself faithfully to the duties of his situation, employing all his leisure in his favorite study of British antiquities. At this time he began to make collections for his great work, the 'Britannia.' In 1582 he traveled through the eastern and northern parts of England, to survey the country. The result of his researches appeared in 1586, when the first edition of his 'Britannia' was published

in Latin. This work, though at first necessarily imperfect, procured the author high reputation at home and abroad. In 1589 and 1590 he went into Wales and the west of England, and obtained materials for the improvement of his book, of which the fourth edition (1594) was enlarged to a quarto volume. In 1593 he became head master of Westminster, for the use of which seminary he drew up a Greek grammar (1597). The same year he obtained the office of Clarencieux king-at-arms, which left him at leisure to cultivate his favorite branches of knowledge. In 1600 appeared the fifth edition of the 'Britannia,' and in 1605 was published 'Remains of a Greater Work Concerning Britain'; and in 1607 a 'Narrative of the Conspiracy Called the Gunpowder Plot,' written in Latin, by the king's command. The same year Camden published the last edition of the 'Britannia' printed during his life, from which was made the English translation of Philemon Holland. After this he undertook to write the history of the reign of Queen Elizabeth, the principal literary labor of his future years. The first part of this work appeared in 1615, entitled 'Annales Rerum Anglicarum et Hibernicarum regnante Elizabetha, ad annum salutis' (1589). The second part was finished in 1617, but not printed till after the death of the author. In 1622 Camden founded a professorship of history at Oxford, which he endowed with the valuable manor of Bexley in Kent. He died at Chiselhurst in Kent, where he had spent the latter part of his life, and was buried in Westminster Abbey. His Chiselhurst home was the residence of Napoleon III. 1871-3. Besides the works already mentioned, Camden published a collection of early English historians, printed at Frankfort in 1603, folio. Hume, in his 'History of England,' ranks Camden's 'History of Queen Elizabeth' among the best historical productions which had been composed by any Englishman. Of the 'Britannia,' which has for three centuries been considered as a standard work, it is unnecessary to say more than that, as subsequently enlarged in Richard Gough's English edition of 1806, so as to extend to four volumes in folio, it constitutes a valuable treasury of British topography and antiquities. The Camden Society, which was established in London in 1838, and has issued a number of valuable works, was named in honor of William Camden. Its publications began in 1847, the first series including 104 volumes. The second series up to 1900 included 63 volumes.

Camden, N. J., city, port of entry, and county-seat of Camden County; on the Delaware River, opposite Philadelphia, with which it is connected by several ferries. The city is situated on a level plain and the streets cross one another at right angles. It is noted for its immense market gardens and manufactures, and is the site of several large ship-building concerns. Area five square miles.

Business Interests.— According to the Federal census of 1900 Camden had 817 manufacturing establishments, employing $16,430,611 capital and 9,677 persons; paying $4,540,032 for wages and $11,499,151 for materials; and having an aggregate output valued at $20,451,874. The most important industries were carpentry, foundry and machine-shop products, shipbuilding, worsted goods, oil cloth, boots and shoes, masonry, and textile fabrics. There were three national banks in 1902 with a combined capital of $560,000 and surplus of $315,000, five trust companies, and several private banking houses. The assessed valuation in 1900 exceeded $16,000,000, and the tax rate was $22 per $1,000.

Public Interests.— In 1899 the city had 120 miles of streets, of which 55 miles were paved, 46 miles of sewers, 110 miles of water mains; and oil, gas, and electric street lighting and waterworks plants, the latter owned by the city. The notable buildings are the city hall, county buildings, and the hospitals and churches. At the close of the school year 1903 there were 21 public school buildings, 11,941 pupils, 241 teachers, and a public and a private high school.

History.— The city was settled in 1681 by William Cooper and was incorporated as a city under an act passed 14 Feb. 1828. Pop. (1830) 1,987; (1840) 3,371; (1890) 58,313; (1900) 75,935.

UPTON JEFFERYS,
Editor Post Telegram.

Camden, Battle of, a battle fought near Camden, 16 Aug. 1780, between the American troops under Gates and the British under Lord Rawdon. Shortly after the British captured Charleston in May, all South Carolina was in their hands except for the guerrilla warfare of Marion, Sumter, and others. Washington had already sent Kalb (q.v.) with 1,400 Maryland and Delaware regulars, among the best troops in the army, to save it, but the new disaster called for fresh efforts and a first-rate new commander of the Southern Department to succeed Lincoln. Washington wished to send Greene; but a popular clamor for Gates, mistakenly credited with the victory over Burgoyne, led Congress to give him the post. He took command at Hillsborough, N. C., where Kalb was vainly waiting for Gen. Caswell and the North Carolina militia to come up from South Carolina. Gates, therefore, determined to march south and join Caswell, and thus reinforced, seize Camden and the Wateree, near which was their camp — the strategic centre of the State, and the converging point of the chief northern roads. It was held by Lord Rawdon with a comparatively small force. A fortnight's starving march of 150 miles, in the course of which he picked up a company of Virginia regulars and the North Carolina men, brought him in front of Rawdon, strongly posted across the road 15 miles northeast of Camden. He might either attack with superior forces or hold Rawdon with a part while he sent the rest around his flank to seize Camden in the rear; but he did neither, and, after waiting two days without apparent object, moved west to Clermont, or Rugely's Mill, a strong position, 13 miles north of Camden. Here he was joined by 700 Virginia militia, but sent off 400 of his splended Maryland regulars to help Sumter cut the British communications far to the southeast, and Cornwallis joined Rawdon, giving the British 2,000 trained men. Gates had no intelligence department, and supposed he still had only Rawdon's small force before him; and about 10 P.M. of 15 August started down the road to surprise Rawdon, Cornwallis at the same hour starting north to surprise him. The vanguards met about 3 A.M. a few miles above Camden, and the Americans were routed; but some British prisoners informed Gates that Cornwallis

was in front with 3,000 men. Gates had 3,052, most of his nominal force being on paper or helpless with dysentery; and over half of them were militia who had never been under fire and did not even understand using a bayonet. Kalb, the brave but judicious officer, wished to fall back on Rugely's Mill; but the other officers thought it too late to retreat, and Gates deployed his men, with as bad judgment as the decision to fight at all. The road ran through a level field flanked by swamps, so that everything depended on the firmness of the front rank; but he massed all the regulars on one wing and all the militia on the other. Kalb held the right opposite Rawdon, with the Delaware regiment and the 2d Maryland brigade in front, the 1st Maryland in reserve; the left wing had the Virginia militia in front and the North Carolina troops in the rear, opposed to Col. James Webster, with the Tarleton's cavalry in reserve. Gates' tactics were as ill-judged as his arrangement; he ordered the first charge made by the Virginia men, who did not even know how to march in order. They became tangled, and, while trying to reform, Webster's onrush broke them in wild panic; they threw down their loaded guns with bayonets set, without firing a shot, and ran to the rear. One regiment of North Carolina men fired several volleys, but all the rest fled like their neighbors, and the one exception soon shared their flight. Meantime, the 2d Maryland twice drove back Rawdon, then broke his ranks with a bayonet charge, and held the field. But Webster and Tarleton, following the routed mob, had flanked the 1st Maryland and after an obstinate fight crowded it off the field; and, taking the 2d Maryland in the rear, compelled it, too, to retire, after a fierce resistance. Kalb fought to the last, and was mortally wounded and captured, with eleven wounds. The stubborn fight of the regulars is shown by the fact that the Delaware troops were nearly annihilated, and the Maryland regiments lost nearly half their number. There were about 1,000 killed and wounded, and as many prisoners taken, with seven cannon and 2,000 muskets. The British lost 324. For the time the American cause in the South was at an end. Gates escaped to Hillsborough, but was shortly supplanted by Greene, who wrought a wonderful transformation in a few months.

Camden Society. See CAMDEN, WILLIAM.

Camden Town, England, a district of London in the parish of St. Pancras, and county of Middlesex. It takes its name from the Earl of Camden who acquired property here by marriage. The houses which are in general of recent erection, are regular and substantial buildings. It lies northeast of Regent's Park and north of the Euston station of the London & N.W. R.R.

Camel, a large ruminant of the genus *Camelus*, family *Camelidæ* (q.v.), two species of which have been domesticated since prehistoric times, and used as riding-animals and beasts of burden in the desert regions of the Old World. They differ from other ruminating animals in the presence of incisor teeth in the upper jaw, and canine teeth in both jaws; other differences are found in the feet, which have two elongated toes tipped with small hoofs, the feet resting upon fleshy pads beneath and uniting the toes. Although much search has been made, no wild species of camel can be found except one small two-humped variety, discovered by Prejevalski, which inhabits central Asia, northward to Siberia, in respect to which it is not certain that it represents an original wild species, or whether, on the contrary, it is not a degenerate race long ago escaped from domestication.

The Arabian camel (*Camelus dromedarius*) has one hump on the shoulders; the Bactrian camel (*C. bactrianus*) two. These are composed of muscle, flesh, and fat, which in times of famine is re-absorbed to a large extent. After it has been exhausted, a rest of three or four months, with abundance of food, is necessary to restore it. The former is the more common species, and is used from Mongolia and northwest India throughout south-central Asia, Asia Minor, Arabia, and northern and eastern Africa, and to a small extent in Spain and elsewhere. At the time of the rush of gold-seekers to California about 1850, efforts were made to naturalize them in the arid regions of the southwestern United States, as a means of carrying supplies to the army posts there, but they proved unsuccessful. The camels were allowed to run loose, and those that survived the mountain lions, Indians, and sportsmen, are still found in small numbers throughout Arizona and Sonora.

The original home of the single-humped camel is uncertain, but as it is better adapted to a sandy region than is the Bactrian species, it is thought to have originated in the Sahara or Arabian desert. Its peculiar adaptability to life in sandy regions is noticeable in many ways. The callous cushions (pads) on its feet are repeated upon the chest and the joints of the legs, upon which it rests when rising, kneeling, or lying down, and protect these parts from abrasion by the sharp sand. Its wedge-shaped, cutting teeth are well fitted for cropping the short, shrubby plants of the desert. Its long eyelashes protect it from the glaring sun and from the drifting sand; and the ability to close the oblique nostrils at will prevents the entrance of dust. The most remarkable provision for life in arid regions, however, is found in the structure of the stomach, the interior of which has no villi on its surface. Both the compartments of the paunch contain a number of pouches or cells in their walls, each of which may be closed and separated from the remainder of the paunch. These are filled and closed when the camel drinks, and by these means it can store more water than is requisite for its immediate use, and so save up a store which may gradually be drawn upon during long journeys over waterless districts. The camel's senses of sight and smell are very acute, and it is capable of discerning water at a great distance. By reason of these qualities it has been a most important factor in the colonizing of the countries that lie south and east of the Mediterranean, Black, and Caspian seas, and such oases or fertile areas as are separated by desert wastes.

The Bactrian camel is of smaller size and heavier build, and, by its harder and more cloven feet, and longer and finer hair, is better adapted to a rocky and cooler region. Its habitat is central Asia. Like the southern species it has wonderful endurance, withstanding the terrific summer heat of Persia and the Tibetan plains, and the Arctic cold of the passes of Hindu-Kush and Mongolia. They have been successfully employed as army transports by the English in northwestern India; and for many years,

through all weathers, trains of these camels, sometimes of many thousands, were the only means by which tea and other merchandise was transported between China and Russia.

There are many breeds of camel, exhibiting great diversity. Some are those bred only for the saddle, others as baggage-carriers or draft animals. Properly, a "dromedary" is any camel of either species of a saddle-breed, distinguished for its speed and ease of gait. As a beast of burden the camel has great powers of endurance. The Arabian species carries twice the load of a mule, while it is not unusual for the Bactrian species to carry half a ton weight upon its back; by reason of which it is sometimes poetically termed the "ship of the desert." Caravans frequently contain as many as 1,000 camels, which move along at a steady and uniform pace of about two and a half miles an hour. When bred especially for the purpose they have been known to carry a traveler 100 miles a day. They move with a pacing motion, lifting the feet on the same side successively. Their money value is about the same as that of horses of similar grade and purpose.

Camel, a water-tight box or caisson used to raise a sunken vessel, or to float a vessel over a shoal or bar. It is sunk by the admission of water, and is attached to the vessel, after which the water is pumped out, and the camel, rising by its buoyancy, lifts the load.

Camel-bird, a book-name of the ostrich (q.v.).

Camel-cricket. See MANTIS.

Cam'elford, England, a village, formerly a parliamentary borough of Cornwall, on the Camel, 28 miles northwest of Plymouth. The streets are spacious and well paved, but the houses are in general very indifferent. It has a town-hall, erected by the Duke of Bedford. Four miles to the northwest of Camelford are the ruins of King Arthur's castle of Tintagel, and about two miles to the north are the celebrated slate quarries of Delabole. The inhabitants are chiefly engaged in agriculture. It was disfranchised by the Reform Act of 1832. Previous to that period it sent two members to the House of Commons, and had done so from the time of Edward VI.

Camelidæ, the camel family, a highly interesting branch of the ruminants, including the Old World camels and New World llamas and guanacos, as the existing remainder of a divergent group formerly closely connected both in structure and in geographical distribution. It forms a distinct section of the *Ruminantia* named *Tylopoda*, in reference to the character of the feet, in which only the third and fourth toes are developed (no traces of any others being present), and these are embedded in a cutaneous pad, forming a broad elastic sole to the foot. The two metapodial or "cannon" bones of each of the long limbs are united for the greater part of their length, though separated for a considerable distance at the lower end. Their distal articular surfaces, instead of being pulley-like, with deep ridges and grooves, as in other recent split-hoofed animals (*Artiodactyla*), are simple, rounded, and smooth. The toes terminate in small nails, and the weight of the animal rests upon the padded sole of the foot, instead of on hoofs, in adaptation to the soft sandy soil of the deserts, in which this race of animals seem to have lived ever since its origin. The dentition of the prolonged jaws has certain peculiarities. The full number of incisors are present in youth, but in the upper jaw these disappear, except the outermost, which persist through life. Canines are present in both jaws, those in the lower jaw being nearly erect and pointed, whereas the incisors in that jaw are procumbent. The molars are of the selenodont type, and one or more of the anterior premolars are usually detached from the series and of a simple pointed form. The neck is very long and flexuous, and its vertebræ have certain peculiarities. The shoulders are high, and the hind quarters inclined to droop. The hinder part of the body, indeed, is much contracted, and the thigh bone is long, and vertically placed, so that the knee-joint is lower in position, and the thigh bone altogether more detached from the abdomen than in most quadrupeds. The tail is well developed and the skin is clothed with long shaggy hair, capable of being woven. The nostrils are high, and may be closed against the admission of dust; and the lips are prolonged and flexible. There are no horns or antlers in either sex. The interior anatomy is peculiar, principally in the character of the digestive organs, described in the article CAMEL. The family includes the camels, of the genus *Camelus*, with two species, which are confined at present to the Old World (see CAMEL) and the genus *Llama* — with two species that are restricted to the New World. See ALPACA; GUANACO; LLAMA.

Camelidæ, Fossil. The evolution of the camel (q.v.) through the Tertiary and Quaternary periods is nearly as completely known as that of the horse, and is hardly less instructive. The camels now inhabit central Asia and northern Africa, the llamas, South America. No fossil camels or llamas are found in these countries in deposits much older than the Quaternary. But in the Tertiary strata of North America have been found a series of animals which appear to be the direct ancestors of this family, and connect them with the primitive hoofed animals of the earliest Eocene. The earliest member of this series, ancestral probably to the camels among other ruminants, is *Trigonolestes* of the Lower Eocene, smaller than a cotton-tail rabbit, with the complete series of incisor, premolar, and molar teeth, the molars of the primitive bunodont type (see BUNODONT) and four complete toes, the side toes very slender (one toe of the primitive five had already been lost), and the metapodials all separate. In the Upper Eocene stage, *Protylopus*, as large as a jack-rabbit, the molars have become selenodont (q.v.), as in modern camels, but with shorter crowns, and the side toes are represented only by splints. In the Oligocene stage, *Poëbrotherium*, as large as a gazelle, the molars have longer crowns, the splints are reduced to small nodules of bone, and the metapodials, though still separate, are closely appressed. In the Miocene stage (*Procamelus*, etc.) the metapodials are sometimes separate, sometimes united; the incisors and premolars are generally reduced in size, and the anterior ones often lost; and the form of the teeth and skull comes closer to the modern type. The Pliocene camels (*Plianchenia*, etc.) are still closer to the

modern type, all with united metapodials and reduced incisors and premolars, and at this epoch they spread to South America and the Old World, the gradual rising of the continents having made land connections between them about this time. During the Pleistocene epoch the camels all became extinct in their original home, although they still survive in the alien continents to which they had wandered.

The most remarkable peculiarity of the camels is the adaptation of the stomach, which enables the animal to go a long time without water (see CAMEL); palæontology gives no direct evidence of the evolution of this character. But the cushioned foot, equally an adaptation to desert life, is not indicated (by the form of the toe bones) in any ancestral camel previous to the Miocene, from which time it became gradually more marked. We may suppose, therefore, that the earlier ancestors of the camel were antelope- or deer-like in their habitat, and were gradually adapted to desert life.

Besides the main line of descent there were, especially in the Miocene, side branches now extinct, one of which (*Alticamelus*) was singularly giraffe-like in proportions, although not related to the giraffes, which were evolved in the Old World at the some epoch.

It is a general law in the evolution of any race of animals that at each succeeding stage in its development the progressive characters appear at an earlier period in the lifetime of the individual. The young individuals of one stage resemble the adults of the preceding stage, while the old individuals take on some of the characters of that next succeeding. This is well illustrated in the camels, especially of the Miocene epoch; in young individuals the metapodials are always separate, as they are in all adult camels of the Oligocene, and they are usually not completely consolidated until a comparatively advanced age. In modern camels and llamas they are consolidated before birth. The anterior incisors and premolars usually drop out in old individuals of Miocene camels; in the later stages they are minute stumps or scales which disappear early in life.

W. D. MATTHEW.
American Museum of Natural History.

Camelina Sativa, căm-e-lī′na sa-tī′va ("gold of pleasure"), a cruciferous annual, belonging to the order *Brassicaceæ*, frequently found in cultivated fields, especially among flax, where it has long been cultivated for its seeds. which contain much oil.

Camellia, ka̤-mĕl′ya̤, a genus of plants belonging to the natural order *Ternstrœmiaceæ*, an order which includes the tea-plant and several species of beautiful flowering shrubs, all natives of China. The name Camellia was given to this genus by Linnæus in honor of Kamel or Camellus, a Moravian Jesuit. The *Camellia japonica*, as it grows in the woods and gardens of Japan and China, is a lofty tree of beautiful proportions, and clothed with a deep green shining foliage, with large, elegant flowers, either single or double, and of a red or pure white color. There are numerous varieties of this species in China, the greater part of which have found their way to Europe and America, while other new varieties have been produced. The double-white, double-striped, and double-waratah, the last so called from the central petals

1. Guanaco.   2. Dromedary.   3. Two-Humped Camel.

1 Alpaca.   2. Vicuna.

resembling those of the waratah plant of Australia, are considered the finest varieties, and both grow and flower well. The peony-flowered and fringed are also much admired. The oil-bearing camellia (*C. oleifera*) is cultivated for its seeds, from which an oil is expressed that is very generally used by the Chinese in their cookery. It thrives best in a red sandy soil, and attains a height of six to eight feet, producing a profusion of white blossoms and seeds. Besides these species the *C. reticulata* and *C. sasanqua* are cultivated.

The single red camellia is propagated by cuttings, layers, and seeds. It forms suitable stocks, on which the others are either inarched or budded and engrafted. The cuttings to be selected are the ripened shoots of the preceding summer; these are taken off in August, being cut smoothly at a joint or bud; two or three of the lower leaves are taken off, and the cuttings then planted firmly in the soil with a dibble. Inarching or engrafting is performed early in spring, when the plants begin to grow. A few seeds are sometimes obtained from the single red and semi-double camellias, and from the single waratah. These require two years to come up, but make the best stocks of any.

Camelopard. See GIRAFFE.

Camelopardalis, one of the northern circumpolar constellations added by Hevelius in 1690. It is a large, irregularly shaped constellation, something like the animal, and is more than 40° in length, with its head close to the North Pole. It borders upon Ursa Minor, Draco, Ursa Major, Lynx, Auriga, Perseus, Cassiopeia, and Cepheus. It contains no stars brighter than the fourth magnitude, and was put in to fill up a part of the sky otherwise uncovered by constellations. Being introduced later than Bayer's time, it has no letters except α, β, and γ, which Baily introduced into the "B. A. C." in 1845. While these have not been universally accepted by astronomers, they will probably be adopted in a general revision of the northern constellations.

Cam'elot, in the Arthurian legends, the city where King Arthur's palace with the Round Table was located. Tennyson, in 'The Coming of Arthur,' describes the city and the royal court, and mentions it in others of the 'Idylls of the King' and in 'The Lady of Shalott.' It is also referred to by Shakespeare in 'King Lear.' The site of Camelot has been much in dispute; Shakespeare supposed it to be in Somersetshire; Tennyson and Capell located it at or near Winchester; and Caxton placed it in Wales.

Camel's Hump, one of the peaks of the Green Mountains, in Vermont, 17 miles west of Montpelier. Its height is about 4,100 feet.

Cam'el's-thorn, a genus of plants belonging to the natural order *Leguminosæ*, and the suborder *Papilionaceæ*. They are herbaceous or half-shrubby plants, with simple leaves, minute stipules, axillary peduncles terminating in spines, and red flowers arranged in racemes. Only three species of this genus are known, the *Alhagi camelorum, A. nipalensis* and *A. maurorum.* They grow in the deserts of Egypt and the East, and their common name is derived from the fact that they afford a food much relished by camels. The first two species (if not

the third) yield a gummy, saccharine exudation like manna.

Cam'eo, in the proper sense, a gem engraved in relief, opposed to intaglio, in which the figure is sunk in the surface. The ancients generally used the onyx for this purpose. The gems were carved according to the layers of the stone, so that the ground should be of a different color from the figure in relief; and it is to gems cut in this way that the word is now generally applied. One of the most famous cameos is an onyx representing 'The Apotheosis of Augustus,' 1 foot high and 10 inches wide. Cameos are often cut in shells having layers of different colors. See GEMS.

Camera Lucida ("light chamber"), an optical instrument employed to facilitate the sketching of objects from nature. It acts by total reflection, and may have various forms, of which that proposed by Wollaston, and represented in the accompanying figures, is one of the commonest. The essential part is a totally reflecting prism with four angles, one of which is 90°, the opposite one 135°, and the other two each 67° 30'.

Fig. 1.

One of the two faces which contain the right angle is turned toward the object to be sketched. Rays falling in a straight line on this face as *x r*, are totally reflected from the face *c d* to the next face *d a*, whence they are again totally reflected to the fourth face, from which they emerge in a straight line. An eye (*p p*) placed so as to receive the emergent rays will see an image of the object in a direction at right angles to that in which the object lies. In practice the eye is held over the corner *a* of the prism in such a position that one half of the pupil receives these reflected rays, while the other half receives light in a parallel direction outside the prism. The observer thus sees the reflected image projected on a real background, which consists of a sheet of paper for sketching. He is thus enabled to pass a pencil over the outlines of the image — pencil, image, and paper being simultaneously visible. It is very desirable that the image should lie in the plane of the paper, not only because the pencil-point and the image will then be seen with the same focusing of the eye, but also because parallax is thus obviated, so that when the observer shifts his eye the pencil-point is not displaced on the image. As the paper, for convenience of drawing, must be at a distance of about a foot, a concave lens, with a focal length of something less than a foot, is placed close in front of the prism in drawing distant objects. By raising or lowering the prism in its stand (FIG. 2), the image of the object to be sketched may be made to coincide with the plane of the paper. The prism is mounted in such a way that it can be rotated about either a horizontal or a vertical axis; and its top is usually covered with a movable plate of blackened metal, having a semicircular notch at one edge for the observer to look through.

Another form of the camera lucida, that of Amici, an Italian optician, is sometimes preferred to that of Wollaston, inasmuch as it allows the observer to change the position of his eye considerably without ceasing to see the image of the object he is tracing. The prism in this case is triangular in shape, and one of the angles is a right angle. In using it, the right angle is turned upward, so that one of the perpendicular faces is turned toward the object in an oblique direction, while the edge of the other perpendicular face meets a transparent glass plate at right angles. The rays from the object falling upon the face of the prism which is turned toward it are, after being more or less refracted, thrown upon the base of the prism, from which they are totally reflected in the direction of the other perpendicular face. In emerging from the prism at this face they are again refracted and thrown upon the transparent glass plate. By this, again, the rays are partially reflected, being thrown upward in the direction of the eye of the observer, who, looking through the plate, sees an image of the object on a sheet of paper beneath, the outlines of which can be traced by a pencil as before.

FIG. 2

Camera Obscura ("dark chamber"), an optical instrument employed for exhibiting the images of external objects in their forms and colors, so that they may be traced and a picture formed. From certain scattered observations in the writings of Friar Roger Bacon, in the 13th century, it would appear that he was acquainted with the principle upon which the camera obscura is constructed, but the first complete description of the instrument is found in the 'Magia Naturalis' of Giambattista della Porta, published in 1569, and Porta is commonly credited with its invention.

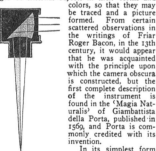

In its simplest form the camera obscura consists of a darkened chamber, into which no light is permitted to enter excepting by a small hole in the window-shutter. A picture of the objects opposite the hole will then be seen on the wall, or a white screen placed so as to receive the light coming through the opening. The images thus obtained become sharper as the size of the hole is diminished; but this diminution involves loss of light, so that it is impossible by this method to obtain an image at once bright and sharp. This difficulty can be overcome by employing a lens. If the objects in the external landscape are all at distances many times greater than the focal length of the lens, their images will all be formed at sensibly the same distance from the lens,

and may be received upon a screen placed at this distance. The images are inverted, and are of the same size whether the lens is in position or not, so long as the screen remains fixed; but they are far sharper and more distinct when the lens is used. As exhibited at seaside resorts and other places of amusement, the camera obscura consists of a small building or of a tent surrounded by opaque curtains, and having at its top a revolving lantern, containing a lens with its axis horizontal, and a mirror placed behind it at a slope of 45°, to reflect the transmitted light downward on a sheet of white paper lying on the top of a table. Images of external objects are thus depicted on the paper, and their outlines can be traced with a pencil if desired. It is still better to combine lens and mirror in one by the arrangement represented in section in the figure. Rays from external objects are first refracted at a convex surface, then totally reflected at the back of the lens (or prism), which is plane, and finally emerge through the bottom, which is concave, but has a larger radius of curvature than the first surface. The two refractions produce the effect of a converging meniscus. The camera obscura, which was formerly chiefly employed for purposes of amusement, has now become well-known from its application to photography.

The instrument employed by photographers (and called simply a "camera") varies in general design according to the use to which it is to be put. It consists essentially, however, of a light-tight box, the length of which can be adjusted by means of a bellows. A lens or objcet-glass is secured to the front end of the box, and the bellows is drawn out until the lens throws a distinct image of the object upon a ground-glass screen at the back of the camera. The object-glass is usually compound, consisting of two single lenses, an arrangement which is very commonly adopted in optical instruments, and which has the advantage of giving the same effective focal length as a single lens of smaller radius of curvature, while it permits the employment of a larger aperture, and consequently gives more light. When the image upon the ground-glass screen has been rendered as sharp as possible, the screen is withdrawn and replaced by a sensitized plate, which is affected chemically by the light rays so as to retain a permanent impress of the image. The impression thus produced upon the sensitized plate is not visible at first, but is brought out, or "developed," by subsequent treatment with chemicals. See PHOTOGRAPHY.

Camera, Photographic, a camera obscura so constructed that sensitized plates or films may be placed at the back and receive the image. There are many styles of camera in use, those of the tripod variety being used for portraits, and landscapes where a long exposure is required, and the hand camera used by tourists on account of its convenient shape and size. See CAMERA OBSCURA; PHOTOGRAPHY.

Camerarius, Joachim, yō'äн-Ĭm kä-mä-rä'-rē-oos, German scholar: b. Bamberg, 12 April 1500; d. Leipsic, 17 April 1574. He contributed to the progress of knowledge, in the 16th century, by his own works as well as by editions of Greek and Latin authors with commentaries, and by a better organization of the universities at Leipsic and Tübingen, and of the gymnasium at Nuremberg. He also took an important part in the political and religious affairs of his time. He was a friend of Melanchthon, and was held in great esteem by the emperors Charles V., Ferdinand I., and Maximilian II. In 1555 he was deputy of the University of Leipsic to the Diet of Augsburg. His proper name was Liebhard, but he changed it to Camerarius, because his ancestors had been chamberlains (late Latin *camerarii*) at the court of the bishops of Bamberg. His son Joachim (1554–98) became known as a botanist.

Camerarius, Rudolph Jakob, roo'dŏlf yä'kŏb, German botanist: b. Würtemberg, 12 Feb. 1665; d. Tübingen, 11 Sept. 1721. To him is ascribed the discovery of the sexual relation in plants. He was in charge of the botanic gardens at Tübingen and was also a medical professor.

Camerino, kä-mä-rē'nō (ancient CAMERINUM), Italy, a town in the province of Macerata, 41 miles southwest of Ancona. It is the seat of an archbishopric, and contains some good public buildings, among which are the archiepiscopal palace and the cathedral. There is a university, founded in 1727. Silk is grown and manufactured here. Pop. (1901) 12,542.

Camerlen'go (It. *camerlingo*, "a chamberlain"), one of the highest officers of the Vatican court. A cardinal Camerlengo, during a vacancy in the holy see, takes charge of all the temporalities, and presides over the apostolic chamber or palace.

Cam'eron, Archibald, American clergyman: b. Scotland, about 1770; d. 1836. After studying at Transylvania Seminary, Lexington, Ky., he was ordained in 1796, and in the same year assumed charge of churches at Big Spring, Akron, and Fox Run. Until 1828 he performed itinerant services, and then became minister of the churches at Mulberry and Shelbyville. The Presbyterian Church in Kentucky owes much to his pioneer labors. His published works include: 'The Faithful Steward' (1806); 'An Appeal to the Scriptures' (1811); 'A Defense of the Doctrines of Grace' (1816); and 'A Reply to Some Arminian Questions on Divine Predestination' (1822).

Cameron, Arnold Guyot, American educator: b. Princeton, N. J., 4 March 1864. He was graduated at Princeton University in 1886, and during the next two years studied abroad. In 1888–91 he was professor of French and German languages and their literatures in Miami University; in 1891–7, assistant professor of French in the Sheffield Scientific School of Yale University; and in 1897 accepted the chair of French at the John C. Green School of Science of Princeton University. He is editor of the text-books: 'Daudet'; 'Mérimée'; 'Loti'; 'Coppée and Maupassant'; and 'The Goncourts.'

Cameron SIR Charles, Scotch journalist and politician: b. Dublin, 1841. He was educated at Madras College, St. Andrews, Trinity College, Dublin, and at medical schools in Paris, Berlin, and Vienna. He edited the *North British Daily Mail* from 1864 to 1874, and from the latter year till 1885 was member of Parliament

for Glasgow. From 1885 to 1895 he sat for the College division, Glasgow, and for the Bridgeton division 1897–1900. The adoption of sixpenny telegrams was the result of a resolution which he introduced in the House, and he was likewise instrumental in the conferring of municipal franchise upon women in Scotland. His publications include many pamphlets on political, social, and medical subjects.

Cameron, SIR Charles Alexander, Irish physician: b. Dublin, 16 July 1830. He was elected public analyst for the city of Dublin in 1862. He was the only one who succeeded in applying the Adulteration of Food Act of 1860. In 1867 he was elected professor of hygiene or political medicine in the Royal College of Surgeons, in Ireland. His lectures on hygiene, open to ladies, were largely attended. He was knighted in 1886, in recognition of his services to public health. He has written: 'Chemistry of Agriculture' (1857); 'Lectures on Public Health' (1868); 'History of the Royal College of Surgeons, Ireland, etc.' (1886); 'Elementary Chemistry and Geology' (1896); etc.

Cameron, Charles Duncan, English soldier: d. 1870. He served in the Kaffir war (1846–7), in the Crimean war, and later at Kars. In 1862 he became British consul in Abyssinia, and having undertaken to deliver a letter from Queen Victoria to King Theodore, was imprisoned by the king for two years on the charge of interfering in the politics of that country. He was released only to be shortly imprisoned again, together with Rassan, agent of the British government, and others, their final release being effected by the advance of English troops upon Theodore's territory. An account of these matters by Cameron was published in the 'Parliamentary Printed Papers' (1868–9).

Cameron, Donald Andreas, English civil servant: b. 1856. He filled the post of consul at Suakin, 1885–8, and at Bengazi, 1888–9. He was judge of the native court of appeals at Cairo 1889–97 and then, returning to the consular service, became consul at Port Said for the Suez Canal. He has published 'Arabic-English Vocabulary' (1892); 'Egypt in the 19th Century' (1898).

Cameron, Emily Lovett, English novelist: b. Walthamstow; married to H. Lovett Cameron, about 1876. Her novels deal mostly with personal complications, and include: 'Juliet's Garden' (1877); 'Deceivers Ever' (1878); 'Vera Nevill' (1880); 'In a Grass Country' (1885); 'The Cost of a Lie' (1886); 'The Dead Past' (1886); 'Pure Gold' (1887); 'A North Country Maid'; 'Jack's Secret'; 'A Sister's Sin'; 'A Bad Lot'; 'A Soul Astray'; 'The Craze of Christina'; 'Bitter Fruit'; 'An Ill Wind.'

Cameron, George Frederick, Canadian poet: b. New Glasgow, Nova Scotia, 1854; d. 1885. He was educated at Queens' University, Kingston, Ontario; resided for a time in the United States; returned to Canada, and edited the Kingston *News*. As a lyrical poet he has received high praise from leading critics, and was accorded an eminent position by some of the great contemporary English poets. See Stedman, 'Victorian Anthology' (1895).

Cameron, Henry Clay, American educator: b. Shepherdstown, Va., 1 Sept. 1827;

d. 26 Oct. 1906. He was graduated at Princeton College in 1847, and at the Princeton Theological Seminary in 1855; and was connected with the department of Greek at Princeton from 1852 to 1906. He was twice chosen to the Presbyterian General Assembly, and wrote 'Princeton Roll of Honor'; 'History of the American Whig Society'; 'Old Princeton: Its Battle, Its Cannon, etc.'

Cameron, Hugh, Scottish artist: b. Edinburgh, 1835. He is a well-known and popular painter of portraits and figure pieces, and among his works are: 'Maternal Care'; 'Age and Infancy'; 'Haymakers Resting'; 'A Lonely Life'; 'The Rivals'; 'The Timid Bather.'

Cameron, James Donald, American capitalist and politician: b. Middletown, Pa., 14 May 1833. He is the oldest son of Simon Cameron (q.v.), and was graduated from Princeton College in 1852. He devoted himself to business pursuits and in 1861 was made vice-president and two years later president of the Northern Central R.R. He remained in this office till 1874. In 1876 President Grant appointed him secretary of war, and in 1877 he succeeded his father as United States senator from Pennsylvania. He was re-elected in 1885 and 1890.

Cameron, John, Scottish scholar: b. Glasgow, 1579; d. 1625. In 1600 he went to the Continent, where his ability and erudition secured for him several appointments at Bergerac, Sedan, Saumur, and other seats of learning. Returning to Great Britain in 1620, he was two years later appointed principal of the university of Glasgow; but in less than a year returned to Saumur, and thence to Montauban, where he received a divinity professorship. Here, as at Glasgow, his doctrine of passive obedience made him many enemies, by one of whom he was stabbed in the street, and he died from the effects of the wound in 1625. Sir Thomas Urquhart styles him a "walking library," and Milton, "an ingenious writer in high esteem." He was considered one of the best scholars of his day; in biblical criticism he was inclined to be perverse; where there was a difficulty he usually chose the opposite view to that held by other divines, especially Beza. His theological opinions were of a somewhat lax character, his eight works, in Latin and French (10 vols., 1616–42), being said to be the foundation of Moses Amyraut's doctrine of universal grace (1634). His followers are sometimes called Cameronites.

Cameron, Richard, Scottish Covenanter: b. Falkland, Fifeshire, 1648; d. Ayrsmoss 22 July 1680. He was at first a schoolmaster, and for a time was tutor in the family of Sir Walter Scott of Harden. Being converted by the field-preachers, he became an enthusiastic votary of the Covenant. On the 20th of June 1680, in company with about 20 other persons, well armed, he entered the village of Sanquhar, and proclaimed at the cross that he and those who adhered to him renounced their allegiance to the king on account of his having abused his government, and also declared a war against him and all who adhered to him, at the same time avowing their resolution to resist the succession of his brother the Duke of York. The privy council immediately put a reward of 5,000 merks upon Cameron's head, and 3,000 upon

those of Cargill and Douglas, his associates; and parties were sent out to waylay them. The little band kept together in arms for a month in the mountainous country between Nithsdale and Ayrshire. But on the 22d of July, when they were lying in Ayrsmoss, near Auchinleck in Ayrshire, Bruce of Earlshall approached them with a party of horse and foot much superior in numbers. A brief skirmish took place, in which the insurgents were allowed even by their enemies to have behaved with great bravery; but nothing could avail against superior numbers. Cameron being among the slain, his head and hands were cut off and carried to Edinburgh, along with the prisoners. The name of Cameron was applied to the small but zealous sect of Presbyterians which he had led in life, and was also used in a wider and looser sense. The 26th Regiment, which was raised at the Revolution out of the west-country people who flocked to Edinburgh, was styled on that account the Cameronian Regiment. It is now known as the Cameronians or Scottish Rifles. Consult Herkless, 'Richard Cameron' (1896). See CAMERONIANS.

Cameron, SIR Roderick William, Canadian capitalist: b. Williamstown, Ontario, 25 July 1825; d. 24 Oct. 1900. He entered mercantile life in New York as a youth and acquired a large fortune as an exporter and importer. He was knighted in 1883. He was well known as a turfman and yacht owner, and was prominent in Canadian-American diplomacy.

Cameron, Simon, American statesman: b. Maytown, Lancaster County, Pa., 8 March 1799; d. there, 26 June 1889. He learned printing and in 1820 he was editor of a paper in Doylestown, Pa., and in 1822 held a similar post in Harrisburg. He then interested himself in banking and the building of railroads, and for a time served as adjutant-general of Pennsylvania. From 1845 to 1849 he was United States senator from Pennsylvania, elected by the Democratic party. He became a member of the Republican party on its formation, and in 1856 was again elected United States senator. He was unsuccessfully supported for the offices of both President and Vice-President in the National Convention of 1860, and in 1861 was appointed secretary of war by President Lincoln. He advocated the arming of fugitive slaves and other extreme measures. In January 1862 he resigned from the Cabinet, and was appointed minister to Russia. He succeeded in gaining the support of the Russian government for the Union. In November of the same year he resigned, and lived in retirement till 1866, when he was again elected to the United States Senate. In 1872 he became chairman of the Committee on Foreign Affairs. In 1877 he retired from the Senate in favor of his son, James Donald Cameron. His influence over the Republican party was strong, and his power in the politics of his State practically absolute. He was a vigorous opponent of civil service reform during the administration of President Hayes.

Cameron, Verney Lovett, English traveler in Africa: b. Weymouth, 1 July 1844; d. Leighton Buzzard, 26 March 1894. He entered the British navy in 1857, and in 1872 was chosen by the Royal Geographical Society of London to conduct an expedition for the relief of Dr. Livingstone. He was only in time to meet the remains of Livingstone at Unyanyembe, but pushed onward to Ujiji on Lake Tanganyika, and partly circumnavigated this great sheet of water, establishing the fact that its outlet was the Lukuga. Not being able to follow the Lualaba River downward, he continued his journey westward to Benguela, and was thus the first to cross tropical Africa from east to west. Returning to England in 1876, he was raised to the rank of a commander. In 1878 he made a journey through Asia Minor and Persia in order to satisfy himself as to the feasibility of a railroad connecting India with the Mediterranean, and in 1882 with Sir Richard Burton explored the country behind the Gold Coast. He published accounts of his journeys in his 'Across Africa' (1877); 'Our Future Highway to India' (1880); and 'To the Gold Coast for Gold' (1883, with Sir R. F. Burton). He died from an accident in the hunting field.

Cameron Highlanders, the old 79th Regiment in the British army, raised in 1793 by Allan Cameron of Erroch. It wears the Highland dress and now forms the first battalion of the King's Own Cameron Highlanders. There is not as yet a second battalion linked with it.

Camero'nian Regiment, a British regiment raised in 1689 among the Cameronians of the west of Scotland to support William III., and long famous as the 26th Regiment. It forms now the first battalion of the Cameronians (Scottish Rifles), the second battalion being the old 90th Regiment.

Camero'nians, a sect of Scotch Presbyterian dissenters, named after Richard Cameron. James I. had enforced on his Scottish subjects a liturgy which the people abhorred, and this led, in 1638, to the formation of the covenant, "in behalf of the true religion and the freedom of the kingdom." The organization of the Scottish presbytery was still further completed in the adoption of the Presbyterian form of Church government, a Calvinistic confession of faith. and the two catechisms, which documents are the standards of the Scottish kirk to this day. Throughout the revolution of 1688 the Cameronians maintained inflexible hostility to the royal usurpation of religious freedom. They supported the Prince of Orange on his assuming the crown of England, but were displeased and disappointed by the form in which the Presbyterian Church was restored. In 1709 they exerted all their influence against the union of Scotland and England. The presbytery of this denomination was not organized until 1 Aug. 1743, when an act of toleration was procured in their favor. They still have a distinctive existence in Great Britain and America, under the name of Reformed Presbyterians.

Cameroons, kä-mē-roon', or Kamerun, a German colonial possession in West Africa extending inland from the Bight of Biafra to the northeast and north as far as Lake Chad, and having an area of 191,130 square miles. It is separated from the British territory on the northwest by a line running northeast from the Rio del Rey to a point on the river Benue east of Yola, and from there northnortheast to the south shore of Lake Chad. From French Congo on the south it is marked off by a line running east from the mouth of the Campo River to the river Sanga, and from

there the eastern boundary proceeds first northwest to lat. 4° N., lon. 15° E., then along that meridian to about lat. 8° 30' N., when it proceeds northwest to the parallel of 10°, which forms the boundary eastward to the Shari River. This river itself to its mouth in Lake Chad serves as the northeastern boundary. The territory receives its name from the Cameroon River, which enters the Bight of Biafra by an estuary nearly 20 miles wide. The swamps along the banks of the river render this district unhealthy for Europeans. Northwest of the river lies the volcanic group called the Cameroon Mountains. which rise to a height of 13,760 feet. The lower slopes of these mountains are more healthy, and are covered with ebony, redwood. and palm-trees. More important than the Cameroon River is the much longer Sannaga or Mbam, entering the Bight of Biafra a little south of the former, and navigable for 40 miles inland to Idia. Among cultivated plants are the banana, oil-palm, cocoanut, groundnut, manioc, yam. sweet-potato, and colocasia; of more recent introduction are cacao, coffee, tobacco, etc. Among the minerals are gold and iron. There is a considerable trade in cotton, ivory, and oil. The inhabitants are almost entirely of the Bantu stock. widely diffused throughout the more southerly portion of the continent, and many of them have almost regular European features. The coast of the Cameroon territory was annexed by Germany in 1884, and the interior has since been acquired, the whole being now a German colony under a governor. The seat of government is at Cameroons, a group of native villages on the estuary of the Cameroon River, but the greater part of the territory is only nominally under German rule. Pop. 4,500,000.

Camil'la, in Roman fable, a virgin, said to have been a daughter of Metabus, a Volscian king, and to have aided Turnus against Æneas (Vergil, 'Æneid.' vii.).

Camille, ka-mēl ("La Dame Aux Camélias"), a novel by Alexandre Dumas the younger, published in 1848, the celebrated play founded upon it appearing in 1852 at the Vaudeville Theatre in Paris. The popularity of both the novel and the play is owing, perhaps, to the fact that the incidents of the story admit of many interpretations of the character of the heroine.

Camil'lus, Marcus Furius, Roman patrician: d. 365 B.C. He is famous as the deliverer of the city of Rome from the Gauls. In 396 B.C. he was made dictator during the Veientine war, and captured the town of Veii after it had defied the Roman power for more than 10 years. In 394 B.C. Camillus besieged the Falerii, and by an act of generosity induced them to surrender. Three years later the envy and jealousy of enemies caused him to exile himself for a time, and he was living in retirement when the Gauls, under Brennus, invaded and captured Rome, with the exception of the capital. Camillus was now appointed dictator a second time, and was successful in repelling the invaders. After he had been four times appointed dictator, a new invasion of the Gauls called him, at the age of 80, once more to that position, and he defeated and dispersed the barbarians. There is a certain amount of myth in the story of his life.

Caminatzin, kä-mĕ-nạ-tsĕn', or **Cacumazin,** Mexican king: d. 30 June 1520. He was nephew of King Montezuma, and reigned over Tezcuco, the principal city of Anahuac. The best citizens of the state, the nobles and priests, saw with indignation the humiliation of their king and kingdom under Cortez and the Spaniards. Caminatzin, with more courage and enterprise than his uncle, proposed to his subjects a declaration of war against the foreigners. The proposal was received with enthusiasm, and Caminatzin called upon the Spaniards to leave the country immediately or to expect to be treated as enemies. Cortez was preparing to march his army against Tezcuco, when the representations of Montezuma concerning the defenses of the town and the daring of the population, induced him to change his plan, and to resort to treason instead of force. At his instigation Montezuma invited his nephew to Mexico to become reconciled with the Spaniards. The answer of Caminatzin was that he could enter Mexico only to destroy the tyrants of his country. Montezuma then despatched secret agents to Tezcuco to get possession of the young prince by whatever means. His first officers and nearest friends were corrupted, and he was delivered by them to Cortez and imprisoned. He was released after the expulsion of the Spaniards, and perished during the evacuation of Mexico by the Spaniards.

Camisards, käm'ĭ-zärdz, Protestants in France (in the Cévennes), who, in the beginning of the 18th century, in consequence of the persecution to which they were exposed after the revocation of the Edict of Nantes in 1685, rose against the royal deputies. The name is usually thought to be derived from "camise," a provincial form of the French word "chemise," signifying a shirt, and it is said to have been applied to them either because their ordinary outer garment was a kind of shirt or blouse, or because on certain occasions they wore their shirts above their other garments. The first occasion on which they broke out into open revolt against the royal deputies was on the night of 24 July 1702, when 50 of them attacked the house of the Abbé du Chayla, one who had signalized himself by his cruelty during the persecutions. They set free the prisoners whom they found confined in the dungeons, and put the abbé himself to death. This was the signal for a general rising of the mountaineers. The government sent troops to punish the authors of these acts. A certain Jean Cavalier, a peasant, whom a fortune-teller had pointed out as the deliverer of Israel, placed himself at the head of the Camisards. His unlimited authority with his adherents, his talents, and courage, enabled him to oppose the measures of experienced generals with so much success that negotiation was substituted for force. The Marshal Villars in 1704 made a treaty with Cavalier, by virtue of which Cavalier himself was received into the royal service as a colonel. This treaty, however, did not satisfy his associates, because it did not concede to them liberty of conscience, and on that account Cavalier was reproached as a traitor who had sacrificed the cause of his coreligionists to his own interest. At the court, too, he was received with coldness, so that in a short time he was glad to go into voluntary exile. He went to England, where Queen Anne gave him a favorable reception. Voltaire, who became acquainted with him in London, speaks of him in high terms. At the time of his death Cavalier was general and governor of Jersey. The name *camisards blancs* (white camisards), or *cadets de la croix* (cadets of the cross), was given to a band of Roman Catholics formed to put down the Calvinistic camisards, who were called *camisards noirs,* or black camisards.

Cam'let, or **Camblet** (in French, *camelot*), a name applied in England to a fabric made of long wool, hand-spun, sometimes mixed with cotton or linen yarn. Various derivations of the word are given. Some consider it to be of the same root with camel, because it was originally made of camel's hair; others derive it from the Arabic *chamal,* signifying fine, because according to them it was originally made of the fine hair of the Angora goat.

Cammerhoff, käm'mèr-hôf, **John Christophe Frederic,** Moravian bishop in America: b. near Magdeburg, Germany, 28 July 1721; d. Bethlehem, Pa., 28 April 1751. He was educated at Jena, and at the age of 25 was consecrated a bishop in London and came to America as Bishop Spangenburg's assistant. He preached in Pennsylvania and New York, but his greatest successes were made among the Indians. The Iroquois adopted him into the Turtle tribe of the Oneida nation, and gave him the name of Gallichwio, or "A Good Message." In 1750 he undertook amid great hardships a tour to Onondaga. It occupied three months, embraced a distance of 1,600 miles and was filled with hair-breadth escapes. He was too weak to endure such enterprises, and died the following year. The Iroquois mourned him as a brother and said of him "He was an honest, upright man, in whose heart no guile was found." Thirty years later Zeisberger heard his name mentioned among them with deep respect and veneration. The memory of his devotion and irrepressible missionary zeal has ever been held in honor by the people of his faith.

Camões, or **Camoens, Luis de,** loo-ĕs dä kä-môṅ'ĕsh, Portuguese poet: b. Lisbon probably 1524, or 1525; d. there, 1579. His father, Simon Vaz de Camoes, was a ship-captain, who perished by shipwreck on the coast of Goa about 1552. Camoes studied at Coimbra. At that time writers were esteemed in proportion as they imitated the ancients. Camoes was inspired by the history of his country, and by the manners of his age. His lyric poems, like the works of Dante, Petrarch, Ariosto, and Tasso, belong to the literature formed under the influence of Christianity. After the completion of his studies he returned to Lisbon, where he fell deeply in love with a lady of the palace, Catharina d'Atayada. Violent passions are often joined with great talents — Camoes had both. He was exiled to Santarem on account of disputes in which his love for Catharina involved him. From despair he became a soldier, and served in the fleet which the Portuguese sent against Marocco. He composed poetry in the midst of battles, and as danger kindled his genius, so genius animated his courage. An arrow deprived him of his right eye before Ceuta. He hoped that his wounds would receive a recompense, though his talents were not appreciated; but envy opposed his claims. Full of indignation at seeing himself neglected, he embarked in 1553 for India. His powerful imagination was excited by the heroic deeds of his countrymen in this quarter, and although he had much reason to complain of them, he could not resist the desire of celebrating their glory in an epic. But this vivacity of mind, essential to the poet, is not easily united with the moderation which a dependent condition demands. Camoes was displeased with the abuses of the government in India, and wrote a satire, which caused his banishment to Macao. Soon after he was removed to the Moluccas, but after three years of captivity a new viceroy recalled the decree of banishment against him, and appointed him administrator of the effects of deceased persons at Macao. His chief poem, the 'Lusiad,' was composed partly during the period of his captivity, and partly while he held the office of administrator. Camoes was at last recalled from his banishment. At the mouth of the river Mekon, in Cochin-China, he was shipwrecked, and saved himself by swimming — holding in one hand above the water the manuscript of his poem, the only treasure which he rescued from the waves. In Goa he encountered new persecutions; was confined in prison for alleged embezzlement of funds intrusted to him during his tenure of office at Macao, and not allowed, until his friends became responsible for him, to embark and return to Lisbon in 1569. King Sebastian, yet hardly past the age of childhood, took an interest in Camoes. He accepted the dedication of his epic (which appeared in two editions, varying both in the text and the orthography, in 1572), and being on the point of embarking on his expedition against the Moors in Africa, felt more sensibly than others the genius of the poet, who, like him, loved dangers if they led to glory. But Sebastian was killed in a battle before Alcaçar in 1578, and with him the royal family became extinct, and Portugal lost her independence. Every source of assistance, as well as every hope of Camoes, was destroyed by this event. So great was his poverty that at night a slave, whom he had brought with him from India, begged in the streets in order to support the life of his master. In this misery he yet wrote lyric poems, some of which contain the most moving complaints. This hero of Portuguese literature, the ornament of his country and Europe, died in a hospital, neglected. In 1596 a splendid monument was erected to his memory. Vasco da Gama's expedition to India is the subject of his great poem. The parts of it which are best known are the episode of Ines de Castro, and the appearance of Adamastor who, by means of his power over the storms, aims to stop Gama's voyage when he is about to double the Cape. In conformity to the taste of the time, Camoes united in this poem a narrative of the Portuguese history with the splendor of poetic description, and Christianity with mythological fables. He pleased himself with tracing the descent of the Portuguese from the Romans, of whom Mars and Venus are considered the progenitors and protectors. Since fable ascribes to Bacchus the first conquest of India, it was natural to represent him as jealous of the undertaking of the Portuguese. If the imitation of the works of classical antiquity has been of any disadvantage to the 'Lusiad,' the injury consists, perhaps, in a diminution of the originality which one expects in a work in which India and

Africa are described by an eye-witness. The general interest of the poem consists principally in the patriotic feeling which pervades it. The national glory of the Portuguese appears here in every form which invention can lend to it, and therefore the countrymen of Camoes must naturally admire this poem more than foreigners. Some critics pronounce the 'Lusiad' a more powerful and pure historical painting than Tasso's 'Jerusalem Delivered.' A valuable edition of the 'Lusiad' (Os Lusiadas, etc.) was published by Joze Maria de Souza-Botelho (Paris 1817). It has been translated into English by Fanshaw, Mickle and Duff; by J. J. Aubertin (with Portuguese text), and by Sir R. F. Burton (with 'Life of Camoes, Commentary,' etc.; 6 vols.). The works of Camoes, besides the 'Lusiad' consist of sonnets, songs, odes, elegies, eclogues, *redondillas,* epigrams, satires, letters, and three dramas 'Amphitryon,' after Plautus, 'King Seleucus,' and the 'Love of Philodemus.' Consult: Adamson, 'Memoirs of the Life and Writings of Luis De Camões' (1820); Braga, 'Historia de Camões' (1873-5); Castello Branco 'Luis de Camões' (1880); Storck, 'Luis de Camoens Leben' (1890).

Cam'omile, or Chamomile (*Anthemis*), a plant belonging to the natural order *Compositæ.* It is perennial, and has slender, trailing, hairy, and branched stems. The leaves are doubly pinnate, with linear pointed pinnæ. The flower is white, with a yellow centre. Both leaves and flowers of this plant have a strong though not unpleasant smell, and a very bitter nauseous taste; but the flowers are more bitter and aromatic than the leaves. The principal use for which camomile flowers are applied is to excite vomiting and promote the operation of emetics. They have likewise been substituted for Peruvian bark in the case of intermittent fevers or agues, but not with much success. Both the leaves and flowers are employed in fomentations and poultices. They are also administered in substance as a powder or electuary, in infusion as tea, in decoction or extract, or in the form of an essential oil obtained by distillation. Camomile flowers are sometimes used by brewers as a substitute for hops. Distilled with water, an essential oil in small quantities is obtained of a greenish color and strong pungent taste. So fragrant is the camomile plant that the places where it grows wild may easily be discovered by the somewhat strawberry-like perfume emitted when it is trodden on. This quality has sometimes induced the cultivation of camomile for a green-walk in gardens. Camomile in the United States is an importation from Europe, the commonest wild varieties being May-weed (*Anthemis cotula*), and corn camomile (*A. arvensis*). The garden camomile is *A. nobiles.*

Camomile enjoys a wide, popular reputation as a diaphoretic and diuretic. The flowers are usually made into an infusion or tea and this is drunk while hot. A poultice is also made of the flowers and applied to painful swellings, such as rheumatic joints, or ear-ache, boils, etc. There is a large amount of fixed and volatile oil in camomile to which its useful physiological and physical properties are due. Volatile oils act as vaso dilators and antispasmodics, diuretics and diaphoretics, the fixed oils permitting of long-continued heat.

Camonica, kä-mŏ-nĕ′kạ, or **Valle Camonica,** a valley in north Italy, formed by two branches of the Rhætian Alps, watered by the Oglio, and stretching about 50 miles from north-northeast to south-southwest as far as Lake Iseo. It is a principal thoroughfare between Italy and the Tyrol.

Camorra, kä-môr′rạ, an association in Naples, the members of which (Camorristi) carried on extortion as a regular business, and were to be found at markets, fairs, and all public gatherings in the exercise of their employment. They might even be hired to commit murder. The association extended its ramifications over the whole of Naples. It had central stations in all the large provincial towns, and 12 in the city of Naples, and it had a regular staff of recruiting officers. Under the former régime it did not aim at concealment; but under the present more powerful government efforts are being made to suppress it. These efforts have not yet been crowned with complete success; but it is not denied that the power of the association has been greatly diminished. The members no longer dare to carry on their business openly. The army, which was formerly infested with them, and is said still to contain a considerable number, is gradually being freed from them, and in every way they are being brought under the power of the law.

Camp, käṅ, **Maxime du.** See DU CAMP, MAXIME.

Camp, Walter, American writer on athletics: b. New Britain, Conn., 7 April 1859. He was graduated at Yale (1880) and soon attained prominence with such writings as 'Book of College Sports,' 'American Football,' etc. He has edited various weekly papers devoted to sports, and is well known as an authority upon college athletics and football.

Camp, in military use, the place and aggregate body of tents or huts for soldiers in the field. In modern times a difference is often made between camp and bivouac, the former signifying the quarters of an army sheltered in tents; the latter the situation of one which dispenses with them, and remains either entirely in the open air, or, when time allows it, in huts built of branches, etc. Camps, in a general sense, are of very ancient origin, since almost all nations in their infancy lived as nomads, dwelling in tents, as is the case with many tribes in Asia and Africa at the present day, for example the Arabs. Among the Greeks, the Lacedæmonians seem to have been the first who devoted attention to the art of forming military camps. The form which they adopted was the circular, that being the form which was best calculated to enable the general, who had his tent in the centre, to have a view of the whole camp, and to despatch assistance in the shortest possible time to any part of the camp that might be attacked. The Romans probably first carried the art of encampment to a high degree of perfection, on account of their many wars in distant and thinly settled regions, where their large armies found no cities to quarter in. Cæsar and several other Roman authors give us much information on their way of constructing a camp, and in Polybius we have a detailed description of the consular camp as it was made in his time. This form of camp, with some modifications, continued to be the usual one

during the whole period of the Roman domination, and down to the time of the invention of gunpowder. The site was chosen by the general himself, or by one of the military tribunes; a spot from which a view of the whole camp could be obtained. This spot was marked by a white pole as the point from which the rest of the camp was measured out, and the place where the general's tent (*prætorium*) was to be erected. The form of the camp was a square, and it was divided into two parts by a street from 50 to 100 feet wide, called the *principia* or *via principalis*, which ran across it. One of these divisions occupied about one third of the whole space, the other, the remaining two thirds; and it was in the former of these that the *prætorium* was situated, with an open area around it extending 100 feet on all sides. On the right of the *prætorium* was the *forum* or market-place, and on the left the *quæstorium*, where were the camp-stores under the superintendence of the *quæstor*. Beyond these again on each side were select bodies of horse and foot taken from the extraordinaries, and behind this whole line of the encampment, and separated from it by a street 100 feet broad, was the place reserved for the main body of the extraordinaries, and for foreigners and occasional auxiliary troops. Immediately in front of the line of the encampment first described the tents of the military tribunes and of the *præfecti*, or officers of the allies, were erected, the former before the *forum* and *quæstorium*, the latter before the select bodies of horse and foot. These tents lined the *principia* on the side of the *prætorium*. On the other side of the *principia* the main body of the army was quartered, the allies being stationed on the right and left, the two Roman legions which belonged to every consular army in the middle. The whole was surrounded with a ditch (*fossa*) and a rampart (*vallum*) at the distance of 200 feet from the tents. On every side of the camp there was a gate. That behind the *prætorium* was called *porta prætoria*, the one on the opposite side *porta decumana*. The other two were at the ends of the *principia*, and were called respectively *porta principalis dextra* and *sinistra*. The camp was improved in strength and convenience according to the time that it was occupied, and in some cases, from the want of fortresses, it was made the basis of their military operations.

Since the invention of gunpowder, intrenched camps, such as that just described, have been of very little service, as they afford no protection against projectiles shot from long ranges. What are usually known as intrenched camps at the present day are much more elaborate affairs and cover a much greater area. They may consist of intrenched areas permanently connected with and under the protection of fortified places; thus they are sometimes attached to certain large cities on the chief roads, partly in order to defend them against the first attack of the enemy, and to prevent his possessing himself easily of the important resources which they afford; partly to give to retreating armies rallying-points for support to numerous soldiers. Camps which, though intrenched, are to be occupied merely for the period of a campaign, or which serve as a refuge for a few days only to a subordinate army, are termed "lines" or "temporary positions.» An example of the former was exhibited by the extensive lines of Torres Vedras. From the perfection of modern artillery strong detached forts form the chief defensive feature of intrenched camps of the present day. For temporary encampments in the field a position is selected such as is not only well supplied with wood, forage, water, and the other necessaries of a camp, but also one that may be easily defended. Rifle-trenches, gun-pits, etc., may be constructed, sentinels being posted to guard against surprise. It has recently become common to form camps in time of peace for the sake of disciplining the soldiers to a camp life, and exercising them in the evolutions connected with camps. These are camps of instruction, of which examples are seen in the United States, where the organizations of the National Guard in the different States are accustomed to annual encampments for these purposes; also in the camp for British troops at Aldershot, and temporary camps throughout Great Britain for the training of the militia and volunteers, and in the like customs and establishments of other countries. The military camp of the United States army is arranged according to directions given in the 'Army Regulations' published by the War Department.

Camp Al'leghany, W. Va., a Confederate camp where an engagement took place 13 Dec. 1861. After the affair at Camp Bartow, 3 Oct. 1861, the Union troops had remained at Cheat Mountain Summit. Gen. R. H. Milroy, who was in command 12 Dec. 1861, determined to attack Camp Alleghany, the summit of Alleghany Mountain, to which the Confederates had fallen back from Camp Bartow, and which was held by Col. Edward Johnson, with 1,400 men and eight guns, partially entrenched. With 1,800 men Milroy marched to Camp Bartow, 12 December, and made his dispositions. One column of 900 men, under Col. James A. Jones, was to ascend the mountain, until near its summit, when, leaving the road, it was to move to the left and attack Johnson's right and rear, while another column of 900 men, under Col. G. C. Moody, was to move down the Greenbank road and by a circuitous route, concealed by heavy forests, assail Johnson's left. The attacks were to be simultaneous at 4 A.M. of the 13th. Jones started at midnight, gained his assigned position on time, and waited for Moody, but his presence being discovered, he was quickly engaged and for a time met with success, driving the Confederates before him, but Johnson rallying his troops on that flank and fighting desperately, Jones was repulsed after a two-hours' contest, leaving his dead and many wounded on the field. While Jones was being driven from Johnson's right Moody was slowly approaching his left. He had been delayed by the difficulties of his route, and it was after 8 o'clock when he became engaged, and was met by such a severe fire of artillery and musketry that he could make no progress, but continued a desultory skirmish until afternoon, when he fell back, and the whole force, reuniting at Camp Bartow, marched back to Cheat Summit. The action was the most severely contested one of the West Virginia campaign of 1861. The Union loss was 20 killed, 107 wounded, and 10 missing; the Confederate loss 20 killed. 98 wounded, and 28 missing. Consult 'Official Records,' Vol. V.   E. A. CARMAN.

Camp Bartow, bär'tō, or **Greenbrier River,** W. Va., a place where an engagement in the Civil War was fought, 3 Oct. 1861. On 2 October the Confederates held Camp Bartow, where the road from Beverly to Staunton crosses the Greenbrier River, with about 2,500 men and eight guns, under command of Gen. H. R. Jackson. Gen. J. J. Reynolds, commanding the Union troops at Cheat Mountain Summit, 12 miles west, concluded to feel Jackson's position and, if possible, force it. He marched at midnight of the 2d with about 5,000 men and 13 guns, drove in a picket post west of the Greenbrier on the morning of the 3d, and coming to within 600 or 700 yards of Jackson's intrenched position beyond the stream, opened on it with his artillery, the Confederates promptly replying. Several guns were disabled on either side, and Reynolds then, under cover of a demonstration on Jackson's left, moved with six regiments to turn his right. The regiment to make the demonstration on the left crossed the stream, but was quickly driven back, and when the six regiments were about to cross the stream on Jackson's right they were met by such a severe fire of artillery and musketry that Reynolds deemed further effort inadvisable and withdrew with a loss of 43 killed and wounded. The Confederate loss was 39 killed and wounded. Consult 'Official Records,' Vol. V.

E. A. CARMAN.

Camp Diseases, disorders common in camp life and more or less incidental to the conditions of active military service, which are often such as to increase the virulence of ordinary diseases. Improper food, exposure to wet and to extremes of temperature, hard muscular labor, unhygienic surroundings, and immoral or intemperate habits, contribute to the general conditions in which disease flourishes. Some of the troublesome infectious diseases of military life are: Asiatic cholera, bubonic plague, cerebro-spinal meningitis, diarrhœa, dysentery, influenza, malaria, measles, mumps, typhoid fever, and tuberculosis. Alcoholism and venereal diseases depend on personal habits; bronchitis, frost-bite, pneumonia, rheumatism, snow-blindness, and sunstroke come from exposure. Scurvy was formerly common, but it is now not often met with. From forced marches or severe exertion the soldier often suffers from heart-trouble.

Camp-meetings, gatherings for religious purposes, held usually in thinly populated districts, and continued for several days at a time, with the view of securing prolonged and uninterrupted spiritual exercises. Assemblies of a like kind have been more or less usual at various periods in the history of the Christian Church; but it was in connection with Methodism in the United States that such meetings became especially prominent. The introduction of the protracted camp-meetings into England in 1799 by Lorenzo Dow led to the separation of the Primitive Methodists from the Wesleyans. See CHAUTAUQUA.

Campa. See ANTI.

Campagna, Girolamo, jĕ-rō'lä-mō käm-pän'ya (called DE VERGNA), Italian sculptor: b. Verona. 1552; d. about 1623. He was a pupil and assistant of Cataneo, many of whose works he completed. Among his own works are the bronze group for the high altar of San Giorgio;

a Madonna and child in San Salvatore; and the altar in the Santi Giovanni e Paolo (all at Venice).

Campagna di Roma, käm-pän'yạ dĕ rō mạ, a territory in Italy which comprehends the greater part of old Latium, from 30 to 40 miles wide and 100 long. By it is usually understood the desert plain which begins near Ronciglione or Viterbo, and including the Pontine Marshes, extends to Terracina. In the middle of this region lies Rome, on its seven hills, and on the Tiber. The lakes of the Campagna are evidently craters of extinct volcanoes. Thus the Lake Regillus above Frascati, lies at the bottom of an inverted cone of hard, black lava, rising in wild and naked masses from 40 to 60 feet high. The craters containing the lakes of Albano and Nemi have a very regular conical form. The Lake of Albano is also remarkable for its aqueduct, or *emissarium,* one of the most ancient and excellent works of the Romans, which discharges the waters of the lake through the mountains. It answers its original purpose even at the present day. There are, also, many sulphur springs here, particularly between Rome and Tivoli, where the water issues almost boiling from the earth, and forms the Lake of Solfatara, which contains floating islands, consisting of a calcareous deposit, that collects round substances thrown into the water. The vapors which rise from the ground all over the Campagna, and especially in the neighborhood of this lake, render the whole district unhealthy. The soil of the Campagna is in general dry, but very fertile in the lower parts. In the middle of the summer, when fevers render a residence in the Campagna very dangerous, all the inhabitants who can do so take refuge in the neighboring towns or in Rome itself; or they may retire with their cattle to the mountains. Besides huts, innumerable ruins of temples, circuses and monuments are scattered over the Campagna, particularly near the Via Appia; and long rows of aqueducts, some in ruins, some in a state of preservation, are overgrown with ivy and other plants. In the winter flocks of sheep pasture in these solitudes; during the summer they are driven up the Apennines. Herds of half-wild cattle remain during the whole year in the Campagna. The herdsmen are mounted, and armed with long lances, with which they manage the cattle very skilfully. Scarcely a ninth part of the Campagna is cultivated, the rest is used for pasturage. In the times of the ancient Romans, this dreary solitude exhibited a smiling picture of abundance and fertility. Yet even in those times the climate was far from being a healthy one. Strabo, Livy, Cicero, Horace, and others agree in describing the districts in the neighborhood of Rome, Ardea, and other towns which stood in what is now the Campagna di Roma, as extremely unwholesome, especially at certain seasons of the year; and it was only through the greatest exertions on the part of the ancient cultivators, and the numerous aids to cultivation that stood at their command, that this tract, now so desolate, was then made so productive. Several of the Popes, particularly Pius VI., have attempted to lessen the insalubrity of the air by the draining of the Pontine Marshes which form the southern portion of the tract. In recent years the Italian government has taken up the problem, and has accomplished much in the way of reclamation, increasing the healthfulness of this historic region.

Campagnola, käm-pän-yō'la, **Domenico,** Italian painter and engraver: flourished about 1520. He was probably born at Padua, where he was a rival of Titian in painting the frescoes in the Scuola del Carmine and in the Scuola del Santa. He is considered one of the best painters of the Venetian school, and his work as an engraver is less important. Of 14 engravings which are known to belong to him, 10 are dated 1517, and one, 'The Descent of the Holy Ghost,' bears the date 1518.

Campaign', in military language, the season during which armies keep the field. Formerly, when war was not carried on with so much impetuosity as at present, campaigns lasted only during the warmer months; and toward winter the troops went into winter quarters, when the officers of the opposing armies often met very amicably at balls and other entertainments; but of late armies have kept the field through the winter till a decisive victory has been gained. Thus the Germans in the war of 1870 with France prosecuted the siege of Paris all through the winter, while at the same time other armies were operating in different parts of France.

Campan, Jeanne Louise Henriette, zhän loo-ēz ŏṅ-rē-ĕt kän-pän (GENEST) : b. Paris, 6 Oct. 1752; d. Mantes, 16 March 1822. She became reader to the daughters of Louis XV.; gained the favor of the wife of the dauphin, afterward Queen Marie Antoinette, who gave her in marriage to the son of her private secretary, M. Campan, and appointed her the first lady of the bed-chamber. Madame Campan gave her patroness many proofs of fidelity and attachment, and wished to follow her into the temple after the 10th of August 1792, which, however, Péthion did not allow. After the fall of Robespierre, Madame Campan established a boarding school for the education of young ladies at St. Germain, which soon acquired a wide reputation. On this account Napoleon appointed her the principal of an institution founded by him for the daughters of the officers of the Legion of Honor, at Ecouen, which she organized and superintended for seven years. After the restoration Louis XVIII. abolished this institution, and Madame Campan lost her situation. Her only son died in 1821, in consequence of ill treatment inflicted because he was a relation of Marshal Ney. She published: 'Memoirs Respecting the Private Life of the Queen Marie Antoinette, with Recollections of the Times of Louis XIV., XV., and XVI.' (1823); 'Journal Anecdotique' (1824); 'Correspondance inédite avec la Reine Hortense' (1835); 'De l'éducation.'

Campana, Pedro, pä'drō käm-pä'ñạ (in the Netherlands known as PETER DE KEMPENEER), Flemish painter of Spanish descent: b. Brussels, 1490; d. there, 1580. In 1530 he went to Italy for study of the Italian masters; he later lived in Seville, Cordova, and other cities of Andalusia, and in 1562 returned to Brussels. In style he combined to some extent the characteristics of the school of Raphael and the Flemish painters. His best known work is in the cathedral at Seville, the 'Descent from the Cross'; other paintings of his are in the same city and he also painted the altar-piece of the Church of Santa Anna in Triana, a suburb of Seville.

Campanella, Tommaso, tŏm-mä'sō käm-pa-nĕl'la, Italian philosopher: b. Stilo, Calabria, 5 Sept. 1568; d. Paris, 1639. He displayed great quickness of parts when quite young, and it the age of 15 entered into the order of the Dominicans. He studied theology and other branches of knowledge with assiduity, but was principally attracted by philosophy. The opinions of Aristotle, then generally taught in the schools, appeared to him unsatisfactory; and in 1591 he published at Naples a work entitled 'Philosophia Sensibus Demonstrata,' intended to show the futility of the prevailing doctrines. This book procured him some admirers, and more enemies. He then went to Rome, and afterward to Florence, where he was well received by the Grand-duke Ferdinand. In 1598 he returned to Naples, and revisited shortly after Calabria, where, in the following year, he was arrested on a charge of conspiracy against the Spanish government, to which Naples was then subject. A scheme was imputed to him of having engaged the Turks to assist him in making himself master of Calabria. On this improbable and apparently unfounded accusation he was imprisoned, and after being repeatedly tortured, condemned to perpetual confinement. In this situation he wrote many learned works, afterward published. At length, in 1626, Pope Urban VIII. procured his removal to Rome, and in 1629 gave him his liberty, and bestowed on him a pension. Dreading some further persecution from the Spaniards, he withdrew in 1634 to France, where he was honorably received by Louis XIII. and Richelieu, and much esteemed by the learned men of that country. He died at the monastery of his order. Among his numerous works may be mentioned: 'Atheismus Triumphatus' (1631); 'Monarchia Messiæ' (1633); 'Defense of Roman Catholicism and the Papal Supremacy'; 'Discorsi della Libertà' (1633); 'Prodromus Philosophiæ Instaurandæ' (1617); 'De Sensu Rerum et Magia' (1620); 'De Monarchia Hispanica Discursus' (1640). A 'Life of Campanella,' by Baldacchini, was published at Naples (1840-3).

Campanero. See BELL-BIRD.

Campani-Alimenis, Matteo, mät-tä'ō kämpä'nĕ ä-lĕ-mä'nīs, Italian mechanician: fl. 17th century. In optics, his greatest achievement was the manufacture of the object-glasses through which Cassini discovered two satellites of Saturn. He wrote 'Horologium solo naturæ motu' (1678), a work on the construction of clocks.

Campa'nia, the ancient name of a province of Italy, in the late kingdom of Naples, which, partly on account of its natural curiosities, including Vesuvius, the Phlegræan fields, the Lake of Avernus, and partly for its remarkable fertility, was a favorite resort of the distinguished Romans, who built there magnificent country houses. Cumæ, Puteoli, Naples, Herculaneum, Pompeii, Baiæ, Stabiæ, Salernum, and Capua, the principal cities of Campania, are names rich in classical associations. The Appian and Latin ways led into the interior of this charming province. Even now Campania, or the province of Caserta, is the most beautiful and fruitful part of Italy, and no traveler can wish for a more delightful country than the fields of Campania, filled in the month of April with barley four feet high, and adorned with lofty poplars, which are connected by luxuriant vines, forming a canopy over the fields. "There," says Goethe, "it is worth while to till the ground."

Cam'panile, a detached tower containing bells. Campaniles are most common in Italy. Several of them have deviated considerably from the perpendicular, in consequence of their great height and narrowness of base. The campanile of Pisa, called *Torre Pendente* (or Leaning Tower), is one of the most remarkable. Its architects were Bonano of Pisa, and Willhelm of Innsbruck, and it was begun in 1174. The tower consists of eight stories, each of which is surrounded by columns, and it inclines nearly 13 feet from the perpendicular. Another celebrated campanile is that which was begun at Florence in 1334, after the designs of Giotto, and finished by Taddeo Gaddi. Its height approaches 300 feet, and it is adorned with 54 bas-reliefs, and 16 statues, representing biblical, pagan, and allegorical subjects. Giotto intended to surmount this tower with a spire nearly 100 feet high, but his intention was never carried out. The Torre degli Asinelli and the Torre Garisenda at Bologna are also remarkable specimens of the campanile. The campanile of St. Mark's Church, Venice, is probably the best known to Americans. Begun as far back as 888 by Pietro Tribuno, it did not assume the form which tourists are familiar with until 1590. For centuries its majestic height dominated the city. Its pinnacle was about 325 feet from the ground.

In 1417 a marble top was put on the old tower. One hundred years later it was crowned with the figure of an angel nearly 16 feet high. Simple in design, the campanile stood out in sharp contrast with the famous belfry of Florence.

The Loggetta at the foot of the campanile was built by the famous Jacopo Sansovino, and was the rendezvous for the nobles of the town. Sansovino adorned it with reliefs and with bronze statues of Minerva, Apollo, Mercury, and Peace. The bronze doors of the vestibule have long been regarded as masterpieces that deserve to rank by the side of the work of the great Italian sculptors. Like many another Italian structure, the Loggetta lost much of its old-time significance. From a meeting-place for the nobles it degenerated into a waiting room for the commanders of the guards during the sessions of the great council. Latterly it was used for auctions and lottery drawings.

The tower was peculiar in that it had no staircase. It was ascended by a winding inclined plane, having 38 bends and ending in a few steps. The tower was always open: but visitors were not allowed to enter alone. For that reason a single traveler was compelled to engage a bystander to accompany him.

From time immemorial a watchman was stationed in the lantern. In the days of the grand maritime Venetian republic it was from the tower that the watchman caught the first glimpse of home-coming war vessels. In modern times the watchman no longer scanned the horizon for vessels, but kept a lookout upon the city for fires.

The campanile served other purposes as well. It was also used for the purpose which its name signifies. According to some authorities, four bells were hung in the olden days in the tower, to be sounded for different purposes. *La marangola* was sounded at dawn to call the laboring classes; *la sestamezzana* opened the official bureaus; *la trotterar* called the councils to duty; and the bell *del malefizio* tolled out the requiem for those who were to be put to death. A fifth bell was later brought from Candia, and tolled only on Ascension Day. In 1518 there hung halfway up the tower a wooden cage, in which prisoners were kept until they starved to death. Scientifically, the tower was of interest by reason of the fact that from it Galileo made many observations. On the morning of 14 July 1902, the campanile collapsed and fell with a great crash into the square. The church of St. Mark and the palace of the Doges were not hurt, but the campanile in falling carried away the Sansovino Loggetta and the library of the Royal Palace. Steps were taken at once to rebuild, and the corner-stone of the new edifice was laid on 24 April 1903. A study of the data provided by the examination of the remains of the fallen tower showed that the bricks had been used for various purposes at a previous stage, in arches, fortifications, tops of walls, etc. The most important fact was that they were not Venetian, but Roman bricks. Moreover, when they were manufactured, they were not manipulated like modern bricks, but formed from slices of clay, as they were found without the natural layers being disturbed. This process resulted in each individual brick being able to support a weight quite four times as great as the modern brick. The bricks examined are of the first century. One bore the impression of a horseshoe, proving the debated point that horseshoes were then in use.

Campanini, käm-pạ-nĕ'nĕ, Italo, Italian singer: b. Parma, 29 June 1846; d. 23 Nov. 1896. His father was a blacksmith. At 14 the boy enlisted in Garibaldi's army and served in two campaigns, after which he worked at his father's trade until the age of 18. Meanwhile, having shown that he possessed an excellent voice, he had taken singing lessons, and after spending a year at the Conservatory in Parma, he appeared in that city as the notary in 'La Sonnambula,' but suffered failure and ridicule. He still continued to sing in public, and in 1869 began to study under Lamperti, a celebrated teacher of Milan. In that city, at La Scala, he sang in 'Faust,' and immediately was acclaimed a great tenor. He appeared in London in 1872, and in the following year made his first visit to the United States, appearing with Nilsson at the Academy of Music, New York, in 'Lucrezia Borgia.' Afterward, in this country and Europe, he sang with great success, and was regarded as the foremost tenor of his time. The partial failure of his voice, mainly through an affection of the throat, caused some interruption of his career, but scarcely diminished his popularity until near the close of his life.

Campan'ula, Bell Flower, or **Bellwort,** a genus of mostly annual, biennial, and perennial herbs of the natural order *Campanulaceæ*. The species, of which there are about 300, are almost all natives of the cooler parts of the northern temperate zone, and among them are some of the most widely grown garden plants which are popular on account of their bell-shaped blue, violet, or white flowers, and the ease with which

they can be cultivated. They do best in a rich, well-drained garden soil, and are readily propagated, the annual and biennial kinds from seeds, and the perennial either from seeds or by division or cuttings. All are hardy. A few species were formerly used in medicine, but are now considered inert For a list of species and for details of cultivation consult Bailey and Miller, 'Cyclopædia of American Horticulture.'

Campanula'ceæ, a natural order of herbaceous and shrubby plants, generally abounding in a bitter, white juice. Their leaves are alternate and entire, rarely opposite. Their flowers form spikes, thyrsi, or heads. They have a monosepalous calyx, with four, five, or eight persistent divisions, and a regular or irregular monopetalous bell-shaped corolla, having its limb divided into as many lobes as there are divisions in the calyx. The stamens are five in number, the anthers free, or brought together in the form of a tube. The ovary is inferior or semi-inferior, with two or more cells, each containing numerous seeds. The style is simple, terminated by a lobed stigma, sometimes surrounded by hairs. The fruit is a capsule crowned by the limb of the calyx, with two or more cells opening either by means of holes which are formed near the upper part, or by incomplete valves. The seeds are very small and very numerous. These plants are chiefly natives of the temperate and colder climates of the northern hemisphere.

Campanula'rians, or **Sertula'rians,** hydroids of the order *Campanularia*. They are always colonial and possess hydrothecæ, and in most cases give rise to a medusa, with auditory organs on the flaps. The ectoderm is protected by a horny or chitinous sheath (perisarc) enveloping the zooids. The hydroids retract, when disturbed, into small cells (hydrothecæ), arranged in opposite rows on the stalk as in *Sertularia*, or singly at the ends of the stalks, as in *Campanularia*, while the sheaths (gonothecæ) protecting the medusa-buds are distinguished by their much larger size and cup-shaped form. The Sertularians abound on seaweeds, and may be recognized from their resemblance to mosses. The medusæ of these and many other hydroids can be collected by a towing-net, and emptied into a jar, where they can be detected by the naked eye after a little practice. It is possible that the extinct palæozoic group, *Graptolites*, belong near the Campanularians, as they have a similar perisarc composed of cells (hydrothecæ). Consult: A. Agassiz, 'North American Acalephæ' (Illustrated Catalogue of the Museum of Comparative Zoology at Harvard College, No. 2, Cambridge 1865); E. C. and A. Agassiz, 'Seaside Studies in Natural History' (Boston 1871); Nutting, 'American Hydroids' ('Special Bulletin of the U. S. National Museum': Washington 1900), contains a full bibliography.

Campardon, Emile, ä-mĕl kän-pär-dôṅ. French writer: b. Paris, 1834. He was educated at the Ecole des Chartes, and then had charge of the archives there. In this position he had opportunity to examine the documents relating to the 18th century and the period of the French Revolution. He has written: 'History of the Revolutionary Tribunal of Paris' (1861); 'Marie Antoinette at the Conciergerie' (1862);

'Madame Pompadour and the Court of Louis XV.' (1867); 'Unpublished Documents of J. B. Poquelin Molière'; 'Voltaire, Unpublished Documents'; 'The Royal Academy of Music in the 18th Century'; and 'Memoirs of Frederic II., King of Prussia' (with E. Boutaric).

Campbell, kăm'bĕl, Alexander, American clergyman: b. near Ballymena, County Antrim, Ireland, 12 Sept. 1788; d. Bethany, W. Va., 4 March 1866. He emigrated to the United States in 1807. He was originally a Presbyterian, but withdrew from that Church in 1812, and received baptism by immersion the same year. In connection with his father, Thomas Campbell, he formed several congregations, which united with a Baptist association, but protested against all human creeds as a bond of union, accepting the Bible alone as the rule of faith and practice. He met with much opposition in the assertion of this principle, and in 1827 was excluded from the fellowship of the Baptist churches. Certain vaguely defined expressions in his writings have been interpreted as implying a belief in baptismal regeneration, a doctrine which the Disciples repudiate. By his discussions on public platforms, and his serial publications, the 'Christian Baptist,' and the 'Millennial Harbinger,' as well as by his assiduity in preaching tours and in training young men for the ministry, Campbell gradually formed a large party of followers, who began about 1827 to form themselves into a sect under the designation of "The Disciples of Christ" (q.v.), but who are most commonly known as Campbellites. In 1841 Campbell founded Bethany College in West Virginia (q.v.). His writings were numerous, and among them are 'The Christian System'; and 'Remission of Sin.' Consult: Richardson, 'Memoir of Alexander Campbell' (1868).

Campbell, Alexander, American politician: b. Concord, Pa., 4 Oct. 1814; d. La Salle, Ill., 9 Aug. 1898. He received a common-school education and entered the iron business, removing to Illinois and attaining prominence in local politics. He was mayor of La Salle, Ill. in 1852, a member of the Illinois legislature in 1858 and a member of Congress in 1875. He was widely known as the "father of the Greenback party."

Campbell, SIR Alexander, Canadian statesman: b. Yorkshire, England, 9 March 1822; d. Toronto, 24 May 1892. He began the practice of law in 1843, and in 1856 became queen's counsel. In 1858 he entered the legislative council, and in 1862 was elected speaker. In 1864-7 he was commissioner of Crown Lands. He was a member of the Quebec Conference in 1864, received an appointment to the Dominion senate (1867), where he was the government leader; became a member of the Queen's Privy Council in 1897, and was postmaster-general in Sir John Macdonald's first federal cabinet. In 1873 he became minister of the interior. With the other cabinet officers, he resigned in the same year, because of the Pacific Railroad scandal. On the return of Macdonald to power, he was minister of militia and defense and again postmaster-general. In 1881 he was minister of justice, and in 1887 lieutenant-governor of Ontario. In politics he was a Conservative, and represented Canada in the imperial federation conference held at London in 1887.

Campbell, Allan, American civil engineer: b. Albany, N. Y., 1815; d. New York, 18 March 1894. He laid out the route of the New York and Harlem R.R.; built a railroad from Callao to Lima, Peru (1855); was appointed engineer of the harbor defenses of New York in the early part of the Civil War; was chief engineer in the construction of the Union P. R. R. He superintended the Harlem R.R. improvement, and became commissioner of public works in New York (1876).

Campbell, Archibald (8th EARL and 1st MARQUIS OF ARGYLE): b. 1598; d. 1661. He was a zealous partisan of the Covenanters. Charles I. created him a marquis in 1641, notwithstanding the opposition he had shown to his favorite object of effecting a conformity between the churches of Scotland and England. It was by his persuasion that Charles II. visited Scotland, and was crowned at Scone in 1651. At the Restoration he was confined in the Tower for five months, and was then sent to Scotland, where he was tried for high treason in connection with the death of Charles I., and beheaded.

Campbell, Archibald (9th EARL OF ARGYLE): d. 30 June 1685. He was the son of the 8th Earl of Argyle, and served the king with great bravery at the battle of Dunbar, and was excluded from the general pardon by Cromwell in 1654, for his exertions in favor of the royal cause. He was afterward made a privy-councilor and one of the lords of the treasury. For refusal to take contradictory oaths, he was tried for treason, and condemned to death, but escaped to Holland, whence he returned with several other disaffected persons, and landed in the Highlands, with a view of aiding the insurrection of the Duke of Monmouth. The plan, however, failed; and he was taken by some country people, who conveyed him to Edinburgh, where he was beheaded.

Campbell, Bartley, American dramatist: b. Allegheny City, Pa., 12 Aug. 1843; d. Middletown, N. Y., 30 July 1888. He engaged in journalism early in his career and established the *Evening Mail* in Pittsburg (1868) and the 'Southern Magazine' in New Orleans (1869). His first drama that met with success in New York was 'My Partner,' appearing in 1879. 'Fairfax, or Life in the Sunny South,' and 'The Galley Slave,' were on the metropolitan boards during the same season. Included in his plays are: 'Matrimony'; 'The White Slave'; 'Siberia'; and 'Paquita.' Several of his plays were brought out in England.

Campbell, Beatrice Stella Tanner (MRS. PATRICK CAMPBELL), English actress: b. London, 1867; married in 1884 Patrick Campbell, killed in 1900 in the Boer war. Her first appearance on the professional stage was made in 1888 at the Alexandra Theatre in Liverpool. She has been particularly successful in such plays as 'The Second Mrs. Tanqueray,' 'John-a-Dreams,' and 'The Notorious Mrs. Ebbsmith.' She has also appeared in such Shakespearean roles as Juliet, Ophelia, and Lady Macbeth. She has frequently visited the United States, playing in most of the leading cities.

Campbell, Charles, American historian: b. Petersburg, Va., 1 May 1807; d. Staunton, Va., 11 July 1876. His life was mainly spent in teaching in his native city. Among his publications are: 'The Bland Papers' (1840-3); 'An Introduction to the History of the Colony and Ancient Dominion of Virginia' (1849); 'Genealogy of the Spotswood Family' (1868). He belonged to the Historical Society of Virginia; was a contributor of the 'Historical Register' and the 'Southern Literary Messenger'; and editor of the 'Orderly Book' of Gen. Andrew Lewis in 1776 (1860).

Campbell, Sir Colin (Lord Clyde), general: b. Glasgow, 20 Oct. 1792; d. 14 Aug. 1863. His father was a carpenter, named Macliver, but the son assumed the name of Campbell. Entering the army in 1808, and serving in the Peninsular war (1809-14), he was severely wounded at the siege of San Sebastian and the passage of the Bidassoa. He took part in the expedition to the United States (1814), and then passed nearly 30 years in garrison duty at Gibraltar, Barbados, Demerara, and various places in England, in 1837 becoming lieutenant-colonel of the 98th foot. He served in India previous to the Crimean war, on the outbreak of which, in 1854, he was appointed to the command of the Highland brigade. The victory of the Alma was mainly his; and his, too, the splendid repulse of the Russians by the "thin red line" in the battle of Balaklava. When, on 11 July 1857, the news reached England of the Sepoy mutiny, Lord Palmerston offered him the command of the forces in India. He effected the final relief of Lucknow, and on 20 Dec. 1858, having five months earlier been created Baron Clyde, announced to the viceroy that the rebellion was ended. Returning next year to England, he was made a field-marshal, and received an annuity of £2,000.

Campbell, Colin, Scottish clergyman: b. Campbelltown, Argylshire, 1848. He was educated at the universities of Edinburgh and Heidelberg, entered the ministry of the Established Kirk of Scotland, and has been minister of the parish of Dundee from 1882. He preached nearly every year from 1883 to 1900 before Queen Victoria at Balmoral Castle and Craithie Parish Church, and has published 'The First Three Gospels in Greek'; 'Critical Studies in St. Luke's Gospel' (1891).

Campbell, Lady Colin, English writer. She is a daughter of Edmond Blood of County Clare, Ireland, and was married to Lord Colin Campbell, youngest son of the 8th Duke of Argyle. She became a widow in 1895. Besides many contributions to journalism, she has published 'Darell Blake'; 'A Book of the Running Brook'; 'A Miracle in Rabbits.'

Campbell, Douglas, American lawyer and writer, son of W. W. Campbell (q.v.): b. Cooperstown, N. Y., 13 July 1840; d. Schenectady, N. Y., 7 March 1893. He practised law in New York (1865-90), but devoted his latest years to historical research. He was the author of 'The Puritan in Holland, England, and America' (1892), which has been widely read.

Campbell, Douglas Houghton, American educator: b. Detroit, Mich., 16 Dec. 1859. He was graduated at the University of Michigan in 1882, and then studied in Europe for four years. Returning he was professor of botany in the University of Indiana till 1891, when he was called to the similar chair in Stanford University. He is author of 'Elements of Structural and Systematic Botany'; 'Structure and

Development of Mosses and Ferns'; and 'Lectures on Evolution of Plants.'

Campbell, George, Scottish clergyman: b. Aberdeen, 25 Dec. 1719; d. 6 April 1796. He was educated at Marischal College, and afterward articled to a writer of the signet at Edinburgh. In 1741 he relinquished the law and studied divinity. In 1759 he was appointed principal of Marischal College. In 1763 he published his celebrated 'Dissertation on Miracles,' in answer to Hume's essay. In 1771 he was chosen professor of divinity, and in 1776 gave to the world his 'Philosophy of Rhetoric,' which established his reputation as a grammarian and critic.

Campbell, Sir George, English statesman: b. 1824; d. London, 18 Feb. 1892. He was educated at Haileyburg for the East Indian service and held several important posts under the Indian government, serving several terms in Parliament also. He published: 'Modern India' (1852); 'India as It May Be'; 'Handy Book of the Eastern Question' (1876); 'White and Black in the United States'; 'The British Empire' (1889).

Campbell, Harry, English physician: b. Margaretting, Essex, England. He studied medicine at Saint Bartholomew's Hospital College and was appointed to the staff of Northwest London Hospital, 1886, and that of Welbeck Street Hospital, 1896. He has published: 'The Physiology of Eyesight' (1885); 'The Causation of Disease' (1889); 'Flushing and Morbid Blushing' (1890); 'Differences in the Nervous Organization of Man and Woman' (1891); 'Headache and Other Morbid Cephalic Sensations' (1894); 'Respiratory Exercises in the Treatment of Disease' (1898).

Campbell, Helen Stuart, American author. b. Lockport, N. Y., 4 July 1839. She was educated at Mrs. Cook's Seminary, Bloomfield, N. J., 1850-8; and very early began contributing to periodicals. From 1881 to 1884 she edited 'Our Continent' (Philadelphia). Her especial interest has been in social and domestic questions, such as the condition of the poor, household management, etc., and her writings for the most part consists of essays and stories illustrating these topics. Chief among them are: 'The Ainslee Series' (1864-7); 'Six Sinners' (1878); 'Unto the Third and Fourth Generation' (1880); 'Under Green Apple Boughs' (1881); 'The Easiest Way in Housekeeping and Cooking' (1881); 'The Problem of the Poor' (1882); 'Mrs. Herndon's Income: a Novel' (1885); 'Prisoners of Poverty' (1887); 'Prisoners of Poverty Abroad' (1889); 'Roger Berkeley's Probation' (1891); 'Anne Bradstreet and Her Time' (1892); 'Women Wage-Earners' (1893); 'In Foreign Kitchens' (1894); 'Some Passages in the Practice of Dr. Martha Scarborough' (1893); 'Ballantyne: a Novel' (1901).

Campbell, Henry Donald, American scientist: b. Lexington, Va., 29 July 1862. He was graduated at Washington and Lee University in 1882; later studied at Berlin and Heidelberg, and in 1887 became professor of geology and biology at Washington and Lee University.

Campbell, James Edwin, American politician: b. Middletown, Ohio, 7 July 1843. After an academic education he was admitted to the bar. During the Civil War he served for a time in the navy and was with the Mississippi and Red River flotillas. He was a Democratic member of Congress, 1883–9; governor of Ohio, 1890–2. He was defeated for re-election by William McKinley, afterward President of the United States. In 1895 he was again a candidate, but was defeated by A. S. Bushnell. His home is at Hamilton, Ohio, where he has a successful law practice.

Campbell, James M., Scottish-American clergyman: b. Scotland, 5 May 1840. He received his education at the universities of Edinburgh and Glasgow and in 1874 came to the United States. He has lectured much on religious themes and has published: 'Unto the Uttermost' (1889); 'The Indwelling Christ' (1895); 'After Pentecost, What?' (1897); 'The Teachings of the Books' (1899); 'Clerical Types' (1900); 'Bible Questions' (1900).

Campbell, James Valentine, American jurist: b. Buffalo, N. Y., 25 Feb. 1823; d. Detroit, Mich., 26 March 1890. When three years old he accompanied his parents to Detroit. He graduated at St. Paul's College, L. I., in 1841; was admitted to the Detroit bar, 1844; practised with success until 1857. He was then elected a judge of the supreme court of Michigan, re-elected at every succeeding election, and was chosen chief justice for nine terms in succession. From 1859 he lectured for 20 years in the law department of the University of Michigan. Much of his leisure was devoted to literary and historical studies, especially the history of Michigan and the northwest territory. Until 1854 he was a Whig, but thereafter acted chiefly with the Republicans. He wrote 'Outlines of the Political History of Michigan' (1876).

Campbell, John, American editor: b. Scotland, 1653; d. 4 March 1728. He was one of a family or kin of Boston booksellers and public officials whose relationships are not determinable, but which included John, in the middle of the 17th century, Duncan, postmaster of Boston from 1694 on, and John (above), who was appointed postmaster — probably succeeding Duncan — in the latter part of 1702. There seems to have been a Thomas also about this time. The later John as postmaster was the news centre of the New England provinces; and in 1703 was writing "news letters" of European news to Gov. Winthrop of Connecticut, and perhaps other governors, made up of information received from arriving travelers, etc., with inferences as to New England policy. In 1704 he concluded to make these public and for sale; and on 24 April issued the first newspaper in America, the Boston *News Letter* (q.v.), which he edited till 1722. In 1719 he was deprived of the postmastership. He was justice of the peace for Suffolk County for some years.

Campbell, John (2d DUKE OF ARGYLE and DUKE OF GREENWICH), British general and statesman: b. Scotland, 1678; d. 1743. In 1706 he served under the Duke of Marlborough, and was a brigadier-general at the battle of Ramilies. He was a promoter of the union, for which he incurred considerable odium in his own country. He commanded at the battles of Oudenarde and Malplaquet, and assisted at the sieges of Lisle and Ghent. For these ser-

vices he was made a Knight of the Garter in 1710, and the year following was sent as ambassador to Charles III. of Spain. He was also appointed commander-in-chief of the English forces there. In 1712 he had the military command in Scotland, of which post he was soon after deprived for opposing the court measures; but on the accession of George I. he was restored, and received additional honors. In 1715 he engaged the Earl of Mar's army at Dunblane, and forced the Pretender to quit the kingdom. In 1718 he was created an English peer with the title of Duke of Greenwich. He filled successively several high offices, of which he was deprived for his opposition to Sir Robert Walpole, but on the removal of that minister he was replaced. In Westminster Abbey, where he was buried, is a noble monument to his memory.

Campbell, John, British historian: b. Edinburgh, 8 March 1708; d. 28 Dec. 1775. His writings before 1742 were published anonymously. From 1755 to the close of his life he was agent of the British government for the province of Georgia. Among his works are: 'A Concise History of Spanish America' (1741); 'Lives of the English Admirals' (1744); 'A Survey of the Present State of Europe' (1750); and 'Trade of Great Britain to America' (1772).

Campbell, John (BARON), lord high chancellor of England: b. Springfield, near Cupar, county of Fife, Scotland, 15 Sept. 1779; d. 23 June 1861. He was educated at the grammar school of Cupar, and at 12 entered the University of St. Andrews (1791) for the purpose of studying for the Church. After remaining, however, for some years at college, he resolved to abandon the clerical profession, and determined to try his fortune in London. In 1798 he quitted his native country for the metropolis, where he became reporter and theatrical critic on the *Morning Chronicle*. In November 1800 he entered as a student of Lincoln's Inn, and in 1806 was called to the bar. He traveled the Oxford circuit, and obtained considerable practice. In 1830 he was elected member of Parliament for Stafford, and in 1832 was appointed solicitor-general. In 1834, on the retirement of Sir William Horne, he became attorney-general, and the same year was elected one of the members of Parliament for the city of Edinburgh, serving till 1841, when he was created chancellor of Ireland, and raised to the peerage as Baron Campbell of St. Andrews. He had scarcely, however, assumed his official duties in Ireland when he quitted office with the Melbourne ministry; and having now more leisure worked on his 'Lives of the Chancellors,' the first series of which was published early in 1846. On the accession of Lord John Russell to power in that year Lord Campbell accepted the chancellorship of the Duchy of Lancaster, but still continued his literary labors, completing, in seven volumes, his 'Lives of the Chancellors,' and adding two other supplemental volumes, entitled 'Lives of the Chief Justices of England.' In 1850, on the retirement of Lord Denman, he was appointed chief justice; in 1859 on Lord Palmerston's resumption of the premiership, Lord Campbell reached the highest legal dignity in the British empire, being raised to the woolsack as lord high chancellor.

Campbell, John, Canadian Presbyterian clergyman: b. Edinburgh, Scotland, 18 June 1840. He was educated in the University of Toronto, and New College, Edinburgh, and in 1868 became pastor of the Charles Street Church in Toronto. In 1873 he was appointed professor of Church history and apologetics in the Presbyterian College, Montreal. Twenty years later he was convicted of heresy by the Montreal Presbytery, but the decision was reversed by the synod. He has published 'The Hittites: Their Inscriptions and Their History' (1890).

Campbell, John Archibald, American lawyer: b. Washington. Ga., 24 June 1811; d. Baltimore, 12 March 1889. He was graduated from the Georgia University in 1826 and was admitted to the bar in 1829 before coming of age, by virtue of a special act of the legislature. Removing to Alabama he soon became prominent in his profession, and in 1853 was appointed associate justice of the supreme court of the United States, resigning in 1861. He was subsequently appointed Confederate secretary of war, and was one of the commissioners named by President Davis to meet President Lincoln and Secretary Seward at the conference in Fortress Monroe in February 1865. He was imprisoned for some months after the close of the Civil War and on his release resumed his legal practice.

Campbell, John Douglas Sutherland. See ARGYLE, CAMPBELLS OF.

Campbell, John Francis, Scotch folklore writer: b. 29 Dec. 1822; d. Cannes, France, 17 Feb. 1885. His first success was 'Popular Tales of the West Highlands' (1860-2), an accurate and discriminating compilation; to which succeeded 'Frost and Fire' (1865).

Campbell, John Lorne, American Baptist clergyman: b. Dominionville, Ontario, 14 Jan. 1845. He was graduated from Woodstock College, Ontario, and from the Baptist Theological Seminary at the same institution, and subsequently from Toronto University. He was ordained to the Baptist ministry in 1868. Since 1889 he has been pastor of the Lexington Avenue Baptist Church in New York. He has published 'Heavenly Recognition and Other Sermons' (1895); 'Sanctification' (1901).

Campbell, John McLeod, Scotch theologian: b. Kilninver, Argyle, 4 May 1800; d. 27 Feb. 1872. Sent to Glasgow University at 11, he was licensed to preach by the presbytery of Lorne in 1821. His views on salvation and the atonement brought upon him a charge of heresy, which led to his deposition in 1831. For years he labored in the Highlands and preached without remuneration. When his health broke down he advised his people to attach themselves to the church of Norman Macleod. He spent the remainder of his life in retirement. In 1868 his university gave him the degree of D.D., and in 1871 a testimonial and address was presented to him by men of nearly every religious denomination in Scotland. He wrote: 'Christ the Bread of Life' (1851); 'The Nature of the Atonement' (1856); and 'Thoughts on Revelation' (1862).

Campbell, John Pendleton, American scientist: b. Cumberland, Md., 20 Nov. 1863. He studied at Johns Hopkins University, and in 1888 became professor of biology at the University of Georgia.

Campbell, John Preston, American lawyer and author: b. Boston, Mass., 8 April 1849. He practised law at Abilene, Kansas, but since 1897 has lived in Washington, D. C. Among his numerous writings are: 'Merl of Medevon and Other Prose Writings' (1888); 'My Mate Immortal'; and 'Queen Sylvia and Other Poems' (1886).

Campbell, John TenBrook, American scientist: b. Montezuma, Ind., 21 May 1833. A carpenter in early life, he enlisted as a private at the outbreak of the Civil War, and rose to the rank of captain. He studied engineering and physical science, and has perfected many surveying implements. He has written 'National Finances,' and pamphlets on mathematical science and astro-physics.

Campbell, Lewis, British classical scholar: b. Edinburgh, 3 Sept. 1830. He received his early education at Edinburgh Academy, and afterward attended the University of Glasgow, and Trinity and Balliol colleges, Oxford, taking the degree of B.A. (with first-class honors in classics) in 1853, and that of M.A. in 1856. Ordained in 1857, he became vicar of Milford, Hants, in the following year, a post which he held till his appointment, in 1863, as professor of Greek in St. Andrew's University. He retired from this chair in 1892, becoming emeritus professor. The 1894-5 series of Gifford Lectures at St. Andrews was delivered by him. As a writer he is known mainly by his editions and translations of ancient Greek authors, the chief of which are: Plato's 'Theætetus' (1861); Plato's 'Sophistes and Politicus' (1867); 'Sophocles — The Plays and Fragments' (1879); 'Sophocles in English Verse' (1873-83); Æschylus in English Verse' (1890); and Plato's 'Republic' (with the late Benjamin Jowett 1894). 'The Christian Ideal,' published in 1877, is a volume of sermons; and his other works include a 'Guide to Greek Tragedy' (1891); 'Life of James Clerk Maxwell' (with W. Garnett 1882); 'Life of Benjamin Jowett' (with E. Abbott 1897); 'Religion in Greek Literature' (1898), the substance of his Gifford Lectures; and the articles, 'Plato' and 'Sophocles' in the ninth edition of the 'Encyclopædia Britannica.'

Campbell, Loomis J., American philologist: b. Oneonta, N. Y., 1831; d. there, 6 Nov. 1896. He was author of a 'United States History,' also of the popular 'Franklin Series' of school books; and edited a 'Young Folks' Book of Poetry' and a 'Hand-Book of Synonyms.'

Campbell, Mrs. Patrick. See CAMPBELL, BEATRICE.

Campbell, Reginald John, English Congregational clergyman: b. London, 1867. After receiving a collegiate training at University College, Nottingham, and Christ Church College, Oxford, he entered the Congregational ministry in 1895. He is pastor of the Union Church, Brighton, and is widely known as a preacher. He has published 'The Making of an Apostle'; 'The Restored Innocence' (1898); 'A Faith for To-day' (1900).

Campbell, Thomas, British poet: b. Glasgow, 27 July 1777; d. Boulogne, France, 15 June 1844. He was educated at the University of Glasgow, where he distinguished himself by the excellence of his poetical translations from the Greek. After leaving the university he resided for a short time in Edinburgh; and all at once attained the zenith of his fame by publishing, in 1799, 'The Pleasures of Hope.' It produced an extraordinary sensation, and soon became a familiar book throughout the kingdom. This was due not more to the graces of its style than to the noble purity of its thoughts. After the publication of this he went to Germany, where he met Klopstock at Hamburg, and visited the scene of the battle celebrated in 'Hohenlinden,' one of the most famous of his poems. The appearance of the English fleet caused him to leave Altona, where he had resided for some time. During this tour several of his best lyrics were written or suggested, among them 'The Exile of Erin,' 'Ye Mariners of England,' and 'The Battle of the Baltic.' In 1803 a new edition of 'The Pleasures of Hope,' with other poems, appeared, and in that year he was married. Settling in London, he devoted himself to literary work, and in 1805 obtained a pension of £200, through the influence of Fox, of whose politics he was an admirer. After this he appears for a time to have given his attention less to poetry than prose, but in 1809 he again made his appearance as a poet, and published 'Gertrude of Wyoming,' which some eminent critics have considered superior to 'The Pleasures of Hope,' though the public appear to have judged differently. In 1814 he visited Paris, and in the following year he received a legacy of over £4,000. In 1819, by his 'Specimens of the British Poets,' accompanied with critical essays, he proved himself the possessor of great critical acumen and an admirable prose style. In 1820 he became editor of the 'New Monthly Magazine,' a position which he held till 1830. In 1824 he published 'Theodoric,' which, though not devoid of fine passages, scarcely sustained his reputation. For some years he took an active interest in the emancipation of Greece and Poland, and in the foundation of the London University, of which he considered himself the originator. He was lord rector of the University of Glasgow from 1826 to 1829. In 1828 his wife died, and thenceforth his vigor, both bodily and mental, began to decline; and though he afterward published 'Letters from the South' (1837), describing a visit which he had paid to Algiers, a 'Life of Mrs. Siddons' (1834-42), and a 'Life of Petrarch,' and either wrote or edited the 'Life and Times of Frederick the Great,' he failed to equal his more youthful efforts. In 1831-2 he was editor of the 'Metropolitan Magazine,' and in 1832 he founded the Polish Association. Among his works not mentioned above are: 'The Advent,' a hymn; 'Love and Madness'; 'Lord Ullin's Daughter'; 'The Wounded Hussar'; 'Gilderoy'; 'The Soldier's Dream'; 'Judith'; 'The Name Unknown'; 'The Turkish Lady'; 'Lochiel's Warning'; 'The Rainbow'; 'The Last Man'; 'Navarino'; 'Pilgrim of Glencoe'; 'Moonlight'; etc. See Beattie, 'Life and Letters of Thomas Campbell'; and Redding, 'Literary Reminiscences of Campbell.'

Campbell, Thomas W., American clergyman: b. Three Rivers, Quebec, Canada, 24 Sept. 1851. He was graduated at Victoria University in 1879, and became a Methodist missionary. Joining the Reformed Episcopal Church, he was elected a bishop in 1891, and presiding bishop

in 1894, and resigned to enter the Presbyterian Church in 1898. Since October 1899 he has been pastor of the Noble Street Church, Brooklyn, N. Y.

Campbell, William, American soldier: b. Augusta County, Va., 1745; d. Rocky Mills, Va., 22 Aug. 1781. He was of Scottish descent. Commissioned a captain in the first regular troops raised in Virginia in 1775, and later becoming a colonel of militia, he distinguished himself greatly in the battles of King's Mountain and Guilford Court-House. His military career was short but brilliant, and on all occasions marked by conspicuous bravery. Lafayette gave him the command of a brigade of riflemen and light infantry. Washington, Gates, and Greene, the Virginia legislature, and the Continental Congress expressed their high sense of his merits and services. He was taken fatally ill a few weeks before the siege of Yorktown. He married a sister of Patrick Henry.

Campbell, William (LORD), English royal governor of South Carolina: b. (?); d. 5 Sept. 1778. He was the youngest son of John, fourth Duke of Argyle. He received a captaincy in the British navy, 20 Aug. 1762; was a member of Parliament in 1764, and governor of Nova Scotia, 1766-73. In 1774 he was appointed governor of South Carolina, entered upon his duties in June 1775, was courteously received by the people, for whom he professed great friendship. The hollowness of his promises was soon proved, however, and finding his residence in Charleston unsafe, he fled on board a British man-of-war, where he was soon joined by his wife, who was a Miss Sarah Izard, sister of the patriot, Ralph Izard, who belonged to the wealthiest family in the province. In 1776 Campbell served as a volunteer on board Sir Peter Parker's flagship, Bristol, in the attack on Fort Sullivan, 28 June, and was severely wounded early in the action, while in command of the lower deck. He ultimately died from the effects of the wounds received at this time. Though not of a very firm character, he possessed of a vigorous courage which frequently displayed itself.

Campbell, William W., American lawyer and historian: b. Cherry Valley, N. Y., 1806; d. there, 7 Sept. 1881. He settled in New York and was a judge of the State supreme court. He wrote 'Annals of Tryon County' (re-issued as 'Border Warfare'); 'Life and Writings of De Witt Clinton'; 'Sketches of Robin Hood and Capt. Kidd'; etc.

Campbell, William Wallace, American astronomer: b. Hancock County, Ohio, 11 April 1862. He was graduated from the University of Michigan in 1886, was professor of mathematics at the University of Colorado, 1886-8; and instructor in astronomy in the University of Michigan 1888-91. Since 1891 he has been astronomer at the Lick Observatory, California, and director there from 1 Jan. 1901. He is a member of several American and foreign learned societies, and besides many professional papers has published 'The Elements of Practical Astronomy' (1899).

Campbell, William Wilfred, Canadian poet: b. Berlin, Ontario, Canada, 1 June 1861. He was educated at Toronto University, and the Episcopal Theological School, Cambridge, Mass., and was for some years in the Episcopal ministry in Canada, retiring from it in 1891 in order to devote himself entirely to literary pursuits. He has published 'Lake Lyrics' (1889); 'The Dread Voyage' (1893); 'Mordred, a Tragedy'; and 'Hildebrand' (1895), the two latter being dramas in blank verse; 'Beyond the Hills of Dream' (1899); and numerous separate poems, among them 'England' (1897). He is cited, in the 'Victorian Anthology,' among the notable poets of Canada.

Campbell. See ARGYLE, CAMPBELLS OF.

Campbell-Ban'nerman, SIR HENRY, English statesman: b. 7 Sept. 1836. He was the son of Sir James Campbell, but added the surname Bannerman, under the will of a maternal uncle. He was educated at Glasgow University and Trinity College, Cambridge. In 1868 he was elected member of Parliament for Stirling Borough. From 1871-4, and from 1880-2, he was financial secretary of the war office; 1882-4, secretary of admiralty; 1884-5, chief secretary for Ireland; 1886 and 1892-5, secretary for war. In February 1899 he became leader of the Liberal party, and on 4 Dec. 1905 succeeded Sir Arthur Balfour as Premier.

Campbell Island, a lonely island to the south of New Zealand, in lat. 52° 34' S., and lon.. 169° 12' E. Though it rises to a height of 1,498 feet, and is only 85 square miles in area, it is yet valuable on account of its harbors. It is also scientifically interesting, being volcanic, and displaying a rich and rare flora. It served as an observatory during the transit of Venus in 1874.

Camp'bellites, followers of Rev. John McLeod Campbell, who was deposed from the Church of Scotland in 1831 for teaching the universality of the Atonement. He established a church at Glasgow in 1833. The name is also applied to members of the church founded in the United States by Alexander Campbell. See DISCIPLES OF CHRIST.

Campbell's Station, Tenn., the scene of an engagement between Federal and Confederate forces, 4 Nov. 1863. Gen. Braxton Bragg, who was besieging Chattanooga, detached Longstreet's corps of 10,000 men and 35 guns, with Wheeler's cavalry force of 5,000 men, to capture Burnside or drive him out of East Tennessee. Longstreet reached the south bank of the Tennessee, near Loudon, on the 13th, and that night and next day laid bridges at Huff's Ferry, two miles below Loudon, and began crossing his infantry. Burnside, who was holding the north bank of the river from Kingston to Lenoirs, concluded to leave one brigade at Kingston and retire the rest of his command to Knoxville, about 30 miles, where he had prepared to make a stand behind defensive works. He skirmished sharply with Longstreet's advance on the 14th, and gradually falling back on the 15th, at night concentrated Hartranft's and Ferrero's divisions of the 9th Corps, and White's of the 23d, at Lenoirs. He had about 5,000 men. Longstreet followed, attacked during the night, and was repulsed. Before daybreak of the 16th Hartranft, with his division and some cavalry, was put on the march to secure Campbell's Station, the intersection of roads coming from the south. After destroying many wagons and contents, taking the teams to assist his artillery over the bad roads, axle-deep in mud, Burnside followed with the other two divisions, artillery and trains, closely pursued by Longstreet, with Hood's division, commanded by Gen. Micah Jenkins, with whose advance his rearguard had several sharp encounters. McLaws' division of Longstreet's corps took a more direct road to the left, the two roads intersecting about a mile southward of Campbell's Station, 15 miles south of Knoxville. Hartranft reached the coveted point in advance of McLaws and, turning west on the Kingston road, deployed his division in such manner as to confront McLaws, and at the same time cover the Lenoir road, along which the trains were moving in advance of the infantry. He had scarcely made his dispositions when McLaws appeared and attacked, but Hartranft held on until Burnside, with the trains and the remainder of the troops, had passed and the troops taken position, when he fell back and formed on the left of White's division, in position half a mile beyond the junction of the two roads, Ferrero's division on White's right, and the artillery on commanding ground sweeping the road and the open country in front. The jaded train continued on the road to Knoxville. McLaws advanced and drew up in the plain, but the forbidding aspect of Burnside's artillery, which opened viciously on him, forbade direct attack with infantry, whereupon he opened with artillery, and Longstreet ordered attacks upon both flanks of Burnside's line, which were made and nicely parried or repulsed; but, largely superior in numbers, Longstreet was able to move around both flanks, especially on Burnside's left, which obliged him to fall back to a ridge nearly a mile in the rear. This he did in a handsome manner, though under a heavy and constant fire, and closely pressed on all sides. It was four o'clock when Hood's division made an attack on Burnside's left, which was repulsed. McLaws attacked his right and was thrown back, and Longstreet then prepared for a general advance of his entire line; but before his preparations were completed it was coming dark, and his train secure and well on the way to Knoxville. Burnside, after dark, resumed his march. His advance reached Knoxville about daybreak next morning, 17 November, Longstreet warily following during the day, and the siege of Knoxville began. In this action at Campbell's Station and the skirmishes preceding it at Huff's Ferry, Lenoirs, and on the march, the Union loss was 303 killed and wounded, and 135 missing. The Confederate loss is not definitely known. Hood's division, the most seriously engaged, lost 174 killed and wounded; the loss of McLaws was much less. Consult: 'Official Records,' Vol. XXXV.; the Century Company's 'Battles and Leaders of the Civil War,' Vol. III.; Woodward's 'Burnside and the 9th Army Corps.'

E. A. CARMAN.

Campe, Joachim Heinrich, yō'äH-īm hīn rīH käm'pě, German author: b. Deensen, Brunswick, Germany, 29 June 1746; d. 22 Oct. 1818. He studied for the Church, acted for some time as a teacher in various positions, and in 1786 was chosen by the government of Brunswick to superintend and reform the schools of that duchy. He became likewise the head of a school-book publishing house at Brunswick, and his own works, which were issued from it, contributed greatly to extend its reputation. These consist principally of educational works and books for youth, the most successful being 'Robinson the Younger,' an adaptation of Defoe's 'Robinson Crusoe.' This attained an immense popularity, being translated into almost all the languages of Europe. He also wrote a 'History of the Discovery of America.'

Campe'che, or **Campeachy,** Mexico, a seaport town in the state and on the bay of the same name, on the west coast of the peninsula of Yucatan, about 100 miles southwest of Merida, to which it is connected by railroad. It contains a citadel, a university with a museum, a hospital, and a handsome theatre. Campeche is an important mart for logwood or Campeachy wood, of which great quantities are exported. Other important exports are wax, cigars, and henequen or sisal-hemp. Owing to the shallowness of the roadstead large vessels have to anchor five or six miles off. There is a lighthouse on the coast at this port. Pop. 16,631. The state of Campeachy has an area of 18,091 square miles. Pop. 84,000. The Bay of Campeachy, part of the Gulf of Mexico, lies on the southwest of the peninsula of Yucatan, and on the north of the province of Tabasco.

Campeggio, käm-pĕj'ō, or **Campeggi,** Lorenzo, Italian ecclesiastic: b. Bologna, 1472; d. Rome, 19 July 1539. He succeeded his father as professor of law in the University of Padua in 1511, and gained a high reputation. When holding this office he married, and became the father of several children, but having lost his wife, took orders. Pope Julius II. made him bishop of Feltri, and Leo X., after giving him a cardinal's hat, employed him on several important missions, the execution of which gave him some prominence in connection with the Reformation. One of his missions was to Germany, for the purpose of regaining Luther; and another to England, to attempt to levy a tithe for defraying the expense of a war against the Turks. He failed signally in both, but ingratiated himself with Henry VIII., and was made bishop of Salisbury. Under Clement VII. he was sent as legate to the Diet of Nuremberg, where he vainly endeavored to unite the princes in opposition to Luther; and to the Diet of Augsburg. He again visited England, with extensive powers to decide in the question of divorce between Henry VIII. and Queen Catherine; but his temporizing measures lost him the confidence of all parties, as well as his bishopric of Salisbury. Notwithstanding his repeated failures, he remained high in favor at the papal court; and at his death was archbishop of Bologna.

Campen. See KAMPEN.

Campen, Jacob de. See KAMPEN, JACOB DE.

Campen, Jan van. See KAMPEN, JAN VAN.

Camper, Peter, pä'tėr käm'pėr, Dutch anatomist: b. Leyden, 11 May 1722; d. The Hague, 7 April 1789. He distinguished himself in anatomy, surgery, obstetrics, and medical jurisprudence, and also as a writer on æsthetics. From 1750 to 1755 he was professor of medicine at Franeker, and from the latter year to 1763 at Amsterdam. Henceforth till his resignation in 1773 he held a professorship at Groningen. His 'Dissertation on the Natural Varieties,' etc., is the first work in which was thrown

much light on the varieties of the human species, which the author distinguishes by the shape of the skull. His 'Treatise on the Natural Difference of Features in Persons of Various Countries and Ages,' and one on 'Beauty as Exhibited in Ancient Paintings and Engravings,' followed by a method of delineating various sorts of heads with accuracy, is intended to prove that the rules laid down by the most celebrated limners and painters are very defective. His general doctrine is, that the difference in form and cast of countenance proceeds from the facial angle.

Cam'perdown (Dutch, *Camperduin*), Holland, a stretch of sandy hills or downs in the province of North Holland, between the North Sea and the small village of Camp, off which the British, under Admiral Duncan, gained a hard-won victory over the Dutch, under De Winter, 11 Oct. 1797. For this victory Admiral Duncan was raised to the peerage as Viscount Duncan of Camperdown. His son became Earl of Camperdown, and this title still belongs to a descendant.

Campero, Narciso, när-thē'sō käm-pā'rō, Bolivian statesman and soldier: b. Tojo (now in Argentina), 1815. He studied and traveled in Europe, and on his return entered the Bolivian army, and rose to the rank of brigadier-general. He was minister of war in 1872. After the overthrow of Hilarion Daza in 1880 he was chosen president of Bolivia. He commanded the combined forces of Peru and Bolivia in Tacna campaign, but was defeated at Tacna, 26 May 1880. Internally, his administration was quiet.

Camphausen, Wilhelm, vil'hĕlm kämp'-how-zĕn, German painter: b. Düsseldorf, 8 Feb. 1818; d. Düsseldorf, 16 June 1885. He was from 1859 professor in the art academy there. He was specially famous for battle-pieces — scenes from Cromwell's battles, the Thirty Years' war, the wars of 1866 and 1870 — and painted many notable portraits of soldiers and equestrian figures.

Cam'phene, or **Camphine',** (1) a general name for those terpenes which are solid at ordinary temperatures (see TERPENE); (2) a purified form of turpentine, obtained by distilling that substance over quicklime in order to remove the resins that the crude product contains, and widely used as an illuminating oil before petroleum was available.

Cam'phol, a substance now better known as borneol (q.v.).

Cam'phor, a white, translucent, crystalline substance occurring in the wood and bark of the laurel-tree (*Camphora officinarum*, *Cinnamomum camphora*, or *Laurus camphora*), from which it is obtained by distillation with steam and subsequent sublimation. It has the chemical formula $C_{10}H_{16}O$, melts at 350° F., boils at 500° F., and sublimes to an appreciable extent at practically all temperatures. It has a strong, pleasant, characteristic odor, and a peculiar, cooling, aromatic taste. Its specific gravity is about 0.992, and it dissolves to a slight extent in water, and freely in alcohol or ether. Small shavings of it exhibit lively motions when thrown upon a water-surface that is absolutely free from oily matter. (See SURFACE TENSION.) It is familiar about the household, on account of its use for protecting furs and woolens from the attacks of moths and other insects. It is also employed in the manufacture of celluloid and various explosives. The chemistry of camphor is very complicated, and numerous substances are known that resemble it closely, and yet differ from it in certain particulars. See BORNEOL.

Camphor'ic Acid, a substance crystallizing in colorless, needle-like, monoclinic crystals, and obtained by boiling camphor with concentrated nitric acid. It has the formula $C_{10}H_{16}O_4$, and a specific gravity of 1.19, and melts at about 370° F. It is almost insoluble in cold water, but is soluble in hot water, alcohol, and ether.

Camphuysen, Dirk **Rafelsk,** dürk räf'ä èlz kämp'hoi zĕn, Dutch painter, theologian, and poet: b. Gorkum, 1586; d. Dokkum, 9 July 1627. He lost his parents at an early age, and was left to the care of an elder brother; who, thinking that he observed in Rafelsk an inclination for painting, placed him as a pupil in the studio of the artist Govitz. He soon distinguished himself by his landscapes, which were generally of small size, but animated with huts, cattle, and human figures, and executed with a skill and delicacy to which no former Dutch painter had attained. His paintings are now very rare, for he abandoned his art to devote himself to theology, which was the reigning passion of the age. He embraced the doctrines of Arminius, and shared in the persecutions under which Arminianism then suffered. He was expelled from the curacy of Vleuten which he had previously obtained, became a fugitive from village to village, a prey to suffering and privation, and often regretted the canvas and brush which had erewhile opened to him so pleasant a career. He found now in writing short poems his only relief and consolation. These are generally upon religious subjects, and are characterized by a remarkable depth of feeling.

Campi, käm'pē, a family of Italian artists who founded what is known in painting as the school of Cremona. Of the four of this name, Giulio, Antonio, Vincenzo, and Bernardino, the first and the last are the best known. Giulio (1502–72), the eldest and the teacher of the others, was a pupil of Giulio Romano, and acquired from the study of Titian and Pordenone a skill in coloring which gave the school its high place. Bernardino (1525–90), was the greatest of the school. He took Romano, Titian, and Correggio in succession as his models, but without losing his own individuality as an artist.

Campion, Edmund, English theologian: b. London, 25 Jan. 1540; d. 1 Dec. 1581. He was educated at Christ's Hospital and St. John's College, Oxford, and distinguished himself greatly, becoming B.A. in 1561 and M.A. in 1564. Though at first a Roman Catholic he adopted nominally the Reformed faith and took deacon's orders in the Church of England. When Queen Elizabeth visited Oxford in 1566 he was selected to make the oration before her, as formerly while at school he had been chosen to deliver an oration before Queen Mary on her accession. He went from college to Ireland, and while there wrote the history of that country and connected himself with the Roman Catholic Church. His enthusiasm leading him to seek to make proselytes to his new faith, he was seized and imprisoned; but after a short time effected his escape to the Low Countries, and soon after joined the English college of Jesuits at Douay, passed his novitiate as a member of that society, and became distinguished for his piety and learning. At Rome in 1573 he was admitted a member of the Order of Jesuits, after which he resided for a time at Vienna, where he composed a tragedy, which was received with much applause and acted before the emperor; and at Prague, where he taught rhetoric and philosophy for six years. Sent by Gregory XIII. on a mission to England in 1581, he challenged the universities and clergy to dispute with him. His efforts were followed by so large a number of conversions as to disquiet the ministry of Elizabeth; and he was arrested and thrown into the Tower upon a charge of having excited the people to rebellion, and of holding treasonable correspondence with foreign powers. Being tried, he was found guilty, condemned to death for high treason, and executed at Tyburn. The insults of the populace attended him to the Tower, where torture was fruitlessly applied to extort from him a confession of treason or a recognition of the supremacy of the English Church, and after his death a fragment of his body was sent to each of the principal towns for exposure. Beside his history of Ireland, he wrote 'Decem Rationes' ('Ten Reasons'), and compiled a 'Universal Chronology,' and collections of his letters and several essays were published after his death. His biography has been written by Richard Simpson (London 1867).

Campion, Thomas, English poet: b. about 1575; d. London, 1 March 1619. He was a physician by profession. He wrote a volume of 'Poems' (1595), being Latin elegies and epigrams. He published (1610–12) four 'Books of Airs,' containing songs written by himself to airs of his own composition: the first book contains 'Divine and Moral Songs'; the second, 'Light Conceits of Lovers'; the third and fourth are not distinguished by any separate sub-title. In his songs the verse and the music are most happily wedded.

Campli, Italy, a town in Naples, in the province of Teramo, and five miles north of the town of Teramo. It has a cathedral, three churches, an abbey, several convents, a hospital, and a mont-de-piété. Pop. 7,236.

Campo Basso, Niccolo, ⟨CONTE DA⟩ Italian soldier: fl. in the latter half of the 15th century. He had first supported the house of Anjou in the kingdom of Naples, but afterward transferred his services to their opponent, Charles the Bold, Duke of Burgundy. By pandering to the prejudices and caprices of that headstrong prince he acquired great influence over his mind, and in the end availed himself of the confidence placed in him by the Duke to sell him to his enemies. While the Duke was engaged in the siege of Nancy, in 1477, on the approach of a superior force under Ferrand, Duke of Lorraine, to relieve the place, Campo Basso deserted to the enemy immediately before battle. The Burgundians were in consequence defeated, and the Duke himself slain. The treacherous Italian was supposed to be the murderer, as the bodies of some of his men were observed near the spot where the unfortunate prince was found killed and stripped the day after the battle.

Campo-Formio, Italy, a town 66 miles northeast of Venice, famous for the treaty of peace between Austria and France which was signed in its neighborhood, 17 Oct. 1797. Its chief provisions were that Austria should cede the Belgian provinces and Lombardy to France, receiving in compensation the Venetian states.

Campo Santo («holy field»), the name given to a burying-ground in Italy, best known as the appellation of the more remarkable, such as are surrounded with arcades and richly adorned. The most famous Campo Santo is that of Pisa, which dates from the 12th century, and has on its walls frescoes of the 14th century of great interest in the history of art. Among more modern Italian cemeteries, that of Genoa is distinguished for its magnificence.

Campo Santo of Dissenters, Bunhill Fields burying-ground, in London; so named by Southey, and with good reason. Among those who lie buried there are John Bunyan; George Fox, the founder of the Quakers; Dr. Thomas Goodwin, who attended Cromwell on his deathbed; Dr. John Owen, who preached the first sermon before Parliament after Charles I. was executed; Susannah Wesley, the mother of John Wesley; Dr. Isaac Watts; William Blake, the painter and poet; Daniel De Foe, and Horne Tooke. On a remnant of land in the neighborhood the Friends have built a coffee tavern and memorial hall.

Campoamor y Campoosorio, Ramon de, rä mōn dä käm-pō-ạ-mōr' ē käm-pō-ō-sō'rē-ō, Spanish poet: b. Navia, 24 Sept. 1817; d. 11 Feb. 1901. He studied medicine at Madrid for a time, but gave it up for literary work. He also entered political life, was governor of Alicante and Valencia and became state counselor under King Alfonso XII. in 1874. In politics he was a Conservative, and his views are expressed in 'Polémicas con la Democracia.' His chief work was in poetry, and he is considered one of the greatest Spanish poets of the 19th century; his attitude of thought is distinctively modern, and the interest of his best writings centres in modern life and problems. His best-known and most characteristic poems are the 'Doloras' (1856), a collection of short pieces which he himself defines as «dramas taken direct from life»; 'Los Pequeños Poemas' (1887), dealing with the «little things» of life; and the 'Humoradas' (1890), a collection of epigrams. He has written also two long narrative poems, 'Colon' (1853) in 16 cantos, and 'El Drama Universal,' and shorter narrative poems which are much more successful, among which are: 'Los Buenos y los Sabios'; 'El Amor y el Rio Piedra'; 'El Trén Express'; 'La Nina y el Nido'; 'Los Grandes Problemas.' His latest poems are 'Licenciado Torralba' (1892); and 'Nuevos Poemas' (1892). He also wrote dramas, which did not prove successful on the stage. These include 'Dies Iræ' (1873); 'El Honor' (1874); and 'Cuerdos y Locos' (1887). Among his prose writings are 'La Filsofia de las Leyes' (1846); 'El Personalisimo' (1850): 'Lo absoluto' (1862), giving most fully his philosophical system; 'El Idealismo' (1883); and 'La Poetica' (1883), summarizing his theory of poetry.

Campobel'lo, New Brunswick, an island, eight miles long, in Passamaquoddy Bay, Char-

lotte County. It is noted as a summer resort. Though copper and lead ores exist, the inhabitants are chiefly engaged in the herring, mackerel, and cod fisheries.

Campodea, a wingless insect of the order *Thysanura*. Owing to its very primitive features it has been regarded by Brauer and by Packard as being the form nearest related to the probable ancestor of all insects. It is a little white insect living under stones. The body is long and narrow, each thoracic segment equal in size, the antennæ long and narrow, while the body ends in two very large, slender, many-jointed appendages. It is very agile in its movements and might be mistaken for a young centipede (*Lithobius*). Though allied to the bristle-tail (*Lepisma*) it is still more primitive. The mouth-parts have undergone some degeneration, being partly withdrawn within the head. It has a pair of short vestigial legs on the first abdominal segment. This and other features suggest its origin from some form with several pairs of abdominal appendages, similar to *Scolopendrella*. It is a cosmopolitan, and this, as well as its structure, suggests that it is an ancient form which has persisted to the present time.

Campos, Arsenio Martinez, är-sā'nĕ-o mär-tē'nĕth käm'pōs, Spanish military officer: b. Segovia, Spain, 14 Dec. 1834; d. 3 Sept. 1900. He was graduated at the Military Staff School in Madrid and appointed a lieutenant in the army in 1858; served on the staff of Gen. O'Donnell and became chief of the battalion in the Morocco campaign of 1859; was on duty in Cuba with the rank of colonel in 1864-70; took part in suppressing the Carlist insurrection and was promoted brigadier-general in 1870; opposed the republic after the abdication of King Amadeus, and was imprisoned as a conspirator. Under a plea for permission to be allowed to serve as a private, he was released and given command of a division in the 3d Army Corps in 1874. In the next two years he was constantly fighting the Carlists, distinguishing himself at Las Munecas and Galdames and causing the noted siege of Bilboa to be raised. With Gen. Jovellar, he called Alphonso XII. to the throne; was made commander-in-chief of the Catalonia district, and crushed Don Carlos at Pena de la Plata in 1876. For these services he was promoted captain-general. In 1877 he was appointed commander-in-chief in Cuba, and brought the revolution to a close chiefly by means of concessions which, as minister of war he endeavored unavailingly to carry out. He was minister of war in 1881 and 1883, commander of the Army of the North of Spain in 1884-5, president of the Spanish senate in 1885: and captain-general of New Castile in 1888. In April 1895 he was appointed governor-general and commander-in-chief in Cuba, and in January 1896 he was recalled to Spain. He found the insurrection more formidable than he had anticipated, and his failure to pursue a vigorous war policy caused much dissatisfaction in Spain. On his arrival in Madrid he repeated his belief that the trouble in Cuba could only be ended by granting reforms.

Cam'pra, An'dra, French composer: b. Aix. Provence. 4 Dec. 1660: d. Versailles, 29 July 1774. He ranks among the most distinguished composers of operas, his themes being classical love stories, notably 'The Triumph of Love'; 'The Amours of Mars and Venus'; 'Hippodamia'; etc.

Cam'pus Mar'tius (known also as *Campus,* merely) was a large place in the suburbs of ancient Rome, consisting of the level ground between the Quirinal, Capitoline, and Pincian hills, and the river Tiber. From the earliest times it seems to have been sacred to the god Mars, from which circumstance it received its name. It was originally set apart for military exercises and contests, as also for the meetings of the comitia by tribes and by centuries. In the later period of the republic, and during the empire, it was a suburban pleasure-ground for the Romans, and was laid out with gardens, shady walks, baths, etc.

Cam'pus Scelera'tus, a name given to a spot within the walls of Rome, and close by the Porta Capeña, where those of the vestal virgins who had transgressed their vows were entombed alive, from which circumstance it took its name.

Camuccini, Vincenzo, vĭn-chĕnt-zo kä-moo-chē'nē, Italian historical painter: b. Rome, about 1775; d. 1844. He followed the pseudo-classical style, and his pictures are of large size. Among his best-known works are 'Death of Cæsar'; 'Death of Virginia'; 'The Incredulity of Thomas'; 'Horatius Cocles'; and 'Death of Mary Magdalene.' He also excelled in portraits.

Camus, Armand Gaston, är-mäṅ gäs-tôṅ, French revolutionist: b. Paris, 2 April 1740; d. 2 Nov. 1804. A zealous and ascetic Jansenist, and a master of ecclesiastical law, he was elected advocate-general of the French clergy, and in 1789 member of the States-General by the people of Paris. He now appeared as the resolute foe of the ancient régime, gained possession of and published the so-called 'Red Book,' with its details of expenditures so disadvantageous to the court and its ministers. He was absent in Belgium during the king's trial, but sent his vote for death. He was made member, and afterward president, of the Council of Five Hundred, but resigned in May 1797, and devoted his time to literature.

Cam'wood, Barwood, or **Ringwood,** a red dye-wood (*Baphia nitida*) obtained in Brazil and also in Africa. It once was common in the neighborhood of Sierra Leone, and was also found in Tonquin and other parts of Asia.

This wood is of a very fine color, and is principally used in turnery for making knife-handles and other similar articles. The dye, mordanted with alum and tartar, obtained from it is brilliant, but not permanent.

Ca'na of Galilee, a town in Palestine, at no great distance from Capernaum, remarkable chiefly as having been the scene of our Lord's first miracle. It was there he turned water into wine (John ii. 1). It was also the city of Nathanael, and the place where Jesus was applied to by the nobleman from Capernaum on behalf of his dying son, and with a word effected the cure. A long-established tradition has identified it with a village bearing the name of Kefr Kenna, which lies about four miles northeast from Nazareth; but this has been disputed.

Canaan, kā'nän, the ancient name of the country west of the Jordan, called also Chanaan, and the Land of Canaan, after one of the sons of Ham. The Greeks applied the term Cana to the entire region between the Jordan and the Mediterranean up to Sidon, afterward termed by them Phœnicia, a name which by degrees came to be confined to the north coast district, or Phœnicia proper. Canaan is generally considered equivalent to the Land of Israel or Palestine. The term is so used in the Pentateuch, and in the early history of the Hebrews it was synonymous with the "Land of Promise." In certain passages in the Prophets the word seems to be restricted in meaning to the maritime plain of Palestine.

Ca'naanites, the general name for the heathen peoples (Jebusites, Hittites, Amorites, etc.) whom the Israelites found dwelling in Canaan (q.v.), west of the Jordan, and whom latterly they utterly subdued, though the subjugation was not quite complete till Solomon's time. They are believed to have been, in part at least, of kindred race with the Israelites; and some authorites find traces of their descendants among the present inhabitants of Palestine. The name Canaanites was also applied in a more restricted sense to one of these peoples.

Canace, kăn'ä-sē (1) In Greek mythology, a daughter of Æolus and Enarete, who was punished by death because of her unlawful passion for her brother; she is mentioned in Gower's 'Confessio Amantis,' and in Chaucer's 'Man of Law's Tale.' (2) In Chaucer's 'Squire's Tale' the daughter of King Cambuscan.

CONTENTS

DEPARTMENT OF

CANADIAN HISTORY AND DEVELOPMENT.

HISTORY

DOMINION OF CANADA;

HISTORY AND MODERN DEVELOPMENT.

1. Canada, Dominion of. Outline History and Political Development (1534 to 1907). When the Dominion of Canada came into existence in 1867 the word "Canada" received a wholly new signification. Its origin is doubtful but it was applied loosely in the early time to the regions occupied by France on the Saint Lawrence, called by the French themselves New France. When in 1763 France surrendered her North American territory to England the term "Canada" was commonly used for the new British dominions. In 1774 these dominions, including part of the Canadian Northwest and what is now the northern tier of western American States, were officially called the "Province of Quebec." Canada does not appear technically until 1791, when the name was used in a constitution given to Upper and Lower Canada, practically the Quebec and Ontario of the present time. Later these Provinces were known as Canada East and Canada West. Not until 1867 did Nova Scotia and New Brunswick become a part of Canada. In considering the history of Canada as we now understand the word, it is important to remember that it includes a separate record of detached provinces, Nova Scotia, New Brunswick, Lower Canada, Upper Canada, etc., until 1867.

In the succeeding articles the epochs in Canadian development are treated in detail. It is sufficient here to outline the chief phases of Canada's history. The first of these, the age of discovery in the 16th and early 17th centuries, has received much attention, but there is still great obscurity as to the range of French effort on the Saint Lawrence. Jacques Cartier (q.v.) and Champlain (q.v.) are the most honored names in this pioneer work. Though few details are known, an extensive fur trade and fishing industry existed in the Saint Lawrence region long before the end of the 16th century. Early in the 17th century French trading companies were fighting for the monopoly of this trade.

The second epoch is that of French colonization and exploration until the final struggle with Britain for the country. When the first pioneer efforts were over France undertook the serious work of colonization, with Quebec as her centre of influence. Her aim was to transplant French social life to North America. Huge grants of land were given to seigniors who were to play the parts of lords in Canada, with vassals looking to them for light and leading and paying rent for the land which they occupied. The system was wholly uncongenial to the new world, but it survived during the whole period of French supremacy and is a picturesque and interesting if not a successful feature of French colonization. See CANADA — SEIGNIORIAL TENURE.

The first permanent settlement apart from trading posts occupied only in the summer was at Port Royal, now Annapolis, in Nova Scotia. Here the French planned really to till the soil and develop the country. From the first the colony had a terrible struggle for life. In 1614 the English from Virginia destroyed it and after it was restored to France in 1632, the adjacent American colonies were always planning to drive out the French. After a chequered history they at last succeeded in 1710, during the reign of Anne, in taking final possession of the Colony, and it became Annapolis. The quiet village of the present day was thus the object of strife between two nations for well nigh one hundred years.

Samuel de Champlain was one of the pioneers at Port Royal, but in 1608 he turned to the Saint Lawrence and made the beginnings of Quebec (q.v.), long the centre of political and commercial life in Canada. By instinct Champlain was an explorer. Like others of that and a later time he hoped that the Saint Lawrence would in some way lead to a water route to China. To Lake Huron and Lake Ontario Champlain penetrated, but the obstacles were enormous. The Iroquois Indians were hostile to the French from the first, and it is hardly strange that with their menace added to the natural difficulties Champlain could do but little to lift the veil from the North American interior.

Nor was he left free from European rivals. The English followed the French to the Saint Lawrence. Quebec they attacked and captured in 1629, and over it the English flag floated for three years. When in 1632 France recovered the place the fortunes of Canada were committed to a great commercial company. This Company of "One Hundred Associates" was to be lord of the land and to have in its hands the work both of trade and of settlement. In France it had the powerful support of Cardinal Richelieu, but when at Quebec in 1635 Champlain died, New France lost its ablest leader, and the Company the most effective exponent of its interests. In the end it failed. Both in India and in America in the 17th century the French commercial companies failed where their English and Dutch rivals succeeded.

After 1635 Canada was the scene of varied activity. It was an age of religious zeal in Europe, and the Jesuit and other missionaries planned to convert and control the savage native tribes of the country. In what is now Northern New York, in Ontario, and in Quebec the missionaries did heroic work. Since the French missionaries were the friends of the Huron tribe, the relentless Iroquois bent on destroying the Hurons, pursued the French too. By 1649 the Huron settlements and the French missions were alike destroyed, and the French were driven back for a time to their base at Quebec. They had founded Montreal in 1640,

1. Sir Wilfrid Laurier. 2. Sir John A. Macdonald. 3. Sir Charles Tupper.
4. Hon. Edward Blake. 5. Hon. Joseph Howe.

but it was long only a fortified outpost to check the Iroquois.

But missions represent only one, if the dominant, phase of French interest. The great interior exercised all the fascination of the unknown upon the chivalrous minds of the French explorers. La Salle, Marquette, Joliet (qq.v.) are only the best known of the leaders who penetrated to the interior before 1700. On Lake Huron, Lake Michigan, Lake Superior, on the Mississippi, even in the Far West of Canada and the United States the survival of French names to this day bears witness to the activity of these explorers. It was a French Canadian, La Vérendrye (q.v.), who first crossed the continent so far as to view the Rocky Mountains, but this was not until 1743.

Between missions and discovery the slow and laborious work of colonization was in danger of being forgotten, but there grew up gradually on both sides of the Saint Lawrence and near the mouths of its tributaries, colonies of French farmers. The river was their highway. For protection from the Indians they lived as close together as possible and so they divided the land into long narrow strips with the houses stretching in a line on the river front. To the present day it is the most conspicuous feature of the French Canadian farms. Colonization was slow work. Adventurous Frenchmen preferred the wild life of the forest, and it was so difficult to attract settlers that in 1700 there were hardly more than 6,000 Europeans in the whole of New France. They enjoyed no semblance of political liberty. Between an aggressive church and a governor with the ideals of Louis XIV., the subjection of the French *habitant* is in striking contrast with the liberty of New England. Towards the end of the 17th century New France was committed to a very able Governor, Frontenac (q.v.). He had a definite programme. He would curb the Church, which aimed to exclude settlement from the interior so that the missionaries might be alone with and continue to control ǂhe Indian tribes; he would hold back the English, build a chain of forts from the Saint Lawrence by the Great Lakes and the Ohio to the mouth of the Mississippi to shut them out from the West, and finally drive them into the sea. It was a great plan, but it required resources beyond anything that France could command. In Europe she was fighting William III. of England and his allies, and needed all the strength she could muster. So Frontenac died in 1698 with his plans unrealized, but he had done a definite work. The mission stage was ended in New France. Entrenched on the Saint Lawrence and soon on the Mississippi France was ready to engage in the supreme struggle to make the interior French and to build up a great transatlantic empire for the glory of the French nation.

The next epoch in Canada's history covers the prolonged struggle resulting in the British Conquest. Probably impossible of realization in any case, the plan of a French empire in America was ended by Louis XIV.'s misfortunes in Europe. With a great alliance against him, he was obliged to make the Peace of Utrecht (q.v.) in 1713. In this he surrendered his claims to Hudson Bay, to Newfoundland and to Nova Scotia. This was the beginning of the end. Though in Cape Breton France built a great fortress, Louis-

bourg, so as to command the Saint Lawrence, and though she still held the country tributary to Quebec, the odds against her were too great. Walpole managed to keep Great Britain at peace until 1744, but when war then broke out France and England engaged in a final struggle for North America. The Treaty of Aix-La-Chapelle (q.v.), in 1748, did not really bring peace. Both sides were preparing steadily for renewed conflict. On the Ohio, on the Atlantic Coast, on the Great Lakes, on the Saint Lawrence, a deadly conflict went on after 1755, and when on a September day in 1759 Wolfe (q.v.) defeated Montcalm (q.v.) before Quebec, the issue was at last decided. By the Treaty of Paris (q.v.) in 1763, France surrendered her dominion of New France to Great Britain.

The fourth epoch in Canadian history covers British rule from 1763 to the Confederation of the Provinces in 1867. After the conquest in 1763, Canada was for a time governed by the British without creating a special constitution for the country, and not until 1774 did the Quebec Act (q.v.) provide for a permanent system. The Quebec Act played a great part in both American and Canadian history. It set up a despotic system of government, and it aimed to bring the whole western country under this despotic régime at Quebec. While introducing British criminal law in the country, it re-established the French civil law. The seigniors retained their feudal rights, the Church was given legal power to collect the tithe.

In the English colonies the Quebec Act caused discontent. They did not desire despotism as a neighbor, they did not wish to be checked in the west, they disliked the legal establishment of Roman Catholicism; and when the colonies revolted the Quebec Act was one of their grievances. They resolved to attempt the overthrow of British rule in Canada and allied, as they hoped, with the conquered French rising against their new masters they planned to make the revolt continental in character. But in 1775 the American army under Benedict Arnold failed to take Quebec; and the French showed fight on behalf of Great Britain. Soon the plan to drive the British from Canada was abandoned and the country remained firm in its British allegiance.

Probably with Arnold's failure the die was cast finally; it is certainly true that the intervening 130 years have never seen any serious prospect of the union of Canada with the United States. When the Loyalists, driven from the United States, found a home in Canada they treasured bitter memories of the revolutionary struggle and rendered the prospect of union even more remote. But once settled in Canada these refugees from the United States demanded the self-government which they had enjoyed at home, and at last in 1791 the British Parliament established Lower Canada and Upper Canada each with a legislature of its own and with some, though not a complete, measure of self-government. In 1812 the United States and Great Britain drifted into war, and the second failure at that time to overthrow British rule in Canada confirmed the results of the defeat of Arnold. Beyond domestic conflicts, more than once resulting in bloodshed, Canada has known no external warfare since 1812–14.

In 1837 there was armed rebellion in the two

Canadas. In Upper Canada the inhabitants claimed the complete control of their own affairs that the Colonial Office in London persistently refused, and to vindicate this demand a few took up arms. In Lower Canada there was a war of races. The French majority demanded that they should dominate in the councils of the country. The English minority, allied usually with the Governor, resisted this claim, and at length some of the French also appealed to arms. Each revolt failed completely, but the risings threw into a clear light the causes of discontent in Canada and in time a remedy was furnished.

Lord Durham, an English radical Whig, sent out to rule Canada with despotic authority and to restore order, in a very able report, published in 1839, urged that the English Province and the French Province should be united under one legislature. This was done. In 1841 Canada received a new constitution, and, joined together for the first time, the people of the two provinces could demand respect and consideration. With more than a million people Canada could no longer be treated as the child of the Colonial Office. After a few doubtful years under the new constitution, the Earl of Elgin, one of the Governor-Generals sent out from England, definitely, amidst some riotous events in 1849, recognized the supreme authority of the Canadian Parliament in regard to Canadian affairs. Since that time political warfare in Canada has been between Canadian parties and not between Canada and the Colonial Office.

But the union of the two provinces contained nothing of finality. Lord Durham had hoped that the English would dominate the French. Instead the French asserted themselves and since each province equaled the other in the number of its representatives, the work of government under the party system proved extremely difficult. A better political temper was growing up throughout British North America. Once free to control their own affairs the provinces saw the advantages of union. Their insight was quickened when in 1866 an advantageous Reciprocity Treaty with the United States came to an end, and in self-preservation it became necessary to increase the commercial and political strength of the provinces. With surprising rapidity negotiations were successfully concluded between 1864 and 1866, and in 1867 the Dominion of Canada came into existence.

The events connected with Confederation furnish a distinct epoch in Canadian history. In the next and concluding epoch the various provinces have been welded together until a real national life has appeared. The development of Federal Government in Canada presents some interesting contrasts with the Federal system in the United States. Sir John Macdonald (q.v.) aimed to make the Federal power strong, the Provincial power relatively weak, and, since his was the master mind that directed Confederation, the Canadian constitution reflected his views. The powers of the provinces are strictly defined, the undefined residue remaining with the Federal Government. Carrying out his views Macdonald frequently tried to curb the provinces, and answering him there was a cry for provincial rights. In spite of Macdonald's desires, development in Canada has been rather in the direction of strengthening the authority of the provinces, but it is still true that a province in Canada falls far short of a State of the Union in political authority. The Federal Government can disallow Provincial legislation; it has done so more than once. But as a result of nearly forty years' experience a fairly stable balance between the two jurisdictions has now been reached. During this time a real unity has grown up in Canada, and it makes Canadians, as it long since made Americans, one in sentiment from ocean to ocean.

Bibliography.— A good, though in some respects defective, bibliography of Canadian history will be found in 'Literature of American History, American Library Association Annotated Guide,' edited by J. N. Larned (1902). Only a short list of the best general histories and of those dealing with special periods need be noted here. Francis Parkman devoted his life to the history of New France and his collected works (12 vols., numerous editions) form the standard history of French rule in Canada. Kingsford's 'History of Canada' (10 vols., 1888–98) covers the whole subject down to 1841. J. C. Dent's 'Story of the Upper Canadian Rebellion' (2 vols., 1885), and his 'Last Forty Years; Canada Since the Union of 1841' (2 vols., 1881), may be used to supplement Kingsford's work to bring the history down to the present time. Roberts' 'History of Canada' (1904) is the best short history. McMullen's (2 vols., 1896) is fuller.

Turning to special periods Biggar's 'Early Trading Companies of New France' (1891), with extensive bibliographies, is the best account of early discovery. Read in connection with Parkman's 'Pioneers of France in the New World,' it gives an adequate account of the early period. For the later period of French supremacy by far the most interesting mass of material is contained in 'The Jesuit Relations and Allied Documents' (73 vols., 1896–1901). Parkman's work is the best connected narrative account of the period. The story of the British conquest of Canada is well told in Bradley's 'Fight with France for North America' (1901), while Doughty and Parmelee's 'Siege of Quebec' (6 vols., 1901), is a unique and exhaustive account of that aspect of the struggle. For a brilliant narrative of the Conquest and its preceding struggles Parkman's account in his 'Half Century of Conflict' (2 vols.), and his 'Montcalm and Wolfe' remains unequaled.

The works of Kingsford and Dent above cited are not rivalled by any special monographs on Canadian history for the period between 1763 and 1840. For recent times Pope's 'Memoirs of Sir John A. Macdonald' (2 vols., 1894), and Willison's 'Sir Wilfrid Laurier and the Liberal Party' (2 vols., 1903), cover the ground adequately. Sir John Bourinot's 'Canada Under British Rule' (1900), is an admirable short sketch, while his 'Constitutional History of Canada' (1901), is the best manual dealing with the subject. 'The Review of Historical Publications Relating to Canada,' edited by the present writer and Mr. H. H. Langton, is an annual bibliography, with extensive critical reviews of the literature of each year relating to Canada (Toronto, The University Library).

GEORGE M. WRONG,
Professor of History, University of Toronto.

2. Canada—The Era of Early Discovery.—
The early history of Canada from 1497 to 1632
may for the sake of convenience be divided into
four periods: (1) The period of the early explorations along the Atlantic seaboard, 1497-
1533; (2) the discovery and occupation by the
French of the gulf and river St. Lawrence,
1534-43; (3) the rise of the fur-trade, 1544-
1612; and (4) the first permanent colonization,
1613-32.

*The Explorations along the Atlantic Sea-
board, 1497-1533.*— The first European to set
foot on British North America after the departure of the Northmen in the 11th century
was John Cabot (q.v.) of Bristol. Though
born in Genoa, Cabot had removed in 1461 to
Venice and by his naturalization in 1476 as a
citizen of that republic had been able to trade
to the Venetian factories throughout the Levant. When on a voyage to Alexandria for
spices he made up his mind to push on to
Mecca, then the great mart for the transfer
of eastern and western goods. He wished to
learn the situation of the region where the
spices grew. On questioning on this subject
those in charge of the spice-caravans at Mecca,
they told him that they received them from
other caravans coming from further eastward
to whom they had in turn been handed over by
others coming from still more remote regions.
It seemed clear to Cabot that the spices must
grow on the very eastern confines of Asia.
In that case would it not be more practical
to bring them direct to Europe by sea across
the western ocean? With this idea in mind
Cabot removed with his family from Venice
to London. In England he learned that in the
summer of 1480 an attempt had been made by
two ships from Bristol to find the island of
Brazil to the west of Ireland. Under Cabot's
direction fresh efforts were made to find both
this island and that of the Seven Cities which
should but form stepping-stones on the new
route to Asia by the west. All was to no purpose. No islands or land of any sort could be
discovered. Suddenly, however, in the summer of 1493 news reached England that another Genoese, Christopher Columbus, had
sailed out into the western ocean with three
Spanish ships and had succeeded in reaching
the Indies. Cabot and his friends were roused
to fresh efforts. During Henry VII.'s visit to
Bristol in the winter of 1495-6 Cabot proceeded to set before him the advantages to
accrue to England could intercourse be opened
between that country and Asia. London
would become in a short time a greater emporium for spices than was then Alexandria
itself. As a result of this interview letters
patent were issued on 5 March 1496, giving
Cabot and his sons permission to sail to Asia
under the English flag. Armed with these
powers Cabot fitted out at Bristol a small vessel
called the Mathew. Her crew consisted of but
18 men. Owing to various delays they were
not able to set sail until Tuesday, 2 May 1497.
Rounding Ireland, they first of all headed north
and then west. After many weeks of varied
winds, land was at length sighted at 5 o'clock
on Saturday morning, 24 June. On the 53d day
after leaving Bristol they had reached the most
easterly point of Cape Breton Island. The
royal banner was unfurled and as the ship's
boat rounded her keel on the beach, perhaps
of Mira Bay, John Cabot stepped ashore and in
solemn form took possession of the land in
the name of King Henry VII. No inhabitants
were seen, but the sailors found snares set
for game and a needle for making nets. It
was, therefore, judged that the country was
inhabited. As the climate was agreeable and
the soil fertile, they were of opinion that they
had reached that portion of the coast of Asia
where grew the spices Cabot had seen at
Mecca. The modern Cape Breton was named
"Cape Discovery" and Scatari Island which lies
opposite, "Saint John's Island," as the day was
the feast of Saint John the Baptist. Sailing
north along Cape Breton Island they gave to
Cape Ray the name of "Cape Saint George,"
and called Saint Pierre, Miquelon and Langley
islands the "Trinity group." Since their provisions were none too plentiful should the return voyage prove a long one, they spent no
time in further exploration and early in July
set sail for home from Cape Race which they
named "England's Cape." Favored by the
westerly winds of the North Atlantic, they
made good progress and on Sunday, 6 August,
the Mathew dropped anchor once more in
Bristol harbor. Cabot hurried to Court and
on the following Thursday, 10 August, was
given a reward of £10 for his successful discovery. According to Cabot's report he had found
some 700 leagues to the west of Ireland the
country of the Great Khan. Although silk and
brazil-wood grew at the spot where he landed,
it was his intention on the next voyage to
proceed on down that coast till he reached
Cipango, for in his opinion this was the region
whence came the spices and precious stones
he had seen at Mecca. Henry VII. was delighted and granted Cabot a yearly pension of
£20. On 3 Feb. 1498 new letters patent were
issued authorizing Cabot to prepare a fresh fleet
of six vessels. In order to secure skilled seamen and probably also to hear news of what
Columbus had done, Cabot about this time
made a trip to Lisbon and Seville. In Lisbon
he came across a certain João Fernandes, called
"Labrador" because he owned land on the island of Terceira. When Cabot informed this
man of his discovery, Fernandes in turn told
him how he himself had also visited a region
to the west of Iceland and north of the point
in Asia reached by Cabot. The latter's curiosity was roused. Here was perhaps a shorter
way of returning to Asia than by crossing
again the dreaded western ocean. On Cabot's
return to Bristol with Fernandes, a brief consultation with the merchants of that town who
had long traded to Iceland convinced everyone
that this was the best route to take. By the
beginning of May the two vessels manned by
300 men were in readiness. Since it was known
that Cabot was taking the route via Iceland,
"in his company sayled also out of Bristowe
three or foure small ships fraught with sleight
and grosse merchandizes, as course cloth, caps,
laces, points, and other trifles." Early in June
they reached the east coast of Greenland a little north of Cape Farewell. As Fernandes had
already told them of this region they named
it the "Labrador's Land." On coasting north
along this desolate shore, they found the ice
to grow steadily thicker and heavier and the

cold to become more and more intense. It was also noticed that the coast trended continually eastward. Finally on 11 June in lat. 67° 30', the crews mutinied and refused to proceed further in that direction. Cabot was thereupon obliged to turn his ships about and to head back to the south. On reaching Cape Farewell, they sailed west and explored the southern and also the western coast of Greenland. On meeting with ice again on the west coast they once more headed west until they arrived off the coast of the present Labrador, near the modern Table Hill in 57° 40'. Since they had not penetrated to the bottom of Davis Strait they naturally supposed it was merely a gulf and that this coast was one with the Labrador's Land in the north. Following on down this coast, which in their opinion was that of Asia, they at length reached Cape Race and the region explored in the previous summer. Proceeding on toward the south they coasted the shores of Nova Scotia and New England until they reached the bay of New York. They were now much struck by the distance westward they had come. The east coast of Greenland lies in 43° while the longitude of Sandy Hook is 74°, which is only three quarters of a degree less than that of Cuba. Cabot could well say, therefore, that he had now "sayled in this tracte so farre towarde the weste, that he had the Ilande of Cuba on his left hande in maner in the same degree of longitude." They continued to coast the shores of New Jersey, Delaware, and Maryland as far as the 38° parallel of latitude, at which point the low state of their provisions and the absence of any traces of eastern civilization induced them to come about and head back to Bristol, where they arrived late in the autumn of 1498. The results of this voyage proved such a disappointment that no fresh expedition was despatched until 1501. Meanwhile João Fernandes returned to Portugal. On the island of Terceira, where he had his home, a Portuguese nobleman named Gaspar Corte-Real (q.v.) possessed considerable estates. This nobleman, who was much interested in the discoveries that were then taking place, seems to have put himself in communication with Fernandes. The result was that early in the spring of 1500 Corte-Real applied for and received letters patent empowering him to undertake an expedition to the northwest. Setting sail from Lisbon early in that summer he reached the east coast of Greenland on 8 June. They proceeded to follow it northward until 29 June, when the ice-floes and icebergs in Denmark strait forced them to head back toward the south. Rounding Cape Farewell they explored the southern and western coasts of Greenland, whence as the season was well advanced they once more returned to Lisbon. In the hope of discovering a region of a less wild and desolate nature, Gaspar Corte-Real fitted out a fresh expedition in the spring of 1501. They left Lisbon on 15 May and were nearing Cape Farewell when they came upon a large pack of field-ice, which forced them to alter their course to the northwest. At the end of several weeks they came in sight of the coast of our present Labrador in 58°. Following this mainland toward the south they came upon a band of Nasquapee Indians, who still inhabit

Labrador. Thinking they would make good slaves they seized 50 of these natives and stowed them under the hatches. Continuing on down that coast they reached Conception bay in Newfoundland early in September. It was then decided that the two vessels with the Indians on board should sail direct from here to Portugal while Gaspar Corte-Real himself should proceed on down that coast in order to discover its connection with the islands discovered near the equator by Columbus. The two caravels reached Lisbon in safety in the second week in October. Though the account of the discovery of this mainland and the appearance of its inhabitants excited considerable interest, more importance was attached to Gaspar Corte-Real's exploration of the region to the south. The autumn passed, however, without anything being seen of him or his vessel. In that summer an English expedition had been dispatched to the same coast by João Fernandes, now a naturalized Englishman, and several other English merchants, but on their return in the autumn with three Indians they reported that they had seen nothing of Gaspar Corte-Real. In January 1502 his rights were transferred to his brother Miguel, who left Lisbon on 10 May with three vessels to search for his lost brother. They reached Newfoundland toward the end of June and on the 24th of that month named the modern Saint John's, "the river Saint John," in commemoration of the feast of Saint John the Baptist. To facilitate the search each ship was ordered to visit a certain portion of the coast and to return to Saint John's by 20 August. Two of the vessels returned at the date fixed but the vessel of Miguel himself was never heard of more. An English expedition also visited the same coast in that year and on 20 September King Henry VII. granted a pension of £10 each to two naturalized Portuguese "in consideracion of the true service which they have doon unto us to our singler pleasure as Capitaignes into the newe founde lande." No trace had been seen by them, however, of either of the missing Corte-Reals. In the hope of finding some trace of them, King Manoel dispatched two vessels to that coast in the summer of 1503, but neither these vessels nor those which were sent out in that year by the merchants of Bristol saw any trace of them. They were thereupon given up for lost. The rich cod-fishing on this coast had now become so well known that in 1504 the French and Bretons began to resort thither. Two years later a tax was laid on the cod from these parts taken to Portugal. The French rapidly increased in numbers and in 1512 when the first Spanish expedition to this coast was fitted out the latter got their pilots in Brittany. By 1519 the French fleet numbered 100 sail and included vessels from Dieppe all the way down to Bayonne. In 1520 Alvares Fagundes of Vianna in Portugal explored the region between Saint Pierre and Miquelon and the coast of Nova Scotia. On his return he received a grant of these regions from the king of Portugal. It is possible that a colony was sent thither in 1525. In this same year the Emperor Charles V. dispatched Estevan Gomez (q.v.), who had sailed with Magellan, to discover in the north a strait similar to the strait of Magellan in the south. Gomez explored the Bay of Fundy and then followed the coast southwards as far as the West Indies. On his return to La Corunna with a ship-load of Indians he was understood to say he had spices. The excitement was great for it was believed he had reached the Moluccas. Ultimately the mistake, which was due to the similarity of the words for slaves and spices in Spanish, was explained and afforded the emperor and his court much amusement. In 1527 two English vessels, the Samson and the Mary-of-Gilford, the latter being a three-masted barque of 250 tons' burden, were sent out to find a northwest passage. On meeting with icebergs at the mouth of Davis Strait they headed south. On 1 July in 52° a storm separated them and the Samson was never heard of more. The Mary-of-Gilford on reaching Saint John's on 3 August found "eleven saile of Normans and one Brittaine and two Portugall Barkes and all a fishing." Finding no news here of the Samson, she continued her course to the south "oftentimes putting her men on land to search the state of those unknowen regions." On one of these occasions the Italian pilot, who may possibly have been Giovanni Verrazano, who had explored this coast for Francis I. in 1524, was killed by the Indians. In the middle of November the Mary-of-Gilford reached the West Indies. Being refused permission to enter San Domingo, she set sail again for England. In the course of her voyage she had met more than 50 French, Portuguese, and Spanish fishing-vessels, which shows the proportions to which the cod-fishing on the Banks had then attained. Each year in fact the numbers increased.

The Discovery and Occupation by the French of the Gulf and River of Saint Lawrence, 1534–43.— Though during the course of the first three decades of the 16th century various English, Portuguese, French, and Spanish expeditions had explored the seaboard of eastern North America none of them had penetrated into the interior. The first to do this were the French in 1534. The French fishermen who resorted every summer to that portion of this main coast which was rich in cod had noticed that a bay, called by them the "Bay of Castles" from the formation of the land thereabout, extended so far inland that not one had ever been able to reach the head of it. It was just possible, therefore, that this might be the entrance to a strait similar to that found by Magellan in the south. On this being reported to the authorities at home an expedition was dispatched from Saint Malo in the spring of 1534 under the pilot Jacques Cartier with orders to explore this opening. Cartier reached Bonne Espérance harbor inside the Strait of Belle Isle (then called the "Bay of Castles") on Wednesday, 10 June. Having discovered on examining the coast beyond this point with the long-boats, that it was completely barren and rocky, sail was made on Monday, 15 June, from Bonne Espérance harbor in order to explore the land seen to the south. Following this south shore of the Strait of Belle Isle they were led steadily down the west coast of what we now call the island of Newfoundland. Off St. George's Bay to the north of Cape Ray they had stormy weather for a week, which forced them to beat up and down. On resuming their course southward they fell in with the Bird Rocks which lie 55 miles north-northwest of Cape Breton Island. The island to the south of these they named "Brion Island" after the Admiral of France. From the currents observed here Cartier surmised that the opening beside Cape Breton Island was a strait and that one could sail from Brion Island directly into the Atlantic. "Should this prove to be the case," added Cartier, "it would mean a great saving both in time and distance should anything of importance be discovered on this voyage." As is well known, this opening, Cabot Strait, is now used quite as much as the Strait of Belle Isle. Leaving Brion Island on Saturday, 27 June, they crossed over to the Magdalen Islands, of which they coasted the northwestern corner until the following Monday, 29 June, when on the wind veering to the south they had to set sail toward the west. They were under the impression that these islands formed the main shore on the south side of the gulf, and when on Tuesday morning, 30 June, they reached Cascumpeque Bay in Prince Edward Island, they believed that this latter formed part of the same main shore with the Magdalens. The western end of Northumberland Strait, which separates Prince Edward Island from the mainland, was mistaken for a bay and called "Saint Leonore's Bay" in memory of a Breton bishop whose festival is celebrated on 1 July. Coasting northward along the New Brunswick shore they believed on reaching Chaleur Bay that they had at last found a passage into the South Sea. On Thursday, 9 July, they discovered that it was merely a deep bay; "whereat," says Cartier, "we were much put out." On account of the heat experienced there they christened it "the Bay of Heat." Pursuing their course northward they entered Gaspé Bay, where they were detained for ten days by bad weather. On Friday, 24 July, the day before they set sail, they set up a cross 30 feet high as a landmark and also seized the two sons of an Indian chief who had come down to the sea with his tribe to fish. Rounding the peninsula of Gaspé, they were heading straight for the mouth of the Saint Lawrence, when one of the mirages so common in those parts led them to believe that this passage between Gaspé and Anticosti was merely a land-locked bay. They consequently crossed over and followed the south shore of Anticosti as far as the eastern extremity of that island. Continuing on along the north shore of Anticosti they at length caught sight of the Quebec coast opposite and saw that they were entering a passage which they called "Saint Peter's Strait." At this point a consultation was held at which it was decided that since there was a great probability of this passage being the one they were in search of, it would be advisable as the season was late to postpone their exploration of it until the following year. They consequently headed east along the north shore of the gulf and were finally brought back to the Strait of Belle Isle or the "Bay of Castles," whence they had set out. The fishermen's statement had been fully confirmed. This narrow opening had turned out to be a great gulf with probably a second entrance into the Atlantic near Brion Island. There was also a prospect that the opening they had just discovered in the north-west corner of this gulf would yet lead them into the South Sea. Setting sail from Belle Isle on Saturday, 15 August, they reached Saint Malo in safety on Saturday, 5 September. As they were in great hopes that the opening in the northwest corner of this large inland gulf would eventually lead them to the South Sea, a fresh expedition consisting of three vessels was sent out under Cartier in the spring of 1535 in order to explore it. Passing through the Strait of Belle Isle and along the north shore of the gulf they anchored on Monday, 9 August, in a small bay on the Quebec shore, opposite Anticosti. As the following day was the feast of Saint Lawrence, this bay was christened "Saint Lawrence's Bay." The name afterward spread by mistake to the whole gulf and was finally extended to the river. The two savages who had passed the winter with Cartier in France, now informed him that the land on the south side of this Saint Peter's Strait was an island and that further west he would come to the mouth of a very large river. Where that river rose they did not know. With this information to help him Cartier proceeded through the passage north of Anticosti and passing on up the gulf entered the river Saint Lawrence or as the savages called it the "River of Hochelaga." On arriving at the mouth of the Saguenay his Indian guides informed him that this river took its name from a kingdom lying toward the northwest which was "rich and wealthy in precious stones." Pleased with this information Cartier pushed on up the "River of Hochelaga" until he reached a large island which he named the "Island of Orleans" after Francis I.'s third son, Charles, Duke of Orleans. On the banks of a small stream which here enters the Saint Lawrence stood the home of the two Indians who had passed the winter in France. For this and other reasons Cartier laid up his two largest vessels in this stream and with his third vessel and two long-boats pushed on westward to visit another Indian village called Hochelaga. The shallow water at the head of Lake Saint Peter, which he named the "Lake of Angoulême" after Charles, Duke of Orleans, checked the further progress of the sailing vessel which had to be left behind here. Pushing on in their long-boats they reached the Huron-Iroquois village of Hochelaga on the island of Montreal at the foot of the Lachine rapids on Saturday, 2 October. On the following morning a visit was paid to this village and an ascent was also made of a mountain near at hand which Cartier named "Mount Royal." From this point they had a magnificent view of the surrounding country. They special-ly noticed the rapids, which checked further progress westward and heard from the savages that there were more such "falls of water" be-yond. Just above the rapids another river en-tered the main stream. According to the sav-ages this was the best route to the kingdom of Saguenay, whose inhabitants were clothed like the French and had great stores of gold and other precious metals.

Cartier made his way back to his vessels on the Saint Charles and in the course of the winter, during which part of his crew was carried off by scurvy, sought to obtain as much information as possible about this northern Mex-ico called by the savages the "kingdom of Sa-guenay." That King Francis might have as much information as possible on this subject Cartier, on the day he had a large cross erected to mark the French possession of this region, ordered his men to seize the chief of this vil-lage and eleven others whom he placed on board his vessels as prisoners. Leaving the Saint Charles with only two of his vessels on Satur-day, 6 May, he passed down the south shore of the Saint Lawrence and through the passage to the south of Anticosti Island, which on his first voyage he had mistaken for a bay. From Chaleur Bay he steered for Brion Island and discovered after leaving it that the coast to the south was not the main shore but a group of islands. Heading still to the east he reached Cape Breton Island and found his conjecture as to the existence of a strait here to be correct. After touching at the islands of Saint Pierre and Miquelon he left one of his long-boats in a small harbor 10 miles north of Cape Race and then on Monday, 9 June, set sail for home. They reached St. Malo in safety on Sunday, 16 July.

Owing to the wars in which France was then engaged, nothing further was done until the winter of 1540-41, when an expedition was organized to proceed to the conquest of this rich kingdom of Saguenay. While Cartier was to act as pilot, the command of the land forces was given to a Picard nobleman named Rober-val, who had distinguished himself in the recent wars. Through a delay about the artillery, the latter was not able to be ready in time, so Car-tier set sail from Saint Malo alone with five vessels on Monday, 23 May. They had a bad passage out and having waited some time in Newfoundland for Roberval did not reach the island of Orleans until the end of August. Car-tier took up his quarters this time at the river of Cap-Rouge, nine miles above Quebec. A week later he sent back two of his vessels to France "with letters unto the king, and to ad-vertise him what had been done and found: and how Monsieur de Roberval was not yet come, and that hee feared that by occasion of contrary winds and tempest he was driven, backe againe into France." Five days later Car-tier set off in two long-boats to re-examine the rapids of Hochelaga and find out what arrange-ments should be made for passing them in the spring with the troops. He was informed by the Indians living alongside the rapids that after passing this one there were several others of the same sort before the Saguenay could be reached. With this information to help him Cartier re-turned to Cap-Rouge, where he spent the winter. Neither in that autumn nor in the spring of 1542 was anything heard of Roberval. The lat-ter did not set sail from France until the middle of April 1542 and was unable to reach New-foundland until the first week in June. When at anchor there in the harbor of Saint John's he was much surprised one morning to see Car-tier arrive. According to Cartier's account "hee could not with his small company withstand the Savages, which went about dayly to annoy him." On being commanded, however, by Roberval to return "he and his company, mooved as it seem-eth with ambition, because they would have all the glory of the discoverie of those partes them-selves, stole privily away the next night and departed home for Brittany." Roberval was thus obliged toward the end of June to make his way up the Saint Lawrence alone. He took up his quarters in the buildings at Cap-Rouge which Cartier had vacated. On 14 September he sent back to France two ships "to carie newes unto the king and to come backe againe the yeere next ensuing furnished with victuals and other things." During the course of the winter 50 of his people were carried off by scurvy, so that when he set off early in June 1543 to conquer the kingdom of Saguenay he had only 8 boats and 40 men. The remainder who only numbered 30 were left in charge of the fort. How far up the Saint Lawrence Roberval penetrated we do not know; for no further account of his movements has come down to us. It seems probable, however, that after penetrating a short distance up the Ottawa and finding no trace of gold he returned to Cap-Rouge where he found Cartier, who had been sent out to bring him home. In the course of the autumn the rest of the men returned. On the failure of this expedition becoming generally known a new proverb was coined. When any object in appearance of value was found to be worthless, it was called a "Canadian diamond."

The Rise of the Fur Trade, 1544-1612.—During the 10 years in which the French had been busy exploring the gulf and river Saint Lawrence and seeking to reach the mysterious kingdom of Saguenay, the number of vessels of various nationalities engaged in the fishing trade along the Atlantic seaboard had been steadily increasing. On his arrival at Saint John's, Newfoundland, on 8 June 1542, Roberval had found "seventeene shippes of fishers," which were six more than Rut had met there in August 1527. Out of this annual fishing trade, which was carried on along the coast from Belle Isle as far south as Cape Cod, gradually grew the fur trade. The fishermen, when riding at anchor in a bay or inlet, found that the savages of the neighborhood were always ready to part with their furs for a mere trifle. Since these furs sold in Europe for a high price, the practice grew up among the fishermen of bringing out each year a supply of trinkets on purpose to barter for furs. The returns were so good that in process of time some vessels made a specialty of the fur trade. Thus in 1569 we hear of a French vessel from Havre that "had a trade with the people of divers sortes of fine furres." In 1581 some Saint Malo merchants sent a small barque of 30 tons into the upper Saint Lawrence, and so successful did the voyage prove that in the following year they despatched a ship of 80 tons. In 1583, in which year the merchants of Saint Malo sent three vessels to the Saint Lawrence, Stephen Bellinger of Rouen "brought home a kynde of muske called castor; divers beastes skynnes, as bevers, otters, martenes, lucernes, seales, buffs, dere skynnes, all dressed and painted on the innerside with divers excellent colours." In the following year the merchants of Saint Malo brought back with them two savages in order that they should learn French and afterward facilitate more extended trading relations. The result was that in 1585 they sent 10 ships into the Saint Lawrence. In January 1588 two of Cartier's descendants obtained a monopoly of this fur trade, but so great was the outcry raised by the other excluded merchants that in May the monopoly was revoked. The trade continued to remain open like the fishing trade until 1599. In addition to cod, some of the vessels fished for furs, and toward the close of the century there was a great development of the walrus-fishing. In the spring of 1591 the Bonaventure of Saint Malo made her way to the Magdalen Islands in the Gulf of Saint Lawrence, where she "slewe and killed to the number of fifteene hundred morses or Sea-oxen," as the walruses were then called. With the 40 tons of train-oil into which these were boiled down she reached the mouth of the English Channel in safety, but was there captured by an English vessel from Bristol. Relying on the information thus obtained, a vessel was sent thither from Falmouth in 1593, and though she "tooke certaine Sea-oxen," it was "nothing such numbers as they might have had, if they had come in due season," for they arrived late in the summer. In the spring of 1594 the Grace of Bristol set sail to Anticosti, "being informed that the Whales which are deadly wounded in the grand Bay (the Gulf of Saint Lawrence), and yet escape the fisher for a time, are wont usually to shoot themselves on shore there." Finding no whales she made her way back to the bay of Placentia in Newfoundland, where she met "fishermen of Saint John de Luz and of Sibiburo [Ciboure] and of Biskay to the number of threescore and odde sayles." After fishing there for some time she made her way to Ferryland on the east coast, where lay "two and twentie sayles of Englishmen." In that port she "made up her fishing voyage" and set sail for home. In the summer of 1597 the Hopewell of London, of 120 tons, was driven away from the Magdalens by two ships of Saint Malo and two others of Ciboure, which united their forces against her. Meeting with a similar hostile welcome from five French ships in a harbor of Cape Breton Island, she repaired to the port of Sainte Marie in Newfoundland, where she found a vessel from La Rochelle and another from Belle-Isle-en-Terre at the mouth of the Loire. Since this latter hailed from a Catholic part of France it was decided to capture her. "We first," says the account, "sent our boat aboord the Rocheller to certifie him that we were his friends and to request him not to hinder our fight with the enemy. This message being sent, we made all the haste we could unto the ship of Belle Isle, which first began with us with three great shot, one whereof hit our maintopsaile, but both the other missed us. And we also sent one unto them; then being approached nere unto them ten or twelve of us went in a shallop to enter them. And when we boorded them in our boat, they betooke themselves to their close fights, playing chiefly upon us with shot and pikes out at two ports, between which we entred very dangerously, escaping meere dangers both by shot and pike. Some of our men were wounded, but no great harme was done." With this prize the Hopewell returned to England. In the following year an unsuccessful attempt was made to establish a colony on Sable Island. The Marquis de la Roche (q.v.) had obtained his first letters patent authorizing him to occupy land in the region of Newfoundland in 1577, and in 1578 he had set sail thither with two vessels. The "pinnace," however, had been obliged to return through "fowell weather," and, though the larger vessel, after being "well beaten by four English ships which this French ship had thought to have robbed," had "taken her course for Newfoundland," we do not know what was done there. It is probable, however, that La Roche merely selected a spot for settlement, since it was not until 1584 that the colonists were embarked. Unfortunately "his greatest ship of 300 tons was caste awaye over against Brouage" on the west coast of France, and so the expedition came to naught. From 1589 to 1596 La Roche was kept a prisoner by the Duc de Mercœur, but on his release he made a fresh attempt to establish a colony. In the summer of 1598 he landed on Sable Island 60 "sturdy male and female beggars," taken from the prisons of Normandy. On returning thither from the mainland he was blown all the way back to France. No fresh attempt was made to continue his colony, and when the remnant was succored by a fishing vessel in 1603, only 11 persons were still alive. On this failure of La Roche's colony, no sign was left that France claimed the region of the Saint Lawrence as her own. To remedy this state of affairs a monopoly of the fur trade for 10 years was granted in the spring of 1599 to a fur trader of Honfleur, who yearly sent out four vessels to the Saint Lawrence. The condition was that he should people the country each year with 50 colonists. In fulfilment of this agreement, on the conclusion of his annual barter with the Montagnais at Tadoussac in the summer of 1599, he left behind 16 men huddled together for warmth in a small log hut at the mouth of the Saguenay. On the return of the vessels in the following summer, no fresh colonists were landed and only five of the former batch were found alive. These had only saved themselves from perishing by taking refuge among the neighboring Indians. In the meantime the remaining traders, who were well aware that the few colonists taken out were only to throw dust in the eyes of the government, loudly complained against their exclusion from the fur trade. To quiet matters, a commission was appointed in the winter of 1602-3, which recommended the admission of certain Rouen and Saint Malo traders on condition they should bear their share of the cost of colonization. Before, however, more colonists were sent out it was deemed advisable to explore the country in detail in order that the best site available might be chosen for the settlement. This survey was carried out in the summer of 1603 by Samuel de Champlain, an officer of the navy, and Dupont-Gravé, one of the fur traders. The result was that in the spring of 1604 a fresh monopoly for 10 years was given to a company formed by the Sieur de Monts (q.v.) on condition that 60 colonists a year should be taken out. The first settlement was formed in the summer of 1604 on the island of Sainte Croix, in the Bay of Fundy. "The Fort hee [De Monts] seated at the end of the Iland, opposite to the place where he had lodged his Canon, which was wisely considered to the end to command the river up and down. And out of the same Fort was the Switzers lodging, great and large, and other small lodgings, representing as it were a suburb. Some had housed themselves on the firme lande neere the brook. But within the Fort was Monsieur de Monts his lodging made with very faire and artificiall Carpentrie worke, with the Banner of France upon the same. At another part was the store-house wherein consisted the safety and life of everie one, likewise made with faire Carpentry worke and covered with reedes

Right over against the said store-house were the lodgings and houses of these Gentlemen, Monsieur D'Orville, Monsieur Champlain, Monsieur Champdoré and other men of reckoning. Opposite to Monsieur de Monts, his said lodging, there was a galerie covered for to exercise themselves either in play or for the workmen in time of raine. And betweene the said Fort and the Platforme, where lay the Canon, all was full of gardens whereunto everie one exercised himselfe willingly." The winter of 1604-5 proved so severe on the exposed island of Sainte Croix, the soil of which turned out to be extremely sandy, that in the following summer the settlement was transported across the Bay of Fundy to the harbor of Port Royal (now Annapolis Basin), where the buildings were put together in the form of a large square. The winter of 1605-6 again proved a hard one, however, and, owing to the late arrival of the company's vessel, not only were all the furs taken by interlopers, but the colonists themselves finally embarked in two small boats in order to find a fishing vessel willing to take them back to France. They fortunately met their own vessel, in which they returned to Port Royal. In the spring of 1607, however, the company's monopoly, which had legally seven years more to run, was suddenly repealed through the intrigues of the Hatters' Corporation of Paris. Nothing remained but to send out a vessel to bring home the colonists at Port Royal, which was done.

On Champlain's recommendation De Monts now turned his attention to the Saint Lawrence. In order that he might retrieve a part, at least, of his losses King Henry IV. allowed him a monopoly of the fur trade there for one year. In the summer of 1608, accordingly, Champlain repaired to that part of the river called Quebec, or "the Narrows," where he constructed a trading-post. It was hoped that this would not only give them an advantage over the other competitors in the years of open trade, but would also hold the warlike nation of the Iroquois in check and allow the Algonquins, who came down every summer with furs from the upper Ottawa, to go backward and forward on the Saint Lawrence in all security. When Henry IV. heard of the construction of De Mont's post at Quebec he renewed his monopoly for another year. Taking advantage of this, Champlain, in the summer of 1609, accompanied the Montagnais and the Algonquins on the warpath against the Iroquois. In order to see the palefaces of which they had heard so much, and also to have their share of the victory over the Iroquois, the Hurons, who dwelt beyond the Algonquins on the shores of Georgian Bay, came down to Quebec, for the first time, in the summer of 1609. This combined expedition surprised a combined force of 200 Iroquois on Lake Champlain. At the sight of the French and the report of their fire-arms the enemy broke and fled. The Hurons were delighted, and promised to come down henceforward every summer to the annual barter. In this same year (1609) the Sieur de Poutrincourt (see POUTRINCOURT, JEAN DE BIENCOURT) established himself with his family in the buildings formerly occupied by De Monts' colony at Port Royal. He continued to reside here until his home was burned by the English in 1613. Although during the winter of 1609-10 De Monts sought to have his monopoly renewed, or at any rate the trade reserved to him, in the region explored by Champlain in his expedition against the Iroquois, all was to no purpose. In the summer of 1610 the fur trade was thrown open to the merchant marine of France to the same extent as the cod, whale, and walrus fishing. The result was that so many traders resorted to the Saint Lawrence in that summer that there was a plethora of goods and many ships found it impossible to get rid of even a portion of their cargoes. There was a similar inroad in the summer of 1611. The results of this competition were soon apparent among the savages. Not only did they ask more for their furs, but they also began to have a poor opinion of the palefaces, whom they saw even strip blood-stained furs off the corpses of dead Indians. De Monts also felt it to be unjust that he should be put to the expense of keeping up the post at Quebec when no advantages were accorded him in return. During the summer of 1612 Champlain was kept in France by a fall from a horse, and he improved the opportunity by seeking to bring about a better order of things in the Saint Lawrence. Through his efforts the system of open trade was brought to an end in the autumn of 1612.

The First Permanent Colonization, 1613-32. — In order that the licentiousness of a few merchants should not spoil the trade in the upper Saint Lawrence and ruin the prospects of exploring, with the help of these Indians, the regions farther to the west, Champlain induced the king's uncle, the Comte de Soissons, to apply in the autumn of 1612 for a monopoly of the fur trade above Quebec. This was granted on condition that, during the 12 years it lasted, six families a year should be taken out by the company. Although Soissons died a few weeks later, the monopoly was transferred, at Champlain's request, to Soisson's nephew, the young Prince de Condé. As no time was left to form the company before the trading season opened, Condé merely issued licenses to seven merchants to barter above Quebec. They were each to place four men at Champlain's disposal in case he had need of them. On account, however, of the licentiousness of some of the traders in the previous summer when Champlain was absent, neither the Algonquins nor the Hurons put in an appearance in 1613 at the rapids. At this Champlain set off up the Ottawa with a few attendants, and by his exertions induced over 80 canoes to come down to the barter. In the same summer of 1613 an English vessel from Virginia destroyed De Poutrincourt's home at Port Royal, and also captured a French vessel sent out by the Jesuits to form a colony at Mount Desert, on the New England coast. In the summer of 1614 Champlain completed the formation of the new company for trade in the Saint Lawrence. On the failure of the La Rochelle merchants to appear, the whole of the shares were divided among the traders of Rouen and Saint Malo. On reaching the annual barter at the Lachine Rapid in the spring of 1615, Champlain found that his absence in previous summer had made the Indians doubt his friendship. In order to regain their confidence, and also explore the regions farther to the west, he set out with the Hurons on their return. He was thus able during the winter of 1615-16 to learn much of the geography of the present western Ontario as well as the region about Lake Ontario, to the southern shore of which he

accompanied a war expedition against the Iroquois. So grateful were the Hurons for the help thus accorded them that they accompanied Champlain in great numbers on his return to the Saint Lawrence in the spring of 1616. For this reason, also, the barters of 1617 and 1618 were extremely well attended. Notwithstanding this increase of trade, the company unfortunately did nothing toward establishing a local source of supply, and paid almost no attention to colonization. Only one family was brought out, and it was treated in an extremely unjust manner. Not only were none of its members allowed to engage in the fur trade, but while paying very high prices for all the stores bought from the company they were obliged to sell their own produce at the very low prices current in France. When Champlain, as the representative of the viceroy, sought to secure the fulfilment of these conditions as to colonists, defense and local sources of supply, he simply made himself disliked. In the spring of 1619 they even refused him a passage to Quebec. At the king's express command he returned there in 1620, only to find the factory so tumble-down that the rain came in on every side. When this was notified to the admiral of France, who had succeeded Condé as viceroy, he at once revoked the monopoly of the company and gave the trade to two Huguenot merchants, William and Emery de Caën. The old company, however, appealed to the king. Pending his decision both parties sent out vessels in the summer of 1621 and each left servants of its own to winter at the factory. In the course of the winter of 1621-2 the two companies amalgamated with a fresh monopoly which was to run until the year 1635. Unfortunately this united company neglected colonization and local sources of supply as much as its predecessor. The result was that in the spring of 1623 when the vessels arrived late they found that for some months all the inmates of the factory had been living on roots and berries. The same state of affairs reoccurred a few years later. Champlain, who was still governor, did his best to keep this united company up to its engagements, but whenever he returned to France everything was allowed to go to ruin. Although on his departure in the autumn of 1624 he left the new factory almost completed, he found on his return two years later that not a single nail had been driven in since he went away. "It could have been finished," said Champlain, "in a fortnight, had they been willing to work, but that is just what they will not do." As little attention was paid to cultivating a local source of supply, and when, in the summer of 1627, the principal supply-ship failed to appear, the outlook for the winter was far from bright. To make matters worse, war broke out between England and France in the spring of 1628 and several English ships were sent into the Saint Lawrence. Although Champlain bravely refused to surrender the factory, the fleet sent out to Quebec by a new company which Richelieu had formed was captured below Tadoussac. At the same time a Scottish colony was founded at De Poutrincourt's old quarters at Port Royal. In the winter of 1628-9 these Scottish and English merchants formed themselves into one company and sent out two fleets in the spring of 1629. While one brought fresh stores to Port Royal, the other entered the

Saint Lawrence and summoned the factory at Quebec to surrender. As no help of any sort had come since 1627 and all the inmates had been living for some time on roots and berries, Champlain was obliged to comply. On 22 July 1629 the English flag was run up on the flag-staff. The new company formed by Richelieu, called the Company of New France, also sent out a fleet, however, which not only succored the small French post at Cape Sable, below Port Royal, but also succeeded in dislodging Lord Ochiltree, who had formed a settlement on Cape Breton Island. He and his people were taken prisoners, and out of the material of their buildings a new French fort was constructed in one of the neighboring harbors. Here a garrison of 40 men was left. In the autumn of 1629 the French applied for the restitution of Quebec, since it had been surrendered after the conclusion of peace on 29 April. King Charles I. acquiesced, but the negotiations dragged on until the spring of 1632. In the meanwhile both companies sent out provisions to their posts; the Company of New France to Cape Sable and Cape Breton Island, and the English and Scottish company to Port Royal and Quebec. Finally, on the conclusion of the Treaty of Saint Germain-en-Laye on 20 March 1632, the post at Port Royal was made over to the Company of New France, while the old United Company was allowed to enjoy the trade at Quebec for one year in order to recuperate itself for its heavy losses. In the summer of 1633 its servants retired and the whole of New France passed into the hands of the Company of New France, which held it until the year 1664. See also EXPLORATION IN AMERICA.

H. P. BIGGAR,
Author of 'The Early Trading Companies of New France.'

3. **Canada — Under French Rule (1632-1755).** When the Treaty of St. Germaine-en-Laye (1632) restored to France (See FRANCE — *History*), her possessions in North America, Acadia and Canada were still savage wastes. Prior to this date Port Royal and Quebec had hardly advanced beyond the status of convenient landing points, while Tadoussac and Three Rivers were mere rendezvous for barter. In theory the profits of the fur-trade were enormous, but disaster or disappointment seemed to follow each venture with dismal regularity. At the same time the attempt to establish permanent colonies had been attended by only a moderate degree of success. Louis Hébert and a few other settlers had maintained themselves at Quebec for twenty-one years before the surrender of that place to the English, but their privations were constant and severe. Those who supported themselves by agriculture were less than a score and the total population barely passed one hundred. As for the missionary efforts which constituted a third form of French activity in Canada, neither Jesuits nor Récollets had gained more than a handful of converts and a certain amount of friction between the two orders already existed. One hopeful sign was indeed visible; for in 1627 the Company of New France took form with Richelieu (q.v.) and other prominent people at its head, but this organization (better known as the Company of the Hundred Associates) was just beginning to show signs of vitality when Quebec fell (1629)

into the hands of Kirke (see KIRKE, SIR DAVID). The general state of the situation can be described in a single phrase. Though individuals had displayed great enterprise and splendid heroism, the French as a nation had not impressed themselves deeply upon the western hemisphere.

Between the Treaty of St. Germain-en-Laye and Wolfe's decisive victory over Montcalm (1759) (see COLONIAL WARS IN AMERICA), lies a period of one hundred and twenty-seven years which is marked by all the features of genuine colonization. It cannot be said that in wealth and population New France kept pace with the English colonies from Massachusetts to Georgia; but while the economic basis of the French was less solid their geographical range was wider and their institutions were equally distinctive. For a century and a quarter France continued to be an active competitor for the control of this continent and maintained a strong foothold upon it. Moreover the Canadian French, the *habitants*, developed feelings of local pride and patriotism which, though they did not beget political restlessness, are not less noticeable to the historian than are the pride and patriotism of the English in America. From 1632 to 1759 New France was a colony peopled by vigorous and resourceful inhabitants. Unfortunately it possessed a defective system of administration, but its annals are adorned by noble deeds and its life represents a characteristic form of civilization.

Of the two regions which France regained in 1632, Canada was destined to be the more important and to be held upon the firmer tenure. Acadia with its long frontier of seaboard lay open to easy attack from the side of New England and after 1621, when James I. gave Sir William Alexander the charter of Nova Scotia, (see NOVA SCOTIA — *History*) its population contained a Scottish element. At the moment when Port Royal fell to the English for the second time (1628) the ablest and most loyal Frenchman in Acadia was Charles de la Tour, but on the formal restoration of the colony four years later Isaac de Razilly, a relative of Richelieu, was appointed royal lieutenant. During his lifetime the French in Acadia proved able to hold their own against New England and even to destroy posts which the English had established on the coast of Maine. De Razilly's death, however, precipitated an acute quarrel between de la Tour and the able, unscrupulous Charnisay who had come to the colony with de Razilly in 1632. The prosecution of the feud between these rivals led, among other things, to a famous siege of Fort Saint John by Charnisay and a spirited but fruitless defense of the stronghold by Mme. de la Tour in her husband's absence. The long and bitter broil ended peacefully enough in the marriage of de la Tour and Mme. Charnisay after the death of Charnisay and Mme. de la Tour, but meanwhile the prosperity of Acadia had been seriously hampered by a domestic feud which unsettled the whole administrative system and raised the issue of Catholic versus Huguenot. In 1654 Acadia was seized by the English for the third time and held till 1667 when France regained it by the Treaty of Breda (see BREDA, TREATY OF). During the greater part of the next twenty years peace between the two nations prevailed along the Atlantic coast, broken by occasional bickerings at points near a frontier which was always in dispute: but with the renewal of hostilities in the reign of William III. Acadia suffered severely and had not repaired her losses when the war of the Spanish Succession (see SUCCESSION WARS) broke out. This time the contest for supremacy reached a final settlement in one part at least of the New World. Nicholson's occupation of Port Royal (which he rechristened Annapolis, 1709) together with Marlborough's victories in Europe combined to secure Acadia to England by the Peace of Utrecht (1713). (See UTRECHT, PEACE OF). But even then the triumph of the English was not complete, for the island of Cape Breton still remained in the hands of France and the guns of Louisburg, guarding the entry to the Gulf of St. Lawrence, declared more plainly than words that the Atlantic seaboard would not be surrendered to England without a further struggle. In marked contrast to their precarious hold upon Acadia, the French built up along the shores of the Saint Lawrence a colony which, whatever its shortcomings, did not change hands with every generation. Canada was far from invulnerable, as the capture of Quebec by Kirke had already proved and as its siege by Phips (see PHIPS, SIR WILLIAM), was to prove once more in 1690; but long stretches of wilderness separated it from the English settlements, while the navigation of the river presented grave dangers to a hostile fleet. The fate of Sir Hoveden Walker, whose powerful fleet was shattered among the shoals of the Egg Islands (1710), shows that sea power could not be brought to bear against Canada so readily as against Acadia, and the fierce raids of Frontenac illustrate with equal force the ability of the French to defend themselves by land. French rule in Canada lasted long enough and was sufficiently secure to furnish a great object lesson in colonial method.

Apart from military history and the pathos which belongs to the loss of an empire, the life of New France is more interesting in the 17th than in the 18th century. The two generations that elapse between the return of Champlain (q.v.) and the death of Frontenac (q.v.) (1633-1698) are marked by a series of striking exploits and the establishment of fixed institutions. Energy and enthusiasm abound; the explorer and the missionary are lavishing their lives on causes which mean infinitely more to them than any form of personal ambition; the colonist is becoming a native, a *habitant,* whose concerns are increasingly associated with America; problems of Church and State are arising to vex the souls of governors and quicken the zeal of prelates. On every side there are signs of that fresh vigor which derives its impulse from the novelty and charm of the wilderness. In dealing with the progress of Canada during the middle and latter part of the 17th century, it is necessary to distinguish between the regions which were claimed by right of discovery and those which were effectively occupied by settlement. Before Frontenac's death lands had been cleared and rendered fit for cultivation at a good many points between Tadousac, where the Saguenay enters the Saint Lawrence, and Montreal. Above Lake Saint Louis there were forts at important strategic points like Kingston (then Fort Frontenac) and Detroit, but for agricultural purposes the colonial zone stopped at the Lake of Two Mountains, an expansion of the Ottawa. Beyond the island of Montreal lay the *pays d'en haut,* a vast territory which was repeatedly traversed by the pioneers, whether adventurers, traders, or missionaries, but which remained almost destitute of settlers. From the Saint Lawrence the French were led inevitably to the Great Lakes and thence by an easy passage to the Mississippi. Thus their explorations belong no less to the history of Illinois, Michigan and Wisconsin than to that of Canada. In the Laurentian valley the river was another Nile with a further element added, since besides being the great local thoroughfare it was a highway that opened the route to the Mother Country. If, unlike the Nile, its waters could not be made to produce a rice crop they abounded in the fish which were so necessary to the food of a Catholic community. The form of land allotment sprang from the one cardinal condition of life on the banks of a central stream. Each peasant had his strip of water frontage, however narrow, and was able at a moment's notice to embark in his own bateau or canoe. The only towns of Canada were Quebec, Three Rivers and Montreal, all situated on the Saint Lawrence, and no permanent settlements were made in any part of the country unless within easy reach of it or its tributaries. The north shore, owing to its rugged character, was less suited to farming than the south, and in the valley of the Richelieu, the outlet of Lake Champlain, many of the best seigneuries sprang up. The settlement of the Richelieu valley was also intended to provide a bulwark against the Iroquois. (See SIX NATIONS, THE.)

Closely connected with the distinction which has just been made between the Laurentian valley and the back or upper country (*pays d'en haut*) is the contrast between peasant and woodsman. According to the system of land tenure that prevailed in Canada under the Old Régime rural society was divided between the *seigneurs* or landlords and the *censitaires* or tenants. In Canada, as in France, gentility and the possession of an estate went together, but there is this important difference between the feudalism of the mother country and the colony, that whereas in France the peasants bore appreciable burdens during the 17th century, in Canada no *censitaire* could be seriously crippled by the taxes or services to which he was bound. Feudalism, an institution of the 9th century could not be transplanted without change to the New World in the age of Louis XIV. The French of Normandy and Brittany made admirable colonists, when once they had been induced to embark; but some prospect of improved conditions must be held out before emigrants would come forward. Moreover in a country of virgin forest it was impossible that peasants should be taxed as their kindred were in a land of ancient cultivation. In view of these considerations the *habitants* received their farms on very reasonable terms. How moderate were the demands of the *seigneur* may be seen from a single instance. A deed of 19 June 1694, concedes a lot of land three arpents in front by forty in depth (about a hundred acres) "in consideration of twenty sous and one good live capon for each arpent of front and one sou of *cens,* payable at the principal manor-house of the seigneury on St. Martin's day in each year so long as the grantee shall occupy the land." The *habitant* had in a certain sense the character of a woods-man, for a large part of his time was devoted to hewing down the forest, but he was not a woodsman in the fullest sense of the word. Besides the stationary peasant who cultivated his stump fields in the valley of the St. Lawrence, the population of New France embraced many restless and adventurous spirits who roved the woods, traded in beaver skins whenever they could elude the monopoly, intermarried with the Indians, and evaded the restraints of civilization without punishment from civil or ecclesiastical law. The *coureur de bois*, ("woodrunner") to give this type of colonist his generic name, was one of the most remarkable adventurers that this continent has ever seen. Though his vices were an object of scandal to the missionaries and his lawless habits an inconvenience to the government, he possessed the virtues of fearlessness and initiative to an exceptional degree. The comrades of Magellan and Drake were no more daring or resourceful than the *coureurs de bois* who pressed on from the valley of the Saint Lawrence into the wilds of the *pays d'en haut* and found amid the dangers of forest or prairie the fullest excitements of a nomadic life. Their names, for the most part, have perished; but legends like that of the *Chasse-gallerie* bear witness to the hold they preserve upon the memory of French Canada.

In passing from these general statements regarding country and inhabitants, it is hard to say whether a place of greater prominence should be given to the government or to the Church. One should be careful not to represent the French Canadians of the 17th century as slaves — a tendency too current among English writers at the present day. The feudalism of New France was feudalism in its most mitigated form and the *habitant* winning a home for himself by courageous toil seems anything but a serf by instinct. Nevertheless French Canada was overshadowed by two institutions which visibly embodied authority as authority was not visibly embodied in New England or New York. Whether or not paternalism was the bane of Canada is an open question to be answered by the historical student in accordance with his own scheme of philosophy. The broad fact is that the Crown and the Clergy divided between them an extremely large part of the world in which the *habitant* lived. From 1632 to 1663 the affairs of Canada were controlled, under the Crown, by the Company of the Hundred Associates. Had this corporation been better managed, or rather had it been actuated by a larger spirit, it might have gained for itself a distinguished reputation and eventually handed over to the King a flourishing possession; but looking only to the greatest immediate return it wasted a fine opportunity and does not merit comparison with either the East India Company (see EAST INDIA COMPANIES) or the Hudson's Bay Company (q.v.). After 1663 executive power in Canada was deputed by the King to the Governor and the Intendant, with whom were associated the Bishop and a board of councillors varying in number from five to twelve. The Governor, who was always a noble, held the highest office in the colony though he did not possess so much real power as the Intendant. He commanded the forces, was the channel of diplomatic intercourse with the English and the Indians, occupied the central place in colonial society and was authorized to follow his own judgment regarding matters of emergency. With finance, however, he had little or nothing to do, and from the whole field of civil administration he was excluded by the presence at his side of the Intendant. This official belonged ordinarily to the middle class and had been trained to law or business. The Crown seems to have acted on the maxim, "Divide and Rule." Both Governor and Intendant were required to send home detailed reports which always included a large amount of criticism and gossip. The Intendant passed judgment on the acts of the Governor and the Governor was not slow to express his opinion concerning the administration of the Intendant. Neither received untrammeled authority, for an autocratic king like Louis XIV. insisted upon reserving the use of his prerogative. The government of New France was less rigid and cumbrous than that of the Spanish possessions under Philip II., but the principle of absolutism carried out at such a distance from the court could not fail to impair the efficiency of administration.

The position of the Church in New France cannot be properly described unless a reference is made to the dominating influence which controlled Europe during the age of colonization. Seventeen years before Cartier's first voyage to the Saint Lawrence (1534) Luther had denounced the sale of indulgences at Wittenberg. In the interval between Cartier's first voyage and his last (1541) the "Institutes" of Calvin (see CALVIN, JOHN) was becoming the foundation of a church and the Company of Jesus (see JESUITS) was arising to stem the tide of heresy. Despite the wars of religion and the national exhaustion which they produced, religion was still the reigning issue in France when Champlain sailed westward to continue the work of Cartier. This may be seen chiefly in two ways; from the missionary zeal of the religious orders and from the anxiety of French Catholics that New France be kept untainted by Huguenot misbelief. With De Monts and Poutrincourt, Calvinism made its appearance at Port Royal and a little later it maintained itself for a while at Quebec under the protection of William and Emery de Caen, who did not carry out their promise to exclude heretics from the colony. But during the sway of Richelieu, the Huguenot cause perishes even more completely in Canada than in France, and a way is left clear for the unchecked ascendency of Rome. No one can read the religious literature of New France without recognizing the sincerity of motive which brought Jesuits, Récollets, Sulpicians, Ursulines, to Quebec and Montreal. The savage races of America had excited the imagination of all Europe, and in France the desire was particularly strong to rescue these heathen from the doom of the unbaptized. The greatest nobles in the realm subscribed funds for the mission and acted as sponsors at the baptism of Micmac or Algonquin converts. First in importance among the religious orders of New France come the Jesuits, whose missionary tradition had been established more than half a century earlier by St. Francis Xavier. Entering Acadia and Canada with a record of brilliant success to give them confidence, they prosecuted their labors among all the nations from the Iroquois to the Illinois and from the Ottawas to the Natchez. Their most heroic deeds of self-sacrifice are bound up with their mission to the Hurons (ending in 1649, when the power of the Hurons was destroyed by the Iroquois), and with their mission to the Iroquois covering the third quarter of the 17th century. It was always the aim of the Jesuits to turn the Indians from the nomadic life to the arts of civilization. In this attempt they were but partially successful. Although certain tribes of the Algonquin family yielded themselves willingly to the guidance of the missionaries, the total number of converts was far smaller in New France than in Paraguay. During the first generation after the restoration of Canada to France the Jesuits published in Paris an annual account of the labors undertaken by members of their order among the American Indians. These "Relations" (see JESUIT RELATIONS AND ALLIED DOCUMENTS, THE), are the best single source of information about the habits of the aborigines and also rank high in the list of our authorities for the history of Canada. Next to the Jesuits in order of prominence stand the Sulpicians, whose efforts centred chiefly in Montreal and the neighboring district. The founding of Ville-Marie de Montreal exemplifies in its purest form the mood of devotion that prompted Frenchmen to leave the civilization of Europe for a life of privation among the barbarous heathen of Canada. Here the colonizing impulse proceeded solely from a desire to spread the faith. With Olier and Dauversière, who founded the Society of Notre-Dame de Montreal, there was no thought of gaining wealth through the fur trade. The charter of the society expressly states that its members detach themselves from all regard to temporal interest and take for their one purpose the conversion of the natives. From 1642 to the close of the century Montreal was an outpost of civilization and Christianity, exposed to frightful dangers, as the exploit of Dollard (1660) and the Lachine Massacre (1689) testify, but defended by men who cared more for religion than for life. In the relations of the Church with the *habitants* friction seldom arose. There is reason to believe that the Jesuits incurred some unpopularity because they did not favor the appointment of *curés* in the outlying districts, but for the most part the attitude of the peasants towards the clergy was one of complete deference. Until 1665 when the Carignan Regiment came to Canada, the social order presented many features of a theocracy. Religion was supported by the state and derived a stronger support still from the energy of the religious. The prevalent mood was pietistic and public opinion sanctioned the ecclesiastical punishments which were called forth even by minor offenses against morals. Apart from church festivals the routine of daily life at Quebec or Montreal made little provision for relaxation or entertainment. Taverns were under the ban, dancing parties were unknown, and the general demeanor of sobriety would have met favor in the eyes of a New England Puritan. The coming of the Carignan Regiment broke in on this religious Arcadia and proved an entering wedge for frivolity, but in the early days the temper of New France was deeply religious, if not ascetic. One other aspect of ecclesiastical affairs deserves emphatic notice. While the clergy had to do with a docile population and were animated by pure enthusiasm in their work among the Indians, the religious life of the colony was not free from friction. The Récollets, and after them the Sulpicians, felt that their interests were threatened by the enmity of the Jesuits. The Jesuits in turn prevented the Abbé de Queylus, an able Sulpician, from being made Bishop of Quebec, casting their influence in favor of Laval (see LAVAL-MONTMORENCY, FRANCIS XAVIER DE), who became the first titular bishop in New France. Laval, once appointed, quarreled with successive governors on different grounds — with Argenson (1661) on the question of precedence, and with Avaugour (1662) on the question of selling brandy to the Indians. The difficulty over precedence brought in the whole issue of Church and state; the quarrel over the brandy question was less lofty but more practical. The position of the Church was that brandy should not be sold to the savages under any circumstances. The general, though not the invariable, position of the government was that if the French did not sell brandy to the Indians the latter would buy rum from the Dutch and English. The Church as a whole and the *habitants* as a whole lived on excellent terms; but there was much friction between the religious orders, the *coureurs de bois* were a thorn in the side of the clergy, and a governor of secular tastes, like Frontenac, might keep up a running feud with the hierarchy for years.

The mention of Frontenac's name recalls a striking personality, for of all the governors who were sent out to New France during the long reign of Louis XIV. he must be called the ablest and most forcible. That his policy towards the Church was judicious or free from prejudice cannot be maintained, nor can it be forgotten that his memory is defaced by the stain of fearful massacres. But he was bold, resolute and thoroughly devoted to the interests of Canada. Throughout both periods of his rule (1672-1682; 1689-1698) he was master of the situation as none of his predecessors had been, and during the seven years of his absence from the colony the failures of La Barre and Denonville served to set off his virtues in the strongest light. The main political problems with which he had to deal were the enmity of the Iroquois, the aggressive policy of the English as suggested by Governor Dongan. and the extension of French influence from the Great Lakes into the valley of the Mississippi. Speaking broadly the Iroquois were the chief menace of Canada in the last part of the 17th century as the English were its chief menace in the first part of the 18th. The most celebrated of the Jesuit martyrs, Jogues and Brébeuf, met death at their hands; the most brilliant deed of courage which the annals of New France contain was Dollard's fight against them at the Long Saut: it was in their face that Madeleine de Verchères shut the door of her father's fort. Whether left to themselves or set on by the English they had every disposition to molest the French. The spirit of conciliation they mistook for weakness and. as Frontenac saw, the only way to impress them was by a show of strength. In 1696 he ravaged their country more thoroughly than De Tracy had done thirty years earlier, burned their palisades, destroyed their corn and convinced them that he had a power which they must respect. The next year their envoys came to Quebec speaking the language of humility. Frontenac's attack upon the

English dates from the beginning of his second term of office. Returning to the colony in 1689 he found that French prestige had vanished almost wholly during his absence. To impress the Indians and terrorize the English he equipped those raiding parties which carried the torch and the tomahawk to Schenectady, Salmon Falls and Casco Bay. As a *tour de force* of endurance, this winter campaign of the French was a remarkable feat, but the atrocities which accompanied it cannot fail to awaken the deepest abhorrence. Parkman finds extenuation for Frontenac in the standards of his age. "He was no whit more ruthless than his times and his surroundings, and some of his contemporaries find fault with him for not allowing more Indian captives to be tortured. Many surpassed him in cruelty, none equalled him in capacity and vigor." Everything considered, this must be called a mitigated sentence, and apart from all considerations of humanity it may be doubted whether Frontenac's policy of carnage was a sound one. Its momentary success in impressing the Indians was not an equivalent for the spirit of vengeance which it awakened among the English. From 1690 forward, New France and New England have their rancorous enmities which continue to exist quite irrespective of peace or war between the mother countries. Phips may be turned back from Quebec but the memory of massacre endures until French power in Canada has been destroyed. A much brighter feature of Frontenac's régime is the progress made by French exploration in the Far West. While the famous journey of Marquette (q.v.) and Joliet (q.v.) down the upper waters of the Mississippi (1673) may be more fitly connected with the names of Courcelle (q.v.), Frontenac's predecessor, and of Talon (q.v.), the good Intendant, the picturesque exploits of La Salle (q.v.) and Tonty (q.v.) fall within the period of Frontenac. It was by favor of Frontenac that the fort at Cataracoui (now Kingston) was placed in La Salle's hands, thus enabling him to establish a fixed base at the east end of Lake Ontario for his operations on the Great Lakes and beyond. As far as the Huron country the French had been on familiar ground ever since the days of Champlain, but their chief triumphs in opening up the *Hinterland* were won under Frontenac.

The 18th century opened for New France with bright prospects which were destined never to be realized. The war that closed at the Peace of Ryswick (1697) had just demonstrated the defensive strength of Canada, and though D'Iberville's (see IBERVILLE, SIEUR D') conquests in Hudson's Bay were restored to England, France did not lose Acadia. Frontenac's chastisement of the Iroquois had brought relief from an ancient scourge and Callières' diplomacy concluded the peace which had been made possible by a decided blow. The War of the Spanish Succession closed less favorably. The success of Vaudreuil's raids was a poor equivalent for Marlborough's victories or even for Nicholson's capture of Port Royal. France lost Acadia and was thrown back for her hope of an Atlantic dominion upon the single fortress of Louisburg (q.v.). The Peace of Utrecht (1713) may be called the beginning of the end. The history of Louisburg is a tale of great effort, enormous expense and complete disappointment. France lavished upon this harbor

in Cape Breton as much money as it would have cost to erect a fortress of the first class in Europe. Until 1745 its strength remained untested, but the French themselves thought it impregnable and the English looked upon it with dread. The political effect of Louisburg was two-fold. Its near neighborhood to Acadia prevented the French of that province from becoming loyal to British rule, and in New England it was regarded as a permanent menace to peace. When the War of the Austrian Succession offered an excuse, Massachusetts was ready for the attack. Governor Shirley (see SHIRLEY, WILLIAM) devised the plan, which was daringly executed by a colonial fleet under William Pepperell (q.v.) in co-operation with four British men of war. The capture of Louisburg by a militia force was the greatest humiliation which France had suffered in America and its restoration by the Peace of Aix-la-Chapelle (1748) (see AIX-LA-CHAPELLE, TREATIES OF PEACE CONCLUDED AT), came to New England as the sorest affront which it had ever received at the hands of the home government.

At the Peace of Utrecht New France contained a population of rather more than 25,000. In 1763 when Canada was ceded to England the number of inhabitants had advanced to about 60,000. It is obvious that this rate of increase was trivial in comparison with the progress of the English colonies during the same period, and when we remember the unusual fecundity of the French Canadians, some special reason needs to be assigned for the slow development of the colony. The cause of this striking phenomenon will be found in the fact that immigration was not spontaneous, as in the case of the English colonies, but controlled by government. Partly owing to the institutions which prevailed in France during the 17th and 18th centuries, and partly owing to gross mismanagement of colonial affairs by the court of Versailles, New France was handicapped in the long race with its southern rivals. This fact must be brought out because it is often erroneously stated that the Frenchman has never made a good colonist. The biography of Canada from Champlain to Montcalm gives the direct negative to such an idea. Maladministration, the lack of local self-government, and excess of loyalty to inherited institutions account for the defeat of the French in America rather than the want of promptness, courage, industry and resource. It must be remembered, moreover, that the English colonies took root in a soil which was better fitted to stimulate rapid growth. The long calm which followed the Peace of Utrecht (1713-1742) was often broken by signs of acute restlessness. As early as 1725 the Marquis de Beauharnois, who had become Governor in succession to Vaudreuil, was busy with schemes for keeping the English within the limits they already occupied. This meant that their expansion northwards should be checked in the vicinity of Lake George and their expansion westward by the range of the Alleghanies. Far from losing their love of exploration, the French pushed farther and farther westward with each decade. Michilimackinac was to Verendrye what Cataracoui had been to La Salle, and just at the moment when Maria Theresa was preparing to recover Silesia from Frederick the Great, one of Verendrye's sons caught a first glimpse of the Rocky Mountains. In America the hostilities which accompanied the War of the Austrian Succession centred at Louisburg and accordingly this conflict affected Canada less than the two preceding wars had done. But every man of colonial origin, English and French alike, saw that the Peace of Aix-la-Chapelle was merely an armistice. Unsettled boundaries suggested endless friction, especially in Acadia and the Ohio Valley. The line which was run by Céloron de Bienville at the instance of France aimed at excluding the English from the Ohio and according to patriotic opinion in such colonies as New York, Pennsylvania and Virginia, amounted to a *casus belli.* Before the development of the western trade the English and French had been separated by a wide zone of wilderness. The expansion of both races brought them face to face at the junction of the Alleghany and the Monongahela. Should the stronghold built in this angle be called Fort Duquesne or Pittsburg? Here was an issue on which hinged the future of a continent. It was the misfortune of the French both at home and in Canada that their administrative system suffered from the worst evils of a corrupt absolutism. At Versailles the folly and extravagance of Louis XV., at Quebec the unblushing thefts of the Intendant Bigot, were but a poor preparation for war. And so the small but valiant race of the Canadian French bore the burden of vices not their own when they entered upon the last act of an irrepressible conflict. See also CANADA — GREAT BRITAIN'S FIGHT WITH FRANCE FOR NORTH AMERICA; CANADA — THE CLERGY RESERVES; CANADA — SEIGNORIAL TENURE.

CHARLES W. COLBY,
Professor of History, McGill University.

4. Canada — Great Britain's Fight with France for North America — 1753-1763. For several years previous to the formal declaration of war between England and France, in 1756 (see CANADA — UNDER FRENCH RULE), the stirring events in the Ohio Valley and in distant Acadia foreshadowed a great crisis, during which territorial disputes, aggressions, and political intrigues would be lost sight of for the moment, and the question paramount would be, the supremacy of France or of England in North America. The policy of France, as dictated from Versailles, had not been broad enough to successfully promote colonization, in the sense of expansion, or even to maintain permanent occupancy, although this was much desired. And the honest designs of her colonial administrator, La Galissonnière, to increase the dominion of his royal master, at an opportune moment, met with no responsive aid. The mother country was wedded to schemes of aggrandizement at home, and was inclined to leave her colony to work out its own future. Besides, the French then, as now, were rather a stay-at-home people. New France was consequently weak in population, and not in a position to retain her empire in the North, and, moreover, her influence was being undermined by official corruption. Great Britain, on the other hand, had the real advantage of superior numbers in the New World, although she had no definite colonial policy, and was already smarting from the effects of an earlier administration, due rather to ignorance than to knavery. The disputes touching possessions in Acadia were of long standing. By the twelfth article of the Treaty of Utrecht (see UTRECHT,

PEACE OF), Nova Scotia, within its ancient boundaries, had been ceded to the Crown of England. A controversy soon arose over the interpretation of a certain clause. Great Britain claimed that her possessions under the Treaty of Utrecht were of the same extent as those acquired by France under the Treaty of Breda; but France protested that the territory she then received was quite distinct from the ancient boundaries, which confined Nova Scotia to a portion of the southern peninsula. At the conclusion of the Treaty of Aix-la-Chapelle (see AIX-LA-CHAPELLE, TREATIES OF PEACE CONCLUDED AT), when Louisburg (q.v.) was restored to the French, the boundary questions were referred to commissioners, each Court agreeing that, until a decision was reached, no fort or settlement should be attempted upon the debatable ground. But the shrewd La Galissonnière, disregarding the stipulation, if he was ever officially acquainted with it, commenced the construction of forts, and favored settlement upon the lands claimed by England. The importance of Nova Scotia in the future development of Canada was apparent to each nation, both from a strategic and commercial point of view, but neither power could furnish from its colonial resources an army of sufficient strength to support its ambition. The policy of Great Britain toward Nova Scotia was most short-sighted. Instead of encouraging the emigration of a desirable class, intended to grow up with the Acadians and form a united and loyal people, she allowed the French, for nearly 40 years, to regard the country in the light of an exclusive settlement. It is true that they were good subjects; but they were French at heart, and it remained to be proved whether, under extraordinary pressure, their sympathies would incline to France or not. The possibility of such a contingency was for years practically ignored, but when it was seriously considered the methods adopted were ill-advised. The lands of the French were divided and sub-divided, until new grants were necessary; but Great Britain decreed that new lands could be acquired only by Protestants. The question of religion, therefore, became a condition of tenure. Shirley (see SHIRLEY, WILLIAM), the energetic governor of Massachusetts, who was largely responsible for the government of Nova Scotia, was firmly convinced that until French influence was exterminated British interests could not flourish; and so he endeavored to effect the conversion of the inhabitants, suggesting that rewards be given to those who renounced their faith. The king favored an assurance that the people should enjoy the exercise of their religion, but Shirley, in a proclamation, omitted the passage as dangerous. The home government then consented to a scheme for promoting the loyalty of the province by the importation of foreign Protestants, to mingle with the Acadians — a fusion possible under the British flag, but doubtful at such a critical moment, when the military organization was insufficient to protect the frontier, or to inspire confidence in the stability of British institutions. Government agents in Geneva, and elsewhere, were active in advertising in the papers for settlers, and bargaining with poor artisans. But the scheme fell through; though at last 3,000 good settlers were landed at Chiboucto Bay in 1749, from which at length sprang the important naval post of Halifax (q.v.). In the meantime, however, a great struggle was impending, which led to the deportation of 8,000 Acadians (see CANADA — THE ACADIAN REFUGEES), whose subsequent misery and suffering contribute the darkest page to the history of Nova Scotia. A new oath of allegiance was demanded by Governor Cornwallis, which from time to time was deferred. While, on the other hand, the fiery zealot, Le Loutre (see LE LOUTRE, LOUIS JOSEPH), backed by the Indians, exercised every effort to retain influence over the people. Le Loutre detested the English, and was generally successful in persuading the unhappy people that an oath of allegiance to a Protestant monarch was very much like being disloyal to their faith, the penalties for which did not cease with their natural existence. But, although the dark· deeds which were being enacted in 1753, concerning Nova Scotia, had a distinct bearing upon the approaching conflict, they were of secondary importance to the great mass of the British colonists, when compared with the prize which both French and English coveted — the possession of the Ohio Valley. The details of the contest in this section cannot be given here. See BRADDOCK, EDWARD; COLONIAL WARS IN AMERICA; FORT NECESSITY; PITTSBURGH, *History;* WASHINGTON, GEORGE. The effect of Braddock's defeat was felt in the expeditions of Shirley against Oswego (q.v.), and in that of Johnson against Crown Point (see CROWN POINT, FORTRESS OF). A body of provincials had been raised, and placed under the command of Johnson for the reduction of Crown Point. But Dieskau intercepted, and almost captured, a detachment of this expedition. Reinforcements arrived at a critical moment, and the tables were turned by the capture of Dieskau. This circumstance was made a great deal of, but, nevertheless, Crown Point was unmolested, and still in the hands of the French. War and bloodshed had desolated the homes of the colonists and destroyed their commerce, and over all of them hung the dread of the tomahawk and the scalping knife of the Indian. Panic-stricken, they could devise no means of defense, and surrender seemed preferable to fight. In Acadia, while the two nations were still at peace, the determination of the British had driven into exile the unhappy Acadians. But their own position there was by no means to be envied. British prestige was indeed at a low ebb in America, when the struggle between the colonists was superseded by a contest between the two powers, which commenced officially when King George II. signed the declaration of war against France in May 1756.

The situation in New France was indeed acute. Agriculture had been neglected, grain was scarce, horses were slaughtered for food, famine was imminent. But it should be borne in mind that this deplorable state of affairs was not the inevitable outcome of the struggles through which the country had passed, but a condition actually created for profit, toiled for and plotted for by Bigot, in order that he might appear as the real savior of the distressed colony. The advice of the Intendant to his somewhat weak-kneed, and certainly dishonest, henchman, Vergor, to "cut and slip, and make hay while the sun shone, in order that he might have the means to build a château

in France," was but an indication of the course he intended to follow himself, though on a grander and more colossal scale. New France was to be pillaged. The people must be subdued, and bodily suffering would prove effective where less persuasive methods might fail. New life was given to the colony for a moment when the Marquis de Montcalm (q.v.) arrived in Canada in the spring of 1756, with 1,200 troops and ample supplies. No better general could have been chosen than Montcalm. In fact, men of his mold were just what New France needed most at this time. He was an excellent soldier and had already won renown. He was loyal to his sovereign, at a time when loyalty was not profitable; he was brave and courteous, and he dearly loved France. Vaudreuil (see VAUDREUIL-CAVAGNAL, MARQUIS DE), the governor, was a Canadian, and attached to the land of his birth, but he despised every form of interference from France. Hence there was constant friction. Bigot, the representative of the king, loved his master and the colony only in proportion to the measure in which they contributed to his needs; and his needs were of abnormal proportions. The conduct of Montcalm throughout the war, until the supreme hour when he yielded up his life in defense of the colony, forms a striking and pleasing contrast to the actions of his two colleagues. He was also fortunate in the chief officers under him.

England was far less happy than France in the choice of the commander-in-chief of her forces. Lord Loudon, who was placed at the head of the 900 regulars sent out to the colonies, was no match for the brilliant Montcalm. Arriving in Albany two months after he was expected by his chief officers, Abercromby and Webb, Loudon was confronted with a condition of affairs similar to that with which Montcalm had to contend — jealousy between colonials and regulars. The War Office had decreed that a colonial officer could not rank above a senior captain of regulars, and consequently well-seasoned officers, experienced in the methods of the enemy, were liable to orders from a man who had never been under fire, and had no knowledge whatever of colonial affairs. The British general seemed unable to decide upon any plan of action, and much valuable time was wasted. In the meanwhile, disaster had overtaken the British at Oswego. By clever tactics Montcalm had surprised the fort, and had 30 guns directed against it before the commander was aware of the danger which threatened him. There was little effective resistance, and capitulation necessarily followed; 1,600 men were made prisoners, and in a few days the fort was razed. The year was passing away without any important move on the part of the British. Loudon desired a change of scene, and induced the home government to agree to an expedition against Louisburg. Large reinforcements were sent out, and in the month of June 1757 he had nearly 12,000 men arrayed against that stronghold. Still unable to decide upon a plan of attack, he wasted a month in exercising the troops, or, as Lord Charles Howe said, "In keeping the courage of His Majesty's soldiers at bay, and in expending the nation's wealth in making sham fights and planting cabbages, when they ought to have been fighting the enemies of the king in reality." On 4 August a movement was set on foot, but intelligence was conveyed to the commander that the French expected reinforcements and were eager for the fray. Thereupon, the noble lord abandoned the enterprise and returned to New York, having covered himself with ridicule, and greatly amused the French.

In the spring of 1757, the region of Lake Champlain was the scene of unusual activity. The Indians from the distant shores of Lake Superior, and from the forests beyond Lake Erie, were rallying around the French standard; and by midsummer a restless band, eager for the fray and only restrained with difficulty, gathered at Fort Carillon as part of the expedition against the British strongholds of Fort Edward and Fort William Henry. Montcalm's army consisted of about 6,000 of the best troops, with the addition of the Indians. The British force was divided between the two forts. Webb was at Fort Edward in command of 3,500 men, and Munro had 2,000 men in Fort William Henry, and 500 entrenched upon a rising ground in the rear of the fort. Montcalm's first move, on approaching, was to occupy the route communicating with the forts, which, at the same time, cut off the British troops upon the rising ground. This was accomplished by de Lévis with 3,000 men. Montcalm strengthened his position and soon had 40 guns bearing upon the fort. From the first it was clear that the British position was untenable. Munro was twice offered terms of capitulation, but he stubbornly refused. At length he was forced to surrender, and the garrison marched out of the fort. Then followed a frightful scene which has unjustly tarnished the memory of Montcalm. The Indians, disappointed of the plunder to which they looked forward at the sack of the fort, fell upon the prisoners with fury, and horribly massacred nearly 100 before any means could be taken to prevent them. Montcalm and Lévis did their best to arrest the fury of the savage hordes, and saved many lives; but the mischief was done, and dire vengeance was threatened. Notwithstanding the dismal failure of Loudon, Pitt was still determined to reduce Louisburg, which was to be made the chief objective in the campaign of 1758. Loudon had been recalled, and the command was entrusted to Amherst, who had already done good service in Germany. The chief officers under him were Lawrence and Wolfe. The force consisted of about 12,000 men. On the second of June part of the fleet anchored in Gabarus Bay, a few miles from Louisburg, Boscawen being the admiral in command. The expedition was a joint one, both naval and military. Wolfe was the most conspicuous figure of all present. His brigade made the real attack from the boats, while Whitmore's and Lawrence's supported him by feints in other places. The landward siege was well pressed home, and Louisburg, the gateway of New France, soon fell, and being shortly after razed to the ground, literally became a thing of the past.

Success had attended British arms in other quarters. Bradstreet at the head of 3,000 men had captured Fort Frontenac, which the unwisdom of Vaudreuil had left inadequately supported, although it was a most important post commanding Lake Ontario and serving as a base for the Ohio forts. De Noyan, the governor, had demanded reinforcements, but, in the place of troops, Vaudreuil had dispatched a one-armed man to his assistance, and, as resistance was futile, capitulation followed. Fort Duquesne had also become a British post, and now bore the name of Fort Pitt. Forbes, in the face of great difficulties, had endured the perils and suffering of a winter's march; and, when at last his bravery and determination had triumphed over every obstacle, and the fort was in sight, he found that it had been evacuated. While Loudon was "planting cabbages," a harmless occupation, Abercromby was making a worse mess of affairs at Ticonderoga (q.v.). The French had been expecting an attack at this vital point, which commanded the route by way of Lake Champlain, and threatened Montreal. A large body of men had been ordered there in the spring by Montcalm; but the withdrawal of so many troops under Loudon, had convinced Vaudreuil that it would be an opportune moment to create a diversion on the Mohawk. Montcalm was opposed to this enterprise; consequently Vaudreuil insisted, and 1,600 men were detached for the purpose. By the middle of June Montcalm had only 3,000 men at Ticonderoga, the battalions of La Sarre, Languedoc, Béarn, Berri, Guienne, and Royal Roussillon, with two good engineers. The place was by no means strongly fortified, but works were hastily thrown up in advantageous positions. In the meantime the formidable army under Abercromby, consisting of regulars and provincials, in all 15,000 men, was encamped about half a mile from the fort. But the real head of the army, Lord Howe, the best soldier in America, as Wolfe had said, had been killed in a preliminary skirmish, and the commander was powerless to act. Something had to be done, however, and Abercromby moved his whole force against Carillon. Montcalm's army had been increased by 500 men under de Lévis; and after a seven hours' blundering assault, Abercromby was completely outgeneralled, and lost no less than 2,000 men. This victory covered Montcalm with glory, and he is frequently referred to as "the hero of Carillon." But although he had won glory for French arms, the victory was a blow to the jealous Vaudreuil, and signalized the farther accentuation of discord which produced serious results in future operations.

In 1759 Pitt was at last in a position to put his greater scheme into practice. The tide of war was almost on the turn, and he seized opportunity beforehand. The Seven Years' war (q.v.) was being waged in many parts of the world; in fact, in a purely military sense, there were several different wars going on at the same time. But there was one great connective force which made them one, and that was the British navy. France and England were now in the very middle of their great imperial war, which began after the fall of the Stuarts in 1688, and was continued as one single age-long and world-wide struggle for the over-sea dominion of the world, down to Trafalgar and Waterloo. The Seven Years' war was the most distinctively imperial phase of the whole of this vast conflict; the heart of it lay in the fight for American dominion; and the central episode of this fight itself is to be found in the expedition against Quebec, which culminated in the renowned battle of the Plains of Abraham. The four real conquerors of New France are Pitt, Anson, Saunders, and Wolfe. The names of Pitt and Wolfe have always been on every tongue; but the equally important ones of Anson and of Saunders have been unduly forgotten. Pitt, of course, was the originator; and in himself, the most important of the four. But as the whole fortunes of the war were really determined by the British command of the sea, it is absolutely necessary to understand the naval side of the campaign, not only for its own sake, but also to fully appreciate the work of the army. In the ever-memorable year of 1759, it was entirely due to the navy that England remained safe at home, and it was more than half due to the navy that she emerged as a conqueror abroad. France had prepared a gigantic scheme of invasion. One fleet was to sail for Ireland, where the troops were to be met on landing by a general rising in their favor. The Jacobites were to be stirred into insurrection by another French fleet destined for Scotland; whilst their third fleet, larger than both the others united, was to convoy innumerable troop-boats across the Channel, as they made a dash for the south of England. To guard against this national danger the navy then developed the first regular system of blockade ever known. Boscawen blockaded Toulon, Hawke blockaded Brest, Rodney cruised off Havre, and Admiral Smith kept the reserve fleet always ready in the Downs. Meanwhile, however, Pitt was preparing a counterstroke; not at France herself—where she would be stronger than England in a campaign fought out on her own home base—but at her over-sea possessions in Canada, from which she was separated by those 3,000 miles of hostile waters, which the British command of the sea had practically made a British possession. Thus Montcalm had to await attack in utter isolation, on the far side of an immense stretch of territorial waters, across which Wolfe advanced in perfect safety to meet him. And it must be remembered that Saunders' squadron was not only a strong one, for it comprised a full quarter of the whole navy, but that it was playing an integral part in a universal scheme of strategy—for all seas are strategically one—whilst Wolfe's little army was only a landing-party on a large scale. There were twice as many seamen as landsmen engaged in the taking of Quebec. Saunders had over 18,000 sailors, more than two thirds of whom belonged to the navy, while Wolfe had less than 9,000 soldiers. The total British force, therefore, amounted to 27,000 men. Saunders and Wolfe received their secret instructions from the King in February, and immediately after sailed for Nova Scotia. The final rendezvous was Louisburg, where over 8,000 men were assembled in May. On 1 June the fleet began its dangerous voyage, with no less than 200 vessels of all sorts and sizes. It was navigated in perfect safety to the Island of Orleans, where it arrived on 27 June, and was not injured by a tremendous gale a day or two later, nor by the costly display of fireworks, in the shape of fire ships, destined to work its destruction. The picket boats met the attack well up stream, and, "taking hell in tow," as a bluejacket forcibly expressed it, put all the enemy's vessels ashore, where they burnt themselves out. Wolfe established three camps.

The principal one was at Montmorency, just beyond the falls. The second was on the Island of Orleans, completely out of range, and thus very convenient for a hospital and stores. The third was at Point Levis, which Vaudreuil foolishly refused to occupy, in spite of Montcalm's sensible advice, and which was consequently left open for Wolfe to build his batteries on. These batteries literally pounded the town to pieces; as a manuscript note on a plan of the siege in the French War Office, truly remarks, "*ce ne fut pas un siège, mais un bombardement.*" Among other projectiles of all kinds, 36,000 solid cannon balls were fired from this coign of vantage. Montcalm's position was still immensely strong, in spite of the loss of the Levis Heights. The Upper Town of Quebec is built upon the extremity of a long promontory which is bounded on the south by steep cliffs, 200 or 300 feet sheer up above the Saint Lawrence, and on the north by lower, but still easily defensible, cliffs overlooking the valley of the Saint Charles. The town was held by 2,000 men under de Ramesay. It had a double tier of batteries, one on the top of the cliffs, the other along the water front below them. The only open ground in the vicinity was round the mouth of the Saint Charles. But this was well entrenched, and the trenches were carried on continuously for seven miles along the Beauport shore to the Montmorency, opposite Wolfe's camp.

Wolfe's first attempt to break through was made some distance up the Montmorency, where he tried to force his way across the fords and so attack the entrenchments in the rear. But he was repulsed with loss, in a bush-fight in which his regulars were at a great disadvantage. His second attempt was a more serious one. On 31 July he tried to carry the Montmorency Heights by storm, a mile on the Quebec side of the Falls. But as his troops had to be collected from several quarters, in full view of the French, Montcalm easily anticipated him at the right spot, before he could deliver the assault. Besides, the faulty British plan could not be carried out even according to Wolfe's intentions, because the grenadiers, 1,000 strong, suddenly broke into a wild charge before being properly formed up, and lost nearly half their numbers in a fruitless effort to scale the heights. Then a terrific thunderstorm burst on the scene of carnage, making the heights more slippery than ever, and so he had no choice but to call off his men at once. After this repulse Wolfe fell seriously ill, and towards the end of August he gave his brigadiers, Monckton, Townshend and Murray, a memorandum of three other plans for assaulting the trenches, and asked them "to consult together for the public utility." Their council of war resulted in a complete rejection of all his suggestions; because, as they well remarked, the storming of such works from open ground would certainly be both difficult and dangerous. Moreover, even if the works themselves were carried, there would still remain the fortified line of the Saint Charles, as well as the heights of the promontory beyond, to keep him out of Quebec, until the lateness of the season would compel him to raise the siege. Their own plan was to take all the available men up the Saint Lawrence, and land at any suitable point between Cap Rouge, which was nine miles, and

Pointe aux Trembles, which was 22 miles, above Quebec. Wolfe informed Pitt, in a dispatch written on 2 September, that he had acquiesced in this plan, and intended to put it into operation at once.

The Montmorency camp was cleverly evacuated, without the loss of a man, by a general naval and military demonstration against the entrenchments, which made the French feel sure that another attempt to storm the position there was about to take place. From 7 to 10 September the rain suspended all operations; and on 10 September Wolfe made his final reconnaissance. He was already well posted on the lie of the land in every direction, and the idea of attacking above Quebec was thoroughly familiar to his mind long before it was mentioned by his brigadiers. On 19 May he had said to his uncle, that he "reckoned on a smart action at the passage of the Saint Charles unless we can steal a detachment up the river and land it three, four, five miles, or more above Quebec." This plan was better than the brigadiers', as it contemplated seizing the ground much closer to Quebec than the nearest objective point they proposed trying. At the final reconnaissance he chose the Foulon, where a path led up to the Plains of Abraham, within two miles of the walls. If he could get up there without any serious check, he saw that he could forestall Montcalm by forming a line less than three quarters of a mile from the city, where the promontory was narrow enough to be commanded by his small army, and where the mixed regulars and irregulars of New France would be forced to meet his homogeneous British red-coats on a flat and open ground. The French were on the alert everywhere along the north shore, from the Falls up to Pointe aux Trembles, a distance of 29 miles — except just at the Foulon itself. They could not tell what Wolfe was about, nor where the bulk of his men were, behind the impenetrable screen of the ubiquitous British fleet. They were naturally very apprehensive of another desperate attack on their trenches; they were well prepared against an assault upon the town, which was so strongly fortified by nature; while the constant movement of the fleet, and occasional landings from it, in the vicinity of Pointe aux Trembles, 22 miles up, made them think that any new plan would probably take the form of an advance in force by land from somewhere thereabouts. One man, indeed, besides Wolfe, was thinking of the Foulon, and that man was Montcalm. On 5 September he had sent the regiment of Guienne to the Heights of Abraham, but Vaudreuil withdrew it on 7 September, and left no defense there, except the puny Samos battery near Sillery Point, and 100 militiamen at the top of the Foulon, under the treacherous Vergor. Even on 12 September, the very eve of the battle, Montcalm had again ordered the same regiment back, this time to the Foulon itself. However, Vaudreuil had again countermanded the order, saying, "We'll see about it to-morrow." But Wolfe himself was up there on that morrow! [For some account of the battle of the Plains of Abraham, see COLONIAL WARS IN AMERICA; MONTCALM; QUEBEC; WOLFE.]

The winter at Quebec, after its capture, was a terribly trying one for the little British garrison; and so many men died of scurvy that, in the following April, when de Lévis marched out of Montreal with 7,260 men, expecting several thousand more to join him on the way, Murray could only muster 3,886 effectives. There was a second battle of the Plains, in which Lévis defeated Murray, who in less than two hours lost over one third of his men. A second investment followed, and Lévis was in the act of advancing to storm the walls, when the vanguard of the British fleet suddenly entered the harbor. The French had now no choice of action. They hurriedly abandoned their camp, and retreated, in all haste, on Montreal, both by land and water. Then, step by step, the final British advance converged on the doomed colony. Murray came up steadily from Quebec, in close touch with Lord Colville's squadron, which the French had absolutely no means of resisting. Haviland advanced from the south by way of Lake Champlain; while Amherst, with the main army, came down the Saint Lawrence from the Lakes. When the united British army, 17,000 strong, actually landed on the Island of Montreal, the few remaining Canadians deserted Lévis in a body, and he found himself left with only some 2,000 of the faithful French regulars. The capitulation of New France occurred two days later, on 8 Sept. 1760. The French troops were deported. The Canadians had already dispersed. The American militia went back to their homes. The fleet sailed away to their stations. The British regulars took up their winter quarters. And the New Régime began. The Seven Years' War was one of the most pregnant events in history; and its results have continued to exert a vast determining influence on the fortunes of every world power, down to the present day. In Europe it foretold the ultimate decline of France and Austria, and the ultimate rise of Prussia to the leadership of Germany. But its significance for the English-speaking people lies mainly in the fact that it was the most truly imperial war they ever waged; and its most dramatic episode — the battle of the Plains of Abraham — will serve to mark forever three vital stages in three great epochs of modern times — the passing of Greater France, the coming of age of Greater Britain, and the birth of the United States.

ARTHUR G. DOUGHTY,
Dominion Archivist, Author of 'The Battle of the Plains," etc.

5. Canada — Under British Rule to Confederation (1760-1864). At the moment when Vaudreuil (see VAUDREUIL-CAVAGNAL, PIERRE) capitulated to Amherst (September 1760) (see MONTREAL — *History*) there were no English in Canada save the troops and a few civilians who had come with them. But, outwardly at least, this act of surrender placed the French Canadians and the English colonists in America on the same basis as subjects of the British crown. One sovereignty was thus established over a vast area where dwelt two races whose origin, sentiments, faith and institutions marked them off from each other in the sharpest contrast. A century later the face of the situation was profoundly changed. The American Revolution had created a second sovereignty in this region at a time when the population of Canada was almost wholly French. and yet by 1860 the Canadian English had come to outnumber the Canadian French. The maintenance of the bond with

Great Britain, the rise of the United States and the influx of English settlers are the broad conditions which have affected the progress of Canada since the cession.

Three years elapsed between Vaudreuil's surrender and the Treaty of Paris, which confirmed Great Britain in the possession of her American conquests. During this interval the country remained under military rule, and though Gen. Murray's relations with the subject population were marked by sympathy and tact, it was impossible that a sense of permanence should be inspired by such a document as the Act of Capitulation. The text of the treaty, in its turn, left many essential points unsettled, especially in the domain of law, and not until 1774, when the Quebec Act was passed, did French Canada receive from the British crown and Parliament a charter upon which it could rely. The first 14 years of British rule were, however, a time of great importance in that the experience gained during this period suggested legislation which continues in force at the present day. The mass of the French population, *seigneurs* and *habitants* alike, accepted the change of masters in a spirit of resignation. Their courageous support of Montcalm and Lévis is proved by a large variety of evidence. They seem to have shown as much daring as the French regulars, together with a superior knowledge of the country and a better grasp of the tactics which were suited to American warfare. That the deportation of the Acadians had stimulated their resistance to the British is more than probable, but in any case loyalty and patriotism would have led them to make a brave defence. Once beaten, they accepted the situation frankly and were not encouraged to rebel by that restlessness of the Indian tribes which took form in the conspiracy of Pontiac (1763-4) (see PONTIAC). The contrast between their docility and the growing disaffection of New England and Virginia did not fail to leave an impression on the official mind both in Quebec and London. The result was that when difficulties arose between them and their English fellow-subjects the government was not disposed to espouse the cause of the latter. Apart from the retention of their property, the guarantee of their religious institutions was the question which came nearest to the hearts of the French Canadians. By Article 27 of Vaudreuil's Capitulation it was agreed that "the free exercise of the Catholic, Apostolic and Roman religion shall subsist entire, in such manner that all classes and peoples of the towns and rural districts, places, and distant posts may continue to assemble in churches, and to frequent the sacraments as heretofore, without being molested in any manner, directly or indirectly." This clause of the capitulation was confirmed at the Treaty of Paris (see PARIS, TREATIES OF) with the condition "as far as the laws of Great Britain permit," but any restriction which might seem to be placed upon religious toleration by the foregoing phrase was nominal rather than real. The communities of nuns were not disturbed even at first, and after a few years of deprivation large estates were restored to the Sulpicians. The Jesuits also would probably have received a confirmation of title but for the special circumstances attending their suppression in France shortly before the Treaty of Paris and their general suppression in 1773. As

it was, the scrupulous care with which governors like Murray and Carleton (see CARLETON, SIR GUY) carried out the policy of toleration reassured the hierarchy and made it a firm supporter of British rule.

Had there been no other factors in the political life of the country than the government and the French Canadians, the first years of the new order would have been peaceful enough. It is true that the commission of Governor Murray (1763) was marked by ill-advised expressions. For example, the members of such an assembly as might hereafter be convened by the governor and council "shall, before their sitting, take the oaths mentioned in the act entitled 'An Act for the further security of his Majesty's person and government, and the succession of the Crown in the heirs of the late Princess Sophia, being Protestants,'" etc. In other words, every French Canadian who aspired to sit in the assembly of the colony must subscribe a declaration against transubstantiation, the adoration of the Virgin and the sacrifice of the mass. Such language (borrowed from the laws of England) would have seemed offensive had political life become active in the colony, but as no assembly was convened till 1791 it remained shorn of practical significance. Real difficulty sprang less from the disaffection of the "new subjects" than from the presence in Canada of certain "old subjects," that is to say, of the English who had come to Quebec and Montreal at the close of the war. Here was a fresh element in the population, small but active and bitterly opposed to the recognition of French institutions. Prior to the outbreak of the Revolution an influential proportion of the English living in Canada were natives of the American colonies who had moved to the northern part of the British dominions with the design of enriching themselves through the fur-trade. Their antagonism to the French was prompted partly by race and religion but also by dislike of French law and contempt for the conservatism of French character. Their plea was that since the fate of war had given Canada to the English the country should be made in the fullest sense a British possession. These "old subjects," but just arrived in the colony, would have uprooted French law, discouraged the use of the French language, destroyed or fettered the hierarchy, and incidentally have made themselves a dominant class. At no time before the passage of the Quebec Act could they have formed more than a fiftieth part of the population, but, owing to the strength with which they raised the cry of the ruling race, they enjoyed a position of great prominence. Unfortunately for the success of their programme, they incurred the dislike of the local authorities by an extreme radicalism of utterance and demeanor. Carleton, in particular, discountenanced them and held them to be infected with the mutinous views which were becoming so increasingly prevalent in the English colonies.

Sir Guy Carleton, afterwards Lord Dorchester, is the most striking figure in Canadian history from the Conquest to the days of responsible government. The close friend and confidant of Wolfe, he began his career as a soldier. Circumstances made him an administrator and he ended by reaching the full stature of a statesman. Those who approve the policy embodied in the Quebec Act will, of course, rank him higher than he will be ranked by those who deny the wisdom of that far-reaching measure, but regarding the quality of his mind, the firmness of his temper, and the justice of his intentions, opinion is undivided. After serving with distinction in the campaigns of 1759 and 1760 he returned to Canada as administrator of the government in 1766. In 1769 he became governor-in-chief; and from this date until his final surrender of office in 1796 he remained among all Englishmen the leading authority on Canadian affairs. The Quebec Act was the fruit of information and advice which he supplied; it was he who repelled Montgomery's invasion, and the Constitutional Act of 1791 which gave the colony its first training in self-government was largely his work. During a formative period of 30 years his policy of generosity towards the defeated race was the policy of the British government. Murray, whose language reflects personal resentment, says of the "old subjects": "I report them to be in general the most immoral collection of men I ever knew." Carleton, though less severe in his strictures, formed a highly unfavorable opinion of them and expressed his preference for the French Canadians with perfect freedom. According to his forecast, which in this respect has not been altogether justified, the valley of the Saint Lawrence was unlikely to be inhabited by any large number of Englishmen. Most of the English who were then resident in Montreal and Quebec had come in the train of the troops and would probably return with them. The traders had not been successful and would soon disappear. To quote his own words, it remained that "barring a catastrophe too shocking to think of, this country must to the end of time be peopled by the Canadian race." The Canadians, he continues, "are not a migration of Britons, who brought with them the laws of England, but a populous and long-established colony." Thus believing that the French could never be supplanted he concluded that their customs, ecclesiastical and legal, should be retained. A detailed statement regarding the Quebec Act will be found elsewhere (see CANADA — THE QUEBEC ACT). Here it need only be said that its territorial provisions were extremely distasteful to the English colonies and that its concessions to the French Canadians have supplied a solid groundwork for their loyalty to the British Crown. Whether Sir Etienne Taché was correct when he said, "The last gun that will be fired for British supremacy in America will be fired by a French Canadian," must be termed matter of conjecture; but the sentiment which prompted him to speak so fervently was gratitude for the Quebec Act. This measure provided an unobjectionable oath of allegiance, sanctioned the Roman Catholic religion in so far as it did not conflict with the king's supremacy, and ordained that "in all matters of controversy relating to property and civil rights, resort shall be had to the laws of Canada as the rule for the decision of the same." Hence English criminal law and French civil law were established side by side in the regions covered by the act. When Upper Canada was constituted in 1791 it received the common law of England unmodified and unlimited, but French civil law still survives in the Province of Quebec.

At the same moment when Great Britain was endeavoring to meet the wishes of her French subjects, the question of Canada was becoming an additional source of friction between the mother country and her older colonies in America. Not only did the English colonies disapprove a policy which heaped such favors upon the French, but some of them resented the king's disposition of the recently acquired territory to the west of the Alleghanies. In the royal proclamation of 1763 nothing was said concerning the government of this valuable region, an omission which disappointed Virginia and other colonies ambitious of expansion. Worse still, the Quebec Act handed over the western country to Canada, shutting out the older colonies and rendering an immense area subject to the operation of French civil law. At any time such action would have provoked remonstrance; in 1774 it quickened the resentment which had been gathering force ever since the passage of the Stamp Act. How prominent Canada was in the eyes of the Continental Congress may be inferred from the decision, speedily formed, to gain control of it by force. The sequel was a severe blow to the Revolutionary cause. Montgomery (see MONTGOMERY, RICHARD), advancing by Lake Champlain and the Richelieu, occupied Montreal and nearly succeeded in capturing Carleton, who was the head and front of the defense. Simultaneously Benedict Arnold (q.v.) made his way through the woods of Maine to the valley of the Chaudière and despite dreadful privations appeared before the walls of Quebec. On the arrival of Montgomery from Montreal a siege was commenced, but the sufferings of the troops proved so intolerable that it was decided to carry the town by assault. On 31 Dec. 1775, the two generals made a desperate attempt to force a passage through the streets of the Lower Town. During the fight which ensued Montgomery was killed and after a sharp encounter Carleton drove out the invaders with heavy loss. The war in Canada dragged on during the greater part of 1776 but before the close of that year the Americans had been repulsed at all points and the issue, so far as it affected Quebec was decided. On the British side the hero of this campaign is undoubtedly Carleton, who maintained his position against heavy odds; but considered historically the attitude of the French Canadians is no less interesting. The clergy and the *seigneurs* used their influence actively on behalf of the British; the *habitants* remained neutral. It seems clear, however. that without the aid which he received from Canadian volunteers, Carleton would have been beaten, and it is also manifest that the French peasantry did not respond with any heartiness to the appeals of the Continental Congress.

While Montgomery's invasion is an exciting and critical episode, the Revolution affected Canada still more profoundly by causing the emigration of the United Empire Loyalists (see LOYALISTS). Into the nature of their differences with the American patriots it is not necessary to go, beyond stating that each party represented a definite point of view and was separated from its opponents by the wide gulf of contrasted ideals. The Loyalists represent the conservative element in the Thirteen Colonies and undoubtedly embraced within their ranks a large proportion of distinguished. educated men. Including those who left their homes while the war was in progress and those who came northwards after its close, we may place the total number of Loyalist emigrants in British North America at nearly 40,000. More than half of these newcomers settled in the neighborhood of the Bay of Fundy, partienlarly in the region which now forms the province of New Brunswick, but at least 10,000 of them made their way to Canada. It is at this period that important settlements are first established upon the northern shore of Lake Ontario, where a population exclusively English possessed itself of lands which the French had explored but never colonized. The population of Canada was further modified between 1783 and 1800 by the opening up of the Eastern Townships, a district situated on the northern border of New Hampshire and Vermont, with a short frontier on the northeastern corner of New York. Here the original settlements were made in part by Loyalists but more largely by emigrants from New England who moved north in quest of cheap land. At the close of the Revolution, then, the race question in Canada begins to assume a very different aspect from that which it had worn before the passage of the Quebec Act. Then the English population constituted a mere handful. Now, through the steady influx of immigrants from the United States fresh portions of the country are developed and a nucleus is formed round which later accessions of English-speaking colonists will range themselves. As the bulk of the new population professed the deepest affection for Great Britain, a separatist movement was not to be thought of, but it was equally certain that disagreement would arise within Canada over the issue of legal and ecclesiastical institutions. As early as 1785 the Loyalists resident on and near Lake Ontario sent a petition to England praying that they might enjoy "the blessings of British laws and British government and of exemption from French tenure of property." Carleton, now Lord Dorchester, was eminently suited to effect an arrangement between the Loyalists and the French Canadians, towards both of whom he was drawn by feelings of strong sympathy. After establishing in 1788 special regulations for the administration of districts inhabited by Loyalists, he assisted in the preparation of the Constitutional Act (1791), a measure which was designed to do away with the grievances of the Loyalists without creating a sense of grievance among the French. Under the Constitutional Act, which in the British Parliament received support from Pitt and Burke, a division was made between Upper and Lower Canada. For each of these provinces the act created a legislative council and an assembly, but no independent power with respect to tariff legislation was granted. Clergymen of whatever denomination were declared ineligible to sit either in the council or the assembly, but freedom of worship was guaranteed to the Catholics in perpetuity and the Protestant clergy received as an endowment one seventh of all waste lands belonging to the crown. Some idea of the relative importance of the two provinces at this date may be gathered from the fact that in Lower Canada the legislative council was to consist of not less than 15 members, while in Upper Canada the minimum number was placed at seven. A still greater disproportion existed between the number of members in the assembly — a minimum of 50 in Lower Canada as op-

posed to a minimum of 16 in the other province. Although grave troubles afterwards arose under the operation of the Constitutional Act, the measure seems to have encountered little opposition in Canada save from the English minority in Quebec, whose leaders looked forward with discontent to the prospect of political inferiority. No tests excluded Roman Catholics from the council or the assembly, and after the elections of 1792 the latter body in Lower Canada contained 34 French as against 16 English members.

Within six months from the day when the first Canadian legislature met, Great Britain joined Austria and Prussia in their war against revolutionary France. While British North America was not drawn into the vortex of England's contest with the Convention, the Directory and the Napoleonic Empire, it felt the influence of that long struggle in more ways than one. Besides Canada's part in the war of 1812, which was a by-product of the larger strife, one must mention the attempt of French republicans to make trouble for England in Lower Canada, and a certain neglect of Canadian issues by the home government which may be ascribed to the pressure of more critical questions in Europe. At about the same time when Genet was endeavoring to raise the United States against Great Britain, agents of the National Convention sought to provoke a disturbance among the *habitants* of Quebec. The execution of McLane and the imprisonment of Fréchette for life are the chief incidents in this abortive undertaking. Of much more consequence was the failure of the colonial office to watch the working of the Constitutional Act in Lower Canada. The council, whose members were appointed by the governor, speedily became a stronghold of English interests. The assembly, whose members were chosen by popular vote, assumed no less speedily a French complexion. As the council considered itself to represent the dominant power and was quite free from the control of the assembly, it tended to assume a tone which was extremely offensive to the French majority in the other house. The Constitutional Act gave representation but did not recognize the principle of ministerial responsibility to the popular branch of the legislature. In an age of mounting democracy, this type of government was open to fierce attack, especially when the question was complicated by racial prejudice. Between 1791 and 1812 the most maladroit governor of Lower Canada was Sir James Craig, who for three years (1808–10) carried on open strife with the assembly and finally had recourse to a *coup d'état*. In his assault upon the 'Canadien,' a nationalist newspaper, he unwarrantably arrested Bedard as the publisher of treasonable articles, dismissed Panet, the speaker of the assembly, from the militia, and eventually imprisoned six of the leading members of the assembly. Craig's action was due to a sincere belief that the French Canadians were disloyal because they criticized the council, but the effect of his measures was most unfortunate, since the Colonial Office could not fail to be identified with them in the public mind. The political life of Upper Canada during the same period was unmarked by any notable dissensions. Through no fault of her own, and simply by virtue of being a British possession, Canada was drawn into the war of 1812 (see UNITED STATES — THE WAR OF 1812). Among the causes of the war, the only one which concerned her directly was the ill-founded contention that English officials were trying to stir up an Indian attack upon the American colonists in the West. From the outbreak of hostilities till the conclusion of peace Canadians of both provinces conducted the defence of their country in a truly patriotic spirit. The Loyalists were stimulated by the memory of their expatriation and fought enthusiastically for the British cause under Brock and Sheaffe. The French Canadians guided by Bishop Plessis (see PLESSIS, JOSEPH OCTAVE) of Quebec, himself the descendant of a New England captive, displayed an attachment to England which had not been so clearly apparent at the time of Montgomery's invasion. De Salaberry's victory at Chateauguay showed that the French peasants had not lost their ancestral courage or their knowledge of the methods to be pursued in guerilla warfare. At Queenstown Heights (see QUEENSTOWN) and Lundy's Lane (see LUNDY'S LANE, BATTLE OF) the Loyalists acquitted themselves well in the open field. The war of 1812 contributed much to the formation of a patriotic sentiment which was independent of provincial bounds.

The political unrest which affected most civilized countries in the generation following the Battle of Waterloo, appeared in Canada under an acute form and was not quieted until after the Rebellion of 1837. The Upper Province, free from the problem of a mixed nationality, had hitherto been undisturbed by violent disputes, but as time went on the Constitutional Act was found unsatisfactory — or rather, the act gave no redress of the grievances which grew up under the existing system of administration. In Lower Canada the claims of the assembly found an eloquent champion in Louis Joseph Papineau (q.v.), the most prominent French Canadian of his generation. It should be clearly pointed out that the grounds of discord were different in the two provinces, but the development of agitation went on simultaneously and the two movements, each proceeding from its own set of conditions reacted strongly on each other. English radicals and French radicals were brought into close sympathy as agitators by their common opposition to the established order. In both cases there were minorities whose privileges depended upon the maintenance of the constitution and the bitterness of the struggle for responsible government was intensified by the presence of these vested interests. In Upper Canada the contest between officialism and reform did not centre round the first principles of politics so much as it did round the exercise of power by certain individuals. The main strife was one of old settlers against new, with several minor issues coming in to complicate the situation and render it disagreeable. A few leading families of Loyalist stock constituted a local oligarchy from which were drawn the chief officials of the colony. As the members of this ruling class belonged almost wholly to the Anglican Church, and used their influence freely to benefit the Anglican clergy, they provoked the opposition of the dissenters who formed a majority of the more recent immigrants. The political solidarity of Anglicanism and the "Family Compact" led both to be denounced by the champions of responsible gov-

ernment — Robert Gourlay, William Lyon Mackenzie, Dr. Rolph and Egerton Ryerson. The clergy reserves were represented as a symbol of government by privilege and Roman Catholics united with Protestant dissenters to demand the application of their proceeds toward the support of schools. It will be seen that these sources of discontent were hardly of a fundamental character, but the population of Upper Canada was not one to bear political grievances lightly. In Lower Canada the situation was more intricate and more serious. When the excitement caused by the War of 1812 had died away, the relations between council and assembly resumed their former rancor, while the assembly and the executive became involved in a protracted dispute over the power of the purse. By the financial provisions of the constitution certain revenues were at the disposition of the crown and the assembly had control of certain other revenues which originally were much smaller. Through the development of the colony, the assembly's share of the revenue kept growing larger in proportion to that of the crown, and at the same time the radicals discovered that they could place the government in a very awkward position by refusing their assent to appropriations. The advantage which the assembly possessed through its power to keep up a perpetual dispute over fiscal matters was used with much tactical cleverness, though perhaps with less genuine patriotism than might have been desired. The fight against privilege (and there can be no doubt that the council had excessive privileges) was accompanied by a revival of racial feeling among the French Canadians. With Papineau for their leader the nationalist majority in the assembly used language which showed that their brightest ideal was not summed up in subjection to British sway. Gradually the English element was eliminated from the ranks of the reformers, and though a few politicians of English and Irish name supported Papineau during the disturbances of 1837 his sole hope of success lay in the support of the French. Under such a system of government as was provided by the Constitutional Act, the role of the governor assumed a degree of importance which it does not possess at present in any self-governing colony of the British Empire. Had abler men than Sir Francis Bond Head and Lord Gosford represented the crown in Upper and Lower Canada during the acrimonious debates of 1836, there might have been no breach of the peace. As it was, risings took place in both provinces, the radicals of Upper Canada being encouraged by some initial successes which the party of Papineau had gained in the autumn of 1837. The Rebellion cannot be dignified by the name of a war since the engagements were accompanied by slight fatalities and the issue was never in doubt. The French Canadian peasants who took the field were defeated at Saint Charles and Saint Eustache, and in Upper Canada the appeal to force collapsed after a farcical skirmish at Montgomery's Tavern, near Toronto. In 1838 fresh disturbances occurred at a few places in Lower Canada, only to be repressed with a promptness which showed the futility of further resistance. Apart from the domestic bitterness occasioned by these outbreaks, they were the cause of a diplomatic crisis, in that the activity of Mackenzie's American sympathizers led to strained relations between Great Britain and the United States. The burning of the Caroline (q.v.) and the fight at Pelee Island (q.v.) were international episodes of the first importance.

The best fruit of the Rebellion was Lord Durham's Report and the transformation of British colonial methods which followed it. In 1838 the Earl of Durham (see DURHAM, J. G. L., EARL OF) was sent to Canada as governor-general and given a commission to investigate the state of the country. The blue-book in which he described the causes of the Rebellion and suggested remedies for obvious evils is held, by common consent, to rank first among the documents of the Colonial Office. Whether the text was written by Durham or Charles Buller, or by both in conjunction with Gibbon Wakefield, the report as it stands is a classic in political literature. The two essential recommendations which it makes are that responsible government be freely conceded and that the provinces of Upper and Lower Canada be reunited with a view to allaying the racial discord which had raged so fiercely in Quebec under the Constitutional Act. The Union Act of 1840 was the immediate sequel of Lord Durham's proposals and a first step towards the political consolidation of British North America. The salient feature of this constitution may be defined as the transfer of political power to an assembly which was chosen on a very democratic basis, though not by universal suffrage. The legislative council, with members appointed by the crown, was retained but real authority centered in the popular branch of the legislature. To the assembly each province contributed 42 members and it was provided that a general election should be held every four years, subject to the chance of a dissolution by the governor-general during the interval. The Union Act had imperfections and inconveniences which finally furnished a strong argument in favor of confederation, but under it (1840-67) Canada gained a political training which was invaluable and escaped from the worst of the anomalies that had provoked the Rebellion. At first the act seemed to favor the English, inasmuch as French ceased to be an official language; but in 1848 it was restored to its former position of parity. With the establishment of democratic principles the party system reached a maturity which before had been unknown in Canada. Lafontaine (see LAFONTAINE, SIR LOUIS H.), Baldwin (see BALDWIN, ROBERT), McNab (see McNAB, SIR ALAN N.), Macdonald (see MACDONALD, SIR JOHN A.), Brown (see BROWN, GEORGE), Cartier (see CARTIER, SIR GEORGE E.), and many other accomplished politicians found free scope for their talents in the ranks of Reformers or Conservatives. Much of the legislation which marks this period (for example, the abolition of seigniorial tenure in 1854) was designed to adjust the life of Canada to modern conditions, even at the cost of parting with a picturesque institution or discarding an ancient view of the relations which should subsist between church and state. The Reformers, however, had no exclusive possession of the liberal spirit, for it was a Conservative administration which abolished the clergy reserves. Education in both provinces began to receive an amount of attention which had not been paid to it hitherto. Judged also by economic results the progress of

Canada under the Union Act was extremely satisfactory.

As the confederation movement is considered separately (see CANADA—THE CONFEDERATION), it will be unnecessary to discuss here the causes which suggested to Canadians a larger political conception than is represented by the Union Act. But in conclusion some reference should be made to the progress of Canada as affected by its relations with England on the one hand and with the United States on the other. From 1840 onwards the country enjoyed self-government in all matters of a local or domestic character, but it remained a colony and never considered itself to be a co-ordinate part of the British Empire. In the second quarter of the 19th century the fixed belief of English ministers was that colonies are a kind of fruit which drops off the parent tree when it has become ripe. The rebellion of 1837 coming when liberal principles were triumphant in the mother country prompted the adoption of a generous colonial policy which has never been abandoned, but its effect upon the rise of imperial sentiment was only indirect. Yet notwithstanding the absence of a full partnership between Canada and England, the loyalty of the colony was signally illustrated during the first century of British rule. Despite friction between races, the pressure of foreign invasion and the existence of political privilege in both provinces, the attachment of an overwhelming majority of the population to British institutions and the British connection remained firm even throughout the decade that preceded the rebellion. The division which the American Revolution created between the United States and British North America, could not fail to affect the fortunes of Canada in the most vital manner. Apart from the importance of the Loyalist immigration, the rise of a new and powerful state on the southern frontier brought into being conditions which thenceforth could never be ignored. As early as 1775 a small but active minority would have preferred membership in the band of revolted colonies, and ever since there have been individual advocates of annexation. But this propaganda has never spread widely or gone beyond the theoretical stage. In addition to the war of 1812 and the irritation caused by the filibustering raids of 1838, the question of boundaries was for long periods together unpleasantly prominent. The Webster-Ashburton Treaty of 1842, though it was received with great dissatisfaction in New Brunswick and Quebec, did good rather than harm by settling an irritating dispute. The Reciprocity Treaty of 1854, which was largely due to the efforts of Lord Elgin, brought the two countries into more direct contact than ever before, promoted friendly intercourse, and was a source of prosperity to Canada during the 13 years of its existence (1854-67). Its repeal by the United States was in large measure due to a resentment which had arisen from Great Britain's attitude during the American Civil War. The fact remains that in its birth year the Dominion of Canada was excluded, by action not its own, from reciprocity in natural products with United States. See CANADA—UNDER FRENCH RULE; CANADA—THE CLERGY RESERVES; CANADA—SEIGNORIAL TENURE.
CHARLES W. COLBY,
Professor of History, McGill University.

6. Canada — The Maritime Provinces to Confederation. The early history of the three eastern sea-board provinces of Canada is an important incident in the long dramatic struggle between France and England for world-empire. (See CANADA.) Their place on the map linked their destinies with those of New France on the one hand, and of New England on the other. The tale of their settlement and organization into communities is part of a greater story, the overflow of European peoples into the New World. They have been profoundly affected by great events outside their borders, European wars, and political changes on this continent; and if they have not as yet reacted on the history of the world, as a nation they are young; their history is yet to make.

Nova Scotia.— In 1604, Sieur de Monts, a Huguenot gentleman adventurer and trusted soldier of Henry IV., made a voyage to the great Atlantic peninsula, which is now called Nova Scotia (q.v.). He was to found a colony in return for his broad patent to trade in furs. After exploring the rugged eastern and southern coast-line, he discovered the beautiful Annapolis Basin, and wintered, suffering terribly, on the island of Saint Croix. The next year, after searching as far south as Cape Cod for a suitable place, he turned back to the Annapolis Basin, and planted his colony on its shores, naming the cluster of huts Port Royal. The colony did not flourish, and, in 1613, it was destroyed by a force under Argall from the newly founded colony of Virginia.

The French name for the country was Acadie, a musical native word, often mistaken for Arcady. It means "abounding in," as in Shubenacadie, and covered an ill-defined tract of wilderness, comprising what is now Nova Scotia, New Brunswick (q.v.), and part of Maine. In 1621, this territory was granted by James I. to Sir William Alexander (q.v.), a Scottish gentleman, to be colonized on a plan distinctly mediæval. Alexander was to parcel out his province in "baronies," six miles long by three deep, to gentlemen, who were to "plant" them with settlers. Each baronet was to have almost regal powers within his own domain, even striking his own coinage, and "repledging" criminals from the King's courts of law to his own. The colony was to be a new Scotland, even by a legal fiction, part of the county of Edinburgh. One small settlement was actually made on the Annapolis Basin in 1629, but it came to nothing, and the whole province was handed back to France in 1632, by the treaty of Saint Germain-en-Laye. Still, to this day, the Baronets of Nova Scotia form a distinct order in the British aristocracy, and the provincial flag bears the azure saltire of Sir William Alexander and the ruddy lion of Scotland ramping in gold.

For 22 years, the French had undisputed possession, and succeeded in planting a colony on the feudal pattern, as far removed as possible in principle from republican New England. The government was military and paternal; the land was held by seigniors and tilled by a docile tenantry. The *habitants* were chiefly unlettered peasants from the country about Rochelle. In Acadie, they found broad marsh lands beside tidal waters, resembling the country they had left. Here they settled, built long dykes of logs and earth on the river banks, and peacefully cultivated the rich fields the salt tides fertilized.

Population grew slowly. In 1671, there were 378 persons in the colony; in 1683, 600, chiefly about Port Royal. An interesting census of Acadie was made in 1686 by de Meulles, intendant of New France, who visited the scattered settlements and numbered the families, acres of cleared ground, boys, girls, fusils, horned cattle, swine and sheep in each. The population had grown to 915, including 30 soldiers at Port Royal. Although thickest about the seat of government, the Acadians had spread along the coasts and as far as Beaubassin at the head of the Bay of Fundy. They were a race of husbandmen, growing wheat, pease and rye; and raising cattle, sheep, swine and poultry; they also built small boats for the shore fisheries. An observer relates that when the manure-heaps beside their barns grew unmanageable, they moved the barns. Few women came with the first settlers, who married with the Indians, and always lived on friendly terms with them. Priests of the Sulpicians and Missions-Etrangères were their trusted guides both before and after the English conquest. See CANADA — ACADIAN REFUGEES.

Throughout this period, the chief interest lies in the shifting fortunes of one family. Claude de St. Etienne, Sieur de la Tour, a ruined Huguenot gentleman of Champagne came out early in the 17th century, with his son, Charles Amador, a boy of fourteen, to better himself in the new colony. After Argall's raid, the two lived for years like Indians among the Indians. Their stronghold was Fort Saint Louis at Cape Sable, on the inlet now known as Port Latour. In 1627, Charles petitioned Louis XIII. to be made commander of the coasts of Acadie, and his father took the petition to the French Court. On his return voyage the next year, he was captured by Kirk's fleet and taken prisoner to England. Here he became a friend of Sir William Alexander, married a maid of honor to Queen Henrietta Maria and was made a Baronet of Nova Scotia, as well as his son, with large grants of land to support their titles. With two men-of-war, he came back to Cape Sable, where Charles held the one solitary post for France in Acadie. By persuasion, and at last, by force, he strove to win his son over. Failing in both, he begged permission to live in Acadie, rather than return to England in shame, or to France and lose his head. This Charles granted, and Claude with his bride, his effects, two valets and two *femmes de chambre* disembarked. In 1635 Denys the historian found them living there in comfort.

Louis XIII. rewarded Charles' loyalty by making him his lieutenant-general in Acadie. In 1632, Isaac de Razilly took possession of the province in the name of France; his chief officers were La Tour the younger and D'Aulnay Charnizay. On the death of de Razilly in 1636, the territory was divided between the two; La Tour established himself in baronial state at the mouth of the Saint John, with his Huguenot bride, while D'Aulnay made Port Royal, across the bay, his headquarters. D'Aulnay intrigued against his rival at the court of France and procured his recall to answer charges of fraud upon de Biencourt, his former commander. La Tour refused to go to France, and tried to enlist the Puritans of Boston on his side. Failing them, he obtained help from Rochelle; the "proud city of the waters" sent him supplies, munitions of war and 140 soldiers in the Clement. When the Clement arrived in the spring of 1643, she found Fort Saint John closely beset by D'Aulnay and 500 men. Being closely pressed, La Tour and his devoted wife slipped through the blockade by night, reached Boston safely, returned with reinforcements and drove D'Aulnay back to Port Royal. But D'Aulnay's hate was not easily tired. He went to France to raise another force against his enemy. At the same time, Madame La Tour went to Rochelle, to gather aid for her husband. D'Aulnay heard of her presence there and tried to have her arrested, but she escaped to England. On her return voyage, she almost fell into his hands a second time, but at last she reached Saint John again in safety. In April 1645 D'Aulnay besieged her here, while La Tour was in Boston. After a gallant defense, the fort was taken by treachery. D'Aulnay, to his everlasting shame, broke the terms of surrender, hanged the garrison and forced Madame La Tour to witness the death-struggles of her faithful soldiers, with a rope about her neck. Three weeks later, the heroine died of a broken heart. La Tour became a wanderer on the face of the earth, exploring and border-fighting in New France, while his rival ruled his province unchecked and built it up with a strong hand until he was drowned in the Annapolis River in 1650. La Tour hastened to France, confuted the old charges against him and obtained his former possessions in Acadie. Returning he married the widow of D'Aulnay and seemed about to enjoy a period of prosperity, when the province was once more taken by a Cromwellian fleet, in 1654. Undismayed by the sudden change of fortune, La Tour sailed for England and secured a joint grant of the territory with two English colonels, Crowne and Temple, to whom he soon sold out his interests. At the Restoration, he was made a baronet of Nova Scotia, and closed his chequered and adventurous career in 1672.

In 1667 Acadie was again restored to France by the treaty of Breda. The story of the French administration is not a pleasant one. It is a tale of incompetence, corruption, pettiness, and is told at length in the pages of Parkman. The priests accuse the officials, the officials accuse the priests. The luckless colony was raided time and again by pirates, and by expeditions from New England to avenge the Haverhill and Deerfield massacres. Canada could only be reached by long and dangerous traverse of the wilderness, but Acadie was only a few days' sail from Boston.

French rule came to an end during Marlborough's wars. In September 1710 a force from Boston, chiefly of provincial troops, under Col. Francis Nicholson, took Port Royal after a brief but gallant defense by Subercase. Port Royal at once became Annapolis Royal, in honor of the reigning sovereign, but it was not until 1713, by the Treaty of Utrecht (q.v.), and surely against the will of Louis XIV., that Acadie became finally a part of the British Empire.

From 1710 to 1749 a small British garrison at Annapolis Royal held the province tenaciously for England. The fort, though well placed, and a Vauban plan, was ruinous; the earthen walls were always crumbling into breaches; the gun-carriages would not bear the guns; the barracks were roofless; for years the men were without bedding, stockings, great-coats or medicines. Supply-ships from England came once a year and brought provisions for nine months instead of twelve. The hostile population would not take New England money for their corn and cattle; the home authorities would not honor the governor's drafts; the Boston merchants refused credit. During Walpole's long peace England seemed to forget the lonely garrison, while the French priests were agents of the French government, undermining English authority. From 1720 on, Louisbourg, the new French city on the island of Cape Breton, was yearly growing in power, millions of livres were spent on its defences, for France was bound to win back her lost province. All the time, convinced of its importance to the empire, one discouraged English governor after another held doggedly to his post.

The government was military, not civil, for the Acadians being Roman Catholics were, by the laws of England, incapable of voting; but at least one official regretted that they could not be given representation. They were governed by their deputies, the "ancientest" and most reputable men of each parish, chosen every year on or about 11 October. These were responsible for the good behavior of their districts and for the execution of orders transmitted by the governor-in-council. Philipps, colonel of the 20th regiment, was governor for almost this entire period. He visited the province twice, but resided mainly in London, while lieutenant-governors, chiefly regimental officers, Armstrong, Cosby, Mascarene, administered the colony. The governor was supreme; but to assist him, he had a small council, whose functions were advisory and executive. These officials did their best to advance British interests, giving the litigious Acadians justice in their endless disputes, and making wise suggestions for the improvement of the colony, which must have been doomed to gather dust in the Duke of Newcastle's closet of unopened despatches.

On the outbreak of the war of the Spanish Succession (see SUCCESSION WARS) the men of Massachusetts rose and by splendid audacity struck down the stronghold of French power, Louisbourg; but that glorious adventure belongs to the annals of New England rather than of Nova Scotia. In the summer of 1744, gallant old Mascarene sustained two hot sieges in his ramshackle fort of Annapolis Royal; the first force was led by young Belleisle and other Acadians; the second, by Du Vivier, a descendant of Charles de la Tour. In 1746, Ramezay encamped against him, awaiting D'Anville's armada, but did not fight. The same winter, he surprised Noble's force at Grand Pré, and killed, wounded, or took prisoner nearly 200 men.

When the war ended by the treaty of Aix-la-Chapelle in 1748, Cape Breton was restored to France, and Louisbourg, the Dunkirk of America, resumed its old attitude of menace to the very life of the English colonies. Then at last, sluggish England moved to save the key to her possessions over-sea. Nova Scotia was to have an effective garrison to counter-check Louisbourg. In June 1749 a fleet of 13 transports, bearing some 3,000 colonists, and escorted by the sloop-of-war Sphinx, reached the great three-fold harbor of Chebucto, long known for its excellence to French and English mariners. The leader of the expedition was Col. Edward Cornwallis, twin brother of the gay Archbishop of Canterbury, and uncle of the Lord Cornwallis, who surrendered at Yorktown. He had seen service at Fontenoy and Preston Pans, and although his military reputation was afterwards clouded by his share in the Rochefort and Minorca fiascos, he did his work as a city-builder well. The new military post, Halifax (q.v.), was quickly laid out, the land cleared, the population organized into a militia and a rough line of stockade and block-house run round the streets of tents and log-huts. In spite of the character of the settlers, trade-fallen soldiers and sailors, and the plague that carried them off in hundreds; in spite of Indian massacres, opposition from local smugglers, extortions of Boston merchants, discouragements from the home government, Cornwallis made Halifax a place on the map of the world. The founding of Halifax brought about the second capture of Louisbourg, leaving the way free for Quebec (q.v.) and the downfall of French power in America. Emigrants from Old and New England flocked to the new city. In 1750 and again in 1752, some hundreds of settlers came from the Palatinate. After a brief stay in Halifax, they were transferred to the island-studded bay of the La Hève, the old headquarters of de Razilly, where they have grown into a race of hardy fishermen, whose town, Lunenburg, is the Gloucester of Canada.

In 1752, Cornwallis returned to England crippled by rheumatism, but his successors, Hopson and Lawrence, built strongly on the foundation he had laid. Their great problem was the growth of French power in the fortress of Louisbourg and in the Acadian population. Under English rule, the *habitants* were far happier than under their old masters. The nominal government at Annapolis Royal had been powerless for good or evil. Its authority did not extend beyond a cannon-shot from the walls of Fort Anne. It was precisely under English rule that the Acadians increased and multiplied and, beginning to press upon the means of subsistence, spread outward, round the Bay of Fundy to the marsh-lands on the further shore. Their law-suits were nearly always over disputed lands, or boundaries. In 1755, they numbered about 10.000 persons. England and France were then mustering all their forces for the coming struggle known to history as the Seven Years War. No one could foretell that it would be final or which country would win. England seemed to be at the lowest ebb of fortune and spirit. Brown's lugubrious *Estimate* predicted her immediate downfall. France seemed strong in the New World; she had hemmed the disunited English colonies in with a chain of posts from the mouth of the Mississippi to Louisbourg. She had never ceased to regret the loss of Acadie or to plan for its recovery. The province was the pivot of the whole situation in the east. In these circumstances, the presence of the alien French population in it constituted a grave danger. The claim has been set up that they were neutrals; they had this idea themselves; but this strange notion was simply due to the impotence of the British government. They were no more neutrals than the people of Alsace and Lorraine were after their transfer to Germany in 1871. They were British subjects by conquest, by treaty, by the formal taking of an oath of allegiance and by the common law of nations, but they refused to consider themselves as such.

They might be French subjects again by another war, or the return of the Pretender. Whether they left the province or remained in it was not a matter of indifference. If they stayed, they afforded a shield to hostile operations; if they were free to go, they would strengthen and feed the garrison of Louisbourg. In this dilemma, the old proposal of Shirley's was renewed, their deportation. In the autumn of 1755, after Braddock's defeat gave the signal for war, this was done. The idea originated in New England and was carried out by New England men, acting under the orders of Gov. Lawrence. At Grand Pré, Pisiquid, Chignecto, and Annapolis Royal, the men were called together and made prisoners, and placed on board the transports; their families followed them. The embarkation consumed long weeks. Finally the ships sailed and distributed the unhappy people among the Atlantic colonies. In all, some 7,000 persons were in this way removed from the province. Opinions differ as to the measure. The French theory is the natural brutality of the English; one writer finds his reason for it in the greed of Lawrence to seize on the belongings of the poor peasantry. The general English view is that it was a war measure, cruel as all war is, but imperative for self-preservation; and this theory has the support of Parkman.

With the deportation of the Acadians came peace with the Indians. In 1761, Argimoosh, "the great witch," and his braves buried the hatchet in Halifax and washed the war paint from their bodies. Now for the first time, settlers were safe outside the pickets of the city; and the country began to fill up. Emigrants from Connecticut occupied the waste lands of the Acadians. Highlanders from Caithness and the Western Isles settled about Pictou harbor. Presbyterians from the north of Ireland found homes in Colchester. Before and after the Revolutionary War, thousands of devoted Loyalists came to the province, some to remain, some to pass on. Shelburne, a city of these exiles, numbering 10,000 at one time, passed away like a gipsy encampment. The long wars of peace began with countless inroads upon the wilderness. In a century the Acadians had scarcely cleared 300 acres. Now farms and settlements were eating into the forest, and hamlets were springing up beside the empty harbors. Before the end of the century, the great industries of shipbuilding and the fishery were in their vigorous infancy. The American Revolution left few marks on the history of the province: efforts were made to bring the colony into revolt with the rest; one daring man planned the capture of Halifax, and some sympathizers with the rebels were tried for treason. There was even something like a tea riot in Halifax; but the conservative forces held the province firm. Halifax prospered, as it always did in war-times, through supplying the army and navy, and the sale of the many prizes brought to port. With the return of peace, the tide of prosperity promptly ebbed. In three great wars since its founding, Halifax was a nest of privateers, which brought large returns to their owners.

Colonial government was at first military. All power was vested in one man, the governor, or his lieutenant-governor, who was usually a soldier. To advise him, he had a council, and his instructions contemplated a legislative assembly. As the Acadians were incapable of representative institutions, they were governed through their deputies. Members of the old council were sworn into the new one by Cornwallis, when Halifax became the seat of government. His large instructions empowered him to summon assemblies and make laws; but the first Assembly was not elected until 1758. From this time, the chief power passed from the govcruor to the council, a small côterie of Halifax officials and merchants, appointed for life, who sat in secret session and were not responsible to the people. The powers of the Assembly were curiously limited, and friction between the two bodies was constant. Governor succeeded governor, almost always an army officer with high Tory views of prerogative and military conceptions of his office. He was gently guided through his unfamiliar civic part by permanent officials in the council like Richard Bulkeley, who came out as aide to Cornwallis and died provinicial secretary in 1800. The tone of society as well as government was conservative, not to say reactionary. This state of things lasted until well into the fourth decade of the 19th century. With its large military and naval population, and the merchants who lived by supplying them, Halifax was in many respects an English garrison town in America. In the first session of the House of Assembly, the Church of England was established by law; the first college was modeled on Oxford, and its statutes required subscription to the Thirty-nine Articles both at matriculation and on taking a degree.

The agitation for reform began outside, for the country was pitted against the city. Jotham Blanchard, editor of the 'Colonial Patriot,' was perhaps the first critic of the existing order. The Rev. T. McCulloch, the Scottish "Seceder" missionary, who founded Pictou Academy and became the first president of Dalhousie College (q.v.), was another early reformer. But the man who brought reform to pass was Joseph Howe (q.v.), Nova Scotia's darling son, perhaps the most interesting personality in Canadian history. He was born at Halifax in 1806 of Loyalist stock. His father was king's printer, and, after some scanty schooling, he was apprenticed to his father's trade. In 1835 he was editor and owner of the 'Nova Scotian' newspaper. On New Year's day it contained a letter signed "The People," accusing the Halifax magistrates, in plain terms, of pocketing public money. Their indignation was extreme and they began a libel suit against the daring editor. If truth is libel, Howe had no case; and no lawyer would undertake it. Howe conducted his own defense, and by a brilliant address to the jury secured a triumphant acquittal. From that hour he was the idol of the people, whose cause he had espoused. On the other hand, several hot upholders of the existing order challenged him; he fought one duel, and, having proved his courage, wisely declined further argument by pistol. Howe was a good example of the popular tribune, emotional, eloquent, social, with the faults of such a nature, but possessing tact withal and the statesman's insight into great problems far beyond the ken of provincial politicians. On such questions as the union of the remaining British American colonies, communication between them, the federation of the empire, Howe was far in advance of his time, and his ideas were formative.

Henceforth, his career was in politics, rather than in journalism. Elected member for Halifax in 1836, he at once attacked existing abuses in a series of resolutions, which served chiefly as a programme of reform. Soon afterward he began an important correspondence with Lord John Russell, the colonial secretary, on the difficulties of local government. As a result, the latter instructed Sir Colin Campbell, the governor, to introduce certain of the changes suggested by Howe. This Sir Colin refused to do, and Howe began an agitation which led to his recall. He was succeeded by Lord Falkland, whose remedy for the trouble was coalition in the council. Four of the old council were dismissed, and four Liberals, Howe among them, took their place. But the two interests were irreconcilable: Howe and his friends soon resigned, and began to lay before the people the evils of the irresponsible system. In the election of 1847 Howe and his party swept the country. The new Assembly passed a vote of want of confidence in the council, which thereupon resigned in disgust. A cabinet was formed of the triumphant liberals and the principle of responsible government was established.

The situation of the colonies remaining to Britain on this continent, in the first half of the 19th century was not cheering. Upper Canada was largely uncleared forest, with struggling towns and widening clearings: Lower Canada was alien in speech and religion; both passed through the throes of rebellion. The great West was supposed to be uninhabitable. The Provinces by the sea were poor, thinly settled, each with its own government and its own tariff wall against the rest. The 20th century dawns on a united and prosperous country stretching from the Atlantic to the Pacific. For years Howe pointed out the value of union, for the object lesson of the Great Republic was hard to mistake. But here, as in the case of the Thirteen Colonies, before and after they achieved their independence, each province had its own pride, interests, and jealousies. Besides these, the geographical barriers to union seemed insurmountable; but the locomotive engine changed the face of affairs and provided the solution of the problem. The universal fever for building railways reached the Provinces. The first railway in Nova Scotia united Windsor, Halifax, and Truro; the first in New Brunswick, Saint John and Shediac. A bolder idea was to join the provinces, inland and seaboard, by an intercolonial railway. If united for commerce, why should not the colonies be united for government?

It cannot be said that anywhere in the Maritime Provinces was there a popular movement in favor of union. It was the thought of a few strong, far-seeing men, with powers of persuasion, like Macdonald in the West and Howe in the East. Nova Scotia has the honor of leadership in bringing about the Charlottetown conference. When the question came up in 1867, Howe was in opposition, and Tupper carried the resolution through the House. By a curious irony of fate, Howe was now led to combat the very measures he had fought for so long. He took advantage of his opponent's failure to submit such an important measure to the verdict of a popular election and he roused the people into fury against confederation. They were bought and sold, he told them, "for 80 cents a head, the price of a sheepskin." In the next election, the great issue was repeal of the union, Howe carried the country, and Tupper was the only Conservative returned. Howe tried every legal means to detach his province from the union, but the British Government refused to reconsider the measure it had just sanctioned, and Howe would not appeal to Washington, or have recourse to arms. He sought "better terms" for his province from the Dominion Government, and entered the Macdonald ministry to assist in working out the problems of the new experiment in government. Though not a consistent, Howe was a great man; with all his faults, he loved Nova Scotia well, and Nova Scotia will long cherish his memory.

New Brunswick.— The waterway of the Saint John as a great Indian road, attracted the attention of the French fur traders early in the 17th century. La Tour fixed his headquarters at its mouth. It is still the main artery of the Province. There were also French settlements on the rivers and harbors, such as the Miramichi, the Restigouche, Baie Verte. Petite Rochelle was partly fortified; the town at Beaubair's Point had 200 houses and a chapel. These settlements were not permanent. There was a small colony from Massachusetts at Maugerville on the Saint John in 1760; but the history of New Brunswick as a political unity begins with the close of the American Revolutionary War.

In some respects, the struggle of the Thirteen Colonies for independence was a civil war: for all the colonists were not of the same mind. Some of the best regiments on the King's side were raised in America. For instance, Fanning, the second governor of Prince Edward Island, at one time Judge of the Supreme Court of North Carolina, raised and commanded "The King's American Regiment." When the British cause was lost, such forces were disbanded, and the citizen soldiers, impoverished by eight years of war, could not or would not live under the new government. Many of the official class, the Episcopal clergy and their humble followers were also on the losing side. For the defeated, there was no mercy; the fierce republicans would not let them live in the country. After the surrender at Yorktown (q.v.) thousands of these unfortunates flocked to New York and other seaports. No provision was made for them in the terms of peace; but public sympathy was aroused on their behalf, the British Parliament took generous measures for their relief, Sir Guy Carleton stood their friend. Ships were provided to carry them away, large grants of land were made to them in the loyal colonies, with tools, supplies and provisions for one, two, or three years. Some went to England, the great majority found homes in the northern wildernesses. There some thirty thousand exiles, many of the educated and cultured classes, found refuge. In American history these are the Tories, traitors to their country; in Canadian history, they are the United Empire Loyalists, the makers of the new Dominion. More than any other class of emigrants, they formed present Canadian sentiment and institutions.

The great emigration took place in 1783. On 18 May a fleet of 19 transports, with some 3,000 Loyalists on board, reached the mouth of the Saint John. Here a great stream of 450 miles pours through a narrow breach in the rocks into a small harbor, where the flood-tide rises 26 feet.

and ebb leaves the great ships aground. All round are desolate hills masking the fertile region beyond. This unpromising site the Loyalists chose for their city. They were men of the 8th, 98th, 194th Regiments, the New Jersey Volunteers, and the Queen's Rangers. The grantees' lists show good substantial English names. The "fall fleet" brought 1,200 more, and Parr-town, so called in honor of Gov. Parr, of Nova Scotia, began its career with a population of 5,000. Politically, it was situated in Sunbury County, Nova Scotia. Soon the Loyalists showed active discontent at Gov. Parr's delay in making out their grants, and in giving them representation in the House of Assembly, and, in spite of his opposition, they succeeded in persuading the British government to erect their county into a separate province with a royal governor, council and House of Assembly of their own. This was done in 1784, and the province of New Brunswick was created by royal charter, with Col. Thomas Carleton, brother of the famous Sir Guy Carleton (q.v.) for governor. His commission and instructions were practically the same as those given to Cornwallis in 1749. This council of 12 members exercised both executive and legislative functions. The first House of Assembly, of 26 members, was elected, not without riot, in 1785, and met for the first time in the following January. In this year, Parr-town was incorporated as Saint John (q.v.); it was the first city in British America to receive a charter. It is modelled on the charter of New York, and gives the Mayor the office of garbling spices and the right to appoint the bearer of the great beam. No emigrant or other person could sell goods without first obtaining the freedom of the city. From the founding of the province until 1832, no changes were made in the constitution. As in Nova Scotia, the prevailing ideas were high Tory; and popular rights received little attention.

New Brunswick's chief wealth is her great forests; and her two chief industries, lumbering and ship-building, soon sprang up: but agriculture languished. Population followed the waterways, the natural timber roads from the interior. Down to the time of the Crimean War, the timber trade was fostered by British legislation. The province grew, but not steadily; periods of prosperity were followed by periods of depression. Many emigrants brought out by the timber-ships simply passed through to the United States. The Reciprocity Treaty of 1852 was a boon to the Maritime Provinces: its abrogation injured trade.

During the War of 1812, the provinces were harried by privateers; but they were not invaded, like Upper Canada, because New England was opposed to the war. In the provincial sea-ports privateering also throve. Dalhousie College was founded with customs money taken at Castine by an expedition from Halifax. After 1815, settlers from the United States began to occupy disputed territory between New Brunswick and Maine. The boundary between the two, left vague by the treaty of 1783 almost led to war. The northwest line was to run due north from the source of the Saint Croix River to the height of land between the Saint Lawrence and the Atlantic. Instead of one chain of high lands, there are two chains: between them lay the disputed territory, comprising some

12,000 square miles. Under the Jay treaty of 1794, a commission was appointed to determine the line. The Americans wished to extend the due-north line to the Métis River in Quebec: the British wished to make Mars Hill the limit, and they could not agree. Another attempt at settlement was made by the Treaty of Ghent. The King of the Netherlands was appointed arbitrator, but his award was not accepted. In 1839, the difficulty became acute. Some lumber-thieves cut timber on the debatable land; the Governor of Maine sent a sheriff and posse to drive them out, and New Brunswick lumbermen resisted the officers of the law. The squabble roused intense feeling on both sides. The governor of Maine called for 10,000 troops to guard the State's rights. The governor of New Brunswick, Sir John Harvey, sent two line regiments with artillery and volunteers to the scene of action. Novo Scotia voted all her militia and £100,000 to aid the sister colony; the Canadas also proffered help. Gen. Winfield Scott took command of the American forces. He and Sir John Harvey had fought against each other in the War of 1812.' They agreed to a joint ocenpatiou of the disputed territory; and the war-cloud blew by. In 1842, Mr. Baring for England, and Webster for the United States, negotiated a treaty that at last delimited the frontier. Of the disputed territory, Maine got 7,000 and New Brunswick 5,000 square miles. Mr. Baring was made Lord Ashburton for his success, and the treaty is known by his title.

One peculiarity of the colonial status was the appointment of colonial officials by the home government. New Brunswick's case is typical. The Governor, the Attorney General, the Provincial Secretary, the Judiciary, the Customs and Crown land officials were all appointed from England and paid out of the revenues arising from the customs and Crown lands. In 1825, the Legislature was given control of the customs, when it soon discovered that nearly all the revenue went out in salaries. Not until 1848 did the province both receive the revenues and fix the salaries of this department. In 1837, the province took over the revenue arising from the Crown lands on condition of paying the Governor, the Judiciary and the other government officials. The last department to come under provincial control was the Post Office.

As in other colonies, the irresponsible Council became an abuse, and many were the contests between it and the Assembly. In 1832, a second Council was established with executive, but not legislative functions. This was done by the home government in its desire for uniformity in the colonial governments; but the parliamentary principle of majority rule with an executive council or cabinet to carry out the will of the majority were slow in being understood. It was six years later before the executive included a member of the elected Assembly. Slowly the province worked out the problem of self-government. In 1839, when Sir John Harvey read to his Legislature, Lord John Russell's despatch on tenure of office, and unlike the Governor of Nova Scotia was in accord with its proposals, the Assembly, after full debate, actually refused the boon of responsible government. In 1848, however, the modern system was in essential particulars recognized by formal resolution. Charles Fisher, and L. A. Wilmot, afterwards Judge and Lieutenant-Governor, were the lead-

ing Reformers, and two of the royal Governors, Sir Howard Douglas and Sir John Harvey, were in complete sympathy with the popular movement.

New Brunswick was represented at the Charlottetown Conference, where the preliminaries of Confederation were discussed. At the Quebec Conference, the leading men of the opposition as well as of the party in power were delegates. The Seventy-two Resolutions then agreed upon were to be submitted to the various Legislatures for their approval. Before the New Brunswick Assembly could vote on them, it was dissolved; and in the new House, a large majority were pledged to oppose them. This led Nova Scotia to withhold the Resolutions, as no vital union could be effected with the upper provinces that left out New Brunswick. However, when the House opened in 1866, the majority committed themselves to the policy of union in the speech from the throne. The House dissolved on the issue, and, sentiment having changed, in the new election, the unionists were returned by a large majority. New Brunswick is one of the four original members of Confederation. See CANADA—CONFEDERATION; NEW BRUNSWICK.

Prince Edward Island.—The large crescent-shaped island in the southern part of the Gulf of St. Lawrence is supposed to have been discovered by Cabot, and afterward by Cartier, who named it Isle Saint Jean. After the conquest, it was still called Saint John's Island until 1780, when the local legislature named it New Ireland, an act disallowed by the British Government. In 1794, it was re-named Prince Edward's Island in compliment to the Duke of Kent, the father of Queen Victoria. After the treaty of Utrecht, Acadians from the main land settled at the southern central harbor and named it Port La Joie, the present Charlottetown. It was governed from Louisbourg. In 1752 the population was 1,354. Three years later, after the fall of Beausejour and the expulsion of the Acadians, many took refuge there. At the fall of Louisbourg in 1758, the population was at least 4,000 souls, in four thriving parishes. The fertile "Garden of the Gulf," as the islanders love to call their little sea-girt province, was even then worthy of th'. name. Casgrain calls it a second Acadie: for hence also the Acadians were expelled. When Capt. Holland made his survey in 1764, he found only 30 Acadian families "on the footing of prison__," and a tiny British garrison in a miserable fofts'

In 1763, the year of its cession to England, Lord Egmont proposed a plan of settlement worthy of Sir William Alexander in its feudal character. One feature was a chain of baronial castles from one end of the island to the other; but the plan was never carried out. In 1767, the entire island was divided into 67 lots or townships, of some 20,000 acres each, and granted, by lot, in one day to a number of influential Englishmen, on the old condition of settling so many emigrants within a certain time; they were to pay a perpetual quit-rent, or land-tax. Here began the curse of the absentee land-lord, which laid the island under a blight for more than a century. At first, it was annexed to the government of Nova Scotia, but in 1768 it was, on the petition of a majority of the proprietors, erected into a separate province. In 1770, the first royal Governor, Col. Patterson, arrived with his official staff, whose salaries were to be paid from the quit-rents. The formative ideas here were also high Tory. Roman Catholics were not permitted to settle; no schoolmaster from England might teach without a license from the Bishop of London. Population grew slowly; for few of the proprietors fulfilled the conditions on which they got the land. In 1773, the first House of Assembly was elected. Its first act was to confirm all the past proceedings of the Governor and the Council.

On the outbreak of the Revolutionary War, two American vessels, sent to cruise in the Gulf for British ordnance store ships, raided Charlottetown and carried away some prominent officials. For this Washington cashiered the delinquent officers and released the prisoners with expressions of regret. Another raiding expedition from Machias came to nothing, and the island remained free from molestation till the close of the war. In 1781, proceedings were begun in the Supreme Court against the townships in arrears with quit-rents, and various holdings were escheated and sold, it was thought, without due notice to the landholders. The unimproved waste land was an obstacle to colonization; the owners neither planted settlers nor paid the quit-rents, on which the revenue depended. The landlords argued for the defense, that some of them were officers on active service, that the war had prevented settlement, and that the lands were sold to persons on the ground at absurdly low prices. In rebuttal, Patterson urged that in the midst of a disastrous war, both money and purchasers were scarce; the Island might have been captured or ceded back to France. He admitted that he bought up escheated land, but held he was within his rights as a citizen in doing so; he had also, at his own risk, saved out of the sales, various lots for the absentee owners. In response to various petitions from the proprietors, the home government granted them relief, and sent a draft bill to Gov. Patterson, making the sales voidable. This he was to submit to the Assembly, but he suppressed it for two years. A new Assembly was elected in 1784. It resolved to complain to the King against the governor for disposing of the lands so hastily, when he dissolved it.

The war was now over; the exiled Loyalists were pouring into Nova Scotia, and Patterson hoped to divert the desirable stream of emigration into his own province. Many Loyalists came; by special favors he secured them to his interest, settled some of them on the lands sold in 1781, and in 1785, secured an Assembly certain to support him. It passed an act approving his conduct in escheating the unimproved estates, but the home government disallowed the act and recalled the disobedient official. In 1786, the governor submitted at last the English draft act, already mentioned, to the Assembly, which passed it with haste, as also another act of the Governor's framing restoring the escheated lands to the rightful owners, but saddling them with heavy expenses; this the home government disallowed and dismissed the members of the Council concerned in it.

The new Governor, Edmund Fanning (q.v.) arrived in November, but Patterson refused to vacate his office, and the winter was spent in the quarrels of these two kings of Brentford: but in the spring, Fanning was firmly established. The escheated lands remained in the quiet possession of their purchasers, some of whom came to terms with the original grantees. Fanning was a native of New York, a graduate of Yale, and a D.C.L. of Oxford. Through the Revolutionary War, he commanded the King's American Regiment and was twice wounded. In his administration, the land question smouldered. The chivalrous Earl of Selkirk, who also planted settlements in Upper Canada and the Northwest, brought out, in 1803, 800 of the Clan Ronald Macdonalds and settled them about Point Prim.

Fanning was succeeded by Des Barres, a Swiss officer in the British service, famous for his amours and his great age; he jumped over a settle when he was more than a hundred years old. His administration was uneventful, but not so that of his successor. Charles Douglas Smith, brother of the famous Sir Sidney, who foiled Napoleon at Acre, was a fine example of the old-fashioned high Tory royal governor. His first address to the Assembly, when it met in November 1813, was insolent and dictatorial. In the following January, he prorogued it and did not convene it again until 1817. Between this and 1820, the Legislature was three times assembled and dissolved, after short sessions, by this exponent of personal rule. His proceedings in regard to the quit-rents were also oppressive. In 1818, in opposition to the express commands of the home government, Smith enforced the payment of quit-rents in arrears. His action, however, the British government disallowed, and ordered part of the exactions to be refunded. Then, for three years, no attempt was made to collect the odious tax; in some instances, payment was refused by the Receiver-General. In 1823, another effort was made by the governor to enforce payment. The Gaelic-speaking Highlanders of King's County were required to pay dues that seemed obsolete, or give promissory notes at 10 days. In the depth of winter, they must haul their farm produce to Charlottetown and sell at a sacrifice to meet these demands. Without a legislature, the people petitioned High Sheriff MacGregor to call public meetings for the discussion of grievances. The gathering at Charlottetown drew up an address to the King, rehearsing a long list of charges against the Governor, and requesting his recall. Smith retorted by opening a libel suit in the Court of Chancery, over which he himself presided, against the committee on the King's address in Queen's County. His object was to prevent the petitions reaching England, but the custodian of them escaped to Nova Scotia. For merely publishing an account of the proceedings, the editor of the local paper was brought into the Court of Chancery for libel. When he revealed the names of the writers, they were admonished by the chancellor-governor in the vein of Judge Jefferies. This energetic ruler, who shook his fist at the Speaker of the Assembly and gave him three minutes by the watch to adjourn the House, was recalled in 1824, when he had brought his long-suffering province to the verge of rebellion.

Governor succeeded governor; the Island grew in population and prosperity; fisheries and husbandry throve; but the land question was an open sore. It had now become complicated by the fact that the original proprietors had died and bequeathed, or had transferred their rights in the Island. In 1859 Sir Samuel Cunard (q.v.), the Halifax merchant who founded the famous line of steamers bearing his name, proposed that the whole question be referred to a commission of three members, one to be appointed by the Crown, one by the Island Assembly, and one by the proprietors. To this all agreed. Howe was the nominee of the Assembly. The commission sat in the Colonial Building in Charlottetown, examined many witnesses, though not on oath, and heard counsel on behalf of both parties. They afterwards visited the shire towns and acquired a vast amount of information on the difficulties. Their report is dated 18 July 1861. It condemns the original method of granting the Island, commends the land purchase act, by which the Selkirk and Worrell estates had been acquired for the people, and considers some such system to be the solution of the vexatious problem. It recommends the British government to guarantee a loan of £100,000, which would enable the local government to enter the open market for the purpose of estates. But the home government refused the loan, and the landlords refused to be bound by the findings of the commission. The old difficulty remained until the Island came into the Confederation in 1873, when the Dominion government placed $800,000 to the credit of the province for the purchase of estates, and the local legislature made the sale of estates, on evolution of commissioners compulsory.

Charlottetown was the scene of the historic conference of delegates from the maritime provinces to discuss union, when the representatives of the Canadas came knocking at the door, but the Islanders were not in favor of any change in their status. There was prejudice, the conception of a new nation was hard to grasp, and the main issue was befogged by parish politics. Although Islanders took part in the Quebec and London conferences also, the Island remained outside Confederation until 1873, when the crippling of the provincial means by extensive railroad building led the people to a reconsideration of the matter. The Dominion Government gave generous terms, and the little province while losing nothing of autonomy, entered into a larger national life. See Canada — Confederation; Canada — Since Confederation; Canada — Constitution; Canada — Agriculture; Canada — Fisheries; Canada — Manufactures; Canada — The Forests and Lumber Industry; Canada — Minerals; Canada — Geography; Prince Edward Island.

ARCHIBALD MACMECHAN,
Professor of English Literature, Dalhousie College, Halifax.

7. Canada — Confederation. In 1837 there took place two rebellions; one in Upper and British, the other in Lower and French, Canada, simultaneous, but almost unconnected, and scarcely united in sympathy, since the British Protestants of the upper province were by no means fraternally linked with the French of the lower. In Upper Canada the rebellion was a rising of a democratic party, including many of the most recent colonists and some from the United States, against the personal rule of the imperial governor and the domination of a political circle nicknamed the Family Compact, and consisting largely of U. E. Loyalists, which monopolized public offices and emoluments. Its leader was Lyon Mackenzie, a man honest and

right in his main aim, if responsible government is right, but wanting in wisdom and capacity as a leader. The object of the extreme wing was an independent republic or annexation to the United States. That of the less extreme wing was responsible government on the British model. The political crisis and the outbreak of civil war were brought on by the indiscretion of an inexperienced governor, Sir Francis Bond Head, who (1836-8) threw himself into the arms of the Family Compact and the Tory party. In Lower Canada the rebellion was a rising of the French, the conquered race, who formed the great majority, against the monopoly of office and power by the British and conquering race, exercised largely through a council appointed by the imperial governor. Its object was the assertion of French equality and right. It had been preceded by a series of angry controversies between the French patriots and the governor with his British councillors and the Colonial Office at their back. Both rebellions were quelled (1838) with ease and without much bloodshed; that in Upper Canada by the loyal militia, that in Lower Canada by the Queen's troops. There were few executions, but some of the leading insurgents were driven into exile. The constitution of Lower Canada was suspended, but that of Upper Canada was not.

The Liberal party in the mother country was now in the ascendant, having carried Parliamentary reform. It looked with sympathy on the struggle of the Canadians for free institutions. Lord Durham (q.v.), son-in-law of the Whig prime minister, Earl Grey, and though an aristocrat a strong Liberal, was sent out (1838) to study the situation. In a report of remarkable ability, which has been regarded almost as the gospel of colonial liberty, he decided in favor of extending to Canada responsible government on the British model, requiring the governor, instead of ruling personally, to be guided, like the British sovereign, by the advice of responsible ministers, who were to be designated by the choice of the people. The report at the same time recommended the reunion of the two provinces, a measure the sure result of which its author imagined to be the complete ascendency of the more powerful race, the destined heir, in his opinion, of the whole North American continent.

Durham, having exceeded the limits of his power, and incurred censure by condemning some ex-rebels to banishment of his own authority, his mission was cut short (1838) but his main recommendations were carried into effect (1839). The provinces were re-united, the measure being carried in the lower province, the constitution of which had been suspended, by the fiat of the Crown; in the upper province, after some debate, by a vote of parliament. Responsible government was introduced. The governor was instructed thenceforth to be guided, like the British sovereign, by the advice of his ministers, who were to be responsible to the people.

In a despatch from Lord John Russell (q.v.) (5 Feb. 1841) the governor-general was instructed to call to his councils "those persons who, by their position and character, have obtained the general confidence and esteem of the inhabitants of the province," and "only to oppose the wishes of the Assembly when the honor of the Crown or the interest of the empire is deeply concerned." There soon followed a general amnesty, with return of exiles, and Lyon Mackenzie sat in Parliament under the new régime.

About the same time, and by the action of the same general forces, including the ascendency of the Liberal party in Great Britain, responsible government on the same model was introduced in the maritime provinces. In Nova Scotia the change was brought about largely by the eloquence of the patriot leader Joseph Howe (q.v.) (1838).

The transition was smoothed by the wisdom of the new governor, Poulett Thompson, Lord Sydenham (1839–42), a man of business, trained in commercial life, who adapted himself steadily and with general success to the introduction and working of the new system. Sir Charles Bagot, who followed (1842–3), though a Conservative, took the same line. But the idea of colonial self-government had hardly taken root in the policy of the Colonial Office or in the minds of British statesmen. Sir Charles Metcalfe (1843–5), the next governor, had been trained in the imperial government of Hindustan, and brought with him the impression that in every dependency the governor was still personally supreme and responsible for the choice of his ministers and for their policy. Acting upon this principle, he attempted to form a ministry (1843) of his own without regard to party designation. A political storm, with furious pamphleteering and ministerial interregnum, were the results. The upshot was failure on the governor's part to form an effective ministry, and his consequent defeat. The colonial secretary, Lord Stanley, however, emphatically endorsed the governor's conduct, and was authorized with his own approbation to convey the personal approbation of the Queen.

The new system was finally installed and brought into order by Lord Elgin (q.v.) (1847–55), one of the best and wisest servants of the empire, who entered fully into the spirit of responsible government, contenting himself with the exercise of an informal influence, rendered important by his character and ability. He could even flatter himself that he did more in this way than he could have done with the formal powers of the governor. He came in, however, for the last of the storm. The Liberal party, now in power, passed an act called the Rebellion Losses Act (1849), indemnifying those who had suffered losses by the destruction of their property in the suppression of the rebellion. This the Tories regarded as the indemnification of the rebels. Their cry was taken up by the Tory party in Great Britain. Elgin gave his assent to the act, reluctantly it seems, in compliance with the rule which required him to be guided by the vote of Parliament and the advice of his responsible ministers. The Tories, now playing the part of insurgents in their turn, rose, burned the Parliament House at Montreal (1849), with its irreplaceable archives, and stoned the governor-general, who had a narrow escape from their fury. Elgin, however, remained firm and was supported by the home government. After this his reign, or rather his term, was peaceful and generally popular, though more popular with the Liberals than with the Tories. The triumph of the free trade policy in Great Britain, depriving Canada of her colonial privileges, while she remained fet-

tered by the Navigation Laws and was excluded from the market of the United States, bred commercial depression and discontent. The consequence was a manifesto signed by leading commercial men and pointing to union with the American republic as a remedy in the last resort. To put an end to this movement by removing its cause, Lord Elgin went to Washington and negotiated a reciprocity treaty with the United States (1854). This, following the repeal of the Navigation Acts and the release of the Canadian trade from the fetters which they imposed, restored prosperity, allayed discontent, and put an end to the desire of annexation. (See CANADA — RECIPROCITY BETWEEN CANADA AND THE UNITED STATES.)

After the Rebellion Losses Bill, the most hotly debated of the political questions was that of the secularization of the clergy reserves (1854) (see CANADA — CLERGY RESERVES), tracts of land which, before the revolution of 1837, when the Church of England was established in Canada, had been set apart for the maintenance of the clergy of the state church. After a long struggle, secularization was carried, and the state church, with its privileges, ceased to exist. King's College, Toronto, which, so far as the teaching staff was concerned, had, like Oxford and Cambridge, been Anglican, was turned into the University of Toronto (see TORONTO, UNIVERSITY OF), and thrown entirely open to all denominations. Under Bishop Strachan, the powerful Anglican leader of the day, high Anglicans seceded from the University of Toronto and founded the University of Trinity College (1852). Other churches, during the continuance of the exclusion, had obtained charters for universities of their own, and dissipation of resources not more than sufficient, if collected, to maintain one great university, was the result.

The abolition of the seigniories (1854) in French Canada (see CANADA — SEIGNIORIAL TENURE), relics of the old Bourbon regime, with the oppressive privileges of the seignior, was another change obviously demanded by the new order of things. It was accomplished peacefully, without violation of the rights of property, and with entire success. Another necessary change was the abolition of the aristocratic custom of primogeniture in succession to land, for which was substituted the democratic principle of equal partition, "gavel-kind," as the movers called it. The Tory party, sympathizing with aristocracy, faintly resisted the change. The progress of democracy was further marked by a change in the constitution of the Legislative Council which formed the Upper House of Parliament. Instead of being nominated by the Crown, as it had hitherto been, it was in 1856 made elective.

The party system of government was now in full play, but the principles and relations of parties were far from being definite or stable. There was a Tory party representing the U. E. Loyalists, and the traditions of the Family Compact under the leadership of Sir Allan MacNab, who opposed the secularization of the clergy reserves and the abolition of primogeniture. There were on the other side moderate Liberals under Baldwin and more advanced Liberals under Hincks. But the lines of political party were crossed and perplexed by the nationality of French Quebec. The French Catholics, instead of succumbing politically to British predominance as Durham had imagined that they would, closed their ranks, showed their force, played on the balance between the British parties, and put a Frenchman, in the person of La Fontaine, at the head of the government. For a time it became an understanding that a government, to hold its ground, must have a double majority; that is, a majority both in the British and the French province. The act of reunion had given to the provinces general representation in Parliament, though the population of the French province was much larger than that of the British. Presently the balance of population turned in favor of the British province. The Liberal leaders of the British province, the most pronounced of them at least, then demanded a rectification in its favor. With the political strife about representation by population, "Rep. by Pop.," as it was called, mingled the religious antagonism of the British Protestants of the upper province to the Roman Catholics of the lower. The great advocate of representation by population, and at the same time the extreme exponent of the feelings of the Protestants against the Catholics, was George Brown (q.v.), a Scotch Presbyterian, and founder of the Toronto *Globe*, the most powerful organ of the British Canadian press in those days. On the other side appeared Mr., afterward Sir, John Macdonald (q.v.), one remarkably gifted with the arts of party management, and with an address in dealing with men which in his chief antagonist, George Brown, was wanting. Macdonald supplanted in the leadership of his party the old-time Tory, Sir Allan MacNab (q.v.), Liberalized it, and set it free from all incumbrances in the way of reactionary principle by which, up to this time, it had been weighted in the struggle for place. It was a stroke of strategy something like that performed in England by Sir Robert Peel (q.v.) when, accepting the consequences of the Reform Bill, he changed his party from Tory to Conservative. Between Macdonald and Brown there was, and to the end continued there to be, enmity, personal as well as political. But Brown was no match for Macdonald in playing the party game. Once for a moment, by a casual defeat of the government of which his rival was a member, he set his foot on the steps of power (1858); but he immediately fell again, Sir Edmund Head, then governor-general (1855-61), having, by an unwonted exercise of the prerogative, which Brown furiously resented, refused him the dissolution and appeal to the country which he demanded (1858). Questions and principles of all kinds were crossed by personal ambitions and connections, as well as by the national sensibilities of Quebec, which naturally carried her to the side of the Conservatives rather than to that of the advocates of representation by population, the hot Protestants and the Orangemen. The end, after a rapid succession of changes of ministry, producing a total instability of government, was a ministry with a majority so narrow that it was said that the life of the government depended on the success of a page in finding a member at the moment of critical division. The upshot was a deadlock. The relation between the two races, owing to the persistent attacks of George Brown's party on the French Catholics, had at the same time become critical and dangerous. From this position an

escape was sought by merging the antagonism of British and French Canada in a confederation of all the British colonies in North America. The credit of proposing confederation has been assigned to different politicians, to George Brown, to Sir John Macdonald, to Sir Alexander Galt. Of the party leaders, it was George Brown who first came forward holding out his hand to his rival, Sir John Macdonald, to propose coalition for the relief of the situation. But Mr. Brown's original proposal was not a confederation of all the provinces, but a substitution of a federal for the legislative union between the British and the French province. What Sir John Macdonald, as a strong Conservative and monarchist, preferred was not a federal but a legislative union of all the North American colonies under the British Crown. What all alike wanted was a relief from the situation, and for this purpose a coalition government comprehending the two rivals and enemies, Sir John Macdonald and George Brown, with followers of both, was formed (1864). The fact is that the real author of confederation, so far as British and French Canada was concerned, was deadlock.

The three maritime provinces, Nova Scotia, New Brunswick, and Prince Edward Island, were inclined to a separate union among themselves, especially with a view to a reduction of the expenses of government. A conference of delegates from those three maritime provinces was held at Charlottetown (1864). To that conference delegates were sent by the coalition government of Canada to propose a wider union. The result was a conference at Quebec (1865), at which 12 delegates were present from Canada, 7 from New Brunswick, 5 from Nova Scotia, 7 from Prince Edward Island, 2 from Newfoundland. That conference sat for 18 days and passed 72 resolutions, on which the act of union was afterward based and which each delegation undertook to submit to its own government.

By the Parliament of the two Canadas the scheme was at once accepted and by a large majority, though there was a long debate, in which a speaker of the opposition glanced at the geographical unfitness of the long and broken line of provinces for political union. New Brunswick, not being adroitly approached, at first rejected the scheme, but presently acquiesced. In Nova Scotia the resistance was very strong, but it still remains a mystery by what arguments a legislature elected expressly to oppose confederation was brought round to its support. Brought round, however, the legislature of Nova Scotia was. Howe, after a vain appeal to the British Parliament to set Nova Scotia free, himself took office in the confederation government. Prince Edward Island held out, but came in at last. British Columbia threatened repudiation of the union, till the construction of the Canadian Pacific Railway, which was the condition of her entrance, was assured. Newfoundland still remains unfederated. But a great addition was soon afterward made to the Dominion by the purchase of the Hudson's Bay country now comprising the province of Manitoba and the Northwest Territories. The accession of Newfoundland alone is wanted to complete the scheme of confederation. The scheme having been framed by the colonial legislature, was laid for revision before the British government, and by it embodied in the British North American Act. (30 and 31 Vict. Cap. 3; 1867.)

When confederation was passed, party lines were drawn again. Brown seceded from the confederation government and the political enmity between him and Sir John Macdonald became as bitter as before.

The Federal constitution was never submitted, like the Constitution of the United States, to the people. It was alleged that in a general election which followed, and in which the confederation government was sustained, the people virtually expressed their approbation. But it is obvious to remark that in this election other issues were submitted and other influences, that of party especially, played their part. So that it cannot be truly said that the constitution of Canada has even been distinctly ratified by the Canadian people.

See CANADA — UNDER BRITISH RULE TO CONFEDERATION; CANADA — THE MARITIME PROVINCES TO CONFEDERATION; CANADA — SINCE CONFEDERATION; CANADA — RELATIONS TO GREAT BRITAIN; CANADA — IMPERIAL FEDERATION; CANADA — CONSTITUTION. See also the history of the different provinces in this work.

GOLDWIN SMITH,
Formerly Regius Professor of Modern History of the University of Oxford, and Emeritus Professor of Cornell University.

8. Canada — Since Confederation. On 1 July 1867 there were great rejoicings in Canada for it was the birthday of the new Dominion. But at that time the work of founding a Canadian nation was only begun; much remained to do. As it stood on 1 July 1867 the Dominion included only four provinces: Nova Scotia, New Brunswick, Quebec, and Ontario, (qq.v.) and of these Nova Scotia was profoundly discontented and, since her people had never voted upon the question, desired to withdraw from the confedcration. Nor did Canada possess the entire East. The two important islands, Newfoundland (q.v.) and Prince Edward Island (q.v.) still held aloof; not until 1873 was Prince Edward Island persuaded to join the Dominion, while Newfoundland still stands apart. The vast Northwest, to-day the chief pride and promise of Canada, was not then included within her territory, nor was its entry brought about without discontent and bloodshed. It had long been a hunting preserve for the Hudson Bay Company, but in 1870 by paying to the company £300,000 to extinguish its rights Canada removed every obstacle to her absorption of those regions. In 1871 British Columbia (q.v.) consented to enter the Union, but was long restless and threatened to withdraw unless a transcontinental railway was promptly built. With all these jarring elements assuredly Canada, when confederated, had no real union, and the subsequent work of her statesmen has been chiefly to consolidate her scattered fragments.

The leader who played the chief part in this work of consolidation was Sir John A. Macdonald (q.v.). In many ways, in wit, in intellectual agility, sometimes in cynical carelessness as to the means he used to secure his ends, he was strikingly like Lord Beaconsfield; but whenever the vital political interests of Canada were concerned, invariably, according to his light, he showed a whole-hearted patriotism. He was filled with passionate devotion to the British Crown and treasured for Canada the ideal that she should be a kingdom modeled on that of Great Britain, taking her place on equal terms as an auxiliary of the United Kingdom. He did not favor federal government, and would have preferred to give Canada one all-powerful legislature like that of Great Britain. But in these respects conditions were too strong for Macdonald. His cherished "Kingdom of Canada" became the "Dominion of Canada" in deference to the supposed prejudices of the American republic against a monarchical neighbor, and he was obliged to assent to a federal system because the French in Canada insisted upon a measure of autonomy only to be secured in this way. It was the pending "Alabama" question that made Britain so anxious at this time to defer to the opinion of the United States. This and questions more directly affecting Canada were settled by the Treaty of Washington, 1871 (q.v.).

Macdonald was Prime Minister of Canada for the long period, 1867 to 1806, with the exception of an interval of about five years, lasting from November 1873 to October 1878. Inevitably he did the work of proving the federal system which he had helped to create. There was trouble from the first. When as a result of the bargain with the Hudson Bay Company Canada assumed jurisdiction in what is now Manitoba, some of the settlers already established there objected to being handed over like cattle to a new government. Surveyors sent in by Canada were turned back; officers going into the country to assert Canadian authority met with a like experience; and at last the half-breed inhabitants under their leader, Louis Riel (q.v.), set up a provisional government at Fort Garry, now Winnipeg (q.v.), and defied the Government of Canada. They tried and summarily executed Thomas Scott, a citizen who opposed their proceedings, and they threw other leaders into prison. See RIEL REBELLION.

In 1870 it was not easy for Canada to assert her authority in the remote settlements on the Red River. She might not use for military purposes the territory of the United States, which offered the most convenient route, and she was therefore obliged to send troops through the vast wilderness lying north of Lake Superior. The present Lord Wolseley, then holding a military command in Canada, was chosen to lead a small army to Fort Garry and did the work with brilliant success. After a toilsome journey through hundreds of miles of wild and barren country Wolseley at length reached Fort Garry only to find that Riel and his provisional Government had fled at the approach of the Canadian force. Rebellion crushed, the work of pacification was conducted partly with the aid of Mr. Donald A. Smith, now Lord Strathcona, an official of the Hudson Bay Company. Manitoba soon became a full-fledged province in the Canadian federation and has since played an important part. In view of the present status of Winnipeg, the third city in Canada, with nearly 100,000 inhabitants, it is interesting to remember that it had not even the telegraph in 1870 and that the railway did not reach the town until 1878.

The trouble in Manitoba settled, Canada had next to pacify her remote Pacific Province, separated from her by an immense and almost unpeopled wilderness. In 1871 British Columbia entered the confederation on the condition that a railway across the continent should be begun within two years and completed within ten. At the time the province contained but a few thousand people of European origin, and there were complaints in eastern Canada that the vast expenditure involved in the bargain would burden too heavily the country's resources. But, on pain of her withdrawal from the union, British Columbia insisted angrily that the bargain should be carried out, and her attitude brought to the front the building of the trans-continental line which was to prove of supreme moment to Canada.

That Canada's small population should spend a hundred million dollars on this undertaking was a stupendous proposal; on the basis of the proportionate cost for each head of population a project for the United States to spend $2,000,-000,000 would be its equivalent. But to build the railway was the condition of national existence in Canada, and in the end the thing was done. Not, however, before the project had long disturbed Canadian political life and threatened to overwhelm its promoters with ruin. When the Canadian Pacific Railway (q.v.) was projected Canada was face to face with the question that has perplexed all the progressive states of modern times. Should the railway be a government or a private enterprise? Though a similar line, the Inter-Colonial Railway, connecting the eastern provinces, was a state enterprise, the cabinet of Sir John Macdonald shrank from saddling the country with so vast a burden as a railway to the Pacific, and it was resolved to hand over the task to a private corporation.

In 1872 there was a general election in Canada, and in the session of Parliament which followed the Canadian Pacific Railway Company with Sir Hugh Allan as president, secured a charter to build the road, and with this went also assurances of assistance from Canada amounting to many millions. But when, as a result of the exposure by the Opposition, the fact came out that Sir Hugh Allan had contributed more than $350,000 to Sir John Macdonald's campaign fund for the recent election, this "Pacific Scandal" brought the downfall ·of the Government, which had accepted the obvious bribe. Amidst huge excitement Sir John Macdonald resigned and the Liberals with Mr. Alexander Mackenzie (q.v.) as prime minister took office in November 1873.

For five years the Liberals remained in power. Throwing less energy into the construction of the Pacific Railway than had been promised, they met naturally with discontent in British Columbia. The menace of withdrawal from the confederation was renewed and at length the matter was referred for arbitration to Lord Carnarvon, the colonial secretary, in London. He decided that the original terms were too onerous and proposed new ones under which a transcontinental railway should be opened by the end of the year 1890. When the Liberal Government thought even this almost impossible of accomplishment, "Carnarvon Terms or Separation" became the war cry in British Columbia. Financial depression overtook Canada in 1876-8 and this heightened the difficulty of the question. But in 1876 the Governor-General of Canada, the Earl of Dufferin, visited British Columbia to soothe her discontent, and he helped to tide over the period of danger. It is interesting to speculate whether an attempt to withdraw from the Canadian union would have been resisted, if necessary, by force of arms. Probably the Canadian and Imperial Governments would have agreed in using coercion.

The financial depression that helped to delay contentment for British Columbia produced effects in Canada even more far reaching, for it led to the cleavage of political parties on the question of Protection (q.v.) or Free Trade (q.v.). In 1878 Canada had a tariff of 17½ per cent, which was hardly sufficient for her growing revenue requirements. During a generation she had tried to secure a free exchange of natural products with the United States and in 1854 her governor, Lord Elgin, had succeeded in making a Reciprocity Treaty on this basis. But the Treaty was not long in force and when abrogated at the close of the Civil War a heavy tariff upon Canadian products was soon imposed by the United States. Over and over again Canada tried to secure the reversal of this policy but always in vain. Meanwhile the low Canadian tariff permitted American manufacturers to supply the Canadian market at prices with which the necessarily smaller producers in Canada could hardly compete, and in time the cry for increased Protection was often heard. Had Mr. MacKenzie's Government taken it up in 1878 probably Sir John Macdonald would have rallied his forces under the banner of Free Trade. But when the Liberal leader refused tenaciously to adopt Protection, Sir John Macdonald proclaimed it as a "National Policy" for building up Canada, and the Canadian electorate, forgetting the discredit which attached to him in connection with the Pacific scandal, returned him to power by an overwhelming majority. Since that time Protection has retained its hold upon Canada, for though the Liberals favored free trade they disturbed the system but slightly on their advent to power in 1896. See CANADA — RECIPROCITY BETWEEN CANADA AND THE UNITED STATES.

An era of great expansion followed the adoption of a protective tariff in 1879. A great many factories were established, and the building of the Canadian Pacific Railway was pushed on with unparalleled energy; in 1885, five years before the time named in the cóntract, the last spike was driven in the line connecting Western and Eastern Canada and British Columbia's grounds for discontent were finally removed. Once completed the road's value not only to Canada but to Great Britain was soon apparent. Not only did it unite the Canadian provinces, it furnished a ready all-British land route to the East. The Canadian Pacific Railway Company in time established lines of steamers crossing both the Pacific and the Atlantic, and the project, looked upon as a doubtful possibility in 1878, has now become one of the chief arteries of world commerce.

The completion of the Canadian Pacific Railway was almost co-incident with a second rebellion of half-breeds in the Canadian West. On the banks of the Saskatchewan, not far from a village called Prince Albert, there was a colony of these people. They had long lived remote from the larger world, and when their country was invaded by the pioneers of modern movement, they began to doubt whether they should be left in permanent possession of the lands they had long occupied. Upon these lands they were technically "squatters" for they had no patents and no surveys had been made. When at length Canadian surveyors came to lay out their fields on a uniform plan, disregarding the divisions which they had established, the half breeds protested and demanded that they should be granted patents for their lands as they stood. At Ottawa their protests were filed but remained unheeded. The official mind was aghast at the prospect of land grants not based upon the usual survey; the half breeds could get nothing done and they grew ever more restless at the supposed menace to their rights. Disinterested observers sent to Ottawa warnings of a probable rising but official supineness was invincible, and the result of neglect and delay was that in March 1885 the despairing half breeds attacked a body of police, killed 12 out of 40 engaged, and defied the authority of Canada. Since it was not unlikely that they would be joined by the Indian tribes the outbreak was serious.

The half breed leader was the same Louis Riel (q.v.) who had caused trouble in 1870. On its hands the Government now had a difficult task. As in 1870 it might not send troops through the United States, and the railway on the north shore of Lake Superior connecting Eastern and Western Canada was not yet completed. In bitter March weather, with the thermometer often below zero, the regiments of militia summoned from Eastern Canada, all unprepared by previous hardship to endure the cold, traversed the desolate shores of that frozen region. Sometimes in open flat cars, for more than a hundred miles on foot, they proceeded over the snow. An experienced officer of the expedition declares that the task was more severe than Napoleon's passage of the Alps, for Napoleon had a beaten road and an abundant commissariat, while both were wanting in the Canadian wilderness. The regiments soon poured into the West in overwhelming force and though the few half breeds made a brave stand against great odds, they were quickly crushed. Their Indian allies the Canadian troops wearily followed to their almost trackless haunts, and so the Rebellion was put down. A few of the rebels were hanged; a good many of the Indians were imprisoned; Riel, the leader, was taken, and then his fate became a question of national concern in Canada.

With Riel the French Canadians had ties of faith and of blood. French Canadians had been pioneers in the Northwest and at times they had dreamed of holding that vast region for their language and faith. If fate was against them, if it was the Anglo-Saxon who was occupying the country and in influence was destined to dominate, none the less was chivalrous support due to the few people who stood in the West for the ideals of France and of the Roman Catholic Church. In 1870 Riel had appealed not in vain to the French in Quebec for help in his time of trouble and it was probably the strength of their sympathy which then saved him from the scaffold. Since in 1885 the men who took up arms had more real grievances the Church espoused their cause. In the Province of Quebec Liberals and Conservatives forgot their quarrels to protest in the name of justice and French Canadian nationality against rigorous treatment of the rebel leader, Louis Riel. On the other hand the English demanded that the law should take its course. Riel had led a revolt in which

law-abiding citizens were shot down. If he was a murderer the penalty of murder was his due. The demand was too urgent to be disregarded. Riel was tried; in the eye of the law the penalty of his crime was death, and in November 1885 he was hanged at Regina, the capital of the Northwest Territories. See RIEL REBELLION; see also CANADA — JESUITS ESTATES ACT for another religious and racial question in Canada in 1888–9.

The Government's course in regard to Riel was a defeat for the French Canadian Bishops who had long played an active part in political life. They claimed that even in secular affairs the authority of the bishops was final and that when they spoke the laity were bound to obey. If the Church chose to indicate her desires in regard to the merits of candidates seeking election, it was the duty of the voter to heed the voice of his spiritual directors. Some of the bishops claimed the right to use spiritual censures to influence electors. Newspapers who opposed the wishes of the hierarchy must not be read by the faithful, and when L'Electeur, a daily newspaper in Quebec, opposed the bishops Mandements in 1896 it was denounced from the altar, and under penalty of grievous sin and the refusal of the sacraments all the bishops forbade formally anyone to read it, subscribe or contribute to it, to sell it, or in any manner whatever encourage it. The denunciation commanded obedience and made the continued existence of the paper under its existing name impossible. It promptly became Le Soleil, and seemed to suffer little real injury, but the incident showed the authority claimed and exercised by the bishops.

With this attitude on their part occasions of strife were not likely to be wanting. In 1890 the Manitoba Government passed an Act establishing a non-sectarian system of education. Owing to the peculiar conditions of older Canada the Protestant minority in the Province of Quebec had secured the constitutional right to devote the taxes paid by them for education in support of their own schools. In Ontario the Roman Catholic minority possessed a similar privilege. For some time Manitoba had followed the example of Ontario, but, impressed by the obvious advantages of a uniform system, the legislature passed the Act of 1890 which deprived Roman Catholics of former privileges. At once a vehement agitation broke out. The Federal Government possesses, within certain limits, the right of disallowing statutes enacted in the provinces and urgent demand was made upon the Government of Sir John Macdonald to disallow the Manitoba School Bill. This, on the ground that Manitoba was acting within its constitutional rights, the Government refused to do. Appeal was then made to the courts to determine the authority of the respective Governments in the matter and the case was finally carried to the Privy Council in London, which decided that the Federal Government possessed the right of intervention in regard to the Manitoba schools.

Extraordinary pressure was then brought to bear upon the Federal Government. The hierarchy of the Province of Quebec took up the question with much heat, while the Protestant Province of Ontario was also aroused in support of the opposite side. In 1891, when Sir John Macdonald died, his successors were left with the legacy of the Manitoba School Question.

The agitation dragged on for five or six years. Retreat from their position the Manitoba Government would not, and finally, in 1896, the Federal Government endeavored to put through Parliament a Remedial Bill for restoring to the Roman Catholics of Manitoba the privileges which had been taken away.

It was this question that brought the downfall of the Conservative party so long dominant in Canada, a process accelerated by evidence adduced in 1891 of a share by responsible leaders in the Province of Quebec in the misuse of public funds. In 1896 Sir Charles Tupper (q.v.) became Prime Minister and in a general election appealed to the country to do justice to the minority in Manitoba. On this question many of his Conservative allies broke away from him and he fought a stern but losing contest. The Liberals too were in a difficult position. When Sir John Macdonald's old rival, Mr. Alexander MacKenzie retired from the leadership of the party in 1880 he was succeeded by Mr. Edward Blake, who, in turn, proved unable to overthrow the Conservative chieftain. In 1887 Mr. Blake retired and was succeeded by Mr., afterwards Sir Wilfrid, Laurier. In personal charm and tact the new leader was not unlike his formidable rival, and he had, besides, remarkable gifts as an orator. French Canadian by birth and also a Roman Catholic, it was not easy for him to lead the Liberal party, which was committed unreservedly against interfering in Manitoba. In Mr. Laurier's own Province of Quebec the hierarchy were still unanimous in demanding intervention to re-establish the Roman Catholic schools. The election of 1896, fought chiefly on this issue, resulted in a conspicuous Liberal triumph and it was in Quebec that Mr. Laurier found his most striking support. Either the issue in regard to Manitoba had been obscured or the "*habitant*" wished to assert his right to pass judgment for himself in political matters independent of the views of the hierarchy. At any rate Mr. Laurier became prime minister of Canada. The Manitoba Government made some minor concessions and the matter passed out of view, but an important warning against interfering with the authority of the Province had been given to the Federal Government.

The Liberal party had long championed the cause of freer trade and declared itself the enemy of Protection; it was therefore committed to some modification of the existing Protective system. But, once in power, it found that, since important industries had grown up under the tariff, this could not be changed in any radical manner without ruin to those concerned. While doing something to reduce Protection the Government took a further remarkable step. The year 1897 saw the completion of 60 years under Queen Victoria's sovereignty, and there was a general desire to draw more closely together the different sections of the empire, and thus to assert British unity. In pursuit of this idea Mr. Laurier's government announced that a preference of 25 per cent (later increased to 33⅓ per cent) would henceforth be allowed to countries whose tariff gave a favorable opening to Canadian products. Since Britain alone gave such treatment the preference was confined to her, though other countries might share in it on the terms laid down. Both in England and in Canada the Preferential Tariff aroused great enthusiasm and no doubt it aided in bringing to a

head Mr. Chamberlain's scheme, announced a few years later, for a Preferential Tariff in the mother country for colonial products. See CANADA — BRITISH PREFERENTIAL TARIFF.

In 1898 the Liberal Government had a renewed opportunity to proclaim its devotion to British connection. When war broke out in South Africa and soon proved more serious than had been thought possible, Canada promptly volunteered to send military contingents in reinforcement of the British troops. The contingents saw some service and a good many Canadian soldiers lost their lives. Naturally the French Canadian showed less enthusiasm for what was in large degree a racial war than did the British element. Only a few French Canadians served in the contingents, and some voices protested against Canada's participating in British wars. But the overwhelming opinion of the country supported the rally to Britain's aid; when the Government appealed to the country in 1900 it gained an easy victory, partly upon this issue.

A little earlier the discovery of gold in remarkable quantities in the Yukon Territory, arousing as it did world-wide interest, naturally attracted attention to a part of Canada hitherto thought of little value. The possession by the United States of the adjacent coast of Alaska (q.v.) through which lay the best route to the new gold country, seriously impaired the value to Canada of the territory. The boundary between Alaska and Canada had long been the subject of dispute, the Canadians contending that since, under the terms of the determining treaty, the line should run from headland to headland, the land at the head of the inlets which furnished the most ready access to the Yukon were in reality British territory. Canada's cause was prejudiced by the fact that (though not without occasional protest) she had acquiesced in the American contention that the boundary line followed the sinuosities of the shore. A disputed boundary is always dangerous. Besides this question there were other matters requiring settlement between the United States and Canada, and at last, in 1898, a Joint High Commission, including prominent representatives of both the American and British side, was appointed and sat for some weeks at Quebec and then at Washington. In addition to the Alaska Boundary the Commission was, if possible, to agree upon a settlement of the differences in regard to the seal fishery in Behring Sea and the Atlantic fisheries; and besides minor matters was to consider the general trade relations between the two countries. Points of variance proving too great, the Commission effected nothing but in the end the two Governments agreed that six jurists of repute, three to represent each side should be appointed with authority finally to settle the Alaska Boundary. In the end a majority of the commissioners gave, in 1903, a decision favorable to the claims of the United States. Lord Alverstone, the British commissioner who supported the American contentions, was severely censured in Canada for an attitude that seemed more diplomatic than judicial, but in spite of a passing irritation there was general satisfaction that a troublesome issue had at last been settled. See ALASKAN BOUNDARY COMMISSION.

If the recent history of Canada has not been dramatic it shows none the less a record of great progress. For a long time the population of the

country increased very slowly. While successive decennial censuses in the United States usually showed increases of about 25 per cent in the population, the increases in Canada were hardly 10 per cent. In recent years, however, an improvement is apparent. Population is increasing rapidly. While formerly there was extensive emigration from Canada to the United States there is now a considerable movement from the United States to Canada and a good many American farmers are occupying the wheat lands of the West. (See CANADA — SETTLEMENT OF THE CANADIAN WEST.) So striking is this Western development that in 1904, further to open up the western country, a second trans-continental line of railway, the Grand Trunk Pacific, was begun, and a third line, the Canada Northern, will probably be completed before many years. These railways will traverse regions far north of Canada's southern frontier, and by extending northward the cultivated area will help to remove from Canada the old reproach that she is "length without breadth." Canada now has confidence in herself to which she was long a stranger. The troublesome domestic issues which played the chief part in her history since Confederation are pretty well solved; the old racial cries are not often heard, and when uttered they usually bring political disaster to those raising them. See CANADA — CONFEDERATION; CANADA — RELATIONS TO GREAT BRITAIN.   GEORGE M. WRONG,
Professor of History, University of Toronto.

9. Canada — The Canadian West. It is doubtful if a British sovereign ever made a more munificent grant to a company of his subjects than did Charles II., in the year 1670, to "The Governor and Company of Adventurers of England trading into Hudson Bay." The sweeping terms of the royal charter defined an area stretching from Hudson Bay to the Rocky Mountains, to which was given the name of Rupert's Land, in honor of the king's cousin, Prince Rupert, the company's first governor. In spite of the hostility of the French Canadian government and the competition of rival traders, the Hudson's Bay Company succeeded in holding this territory down to the date of its cession to Canada two centuries later. Although a century had elapsed since Sir Francis Drake had sighted the snowy peaks of the Pacific coast, and half a century since the ill-fated Henry Hudson had discovered the bay which became at once his grave and the monument of his achievement, yet the history of the Canadian West may be said to date from the founding of the Hudson's Bay Company. See CANADA — THE HUDSON'S BAY COMPANY.

The presence of the English company upon the shores of Hudson Bay was from the outset a serious menace to French Canadian influence in the Northwest. The newcomers were drawing off the trade of the northern tribes. English and French were face to face in a struggle for commercial supremacy in the West, and their rivalry was bound sooner or later to break into a clash of arms. The Hudson's Bay Company had strengthened its position by the establishment of four trading-posts: one upon the west shore near the Nelson, and the other three, Forts Albany, Hayes, and Rupert, on the south arm of the bay. In the spring of 1686 the progress of trade was rudely interrupted. Chevalier de

Troyes and a company of 80 adventurous Frenchmen, ascending the Ottawa, worked their way slowly by stream and lake over the height of land to the neighborhood of James Bay. So sudden was their coming, and so spirited their attack, that the three lower forts fell almost without resistance.

In 1697 Pierre le Moyne D'Iberville, who had been De Troyes' right-hand man, entered Hudson Strait, under orders from Quebec, to attack Fort Nelson, the most important trading-post on the bay. The Pelican, which carried the commander, became separated from the rest of the fleet, and fell in with three English ships belonging to the Hudson's Bay Company. In the encounter which followed the Pelican sank one of the company's ships and disabled a second, while the third made off under full sail. Rejoined by his missing ships, D'Iberville soon forced Fort Nelson to surrender. In 1713 the Treaty of Utrecht put an end to hostilities and left the English traders in undisturbed possession of their posts.

Meanwhile French Canadian traders were extending their trade beyond Lake Superior. With these there was ever present the desire to find *La Mer de l'Ouest*, which they thought could not be far distant. The ambition to discover this "Western Sea" possessed the mind of Pierre Gaultier de Varennes de la Vérendrye, the commander of a little post on Lake Nepigon. It was late in August 1731 that Vérendrye and his party passed over Le Grand Portage leading over the height of land to the waters flowing toward Lake Winnipeg. The mouth of the Maurepas (Winnipeg) River had been reached when troubles began to crowd upon the unfortunate explorer. The merchants who were to forward supplies failed to do so; his nephew died; and, as a climax to his misfortunes, 21 of his company, including his eldest son, were butchered by a band of murderous Sioux. It was not until six years later that Vérendrye again turned his face westward. The course of his travels was marked by a series of trading-posts built at successive stages. Among these were Fort La Reine, near the site of the present town of Portage la Prairie, and Fort Rouge, whose name still clings to a suburb of the city of Winnipeg.

During the last century of the French régime the Hudson's Bay Company had held its own throughout the dangers of war and the competition of trade. Its forts had fallen into the hands of De Troyes or D'Iberville, but had been restored by the Treaty of Utrecht (q.v.). Though the dangers of war were past, the rivalry of the Canadian traders had still to be met. Despite the long overland journey, the latter penetrated to the neighborhood of Hudson Bay, attracting the Indians with showy trinkets, and too often with brandy. The majority of the natives, however, were not easily drawn away from the old company's forts. Every spring the rivers and lakes were dotted with fur-laden canoes making their way to Lake Winnipeg, the meeting place of the hundreds of natives who journeyed annually to Hudson Bay. As many as 500 canoes in a year made the long and toilsome journey to York Factory. Here they exchanged their dearly-earned furs for coats, blankets, kettles, and tobacco, or for necessities of the hunt, such as guns, powder, powder-horns, shot, hatchets, and knives.

The conquest of Canada by Great Britain brought about an immediate and complete change in the fur trade. With the passing of the French régime, monopoly and licenses disappeared. The officers of the French company withdrew from the country rather than live under the British flag. The *coureurs de bois*, suddenly cast adrift, lacked the capital necessary to continue the fur trade. New employers, however, were soon at hand. The old route from the East, up the Ottawa and across Lake Superior to Grand Portage, had scarcely forgotten the passing of the French traders when it was traversed afresh by British merchants from Montreal. Alexander Henry, Thomas Curry, James Finlay, and the Frobisher brothers were the hardy forerunners of a new race of traders, whose enterprise and daring soon carried them into the Saskatchewan and Athabasca districts. In order to compete the more successfully with their long-established rivals, the newcomers, who at first traded individually, decided upon union, a decision which led to the founding in 1783 of the Northwest Company. Under the stimulus of competition the operations of both companies quickly extended northward to Lake Athabasca and westward to the foot-hills of the Rockies.

The necessity of enlarging the field of trade gave a remarkable impulse to exploration. In penetrating the unknown lands, north and west, the pioneer traders rendered invaluable service to their country. The honor of leading the way into the northland belongs to Samuel Hearne, a servant of the Hudson's Bay Company. Setting out from Prince of Wales Fort, Hearne succeeded, after two failures, in reaching the Coppermine River. He was the first white man to arrive at the Arctic shores from the interior. The men of the Northwest Company were not slow to follow the example of their rivals. No name holds a prouder place in the annals of American travel than that of Alexander Mackenzie. Fort Chipewyan, situated upon the shores of Lake Athabasca, the trade centre of the north, was the starting point of his two great journeys. The "Western Sea," the elusive goal of Vérendrye's travels, was the object of Mackenzie's quest. His first journey, made in 1789, terminated at the Arctic Ocean. Choosing a more westerly stream for his second attempt, Mackenzie ascended the Peace River to its source in the Rockies, crossed the height of land, and, after descending the Fraser River a short distance, struck out across country for the sea. The successful issue of the journey was proclaimed by the following words inscribed upon the face of a rock overlooking the waters of the Pacific: "Alexander Mackenzie from Canada by land, the twenty-second of July, one thousand seven hundred and ninety-three." Two other Nor'westers, Simon Fraser and David Thompson, also made their way to the Pacific Ocean, the former in 1808 by the river which bears his name, the latter in 1811 by the Columbia.

While British explorers were forcing a way across the continent, British seamen were making good their country's claim to the Pacific coast. In 1778 Captain Cook touched at Nootka, on Vancouver Island. At this centre of trade Captain John Meares 10 years later established a settlement, which unfortunately was soon destroyed by the Spaniards. In 1792 Captain George Vancouver, being sent out to inquire into the action of the Spaniards, forced the latter to withdraw from the scene of their outrage. As the result of arbitration Great Britain received the entire coast line.

Down to the close of the 17th century the ruling interest of the West centred in the fur trade. Lord Selkirk it was who first conceived the idea of planting a settlement at the heart of the continent. From the Hudson's Bay Company he secured a grant of 110,000 square miles in the valley of the Red River, a district henceforth called Assiniboia. Settlers were hurried out from Scotland, and in 1812 a small company, 70 in number, made its way inland from York Factory.

The newcomers were looked upon as intruders by the Nor'westers, who suspected that Lord Selkirk, being a shareholder in the Hudson's Bay Company, had planted his colony to interfere with the trade of the Canadian company. The early years brought trying experiences to the settlers. So great was the scarcity of food that the governor, Miles Macdonell, issued a proclamation to the effect that "no provisions, flesh, fish, grain, or vegetables were to be taken out of the lands of the settlement for a year." This action brought the hostility of the Nor'westers to the point of violence. Some of the colonists were bribed to desert, the remainder were driven out by a band of Métis, or half-breeds. Almost immediately, however, the refugees returned, reinforced by another company of immigrants. With the new arrivals came Robert Semple as governor.

Meanwhile Lord Selkirk had arrived in Canada. Hearing at Montreal of the misfortunes of his colonists, he had engaged the services of 100 discharged soldiers and set out for the West. While he was yet on the way, stirring events were happening in the Red River Valley. The Nor'westers, angered by the destruction of their fort on the Red, bestirred themselves to destroy the settlement. A strong band of half-breeds was gathered at Portage la Prairie, under the leadership of Cuthbert Grant. Upon 19 June 1816 Governor Semple was informed that a body of horsemen was approaching over the prairie. Taking a small force, he marched out to inquire the purpose of the intruders. This move precipitated a skirmish at a spot now marked by the Seven Oaks monument. When the firing ceased Semple and 21 of his followers lay dead or mortally wounded. By this disaster the settlers were forced to again leave their homes.

The news of Seven Oaks was the signal for great rejoicing at Fort William, the headquarters of the Northwest Company. The joy of the Nor'westers, however, was rudely dispelled by the sudden arrival of Lord Selkirk. The latter, acting in the capacity of magistrate, arrested several of the leading partners, and sent them down to York, Upper Canada. In the following spring he pushed on to the Red River, where he promptly restored the ejected colonists to their farms, settled his soldiers about Fort Douglas, and made a treaty with the Indians.

When the news of the tragic death of Semple and his men reached England, the Imperial government at once interfered. Both parties to the quarrel were ordered to give up all posts and property seized. The death of Lord Selkirk in the year 1820, though to be regretted, was beneficial to the West, removing as it did the last obstacle in the way of a union of the fur companies.

After the union, which took place in 1821, the management of the company's affairs rested with an official known as the governor of Rupert's Land, assisted by a council of chief factors and traders. A strong man was needed for the governorship, and such an one was found in the person of a young Scotchman named George Simpson, who ably guided the fortunes of the company during the next 40 years. To the enterprise of the Hudson's Bay Company, in no small measure, Great Britain owes her control of the Pacific coast. From the north Russia, from the south the United States, were pressing rival claims which threatened to shut out Great Britain entirely from the sea. Under Simpson's aggressive administration the country between the Rockies and the Pacific was occupied. A fleet of six armed vessels protected the company's coast trade, of which Fort Vancouver was the centre.

Meanwhile the Selkirk settlement, clustering about the historic walls of Fort Garry, was winning its way to prosperity. The hardships of pioneer life in the East were here repeated. Spade and hoe, sickle and cradle, flail and quern, all told of the day of small things. A series of disasters, in the form of grasshoppers and floods, failed to shake the courage of the sturdy settlers. The growth of the colony made necessary a change of government. The people complained that the members of the council of Assiniboia were paid servants of the company, and did not, therefore, represent the popular will. Discontent was a sign of progress, a sign that the settlement was growing beyond the control of a fur company.

The steadily growing importance of the Pacific country made it imperative to determine the boundary line between American and British territory in the West. The 49th parallel was the accepted line as far as the Rockies, and it was agreed that for the time being the country beyond the mountains should be "free and open" to both nations. In 1846 the Oregon treaty continued the boundary line along the 49th parallel to the channel separating Vancouver Island from the mainland. The line was to follow this channel southwesterly to the Pacific Ocean. For several years the ownership of the Island of San Juan was in dispute. The question was finally referred for settlement to the emperor of Germany, who gave his award in favor of the United States.

To maintain order among the lawless miners whom the discovery of gold had drawn to the Pacific coast, a separate government was established on the mainland. New Westminster, on the Fraser River, became the capital. This arrangement, however, proved unsatisfactory; and at times there was talk of annexing Vancouver Island to the United States. Fortunately a strong British sentiment prevailed, which led to the reunion, in 1866, of the island and the mainland, to form the province of British Columbia. Victoria was chosen as capital.

The British North America Act made provision for the admission to confederation at any time of British Columbia, Rupert's Land, and the Northwest Territories. The first Dominion parliament petitioned the British government to hand over to Canada Rupert's Land and the Northwest. It was claimed that the rule of a fur company did not tend to the general development of the country, and, moreover, that the extension of the Dominion westward would be a safeguard against any aggression on the part of the United States. The Hudson's Bay Company finally surrendered to Canada its control of Rupert's Land and its monopoly of trade. The company, in return, received the sum of £300,000, one-twentieth of all land thereafter surveyed for settlement, and also retained its posts and trading privileges.

At the time of confederation (q.v.), the only occupants of the land beyond Lake Superior were roving bands of Indians, a few scattered traders, and 12,000 settlers in the valley of the Red River. Ten thousand of these 12,000 were half-breeds, Scotch and French. Into this community, without warning, flocked Canadian surveyors to lay out roads and townships. The country had been handed over to Canada and the interests of the natives were to be sacrificed. Such was the thought of the half-breed element. The storm centre was the French half breed party, the Métis, led by Louis Riel (see RIEL REBELLION). There was no one in the colony to restrain the latter's madness. Fort Garry was seized and a "provisional government" established. There was every prospect, however, of a bloodless settlement of the situation, when suddenly Riel, in a moment of recklessness, ordered the execution of a young Ontario immigrant named Thomas Scott. The news of this brutal murder raised a storm of indignation in the East. In a remarkably short time a volunteer force under the command of Col. Garnet Wolseley, reached Fort Garry, only to find that the instigators of the rebellion had fled across the American border.

Out of the strife of rebellion arose a new province. Even while Wolseley's force was on its way up from the East, the Manitoba Act passed the Canadian Parliament. Manitoba was admitted into Confederation as a full-fledged province. The claims of the half-breeds were fully met by a generous land grant. Many of Wolseley's men remained in the new province to share in its making. The little settlement about Fort Garry was soon transformed into the populous city of Winnipeg. Manitoba drew her first governor from the far East, in the person of a distinguished Nova Scotian, Adams G. Archibald.

A year later the westward expansion of confederation was continued. British Columbia became part of the Dominion, subject to a very important condition, namely, that a transcontinental railroad should be begun within two years and completed within ten years from the date of union. In 1872, therefore, Sir John A. Macdonald introduced the question in Parliament. The great enterprise was well under way when the ministry, charged with corruption, was forced to resign. Alexander Mackenzie, who succeeded Sir John, proposed to construct the road gradually, as the finances of the country allowed. This delay put a severe strain upon British Columbia's loyalty to the Dominion. The Macdonald government, returning to power in 1878, immediately took up again the railway question. Construction was begun from both ends; and with such vigor was the work pressed forward that the last spike was driven by Lord Strathcona in November 1885. The completion of a transcontinental railway cemented the bond binding the East and the West.

No sooner was order restored after the Riel rebellion than settlers began to flock into Manitoba. Many farmers from eastern Canada moved west, while from Europe came an ever increasing number of colonists, of British, Scandinavian, and German stock. The newcomers spread beyond the limits of Manitoba, many finding their way into the valley of the Saskatchewan, a few even to the foothills of the Rockies. This Northwestern Territory was governed by the lieutenant-governor of Manitoba, and a council of 11 members. In 1876 a change took place. The eastern section of the country, called Keewatin, was placed under the personal control of the lieutenant-governor of Manitoba, while the western was given a resident governor and a council of five members. A few years later four districts were organized, Alberta, Assiniboia, Athabasca, and Saskatchewan. Regina, being situated upon the main line of the Canadian Pacific Railway then under construction, was chosen as the seat of government.

The advent of the railway gave promise of peaceful and rapid progress, when suddenly a second rebellion broke out. At the close of the Red River rebellion many of the Métis withdrew westward and settled upon the banks of the Saskatchewan, among their near relatives, the Cree Indians. Here they were disturbed by the encroachment of a hated civilization. Their unrest was increased by a fear of losing their lands through the failure of the Dominion government to issue title deeds. The sudden return from exile of Louis Riel was all that was needed to provoke rebellion. Near Duck Lake, within the angle formed by the North and South Saskatchewan, the first clash took place, between a band of Métis and a force of mounted police and volunteers.

The position of the white settlers of the Saskatchewan valley was serious. The real danger lay, not in a revolt of the Métis, but in the possibility of a general rising of the Indians, of whom there were over 30,000 in the Northwest. Prince Albert, Battleford, and Fort Pitt lay exposed to attack. The most serious risings of the Indians took place near Battleford and Fort Pitt, among the followers of Poundmaker and Big Bear. The heart of the rebellion was the village of Batoche, the centre of the Métis settlements. The news of the fight at Duck Lake was the signal for an outbreak among Big Bear's warriors, who massacred the male inhabitants of Frog Lake and then drove out the garrison of Fort Pitt. When the report of the rebellion reached Ottawa, the Dominion government took prompt action. The call for volunteers met with an eager response on all sides. In spite of the great distance, within less than two months 4,400 men were placed in the field, all save the Winnipeg contingent being from eastern Canada.

General Middleton, commander-in-chief of the Canadian militia, who arrived at Qu'Appelle in advance of the main force, made the Canadian Pacific Railway the base line of his operations, and prepared to crush the rebellion in all its centres at once. Three places were in immediate danger: Prince Albert, Battleford, and Fort Pitt; three relief expeditions were provided for in the plan of campaign. General Middleton was to advance from Qu' Appelle to Batoche, Riel's headquarters, Colonel Otter from Swift Current to Battleford, and General Strange from Calgary to Edmonton. The three movements were successfully carried through, the divided forces converging upon Battleford. The bulk of the fighting fell to Middleton's column, which met with determined opposition at Fish Creek and Batoche. With Riel, Poundmaker and Big Bear finally in custody, the rebellion was at an end. Riel and eight Indians suffered the death penalty.

The rebellion was not without its good results. In recognition of their growing importance, the Northwest Territories were granted representation in the Dominion Senate and House of Commons. The need of a stronger government in the Northwest became obvious. The old council was abolished and its place taken by an elective assembly, which first met in 1888, at Regina. But this was not, of course, a final settlement and in 1905 the vast district between Manitoba and British Columbia was divided into two self-governing provinces — Saskatchewan and Alberta.

The discovery in 1897 of rich deposits of gold in the Yukon (q.v.) was the signal for an influx of fortune-hunters. As a result the long standing dispute over the Alaskan boundary gathered new importance. In taking over Alaska from Russia in 1867, the United States secured all the rights of that nation as laid down in the treaty of 1825, between Russia and Great Britain. The interpretation of the terms of the treaty was left to a commission, composed of three representatives from the United States, two from Canada, and Lord Alverstone, the chief justice of England. The commission met in London in September 1903. The decision was, upon the whole, favorable to the American claims. See ALASKAN BOUNDARY COMMISSION.

The growth of the West during the last quarter of a century has been very marked; the inevitable result of the expansion of the Canadian railway system. The Canadian Pacific Railway (q.v.) worked a marvelous change. At the terminus of the road there sprang up, as in a night, the bustling city of Vancouver, while the line throughout was soon dotted with villages. Many of these have now risen to the dignity of towns, a few even aspire to take rank with the cities. To north and south the road has thrown out branch lines, everywhere developing new districts. No sooner has one transcontinental railway opened up a broad belt of land than a second is suggested. Already a new company, the Grand Trunk Pacific, has entered into a contract with the Dominion government to build another railway from coast to coast. When this contract is carried out, the second line will run parallel with the Canadian Pacific, and will open a new Northwest.

DAVID M. DUNCAN,
Author of 'The Story of the Canadian People,'
Collegiate Institute, Winnipeg.

10. Canada — The Settlement of the **Canadian West.** Without a just appreciation of the attractions and possibilities of the "Canadian West," as the larger half of the Dominion situated west of Lake Superior has commonly been called, neither the Canada of to-day nor that of the future will ever be understood. One of the first acts of statesmanship after the consummation of Confederation (see CANADA — CONFEDERATION) was the purchase by the Canadian government from the Hudson's Bay Company (see CANADA — HUDSON'S BAY COMPANY) of the immense territory forming the basin of Hudson Bay and known as Rupert's Land, over which that company held proprietary rights. British Columbia, in 1871, entered the Dominion thus brought up to her borders. Some 14 years later followed the completion of the Canadian Pacific Railway (q.v.), an enterprise of splendid self-confidence in so young a country. A railway was needed to fulfil the conditions upon which British Columbia had joined the Confederation, and without it the vast territory between that province and Ontario could not be developed nor preserved to Canada. The purchase of Rupert's Land created the conditions which brought about and justified the building of the first transcontinental railway, and the prolonged discussions over the policy of the government of the day in respect to the public assistance given to that road began the process of popular education in eastern Canada in the extent and resources of the West. A seemingly limitless sphere for internal development has gradually been revealed, and the necessity on two occasions for the employment of armed force against half-breed rebellions, with some sacrifice of blood, has sealed the sense of possession. Pioneers proved the fertility of the soil and the richness of the mines, and with the assurance of a rapidly increasing population the whole national life has received an access of vigor and hopefulness. External policy, as well as internal, has been influenced. A country that can produce and export staple foodstuffs in quantities capable of indefinite multiplication, and has vast stores of timber, coal, and metals, can support great home industries and also be a prominent factor in international trade. It can work at home and bargain abroad. It can make choices. The idea of a trade union of the British empire, for example, has presented itself in practical form largely because of the potentialities of the Canadian West. Population only has been needed to show results, and the movement of population into this part of Canada is therefore a subject of interest and importance.

The country lying west and northwest of Lake Superior in Canada is of vast extent and great variety. It includes the extreme western end of the province of Ontario, the provinces of Manitoba, Saskatchewan, Alberta, and British Columbia, while beginning again at the east and lying to the north of these districts are the Northwest Territories and Yukon. Prior to 1905 the only provinces were Manitoba and British Columbia. The remainder constituted the "Territories." Now "the Territories" signify the vast northern region stretching from Labrador to Yukon. The land area in these districts in acres is:

District	Area in acres
Ontario (western end) approx.	20,000,000
Manitoba	41,169,098
Saskatchewan	155,092,480
Alberta	160,755,200
British Columbia	227,302,400
North West Territories (Labrador to Yukon)	1,197,475,200
Yukon	132,113,280

For present purposes the northern Territories, with the exception of Yukon, may be disregarded, since they have not yet attracted population to any marked degree. The western end of the province of Ontario is rich in timber and minerals, and possesses stretches of good agricultural land. The prairie region begins at the eastern boundary of Manitoba and extends to the Rocky Mountains, embracing the provinces Manitoba, Saskatchewan, and Alberta: wooded prairie and open prairie, rolling and flat, broken by hills and some rocky ridges and drained by great rivers that flow eastward and northward into great lakes with outlets into Hudson Bay. No richer agricultural lands and no better grazing ranges exist than are here found. Of the 350,000,000 acres in this combined district it would be idle to estimate the proportion of good grain land. It is very large, as attested by the successful farms now scattered throughout the whole region. In 1903 only 5,073,424 acres had yet been put under crop. It is known, moreover, that the fertile belt extends up into the northern tier of Territories. British Columbia is a land of magnificent mountains rich in minerals, and of valleys of the very highest agricultural possibilities, nearly the whole clothed with splendid forests. See CANADA — AGRICULTURE; CANADA — MINERALS; CANADA — THE FORESTS AND LUMBER INDUSTRY.

In 1901 the Canadian West, not including the portion of Ontario, was shown by the census to have a population of 645,517. Out of this number 250,901, or 38.87 per cent, had been born in the West; 154,581, or 23.94 per cent, had been born in the eastern provinces of Canada; 83,579, or 12.94 per cent, had been born in the British Isles; and 145,369, or 22.52 per cent, had been born in foreign countries, while 8,299, or 1.28 per cent, had been born at sea or failed to give their birthplace. Indians numbered 61,518 and half-breeds 28,255. By origin 356,411 were of British stock, 29,579 of French stock, 54,714 of German, 23,836 of Scandinavian, 23,460 of Russian, 16,949 of Austro-Hungarian, and 20,073 of Chinese and Japanese. All the leading nationalities and races of Europe were represented. To understand the nature and the rate of the movement of population into the Canadian West indicated by these figures, many general considerations must be borne in mind. Conditions as they have existed in the United States are among the most important of these considerations. Until the closing years of the last century the United States was an irresistible magnet. It drew the best, as well as much that was not the best, of the movable population of all countries. From Canada itself it attracted a larger proportion of the native population than from any other country. Its relative advantages over Canada, in the eyes of those who sought to better their condition, consisted in its advanced stage of development. Not only were there more varied employment and larger opportunities in industrial and commercial life, but its fertile lands were opened up by railways from ten to forty years before those in the Canadian West and the mineral wealth of its western mountains was discovered and advertised to the world years before the riches of Canada in this respect were even suspected. The prairie regions of the Canadian West had to wait for transportation facilities, and then they had to wait until their profitableness was established. Since people are not predisposed to believe in the security of agriculture in northern latitudes, this meant, practically, that they had to wait until the prairies in the United States were tested right up to the border. Before that time even official crop returns could not be widely effective as inducements to immigration. Moreover streams of migration are not easy to divert. Where many have gone others tend to follow.

To what extent the United States drew upon Canadians up to 1900 is shown in the census returns of that year which record the residence in that country of 1,181,255 persons born in British North America, that is, in Canada and Newfoundland. How little the United States had given in return appears from the comparatively small number of 127,899 natives of the United States resident in Canada when the Canadian census was taken in 1901. But conditions have changed. The flow of population from Canada to the United States has been checked and the tide has turned. Canada has made steady and substantial progress and her industries now provide opportunities for all her own people who desire industrial employment, while the large immigration into the cities of the United States from Eastern and Southern Europe has rendered industrial life in the United States less attractive. But what is of more direct importance to the present subject, the cheap, good lands in the United States are now very largely occupied. Prosperity and a good birthrate among the farming population have created a host of landseekers of native birth apparently more than numerous enough to take up, within a few years at least, what good land is still easily available: and the price of land has rapidly risen. In the Canadian West, on the other hand, millions of acres of the most fertile land are obtainable at low cost; this land has been proved; and railway facilities and railway rates put the crops within profitable reach of the markets.

The history of the settlement of the Canadian West may conveniently be divided into three periods: the first embracing the time before railway facilities existed or, say, up to 1885; the second from 1885 to 1901; and the third beginning in 1901. So far as the prairie division is concerned fur traders visited it and dwelt in it from early times, but no attempt was made at colonization previous to that of Lord Selkirk in the decade succeeding 1812. That his venture, beset with misfortunes though it was, left a permanent result was shown by the fact that in 1873 as many as 530 of the original Selkirk settlers or their white children were found to claim the grants of land offered by the Canadian Parliament. Other independent colonists had made their way into the country and there were, of course, the employees of the Hudson's Bay Company, but in 1869, when the purchase by Canada was made, the total white population numbered only a few hundreds. Some members of the military expedition of 1870 remained as settlers and other accessions

were received at about the same time. In 1871 the Dominion Government appointed the first immigration agents in the West, one in Manitoba and another in the Territories, and authorized the establishment of an "immigration shed" at Winnipeg, a hamlet then possessing 241 inhabitants. The work of promoting immigration to Canada had been undertaken by the Federal Government in 1868, the provincial governments co-operating, and the appointment of agents in the West brought that section into direct touch with the general system having agents in Great Britain and Europe. It is interesting to note that in his annual report to the department for 1872 the agent at Winnipeg estimates the arrivals during the year at 1,400, of whom 954 came from Ontario, 78 from Quebec, and 115 from the United States. During 1872 and 1873 the Dominion Government entered into negotiations with a colony of German Mennonites living in southern Russia who desired to emigrate. Delegates visited Canada and in 1874 1,349 of these people settled in southern Manitoba. This is important, not only because it led to further immigration from the same source but also because the attention of the Dominion Government was thus directed to the question of special colonization in the West. In 1874 Scandinavian and Icelandic delegates were shown through the country and a small beginning was made in Icelandic settlement through the moving up from Ontario of 285 Icelanders. The years 1874 and 1875 may be noted also because the Dominion Government then first appointed Canadian immigration agents in the United States, chiefly for the purpose of effecting the repatriation of Canadians. Results were at once obtained and agents reported some 400 repatriated Canadians as immigrants into the West in 1876 and some 800 in 1877. In 1879 a delegation of tenant farmers of Great Britain visited the country and their reports resulted in an increase in immigration from the British Isles. The projected transcontinental railway had met with difficulties and delays, but in 1875 work was begun at Thunder Bay, the head of Lake Superior, on the section to Winnipeg, and in 1878 a line from the United States border at Pembina was completed to St. Boniface, opposite Winnipeg across the Red River. Although the line from Lake Superior was not completed until 1883, the line from Pembina increased the facilities for reaching Winnipeg (q.v.), and the railway building combined with other not unnatural causes led to a "boom" in real estate, accompanied by a rush of speculators and prospective settlers. In 1881 the immigration agents estimated the arrivals in Manitoba at about 25,000, in 1882 at almost 70,000, and in 1883 at 50,000. Eastern Canada and the United States contributed the great proportion of these visitors, as most of them proved merely to be. The boom "burst" in 1883. By the census returns for 1881 some estimate of what was permanent in the immigration of the previous years can be reached. Manitoba was given a total population of 65,954, of whom 18,020 were born in Manitoba itself, and 6,422 in the Territories. Of these two classes 6,767 were Indians, but the halfbreeds were not separately enumerated. From outside the largest number was furnished by the province of Ontario, namely 19,125, Quebec supplying 4,085 and Nova Scotia 820. Natives of England and Wales numbered 3,457, of

Scotland 1,836, and of Ireland 2,868. Russia supplied 5,651, chiefly Mennonites; Germany, 220; Norway, Sweden and Denmark, 121; and France, 81. The United States had contributed 1,752. In the same year the white population of the Territories was 6,974, of whom 517 were born in Ontario, 101 in Quebec, 98 in England and Wales, 136 in Scotland, 62 in Ireland, 27 in France and 116 in the United States. As the Canadian Pacific Railway was pushed through real settlement followed at a faster rate than ever before and in 1886 when the first train was run from Montreal to the Pacific coast the net gain in population from the principal sources, over the figures just given for 1881, was: From Ontario 14,996, from Quebec 1,891, from Nova Scotia 497, from New Brunswick 363, from England and Wales 6,865, from Scotland 4,146, from Ireland 753, from Iceland 1,500, from the United States 570; while each of the other countries showed small gains. The chief sources of increases in the Territories were Ontario 8,300, Quebec 1,200, England and Wales 3,750, Scotland 2,000, and the United States 890.

It will not be necessary to follow in detail the records of the succeeding years up to 1901, which form the second period. The Canadian Pacific Railway Company, which had received large grants of land, became an additional agency in the organizing of immigration movements as also to a limited extent did the colonization societies which had purchased tracts of land in 1882, 1883 and 1884. A movement which began in 1889 and 1890 and ultimately attained considerable proportions was that from Austria-Hungary. The year 1890 was marked by a considerable immigration from Great Britain. Migration from the eastern provinces of Canada remained moderate until 1898. In 1899 over 7,000 Doukhobors were brought in and established in colonies. According to the census of 1901 Manitoba had a population of 238,-934, not counting Indians and half-breeds. Those born in Canada numbered 164,582. Of the Canadians 67,566 were born in Ontario, 8,492 in Quebec, 1,536 in Nova Scotia, 820 in New Brunswick, 419 in Prince Edward Island, and 167 in British Columbia. In England there were born 20,036, in Scotland 8,099, in Ireland 4,537, and in Wales 356; in Austria-Hungary 11,570, in Russia 8,854, in Iceland 5,403, in Germany 2,285, in Norway, Sweden and Denmark 2,090, in France 1,470, and in the United States 6,922. The Territories had a population of 185,335, exclusive of Indians and half-breeds. Of the 65,231 born in Canada, Ontario was the birthplace of 28,229, Quebec of 4,075, Nova Scotia of 1,169, New Brunswick of 669, and Prince Edward Island of 488. Those born in England numbered 10,752, in Scotland 4,226, in Ireland 2,158, and in Wales 186; in Austria-Hungary 13,407, Russia 14,585, Norway, Sweden and Denmark 2,462, Germany 2,170, France 1,023, Iceland 424, and the United States 13,877.

Before touching the movement of the past three years into the prairie region a few words may be said of the progress of settlement in British Columbia. In 1901 the population of that province was 149,708, again excluding Indians and half-breeds. The composition of the population of British Columbia differs from that of the districts we have just been considering in several interesting respects. In the first place, it contained in 1901 relatively a larger number born in the United States, namely, 17,164. Then there were 14,576 Chinese and 4,515 Japanese. Ontario contributed 23,642, but Nova Scotia came next among the provinces with 4,603. These features are easily explainable. The chief attractions of British Columbia have been its mines, its forests, and its fisheries. The first named have in many different years caused rushes from the United States and they have been an added attraction to the people of the province of Nova Scotia. The man from Ontario is a good pioneer under any conditions. And the same causes that drew Chinese to California have operated in the case of British Columbia. The first gold rush to British Columbia occurred in 1858, nine years after the memorable rush to California. It is said that between 20,000 and 30,000 prospectors from California invaded the province in that year. Systematic exploration, however, was not attempted and the mining population came and went in waves, the years 1858, 1861, 1864, 1865, 1869, and 1872 marking the influxes. Up to 1893 nearly all the gold produced was placer gold and the values ran from $705,000 in 1858 to $3,913,563 in 1863, continuing at an average of over $3,000,000 until 1868, when with variations a decline set in. The working of lode mines since 1893 has given an element of permanence to the mining population and the product of gold has risen in 1902 and 1903 to $5,900,000. The copper, silver and lead mined exceed gold in their total value. Coal was known to exist from early times and seems to have been mined since 1836, but it was not until 1875 that the annual production exceeded 100,000 tons. The increase has been steady and the product in 1903 exceeded 1,600,000 tons. The magnificent timber resources of the province have given employment to an increasing number of men and the yield of the fisheries has grown from $100,000 in 1876 to $7,900,000 in 1901. In 1871, when British Columbia became a province in the Dominion, the population was 36,247, of whom 25,661 were Indians. In 1881 it had increased to 49,548, in 1891 to 98,173, and in 1901 to 178,657.

The Yukon territory might perhaps be classed with British Columbia. In 1896 the gold discoveries were made there which caused the famous rush in 1897. The census of 1901 gave the Yukon a population of 24,357, exclusive of Indians and half-breeds. Natives of the United States numbered 6,707, of Ontario 1,940, of Quebec 1,349, of Norway and Sweden 1,265, of England 1,153 and of Germany 746; not specified 6,573.

The part of Ontario included in the Canadian West has interests of its own in mines and fertile land, but its progress in settlement has been largely bound up with that of the prairie region to the west. The mines in the Lake of the Woods district caused the establishment of the town of Rat Portage, now Kenora, the continued prosperity of which, however, came to depend to a great extent on the lumber industry for the supply of the demand in Manitoba and the territories. Port Arthur and Fort William on Thunder Bay, Lake Superior, are at the head of lake navigation on the Canadian route, and the summer traffic in goods for the West and in grain and flour from the West is there transhipped, the towns possessing immense storage and shipping grain elevators. These towns are growing rapidly, particularly since 1901, and their growth will keep pace with the development of the West. The completion of the Canadian Northern Railway between Port Arthur and the wheat fields, running through the southern part of the province, has not only assisted Port Arthur but has opened up the valley of the Rainy River and new centres for the lumber industry. In 1901 Rat Portage, now Kenora, had 5,202 people, Fort William 3,997 and Port Arthur 3,212. Since that date the population, especially of the two last mentioned towns, has greatly increased and new towns have sprung up along the line of the Canadian Northern.

The third period in the settlement of Manitoba and the Territories began in 1901. Conditions to which reference has previously been made had developed and the time was ripe. In the United States a greater movement of landseekers was taking place than at any previous time, with the exception perhaps of the early eighties, and good available lands for pioneers were fast becoming occupied. This movement was not directly from the more thickly settled Eastern and Middle States to new lands, but from these States to the Northwestern and Southwestern States. The newcomers were willing to buy lands under cultivation at prices which were comparatively large to the men who had broken them. It was the men who had entered the Northwestern States as pioneers ten, fifteen or twenty years before who were offered tempting prices, and in thousands decided to become pioneers again. This movement of population was directed by the railway companies and by private land companies, the managers of which had their connections in all parts and thoroughly understood the business of land settlement. The new feature in the history of immigration into the Canadian West in 1901 was the advent of these United States land companies. As soon as prospects seemed to indicate a good crop in that year, their agents appeared in considerable numbers and purchased large tracts. This continued in 1902. To show the magnitude of the operations it may be mentioned that one of these companies purchased in one block about 1,100,000 acres. The lands thus secured could be offered to land-seekers in the United States at from $4 to $10 per acre. In certain localities, or in the case of improved farms, the price was higher. The man who could sell his farm in the Dakotas, Minnesota, or Iowa, for example, at from $30 to $75, or even $100 per acre was offered land in Canada, which returns showed was capable of producing more bushels to the acre, for a price which would not only pay the expenses of the transfer but leave him with a bank account. In most cases the large blocks of land purchased were sold in smaller lots to middlemen and the number of agents thereby largely increased and distributed. Enterprising Canadian land companies also existed and greatly increased in numbers. By 1903 the first phase of this new development, that is, the purchase of large blocks of land by speculating settlement companies, had almost come to an end. The policy of the government is opposed to selling except to the actual settler and the Canadian Pacific Railway Company, the Hudson's Bay Company and the Canada Northwest Land Company, the other largest owners of land, were likewise unfavorable to the too extensive operations of speculative middlemen.

It was to the interest of the railway company, particularly, to secure the actual settler as soon as possible and it was believed that prices could most effectually be kept at an attractive level by retaining the retail selling of the lands in the hands of the company. Large sales were, however, made by these Canadian companies in blocks as well as in farms during 1901 and 1902. Their returns show these total sales:

CANADIAN PACIFIC RAILWAY COMPANY.

Year	Acres	Value	Average price
1901........	831,732	$2,646,237	$3.18 per acre
1902........	2,420,265	8,140,598	3.36 per acre

HUDSON'S BAY COMPANY.

Year	Acres	Value	Average price
1901........	71,703	$351,487	$4.90 per acre
1902........	196,844	999,685	5.08 per acre

CANADA NORTHWEST LAND COMPANY.

Year	Acres	Value	Average price
1901........	121,069	$ 629,130	$5.19 per acre
1902........	515,800	2,518,000	4.88 per acre

The elimination of speculative buying caused smaller returns for 1903. The Canadian Northern Railway Company, which possesses a land grant of considerable size, has recently handed over the selling of its lands to a powerful private company. The government still has millions of acres of homestead lands, as well as lands held for sale, and the following returns of homestead entries for the last four calendar years will indicate the demand existing:

Year	Entries
1900....................................	7,850
1901....................................	9,108
1902....................................	22,215
1903....................................	32,682

Among the factors at work during this period, the immigration department of the government must be given a chief place. The number of agents in Europe and the United States had been increased and more money than ever before was spent in advertising Canada. In January 1904 the United States and Canadian land companies interested in Western Canada and leading business men in Winnipeg and elsewhere organized what is called the Western Canada Immigration Association and raised a fund of $50,000 for a two years' campaign of education through the press of the United States. To this fund the Dominion Government, the government of the province of Manitoba and the city of Winnipeg gave contributions. The effect of the increased immigration from the United States was not alone in additions to population from that source, but the fact that United States farmers were seeking Canadian lands was an excellent advertisement in Europe. The most telling advertisements of all, however, were the splendid crops of 1901 and 1902. The government returns for Manitoba and the territories for the six years up to 1903 are as follows:

MANITOBA

WHEAT

Year	Acres	Bushels	Yield per acre
1898	1,488,232	25,313,745	17.01
1899	1,629,995	27,922,230	17.13
1900	1,457,396	13,025,252	8.90
1901	2,011,835	50,502,085	25.10
1902	2,039,940	53,077,267	26.00
1903	2,442,873	40,116,878	16.42

OATS

Year	Acres	Bushels	Yield per acre
1898	514,824	17,308,252	33.6
1899	575,136	22,318,378	38.80
1900	429,108	8,814,312	20.50
1901	689,941	27,796,588	40.30
1902	725,060	34,478,160	47.50
1903	855,431	33,035,774	38.62

BARLEY

Year	Acres	Bushels	Yield per acre
1898	158,058	4,277,927	27.06
1899	182,912	5,379,156	29.4
1900	155,111	2,939,477	18.9
1901	191,009	6,536,155	34.2
1902	329,790	11,848,422	35.9
1903	326,537	8,707,252	26.66

THE FORMER TERRITORIES
WHEAT

Year	Acres	Bushels	Yield per acre
1898	307,580	5,542,478	18.01
1899	363,523	6,915,623	19.02
1900	412,864	4,028,294	9.75
1901	504,697	12,808,447	25.37
1902	625,758	13,956,850	22.30
1903	837,234	16,029,149	19.14

OATS

Year	Acres	Bushels	Yield per acre
1898	105,077	3,040,307	28.93
1899	134,938	4,686,036	34.81
1900	175,439	4,226,152	24.08
1901	229,439	11,113,066	48.43
1902	310,367	10,661,295	34.35
1903	440,662	14,179,705	32.18

BARLEY

Year	Acres	Bushels	Yield per acre
1898	17,092	449,512	26.19
1899	14,276	337,521	23.62
1900	17,044	353,216	20.72
1901	24,702	795,100	32.18
1902	36,445	870,417	23.88
1903	68,974	1,842,824	26.72

No Government crop reports were issued for the Territories before 1898, but in Manitoba they have been issued for 20 years. For that period the average yield per acre in Manitoba has been 19.05 bushels of wheat. The yield in 1900 was much the smallest on record and when the total production of wheat for the Canadian West jumped from 17,000,000 bushels to 63,000,000 bushels in a single year the attention of the world was startlingly attracted. The unsurpassed excellence of Manitoba hard wheat had been recognized, but a yield of 63,000,000 bushels for the first time gave the Canadian West a regulating influence in the world's markets. If a comparison of the above figures of yield per acre is made with the returns for Minnesota and North Dakota it will be seen what a powerful aid they became to the various advertising agencies. For the last four years the yield per acre in bushels of wheat in these two States and the average yield for the whole United States have been:

	1900	1901	1902	1903
Minnesota	10.5	12.9	13.9	13.1
North Dakota	4.9	13.1	15.9	12.7
United States	12.3	15.0	14.5	12.9

As to the results accomplished during the past four years it is impossible to present complete or reliable statistics. The figures given by the immigration department for the total immigration to Canada, during the fiscal years ending June 30, are:

	1903	1902	1901
English and Welsh	32,510	13,095	9,401
Scotch	7,046	2,853	1,476
Irish	2,236	1,311	933
United States	49,473	26,388	17,987
Galicians	10,141	6,550	4,702
Germans	1,887	1,048	984
Hungarians	2,156	1,048	546
Austrians	798	320	228
Scandinavians	5,448	2,451	1,750
French and Belgian	1,240	654	492
Russians, Finlanders	7,217	3,759	1,726
Miscellaneous	8,152	7,902	8,924
Totals	128,364	67,379	49,149

The unrevised figures for the fiscal year 1904 give a total of 130,329, of whom 50,915 came from the British Isles, 36,241 from the continent of Europe and 43,173 from the United States. The greater part of this total immigration was directed to the Canadian West and there was also a large migration from eastern Canada, estimated by the immigration commissioner at Winnipeg at 8,604 in 1901, 12,530 in 1902, and 17,286 in 1903. By the same authority the increase in the population of the Canadian West in the fiscal year ending June 30, 1903, from the above sources, was 115,000 and in 1904 about 110,000. See CANADA—THE CANADIAN WEST. W. SANFORD EVANS,
Editor of 'The Telegram,' Winnipeg.

11. Canada—The Constitution. In the Canadian draft of the bill, Canada was styled a "Kingdom." For that title "Dominion" was substituted at the instance of Lord Derby, who thought that the title "Kingdom" might be offensive to the Americans. Sir John Macdonald, as a strong monarchist, deplored the change, feeling that had the title "Kingdom" been adopted the Australian colonies would have been applying to be placed in the same rank as the kingdom of Canada. As it is, the Australian colonies have adopted the title "Commonwealth," suggestive rather of progress in democratic sentiment.

The term Confederation has been applied to two forms of polity materially different from each other. One is confederation proper; the other is nationality with a federal structure. The instance of confederation proper in ancient history is the Archæan League; in modern history, instances are the original Swiss Bund, the United Netherlands, and the Union of the American colonies during the Revolutionary War. Instances of a nation with a federal structure are the United States of America under their present constitution and the present Swiss Bund. A confederation proper is formed for a special object, usually that of common defense. The several States entering into it do not resign their sovereign power. Nor does the federal council exercise, like a national government, authority over the individual citizen, but only over the States. Its legislative power is confined to the fulfilment of the special object of the federation. Nor has it any power of taxation, but only a power of requisition. In the case of a federation proper, the Federal government is an organ of the States governments collectively. In the case of a nation with a federal structure, the States are severally organs of the federal government. The Canadian confederation belongs, as its name Dominion of Canada imports, to the class of nations with a federal structure. So does the newly formed Commonwealth of Australia.

The Canadian constitution is embodied in the act of the British Parliament called the British North America Act, which can be amended only by the power by which it was passed. In common with the other colonies, self-governed as they are styled, Canada remains in the allegiance of the British Crown, retains the constitutional forms and nomenclature of the monarchy, and is, to a certain, though of late years diminishing, extent, under the actual control of the Imperial government. The legislation of the Imperial Parliament is in all things binding upon Canada. To the king's government under the control of the Imperial Parliament belong the treaty-making power and the power of peace and war. By the Imperial government the governor-general, the legal head of the Dominion, is appointed. The supreme jurisdiction is still the British Privy Council, and in it is vested the interpretation of the Canadian constitution. The command of the army is still Imperial. So is the fountain of honor. The territory of the Dominion is part of the domain of the empire, at the disposal of the Imperial government, which has exercised its power in boundary cases. The tendency, however, since confederation, has been constantly toward practical independence. The veto power has been very sparingly exercised, and only in special cases, as in that of copyright where the colonial act conflicted with the Imperial law. Appeal from the colonial courts to the Privy Council has been restricted. Military occupation has ceased. Though the command of the army remains in the Crown, the military administration has passed, not without friction, into the hands of the Canadian minister of militia. The dispensation of titles and decorations, to which great influence is attached, still remains Imperial, though even in this the wishes of the Canadian government probably make themselves felt.

The Dominion of Canada and the other self-governing dependencies of the British Crown faithfully reproduce the forms of monarchy. The governor-general of Canada, as the representative of the British sovereign, has the prerogative of calling and dissolving Parliament, of appointing the members of the Privy Council, of nominating the Senate. Parliament is opened by him with a "speech from the throne." But, like the monarch whom he represents, he reigns but does not govern. Very rare have been the instances since the confederation, and those not cases of general policy, in which he has exercised his personal power. Only of the pageantry of his office and of his assumption of state has there since confederation been an increase, favored by those who desire to foster the monarchical sentiment. The lieutenant-govern-

ors of provinces, nominally appointed by him, are really appointed by his ministers, and invariably from the ranks of their own party. When one of them was dismissed it was apparently against the wish of the governor-general and manifestly on party grounds; yet on reference to the home government the governor-general was directed to conform to the opinion of his constitutional advisers.

The legislative power is divided between the central legislature and those of the provinces, the subjects of legislation assigned to each being set forth in the Act: The exclusive legislative authority of the Parliament of Canada extends to (1) The public debt and property; (2) The regulation of trade and commerce; (3) The raising of money by any mode or system of taxation; (4) The borrowing of money on the public credit; (5) Postal service; (6) The census and statistics; (7) Militia, military and naval service, and defense; (8) The fixing of and providing for the salaries and allowances of civil and other officers of the Government of Canada; (9) Beacons, buoys, lighthouses, and Sable Island; (10) Navigation and shipping; (11) Quarantine and the establishment and maintenance of marine hospitals; (12) The coast and inlet fisheries; (13) Ferries between a province and any British or foreign country, or between two provinces; (14) Currency and coinage; (15) Banking, incorporation of banks, and the issue of paper money; (16) Savings banks; (17) Weights and measures; (18) Bills of exchange and promissory notes; (19) Interest; (20) Legal tender; (21) Bankruptcy and insolvency; (22) Patents of invention and discovery; (23) Copyright; (24) Indians, and lands reserved for the Indians; (25) Naturalization and aliens; (26) Marriage and divorce; (27) The criminal law, except the constitution of courts of criminal jurisdiction, but including the procedure in criminal matters; (28) The establishment, maintenance, and management of penitentiaries.

To the provincial legislatures are assigned (1) The amendment from time to time, notwithstanding anything in the act, of the constitution of the province, except as regards the office of the lieutenant-governor; (2) Direct taxation within the province in order to the raising of a revenue for provincial purposes; (3) The borrowing of money on the sole credit of the province; (4) The establishment and tenure of provincial offices, and the appointment and payment of provincial officers; (5) The management and sale of the public lands belonging to the province, and of the timber and wood thereon; (6) The establishment, maintenance, and management of public and reformatory prisons in and for the province; (7) The establishment, maintenance, and management of hospitals, asylums, charities, and eleemosynary institutions in and for the provinces, other than marine hospitals; (8) Municipal institutions in the province; (9) Shop, saloon, tavern, auctioneer, and other licenses, in order to the raising of a revenue for provincial, local, or municipal purposes; (10) Local works and undertakings other than such as are of the following classes: (a) Lines of steam or other ships, railways, canals, telegraphs, and other works and undertakings connecting the province with any other or others of the provinces, or extending beyond the limits of the province; (b) Lines of steamships between the province and any British or foreign country; (c) Such works as, although wholly situate within the province, are before or after their execution declared by the Parliament of Canada to be for the general advantage of Canada or for the advantage of two or more of the provinces; (11) The incorporation of companies with provincial objects; (12) The solemnization of marriage in the province; (13) Property and civil rights in the province; (14) The administration of justice in the province, including the constitution, maintenance, organization of provincial courts, both of civil and of criminal jurisdiction, and including procedure in civil matters in those courts; (15) The imposition of punishment by fine, penalty, or imprisonment for enforcing any law of the province made in relation to any matter coming within any of the classes of subjects enumerated in this section; (16) Generally all matters of a merely local or private nature in the province.

Powers not specifically given to the provinces are reserved to the Dominion, whereas under the American constitution powers not specifically given to the Federal government are reserved to the States or to the people.

The judges are appointed by the Federal government and, as in Great Britain, for life or during good behavior, in contrast with the practice of the United States, where judges are elected for a term of years. They can be removed only by the governor-general on an address from both houses of Parliament,

The Canadian Parliament consists, like the British, of two houses. The House of Commons, in which supreme legislative power practically resides, is elected almost by manhood suffrage. The North America Act apportions representation to the several provinces on the principles of population and provides for decennial readjustment to meet changes in the balance of population. Members are paid, whereas in Great Britain they are unpaid, and non-payment of members there forms a strong conservative institution. The Senators are appointed nominally by the Crown, really by the head of the party in power, and almost invariably on party grounds. Senatorships are for life, not hereditary like seats in the House of Lords, so that the political analogy is imperfect. On the other hand, party, which appoints the Canadian Senate, controls it. It might otherwise block legislation and there would be no remedial force; while the British House of Lords, it is well understood, must give way to the will of the nation when persistently declared. As it is, when the outgoing party happens to retain a majority in the Senate, there is danger of a block. The House of Commons is elected for a term of five years, subject, however, to the prerogative of dissolution.

The provincial legislatures are miniatures of those of the Dominion. The forms like those of the Dominion Parliament are monarchical, the lieutenant-governor formally nominating the ministers, as does the governor-general those of the dominion The practical working is popular, elective, and partisan. The party divisions run through the provinces severally as well as through the Dominion at large. Quebec and Nova Scotia, like the Dominion Parliament, have each two chambers; the rest have only one. The Federal government has a veto on provincial legislation.

The treatment of the Northwest Territories, as provinces, presents a certain analogy to that of the Territories of the United States, executive and legislative powers being given to a lieutenant-governor with an elective council subject to instructions by order under Federal council or by the Canadian secretary of state.

The Parliament is by law bilingual: the French language as well as the English being recognized, though practically English prevails. The civil law, in which the *Coutume de Paris* and the Code Napoleon are blended with the common and statutory law of Great Britain, remains the law of Quebec.

In its generally democratic character the Canadian constitution approaches to that of the American republic, but in their structure they materially differ. The American constitution, in accordance with the principle laid down by Montesquieu (q.v.), separates the Executive from the Legislative. The members of the President's council, miscalled a cabinet, have not seats in the Legislature, nor is their continnance in office dependent on its support. They are the nominees of the President alone. Under the Canadian constitution, as under the British, the members of the cabinet have seats in the Parliament, on the confidence of which their tenure of office depends, and in which they initiate and control legislation. The head of the American republic is elected for a term certain. The terms of members and the times of election are fixed by law, whereas the Canadian Parliament is called in the name of the Crown by the prime minister, the head of the party in power, who wields in the interest of his party the prerogative of summoning and of dissolution. The members of the Canadian Senate are chosen by the head of the party in power, whereas the American Senate is elected by the legislatures of the several States. Thus the Canadian constitution lends itself more aptly to the working of the party system of government, which, with all its accessories, political and moral, has prevailed, though the general influence of party cannot be stronger than it is in the United States.

In Great Britain the cabinet, in which the real power of government resides, is a growth of political party unrecognized by law, while the Privy Council, recognized by law, has become honorary. In Canada the Privy Council is the cabinet, at the same time conferring the honorary rank, but the relation to the Crown, the relation to Parliament, and the working of the system in both cases are the same.

The British North America Act does not, like the American constitution, prohibit the establishment of a particular religion by the state. It leaves untouched to the Roman Catholic priesthood of Quebec the power of levying tithes on the people of their own communion. In the section respecting education it perpetuates the privilege of denominational schools. Since confederation the government of Ontario has practically aided a denominational university. But since the secularization of the clergy reserves and the opening of the University of Toronto, non-interference of the state with religion may be said to have been established as a general principle and may be regarded as practically part of the constitution.' See CANADA — CONFEDERATION; CANADA — LOCAL GOVERNMENT; CANADA — IMPERIAL FEDERATION; CANADA — UNDER FRENCH RULE; CANADA — UNDER BRITISH RULE.

GOLDWIN SMITH,
Formerly Regius Professor of Modern History in the University of Oxford, and Emeritus Professor of Cornell University.

12. **Canada — Local Government.** Under the British North America Act of 1867, which is virtually the constitution of the Dominion of Canada, the organization of local government is placed within the jurisdiction of the different provinces. There is consequently considerable variety in the structure of rural and urban government in the different parts of the Dominion. Certain general features are, however, to be observed. The fundamental principle of organization is that of local autonomy by the means of representative elected bodies. The provinces are divided into counties, subdivided into townships, in which again school sections are formed. The county and the township are not everywhere found side by side. Indeed, the provinces of Canada present the same contrast between the predominance of the township and the county as is found in the United States. In Nova Scotia and New Brunswick the county is the unit of local government; in Ontario and Quebec both township and county are found; throughout the West the township system prevails, the county being only a judicial area. In addition to these rural areas of government, there are found incorporated villages, towns, and cities. In Ontario and Manitoba incorporation takes place by virtue of a general statute; elsewhere it is done by special legislation. The details of local government may best be understood by first passing in review the organization and powers of rural governing bodies in the different provinces, and treating separately the question of town and city government and municipal franchises. Ontario, the most populous of the provinces, contains 43 counties and 423 townships. Both of these divisions vary greatly in size and population. The largest county (Grey) contains 1,071,642 acres, the smallest (Brant) only 196,800 acres. Thirty-two townships contain less than 20,000 acres, 11 of them more than 80,000 acres each. There are in addition the districts of Muskoka, Parry Sound, Nipissing, Manitoulin, Algoma, Thunder Bay, and Rainy River, not yet organized as counties, but in the settled portions of which 83 townships have been incorporated. The affairs of the townships are managed by a reeve and four councillors elected yearly. For the county there is a county council, varying in number from 8 to 18, two members being elected from each of the districts into which the county is divided. The cumulative system of voting was introduced in 1896. The franchise for all local elections is extremely wide. It includes all men, widows, and spinsters of 21 years and upward, rated for real property to an extent varying from $100 in the townships to $400 in the cities; those assessed for an income of $400 and farmers' sons of full age living at home. The township council is chiefly concerned with the maintenance of roads and bridges, the levy and collection of school taxes and the collection of the county tax. Assessors

appointed annually by the township council make a valuation of real and personal property. The other principal officers of the township are the treasurer and the township clerk. The latter, though legally holding office at the pleasure of the council, enjoys a practically permanent tenure. He prepares the collector's rolls, statute labor lists, voters' lists, etc., registers births, deaths, and marriages, and performs many other duties assigned to him by separate statutes. The county council meets at the "county town," under the presidency of a warden whom it elects annually. It acts largely through committees, both standing and special. It appoints a treasurer, a county clerk, an engineer, a public school inspector, and two auditors. The county council provides accommodation for the courts of justice, maintains county buildings, roads, and bridges, houses of refuge, etc. The county rate is collected with the local taxation, but the county council has power to "equalize" the valuations of the local assessors if it thinks necessary. For organization of school districts, and control of schools in Ontario and elsewhere, see article on PUBLIC EDUCATION IN CANADA. Local government in the province of Quebec is organized under a municipal code enacted by the legislature (24 Dec. 1870), and revised in 1888. The larger towns and the cities are incorporated under special charters granted by the legislature. Of the counties some are divided into parishes, others into townships. For each county there is a council composed of all the mayors of the included municipalities. At its head is a warden (préfet) whom it annually elects. The county council meets in regular session four times a year; its duties consist chiefly in the construction and maintenance of roads, bridges, etc., the locating of the circuit court, provision against forest fires, etc. The subordinate local councils (parish, township, united township, village, and town) consist of seven councillors elected annually throughout the province, each council having a mayor as its head. The powers of these minor councils extend to highways, bridges, ferries, regulation of public health, etc. For all local purposes direct taxes are levied on all real estate, except the property of the government and that of religious and educational institutions. (For organization, etc., of schools, consult article on PUBLIC EDUCATION.) The seigniorial tenure of land, which once carried with it certain powers of local administration, is also treated in a separate article. The local government of New Brunswick is regulated by a consolidated statute of 1898. Each county has an elected council, meeting twice a year. The larger cities have a representative in the county council as well as their own local council. The officers of the parishes are appointed by the county council. In Nova Scotia there are elective county councils, choosing its own wardens. Their by-laws are subject to the approval of the legislature. The counties of Prince Edward Island are electoral and judicial areas, but, owing to the small size of the province the legislature itself acts as the organ of local government; villages and towns are, however, incorporated with elective councils. In Manitoba, in the Northwest Territories, and British Columbia local government centres in the township, administered by a council of four to six members, with a reeve at its head. The unorganized territories (Yukon, Mackenzie, Keewatin, and Ungava) are

1. Sir William Dawson.
3. Sir Gilbert Parker.
2. Goldwin Smith.
4. Louis H. Fréchette.

controlled by the Dominion government, and have no representative institutions. The government in Canadian cities is regulated by statutes of the provincial legislatures. This fact permits of frequent change, and a continuous development of organization to meet the circumstances of the hour. In Toronto, for example, and in many other cities, it is the practice to suggest to the Parliament from year to year such alterations of the municipal act as seems advisable. In the majority of the Canadian provinces towns and cities are incorporated by special legislation; in Ontario and Manitoba, by virtue of general statutes on proclamation by the lieutenant-governor. Even in these provinces, however, special declaratory acts are usually passed announcing the incorporation and making provision for liabilities, etc. The typical form of Canadian urban government consists of a single chamber of aldermen (varying in number from 9 to 26) with a mayor. Both the mayor and council are generally elected for one year. In Montreal and Quebec the mayor is elected for two years, and in the latter city is chosen from among the aldermen. In Montreal, Quebec, Winnipeg, Brandon, and Vancouver the aldermen are elected for two years. A board of control (the mayor with four aldermen), whose function it is to prepare the annual estimates, has recently (1897) been adopted for the cities of Ontario (except Hamilton) having a population of more than 45,000. Municipal offices are, in most cases, filled by appointments made by the mayor or the council. In the cities of Ontario and British Columbia, in Winnipeg, Charlottetown, and Saint John, police appointments are made by commissioners independent of the civic government. The liquor licenses are almost everywhere under the control of the provincial authorities. The municipal suffrage in Canada is more restricted than the rural or parliamentary. Throughout Ontario, in Montreal, Quebec, Calgary, and the four largest cities of British Columbia a special qualification of real property or income is demanded. The chief sources of civic revenue are found in taxes on real property (averaging 21.8 mills on the dollar in Ontario 1898), betterment taxes, and, in some cases, license taxes and percentage receipts from city franchises. Municipal indebtedness, incurred mainly for waterworks and education, has much increased of late years, but the rate of interest on city debentures, which formerly stood at 6 and 7 per cent, has now in many instances fallen to 3 or 4. The total debt of Montreal in 1902 was $27,000,000, of Toronto in 1901 about $22,000,000. Except for waterworks there is but little municipal management of public works. Winnipeg, New Westminster, Three Rivers, and a number of minor towns in Ontario own and operate electric plants. Street railway franchises are granted for periods varying from 15 to 30 years; in Toronto, Montreal, Hamilton, Ottawa, and Halifax the city receives a percentage of gross receipts.

Bibliography.— Biggar, 'Municipal Manual' (Ontario 1900); University of Toronto Studies, Vol. II., Nos. 1-2; Report of Ontario Assessment Commission (1901-2); Bourinot, 'Local Government in Canada'; Johns Hopkins University Studies in History; Municipal Undertakings: Provincial Report (1904).

STEPHEN LEACOCK,
Lecturer in Political Science, McGill University.

13. Canada — Relations to Great Britain. When the Canadian Confederation was formed its founders believed that they were establishing a nation. Their hopes have been slow of fulfilment, for, though the phrase "The Canadian Nation" is frequently used, that *status* Canada has not really attained. She is still under tutelage. Her Parliament exists not by the will of her own people, but under an enactment of the Parliament of Great Britain, which, in theory, may at any time change the Canadian constitution without reference to the Canadians themselves. Canada possesses no treaty-making powers. She has no authority to make either war or peace. She does not even control her own copyright laws. (See COPYRIGHT, CANADIAN.) There is an appeal from her courts to the king's privy council in London. But while on these lines a formidable list of restrictions could be drawn up, the will of the Canadian people is in fact supreme in regard to Canadian affairs. Authority once granted, the Imperial Parliament would never venture to revoke, though from time to time in the borderland of rival jurisdiction the cabinet at London has caused annoyance in Canada by what seem unreasonable checks. Again, British statesmen vie with each other in generous statements as to Canadian autonomy.

It is becoming more and more obvious that to Great Britain's policy and needs in the present day the co-operation of Canada is necessary. The Dominion occupies the middle ground between the East and West, and has in geographical situation the advantages possessed by the United States. The Canadian wheat fields are increasingly necessary for Britain's food supply. While in Canada there is striking devotion to the political tie with Great Britain, it goes hand in hand with a resolute conviction that her own domain Canada must rule for herself. No coercion of Canada by Great Britain would have any prospect of success. Probably the thought of coercing Canada would never occur to British statesmen. In any case the Dominion has her destiny in her own hands.

When Canada is called a "colony" the epithet is resented by the Canadian people; and Mr. Chamberlain, Lord Rosebery, and other British statesmen have avowed their sympathy with this dislike, since the title carries the brand of inferiority. It is sometimes suggested that the word "Dominion" in Canada's title should be changed to "Kingdom," since "Dominion" implies possession by some other power, while "Kingdom" asserts an equal status with England, Scotland, and Ireland. It is not improbable that in the future increased attention will be given to this proposal. There is no doubt that Canada is a little restless in her present situation and resents the patronizing attitude often adopted toward her in Great Britain. But to become a kingdom she must assume the full burdens of equal *status*. At the present time the British government spends considerable sums in maintaining fortifications in Canada and in keeping up military and naval establishments on the Atlantic and the Pacific. Canada's excuse for permitting these things to be done for her are two-fold: she has been spending enormous amounts in building railways that among other things serve military purposes, and she claims, too, that since she has no voice in regard to war or peace, those who control these issues may properly bear the expense of defense.

The relations of Canada to the United States are hardly less important to her than those of Great Britain. It has been difficult for many to understand why Canada, with so many ties in blood and ideals to the United States, with so much to be gained commercially by the step, should not join the Union. It may be answered that smaller nations have always been jealous of absorption by great neighbors. During centuries Scotland fought the proposals for union with England. At the present time little Holland, linked in blood with Germany, dreads the prospect of any political tie. There were periods when Canada seemed likely, to a superficial observer, to consent to annexation. In 1849, from the depths of great commercial depression, some of her political leaders, one of whom, Sir John Abbott, afterward became prime minister, openly proclaimed their desire for annexation. From 1888 to 1891, in a similar time of distress, commercial union with the United States, which would almost certainly have involved political union, was strenuously advocated by a powerful wing of the Liberal party. In spite of this the calmer judgment of the Canadian people has always been that it is best to remain a separate state. The United States and Canada together would be continental in size; if it is desired to prove that a state may become too big, the present condition of Russia need only be pointed to.

While this is true there is no doubt that throughout Canada a better feeling than was formerly apparent towards the United States now exists. Traces of hostility are still often found. The American commercial policy of a high tariff has hit Canada very hard and every attempt to soften its rigor has met with failure. With this present fact and the other fact that English-speaking Canada is in large degree descended from Loyalists driven out at the period of the revolution, it is not strange that hostile utterances should occasionally be heard. But though family traditions serve to perpetuate the old *animus* the issues of the revolution and of the War of 1812 are very, very ancient, with hardly more reality now than has Jacobite sentiment in England. When Canada was less important she was more sensitive and touchy and differences with the United States aroused greater feeling. Her present self-reliance has encouraged a better temper. Moreover the troublesome questions between the two countries have been for the most part settled. The only conflict possible is the commercial war involved in high tariffs and this is not likely soon to cease. Canada despairs of reciprocity in trade with the United States and has found markets elsewhere. See CANADA — RECIPROCITY BETWEEN CANADA AND THE UNITED STATES.

No party in Canada favors any radical alteration of her present position. The more thoughtful Canadians undoubtedly dislike the existence of an even nominal subservience to the Parliament at Westminster. They want complete independence, but it is "Independence within the Empire," that is to say, independence which involves perpetual alliance between Canada and Great Britain for all national purposes. When Edward VII. was crowned his title was changed to that of "King of the United Kingdom of Great Britain and Ireland and of the British Dominions beyond the Seas." This proposal was not found as soothing in Canada as it was intended to be. "I claim independence of the Parliament of Great Britain," says a Canadian publicist, Mr. J. S. Ewart, K.C., "and I object therefore to Canada being called a 'Dominion,' for the word implies subjection. Further, I object to being called a British Dominion, for I assert that Canada belongs not to the British but to Canadians. . . . And I resent being lumped with Trinidad and Guiana and Barbadoes as 'British Dominions over the Sea.'" The writer then proceeds to give his ideal for Canada: "Canada's Parliament shall be as omnipotent as that at Westminster. The king's Canadian ministers shall advise him upon all things Canadian with the same constitutional authority as that of British ministers to advise their sovereign about all things British; our own men shall decide our own law suits and command our own forces; and our own money shall provide for our own defence and for such mutual aid as we ourselves may approve." This is far removed from the ideal of what is called "Imperial Federation." (See CANADA — IMPERIAL FEDERATION.) Imperial Federation implies a central parliament clothed with at least some power, but Canada, which for generations has been struggling to increase her powers of self-government, will not consent to surrender any of the autonomy that she has won.

GEORGE M. WRONG,
Professor of History, University of Toronto.

14. Canada — Imperial Federation. Imperial federation is the name given to the various projects for revising the relations between Great Britain and her colonies, so as to give to the latter a share in the government of the empire. The growth of the colonies, and the increasing burden of national defence, naturally suggest that the colonies should contribute to the imperial revenue; on the other hand, such a contribution, unless accompanied by a voice in the councils of the mother country, would constitute that "taxation without representation" so abhorrent to Anglo-Saxon ideas. Such was the situation during the great controversy of the 18th century between Great Britain and her North American dependencies, and such is again the situation at the present day. Even in the 18th century various proposals were made for solving the colonial difficulty by admitting American representatives to the British Parliament. Governor Pownall (see POWNALL, THOMAS), Edmund Burke (q.v.), and Adam Smith (q.v.) made suggestions of this sort. But the difficulty of communication rendered any such federation impracticable. During the middle period of the 19th century it was currently believed that the manifest destiny of the colonies was independence. With the passing of that idea has arisen the demand for a closer bond of union. The imperial federation movement originated in the early '70s, an informal conference for discussing the subject being held in 1871. In 1884 the Imperial Federation League was founded, its first chairman being the Right Hon. W. E. Forster (q.v.). Lord Rosebery (q.v.), the Right Hon. Ed. Stanhope (sometime secretary of state for the colonies), and Sir Frederick Young (q.v.) (whose work, 'Imperial Federation,' had appeared in 1876) were interested in the movement from its inception. A significant event was seen in the London colonial conferences of 1887, to which representatives of both the self-governing and the crown colonies were summoned, and at which the subjects of imperial defense and trade were discussed. In 1892 a committee of the Imperial Federation League presented a practical scheme of federation. It recommended the institution of a council of the empire, to which delegates should be summoned from the self-governing colonies, the crown colonies, and India. The function of the council was to consist in the regulation of imperial defense. It was recognized, however, even at this stage of the movement, that there was no sufficient unanimity among the members of the League in reference to the details of the plan to be adopted to enable them to work effectively toward a common end. The League, whose work was declared to be only preliminary and preparatory, was dissolved in 1893 and its place was taken by a number of organizations having each a more definite purpose. Of these the United Empire Trade League became the advocate of the commercial union of the empire by means of protective duties. The Imperial Federation (Defence) Committee urges combined action for defensive purposes, the establishment of a navy supported by joint contributions being its immediate object. Most important, perhaps, is the British Empire League, established in 1894 and extended to the Dominion of Canada. The programme of the League aims at the permanent unity of the empire, the promotion of trade and inter-communication, the holding of periodic conferences, and co-operation in national defense. In Canada, indeed, the movement had already made considerable progress. The Imperial Federation League in Canada had been formed at Montreal in 1885, with branches subsequently established at various places in the Dominion. Under the auspices of the organizing committee of the League a distinguished Canadian, George Parkin, delivered addresses throughout Canada, and in 1889 was sent, on behalf of the parent league, on a tour of the Australasian colonies. In 1894, at the instigation of the Canadian government, a conference was held at Ottawa to discuss intercolonial trade and communication. The Imperial government, Canada, Cape Colony, and the Australasian colonies were represented. Resolutions were adopted in favor of reciprocal preferential duties among the colonies. A still more important conference was held in London in 1897 on the occasion of the jubilee celebration of that year. At this meeting the premiers of Canada, Newfoundland, New South Wales, Victoria, Queensland, South Australia, West Australia, Tasmania, New Zealand, Cape Colony, and Natal discussed with the Right Hon. Joseph Chamberlain (q.v.), secretary of state for the colonies, both the commercial and political relations of the mother country with the colonies. In reference to the former, a resolution was unanimously adopted favoring the "denunciation at the earliest convenient time of any treaties which now hamper the commercial relations between Great Britain and her colonies." The premiers also undertook to confer with their colleagues to see whether a preference could advantageously be given by the colonies to the products of the United Kingdom. In reference to political relations, the majority of the premiers endorsed the following resolutions: (1) "That the present political relations between the United Kingdom and the

self-governing colonies are generally satisfactory under the existing condition of things." (2) "That it is desirable, whenever and wherever practicable, to group together under a federal union those colonies which are geographically united." (3) "That it would be desirable to hold periodical conferences of representatives of the colonies and Great Britain for the discussion of matters of common interest." From the first of these resolutions Seddon of New Zealand and Sir E. N. Braddon of Tasmania dissented, on the ground that the time had already come for a reconstruction of political relations. The Canadian government in the next year (1898) extended to Great Britain and to such British colonies as should reciprocate, a tariff preference of 25 per cent, increased in 1900 to 33⅓ per cent. In the summer of 1902, on the occasion of the coronation of King Edward VII., a further colonial conference was held between Secretary Chamberlain and the premiers of the self-governing colonies. The meetings of the conference, of which there were 10 in all, were also attended by several ministers of Australia and Canada then present in London, and by the members of the British cabinet whose departments were concerned in the discussion. Chamberlain submitted a paper showing the disproportionate share of the burden of imperial defense at present borne by the United Kingdom. "If you are prepared at any time," he said, "to take any share, any proportionate share, in the burdens of the empire, we are prepared to meet you with any proposal for giving to you a corresponding voice in the policy of the empire." No definite conclusion was reached for the alteration of present political relations beyond the following resolution: "That it would be to the advantage of the empire if conferences were held, as far as practical, at intervals not exceeding four years, at which questions of common interest affecting the relations of the mother country and His Majesty's dominions over the seas could be discussed and considered as between the secretary of state for the colonies and the prime ministers of the self-governing colonies. The secretary of state for the colonies is requested to arrange for such conferences after communication with the prime ministers of the respective colonies. In case of any emergency arising upon which a special conference may have been deemed necessary, the next ordinary conference to be held not sooner than three years thereafter." On behalf of the commonwealth of Australia £200,-000 a year was offered toward the cost of the Australian Naval Squadron and naval reserve, from New Zealand £40,000 for the same purposes, from Cape Colony £50,000, and from Natal £35,000 for the imperial navy generally, and from Newfoundland £3,000 for maintaining a branch of the Royal naval reserve. The grants were subject to ratification by the colonial legislatures. Resolutions of a general character in favor of preferential trade were also adopted by the congress. The Australian contribution met with sharp criticism from the Melbourne *Age* as involving taxation without representation. In February 1903 the British Empire League in Canada passed a resolution against the abstention of Canada from naval contributions, and declared that "it would be proper for her . . . to contribute a fair and reasonable share toward the annual cost of the navy of the United Kingdom."

The question of imperial defense and colonial contributions has been under constant discussion in the colonies, especially in Canada and Australia, during the last two years. The general arguments in favor of a reconstruction of present imperial relations are very strong. The rapid growth of the population of the great self-governing colonies renders their exclusion from the government of the empire more and more at variance with the spirit of Anglo-Saxon institutions. The population of the United Kingdom (estimated June 1902) is 41,952,510, that of Canada (1901) 5,371,315, of Australia (1901) 3,771,715, of New Zealand 815,000, of Newfoundland 220,984, and the white population of the South African colonies about 850,000. The great discrepancy between the contributions made toward imperial defense by the people of the United Kingdom and those of the colonists is also very striking. The figures presented by Mr. Chamberlain at the conference of 1902 showed the per capita yearly expenditure for military and naval defense to be: for the United Kingdom, $7.12; for Canada, 49 cents; for New South Wales, 83 cents; for Victoria, 79 cents; for New Zealand, 81 cents; and for the Cape and Natal, from 50 to 75 cents. A further general argument in favor of imperial federation is based on the fact that, though politically united, the various parts of the British empire do not form a commercial unit. The grant of representative institutions to British colonies in the middle of the 19th century carried with it the right to set up a protective tariff against the mother country, a right of which the colonies have made full use. The preferences recently granted by Canada, New Zealand, and South Africa are far from amounting to commercial unification. The cogency of these general arguments is undoubtedly great, but when one passes from general considerations to explicit schemes of federation, difficulties of the gravest character are encountered. This is seen in the great variation in the different plans proposed. The League of 1892, as already said, proposed a council of empire supplementary to the British Imperial Parliament. Here difficulties at once occur. If the council is supreme over the British Parliament, then it would be necessary to effect a radical reconstruction of the sphere occupied by the latter. If it is inferior, it becomes merely an advisory body and represents no real colonial participation in imperial power. To meet this objection plans are proposed for the admission of colonial representatives to the British Parliament. As against this it is urged that the House of Commons, with its 670 members, is already too unwieldy for its work, and is already in a state of chronic congestion from the press of business, both British and imperial, with which it is compelled to deal. The question, moreover, arises as to whether the colonial representatives would be allowed to vote on all matters before the House or only on those of imperial import. The former system would obviously appear unjust to the people of Great Britain, the latter would introduce the cumbrous device of an "in-and-out" parliament, an arrangement notoriously difficult in operation. These objections seem logically to lead imperial federation toward such plans as those of Granville Cunningham ('Imperial Federation,'

1895) and Sir Frederick Young. By these writers a complete scheme of federation is proposed with an Imperial Parliament and local assemblies. Cunningham assigns a single local parliament for England, Ireland, and Scotland, with a viceroy representing the sovereign. Sir Frederick Young proposes a separate local parliament for each of the three divisions of the United Kingdom. A division of jurisdiction is suggested by Sir Frederick Young (address on 'Imperial Federation,' London 1903) as follows: "Imperial questions would comprise foreign relations, peace and war, national defence, revenue and expenditure for national, as distinguished from local, purposes, extensions of empire, the government of India, and generally all that comes within the department of international law." Such subjects as marriage, domicile wills, coinage, copyright, patents, railroads, might be left, the author thinks, "either to the Federal or Provincial governments without impairing the strength or efficiency of the imperial organization." Such a division of power would, however, introduce into British legislation the question of constitutional limitations and fundamentally alter the nature of parliamentary statutes and the relation of the judicial and legislative organs of government. The system of representation suggested by Cunningham would distribute the 300 members of the proposed Imperial Parliament as follows: England 185, Scotland 25, Ireland 40, the colonies 50. Of the colonial members he would allot 20 to Canada, 15 to Australia, and 5 each to New Zealand, the Cape settlements, and the West Indies. Such schemes of colonial representation at once meet with the difficult question of the extension of the franchise to the native races. "What," asks Prof. Goldwin Smith ('Saturday Review,' February 1897), "are they going to do with the West Indies? Are they going to import the negro vote into the political and diplomatic councils of the empire?" The same writer considers that colonial representation would carry with it the danger of the obtrusive influence of colonial party politics on the Imperial Parliament, the colonial members voting "in the Imperial councils with their eyes fixed on the ballot-box at home." A serious difficulty is also presented by India, whose population of 287,000,-000 seems admittedly to be outside of the imperial representation. Whether or not the government of India would fall within the sphere of the Imperial Parliament is a matter of divergent opinion. If it did not, the relations of India with the separate parliaments of England, Ireland, and Scotland would be difficult to adjust. Further trouble is presented by the question of the House of Lords. Would the Imperial Parliament be composed of a single chamber or of two? Mr. Cunningham, who makes the House of Lords the upper chamber of his Imperial Parliament, suggests that it would be necessary to add a few life peers (perhaps 20) to represent the colonies. It is not stated why they should be "few" or why they should only be life peers. Perplexing also is the question of the public finance of the reconstructed empire. The national debt of the United Kingdom and the debts of the colonies would have, in some way, to be adjusted to the new relations. The consideration of revenue raises the question whether imperial federation would necessitate a customs union; in this case either Great Britain must abandon free trade, or the colonies must abandon protection. These and other difficulties which beset any practical scheme of federation serve for the present to keep the political problem of imperial relations in suspense and postpone its solution until the pressure becomes more intense. To the commercial aspect of the question renewed interest has been directed by Mr. Chamberlain's present agitation in favor of a revision of the British fiscal policy. Consult: Parkin, 'Imperial Federation' (1892); Cunningham, 'Scheme for Imperial Federation' (1895). See also CANADA — SINCE CONFEDERATION; CANADA — RELATIONS TO GREAT BRITAIN; CANADA — THE BRITISH PREFERENTIAL TARIFF.

STEPHEN LEACOCK,
Lecturer on Political Science, McGill University.

15. Canada — Primary Education. According to the British North America Act. education within the Dominion was entrusted to the several Provinces. One reason for this was doubtless the fact that in language and creed the Provinces differed so widely. Each Province has worked out a system suited to its own particular needs and conditions, and though there are striking similarities in aims and methods, yet there are great diversities in details of administration and in results attained.

Education Free. — Speaking generally, primary education is free to all pupils of school age, that is, from 5 or 6 years to 18 or 21. In one of the Provinces a fee may be charged, but this is merely nominal. In kindergarten schools and secondary schools, the payment of fees as supplementary to state, municipal, and district aid is sometimes permitted.

The Central Governing Bodies. — In every case the system is administered by a central authority. In Prince Edward Island the Board of Education consists of the executive council, the principal of Prince of Wales College and Normal School, and the chief superintendent of education, the last-named officer being appointed by the lieutenant-governor in council. In New Brunswick the Board of Education consists of the executive council, the chancellor of the provincial university, and the chief superintendent of education, who is appointed by the lieutenant-governor in council. In Nova Scotia the Council of Public Instruction consists of members of the executive council, of whom five shall form a quorum, and the chief officer is a superintendent of education appointed by the lieutenant-governor in council. In Quebec the Council of Public Instruction consists of (1) the Roman Catholic bishops of the Province, (2) an equal number of Roman Catholic laymen, (3) an equal number of Protestants. The last two classes are appointed by the lieutenant-governor in council. This Council of Public Instruction is divided into two committees known as the Roman Catholic and the Protestant committee, each being concerned with the administration of schools of its own kind. The practical administration of schools is carried on through a superintendent of education, who is appointed by the lieutenant-governor in council, and through two secretaries, one for each section of the Council of Public Instruction. In Ontario the Department of Education consists of the executive council or a committee

thereof, and the head of this department is known as the minister of education. In the matter of examinations the department is advised by an educational council of 12 persons, 6 of whom are appointed by the senate of the university. In Manitoba the executive council forms the Department of Education, and an advisory board, consisting of members chosen by the government, the university and the teachers of the Province, has authority in such practical matters as the framing of a programme of studies, the certification of teachers, the authorization of text-books. In the Northwest Territories the Department of Education is presided over by a member of the executive council known as the commissioner of education who is assisted by an educational council of five persons, at least two of whom shall be Roman Catholics. In British Columbia the Council of Public Instruction is composed of the executive council, and the work under its direction is carried on by a superintendent of education.

Local Self-Control. — Though the governing bodies just mentioned regulate education as regards the organization, government, examination, and inspection of schools, the certification and training of teachers. the authorization of text-books, and other matters of like importance, yet much power is given in most of the Provinces to local school boards. Each district selects its own teacher, but must not take any one who has not a certificate to teach in the Province. Within limits each district erects the building it considers most suitable under the circumstances and equips it as it may desire. There is wise supervision in matters of this kind to prevent undue expenditure and to guard against overcrowding of pupils and lack of apparatus. In British Columbia the Council of Public Instruction is supreme in all matters, virtually doing away with district control, except in the selection of teacher.

The Religious Difficulty. — The constitution of the governing bodies in education indicates that there has been difficulty in establishing and administering school systems because of the conflicting religious beliefs of the people. A closer examination emphasizes this fact. In Quebec there are two systems of schools — one for Roman Catholics, one for Protestants. In Ontario there is a system of separate schools. In New Brunswick after a struggle lasting for many years a compromise has been effected whereby separatists have practically all they demand, though they have not separate schools in name. In the Northwest Territories separate schools are supported by the state. In Manitoba, which until 1890 had Protestant schools and Roman Catholic schools, there is now but one system.

Religious Exercises. — Closely connected with the separate school question is that of religious teaching and religious exercises. In British Columbia, schools must be conducted on strictly secular and non-sectarian principles. No religious dogma or creed shall be taught. The Lord's Prayer may be used in opening or closing school. No clergyman of any denomination shall be eligible for the position of superintendent. teacher or trustee. In the Northwest Territories no religious instruction shall be given until half an hour previous to school closing in the afternoon, after which time any such instruction permitted or desired by the board may be given. It is not compulsory on any pupil to attend during this period. Any school may be opened by the recitation of the Lord's Prayer. In Manitoba, schools may close with the reading of the Bible without comment and the recitation of the Lord's Prayer, and it is possible for clergymen or their appointees after half an hour before closing to give religious teaching to those of their own denomination. In Ontario every public school shall be opened with the Lord's Prayer and closed with the reading of Scriptures and the Lord's Prayer, or the prayer authorized by the Department of Education. Teachers who have conscientious scruples in this matter may be relieved. Attendance during religious exercises is not compulsory. Religious teaching may be given by the clergy or their representatives after the regular hours of school. In Quebec, in the Roman Catholic schools, there is daily prayer and systematic daily instruction in the catechism. In Protestant schools the first half hour is devoted to prayer, Scripture reading, instruction in morals, and Scripture history. No denominational teaching may be given. A conscience clause is operative. In New Brunswick the teacher may open and close the school by the reading of Scripture and by offering the Lord's Prayer. In Prince Edward Island the school is opened with Scripture reading, but no comment or explanation is permitted. In Nova Scotia the law is practically the same as for the last two provinces, local option being permitted.

The Support of Schools.— The schools of the Dominion are maintained by a fund drawn from three sources — a state fund, a municipal or county fund, and a fund yielded from district assessment. The government aid is distributed in different ways. In Prince Edward Island and New Brunswick the grant depends upon the sex and the grade of certificate of the teacher. In Nova Scotia it depends upon grade of certificate and the number of days school is open. In Quebec the sum depends upon the population of the district, and in Ontario it is divided among the counties, townships, cities, and towns in a similar manner. In Manitoba a definite sum depending upon the total grant available is given to each school open the full year, and a proportionate sum to schools open for less time. In the Northwest Territories the grant depends upon the size of the district, the number of days school has been kept open, the grade of certificate held by the teacher, and the percentage of attendance. In British Columbia the government meets practically all the expense of education except in the case of cities. Here a per capita grant is given. In Manitoba and the Territories no less than one-eighteenth of the whole land is set aside for school purposes. It is doubtful if any other country has made such ample provision for education.

The Salaries of Teachers.— In the older Provinces, when free schools were introduced and districts began to be formed, it was natural that every settler should wish to be near the school-house. This led to small school districts. When the burden of supporting the small district fell upon the small district there was a tendency to reduce the salary of the teacher to the lowest amount possible. The result has been most unhappy. In spite of excellent provision for the instruction and training of teachers it is now impossible to get as many who are fully-qualified for their work as there are schools; and the male members of the profession are becoming fewer every year. This is particularly true in those communities where there is great industrial activity and consequent openings for men. The question of consolidation of rural schools is now under discussion. In the more thickly settled parts of the older provinces consolidation may in time help to solve one of the greatest problems of elementary education in Canada. But it can never be more than a very partial solution. In the west the districts are about as large as they can be made. Consolidation in most cases is an impossibility. Relief can come about in only two ways: (1) There must be an increase of legislative aid; (2) there must be increased local support. The former is probably an impossibility because of the limited resources of the Provinces; the latter will come only as a matter of education. No people are in a better condition financially than the Canadian farmers. The burdens of taxation are comparatively light. Yet the salaries paid to teachers are very meagre. In Prince Edward Island the average salary in 1902 was $216.09, and a number were living on $130. In Nova Scotia the salaries vary from $438 for male teachers of the "B" grade and $293 for female teachers of the same grade, to $184 for males of "D" grade to $167 for females of the same grade. In Ontario the salaries average $436 for males and $313 for females. In Manitoba the average for all is $488. In the Territories the average is $47.67 per month.

Wherever salaries are small two things are noticeable: (1) The percentage of female teachers is large; (2) the percentage of trained teachers is small. In the Northwest Territories not over 5 per cent of the teachers are untrained; in Manitoba conditions are almost equally satisfactory. In Nova Scotia about 43 per cent of the teachers have taken normal training. In New Brunswick where salaries are small less than 20 per cent of the teachers are men; in Nova Scotia about 18 per cent; in Ontario 24 per cent; in Manitoba 30 per cent; in the Northwest Territories about 43 per cent. The small salaries, therefore, affect the schools in two very important respects, and this is being felt from one end of the Dominion to the other.

Training of Teachers.— The training of teachers is something to which all the Provinces have given much attention, though the system adopted is not uniform throughout. In Ontario, Manitoba, and the Northwest Territories the course is purely professional and based on a definite academic course. In other Provinces the academic and professional work are carried on simultaneously as in many of the normal schools of the United States. (See TEACHERS, PROFESSIONAL TRAINING OF; SCHOOLS, COUNTY TRAINING.) The tendency in professional training seems to be toward a short course for beginners, followed by actual experience in a schoolroom and then a longer and more philosophic course leading to a permanent license. The fact that all certificates are granted by provincial rather than local authorities does much to elevate the standard of the profession.

Teachers' Institutes.— The work of the normal schools is supplemented by teachers' institutes which are of two kinds, (1) Those arranged for and carried on under the direction of the Department of Education; (2) those which are purely voluntary on the part of the teachers. These institutes do much toward developing a professional spirit, toward bringing teachers into touch with educational progress in other lands, and toward bringing school and home into closer relationship. The greatest of these gatherings of teachers is the Dominion Educational Association, which meets every two or three years. All departments of education are here represented. As yet this association is in its infancy, just having held its fourth meeting, but it promises to be to the Dominion what the National Educational Association is to the United States. See COLLEGES FOR TEACHERS.

School Libraries.— It is recognized throughout Canada that school libraries are a necessity in education. In most of the Provinces grants are made to supplement the grants of trustees. The Northwest Territories has made the most complete provision by making it compulsory for trustees to spend annually a portion of the regular grant in the purchase of books for library purposes.

Coeducation.— A distinctive feature of Canadian elementary schools is the coeducation of the sexes. There are exceptions to this rule in Quebec and in a few leading cities of the other provinces. In all rural communities coeducation must continue to be the practice, and it is doubtful whether there will be any departure from customary procedure in cities and towns. The results morally and intellectually under present conditions seem as satisfactory as in lands where separation of the sexes is considered a necessity.

Courses of Study.— The course of study pursued in the various provinces does not differ very greatly from that followed in other civilized lands, though emphasis may not be placed on the same subjects. Though direct moral instruction is not systematically given in all the Provinces, it is doubtful if anything could be more salutary than the influence of the schools. The high moral standing of the Canadian citizen must be attributed in a measure to the faithful labor and supervision of the public school teacher. In addition to the study of the five central subjects,— language, literature, mathematics, geography, and history,— emphasis has of late been given to manual training (q.v.), and nature study (q.v.). The former branch received prominent notice owing to the liberality of one of Canada's most worthy citizens — Sir William McDonald. The work in nature study is carried on successfully in several of the Provinces and with excellent results. In the cities and towns particularly music and drawing are taught. The play impulse is recognized in the games of the school. In these the teacher frequently takes a prominent part. Though physical exercises are usually conducted for a few minutes each day and serve as a relaxation from mental labor, there is lacking that medical supervision in all things pertaining to bodily welfare, which is so necessary.

It is generally recognized in elementary schools that the method of study, and the mental attitude developed in pupils, are of as much importance as the facts learned. The power for self-direction developed in Canadian youth, is amply proven by the behavior of manhood. The method of classification, even in the large city schools, does not appear to have crushed out the individuality of the pupils. It may have removed idiosyncrasies, but it has still left power for independent action. The ideal of school government in Canada, though not fully realized in many cases, is that of a kindly authority which induces power of self-control. In this, the temper of the Canadian people is expressed. However, in the home as well as in the school, well-meant liberty often develops into license. Intelligence, right habits of thought, and good morals are often noted where manners and good taste are in a marked degree lacking. Yet on the whole the type of life represented in Canadian elementary schools is of a very high order.

Canada may be considered the land of the common school. With the one unfortunate exception already noted, there is nothing in the public school system which recognizes class, race, or creed. The school is the most potent agency for unifying the diverse elements of the population. With the exception of the foreigners who are entering the west, practically all children can read, write and calculate. Nearly all go to school for at least a portion of the school year. Probably for this reason no vigorous steps are taken to enforce the compulsory education clauses of the school acts. See ELEMENTARY EDUCATION; CANADA — SECONDARY EDUCATION; CANADA — HIGHER EDUCATION; CANADA — CATHOLIC EDUCATION. See also the section *Education* in the articles on the different Provinces.

W. A. McINTYRE, B.A.,
Normal School, Winnipeg.

16. **Canada — Secondary Education.** The public high schools of the English-speaking provinces have been modeled more or less upon those of Ontario, which was the first (1844) to organize a system of public instruction. As a result, there is a very general similarity amongst them. Quebec, however, which is largely French and Roman Catholic, with an English-speaking Protestant minority, has organized its high, as well as its elementary schools, in accordance with its exceptional conditions.

Secondary education in Canada is provided for in three classes of schools which are well distributed geographically and are known sometimes by different names in the different provinces:

(1) Public high schools, in which secondary education alone is provided for. A few do also the first year or the first and the second year work of the universities.

(2) Public high school grades in connection with the elementary schools. Sometimes such grades are as good as the high schools, and often gradually develop into separate institutions.

(3) A small number of private secondary schools. These have usually elementary grades attached and occasionally do the work of the earlier years of the universities. Their fewness is due chiefly to the efficiency of the public systems, which were organized early in the history of most of the provinces. As, however, the

wealth increases, more of such schools are established, but they are now, and will likely continue to be, comparatively unimportant factors in the education of the Dominion.

The public high schools differ markedly from those of the United States in being organized into one system in each province and in being controlled and supported by the province as well as by the locality. The causes which thus tend to uniformity in the individual systems have in most been reinforced by uniform examinations of the different grades, conducted by the central authority. The State-control is exercised by a minister of education, who is a member of the provincial cabinet, or by a superintendent of education, responsible to the cabinet, or by both. Such controlling officers have associated with them an advisory council, variously constituted, with more or less important powers. The functions of the State are legislative and general. Subject to this oversight, which is exercised directly and through government inspectors, and which prescribes text-books, courses of study, and school regulations, local boards of trustees or commissioners have complete control, appointing the teachers and managing the finances. The boards are thus able to deal with local conditions, while the State connection has secured a measure of uniformity and general efficiency of courses and standards. The State contributes often very liberally to the support of the public high schools, the expense of establishment and the rest of the expense of maintenance being provided for by local taxation. Sometimes small fees are also charged.

The private schools are generally proprietary and of denominational origin; and, as a result, nearly all of them are under denominational control. Although affected in their courses and organization by the denominating public systems, they have no connection with the State, except in the case of a few which are affiliated with State universities, or of some Quebec schools which are subsidized under certain conditions. Except also in Quebec, the public high schools are open to and attended by all denominations. The private schools, on the other hand, are usually sectarian, but the religious training given in most of the Protestant schools is such that they are patronized by the adherents of other churches than those with which they are connected.

All the secondary schools have more or less extended curricula, corresponding to those of the United States high schools; but, as there, the entrance and the leaving standards vary according to the system of organization, the efficiency of the elementary schools, the requirements of the universities, and the wealth and population of the different provinces. The Ontario high schools are the best developed and the most efficient, being, as regards standard, on a par with the best in the United States. Besides providing a general education, the Canadian high schools prepare for university matriculation, for commercial pursuits, and for teachers' non-professional certificates. In one important and far-reaching respect they differ from the high schools of the United States: their teachers must all hold certificates of scholastic and professional competency, authorized by the respective education departments, and varying in standard and character according to the conditions of the system. Such teachers are usually obliged to attend professional schools. Ontario, however, is exceptional in having a normal college, in the city of Hamilton, with a practice school attached, the former being controlled and supported by the government. Here are trained for one year the highest grade of public school and high school teachers. In the other provinces the normal schools provide the general professional training for all grades.

Following are additional details in regard to each of the provinces:

Ontario. — Here the special secondary schools are of two classes, high schools and collegiate institutes. The principal of each must be a graduate in arts of a university in the British dominions, with at least two assistants for a high school, and three for a collegiate institute. The staff of the latter must be specialists (usually with honor university degrees) in Classics, Mathematics, Moderns and History (including English), and Science, with a specialist in art and in the commercial subjects, some having as many as 20 teachers. Both classes of schools must have good accommodations and a minimum equipment — $800 for a high school, and $1,600 for a collegiate institute. The latter must also have a gymnasium, for which each school receives a maximum grant of $160 a year; a special grant of $80 a year may also be made to a high school which has one. Besides the separate high schools, there are, in connection with the elementary schools in localities where there are no high schools, fifth forms or continuation classes, which also do high school work of a character sometimes as good and as comprehensive as is done in the high schools. The teachers of these grades must hold first class certificates or other professional certificates satisfactory to the inspector and in accordance with the character of the work undertaken, but many of them are university graduates. Pupils pass from the fourth grade of the elementary (called public) schools (age 12 to 14) into the secondary schools, on uniform examination papers set by the education department and valued by local boards. Just recently, however, city boards have been given the right to set their own papers or to accept, under certain conditions, the promotion examinations of the public school staffs. The standard of entrance in Ontario is at least equal to that of the best United States high schools. Besides the usual courses, these schools may have special art, commercial, manual training, household science, and agriculture departments. These departments are not yet well developed. Already, however, the city of Toronto (q.v.) has a separate technical high school; and there are technical high school departments, with manual training and household science, in six or seven other centres of population. A high school is established by a county (or city) municipal council with the concurrence of the government, and its establishment involves a legislative grant of from $450 to $1,600 according to the grade, as well as its proper maintenance by the county and by the municipality in which it is situated. After providing for a minimum grant of $375 the rest of the legislative grant is distributed on the bases of the attendance, the value of the equipment, the amount of the teachers' salaries, and the character of the accommodations, a system which has greatly stimulated local expenditures and has done much to secure the efficiency of the schools. Some of the boards of trustees are separate from those of the public schools, and others have charge of both classes of schools as in the United States. In constitution they are peculiar in containing a representative of the Roman Catholic separate elementary school, if there should be one in the municipality (the city of Toronto has two). Until recently, as in the other provinces, the education department held uniform leaving examinations at the end of the course in each form. Now, however, as the consequence of evils associated with so much uniformity, these examinations have been discontinued and the department itself holds only those that are necessary for teachers' certificates. It continues, however, to conduct, through its educational council, the uniform matriculation examinations authorized by the universities of the province. In other matters also the educational policy of Ontario is now one of decentralization. Total number of high schools 138, of which 41 are collegiate institutes and 52 are free. Number of teachers 600, of whom 489 are university graduates (chiefly Canadian), and 368 hold honor degrees or the equivalent. Highest salary, $3,000; average for principals, $1,220; for assistants, $699. Number of pupils, 24,472; total legislative grant, $112,650; total county grant, $130,125; total local grant, $384,401; total fees, $105,801; total expenditure, $769,680. Total number of continuation classes (public school and Roman Catholic here separate) 480, of which 65 have each one or more classes doing high school work alone; total number of pupils, 4,864.

The public secondary school system is so efficient and so popular with all classes that there are very few private schools. Of these the chief is Upper Canada College (which, however, is only semi-private), an old historic residential school, at one time under government control, but now under a board of governors partly elected by the "Old Boys," and partly nominated, the State connection being maintained through the minister of education who is an *ex-officio* member. This college has still a small endowment, but is supported chiefly by fees. It does general and university matriculation work for boys, and is attended by pupils from all parts of the Dominion and even from the United States. Besides ladies' colleges which have been established in some of the cities, there are a few other colleges for boys, doing elementary and general work and that for university matriculation. One or two also have mixed classes, the chief being Albert College, Belleville, which was at one time a university but is now affiliated with the University of Toronto (q.v.), providing courses of various kinds and grades, as far as the end of the university work of the first year. With only one or two exceptions all the private schools are connected with denominations.

Quebec.— As has already been stated, the public secondary schools of Quebec differ from those of the other provinces in being denominational, Protestant and Roman Catholic, the latter being French. Of both classes, there are two grades called model schools and academies. The Protestant model and academy courses each extend over three years. On completing the first academy grade, pupils may enter McGill (Montreal) Normal School for teachers, and on completing the academy courses (pass matriculation) they may enter the universities. The Roman Catholic model and academy courses, on the other hand, extend each over two years and have no classical departments. On completing the four years' courses, pupils enter the Roman Catholic classical colleges to prepare for the universities. These colleges furnish good courses in philosophy, languages and literature, but are defective in science. They confer certain degrees and are a combination of high school and college, attended by boys and young men. Most of them are affiliated with Laval (the chief Roman Catholic) University (q.v.). The model schools of both denominations correspond generally to the United States grammar grades, so that they are not really high schools of the usual type. Occasionally they have grades which overlap the academy and the elementary schools. The Quebec secondary system, although superior in character to its elementary system, is inferior to those of most of the other Provinces, and to the best in the United States. As regards relation to the State, some of the secondary schools are dependent, some are wholly independent, and others are partly so. The dependent schools are controlled and supported similarly to those in Ontario. The independent schools are supported chiefly by fees and are controlled generally by Roman Catholic ecclesiastics; but, when schools of this class follow the authorized courses of study, they are subsidized by the province. Most of the classical colleges have endowments, and some of them are comparatively wealthy. Lay teachers are required to hold professional State certificates; the religious teachers are exempt; but the law in regard to the lay teachers is not well enforced. A model school is established by agreement amongst the school boards of two or more municipalities, and is under the control of the board of the municipality where it is situated. The establishment of an academy (three teachers the minimum) is authorized by the superintendent of public instruction on application of the commissioners of two or more municipalities. Such schools are controlled by trustees appointed from their own members by the commissioners on whose initiative they were established. The principals of the Protestant academies are, with one exception, men, almost all being university graduates. Besides the ordinary model schools and academies, there are certain special secondary schools which do work of a higher character, the Boys' and Girls' High School of the city of Quebec, Stanstead Wesleyan College School, Bishop's College School, Westmount Academy, the High School of Montreal, and one or two others. At the close of the session of the Protestant schools, each grade except the third academy (examined by the university for matriculation) is subjected to a uniform examination on papers prepared under the supervision of the inspector of superior schools.

Of the model schools under control of commissioners, 367 are Roman Catholic, 47 Protestant, and of the academies, 44 are Roman Catholic and 27 Protestant. Of the independent or partly independent schools, 144 are Roman Catholic model schools, 105 are Roman Catholic academies, and 2 are Protestant; there are also 18 Roman Catholic classical colleges. Of 121,126 pupils in attendance, 111,724 are Roman Catholic and 9,402 are Protestant. Of the Roman Catholic lay teachers, 564 hold professional certificates; 109 have none. Of the Protestant lay teachers 306 hold professional certificates. 27

have not. The total number of Roman Catholic religious teachers is 3,242.

Nova Scotia.— There are twelve grades in the public schools of Nova Scotia, grades eight, nine, ten, eleven and twelve being high school. Very many of the rural elementary schools have superior grades which do the first and the second year and even the third year work of the high schools. In the towns and larger villages the high school departments are separate. The law allows one high school, called the county academy, in each county, to share in the $10,000 which the Legislature grants for secondary education, in addition to the other grants to which they are entitled in common with the high school grades generally; provided the county academy is free to each pupil of the county who passes the uniform departmental entrance examinations. Should, however, the shire town fall below the superior school in equipment and accommodations, the latter may be made the county academy by the council of public instruction. Besides the uniform entrance examinations the education department holds uniform examinations in the courses of all the high school grades, and the universities and colleges of the provinces accept for matriculation the certificate of having passed grade eleven when it indicates a pass in the subjects they prescribe. There are 19 county academies with 59 teachers, of whom 20 are university graduates, class A (the highest) being the necessary professional qualification for the high school teachers of all grades of school. In 1903 the total enrollment was 7,081, of which 822 belonged to grade eleven, and 112 to grade twelve. Of the total attendance about 1,700 belonged to the county academies. Nova Scotia has 16 private schools which report an attendance of 476 as doing high school work.

New Brunswick.— Secondary education in New Brunswick is provided for in grammar and superior schools. The number of the former is 13, with 37 teachers and an enrollment of 1,084. Teachers holding license of the grammar school class receive from the government $350 a year provided the district also pays the teacher at least an equal amount; but not more than four teachers in any one grammar school can receive this legislative grant. These schools are free to all pupils in the county in grades eight to twelve. Their work is of the usual character. Superior schools may be established in each county, one for every 6,000 inhabitants. The principal must hold a first-class superior license, and receive from the government a grant of $250 a year. In this case also the trustees must add an equal amount. Superior schools in grades seven and upwards are free to all pupils residing within and belonging to the parish in which the schools are situated. As in the other provinces, many of these schools are high schools in everything except the name, and do the same class of work.

Prince Edward Island.— This province has no high schools proper, but provision for the work has been made in about 30 schools with high school departments, in 34 graded schools, and in some of the best conducted primary schools. In these grades about 1,400 pupils are prepared for entrance into Prince of Wales College and Normal School in Charlottetown (the capital) in a course which corresponds to that of the first two years of a high school. All the schools are supported by legislative aid and district assessment, of which the former constitutes about three-fourths of the expenditure. No special grant is made for high school purposes. Whatever is paid extra comes by voluntary vote of the rate-payers of the district.

Manitoba.— In Manitoba, a recently settled province, the high school work is done in intermediate schools, of which there are 46 with 124 pupils, and in collegiate institutes, of which there are three, with 1,160 pupils. The intermediate schools are elementary schools with a high school grade. They do general work and prepare for third and second class non-professional teachers' certificates, but they rarely take up the languages. Such schools receive a special legislative grant of $300. The collegiate institutes at Winnipeg, Brandon, and Portage la Prairie, in addition to the high school work by the intermediate grades, prepare for first class certificates and matriculation into Manitoba University with occasionally the work of the first year. (See MANITOBA — EDUCATION.) The legislative grant to these three schools is a liberal one, $8,400 being distributed on bases that recognize their efficiency. Principals of intermediate schools must hold first class certificates; principals of collegiate institutes must in addition be university graduates. The assistants also of both classes of schools must hold professional certificates.

Northwest Territories.— The territories have not as yet developed a high school system. This work is done in grades six, seven and eight of 16 of the elementary schools, with an attendance of 88 in the rural districts and of 493 in the towns and villages. Grade six prepares for third class certificates, grade seven for university pass matriculation and second-class certificates, and grade eight for senior matriculation or the first year examination of the University of Manitoba and for first class certificates. When the languages are taught the principals are university graduates who have had a course of training in a normal school or college. These schools are supported by local taxation and by liberal legislative grants distributed on various bases in accordance with their size and efficiency. A private college has been established at Edmonton (Methodist), that does matriculation and first year work, and there are others at Calgary and Kamloops (both Presbyterian), but as yet these have not developed regular high school courses.

British Columbia.— In this, the most westerly province, there are 8 high schools with 856 pupils and 27 teachers, of whom 17 belong to the high schools at Vancouver and Victoria. (In 1903 two more were established.) These schools do the usual work of the other Dominion high schools. Vancouver high school and college, however, has two divisions which take up the first and second years' courses of McGill University (q.v.) (Montreal) with which this school and Victoria high school are affiliated and which conducts the examinations of the university grades. In cities where high schools are in operation and where the buildings and accommodations are satisfactory to the council of public instruction, a special legislative grant of $300 is made for each teacher employed. In this province not only is the school system non-sectarian, but no clergyman is eligible for the position of superintendent, inspector, teacher, or trustee. The Methodist Church maintains Columbia College at New Westminster. This college has affiliation relations with Toronto University and does both secondary school work and the work of the first year of the university, the examination papers being sent from Toronto and valued by the university examiners. See CANADA — PRIMARY EDUCATION ; CANADA — HIGHER EDUCATION ; CANADA — CATHOLIC EDUCATION ; CANADIAN UNIVERSITIES ; EDUCATION ; EDUCATION IN LATIN AMERICA ; EDUCATION IN THE UNITED STATES ; EDUCATION, CATHOLIC ; EDUCATION, SECONDARY.

JOHN SEATH,
Inspector of High Schools and Collegiate Institutes for Ontario.

17. Canada — Higher Education. The history of higher education in Canada is by no means a homogeneous development in all the provinces. Each province, possessing its own machinery of local government and peculiarities of social and economic condition, has, as might be expected. evolved its own system of higher education. It is, therefore, the more remarkable that the beginnings of university education were almost identical in all the older provinces. This was due to the enlightened policy of the British government, which through the executive heads of the colonies began very early to make provision for future educational needs. In Upper Canada (now Ontario) and New Brunswick this provision took the form of an endowment out of Crown lands for the purposes of higher education. In Nova Scotia, already a self-governing colony, the Legislature was encouraged to devote a special grant of money to establish a university and to make an annual appropriation in support of it thereafter, while the Imperial Parliament endorsed this action by voting much more substantial sums both· for establishment and for annual maintenance. In Lower Canada (now Quebec) a proposal was made to create an undenominational state university, but the uncompromising hostility of the Roman Catholic Church to the idea prevented it from being carried out. Thus in each of the four colonies or provinces which at the end of the 18th century made up the settled portion of British North America the policy was inaugurated of establishing State universities, either with large land endowments or with the pledge of support by the provincial Legislature. The next stage was also alike in all the provinces of older Canada except Lower Canada. In these a narrower view prevailed, and the State college in each, when established, discriminated in favor of the Church of England against other religious denominations. It was an attempt to implant in the colonies the English institution of an established Church. but the conditions in Canada were very different from those in England ; the Church of England was numerically hardly stronger than the Presbyterian, Methodist, or Baptist bodies separately, and certainly no exclusive right to control the State universities should have been given. The other denominations accordingly, seeing the doors of the State institution closed to their members, or open perhaps but with reservations in favor of a rival Church, established their own institutions of higher education. Thus, instead of a single well-supported university in each province there were several universities of a small calibre, none of them, not excepting the State university, coming up to the standard that had been anticipated when the policy of a single State-supported institution

for each province was framed. In course of time the disadvantages of division became more apparent. The denominational character of the State universities was altered and negotiations for alliance were seriously begun. Up to the present time these negotiations have had no result in Nova Scotia or New Brunswick. But in Ontario a third stage has been reached, and the movement to combine resources has met with partial success. In western Canada the history of higher education is different. Profiting, perhaps, by the experience of the older provinces, the State university in Manitoba has been established under conditions that prevent it from being controlled in the interests of any denomination, and at the same time the foundation of denominational rivals has been guarded against. A State university for the Northwest Territories has just been established by act of the Legislature, and it is probable that it will develop on similar lines.

Nova Scotia.— Taking each province in turn, for a more detailed account, we begin with Nova Scotia, the earliest settled of the English-speaking provinces of Canada. The first attempt at establishing a university was made by act of the Legislature in 1789 incorporating King's College at Windsor, where a seminary had been founded a year before by legislative aid. A grant of £500 for a site was also made and an annual appropriation of £400 for maintenance. In the following year the British Parliament gave £4,000 in further aid of the infant institution. It does not appear that actual university powers were obtained until 1802, when a royal charter was granted. At the same time an annual subsidy of £1,000, which was not discontinued until 1835, began to be made by the British Parliament. The charter gave control of King's College to the authorities of the Church of England in the province, and at the beginning of its career the governing body unwisely restricted to members of that Church the right of entering the college as students, thus completely establishing the sectarian character of the State institution. A majority of the inhabitants of the province were now debarred from sharing in the benefits to which they had looked forward, and agitation began for a freer system. In response to this demand Dalhousie College was founded at Halifax in 1821 out of funds at the disposal of the governor for provincial purposes. Attempts at fusion of the two State-endowed colleges were subsequently made from time to time but without success. It was as a result of the refusal in 1835 of the governors of King's College to surrender their charter and amalgamate with Dalhousie College that the imperial grant of £1,000 was withdrawn. Dalhousie College, though founded in 1821 and soon afterward provided with a building, was not opened for academical instruction until 1838, when sufficient funds had accumulated to enable a beginning to be made. In 1841 university powers were conferred by act of Legislature and control was vested in a board appointed by the lieutenant-governor. But a similar mistake had been made as in the case of King's College, and Presbyterian influences had been allowed to preside at the organization in 1838. The Baptist body, therefore, seeing one of the State institutions avowedly under Anglican control, the other practically Presbyterian, pro-

ceeded to establish a college of its own at Wolfville. It was named Queen's College, and was
formally opened in 1839. The act of incorporation conferring university powers was not passed
however until 1840, and another act in 1841
changed its name to Acadia College, which it
still retains, with the alteration of "university"
for "college." The Roman Catholic Church,
which had always stood apart from any system
of higher education under State control, established somewhat later St. Francis Xavier's College at Antigonish, in the year 1855. Under
varying conditions higher education in the province continued to be carried on for a number
of years by the institutions named, two of them
being the recipients of government bounty. Dalhousie College, indeed, for want of funds was
closed from 1845 to 1863, and on reorganization
at the latter date was given a strictly non-denominational character. But the hope of uniting all
the existing colleges in a single State university had not been given up. In 1876 an act of
the Legislature established the University of
Halifax, which should examine and confer degrees upon candidates sent up by the colleges.
The latter, however, gave it no support, and
continued to exercise their university functions.
In 1881 the Legislature withdrew its financial
support and at the same time discontinued the
annual grant which had hitherto been made to
King's College. University federation in Nova
Scotia had proved a failure, and no scheme to
that effect has since been proposed. At present Nova Scotia possesses five institutions with
university powers, a second Roman Catholic
college, Saint Anne's College, in the county of
Digby, having been established in 1890 The
numbers of members of faculties and of students
in the several colleges are as follows for the
latest year for which statistics have been issued:

character of the new college was strongly opposed by other religious denominations. In 1842
the Wesleyan Methodists succeeded in establishing an institution of their own, Mount Allison
Academy, at Sackville. At first only a secondary school, it received in 1858 university powers, which came into operation four years later.
Meanwhile agitation against the existing constitution of the provincial college began to bear
fruit. In 1845 religious tests were abolished,
and in 1859 reorganization on a non-denominational basis was effected and the name changed
to University of New Brunswick. A third university for the province was added in 1864, when
the Roman Catholic College of St. Joseph was
founded at Memramcook. The latest statistics
(1903) for the three universities of the province
are as follows:

	Prof. etc.	Stud.
University of New Brunswick	7	193
Mount Allison College	10	175
Saint Joseph's College	10	48

Quebec.— Before the cession of Canada to
Great Britain in 1763 the control of all education in the French colony had been in the hands
of the Roman Catholic religious orders. Laval,
first bishop of Quebec, had established the Grand
Séminaire at Quebec in 1663, which is perpetuated as Laval University of the present day.
The Grand Séminaire, however, was not a university, but a theological training college for
the priesthood. The first suggestion of a university in the province was made in 1789, when
a committee of the executive, in reporting on
the condition of education in the province of
Lower Canada (now Quebec), recommended
the establishment of a non-denominational university at Quebec. The opposition of the Roman Catholic bishop prevented the suggestion
from being carried out, and though the hope
was long cherished that the project would be

	Fac. of arts and sciences		Fac. of medicine		Faculty of law		Faculty of divinity	
	Professors and lecturers	Students	Prof. etc.	Students	Prof. etc.	Students	Prof. etc.	Students
King's College	7	24	....	....	14	16	6	1
Dalhousie College	25	231	23	80	5	57	....	....
Acadia University	12 (All faculties)	131	....	....	....	....	....	....
St. Francis Xavier's College	12 (All faculties)	122	....	....	....	....	....	....
St. Anne's College	University work not yet undertaken							

New Brunswick.—As early as 1786 an endowment of 2,000 acres near Fredericton, the capital,
was set aside for the foundation of a provincial
Academy of Arts and Sciences, which became
incorporated in 1800 as the College of New
Brunswick. In 1805 an act was passed authorizing an annual grant of £100 in addition, which
was subsequently increased from time to time up
to $8.844, at which sum it has stood since 1829.
In 1828 the provincial charter was surrendered
and a Royal charter obtained incorporating the
institution under the favorite name of King's
College, with university powers. In the following year a suitable building was erected and
academical work begun. The Royal charter contained, however, the same provision for Church
of England control which had already begun to
work so disastrously in Nova Scotia, and almost
from the moment of its inception the sectarian

renewed under more favorable conditions, no
subsequent proposal to that effect was ever formally made. It was left to private enterprise
to establish the first university in Lower Canada.
In 1813 the Hon. James McGill of Montreal
died, leaving by will a piece of land as a site for
a university or college and the sum of £10,000
for maintenance. A Royal charter was obtained
in 1820, but the college, bearing its founder's
name, was not opened until 1829, and on the day
of its inauguration the Montreal Medical Institute was united to it as its medical faculty. For
more than 20 years the college had a precarious
existence, its expansion being, to a certain extent, hampered by the constitution of its governing board, but a new charter was obtained in
1852 entirely freeing it from official control. The
history of McGill University (q.v.) since that
time is a record of steady improvement. It is

not identified with any religious body, nor is it dependent upon any form of state assistance. It owes its present position as one of the leading universities, not only of Canada but of the continent of America, to the generosity of the merchant princes of Montreal, and to the wise and able guidance of Sir J. W. Dawson, principal from 1855 to 1893, and of his successor, Dr. Peterson.

The second university to be established in the province in the interests of the English-speaking inhabitants was the Church of England institution at Lennoxville, called Bishop's College. It was incorporated in 1843, but a Royal charter conferring university powers was not obtained until 1853. In the previous year, 1852, a Royal charter had also issued to the corporation of the Grand Séminaire of Quebec empowering it to confer degrees and exercise other university functions, under the name of Université Laval. The university thus established remains the sole Roman Catholic university of the province, with faculties of divinity, law, medicine, and arts, having affiliated colleges and seminaries in various towns, and an integral branch of itself at Montreal under the name of "Succursale de l'Université Laval." Other colleges in the province without separate university powers, but carrying on university instruction, are Morrin College at Quebec, founded in 1860 under Presbyterian control, affiliated to McGill University since 1862, and St. Mary's College at Montreal, under control of the Jesuit order, incorporated in 1852, and since 1889 entitled by papal brief to confer the degrees of Laval University. There are numerous Roman Catholic colleges affiliated to Laval University, some of them of considerable antiquity. The oldest are Saint Raphael's College at Montreal, established by the Sulpicians in 1773; those at Nicolet, founded in 1804; Sainte Hyacinthe, in 1812; Sainte Thérèse, in 1824; Sainte Anne de la Pocatière, in 1827; and L'Assomption, in 1832. The higher education given at these colleges is chiefly theological. The statistics for 1903-4 of the three universities of the province are as follows:

1840 the charter for Queen's College at Kingston, the Presbyterian institution, was secured and the college was opened in 1842. In 1841 the Methodist theological seminary already established at Cobourg was reorganized as a university. It was not until after the establishment of these rival institutions that the work of teaching was begun in King's College, in 1843. Continued political agitation against the privileges accorded to members of the Church of England in the state university brought about a complete reconstitution in 1849, when the non-sectarian character of the University of Toronto (see TORONTO, UNIVERSITY OF), as it was then named, was firmly established. The chief result of this overthrow of Anglican control was the establishment in 1852 of a strictly Anglican university, Trinity College, through the exertions of the same bishop who had been instrumental, 25 years earlier, in procuring the charter for King's College in the interests of his communion. The only apparent effect of broadening the character of the state university had been to erect another rival. In 1853 reorganization of the University of Toronto took place again on a narrower basis; the teaching faculties of law and medicine were abolished, and the faculty of arts was constituted a separate corporation as University College, while the University of Toronto itself became, after the pattern of the University of London of the day, a mere examining and degree-conferring corporation. The next 30 years saw five more denominational colleges founded in the province, Albert College at Belleville in 1866 (Wesleyan Methodist); Ottawa College in 1866 (Roman Catholic); Regiopolis College at Kingston in 1866 (Roman Catholic); the Western University at London in 1878 (Church of England); and McMaster College in 1881 (Baptist), the last-named at first a theological college only, but in 1887 given full university powers. In spite of this multiplication of small colleges with university powers, a change of sentiment was gradually coming about. The needs of modern education in science called for considerable expenditure on laboratories and instruments. A

	Arts		Medicine		Law		Applied sci.		Divinity	
	Prof. etc.	Stud.	Prof. etc.	Stud.	Prof. etc.	Stud.	Prof. etc.	Stud.	Prof. etc.	Stud.
McGill University	46	356	74	420	11	40	23	280	....	....
Laval University (Quebec)....	16	90	15	119	11	78	....	....	7	112
Laval University (Montreal)...	18	48	48	180	12	108	7	48	12	300
Bishop's College	5	33	....	....	....	....	....	....	2	6

Ontario. — In Upper Canada (now Ontario) an endowment of 500,000 acres of Crown lands was set aside in 1798 for the purposes of higher education in the province, but not until 30 years later, in 1827, was a Royal charter obtained for the establishment of a university upon this endowment. The name of the institution, as in the provinces of Nova Scotia and New Brunswick, was King's College, and the unfortunate example set by the older provinces was also followed in providing for the Church of England control. The Methodist and Presbyterian bodies protested against the terms of the charter, and some modifications were secured in 1837, before actual organization of the college, but the concessions made were not sufficient, and these denominations proceeded to establish colleges of their own. In

strong state university in alliance with the denominational institutions could adequately supply the instruction in scientific subjects for them all, while they in turn might maintain their own faculties for teaching languages, philosophy, history, and theological subjects. The federation idea, as it was called, rapidly gained ground, and in 1887 an act of the legislature was passed reorganizing the University of Toronto once more, this time to broaden instead of to narrow the scope of its activity. The scientific subjects and one or two others were assigned to a teaching faculty of arts, the instruction being free to all students of the federated colleges. These, including the state college (University College), were concurrently to give instruction in languages and literature and certain branches of philosophy and history. Teaching faculties of medicine and law were also established in the university. Under this arrangement Victoria College, the Methodist university, became a federated institution in 1891, renouncing its right to confer degrees in any faculty except divinity; and Trinity College, the Church of England university, has taken similar action within the last year (1903). In pursuance of the policy outlined when the federation plan was under discussion, the University of Toronto has added largely to its facilities for teaching the sciences. In 1901 the School of Practical Science, a provincial school of engineering and applied chemistry, founded in 1878, was incorporated in the circle of University institutions by its staff of teachers becoming the faculty of applied science and engineering of the University of Toronto. The provincial colleges of dentistry, pharmacy, agriculture, and veterinary science have been affiliated, and the University holds examinations and confers degrees upon their students. Colleges of music have also been affiliated, and local examinations are held and degrees conferred in music. The expansion of the University of Toronto since 1887, as outlined above, is the most notable event in the history of higher education in Canada. It has been the justification of the far-sighted policy of the British governors of the colony at the end of the 18th century, when they made provision for a single university in each province to be the head of a state-supported system of education. Within a comparatively few years the University of Toronto has developed into the largest university of Canada and has reached the front rank of universities on the continent of America. Its importance is measured not only by the number of its students, but by the place which they take in the estimation of the academic world.

Victoria College and Trinity College having both federated with the provincial University, there remains independent but one of the three early rival denominational institutions, Queen's University (q.v.) at Kingston. Although still recognized as the Presbyterian university of the province it imposes no religious tests upon professors or students. Of the other denominational colleges founded later, Albert College has resigned its university powers and become affiliated with the University of Toronto, Regiopolis College was closed in 1869, and Ottawa College became the Catholic University of Ottawa in 1889.

The statistics of the existing universities of the province for 1903 are as follows:

with the sole power of conferring degrees in arts, law, and medicine in the province; degrees in divinity may only be conferred by colleges affiliated with the university. Up to the present year the university has been an examining and degree-conferring body only, all teaching being left to the affiliated colleges. Recently, however, a grant of land has been made by the provincial government for the erection of a building for purposes of instruction in the departments of science and for a university library. Three university lecturers in science have already been appointed, so that a new departure in the university system of the province has fairly begun, the further development of which will be watched with great interest. There are at present four arts colleges and one medical college affiliated with the University of Manitoba. Saint Boniface College is a Roman Catholic institution and was established as a small school so early as 1818; Saint John's College (Church of England) was founded in 1866; Manitoba College (Presbyterian) in 1871; Wesley College (Methodist) in 1888; Manitoba Medical College in 1883. All are in Winnipeg except Saint Boniface College, which remains at the town of Saint Boniface, where it was first established. The numbers of members of faculties and students are as follows for 1903:

University of Manitoba — Students registered in Arts, 184; in Medicine, 100; in Law 18.

	Faculty	Students
Saint Boniface College	23	187
Saint John's College	10	52
Manitoba College	12	177
Wesley College	12	163

Up to the present time no university has been organized in western Canada except the University of Manitoba. Local examinations are conducted in various centres of British Columbia by the University of Toronto and by McGill University. In the chief centres of population in that province denominational colleges and schools are found, such as Vancouver and Columbian colleges, which undertake some teaching of a university course in arts. The legislature of the Northwest Territories passed an act in the autumn of 1903 to establish a territorial university. The constitution of the governing body is much the same as obtains in the University of Manitoba or the University of Toronto. The power to affiliate colleges and to establish faculties is given to the university senate; but this body has not yet commenced its functions. See CANADA — CATHOLIC EDUCA-

	Arts		Medicine		Law		Applied sci.		Divinity	
	Prof. etc.	Stud.	Prof. etc.	Stud.	Prof. etc.	Stud.	Prof. etc.	Stud.	Prof. etc.	Stud.
University of Toronto.	101	1,012	70	721	......	......	20	402	......	......
(Univ. Coll.)	14)									
(Victoria Coll.)	14)									
(Trinity Coll.)	14)									
Queen's University	19	495	19	200	......	......	12	129	5	33
McMaster University	12	136	......	......	......	......	......	......	3	40
		61								
Western University	10 (All faculties)	......	......	......	......	......	......	......	......	......
Catholic Univ. of Ottawa	46	473	......	......	......	......	......	......	......	......

Manitoba.— Higher education in Manitoba is of recent date. By act of legislature in 1877 the University of Manitoba (q.v.) was established,

TION; CANADIAN UNIVERSITIES; HIGHER EDUCATION; UNIVERSITIES.

JAMES LOUDON,
President of University of Toronto.

18. Canada — Catholic Education. By the British North America Act of 1867 (see CANADA — CONFEDERATION) it was enacted, "That the local legislature of each province shall have power to make laws respecting education saving the rights and privileges which the Protestant or Catholic minority in both Canadas may possess, as to their denominational schools, at the time when the Union goes into effect." As therefore education belongs primarily to the different provinces, we shall consider each province separately.

Ontario. — One of the earliest tasks undertaken by the United Legislature of Upper and Lower Canada, in 1841, was the improvement of the primary schools. An act was passed in that year providing for denominational schools in both provinces. Taxes were levied uniformly upon all; and these taxes, with the legislative grant, were divided between the two classes of schools in proportion to the number of their supporters. Separate, or parochial, schools were not authorized in towns or cities, where a joint board consisting of an equal number of Catholics and Protestants controlled all schools. To the Catholic section was given full jurisdiction over Catholic schools. This act, on account of the dissimilar educational interests in Upper and Lower Canada, soon proved unsatisfactory. Two years afterward it was repealed, and an act for each of the Canadas was passed, duly recognizing the principle of religious education. The difficulty of adjusting the demands of Catholics, and of legislating for a systematic respect for all concerned, continued for many years with much acrimony, which religious, racial, and political differences tend so seriously to aggravate. A new turn was given the controversy in 1846, when the provincial secretary was relieved of his duties as chief superintendent of education, and a person appointed by the governor of Upper Canada for this position. The first, and indeed only, chief superintendent of education in Upper Canada was the Rev. Egerton Ryerson (see RYERSON, A. E.). The contest was in no way diminished by thus withdrawing the chief from the ministerial ranks and legislative hall. It continued unabated until 1863, when what is known as the Scott Act was introduced and passed. This act, being in operation at the time of confederation, remained the anchorage and basis for parochial education. The following are among the chief benefits of the act "(1) Permitting the union of adjacent rural sections, and allowing any Catholic within three miles of the school to become a supporter; (2) Requiring of lay teachers the same qualifications as for common schools; (3) Giving a share in all public appropriations for elementary education. The schools were at the same time made subject to inspection and to such regulations as the chief superintendent might impose." After remaining unchanged for 14 years some amendments to this act were introduced in regard to the trustees and supporters of the Catholic schools. One important clause was introduced, providing that a "separate school may become a model school for the preliminary training of Catholic teachers." The inspection of separate schools in cities and towns was confided to the high school inspectors, while in rural districts the duty devolved upon public school inspectors. The work of

the former increased so much, and the incompatibility of inspecting schools so different gave no satisfaction. The office of Separate School Inspector was created in 1882, and James F. White appointed. Since that time two others have, on account of the increase of work, been added, so that separate schools are regularly visited and systematically inspected. We quote the following points in regard to the support and teachers' qualifications from 'The School System of Ontario,' by G. W. Ross: "Separate schools are supported (a) by a grant from the provincial treasury, paid upon the basis of average attendance; (b) by a rate levied by the trustees upon the taxable property of the supporters of the school; (c) by fees from the pupils attending separate schools." Practically speaking, no fee is charged. "There are two classes of teachers employed in separate schools: one class, known as lay teachers, who are subject to the same examinations and receive their certificate of qualification in the same way as public school teachers; the other class known as religious teachers — members of religious communities — who are not, by the Separate School Act, subject to any examination." It is just to add that the religious communities are striving earnestly and with marked success to have their postulant and young members qualify in the normal and other technical schools. With regard to religious instruction, the separate schools are supervised by the clergy. "The Department of Education lays down no regulations and exercises no jurisdiction upon the subject."

TABLE OF ROMAN CATHOLIC SEPARATE SCHOOLS FOR THIRTEEN YEARS — 1890 TO 1902.

Year.	Schools.	Pupils.	Average Attendance	Receipts.	Expenditures.
1890....	259	34,571	18,395	$313,326	$289,703
1891....	289	36,168	20,795	320,386	278,687
1892....	312	37,466	21,560	326,035	289,838
1893....	313	38,067	21,863	305,767	270,729
1894....	328	39,762	23,328	392,393	337,307
1895....	334	39,773	24,090	331,501	296,055
1896....	339	40,846	24,630	337,030	303,147
1897....	340	41,620	24,996	335,324	302,169
1898....	345	41,667	25,671	389,185	349,481
1899....	352	41,796	25,767	401,155	352,012
1900.....	355	42,397	25,875	396,137	338,551
1901....	372	43,987	26,026	436,721	391,628
1902....	391	45,964	28,817	485,503	435,441

The work of secondary and higher education devolves upon the voluntary institutions conducted by the religious communities. These institutions, chiefly residential, range from the academy and select school to the college and university. Their programme of studies includes a liberal education based upon the programme of studies provided for by public institutions of a similar grade. Throughout Ontario there are 36 academies for young ladies. There is a Catholic university at Ottawa under the direction of the Oblate Fathers. The Most Rev. the Archbishop of Ottawa is apostolic chancellor. At present the Very Rev. Father Emery, D.M.I., is rector. There are faculties in theology, arts, and law, and a commercial department. The Grand Seminary for the Diocese of Ottawa is in connection with the University, as is also Saint

Joseph's College. It was unfortunately destroyed by fire on 1 Dec. 1903. The new plans (1904) foreshadow a building of exquisite design and magnificent proportions, which, when completed, will admirably fulfil its purpose as an educational institution and be an ornament to the capital of the Dominion. In Toronto, the educational centre of Ontario, is Saint Michael's College, in federation with the University of Toronto. It was founded in 1852, and is under the charge of the Fathers of the Community of Saint Basil. It conducts the course of Catholic philosophy and history as prescribed by the University of Toronto. Its course includes a commercial, a classical, and a philosophical course. The Basilian Fathers also conduct a large college at Sandwich, just opposite Detroit, entitled Assumption College. This institution was first founded in 1855; but it was not until 1870 that it was entrusted to the Basilian Community, under the superiorship of the Rev. D. O'Connor, now archbishop of Toronto. The present rector of the College is the Very Rev. Robert McBrady. The Diocese of Kingston has Regiopolis College, whose history is in two volumes, the first closing in 1869; the second opened in 1896, when, by the provision of the late Most Rev. James Vincent Cleary, archbishop of Kingston, an endowment was secured for its reestablishment. At present the work of the College terminates with the requirements for the honor matriculation examinations in either the University of Toronto or of Queen's University, Kingston. Saint Jerome's College is situated in the town of Berlin, in the county of Waterloo. It was established by the Very Rev. Father Louis Funcken, a member of the Congregation of the Resurrection. Originally it was intended for the education of young men of German descent. Its usefulness has widened, its professors have increased, and its students multiplied. Since its start in 1865 over 100 priests and a large number in the secular professions are counted among its graduates.

Quebec.— Catholic education in Quebec, the pioneer province of the Dominion, clusters around the Seminary of Montreal and the University of Laval at Quebec, whose early foundations are associated with the dawn of civilization and evangelization of Canada by the intrepid religious of France. The former was founded in 1649, and the latter in 1663 as a Grand Seminary, by François de Laval (see LAVAL-MONTMORENCY, F. X. DE). Even before — in 1615 — four Recollect Fathers taught an Indian school on the banks of the Saint Charles. In 1632 the Jesuits established a college in Upper Town (Quebec), which three years after began to receive pupils. The first school for girls in the colony was the Ursuline Convent of Quebec. This was followed in 1653 by the establishment of a convent in Montreal by Margaret Bourgeois, the saintly foundress of the Sisters of the Congregation. These institutions still remain. Progress marks their history — enlarged buildings and commodious show their success and the confidence in which their teachers are held; but the discipline and spirit is much the same, exercising a most beneficial influence of contentment and steadiness in an age of change and restlessness. Their further advance is marked by their multiplication. In 1773 the Sulpicians founded Montreal College, which they first named Saint Raphael's College. The Petit Seminaire de Quebec had been founded over 100 years before (1668). This first served as a preparatory school to the Jesuit College, and afterward took its place. Nor should it be supposed that under the French régime primary education was neglected. Chauveau says: "From the very beginning a large number of those who settled in the country had received a fair education, and the old parish registers still preserved at Quebec and Montreal show that a large proportion of the population could write."

At the beginning of the 19th century the number of schools in operation was 1,321, with 36,000 pupils. This does not include colleges, academies, or kindred schools. Garneau gives a total of 57,000. To advance primary education, Lieutenant-Governor Milnes, in 1801, urged the legislature to vote land, the revenue of which should be expended on education. An act was therefore passed, and the government formed a corporation for educational purposes under the name of the Royal Institution. This institution was neither successful nor satisfactory. After a trial of 20 years it proved so detrimental that Lord Dalhousie entertained the idea of forming two distinct Royal Institutions. This idea was not carried out. Eventually, however, but only after many years — in 1875, and when the Council of Public Instruction had taken the place of the Royal Institution — this idea was modified by the council being composed of two committees, one for Catholics and the other for Protestants. In spite of difficulties arising from legislation and from the disturbed state of the country in 1837-8, education advanced through the redoubled efforts of the clergy. The following colleges owe their existence to this period: Nicolet, founded in 1804; Saint Hyacinthe, in 1812; Sainte Thérèse, in 1824; Sainte Anne de la Pocatière, in 1827; and L'Assomption in 1832. Two Catholic normal schools were established in 1857: that of Jacques Cartier at Montreal, and Laval at Quebec. The support of these normal schools is taken partially from the superior education income fund and the common school fund. They are regulated by the Roman Catholic committee of the Council of Public Instruction, with the approval of the lieutenant-governor in council. These regulations include: (1) their management; (2) the terms and conditions upon which students shall be received and instructed; (3) the course of instruction to be followed; (4) the manner in which registers and books shall be kept; and (5) diplomas granted to students. The professors, directors, and principals are appointed or removed by the lieutenant-governor upon the recommendation of the Catholic committee of the Council of Public Instruction. In 1852 the Seminary of Laval enlarged its courtyards by securing a royal charter as a university. Its privileges were further extended in 1876 by Pope Pius IX., who bestowed upon the University canonical status as such, having for its protector at the Holy See the Cardinal Prefect of the Propaganda. The supervision of "faith and morals" is entrusted to a superior council of the University consisting of the archbishops and bishops of the province of Quebec, under the presidency of the archbishop of Quebec, who is the apostolic chancellor of the University. The ordinary council of the University consists of the rector, the directors of the Seminary of Quebec, and the three senior professors of each of the faculties of theology, law, arts, and medicine.

The superior of the Seminary is *ipso facto* rector of the University; and the visitor of the University is always the Catholic archbishop of Quebec. This council has full authority concerning the government and advancement of the University. It has power to nominate the professors of the faculties of law, medicine, and arts, and, upon sufficient and just cause, to revoke and annul its own nominations. It has the right to propose names suitable for the faculty of theology as professors, but it is the visitor who makes these appointments. The University is maintained by the Seminary of Quebec, which is still obliged to add more than $10,000 a year in order to make up the University deficit. A Succursal to Laval was established at Montreal some years ago with the same faculties of theology, law, arts, and medicine. The faculty of theology consists of the Grand Seminary of Montreal, which is under the direction of the priests of Saint Sulpice. The functions of the University are, in this question, limited to the granting of certificates after special examinations at the Grand Seminary. "The public schools of the province of Quebec are divided into elementary schools, model schools, and academies. Some of the public schools are said to be 'under control,' the others are said to be 'subsidized.' Schools under control are those whose teachers are engaged and paid by the school commissioners or trustees." The elementary school course consists of four years, and corresponds to the first four or five years of the public schools in the United States. According to the report of the superintendent of public instruction the Roman Catholic schools under control in 1901 contained 176,799 Roman Catholic pupils, and 587 Protestant pupils. Of these 171,446 were French and 5,940 were English. The next higher grade of school is the model school, which may be established by the union of two or more municipalities. In these cases the school is under the control of the municipality in which it is situated. Next to these are ranked the academies, which have their official origin in a petition signed by delegates who are chosen by the chairmen of the boards of trustees desiring the academy. This petition, addressed to the Council of Public Instruction, is, upon the approval of the Catholic committee of the Council, forwarded by the superintendent of education to the lieutenant-governor, with whom rests the final authorization. When established, an academy is under the control of three trustees. To provide for the building and maintenance of an academy a limited amount may be raised by a tax upon the taxable real property of the school municipality. Each academy fulfilling the required conditions is entitled to a share in the legislative grant for superior education. The course includes, besides religious instruction, grammar, composition, algebra to equations of the second degree, bookkeeping, history, political economy as applied to Canada, and elements of philosophy, geology, and botany.

STATISTICS OF ROMAN CATHOLIC MODEL SCHOOLS AND ACADEMIES, FROM THE REPORT OF EDUCATION FOR 1902.

I. MODEL SCHOOLS.
Number of schools under control of school commissioners, ... 367
Number of pupils attending the above schools, 62,314
Number of schools partly under control and partly independent 7

Number of pupils........................... 902
Number of independent schools.............. 137
Number of pupils........................... 14,957

To a number of schools................. 511
Total number of pupils................. 78,173

II. ACADEMIES.
Number of academies under control of school commissioners 44
Number of pupils........................... 16,185
Number of academies partly under control and partly independent 8
Number of pupils........................... 1,623
Number of independent academies.......... 97
Number of pupils........................... 15,743

Total number of academies............. 149
Total number of pupils................. 33,551

III. ROMAN CATHOLIC COLLEGES.
Number 19
Pupils in classical course................... 3,757
Pupils in commercial course............... 2,417
Total 6,174
Ecclesiastical (including religious) professors, 527
Lay professors 32

IV. ROMAN CATHOLIC NORMAL SCHOOLS.

	(a) Laval	(b) Jacques Cartier
Professors	10	11
Associate professors	6	5
Female pupil teachers who obtained diplomas	74	40
Male pupil teachers who obtained diplomas	39	41

V. LAVAL UNIVERSITY

	(a) Quebec	(b) Montreal
Professors in theology	7	11
Professors in law	11	11
Professors in medicine	14	48
Professors in arts	20	16
Students in theology 124		300
Students in law	90	108
Students in medicine 108		180
Students in arts	98	48
Students in pharmacy	6	...

Nova Scotia. — There are two means used by Catholic educationists in Nova Scotia for keeping in touch with the public school system. The first method is by ranking an institution as a county academy. "The county academy is that high school within the county which receives a special grant on account of its agreement to admit free any students from the county who are able to pass the county academy entrance examination." The Saint Francis Xavier College at Antigonish and the French College of Sainte-Anne in the county of Digby avail themselves of this opportunity, and function under the law as county academies, receiving therefor a due share of the academic grant. Both these universities have the power of conferring degrees. Saint Francis Xavier College was founded at Antigonish in 1854, and had for its first president the Rev. Dr. John Cameron, afterwards bishop of Antigonish. Its president for 1902-3 was the Rev. Dr. Alexander Thompson. The College of Sainte-Anne was founded in 1890, and in 1892 was incorporated and chartered as a university. The university was destroyed by fire in 1898, but a larger and more commodious has replaced it. The archbishop of Halifax is (*ex officio*) chairman of the board of governors. The fact that the trustees of public schools "can rent the school rooms of denominational schools, gives rise to the second method by which several Catholic schools are affiliated to the public school system. In some districts the due consent of the town councils and school boards in these localities having been obtained, several Catholic schools were thus affiliated, their work acknowledged, and "they participated in the public grant." The chief voluntary educational institutions other than those already mentioned, are Saint Mary's College, Halifax, of which Rev. Edmund Kennedy is superior; La Salle Academy, Halifax; Convent of the Sacred Heart, Halifax; and Saint Vincent Academy. The following educational statistics in Halifax and Antigonish are taken from the Church 'Directory' for the year 1904:

HALIFAX

College and academies for boys,	2,	students 210
Academies for young ladies.....	4,	students 420
Parochial schools	10,	pupils in the city—Halifax 3,750
Industrial and reform schools..	2,	inmates 90

ANTIGONISH.

College	1,	students 150
Boarding schools for young ladies	4,	students 610
Parochial schools	11,	pupils 2,700

New Brunswick.— Catholic education in New Brunswick is more the history of devotion and struggle than of an organized system. At the time of the passing of the British North America Act (1867), Catholics had their schools established and maintained in their more thickly settled districts. These received legislative grants in proportion to local contributions. Matters went on quietly and satisfactorily until 1871 when an act was passed taxing all the property of the country for schools of a non-sectarian character. This act aroused a strong feeling among the Catholics, who claimed that to them it meant double taxation for school purposes, that thus their condition was worse than before confederation. The courts were appealed to, the Dominion Parliament asked to intervene, and the Crown petitioned. As a result, although the act was maintained, some concessions were made by the legislature in 1875. "Local trustees in cities and towns were permitted to lease from the authorities of the Roman Catholic Church the buildings in which the separate schools had up to that time been conducted, to open public schools in these buildings, and to employ as teachers in such schools members of religious communities and others having the confidence of the Catholic clergy, provided, however, that all such teachers should undergo examination in the regular way as to their qualifications and receive a licence from the Board of Education." Under this arrangement matters, if not altogether satisfactory, quieted down. Schools increased in number and advanced in progress. Large schools exist in most of the missions. Besides 12 academies for the higher education of young ladies, there are two colleges for the classical and secondary education of young men. Saint Joseph's College at Memramcook, under the direction of the Fathers of the Holy Cross, has both a classical and a commercial department, and ranks as a university in conferring degrees. Within the past few years (1899) a college has been opened at Caraquet, conducted by the Eudist Fathers.

Prince Edward Island.— In Prince Edward Island the Catholic institutions of education are all voluntary. They consist of eight academies for girls and several other schools located in various parts of the island. There is one college — Saint Dunstan's — situated at Charlottetown, in charge of the secular clergy. The Sisters of Notre Dame conduct a school in the Magdalen Islands.

Manitoba.— In the early days of Manitoba the work of Catholic education was as zealously carried on as circumstances would permit. Settlements were sparsely scattered over a vast extent of country; teachers were few, and what few there were shared poverty and hardship, the common lot of all. The first legislation upon education in the province was passed in 1871. So far as Catholic education is concerned, the main features of the act were as follows: (1) The Central Board of Education, in whose power the whole education was placed, was divided into two sections — one Catholic, the other Protestant, equal in number. (2) Between these two sections the annual legislative grant was equally divided. (3) It was arranged that 12 of the school districts into which the province was divided should be Catholic schools, under the Catholic section of the Central Board. This act was denominational in its principle and action. All was reversed by the Act of 1890. Only one school was recognized. The instruction was non-sectarian; and the taxes for the support of these schools were raised from all the rate-payers alike. This change produced a bitter feeling and roused prolonged opposition. The Catholics of Manitoba strove by every legitimate means in their power to effect a change. At length the Federal and Provincial governments agreed to certain measures calculated to diminish the grievances. An able-gate, Mgr. Merry del Val, was sent out by the Holy See to report upon the whole question. After receiving the report the Sovereign Pontiff wrote in an encyclical: "We have no doubt that these measures have been inspired by a love of fair dealing and good intention. But we cannot conceal the truth. The law made to remedy the evil is defective, imperfect, insufficient." The Catholic schools of the diocese of Saint Boniface number 126, attended in all by about 5,000 children. There is at Saint Boniface a large college conducted by the Jesuits, in affiliation with the University of Manitoba.

Northwest Territories.— In the Northwest Territories the principle of separate schools was recognized. The statistics give for 1898, 44 Roman Catholic public schools and 11 separate school districts, with a total attendance of nearly 2,000.

Catholic Industrial Schools.— A great deal has been done for children who are placed in these schools. Provincial help is given in both Ontario and Quebec. Besides these provincial institutions there are many industrial schools for the education of Catholic Indians, conducted by religious, and supported by public aid. See also EDUCATION, ROMAN CATHOLIC; CANADA — RELIGIOUS CONDITION.

J. R. TEEFY, LL.D.,
President of Saint Michael's College, Toronto.

10. Canada — Public Education. Under the provisions of the British North America Act, control of public education in Canada is vested in the provincial governments. The position of dissentient denominational schools is, it is true, specially safe-guarded under the act (30–31 Vict. c. 3 § 93), and on their behalf the Dominion Parliament may interpose remedial legislation, but with this exception the whole organization, conduct, and maintenance of education lies with the provinces. At the time of confederation the provinces then existing had already in operation a system of free elementary schools, which has since been expanded into the present effi-

cient organization. The figures of the census of 1901 show the high standard obtained in public education in Canada. In a population of 4,728,631 persons over five years old, only 14.4 per cent are illiterate; in the Province of Ontario of the persons over five years old, the illiterates number 8 per cent. There are now nearly 1,000,000 pupils in 19,891 primary and secondary schools of Canada, with about 25,000 teachers. Except in the Province of Quebec all but a small fraction of these schools are government institutions. Throughout the Dominion elementary education is free, compulsory, and co-educational, and the schools controlled (within the scope of provincial statutes and regulations), by locally elected trustees. There are provincial secondary schools everywhere except in the Northwest Territories, and provincial universities in Ontario, New Brunswick, and Manitoba. The following table, compiled from the Statistical Year Book of Canada (1903) and the Annual Provincial Reports illustrates the status of public education in the provinces of Canada:

ing, object lessons, etc. Above these are the public schools of the provinces, whose organization (first placed on a comprehensive basis in 1844 by Egerton Ryerson, superintendent of education), owes much to the educational system of the State of New York. Every township is divided by its council into school sections, and for each section, each incorporated village, town, and city there is a board of trustees. The latter are elected by the rate payers, both male and female. Within the provisions of the statutes of the province, and the regulations of the education department, the trustees appoint the teachers, determine the salaries, and provide and maintain buildings and equipment. The provincial government makes an annual grant of money to each school according to the average number of pupils in attendance. For the rural schools the county council adds an equal grant, the township council contributes $100 ($150 for a school with two teachers), and the remaining funds needed are raised from the rate payers. In cities, towns, and villages the legislative grant is supplemented by funds raised by the municipal

Provinces	No. of public (primary) schools	Teachers in public schools	Pupils in public schools	Average attendance	Average salaries of teachers in public schools	Public school expenditure per head of population	Percentage paid by provincial government	No. of high schools, collegiate institutes, academies, and grammar schools	No. of pupils in ditto	Total school expenditure	Grants from provincial governments
					$	$				$	$
Ontario pop. (1901) 2,182,947	6,062	9,367	454,088	261,480	{436 (males) 313 (females)}	2.20	8.83	134	24,472	4,825,160	1,806,590
Quebec pop. (1901) 1,648,898	5,379	6,301	205,057	143,044	{500 (males) 135 — 400 (females)}	1.40	10.83	*178	*39,334	2,355,087	419,974
Nova Scotia pop. (1901) 459,574	2,395	2,494	98,768	55,213	{188 — 809 (males) 166 — 456 (females)}	2.03	28.09	18	1,688	936,458	263,092
New Brunswick pop. (1901) 331,120	1,726	1,815	58,863	37,552	....	1.89	30.59	13	1,019	629,991	192,735
Manitoba pop. (1901) 255,211	1,584	2,094	57,409	36,479	{440 (rural) 570 (urban)}	5.22	12.72	3	711	1,509,276	191,991
British Columbia pop. (1901) 178,657	338	580	23,643	16,000	396	2.96	78.40	8	856	604,358	473,802
Prince Edward Island pop. (1901) 103,259	572	572	19,956	12,112	....	1.63	74.37	1	160	166,617	123,919
Northwest Territories pop. (1901) 158,440	743	1,152	33,191	16,321	....	......	......	......	......	213,764	213,764
Total for Canada pop. (1901), including unorganized territory, 5,371,315	18,799	24,375	950,975	574,201	....	2.03	....	355	68,856	11,240,711	3,685,865

* Includes 105 independent Roman Catholic Academies and 2 independent Protestant.

For the organization of education it is necessary to consider the provinces separately. Ontario, the most populous of the provinces and the most advanced in matters of education, having largely influenced the educational systems of the other Protestant parts of Canada deserves the most detailed treatment. The system of public education in Ontario includes, kindergartens, public (primary) schools, high schools and collegiate institutes, and a provincial university, the whole forming an organic unit. Kindergarten schools, admitting children between the ages of four and seven, may be organized at the option of boards of school trustees in cities, towns and incorporated villages. There are at present 120 such schools in the cities and towns of Ontario, with an enrollment of 11,300 pupils. The exercises consist of singing, marching, sew-

council. All the public schools are free, and under an act of 1891, trustees are empowered to supply text books either free or at reduced prices. In the uniform course of study prescribed by the education department chief stress is laid on reading, writing, arithmetic, grammar, geography, and drawing. In the upper forms British and Canadian history and commercial subjects are taught; agriculture is taught in rural schools. Periodic talks are given on temperance and hygiene. Only text books authorized by the education department are allowed. Attendance is obligatory for all children between the ages of 8 and 14 years, not attending separate schools and not under efficient instruction at home. The public schools are strictly non-sectarian, but the schools are opened and closed with the reading of the Lord's prayer and portions of the Scriptures are read daily. The clergy of any denomination may arrange with the trustees to give religious instruction in the school after the regular hours. Any group of five or more heads of families may, upon giving notice to the municipal clerk, cease to pay school rates, and become supporters of a separate school. This privilege may be used by any religious sect or by persons of color; in actual fact, of the 397 separate schools existing in Ontario all but 6 are Roman Catholic institutions. The course of instruction given in the separate schools is almost identical with that of the public schools, with the addition of special religious teaching. Separate schools share in the legislative grant. For secondary education Ontario has an admirable system of high schools and collegiate institutes; these are almost identical in character, the collegiate having a larger and more highly qualified staff, special facilities in regard to apparatus, etc., and receiving a larger government grant. Any high school may become a collegiate institute on fulfilling the requirements. High schools and collegiate institutes are created by municipal and county councils, and managed by elective boards of trustees. The original cost, and the cost of permanent improvements are defrayed by the local authorities. For current expenditure, the provincial government contributes a yearly grant varying according to situation, attendance, etc., but with a fixed minimum. The grants average from $500 to $800. The county contributes an equal amount. The remaining expense is met by the municipality. About one third of the schools are free, in the others the annual fee varies from $2.50 to $26. A uniform examination is prescribed for admission. A graded series of four forms leads to the uniform "leaving" examinations (Junior and Senior) conducted by the department, on the results of which certificates are granted for public school teachers. The matriculation examination for the provincial university is almost identical with the junior leaving examination. In 1902 there were in in Ontario, 134 high schools and collegiate institutes, with 593 teachers and 24,472 pupils. Coeducation obtains in all of them, 12,843 of the registered pupils being girls. The total expenditure was $769,680. Special attention is paid in Ontario to the uniform qualification and training of teachers. The lowest grade of public school teachers (third class) must pass the high school primary examination (Forms I. and II.) and attend a county model school. Teachers of the second class must pass the junior leaving and attend the provincial normal school. Teachers of the first class must pass the senior leaving examination, and attend the school of pedagogy in Toronto. To hold a position in a high school a teacher must hold a first class public school certificate, or have passed at least equivalent university examinations. For specialist positions in collegiates, higher university standing is demanded, varying according to the subject. Unless by special permission of the department, only the certificates of the universities in Ontario are accepted. At the head of the system is the minister of education, a member of the provincial cabinet.

The problem of public education in the Province of Quebec, owing to the division of the population between the French and English races, and the Roman Catholic and Protestant religions is one of peculiar difficulty. The difference of creeds has led to the establishment of a dual system of elementary, secondary, and superior schools. The Roman Catholics of the province, numbering (census of 1901) 1,429,186, have 5,180 schools of all kinds, the Protestant population of 219,712 have 964. At the head of the educational system is a superintendent of public instruction with a council of 35 members, both Protestants and Roman Catholics being represented. Within the council are a Protestant committee and a Roman Catholic committee which control the schools of their respective denominations. Each has its elementary, model, and normal schools and academies. In each parish or township there is a board of school commissioners elected by the owners of real estate. These erect and maintain schools, appoint teachers, and levy the school tax, which falls on real property only. But in any such district a dissentient minority, professing a religious faith different from that of the majority, may organize themselves separately, elect a board of trustees, and conduct a school of their own. In the cities and towns there are separate Protestant and Roman Catholic boards of school commissioners. Real estate is taxed for school purposes according to the religious faith of its owners. Attendance at the elementary schools is free and is compulsory for children between the ages of 5 and 16 years. The cost of elementary schools in 1903 was $2,270,113, of which $235,000 was covered by the annual grant of the provincial government, and, $1,935,113 by local taxation.

In each of the three maritime provinces (New Brunswick, Nova Scotia, and Prince Edward Island) there is a system of public elementary schools, normal schools and academies, grammar schools in New Brunswick), whose organization closely resembles that of the Ontario schools. In each province the executive council, acting through its superintendent of education is at the head of the system. The elementary schools are free, coeducational, non-denominational, with compulsory attendance, placed under trustees elected in each school district, and supported partly by provincial, county, and municipal grants, partly by local assesments. In both Nova Scotia and New Brunswick the annual "school meeting" of rate payers which elects the trustees votes the amount of money to be locally assessed. New Brunswick has separate schools for Roman Catholics in the towns and in some French-Canadian settlements. New Brunswick has a provincial university (see article CANADIAN UNIVERSITIES), whose president is adjoined to the executive council in its capacity of board of education. In Prince Edward Island, the Prince of Wales College at Charlottetown is a secondary school with governmental support.

In Manitoba the executive council, or cabinet, is at the head of public education. There is a minister of education. An advisory board, partly appointed, partly elected by the teachers, aids the government in organizing the school curriculum, establishing teachers' qualifications. etc. The provincial system includes public (primary) schools, a higher grade of which are called intermediate schools, and three collegiate institutes, at Winnipeg, Brandon, and Portage la Prairie. Schools are free and are supported by provincial grants, municipal grants, and a local school tax levied by the trustees. School districts are erected by local municipalities, and trustees are elected therein. The whole system closely resembles that of Ontario. For the provincial university see article CANADIAN UNIVERSITIES. The question of separate schools for Roman Catholics was long a subject of acute controversy. Established in 1871, they were abolished in 1890. The agitation in favor of their restoration reached an alarming crisis in 1895. A compromise was made in 1896 whereby religious instruction may be given during the last half hour of the school day, and which permits the Roman Catholic school children of a district, if numbering 25 or more, to have a teacher of their own denomination. British Columbia has a system of free, non-denominational public schools, controlled by the provincial government through a superintendent of education. The expenses of the schools are defrayed by the government, except in the towns of Victoria, Vancouver, Nanaimo, and New Westminster, which supplement the provincial school grant of $10 per capita by local assessment. There are eight high schools, controlled by local boards of trustees, and a normal school, but no provincial universities. The Northwest Territories have a system of public schools administered by a commissioner of education who is a member of the executive council. The organization is similar to that of Ontario. There is a normal school at Regina, but as yet no high schools.

See CANADA — PRIMARY EDUCATION; CANADA — SECONDARY EDUCATION; CANADA — HIGHER EDUCATION; CANADA — CATHOLIC EDUCATION; PARISH SCHOOLS; PUBLIC SCHOOLS.

STEPHEN LEACOCK,
Lecturer in Political Science, McGill University.

20. Canada — Canadian Universities. See CANADIAN UNIVERSITIES.

21. Canada — Canadian Literature. See LITERATURE, CANADIAN.

22. Canada — Racial Population. The last census of Canada stands for the date of 31 March 1901. In the enumeration count was made of the people by family, sex, conjugal condition, religion, origin or race, nationality, birthplace, citizenship, occupation or profession, education and language. The races of men were classed under the general heads of color and racial or tribal origin, without any attempt at classification by physical types, which is a work for experts. In the instructions given to enumerators, only four colors were recognized, viz., white for the Caucasian race, red for the American Indian, black for the Ethiopian or Negro, and yellow for the Mongolian. "Only pure whites will be classed as whites; the children begotten of marriages between whites and any one of the other races will be classed as red, black, or yellow, as the case may be, irrespective of the degree of color." In making the record of racial or tribal origin, enumerators were told that among whites such origin is traced through the father, but that care should be taken not to apply the terms "American" or "Canadian" in a tribal sense. In the case of Indians, the names of their tribes were required to be given; and persons of mixed white and red blood, usually called half-breeds, were to be described in addition to the tribal name with the name of the white race infused in the blood. For example, "Cree, f. b." would denote that the person is racially a mixture of Cree and French; and "Chippewa, s. b." would denote that the person is Chippewa and Scotch. "A person whose father is English, but whose mother is Scotch, Irish, French, or any other race, will be ranked as English, and so with any others — the line of descent being traced through the father in the white races."

The census of 1891 omitted the enumeration of the people by races and origins, and to obtain a comparison with 1901 it is necessary to go back to 1881, in which year the population of the Dominion was 4,324,810. The following table gives the classification by color for 1881 and 1901:

Color	1881	1901
White	4,190,486	5,293,896
Red	108,547	127,932
Black	21,394	17,437
Yellow	4,383	22,050
Total	4,324,810	5,371,315

In 1881 the white race was 96.89 per cent of the whole population, the red 2.59, the black 0.51, and the yellow 0.01 per cent. In 1901 the white race was 96.88 per cent of the whole, the red 2.38, the black 0.33, and the yellow 0.41 per cent. The increase of the white population in the 20 years was 1,013,410, of the red 19,385, and of the yellow 17,667, while the black population showed a decrease of 3,957.

The population of the country by principal national or tribal races in 1881 and 1901, and the increase or decrease of each race during that period of 20 years, is shown in the next table:

Race	1881	1901	Increase
English	881,301	1,260,899	379,598
Irish	957,403	988,721	31,318
Scotch	699,863	800,154	100,291
Others of British origin..	9,947	13,421	3,474
French	1,298,929	1,649,371	350,442
German	254,319	310,501	56,182
Dutch	30,412	33,845	3,433
Scandinavian	5,223	31,042	25,819
Russian	1,227	28,621	27,394
Italian	1,849	10,834	8,985
Jewish	667	16,131	15,464
Swiss	4,588	3,865	*723
Indian and half breed...	108,547	127,932	19,385
Chinese and Japanese...	4,383	22,050	17,667
Negro	21,394	17,437	*3,957
Various origins	3,952	24,952	21,000
Unspecified	40,806	31,539	*9,267
Total	4,324,810	5,371,315	1,046,505

* Decrease.

The number of people of the British races in 1881 was 2,548,514, and in 1901 it was 3,063,195, being an increase in the 20 years of 514,681, or 20.19 per cent. The French, who were the pioneers of Quebec and the Maritime Provinces (the old Acadia), numbered 1,298,929 in 1881, and 1,649,371 in 1901, being an increase of 350,442, or 27.75 per cent. In Quebec the French race has grown in the 20 years from 1,073,820 to 1,322,115, in New Brunswick from 56,635 to 79,979, in Nova Scotia from 41,219 to 45,161, in Prince Edward Island from 10,751 to 13,866, in Ontario from 102,743 to 158,671, in Manitoba from 9,949 to 16,021, in British Columbia from 916 to 4,600, and in the Northwest Territories from 2,896 to 7,040. (See CANADA — THE FRENCH CANADIANS.) During the same period the British races grew in Ontario from 1,548,030 to 1,732,144, in Quebec from 260,538 to 290,169, in Nova Scotia from 342,238 to 359,064, in Manitoba from 38,285 to 164,239, in British

Columbia from 14,660 to 106,403, and in the territories from 2,873 to 85,769. In New Brunswick the number of the British races fell from 245,974 to 237,524, and in Prince Edward Island from 95,916 to 87,883.

A noticeable feature of the five older provinces of Canada is the relative standing of the British races at the beginning and close of the 20 years' period. The English increased from 861,127 to 1,104,602, or 28.27 per cent, while the Scotch only increased from 678,248 to 693,043, or 2.09 per cent, and the Irish decreased from 943,777 to 899,260, or 4.95 per cent. The English increase is mostly in Ontario (165,578); in New Brunswick and Nova Scotia the increase was 42,063. The Scotch increased 26,139 in Ontario and Quebec, but decreased 11,344 in the Maritime Provinces, and the Irish decreased in all the provinces. In Manitoba, British Columbia, and the Northwest Territories the English race increased in the 20 years by 136,123, the Irish by 75,495, and the Scotch by 85,496. An obvious cause of these results in the older provinces is found in this record of population by birthplaces, which is shown for the principal British islands in the following table for the whole of Canada:

Born in	1881	1901
England	169,504	201,285
Ireland	185,526	101,629
Scotland	115,062	83,631
Total	470,092	386,545

There was an increase of 31,781 in the number born in England, but a decrease of 83,897 in the number born in Ireland and 31,431 in the number born in Scotland, and a net decrease of 83,547 in the number born in the three countries. Consequently there was a large falling off during the period of 20 years in the number of immigrants arrived in Canada from the British Islands as compared with years preceding 1881. The growth of the French race in Canada appears to be due almost wholly to natural increase, for the census tables show that in 1881 the number of persons in the country who were born in France was only 4,389, and in 1901 only 7,944. The other races of Continental Europe making up part of the population of Canada comprise German, Dutch, Scandinavian, Russian, Italian and Swiss. In 1881 these peoples together with Jews numbered 298,285, and in 1901 they were increased to 434,839. But to them are to be added for the latter year 18,178 Austro-Hungarians and 2,994 Belgians, which in the table of population by races are included under the head of "various origins." The remaining 3,780 under the same head embrace 1,637 Syrians, 861 Spaniards, 442 Portuguese, 225 Greeks, 225 Flemings, 73 Arabians, 57 Rumanians, 39 Turks, 34 Armenians, 16 Persians, and 9 Bulgarians, and nearly 100 of the minor races.

The Scandinavian race includes 10,594 enumerated as Swedes, 5,324 as Norwegians, 3,161 as Danes, 9,297 as Icelanders, and 2,666 as Scandinavians in general. The Icelandic race is found chiefly in Manitoba, where a colony was established a quarter of a century ago. But there are a few in Ontario and British Columbia and nearly a thousand in the territories, whence they have migrated from Manitoba.

The Russian race is made up largely of the religious body known as Doukhobors, who came to Canada to escape persecution in the closing years of the 19th century. They have settled as colonies in Manitoba and the territories. Counted with the Russian race also are 5,726 Poles and 1,929 Finns.

The Austro-Hungarian races are composed largely of Galicians, Bohemians, and Slavonians who have settled in the Northwest.

A scientific classification of the European races in Canada's population would no doubt make many changes in the groups as given here, which are arranged generally in the national order. No other arrangement would be intelligible to most of the enumerators employed on the census, and it would happen but rarely that stature, or facial features, or form of the head, or texture of the hair, or spoken language would enable anyone concerned in the work to give or record a scientific answer. In an instance so apparently simple as the determination of race in the descendants of Highlanders who crossed the Grampians to the Lowlands of Scotland a century and a half ago the experts themselves are not infrequently perplexed even on Scottish ground. But much greater the problem becomes in a new world, where climate, environment and other conditions have reconstructed the physical man, in spite of the prepotency of racial characteristics.

The Indian races, including half-breeds, increased in the 20 years from 108,547 to 127,932, or 17.86 per cent. In 1901 there were 93,459 pure Indians and 34,473 half-breeds,— the latter term being officially used to describe a person of Indian and other blood in any degree of strain.

The census record of Indians for British Columbia is not very satisfactory, inasmuch as most of the bands have been described by enumerators by the name of the district they occupy instead of by their tribal names. In the other provinces and territories of the Dominion they have been properly described by tribal names, and the population of the principal ones is given in the following table:

Tribal Name	Population
Abnakis	385
Algonkin	2,369
Amalecite	520
Assiniboin	258
Blackfoot	2,193
Chippeway or Ojibway	13,231
Cree	15,279
Dakota	231
Delaware	432
Dog Rib	697
Huron	228
Iroquois	8,608
Micmac	2,177
Montagnais	1,455
Ottawa	1,039
Peigan	513
Salteaux	600
Sarcee	173
Sioux	366
Slave	620
Stoney	435
Total	51,809

This table includes 22 Chippewas and 10 Crees in British Columbia, leaving for that province 25,456 Indians not described by their tribal names. The remaining 16,194 Indians consist of 3,302 in Yukon and 12,153 in the other far northern territories not described by tribal names, and 739 made up of small tribes or bands in the old provinces — among which are Mistassinis, Nipissings, Tête de Bull and Wapenakis in Quebec, Kioways in Nova Scotia, and Mississagas, Munsees, Shawnees, Wyandottes and one 'last of the Mohegans' in Ontario. The Abnakis are almost all in Quebec, and four-fifths of the Al-

gonkins are in the same province. The Amale-
cites are in New Brunswick, but a few scattered
ones are in Nova Scotia and Quebec. The Chip-
peways are in all the provinces except Nova
Scotia and Prince Edward Island, but 10,126 are
in Ontario, 1,035 in Manitoba, and 1,950 in the
Northwest Territories. The Iroquois or Six
Nations are in Ontario and Quebec,— 5,660 in
the former and 2,880 in the latter, with a few
scattered ones elsewhere. The once powerful
Hurons now exist as a small remnant at Ancienne Lorette, near the city of Quebec, but 15
out of the 228 are yet in Ontario. The ruins of
their forts and the midden heaps of their camps
in the rich farmland that lies between Lake Simcoe and Georgian Bay have been for the last
50 years interesting spots of research for the
tireless antiquarian. The Crees are the most
numerous of all the Indian tribes in Canada, but
four fifths of them are in the Northwest Territories. Manitoba has 1,246, Ontario 585, and
Quebec 628. The Montagnais are in Quebec,
and the Ottawas and Delawares in Ontario.
The last named, a branch of the old Lenapes,
were brought to Canada by the Moravian missionaries late in the 18th century, and half a
township of fine land was given to them by the
government. The Blackfoots, Peigans, and Sar-
cees are in Alberta, and the Slaves and Dog
Ribs in Mackenzie of the Northwest Territories.

The records of half-breeds show the Indians
to be crossed with nearly all the races of the
country, including Ethiopians and Mongolians,
and there are some "breeds" in all the tribes.
Following is the number under five classes:

Classes of Half-breeds   Population
English 4,447
French 17,886
Irish 1,132
Scotch 5,931
Other 5,055

Total 34,451

The French "breeds" are the most numerous,
for the reason that for more than 300 years the
French traders and trappers have been coming
and going among the Indians, and occupying
posts where business of the kind in which they
were employed might be carried on in the easiest
and best way. The *coureur de bois* or bush
ranger sought trade in all the Indian country
from Quebec to the Pacific Ocean, and wherever
he went he became a member of a family or
was adopted into a tribe. The Scotchman and
the Englishman came in later as employees of
the Hudson's Bay Company, and they, too, became tribesmen through adoption. As a rule
the children did not take up the father's language, but they inherited his vices, and the
Indian character was not improved by the new
cross of blood. The "breed," however, acquired
a few words of French, or English, or Gaelic,
which helped him in trading, and so made him
a useful means of communication between the
white and the red races. But often in the far
north it is noticeable by phrase and accent that
his English has been learned from a Highlander
or an Orkney man.

A few words may be said of the Eskimo
race, whose habitat is portions of the mainland
around Hudson Bay, in the Territories of Ungava and Keewatin, parts of Mackenzie and
Yukon near the Arctic Ocean, and the islands
in that ocean comprising Franklin. Their number is not accurately known, for a census of only

a part of them was taken at trading posts and
mission stations when the yearly visit to these
places was made. The chief occupations of the
Eskimos are hunting and fishing, upon which
their subsistence depends. They are a square-
built folk, powerful and hardy; yet it is rare to
find more than four or five in a family. Many
of them can read well, and write in the syllabic
form, although the census records of the East
Main show that their whole time at school
ranges only from 3 to 10 days. The same remark also applies to the Indians around Hudson Bay, most of whom can read and write
and speak English. Like the Indian, the
Eskimo finds his chief social pleasure in telling
and hearing salacious stories, over which he will
laugh uncontrollably. The mother tongue is
Eskimo or Innuit, and a few proper names of
persons in a family will serve as examples:

Nåpårktôk................ male   head of family
Evidlak .... female   wife
Apåluktak .... male   son
Pookta .... female   daughter
Kingnaroåk .... male   son
Kaukelak .... female   boarder

The following table gives by provinces the
number of the Chinese and Japanese races in 1881
and 1901, but separately only for the latter year:

PROVINCES	1881	1901	
	Chinese and Japanese	Chinese	Japanese
British Columbia	4,350	14,938	4,544
Manitoba	4	206	4
New Brunswick		59	
Nova Scotia		106	1
Ontario	22	732	29
Prince Edward Island		4	
Quebec	7	1,037	9
The Territories		286	95
Totals	4,383	17,368	4,682

The increase of the two races in the 20 years
is 17,667 or 400 per cent, and has been almost
wholly by immigration. A capitation tax of $50
was imposed by the Canadian Parliament on
Chinese immigrants in 1886, which on 1 Jan.
1901, was increased to $100. But neither the
first nor the second tax had any effect upon arrivals. On 1 Jan. 1904, the tax was further increased to $500, and from that date to the end of
the fiscal year, 30 June, only one Chinaman
landed in the country. This tax does not apply
to the Japanese, who continue to come in at a
moderate rate. In 1901 they had adopted Canadian citizenship to the number of 1,070 or 22.85
per cent, and the Chinese to the number of 993
or only 5.72 per cent.

Canada has by its constitution two official
languages, English and French, and its population five years of age and over is 4,728,631. Of
this number 3,709,370 speak English, 1,514,977
speak French, 126,978 English speak English
and French, and 529,552 French speak French
and English. There are 1,019,261 who cannot
speak English, 3,213,654 who cannot speak
French, and 160,814 who cannot speak French
or English. The third lot comprises many
Indians and recent immigrants.

ARCHIBALD BLUE,
Census Commissioner, Ottawa.

23. Canada — The French Canadian. *Geographical Distribution.*— In 1901, according to
the last Dominion census, 1,650,000 inhabitants
of Canada, that is, a little more than one third
of the whole population, were of French origin.

Of these, by far the greater part, namely, over 1,300,000, were settled in the province of Quebec, forming 80 per cent of the total population of that province. But considerable numbers were located in some of the other provinces: nearly 159,000 in Ontario, 80,000 in New Brunswick, 45,000 in Nova Scotia, 14,000 in Prince Edward Island, while 16,000 were to be found in Manitoba, 7,000 in the Northwest Territories, 4,600 in British Columbia, and about 2,000 in the unorganized territories, principally the Yukon. Then, according to the last United States census, there were, in 1900, throughout the Union, nearly 400,000 Canadian-born French; and the total number of people of French Canadian extraction in the United States, if local statistics are to be credited, would exceed 1,000,000. From the point of view of physical and social geography, the French Canadian element in North America is made up as follows:

(1) The main body, 1,500,000 strong, extends uninterruptedly over Quebec, eastern and northern Ontario, and northern New Brunswick. The nucleus of this main body is a compact community of farmers occupying the banks of the Saint Lawrence and the valleys of its tributaries. On the outskirts of this central group, over the wooded and rocky highlands, north and south of the great river, but more especially throughout the plateaus of northern Quebec, northeastern Ontario, and northern New Brunswick, farming is largely supplemented by lumbering, and not infrequently by mining; while along the Gulf and sea-coast of Labrador, the Gaspé Peninsula, Chaleurs Bay, and eastern New Brunswick it is more or less superseded by fishing.

(2) Then, hardly separated from these, and from one another, we have, off the extreme eastern limit of this central group, the French-speaking communities of fishermen of Nova Scotia and Prince Edward Island; while, as a projection from the opposite extreme western border, in Ontario, we find, along the shores of the Saint Lawrence and the Great Lakes, a string of small settlements of French Canadian rivermen, boatmen, and woodsmen, forming an almost continuous chain around that province and connecting, as it were, the two large French groups of Detroit River and Georgian Bay with the still larger one occupying the western bank of the Ottawa. Over one third, namely, about 560,000, of the total French element composing this main body and its projections are congregated in villages, towns, or cities, where they make a living through physical labor, trading, the crafts, and the liberal professions.

(3) As distinct outlyers from the above main group, we have, in the first place, the many French-speaking communities of urban population, which, in very large, though fluctuating numbers, are spread throughout the manufacturing towns of the North Atlantic States of the Union, principally Massachusetts; in the second place, smaller and sparser groups of French-speaking farmers (at times woodsmen and miners as well), to be found in the Western country, in Manitoba, Alberta, and in some States of the North Central division of the Union, especially Michigan, Wisconsin, Minnesota, and Illinois; in the third place, still smaller and sparser groups of French Canadian prospectors or miners, spread in the camps and towns of British Columbia, the Yukon, and some of the States of the Western division of the Union, principally Montana and California. Lastly, French Canadian families or individuals are to be found in every part of the Union, though in the States of the South Atlantic, South Central, and Western divisions they aggregate in most cases a few units or a few hundred only. About 40 per cent of the total French Canadian element in the United States are located in 160 principal cities.

Social Features.— The most widespread, fundamental, and characteristic type of the French Canadian is the habitant, or farmer, of the province of Quebec (q.v.). From a study of his conditions there may be gathered the clearest idea of the capabilities and limitations of the race as a whole. Three main groupings are distinctive of social life in the French Canadian country: the habitant's household, the range, the parish.

(1) The habitant's household normally consists of two families, that of the senior householder, and that of an associate son and heir; it includes generally sisters and younger brothers of the heir, children of the younger couple, and, in some cases, sisters of the senior father of family. We have thus a group of some 10 or more persons, closely bound together, not only by ties of kinship and family love, but by co-operative effort, community of interest and habits of mutual dependence, which extend, in a measure, even to those members of the group who have settled outside of the family circle. The habitant's household is primarily a labor organism, a workshop. Agriculture is its mainstay; but it is of a type neither extensive nor intensive, its scope being narrowed down to the task of satisfying directly the household's needs, and limited by the household's internal supply of labor. The farms seldom exceed 100 acres in area, and outside hired help is resorted to in very exceptional cases only. To avoid this contingency, women and children are called upon to work in the fields, especially in haying and harvesting time. On the other hand, the object being to provide directly, as far as circumstances will permit, for all the requirements of the family, habitant farming is greatly diversified. On almost every farm there are to be found, beside the kitchen-garden and its few fruit trees, small patches of flax, tobacco, potatoes, Indian corn, buckwheat, and barley, while larger areas are given to other cereals, hay, and pasturage. Similarly, all kinds of stock are kept on each farm, though seldom any in large numbers or of excellent quality. Various home industries, such as the spinning and weaving of both flax and wool, the manufacture of maple syrup and sugar, carpentry, joinery, cooperage, brushmaking, leather-working, etc, are an important factor on many farms. Agriculture is seldom the sole means of living of the habitant, since in the newer settlements the mere gathering of natural products, such as fish, game, wild fruits, and wood is largely resorted to, while in the older and more densely populated sections by-industries are conspicuous. Then again temporary emigration to and employment in the manufacturing, mining, and lumbering centres of Canada and the United States is, in all situations, an occasional means of securing capital to start out in life or of bridging over hard times. The methods of farming of the habitant, his rotation of crops, his processes of retting

and breaking flax, dyeing wool, making candles, etc., are traditional and have been in use for centuries in certain provinces of France. However, in recent years, the wave of modern progress has been felt, agricultural machinery has come into fairly general use, co-operative butter and cheese factories have been established, and, especially in the vicinity of railways, improved methods and a more specialized type of farming have been adopted. Through hard work and close economy a capable habitant will succeed, with the help of his family, in building up a homestead of sufficient area to meet the wants of the household. Should his acquisitions of land during his lifetime remain within that limit, then the homestead will be transferred in its entirety to the associate son or heir, who in turn will be charged with providing for the whole family, in the same way as the testator would have done. On the other hand, should the acquisitions of the father of family exceed the area required for the support of an ordinary household, the lots in excess are freely used in helping out other sons who, after contributing to the sustenance and welfare of the paternal household in their early life, undertake to make an independent living through agriculture. Girls receive very little aid from the family estate, as it is considered they will be provided for either through remaining as members of the paternal household, or through marrying into some neighboring family. Likewise, sons who are sent to college and enter the liberal professions or the priesthood, receive very little else from their parents. In the management of the family affairs, the influence of the mother is about on a par with that of the father. As a rule she is better educated than her husband, sees to the correspondence and accounts, is consulted in all matters of importance, and leads in the family worship. Through working with their parents on the farm the children acquire a variety of aptitudes, but no particular proficiency in any of the arts, nor any strong desire of attaining eminence in the various walks of life, barring possibly priesthood and politics. Education is reserved for the few who take to the liberal professions and the Church. The style of living is plain, and in many respects old-fashioned. Food is in abundance, though lacking in delicacy. The house, usually of wood and whitewashed, is often rather small for the accommodation of its inmates, but as a rule kept clean and tidy. Homespun, still in use in a few families in isolated sections, is fast being replaced by the cheap cotton and woolen goods supplied by the trade. Births are numerous, but owing to defective hygienic conditions, or to overwork on the part of mothers, this advantage is partially offset by the high proportion of deaths among infants. Amusements are simple, pertaining to the daily work, the family circle, church festivals. Many of the songs and dances are importations or adaptations from Old France. However, here, as throughout the whole range of social phenomena, outside influences are apparent, and features of recent origin are found grafted on old and quaint usages.

(2) The farms are in the shape of long, narrow rectangles, 20 or 30 arpents in length, by 2 or 3 in breadth. The farm buildings are all built at one end of these rectangles, along the public road, which crosses them at right angles, thus giving a close succession of houses and barns. Not infrequently the buildings of two abutting ranges are situated on opposite sides of the same road, making a double row of almost contiguous houses, somewhat like a village street. The ranges, of which there are four or five in parallel line in every parish, connect with one another and with the village by means of "routes" or transverse roads, along which no buildings are erected; so that each range is isolated from the rest and forms a distinct grouping within the parish. This type of settlement, which differs from that of the isolated homestead to be found in some parts of France and throughout the Anglo-Saxon world, and also from the central village type observed in other parts of France and Europe, is a distinctly French Canadian creation, which the habitant takes with him wherever he settles in numbers. The range seems to have been the outcome of the desire on the part of the habitant, while residing on his own farm (which the village settlement would not allow him to do), to secure the benefit of his neighbor's assistance and company in a more effective way than the isolated homestead would permit. What the habitant cannot accomplish with the help of his family he endeavors to do through the free help of his neighbors. However, while the nearest neighbor, on either side, may be called upon now and then to lend a hand in the ordinary work of the farm, the summoning in numbers of the near-by farmers is resorted to in exceptional cases only, such as the clearing of land, the "lifting" of a barn, or the relief of some destitute family. Each range looks after its poor, by means of voluntary contributions, principally in kind. Each range has its cheese or butter factory, its school house, also its large wooden cross along the highway, in commemoration of some religious revival.

(3) The roads leading from the various ranges all centre toward a village, generally small, comprising a few lodgings, workshops, and stores, besides the priest's house and the church. A community wherein the highest aim of the farmer, the basal element, is to cater to all the needs of his household directly through the labor of his own family and the occasional assistance of his neighbors, does not leave much scope for the development of other social factors. The ambitions and efforts of the most capable being restrained within that limit, equality and similarity of condition is the rule. Commerce, industry, the liberal professions remain embryonic. In the absence of leaders in agriculture, industry, and commerce, learning becomes the standard of distinction. A few wise old farmers, the doctor, the notary, the lawyer, are looked up to; but, on account of the exalted nature of his function, the parish priest is decidedly the dominant factor. Like the family and the range, the parish is primarily an organism for mutual support, both in the physical and moral order. It plays to a certain extent the part of an insurance company, as barns, for instance, destroyed by fire are restored through contributions from all the parishioners in material or labor. On Sundays and feast days the habitant meets at church his co-parishioners, who are all relatives or close acquaintances, the doctor, the notary; he listens to the admonitions of the "curé," to the announcements made by the public crier, and receives the intelligence and impressions which will be his mental

food for the remainder of the week. To all intents, the parish may be considered as an enlargement of the family, with the parish priest as its patriarchal head. Then, the parish is the main organ of local government in the French Canadian country, the school commission and the municipal corporation, of British origin and of comparatively recent introduction, remaining mere adjuncts, only partially developed, of the parish proper. The revenues of the latter often exceed those of the school commission and municipal body put together. Many localities have no town-hall other than the vestry. In practice the curé is much more the maintainer of the peace and the arbitrator of disputes within the parish than are the mayor, the local magistrates, and court. His powers extend even to a close supervision of family affairs. The law of the province allows him the 26th bushel of all cereals grown by his parishioners within his territory, and his influence over the church wardens and flock generally enables him to obtain from close-fisted farmers the expenditure of comparatively large sums of money on church buildings. His influence is exerted as well over the school commission and municipal council, whose policy and decisions are usually made to conform to his wishes. On the other hand, practically the only check on the curé is the far-off bishop, who visits the parish and inspects the books every third year, and may remove him at will. The school commission and municipal corporation are administered in a spirit of parsimony. School buildings are inadequate, and the teachers, generally girls, receive very little pay and give correspondingly poor results. Illiterates are still in large numbers. As each individual farmer is required to look directly after that part of the public highway which faces his property, and to contribute his share of the labor necessary for the maintenance of the cross-road leading to the village, the municipal council has little to do apart from supervising, in a general way, the repairing of roads or the occasional building or repairing of bridges within the limits of the parish. Similarly, county councils have not acquired in the French country anything like the importance which they have in English sections, and are content with looking after roads, bridges, or water courses common to two or more parishes. On the other hand, Provincial and Federal politics have taken quite a hold on the habitant; but the interest which he takes in them is more the outcome of his inclination for clannish warfare and oratory, and of his craving for the petty favors of officialism, than the result of a desire on his part to insure the proper management of public affairs, which he does not always grasp. These are the prey of organized political parties, whose leaders are recruited mainly from the liberal professions and the cities. Church and politics are, in the mind of the habitant, the only avenues open to those desirous of rising in the world. And this accounts for a rather remarkable development of institutions of classical and literary teaching in a community wherein common schools are markedly deficient and technical and business training neglected.

Evolution.— On the basis of the classification of societies proposed by F. LePlay and his followers, H. de Tourville and the French school of social science, the French Canadian is a semi-patriarchal or semi-communistic type; that is one in which social organization and life, while swayed by tradition and habits of mutual dependence to a less degree than in the purely patriarchal or communistic types of the Orient, still are not permeated and uplifted by that spirit of private independence and enterprise distinctive of the individualistic or "particularistic" types, as exemplified in the Anglo-Saxon races. His semi-communistic training the French Canadian holds from France. His social ancestors were mainly the Gaul, on the one hand, the Frank on the other. The former, with his clan organization, village life, and neglect of agriculture, was a distinctly communistic type. The particularistic Frank broke up, to some extent, the clannish and communistic spirit and institutions of the Gaul, and gave a strong impulse to agricultural pursuits; but his influence, for reasons which it would be too long to set forth here, was not so lasting nor so far-reaching in France as was that of his duplicate, the Saxon, in England. Thus there sprung up an intermediate type presenting many of the qualities and defects of the Celt, with something of the qualities of the Saxon. A farmer, an artisan, a trader, though generally in a small way and still conserving a fondness for nature and primitive, easy-going occupations; a race lacking ambition and ability to risc in the ordinary callings of life, having for its sole leaders the clergy and the military or civil officers of the Crown; and these leaders, though in many cases sprung from the people, isolated from them by class interests and training and unfit to lead adequately in practical pursuits. Under the trying conditions of New France — the dense forest to clear, the rigorous climate to provide against, the lurking Iroquois to evade — the peasant from north central France, single-handed, made rather slow progress at colonization. Agriculture was neglected, while the more attractive, more remunerative, though deceptive, fur trade became the means of sustenance of both the individual and the colonial government, with a consequent rapid but superficial expansion of the colony and constant warring. The French settler, fond of home and of quiet, evolved into the adventurous and hardy type of the *coureur des bois*. Under British rule, and especially in the course of the 19th century, through the restoration of peace and the advent from Great Britain of a class of business men, the fur trade, carried on by large companies, receded toward Hudson Bay and the Far West, vast lumbering operations were carried on, with a consequent impulse to agriculture, extension of settlements, increase in population; a period of unprecedented prosperity for French Canada. Then, in the latter half of the 19th century, the world-wide evolution of commerce and industry set in, with its marvelous applications of steam and electricity, its powerful machinery and means of transportation, the progress of manufacturing centres; and the French Canadians developed a class of factory operatives, together with a vigorous undergrowth of artisans and traders in the large cities. See also CANADA — UNDER FRENCH RULE; CANADA — THE RACIAL ELEMENTS; CANADA — CATHOLIC EDUCATION.

LÉON GÉRIN, LL.B., F.R.S.C.,
Membre de La Société Internationale de Science Sociale.

24. Canada — Religious Conditions. The religious and ecclesiastical life of Canada cannot be understood without some reference to the sources from which it sprang. The same great forces and influences which molded the history of the Old World re-appear here, but modified in their action and combinations by the new and freer environment in which they work.

General History.— The Roman Catholic Church is the oldest and largest of the ecclesiastical bodies in Canada. It has its chief seat in the province of Quebec. In Canada, under French rule, it was all-powerful. In its origin it was distinctively missionary. The Jesuits were the pioneers and, from the Saint Lawrence to the Rockies, have left an imperishable record. Mgr. Laval (see LAVAL-MONTMORENCY, FRANÇOIS XAVIER DE) in 1674 obtained the erection of the diocese of Quebec and laid the foundations of a regular system of ecclesiastical government. Parishes were established and provision made for the support of the clergy and for the performance of divine worship. The system of tithes was inaugurated in 1663. The Church grew in wealth. Of all the lands, exclusive of islands, granted by the French government previous to the cession to England, at least one fourth came into the possession of the Church. The Jesuits acquired extensive estates, which subsequently became the subject of litigation and political agitation. By the Treaty of Paris (1763) (see PARIS, TREATIES OF) the French Canadians were allowed full liberty "to profess the worship of their religion according to the rites of the Romish Church, as far as the laws of Great Britain permit." This was confirmed by the Quebec Act of 1774, by which also the tithes and rights of the Roman Catholic clergy were secured. The Church in Canada, under the French dominion, was modeled after the National Church of France. The ecclesiastical laws of France were extended to Canada, and with them the so-called Gallican liberties (see GALLICANISM). After the conquest these continued for some time to be more or less observed, along with the assertion of the rights of the sovereign, from which, in France, they had never been separated. It was evidently the intention of the British government to maintain in Canada the previously existing relations between Church and State as defined in Gallicanism, subject only to such changes as the laws of England might necessitate. After many futile attempts to secure some form of concordat with the Papal authorities, it became evident that this Anglo-Gallican policy was impracticable. The more stringent regulations fell into abeyance. In 1806 the Pope appointed M. Plessis (see PLESSIS, JOSEPH OCTAVE) to the See of Quebec, which had been vacant for some time on account of difficulties with the government. From this time the Roman Catholic Church, while richly endowed by the state and practically established by law, was independent in its internal government and as free from state control as other Churches. Besides the political causes which contributed to the failure of the British attempt to perpetuate the Gallican policy, account must be taken of the change within the Church itself by which Gallicanism was rapidly supplanted by Ultramontanism, just as it was in France. The French ecclesiastical law was superseded by the Roman canon law, the Gallican liturgy gave place to the Roman liturgy, and the attitude of the clergy generally toward the civil power changed greatly. This development was accelerated by the publication of the decrees of the Vatican Council (q.v.) in 1870. In Canada, as in France, Gallicanism is a mere matter of past history. But during the last decade not a few significant indications have appeared of a reaction towards a more tolerant and liberal spirit especially among the laity. In the other Provinces the Roman Catholic Church holds a strong position. In the Maritime Provinces there is a large French population, especially along the shores of the Gulf of Saint Lawrence and the Straits of Northumberland. In Cape Breton and the contiguous districts of Nova Scotia many Roman Catholics from the highlands of Scotland settled. Irish Roman Catholics are numerous, especially in the cities of Halifax and Saint John. In all, there are not less than 300,000 members of the Roman Catholic Church in the Provinces by the Sea. The French Canadians have flowed over the boundary from Quebec into Ontario; and they have emigrated extensively into Manitoba and the Northwest Territories. In all these districts are also found both Irish and Scotch Roman Catholics. In Ontario there are, in all, nearly 400,000 Roman Catholics out of a population of upward of 2,250,000. In Manitoba and the West there are about 110,000. The total Roman Catholic population of the Dominion is about 2,230,000.

The Church of England in Canada may be traced back to the few and scattered settlers who followed the British regiments into Nova Scotia and Quebec in the latter part of the 18th century. It received its first accession of strength in the Loyalist refugees who flocked into Canada in 1783-4, many of whom were attached members of the Episcopal Church. The organized life of the Church began with the consecration of the first bishop of Nova Scotia, Dr. Charles Inglis (q.v.), 12 Aug. 1787. In 1798 Dr. Jacob Mountain was consecrated bishop of Quebec. The diocese of Montreal was set apart in 1850. In 1838 Dr. John Strachan was consecrated bishop of Toronto, with the whole of Upper Canada as his diocese. So far the Church had been chiefly dependent for its support upon the English societies, especially the Society for the Propagation of the Gospel. An important step toward self-support was taken in 1842 by the inauguration of the Church Society of the Diocese of Toronto, for the purpose of collecting and disbursing funds for the support and extension of the Church's work. The year 1851 was signalized by a notable advance in the development of the Church. Hitherto the bishops had been appointed by the Crown and the chief ecclesiastical superintendence was in the hands of the archbishop of Canterbury. Now the Church was given self-government in each diocese, by a synod consisting of the clergy and duly elected representatives of the laity, with the right to elect its own bishops. As the Church grew, the diocese of Toronto was gradually subdivided, until now it comprises within its former limits the five dioceses of Toronto, Huron, Ontario, Ottawa, and Niagara, and also the missionary diocese of Algoma and the greater part of the dioceses of Keewatin and Moosonee. In 1845 the diocese of Nova Scotia was subdivided, and that part of it which now forms the province of New Brunswick was erected into the new diocese of Fredericton.

For many years each diocese was independent; there was no organic connection binding them together, beyond their common relations to the Church in England. In 1861 the Provincial Synod was constituted, and comprised within its jurisdiction all the then existing dioceses of Eastern Canada. But there had grown up in the Far West another distinct organization. In 1820 the Hudson's Bay Company (see CANADA — THE HUDSON'S BAY COMPANY) sent out to Fort Garry the first missionary, who ministered assiduously to the servants of the company and the few settlers, both Church of England and Presbyterian, and made some feeble efforts to evangelize the heathen Indians. Others followed. The work was so far advanced in 1849 that the diocese of Rupert's Land was created. It was, for many years, chiefly a missionary work, sustained by the Church Missionary Society, but the federation of all the Provinces into the Dominion of Canada and the opening up of the vast territories hitherto traversed only by the Indian and the trapper led to the rapid influx of population and gave a strong impetus to the work of the Church. The dioceses of Saskatchewan, Calgary, and Qu'Appelle were created. There were also set apart the missionary dioceses of Mackenzie River and Athabasca, and on the Pacific coast the dioceses of New Westminster, Kootenay, Caledonia, and Selkirk. In 1890 an important conference was held in Winnipeg, the object of which was to adopt a scheme for the unification of the Church throughout Canada. This scheme, with little change, became the basis of the constitution of the General Synod, which first met in Toronto in 1893. The Church of England in Canada, from the Atlantic to the Pacific, was now one organized body, possessed of all the powers of self-government.

The Presbyterian Church of Canada traces its descent to several distinct sources. The attempt made in the 17th century to found Huguenot settlements failed disastrously and few traces remain of their existence. Among the Presbyterian Loyalists who came to Canada at the close of the Revolutionary War there was a goodly number of descendants of Huguenots. In 1749 Protestant colonists were brought into Nova Scotia from England and the Continent, in order to counteract the disaffection of the Acadians. Again in 1755, after the expulsion of the Acadians, many Protestants from Great Britain and older colonies along the Atlantic coast were induced, by the promise of liberty of conscience and of worship, to occupy the vacant lands. Then there was a large influx of immigration from the north of Ireland and from Scotland. Some districts, such as the county of Pictou, were almost exclusively occupied by Scotch Presbyterians. These people naturally clung to the various ecclesiastical bodies into which Scotch Presbyterianism was divided. And accordingly there were Presbyteries constituted with relations to the Kirk of Scotland and the Secession Church in its two subdivisions of Burgher and Anti-Burgher, and also adherents of the Reformed Presbyterians, or Covenanters. The great disruption of the Church of Scotland in 1843 extended to the colonies and added to the existing divisions the Free Presbyterian Church. But in 1861 the process of reunion

began with the union of the United Secession Church (inclusive of both Burgher and Anti-Burgher) and the Free Church of the Maritime Provinces into one synod.

The history of the Presbyterian Church in the Western provinces followed similar lines but with new complications. Soon after the conquest, Presbyterian congregations were organized in the cities of Quebec and Montreal. Among the Loyalists were not a few Presbyterians. But there was scanty provision for their religious needs. Applications for ministers made to the churches in Scotland met with no response for many years. A similar appeal made to the "Associated Reformed Church" in the United States resulted in the incoming of a number of ministers from that country. Other ministers followed from Scotland and Ireland. In 1818 was organized "The Presbytery of the Canadas." In 1831 there was organized a synod in connection with the Church of Scotland. In 1840 the two synods were united into one. But in 1843 the great disruption in Scotland again rent it asunder and two synods resulted, one in connection with the Established Church of Scotland and the other in connection with the Free Church of Scotland. Besides these there were other independent Presbyteries, one at Niagara and the other at Stamford, composed of ministers from the United States, and a third originated by ministers from Scotland and from Nova Scotia, connected with the "United Presbyterian Church." The first two were disbanded and absorbed into the larger bodies. The third, in 1861, united with the Free Church and the combined body received the name of the Canada Presbyterian Church. In 1875 the greater union was consummated by which all the Presbyterian bodies throughout Canada from east to west, were united in one great Canadian Presbyterian Church.

Until the greater union was consummated little had been attempted by the Presbyterians in the evangelization of the Northwest. In 1812 and 1816 a large body of Highlanders had settled in the Red River district, but the only ministers they had were those of the Church of England until 1852, when the Rev. John Black, a devoted missionary, organized them into a congregation. Little more was done until after the federation of Canada and the complete union of the Canadian Presbyterians. In 1881 the General Assembly appointed the Rev. Dr. James Robertson to be superintendent of Presbyterian missions in the Northwest. This remarkable man laid the foundations of Presbyterian organization throughout those vast territories and covered the whole country with a network of Presbyterian missions.

The Methodist Church in Canada traces its origin to two distinct sources, England and the United States. In 1770 Lieutenant-Governor Franklin sought English settlers for the province of Nova Scotia in the East Riding of Yorkshire. Among them were the earliest Methodists of Canada, one of whom was the noted preacher and evangelist, John Black. In 1784 he went to the United States, and his appeal to the Baltimore conference led to the coming of a number of Methodist ministers to the Maritime Provinces. In Quebec the first Methodist preachers were connected with the British regiments. As early as 1778 Methodists from New York State came to the Eastern Townships and to Upper Canada. The Methodists did a noble work in laying the foundation of religious life and worship in many districts in Canada, especially in the province of Ontario. Until the War of 1812 Canadian Methodism was closely connected with that of the United States. Negotiations were then entered into with the British Wesleyans. Unhappy dissensions followed. While one party was anxious to maintain the American connection, the other insisted that, as loyal British subjects, they should look to the mother land. A compromise was arrived at by which the American connection was to be observed in Upper Canada, while the British missionaries were to be free to enter Lower Canada. This compromise was of short duration; for when, in 1828, the American conference relinquished its jurisdiction over the Canadian conference and the latter was independently organized under the name of the Methodist Episcopal Church in Canada, the British conference decided not to confine its work to Lower Canada. After much controversy, in 1833 a union between these two branches of Methodism was consummated under the name of "The Wesleyan Methodist Church in North America." But, notwithstanding this union, the Methodist Episcopal Church survived in a new form and increased very rapidly.

Methodist missionary work in the Northwest began about 1840. Its annals abound with noble achievements. There now existed in Canada five principal Methodist bodies. In addition to the two main bodies already mentioned, different branches of British Methodism had been brought into the country, namely, the Methodist New Connection, the Primitive Methodist body, and the Bible Christians. All these became firmly rooted in Canada and developed into strong bodies. The need of unification began to be earnestly discussed as early as 1866; but it was not until 1883 that, at a general conference held in Belleville, the union was consummated. Then all the Methodist bodies, hitherto locally or ecclesiastically separated, were brought together; and, from the Atlantic to the Pacific, there is now one great Methodist Church of Canada.

The *Baptist Church* derived its origin from the American Baptists. From 1760 onward there are traces of individual Baptists in different localities in Nova Scotia. In 1820 the first Baptist association was formed for the Maritime Provinces. The first Baptist Church in Lower Canada was formed in 1794, and consisted chiefly of Loyalist refugees from Connecticut. In 1795 another was organized in Upper Canada. The first Baptist Church in Montreal was not organized until 1830. The Baptists in Canada are chiefly close communion. There is a body of "Free Baptists" which maintains open communion as in Britain, and welcomes all Christians, by whatsoever mode baptized, to the Lord's table.

Congregationalism has never found a strong footing in Canada. A few scattered adherents came from New England to Nova Scotia in 1758. In the eastern townships Congregationalism was founded in 1811 by settlers from Massachusetts, and in Ontario some 10 or 12 years later. Nothing was done west of Ontario until 1870, when work was begun in Winnipeg.

The *Lutheran Church* in Canada dates from the middle of the 18th century. The first German Lutheran landed at Lunenburg, Nova Scotia, in 1749. The first Lutheran congregation in Upper Canada was founded in 1775. Others came in with German immigration. In 1853 the Canada Conference of the Lutheran Church was founded.

There are a number of small religious bodies in Canada, none of which exercises any appreciable influence upon the religious life of the country; chief among them are The Disciples and The Brethren. There are a few Unitarians and Quakers. The Salvation Army has acquired a considerable foothold in the larger cities and towns.

There are four paramount considerations which have profoundly affected the whole religious history and development of the country, namely, the relations of the Churches to the state and to education, their beneficent and missionary activities, and the problem of church union.

Church and State.— In the 18th century neither the principles of responsible government nor the special conditions of Canada were rightly understood by its rulers. It was believed that an Established Church was necessary in order to secure the loyalty of the colonists, and it was, without doubt, the intention of the British government to maintain an Anglican establishment in Upper Canada the counterpart of the Roman Catholic establishment in Lower Canada. In 1792 Lieutenant-Governor Simcoe urged upon the home government the necessity of establishing the Church of England in Upper Canada, as the only means of fostering the spirit of loyalty in that Province. There was nothing in the conditions of the country to warrant the monopoly of religious functions and privileges by any denomination, but the Anglicans had the prestige of their relations to the Established Church in England. The Constitutional Act of 1791 reaffirmed the provision of previous legislation, giving the king the right to set apart for the support of the "Protestant clergy" the seventh part of all ungranted Crown lands. This was the origin of the "clergy reserves" (see CANADA — THE CLERGY RESERVES). The ambiguity of the term "Protestant clergy" admitted of a variety of interpretations. The Anglican clergy maintained that they alone were intended by the designation. The few clergy connected with the Established Presbyterian Church of Scotland contended that they had an equal right to it, and their claim was supported by eminent legal authority in England. The Methodists, in general, resisted such an appropriation of the public lands, but the British Wesleyans urged an acceptance of a portion of the "clergy reserves." This, for a time, created a division among them. Their resistance and the disruption of the Presbyterians hindered the carrying-out of the scheme. In 1836 the lieutenant-governor, Sir John Colborne, erected and endowed 44 rectories in Upper Canada. Futile endeavors were made to secure the lands for educational purposes. Acts to that effect were repeatedly passed by the House of Assembly and rejected by the Legislative Council. At last, in 1854, in the face of the protests of Bishop Strachan and other Anglican leaders, the act was passed by the legislature of Upper Canada, by which the lands were handed over to the municipal corporations of the province for secular purposes, provision being made to satisfy the claims of existing incumbents. In lieu of these claims there was paid over to the Church of England the sum of $1,103,405; to the Church of Scotland, $509,739; to other Presbyterians, $8,962; to the Wesleyan Methodists, $39,074; and to the Roman Catholics in Upper Canada, $83,731. The Anglican Church was thus delivered from what threatened to be its ruin, and the people of the Province released from a grievous injustice and a source of political discontent and strife.

The representatives of the Churches of England and Scotland, especially the former, had a certain status accorded to them, denied to other denominations. The Methodists were most unjustly charged with disloyalty, to which their connection, in origin and government, with the United States gave some color of plausibility. Until 1830 the Methodists and other dissenters had no right to hold land for places of worship or for the burial of their dead, nor had the Methodists and their ministers the right to solemnize matrimony, even among their own people. It was only after long and bitter controversy that laws were passed authorizing the various religious bodies to hold land for churches, parsonages, and burial grounds, and empowering their ministers to celebrate marriages. The struggle in the other provinces was less acute, but of a similar character. The Northwest was singularly free from these difficulties. The outcome of this controversy throughout Canada was the complete separation of Church and State, with the exception of the peculiar position held by the Roman Catholic Church in Quebec, secured by treaty and the terms of British occupancy of that province.

The Church and Education.— So long as France held Canada, education was entirely in the hands of the Roman Catholic Church. The Jesuits, Franciscans, and other orders laid the foundations of the colleges and seminaries which hold an important place in the education of Lower Canada. Thus the system of education was entirely ecclesiastical. Under British rule the attempt was made to establish free schools common to the whole population and unsectarian in character. This was found to be impracticable. With the union of the two provinces in 1841 separate schools had to be conceded to the Protestants in Lower Canada because the public school system was essentially Roman Catholic; and when, in the same year, the first attempt at a general system of public schools was made in Upper Canada, the Roman Catholies there secured the concession of separate schools, but in a very limited way. This, for many years, was a subject of controversy, political as well as religious, the Liberal party demanding the abolition of separate schools and the Roman Catholic authorities seeking the complete control of the education of their children. Finally, on confederation in 1867, the separate school system was bound upon the province of Ontario; although, as is noteworthy, there are more Roman Catholic children in the public schools of Ontario than in the separate schools. In the Maritime Provinces and in northwestern Canada there are no separate schools.

While public school education has been removed from the control of the churches (except in Quebec) the great body of the people are anxious that it should not be divorced from the sanctions and influences of religion. In the Province of Ontario, the public schools are, with few exceptions, opened daily with prayer and the reading of the Scriptures. In not a few, the Bible is carefully taught. But much depends not only upon the character of the teachers, but also upon the disposition of the school trustees, to whom the law gives a large discretion in this matter. There is a strong feeling growing in the community at large and expressed by resolutions of the different church legislatures that there is urgent need of more ethical and Biblical teaching in the schools and, that it is possible to secure it upon lines acceptable to the great majority of the people and with proper regard for the conscientious convictions of those who may differ from them.

Sectarian jealousies greatly hindered the development of higher education in all the older provinces. The struggle in Ontario occupied a very large place, both in the politics and the religious life of the province. The attempt to create a national university was for a long time prevented by the exclusive policy of the Anglican authorities, who used public funds for the establishment of King's College in 1843 (the charter was obtained ·in 1827) upon an exclusively Anglican basis. In 1849 King's College was secularized and became the University of Toronto, upon a broad undenominational basis, but not until the Church of Scotland, shut out from King's College, had established Queen's University, and the Methodists founded Victoria University, afterward federated with the University of Toronto. Other denominational colleges sprang into existence. After the secularization of King's College, Trinity University was established by Bishop Strachan, upon an exclusively Anglican basis. The leaders of the broader policy had been broad-minded Anglican laymen, and it was laymen of the same type who, in 1877, established Wycliffe College, federated with the University of Toronto and upon a distinctively evangelical or "Low Church" basis, as opposed to the High Church position of Trinity University. The latter has not realized the expectations of its founders, and now, in 1904, has abandoned its position of isolation and connected itself with the University of Toronto as a federated college. The result is that, in Ontario to-day, there are Church of England, Presbyterian, Methodist, and Roman Catholic colleges federated with the Provincial University; while, apart from it, there still stand the Presbyterian University of Queen's, the Baptist University of McMaster, and several Roman Catholic institutions. In Montreal, McGill is virtually a Protestant university, and ' has affiliated with it Presbyterian, Methodist, Congregational, and Anglican schools of theology. In Quebec, Laval University is a Roman Catholic institution and the oldest in Canada. In each of the provinces of Nova Scotia and New Brunswick a university was founded under the name of King's College and sustained by means of land and money from the public treasury, but upon an exclusively Anglican basis. The one in Fredericton was remodeled and became the University of New Brunswick, upon a broad, undenominational basis; the other, in Windsor, Nova Scotia, ceased to receive provincial support but remained an Anglican university and theological college. Dalhousie University, in Halifax, while undenominational, has not the status of a provincial university. The Presbyterians have a theological college in connection with Dalhousie. The Baptists have a university in Acadia, Nova Scotia; and the Methodists a university and theological college in Sackville, New Brunswick.

The Work of the Churches.— The Roman Catholic Church carries on a great variety of charitable work in asylums, houses of refuge, and reformatories. In the Province of Quebec all the provincial institutions are under Roman Catholic control. In the cities the Protestants have distinct institutions controlled by boards representative of the chief Protestant churches. In Ontario, the Roman Catholics are upon the same footing with Protestants in the provincial institutions. In many cities and towns the former have their own hospitals and reformatories, which receive provincial aid in proportion to the number of patients treated. This plan also prevails in the other provinces to a less extent. In other cases, special provision is made for Roman Catholic religious services in addition to the Protestant services.

The charitable work of the Roman Catholic Church is carried on by the various religious orders, many of which are specially devoted to the relief of the poor, the sick, and the fallen.

The work of home missions within the Dominion in connection with the different churches reaches out to every corner of the land, and to the Indians and Eskimos. Foreign missionary work is prosecuted with great vigor by all denominations. Among other good works of an undenominational character may be mentioned the Bible Society, the Religious Tract Society, the Evangelical Alliance, the Young Men's Christian Association, the great Christian movement organized by Mr. Mott among university students, the Young People's societies, such as the Christian Endeavor, the Epworth League, and the Saint Andrew's Brotherhood. The organization of women in the home and foreign missionary work of all the churches and in various other associations has greatly stimulated religious life and work. The reverent observance of the Lord's Day throughout Canada has been a marked feature in its religious life. Church attendance has, on the whole, been well maintained. The laws against Sunday excursions and other violations of the Sabbath rest are effectively enforced. The Lord's Day Alliance has the co-operation of the labor unions as well as of the churches in the protection of the Lord's Day. The Protestant churches in Canada exercise a very strong influence upon legislation, education, and the press. While not unaffected by modern controversy, their attitude generally has been, on the whole, conservative, while the general tone is more liberal and less aggressive than in the past.

Many old prejudices have passed away. A noteworthy illustration of this is furnished in the public worship of the Presbyterian Church, one section of which refused to use anything except the metrical version of the Psalms, regarding even the use of the paraphrases as a serious and hurtful innovation. Now all are united in the use of a hymn book which contains hymns of all sections of the Church of Christ. In many cases the worship has become more liturgical even in non-liturgical churches. Old controversies have passed into oblivion. Greater liberty both in action and in thought is found in all communions.

It is more than possible that with this enlargement and liberty, there has been a corresponding diminution in the intensity of the religious spirit and a growing laxity within the churches which many regard with apprehension. Family worship is not observed as it once was, the children are not as familiar with the Scriptures as were their parents, and many things are tolerated in professedly Christian families which would a generation ago have been rigidly excluded. It is a time of unrest and transition. But in the midst of much change, the churches in the main hold firmly to the fundamentals of the Christian faith, and in all are found devoted men and women who earnestly follow after the ideals of truth, purity, and righteousness.

Among the Anglicans, while the Oxford or Tractarian movement has exercised considerable influence, especially among the clergy, it has seldom reached the extremes seen in England. The majority of the laity have only been slightly affected by it, and they have continued decidedly Protestant. The Presbyterians have exercised a strong influence upon the national ideals of righteousness, and have set a high standard in the education of the ministry. The Methodists have been leaders in Christian liberality and in benevolent enterprises. The Baptists and Congregationalists have borne consistent testimony to the supremacy of the individual conscience and the independence of the Church from state control. Thus each denomination has contributed essential elements to the general religious well-being of Canada, each has in its own sphere accomplished a good work and manifested distinctive excellences, the value of which is coming, more and more, to be recognized by all.

Church Unity.— The general tendency among the Protestant denominations has been toward the unifying of the Christian churches, and this appears the more remarkable when the present religious condition is compared with that of 100 or even 50 years ago, with its polemics and antagonisms. There has been a breaking down of barriers and a marked diminution of the jealousies and rivalries of the past. The old sectarian spirit has, to a large extent, disappeared and a cordial spirit of good-will has manifested itself even in those bodies which special privileges or exclusive theories had tended to separate from others. This is seen in the increasing co-operation in good works, in the frequent inter-denominational comity, and in the general attitude of the churches toward each other. It is remarkably manifested, as we have seen, in the changed attitude of most of the churches in regard to higher education. Federation of denominational colleges in a common state university has been accepted by many who were once strenuously opposed to it, as the best solution of our educational problems. In the three chief Protestant churches of Canada, the Methodist, the Presbyterian, and the Anglican (they are named in the order of their numerical strength), which are each now a unit throughout the Dominion, the tendency is toward a still larger union. Negotiations are at the present time (1904) in progress, looking toward the union of the Methodist, the Presbyterian, and the

Congregational churches in Canada, and there is a reasonable possibility of some substantial result flowing from them. The very fact of the consideration of such proposals by the different bodies concerned is a striking proof of the strong tendency that exists toward the unification of the Protestant churches of Canada.

JAMES P. SHERATON, D.D., LL.D.,
Principal of Wycliffe College, Toronto.

25. Canada—The Roman Catholic Church. See ROMAN CATHOLIC CHURCH IN CANADA.

26. Canada — Military Equipment. The military defense of Canada, so far at least as a resident garrison is concerned, is entrusted entirely to Canadian troops, with but two exceptions, to-wit, the Imperial forces stationed at Halifax and Esquimault, and the reason for their employment in the Dominion is found in the fact that these two ports are important British naval bases, and as such of joint importance to Canada and the motherland. In both stations the resident militia drill each year with the British regulars, so that they may form a well-trained auxiliary force to the latter if attacked. In the case of Esquimault the Canadian government bears one half the annual expenditure for maintenance, under an arrangement with the home government. Up to this date, 30 June 1904, the end of the Canadian fiscal year, there has been practically no naval defensive force in the Dominion, the strength of the country in this respect being confined to a small number of fishery protective service and customs craft, for while the old Militia Act made certain provisions for a naval service, nothing had been done to convert the paper force into an actuality. The government of the day, however, has decided entirely to separate the land and naval militia hereafter, and a bill will shortly be introduced by the Minister of Marine and Fisheries which will be the starting point for a real defensive force operating upon Canadian waters. With regard to the land forces a very important bill has been introduced, and will this session become law; we cannot do better than deal with some of its provisions to show the present legal status of the Canadian army, and the liability of citizens to service therein.

The command in chief is vested in the king, and will continue to be exercised by His Majesty, or by the governor-general as his representative. The actual military command, however, may be given to an officer who shall hold rank not below that of a colonel in the militia or in His Majesty's regular army, subject to the regulations and under the direction of the minister of militia. Here we find a change in the law which opens the door to the highest command for officers of the Canadian militia; formerly only officers of the regular army were eligible. The new bill also gives power to appoint an inspector-general, to be charged with the general inspection of all the military forces in the country. We thus have a continuation of the old power to appoint a general officer commanding, and with it a new power as to an inspecting general, in the latter case following the recent change in army administration in Great Britain.

The general supervision and administration of the military affairs of the country is entrusted to the Minister of Militia and Defense, who must be a member of Parliament, and responsible to that body. Power is taken in the new act to appoint a militia council to advise him in this once again following British precedent in the establishment of an army council there. This body will consist of four military and three civil members, including the Minister, who will be chairman, and will sit at the capital for the transaction of business.

All the male inhabitants of Canada from 18 to 60 years of age, the former only inclusive, are liable to military service. To this general rule there are some few exceptions, for example, judges, clergymen, professors in colleges, policemen and firemen in permanent employ as such, etc. The exempted classes would not muster more than a few thousand men in all, so this provision practically gives the males of 6,000,000 people as a supply to the militia. More than this — in cases of great emergency a *Levee en Masse* may be ordered, when all male inhabitants capable of bearing arms can be called out. Those ordinarily liable to service are divided into four classes. (1) Those 18 years of age to 30, unmarried, or widowers without children; (2) 30 years of age to 45, unmarried, or widowers without children; (3) 18 to 45 who are married, or widowers with children; (4) 45 and upward but under 60. It is in this order the male population may be summoned to the colors.

The active militia of Canada, by which is meant those actually equipped and enrolled, consists of about 42,000 men. Of these a little more than 1,000 constitute a permanent force, the main duty of which is to provide instructors for the balance of the militia in the different arms of the service at a number of schools located in various parts of Canada. On account of the rapid growth of population, especially in the West, this permanent portion of the militia is soon to be doubled in strength, the government having given formal notice of its intention in this regard. The non-permanent portion of the active militia may be called out each year for drill, for a period not exceeding 30 days; as a matter of fact, the usual annual term of instruction is 12 days. A new establishment for the militia has recently been authorized. Under this scheme the peace establishment will be greatly increased, as far as the number of officers and non-commissioned officers is concerned, and while the total number to be drilled annually will still be under 50,000 men, provision will be made to increase that number at short notice to a war strength of 100,000, as a first line of defense, with a second line of equal strength organized on paper for a somewhat slower mobilization. The increase in the peace strength of officers and non-commissioned officers above referred to will be sufficient for the war strength of the first line, with enough in excess to form the basis of the second line. In connection with this point we may state that the militia may be sent on active service "anywhere in Canada and also beyond Canada for the defense thereof," and when in time of war the "militia is called out for active service to serve conjointly with His Majesty's regular forces, His Majesty may place in command thereof a senior general officer of his regular army."

Since the conclusion of the South African war the government has been actively promoting rifle shooting throughout Canada. Rifle clubs are formed under government regulation, the members enrolling therein doing so on the condition that in "case of emergency" they shall at once become members of the active militia. At present the membership in these clubs has passed the 20,000 mark. They are steadily growing in numbers, and as suitable locations for ranges are found these are provided. The government supplies a limited number of rifles to each club, with a fair proportion of free ammunition. It is confidently expected that in a few years these clubs will have a sufficient membership to fill the active militia to war strength.

For a similar purpose, that is, to serve as a feeder to the militia proper, the formation of cadet corps in the schools is being vigorously fostered. The boys in these organizations are given the rudiments of drill, and are instructed as far as possible in rifle shooting, miniature ranges being employed for this purpose. This movement, like that of the rifle clubs, is steadily growing. Since matters of education are under the control of the Provincial governments, the work can be carried on only with their assistance and consent; so far they have very willingly co-operated with the Dominion government. The supply of modern rifles at present in Canada is barely sufficient to arm the militia on a peace footing. To provide for the expansion of war time the government has entered into contracts for the purchase of more arms, and has even succeeded in inducing British capitalists to establish a rifle factory at the city of Quebec. This manufactory has a capacity of 12,000 rifles a year, or double that number if working night and day. Already the first of these weapons are being turned out; they are proving satisfactory. To meet the increased demand for ammunition consequent upon the extension of rifle shooting, and to provide a supply in case of war, the Dominion arsenal has been largely extended, its capacity now being six-fold what it was three or four years ago.

With a rural population very large in proportion to the whole, and chiefly engaged in farming pursuits, Canada has perhaps the best supply of material for mounted troops that can be found in any country containing an approximate number of inhabitants. Knowing this, and recognizing that numbers can, so to speak, be multiplied by speed, the government has recently converted several infantry regiments into mounted corps, and in the formation of new bodies this principle will not be lost sight of.

With the large demands which a new and expanding country always makes upon a national treasury for public works and the increase of transportation facilities, it is impossible to spend large sums upon military development. This being the case, the question arises as to how best to spend the moneys available for defense purposes. It has been felt that the solution is in establishing and perfecting, as far as possible, those more technical and scientific branches which it would be absolutely impossible rapidly to improvise. As a consequence, much attention has been devoted of recent years to the establishment of the subsidiary services. To this end the engineer corps have been increased in number and perfected in equipment, and an establishment thereof added to the permanent force. An excellent army medical corps has been created; schools of signaling are now in course of preparation; an army service corps is in being and well under way; an intelligence branch, with a thoroughly organized corps of guides, is on the establishment; an ordnance corps has displaced the civil administration of the stores department, and a school of musketry, modeled upon the British institution at Hythe, is doing excellent and rapidly increasing service.

For complete professional training the Royal Military College at Kingston, founded in 1876, has proved of immense usefulness. While this seat of military learning is used chiefly for the instruction of cadets, long courses are also held in connection with it for officers of the militia who desire to perfect themselves in a technical knowledge of their work. Officers of the permanent force in its various branches are sent to England for courses there which the limited military resources of Canada would make it impossible to obtain in the latter country.

In conclusion, we may summarize by saying that the last decade has witnessed a very marked advance in the strength and technical training of Canada's military forces, while everything seems to point to a still further and constant improvement in the future, since the national revenues are increasing by leaps and bounds and the spirit of the people demands that a fair proportion shall be devoted to insure the safety of the country.

ANDREW T. THOMPSON, M.P.,
Lieut.-Col. Canadian Militia.

27. Canada — The Acadian Refugees. After the conquest of Acadia in 1710 — the first and only fruit of Samuel Vetch's grand design for the conquest of Canada,— the Treaty of Utrecht (see UTRECHT, PEACE OF) provided for the free exercise of the Roman Catholic religion by such of the French inhabitants as were willing to remain there, but also stipulated that any who should choose might remove within a year. Nearly all remained; but, under various excuses, in the hope of a return of French power, they postponed taking the oath of allegiance to the British crown until 1730. In 1745 war broke out again, and in 1749 the founding of Halifax (q.v.) by several thousand British emigrants excited the jealousy of the officials of Canada and priests of Acadia. The people were a simple and densely illiterate peasantry, taught to obey their missionaries in everything. These missionaries were chosen and directed by the bishop of Quebec and the governor of Canada as agents of French policy, and hence a very difficult position existed, both for the English and for the Acadians. Through the promptings of the fanatical Abbé Louis Joseph Le Loutre (q.v.), and the duplicity of Governor La Jonquière of Canada and the court of France, the Indians were encouraged to murder English settlers and commit other outrages, some of the Acadians even taking part in these crimes. These charges are proved by the citations from French secret documents given in Parkman's 'Montcalm and Wolfe'; and have not been effectively answered. Le Loutre, who was vicar-general of Acadia and missionary to the Micmacs, even paid 100 livres each for English scalps in time of peace; and the money was reimbursed to him by the intendant of Louisbourg. He held constant threats of Micmac massacre over the Acadians themselves. compelling them to acts antagonistic to the English, and moving many of them from their farms and possessions to suit his plans. Yet his inhumanities were evidently justified in his own warped heart and intellect

as services to his Church and country. The people, as a whole, would have been quite content to live in peace, being very well treated. In 1751, La Jonquière issued a proclamation commanding all Acadians to enroll themselves in the French militia. A claim was put forward that only a small part of the province was "Acadia," as ceded to the British under the Treaty of Utrecht, and consequently that all the rest was still under the rule of the French. The latter now conceived the definite design of reconquering the province; but the English, obtaining exact information through the spy Pichon, struck first by capturing Fort Beauséjour, on the neck of the Acadian peninsula, on 16 June 1755. Fort Gaspereau, 12 miles distant, then surrendered, and the French fort at Saint John being burnt and abandoned on the approach of an English force, the whole country was left under British control. This entire plan of re-establishment was due to the forethought of Governor Lawrence, aided with due vigor by Governor Shirley (see SHIRLEY, WILLIAM) of Massachusetts.

The chief interest in the Acadians will always, however, be centered in the incidents of the famous dispersion, which were now about to begin. The projected French invasion had aroused the apprehension of the small British population and authorities, an apprehension deepened by the Indian outrages of Le Loutre and the fear of the neighboring stronghold of Louisbourg. The whole of the Acadians also persistently refused the oath of allegiance. In this state of affairs, which not only seemed a great danger but appeared to imply a great ingratitude, after the mild treatment and privileges of property and religion so long extended to them, it was determined by Governor Lawrence that the only safety lay in removing the Acadian population and replacing them by New Englanders. That view had been held for some time by Governor Shirley of Massachusetts and others. Lawrence had complained bitterly to the Lords of Trade before the capture of the French forts "that this lenity has had so little effect, and that they still hold the same conduct, furnishing them [the French] with labor, provisions, and intelligence, and concealing their designs from us." On the capture of Beauséjour, Lawrence exacted an unqualified oath of allegiance from the Acadians; and in response two successive deputations came to Halifax, representing together nine tenths of their entire population. Both absolutely refused to take the simple pledge of fidelity and allegiance to the British sovereign. The governor and council therefore resolved that it was necessary to deport their people, and in order that they should not strengthen the enemy, they were to be distributed among the English colonies. Lawrence now ordered Colonels Moncton and Winslow and Major Handfield,— at Beauséjour, Basin of Minas, and Annapolis, respectively,— to seize the inhabitants, and if necessary to burn their houses. The principal scenes of the expulsion took place under Winslow at Grand Pré and Fort Edward, in the Basin of Minas, just after completion of the harvest at those fair and populous settlements. At Grand Pré all the males over 10 were ordered to the parish church, where Winslow read them the order of removal and detained them as prisoners. They were kept several weeks before deportation, and the

year was nearly ended before all were gone. Tragic scenes of lamentation and distress accompanied the leaving, although it was carried out as humanely as possible. The whole number removed from the province is usually stated as a little over six thousand, although Richard and others place the figures much higher. Some took refuge in the forests or fled to the French territories. Lawrence sent the ships deporting them to the different colonies from Massachusetts to Georgia, where they became a charge on the people and their gradual departure was connived at. Many in the South eventually reached the French settlements of Louisiana, where their descendants are still found in certain parishes and were estimated at 40,000 a few years ago. The sorrows of the dispersion were great, and the death rate considerable. It is regrettable that those who reached Canada and the French West Indies suffered perhaps the most terrible miseries of all from neglect and ill-treatment. Most of the refugees at length found their way back to Nova Scotia and were progenitors of the greater part of the present French population. Their woful story was told in an idealized form in the pages of Haliburton, from whom, passing through a medium of feminine sentimentality in the pages of a lady writer, it reached Longfellow and was immortalized in his 'Evangeline.' The unhappy facts were afterward the subject of heated recriminations, especially by French writers such as Abbé Casgrain and Rameau, against the New Englanders, whose leading defenders are Parkman and Hannay. Edouard Richard in his 'Acadia' ascribes all to Lawrence personally. The dispassionate view would seem to lie in fair allowances for the difficult situation and training of the actors on both sides. In this light the Acadian population must be remembered as a densely ignorant people. Without some education, the measure of natural shrewdness they possessed could not be expected to clear up for most of them the moral problems connected with allegiance to the British crown, and the political problem of the ownership of Acadia as it was represented to them. Most of them were undoubtedly trying to be loyal to France and ready to return, the country into its possession, and duplicity did not seem to them improper. This is not only deducible from all the events but plainly set forth in the petition of 3,500 Miramichi refugees to Governor de Vaudreuil in 1756.

For the Indian atrocities, to which some of them gave support, we cannot hold the Acadians as a whole responsible. In view of these considerations the Acadian people must be regarded as unfortunate and misled, and their condition as a conquered people, torn from their compatriots and coreligionists by the fortune of war, as they hoped only temporarily, must be considered. As in the case of ignorant populations generally, it is chiefly their leaders and advisers — Le Loutre, Jonquière, and the bishop of Quebec — who must be held responsible. Regarding Le Loutre, although his character of the peculiarly savage and relentless fanatic led him into acts which place him among the class of murderous criminals, his guiding motives appear to have been a distorted patriotism and allegiance to his religion. These are in a different class from the mean duplicities and false quibbles of La Jonquière and the French ministry, who were well aware both of the untruth of their pretensions concerning the extent of Acadia, and of the dangerous position in which they were placing the Acadian people. When we examine the motives of the British side, we have to deal with practically only Lawrence and his council at Halifax. A state of war existed, and in their judgment desperate measures were necessary for the safety of the little British colony. The British settlers were greatly outnumbered and held but a small part of the country. Le Loutre and the French authorities were pursuing a treacherous course of savage murder against them, with Acadian participation. The entire people absolutely refused to take a simple oath of allegiance, although repeatedly and plainly warned of the consequence. In Lawrence's judgment no other course than deportation then seemed safe; and although a harsh measure, like its modern analogue, Reconcentration, it proved effectual in removing all doubt respecting the security of the colony. Harsh and drastic as his measures were, he is entitled to be judged, in part at least, as a military man bound to perform a duty; and his freedom of discretion at a difficult juncture must be respected even if it may have been badly used. On the side of France, two instances of a similar deportation policy are cited in defense — the proposal of Governor de Callières, endorsed by the French king in 1689, to seize the Province of New York and deport all the Protestant population (Doc. Hist. N. Y., Vol. I., pp. 285-297); and the actual deportation of the English settlers from the Island of St. Kitts in 1666, to the number of 2,500, an occurrence marked by the striking of a medal by Louis XIV., inscribed "Ang. Ex Insula St. Christoph Exturbat."

Bibliography.— Abbé Raynal, 'Histoire des Indes,' 2d ed.; Haliburton, 'History of Nova Scotia' (1829); Rameau, 'La France aux Colonies' (1859); 'Une Colonie Féodale en Amérique' (1889); Murdoch, 'History of Nova Scotia' (1865); Akins, 'N. S. Archives' (1869); Campbell, 'History of Nova Scotia' (1873); Moreau, 'Histoire de l'Acadie' (1873); Hannay, 'History of Acadia' (1879); and 'The Story of Acadia' (1904); Smith, 'Acadia' (1884); Casgrain, 'Pèlérinage au Pays d'Evangeline' (1888); Parkman, 'Montcalm and Wolfe' (1884); Hart, 'Fall of New France' (1888); Richard, 'Acadia' (1894). See also NOVA SCOTIA — *History.*

WILLIAM DOUW LIGHTHALL,
Author of 'The False Chevalier': Founder of Chateau de Ramezay Historical Museum; etc.

28. Canada — The Quebec Act. From the capitulation of Montreal in 1760 down to the ratification of the Treaty of Paris in 1763 Canada was without any form of civil government, the affairs of the colony being administered by the officer in command of the British armies of occupation. But with the conclusion of peace and the definite cession of the colony to the British Crown this tentative arrangement came to an end and in the autumn of 1763 a royal proclamation decreed the establishment of a civil government in the newly-acquired colony, promising that as soon as circumstances would permit, representative assemblies would be convened. In the meantime the laws of England were to be in force. In virtue of this arrangement General James Murray (q.v.) was appointed to the gov-

ernorship of the colony and a council of eight members was nominated to assist him in the work of administration. For the time being, justice continued to be administered by the military courts at Quebec, Three Rivers and Montreal but in September 1764 a proclamation was issued by the Governor-in-Council establishing a court of King's Bench for the trial of all causes, both civil and criminal, agreeably to the laws of England which the royal proclamation of the preceding year had declared to be in force. At the same time a court of Common Pleas was established for the trial of actions which had arisen before the publication of the proclamation of 1763 and in regard to which the old French law had to be applied.

The immediate result of this change was to inaugurate a régime of utter judicial chaos, for the new judges were completely at a loss to apply the principles of English common law to the causes which came before them, especially where questions of real property were concerned. Accordingly, the Governor-in-Council during the month of November 1764 issued a further proclamation declaring that "in all actions relative to the tenure of land or the rights of inheritance, the French laws and usages shall be observed as the rule of decision." But in all other civil cases and in all criminal cases the common law of England was to be applied. This change improved matters but slightly for the new English judges were slow to master the intricacies of French law and applied it very imperfectly where they endeavored to make it apply. To the application of the English criminal law the French inhabitants of the province made no great objection, although for the time being many of them failed to take kindly to the institution of trial by jury; but there was a widespread demand for the extension of French law to all civil causes. Complaints were likewise made that the judicial officers were for the most part ignorant of the French language; that they were often dishonest and that the legal fees charged the inhabitants were exorbitant. For all of these complaints there seems to have been considerable foundation and in fact the law officers of the Crown in England reported a recommendation that the French language should be restored in judicial proceedings and that the old French law should be extended to all civil cases.

Matters rested as they were until the appointment of General Sir Guy Carleton (q.v.) to the post of Governor in 1767. The new Governor was not long in grasping the situation and in deciding that the restoration of the whole fabric of French civil law would be advisable. To this end he had the *coutume de Paris* of the old régime carefully re-edited by several colonial jurists of acknowledged ability and the revised text at once became the acknowledged source of law in all cases of land tenure and inheritance. Carleton pressed his proposal on the home authorities and in 1770 went to England to urge its adoption. There he managed to secure the appointment of a commission to examine into the merits of the whole matter and the report of this body, although it was not presented until the closing days of 1772, was on the whole in favor of the Governor's recommendation. In the meantime, however, there was a growing demand among the British inhabitants of the colony for the establishment of a representative assembly in accordance with the promise made in the proclamation of 1763. At meetings of the British inhabitants resolutions calling upon the Home authorities to take steps in this direction were passed and forwarded to England. But to the adoption of such a step there was grave difficulty, namely, the decision of the question as to whether Roman Catholics would be permitted to sit in the new Assembly. The disabilities of Roman Catholics had not been removed in England at this time and it was hardly to be expected that Parliament would extend to Roman Catholics in a colony privileges which it denied them at home. On the other hand, an assembly from which Roman Catholics were excluded would be very far from representative in a colony where nine-tenths or more of the population professed that religion. This difficulty, together with the fact that the position assumed by the representative assemblies in the British colonies on the Atlantic seaboard at this time was not calculated to inspire the Home authorities with a favorable regard for popular colonial representation, seems to have determined the Ministry in its decision that Canada, for the time being, should not be trusted with an assembly representing the people. On some other points, however, the home authorities evinced a desire to meet the wishes of the colonists.

On 2 May 1774 a bill, popularly known as the Quebec Bill, was introduced into the House of Lords where it passed with little opposition. In the House of Commons the measure was vigorously opposed by a strong minority, but with some amendments was eventually passed, and towards the end of June received the royal assent. By the provisions of the Act the boundaries of the Province of Quebec were extended to include all ancient Canada, including Labrador, and all the territory lying north of the Ohio and west of the Mississippi. Roman Catholics were released from all penal restrictions; the obligation of the tithe was reimposed in favor of the Church, and all classes, with the exception of the religious orders were confirmed in the full enjoyment of their proprietary rights. French law was hereafter to be applied in *all* civil cases while the law of England was retained for the decision of all criminal causes. Both, however, might be modified by ordinances of the Governor and Legislative Council. Inasmuch as it was "inexpedient to call an Assembly" the Act provided for the establishment of a Legislative Council to consist of not less than 17 nor more than 23 members nominated by the Crown. To this body in conjunction with the Governor was given a limited power of internal administration including the right to levy internal and local taxes. But Parliament expressly reserved to itself the right of external taxation and every ordinance passed by the Council was to be transmitted to England where it might be disallowed if the home authorities deemed advisable.

In the New England colonies the passage of the Quebec Act was bitterly resented, partly because of the privileges which it granted a French and Roman Catholic population but more especially because it placed under the almost complete control of the British authorities the vast expanse of territory west of the Alleghanies in the conquest of which the seaboard colonies had borne a heavy share. In Quebec the French inhabitants, while many regretted that provision

had not been made for the establishment of a popular assembly open to Roman Catholics, for the most part welcomed the substantial concessions which the Act conveyed. There is little doubt that these concessions served in some measure to assure the British authorities of at least their neutrality during the turbulent days of the next few years. The British inhabitants of the province, on the other hand, were naturally disappointed but the course of events during the next half-decade was such as to prelude any important manifestation of their feelings. Under the provisions of the Quebec Act the administration of the province was carried on for the ensuing 17 years.

Bibliography.—Coffin, 'The Province of Quebec and the American Revolution' (1896); Hart, 'The Quebec Act' (1885); Kingsford, 'History of Canada,' passim; Marriot, 'Plan of a Code of Laws for the Province of Quebec,' (London 1774); Maseres, 'Projet des Lois pour Quebec' (Quebec 1770).

WILLIAM BENNETT MUNRO,
Instructor in Government, Harvard University.

29. Canada — The Ashburton Treaty. The Ashburton Treaty (also called Treaty of Washington), a treaty between the United States and Great Britain, signed 9 Aug. 1842, is chiefly important for its settlement of the Northeastern boundary question. The boundary between Massachusetts (subsequently Maine) and British North America had been in dispute since 1783. The treaty of that year (Art. 2) had made the following provision: "And that all disputes which might arise in future on the subject of the boundaries of the said United States may be prevented, it is hereby agreed and declared, that the following are and shall be their boundaries, namely, from the northwest angle of Nova Scotia, namely, that angle which is formed by a line drawn due north from the source of the Saint Croix River, to the Highlands; along the said Highlands which divide those rivers that empty themselves into the river Saint Lawrence from those which fall into the Atlantic Ocean, to the northwesternmost head of the Connecticut River; east, by a line to be drawn along the middle of the river Saint Croix, from its mouth in the Bay of Fundy to its source, and from its source directly north to the aforesaid Highlands which divide the rivers that fall into the Atlantic Ocean from those which fall into the river Saint Lawrence." The article was doubtless drawn in good faith, but owing to the imperfect knowledge of the geography of the territory concerned, its meaning was soon involved in doubt. The identity of the river Saint Croix, the location of the Highlands referred to, and the ownership of the Passamaquoddy Islands became matters of dispute. The identity of the Saint Croix was settled by a commission in 1798, appointed under the Treaty of 1794. Under the Treaty of Ghent (see GHENT, TREATY OF) (1814) a commission was appointed which settled the Passamaquoddy question by compromise (1817). But the demarcation of the inland boundary seemed long impossible of solution. The American claim located the "northwest angle" at the point where the line due north from the source of the Saint Croix met the Highlands between the rivers flowing into the Saint Lawrence and those flowing into the Atlantic; this established the angle in question "at a place about 144 miles due north from the source of the River Saint Croix, and about 66 miles north of the River Saint John" (United States commissioner, 4 Oct. 1821). The extreme British claim (at any rate after 1814) placed the angle "at or near the mountain or hill called Mars Hill, distant about 40 miles on a due north line from the source of the River Saint Croix, and about 37 miles south of the River Saint John" (note of British commissioner 4 Oct. 1821). In each case the boundary proceeded westward and southward along the Highlands to the head-waters of the Connecticut. Between the two there thus lay a disputed territory of 12,000 square miles. After fruitless negotiations a convention of 27 Sept. 1827 referred the boundary to the arbitration of the king of the Netherlands. His award, however, in 1831 was rejected by the United States.

Meantime the district of Maine had become (1820) a State, and was eager in the defence of its claim to the disputed region. The progress of settlement naturally led to conflict and disturbance on the border line, known as the "Aroostook War." By the year 1840 matters had reached an apparent deadlock in which the adoption of a conventional line seemed the only solution. In addition to the northeastern boundary, various other matters of controversy were outstanding between the two nations. The English claim of a "right of search" for the suppression of the slave trade created a standing difficulty. The destruction of the Caroline (q.v.), an American vessel, by a party of Canadians during the revolt of 1837 had led to a demand for redress. The British government had met this claim by asserting that the destruction of the vessel was a legitimate act of war, the Caroline having carried supplies for the insurgents. A Captain McLeod, a Canadian, accused of participation in the affair, was arrested and brought to trial in New York; in all probability nothing but his acquittal prevented actual hostilities. A further complication had arisen in the case of the Creole, a slave ship on which the negroes had revolted (1841), and which they had carried to a British port in the West Indies, where they were allowed to go unmolested. There was also in question the boundary of Oregon. To settle these various points at issue, Lord Ashburton (see ASHBURTON, ALEXANDER BARING, LORD) was sent to Washington (April 1842) and in conjunction with Daniel Webster, secretary of state, arranged the treaty commonly known by his name. Ashburton, formerly Mr. Alexander Baring, a prominent financier, and for nearly 20 years a member of the House of Commons, had previously resided in America, where he married a daughter of Senator Bingham. His known desire for a good understanding between Britain and America rendered his relations at Washington most cordial. He was widely entertained, and is said to have "spread a social charm over Washington, and filled everybody with friendly feelings toward England." With Webster his relations were especially amicable, and their negotiations assumed an altogether informal character. (See Schouler, 'History of the United States,' Vol. IV., ch. xvii.) To this fact has been partly due the impression ever since prevalent in Canada that the interests of that country were sacrificed to the expansiveness of Lord Ashburton's feelings. Under the terms of the treaty, the northeast boundary was settled thus (Art I.): "It is hereby agreed and declared that the line of boundary shall be as follows: Beginning at the monument at the source of the River Saint Croix, as designated and agreed to by the commissioners under the fifth article of the treaty of 1794, between the governments of Great Britain and the United States; thence north, following the exploring line run and marked by the surveyors of the two governments in the years 1817 and 1818, under the fifth article of the Treaty of Ghent, to its intersection with the River Saint John, and to the middle of the channel thereof; thence up the middle of the main channel of the said River Saint John into the mouth of the River Saint Francis; thence up the middle of the channel of the said River Saint Francis, and of the lakes through which it flows, to the outlet of the Lake Pohenagamook; thence southwesterly in a straight line to a point on the northwest branch of the River Saint John." This locates the main part of the boundary; for details of the further extension of the line, the text of the treaty may be consulted ('Treaties and Conventions,' Washington 1889; 'Annual Register,' 1842). The treaty provided further for the survey and permanent marking of the boundary, which was completed in 1847. Of the disputed territory the United States received about seven twelfths and Canada five twelfths. Rouse's Point, on Lake Champlain, was also declared to belong to the United States, the government of that country binding itself to pay to Maine and Massachusetts $300,000 on account of the relinquished territory. The right to carry timber down the Saint John River was granted to the United States. By Article 8 of the treaty, it was agreed that each country should maintain on the coast of Africa a sufficient naval force, carrying not less than 80 guns for the purpose of enforcing, separately and respectively, the laws, rights, and obligations of each contracting party for the suppression of the slave trade. The treaty passed over the Caroline and Creole cases (see CREOLE CASE), but declared (Art. 10) that "each party, on requisition from the other, shall deliver up to justice persons charged with murder, assault with intent to murder, piracy, arson, robbery or forgery, upon sufficient proof of their criminality." The question of the Oregon boundary was also omitted.

The boundary award of the treaty met with great dissatisfaction in Canada. It was currently believed, and the belief largely persists, that the interests of Canada had been unduly sacrificed. The Canadian view of the case is presented in Dent's 'Last Forty Years of Canada' (1881), and in more extreme form in Coffin's 'Quirks of Diplomacy' (1874). The supposed sacrifice of Canada by Lord Ashburton has become a commonplace of Canadian political discussion. Later investigation, however, is strongly in favor of the American claim. The whole subject of the boundary has recently been exhaustively treated in an admirable paper by Dr. William Ganong of Smith College ('Proceedings of the Royal Society of Canada,' 2d series, Vol. VII., 1901). Dr. Ganong, though a Canadian, decides that Maine was right and New Brunswick wrong in the

northwest angle controversy. He bases his decision on the text of the treaty of 1783, on the maps of the time, on the admissions of Governor Carleton and others, and on a petition of the New Brunswick legislature of 1814, virtually admitting the American claim. The Mars Hill boundary line was not advanced, he says, until 1814. In the controversial discussions of the treaty the episode of the "red line" map has played a considerable part (see 'North American Review,' April 1843, and Winsor's 'America,' VII. 180). This was a map found in the French archives and supposed to have been given to Vergennes by Franklin in connection with the treaty of 1783. A boundary line favoring the English claim was marked upon it in red ink. A copy of this map was in Webster's possession during the negotiations but was not shown by him to Lord Ashburton. It was shown by him to the Maine commissioners; played some part in securing their assent to the Ashburton Treaty.[9] But it is not proved that the marking of the map was by Franklin, and it is also possible that it was wrongly marked with intent to deceive (see Hinks, 'Boundaries Formerly in Dispute,' 1885). To offset this map, the original of which has disappeared, there is still in the British Museum an English map favoring the American claim. See also UNITED STATES—DIPLOMACY 1815–61; TREATIES OF THE UNITED STATES WITH FOREIGN NATIONS.   STEPHEN LEACOCK,
Lecturer in Political Science, McGill University.

30. **Canada — The Clergy Reserves.** The clergy reserves were lands set apart, by virtue of the constitutional act of 1791, for the maintenance of the Protestant clergy in Upper and Lower Canada. The intention of the act was to reproduce in the colony an episcopal establishment similar to that of Great Britain, to whose primate it was to be subordinate. The provincial governors were directed under the act to reserve one seventh of the land for the support of the Protestant clergy. The reserved blocks of land were to be distributed among those granted to settlers. In Upper Canada a full seventh of all the land was to be granted. In Lower Canada reserves were to be made only in proportion to new settlement and not in respect of lands already occupied. No reservations were made in the latter province until 1796. Reservations were made each year until 1838 (except in 1813). The total reservations made in Lower Canada amounted to over 930,000 acres: in the Upper Province to about 2,400,000 acres. The crown was also empowered to authorize the lieutenant-governor of each province from time to time to erect parsonages, to endow them with a portion of the reserve lands and to present incumbents to them (constitutional act, Secs. 38, 39, 40). The operation of the system thus established was not at first felt as a serious grievance. Land being still plentiful, the reservations remained unsold and were leased at extremely low rentals (10 shillings for 200 acres during first seven years). With the progress of settlement however the rentals constantly rose. The question of the clergy reserves became a subject of increasing complaint. The members of the Church of England were in a decided minority, not only in the Lower Province, but in Upper Canada itself. The ques-

tion early arose whether the wording of the act, — "allotment and appropriation of lands for the support of a Protestant clergy" — could not be construed in favor of the Presbyterian and Dissenting denominations. The matter being referred to the home government, the law officers of the crown decided (November 1819) that the Scotch Church had a claim for a share of the rentals, but that no other denominations had a claim at all. The irritation thus caused rendered the question one of acute difficulty during the succeeding thirty years, and has been designated by Dr. Bryce, the Canadian historian, the "Thirty Years' Religious War in Upper Canada." The distribution of the population of Upper Canada among the different denominations in 1839 was as follows: Church of England, 79,754; Methodists, 61,088; Presbyterians, 76,383; Roman Catholics, 43,029; Baptists, 12,968; others, 57,572. The claims of the Church of England were stoutly upheld by the Rev. John Strachan, subsequently Bishop of Toronto (1839). Egerton Ryerson (see RYERSON, A. E.), a young Methodist minister, strove with equal zeal on behalf of the Methodist Church.

In 1827 the assembly of Upper Canada asked the crown to devote the reserves to the creation of schools and of churches of all denominations. The same request was repeated in each of the three following years with considerable popular agitation. Meantime the endowment of rectories as provided by the act of 1791, was authorized by instructions from the crown in 1825. The excited state of public feeling delayed for some years the execution of this project, but in 1836, 54 rectories were endowed with 400 acres each. The discontent thus caused helped to precipitate the rebellion of 1837. With the suppression of that movement the question of the clergy reserves still earnestly demanded solution. An act of the legislature of Upper Canada in 1839, proposing to re-invest the reserves in the crown, was disallowed by the home government. In the following year the legislature passed an act for the sale of the reserves, one half of the proceeds to go to the Churches of England and Scotland, and the other to be divided among the other religious denominations. This again was abortive, the British judges, on question by the House of Lords, deciding that the provincial legislature had exceeded its authority. The Imperial Parliament now intervened and passed an act (7 Aug. 1840) for the settlement of the question. Part of the reserves had already been sold by authority of a statute of 1827. The proceeds of these sales were to be divided between the Churches of England and Scotland, the former receiving two thirds: the unappropriated lands (1,800,000 acres) were to be sold, and the amount realized to be invested, one half of the interest being given to the two above churches, in the proportion already mentioned, the other half to be applied by the governor and executive council for public worship and religious instruction. The income thus accruing was divided in the ensuing years among the churches of England and Scotland, the Wesleyan Methodist, Roman Catholic and Synod Presbyterian churches and the United Synod Presbytery. The question was still far from settled. It was claimed that the lands were sold by the crown at insufficient prices, and Bishop Strachan led an agitation for the sharing up of the lands themselves. The assembly refused to petition the

crown to this effect, but demanded the repeal of the act of 1840. The Imperial Parliament complied by a statute of 1853, which placed the reserves in the control of the Provincial Parliament (the two Canadas being now united). The Canadian Parliament elected in 1854 strongly reflected the general public feeling in favor of secularization. A statute to that effect was passed. A lump sum of £188,342 was paid to the Church of England, representing the guarantee of stipends then charged on the reserve fund, called for by the imperial act. The reserved lands were sold and the proceeds given to the municipal authorities for education and local improvements. Consult: Lindsay, 'The Clergy Reserves' (1851); 'Memoir of Bishop Strachan' (1870); Ryerson, 'Story of My Life' (1883).   STEPHEN LEACOCK,
Lecturer in Political Science, McGill University.

31. Canada — Seigniorial Tenure. The system of Seigniorial Tenure was that system of public and private relations based upon the tenure of land which the French government undertook, during the course of the 17th and 18th centuries, to introduce into its North American colonies, and more especially into the colony of New France, now Canada. The system of feudal — or as in its later stages it came to be called — seigniorial tenure, was deeply rooted in France, and it is easy to understand how its introduction into the colonies appealed to Richelieu as a means of providing estates for many of the landless aristocrats of France. Moreover as feudalism was now so far advanced in decay as to be no longer a menace to the central power, it is easy to see how the system appealed to the Bourbon monarchs as likely to permit, in the colonies, of that centralization of authority which characterized France at this time.

As regards Canada, the seigniorial system had its origin in 1627 when the French King granted to the Company of New France, more commonly known as the Company of One Hundred Associates, the whole of the French possessions in North America as one immense fief with full power to sub-grant it in seigniories to settlers. During the whole 35 years of its existence, however, this Company devoted almost its entire attention to the development of the lucrative fur trade; very few settlers were sent out to the colony, with the result that while over 60 *in extenso* grants of seigniories were made, almost none at all were ever taken possession of by the grantees. But in 1663 the Company was compelled to surrender its charter and extensive territorial rights, the Crown taking into its own hands the supervision of colonial affairs and providing New France with a royal government corresponding roughly to that established in the French provinces at home. From this time on settlers came in increasing numbers; power was given the colonial Governor and Intendant to make grants of seigniories subject to royal ratification, and during the last quarter of the 17th century these were made freely. In no case were grants made to absentees: each applicant for a seigniorial grant had to prove himself a *bona fide* colonist. Large numbers of the settlers were sent over at the royal expense and once in the colony, every inducement was given them to remain. Even the detachments of French regular troops sent out to the colony

Vol. 3 — 38.

were disbanded there and both officers and men were encouraged, by liberal grants both of land and money, to become permanent residents of New France.

As to the size of the seigniories granted, there was no fixed rule: they varied from small plots containing a few square *arpents* to huge tracts ten by twelve leagues in area. Much depended on the position occupied by the settler before his immigration to the colony and upon the available means which he had for the development of his grant. But whatever the area of the grants, they almost invariably assumed the same shape,— that of a parallelogram with the shorter end fronting on the river. On receiving his grant the new seignior was under obligation to repair at once to the Château de St. Louis in Quebec, there to render his fealty and homage to the Governor as the representative of the Crown. Within the next forty days he was required to file with the Registrar-General his *aveu et dénombryment,* or statement showing clearly the location, extent and nature of his seigniory. A similar statement containing full information regarding the development of the holding was required every time the seigniory changed owners. No payment was exacted from the seignior in return for the original grant, but an exaction known as the *quint* became payable on each mutation of ownership by sale, gift, or inheritance other than in direct succession. This amounted to one fifth of the estimated value of the seigniory, but of this amount it was the custom of the Crown to give a rebate of one third. As the seigniories increased in value very slowly this burden was never an onerous one. In making the grants, the authorities usually reserved the right of taking, from the granted seigniories such locations as might at any time be found necessary for the construction of fortifications or other public works, such oak and pine timber as might be found suitable for use in the royal shipyards and the right to a share in all mines and mineral deposits found in the seigniory.

In France the seignior was under no obligation to sub-grant the lands within his seigniory, but by a series of royal edicts,— more notably the Edict of Marly (1711), this obligation was imposed upon the seigniors of New France in the interest of colonial development. From 1711 onwards it was incumbent on all seigniors in Canada to sub-grant portions of the unoccupied lands of their seigniories to any settlers who applied for such grants, on whatever terms were customary in the neighborhood without exacting any bonus or *prix d'entrée.* If the seignior refused to do this, power was given the Governor and Intendant to step in and to make the grant, the seigniorial dues in such case to become payable to the Crown. Furthermore, from time to time various edicts revoked or curtailed the grants made to such seigniors as did not seem to be showing sufficient zeal in having their lands granteu to settlers. In this way every seignior was compelled to become, after a fashion, the immigration agent of the colonial authorities, and it was this particular feature which serves most prominently to differentiate the seigniorial system in Canada from its prototype at home.

Grants made by the seigniors to settlers were called grants *en censive.* These likewise varied considerable in size, but almost invariably assumed the same shape as the seigniory within which they lay. Over them the seignior retained a variety of rights, some financial, some judicial, and some merely ceremonial or honorary in their nature. Among the former was the annual payments known as the *cens et rentes*, the former payable in money, the latter usually in produce. The *cens* was a very small due, amounting usually to a few *sous* per superficial *arpent* and valuable to the seignior mainly as establishing his claim to other and more important rights. The *rentes* was payable annually in grain, cattle or poultry but might be commuted by agreement of the parties into a fixed money payment. Then there was the *lods et ventes*, a mutation fine payable at every change of ownership. This amounted to one twelfth of the mutation price, and of it the seignior usually remitted one fourth, although he was under no legal obligation so to do. To guard himself against loss of his proper *lods et ventes* through sales of *en censive* holdings at less than their actual value, the seignior possessed the *droit de retraite* by virtue of which right he might pre-empt any holding thus sold by payment to the purchaser of the mutation price, within forty days from the date of the sale. Then there was the *droit de banalité* or the exclusive right of the seignior to erect a grist mill within the limits of his seigniory and to compel his *censitaires* to have their grain ground there and not elsewhere on pain of confiscation. The amount of toll receivable for this service was fixed by a royal edict at one fourteenth of the grain ground. During the greater part of the French régime this incident bore more heavily upon the seignior than upon his *censitaires*, for except in the more populous seigniories, the amount of toll received rarely sufficed to pay expenses. At the same time the colonial authorities compelled the seigniors to provide mills in their seigniories on pain of losing the right for all future time. Finally, there was the much-detested *corvée*, or right of the seigniors to exact from their *censitaires* a certain quota of labor on the seigniorial lands without compensation. The amount allowable varied in different seigniories but as a rule the *censitaires* were permitted to commute it into a fixed money payment. An ordinance of the Superior Council in 1716 forbade the exaction of *corvée* during seed time and harvest. In addition to the foregoing main rights the seignior ordinarily reserved for himself the privilege of taking from the lands of the *censitaires* such wood and stone as might be found necessary in the erection of the seigniorial manor house, mill or church, and in some cases the right of taking wood for fuel. In many cases he likewise reserved the right of claiming a share in all the fish caught by his *censitaires* in the waters of the seigniory.

Most of the seigniors possessed certain judicial rights. These, however, were not inherent in the ownership of a seigniory, but were specifically granted by the Crown. This grant might convey merely the right of *basse justice* in which case the seignior was empowered to deal with minor causes in which the amount in dispute did not exceed a few *sols*. The grant of *moyenne justice* gave him a large jurisdiction, while the grant of *haute justice* gave full judicial power in all cases except those such as

treason and counterfeiting in which the Crown was directly concerned. As a rule all three degrees of judicial power were conferred on the seignior. But in every case an appeal lay to the royal courts of the colony. As the exercise of his judicial powers brought the seignior very little profit the seigniorial courts never became a very important element in the colonial judicial system.

The remaining rights of the seignior were merely honorary and afforded him no financial return. He was entitled to the fealty and homage of his *censitaires*, to a front pew in the parish church, to certain precedence at the Sacraments, to the erection of a Maypole at his door each Mayday and, in general, to the respect and deference of his dependents. A number of seigniors who showed zeal in the development of their holdings received patents of nobility but it must be borne in mind that the possession of a seigniory in New France did not of itself give noble rank. Herein Canadian feudalism again differed from its prototype in France. The French seignior was always a noble; the Canadian very rarely.

At the close of the French régime nearly eight million *arpents* of land had been granted out to be holden under the seigniorial tenure. The system had become so deeply rooted in the colony that the English authorities, after the Conquest, did not venture to take the drastic step of supplanting it in favor of the English system of tenure in free and common socage. The old system was allowed, therefore, to remain intact but as the colony became more thickly settled, many of the seigniorial exactions became burdensome. The *droit de banalité* became especially so. Moreover, the new English courts failed utterly to afford the *censitaires* that protection against the seigniors which the authorities of the old régime had given. From time to time the Legislature of Lower Canada sought to deal with the growing complaint that the operation of the system was retarding the development of the province but found it extremely difficult to devise any plan which would be satisfactory to the tenants and at the same time protect the vested interests of the seigniors. In 1825 an Act was passed giving to the parties concerned the right to commute all seigniorial dues into a lump sum by mutual agreement but very few took advantage of the legal permission thus accorded. It was not until 1854 that by the Seigniorial Tenures Abolition Act a general scheme for the compulsory commutation of all seigniorial obligations received the assent of the Canadian Legislature. This Act provided for the establishment of a Special Court to determine just what seigniorial claims were justifiable and on a basis of its decisions each seignior was awarded a certain indemnity for the loss of his rights. Part of the amount was paid him from the public treasury; the balance became an annual rent charge on the lands of the tenants, which annual charge, again, might be commuted into a lump sum if the tenant so desired. In any case all lands formerly holden *en seigneurie* or *en censive* were thereafter to be holden in fee simple. Thus by one stroke of legislation the whole system of territorial law in Lower Canada was revolutionized and the last vestige of Canadian feudalism disappeared.

Bibliography.— Parkman, 'The Old Régime

in Canada,' Kingsford, 'History of Canada,' Vol. X.; Weir, 'The Administration of the Old Régime in Canada'; La Fontaine, 'Judgments and Deliberations of the Special Court for the Abolition of the Seigniorial Tenure;' .Lareau, 'De la Féodalité en Canada' (in his 'Melanges historiques et litteraires'); Doutre et Lareau, 'Histoire du droit Canadien'; Titles and Documents relating to the Seigniorial Tenure (1854); Daniels, 'Histoire des Grandes Familles Canadiens-Français'; Munro, 'The Droit de Banalité' during the French régime in Canada.

WILLIAM BENNETT MUNRO,
Lecturer Political Economy, Harvard University.

32. Canada — The Hudson's Bay Company.* This great trading company has been in operation under its present charter for two and one third centuries. Its charter, which is a very generous one, was given by easy-going Charles II. The company owes its origin to the adventures in the New World of two French Huguenots, Pierre Esprit Radisson and Medard Chouart (afterward Sieur de Groseilliers, or familiarly "Mr. Gooseberry"). It is claimed that in 1662 these daring spirits reached James Bay, the southern lobe of Hudson Bay. This is entirely improbable, as in that year they are known to have been in Lac des milles Lacs, now northern Minnesota. (See the discussion on this matter in the author's 'Remarkable History of the Hudson's Bay Company.') Persecuted in French Canada, the adventurers fled to New England and thence to England, where they had an audience with the king, and through the influence of Prince Rupert (see RUPERT, PRINCE), the king's cousin, a strong company was afterward formed, being created by royal charter. The first expedition to Hudson Bay was made for the adventurers in the ship Nonsuch Ketch, Capt. Zachariah Gillam, a New England mariner. Arrived at the destination, a fortress was erected on James Bay (lat. 51° 20' N., lon. 78° W.), called Charles Fort. On the return of the vessel to England the charter was granted (1670). Prince Rupert was made the first governor, and the vast territory covered by the charter became known as Rupert's Land. He was followed by the king's brother, James, Duke of York, and the third governor was the famous Duke of Marlborough, who has left his family name on Fort Churchill. England's great rival, "La Belle France," immediately began to lay claim to the bay as a part of Canada. Several expeditions were sent out to drive off the English, the most notable being that under Pierre Le Moyne d'Iberville. See IBERVILLE, PIERRE LE MOYNE D'.) He achieved so great a naval victory that the whole bay fell into French hands, comprising at that time seven forts, of which Charles, Nelson, Moose, and Albany were the chief. The territory under dispute was restored to England by the famous treaty of Ryswick, 1697. Up to the time of the French forays rich dividends had been declared by the partners, that of 1690 being 75 per cent of the original stock, and the king's share was rendered in guineas instead of pounds. The com-

*The charter of this company is given to the "Governor and Company of Adventurers of England trading into Hudson's Bay." From this it has been usual to employ the title "Hudson's Bay Company," using the possessive form of the name of Hudson, the discoverer. The bay itself, as in the case of Hudson River, has its name spelt by the geographers without the apostrophe and s.

pany, which included many distinguished men, such as the Duke of Albemarle (Gen. Monk), (see MONK, GEORGE), and Sir George Carteret (see CARTERET, SIR GEORGE) was very influential. Prince Rupert presided at the London meetings, and a sub-committee met regularly to buy and sell, went to Gravesend to see the goods shipped, the men paid, and the like, in the good ships Prince Rupert, Wyvenhoe, or Bark Craven, which sailed around the north of Scotland and thence to Hudson Bay. Every year, about 1 June, for more than two hundred years, one ship at least has cleared for its northern' port on the bay, latterly generally York Factory. How small the beginnings of trade were may be seen in the inventory of goods sent out in 1672: "Two hundred fowling-pieces, and powder and shot; 200 brass kettles, size from 5 to 16 gallons; 12 gross of knives; 900 or 1,000 hatchets." In October the ship returned with its valuable cargo of furs, which was sold in London, often by auction.

The second period of Hudson's Bay Company history is that involving the local opposition in England to the traders. Between the treaties of Ryswick (1697) and Utrecht (1713), the menaces of the French destroyed the fur trade, but after the latter treaty, from which time the bay has remained continuously English, the affairs of the company improved. This roused the envy of a number of merchants, the leader among them being an Irish gentleman named Arthur Dobbs. He advocated an expedition to explore the Northwest Passage, raised by subscription a large sum to send out a ship to rival the company, and though his expedition did not accomplish much, yet the Hudson's Bay Company was disturbed, was put on its mettle, and the struggle as recorded in the Government bluebook of 1749 became very interesting. A more serious movement, however, began in French Canada. The charter of the company gave it the trade of all the lands and streams within "Hudson's Streights," with one most important limitation, namely, except those "which are not now actually possessed by any of our subjects, or by the subjects of any other Christian prince or state." Long before the Hudson's Bay Company penetrated Rupert's Land, the French ascended the Great Lakes, and 20 or 30 years before the English had reached the Saskatchewan River from Hudson Bay, explored the river system of Rupert's Land and came in sight of the Rocky Mountains. This feat was accomplished by Sieur de la Verandrye, who in 1738 caused a fort to be erected on the site of the present city of Winnipeg, and took possession of the country for the king of France. The conquest of Canada by Wolfe put an end to this French occupation, but as later discussions show left it a part of Canada. Soon after the conquest of Canada, however, a critical movement took place in the effort of the Hudson's Bay Company to penetrate the interior from the bay, on whose shores for nearly a century it had lain in slumber. This advance was under the leadership of one of the captains of exploration. Samuel Hearne, a Hudson's Bay Company officer, sometimes called the "Mungo Park of Canada." Hearne discovered the Coppermine River and followed it to its mouth on the Arctic Sea. He, too, first of white men saw Great Slave Lake. But, also, shortly after the transfer of Canada from France to England,

Scottish traders from Montreal began to ascend the waterways of Canada, and to pass from Lake Superior on to Lake Winnipeg and the Saskatchewan River, the very centre of Rupert's Land. Alexander Henry (1760), Thomas Curry, James Finlay, and the brothers Frobisher, traders from Montreal, led the way and reached the Saskatchewan. Hearne from Hudson Bay heard of the Canadian traders having built a fort at Sturgeon Lake, and two years later (1774) accepted the gage of battle, and built Fort Cumberland alongside of his rivals on the Saskatchewan. The war of the giants had now begun, and for well-nigh 50 years it raged with increasing rancor and bitterness. Out of the movement of the Scottish merchants named, from Montreal, grew the union of traders (1783-4) known as the North-West Company. Its leading traders were Frobisher, Mackenzie, McLeod, McGillivray, Grant, Cameron, and greatest of all Simon McTavish — familiarly called "Le premier," and the founder of the North-West Company. The magnates of this great company Washington Irving has characterized as the "Lords of the Lakes and Forests." Their trade was enormous and extended to the coast of the Pacific Ocean itself. Toward the end of the century (1795-9) one year's production of furs was 106,000 beavers, 32 martens, 11,800 mink, 17,000 musquash — counting altogether 184,000 skins. At this time the North-West Company employed besides officers and partners, 50 higher clerks, 71 interpreters and clerks, 1,200 canoemen, and 35 guides. But the Hudson's Bay Company was not to be beaten. They were able to carry goods from the seacoast of Hudson Bay to the inland parts of Rupert's Land earlier in the season, even in the Red River districts, than the Nor'-Westers were able to do by the long river and lake route from Montreal. They duplicated all the forts of the North-West Company. The confusion became worse confounded when the North-West Company divided (1796) into two rival factions, the rebels forming themselves into the "New North-West Company" or "Alexander Mackenzie and Company," more familiarly, however, known as the "XY," the name being from the letters of the alphabet following the initials of the old company N.W. The young company was intensely active, and about this time, but only for a short period, the introduction of dangerous amounts of strong drink took place among the Indians. After eight years of unprofitable trade the two sections were reunited as the "North-West Company."

Early in the 19th century a new problem arose. A Scottish nobleman, the Earl of Selkirk, obtained control of the stock of the Hudson's Bay Company and proceeded to settle up the fertile lands along the Red River, bringing his colonists chiefly from Scotland by way of Hudson Bay. This invasion of the fur-country (1812-15) by farmers the Nor'-Westers strongly resented. They several times drove out, or inveigled away many of the Highland settlers, who were beginning to till the soil within two or three miles of the site of the present city of Winnipeg. Two forts represented the opposing parties — Fort Gibraltar, the North-West Company fort — Fort Douglas, the Lord Selkirk stronghold. The descendants of the Nor'-Wester French voyageurs, whose mothers were Indian women, were now becoming numerous and went

by the name of Metis (Halfbreeds) or Bois-Brûlés (Charcoal faces). They were chiefly in the employ of the Montreal company, while the servants of the Hudson's Bay Company, largely Orkneymen, were called by their opponents "Les Orcanais." Attacks on the forts were begun by the hostile factions, and in 1816 Gov. Semple and 20 of his officers were killed by the Bois-Brûlés, and Fort Douglas was captured. In the next year Lord Selkirk arrived supported by a band of several hundreds of discharged mercenary soldiers who had fought in the war of 1812-15 in eastern Canada. These his lordship had hired and with their aid Fort Douglas was retaken and the colonists re-established, in their farms. About the year 1811 John Jacob Astor of New York engaged a number of men who had been in the North-West Company and with these established Astoria, a trading post, on the Columbia River. This movement took place by way of the Cape Horn route and the rendezvous was in what was known as the Oregon region. The Nor'-Westers taking advantage of the state of war between Great Britain and the United States seized Astoria and employed the greater number of the Astorians in their posts in New Caledonia, as the region of British Columbia was then called. The conflicts of the various companies in different parts of Rupert's Land, the Mackenzie River district, and New Caledonia well-nigh destroyed the fur trade. Now arose a man who was to be the pacificator and leader of all the fur-traders. This was a young Scottish clerk in the Hudson's Bay Company — George Simpson (See SIMPSON, SIR GEORGE.) On the union of the worn-out companies in 1821, Simpson was made chief officer and in time he became "Emperor" of the fur country. For 40 years he built up the united company, and spent a portion of his time at Fort Garry, the chief point in Rupert's Land, as it was also the capital of Assiniboia, as the Selkirk colony was legally called. In Assiniboia a community of 12,000 grew up, 5,000 Metis, 5,000 English-speaking or locally called Scotch halfbreeds, and some 2,000 whites. Not only in this chief settlement, but from Labrador in the Atlantic Ocean to Vancouver Island on the Pacific did the little despot rule. Great forts were scattered over this wide domain, such as Fort Victoria on the Pacific shore, Fort Simpson in the Mackenzie River district, Fort Chipewyan on Lake Athabasca, Fort Edmonton on the Saskatchewan River, old Fort Cumberland on the same river, Norway House on Lake Winnipeg, York Factory, and Fort Churchill on Hudson Bay, Fort William on Lake Superior, Sault Sainte Marie, between Lakes Huron and Superior, the king's posts on the lower Saint Lawrence River, and Rigolette in extreme Labrador. From Lachine, his residence, Sir George Simpson dictated law throughout this vast extent of country, and compelled order and industry. The company quoting its charter-rights was from the first repressive in dealing with its territory with traders other than its own. The usual metaphor for describing Rupert's Land was that it was "surrounded by a Chinese wall." After a revolt of the Metis in 1849 this largely ceased to be the case. The company always retained the confidence of the Indians, and with practically no police or military, maintained a fair state of law and order. The fertile plains of Rupert's Land were visited by several exploratory expeditions shortly after the middle of the 19th century. Some of these were that of Palliser and Hector, 1857, of H. Y. Hind in the same year, and of Milton and Cheadle a few years afterward. A famous parliamentary investigation took place in London in the year of Palliser's expedition. Canada was at this time becoming alive to the importance of the Northwest. Negotiations took place between the British and Canadian governments which culminated in 1868-70 in the virtual decision that Rupert's Land, and the Northern and Western territories which were leased to the Hudson's Bay Company, should become Canadian. Unskilful dealing on the part of the Dominion Government with the people of Red River Settlement led, however, to the Riel rebellion, 1869-70. A military expedition of British troops and Canadian volunteers was sent by the old fur traders' route to Red River, but the rebels disappeared before the arrival of the troops. In 1870 the sum of $1,500,000 was paid by Canada to the Hudson's Bay Company to satisfy its claims, the new province of Manitoba was formed by the Canadian Parliament, and thenceforward the West as far as the Rocky Mountains became a part of Canada. Several years afterward British Columbia came into the Dominion as a province.

The Hudson's Bay Company, though shorn of all political power, still survives, and is vigorous. It still seeks for furs in the far North, and is the largest land company in Canada, owning one twentieth of every new township, which the government surveys. This serves to give the Hudson's Bay Company a strong interest in building up and developing the newer portions of the country. · In addition to this the company has largely devoted itself to conducting large shops in the leading business centres of western Canada. The largest of these is the store in Winnipeg. This with its different departments does an enormous trade not only in Winnipeg, but in supplying by the use of the mails the needs of all parts of the country. Important stores are maintained by the company in Portage la Prairie, Rat Portage, Fort William, Calgary, Vancouver, Edmonton, and Prince Albert. The present governor of the Hudson's Bay Company is the predominating figure, Lord Strathcona, the Canadian commissioner in London. As the writer has elsewhere said, "for the last 15 years the veteran of kindly manner, warm heart, and genial disposition, Lord Strathcona and Mount Royal (q.v.), has occupied this high place. The clerk, junior officer, and chief factor of 30 hard years on the inhospitable shores of Hudson Bay and Labrador; the commissioner who, as Donald A. Smith, soothed the Riel rebellion, and for years directed the reorganization of the company's affairs at Fort Garry and the whole Northwest; the daring speculator who took hold, with his friends, of the Minnesota and Manitoba Railway, and with Midas touch turned the enterprise to gold; the projector and a builder of the Canadian Pacific Railway; the patron of art and education, and the patriot who sent out at a cost of between $1,000,000 and $2,000,000 the Strathcona regiment of horse to the South African war has worthily filled the office of governor of the Hudson's Bay company, and with much success reorganized its administration and directed its affairs." See also CANADA — THE ERA OF EARLY DISCOVERY; and CANADA — COMMERCE, TARIFFS, AND TRANSPORTATION. GEORGE BRYCE, *Author of 'History of the Hudson's Bay Company.'*

33. Canada — The Washington Treaty. The Treaty of Washington, between the United States and Great Britain, was signed on 8 May 1871, and had reference to the Alabama claims (q.v.), the fisheries question, the lake, river and canal navigation, the bonding privilege, and the Vancouver water boundary question. In the years immediately following the Civil War several causes of acute friction existed between the two countries. Of these the principal was the question of indemnity for the depredations committed by the Alabama and other southern cruisers, whose construction in England was claimed by the United States to be a violation of neutrality. The second main cause of contention was the question of the coast fisheries. Under the Reciprocity Treaty of 1854, the fishermen of each nation were admitted to the inshore coast fisheries of the other. With the expiration of the treaty in 1866 the rights of American fishermen on the Atlantic coast of Canada were limited to the privileges secured under the convention of 1818, with a modification of 1845 admitting them to the Bay of Fundy. By this they were excluded from taking fish within three marine miles of any coasts, bays, creeks, or harbors of British North America, except in special parts of the Newfoundland and Labrador coast, and off the Magdalen islands. The proper interpretation of this three mile limit had been a standing subject of controversy. It was claimed by Great Britain that the terms of the treaty precluded entrance into the bays: by the United States that it merely forbid a nearer approach to the shores of the bay than a distance of three miles. This left in dispute the right to fish in the Bay of Chaleurs and other important places. (See Cushing, 'Treaty of Washington,' ch. v.) As a temporary expedient since 1866, the Canadian government had sold licenses to American fishermen for a nominal fee. This scheme had proved abortive, for the raising of the license fee in 1868 had resulted in an almost complete cessation in their use, only 25 being taken out in 1869. The Dominion government, in consequence, by an order in council (8 Jan. 1870) abandoned the system of licenses and equipped cruisers to protect its claims in the coast fisheries. The Alabama claims and the fisheries had been for some time a standing subject for negotiations. A treaty of January 1869 (known as the Johnson-Clarendon Treaty) was rejected by the Senate. Negotiations were renewed under President Grant and, at the suggestion of the British government, it was finally decided to appoint a joint high commission to meet at Washington to settle outstanding matters of dispute. The commissioners for the United States were Hamilton Fish, secretary of state; Gen. Robert Schenck, Judge Nelson of the Supreme Court, Ebenezer Hoar, and George H. Williams. The British commissioners were Lord de Grey, Sir Stafford Northcote, Sir Edward Thornton, Professor Montague Barnard, and Sir John Macdonald, prime minister of Canada. Their deliberations lasted from 27 Feb. until 6 May 1871. Of the different points in the treaty agreed upon the most important is that in reference to the Alabama claims, on account of its bearing upon international law. The matter at issue here was the extent to which Great Britain had been guilty of a breach of neutrality. The Alabama had been built in Birkenhead. The purpose of her construction had been a matter of general notoriety The British government had refused to listen to any representations that fell short of being technical evidence. Even when the American consul at Liverpool furnished the needed proof, the dilatory action of the government per- mitted the cruiser to depart unmolested. The question was whether, in reference to the Ala- bama and other Confederate cruisers, the gov- ernment of Great Britain had shown the dili- gence demanded of a neutral power (see 42d Congress, 2d Sessn. Senate Exec. Doc. 31 No- vember, pp. 146–51). The commission decided that the claims thus arising "shall be referred to a tribunal of arbitration to be composed of five arbiters," one to be named by the President of the United States, one by Her Britannic Ma- jesty, one by the king of Italy, one by the presi- dent of the Swiss Confederation, and one by the emperor of Brazil. The questions considered were to be decided by a majority. Article 6 of the treaty declares: In deciding the matters submitted to the arbitrators they shall be gov- erned by the following three rules, which are agreed upon by the high contracting parties as rules to be taken as applicable to the case, and by such principles of international law not incon- sistent therewith as the arbitrators shall de- termine to have been applicable to the case: A neutral government is bound: First, to use due diligence to prevent the fitting out, arming or equipping, within its jurisdiction, of any vessel which it has reasonable ground to believe is intended to cruise or to carry on war against a power with which it is at peace; and also to use like diligence to prevent the departure from its jurisdiction of any vessel intended to cruise or carry on war as above, such vessel having been specially adapted, in whole or in part, within such jurisdiction, to warlike use. Sec- ondly, not to permit or suffer either belligerent to make use of its ports or waters as the base of naval operations against the other, or for the purpose of renewal or augmentation of military supplies or arms, or the recruitment of men. Thirdly, to exercise due diligence in its own ports and waters, and, as to all persons within its jurisdiction, to prevent any violation of the foregoing obligations and duties." The tribunal thus arranged met at Geneva (December 1871) and in September 1872, rendered its decision "that the British government had failed to use due diligence in the performance of its neutral obligations," and awarded an indemnity of $15,500,000 to the United States. In regard to the fisheries, the treaty practically re-estab- lished the status under the Reciprocity Treaty of 1854, throwing open the inshore fisheries of the Atlantic coast north of latitude 39° to the fisher- men of both nations (Art. XVIII., XIX.). It also established reciprocal free trade in fish and fish oil (Art. XXI.) and decided that commis- sioners should be appointed to determine what extra compensation, if any, should be paid by the United States for the privileges thus acquired. A compensation of $5,500,000 was subsequently awarded by the Halifax Fisheries Commission (1878). The location of the north- western boundary (see NORTHWEST BOUNDARY

DISPUTE) which under the treaty of 1846 was declared to follow the 49th parallel "to the mid- dle of the channel which separates the continent from Vancouver's Island and thence southerly through the middle of the said channel and Fuca Straits to the Pacific Ocean," was left (Art. XXXIV.) to the decision of the Ger- man emperor. It was further agreed (Art. XXVI.) that the navigation of the river Saint Lawrence shall forever remain free and open for the purpose of commerce to the citizens of the United States. The United States in re- turn declared the Yukon, Porcupine and Stikine open to British commerce, (Art. XXVI.) granting also to British subjects the right of navigating Lake Michigan, the use of the Saint Clair Flats Canal on terms of equality with inhabitants of the United States. The bonding privilege (Art. XXIX.) was mutually conceded. The fisheries provisions were not to go into effect until the "laws required to carry them into operation" should be passed by the British and Canadian Parliaments, the legisla- ture of Prince Edward Island, and the Congress of the United States. The entire treaty was to remain in force for 10 years, after which certain articles — the fisheries arrangement, the right of navigating Lake Michigan, and the bonding privilege — might be terminated on two years' notice from either party. The fisheries clauses of the treaty were subsequently renounced by the United States, and after due notice, ex- pired 1 July 1885. For further details the work of Cushing (mentioned above) may be con- sulted. The text of the treaty is in 'Treaties and Conventions of the United States' (1889). For the part played by Sir John Macdonald (q.v.) in the negotiations and their relation to Canadian politics, see Pope, 'Memoirs of Sir John A. Macdonald,' Vol. II., ch. xix.–xxi. See also UNITED STATES — FOREIGN AFFAIRS, 1861– 1904; TREATIES OF THE UNITED STATES WITH FOREIGN NATIONS.   STEPHEN LEACOCK, *Lecturer in Political Science, McGill University.*

34. Canada — Jesuit Estates Act. This measure passed by the legislature of Quebec in 1888, gave rise to an agitation which occupied public attention throughout all parts of Canada during the following year and for a time threat- ened to bring about a reconstruction of political parties. Under the French régime, which ended in 1763, the Jesuits had owned considerable landed estates at various points in the valley of the Saint Lawrence — particularly at Quebec, Montreal, and Laprairie. After the conquest of Canada by the English the religious orders were permitted to retain the property which they held under grant from the French crown or by other legal title, with the exception of the Jesuits. This order had been banished from France, 1767, and was suppressed generally by the papal brief *Dominus ac'Redemptor* (1773). Although Gen. Amherst brought influence to bear upon the gov- ernment to secure for himself the estates of the Jesuits in Canada, his efforts proved unsuccess- ful. Despite personal pressure and the papal brief the "black robes" at Montreal and Quebec were not immediately molested by the British authori- ties, who refrained from taking over their prop- erty until the death of Father Casot, the last remaining member of the society. This event occurred in 1800. Once possessed of the Jesuits' estates the Crown had to determine what should

be done with them, and after a certain amount of indecision it was decided that their income should be used for the support of education in the province of Lower Canada. In vain the Roman Catholic bishops maintained the legality of the Church's claim to the property. The government stood its ground and appropriated the revenues.

From having been originally assigned to Lower Canada, the Jesuits' estates passed at Confederation (1867) into the hands of the province of Quebec. It was found, however, by the local government that their actual value was impaired by the ecclesiastical claims which stood against them. The bishops did not cease to protest against their retention by the state and the Jesuit order, revived under papal warrant, defended the justice of its own title. Had these lands been situated in a Protestant community the representations of bishops and Jesuits might have carried little weight, inasmuch as they could not be vindicated by an appeal to the courts, but where the mass of the population was Catholic the reiterated claims of the Church had their effect upon the market. After Confederation the rent of the property decreased until it became almost negligible in comparison with the valuation, and when the government sought to effect a sale no purchaser could be found. In 1887, after the question had been put off by several preceding administrations, Mr. Mercier, a French Nationalist of pronounced views, endeavored to effect a final settlement of it. Whatever the motives which actuated him, to criticize them would be to raise a matter of opinion. He introduced a bill which gave $400,000 to the Roman Catholic Church as compensation for the property which the Crown had seized in 1800. This sum was, for the moment, to constitute a special deposit which eventually should be distributed by the Pope in return for a relinquishment of all claims to the Jesuits' estates that had been advanced by the bishops or by the Jesuits themselves. As a matter of fact the Pope divided the money between the Jesuits, the bishops, and Laval University, but in the meantime this recognition of his right to allot what were considered public funds among members of his own Church, drew forth cries of remonstrance from a large number of Protestants. A simultaneous grant of $60,000 to Protestant schools in Quebec did not allay the feeling of hostility.

It should be observed that two distinct questions were raised by the agitation which proceeded from the Jesuits' Estates Act. The first had its root in the opposition of religious systems; the second was due to the federal character of the Canadian constitution. In 1888, Col. O'Brien, a Protestant member of the House of Commons, proposed that the Dominion Parliament should disallow the action of the Quebec Legislature in appealing to the Pope and setting aside $400,000 as a subsidy to Roman Catholic institutions. The debate which followed was marked by a series of able and aggressive speeches from all quarters of the House. The chief supporter of Col. O'Brien's motion was Mr. Dalton McCarthy, while against him were ranged the premier, Sir John Macdonald, and Mr. Laurier, the leader of the Opposition. On the one side an appeal was made to the alleged political misdeeds of the Jesuits throughout the whole course of their history and to

their expulsion from the chief countries of the civilized world. On the other, it was maintained that the Dominion Parliament could not, without extreme danger, disallow provincial legislation and that "the subject-matter of this act was one of provincial concern, only having relation to a fiscal matter entirely within the control of the legislature of Quebec." The vote of 188 to 13 against Col. O'Brien's motion conveys but a faint idea of the public interest in this debate and in the issues which lay behind it. The fundamental claim of the extreme Protestant party was that recognition of papal authority and the encouragement of the Jesuits were direct blows at British freedom; while the leaders of both parties united to point out the constitutional dangers which would accompany disallowance.

Outside the House of Commons the agitation caused by the Jesuits' Estates Act led to the formation an "Equal Rights" party, which was recruited from the ranks of the more pronounced Protestants. It proved impossible, however, to break down existing political lines by giving central importance to an anti-Catholic movement. Despite many public meetings and an active campaign in the newspapers, the attack upon the Jesuits' Estates Act has left no lasting trace upon party organization in Canada.

CHARLES W. COLBY,
Professor of History, McGill University.

35. Canada — Geography. I. GENERAL.— *Area and Boundaries.*— With the exception of Alaska, Greenland, Newfoundland, and the two small islands of Saint Pierre and Miquelon, all the northern half of the North American continent is comprised in the Dominion of Canada. Alaska, the great peninsular projection at the northwest corner of the continent, with a narrow strip of coast depending from it southward, belongs to the United States; Greenland, a huge island at the northeast corner, is Danish; Newfoundland, another island blocking the mouth of the Saint Lawrence estuary on the east coast, is British, and Saint Pierre and Miquelon, lying off Newfoundland, are French. To the north of the continent there is a cluster of large islands, divided from the mainland and from one another by comparatively narrow channels. All of these form part of Canada and are included in its area, but as yet they have been only partially explored, and their exact dimensions are not known. The official estimate, as nearly accurate as it can be made at present, gives the total area of Canada, including the great fresh-water lakes wholly within its boundaries, as 3,729,665 square miles. The boundaries separating Canada from its only continental neighbor, the United States, are to a great extent meridians of longitude or parallels of latitude. Between Canada and Alaska, beginning from the north, the boundary follows lon. 141° W. from the Arctic Ocean to Mount Saint Elias, within 20 miles of the Pacific, from which point it is an irregular line running about parallel with the coast round the heads of all bays and inlets of the sea at a distance of 20 to 30 miles inland. It reaches tide-water again at the head of Portland Channel, down which it passes, terminating in the Pacific Ocean. All the islands of the coast south of lat. 54° 40' belong to Canada as far as the southern extremity of Vancouver Island.

The international boundary begins again in Juan de Fuca Strait. It takes a devious course from Vancouver Island to lat. 49° on the coast of the continent, and then follows the 49th parallel as far east as Lake of the Woods. A water boundary here begins, up Rainy River and its head-water series of lakes, cutting across the height of land to another chain of small lakes and following Pigeon River to its mouth in Lake Superior. From this point the boundary is the chain of Great Lakes and the Saint Lawrence River to its intersection with lat. 45°. The line now follows a more or less arbitrary course along the 45th parallel for some distance, then rising irregularly to the north almost to lat. 47° 30', then down the upper course of the Saint John River, then due south to the head-waters of the Saint Croix River, which it follows to its final termination in the Bay of Fundy.

The areas in square miles of the individual provinces and territories are as follows:

	Land	Water	Total
Nova Scotia	21,068	360	21,428
New Brunswick.......	27,911	74	27,985
Prince Edward Island.	2,184	....	2,184
Quebec	341,756	10,117	351,873
Ontario...............	220,508	40,354	260,862
Manitoba.............	64,327	9,405	73,732
Saskatchewan	242,332	8,318	250,650
Alberta	251,180	2,360	253,540
British Columbia......	355,160	2,440	357,600
Yukon................	206,427	640	207,067
North West Territories	1,871,055	51,680	1,922,735
Total..............	3,603,908	125,748	3,729,656

Main Physical Features.—The four principal surface divisions are: (1) The Appalachian region, forming the extreme southeastern corner; (2) the Laurentian plateau or peneplain, with its fringes and outliers of lowlands, comprising the remainder of the eastern half of Canada; (3) the central plain; and (4) the mountain region to the west. Each of these divisions represents, on the whole, a different geological formation and has its own peculiar physical features. I. The Appalachian region of Canada is the northern extremity of the system of parallel ranges of mountains pushed up, as it were, from the southeast against the great archæan, or Laurentian, area. The ranges all run from southwest to northeast, the Nova Scotian peninsula being without a corresponding extension in the United States. The hills are composed of older rocks, rising out of the carboniferous strata which once overlay the whole district, but of later formation than the Laurentian plateau to the north. They are much weathered and the river valleys have been comparatively well eroded. II. The Laurentian plateau or peneplain which covers about half the entire area of Canada is, geologically speaking, the nucleus of the continent. It presents a shield-shaped surface of archæan rocks, broken into on the north by Hudson Bay, and extending south to the Saint Lawrence River. As is implied by calling it a peneplain, it is a much-weathered surface, nowhere rising to any great height, but maintaining a fair elevation above the sea-level, except along the west shore of Hudson Bay. It is a country of hard, crystalline rocks, everywhere scored by glacier action, and sparely covered with soil in which pine, spruce, and other northern trees grow more or less densely, giving place in the higher latitudes to mosses and lichens. As a result of the melting of the glaciers which covered this region in the last geological period, the whole surface is a net-work of small lakes and streams. The latter have been unable to wear down the hard rocks to any appreciable extent, and consequently present all diversities of level with many falls and rapids in their course. The western limit of the plateau is marked by a series of great lakes, from Great Bear Lake in the north to Lake Huron near the southern extremity. Adjoining the Laurentian plateau on the north and south there is, as it were, a fringe of later geological formations. Most of the large islands north of Hudson Bay as of the mainland west of it appear to consist chiefly of older sedimentary rocks in undisturbed arrangement, but the partial glaciation of these islands has hitherto prevented any detailed geological or other survey. South of the Laurentian plateau again occurs a lowland area, consisting of the valley of the Saint Lawrence River and the peninsula enclosed by the three lower members of the chain of great lakes. It is small in extent, but of great importance in the history of Canada, because the first European settlements were established mainly within its limits and it still contains the greater part of the population. III. The central plain is of vast extent, reaching from the Arctic Ocean to the Gulf of Mexico, so that only its northern portion lies in Canada. It is the elevated bed of a carboniferous sea, and from a breadth of 800 miles at the international boundary it is gradually narrowed toward the north by the westerly trend of the Laurentian plateau and broken into by subsidiary ranges of the Rocky Mountains. Still farther north, where it terminates at the Arctic Ocean, it again expands to a width of about 300 miles. There are three steppes of different elevations in this great plain, rising from east to west, and the general slope is from the southwest downward to the east and north. The fourth great region, the mountain belt, is also of vast extent, being traceable in greater or lesser width from the Tierra del Fuego, at the extremity of South America, to the farthest western point of Alaska. In Canada this mountain, or Cordilleran, region attains a breadth of about 400 miles, the greatest average elevation being in the southern portion. The Rocky Mountains, the most easterly range, are paralleled by a succession of smaller ranges, the most westerly of which is represented by the mountains of Vancouver Island and the Queen Charlotte Islands. The geological age of this division is more ancient than that of the central plain, and the changes in the crust have been violent and recent, resulting in the upheaval of the Rocky Mountains, the youngest of the ranges of the Cordilleran System.

Altitudes and Slopes.—The greatest altitudes in Canada are in the Saint Elias range of mountains, a small group near the Alaska frontier, not far from the Pacific Ocean. Mount Logan is the highest of these and is estimated at 19,539 feet. The next greatest elevations are

DOMINION
OF
CANADA

i.i the southern portion of the Rocky Mountains and the parallel ranges immediately to the west, where several peaks exceed 12,000 feet, although only one, Mount Robson, possibly reaches 13,500. The height of the ranges west of the Rocky Mountains becomes less and less as they approach the Pacific Ocean, and in Vancouver Island the highest peak is under 7,500 feet. The next greatest altitudes are in the extreme east of the Laurentian plateau, in northern Labrador, where a range of hills occurs, bordering on the Atlantic Ocean, which attains a height of 6,000 feet. Elsewhere in Labrador the Laurentian plateau seldom exceeds 1,800 feet, and on the west side of Hudson Bay the Laurentian area is lower and gradually merges in the central plain. The Appalachian region contains ranges of low hills nowhere exceeding 4,000 feet, which is only reached in the extremity of the Gaspé peninsula. The central plain rises in three steppes from the valley of the Red River, about 800 feet above sea-level, to the foothills of the Rocky Mountains, where it has an extreme elevation of 4,200 feet and an average elevation of about 3,000 feet. The Saint Lawrence lowlands are nowhere much higher than 1,000 feet, or about 500 feet above Lakes Huron and Erie, and sink gradually with the Saint Lawrence River to its mouth.

Water Ways.— The distribution of land and water in Canada has rendered the interior continental area peculiarly accessible. The Gulf of Saint Lawrence is a large arm of the sea affording ready means of entrance from the east, and leads to the broad estuary of the Saint Lawrence River. Exploration naturally followed this highway. No mountain barriers occur to obstruct or divert approach by the rivers Saint Lawrence and Ottawa to the chain of great lakes that extend to the very centre of the continent. The length of continuous waterway from the Atlantic Ocean at the Straits of Belle-Isle to the head of Lake Superior is 2,388 miles. Similarly Hudson Bay, a huge landlocked sea, communicating with the Atlantic by Hudson Strait, reaches even farther west than Lake Superior to the south of it. It was by way of Hudson Strait and Hudson Bay that the English explorers arrived at the great interior plains, just as the French *voyageurs* penetrated to the same region by the Saint Lawrence and the Great Lakes. The first systematic attempt at settlement of what is now the province of Manitoba, where the prairies begin, was by way of Hudson Bay, when Lord Selkirk established his colony of Highlanders at the junction of the Assiniboine and Red rivers in the first years of the 19th century. Two great waterways are found in the central area leading up from Hudson Bay and from the Arctic Ocean to the very base of the Rocky Mountains. These are the Nelson-Saskatchewan and the Mackenzie-Athabasca river systems, both of which were well-traveled highways for *voyageurs* and fur-traders long before settlements along the Saint Lawrence Valley had reached the Ontario peninsula. In the Appalachian region there is one river of considerable length, the Saint John, which flows across the ranges into the Bay of Fundy. The mountain region possesses its great rivers in the Columbia, the Fraser, and the Yukon, all of which originate at the western base of the Rocky Mountains and empty into the Pacific. But the rivers of this region are obstructed by numerous and fierce rapids and have not afforded the same facilities for navigation as the rivers of the central and eastern areas. In recent years, however, the Yukon has become a great highway leading to the goldfields of Alaska and the Yukon Territory.

Climate and Vegetable Productions.— The climate of Canada has the usual characteristics of a continental climate in its extremes of heat and cold, but the presence of vast bodies of water, Hudson Bay and the Great Lakes, in the very heart of the continent, has introduced modifications of temperature which differentiate Canada from other great continental areas. Thus, the Laurentian lowlands enjoy a temperate and fairly equable climate, and are wholly free from periods of drought. The central prairies, moreover, though subject to extremes of temperature, obtain sufficient moisture for growing wheat, except in the extreme southwest portion. Here an area of about 20,000 square miles forms part of the semi-arid region which has so great an extension south of the international boundary. The grassy plains are liable to frosts in the early and late summer, perhaps in consequence of the general slope down toward the Arctic Ocean, with no intervening chain of mountains. It has been found, however, that where the ground has been broken up for agriculture over considerable areas these unseasonable frosts do not occur, and at the same time there is a marked tendency to an increase in the average precipitation. The western portion of the central plain enjoys milder winters than the eastern, and this contrast is even more marked in the north than in the south of the area. In the mountain region great variations are presented both in temperature and humidity. The islands and the coast of the mainland up to the crest of the first range of mountains upon it have a very mild and very moist climate. The western slopes of the ranges farther inland also receive abundant rainfall and are clothed with dense forests. But the interior plateau receives very little moisture, and its altitude and dryness combine to give it extremes of temperature in summer and winter. The northern part of the Laurentian plateau on either side of Hudson Bay is, for climatic reasons, uninhabitable. The forests that clothe the southern portion of the same plateau give place to grasses, sedges, and mosses, and ice remains in the rivers and lakes throughout the brief summer. This tundra region, some of which has not yet been explored, covers an area of perhaps 200,000 square miles west of Hudson Bay, where it goes under the name of "the Barren Grounds," and half as much east of Hudson Bay, in the Labrador peninsula. The climate of the Appalachian region is influenced by its proximity to the Atlantic Ocean, and presents no peculiarities. There are three well-defined belts of vegetation in eastern and central Canada. The southern part of the central plain is a region of treeless, grassy prairies, once the home of countless buffalo. In the extreme north, on either side of Hudson Bay, are the Arctic tundras, the Barren Grounds, where only mosses and other lower forms of vegetable life can exist, affording food to enormous herds of caribou and a smaller number of musk-oxen. Between these two treeless regions is the great forest belt which covers the whole of eastern Canada and extends across the central plain to the mountains, verging continually north in consequence of the decreasing severity of the winters, until in the valley of the Mackenzie River it reaches beyond the Arctic circle. In the northerly latitudes the forest is composed chiefly of pine, spruce, tamarack, and aspen poplar, but in its southern extension, and especially in the Saint Lawrence lowlands and the Appalachian region, deciduous trees, such as the maple, beech, and ash, are mingled with the conifers and even replace them in the river valleys. Before the advent of the white men, a dense growth of forest covered the Appalachian region and the Laurentian lowlands, which have since been cleared to a great extent and agriculture introduced. The process is still going on, settlement is pushed farther and farther north, and forest is giving place to farms wherever the soil is suitable. The prairie region is being rapidly converted to agricultural uses, even the semi-arid corner being capable of cultivation by the aid of irrigation. The mountain region, throughout almost its entire extent, is heavily wooded near the coast and on the western slopes of the inland ranges. The enormous height and girth to which trees of some species, such as the Douglas fir and western cedar, may attain are well known. The river valleys and alluvial flats of the southern portion are suitable for agriculture, but the interior plateau does not receive enough moisture and is given over to ranching.

II. THE PROVINCES. — [For the sake of convenience and completeness, the physical features and topography of the provinces comprising the Dominion are here briefly treated. The articles in this work on the individual provinces should be consulted for further information.]

Nova Scotia. — The province of Nova Scotia, the most southerly member of the Appalachian region in Canada, consists of a peninsula about 250 miles long and 100 at its greatest breadth, and its continuation, the island of Cape Breton, which is separated from Nova Scotia proper by a narrow strait, the Gut of Canso. More or less parallel to the length of the peninsula run ranges of low hills, which near the Atlantic become mere ridges of rock. The country on this, the southern side of the province, is wild and rocky, covered with forests and dotted with small lakes. Agriculture is confined to the alluvial land along the river valleys, and the villages and towns for the most part are situated on the coast at the heads of the numerous bays which here indent it. The north shore of the peninsula is of a totally different aspect. The extended ridge of trap which forms the southern shore of the Bay of Fundy is broken into in a few places only, and long narrow bays are thus formed, into which the tide rushes with great force. The chief agricultural district of the province is behind this protecting wall of trap, and the hills beyond are covered with fertile soil and clothed to their tops with dense hardwood forests. The marshes formed by the enormous tides of Minas Basin and Chignecto Bay, the two heads of the Bay of Fundy, have been reclaimed and diked, and form a rich pasture country. The orchards of the sheltered valleys on this side of the peninsula are celebrated. The chief region of mining and industrial development is the northeast portion, facing Northumberland Strait and the Gulf of Saint Lawrence. Here coal and iron are extensively worked; gypsum also occurs in large quantities and is exported principally from the district around Minas Basin. Gold, on the other hand, is found in the wild rocky region along the southern or Atlantic coast, and is mined on this side from one end of the peninsula to the other. The fisheries of Nova Scotia have always been an important industry, carried on from every harbor of the province. Cape Breton Island, of irregular shape, about 100 miles long by 80 broad, forms part of the province of Nova Scotia. An arm of the sea, entering from the northeast, almost divides the island in two; actual division is accomplished by a canal across the narrow neck of land. A great part of the island to the north is a high forest-covered table-land, and the centre about the Bras d'Or channel is the most picturesque district in the province. At the east side occur the coal and iron ore deposits which are making Sydney, its chief town, one of the industrial centres of Canada.

New Brunswick. — The second in importance of the maritime provinces is New Brunswick, occupying the centre of the Appalachian region of Canada. It forms an irregular square of about 200 miles in extreme length and breadth, bounded on the north by the Bay of Chaleurs and the province of Quebec, on the east by the Gulf of Saint Lawrence and Northumberland Strait, on the south by Nova Scotia (at the isthmus) and the Bay of Fundy, and on the west by the State of Maine and the province of Quebec. Two lines of hills traverse the province; one follows the coast-line of the Bay of Fundy, the other, starting from the same southwestern angle, runs diagonally across the province to the northeast. Between the two lies a triangular low-lying plain, sloping down to the east coast, and beyond the diagonal range of hills the northwest region of the province is a rolling country, fertile and well suited for agriculture, but at present covered with forests. New Brunswick is a country of fine rivers, which have cut broad valleys through the soft rocks of the interior and afford access from the sea-coast to the innermost recesses of the province. The Saint John River flows south from the extreme northwest angle, entering the Bay of Fundy not much more than 50 miles from the international boundary. The Saint Croix, forming the boundary, also falls into the Bay of Fundy. The Restigouche, flowing into the Bay of Chaleurs, the Mirimachi into Mirimachi Bay in the Gulf of Saint Lawrence, and the Richibucto, into Northumberland Strait, are the other large rivers. A dense forest, chiefly spruce, still covers most of the province, and lumbering is the principal industry. The fisheries are second in importance. Agriculture follows the river valleys mainly, but the marsh lands at the head of the Bay of Fundy have been converted into rich pastures, and new land in the interior is continually being brought under cultivation. In time, no doubt, the whole of the level area in the centre of the province will be devoted to agriculture, when the forest wealth has been exhausted in that region. The mineral resources of New Brunswick have not yet been developed to any extent.

Prince Edward Island. — Prince Edward Island, the smallest province of the Dominion,

1. Mount Sir Donald, and the Illecillewat Glacier, Selkirk Mountains.

2. Lachine Rapids, St. Lawrence River.

is an island in the Gulf of Saint Lawrence, 145 miles long, with an extreme breadth of about 30 miles, separated from New Brunswick and Nova Scotia by Northumberland Strait, which varies from 9 to 30 miles in width. The curving coast on the north side of the island is broken by a deep bay with a narrow entrance, and terminates in long, narrow points. The south coast is very irregular, presenting a succession of bays and inlets. The island has a uniform, gently undulating surface, everywhere fertile, and for the most part cleared of woods and brought under cultivation.

Quebec.— The oldest province, Quebec, formerly a French colony, is still largely inhabited by French-speaking people, although in the extreme south a group of counties, commonly known as the Eastern Townships, were settled almost exclusively by English-speaking colonists. The province of Quebec is one of the largest in Canada. It extends north and east into Labrador, bounded in the latter direction by the strip along the Atlantic coast which belongs to Newfoundland. Its extreme northwest corner touches James Bay, from which its western boundary runs due south to the Ottawa River. The southern boundary is irregular, consisting of the Ottawa River nearly to its mouth, then the 45th parallel of latitude, and the rest of the international boundary eastward as far as New Brunswick, and finally the Restigouche River and the Bay of Chaleurs separating it from that province. The island of Anticosti and the Magdalen group in the Gulf of Saint Lawrence belong to Quebec. The whole of the valley of the Saint Lawrence River, from a short distance above Montreal, lies within its boundaries and constitutes, with the Eastern townships, the chief agricultural district. The valleys of the principal affluents of the Saint Lawrence are also cultivated, and two new agricultural districts, that watered by the upper Ottawa and the country about Lake Saint John, out of which flows the Saguenay River, are receiving a great influx of settlers. Except for the area in the extreme northwest of the province, which drains into James Bay, all the rivers empty into the Saint Lawrence River or Gulf. From the north come the Ottawa, the Saint Maurice, the Saguenay, and many others of less note farther east, while from the south the only ones of importance are the Richelieu, flowing from Lake Champlain, and the Saint Charles, emptying nearly opposite the city of Quebec. The general slope of the country is thus apparent. The southern edge of the Laurentian plateau, which runs not far from the Ottawa and Saint Lawrence rivers, comes quite down to the coast of the Gulf. South of the Saint Lawrence River the fertile lowlands are bounded by the ranges of the Appalachian system, which approach ever nearer to the river until, in the Gaspé peninsula, they also reach the water's edge. Next to agriculture the chief industry of the province is lumbering. The immense extent of the forests on the Laurentian plateau provides a source of supply that is virtually inexhaustible, and the recent development of the manufacture of pulp-wood has given new value to the smaller and softer trees such as the spruce. The mineral wealth of Quebec is not so great as that of Nova Scotia, but it is considerable, nevertheless. Asbestos of the best quality is found in the southeastern part of the province,

and virtually constitutes the world's sole supply of the mineral. Mica is also extensively mined, and gold, copper, and iron to a lesser extent.

Ontario.— The province adjoining Quebec on the west, Ontario, is the most populous and wealthy of Canada. It extends from the province of Quebec to Lake of the Woods; its northern boundary is the Albany River, which flows from west to east into James Bay, and its southern limit is the international boundary from Lake of the Woods to Lake Superior and the chain of Great Lakes and the upper Saint Lawrence. The whole of the province is thus to the north of the great waterway, but as both the lakes and the river in its upper course lie at the very southern limit of the area which they drain, Ontario contains all the tributary rivers of the Saint Lawrence system as far down as the Ottawa River. These, however, are not as numerous as might be expected, for the height of land between the Hudson Bay and Lake Superior slopes runs very near to the lake. Almost all the northern part of the province, therefore, drains into James Bay by the Albany and Moose rivers and their tributaries. The Nipigon, issuing from Lake Nipigon, flows south, exceptionally, into Lake Superior. In the extreme west a corner of the province belongs to the Lake Winnipeg drainage area. There are no ranges of mountains in Ontario. The Laurentian plateau includes the northern half of the province, while the rest is part of the Saint Lawrence lowlands. The lowlands, and especially their western extremity, the peninsula between Lakes Huron, Erie, and Ontario, are the chief agricultural district. The peninsula is favored with an excellent climate and soil, and its southern portion is the principal fruit-growing district in Canada, the chief products being peaches, grapes, strawberries, and apples. Hops, tobacco, and flax are also cultivated successfully in this part of Ontario. The northern part of the province beyond Lakes Huron and Superior has recently begun to be opened up, and its agricultural possibilities are being developed with great rapidity. Lumbering has always been an important industry, but the available timber limits producing pine have begun to show signs of exhaustion. The increasing demand for wood-pulp has however given new value to the great northern belt of forest, which is mainly spruce and practically inexhaustible. Ottawa is the chief centre of the manufacture of lumber; its situation on the Ottawa, the great log-carrier of two provinces, and the magnificent waterpower of the Chaudière Falls, utilized for operating the saw-mills, give it advantages over all competitors. The mineral resources of Ontario have begun to be turned into account. Gold is found in various places, chiefly in the Lake of the Woods or Rainy River district. Iron is found in many different localities but the ore is principally mined in the Algoma district, northeast of Lake Superior. The water-power of the rapids in the Saint Mary River connecting Lakes Superior and Huron has been utilized, and great iron and steel manufactures have been established at the town of Sault Ste. Marie. The Sudbury district north of Lake Huron is rich in copper and nickel, the latter metal being found in quantity only there and in New Caledonia in the Southern Pacific Ocean. In the western part of the Ontario peninsula petroleum wells have long been worked.

Manitoba.— The next province westward is Manitoba, a square of 270 miles to a side. It has Ontario and the North-west Territories to the east, the North-west Territories.also to the north, Saskatchewan to the west and the international boundary on the south. The southern part of the province is at present the chief wheat-growing district of Canada. It consists of a perfectly level plain, the alluvial bed of a former lake, through which winds the Red River. This first prairie steppe is bounded on the east by the Laurentian plateau which covers all the eastern part of Manitoba beyond Lake Winnipeg. Westward, an escarpment, nowhere rising higher than 500 feet above the level of the first steppe, runs in a northwesterly direction and marks the beginning of the second prairie steppe, which presents a more undulating surface. More than two-thirds of Manitoba is thus prairie land, for the northern belt of forest only covers a small corner of the province. The area covered by water is considerable. Lake Winnipeg, a very large lake, is mainly within the boundaries of Manitoba, as are also Lake Manitoba and Lake Winnipegosis, with others of smaller size. The chief river of the province is the Red River which enters Manitoba from the south and empties into Lake Winnipeg. At Winnipeg the Red River is joined from the west by the Assiniboine, which with its affluents waters all the western part of the province.

Saskatchewan.— The province of Saskatchewan, established by Act of Parliament in 1905, is bounded on the south by the international boundary and on the north by the 60th parallel of latitude, and extends from the Manitoba boundary, and a straight line running north in continuation of it, westward as far as the 110th meridian. It is thus a huge rectangle about equally divided between prairie and wooded country, the limit of each lying north-west and south-east across the province. Most of the north-eastern half is comprised within the Laurentian area, where the forest is scantier and the trees more stunted than in the belt of woodland contiguous tò the prairie section. In the northern portion there are several very large lakes, such as Lake Athabasca, Rein Deer Lake, Wollaston Lake, and the chain of lakes which constitute the head waters and upper course of the Churchill river.. The Saskatchewan river flows through the middle region of the province, and the Qu'Appelle river waters the prairie section farther south. The general slope being from west to east, all the rivers flow across the province to the east or north-east, except in the ext₁.me north-west where the slope is north toward Lake Athabasca and the Mackenzie river basin. The prairie section comprises all of the second prairie steppe not included in Manitoba and a portion of the third and highest. The escarpment of the latter runs north-west, appearing from the lower level like a range of low hills. When the crest is reached this third so-called steppe is found to be a much more irregular surface than the rolling plain below. Certain portions of it form small isolated plateaus, standing as high as 2,000 feet above the surrounding country.

Alberta.— Adjoining Saskatchewan on the west is a second province, Alberta, established by Act of Parliament in 1905. Like Saskatchewan it extends from the international boundary to the 60th parallel of latitude. Its western limit is the summit line of the Rocky Mountains from the international boundary to the point where that line crosses the 120th meridian of longitude, very nearly in lat. 54°, and from this point the 120th meridian to lat. 60°. Alberta, like Saskatchewan, is divided almost equally between prairie in the south and woodland in the north. Its prairie land is altogether within the limits of the third prairie steppe described above; much of it constitutes a semi-arid district, not suitable for agriculture except by the aid of irrigation, but making excellent pasture-land. The extreme north-eastern corner of the province touches upon the rocky Laurentian area, but the rest of the northern half of the province is well-wooded country, broken by prairie openings, with abundant streams and small lakes, suitable alike for grazing or crops. The Peace and Athabasca are the main rivers in this half of the province, while the North and South Saskatchewan rivers with numerous small affluents rising amid the mountains and foothills cut their channels deeply into the rolling prairie of the southern portion. The climate of Northern Alberta is much milder than the latitude would indicate, and wheat can be grown successfully in the valley of the Peace river near the northern boundary of the province. Besides agricultural possibilities, both Saskatchewan and Alberta, and especially Alberta, have a valuable asset in extensive coal fields.

British Columbia.— The largest of the provinces is British Columbia, occupying the whole of the mountain region from the international boundary to lat. 60°. It also cuts off a portion of the central plain, where the eastern boundary of the province leaves the Rocky Mountains and runs north along long. 120°. Vancouver Island and the other islands off the mainland are included in the bounds of the province. West of the broad chain of the Rocky Mountains, which form the eastern boundary, three older ranges run approximately north and south and are thus confined to the southern part of the province, being extinguished northward by the more recent upheaval of the Rockies, whose axis inclines to northwest. These smaller and lower ranges are, in order from east to west, the Purcell, the Selkirk, and the Gold ranges. Near and parallel to the Pacific coast another broad mountain system, .the Coast Range, extends northward into Yukon Territory and Alaska, where it reaches its greatest elevation. Between the Coast and Gold ranges there is the interior plateau, about 100 miles in breadth and from 2,000 to 3,000 feet in elevation. To the north it is cut off by transverse ranges of mountains. Vancouver Island and the Queen Charlotte islands are the unsubmerged remains of a subsidiary mountain range west of the Coast Range. The rivers and lakes of British Columbia occur in deep valleys between the ranges. The Columbia River and its chief affluent, the Kootenay, take a remarkable course through the valleys between all the eastern ranges, running north and south in great loops. The lake-like expansions of both rivers form the chief navigable inland waters of British Columbia. The Fraser River which rises in the Rocky Mountains flows at first north, but soon turns westward round the head of the Gold Range, and finally runs almost due south cutting a deep channel in the interior plateau. It breaks through the Coast Range and reaches the sea not far from the international boundary. Its chief affluent is the Thompson. Both are very turbulent streams and form an additional obstacle rather than an assistance to inland communication. The northern half of the province is still very imperfectly explored. In a central elevated plateau many rivers take their rise, some flowing south to join the Fraser, others, such as the Liard, east into the Mackenzie basin, others again like the Skeena and Stikine westward into the Pacific Ocean. What British Columbia lacks in a system of navigable inland waterways is more than made up by its deeply indented coast line, where many magnificent harbors for sea-going vessels of any draught are available, from Port Simpson at the north to Burrard Inlet at the south extremity. The coast of Vancouver Island is also well supplied with harbors. British Columbia, although so mountainous, is not without its agricultural industries. The interior plateau forms a good ranching country, and in the sheltered valleys, where irrigation can be introduced, fruit farms are very successful. Lumbering is one of the great industries of the province, and the mineral wealth is very great. Gold has been found in many localities from the international boundary to Atlin district on the borders of Yukon Territory. Placer mining alone has been carried on in most of these places, but in the Kootenay district in the extreme south, where communication by railway and water is easy, scientific treatment of ores has been practised for some years. The metals, besides gold, produced by this method are silver, lead, and copper. The exceedingly heavy growth of timber has added to the difficulty of making roads and even of prospecting. Iron ore has been found both on the mainland and on Vancouver Island, but is mined principally on Texada Island in the Strait of Georgia. Coal is obtained chiefly on Vancouver Island at Nanaimo and Comox and in the Rocky Mountains at Crow's Nest Pass. Another great industry of British Columbia is the salmon-fishery, which is carried on chiefly at the mouth and in the lower reaches of the Fraser River. Canneries are also established at the mouths of the Naas, Skeena, and other rivers.

Yukon.— The Territory of Yukon, under the government of a Commissioner and an Executive Council, lies north of British Columbia and is bounded on the west by Alaska. It has also a northern coast-line on the Arctic Ocean, but a comparatively short one, its eastern boundary being an irregular line sloping from south-east to north-west, for the most part following the easternmost range of the Rockies. It does not lie entirely outside of the Mackenzie river basin, f the mountain boundary is low and the upper waters of many streams tributary to the Liard river, which flows into the Mackenzie river, take their rise in the south-east part of the Territory and flow south. In the north portion also the Peel river, flowing parallel to the Mackenzie, is contained within the boundaries of the Territory for most of its course, but bursts through the mountain barrier near its mouth and empties into the Mackenzie where the delta of the latter begins. The greater part of the Territory, however, is watered by the Yukon and its tributaries, the Teslin, Lewes, Pelly, Stewart, and

Klondike rivers, all flowing from south-east or east, and in the northern portion the Porcupine, which begins by flowing north-east as if to join the Mackenzie, but turns sharply and flows due west until it crosses the boundary into Alaska. The mountain system of the territory is the series of parallel ranges of the Rockies, decreasing in elevation as they run further north and turning eastward into the Alaskan peninsula.

The North-west Territories.— The remainder of Canada, north of the provinces and east of the Yukon Territory, including the islands in the Arctic Ocean and the peninsula of Labrador, except the strip of coast along the Atlantic which belongs to Newfoundland, is broadly described as the North-west Territories, the former provisional districts of Mackenzie, Keewatin, Ungava, and Franklin having been discontinued. This vast country is under the direct control of the Dominion Government. It is very sparsely populated by Indians and Eskimos, together with a few white trappers and traders in the employ of the Hudson's Bay Company, and missionaries. The valley of the Mackenzie river in the west is fertile and covered with trees almost to the very mouth of the river in the Arctic Ocean. The climate in that region is not so severe as the high latitudes would seem to imply; the summers, though short, are hot and the summer days long, and vegetables and some cereals have been raised by Hudson's Bay Company's agents at most of their posts in the district. Coal moreover occurs and possibly petroleum. The region immediately to the south-west and south-east of Hudson Bay has also possibilities of settlement on account of the magnificent water power of the rivers flowing through it into the Bay. The opportunity these afford for cheap development of electrical energy may yet be turned to account for manufacturing purposes, especially if it is found practicable to make exports by way of Hudson Bay. The fur-trade, which is still a considerable industry, is carried on over the whole area covered by the sub-Arctic forest, and much of this vast northern territory will remain the home of many species of fur-bearing animals as long as that forest remains to shelter them. But the northern portions of the country on each side of Hudson Bay must remain a hunting country only. The Arctic archipelago has at present only a sentimental value. The series of daring British explorers who, in their search for a northwest passage, discovered the various islands and claimed them for British territory, are commemorated in the names given to the islands themselves and to the principal bays, straits, and headlands. For ordinary purposes and for men of the white race they are utterly uninhabitable.

H. H. Langton,

Editorial Staff, 'Review of Historical Publications Relating to Canada.'

36. Canada — Agriculture. Fish and furs were the earliest products of Canada. Agriculture, however, in time became the chief industry of the people, and to-day far outweighs the other three great natural products, furs, fish, and minerals. Canada possesses a unique record of national growth in the various census enumerations that cover nearly two and a half centuries. The earliest is that for 1665. Students of statistics will find the successive records from 1665 to 1871 in Vol. 4 of the Census of Canada for 1871. The following table has been compiled from the last three census takings, and, while valuable for reference as to the main items in the agricultural industry, it is also a statistical statement of 20 years' growth.

DOMINION OF CANADA — CENSUS STATISTICS OF AGRICULTURE.

Items	1881	1891	1901
Acres occupied......	45,358,141	60,287,730	63,422,301
Acres improved.....	21,899,181	28,537,242	30,163,496
Acres in field crops..	15,112,284	15,662,811	19,763,740
Acres in pasture, orchards, gardens, etc.	6,786,897	15,748,250	16,138,505
FIELD CROPS.			
Wheat, bushels......	32,350,269	42,223,372	55,572,368
Barley, bushels.....	16,844,868	17,222,795	22,224,366
Oats, bushels......	70,493,131	83,428,202	151,497,407
Rye, bushels........	2,097,180	1,341,125	2,316,793
Corn in ear, bushels.	9,025,142	10,711,380	25,875,919
Buckwheat, bushels..	4,901,147	4,994,871	4,547,159
Peas and beans, bush.	13,749,662	15,623,779	13,208,270
Mixed grains, bushels	no census	no census	7,267,621
Flax seed, bushels...	108,694	138,844	172,222
Grass and clover seed, bushels.....	324,317	346,036	288,275
Potatoes, bushels....	55,768,227	53,490,857	55,362,635
Field roots, bushels..	48,251,414	49,679,636	70,075,642
Tobacco, pounds....	2,527,962	4,277,936	11,266,732
Hops, pounds......	905,207	1,126,230	1,004,216
Hay, tons..........	no census	7,693,733	7,852,731
Forage crops, tons...	no census	no census	1,251,327
Tree fruits, bushels.	7,659,576	11,477,363	20,668,460
LIVE STOCK.			
Horses, number.....	1,059,358	1,470,572	1,577,493
Dairy cows, number.	1,595,800	1,857,112	2,408,677
Other cattle, number	1,919,189	2,263,474	3,167,774
Sheep, number.....	3,048,678	2,563,781	2,510,239
Swine, number.....	1,207,619	1,733,850	2,353,828
Poultry, number....	no census	14,105,102	17,922,658
ANIMAL PRODUCTS.			
Cattle (killed or sold) number	657,681	957,737	1,110,209
Sheep (killed or sold) number	1,496,465	1,464,172	1,342,288
Swine (killed or sold) number	1,302,503	1,791,104	2,555,413
Wool, pounds.......	11,300,736	10,031,970	10,657,597
Butter, pounds.....	104,252,559	115,938,165	141,409,815
Cheese, pounds.....	63,901,152	114,981,514	220,833,269

given only for Canada, not by Provinces. In the Government returns the exports are entered under the provinces whence they are shipped. Students are cautioned against considering these as the provinces of production. For example, as Montreal (Quebec) is the main port of export for Ontario, most of the Ontario agricultural exports are entered in the Blue Book as shipped from Quebec Province.

TOTALS OF EXPORTS — FIELD PRODUCTS AND ANIMAL PRODUCTS. 1868-1903.

	Animals and products of	Field products, etc.	Total
1868..........	$ 6,893,167	$12,871,055	$19,341,387
1869..........	8,769,407	12,182,702	20,584,552
1870..........	12,138,161	13,676,619	25,504,703
1871..........	12,608,506	9,853,924	22,146,808
1872..........	12,706,967	13,378,891	25,494,393
1873..........	14,243,017	14,995,340	28,302,384
1874..........	14,679,169	19,590,142	32,035,810
1875..........	13,700,507	17,258,358	28,634,859
1876..........	13,614,569	21,139,665	32,878,281
1877..........	14,220,617	14,689,376	27,587,236
1878..........	14,019,857	18,008,754	30,802,010
1879..........	14,100,604	19,628,464	32,537,712
1880..........	14,607,577	22,294,328	38,686,280
1881..........	21,360,219	21,268,327	40,645,450
1882..........	20,454,759	31,035,712	50,212,131
1883..........	20,284,343	22,818,519	42,015,339
1884..........	22,946,108	12,397,843	34,224,195
1885..........	25,337,104	14,518,293	38,228,571
1886..........	22,005,433	17,652,779	38,062,008
1887..........	24,240,937	18,826,235	41,357,870
1888..........	24,719,297	15,436,360	38,187,456
1889..........	23,894,707	13,414,411	35,472,541
1890..........	25,106,995	11,908,030	35,443,629
1891..........	25,967,741	13,666,858	38,205,270
1892..........	28,594,850	22,113,284	49,153,010
1893..........	31,736,499	22,049,490	52,302,906
1894..........	31,881,973	17,677,649	47,802,859
1895..........	34,387,770	15,719,128	48,531,344
1896..........	36,507,641	14,083,361	48,791,344
1897..........	39,245,252	17,982,646	55,933,592
1898..........	44,301,470	33,063,285	75,834,858
1899..........	46,743,130	22,952,915	68,140,758
1900..........	56,148,807	27,516,609	81,858,450
1901..........	55,495,311	24,781,486	78,630,966
1902..........	59,161,209	37,152,688	94,517,019
1903..........	69,817,542	44,624,321	114,441,863

In the above table the years end 30 June: they are fiscal years, not calendar years.

Having given the above totals for Canada as a whole, it may now be interesting to give details by provinces. The following tables compiled from the same sources as the preceding will enable the reader to compare the various provinces. The following conclusions may be drawn; farms west of Lake Superior are more than twice as large as those east of the lake; from eighty to ninety per cent of the farms of Canada are owned by the occupiers; Ontario possesses nearly one half of the farm wealth of Canada; while mixed farming is followed in Ontario, the live stock industry is paramount and far exceeds that of all the other provinces combined; Manitoba has become the chief wheat-producing province of the Dominion.

The agricultural growth of Canada has far outstripped its increase in population. The confederation of provinces took place in 1867. The following table gives the year by year exports of agricultural products taken from the Trade and Navigation Returns wherein they are arranged under two groups; animals and their products, and field products. These totals can be

Having given the totals as showing the steady upward movement in surplus products, it will next be in order to give some details that we may see the causes of the main increases. The following table shows that in field products the increase is due mainly to wheat and flour, and the recent increase of wheat farming on the prairies of Manitoba and the North West Territories is the key to this. The export of live animals has not changed much in the past twenty years. In animal products, cheese, bacon and butter largely account for the increase. The total of the exports of these three products in 1891 was $10,701,907, whereas in 1903 the total was $47,122,735. When it is considered that these are concentrated products, the result of higher agricultural skill, the secret of Canadian agricultural prosperity in recent years may be readily understood.

The Minister of Agriculture for Canada is a member of the Dominion Government and Parliament. He has under his control a well-organized department with specialists in charge of the various branches. The transportation and marketing of farm products is a matter that comes particularly under his

CANADA—AGRICULTURE

AGRICULTURAL STATISTICS, TAKEN FROM CENSUS OF 1901.
Provinces of the Dominion.

PROVINCE	Number of occupiers of farms containing			Total No. of farms	Average size of farm	Per cent of farms owned by occupiers
	50-100 acres	100-200 acres	Over 200 acres			
Nova Scotia............	14,234	11,073	4,483	47,497	106.64	97.92
New Brunswick.......	12,894	8,775	4,257	35,051	126.64	96.10
Prince Edward Island.	5,380	3,030	581	13,149	90.74	97.23
Quebec	45,813	44,216	16,374	130,158	110.82	93.18
Ontario	76,164	52,534	14,331	185,415	114.91	85.14
Manitoba ....:......	1,254	14,394	7,771	31,812	288.	91.30
N. W. Territories.....	226	14,618	15,204	22,813	278.	80.
British Columbia.....	813	2,186	1,654	5,938	252.	86.04
				471,833		

PROVINCE	Total acreage of occupied land	Percentage of improved land occupied	Total value of farm property	Land in wheat acres	Land in hay and forage acres	Total value field products	Total value fruit and vegetables
Nova Scotia............	5,080,901	24.57	$ 70,694,395	18,485	8,458	$ 9,764,493	$ 1,407,369
New Brunswick.......	4,443,400	31.67	50,506,018	26,990	553,676	8,110,918	394,337
Prince Edward Island.	1,194,508	60.76	30,434,089	42,318	184,023	4,764,674	139,004
Quebec	14,444,175	51.45	430,154,421	139,826	2,588,190	46,993,237	2,504,801
Ontario	21,349,524	62.06	1,001,323,296	1,487,344	2,772,866	109,182,192	87,809,084
Manitoba ....:......	8,843,347	45.18	149,017,965	1,965,200	521,426*	16,815,964	7,163,958
N. W. Territories.....	6,569,064	24.31	76,331,742	530,274	16,838*	7,294,283	80,553
British Columbia.....	1,497,382	31.59	323,465,512	15,967	103,294	3,479,682	435,794
	63,422,301		$2,132,527,438			$203,405,443	$99,994,900

PROVINCE	Total value animals and products	Per cent of crop to total produce	Per cent animal products	Per cent the total on investment	Chief crops (named in order of importance).
Nova Scotia........	$ 5,846,390	62.55	37.45	22.08	Hay, oats, wheat, potatoes.
New Brunswick.....	4,510,657	64.26	35.74	21.99	Hay, oats, buckwheat, potatoes, wheat.
Prince Edward Island	2,648,623	64.27	35.73	24.36	Hay, oats, wheat, potatoes.
Quebec	35,456,171	57.	43.	19.17	Hay, oats, wheat, barley, obacco, potatoes.
Ontario	83,684,111	56.61	43.39	20.94	Hay, oats, wheat, peas, barley, corn, potatoes, roots.
Manitoba	7,221,883	69.96	30.04	16.07†	Wheat, oats, barley, flax, potatoes, and forage crops.
N. W. Territories...	5,508,013	56.98	43.02	16.77	Wheat, oats, barley, potatoes, and forage crops.
British Columbia....	2,740,079	55.95	44.05	19.16	Hay, oats, wheat, roots.
	$147,615,827				

* Hay not included (forage only) as it is got from the prairie grass. Some timothy is grown in Manitoba.
† Low average due to failure of grain crop in census year.

care. The starting of various lines of work in the newer provinces, such as dairying and stock raising, has received special attention, the practice being to hand this work over, when successfully going, to the local Provincial Departments. The Dominion Department has a well arranged series of experimental farms. The central farm is at Ottawa, Ont.; the branches are at Nappan, N. S.; Brandon, Man.; Indian Head, N. W. T.; and Agassiz, B. C. All are under the control of one Director and each farm is interested in carrying on experiments profitable to the Province in which it is situated.

Ontario.—The settlement of Ontario began in 1784, when several thousand Loyalists, mainly from New York and New Jersey, moved in at the close of the Revolutionary War. They were of mixed nationality and took up land on the frontier from Detroit in the west to the present eastern limits of the Province on the St. Lawrence a few miles above Montreal. In the clearing away of the forests timber and potash were the two marketable farm products. As the cleared land increased wheat became a surplus product. The over-sea immigration began in 1816 after the close of the Napoleonic wars, became quite large about 1825, and continued down to the middle of the century. Up to this time the population was mainly rural; the following statement of population, therefore, will fairly indicate the growth of the farming population.

1784........about 10,000   1841........about 500,000
1812........about 75,000   1848........about 726,000
1824........about 157,000   1851........about 952,000

The middle of last century was the "growing time" in Ontario, and at that time wheat was king. This branch of farming received a remarkable impetus during the Crimean War, 1854-6 and at the same time the Reciprocity Treaty between Canada and the United States permitted the interchange of the natural products of the farm. (See CANADA — RECIPROCITY BETWEEN CANADA AND THE UNITED STATES.) This period of inflated prices was prolonged by the Civil War in the United States and continued down to 1865. The year 1866 marks a new era in Ontario agriculture. The Reciprocity treaty was discontinued and a tariff wall erected in its place. European grain prices had come down and wheat growing in Ontario suffered as a consequence. The British settlers that had been coming in a steady stream across the Atlantic during the pre-

VALUES OF EXPORTS OF (A) FIELD PRODUCTS. (B) ANIMAL PRODUCTS, 1873-1903.

(a) Field products:	1873	1881	1891	1901	1902	1903
Wheat and flour	$ 8,927,330	$ 4,766,928	$ 2,971,662	$10,887,165	$22,656,942	$29,266,116
Barley	2,956,106	6,260,183	2,929,873	1,123,055	231,199	457,233
Oats	217,028	1,191,873	129,917	2,490,521	2,052,559	2,583,151
Peas and beans	1,000,301	3,595,711	2,528,369	3,092,873	2,031,531	1,132,364
Other bread stuffs	674,935	1,092,036	499,072	1,398,072	1,187,590	1,295,158
Fruit	264,015	645,658	1,073,890	2,006,235	1,922,304	3,689,662
Other field products	955,625	3,715,848	3,534,075	5,789,800	7,070,563	6,200,637
Totals	$14,995,340	$21,268,327	$13,666,858	$24,781,486	$37,152,688	$44,624,321
Horses	$922,233	$ 2,099,724	$ 1,572,564	$ 910,273	$ 1,457,173	595,921
Cattle	655,594	3,489,611	8,774,769	9,064,562	10,663,819	11,342,632
Sheep	937,721	1,375,043	1,150,865	1,625,702	1,483,526	1,655,681
Swine	84,531	11,841	1,954	8,301	84,019	319,762
Poultry and others	88,942	134,063	63,403	85,091	50,576	58,600
Total animals	$ 2,709,021	$ 7,110,282	$11,563,555	$11,693,929	$13,739,113	$13,972,596
(b) Animal products: *						
Bacon }	$ 2,323,299	$ 717,589	$ 590,852	$11,493,866	$12,162,953	$15,455,174
Ham }		40,745	37,617	284,578	240,840	451,160
Pork	267,720	113,694	4,089	51,374	540,070	122,935
Lard	204,222	19,882	3,174	58,602	22,186	236,007
Beef	113,390	83,738	16,051	813,343	414,095	206,563
Mutton	....	8,184	23,993	5,712	6,135	7,794
Canned meats	....	....	271,184	419,959	881,578	619,299
Other meats	1,165	108,154	16,258	420,388	122,414	260,502
By products	1,984,941	1,082,385	893,501	2,400,887	2,898,953	4,149,991
Eggs	509,447	1,103,812	1,160,359	1,691,640	1,733,242	1,436,130
Butter	2,808,979	3,573,034	602,175	3,295,663	5,600,541	6,954,618
Cheese	2,280,412	5,510,443	9,508,880	20,696,951	19,686,291	24,712,943
Total Animal products	$10,493,575	$12,361,660	$13,128,133	$41,632,965	$44,369,298	$54,613,116
Total Animals and products	$13,202,596	$19,471,942	$24,691,688	$53,326,894	$58,108,411	$68,585,712
Total farm products	$28,197,936	$40,740,269	$38,358,546	$78,108,380	$95,261,099	113,210,033

* This list does not include Furs, as they are not agricultural products. This accounts for the totals of this table being somewhat less than those of preceding.

vious two decades had introduced a new element —they brought with them an acquaintance with and love of high class stock of all kinds. Dairying, sheep breeding, the rearing of pure bred beef animals and of heavy horses, now brought some relief to the farmer. Gradually he built up also a big barley trade that was temporarily very profitable but ultimately ruinous to the farm lands. The competition of the rich cheap farm lands of the Western States now began to tell upon Ontario farming and the struggle was acute. Here and there a bright year intervened. The 6th of October 1890 started a new era, apparently worse than the preceding, for then the McKinley Tariff came into operation and at one sweep the agricultural trade with the United States completely disappeared. Barley, eggs, butter, mutton, poultry, horses and many other products that had been shipped to the South, dropped in value and the farmer was face to face with the most serious situation he had known since the days of pioneer hardship.

The tale as told in figures is interesting. In the three years prior to the McKinley Tariff (1888, 1889 and 1890) the Canadian Agricultural exports to the United States amounted to $46,500,000; in the three years following the same, (1892, 1893 and 1894) they amounted to only $20,400,000. There is, however, another side to the story and this is an interesting part of Canadian history. In the three years, 1888, 1889 and 1890, Canada's exports to Great Britain averaged $20,000,000 a year; for the three years, 1900, 1901 and 1902 they averaged $71,500,000. The loss in the United States market has thus been made up over and over again in the British market. This forced seeking for a new market has brought about a very important change in Ontario farming, and the progress made in the past six years is most remarkable. The following statement briefly tells the story. It is taken from the annual reports of the Ontario Department of Agriculture.

PRODUCTION OF ONTARIO FARMS.

	1896	1902	Increase
Beef	$12,000,000	$23,000,000	$11,000,000
Bacon and pork	10,000,000	20,000,000	10,000,000
Cheese	9,000,000	15,000,000	6,000,000
	$31,000,000	$58,000,000	$27,000,000

If we add other products, we may state that in 1902 and 1903 the farm products of Ontario were worth from $35,000,000 to $40,000,000 more than they were six to ten years ago. In other words, the average income of the 175,000 farmers in 1903 was at least $200 more than six years ago. As it cannot be supposed that all farmers have participated equally in this gain, it will be seen that the increased profits of the more progressive among them must have been very great. Therein is the explanation for the continuance of good times in Ontario down to the middle of 1904, when this article is being written. The steady increase in the numbers of live stock kept on Ontario farms has resulted in a steady improvement in the production of grain and forage crops, but these have not been marketed as crude products but have been turned into beef, bacon, and cheese. The above table, in brief, represents the greatest and most important factor in the Ontario agriculture of recent years.

Fuller details cannot be given here, but those who may desire a more minute study of this question will find full information in the annual reports issued by the Ontario Bureau of Industries, the statistical branch of the Department of Agriculture, Toronto, Ont. The breeding of pure bred stock is an important part of Ontario agriculture. Clear air, clean water in abundance and good pasture are there found, while as stated above a large number of the farmers have come from the British Isles where live stock breeding and feeding form so important a part of farm work. Fruit growing is steadily increasing in the Province. The most southern point of Ontario is in the same latitude as Chicago and Boston, and Southern France and Central Italy. The Great Lakes have a modifying and controling influence on the climate. The consequence is that while apples grow to perfection in nearly all parts of the Province, cherries, plums, pears, peaches and grapes are very profitably grown along the borders of the lakes. As a rule the fruits of Ontario are of high flavor. Probably the greatest surprise that comes to a stranger in making a personal study of Ontario is the finding of such a wide range and great abundance of sub-tropical fruits of large size and fine flavor. As an outcome of this there are many extensive fruit canning plants in Ontario. Dairying has for many years been a leading industry. Butter making in creameries has not been so extensive as cheese making in factories. In 1883 there were 635 cheese factories: in 1902 the number was 1,127. The output in the same time increased from 53,500,000 lbs. to 146,800,000 lbs. Most of these factories are conducted on the co-operative plan. The improvement in agricultural methods and the increasing production of concentrated high class products should show an effect in increasing farm values. The following table is therefore interesting as summing up in a condensed form the farm progress of the past few years. It is compiled from the annual reports of the Provincial Department of Agriculture.

ganized along all lines of agricultural work having, under the Deputy Minister, specialists in charge of the various branches. Through it is directed the Agricultural College and Experimental Farm at Guelph; Farmer's and Women's Institutes, that hold about one thousand meetings every year; three dairy schools at Guelph, Kingston and Strathroy; thirty instructors who give instruction at the cheese factories and creameries; six live stock associations that are interested in the breeding and exporting of pure bred stock and the holding of Winter Shows at Guelph and Ottawa; the direction of twelve fruit experiment stations; the superintendence of 300 Agricultural Societies; and many other lines of work. The Department prints and publishes all the bulletins and reports prepared at the Agricultural College and by the various Societies and Associations, and also collects, compiles and publishes annually bulletins and reports on crops and farm statistics.

Quebec.— The rural population of Quebec consists of two classes or nationalities. The original settlers from France were located as tenants on the seigniories along the Saint Lawrence River; while the English-speaking settlers from Vermont, New Hampshire, and other northern States, coming in by way of Lake Champlain, settled in the district adjacent to the Lake, still known as the Eastern Townships. These two classes carry on agricultural work of an entirely distinct nature. The French Canadian farms are long and narrow; their houses and outbuildings are peculiar; their cattle and horses trace back to Norman and Breton types, and their methods of work are characteristically French. The English-speaking farmers of the Eastern Townships make specialties of live stock and dairying and their style of farming is quite similar to that of Ontario.

The Minister of Agriculture at Quebec has a department to carry out his work. He is assisted also by a representative Council of Agriculture. Agricultural Societies exist in all the counties. There is a vigorous Provincial Dairy Association, having supervision of a Dairy School at Saint Hyacinthe. There are agricultural schools or colleges in various parts of the Province conducted by religious orders that are assisted by the government.

Nova Scotia.— This Province has 172 agricultural societies with about 10,000 members. Through these societies pure bred animals are imported and distributed. Dairying is increasing,

VALUES OF FARM LANDS, BUILDINGS, IMPLEMENTS AND LIVE STOCK.

	Land	Buildings	Implements	Live stock	Total
1894	$587,246,117	$204,071,566	$51,530,172	$111,547,652	$954,395,507
1895	572,938,472	204,148,670	50,044,385	103,958,047	931,089,574
1896	557,468,270	205,235,429	50,730,358	96,817,566	910,201,623
1897	554,954,552	206,090,159	51,209,008	93,640,804	905,003,613
1898	556,246,569	210,054,306	52,977,232	103,744,223	923,022,420
1899	563,271,777	213,440,281	54,994,857	115,806,445	947,513,360
1900	574,727,610	219,488,370	57,324,130	123,274,821	974,814,931
1901	585,354,294	226,575,228	59,807,513	129,496,261	1,001,233,206
1902	604,860,063	237,289,668	62,199,787	140,514,814	1,044,804,382
1903	620,869,475	247,629,153	63,996,190	154,327,267	1,086,822,085

The public direction of agricultural work in Ontario is by the Provincial Department of Agriculture at Toronto, presided over by the Minister of Agriculture, who is a member of the Provincial Government. This Department is or-

Vol. 3 — 39.

there being in 1903, 18 creameries, 13 cheeseries and 4 condensers. Fruit growing, however, is the most advanced branch of Agriculture. The apples of the Annapolis and other valleys have a world wide reputation. In order to extend this industry the Provincial Department of Agriculture has started model orchards in various counties. The Province exports from 500,000 to 1,000,000 barrels of apples in good yielding years. There is a school of horticulture at Wolfville. A school of agriculture is now being organized at Truro. Agriculture is taught in the public schools of this Province.

New Brunswick.— Like Nova Scotia, New Brunswick has derived its wealth from fisheries and forests rather than the cultivated field. Agriculture, however, is improving. Dairying is extending: there being now 40 butter factories and 55 cheese factories. A very successful dairy school has been conducted for some years at Sussex, N. B.

Prince Edward Island.— This is a fertile province with mild summer climate and possessing all the requirements for a fine stock country. Potatoes and mutton are the two special products. There are 52 cheese factories. Agriculture is taught at the Prince of Wales College, Charlottetown, the Professor of Agriculture having charge of experimental work for the whole Island.

British Columbia.— The largest Province of Canada, derives its wealth from forests, mines and fisheries. Agriculture as a serious business is of comparatively modern origin. The long valleys of the south and west possess a very rich alluvial soil and have a mild climate. Fruit culture is one of the most promising branches; the trees mature early and yield heavily. There is now a limited quantity of fruit available for export. The more progressive farmers are, with the help of the Provincial Department of Agriculture, importing pure bred breeding stock from Ontario, the great centre of live stock for all Canada.

Manitoba and the North West Territories.— The agricultural story of this great region is told most briefly in the following tables

	Acreage prepared for crop 1904	Total suitable for cultivation
Manitoba	2,385,505 acres	27,000,000 acres
N. W. Territories	1,706,100 acres	144,000,000 acres
Totals	4,091,605 acres	171,000,000 acres

Land cultivated in 1904 is therefore 2.3 per cent of the cultivable land.

THE TERRITORIES — CROP STATISTICS.

Wheat

Year	Bushels	Acreage	Yield per acre	Average
1898	5,542,478	307,580	18.01	
1899	6,915,623	363,523	19.02	
1900	4,028,294	412,864	9.75	19.42
1901	12,808,447	504,697	25.37	
1902	13,956,850	625,758	22.30	
1903	16,029,149	837,234	19.00	

Oats

Year	Bushels	Acreage	Yield per acre	Average
1898	3,040,307	105,077	28.93	
1899	4,686,036	134,938	34.81	
1900	4,226,152	175,439	24.08	
1901	11,113,066	229,439	48.43	34.32
1902	10,661,295	310,367	34.35	
1903	14,179,705	440,662	32.17	

Barley

Year	Bushels	Acreage	Yield per acre	Average
1898	449,512	17,092	26.29	
1899	337,421	14,276	23.62	
1900	353,216	17,044	20.72	
1901	795,100	24,702	32.18	25.36
1902	870,417	36,445	23.88	
1903	1,741,209	69,667	24.65	

See Reports Dept Agriculture Regina N. W. T. 1902-3.

MANITOBA — CROP STATISTICS.

Wheat

Year	Bushels	Acreage	Yield per acre
1889	7,201,519	623,245	12.4
1890	14,665,769	746,058	19.65
1891	23,191,599	916,664	25.3
1892	14,453,835	875,990	16.5
1893	15,615,923	1,003,640	15.56
1894	17,172,883	1,010,186	17.0
1895	31,775,038	1,140,276	27.86
1896	14,371,806	999,598	14.33
1897	18,261,950	1,290,882	14.14
1898	25,313,745	1,488,232	17.01
1899	27,922,230	1,629,995	17.13
1900	13,025,252	1,457,396	8.90
1901	50,502,085	2,011,835	25.10
1902	53,077,237	2,039,940	26.00
1903	40,116,878	2,442,873	16.42

Average for 15 years 1889–1903 = 18.29

Oats

Year	Bushels	Acreage	Yield per acre
1889	3,415,104	218,744	16.8
1890	9,513,443	235,534	40.2
1891	14,762,605	305,044	48.3
1892	11,654,090	332,974	35.0
1893	9,823,935	388,529	25.28
1894	11,907,854	413,686	28.8
1895	22,555,733	482,658	46.73
1896	12,502,318	442,445	28.25
1897	10,629,513	468,141	22.7
1898	17,308,252	514,824	33.6
1899	22,318,378	575,136	38.80
1900	8,814,312	429,108	20.50
1901	27,796,588	689,951	40.30
1902	34,478,160	725,060	47.50
1903	33,035,774	855,431	38.62

Average for 15 years 1889–1903 = 34.5

Barley

Year	Bushels	Acreage	Yield per acre
1889	1,051,551	80,238	13.1
1890	2,060,415	66,035	31.33
1891	3,197,876	89,828	35.6
1892	2,831,676	97,644	29.0
1893	2,547,653	114,762	22.11
1894	2,981,716	119,528	25.87
1895	5,645,036	153,839	36.69
1896	3,171,747	127,885	24.8
1897	3,183,602	153,266	20.77
1898	4,227,927	158,058	27.06
1899	5,379,156	182,912	29.4
1900	2,939,477	155,111	18.9
1901	6,536,155	191,009	34.2
1902	11,848,422	329,790	35.9
1903	8,707,252	326,537	26.66

Average for 15 years 1889–1903 = 27.63

Average wheat 1889–1897	18.14
Average wheat 1898–1903	18.43
Average oats 1889–1897	32.45
Average oats 1898–1903	36.55
Average barley 1889–1897	26.58
Average barley 1897–1903	28.68

See Statistical Year-Book of Canada, Ottawa, 1902; and Manitoba Crop Report, Winnipeg, December 1903.

Manitoba has a vigorous Department of Agriculture, collects and publishes crop bulletins, maintains a dairy school, and is just now establishing an agricultural college near Winnipeg. See CANADA — THE GRANGER MOVEMENT; CANADA — COMMERCE, TARIFFS, AND TRANSPORTATION; AGRICULTURE.

C. C. JAMES,
Deputy Minister of Agriculture for Ontario.

37. **Canada — Minerals.** From a country so vast and of such varied geological structure as Canada one expects a wide range of mineral deposits, and the expectation is not disappointed, for already most of the minerals known to exist elsewhere have been found in the Dominion, and often in important deposits, though only its southern fringe has been explored. However, up to the present, Canada's mineral production must be looked on as at the stage of promise rather than performance, except in a few substances where nature has given her the lead. For example, the world's supply of asbestos comes from the province of Quebec, and more than half of its supply of nickel is obtained from a single mine in Ontario, while the richest placer gold region is in the Yukon territory (see KLONDIKE, THE; ALASKA). On the other hand, Canada is backward in the production of iron and steel, basic factors in the development of a country, and stands low as a producer of coal, though the fact that the only deposits of good coal on tide-water in America, both on the Atlantic and Pacific, are Canadian is a fact of much importance which has produced great metallurgical industries in Nova Scotia.

Until recently the exploitation of Canadian mineral resources has been largely due to foreigners, especially Americans; but Canadian skill and capital are now turning in this direction. In 1903 the total value of the mineral products of Canada was $63,222,510, about $11 for each inhabitant, as compared with $15 per capita in the United States, where the total reached $1,250,000,000 in 1902. The area of Canada is about equal to that of the United States, and in the parts best explored its mineral resources give promise of equaling in value those of corresponding States of the Union; so that an immense expansion in mining is to be looked for in the next generation.

The mineral production of Canada is very unequally distributed among the provinces, British Columbia coming first, followed by Ontario, the Yukon and Nova Scotia, with the remaining provinces far in the rear. In per capita production the order is different, Yukon territory, with its tiny population of 20,000 or 30,000, almost equaling Ontario with more than 2,000,000 inhabitants, while British Columbia stands second and Nova Scotia third.

Of the maritime provinces of eastern Canada only Nova Scotia can be described as a mining region, gold and coal having been produced there for nearly half a century. Quebec is not of great importance except for its asbestos mines. Ontario produces a variety of minerals, nickel being the foremost, while British Columbia provides gold, silver, copper, lead, and coal; and the Yukon gold.

Following the usual classification, the minerals of Canada may be taken up under three heads, metals, non-metallic minerals, and structural materials.

METALS.

Ores of 13 metals have been mined in Canada, antimony, chromium, cobalt, copper, gold, iron, manganese, mercury, molybdenum, nickel, platinum, silver, and zinc, and minerals containing a number of other metals have been found, though they have not yet been mined. Only six of these metals are prominent economically, gold, silver, nickel, copper, lead, and iron, and attention will be directed mainly to them.

Gold.— The gold areas of Canada are widespread but the production has been very fluctuating, the value in recent years varying from $907,601 (in 1892) to $27,908,153 (in 1900), and standing at $18,834,490 in 1903. In 1900 Canada was third in rank as a producer of gold, being surpassed by the United States and Australia only; but has dropped to the fifth place since then, yielding to South Africa (see AFRICA — *Geology, Minerals;* TRANSVAAL) and Russia (see RUSSIA — *Minerals*). Three provinces and one territory are gold producers at present. Nova Scotia has carried on quartz mining, on "saddle reefs" like those of the famous Bendigo region in Australia, for more than 40 years, and of late has exceeded $500,000 per annum, the value reaching $627,357 in 1902. Ontario also produces gold from quartz mines, but with less steadiness than Nova Scotia, the value running from $421,591 in 1899 to $188,000 in 1903. Before the sudden rise of the Klondike, British Columbia was the greatest gold region of Canada, its history beginning with the times of wild excitement in the '60s, when thousands of miners from California swarmed into the rich placers of the Fraser and Columbia rivers and washed out millions of dollars worth, reaching the climax of $3,913,563 in 1863. The easily available placers were gradually exhausted, the value falling in 1893 to $379,535, a little less than the output of Nova Scotia in the same year; but the production of lode gold, especially from the smelting ores of Rossland, on the southern edge of the province, has once more placed British Columbia in the first rank. In 1902 the yield was $5,961,409, of which $1,073,140 came from placer mines, mostly in the Cariboo and Atlin districts in the north, the rest from smelting ores and a few quartz mines in the south.

The territories have furnished a small amount of placer gold from bars on the Saskatchewan and other rivers for a number of years, but it was not until the working of the Klondike placers in 1897 that gold mining assumed importance in the north. This region, in lat. 64°, 500 miles below the head-waters of the great Yukon River, is unique as a placer mining country, reminding one of the famous placers of California and Australia, but surpassing them in difficulty of access and of working conditions, as well as in richness. For its length Eldorado Creek, a tributary of Bonanza Creek, was the most productive ever mined, but its gravels are nearly worked out, and the yield of gold, though still great for so small a region as the Klondike, which is about 40 miles square, has fallen since 1900, when it was estimated at $22,275,000, to $12,250,000 in 1903. The gold-bearing gravels are perpetually frozen and usually buried under several feet of frozen muck, so that the ground must be thawed before it can be worked. At first this was done by building fires, but more recently steam delivered from steel pipes driven into the ground has been employed, and it is found, also, that when stripped of moss the warm summer's sun thaws layer after layer, which may then be sluiced off in the ordinary way. As methods are improved and the cost of living diminishes, much poorer gravels can be worked profitably, so that the placers of Yukon territory will no doubt be productive for a generation to come, even if no important new finds are made. It is probable, however, that the Klondike output will slowly diminish or only hold its own in the future, and that the British Columbian production will increase, leaving the total for Canada not very different from what it is now. See Gold — *World's Production.*

Silver.— A generation ago Ontario was the chief province for silver, the Silver Islet mine near Thunder Bay, on the north shore of Lake Superior, being credited with a production of $3,250,000, while several other mines were worked west of Thunder Bay; but in recent years British Columbia has taken the lead, beginning in 1895 and culminating in 1897 so far as value is concerned, with more than $3,000,000 worth. The fall in the price of silver, and also of lead, with which it is always associated in British Columbian ores, has caused a serious shrinkage in production, only 3,182,000 ounces, valued at $1,700,779, having been reported from the whole of Canada in 1903. Of this a small amount was derived from the gold of the Yukon and trifling quantities from Ontario and Quebec, the rest from British Columbia, where the mines of the Slocan region in the south are most important. See Silver — *Silver-producing Districts.*

Nickel.— This metal has become of practical value only within the last 20 years, and methods of reducing its ores are still somewhat in the experimental stage. The world's supply comes almost entirely from two regions, the Sudbury district in northern Ontario and the French penal colony of New Caledonia. Until the last year or two New Caledonia was somewhat in advance, but in 1903 Sudbury passed it in production and seems likely to hold its position in the future. The mines are all situated round the edge of a basin-shaped sheet of eruptive rock 37 miles long and 15 broad, and among them the Copper Cliff, which is about 1,000 feet deep, produces the richest ore, while the Creighton, a few miles to the west, is the greatest nickel mine in the world, supplying 18,000 tons of ore per month. Nearly as much copper as nickel is produced in these mines, and also small amounts of cobalt, gold, and platinum, the last metal occurring in the rare arsenide sperrylite, first found in the district. In 1903 matte smelted from the roasted ore contained 6,998 tons of nickel, mostly mined and treated by the Canadian Copper Company. The value of the nickel in the matte was placed at $2,499,068, while the refined metal was estimated to be worth $5,000,000. See Nickel.

Copper.— Copper has been mined in Newfoundland, Nova Scotia, New Brunswick, Quebec, Ontario, and British Columbia, but only the last two provinces are important producers. The copper of Quebec is a by product of the iron pyrites of the Eastern Townships; and most of the copper from Ontario is, as shown above, produced as an accompaniment of the Sudbury nickel ores; though mines of copper alone are worked at Massey and one or two other points in western Ontario, not far from the once well-known Bruce mines, north of Lake Huron, which were prosperous half a century ago but are no longer worked. British Columbia supplies more than three fourths of the copper mined in Canada, chiefly from the gold-copper ores of the Rossland region and the large low grade deposits of the Boundary district, but numerous other deposits are known along the Pacific coast of the province and in the White Horse district of Yukon territory. The total production of copper in the Dominion in 1903 was 21,640 tons, valued at $5,728,261. See Copper, World's Output of.

Lead.— Almost the whole of the lead mined in Canada comes from the silver-lead ores of southern British Columbia, which began to be opened up extensively in 1893 and furnished 31,500 tons in 1900, but sank in 1903 to 9,000 tons with a value of $762,660. The falling off is attributed to adverse conditions imposed by the smelters of the Western States, which had bought the ores at advantageous rates in former years. To stimulate lead mining and smelting in British Columbia the Dominion government has provided a bounty on lead smelted and refined in Canada, and it is expected that lead mining will recover some of its former prosperity. See Lead.

Iron.— In regard to the most important of all metals, iron, Canada is backward, largely from the fact that the ore deposits and the fuel for treating them are generally widely sundered. Nova Scotia, Quebec, and Ontario are producers of iron and steel, the first province having the great advantage of supplies of coking coal on the seaboard, at Sidney in Cape Breton Island and other points, so that two large iron and steel plants are in operation there. Most of the ore smelted is, however, in a sense foreign, coming from Bell Island, off the coast of Newfoundland. The province of Quebec has for generations smelted a small amount of bog iron ore in charcoal furnaces near Three Rivers, the product being of high grade and used for special purposes. Charcoal iron furnaces were operated on a small scale in different parts of Ontario, also, from 50 to 100 years ago, but when railways began to bring in British iron the industry ceased. Within the last few years large furnaces using American coke, and in part American ore, have sprung up at Hamilton, Midland, and the Sault Sainte Marie, and some charcoal furnaces have come into operation.

Deposits containing millions of tons of fair grade ore have been found in Hutton township, Michipicoton, and other points in northern Ontario in rocks similar to those of the great iron regions of Michigan and Minnesota, so that iron production is likely to increase in the future, particularly since the governments of the Dominion and of the province have provided bounties for iron and steel of home production. British Columbia also possesses large deposits of iron ore and excellent coking coal, so that an iron industry like that of Nova Scotia may be expected to grow up as the province becomes more populous. In 1903 the amount of pig iron produced in Canada was 297,885 tons, valued at $3,742,710, of which, however, only 42,052 tons were from Canadian ore, the rest being from Newfoundland and American ores. The quantity of steel produced is not given, but in the previous year it was 182,037 tons. See Iron and Steel Industry in America.

NON-METALLIC MINERALS.

Twenty-three non-metallic minerals are reported in the statistics for 1903, and several others occur in lists of former years, but attention may be confined to a few of the more important ones, beginning with the mineral fuels.

Coal.— In 1903 the coal raised in the Dominion amounted to 7,996,634 tons, valued at $15,957,940, Nova Scotia producing more than 5,000,000, and British Columbia most of the remainder, though the territories are credited with about 500,000 tons. The coal supply of the great manufacturing province of Ontario comes entirely from the United States; but, on the other hand, Nova Scotia exports 500,000 tons to the New England States and British Columbia 750,000 to California and other Western States. Besides the rich bituminous coal beds of Nova Scotia and of Nanaimo and the Crow's Nest Pass, in British Columbia, which are the most important producers in Canada, lignite or lignitic coal of poorer quality is mined at numerous points on the prairies, which are largely underlain with seams of the kind, and valuable mines are worked in the foot-hill region near the Rockies. A few small areas in Bow Pass, nipped in during mountain building, approach anthracite in quality. Great coal fields are known to exist near the Skeena River and at other points in northern British Columbia and the territories to the north and east. The coal fields of western Canada are mainly of Cretaceous age, unlike those of Nova Scotia and the Eastern and Southern States, which are Carboniferous. In all there are probably not less than 100,000 square miles of coal fields in Canada, and the extent may prove to be much greater than this. See COAL — *Coal Fields of the World.*

Petroleum and Natural Gas.— At present Ontario is the only producer of petroleum, which comes from a small area in its southwestern peninsula. Crude oil and its products to the value of $1,586,674 are reported in 1903, but the supply is slowly diminishing and before long will be exhausted unless other pools are struck. Petroleum is known from Gaspé in Quebec and from the Crow's Nest Pass in the Rockies, and great stretches of "tar sands" along the Saskatchewan and Athabasca suggest oil deposits, though productive wells have not yet been sunk in these regions. (See PETROLEUM INDUSTRY, THE.) Natural gas has been exploited in Essex and Welland counties of southwestern Ontario, but the yield of the Essex field has greatly fallen off in the last two or three years. In 1903 the wells of Ontario furnished gas to the value of $196,535. Gas is known also and slightly put to use at Medicine Hat and Langevin, on the prairies. (See GAS, NATURAL.) Peat bogs exist over thousands of square miles of northern Ontario and Quebec, a reserve of fuel that may some day be drawn upon, but which is barely touched at present, though a few plants have been operated for drying and compressing peat to serviceable briquettes.

Minor Economic Minerals.— After the fuels come several less important minerals, asbestos being the chief one, with an output of 42,328 tons, valued at $904,853. The whole product, which means practically the world's supply, comes from a few mines in serpentine rocks in the Eastern Townships of Quebec. The value of this beautiful silky-fibred mineral depends on the fact that it is an incombustible material which can be spun and woven. Next in value is gypsum, the raw material of plaster of paris, of which 307,489 tons are reported, worth $384,259, mainly from New Brunswick and Nova Scotia. Salt is produced to the amount of 53,537 tons, valued at $334,088, from wells in southwestern Ontario; and mica is mined in the provinces of Ontario and Quebec, to the value of $159,473, Ontario being the largest producer in the world of this mineral, so important as an insulator in electric machinery. Pyrites, used chiefly in the chemical industries, is produced to the value of $126,133 in Quebec; and a new item has recently appeared in the statistics of Ontario, corundum, the hardest mineral next to diamond. In 1903 the output was valued at $87,600, and the crushed material is beginning to replace emery as an abrasive. Although these deposits of corundum are the largest known, the gem varieties, ruby and sapphire, have not yet been found in the province. Among minor non-metallic minerals may be mentioned chromite, mineral paints, graphite, feldspar, diatom earth, and arsenic, having an annual value of from $15,000 to $35,000 each.

STRUCTURAL MATERIALS.

Building-stone, clay for brick-making, and marl or limestone and clay for the manufacture of cement are, of course, found in all the provinces; but the greater part of the clay products and almost all the cement are manufactured in Ontario, which in 1903, according to the Bureau of Mines, made brick, tile, etc., to the value of $2,185,509, and Portland and natural rock cement worth $1,252,118. Quebec is the greatest producer of granite and other building and ornamental stones, but definite statistics regarding them are hard to obtain. In 1903 the Geological Survey gives the following statistics of structural products of the Dominion:

Cement, natural rock	$ 75,655
Cement, Portland	1,099,842
Granite	150,000
Pottery	200,000
Sands and gravels (exports)	124,006
Sewer pipe	317,970
Slate	22,040
Terra-cotta, pressed brick, etc	386,532
Bricks, stone, lime, etc	5,650,000
Total	$8,017,045

It will be noticed that the Ontario Bureau of Mines shows a greater value for the cement manufactured in that province than the whole Dominion is credited with in the table just given, showing the uncertainty of the statistics of this class of products.

Summing up the mineral production of Canada in 1903, we have the following results as shown by the Geological Survey:

Metals	$33,707,403
Mineral fuels	18,716,543
Other non-metals	2,485,519
Structural materials	8,017,045
Estimate of minerals not reported	300,000
Total	$63,226,510

This shows a falling off since 1901, when the total was $66,339,155, but the difference is much more than accounted for by the diminished production of gold in the Klondike. In all other departments, except the mining of silver and lead, there has been a steady advance, which may be expected to remain.

The following table, showing the production at five-year intervals, illustrates the rapidity of the increase since statistics have been kept by the Geological Survey:

1886 (first year of statistics)................$10,221,255
1888 12,518,894
1893 29,035,082
1898 38,697,021
1903 63,226,510

It will be seen that the mineral production has nearly doubled every five years, and has increased at a very much. more rapid ratio than the population, which has been far from doubling since 1886, though the mining industry has gained six-fold. The prospects of advance in the future are bright.

Statistical information as to the mineral production of the country as a whole may be found in the annual reports of the Geological Survey of Canada (Section of Mines, compiled by Elfric Drew Ingall), and in the annual volumes of the 'Mineral Industry.' The mining departments of the provinces of Nova Scotia, Ontario, and British Columbia also publish annual reports of much value, in which information is given as to their special mining industries. The statistical materials for this paper have been largely drawn from these sources.

A. P. COLEMAN,
Professor of Geology, University of Toronto.

38. Canada — The Forests and Lumber Industry. Until further explorations are made it will be impossible to give more than a rough estimate of the vast extent and value of the forests of Canada. The total area of the Dominion is estimated at 3,315,647 square miles. Of this about 40 per cent, or 1,326,258 square miles, is supposed to be in forest. Not only is the area of vast extent, but the varieties of trees are very numerous, and among them are found some of the most valuable species. Professor John Macoun gives 121 as the total number of indigenous species. Among these are the different varieties of the pine, spruce, fir, hemlock, cedar, oak, maple, beech, birch, poplar, basswood, elm, ash, hickory, walnut, and various others of more or less commercial value. The white pine is the tree that has brought most wealth to the people of the eastern provinces, while the fir, the cedar, the hemlock, and the spruce are the varieties of greatest value west of the Rocky Mountains. Within recent years the development of the pulp industry has brought into more general use the wood of the spruce, it being particularly well adapted for that purpose, and as it is one of the most widely distributed of Canadian trees, extending from the Atlantic on the east to Alaska on the west, and from about lat. 45° N. to the limit of tree growth, the Dominion holds an almost unlimited supply for this purpose. The Federal government has charge of the forests on Dominion lands proper. These embrace the province of Manitoba, the Northwest Territories, and also a part of British Columbia known as the Railway Belt, the last named consisting of a district 40 miles wide, 20 miles on each side of the main line of the Canadian Pacific Railway, and containing about 20,000 square miles. It is estimated that the area of forest thus under Dominion control (not including the Indian reserves in the old provinces or those in British Columbia) is 742,578 square miles, while that under the control of the Provincial governments is 506,220 square miles. It has been the policy for many years of both the Federal and Provincial governments to grant licenses permitting the holders to cut timber on certain areas of the Crown domain. These licenses are obtained by public competition, and only give the owners the exclusive right to cut within the areas specified. They get no rights to the land, and in addition to the bonus paid at the time the license is given a specified annual ground rent is collected, and also in most cases stumpage dues of a stated amount per thousand feet when the timber is cut.

The report of the Department of Trade and Commerce for the year ending 30 June 1903, shows the value of the exports of forest products of the Dominion for that year to be $36,-386,015. The figures also show an average increase for the past five years of nearly $2,000,-000 per annum, while the increase of last year over the preceding one is over $4,000,000. This trade is at present mostly confined to Great Britain and the United States, the exports to the former last year being valued at $16,742,435, and to the latter at $16,977,232; while those to all other countries only amounted to $2,666,348. But with the increased demand for lumber in foreign countries, and especially of those bordering on the Pacific Ocean, both in South America and eastern Asia, and the ability of British Columbia to furnish a large supply, it is improbable that these proportions will be long maintained. This province is destined in a few years to take a prominent, if not a leading, place with her sister provinces of the East in the lumber trade of the country. It should be noted that the exports give only a comparatively small part of the total products of the forests, and as the census returns for 1901 are not yet (1904) fully tabulated it is impossible to give as full information as is desirable. These returns, however, give the value of the products of the saw- and pulp-mills alone for the previous year as $53,051,865, while the capital invested was $67,164,226, the number of employees 54,726, and the wages paid $12,198,914. They also show the raw products to amount to $51,-082,695, made up as follows: From Ontario, $21,351,898; Quebec, $18,969,716; Nova Scotia, $3,409,528; New Brunswick, $2,998,038; British Columbia, $2,634,157; Manitoba, $950,057; Northwest Territories, $484,263; Prince Edward Island, $285,038. But all these figures together give only a part of the value that the inhabitants derive from their timber. It is used by the backwoods pioneer in a rough state for his dwelling and other farm buildings, for fencing and fuel, and for numerous implements in his daily use, and it furnishes employment to a large section of the population in the manufacture of articles in which wood is the chief ingredient. Not only are the forests of Canada of vast extent, but the facilities for floating logs to the mills for manufacturing are perhaps unequaled in any other country. It is pre-eminently a land of forest, lake, and stream. Great stretches of country form the basins from which certain large rivers derive their waters. Within each of these is an almost endless number of lakes of all dimensions, connected by streams of varying sizes, but all serving as feeders to the great river which serves as their outlet. The timber is usually cut in the winter and drawn to one of these streams. There it remains till the spring opens, when it is carried by the current down to its destination. In many cases no rafting or towing is necessary. All that is required is that a few river men watch the "drive" till it reaches the boom at the mill. The facilities afforded for the development of water-power are very great, and many of the saw-mills, pulp-mills, and various other industrial establishments are run by such power. While the percentage of land in forest in Canada as a whole is very large, there are many districts in the older provinces where the denudation has gone far beyond what good economic conditions demand, and the yearly destruction caused by spring floods is followed by the consequent summer drought. The census of 1901 gives the percentage of woodland on the farms in the five eastern provinces as follows: Ontario, 22 per cent; Quebec, 38 per cent; New Brunswick, 57 per cent; Nova Scotia, 56 per cent; and Prince Edward Island, 30 per cent. But this favorable condition is made by the large proportion of forest still existing on the farms of the pioneer settlers in the newer districts, counterbalancing the prairie-like condition of many of the older settlements, in some of which 5 per cent of woodland would be an over-estimate.

The practice of reserving from settlement certain areas of land for timber reserves has been adopted within recent years in Dominion territory, and also in the provinces of Ontario and Quebec. The object of reserving these tracts is not only for the supply of timber they will afford, but more especially to conserve the water supply at the sources of rivers and streams. These reserves are nearly all in elevated situations, such as the Rocky Mountains, the Riding and Moose mountains, on Dominion lands; the Algonquin Park, the Temagami and Mississaga reserves, which embrace large tracts of land at the sources of several of the large streams of northern Ontario, in Ontario; and the Laurentides National Park, at the summit of the Laurentian range of mountains, in Quebec. In 1903 the areas set aside for such purposes by the Dominion government aggregated 9,686,880 acres, while those in Ontario contained 6,928,383 acres, and in Quebec 1,619,383 acres. Forest fires have destroyed vast quantities of timber in all parts of the country, but more especially in the coniferous regions extending from Nova Scotia and New Brunswick to British Columbia. Within the last few years, however, public attention has been awakened to the necessity of greater attention being given to the subject of forestry, and the Province of Ontario and the Dominion have now each established a forestry office as a branch of the public service. The Dominion office was started in 1899. The officials consist of a superintendent, assistant superintendent, inspector, several supervisors of tree planting, and a number of forest-fire rangers. The rangers are employed for a longer or shorter time each summer, as the necessities of the case require. The Ontario Bureau of Forestry is presided over by a director, and the work of the large staff of fire rangers employed has been the means of lessening the loss of timber to a very marked extent.

Similar results have followed the work of the government fire rangers on Dominion lands, and also in the Province of Quebec.

Co-operation with the settlers in forest planting on the prairie lands of Manitoba and the Northwest Territories has been established within the last three years, and is now assuming large proportions. The system adopted may be briefly stated as follows: Any land owner desiring to avail himself of the co-operation of the government applies to the Forestry Branch at Ottawa. These applications are tabulated and the land of the applicant is visited by one of the supervisors the following summer, when a plan of the proposed plantation is made. The next spring seedling trees are sent by express from the government nurseries free of charge. The settler enters into an agreement to set aside a certain portion of his land as a permanent forest plantation, to carefully prepare his soil according to the directions of the supervisors, to plant the trees on their arrival, and to cultivate and keep the ground clean till such time as the trees are of sufficient size to no longer need such attention. The varieties planted will vary according to the district of country where planted and prevailing soil and climatic conditions. The work is also designed to be educative and to furnish practical object lessons of the possibilities of tree culture on the open plains. In 1901 44 settlers received an aggregate of 58,800 trees; in 1902, 415 an aggregate of 468,900 trees; in 1903, 616 an aggregate of 920,000 trees; in 1904, 1,026 an aggregate of about 2,000,000 trees. Heretofore the seedling trees for distribution have been grown on the Government Experimental Farms at Brandon and Indian Head, but it is now proposed to centralize the work, and 160 acres of land have been obtained for a forest nursery station near Indian Head, Assiniboia, where buildings are being erected and preparations made by which the supply for the whole country will be grown in, and distributed from, that place. The Agricultural Department of Ontario has also this season (1904) started to grow forest trees at the Experimental Farm at Guelph for distribution to the farmers of that province.

A Canadian Forestry Association was organized in 1900, which is proving a very useful institution and doing much in the interests of forestry. Its purposes, as stated in its constitution, are: (1) To advocate and encourage judicious methods in dealing with our forests and woodlands. (2) To awaken public interest to the sad results attending the wholesale destruction of forests (as shown by the experience of older countries), in the deterioration of the climate, diminution of fertility, drying up of rivers and streams, etc. (3) To consider and recommend the exploration, as far as practicable, of our public domain and its division into agricultural, timber, and mineral lands, with a view of directing immigration and the pursuits of our pioneers into channels best suited to advance their interests and the public welfare. With this accomplished, a portion of the unappropriated lands of the country could be permanently reserved for the growth of timber. (4) To encourage afforestation wherever advisable, and to promote forest tree planting, especially in the treeless areas of our northwestern prairies, upon farm lands where the proportion of woodland is too low, and upon highways and in the parks of

our villages, towns, and cities. (5) To collect and disseminate, for the benefit of the public, reports and information bearing on the forestry problem in general, and especially with respect both to the wooded and prairie districts of Canada, and to teach the rising generation the value of the forest with the view of enlisting their efforts in its preservation. The officers embrace leading men from all parts of the Dominion, and reports of the annual meetings are printed in attractive form and widely distributed. The Association is now about taking another forward step in publishing a quarterly periodical, which will be devoted entirely to forestry. Action is also being taken to establish a course of study in forestry in certain colleges in the country. Altogether, the attention of the general public is now being directed in various ways to the necessity of greater attention being given to this subject than has been the case in the past.   E. STEWART,
Dominion Superintendent of Forestry.

39. Canada — Fisheries. Among the great industries of Canada the fisheries stand fifth in the order of value. The farming industry (mainly grain-growing) is estimated to yield $208,000,000 per annum; the lumber industry $80,000,000; stock-raising $75,000,000; mining $65,000,000, while the fishing industries are estimated to produce, on the whole, $35,000,000 to $36,000,000 annually. This estimate is much in excess of that reported in official returns. The latest report of the Marine and Fisheries Department, which gives the value for 1902, places it at $21,959,433; but when account is taken of the amount of fish consumed by wandering tribes of Indians and Eskimo, with their hordes of fish-eating dogs, as well as the amount used as food by isolated settlers, miners, prospectors, lumberers and sportsmen and, above all, the employees at the Hudson's Bay Company's posts in the remoter parts of northern Canada, the total amount must be greatly in excess of official statistics.

Completely accurate returns are hardly possible, admirable as the Canadian system of gathering statistics is, so admirable that the late Prof. Brown Goode, head of the United States Fish Commission, declared in a fisheries conference in 1883 that ". . . other countries ought to study it with a great deal of care." The domestic consumption of fish in the Dominion is stated, on high authority, to be not less than 100 pounds per head annually, as compared with 30 pounds in Britain.

The expansion of the Canadian fisheries since 1870 is sufficiently shown by the figures given below:

1870	$6,577,391	1887	$18,386,103
1871	7,573,199	1888	17,418,510
1872	9,570,116	1889	17,655,256
1873	10,754,097	1890	17,714,902
1874	11,681,886	1891	18,077,878
1875	10,350,385	1892	18,941,171
1876	11,117,000	1893	20,686,661
1877	12,005,934	1894	20,719,573
1878	13,295,678	1895	20,199,338
1879	13,529,254	1896	20,407,425
1880	14,499,079	1897	22,783,546
1881	15,817,162	1898	19,667,121
1882	16,824,092	1899	21,891,706
1883	16,958,192	1900	21,557,639
1884	17,766,404	1901	25,737,153
1885	17,722,973	1902	21,959,433
1886	18,679,288		

Number of Boats, Fishermen, etc.— Over 1,200 vessels (valued at $2,620,661) and 41,667 boats (valued at $1,199,598) are employed, while the fishing gear used, including nets, lines, lobster-traps, etc., is valued at over $3,000,000. Certain branches of the fisheries have developed in a special degree, such as the salmon canning industry on the Pacific coast, and lobster packing on the Atlantic coast. The former, embracing about 80 canneries, represents an investment of about $3,000,000, while the Atlantic lobster canneries, in Quebec and the three maritime provinces, numbering over 750, are valued at about $450,000. Smoke-houses, curing and refrigerating establishments, in operation, are officially recorded at $3,153,838 in value. In other words, a capital of over $12,000,000 is employed in these various branches of the fisheries.

The total number of persons engaged either in fishing or in handling fishery products in Canada reaches about 80,000, of whom 60,000 take part in Atlantic fishery enterprises. On the Pacific coast 4,000 or 5,000 fishermen follow salmon netting, and 10,000 or 12,000 hands find employment as cannery workers, etc. The inland (fresh-water) fisheries engage a considerable number of fishermen, over 2,000 being employed in the Ontario or Great Lake fisheries, while, in Manitoba and the northwest territories, 3,000 or 4,000 men take part in the fishing operations.

Seven Fishery Districts.— Seven territorial divisions may be distinguished in a general survey of the fisheries of the Dominion, viz.:

1. The Atlantic division, from Grand Manan in the south to the coast of Labrador, including the Bay of Fundy (8,000 square miles) and the Gulf of Saint Lawrence (80,000 square miles), and characterized by deep-sea and inshore fisheries for cod, mackerel, haddock, halibut, herring, hake, lobsters, oysters, seals and white whales (*beluga*). Annual value, $10,000,000.

2. The estuarine and inland waters of Quebec and the Maritime Provinces, including fisheries for salmon (by stake-nets, drift-nets and angling), striped bass, smelt, shad, gaspereau (alewife); and in the lakes, ouananiche or land-locked salmon, lake trout, togue or lunge, etc. Annual value, $3,000,000.

3. Great Lakes division, including Lakes Ontario, Erie, Huron, and Superior, which Canada shares with the United States, the international boundary passing practically through the centre of these vast inland seas, all of which finally empty into the river St. Lawrence. This complex system of waters, with innumerable subsidiary lakes and rivers, abounds in lake whitefish (*Coregonus*), great lake trout (*Cristivomer namaycush*), lesser whitefish (erroneously called lake herring), sturgeon, pike-perch (doré or pickerel), black bass, brook-trout, maskinongé, pike, and numerous carpoid suckers, and bearded catfish. Annual value, $2,000,000.

4. Manitoba and northwestern division, including Keewatin, etc., whose wide expanses of fresh water, such as Lake Winnipeg, Great Bear Lake, and Great Slave Lake, yield enormous quantities of whitefish, sturgeon, pike-perch, tullibee (a peculiar lesser whitefish), pike, gold-eye (a true fresh-water herring), large river-trout and catfish. Value, inclusive of an extensive "caviare" or sturgeon-roe industry, over $1,000,000.

5. Pacific Interior division, extending from the Okanagan, Kootenay, and Arrow waters, in

the south, to the Yukon district, in the north, and covering an area of plain, valley and mountain 1,000 miles north and south, by about 500 miles east and west, intersected everywhere by rivers and lakes, and comprising limited fisheries for lake-trout, whitefish, land-locked salmon, river-trout, grayling, and numerous carps or suckers, not identical, for the most part, with eastern species. Annual value probably not exceeding $500,000.

6. Pacific Coast division, the fisheries of which are little developed, if we except the estuarine and coastal salmon fisheries. The various species of salmon (belonging to the genus *Oncorhyncus*) include the blue-back or sockeye, the spring salmon or quinnat, the coho, dog-salmon, humpback salmon, and a true *Salmo*, namely, Gairdner's salmon or steel-head. Halibut, skill or black cod, oolachan (candle-fish), anchovy, herring, sardine, smelt, and a great variety of other fishes, abound, which are not to any adequate extent utilized. Shark, dog-fish, rat-fish or chimæra, and whale fisheries exist, and there are limited oyster fisheries, while the famous fur-seal fishery (value $400,000 to $500,000 per annum, and employing nearly 1,000 men) is of importance, and is mainly an oceanic industry. Annual value, $6,000,000, though in special years that amount may be exceeded.

7. Hudson Bay and Peri-Arctic division, from Ungava Bay, Labrador, to the Mackenzie River, or rather Herschell Island, Yukon distriet. Whale, walrus, sea-trout, Hearn's salmon, (a great spotted trout), the inconnu (resembling a river whitefish), pike, suckers, sturgeon, and possibly, salmon and cod, occur in these vast northern waters, of which Hudson Bay alone exceeds the Mediterranean in extent and has an estimated drainage area of 2,700,000 square miles. The richest whaling grounds in the world are in these remote regions of the Dominion, whose tidal channels, as the late Sir John Schultz declared, "are destined to be the last home of the leviathans which within the memory of living man have been driven from Newfoundland latitudes to the places where their survivors have now sought retreat." Hair-seals of various species, and white whales (*Beluga*), abound in these sub-arctic waters, and constitute valuable fisheries; one station, according to Dr. Robert Bell, securing no less than 2,800 of these small whales in one season.

Marine Fishing Grounds: Area, Kinds of Fish, etc.— The waters grouped in this sevenfold manner afford a field, hardly to be surpassed, for the development of extensive fisheries. The grounds, where fishing can be remuneratively carried on, off the eastern and western sea-board, embrace a total area of no less than 200,000 square miles, the Atlantic shore being over 5,000 miles in length, while the Pacific shore (British Columbia) exceeds 7,000 miles. On this latter coast, Hecate Straits (20,000 square miles) and the straits between Vancouver Island and the mainland, namely, the straits of Georgia and Fuca (15,000 square miles) afford the most remarkable sheltered fishing grounds in the world, being for the most part shielded from the open ocean, and extending inland as placid fiords and deep, salt-water inlets, the total area of these inshore waters being no less than 40,000 square miles in extent. The Canadian fishing banks on the Atlan-

tic coast are historic. They stretch from Labrador, Anticosti, and Gaspé in the north to the West Isles in the southern Passamaquoddy waters, including famous areas like the Bay of Chaleurs, off Quebec Province, Northumberland Straits, off Prince Edward Island, and New Brunswick, and Chedabucto Bay, off eastern Nova Scotia. Between the outer edge of the Atlantic areas and the deep-sea waters of the inshore areas and the deep-sea waters occur for cod, haddock, mackerel, and other valued edible fishes. "There is probably no part of the world," said Mr. P. L. Simmonds, the well-known fishery authority, "where such extensive fisheries are to be found, as in the Gulf of Saint Lawrence." Among the series of banks mainly resorted to by Canadian fishing boats are (passing from north to south) Great Bank, Green Bank, Bank Saint Peter, Misaine, Canso, Quero, Howe, Roseway, La Havre, and George's Banks, apart from the great fishing areas in the open Atlantic, such as the Grand Banks, which are not really in Canadian limits and are indeed mainly exploited by fishermen from more distant countries.

Fresh-water Fisheries.— If, owing to the superficial extent, and, no less, the coldness and purity of the marine waters of Canada, as well as the abundance of natural food, upon which cod, mackerel, halibut, herring, etc., subsist, the sea fisheries rank amongst the best in the world, it may be said of the fresh-water fisheries, that they are hardly inferior in these characteristics. The total area of the fresh waters of the Dominion (lakes and rivers) is estimated at 140,-000 square miles. From a fisheries' point of view, the lake systems of Canada may be arranged under five principal heads, namely:

Five Lake Systems.— 1. The maritime lakes, embracing the numerous lakes of Labrador, Quebec, and the Atlantic provinces. Certain of these, notably, Lake Saint John, Quebec (366 square miles), and the Chamcook Lakes, N. B., are famous for land-locked salmon, so prized for their unique game qualities. Black bass, pickerel or doré, lake-trout, red and speckled trout, abound in these waters, while Clear Lake, Little Seal, Mistassini, and most of the northern lakes swarm with whitefish and sub-arctic varieties of trout.

2. The central lake system, including the Great Lakes (76,562 square miles in total area) and innumerable subsidiary lakes, all utilized for commercial purposes and for sport. The areas and maximum depths of the more important of these lakes are as follows: Superior, 31,-200 square miles, 160 fathoms deep; Huron, 23,-800 square miles, 145 fathoms deep; Erie, 10,030 square miles, 35 fathoms deep; Ontario, 7,330 square miles, 123 fathoms deep; Lake Nepigon, 1,450 square miles; Lakes Saint Clair and Simcoe, 300 square miles each.

3. The Manitoba and Keewatin system, the principal waters of which are Lake Winnipeg, 9,400 square miles; Lake Winnipegosis, 2,030 square miles; Lake Manitoba, 1,900 square miles; and Lake of the Woods, 1,500 square miles; and in these waters enormous fishing operations are carried on for whitefish, pickerel, or doré, sturgeon, pike, etc.

4. The Athabasca and Mackenzie system, extending from Reindeer Lake to Great Bear Lake, the latter lake no less than 11,200 square miles in area, while Great Slave Lake is 10,100

square miles, and others are: Athabasca 4,400 square miles; Reindeer Lake, 4,000 square miles; Woolaston and Doobount lakes, each over 2,000 square miles in extent. These waters have been little fished, excepting by Indians, Hudson's Bay Company employees, and the like, but being prolific in whitefish, sturgeon, etc., the development of great commercial fisheries in the near future is assured.

5. The Pacific Interior system from Lakes Labarge and Atlin to Shuswap Lake, and the Kootenay, Arrow and Okanagan lakes near the United States boundary. None of the lakes in this western series are comparable in area to the vast inland seas referred to above; but such waters as Babine Lake (250 or 300 square miles) at the head of the Skeena River, and Stuart Lake, and Quesnelle lakes (respectively 100 and 750 square miles in area) at the head of the Fraser River, have an importance wholly disproportionate to their size, owing to the fact that their creeks and tributary streams are the great spawning resorts of various species of Pacific salmon. Whitefish, lake-trout, Pacific trout of various species, and grayling occur in these waters.

Rivers of Canada.— Fisheries are also conducted upon the rivers, which almost without exception, are abundantly supplied with the most esteemed fishes. Apart from a great stream like the river Saint Lawrence, whose drainage area is estimated to be 367,000 square miles, there are rivers, like the Mackenzie (2,400 miles long); the Great Saskatchewan (1,900 miles); the Churchill and Back rivers (each 1,500 miles); the Fraser (750 miles long and draining 100,000 square miles); the Red River (600 miles), and others like the Peace, Nelson, Albany, Great Whale, Skeena (300 miles); Ottawa (600 miles); Saint John (500 miles); Restigouche, Saguenay, and Miramichi; all of which are great rivers, presenting for the most part unsurpassed scenic grandeur, and affording notable sport and extensive commercial fishing. It would indeed be difficult to parallel the Fraser River, with its incredible multitudes of salmon, while the Restigouche and other famous angling rivers emptying into the Atlantic Ocean have no peers in the annals of sport. "Canada," as Prof. Elwyn said, "is the paradise of the angler."

Minor Fisheries, Oysters, Smelts, etc.— The shores of Prince Edward Island, New Brunswick and parts of Nova Scotia furnish oysters of unequalled flavor and comestible qualities. Owing to over-fishing and inadequate protection the yield has seriously declined from 70,000 or 80,000 barrels per annum to half that quantity, valued at about $140,000 yearly. On the other hand, such an industry as the smelt fishery, mainly carried on through the ice in December, and the early months of the year, has grown from $117,000 in 1881 to $400,000 or $500,000 in value. These dainty fish formerly used as fertilizing material on farm lands, are now shipped, four or five thousand tons per season, in a frozen condition, mainly to the United States markets. The estuaries of the Miramichi, Restigouche and other New Brunswick rivers are the centres of this remarkable fishery.

The sturgeon fishery has witnessed a great development recently, and has much greater possibilities before it. This fish became commercially valuable in Canada, first on the Saint John River, N. B., in 1880, when 602,500 pounds were shipped to New York. In four years the catch fell to 126,000 pounds, and in 1895 barely 27,000 pounds were secured; but in Lake of the Woods, and on the Great Lakes, and above all, in the illimitable waters of Manitoba, the Northwest, and British Columbia, the sturgeon fishery has received a great impetus during the last five or six years. In 1902 the yield of sturgeon was valued at $173,315, as compared with $90,000 20 years ago. Canada, in the opinion of some authorities, is now one of the chief producers of "caviare," which formerly brought 10 cents to 15 cents per pound, and now sells in the cleaned, partly prepared condition at 90 cents to $1 per pound. Catfish and similar species, as well as eels and coarse fish generally, formerly little valued, are now in demand, bringing to the fishermen from $750,000 to $1,000,000 per annum.

Fishing Bounty.— For the encouragement of the Atlantic deep-sea fisheries a bounty system is carried out, the fund for which ($4,490,882) was provided by the Halifax Award, 1877. The bounties paid annually to vessel owners, vessel-fishermen, and boat-fishermen, amount to about $160,000.

Government Hatcheries.— An important adjunct to the natural reproduction of fish, aided by close seasons, size limits, etc., is the artificial culture of fish under the Dominion commissioner of fisheries. Twenty-two hatcheries are in operation, and four or five are in course of erection. The output of fry in 1903, amounted to 314,511,500, including Atlantic and Pacific salmon, lake trout, brook trout, whitefish, pickerel or doré, lobsters, etc. The total number of young fish planted in Canada during the last 30 years is no less than 3,704,546,000. Several of the Provincial Governments (Ontario, New Brunswick, and British Columbia) also aid in fish-culture to a limited extent.

Scientific Stations.— Two scientific biological stations are maintained by the government for the study and solution of fishery problems. The Canadian Marine Station, founded in 1898, can be floated from one part of the coast to another, and the staff have been engaged in the investigations of marine life at St. Andrews, N. B., Canso, N. S., and Malpeque, Prince Edward Island. It publishes, at intervals, a scientific bulletin. The Georgian Bay Station, Lake Huron, confines its work to the fisheries of the inland waters. The staff at both institutions, consists of professors and specialists from the Canadian universities.

Bait Freezers, Guano Works, etc.—In the fall of 1900 the Canadian government inaugurated a system of State-aided bait freezers in order to meet the needs of the fishermen, who have suffered much from irregular supplies of bait. Local fishermen's associations can, under conditions, secure a government grant covering half the cost of construction, and an annual payment of $5 per ton for bait preserved in the State-aided freezers. Twenty-four of these buildings have been built, varying in capacity from 10 tons to 50 tons. Larger freezers, to supply the Canadian "banking" fleets, are included in the scheme, one at Canso, costing $50,000, having a capacity of 2,000 tons. Government fish-dryers are also at work aiding the fishermen in preparing their products for the market independently of unfavorable weather. The initial drier was erected at Souris, Prince Edward Island. Further the government have imported Scottish experts, and a staff of Highland girls, to cure herring on the most approved methods. The scheme has proved most successful, and the Canadian fishermen receive instruction, and are enabled to improve the quality of cured herring sent into the markets. The incursions of hordes of destructive dog-fish and the injury to the fisheries resulting from the dumping of fish-offal, etc., in the sea, have moved the government to start fish-waste reduction works at various localities on the coast. These works conducted on the most approved methods, purchase dogfish, cod-heads, etc., from the fishermen, and convert them into guano, fish-oil, etc., under qualified government management.

Fishery Cruisers.— The Fisheries Protection fleet of about a dozen vessels, including a number of armed cruisers under trained naval officers, patrol the sea-coast and the Great Lakes. They enforce the fishery laws, and are under the direction of the commander of the Fisheries Protection Service.

Central Administration.— For the administration of fishery affairs, a special government Department of Marine and Fisheries was created at Confederation (1867) under a minister of the crown, and aided by a large staff of officials (inside and outside service) at Ottawa. A deputy minister, a commissioner of fisheries, about 20 inspectors, and numerous lesser officials carry out the duty of regulation which falls to the Federal authorities. The Dominion expenditure on fisheries approaches $600,000 per annum. Up to 1898, the Dominion government exercised sole administration; but by a recent judgment of the Imperial Privy Council (London, June 1898) it was decided that most of the Provinces have "property" in the fisheries, and in them is vested the right of issuing licenses, collecting revenue, and enforcing fishery laws, while it falls to the Dominion to frame regulations, exercise jurisdiction and carry out a general supervision in the interests of the fisheries as a whole.

EDWARD E. PRINCE,
Dominion Commissioner of Fisheries.

40. Canada — Manufactures. Canada has become year by year increasingly important as a manufacturing country. In the vast agricultural wealth, the fish, timber, mineral and other resources, her industries have a sure foundation, while the practically unlimited supply of water-power, supplemented by extensive coal areas, have combined with an increasing home and export trade to give manufacturing a development which has been phenomenal.

The grain produced forms the basis of a large milling industry. Much Canadian wheat is shipped direct to Europe, but in addition nearly 6,000,000 bushels are ground yearly in Canada and exported. In 1903, 1,228,000 barrels of flour, 145,000 barrels of oatmeal, and 11,251 barrels of other meal were exported. Other mills manufacture cereal foods. Co-operative butter factories or creameries have become a most important manufacturing industry among the farmers, the factory method of manufacture having, for trade purposes, entirely superseded the home method. In 1903 Canada exported 229,100,000 pounds of cheese and 34,128,944 pounds of butter. Pork-packing (including bacon, ham, and pork) is an important industry which is rapidly developing. In 1903 the exports of pork aggregated 143,288,402 pounds. Beef and mutton are also the basis of important dressed meat enterprises. The raw material of flour and grist mills, butter and cheese factories, meat-packing and slaughtering establishments is almost wholly of the products of agriculture. Their aggregate value in 1901 was $71,173,295.

Exports of canned meat, fruit, and vegetables have increased rapidly in value from year to year, totaling in 1903 more than $6,000,000, as compared, for example, with a total of $3,700,000 10 years previous. The tanning industry, the manufacture of boots, shoes, harness, saddlery, and leather goods are all enterprises more or less directly concerned with the products of the farm, which have shown steady and increasing development.

Connected with the fisheries is the fish-canning industry, a most important one, in which alone it is estimated that 80,000 men and a capital of $11,000,000 are employed. The fish are smoked, canned, or pickled for export, or shipped in cold storage to Canadian cities, the United States, and the West Indies. The exports for 1902 of the salmon canning industry on the Pacific coast aggregated over 49,000,000 pounds. Lobster canning is a considerable industry on the Atlantic coast.

Lumbering has always been an important industry in Canada. The total value of lumber exports in 1903 was $36,386,015. Canadian forests are looked upon as a great source of supply of pulp wood, and several mills have in recent years been put in operation for the purpose of converting spruce into pulp wood. The manufacture of furniture, vehicles, matches, and other wood products besides paper, is making rapid progress. The following estimates of the raw material in the several provinces may serve to indicate the basis for future development of this important industry: In 1900 there were in the province of Nova Scotia about 75,000,000 acres of ungranted crown lands covered with forest; in New Brunswick about 12,000 square miles of forest in possession of the crown, of which over 9,000 square miles are under license to lumbermen. In the province of Quebec, standing timber, exclusive of pulp wood and under-sized trees, would produce at least 60,000,000,000 feet of lumber. The northern portion of Manitoba and the Northwest Territories is covered with a sub-arctic forest, and the forests of British Columbia probably cover about 1,500,000 acres. Ontario contains the greatest variety of useful trees, and the greatest number of industries depending upon wood of all of the provinces.

Manufacturing based upon the mineral resources of the Dominion has been of a later development than manufacturing in other lines, but promises to become increasingly important. The bituminous coal of Nova Scotia is well adapted to the manufacture of gas and coke. All varieties of iron ore are found in that province, and are being extensively developed. Asbestos is an important mineral in the province of Quebec. Copper, iron, and mica are also extensively produced. Nickel is the most important mineral in Ontario. In 1903 its production was 6,999 tons, valued at $2,499,681. In the province of Ontario during the same year there were mined 208,154 tons of iron ore, and there were produced 87,400 tons of pig iron and 15,229 tons of steel. The total mineral production of the province for the year amounted to $12,870,931, including the non-metallic minerals, the chief of which were common brick to the value of $15,615,700, petroleum to the value of $1,586,674, and Portland cement to the value of $1,182,979. British Columbia is particularly rich in minerals, the chief of which are gold, silver, copper, and lead. While manufacturing has not developed to any considerable extent in the province of British Columbia, a very great development may be expected. A large amount of capital has been invested at Sydney, N. S., and at Sault Ste. Marie, on Lake Superior in Ontario, in the iron and steel industry. There are also important rolling mills and foundries; and special lines of machinery are largely manufactured in different parts of Canada, especially in the province of Ontario. Among other important industries in the Dominion are cotton and woolen mills, tobacco factories, sugar and petroleum refineries, breweries, and distilleries.

The water-power of Canada is not equaled by that of any other country, and its presence is attracting much capital for manufacturing purposes to the Dominion. Some of the largest industries are being operated by water power. In Sault Ste. Marie the largest pulp mill in Canada and a number of important industries are operated by electricity, developed by the local rapids, 175,000 horse-power having been developed thus far. It is reported that Winnipeg, which is 100 miles west of Rat Portage, with its industries, as well as other places, will be supplied with power from a dam across the Winnipeg River at Rat Portage, with a capacity of about 30,000 horse-power. At Niagara Falls extensive power companies and many large chemical industries have been established, with an aggregate capital of about $20,000,000, the horse-power to be developed at this point to be 424,000. Large electrical works have also been constructed at Lachine Rapids, above Montreal, and at Chambly, on the Richelieu River. These plants supply electricity for the operation of a street railway and for domestic and street lighting in Montreal. The streets of Quebec are lighted and the Quebec street railway operated by electricity developed at Shawinigan Falls on the river Saint Maurice. The Chaudiere at Ottawa, with a fall of about 40 feet at low water, has been used for many years for driving mills, pumping the city water supply, and generating electricity for light and operating the street railway, 8,000 horse-power being developed. Within a radius of 50 miles from Ottawa there is available water-power energy equivalent to 900,000 horse-power. These are only instances. It is estimated that the Saint Lawrence system places 10,000,000 horse-power at the disposal of Canadian industry.

The favorable conditions for skilled workmen in the manufacturing industry in Canada are reflected by the constant demand for labor which has been general for many years, the comparatively high rates of wages paid to workmen, and the reasonable length of the working day. The several trades are partially organized, their members belonging to unions having for the most part international affiliation with the unions in the United States. During 1903 it was estimated that there were between 1,500 and 1,600 local labor organizations in Canada. Unemployment on any noticeable scale has been practically unknown in the manufacturing industries in Canada since the industrial depression in the '70s, and at the rate at which manufacturing development has been proceeding, is unlikely that the large demand for labor will cease for some time to come. On the other hand, the favorable condition of the labor market to employers is reflected by the comparatively small number of strikes and lockouts arising throughout the year, and the fact that in many industries, notwithstanding that wages have shown a tendency to increase, profits have been such as to attract a rapidly increasing amount of capital. During the three years 1901, 1902, and 1903, there was an average of only 130 strikes a year in all the trades and industries throughout the Dominion, and of this number only one half were connected with manufacturing establishments.

A comparison of the figures given in the returns of the census for the year 1901 (*) and the returns of previous censuses will indicate the great development which has taken place in manufacturing in Canada during recent years, as well as the nature of the chief manufactures.

It is estimated that in 1891(†) there were in manufacturing establishments employing five hands or over, in all, 272,033 employees. In 1901 this number had increased to 344,095. The amount paid in yearly wages in 1891 was $79,234,311. In 1901 it had increased to $113,283,146. According to the first Dominion census, which was taken in 1871, there were in that year employed altogether in manufacturing establishments in the Dominion 187,942 persons; the amount paid in wages was $40,851,009. These figures would indicate that the total number of persons employed in manufacturing in Canada has almost doubled during the past 30 years, while the amount paid in wages has nearly trebled in the same time.

Equally interesting by way of comparison are the figures which show the total value of articles manufactured. According to the returns of 1891 the value of the articles manufactured in establishments employing five hands and over was $368,696,723. This amount had increased to $481,053,375 in 1901. Compared with the total value of articles manufactured in 1871, which is estimated at $221,617,773, it will be seen that the total value of articles manufactured has more than doubled in 30 years.

According to the original figures of the census of 1891, in which account was taken of all kinds of manufactures, no matter how few persons were employed, the estimate given of the amount of capital invested in manufactures in Canada is $354,620,750. In the census of 1901, which relates exclusively to establishments employing five hands or over, the estimated capital invested is placed at $446,916,487. In the

*The figures made use of in these comparisons are taken from the tables of the 1901 Census, the compilation of which has just been completed. The figures have not, as yet, been published.
†The figures quoted for 1891 are the figures of the Census of that year as revised for comparison with the 1901 Census, a different basis of calculation having been employed in previous years. The Census of 1901 took account only of establishments employing 5 hands and over.

1. Lord Mount Stephen   3. Sir William Van Horne   5. Sir Thomas Shaughness)
2. Sir George A. Drummond   4. Lord Strathcona, and   6. Charles M. Hays
                      Mount Royal

census of 1871 the amount of capital invested in manufactures is placed at $77,964,020. A comparison between the years 1871 and 1901 indicate that the capital invested in manufactures in Canada has increased between five-and six-fold during the period of 30 years.

The following table gives the development during 10 years in the most important of Canada's industries:

INDUSTRY*	1891		1901	
	Establishments Number	Value of Products	Establishments Number	Value of Products
Agricultural implements	95	$ 7,252,005	114	$ 9,597,389
Boilers and engines	42	2,433,878	59	4,626,214
Boots and shoes	269	12,706,215	179	18,481,216
Bread, biscuits and confectionery	269	8,364,306	258	11,637,808
Brick, tile and pottery	524	3,852,021	573	3,299,917
Bridges, iron and steel	6	728,075	6	1,693,000
Butter and cheese	1,735	10,697,879	3,576	29,462,402
Carriages and wagons	367	5,942,559	349	6,650,912
Car works	18	9,450,525	33	11,500,816
Cement (Portland)	11	227,275	7	765,876
Cottons	23	8,741,724	20	12,033,052
Clothing, men's	1,373	18,669,652	735	8,775,439
†Clothing, men's (factory product)........	....	....	538	8,980,291
Clothing, women's	....	....	334	4,368,380
Clothing, women's (factory product).......	768	4,931,779	26	2,190,627
Electrical apparatus and supplies...........	13	801,752	25	3,032,252
Electric light and power..................	23	845,134	58	2,008,017
Evaporated fruits and vegetables	30	142,436	50	395,549
Fish, preserved	805	5,661,144	1,097	8,025,630
Flouring and grist mills	230	30,721,846	400	31,835,873
Foundry and machine shop products........	383	16,111,352	315	15,292,445
Fruit and vegetable canning..............	43	887,578	58	2,831,742
Furniture and upholstered goods	234	6,025,811	169	6,949,384
Harness and saddlery.....................	112	1,502,753	95	3,427,255
Hosiery and knit goods...................	51	1,747,785	52	3,857,519
Iron and steel products	23	4,356,730	29	6,912,457
Leather, tanned and finished	170	9,711,781	143	12,068,600
Liquors, distilled	8	2,199,600	9	1,620,418
Liquors, malt............................	100	5,484	96	6,204,250
Log products	2,148	46,774,896	2,075	50,805,084
Lumber products.........................	420	13,443,802	467	10,754,959
Oil	43	2,128,112	14	3,519,493
Paper	32	2,570,722	28	4,380,776
Patent medicines	14	421,100	35	1,350,993
Printing and bookbinding	66	1,966,653	84	2,748,356
Printing and publishing	349	7,671,310	419	10,319,241
Rubber goods	9	2,040,000	7	1,173,422
Ships and repairs	132	3,067,475	39	1,899,836
Slaughtering and meat markets............	62	5,264,143	57	22,217,984
Smelting	15	3,016,240	12	7,082,284
Soap	30	1,909,390	23	2,143,945
Sugar refining	7	11,627,100	4	12,595,000
Tobacco, chewing and smoking	31	2,347,651	22	6,469,961
Tobacco, cigars	93	3,280,114	138	5,332,151
Wood-pulp	23	1,053,842	25	4,246,781
Woolen goods	213	7,845,386	157	7,359,541

*Note—Figures supplied by Mr. A. Blue, census commissioner.
†Note—Factory and home product not distinguished in Census of 1891.

See CANADA — AGRICULTURE; CANADA — FISHERIES; CANADA — FORESTS AND LUMBER INDUSTRY; CANADA — MINERALS; CANADA — COMMERCE, TARIFFS, AND TRANSPORTATION; CANADA — RECIPROCITY BETWEEN CANADA AND THE UNITED STATES.

W. L. MACKENZIE KING,
Deputy Minister of Labor, Ottawa.

41. Canada — Commerce, Tariffs, and Transportation. In their earlier condition the various provinces of British North America, now forming the Dominion of Canada, were all alike subject to those general laws which embodied the principles, if not always the practice, of the British Colonial System. Owing, however, to variations in location, natural resources, and the character of the inhabitants, the commerce and tariffs of the various provinces were more or less adapted to their special conditions.

Before the conquest of Canada, the Maritime Provinces, under the general name of

Nova Scotia, were valued as a market for British goods and as a field for the furnishing of naval supplies, chiefly sailors, fish and timber. Nova Scotia's trade was almost entirely developed in connection with New England and the West Indies. Trade with French Canada was illegal on both sides, and for the most part unprofitable, except for furs in exchange for British manufactures. It was but natural, therefore, that, after the conquest of Canada and the independence of the United States, Nova Scotia should still continue to trade chiefly with the New England States and the West Indies, and only to a limited extent with Canada.

Owing to their extensive coast line and numerous harbors, New Brunswick being also well supplied with river navigation, the question of transportation was long a simple one for the Maritime Provinces. For Canada, the Saint Lawrence and its tributaries had always furnished the great highway of the country. But above Montreal the river was greatly obstructed by rapids, hence the trade to the West first developed along the easier Ottawa route, which passed by way of Lake Nipissing to the Georgian Bay. There it followed the sheltered northern channel and the Saint Mary River, with a portage at Sault Sainte Marie, up to Lake Superior, and on, by numerous lakes and streams, to the vast Indian country beyond.

The coming of the Loyalists, as the first

settlers in what is now the Province of Ontario, rendered necessary a regular traffic up the Saint Lawrence and along the lower lakes. From Montreal to Prescott and Kingston this traffic was carried on by means of various forms of large flat-bottomed boats, known as bateaux, which were towed up the rapids, later with the aid of horses. These bateaux brought up limited supplies of European imports, chiefly British goods, and took down the furs and, so far as their space would allow, the potash and flour of the Western settlements. The Revolutionary War had led to the building of the first British vessels on the Lakes. After the peace, several of these became trading vessels and others were built, the number steadily increasing with the growth of the Canadian and American settlements on either side of the Lakes. The presence of lake vessels diverted the greater part of the Indian trade from the northern to the southern route.

At first most of the surplus produce of the Western settlements found a ready local market in supplying the temporary needs of new settlers, and in furnishing provisions for the Indian posts and the British garrisons. With increasing crops, however, there soon arose a necessity for export, especially of such articles as wheat, flour, peas, salt meat, and various minor provisions. About the beginning of the 19th century the amount of provisions exported from western Canada was nearly equivalent to the amount purchased by the British Government for consumption at the garrisons and posts. In 1801 the total exports of Canada amounted to $4,800,000. This growing trade required a more extensive and economical means of conveyance than that afforded by the bateaux. A trade in staves and various forms of timber having developed about the same time, and being sent to market in the shape of rafts, these were utilized to convey such provisions as might suffer a little exposure. Large square scows were also built for the purpose of taking provisions to market in bulk.

As regards tariffs and trade regulations in the earlier Colonial period, nothing was left to the Provincial authorities; all was regulated by British statutes and administered by imperial officers. In the matter of taxation, after the American Revolution the British North American colonies had little to complain of, for instead of being taxed to assist Britain the British people were taxed to assist the colonies. In return for her freedom to determine the commercial policy of the colonies and to appoint their officials, Britain had to meet their deficits, besides furnishing the whole of the naval and military services.

The first important change in colonial commercial relations resulted from the recognition of the independence of the United States in 1783. Pitt and Shelburne had desired to continue practically the same commercial relations with the late colonies after the separation as had existed before it, considering that political independence did not alter the value of a profitable mutual trade. Technically, however, such a policy would do violence to the whole commercial and colonial system, including the Navigation Acts,—the system of "ships, colonies and commerce," upon which the whole British empire was supposed to rest—and this could not be permitted.

Canadians were for a long time too completely absorbed in questions connected with the control of their internal affairs to be much concerned with the fiscal policy of the country. Indeed they rather looked upon Britain's control of the fiscal policy as a means of obtaining increasing assistance from the mother country. The earlier tariffs were simple affairs, the revenue was derived chiefly from duties on spirituous liquors and the molasses from which rum was distilled. The sweeping prohibitions of the Navigation Acts simplified matters very much. There was no trouble with foreign European goods, because they were forbidden to be admitted to the colonies even in British ships, except when they had passed through British ports. It was in Britain, therefore, that the tariff dealt with them and qualified them for entrance to the colonies. In the matter of spirits and such things as were dealt with in colonial tariffs, a variety of preferential duties favored the more as against the less direct trade with Britain and the colonies. After the granting of representative legislatures in the colonies (1791 in Canada) they were permitted to impose customs duties on imports, for revenue purposes only. The right of disallowance exercised by the Crown prevented any unfavorable treatment of British goods.

By the Act of 1778 the British Parliament maintained and freely exercised the right to regulate, by tariff or other restrictions, the commerce of the colonies, but explicitly stated that all revenue incidentally obtained, after paying the expenses of its collection, should go to the treasury of the colony in which it was collected. There was thus a double jurisdiction in the matter of tariffs, the Imperial and the Colonial. But, so far as the colonial and imperial tariffs covered the same ground, only the colonial tariff was enforced. The imperial tariff applied only where its rate of duty exceeded that of the colonial. The colonial tariff was practically only for revenue purposes; the imperial tariff was entirely for the regulation of commerce in the interests of imperial trade.

The first legally recognized trade between the United States and Canada was provided for in the Quebec Ordinances of 1787-8, which permitted the free export of all goods except furs and peltries, and the import of all forms of timber and naval stores, all kinds of grain and other natural products, and settlers' effects. Rum, spirits and manufactured goods were entirely prohibited, but in 1790 pig iron was added to the list of permissible imports. Pitt's commercial treaty with the United States in 1794 greatly promoted trade between the British American provinces and that country. In this he partly realized his earlier idea of permitting a free mutual trade in all ordinary goods between the United States and the British colonies. But, in deference to the Navigation Acts, so far as the trade was conducted by sea it must be in British ships. A direct trade to the East Indies was also permitted to the United States, and later this led to several important relaxations of the British colonial policy.

The Canadian merchants at such western points as Kingston and Queenston (Niagara), sent their orders for British goods to their Montreal correspondents, who imported them from London, guaranteeing payment there, and forwarded them to the western centres, whence they were distributed to the local dealers in Canada and the United States. The same agents were employed in collecting and forwarding the western produce, consisting of grain, provisions, potash and staves, as well as some of the cash which the original settlers had carried with them to meet their first wants. By these means payments to the Montreal merchants were partly made, the balance being met chiefly by commissariat and other bills of the British Government, for supplies and salaries.

The United States was the first to interfere with the freedom of this trade, duties being imposed in 1801 in the interest of eastern American traders. However, custom houses did not flourish in the wilderness, and for many years trade with the United States was not greatly hampered by tariffs. In 1805 duties were imposed, in Lower Canada, on certain goods coming from the United States, but in practice this applied to the Lake Champlain route only.

The trade relations of the Maritime Provinces, as we have seen, were well established before the United States secured its independence, but, while the United States enjoyed great freedom of trade with all countries, the Maritime Provinces still remained under the close restrictions of the Navigation Acts and the Colonial System. Thus general merchandise, even British and East Indian goods, was cheaper in the United States than in the British American ports. As a natural result there was extensive smuggling along the coasts of Nova Scotia and New Brunswick, and especially among the islands of Passamaquoddy Bay. American vessels supplied the colonists with liquor, tea, tobacco, molasses and other East and West Indian produce, and the chief lines of European and American goods, and received in return furs, fish, lumber, grain, etc., which they carried to their own ports and to the West Indies. Thus the restrictions designed to give Britain a monopoly of the colonial trade and shipping worked to the opposite purpose. Plainly the system had either to be given up or enforced by quite drastic measures. On the death of Pitt the latter policy was adopted, beginning with the Orders in Council, which in turn induced the non-intercourse policy of the United States, and ultimately the war of 1812-15.

While disastrous to the West Indies and most injurious to great Britain, yet the troubles between Britain and the United States were immensely profitable, for the time being, to the British North American colonies. To insure the carrying of the West Indian supplies in British ships, American produce was collected in ports of the Maritime Provinces and Canada, where it might be taken by sea in either American or British vessels, by overland transport, or by inland navigation. This stimulated the trade and shipping of the Canadian and Maritime Provinces and enriched the colonial produce dealers. The ultimate benefit, however, of these and later abnormal conditions was more than doubtful. After the Peace of 1815, Canada suffered a severe reaction, emphasized by an unfortunate land and emigration policy.

The enormous preference in the British market on British North American timber, which had been built up during the Napoleonic wars, was retained and developed because it enriched British shipowners and timber merchants.

By the new Corn Law of 1815 a preference was granted to Canadian grain, but it was very uncertain in its operation, since the grain was not admitted at all until the price had risen to quite a high level, in the case of wheat to about $2.10 a bushel.

The international restrictions necessary to preserve a fair equality for British shipping, under the disadvantages of her Colonial System, involved further trouble with the United States. Britain admitted a reciprocal shipping trade between the home country and the United States, and between her colonial possessions and the United States in the inland waters of North America, but denied corresponding reciprocity by sea between the United States and her American colonial possessions. In 1818 the United States retaliated, and direct trade with the West Indies was again suspended. Halifax in Nova Scotia and Saint John in New Brunswick, were then made free ports for American vessels bringing certain lines of goods necessary for the suppy of the West Indies. In 1823 American vessels were admitted to the colonial trade generally for all direct dealings between the United States and the colonies. Once more the trade of the Saint Lawrence languished, and complaints poured in upon the home government.

In 1825 Mr. Huskisson, who had revived the policy of Pitt, sought to promote freer trade in America. But he found it impossible as yet to grant perfect reciprocity in shipping. Differential duties were imposed in favor of British shipping in the trade between the United States and the West Indies. The Americans applied the same differentials on their side, and there resulted another period of non-intercourse, from 1826 to 1831, with corresponding activity and prosperity for the Saint Lawrence route and the British North American ports. By admitting to the colonies provisions from the northern nations of Europe in their own ships, Huskisson managed to prevent the Americans from forcing his hand. They came to terms in 1831 and normal trade was once more resumed. But by this time the Colonial System was badly shattered, and almost the only thing left of the Navigation Acts was the British monopoly of the domestic shipping of the empire. The way was being gradually prepared for the final stroke of colonial economic emancipation.

In 1825 Huskisson weakened the corn laws by greatly increasing the preference on Canadian wheat. Regardless of the local price, Canadian wheat was to be admitted at a uniform duty of five shillings per quarter. For a time the exports of wheat were greatly stimulated, but the benefit was not permanent, and the cry for additional preferences was soon resumed.

The prosperous period of 1826-31, augmented by large expenditures on Canadian public works and an increased emigration, continued for a couple of years after the resumption of normal relations with the United States. But trade depression and political troubles brought Canada to a very low ebb in 1837-8. In 1840 the two Canadian provinces were united, their political freedom was greatly enlarged, and trade revived.

In 1843, after urgent petitions, which more or less coincided with the rising demand in Britain for free food, Canada obtained the ominously liberal concession of access to the British market, at the nominal rate of one shilling per quarter, for all the flour she could grind from her own, or imported American wheat, while the corn laws still stood against the rest of the world. Bad harvests and higher prices in Britain tended to enrich the Canadian merchants and millers, but precipitated the repeal of the corn laws, in 1846, and the adoption of a free trade policy generally.

Free trade carried with it important changes for Canadian commerce, tariffs, and transportation. The preference on Canadian grain had gone, and the preference on British North American timber soon followed. In 1847 Britain renounced the right to regulate Canadian trade, and in 1849, by the final repeal of the Navigation Acts, she gave up her monopoly of the domestic carrying trade of the empire. The general result was that the colonies were left to face the world on much the same terms as other countries. Though lacking in the experience which breeds prudence, those interests which had not been specially pampered entered upon their new career with much zest and enterprise, tending sometimes to rashness.

At this stage questions of transportation began to be of vital importance to Canada. After the war of 1812 attention had been directed to the necessity for improving the Saint Lawrence route between Montreal and the lakes. A canal to surmount the Lachine Rapids had long been talked of, even abortively attempted. Finally, in 1821, the work was seriously undertaken by the government of Lower Canada, and completed in 1825. This was the year of the opening of the Erie Canal, which, coming at the beginning of a decade of unusual expansion and prosperity for the lake regions, proved a phenomenal success, commercially and financially. This gave an immense impetus to canal building in Canada and the United States. Canals, instead of building public debts, were to abolish them and support States and provinces without taxation. See CANALS.

In 1824 the Welland Canal was undertaken by a joint stock company with a capital of only $150,000, mostly subscribed in the United States. After many vicissitudes and appeals for both imperial and provincial assistance, it was opened for traffic in 1832. The locks were of wood, 100 x 22 feet with 7 feet of water. However, neither the Lachine nor the Welland Canal could be of much more than local importance until the remaining Saint Lawrence rapids were surmounted. This task the Imperial Government was prevailed upon to undertake. But, in doing so, it disregarded all commercial considerations and followed a short-sighted but very round-about military idea. The Rideau Canal was the result, extending from Kingston to Ottawa, which was afterward connected with Montreal by improvements of the Ottawa River navigation. The locks as constructed were 134 x 33 feet with 5 feet of water. It was opened in 1832 and cost the Imperial Government about $4,000,000, or between six and seven times the original estimate. Though of necessity carrying considerable traffic, it soon proved that it was not to be a commercial success, since it could not compete with the Erie Canal and did not even supercede the bateaux on the Saint Lawrence. The Upper Canadian legislature determined to complete the Saint Lawrence system, and the Cornwall Canal was begun in 1834. But the financial crisis and political troubles of 1837 suspended operations.

The union of the provinces in 1841 brought with it an imperial guaranteed loan for $7,500,000, with which to complete the public works already planned and partly undertaken. The Welland Canal was taken over by the government and reconstructed. The new locks were 150 x 45 feet, with 9 feet of water, afterward increased to 10½ feet. These were smaller than the locks of the Cornwall Canal, which were 200 x 45 with 9 feet of water. The latter was opened in 1843. The Beauharnois and Williamsburg canals completed the Saint Lawrence system. They were built on the same scale as the Cornwall Canal, and the last lock was opened in 1847. The completing of these canals necessitated the enlargement of the Lachine on the same scale, which was completed in 1848. Thus, in 1849, after the expenditure of upward of $20,000,000, the new Canadian canal system was prepared to accommodate vessels drawing 9 feet of water, and Canada expected to realize her eagerly awaited control of the growing traffic of the great basin of the lakes.

But many changes in commerce and transportation had taken place between the opening of the Erie Canal and the opening of the Saint Lawrence system. The British protective and colonial system had been abandoned, and grain from the ports of the United States entered Britain as freely as from those of Canada. Moreover, railways were transforming the carrying trade, making time and continuous service essential features in commerce. While the Canadians were preparing their canals to capture the American carrying trade of the West, the American government was induced, in 1846, to establish the drawback or bonding system. This enabled the American railroads and other transportation companies to make a successful bid for a large share of the western Canadian carrying trade to Atlantic ports. Finally, though after 1849 western produce could be landed at Canadian seaports much more cheaply than at American ports, yet this advantage was lost through higher ocean freights and higher insurance from Canadian ports. The total suspension of shipping for half the year also discounted the natural advantages of the Canadian route, especially in competition with the railroads.

Nothing daunted, the Canadians with their new energy and self-reliance grappled with the changed conditions. On the one hand the government undertook the improvement of the navigation of the Saint Lawrence below Montreal, especially by deepening the channel of the river. The depth of 11½ feet at the time was increased to 18½ by 1860, and has since been increased to 27½ feet as far as Montreal. The navigation of the gulf was also improved.

About 1850 the ocean steamer was rapidly replacing the sailing vessel. The Cunard line of steamers, running to New York and Boston, was subsidized by the British government, doubtless a profitable venture for Britain, but appearing to Canadians as an additional handicap for the Saint Lawrence route. Canada was constrained to subsidize a line of its own, — the Allan — for weekly service, at an annual cost to the country of $225,000.

The American boom in railroad building, starting from 1849, convinced the Canadians that they, too, must have railroads to supplement their canals. They desired independent winter outlets on the Atlantic, and connection with American markets to which the attention of Canada was now turning. While absorbed in their canals the Canadians had given little practical attention to railroads. Hence, before 1840 only 16 miles of railroad had been built, connecting Montreal with Saint John's on the Champlain route to New York. Much discussion took place and many charters were obtained during the forties, but little of a serious nature was attempted. In 1849 the Canadian government, chiefly under the influence of Mr. (afterward Sir) Francis Hincks, adopted a vigorous railroad policy by undertaking to guarantee 6 per cent interest on a sum not to exceed half the cost of any railroad of not less than 70 miles in length. Among the first lines to be undertaken was the Saint Lawrence & Atlantic, connecting Montreal with Portland, and opened in 1853. In western Canada the Northern railway, from Toronto to Collingwood, was the first to be built, being begun in 1850 and opened in 1853. The Great Western railway, between Niagara and Detroit, was the next to be undertaken, and was opened in 1854. Under the fostering direction of Mr. Hincks, the Grand Trunk railroad was chartered in 1852, as the great central line of Canada. In 1853 it leased the Saint Lawrence & Atlantic, and when, in 1856, the main line was opened from Toronto to Montreal, the chief commercial districts of Canada were connected with the Atlantic by a Canadian line.

The railroad boom lasted from 1849 to 1857, involving an immense outlay of capital, chiefly British. Both the central government and the municipalities were deeply pledged in support of the numerous lines undertaken. The crisis of 1857 brought the movement to a close, and the pecuniary embarrassments of most of the lines effectively discouraged further railroad enterprises for the next 10 years. In Nova Scotia and New Brunswick large projects were also afoot to connect Halifax and Saint John with the New England States, and also with Canada. But, beyond small sections of these plans, chiefly for local traffic, little was accomplished before Confederation. The general situation is reflected in the following figures. In 1840 there were in the British North American Provinces 16 miles of railroad; in 1850, 66 miles; in 1860, 2,065 miles, and in 1870, 2,617 miles.

With regard to tariffs, the central feature of the period between 1850 and Confederation, in 1867, was the Reciprocity Treaty with the United States, signed in 1854 and abrogated in 1866. It established reciprocal free trade between the British North American Provinces and the United States, in all natural products. This secured free entry to the United States for practically everything which the British provinces had to sell. (See CANADA — RECIPROCITY WITH THE UNITED STATES.) The special attraction for the United States was the freedom of access to the Canadian fisheries (q.v.); though the Americans also enjoyed large local markets for agricultural products, in many parts of the eastern provinces. According to the statistics of trade, Canada appeared to have the best of the bargain. But the statistics require interpretation. Much of the Canadian export to the United States was really only a transit trade; either the same goods, or their equivalent,

being shipped from Atlantic ports. Again, between 1854 and 1858 the decline in the amount of manufactures imported from the United States was due to the financial crisis of 1857 and the cessation of public works in Canada. Then, during the Civil War the United States was extensively purchasing supplies, and had little to sell. The Canadians themselves have been greatly deceived by the figures of the reciprocity period, and have imagined that a like result would flow from the renewal of reciprocal trade.

The other feature of importance in this period was the increase in the Canadian tariff on manufactured goods, in 1858 and 1859. Owing to the large public debt contracted for the building of the canals, the interest on which was not offset by tolls as expected, and, more immediately, owing to the great obligations incurred in guaranteeing railroad investments, the Canadian government was in great financial straits after 1856 and was therefore forced to seek a larger revenue. Accordingly, in 1858 the tariff on imports was raised, the general rate being increased from about 12½ to 15 per cent, and in 1859 it was still further increased to 20 per cent. The British merchants and manufacturers vigorously protested against such an increase of duties on the goods of the Mother Country, and the manufacturers of the United States considered the increase of duties a breach of faith, inasmuch as they had expected their advantage from reciprocity to come from the sale of manufactured goods. The Canadian government replied that its sole object was to relieve its obligations, not to check imports.

The abrogation of the Reciprocity Treaty in 1866 produced a strong effect upon the British North American Provinces and undoubtedly precipitated Confederation. The Canadian tariff of 1866 was lowered to a 15 per cent standard, as a concession to the freer trade leanings of the Maritime Provinces, and became the first tariff of the Canadian Dominion. Canada retained the general principles of a tariff for revenue until, in common with other countries, she suffered from the world-wide depression of 1875-8. An effort was made to secure the renewal of the Reciprocity Treaty. This failed, however, and a change of government took place on a promise of relief by means of a protective tariff. This new tariff of 1879 raised the general standard of duties from 17½ to 20 per cent. Times revived throughout the world and the relief promised actually came. The tariff, however, did not prevent the country from suffering with all others during the next period of depression, from 1884 to 1886, though the tariff had been raised somewhat in the interval. Nor did the country escape during the next depression, from 1894-6, when another change of government took place after a general election. The Liberal party, being more or less pledged to a reduction of duties, found it more difficult to accomplish than to promise. In 1897, however, the tariff was considerably amended in the interest of the consumer, and the happy expedient was devised of offering to the world at large a reduction of 25 per cent on the general tariff, wherever Canada was treated with equal favor. As Britain was practically the only important country fulfilling these universal conditions, the policy which was entered upon as a redemption of the party pledge ended in the preferential treatment of

British goods only. This limitation was explicitly recognized in 1900, when the preference on British imports was increased to 33⅓ per cent. Since, for various reasons, Canadian imports from Britain were declining, relatively at least, this concession did not adversely affect important Canadian industries except in the department of textiles. Accordingly in 1904 this part of the preferential tariff has been amended and the duties raised. At the same time a new principle of maximum and minimum tariffs has been outlined for the future.

As a condition of Confederation, in the East, the Intercolonial railway, connecting the Maritime Provinces with Canada, was constructed by the government at a cost of upward of $20,000,000. A corresponding condition of western federation was the construction of a transcontinental line to British Columbia. This was ultimately realized in the Canadian Pacific railway, begun in 1881 and completed in 1885 at a cost to the country of $62,000,000 in cash and 25,000,000 acres of land.

Confederation also directed attention to the renewed importance of the Saint Lawrence route and the economy of large vessels for the carrying trade. It was determined to enlarge and deepen the canal system. The new movement was once more begun at Cornwall, in 1876. The dimensions of the new locks were 270 x 45 feet with 14 feet of water. The other canals were enlarged or quite new ones constructed on at least the same scale. The Soulanges Canal, the last to be built, has locks of 280 x 45 feet with 15 feet of water. In 1895 a Canadian canal at Sault Ste. Marie was opened with one lock of 900 x 60 feet and with 20 feet of water. There is now, therefore, a continuous waterway with a minimum depth of 14 feet from Lake Superior to the sea. It is not yet possible to say what the full effect of this will be on the carrying trade of the lakes, but much more grain is already following the Saint Lawrence route.

Meantime, railroads have been steadily expanding into the newer regions of the West and North, for now, as a rule, the railroad precedes regular settlement. The tendency to multiply independent lines, in steam railroads at least, has almost ceased, while the smaller roads are being consolidated into a few large systems, of which the Canadian Pacific railway and the Grand Trunk railway are the chief. Following modern American developments the railroad companies show a tendency to acquire lines of steamships connecting with their ocean terminals, the Canadian Pacific railway being the pioneer in this respect. Since 1870 the mileage of the railroads has increased as follows: 1870, 2,617; 1880, 6,858; 1890, 13,151; 1900, 17,657; and in 1904 nearly 19,000 miles. In the near future the mileage will be greatly increased, since the Dominion government has entered into an agreement with the Grand Trunk Pacific Company to construct another transcontinental line. This will extend from Monckton, N. B., through Quebec to Winnipeg, by a more northerly route than that of the present lines, and on, by the Saskatchewan Valley and Edmonton, through Northern British Columbia to the Pacific. This will involve new branch and connecting lines. Already, Canada as a nation has spent about $80,000,000 on her canals and has contributed, in construction and subsidies for railroads, $178,-022,186 of Dominion money, while the provincial governments and municipalities have aided to the extent of $36,554,792, and $18,662,897, respectively.

That Canada has now begun to reap the benefit of these large outlays, which constitute the bulk of her national debt, is evident. For five or six years after Confederation, Canadian trade rapidly expanded, rising from $131,027,000 in 1868 to $217,801,000 in 1873. But it did not attain to these dimensions again before 1890. After rising and falling somewhat until 1896, it began to rapidly expand and in 1903 had risen to $467,064,685, having more than doubled in eight years.

The most noteworthy feature of Canadian foreign trade is that it has always been confined chiefly to two countries, Great Britain and the United States. Canada exports chiefly to Great Britain and imports chiefly from the United States. However, the expansion of exports to Britain is to some extent due directly or indirectly to the expansion of imports from the United States. In 1902, of the total imports, 58.4 per cent came from the United States and 24.9 per cent from Great Britain, leaving only 16.6 per cent to be obtained from all other countries, within or without the British Empire. Of the exports, 33.1 per cent went to the United States and 55.8 per cent went to Great Britain, leaving only 11 per cent for all other countries. Of the free imports to Canada, over 70 per cent come from the United States, while, taking one year with another, nearly one half of the whole imports from the United States are free goods. Practically all of the free goods from the United States are essential to Canadian trade and industry. But a very considerable proportion of the dutiable goods from the United States are likewise employed as raw materials or instruments in Canadian industry. As Britain and the United States are the chief markets for the most rapidly expanding sections of Canadian industry — agricultural and mineral — there is no immediate prospect of a change in the direction of the main volume of Canadian trade. See CANADA — AGRICULTURE OF; CANADA — FISHERIES OF; CANADA — LUMBER INDUSTRY; CANADA — MANUFACTURES OF.   ADAM SHORTT, *Professor of Economics and Politics, Queen's University, Kingston.*

42. Canada — Financial System. The first banking establishment in Canada was a private bank founded in Montreal in 1792, under the name of the Canada Banking Company, and evidently intended to be modeled after the English private banks. It opened for business and issued notes, but its life was very short. In 1807-8 an unsuccessful attempt was made to obtain from the Legislature of Lower Canada a charter for the Bank of Canada, which would have been a semi-government bank, resembling in many respects the first Bank of the United States, though naturally on a much smaller scale. In 1817 the "Montreal Bank" began business in Montreal as a private partnership, this being the origin of the Bank of Montreal, which was for many years, and still in some respects remains, the most important bank on the continent, while from its "Articles of Association" there has been developed, with steady continuity, the scientific system of banking law which exists in Canada to-day. In the following year two similar associations — the Quebec Bank and the Bank of Canada — were formed, on almost identical lines, and in 1822 all three obtained legislative Charters of Incorporation, valid for ten years, which followed the Articles of Association in almost every important particular. They differed very considerably, however, from the abortive bill of 1808. Framed to give legal recognition to associations of merchants already actively engaged in commercial banking, they were throughout designed to meet ordinary commercial requirements, and although they are perhaps more remarkable for what they omitted than for what they included, most of their provisions were sound. They confined the bank's business to legitimate lines, they prohibited lending upon pledge of goods or upon mortgage, or dealing in real estate, and they provided that all notes issued were to be redeemable on demand in specie. Power to open branches was not expressly given, but as it was not denied, its existence was assumed, and the banks did, as a matter of fact, open branches or agencies in both Lower and Upper Canada. The English private banks and the Scottish chartered banks were the joint parents of these Lower Canadian charters, and of the Canadian banking system which has sprung from them, but various changes and additions were made to suit Canadian requirements. In the phraseology used, as well as in some of the internal regulations, the influence of the chartered banks in the United States may be seen, but it may safely be said that practically everything which has proved of permanent value was derived from English, Scotch or native sources.

In Upper Canada the earliest banking legislation was on political, rather than commercial lines, and the first charter, that of the Bank of Upper Canada, granted in 1821-2, followed the Lower Canadian bill of 1808 rather than the Articles of Association of the «Montreal Bank.» The plan as first adopted was not sound, and as it had little permanent influence upon later legislation no description of it is necessary. The Imperial authorities, by pressure persistently exerted, succeeded in securing the adoption of two important amendments which are still part of Canadian banking law. In 1832 banks were prohibited from holding, or lending on, their own stock, while in the charter of the Gore Bank, granted in 1835, it was provided that the shareholders should be individually liable for the debts of the bank to an amount equal to their respective holdings of subscribed stock. The prohibition of the lending of money on mortgage, which from the first had been embodied in Lower Canadian charters, was never adopted in Upper Canada, although strongly urged by the Colonial office.

The Union of the two Canadas took place in 1840, and at its first session in 1841 the legislature of the Province of Canada adopted the report of a Select Committee, favoring a uniform system of banking, and approving a number of important regulations emanating from the Colonial Office, some of which already existed in individual charters. All notes were to be payable on demand in specie, they were not to be issued to an amount exceeding the bank's paid up capital, and suspension of specie payments for a given number of days (not in any case exceeding sixty) either consecutively, or at

intervals within any one year, was to forfeit the charter. The bank was not to hold its own stock, or to make advances against it, nor was it to lend money on security of lands or houses, or ships, or on pledge of merchandise. These and a few less important regulations were incorporated in every new and renewal bank charter thereafter granted, the double liability clause was made applicable to every bank, and one bank was prohibited from holding stock in another, except such as might be taken for *bona fide* debts, contracted in the usual course of business. In this Act we have the first attempt to deal with banking in a systematic way and to lay down general rules to which all banks must conform.

Only a passing mention need be made of the free banking law which, avowedly an imitation of the free banking laws of the State of New York, was passed in 1850. By 1854 its failure was evident, the free banks gradually died out or obtained charters, and the Act was repealed in 1866. The only vestige of it now to be found is the provision, revived in the Dominion Act of 1880, that notes issued by a bank should be the first charge upon its assets.

Up to 1859 banks had been prohibited from lending money upon the pledge of goods, but in that year an Act was passed authorizing a bank to take bills of lading, warehouse receipts, etc., as collateral security for the payment of any bill or note discounted by it, providing the security was taken at the time the bill was negotiated.

Little need be said as to the banking history of the other Provinces. The charters in the Maritime Provinces were very similar to those of Lower Canada, Manitoba had no existence as a Province before it joined the Confederation, while British Columbia had passed no banking legislation, its only bank having been incorporated under an Imperial charter, which has now been surrendered.

Ever since Confederation in 1867, all right to legislate regarding banking has been vested in the Federal Government. The first important act passed after that date was that of 1871, which embodied all the provisions of any charter or general act then in force which it seemed desirable to perpetuate, making them applicable immediately to all new banks, and to all the then existing banks as soon as their respective charters expired. A few small banks in the Maritime Provinces continued for several years under their old charters, the last one coming under the operation of the Act on 1 March 1892. While each bank retained the necessarily individual features of its own charter — those relating to its name, capital, chief place of business, etc., — and while it still remained necessary for every new bank to obtain a special act of incorporation (which it could do as a matter of course during any session of Parliament, if it conformed to the prescribed conditions) the new Act made all other regulations uniform, with some unimportant exceptions in the case of the Bank of British North America, which was incorporated under an Imperial charter, and La Banque du Peuple, which has since passed out of existence. Except for fixing a minimum subscribed and paid up capital for every new bank, and for the express right given to a bank to make advances on the stock of other banks (a most objectionable enactment, repealed in 1879) no new features which call for extended notice were introduced. It provided that no bank obtaining a new or renewal charter should issue notes of less than $4 each, and that every bank should

bankers in Canada, and their operations are on quite a small scale.

The following tables give the principal items in the combined balance sheets of the banks at different dates since Confederation:

(ooo omitted)						Liabilities (ooo omitted)			Assets (ooo omitted)			
Dec. 31	No. of banks	No. of br'ch's (a)	Paid up capital	Surp's	Av'r'ge capital per b'k	Notes issued	Deposits	Total Liabilities	Specie & Dominion notes	Securit's	Loans & disc'nts	Total Assets
1870....	(b)20	(g)	$33,449	(g)	$1,672	$18,526	$ 52,056	$ 72,494	$14,018	(e) $4,847	$ 78,064	$110,973
1880....	(c)36	(g)	59,819	(g)	1,661	27,328	90,387	121,471	16,485	(e) 2,687	124,869	192,537
1890....	(d)38	(g)	60,057	$21,940	1,580	35,006	139,701	178,826	16,328	(e) 8,603	202,056	260,137
1900....	36	(g)	67,087	34,501	1,863	50,758	325,824	392,150	31,558	50,248	362,043	501,542
1901....	34	740	67,591	37,364	1,988	54,372	374,781	449,091	32,976	56,290	410,130	562,077
1902....	35	897	72,795	44,517	2,079	60,574	416,926	499,508	37,622	61,259	458,087	625,388
1903....	33	1,048	78,563	50,598	2,380	62,539	442,171	525,924	47,042	63,590	481,992	663,145

(a) Does not include branches outside Canada, now about 23 in number.
(b) Five other small banks not reporting.
(c) Eight other small banks not reporting.
(d) Two other small banks not reporting.
(e) Government securities only.
(g) Exact figures not available.
The dividends paid vary from 5 to 12 per cent, the average rate being about eight.

hold as nearly as practicable one-half, and never less than one-third, of its cash reserves in Dominion notes, but the importance of the Act rests on the fact that it established the uniformity of the banking system which now prevails throughout the length and breadth of Canada.

Space will not permit of the subsequent development being traced in detail; it may be noted, however, that in 1900 a charter was given to "The Canadian Bankers' Association," a voluntary association of which practically all the chartered banks were members. It was now incorporated, and given certain definite legal duties and powers. For the rest, it must suffice to describe the Canadian banking system as it now exists.

The Bank Act is really the charter of every bank; the Bank of Montreal with a paid up capital and surplus of $24,000,000, and the Saint Stephen's Bank, which has a paid up capital and surplus of only $245,000, have exactly similar rights, privileges and limitations. The present practice is to enact the Bank Act for ten years only, and in this way a periodical discussion of the whole theory and practice of banking is ensured. During the intervals, the banks, as a rule, have peace.

The minimum subscribed capital necessary before a new bank can begin business is $500,000, of which $250,000 must be actually paid up in cash. Those banks which are on a smaller scale were in existence before 1890, at which date the minimum of paid up capital was raised from $100,000 to $250,000. After the bank is in operation the shareholders may, by passing a by-law at a general meeting, and afterward obtaining the approval of the Treasury Board, increase or reduce the capital stock, but it must not be reduced below $250,000. Before a bank may begin business, it must obtain from the Treasury Board a certificate that it has complied with all the requirements of the law. The Treasury Board is the financial committee of the Privy Council for Canada. No person or corporation may assume the title "bank," "banking company," "banking house," "banking association," or "banking institution" without being authorized to do so by the Bank Act or by some other Act. There are now very few private

The chief place of business of most of the banks is at either Montreal (q.v.), or Toronto (q.v.). The right to establish branches is specifically granted, and while two or three of the banks have not availed themselves of this right; most of them have numerous branches, several being represented in nearly every Canadian town of any importance. Two or three have branches or agencies in London and in some of the more important cities in the United States, as well as in Newfoundland and the West Indies. Those represented in New York are among the largest dealers in foreign exchange there. Each bank is administered by directors, not less than five nor more than ten in number, who are elected annually by the shareholders, each share carrying one vote. Directors must each hold paid up stock of from three to five thousand dollars, according to the total amount of the capital stock; the majority of them must be British subjects. A general meeting of shareholders must be held annually, at which the directors must submit a clear and full statement of the affairs of the bank. Detailed statements must be sent monthly to the Minister of Finance, by whom they are published in the 'Canada Gazette.' The Minister of Finance has power to call for special information from any bank. No system prevails either of audit by the shareholders or of examination by the Government, but the banks make a practice of having all their branches and departments inspected at least once a year by their own inspectors.

In the United States the bank's president is generally its chief executive officer, but in Canada this is not the case. British precedent is followed, and the bank is managed by a general manager, who accepts the fullest responsibility for the conduct of its business. The Board of Directors deliberate on all important transactions and all applications for large credits which have been approved by the general manager are submitted to them. The branch managers are responsible for the general business of their respective branches, and, as a rule, are allowed to use their own discretion in making advances up to certain amounts, varying according to the importance of the particular branch. Any loans applied for in excess of the limit fixed must be referred to the General Management at the Head Office.

By means of the branch system credit is distributed throughout the whole country; money borrowed from depositors in the rich but less progressive portions of Ontario may be lent out again in the newest parts of the Northwest, and interest tends toward a common level. The *average* rate obtained in Manitoba and the Northwest is only about 1 per cent more than in Ontario. The banks being large, and under no restrictions as to the amount which they may lend to any one customer, are able to supply the total needs of any person with whom they are willing to do business. They grant yearly credits, and practically undertake to supply their customers' wants up to the limit fixed at any time during the continuance of the credit. As a corollary to this they usually require that each customer shall borrow from only one bank.

No special percentage of cash reserves is required to be kept — in fact, the banks are not required by law to keep *any* cash or other reserves — but of whatever cash reserves are kept, at least 40 per cent must be in Dominion notes. Percentages of cash reserves to total liabilities to the public held by all banks on 31 December in each of the last five years are as follows:

(000 omitted)

Year	Specie	Domin'n Notes	Total	Perc'tage to liabilities to public
1903	$16,101	$30,941	$47,042	9.32
1902	12,892	24,730	37,622	7.87
1901	11,571	21,405	32,976	7.68
1900	11,773	19,785	31,558	8.38
1899	9,584	17,910	27,494	8.42

It must not be forgotten that the banks' cash reserves are only their first line of defense. Their real reserves are in the shape of call loans in New York against stocks and bonds, balances in the hands of their correspondents, and securities lodged with their agents in London and elsewhere, against which they are entitled to draw at any moment. New York and London are the final settlement points, and it is there that real strength is most necessary and most effective.

Clearing Houses exist at Montreal, Toronto, Halifax, St. John, Winnipeg, Vancouver, Victoria, Quebec, Ottawa, London (Ontario), and Hamilton. By local custom settlement of balances at the eight places first mentioned is made in Dominion notes; at the other points by drafts on Montreal or Toronto.

The total clearings during the last five years have been as follows: 1903, $2,690,000,000; 1902, $2,540,000,000; 1901, $1,871,000,000; 1900, $1,590,000,000; 1899, $1,626,000,000.

The bank may issue and re-issue notes of $5 and multiples thereof, but the total amount in circulation at any one time must not exceed its paid up capital. These notes must be redeemed in specie or Dominion notes on demand at the place of issue, and they must be accepted in payment at par at any office of the bank. Arrangements must be made under which they will circulate at par in every part of the country, and for this purpose the bank must establish agencies for their redemption and payment at Halifax, St. John, Charlottetown, Montreal, Toronto, Winnipeg and Victoria, and at such other places as are from time to time designated by the Treasury Board. The right to issue notes intended for circulation is confined to the chartered banks. Very heavy fines are imposed in the case of over-issue, these fines varying from the amount of the excess circulation, if the excess is under $1,000, up to $100,000, if the excess should be $200,000 or over. The notes issued by a bank are a first charge upon all its assets, but they are not specially secured by a deposit of bonds or cash, except by the "Bank Circulation Redemption Fund," to which all the banks have contributed 5 per cent on their average circulation, and which is held by the Government for the purpose of redeeming with interest at 5 per cent any notes of a suspended bank which the bank or its liquidator is not ready to redeem within two months after the date of suspension. The result of this is that the other banks readily accept at par the notes of a suspended bank, the notes remaining in their hands earning interest at 5 per cent until they are redeemed. As the banks are obliged to replenish the Redemption Fund gradually if it ever becomes depleted, they are all practically guaranteeing the notes of each. The amount at credit of this fund on 30 April 1904 was $3,130,844, bearing interest at 3 per cent. No call has yet been made on it. The Canadian Bankers' Association has power to supervise and control all details connected with the issue of notes.

The bank's unissued notes cost it nothing, except for paper and printing, and it is thus enabled to keep at each of its branches a sufficient supply of currency for ordinary requirements, without any loss of interest except on a trifling amount of change-making currency. This has an important bearing upon the cost of establishing and conducting small branches. As the note issue is a source of profit, each bank pays out only its own notes and sends in for redemption the notes of other banks which it receives. Daily exchanges are made at every point where two or more banks are represented, each bank sending in to the other all the notes issued by the other bank which it received the previous day. The resulting balances are settled at the smaller places by drafts on the Clearing House centres. In this way an automatically elastic currency is obtained, and the banks are enabled, up to the extreme limit of their issuing power, to meet the annual demand for currency to "move the crops"—a demand which in an agricultural country like Canada is very urgent—while at the same time the daily redemption provides that the extra supply of notes will be forced out of circulation as soon as the need for them has passed. The elasticity of the note issue is shown by the following table:

TOTAL NOTE ISSUE OF THE CHARTERED BANKS.

Year	Lowest point reached		Highest point reached		Percentage of increase
	Amount (000 omitted)	Date	Amount (000 omitted)	Date	
1903	$55,040	January	$70,480	October	28.05
1902	48,586	January	65,928	October	35.69
1901	45,025	January	57,954	October	28.71
1900	41,320	January	53,198	October	28.75
1899	36,916	January	49,588	October	34.33

The merits of the Canadian bank note may be thus summed up: First, it is safe; nothing but national insolvency could make its ultimate redemption doubtful. Second, it is redeemable on demand in specie or Dominion notes; if suspension of payment occurs, the note bears interest at 5 per cent. until it is redeemed, and if not redeemed by the bank within two months, it will be paid out of the Redemption Fund. Third, it passes at par from one end of Canada to the other. Fourth, the amount in circulation is always the exact amount demanded by the industrial activity of the country.

The bank is obliged to confine its business within the limits which are almost universally assigned to the banker. Speaking generally, it may not deal in merchandise, or be engaged in any trade; it may not lend money upon the security of goods, or ships, or land and other immovable property, nor may it advance against its own stock, or the stock of any other bank. It may, however, under certain conditions, lend money to wholesale manufacturers, and to wholesale purchasers, shippers of or dealers in various products, on the security of the goods they manufacture or deal in, and it may lend to any person on the security of a bill of lading or of a warehouse receipt. It may also lend money on the security of standing timber, and may make advances for shipbuilding, taking security on the ship. As additional collateral to a debt already contracted it may take security of almost any kind, and it has a first lien on its own stock for any liability due to it by a stockholder. It cannot recover by process of law any interest in excess of 7 per cent, but no penalties for usury now exist.

In addition to carrying on the ordinary business of a commercial bank, the Canadian banks receive money on deposit at interest, the prevailing rate at present being 3 per cent. Out of total deposits in the Canadian chartered banks of $448,000,000 about 65 or 70 per cent would in the United States be deposits in Savings Banks. No securities are specially set aside against any deposits. Deposits due to the Dominion Government are a second charge on all the assets of the bank (the notes being the first) and those due to any Provincial Government are a third charge.

One bank may sell out all its assets to another bank, proper provision being made for the assumption of the liabilities of the selling bank. The purchase price may be in stock of the purchasing bank, or in such other form as may be arranged.

In the event of a bank suspending payment, it is taken in charge by a curator appointed by the Canadian Bankers' Association, who will control and supervise it until it either resumes payment or goes into liquidation. Suspension for ninety days, consecutively or at intervals within twelve consecutive months, constitutes the bank insolvent. If it becomes insolvent the shareholders are each individually liable for an amount equal to the amount of their respective holdings of subscribed stock in addition to any amount not paid up on such stock. This double liability does not exist in the case of the Bank of British North America, and its ordinary note issue is therefore confined to 75 per cent of its paid-up capital. Against any portion of the other 25 per cent which it may desire to issue,

it must make a special deposit with the government.

The giving of a fraudulent preference to any creditor, or the making of false returns, etc., on the part of any director or officer of a bank, is punishable by heavy fines or by terms of imprisonment.

Since Confederation sixteen banks working under Federal laws have gone into liquidation, their paid up capital at the time of suspension aggregating some $9,000,000 and their total liabilities about $25,000,000. Eight paid both noteholders and depositors in full, six paid noteholders in full, but not depositors, while two paid neither in full. Both of the last two failed before notes were made a first charge on assets, while one of them was a fraudulent affair, which was only in operation for a few months. The total liabilities of these two banks were only $654,000. The total loss to creditors of insolvent banks has been about $4,000,000.

No description of Canadian finances would be complete without some mention of Mortgage and Loan Companies, Public Savings Banks, and the incorporated Savings Banks, but a few lines only can be devoted to each. Mortgage and Loan Companies date from about 1845, and have played a not unimportant part in the development of Canada. Unlike the banks, they are not governed by one general Act, and whether they should be under the jurisdiction of the Federal or the Provincial Governments has not yet been decided. It has therefore come about that General Acts, and also Special Acts, have been passed both at Ottawa and in some of the Provincial Legislatures, and the Special Acts are not always in accord even with the General Acts passed by the same authority. Three or four companies owe their existence to Imperial legislation. The specific purpose, however, for which all these companies are supposed to be incorporated is the making of loans on real estate, and they are sometimes restricted to this class of security. In many cases they are also allowed to lend on the security of stocks, bonds, etc., and one or two charters give powers of *dealing in* such securities, but over 70 per cent of their total assets are loans on real estate. They are allowed to borrow from the public by taking deposits and by issuing debentures, about two thirds of the debenture issue being held outside Canada, principally in Scotland. The rate of interest paid varies, from about three and a half to four and a quarter per cent. The total amount which may be borrowed from the public is generally limited, and, as a rule, is made to bear some proportion to the paid up capital, or to the capital and cash combined, but no general principle exists. Until the last year or two the loan companies had an extremely good record, very few having failed and their creditors always having been paid in full. Recently, however, there have been one or two bad failures.

The following figures show the approximate extent of the operations of the loan companies during the last few years. In consequence, however, of there being no one authority which can compel uniform returns from all the companies, it is not pretended that they are complete.

Savings banks under the management of the Government are of two kinds: "Government Savings Banks," under the control of the Fi-

Year	(ooo omitted)			Liabilities (ooo omitted)			Assets (ooo omitted)		
	No. of Companies	Capital paid up	Surplus	Deposits	Debentures	Total liabilities	Current loans on real estate	Property owned	Total assets
1880	83	$24,496	$ 4,618	$11,714	$23,213	$39,404	$ 56,612	$15,848	$ 69,989
1890	76	34,659	9,801	17,894	53,424	77,270	118,119	31,610	122,887
1900	97	48,894	10,290	19,959	50,695	93,455	113,291	32,635	152,640
1901	98	50,383	10,708	20,756	51,763	97,432	112,686	29,221	158,523
1902	92	47,667	11,479	21,069	52,848	95,941	105,536	14,061	162,532

nance Department,» and «Post-office Savings Banks,» which are part of the post-office system. The former were in existence in the Maritime Provinces for several years previous to 1867 and were taken over by the Federal government when the provinces entered into Confederation. In British Columbia Savings Banks controlled by trustees existed before Confederation, and these banks were wound up and «Government Savings Banks» established in their stead. A Government Savings Bank was opened in Winnipeg in 1871 and another in Toronto in 1872. In 1888 there were 50 offices with 57,367 depositors having $20,682,025 to their credit, an average of $360 for each depositor. It has now been recognized that these banks are no longer necessary, and whenever the position of superintendent of any office becomes vacant, the deposits in that office are transferred to the Post-office Savings Bank. We accordingly find that on 30 June 1903 there were only 23 offices still open, with 46,615 depositors and a total of $16,515,802 on deposit, the average for each depositor being $354.

In 1868 the system of Post-office Savings Banks which had proved so successful in Great Britain was introduced into Canada, 81 offices being opened on 1 April in that year. On 30 June 1903, 934 offices were open, the total number of depositors being 167,023, having $44,255,327 to their credit, an average of $265 for each depositor. In order to give some practical effect to the theory that both kinds of Public Savings Banks are intended as safe places of deposit for the poor and ignorant, the net amount which may be received from any person during one year is $1,000, while the total amount which any depositor may have at his credit is $3,000. The rate of interest paid in both classes of savings banks was formerly 4 per cent, but on 1 Oct. 1889 it was reduced to 3½ per cent, and on 1 July 1897 to 3 per cent. There is, however, no justification for even 3 per cent being paid. Canada is now able to negotiate term loans (against which no reserves need be kept) at a net interest rate of about 2.86. By an Act passed in 1903 the Department of Finance is obliged to hold as reserves against Savings Banks deposits an amount in gold, or in gold and Canada securities guaranteed by the government of the United Kingdom, an amount equal to not less than 10 per cent of the deposits. When to the rate actually paid on these deposits is added cost of reserves and expense of management (from one fourth to one half of 1 per cent per annum), the money held on deposit actually costs the country about 3.75 per cent. This fact is fully recognized by the government, and they recently proposed to reduce the rate paid to 2½ per cent, but, for political reasons, the proposal was withdrawn. Amounts held on deposit by the government in certain years are as follows:

Year	Government savings bank	Post office savings bank	Total
1870	$ 1,822,570	$ 1,388,849	$ 3,411,419
1880	7,107,287	3,945,669	11,052,956
1890	19,021,812	21,990,653	41,012,465
1900	15,642,267	37,507,456	53,149,723
1901	16,098,146	39,950,813	56,048,959
1902	16,117,779	42,320,209	58,437,988
1903	16,515,802	44,255,327	60,771,129

Apart from the Public Savings Banks the only savings banks of any importance are the City and District Savings Bank of Montreal and La Caisse d'Economie de Notre Dame de Quebec. The former has a paid-up capital of $600,000, its deposits are about $16,000,000, it holds securities of about $8,000,000 and has loans against securities of about $7,000,000. The latter has a paid-up capital of $250,000, and deposits of about $7,000,000. It holds securities of about $4,000,000 and has loans of about $3,-000,000 against securities. These banks may invest not more than three fourths of their deposits in certain approved securities, including the stock of chartered banks, and may make advances against such securities. These are the only classes of investments which they may make. They are specially prohibited from lending on real estate.

It may be convenient to summarize here the approximate amount of public money held on deposit in Canada by the government and by the various institutions which accept deposits. Except in the case of the Mortgage and Loan Companies, the figures are as on 30 April 1904:

Government savings banks..............$ 16,291,400
Post-office savings banks.................. 44,393,438

Total held by government.............$ 60,684,838
Chartered banks —
Public deposits, payable on
demand $104,112,729
Public deposits, payable after
notice 301,044,721
                                    $405,157,450
Quebec savings banks —
Public deposits 23,056,357
Mortage and loan companies (1902) —
Deposits $21,069,000
Debentures 52,848,000
                                    $ 73,917,000
                                    $562,815,645

In addition, some deposits are held by private bankers. It is impossible to give an estimate of the amount, but it is quite inconsiderable. See CANADA — PUBLIC FINANCE; BANKS AND BANKING; FINANCE; MONEY.

Bibliography.— Articles of Association, Montreal Bank; Dominion and Provincial Statutes, including the earlier charters; Journals of Upper Canada; R. M. Breckenridge, 'The Canadian Banking System'; B. E. Walker, 'A History of Banking in Canada'; 'Banking in Canada'; Adam Shortt, 'The Early History of Canadian Banking'; Massey Morris, 'The Land Mortgage Companies, Government Savings Banks, and Private Bankers of Canada'; 'Journal of the Canadian Bankers' Association'; 'The Statistical Year Book of Canada.'

F. G. JEMMETT,
(Secretary, The Canadian Bank of Commerce.)

43. Canada — Public Finance. When the federation of provinces, forming the Dominion of Canada, was achieved in 1867 (see CANADA — CONFEDERATION) the powers assigned to the provincial governments included the right to borrow money on the sole credit of the province, and right of direct taxation within the province in order to the raising of a revenue for provincial purposes. The right of management and the sale of the public lands belonging to the province, and of the timber and wood thereon, was also assigned to provincial governments, and, as will be seen later, has proved an important source of revenue (cf. Brit. N. America, Act, Sec. 92). To the Dominion Parliament all powers not specifically reserved to the provinces were given, and particularly control of the public debt and property, the borrowing of money on the public credit, and the raising of money by any mode or system of taxation. Thus the rights of the provinces to levy taxation for their own purposes are restricted in the mode in which they may be exercised, and cannot be so employed as to exclude the Dominion government from the use of any form of taxation found desirable. All the ordinary revenue of the Dominion is credited to a consolidated revenue fund, and on this fund are chargeable: (1) The expenses of collecting the public revenues; (2) interest on the debts of the provinces which the Dominion assumed; (3) the salary of the governor-general; the remainder of the fund being available for covering such appropriations as may be made by Parliament. Thus all ordinary revenue and ordinary expenditure are included in the consolidated fund accounts, and any balance of available funds may be used for capital outlay in place of covering such outlay by extraordinary revenues, such as loans. The progress of the revenue and expenditure of the Dominion is exhibited in the following summary:

REVENUE AND EXPENDITURE OF CANADA.

FISCAL YEAR ENDING 30 JUNE	Consolidated fund		Total Revenue $,000	Total Disbursements $,000
	Revenue $,000	Expenditure $,000		
1868...........	13,688	13,486	13,688	14,072
1878...........	22,375	23,503	22,406	30,546
1888...........	35,908	36,718	35,908	45,064
1893...........	38,169	36,814	38,209	40,854
1898...........	40,555	38,833	40,556	45,334
1903...........	66,037	51,692	69,348	61,747

Of the 36 years since confederation, in only 12 has the consolidated fund revenue failed to exceed the expenditure chargeable to that fund, namely in the years 1875–6 to 1879–80, in 1884–5, 1885–6, 1887–8 and 1893–4 to 1896–7. The aggregate revenue of the consolidated fund has been

$1,186,500,000, and the expenditure chargeable on it $1,127,800,000, thus leaving a surplus of $58,700,000. Taking total revenue and total disbursements, the years 1870–1, 1881–2 and 1902–3 alone have shown surpluses. In addition, the expenditure of 1899–1900, apart from sinking-fund charges, showed a surplus, which, however, was barely one-third of the amount needed to meet the year's payments on account of sinking-funds. The aggregate deficit of the 36 years has been $238,976,000, and the amount of $53,098,000 has been paid to sinking funds and debt redemption in the period; so that the net outstanding debt has been increased by $185,878,000, or about 15 per cent of the ordinary revenue raised during the period. It may be noted that capital expenditure on railways and canals, during these 36 years, has amounted to over $188,000,000, or a sum exceeding the increase in the net debt. The chief source of the revenue of the Dominion is found in customs and excise duties. The progress of these items is exhibited in the following:

SOURCES OF REVENUE.

Fiscal year ending 30 June.	Customs $,000	Excise $,000	Total taxes $,000	Post office and public works, including railways and canals $,000	Various other sources $,000
1868	8,578	3,003	11,701	1,427	560
1878	12,783	4,859	17,842	3,242	1,291
1888	22,106	6,071	28,177	5,935	1,796
1893	20,954	8,367	29,321	6,535	2,312
1898	21,705	7,871	29,576	7,401	3,578
1903	37,002	12,014	49,016	11,486	5,535

The great growth of tax revenue, over the whole period, its stagnancy from about 1880 till 1898, and the rapid increase of recent years are noteworthy features of the tables of which the above is an abstract. Till the year 1881–2 the tax revenue included an item, derived from bill stamps, since discontinued. The revenue from the post office and from railways and canals is required to maintain the services rendered by these enterprises, so that the public receipts and expenditure are swelled by the inclusion of items approximately balancing each other on both sides of the account. The principal of the various sources of revenue covered by the last column of the table are Dominion lands and interest on investments. These two items comprised, in 1902–3, two-thirds of the amount shown in the last column of the table. The dependence of the public revenue on the productiveness of the customs and excise is seen to be very great. From these sources chiefly are derived the funds needed to carry on the government. The response of the volume of the revenue to changes in the tariff cannot be treated in this place. The influence of the wave of business activity, which has, since 1897, swelled in most countries, and especially in America, is the most important element contributing to the expansion of revenue since that date.

Among the heads of expenditure, the debt charges form the largest single item. At the date of the formation of the Dominion the provincial debts were transferred to the Dominion, equitable arrangements being made by which Nova Scotia and New Brunswick might be favored in a degree corresponding to that represented in the transfer of the debt of the old province of Canada to the Dominion. Subsequently to the date of federation, responsibility for, in round figures, $32,000,000 of provincial borrowings, additional to the $77,500,000 of debt taken over at that date, has been assumed by the Dominion. The annual charges on account of debt increased rapidly up till about 1885, approximately doubling in amount between 1867 and that date; since 1885 the aggregate increase has been only about 10 per cent. The contrast between the earlier and later halves of the interval since federation is very striking. It is only in part due to a slower increase of the amount of the debt. The lower rates at which borrowing has been effected, as old loans fell due for renewal, have been very helpful to Canadian finance. An increasingly large amount of revenue is required for sinking-fund purposes, though the increase has been slower, and less as a total, in the second than in the first half of the period since the formation of the Dominion. A sum equal to nearly one fourth of the annual interest is now needed for meeting sinking-fund obligations. More recent loans have not had definite sinking funds attached to them.

The principal items of ordinary expenditure in the year 1902–3 were as follows:

Interest on public debt....................$11,068,000
Sinking funds 2,621,000
Public works.............................. 4,628,000
Post-office 4,105,000
Railways and canals....................... 7,550,000
Collection of customs and excise.......... 1,708,000
Militia 1,963,000
Mounted police 990,000
Administration of justice................. 960,000
Civil government 1,555,000
Legislation 789,000
Mail subsidies and steamship subventions... 799,000
Subsidies to provinces.................... 4,402,000

This table includes items of smaller amount than some of those omitted. Those of greatest general importance are shown, and the table includes five sixths of the ordinary expenditure. This expenditure, which was about $4.00 per head of the population in 1867–8 reached about $9.40 per head in 1902–3. The last item in the preceding list represents a financial adjustment between the federating provinces and the federal government. The latter pays to the former an amount made up of two principal items, one an allowance for the expense of government, the other a payment based on population. The former allowances were fixed as follows: Ontario, $80,000 per annum; Quebec, $70,000; Nova Scotia, $60,000; New Brunswick, $50,000. The further annual grant in aid is at the rate of 80 cents per head of the population, as enumerated at the census of 1861 for Ontario and Quebec, and as enumerated at subsequent censuses for the other two provinces, until the number in each case reaches 400,000. New Brunswick has not yet reached this limit. Some additions to these subsidies and allowances have since been made, and the same general principle of computing the amount to be paid has been applied to other provinces as admitted to the Dominion. The allowances for government are: Manitoba, $50,000 per annum; British Columbia, $35,000; Prince Edward Island, $30,000. The latter three

provinces received additional allowances in lieu of lands, amounting to $100,000 per annum for each of the first two, and $45,000 for the last. Other adjustments have been effected from time to time, and the aggregate of subsidies, for 1902–3, amounted, as stated above, to $4,402,000, or about 85 cents per head of the present population of the provinces. The position of the provincial revenue and outlay, for the past quarter of a century, is shown, in summary form in the following table:

REVENUE AND EXPENDITURE OF THE PROVINCES.

AVERAGE OF FISCAL YEARS	Subsidies to provinces	Aggregate ordinary provincial	
		Revenue	Expenditure
1877–8 to 1881–2....	$3,466,587	$7,115,785	$7,882,388
1882–3 to 1886–7....	3,904,316	8,288,856	8,929,119
1887–8 to 1891–2....	3,996,907	10,472,029	11,303,506
1892–3 to 1896–7....	4,173,363	11,422,476	11,825,931
1897–8 to 1901–2....	4,278,264	13,247,135	13,668,388

It will be seen that the aggregate of the provincial subsidies has grown, roughly, in about the proportion of the population of the Dominion, and that, whereas, in the first period shown in the table, they formed nearly one half the revenue of the provinces, in the last period they fell short of one third of the provincial revenues. In the light of this fact, the agitation for an increase in these subsidies can be readily understood. It must be added that the wording of the contract which determined the amounts of the subsidies at federation is explicit, and expressly excludes future claims for increase. The fact of a deficit in the provincial accounts, taken in the aggregate, is clearly shown in the above table. So far as Ontario is concerned, this unfavorable balance appears only in the first two of the five periods of the table. Quebec had an unfavorable balance in each of the first four periods, a small favorable balance in the last. New Brunswick, too, had a favorable balance only in the last period, while Nova Scotia achieved a favorable balance in each of the last two periods. Manitoba and British Columbia fail throughout to cover ordinary outlay out of ordinary revenue, and the deficit of the Pacific province outweighs the surplus of the four provinces already named as having a surplus in the last of the quinquennial periods dealt with. The Prince Edward Island accounts show a small deficit in each period, but they include capital outlay except in the years 1899–1900 and 1900–1. In the case of British Columbia, the accounts exclude charges on account of ·sinking funds and debt redemption from ordinary expenditure, and the real situation is consequently even less favorable than that shown. It may be noted, however, that from one fifth to one fourth of the ordinary expenditure of British Columbia in recent years has been on roads, streets, bridges, and wharves. It is possible that the charging of the whole of this on current revenue may more or less offset the considerations which gave rise to the preceding reflection.

The accounts of the provinces are not all made up to the same date, and changes in the date at which the fiscal year ends have been made from time to time in some of them. Ontario, Manitoba, and Prince Edward Island make up their accounts for calendar years; Nova Scotia and British Columbia for a fiscal year ending 30 September. New Brunswick closes its financial year on 31 October, and Quebec on 30 June. The relative amounts of the budgets of the different provinces are shown in the following statement relating to financial years ending in 1902, the ordinary revenues and expenditures only being shown:

1901-2	Revenue		Expenditure	
	Amount	Per Head	Amount	Per Head
Ontario	$4,291,083	1.96	$4,345,004	1.98
Quebec	4,515,170	2.70	4,490,677	2.69
Nova Scotia...	1,140,217	2.47	1,087,403	2.36
New Brunswick	826,066	2.48	845,637	2.54
Manitoba	1,443,256	5.28	1,248,128	4.56
British Colum'a	1,807,925	9.38	2,537,374	13.17
P. E. Island...	324,670	3.17	324,185	3.16
Total	14,348,387	2.75	14,878,408	2.85

In view of repeated annual deficits on the ordinary budgets, as well as on account of capital outlay, the provincial debts have been substantially increased in the period covered by the statement given above. Between 1897 and 1902 the additions to debt exceeded 25 per cent of the ordinary revenue, taking all the provinces together. This mode of statement, however, obscures the actual fact, namely, that the chief increases of debt have been incurred by Manitoba and British Columbia, a fact entirely in accord with preceding statements as to the relation of revenue to outlay in the different provinces. The debt of Manitoba has been increased by nearly $11,000,000 in the five years, which has nearly trebled it. British Columbia has added about $4,000,000, or half the amount of the ordinary revenue of the period, to its debt. The differences in the mode of statement of accounts in the various provinces render summaries of outlay for special ends very difficult. On education, about $2,500,000 was expended by the provinces in 1901-2. It must be borne in mind that the principal expenditure on education is that of the municipalities, not that of the provinces. On the side of income, the leading item, exceeding in aggregate amount the subsidies from Dominion funds, is the revenue from leases and sales of lands, timber and mining rights. These receipts from the public domain amounted to over $4,600,000 in 1901-2. All the provinces, without exception, levy succession duties among the taxes levied. These inheritance taxes yielded revenues totaling a little over $600,000 in 1901-2. The taxation of corporations finds a place among the sources of revenue of most of the provinces, and so do license taxes on businesses of various kinds. British Columbia and Prince Edward Island make use of income taxes, and the former has taxes on real and personal property in operation in addition. Royalties on minerals and land taxes also find a place among the sources of provincial tax-revenue. No summary of municipal finance for the entire Dominion can be given. As an example of the comparative magnitude of provincial and municipal revenues and expenditures, the figures published for the province of Ontario may be quoted. The ordi-

nary revenue of municipalities of all grades in that province amounted in the aggregate to $17,200,000 in 1901, of which $13,600,000 was tax-revenue. The ordinary municipal revenue was thus, in this case, four times as great as the ordinary provincial revenue. In the course of the last 15 years the taxes imposed by municipalities for all purposes have increased in amount by 50 per cent. The principal mode employed in raising municipal revenue is to levy an assessment on the value of property, either real property, or all property, real and personal, while income is also made assessable with property in some cases. The municipalities of Ontario subject all these to assessment. The aggregate revenue of municipalities stated above includes $1,445,000 derived from water, gas, electric, etc., enterprises in 1901. As large expenditures were required for the provision of the corresponding services, this was not net revenue, available for general purposes. The municipalities have, in every year, contracted new loans, but the repayment of old loans has, in the aggregate, nearly offset the new borrowings. The aggregate debenture debt has increased, in the five years to 1901, by $7,600,000, while the borrowings on debentures have amounted to $20,600,000 in that period. Loans for current purposes have amounted to $28,-700,000 in these five years, but less than $1,400,-000 has been added to the amount of such loans outstanding. The total amount of debt, for all municipalities in the province, was about $59,500,000 of debenture debt and $7,200,000 of floating debt, in 1901. These few references to Ontario municipalities may serve to illustrate the subject of municipal finance in Canada generally, especially affording an example of the relative extent of taxation for public purposes by the municipal, provincial, and federal (Dominion) authorities.

In connection with the subject of Canadian public finance, it is of importance to note that the mode of preparation and discussion of financial legislation is practically that followed in Great Britain, and contrasts in many points, and in marked degree, with that followed in the United States (see UNITED STATES — FINANCES, 1775-89, 1789-1861, 1861-1904). The estimates of expenditure are prepared by the government departments concerned, and, when approved by the ministry, are considered by the House of Commons sitting as a committee of supply. The responsibility for the amount and distribution of expenditure thus rests, originally, with the executive government, and its proposals need the approval of, and are presented for discussion by, the body of popularly-elected representatives. Similarly, the plan of taxation (or borrowing) by means of which the necessary funds are to be secured is submitted to the House of Commons, sitting as a committee of ways and means. The entire House constitutes each of these two important financial committees. The responsibility for the two sides of the year's finance is not divided between differently constituted committees. The proposals by which financial equilibrium is to be maintained are the proposals of the ministry, put forward by the Finance Minister. The stability of the administration is involved in the production of a plan for the coming year's finance which shall be acceptable to the House of Commons. The consideration of the balance of revenue and expenditure is an essential feature involved in the presentation, at a definite period of the year, of a statement setting forth the expenditure proposed and the means by which it is intended to cover it. In Provincial, as well as in Dominion, finance, the same principles are applied, of the presentation of an annual balance-sheet of income and expenditure, and of ministerial responsibility for the financial scheme involved in that balance sheet. It may be added, in conclusion, that the Dominion of Canada is entirely autonomous in financial matters. It is true that a small subsidy is paid by the Imperial government in respect of Sable Island, that is, the outlay there is recouped, in view of its being for purposes non-Canadian. Apart from this insignificant item, the finance of the Dominion is not involved in any way with that of Great Britain. No subsidy is received by Canada, no contribution in money is made by Canada for Imperial purposes. The share of financial responsibility assumed by the Dominion government in connection with the Pacific cable is of an entirely different nature from such subsidies or contributions, though it may aid in effecting purposes which are sought by some through these financial expedients. See also CANADA — THE FINANCIAL SYSTEM; and the paragraph *Finances* in articles on the provinces.

ALFRED W. FLUX,
Professor of Political Economy, McGill University.

44. Canada—Currency, Coinage and Legal Tender. Interesting as it would be to trace the history of the currency and coinage of the various British provinces from the time when grain and furs were the actual currency, down through the card money of de Meulles, the *ordonnances* of Bigot and the Army Bills of 1812 to the present satisfactory system, such a task is quite impossible within the limits set for this article. "Broadly speaking," says Chalmers, "the currency history of Canada consists in the transition from the French *écu* to the silver Spanish dollar, and from the Spanish dollar to the gold dollar of the United States. But this transition has reference exclusively to the standard coin; the characteristic feature of Canadian currency, both in the 17th century and at the present day, is paper." During the French régime a special colonial coinage was struck in France, but until the period when the chartered banks began to provide a stable medium of exchange, we find a large proportion of the currency consisting of the gold and silver coins of various countries, passing current and made legal tender at rates which were changed from time to time in the hope of keeping coin within the country. British, French, Spanish, Portuguese, German, Mexican and American coins were all legal tender, while for the first 50 or 60 years after the British conquest the actual currency of old Canada consisted chiefly of Spanish silver and some British gold, together with paper, more or less doubtful in value, issued by merchants, private bankers and others.

By ordinance of 1777, followed up by Acts of the legislatures of Upper and Lower Canada in 1796, the Halifax currency, with the Spanish dollar valued at 5 shillings, or four to the pound currency, was made the standard of the country, and new rates were established at which differ-

ent coins should pass current. The British guinea, which appears to have been the gold coin most in use, was worth £1 3s. 4d. currency. The Halifax currency, it will be observed, was to sterling money in the proportion of 10 to 9, £10 currency being the equivalent of £9 sterling. In Lower Canada, however, accounts were for many years afterwards kept in livres and sols, 6 livres being equal to one Spanish dollar, while in Upper Canada the York (or New York) currency was more or less in use, its basis being the Mexican *real*, known in North America as the York shilling, eight of which went to the dollar. Its use, however, was prohibited after 1 July 1822. With many attempts at change, and with variations in the ratings of different coins from time to time, the Halifax currency, which, it must be remembered, was a money of account only, remained as the legal currency system until 1853, when a decimal system having as its unit a dollar equal in value to the American dollar was introduced, and placed on an equal footing with the Halifax currency. On 1 Jan. 1858, the decimal system was finally adopted as that in which all public accounts should be kept, and since that date Canadian currency has really been on a gold monometallic basis, with a unit of value equal to the gold dollar of the United States.

The first Act of the Dominion Parliament dealing with the standard of value and the metallic currency was passed in 1868. It declared that it was desirable that the currency of Canada should be assimilated to the basis agreed on at the monetary conference held in Paris earlier in the year, and also that it should be of the same value as the metallic currency of the United States. It provided, however, for the continued use of the old "pound currency" when this was desired. This Act was repealed by the Act of 1871, which established the metallic currency on its present basis, the extension of the system to the whole Dominion being effected in 1881. In 1886 a Consolidating Act was passed, which reads in part as follows:

> The denominations of money in the currency of Canada shall be dollars, cents and mills,—the cent being one hundredth part of a dollar, and the mill one tenth part of a cent.
> The currency of Canada shall be such, that the British sovereign of the weight and fineness now prescribed by the laws of the United Kingdom, shall be equal to and shall pass current for four dollars eighty-six cents and two-thirds of a cent of the currency of Canada, and the half sovereign of proportionate weight and like fineness, for one half the said sum.
> Any gold coins which Her Majesty causes to be struck for circulation in Canada, of the standard of fineness prescribed by law for the gold coins of the United Kingdom, and bearing the same proportion in weight to that of the British sovereign, which five dollars bear to four dollars eighty-six cents and two-thirds of a cent, shall pass current and be a legal tender in Canada for five dollars; and any multiples or divisions of such coin, which Her Majesty causes to be struck for like purposes, shall pass current and be a legal tender in Canada at rates proportionate to their intrinsic value respectively.

It will be observed that although the Canadian currency has a unit of value equivalent to that of the United States, the standard of value is the British sovereign.

Power was taken to make any foreign gold coins legal tender in Canada, and the American gold eagle of the weight and standard of fineness then existing, together with its multiples and halves, was made legal tender, each coin at its face value.

CANADA — CURRENCY, COINAGE AND LEGAL TENDER

The actual currency of the country consists almost entirely of paper (see BANKING SYSTEM), and as this has been found most satisfactory, no Canadian gold coinage has ever been struck. The silver and bronze coinage has hitherto been obtained through the royal mint, an arrangement which has proved most cheap and satisfactory. Influenced, however, by the large production of gold in the Yukon Territory, the government took authority during the session of 1901, with the concurrence of the Imperial government, to establish a branch of the royal mint at Ottawa, and as soon as this is in operation it is intended to inaugurate a Canadian gold coinage. However, no active steps toward the erection of the mint have yet been taken, and it is to be hoped that the proposal will.be allowed·to drop. Practically no gold is in circulation in Canada, all that there is in the country (about $37,000,000 or $40,000,000) being held as reserves by the Government and the banks. These stores are drawn upon for settlement of international balances, and for this purpose the British and American gold which is at present held is far more useful than any Canadian gold could be.

The subsidiary coins are five, ten, twenty-five and fifty-cent pieces, all silver, and one cent, bronze. These are tokens only, and the silver coins are legal tender up to ten dollars only, bronze up to one dollar. The total amount of silver coined and put into circulation in Canada since Confederation up to the end of 1903 is $9,795,000, and of bronze $449,000. None has ever been redeemed, and it is estimated that the amount now in circulation is from one half to one third of the total coined.

The history of the paper obligations of the Dominion Government really begins before Confederation, when in 1866 the Legislature of the Province of Canada sanctioned an issue of provincial notes to an amount not exceeding $8,000,000. At Confederation this issue (as well as a small issue of Nova Scotia) was assumed by the Dominion, and the "Dominion Note" system was thus inaugurated. In 1868 provision was made for securing the note issue up to $5,000,000 and 25 per cent of any excess by specie, the balance up to the limit of $8,000,000 to be covered by Provincial or Dominion debentures. In 1870 the issue limit was raised to $9,000,000, secured by 20 per cent of specie and 80 per cent of debentures, with authority to increase to any amount, providing the excess above $9,000,000 was covered by specie. In 1872 it was provided that only 35 per cent of this excess need be so covered, while in 1875 it was enacted that for any issue between $9,000,000 and $12,000,000 specie to the extent of 50 per cent must be held, any excess above $12,000,000 being entirely covered by specie. In 1880 the maximum issue was raised to $20,000,000, to be covered to the extent of at least 15 per cent by gold, an additional 10 per cent by gold or Dominion securities guaranteed by the Imperial Government, and the remaining 75 per cent by ordinary Dominion securities. The issue might exceed $20,000,000 to any extent, provided the whole of any excess was covered by gold.

The Act now in force was passed in 1903 and provides that:

Notes of the Dominion of Canada may be issued and outstanding at any time to any amount, and the notes issued and outstanding under the authority of this Act shall be known as "Dominion notes," and

shall be a legal tender in every part of Canada except at the offices at which they are redeemable. Such notes shall be redeemable in specie on presentation at branch offices established or at banks with which arrangements are made for the redemption thereof as hereinafter provided.

The Minister of Finance and Receiver General shall always hold as security for the redemption of Dominion notes issued and outstanding at any one time, up to and including thirty million dollars, an amount in gold, or in gold and securities of Canada, the principal or interest of such securities being guaranteed by the Government of the United Kingdom, equal to not less than twenty-five per cent of the amount of such notes so issued and outstanding, provided that the amount so held in gold shall be not less than fifteen per cent of the amount of such notes so issued and outstanding, and as security for the redemption of Dominion notes issued in excess of thirty million dollars an amount in gold equal to such excess.

The Act also enacts that any provincial notes still outstanding shall be held to be Dominion notes, and provides for redemption offices at Montreal, Toronto, Halifax, St. John, Winnipeg, Charlottetown, and Victoria. Under the authority of this Act the following notes were outstanding on 30 April 1904:

Fractionals	$ 359,883
$1 and $2	11,235,200
$4	430,477
$5, $10 and $20	7,877
$50 and $100	157,200
$500 and $1,000	6,837,000
$5,000	20,665,000
	$39,692,637

A very large proportion of the large notes in circulation is held by the chartered banks for reserve purposes, and also as a medium in which to make their daily settlements with each other. A special form of note has therefore been issued, negotiable only between banks, and of no value except to a bank. This materially lessens the risk of loss by robbery when large amounts are being carried from one bank to another, or at any other time. Of the $27,000,000 in large notes in circulation as above, $23,926,000 were the special notes for the banks, and were therefore held by them. Of a total issue of $39,692,637, $30,251,958 were held by the banks, only a little over $9,000,000 being in the hands of the public.

As security for the note issue, the following specie and debentures were held by the Minister of Finance:

Specie	$21,507,688
Guaranteed Sterling Debentures, £400,000 stering	1,946,667
	$23,454,355
Specie and Guaranteed Debentures required to be held, 25% on $30,000,000	$7,500,000
Specie held in excess of $30,000,000	9,692,637 … 17,192,637
Excess of Specie and Guaranteed Debentures	6,261,718

The following table shows the average amount in circulation each year during recent years:

1884	$16,434,385	1901	29,052,769
1890	15,501,360	1902	32,041,413
1895	21,397,750	1903	38,163,460
1900	26,550,465		

Legal Tender in Canada is: Full legal tender: (1) The British sovereign and half sovereign, at $4.86⅔ to the £. (2) The American gold eagle, with its multiples and halves. (3) Notes of the Dominion Government, redeemable in specie on presentation.

Limited legal tender: (1) Silver coinage of Canada, up to $10. (2) Bronze coinage of Canada, up to $1.

Potential legal tender: (1) Any gold coin

for five dollars (or its multiples and divisions) of the British standard of fineness, which the Government may strike for circulation in Canada. (2) Any foreign gold coin, at rates to be fixed by proclamation. See CANADA—FINANCIAL SYSTEM; CANADA—PUBLIC FINANCE.

F. G. JEMMETT,
Secretary The Canadian Bank of Commerce.

45. Canada—The Granger Movement. The Granger Movement in Canada closely resembles in its economic and social features the movement of the same name in the United States from which it derived its initial inspiration. The Grange was first established in the province of Quebec in 1872 by Eben Thompson, a deputy from the United States. Two years later representatives from several Canadian Granges met at London, Ont., and organized the Dominion Grange of the Patrons of Husbandry. In the declaration of principles then adopted the motto, «Unity, Liberty, and Charity,» was heartily endorsed. The objects of the organization were declared to be to develop a higher and better manhood and womanhood among the agricultural class; to enhance the comforts and attractions of their homes; to encourage farmers to buy less and produce more; to diversify their crops; to condense the weight of exports, selling more on hoof and in fleece, and less in the bushel. The society expressed itself as opposed to the credit system, and the mortgage system. It declared itself to be independent of political organizations, and dissociated from political parties. At the same time it was "reserved for every patron as his right as a freeman to affiliate with any party that will best carry out his principles." The declaration of principles laid stress upon the importance of the abilities and sphere of women, who were admitted both to membership and to office in the order. The growth of the Grange during the next few years was very rapid. With the Dominion grange as its center, it was organized in provincial granges, division granges and subordinate granges. In 1876 the secretary reported a total membership of 17,500 patrons, with 33 division and 530 subordinate granges. Of the latter 4 were in Nova Scotia, 7 in New Brunswick, 16 in Quebec, and 503 in Ontario. There were also six subordinate granges in Quebec, organized under the National Grange of the United States. In the following year the Grange was incorporated by the Dominion parliament, and in 1879 its membership reached 31,000. The Grange not only sought to exert an educative influence on the farming population by the distribution of literature, etc., but also set on foot, directly or indirectly, various economic enterprises of a co-operative nature intended to enable the farmers to buy and sell more cheaply by acting in union. Of these the most important was the Grange Wholesale Supply Company of Toronto, with a branch establishment at Halifax. This was a joint stock company whose capital was supplied by members of the society, and which sold farmers' supplies, seeds and minor machinery to the patrons at greatly reduced prices. The local distribution was effected by the members of the subordinate granges. The company issued for some years a paper devoted to the interests of the patrons under the title of the 'Grange Bulletin.' In this were printed extensive price lists of farmers' supplies offered

for sale. A similar undertaking was established in the form of the People's Salt Company of Kincardine. The economic enterprises of the Grange have not, however, met with marked success. The demands made thereby upon the initiative of the co-operative purchasers have proved too exacting. After some 10 years of successful existence the enthusiasm which the institution of the Grange had at first aroused began to cool, and many of the subordinate granges died of inanition. In the year 1876, 271 new granges had been reported in Ontario alone; in 1891 only two subordinate granges were organized in Canada, and in 1898 no new organizations were reported. Meantime the constant lapse of those in existence, through the apathy of their previous supporters, greatly reduced the numbers of the active patrons. The total number of granges instituted had reached about 1,000, but at the twenty-ninth annual meeting (2 and 3 Feb. 1904) the secretary's statement shows that only 13 division granges and 30 subordinate granges (with a membership of 411) had reported during the last year. The receipts of the treasury of the Dominion grange, which amounted to $6,900 in 1876, fell to $129 in 1904. Many persons had been led to join in the movement from the sanguine hopes of profit to be derived from the co-operative side of the enterprise, and fell away when these were not realized. On the whole, the grange movement must be regarded as a failure in the direction of its economic enterprises, but its influence for the social and educational advancement of the farming class has undoubtedly been great. During the flourishing period of the movement literary exercises alternated with the conduct of business matters at the local meetings. It has especially been instrumental in promoting various legislative measures in the interests of the farming class. Among these may be mentioned the Provincial Drainage Acts (R. S. O. C. 37, 38), the Dominion statute known as the Butter Act, etc. On the tariff question the opinion of the patrons has been divided: it has been difficult for the grange to adopt any decided position in the matter without identifying itself with party politics. The grange was, however, instrumental in securing the repeal of the duty on binder twine. The patrons have constantly sought to foster the cheese industry and the cattle trade with Great Britain; have succeeded in having agriculture taught in the public schools; and have strongly supported the agricultural college at Guelph. The grange has also agitated in favor of the inflation of the Dominion paper currency, the reduction of railroad rates, and the appointment (now effected) of a railroad commission. The Dominion grange sends annually a fraternal delegate to the meeting of the National Grange. See also GRANGERS; CANADA—*Agriculture.*

STEPHEN LEACOCK,
Lecturer on Political Science, McGill University.

46. Canada—The British Preferential Tariff. Canada was the first of the British colonies to secure the right of self-government, including fiscal autonomy. The last tariff made in Great Britain for Canada was that of 1842. The freedom of Canada to frame her own financial and trade policy has, since that date, become gradually more absolute. Formerly, the commercial treaties of the mother country were applicable also to the colonies, whether they would or not. The newer practice has been to leave the self-governing colonies free to accept or reject such treaties, so far as they are themselves concerned. Some of the older treaties remain, not having been revised since the introduction of this policy. The treaties with Belgium and the German Zollverein (see ZOLLVEREIN), dating from 1862 and 1865, respectively, even required the granting to these countries by British colonies of terms as favorable as those accorded to the mother country. The most-favored-nation clause in other treaties extended these privileges to other countries. The stipulations of these treaties, then, deprived Canada of power to grant preferential terms to the mother country, thus limiting her complete fiscal freedom. In 1897 Canada took a step which led to the removal of this restraint. The accession to power of a new government, under Sir Wilfrid Laurier (q.v.), was followed by a revision of the tariff. This revision was characterized by two leading principles. The first was the reduction of all duties (except those on spirits and tobacco) of excessive amount, so that the standard maximum rate became 35 per cent ad valorem. The second was a further special reduction of duties on imports from any country which might offer to Canada equally favorable tariff rates in return. Excluding spirits and wines, and tobacco, cigars and cigarettes from the operation of the reduced tariff, a deduction of one eighth (12½ per cent) of the duty payable was to obtain for the first year, and thereafter a deduction of one quarter of the duties (25 per cent). Practically, the preferential rates of duty thus instituted affected no other country than Great Britain and certain of the British colonies. In form, the advantages were open to all, not to the mother country exclusively. In spite of this, the decision was reached that the treaties with Germany and Belgium compelled the extension to those countries of whatever remission of duties was accorded to the United Kingdom. The government of the United Kingdom duly notified the governments of Germany and Belgium that the treaties in question would be terminated, and from 31 July 1898 they ceased to be in force. When this had been accomplished, the form of the preferential clause in the Canadian tariff underwent a change. It no longer offered reciprocal advantages to all countries, but only to the other divisions of the British empire. The title of the schedule setting forth the amount and conditions of the rebate of duties changed from that of "Reciprocal Tariff," adopted in 1897, to that of "British Preferential Tariff." That it should be the latter in fact had been intended from the first, and no time was lost in making its form correspond with its purpose. It would appear that the form originally adopted was selected with a view to avoid collision with the obnoxious treaties. The appearance of deliberately forcing the hands of the British government was not afforded prominence, but the pressure actually exerted proved sufficient to secure the denouncing of the treaties. A further step in developing the preferential treatment of British imports into Canada was taken two years later, when the rebate of duties was raised from one fourth to one third. When the preferential tariff was first instituted, the severity of the consequent pressure on certain home industries was modified by advancing a few of the duties of the general tariff, so that the net rates, after deducting the rebate on British goods, might not become so low as to threaten home interests. When the rate of the rebate was increased in 1900, its effect was not qualified by any such preliminary adjustment of duties. The further development of preferential trade within the British empire was discussed by representatives of the colonies and of the home government at the Colonial Conference of 1902. So far as Canada was concerned, a willingness to extend the preference, in response to reciprocal favors, was indicated. The nature of such possible extension was sketched as follows: (1) Increase of preference on particular goods. (2) Raising of the general tariff on various articles. (3) Imposing duties on foreign imports hitherto admitted free of duty. These proposals and the general discussion of the subject have made fairly clear the direction in which changes of the Canadian preference are likely to take place. The indications afforded are entirely confirmed by the utterances of the Finance Minister in introducing the budget of 1904. The uniform rate of preference is to give way to two tariffs, the one applicable to ordinary foreign trade, the other, with lower rates, applicable to British trade. The minister further foreshadowed a special tariff, with rates higher than those of the general tariff, to be applied in the case of the nations not granting Canada most-favored-nation treatment. By thus elaborating the tariff schedules, the pressure felt by particular industries as a result of the preference will be modified. A simple increase of the rate of preference would either make the reduced rates on some goods so low as to provoke an outcry which could not be ignored, or would require the rates of the general tariff to be raised to an almost prohibitive level, contrary to the spirit in which the authors of the preference set about the revision of the tariff. The employment of a rate of preference varying from one class of goods to another is the obvious solution of the difficulties of the situation. After the expiration of the treaty of 1865 between the German Zollverein and the United Kingdom, some arrangements were necessary pending the negotiation of another treaty. Germany arranged to grant most-favored-nation terms to the whole of the British empire, with the exception of Canada. To Canada the German general tariff was applied, in view of the fact that Canada was favoring British trade more than German trade. Vain attempts were made by Canada to procure a modification of Germany's action toward her, and, failing in these attempts, Canada retaliated in 1903 by imposing a surtax of one third of the duties otherwise payable on all German goods imported into the country. This surtax corresponds to the higher rates of the third division of the elaborated Canadian tariff which is foreshadowed.

Canada claims that the tariff arrangements between different divisions of the British empire are domestic affairs of that empire, and do not justify a foreign nation in imposing disabilities on particular parts of the empire. The claim, and the principle on which it rests, are apparently reasonable. It is true that no other country than Great Britain grants fiscal autonomy to its colonies. This fact is held to deprive of force the citation of the example of other cases where preferential arrangements between colonies and their motherlands have not affected the interpretation of most-favored-nation clauses. So long as the Belgian and German treaties remained in force, this might be contended with reason. Hence the irritation which led to their denunciation. Before passing to consider the effect of the preferential tariff on Canadian trade, it may be noted that the effect of the German surtax has been remarkably clearly shown in the trade returns. In the first 10 months of the fiscal year 1903-4, the dutiable imports from Germany into Canada were $3,281,000, or 38 per cent, less than in the like period of the preceding year, when they amounted to $8,648,000. But whether from the delay in the full application of the surtax, or from the fact of the importation of goods through Germany from other countries, $3,211,-000 of the imports from Germany, in the 10 months in question, were not subject to the surtax. Deducting this amount from the preceding year's figures, the reduction of $3,281,000 has taken place on a total of $5,437,000. The imports of free goods had slightly increased, namely, from $1,359,000 to $1,618,000. Of the imports from Germany in the 10 months ending April 1903, $3,271,000 were sugar. In 1903-4 no sugar was imported subject to surtax, and the value of sugar imported from Germany under the general tariff was $577,000. Thus, of the total reduction of imports, amounting to $3,281,000, not less than $2,694,000 may be assigned to the cessation of sugar imports. The reduction in other goods may be placed at $587,000, on a value of $2,773,000 subject to surtax on direct importation from Germany, or about 20 per cent. What the effect on the indirect importations of German goods has been cannot be seen, as the records of earlier years do not show the extent of these importations. As the amount of imports from Germany had been increasing rapidly in preceding years, the reduction in the trade figures is more likely to give an under-estimate than an over-estimate of the effect on the trade. The entire destruction of the export of German sugar to Canada, and the transfer of this trade to the British West Indies and British Guiana, is a notable result of the surtax policy.

Turning now to the examination of the trade records for the purpose of determining the effect of the preference on the import into Canada of British goods, we find that, in the year preceding the institution of the preferential tariff, namely, 1896-7, the dutiable imports into Canada from Great Britain were valued at $20,200,000. In 1902-3, the sixth year of the preference, they reached $42,200,000. Meanwhile, free imports from the same quarter had increased in value from $9,200,000 to $16,600,-000. To find figures of imports from Great Britain exceeding those of 1902-3, we must go back to 1874-5, when price-inflation exaggerated the nominal values entering into trade. In absolute magnitude, therefore, the trade has grown largely under preference, and that after a long period of decrease. But it is not only the trade of Canada with Great Britain which has grown rapidly in these years. The total trade of Canada has also increased with great rapidity. In 1896-7, the year before the pref-

erence was instituted, 30.53 per cent of Canada's dutiable imports, 22.73 per cent of her free imports, were obtained from Great Britain. In 1902-3 the corresponding figures were 30.85 and 18.84 per cent. The smallest proportion of dutiable goods which has ever been recorded as supplied from Great Britain was in 1901-2; the smallest proportion of the aggregate imports was reached in 1900-1. The imports from Great Britain were 26.15 per cent of the total imports of Canada in 1902-3; they were 27.58 per cent of the total in 1896-7, and had never previously been below 30 per cent of the total. The check which has apparently been placed on the process of diminution of the proportional share of Great Britain in Canada's import trade is certainly a distinct advantage accruing to Great Britain from the operation of the preferential tariff. But the advantage due to the preference appears much less, when measured by the proportional share of Canada's imports supplied by the mother country, than when measured by the change in the aggregate amount of those imports. The increase in aggregate amount is part of a general increase in Canadian trade since 1897. The United States supplied 53.5 per cent of Canada's imports in 1896-7, and 57.3 per cent in 1902-3, so that, in this case, the advance has been one, not merely of total value of goods supplied, but of proportionate share in the trade. It can readily be understood that the United States is able to supply goods adapted to the needs of Canadian consumers more readily than can be done by British manufacturers. In many lines the conditions to be met in Canada and in parts of the United States are closely similar, so that the goods which suit the latter market are well adapted to the needs of the former. This consideration appears to have had great weight even against the advantages offered by preferential rates of duty. A good illustration is afforded by the case of many classes of iron and steel goods, the proportion of which supplied by the United States continues to increase, while the proportion supplied by Great Britain decreases. The extent of the rebate of duties under the preference clauses of the Canadian tariff is shown in the following table:

DUTIES ON IMPORTS UNDER THE PREFERENTIAL TARIFF, AND AMOUNT OF THE PREFERENTIAL REBATE, 1897–8 TO 1902–3.

ON IMPORTS FROM	Duty collected	Rebate of duty	Value of goods
	Thousands of dollars		
Great Britain............	32,571	12,707	158,400
British Empire, other than Great Britain..........	1,526	693	8,020
All other countries.......	1,987	406	7,981
All countries.............	36,084	13,806	174,401

The figures of the middle column, showing the rebate, are calculated from the rates at which rebate has been granted from year to year. It will be observed that, during the short period when the preference was extended to foreign countries enjoying most-favored-nation treatment, the advantage taken by those countries was very great. The imports from Great Britain are only entitled to preferential treatment when they are British goods, and wine, spirits, and manufactured tobacco are not in any case granted rebate of duty. About one sixth in value of imports from Great Britain fail thus to secure a preferential rebate of duty, and the duties on these amounted, in the six years to which the above table refers, to no less than $15,593,000 on a value of $32,215,000. The high duties on spirits and tobacco are responsible for the high proportion of duties to values in this part of the trade with Great Britain. If we were to note simply the average rate of duty charged on goods imported from Great Britain, it would appear that some preferential rebate is needed to offset a special burdensomeness of the tariff on this section of imports. If we exclude wines and spirits and tobacco from the account, and calculate the average rate of duty levied on other dutiable imports, we find that it was close to 24 per cent in each of the years 1901-2 and 1902-3. Adding to the duties actually collected the amount of the preferential rebate, the result shows the average rate of the general tariff, namely, 26½ per cent to within a small fraction. On goods from Great Britain securing preferential treatment, the actual duties collected were 18.8 per cent of the aggregate value in 1901-2, and 18.5 per cent in 1902-3. The rates of the general tariff on these goods were, therefore, about 28 per cent, as an average, compared with 26½ per cent on all goods with the exception of spirits and tobacco. On imports from the United States, the average rate charged was approximately 25 per cent. The comparative lowness of this rate, like the large proportion of free goods supplied by the United States, is not difficult to explain. Raw materials and instruments of industry are rated at moderate duties when they are not admitted free. The fact that goods from the United States are charged to duty at rates lower than those imposed, apart from the preference, on goods from Great Britain, with the fact that so large a part of the imports from the United States are free of duty, has led to some suspicion of the *bona fide* nature of the British preference. It is clear from the foregoing that the difference of the rates charged on goods properly comparable is but little in favor of the United States, and the reason for the difference is obvious, and implies no reflection on the makers of the tariff. It is a point worthy of attention that approximately one half of the preferential rebate is accounted for by two items, woolen manufactures and cotton manufactures. The tariff rates on these are higher than on most goods. Calculations similar to the preceding show that the general tariff on woolens entitled to the preference stands at an average rate of 34 per cent, while for cottons the rate is 31 per cent. The rebate is therefore in excess of 10 per cent of the value of the goods, and it would be a fair conclusion from the figures that the classes of goods imported most largely are those on which the general tariff rate, and therefore the preferential rebate, is highest. About 70 per cent in value of woolens imported come under the preferential tariff, and about 60 per cent of cotton manufactures. The import of the latter has grown steadily during the whole of the six years since the institution

of the preference, but the part affected by the preference has not increased more rapidly than the part not so affected. In regard to woolens, the proportion affected by preference was larger during the period when the preference was not confined to the British empire than it has since been. It is true that, since the rate of preference was increased in 1900, woolen imports have increased faster than before, but again the figures show that the growth is not confined to, not more marked in, the trade under preferential tariff rates, than in the rest of the woolen imports. Of all goods imported under the preferential tariff, about 27 per cent by value are woolen goods, about 15 per cent cotton goods. The cotton and woolen industries are therefore largely affected by the preference. That their representatives should cry out for a reduction of the preference is intelligible enough at first sight, and that the rate of the rebate on woolen goods should be reduced in response to that cry is readily understood. But the reasonableness of the outcry, and of the concession to it, are less obvious when we regard the fact that the proportion, of woolens favored by the preference to the total of woolens imported, is not growing.

It remains to consider briefly the attitude of the Canadian people toward the preferential idea. At its introduction in the tariff of 1897, it formed the most prominent feature of a change in the tariff in the direction of moderation. Other readjustments of the tariff about compensated each other, though the elimination of prohibitive rates of duty is a move toward freer trade, even though the average duties actually levied do not decrease in proportion to the value of goods subject to them. In actual reduction of rates of duty, the preferential rebate represents the net concession of the 1897 tariff. It was thus not only, or, perhaps, even chiefly, an advantage to trade with the mother country, but a method of tariff reduction. Canada's advantage was sought, and continues to be sought, in the arrangements of the tariff, and the modification of particular rates of duty, or of preferential rebate, is aimed at securing the advantage, real or supposed, of Canada. Another point of view was, and is, found, namely, that the rebate is a sacrifice of Canadian interests to those of the mother country, or of the empire. This sacrifice is believed to require, as justification and compensation, preferential terms for imports of Canadian products into the United Kingdom. The two great political parties of the Dominion appear to differ slightly on this point in their attitude to the policy of preference. Both would gladly welcome a British tariff which granted a preference to colonial products. The one party is content to grant concessions to trade with the mother country, in Canada's interest as well as that of the mother country, leaving it to Great Britain to determine whether reciprocal advantages can be offered, though strongly desirous of such reciprocity in preferences. The other party is inclined to represent the Canadian preference as only to be justified by a reciprocal British preference, and to openly declare its sympathy with the active supporters in Great Britain of tariff changes which should include preferential treatment of colonial imports. The belief is very widespread in Canada that the country would gain largely by such

a system of colonial preferences in Great Britain. It seems hardly possible, however, that such preferences can touch raw materials, or anything but food products. So far as Canada is concerned, a preference on grain appears likely to stimulate the development of the Canadian West, to the advantage of manufacturing industry in the East. The growth of population engaged in cultivating the soil means an enlarged market for manufactures, but if this market be secured by Canadian manufactures, two results must follow. Immigrants must be employed in manufacture, thus decreasing the flow to the western prairies; and to the extent to which the new market is held by Canadians, it will not afford the enlarged outlet for British manufactures in anticipation of which British voters are being urged to support the policy of a tariff with colonial preferences. The currents of trade in Canada are more and more flowing east and west. The nature of Canada's natural products, and the trade policy of the United States, as well as the political relation of Canada to the United Kingdom and the institution of preferential trade, tend to produce this result. Whatever the advantages of freer trade intercourse with the United States, it appears unlikely that Canada will be willing to pay a high price for them or to prejudice her imperial trade relations for their sake. Even had no other advantage been secured by the Canadian Imperial Preferential Trade policy, it has aided powerfully in establishing Canadian goods in the English market. See also CANADA — *Commerce, Tariffs, and Transportation.* ALFRED W. FLUX,
Professor of Political Economy, McGill University.

47. Canada—The Trade of the British Empire. It is often said that the British empire was built up by trade, and the opinion that the development of trade between its different parts is the surest means of consolidating it for political purposes is widely held. How best to de-

and comparing them with a recent and a fairly distant date, so as to show the tendency of movement.

TRADE OF THE BRITISH EMPIRE.
(Millions of Dollars.)

AVERAGE OF YEARS	Imports			Exports		
	Total	From the Empire	From foreign countries	Total	To the Empire	To foreign countries
1867–71	2,003	736	1,267	1,729	697	1,032
1892–96	2,852	1,020	1,732	2,323	962	1,361
1898–02	3,634	1,299	2,335	2,835	1,261	1,574

This table shows that, in 30 years, the total foreign trade of the empire has increased from 3,732 millions of dollars to 6,469 millions, and that the part of it which consists of trade with other parts of the empire has increased from 1,433 millions to 2,560 millions. The proportion of inter-imperial trade has increased from 38 per cent of the whole to 39 per cent. Imports from other parts of the empire have fallen from 37 per cent of total imports to 36 per cent. Exports to other parts of the empire have increased from 40 per cent of total exports to 44 per cent. In these computations the trade between the different colonies of what is now federated Australia has been omitted from the reckoning throughout. In some degree, then, it seems that the empire purchases more largely from outside than formerly, though its sales are made more exclusively within its own bounds. As the course of development has, naturally, not been uniform, the trade between the United Kingdom and various portions of the colonies and dependencies may be examined in a little greater detail. First, considering imports into the colonies, the position is found to be as follows:

In examining this table, the exceptional situation of the Straits Settlements is manifest. The fact that the trade of Singapore is very

TOTAL IMPORTS OF BRITISH COLONIES.
(Millions of Dollars.)

	Average of 1867–71			Average of 1892–96			Average of 1898–1902		
	Total of Imports	Imports from Britain	Per cent from Britain	Total of Imports	Imports from Britain	Per cent from Britain	Total of Imports	Imports from Britain	Per cent from Britain
India	224	155	69	257	185	72	334	221	66
Straits Settlements	42	11	27	103	13	13	139	15	11
Self-Governing Colonies	208	120	58	364	215	59	581	292	50
Other colonies and protectorates	70	27	39	92	38	41	122	45	37
Total	544	313	58	816	451	55	1,176	573	49

velop the trade is matter for strong differences of opinion. Other countries regard the large and profitable trade between the British Isles and the outlying parts of the British empire as something to be imitated, if the proper procedure to that end could but be accurately ascertained. The actual status of the trade between the different parts of the empire, and the general direction of any changes which are taking place, will be briefly indicated in what follows. A summary of the situation is given in the following table, setting forth the data for the latest years for which complete returns are available,

largely an *entrepôt* trade sufficiently explains the apparently exceptional condition of affairs. It must be noted that the trade of Hong Kong, of Malta, and of Gibraltar cannot be included in the above, for want of returns. Especially conspicuous in the record of expansion of trade during the past generation are the figures relating to the self-governing colonies. This designation in the table applies to the same colonies throughout. though not all of them have been entitled to that description throughout the period covered. The differences between the different colonies are shown in the next table.

The proportion of imports from Great Britain has decreased in every case, though the value of these imports has increased in every case except that of Newfoundland. The nature of the goods the colonies from other colonies have increased much more than imports from foreign countries, though the latter have increased more than imports from Great Britain. How far the growth

IMPORTS OF THE SELF-GOVERNING COLONIES.
(Millions of Dollars.)

	Average of 1867–71			Average of 1892–96			Average of 1898–1902		
	Total of Imports	Imports from Britain	Per cent from Britain	Total of Imports	Imports from Britain	Per cent from Britain	Total of Imports	Imports from Britain	Per cent from Britain
Canada	79.3	39.6	50	113.9	37.6	33	184.2	46.4	25
Newfoundland	5.7	2.2	38	6.8	2.2	32	6.9	2.1	30
Australia	86.1	55.3	64	125.5	89.1	71	185.7	113.9	61
New Zealand	23.5	11.7	50	33.4	21.4	64	49.6	30.2	61
Cape Colony	11.7	9.2	79	68.9	54.1	78	111.1	72.4	65
Natal	1.8	1.5	82	15.7	11.2	71	43.6	27.0	62
Total	208.1	119.5	58	364.2	215.6	59	581.1	292.0	50

required by the colonies has been one cause of the decreasing share obtained from the mother country, though this is due also, in part, to the activity of the competition of other nations in colonial markets. The agitation in favor of preferential treatment of British goods by the colonies (see CANADA—THE BRITISH PREFERENTIAL TARIFF) is, in part, due to the consideration of such facts as are suggested by this table. A preceding table showed that, in the empire as a whole, the inter-imperial trade had been fairly well maintained. The growth in foreign imports is exaggerated by increased accuracy of the returns of countries of origin, cannot be ascertained. It is certain that goods are now obtained directly from some countries whence they were formerly obtained via Great Britain and thus included in the record with British goods.

Turning to the returns of exports from the colonies, and, in particular, of the self-governing colonies, the following tables show, in a form similar to that adopted for imports, the amounts and changes of the trade:

EXPORTS OF THE SELF-GOVERNING COLONIES.
(Millions of Dollars.)

	Average of 1867–71			Average of 1892–96			Average of 1898–1902		
	Total of Exports	Exports to Britain	Per cent to Britain	Total of Exports	Exports to Britain	Per cent to Britain	Total of Exports	Exports to Britain	Per cent to Britain
Canada	65.5	20.6	31	117.3	64.5	55	191.6	112.1	53
Newfoundland	5.7	1.9	33	6.3	1.6	25	7.7	1.7	22
Australia	98.2	69.1	70	162.3	111.6	69	222.8	118.1	53
New Zealand	22.9	11.1	49	44.6	36.1	81	60.8	45.6	75
Cape Colony	13.0	10.7	83	71.3	68.8	96	83.5	78.3	94
Natal	1.8	1.2	67	6.0	4.3	71	9.8	4.8	50
Total	207.1	114.6	55	407.8	286.9	70	576.2	360.6	63

TOTAL EXPORTS OF BRITISH COLONIES.
(Millions of Dollars.)

	Average of 1867–71			Average of 1892–96			Average of 1898–1902		
	Total of Exports	Exports to Britain	Per cent to Britain	Total of Exports	Exports to Britain	Per cent to Britain	Total of Exports	Exports to Britain	Per cent to Britain
India	276	145	53	333	111	33	413	121	29
Straits Settlements	38	7	20	91	16	18	118	23	20
Self-Governing Colonies...	207	115	55	408	287	70	576	361	63
Other colonies and protectorates	74	45	60	88	37	42	94	31	33
Total	595	312	52	920	451	49	1,201	536	45

of colonial imports has, it is clear, therefore, been from other colonies rather than from the mother country; only in part has it been from foreign countries in substitution for British trade. In particular, in the interval between the last two periods of the tables, the imports into

A striking feature of this exhibit is the fact that in the case of the self-governing colonies alone has the proportion of exports to the mother country increased, though this is not true of all of them. What was stated of imports applies also to exports, namely, that exports to other colonies have grown with great rapidity in recent years, while, as far as the records go, the exports to foreign countries have grown somewhat more in proportion than those to the mother country. The comparison of the trade between the colonies and the mother country with the total trade on the two sides respectively, is set forth below:

The relative importance of the trade between the colonies and Great Britain is clearly much

48. Canada — Reciprocity between Canada and the United States. The question of mutual tariff concessions between the United States and Canada, has been a subject of constant interest. But at no time in the history of the two countries, except in the brief interval between 1854 and 1866, has there been any serious adoption of the principle of reciprocal lowering of duties. Previous to 1846 the tariffs and trade of the British colonies were regulated

TRADE BETWEEN GREAT BRITAIN AND ITS COLONIES.

(Millions of Dollars.)

FROM THE COLONIAL STANDPOINT.

COLONIAL	Average of 1867–71			Average of 1892–96			Average of 1898–1902.		
	Total	From or to Britain	Per cent British	Total	From or to Britain	Per cent British	Total	From or to Britain	Per cent British
Imports	544	313	58	816	451	55	1,176	573	49
Exports	595	312	52	920	451	49	1,201	536	45
Aggregate trade	1,139	625	55	1,736	902	53	2,377	1,109	47

FROM GREAT BRITAIN'S STANDPOINT.

GREAT BRITAIN'S	Average of 1867–71			Average of 1892–96			Average of 1898–1902		
	Total	From or to colonies	Per cent colonial	Total	From or to colonies	Per cent colonial	Total	From or to colonies	Per cent colonial
Imports	1,456	328	22	2,046	461	23	2,470	516	21
Exports	1,190	264	22	1,411	396	28	1,636	505	31
of which Re-Exports......	239	37	15	310	30	10	315	37	12
Aggregate trade	2,655	592	22	3,457	857	25	4,106	1,021	25

greater from the standpoint of the colonies than from that of Great Britain. Proposals looking to reduced taxation on trade within the empire as compared with external trade must be considered in the light of actual facts. If interimperial trade is to be made to contribute but lightly to colonial revenues, the basis of revenue-taxation is very much narrowed. The question cannot be considered adequately without an examination of the classes of goods concerned, on which taxation is actually levied, in greater detail than is proposed here. The general tendency of the trade figures set forth is to show a marked contrast between the British and colonial aspects of the problem. To grant colonial preferences in Britain would mean imposing taxation which would affect the stability of the foreign trade, whose magnitude relative to the colonial is shown above. Were it possible to admit British goods to the colonies at nominal tariff rates, Great Britain might find some compensation for interference with her foreign trade. Fiscal needs at present render it impossible for the colonies to abandon duties on inter-imperial trade, while vested interests in many places would prove obstacles to such a movement, even if the fiscal situation permitted a practical abandonment of the customs duties on British goods. See also GREAT BRITAIN — Commerce, Export Statistics; CANADA — THE BRITISH PREFERENTIAL TARIFF; CANADA — COMMERCE, TARIFFS, AND TRANSPORTATION.

ALFRED W. FLUX,
Professor of Political Economy, McGill University.

by the mother country. After the Peace of 1783, the British Navigation Acts in restriction of colonial trade, and the British discriminating duties in favor of the mother country were applied against the United States. Congress early adopted a mildly protective tariff (1789) and enacted navigation laws. But in the era following the War of 1812-15, public feeling on both sides of the Atlantic increasingly condemned this restrictive policy.

By a statute of 1846 (9 and 10 Vict. c. 94) the British colonies in North America were empowered to repeal the existing differential tariff made for them by the Imperial Parliament. The Province of Canada availed itself of this permission to enact (1847) a uniform tariff of 7½ per cent against British and American manufactures alike. Nova Scotia adopted the same course. New Brunswick maintained a discriminating tariff against the United States. The remaining parts of the Navigation Acts were repealed in 1849 (12 and 13 Vict. c. 29). Meantime public feeling in Canada and the United States favored still greater freedom of intercourse. The general prevalence of the doctrine of free trade, its triumph in England (1846), and the adoption by the United States of the low tariff of 1846, set strongly in this direction. Attempts were first made to establish reciprocity by means of concurrent legislation in Congress, and the Canadian legislature. It was hoped in this way to avoid the constitutional question that might arise should the President exercise his treaty-making power for the regulation of customs duties. The Canadian Parliament passed an act to the desired effect in 1849. But the legislation introduced in Congress in 1848 and 1850 failed to pass, Congress being unwilling to concede reciprocal lowering of duties without obtaining the free navigation of the Saint Lawrence. Finally Congress adopted a resolution (1853) asking the President to settle both these matters, together with the coast fisheries, by treaty. A like wish having been communicated from Canada to the Crown, Lord Elgin, the governor-general of Canada, was sent to Washington to arrange a treaty. William Marcy, the secretary of state, conducted the negotiations for the United States. The result was the Reciprocity Treaty signed 6 June 1854. It was duly ratified, and an act of Congress passed (Approved 5 Aug. 1854) to carry out its provisions, which came into effect by proclamation 16 March 1855. The terms of the treaty were as follows. An enumerated list of natural products (Art. 3) were to be admitted free of duty between British North America (Canada, New Brunswick, Nova Scotia, and Prince Edward Island) and the United States. According to these specifications no manufactured articles were to be admitted. The treaty further provided for the free navigation of the Saint Lawrence and the opening of the coast fisheries of each country to the fishermen of the other. It was to remain in force for 10 years and further "until the expiration of 12 months after either of the high contracting parties shall give notice to the other of its wish to terminate the same." The reciprocal relations thus established lasted for 11 years. The economic effect of the treaty is still a matter of controversy. The following figures illustrate the course of trade between the United States and British North America before, during, and after the Reciprocity Treaty:

Year	Imports United States from British North America	British North America from United States
1852	$ 5,469,445	$13,993,579
1853	6,527,559	19,445,478
1854	8,784,412	26,115,132
1855	15,118,289	34,362,188
1856	21,276,614	35,764,980
1857	22,108,916	27,788,238
1858	15,784,836	22,210,837
1859	19,287,565	26,761,618
1860	23,572,796	25,871,399
1861	22,724,489	28,520,733
1862	18,515,685	30,373,212
1863	17,191,217	29,680,955
1864	29,668,736	7,952,401
1865	33,264,403	27,269,158
1866	48,528,628	27,905,984
1867	25,044,005	25,239,459
1868	26,261,378	22,644,235
1869	29,293,766	21,680,062

Complete statistics illustrative of the operation of the treaty can be found in the appendix to an article thereon by Professor Haynes in the publications of the American Economic Association, Vol. VII. The stimulus it afforded to trade between the two countries is undoubted, but it must be remembered that the situation during a large part of the treaty period was quite exceptional. The inflated prices of agricultural products due to the Crimean War stimulated the farming industry. The strain of the American Civil War naturally led to an increased importation of Canadian products. The great increase for the fiscal year ending 30 June

1866 ($48,528,628), was partly due to the rush of importation in view of the prospective abrogation of the treaty. During the earlier years of the operation of the treaty, it met with a general approval. But unfortunately for its continuance it was presently claimed on the part of each country that the existing arrangement unduly favored the other, and that the provisions of the treaty had not been faithfully observed. The American contention can be found in detail in the report made by Mr. Israel T. Hatch 28 March 1860 (House Executive Document No. 96, 36th Congress, 1st Session, Vol. 3, pp. 1–48), in the concurrent resolutions in the New York legislature early in 1862, and in a report made to the House by Representative Ward on behalf of the Committee on Commerce (House Committee Reports, 37th Congress, 2d Session, Vol. III., No. 22). It was here claimed that the increase of duties on manufactured articles adopted by Canada since 1854 was a virtual violation of the treaty. The navigation rights secured by the treaty were argued by Mr. Hatch to have been of little actual benefit, only 40 American vessels with a gross burden of 12,550 tons, having gone down the Saint Lawrence during the first six years of the treaty. "Our railroads," he said, "suffer from a British competitor (the Grand Trunk) supported by privileges equivalent to the taxation on their business with the Canadian Province, and the interior of our own country." The New York resolutions denounced the "gross inequality and injustice existing in our present intercourse with Canada," and called for a revision of the treaty. As against these contentions the Canadian side of the controversy appears in a report made by Mr. A. T. Galt, Canadian minister of finance (March 1862). The increase of Canadian duties on certain manufactures, from 15 to 20 per cent, he declared to be due solely to financial exigencies, and to be a quite legitimate step since the "treaty contains no reference to manufactured articles whatever." To show Canada's sincerity, he instanced the "repeal of tonnage dues on Lake Saint Peter," and "the abolition of tolls on all vessels, whether American or Canadian." He argued further that the "spirit of the treaty," had been "infringed by the United States by the imposition (though removed on protest) of heavy consular fees on proof of origin, tantamount to a duty." The ill-feeling thus engendered in regard to the treaty was still further aggravated by the strained relations of the war period. Indeed competent authorities on both sides attribute its final abrogation to the violence of partisan feeling, rather than to commercial reasons. Charles Francis Adams, minister to Great Britain, wrote (February 1865) that the measures for abrogation "were the result rather of a strong political feeling than of any commercial considerations." As a result Congress (16 Jan. 1865) passed resolutions calling on the President to give notice of the termination of the Reciprocity Treaty. This having been done, the treaty expired in 12 months (17 March 1866). The British government made no attempt to preserve reciprocity, but efforts were made in its behalf both in the United States and in Canada. A convention was held at Detroit (July 1865) consisting of representatives of boards of trade, etc., of the leading American cities and Canadian provinces. The hope that had been freely expressed in the United States that the desire for renewed reciprocity might lead to annexation, was defeated by the action of the Canadian delegates, but the convention, while approving the abrogation of the present treaty, passed a unanimous resolution in favor of a new one. At the eleventh hour (January 1866) a Canadian delegation of provincial cabinet ministers came to Washington and endeavored fruitlessly to arrange a new basis of agreement. Since the expiration of the treaty in 1866, reciprocal trade relations (except in fish under the Washington treaty of 1871 [q.v.]) have never again been adopted.

Repeated efforts have, however, been made on both sides of the line for their re-establishment. The federation of the Dominion of Canada (1867) was followed by the adoption of a tariff which contained a standing offer for a resumption of reciprocity. Meantime the Canadian minister of finance, Sir John Rose, visited Washington in 1869, with a view to arranging a renewal of tariff concessions. It is thought that he even proposed a complete customs union (see 'Canadian Magazine,' March 1897). Further efforts were made by the Liberal party on their advent to power (1873). Mr. George Brown visited Washington as Canadian commissioner, acting in conjunction with Sir Edward Thornton, the British minister. They, with Mr. Hamilton Fish, secretary of state, drafted a new reciprocity treaty (June 1874). Its terms referred not only to natural products, but a number of manufactured articles,— agricultural implements, boots and shoes, cottons, iron, leather, engines, etc. Duties were to be diminished by one third each year, until a basis of free exchange was reached. The treaty was rejected by the United States Senate. Shortly after this the Conservatives returning to power (1878) adopted the high tariff schedule of the so-called "national Policy"; this and the American tariff act of 1883 rendered the chances of renewed reciprocity still more remote. But towards the close of the 80's, the question again assumed great prominence, especially in Canada. It now took the form of a movement in favor of "commercial union," advocated by Mr. Erastus Wiman, Prof. Goldwin Smith, and others. This meant the abolition of customs duties between Canada and the United States, and the erection of a common tariff. A modified form of this policy known as "unrestricted reciprocity," was adopted by the Canadian Liberals as the main issue in their unsuccessful election campaign of 1891. The term was generally understood to mean a large measure of free trade both in manufactures and products, but not of necessity a complete customs union (see address of Sir W. Laurier, Quebec, 12 Feb. 1891). Meantime in the United States Representative Butterworth introduced a bill (December 1888) in favor of complete reciprocity. Representative Hitt in 1889, presented a resolution in favor of commercial union. Neither of these measures was carried, and the McKinley Tariff (1890) considerably raised the duties on barley, peas, potatoes, and various other natural products. After their successful re-election in 1891 the Canadian Conservatives opened negotiations with Mr. Blaine, secretary of state, for renewal of partial reciprocity. The negotiations came to nothing,

Mr. Blaine refusing to consider a treaty which should include only natural products. An international convention at Saint Paul, Minn., 1893, passed a resolution in favor of "a treaty providing for the free interchange of those classes of the products, both natural and industrial, of each [nation] that are most generally in demand . . . in the markets of the other." The Wilson Tariff (1894) lowered many duties in the agricultural schedule and placed lumber on the free list, but the Dingley Tariff (1897) raised the duties on cattle, wheat, flour, etc., and put a duty on lumber of $2.00 per 1,000 feet. Mr. Osborne Howes of the Boston Chamber of Commerce, gave evidence before the recent Industrial Commission (Report Ind. Comm., Vol. IX., 1901) in favor of adoption of reciprocity. He showed that the Canadians are, per capita, the best customers of the United States, and that the 6,000,000 people of Canada purchase from the United States more than the 60,000,000, south of the Rio Grande. The balance of trade between the two countries is strongly favorable to the United States. Such a trade should, therefore, be developed by reciprocal concessions, especially as there is a possibility that the present Canadian preferences (33⅓ per cent) in favor of British goods may develop into a commercial federation of the empire. The balance of trade for recent years is seen by the following figures:

Year	Exports from Canada to the United States	Imports for consumption into Canada from the United States
Ending June 30, 1900...	$68,619,023	$109,844,378
Ending June 30, 1901...	72,382,230	110,485,008
Ending June 30, 1902...	71,197,684	120,814,750
Ending June 30, 1903...	71,783,924	137,605,195

The lumber interest in the United States is strongly opposed to reciprocity. Canadian lumber would have nearer access to the markets of New England, and the Middle States than the lumber of Minnesota or Wisconsin. The bituminous coal of Nova Scotia is mined at the same cost as in Maryland and West Virginia, but the Nova Scotia mines are on the sea board, whereas the railroad haul from the States mentioned, to tidewater, costs $1.25 a ton. Without a tariff New England would look to Nova Scotia for her supply of bituminous coal. It thus appears that at the present time New England is the territory most interested in securing reciprocity. A considerable movement in that direction is now on foot. Various public meetings in Boston and elsewhere, in the spring of 1904, passed resolutions in favor of reciprocity with Canada. In Canada on the other hand the question is at present very much in the background. The absorbing interest in the outcome of Mr. Chamberlain's recent proposals of inter-imperial preferential trade (see CANADA — BRITISH PREFERENTIAL TARIFF) naturally suspends action in other directions. See CANADA — COMMERCE, TARIFFS AND TRANSPORTATION; FREE TRADE; PROTECTION: TARIFF; UNITED STATES — HISTORY OF THE TARIFF; UNITED STATES — RECIPROCITY.

STEPHEN LEACOCK,
Lecturer in Political Science, McGill University.

Canada Balsam, a pale balsam, resin, or oleoresin, obtained by incision from a Canadian tree, the American silver-fir, sometimes called the balm-of-gilead fir (*Abies balsamea*). Canada balsam is of the consistence of thin honey, drying slowly by exposure to the air into a transparent adhesive varnish. It is used to mount objects for the microscope, and for other optical purposes, its refractive and transparency being equal to glass. Thus, when it is sought to cut thin a piece of fossil wood, or anything similar, so as to subject it in favorable circumstances to microscopic examination, it is affixed to a more massive body by Canada balsam.

Canada — Grand Trunk Pacific Railway Company. This company was incorporated by act of the Dominion Parliament 24 Oct. 1903, for the purpose of constructing a railway from Moncton, in the Province of New Brunswick, to some suitable port on the Pacific Coast, in the northern portion of British Columbia. No part of the railway has at this date (January 1, 1905) been constructed, although much of the preliminary survey work has been accomplished. The approximate route of the line from Moncton to Quebec will skirt the northern extremity of the State of Maine; from Quebec the line will run in a westerly direction to a point on the boundary line between the Provinces of Ontario and Quebec, south of and near Lake Abittibi, thence in a westerly and northwesterly direction passing to the north of Lake Nipigon, to a point at or near the city of Winnipeg, thence westerly passing Edmonton, and by way of the Peace or Pine River Passes, or any other convenient pass through the Rocky Mountains, to Port Simpson or Bute Inlet, or some other accessible port on the Pacific Coast. The company has power to construct branch lines from points on the main line to Montreal, North Bay, Port Arthur or Fort William, Brandon, Regina, Prince Albert, and Calgary, also a branch line to Dawson in Yukon Territory. The company also has authority to own, control, and operate steamships or other vessels, on any of the navigable lakes and rivers of Canada, and upon the Atlantic and Pacific Oceans; it may also own hotels, telegraph and telephone lines, and generally enter into any business incidental to an undertaking of such magnitude.

By an agreement entered into with the Canadian Government, the latter undertake to build the section from Moncton, N. B., to Winnipeg, Man., and lease it to the Grand Trunk Pacific Company for a period of 50 years at rental of 3 per cent on cost of construction. For the first seven years the company is subject to payment of working expenses only (the Government waiving the rental). For the remainder of the period, the company pays rental at the rate of 3 per cent on the cost of construction, except that in the event the company fails to earn the rental due for the first three years, following the period of seven years during which the company pays no rental (the 8th, 9th, and 10th years of the lease), then the rental so unpaid shall be added to the capital account and interest paid thereon at the same rate — 3 per cent.

On the section Winnipeg to the Pacific Coast the Canadian Government guarantees for 50 years the payment of 75 per cent of the principal and interest of an issue of bonds not exceeding $13,000 a mile for the prairie portion (Winnipeg to the foot-hills of the Rocky Mountains, a distance of about 1,200 miles) and $50,000 per mile through the Rocky Mountains. The remaining 25 per cent is guaranteed by the Grand Trunk Railway Company of Canada. The Grand Trunk Pacific Railway is to provide the equipment for the entire line. The capital stock of the company is fixed at $45,000,000, of which $20,000,000 is preferred stock. The $25,000,000 of common stock is held by the Grand Trunk Railway Company of Canada.

It is anticipated that work on the surveys of certain portions of the line will have so far advanced as to enable construction to be commenced in the spring of 1905.

The railway, — although located in a more northerly latitude than any of the existing transcontinental lines, — passes through a territory in a lower altitude, and it is quite certain that the grades will be much more favorable, considerably lessening the cost of operation. It is anticipated that the maximum grade across the Rocky Mountains will not exceed 52 feet to the mile — while that across the prairies will be about 21 feet, and on the Lake Superior section 16 feet per mile.

The line will cross the extensive region of the Canadian northwest, which is enormously rich in agricultural and mineral products, at or about latitude 55°. Approximately, the distances arr as follows: Moncton to Winnipeg, 1,840 miles; Winnipeg to Port Simpson, 1,400 miles.

CHARLES M. HAYS,
Second Vice-President and General Manager Grand Trunk Railway System.

Canada — Grand Trunk Railway System. An international system of railways extending from Portland, Me., to Chicago, Ill., traversing the States of Maine, New Hampshire, and Vermont, the Provinces of Quebec and Ontario in Canada, and the States of Michigan, Indiana, and Illinois. The system now comprises 4,200 miles of railway, of which 921 miles of the main lines are double-tracked, practically the entire distance between Saint Johns, Que., and Chicago, Ill., and (from Hamilton) to Niagara Falls. The Grand Trunk Railway Company was incorporated 10 Nov. 1852, by act of Parliament of the Dominion of Canada for the purpose of acquiring and operating as a unit various sections of railway then built, or in course of construction. The section between Portland, Me., and Montreal, Que., was opened in 1853, and the section Montreal, Que., to Sarnia, Ont., via Toronto and Stratford; and the section from Richmond, Que., to Point Levi, Que., the same year. In 1863 the line from Port Huron, Mich., to Detroit, Mich., was completed, thus providing a through route between Detroit, Mich., and Portland, Me. In 1880 the line from Port Huron, Mich., to Chicago, Ill., was completed and opened for traffic.

In 1882 the Grand Trunk acquired control of the Great Western Railway of Canada extending from Suspension Bridge, N. Y., to Windsor, Ont., with several branches north and south of the main line, and also the Detroit, Grand Haven and Milwaukee Ry., whose line extended from Detroit, Mich., to Grand Haven, Mich. In 1883 the Midland Railway of Canada was acquired, which included the branches north of the Grand Trunk Railway main line, extending from Belleville to Peterboro, Haliburton, and Midland, in Ontario.

In 1888 an amalgamation was effected with the Northern and North Western System of railways extending from Port Dover and Hamilton to Collingwood. Meaford, and Nipissing Junction. thus completing a network of railways under one management, reaching every town and village of importance in the Southern peninsula of Ontario, and forming the consolidation of lines now known under the title of the Grand Trunk Railway System.

The Central Vermont Railroad and its leased lines, aggregating a total of 531 miles, is also controlled and operated in the interests of the Grand Trunk Railway System.

Arrangements have been recently concluded by which, in return for a guarantee of the interest and principal of a new issue of bonds, the Canada Atlantic Railway, extending from Swanton, Vt., to Ottawa. Ont., — the capital of the Dominion, — and Parry Sound, on Georgian Bay, will hereafter be controlled by the Grand Trunk Railway System; as also the Canada Atlantic Transit Company, operating a line of steamers from Parry Sound to Fort William, Duluth, Milwaukee, and Chicago.

SUMMARY OF MILEAGE.

	Miles.
Grand Trunk Railway system	4,177
Central Vermont R. R. and leased lines	531
Canada Atlantic Railway	468
Total owned and controlled lines	5,176

At Portland, Me., the Grand Trunk Railway owns extensive wharf and elevator facilities, the capacity of the latter being 2,500,000 bushels. Sea-going vessels can dock at any stage of the tide, and trains can be run alongside at any hour of the day. At Montreal the elevator capacity owned by the company is 2,250,000 bushels, while at the various lake ports reached by the company, viz., Midland, Collingwood, Meaford, Goderich, Parry Sound, and Point Edward, there are large transfer and storage elevators with a combined capacity of about 5,000,000 bushels.

Several engineering works of considerable magnitude are numbered among the undertakings of the company, those particularly worthy of mention being: (1) The Victoria Tubular Bridge across the Saint Lawrence River at Montreal, one and a half miles in length, originally opened for traffic in 1860 by the present King, Edward VII., then Prince of Wales. This bridge cost $7,000,000. In 1897–8 it was entirely rebuilt at a cost of $2,000,000. and is now a modern open truss double-track structure, having carriage-ways and foot-walks on each side, and is known as the Victoria Jubilee Bridge. (2) The Niagara Falls double-track Steel Arch Bridge spanning the gorge, completed in 1897, and replacing the old original Suspension Bridge, which was for over 40 years a land-mark to travelers and tourists. This is the largest single-arch railway and vehicle bridge in the world, having a clear span of 555 feet. (3) The International Bridge between Fort Erie, Ont., and Black Rock, N. Y., a distance of over a mile, which formerly consisted of iron single-track trusses across the main river and harbor at Black Rock, opened for traffic in 1873. This bridge was entirely reconstructed in 1901. and is now capable of carrying the heaviest loads. (4) The Saint Clair Tunnel, under the Saint Clair River from Sarnia, Ont., to Port Huron, Mich., a distance of two and a quarter miles, commenced November, 1888; finished August, 1890. The length of the actual tunnel under the river is 6,026 feet. It is lined with solid cast-iron plates two inches thick, bolted together in segments, and cemented throughout. The interior diameter of the tunnel is 20 feet. The roadbed through the tunnel is laid in the most substantial manner with steel rails weighing 100 pounds to the lineal yard.

For the year ending 31 Dec. 1903, the gross earnings of the Grand Trunk Railway System were $35,710,107, of which the freight receipts amounted to $23,680,685, and the passenger receipts to $11,296,229.

The total miles run by engines hauling passenger and freight trains during the year 1903 was 24,357,080. The number of passengers carried was 11,152,513, and the number of tons of freight handled was 14,615,031. There are in use on the System 990 locomotives, 932 passenger cars and 30,202 freight cars, and in addition a large number of " service " cars, snow plows, derrick cars, etc.

The following constituent companies form the Grand Trunk Railway System :

	Miles.
Grand Trunk Railway	3,483
Grand Trunk Western Railway	336
Detroit, Grand Haven and Milwaukee Railway	189
Toledo, Saginaw and Muskegon Railway	116
Cincinnati, Saginaw and Mackinaw Railway	53
Total	4,177

CHARLES M. HAYS,
Second Vice-President and General Manager Grand Trunk Railway System.

Canada Hemp, Indian Hemp, or Amy-root, a perennial herb *Apocynum cannabinum* of the dogbane family (*Apocynaceæ*). a native of North America (British Columbia, Florida, and Lower California) generally found growing along the banks of streams or in moist ground. It has a strong fibre used by the Indians for twine, nets, woven fabrics, etc. They root deep, the stem and branches are upright and the leaves oblong, lancerlate–oblong and ovate-oblong, acute or obtuse and mucronate at the apex but narrow and rounded at the base. Above they are glabrous and sometimes pubescent beneath and range from two to six feet in length and six inches to three feet in width. The cymes are dense: the pedicels short and bracteolate at the base; and the flowers are from two and one-half to three inches broad. The calyx⁻ segments are nearly as long as the tube of the greenish–white corolla. Consult: Britton 'Illustrated Flora of the Northern United States and Canada' (New York, 1897); Gray 'Manual of Botany' (New York, 1889); etc.

Canada—Immigration to. The Dominion has witnessed within recent years a great increase of immigration, more especially from Great Britain and the United States, but also from the Scandinavian kingdoms, from Germany and other countries of Europe. Within the past decade the Dominion has received more than half a million immigrants, nearly all of a most desirable class, and the large majority devoted to agriculture, and ready and able to do their part in developing the practically unlimited wealth of Canada's vast wheat-growing area. This area is estimated at 171,000,000 acres, of which about 5,000,000 are under cultivation. It is estimated by high Canadian authority that within 10 years 10,000,000 acres will be under wheat, yielding 200,000,000 bushels, a quantity equal to Great Britain's annual wheat importation.

The cheapness of land, its unparalleled productiveness, the certainty of comfort and independence as the reward of industry and thrift, and the security of life and property under a well-regulated administration, are the chief inducements which have already attracted hundreds of thousands of Britons and of Americans to the Canadian Northwest, and which are continuing to bring them in an ever-increasing flood. For every British immigrant there is one American, the latter from nearly every section of the Union.

While these English speaking settlers form the much greater part of the new population, the Scandinavians, Germans, Hungarians, Galicians, Russians, French, and Belgians and other nationalities are represented in the arrivals. The Doukhobors, from Russia, have proved an industrious and valuable addition to Canada's population, and hold 422,700 acres of land, of which 180,000 have been taken up by them as homesteads.

The lands offered to settlers by the Canadian government are situated west of Lake Superior, and to the north of Minnesota, North Dakota, and Montana, and east of the Rocky Mountains, in the Provinces of Manitoba, Saskatchewan, and Alberta. The land is for the most part prairie, and can be secured absolutely free from timber and stones, if desired, the soil being the very best alluvial black loam, from one to two feet deep, with a clay subsoil. It is just rolling enough to give it good drainage, and in a great many places there is plenty of timber, and in other places it is underlaid with good coal. The land can be secured by homesteading. The entry fee for a homestead of 160 acres is $10, there being no further money consideration. The settler, before receiving his patent, must live upon the land for three years, a residence of six months in the year being necessary, and he must also do a small amount of cultivation. A foreigner — that is, a person not a British subject — may enter land for a free homestead at once on his arrival in Canada, but he must become naturalized before he can obtain a patent for the land, and he must reside three years in the country to become naturalized. Meantime he can hold possession of the land, live upon it, and exercise every right of ownership.

Though there are tracts of forest in the Canadian Northwest, there are localities where the quantity of building timber and material is limited, and the government has made provision for such cases. Should a man settle on a quarter section of land devoid of timber, he can, by making application to the Dominion Lands Agent in the locality, obtain a permit to cut on the Government lands free of charge the following: (1) 1,000 lineal feet of building timber, measuring no more than 12 inches at the butt; (2) 400 roofing poles; (3) 2,000 fencing rails and 500 fence posts seven feet long and not exceeding five inches in diameter at the small end; (4) 30 cords of dry fuel wood or firewood. The settler having all these free of charge has only the expense of the cutting and hauling them to his homestead, which cannot cost him a great deal. He is also very likely to have the benefit of cheap coal. There are areas of coal in Western Canada of such an extent as to be practically inexhaustible. The principal districts of Western Canada are within easy reach of firewood, while the settlers of Alberta and Saskatchewan are particularly favored, especially along the various streams, at which they can get all the coal they require, very frequently at the cost of handling and hauling it home.

If a settler should desire to go into stock raising, and his quarter-section of 160 acres should not prove sufficient to furnish pasture for his stock, he can make application to the Land Commissioner for a lease for grazing lands at a very low cost.

The public school system is established all through the country, and there are schools in all the organized school districts. There is a ready market for cereals and other produce; the climate is healthy and agreeable, and pulmonary complaints are unknown, except in the cases of invalids sent there for the sake of the dry and bracing air.

The aim of the Dominion Government is to attract to Canada industrious, intelligent, and energetic immigrants, with the purpose and the ability to do their part in building up a nation imperial in its natural resources and in the extent of its magnificent territory, and in carrying out this policy the Government is meeting with eminent and ever-increasing success.

W. D. SCOTT,
Superintendent of Immigration, Ottawa, Canada.

Canada — Intercolonial Railway. This railway and the Prince Edward Island Railway are owned and operated by the Government of Canada, and together form the Government Railways.

They are under the charge of a department of the Government called the Department of Railways and Canals, which is presided over by the Minister of Railways and Canals. He is a member of the Government and has a seat in Parliament.

The Intercolonial extends through the Provinces of Quebec, New Brunswick, and Nova Scotia, connecting the cities of Montreal and Quebec with the cities of Saint John, Halifax, and Sidney on the Atlantic Coast. Its length, including branches, is 1446 miles.

The history of the Intercolonial is interesting, but there is space here for only a brief outline.

The construction of a railway from the Atlantic Ocean to the Saint Lawrence River at Quebec, through the British Provinces, was proposed in

1832. An exploratory survey from Point Levis, opposite Quebec, to Saint Andrews on the Bay of Fundy was made, with the assistance of the British Government, in 1836, and a practicable route was found, but nothing further was done at that time, because of representations from the United States Government, that part of the surveys were in territory claimed by the State of Maine. Other explorations were subsequently made until 1846, when the Royal Engineers, under instructions from the British Government, commenced the survey of several routes from Halifax to Quebec. These surveys were completed in 1848, and the route recommended by the Engineers was, generally speaking, that adopted when the Intercolonial was constructed many years afterwards. The surveys showed that there were several routes by which such a railway could be constructed, but the Provinces considered that the work was too great and costly for their unaided resources ; under these circumstances the greater project was laid aside for a time, and each of the Provinces in its own way, and independently of the others, turned its attention to the construction of railways which were destined afterwards to form parts of the Intercolonial.

The Province of Canada in 1849 passed an Act affording assistance to railway companies by guaranteeing their bonds, and the Halifax and Quebec Railway was particularly mentioned in this Act. In 1852 the Grand Trunk Railway Company was incorporated and subsidized. Another company was also incorporated and subsidized, in the same year, to build a railway from opposite Quebec to Trois Pistoles. This company was amalgamated with the Grand Trunk Railway Company, and the latter built the line from Point Levis, opposite Quebec, to Rivière du Loup, 126 miles, which was opened in 1860. The company did not build as far eastward as Trois Pistoles.

The Province of New Brunswick in 1853 also commenced railway construction, and built, as a Government work, a line from Saint John to Point du Chene on the Gulf of Saint Lawrence, 108 miles. It was opened in 1860, and was called the European and North American Railway. In 1865 the Province entered into a contract for an extension of this railway eastward to the boundary of Nova Scotia, and this was completed and opened in December 1870.

The Province of Nova Scotia commenced in June 1854 the construction of a Government railway, and in December 1858 it was opened from Halifax to Truro, 61 miles, with a branch to Windsor, 32 miles. This was called the Nova Scotia Railway. The Province afterwards extended this railway from Truro to Pictou on the Gulf of Saint Lawrence, 52 miles, this extension being opened in May 1867.

The people still desired complete railway communication between the Provinces, and in 1864 and 1865 a survey was made of a route to connect Truro, Nova Scotia, with Rivière du Loup, Quebec, the link which remained to be constructed.

On 1 July 1867 the Provinces of Canada, Nova Scotia, and New Brunswick were, by an Act of the Parliament of Great Britain, united in a confederation called the Dominion of Canada. By that Act the railways already mentioned, owned by the Provinces of Nova Scotia and New Brunswick, became the property of the Dominion. That Act also provided that an Intercolonial Railway connecting the River Saint Lawrence with the city of Halifax should be immediately constructed by the Government of Canada ; and by another Act of the same Parliament, in the same year, the British Government was authorized to guarantee the interest on a loan, not exceeding three million pounds sterling, to be raised by Canada, for the purpose of constructing the railway between Rivière du Loup and Truro. These arrangements were carried out, the work of construction of the Intercolonial was commenced without delay, and prosecuted without intermission, and on 9 November 1872 the division extending from Truro to Amherst, 76 miles, was opened. This division formed the connection between the Nova Scotia Railway and the European and North American Railway, and completed railway communication between Halifax and Saint John. The three railways, a total of 370 miles, were on the above date consolidated under the name of the Intercolonial Railway. These three railways forming the Intercolonial had been built with a gauge of 5 feet 6 inches, and they remained that gauge until 18 June 1875, when they were changed to 4 feet 8½ inches, the gauge in general use on this continent, and which had been adopted for the Intercolonial.

The next division opened was that connecting with the Grand Trunk at Rivière du Loup and extending eastward to Ste Flavie 83 miles. This was opened in August 1874. In November 1875 the division from Moncton to Campbellton, 185 miles, was opened, and on 1 July 1876 the division from Campbellton to Ste Flavie, 105 miles. On the latter date the work of providing direct and continuous railway communication between Quebec and Saint John and Halifax was completed.

The length of the Intercolonial on 1 July 1876 was 746 miles. Since that date it has been extended by construction and by purchase. The more important additions are the following : —
In August, 1879, the portion of the Grand Trunk Railway between Rivière du Loup and Point Levis, 126 miles, was purchased ; in January 1884 the railway from New Glasgow to Mulgrave on the Strait of Canseau, 80 miles, was purchased.

The following were constructed : from Oxford Junction to Pictou, 72 miles, opened July 1890 ; and in the Island of Cape Breton, from the Strait of Canseau to Sydney and North Sydney, 96 miles, opened January, 1891.

On 1 March 1898 it was extended to Montreal by the purchase of the Drummond County Railway, 130 miles, and by a one-half leasehold interest in the Grand Trunk from Ste Rosalie to Saint Lambert, with the right to use the Victoria Bridge and the terminals of the Grand Trunk in Montreal, distance 38 miles.

On 1 Oct. 1904 the Canada Eastern Railway, extending from Fredericton, the Capital of New Brunswick, to Chatham, 125 miles, was purchased.

The total length of the Intercolonial on 30 June 1905, not including the Windsor Branch, which is leased to the Dominion Atlantic Railway, was 1446 miles.

The Government spared no expense in its construction and equipment, and has from time to time made improvements so as to keep it up to the highest standard of railways.

It is built in the most substantial manner, all bridges being of stone and iron or steel. The track is laid with heavy steel rails weighing 80 pounds to the lineal yard. The station accommodation is ample and convenient. It is fully equipped with the best modern rolling stock for both passenger and freight traffic, including sleeping, parlor, and dining cars which are owned and operated by the railway.

Its tracks connect with the wharves in Montreal, it has an extensive water front and wharves in the harbor of Quebec, also wharves at Rivière du Loup and Rimouski, all on the Saint Lawrence River. It has wharves at Campbellton on the Restigouche River, at Dalhousie on the Bay Chaleur, at Newcastle, Chatham, and Loggieville on the Miramichi River, at Gibson on the Saint John River, at Moncton on the Petitcodiac River, at Dorchester and Sackville on arms of the Bay of Fundy, at Point du Chene, Pugwash, and Pictou on the Gulf of Saint Lawrence, at Mulgrave and Point Tupper on the Strait of Canseau, and at Sydney, North Sydney, Halifax, and Saint John on the Atlantic Ocean.

At these various ports the railway has provided accommodation for shipping, and at Halifax and Saint John this is extensive, including grain elevators at both places.

At Rimouski, in summer, ocean steamers when passing on the voyage between Montreal and Europe in both directions land and embark mails and passengers, which are carried by fast trains to and from points east and west of Rimouski.

At Point du Chene and Pictou, in summer, steamers run daily to and from Prince Edward Island. In winter this communication is made from Pictou by strong and powerful steamers, built for the purpose, which force their way through the ice.

At the Strait of Canseau, between Mulgrave and Point Tupper, a distance of about one mile, there is a steam car ferry connecting the lines in Nova Scotia with those in the Island of Cape Breton. This steamer runs both in summer and winter, and is capable of transporting an entire train of cars at each trip.

At North Sydney there is steamboat communication both winter and summer with New Foundland.

In winter the Canadian mail steamers land and embark mails and passengers at Halifax, and these are carried from and to Montreal by fast trains. In winter also a considerable portion of the exports and imports of Canada pass through the ports of Saint John and Halifax.

The cost of the railway and equipment to 30 June 1905 was $77,474,272.03.

The gross earnings for the year ended 30 June 1905 were $6,783,522.83, of which $2,105,066.75 came from passenger traffic and $4,678,456.08 from freight traffic.

The number of passengers carried was 2,810,960, and the number of tons of freight 2,782,257. The number of miles run by trains was 7,296,745.

The rolling stock consists of 332 locomotives, 41 first-class sleeping cars, 35 second-class sleeping cars, 9 parlor cars, 9 dining cars, 270 passenger cars, 60 baggage cars, and 10,185 freight cars of various kinds. There are also auxiliary cars, vans, snow and wing ploughs, travelling cranes, etc., to the number of 212, used exclusively in the service of the railway.

Prince Edward Island Railway. The Province of Prince Edward Island became a part of the Dominion of Canada on 1 July 1873, and one of the terms of union was, that the railway under contract and in course of construction for the Government of the Island should become the property of the Dominion. This railway extended from Charlottetown, the capital, westward to Tignish and eastward to Georgetown and to Souris, a total distance of 198 miles. It was completed and transferred to the Dominion 29 Dec. 1874, and was opened for traffic 12 May 1875. A branch from Emerald Junction to Cape Traverse, 11 miles, was opened 22 Jan. 1885. A branch from Charlottetown to Murray Harbour, 48 miles, including a bridge half a mile in length across the Hillsborough River at Charlottetown, was opened 1 Nov. 1905, making the total length 257 miles. This bridge is of the most substantial character, the piers and abutments being of masonry and the superstructure of steel. It is an important engineering work; the depth of water and of mud, and the tides and currents, made the undertaking difficult. A number of the piers were constructed by the pneumatic process, and the height of these from the rock, where the foundation rests, to the floor of the bridge is 110 feet.

Two other branches are under construction, one to Port Vernon, 4 miles, and one from Cardigan to Montague Bridge, 6 miles.

The gauge of the railway is 3 feet 6 inches. It is well constructed and equipped, and is provided with suitable conveniences for business, including wharves at Charlottetown, Summerside, Georgetown, Mount Stewart, Souris, Alberton, and Murray River.

There is daily steamboat communication with the mainland during the season of navigation, between Charlottetown and Pictou, and between Summerside and Point du Chene; and in winter passengers and freight are carried from and to the Island by powerful ice-breaking steamboats, owned and operated by the Dominion Government, which run between Georgetown and Pictou, making daily trips with considerable regularity during the greater portion of the winter.

The cost of the railway and equipment to 30 June 1905 was $6,719,463.80.

The gross earnings for the year ended 30 June 1905 were $217,330.61, of which $102,505.55 were for passenger traffic, and $114,825.06 for freight traffic.

The number of passengers carried was 235,194, and the number of tons of freight 73,969. The number of miles run by trains was 343,301.

The rolling stock consists of 27 locomotives, 64 passenger train cars, 416 freight cars, and 23 service cars and snow ploughs.

DAVID POTTINGER,
General Manager, Government Railways.

Canada, Literary Conditions in. It is probable that for years to come Canada must continue to find her literature in the columns of the daily and weekly press of the country. Writers the Dominion has in plenty, of course; but the author, in the highest sense of the term, she has not. Of men and women who have made their living at authorship, it is impossible to name even one. Of successful books which have repaid their publishers and left something for the author, the list is exhausted when half a dozen are put down. Canada has her fair share of ably-conducted newspapers, the writing in which is vigorous and thoughtful. She has also a press in the smaller towns, where the political controversies of the day are still carried on with that "peculiar animation" which Lord Dufferin noticed before he had been three weeks in the country. The weekly newspaper, as a rule, is a mere eclectic, compiled from the daily issues of the particular journal whose title it bears. Several attempts have been made to establish an English magazine of general literature, but in almost each instance failure has proved the result of the enterprise. The Canadian Magazine, published at Toronto, alone survives. The French-Canadian writers have been more fortunate. They have succeeded in maintaining a creditable monthly and quarterly press, largely made up of original matter, for quite a number of years. And yet the constituency from which they must draw their support is limited to but one province, Quebec; Eastern Ontario, which has a large French-Canadian population, and Manitoba, which has nearly 10,000 French Canadians, offering but slight encouragement.

Has Canada a literature of her own? The question is often asked, but the answer can only be given when the sense in which the word "Canadian," as applied to letters, is made clear. Does Canadian literature mean a body of literary work not merely dealing with Canadian subjects, but called forth by Canadian social, political, religious or other conditions. If that is the true definition of the term, points out that eminent scholar, William Houston, Librarian of the Ontario Legislature, in a letter to me, "then we have no Canadian literature worth boasting about." "If we mean," the same writer continues, "a body of literary work produced in Canada, then we have a respectable amount of average product to show, and some of it is of rare excellence. If by Canadian literature we mean all the writings produced by Canadians in every language, then we can make a passable exhibit; but what we have produced in French is mainly French literature, and what we have produced in English is not essentially different from English literature produced in England or the United States. There is sometimes a tinge of local color about it, but often there is not even that." Mr Charles Dudley Warner, the engaging satirist and observer, thinks that the lack of intellectual activity of the Canadians is due to the fact that they have to put forth so much of their physical energy in an endeavor to keep warm. But Mr. Warner's delicious raillery is always extravagant, and to point a phrase, it troubles him little if he discards a fact. A Canadian writer, taking him sharply to task, on surveying the field, felt at the last constrained to admit that in Canada there really was considerable "literary feebleness." The cause of this he attributes to "our humble political status." "As a colony," he writes, "Canada possesses neither the higher attributes nor the greater responsibilities of national existence, and where such attributes and responsibilities are wanting, national life and feeling, the source and inspiration of all literary achievement, will be equally wanting." Now this simply means that the colonial position is fatal to the development of

the higher intellectual life and movement — literary genius, in fact — and that the only hope for Canada is to rid herself of the slender thread which binds her to the mother country, and the Colonial office. Something of the sort has been said before and the politicians spasmodically employ the phrase when questions involving treaty-making with foreign countries come up in Parliament But independence, though a suggestive topic, has, so far, no very strong foothold in Canada, many of the more prominent public men looking upon it merely as a short cut to annexation to the United States. The idea, however, may be discussed.

American letters during the colonial period in the United States were feeble and insignificant enough; and it was not until after a season of tracts, sermons and pamphlets, that poetry, history and the novel began to appear. Bryant and Poe. Prescott and Motley followed; and in Hawthorne the continent possessed her strongest and most brilliant romancer. From New England came the great ones, whose names it is not necessary to repeat here. The Civil War stimulated rather than stifled the literary spirit, and since 1864 literature in the United States has kept even pace with the growth of material progress. American novelists have formed a distinct school of their own, and American books have a vogue everywhere. But has this condition of things been reached by independence merely? Must Canada pursue a similar course of political advancement if she would have a literature of individuality, color and strength? Nor must the significant fact be lost sight of, American letters have largely influenced those of Canada.

The want of a large leisure class has, in all probability, helped to retard literary effort in the Dominion; but that cannot be the only reason why a great genius in letters has not arisen in British America. Principal Grant, a singularly graceful and sagacious writer, said, not long since, that the Dominion had not even given the world a single scientist of the first class. In science, however, the Dominion has done very well, better, in fact, than she has done in literature, and the names of Sir William Dawson and his gifted son, Dr. George M. Dawson, rank deservedly high as "scientists of the first-class." Sir Daniel Wilson, of Toronto, the archæologist, was not a Canadian by birth, but the greater part of his life was spent in Canada, the land in which his best work was accomplished.

But if no great genius in letters has been developed in Canada, there is at least a very respectable showing of good writers to point to, though the departments to which they have devoted their pens have not been extensive. Political economy has been untouched by the Canadian thinker, save in the most general and perfunctory way, though the subject is both fascinating and inviting. The novelist, too, is yet to appear, as well as his younger brother, the short story writer. Of course, the Canadian novel has been attempted in both the English and

French languages; but success, it may be said with truth, has not rewarded the authors. One story, dealing with life and adventure in Quebec, and having a picturesque background, has the reputation of being the best Canadian novel yet written. This, however, cannot be considered as very high praise, when the other Canadian novels have been looked into. Canadian writers who have attempted fiction seem to lack the creative faculty entirely. They have failed to produce work of high imagination, and, apparently, they are out of touch with human sympathy and life. The characters they delineate are, as a rule, colorless, the conversations are insipid, and the movement is slow. No improvement on Haliburton or De Mille has been made since those men delighted growing audiences. But the former was a humorist rather than a novelist, and the latter was only beginning to show what was in him when he died. The one prominent Canadian novel to which reference is made here is read because it touches a most dramatic series of incidents in early Canadian history, and the *locale* is familiar to the summer tourist seeking recreation in the old capital town of Canada. But as a novel it lacks action, and the art of the novelist is wanting.

If the novels of Sir Gilbert Parker do not betray the true French-Canadian flavor always, they are distinguished for their thorough workmanship and fine literary execution. The stories, short and long, of the late William McLennan in quick succession showed great improvement, and he died just as his pen was giving us what the public demanded. In collaboration with Miss McIlwraith he wrote 'The Span o' Life,' — a book which promised much. On her own account, Miss McIlwraith wrote, with much acceptance, several short stories, the scene of which was laid along the banks of the Lower St. Lawrence. "Ralph Connor," Rev. Charles W. Gordon, wrote 'The Man from Glengarry.' Since then his pen has not been idle and much good work has issued from it. Prof. Charles G. D. Roberts is not only a poet, but a novelist of much power. His subjects deal principally with wild life. Miss Agnes Laut is a novelist also of growing force.

To stimulate art, science and letters in Canada, Lord Lorne (now the Duke of Argyll), during his reign, established two societies. The Academy of Arts, leaping into popularity at a bound, is doing very well. The Royal Society, which combines, perhaps, the best features of the French Academy and the British Association, was not so well received at first, and in certain quarters it provoked hostile criticism. The membership was limited to 80 Fellows. It has since been increased to 120 Fellows. The first two sections of 30 Fellows each concern themselves with history, archæology, ethnology and general literature. The first section is composed of Frenchmen and the second of Englishmen; the remaining two sections are devoted to science in all its branches, nearly every department being represented. It must be confessed that the latter make by far the better exhibit, but the literary sections show yearly signs of great vitality. The French members conduct their department in the annual volume of 'Proceedings and Transactions,' as if it were part of a popular review. They admit poetry, stories, dramas and fragments of comedies, though, of course, philology and history are not excluded. The English are more conservative, and though poems are sometimes read at the meetings, they find no place in the published volume. Tales and the play are likewise absent. The section is strong in archæology, history and ethnology, and in the development of those studies it has a mission of usefulness to perform. Parliament grants the Royal Society $5,000 per annum, for the purpose of publishing the transactions of the body, and it is not too much to say that its collections of papers are in every way creditable and valuable.

Versifiers the Dominion has by the score; but of poets there are not more than half a dozen who write in English, and two or three who write in French. Their work is good, much of it is strong and robust; and though their muse is largely influenced by the old-world masters of song, such as Tennyson, Keats, Hugo and Beranger, and such American poets as Longfellow and Poe, there is enough originality shown in the way of ineident and locality to prove its unmistakable origin. The younger, and it may be admitted, the better poets of Canada, have uttered notes of a distinctly patriotic tone. Roberts' lines addressed to "Canada," are especially spirited, and when first published they sent a genuine thrill through the land. Another Canadian poet, who has sounded a bold note, is Bliss Carman, whose workmanship is artistic and original. He excels in the lyrical form of poetry, and his place is undoubtedly among the best of the Canadian poets. He has produced no long poem, and he does not readily turn to narrative; but his songs are cheery, musical and emiently patriotic. Canadian fruit, flower, manhood and incident are the well-chosen subjects he beautifies, and some of these he has invested with true grandeur. 'Low Tide on Grand Pré' is the most ambitious of his performances. Much in the way of praise may he said of Archibald Lampman, whose 'Among the Millet' made his fame. One reads his verses with fresh surprise and delight; for the range of his thought and the gentleness of his treatment are alike admirable. George Murray's 'Verses and Versions' reveal that distinguished poet at his best. His taste is catholic and pure, and his manner is delicate and thoughtful. He and Sir Edwin Arnold were educated together at Oxford, and both were earnest students. The one went to Canada, the other to India. From John Reade we have the tuneful 'Prophecy of Merlin,' a poem constructed on the lines set down by Tennyson in his 'Idyls of the King,' charming in conception, almost faultless in measure and very even in texture. William Wilfred Campbell, the Lakeside poet, has done much to popularize the beauty and pictur·

esqueness of Canadian lake scenery, and his lake lyrics are very sweet and full of life and poetic power, while their wealth of description stamps him as a true observer of nature in her various and varied moods. Dr. William Henry Drummond in his dialect poems and ballads has blazed a new trail, and his 'Habitant' establishes his pre-eminence in that department of polite letters.

The drama has met with fair success, two or three acting plays — notably, Frechette's 'Papineau,' and Le May's 'Rouge et Bleu,' — having been produced before admiring audiences. But the dramas which have not found their way to the stage have proved the more successful performances from a literary point of view. Charles Mair and Hunter Duvar have given us two Canadian dramas of very great importance and merit; and Heavysege's 'Saul,' is, all things considered, a marvellous piece of work from the first line to the last. Heavysege, however, was an Englishman, and his poetry was never distinctively Canadian.

Many histories of Canada have been written, all Canadians who write evidently feeling it to be at once their duty and their mission to set down the annals of the rise and progress of their country. They are good, bad and indifferent. Of critical and analytical historical writers, the Dominion can count but few. Some have tried to tell the story with a well-meaning desire to be exact and correct; most of them, however, have only succeeded in repeating the errors of their predecessors. Few have gone to original sources for information, though the records are available in copious richness. Those historians who have devoted their energies and their pens to the treatment of special events in Canadian political, historical and social life,— such as Dr. Doughty's 'Siege of Quebec;' Major Wood's 'Fight for Canada;' Dent's 'History of the Upper Canadian Rebellion' — have made a better exhibit, and we have, therefore, several satisfactory recounts of instructive and interesting periods in the history of the colony, from early times down to the era of confederation, by as many as ten or a dozen different hands.

French Canada, notwithstanding its limited opportunities, has done very well in letters. Poetry, history and the *chronique* — the latter borrowed from France — are prosecuted with industry and ability. Against following implicitly the teachings of French Canada's historians, however, the public may be warned, for the majority have written their books with a special object in view. Thus, Le Clercq wrote his remarkable volume as a protest in behalf of the Recollet Fathers, and to offset the encroachments of the Jesuits. Charlevoix, on the other hand, smiles on the Society of Jesus, and presents the Recollets of Frontenac in a less estimable light. Ferland wrote his history from the severely ecclesiastical side, and Garneau contributes his narrative from the National standpoint. The Abbé Casgrain, a voluminous and brilliant writer, is the chief French-Canadian questioner of Dr. Francis Parkman; and

Benjamin Sulte stands high among the lay historical writers, and though he courts the muse with some success, his fame will rest on his prose.

The French-Canadian romance is devoid of promise. It is, of course, historical in tendency, but in plot it is poor, and in character-drawing it is lamentably weak. It has no humor. The first principles of novel writing seem to be unknown, and with the exception of Chauveau's 'Charles Guerin,' and Bourassa's 'Jacques et Marie,' no appreciable attempt has at all been made to cover a field which is emphatically rich in material. Fair copies of verse, the French-Canadians frequently turn out, but of poets worthy of the name, there are only Cremazie and Frechette, and one other possibly. Biography the French do very well.

In one branch of writing Canada, it may be said, has surpassed her sister colonies. In works treating of the Constitution of the Country, and Parliament in action, there are the notable volumes of Alpheus Todd and Sir John George Bourinot. For many years Dr. Todd's monumental work on 'Parliamentary Government in England,' occupied a place in the Parliaments of Her Majesty's possessions equal to that of Erskine May. Even in the United States, where the system is so different from that of Britain and her Colonies, Todd is recognized as an authority, and frequently quoted. A few years before his death, the author produced his companion volume, dealing exhaustively with Parliamentary Government in the British Colonies. It at once became an indispensable authority. Sir John Bourinot has published an able treatise on 'Parliamentary Procedure and Practice,' which shows the Canadian system of responsible government in full operation, and is the result of twenty years' close observation and study of Parliamentary methods. These books, creditable to Canada as well as to their authors, are used in the Legislatures of the British Colonies and possessions throughout the world, and are a real and clearly defined contribution to the literature of politics and statesmanship. One word more in regard to Canadian authorship may be said: Colonel Denison, of Toronto, a distinguished officer of volunteer cavalry, gave a text-book to the troopers of Russia, Germany and Hungary, and won the Czar's prize of 5,000 rubles with his 'History of Cavalry,' the first specific work on the subject ever written. See LITERATURE, CANADIAN.

GEORGE STEWART,
Author of 'Canada Under the Administration of the Earl of Dufferin,' etc.

Canada—Loyalist Settlers in. In this 20th century it is easy to review without prejudice the motives and sacrifices of those Americans who chose to adhere to British allegiance when the 13 colonies declared themselves independent States. That the great majority of the Loyalists, or "Tories," as they were called by their enemies, were sincerely devoted to the royal cause there can be no sensible doubt, and official records recently brought to public notice present a pathetic picture of the sufferings and losses endured by the unfortunate supporters of British rule in the War of the Revolution. While as a result of that struggle the United States secured their independence, they also lost a host of valuable citizens who emigrated chiefly to Canada, where they established new homes, and helped to strengthen Great Britain's hold on that portion of her empire. The descendants of those emigrants compose a large and influential part of Canada's population, and the names of men prominent in the politics, the professions, and industries of the Dominion can be traced back to time-worn folios which tell the story of the plea of the poverty-stricken refugees for aid from the motherland.

The migration of Loyalists to Canada began as early as 1774, before the actual clash between the colonies and British authority. This was due to the fact that families which found themselves menaced and beset on account of their unpopular opinions saw no safe refuge nearer than Canada. The movement continued throughout the war, varying in degree with British success and defeat, until the surrender of Cornwallis extinguished any remnant of hope in the breasts of the royal adherents, who hastened in multitudes, by land and sea, to seek shelter and protection in the Canadian provinces. Many who tried to live down the past, trusting that, with hostilities over, their former attitude would be pardoned, if not forgotten, found their situation intolerable, and followed in the footsteps of earlier refugees, and this went on until 1789, when the Loyalist migration ceased.

The total number of Loyalists who settled in Nova Scotia, New Brunswick, Cape Breton, and Prince Edward Island is estimated at not less than 35,000, of whom about 30,000 went from New York, although probably the homes of many of these had been elsewhere before they sought shelter in that final stronghold of the British. In 1791 the English-speaking population of Lower Canada had increased to about 20,000, owing chiefly to the Loyalist arrivals, and in Upper Canada 10,000 Loyalists settled in 1783 alone, the next year the population had doubled, and in 1791 it was estimated at 25,000. The province of Ontario may be said to owe its foundation to American Loyalists.

The British Government and the provincial authorities extended cordial and liberal aid to the exiles. Those who were transported at the expense of the government received provisions for one year on leaving New York, and were supplied with rations regularly as long as their necessities continued. They also received clothing, grants of land, and assistance in stocking their farms, building homes, and clearing and cultivating the farms. Tools and arms were also distributed.

The British Crown and Parliament took steps in July 1783 to compensate the refugees from the United States for injuries suffered through their loyalty, and a commission consisting of five members was appointed to examine into and classify the losses and services. The following were held to be entitled to compensation: (1) Those who had rendered services to Great Britain; (2) Those who had borne arms against the Revolution; (3) Uniform Loyalists; (4) Loyalists resident in Great Britain; (5) Those who took oaths of allegiance

to the American States, but afterward joined the British; (6) Those who armed with the Americans and later joined the British army or navy.

Compensation was not allowed for anticipated professional profits, losses in trade or through depreciated paper money, or losses caused by the British army, which were accounted as obligations of the British Government outside the province of the Commission. By the treaty of peace between the United States and Great Britain it was stipulated that Congress should earnestly recommend to the States the restoration of the rights and possessions of "real British subjects," and of Loyalists who had not borne arms. The recommendation was without effect. Nevertheless the Commission required evidence in support of the claim that property had been confiscated, and had not been restored. Notwithstanding the bitter feeling in the United States toward the Loyalists, the requisite evidence appears to have been readily supplied to claimants by American local authorities.

Apart from the expenditures already noted in supporting and establishing Loyalists on their farms, and which amounted in Upper and Lower Canada to probably $4,000,000, the British Government paid $9,448,000 on 1,680 claims examined and allowed by the Commission appointed under the Act of 1783. This Commission sat in London. In 1785 two commissioners were sent to Canada to examine claimants who had failed, through ignorance, inability, or other causes, to present their claims in London. This Commission allowed $2,745,000 on 1,401 claims. After the departure of the Commission claims continued to be sent to Great Britain, where many more were allowed. The claims ranged in amount from $60 to $777,000, and the sums allowed from $50 to $221,000, the latter amount having been granted to Sir John Johnson, the noted "Tory" commander. Every one of the 13 States — or 14, including Vermont — was represented in the number of claimants, as follows: New York, 941; South Carolina, 321; Massachusetts, 226; New Jersey, 208; Pennsylvania, 148; Virginia, 140; North Carolina, 135; Georgia, 129; Connecticut, 92; Maryland, 78; Vermont, 61; Rhode Island, 41; New Hampshire, 31; Delaware, 9; total, 2,560.

It is estimated that the British Government expended in all about $30,000,000 during the Revolution and afterward in aiding Loyalists in America and Great Britain. Those who settled in Canada soon became self-supporting and, as a rule, prosperous. In 1789 it was decreed that all Loyalists should be "distinguished by the letters U. E. affixed to their names, alluding to their great principle, the Unity of the Empire." This distinction has fallen into disuse, although occasionally recalled when some eminent Canadian of old Loyalist stock passes away.   HENRY MANN,
Author of 'The Story of Our Country,' etc.

Canada, Northwest Territories of. — An immense tract of country covering 2,634,880 square miles and governed, since its purchase from the Hudson's Bay Company, in 1870, by the federal authorities of Canada in varying degrees of responsibility and executive author -

ity. Population in 1891 was 98,967; in 1901, 211,649; in 1905 (estimated), 500,000. The districts of which it was composed were created at different dates and, with their respective areas, may be seen in the following table:

DISTRICT	Date of Organization	Area
Keewatin	April 12, 1876	470,416 sq. miles
Assiniboia	May 17, 1882	88,879 sq. miles
Saskatchewan	May 17, 1882	107,618 sq. miles
Alberta	May 17, 1882	101,883 sq. miles
Athabaska	May 17, 1882	251,965 sq. miles
Yukon	June 13, 1898	196,976 sq. miles
Mackenzie	Oct. 2, 1895	562,182 sq. miles
Ungava	Oct. 2, 1895	354,961 sq. miles
Franklin	Oct. 2, 1895	500,000 sq. miles

By order-in-council, 18 Dec. 1897, the boundaries of Ungava, Keewatin, Franklin, Mackenzie and Yukon were somewhat changed. In 1898 the Yukon was made a separate territory. The District of Franklin, it may be added, is a somewhat indeterminate phrase, the area being estimated and its northern boundaries not fully settled. The government of these territories, in a local sense, was centred in Regina (1882) before the people were given even the partial privilege of governing themselves. The first lieutenant-governor was Hon. A. G. Archibald, appointed on 10 May 1870, and for many years the government was carried on by him and his successors, the lieutenant-governors of Manitoba, without popular control. In 1880 they were given a separate lieutenant-governor and council. In 1886 the territories were accorded representation in Parliament; in 1888 a local legislature was established and the first elections held and an advisory council formed for dealing with matters of finance; in 1891 additional powers were given to the legislature and, in 1897, by special federal enactment, an executive council was established responsible to the legislature.

The first appointments to this body were made in 1898 with Mr. F. W. G. Haultain as premier, attorney-general and treasurer. He had already been for ten years the practical head of the local government. In this position he remained until 1905 when the new provinces were created. His successive assistants during this long period were Messrs. Hillyard Mitchall, C. A. Magrath, J. H. Ross, G. H. V. Bulyea, A. L. Sifton and W. Elliott. In 1902 there began a practical and insistent demand for full provincial powers including control of lands and mines, taxation and the right to borrow money. This continued actively until its settlement in the autonomy events of 1905. An important incident in the history of the territories was the Federal Act of 1875 defining certain powers and conditions and including the following reference to education:

When, and so soon as any system of taxation shall be adopted in any district, or portion of the Northwest Territories the lieutenant-governor, by and with the consent of the Council, or Assembly, as the case may be, shall pass all necessary ordinances in respect to education; but it shall therein always be provided that a majority of the ratepayers of any district or portion of the Northwest Territories, or any lesser portion, or sub-division thereof, by whatever name the same may be known, may establish such schools therein, as they may think fit, and make the necessary assessment and collection of rates therefor; and further, that the minority of the ratepayers therein, whether Protestant or Roman Catholic, may establish separate schools therein and that in such latter case the ratepayers establishing such Protestant or Roman Catholic separate schools shall be liable only to assessment of such rates as they may impose upon themselves in respect thereof.

Under this law a system of Roman Catholic separate schools gradually grew up, not very important in number, as the population was small, but considered to be very important in their basic principle. In 1892 and 1893 and 1901, however, ordinances were passed by the legislature practically eliminating this system and giving the Roman Catholics only the right to separate buildings, appointment of teachers of their own faith and half-an-hour at the close of the school day for purposes of religious instruction — subject, however, to complete supervision by the department of education, the use of uniform text-books and the possession of regulation teaching qualifications. In 1901 the Protestant population of the territories was 92,760 and the Roman Catholic 30,073; in 1904 there had been 1,360 school districts erected since 1884 and only 16 separate school districts, of which two were Protestant. After the passage of the Acts of 1905, carving the new provinces out of this region, a reorganization of the territories took place, under the old designation.

By the terms of this legislation they were to now comprise the region formerly known as Rupert's Land and the Northwestern Territory, with the exception of Manitoba, the new provinces, Keewatin and the Yukon; including, also, all other British territories and possessions in Northern Canada and all islands adjacent thereto with the exception of Newfoundland and its dependency of Labrador. The federal authorities were given power to appoint a commissioner for the Northwest territories, who should administer its government "under instructions from time to time given him by the governor-in-council or the minister of the interior." A council of not more than four persons was also authorized for appointment by the federal government to aid the commissioner and the latter, in council, was given the same power to make ordinances as had been vested in the legislative assembly of former territories.

Establishment of the New Provinces. — During the three years prior to 1905 the question of provincial autonomy for the Northwest territories of Canada had only excited a languid interest at Ottawa, although it had been pressed with much vigor by the western premier, Mr. Haultain, and was keenly discussed at more than one territorial general election. It was noteworthy, however, in these preliminary discussions, that the separate school or educational question was almost eliminated, that in the many dispatches passing between the territorial and dominion governments it was never directly mentioned, that so far as the public is aware, it was not discussed in the occasional conferences between the two governments, and that it was not an issue in the territorial elections of 1902 or in the dominion contest of 1904.

Prior to the latter event Sir Wilfrid Laurier had written Mr. Haultain that his government would, if returned to power, be prepared to take up the question after the general elections. Accordingly on 5 Jan. 1905 a conference commenced at Ottawa between Mr. Haultain and Mr. G. H. V. Bulyea representing the territories and Sir Wilfrid Laurier and other members of the federal government. On 21 February following, the dominion premier introduced in the house of commons his bill establishing the province of Alberta with a similar one creating the province of Saskatchewan. These provinces were each to have an area of about 270,000 square miles and a population of some 250,000. The financial terms were to be generous. In 1904 there had been appropriated by the dominion for territorial purposes, and in a very small measure raised by local taxation, a total sum of $1,636,000 or an average of $818,000 for each of the regions now being made into separate provinces. It was now proposed to grant Alberta and Saskatchewan each $50,000 a year for civil government; $200,000 for capitation allowance upon a present basis of 250,000 population which would increase *pro rata* until the population reached 8,000,000 souls; a debt allowance of $405,375, and a compensation allowance, for retaining the public lands, of $375,000 — a total of $1,030,375 per annum. To this would be added, in each case, for five years, an allowance of $62,500 per annum for the construction of buildings and public works.

The public lands, officially estimated at 25,-000,000 acres, and by the opposition at twice that number of acres, the government proposed to retain under federal control. As to education the premier announced that it was the intention to protect the Catholic minority in establishing, permanently, the existing separate school system. This was the vital point of the violent controversy which ensued. Mr. Haultain at once took strong ground against the policy. His position, as defined in an open letter on 12 March, addressed to Sir Wilfrid Laurier, was that "the province should be left to deal with the subject, exclusively, subject to the provisions of the British North America Act." Parliament, he claimed, was bound and restricted in its powers by those provisions, and he quoted Mr. Edward Blake, the former liberal leader, as declaring that the basis of union was not "capable of alteration by act of Parliament." The only jurisdiction possessed in this respect was that of remedial legislation conferred by the act itself.

Mr. Haultain then proceeded to contend that these new provinces were not now being admitted to the union. They were admitted on 15 July 1870 under territorial conditions, when "as a matter of indefeasible right" they

clares territorial school laws passed under the restrictions imposed by the Northwest Territories Act to be provincial school laws. It clothes laws imposed by the federal parliament with all the attributes of laws voluntarily made by a free province. It ignores territorial limitations and conditions. It denies facts and abolishes time." He demanded, therefore, on behalf of the territories that "the same terms, and no others," imposed by the queen-in-council on the admission of Prince Edward Island and British Columbia be granted in this case. These had been included in his draft bill of three years before, and to impose more or prescribe less in the present case would, he contended, be equally contrary to the law and to the constitution. He maintained that the fact of dominion legislation having in previous years dealt with territorial matters did not involve any principle or necessity of perpetuation. In this respect, laws affecting education were no different from any other legislation.

During the next few weeks the discussion in and out of Parliament took the form of most strenuous agitation in certain important Ontario circles; resulted in the resignation of Mr. Sifton, minister of the interior and a strong member of the government; and caused prolonged and sometimes heated debates in Parliament. Eventually the premier consented to modify his education clause by making it quite plain that the system perpetuated in the new provinces would be that established under the territorial ordinances of 1901 and no other. Meanwhile, there had been no particular excitement in the northwest over the matter, and when Mr. Oliver, the new minister of the interior, returned to his constituents at Edmonton he was re-elected by acclamation. The second reading of the bills — the vital point in the procedure through Parliament — passed by 140 to 59 and thence the measures went through both houses with slight amendment and, finally, became law. On 1 September following the two new provinces came into legal existence. Col. Fred. White, C. M. G., was appointed the first commissioner of the afterwards reorganized territories. The crop production of the original territories during recent years will be seen in the following (official) figures — the average product over the whole period for spring wheat being 18.95 bushels; for oats 33.46 bushels; for barley 25.44 bushels:

	SPRING WHEAT		OATS		BARLEY	
YEAR	Bushels	Yield Per Acre	Bushels	Yield Per Acre	Bushels	Yield Per Acre
1898	5,542,478	18.01	3,040,307	28.93	449,512	26.29
1899	6,915,628	19.02	4,686,036	34.81	337,421	23.62
1900	4,028,294	9.75	4,226,152	28.08	353,216	20.72
1901	12,808,447	25.37	11,113,066	48.43	795,100	32.18
1902	13,956,850	22.00	10,661,295	34.35	870,417	23.88
1903	16,029,149	19.00	14,179,705	32.17	1,741,209	24.65
1904	16,723,412	17.47	16,335,519	31.19	2,205,434	25.59

received the privileges of section 93 of the British North America Act. Present legislation proposed to create provinces retroactively. "It de-

J. CASTELL HOPKINS,
Editor 'The Canadian Annual Review of Public Affairs.'

Canada — The South African War. When trouble was seriously threatened in the Transvaal in 1899 a very general feeling developed in Canada outside of Quebec, that the Dominion should in some manner aid the mother-country in the event of war resulting. The progress of the negotiations was very closely watched and the policy of the British government upon the whole approved, although, as in Great Britain itself, there were some diversities of opinion. Amongst military men there was a strong undercurrent of desire to raise a volunteer force for active service and, in this connection, Col. S. Hughes, M. P., was particularly enthusiastic. He introduced the subject into Parliament on 12 July 1899, while the negotiations were still pending between President Kruger and Mr. Chamberlain. It was, however, thought best not to take any immediate action, and the premier, Sir Wilfrid Laurier, expressed his hope and belief that, in view of the absolute justice of the Uitlanders' claims, recognition would eventually be given to them and war averted. On 31 July more definite action was taken and the following resolution, moved in the House of Commons by Sir Wilfrid Laurier and seconded by the Hon. G. E. Foster in the absence, but with the approval of, Sir Charles Tupper as leader of the opposition, was carried unanimously:

That this House has viewed with regret the complications which have arisen in the Transvaal Republic of which her majesty is suzerain, from the refusal to accord to her majesty's subjects now settled in that region an adequate participation in its government. That this House has learned with still greater regret that the condition of things there existing has resulted in intolerable oppression and has produced great and dangerous excitement among several classes of her majesty's subjects in her South African possessions. That this House, representing a people which has largely succeeded, by the adoption of the principle of conceding equal political rights to every portion of the population, in harmonizing estrangements and in producing general content with the existing system of government, desires to express its sympathy with the efforts of her majesty's imperial authorities to obtain for the subjects of her majesty who have taken up their abode in the Transvaal, such measure of justice and political recognition as may be found necessary to secure them in the full possession of equal rights and liberties.

Public Opinion Favors Action. — The members, after passing the motion, sprang to their feet and sang "God Save the Queen" amid a scene of striking enthusiasm which was duplicated a little later in the senate. Leading papers took up the subject and approved the sending of a force in case of necessity and, on 2 October, a few days before the war began, a large and representative meeting of militia officers was held in Toronto and the following resolution passed with unanimity:

That the members of the Canadian Military Institute, feeling that it is a clear and definite duty for all British possessions to show their willingness to contribute in the common defense in case of need, express the hope that, in view of the impending hostilities in South Africa, the government of Canada will promptly offer a contingent of Canadian militia to assist in supporting the interests of our empire in that country.

On the following day the prime minister was interviewed at Ottawa and expressed the opinion that it would be unconstitutional for the militia, or a portion of it, to be sent out of Canada without the permission of Parliament; and pointed out that it would take some weeks to call that body together.

Public sentiment in Canada soon proved too strong for what might have been, in other circumstances, a legitimate constitutional delay. On 27 September, Sir Charles Tupper, in a speech at Halifax, offered the government the fullest support of the conservative opposition in the sending of a contingent, and, on 6 October, telegraphed the premier to the same effect. There was, inevitably, some opposition to such action, and it was largely voiced by the Hon. J. Israel Tarte, minister of public works, in the Dominion government. It was not apparently a note of disloyalty; it was simply the expression of a lack of enthusiasm and the magnifying of constitutional dangers or difficulties. No one in Canada expected the French-Canadians, amongst whom Mr. Tarte was a party leader, to look upon the matter with just the same warmth of feeling as actuated English-Canadians; and very few believed that the absence of this enthusiasm indicated any sentiment of actual disloyalty to the crown or the country.

The Troops Leave for the Front. — The first contingent of 1,000 men was accepted by the imperial government early in October. On 30 October, after farewell banquets to the officers and an ovation from immense crowds in the gayly decorated streets of Quebec, it left for the seat of war. The principal officers of the contingent were its commander, Lieut.-Col. W. D. Otter, who had seen active service in the Northwest Rebellion, Lieut.-Col. Lawrence Buchan, Lieut.-Col. O. C. C. Pelletier, Maj. J. C. McDougall and Maj. S. J. A. Denison, who was afterwards appointed to Lord Roberts' staff. The troopship *Sardinian* arrived at Cape Town 29 November and the Canadians were given a splendid reception. Meanwhile, public feeling in Canada seemed to favor the sending of further aid, and its feasibility was more than shown by the thousands who had volunteered for the first contingent, over and above those selected. But it was not until some of the earlier reverses of the war took place that the offer of a second contingent was pressed upon the home government. On 8 November, however, it was declined, for the moment, and a week later Mr. Chamberlain, the colonial secretary, wrote as follows:

The great enthusiasm and the general eagerness to take active part in the military expedition which has unfortunately been found necessary for the maintenance of British rights and interests in South Africa have afforded much gratification to her majesty's government and the people of this country. The desire exhibited to share in the risks and burdens of empire has been welcomed not only as a proof of the staunch loyalty of the Dominion and of its sympathy with the policy pursued by her majesty's government in South Africa, but also as an expression of that growing feeling of the unity and solidarity of the empire which has marked the relations of the mother-country with the colonies during recent years.

A second contingent was accepted on 18 December; events in South Africa and the pressure of loyal proffers of aid from Australia, and elsewhere, inducing the imperial government to change its mind. The first troops had been composed of infantry, the second were made up of artillery and cavalry. Eventually, it was decided to send 1,220 men, together with horses, guns and complete equipment, and they duly left for the Cape, in detachments, toward the end of January, and in the beginning of February 1900. A third force of 400 mounted men was recruited in the latter month and sent to the seat of war fully equipped, and with all expenses paid, through the personal and patriotic generosity of Lord Strathcona and Mount Royal, the Canadian high commissioner in London. In addition to "Strathcona's Horse" another independent force of 125 men was offered in similar fashion by the British Columbia provincial government and duly accepted at London and Ottawa, though for local reasons of political change it was never despatched; while a movement was commenced to offer an organized Dominion brigade of 10,000 men, if required.

Active Service of the Canadian Troops. — The men of all these forces saw much service and experienced much privation. The Royal Canadian regiment, or portions of it, shared in the skirmish at Sunnyside, in the far more important battles around Paardeburg and in the capture of Cronje. For their gallantry in this latter fight, the impetus which they gave to the Boer general's surrender and the position they took and held beside the great historic regiments of the mother-land, the Canadians won a pronounced reputation. Lord Roberts eulogized them publicly, cables of congratulation came to Canada from the Queen and Lord Wolseley, Mr. Chamberlain and Sir Alfred Milner and, as it were in an hour, Canada appeared to take a prominent place in the defense system of the empire. The regiment also took part in the march to Bloemfontein and in the further campaign toward Kroonstadt and Johannesburg into Pretoria. They were brigaded with the Gordons and other Highland regiments for a time and were then placed in the 19th brigade under Maj.-Gen. H. L. Smith-Dorrien who, on 16 July, issued an official order of historic interest in which he stated that:

The 19th Brigade has achieved a record of which any infantry might be proud. Since the date it was formed, namely, the 12th of February, it has marched 620 miles, often on half rations and seldom on full. It has taken part in the capture of 10 towns, fought in 10 general actions and on 27 other days. In one period of 30 days it fought on 21 of them and marched 327 miles. The casualties have been between four and five hundred and the defeats *nil*.

Meanwhile the Canadian Mounted Rifles of the second contingent had been attached to Sir Redvers Buller's force and under the more immediate command of Maj.-Gen. E.T. H. Hutton. They took part, and later on the Strathcona's, in the conflicts and incidents of the march from Natal to Pretoria and the north and upon several occasions won distinguished mention from their commanders. Early in 1901 Canadian volunteers for the South African constabulary to the total number of 1,208 left for the seat of war under command of Col. S. B. Steele, C. B., M. V. O. On 25 November, following, the colonial secretary telegraphed the governor-general that the imperial government would gratefully accept the offer of another contingent of not less than 600 men. Action was at once taken by the militia department and in January 1902, the Second Regiment Canadian Mounted Rifles sailed for South Africa, 900 strong, under command of Col. T. D. B. Evans and Maj. W. Hamilton Merritt. They were attached to Col. Cookson's Column and took part in the following events:

(1) The night ride of 45 miles to Witpoort Ridge followed by the "drive" at daybreak next morning — the Regiment covering 85 miles in 23 hours.
(2) The operations ending with the Battle of Boschbult near Hart's River, on 31 March.
(3) The "drive" commencing 10 April, culminating with the attack of the Boers on General Kekewich's column and their defeat with heavy losses.
(4) The "drive" from Driekuil to Klerksdorp on 14–15 April.
(5) The operations between 23 April and 2 May, west of Klerksdorp, in which a large amount of the standing crops of the enemy were taken or destroyed.
(6) The "drive" commencing 5 May, and ending 23 May, to Vryburg, in Cape Colony and return, resulting in large captures of prisoners and stock.

On 29 May, following, the imperial government signified its willingness to accept another 2,000 men. Those offering were, as usual, largely in excess of the number required and in May the Third, Fourth, Fifth and Sixth Regiments, Canadian Mounted Rifles, started for the front — under the respective commands of Lieutenant-Colonels V. A. S. Williams, T. de L. Boulanger, A. C. Macdonell and J. D. Irving. The establishment of each regiment was 509 officers and men and 539 horses. They arrived too late to see any active service, as peace had been made on 31 May. Outside of Paardeberg the most memorable incident of Canada's share in the war was the stand taken at Hart's River on 31 March 1902 by a small force of the Second Canadian Mounted Rifles. Lord Kitchener's official report of the affair was as follows:

The heaviest loss in this engagement fell upon the Canadian Mounted Rifles, who in this their first fight of importance since landing, displayed the utmost bravery and determination, Lieut. Bruce Carruthers of the Regiment especially distinguished himself. Being in command of a detachment of the rear guard when coming into camp, he remained out in a position of observation, in which he eventually found himself isolated and surrounded by a large body of the enemy. Rejecting all idea of surrender, however, his small patrol of 21 men fought stubbornly on, to the end, no less than 6 of their number being killed and 12 wounded. There have been few finer instances of heroism in the whole course of the campaign.

Result of Canada's Action. — Such is the story of the share taken by Canada and Canadian troops in an eventful struggle. It was an important share and one entirely out of proportion to the number of men sent to the front from the Dominion. But the assertion of a new and great principle of imperial defense; the revolution effected in methods of war by the proved and superior mobility of colonial forces in the contest; the actual achievements of the men themselves in steadiness, discipline and bravery; reveal ample reasons for considering the participation of Canada in this war as one of the great events in its history. The total number of officers and men whose services were accepted was 8,372; the deaths from wounds or disease were 224; the wounded numbered 252; the cost to Canada was $2,-830,965. It may be explained that the first contingent only went at the expense of the Dominion; the cost of the others was defrayed by the imperial government. Three Canadian officers were decorated with the Victoria Cross for conspicuous gallantry and a number of others were given the Distinguished Service Order.

J. CASTELL HOPKINS,
Author (with Halstead) of 'History of the South African War.'

CANADIAN CANALS

Canadian Canals. The inception of the Canadian canal systems, now so important a factor in carrying on extensive Canadian inland communication, dates back to the 18th century, when locks and canals were constructed in a crude way to overcome the difficulties of ascending the Saint Lawrence river.

In 1826, the Imperial Government began the work of connecting the waters of the Rideau and Cataraqui rivers. Since that time every advantage has been taken of the facilities for water highways provided by the Saint Lawrence and the Great Lakes. The latest triumph in modern canal-lock construction, at Peterborough, in the Province of Ontario, represents the culmination of experiments and trials made with a view to overcome serious deviations in the land level.

Engineering skill of the highest order has been brought into play in solving the problem of freight transportation by means of large vessels on deep and shallow canals. From the beginning of the canal movement in Canada until the perfecting and opening of the Peterborough hydraulic lift-lock in 1904 a series of engineering feats marvelous in their intricacy marked the progress of Canadian canal expansion.

The cutting of canals to complete a continuous waterway from the head of Lake Superior and from Lake Michigan to the Seaboard at Quebec, via Montreal for vessels up to 14 feet draft is now an accomplished fact. The total length of route covered in this gigantic enterprise is nearly 1,860 miles, of which distance 73 miles of canals were excavated. No less than 48 locks were necessary to overcome the 600 feet of difference between Lake Superior and tide-water. This waterway has cost at least $90,000,000 to construct and improve. The maintenance expenses per annum are, approximately, $20,000,000.

Saint Lawrence Route.— The Saint Lawrence route, nearly 1,000 miles in length, from the Strait of Belle Isle to Montreal, formerly accessible only to vessels drawing a maximum of 10 feet of water, has been vastly improved. Within the past 20 years the shoals between Montreal and Quebec have been dredged to a minimum depth of 27½ feet, providing a submerged depth of 39¼ miles.

Lachine Canal.— The Lachine Canal, above Montreal, has been twice enlarged. From 4½ feet depth at the locks an increase has been made to 14 and 16 feet.

Soulanges Canal.— The Soulanges Canal, 14 miles long, 100 feet wide at the bottom, 164 feet at surface and with a wide macadam pathway, reconstructed in 1892, is another engineering triumph. This feat is in every way modern, the most improved lock appliances being in use, including an electric gate opening and closing system.

Cornwall Canal.— The Cornwall Canal, built to overcome the Long Sault Rapids, has been deepened from 9 to 14 feet. The Williamsburg Canals have also been extended and improved.

Welland Canal.— This is probably the most extensive of the public works of this character undertaken by the Canadian government. It has practically been twice constructed, and now extends in a nearly straight line from Port Dalhousie, on Lake Ontario, to Port Colborne, on Lake Erie, a distance of 26¾ miles. Within the length of this canal there are 25 lift-locks and one guard lock to overcome a difference in level of 326½ feet.

Richelieu and Lake Champlain System.— The Richelieu and Lake Champlain system, extending from Sorel, at the confluence of the Richelieu and Saint Lawrence rivers, to the international boundary, covers a distance of 81 miles and forms part of a complete water route, more than 400 miles long, from Montreal or Quebec to New York. This system has been much improved since its construction.

Rideau Canal.— This system was built by the British government, early in the last century and primarily for military purposes. It forms communication by connecting navigable water stretches lying between Kingston, on Lake Ontario, and Ottawa, (then known as By-town) on the river of that name. It is used for barge and small steamer purposes.

Trent Navigation System.— Another important system of canals in Canada, and one that has been greatly developed since its inception, is known as the Trent Navigation System. Active steps are now in progress to complete a waterway of over 200 miles, by stretches of canals connecting rivers and lakes that abound in this district of the Province of Ontario. The terminal points of the system are Newton, on Lake Ontario, and Midland, on the southeastern side of Georgian Bay. The Trent system, includes the new hydraulic lift at Peterborough, 100 miles northwest of Trenton.

Original Purpose of the Canals.— When canals were first provided in the Dominion, the aim was to float flat-bottomed boats such as could be hauled in very shallow water, and as was purposed to do when the first, the Rideau canal was built. The locks used were 13 feet in width and 30 feet in length. On the sills the water was usually a trifle over four feet in depth. Boats could not carry a cargo of more than 35 tons. Many years elapsed before any serious effort was made to develop the original canal system in such a way as to admit the passage of boats or vessels of considerable tonnage.

The Use of Locks.— The use of locks is by no means a modern device. From the earliest days some method has been necessary to overcome differences of level. From time to time, as the pressure of transportation became greater, numerous plans were tested to substitute for the old-fashioned canal-locks a scheme giving, among other things, a more rapid means of transfer from one level to another.

Various Methods to Facilitate Transfer.— The contrivances to overcome delay include inclined planes, up which the boat is hauled; cylindrical tanks in which the boat can be rolled up hill; pneumatic lifts; hydraulic lifts; screw lifts and modifications of each of these methods. While all forms of locks are termed hydraulic, in the sense that the burthen is sustained in raising or lowering by the flotative power of the water, the last few years have seen perfected what is known as the "Hydraulic Lift Lock," and which in principle is that both the barge or boat, the water in which it floats, the tank or chamber containing the water are all raised or lowered by means of one or more powerful hydraulic rams, operating vertically. The practical application of each and all of these methods, with their modification, reveals the fact that the hydraulic lift is best fitted for extensive canal systems such as exist in Canada.

Lock of Ordinary Type.— The first canal-lock lift on record is said to have been invented in 1481, by two brothers, Dionisio and Pietro Domenico of Viterbo, Italy. Their invention was put into use during that year on the Pie-vega, a canal running from Pagua to Stra. About fifteen years later the plan of these two brothers was copied by Lonarto da Vinci. He constructed 6 locks similarly operated on the Milan Canal in 1497. The use of locks then became general in Italy and, subsequently, throughout Europe, but nearly four centuries elapsed before any serious effort was made to improve canal facilities in matters of speed and capacity for sea-going ships and other vessels carrying heavy freightage.

The Hydraulic Lift-Lock.— Referring to mechanically operated lift-locks of the hydraulic ram type, of which the example at Peterborough, Ont., Canada, is the first constructed and brought into use on the American continent, it is the outcome of many evolutionary processes. The first of these ingenious contrivances was built at Anderton, England, connecting the river Weaver with a series of local canals. It lifts about 50 feet, but its barge capacity is limited, the chambers being only 70 feet long and 14 feet wide.

The second lift was built at Les Fontinettes, France. It, too, was of very moderate dimensions, the third lift built, according to the records, was at La Louviere, Belgium, with guide towers, of the truss girder pattern. Each of these lift-locks has been operated with fair success. It has been demonstrated from their use that the principle on which they were constructed is correct. Many defects were brought to light, however, after their completion. These defects have now been overcome.

Purpose of the Peterborough Lift-lock.— The Peterborough lift-lock was projected partially to connect Lake Huron and Lake Ontario. It was intended to facilitate the transportation of western freight between Georgian Bay and Lake Ontario. By the use of this lift the length of the Lake route is shortened by 250 miles. The highest point on the new route is 600 feet above the level of Lake Ontario. To overcome this, a series of drops at the eastern end of the route were necessary. The largest of these drops is at Peterborough. At that place the canal makes a cut of four miles through the country, with a drop of 65 feet.

The building of the Peterborough lift-lock has removed what would otherwise have been an insurmountable obstacle. In the construction of this lock four things were aimed at. (1) To overcome the elevation; (2) to reduce the time for lock operation; (3) to furnish ample capacity for a maximum number of lockages, thus preventing a congestion of traffic; (4) to provide for future increased traffic.

If locks of the ordinary type had been used, five of them would have been necessary, and it is probable that five pairs of locks would have been required to reduce the periods of delay. With locks in single series (one above the other), every barge must wait until the barge preceding has passed through the whole series.

Principle on which the Lock Works.— The principle applied is very simple in its details. Two tanks are placed side by side and supported on plungers working in hydraulic cylinders. The two cylinders are connected by a pipe so that water can flow from one to the other, and when one plunger with its tanks is at the top of its stroke, the other is at the bottom, the two tanks balancing each other, with the exception of the surcharge of water in the descending tank, and which surcharge forms the propelling power to raise or elevate the other tank. The movement of the lock proper is based on hydraulics and hydrostatic principles. If a cube of iron, say four inches square each way, is dropped into a pail quite filled with water, the iron will sink and displace exactly as much water as will be equivalent to the metal's bulk. If the iron is hammered or spun into some form of vessel or dish that will float, the iron in its new form would displace water exactly equivalent to its weight. Anything that sinks displaces its bulk of water. And anything that floats displaces its weight of water. This is practically illustrated in the filling of the chambers with water or with boat and water. If one chamber is filled with water to the depth of 8 feet and in the other chamber is placed a barge and water to the same depth, the load in both chambers will be exactly the same. Lockages may therefore be effected with one barge or boat in a chamber, with barges in each chamber, or with the chambers containing water only. At the bottom of each well, to receive the base of the cylinder is placed a foundation of large blocks of Stanstead granite, in three courses, two of 30 and one of 40 inches in thickness. The wells are lined with concrete, making the walls practically smooth and watertight.

Foundation.— Much labor was involved in preparing for a proper foundation for this lift-lock. More than 120,000 cubic yards of earth was removed. The excavation was completed in 1899. The entire task of building the lock and erecting the steel superstructure occupied seven years.

Details of the Task.— Some interesting details have been made available regarding this work. The substructure of the lock represents the largest monolithic mass of concrete in the world; over 26,000 barrels of cement being used in making the concrete. The breast wall of the lock is 40 feet thick, 80 feet high and 126 feet long at the base. The dimensions of the chambers, which are built of steel plates, give a space in each of the two chambers of 140 feet in length, 33 feet in width and a depth of 9 feet 10 inches. The guide towers rise 100 feet from the foundation. The base of the tower measures 26 feet 6 inches by 40 feet 8 inches. The depth of water in each chamber is 8½ feet, weighing, approximately, 1,300 tons. There is a pressure in the presses, during operation, of 600 pounds to the square inch. The external diameter of the cylinders is 8 feet 3½ inches, the diameter of the ram being 7 feet, 6 inches, with a working stroke of 65 feet. The presses are the largest thus far constructed. The work of excavation occupied four years. This was followed by the concrete work, which took a considerable time to perfect before the erection of

HYDRAULIC LIFT LOCK, PETERBOROUGH, CANADA.

the steel superstructure, which was erected in 1902-3. The lock proper is automatic. The gates and capstans are worked by hydraulic power. The actual time of lockage is twelve minutes and of vertical motion, 1½ minutes.

Route.— The route of the canal is now open for continuous navigation from Heeley's Falls on the Trent River to beyond the shores of Balsam Lake, a distance of over 126 miles, and by the completion of a second hydraulic lift-lock, near Kirkfield, Ont., early this year (1906), will give access to the waters of Lake Simcve, embracing a rich agricultural district, several centres of large and important industries, the limestone and granite quarries of Ciear and Stony Lakes, extensive lumber and timber locations and the promising stone and granite area above Coboconk. See CANALS.

F. H. DOBBIN,
Peterborough, Canada.

Canadian Commerce. See CANADA.— COMMERCE, TARIFFS, AND TRANSPORTATION; THE BRITISH PREFERENTIAL TARIFF; THE TRADE OF THE BRITISH EMPIRE; RECIPROCITY BETWEEN CANADA AND THE UNITED STATES; etc.

Canadian Copyright. See COPYRIGHT, CANADIAN.

Cana'dian Embroidery, a kind of embroidery formed from small pieces of snake skin, fur, etc., intermingled with flexible pieces of split porcupine quills dyed in various colors.

Canadian Indians. There has been no figure in all history so picturesque and peculiar as that of the North American Indian. The storm-tossed life of the various nations, or tribes, the concentrated cruelty of individual character, combined with loyalty and honor in tribal relations; the constant and bloody struggles between each national unit and the prolonged conflict with the white invaders of a continent; the complexity of the savage temperament in its mingled simplicity and guile, its courage and endurance, its treachery towards foes and cruelty in war, its pride and prudence combined with periods of insane recklessness and a humility akin to that of a beggar, its self-restraint and moments of unbridled rage, its strange conjunction of greatness and littleness; stamp the American aborigine as the most extraordinary product of the vast wilderness and forest home of his wandering race. See INDIANS.

Character of the Indian. — History has yet to do him justice. The pen of the poet, the voice of the preacher, or the thought of the philosopher seem alike unfitted to cope with his difficult environment and curious character. Cold and hard, passionate and revengeful, ignorant and superstitious, keen and quick in thought he has yet in pre-civilization days never been guilty of the effeminate and meaner vices which destroyed peoples such as the Roman or the Aztec. Love of liberty in its wilder forms, and contempt for all arbitrary rule or personal control, he carried to an extreme greater than can be elsewhere paralleled. Sleepless suspicion of others was a part of his surroundings of war and treachery. As with nearly all savage races his warfare was one of sudden and secret surprise, ruthless and unhesitating slaughter. A native of the wilds, a product of primeval conditions, he could not change his character without deterioration, or his mode of life without physical and mental injury. Civilization, indeed, has destroyed the Indian. In curbing his wilder passions it has usually developed the meaner ones, and in destroying the environment which made him the barbarous yet noble owner of a boundless continent it has cramped his intellectual acuteness, dulled his powers of perception, starved his wonderful physical qualities, and fatally affected the peculiar morality which he undoubtedly possessed. Christianity and agricultural pursuits may fit the survivors for life amidst new conditions, but the result of this development in Canada, at least, is no more the Indian of past centuries than the Greek of to-day is the true heir of Leonidas at Thermopylæ, or the modern native of Rome the just inheritor of imperial valor.

Distribution of the Indian Tribes.— When the first discoverers and explorers found their way amidst the wilds of Canada, they came into collision with various Indian nations. The great family of the Algonquins extended right up through the centre of the continent. They formed the chief central race of early Canada, and reached in scattered masses from the Atlantic to Lake Winnipeg and from the Carolinas to Hudson's Bay. Cartier met them when he ascended the Saint Lawrence, the early English settlers met them along the coasts of Virginia, the people of New England fought them under King Philip. William Penn made peace with them under the trees of the Keystone State and the French Jesuits and furtraders found the same race in the valley of the Ohio, on the shores of Lake Superior, and at the rapids of Sault Ste. Marie.

Of this race were the Delawares and the Shawnees. The latter were a strange and wandering people, whose location it was always difficult to fix, but who are known to have more than once come into conflict with the French of Quebec. They eventually settled on Canadian soil and played a brief but important part under Tecumseh in the War of 1812. The former were at one time conquered by the Iroquois and compelled to bear the opprobrious Indian name for women, but in one of the French and English wars they recovered at once their courage and their position by espousing the side of the French. Other branches dwelt along the Canadian shores of the Atlantic and in the wastes north of Lakes Michigan. Superior, and Huron. The latter tribes included the Ojibiways, Pottawatamies and Ottawas, who at one time formed a sort of loose union and offered a yielding but efficient check to the course of the Iroquois conquest. In this region also were the Sacs, the Foxes, and other smaller divisions of the Algonquin race. Other branches in Nova Scotia were known as the Micmacs, in western New Brunswick as the Etchemins, in Quebec as the Montagnais, and in the far North as the Nipissings.

The Iroquois stretched across what afterwards became the State of New York into Ontario and Quebec, and included the Mohawks, Oneidas, Onondagas, Cayugas and Senecas. Though united in a sort of loose confederacy and by a system of clanship, they seem to have had no clearly defined and continuous ruler, but to have trusted their joint affairs to the central council at Onondaga. And, though numbering only about four thousand warriors in their day of greatest power, they were able to make the name of the Five Nations a word of terror to all the tribes from Quebec to the Carolinas and from the far West to the Atlantic shores. To the French and the American colonists they were a continuous source of dread, while to the English forces in Canada at a later period they became an arm of military strength a little difficult to define in degree.

A people not inferior in courage but not nearly so aggressive in character as the Iroquois were the Hurons, whose name is so well known through their intercourse with the French Jesuit missionaries. Their population is estimated by Parkman as having been about 10,000 souls, though other writers place the number at double that figure. In the superior nature of their dwelling houses, in their manners and customs and superstitions, they closely resembled the Iroquois. They met destruction at the ruthless hands of that great confederacy, and after 1680 disappear from view, except in a few isolated settlements under French protection. The Neutral nation, living along the north shore of Lake Erie and remaining for a long period neutral between the Hurons and the Five Nations; the Andastes, dwelling in fortified villages in the valley of the Susquehanna; the Eries, living in the vicinity of the lake which bears their name; were all of kin to the Iroquois and were all conquered and practically destroyed in time by that most powerful of the savage nations of North America. Then followed the conquest of the Delawares, or Lenapes, and the expulsion of the Ottawas from the vicinity of the great river which now runs by the capital of Canada and onward through the towns and villages of a peaceful civilization. In 1715 the Iroquois were strengthened by the admission of the Tuscaroras, a warlike people of admitted kinship, to the confederacy, as a sixth nation.

The original population of these various tribes and races and nations of kindred origin, can, of course, only be estimated. Garneau, in his 'History of French Canada,' puts the Algonquin total at 90,000 souls, the Hurons and Iroquois together at about 17,000, the Mobiles of the far south at 50,000, and the Cherokees, of what is now the centre of the United States, at 12,000. His total is 180,000 for the greater part of the continent, and in view of the constant condition of warfare in which they were involved, and the statements of travelers like Cartier, Joliette, Marquette, De la Jonquiere, etc., it is probable the estimate is not too small. Even as it is, however, the fact of the dominating power of a few thousand Iroquois during so many years affords an interesting illustration of savage strength and superiority.

Habits, Customs and Appearance. — In conduct it should be remembered the early Indian was kind and hospitable to the exploring European. The Jesuit and Recollet missionaries, in what is now Canada, bear testimony in many cases to this fact. Hakluyt, in his account of Cartier's first visit to Hochelaga (1535), says that "the Indians brought us great store of fish and of bread made of millet, casting them into our boats so thick that you would have thought

it to fall from Heaven." Indian appearance, customs and beliefs have been often described and with most varying degrees of accuracy or the reverse. The fact is that changing conditions brought about frequent changes in manners and appearance. The Huron, or Wyandotte, in days when he was a successful rival of the Iroquois could hardly be recognized in the fearful and unaggressive convert of the missionaries during the years of his final struggle and disappearance. The Delawares, in their period of active life and power, were not the same people as the subject slaves of the Iroquois, nor were the latter in their earlier times of peace and trade like the fiery savages whose conquering warwhoop became a signal of death from the great lakes to the Mississippi.

The Indian races of Canada were emphatically the product of nature, however, and amongst them all were similarities which stamped them as of the same origin and as possible descendants of migrating Tartars from the Steppes of Central Asia. They were as a rule tall and slender and agile in form, with faces bronzed by sun and rain and winds. Their expression was stern and sombre, seldom or never marked with a smile. Their heads had high cheek bones, small sunken and keenly-flashing eyes, narrow foreheads, thick lips, somewhat flat noses and coarse hair. The senses of sight, and sound, and feeling were developed into a sort of forest instinct which seemed almost supernatural to the first white settlers. Their costumes of deer-skin and moccasins, their necklaces of wampum, beads, or shells, their ornaments of feathers and claws and scalps are well known, as is the vermilion paint with which they delighted to daub their faces and bodies. The only weapons they possessed before the Europeans came were the arrow and tomahawk. Hunting or fishing was their occupation, war their pastime. All these pursuits made permanence of dwelling very difficult and involved naturally a life of ceaseless wandering.

Religions and Superstitions of the Indian. — Their religion was always a peculiarly mixed quantity. Champlain states that the Micmacs had neither devotional ideas nor ceremonies. Other tribes assured him that each man had his own god whom he worshipped in silence and secretness. They seem, however, to have all worshipped something — whether the spirit of good, the spirit of evil, the spirit of storm, the god of war, the spirit of the mountains, or a spirit of the waters. Sacrifices were not uncommon, and Father Jogues is authority for having seen at least one human sacrifice amongst the Iroquois. How far they really worshipped one Great Spirit is a matter of uncertainty and it has been claimed that the early missionaries suggested to their minds an idea which they were quick to absorb through the questions and answers naturally given. However that may be, there can be no doubt of their intense belief in spiritual manifestations and interventions. They peopled the very air with friendly or hostile spirits and created amongst themselves those powerful manipulators of superstition — the medicine men — to control the surrounding demons of storm and famine, and disease and death. To the same men were given the care of the sick, and, mixed up with much that was harmful, there were no doubt many simple remedies used amidst a mass of incantations and superstitious mummery. Dreams they put great faith in, and oratory was almost as much a factor in success as bravery. But the chief of all important customs of the Indians turned upon war and its occasionally brief concomitat, peace. A struggle between two tribes or nations could be brought on by the most trivial cause, or by almost any ambitious and restless individual. When determined upon, it became the source of uncontrollable joy, of wild dances, of eloquent harangues, of multitudinous prayers and sacrifices, of feasts and endless bravado and boasting.

Relations with the French and English. —In the wars between the French and English and Americans which devastated parts of North America during nearly 300 years, the Indians exercised a large influence and, had they been united, might more than once have expelled the white invader altogether. Roughly speaking, the Algonquins and Hurons stood by the French, the Iroquois and some minor nations by the English. When the Five Nations had beaten the Algonquins and destroyed the Hurons, they turned their attention to the French, and several times brought the settlements on the Saint Lawrence to the very verge of destruction. After the supremacy of England seemed finally established there existed for some years a sort of brooding trouble. The New England colonists had never treated the Indians upon their borders well, and the result had been a long series of reprisals and wasting war. Greedy traders and unscrupulous speculators in land had robbed the Indians of their intellect by brandy, and of large tracts of land by fraud. The American colonies, indeed, claimed the whole soil, and without British permission, though in the King's name, made frequent and large grants of Indian territory and then seemed surprised when the tomahawk and scalping-knife were used in response by the untutored savage. Finally, land regulations were made by the Home Government which to some extent stopped this sort of lawlessness, and were respected in Canada, though more or less disregarded in the Thirteen Colonies as the spirit of local revolt developed. Sir William Johnson, of the Mohawk Valley, in New York, was appointed Superintendent-General of Indian Affairs, and he did his best to enforce these regulations.

When the Thirteen Colonies plunged into revolution the bulk of the Indians stood by Great Britain. Those who did not take an active part with the Iroquois stood aloof — with the exception of the Oneidas and Tuscaroras — and refused all the efforts of Congress to obtain their co-operation. At the close of the war (1783) the Iroquois were given large grants of land by the British government and, under the guidance of Joseph Brant — Thayendanegea — the brilliant chief who had led them throughout this period, they settled in various parts of the new province of Upper Canada. In 1812 many served again under the British flag, while other nations and tribes were brought together by the martial spirit and influence of Tecumseh — a leader who fills an interesting page in Canadian history. Since

then, the Indians of Canada, with the exception of a very few who were led astray by Louis Riel in the Northwest troubles of 1885, have lived at peace amongst themselves and with the white men, and have been trying to become accustomed to a life of monotonous civilization, and, to them, somewhat degrading labor.

Indians of the West. — The Western Indian, under the long and reasonably wise administration of affairs in what is now the provinces of Manitoba, Saskatchewan and Alberta, by the Hudson's Bay Company, acquired characteristics different from those of other parts of the Dominion. They were not in quite such a state of tutelage as in Ontario; they were trusted in the matter of supplies and the trust was rarely abused; they became an easy-going, light-hearted people, with something of the white's shrewdness in trade and all of the native agility on foot or in a canoe When the old order passed away in 1871 and the country was acquired by Canada, there was much ferment, but it gradually gave way before the wise treaties, made from time to time, allotting on behalf of the crown certain reserves which were selected by joint action, on a basis of 640 acres for each family of five, and administered with, upon the whole, fairness and justice by government officials. These treaties were as follows:

No.	Year	District, etc, Dealt With Indians Concerned	
I.	1871	Province of Manitoba	3,270
II.	1871	Lake Manitoba, Souris, and Moon Mountain	2,185
III.	1873	Lake of the Woods, etc. (55,000 square miles)	2,673
IV.	1874	Lake Winnipeg to Cypress Hills (75,000 square miles)	6,886
V.	1875	Lake Winnipeg and River Saskatchewan (100,000 square miles)	3,182
VI.	1876	Plain and Wood Crees. Upper Saskatchewan (120,000 square miles)	6,622
VII.	1877	Blackfeet of Bow River (35,000 square miles)	7,681

These western Indians were, and are to some extent, divided into a series of loose confederacies — the Blackfeet, including the Bloods, Piegans and Blackfeet; the Sioux, including the Stoney or Assiniboine tribe and various branches of the Sioux; the Cree, including the Plain Crees, the Wood Crees and the Muskegon Crees; the Ojibiway Confederacy. In British Columbia the Indians at the present time number about 25,000 and are lowest in the scale of the Canadian tribes. They include the Coast Indians and the Mountain Indians and are divided chiefly into the Tinne and Thlinkit tribes and various sub-divisions such as the Shuswaps, the Tahlkill, the Tahltan, the Taku, the Kaska, etc. With the Indians of Canada, as a whole, there have been some 1,540 treaties made from time to time and involving the exchange, or sale, of lands, or the relinquishment of claims. The Indian population of Canada in 1903 was 198,233, divided as follows:

Ontario	21,003
Quebec	11,066
Nova Scotia	1,930
New Brunswick	1,699
Prince Edward Island	301
British Columbia	25,582
Manitoba	6,829
Northwest Territories	17,649
Athabasca	1,239
Outside Territorial limits	20,845

J. Castell Hopkins,
Author of 'The Canadian Annual Review of Public Affairs.'

Canadian Literature. See LITERATURE, CA-NADIAN; CANADA, LITERARY CONDITIONS IN.

Canadian Northern Railway. The construction of the Canadian Northern Railway was commenced in 1896 by building the Lake Manitoba Railway & Canal Company's line, a local road commencing at Gladstone, Manitoba, to the Dauphin country in the northwest part of the Province of Manitoba. Temporary running powers were secured over the Manitoba & Northwestern Railway from Gladstone to Portage la Prairie, where a connection was made with the Canadian Pacific and the Northern Pacific & Manitoba railways. This company was then amalgamated with the Winnipeg Great Northern Railway, and called the Canadian Northern Railway Company.

The following lines were built and absorbed: The Manitoba & Southeastern, The Minnesota & Manitoba, the Ontario & Rainy River, the Port Arthur, Duluth & Western, the Modern & Northwestern, and the Western extension Railway Companies.

The Northern Pacific & Manitoba Railway Company with a mileage of 354 miles was leased for 990 years with an option to purchase at any time. The total mileage is 2,100 miles.

At the commencement of construction in 1905 there were 141 miles grade and 312 miles of track to lay to complete the main line to Edmonton, which the management expect soon to have in operation, together with 165 additional miles of branch lines, making a total at the end of 1905 of 2,557 miles.

From 50 miles east of Winnipeg, where the prairie section commences, to 50 miles beyond Edmonton, where the timber country at the foothills is reached, a distance of over 900 miles of main line through the provinces of Manitoba, Saskatchewan and Alberta, all the stations will be wheat-producing points.

As the distance between Lake Superior and the Rocky Mountains on the northern part of the continent is greater than at any point in America from east to west, it affords an opportunity to give the best possible grades. The maximum grade with the traffic, along the main line, from 50 miles west of Edmonton, a distance of 1,315 miles, is 26 feet per mile. On the prairie divisions the same grade practically exists westward. On the Lake Superior division the maximum grade westbound is 52 feet per mile. The company has built an elevator plant at Port Arthur on Lake Superior, with a capacity of 7,000,000 bushels, 5,000,000 bushels of which is storage and absolutely fireproof.

Prior to 1896 the system adopted by both Dominion and Provincial governments in Canada for aiding in the construction of railways in the unsettled parts of the country was to grant assistance in the shape of a cash bonus to the company of a certain amount per mile, and in some cases to make a land grant as well. It is an interesting fact that the assistance given by the government of Manitoba to the Lake Manitoba Railway & Canal Company took the form of a guarantee by the government of the principal and interest of the company's bonds secured by first mortgage upon its undertaking. This was an experiment in the way of aiding railways which caused a great deal of discussion at the time, and doubts were expressed about the expediency of the change. Time, however, has proved the wisdom of the Manitoba government in this respect, as other governments since 1896 have in a good many cases followed its lead greatly to the advantage of the railway companies and of the government itself. The advantage to the company is that guaranteed securities bearing a low rate of interest can be disposed of at a higher price than it was possible to obtain for unguaranteed securities issued by a new railway company.

With the exception of an issue of 4 per cent unguaranteed debenture stock practically all the securities issued by the Canadian Northern Railway Company have been guaranteed, both as to principal and interest, either by the government of Manitoba or the government of Canada. The highest rate of interest on the guaranteed securities is 4 per cent and on those issued in aid of the construction of the 720 miles of the line in the provinces of Saskatchewan and Alberta and guaranteed by the Dominion government, the rate is 3 per cent.

The fixed charges of the road on its bonds and leased lines is $467 per mile per annum. £1,000,000 of Consolidated Debenture stock has been issued, which should be added to the above, making a total of $544 per mile per annum for the entire system.

The common stock is not on the market, and is controlled by Mackenzie, Mann & Company, Limited, who also control in Eastern Canada, the James Bay Railway, Great Northern Railway of Canada, the Chateauguay & Northern Railway, Halifax & Southwestern Railway and the Inverness Railway & Coal Company, making a total mileage in operation at present in the east of over 500 miles. An additional 500 miles of these latter lines are under construction, 300 miles of which will soon be in operation, making a total mileage of 3,350 miles in operation in 1905.

In pursuance of the plan to afford the Canadian Northern Railway System connection with Eastern Ontario and Quebec, Mackenzie, Mann & Company, Limited, acquired the charter of the James Bay Railway Company, which had power to build a line from Port Arthur to Sudbury and Toronto, Ottawa and Montreal, making connection at Hawkesbury, on the Ottawa River with the Great Northern Railway of Canada. Tracks were laid for the construction of this line in 1904, and construction is now being rapidly proceeded with. It is expected that the line will be opened from Toronto to Parry Sound Harbor on the Georgian Bay during this present fall of 1905. The name of the James Bay Company will be changed and its lines will form part of the Canadian Northern System.

The company also secured control of the Chateauguay & Northern Railway Company and of the Great Northern Railway of Canada. The line of the former runs from Montreal to Joliette, a distance of thirty-seven miles, and there connects with the line of the latter company. The line of the latter company runs from Hawkesbury, a point on the Ottawa River, about 60 miles below the city of Ottawa, to a point on the Quebec & Lake Saint John Railway, a distance of about 208 miles, passing through Shawinigan on the Saint Maurice River, where extensive water power exists, which is made use of to generate power for pulp mills, carbide works and other works at Shawinigan and to generate electricity which is taken into the city of Montreal for the street railway electric companies there. The company has fine terminal facilities in the city of Quebec, including a grain elevator there. These terminals are reached at present over the lines of the Quebec & Lake Saint John Railway, but a direct line from a point near Shawinigan into the city of Quebec will be constructed at an early date. The Chateauguay & Northern line has been leased to the Great Northern Railway of Canada and these lines will form part of the Canadian Northern system and will be connected therewith by an extension of the James Bay Company's line to Hawkesbury, connecting with the city of Ottawa en route, thus making the Canadian Northern Railway system extend from Quebec to Edmonton with entrances into and terminals in the cities of Quebec, Montreal, Ottawa, Toronto and Winnipeg. Extensive properties for terminal facilities have been acquired in Montreal.

The Canadian Northern Railway has charter powers to build to Hudson Bay and the Pacific coast, and their eastern lines have charter powers to build from its terminals at Port Arthur to the Atlantic coast.   D. D. MANN,
Vice-President.

Canadian Pacific Railway, The. A Canadian railway running across the continent from Saint John, N. B., on the Atlantic, to Vancouver, B. C., on the Pacific, with lines owned or leased, running from Montreal to Quebec, Ottawa, Toronto, London, and Windsor, on the Detroit River, and branch lines throughout the Provinces of Ontario and Quebec; with other branch lines to various points in New Brunswick; with a network of lines throughout the Canadian West and British Columbia, including the Souris Branch, the Manitoba South Western, The Manitoba & North Western, the Great North West Central, the Crow's Nest Pass and Columbia & Kootenay Lines, the Calgary & Edmonton, the Columbia & Western, and many others; making a total mileage of 8,332 covered by the traffic returns of 30 June 1904. Other lines worked by the railway at that date aggregated 438 miles, and there were under construction 338 miles, while the mileage of the Minneapolis, Saint Paul and Sault Ste. Marie Railway and the Duluth, South Shore and Atlantic Railway (lines controlled by the Canadian Pacific) was 1,648 and 565 miles respectively; a grand total of 11,321 miles of road built, acquired, leased, or controlled since the company was chartered early in 1881. Construction of the main line was commenced in June, 1881, and completed on 7 Nov. 1885.

By the terms of the Government contract with a company whose directorate included George Stephen, Esq., now Lord Mount-Stephen, and Donald A. Smith, Esq., now Lord Strathcona and Mount Royal, Richard B. Angus, Esq., and others, it was agreed to build a railway from Callander, in Northern Ontario, to the Pacific, for a consideration of $25,000,000 in money, and 25,000,000 acres of selected land, together with various privileges as to right of way, etc.

The original share capital of the company was $5,000,000, increased in 1882 to $25,000,000, and then to $100,000,000, of which $35,000,000

was cancelled in 1885. Various financial changes and difficulties occurred during construction, and it became necessary to secure government loans of $30,000,000 in 1884, and $5,000,000 in 1885; these loans were repaid in full and the efforts of the promoters and management of the railway were eventually crowned with success.

By owning and operating all of the adjuncts of the railway service — telegraphs, express, sleeping cars, dining cars, grain elevators, as well as hotels at the leading points, steamship lines on the lakes and on the Pacific and Atlantic Oceans, the Canadian Pacific adopted special methods of management which have worked out to the material advantage of the company.

According to its statement of 30 June 1904, the cost of the railway and equipment was $256,665,689; of its various steamship lines, $14,027,345; and of its hotels, buildings, etc., $2,724,417. It then held in Manitoba and the Territories 11,338,350 acres of land, and in British Columbia 3,744,324 acres. Its capital stock was $84,500,000, receiving dividends at the rate of 6 per cent per annum; its 4 per cent preference stock, $33,473,333; its 4 per cent consolidated debenture stock, $82,355,217; its mortgage bonds, $47,238,086; its total cash subsidies received, $30,673,283; and its land grant sales, $41,160,443.

The company issued $25,000,000 5 per cent land grant bonds in 1881, which have been paid off. In 1888 a further issue of $15,000,000 3½ per cent land bonds was made, and of these $3,500,000 had been provided for at 30 June 1904 by payment of that amount to the Government out of the proceeds of land sales in terms of the mortgage, leaving $11,500,000 outstanding. The deferred payments on lands sold amounted at 30 June 1904 to $15,252,308.

The following table illustrates the diversified nature of its traffic during the three years, each ending June 30:

Description of freight carried.	Year ended June 30th,		
	1902.	1903.	1904.
Flour, barrels....	4,921,993	5,110,757	5,270,432
Grain, bushels...	52,719,706	63,822,710	52,090,151
Live stock, head.	963,742	1,103,686	1,314,814
Lumber, feet	1,033,569,377	1,190,378,217	1,267,804,321
Firewood, cords.	204,963	268,401	270,803
Manufactured articles, tons.....	2,288,234	2,665,260	3,119,569
All other articles, tons...........	2,571,136	2,942,736	3,620,515
Freight traffic.			
Number of tons carried	8,769,934	10,180,847	11,135,896
Of tons carried 1 mile	3,247,922,167	3,862,242,903	3,809,801,95
Earnings per ton per mile.......	$0 75	$0 74	$0 7
Passenger traffic.			
Number of passengers carried .		5,524,198	6,251,47
Number of passengers carried 1 mile		635,855,533	677,940,49
Earnings per passenger per mile		$.0473	$.0183

The gross earnings of the system for the year ending 30 June 1904 were $46,469,132, and the working expenses, $32,256,027, with net earnings of $14,213,105.

Lord Mount-Stephen resigned the presidency of the company in 1888, and was succeeded by Sir William C. Van Horne, who retired in 1899, and was succeeded by the present president of the company, Sir Thomas G. Shaughnessy. The general offices of the company are at Montreal, Canada.

C. DRINKWATER,
Secretary Canadian Pacific Railway Company.

Canadian River, a river that rises in the northeast part of New Mexico, and runs generally east through Texas and Indian Territory to the Arkansas. Its length is about 000 miles, but it is rather shallow and not important for navigation. Its largest tributary is the Rio Nutria, or North Fork of the Canadian, which runs parallel to the main stream for about 600 miles.

Canadian Series, the lower of the two series into which the rocks of the Ordovician system are divided by American geologists. It comprises the Chazy and calciferous stages, principally limestones, and grades upward into the Trenton. See ORDOVICIAN.

Canadian Turpentine. See CANADA BALSAM.

Canadian Universities. There are in Canada 15 universities, several of which have various federated and affiliated colleges. Three of them (the universities of Toronto, New Brunswick, and Manitoba) are provincial institutions. Of the rest 10 are denominational and 2 are non-denominational. The list of the universities, with their endowments, etc., is as follows:

institution dating from 1668) in 1852, being granted a royal charter defining its organization and powers. At the head of the university is the archbishop of Quebec as visitor and apostolic chancellor. The superior of the Quebec Seminary is ex-officio rector of Laval. The directors of the Quebec Seminary, and the three senior professors of each faculty form the council of the university. A bull of Pope Pius IX. (15 April 1876) gave to the university the requisite acknowledgment from the Holy See and appointed the cardinal prefect of the propaganda its protector. The direction of faith and morals is thereby placed under a council composed of the archbishops and bishops of the Province of Quebec. There are four faculties: Theology, Law, Medicine, and Arts. Appointments in the Faculty of Theology are made by the visitor, in the other faculties by the council. The academic year extends over nine months, beginning in September, and is divided into three terms. In each faculty there are granted the degrees of Bachelor, Master or Licentiate, and Doctor. The course in Theology covers four years, the lectures and examinations being held in Latin; the other courses at Laval are conducted in French. No student is admitted without a recommendation from the Roman Catholic bishop of his place of residence. In the Faculty of Law, the course covers three years, and includes instruction in Roman and civil law, civil procedure, commercial and maritime law, criminal, administrative, and international law. At the end of the course the degree of Licentiate, or of Bachelor of Laws may be awarded, according

UNIVERSITIES	Date of foundation	Endowment	Value of property owned	Income	Number of students (about)
University of King's College, Windsor, N. S.	1790	$ 140,000	$ 250,000	$ 8,500	25
University of New Brunswick, Fredericton, N. B.	1800	8,964			134
McGill University, Montreal, Que.	1821	2,074,504	1,874,937	346,448	1,100
Dalhousie College and University, Halifax, N. S.	1818	420,000	100,000	2,800	350
University of Toronto and University College, Toronto, Ont.	1827	3,700,000	2,922,250	200,000	2,125
University of Acadia College, Wolfville, N. S.	1838	241,970	130,000	18,528	113
University of Queen's College, Kingston, Ont.	1841	500,000	200,000	54,000	875
University of Bishop's College, Lennoxville, Que.	1843	192,918	154,200	16,388	40
University of Ottawa, Ottawa, Ont.	1848		300,000	50,000	500
University of Trinity College, Toronto, Ont.	1852	490,000	380,000	31,500	140
Laval University, Quebec and Montreal	1852	none	180,000	none	11,304
University of Mount Allison College, New Brunswick	1862	120,000	150,000	15,000	125
University of Manitoba, Winnipeg, Man.	1877	150,000	70,000		368
Victoria University, Toronto, Ont.	1836	487,455	464,740	44,013	335
McMaster University, Toronto, Ont.	1887	900,000	250,000	75,000	200
University of Saint Joseph's College, Saint Joseph, N. B.	1864		80,000		25,000	200

Of the above institutions Laval and McGill universities, and the universities of Toronto and of Queen's College may be considered, in respect to the number of their students, value of property, etc., as constituting the first class. Laval University, Quebec, was founded by the Seminary of Quebec (a private Roman Catholic to excellence. The degree of Doctor (LL.D.) is obtained one year later on presentation of a thesis, publicly discussed by a board of examiners. The course in Medicine covers four years, with a primary examination at the end of the second year, and a final examination at the end of the course. The arrangements in the

Faculty of Arts resembles rather the practice of European than American colleges. The degrees B.A., B.L., and B.Sc. are given at the end of an eight-years' course, the commencement of which is quite elementary. The first six years are devoted to Classics, French, English, Mathematics: in the last two years, Philosophy and Natural Science are studied. An examination is held on the completion of each of these portions of the work. The three degrees represent merely three grades of excellence. The teaching in the arts branches is given by the various affiliated colleges (Ste. Anne, Three Rivers, Saint Hyacinthe, etc.), in different parts of the province. The university, however, offers courses in the philosophical and scientific subjects, attended by the pupils of the Quebec Seminary. The expenses of the university are paid by the Quebec Seminary. The Laval charter was granted on condition that it should remain the sole Roman Catholic university of the province. The attempt to establish a separate university at Montreal was discountenanced by the Holy See, which permitted, however (1876), the establishment of branch faculties, with identical teaching. This was confirmed by provincial legislation (1881), and the Montreal branch of Laval acquired a practical independence by a Papal brief of 1889, and by the separate incorporation of its legal and medical faculties. But the Montreal professors (except in medicine are appointed by the council at Quebec. McGill University (Montreal) originated in a private endowment by the Hon. James McGill, in 1813. It received a royal charter in 1821, and commenced the work of teaching, in arts and medicine, in 1829. McGill expected his foundation to form part of a provincial government university, a scheme which proved impracticable. It results from this, however, that the supreme authority lies with thé crown. The actual control is vested in a board of 15 governors selected by co-optation with the approval of the governor-general of Canada. These appoint the principal, and together with him and the Fellows form the corporation, the highest academical body of the university. There are four faculties, Arts, Applied Science, Law, and Medicine. In Arts, and Applied Science, the undergraduate course extends over four sessions of seven and one half months each, in Law it covers three sessions of eight months each, and in Medicine four sessions of nine months each. A combined course in Arts and Medicine can be taken in six years. The Faculty of Arts has a teaching staff of 53, with 356 students (session of 1902–3). In the first two years of the course leading to the degree of B.A. the subjects are closely prescribed with but little option. In the third and fourth year there is a wide range of selection among literary and scientific subjejcts: students may here specialize so as to obtain honor standing in a particular study or group of studies. The degree of M.A. is given on a special examination with presentation of a thesis. The fee for under-graduates is $61 per session, for partial students $22 per course. Summer courses are held during May and June in the subjects of the first two years for which special fees are paid. Women are admitted to this Faculty, but to no other. In the first two years they take their lectures in the Royal Victoria College, a residential college erected and en-

dowed by Lord Strathcona and Mount Royal (1883) for the women students at McGill. In the third and fourth years complete coeducation obtains. The Faculty of Applied Science has a staff of 40, with 280 students. It enjoys especial facilities owing to its exceptionally complete apparatus and equipment. It gives instruction in architecture, chemistry, surveying, civil, electrical, mechanical and mining engineering, and metallurgy. It grants the degree of B.Sc., and the higher degrees of M.Sc. (for special examination) and D.Sc. (for special research). The undergraduate yearly fee is $175. The Faculty of Medicine has a staff of 76 with 420 students. Its clinical teaching is conducted in the Montreal General Hospital, the Royal Victoria Hospital, and the Montreal Maternity Hospital. The annual fee is $125. Graduate courses in clinics and laboratory instruction are given during the month of June. The Faculty of Law has a teaching staff of 11 with 40 students. Students are instructed, as at Laval, in the subjects prescribed by the general council of the bar of the Province of Quebec. The annual fee is $60. Several colleges in Montreal and elsewhere are affiliated with McGill. The Stanstead Wesleyan College (Stanstead, P. Q.), and Vancouver College (Vancouver, B. C.), are affiliated for the work of the first two years in arts: Victoria College (Victoria, B. C.), for the first year in arts. The Congregational College of Canada, the Presbyterian College, the Wesleyan College of Montreal, the Diocesan College of Montreal (Church of England), are theological institutions affiliated with McGill. The McGill Normal School (Montreal) gives pedagogic training for elementary and secondary schools, and awards provincial diplomas. The university possesses a fine library building with about 100,000 volumes. The theological colleges, and the Royal Victoria College provide residential accommodation, but there is no university residence. The University of Toronto is a provincial institution, whose constitutional powers and functions are defined in the University Act (Ontario, 1901). Its only college is University College (one of the most beautiful buildings on the continent), but with the university are federated a number of denominational colleges, Victoria (Methodist), Trinity (Anglican), Knox (Presbyterian), Wycliffe (Anglican), and Saint Michael's (Roman Catholic). The supreme authority is vested in the crown, acting through the lieutenant-governor of Ontario. Annual appropriations receive his ratification. Expenditures of endowments are ratified by the legislative assembly of Ontario. The professors of the university and of University College are appointed by the crown. The property of the University and of University College is vested in a board of nine trustees, four of them dignitaries of the university acting ex-officio, and five appointed by the lieutenant-governor. The university has Faculties of Arts, Law, Applied Science, and Medicine. The course in each Faculty extends over four years. In the Faculty of Arts instruction is given partly by professors, etc., attached to the University of Toronto, partly by the professoriate of University College. The federated Victoria and Trinity colleges also instruct their students in arts in the same subjects as University College. The students in arts may take either a general course, or select one of the fourteen honor courses (Classics, Mathematics, Modern Languages, etc.). The system favors a high degree of specialization on the part of capable students. The degree of M.A. is obtainable by special examination and presentation of a thesis one year after graduation. The degree Ph.D. is granted after two years of postgraduate work under the direction of the professoriate. The four years' course in the Faculty of Law leads to the degree of LL.B. The Faculty of Applied Science and Engineering grants degrees in Applied Science (B.A.Sc.) and in different engineering branches. The four years' course of instruction given by the Faculty of Medicine leads to the degree of M.B. To receive license to practise in Ontario students must pass the final examination prescribed by the Ontario Medical Council for which a fifth year of study is required. Clinical instruction is given at the Toronto General Hospital and other places. By the recent federation of Trinity University with the University of Toronto (in effect 1 Oct. 1904) the medical faculties of the two are now amalgamated. The university holds examinations and grants degrees in Dentistry, Pharmacy, Agriculture, Music, Pedagogy and Household Science, the preparation for which is mainly done in affiliated colleges such as the Royal College of Dental Surgeons, Ontario College of Pharmacy, etc. The number of students in 1903 attached to the University of Toronto (exclusive of theological students in federated colleges) was 2,135: of these 653 were students in Arts at University College, 300 in Arts in Victoria College, 721 in Medicine, and 402 in Applied Science. The University of Trinity College (previous to federation) had 140 students. The theological colleges are residential, and University College has a dining hall. Queen's University (Kingston, Ont.) was founded by Royal charter in 1841, its funds being raised by the Presbyterian church. For many years the university received a provincial grant of $5,000, which, however, was withdrawn in 1868. In spite of financial and other difficulties Queen's University rose under the distinguished Principal Grant (1877–1902) to a foremost place among Canadian universities. It has now a staff of 55 with 875 students. It has Faculties of Theology, Arts, Law, Medicine, and Practical Science. It confers also the post-graduate degrees of Ph.D. and D.Sc. These degrees are given four years after the degree of M.A. An approved thesis must be submitted, but residential study is not compulsory. Women are admitted to all except the theological faculty at Queen's on an equal footing with men. The university possesses an observatory, a museum, and a library of about 37,000 volumes. Degrees in Arts are awarded on examination to extramural students. There is no university residence. The University of Ottawa is a Roman Catholic institution, founded by the Oblate Fathers in 1848 as the College of Bytown, and erected into a university in 1866. Unlike Laval it is an English-speaking institution, and draws a considerable number of students from the Eastern States. It offers a four years' course in theology, the degree of Bachelor of Divinity being granted at the end of the second year, that of Licentiate a year later, the final degree being Doctor of Divinity. There is a four years' course in Arts, largely classical and lit-

erary, and courses of three years in Law, and Science. The university had 500 students in 1903 with a teaching staff of 52. The University of Manitoba, established 1877, by act of the local legislature, is a provincial institution, having sole power to confer degrees in Arts, Law, and Medicine, in Manitoba. The university gives instruction only in the departments of Natural and Physical Science: in respect to other subjects it is an examining body only, with examiners but no teaching professoriate. The educational work of the university is conducted in the affiliated colleges, Saint Boniface (Roman Catholic), Saint John's (Anglican), Manitoba (Presbyterian), the Wesleyan College (Methodist), and the Manitoba Medical College, all situated in Winnipeg except the first, which is in the suburb of Saint Boniface. Degrees in Divinity are granted by the affiliated colleges. The university had 368 students in 1903. Dalhousie College (Halifax), founded in 1821, is a non-residential, non-denominational institution, having full university powers. Women are admitted on terms of equality with men. It has a staff of 30 members with 350 students, in 1903. It has Faculties in Arts, Science, and Medicine, the course in each covering four years, and in Law with a three years' course. The course in arts follows the elective system. Medical instruction is given in the Halifax Medical College. It has a library of over 12,000 volumes. McMaster University (Toronto) is a Baptist establishment, with courses in Arts and Theology. It had in 1903 a staff of 16 instructors and 200 students. The University of Saint Joseph's College (Memramcook, N. B.) was established by the (Roman Catholic) Fathers of the Holy Cross for the higher education of the French population of the maritime provinces. It has Theological and Art courses, and had 200 students in 1903. The University of New Brunswick (Fredericton) was founded as a college under provincial charter and endowed with crown lands in 1800, and erected into a university in 1859. Since 1845 it has been non-sectarian. The university has Faculties in Arts, and Engineering: the course in each covers four years. There is accommodation for resident students. Women are admitted to the university. The number of students in 1903 was 134, with a staff of 9 instructors. Acadia College, a Baptist institution Until recently instruction was given only in Divinity and Arts, but a course in science has just been inaugurated. The University of Mount Allison College is a Methodist institution at Sackville, N. B., with Faculties in Arts and Theology. It has also an engineering course leading to entrance to the third year in Applied Science at McGill. It covers also a part of the work required for the Dalhousie Law School. The college has a staff of 10 instructors with 125 students in 1903. Bishops College, Lennoxville, is the Anglican University of the Province of Quebec. It has a Theological and Arts Faculty with 40 students, in 1903. The University of King's College, Windsor, N. S., founded in 1790, is the oldest of Canadian universities. It is a denominational institution, connected with the Church of England. It had 25 students in 1903. The Western University (London, Ont.) is also controlled by the Church of England. In addition to a divinity school of about 20 students, it has a medical faculty and a few stu-

dents in arts. See CANADA — HIGHER EDUCATION; CANADA — SECONDARY EDUCATION; CANADA — PRIMARY EDUCATION; CANADA — PUBLIC EDUCATION. STEPHEN LEACOCK,
Of McGill University.

Canaigre, kăn-ā'gr, a species of dock (*Rumex hymenosepalus*) indigenous to the arid region of southern California, Arizona, New Mexico, northern Mexico, and western Texas. It is a perennial herb with tuberous roots from which a reddish or green stem rises to a height of about two feet and bears rather large leaves resembling those of other docks. The tubers, which resemble those of dahlia, have long been used locally as a source of tannin, and fairly successful attempts have been made to grow them upon a commercial scale for this purpose. Propagation is easily effected by means of the tubers, about 2,000 pounds of which are required to plant an acre.

Canajoharie, kăn'-a-jo-hă're, N. Y., an Indian word, meaning, "The pot that washes itself." A village on the south bank of the Mohawk River in Montgomery County, 55 miles west of Albany, in the most picturesque part of the Mohawk Valley. Canajoharie was first settled about 1740 by the Dutch and Germans. It was the home of Brant, Chief of the Six Nations, and place of departure from the Mohawk to the southern interior. The Erie Canal, the New York Central and West Shore railroads pass through the village. The village has two banks, with a combined capital of $275,000, a library, six churches, and a school of very high standing. Two weekly local newspapers, and one hay trade publication; national, flour mills, limestone quarries, paper and cloth bag manufactory and meat and fruit packing-houses. Is equipped with electric light and power, sewers and an abundant water supply. It is governed by a board of trustees and a council of five members, elected annually. Pop. 2,500.

Canal Dover, Ohio, a city of Tuscarawas County, situated on the Tuscarawas River and the Ohio Canal, and on the Pennsylvania and other railroads. There are deposits of coal, iron, and building-stone in the vicinity. The chief industries are in iron and steel, and the manufacture of racing-sulkies, baby-carriages, roofing, etc. Pop. (1900) 5,422.

Canal Du Mide. See CANALS.

Canal Ring. See TILDEN, SAMUEL J.

Canale, Nicolo, nĕ-kō-lō' kä-nä'lĕ, Venetian admiral, who flourished in the second half of 15th century. In 1469 he was commander of the Venetian fleet at Negropont (the ancient Chalcis), and succeeded in seizing the Turkish town of Enos. The cruelties perpetrated upon the inoffensive inhabitants created great indignation at Constantinople, and Mohammed II., with a view of resenting the outrages, besieged Negropont with a force of 120,000 men, and after a violent contest expelled the Venetians. Canale, to whom this defeat was attributed, was sentenced to death by the council of ten, but at the instance of Pope Paul II. and of other influential persons, his punishment was commuted to exile for life.

Canaletto, kä-nä-lĕt'tō, or **Canale,** Antonio, Venetian painter: b. Venice, 18 Oct. 1697; d. there, 20 Aug. 1768. He is celebrated for his landscapes, which are true to nature, and his architectural paintings. He is said to have first used the camera obscura for perspective.

Canaletto, Bernardo Belotti, bĕr när'dō bĕ-lōt'tĕ, Venetian painter: b. 1724: d. Warsaw, 1780. He was nephew of Antonio Canaletto (q.v.), who was likewise a good artist, and painted many Italian landscapes. He lived in Dresden, where he was a member of the Academy of Painters.

Canals. Navigation canals, as distinguished from power or irrigation canals, may be classified in various ways. One is according to their magnitude, and the consequent traffic for which they are intended; as boat and barge canals, or ship canals. Or again, according to their source of supply; as pure canals, mere artificial cuts with no water but what is turned into them; tidal canals, varying with ebb and flow; and canalized rivers, with weirs to increase depth and a lock at one end, and if necessary, lateral cuts around falls or other obstructions. Or according to their geographical purpose: as isthmian canals, like those across Suez, Panama, and Corinth; peninsular, to save distance or a stormy passage, as those across Jutland, the Languedoc Canal from the Bay of Biscay to the Mediterranean, the Caledonian, the Chesapeake & Delaware (bays) across Delaware, etc.; canals around falls, as the Welland, Sault Ste. Marie, Ohio Falls, etc.; system-joining canals, as those connecting the Danube and Rhine, the Seine and Loire, Lake Erie and the Ohio or the Hudson, Lake Michigan and the Mississippi, the St. Lawrence and the Ottawa or Lake Champlain, etc.; or artificial-seaport canals, as the Manchester & Liverpool, to give inland cities access to the sea. Practically, however, the first is the only very useful one.

The chief problems in the construction and operation of a canal are: (1) To proportion its dimensions to the probable volume of traffic, in order to save interest, maintenance, and operation charges. (2) To give it the shortest and most easily constructed route, and the best lines and form, consistent with the cheapest maintenance and operation. (3) To provide and regulate a constant supply of water. (4) To shift vessels from one level to another most speedily and cheaply and with the least waste of water. (5) To gain the maximum of speed with the least injury to the embankment.

1. American and English barge canals have very largely gone out of use since the advent of railroads; and it is agreed that a principal reason is the small cargo they can float, making the expense of freightage heavy in proportion. As the operating expense of canals with thrice the carrying capacity is less than half as much again, it is certain that with enlarged size and a full business a great reduction in freight rates would be possible. But the latter clause is the dubious part: if the traffic were not commensurate, the added expense would still further handicap them as business ventures. It is therefore a very nice question exactly how large to make a canal; and has hitherto proven insoluble, except to large communities, which can afford to sink a part of the expense in the general "plant" of their industrial appliances.

2. A canal cannot, like a highroad or a railroad, have "grades." Each level must be absolute until a new one is established; and it

must follow hills and valleys as it finds them, tunnel the former and build aqueducts across the latter or the river-courses, and change levels when needed. But locks are expensive both to build and operate, and delay traffic; the fewer the better on all grounds. It is therefore often thought cheaper in the long run, and a saving of time in transit, to take a longer route and save locks. The soil is also to be considered: rock or hardpan costs more to excavate, and a longer route may furnish cheaper cutting. On the other hand, in hard ground, the cut can be more nearly vertical and less excavation be needed. In soft ground the sides must have a heavy slope or they will cave, so that the top may be from two to two and a half times as wide as the bottom; in all ordinary ground some slope is needed; in rock cutting the sides are nearly or quite vertical, as also in passing through towns, where the sides are of masonry and space is a desideratum. The question of route is therefore anything but a simple one, and is complicated with many business and mechanical ones. The number of bridges, aqueducts, culverts, etc., to be built is an important consideration. The width must be sufficient to allow two of the largest vessels to pass abreast without fouling, and the narrower the way the more traction power is needed. The width of bottom is usually fixed at the beam width of two vessels, and the depth at 18 inches more than their draft. The excavation of canals is carried on like other large excavations, with machinery from the ordinary pick and shovel, scraper, and cart, to great steam excavators and dredges, powder and dynamite for rock blasting, and portable railroads for carrying off the material excavated, etc. Aqueducts have always masonry foundations or piers, supporting a trough of masonry, wood, or steel. When the interfering stream is small, it is carried under the canal by a culvert.

3. The provision of a supply of water might well be placed first, as the canal would be useless without it. If possible, the location is chosen so as to fill its summit levels from sufficient lakes or streams. Otherwise artificial reservoirs must be constructed, with all the care needed for the water supply of towns except as to quality. The drainage basin must be ample to supply loss of water by evaporation, leakage, and lockage, with reference to length of canal, number and size of locks, and volume of traffic; and the feeders properly calculated as to length and size. When an elevated supply is not to be had, pumping works take their place. Of the causes of wastage mentioned above, evaporation cannot be lessened. Leakage is prevented in porous soil by cementing or puddling the sides of the canal. But lockage is the constant drain on the supply, which has exercised much ingenuity in minimizing. One method of preventing waste is also connected with the regulation of overflow: to keep a "ladder" of locks far enough apart, say 100 yards, so that the discharge from upper to lower level shall not overspill: or an intervening pond must be formed. As overflow not only wastes, but may cause heavy damages and suits, and also injures the towpath, waste-weirs should be provided at convenient distances; and as a break would drain the entire reach before it could be repaired, these must be localized by stop-gates at short distances, making only a small basin to

waste and do damage with its water. The towpath must also be so sloped and prepared as to prevent its soaking and miring or crumbling.

4. The lock is the chief agency for shifting boats from one level to another. Its principle is to open a small basin with one closed end into a larger one, thus raising or lowering the water of the smaller to the level of the larger without much affecting the latter. In practice, the lock is a chamber with its sides at the upper level and its bottom at the lower; and to save water, it is made as nearly as possible the size of the largest vessel that is to use it, with six inches to a foot of play at each side and end. The lateral walls in the more important canals are of stone. The ends are wooden or iron folding gates, opening up-stream; each made of two leaves pivoted in the walls, each leaf a little more than half the width of the lock, so that they shut together at an obtuse angle against the current, the weight therefore only serving to close them still tighter. When a vessel is to be brought from one level to the other, it is floated into the basin or "pound," and the gate shut behind it. A sluice or valve in the upper gate then admits water and slowly raises it to the upper level, or the one in the lower gate lets it down to the lower level, as the case may be. The total lockage takes all the way from 6 to 20 minutes. These sluices are worked by rack and pinion in the gate, or revolve on an axis; they are managed by long levers set in the top of the gate, and reached by a "running board" projecting over it. The gates themselves are also managed by levers except in the better equipped and important ones, where they are often worked by steam machinery, at a saving of half the time. To save time and expense of superintendence, the reaches are made as long as possible, and the locks bunched in one spot in "ladders" of several close together, like a flight of steps, with a high lift, rather than scattered along the route. As said above, these should be some way apart to prevent overflow. As the pressure on the gates and sides is very great, the limit of "lift" in a lock, or the vertical height to which the water is raised, averages not over eight or nine feet, and may be only three or four; though 12 is not very uncommon, and 18 has been attained at the Sault Ste. Marie. On the largest locks the water is admitted through a culvert parallel to the side wall of the lock, and opening into the centre through a tunnel; this is said to reduce the time of lockage considerably. Of course too sudden an admission of water would injure the boat. Pipes are also used.

It is evident that at each passage of a boat, the upper level has to supply water enough to fill the lock between it and the lower. It may be noted that the ascending traffic takes far more than the descending, because in the latter case the water displaced by the boat itself flows back into the upper reach, and remains there after the gates are shut. A 25-ton boat with an eight-foot lift costs 163 tons of water going up and 103 coming down. To economize this supply where water is scarce, two chief plans have been devised. One is to form at the side of the lock a reservoir equal in size. When the lock is to be emptied, the water is run into the reservoir until it and the lock are at the same level, which of course will be half height. The reservoir is then closed, and the remaining water in

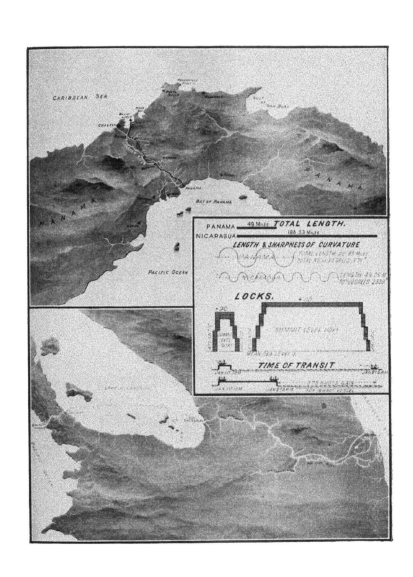

the lock run off through the lower sluices in the usual way. On refilling the lock, before opening the upper sluices, one fourth the quantity required can be obtained from the reservoir, thus saving 25 to 40 tons of water at each passage. This delays the traffic, however, and has not been much used. Another method is now coming into use in the canals of largest traffic, at the spots where a number of locks are bunched, and therefore a great amount of water used and time consumed. This is a reversion to the oldest historic type, of lifting the boats by machinery instead of floating them up; except that instead of inclined planes for hauling up and gravity for letting them down, hydraulic vertical lift locks are used. In this system the lock is a chamber with gates and water, as in the other; but it is movable, and when the boat is run into it, is raised or lowered to level. Counterweights and flotation tanks are sometimes used to aid the hydraulic power. The first of these was built at Anderton on the Weaver River, England, in 1876; lift, 50 feet 4 inches; two troughs 75 by 15 by 5; hydraulic ram, with three-foot plunger. This lets through a 100-ton boat in a total lockage time of eight minutes, and takes the place of six ordinary locks, which would take at least an hour, and on an average considerably more. The next was at Les Fontinettes, northwest France, on the Neufossé Canal, connecting the North Sea ports with Paris; lift, 43 feet 1 inch; two troughs 139 feet 7 inches by 18 feet 4½ inches by 6 feet 10⅝ inches; hydraulic ram, 6 feet 6¾ inches plunger. This lets through a 300-ton boat in 20 minutes, and replaces five locks taking two hours. At La Louvrière, Belgium, on the Canal du Centre, connecting Mons with Brussels, there is a fall of 293 feet in 17 miles, and 213 of it in five miles. This has been overcome by five lifts, with hydraulic rams having plungers of 6 feet 6¾ inches, operated by turbines turned by the upper-level water; height of lift from 50½ to 63⅔ feet. Each of these has two troughs of 141 feet 1 inch by 19 feet ¼ inch by 8 feet 6 inches, and takes 400-ton barges in 15 minutes. At Lockport, N. Y., on the Erie Canal, the original nine and later five double locks, with a lift of 54 feet 5 inches, have been replaced by a hydraulic balance, working two troughs 225 feet by 19 feet 2 inches by 9 feet, and raising 400-ton boats in 15 minutes of lockage, against half an hour to an hour and a half of old. Others are either built or building.

5. The maximum of speed thus far found compatible with safety and economy on canals is from three and a half to four miles. Higher speed not only involves much greater proportionate power for traction on account of the resistance in a narrow way, but injures the embankment by the wash of the waves. Even on a navigable small river, a steamer at eight or nine miles an hour will cut the banks badly; and it would destroy those of a canal, unless faced more solidly than is commercially practicable. Furthermore, if the canal were worked to its full capacity, the traffic would not be expedited unless lockage could be shortened. The question of power for hauling the boats has been variously solved. Sometimes men draw the boats by ropes from the towpath, sometimes they row the boats direct,— this mostly in China; most often animals on the towpath draw them with ropes, singly or in tows; sometimes loco-

motives replace the animals, and in one place (the Muscle Shoals Canal on the Tennessee) the locomotives exchange boats when they meet; on the Erie and the Delaware & Raritan, steam propellers are used; in still others, especially on the continent of Europe, the power is from a cable or an endless chain along the bottom of the canal. either gripped by the boat or wound over a drum on the bottom of the boat.

Historical.— The earliest artificial water channels were for irrigation and drainage; not to reclaim swamp land, other soil being too plentiful, but to regulate the overflow of rivers. These date from an immemorial past, certainly 3500 B.C. in Babylonia and Egypt, more probably 7000 at least. Very early also the larger ones must have been used for boat navigation, to transport agricultural and building materials; these combined drains and canals still exist in England, called "navigations," and the workers on them "navigators," and have given to the language the word "navvy" for construction laborers. At what period the first ones were dug primarily for navigation, and incidentally for irrigation, cannot be told. There is a tradition that the Suez Canal was dug under the Old Kingdom of Egypt before 2000 B.C.; it was certainly opened or reopened for small boats by Necho, about 600 B.C. About this time also Nebuchadrezzar of Babylon opened the Royal Canal between the Tigris and Euphrates, but Mesopotamia had been well canalized before. These two countries, indeed, invited canals, with their flat surface and long levels, and easy digging in sand or clay. It is probable that China also had canals before the Christian era, but evidence is wanting. The first canals were of course on one level; but with the light boats and great engineering skill of the ancients the step was not long to damming the water at different levels and hauling the boat over. The first system, not yet disused, was to pull the boat up an inclined plane and let it down by gravity; and this remained the only available method till modern times. Under Alexander and his successors in Egypt and the Seleucid empire, canals were much used: an important one was from Alexandria to the Nile, whose mouths were shut off by sandbars. Marius had one constructed 102 B.C. from the lower Rhone to the Mediterranean. Under Claudius there was one from the Tiber to the sea; and in Great Britain there are two which date from the Roman time. the Foss Dyke and the Caer Dyke, in Lincolnshire, of 40 and 11 miles respectively. In the 4th century Lombardy was canalized.— a very favorable spot from its great plain and many rivers; and near the end of the 5th century, Odoacer carried one from the Adriatic to Mentone above Ravenna. The downfall of Roman civilization stopped their development for a while; but under Charlemagne a fresh extension began, that monarch building canals to connect the Danube both with the Rhine and the Black Sea. In the Netherland bogs the system is that of nature itself, and began very early; here the canal is not so much an artificial channel as a remnant of the original sea, around which the land is built. In Britain as early as 1121, Henry I. deepened and made navigable the old Foss Dyke. The Grand Canal of China, about 1,000 miles long, a large part of it made up of canalized rivers, was completed in 1289. That country has many other great systems connecting its internal waterways.

But obviously the boats transferable by such machinery must be small and lightly loaded; and the modern canal system, with long heavy boats and large cargoes, was first made possible by the invention of the lock. This doubtless developed out of putting dams close together with gates in them; but neither inventor nor even country of first use is certain. It has been claimed for two brothers, engineers of Viterbo in Italy, in 1481; also for Leonardo da Vinci the universal genius; and again for Holland a century earlier. The one certain fact is, that in the latter part of the 15th century they were in use in both countries, and spread rapidly through Europe. The first country to undertake on a large and systematic scale the connection of its leading systems by canals was France, in the 17th century. The Brière Canal, connecting the Seine and Loire, was begun in 1605 under .Henry IV., and completed 1642 under Louis XIII. The Orléans Canal, uniting the same basins by the Loing, was completed 1675, under Louis XIV. The greatest of all, the Languedoc Canal, to connect the Bay of Biscay with the Mediterranean, was finished 1681. It is 148 miles long, 6½ feet deep, with a summit level of 600 feet; has about 119 locks and 50 aqueducts, and floats barges of 100 tons. France in 1879 passed a law making all its canals uniform at 6½ feet deep, with locks 126½ feet long by 17 wide. England was much later in taking up the system on a large scale, but when it did so, carried out a remarkable one, with great feats of engineering. The fathers of it were Francis Duke of Bridgewater and his famous engineer, James Brindley; and the beginning was the charter for the Bridgewater Canal in 1759. The names of Watt, Telford, Nimmo, Rennie, and other noted engineers are associated with it. The last inland canal in Great Britain was built in 1834. Among the leading ones are the Grand Junction, 128 miles; Leeds & Liverpool, 128; Trent & Mersey, 93; Kennet & Avon, 57. The great Irish canals are the Grand Canal, from Dublin to Ballinasloe, 164 miles, uniting the Irish Sea to the Shannon; and the Royal Canal nearly parallel to it for the same traffic, from Dublin to Torinansburg, west of Longford. The great canals of Scotland are the Caledonian and the Forth & Clyde, spoken of under *Ship Canals.* Early in the 18th century Peter the Great constructed a great system of canals and canalized rivers, 1,434 miles long, to connect St. Petersburg with the Caspian. The Danish Canal, 100 miles long, from the North Sea to the Baltic, was finished in 1785. The Gotha Canal, 280 miles long, connecting Stockholm with Gothenburg across Sweden, was planned 1716, but opened the first part 1810, the whole 1832. In 1836-46 Louis of Bavaria revived Charlemagne's old plan, connecting the Main (and so the Rhine) with the Danube, by a canal 108 miles long, 650 feet above the Main, and 270 feet above the Danube.

United States Boat Canals.— The first canal in this country was built in 1793, around the falls of the Connecticut River at South Hadley Falls, Mass.; the engineer was Benjamin Prescott of Northampton, afterward superintendent of the Springfield Armory. The lift was not by locks, but by inclined planes, the boats being run into a movable caisson, filled with water

and hauled up by cables operated by waterpower; locks were introduced later. In 1796 a canal was completed around Turner's Falls farther north in the same river, at Montague. "The Proprietors of the Locks and Canals on Merrimack River" were incorporated 1792, and opened their canal around the falls at Lowell to the mouth of the Concord, one and a half miles long and with four locks, in 1797; it was for the lumbering business, rafts, masts, etc. But the first general canal for passengers and merchandise opened in the United States was the Middlesex, a rival to the last, incorporated 1793, and completed 1804 at a cost of $700,000; it ran to Charlestown, 31 miles, was 24 feet wide and 4 feet deep, and fed by the Concord. A packet boat, the Governor Sullivan, plied regularly between Boston and Lowell, taking nearly a day. The first boat voyage to Concord, N. H., was made in 1814, and a steamer began passages in 1819. The canal was disused 1851. But much broader projects had been set on foot about the time of these local ventures; and several of the greatest afterward carried out, as well as some which have been chimeras rather from political developments than from any inherent impracticability, were broached even before the Revolution. Washington was deeply interested in canal schemes all through his life, and favored canals to connect all the great American water systems. The Potomac and Ohio, the James and Ohio, and the Mohawk Valley and Great Lakes connections, were all examined by him. The last named he looked over during the Revolution. In 1792 the Western Inland Navigation Lock Company was formed, and by 1797 had finished six miles of canals around the rapids at Little Falls, making a navigable way for 15-ton barges to Lake Ontario. Pennsylvania built several small canals in the two decades from 1790 to 1810, but they had little success. In 1784 Maryland and Virginia jointly granted a charter for a canal from Georgetown on the Potomac to the Alleghanies, under which up to 1822, when it was abandoned, some three quarters of a million dollars were spent in excavations, dams, and locks. But the great era of American canal-building, and of furious and losing canal speculation, was from 1810 to 1840; its definitive close was about 1850, since which year no boat canal has been built in this country except the Illinois and Mississippi. The entire system in the United States aggregates about 4,200 miles, nearly all in the belt from New York south to Virginia and west to Indiana. There are at present about 40 large canals in the United States, of which 14 are in Pennsylvania, 13 in New York, and 5 in Ohio. Some of the lines most important in their early days, and which gave great cities their start since confirmed by railroads, are now entirely disused; and a history of their fortunes would be of no more importance than of other bygone business ventures. Some of the leading existent ones, or those which may be only dormant, will be described.

Chesapeake & Ohio.— The fortunes of this system have shown how difficult it is to forecast business developments. As designed by Washington, it was to connect the Chesapeake and ocean navigation, by way of the Potomac, with that of the Ohio, by portages and highroads from its terminus Cumberland at the foot of the Alleghanies; as a fact, its use has been

SAULT STE. MARIE CANAL.

mainly from the accidental fact that Cumberland is near the Pennsylvania coal fields. The fortunes of the first company have been described. In 1823 commissioners appointed by Maryland and Virginia reported in favor of a new route in place of attempting to complete the old one; in 1824 the national system of internal improvements was inaugurated by act of 30 April, and a board of engineers in October 1826 reported on a canal from Georgetown to Pittsburg. As the cost was over $22,000,000, it was considered prohibitory then; and in 1829 the "eastern division" to Cumberland was authorized, by national, State, municipal, and private stock subscriptions. But the work had been inaugurated on 4 July 1828 by President J. Q. Adams, who struck the first spade; and it was fully opened in 1850. It is 184 miles long and 6 feet deep, 60 feet wide from Georgetown to Harper's Ferry, and 70 on an average from thence to Cumberland. It is fed from the Potomac by seven dams. The aqueduct at Georgetown over the Potomac was a very considerable engineering feat for its time; it rests on 12 masonry piers constructed by coffer-dams on rock 28 to 40 feet below the surface. At Paw Paw Bend, 27 miles east of Cumberland, the canal saves six miles by a cut-off and tunnel through the mountain, 3,118 feet long. The summit level is 613¾ feet above tidewater; the rise is accomplished by 74 locks of 6 to 10 feet lift. The whole work had cost over $9,500,000 when opened, and its total capitalized outlay had been over $15,000,000 when the bondholders foreclosed in 1890.

Erie Canal.— The State of New York finally bought the works of the Western Inland, above mentioned. In 1803 Gouverneur Morris suggested or re-suggested a broader plan, to make a navigable way not to Ontario but to Erie, and therefore from the new West to New York. De Witt Clinton eagerly took up the idea, threw his whole energies into pushing it, and made it a foremost part of his political programme, bitterly opposed by the Tammany and Van Buren wing. In 1808 Simeon De Witt was appointed to survey the Mohawk route. On 3 March 1810 a commission was appointed, with Gouverneur Morris at the head and Clinton a member; it made several reports urging the feasibility and business advantage of the canal, and Clinton's memorial to the legislature in 1815 is said to have carried conviction. At any rate, on 7 April 1816 an act was passed authorizing the construction of the Erie and Champlain canals; on 4 July 1817 the first ground was broken, at Rome; and on 4 Nov. 1825, during Clinton's governorship, the canal was formally opened from Albany to Buffalo, 352 miles. It had cost $7,602,000, but it reduced the freightage time between the termini from 20 days to 10, and the passenger time shortly to 3½, by a line of light packet boats with relays of horses at a trot; and reduced freights at once from $100 a ton to $10, and then to $3. It made central New York, largely uninhabited, at once a district of potential empire with settlers flocking in; secured for New York the domination of the American seaboard; and created or solidified the prosperity of the remarkable line of cities in its path. Its construction was justly considered a triumph of engineering ability: several of the stone aqueducts by which it was carried over the streams (it crosses the Mohawk twice) presented peculiar difficulties, and in places it was cut through solid rock. It was at first 40 feet wide and 4 feet deep; later enlarged to 70 feet at top, 56 at bottom, and 7 feet deep; still further deepened as below. It has 72 locks, 110 by 18, 57 of them double. The chief lifts are at West Troy, 188½ feet, surmounted by 16 double lift-locks; at Lockport, 54½ feet, at first by nine double locks, then by five higher ones, since 1895 by a hydraulic balance lift (above described); and at Albany, 20 feet. It is fed from Lake Erie, the Black River, and several lakes in its course. The total rise to Buffalo is 568 feet, which means that the general fall of water is to the eastward. After the New York Central paralleled it, the business declined, and for many years after the war seemed doomed to extinction. In 1883 all tolls were removed on the State's canals, and the navigation made free; but even this did not wholly arrest the decline, due to reasons heretofore stated. It being evident that the Erie must be enlarged to be an effective competitor of the railroads, in 1896 a referendum was taken on an expenditure of $9,000,000 for deepening it to nine feet. In little more than a year from the time that work was begun, this money was exhausted, and the task but partly completed. Elaborate plans were devised for turning it into a great barge canal, navigable for vessels of 800 to 1,000 tons.

The report of the New York Legislative Special Committee on the canal, made to Governor Roosevelt early in 1900 recommended that the Erie Canal be enlarged to accommodate boats of 1,000 tons burden. The recommendation was for the construction of a new canal from Lake Erie to the Hudson River following the present canal for about two-thirds of the distance and new routes for the remaining distance, and utilizing as far as possible the existing structures and canals. The proposition was for a canal 12 feet deep, 75 feet wide at the bottom and 122 feet wide at the surface, as against a depth of 9 feet, a bottom width of 49 feet and a surface width of 73 feet. It would accommodate boats 150 feet in length, 25 feet in width and 10 feet in draught, capable of carrying 1,000 tons of freight, and would have a capacity of 20,000,000 tons per annum. On that tonnage the saving as compared with the present canal would be $12,200,000 per annum. It could transport freight at one-third the cost of transportation by rail, and as compared with the lowest rail rate ever quoted across the State of New York, the saving on a tonnage of 20,000,000 would be nearly $18,000,000 per annum.

The issue at stake was not merely the commercial prosperity of the State at large and the Port of New York in particular, but was a question as to whether the great and enormously valuable wheat-carrying trade of the West should be retained in the United States or drift over the border into the hands of the Canadians. The last link in the chain of improvements by locks and canals of the St. Lawrence River has just been completed, with the result that vessels 255 feet long, of 12 to 14 feet draught and 2,200 tons capacity, can now pass from the lakes to Montreal. Chicago and Buffalo capitalists have made a proposition to the harbor commissioners of Montreal involving the immediate construction of fifteen 2,200-

ton barges, besides grain elevators and wharf facilities at Montreal to cost $4,000,000, the result of which would be to divert about 35,-000,000 bushels of grain from the New York route. Add to this that the railroads are discriminating in favor of other Atlantic ports, and it can be seen that the construction of the proposed canal is of vital importance to the future development of the Empire State.

The details of the proposition voted on at the election in November, 1903, and now being worked out in practical shape show that the new Erie Canal follows the Hudson River to Waterford; then passes by locks to the Mohawk River above Cohoes Falls. From the Falls to Rome the bed of the river is utilized, the river being canalized. Beyond Rome there is a summit level connecting with Wood Creek, and the canal then continues over the old pioneer water route up the Seneca River to the vicinity of Clyde. From Clyde the new canal will follow the route of the present canal to the Niagara River at Tonawanda. Of the other two branches, the Oswego barge canal leaves the Erie canal at Three Rivers Point, and utilizes the canalized Oswego River to Lake Ontario. The new Champlain canal will not parallel the Hudson River on the bank of the same as at present, but will utilize the river itself from Waterford to Fort Edward, and from Fort Edward to Lake Champlain the present location will be followed.

The estimated cost of this great work is $101,000,000, and the whole plan of the work has been laid out to accommodate a tonnage of 10,000,000, while at a slight increase in cost, accommodation can be provided for a very much larger tonnage. The commerce of the upper Great Lakes is between 90 and 100 million tons per year, and the importance of the canal lies in the fact that it will provide a means for connecting this huge commerce with the seacoast by a direct route, on which freight can be carried at a cost below that which is possible on the railroad. The original canal had a depth of 4 feet, and accommodated boats of only 80 tons capacity. In 1835 it was enlarged to take boats of 240 tons. Then in 1894 came the agitation for deepening to 8 feet draft, instead of 6 feet, and the absurdly inadequate appropriation of $9,000,000 was made for doing this work. The present scheme, which owes its success not a little to the efforts of President Roosevelt when he was Governor of the State, provides a 12-foot depth throughout and locks of sufficient length to take two 1,000-ton barges at one lockage, which is about eight times the capacity of the present canal.

At the present time the United States has under construction two great engineering works which, in point of magnitude and cost, far exceed anything under construction or projected elsewhere. One of these is being carried out by the Federal government, the other by the enterprise of a single State, and each is destined to exert a widely-extended influence upon the commerce not merely of the country and state affected, but of the whole world. We refer to the 46-mile ship canal which is to be opened across the Isthmus of Panama, and the 350-mile barge canal which is now being built across the State of New York. The Federal project, for many reasons, looms so large in the pub-

lic eye that the general public, and probably the majority of the people in the State in which the Erie barge canal is being built, will be surprised to know that in the mere magnitude of the work to be done the New York canal exceeds that at Panama. Furthermore, it is due only to the fact that the unit prices that must be paid for work at Panama are so much higher than those for work done at home, and in a temperate zone, that the cost of the Panama project will exceed that in New York State, although the latter will reach the great total of $101,000,000. This comparison, it must be understood, is based upon the project for a 68-foot summit level canal at Panama, which was the one in contemplation and under construction at the time the canal was taken over by the United States government. If the attempt be made to cut the canal at sea level, all the elements of time, quantities of excavation, and cost will be so greatly augmented, as to place the Panama enterprise beyond comparison with the barge canal.

At present, however, if the State and Federal canals are compared on the mere basis of quantity to be excavated and masonry and dams to be built, the remarkable fact is established that the completion of the Erie barge canal on the present plans calls for more work than the completion of the canal at Panama. This fact is mentioned as suggesting that the magnitude of the New York State project is little appreciated, not merely by the general public, but by the people of the State that it concerns.

Illinois & Michigan Canal.—This route connects the Mississippi system with the Great Lakes, and by the Welland Canal with the St. Lawrence. Its inevitability was plain by reason of the extensive use of the Chicago portage (from the Chicago River to the head-waters of the Kankakee, an affluent of the Illinois) by the Indians and trappers, it being only half a mile for boats, the shortest important portage on the continent. Chicago was one of the best trodden sites in America before white men came here. As early as 1822 Congress granted a right of way for such a canal, and in 1827 and 1854 made further grants. For some reason it hung fire for many years, though a host of surveys and estimates were made by the State and the nation. Work was prosecuted on it 1836–41, then suspended till 1845, and the canal was finally opened in April 1848. It had then cost $6,170,226. The western terminus is La Salle, at the head of steamer navigation on the Illinois River; its eastern is on the south branch of the Chicago, about five miles from its mouth in the city. The entire length is 96 miles, and the rise from La Salle to Lake Michigan is 145 feet, surmounted by 17 locks, 110 by 18; the capacity of boats is 150 tons. The original intention was to make a straight cut from Lake Michigan to the Des Plaines River, the chief branch which with the Kankakee forms the Illinois; but to save expense it was decided to use the Chicago River instead. Thence it runs to Summit on the Des Plaines, 8 miles; then 42 miles to the junction with the Kankakee; thence through the Illinois valley to La Salle. It has five navigable feeders, the Calumet, Des Plaines, Du Page, Kankakee, and Fox; and five large storage basins. The summit level at Bridgeport required pumping for supply; and two steam engines, delivering 15,000 cubic feet of water per minute, were used till 1870. These were also used for many years to help draw off the sewage of Chicago, which empties for miles into the river. By supplying the canal from the river, the lake water was drawn in to fill the vacancy, and so kept the river comparatively sweet. But the system was expensive, and the canal was deepened for some years, ending 1870, to carry the sewage by its own flow to the Des Plaines, reversing the current of the river. It proved insufficient, and in 1892 the Chicago Drainage Canal (q.v.) was begun, which was finished in 1900. It is 40 miles long to Joliet, 22 feet minimum depth, and 162 to 290 feet wide at top. A scheme has been mooted for years, to convert this into a huge ship canal to enable ocean-going steamers to ascend from New Orleans to Chicago, and so through the Great Lakes and to the St. Lawrence; but it depends on the co-operation of the national government. Another canal to connect the Mississippi and Lake systems, which has been under construction since 1892, is the Illinois & Mississippi, the only barge canal started for over half a century. It is a supplement to the Illinois & Michigan; running from Hennepin on the Illinois River, a little beyond La Salle, to the Rock River, 50 miles, and then by 27 miles of slack-water navigation down that river to Rock Island, Ill. It is to be 80 feet wide and 7 feet deep, with 37 locks.

James River & Kanawha Canal.— This is a line partly existent and partly on paper, but interesting as probably the oldest North American canal scheme. The idea is accredited to Gov. Spotswood in 1716, when he explored the Blue Ridge; but the first active part was taken, as in all these early ventures, by Washington, who saw from his backwoods days the necessity of joining the eastern seaboard to the trans-Alleghanian territory by lines of communication. He personally explored the James River route in 1784, and induced the Virginia legislature on 5 Jan. 1785 to pass an act for improving the navigation of the James. Under this the James River Company was organized, 25 Jan. 1785, with Washington as president. No work was done, and in 1835 another company of the same name took up its task; beginning the construction of the section from Richmond to Lynchburg in 1836, and completing it near the end of 1841. The second division, from Lynchburg to Buchanan on the upper James, was begun before this was opened, and completed in 1851. In 1853 an extension of 47 miles to Covington on Jackson River was begun, but the war interrupted it, and it has never been resumed. In 1874 the cost of completing it to the Kanawha, including an improvement of the navigation of that river, was estimated at $60,000,000.

The Ohio Falls Canal.— This is a short canal, but from its location a very important one; it makes continuous navigation in one of the chief waterways of the continent. The first canal was built 1825-30, and called the Louisville & Portland. It was 1 7-10 miles long, 64 feet wide, had 8⅔ feet lift, and three locks, one at the head and two at the foot. An enlargement was begun in 1861, but interrupted by the war; in 1868 the national government included it in its river and harbor appro-

priation, and it was opened February 1873, having cost about $4,000,000. It runs west from in front of Louisville, Ky., to Portland; is a little over 11,000 feet long and 86½ feet wide, with a minimum depth of 6 feet assured by a dam at the falls. The water in the river varies from 6 to nearly 43 feet, and earthen parapets on the sides of the canal rise to 44 feet, based on stone walls, themselves built on the limestone rock through which the canal is cut. The upper lock has been raised, the lower two left as they were, but a branch with two locks has been added. At the head are flood-gates 46 feet 11 inches high. The upper entrance is 400 feet wide.

Among others existent or of past importance are the canal between the Chesapeake and Delaware bays, across the Delaware isthmus, built 1824-9; 13½ miles long, and supplied by pumps for 10 miles of it. An enlargement has been projected. The Morris Canal, 101 miles long, built in 1830, connects the Hudson at Jersey City with the Delaware at Phillipsburg, N. J.; it is owned by the Lehigh Valley R.R. The Delaware & Raritan, 43 miles long, built 1831-4, connects those rivers, and therefore New York and Philadelphia. The Delaware & Hudson, completed 1820, was once the great coal freight route between New York and the Pennsylvania mines; its company transformed itself into the railroad company of the same name, and has abandoned the canal. The Schuylkill Coal & Navigation Company's canal is 108 miles long. The Ohio & Erie Canal from Portsmouth, Ohio, to Cleveland, and the Wabash from Toledo, Ohio, to Evansville, Ind., were once of importance in building up these sections. For the Sault Ste. Marie, see *Ship Canals* below.

Canadian Canals.— Canada has a very extended and important set of canal systems, which may be classified as follows: (1) The St. Lawrence and Great Lakes system; which includes the Welland across the neck of land to the west of Niagara Falls, carrying continuous navigation from Lake Superior to Lake Ontario, and the canals around the rapids on the St. Lawrence, between the Thousand Islands and Montreal, making unbroken passage from Duluth to the ocean. The Welland will be spoken of below. The system also comprises the Burlington Bay Canal, through a bar at the head of Lake Ontario; (2) the two Ottawa River systems, one around the falls on the river between Ottawa and Montreal, the other by the Rideau and Cataraqui rivers and the connecting Rideau Canal to the lower St. Lawrence; (3) the Lake Champlain and St. Lawrence navigation, by the St. Ours & Chambly, along the Richelieu River; (4) the Trent River system, intended to connect Ontario with Huron through the Trent, but not completed; (5) St. Peter's Canal, connecting the Bras d'Or in Cape Breton with St. Peter's Bay on the south coast. Several others are projected. See CANADIAN CANALS.

Ship Canals.— Great ship canals across isthmuses or peninsulas, to make shorter sea routes or avoid stormy passages, or surmount falls, or to make seaports of inland cities, have been the speculations of dreamers for ages; but the developed and hurried commerce of this age has made some of them imperative. The ship canals of the world are nine in number, as follows:

CANALS

1. The Suez Canal, begun in 1859 and completed in 1869.

2. The Cronstadt and St. Petersburg Canal, begun in 1877 and completed in 1890.

3. The Corinth Canal, begun in 1884 and completed in 1893.

4. The Manchester Ship Canal, completed in 1894.

5. The Kaiser Wilhelm Canal, connecting the Baltic and North seas, completed in 1895.

6. The Elbe and Trave Canal, connecting the North Sea and Baltic, opened in 1900.

7. The Welland Canal, connecting Lake Erie with Lake Ontario.

8 and 9. The two canals, United States and Canadian, respectively, connecting Lake Superior with Lake Huron.

The Suez Canal is usually considered the most important example of ship canals, though the number of vessels passing through it annually does not equal that passing through the canals connecting Lake Superior with the chain of Great Lakes at the south. In length, however, it exceeds any of the other great ship canals, its total length being 90 miles, of which about two thirds is through shallow lakes. The material excavated was usually sand, though in some cases strata of solid rock from 2 to 3 feet in thickness were encountered. The total excavation was about 80,000,000 cubic yards under the original plan, which gave a depth of 25 feet. In 1895 the canal was so enlarged as to give a depth of 31 feet, a width at the bottom of 108 feet and at the surface of 420 feet. The original cost was $95,000,000, and for the canal in its present form slightly in excess of $100,000,000. The number of vessels passing through the canal in 1870 was 486, with a gross tonnage of 654,915 tons; in 1875, 1,494 vessels, gross tonnage, 2,940,708 tons; in 1880, 2,026 vessels, gross tonnage, 4,344,519 tons; in 1890, 3,389 vessels, gross tonnage, 9,749,129 tons; in 1895, 3,434 vessels, gross tonnage, 11,833,637 tons; and in 1900, 3,441 vessels, with a gross tonnage of 13,699,237 tons. The revenue of the canal is apparently large in proportion to its cost, the Statesman's Yearbook for 1901 giving the net profits of 1899 at 54,153,660 francs, and the total amount distributed among the shareholders 51,538,028 francs or about 10 per cent of the estimated cost of $100,000,000. The canal is without locks, being at the sea level the entire distance. The length of time occupied in passing through the canal averages about 18 hours. By the use of electric lights throughout the entire length of the canal passages are made at night with nearly equal facility to that of the day. The tolls charged are 9 francs per ton net register, "Danube measurement," which amounts to slightly more than $2 per ton United States net measurement. Steam vessels passing through the canal are propelled by their own power.

The canal connecting the bay of Cronstadt with Saint Petersburg is described as a work of great strategic and commercial importance to Russia. The canal and sailing course in the bay of Cronstadt are about 16 miles long, the canal proper being about 6 miles and the bay channel about 10 miles, and they together extend from Cronstadt, on the Gulf of Finland, to St. Petersburg. The canal was opened in 1890 with a navigable depth of 20½ feet, the original depth having been about 9 feet; the width ranges from

220 to 350 feet. The total cost is estimated at about $10,000,000.

The next of the great ship canals connecting bodies of salt water in the order of date of construction is the Corinth Canal, which connects the Gulf of Corinth with the Gulf of Ægina. The canal reduces the distance from Adriatic ports about 175 miles and from Mediterranean ports about 100 miles. Its length is about 4 miles, a part of which was cut through granite soft rock and the remainder through soil. There are no locks, as is also the case in both the Suez and Cronstadt canals, already described. The width of the canal is 72 feet at bottom and the depth 26¼ feet. The work was begun in 1884 and completed in 1893 at a cost of about $5,000,000. The average tolls are 18 cents per ton and 20 cents per passenger.

The Manchester Ship Canal, which connects Manchester, England, with the Mersey River, Liverpool, and the Atlantic Ocean, was opened for traffic January 1, 1894. The length of the canal is 35½ miles, the total rise from the water level to Manchester being 60 feet, which is divided between four sets of locks, giving an average to each of 15 feet. The minimum width is 120 feet at the bottom and averages 175 feet at the water level, though in places the width is extended to 230 feet. The minimum depth is 26 feet, and the time required for navigating the canal from 5 to 8 hours. The total amount of excavation in the canal and docks was about 45,000,000 cubic yards, of which about one fourth was sandstone rock. The lock gates are operated by hydraulic power; railways and bridges crossing the route of the canal have been raised to give a height of 75 feet to vessels traversing the canal, and an ordinary canal whose route it crosses is carried across by a springing aqueduct composed of an iron caisson resting upon a pivot pier. The total cost of the canal is given at $75,000,000.

Two canals connect the Baltic and North seas through Germany, the first, known as the Kaiser Wilhelm Canal, having been completed in 1895 and constructed largely for military and naval purposes, but proving also of great value to general mercantile traffic. Work upon the Kaiser Wilhelm Canal was begun in 1887, and completed, as above indicated, in 1895. The length of the canal is 61 miles, the terminus in the Baltic Sea being at the harbor of Kiel. The depth is 29½ feet, the width at the bottom 72 feet, and the minimum width at the surface 190 feet. The route lies chiefly through marshes and shallow lakes and along river valleys. The total excavation amounted to about 100,000,000 cubic yards, and the cost about $40,000,000. The number of vessels passing through the canal in 1900 was 21,571, with a tonnage of 4,282,258, and the dues collected amounted to 2,133,155 marks.

Three ship canals intended to give continuous passage to vessels from the head of Lake Superior to Lake Ontario and the St. Lawrence River are the Welland Canal, originally constructed in 1833 and enlarged in 1871 and 1900; the St. Mary's Falls Canal at Sault Ste. Marie, Mich., opened in 1855 and enlarged in 1881 and 1896; and the Canadian canal at St. Marys River, opened in 1895. In point of importance, measured at least by their present use, the canals at the St. Marys River by far surpass that of the Welland Canal, the number of vessels passing through the canals at the St. Marys River being eight times as great as the number passing through the Welland, and the tonnage of the former nearly forty times as great as that of the latter. One of the important products of the Lake Superior region, iron ore, is chiefly used in the section contiguous to Lake Erie, and a large proportion of the grain coming from Lake Superior passes from Buffalo to the Atlantic coast by way of the Erie Canal and railroads centering at Buffalo. The most important article in the westward shipments through the Sault Ste. Marie canals — coal — originates in the territory contiguous to Lake Erie. These conditions largely account for the fact that the number and tonnage of vessels passing the St. Marys River canals so greatly exceed those of the Welland Canal. The Welland Canal connects Lake Ontario and Lake Erie on the Canadian side of the river. It was constructed in 1833 and enlarged in 1871 and again in 1900. The length of the canal is 27 miles, the number of locks 25, the total rise of lockage 327 feet, and the total cost about $25,000,000. The annual collection of tolls on freight, passengers, and vessels averages about $225,000 and the canal is open on an average about 240 days in a year.

Canaletto (proper name BERNARDO BELOTTO), Venetian painter: b. Venice 1724; d. Warsaw 1780. He was a pupil of his uncle, Antonio Canaletto, whose style he imitated perfectly. He worked in Dresden, London, and other places, and painted principally suburban buildings and scenes. He excelled in perspective.

Canaletto, Antonio, Italian painter of perspective views: b. Venice 1697; d. there 1768. In early life he was a scene painter, but having studied in Rome he returned to his native city and became an artist of note. He is said to have been the first who used the camera obscura in painting. His principal subjects, which are highly prized, are mostly views of the palaces and canals of Venice. As he was an extremely rapid worker and very industrious, he left a great number of works. His pictures of Venetian palaces and scenery, while greatly admired by some critics, are harshly censured by others, who consider his art as mere mechanism.

Canandaigua, N. Y., a village of Ontario County, 29 miles southeast of Rochester; at the northern end of Canandaigua Lake, and on the New York C. & H. R. and Northern C. R.R.'s. It is finely situated, on high ground, with a commanding view of the lake. The fishing and boating accommodations are excellent.

Industries, etc.— The chief manufactures are those of ale, pressed brick, and anti-rust tin and enameled ware. The Lisle Tin and Enamel Works have 600 employees, the Empire Pressed-Brick Works 159, the brewery 75. The power-house and shops of the Rochester & Eastern Interurban Electric railway, with 100 employees, are also located here.

Public Institutions, Buildings, etc.— The churches are Congregational, Episcopalian, Methodist Episcopal, Baptist, Presbyterian, Roman Catholic, and Wesleyan Methodist. There are two banks, with a combined capital of $200,000 and deposits of $1,200,000. Here are also located the Thompson Memorial Hospital, the Ontario Orphan Asylum (private), a private insane asylum. and an association library.

It is also the seat of Canandaigua Academy, a public high school, and of the Granger Place School for Girls, a private secondary school.

Government.— The government is administered by a president, and a board of trustees of eight members, elected annually.

History.— Canandaigua was settled by New Englanders in 1789, and became a village in 1815. The name was originally Canandarqua, an Indian word signifying "the chosen spot." Pop. (1890) 5,868; (1900) 6,151.

Canandaigua Lake, N. Y., a body of water lying chiefly within the limits of Ontario County. It is 668 feet above the sea and 437 feet above Lake Ontario, and has an extreme length of 15 miles and an average width of one mile. Its outlet is the Clyde, a tributary of Seneca River.

Canani, Giovanni Battista, jō-vän'nē bät-tēs'tä kä-nä'nē, Italian anatomist: b. 1515; d. 1597. He discovered certain of the hand muscles, and was the first to observe the use of the valves in the veins.

Cananore. See KANANUR.

Canar, kä-ñär', Ecuador, a small province situated among the Andes, between the provinces of Chimborazo and Azuay; capital, Azogues. Pop. of province, 64,000.

Canard, kạ-närd', or kạ-när', a false report; a silly rumor. The origin of this use of the term is not known. It is the French word meaning "a duck," and is thought by some to be derived from the old phrase, *Vendeur de canard a moitie,* one who half-sells a duck or cheats in such a transaction; hence a liar, a guller, eac. According to an account of wide currency in different versions, the usage arose from a story of cannibalism among a flock of ducks that ate one of their number each day until they were reduced to a single survivor, who, it was argued, had eaten all his companions. The story became common in Paris, and afterward, when any marvelous recital was heard, the listener would shrug his shoulders and exclaim, *C'est un canard!* ("That's a *canard,* or duck!").

Canaries. See CANARY ISLANDS.

Canarium, kǎn-ā'rǐ-um, a genus of plants of the order *Amyridaceæ.* The gum of *C. commune* has the same properties as balsam of copaiva. The nuts are eaten in the Moluccas and Java, but are apt to bring on diarrhœa. An oil is expressed from them, used at table when fresh and burned in lamps when stale.

Canary, a small, domesticated finch (*Carduelis canaria*), closely allied to the goldfinch, (q.v.), and found throughout the Canary Islands, Cape Verde, and Madeira. Domestication, besides having modified the size and colors of this bird, has developed its power of song. It was introduced into Europe as a cage-bird early in the 16th century, and is now familiar in all parts of the world. Canaries in their wild state are about five inches long, and, like other finches, live mainly upon seeds, seldom eating insects. They build nests of moss and feathers in bushes and trees, often near dwellings; and their pale-blue eggs number four or five. Canaries are bought, bred, and sold in large numbers in England, Scotland, Belgium, and in the Hartz

Mountains, where their breeding forms an important household industry. The varieties are named, to a great extent, from the localities in which they are bred. Among birds valued for their beauty rather than for their power of song are: the British crested Norwich canary, the Manchester canary, which is noted for its abnormal size, it sometimes reaching a length of eight inches. The Scotch Fancy is a slender bird with long neck, its body, trunk, and tail, when in certain positions, curving into almost a half circle. The gold- and silver-spangled canaries are considered the handsomest. Their ground color is dull, spotted with gold or silver markings. The Belgian or humpback canaries are also bred for their beauty of plumage, and are remarkable by reason of the peculiar appearance they present by their broad shoulders, short neck, and small head.

Canaries bred for their power of song, and selling from $1 to $75, are those of the Hartz Mountains, which vary in color from a clear yellow to a bright green. The most valuable of these varieties is the South Andreasberg bird, bred solely for their power of song. Single birds are frequently utilized for the instruction of young birds, and are known as "campaninis." Other varieties are the cinnamon canaries and the cayernus, the brilliant red and scarlet of the latter being due to judicious feeding with red pepper.

Canaries are easily cared for, the only essentials being cleanliness, food, and water. The principal danger to the bird is a cold draught. The best food consists of canary-grass seed, hemp-seed, and a certain amount of greens. Acids are to be avoided, but sugar is beneficial in small quantities. Lime is essential to its welfare, and is most easily obtained in cuttle-fish bone. If their nails grow so long as to be troublesome to the bird, they should be occasionally cut with a very sharp scissors, thus running no chance of injuring the foot. Consult: Wallace, 'The Canary Book'; Belts, 'The Pleasureable Art of Breeding Pet Canaries.'

Canary-flower, an annual climbing plant (*Tropæolum peregrinum*), of the Indian cress family, a native of New Granada, cultivated for its showy yellow flowers.

Canary-grass. See CANARY-SEED.

Cana'ry Islands, or **Canaries,** a cluster of islands in the Atlantic, considered as belonging to Africa, the most easterly being about 150 miles from Cape Non. They are 13 in number, 7 of which are of considerable size, namely Palma, Ferro, or Hierro, Gomera, Teneriffe, Grand Canary (Gran Canaria), Fuerteventura, and Lanzarote. The other six are little more than mere rocks. The population in 1897 was 334,521, the area being about 2,808 square miles. The Canaries form a Spanish province. Lanzarote and Fuerteventura lie in the northeast of the group, Ferro is the farthest southwest. Through Ferro the first meridian used to be drawn. All are rugged and mountainous, frequently presenting deep ravines and precipitous cliffs to the sea, though having also fertile valleys and verdant slopes. The principal peaks are that of Teneriffe, 12,182 feet, and La Cruz, in Palma, 7,730 feet. Fuerteventura and Lanzarote, which are nearest the African coast, are less elevated and also less fertile than the others, and have much of an African character. Evidence of volcanic action is almost everywhere present, and volcanic disturbances have taken place on some of the islands in quite modern times. The flora generally resemble that of the Mediterranean region, the trees and shrubs including the oak, chestnut, pine, cedar, laurel, heather, etc.; but there are also plants that belong to the African region, such as the dragon-tree and euphorbias. Among the fauna may be mentioned the canary, the red partridge, and several kinds of lizards; there are no snakes. The goat is the chief domestic animal. The islands are somewhat deficient in moisture and severe droughts sometimes occur; tornadoes also are not infrequent. The climate is hot on the low grounds, temperate higher up, and generally healthy. The soil where suited for cultivation readily produces all kinds of grain, fruits, and vegetables in abundance; so that the name of "Fortunate Islands," which the ancients gave the Canaries, was well deserved. Some of the islands furnish good wine, especially Teneriffe and Palma. The Canaries constitute a valuable possession of Spain, and they serve as a winter resort for invalids from colder regions. This has led to the erection of hotels specially intended for visitors, to the making or improvement of roads, and to the providing of attractions of various kinds, including golf-courses, lawn-tennis grounds, etc. There are several places of worship for English-speaking visitors. The exports at present consist chiefly of bananas, tomatoes, and potatoes, shipped in great quantities to London and Liverpool, cochineal, sugar, wine, etc. The imports chiefly consist of textiles and other manufactured goods, cereals, coals, etc. Peaches, oranges, lemons, figs, and other fruits are cultivated. Teneriffe and Grand Canary are the two chief islands. Santa Cruz, the capital of the islands (pop. about 20,000), is a port on the northeast coast of the former, which also contains La Laguna, the old capital, Orotava, and other towns or villages. Orotava is a favorite resort of foreign visitors. Las Palmas, on the northeast coast of Grand Canary, is a more important place, with its new harbor, Puerto de la Luz, between three and four miles distant, protected by a breakwater. The city is rapidly extending, its streets have been improved and lighted by electricity. Numerous steamers engaged in the trade between Europe and Africa call here, and also at Santa Cruz. Though the Canaries were known to the ancients they fell out of the knowledge of Europeans till they again became known from the 12th or 13th century onward. They were claimed by the Spaniards in the 14th century, and in 1402-5 Jean de Bethencourt, a Norman adventurer, conquered Lanzarote, Fuerteventura, Gomera, and Ferro. By the end of the 15th century the Spaniards had subdued the original inhabitants entirely; and they almost extirpated them at a later period. These early inhabitants, who are known as Guanches, had attained some progress in civilization, as shown by remains still extant. They were no doubt of Berber stock. The present inhabitants are mainly of Spanish blood, though it is said the Guanche element may still be detected. See the separate articles on Teneriffe, Grand Canary, Palma, Ferro, and Lanzarote.

Canary-seed, the seed of a plant (*Phalaris canariensis*), belonging to the order of *Graminaceæ*, cultivated for its seed, which is used principally as food for birds. In its early growth it is scarcely distinguishable from oats or wheat. With good cultivation it attains a height of three or four feet, and terminates in egg-shaped heads or ears, each containing upward of 100 seeds. The straw is of little value, either as fodder or litter, but the ears, especially when mixed with other kinds of chaff, are good food for horses. It requires a deep adhesive soil, and its produce per acre is about the same in quantity as wheat. It is a native of the Canary Islands, but is successfully cultivated elsewhere.

Canary Wine, a wine that comes from the Canary Islands, chiefly from the island of Teneriffe. It is not unlike Madeira.

Canary-wood, the light orange-colored wood of *Persea indica* and *P. canariensis*, trees of the laurel family.

Canas'ter, or **Kanaster,** originally, the rush-basket in which South American tobacco was packed and exported, and hence applied to a kind of tobacco consisting of the leaves coarsely broken for smoking.

Canastota, N. Y., village in Madison County, on the Erie Canal, and on the New York C., the West Shore and the Lehigh Valley R.R.'s. It is the centre of an agricultural district and manufactures agricultural implements, gasoline engines, boats, canned goods, etc. It has two banks, public library, churches, high school and two grammar schools. Pop. (1900) 3,330.

Can'by, Edward Richard Sprigg, American army officer: b. Kentucky, 1817; d. 11 April 1873. He graduated at West Point in 1839; served in the Mexican war, 1846–8; commanded the United States troops in New York during the draft riots of 1863; succeeded Gen. Banks in the command of the army in Louisiana, 1864; became brigadier-general United States army, and major-general of volunteers, 1866. After the war special duties were assigned to him, and in 1869 he took command of the department of the Columbia. He was treacherously shot by an Indian chief, while negotiating for the removal of the Modocs from northern California, in the "Lava Beds."

Canby, William Marriott, American botanist: b. Philadelphia, Pa., 1831; d. 1904. He was educated privately, and though a business man, devoted much time to the study of botany. He gathered a fine herbarium of over 30,000 species of plants, which is now owned by the New York College of Pharmacy. A smaller collection was brought together for the Delaware Society of Natural History. He was one of the botanists attached to the Northern Pacific Transcontinental Survey.

Can'can, a dance, something of the nature of a quadrille, but accompanied by violent leaps and indecorous contortions of the body. The earlier and usual meaning of the word in French is noise, racket, scandal; and is derived, oddly enough, from the Latin conjunction *quamquam,* "although,"— a great squabble having arisen in the French mediæval law schools as to the pronunciation of this word.

Cancella'ria, a genus of univalve *Testacea,* belonging to the family *Muricidæ,* and Swainson's sub-family *Scolyminæ,* in which the shell is turbinate, scabrous, and generally reticulated, the spire and aperture nearly equal, and the

body ventricose. Tate in 1875 estimated the known recent species at 71, and the fossil ones at 60, the latter from the Upper Chalk till now.

Cancellation, a method of abbreviating certain arithmetical and algebraic operations. When the product of several numbers is to be divided by another such product, any factors common to both products may be left out, or "cancelled." If divisor and dividend do not appear *in extenso* as products, the process of cancellation may yet be applied if common factors exist and can be detected. The work is substantially the same as that of reducing fractions to their lowest terms.

Can'cer (Lat. *cancer,* "a crab"), **Carcinus,** kär'sǐ-nŭs (Gr. καρκίνος, "a crab"), or **Carcinoma,** kär-sǐ-no'ma (Gr. καρκίνωμα, "cancer"), a disease so called from its hideous appearance or on account of the enlarged veins which surround it and which the ancients compared to the claws of the crab. It is called malignant because its symptoms are so aggravated and destructive to human life.

The causes of cancer are more or less obscure, but persistent local irritation and injuries are the established causes in a large majority of the cases. Hereditary influence has usually been considered a very powerful factor in the production of the disease. The consensus of opinion is opposed to the theory that cancer is of parasitic origin. It always begins as a local disease and is essentially a new growth and composed of tissue unlike that in which it grows. It is a disease of adult life as a rule, though it is frequently found in the young. In a general way it is most likely to attack an organ that has passed through its active period of existence, as the breast or womb. The womb and stomach are the organs in which primary cancer is most frequently found, though the disease may make its appearance in any organ or tissue of the body. When the disease begins it grows rapidly; there is loss of flesh, the neighboring lymphatic glands are involved through the absorbent glands; the tissue is infiltrated; and the body is affected generally. There is more or less pain, and the tumor is composed of cells and fibrous tissue in varying amounts, with more or less white fluid.

There are several varieties of cancer:

Hard or *Scirrhous Cancer,* or *Carcinoma Fibrosum.*— This is the usual form seen in the female breast, on the testicle, tonsil, skin, bone, eye, rectum, or any tissue, and is more frequent in women than in men. The disease spreads, and soon takes possession of the neighboring structures by infiltrating them. In this way it becomes gradually less movable and finally fixed. No tissue is able to resist its influence, muscles, skin, fat, and bone becoming filled with cancerous deposits as the disease advances. When the glands become enlarged they may press upon nerves, causing pain, and upon veins, causing swelling. In many cases the skin over the cancer contains small hard tumors known as tubercles; these are always indicative of cancer. Sometimes the skin becomes swollen and of a brawny appearance, indicating the most rapid form of the disease. When it attacks the female breast there is generally some slight pain, and as it advances there is a depression over the growth. Soon the nipple retracts, and if let alone it will ulcerate or break down and have an offensive discharge. This form of the disease destroys life in from three to five years.

Medullary, Encephaloid, or *Soft Cancer,* in which the cell elements predominate, has all the cancerous peculiarities. Medullary cancer is the form which sometimes appears as a congenital tumor, and which attacks young adults and children, and is the cancer of young life. It grows rapidly, and runs its course much sooner than the hard form. It is found most frequently about the periosteum, bones, eye, uterus, tonsil, testicle, and ovary. It is specially liable to occur about the cavities and bones of the head and face. This form of cancer is so soft that it often seems like a sac of fluid.

Epithelioma is a term applied to cancers of the skin, because the composition of the cancer is similar to the epithelial elements of the true skin. These tumors affect the skin and mucous membrane, and never originate in any other tissue. They are called local cancers by many. Epithelioma first appears as a wart or small ulcer about the lips or face. It is also found in the tongue, scrotum, throat, rectum, penis, and clitoris. It grows slowly and is not liable to return when removed.

Rodent ulcers are forms of epithelial cancer, with the exception that the cells are smaller and do not extend the lymphatics or have any secondary deposits. They usually begin on the face as dry warts and spread very slowly. They attack healthy people as well as weak or sick ones, and appear after middle age.

Colloid or *Alveolar Cancer* is one in which the intercellular spaces are filled with a glairy fluid like glue or mucus. It is most frequently found in the wall of the intestines or rectum and may be seen about the angles of the jaw, or in ovary and breast.

Melanosis, or *Black Cancer,* is a tumor containing pigment originating from a natural tissue which contains pigment, such as a mole or the choroid of the eye. Such tumors frequently appear in groups; the coloring matter being distributed throughout the mass in varying degrees. The secondary deposits are also distinguished by the presence of pigment. It is of the soft variety and runs a rapid course.

Treatment of Cancer. — There is no subject, perhaps, in the medical and surgical world, to which so much thought has been given in the last half-century as the treatment of this most formidable and alarming disease. A few years ago, when animal therapy was introduced, many of the preparations were extensively used in the treatment of cancer, and many persons proclaimed that a new era in the management of this disease had dawned upon the world, and in a little while no one would think of such a thing as a surgical operation in a case of cancer. While it has done some good, the beneficial results have not been satisfactory up to this time. Radiotherapy and phototherapy have been introduced recently in the treatment of cancer, and there are many experiments going on at this time, and much good has been accomplished in the treatment of cancers of the skin; but as yet there are no definite conclusions drawn from the use of these two agents. Perhaps in superficial carcinoma, involving large areas, radiotherapy is preferable to all other methods of treatment. Small superficial circumscribed areas are amenable to treatment with X-rays. In many cases it is best to remove the growth with a knife, and then follow it with the X-ray treatment. Some of those using this method say it is preferable. There seems to be some danger, in the treatment of carcinoma, of causing an inflammation which might carry the cancer cells to normal or inflamed tissue surrounding the growth. Another condition to be feared is the very great danger of burning the healthy skin. The use of the X-rays as a curative agent in the treatment of cancer of the skin is, too, in its experimental stage, and the weight of evidence is not sufficient to warrant any fixed conclusions, either for or against it, other than to say the trend of the medical mind is in its favor. Destruction by the use of caustics is a time-honored method of treatment and will continue to be employed by many. The agent used for that purpose is the chloride of zinc. The most highly scientific and satisfactory treatment for all forms of cancer, if seen early, is removal by the use of the knife. All the glands involved should be removed at the same time, as well as the neighboring ones, whether they are affected or not. Early recognition and prompt treatment are the only ways in which this disease can be cured.

Cancer, in astronomy, the fourth sign in the zodiac, marked thus ♋. The sun enters this sign on or about the 21st of June. He is at his greatest northern declination on entering the sign, and the point which he reaches is called the summer solstice, because he appears for the moment to stop in his progress northward and then to turn south again. The sun is then $23\frac{1}{2}°$ north of the equator, and a small circle of the sphere parallel to the equator at $23\frac{1}{2}°$ distant from it is called the Tropic of Cancer. The sun leaves this sign about the 22d of July. The constellation Cancer is no longer in the sign of Cancer. At present it occupies the place of the sign Leo.

Cancer-root, or **Beech-drops,** a branched parasitic plant (*Epiphegus virginianus*), of the order *Orobanchaceæ,* with brownish scaly leaves, indigenous in America, growing almost exclusively on the exposed root of the beech tree. The whole plant is powerfully astringent, and the root of a brownish color, spongy, and of a very nauseous bitter taste. It has been applied more externally than internally to the cure of cancer. Other plants of the same order are also called cancer-root.

Cancrin, Georg, gä örg′ kän-krēn′, COUNT. Russian general, statesman, and financier: b. Hanau, Prussia, 8 Dec. 1774; d. Saint Petersburg, 22 Sept. 1845. He served with distinction against the French (1812-15); was minister of finance from 1823 to 1844; and wrote on military and economic subjects, his most noted work being 'Military Economy in Peace and War.'

Cancrum Oris, or **Noma,** gangrene of the cheek, due to bacterial infection and mostly occurring in sickly children, especially those with scarlet fever or measles. It begins as a red spot on the cheek or at the angle of the mouth, spreads rapidly, and soon eats away the whole cheek, even the bone. There is fever, and death usually results. As soon as the disease is recognized it should be freely cauterized and the parts kept bathed in antiseptic solutions.

Candace, kăn'dạ-sē, a name apparently common to the warrior queens of Ethiopia (Upper Nubia), between the Nile and the Atbara, in the later period of the kingdom of Meröe. The most distinguished of them invaded Egypt 22 B.C., was defeated by the Romans and obliged to sue for peace, which she obtained with a remission of the tribute imposed on her by Petronius. One of her successors is mentioned in Acts viii. 27; her high treasurer was baptized by Philip the Deacon on the road to Gaza.

Candahar'. See KANDAHAR.

Candaules, kăn-dô'lēz, king of Lydia, who lost his throne and life through his besotted admiration of the beauty of the person of his queen, in 718 B.C.

Can'dee, Helen Churchill, American journalist: b. Brooklyn, N. Y., 1861. She is an editorial writer on the New York *Evening Mail,* and has published: 'Susan Truslow' (1900); 'How Women May Earn a Living' (1900); 'Not on the Flag' (1901); 'An Oklahoma Romance' (1902).

Candeille, Amelie Julie, ăm-ā-lē zhü-lē kän-dā-yē, French actress and composer: b. Paris, 31 July 1767; d. there, 4 Feb. 1834. She wrote libretto and music of the very successful operetta, 'The Beautiful Farmer.'

Candeish'. See KHANDESH.

Candela'brum, a word originally signifying candlestick, but usually denoting a support for a lamp or lamps among the Romans. The candelabra were of considerable size and often intended to stand upon the ground. They were made of wood, bronze, silver, or marble, and were often elaborately and beautifully adorned. Sometimes they had shafts in the shape of columns, which could be shortened or drawn out; sometimes the luxuriant acanthus formed a part of them; sometimes they represented trunks of trees entwined with ivy and flowers, and terminated by vases or bell-flowers at the top, for the reception of the lamps; and not infrequently the lamps were supported by figures. In ancient times Tarentum and Ægina were famous for their elegant candelabra, and Corinth also manufactured them. The Etruscan candelabra of bronze were celebrated.

Can'dia, or **Megalokastron,** Crete, a fortified seaport and capital of the island, situated on the north coast, 65 miles east of Canea. Its harbor admits only vessels of small draught. The governor and the Greek archbishop reside here. Soap is manufactured and exported. The fortifications of the city date from the time of the Venetian occupation, and in 1669, after a prolonged siege, it submitted to the Turks. Pop. estimated at 20,000.

Candia. See CRETE.

Can'didate, an applicant for an office, from the Latin *candidatus,* "white-robed," because, among the Romans, a man who solicited a public office appeared in a white garment — *toga candida* — and wore this during his candidature, which lasted for two years. In the first year the candidates delivered speeches to the people, or had them delivered by others. After this year they requested the magistrate to enter their names on the list of candidates for the office sought for. Before this was done the previous life of the candidate was subjected to a scrutiny in the senate, after the prætor or consul had received his name. If the senate accepted him he was permitted to offer himself on the day of election as a candidate. The formula by which permission was granted was *"Rationem habebo, renuntiabo"*; if he was not accepted he received the answer, *"Rationem non habebo; non renuntiabo."* The tribunes often opposed a candidate who had been accepted by the senate. The morals of the aspirants, in the purer ages of the republic, were always severely examined. In the later period of the republic, nobody could obtain an office if he was not present and if he had not offered himself on three market days. On these days the candidates tried to insinuate themselves into the favor of the people. They went from house to house (*ambitio,* whence the word ambition), shook hands with everybody whom they met (*prensatio*), addressed each one by his name, for which purpose they generally had a nomenclator with them, who whispered the names of those whom they met into their ear. Cicero, therefore, calls the candidates *natio officiosissima.* They placed themselves on market days in elevated places in order to be seen. On the day of election they did the same. Favorites of the people accompanied them (*deductores*); some of their suite (*divisores*) distributed money among the people, which, though prohibited. was done publicly. *Interpretes* were employed to bargain with the people, and the money was deposited in the hands of *sequestres.* Sometimes a number of candidates united into parties (*coitiones*), in order to defeat the endeavors of the others. At last the grounds on which each candidate rested his claims to the office were read, and the "tribes" delivered their votes. The successful candidate then sacrificed to the gods in the capitol. To oppose a candidate was called *ei refragari;* to support him, *suffragari,* or *suffragatores esse.* In the early Church newly baptized Christians were called candidates, on account of the white robes worn by them for a certain period after celebrating the rite. The word "candidate" is also used by Protestants to designate a theologian who, having finished his studies at a university, is waiting for an appointment in the Church.

Candide, ou l'Optimisme, a famous novel by Voltaire. forming an epoch in French literature. In this book he ridicules the system of optimism with his usual spirit, and attacks revelation with plausible but superficial arguments. aiming to controvert the celebrated maxim of Leibnitz, "All is for the best in the best of all possible worlds." Among the descriptions in this work, that of the carnival at Venice is notable.

Candle, a solid cylindrical rod composed of beeswax. tallow, paraffine. or some other fatty substance, with a wick running longitudinally through its centre, designed for slow combustion with illumination. The wick is generally composed of a few threads of cotton yarn lightly twisted or plaited; but formerly, in home-made candles, dried rushes (*Juncus effusus*) were employed for this purpose. The process of making rushlights is described at length by the Rev. Gilbert White in his well-known 'History of Selborne.'

Candles are mentioned in several places in the Bible, but no direct evidence is given as to their form or of what they were made. There seems to be a distinction, however, between candles and lamps,—the latter specifically calling for oil, while the candle is spoken of as being lighted and placed on a candlestick.

Considerable modern improvements have been made in the manufacture of candles. One of the most important of these consists in not employing the whole of the fatty or oily substances, but in decomposing them, and then using only the stearine or stearic acid of the former, and the palmitine of the latter class of substances. The animal fats are combinations of glycerine and fatty acids, principally stearic and palmitic, both solids, and oleic acid, which is liquid. If the latter be in excess, the fat will be a liquid and constitute an oil; if, on the contrary, the solid acids predominate, we shall have a more or less concrete fat, such as the tallow of the ruminants and lard of the hog. Stearic acid now constitutes the principal raw material for the manufacture of candles. The chief chemical agents employed to obtain the stearine are caustic lime, which, setting free the glycerine, produces stearate, margarate, and oleate of lime, in the form of a solid soap; and dilute sulphuric acid, by which this solid soap, after being reduced to powder, is effectually freed of its lime. By means of a subsequent bleaching process cakes of a perfectly white color, free from impurities, and fit for the manufacture of candles, are obtained.

Candles are commonly made by dipping, molding, or rolling. The former is the older method, and consists in arranging in a frame a number of wicks of the proper length and thickness, and dipping them a number of times successively in a tank of melted tallow or other fatty composition, with intervals for the incipient forms to cool and harden. These dippings are repeated until the candles have assumed the requisite thickness and weight.

Molded candles, as their name implies, are formed in molds. These are generally made of pewter, or an alloy of 20 parts of tin and 10 of lead, though glass has also been introduced. They are hollow cylinders of the length of the candle, and open at both ends, but provided at the upper end with a conical cap, in which there is a hole for the wick. A number of these molds are inserted in a wooden frame or trough with their heads downward; the wick is then drawn in through the top hole by means of a wire, and kept stretched and in the centre by a peculiar arrangement. The molds thus prepared are filled by running melted tallow of the proper temperature from a boiler into the trough. The candles remain in the molds for about 24 hours, but, as they improve by keeping, generally remain in

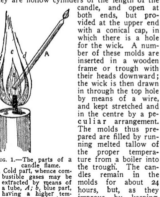

FIG. 1.—The parts of a candle flame. a, Cold part, whence combustible gases may be extracted by means of a tube, A; b, blue part, having a higher temperature; c, luminous part.

the storehouse for a few months before they are exposed for sale.

The rolling of candles is confined principally to those made of wax. Although the bleaching of wax was described by Pliny, the use of this material for the manufacture of candles dates back only to the beginning of the 4th century. From its tenacity, and the contraction which it undergoes in cooling, wax cannot be formed into candles by melting it and then running it into molds. Instead, wicks, properly cut and twisted, are suspended by a ring over a basin of liquid wax, which is poured on the tops of the wicks, and, gradually adhering, covers them. Or the wicks may be immersed, as in the case of tallow "dips." When a sufficient thickness is obtained, the candles, while hot, are placed on a smooth table kept constantly wet, and rolled upon it by means of a flat piece of wood. In this way they assume a perfectly cylindrical form. Machines have been constructed, however, for the manufacture of such products. The large wax candles used in Roman Catholic churches are merely plates of wax bent round a wick and then rolled.

For preparing wax tapers, the wick is wound around a drum and is then made to pass into the melted wax under a hook placed at the bottom of the kettle. The wick, coated with wax, traverses a draw-plate which gives it the desired diameter, and then winds around a second drum. A little tallow, resin, and turpentine is often added to the wax in order to give it greater ductility.

Wax matches, also, which are generally of paraffine, are made with the draw-plate. They are afterward cut to the proper length and tipped with a paste of inflammable material. The use of wax for candles, by reason of their cost, was never very widely diffused, and of course at the present day is likely to diminish greatly. See WAX.

Hollow candles are provided with three apertures extending throughout their entire length. They offer the advantage of not guttering when burning. They are manufactured by means of a special machine, the molds of which contain three solid rods, which are withdrawn before the solidification of the mass.

At the beginning of the 18th century, spermaceti, a product of the cachalot, or sperm whale, came largely into use for the manufacture of candles. The competition of other materials and the decline of the whale fisheries limit its use at the present day.

Cetin, a form of spermaceti, is too brittle and lamellar in texture to use alone in candle-making. These defects are corrected by the addition of about three per cent of wax.

Paraffine candles came into general use about 1850. When crude petroleum is distilled the products obtained consist of light oils employed for illuminating purposes, and heavy oils used as lubricants. These latter, upon cooling, yield a solid substance of waxy consistence and deep color, called paraffine. This material, when purified, gives a white, odorless combustible substance, which is made into candles which give a brilliant but slightly smoky flame. Objections to their use are that at the moment of extinction they emit a disagreeable odor, and that they are too fusible and apt to become distorted in a warm atmosphere. For these reasons paraffine is generally mixed with stearic acid. The use of paraffine candles is most common in Great Britain. See PARAFFINE.

Ozokerit, or *cérésine*, which is also used in the manufacture of candles, resembles paraffine in appearance. It is obtained by purifying a sort of natural mineral wax, the principal deposit of which is found in Galicia. It is not much used except in Germany and Austria. Since cérésine candles melt at a higher temperature than paraffine, they undergo no deformation when used.

Palm-oil is obtained from the west coast of Africa, especially the neighborhood of Lagos. The palm which yields it is the *Elais guineensis*, which produces a golden-yellow fruit of the size and shape of a pigeon's egg. By detaching its pulp from the kernel, bruising it into a paste, and then agitating it in boiling water, the oil is separated, and, rising to the surface, concretes as the water cools. About two thirds of it in weight consists of a peculiar white solid fat, called palmitine; the remainder is chiefly oleine.

The manufacture of candle-wicks is fully as important as the treatment of the combustible fats, and candle-makers have studied the principles of combustion with a view to discovering methods of producing the clearest light with the minimum of smoke, odor, and trouble in snuffing.

A flame is the result of the combustion of a gas. In a burning candle the fatty or other substances are melted and carried by the wick into the interior of the flame, where they are continuously converted into gas. We may compare the combustion of a candle to a microscopic gas-works, and, just as the gas-burner gives more or less light according as the pressure is varied, or the tip is more or less foul, or the proportion of air that reaches the gas is greater or less, just so a candle will give a different light according to the draft of air or the size and nature of the wick. Too large a wick would absorb the melted material too rapidly, the flame would be unduly increased, and the feeding of it would be effected under unfavorable conditions. Too small a wick would produce the opposite effect; around the periphery of the candle there would form a rim, which, no longer receiving a sufficient quantity of heat, would remain in a solid state; the cavity that serves as a reservoir for the liquefied material would become too full; and the candle would gutter. So the section of the candle, the size of the wick, and the draft of air in the flame must be apportioned in such a way that there shall always be an equilibrium between the quantity of material melted and that decomposed by the flame. The purity of the air, too, must be taken into account, for, just as a man needs pure air in order to live in health, so a candle has need of the same in order to burn well. During an evening party it may be observed that the brilliancy of the candles diminishes in measure as the air becomes impoverished in oxygen and enriched with carbonic acid.

In the flame of a candle four parts may be distinguished. The dark nucleus, *a* (Fig. 1), is formed by the gas resulting from the gasification of the combustible bodies. This gas may be ignited at the point of a glass tube, *A*, introduced into the flame. Since the air directs itself especially toward the axis of the flame,

the azure-blue part, *b*, presents a comparatively low temperature in the illuminating envelope, *c*. The oxygen but partially suffices for the combustion, while in the non-illuminating part, *d*, products of the incomplete oxidation burn in the air in excess.

The wick must be placed in the centre of the candle, or else it will remain too long, produce smoke, and darken the flame. If the end remains exactly in the centre the air will not reach it, and the wick will carbonize and form a «thief» or «waster,» which, falling into the cavity at the top of the candle, will make the latter gutter, and end by obstructing the wick.

FIG. 2.   FIG. 3.   FIG. 4.

FIG. 2.—Tallow candle before snuffing. The wick becomes incrusted, and the flame becomes unsteady and smoky.
FIG. 3.—Tallow candle after snuffing. The flame is normal.
FIG. 4.—Wax candle. The wick curves, and a bead forms on its end inside the flame.

It then becomes necessary to snuff it. In order to do away with this inconvenience, Gay-Lussac and Chevreul, in 1825, recommended the use of flat or cylindrical wicks of an uneven texture, having the property of curving over. In the same year Cambacérès proposed the use of hollow plaited wicks, which, in measure as the candle burned, had the property of curving toward the white part of the flame. But ashes nevertheless formed, and, obstructing the wick, affected the light. In the month of June 1826 De Milly finally succeeded in solving the problem by impregnating the wick with boric acid. This latter, uniting with the ashes of the wick, gives rise to a fusible body, which is rejected in the form of a drop or bead toward the extremity of the wick. In Austria, wicks are impregnated with phosphate of ammonia, which gives analogous results. Balley has proposed a solution of sal-ammoniac of 2° or 3° Baumé.

Candle, Electric. See ELECTRIC LIGHTING.

Candle-fish, Oolakan, oo'la kăn, Oulachon, -kŏn, or Eulachon, ū'la-kŏn, a sea-fish (*Thaleichthys pacificus*), of the salmon family, frequenting the northwestern shores of America, of about the size of the smelt, to which it is allied. It is converted by the Indians into a candle simply by passing the pith of a rush or a strip of the bark of the cypress-tree through it as a wick, when its extreme oiliness keeps the wick blazing. Oulachon oil, a substitute for cod-liver oil, is obtained from it. This fish is a favorite article of food in British Columbia.

Candle-fly, or **Lantern-fly,** a hemipterous insect of the group *Homoptera,* family *Fulgoridæ.* The large Chinese candle-fly (*Fulgora candelaria*) is remarkable for its greatly prolonged head, which was formerly believed to be luminous. Compare LANTERN-FLY.

Candle-nut, the nut of *Aleurites triloba,* the candleberry-tree, a native of the Moluccas, Pacific islands, etc., belonging to the natural order *Euphorbiaceæ.* It is about the size of a walnut, and yields an oil used for food and for lamps, while the oily kernels are also strung together and lighted as torches.

Candleberry, Bayberry, Candleberry Myrtle, Tallow-tree, or **Wax Myrtle,** a shrub (*Myrica cerifera*) common in North America, where candles are made from the waxy substance collected from a decoction of the fruit or berry. It grows abundantly in a wet soil, and seems to thrive particularly well in the neighborhood of the sea, nor does it ever seem to be found far inland. The berries intended for making candles are gathered late in autumn, and are thrown into a pot of boiling water, where the fatty or waxy substance floats on the top and is skimmed off. When congealed this substance is of a dirty-green color, somewhat intermediate in its nature between wax and tallow. After being again melted and refined it assumes a transparent green hue. Mixed with a proportion of tallow it forms candles, which burn better and slower than common tallow ones, and do not run so much in hot weather. They have also very little smoke and emit a rather agreeable odor. Soap and sealing-wax are also made of this substance. The plant has been cultivated in France and Germany, where it grows in the open air. Another plant belonging to the same genus is the sweet-gale (*Myrica gale*), which grows abundantly in bogs and marshes in Scotland. It is a small shrub with leaves somewhat like the myrtle or willow, of a fragrant odor and bitter taste, and yielding an essential oil by distillation. It was formerly used in the north of Europe instead of hops, and in some places it is still so used. The catkins or cones boiled in water throw up a scum resembling beeswax, which, collected in sufficient quantities, would make candles. The plant is used to tan calf-skins. Gathered in the autumn, it dyes wool a yellow color, and is thus used both in Sweden and in Wales. The dried leaves are used to scent linen and other clothes.

Can'dlemas, an ecclesiastical festival instituted by Pope Gelasius I. in 492, in commemoration of the presentation of Christ in the temple, and of the purification of the Virgin Mary. It is celebrated on 2 February, and has its name from the fact that in the Roman Catholic Church candles are blessed and carried in procession, in allusion to the words of Simeon, spoken of the infant Christ, "a light to lighten the Gentiles." See PURIFICATION.

Can'dler, Warren A., American clergyman: b. Carroll County, Ga., 23 Aug. 1857. He was graduated from Emory College, Oxford, Ga., in 1875, being licensed to preach and entering the North Georgia Conference of the Methodist Episcopal Church in that year. He was in the pastorate until July 1886, when he became editor of the Nashville 'Christian Advocate' (the organ of the M. E. Church South), serving in that capacity until 1888. In the latter year he became president of Emory College, but resigned in 1898 when he became a bishop of the M. E. Church South. He has written: 'History of Sunday Schools' (1880); 'Georgia's Educational Work' (1893); 'Christus Auctor' (1899); 'High Living and High Lives' (1901); 'Great Revivals and the Great Republic' (1904); etc.

Cand'lish, Robert Smith, Scottish clergyman: b. Edinburgh, 23 March 1806; d. Edinburgh, 19 Oct. 1873. He was educated at Glasgow University; in 1828 was licensed as a preacher, and in 1834 was transferred from Bonhill to St. George's, Edinburgh. In 1839 he threw himself into the conflict with the civil courts in the matter of the congregational right of election and independent church jurisdiction in matters spiritual, and soon became, next to Chalmers, the most prominent leader of the "non-intrusion" party and of the movement that culminated in the Disruption of 1843, and the formation of the Free Church of Scotland. From the death of Chalmers till his own death, Candlish was the ruling spirit in the Free Church. In 1862 he was made principal of the New College (the theological college of the Free Church), Edinburgh. He was the author of 'Contributions Toward the Exposition of the Book of Genesis' (1842); 'Reason and Revelation' (1859); 'The Fatherhood of God'; 'The Two Great Commandments' (1860); etc. See 'Life,' by Wilson (1880).

Candolle, Alphonse Louis Pierre Pyramus de, äl-fôns loo-ē pē-är pē-rä-mü dĕ kän-dôl, Swiss botanist: b. Paris, 28 Oct. 1806; d. 4 April 1893. He was son of Augustin de Candolle (q.v.). He was professor of botany and director of the Botanical Garden at Geneva, published numerous works on botanical subjects, and continued his father's 'Introduction to a Natural System of the Vegetable Kingdom.'

Candolle, Augustin (ô-güst-ăṅ) **Pyramus de,** Swiss botanist: b. Geneva, 4 Feb. 1778; d. there, 9 Sept. 1841. He studied at Paris, where he made his reputation by his 'History of Succulent Plants,' and 'Essay on the Medicinal Properties of Plants.' In 1808 he took the chair of botany at Montpellier, where he replaced the artificial method of Linnæus by the natural method of Jussieu, and published the remarkable 'Elementary Theory of Botany.' After the Restoration of 1815, he returned to Geneva, where he devoted the rest of his life to his great work, 'Introduction to a Natural System of the Vegetable Kingdom,' the continuation of which he entrusted to his son, together with an herbarium of 70,000 species of plants.

Candon, kän-dōn', Philippines, a town of the province of Ilocos Sur, situated in the northwestern part of the Island of Luzon, very near the coast. Pop. about 16,000.

Candy, or **Kandy,** a measure of weight in the East Indies. In Madras the candy is equal to 493.7 pounds, in Bombay it is 560 pounds, and in Ceylon it is equal to 500 pounds. It is divided into from 20 to 22 maunds. In Bombay there is a unit of capacity called the candy equal to 8.2 imperial bushels, and elsewhere a dry-measure candy is found varying from 15 to 30 bushels.

Can'dy. See CONFECTIONERY.

Candy Ceylon. See KANDY.

Candytuft, a genus of plants (*Iberis*), of the natural order *Cruciferæ*, flowering in dense corymbs, and distinguished by an emarginate pouch with keeled and winged valves. It is indigenous to the countries bordering on the Mediterranean, and several species, as *Iberis umbellata, Iberis odorata,* and others, are cultivated in gardens.

Cane, kān, or Ken, a river in Bundelcund, British India, a tributary of the Jumna River. It follows a northeast course and is about 250 miles long.

Cane-brake, a term applied to the extensive growths of the *Arundinaria macrosperma,* the most gigantic of the grasses, which occur in the southern portions of the United States, and are to be found covering vast extents of country in the alluvial bottoms of Central and South America. The plant is not unfamiliar in the temperate zones, as its stalks are much used for fishing-rods. Cane-brakes are indicative of rich land, as they are only to be found in perfection in the most inexhaustible soils, where, having obtained a foothold, by their more rapid growth they usurp the place of the timber. In the southern portions of the United States the plant often reaches the height of 15 and 18 feet, with a base of one to one and a half inches diameter. In more southern latitudes it is very much larger. It grows as straight as an arrow from the root, tapering off finally in a beautiful, thread-like, feathery top. The leaves commence at about two thirds of the height of the plant, and seem to be attached directly to the stalk, as the branches on which they grow, save the very top ones, are not perceptible to ordinary observation. To the hunter, progress through a cane-brake is one of the most toilsome journeys that can be undertaken. Each step is disputed by the dense vegetation which rises before the intruder like a wall. In places, the cane is sometimes pressed down and interlaced, and then it becomes quite impenetrable. Under the most favorable circumstances the knife has to be freely used. Cane-brakes are often many miles in extent, always lessening in density as they reach high ground. They are favorite haunts for all kinds of game, which seek their solitudes either for protection or for the leaves for food. The deer and bear are particularly fond of the young green leaves, and upon them often become exceedingly fat. Cane-stalks being hollow, having no pith, and being divided inside every few inches into sections, they are very combustible when dried in the sun; and the air confined within the hollow sections, warming by the external heat, explodes with very considerable force, so that a cane-brake on fire gives the idea of a continued roar of distant musketry.

Cane Ridge Revival. See REVIVALS, AMERICAN.

Cane Sugar. See SUGAR AND SUGAR-MAKING.

Canea, kä-nē'ą (Greek KHANIA), Crete, the chief commercial town of the island, situated on the northwest coast, with a good harbor. It occupies the site of the ancient Cydonia, but the present town is due to the Venetians, from whom it was wrested by the Turks, after a two years' siege in 1669. Canea is the principal mart for exporting the productions of the island. Pop. about 20,000. See CRETE.

Canella, a genus of plants belonging to the order *Guttifcræ,* but of which the affinities are so doubtful that it has been made the type of a distinct order, *Canellaceæ.* They are ornamental shrubs or trees. *C. alba,* the wild cinnamon, is a common West Indian aromatic evergreen tree, growing to a height of from 10 to 50 feet, with a straight stem branched only at the top. It is covered with a whitish bark, by which it is easily distinguished at a distance from other trees; the leaves are placed upon short footstalks and stand alternately. They are oblong, obtuse, entire, of a dark, shining green hue, and thick like those of the laurel. The flowers are small, seldom opening, of a violet color, and grow in clusters at the tops of the branches on divided foot-stalks. The fruit is an oblong berry containing four kidney-shaped seeds of equal size. The whole tree is very aromatic, and when in blossom perfumes the whole neighborhood. The berries, when ripe, are greedily eaten by the wild pigeons of Jamaica, and impart a peculiar flavor to their flesh. The canella of commerce is the bark of the tree freed from its outward covering and dried in the shade. It is brought to Europe in long quills, which are about three fourths of an inch in diameter, somewhat thicker than cinnamon, and both externally and internally of a whitish or light-brown hue, with a tinge of yellow. This bark is moderately warm to the taste, and aromatic and bitterish. Its smell is agreeable, and resembles that of cloves. In distillation with water it yields an essential oil of a dark-yellowish color, and of a thick tenacious consistence, with difficulty separable from the aqueous fluid. The remaining decoction, when evaporated, leaves a very bitter extract composed of resinous and gummy matter imperfectly mixed. It has been supposed to possess a considerable share of active medicinal powers, and was formerly employed as a cure in scurvy. Now it is merely esteemed as a pleasing and aromatic bitter, and as a useful adjunct in correcting more active though nauseous medicines. The powder is given along with aloes as a stimulating purgative.

Caneph'orus, a term applied to one of the bearers of the baskets containing the implements of sacrifice in the processions of the Dionysia, Panathenæa, and other ancient Grecian festivals. It was an office of honor, much coveted by the virgins of antiquity. The term is often applied to architectural figures bearing baskets on their heads, and is sometimes improperly confounded with caryatides.

Canes Venatici, kā'nēz vĕ-năt'ĭsĭ ("the hunting dogs"), one of the northern constellations added by Hevelius in 1690, between Boötes and Ursa Major. Coming in after the time of Bayer, it has none of his assigned letters; but Baily, in the "B. A. C." in 1845, assigned the letters α and β to the two brightest stars, and they will probably stand, though they have not been universally accepted by astronomers. The former of the two stars is a well-known double. On the maps, the two dogs, Asterion and Chara, are represented as held in leash by Boötes, and pursuing Ursa Major and the celestial pole, but this change in the figure of Boötes has of course been made since the introduction of Canes Venatici into the celestial train. The constellation is surrounded by Ursa Major, Boötes, and Coma Berenices.

Cañete, Manuel, mä'noo-el kän-yä'tä Spanish author: b. Seville, 6 Aug. 1822; d. 4 Nov. 1891. He was educated in Cadiz. For a long time he was an official in the ministry of the interior, and was later chamberlain to King Alfonso XII. His lyric poems, published under the title, 'Poesias,' are highly esteemed, and his dramas, also successful, include 'Un Rebate en Granada'; 'El Duque de Alba'; 'La Flor de Besalu'; and 'La Esperanza de la Patria' (with Tammayo). He is best known, however, as a dramatic critic and a writer on the history of the Spanish stage. His writings in the field of criticism had much influence in the reform, of the stage, which at that time was badly corrupted. Among his other works are: 'Farsas y Eglosas de Lucas Fernandez' (1867); 'La Tragedia Llamada Josefina' (1870); 'Escritores Españoles é Hispano-Americanis' (1884); and 'Teatro Español del Siglo XVI.' (1884).

Canfield, James Hulme, American educator: b. Delaware, Ohio, 18 March 1847. He was graduated from Williams College in 1868; admitted to the Michigan bar, 1872, and practised law at St. Joseph, Mich., 1872–7. He was professor of history in the State University of Kansas, 1877–91; chancellor of the University of Nebraska, 1891–5; president of the Ohio State University, 1895–9, when he was appointed librarian of Columbia University, New York. He was secretary of the National Educational Association for five years, and its president for one. Besides numerous papers and addresses he has published: 'Taxation: Plain Talk for Plain People' (1883); 'The College Student and His Problems' (1902).

Cang, Cangue, or **Kia,** the wooden collar or portable pillory, weighing from 50 to 60 pounds, and fitting closely round the neck, imposed upon criminals in China. It renders the wearer unable to feed or otherwise care for himself.

Canga Arguelles, José, hō sä kän'ga är-gwēl'yēs, Spanish statesman: b. Asturias, 1770; d. 1843. In 1812 he was a member of the Cortes from Valencia, and rapidly rose to the leadership of the constitutional party; became on the accession of Ferdinand VII. he was banished. Recalled in 1816, he became minister of finance in 1820, when the constitution was restored. Through the abolition of certain direct taxes, he caused financial disorder, and was forced to resign in 1821; was a member of the Cortes in 1822, but fled to England at the time of the revolution of 1823. Returning in 1829, he again was elected to the Cortes, where he remained true to his liberal principles. He wrote 'Memoria sobre el Credito Publico' (1820); 'Elementos de la Ciencia de Hacienda' (1825); and 'Diccionano de Hacienda' (1827–8).

Caniapuscaw, kăn-ĭ-ăp'ŭs-kạ, a river in Labrador, outlet of a lake of the same name, flowing northwest into Hudson Strait; length, 400 miles.

Canicatti, kä-nē-kät'tē, Sicily, a city in the province of Girgenti, situated in a grain and fruit region. Here are also sulphur mines. The inhabitants are mostly engaged in agriculture. Pop. about 25,000.

Canic'ula, the Dog-star or Sirius (qq.v.); hence the term, "Canicular days," the dog-days (q.v.).

Cani'dæ, the dog tribe, comprising wolves, foxes, jackals, dogs, and the like, a family of carnivores, intermediate in structure and phylogeny between bears and hyenas. Their legs are long; the claws non-retractile, and in all except the lycaon there are five toes in front and four behind. The dentitions usually consist of three incisors, a great canine (a tooth which takes its name from its prominence in the dog, and is the seizing and tearing instrument).; two small premolars, and two molars on each side of each jaw; but in the lower jaw there are three molars. All these teeth have the carnivorous characteristic of sharp-cutting crowns rather than broad, grinding surfaces, such as characterize the molar teeth of vegetable-eaters. Dogs are mainly diurnal and live in open uplands rather than in forests, where they obtain their prey by chasing it down; they occupy dens and burrows, and possess keen senses and great intelligence. See DOGS. For the fossil history of the family, see CARNIVORA.

Canid'ia, a Neapolitan woman (real name probably Gratidia), whom Horace loved, and who deserted him. Horace, in an epode and the Satires, gives her name to a sorceress.

Canigou, kä-nē-goo', one of the peaks of the Pyrenees in France. It is in the department Pyrénées-Orientales, 24 miles from Perpignan; height, 9,137 feet.

Canina, Luigi, loo-ē'jē kä-nē'nä, Italian archæologist and architect: b. Casale, Piedmont, 23 Oct. 1795; d. Florence, 17 Oct. 1856. He was for some time professor of architecture at Turin, and afterward lived in Rome, where he published works of great value on the antiquities of Rome, Veii, Etruria, and Tusculum, among them 'Ancient Architecture Described and Illustrated by Monuments' (1844).

Caninde, kä-nēn'dä, a river of Brazil, flowing into the Parnahiba; length, 200 miles.

Ca'nis Major ("the greater dog"), a constellation of the southern hemisphere, remarkable as containing Sirius, the brightest star in the heavens.

Canis Minor ("the lesser dog"), a constellation in the northern hemisphere, immediately above Canis Major, the chief star in which is Procyon.

Canisius, Petrus, pä'trŭs kä-nĭsh'ĭ-ŭs, Dutch theologian: b. Nimeguen, 8 May 1524; d. Freiburg, Switzerland, 21 Dec. 1597. He was the first man in Germany who entered the order of the Jesuits, of which he became a very active member. In 1549 he was made professor of theology, rector and vice-chancellor of the university at Ingolstadt, and in 1551 court preacher at Vienna. He afterward reformed the University of Vienna, according to the views of the order. His catechism, which has passed through more than 400 editions, is yet in use. He persuaded Ferdinand I. to adopt stringent measures against the Protestants, and founded the colleges at Prague, Augsburg, Dillingen, and Freiburg in Switzerland. He was beatified 20 Nov. 1864.

Canisius College, an educational institution in Buffalo, N. Y.; organized in 1870 under the auspices of the Roman Catholic Church; reported in 1903: Professors and instructors, 31; students, 283; volumes in the library, 24,000; value of property (including endowment) $385,000.

Can′ities (Latin *Canus*, "hoary or grayhaired"), whiteness or grayness of the hair. When occurring in consequence of old age it is not a disease. Sometimes it happens suddenly, as a result of severe mental emotion.

Canitz, Friedrich Rudolf Ludwig, frĕd′-rĭh roo′dŏlf lood′vĭg kä nĭts (BARON), German poet and diplomat: b. Berlin, 27 Nov. 1654; d. there, 16 Aug. 1699. He studied law at Leyden and Leipsic, and was made state counselor in 1697 under Frederick I. of Prussia; in 1698 he was given the rank of baron. His poems were first published anonymously after his death (1700) under the title 'Nebenstunde unterschiedener Gedichte'; the second edition with the name of the author appeared in 1719. They had influence on style in opposition to the mannerisms of Lohenstein and other writers of the time. Those most popular with his contemporaries are the satires and an elegy on the death of his first wife.

Canker, a disease of plants. See APPLE.

Cankerworm, a caterpiller of a geometoid moth of the genus *Anistopteryx*, destructive to fruit-trees, especially apples. See APPLE.

Canlassi, Guido, gwĕ′dŏ kän-läs′sē, Italian painter: b. near Rimini, 1601; d. Vienna, 1681. He studied under Guido Reni at Bologna, and lived at Venice as court painter under the Emperor Leopold I., and later at Vienna. He is to some extent an imitator of Guido Reni, but is especially distinguished for his use of color. His chief works, mostly biblical or mythological subjects, are in Vienna, Munich, and Dresden.

Can′na, one of the Hebrides, 12 miles southwest of Skye, and 3 miles northwest of Rum. It is four and a half miles long, one mile broad, and four and a half square miles in area. The surface, nowhere higher than 800 feet, consists of trap. A hill here of basalt, called Compass Hill, reverses the magnetic needle.

Can′na, a genus of plants, some species of which have fine flowers, and some, from their black, hard, heavy seeds, are called Indian shot. There are about 30 species in tropical America, with ornamental leaves, creeping rootstocks, and panicles of red or yellow flowers. *C. indica* is the best-known species, and *C. edulis* yields *tous-les-mois*.

Can′nabis. See HEMP.

Cannæ, kăn′ē, Italy, an ancient town in Apulia, on the river Aufidus. Its site was between the modern Canosa and Barletta, and was famous for the battle in which the Romans were defeated by Hannibal (216 B.C.). The Roman army under the consuls Æmilius Paulus and Terentius Varro consisted of 87,000 men, while that of the enemy amounted only to 50,000,

among whom were 10,000 horse. The battle was brought on by Varro against the better judgment of his colleague. The Romans left their strong position at Canusium on the banks of the Aufidus, and the whole army crossed the river. Varro drew up his troops on the plain, with his right wing protected by the river. At the same time Hannibal forded the Aufidus and led his small army to the attack. The battle was long, and the Romans fell in great numbers, among them the consul, Æmilius Paulus, and both the proconsuls Servilius and Atilius. Hannibal's Numidian horse destroyed those who fled from the field. The victor made 13,000 prisoners. The Romans lost, according to their own lowest statements, 45,000 men; according to the highest, 70,000. Hannibal collected the gold rings of the knights who had fallen and sent some pecks thereof to Carthage.

Can′nel Coal. See COAL.

Cannes, kän, France, a seaport and health resort on the shore of the Mediterranean, in the department of Alpes-Maritimes. It is beautifully situated in a rich fruit district, has a mild and equable climate, and attracts numerous winter visitors. There are many hotels and fine villas, charming public walks, etc. Perfumes and soap are made here. Near Cannes, 1 March 1815, Napoleon landed on his escape from Elba. Pop. about 20,000.

Cannibalism, the act or practice of eating human flesh by mankind; anthropophagy; also the eating by an animal, or animals, of a member of the same race; as, of a wounded wolf by others of the pack. In the 'Odyssey' of Homer we have the story of Polyphemus devouring human flesh; and in Herodotus, the Massagetæ (i. 216) are said to eat their aged parents. The Padæi of India (Herodotus iii. 99) were in the habit of killing and eating their relations when they fell ill. Modern facts, the truth of which is put beyond all doubt, confirm the statements of Herodotus. Among the ancient Tupis of Brazil, when the *pajé* (chief) despaired of a sick man's recovery, he was by his advice put to death and devoured. Herodotus (iv. 26) also says that among the Issedones, when a man's father dies, his relations come and help to eat the dead man, whose flesh they render more palatable by mixing it with that of some animal.

In the Middle Ages these stories were wonderfully enlarged, and people who had not yet embraced Christianity were pretty generally set down as anthropophagi. When the Lombards invaded Italy at the end of the 6th century it was reported of them that they ate human flesh; and a century later the same aspersions were cast on the Slavonian tribes. It became the fashion to bandy the accusation between enemies: thus, during the Crusades, the Saracens said the Christians ate human flesh as well as the unclean flesh of swine; while the Christians on their side maintained that the Saracens ate men, women, and children, and were particularly fond of a sucking Christian babe torn fresh from the breast of its mother. The old travelers' narratives abound in stories of cannibalism, which we may almost invariably pronounce to be false. Few persons would now credit that the Indians and Chinese sold human flesh in the market, or that the Grand Khan of Tartary fattened his astronomers and magicians with carcasses of condemned criminals; but the statements of Marco Polo regarding the Battas, a people of Sumatra, have been confirmed.

When America was discovered, cannibalism was found to prevail to a very great extent, and as late as the year 1866 it is well known that two Brazilian officers exploring the Pachitea River were eaten by the natives. The practice was also common in Malaysia and Polynesia,— the case of Capt. Cook in the Sandwich Islands is well known. In many parts of Africa cannibalism is systematically practised; human flesh being regarded as a great delicacy, and even preferred to every other kind of food.

Cannibalism has been ascribed to various causes — to hunger, desire for revenge, and to various superstitions. Among the latter is the belief that the spirit of a brave enemy would pass into the body of the eater and thereby strengthen him for battle. More especially is this the case in regard to eating the heart. The former cannibals of the Sandwich and other Polynesian islands called to give to a human body destined to be eaten the equivocal term "long pig."

Cannibalism has been practised by members of civilized nations from time immemorial, when in dire distress from want of food. Travelers in desert lands and shipwrecked sailors have often resorted to this method of preserving the lives of many at the expense of the few, and perhaps as a general rule this has been done by mutual agreement to abide the hazard of a lottery to decide who should be the victim. Despite such agreement, the killing of a comrade in this manner is generally held to be murder and punishable accordingly. Several years ago, the survivors of the shipwreck of a British vessel resorted to this plan. They were subsequently rescued, and on their return to England were tried for murder, convicted, and sentenced to death. This sentence was afterward commuted to imprisonment, and later the prisoners were pardoned.

Canniff, William, Canadian physician: b. Thurlow, near Belleville, Ontario, 1830. He was educated at Victoria College, Cobourg, and studied medicine in Toronto, New York, and London, England, where he took the degree of M.R.C.S. He served in the Crimean war, 1856; returned to Canada, became professor of surgery in Victoria College; visited the Washington hospitals during the Civil War, and finally settled in the practice of his profession at Toronto. He was one of the originators of the "Canada First" movement. Besides many periodical articles, he has written 'Manual of the Principles of Surgery, Based on Pathology' (1866); 'The Medical Profession in Upper Canada, 1783-1850: An Historical Narrative' (1894); 'The Settlement of Upper Canada.'

Can'ning, Albert Stratford, English writer: b. 24 Aug. 1832. He is the second son of the first Baron Garvagh. He has been a prolific writer, and among his works may be mentioned 'Christian Toleration' (1874); 'Intolerance Among Christians' (1876); 'Religious Strife in British History' (1878); 'British Rule and Modern Politics' (1898); 'British Power and Thought' (1901).

Canning, Charles John (Earl), English statesman, son of George Canning (q.v.): b. near London, 14 Dec. 1812; d. London, 17 June 1862. He was educated at Eton and Oxford.

He entered Parliament in 1836 as member for Warwick, and in the following year succeeded to the peerage, on his mother's death, as Viscount Canning. In 1841 he was appointed under-secretary of state for foreign affairs in Peel's government, and in 1846 commissioner of woods and forests. In the Aberdeen ministry of 1853, and under Palmerston in 1855, he held the postmaster-generalship, and in 1856 went out to India as governor-general. Throughout the mutiny he showed a fine coolness and clear-headedness, and though his carefully pondered decisions were sometimes lacking in promptness, yet his admirable moderation did much to re-establish the British empire in India. In 1858, when the government of India was transferred from the East India Company to the Crown, Canning became the first viceroy; and in the succeeding year he was raised to the rank of earl. From that time till his retirement in March 1862, the arduous task of undoing the mischief wrought by the mutiny devolved upon him, and his great success was a witness to his ability. See Cunningham, 'Earl Canning' (1891).

Canning, George, English orator and statesman: b. London, 11 April 1770; d. Chiswick, 8 Aug. 1827. His father offended his family by marrying a lady of beauty and accomplishments, but without fortune, and died in 1771, leaving her destitute. She however lived to see the success of her son, from whom she ever received the tenderest marks of filial love. Canning, who had inherited a small estate in Ireland, was educated at Eton. In 1787 he was entered at Oxford. His vacations were passed with Sheridan, by whom he was introduced to Burke, Fox, and other distinguished Whigs. But although Sheridan had already announced him in Parliament as the future ornament of his party, Canning entered into terms with Pitt, by whom he was brought into Parliament in 1793. During the first session he remained silent. In 1796 he was under-secretary of state. In 1797 he projected, with some friends, the 'Anti-Jacobin,' of which Gifford was appointed editor. Canning contributed many poetical and other articles to this periodical, the happiest of his efforts in this direction being the 'Needy Knife-grinder.' In 1798 he supported Wilberforce's motion for the abolition of the slave-trade. In July 1800 Canning increased his fortune and influence by a marriage with Joanna, daughter of Gen. Scott, a lady with a large fortune. The administration being dissolved in 1801, Canning became a member of the opposition until the restoration of Pitt in 1804. In 1807 he was appointed secretary of state for foreign affairs, in the Portland administration. A political misunderstanding with Lord Castlereagh led to a duel between that minister and Canning, in which the latter was slightly wounded. This dispute occasioned the dissolution of the ministry. In 1810 he opposed the reference of the Roman Catholic claims to the committee of the whole House, on the ground that no security or engagement had been offered by the Roman Catholics. Some of his most brilliant speeches were on this subject. The adoption of the measure being a matter of policy, the state of opinion, the condition of affairs, and the securities with which it should be accompanied, were with him elements of the question. He proposed securities in 1813, which, with the bill, were rejected. He supported in 1812 and 1813 the same motion which he had opposed in 1810. To Canning was principally owing the first blow which shook the throne of Napoleon: the British policy in Spain was directed and animated by him. In 1812 he was elected member for Liverpool. from which he was also returned in 1814, 1818, 1820. In 1814 he was appointed minister to Portugal, and remained abroad about two years. In 1819 he declared his decided hostility to parliamentary reform in whatever shape. On the occasion of the proceedings relative to the queen. he declared that "toward the object of that investigation he felt an unaltered regard and affection"; and soon after resigned the presidency of the board of control, and went abroad. Having been nominated governor-general of India, he was on the point of embarking when the death of the Marquis of Londonderry called him to the cabinet as secretary for foreign affairs, 16 Sept. 1822. One of his earliest acts in this situation was to check the French influence in Spain, the French having sent an army into that country to put down the revolutionary party. By way of withdrawing the Spanish-American colonies from French influence he decided to recognize their independence; thus, as he afterward phrased it, "calling the New World into existence to redress the balance of the Old." He continued to support the propositions in favor of the Roman Catholics, and in 1825 communicated to foreign ministers the determination of the government to appoint chargés d'affaires to Colombia, Mexico, and Buenos Ayres. In consequence of the attempts made by Spain to assist the malcontents of Portugal, it was immediately determined by the ministry to support the regency of that country, and troops were sent to Lisbon in January 1827. On 12 April 1827 his appointment to be prime minister was announced. His administration was terminated by his death, but not until it had been crowned by the Treaty of London (6 July), for the settlement of the affairs of Greece. As an orator Canning was showy and graceful, with a brilliant wit and caustic satire, though neither formed on a very masculine taste. During his career the leading domestic subjects on which the British Parliament was called upon to legislate were the following: the liberty of the press, the emancipation of the Roman Catholics, the test and corporation acts, the corn-laws, and reform in Parliament. Those of a foreign nature were, among others, the various overtures of peace between Britain and France. the settlement of Europe on the overthrow of Napoleon, the treatment of Italy by the Austrians, the Spanish revolution, and recognition of the South American republics. On all these questions. with one or two exceptions, he supported the high Tory side. The chief exceptions were the emancipation of the Roman Catholics, and the recognition of the South American republics. He was also desirous of amending the corn-laws. Consult Stapleton, 'Political Life of Canning' (1831); Stapleton, 'Canning and His Times' (1835); Lord Dalling, 'Historical Characters' (1867).

Canning, Sir Samuel, English civil engineer: b. Wiltshire, 1823. He is best known in connection with the laying of the Atlantic cables in 1865-6 and 1869, and those in the Mediterranean and North Seas. He was knighted in 1866.

Canning, Stratford (Viscount Stratford de Redcliffe), English diplomatist, cousin of George Canning (q.v.): b. London, 4 Nov. 1786; d. 14 Aug. 1880. His father, Stratford Canning, who had been disinherited owing to an imprudent marriage, and had gone into business as a merchant, died a few months after his son's birth, and in consequence young Stratford and his mother removed to Wanstead. He went to Eton, and in 1805 he was elected to a scholarship at King's College. Cambridge. Before graduating he was in 1807 appointed by his great cousin, then foreign secretary, to be his précis writer, and in the latter part of that year was sent as second secretary with a mission to Denmark. In the following year he accompanied as first secretary an important mission to Constantinople, which resulted in the conclusion of a treaty of peace with the Porte on 5 Jan. 1809. In the summer of 1810 his chief, Sir Robert Adair, was transferred to Vienna, and Canning temporarily succeeded him as ambassador at Constantinople. Before the arrival of Adair's successor, Canning made his reputation as a diplomatist by the masterly way in which he conducted the difficult negotiations which led to the signing of the Treaty of Bucharest on 28 May 1812. This treaty put an end for the time to the war between Russia and Turkey, and thus left Russia free to resist the advance of Napoleon. Moreover, it firmly secured English predominance at Constantinople, and was in this respect the first notable triumph in the traditional British policy on the Eastern Question. In 1812 Canning returned to London, and after declining in 1813 the offer of the chief secretaryship to Lord Aberdeen's Vienna mission, accepted in the following year the post of envoy extraordinary and minister plenipotentiary in Switzerland. He held this post till 1818, and was completely successful in his endeavors to free Switzerland from French domination, and to erect it into a neutral federal republic. Shortly after his return he was appointed ambassador to the United States, and he arrived at Washington in the autumn of 1820. He was again in London in 1823. The diplomatic agreement arrived at in 1824 was however, thrown out by the United States Senate. After a brief but important mission to the Russian capital he was again sent to Constantinople in October 1825 as ambassador. In the following year he succeeded in again patching up a peace between Russia and Turkey, and thus prepared the way for a joint representation by England. France, and Russia on behalf of insurgent Greece. Negotiations were, however, abruptly broken off by the Sultan's indignation on learning of the battle of Navarino, and Canning was later in the same year engaged, along with the representatives of France and Russia, in drawing up proposals for establishing a Greek kingdom. These were ultimately forced on the acceptance of Turkey in a more stringent form as part of the peace treaty which ended the Russo-Turkish war of 1828-9. In 1829 he resigned his position and returned to England, where he was created G.C.B. He entered Parliament as member for Old Sarum, but he ultimately secured election for King's Lynn. After acting as special envoy to the Porte in 1831-2, and to Portugal in 1832-3, he was in 1841 appointed for the third time ambassador at Constantinople. For a considerable period he was mainly engaged in assisting and encouraging the Sultan, Abd-el-Mejid, in his policy of reform, but after a visit to England in 1852, during which he was raised to the peerage, his efforts had to be directed to thwarting Russian designs. His diplomatic triumph over Prince Mentchikoff caused the czar in a moment of irritation to precipitate the Crimean war. He resigned in 1858, and the remainder of his career was passed mainly in retirement. In addition to a few volumes of poetry, he published works entitled 'Why am I a Christian?' (1873), and 'The Greatest of Miracles' (1876). A selection of his articles on eastern affairs was published in 1881 under the title of 'The Eastern Question.' See 'Life' by Stanley Lane-Poole (1888).

Canning Industry in America. The hermetical sealing of food, generally termed "canning," has long since passed the experimental stage and is now one of the leading industries of the country. The inventive genius of man has from the earliest times turned toward some method of preventing articles of food from deteriorating, and toward some way of preserving food so that it will be palatable at some future time. "Desiccation" or drying was probably the first method used, but the food thus preserved lost its natural flavor and became tough in texture. Prior to 1750 this method of drying, and that of using salt and sugar, were the only methods in use for preserving food. From 1809-10 a Frenchman, Nicholas Appert (b. 1750; d. 1841), devolved a plan for hermetically sealing foods for use at sea and his process was purchased by the French government, who gave it to manufacturing firms in France and England for use in producing canned goods. Appert described his invention as an expensive and simple method of preserving various sorts of animal and vegetable food in perfect condition for an indefinite period. He gave to the world one of the principles involved in the art of canning and since his time there have been several new principles discovered equally as important as his sterilizing process, which did not take in the prevention of souring prior to sterilization. There have also been other improvements in machinery especially adapted to the principles involved, whereby cost has been enormously reduced, so that food preserved in tins is within reach of all classes of consumers. He was later awarded a prize of 12,000 francs by Napoleon, but spent most of this money for further experiment and died when over 90 years of age, after having seen his processes thoroughly tested and put into operation.

In 1810 the English government granted a patent to Peter Durand for the preservation of fruits, vegetables and fish in hermetically sealed cans, made of tin, glass, or other fit material. He made no claims to the discovery of the process, and it was stated at the time that he received his information in regard to it from a "foreigner residing abroad." The methods, despite the secrecy in their use, gradually became known, and in the course of time, came to America. It is believed that a man by the name of Ezra Daggett was the first to put the practice of canning goods into actual use in this country, in the years from 1815 to 1818. He, with his son-in-law, Thomas Kensett, began to manufacture hermetically sealed goods, on a large scale, in the year 1819, and the principal foods thus packed were salmon, lobsters, and oysters. A patent was granted them in 1825 on the use of the tin can, or "case" as it was then called, and they immediately started the use of this process in their factory. Glass jars were thereafter little in use, because of their costliness, bulk, and inability to withstand the extremes of temperature.

In 1820 William Underwood and Charles Mitchell combined, in Boston, for the purpose of manufacturing foods in hermetically sealed cans. The principal business engaged in during the early days of the combination was the preparation of pickles, jams, jellies, sauces, and mustard; but they also put up quinces, cranberries, currants, etc. About the same time, Allen Taylor and M. Fallagher, who had learned their trade in Ireland, came to this country and were for some time employed in New York. They with Kensett did much to put the industry on a permanent basis. In 1839 William Underwood began to substitute tin for glass, though it was a number of years before the jar and the bottle gave way entirely to the "tin can." The methods of can-making were for many years very slow and primitive. A tinker who could turn out 60 cans a day was a master workman, for every can was made by hand. The body for each had to be measured, marked and cut out from the plate by hand shears, and, to make the seam or lap secure and air-tight, it was thought necessary to pile on the solder until a ridge an eighth of an inch thick was built up from end to end. It was also a slow and difficult operation to make the covers and bottoms. Each one had first to be drawn on the tin with compasses and then cut out with the shears, and finally, with a mallet, the edge struck up or bent, over an upright piece of iron called "a heading stake.[1] The tops and bottoms, like the seams, were soldered on with a heavy beading of metal, and enough solder was used on one can to make a dozen of to-day's manufacture.

So was born the tin can that now is scattered in every direction, along the paths of travel and progress; but, strange enough, this growing infant had, in its younger days, another name, one which more became its infantile and clumsy form — "The Tin Canister.[2]

In all the correspondence for the next 10 or 15 years, cans or canned goods never seem to be mentioned. They were always spoken of as hermetically sealed goods in canisters or tin cases. In the salesbook or "Waste,[3] as it was then called, canisters were abbreviated thus, "Cans," and probably by such abbreviations, tin packages for food came ultimately to be known as cans.

The stamp-can was invented in 1847 by Allen Taylor and was a decided improvement over any previously made. Two years later, 1849, Henry Evans, Jr., of New Jersey, brought forth the "pendulum" press for making can tops and so the improvement in the manufacture of cans has gone on till now we have the key-opened can, the invention of a Mr. Zimmerman. While the manufacture of cans has become a distinct industry and not now generally connected with the canning industry, nearly 10 per cent of those now in use are made by the canning establishments. Those cans are made from sheets of Bessemer steel, 14x20 inches in size and weighing about one pound. The objection to tin cans as containing poisonous acids or injurious substances has caused the methods of manufacture to be carefully scrutinized, so that now all cans are subjected to an acid preparation for removing dirt, grease, etc., and then coated with pure tin by the acid process or palm-oil process, the latter of which is considered the safer.

In the methods of cooking there have been many improvements, the slowness and low temperature of 212° F. allowable in the Appert process, being gradually raised by the use of chloride of calcium, till now a temperature of 250° F. is possible, although this process is more expensive, as the cans become discolored and have to be cleaned before they can be put on the market. The "closed-kettle" process of cooking goods by means of superheating water with steam was invented by A. K. Shriver of Baltimore, and about the same time, the invention of the patent-process kettle, securing similar results by the use of dry steam, was brought out by John Fisher of the same city. One of the latest systems for sterilization is the Continuous Calcium Process system, patented by the Sprague Canning Machinery Company, of Chicago. Another is the Continuous Process system in oil, used by the packers of canned meats. The latest is the Polk Agitating System, patented by Ralph Polk, of Greenwood, Ind. By this system the time of sterilization is materially shortened.

The canning industry, although established in the United States as early as 1825, did not become of much importance until the middle of the century, but from 1850, came to the front by leaps and bounds. As the history during the period between '55 and the present is, as yet, too familiar to be of especial interest, nothing further need be said of it: though, before leaving the subject, it may be of interest to learn something of the trials and tribulations which beset the pioneers.

Many unaccountable losses were sometimes met with, when, in certain years, the goods would not all keep. Numerous theories were hunted down, in vain efforts to learn the cause of these mysterious deteriorations. The year of 1850 seems to have been one of vexation to all, as the following quotation from a letter written a year later, will show:

"The season, ending last year, has been a very strange one, and some of our hermetically sealed goods have spoiled: although they were put up with great care and of the best quality, and we can only suspect that the whole atmosphere has been impregnated with cholera that acted upon animal matter as it did upon vegetable. Our process has been the same for a number of years, with the exception of a little more care, in that process, last year than heretofore; because we had known of others having the same trouble. We wish to be very particular and not suffer any of our hermetically sealed goods to go out of your hands until you have opened a few packages of each case."

At another time, when trouble was prevalent, a new theory was advanced. It seemed certain that this spoiling was caused by freezing. Some salmon had been stored in a warehouse, which, during the winter, had not been constantly heated. Many cans of this lot went bad; so the freezing theory was accepted and held good, until some other cans from the same packing spoiled, which could not possibly have frozen. To explain this new phase of the situation, another theory had to be manufactured.

In searching for the probable origin of these mysterious losses, the real cause was not suspected. The exclusion of air was thought to be one of the most important factors in keeping the goods, and, until recently, this opinion has prevailed.

The researches in bacteriology in 1895-9 at the Massachusetts Institute of Technology brought out the fact that in some cases the spoilage of canned goods was due to imperfect sterilization through lack of sufficient heat to destroy all bacteria. This, however, accounted for only a small per cent of the spoilage cases. There are several other causes which have been brought out by the research work of Edward W. Duckwall, M.S., in the Sprague Canners' Laboratory, an institution which was founded in August, 1903, by Mr. Daniel G. Trench of Chicago. (The name of this laboratory has since been changed to the National Canners' Laboratory.) It was discovered that a large per cent of what is known as "sour" corn and peas was due, not to insufficient sterilization, but to souring which had been accomplished by bacteria in the raw product prior to the sterilizing process. It was also discovered that some of the spoilage was due to the evolution of carbonic acid gas from the seeds of certain fruits and vegetables. The germ life of the seeds was not destroyed by the heat, and carbonic acid gas was liberated when the seeds sprouted in the cans. There are many important problems coming up for solution and the National Canners' Laboratory is constantly engaged in this work; but gradually all obstacles are being overcome; new processes have been invented, the purity of the canned article has been proven by expert chemists and the manufacture has become general in every part of the United States where fruits or vegetables are grown or where the supply of fish and oysters is nearby. The California gold fever gave canning a great impetus, as did also the Civil War, and hundreds of firms sprang up during these years, some of them canning meat on government contracts for the army.

The installation of labor saving machinery, the remarkable growth in the number of firms, the decline in the market value of the goods, made necessary uniform grades and rates of sale throughout the country. In October 1872 the first organization of canned goods packers met in Philadelphia, but this was only short-lived, and it was not until February 1883, that a permanent exchange was established. The "Canned Goods Exchange" of Baltimore was at that time organized, with the intention of having sales on the floor daily, but after a thorough trial, they abandoned that plan and adopted grades for goods, and rules and terms governing transactions. These exchanges began rapidly to come into existence. In 1885, the "Western Canned Goods Packers Association" was formed, composed of those doing business in the Mississippi Valley. In the same year the New York State packers organized and two years later those of New Jersey and Virginia. In May 1889 the National Association was formed at Indianapolis, followed by the "Peninsula Packers' Association" of Delaware, formed in 1894, and the "Atlantic States Canned Goods Packers' Association" of Baltimore, organized in the fall of the same year. During the winter of 1898, at a convention of canned goods packers held in Buffalo, N. Y., and again in 1899 in Detroit, at the largest gathering of preservers of food ever assembled in the United States, unusual interest was manifested in papers, read by William Lyman Underwood and Prof. Samuel C. Prescott, of the Massachusetts Institute of Technology, Boston, in which they gave an account of their researches to discover, if possible, why canned corn turned sour.

And they were successful in proving that bacteria were responsible in some cases, but it remained for Edward W. Duckwall, of the National Canners' Laboratory, to bring out the fact that spoilage of canned goods was also due to other causes. These facts were brought out in addresses delivered before the Canners in Columbus, Ohio, in 1904 and 1905. The papers read before the Canners' conventions by these gentlemen were published in the 'Canned and Dried Fruit Packer,' the 'Trade' and the 'American Grocer.' The reports of the National Canners' Laboratory have been published monthly for the last two years in the 'Canner.'

The localization in the canning industry is principally due to climatic conditions. Thus we have Maine, New York, Maryland, Illinois, Iowa, and Kansas as the principal corn packing States; New Jersey, Maryland, Virginia, Kentucky and Indiana as the tomato canning States; New York, Illinois, and Ohio produce the largest amount of canned milk and the Central States monopolize the beef trade. Maine is the principal packer of sardines, while Alaska and the Pacific States monopolize the salmon canneries. Peaches are principally canned in Delaware, California, Maryland, Michigan and Georgia; New York, Maine, Maryland, Iowa, Illinois, Ohio, and Kansas put up the major portion of the apples packed, though the industry is carried on to some extent in Washington and Oregon. Pears are packed mainly in New York, New Jersey, Delaware, Maryland, and California, while pineapples are almost wholly packed in Baltimore, Md., Bahama, Porto Rico, Hawaii. Pear canneries are most numerous in New York, Maryland, Indiana, and Ohio, while pumpkin is almost entirely packed in the Northern States. as are soups, which are packed mainly in New Jersey, New York, Illinois, Massachusetts and Ohio.

For general purposes of comparison, the canning industry may be divided into three distinct classes: fruits and vegetables, fish, and oysters, and under these headings the industry may be more comprehensively discussed.

Fruits and Vegetables.—Fruits were the first foods to be successfully canned, as the low temperature used in the early methods was more easily applied to this class of goods because less heat is required to preserve them than all others. Glass bottles were filled up to the neck, loosely corked, and then placed in tepid water, the temperature of which was gradually raised from 170° to 190° F., remaining there for a period varying from 30 to 60 minutes according to the

article being preserved. In 1823 Pierre Antoine Angilbert made an improvement on this method by placing the fruit in a tin can containing water, then placing on the cover in which there was an aperture to allow for gas escape. It was then placed in water and heat applied; after boiling a sufficient length of time, the aperture was closed by a drop of solder.

Not much is known of this branch of the canning industry between the years 1820–45 and it probably was not very extensive and it is certain that tomatoes and corn were not put up to any great extent during these years. It appears from a narrative presented by William Lyman Underwood that his grandfather William began to use the Appert process about 1820, and exported preserved goods to Manila in 1821. In 1830 he packed pie fruit in bottles, and in 1830 imported tomato seed. His son, William J., has a label used in 1845 on "hermetically sealed tomatoes," and which contain the following: "This is prepared by straining the skins and seeds from the tomatoes, evaporating the particles by slow heat. The bottles contain the substance of about two dozen tomatoes, and it will keep good any length of time." The style of the label is in marked contrast to those now in use. In 1847 Harrison W. Crosby, when he was steward of Lafayette College, at Easton, Pa., first used tin cans to hermetically seal tomatoes, and in 1839 the canning of corn was begun by two firms, one in Baltimore, Md., and one in Portland, Me. The establishment in Portland gained little headway until 1852, in which year Isaac Winslow, who was in charge, applied for a patent on his process, but which was not granted him until 8 April 1862. His method was substantially the same as the Appert process with the exception that the first cooking was done away with by the introduction of "cookers," which are steam retorts used to cook the corn before placing it in the can. Prior to 1846 numerous canneries were in operation in New York, Boston, Baltimore, Portland, and Eastport, Me., and in Newark, N. J., and it was in the latter place that the fruits and vegetables were prepared for Kane's Arctic Expedition.

In 1860 factories began to spring up in all the great fruit and vegetable raising sections of the country. The Middle West loomed up as a manufacturing centre. Thomas Duckwall erected the first canning factory in Claremont County near Cincinnati, and Albert Fisher followed at Cincinnati. A few years later a cannery was started at Circleville, Ohio, and at Indianapolis, Ind. From that time up until 1880 factories sprung up all over the Middle States like mushrooms.

California then began to be heard of and rapidly came to the front as a producer of canned fruits, now being in the lead in the preserving and canning of small fruits, such as the plum, pear, peach, and cherry, and such vegetables as tomatoes, asparagus, and peas.

The canning of fruits and vegetables has grown more rapidly in the last 30 years than any other branch of the industry, due to the greater territory in which it may be carried on and to the unlimited cultivation of these articles. The growth of this industry may be seen from a perusal of the table at the top of the following page:

CANNING INDUSTRY IN AMERICA

	Date of Census				Per cent of Increase		
	1900	1890	1880	1870	1890 to 1900	1880 to 1800	1870 to 1880
Number of establishments	1,808	886	411	97	104.1	115.6	323.7
Capital	$27,743,076	$15,315,185	$8,247,488	$2,335,925	81.1	85.7	253.1
Salaried officials, clerks, etc.	1,741	1,119	....	....	55.6	....	....
Salaries	$1,277,028	$592,390	....	....	115.6	....	....
Wage earners..........	36,401	49,762	31,905	5,689	* 26.8	56.0	443.6
Wages	$8,050,793	$4,651,317	$2,679,960	$771,643	73.1	73.6	247.3
Miscellaneous expenses..	$2,423,623	$1,289,681	....	....	87.9	....	....
Cost of materials used..	$37,527,297	$18,665,163	$12,051,293	$3,094,846	101.1	54.9	289.4
Value of products	$56,668,313	$29,682,416	$17,599,576	$5,425,677	89.8	69.7	244.4

* Decrease.

Notwithstanding the increase in the number of establishments, the average capital per establishment decreased from $24,082 to $15,345, a decrease of $8,737, or 36.3 per cent. The average product has also shown a decrease from $55,935 to $31,343, or, in other words, in 1900 was just a little more than half that reported in 1870. These conditions were caused by the large number of small canneries which sprung up during this time, and by the great decrease in cost of production brought about by the installation of improved machinery, and the system introduced into every branch of the business. In all the other branches the industry shows substantial gains. Climatic conditions largely regulated the locality and amount of fruit and vegetables packed, as shown by the fact that in 1900 the value of canned products in the 10 leading States was as follows: California, $13,081,829; Maryland, $11,996,245; New York, $8,975,321; Illinois, $3,730,030; Indiana, $2,589,908; New Jersey, $2,199,176; Ohio, $1,941,398; Delaware, $1,570,790; Iowa, $1,359,958; and Maine, $1,335,671. In exports of fruit the value of products has increased from $1,207,481 in 1891 to $5,438,577 in 1900, an increase of $4,231,096, or 350.4 per cent. The value of canned vegetables exported in 1891 was $466,494, and in 1900 reached the sum of $1,099,530, an increase of 135.8 per cent.

Fish.—All the known processes are used in the preservation of fish, of which all foods is the most rapid to putrefy. The Hollanders put up fish in cans long before the Soddington and Appert methods were known. About 1845, sardine canning was successfully established on the coast of France. Prior to 1843 the canning of fish in the United States was little known, but in that year lobster and mackerel canneries were successfully established at Eastport, Me., and the business grew rapidly till 1860, when the supply of lobsters decreased and the prejudice against the canneries resulted in the enactment of strict laws restricting the time of operation of canneries and the canning of short lobsters, so that in 1895 the last factory so engaged suspended, and in 1900 there were no lobsters canned. Mr. Underwood established the first lobster-packing factory in this country at Harpswell, Me., in 1848, and in 1853 started a factory for packing salmon at Bathurst, N. B., at one time the only source of supply. Quantities of this fish were sent to California prior to salmon being taken from the Columbia River. He died in 1864, and was succeeded by the firm of William Underwood Company, of which his grandson, H. O. Underwood, is president. Prior to

1864 salmon-canning was carried on to a small extent, but after that year the industry grew rapidly; factories were established on the Pacific coast, at Washington, Cal., on the Sacramento River, and in 1866 on the Columbia River. Perhaps the most striking illustration of the growth of this business is in that almost universally used article, canned salmon. In 1864 the firm of Hapgood, Hume & Company, consisting of William Hume, G. W. Hume, and A. S. Hapgood, canned a few cases of salmon on the Sacramento River, where William Hume had been a hunter and fisherman for several years. William Hume carried the samples around to introduce them, using a basket for that purpose, from which the salmon were sold. In 1866 the business was transferred to Eagle Cliff, Wash., on the Columbia River, where William Hume had been prospecting the year before, and there (in 1866) the first Columbia River Royal Chinook salmon were packed, thus introducing to the trade what is unquestionably the finest food-fish known. That year they packed about 4,000 cases of 48 1-pound cans each, or 192,000 cans. Most of this was shipped to Australia, selling at about $4 in gold (which was at a heavy premium at that time), and a small amount was shipped to New York, around Cape Horn, bringing $5 per dozen there at wholesale. In 1883 there were in Alaska 5 canneries, which in six years increased to 37 with an output of 714,196 cases.

Next in importance comes the sardine canning of Maine, which did not come to a point of success until 1875, and this branch of the business outranked all others. The process of putting up fish is extensive and complicated, and since the beginning of the industry many changes have been made, more especially in the time allowed for cooking, softening the bones of the fish, and in filling, capping, labeling, and boxing the same. Up to 1880 the business done in this line was very small, but gradually grew after that, and the establishments at Eastport, Robinson, Lubec, Jonesport, East Lamoine, and Camden, all in Maine, are now thriving.

Besides the fishes named, smelt, sturgeon, menhaden, halibut, Spanish mackerel, eels, and herring are put up in large quantities. The canning of fish is generally divided into five classes: (1) those plain boiled or steamed, which include salmon, mackerel, halibut, lobsters, etc.; (2) those preserved in oil, of which sardines constitute the major portion; (3) those preserved with vinegar, sauces, spices, etc., among which are herring, eels, and sturgeon; (4) those cooked with vegetables, namely, fish chowder, clam chowder, and codfish balls; (5) those preserved by any other process, such as smoking and salting, and which are put into cans for convenience. Smoking and salting of fish is principally confined to the Eastern States lying along the Atlantic coast, although the industry is carried on to some extent in the Pacific States.

It is interesting to note some of the prices of that time. One-pound peas and corn were selling at $3; tomatoes in two-pound canisters brought $3.25. In 1855 one-pound lobsters sold at $2.75 and salmon at $4 a dozen. No one believed him when William J. Underwood made a prediction that the prices of salmon and lobsters would cross each other during his generation, the lobster tending upward and the salmon dropping down, a situation which has come about even earlier than he anticipated.

The remarkable increase in the number of canneries and the value of their output from 1890 to 1900 may be observed in the following table, the periods for comparison being limited to those two census years from the fact that the industry was carried on in connection with the canning of fruits and vegetables, and statistics for this separate branch do not appear previous to the census of 1890.

	1900	1890
Number of establishments..	348	110
Capital	$19,514,215	$3,186,975
Salaried officials, clerks, etc.	618	182
Salaries	585,160	120,253
Wage earners, average no...	13,410	5,030
Total wages	4,229,638	1,128,143
Miscellaneous expenses.....	$883,363	280,660
Cost of materials used......	$13,232,001	$4,710,709
Value of products..........	$22,253,749	$6,972,268

As in the fruit and vegetable industry, there is the same tendency to centralize in points nearest to the source of supply, and the States and Territories which have produced the most in value are ranked as follows: Washington, $4,831,038; Maine, $4,779,733; Massachusetts, $4,619,362; Alaska, $3,821,136; Oregon, $1,788,-809; California, $866,432. The total number of pounds of fish canned in 1902 was 172,856,178, valued at $14,589,127; of smoked fish, 21,723,426 pounds. with a valuation of $986,003; and of salted fish, 125,669,131 pounds, valued at $5,260,-927. In the total number of pounds of fish canned, Alaska ranks first with 52,011,552 pounds, or 30.1 per cent of the total number; Maine ranks second, with 48,451,808 pounds; Washington comes third, with 43,195,262 pounds; Oregon fourth, with 16,469,602 pounds; and California fifth, with 3,860,124 pounds.

Oysters.—The oyster is a lamellibranch or bivalve mollusk of the genus Ostræa, the most important in commercial value to be found in American waters being the Ostræa virginiana, and which are generally found attached to some solid substance in the moist, brackish waters at the mouth of rivers or in the shallow waters along the seacoast, the depths of the water in which they lie varying from 15 to 180 feet, according to temperature. The principal and most productive beds in which they were found in the early history of the industry were in Chesapeake Bay, Cape Cod, and Long Island Sound, but the constant fishing up to 1860 soon depleted these, and the supply in the public beds along the coast of Connecticut, New York, New Jersey, and Delaware is now nearly exhausted, and at best irregular and uncertain, and the oyster found is very small. Oysters are found in the Gulf of Mexico, and to a small extent along the Pacific coast, and unless some method for rapidly propagating the species be found, the industry will soon find itself in the same sphere as the lobster industry; that is, extinct.

The canning of oysters has grown simultaneously with the canning of fish, and the two were generally carried on, in the early days of the industry, under the same roof. Thomas Kensett was probably the pioneer of oyster canning, and commenced operations in Baltimore as early as 1820, later being followed by others, but it was not until 1850 that the industry was put on a permanent basis. Originally, the oysters were opened by hand, but Louis McMurray, of Baltimore, introduced, in 1858, a new method, that of scalding the oysters before removing the shells, and this method made the removal of the oyster from the shell much easier. Two years later steaming took the place of McMurray's method, and this process consisted of placing the oysters in baskets having a capacity of three pecks or more, and then putting these baskets into a box through which steam was passed. In 1862 Henry Evans introduced the method of "shucking," his process being as follows: The oysters were placed in cars of iron framework, 6 to 8 feet long, which held about 20 bushels of unshucked oysters; the cars were then run on a track from the wharf to an air-tight and steam-tight box; after steaming for about 15 minutes, the cars are run into the shucking shed and opened; after shucking they are washed in cold water, packed in air-tight cans, hermetically sealed, and weighed; the cars were then run on a track from the steamed to a sufficient degree to kill all germs of fermentation, and then cooled off in a vat of cold water. The total cost of handling a bushel of oysters by this method was estimated at 29 cents, while the modern method averages 55 cents. In canning the variety of oysters found in the Gulf of Mexico, the following process was introduced in 1880 by William T. J. Mayburg: "To 10 gallons of pure water add one half gallon of good commercial vinegar and one tenth gill of a saturated aqueous solution of salicylic acid, to which mixture sufficient common salt is added to impart the requisite salty flavor to the oyster. The mixture is boiled a few minutes and poured over the oysters in the cans, which are at once sealed and placed in a steam bath, the temperature of which is 202° F. This temperature is gradually raised to 240°, and maintained at that degree for about 40 minutes. The cans are then vented, resealed, and steamed as before for about 30 minutes, after which they are ready to be labeled and packed."

It seems rather extraordinary, but in 1850 oysters were packed in Boston, which found a ready sale in direct competition with Baltimore goods, and for a number of years there was considerable rivalry between the two markets. The oysters were brought from the coasts of New Brunswick and Prince Edward Island, and were said to have a finer flavor and to keep much better than those from the warmer waters of the South. They were packed in one- and two-pound canisters, and large sales were made in Saint Louis at $4 and $7.50 per dozen. six months: 5 per cent off for cash.

The following table gives a comparative summary of the statistics of the industry for the years 1890 and 1900:

	1900	1890
Number of establishments...	39	16
Capital	$1,240,696	$1,106,692
Salaried officials, clerks, etc.	119	61
Salaries	$112,879	$69,891
Wage earners, average no...	2,779	3,453
Total wages...............	$630,016	$642,610
Miscellaneous expenses.....	$93,707	$80,199
Cost of materials used.....	$2,608,757	$2,088,867
Value of products..........	$3,670,134	$3,260,766

In 1900 there were 33,356,677 pounds of oysters canned, valued at $2,380,711, making the average value of a pound $.071. Maryland ranked first in quantity and value of production, showing over 50 per cent of the total; Mississippi followed Maryland with 25 per cent of the total; and Florida and Louisiana came in the order named, their combined output being 9 per cent of the total. The apparent discrepancy in the figures is accounted for by the fact that several of the largest firms handle the fresh oysters in bulk in connection with the canning business, and, as it is impossible to segregate the amounts directly chargeable to the manufacturing end of the business, the value of raw oysters sold must be included in the table.

From the foregoing tables it will be seen that in 1900 there were 2,000 known firms engaged in the canning industry, operating 2,195 canneries, distributed over 42 States, of which 25 per cent were in Maryland, 7 per cent in Maine, 6 per cent in New York, 3½ per cent each in Virginia, Illinois, and Ohio, 5 per cent in California, 3 per cent in Indiana, and the remainder scattered through the other States.

Such are the vast proportions to which the canning industry of America has grown: an industry developed by the ingenuity and ability of the American, from mere nothingness to a position of great influence and import in our industrial life.

Revised by EDWARD W. DUCKWALL, M.S.,
Bacteriologist of the National Canners' Laboratory, Aspinwall, Pa.

Cannizzaro, Stanislao, stän ĭs lä'ō kän-nē-tsä'rō, Italian chemist: b. Palermo, 16 July, 1820. He studied medicine at Palermo, and chemistry at Pisa. In 1848 he was a member of the Sicilian Parliament and had part in the revolution in Sicily. In 1852 he became professor of chemistry in Alessandria; in 1857 in Genoa; in 1860 in Palermo; and in 1870 in Rome. He emphasized by clear definition the difference between atomic and molecular weights, and was one of the most influential in establishing Avogadro's law as a maxim of chemical science. He also discovered benzyl-alcohol and cyanamide. He wrote 'Sunto di un Corso di Filisofia Chemica, e Nota Sulle Condensazioni di Vapore' (1880); 'Relazione Sulle Analisi di Alcune acque Potabili' (1882); and 'Abriss eines Lehrganges der theoretischen Chemie,' which appeared in Ostwald's 'Klassiker der exakten Wissenschaften.'

Can'nock, England, a town in West Staffordshire, seven and one half miles northwest of Walsall, in the district known as Cannock Chase, which is rich in coal and ironstone.

Manufactures of boilers, edge-tools, bricks, and tiles, are carried on, and there are numerous collieries. Pop. (1901) 23,992.

Can'non, Frank Jenne, American politician, son of George Q. Cannon (q.v.): b. Salt Lake City, Utah, 25 Jan 1859. He was graduated from the University of Utah in 1878, and has since been engaged in journalism. He was United States senator, 1896–9, and has been prominent as a Silver Republican.

Cannon, George Lyman, American geologist: b. New York, 10 March 1860. He was educated at the University of Colorado and the Colorado State School of Mines, and has been an instructor in geology and biology in the Denver High School from 1887. He has published 'Geology of Denver and Vicinity' (1894); 'Outlines of Geology' (1895); 'Nature Study for Denver Schools' (1895); 'The Protection of Colorado Birds' (1899).

Cannon, George Q., American politician: b. Liverpool, England, 11 Jan. 1827; d. Monterey, Cal., 12 April 1901. He went with his parents to Nanvoo, Ill., in 1844, and was one of the earliest settlers in Salt Lake City. He was a member of the Legislative Council of Utah in 1865–6 and 1869–70, and was a delegate to Congress from 1865 to 1881. At a Constitutional Convention at Salt Lake City in 1872 he was chosen to present the constitution and memorial to Congress for the admission of the Territory into the Union as a State. He translated the 'Book of Mormon' into the Hawaiian language. His son, Frank J. Cannon, was elected one of the first two United States senators from Utah in 1896.

Cannon, Henry White, American bank president: b. Delhi, N. Y., 25 Sept. 1850. He was educated at Delaware Academy in his native town and engaged in banking. He was comptroller of the currency, 1884–5, and was a member of the International Monetary Conference at Brussels in 1892. He is a director of several important railroads and of the Manhattan Trust Company, and president of the Chase National Bank in New York.

Cannon, Joseph G., American politician: b. Guilford, N. C., 7 May 1836. Admitted to the Illinois bar, he was State's attorney of Vermillion County, 1861–8. He was a member of Congress from 1873 to 1891, and again, 1893–1903. He was 20 years on the Committee on Appropriations, and its chairman in the 55th and 56th Congresses. He was Speaker of the House of Representatives in the 58th and 59th Congresses.

Cannon. See ORDNANCE.

Cannon-ball Tree, a large tree (*Couroupita guianensis*) of the order *Lecythidaceæ*, a native of Guiana, with a hard, woody, globular fruit six or eight inches in diameter — whence the popular name of the tree. It has large white or rose-colored flowers growing in clusters on the stem and branches. The pulp of the fruit is pleasant to eat when fresh.

Cannstadt, kän'stat, **Cannstatt,** or **Kanstatt,** Germany, a town in Würtemberg, in a beautiful and fertile district on the Neckar, two miles northeast of Stuttgart. Its antiquity is proved by the Roman remains found. It has celebrated and much-frequented mineral springs, active and varied industries, including the manufacture of cotton and woolen goods, machinery, etc. Here are also railroad shops and dye works. The Neckar is here crossed by two bridges. Pop. (1900) 26,500.

Cano, kä'nō, **Alonzo,** Spanish painter, sculptor, and architect: b. Granada, 19 March 1601; d. 5 Oct. 1667. He became so distinguished in each of these arts that his countrymen called him the Michael Angelo of Spain, although the title is due more to his versatility than to any resemblance in point of genius to the great Florentine. His 'Conception of the Virgin,' in the church of San Diego, at Granada, is considered his masterpiece. His works in sculpture and architecture are also numerous. He was a contemporary of Velasquez, and in 1639 was appointed court painter to Philip IV. His ungovernable temper on various occasions brought him in danger of the inquisition, and he was once put on the rack on suspicion of having killed his wife in a fit of jealousy, but was subsequently absolved from the charge. On this occasion his right arm was exempted from torture, as being *excellens in arte.* As an illustration of his whimsical character it is related that on his deathbed he refused to take the crucifix from the priest on account of its bad workmanship.

Cano, Juan Sebastian del, hoo-än' sä-bäs'-tē-än dĕl, Spanish navigator: b. Guetaria, Guipuzoca, about 1460; d. on the Pacific, 4 Aug. 1526. He was one of the first to circumnavigate the globe (1522), as captain of one of Magellan's fleet, which he afterward commanded. In 1525 he was placed second in command of a similar expedition and became its commander by the death of Loaisa.

Cano, Melchior, mĕl'kē-ôr, Spanish theologian: b. Tarrancon, 1523; d. Toledo, 30 Sept. 1560. He was a member of the Dominican order and an opponent of the Jesuits. He was professor at the universities of Alcantara and Salamanca, and was made bishop of the Canaries, but did not live in his see. He wrote 'De Locis Theologicis,' and many other theological works.

Cano y Masas, Leopoldo, lä ō pold o kä'nō ē mä'säs, Spanish poet and dramatist: b. Valladolid, 13 Nov. 1844. He graduated from the Spanish Military Academy at Madrid (1865), and was appointed professor of analytical and descriptive geometry there in 1867, retiring in 1885. His first comedy was 'Laurels of a Poet' (1852). His many other plays include: 'The Code of Honor'; 'Modern Idolatry'; and 'The Death of Lucretia.' He is the author of a volume of poems, entitled 'Arrows.'

Cano'ba, the Indian Apollo, or god of inspiration.

Canoe, ka̤-noo', a light boat designed for propulsion with a paddle or paddles. The term is very commonly used to designate the small vessels used by uncivilized people living near the water. The name is of West Indian origin, the Carib word being *canŏoa.*

Canoes are built in divers forms and of various materials. Doubtless the most primitive form is the hollowed tree-trunk; the excavation, before the advent of adequate cutting-tools, being accomplished by means of fire. This

form is of wide distribution, being found in Africa, South and Central America, China, and the islands of the South Pacific and Indian oceans. In the form known as a "dugout" it is common in the United States. Among the island races of the Pacific the stability of the canoe is largely increased by the adoption of an outrigger, which, of varying forms, prevents capsizing on the one side by its weight and leverage, and on the other by its buoyancy. Many of these islanders sew planks together to form their canoes, making the joints water-tight by means of gums, etc. Others use double canoes united by a strong platform. Such a vessel is capable of carrying a number of persons and a considerable lading. In South America, where large trees are abundant, very large canoes are constructed. The same is true of Africa, where the war-canoes of the native kings carry very large crews. They are often fantastically carved and ornamented.

As stated above, the propelling force of the canoe is usually the paddle, but sails are often used, particularly on sea-going craft.

The Esquimaux canoe is known as a *kayak.* This consists of a light wooden or bone frame covered with seal-skins sewed together with sinews. The skin covering extends across the top, forming a water-tight deck with but one opening amidships to admit the boatman. A hoop is fitted to this opening, and after the boatman has entered he fastens himself in by means of an apron so that the whole boat is water-tight, and he becomes, as it were, part of the craft. So intimate is this union, and so skilful are the Esquimaux in the management of their kayaks, that the boatman can with a twist of his paddle capsize the craft and turn completely around under water, coming up again on the opposite side to that he went over. The paddle is about 10 feet long and double-bladed. The *oomiak,* or women's boat, is also made of seal-skins sewed over a framework; but it is of large, even clumsy build, and but for its propulsion by paddles might be classed as a boat rather than as a canoe. It is designed as a transport for women, children, and household goods rather than for the chase, for which the kayak is principally used.

The Aleuts build large skin boats, somewhat resembling the Esquimaux oomiak, which are propelled by paddles. Such a boat is known as a *bidarkee.* Other tribes of the west coast build large canoes of wood, the war-vessels being, like those of Africa, curiously decorated.

A peculiar form of canoe is found in the Kootenai district and on the Columbia River. While most canoes are constructed with the bow and stern either perpendicular or with a flaring overhang, these Kootenai craft are shaped, both at bow and stern, like the ram of a warship. In other words, the greatest length is along the bottom. These canoes are generally about 15 feet long and are constructed with a light framework of cedar covered with spruce or white-pine bark. This bark is cut off in one piece in the spring, when the sap is running, and is turned inside out, bringing the smooth side in contact with the water. The canoes are sewed with rawhide or tendons, and cracks and knot-holes are stopped with resin. Two squaws will make a canoe in four or five days; the chief difficulty being to get the bark off whole and to turn it wrong side out successfully.

The North American Indians have brought the canoe to its highest state of perfection. With the most frail material, birch bark, they construct a craft so light that it may be carried by one man, and yet so strong and buoyant that it will carry a very considerable load. A framework of light but tough wood is covered with sheets of birch bark, which are sewed together; the seams being waterproofed with resinous gums. They are propelled by means of a single-bladed paddle, which is dipped on one side only (a slight twist correcting the tendency to swerve from a straight line), or alternately on either side. The use of the birch-bark canoe by the Indians of the United States is rapidly becoming a thing of the past; but the art of building them has been preserved by their construction as pleasure-craft.

A form of canoe of recent invention is used solely for pleasure. About 1865 John Macgregor, impelled by a love of adventure, sought recreation on the rivers and fjords of Europe as well as on the waters of Egypt and Palestine. He developed his model from the Esquimaux kayak, and evolved a clinker-built craft of cedar, about 14 feet long and 2 feet in beam, entirely decked over with the exception of a "well" in which the canoeist sits. This is propelled by means of a double-bladed paddle, but a short mast enables the carrying of a sail. In a canoe of this type, which he named the Rob Roy, Macgregor cruised on the Danube, the Jordan, the Nile, the Seine, and on Norwegian fjords. From this early model other forms have been evolved, notably the Nautilus and Shadow types. Water-tight compartments ensure permanent buoyancy. Centre-boards counteract leeway when under sail on a wind. The interior space is so arranged as to provide a sleeping-place for the cruiser.

There are many canoe clubs in the United States, England, and Canada, and the canoe may be seen on all the coastwise and inland waters of those countries, as well as on the continent of Europe.

See article by W. Baden-Powell in the 'Encyclopædia of Sport' (1897) ; Hicks, 'Yachts, Boats, and Canoes' ; Powell, 'Canoe Traveling' ; the works of J. Macgregor ("Rob Roy") ; Hayward, 'Canoeing with Sail and Paddle' ; Field, 'Canvas Canoes.'
ELFORD E. TREFFRY.

Canon, Johann, yō'hän kä'nōn, Austrian painter: b. Vienna, 13 March 1829; d. there, 12 Sept. 1885. He entered the Austrian army and in 1848-55 was lieutenant of cuirassiers, but even while in the army had given much attention to painting, and finally devoted his whole time to it. His name first became known through his picture 'The Fishermaiden,' exhibited in 1858. His work includes genre pictures, historical paintings, and portraits; the latter are thought to resemble Rubens or Van Dyck in style. Among his other paintings are 'Cromwell Beside the Corpse of Charles I.' ; 'The African Lion Hunt' ; 'Flamingo Hunt' ; and the 'Fish Market.'

Cañon, or **Can'yon,** in physical geography, a great ravine or gorge; a deep, trench-like river valley with nearly vertical walls. It is the simplest type of river valley and is formed by a young stream in its torrent stage. Thus a cañon is, geologically speaking, of recent date, and is more likely to be found in an arid region than in one of average rainfall, since its growth is due to the down-cutting action of the stream being faster than the general lowering of the land surface by rock-weathering and rain erosion. In southern Arizona, New Mexico, southern Utah, and Colorado, a great plateau 7,000 to 8,000 feet high has been elevated since Tertiary time, as shown by the latest rocks being of Tertiary age. They lie in horizontal strata, and the streams crossing the plateau have cut deep trenches with nearly vertical walls, exposing rocks of all ages down to the basement granite. Here the drainage is several thousand feet below the surface of the plateau. The Grand Cañon of the Colorado is 300 miles long. The average width from rim to rim does not exceed 10 miles throughout the widest portion of the cañon, and it frequently narrows to eight miles. The river does not occupy the middle of the gigantic trough, but flows at a distance varying from one to three miles from the south side. Practically all of the magnificently sculptured pinnacles and so-called temples lie north of the river at distances of from five to seven miles from view-points usually visited by tourists. The depth of the Grand Cañon measured from the south rim is considerably less than a mile. From the rim at the Bright Angel Hotel, where the altitude is 6,866 feet above sea-level, to the high-water mark of the river at the foot of the tourist trail, the drop is 4,430 feet. The highest point on the south rim at the Grand View Hotel is 7,496 feet, about 4,900 feet above the river. From the north side, however, the drop to the water level averages considerably over a mile and in places exceeds 6,000 feet. In a general way it may be said that the north rim is 1,000 to 1,200 feet higher than the south, thus producing the high, even sky-line so impressive to the tourist. It is altogether unlikely that such a chasm could have been carved through similar rocks in a region of average rainfall, as lateral torrents would have greatly widened the valley. Of other cañons and gorges in the Western States may be mentioned the gorge of the Columbia, where it breaks through the lava flows of the Cascade Mountains, 2,500 to 3,000 feet deep. It was eroded in Quaternary time. In California the gorges of the north and south forks of the American River are 2,000 to 3,000 feet deep; the cañon of the Merced River, including the Yosemite valley, is 3,000 to 5,000 feet deep, and the Grand Cañon of King's River 3,000 to 7,000 feet. In some of these cases the stream has cut its way down rapidly enough to form a cañon by following a fault-plane or other line of weakness in the rocks. In parts of the West the word cañon is used very loosely, being applied to almost a ravine or even a gulley.

Can'on (Greek, a rule, measure, or standard). 1. In the arts: When art has succeeded in producing beautiful forms the question arises, with what proportions beauty of form is united. Artists of genius first started this question, and imitators, inferior to them in talents, scrupulously followed their results, and naturally exalted some existing work into a model for every performance. Among the Greeks the celebrated statuary Polycletus (452–12 B.C.) first instituted such inquiries; and as he generally represented youthful, pleasing figures, it is probable that he fixed the standard of beauty in the youthful form. The canon (the model statue) of Polycletus was accordingly a statue which was made principally for the purpose of showing the beautiful proportions of the human form in a youth just ripening into manhood. No copy of it is known to exist; the artist probably gave his model of proportion a quiet, simple attitude, without any strong distinguishing marks. His successors imitated it without deviation. Polycletus was not the only Greek artist who pursued such investigations respecting the proportions of form. Among the moderns, Dürer and Leonardo da Vinci have devoted themselves to similar inquiries.

2. In Scriptural literature, a term employed to designate the collection of books containing the rule or standard of primitive Christianity; that is, the canonical books of the Holy Scriptures. The canon of the books of the Old Testament, as contained in the Hebrew Bible, receives in this form equal respect among all Christians, because Christ and the apostles have expressly appealed to them, and in this way pronounced them writings inspired by God. There are certain books, however, belonging in subject to the Old Testament, but whose canonical character the Jews did not acknowledge, and which Protestants class together under the head of Apocrypha, and reject from the canon. For these there is only a Greek, and not a Hebrew text. The Western Church accepted them as canonical in the African Council, about the end of the 4th century; but the opinions of the clergy respecting them remained for a long time divided. St. Jerome denied their canonicity, and many theologians coincided with him. The Roman Catholic Church finally declared them canonical in the Council of Trent. (See Apocrypha.) Respecting the number of books belonging to the canon of the New Testament, the opinions of Christians were much divided till the 6th century. As early as the 2d century the separation was made into the Evangelicon (the four Evangelists) and the Apostolicon (the Acts and Epistles of the Apostles). The five historical books, the Epistles of Paul, the First Epistle of Peter, and the First Epistle of John were universally acknowledged to be genuine in the 3d century; hence Eusebius, in his 'Ecclesiastical History,' written about 325 A.D., calls them Homologoumena (universally received). The other five catholic epistles (Second of Peter, Second and Third of John, Jude, and James) he calls Antilegomena (doubtful, not universally received). At that time the Epistle to the Hebrews was considered genuine by most persons, and the Apocalypse by many. These books were received in the second half of the 4th century in the Egyptian Church (where Athanasius first used the term canonical), and in the Western Church. In the Eastern Church, properly so called (the dioceses of the patriarchs of Constantinople, Antioch, and Jerusalem), only the catholic epistles were of canonical authority at that time; the Apocalypse not till the 6th century. The canon of the New Testament has since remained unaltered, and the Protestant churches hold it in common with the Greek and Catholic churches. The results of critical examinations of the genuineness and canonical character of the single books of the Bible, even when they were unfavorable to the books, have produced no alteration in the established canon. The reasons of the ancient fathers of the Church for or against the canonical character of the biblical books were merely historical and traditional, and built on philological criticism; they are still the most tenable and rational; the philosophical grounds are more subject to be affected by extraneous influences.

3. In ecclesiastical use, a rule or law of doctrine or discipline as established by ecclesiastical authority. The term is farther applied to various matters of church organization and ceremony; also to books containing the rules of religious orders, etc., and to a list or catalogue of acknowledged and canonized saints in the Roman Catholic Church.

Another distinctive ecclesiastical use of the term is that which designates a dignitary possessing a prebend, or revenue allotted for the performance of divine service in a cathedral or collegiate church. Canons were originally priests who lived in community, appointed to assist the bishop in his duties, and supported by the revenues of the bishopric. Secular Canons are those who, in progress of time, have left off the custom prevalent in monasteries of living a community life, and have the privilege of enjoying the returns of their respective benefices. The obligations of the canons are contained under three heads: (1) the duty of residing in the place where the church they belong to is situated; (2) assisting at the canonical offices which are celebrated in the church; and (3) attending the meeting of the chapter at the appointed times. They cannot be absent from their benefices for a longer period than three months, and are obliged to sing or recite their office in choir. In their collective capacity they are called a chapter, and form the council of the bishop. In each chapter there are dignitaries. The name was originally applied to all the clergy, but was afterward confined to those who were connected with the cathedral church, or to specially privileged churches.

4. In music, with the ancient Greeks, the term canon signified what now is called monochord. At present it signifies a composition in which the several voices begin at fixed intervals, one after the other, and in which each successive voice sings the strain of the preceding one. In Italian, therefore, it is called fuga di conseguenza; in Latin, canon perpetuus, or continuous fugue; in German, Kreisfuge (circulating fugue). Sometimes each voice begins with the same, sometimes with different notes. The phrase or passage for imitation is called the theme or subject, the imitation the reply. Canons may be finite or infinite. The former end, like any other compositions, with a cadence, while the infinite canon is so contrived that the theme is begun again before the parts which follow are concluded. A canon may consist of two, three, four, or more voices. Canons differ from ordinary fugues; for, in the latter, it is sufficient that the subject be occasionally repeated and imitated according to the laws of counterpoint; but, in the former, it is essential that the subject be strictly repeated by all the succeeding parts; which repetition may be made in the unison or octave, the fourth, or the fifth, or any other interval of the scale. There are several other canons, as canon polymorphus, canon per diminutionem, and canon per augmentationem. Sometimes, also, a musical passage of a composition in which one voice repeats for a short time another, is called, improperly, a canon.

5. In printing, canon is the name given to a large type which is so called from the early use of it for printing the canon of the mass and the Church service-books.

Cañon City, Col., a city and county-seat of Fremont County, situated on the Arkansas River, near the mouth of the Grand Cañon, and on the Denver & R. G., and the Atchison, T. & S. F. R.R.'s. It is a well-known health resort, over 5,000 feet above the sea-level, with an excellent climate and hot and cold mineral springs. In the vicinity there are valuable deposits of limestone, coal, and iron. The river furnishes abundant water-power. Pop. (1900) 3,775.

Canon Finch, Towhee, **Wren**. See FINCH, TOWHEE, WREN.

Canon Law. Canon law is so named because it consists of rules or canons, which are established to guide the faithful to eternal happiness. In a strict sense, canon law comprises only those laws which emanate from an ecclesiastical authority that has supreme and universal jurisdiction. In a wide sense, it takes in also those laws enacted for the good of the faithful by anyone having ecclesiastical authority. The sources or fountains from which canon law has originated are: Sacred Scripture; divine tradition; laws made by the Apostles; teachings of the Fathers; decrees of the sovereign pontiffs; ecumenical councils; certain congregations of cardinals under orders of the Pope; custom, which, however, could in no case be contrary to divine law, common sense, good manners, public order, or the spirit and the rights of the Church. The Old Testament contains three sorts of precepts, moral, ceremonial, judicial. The moral code remains in full force under canon law; the ceremonial and judicial laws have lapsed. The New Testament is the chief source of ecclesiastical law. It contains also dogmas of faith, but with these canon law does not deal except indirectly. By tradition is meant a doctrine not written by its first author, but conveyed by word of mouth. Usually it is subsequently put into writing. Traditions, considered in their source, are divine or human. Divine are those which have God for their author, and which the apostles received either directly from Christ or by the suggestion of the Holy Ghost. Human traditions are termed apostolic if they originate with the apostles, or ecclesiastical if they come from the successors of the apostles, called bishops of the church. Divine traditions bind all the faithful; human only those of the localities and times to which they are applicable. Some of the enactments attributed to the apostles are: the Apostles' Creed; abstinence from things sacrificed to idols, and from blood and from things strangled, part of which prohibition has lapsed; the substitution of the Sunday for the Sabbath of the Jews; the institution of certain feast days; the fast of Lent. The sentences of the fathers, approved by the Church and made into universal laws by councils or the Roman pontiffs, are part of canon law. These sayings were not inserted in the collection of canons before the 6th century, John Scholasticus being the first to do this in the East in that century, and Regino first in the West in the beginning of the 10th century. To the student it is evident that the constitutions or decrees of the Roman pontiffs constitute the chief source of canon law; in fact, the entire

canon law in the strict sense of the term is based upon the legislative authority of the Pope. To understand this it is necessary to recall that in the Catholic doctrine all authority in the Church comes from above, not only in the office of priesthood, but also in the matter of jurisdiction or power of ruling. Catholic writers hold that the primacy or headship in the Church was established by Christ in Peter before the priesthood was conferred on him and the other apostles, the purpose of the Savior being to effect unity in his organization. The church thus organized is a spiritual monarchy; elective it is true, but not an aristocracy or democracy. Other religious organizations hold quite the opposite doctrine and would make their unity be a coalition of equal parts. This point of primacy of the Roman pontiff is also the line of separation between the canon law of the west and that of the separated Greek and the Russian churches, the review of which is given later in this article. Ecumenical councils, whose decrees are a source of canon law, are those meetings of the bishops of the church throughout the world, which are held under the presidency of the pope or his legates, and whose acts are by him confirmed. There are twenty councils recognized as ecumenic; the first being that of Nicæa in 325; the latest that of the Vatican in 1870.

During the first three centuries, the church was administered according to the scriptures only and the rules laid down by the apostles and bishops, as occasion required. Thus Clement, the disciple and successor of Peter, mentions the rule given by the apostles concerning the succession of bishops, and Ignatius the Martyr, in his epistles, exhorts his followers to diligently and tenaciously observe the traditions of the apostles. Thus, too, in the controversy concerning the celebration of Easter, the contestants on each side alleged the apostolic tradition. But councils were held at Ancyra and Neo-Cesarœa in 314, at Nicæa in 325, at Antioch in 322, at Sardica in 347, at Gangra from 362 to 370, at Laodicæa between 337 and 381, at Constantinople in 381, at Ephesus in 431, and in the council of Chalcedon in 451 a collection of canons made up from these previous councils was read and partly authorized for the entire church. With the exception of those of Sardica, which are in Latin, the canons of all these early councils were formulated in Greek. The name of the compiler of this first collection is unknown and few of these early canons have reached our times, only their tenor being known through subsequent use in the western church, especially in Spain. After the emperors assumed the Christian religion, ecclesiastical legislation became important, and the laws of the church were therefore in the year 438 inserted in his collection by the emperor Theodosius II. Valentinian III. afterwards adopted this collection for the West. About this time — the latter half of the 5th century — a compilation was made of the so-called apostolic canons and constitutions together with decrees of some of the councils. Originally there were 50 canons called apostolic, but their number was afterwards increased to 85, some of which are certainly spurious. In the East these were received as having the stamp of authority, but not so in the West, where their origin was doubted. However, Dionysius adopted the smaller collection of 50,

CANON LAW

considering them useful for discipline, and thereby without determining their origin procured for them in Rome the stamp of authority. John Scholasticus made a collection of canons for the Greek church in 564, to which he added 68 canons taken from Saint Basil. He divided the work into 50 titles. To this he later added the laws of the empire which had relation to the laws of the church, and the new compilation became known as Nomo-canon. The emperor Justinian II. in 692 assembled a council in his palace at Constantinople, called the Trullan Council from the room in which it was held, and 102 canons were enacted. When the acts and canons of this council were submitted to Pope Sergius at Rome for approval he refused even though the emperor ordered his armor-bearer to bring the Pope to Constantinople. The Trullan compilation consisted of the so-called Canons of the Apostles, those of the ten councils previously mentioned, the canons of the synod of Carthage, the decrees of a synod in 394 at Constantinople under Nectarius, the canonical decisions of the twelve Eastern patriarchs and of some bishops from the 3d to the 5th centuries, the canon of a council held at Carthage under Cyprian in 256, to all of which were added the 102 canons drawn up by the Trullan council itself. Afterwards 22 canons of the second council of Nicæa held in 787 were added. On this foundation the church law of the East was based up to the middle of the 9th century. By the Trullan synod, priests were allowed to marry, which up to that time was against the canon law of both the Eastern and the Western church. The Trullan synod also sanctioned the Canons of the Apostles, one of which teaches the doctrine of the re-baptisers, which had been previously repudiated by Pope Gelasius. Herein is noticed the first real divergence between Eastern and Western canon law. Photius, who was intruded into the see of Constantinople, called a council against the patriarch Ignatius in 861, and 17 canons made by this council were added to the codex of the Greek church. He also formulated a new collection, in which the second part, called the Nomo-canon remained unchanged. The emperor Leo the Philosopher, who deposed Photius, rescinded his collection of laws, but nevertheless the seeds of the separation of the Greek church from that of Rome had been implanted by the work, although a complete schism took place only later in 1054 under Michael Cerularius. From time to time new ecclesiastical constitutions issued from the emperors, as from Leo Philosophus in 911, from Constantine Porphyrogenitus in 961, from Alexius Comnenus in 1118, from Isaac Alexius in 1185–90. The resolutions of synods summoned by the patriarchs of Constantinople, epistles of renowned bishops and their decisions, formed another addition to the canon law of the eastern church. The first commentary on the Greek codex was undertaken by Theodore Prodromos in the 8th century. The second, containing the text with a commentary, is the Nomo-canon of Doropater. The monk John Zonares composed a comprehensive verbal interpretation in 1120, using the collection of Photius as a basis. Fifty years later, Theodore Balsamon made a commentary with a view to practical questions, comparing the canons with the civil law and insisting that Justinian's maxims only applied when comformable to the Basilics. He added many matters

not found in the collection of Photius. Epitomes of canon law were composed at a comparatively early period, the author of the first of which appears to have been Stephen of Ephesus in the 5th century. There is a synopsis by Aristenus augmented by Alexius Aristenus in 1160, and another by Arsenius, a monk of Mount Athos, in 1255. Constantine Harmenopoulos in 1350 composed an epitome of the spiritual law in six parts, using, with some omissions, the collection of Photius as altered by Zonares. In order to reduce canon law to a more practical form than it appeared in the collection of Photius and at the same time present a more comprehensive work than these epitomes, Matthæus Blastares drew up his syntagma in 1335, divided into chapters of different lengths and arranged according to the principal word of these rubrics, the numbers of the chapters commencing anew under each letter. Each chapter begins with the ecclesiastical law, followed by the civil law applicable to it, without, however, mentioning the source of the latter. This work came into very general use among the clergy. The collection of Photius and the syntagma of Blastares continued still in use under the Turkish rule and were alike termed Nomo-canon and, metaphorically, the 'Rudder.' The collection and interpretation of Zonares also obtained canonical authority. From these materials many extracts were translated into modern Greek up to the 18th century, and several text books composed for the use of the clergy, some of which were printed in Venice. Lastly a comprehensive collection was published in 1800 at the instance of the patriarch and synod. It contains the old Greek text of all the authentic canons of councils since Photius and Zonares, to which are added interpretations of the authentic commentators in modern Greek, especially those of Zonares and Balsamon. In the interpretation, the canons of those fathers are taken into account which had not been confirmed by any general synod, but had obtained a canonical authority. Nothing was inserted from the municipal law works which did not agree with the canons. Several appendices were added, including formulas for ecclesiastical business, and upon these and similar collections is founded the present law of the Greek separate church. The Russian followed the Greek church in adopting compilations of church law up to the end of the 15th century. In 1550 certain regulations respecting the jurisdiction of bishops were introduced. Some canonical epistles and rules drawn up at councils are used in addition to the Greek codex, and manuals adapted to the country have been compiled therefrom. Peter the Great in 1721 changed the chief executive authority in the church from a patriarch into the Holy Synod, by decrees of which the church to-day is ruled. By an arrangement lately made with the Roman pontiff the bishops and priests under Roman jurisdiction are ruled by the canon law of Rome, subject to the civil laws of the Russian Empire, and to prevent complications, Russia, besides a resident minister and two secretaries, has at the Vatican a representative agent for ecclesiastical affairs.

In the Western or Latin Church the canons of Nicæa and Sardica were the only code publicly received up to the end of the 5th century. About this time the Spanish translation of the Greek code was turned into barbarous Latin, and became known as the Prisca. The decretals of the Roman pontiffs were added to the canons of the Greek code, as found in the Prisca, but it seems that Dionysius the Little, about the year 500, was the first to formulate a collection of the councils and the decretals. He had previously made a collection of the concilia for Stephen, the bishop of Dalmatia. The deacon Theodosius later made a new collection founded on the old Spanish and the Dionysian. A third collection termed the Avellanian, valuable for the historical documents it contains, appeared in the latter half of the 6th century. These, however, were superseded by a second edition of Dionysius, made probably in 731 under Pope Gregory II. In this edition some decrees overlooked previously were added, together with an appendix consisting of the statutes of the Roman pontiffs from Linus downwards, those up to Sericins, however, being given only in an historical form as no longer actually in existence. The German conquerors of Italy in 476 did not, although Arian, interfere with the laws by which the church was governed, but when Justinian reconquered Italy he introduced the Novellæ in the Julian translation in place of the codex of Theodosius II., and this order of things was later upheld by the Lombard kings in their edicts. In Africa the deacon Fulgentius Farrandus made the first collection in 547, termed Breviatio. This was an excerpt in 232 numbers of nearly all the Greek canons, including the Nicæan, to which was added the African concilia under Gratus in 348-9, under Genethlius in 390, and that of Carthage in 419 with its 33 canons, together with 304 taken from synods as well as an extract from the canons framed at Hippo in 393. The second African work was the Concordia of Bishop Cresconius in 690, founded upon Dionysius, but arranged in 300 titles instead of in chronological order. This work was incorporated with Dionysius and appeared under the name Breviarium. But the Arabs now put a sudden stop to all further development of canon law in this quarter. As early as the 5th century, as noted above, there was in Spain a translation of the Greek canons; in the 6th century Martin of Braga made a collection of canons, but in the 7th century Isadore of Seville held two councils, half church, half civil, the canons of which may be said almost to have formed the basis of the constitutional law of Spain in both church and state down to the 15th century. The collection of canons known as Collectio Isadoriana or Hispana was divided into two parts; the first containing the classified series of Greek, African, Frankist and Spanish canons, and the second the decretals from Pope Damasus in 366 to Gregory the Great in 604. In the 5th century an extensive but confused collection of councils and decretals was compiled in Gaul under Gelasius. It was founded upon the old Spanish version and some peculiar version of the canons of Nicæa and the Prisca. Out of it sprung several other collections; the first in the middle of the 6th century, containing the councils of Nicæa, and of Sardica, some Frankist concilia and papal decretals; the second of the same date containing Greek, African, and Gallic canons, and papal decretals in a confused order; the third in the 7th century, containing 103 numbers, many decretals, Frankist, Roman, and Italian concilia. A fourth and a fifth collection of the same century contained chiefly Frankist and Spanish conciliar decrees. After Charlemagne in 774 on his first visit to Rome had received from Pope Hadrian a copy of the Dionysian collection with some additions, he had it sanctioned in a synod at Aix-la-Chapelle as the *codex canonum* for the Frankist empire. In addition to these principal works many of the bishops composed capitularies for their own dioceses, as Boniface of Mayence, Theodulph of Orleans, Hincmar of Rheims. The 'Hispana' circulated among the Franks in a more or less corrupt form. One edition, which appeared between the years of 829 and 857, has caused great controversy, and is known as 'Collectio Pseudo-Isadoriana,' or False Decretals. The author called himself Isadore Mercator, and the name led many to believe the work that of Isadore of Seville. The best evidence shows that Levites Benedict of Mainz was the compiler, but no purpose for the forgeries in the work has been conclusively shown. After the preface and some minor apocryphal documents, the first part contains 50 of the apostolic canons taken from 'Hispana' and 60 supposed decretals of the popes from Clement in 92 to Melchiades in 314, arranged chronologically. The second part consists chiefly of canons taken from the 'Hispana.' In the third part, founded also on the 'Hispana,' the compiler has interpolated 35 decretals. A supplement contains some brief regulations regarding processes against bishops, said to be by Capitula Angilramni, a bishop of Metz. The collection was regarded as genuine by all canonists and theologians for 700 years from the 9th to the 15th century. Cardinal Nicholas of Cusa in the 15th century first expressed doubts of the genuineness of some of its contents. In the following century religious bitterness overshadowed scholarly inquiry, but it is now admitted by Protestant writers that the compilation was produced, not in the interest of the pope but of the Frankist bishops in order to protect themselves against oppression by temporal rulers on the one hand and church councils on the other. For this reason such insistence is found in the collection on the right of appeal to the pope in every major cause of a bishop and also that the pope's permission is necessary to the holding of a provincial synod. The sources from which the compiler chiefly borrowed his materials were the Bible, the fathers, genuine canons and decretals, Roman law, the works of Rufinus and Cassiodorus on church history and the lives of the popes in 'Liber Pontificalis.' Of the supposed decretals a large number are authentic although antedated and ascribed to earlier popes to give them the value of antiquity, while others embody the traditional contents of actual but lost decretals. The influence of the pseudo-Isadorian collection has been much exaggerated for it wrought no material change either in the faith or the discipline of the church, since it merely put into enactments the prevailing ideas and doctrines of that period on church government. Had it introduced a violent change the innovation would have caused a speedy inquiry into the genuineness of the work. However, it cannot be doubted that a written text often in controversy is a more forcible argument than traditional law, and hence the false decretals naturally exerted some influence.

To meet the necessity of rendering canon law more accessible from the 10th to the 12th century at least 36 compilations were made, only the authors, titles and dates of which seem necessary for this article. The first was a manuscript under twelve heads, divided into 354 chapters, abstracted from Cresconius. The second was extracted from Dionysius and the pseudo-Isadore collection. The third is very voluminous, and taken from Hadrian's codex with numerous additions. The fourth, by an unknown author, contains portions of concilia, decretals, and extracts from the Fathers. The fifth, made by Regino, abbott of Prum, between 906 and 915, is founded on three Frankist collections, the Fathers and the West Gothic Breviary. The sixth is a Leipsic codex; the seventh a Darmstadt codex. The eighth is attributed to Rotger, Bishop of Treves in 922. The ninth is a Viennese manuscript. The tenth is also a manuscript of five books, composed in Italy in the middle of the 10th century, and is founded upon the Irish collection in 65 titles, on fragments of the Fathers, lives of the saints, decretals, Julian's 'Novellae,' with capitularies of the emperors added up to Henry I. The eleventh was addressed by Abbo, abbot of Fleury, to King Hugo and his son Robert, and consists of a treatise of 52 chapters on the church and clergy. The twelfth was composed by Burchard, bishop of Worms, in 1012–23, and contains the canons of the apostles, the transmarine, German, Gallic and Spanish councils, papal decrees, and other passages. The 13th is a manuscript in 12 books made in Germany or France. The 14th is a Terraconian manuscript belonging to the 11th century. The 15th is an introduction to discipline. The 16th is a collection taken chiefly from Halitgar, Rasbanu, Maurus and Burchard. The 17th is a rich collection in manuscript by Anselm, bishop of Lucca in 1086. The 18th is 74 titles taken from the above work, and the 19th and 20th appeared about the end of the 11th century, both taken from the works of Anselm and Burchard. The 21st is a work in 13 books. The 22d is the capitularies of Cardinal Atto in 1081 and excerpts from decretals. Cardinal Deusdedit composed the 23d in 4 books, at the end of the 11th century, from Dionysius, the Greek canons, the old Italian and Spanish-Saxon and Roman records. The 24th is by Bourgo, bishop of Satrim in 1089, and is in 10 books. The 25th is in two books and belongs to the 11th or the 12th century. The first chapter is inscribed from the Primate of the Roman church and is published with the Dionysian collection. The 26th is the decree attributed to Ivo, bishop of Chartres, and the 27th is the Pannormia in eight parts by the same author in 1090. The 28th is a large manuscript collection; first of decretals, second of councils, third of fathers, then Roman and Frank legal collections. The 29th was made under Pascal II. in 1102–18 in seven books. The 30th is attributed to Hildebert, bishop of Tours, in 1134, and may be the same as the ten books attributed to Ivo. The 31st is a manuscript in 15 books called the collection of Saragossa. The 32d is wholly extracted from the above. The 33d is taken from Burchard and Ivo. The 34th is a penitential book in nine titles belonging to the 12th century. The 35th belongs to the middle of the 12th century and is taken chiefly from Anselm of Lucca and the collection dedicated to Anselmus. Gregory, a Spanish priest, is the author. Lastly, Algerius of Liege in the

beginning of the 12th century compiled a work on 'Justice and Mercy,' which contains a treatise on church discipline in three parts, taken from Anselm and Burchard for the most part. Gratian, a Benedictine monk, composed at Bologna in the middle of the 12th century a scientific and practical work on the canon law with references and proofs. The first part treated of ecclesiastical administration, the second contained 26 legal positions, with their answers, the third part concerned the liturgy of the church. The whole work is founded on previous collections and contains many mistakes. It was never approved by the church though it obtained great authority and superseded all other collections. Other collections are by Cardinal Laborans in 1182, that of Bernard of Pavia in 1190, that by Gilbert, an Englishman, in 1203. The universities of Bologna and Paris at an early period began to exercise great influence on canon law and their opinion in controverted questions was considered decisive, and was termed the authority of the schools. Gratian's collection was made the basis of lectures in Bologna and teachers of the canons were called *magistri* and *doctores decretorum*. Their teachings were soon gathered together in books of commentaries. Soon after the collection by Gratian, the Extravagantes, or decrees not yet collected, were gathered together, there being between the years 1179 and 1227 14 different compilations, only five of which received the stamp of authority. Pope Gregory IX. ordered a code to be published in which the entire body of law should be properly arranged. What was useless should be cut out, what was ambiguous should be corrected. Raymond of Pennafort was intrusted with this task, which he finished in the year 1233, and the collection was sent to the universities of Bologna and Paris with instructions that it was to be the sole authority. The whole work is divided into five books. The first treats of ecclesiastical judicature and of prelates; the second of civil suits; the third of civil causes before the episcopal forum; the fourth of betrothals and marriage; the fifth of judicial proceedings in criminal matters and of punishments. To these five books was added by Pope Boniface VIII., in 1298, a sixth book of decretals. This was followed in 1334 by the Clementinæ or collection of decretals by Pope Clement V. The Extravagantes of John XXII. in 1334 and the Extravagantes Communes (73 decretals from Boniface VIII. to Sixtus V.) were gathered by authority and made part of the code or 'Corpus Juris Canonici.' Commentaries on the 'Corpus' were made by the doctors, and systematic works for the use of courts were published. In the 15th century legal literature seems confined to these efforts. But in the 16th century Pope Paul IV. confided to a congregation of cardinals, with canonists as consultors, the work of revising and correcting the 'Corpus Juris.' Gregory XIII. approved the work of the committee and an authentic edition was published in 1580, in which the glosses are retained, and on which all subsequent editions have been based. The corrections made by the commission are marked *"cor. Rom."* in the text. Two appendices were added, one the Institutiones Lancelotti, the other Septimus Decretalium, which contained the Extravagantes to Sixtus V. in 1590. Neither is of public authority, but both are very useful and recognized by scholastic approval. Since then the Bullarium Benedicti XIV., which contains the constitutions of that pope, has been made of public authority. There is also a collection of papal bulls, called Bullarium Magnum Romanum, made up in 14 volumes, which was published in 1744 and continued in 1840; but it is very imperfect and only a private collection. Anyone who desires to know canon law must learn the 'Corpus Juris,' even though to-day many parts have been changed by the councils of Trent and the Vatican and by new papal decrees. In the 'Corpus' itself the different portions stand as *lex prior* and *lex posterior*, so that in cases of contradiction the latest is preferred. With certain modifications the 'Corpus' still has the force of law in matters relating to ecclesiastical judicature, to divine worship, to doctrine and discipline. It is the code still followed in the schools and used in church courts, not only as the source of argument but also as the method of procedure in many cases. The 'Jus Novissimum' in canon law consists of laws published from the time the 'Corpus Juris' was closed, that is, since the Extravagantes were inserted down to the present day, and includes the decrees of the councils of Trent and the Vatican. Except the Bullarium of Benedict XIV., mentioned above, no authentic collection has been made of the various constitutions and laws made by the Roman pontiffs since the close of the 'Corpus.' Still every genuine decretal is part of the canon law. The same may be said of the decisions of certain congregations of cardinals which have the force of law, especially that of the Council which authoritatively interprets the decrees of the Council of Trent. So evident was the need of a revision of canon law that at the ecumenic Vatican Council, held in 1870, proposals were made by a number of bishops to have a committee appointed, consisting of the most eminent canonists, to revise the 'Corpus Juris' or rather prepare a new one, omitting whatever owing to changed times was no longer applicable. Nothing was done before the adjournment of that council, but Pope Pius X. by a *motu proprio* in the year 1904 appointed a special committee of cardinals, with a number of consultors, and a canonist from each nation, to thoroughly revise not only the 'Corpus Juris' but all the canon law of the church, that general for the world and that special to the various nations. He himself is president of the committee to which he assigned the following cardinals: Seraphin Vanutelli, Agliardi, Vincent Vanutelli, Satolli, Rampolla, Gotti, Ferrata, Cassetta, Mathieu, Gennari, Cavicchioni, Merry del Val, Steinhuber, Segna, Vives y Tuto, and Cavagnis. Archbishop Gasparri was appointed secretary. At least five years will be consumed in the work, and the code thus established will hereafter be the only authorized canon law of the Latin church.

It will have been noticed that canon law is not traceable to any original code, but is a development founded on the general moral rules laid down in the Scriptures and especially in the New Testament. Neither is the Roman civil law traceable to any code, but is a gathering of principles suggested by good reasoning for promoting the civil interests of its subjects. Compared to the Jewish law, the principle upon which Roman jurisprudence was founded was very different — the former treats

principally of criminal matters and is most severe in its penalties; the latter on the contrary, treats all questions as civil, and prefers restitution to punishment. When the Roman emperors had been converted to Christianity, in promoting its progress by special constitutions which then became part of the canon law, they necessarily gave to canon law much of the spirit of their civil law. Thus it happens that in the canon, as in the Roman civil law, there was little severity in criminal matters, and many cases which other peoples than the Romans treated as criminal were cognizable by a civil tribunal and an indemnification was effected by damages. Generally no crime was punished capitally, especially where no force or violence was employed. This spirit of leniency is manifest throughout canon law to the present day. During and after the 4th century wherever Roman power conquered the nations and wherever Christian missionaries converted the pagans canon law was introduced through the influence of the pope and the emperor. It permeated and modified the laws of the peoples of northern Europe, as well as those of England to a certain extent. With it necessarily came the principles of Roman civil law. The rules for the application of canon law were as follows: (1) In cases not contained in the civil law, or the rule for which was obscure, open to doubtful interpretation, or not expressly determined, if expressly and clearly resolved by the canon law, this latter formed the basis of the decision; and on the contrary, if the case was not provided for, or ambiguously resolved by canon law, when it was expressly met or its solution more clearly indicated by the civil law, this latter was to be preferred. (2) In cases of conflict, the civil law formed the rule for courts of civil, and the canon in those of ecclesiastical jurisdiction. Thus, when a matter of canon law cognizance arose in the civil courts the decision was given according to the rules of the canon law; and *vice versa*, when a question of civil cognizance occurred before an ecclesiastical tribunal. (3) Within the imperial states the civil law formed the basis, and the canon law in the papal states. (4) In matters of a feudal nature the civil was preferred to the canon law. (5) In forensic causes the canon is not presumed to differ from the civil law. When the Western empire passed under the rule of a barbarian race the Roman and the canon law were not only preserved, but to a great extent they influenced the legislation of the conquerors. Alaric, Attila, Ricimir did not disturb the outward form of Roman government. In the collection of west Gothic laws, gathered in 672 A.D., there are evident traces of the part which the Roman clergy took in the compilation. The Burgundian laws also show literal excerpts from the Roman law. Roman law is found also in the Bavarian code composed in the 7th century, as well as in the capitularies of the Franks, which commence in the year 560 and are introduced by a literal transcript of a novel of Valentinian. It is noteworthy that the German tribes did not force their laws upon their subjects in those portions of their conquests where the Roman law was acknowledged. It was natural, too, that the churches, as juristical persons, should follow the Roman law, not only on account of its connection with religion and the great degree of favor it manifested toward the Church, but also of the accuracy of its provisions in this respect. Like the law of the Teutonic tribes, that of England is an accumulation of individual laws. While Britain was conquered by Julius Cæsar in 54 B.C., still it was only at the end of the 1st century of the Christian era that Roman manners, arts, architecture, language, and laws were introduced. The Roman law superseded the customary laws of the island and remained in force until the year 455, when Britain became derelict because of the removal of the seat of empire to Constantinople and the impossibility of the emperors defending it against the Picts and Scots. Christianity was introduced into Britain under the Roman dominion and was preached in Scotland and Ireland before the year 430. Roman literature, arts, and law, however, received a sudden check by the Saxons, who, when they invaded Britain, imposed their law upon the conquered people. The Danes subsequently did the same. Still we are informed by the Venerable Bede that Ethelbert, king of Kent, in 613, with the assistance of his wise men, made certain decrees and gave judgments between his subjects in conformity with the principles of Roman and canon law, at least so far as regarded sacrilege, bishops, and the like. Indeed, it is not surprising that the Saxons and Danes, whose codes contained a great admixture of Roman law, should carry the same principles with them into their new settlement in England. Traces of a Roman original may be seen in the laws of Ina, king of the West Saxons, Offa, king of the East Angles, and in the laws published by Canute which were translated into Latin. Thus it happened that, when Edward the Confessor compiled a code out of the materials then at hand, much of the Roman and canon law was inserted and thus became the basis of much of the common law of England and the United States. During the dominion of the Saxons and Danes, those Britons who had fled to Wales were governed by their own princes. Howel Dha, in 940, is said to have assembled his bishops and the more literate among the laity for the purpose of revising the law which was translated into Latin at his command. In the 85th article he approves the Roman rule of two witnesses being sufficient in cases where no specific number is stated, and for holding the testimony of one to be insufficient, except of a woman in cases of rape, of a lord between two tenants, an abbot between two monks, a father between two of his children, a priest in a matter attested in his presence, and a thief turning king's evidence in the place of execution. Most of the Roman laws of this age seem to have been taken from the Theodosian code. Although the foot of the Roman soldier never trod on the bosom of Ireland, nor did a Roman general have a chance to introduce the Roman law, still the principles of canon law were enforced throughout Ireland and Scotland by Saint Patrick in his canons. One of them, translated by the Anglican Bishop Usher, reads: "Wherever any cause that is very difficult and unknown to all the judges of the Scottish nation shall arise, it is rightly to be referred to the see of the archbishop of the Irish (that is, of Saint Patrick) and to the examination of the prelate thereof. But if there, by him and his wise men, a cause of this nature cannot easily be made up, we have decreed it shall be sent to the see Apostolic, that

is, to the chair of the Apostle Peter, which hath authority of the city of Rome." In 680, at the command of Ethelred, Egfrid, king of Northumberland, Aldwulf, king of the East Angles, and Lother, king of Kent, Theodore, at that time archbishop of Canterbury, summoned a synod at Hatfield, in which the canons of the five general councils of Nicæa, Constantinople, Ephesus, Chalcedon, the second of Constantinople, were enforced, together with the Concilia drawn up under Pope Martin at Rome in 648. He also collected in his capitularies the most important points of church discipline. Later he wrote his 'Book of Penances.' In the latter half of the 8th century, Egbert of York made an extensive collection of canon law from the sources then existing. He also wrote the book 'De Remediis Peccatorum.' In the 8th century a collection was made in Ireland in which the Dionysian collection and Roman, Gallic, and Irish councils are used. King Henry I., in 1100, endeavored to repudiate a number of church laws and ordered that Peter's Pence was to be paid to the king instead of the Pope. Henry II. entered into a controversy over the enforcement of canon law with Thomas à Becket. In 1215, by the Magna Charta, King John confirmed to the prelates and barons of his kingdom the freedom of election of the clergy, and this acted as a general acknowledgment of ecclesiastical rights and liberties. In 1230, Otho, the legate of Pope Gregory IX., held a national synod, and in 1268 Othobon, the legate of Pope Clement IV., held a second, both of which, as Blackstone says, had a great effect on the ecclesiastical jurisprudence of England. Under King Henry III., Boniface, archbishop of Canterbury, enacted several canons which seemed against the existing laws of the realm, and under Stephen an ecclesiastical and a secular party were formed, the latter adhering to the common law as tenaciously as the clergy and nobility did to the canon and civil law. In the parliament of Merton, however, the adherents of the canon and civil law were defeated on the proposition to make *legitimatio per subsequens matrimonium* legal also in England as it was under canon and civil law. Under Richard II., more than 100 years later, the feud still existed. Anglo-canon law was further augmented by the decrees of provincial councils held under the archbishops of Canterbury, from Stephen Langton to Henry Chichiley, which were glossed by William Lindwood, and later enforced also by the archbishops of York. The kings meantime had also enacted many statutes on the relations between secular and ecclesiastical jurisdiction. A statute of Henry VIII. rendered void all canons which were contrary to the law of the realm or hurtful to the royal prerogatives, and provided a commission to revise them. Edward VI. renewed the commission, but the code was not confirmed before his death. Mary repealed all these acts, but Elizabeth revived the first act of Henry VIII. In 1603 some canons were made in the convocation of the province of Canterbury and confirmed by the king but not by Parliament. It is held that, therefore, these bind the clergy in church matters, but not the laity, except in so far as not repugnant to the laws of the realm. By acts of Parliament (26 Henry VIII., 1; 35 Henry VIII., 3: 1 Elizabeth, 1) the king was declared the supreme head of the Church, and it became treason (1 Ed. VI., 12; 5 Eliz., 1) to doubt it or to defend the supremacy of the Pope as head of the Church. These acts and subsequent ones reversed canon law in England, Ireland, and Scotland. Speaking of the courts of the archbishops and bishops of the English Church to-day, Blackstone says: "An appeal lies from all these courts to the sovereign in the last resort, which proves that the jurisdiction exercised in them is derived from the crown of England. . . . It appears beyond a doubt that the civil and canon laws, though admitted in some cases by custom in some courts, are only subordinate and *leges sub graviori lege.* They are by no means with us a distinct, independent species of law, but are inferior branches of the customary or unwritten laws of England." In Scotland many of the provisions of canon law became the law of the land. During the 16th and 17th centuries canon law was taught in the Scottish universities, and from very early times many of the youths of Scotland attended the schools of the Continent, whence not a few returned as doctors *in utroque jure,* that is, canon and civil law. The canons of provincial councils, held yearly, and at whose meetings representatives of the king were present, constituted a national canon law which was recognized by the Pope and by Parliament and enforced in the courts of law. Even to this day, though the ecclesiastical system of the country is Presbyterian, the old canon law still prevails to a certain extent. "So deep hath this canon law been rooted," says Lord Stair in his 'Institutes of the Law of Scotland,' "that even where the Pope's authority is rejected yet consideration must be had to these laws, not only as those by which the Church benefices have been erected and ordered, but as likewise containing many equitable and profitable laws which, because of their weighty matter and their once being received, may more fitly be retained than rejected." In two old acts of the Scotch Parliament, made in 1540 and 1551, the canon and Roman law are mentioned as the common law of the country, the clause used being "the common law, baith canon, civil and statutes of the realme." Since the restoration of the Catholic hierarchy in England in 1850, and in Scotland in 1878, the churches under Roman jurisdiction have held various councils and enacted laws to fit the changed conditions. These laws, having been examined by the committee of cardinals in Rome appointed for such purpose, have become, as it were, a national canon law for the Catholics of those countries. In a similar way the Catholics of newly established nations, owing to various reasons, are ruled by a modified canon law which gives the bishops and superiors a very extensive authority. Such is the case at present in Canada, Australia, and the United States. These modifications pertain chiefly to the election of bishops, the appointment and removal of parish clergy, the tenure and administration of church property. The second and third plenary councils of Baltimore contain special modifications for the United States. For Canada a preparatory meeting for a plenary council was held in 1903 under the presidency of the apostolic delegate. For Mexico, West Indies, and South America a council was held in Rome of the bishops of those countries, and its decrees were published

Vol. 3—45.

in 1901. Other national modifications of canon law in the course of time have been introduced by concordats made by the Pope with the rulers of Christian nations by which he grants them certain concessions. As a nation Spain enjoys the greatest concessions, France up to the present coming next. The councils held in Gaul in the 4th and following centuries show the beginning of a national canon law for France. The fourth canon of the Council of Arles, convoked by King Clovis in 511, prohibited certain laymen and teachers from receiving holy orders without the king's consent. The Council of Orleans, in 549, shows that at that time the king's consent was necessary for the election of bishops. Many points regarding a special liturgy, the administration of the sacraments, the matter and forms of ecclesiastical trials are to be found in these same early councils. The laws of Dagobert, in 620, show special protection given the Church but also lay the foundation for future subjection; for councils could not be held without consent of the king, and bishops were elected not unfrequently at the dictation of royalty. But the capitularies of Charlemagne and his successors, collected in 825 by the abbot Ansegiso, were very favorable to the Church. Under the third dynasty, especially because of the feudal law, bishops, abbots, and chapters exercised almost complete civil authority over the people in their charge; but the oath of fealty was imposed on the prelates as vassals of the king. On the other hand, the kings took upon themselves the defense and guardianship of the Church, and on the pretext that at the death of the prelate they were the guardians of the vacant see, they performed many acts of ecclesiastical jurisdiction, among which was the administration of the temporalities of the vacant church. This was not done, however, without the assent of the sovereign pontiffs. Herein is found the origin of *jus Regaliæ* which later caused such trouble. In the year 1268 a pragmatic sanction was issued by Saint Louis which gave liberty of election of bishops and ordered that the general canon law should be observed throughout France. However, the genuineness of this law has been seriously questioned. Under Philip the Fair the seeds of absolute independence of the secular from the spiritual authority were sown; and about the same time serious contests arose between clerical and lay judges concerning their jurisdiction. On appeal to the king the clergy won; but the jurisdiction of the Church was gradually lessened, and at this time the appeal "as from abuse" was introduced, that is, a clergyman might appeal to the king from an abuse of the power exercised by a bishop. This was diametrically opposed to general canon law. The great schism of the West brought out the question whether the Pope or an ecumenical council was superior, and the controversy became especially bitter in France. Charles VII. selected certain passages from the Conciliabule of Basle, and in 1438 issued a pragmatic sanction in which the superiority of the council over the pope was declared, and elections both to episcopal sees and in monasteries were to be held after the ancient law of France. Louis XI. suppressed this decree, but it was revived after his death until finally condemned by the Fifth Lateran Council, and changed by

CANON LAW

the concordat made between Leo X. and Francis I. In this concordat many of the dispositions of the pragmatic were preserved; but the concordat differed from the pragmatic in this: that in place of the election of bishops and prelates in case of vacancy the king was given the right to present to the sovereign pontiff, within six months, a doctor or licentiate in theology who should be at least 27 years of age and otherwise competent. The pontiff would grant institution. The parliament, after a long contest, agreed to the execution of this concordat. Herein is seen the beginning of the system of government nomination of bishops, concerning which, in 1903–4, the Pope and the French government were at variance. In the 16th century the government long opposed the publication of the decrees of the Council of Trent, but finally, without mentioning the source, the chief decrees, word for word, were published in 1579 by royal order. In 1681 the Gallican clergy, at the instance of the government, met in extraordinary convention and adopted a declaration favoring the extension of the *Regalia* to all France. This was repudiated by Pope Innocent XI. The next year the Gallican clergy adopted four propositions in which they attacked the Holy See in administrating temporal matters, and declared that the judgment of the Pope on a matter of faith was not irreformable except when the consent of the Church had been added. The king ordered the observance of this declaration, but it was condemned by Alexander VIII. Later, King Louis XIV. wrote the Pope that he had ordered that the decree should not be observed. Nevertheless, the *Regalia* was observed up to 1789 throughout all France, and the government continued taking the revenues of all vacant bishoprics and appointing to benefices during the interregnum. In an edict of 1695 a code of ecclesiastical law as observed in France was enacted, and in it was the appeal "as from an abuse," that is, from the ecclesiastical to the civil authorities. The national convention in 1790 passed a civil constitution for the clergy by which dioceses and parishes were suppressed and the Church made subject to the state. In 1801 Napoleon, as first consul, and Pope Pius VII. made a concordat in which the Catholic Church was acknowledged as the state Church, and by which new limits were assigned to dioceses and parishes, and by which especially the right of nominating bishops was given to the ruler of France. To the nominees the Pope would grant institution. Various other regulations were made, and the French government took upon itself the support of the bishops and parish priests in place of restoring the immense church properties which had been confiscated. During the year 1904 a great agitation occurred for the suppression of this concordat because of controversies over some bishops held delinquent and suspended by the Pope. With the abrogation of the concordat the state will not longer support the clergy, nor can it nominate to bishoprics. During the 19th century the liturgical worship of the Church in France was made conformable to that of Rome, and other matters of discipline were brought under general canon law.

Undoubtedly canon law has exerted a wide and lasting influence on the nations of Europe and America. It made them Christian states and directly or indirectly modified their constitutions. State legislative assemblies based their proceedings on the methods of Church councils. The law of nations is simply the application to nations of the principles of Christian law taught to individuals. The ancient Romans as well as barbarous tribes considered all foreigners enemies; the Church taught the brotherhood of all men. The Pope, as the common father of all Christians, acted as arbitrator in the disputes between nations, and so noteworthy became the Roman Rota, to which the Pope referred international disputes, that at times much of its work was deciding important questions for rulers of nations. The system of Church administration served as a model for that of states, and the clergy, especially in the earlier and Middle Ages, being the educated class and following canon law, naturally introduced many of its rules into everyday life. The elevated condition of woman is due to the canon law prescriptions regarding marriage, which the Church enforced on all nations converted to Christianity. Questions relating to widows and orphans were within the jurisdiction of canon law and Church courts. The incorporation of Church bodies, from which other corporations took their origin, had its foundation in the law of Justinian and was imported into England with the civil and canon law. As in the Roman law, the charter of the sovereign is always expressed, or at least implied. From England the idea of corporation and corporation sole came into American law. The writ of habeas corpus had its origin in the Roman law *"interdictum de libero homine exhibendo."* Inheritance by will and the rule for the descent of real property came from Roman law, while trial by jury, with challenges of the jurymen, was determined in the Roman Lex Servilia and Lex Cornelia. While in England "Christianity is part of the law of the land," in the United States this "is true only in a qualified sense" (33 Barber 548), and wholly only to "the fact that it is a Christian country and that its constitution and laws are made by a Christian people" (23 Ohio St. 211). Nevertheless "the decision of ecclesiastical courts or officers having, by the rules or laws of the bodies to which they belong, jurisdiction of such questions, or the right to decide them, will be held conclusive in all courts of civil administration, and no question involved in such decisions will be revised or reviewed in the civil courts, except those pertaining to the jurisdiction of such courts or officers to determine such questions according to the laws or usage of the bodies which they represent." (Quoted with approval in 98 Penn. 213.) "Civil courts will not review the action of ecclesiastical tribunals except where rights of property are involved" (62 Iowa 567; 23 Ill. 456). Justice Strong, in 'Relations of Civil Law to Church Policy,' concludes: "I think it may be safely asserted, as a general proposition, that whenever questions of discipline, of faith, of church rule, of membership, or of office have been decided by the Church in its own modes of decision, civil law tribunals accept the decisions as final and apply them as made." See also Law; Catholic Church, Roman.   P. A. Baart, S.T.L., LL.D., *Author of 'Church and State in the United States of America,' 'The Roman Court,' 'Legal Formulary,' 'Tenure of Church Property in the United States.' etc.*

Canon of the Mass, that part of the mass following the sanctus. The rule of the Roman Catholic Church for celebrating the Eucharist is contained in this canon.

Canon of Scripture. See CANON; BIBLE.

Can'oness. At the close of the 8th century the title of canoness was given to a class of women who took the vows of chastity and obedience, but not that of poverty, and were not cloistered, though they had a common table and dormitory, and were bound to the recitation of the breviary, as were nuns. They derived their name from their being enrolled in the canon or official list of the church. Their occupations were chiefly education of girls, transcription and embellishment of church office-books, and embroidery of vestments. The advantages of such institutions as asylums in a rough age were soon visible, and they multiplied in consequence, but as in many houses the religious motive had little to do 'with entrance, a distinction was drawn ere long between canonesses regular and secular. The secular canonesses were for the most part members of princely or noble families, practised much state and luxury, and retained none of the rule save the common dormitory and the recitation of the Hours in choir. In Germany, several abbesses of canonesses were princesses of the empire, kept up feudal state, and furnished contingents to the imperial army from their vassals; and at the Reformation some chapters adopted the new opinions, and subsist to the present day as Protestant foundations, enjoying the revenues, and admitting to membership only ladies of noble birth or daughters of distinguished members of the military and civil services, whose sole obligation is celibacy during membership. The institute never spread beyond the limits of the empire, and the non-German houses were chiefly in Hainault, Flanders, and Lorraine.

Can'ongate, The, the principal street in the Old Town of Edinburgh. It is upward of one mile in length, rising gradually with a regular and steep incline from a small plain at the east end of the town, on which stands the palace of Holyrood, and terminating at the castle. The appearance of this street, the scene of many interesting historical incidents, is rendered remarkable by the loftiness and antique aspect of the houses with which it is lined, most of them ranging from five to seven stories in front, and often more behind. At different points it is known by other names, High Street, Lawnmarket, etc.

Canon'ical Books, the books of Scripture belonging to the canon. See CANON: BIBLE.

Canonical Hours, certain times of the day set apart by ecclesiastical law in the Roman Catholic Church to the offices of prayer and devotion, namely, matins with lauds, prime, tierce, sext, nones, even-song or vespers, and compline. The day was divided into seven parts and the observance of the canonical hours was as follows: prime, tierce, sext and nones at the first, third, sixth and ninth hours of the day, counting from six in the morning; vespers at the eleventh hour, compline at midnight and matins shortly after midnight. These times are no longer strictly adhered to. In England the canonical hours are from eight to twelve in the forenoon, before or after which the marriage service cannot be legally performed in any parish church.

Canonicals, the prescribed dress or vestments worn by the clergy of the Roman Catholic, Protestant Episcopal, and other churches when officiating at religious services. The wearing of vestments is of ancient origin. In all the pagan religions the priests wear symbolic garments, and in the Jewish system the priestly robes were very elaborate and significant. The modern Jewish system retains these ecclesiastical vestments and the ministers of many Protestant denominations wear such attire. See CHASUBLE; STOLE, etc.

Canon'icus, Indian chief: b. about 1565; d. 4 June 1647. When the Pilgrims landed, he and his nephew Miantonomo (q.v.) were associate sachems of the fierce Narragansetts, mustering some 3,000 warriors. In the winter of 1621-2 he sent to the little colony, with about 50 fighting men, a bundle of arrows bound with a snakeskin, either as a preliminary of war or a demand of gifts to avert it. They returned the skin stuffed with powder and ball, and the frightened savages did not dare keep it, but saw that it got back to the colony. A lasting treaty was negotiated, and it was partly owing to the influence of Canonicus that the tribe never made war against the English, even many years after his death, till "King Philip's War" of 1675. In 1636 the septuagenarian chief was succeeded as head sachem by Miantonomo, but still retained the prestige of age and experience. In that year Roger Williams and his company, who had first sought refuge from the Massachusetts authorities among the Pokanokets, thought it best to go farther, and applied to the Narragansetts. They were kindly received, and to them was granted the peninsula where Providence stands. According to Williams, Canonicus was always most friendly and helpful till his death. In 1637 the Pequots of Connecticut were attempting to form a general Indian league to exterminate the English settlements. and the Massachusetts government sent an embassy to prevent the Narragansetts from joining it. Canonicus received them with great Indian pomp in his wigwam of poles and mats, surrounded by his "mugwumps" and leading warriors, gave them a feast with boiled chestnuts and huckleberry Indian pudding for dessert; and probably more from kind regard for Williams than through the embassy's persuasions — kept the peace, and even furnished a couple of hundred warriors to help the English. These allies, however, played the usual ambiguous Indian part, ready to massacre the beaten side. In 1644 the Gorton (q.v.) party succeeded in persuading the chiefs that it was under the protection of irresistible powers in England; and on 9 April Canonicus, his son Mixan, and his nephew Pessacus, brother and successor of Miantonimo, signed two astonishing documents, of whose purport it is very unlikely that they had been correctly informed. One of them ceded the land and people of the Narragansetts to his Majesty of Great Britain, placing the Indians themselves under his protection, and appointing Gorton and three others their attorneys to carry the instrument to him. The other, addressed to the Massachusetts authorities, was the refusal of their invitation to visit Boston. It also menaced the authorities on account of Miantonimo's death, and threatened to revenge it on Uncas. Finally, however, a truce was signed, and three years later Canonicus died.

Canonization, a rite in the Roman Catholic Church by which a deceased person is inscribed in the catalogue of the saints and by which it is publicly, solemnly and canonically declared that such person is to be honored as a Saint by all the faithful.

The desire to honor the dead is an instinct of human nature. The state picks out its great ones for civil honors; the Church holds up to the veneration of its members those who by the sanctity of their lives and their love of God and their fellow-men merit imitation.

The state honors its heroes on account of intellectual ability, oratorical gifts, courage, or patriotism; the Church demands purity of life and eminent virtue in her spiritual heroes. As a proof of that virtue she requires miracles wrought by or through their intercession. The virtues, which must be heroic, and the miracles are proved by a process most minute and searching.

During the early centuries the deeds of the martyrs were recorded by Christian notaries. For this purpose Pope Clement divided the city of Rome into seven quarters with a special notary for each quarter. The letters of Saints Cyprian, Jerome, Augustine, and Epiphanius, tell us of the efforts of the bishops to collect the deeds of the martyrs and to have them venerated.

In the early times individual bishops sifted the testimony regarding those brought to their notice as worthy of veneration and declared for or against it. But this gave rise to inconveniences and the necessity of a central authority for judging in such cases was made manifest.

As early as the 4th century the case of Saint Vigilius, bishop of Trent, who was martyred A.D. 399, was brought to Rome to secure the consent of the Pope for his veneration as a Saint.

Gradually the procedure in these matters was elaborated and in 1587 the Congregation of Rites was charged with the duty of investigating the causes of Beatification and Canonization.

Beatification precedes Canonization, and is a decree which permits the honoring of a servant of God by public worship in a certain place. It differs therefore from Canonization in that the latter not only concedes but *declares* that veneration be paid by the universal Church to the canonized one whilst Beatification *permits* only in a certain place the honoring of the beatified.

The process by which Beatification is reached is a lengthy one. "The fierce light which beats upon a throne" is nothing to the minute and protracted inquiry which turns upon the every-day life of the person submitted to it.

Thirteen or fourteen steps may be distinguished in the process of Beatification. The bishop of the diocese first inquires as to the reputation of the person proposed for virtue and miraculous powers. Then the question of *"non-cultus"* is examined; namely whether any veneration was paid to the servant of God or whether anything was done contrary to the decrees of Urban VIII. which prescribe the form of Beatification and Canonization.

As a third step the minutes of these two inquiries are sent to Rome. The process is then opened before the Congregation of Rites. See CONGREGATIONS, ROMAN.

The Promoter Fidei (called in popular language the "devil's advocate") is appointed. His duty is to raise objections against the process and person. All the works printed or in manuscript, if the person were an author, are then examined. If a favorable report is made, then begins what is called the Apostolic Process. A commission is given to the Congregation of Rites to investigate the notoriety, reality and nature of the virtues and miracles ascribed to the one to be beatified.

Three bishops are appointed to deal with the case systematically. Their findings are sent to the Congregation of Rites and examined and arguments are heard pro and contra.

A new delegation makes another and more searching inquiry if the result of the last examination is favorable. The process is again returned to the Congregation of Rites to be again examined. In three successive meetings, at the last of which the Pope is present, the virtues and miracles of the subject for beatification are again discussed.

Having sought to know the will of God by prayer the Pope confides his judgment to the Secretary of the Congregation.

In a new general assembly the question is considered whether the Beatification may proceed without further delay. In the event of an affirmative decision the Pope appoints a day for the ceremony, and orders a brief to be prepared setting forth the Apostolic sentence.

The Beatification takes place in St. Peter's with ceremonies appropriate to the occasion. Proof of at least two miracles is necessary in the case of Beatification, and before proceeding to Canonization it must be proven that at least two more miracles were wrought through the intercession of the "Blessed" person.

So strict is the examination of these miracles, that according to an Italian proverb, "It is next to a miracle to get a miracle proved in Rome." To prove the truth of miracles worked after Beatification, the same formality and rigorous conditions are required as are necessary in the case of miracles before Beatification.

The three congregations or assemblies which were required before Beatification are again convoked and after mature deliberation if everything is favorable to the Cause, declare for it. A decree is drawn up by the direction of the Pope expressing that decision. Canonization then takes place in St. Peter's.

Most solemn ceremonies mark the event and never does the venerable Basilica with its thousands of worshipers look so grand and inspiring as when the Pope declares and ordains that the servant of God in question shall be inscribed in the register of the Saints ("Canon Sanctorum") and that his (or her) memory shall be celebrated on a given day in every Church.

Consult the celebrated treatise of Pope Benedict XIV. 'De Servorum Dei Beatificatione et Beatorum Canonizatione' (1734-8), the standard work on the subject; a portion of it has been translated under the title 'Heroic Virtue' (3 vols., 1856); also Addis and Arnold, 'The Catholic Dictionary' (1893); Aichner. 'Compendium Juris Ecclesiastici' (1900); Baart, 'The Roman Court'; Bargilliat, 'Prælectiones Juris Canonici,' Vol. I, p. 344-5 (1903); Bouix, 'Tractatus de curia Romana,' 180 p. 183 (1880).

DAVID J. O'HEARN,
Saint John's Cathedral, Milwaukee, Wis.

Canons, Book of, a system of canons or rules prepared for the Church of Scotland by its bishops, in accordance with the direction of Charles I. It was published in 1636, having undergone revision at the hands of Archbishop Laud. In Scotland its promulgation was felt to be arbitrary, and the strongest objections were made against it.

Canons of the Church of England, the "constitutions and canons ecclesiastical" drawn up in convocation in 1604 by the synod in London. These canons, still in force as revised, number 141, and were designed to confirm the established system of the Church of England, particularly through the test oath, aimed at the Puritan party, in which the clergy were sworn to subscribe willingly to the supremacy of the sovereign, to the Articles, and to the Prayer-book.

Canons of Hippolytus, The, a book divided into 38 canons, believed to have been written by Hippolytus, archbishop of Rome, about the middle of the third century. It contains instructions in regard to the selection and ordination of Christian ministers, conversion and baptism of the heathen, rules for the celebration of the Eucharist, for fasting, etc. The book originally was made from a Coptic version of the Greek but has been handed down only in Arabic. It first attracted attention in the 17th century, was published in 1870 by Haneberg, who added a Latin translation, and was revised by Achelis in 1891. A German translation was made by Riedel in 1900 from new manuscript, which showed that the book had been previously thrown into disorder by the displacement of two pages, and which also removed other difficulties upon which the theory of interpolation was based. There has been much controversy about the authorship of the book and as to whether the canons were the original form from which the Egyptian Church Order was derived, but all documents, as well as the general style of writing, point to Hippolytus as the author.

Cano'pic Vases, or **Cano'pi,** certain large-bellied vessels found in tombs in Egypt, containing the embalmed intestines of bodies that had been converted into mummies. Four of these were placed in a tomb, each appropriated to a particular deity, and surmounted by the effigy of the head of such deity, as of a man, an ape, a jackal, or a hawk. It is to those with the human head that the term canopi has been more particularly applied. They were frequently made of basalt, and decorated with figures in relievo or paintings; or of costly white alabaster, with spiral flutings; or they were formed from black burned clay. The name is derived from the town Canopus.

Canoppi, Antonio, än-tõ'nē-ō kä-nō'pē, Italian scene-painter: b. 1773; d. St. Petersburg, 1832. He received his first education from his father, who was employed as civil engineer by the Duke of Modena, and after occupying himself for some time with fresco-painting, was subsequently employed as scene-painter in Venice and Mantua. Compelled to resort to flight at the time of the French invasion, he first betook himself to Vienna and afterward to Moscow, where he was engaged in the decoration of many palaces, which, however, were burnt in the great fire of 1812. From that time until his death he was engaged as scene-painter of the imperial theatre of St. Petersburg. His most admired efforts in that branch of art were his architectural scenes for Mozart's 'Magic Flute,' and for 'Semiramis.'

Cano'pus, or **Cano'bus,** a bright star of the first magnitude, belonging to the southern constellation Argo, and invisible in the north or middle parts of the United States, on account of its nearness to the South Pole.

Cano'pus. 1. In Egyptian mythology, a water-god, represented on vessels of a spherical shape. These vessels were used by the ancient Egyptians to keep the water of the Nile in good drinking condition. The worship of Canopus was superseded under the first Ptolemy by that of Serapis — a Greek inscription in honor of Serapis at Canopus having been discovered by Mr. Hamilton amid the ruins of Alexandria. 2. In ancient geography, one of the most remarkable towns of lower Egypt, near the most western mouth of the Nile. The name of the town is variously ascribed to the divinity of the same name and to Canopus, or Canobus, the helmsman of Menelaus, who died in Egypt of the bite of a serpent, after his return from Troy, and who was buried on the site of the town. It was the seat of a temple of Serapis, whose oracle was celebrated, especially among the sick seeking for restoration to health. 3. In astronomy, the name of the brightest star, except Sirius. It is in the constellation Argo.

Can'opy, a net of very ancient use, as in Greece and Egypt, for protection against mosquitoes, gnats, etc.; hence any net or hanging placed over a bed for like purpose; also such a hanging or a projection over a bed, a door, a window, an altar, a pulpit, throne, niche, tomb, or other architectural structure. Canopies are also borne over the heads of kings or other personages and over sacred objects in ceremonial processions.

Canosa (kä-nōs'sä) **Di Puglia,** Italy, a city in the province of Bari, 14 miles to the southwest of Barletta on the Adriatic. It was the ancient Canusium, and various relics of Roman times, including an amphitheatre, have been found. Between Barletta and Canosa was the ancient Cannæ (q.v.), where in 216 B.C. Hannibal defeated the Romans. Tombs cut in rock on a hill have been found in the neighborhood, and in 1813 a beautiful burial-chamber was opened, which contained the corpse of a warrior in armor. A copper lamp and a number of beautiful vases were also found here. The paintings upon the vases were the most important part of this discovery. They refer to the Greek-Italian mysteries. Pop. about 25,000.

Canossa, a ruined mountain castle of northern Italy, 12 miles southwest of Reggio. In the 11th century it belonged to Countess Matilda of Tuscany, with whom Pope Gregory VII. resided in 1077, when he imposed a severe penance upon the excommunicated Emperor Henry IV. (q.v.). The phrase "to go to Canossa" has come to be proverbial for some humiliating surrender, withdrawal, or the like.

Canot, kä-nŏ', Theodore, Italian adventurer and slave trader: b. Florence, 1807; d. 1850. His father was a captain and paymaster in the French army; his mother a native of Piedmont. He made his first voyage in 1819, in the American ship Galatea, of Boston, from Leghorn to Calcutta. He visited Boston, sailed to various parts of the world, was shipwrecked near Ostend, and again on the coast of Cuba, where he fell into the hands of a gang of pirates, one of whom claimed to be his uncle, befriended him for some time, and finally sent him to an Italian grocer at Regla, near Havana, who was secretly concerned in the African slave trade. Canot made his first voyage to Africa in 1826, landing at the slave factory of Bangalang, on the Rio Pongo, Senegambia. After quelling a mutiny on board and helping to stow away 108 slaves under 15 years of age, in a hole 22 inches high, the young adventurer entered the service of the owner of the factory. He soon became a favorite with the native chiefs, whose proposals of matrimonial alliance were exceedingly embarrassing. He visited various parts of the neighboring country, improving every opportunity to study the workings of the trade in which he had determined to engage, and collecting by the aid of the African princes a stock of slaves for his newly established depot at Kambia near Bangalang. In May 1828 his factory and goods were destroyed by fire. He afterward purchased a vessel at Sierra Leone, in which with a cargo of slaves wrested from a trader in the Rio Nunez, he sailed to Cuba. Three more expeditions soon followed; in the first he lost 300 slaves by smallpox; in the last he was taken by the French and condemned to 10 years' confinement in the prison of Brest, in France, but after a year's durance was pardoned by Louis Philippe. Resolved still to pursue his dangerous occupation, he returned to Africa, and was the pioneer of the slave traffic at New Sestros. After meeting with various adventures here in his expeditions among the surrounding tribes, we hear of him in 1839 on a pleasure trip to England. He returned to New Sestros and in 1840 shipped to Cuba 749 slaves. He now resolved to abandon his illicit course, and obtaining from an African chief a valuable grant of land at Cape Mount, established there in 1841 a trading and farming settlement under the name of New Florence. In March 1847 New Florence was destroyed by the British, who suspected it to be a slave station, and Canot subsequently removed to South America, where he engaged in legitimate commerce. He resided for some time in Baltimore, Md., and finally received from Napoleon III. an office in one of the French colonies in Oceanica. Consult Mayer, 'Captain Canot, or Twenty Years of an African Slaver' (1854).

Canova, Antonio, än-tō'nĕ-ō kä-nō'vä, Italian sculptor: b. Possagno, Venetia, 1 Nov. 1757; d. Venice, 13 Oct. 1822. Canova may be considered as the restorer of the graceful and lovely style, and the founder of a new school, as far as it respects softness and delicacy of execution, and excellent handling of the marble. He was sent as an apprentice to Bassano, where he acquired skill in the mechanical part of the art. His first work, executed in his 17th year, was an Eurydice in soft marble, of half the natural size. He was now sent to the Academy of Venice, where his proper study commenced. He gained several prizes, and excited expectations which he more than equalled in the sequel. The first work which he was commissioned to execute was the statue of the Marchese Poleni, of the natural size, for the city of Padua. In his 25th year he finished the group of Dædalus and Icarus, of the natural size, in Carrara marble, a remarkable juvenile work. The senate of Venice sent him, in 1779, to Rome, with a salary of 300 ducats. A group as large as life — 'Theseus Sitting upon the Slain Minotaur' — was the first large work by which Canova made himself known in Rome (1783). In 1783 he undertook the execution of the tomb of Pope Clement XIV., in the church Degli Apostoli. He retained the usual style of composition, and only improved on the depraved taste of the school of Bernini. He next executed the group of 'Cupid and Psyche,' where he first displayed his own peenliar style, of which loveliness is a striking characteristic. The figures are exceedingly delicate and graceful. He was employed on a second public monument, the tomb of Pope Clement XIII., in St. Peter's. It was finished in 1792, and is distinguished by its colossal size and simple style. Meanwhile the fame of the artist continually increased. He established in the palace of the Venetian ambassador a school for the benefit of young Venetians. His next works were a winged Cupid, standing; another group of 'Cupid and Psyche'; a group of 'Venus and Adonis' for the Marchese Verio, in Naples; the tomb of the Venetian Admiral Emo, for the Republic of Venice. This is a combination of bas-reliefs with figures in full relief. Canova also produced a very lovely 'Psyche,' standing, half-dressed, with a butterfly in her left hand, which she holds by the wings with her right, and contemplates, with a calm, smiling mien. A 'Repentant Magdalene,' of the natural size, belongs to the works in marble in which he has carried the expression of the melting and the soft to the highest degree. His 'Hebe' is a delightful figure. In an easy and animated attitude the smiling goddess of youth hovers upon a cloud, pouring nectar with her right hand into a bowl which she holds in her left. Both vessels, as well as the coronet of Hebe and the edges of her garment, are gilt. Canova is fond of a variety of material, and often endeavors to give to his statues the effect of pictures. He next displayed his talent for the tragical in the raging 'Hercules Hurling Lichas into the Sea.' The group is colossal, and Hercules somewhat larger than the Farnesian; but it makes a disagreeable impression, which proves that the genius of Canova was not adapted to such subjects. His representation of the two pugilists, 'Kreugas and Demoxenos,' is much more successful. A standing group of 'Cupid and Psyche' was the triumph of his art. Psyche here appears again holding the butterfly. In 1796 and 1797 Canova finished the model of the celebrated tomb of the Archduchess Christina of Austria, wife of Duke Albert of Saxe-Teschen, which in 1805 was placed in the church of the Augustines at Vienna. In 1797 he made the colossal model of a statue of the king of

Naples, one of his finest works. This statue, 15 palms high, was executed in marble in 1803. During the revolution of 1798 and 1799 Canova accompanied the senator prince, Rezzonico, on a journey through Germany. After his return he remained for some time in the Venetian territory, and painted for the church of his native village an altar-piece, in which are represented the dead Christ, the Maries, Nicodemus, and Joseph, and, on high, God the Father. He afterward executed in Rome his 'Perseus with the Head of Medusa,' which, when the Apollo of Belvidere was carried to France, occupied its place and pedestal. This statue increased the fame of Canova more than any of the preceding works. But Perseus is only an imitation of the Apollo. The separate parts are of exquisite beauty in form as well as in masterly, delicate finishing. In 1802 he was invited by Bonaparte to Paris to make the model of his colossal statue. In the beginning of 1803 the model of the emperor's bust, and afterward that of his statue, was to be seen in the workshop of the artist. There is not a more successful work of the kind than this bust: the figure of the statue is not so good. Among the later works of the artist are a Washington, of colossal size, in a sitting attitude; the tombs of the Cardinal of York and of Pius VII.; an imitation of the Medicean Venus; a 'Venus Rising from the Bath'; the colossal group of 'Theseus killing the Minotaur,' far surpassing his earlier works in the heroic style; the tomb of Alfieri, for the Countess of Stolberg, in Florence, and erected in that place (the 'Weeping Italia,' a colossal statue in marble, is particularly admired); the 'Graces Rising from the Bath'; the monument of the Marchioness of S. Croce; a 'Venus'; a 'Dancing Girl,' with almost transparent garments; a colossal 'Hector'; a 'Paris'; a 'Muse,' larger than the natural size; a model of a colossal 'Ajax'; and the model of a sitting statue, in rich robes, of the Archduchess Maria Louisa of Austria. After the second fall of Napoleon, in 1815, Canova was commissioned by the Pope to demand the restoration of the works of art carried from Rome; went from Paris to London, and returned to Rome in 1816, where Pius VII. inscribed his name in the golden book of the capitol, declared him "to have deserved well of the city of Rome," and made him Marquis of Ischia, with a pension of 3,000 scudi.

As a man Canova was active, open, mild, obliging, and kind toward everybody. His opinion of himself was very modest, notwithstanding his fame was spread through all Europe. He assisted promising young artists, and established prizes for the encouragement of the arts. When the Pope conferred upon him the title of Marquis of Ischia, with a pension, he dedicated the whole of the latter to the support and encouragement of poor and deserving artists. Canova was also an agreeable painter, but, strangely enough, more of a colorist than a correct designer. See lives of Canova by Ciognara (1823); Missirini, (1824); the biographies of Rosini (1825); D'Este (1864). Engraved representations of all his works have appeared in Italy and at Paris.

Canovaï, Stanislao, stän-ïs-lä'ō kä-nō-vä'ē, Italian ecclesiastic and historian: b. Florence, 27 March 1740; d. there, 17 Nov. 1811. Having

taken holy orders, he officiated afterward as professor of mathematics at Parma. In 1788, as a member of the academy of antiquities, he contended for the prize which was offered for an essay on Americus Vespucius. He opposed the common opinion that Columbus was the first discoverer of the new world, claiming that Vespucius one year before him had touched upon the northern part of the continent and had landed in Brazil. His paper gained the prize, but produced much discussion.

Canovas del Castillo, Antonio, än-tō'nē-ō kä'nō väs dĕl käs tēl'yō, Spanish statesman and man of letters: b. Malaga, 8 Feb. 1828; d. Santa Aquedo, 8 Aug. 1897. He was editor of the Conservative journal, 'Patria,' and in 1854 entered the public service as member of the Cortes; thereafter he held various posts in the government. At his death he had been for two years prime minister, and had held the same position three times previously. He is author of 'Literary Studies' (1868); 'History of the Austrian Dominion in Spain' (1869); 'Problems of the Time' (2 vols. 1884); 'Studies on the Reign of Philip IV.' (3 vols. 1888-90). He was editor-in-chief of a 'General History of Spain,' consisting of monographs by sundry writers (1890-7). He was assassinated at the baths of Santa Aqueda. See Pons y Humbert, 'Canovas del Castillo' (1901).

Canrobert, François Certain, fräṅ swä sĕr-täṅ käṅ-rō-bär, marshal of France: b. St. Cere in Lot, 27 June 1809; d. Paris, 28 Jan. 1895. He was educated in the military academy of St. Cyr, and in 1828 entered the army. He had seen nearly 20 years' brilliant service in Algeria, and had actively supported the future emperor at the coup d'état of 1851, when he received the rank of a general of division in 1853. As such he commanded the first division of the French army under Marshal St. Arnaud, sent to the Crimea in 1854; and at the battle of the Alma was wounded in the breast and hand by the splinter of a shell. On St. Arnaud's death, nine days later, Canrobert assumed the chief command of the French army. According to the historian Kinglake, he deliberately retarded the progress of operations, let slip many opportunities, and hampered the English — his object being to forward Napoleon's design of coming out to head a final and victorious campaign. In the war in Italy against the Austrians (1859) Canrobert had the command of the third division of the French army, and at the battles of Magenta and Solferino his corps d'armée was engaged. In the Franco-German war of 1870 he was shut up in Metz with Bazaine, and became a prisoner in Germany. He was an ardent Imperialist till the death of the Prince Imperial (1879). In 1876 he became a member of the Senate. See Martin, 'Le Maréchal Canrobert.'

Can'so, Gut or Strait of, a narrow strait or channel, about 17 miles long and 2½ miles in width, separating Nova Scotia from Cape Breton island. It is navigable by the largest ships, and its scenery is very beautiful.

Canstadt, kän'stät, the name given, from Cannstatt or Canstadt, Germany, to the dolichocephalic or long-headed man of the Quaternary age, whose existence was inferred from a piece of skull found near there in 1700.

Canstein, Karl Hildebrand von, kärl hĭl'-dĕ-bränt fôn kän'stĭn, German founder of a famous establishment for printing Bibles: b. Lindenberg, 1667; d. 1719. He studied at Frankfort-on-the-Öder, traveled much in Europe, went in 1688 to Berlin, where he was appointed page of the Elector of Brandenburg, and served as a volunteer in the Netherlands. A dangerous sickness obliged him to leave the military service. He went to Halle, where he became familiarly acquainted with Spener and Francke, and became eager to spread a knowledge of religion among the common people. He was especially anxious that the poor should have Bibles at as low rate as possible, and thus originated the famous institution, called the Canstein Bible Institution, which after the death of Canstein in 1719 became associated with the institutions founded by Francke, and still continues its benevolent operations.

Cant-timbers, in ship-building, those timbers which are situated at the ends of a ship. They derive their name from being *canted,* or raised obliquely from the keel, in contradistinction from those the planes of which are perpendicular to it.

Cantabile, kän-tä'bĭ-lä, in music, a term applied to movements intended to be performed in a graceful, elegant, and melodious style.

Cantabri, kän-tä'brē, the rudest and most valiant of all the Iberian tribes, who dwelt in the ancient Hispania Tarraconensis, and inhabited the greater part of what is now La Montana and the northwest part of the present province Burgos. In ancient history Cantabri is generally used to denote all the inhabitants of the northern mountains of Spain. Cantabria is the name which was given to the country they inhabited. Oceanus Cantabricus is the ancient name of the Bay of Biscay. Cantabrian Mountains is the general name of the various mountain ranges extending from the western Pyrenees along the north coast of Spain to Cape Finisterre. The highest of the ranges, the Sierra d'Aralar, attains an altitude of 7,032 feet. These mountains are imperfectly known, but in parts they are covered with magnificent forests, and from those of Santander the snow never entirely disappears.

Canta'bria. See CANTABRI.

Canta'brian Mountains, the general name of the various mountain ranges extending from the western Pyrenees along the north coast of Spain to Cape Finisterre. They attain in some parts a height of about 9,000 feet, and are rich in minerals, especially copper, lead, iron, and gold. Large forests of oak, chestnuts, and other trees are also found on their slopes.

Cantacuzenus, kän-tä-koo-zā'noos, **John,** Byzantine emperor and historian: b. about 1300; d. about 1383. While minister of Andronicus III. he negotiated a favorable peace with the Genoese in 1336, and repelled the encroachments of the Turks in 1337. On the death of Andronicus in 1341 Cantacuzenus became regent during the minority of the young emperor, John Palæologus. He defeated the Bulgarians and Turks, assumed the diadem, and entered Constantinople, victorious over his rivals, in 1346. He used his power with moderation, and endeavored to heal the wounds which five years of civil war had inflicted on the state; but religious disputes, civil dissensions, and foreign enemies soon disturbed his government; and the jealousy of Palæologus, the rebellion of his own son, war, plague, the frightful disorders which prevailed in the empire, and his own loss of popular favor, induced him to renounce the crown. He retired to a monastery (1355), where he employed himself in literary labors. He is considered one of the greatest among the successors of Constantine. His ‹Four Books of Byzantine History› were printed in 1645, and belong to the collection of the Byzantine historians. His other works, principally theological, are partly printed and partly in manuscript.

Cantal, kän täl, France, a central department, area, 2,217 square miles; capital, Aurillac. It is named from its highest mountain, the Plomb du Cantal, Mons Celtorum of the ancients, which rises to the height of 6,094 feet. The department is one of the poorest and least productive districts of France. The climate is rather severe near the mountains. Agriculture is in a backward state. The principal crops are rye, buckwheat, potatoes, and chestnuts, and some hemp and flax. Of wheat and oats the product is insufficient for the consumption. Cattle, sheep, horses, and mules are raised in large numbers; and on the refuse of the dairies numerous pigs are fed. The fat cattle from this department are much esteemed, and are sent to all parts of the country. Large quantities of cheese are made, and sold principally in the south of France under the name of Auvergne cheeses. The minerals, as a whole, are unimportant. Hot mineral springs are abundant, those of Chaudes-Aigues being the most frequented. The manufactures are of trifling importance. Cantal is divided into four arrondissements, containing 23 cantons and 267 communes. Pop. (1901) 218,941.

Can'taloupe, a small round variety of musk-melon, globular, ribbed, of pale-green or yellow color and of delicate flavor; first grown in Europe at Cantalupo, in Italy. See MUSK-MELON.

Cantalupo, kän-tä-loo'pō, Italy, a town of Naples, province of Sannio or Molise, memorable for a French victory over the Neapolitans in 1798, and for a destructive earthquake, in which many lives were lost, in 1805.

Cantani, kän-tä'nē, **Arnoldo,** Italian physician: b. Hainsbach, Bohemia, 15 Feb. 1837; d. Naples, 7 May 1893. He was educated at Prague, and was physician in the general hospital there. In 1864 he became professor of pharmacology and toxicology at Pavia; in 1867 he was director of the clinical institute at Milan, and in 1868 of that at Naples. In 1889 he became a senator of Italy. He investigated chiefly malaria, typhus, and tuberculosis; and was influential in introducing the methods of German medicine into Italy. He wrote ‹Manuale di Materia Medica e Terapeutica› (1865); ‹Manuale di Farmacologia Clinica› (1885-90).

Cantarini, Simone, sē mō nä kän-tä-rē'nē, also known as IL PESARESE, Italian painter: b. Pesaro, 1612; d. Verona, 1648. He studied under Guido Reni at Bologna, where he afterward painted a large number of pictures, all much in the style, but without the grace and delicacy, of his master's work. His 37 etchings more closely resemble those of Guido. Throughout his life Cantarini's intolerable arrogance made him numerous enemies; and after a quarrel with his chief patron, the Duke of Mantua, he died in Verona. Among his best-known paintings are an 'Assumption'; 'A Holy Family'; and 'Joseph and Potiphar's Wife.'

Cantata, kăn-tä'tạ, in music, a species of vocal composition, consisting of an intermixture of air, recitative, duet, trio, quartette, and chorus. According to some, it was invented by Carissimi about the middle of the 17th century. By others its invention has been ascribed to Barbara Strozzi, a Venetian lady, in the 18th century. The subject may be sacred, pastoral, or amatory, and in the hands of some composers it takes the dimensions of a short oratorio or opera, but without acting.

Canteen, in the United States army, (1) a soldier's tin flask, containing two to three pints, and covered with a woven fabric; (2) a cooperative store, at a camp or garrison, where spirituous liquors are on sale under certain regulations. In British use the canteen is not a refreshment-bottle, but a sort of combination pan, dish, and plate, for use at mess. The departments of the British garrison store are usually divided into a dry canteen and wet canteen, the former being for general groceries and provisions, and the latter for liquid refreshment, excluding spirituous liquors.

Previous to 1901, beer and wine were allowed to be sold at the canteens in the United States army, though spirits were prohibited. In that year an anti-canteen law went into effect, as the result of temperance agitation. There has been wide discussion as to the merits and demerits of this law.

The United States Congress in 1902 appropriated $500,000 to build and maintain suitable buildings at army posts, for the recreation and sociability of the men, and also increased the rations five cents per day, to enable them to procure more delicacies without depending upon the profits of a liquor-selling canteen. When these buildings come into general use, and statistics can be had for a longer period, it will be possible to form a more accurate opinion as to the wisdom of abolishing the canteen.

Canterbury, England, a cathedral city, a parliamentary and a municipal borough, and a county borough under the Local Government Act of 1888. It is situated in the eastern division of the county of Kent, 55 miles distant by road from London and 62 by rail. It stands on the banks of the river Stour, is 14 miles from Margate and 16 from Dover. It is connected with Whitstable by means of a special line of railway about 7 miles in length. The parliamentary city has an area of 3,837 acres, while the municipal area contains 3,976 acres. The town is on the lower London tertiaries.

Industries.—The district is chiefly agricultural. Canterbury was formerly noted for its silks, velvet, and brocade manufacture. Leather, bricks, and lime are the important manufactures at the present day. There are also several large breweries in the city. Market days are on Mondays and Saturdays. Grain markets are also held on the 2d and 4th Mondays in each month, the principal articles of produce being corn and hops. Excepting the supply of electric light,

there are no great municipal undertakings, not only the gas and water-works but also the swimming baths being managed privately.

Churches, Buildings, Educational Institutions, etc.—There are 14 parish churches and various chapels. In addition to the churches, of which the most historic is Saint Martin's, built originally by the Romans, Canterbury contains a number of interesting buildings, the principal of which are "The Guildhall" (built 1439, rebuilt 1697), Market House, Saint Augustine's College, Chaucer's Inn, the 'Chequers of the Hope (1477), and the Crown Inn, erected by Prior Chillenden in the 15th century. The only remaining city gate is the West Gate, rebuilt by Archbishop Sudbury, 1380, and now used as a Museum of Arms and Armory. Saint John's Hospital, East-bridge Hospital, and Saint Nicholas Hospital at Harbledown are picturesque survivals of ancient charitable foundations.

The public library was established in 1858. It has a total stock of over 9,000 volumes, and an annual issue of about 55,000. The Museum, which has been in existence since 1825, is, together with the public library, housed in the Beaney Institute. This institute was partially paid for out of a legacy of £10,000, left to the city by the late Dr. Beaney, a native of the city, who amassed a large fortune in Australia. The Cathedral library, which was founded in 1660, contains about 13,000 volumes, and the library at Saint Augustine's College has about 18,000 volumes. An art gallery was presented to the town in 1882 by Mr. T. Sidney Cooper, the famous artist, who was born in the city. Attached to the cathedral is a school founded by Henry VIII., and until recently a bluecoat school founded by Queen Elizabeth, which has recently been merged into a scheme called the Simon Langton schools. Saint Augustine's Monastery has been restored and enlarged and is now used as a Church Missionary College.

Canterbury Castle, one of the largest in England, is of Norman construction. For many years it has been in use by the local gas company as a coal store. Negotiations are now proceeding by which the gas company, for some pecuniary consideration, will hand over this grand old keep to the civic fathers for future preservation.

The Cathedral.—The most remarkable object in the city is the cathedral, which is one of the finest ecclesiastical structures in England, of which, however, no part of the original now remains. The present edifice is 537 feet in length, east to west, and 154, exterior, feet in breadth. It has been built in various times (oldest part in the 11th century), and, although it represents various styles of architecture, it has a most imposing appearance. The crypt is the largest in England. It contains fragments of Roman and Saxon work, and is replete with every form of historic interest. The central tower, which is called the Bell Harry tower, is 235 feet high and 35 feet in diameter. It is in the perpendicular style and was erected in 1495. The cathedral is built on the site of a Roman church, which was re-named Christ Church by Saint Augustine when he was elected Archbishop of Canterbury. The church was destroyed by fire the year after the Norman Conquest, 1067, but rebuilding was commenced three years afterwards and was completed in 1130. This was again destroyed by fire four years afterwards. It contains the tomb of Edward the Black Prince, 1376, also that of Henry IV. and his queen in the Trinity Chapel; the stone chair in which the archbishops are enthroned; and some beautiful 13th-century stained-glass. The principal historical connection with Canterbury cathedral will always be the murder of Thomas à Beckett, which took place in 1170, and eventually caused a considerable number of pilgrims to go to Canterbury. The Archbishop of Canterbury is Primate of all England and Metropolitan Bishop for all the dioceses south of the Trent.

Government.—Until 1885 Canterbury sent two members to the House of Commons, but now it only sends one. The town is governed by a mayor, six aldermen, and eighteen councillors. The rateable value of the borough is £125,469. Several charters have been granted from time to time. The first by Henry II. and the last by Charles II., who granted a charter of incorporation in 1686. It has the privilege, granted by charter of James I., in 1607, of a sword and mace. The first mayor was elected in the year 1448.

History.—Canterbury is supposed to have been a place of importance before the Roman invasion, the Roman name *Durovernum* showing apparently the British prefix *Dwr*, water, although antiquaries differ as to the remainder of the compound. Druidical remains have been found here, together with the British weapons termed celts. Its importance under the Roman dominion is proved by many circumstances; and especially by the discovery of a great variety of remains of that people; added to which, Roman bricks have been found in certain portions of the remaining walls. It derives its present name from the Saxon *Cant-wara-byrig*, the Kentishmen's city. During the residence of Ethelbert, king of Kent, the memorable arrival of Saint Augustine took place in 597; an event rapidly followed by the conversion of this king and his people to Christianity; and the foundation of the archiepiscopal see of Canterbury. In the 8th and the three following centuries, the city was dreadfully ravaged by the Danes, and on one occasion, in 1011, nearly the whole of the inhabitants, including women, children, and the archbishop himself, were barbarously massacred, and the cathedral burned to its bared walls. It gradually, however, recovered, and at the Conquest its buildings exceeded in extent those of London. The ecclesiastical importance of the place, in particular, advanced with great rapidity, which was consummated by the murder of Thomas à Beckett, whose canonization by the Pope rendered Canterbury the resort of pilgrims from every part of Europe. Not only were the priory and see benefited by the offering of the rich devotees, but the prosperity of the town itself was greatly advanced by the money spent in it by so many wealthy strangers. Erasmus describes the church, and especially the chapel in which he was interred, as glittering with the gold and jewels offered up by the princes, nobles, and wealthy visitors of his shrine; all of which Henry VIII. appropriated to himself on the dissolution of the priory in 1539, when he ordered the bones of Beckett to be burned to ashes. Several of the English monarchs have made a temporary residence at Canterbury, which was also occupied by Oliver Cromwell in the civil wars, whose troopers made

a stable of the cathedral. Pop. (1901) 24,868; (1907, estimated) 25,000.

Bibliography.—Willis, 'Architectural History of Canterbury Cathedral' (1845-69); Stanley, 'Historical Memorials of Canterbury' (1883); Hook, 'Lives of the Archbishops of Canterbury'; R. Jenkins, 'Diocesan History of Canterbury' (1880); J. Charles Cox, 'Canterbury: A Historical and Topographical Account of the City' (1905).

H. T. MEAD,
Librarian of the Public Library.

Can'terbury, New Zealand, a provincial district occupying the centre of South Island; capital, Christchurch. The famous Canterbury Plain, of 2,500,000 acres, slopes gradually down over a descent of 40 miles toward the sea. A rich loamy tract, admirably adapted for agriculture and cattle grazing, extends along the east coast, while the interior is a true pastoral country, well watered by numerous streams, and covered with a perpetual herbage of various grasses. A vast coal-field seems to underlie the whole country, and coal is worked in the districts of Timaru and Malvern. Good fire-clays, quartz, sand for glassmaking, marble, limestone, etc., are also found. The productions include wool, grain, frozen meat, skins and hides, butter, cheese, and some silk. Pop. (1901) 143,040.

Canterbury-bell, a name given to species of *Campanula* (q.v.), especially *C. medium* and *C. trachelium.*

Canterbury Tales. See CHAUCER.

Cantharel'lus. See FUNGI, EDIBLE.

Cantha'rides, kăn-thă'rĭ-dēs, blister-beetles (q.v.) when prepared for medical use. Our native American blister-beetles (especially *Epicauta villata* and *cinerea*) are not inferior to the Spanish-fly in vesicant qualities. By a strange misconception the presence of the brilliant green particles of the wing-cases in the powdered imported insect has been associated with their activity, and any sample of powdered cantharides or of prepared emplastrum where these brilliant particles are wanting would be condemned by many physicians. The recent introduction of the Chinese beetle (*Mylabris cickorii*) has done much to remove this misconception, for it has been shown that the *Mylabris* is much stronger than *Lytta vesicatoria*, yielding, according to analysis, fully double the quantity of cantharidin. Our native blister-beetles, when powdered, nearly resemble the *Mylabris* in color.

Cantha'ridin ($C_{10}H_{12}O_4$), the vesicating principle of cantharides. The methods of obtaining it consist in treating the powdered insects with a solvent, such as alcohol, ether, or chloroform, the last being preferable. The solution is evaporated, and the residue is purified from a green oil which adheres to it obstinately, by digesting with bisulphide of carbon or by redissolving in alcohol. Purification is further affected by animal charcoal, and the cantharidin is crystallized from hot alcohol or chloroform.

Can'thoplasty (Gr. *kanthos*, "the angle of the eye," and *plastikos*, "formative"), the formation by plastic operation of the angle of the

CANTERBURY CATHEDRAL.

eye, an operation proposed by Ammon when the eyelids are not sufficiently cleft, or when the eyelids produce tension on the eyeball, as in inflammatory processes.

Can'ticles, or **Song of Songs** (*Shirhashirim* in Hebrew, the *Canticum Canticorum* of the Vulgate), the fourth book of the Hagiographa, and the first of the so-called Megilloth, has its name of Song of Songs, from the superior beauty of its language and poetry. In a number of dialogues and soliloquies, written in most harmonious verses, it gives a glowing description of the tender, chaste, and faithful love, as well as of the beauty of two lovers betrothed, or bride and bridegroom ; of rural scenes among the mountains of Lebanon and Hermon, among the hills and vineyards of Engedi, and in the environs of Jerusalem and Thirza ; and of love itself, sweeter than wine, more fragrant than ointments, which cannot be bought, nor quenched by waters, nor drowned by floods. It is ascribed to Solomon, whose palaces, gardens, chariots, horses, guards, and wives are mentioned, enhancing by the contrast, the charms of calm rural life, full of song, innocence, and love. In regard to its form, its plot, and the order of its parts, as well as to its subject, it has been variously classified by ancient and modern writers ; by Origen, in the preface to his comments, as an epithalamium in the form of a drama, which is also the opinion of Lowth and Michaelis ; by Bossuet as a regular pastoral drama of seven acts, giving the scenes of seven days, of which the last is the Sabbath ; by others as a collection of songs or idyls. Dr. Adam Clarke regards it as a poem *sui generis*, composed for the entertainment of marriage guests. Its canonicity has also been a matter of controversy ; it seems to have been in question with the Jews at the time of the Mishna. Theodore of Mopsuestiæ, the friend of St. Chrysostom, attacked it most vehemently with arguments derived from the erotic character of the book, and was severely condemned for his attacks. Origen, who is said to have written 10 books of comments on the Canticles, containing no less than 20,000 verses, and his admirer Jerome, are among its most prominent defenders, supported by the circumstance that the book is contained in all the Hebrew copies of the Scriptures, in the translations of the Septuagint, of Symmachus the Jew, and of Aquila, and is mentioned in the most ancient catalogues of the Church, commencing with that of Melito, bishop of Sardis, who lived in the 2d century, though not expressly by Josephus. Modern criticism has also questioned the authorship of King Solomon, and several Aramaic words, the *yod* in the word David, and the abbreviation of the relative *asher*, etc., have been quoted as evidences against the generally accepted antiquity of the book. though none of these is conclusive. But no subject has excited more and livelier controversies, or has been a source of more learned and contradictory disquisition and scrutiny, than the question of the literal or allegoric and mystic sense of the book. Many modern · critics both among Jews and Christians, not unsupported by the opinions of ancient and grave authorities, contend for the literal sense. They widely differ in the interpretation of the meaning and object of the book. These writers account for its reception into the canon on the ground of its praise of faithful love, of conjugal affection, and the chastity of monogamy, or of a misunderstanding of the collectors. The more ancient opinion, on the other hand, which is alone regarded as orthodox in both Church and synagogue, defends the allegorical, religious, and sacred character of the songs. Thus, on the one side the subject is the love of a shepherd, of a youthful king, etc., and the beloved is a shepherdess, an Ethiopian princess, or, according to Grotius and others, the daughter of Pharaoh, wife of Solomon ; while, on the other side, love appears as a spiritual affection, as the love of the God of Israel for his chosen but abandoned people, according to the Chaldee paraphrast, the rabbis, and even Luther; of Christ for the Church, between the soul of the believer and Christ, or as the connection between the divine and human nature, according to views current in the Church. Aben Ezra, a Jewish philosopher of the 12th century, finds in the book the hopes of redemption for oppressed Israel ; Keiser, the restoration of the Mosaic law by Zerubbabel and Ezra ; Hug, an attempt made in the time of Hezekiah to reunite the remnant of the 10 tribes to Judah ; others, the love of wisdom ; the alchemists, even the search for the philosopher's stone. Dr. Kirschbaum, of Cracow, brings the book down to the time of Hadrian, finds in it the last outbreak of Jewish patriotism and love of liberty, and in the *harai bather* the mountains of Bethar, so heroically defended by Bar-Cokeba. Besides the authors above mentioned who have written upon the Canticles, the names of Erasmus, Le Clerc, Rosenmüller, Eichhorn, Jahn, De Wette, Ewald, Robinson, Stuart, Delitzsch, Renan, Siegfried, Cheyne, and Black, must be mentioned. Mendelssohn and Dr. J. Mason Good have published admirable translations. Of those of Jerome only one is extant.

The name of canticles is also given to certain detached psalms and hymns used in the service of the Anglican Church, such as the Venite exultemus, Te Deum laudamus, Benedicite omnia opera, Benedictus, Jubilate Deo, Magnificat, Cantate Domino, Nunc dimittis, Deus misereatur, and the verses used instead of the Venite on Easter Day.

Can'tilever, a wooden or iron block framed into the wall of a house, and projecting from it to carry moldings, eaves, balconies, etc. The name is given also to a large projecting framework forming part of an iron bridge. See BRIDGE; BRIDGE CONSTRUCTION.

Cantium, căn'tĭ-ŭm, England, an ancient territory in South Britain, whence the English word Kent is derived, supposed to have been the first district which received a colony from the Continent. The situation of Cantium occasioned its being much frequented by the Romans, who generally took their way through it in their marches to and from the Continent. Few places in Britain are more frequently mentioned by the Roman writers than Rutupiæ (now Richborough). Portus Dubris (now Dover), Durobrivæ, and Durovernum (now Rochester and Canterbury) were also Roman towns and stations. Cantium made a part of the province called Flavia Cæsariensis. See KENT.

Canto Figurato, fē-gṓ-rä'tō, a term applied by the old Christian ecclesiastics to the chant in its more florid forms, or in which more than one note was sung to a syllable.

Canton, John, English electrician: b. Stroud, 31 July 1718; d. 22 March 1772. He settled as a schoolmaster in London, and was elected a Fellow of the Royal Society in 1749. He invented an electroscope and an electrometer; originated experiments in induction; was the first to make powerful artificial magnets; and in 1762 demonstrated the compressibility of water.

Can'ton, William, English writer: b. Isle of Chusan, China, 27 Oct. 1845. He was educated in France for the Roman Catholic priesthood, but decided upon a secular career and was for many years on the staff of the Glasgow *Herald.* Since 1890 he has been sub-editor of the 'Contemporary Review' and manager of the London publishing house of Isbister & Company. He is author of 'A Lost Epic and Other Poems' (1887); 'The Invisible Playmate,' a strikingly original piece of work (1894); 'W. V., Her Book, and Various Verses' (1896); 'The Invisible Playmate, and W. V., Her Book' (with final chapter) (1897); 'A Child's Book of Saints,' republished in the United States as 'W. V.'s Golden Legend' (1898); 'Children's Sayings' (1900).

Canton', China (more correctly *Quang-chow-foo*), a large and important city, situated on the Pearl River, at a distance of 80 miles from the sea. It is situated in the province of Quang-tung (of which name Canton is a corruption), and consists of the city proper and of many suburbs, and its total population is estimated at from 500,000 to 2,500,000. The city proper is enclosed by walls, forming a circuit of six miles, and is divided into two parts by a partition wall running east and west; the portion north of this wall, which is much the larger, being called the old, that on the south of it the new city. The walls, mainly of brick, rise to the height of 25 feet, with a thickness of about 20. There are 12 gates, all of which are shut at night. The streets are long and straight and in general paved with flat stones, but they are very narrow, the average breadth not exceeding eight feet. The houses of the poorer classes are mere mud hovels; those of the shop-keeping class are commonly of two stories, the lower of which serves as the shop. The streets are to a great extent lined with these shops, in which are to be found the productions of all parts of the globe. Neat and gaudily painted signs and names give a gay appearance to the narrow streets; in most cases there are no windows in front, but the whole is thrown open by day and closed at night. Temples and other religious edifices are very numerous, but few of them are in any way remarkable. There are two lofty pagodas, forming a notable feature in any general view of the city. One of these, 170 feet high, is about 1,300 years old, the other, 160 feet high, about 1,000. Among the chief temples, which are far from attractive buildings, may be mentioned those of the Ocean Banner, of the Five Hundred Gods, of Longevity, of the Five Genii. Among other buildings may be mentioned the residences of the governor-general, the commander-in-chief, the treasurer, the prefect, etc. There are four large prisons, one of them capable of holding 1,000 prisoners. In the European quarter are churches, schools, and other buildings in the European style. Wheeled carriages are not in use in Canton; goods are transported on bamboo poles laid across the shoulders of men, while people who can afford it have themselves carried about in sedan-chairs. The river opposite the city for the space of four or five miles presents a most interesting scene. The prodigious number of boats with which it is crowded is the first thing that strikes the eye. A large number of these — as many, it is said, as 40,000, containing a population of 200,000 — are fixed residences, and most of them moored stem and stern in rows. The inhabitants are called tankia or boat-people, and form a class with many customs peculiar to themselves. Millions are born and live and die in these floating dwellings without ever having put foot on dry land; while their ancestors for generations were all amphibious like themselves. The family boats are of various sizes, the better sort being from 60 to 80 feet long, and about 15 feet wide. A superstructure of considerable height, and covered with an arched roof, occupies nearly the whole of the interior of the boat. This structure is divided within into several apartments, devoted to different domestic purposes, all of them being kept very clean. The smaller boats of this description are not above 25 feet long, and contain only one room. By far the handsomest boats are the hwa-ting or flower-boats, which are graceful in form and have their raised cabins and awnings fancifully carved and painted. These are let to pleasure-parties for excursions on the river. The foreign mercantile houses, and the American, British, and French consulates have as their special quarter an area in the suburbs in the southwest of the city, with water on two sides of it. The river banks are faced with a granite wall; handsome hongs or factories have been built, and much money has been spent on improvements. The manufactures and other industries of Canton are varied and important, embracing silk, cotton, porcelain, glass, paper, sugar, lacquered ware, ivory carving, metal goods, etc. The direct trade between the United States and Canton is constantly growing, the exports and imports for 1902 being upward of $15,000,000 and $10,000,000 respectively. Its foreign trade has been known for three centuries throughout the world, and it was the chief foreign emporium in China until 1850, when Shanghai began to surpass it. Since then the opening of other ports and different causes have interfered with its prosperity, but it still carries on a large traffic, its exports and imports together often amounting to about $40,000,000. Business transactions between natives and foreigners are transacted in a jargon known as "pidgin-English." Since the establishment of the colony of Hong Kong there has sprung up quite a flotilla of river steamers, which ply daily between Canton, Hong Kong, and Macao, and convey the greater part of the produce and merchandise for native and foreign consumption. These steamers equal the best river boats of Europe, and carry large numbers of passengers. The climate of Canton is healthy; in July and August the thermometer may rise to 100° F. in the shade, and during winter it is at times below the freezing-point. Canton was first visited by English vessels in 1634. From 1689 to 1834 the East India Company had a monopoly of the English trade. In 1839 war was declared by Great Britain against China, and Canton would have been occupied but for being ransomed by the Chinese. In the war of 1856 the foreign factories were pillaged and destroyed, and about a year after this Canton was taken by an English force. From this time to 1861 it was occupied by an English and French garrison. Since then it has been open to foreign trade.

Can'ton, Ill., city of Fulton County, situated on the Chicago, B. & Q. and the Toledo, P. & W. R.R.'s. It is the centre of trade of a fertile agricultural region; and has numerous industrial interests, including a large manufactory of agricultural implements, cigar factories, etc.; a public library and a high school. There are coal mines within the city limits. Pop. (1900) 6,564.

Canton, N. Y., a village and county-seat of Saint Lawrence County, on Grass River, and the Rome, W. & O. R.R., 59 miles northeast of Watertown. It is the seat of St. Lawrence University, and has large flour and lumber interests, a national bank, weekly newspapers, several churches, and an assessed property valuation of over $3,000,000. Pop. (1900) 2,757.

Canton, Ohio, city and county-seat of Stark County, on Nimisilla Creek and the Pennsylvania, the Baltimore & O., and the Cleveland, C. & S. R.R.'s; 60 miles south of Cleveland. It is in a fine fruit and wheat-growing district, with coal, limestone, and pottery clay in the vicinity, and was for many years the residence of President McKinley whose tomb is here. It is a manufacturing city of considerable importance. The principal industries are the manufacture of agricultural implements, brick and tile, foundry and machine-ship products, iron bridges, steel goods, and stoves. There are three national banks, besides several State and savings banks. The city has an electric light and street railway system, and well-paved streets. Among the notable buildings are the post-office, high school, public library, the United States signal service station, and several churches. Pop. (1900) 30,667.

Canton, S. D., the capital of Lincoln County, on the Sioux River, 20 miles from Sioux Falls. It is on the Chicago, M. & St. P. R.R., and is the seat of Augustana College. The town contains eight churches, public schools, and important manufactories, is lighted by electric light, and has other public improvements. Pop. (1900) 1,943.

Canton, a small division of territory, constituting a distinct state or government, as in Switzerland, where each of the 22 states is so designated. In France judicial districts are called cantons.

Cantoni, kän tō′nē, **Carlo,** Italian philosopher: b. Gropello, 1840. He studied law and philosophy at Turin, and philosophy at Berlin and Göttingen (under Lotze). He was professor at the lyceum at Turin, and in Milan; since 1878 he has been professor of philosophy at the University of Pavia. In his philosophical theory he agrees in general with Kant. He wrote: 'G. Battista Vico, studii Virtu e Comparazione' (1867); 'Corso Elementare di Philosofia' (1870); 'Guiseppe Ferrari' (1878); 'Emanuele Kant' (1879–84).

Canton′ment, the district in which troops are quartered when they are not collected into a camp, but detached and distributed over the neighboring towns and villages. The object of sending troops into cantonments is to be able to concentrate them as quickly as possible on one spot, when circumstances do not admit of a camp being formed, or do not render it advisable to form one. In India the permanent military stations erected in the neighborhood of the principal cities are so called.

Cantu, Cesare, chä-zä-rĕ kän′too, Italian historian, poet, and philosopher: b. Brisio, 5 Sept. 1805; d. 11 March 1895. He was educated at Sondrio in the Valtellina, where he taught belles-lettres at a youthful age, resided afterward in Como, and next at Milan until 1848. One of his earliest works, entitled 'Ragionamenti sulla Storia Lombarda nel Secolo XVII.' ('Lectures on the History of Lombardy in the 17th Century'), appeared in a second edition in 1842–4, and contained liberal ideas that brought upon the author the animadversion of the Austrian government, which condemned him to a year's imprisonment. During his confinement he composed a historical romance, entitled 'Margherita Pusterla' (1845), which became very popular. His great work, on which his reputation will chiefly rest, 'Storia Universale' ('Universal History'), appeared first in 1837, at Turin. It has been since revised and reprinted at Palermo and Naples, and translated into German. A French translation by Aroux and Leopardi, was published in Paris in 1843. Other works of his are: 'Storia degli Italiani' (1854); 'The Last One Hundred Years' (1864); 'The Italian Heretics' (1866–8). See Bertolini, 'Cesare Cantu e le sue opere' (1895).

Cantus Firmus, an ancient chant of the Roman Catholic Church. These chants were adopted as standing melodies, and until counterpoint was discovered, were unaccompanied, or only harmonized with octaves.

Canuck′, a term sometimes used in the United States to denote a Canadian.

Canute IV., Saint, king of Denmark 1080–6. He suppressed the ancient heathen customs of his people, and thus aroused opposition; in 1085 he started on an expedition against William the Conqueror, but was murdered by rebels in his own army. He was canonized in 1101 and in the Middle Ages was considered the patron saint of Denmark.

Canute (kä-nūt′) **the Great,** Knud, or Knut, the second king of Denmark of that name, and first Danish king of England: b. in the former country, about 995; d. Shaftesbury, England, 1035. He was the son of Sweyn, king of Denmark, and accompanied his father in his victorious campaigns in England. Sweyn, having proclaimed himself king of England, died in 1014, before his power was established, and appointed Canute his successor there. The latter was immediately driven out by Ethelred, the representative of the Saxon line, and fled with 60 ships to the court of his brother, Harold, king of Denmark. Harold enabled him to collect a large fleet in the north to prosecute his cause in England. He invaded that country anew in 1015. He fought many battles with Edmund Ironside, who had succeeded his father, Ethelred, in 1016, and was finally victorious at the battle of Assington. After this battle, Edmund and Canute agreed upon a division of the kingdom. To Canute were assigned

Mercia and Northumbria, while the Saxon prince preserved West and East Anglia. By the death of his brother, Harold, he obtained the crown of Denmark (1016). In the same year, and but one month after the ratification of the treaty of partition, Edmund died, and Canute became sole king of England without further resistance. He refrained from murdering the children of his late rival, and sent them to his half brother, Olave, king of Sweden. He put away his wife, Alfgive, the daughter of the Earl of Northampton, and espoused Emma, the widow of Ethelred, the Saxon monarch (1017), on the condition that their children should succeed to the throne of England. He made the greatest exertions to gain the affections of his English subjects, to whom his Danish origin was no recommendation. He accordingly disbanded his Danish army, retaining only a body-guard. He endeavored to blend the two races as far as possible, and to induce them to live in harmony with each other. He erected churches, and made donations to abbeys and monasteries on the scenes of former conflicts and massacres. In a witenagemote at Winchester, he compiled a code of laws which is still extant. In this code he denounced those who kept up the practice of pagan rites and superstitions, and forbade the sending of Christian slaves out of the country for sale. Although Canute generally resided in England, he made frequent visits to Denmark. He carried with him on these occasions an English fleet, English missionaries, and English artisans. He promoted three Englishmen to the newly erected bishoprics of Scania, Zealand, and Fionia. In 1025 he was attacked by the king of Sweden and defeated; but in the night, Earl Godwin, at the head of the English contingent, surprised the Swedish camp and dispersed the enemy. His absence from Denmark, and the bestowal of so many diguities in Denmark upon his English subjects, made him unpopular in that kingdom. To appease this discontent, he left behind in Denmark his son, Hardicanute, then aged 10 years, under the guardianship of his brother-in-law, Ulf (1026). In this year he made a pilgrimage to Rome. He was well received there by the Pope John, and by the Emperor Conrad II., who gave up to the Danish king all the country north of the river Eider. From the Pope he obtained privileges for the English school established in Rome, and an abatement of the sums demanded from his archbishops for the pallium; and from the various princes, relief for all English and Danish pilgrims and merchants from all illegal tolls and detentions which they had endured on their route to Rome. He returned from Rome to Denmark. In 1028 he made an expedition into Norway, expelled Olave, and restored Haco, who swore allegiance to him. In 1029 he returned to England, and his Danish subjects proclaimed Hardicanute king of Denmark. Canute immediately returned to Denmark, put down the revolt, and executed the traitor, Ulf. In 1031 Canute was acknowledged king of Norway, and laid claims to the crown of Sweden. On returning again to England, he allowed his son, Hardicanute, to share with him the Danish crown. His reign is very important in the constitutional history of Denmark. Canute issued the first national coinage of Denmark, and published the first written code of Danish law, wherein the custom of private vengeance was prohibited. He raised the clergy in their corporate capacity to a separate estate of the realm, and instituted the Thinglith or royal guard of 3,000 men. The members of this body were all men of good family, and rich enough to equip themselves at their own expense. From them sprang the Danish order of nobility; they were tried only by their peers, and formed with the king the highest court of justice. Canute's last campaign was against Duncan, king of Scotland, respecting the possession of Cumberland, but before the armies could engage the two kings were reconciled, and ancient stipulations concerning the tenure of Cumberland were renewed (1033). Canute was buried at Winchester. By Emma he had two children, namely, Hardicanute or Canute the Hardy, and a daughter, Gunhilda, married to Henry, the son of Conrad II., of Germany, emperor. By Alfgive he left two sons, Sweyn and Harold. To Sweyn was given the crown of Norway; Hardicanute retained that of Denmark, and Harold, surnamed Harefoot, took possession of that of England. Canute is most popularly known, not by his extended rule and legislative enactments, but by the familiar story of the monarch, the courtiers, and the disobedient sea.

Can'vas, a textile fabric made of the fibres of hemp; or any strong, firm cloth, whether of hemp or flax. It is chiefly used for tents, and for the sails of sailing vessels, for which its strength makes it well adapted. Varieties of it are also used as the ground of tapestry work and of oil paintings. A finer description is used for many common domestic purposes, as for towels, table-cloths, etc. Canvas for sails is made from 18 to 24 inches wide, and numbered 0 to 8, No. 0 being the thickest. A bolt is 39 to 40 yards long, and weighs 25 to 48 pounds.

Canvas-back, a widely distributed freshwater duck (*Aythya vallisneria*), much sought as a table luxury, as its flesh is considered superior to that of all other ducks. It is about 22 inches in length and its reddish-chestnut head and neck are much shaded with dusky hues; the lower neck, breast, and forepart of the back, with the rump and tail-coverts, are black; and the back and sides gray, covered with fine lines and dots, so that the plumage resembles canvas. By reason of its similarity, this duck is frequently confounded with the red-head (q.v.). "The canvas-back is larger, its head darker, and its bill a deep black, while that of the red-head is deep blue, or a slatish color. The shape of the bill of the canvas-back is wedged and long; of the red-head moderately long and concave. . . . They are very tenacious of life, their bump of stubbornness being fully developed, and they will dive long distances, and prefer death by any other means than human agency. When one is crippled it will usually look around for an instant, to see where the danger lies, then down it goes, and if rushes or cover are near, it is good-bye to that duck,— it will not be seen again. When one is crippled it should be shot again, and at once." The food of the canvasback consists chiefly of the roots of wild celery (*Zostera vallisneria*), which resembles the cultivated celery in appearance. It grows densely in the shallow parts of the Chesapeake Bay and Susquehanna River, about the Great Lakes, and in the Mississippi valley. Few canvas-backs are found east of the Hudson and Delaware rivers. It is almost safe to say that where the plant grows in abundance, the canvas-back is almost sure likewise to be found; consequently the peculiarly delicate flavor of its flesh, and the market value of this duck, increase with the amount of celery it consumes, as otherwise it is hardly distinguishable from the red-head in flavor. The canvas-back breeds north of Dakota, building its nest on the ground, in a marsh, and laying from 6 to 10 greenish-buff eggs. Consult: Elliot, 'Wild Fowl of North America'; Job, 'Among the Wild Fowl.'

Canzone, kän-tsō'nä, a lyric poem, of Provençal origin. It is found in the Italian poetry of the 13th century. At first it was quite irregular, but was confined by Petrarch to more fixed and regular forms. Hence it is called canzone Petrarchesca; it is also called canzone Toscana, because it originated in Tuscany. It is divided into several stanzas, in which the nature and disposition of the verses, which are of 11 and 7 syllables, and the place of the rhymes, are uniform. The canzone usually concludes with a stanza which is shorter than the others, and is called ripresa, comgedo, comiato, signifying dismission or taking leave. There are different kinds of canzoni, and different names are given to the different parts. The canzone Anacreontica is divided into small stanzas, consisting of short verses, with a regular disposition of the rhymes through all the stanzas. Not only light, pleasing songs of love, gaiety, and mirth, but poems on solemn and lofty subjects, and of an elevated dithyrambic strain, are included under this name. The latter subjects, however, are better adapted to the canzone Pindarica, which was first introduced in the 16th century, by Luigi Alamanni, and owes its perfection chiefly to Chiabrera. It is distinguished from that of Petrarch by a bolder flight, loftier ideas, greater freedom in the choice and disposition of the verses, and by the form of the stanzas, which is borrowed from the Greek chorus. The Pindaric canzoni are divided into strophe, antistrophe, and epode, and are called canzoni alla Greca. Those divisions are sometimes called ballata, contraballata, and stanza; or volta, rivolta, and stanza; the Greek names are the most common. There is also the canzone a ballo, an old Italian poem, originally intended to be sung at a dance (ballo). It is called also ballata. It is not employed by the Italian poets later than the 16th century.

Canzonet, kän-tsō-nĕt', **Canzonetta,** in Italian poetry a canzone (q.v.), consisting of short verses, much in use with the poets of the 15th century. Rinuccini, and after him Chiabrera, have used it in modern times, and given it more grace. Canzonets are generally expressive of tender feelings. In music, canzonet signifies a song, shorter and less elaborate than the aria of the oratorio or opera.

Caonabo', kä-o-nä-bō', Indian chief of Hispaniola (Haiti) at the time of its discovery by Columbus. The latter built a fort which he called La Navedad, and in which he left, when sailing for Spain early in 1493, a garrison of 40 men — among them one Irishman and one Englishman, as shown by Navarrete's list. Returning before the end of the year, he found that Caonabó had burned the fort and killed the garrison. According to the account of a friendly native, the Spaniards had drawn this fate upon themselves by their evil conduct. It has been suggested, as a reason for special regret, that we might otherwise have had from the Englishman or the Irishman an eye-witness's description of the first voyage of Columbus, in our own language. In 1494 the Indians in great numbers attacked the Spaniards, having been provoked by the misconduct of one of the lieutenants of Columbus, Pedro Margarite. Columbus overthrew them, first at Magdalena, and later (1495) on the plains of the Vega Real — where, tradition has it, 100.000 hostiles were assembled. Caonabó meanwhile threatened the garrison of St. Thomas. Alonso de Ojeda was sent by Columbus to cajole Caonabó into coming to a conference. Ojeda went alone among the hostiles. As presents he took gyoes and manacles of shining metal; treacherously persuaded the prince to show himself to his subjects wearing these novel ornaments, and even, while thus adorned, to ride Ojeda's horse; then, mounting also, he dashed through the crowd of savages and carried his victim into the presence of Columbus. Sent to Spain for trial, Caonabó died in 1496.

Caoutchouc, koo'chook, an elastic, gumlike substance, obtained from the juice of certain tropical trees and shrubs, and commonly known as India-rubber or "rubber." The best caoutchouc comes from the Para region, in Brazil; but supplies are also obtained from Central America and the West Indies, from Africa, and from tropical Asia. The details of collecting the juice and preparing it for market vary somewhat according to the locality, and with the nature of the trees or shrubs from which the juice is obtained. In the Amazon region, when the source is a tree, incisions are made in the bark each morning, and the milky sap that exudes is collected in little tin or clay cups that are secured to the tree for the purpose. At the end of about 10 hours these are emptied into larger collecting vessels, and on the morning of the following day new incisions are made in each tree, some eight inches below the first ones. This process is continued until incisions have been made in the bark from a height of about six feet down to the ground. The poorest quality of sap is obtained from the highest wounds, and the best from the lowest ones. To evaporate the juice, a fire is first built of materials that yield dense volumes of smoke. A workman then dips a wooden paddle into the collected sap, after which he holds it in the smoke until the sap solidifies and acquires a slight tinge of yellow. He then dips the paddle into the sap supply again, repeats the smoking process, and so proceeds until the paddle is covered with a layer of the dried gum that is perhaps an inch and a half thick. He then slits this layer, removes it from the paddle, hangs it up to dry, and starts a fresh evaporation.

Pure caoutchouc from Para is light-colored below the surface, but superficially it is dark brown from oxidation. It has a specific gravity of about 0.92, and consists chiefly of carbon and hydrogen in the proportion of about 87 per cent of carbon to 13 of hydrogen. Small quantities of oxygen are always present, however, as the best of the Para product contains as much as one half of 1 per cent of a sort of resin that contains oxygen, and is undoubtedly produced by the oxidation of the gum. In fact, it is known that caoutchouc will oxidize slowly in damp air, even after it is vulcanized, and particularly when exposed to the action of light. Caoutchouc consists, apparently, of two different kinds of gum, one of which is fibrous, while the other is viscous, though the two are chemically identical. It is slightly soluble in ether, turpentine, chloroform, petroleum, naphtha, benzene, and carbon disulphide, the viscous portion being more soluble than the fibrous part. At 250° F. caoutchouc begins to melt, and becomes permanently transformed into a sticky substance which retains its peculiar consistency almost indefinitely. At 400° F. the transformation is more complete, and the black, adhesive mass that results makes an excellent lute for sealing glass bottles and jars if it is thoroughly incorporated with 50 per cent of its own weight of dry slaked lime. By careful destructive distillation caoutchouc is resolved into a number of hydrocarbon oils that are of interest to the chemist.

As early as 1615 the Spaniards used the crude gum "for waxing their cloaks, which were made of canvas, so as to make them resist water." But it was not until about 200 years later that caoutchouc began to attract general attention in such ways. At first it was applied to cloth by the aid of heat; but improved methods followed the discovery of solvents for the gum, and the invention, by an Englishman named Thomas Hancock (about 1820), of the "masticator," a machine by which the caoutchouc is thoroughly worked over and brought to a uniform consistency. But the greatest step in the development of the rubber industry was the discovery of the process of vulcanization,—a discovery that appears to have been made independently and at about the same time (1843) by Charles Goodyear, of New Haven, Conn., and Thomas Hancock, to whom reference has previously been made. The credit of priority belongs to Goodyear, but Hancock did a great deal to make the discovery a commercial success. Unvulcanized caoutchouc is softened by heat, and is made hard and inelastic by cold; but upon being vulcanized the gum becomes comparatively insensible to ordinary extremes of temperature, and also has its elasticity materially increased. The process of vulcanization depends upon the fact that the crude rubber will absorb sulphur, and combine with it at a temperature that is easily attainable without injury to the product. The details of the vulcanization differ somewhat, according to the nature of the article that is being manufactured. If sheet rubber is submerged for a few moments in melted sulphur at a temperature of 250° F., it absorbs about one tenth of its weight of that element; but although its color changes somewhat it is otherwise apparently unaltered. Upon exposure for a somewhat longer time to a temperature of 285° F., however, true combination of the sulphur and caoutchouc ensues, and the gum is said to become "vulcanized." It is not necessary that the sulphur should be actually melted in order that the sheet rubber may absorb it, for sheets that are laid in powdered sulphur that is heated nearly to its melting-point will absorb the proper amount for good vulcanization in the course of a few hours.

Vulcanization of rubber sheets can even be brought about without the action of heat, by dipping the sheets for a few seconds in a solution of chloride of sulphur in carbon disulphide. It is more common, however, to knead the requisite amount of sulphur directly into the caoutchouc by mechanical means. The article to be manufactured is then brought into shape by the action of pressure and moderate heat (or in any other manner), and the final operation consists in heating it to the vulcanizing temperature by the aid of a steam bath. Chemically considered, the process of vulcanization appears to consist in the substitution of one or more sulphur atoms for a portion of the hydrogen of the hydrocarbons of which the caoutchouc is composed. See INDIA RUBBER; RUBBER MANUFACTURE.

Cap, the cover of the end or head of anything. Caps were not worn by the Romans for many ages. When either the rain or sun was troublesome the lappet of the gown was thrown over the head; and hence all the ancient statues appear bareheaded, excepting sometimes for a wreath or the like. The same usage prevailed among the Greeks, to whom, at least during the heroic age, caps were unknown. The sort of caps or covers of the head in use among the Romans on divers occasions were the *pitra, pileus, cucullus, galerus,* and *palliolum,* which are often confounded by ancient as well as modern writers. The general use of caps and hats is referred to the year 1449. The first seen in Europe were used at the entry of Charles VII. into Rouen. From that time they began to take the place of *chaperons* or hoods. When the cap was of velvet they called it *mortier;* when of wool simply *bonnet.* None but kings, princes, and knights were allowed to use the *mortier.* The cap was the head-dress of the clergy and graduates. Pasquin says that it was anciently a part of the hood worn by the people of the robe; the skirts whereof being cut off, as an incumbrance, left the round cap an easy commodious cover for the head; which cap, being afterward assumed by the people, those of the gown changed it for a square one, first invented by a Frenchman called Patrouillet. He adds, that the giving of the cap to the students in the university was to denote that they had acquired full liberty, and were no longer subject to the rod of their superiors, in imitation of the ancient Romans, who gave a *pileus* to their slaves in the ceremony of making them free: whence the proverb *vocare servos ad pileum:* hence, also, on medals, the cap is the symbol of Liberty, who is represented holding a cap in the right hand by the point.

Cap of Maintenance, one of the ornaments of state carried before the sovereigns of England on the occasion of their coronation. It is also applied to an ornament borne before the mayors of certain cities on state occasions, and to a device in heraldry.

In ship-building a cap is a square piece of timber having two holes cut through it,—one square to fit on the squared or tenon head of the lower mast; the other round, to take the heel of the upper mast. Also a similar contrivance affixed to the end of the bowsprit, through a round hole in which the jib-boom is rigged.

In mining, a mass of unproductive rock overlying valuable ore; and in physical geography, a similar mass, as of ice overlying the surface of a country; as, the ice-cap of Greenland.

For the term as used in military parlance, see PERCUSSION CAP.

Capacity, Specific Inductive, a term introduced by Faraday, the discoverer of the property, to denote the relative powers or capacities of insulating media, called by him dielectrics, for transmitting electrostatic inductive influence. When an electrified body is brought near to a non-electrified conductor, an electric disturbance takes place at the surface of the latter, electricity of the kind opposite to that which the charged body possesses being attracted and the opposite kind being repelled. This disturbance is said to be due to *induction*. (See INDUCTION, ELECTROSTATIC.) Faraday discovered that it depends for intensity on the nature of the insulating medium between the two bodies, showing that, other things remaining the same, the disturbance is greater with some media than with others. The view that Faraday took of induction was altogether opposed to that which was held previous to the time of his investigations, and which was expressed by speaking of induction as action of electricity at a distance: and by experiments on liquid insulators, and in other ways, he proved that what was looked on as influence at a distance is really an influence transmitted by means of the intermediate particles of the insulating substance. The medium he termed the *dielectric*. He showed that the particles of the dielectric are in a polarized condition when it is exposed to electric force. (For a full exposition of Faraday's theory of induction see INDUCTION, ELECTROSTATIC.)

In order to compare the inductive capacities of various substances, Faraday made use of the fact that the capacity for electricity of a Leyden jar depends on the inductive capacity of the insulator which separates the interior and exterior coatings. He constructed two spherical Leyden jars precisely similar, so far as the conductors were concerned, but arranged so that the insulating medium might be varied. Having charged one of the jars he connected the other to it, the inside coatings together and likewise the outside coatings. Part of the electricity in the charged jar under these circumstances passes into the uncharged jar; and the jars being identical in form, it is divided between the two jars in proportion to the inductive capacities of their respective insulators. By determining the quantity in each jar the inductive capacities of the insulators are compared.

Faraday found that all the gases he experiment d on have the same inductive capacity. He took common air as the standard of reference, and found the following numbers to represent the specific inductive capacities of the various substances compared with it:

Air	1.00	Wax	1.86
Spermaceti	1.45	Glass	1.90
Resin	1.76	Shell-lac	2.00
Pitch	1.80	Sulphur	2.24

Later investigations on specific inductive capacity have been made with a "platimeter," devised by Sir William Thomson (Lord Kelvin), and are far more accurate than any that could be made with Faraday's apparatus.

Capa'neus, one of seven legendary heroes who warred against Thebes, killed by Jupiter.

Cap-à-pie, kăp-a̱-pē (O. Fr. *de cap à pie;* Mod. Fr. *de pied en cap*), a term signifying from head to foot, and used with reference to a complete suit of armor covering the body of a knight at all points; as, "He was armed cap-à-pie for the encounter."

Cape Ann, Mass., the southeast point of the town of Gloucester, Mass., the northern limit of Massachusetts Bay; in lat. 42° 38′ N., and lon. 70° 34′ W. The whole of the rocky peninsula forming this part of Gloucester is also called Cape Ann, including the village of Squam in its northeastern part. This peninsula is a headland of sienite, which forms low hills, over the surface of which the rock is very generally exposed to view. Valuable quarries of sienite for building purposes are worked most conveniently for shipment. The place is much exposed to the prevalent northeast storms; but it offers a small, well-sheltered harbor among the rocks, where coasting vessels often take refuge. There are on the shores of this harbor two fixed lights.

Cape Ann Settlement, the first within the limits of the Massachusetts Bay territory. In 1622, the New England Company, to push the settlement of its grant and give it some value, divided the land in severalty among its members. The region about Cape Ann fell to Edmund, Lord Sheffield, who sold a patent for it in 1624 to Robert Cushman and Edward Winslow of the Plymouth colony. They found some English hunters and fishers who had been there since the year before; these acknowledged the rights of the Plymouth people, and the two parties planted and fished amicably; but shortly after a London vessel which had taken up the quarrel of the firebrand, Rev. John Lyford, seized the Plymouth men's fishing stage. Miles Standish came up from Plymouth to settle the trouble by force, but against his wish, the settlement compromised the matter by the crew agreeing to build them another stage. In 1624 Winslow's company sold the site of Gloucester to the "Dorchester Adventurers," an unincorporated English joint-stock company recently formed. These had anticipated the bargain by sending out a band of settlers the fall before, with live stock, implements, etc., and they made Thomas Gardner overseer. The attempt was unsuccessful, and in 1625 the Dorchester company engaged Roger Conant, then at Nantasket with Lyford, to be governor, Lyford to be minister. But the next year the "Adventurers" dissolved, and most of the settlers went home; the few remaining ones, however, removed to "Nahumkeike" (Naumkeag), where they founded Salem.

Cape Ar'ago, a cape on the western coast of Oregon, on the south of Coos Bay. Its lighthouse, which is on a small island, is in lat. 43° 20′ 38″ N., and lon. 124° 22′ 11″ W., and shows a white, flashing light.

Cape or Point Barrow. See BARROW, CAPE OR POINT.

Cape Blanco, Africa. See BLANCO, CAPE.

Cape Blanco, Oregon, a cape forming the most western point of the State, situated in lat. 42° 50′ N., and lon. 124° 32′ W. It has a lighthouse with a white fixed light, 256 feet above sea-level.

Cape Boeo, bō-ā'ō, the ancient *Lilybæum Promontorium*, a cape, on the western coast of Sicily, one mile from Marsala. It is the point of Sicily nearest to ancient Carthage, and at an early period became an important naval station. The naval victory of the Romans over the Carthaginians, which put an end to the first Punic war, was gained near this point.

Cape Bojador, bŏj-ạ-dōr'. See BOJADOR, CAPE.

Cape Bon, or **Ras Adder**, a headland of Tunis, on the Mediterranean, forming the northernmost point of Africa, in lat. 37° 6' N., and lon. 11° 3' E.

Cape Breton, bret'ŭn, Canada, an island of the Dominion of Canada, separated from Nova Scotia, to which province it belongs, by the narrow Gut or Strait of Canso; area 3,120 square miles; length about 110 miles. It is of very irregular shape, the Bras d'Or, an almost landlocked arm of the sea (with most picturesque scenery), penetrating its interior in various directions, and dividing it into two peninsulas connected by an isthmus, across which a canal has been cut. The surface is rather rugged, and only small portions are suited for agriculture; but it possesses much timber, valuable minerals (several coal mines being worked), and the coast abounds in fish. Timber, fish, and coal are exported. The island belonged to France from 1632 to 1763, and Louisburg, its capital, was long an important military post. It was separate from Nova Scotia between 1784 and 1820. The chief towns are Sydney and Arichat. Pop. (1901) 97,190.

Cape Canav'eral, a cape on the eastern coast of Florida, in lat. 28° 27' N., and lon. 80° 33' W. There are dangerous shoals at this point, and navigation is protected by a revolving light.

Cape Canso, the eastern extremity of Nova Scotia, at the entrance of Chedabucto Bay, in lat. 45° 19.5' N., and lon. 60° 55' W.

Cape Car'thage, a headland on the northeast coast of Tunis, jutting out into the Mediterranean. Traces of the ancient city of Carthage are found on it to the north of the Tunis lagoon.

Cape Catoche, kä-tō'chä, a headland at the northeastern extremity of the peninsula of Yucatan, Central America, in lat. 21° 34' N., and lon. 86° 57' W. It was here that the Spaniards first landed on the American continent.

Cape City. See CAPE MAY, N. J.

Cape Charles, a cape at the northern entrance of Chesapeake Bay, forming the southern extremity of Northampton County, Va., in lat. 37° 07' N., and lon. 75° 53' W. Northeast of it, on Smith's Island, is a lighthouse with a revolving light.

Cape Clarence, a headland at the northern extremity of Jones' Sound, Baffin Bay. It is surrounded by inaccessible mountains whose summits are covered with perpetual snow.

Cape Clear, a headland forming the southernmost extremity of Ireland, in lat. 51° 26' N., and lon. 9° 29' W. It is on an island of 1,506 acres, with a lighthouse on an abrupt cliff 455 feet high.

Cape Coast Castle, a town and fort of western Africa on the Gulf of Guinea, in British colony of the Gold Coast, in lat. 5° 5' N., and lon. 1° 13' W. The place lies in a chasm, and is defended by the great castle near the water's edge, and by three small forts on the hills behind, one of which serves as a lighthouse and signal station. With the exception of a few houses for Europeans, the town consists of straggling lines of mud huts, with clusters of palm-trees and an occasional tamarind attached. It is a principal mart for native trade. It is connected by telegraph with Accra (the capital), and by road with Prahsue. The climate is unhealthy; mean temperature, 78°. The principal exports are gold-dust, ivory, and palm-oil. Cape Coast Castle was ceded by the Dutch to the English in 1665, and from 1672 was possessed by several British African companies till 1843, when it was taken over by the British government. Pop. about 12,000.

Cape Cod, a cape and peninsula on the coast of Massachusetts, on the south side of Massachusetts Bay, forming the county of Barnstable; lat. of the cape, 42° 3' N., lon. 70° 15' W. The peninsula is 65 miles in length and from 1 to 20 in breadth, and is in the form of a man's arm, bent inward both at the elbow and the wrist. Though mostly sandy and barren, it is nevertheless populous; and the inhabitants derive their subsistence chiefly from the sea. The best harbor on the peninsula is at Provincetown. There is a lighthouse known as the Highland Light, on the northeast shore and one at Race Point almost directly west of the former. The navigation around the cape is peculiarly baffling and hazardous, and the saving to commerce and human life which would result from a short-cut waterway would be great. A proposition to cut a canal from Buzzard's Bay to Barnstable Bay dates from the early part of the 17th century, but nothing was actually done until 1878, when a charter was granted by the legislature of Massachusetts, a company was formed, and work begun. The cape was discovered 15 May 1602 by Bartholomew Gosnold, who gave it its name from having taken a great quantity of codfish near it. In 1620 the Pilgrims of the Mayflower made a temporary landing at the site now occupied by Provincetown.

Cape Cod, a book of travel and description by Henry D. Thoreau, published in 1865. Until Thoreau arrived to make acquaintance with its hard yet fascinating personality, Cape Cod remained unknown and almost unseen, though often visited and written about by tourists and students of nature. Something in the asceticism, or the directness, or the amazing keenness of Thoreau's mind brought him into sympathetic understanding of the thing he saw, and he interpreted the level stretches of shore with absolute fidelity. In this, as in his other books, Thoreau rises from the observation of the most familiar and commonplace facts, the comparison of the driest bones of observed data, to the loftiest spiritual speculation, the most poetic interpretation of nature.

Cape Colon'na. See SUNIUM.

Cape Colony, a British colony at the southern extremity of Africa, washed on the west, south, and east by the ocean, and having on the north and northeast the German terri-

tory of Great Namaqualand, the British territory of Bechuanaland, the Orange River Colony,
Basutoland (British), and the colony of Natal.
A considerable portion of the boundary on the
north is formed by the Orange River. The
colony extends about 450 miles from north to
south, and 600 from east to west; the coast
line is about 1,300 miles. The area is 276,000
square miles. The principal indentations of the
coast are St. Helena, Saldanha, Table, False,
Walker, Mossel, Plettenberg, St. Francis, and
Algoa bays.

In the interior almost every variety of soil
and surface is found, but a great part of the
colony is arid and uninviting in appearance.
Several ranges of mountains, running nearly
parallel to the southern coast, divide the country into successive terraces, rising as they re-
cede into the interior, between which lie belts
of fertile land, or vast treeless and barren-
looking plains. One of these, called the Great
Karoo, is 300 miles long and 100 broad, and
presents a desolate appearance, having a dry and
often baked soil, with small shrubby plants
scattered over it. Yet these plains make valuable sheep-walks, the flocks thriving exceedingly well upon the scanty vegetation; and the
soil, where water can be obtained by collecting
the rain, is generally very fertile. Large reservoirs have been constructed in many places, and
permanent homesteads established where formerly flocks could only be maintained for a
month or six weeks at a time. The principal
and farthest inland mountain terrace averages
6,000 or 7,000 feet in height, and, commencing in Namaqualand, runs eastward under the
names of Roggeveld, Nieuwveld, Sneeuwber-
gen, Stormbergen, etc., to the northeast frontier. The culminating point is the Compass
Berg, over 8,000 feet high. The Table Mountain at Cape Town is a stupendous mass of
naked rock, rising almost perpendicularly, about
3,585 feet in height. The colony is deficient in
rivers, though in this respect the eastern half is
more favored than the western. The Orange
River is the largest in this part of Africa, but
is of little or no use for navigation. Others are
the Elephants or Olifants River, flowing into
the Atlantic; the Gauritz, Gamtoos, Great Fish,
Sunday, and Great Kei, emptying themselves
into the sea on the south and southeast.

The most valuable mineral product is diamonds; copper ore is largely exported; coal is
mined, and iron ore, gold, amethysts, agates, etc.,
are found. The bulk of the diamonds that come
into the markets of the world in the rough state
are now obtained from Cape Colony. The great
mining centre is Kimberley, in the far north of
the colony, about 10 miles from the Vaal River,
and near the frontier of the Orange River
Colony. So far as is known, the first of the
South African diamonds was casually picked up
in 1867, and soon after several others were
found, including a fine large stone known as
the "Star of South Africa." By the early part
of 1870 so many diamonds had been found that a
rush of people to the diamond district began
to take place, and the banks of the Vaal were
soon covered with thousands of diggers. At
first the precious stones were found on or near
the surface, but subsequently it was discovered
that they were to be found deeper down, and
latterly they have been obtained many hundreds

of feet below the surface, great open excavations
having been made at the localities where they
are plentiful. The richest mine has been the
Kimberley mine, situated in the centre of the
town of the same name, which sprang up around
it. For the first hundred feet in depth the diamonds were found embedded in a soft, friable,
yellowish earth; below that the soil changed
to a slaty-blue color, and was of a firmer consistency, and the diggers then thought that the bottom of the mine had been reached. It was soon
discovered, however, that the blue ground
yielded as many diamonds as the yellow, if not
more, and this productivity has still continued.
Another famous mine is the De Beers mine.
Both these mines have yielded a remarkable
number of large stones, but a great many of
the diamonds have been "off-color," that is, yellow, spotted, or otherwise defective in water or
lustre. One of the finest yet found in South
Africa is the "Porter Rhodes," a beautiful stone
weighing 150 carats, and valued at $300,000.
One much larger, a yellow stone, weighing 302
carats, was found in 1884, and a still larger,
weighing 428½ carats, was found in the De
Beers mine in 1888. The largest in the world,
weighing 971 carats, but with a large flaw, was
found in the Orange Free State in 1893. Although mining operations have been carried on
at great expense, owing to the depths to which
the workings have been sunk (some 600 feet or
more), the profits of the companies which latterly have owned the mines have been enormous.
The rough work has been done almost entirely
by the native Africans, of whom 10,000 or 11,000
have been in employment in the mines at one
time. Very stringent regulations have had to
be enforced to prevent theft of the precious
stones, and also illicit dealing in stones unlaw-
fully acquired.

The climate is very healthy and generally
pleasant, though in summer the heat is great in
some parts. The mean temperature for the year
at Cape Town is about 62°. The climate of the
dry and elevated inland districts is considered
remarkably suitable for persons of consumptive
tendency, and many have been attracted to the
colony on this account.

Except along the coast line, especially the
southeast coast district, where there are extensive forests, timber is scarce. There are upward of a hundred different kinds of woods,
however; many of them extensively employed
for such purposes as house-building, wagon-
making, and furniture- and cabinet-work. With
irrigation, trees can be grown anywhere. The
aloe and the myrtle attain a great size.

The quadrupeds of the colony comprise the
African elephant, still found in the forests of the
south coast region; the buffalo, equally restricted in locality; the leopard, jackal, hyæna,
numerous antelopes, baboon, aardvark, etc.
Lions, at one time numerous, are not now to be
met with in the colony, nor is the giraffe. The
birds include vultures, eagles, and other *Rap-
tores* (the most remarkable of which is the
serpent-eater), pelicans, flamingoes, and most
important of all, the ostrich, now bred as a domestic animal for the sake of its feathers, those
plucked from an adult bird in a season being
sometimes worth from $50 to $90. Other native animals are large snakes, the venomous
cobra di capello, and the scorpion. Along the

coast whales and seals abound, and salt- and fresh-water fish are plentiful.

The colony is better adapted for pasturage than for agriculture, but wheat, maize, and other cereals can be grown almost everywhere, the only drawback to their cultivation being the want of moisture in certain localities and in certain seasons. In some years a surplus of grain is left for exportation; in others grain has to be imported. All kinds of European vegetables and pot-herbs, and all the fruits of temperate climates, such as apples, pears, plums, peaches, melons, apricots, walnuts, almonds, oranges, limes, etc., thrive excellently, and fruits, dried and preserved, are exported. The vine is cultivated, and some excellent wines (notably those of Constantia) are made. The colony is said to be particularly well suited for grape-culture, and the vines produce heavier crops than are known almost anywhere else. Viticulture, it is believed, is yet only in its infancy, though there are already over 90,000,000 vine-stocks. The colonial government has up to 1899 disposed of 128,000,000 acres of land, the quantity remaining undisposed of being 49,564,000 acres.

Sheep-raising is the most important industry, and wool the chief export (although surpassed in value by diamonds). The amount of this article exported to the United Kingdom in 1899 was 84,032,536 pounds. Most attention is now devoted to the breeding of pure merinoes, the consequence being a great improvement in the wool. Goats are also bred, both the native and the Angora, and the export of goats' wool or hair to Great Britain has increased from 102,570 pounds in 1868 to 12,948,574 pounds in 1899. Cattle-breeding is carried on to some extent, especially along the coasts and in the eastern and northern districts.

There are no manufactures of any importance, and consequently the imports of the colony consist largely of manufactured goods, chiefly from Great Britain. The total imports in 1898-9 were of the value of $83,652,000; in 1871 their value was $15,173,014; exports in 1898-9 amounted to $131,265,250, in 1871 to $16,422,083. The value of the gold exported in the year 1898-9 was $83,735,250; of diamonds, including those sent through the postoffice, $22,145,100. The total value of the diamonds exported from 1867 to 1898 was $226,800,000. The other exports of importance, besides wool, are ostrich feathers, copper ore, skins, and hides. The exports of merchandise to Great Britain in 1899 amounted to $45,274,887, the imports of British produce to $40,645,654. To facilitate the inland traffic numerous roads have been made (the total length within the colony proper amounting to 8,000 miles), while 2,700 miles of railway and 7,500 miles of telegraph have been opened. Lighthouses have been built round the coast, and harbor works constructed.

The coinage is that of Great Britain, as are also the weights and measures, except that for land the *morgen* = 2.116 acres is employed.

The constitution formed under the acts of 1853, 1865, and 1872 vests the executive in the governor (who is also commander-in-chief of the forces) and an executive council or ministry composed of certain office-holders appointed by the Crown. The legislative power is in the hands of a legislative council of 23 members, elected for seven years, over which the chief justice presides *ex officio*, and a House of Assembly of 95 members, elected for five years, representing the country districts and towns of the colony. The public revenue for 1897-8 was $34,979,292; the expenditure, $40,891,280; the public debt amounts to about $145,500,000. The revenue is chiefly derived from railways, customs duties, and taxes. Much the greater portion of the debt represents money spent on the construction of railways.

The European population consists in part of English, Scottish, and Irish settlers and their descendants, but the majority is of Dutch origin (see BOERS), with a considerable number of German origin. The colored people are chiefly Hottentots, Kaffirs, Bechuanas, Basutos, Griquas, Malays, and a mixed race, the offspring of black women and white fathers. The laborers are chiefly Hottentots and Kaffirs. The prejudices and ill feeling once subsisting between the different nationalities of which the population is made up are now fast disappearing. Education is advancing, though it is not compulsory. The returns show a steady increase in the numbers of children of all classes receiving instruction. For the higher education there are seven colleges, besides a university (at Cape Town) incorporated in 1873. The colleges have each a staff of instructors in classics, mathematics, science, etc., but the university is merely an examining and degree-conferring institution. The religious bodies in the colony with the greatest number of adherents are the Dutch Reformed Church, the Church of England, the Methodists, Independents, and Presbyterians, in the order here given. There is no Established Church.

The chief towns of the colony ranking after Cape Town are Port Elizabeth, Kimberley, and Graham's Town (qq.v.).

The Dutch, who had early fixed upon the Cape as a watering-place for their ships, first colonized it under Van Riebeek in 1652. Reducing the Hottentot inhabitants to slavery, or driving them beyond the mountains, they extended the Cape settlement over a pretty large area. But the colony was under the rule of the Dutch East India Company, and owing to their regulations, made very slow progress. It was captured by the British in 1795, restored at the Peace of Amiens (1802), and again taken in 1806, Sir David Baird being sent at the head of an expedition to take possession of it, and so prevent it from falling into the hands of the French. From this time it has remained in the possession of the British, to which it was formally assigned in 1815, along with Dutch Guiana, Holland receiving in return £6,000,000. It now began to advance in prosperity, but the progress of the colony was greatly retarded by the Kaffir wars of 1834, 1846, and 1851-3, the result of the depredations of this warlike race. Subsequently the area of the colony was gradually enlarged by the annexation of surrounding districts. The most important of these annexations were British Kaffraria (annexed 1866); Griqualand West (1876); Kaffraria proper, or the Transkeian districts (Transkei proper, Griqualand East, and Tembuland), including nearly the whole of the region between the Kei and the Natal border (1875-80); Pondoland (1894); and part of Bechuanaland (1895). Its most recent history has been connected with the war between Great Britain and the Boer republics. See BOERS; SOUTH AFRICAN WAR.

Cape Comorin, kŏm'ō-rĭn, the most southern extremity of the peninsula of Deccan, British India, in lat. 8° 5′ N., and lon. 77° 30′ E., forming a circular, low, sandy point, which is not discernible above the distance of 12 to 16 miles from the deck of a large ship. Eighteen miles north from the cape is a bold summit called Comorin Peak, the southern termination of the western Ghauts, which has, from a distance, been often taken for the cape itself. Within a short distance of the cape lies a rocky islet, high above water; and about three miles from this islet are a fort and a village, a few fishermen's houses, a church, and some ancient temples, being the remains of the once famous town of Cape Comorin.

Cape Diamond, the extremity of an abrupt promontory in the province of Quebec, Canada, at the junction of the St. Charles and St. Lawrence rivers. On the promontory stands the citadel of Quebec, and on the west and nearly on a level with the ramparts lie the Plains of Abraham. Here was gained in 1755 the memorable victory by the English under Wolfe, over the French under Montcalm.

Cape Disappointment, or **Cape Hancock,** a cape at the mouth of the Columbia River, forming the southwest point of the State of Washington, in lat. 46° 16′ N., and lon. 124° 2′ W. There is a lighthouse at this point with a fixed light.

Cape Ducato, doo-kä'tō, the southern extremity of Santa Maura, one of the Ionian islands. It is identical with the ancient promontory of Leucadia, commonly called the Lover's Leap, or Sappho's Leap. The famous Greek poetess, according to an ancient tradition, threw herself from the top of this promontory.

Cape Elizabeth, a headland projecting into Casco Bay, between Portland harbor in Maine and the Atlantic Ocean, in lat. 43° 33′ N., and lon. 70° 11′ W. The coast is rocky, made up of ledges of talcose slate, traversed by dikes of trap. There are two lighthouses on the outer point, which stand 300 yards apart, the lights being 140 feet above the sea.

Cape Espichel (probably the ancient *Barbarium Promontorium*), a cape on the western coast of Portugal, 121 miles southwest of Lisbon. It rises abruptly from the sea, and is crowned by a small chapel and a lighthouse.

Cape Farewell, the southern extremity of Greenland, at the eastern entrance to Davis Strait. A strong current sets around this cape, and continues north along the eastern coast of the strait.

Cape Faro, fä'rō, the northeast extremity of the island of Sicily, known to the ancients as *Pelorus.* It is at the narrowest part of the strait of Messina, opposite the rock of Scylla on the coast of Italy.

Cape Fear, the south point of Smith's Island, near the mouth of Cape Fear River, N. C. About one mile from the shore stands Bald Head lighthouse.

Cape Fear River, a river of North Carolina; navigable for steamboats for 120 miles from its mouth. Its length, including one of the head branches, is about 300 miles. Formed by the junction of the Deep and Haw rivers, its course is generally southeast till it reaches the Atlantic Ocean. This is the largest and most important river which lies wholly within the State.

Cape Finistere, fĭn-ĭs-tär', the western-most point of Spain, in the province of Corunna, extending southwest into the Atlantic, in lat. 42° 54′ N., and lon. 90° 21′ W. Several naval battles were fought off this cape.

Cape Flattery, the most westerly point of the State of Washington, at the entrance to the Strait of Juan de Fuca, in lat. 48° 23′ N., and lon. 124° 44′ W. On the island of Tatoosh, opposite the cape, there is a lighthouse.

Cape Florida, the southern extremity of Biscayne Key off the southeast coast of Florida, at the north entrance to Biscayne Bay, in lat. 25° 39′ N., and lon. 80° 9′ W. There is a lighthouse on the shoals opposite this point.

Cape Foulweather, a cape projecting into the Pacific Ocean from the coast of Oregon, in lat. 44° 50′ N., and lon. 124° 5′ W.

Cape Fox, or **Lalande's Dog,** a peculiar canine animal (*Otocyon lalandii*), differing from other dogs principally in the possession of an additional molar in each jaw. Other characters in the structure of the jaw and dentition suggest that *Otocyon* is a persistent creodont-like form, which has developed from a primitive arctoid stock in a direction curiously parallel to that of the true dogs. No other mammal outside the marsupial order ever has four molar teeth in both jaws, and this may indicate a still more remote marsupial ancestry. This wild dog is generally found in open country, dwelling among small bushes in pairs, exceedingly shy, and not gathering into packs. It is rather smaller than a fox and resembles a fennec in having enormous ears and a thick, bushy tail. In general color it is brownish or iron gray, mottled with yellow and with the limbs nearly black.

Cape Frio, frē'ō (Port. *Cabo Frio,* "cool cape"), a promontory on the coast of Brazil, in the State of Rio de Janeiro. It forms the terminus of a range of mountains running parallel to the coast, and consists of a huge oval mass of granite. There is a lighthouse at this point.

Cape Froward, the southern extremity of the continent of South America, lying northwest of Cape Horn, in lat. 53° 53′ S., and lon. 71° 18′ W. It is a bold promontory of dark slaty rock.

Cape Gaspé. See GASPÉ.

Cape Gata, gä'tä, or **Cape de Gatte,** a promontory of Spain, on the coast of Granada, 24 miles in circuit and 13 miles broad. It was formerly a resort of Moorish pirates.

Cape Girardeau, jē-rär-do', Mo., a city of Cape Girardeau County, on the Mississippi River, the Illinois Cent., and the St. Louis, C. G. & F. S. R.R.'s; 150 miles southeast of St. Louis. It is the seat of St. Vincent's College and the Southeastern Missouri State Normal School, and has a national bank and several newspapers. Pop. (1900) 4,815.

Cape of Good Hope, a promontory near the south extremity of Africa, in lat. 34° 21′ S., and lon. 18° 3′ E., at the termination of a small peninsula extending south from Table Mountain, which overlooks Cape Town. This peninsula forms the western side of False Bay, and on its inner coast is Simon's Bay and Simon's Town, where there is a safe anchorage and a British naval station. Bartholomew Diaz, who discovered the Cape in 1487, called it Cape of Storms; but John II. of Portugal changed this to its present designation. It was first doubled by Vasco de Gama in 1497. Here is one of the principal astronomical institutions of the world. About the middle of the 18th century the French astronomer, Lacaille, made an exceedingly valuable series of observations at the Cape. Ever since the English have had a colony there they have kept up astronomical work, the Cape having been the scene of the labors of several celebrated English astronomers, among them Sir John Herschel.

Cape Grisnez, grē-nā, a headland of France in the department of Pas-de-Calais, the nearest point of the French coast to Great Britain. It has a revolving light 195 feet high.

Cape Guardafui, gwär-dä-foo-ē′, or **Gardafui,** a cape on the east coast of Africa in Somaliland, situated in lat. 11° 50′ N., and lon. 51° 16′ E.

Cape Haitien, ä-ē-tē-ăṅ, or **Cape Haytien,** Haiti, a town on the north coast of the island. It was formerly known as Cap Français, Le Cap, or Guarico, the latter being the native name. It has an excellent harbor, but has declined in importance in recent years. Pop. about 29,000.

Cape Hat′teras, the easternmost point of North Carolina, a sandy insular spit, or narrow beach, separated from the mainland by the broad bay called Pamlico Sound. South of the capes of the Delaware, no land stretches so far out into the Atlantic as Cape Hatteras. The Gulf Stream, in its eastern and western vibrations, often flows within 20 miles of the cape, crowding toward the shore coasting vessels bound south. The difference of temperature between the hot airs of the Gulf and the breezes along shore and from the land engender frequent commotions in the atmosphere at this place; and no point on the coast is more noted for its frequent and dangerous storms. A lighthouse is kept a little over a mile north of the outermost point.

Cape Henlo′pen, a cape on the eastern coast of Delaware at the south side of the entrance to Delaware Bay, in lat. 38° 47′ N., and lon. 75° 5′ W.

Cape Henry, a cape on the coast of Virginia at the southern entrance of Chesapeake Bay. It has a fixed light 120 feet above the level of the sea.

Cape Horn, the southern extremity of an island of the same name, forming the most southerly point of South America. It is a precipitous headland, 500 to 600 feet high, and running far into the sea. Sailing vessels often encounter dangerous tempests in passing round the Horn; steamers generally pass through the Straits of Magellan. The cape was first doubled in 1616 by the navigator Schouten, a native of Hoorn, Holland, whence its name.

Cape Hunting-dog, a wild dog of Africa (*Lycaon pictus*), which is placed in a separate genus because it differs from all other dogs in having only four toes on each limb, in lacking one pair of molars in the upper jaw, and in certain other features. It resembles a hyæna in

form, and is yellowish-gray, with irregular, black markings. It hunts in packs, and is one of the enemies most dreaded by all the African antelopes. Since the decrease of this, its natural game, it has played havoc with domestic cattle and sheep, and is killed off by the settlers wherever found.

Cape Island City. See CAPE MAY, N. J.

Cape de la Hague, häg (written also, but less correctly La Hogue), a headland of Normandy, France, opposite the island of Alderney, and forming the northwestern extremity of the peninsula of Cotentin, in the English channel. It is often confounded with Fort La Hogue or La Hougue, on the opposite side of Cotentin. Near this latter promontory the united English and Dutch fleets defeated the French, 19–24 May 1692.

Cape Linguetta, lĭn-gwĕt′tą, a headland of European Turkey, 2,290 feet high. It forms the termination of the Chimara, or Acroceraunian Mountains, and bounds the east entrance into the Adriatic.

Cape Lookout, a cape situated on an island off the southeast coast of North Carolina, in lat. 34° 37′ N., and lon. 76° 31′ W. There is a lighthouse at a considerable height above the sea.

Cape Lopa′tha, the southern extremity of Kamchatka. At the northern part of the headland is a mountain, bearing the same name, whence the land gradually slopes and narrows until it terminates in a low and barren tongue.

Cape Lopez, lō′päth, the southern extremity of the Bight of Biafra, on the west coast of Africa. It is situated in lat. 0° 36′ S., and lon. 8° 44′ E.

Cape Matapan, mà-tą-pän′, a promontory of Greece, forming the southern extremity of the Peloponnesus, in lat. 36° 23′ N., and lon. 22° 29′ E. The name *Tænarum*, or *Promontorium Tænarium*, was applied by the Greeks to the headland, and to the small peninsula north of it, connected with the great Taygetic peninsula by a narrow isthmus.

Cape May, N. J., a city and watering place in the southern part of Cape May County, having good railroad and water communication. It has a fine beach and is very popular as a seaside resort, providing accommodations in hotels and boarding-houses for guests 10 times exceeding in number the permanent inhabitants. The place is sometimes called Cape City or Cape Island City. Pop. (1900) 2,257.

Cape May, the southern extremity of New Jersey, at the entrance to Delaware Bay, situated in Cape May County, in lat. 38° 56′ N., and lon. 74° 57′ W. It has a revolving light about 150 feet above sea-level.

Cape Mendocino, mĕn-dō-sē′no, the westernmost point of the coast of California, projecting onto the Pacific Ocean in lat. 40° 25′ N., and lon. 124° 25′ W. It has a very high lighthouse with a flashing light.

Cape Ned′dock, Maine, a promontory 35 miles southwest of Portland, with a lighthouse on Goat Island near it, containing a fixed light, 33 feet above the sea.

Cape Nome, nōm, a cape on the south coast of the peninsular projection of Alaska, which separates Kotzebue Sound on the north from Bering Sea on the south, and terminates on the west in Cape Prince of Wales. In the vicinity of the cape is a remarkably rich gold mining region. In a direct line of navigation, it lies about 2,500 miles northwest of Seattle, and 175 miles southeast of Siberia. The nearest settlement of consequence, prior to 1899, was St. Michael, 100 miles to the southeast, the starting point of the steamers for the Yukon River; but during the year various aggregations of mining population had built themselves up in closer range and reduced the isolation from the civilized world by some 60 miles. The Nome district as settled centres about the lower course of the Snake River, an exceedingly tortuous stream in its tundra course, which emerges from a badly degraded line of limestone, slaty, and schistose mountain spurs, generally not over 700 to 1,200 feet elevation, but backed by loftier granitic heights, and discharges into the sea at a position 13 miles west of Cape Nome proper.

The first discovery of gold was made in September 1898, when a party of Swedes found it on the creeks and the gulches. It was not until July 1899 that the beach gold was discovered. In the middle of October following, Nome City had 5,000 inhabitants all living in tents on the hitherto barren shore. The rapidity of the growth of this town has probably never been equaled. The region is wholly within American territory, and early prospecting indicated that it would rival in richness the famous Klondike district. During the season of 1901 $7,000,000 in gold was taken from the Cape Nome region.

Cape North, the northeast point of Cape Breton, projecting into the Gulf of St. Lawrence.

Cape North, or Otoo, Otou, a peninsula at the northern extremity of New Zealand, about two miles long, and terminating in a bluff head flat at the top.

Cape North, northernmost promontory of Europe. See NORTH CAPE.

Cape Nun, noon, a headland on the west coast of Morocco, extending into the sea at the southwestern extremity of the Atlas range, in lat. 28° 45′ N., and lon. 11° 5′ W.

Cape Ortegal, ôr-tä-gäl′, a rugged promontory forming the northern extremity of Spain, extending into the Bay of Biscay, in lat. 43° 45′ N., and lon. 7° 56′ W.

Cape Pal′mas, a cape on the western coast of Africa, situated in the southern part of Liberia, in lat. 4° 22′ N., and lon. 7° 44′ W.

Cape Petrel, or Cape Pigeon, a large petrel (*Daption capensis*), about the size of a pigeon, exceedingly numerous about the Cape of Good Hope, and widely distributed throughout the Southern Ocean.

Cape Pillar, a high mass of rocks terminating in two tower-shaped cliffs on the northwest coast of Tierra del Fuego, at the southwest entrance from the Pacific Ocean into the Straits of Magellan.

Cape Poge, a cape on the coast of Massachusetts, in lat. 41° 25′ N., and lon. 70° 26′ W. It has a lighthouse with a fixed light.

Cape Prince of Wales, a promontory on Bering Sea, the most northwest point of North America. It terminates in a peaked mountain, presenting a bold face to the sea, and is a dangerous point on account of a shoal which stretches to the northeast.

Cape Race, a promontory at the southeastern extremity of Newfoundland, in lat. 46° 39′ N., and 53° 4′ W. The fogs of this part of the coast make navigation hazardous. The British government maintains a light here.

Cape River, or Rio de Segovia, known also as Coco or Wanx, a river of Nicaragua, Central America, which after a generally northeast course of nearly 300 miles enters the Caribbean Sea at Cape Gracias a Dios. It is navigable for a considerable distance from the sea, but the upper part of its course is obstructed by cataracts and shallows. It forms part of the boundary between Honduras and Nicaragua.

Cape Romain′, a low and barren point of land, with a lighthouse, 37 miles northeast of Charleston, S. C.

Cape Sable, the name of two capes in North America: (1) The southernmost point of the mainland of the United States at the extremity of Florida, in lat. 25° 8′ N., and lon. 81° 9′ W. (2) A point at the southwest extremity of Nova Scotia, in lat. 43° 23′ N. and lon. 65° 37′ W.

Cape San Antonio, sän än-tō′nĕ-ō, the name of two capes: (1) A high, barren, and precipitous headland, on the coast of Valencia, Spain. On its summit are a convent, a watch tower, and several windmills. (2) A lofty and nearly perpendicular promontory, at the mouth of the Rio de la Plata, in the territory of Buenos Ayres.

Cape San Blas, sän blä, a low point of land, about two miles long, on the south coast of Florida, 123 miles east-southeast of Pensacola. It has a revolving light 65 feet high.

Cape San Lucas, loo′käs, the southern extremity of the peninsula of Old California, in lat. 22° 44′ N., and lon. 109° 54′ W.

Cape St. Roque, rō′kä, San Roque, or São Roque, a cape on the east coast of Brazil, in lat. 5° 29′ S., and lon. 35° 14′ W. See BRAZIL.

Cape St. Vincent, a headland at the southwestern extremity of Portugal, in lat. 37° 3′ N., and lon. 8° 58′ W. Off this cape, 14 Feb. 1797, an English naval force, consisting of 15 ships of the line, under Admiral Jarvis, defeated a superior Spanish fleet. This point was known to the ancients as *Promontorium Sacrum.*

Cape Spartiven′to, the ancient *Herculis Promontorium,* a promontory of southern Italy, forming the southeastern extremity of Calabria, in lat. 37° 57′ N., and lon. 16° 5′ E.

Cape of Storms. See CAPE OF GOOD HOPE.

Cape Tindaro, tĭn-dä′rō, a headland of Sicily, extending into the Gulf of Patti. The remains of the ancient Tyndaris are in its neighborhood.

Cape Town, Africa, capital of the Cape Colony, situated in the midst of striking scenery, rather more than 30 miles from the Cape of Good Hope, at the head of Table Bay, which opens into the Atlantic on the northwest, and at the foot of Table Mountain. It is regularly laid out and has some good streets, with well-built business premises and other buildings, and is furnished with most of the institutions and conveniences of a European town (including tramways). The finest edifice is that which accommodates the legislature, a handsome structure of modern erection; another good edifice is that containing the public library (40,000 volumes) and museum, in the Roman-Corinthian style. The Standard Bank of South Africa also occupies handsome premises. Other buildings are the government house, the courts and government offices, the town house, the gallery of fine arts, the railway station, the post-office, the exchange, etc. The best ecclesiastical building is the Roman Catholic Cathedral; there is also an English Episcopal Cathedral, and Dutch, Presbyterian, Lutheran, Independent, and Methodist churches. There is a well-equipped college, the South African College, which trains students for the degrees of the Cape University, which is merely an examining body. There are beautiful botanic or government gardens in the town, occupying 14 acres, and forming a fine promenade. The Cape Observatory is a celebrated institution supported by imperial funds. A railway runs from Cape Town into the interior of the colony, connecting the town with the Orange Free State and Transvaal. The port has been provided with a breakwater 3,554 feet long, inside of which ships can safely ride at anchor protected from the northwest gales; and there are two docks 16 acres in area, an outer harbor of 62 acres, a large graving dock, etc. The population is very mixed, a large number consisting of colored people of negro or other African descent. About 14,000 are Malays, descendants of those who were brought from the Dutch East Indies; they constitute the chief fishing and working population of the town and environs. They number altogether about 86,000, more than half of the whites being of Dutch descent.

Cape Trafalgar, trăf äl gär, or trä-fäl′gär, a headland on the coast of Cadiz, Spain. It is memorable for the naval battle fought near it, 21 Oct. 1805, between the English under Nelson, and the combined fleets of France and Spain. The English gained a complete victory, though with the loss of their commander. It was known to the Romans as *Promontorium Junonis.*

Cape Verde, the most westerly headland of Africa in Senegal, jutting out into the Atlantic Ocean, between the rivers Gambia and Senegal, in lat. 14° 43′ N., and lon. 17° 30′ W. It was discovered by the Portuguese navigator, Fernandez, in 1445, and is said to have derived its name from a group of gigantic baobab trees adorning its summit.

Cape Verde Islands, a group of islands west of Africa, in the Atlantic Ocean, so called from Cape Verde, opposite to which they are situated; 320 miles west of Cape Verde, and between lat. 15° and 18° N. They belong to Portugal. As to their number, some reckon 10, others 14 or more, by giving the name of islands to masses which are only rocks. They are, in general, mountainous. The island of Fogo, one of the group, consists of one single mountain, a volcano, sometimes active, about 10,000 feet above the level of the sea. Some of the islands are very bare; in others the lower hills are covered with a beautiful verdure, as well as the

valleys between; but there is little water, except what is found in ponds and wells. Long droughts have occurred, sometimes causing great loss of life. The climate is hot and unhealthy in most of the islands. The soil is, for the most part, not very fertile; nevertheless, some parts produce sugar, coffee, rice, maize, etc., with bananas, lemons, oranges, citrons, grapes, and other fruits. The total population amounts to about 148,000, of whom about 4,000 are white, the rest being chiefly negroes. The chief town is Porto Praya on São Thiago (Santiago), and Porto Grande on São Vicente is a coaling station for steamers. Salt is an export of importance. Coffee, hides, and physic-nuts are also exported.

Cape Wrath, a pyramidal promontory of unrivaled wildness and grandeur, forming the northwest extremity of Scotland and running out into the Atlantic; in lat. 58° 38′ N., and lon. 4° 58′ 5″ W. It presents deep fissures and tall pinnacles. From it a reef of rocks, perforated with arches and caverns, juts out into the sea. Off the cape is Stag Rock, a pillar 200 feet high. Cape Wrath is 600 feet high, and there is a lighthouse near it, 400 feet above the sea, visible 25 miles off.

Capecelatro, Alphonse, äl-fôns kä-pä-che-lätrō, CARDINAL, Italian pietist biographer and controversialist: b. Marseilles, 5 Feb. 1824. He has won distinction as Italy's leading contemporary Church writer, with a 'History of St. Catherine of Siena and of the Papacy of Her Day' (1856); 'The Errors of Renan'; a 'Life of Jesus'; and a 'Life of St. Philip of Neri' (1882).

Capefigue, Baptiste Honoré Raymond, bäp-tēst ō-nō-rä rä-môn käp-fēg; French historian and journalist: b. Marseilles, 1802; d. Paris, 23 Dec. 1872. His contributions to historical science are the 'History of Philip Augustus' (1829); and 'History of the Restoration and of the Causes that Led to the Fall of the Elder Branch of the House of Bourbon' (1831-3).

Cap′el, Arthur, LORD, English soldier: b. about 1610; d. 9 March 1649. He was son of Sir Henry Capel; was raised to the peerage as Lord Capel, of Hadham, by Charles I. in 1641. During the revolutionary war he fought bravely as one of the royalist generals in the west in the engagements at Bristol, Exeter, and Taunton. Having been at length forced to surrender at Colchester to Gen. Fairfax, he was imprisoned, and after some vicissitudes, executed. His 'Daily Observations or Meditations' was published posthumously with a memoir.

Capel, Arthur, VISCOUNT MALDEN and EARL OF ESSEX, English statesman, son of the preceding: b. January 1631; d. July 1683. In 1661 he was created Viscount Malden and Earl of Essex and appointed ambassador to Denmark in 1670. He served as lord-lieutenant of Ireland, 1672-7, and was for a few months in 1679 head of the treasury commission. Arrested for his connection with the Rye House Plot, was sent to the Tower, and is supposed to have committed suicide there.

Capel, Thomas John, MONSIGNOR, English Roman Catholic ecclesiastic: b: London, 28 Oct. 1835. He was educated at the Roman

Catholic College at Layston and was ordained to the priesthood in 1860. He devoted himself to education, establishing a Roman Catholic public school at Kensington in 1873, and was given the title of Monsignore by Pope Pius IX. He came to the United States in 1883, and after a lecture tour settled to private life in California. He is the author of 'The Holy Catholic Church'; 'Confession'; 'The Name Catholic'; 'The Pope the Head of the Church.' As Catesby he is supposed to be portrayed in Disraeli's 'Lothair.'

Ca'pel, or **Ca'ple,** a term used by miners to indicate the wall of a lode, especially in a tin or copper mine. It is generally of quartz, black tourmalin, and hornblende. The capels sometimes contain sufficient metallic particles to make it worth while to work them. In these cases they may be considered as forming part of the lode. The word "cab" is an equivalent used by Cornish miners. In the United States, "casing" is nearly synonymous.

Capeline, or **Capelline,** a small piece of armor, consisting of a skull cap of iron, worn in the Middle Ages by light armed men such as archers.

Cap'ell, Edward, English Shakespearean scholar: b. Throston, Suffolk, 1713; d. London, 24 Feb. 1781. He was deputy inspector of plays, and published 'Mr. William Shakespeare, His Comedies, Histories, and Tragedies'; 'Notes and Various Readings of Shakespeare'; and 'The School of Shakespeare.'

Capel'la, Martianus Mineus Felix, Latin writer of the 4th century: b. probably in Africa. His extant work, 'Satiricon,' consists of nine books, the first two under the title, 'De Nuptiis Philologiæ et Mercurii,' being an introductory allegory, while the others treat of grammar, logic, metaphysics, geometry, arithmetic, astronomy, and music. His statement of the heliocentric system of astronomy in the eighth book may possibly have given hints to Copernicus, who quotes him occasionally.

Capella, a star situated in the constellation Auriga, on the "Charioteer's" left shoulder. It is of remarkable brilliancy, only four stars exceeding it in that respect. Its color is nearly that of solar light.

Capellini, Giovanni, jō-vän'nē kä-pĕl-lē'nē, Italian geologist and paleontologist: b. Spezia, 13 Aug. 1833. He studied at Pisa, and traveled widely. In 1860 he became professor at Genoa, and later at Bologna. He has emphasized the importance of prehistoric discoveries which related archæology to paleontology and defended the Darwinian theory. He was influential in calling the International Congress of Anthropology and Prehistoric Archæology in 1865.

Capello, Bianca, bē-änk'ä kä-pĕl'lō, Italian adventuress: b. Venice, 1542; d. in the Castle Paggio di Capano, 11 Oct. 1587. In 1563 she eloped with a banker's clerk named Pietro Buonaventuri, who put himself under the protection of Francesco de Medici at Florence. The latter made Bianca his mistress and her husband his steward, but had him put to death in 1570, and after the death of his wife, Joanna of Austria, married Bianca in 1578. She and Francesco are supposed to have been poisoned by his brother and successor, Cardinal Fernando.

Capello, Hermengil'de, Augus'to de Brito, brē'tō, Portuguese African explorer: b. Lisbon, 1839. He entered the navy in 1858, and rose to the rank of captain. In 1877–9 he, with Robert Ivens, conducted an expedition which explored the sources of the Kuanga. In 1885 he set out on a second expedition with Ivens, traveling through the southern part of Africa from Mossamedes to Mozambique, thus exploring the sources of the Congo and the Zambesi, a country entirely unknown before. He wrote with Ivens 'De Benguella a sterras de Jacca' (1881); and 'De Angola a Contra-Costa' (1886).

Capen, Elmer Hewitt, American educator: b. Stoughton, Mass., 5 April 1838; d. Medford, Mass., 22 March 1905. He graduated at Tufts College in 1860, and was elected to the Massachusetts legislature while still an undergraduate, 1859. After studying at the Harvard Law School, he was admitted to the bar, and practised at Stoughton for a short time; began the study of theology, became a Universalist clergyman, held pastorates at Gloucester, Mass., and Providence, R. I., 1865–75, when he was elected president of Tufts College, a position he held till his death. His administration was most successful in every way, and under him the institution grew to be one of the most progressive of American colleges. His collected addresses appeared, entitled 'Occasional Addresses' (1902).

Ca'pen, Nahum, American historical writer: b. Canton, Mass., 1804; d. 4 Jan. 1886. He was postmaster of Boston, Mass. (1857–61); introduced street letter-box collections; wrote 'The Republic of the United States'; 'History of Democracy' (1874); etc. He also wrote and edited works on phrenology.

Capen, Samuel Billings, American missionary commissioner: b. Boston, Mass., 12 Dec. 1842. He was educated in the public schools, and after leaving the English High School in 1858 entered the carpet store in which he became a partner in 1864. He is best known to the public through his close association with the missionary work of the Congregational Church. He was president of the Boston Municipal League, 1894–9; of the Congregational Sunday School and Publishing Society; and of the American Board of Commissioners for Foreign Missions.

Capena Porta. See CAMPUS SCELERATUS.

Capercailzie, kăp-ĕr-kā'lī, **Capercaillie,** or **Cailzie,** kā'lī, a readily domesticated, polygamous grouse (*Tetrao urogallus*), about the size of a turkey, widely distributed throughout the pine-covered mountains of Europe. Formerly it inhabited Ireland and Scotland, where it was known as "blackcock," but it was entirely extirpated toward the end of the 18th century. It has since, however, in small numbers, been restored to Scotland by stock imported from Scandinavia. The ground color of the cock is muddy black, spotted with gray and brown; quill feathers dark brown; tail feathers nearly black; a glossy dark green chest; whitish bill and a small patch of naked skin above the eye, which is scarlet. The feet are feathered to the toes. The hen and young are dark brown, covered with freckles of a lighter shade; neck and chest yellowish chestnut, and the feathers of the under part usually edged with white. It feeds chiefly upon berries, seeds, insects, and the young shoots of the pine and other trees, which give its flesh a delicate turpentine flavor. They are hunted with the aid of dogs, which "tree" them, when they are easily shot. In the early spring, at the approach of the breeding season, the cocks meet at an accustomed place to give the hens the benefit of their annual "dances," at which assemblies the hens seem to choose their mates by the amount of plumage, colo·, daring, and extraordinary gestures which each displays. On such occasions the cock is oblivious to all else save the winning of his mate, and may easily be approached and killed. The female bird builds her nest on the ground among the pines, generally laying from 6 to 12 eggs, few of which reach maturity, owing to the carelessness of the mother. They are spotted red or yellowish brown, and are over two inches long. Consult: Lloyd, 'Game Birds of Sweden and Norway'; Morris, 'British Game Birds'; and Darwin, 'Descent of Man.'

Ca'pern, Edward, English minor poet: b. Tiverton, Devonshire, 29 Jan. 1819; d. 1894. He was long in the mail service in his native county, and was often styled "The Postman Poet." The poet Landor, attracted by the verse of Capern, procured him a pension from the civil list. His published works include: 'Poems by the Biddeford Rural Postman'; 'Ballads and Songs'; 'Wayside Warbles'; 'Sun-gleams and Shadow Pearls.' His verse is mainly descriptive of Devon life and character and several of his lyrics were set to music by the poet himself.

Caper'naum, a city of ancient Palestine, on the west or northwest side of the Sea of Tiberias. This place is famous in Christian history, because Jesus often visited it during the time of his ministry, and in its vicinity he delivered the Sermon on the Mount. Nothing of the city now remains.

Ca'pers, Ellison, American Protestant Episcopal bishop: b. Charleston, S. C., 14 Oct. 1837. He graduated at the South Carolina Military Academy 1857, and was a professor there, 1858-60. He entered the Confederate army, was successively major, lieutenant-colonel, and brigadier-general, and received severe wounds at Jackson, Miss., Chickamauga, and Franklin, Tenn. He was secretary of State of South Carolina in 1867-8, then entered the Protestant Episcopal ministry, and was rector of Christ Church, Greenville, S. C., for 20 years, and at Columbia, S. C., for six years. In 1893 he was consecrated seventh bishop of South Carolina.

Capers, the unopened flower-buds of a low shrub (*Capparis spinosa*), which grows from the crevices of rocks and walls, and among rubbish, in the southern parts of France, in Italy, and the Levant. The stems of the caper-bush are trailing, and two or three feet long. In the south of France the caper-bush is very common. It grows wild upon the walls of Rome, Sienna, and Florence, and, when trained against a wall, flourishes even in the neighborhood of Great Britain as an exotic as early as 1596. Modern horticulturists are of opinion that with care it might be raised in the open air in England, but this has never been accomplished to any practical extent. It is cultivated on a large scale between Marseilles and Toulon and in many parts of Italy. In the early part of summer it be-

gins to flower, and the flowers continue successively to appear until the commencement of winter. The buds are picked every morning before the petals are expanded; and as they are gathered they are put into vinegar and salt. When a sufficient quantity is collected they are distributed, according to their size, into different vessels, again put into vinegar, and then packed up for sale and exportation. The smallest capers are the dearest, simply from the reason that they are more troublesome to gather. This pickle is much used in sauce for boiled mutton. To persons unaccustomed to it the taste of capers is unpleasantly sharp and bitter, but after a little while the palate becomes reconciled to it. The flower-buds of the marsh-marigold (*Calthapalustris*) and the seeds of nasturtiums are frequently pickled and eaten as a substitute for capers. The bark of the root of the caper, cut into slices and dried in small rolls or quills, is sometimes used in medicine as a diuretic and in cases of obstruction of the liver.

Capes, Bernard, English novelist. His works include: 'The Lake of Wine' (1898); 'The Adventures of the Comte de la Muette' (1898); 'Our Lady of Darkness'; 'At a Winter's Fire' (1899); 'From Door to Door' (1900); 'Joan Brotherhood' (1900); 'Love Like a Gipsey' (1901); 'Plots' (1901). The majority of these have been republished in the United States.

Capes, William Wolfe, English historical writer. He has published: 'The Early Roman Empire'; 'Roman Empire in the 2d Century' (1876); 'University Life in Ancient Athens' (1877); 'Livy' (1879); 'Stoicism' (1880); 'History of the Achæan League,' a translation from Polybius (1888); 'The English Church in the 14th and 15th Centuries'; 'Rural Life in Hampshire.'

Capet, kȧ-pā, or kăp'ā, the name of the French race of kings, which has given 118 sovereigns to Europe, namely, 36 kings of France, 22 kings of Portugal, 11 of Naples and Sicily, 5 of Spain, 3 of Hungary, 3 emperors of Constantinople, 3 kings of Navarre, 17 dukes of Burgundy, 12 dukes of Brittany, 2 dukes of Lorraine, and 4 dukes of Parma. The history of this royal race is, at the same time, the history of the rise and progress of the French monarchy. The fate of one of the most interesting countries and nations in Europe is connected with the name of Capet. After having been deprived of four thrones, and again restored to them, this family stood forth as the first and most ancient support of the European principle of political legitimacy, that divine right, which in this house commenced with treason. Its origin is remarkable. Pepin the Short, the father of Charlemagne and mayor of the palace under the Merovingian dynasty, had displaced that royal house, and usurped the throne of the ancient kings of the Franks. After a space of 235 years his own descendants, the Carlovingian monarchs, experienced a similar fate. Under the last Carlovingians, destitute alike of energy and wisdom, Hugh the Great, Duke of France (by which was then understood the Isle of France), Orleans, and Burgundy, exercised a power as unlimited as that of the mayor of the palace under the Merovingians. On the death of Louis V., without children, in 987 his uncle,

Charles, Duke of Lower Lorraine, laid claim to the throne, which the Franks had sworn to preserve to the family of Charlemagne. The French nobility, disgusted at the German leanings of the Carlovingians, whose domains and influence lay in the eastern provinces, preferred that a member of their own class, whose possessions were situated in the centre of the country, and whose power was so great as to outrival that of the old dynasty, should rule over them, and accordingly chose as their king Hugh, son of Hugh the Great, Duke of France and Count of Paris, and had the support of the Church in their favor. The valiant Charles of Lorraine was surprised in Laon by the treachery of a bishop, and made prisoner. He died soon afterward in prison, and his son, Otho, Duke of Lower Lorraine, died in 1006. Both his younger brothers died childless in Germany. Thus the race of Capet was left in possession of the throne of France. According to some historians, Hugh Capet was descended from a Saxon family. He was married to a German princess, Adelaide, daughter of King Henry I. of Germany (Duke of Saxony). Hugh was crowned at Rheims, and swore to preserve to the nation, and particularly to the powerful feudal nobility and clergy, all their existing privileges. By his wise measures he gave permanence to his dynasty, which, next to the family of Guelph, is the oldest royal line at present existing. Hugh and the succeeding monarchs, till Louis VII., took the precaution to have their successors invested with the royal title during their own lifetime. Thus Hugh had his son, Robert, crowned and anointed as his colleague as early as 1 Jan. 988. He abolished by law the partition of the hereditary estates among the sons of the kings and forbade the alienation of the family domains. The daughters of the kings were endowed from that time with money, and the appanage which was given to the princes of the blood returned to the crown in default of male heirs. Both these principles were more fully confirmed by later laws. Thus Hugh Capet, by uniting his hereditary duchy, consisting of Paris, Isle de France, and Burgundy, inalienably with the crown, may be regarded as the founder of the French monarchy. What he had begun was completed by his successors, particularly in the times of the Crusades, and by the establishment of standing armies. On the failure of the direct line at the death of Charles IV., the French throne was kept in the family by the accession of the indirect line of Valois, and in 1589 by that of Bourbon. Capet being thus regarded as the family name of the kings of France, Louis XVI. was arraigned before the National Convention under the name of Louis Capet.

Cap'grave, John, English historian: b. Lynn, Norfolk, 1393; d. there, 1464. The most of his life was passed in the Augustinian friary of his native place. He was provincial of the order of Austin Friars in England, and was one of the most learned men of his day. He wrote in Latin numerous commentaries, sermons, and lives of the saints. His most important work was his 'Chronicle of England,' in English, extending from the creation to the year 1417. Other works were a 'Liber de Illustribus Henricis' and a 'Life of St. Katherine.' Many of his works are lost, others have never yet been printed. His 'Chronicle' and his 'Liber de Illustribus Henricis' have been printed in the Rolls series.

Caphtor, kăf'tŏr, the country in which the Philistines originated; mentioned in Deut. ii. 23; Jer. xlvii. 4; and Amos ix. 7. The location of Caphtor is not certain; it has been variously identified with Cappadocia, Cyprus, Crete, and Cilicia. It is most generally supposed to have been Crete, on account of the frequent connection of the Philistines with the Cherethites (or Cretans).

Capias, kăp'ē-ăs ("that you take"), a writ or process whereby the sheriff is ordered to arrest the body of the defendant. The writ so framed as to call for the arrest of the defendant before judgment, in order to compel him to answer to a suit, is called a *capias ad respondendum;* if after the judgment, to compel him to satisfy the judgment, it is called a *capias ad satisfaciendum,* commonly abbreviated *ca. sa.* In case of injuries without force, the civil law, and originally the common law, did not authorize the arrest of the defendant before judgment, that is, the arrest to answer; and upon feudal principles, says Sir William Blackstone (3 Com. 281), "the person of a feudatory was not liable to be attached for injuries merely civil, lest thereby the lord should be deprived of his services." The first writ of *capias ad respondendum* was given by act of Parliament in 1267, 52 Hen. III, c. 23, § 1, which provided that "if bailiffs, which ought to make account to their lords, do withdraw themselves, and have no lands nor tenements whereby they may be distrained, they shall be attached by their bodies, so that the sheriff shall cause them to come to make their account." This act applied to a particular description of receivers, and supposed them not only to be debtors, but also to have in their own hands the evidence of the amount of the debt, the production of which was one object of the process. The statute of 13 Edw. I., c. 11, passed in 1285, 18 years after the former, extends this process to "all manner of receivers bound to yield account," and provides "if they be found in arrearages upon this account, their bodies shall be arrested, and, by the testimony of the auditors, shall be sent into the next jail, and be imprisoned in irons under safe custody, and remain in prison at their own cost until they have satisfied their master (the creditor) fully of their arrearages." It would appear that the practice of arresting on mesne process, that is before judgment, to answer in civil suits, grew out of these statutes; for the subsequent statutes of 25 Edw. III., c. 17 (1350), providing that "such process shall be made in writ of debt, detinue of chattels, and taking of beasts, by writ of *capias,* as is used in writ of account"; and of 21 Hen. VII., c. 9 (1503); evidently have reference to an arrest to answer. Formerly, a writ upon which a suit was commenced was either a *capias,* distress, or summons; either the person of the defendant was seized, and (unless he was bailed) imprisoned until the trial, or his goods or lands were seized as a guarantee of his appearance to answer; and more often, in modern times, to obtain a lien to secure satisfaction of the judgment; or he was only summoned, that is, merely had notice that a suit had been commenced before such a court, by such a plaintiff, and was to be heard at such a time. The commencement of an action by summons is now the usual course of procedure; recent legislation, and especially the practical abolition of imprisonment for debt, having greatly restricted the use of writs of *capias* of any kind. By the Debtors' Act, 1869 (32 & 33 Vict. c. 62), the writ of *capias ad satisfaciendum* is abolished, except in cases in which the defendant can pay, but will not. The same act provides that when a plaintiff has good cause of action against a defendant to the amount of £50 or upward, and the defendant is about to quit England, and the absence of the defendant from England will materially prejudice the plaintiff in the prosecution of his action, a judge may order the defendant to be arrested unless or until security be found.

Capillaries, kăp'ĭ-lă-rĭz, or ka-pĭl'ạ-rĭz, extremely minute blood vessels that make the connection between the arteries and the veins. They are extremely abundant, being present in practically all parts of the body and in enormous numbers. It is by means of the capillaries that most of the interchange of nutrition takes place in the various tissues of the body. The arteries bring the fresh oxygenated blood to the parts, to which it is distributed by the rich network of capillaries, through the walls of which the waste products pass and are carried on by the blood pressure into the veins, to be eliminated by some one of the large excretory organs, the liver, etc., or carried to the lungs to be thus modified or cast off. The arrangement, width, and capacity of the capillaries varies in every tissue of the human body. In general they are arranged as a close network about the parts to which they are distributed, and in width they vary from one two thousandths to one two hundredths of an inch in diameter. See ARTERY; CIRCULATION.

Capillarity. The subject of capillarity takes its name from the circumstance that it was first studied in connection with the rise of liquids in tubes having a bore so fine as to be comparable in diameter with a hair (*capilla*). When one end of such a tube is immersed in water, the water rises in the tube above the general level of the surface outside it, in a way which is not in accord with the general law of hydrostatics, that a liquid will stand at the same level in two communicating vessels. Many other instances can be found in which liquid surfaces, especially in the neighborhood of solid bodies, assume shapes and positions which are equally at variance with the laws of hydrostatics. All such cases are now treated as belonging to the general subject of capillarity. Examples of capillary actions are the soaking up of water by a sponge; the penetration of varnish into wood; the rising of oil in a lamp wick; the clinging of ink to a properly nibbed pen; the running off of the ink from pen to paper; the soaking up of the superfluous ink in blotting paper; the falling of drops of uniform size from the lip of a bottle or from a medicine dropper; the rounding of drops of melted lead into pellets of shot as they fall in a shot-tower. When we consider such examples as these, it becomes clear that they are to be explained as the result of forces acting between the parts of the liquid, or between the liquid and the solid with which it is in contact. These forces are often called the forces of cohesion and adhesion. Very little is known about them. The one thing definitely known is that they are very great when the parts of the body or bodies between which they are exerted are so near together that they are said to be in contact, and fall off rapidly in magnitude as the parts are separated, so as to become inappreciable when the distance between the parts becomes discernible. It is customary to think of these forces as exerted between the molecules of matter, and so to call them molecular forces. The very small distance within which the action of a molecule on its neighbors is appreciable is called the range of molecular action.

By reflection upon the effects of such molecular forces acting in a liquid, Young (1804) was led to assume that a tension exists in a thin layer of molecules at the surface of a liquid, comparable in general to the tension in a stretched membrane. The magnitude of this surface tension depends upon the nature of the liquid, or, more exactly, upon the nature of the two media, of whatever sort they may be, separated by the surface. It is independent of the shape of the surface, provided that its radii of curvature are always great in comparison with the range of molecular action or the thickness of the surface layer. Young added to this hypothesis the observation that the angle of contact between a liquid surface and a solid is always the same for the same pair of substances. The angle of contact is generally measured, at the line of contact, between the external normals to the solid and the liquid surfaces. In the case of mercury and glass, which Young particularly observed, this angle is obtuse, and seemed to him to be about 135°. In the case of water and glass it is acute, and so small as to seem evanescent, or equal to zero. Young assumed that the like is true for all contacts of liquids with solids which are wetted by them.

Young's two principles are clearly not proved to be consequences of the more fundamental hypothesis of molecular force; but, accepted as generalizations from observation, they may be used to explain all the forms of liquid surfaces. For example, let us consider the rise of water in a glass tube. The water wets the inner wall of the tube, and so meets it everywhere in the circle of contact at an angle equal to zero. Owing to this, the surface of the water in the tube will be concave upward. In a tube of very small bore, it will be approximately hemispherical. The tension strives to straighten out the surface, and since the contact condition prevents its doing this, it lifts a column of water up the tube, to a point such that the weight of the uplifted column is sustained by the upward force due to the tension, while at the same time the curvature of the surface is consistent with the contact condition.

When the column is stationary, the tension in the surface can be considered as acting vertically upward at all points in the circle of contact of the surface with the wall of the tube. Representing by T the tension in the surface, or the force acting in the surface across a line of unit length, and by r the radius of the tube, we have the expression $2 \pi r T$ for the upward force acting on the column. Representing by P the density of water, by g the acceleration of gravity, and by h the height of the column above the general level of the water surface outside the tube, we have the expression $\rho g \pi r^2 h$ for the weight of the column. Setting the two forces equal, we obtain $2T = \rho g r h$, and conclude that the height of the column is inversely as the radius of the tube. This law was made known by the experiments of Jurin (1718), and is generally known as Jurin's law.

By a slight extension of Young's conception of surface tension, we may deduce from it the constancy of the contact angle. We need only to suppose that a tension exists, in any surface separating two substances, which has a particular value for each pair of substances. Consider then three fluids in contact along a line. It is evident that the line of contact will be at rest when the angles made with each other, at that line, by the three surfaces in which the fluids meet in pairs, are such that the tensions in the three surfaces are in equilibrium. These angles are therefore obtained by constructing the triangle of forces, with the three tensions as sides, and they are constant, for the three substances.

We may consider more particularly the special case in which one of the three substances is a solid. Suppose, for convenience in statement, that the three substances are a liquid, air, and a solid. Represent by T_{12}, T_{13} and T_{23} the tensions in the surfaces separating the liquid from air, the liquid from the solid, and air from the solid, respectively. Denote the angle of contact of the liquid-air surface with the solid by ϕ. The line of contact will be at rest when the sum of all the tensions or components of tension in the plane of the solid is equal to zero, or when

$$T_{12} \cos \phi + T_{13} - T_{23} = 0.$$

The angle of contact is therefore given by

$$\cos \phi = \frac{T_{23} - T_{13}}{T_{12}},$$

and is constant. It is acute or obtuse, according as T_{23} is greater or less than T_{13}. In the case of mercury and glass, T_{13} is the greater, and ϕ is obtuse. In the case of most liquids and glass, the tension corresponding to T_{23} is the greater, and ϕ is acute. When T_{23} equals or exceeds $T_{12} + T_{13}$, the angle ϕ becomes evanescent.

Almost contemporaneously with Young, Laplace (1805) formally applied the hypothesis of molecular forces to the study of the forms of liquid surfaces. He considered the pressure at the end of a liquid filament, beginning in the surface and drawn normal to it, and terminating in the interior of the liquid. He proved that it may be expressed by the sum of two pressures. One of these, called the molecular pressure, is very great, and is constant at all points of the liquid that are not in the surface layer. This pressure is eliminated from all equations of equilibrium of liquid surfaces, and plays no part in determining the forms of liquid surfaces. The other pressure depends upon the shape of the liquid surface, and is given by the formula $\dfrac{H}{2}\left(\dfrac{1}{R} + \dfrac{1}{R'}\right)$, in which H is a constant, and R and R' the two principal radii of curvature of the surface. This pressure, at any point under the surface layer, is in equilibrium with the hydrostatic pressure at that point. Under a flat surface, and therefore under the level surface of a large expanse of liquid, the radii of curvature are infinite and this

pressure vanishes. If h is the height of a point in the curved surface above the general level, we then have for equilibrium the condition $\dfrac{H}{2}\left(\dfrac{1}{R} + \dfrac{1}{R'}\right) = \rho g h$. This relation may be deduced from Young's hypothesis of surface tension, and it is found that Laplace's constant H is equal to $2T$. As an example of the use of this equation, consider again the rise of water in a tube. The surface in the tube, if its bore is small enough, may be considered a hemisphere, and therefore $R = R' = r$, the radius of the tube. Accordingly we have $H = \rho g r h$, as we obtained before by Young's method.

Laplace's theory did not suffice to demonstrate the constancy of the contact-angle, and Laplace was forced to assume it as a fact of observation.

A more profound and successful application of the hypothesis of molecular forces to the problem of capillarity was made by Gauss (1829). He showed, by means of the principle of virtual work, that a system of substances in contact possesses a certain amount of potential energy arising from the molecular forces. For each pair of substances the energy is proportional to the extent of surface separating them, and the factor of proportion is a characteristic constant for the two substances. This constant is called the surface energy. The existence of such a surface energy may readily be deduced from the hypothesis of molecular forces. Consider, for example, a mass of liquid surrounded by another liquid of the same specific gravity. If its surface is enlarged, it can only be by the movement of some of its parts out of its interior into the surface layer, and it is evident that, as they move out through the layer, work is done against the molecular forces, which will be proportional, generally, to the area by which the surface is increased. The liquid acquires potential energy equal to the work done in increasing its surface. As the potential energy of a system in equilibrium is always a minimum, the condition of equilibrium of such a mass of liquid is, therefore, that the area of its surface shall be a minimum. If the liquid is entirely free, its surface will be spherical. If it is subject to conditions, so that portions of the surface are limited by certain fixed boundary lines, it may be proved that the forms of the various portions of the surface, which will make the surface energy a minimum, are such that the sum of the reciprocals of the principal radii of curvature is the same for all parts of all the surfaces. We are thus led to the same rule for the form of a liquid surface as that reached by Laplace.

It may be shown that the constants denoting the surface energy and the surface tension are the same. To do this, consider a film of liquid bounded by the sides of a rectangle, one of which can be moved so as to increase or diminish the area of the film. Since both faces of the film act alike, we need consider only one of them. The force applied by the tension T in the film to the movable side, the length of which is represented by s, is Ts; and if the movable side moves in toward the opposite side through the distance r, the work done by the surface tension is Tsr. This is, therefore, the measure of the change in the energy of the film, and since sr is the change of area, T equals the energy per unit of area, or the surface energy.

The method of Gauss furnishes a proof that the contact-angle should be constant. If we consider that the potential energy of the system is a minimum, when the surface tensions which arise from the surface energies are in equilibrium, this may be proved in the way already indicated; or a direct proof may be given.

A very interesting set of verifications of the theories of capillarity was devised by Plateau. In order to be able to examine a liquid taking shape under its surface tension only, he prepared a mixture of alcohol and water having the same density as olive oil, in which the oil could be suspended. A mass of oil, freely floating in this mixture, assumed a spherical form. This form is manifestly that which would be produced by a tension acting uniformly in all parts of the surface; it is also that for which the internal pressure represented by $\dfrac{H}{2}\left(\dfrac{1}{R}+\dfrac{1}{R'}\right)$ is the same everywhere; and also that for which the surface, and consequently the potential energy, is a minimum. When the oil was suspended in a wire frame, it assumed various forms, depending on the shape of the frame and the quantity of oil, which were always such that the internal pressure, determined by Laplace's equation, was the same everywhere.

A similar set of verifications was afforded by the use of films of soapy water. Such films are so thin and light that their weight hardly distorts them at all, and the positions they assume are due almost solely to the surface tension. Such a film, blown into a bubble, is spherical. When formed on a wire frame lying in a plane, the film is a plane. When the frame is twisted out of the plane, the surface of the film is the least that can be constructed with the edges of the frame as a boundary. It is one of the so-called minimal or ruled surfaces. Various films of this sort were examined by Plateau, and found to fulfill the geometrical conditions of the minimal surface.

Observers have ordinarily tested the theory by determining, from Laplace's equation, the various forms and dimensions of liquid surfaces, subject to various boundary conditions, and comparing the actual forms obtained by experiment with those deduced from the theory. For example, rough observations show that for any one liquid that wets glass, the heights to which it rises in various capillary tubes are inversely as the radii of the tubes, as the elementary theory declares they should be. More refined observations show that this statement is not strictly accurate, and a more complete theory leads to certain corrections of the statement, to which the better observations conform. In a similar way, the rise of a liquid between parallel plates, the forms of large drops of mercury on a horizontal plate, or of large bubbles of air in a liquid under a horizontal plate, the force needed to lift a horizontal plate from the surface of a liquid which wets it, the maximum pressure exerted in a small bubble as it is enlarging and is liquid at the end of a tube, have all been used as means of testing the theory. Generally the observations are used in the appropriate formula to obtain a value for the surface tension T, or

for the constant $a^2 = \dfrac{2\,T}{\rho\,g}$ (called Poisson's constant) and the verification of the theory is found in the fact that the values of these quantities obtained by different methods are in good agreement with one another.

The determination of the surface tension is complicated by the fact that many of the formulæ containing it involve the contact-angle also. In such cases the contact-angle may be determined by an independent observation, as was done by Young in the case of mercury in contact with glass; but in most cases the liquids examined wet, or seem to wet, the solid walls, and it is then assumed that the contact-angle is evanescent or zero. The results obtained on this assumption may be compared with those obtained by methods in which the contact-angle is not involved, to test the validity of the assumption, and if it is found in error, to determine the magnitude of the contact-angle.

It is of interest to consider some examples of the constants of capillarity. The units commonly employed are not those of the absolute c. g. s. system. It has been found more convenient to use the millimetre as the unit of length, and the weight of a milligramme as the unit of force. Poisson's constant a^2, being always expressed, as in the example given of the rise of a liquid in a tube, by the product of two lengths, is a number of square millimetres. The surface tension T, or the force which acts across a unit of length in the surface, is expressed in milligramme weights per millimetre. In these units Poisson's constant for mercury is about 6.75, and the surface tension 45.7. For water at 20° C. we may take $a^2 = 15.0$ and $T = 7.5$; for chloroform at 23° C., $a^2 = 3.7$, $T = 2.73$; for refined petroleum at 22° C., $a^2 = 6.75$, $T = 2.64$. These numbers are simply cited as examples of the magnitude of the two constants in typical cases. Their exact determination is beset with such difficulties that it is doubtful whether any results have been obtained which can be accepted as definitive.

The constant contact-angle of mercury with glass is about 135°, or a little larger. Most liquids wet glass, and their contact-angles are assumed to be 0°. Evidence has been adduced to show that in some cases, with water or petroleum, for example, the contact-angle with glass is not 0°, but has a finite, though not a large, value. This question is not yet definitely settled.

The principal difficulty in determining the constants of capillarity with accuracy lies in the effect of impurities on the surface tension. This is especially felt with the liquids which have high surface tension, like mercury or water. The least trace of oil or grease will spread out over a water surface in a thin film, and alter its surface tension very considerably. It is very difficult to get the vessels clean, which are used in the experiments, and much more difficult to keep them clean, so that the constants obtained for any liquid are always open to a certain degree of suspicion. Impurities dissolved in the liquid affect the surface tension also, though not to so great a degree as those which spread over its surface.

The surface tensions, of all liquids which have been tested, become less as the temperature rises. Selby has shown it to be a consequence of the principles of thermodynamics that the amount by which the surface tension changes should be proportional to the change in the absolute temperature. Most of the older measurements of the temperature coefficients do not confirm this conclusion, but the recent observations of Knipp on water, and of Feustel on various organic liquids are in agreement with it. The magnitudes of the constants of capillarity manifestly depend on the magnitudes of the forces between molecules and on the range of molecular action. The theory of van der Waals leads to an estimate of the molecular pressure within a liquid, the values obtained for it ranging from 1,430 atmospheres in the case of ether to 10,700 atmospheres in the case of water. The same theory indicates that the range of molecular action is proportional to the linear dimensions of the molecule, and is of about the same magnitude as the radius of the molecule. By the help of a modified form of this theory, Eötvös came to the conclusion that the rate of variation with the temperature of the product of the surface tension and the two-thirds power of the molecular volume should be constant, and the same for all liquids, within a certain temperature range, if their molecules are single, and not double or compound. Observation shows that this law holds true for many liquids, and in cases in which it fails, there are often other reasons to support the conclusion that the molecules of the liquid are compound.

Before closing, we may consider a few examples of the effects produced by surface tension.

When waves are set up on the surface of water, they are transmitted across the surface at a rate which depends on the hydrostatic pressure and on the surface tension. The surface tension is practically the only agent in transmitting the waves when they are very short. Such waves may be set up by the use of a vibrating tuning fork, and the measurement of their lengths furnishes a means for the determination of the value of the surface tension. The ripples set up on the smooth surface of a pond by a breath of air, or which proceed in front of a slowly moving boat, are largely due to surface tension.

When a glass tumbler is partly filled with water, the surface tension draws the water up the sides. As more water is carefully poured in, the line of contact rises until it reaches the edge of the glass. It often happens that the line of contact is checked at the edge, so that the water does not run out over the top of the glass. In this case the glass can be filled above the level of its edge, and the water will stand in it under a surface that is convex upward, the surface tension in which keeps the water from running out.

The surface tension in the convex surface of the mercury in the tube of a barometer produces a pressure downward, which has to be estimated and allowed for when accurate observations are to be made.

A fine needle that has been slightly oiled or greased, if laid gently down on the surface of water, will float there. It lies in a concave trough formed in the water surface. The water cannot wet the needle, because of its coating of oil, and so the needle is supported by the uplift due to the surface tension acting in the concave surface in which the needle rests. In a way generally similar, the insects which run over the surface of water are supported in little hollows in the water surface. Their feet are not wetted by the water.

When two light bodies, floating on the surface of a liquid, are moved toward each other until the curved parts of the liquid surface near them intersect, they seem to exert forces on each other. If they are both wetted by the liquid, or are both not wetted by it, they move together and adhere to each other. If one of them is wetted by the liquid and the other not, they move apart. If water is run in between two parallel sheets of plate glass, they are drawn closely together and adhere very strongly to each other. These actions are ascribed to differences in the pressures on opposite sides of the bodies. In case the bodies are wetted by the liquid, the pressure in the region between them, in the elevated portion of the liquid under its concave surface, is less than the pressure on their outer sides, and they are pushed together. This action takes place even in a vacuum, in which case the pressure under the concave surface is a negative pressure or tension. In case the bodies are not wetted by the liquid, the liquid is depressed between them, and the pressure inward on their outer sides is greater than that acting outward, and they are pushed together. A curious effect, predicted by Laplace from the theory of capillarity, and verified by experiment, is exhibited by two bodies, one of which is wetted by the liquid and the other not. These bodies, as the distance between them is diminished, at first appear to repel each other, but as the distance is reduced the repulsion changes to an attraction and the bodies come together.

If a small lump of camphor is dropped on clean water, it begins to move about over the surface in an irregular way, and continues to do so, generally, for some time. These motions are explained by noticing that one part of the lump of camphor dissolves more freely than the rest, and so, near it, the surface tension of the water surface is lowered below that near the other parts of the lump. The camphor is accordingly drawn toward that part of the surface in which the tension is greatest.

If a thread of water is at rest in a horizontal capillary tube, and one of its two end surfaces is touched by a wire that has been dipped in turpentine or benzine, the tension at that end will be diminished, and the greater tension of the other end will draw the water along the tube. This effect is taken advantage of in cleaning off grease spots from cloth. The surface tension of benzine is very low, and when benzine is applied in a gradually narrowing ring around the spot of grease, the grease is drawn in toward the centre of the ring, and if the cloth is laid on a piece of blotting paper, the grease will be taken up by it. This action is promoted if a hot iron is applied to the other side of the cloth, for the heat lessens the tension in the ends of the pores nearest the iron, and the greater tension at the other ends draws the grease into the blotting paper.

WILLIAM FRANCIS MAGIE,
Professor of Physics, Princeton University.

Capilupi, Camillo, Italian poet: b. Mantau in the early part of the 16th century. He was the author of a work issued in 1572 entitled 'The Stratagem of Charles IX. against the Huguenots,' in which the Massacre of St. Bartholomew was justified, and made it appear that the action was premeditated. Cardinal Lorraine, who at the time was attending the Pope in Rome, endeavored to suppress the book from motives of policy.

Capistrano, Giovanni di, jō-vän'nĕ dē kä-pē-strä'nō, or **Capistranus,** Johannes, Saint, Italian monk: b. Capistrano, a small Neapolitan town of the Abruzzi, 24 June 1386; d. Illock, Slavonia, 23 Oct. 1456. He at first studied law, but in his 30th year, impelled by a vision, entered the Franciscan order, and was soon distinguished by the austerity of his manners, and a great zeal against the numerous heretical sects in Italy. The Popes Martin V., Eugene IV., and Felix V., often employed him as legate and inquisitor in suppressing the sect of the Fraticelli, which had spread widely over Naples and the Papal States. In 1444 he became vicar-general of the strict order of Franciscans called Observants, and in 1450 proceeded as legate to Germany with a view to suppress the Hussites, and rouse the Germans to a crusade against the Turks. Although he was successful in his opposition to the Hussites in Moravia, he was expelled from Bohemia by George Podiebrad. His fanaticism often led him into many acts of cruelty, one of the worst being the racking and burning of 40 Jews in Breslau, on the charge of profaning the Host. His harangues in favor of a crusade against the Turks failing to make much impression on the German princes he resolved to try their effect on the populace, and easily persuaded great numbers to join him in marching against the Turks, who were advancing under Mohammed II., and had closely invested Belgrade, the key of Hungary, with an army of 150,000 men. At the instigation of Capistranus, John Corvinus Hunnyades furnished a force of 60,000, destroyed the Turkish fleet on the Danube, and threw into Belgrade succors both of men and provisions. On this expedition Capistranus in person commanded the left wing of the party, forced his way into Belgrade, repulsed a general assault by the Turks, and on 6 Aug. 1456, in conjunction with Hunnyades, signally defeated the whole Turkish host. His exertions, and the pestilential atmosphere caused by the dead bodies lying unburied around Belgrade, laid him on a sick-bed, and he died in the same year in the Franciscan monastery at Illock. He was canonized in 1690. He was the author of 'Speculum Conscientiæ.'

Capisucchi, kä-pe-sook'kĕ, or **Capizucca,** Biago, or Biasio, MARQUIS OF MONTERIO, Italian general: b. Rome about the middle of the 16th century; d. 1613. He was in the service of Spain in the Low Countries, under the Duke of Parma, in 1584, afterward becoming lieutenant-general and commander of the army of Ferdinand I. de Medici, duke of Tuscany.

Capisucchi, Paolo, Italian ecclesiastic: b. Rome 1479; d. there 1539. Having become bishop of Neocastro he was summoned to Rome by Clement VII., who referred to him the question of a divorce between Henry VIII. of England and Queen Catherine. In this matter Capisucchi made a report against Henry.

Capital, in architecture the uppermost member of a column, that is to say, a separate piece of stone set upon the shaft and capital an epistyle or the abutment of an arch — in short the mass of the building which is imposed upon the column.

A column must always have a shaft and a capital; without these features it would be a post, perhaps a pillar or a pier, but would have no architectural character. The capital, moreover, has generally received the most elaborate decorative treatment of the whole composition. Thus in Egypt, while the shaft might be cylindrical or conical, the capital would spread out immediately in curves either concave or convex, and would be carved and painted. It is even practicable to divide Egyptian columns into four orders by their capitals, which spread in different ways, and are ornamented by different sculpture, more or less imitative of nature. The idea of the spread given to the capital is, of course, that in this way the superstructure is taken more easily, as it is always and of necessity much larger horizontally than the column itself.

The stone uprights left in rock-cut temples in India and called ordinarily pillars, because of their varied forms — octagonal, square, and the like — are still divided into shaft and capital, though the forms of these are entirely remote from Egyptian or later European examples. Thus, some capitals consist of a mere enrichment of the uppermost band of the shaft and a superincumbent block very elaborately carved. In some cases this upper block gives off corbels and consoles which help to carry the roof by their greater spread.

The capitals which have excited the most interest among European students of art are those of the three Greek orders and of the five Renaissance orders which were deduced from the first three. The capital of the Grecian Doric is a reversed cone rounded off at top and carrying a square plinth or die; this plain echinus was richly painted in bright colors. The capital of the Ionic order is a curious device consisting of scrolls or volutes, two on each of the two opposite sides, so that this capital, almost alone, has not the same appearance from every point of view. The capital of the Corinthian order is a circular bell, surrounded by acanthus leaves and having at each corner a couple of projecting scrolls not unlike those of the Ionic order but small. This Corinthian order received many modifications in ancient Roman practice, and one of these was erected by the Renaissance men into a separate order, the so called Composite. From the Grecian Doric the Roman Doric took shape, and this was used by the Renaissance men, while a still simpler order was made from it and called the Tuscan. The capitals of these two orders are very thin and low in vertical measurement, and consist of moldings running round the continuation of the shaft, and either plain or slightly carved into the simplest of the egg and dart moldings or the like.

In mediæval architecture, both Romanesque and Gothic, the capitals are almost infinitely varied. The strong tendency of the time toward elaborate carving made this block of stone, from 5 to 20 feet above the aisles and in a prominent place, a most tempting vehicle for sculpture, and

member of a column, that is to say, a separate
piece of stone set upon the shaft and supporting
an epistyle or the abutment of an arch — in short
the mass of the building which is carried upon
the column.

A column must always have a shaft and a
capital; without these features it would be a
post, perhaps a pillar or a pier, but would have
no architectural character. The capital, moreover, has generally received the most elaborate
decorative treatment of the whole composition.
Thus in Egypt, while the shaft might be cylindrical or conical, the capital would spread out
immediately in curves either concave or convex,
and would be carved and painted. It is even
practicable to divide Egyptian columns into four
orders by their capitals, which spread in different ways, and are ornamented by different
sculpture, more or less imitative of nature. The
idea of the spread given to the capital is, of
course, that in this way the superstructure is
taken more easily, as it is always and of necessity much larger horizontally than the column
itself.

The stone uprights left in rock-cut temples in
India and called ordinarily pillars, because of
their varied forms — octagonal, square, and the
like — are still divided into shaft and capital,
though the forms of these are entirely remote
from Egyptian or later European examples.
Thus, some capitals consist of a mere enrichment
of the uppermost band of the shaft and a super-
incumbent block very elaborately carved. In
some cases this upper block gives off corbels and
consoles which help to carry the roof by their
greater spread.

The capitals which have excited the most interest among European students of art are those
of the three Greek orders and of the five Renaissance orders which were deduced from the
first three. The capital of the Grecian Doric
is a reversed cone rounded off at top and carrying a square plinth or die; this plain echinus was
richly painted in bright colors. The capital of
the Ionic order is a curious device consisting of
scrolls or volutes, two on each of the two opposite sides, so that this capital, almost alone, has
not the same appearance from every point of
view. The capital of the Corinthian order is a
similar bell, surrounded by acanthus leaves and
carrying at each corner a couple of projecting
scrolls not unlike those of the Ionic order but
thinner. These Corinthian order received many
modifications in ancient Roman practice, and one
of these was erected by the Renaissance men
into a separate order, the so called Composite.
From the Grecian Doric the Roman Doric took
shape, and this was copied by the Renaissance men,
while a new order was made from it
.... The capitals of these two
.... but few in vertical measurements .... of mouldings running round
.... of the shaft, and either plain
.... into the simplest of the egg
.... and of the like.
.... architecture, both Romanesque

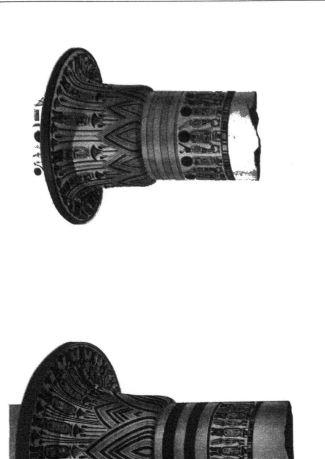

BELL-SHAPED CAPITAL FROM THE HYPOSTYLE HALL
KARNAK, EGYPT

BELL-SHAPED CAPITAL FROM THE RAMESEUM
THEBES, EGYPT

CAPITAL

the abandonment of the classical orders left every artist free to design his own system of leafage, animal forms and the like. In this way mediæval capitals are often of extraordinary beauty; but no attempt has been made to classify them except as they form part of a style. See COLUMN. RUSSELL STURGIS.

Capital, in political economy, the accumulated wealth, in possession of individuals or of a community, which is available for use in further production. In estimating the capital of any individual we necessarily take into consideration the debts due to and from him; and many men of large capital are only possessed of claims upon others; their whole stock is in the hands of others at interest; and they have only promises for a certain amount of money, and actually possess neither lands nor goods to any considerable value; while others possess large quantities of both, and yet have little or no capital, since they owe in money the value of the greater part or the whole of their possessions. Now it is plain that no individual can undertake production, to any large extent, without an extensive stock. He must have land to cultivate, or materials to work up, and implements to work with. Even a savage must have a capital, such as his hut, clothes, cooking utensils, food enough to support him until he can obtain a new supply, and implements, such as a hatchet, gun, canoe, fishing gear, to procure this supply. The first effort of industry is to supply the implements, apparatus, and machinery for his own employment; and as society and the arts advance, and the operations of industry are extended, the implements, apparatus, machinery, and materials requisite in conducting the processes of production must be proportionally accumulated; and these will constitute a part of the capital of a community, and also of an individual, which is essential to success in productive processes. And these can be commanded by any one in proportion to the extent of his individual capital; or, if he have credit, then his resources for production will depend upon the capital of others—in other words, that of the community to which he belongs.

In considering the aggregate capital of a community we may put out of the question all the debts due from any of the members to others; for, whether these be great or small—and they will vary according as the practice of giving credit is more or less in use—still the capital of the community will consist in its lands, buildings, ships, machinery, materials on hand, implements; in short, in all those things which bear a value in the market. Provided the community owes no debt abroad, these will constitute its aggregate capital; and, if its members are indebted abroad, we find its actual net capital, as in the case of an individual, by deducting the amount of its debts from the value of its possessions, without regarding the debts due from some of its members to others.

Capital has long been recognized as necessary as an auxiliary to labor, despite the fact that in more recent times it has been urged by unscholarly writers and by demagogues that capital is really the tyrant of labor and that the latter could readily dispense with it. The cultivator of the soil demands a spade or a plow, the blacksmith an anvil, hammer, and bellows, etc. All trades and industries demand certain instru-

ments,—tools, raw material, every kind of supplies, and all these are capital. This, being true on a more primitive basis, is proportionately truer in a civilized state, where labor is complicated and returns are not immediate. "In that rude state of society," says Adam Smith, "in which there is no division of labor, in which exchanges are seldom made, and in which every man provides everything for himself, it is not necessary that any stock should be stored up in order to carry on the business of the society. . . . But when the division of labor has once been thoroughly introduced, the produce of a man's own labor can supply but a very small part of his occasional wants. The far greater part of them are supplied with the produce of other men's labor, which he purchases with the produce, or, what is the same thing, with the price of the produce of his own. But this purchase cannot be made till such time as the produce of his own labor has not only been completed but sold. A stock of goods of different kinds, therefore, must be stored up somewhere sufficient to maintain him and to supply him with the materials and tools of his work." At any given time, capital may be arranged under the three heads above indicated—subsistence, tools, and materials.

An owner of capital, possessing an amount larger than he is capable of using in his own work, obtains the labor of others. He either attempts an industry with the assistance of workmen to whom he pays a remuneration agreed upon, or diverts a portion of his capital as a loan, or as stock, or in some other way, such capital being made effective by others. On such, contrary one not possessing capital adequate to the useful employment of his activities, undertakes the combination of his labor with the capital of another. This combination may vary according to circumstances, and may of course be at times unfavorable to labor.

Capital is distinguished into floating or movable, and fixed; the former consisting of things that may be transferred by delivery of any kind from place to place, the latter of land, houses, and other property which must be taken delivery of in the place where they stand. Another use of the distinction is made to represent the difference between the permanent plant of a business and the current capital necessary to carry it on. Capital may thus be said to be fixed either when it is physically incapable of being moved, or when it is rendered immovable by the permanent arrangement of its parts. Thus one carrying on a flour-mill wants a floating or disposable capital, over and above the cost of his works, to be invested in wheat to be floured, and flour not yet disposed of. This instance illustrates what is meant by the floating or disposable capital of a whole community, being that movable exchangeable stock of things on hand, over and above the fixtures and apparatus of production, including lands, buildings, ships, working animals, all the implements of the arts, with necessary food. clothing, and a stock of seed sufficient for the time requisite for reproduction. What remains over these is the disposable capital. and, in a flourishing community, the disposable floating capital is constantly invested in new fixed capital. implements and apparatus of production. A declining community. on the contrary. consumes a part of its implements and apparatus of industry; or what is in effect the same thing, it does not repair and replace the damage of use and decay. The idea is held out in many economical treatises that a community cannot have a surplus capital; that is, it cannot have more capital than it can make use of in its consumption and reproduction. As no grounds whatever are given for this doctrine, it seems to be hardly entitled to a consideration; for the position is certainly, at the first view, very improbable, since we know very well that men may accumulate; and why they may not, in any possible case, accumulate a surplus, does not appear by any plausible reason, and whether such surplus accumulation may be useful or not will depend entirely upon the kind of articles of which such accumulation consists. If it consist in articles the value of which depends on the prices in foreign markets the excess may be of no value at all; for it may so depress the foreign prices as to countervail all the direct advantage arising from the cheaper supply, for a time, of the domestic demand.

Fictitious capital generally means nothing more nor less than excessive credits, which throw the management and disposition of a great deal of property into the hands of persons who are not able to answer for the risks of loss from its bad management, or other causes. A whole community, in the aggregate, can have fictitious capital only in case of its members having an excessive credit in a foreign country. But the members may, among themselves, have a fictitious capital by too great credits in their dealings with each other, and the fiction, in this case, is in their false promises of payment. See POLITICAL ECONOMY; TRUSTS; WAGES.

Capital (*Das Kapital*), a noted work by Karl Marx, published in 1867. English translation edited by Fred Engels, 1887. A book of the first importance, by the founder of international socialism. The conservative aspect of Marx's teaching is in the fact that he honestly seeks to understand what, apart from any man's opinion or theory, the historical development actually is; and that he does not think out and urge his own ideal programme of social reform, but strives to understand and to make understood what must inevitably take place.

Capital Punishment (Latin, *caput*, "the head"; hence *capitalis*, "pertaining to or affecting the head"; hence "affecting the life"), the punishment of death. The questions most commouly discussed by philosophers and jurists under this head are: (1) as to the right of governments to inflict the punishment of death; (2) as to the expediency of such punishment; (3) as to the crimes to which, if any, it may be most properly confined and limited; (4) as to the manner in which it should be inflicted.

1. As to the right of inflicting the punishment of death. This has been doubted by some distinguished persons; and the doubt is often the accompaniment of a highly cultivated mind, inclined to the indulgence of a romantic sensibility, and believing in human perfectibility. The right of society to punish offenses against its safety and good order will scarcely be doubted by any considerate person. In a state of nature individuals have a right to guard themselves from injury, and to repel all aggressions by a force or precaution adequate to the object. This results from the right of self-

preservation. If a person attempts to take away my life, I have, doubtless, a right to protect myself against the attempt by all reasonable means. If I cannot secure myself but by taking the life of the assailant, I have a right to take it. It would otherwise follow that I must submit to a wrong, and lose my life rather than preserve it by the means adequate to maintain it. It cannot, then, be denied, that in a state of nature men may repel force by force, and may even justly take away life, if necessary, to preserve their own. When men enter society, the right to protect themselves from injury and to redress wrongs is transferred generally from the individuals to the community. We say that it is generally so, because it must be obvious that in many cases the natural right of self-defense must remain. If a robber attacks one on the highway, or attempts to murder him, it is clear that he has a right to repel the assault, and to take the life of the assailant if necessary for his safety; since society in such a case could not afford him any adequate and prompt redress. The necessity of instant relief, and of instant application of force, justifies the act, and is recognized in all civilized communities. When the right of society is once admitted to punish for offenses, it seems difficult to assign any limits to the exercise of that right, short of what the exigencies of society require. If a state have a right to protect itself and its citizens in the enjoyment of its privileges and its peace, it must have a right to apply means adequate to this object. The object of human punishments is, or may be, threefold: (1) to reform the offender; (2) to deter others from offending; and (3) to secure the safety of the community, by depriving the offender of the power of doing mischief. The first consideration rarely enters into human legislation, because of the inadequacy of our means to produce great moral results by the infliction of punishment. The two latter considerations enter largely into the theory and practice of legislation. Who is to be the judge in such cases? what is the adequate punishment for any offense? Certainly punishments ought not to be inflicted which are utterly disproportionate to the offense, and beyond the exigencies of society. No government has a right to punish cruelly and wantonly and from mere revenge; but still, the discretion must be vested somewhere, to say what shall be the degree of punishment to be adapted to a particular offense. That discretion must be, from its nature, justly a part of the legislative power, and to be exercised according to the actual state of society. It may,— nay, it must,— be differently exercised in different ages and in different countries; for the same punishment which in one age or country may be sufficient to suppress an offense, or render it comparatively harmless, may, in another age or country, wholly fail of the effect. If mild punishments fail of effect, more severe ones must be resorted to if the offense be of a nature which affects society in its vital principles, or safety, or interests. The very frequency of a crime must often furnish a very strong ground for severe punishment, not only as it furnishes proof that the present punishment is insufficient to deter men from committing it, but from the increased necessity of protecting society against dangerous crimes. But it is often said that life is the gift of God,

PIERS WITH CAPITALS

CAPITAL PUNISHMENT

and therefore it cannot justly be taken away, either by the party himself or another. If he cannot take it away, he cannot confer that power on others. But the fallacy of this argument is obvious. Life is no more the gift of God than other personal endowments or rights. A man has, by the gift of God, a right to personal liberty and locomotion, as well as to life; to eat and drink and breathe at large, as well as to exist, yet no one doubts that, by way of punishment, he may be confined in a solitary cell; that he may be perpetually imprisoned or deprived of free air, or compelled to live on bread and water. In short, no one doubts that he may be restrained in the exercise of any privileges or natural rights short of taking his life. Yet the reasoning, if worth anything, extends to all these cases in an equal degree. If, by his crimes, a man may justly forfeit his personal rights, why not his life? But we have seen that it is not true, even in a state of nature, that a man's life may not be taken away by another if the necessity of the case requires it. Why, then, may not society do the same if its own safety requires it? Is the safety of one person more important than the safety of the whole community? Then, again, as to a man's inability to confer on others a right which he does not himself possess. Suppose it is so; the consequence which is deduced from this does not, in fact, arise. Blackstone, indeed, seems to deduce the right of society to punish capital offenses in certain cases (that is, in cases of *mala prohibita* and not *mala in se*) from the consent of the offenders. The Marquis Beccaria, on the other hand, denies than any such consent can confer the right, and therefore objects to its existence. But the notion of consent is, in nearly all cases, a mere theory, having no foundation in fact. If a foreigner comes into a country and commits a crime at his first entrance, it is a very forced construction to say that he consents to be bound by its laws. If a pirate commits piracy, it is absurd to say that he consents to the right of all nations to punish him for it. The true and rational ground on which the right rests is not the consent of every offender, but the right of every society to protect its own peace, interests, property, and institutions, and the utter want of any right in other persons to disturb, or destroy, or subtract them. The right flows, not from consent, but from the legitimate institution of society. If men have a right to form a society for mutual benefit and security, they have a right to punish other persons who would overthrow it. There are many cases where a state authorizes life to be taken away, the lawfulness of which is not doubted. No reasonable man doubts the right of a nation, in a just war, especially of self-defense, to repel force by force and to take away the lives of its enemies. And the right is not confined to repelling present force, but it extends to precautionary measures which are necessary for the ultimate safety of the nation. In such a war a nation may justly insist upon the sacrifice of the lives of its own citizens, however innocent, for the purpose of ensuring its own safety. Accordingly we find that all nations enrol militia and employ troops for war, and require them to hazard their lives for the preservation of the state. In these cases life is freely sacrificed by the nation; and the laws enacted for such purposes are deemed just exercises of power. If so, why may not life be taken away by way of punishment if the safety of society requires it? If a nation may authorize, in war, the destruction of thousands, why may it not authorize the destruction of a single life, if self-preservation require it? The mistake, however, is in supposing that life cannot be taken away without the consent of the party. If the foregoing reasoning be correct, such consent is neither supposed nor necessary. In truth, the supposition of an original compact between all the persons who are subject to the society, as the necessary and proper basis on which all the rights of such society depend, is at best a gratuitous supposition, and it sometimes leads to very incorrect results. It may be added that the Scriptures most clearly recognize and justify the infliction of capital punishments in certain cases.

2. As to the expediency of capital punishment. This opens a wide field for discussion. Some able men who do not doubt the right do still deny the expediency of inflicting it. It may be admitted that a wise legislature ought to be slow in affixing such a punishment to any but very enormous and dangerous crimes. The frequency of a crime is not of itself a sufficient reason for resorting to such a punishment. It should be a crime of great atrocity and danger to society, and one which cannot otherwise be effectually guarded against. In affixing punishments to any offense, we should consider what are the objects and ends of punishment. It is clear that capital punishment can have no effect in reforming the offender himself. It may have, and ordinarily does have, the effect of deterring others from committing a like offense; but still, human experience shows that even this punishment, when inflicted for small offenses, which are easily perpetrated, and to which there is great temptation, does not always operate as an effectual terror. Men are sometimes hardened by the frequent spectacles of capital punishments and grow indifferent to them. Familiarity deprives them of their horror. The bloodiest codes are not those which have most effectually suppressed offenses. Besides, public opinion has great weight in producing the acquittal or condemnation of offenders. If a punishment be grossly disproportionate to the offense, if it shock human feelings, there arises, insensibly, a sympathy for the victim and a desire to screen him from punishment; so that, as far as certainty of punishment operates to deter from crimes, the object of the legislature is often thus defeated. It may be added that a reasonable doubt may fairly be entertained whether any society can lawfully exercise the power of punishing beyond what the just exigencies of that society require. On the other hand, a total abolition of capital punishments would, in some cases at least, expose society to the risk of deep and vital injuries. A man who has committed murder deliberately has proved himself unfit for society and regardless of all the duties which belong to it. The safety of society is most effectually guarded by cutting him off from the power of doing further mischief. If his life be not taken away, the only other means left are confinement for life or transportation and exile for life. Neither of these is a perfect security against the commission of other crimes, and may not always be

CAPITAL PUNISHMENT

within the power of a nation without great inconvenience and great expense to itself. It is true that the latter punishments leave open the chance of reform to the offender, which is indeed but too often a mere delusion; but, on the other hand, they greatly diminish the influence of another salutary principle, the deterring of others from committing like crimes. It seems to us therefore that it is difficult to maintain the proposition that capital punishments are at all times and under all considerations inexpedient. It may rather be affirmed that in some cases they are absolutely indispensable to the safety and good order of society. Some states have, however, entirely abolished capital punishment, as is the case in Holland, Rumania, Portugal, a certain number of the Swiss cantons, and some States of the American Union. It was entirely abolished in Switzerland in 1874, but a few years after, owing to the increase of murders, it was again made permissible. It was also for a time done away with in Austria and in one or two of the States of this country.

3. As to the crimes to which capital punishments may most properly be limited. From what has been already said it is plain that this must depend upon the particular circumstances of every age and nation; and much must be left to the exercise of a sound discretion on the part of the legislature. As a general rule humanity forbids such punishments to be applied to any but crimes of very great enormity and danger to individuals or the state. If any crimes can be effectually suppressed by moderate means, these ought certainly to be first resorted to. The experience, however, of most nations, if we may judge from the nature and extent of their criminal legislation, seems to disprove the opinion so often indulged by philanthropists that capital punishments are wholly unnecessary. The codes of most civilized nations used to abound with capital punishments. That of Great Britain long continued to be very sanguinary. Blackstone, in his 'Commentaries,' admits that in his time not less than 160 crimes were by the English law punishable with death. Forgery was one of these up to the reign of William IV. The only crimes for which capital punishment may now be inflicted, according to the law of England, are high treason and murder. The law in Scotland is substantially the same, a sentence of capital punishment now being competent only in cases of treason, murder, and attempts to murder in certain cases. By United States statutes nine crimes are so punishable, including treason, murder, arson, rape, piracy, and robbery of the mail. In several States of the Union still fewer crimes are generally punishable with death. Beyond treason, murder, arson, piracy, highway robbery, burglary, rape, and some other offenses of great enormity and of a kindred character, it is extremely questionable whether there can be necessity or expediency in applying so great a severity. Beccaria, with his characteristic humanity and sagacity, has strongly urged that the certainty of punishment is more important to deter from crimes than the severity of it.

4. As to the manner of inflicting the punishment of death. This has been different in different countries, and in different stages of civilization in the same countries. Barbarous nations are generally inclined to severe and vindictive punishments; and, where they punish with death, to aggravate it by prolonging the sufferings of the victim with ingenious devices in cruelty. And even in civilized countries, in cases of a political nature or of very great atrocity, the punishment has been sometimes inflicted with many horrible accompaniments. Tearing the criminal to pieces, piercing his breast with a pointed pole; pinching to death with red-hot pincers; starving to death; breaking his limbs upon the wheel; pressing to death in a slow and lingering manner; burning at the stake; crucifixion; sawing to pieces; quartering alive; exposure to wild beasts; and other savage punishments, have been sometimes resorted to for the purposes of vengeance, public example, or public terror. Compared with these the infliction of death by drowning, strangling, poisoning, bleeding, beheading, shooting, or hanging is a moderate punishment. In modern times public opinion is strongly disposed to discountenance the punishment of death by any but simple means; and the infliction of torture is almost universally reprobated. Even in governments where it is still countenanced by the laws it is rarely resorted to; and the sentence is remitted, by the policy of the government, beyond the simple infliction of death. In Prussia, where atrocious criminals were required by the penal code to be broken upon the wheel, the king latterly used always to issue an order to the executioner to strangle the criminal (which was done by a small cord not easily seen) before his limbs were broken. So in the same country, where robbery attended with destruction of life was punished by burning alive, the fagots were so arranged as to form a kind of cell in which the criminal was suffocated by the fumes of sulphur, or other means, before the flame could reach him. Not only is torture now abolished by civilized nations, but even the infliction of capital punishment in public has been given up by most of them. In England, in high treason, the criminal is sentenced to be drawn to the gallows, to be hanged by the neck until he be dead, to have his head cut off, and his body divided into four parts, and these to be at the disposal of the Crown. But, generally, all the punishment is remitted by the Crown, except the hanging and beheading, and these too may be altogether remitted according to circumstances. In other cases the punishment is now simply by hanging, or, in the military and naval service, by shooting. In France formerly the punishment of death was often inflicted by breaking the criminal on the wheel. The usual punishment now is beheading by the guillotine. In 1853 a kind of guillotine (*Fallschwert*) was introduced into the kingdom of Saxony, and it has since been adopted as the means of execution in several other German states. In Austria the general mode of punishment is by hanging. In Prussia hanging is rarely inflicted; but the usual punishment is beheading with a heavy axe, the criminal's head being first tied to a block. In one or two German states execution by the sword still exists. It should be remarked, however, that in Germany hanging has always been deemed the most infamous sort of punishment; and the sentence has often been commuted for beheading by the sword as a milder or less dishonorable mode of punishment. In the United States of America hanging is the almost universal mode of capital punish-

ment, though electricity has recently been tried. The Constitution of the United States contains a provision against "cruel and unusual punishments." In China decapitation by the sword is the usual form: murderers are cut to pieces; robbers not. In Russia the punishment of death has been frequently inflicted by the knout. In Turkey strangling and sewing the criminal up in a bag, and throwing him into the sea, are common modes of punishment. In the Roman code many severe and cruel punishments were prescribed. During the favored times of the republic many of these were abolished or mitigated. But again, under the emperors, they were revived with full severity. In the ancient Grecian states the modes of punishment were also severe and often cruel. The ancient Greek mode of capital punishment by taking poison at such hour as the condemned party should choose, seems never to have been in use among any Christian people.

Whether execution ought to be public or private has been a question much discussed, and one upon which a great diversity of opinion exists among intelligent statesmen. On the one hand, it is said that public spectacles of this sort have a tendency to brutalize and harden the people, or to make them indifferent to the punishment; and the courage and firmness with which the criminal often meets death have a tendency to awaken feelings of sympathy, and even of admiration, and to take away much of the horror of the offense as well as of the punishment. On the other hand it is said that the great influence of punishment in deterring others from the like offense cannot be obtained in any other way. It is the only means to bring home to the mass of the people a salutary dread and warning; and it is a public admonition of the certainty of punishment following upon crime. It is also added that all punishments ought to be subjected to the public scrutiny, so that it may be known that all the law requires, and no more, has been done. Since 1868 the law of the United Kingdom has required all executions to take place privately within the prison walls, and this system seems to have given general satisfaction. The same method is also practised in various other countries. In 1870 a similar measure was proposed in the French Assembly, but the war prevented it being passed and it is not yet law.

In England, the court before which the trial is held declares the sentence and directs the execution of it. In the courts of the United States there is a like authority; but in the laws of many of the States there is a provision that the execution shall not take place except by a warrant from the governor, or other executive authority. In cases of murder and other atrocious crimes the punishment in England is usually inflicted at a very short interval after the sentence. In America there is usually allowed a very considerable interval, varying from one month to six months. In Great Britain there lies no appeal from the verdict of a jury and the sentence of a court, in capital cases, and the very fact that the verdict and sentence are final produces great caution and deliberation in the administration of criminal justice, and a strong leaning toward the prisoner on trial. In the United States there is considerable latitude of appeal. In France there may be a review of it in the court of cassation. In Ger-

many there is, in criminal as in civil cases, a right of appeal; hence, in that country, few innocent persons have suffered capitally since the 16th century. Capital punishment cannot be inflicted, by the general humanity of the laws of modern nations, upon persons who are insane or who are pregnant, until the latter are delivered and the former become sane. It is said that Frederick the Great required all judgments of his courts condemning persons to death, to be written on blue paper; thus he was constantly reminded of them as they lay on his table among other papers, from which they were readily distinguished. He usually took a long time to consider such cases, and thus set an excellent example to sovereigns of their duty.

Capitals (*majuscula*), the large letters used in writing and printing, most commonly as the initial letters of certain words, or of all words in certain positions, and distinguished from the small letters (*minuscula*). As among the ancient Greeks and Romans, so also in the early part of the Middle Ages, all books were written without any distinction in the kind of letters used; but gradually the practice became common of beginning a book, subsequently, also, the chief divisions and sections of a book, with a large capital letter, usually illuminated and otherwise richly ornamented. In legal or state documents of the 13th century capital letters are found dispersed over the text as the initial letters of proper names, and of the names of the Deity, and in the next century the same usage was followed in ordinary manuscripts. The practice with regard to the use of capitals varies in different countries. Sentences and proper names begin almost universally with capitals, but there are several other cases in which the usage is not so general. In English there cannot be said to be any invariable rule regulating their use. The first personal pronoun is always written and printed with a capital letter, and it is common also to begin titles and the names of well-known public bodies, societies, institutions, etc., with capitals. Formerly, it was a frequent practice to begin all substantives in English with a capital, which is still the rule in German. The Germans also begin all titles and pronouns of address with capitals, but not the first personal pronoun. One point in which the English practice differs from that of Germany, France, Italy, and other continental countries, is in beginning adjectives derived from proper names, such as Spanish, Italian, etc., like proper names themselves, with capitals, such adjectives being printed in other countries entirely with small letters.

Capitanis, kăp-ĭ-tä′nĕs. See ARMATOLES.

Capitation is applied to anything that concerns a number of persons individually. Thus a capitation-tax is a tax imposed upon all the members of a state, each of whom has to pay his share, and is distinguished from taxes upon merchandise, etc. A capitation-grant is a grant given to a number of persons, a certain amount being allowed for every individual among the number.

Capito, or **Kopfel**, Wolfgang Fabricius, vôlf′gäng fä-brĕt′sĕ-oos cä′pē tō, or kĕp′fĕl, Alsatian reformer: b. Haguenau, 1478; d. Strassburg, November 1541. Entering the Benedictine order, he became professor of theology at Basel, where he showed in his lectures a tendency to shake off the trammels of the scholastic writers. He approved of Luther's action, but nevertheless in 1519 entered the service of Albert of Mainz; and it was not till some years later that he finally declared for the Reformation. He then entered zealously into its work, shared with Bucer the composition of the Confessio Tetrapolitana, and took part in the Synod of Bern in 1532.

Cap'itol, now *Campidoglio*, the citadel of ancient Rome, standing on the Capitoline Hill, the smallest of the seven hills of Rome, anciently called the Saturnine and the Tarpeian Rock. It was planned and said to have been begun by Tarquinius Priscus, but not completed till after the expulsion of the kings. At the time of the civil commotions under Sulla it was burned down, and rebult by the senate. It again suffered the same fate twice, and was restored by Vespasian and Domitian. The latter caused it to be built with great splendor, and instituted there the Capitoline games. Dionysius says the temple, with the exterior pillars, was 200 feet long and 185 broad. The whole building consisted of three temples, which were dedicated to Jupiter, Juno, and Minerva, and separated from one another by walls. In the wide portico triumphal banquets were given to the people. The statue of Jupiter, in the capitol, represented him sitting on a throne of ivory and gold, and consisted in the earliest times of clay painted red. Under Trajan, it was formed of gold. The roof of the temple was made of bronze; it was gilded by Quintus Catulus. The doors were of the same metal. Splendor and expense were lavished upon the whole edifice. On the pediment stood a chariot, drawn by four horses, at first of clay, and afterward of gilded brass. The temple itself contained an immense quantity of the most magnificent presents. The most important papers were preserved in it. The Capitoline Hill consists of three parts, namely, the northern summit, now occupied by the church of Santa Maria in Aracœli; the southern summit, crowned by the Palazzo Caffarelli, now occupied by the German ambassador; and the depression between these, in which is now the Piazza del Campidoglio. The above church, which is approached from the northwest by a lofty flight of steps, is of great antiquity. In 1888 the Franciscan monastery which was connected with it was replaced by a large monument of Victor Emmanuel II. The Piazza del Campidoglio was designed by Michael Angelo. In its centre is a fine equestrian bronze statue of Marcus Aurelius. On the southeast side there is the Palazzo del Senatore, with a fine flight of steps erected by Michael Angelo. The Palace of the Conservatori occupies the southwest side of the square, and contains valuable collections in art and antiquities. Directly opposite is the Capitoline Museum, founded by Innocent X. The southern summit of the hill is now called Monte Caprino, and on it, beside the Palazzo Caffarelli already mentioned, stands a hospital and a German archæological institute. (See ROME.) Besides the edifice in Washington where Congress assembles, some of the statehouses in States of the Union are officially called capitols.

Capitol at Washington, History of the. After the national capital had been located on the Potomac in 1789, Washington and Major

P. C. L'Enfant selected sites for the public buildings. On the first map (1791), the "Congress House" is situated as now, on a low hill commanding the best view in Washington, with 12 broad streets radiating from it, so that it closes the vista of every main avenue. On the decision of a board of three commissioners, with Washington and Jefferson, the plans of the capitol and the President's house were given out in 1792 to public competition, for a prize of $500 or a medal of that value, at the winner's option. For the President's house James Hoban's plans were accepted at once, and he was made superintendent of its erection. For the capitol none were satisfactory, but the three foremost competitors were given another trial, and one, Stephen Hallet, a French artist living in Philadelphia, was employed at a salary and indemnity to revise his plans under the commissioners' criticism. But later in the year Dr. William Thornton (q.v.) of Tortola Island, W. I., submitted plans whose "grandeur, simplicity, beauty, and convenience" forced the committee to accept them. They were too grand for the commissioners' ideas of national needs or resources at the time, however, and specified too costly materials. Thornton wished marble and mahogany and the best of construction, and under a bitter assault from several of his rejected competitors, headed by Hallet, whom the commissioners had joined with Thornton in a revising board, he was forced to reduce its scale and material greatly. Their suggested modifications of his general plan were, however, disapproved. These plans were for what is now the central portion of the capitol.

Work was begun about 1 August. The corner-stone was laid 18 September in the southeast corner of the old north wing, now the supreme court section, with imposing ceremonies, Masonic rites and procession, and a barbecue. Hoban was made superintendent, and Hallet his assistant; but Hoban gave his whole time to the White House, as the President's house came to be called, and Hallet was the real manager. He proceeded to change Thornton's plans and specifications at will, was repeatedly censured for it, and at last ordered to stop it. He resigned, but refused to give up the drawings; the commissioners at last secured them and discharged him, 15 Nov. 1794. Thornton, now one of the commissioners of the District of Columbia, was asked by Washington to obliterate Hallet's changes as injurious, and did so. Hoban now acted as superintendent until George Hadfield, an English architect, was engaged to succeed Hallet, on Jonathan Trumbull's recommendation of him as a modest man and good artist. He outdid Hallet; spent his whole energy in fighting Thornton and Hoban (who always worked in harmony), and after repeated resignations and reconsiderations, was discharged for practical incompetence 10 May 1798. Hoban again took charge. On 17 Nov. 1800 the second session of the sixth Congress met in the north wing of the building. Much of this early construction was of wood or poor material. This was on account of haste, the local interests being very urgent for the coming of the government to that seat. A few years later more durable material was substituted. The commissionership was abolished May 1802, and Thornton and Hoban ceased direct superintendence, though often called in

THE NATIONAL CAPITOL, WASHINGTON, D. C.

consultation. At this time the north wing was complete, the foundation of the central rotunda and dome in place, and the basement story of the south wing partly done. These are still as Thornton planned them.

On 6 March 1803 Jefferson appointed Benjamin H. Latrobe (q.v.) "surveyor of public buildings." He at once began, like the others, to besiege the President with the bitterest assaults on Thornton's designs, and when the former declined to interfere, appealed to Congress. Thornton, however, now in charge of the patent office, though he defended himself with severity, made no further attempt to prevent the alteration of his plans; and Latrobe made many serious changes, some of them since judged harmful to beauty and utility. Thus, the Representatives' hall was changed from a graceful, ellipse to a square with semicircular ends; a bad echo gave trouble for many years, caused by the changes. The number and size of entrances to the rotunda were curtailed, the splendid open staircases, cut down and placed in obscurity, were difficult for strangers to find; and the grand semicircular western portico was abolished. The principal entrance was also changed from the west front, facing the White House, to the eastern side. Latrobe was constantly in hot water with both Jefferson and Congress, and published a pamphlet against them in 1806; but till 1811 had pretty much his own way. When the War of 1812 broke out, the capitol consisted of the north and south wings, connected by a corridor of rough boards over the central foundations. On 24 Aug. 1814 the British burnt it as far as possible, piling the furniture and platforms in the rooms with rocket stuff and igniting them; the interior was dreadfully damaged, but the outside walls remained, also the inside brickwork and some stone. A strong movement arose for removing the capital elsewhere; but the same considerations prevailed against it as later. In fear of such a result, however, the local interests formed the "Capitol Hotel Company," and erected a building for government occupancy till the repairs on the capitol were finished. It was occupied, 1815-19, and was afterward known as the "Old Capitol," and used in the Civil War as a military prison. In the reconstruction the House wing was entirely altered.

Near the end of 1817 Latrobe became embroiled with a new commissioner of the Federal building, Samuel Lane, and resigned. In his place was appointed Charles Bulfinch (q.v.), from 1 Jan. 1818; he remained supervising architeet for the next decade. In the winter of 1819-20 Congress took its seat in the new hall. The centre was pushed forward to completion, and on 10 Dec. 1824, the entire interior was finished. In 1825 a public competition was held for the figures on the pediment of the eastern portico. From 1826 on Bulfinch was employed on special detail, and the landscape gardening and work on the grounds, which were of his designing. The capitol was set in a park of 22½ acres, encircled by an iron railing somewhat taller than a man, affixed in the sandstone coping of a low wall. There were four carriage and five pedestrian entrances. On 2 March 1828 the position of architect of the capitol was abolished; but Bulfinch remained in employment till the end of June 1829, when Jackson dismissed him. He designed and planned the modern

form of the then west extremity of the building, the Senate galleries, and the terraces on the east; and made the dome higher than in Thornton's plan. Among others who should have great credit for the beauty of the capitol are Peter Lenox, clerk of works under Latrobe; George Blagden, superintendent of stonecutters; and Giovanni Andrei, an Italian, superintendent of carvers. That so beautiful and harmonious a structure should have emerged from the contentions of so many different minds is due partly to the really great ability of the three chief architects, Thornton, Latrobe, and Bulfinch, and partly to the determination of successive Presidents that the changes should harmonize with the original design. Latrobe's material external alterations of Thornton's plan have been mentioned; Bulfinch designed the western central portico as it now stands.

From 1829 to 1836 there was no architect of the capitol. On 6 June 1836, Jackson appointed as Federal architect Robert Mills (q.v.), who had studied under Latrobe; and he held the place till 1851. Thomas U. Walter (q.v.) then took the post, having drawn the plans for the two modern wings that extended the original capitol, which the government needs had outgrown, into the modern one. The corner-stone of the extension was laid by President Fillmore, 4 July 1851; the new Representatives' hall was occupied in 1857; the Senate hall in 1859. The great lengthening of the dimensions required a correspondent heightening of the dome; and Mr. Walter designed a new one, which was constructed during the Civil War, and completed at the close of 1863, the statue of Freedom being then lifted into place. Mr. Walter, however, had foreseen a future need of still further extension, and had drawn plans for it while the other work was going on. These have been awaiting their time since; and Congress in the spring of 1903 authorized their execution, at a probable expenditure of $2,500,000 and three years' time, under the supervision of the present Federal architect, Mr. Woods. This extension is to the eastward, and involves the removal of Latrobe's portico at the east front, but none of the old walls. The present front wall will become the rear wall of an open court, which is to light the west side of the addition. This will contain 66 new and handsome rooms, divided equally between the Senate and the House. (For a minute history of the capitol down to 1851, see Glenn Brown in the 'American Architect,' Vols. LXII.-LXV.).

Capitoline Games, games held in ancient Rome in celebration of the deliverance of the city from the Gauls, and in honor of Jupiter Capitolinus, to whom the Romans ascribe the salvation of the capitol in the hour of danger. They were instituted 387 B.C., after the departure of the Gauls.

Capitoli'nus, Julius, Roman historian, who lived toward the end of the 3d century, and wrote the lives of nine emperors. He is one of the writers of the 'Historia Augusta,' in the editions of which his works are to be found.

Capitulary, ka-pĭt'ū-la-rĭ (Lat. *capitula*, "chapters"), a writing divided into heads or chapters, especially a law or regal enactment so divided into heads. Laws known by this designation were promulgated by Childebert, Clothaire, Carloman, and Pepin, kings of France;

but no sovereign seems to have put forth so many of them as the Emperor Charlemagne, who appears to have wished to effect, in a certain degree, a uniformity of law throughout his extensive dominions. With this view it is supposed he added to the existing codes of feudal laws many other laws, divided or arranged under small chapters or heads, sometimes to explain, sometimes to amend, and sometimes to reconcile or remove the differences between them. These were generally promulgated in public assemblies composed of the sovereign and the chief men of the nation, both ecclesiastical and secular. They regulated equally the spiritual and temporal administration of the kingdom; and the execution of them was entrusted to the bishops, the courts, and the *missi regii*, officers so called because they were sent by the French kings of the first and second race to dispense law and justice in the provinces. Many copies of these capitularies were made, one of which was generally preserved in the royal archives. The authority of the capitularies was very extensive. It prevailed in every kingdom under the dominion of the Franks, and was submitted to in many parts of Italy and Germany. The earliest collection of the capitularies is that of Anségise, abbot of Fontenelles. It was adopted by Louis the Debonnaire and Charles the Bald, and was publicly approved of in many councils of France and Germany. But as Anségise had omitted many capitularies in his collection, Benedict, the Levite or deacon of the church of Mentz, added three books to them. Each of the collections was considered to be authentic, and of course was appealed to as law. Subsequent additions have been made to them. The best editions of them are those of Baluze (two volumes, Paris 1677), and of Pertz in the 'Monumenta Germaniæ Historica' (2d div. Vols. I. and II.; Hanover 1835-7). The capitularies remained in force in Italy longer than in Germany, and in France longer than in Italy. The incursions of the Normans, the intestine confusion and weakness of the government under the successors of Charlemagne, and above all the publication of the epitome of canon law termed the Decretum of Gratian, about the year 1150, which totally superseded them in all religious concerns, put an end to their authority in France.

Capitula'tion ("a writing drawn up in heads"), in military language, the act of surrendering to an enemy upon stipulated terms, in opposition to a surrender at discretion.

In the 15th century capitulations, as they were called, were presented by the ecclesiastical establishments in Germany to their newly chosen abbots and bishops, who were obliged to swear to observe them as laws and conditions for their future rule. The ecclesiastical Electors obtained, after the fall of the Hohenstaufen family, certain advantageous promises from the new emperors, which were called capitulations. When Charles V. was proposed as emperor, and it was apprehended, on account of his foreign education, that he would disregard the German constitution, he was obliged to make oath that he would not reside without the German empire, nor appoint foreigners to office in the empire, etc. This was called his "election capitulation." Such a *Wahlcapitulation* was afterward presented to every new emperor as a fun-

damental law of the empire. In this way the authority of the German emperors was constantly more and more diminished, so that at last it became merely nominal, since the electors, at the choice of every new emperor, made some new infringement on the imperial privileges. The *Wahlcapitulationen* were acknowledged bargains, certainly unique in history.

Capiz, kä pēth', Philippines, capital of the province of Capiz, situated in the northern part of the island of Panay, four miles from the mouth of the Panay or Capiz River. The river is navigable to the city, and there is also an excellent roadstead at its mouth. There is a large local trade, particularly in rice, and connection by steamer with Manila. Capiz is also a telegraph and military station. Pop. 13,676.

Cap'lin, or **Capelin,** a small savory smelt (*Mallotus villosus*), found in large numbers on the Arctic coast as far south as Cape Cod. The inhabitants of Newfoundland and Labrador catch it in large quantities at certain seasons, and many are dried and exported to Great Britain.

Capmany y Montpalau, Antonio de, än-tō'-nē-ō dä käp mä nē ē mōnt-pạ-län', Spanish critic and historian: b. Barcelona, 24 Nov. 1742; d. Cadiz, 14 Nov. 1813. He served in the wars with Portugal in 1762, left the army in 1770, and joined Olavide in his scheme for colonizing and cultivating the Sierra Morena. This enterprise terminated disastrously, and Capmany removed to Madrid, where he was chosen secretary of the Royal Historical Academy of Spain in 1790, and filled several offices in the gift of the government. He traveled in Italy, Germany, France, and England. When the French entered Madrid in 1808, he fled to Seville, arriving there destitute and in rags. He was chosen a member of the Cortes of Cadiz, in which capacity he made himself conspicuous by his patriotism and active opposition to the new rulers. His works, which enjoy a high reputation in Spain, are numerous; among them are 'Memorias historicas sobre la Marina, Commercio y Artes de la antigua Ciudad de Barcelona'; 'Questiones criticas sobre varios puntos de historia, economica, politica y militar'; 'Teatro historico-critico de la Elocuencia Española'; and 'Dictionario Frances-Español.'

Cap'nomancy, divination by smoke, one of the modes of divination resorted to by the ancients. They used to burn vervain or some other sacred plant, and observe the form and direction which the smoke took in escaping, and from these circumstances they drew their auguries. Sometimes the smoke of sacrifices was observed instead of that of vervain. When this smoke was thin and transparent, it was considered a good omen; if, on the contrary, it was thick and opaque, the omen was bad. Another method of acquiring a knowledge of the future by capnomancy was to throw the seeds of jasmine or poppy on burning coals, and to observe the smoke which rose from them.

Capo d'Istria, Austria (the ancient ÆGIDA, later JUSTINOPOLIS), a seaport on the Gulf of Trieste, nine miles south of Trieste. It is connected with the mainland by a causeway rather more than half a mile long. It is defended by an old fort now going to decay. It contains a cathedral, a lofty edifice, faced in the Venetian style with marble, and containing some fine paintings, sculptures, and arabesques. It is the seat of a bishop, and has six monasteries and two nunneries, a gymnasium, several hospitals, and a penitentiary. There are manufactories of soap, candles, leather, and sea-salt; and there is also a considerable trade in wines, oil, and fish. After the 10th century Capo d'Istria belonged, alternately, to the Venetians and Genoese, till finally, in 1478, it succeeded in making itself independent of the latter with the aid of the former. Capo d'Istria now became the capital of Istria, and along with it came into the possession of Austria in 1815. Pop. (1903) about 12,000.

Capo d'Istrias, or **Capo d'Istria, Ioannes Antonios,** yō-än'nēs än-tō'nyōs kä-pō-dēs'-trē-as, Count, Greek statesman: b. Corfu, 11 Feb. 1776; d. Nauplia, 9 Oct. 1831. His family had been settled in Corfu since 1373, but originally came from the Illyrian town of Capo d'Istria. He devoted himself to political life, and in 1809, after holding a high place in the Ionian Islands, entered the diplomatic service of Russia. Here his policy tended to· the separation of Greece from Turkey. In 1828 he entered on a seven years' presidency of Greece; but whether from his attachment to Russian interests, or from the jealousy and impatience of restraint of the chiefs, he speedily became extremely unpopular. Several of these unruly chiefs belonging to the islands and to the province of Maina at last, in the spring of 1831, rose in open rebellion against him, demanding a convocation of the national assembly, the establishment of the liberty of the press, and the release of certain state prisoners, especially of Petros Mauromichalis, one of their own number whom D'Istrias had arrested and imprisoned. The president obtained the aid of Russia, but before the insurrection could be quelled he was assassinated in a church at Nauplia, by Constantine and George Mauromichalis, the brother and nephew of Petros Mauromichalis.

Caponière, kä-pō-nyär, or **Caponnière,** in fortification, a place covered against the fire of the enemy on the sides, sometimes also above, and serving for the connection of two works or for maintaining an important point. In particular:

1. A passage secured by two parapets, in the form of glacis, which leads through the dry ditch from one work to another; for instance, from the chief wall to the ravelin. If danger is to be apprehended only from one side, and consequently only one parapet is made, it is called a demi-caponnière; if it is covered above with hurdles or with wood, it is called a coffer: but this word is often used indifferently for caponnière.

2. Small block-houses in the covered way, for its defense. Coehorn laid out similar but less useful works below the glacis, and Scharnhorst proposes them, under the name of field-caponnières, for the salient angles of field fortification.

Capote, Domingo Mendez, dō-mēng'gō mēn-dāth' kä-pō'tä, Cuban statesman: b. Cardenas, 1863. He was graduated at the University of Havana, and became one of the best-known lawyers in Cuba. Susequently he was a professor in the University of Havana for many years. In December 1895 he joined the insurgents under Gen. Maximo Gomez; became a brigadier-general; and was appointed civil governor of Matanzas and of Las Villas. In November 1897 he was elected vice-president of the Cuban republic. When the Cuban Constitutional Convention appointed a commission of five members to confer with President McKinley and Secretary Root concerning the future relations of the United States and Cuba. he became its leader. The conference was held in Washington, D. C., in April 1901.

Capoul, Joseph Amédée Victor, zhō-zēf a-mā-dā vēk-tōr kä-pool, French tenor singer: b. Toulouse, 27 Feb. 1839. He was educated at Paris; and sang there in the Opéra Comique, 1861–72· where he was very popular, especially in his role as Gaston de Meillagré in Auber's 'Premier Jour de Bonheur.' He has also sung in New York, London, Vienna, St. Petersburg, and other cities, being everywhere very successful.

Cappadocia, kăp-pä-dō'shĭ-a, in antiquity, one of the most important provinces in Asia. once a famous kingdom; in its widest extent bounded west by Lycaonia, south by Cilicia and Syria, east by Armenia, and north by the Pontus Euxinus. In the period of the Persian government Cappadocia comprehended all the country between the Halys and Euphrates. By the former river it was separated from Phrygia and Paphlagonia; by the latter, from Armenia: therefore the region afterward called Pontus was comprehended in this territory. The Persians divided it, according to Strabo, into two satrapies, which bore the name of Cappadocia Magna, afterward Cappadocia Proper; and Cappadocia Minor, afterward Pontus. This division, however, was not always strictly observed. The Persian satraps governed, at a later time, under the title of kings, and sometimes made themselves independent. At the time of the famous retreat of the 10,000 Greeks, both the Cappadocias seem to have been under the rule of Mithridates I., who had participated in the conspiracy of Cyrus the Younger, but retained his government and became, after the defeat of Cyrus, again dependent upon the kings of Persia. It became a Roman province in 17 A.D. Cappadocia Magna was a good grazing country, and also well adapted for the cultivation of grain, especially wheat: but wood was scarce. Mazaca, afterward Cæsareia. now Kaisariyeh, was the residence of the kings of Cappadocia. The name of Leukosyri (White Syrians) is said by Strabo to have been applied to the Cappadocians, as if to distinguish them from the dark Syrians who dwelt to the east of Mount Amanus.

Cappel, kä'pĕl, Switzerland. a village in the canton of Zürich, and 10 miles from the town of Zürich. It contains an old Cistercian convent, founded in 1185. and a simple monument erected in 1838 to the reformer Zwingle, who was killed 11 Oct. 1531.

Cap'pon, James, Canadian educator: b. Scotland, 8 March 1854. He was educated at Glasgow University, and since 1888 has been professor of English language and literature at Queen's University. Kingston. Ontario. He has published 'Victor Hugo: a Study and a Memoir'; 'Britain's Title in South Africa.'

Capponi, Gino, MARCHESE, gē'nō mär-kä'zĕ kăp pō'nē, Italian scholar and historian: b. Florence, 14 Sept. 1792; d. there, 3 Feb. 1876. He traveled widely and devoted himself almost entirely to his studies in spite of the fact that he became blind early in life. For a short time in 1848 he was at the head of the Tuscan government; in 1859 he was a member of the Constitutional Convention of Tuscany; he was also made a senator of Italy; and in 1862 was at the head of the Historical Commission for Tuscany, Umbria, and the Marches. He wrote 'Storia della Repubblica di Firenze' (1875); and had a part in the preparation of a lexicon by the Accadamia della Crusca, and in the editing of texts of Dante's 'Divine Comedy.'

Capps, Edward, American philologist: b. 21 Dec. 1866. He was graduated from Illinois College, 1887; took his doctor's degree at Yale, 1891; and was tutor in Latin at the latter place, 1890-2. Since then he has been successively associate professor and professor of Greek in the University of Chicago. Besides a number of philological papers, he has written 'From Homer to Theocritus' (1891).

Caprara, Giambattista, jäm-bät-tēs'tä käprä'rä, CARDINAL, Italian ecclesiastic: b. Bologna, Italy, 29 May 1733; d. Paris, 21 June 1810. He studied theology, became vice-legate of Ravenna in 1758 under Benedict XIV., and in 1785 was sent by Pius VI., as nuncio to Vienna, to remonstrate with the Emperor Joseph on his conduct in relation to Church matters. His remonstrance proved ineffectual, but in 1792 he was appointed a cardinal, shortly afterward a member of the state council, and in 1800 bishop of Jest. In 1801 he went to Paris as legate of Pius VII., and conducted the negotiations with the French republic with so much success that in 1802 the first concordate was concluded. Shortly after he was appointed archbishop of Milan, and in 1805 he crowned Napoleon king of Italy.

Caprera, kä-prā'rạ, a small island in the northeast of Sardinia, and separated from it by a narrow strait. It is six miles long from north to south, and two miles broad. It is fertile, and produces both corn and good pasture. It is well known as the ordinary residence of Garibaldi, who since 1854 possessed a dwelling-house on the island, along with a piece of ground which he farmed until his death here in 1882.

Capri, kä'prē, an island in the beautiful Gulf of Naples, which contributes not a little to the charms of this favorite scene of nature. Capri, five miles long and two broad, lies at the entrance of the gulf, and consists of two mountains of limestone, remarkable for their picturesque shape, and a well-cultivated valley. The inhabitants, amounting to 4,600, are occupied in the production of oil and wine, in fishing, and in catching quails, which come in immense numbers from Africa to the shores of Italy. Every spot on the island which can be made productive is cultivated. In fact, agriculture all around Naples is in the highest state of perfection. The town of Capri is the seat of a bishop, to whom all the quails belong. A high rock separates Capri from the little town of Anacapri, which is reached by 522 steps cut in the rock. With the Romans Capri was called Capreæ. Augustus obtained it from the Neapolitans in exchange for Ischia, and made it a place of agreeable retreat, but never made use of it. Tiberius spent here the last seven years of his life in degrading voluptuousness and infamous cruelty. The ruins of his palaces are still extant, and other ruins are scattered over the island. The island of Capri is remarkable for several remarkable caverns or grottoes in its steep, rocky coast. By far the most remarkable of these is unquestionably the celebrated Grotta azzurra (Blue Grotto), which was discovered by a singular accident in the summer of 1832, an Englishman while bathing having observed the opening in the rocks which forms the entrance to the grotto, and swum into it. It gets its name from the fact that, while the sun is shining outside, all the objects within the cavern — rocks, water, and sand — are tinged with a beautiful blue color, very soft and agreeable to the eye. The cavern is elliptical in form, measuring about 1,200 or 1,300 feet in circumference; its height is considerable, and its roof and sides bristle with stalactites. The blue color within the grotto is supposed to be caused by the refraction of the rays of light in passing through the water before entering the cave. The blue rays, with those next to them, the violet and the indigo, being the most refrangible, are the only rays that are admitted, the others — red, orange, etc., being dispersed in the water. In another part of the coast there is another grotto which exhibits phenomena precisely similar, except that the objects in this one are clothed with a green instead of a blue color. It is called the Grotta verde (Green Grotto)hence

Cap'ric Acid. See DECOIC ACID.

Capriccio, kä-prē'chō (*Caprice*), is the name applied to a musical composition, in which the composer follows the bent of his humor. The *capriccio* may be used with propriety in pieces for exercise, in which the strangest and most difficult figures may be introduced, if they are not at variance with the nature of the instrument or of the voice.

Capricor'nus (Lat. *caper*, "a goat," and *cornu*, "a horn"), "the goat," one of the 12 signs of the Zodiac, between Sagittarius and Aquarius; also the corresponding zodiacal constellation, one of Ptolemy's original 48. One of its brightest stars, Alpha, is a wide double, easily separated by the naked eye by any one with good eyesight. Capricornus is surrounded by Aquila, Aquarius, Piscis Austrinus, Microscopium, and Sagittarius.

Caprification, kăp-rĭ-fĭ-kä'shŏn, the fertilization of the flowers of the Smyrna fig with pollen derived from the wild fig, or caprifig. From time immemorial it has been the custom of Orientals to break off the fruits of the caprifig, bring them to the edible-fig trees, and tie them to the limbs. From the caprifigs thus brought in there issues a minute insect, which, covered with pollen, crawls into the flower receptacles of the edible fig, fertilizes them, and thus produces a crop of seeds and brings about the subsequent ripening of the fruit. It has been shown that the varieties of the wild fig or caprifig are the only ones which contain male organs, while the varieties of the Smyrna fig are exclusively female. In the 'caprifig there are said to exist in Mediterranean regions three crops of fruit,—the spring crop, a summer crop, and a third, which remains upon the trees through the winter. The fig-insect (*Blastophaga grosso-rum*) over-winters in the third crop, oviposits in the spring crop, develops a generation within it, each individual living in the swelling of a gall-flower (a modified and infertile female flower), and, issuing from it covered with pollen, enters the young flower receptacles of the young Smyrna fig, which are at that time of the proper size, and makes an attempt to oviposit in the true female flowers, fertilizing them at the same time by means of the pollen adhering to their bodies. The life history of the insect from that time on is not well understood, but the *Blastophaga* has been known to occur again in the over-wintering crop of figs. The effect of caprification on the young Smyrna figs becomes readily visible within a few days; before the *Blastophaga* enters the fig the latter is transverse and strongly ribbed, while a few days after fertilization the fig swells up and becomes rounded and sleek. The male *Blastophaga* is always wingless. It has no ocelli, and its compound eyes are greatly reduced in size. The fact that the male rarely leaves the fig in which it has hatched might almost be inferred from these facts of winglessness and partial blindness. When this wingless male issues from the seed-like gall in which it is contained, it seeks a female gall in the interior of the same fig, gnaws a small hole through its cortex, inserts its extremely long, almost telescopic, abdominal extremity through the hole, and fertilizes the female. The female subsequently, with her powerful jaws, gnaws the top of the gall off and emerges, crawling around the interior of the fig, and eventually forcing her way through the ostiolum, almost immediately seeking for young figs which she enters, and, should the fig entered prove to be a caprifig, lays her eggs at the base of as many flowers as she can find, and then dies. Should the fig entered, however, be a Smyrna fig, either through the fact of the caprifig from which she issued having been hung in the branches of a Smyrna-fig tree, or from the fact that she has flown to an adjoining Smyrna-fig tree, she walks around among the female flowers seeking for a proper place to oviposit. It is this futile, wandering search, when her body is covered with pollen from the caprifigs, that produces the extensive and almost perfect fertilization of the entire number of female flowers. The young larva is a delicate little maggot curved upon itself and showing no visible segmentation. In the full-grown larva the segments are more apparent, and with the growth of the larva the gall at the base of the male florets becomes hard, and greatly resembles a seed, turning light brown in color. The male and the female pupa each occupies a greater portion of the interior of the gall. Consult: 'The Fig' (United States Department of Agriculture, Washington 1901).

Although figs are raised in California and the southern States they have long been inferior to the Smyrna fig, the standard kind of commerce, which owes its peculiar flavor to the number of ripe seeds which it contains. These seeds are obtained only by the process described above, and the United States Department of Agriculture has recently devoted much attention to caprification, with a view to the development of the American fig industry.

Caprimulgidæ, kăp-rĭ-mŭl'jĭ-dē, the goatsuckers (so called from a superstition regarding their habits), a family of birds of puzzling affinities, but nearest to the swifts (*Cypselidæ*), with which, and the humming-birds, they are often considered to constitute an order, *Macrochires*. The family is characterized by a small bill, enormous gape fringed with elongated, stiff bristles, elongated tail of 10 soft rectrices, long pointed wings, very small feet with the middle claw pectinate, and very lax plumage. Two subfamilies, the *Caprimulginæ* or true goatsuckers, and the *Nyctibiinæ* of tropical America, are recognized, to which the oil-birds (*Steatornis*), and *Podargus* and its allies, are sometimes added as two more. The family is nearly cosmopolitan, and comprises 12 or 15 genera and perhaps 100 species, all birds of more or less crepuscular habits, which catch insects on the wing like swallows. The "night-hawk" and "whip-poor-will" are the common species of the eastern United States.

Caprivi, Georg Leo, gä örg lā ō kä-prē'vě, GRAF VON, sometimes called CAPRIVI DE CAPRARA DE MONTECUCULI, German soldier and statesman: b. Charlottenburg. 24 Feb. 1831; d. Skyren, 6 Feb. 1899. He entered the army in 1849; fought in the campaigns of 1864 and 1866; and in the Franco-German war of 1870 was chief of staff to the 10th Army Corps. In 1883–8 he was at the head of the Admiralty; in 1888 he became commander of his old army corps. Hence he was removed, on the fall of Bismarck, in 1890, to become imperial chancellor and Prussian prime minister. His principal measures were the army bills of 1892 and 1893, and the commercial treaty with Russia in 1894, in which year he retired.

Capro'ic Acid. See HEXOIC ACID.

Capron, Allyn, American soldier: b. Tampa, Fla., 27 Aug. 1846; d. Fort Myer, Va., 18 Sept. 1898. He was graduated at West Point, 1867, and entered the 1st Artillery, receiving his captaincy 4 Dec. 1888. During the Sioux campaign of 1890 he made a brilliant record at the battles of Wounded Knee and Drexel Mission. During the war with Spain, 1898, he opened the fight at El Caney, Cuba, and shattered the first flagstaff in Santiago. During this campaign he was taken ill with typhoid fever, and succumbed to its attack. He was a fine mathematician, and a recognized authority on artillery and tactics. His father, Erastus Allyn Capron was killed at Churubusco, in the Mexican war, 20 Aug. 1847.

Ca'pron, Allen Kissam, American military officer (son of Allyn Capron, q.v.): b. Brooklyn, N. Y., 24 June 1871: d. Las Guasimas, Cuba, 24 June 1898. He enlisted as a private (1890), and rose to a second lieutenant (1893), joining the "Rough Riders" on the outbreak of the war with Spain. He was made a captain for bravery, and was the first American army officer who fell in that war.

Capryl'ic Acid. See OCTOIC ACID.

Cap'sicin, kăp'sĭ-sĭn, a name given to two apparently different substances. One described by Braconnot, obtained from chilli pepper, is an acrid oil or oleoresin, of a reddish-brown color, the vapor of which excites sneezing and coughing. It is probably a mixture of different bodies. The other is a resinoid substance obtained from cayenne pepper; it is brown with a golden tint, has the consistence of tar, an aromatic smell and pungent taste, and is used in America as a powerful stimulant in influenza, fever, indigestion, and other disorders, and externally as a rubefacient. Quite recently a volatile alkaloid has been obtained from chilli pepper, by first removing the acrid resin, then making the fluid alkaline, and extracting with petroleum spirit. On evaporating, a substance is produced with an odor like that of conia. It is distinguished from conia and nicotine by a variety of reactions.

Capsicum, a genus of plants of the order *Solanaceæ,* consisting of annual or biennial plants, bearing membranous pods containing several seeds, noted for their hot, pungent qualities. *C. annuum,* a native of South America, furnishes the fruits known as chillies. These, as well as the fruits of *C. frutescens* and other species, are used to form cayenne pepper. For this purpose the ripe fruits are dried in the sun or in an oven, and then ground to powder, which is mixed with a large quantity of wheat flour. The mixed powder is then turned into cakes with leaven; these are baked till they become as hard as biscuit, and are then ground and sifted. Cayenne pepper is largely adulterated with red lead and other substances. *C. fructus* is the dried ripe fruit of *C. fastigiatum,* imported from Zanzibar. It is a small, oblong, scarlet, membranous pod, divided internally into two or three cells containing numerous flat, white, reniform seeds. It has no odor; its taste is hot and acrid. Capsicum fruits are used medicinally, in powder or as a tincture, externally, or as a gargle in cases of malignant sore throat, and internally as a stimulant in cases of impaired digestion.

By reason of the resin-like body, capsicin, which is contained in the fruits of these plants, they possess very active irritant properties. The pure crystals of capsicin are extremely virulent, and readily cause severe poisoning; but the ground fruit is less active, and is of service in medicine, both for external and internal medication.

Externally, capsicum is used as an irritant to cause redness of the skin or to blister, thus affecting related visceral areas within the body. It is thus employed in bronchitis, in early stages of pneumonia, in pleurisies, and in joint and nerve affections. Internally, capsicum is used to stimulate the appetite and to increase the amounts of gastric and intestinal juices. It is particularly serviceable in the gastritis of alcoholism. All capsicum should be excluded from the diet of patients with disease of the kidneys or acute disease of the genito-urinary system.

Cap'stan (Fr. *cabestan,* probably from a derivative of Lat. *capistrum,* a halter, from *capere,* to hold), an apparatus constructed on the mechanical principle of the wheel and axle, used for moving heavy weights and by various methods for the application of power. Its axis, unlike that of the windlass, is vertical. The capstan may be operated either by steam-power or by means of a lever set in its socket and worked by horses or pushed by hand, the last method usually requiring several men. When used elsewhere than on shipboard, the capstan generally has some specific name. Thus, when employed for raising coal from pits it is com-

mouly called a gin; if worked by horses, it is known as a whim-gin. Capstans were formerly made of wood, but are at present almost universally of iron. The upright barrel of a capstan is constructed around a spindle. The barrel is sometimes smooth, and sometimes for increase of friction has, running up and down its surface, ribs or ridges called whelps. In the capstan-head or drum-head, surmounting the barrel, are holes for the levers or capstan-bars used to revolve the barrel. Being smaller at its centre than at the top or bottom end, the barrel has a curve from above and below, whereby a rope wound by working the capstan slips toward the concave part so formed. By this device a length of rope may be compactly and securely wound and kept in place for repeated use. On the circumference of a pawl-head at the bottom of the barrel are pivoted pawls which catch a pawl-rim or ratchet-ring fastened to the platform or floor on which the capstan is fixed. There are various other devices for increasing friction, the prevention of slipping, and reverse operation of the mechanism.

Cap'sule, in botany, a dry fruit containing several seeds, sometimes a large number, and opening of itself by means of valves or pores when it comes to maturity. According as it contains one, two, three, or more cells, the capsule is called unilocular, bilocular, trilocular, etc., and when it has many cells it is called multilocular.

In anatomy a capsule is a mass of fibrous, connective tissue cells surrounding or supporting an organ, either as a bag, as is the case in the kidneys; or as a framework, as in the liver. The capsule is usually an integral portion of the structure of an organ.

In pharmacy gelatin capsules are widely used for purposes of rendering medicines tasteless.

Captain. This is one of those many words derived from the Latin of the Middle Ages, and now to be found in all the different idioms of Europe. Captain comes from the Latin *capitaneus,* from *caput,* head, and signified, first, a governor of a province, who in the first half of the Middle Ages was generally a military man. Thus the word captain soon came to be used chiefly to denote a high, or rather the highest military officer. Like many other words, however, this has in the course of time lost much of its dignity, and in military technology now signifies the commander of a small body, a company, and in maritime language the master of a vessel. In the navy it indicates a specific rank, the captain being distinctively the officer commanding a war-vessel. In the latter part of the Middle Ages, when armies were not yet so regularly divided and subdivided as at the present time, captains were the commanders of those small bodies of which the armies consisted. These were generally collected by their commander, who entered with his company into the service where most pay or most booty could be obtained. The practice of carrying war by troops collected in this manner prevailed to the greatest extent in Italy, where the continual quarrels of the numerous small states afforded ample employment to the unsettled and the dissolute. These companies play an important part in the history of the Middle Ages, particularly that of the two centuries preceding the Reformation, and had a very important influence on the manners and morals of the south of Europe. They are further interesting to the student of history, because they are so unlike anything at present existing.

CAPTAIN, in modern armies, is the commander of a company of foot or a troop of horse. In the United States army he nominates the sergeants, corporals, and lance-corporals of his company, who are appointed by the commander of the regiment.

CAPTAIN, in the navy, an officer commanding a ship of war. The naval captain is next in rank above the commander, and in the United States ranks with a colonel in the army.

CAPTAIN-GENERAL, the commander-in-chief of an army or of all the military forces of a country. In France it was an ancient title which conferred an almost unlimited power on the person who possessed it in the district where he commanded. But it never corresponded to that of generalissimo except in the case of the Duke of Savoy, in 1635, in the time of Louis XIII. The title is not in use at present, nor would it agree with the existing organization of the administration. In Spain the rank of a captain-general corresponds with that of a marshal of France, the captain-general having command of an army or army-corps. The title was also given to the head of a province in the Spanish colonies in South America, which were divided into viceroyalties and captain-generalships (*capitanias-generales*); thus Chile used to be a captain-generalship. The captains-general were not placed under the viceroys, but accountable only to the king through the council of the Indies. The captain-general of Venezuela, for instance, had no connection with the viceroy of New Granada. They decided, in the last instance, on all legislative, judicial, and military affairs, and presided in the *real audiencia*. The time during whch these governors remained in power was limited to a few years, probably in order to prevent them from becoming too powerful. The consequence was, that the colonies were oppressed the more to enrich the governors, for rich every one was when he left his office.

CAPTAIN of a merchant ship, he who has the direction of a ship, her crew, lading, etc. In small vessels he is more ordinarily called master, which indeed is the correct title.

Caption, in law, signifies that part of a legal instrument such as an indictment or commission, which states when, where, and by what authority it is executed. In Scotch law it signifies a warrant of imprisonment issued against a party to enforce an obligation, being now confined to a warrant served upon a party who has illegally retained papers in a lawsuit that had been borrowed by him, and intended to compel the return of the papers.

Capua, kä′pō-ä, Italy, a city in the province of Caserta, 18 miles north of Naples, on the Volturno, which is crossed by a handsome bridge. The district is very fertile, but somewhat unhealthy. It is the seat of an archbishopric, and is the principal fortress that covers the approach to Naples. It has two magnificent gates, three principal streets, two handsome squares, and three public fountains. The town is dirty and badly built. The principal public buildings are the cathedral, with a cupola supported by 18 columns, entirely modernized;

the church of the Annunciation; the governor's palace, the town-hall, a museum with many ancient works of art, etc. The ancient city was situated two and a half miles southeast from the modern town, which was built from its ruins on the site of the ancient Casilinum by the Lombards in the 9th century. The site is now occupied by a considerable town, called Santa-Maria-di-Capoa-Vetere. The ancient Capua, one of the finest and most agreeable cities of Italy, was of such extent as to be compared to Rome and Carthage. Hannibal wintered at ancient Capua after the battle of Cannæ, and thus not only lost time, but also is commonly said to have rendered his army unfit to follow up the advantage he had gained. It was a favorite place of resort of the Romans, on account of its agreeable situation and its healthy climate; and many existing ruins attest its ancient splendor. In 456 A.D. it was devastated by the Vandals under Genseric, and in 840 the Saracens completely destroyed it. Pop. about 14,000.

Capuana, Luigi, loo-ē′jē kä-poo-ä′nä, Italian poet, novelist, and critic: b. Mineo, Sicily, 27 May 1839. Having devoted himself to journalism, he settled in Florence in 1864, where he wrote dramatic criticisms; from 1868 until 1877 he lived in his native town, then in Milan, again as a journalist. His best-known work is 'Giacinta' (1879), a naturalistic novel. Besides this he has published several volumes of short stories, among them: 'Profiles of Women' (1881); 'Homo' (1883); and two collections of charming fairy tales: 'Once upon a Time' (1882) and 'Fairy Land' (1883). A curious specimen of rhythmical prose is his 'Semi-Rhythms' (1888), in praise of worldly joy and beauty.

Capuchin, kăp ū shĕn or kap ū chĕn, the name of several animals in which the growth of the hair or feathers upon the head forms a sort of hood suggesting that of a Capuchin friar. Certain monkeys are so called, especially the South American sapajous (q.v.) and one or more of the macaques (q.v.). A breed of domestic pigeons is also so called.

Capuchins, an order of mendicant friars in the Roman Catholic Church founded in 1528 in virtue of a bull of Clement VII. Its founder, Matteo Barro, was a member of the rigorist section of the Observantine Franciscans, who sought to restore the rule of perfect poverty and humility, and to be of aid to parish priests in the cure of souls. The Capuchin friars obtained their name from the capuerce, cowl, or hood which they wore. They were vowed to live according to the rule of St. Francis in hermitages and to labor for the conversion of notorious sinners. Their churches were to be bare of ornament. Soon after their foundation they did heroic service in ministering to those stricken by the plague which at that time ravaged all Italy. The third vicar-general of the order, Bernardino Ochino (q.v.) brought the Capuchins into discredit by his notorious leanings toward protestantism, and the fraternity was interdicted from preaching and would have been suppressed had not Cardinal Sanseverino, archbishop of Naples, interceded for them. Paul also forbade them to establish any convents beyond the Alps, but his successor, Gregory XIII., revoked that decree. Again, Gregory XIV. in 1591 withdrew from them the faculty of ministering in the confessional; but it was restored to them 10 years later by Clement VIII. Finally, in 1619 the fraternity was restored to good standing, and was even erected into an order administratively independent of the general of the Franciscans, and their vicar-general assumed the style of minister-general. Ever since, the Capuchins have been recognized as eminently useful servants of the Church. The order conducts missions in all quarters of the globe, and has the reputation of being very successful in winning converts.

Cap'ulets and Mon'tagues, the English spelling of the names of the Cappelletti and Montecchi, two noble families of northern Italy, according to tradition of Verona, chiefly memorable from their connection with the legend on which Shakespeare has founded his tragedy of 'Romeo and Juliet.'

Ca'put Mor'tuum (Latin), literally, a dead head; a fanciful term much used by the old chemists to denote the residuum of chemicals when all their volatile matters had escaped; hence the word is figuratively used of anything from which all that rendered it valuable has been taken away.

Caputiati, kă-pū-shĭ-ā'tĭ, a Christian sect which arose in France in the 12th century. They wore on their heads a leaden image of the virgin Mary. They wished liberty, equality, and the abolition of all civil government. Hugo, bishop of Auxerre, suppressed them by military force.

Capybara, kă-pē-bä'rạ, an aquatic rodent (*Hydrochoerus capyoara*), of the family *Caviidæ*, native to South America. It is the largest rodent known, being four feet long, and weighing nearly 100 pounds. It has a rough brown coat, a heavy flat head, small, pig-like eyes and ears, and a blunt muzzle. Its feet are supplied with hoof-like claws, and its tail, unlike that of most rodents, is very short. The animal is herbivorous, browsing on grass along river banks, and often creating havoc in sugar plantations. It is awkward on land, but swims and dives well, and can remain under water a long time. The flesh is edible, except that of very old males.

Carabao, kä-rạ-bä'ō. See BUFFALO.

Car'abas, Marquis of, the exalted personage who figures in Perrault's story of 'La Chat Botté' ('Puss in Boots'). The name is often applied to an extremely conservative aristocrat. In Disraeli's 'Vivian Grey' the Marquis of Clanricarde is satirized as the Marquis of Carabas.

Carabidæ, the family of *Coleoptera*, comprising the ground-beetles. In form the species vary greatly; the antennæ are inserted behind the base of the mandibles under a frontal ridge; maxillæ with the outer lobe palpiform, usually biarticulate, while the inner lobe is usually curved, acute, and ciliate, with spines. The epimera and episterna of the prothorax are usually distinct; the three anterior segments of the abdomen, usually six, rarely seven or eight in number, are connate. The legs are slender, formed for running; anterior and middle coxæ are globular, posterior ones dilated internally, and the tarsi are five-jointed. They are, with few exceptions, predaceous and carnivorous beetles; they are runners, and do not fly, the hind wings

being often absent. Their colors are dull metallic or black. They run in grass, or lurk under stones or the bark of trees, whence they go out to hunt in the night-time. The larvæ are found in much the same situations as the adult beetles, and are generally oblong, broad, with the terminal ring around, with two horny hooks or longer filaments, and with a single false leg beneath. *Carabus serratus* and *Calosoma calidum* are common examples.

Car'abine, or Carbine. See RIFLE.

Carabobo, kä-rạ-bō'bō, a state of Venezuela, bounded on the north by the Caribbean Sea; area, 2,984 square miles. The capital is Valencia, and the chief port Puerto Cabello. Coffee, cacao, and sugar are cultivated. The village of Carabobo, 20 miles southwest of Valencia, was the scene of the battle fought 24 June 1821, which was decisive of the independence of Colombia. Caracas, La Guayra, Carthagena, Cumana, and all that portion of Venezuela which is dependent upon them, were permanently secured to the patriots by this victory. Pop. (1900) 225,000.

Caracal, kär'ạ kăl, a lynx-like wild cat of Africa and southern Asia, slender in form and usually red-brown in color. See LYNX.

Caracal'la, Roman emperor: b. Lyons, 188 A.D.; d. 217. His real name was MARCUS AURELIUS ANTONINUS BASSIANUS, and he was the eldest son of Septimius Severus. On the death of his father he succeeded to the throne with his brother, Antoninus Geta, whom he speedily murdered. To effect his own security upward of 20,000 other victims were butchered. He was himself assassinated by Macrinus, the pretorian prefect, near Edessa, in 217. Among the buildings of Caracalla in Rome, the baths—*Thermæ Caracallæ*—near Porta Capena, were most celebrated, and their ruins are still magnificent.

Caracara, kä-rạ-kä'rạ, a genus of large carrion-eating hawks of the tropical parts of America, with black and white plumage, the head somewhat crested, legs long and naked and the general aspect vulture-like. They have increased greatly with the spread of the cattle-raising industry in South America, and have proved of much service as scavengers about the ranches and villages. The species to which the name most strictly applies is *Polyborus cheriway*, which is found from Venezuela to Texas and southern California. Another prominent species is the carancho (*P. tharus*) numerous and well known all over Brazil and Argentina. Darwin gives interesting facts in regard to this and related vulture-hawks in his journal. Compare CHIMANGO.

Caracas, kä-rä'käs, city and capital of the United States of Venezuela, was founded in 1567 by Diego de Lozada, who called the city Santiago de Léon, but in popular usage a more distinctive name was adopted—that of the Caracas tribe of Indians, formerly inhabiting the valley in which the city is built. Its altitude being about 3,000 feet above sea-level, the climate is generally mild and agreeable, the temperature seldom rising above 82° F. (with 84.2 as a maximum), or falling below 65° F. (with a minimum of 48.2). Toward the end of December the temperature is lowest, and it is highest from June to September. Mean temperature, 66.2° F. Lat. 10° 32' N., lon. 67° 4' 45" W.

The streets cross each other at right angles, running due east and west, or north and south, and the principal thoroughfares are paved with stone, and have sidewalks of cement. The capitol building occupies an entire square, an area of more than two acres. It includes the halls in which both chambers of the national congress hold their sessions. The rooms of the high federal court, and the departments of public instruction and the interior are in the galleries on the east and west sides of the capitol. *La Casa Amarilla* (the Yellow House), official residence of the president of the republic, is situated west of the Plaza Bolivar. On the north side of the same square is the main post-office. Near by are the archbishop's palace, the cathedral, and the municipal palace. Opposite the southern façade of the capitol are the university buildings (Gothic architecture, with interior gardens) ; the old temple of San Francisco, and the Exposition Palace, the western wing of which contains the Bolivar Museum, the headquarters of the Academy of History, and the corresponding branch of the Spanish Royal Academy. The national library and museum are housed by the university. Other characteristic buildings are: The National Pantheon, the Masonic Temple, the three markets, the National Benevolent Institute, the Arsenal, the Institute of Arts and Trades, and the Municipal Theatre. Besides the Plaza Bolivar, the principal public squares are the Washington, Pantheon, and Fifth of July (Independence Day). The cathedral, dating from 1614; the Basilica de Santa Ana, and the Santa Capilla, are noteworthy among the churches of the city. Interesting relics of the heroes of the struggle for liberty, Miranda, Bolivar, and Páez, are shown in the National Museum. There are several promenades (called "Iron Bridge," "Paradise Avenue," and "Independence"), and among the places of amusement are a Plaza de Toros, baseball grounds, and a bicycle park. An important institution supported by the government is the Vargas Hospital. The Linares Hospital for children is maintained by private contributions. Leading clubs are the Union, German, Italian, and Agricultural. Street railways are controlled by the Caracas and Bolivar companies. The city has cheap telephone service, furnished by two companies, and is lighted by gas and electricity. All telegraph lines throughout the republic are owned by the government. Four lines of railway start at Caracas, three of which are designed to place the capital in communication with the interior, while the most important runs to Port La Guayara. Pop. including the six suburban parishes making up the federal district is about 90,000.

Caracci. See CARRACCI.

Caraccioli, Francesco, från chês'kö kä-rä-chö'lö, Italian admiral: b. Naples, 1752; d. 29 June 1799. He was distinguished in the Neapolitan service, but entered the service of the Parthenopean Republic set up by the French republicans in 1799, and repelled a Sicilian-English fleet. When Ruffo took Naples, Caraccioli was arrested, and being tried by court-martial was condemned to death, and hanged at the yard-arm of a Neapolitan frigate. The court-martial was ordered by Nelson, to whom the king had given command of the Neapolitan navy.

Carac'tacus, British king. He was a son of Cunobelin, king of the Trinobantes, and in 43 A.D., when Plautius landed, was at the head of the Catuvellauni. Plautius and his lieutenant Vespasian, who afterward became emperor, defeated the British forces under Caractacus on several occasions, the chief battle probably taking place about Wallingford. When the Romans had pushed well down the Thames the Emperor Claudius arrived and took part in further military operations, but his stay was a very short one. Caractacus now established himself in South Wales among the Silures, whence he took every opportunity of harassing the Romans. In 47 A.D. Plautius was replaced by Ostorius Scapula, and that commander completely defeated Caractacus in a battle somewhere about Shropshire, probably at Caer Caradoc. The wife, daughter, and brothers of the British leader were captured, and Caractacus himself fled to the country of the Brigantes in the north, only to be delivered up by their queen Cartismandua into the hands of the Romans. He was taken to Rome and made to take part in a triumphal procession. Here he was led before the Emperor Claudius and an assembly of the people. When he came to the seat of the emperor he stopped and addressed him, and so won upon the monarch by his noble behavior and pathetic speech that the other pardoned him. According to the Welsh Triads he lived four years longer, and his children became Christians and introduced Christianity into Britain. He is introduced among the dramatis personæ of Beaumont and Fletcher's play, 'Bonduca.'

Caradoc Sandstone, the name given by Murchison to a thickness of about 4,500 feet of sandstones, shales, grits, flags, and sandy limestones on the border between England and Wales, which he made a separate series. Subsequent investigation has shown that the Caradoc series is of the same age as the Bala, and the series is sometimes called Bala and Caradoc by English geologists. The rocks are of the Ordovician system. See ORDOVICIAN.

Carafe, kă-raf', the French name for an ordinary glass bottle or decanter for holding drinking water.

Caraffa, kä räf'fä, a celebrated Neapolitan family, which has produced several distinguished commanders and statesmen: 1. OLIVIERO, b. 1406; d. Rome, 1511. He was made a cardinal by Pope Paul II. in 1467. Sixtus IV. appointed him his legate to Alfonso of Naples, and in 1472 made him admiral of his fleet against the Turks, from whom he captured Smyrna, and the port of Satalia in Asia Minor. 2. CARLO, b. Naples, 1517; d. 1561. He served first in the Netherlands under the Spaniards, then entered the order of Malta, and was made a cardinal by his uncle Pope Paul IV., who, for his sake, stripped the Colonnas of their possessions. This involved them in a war with Philip of Spain, but the result proved favorable to the Caraffa family. Paul IV. who succeeded Pius IV. appointed a commission of eight cardinals who tried Carlo and on 3 Mar. 1561 put him to death for high treason. 3. ANTONIO, b. Naples, 1538; d. 1591. He was made cardinal by Pius V., and intrusted with the superintendence of the congregation for the revision of the Bible, and an Exposition of the Canons of the Council of Trent. Under Gregory XIII. he became librarian of the Vatican. He translated Theodoret's Commentaries on the Psalms, and the Orations of Gregory Nazianzen from Greek into Latin. 4. ANTONIO, another member of the family, distinguished himself in Hungary in the service of Austria, but made himself universally hated by his cruelty. D. Vienna, 1693.

Carambola, kä-ram-bō'la, the fruit of an East Indian tree of the same genus as the bilimbi, the *Averrhoa Carambola,* order *Oxalidaceæ.* It is of the size and shape of a duck's egg, of an agreeable acidulous flavor.

Car'amel. When sugar is gradually heated, it loses water and other substances, and is converted into a dark mass with a characteristic smell and taste. This is crude caramel, which is used in cookery as a coloring and flavoring ingredient. It is a mixture of several bodies, of which three have been described: Caramelane, a brown bitter body, soluble in water; Caramelene, a dark brown body, also soluble in water, and possessed of great tinctorial power; and Caramelin, a black substance, of intense coloring power, which exists both in a soluble and insoluble modification.

Carangidæ, kä-răn'jĭ-dĕ, a family of marine fishes, the pompanos. Among the more widely known members of the family are the leather jackets, pilot fishes, amber fishes, runners, horse mackerels, crevallés, moonfishes, and pompanos. There are about 200 species in the family, and nearly all are good for food. They abound in the warmer seas, and many of them are remarkable for their graceful or strange forms.

Car'apa, a small genus of tropical trees of the natural order *Meliaceæ,* with mostly imparipinnate leaves and regular flowers. A South American species (*C. guianensis*) is a fine large tree, whose bark is in repute as a febrifuge. Oil made from its seeds (called carap-oil or crab-oil) is used for lamps, and masts of ships are made from its trunk. The wood is called crab-wood. The oil of the African species (*C. tolucana*), called *coondi, kundah,* or *tallicoona* oil, is used by the negroes for making soap and anointing their bodies in order to protect them against insects. The oil of the South American carapa is used for the same purpose also.

Car'apace, the upper part of the hard shell or case in which reptiles belonging to the order of the *Chelonia* are enclosed, the lower part being called plastron. The same name is also given to the upper part of the shell of the Crustacea, and to the case inclosing certain of the *Infusoria.*

Car'at is said to have derived its name from *qirrât,* which in Arabic signifies the pod of a leguminous plant, the seeds of which have, from time immemorial, been used in the East in weighing gold, because they never vary in weight when once dry. It is a weight of three and a sixth troy grains, used in weighing pearls and precious stones, and also serves to express the relative fineness of gold. Twenty-four carats being assumed as the standard of gold perfectly free from alloy, every specimen, in proportion as it falls short of this purity, has a fineness of less than 24 carats — for example, if the alloy amounts to a sixth of the whole, it is 20 carats fine; or to a fourth, it is 18 carats fine.

Carausius, kä-rô'shǐ-ŭs, Roman general: b. among the Menapii, in Gallia Belgica. He was sent by the Emperor Maximian to defend the Atlantic coasts against the Franks and Saxons; but being suspected of permitting those pirates to commit their ravages in order to increase his own plunder when he afterward captured their vessels, and foreseeing that he was likely to fall into disgrace, he landed in Britain and had himself proclaimed emperor by his legions (287 A.D.). In this province he was able to maintain himself six years, when he was assassinated by one of his officers named Allectus (293 A.D.).

Caravaca, kä-rä-vä'kä, Spain, a town in the province of Murcia, and 43 miles west by north of the town of Murcia. It occupies the side of a hill crowned by an ancient castle, and overlooking the river Caravaca, here crossed by a stone bridge; is well built, and has a handsome town-house and church, the latter with a lofty tower and some good sculptures and paintings. Its trade is chiefly in cattle, grain, and manufactures of woolen and hempen goods, paper, soap, earthen and copper ware. Pop. 16,000.

Caravaggio, da, Michelangelo Amerighi, or Merighi, mē'kĕl än'yō lō ä-mĕr-ē'jē or mēr'ē jē kä rä väd'jō, Italian painter: b. Caravaggio, in the Milanese, 1569; d. near Porto Ercole, 1609. He was at first a journeyman mason, but soon applied himself to the study of painting, studied in Milan and Venice, and afterward went to Rome, where he distinguished himself. He may be considered as the inventor of a manner which has had a crowd of imitators. His characteristic traits are vigor and truth of *chiaroscuro,* combined with excellent coloring. He was fond of introducing broad and deep masses of shade, whereby a great effect is given to the light. To aid him in producing this effect the room in which he worked was illuminated by a skylight, and the walls were painted black. He excelled in the painting of naked figures. His faults are obvious. Narrow and servile imitation of nature was his highest aim. Annibale Caracci and Domenichino were, perhaps, less distinguished than Caravaggio during their lives, but after their death were ranked higher; because, without neglecting coloring and the study of nature, they aimed at correctness of design and dignity of conception. His violent character involved him in many difficulties. He died in consequence of wounds received in a quarrel in which his violent nature had involved him. The painters who have imitated him most are Manfredi, Valentin, and Ribeira, called *Espagnolet.*

Caravaggio da Polidoro, Italian painter: b. Caravaggio, 1495; d. 1543. His real name was CALDARA, but he was surnamed CARAVAGGIO from his birthplace. He went to Rome in his youth and carried bricks at first for the masons who worked in the Vatican. He first felt a great desire to become a painter from seeing Giovanni da Udine and the other painters who were occupied in the Vatican. He formed a close friendship with Maturin of Florence, who assisted him with his advice. Caldara soon surpassed him, and exerted himself to introduce improvements in drawing, having always in view the antiques. Raphael employed him in the galleries of the Vatican, where he painted, under his direction, several excellent friezes. At Messina he executed an oil-painting, representing Christ bearing the cross, which contains a number of beautiful figures, and proves his ability to treat the most elevated subjects. He has approached more than any one to the style and the manner of the ancients, particularly in imitating their bas-reliefs. His figures are correct, well distributed and arranged; the positions are natural, the heads full of expression and character. It is evident that he would have acquired great celebrity if he had undertaken greater works. He applied himself to the *chiaroscuro*, particularly to that kind of it which is called *sgraffiato*. He showed, also, much talent in his landscapes. At the sack of Rome in 1527 he fled to Naples, and on his return from that place to Rome, in 1543, he was murdered by his domestic.

Caravaggio, Italy, a town and commune in Lombardy, 24 miles east of Milan, on the Gera d'Adda. It is celebrated as the birthplace of the two great painters, Polidoro Caldara and Michelangelo Amerighi, both called *da Caravaggio*. It was formerly surrounded by walls and defended by a strong castle. Its principal church has some good paintings. The commune is famous for its melons. Pop. about 10,000.

Car'avan, or **Karavan,** a Persian word, used to denote large companies which travel together in Asia and Africa for the sake of security from robbers, having in view, principally, trade or pilgrimages. Such a company often have more than 1,000 camels to carry their baggage and their goods. These walk in single file, and the line is often four or five miles long. To avoid the excessive heat, they travel mostly early in the morning. As every Mohammedan is supposed to visit the tomb of Mohammed once at least during his life, caravans of pilgrims go to Mecca every year from various places of meeting. Of the various caravans which proceed to Mecca every year, the most important has always been the Syrian. The place at which it meets is Damascus, and here the pilgrims and merchants assemble many weeks before the day of departure, which is always fixed according to the season of the year in which the feast of Bairam occurs, the pilgrims requiring to be at Mecca on the day of the feast. As these caravans serve mercantile as well as religious purposes, Mecca, on the arrival of the caravans, resembles a great fair, and this fair is indeed the most important in all the East. The journey from Damascus to Mecca and back occupies about four months. The leader of such a caravan to Mecca, who carries with him some cannon for protection, is called *Emir-el-Hadj* (Prince of the Pilgrims). Trading caravans choose one of their own number for a leader, whom they call Caravan Bashi. Much information on the subject of caravans is to be found in the travels of Niebuhr, who made many journeys with them, and describes them, as it is well known, minutely and faithfully.

Caravansari, kä-ra-văn'sạ-rĭ, in the East, a sort of inn, situated in countries where there are no cities or villages for a considerable extent, to furnish travelers with a shelter. Some of them are built with much splendor, though they are generally unfurnished, and the traveler is obliged to bring with him not only his bed

and carpet, but also all his provisions and necessaries. In many, the hospitality is gratuitous. It is common for a pious Mohammedan to establish, during his life or by will, one or several of such caravansaries. This kind of benevolence is considered peculiarly agreeable to the deity, and promotive of the eternal happiness of the founder. Sometimes persons are kept in these establishments to guide the caravans for some distance. See KHAN.

Car'avel, formerly the name of different kinds of vessels; one used in Portugal of 100 to 150 tons burden, another a French fishing vessel used on the coasts of Normandy and Picardy of 10 to 15 tons, and a third a large Turkish ship of war.

Carawala, kä-ra-wä'la, a large viper (*Hypnale nepa*) of Ceylon and southern India, numerous, and greatly dreaded by the natives, especially those who work in the pineapple plantations. Its poison has the peculiarity of not affecting the system until several days after the bite, so that proper remedies immediately applied will counteract the venom.

Car'away, an umbelliferous biennial plant (*Carum carui*), with a tapering fleshy root, a striated furrowed stem, and white or pinkish flowers. It produces a well-known seed used in confectionery, and from which both a carminative oil is extracted and a spirit cordial distilled. The two species found in America are the descendants of naturalized European plants, that have escaped from cultivation. It is largely grown in England, on strong and rich clays, and is sometimes sown with beans, but more usually with coriander and teazel, or coriander alone. After the coriander, which is only a preparatory crop, has been removed, the plants of the caraway are singled out and repeatedly hoed and cleaned. It is cut about the beginning of July, and produces on an average about 900 pounds per acre. It is a favorite crop with the Dutch. The volatile oils in caraway render it of much service in medicine. The action of these oils is to stimulate peristalsis and thus overcome flatulency. They are further antiseptic and check excessive intestinal putrefaction. They act also as mild local anæsthetics and are useful in nausea and vomiting.

Carayon, Auguste, ô-güst kä-rä-yŏn, French historian: b. Saumur, 31 March 1813; d. Poitiers, 15 May 1874. A distinguished Jesuit, he wrote: 'First Canadian Missions of the Jesuits' (1864) ; 'Banishment of the Jesuits from Louisiana' (1865) ; and similar studies.

Carbajal, Francisco, frän-thěs'kō kär-bä-häl', Spanish soldier: b. Alavaro, 1464; d. near Cuzco, 10 April 1548. He served in the army in Europe; went to Mexico in 1528; and when Pizarro appealed for help against the Inca uprising he was one of the force sent by Cortez to Peru. He was marshal under Vico de Castro, in the battle of Chuas. He later took office under Gonzalo Pizarro, in the war against Diego Centeno and De la Gasca. At first he was triumphant over Centeno in the Collao, but at the battle of Sacsahuana, 8 April 1528, he was taken prisoner with Pizarro and executed. He was extremely cruel in his treatment of his enemies, but was not less noted for his humor which never failed him, not even at his own execution.

Carballo, kär-bäl'yō, Spain, a town in the province of Corunna, situated 24 miles northwest of Santiago. It has warm mineral springs and baths. Pop. 13,500.

Carbazo'tic Acid. See PICRIC ACID.

Car'berry Hill, Scotland, a rising ground in Mid-Lothian, about seven miles southeast of Edinburgh, between Musselburgh and Ormiston, where Mary, Queen of Scots, surrendered herself to the confederate nobles of the kingdom, 15 June 1567, just before her confinement in Loch Leven Castle.

Car'bide, in chemistry, a binary compound of carbon with a metallic element, or with certain of the non-metallic elements. Of the known carbides those of iron and calcium are most important. Carbide of iron occurs in steel, and is undoubtedly concerned in some manner, with the hardening of that metal; although the authorities are not agreed as to the precise role that it plays. The best known carbide of iron is the one having the formula CFe_3; but Campbell has shown ('American Chemical Journal,' XVIII., 836) that a series of iron carbides probably exists, having the general formula C_nFe_{3n}, and corresponding in a certain sense to the hydrocarbon series C_nH_{2n}; so that when any one of the carbides of iron is treated with an acid, the corresponding hydrocarbon is set free. Calcium carbide is formed by the action of carbon upon lime at the temperature of the electric furnace. It has the formula CaC_2, and its commercial value depends mainly upon the fact that it is readily decomposed by water, with the copious liberation of acetylene gas (q.v.). Carbide of magnesium is not formed at the temperature of the electric furnace, probably because it is not stable at that temperature. It may be prepared, however, by the action of calcium carbide upon magnesium fluoride, in accordance with the equation $CaC_2 + MgF_2 = CaF_2 + MgC_2$. Like calcium carbide it is decomposed by water with evolution of acetylene gas, the yield being 50 per cent greater, per pound of the carbide, in the case of magnesium carbide. It is not unlikely that magnesium carbide will one day replace calcium carbide for the production of acetylene gas, on account of the larger yield; but this substitution cannot be made on a commercial scale until some cheaper mode of manufacture is found. The chemistry of the carbides is still in its infancy, but within the past few years, and largely owing to the splendid work of Moissan, many new bodies belonging to this class have been discovered. Gold, bismuth, lead, and tin do not form carbides at the temperature of the electric furnace, nor do they dissolve carbon at that temperature. Platinum and iridium dissolve carbon freely, but deposit it again, upon cooling, in the form of graphite. Aluminum absorbs carbon freely, with the formation of Al_4C_3, and similar results are obtained with many other metals and metallic oxides. The carbides of chromium, molybdenum, titanium, tungsten, and zirconium do not decompose water. Those of calcium, strontium, barium, and lithium decompose it with liberation of pure acetylene; but the carbides of aluminum and beryllium yield pure methane, and carbide of manganese gives a mixture of equal parts of methane and hydrogen. Other carbides decompose water with more complex results. Thus the carbides of the rare metals of

the cerium group yield complicated mixtures of hydrogen, acetylene, methane, and ethylene, and the carbide of uranium gives all these products (except, perhaps, acetylene), and, in addition, copious quantities of various liquid and solid hydrocarbons. The carbides of sodium and potassium, which are best prepared by passing dry acetylene gas over the corresponding metals at a temperature of about 450° F., decompose water with liberation and acetylene. The carbides of titanium and of silicon are characterized by extreme hardness, and it is said that they will even cut the diamond with facility. Carbide of silicon is an exceedingly stable substance, and is now largely used, under the trade name of "carborundum," as an abrasive material in the manufacture of grinding-wheels, whetstones, and polishing-cloth.

Moissan's researches with the electric furnace are reported chiefly in the 'Annales de Chimie et de Physique,' and useful reviews of them have been printed at frequent intervals in 'Nature.' Moissan claims to have been the discoverer of the crystalline carbide of calcium that is now commercially familiar; but in the United States this honor is usually accorded to Mr. Willson, whose labors were certainly quite independent of those of Moissan. See ACETYLENE; CALCIUM; CARBIDE; CARBORUNDUM.

Carbohy'drate, in chemistry, a compound consisting of carbon, hydrogen, and oxygen, and having the general formula $C_{6n}H_{2p}O_p$. As will be seen, the number of carbon atoms in a carbohydrate is always divisible by six, and the oxygen and hydrogen are present in the same proportion in which they occur in water. It is not implied, however, that the compound contains water as such, but only that the oxygen and hydrogen atoms are present in the proportion of two atoms of the latter to one of the former. It will also be observed that a carbohydrate and a hydrocarbon are two essentially different things, inasmuch as a carbohydrate contains oxygen, while a hydrocarbon is a compound containing no element but carbon and hydrogen.

The carbohydrates constitute a large and very important class of substances, embracing the starches, sugars, glucoses, and gums. Their chemical relations are intricate, and are far from being thoroughly understood. Several schemes have been proposed for their classification, but owing to the present imperfection of our knowledge none is entirely satisfactory. The classification proposed by O'Sullivan is convenient, however, and will be adopted here.

Class 1.—S A C C H A R A N S: Amorphous substances, having the general formula $nC_6H_{10}O_5$, soluble in water but insoluble in alcohol, and further characterized by the fact that when they are treated with acids they yield substances of the type $nC_6H_{12}O_6$, directly, and without the formation of intermediate compounds. Dextran, lævulan, the amylans and the galactans are examples. (These bodies are gums.)

Class 2.— SACCHARENS: Substances possessing a certain amount of structure, having the general formula $nC_6H_{10}O_5$, insoluble in either water or alcohol, and transformed by the action of acids and certain ferments first into $nC_{12}H_{22}O_{11}$, and finally, by the action of acids, into $nC_6H_{12}O_6$. Cellulose, starch, inulin, and tunicin are examples; the first two falling under "amylose" in the less elaborate classification which divides the carbohydrates merely into amylose, saccharose, and glucose.

Class 3.— SACCHARINS : Amorphous substances, having the general formula $nC_6H_{10}O_5$, soluble in water, but insoluble in alcohol; converted by acids first into $nC_{12}H_{22}O_{11}$, and finally into $nC_6H_{12}O_6$; and by certain ferments into $nC_{12}H_{22}O_{11}$. Glycogen, dextrin, and malto-dextrin are examples.

Class 4.— SACCHAROSES (sugars).

Group (a).— SACCHARONS : Sweet, crystallizable bodies, soluble in water and in moderately strong alcohol, having the general formula $nC_{12}H_{22}O_{11}$, and convertible by acids and sometimes by ferments into $nC_6H_{12}O_6$. Sucrose (cane sugar), lactose (milk sugar), maltose, and raffinose are examples.

Group (b).— GLUCOSES : Substances crystallizing, though not so readily as the members of the preceding group; having the general formula $nC_6H_{12}O_6$; soluble in both water and alcohol; and converted by the prolonged action of acids into substances that are no longer carbohydrates. Some of these, such as dextrose, lævulose, and galactose, are fermentable by yeast; while others, such as sorbinose, are not fermentable.

Group (c).— Certain substances, such as inosite and scyllit, which probably belong in the aromatic series and bear no special resemblance to the other members of the carbohydrate family.

O'Sullivan has also a fifth class, including those substances which, though they may not be carbohydrates in the strict sense, are nevertheless closely allied to the carbohydrates and are easily converted into them. In this class he places the glucosides and certain of the gums, mucilages, and pectins.

The carbohydrates are exceedingly important elements in the world's food supply, and may indeed be said to be essential to the maintenance of life. They are practically all of vegetable origin, and are derived ultimately from certain simple fundamental substances that are formed in the green leaves of plants. Under the influence of sunlight the chlorophyll contained in the leaves is competent to split up the carbon dioxide of the air, retaining the carbon and setting the oxygen free. The carbon that is abstracted in this way is caused to combine with the water that the leaves contain, with the production of carbohydrates; but the identity of the carbohydrate that is first formed in this way, and which serves as the starting-point for the others, is not yet established. According to the views of Sachs the "first obvious product" is starch, the formation of which he explained by the equation

$$6CO_2 \ + \ 5H_2O \ = \ C_6H_{10}O_5 \ + \ 12O$$
Carbon   Water   Starch   Free
Dioxide   Oxygen

It appears more likely, however, that formic aldehyde, CH_2O, is the first product, as is indicated by the equation

$$H_2O + CO_2 = CH_2O + 2O,$$

and that the subsequent products are built up by polymerization.

Carbohydrate metabolism is one of the most important physiological processes of the animal body. The carbohydrates are the chief source of energy and heat in the body. Most of the carbohydrates are converted into maltose by the digestive processes. This, by the action of absorption and assimilation, becomes dextrose, which sugar is the only normal sugar of the circulating fluids and the tissues. The dextrose is taken up by the blood, conveyed to the liver by the portal vein and stored up in the liver cells. Some of the dextrose is also stored in muscle, and certain portions of it are utilized by the nucleoproteids of the body. The fate of the glycogen of the body is to be oxidized into carbon-dioxide and water. The steps of this process of oxidation are very much involved, but it seems certain that an oxidizing ferment, perhaps from the adrenal glands, acting in conjunction with the pancreas, is largely influential in the process. A failure to bring about sufficient oxidation of the sugar in the body causes the well-known symptom of glycosuria, one of the features of diabetes (q.v.).

Carbol'ic Acid, a substance having a formula $C_6H_5.OH$, possessing feebly acid properties, and occurring chiefly in that part of the distillate from coal-tar which passes over at temperatures between 330° F. and 375° F. Chemically, carbolic acid has the structure of an alcohol (q.v.), and is an aromatic compound derived from benzene by the substitution of the hydroxyl group, OH, for one of the typical hydrogen atoms. It is also known as phenol, phenyl hydrate, or phenyl alcohol.

Carbolic acid, in the pure state, crystallizes in white, deliquescent needles, having a strong characteristic smell slightly suggestive of tar. It melts at 106° F., and boils, under ordinary atmospheric pressure, at about 360° F. Its specific gravity is about 1.07. It dissolves in alcohol, ether, and many other organic liquids, but is only moderately soluble in water under ordinary atmospheric conditions. It readily absorbs a small quantity of water from the air, forming a hydrate which is fluid at temperatures above 63° F. If the liquid so formed is shaken with water, the greater part of the carbolic acid separates out upon standing, and the vessel is found to contain an upper layer consisting of water in which a small amount of carbolic acid is dissolved, and a lower layer of carbolic acid in which a little water is dissolved. It does not exhibit very marked acid properties, but dissolves in the alkalis with the formation of salts called phenates. It does not have a strong affinity for the alkaline bases, however, and from a strong solution of sodium phenate (for example) it may be again separated in the form of an oily liquid by the addition of another acid; the new acid appropriating the base to itself, and setting the carbolic acid free. A solution of carbolic acid, even when very weak, develops a red color when boiled with a solution of mercurous nitrate and nitrous acid. This reaction, which serves for the detection of carbolic acid, is said to be delicate enough to indicate one part of the acid in more than 100,000 parts of water.

In medicine, carbolic acid has many uses. It is highly poisonous to living matter, and is used extensively to kill bacteria. In surgery it is used an an antiseptic dressing in proportions of from ⅛-2 parts of acid to 100 of water. It, or some of its derivatives or allies, is used to sterilize instruments and to disinfect wounds, rooms, and dejecta. Internally, carbolic acid is used as a bactericide, limiting excessive intestinal putrefaction. It is also an anæsthetic, and is at times of service in irritability of the stomach. When used in too concentrated a solution it is an active caustic, causing a white, painless burn. Alcohol is an excellent antidote. Taken internally in pure form in doses over two to three drops it causes poisoning with a characteristic series of symptoms. There is burning in the mouth, fauces, œsophagus, and stomach. The whitish scars of the lips and mouth are characteristic. There is great pain, with vomiting of large quantities of mucus. There is usually ringing in the ears, headache, vertigo; the urine may be suppressed, reddish or greenish; and death results with small, rapid pulse, collapse, and, may be, convulsions. Similar symptoms may develop slowly in sub-acute forms of poisoning. The urinary symptoms usually lead to the diagnosis. The treatment of the acute form of poisoning is the free use of gastric lavage, ingestion of alcohol, and the use of lime water. Symptomatic treatment and careful nursing are necessary for other symptoms.

Carbolineum, derived from the Latin words *carbo*, coal, *oleum*, oil, to form a fancy name for a new commodity, is a distillation from coal-tar or bituminous shale, containing phenoloid hydro-carbons of a highly preservative nature. Extensive deposits from which carbolinuem is obtained are found in the grape-growing countries bordering on the Rhine, various other parts of Europe and some places in America. The liquid in its commercial form is of a nut-brown color, but it is a stain rather than a paint. However, it can be washed off a person's hands with cold water without leaving any stain. Tests made with it prove that it has many times greater penetrating power than linseed-oil. It never crystallizes. When it has been painted upon wood and has become apparently thoroughly dry, its action does not cease. If the wood is then painted with a heavy coat of white-lead mixed with linseed-oil, the carbolineum will make its appearance through the paint in a short time. Consequently, any wood that is first treated with carbolineum cannot be painted without previous sizing. Owing to carbolineum being composed of comparatively heavy hydrocarbons, it is only slightly inflammable; but when ignited by holding a match in contact with the carbolineum for a short time, it burns with a bright red light and gives off considerable carbon in the form of a dense smoke. Workmen when painting roofs on bright warm days have had their hands and faces blistered by vapors given off by the carbolineum. Carbolineum first came into use about the year 1876. The grape-growers of the Rhine valley were much annoyed with insects and sustained considerable loss by the rotting of the posts and poles used in their wine industry. It is said that Richard Avenarius, who was an officer in the German army, first suggested the use of carbolineum as a wood preservative. No doubt the insects and fungi were as much accountable for the destruction of the poles and posts used for supporting the vines as any chemical action of the elements; and, conse-

quently, the use of carbolineum was particularly adapted to preserve wood used in grape-growing. Very soon after the first use of carbolineum, its merits were advertised broadly and its manufacture was begun in various countries of Europe under different names, as "Presser's Carbolineum," "Carbolineum-Anthracen," "Wollner's Carbolineum," "Floria-Carbolineum," "Carbolineum Für Farbenanstriche," "Carbolineum Van Baerle," "Carbolineum Avenarius," etc.

A chemical analysis of Presser's Carbolineum gave the following results:

Specific gravity at 15° C 1.0864
Flashing point .... 90° C = 194° F
Ignition point .... 138° C = 280° F
Begins to distill at.................. 150° C = 300° F
Residue of distillation (tarry substance) 8.79 %
Tarry acids .... 0.09 %
Congealing point .... — 20° C = — 70° F

In the manufacture of carbolineum some concerns attempt to distinguish their products from the products of others by adding coloring matter. Others try to improve it by the use of chloride of zinc, and other antiseptics.

Carbolineum is usually shipped in barrels and then put in small packages to accommodate the retail trade. It is retailed at about 75 cents per gallon. The most extensive users are the tanners, railroad companies, malsters and farmers. Railroad ties and posts are dipped in it before setting, which preserves the wood for a longer time without decay than it would otherwise last in its natural state.

Some of the railroad companies after due experiment have made extensive use of it, even "painting" parts of the woodwork of their freight cars with it. It is used in a modified form by dyers. Farmers use it for painting hog-pens, chicken-coops and barns for the purpose of destroying lice and other vermin. The carbolineum may be applied directly to the skin of animals without injury.

Considerable litigation has grown out of the use of the word "carbolineum" as a trade-mark. Richard Avenarius did not obtain a trade-mark on the word "carbolineum" when he first used it, and never obtained a patent on carbolineum, and many others began its manufacture under that commercial name. Eventually he filed the word "carbolineum" as a trade-mark in Austria, but subsequently his trade-mark was revoked and protection refused on the ground of the general use of the word. Also, he registered the word "carbolineum" as a trade-mark in the Patent Office of the United States, as No. 14,048, dated February 8, 1887. A suit concerning his right to such use is now pending.

CHARLES M. SCANLAN,
Milwaukee, Wis.

Car'bon, a non-metallic element, existing in nature in large quantities, both in the free and combined states. It exhibits marked allotropy, at least three distinctly different forms of it being known. These are (1) amorphous carbon; (2) graphite; and (3) diamond. Amorphous carbon is formed when wood or coal or almost any vegetable matter is heated strongly, out of contact with the air, and is familiar to everybody as charcoal, coke, and lampblack. Graphite (q.v.) occurs native, and may also be artificially prepared in various ways. Diamond (q.v.), which is crystallized carbon, also occurs native in certain regions, and pure specimens that are devoid of color, or which have certain special tints, are highly esteemed as gems.

Carbon has the chemical symbol C, and an atomic weight of 12.0 if $O = 16$, and 11.91 if $H = 1$. The specific gravity of diamond is 3.51, that of graphite is from 2.11 to 2.26, and that of hard gas-coke is about 2.35. The linear coefficient of expansion of diamond (Fahrenheit scale) is 0.00000066 at ordinary temperatures, and that of graphite is 0.00000.44. Graphite has an electrical conductivity of about one twelfth, and hard gas-coke about one one-hundredth, when the corresponding conductivity of mercury is taken as the unit. Diamond is practically a non-conductor. The specific heats of diamond and graphite are quite different at ordinary temperatures. Thus at 50° F. diamond has a specific heat of 0.113, graphite 0.160, and wood charcoal about 0.165. These values increase as the temperature rises, and at about 1,100° F. all three varieties have a common specific heat of about 0.44.

Carbon is infusible, and insoluble in any known liquid at ordinary temperatures. It dissolves to a limited extent in melted cast iron, and in melted platinum it dissolves freely, separating out again in the form of graphite upon cooling. It is unaltered by the action of acids, except when some powerful oxidizing agent like chlorate of potassium or bichromate of potassium is also present. Chemically it is tetravalent in nearly all of its compounds. It combines with oxygen in two different proportions, with the formation of a monoxide CO, and a dioxide CO_2. It also forms, with hydrogen, a great number of compounds known as hydrocarbons (q.v.); and it combines with many of the metals to form carbides (q.v.). With hydrogen, oxygen, nitrogen, and small quantities of other elements, it constitutes the entire substance of animals and plants; and the coal beds that make our modern civilization possible are composed of vegetable remains from which the elements other than carbon have been mostly expelled by the combined action of heat and pressure.

For further information concerning carbon, see AROMATIC COMPOUNDS; CARBON COMPOUNDS; CHARCOAL; COAL; DIAMOND; FATTY COMPOUNDS; GRAPHITE.

Carbon Black. This is the trade term given in this country to black made from gas. It was originally called hydrocarbon gas black, and a black of a similar nature to that now made was manufactured both in this country and in Europe from artificial gas. The industry did not, however, assume any importance before 1872, when the first patent was obtained for producing this black from natural gas. Since this date, innumerable patents have been taken out for the manufacture of this black from natural gas, and at the present time there are 10 distinctly different processes in operation.

The various methods of making the black from natural gas are fundamentally the same, the black in every case being produced by allowing the flame to strike a metal surface, upon which the carbon is deposited in the form of a black flocculent powder. Carbon black is of a similar nature to lampblack made from oil. It is an exceptionally pure form of carbon, varying from 98 per cent to 99½ per cent pure. The color is absolutely permanent, and it is the blackest and most brilliant permanent black produced.

The difference in the qualities are principally due to the amount of air supplied to the flame, and the shape of the plates or rollers upon which the black is collected. All of the works now operated are automatic, for the gas not only converts itself into the black, but also furnishes the power that scrapes it off the plates and collects and packs it in barrels, ready for shipment, the black not being seen or touched until it is used by the consumer.

The principal use for the black is in the manufacture of printing inks, paints, rubber goods, oil cloth, blackings, etc.; the finest qualities are used in the manufacture of lithographic and half tone inks; the cheaper in news inks.

The abundance of natural gas in the United States, and the automatic method of making the black have enabled the manufacturers in this country to produce it at so much lower prices that little of this black is now made from artificial gas, and large quantities of the product are exported annually. The total production of carbon black in this country is (1905) 12,000,000 pounds per annum, of which one-fifth is exported. C. HAROLD SMITH,
Of the Binney & Smith Co., New York.

Carbon Compounds, in chemistry those compounds which contain the element carbon; and since carbon is an essential constituent of nearly all organic substances, the chemistry of its compounds is practically synonymous with "organic chemistry." Until within the past half-century it was thought by many authorities that the compounds that occur in animals and plants are essentially different in nature from those that are produced in the laboratory, and that they cannot be obtained without the action of the "vital principle." This idea received its first blow in 1828, when Wöhler prepared urea from substances that had been previously considered to be inorganic; yet as late as 1849 a great chemist, Berzelius, defined organic chemistry as "the chemistry of compounds formed under the influence of life." A vast number of substances that were formerly classed as organic have now been prepared in the laboratory, and the old classification of chemistry into organic and inorganic branches has broken down, the organic division being now more correctly called the "chemistry of carbon compounds."

The carbon compounds form a group of great complexity, and are apparently unlimited in number. The reasons for this are that carbon is quadrivalent: that it forms multitudes of compounds with hydrogen alone, in many of which more or less of the hydrogen can be replaced by other elements, with the formation of new and altogether different substances; that its chemical bonds are apparently powerful; and that it unites with elements of the most widely different nature.

In a general way, the better-known carbon compounds are mostly divided into two great classes, according to the type of the "graphical" or "structural" formula that must be used in order adequately to represent their chemical relations. The first class includes all those bodies whose structural formulæ are distinguished by the fact that the atoms (or radicals) that are present form "open" chains, which do not anywhere return into one another. The hydrocarbon "propane," which has the structural formula

$$H-\underset{\underset{H}{|}}{\overset{\overset{H}{|}}{C}}-\underset{\underset{H}{|}}{\overset{\overset{H}{|}}{C}}-\underset{\underset{H}{|}}{\overset{\overset{H}{|}}{C}}-H,$$

is an illustration of this class. The "open chain" compounds are called fatty compounds, and are treated under that heading. The name was originally given because many of the substances that are included in the class have long been known in connection with fats and allied bodies; but it would be more logical to call them "methane derivatives," since they may be considered to be obtainable from the hydrocarbon methane, CH_4, by a process of substitution. The second great class of carbon compounds is distinguished by the fact that the structural formulæ that are required in order to exhibit the chemical properties of its members return into themselves, so as to form "closed" chains or rings, which (at least in the fundamental forms) contain six carbon atoms. Benzene is a familiar example. From the fact that many of the first known representatives were balsams, oils, and resins, these substances are known collectively as aromatic compounds, and are described under that heading. A better name would be "benzene derivatives," since all the members of the class are derivable from benzene by substitution.

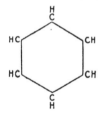

In addition to the aromatic and fatty compounds, others are known which do not properly come under either heading. Thus the structural formula of furfuran contains a closed ring, formed by the union of four atoms of carbon and one of oxygen. Closed rings, consisting of three, four, and five atoms of carbon, are also known. The pronounced analogies and affinities that exist among the members of the aromatic and fatty groups, respectively, have forced those two groups upon the attention of chemists. Those compounds of carbon which are not strictly included within either have not yet been classified upon a similarly broad basis.

The principal phenomena of the carbon compounds are given under special headings. In addition to those already given, see, particularly, Isomerism; and Radical.

For an excellent presentation of the whole subject, see Hjelt, 'Principles of General Organic Chemistry.'

Carbon Dioxide, Carbonic Acid Gas, or Carbonic Anhydride, CO_2, is formed whenever carbon is burned in the presence of excess of oxygen or air. It is a colorless, odorless gas, soluble to a considerable extent in cold water, especially when subjected to pressure. Its solution possesses feebly acid properties, and has a peculiarly pungent taste, on account of which the aqueous solution of the acid is greatly used as a constituent of various beverages. The ef-fervescence accompanying the opening of a bottle of beer, soda-water, or champagne, is due to the escape of the carbon dioxide that was previously held in solution. Carbon dioxide occurs in great abundance in nature, both free and in combination with various elements, in the form of carbonates. Carbonate of lime, $CaCO_3$, is one of the most common carbonates. It is formed when the gas is allowed to bubble up through a solution of lime water, and exists in nature in vast masses, as limestone and marble. (Other carbonates are described under the metals that constitute their bases.) Carbon dioxide is a constant constituent of the atmosphere (see Air), occurring even at the tops of mountains and in the air collected from balloons. It is generated by the combustion of fuel, by respiration, by fermentation, and by the decay of animal and vegetable matter. In some localities, too, immense quantities of the gas are emitted from the ground, or from mineral springs and wells, as in the Grotto del Cane, the Cave of Montjoly in Auvergne, in the valley of Wehr, in the Eifel, and at many other places. It is being simultaneously abstracted from the air by plants, which in the sunlight decompose the gas, fixing the carbon that it contains, and setting the oxygen free. Carbon dioxide has but feeble affinity for the bases with which it combines, and is readily replaced by almost any other acid. In preparing the gas for experimental purposes. the usual method is to add a dilute mineral acid to pulverized marble or other carbonate, the carbon dioxide then being liberated continuously and in large quantities. The gas is about 1.53 times as heavy as an equal bulk of air. Its critical temperature is about 90° F., and at any temperature lower than this it can be reduced to a liquid by the application of pressure.

Poisoning by this gas frequently results in closed rooms crowded with people. The symptoms may be very slight, consisting of a mild indisposition, or they may be severe — headache, nausea, vomiting, etc. In poisoning in the severer grades there is cyanosis, coma, and unconsciousness. Carbon dioxide alone is not a fatal poison; it is rendered so usually by the diminution of oxygen supply.

Carbon Disulphide, CS_2, a liquid formed when the vapor of sulphur is passed over red-hot charcoal. Under normal conditions it is a very volatile, inflammable liquid, having a specific gravity of 1.29, and boiling at 115° F. The commercial disulphide has an exceedingly disagreeable smell, but this is due to the presence of impurities. The pure liquid has a pleasant, ethereal smell. Carbon disulphide (or bisulphide) does not mix with water, but it dissolves sulphur, phosphorus, caoutchouc, and many other organic bodies that are difficultly soluble in other menstrua, and it is to this property that it owes its commercial value.

Poisoning by carbon disulphide is becoming very prevalent since the use of rubber goods has become so extensive. The symptoms of acute poisoning are due to a poisoning of the blood and a central paralysive action on the nervous system. The blood action is that of a breaking up of the red blood cells, hemolysis. This results in cyanosis, pains, headache, coma, vertigo, nausea, vomiting, weakness, unconsciousness, coma, and death. Such symptoms are rare, the poisoning developing as a rule much less rapidly. In workers in rubber factories, in which there is much vapor of CS_2, there develop disturbances of temper, pressure feelings on the head, heat, and the feeling as if the blood would burst through the skull, with headache. There may also be symptoms of irritation of the bronchi, coughing, and roughness of the voice, etc. Treatment is fresh air and symptomatic.

Carbon Monoxide, or Carbonic Oxide, CO, is produced, in addition to the dioxide, when carbon is burned with a limited supply of air or oxygen. It is also generated by passing carbon dioxide through a red-hot bed of carbon, in accordance with the equation $CO_2 + C = 2CO$. For experimental purposes the gas may be generated by decomposing oxalic acid by heating it with strong sulphuric acid, and passing the gases that are evolved through a solution of caustic soda to absorb the carbon dioxide that is present. Carbon monoxide is colorless, and has a density about 0.97 times that of air. It burns with a lambent, blue flame that is often seen in coal fires that have been freshly supplied with fuel.

Carbon Oxychloride. See PHOSGENE.

Carbonado, or Carbon, a massive, black or dark-gray variety of diamond, also called "black diamond." Though possessing the adamantine or resinous luster of the crystallized variety, it is opaque and, therefore, of no value as a gem. It is the hardest substance known and this fact makes it the most desirable for use in diamond drills; it therefore sells for as high a price per carat as one carat rough gem diamonds (q.v.). Being without cleavage it is less brittle than the crystals, and owing to its somewhat porous structure, its specific gravity is less, 3.15 to 3.29. The commercial supply comes exclusively from the province of Bahia, Brazil, where it occurs in angular fragments which occasionally show a rough cubic outline.

Carbonari, kär-bō-nä'rē (colliers, or more strictly, charcoal-burners), the name of a large political secret society in Italy. According to Botta's 'Storia d'Italia' the Republicans fled, under the reign of Joachim (Murat), in the recesses of the Abruzzi, inspired with an equal hatred of the French and of Ferdinand. They formed a secret confederacy, and called themselves carbonari. Their chief, Capobianco, possessed great talents as an orator. Their war-cry was "Revenge for the lamb mangled by the wolf!" When Murat ascended the throne of Naples he employed Maghella, a Genoese, in the department of police, and afterward as minister. All his efforts were directed to the union and independence of Italy, and for this purpose he made use of the society of the Carbonari. The ritual of the Carbonari was taken from the trade of the charcoal burner. Clearing the wood of wolves (opposition to tyranny) was the symbolic expression of their aim. By this they are said to have meant at first only deliverance from foreign dominion; but in later times democratic and anti-monarchical principles sprang up. They called one another good cousins. The general union of the order under a common head seems to have been effected. The separate societies in the small towns entered into a connection with each other, but this union extended

no farther than the province. The place of assembly was called the hut (*barraca*); the surrounding neighborhood was called the wood; the meeting itself was distinguished as the sale (*vendita*). The confederation of all the huts of the province was called the republic, generally bearing the ancient name of the province. The chief huts (alta vendita) at Naples and at Salerno endeavored to effect a general union of the order, at least for the kingdom; but the attempt appears to have been unsuccessful. The order, soon after its foundation, contained from 24,000 to 30,000 members, and increased so rapidly, that it spread through all Italy. In 1820, in the month of March alone, about 650,000 new members are said to have been admitted; whole cities joined the society. The military, in particular, seem to have thronged for admission. The religious character of the order appears from its statutes: "Every Carbonaro has the natural and inalienable right to worship the Almighty according to the dictates of his conscience." After the suppression of the Neapolitan and Piedmontese revolution in 1821, the Carbonari throughout Italy were declared guilty of high treason, and punished by the laws. Meantime societies of a similar kind had been formed in France, with which the Italian Carbonari amalgamated, and Paris became the headquarters of Carbonism. The organization took on more of a French character, and gradually alienated the sympathies of the Italian members, a number of whom dissolved connection with it, in order to form the party of Young Italy.

Car'bonates. See CARBON DIOXIDE.

Car'bondale, Pa., a city of Lackawanna County, situated on the Lackawanna River, 110 miles north-northwest of Philadelphia; and on the Erie, the Delaware & H., and the New York, O. & W. R.R.'s. It is the centre of an important anthracite coal-field, and the principal industry is mining. There are also machine-shops, foundries, etc. As it is in a mountain region with fine scenery, it is also a summer resort. Pop. (1900) 13,536.

Carbonear, kär'bŏn-ēr, Newfoundland, a port of entry on the eastern side of the peninsula separating Trinity Bay from Conception Bay 25 miles in a northwesterly direction from St. John's. Pop. (1901) 3,703.

Carbonic Acid, or Carbonic Acid Gas. See CARBON DIOXIDE.

Carbonic Anhydrid. See CARBONIC DIOXIDE.

Carbonic Oxide. See CARBON MONOXIDE.

Carboniferous Limestone, or Mountain Limestone, certain limestones of Lower Carboniferous age, as named by Murchison and other English geologists. In the United States the silver-lead ores of Leadville and other Rocky Mountain camps, and the zinc and lead ores of southwestern Missouri, are in limestones of Carboniferous age. See CARBONIFEROUS SYSTEM.

Carboniferous Period, the last of the great time divisions of the Palæozoic Epoch. During it were laid down vast beds of plant-remains now turned to coal, whence the name. It is true that coal fields of later age than Carboniferous are known, particularly in North America, but the important coal fields of Europe and of eastern North America are of Carboniferous age. In North America, when the

CARBONIFEROUS SYSTEM

Carboniferous Period began, most of New England, eastern Canada, and Newfoundland was land, though two long, narrow arms of the Gulf of St. Lawrence extended to Narragansett Bay. West of the Blue Ridge Mountains, or Appalachian uplift, was a great interior sea, in places quite deep and extending to the Rocky Mountains. During Carboniferous time, by a gradual uplift, the northeastern part of this sea was divided into two bays, one covering nearly all of Pennsylvania, West Virginia, eastern Ohio, and Kentucky, the other covering southern Michigan. In the west the old land surfaces sank, and great areas along the whole Rocky Mountain region and beyond were covered by the sea. In general, the Carboniferous in North America was a period of slow changes of land surface with no volcanic outbursts. In the eastern part of the continent the land sank, then gently rose, over great areas, forming vast swamps, with numerous oscillations following. The sea covered most of the land west of the Mississippi. In Europe a clear sea stretched from inland to central Germany at the beginning of Carboniferous time, but later this area was a series of swamps. In Russia the land, after several changes of level, sank, and a great area, comprising southern Europe and Asia and part of northern Africa, was covered by the sea.

The plant-life of the Carboniferous Period — entirely gymnosperms and angiosperms — showed some advances from the Devonian. The ferns were most abundant, some being like tall trees, others as small as the maidenhair fern of to-day. The most conspicuous growths in the Carboniferous forests were the Lycopods or club-mosses, now represented by insignificant forms, but then growing sometimes 75 feet or more high, with trunks three feet in diameter, and spreading branches (*Lepidodendron*). Other Lycopods (*Sigillaria*) had short, thick trunks with few if any branches. Still another group of cryptogams, the *Equisetæ* or horse-tail rushes, were of far greater importance in Carboniferous time than now. Of these the *calamites*, with their tall, slender stems, must have been one of the commonest plant forms of the Carboniferous forest. No plants with conspicuous flowers existed, the flowering plants being gymnosperms of which one of the commonest was *Cordaites*. The Carboniferous forests were probably gloomy and featureless. The singularity of the flora over the whole world from Siam to Spitzbergen indicates a uniform climate without temperature zones.

Of animal life, corals, especially the genus *Lithostrotion*, were abundant; and the *Foraminifera*, especially the genus *Fusulina*, became of importance. Of the echinoderms the extinct blastoids, particularly the genus *Pentremites*, were abundant, and the Carboniferous is the period in which the crinoids, or sea-lilies, reached their highest development. Sea-urchins (echinoids) were more plentiful than in the Devonian, but the trilobites were slowly dying out. Of the land arthropods, scorpions were fairly abundant, and the first true spiders appeared. The brachiopods were less abundant than in the Devonian, the genus *Productus* being of most importance. Bivalve mollusks were numerous, among them being the first land shell. Of the fishes, the sharks, notably the orders *Pleuracanthus* and *Acanthodes*, were remarkably developed. Amphibians, which probably existed in

Devonian, increased greatly in Carboniferous time, but belonged to an order now extinct, *Stegocephala*, and were of small or moderate size, no species being over eight feet long.

Carboniferous System. As the rocks laid down in Carboniferous time furnish by far the greater part of the world's supply of coal, they have been very carefully studied in many different places and accurately mapped, so that more is known of the Carboniferous rocks than those of any other Palæozoic system. By American geologists the rocks are divided into two series, an upper and a lower, which differ greatly in Nova Scotia, the Appalachian States, the Mississippi valley, and the Rocky Mountain States.

The Lower Carboniferous series, in what is called the Acadian province, Nova Scotia, and New Brunswick, is made up of thick beds of sandstone and limestone overlaid by limestones containing masses of gypsum. The total thickness of the series is 6,000 feet. In Pennsylvania the Lower Carboniferous series is divided into the Pocono sandstone and the Mauch Chunk shales, with a total maximum thickness of 4,000 feet. Westward there are in Ohio the Waverly beds, shales with some limestone, and in Michigan the marshall beds, sandstone and gritty shales, with limestone and gypsum above. Farther west the Lower Carboniferous is represented by the Mississippi series, including the Kinderhook, Osage, St. Louis, and Chester stages, all limestones, with a maximum thickness of over 1,200 feet in southern Illinois. These limestones underlie the eastern and western interior coal fields (see Coal). In southwestern Virginia are limestones, sandstones, and shales of Lower Carboniferous age, 2,000 feet thick, and containing a few workable beds of coal. In the Rocky Mountains the Lower Carboniferous rocks are, with few exceptions, limestones.

The rocks of the Upper Carboniferous include the great coal fields of eastern North America. (For the origin of coal fields, see Coal.) The rocks of the coal measures are sandstones or conglomerates, grits, shales, clays, limestones, and seams of coal. A coal seam is usually underlaid by a bed of fire-clay, representing an old soil, and overlaid by shale. The total thickness of the Nova Scotia coal measures is 7,000 feet, and 76 distinct seams of coal are known. In Pennsylvania the coal measures have been separated into the millstone grit, lower productive, lower barren, and upper productive stages, and have a total thickness of 4,000 feet. In Michigan the coal measures are about 300 feet thick; in the eastern interior (Illinois-Indiana) field 600 to 1,000 feet, and in the western interior field the thickness varies widely, reaching a maximum in Arkansas.

The Upper Carboniferous is therefore the areas in Utah, Colorado, and Arizona; they also occur in the Black Hills in South Dakota, and in California, and British Columbia. They are generally limestones or sandstones, and contain no coal beds. The distinction between Upper and Lower Carboniferous is not as sharp as in the Mississippi valley. The total thickness of the whole Carboniferous series in Nevada and Utah is about 13,000 feet.

In western Europe the Lower Carboniferous limestones reach from Ireland to central Germany, with a maximum thickness in England of 6,000 feet. In southeastern Germany the Lower

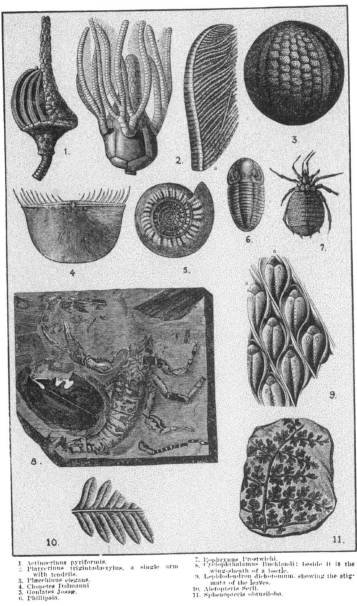

1. Actinocrinus pyriformis.
2. Platycrinus trigintadactylus, a single arm with tendrils.
3. Plæcchinus elegans.
4. Chonetes Dalmanni
5. Goniates Jossæ.
6. Phillipsia.

7. Eophrynus Prestwichi.
8. Cyclophthalmus Bucklandi; beside it is the wing-sheath of a beetle.
9. Lepidodendron dichotomum, showing the stigmata of the leaves.
10. Aletopteris Serli.
11. Sphenopteris obtusiloba.

1. The Tooth-Fern — Odontopteris.
2. The Scale Tree — Lepidodendron.
3. Cordaites Borassifolia.
4. Pecopteris Cyathea.

5. Calamites.
6. Sigillaria.
7. Rhizome of Sigillaria in Water.
8. Foliation of Aunularia.

Carboniferous rocks are sandstones and slates, while in Russia the coal measures of Lower Carboniferous age are overlaid by a great thickness of Upper Carboniferous limestone. In Asia the Chinese coal measures are of Upper Carboniferous age, and are underlaid by Lower Carboniferous limestone. In South America the Lower Carboniferous is mostly made up of sandstones, and the Upper of limestones, with very few coal seams.

See Dana, 'Manual of Geology'; Giekie, 'Text Book of Geology'; 'Report of the United States Geological Survey' (1900–01, Part III.).

Carborun'dum, a trade name for carbide of silicon, SiC. This compound is produced by heating sand and carbon together in the electric furnace. It is characterized by extreme hardness, and is used for abrasive purposes as a substitute for corundum and emery. It was discovered in 1891 by E. G. Acheson, and is now manufactured in large quantities at Niagara Falls. The production amounts to no less than 4,092 tons per annum. Carborundum in a fine form is placed on the market in considerable quantities as carbide of silicon for the introduction of silicon into iron, the material being very readily dissolved by the fused metal. Since carborundum is infusible and is only oxidizable at extremely high temperatures in a large amount of free oxygen, it follows that the temperatures ordinarily generated for smelting of ores and metals are much below its point of destruction. Finely powdered carborundum is made up into a paste with sodium silicate or some similar binding substance; and the paste is applied by means of a brush or otherwise to bricks which are intended to be used for building a furnace, or the bricks are actually immersed in the viscous liquid for a certain time. If the furnace has already been built, the paste can be painted on the exposed surfaces. It is stated that a layer one twelfth inch thick will protect the bricks from the attack of the highest temperature that is ever produced by combustion methods in ordinary work.   E. G. ACHESON.

Car Building Industry. The memory of men still living is sufficiently elastic to stretch back to the beginnings of steam railroads in this country, and to comprehend the various changes by which the modern railway has become a highly organized and elaborately equipped mechanism. We borrowed the railway from England, but developed it on our own lines. The invention of the locomotive at first simply furnished a mechanical power to transport freight in cars that had formerly been hauled by horses. Tramways were in use in the Hungarian mines during the 16th century; and Ralph Allen's English stone-car of 1734, with its flanged wheels and its hand-brake, is clearly the forerunner of the freight-cars of to-day.

The term "railway" was invented in 1775, when it was first used in Smeaton's reports on English transportation, a quarter of a century before steam was applied to locomotion. Thanks to the recent researches of Mr. Clement E. Stretton, we now know that the first persons ever conveyed by a locomotive on rails traveled, on 24 Feb. 1804, behind Trevethick's locomotive on the Pennydarran cast-iron plateway or tramroad to Merthyr-Tydvil, in Wales, a distance of nine miles. In order to transport long bars of iron and timber, the cars were made in pairs, coupled together by an iron drawbar having a joint at either end. The cars had no sides, but in the middle of each was fixed a centre-pin upon which worked a cross-beam or bolster, and upon this cross-beam the timber or bars of iron were placed. On the occasion referred to the trucks were loaded with 10 tons of iron bars, and 70 persons stood on the iron. Here we have the origin of the bogie or truck, the invention of which has been claimed for this country, as we shall see hereafter. Also the capacity of the freight-car, fixed at the beginning at 10 tons, remained at that figure for half a century or more.

In 1812 John Blenkinsop of Leeds had a private car built to carry himself and his managers to his Middleton colliery, while the workmen rode on the coal-cars. On 27 July 1814, George Stephenson's first locomotive, Blucher, drew over the Kenilworth colliery line a passenger-car made by placing the body of Lord Ravensworth's four-in-hand coach on a wooden frame fitted with flanged wheels. This car was used for 20 years. On 27 Sept. 1825, the Stockton & Darlington Railway was opened, and trains of coal-cars were run, with one passenger-coach named the Experiment. This was the first passenger-car to be run regularly for the use of the public. It was placed on four wheels, and had a door at each end, with a row of seats along either side and a long deal table in the centre. This car was operated 10 days, until the novelty was worn off; and then the faster stage-coaches carried the passengers. It was not until 15 Sept. 1830 that the Liverpool & Manchester Railway opened its line with a train carrying 600 passengers, and immediately thereafter began to run the first regular passenger-trains.

It is a striking fact in the history of car construction that the English invented both the truck and the long passenger-car with the door at each end; and that these forms, once invented, were almost immediately discarded in England, so that it was left for this country to reinvent them and to make them the distinguishing features of American car building as contrasted with English construction. Indeed, it has been with great reluctance that we have ceased to claim them as original discoveries.

The fact that passenger-trains, by displacing stages, threw out of use many of those vehicles, coupled with the other fact that the stage owners, submitting to the inevitable, often became railroad promoters, furnishes a reason why the early masters of transportation both used the stage-coach body as a matter of economy, and also built their new cars on the model in which the conveniences of travel had been most highly developed. The first passenger-coach used in Pennsylvania in 1832 was a stage-coach slightly enlarged. To be sure, the early prints show that in 1830 Peter Cooper's first locomotive hauled an open boat-shaped car from Baltimore to Ellicott's Mills, on the Baltimore & Ohio Railroad; but this model must have been adopted for economy's sake, because in 1833 that railroad placed in service the Ohio, a car, stage-coach in shape, with seats on top as well as inside.

As President Mendes Cohen well observed in his address before the American Society of

Civil Engineers in 1892, the first important modifications in car building were called forth by the speed developed in the locomotive. Naturally the wheels first demanded attention. The names of four men are connected with early wheel improvement. Mr. Knight improved the shape of the tread and flange; John Edgar and Ross Winans developed the chilled features; and Phineas Davis further improved and perfected the wheel by altering the disposition of the metal in the tread and the angle of the flange, and by introducing within the cast-iron wheel a wrought-iron ring of five eighths or three quarters of an inch round iron, both perfected the chill and added strength to the wheel. Mr. Winans' shops turned out thousands of these wheels for use not only in this country, but also in Germany and Switzerland. From 30,000 to 50,000 miles represented the capabilities of a Winans wheel.

With increased speed came the need for increased steadiness, and it occurred to Ross Winans that by adopting the device of the bogie, or swiveling truck used in the transportation of freight, he could build an easy-riding passenger-car. In 1833 Mr. Winans constructed three long houses on wheels, each capable of seating 60 passengers. Having patented his invention, he was confronted by the fact that the principle he had used was one that had been utilized frequently on tramways, and particularly on the famous Quincy granite railroad, built to transport stone for the Bunker Hill Monument. At the end of protracted litigation the courts annulled the patent.

We now know that prior to 1830 England had three bogie-engines at work; that in 1831 Stephenson's John Bull, built for the Camden & Amboy road, was made into a bogie after it reached this country — a fact made patent by the famous run of that engine from New York to Chicago in 1893; that Horatio Allen used a bogie-engine on the South Carolina Railroad in 1832, the same year in which the bogie-locomotive Experiment was built for the Mohawk & Hudson Railroad. Moreover, the bogie principle was patented in England in 1812. Yet, whatever may be the legal aspects of the case, it is certain that the American passenger-car of to-day originated with the three passenger-coaches built in Ross Winans' shops in 1833. England discarded the bogie principle for engines in 1830, and did not return to it until 1876; and that country to this day has not adopted the bogie for passenger- or freight-cars. In 1889, the Paris, Lyons & Mediterranean Railway adopted the bogie for certain passenger-cars; and in 1895 the Great Western Railway of England began to experiment with the bogie-truck. In America the Winans passenger-coach almost immediately supplanted everywhere the stage-coach form, which England still retains in a modified shape, excepting only on the Pullman cars, introduced into that country in 1874. With us not only the passenger-cars, but the baggage, mail, and freight-cars, all were placed on swiveling trucks.

That the early railroads of this country were designed to carry passengers rather than freight is to be seen by their reports. The Baltimore & Ohio road, from 1 Jan. 1831, to 1 October carried over its 13 miles of track 5,931 tons of freight and 81,905 passengers; and so late as 1839 the Camden & Amboy carried only 13,520

tons of merchandise as against 181,479 passengers. In fact, the railways as freight carriers could not compete with the canals, which in those days were the traffic routes. In 1831 the Tuscarora & Port Carbon Railroad could not meet canal rates by 39¼ cents per ton, the railway charges being 40 cents, plus a toll of 15 cents per ton, while the canal rates were 10¾ cents, plus 5 cents toll.

Mr. John Kirby, describing from memory the freight-car of 1848, says that it was the same square box it is to-day; its capacity was from six to ten tons; the roof was covered with cotton duck painted and sanded. The hot sun cracked this covering and let the water in on the freight, an annoyance common also to passenger-coaches of that day. Few freight-cars were used in New York State at that date, the Erie Canal being sufficient for summer freight. Wood was the universal fuel, so there was no coal transportation. Wooden brake-heads were used, and it required three men to turn the screw that pressed the wheels on and off the axles. The ripping of planks was done by hand, as was also the dressing up; and when one man had tools to grind, a fellow-workman turned the stone. Carpenters and car builders of six years' experience commanded $1.12½ a day wages.

Viewed from the standpoint of to-day, the passenger-car of the early 'fifties, built at a cost of about $2,000, was a combination of inconveniences. The cast-iron stove in the centre of the car broiled those who sat immediately around it, while the unfortunates one seat removed from its satanic glare shivered and froze. In summer the dust was intolerable, and, notwithstanding elaborate devices for ventilation, the dust problem did not begin to be solved before the appearance of the monitor roof in 1860. Hot-water heating and the abolition of the deadly car-stove came with the Pullmans.

In 1856 Captain (now Sir) Douglas Galton, of the Royal Engineers, was sent to America to investigate our railways. His report to the lords of the Privy Council for Trade gives a straightforward and unbiased account of his investigations. Perhaps there is extant no other report which so comprehensively discusses the railway situation in the United States about that date. "The practice of constructing railways [in America] in a hasty and imperfect manner," says Capt. Galton, "has led to the adoption of a form of rolling stock capable of adapting itself to the inequalities of the road; it is also constructed on the principle of diminishing the useless weight carried in a train. The principle is that the body of the car is carried on two four-wheeled trucks, to which the body is attached by means of a pintle in the centre, the weight resting on small rollers at each side. The framing of the truck is supported on springs resting on the axles, and the pintle and rollers are fixed to a cross-beam, which is attached by springs to the main framing; so that between the body of the car and the axles are a double set of springs. India-rubber springs are in general use, but they often become hard; consequently sometimes steel springs are used, with great advantage. Any side movement which might result from the slight play allowed to the cross-beam is counteracted by springs placed between its ends and the framing. An iron hoop attached to the framing passes under the axle on each side, so as to support the axle in case it should break."

The bearings Capt. Galton found not unlike those used in England, but the use of oil as a lubricator was novel. He was told that under favorable circumstances the oil in an axle-box needed to be renewed but once a month; but that it was difficult to obtain good oil. The wheels were of cast-iron, with chilled tires; they were from 30 to 36 inches in diameter, weighed rather more than 500 pounds, and were without spokes. When made by the best makers they would run from 60,000 to 80,000 miles before the tires were worn, and they cost from $14.50 to $17.00 each. The iron used in making wheels was of very superior quality; and so great was the practical skill required that but three firms in the United States could be relied on to furnish wheels of the first grade.

The most approved form of draw-bar was continuous under the car, and was attached to the elliptic springs, acting in both directions. The iron shackle was in general use, but some railways preferred an oak shackle 18 inches long, two inches thick, and six inches broad. This block was bound with an iron band divided on each side at the centre, so that a car on leaving the rails would break the shackle transversely.

Already the automatic coupler for freight-cars was prefigured in a device by which the pin in the bumper of one of the cars was supported by means of a ball, so that the shackle of the on-coming car pushed back this ball and let the pin fall into its place. All passenger-cars and most freight-cars were supplied with brakes; and the Philadelphia & Reading Railroad was endeavoring to anticipate the air train-brakes by an invention whereby a sudden check in the speed of the engine applied the brakes to the wheels of all the cars. The saloon, the car-stove, and the ice-water tank all had established themselves in the best cars, and were novelties to the visiting Englishman.

On the Illinois Central, between Cairo and Dubuque, some of the cars were filled with compartments in which the backs of seats turned up and so formed two tiers of berths or sofas, for the accommodation of persons who might wish to lie down and were willing to pay for the privilege. The passenger-car had attained a length of 60 feet, though the 30- and 45-foot cars were more common; the baggage-cars, with their compartments for mail and express, were 30 feet long, and the freight-cars from 28 to 30 feet. In those days the freight-cars were constructed more strongly than were the passenger-coaches; a Baltimore & Ohio freight-car 28 feet long, and with a capacity of nine tons, itself weighed six tons.

In summing up the result of his observations as to the rolling stock in this country, Capt. Galton notes that the Americans appear to have taken their ideas more from a ship than from an ordinary carriage, and to have adopted the form best calculated to accommodate large masses, with a minimum of outlay for first cost; and that while the cars had been designed with a view to avoid every appearance of privilege or exclusiveness, or of superiority of one traveler over another, they had been constructed so as to secure to every traveler substantial comfort and even privacy.

"There is but one class," he said; "but as the cars are designed with more regard to comfort than English railway carriages, this class is much superior to our second and third classes, and is inferior only to the best first-class English carriages. Notwithstanding the superior comfort of the American railways, the rates of fare averaged lower than the second- and sometimes even the third-class fares in England."

Of necessity progress in car-building had to wait for the development of the railroads. The original roads were not constructed as through lines between the larger cities, but as the connecting-links between natural waterways, answering to the portages or carrying places of the old days when commerce was conducted in canoes. Often built as the result of local or State enterprise, a short line was sufficient to use up the scanty capital available, or to exhaust the willingness of the people to be taxed for public improvements. The great systems of to-day represent survivals of the fittest early ventures, and developed according to environment. Thus the various small roads which traversed the present main line of the New York Central were not consolidated until 1853, and the same year the roads between Philadelphia and Pittsburg came under one control. So late as 1862 there were five separate companies operating the lines between Lake Erie and Lake Michigan; and as each road had a gauge of its own, it was regarded as a triumph in car construction when freight-cars of compromise gauge were built to run over all five roads. In 1869, however, the Lake Shore & Michigan Southern lines came under a single head.

When, in October 1865, a combination was formed among eight railroads to establish a fast freight line between New York and Boston and Chicago, the maximum difference in the gauges of the several lines was one inch; and this was compensated for by a broad tread wheel. Each company contributed a number of cars proportionate to its mileage, one car for every three (afterward increased to one for every two) miles. In 1865 the quota of the Lake Shore & Northern Indiana was 179 cars; while in 1894 that road's quota of Red Line cars was 2,200.

In 1862 the United States government conducted the greatest railroad business known up to that time. With headquarters at Nashville, the government operated 1,500 miles of road with 18,000 men, whose monthly wages amounted to $2,200,000. The rolling stock consisted of 271 engines and 3,000 cars. No entirely new locomotives were built, but the 3,000 men employed in the locomotive repair shops pieced out fully equipped engines founded on a serviceable boiler or a pair of sound driving-wheels. Among the triumphs of the national car-shops were, first, a headquarters car for Gen. Thomas, the car being 50 feet long, iron-plated, and provided with a kitchen, a dining-room, a sleeping apartment, and an office; and, secondly, the hospital-trains, in which the jars and jolts were reduced to a minimum. It was during the year 1864 that Gen. McCallum and Col. Wyman came to Detroit and summoned the managers of the Michigan Car Company to stop all building then in progress and to work solely for the government. They gave a contract for a number of box- and flat-cars to be operated on southern roads; and inasmuch as the gauge differed from that of the northern roads, the new cars were loaded on flat-cars and sent to Cincinnati. The government officials fixed the price of the cars and made payment in certificates, some of which the company exchanged for materials, and the remainder were held until money could be obtained for them.

The enormous transportation business developed by the war, together with the labor conditions and the paper-money issues, combined to raise the price of cars; so that the standard freight-car of 1864, a car 28 feet long and with a capacity of 10 tons, cost $1,000 or more. About 30 years later a car 34 feet long, with a capacity of 30 tons, and provided with automatic couplers, air-brakes, and other improvements, could be purchased for about $500.

.When the war ended the managers of railways were called on to face a heavy decline in both freight and passenger traffic, due to the disbanding of the armies. Money was not plentiful, cars were very expensive, and the mania for extending lines into new territory had begun. Under these conditions the roads began a system of borrowing cars from the builders or from car-trust companies. The Michigan Car Company was probably the first to make contracts on a car-loaning basis; be that as it may, this company had at one time loaned to railroads between 6,000 and 7,000 cars, payment being made according to the car's mileage. With better times and better credit the roads began to buy cars for cash or on long time, as was most convenient; and loaning freight-cars to railroads on a mileage basis was practically discontinued. A majority of the refrigerator-cars, however, continued to be owned by private parties and run on a mileage basis. The reduction in the mileage rate practically killed the business of private ownership, since the new rate did not much more than pay for the repairs.

The sleeping-car had its beginnings as early as 1838. The Baltimore *Chronicle* for 31 October of that year described one such car that had been put on the line between Baltimore and Philadelphia. The enthusiastic reporter related that the car had berths for 24 persons, and that for a small consideration the weary passenger might spend the six hours of travel between those cities as pleasantly as if he were asleep in his own bed. Nothing then seemed to be wanting except dining-cars, and those were promised for the near future — a promise, alas! not fulfilled for many a long year.

Twenty years later, in 1858, George B. Gates invested $5,000 in two sleeping-cars to run between Cleveland and Buffalo; but passengers could not be persuaded to use them. The same year the line between Toledo and Chicago was equipped with two sleeping-cars built by the Wason Company, of Springfield, Mass., and owned by Mr. Bates, of Utica, N. Y. These cars were 50 feet long, with 16 sections in summer and 14 in winter. When not in use the bedding and curtains were stored in an end section; and a single wash-basin and one saloon furnished the toilet conveniences for the 48 persons the car was expected to carry. A sofa along the side of the car formed the lower berth, the middle one was hinged to the window-casing, and the upper berth rested on cleats fastened to permanent cross-partitions. It was

while traveling in one of these cars, in 1858, that Mr. George M. Pullman began to plan the sleeping-cars that have revolutionized railway travel in this country, and are making their way in Europe, where comfort is less an essential to the traveler than it is in America.

In 1859 Mr. Pullman transformed two Chicago & Alton coaches into better sleeping-cars than any others; but it was not until 1863 that the Pioneer, the first Pullman, was placed on the road. The car cost $18,000 — an astounding price in those days. It was higher and wider than most roads could admit, and it was not until President Lincoln's funeral that the roads between Chicago and Springfield narrowed their platforms and adapted their bridges so as to allow the Pioneer, carrying the funeral party, to pass over their lines. Shortly afterward Gen. Grant's trip from Detroit to Galena, Ill., in the same car, opened those lines to the Pioneer. After that time progress was rapid. The Pullman Company was organized in 1867, and its success is too well known to need comment here. From the palace sleeping-car to the parlor- and the dining-room car is a short step. But a long jump was taken in the vestibule, invented by Mr. Pullman in 1887, by which trains are made solid and the platform is robbed of the last of its terrors.

In the winter of 1868-9 the first Westinghouse air-brake was used on the Steubenville accommodation train running on the Pittsburg, Cincinnati & St. Louis Railroad. The Pennsylvania road adopted it, and since the automatic feature was added, in 1873, it has come into almost universal use on passenger-trains, while by far the larger proportion of new freight-cars built are equipped with it. In 1887 a train of 50 freight-cars made a triumphal tour of the great lines, and by repeated tests, under varying conditions, proved that the Westinghouse brake can stop a train in one tenth the space required by the hand-brake. In 1867 Col. Miller placed his patent platform, buffer, and coupler on three cars building in the shops at Adrian, Mich.; and with great rapidity the dangerous old platform, with its loose link coupling, disappeared. In 1860 the Post-Office Department began to demand more room from the railroad companies, and year by year the mail-cars were increased from 17 to 20 feet in length, then to 35, and finally to 60 feet.

The interchange of cars among the various roads made it necessary to adopt standards in car construction, in order to facilitate repairs to cars when away from the home road. Some authority, too, was needed to settle disputes between roads, arising from charges for repairs; to investigate new brakes and couplers; and, in general, to keep the work of construction fully abreast of the times. The Master Car Builders' Association, organized in 1867, amply fills this need; and the reports of its annual meetings contain the latest word on all subjects relating to car-building. Its arbitration committee also acts as a court of conciliation for the various roads.

Prior to the panic of 1873 all the car-works were busy. That panic caused the failure of a large number of new railroads, which in turn, forced into bankruptcy and eventual reorganization many car companies. From 1873 to 1879 the car-shops throughout the country were practically idle; but with the revival of business in

CAR BUILDING INDUSTRY

1878–9 the car-works again became busy, and with the exception of a slight dullness in 1883–4, did a large and profitable business until 1893. The effect of business depression on car-building may easily be seen from the fact that in 1890, 103,000 freight-cars were built by 50 companies; in 1893 the output of 43 companies was only 51,216 cars; and in 1894 the 27 companies operating their plants turned out 17,029 cars. Fifteen companies that built 3,000 freight- and 300 passenger-cars in 1893 built not a single car in 1894. The increase in the total number of cars during the fiscal year 1894 was but 4,132, as against 58,854 in 1893. The rapid increase since that date may be judged from the fact that the capacity of car-building factories in the United States on 1 June 1903 was estimated as follows: Freight-cars, 270,200 per annum; passenger-cars, 2,700; street-cars (including electric and interurban), 17,850.

CAPACITY OF CAR FACTORIES FOR OUTPUT JUNE 1, 1903.

	Freight cars	Passenger cars
American Car & Foundry Co......	125,000	800
Pressed Steel Car Co............	35,000	
Southern Car & Foundry Co.......	20,000	
The Portland Co.................	300	
The Laconia Car Co..............	1,200	50
Keith Mfg. Co..................	600	
Osgood Bradley Car Co..........	700	100
Wason Mfg. Co.................	1,800	100
Cambria Steel Co...............	4,000	
Erie Car Works.................	2,400	
Lehigh Car, Wheel & Axle Works..	4,000	
Middletown Car Works...........	2,400	
Standard Steel Car Co...........	18,000	
M. H. Treadwell & Co..........	1,200	50
Billmeyer & Small Co...........	1,200	100
Harlan & Hollingsworth Co......		200
South Baltimore Car Works.....	3,600	
Chattanooga Car & Foundry Co....	800	
KnoXville Foundry & Mach. Co....	700	
Georgia Car & Mfg. Co.........	2,400	
Barney & Smith Car Co.........	5,000	300
The Niles Car & Mfg. Co........		50
Lima Locomotive & Machine Co...	2,500	
The Jewett Car Co.............		150
The Youngstown Car Mfg. Co....	2,000	
Haskell & Barker Car Co........	10,000	
Mt. Vernon Car Mfg. Co.........	4,500	
The Pullman Co.................	10,000	700
Western Steel Car & Foundry Co..	10,000	
California Car Works............	900	100
	270,200	2,700

	Street and Electric cars
American Car & Foundry Co................	150
The Laconia Car Co.......................	900
Briggs Carriage Co.......................	300
Newburyport Car Mfg. Co..................	300
Osgood Bradley Car Co....................	300
Wason Mfg. Co...........................	500
The Graham Co...........................	600
J. M. Jones Sons.........................	600
John Stephenson Co.......................	700
J. G. Brill Co...........................	3,000
Barney & Smith Car Co...................	1,000
The Jewett Car Co........................	700
The G. C. Kuhlman Car Co.................	800
The Niles Car & Mfg. Co.................	800
American Car Co..........................	1,000
Laclede Car Co...........................	1,000
St. Louis Car Co.........................	4,000
Woeber Carriage Co.......................	300
California Car Works.....................	800
	17,850

The average life of a freight-car being from 12 to 15 years, at least 125,000 cars must be built each year to repair the ravages of time; besides the cars required to make good the losses by accidents and for the increase in mileage and business. The transportation of various kinds of products, such as live-stock, dressed meat, oil, timber, etc., has called into being cars especially adapted to each class of freight, so that scores of different kinds are now constructed to answer the demands of the shippers. Among the different makes may be named: flat or platform cars; the ordinary box-car, the gondola or coal-car, the hopper gondola coal-car, which has a gate in the bottom of the car for emptying the car without handling the contents; the hopper-car, which has a number of gates in the bottom for emptying the car rapidly; side dumping-cars, coke-cars, stock-cars especially prepared for different kinds of stock; horse express-cars, for transporting fine horses; furniture or vehicle-cars; refrigerator-cars; ventilated fruit-cars; special construction or repair-cars, and caboose-cars for trainmen. Steel-cars are used for the transportation of heavy material such as coal and ore. See STEEL CAR INDUSTRY.

Passenger-cars are divided into the ordinary passenger-car, the combination cars for baggage, mail, express and passengers, each style being of different construction; chair-cars, parlor-cars, dining-cars, combination parlor and café-cars; library- and buffet-cars; private cars containing business office, sleeping apartments, dining-room, kitchen, and observation room; and sleeping-cars. Street-cars are divided into electric, cable, horse, and parlor-cars.

According to the census of 1900 there were 65 establishments turning out street-cars (some of which also constructed street railway cars); and 1,296 car-shops belonging to the various steam railways, and engaged in the building as well as the repairing of cars, making a total of 1,361 establishments, with a capital of $207,904,125, employing 215,567 wage-earners and salaried officials, with wages and salaries aggregating $120,798,002. The materials used cost $171,281,760 and the value of products aggregated $308,748,457.

The 1,296 establishments operated by railroad companies, reported an invested capital of $119,580,273, or 57.5 per cent of the capital of the combined industry.

The 10 states leading in the construction and repair of steam railway cars in 1900 were: Pennsylvania, with a capital of $62,326.081; Illinois, with $41,426,030; New York, with $21,423,201; Indiana, $19,248,999; Ohio, $16,917,-554; Michigan, $14,253,707; Missouri, $14,246.889; Texas, $8,314,691; California, $7,553,626; and Kansas, $6,816,816. The aggregate value of the products for these States $212,527,504, or 68.8 per cent of the total value for the United States. The products for the first five States aggregated $161,341,865, or 52.3 per cent of the total value.

The constantly increasing traffic in this country rapidly absorbs the product of the car-shops, but there is also a foreign demand of considerable magnitude for American-built cars. This demand changes with the varying industrial conditions and commercial activity of the countries importing these products, as well as with the economic conditions existing in this country.

In 1890 and 1891 the value of exported cars exceeded the value in 1900. During the business depression which followed there was a marked decrease in the number of cars constructed, both for foreign and domestic use. The construction of freight-cars was the first to be affected. The number of passenger-cars constructed in this country did not decrease materially until after the Columbian Exposition in 1893. The foreign demand and the exposition were potent factors in keeping many of the shops running during 1893. A year or two later the demand for freight-cars began to increase, and since 1897 the demand for both passenger- and freight-cars for foreign and domestic use has shown a constant growth. The exports for 1900, aggregating $2,558,323, exceeded the average yearly exports from 1880 to 1890 by $1,581,872; those from 1890 to 1900 by $756,484; and the average for 20 years by $1,169,178.

Among foreign countries importing American cars for steam railroads in 1900, Mexico led, purchasing to the amount of $714,329. Egypt followed with imports aggregating $401,151. The next six countries in the order of amounts expended are: France, $280,939; Brazil, $133,378; Great Britain and Ireland, $124,585; Argentina, $105,147; British Australasia, $50,754; Cuba, $79,723. No cars or parts of cars were exported to Asia or Africa in 1890, but in 1900 these exports to Asia were valued at $33,492 and to Africa at $405,895.

W. J. McBRIDE,
Vice-President American Car & Foundry Co.

Car'buncle, a very severe form of boil (q.v.). Also the lesion of malignant pustule, or anthrax (q.v.).

Carbuncle, a general term used to describe any red garnet when cut *en cabochon.* Pliny and other early writers apparently applied the name "carbunculus" indiscriminately to ruby, ruby spinel and garnet. The best usage at the present time confines it to the almandite garnet when cut *en cabochon,* that is, with a rounded convex surface. Usually such stones are hollowed out at the back and a piece of metal foil is inserted in order to lighten the otherwise too dense red color.

Carburetor. An apparatus employed to increase the illuminating power of a gas, such as coal-gas, hydrogen, or air, by passing it over liquid hydrocarbon. All forms are practically similar in construction, being designed to force the gas into contact with the hydrocarbon liquid held in a series of overflow pans, cylinders, or troughs formed of inclined plane bottoms dovetailing into each other, and making a sinuous course through which the gas passes and emerges from the retort highly impregnated with the volatilized hydrocarbon vapor.

When employed for enriching gas, a poorer quality of coal may be used initially and the product thus obtained subsequently carbureted into a medium of a high illuminating power, and when gas is not available, air may be carbureted or saturated with the inflammable hydrogen vapor by passing it through the liquid and thus obtain a good illuminant. See AUTOMOBILE.

Carcanet, kär'kạ nĕt, a jeweled necklace or chain, an ornament referred to by Shakespeare, and by Tennyson in 'The Last Tournament.'

Carcano, Giulio, joo'lĕ ō kär-kä'nō, Italian poet: b. Milan, 1812; d. 1884. He wrote a narrative poem, 'Ida Della Torre,' while a student at Pavia (1834). His next work, 'Angiola Maria' (1839), had extraordinary success; it is a deeply sympathetic story of Italian family life, and is regarded as the highest type of that class in Italian. In the same vein is the volume 'Simple Narratives' (1843). He wrote also 'Damiano, the Story of a Poor Family,' and other works. See Prina, 'Giulio Carcano' (1884).

Carcar, kär'kär, Philippines, a city on the northern coast of the island of Cebu, situated on the Bay of Carcar, 23 miles from the city of Cebu. It is near the head of the bay and on the road running along the eastern coast of the island. Pop. about 30,000.

Car'cass, in military language, an iron spherical case filled with combustible materials, which is discharged from a mortar, howitzer, or gun. It does not burst, but has three fuse-holes through which the flame rushes, firing everything within its influence. Carcasses are of considerable use in bombardments for setting fire to buildings, vessels lying in harbors, etc. They will continue to burn for 8 or 10 minutes, and are not even extinguished by water.

Carcassonne, kär-kạ-sŏn', France, capital of the department of Aude, on both sides of the river Aude and on a branch of the Canal du Midi, 53 miles south of Toulouse. It consists of an old and a new town, which communicate by a bridge of 12 arches spanning the river. The old town is surrounded by a double wall, part of it so ancient as to be attributed to the Visigoths, and is defended by a castle. Its streets are narrow, dirty, and desolate, forming a striking contrast to those of the new town, which is regularly built, and has many handsome modern houses. The boulevards are finely planted. The chief manufacture is that of woolen cloth, which is exported chiefly to the Levant, the Barbary states, and South America. There is also trade in wine, grain, brandy, fruit, and leather. Pop. 31,000.

Carchar'odon, an extinct genus of sharks of the Tertiary Period, nearly related to the modern white "man-eater" shark, but of gigantic size. The flat, triangular, sharp-edged teeth found commonly in the marl-beds of the Atlantic coast, are sometimes six inches wide, indicating that the animal was not less than 60 feet in length.

Carchemish, kär'kĕm-ĭsh, an ancient city on the Euphrates, formerly thought to be the same as the Roman Circesium, but now is more generally located near Jerabis, a village on the west bank of the Euphrates. It was the northern capital of the Hittites; was once captured by Tiglath-Pileser I., and made to pay tribute by Asurnazirpal; but was not finally subdued by the Assyrians until taken in 717 B.C. by Sargon II., who deported the inhabitants and settled Assyrians in the city. In 608 B.C. it was captured by the Egyptian Pharaoh Necho. At this time Josiah, king of Judah, was killed (mentioned in 2 Chron. xxxv.); but the city was retaken by Nebuchadnezzar in 605.

Carcinoma. See TUMOR.

Card, Henry, English miscellaneous writer: b. Egham, Surrey, 1779; d. Great Malvern, 4 Aug. 1844. He was educated at Westminster School and Pembroke College, Oxford. In 1815 he was presented to the vicarage of Great Malvern, Worcestershire, and in 1832 to that of Darmington, Herefordshire. He was elected a Fellow of the Royal Society, 2 March 1820, and also a Fellow of the Royal Society of Antiquaries and of the Royal Historical Society. He was a prolific writer and some of his published works are: 'The History of the Revolutions of Russia' (2d ed. 1804); 'Historical Outline of the Rise and Establishment of the Papal Power' (1804); 'Thoughts on Domestic or Private Education' (1807); 'The Reign of Charlemagne, Considered Chiefly with Reference to Religion, Laws, Literature, and Manners' (1807); 'Literary Recreations' (2d ed. 1811); 'Beauford, or a Picture of High Life,' a novel (2 vols. 1811), etc.

Card Indexing, Commercial, the adaptation of the principle of the modern library card catalogue to the multifarious uses of industrial, mercantile, and commercial life. Following the practical American development and improvement of the various old-world principles and rules laid down for the cataloguing of libraries, and the establishment after 1876 of library bureaus for furnishing standard supplies, it was speedily recognized that card systems for facilitating the record of the affairs of business life and their multitudinous details, were henceforth to be — as in the case of the telephone, the typewriting machine and accessories — indispensable adjuncts to the equipment of every well-appointed office, store, factory, or institution throughout the world.

The invention of time and labor-saving systems and devices of all kinds speedily followed, and now, any branch of any kind of business, from the simplest to the most complex, can advantageously install and use a card system, and procure standard supplies of blank or special printed and ruled forms with full information as to their application for the keeping of accurate records of all affairs in the most practical way.

The development of commercial card systems also led naturally to a corresponding and commensurate growth of office furniture, fixtures, and accessories for their accommodation, which include: box, tray, and drawer cases for card indexes; various kinds of folders, guides, indexed storage and binding cases for vertical files; indexed transfer cases for flat files; elastic or expanding filing and other cabinets for document, check, and mercantile reports, etc.; specially devised stands, tables, desks, etc.

For classifying work by separating miscellaneous information — grouping information of the same kind together — no other method has been found to equal the card-index system, the impossibility of keeping different facts about the same business or profession recorded in a bound book with any degree of sequence or order, being now universally recognized. The card indexing system has proved of especial advantage, and is now extensively utilized in the offices of government, state, and municipal departments, of railroad, telegraph, telephone, electric light, gas, and waterworks companies, real estate and trust corporations, building and loan associations, fire, life, and accident insurance companies, solicitors' and underwriters' agencies, benevolent societies, lodges, banks and other financial institutions, factories, wholesale commercial and mail order houses, publishers, advertising agencies, professional men, clergymen, lawyers, physicians, oculists, dentists, specialists, etc.

By means of the card index system, names, facts, figures of any description, recorded on cards of uniform size, are arranged alphabetically, numerically, territorially, chronologically, or according to any suitable defined order in boxes, trays, or drawers of cabinets of special design. Various plans, ranging from simple to complex, are used for special indexing. All, however, are transparently concise in arrangement and of facile adaptation for reference. The most simple form of card-indexing is the alphabetical-subject plan in which the name is indexed alphabetically, and the subject indicated by different tab cards. In territorial card-indexes the names are first classified by states, with alphabetical guides for each city or commercial community in the state, the cards bearing the records of firms or individuals being filed back of the alphabetical guides. Chronological card-indexes are divided into monthly, daily, and alphabetical sections, distinguished by different colored cards, and back of each monthly guide is arranged a set of blank daily guides, so that cards may be filed in advance for attention on any day of any month. Each card with its record has an individual existence in its relations to others of the system, and is always to be found in its place, notwithstanding the cumulative and expansive principle of the index, which allows cards to be added or withdrawn as needed. Guide or signal cards of different colors with projecting edges or tabs facilitate the immediate finding of the card for rapid reference; the liberal use of these signal cards, carefully inserted in long lists of the same surnames, also obviates a considerable amount of handling, and saves time, labor, and the wear and tear of the cards.

One of the most ingenious uses of the card system for commercial purposes is its application to the keeping of ledgers, of which the loose-leaf ledger is an offshoot in the developing process of commercial card-indexing. The card ledger does away with the necessity of purchasing books, ledgers, or binders, and accounts can be posted, checked up, trial balance taken off, and statements mailed in approximately half the time required for a book ledger. Accuracy is also promoted by each card representing one account only, which can be laid on the sales sheet or other original record, thus lessening the liability to error in posting. Each account being on a separate card is easily indexed, and no separate or cross-index is required; more perfect indexing is thus insured; as the number of accounts increase year by year, sets of index cards, with as many subdivisions of the alphabet as desired to facilitate quicker reference, may be substituted for the original set. Statements can be taken off promptly at the first of the month, and where necessary, several clerks can do the billing at the same time, which is impossible with the book ledger. Open accounts only are kept on the regular file; all closed accounts are removed and indexed in a separate file, the only practical method of providing for closed accounts, which can be as easily referred to as open ones. The card being removed from the files when the account is closed, and replaced when opened, also obviates the former necessity of transferring accounts from one ledger to another, at the end of each year. Finally the card index ledger can be profitably used for mailing and circular lists.

Other notable commercial adaptations of the card index system are: Follow-up cards for keeping a record of prospective purchasers and customers; customers' list cards for traveling representatives and especially useful for the request to "duplicate a previous order"; quotation-made and -received cards; catalogue cards for price-lists, business catalogues and prospectuses; stock record cards to afford an estimate of the amount of merchandise stock carried, its maximum and minimum quantity; savings bank account cards which, at a glance, give amount deposited, withdrawn, and balance on hand. See also LITERARY LABOR-SAVERS, LIBRARY UTENSILS, and MERCANTILE OFFICE-FIXTURES.

Cardamine, kär'dȧ-mĭn, a genus of plants of the natural order *Cruciferæ*, containing about 60 species with a very wide distribution. They are herbaceous plants with usually pinnate leaves, white or lilac flowers of the usual cruciferous type, and the siliquose fruit which characterizes a section of the order. One of the best-known American species is the cuckoo-flower (*C. pratensis*), growing in wet places from Vermont to New Jersey, westward to Wisconsin, and northward. *C. hirsuta* is a common weed everywhere, varying in size, according to soil, from 6 to 18 inches in height. The leaves and flowers of this species form an agreeable salad. This species produces young plants from the leaves, all that is necessary being to place them on a moist grassy or mossy surface. These species were imported to this country from Europe. The indigenous American species are *C. rhomboidea*, spring cress, and *C. rotundifolia*, mountain water-cress, common throughout the eastern part of the United States. *C. amara*, the bitter-cress, is not unlike the water-cress, but may be readily distinguished by its dark-colored anthers.

Car'damom, the capsule and seed of several species of plants of the order *Zingiberaceæ*, perennial plants, growing in the East. The fruit is used as a stimulant and aromatic. Triangular capsules, from four to five lines in length, contain the seeds, which are of a brown color, a pleasant, aromatic smell, and a warm, pepper-like taste. The cardamoms known in the shops are produced by *Amomum angustifolium*, a Madagascar plant, *A. cardamomum*, a native of Sumatra, and other eastern islands. Those recognized in the United States pharmacopœia, called true or officinal cardamoms, and known in commerce as Malabar cardamoms, are the produce of *Elettaria (Alpinia) cardamomum*, a native of the mountains of Malabar and Canara. The seeds of cardamom are widely employed in medicine as the basis of vehicles for carrying disagreeable drugs, and also as carminatives and digestants. The volatile oils of cardamom act like other volatile oils in stimulating peristalsis, thus expelling excess of intestinal gases, but they also increase the gastric and intestinal secretions.

Cardan, or **Cardano, Girolamo**, jĕ-rō'lä-mō kär dän or kär-dä'nō, Italian philosopher, physician, and mathematician: b. Pavia, 24 Sept. 1501; d. Rome, 21 Sept. 1576. He was educated from his fourth year in the house of his father. At 20 he went to the Pavia to complete his studies, and after two years began to explain Euclid. He was subsequently professor of mathematics and medicine in Milan (1534). His biographers differ with regard to his religious opinions, but he was lost in cabalistic dreams and paradoxes, and pretended to have a familiar demon from whom he received warnings, etc. All this excited the theologians against him, who even accused him of atheism, though the charge was without foundation. He believed so implicitly in astrology that he drew his own horoscope several times, and ascribed the falsehood of his predictions, not to the uncertainty of the art, but to his own ignorance. His two works, 'De Subtilitate Rerum,' and 'De Varietate Rerum,' contain the whole of his natural philosophy and metaphysics. Cardan wrote also on medicine, and his fame as a physician was very great. His highest claims to the gratitude of the learned rest on his mathematical discoveries. Cardan, it is said, was told that Tartaglia had discovered the solution of cubic equations, and obtained the secret from him by stratagem and under promise of silence, but published the method in 1545, in his 'Ars Magna.' The honor of giving his name to the invention has remained to him who first made it known, and it is still called the formula of Cardan. It is universally believed that Cardan discovered some new cases, which were not comprehended in the rule of Tartaglia; that he discovered the multiplicity of the roots of the higher equations, and finally the existence of negative roots, the use of which he did not, however, understand. All his works, to the number of more than 50, are contained in the standard edition of Sponius (Lyons 1663).

Card'board, a thick paper, or aggregation of paper or paper-stock, made by pasting several sheets of paper together and compressing the product between rollers. The finest cardboard, or Bristol board, such as is used for visiting-cards and in the arts, is so made of white paper only. It is known as three-, four-, six-, or eight-sheet board, according to the number of layers of paper. A cheaper grade of white cardboard is composed of coarse white paper for the inner layers, and a finer facing paper on the outside. Another variety of cardboard is that used by boxmakers, and is made from coarse brown paper glued and rolled, and faced with white or colored paper, or unfaced, according to the use to which it is to be put. A coarser grade yet is known as millboard. This is used by bookbinders for the covers of books, by boxmakers, and for other work in which strength is of more value than appearance. Fine qualities of millboard are also made to some extent. See PAPER AND PAPER-MAKING.

Cardenas, Bernardino, bĕr-nar-dē'nō kär'-dä-näs, Peruvian ecclesiastic: b. Chuquisæa, about 1595; d. Santa Cruz de la Sierra, about 1667. Entering the order of Franciscans he became a missionary among the Indians, being made bishop of Paraguay in 1640. On account of differences with the Jesuits he was twice expelled from his diocese. When Osorio, then governor, died in 1649, Cardenas was elected to fill the vacant position and immediately expelled the Jesuits from Asuncion. He was then deposed, imprisoned and excommunicated, but restored in 1662, and in 1666 made bishop of Santa Cruz de la Sierra. He wrote a defense of his career entitled 'Manuel y relacion de las Cosas del Reyno del Peru.'

Cardenas, kär'dä näs, Cuba, a seaport in the northern part of the province of Matanzas, situated on Cardenas Bay. It is connected with Havana by rail, and has a large trade in sugar and molasses. On 11 May 1898 the Spanish shore batteries and gunboats at Cardenas attacked the United States vessels blockading the port, and in the engagement the United States torpedo-boat Winslow was disabled, and Ensign Worth Bagley (q.v) and four sailors were killed.

Cardenas y Rodriguez, Jose (hō-sä') M. **de**, Cuban poet and prose-writer: b. Matanzas, 1812; d. 1882. Many of his humorous sketches of Cuban life have been translated into French and published in the 'Revue des Deux Mondes.' Besides a good comedy, 'A Deaf Uncle,' he has written a collection of fables, some of which have been translated into English; and numerous poems.

Cardenas y Rodriguez, ē rō drē'gäth, **Nicolas de**, nē'kō-lä dä, Cuban poet and novelist: b. Havana, 1814; d. 1868. His works comprise: 'Poetical Essays' (1836); 'Scenes from Life in Cuba' (1841); 'The Two Weddings,' a novel (1844); 'Diego de Velazquez,' a drama. He was also a regular contributor to periodicals.

Cardi, Lodovico, lō-dō-vē'kō kär'dē, surnamed CIVOLI, or CIGOLI, Italian painter and architect: b. 1559; d. 1613. He studied painting under Allori and S. di Titi, and afterward formed his style on the works of Andrea del Sarto and Correggio, but more especially on the noble and spirited productions of Baroccio at Florence. His architectural works, in which he followed Michael Angelo, possess considerable merit. His most celebrated picture is 'The Lame Man Cured,' which is in St. Peter's at Rome. Sacchi considers it entitled to hold the first place among the pictures in Rome, after 'The Transfiguration' of Raphael, and the 'St. Jerome' of Domenichino. His 'Martyrdom of St. Stephen,' executed for the convent of Monte Domini, and his 'Tobias Entertaining the Angel,' now in the Hermitage at St. Petersburg, are also noble paintings.

Car'dia, the upper or cardiac orifice of the stomach, as distinguished from the intestinal opening or the pylorus.

Car'diac Medicines, medicines which act upon the heart. They may be roughly classified into those which stimulate the heart; heart tonics which brace or tone the heart; and heart sedatives or depressants, which quiet or soothe the heart. To the first group belong ammonia, ether, camphor, and alcohol; to the second, digitalis, squills, lily of the valley, and strophanthus; and to the last aconite. Several of these must be administered with great care.

Cardial'gia, an intense pain over the general heart region. It is usually due to stomach disturbance, heartburn, and is often accompanied by pains in the œsophagus. Heartburn is nearly always due to the presence of large amounts of gas, causing pressure. These gases usually accompany and cause an indigestion.

Cardiff, Wales (Welsh, Caerdydd, perhaps the fortress on the Taff, but derivation uncertain), a municipal and parliamentary borough, raised to the rank of a city (with the title of Lord Mayor for its chief magistrate) by royal charter in 1905, a seaport on the Bristol channel, the capital of Glamorgan and the largest town in Wales. The city is built on both banks of the river Taff, a mile above its junction with the estuary of the Severn (known as the Bristol channel) and extends to the rivers Rhymney on the east and Ely on the west. It is 135 miles west of London, on the Great Western main line from London to New Milford and Fishguard (for Ireland), distance by rail 145 miles, fast trains three hours.

Geology.—Almost every geological formation from the Silurian up to the coal measures is found in the ring of higher ground surrounding the plain of recent alluvial deposits on which the city stands.

Trade and Development.—The rapid increase of the last half century is due to the development of the coal trade consequent upon the construction of the Bute docks. The first dock, completed in 1839, was built by the second Marquess of Bute, further docks being constructed by the Bute trustees as the trade expanded, These properties have now been merged into a company, the Cardiff Railway Company. This company has a fourth dock, larger than all the others, approaching completion, with a deep water entrance through which vessels can enter at any state of the tide. The total water area of the docks is about 200 acres, and the shipments of coal 16,000,000 tons per annum. There are also docks at the adjoining ports of Penarth and Barry.

The coal is worked in collieries to the north (nearest colliery nine miles), and shipped at the docks below the city, which is singularly free from any evidence of the staple trade. The fine, wide streets, abundance of trees, and freedom from smoke and other evidences of industry, are a surprise to visitors. Besides the dock operations, the most important works are the Cardiff Dowlais steel works (Guest, Keen & Co., Limited), the Tharsis Copper Works, numerous ship repairing yards, extensive flour mills (Spillers & Bakers, Limited), biscuit works (Spillers' Nephews, Limited), ice and cold storage (with large import trade), and steam trawlers for the fishing industry. The import trade has been developed of late years, and Cardiff is now the chief wholesale centre for supplying the teeming populations of the mining valleys of Glamorgan and Monmouth.

Railways.—The Great Western Railway and its connections provide a good and quick service to distant places, while the local railways constructed primarily for mineral traffic, the Taff Vale, Rhymney, and Barry respectively, communicate with the districts adjacent. The Midland and London & North Western companies have goods depots.

Government and Public Works.—The government of the city is vested in the Lord Mayor, aldermen (10), and councillors (30). The oldest surviving charter, granted sometime before 1147, evidences the existence of rights and privileges extending to a much earlier time. Other charters were given by the feudal lords, and later by the crown. The area of the city is 8,408 acres. One member is returned to parliament jointly with the small contributory boroughs of Cowbridge and Llantrisant; number of voters (1906), municipal, 24,832; parliamentary, 24,146. Number of buildings rated, 34,469; rateable value, £1,028,146. Parks and open spaces, 291 acres (cost, £326,426). Gas is supplied by a company; the water supply (cost, £1,278,537; revenue, £64,979); electric light (cost, £242,721; revenue, £35,962); electric trams (cost, £747,308; revenue, £113,903; tracks laid, 28.84 miles); the fire brigade, markets, and cemeteries are municipal undertakings. The asylum for the city, 650 patients (cost, £300,000), is at Whitchurch (3½ miles). The police force comprises the head constable, 42 officers, and 195 men. A special police force is employed for the dock properties by the Cardiff Railway Company.

Public Buildings.— The public buildings are being grouped in a park of 50 acres. The town hall and law courts (cost, £330,000) are completed, as are also the offices of the University of Wales (cost, £6,000), and new buildings for the University College of South Wales and Monmouthshire, a constituent college of the University of Wales (to cost £250,000), are being erected. The secondary and elementary schools are modern, and efficiently equipped and administered, and special provision is made for blind, deaf and dumb, and defective children. Other public buildings include the post-office, custom-house, offices of the Board of Trade and Mercantile Marine, a general hospital, a hospital for seamen, a sanatorium for infectious diseases, Coal Exchange, barracks, County Gaol, theatres, and numerous others. The Castle, restored and extended at great cost by the late Marquess, is one of the residences of the Marquess of Bute.

Libraries.— The public libraries (Central, cost, £30,000, and six branches), contain 156,000 volumes, and include the largest collection of Welsh books and manuscripts in existence. The school library system of the city is one of the best in existence. The Museum and art gallery, about to be merged in the National Museum of Wales with a government grant of £8,000 per annum, contains modern paintings and sculpture; Swansea, Nantgarw, and other poreelain, and examples of pre-Norman sculptured stones and crosses.

Churches.— The only ancient church is Saint John's with a fine decorated tower, built in 1473, by Anne Nevill, who inherited the lordship of Glamorgan. She was the wife of Richard Nevill, Earl of Warwick ("the kingmaker") and mother of Ann, wife of Richard III. There are numerous modern Episcopalian, Roman Catholic, and Nonconformist churches. The ancient cathedral of Llandaff is just outside the city boundary.

Societies, etc.— Consuls and vice-consuls for almost every country are stationed here, and important societies such as the Chamber of Commerce, South Wales Coal Owners' Association, and South Wales Institute of Engineers, have their headquarters. The offices of the Glamorgan County Council, the Welsh Central Board of Intermediate Education, and similar bodies, are included in the city.

There are two morning, two evening, and two weekly newspapers, and several minor periodicals.

History.— The Romans had an important station here, extensive remains of their fortifications having recently been discovered in the Castle grounds. According to tradition, Cardiff was an important place under the Welsh princes before the Roman occupation; it was certainly a stronghold of the Welsh after the departure of the Romans, and was ravaged by Danes and Norsemen. After the Norman conquest the district was subdued by Robert Fitzhamon and his followers, who established a powerful Marcher Lordship with Cardiff as the capital. The Castle Keep was erected inside the Roman fortification by the Norman lords. The town and district were in the hands of the feudal lords for centuries, and the scene of several bitter contests between the Welsh and their alien masters. Cardiff was at this time surrounded by a high and massive wall and a moat, while the Castle, with its law courts and other appanages of feudalism, was a very strong place, guarded by relays of soldiers, supplied in rotation from the forces of the under lords, who had castles in the surrounding districts. The lordship reverted to the king in 1495 and was in 1550 granted, stripped of its feudal privileges, to Sir William Herbert, afterward first Earl of Pembroke, from whom it has descended to the Marquess of Bute.

During the Civil War Cardiff was an important centre of operations, and was held by the forces of the king and of Cromwell in turn. It was visited by Charles I. in 1645, who sought to revive the loyalty of his followers, but with poor success. The decay of feudalism stripped the town of its importance and it continued to decline until the dawn of the era of coal and iron.

Population.— In 1801 the population was 1,870, and 50 years later, 18,351. It is now (1906), about 170,000.

Bibliography.— 'The Cardiff Records' (six volumes, published by the city council); 'Cardiff,' an illustrated hand-book, edited by Ballinger (1896). JOHN BALLINGER,
Librarian of the Public Libraries.

Car'diff Giant, the name given to a roughly carved statue of a man exhibited in various parts of the United States in 1870 as a "petrified man." It was originally carved in California from a block of gypsum and subsequently buried in Onondaga County, N. Y., near the village of Cardiff, and hence its name. It was alleged to have been accidentally discovered there in October 1869.

Cardigan, James Thomas Brudenell, EARL OF, English general: b. Hambleton, 16 Oct. 1797; d. 28 May 1868. He was educated at Christ Church, Oxford, and was gazetted 6 May 1824, as cornet in the 8th Royal Irish Hussars, under the courtesy title of Lord Brudenell. His family influence and wealth in England procured for him a rapid promotion, and in a few years he had attained the rank of major. Lord Brudenell was next, 3 Dec. 1830, made lieutenant-colonel of the 15th Hussars. He was a member of the House of Commons from the period of his coming of age in 1818, until 14 Aug. 1837, when on the death of his father, he became Earl of Cardigan. After his regiment returned from India Lord Cardigan got himself into difficulties with the officers, who, one by one, had to sell out until the feeling of the regiment broke into mutiny

In what was known as the "black bottle quarrel." This quarrel arose in 1840, while Lord Cardigan's regiment was stationed at Canterbury. One of his officers, Capt. Reynolds, having caused wine to be placed on the table in a "black bottle," Lord Cardigan accused him of degrading the mess to the level of a pot-house. This led to angry words: Capt. Reynolds was placed under arrest, demanded a court-martial, but this privilege was withheld from him, and, as the public thought, unjustly. The excitement created by this affair and by his subsequent misunderstanding with another officer also of the name of Reynolds, had hardly subsided, when he fought a duel with Capt. Harvey Tuckett because this officer had censured his conduct in the *Morning Chronicle*. Capt. Tuckett was wounded, and Lord Cardigan tried before the House of Lords, but, although acquitted, public opinion was against him. His reputation, however, as an accomplished cavalry officer, and the satisfaction which the Duke of Wellington expressed in 1848, with the efficiency of the 11th Hussars' Regiment, which was under Lord Cardigan's charge, led to his promotion. On the outbreak of the Crimean war Lord Cardigan was raised to the rank of major-general, and appointed brigadier in command of the light cavalry brigade. This brigade constituted the celebrated "Six Hundred," whose charge at Balaklava will long be remembered as one of the bravest yet wildest feats, perhaps, ever told of in the history of war. On that occasion (25 Oct. 1854), Lord Cardigan is said to have received from Lord Lucan, his brother-in-law, an order to capture certain guns from the Russians. A mile and a half had to be traversed, under fire, before the enemy could be met, and the Russian forces stood in formidable array in every direction. The enterprise seemed hopeless. Cardigan, however, led on the charge, and actually took the guns, his men cutting their way through the infantry support and through the cavalry, and then back again, under the play of the Russian batteries, but with fearfully diminished numbers, the survivors not exceeding 150. As the hero of this daring exploit, Lord Cardigan was received with great enthusiasm on his return to England, and appointed inspector-general of the cavalry. The charges, however, subsequently alleged by the Crimean commissioners, tended to reduce the high estimate placed upon his services.

Car'digan, Wales, a seaport town, municipal and formerly a parliamentary borough, capital of Cardiganshire, on both banks of the Teifi, about five miles from its mouth, and 200 miles west-northwest of London. The most noteworthy buildings are St. Mary's Church, upward of 200 years old; several dissenting chapels, all fine edifices; the shire hall, Cardigan county school, the national and board schools, etc. Cardigan Castle, famous in Welsh history, stands at the foot of an eminence near the bridge, two circular bastions only now remaining of it. Brick, tile, and pottery works are here, and two iron-foundries are employed chiefly in the manufacture of agricultural implements. The salmon fishery is extensively carried on in the neighborhood, and many of the male population are engaged in the mercantile navy. Pop. (1901) 3,511.

Car'diganshire, Wales, a maritime county, having Cardigan Bay on the west, and on the land side chiefly Carmarthen, Brecknock, Radnor, and Montgomery; area, 443,387 acres. The northern and eastern parts are mountainous, the southern and western districts more level. The soil in the vales is chiefly peat, capable of growing either grain or grass, by the application of lime; the higher grounds consist of a light sandy loam, and the mountains are composed chiefly of clay-slate. The agricultural produce is comparatively small. Cattle, sheep, and wool are the staple commodities. The chief crops are barley and oats, very little wheat being grown. The lead-mines still yield largely, and zinc is obtained in several places. The coast-line is long, and many of the male population are sailors and fishermen. The principal towns are Cardigan, the county capital, Aberystwith, Lampeter, Tregaron, and Aberaeron. There are few manufactures. Pop. (1901) 60,237.

Cardinal von Widdern, Georg, gä örg kär'dĕ näl fŏn vid'dĕrn, German military historian: b. Wollstein, 12 April 1841. He entered the army in 1859; was engaged in the war of 1866 and the Franco-Prussian war; and was professor at the military school at Neisse. He retired in 1890 and has since lived in Berlin. He wrote 'Der Rhein und die Rheinfeldzüge' (1869); 'Belgien, Nordfrankreich, der Niederhein und Holland als Kriegsfeld'; 'Die Russischen Kavallerie-divisionen und die Armeeoperationen in Balkanfeldzuge' (1878); 'Das 76 Armeekorps und die 7 Kavallerie-division während ihrer selbständigen Operationen in Moselfeldzug bli Metz' (1886); and a number of works on military tactics.

Cardinal-fish, a fish of the family *Cheilodipteridæ,* characterized by two dorsal fins, the anterior of which consists of from six to nine spines. The anal fin is short and has only two spines. The scales are large, and the color is often bright red, whence the name. They are especially abundant in the East Indian seas; but several species are found in America, one of which is known as "king of the mullets."

Cardinal Flower, the name commonly given to *Lobelia cardinalis,* because of its large, very showy, and intensely red flowers. It is a native of America, growing on the muddy banks of streams. Stems two to three feet high, the flowers in racemes. It admits of cultivation, and is much prized abroad, particularly in England.

Cardinal Grosbeak, or **Red**-bird, a large song-bird (*Cardinalis cardinalis*) of the finch family, very numerous in the southern United States. It is particularly distinguished for its loud, clear, sweet song, whose quality makes it popular as a cage-bird. It is a brilliantly red bird, with a vermilion head, its bill surrounded with a small band of glossy black, and having the long feathers of the crown erected into a comical crest. The female builds her nest, which is made of twigs, grasses, roots, etc., in bushes, and frequently breeds twice in a season, her bluish, brown-spotted eggs numbering about four. This bird is migratory only to a small degree, moving southward only along the northern limits of its range, and occasionally passing the winter in village gardens even in New England.

Cardinal Points, the four intersections of the horizon with the meridian and the prime vertical circle. They coincide with the four cardinal regions of the heavens, and are, of course, 90° distant from each other. The intermediate points are called collateral points. See COMPASS.

Cardinal Virtues, in morals, a name applied to those virtues to which all the rest are subordinate, or which comprehend all the others. The distribution of the virtues, which lies at the foundation of this notion, had its origin in the old Grecian philosophy, and the same number is found here as in the elements of nature. These principal virtues, as enumerated by Plato, are prudence, temperance, fortitude, and justice. The first three seem to relate to the duties of man toward himself, and to correspond with the triple division of the soul into the intellectual, the irrational (the seat of the sensual desires), and the seat of the affections. Justice either relates to our duties to others (God and men), or is the union of the three first virtues. This division appears to be peculiar to the old Pythagoreans. Aristotle divided them still farther. The Stoics, too, made the same division in their system of morals, and Cicero introduced it into his 'De Officiis.' Plotinus and many New Platonists divide the virtues into four classes — civil or political, philosophical or purifying, religious, and lastly, divine or pattern virtues: a division coinciding with the rest of his philosophical views. The influence of the ancient philosophers has made these cardinal virtues also a part of the Christian code. Some add to them the three "Christian virtues," faith, hope, and charity, and call the former philosophical. The imagination of artists has represented the cardinal virtues under sensible images. In modern times this division is regarded as useless in treating of ethics.

Cardinals, College of, an ecclesiastical body consisting of the highest dignitaries in the Roman Catholic Church. The name cardinal is applied to one of the principal advisers of the supreme pontiff as it is to the principal virtues or to the four points of the compass; etymologically cardinal is from *cardo,* linige, pivot, tenon, point around which anything turns. In the 11th century the term cardinal appears to have come into use to designate the "bishops collateral to the Pope," those whose sees are in the neighborhood of Rome, and to the clergy of the principal churches, parishes or *tituli* of the city; but probably *cardinalis* was at first said of a principal church rather than of its ministers. Nor was the term cardinal at first restricted to designation of churches and their clergy in Rome and its vicinity; for a long time, even down to 1585, date of the bull *Postquam* of Sixtus V., which forbade the application of the term to any but members of the sacred college, it was customary to call the ecclesiastics attached to mother-churches or to all cathedrals even, *cardinales.* The use of the word *cardo,* or its equivalent to express the relation of a bishop to his clergy and people, is very ancient: Saint Ignatius, bishop of Antioch (d. about 202), speaks of the bishop of a church as the pivot on which it turned. Till the issuance of the bull *Postquam* the title of cardinals was currently bestowed, but not by authority from the centre, upon the clergy of cathedral chapters in countries beyond the Alps, as those of the sees of Bourges, Metz, Cologne, Compostella, and other cities in Germany, Spain, and France; even in Italy the same usage was common; for it was with the name *Cardinalis* as with the name *Papa:* they both were originally applied to church dignitaries, to pastors, and church officers generally; later their application was restricted.

Ever since the reign of Nicolas II. the cardinals have possessed the privilege of electing the Pope. The decree of Pope Nicolas (1059) provides that on the death of the Pope the cardinal-bishops shall assemble in council and then the rest of the sacred college shall join them. In naming the Pope the college must take into account the choice of the clergy and people; only in case no Roman priest is found eligible in every way, shall the choice fall upon one that is not a Roman. In the 12th century the sacred college comprised seven cardinal-bishops of the "suburbicarian" churches, Ostia, Rufina, Porto, Albano, Tusculum, Sabina, and Palestrina; the cardinal-priests were 28, and were the rectors of as many churches in the city; there were 18 cardinal-deacons, of whom 14 belonged to the clerical staff of churches in the city, and 4 to the papal court or household. The members of the sacred college are yet styled by the titles of churches in the city, but are no longer in any sense ministers of those churches or parishes. And, like other church offices and church dignities the cardinalate became an object of ambition or of cupidity; popes bestowed the honor, princes and popes bestowed the dignity and the emoluments of episcopal and primatial sees, with the cardinalate annexed, upon minors and infants; thus, John de Medici was raised to the cardinalate at the age of 14 years, being already vested with a number of highest church dignities; and as late as 1740 a prince of the house of Bourbon was archbishop of Toledo and cardinal at the age of eight years.

According to the present constitution of the sacred college that body consists of 70 members — though very rarely indeed, if ever, are all the places filled. Of the 70 six are cardinal-bishops, and they are the ordinaries of sees in the neighborhood of Rome; 50 cardinal-priests, and 14 cardinal-deacons. In the year 1903, the cardinal-bishops numbered five, all Italians; the cardinal-priests 52, and of these four were Spaniards, seven were Frenchmen, one German, one Belgian, one Pole, one American, three British and Irish, two Austrians, two Hungarians, one Bohemian; the rest were Italians. There were eight cardinal-deacons, among them one German and one Spaniard; the rest were Italians.

The scarlet hat is distinctive or the cardinalitial dignity, and above the double cross in the arms of an archbishop who is a cardinal is the figure of the scarlet hat with its tasseled pendants. The gown of the cardinal is scarlet (*purpura,* commonly rendered purple, but our "purple" in the language of the ritual is violet *violaceus*). Hence "to receive the hat" means to be made a cardinal; and to aspire to the purple is to aim at the cardinalitial dignity. Etiquette requires that a cardinal be addressed as Eminence; in English usually "your eminence," and every cardinal is *eminentissimus.* A bishop or archbishop who is a cardinal, uses such a formula as the following in official instruments (the example is taken from the approbation of a book by an archbishop of Mechlin or Malines in Belgium) :

"Engelbert, by the divine mercy, cardinal-priest of the holy Roman Church, of the title of Saint Bartholomew in the Island, archbishop of Mechlin, primate of Belgium," etc.

Carding, the process which wool, cotton, flax, etc., are made to undergo previous to spinning, to lay the fibres all in one direction, and remove all foreign substances. The card formerly consisted of a number of iron teeth arranged in a piece of leather of various lengths, and the material was combed by hand. For many years this work has been done by machinery, the cards being fine, long teeth fixed on leather strips called card-clothing, which are arranged on a series of cylinders so placed that the material is carried from one to another, until removed by still another and much smaller cylinder called the doffer, from which it is stripped by a moving comb, and then by a series of rolls is delivered in the form of a ribbon into a can, when it is ready for the drawing-frame, on which it is prepared for spinning.

Car'dioid, a heart-shaped curve. It is produced by drawing a great number of chords from a single point of the circumference of a circle, prolonging each beyond the further crossing of the circumference to a distance equal to the diameter of the circle, and joining the free ends by a smooth curve. It is a special case of the limaçon, in which the extension of the chords is of any uniform length. The limaçon was invented by Pascal.

Carditis, kär-dï'tïs, an inflammation of the heart. The word is not now used, since more definite terms are accessible to designate particular types of inflammation. Thus myocarditis is an inflammation of the heart muscle, endocarditis, of the lining membrane, the endocardium; pericarditis, of the external membrane, the pericardium.

Cardona, kär-dō'nä, Spain, a town in the province of Barcelona, on the right bank of the Cardoner, 50 miles north-northwest of Barcelona. It has a castle. In its vicinity is a hill of rock salt 500 feet high, which affords inexhaustible supplies of salt. Pop. (1887) 3,708.

Cardoon', a garden vegetable (*Cynara cardunculus*), of the natural order *Compositæ*. It so closely resembles the artichoke (*Cynara scolymus*) that some botanists consider the two species merely as horticultural varieties. The plant, which is a native of southern Europe, is a thistle-like, tender perennial which is cultivated as an annual. Seed is usually sown in spring in a hotbed ; the young plants are transplanted to the rich soil of the garden about four feet apart each way, and kept cleanly cultivated until the leaves are nearly full grown, when the plant is tied up, covered with straw and earth, to blanch for two or more weeks. The thick leaf-stalks and the mid-ribs are the parts desired. In America the plant is not very popular except with the foreign population.

Cards, pieces of cardboard, oblong in shape, bearing certain figures and spots ; specifically, playing-cards used in various games of chance and skill. Playing-cards are probably an invention of the East, and some assert that

the Arabs or Saracens learned the use of cards from the gypsies and spread them in Europe. The course that card-playing took in its diffusion through Europe shows that it must have come from the East, for it was found in the eastern and southern countries before it was in the western. The historical traces of the use of cards are found earliest in Italy, then in Germany, France, and Spain. The first cards were painted, and the Italian cards of 1299 are found to have been so. The art of printing cards was discovered by the Germans between 1350 and 1360. The Germans have, moreover, made many changes in cards, both in the figures and the names. The lanzknechtsspiel, which is regarded as the first German game with cards, is a German invention. Of this game we find an imitation in France, in 1392, under the name of lansquenet, which continued to be played there till the time of Molière and Regnard, and perhaps still longer. The first certain trace of card-playing in France occurs in the year 1361, and Charles VI. is said to have amused himself with it during his sickness at the end of the 14th century. The modern figures are said to have been invented in France between 1430 and 1461. It has been said that cards were known in Spain as early as 1332 ; but what is certain is that card-playing must have become prevalent in the course of the century, seeing it was prohibited by the king of Castile, John I., in 1387. Mr. De la Rue, the most extensive manufacturer of cards in England, obtained in 1832 a patent for various improvements in manufacture. The figures on cards had been generally produced by the outlines first being printed from copper plates, and the colors then filled in by stencilling. Mr. De la Rue's process was to print them from colored types or blocks exactly in the same way as calico-printing, but all the colors being in oil.

As early as the 15th century an active trade in cards sprung up in German, and was chiefly carried on at Nuremberg, Augsburg, and Ulm, the demand from France, England, Italy, Spain, and other countries producing great prosperity among the manufacturers. In England the manufacture of cards flourished especially under Elizabeth. But no sooner had cards come to be generally used in Europe, than they were prohibited by several governments, partly from moral considerations, the first games being games of chance ; partly from considerations of political economy, as in England, where the importation of foreign cards was considered injurious to the prosperity of home manufacturers. The prohibition, however, only tended to increase the taste for cards. In England, under Richard III. and Henry VII., card-playing grew in favor. The latter monarch was very fond of the game, and his daughter Margaret was found playing cards by James IV. of Scotland, when he came to woo her. The popularity which cards gradually obtained in England may be inferred from the fact that political pamphlets under the name of "Bloody Games of Cards," and kindred titles, appeared at the commencement of the civil war against Charles I. One of the most striking publications of this kind was one in 1660 on the royal game of ombre. Pepys, in his 'Diary,' under the date of 17 Feb. 1667, states that on Sabbath evenings he found "the Queene, the Duchesse of York, and another or two, at cards, with the rooms full of ladies and great men.» The modern pack of cards, used in most of the familiar games, is 52 in number, containing four suits; clubs and spades (black), and hearts and diamonds (red). Thirteen cards compose a suit, consisting of king, queen, knave or jack, and ten pip-cards ranging in number of spots from one (ace) to ten. The figures of the four suits are supposed to have been originally intended for symbolical representations of the four great classes of men, and the names attached to these figures in England arose from a misapprehension of the names originally assigned to them. Thus, by the hearts are meant the gens de chœur (cœur), the choir-men or ecclesiastics, and hence these are called copas, or chalices, by the Spaniards; whose word espada, sword, indicating the nobility and warriors of the state, has been corrupted into the English spade. The clubs were originally trèfles (trefoil leaves), and denoted the peasantry; while the citizens and merchants were marked by the diamonds (carreaux, square tiles). The word knave (German, knab, boy), was used,.of course, in its older sense of servant, or attendant on the knights. The natural rank of the cards in each suit is, king highest, and so on down to ace lowest; but in many games this rank is varied, as in whist, where the ace is put highest of all, above the king; in écarté, where it is put between the knave and the ten; and in bézique, where it is made the highest, but where the ten is put between it and the king; in quadrille, the rank of some of the cards is variable in every hand. Sometimes the pack of cards is reduced to 32, by excluding the six, five, four, three, and two of each suit; it is then called a "piquet pack.» An immense variety of games may be placed with cards, some involving chance only, others combining chance and skill, the best furnishing intellectual amusement. There are round games, in which any number of persons may join, as poker, hearts, loo, etc.; games for four persons, as whist, in its different forms, and euchre; for two, as piquet, écarté, bézique, cribbage, and penuchle, closely resembling bézique, and at present much played in the United States; and there is one game, solitaire, played in many ways, at which a single person often finds ·both restful diversion and pleasant occupation for the mind.

Carducci, or **Carducho,** Bartolommeo, bär-tō-lóm-mä'ō kär-doo'chē or kär-doo'chō, Italian artist:· b. Florence, 1560; d. Madrid, 1608. He studied in Rome as a pupil of Zuochero, and later went to Spain, where he was a favorite of Philip III. Among his best works are 'Descent from the Cross,' and the 'Adoration of the Magi.'

Carducci, kär-dö'chi, **Giosuè,** Italian poet and philologist: b. Valdicastello, Tuscany, 27 July 1836; d. Bologna 15 Feb. 1907. He became professor of Italian literature in the University of Bologna in 1861. He had previously written essays on the history of literature; and a small volume of lyrics, 'Rimes' (1857). But his poetical genius was better shown in 'Inno a Satana' (1863); and 'Odi Barbare'; 'Nuove odi Barbare'; and 'Terze odi Barbare.' His employment of original poetic forms in the 'Odi Barbare' series aroused much literary discussion. Carducci also published 'Studii

leterarii' (1875); 'Bozetti critici e discorsi letterarii' (1875). In November 1906 he received the Nobel prize for literature.

Carducci, or **Carducho, Vincenzo,** vīn-chěnt'sō, Italian artist: b. Florence, 1568; d. Madrid, Spain, about 1638. He was a brother of the preceding and was patronized by both Philip III. and Philip IV. of Spain, where his most important works are to be found. He was the author of 'Dialogos de las excelencias de las pintura' (1633).

Carduus, kär'dū-ŭs, a genus of plants belonging to the natural order *Compositæ*, resembling the thistles, common along the Mediterranean. They are almost all troublesome weeds, though some of them are said to possess medical properties which make them useful in fevers. Among the more common of them are the arvensis (corn-thistle, way-thistle, or creeping-thistle), which has strong fleshy roots extending underground, and difficult of extirpation; and *C. lanceolatus* (spear-thistle), which both from its size and rough feeding, is a great robber of the soil, but from being only a biennial is more easily managed.

Card'well, John Henry, English clergyman: b. Sheffield, England, 20 June 1842. He was educated at Caius College, Cambridge, was ordained in the Established Church 1865, and was incumbent of St. Andrew's, Fulham, 1868–91. Since 1891 he has been rector of St. Anne's, Soho, London, and has been prominent in municipal politics and civic reforms. He has published 'The Story of a Charity School'; 'Two Centuries of Soho'; 'Men and Women of Soho, Famous and Infamous.'

Care Sunday, sometimes taken to be the Sunday immediately preceding Good Friday; but generally used to signify the fifth Sunday in Lent. Same as Passion Sunday.

Careen'ing, the process of heaving a vessel down on one side by applying a strong purchase to the masts, so that the bottom may be cleansed by breaming, that is removing by means of fire any growth which adheres to it, or any other necessary work effected. A half careen may take place when it is not possible to come at the bottom of the whole ship. Very few ships are now careened, more especially since the introduction of copper sheathing.

Carême, Marie Antoine, mä-rē än-twän kä räm, French cook: b. Paris, 8 June 1784; d. there, 12 Jan. 1833. He wrote 'Le pâtissier pittoresque' (2d ed. 1842); 'Le maître d'hotel française' (2d ed. 1842); 'Le pâtissier royal parisien' (1828); 'L'art de la Cuisine française aux XIX. siécle' (1833).

Caret, kärä', a turtle. See HAWKSBILL.

Carew, ka-roo', Richard, English antiquarian and poet: b. East Antony, Cornwall, 17 July 1555; d. there, 6 Nov. 1620. He was a member of the House of Commons, high sheriff of Cornwall in 1586, and the author of a much valued 'Survey of Cornwall' (1602), and an English translation of a portion of Tasso's 'Jerusalem Delivered.'

Carew, Thomas, English poet; b. 1598; d. 1639. He was educated at Corpus Christi College, Oxford. Cultivating polite literature in the midst of a life of affluence and gaiety,·he was the subject of much eulogy by Ben Jonson,

Davenant, and other writers of the period. In him was exhibited the not unusual transformation of the courtly and libertine fine gentleman into the repentant devotee. Carew is coupled with Waller as one of the improvers of English versification. The first collection of his poems was printed in 1640, and the last in 1824. His elegant masque of 'Cœlum Britannicum' was printed both in the early edition and separately in 1651, and the whole were included in Chalmers' 'British Poets.' Carew was much studied by Pope, and Dr. Percy also assisted to restore him to a portion of the favor which he has come to be regarded. Specimens both of the sublime and the pathetic may be found in his works; the former in his admirable masque, and the latter in his epitaph on Lady Mary Villiers.

Carex, kār'ĕks, a genus of plants, belonging to the natural order *Cyperaceæ*, or sedges, and containing numerous species, which are found in all parts of the world where vegetation can exist, on the driest upland as well as the wettest marsh. The plants are perennial, often creeping, with sharp-keeled leaves and solid triangular stems. The flowers are without perianth and unisexual, being grouped in spikelets. The male flowers have usually three stamens, the female having a single style with three stigmas. The number of known species is above 2,500, and of these the United States has nearly 300. Hardly any of them have any agricultural value, but *C. arenaria*, the sand-sedge, is of use in binding the sand on many sea-shores. In parts of the United States a poor quality of hay is made from some of the sedges. *C. japonica variegata* is an elegant variety cultivated by florists.

Ca'rey, Henry, English composer and poet: b. London, 1696; d. there, 1743. He is supposed to have been a natural son of George Saville, Marquis of Halifax. His first instructor in music was a German, named Linnert, but he was afterward more thoroughly trained under Roseingrave and Geminiani. He was inexhaustible in the invention of new, pleasing, and often deeply pathetic melodies, to which he not unfrequently furnished the words. His 'Sally in Our Alley' is still a well-known song. He has also been said to be the author of 'God Save the King,' but this appears to be doubtful. He supported himself by public and private teaching, but his whole life was a continued struggle with poverty, and it has been said that at last, in a fit of despair, he committed suicide (1743). His collected songs were published in 1740. Among other works are: 'Teraminta' (1732) and other operas; 'Chrononhotonthologos,' "the most tragical tragedy ever yet tragedized" (1734), a burlesque; 'The Wonder, or An Honest Yorkshireman' (1735); and 'The Dragon of Wantley' (1737). His dramatic works were published together in 1743.

Carey, Henry Charles, American political economist: b. Philadelphia, 15 Dec. 1793; d. there, 13 Oct. 1879. He was the eldest son of Mathew Carey, and in 1814 became a partner in his father's bookselling and publishing firm, where he continued until 1835. In that year he published an essay on 'The Rate of Wages,' which he afterward expanded into 'The Principles of Political Economy' (1837-40). His other important works are: 'The Credit Sys-

tem in France, Great Britain, and the United States' (1838); 'The Past, the Present, and the Future' (1848); 'The Principles of Social Science' (1858-9); 'Letters on Political Economy' (1860 and 1865); 'The Unity of Law' (1872). Originally a free-trader, he became an advocate of protection on the ground of temporary expediency: held that the growth of population was self-regulating; and was opposed to the theories of Ricardo and others on the law of diminished returns from the soil and on rent. He was also opposed to any arrangement on the subject of international copyright. Some of his works have been translated into other languages, and his writings have had considerable influence on economical speculation.

Carey, James F., American socialist leader: b. Haverhill, Mass., 19 Aug. 1867. He received a common school education and learned the shoemaking trade. In 1895 he was chairman of a convention at Boston, which amalgamated three national organizations of shoemakers into one union. In 1894 he was one of the leaders in the agitation of the unemployed on Boston Common, and the governor appointed him a commissioner of the unemployed, but he was not confirmed. He was later elected president of the Haverhill common council. In 1898, 1899, and 1900 he was elected to the Massachusetts House of Representatives, twice defeating a combination of the Democratic and Republican parties. He was the first Socialist ever elected to political office in New England.

Carey, Mathew, Irish writer and bookseller: b. Dublin, 28 Jan. 1760; d. Philadelphia, 16 Sept. 1839. After a varied experience, including imprisonment for offending publications, he came to the United States in 1784, and in Philadelphia began to publish the *Pennsylvania Herald*. A few years later he became a bookseller, and an extensive publisher. The best known of his political writings was his 'Olive Branch' (1814). It was an effort to promote harmony among political parties during the War of 1812. It passed through 10 editions. In 1819 he published his 'Irish Vindications,' and in 1822, 'Essays on Political Economy.'

Ca'rey, Rosa Nouchette, English novelist: b. London. She began writing novels in 1868, and her fictions, in which the literary element is not a very strong feature, have been very popular with the average, uncritical reader who demands only to be entertained and cares little or nothing for literary style. They include 'Wee Wifie' (1869); 'Nellie's Memories' (1868); 'Barbara Heathcote's Trial' (1871); 'Robert Ord's Atonement' (1873); 'Wooed and Married' (1875); 'Heriot's Choice' (1879); 'Queenie's Whim' (1881); 'Mary St. John' (1882); 'Not Like Other Girls' (1884); 'For Lilias' (1885); 'Uncle Max' (1887); 'Only the Governess' (1888); 'Basil Lyndhurst' (1889); 'Lover or Friend' (1890); 'Sir Godfrey's Grand-daughters' (1892); 'Men Must Work' (1892); 'The Old, Old Story' (1894); 'Mrs. Romney' (1894); 'The Mistress of Brae Farm' (1896); 'Other People's Lives' (1897); 'Mollie's Prince' (1898); 'Twelve Notable Good Women'; 'My Lady Frivol' (1899); 'Rue with a Difference'; 'Life's Trivial Round' (1900); 'Herb of Grace' (1901); 'The Highway of Fate' (1902).

Carey, William, English Orientalist and missionary: b. Paulerspury, Northamptonshire, 17 Aug. 1761; d. Serampore, India, 9 June 1834. He was early apprenticed to a shoemaker, and continued to work at his trade till he was 24. With what assistance he could procure he acquired Latin, Greek, and Hebrew, and studied theology. In 1786 he became pastor of a Baptist congregation at Moulton, and in 1787 was appointed to a similar situation in Leicester. In 1793 he sailed for the East Indies as a Baptist missionary, but became overseer of an indigo factory. He studied languages and natural history, and collected a rich store of Oriental knowledge. In 1800, in conjunction with Marshman, Ward, and others, he founded the missionary college at Serampore; the year following he became professor of Sanskrit, Bengali, and Mahratta at the newly erected Fort William College, Calcutta. In Serampore he had a printing-press for more than 40 different Indian languages, and issued various translations of the Scriptures. His first work was a Mahratta Grammar. It was followed by other works, including a Bengali 'Lexicon,' in which he was assisted by Felix Carey, his son. Under his direction the whole Bible was translated into 6, and the New Testament into 21 languages or dialects of Hindustan; and considerable progress was made with the translation of the whole Scriptures into Chinese. He also edited Shroeder's Lexicon of the Thibetan language, and Roxburgh's 'Flora Indica,' in which a genus of plants which he discovered is named after him, Careya. He established an agricultural society at Calcutta, and a botanical garden, at his own expense, at Serampore. See his 'Life' by Dr. G. Smith (1885).

Cargill, kär'gĭl, Donald, Scotch covenanting preacher: b. Rattray, Perthshire, about 1619; d. Edinburgh, 27 July 1681. He was educated at Aberdeen and St. Andrews, and became minister of the Barony Church in Glasgow in 1655. At the Restoration he refused to accept collation from the archbishop, and was exiled beyond the Tay. In 1679 he took part in the battle of Bothwell Bridge, where he was wounded, but succeeded in escaping to Holland. In 1680 he published, along with Richard Cameron, the 'Sanquhar Declaration.' In September of the same year he formally excommunicated King Charles II., Duke of York, and other great personages. After avoiding pursuit for several months, in May 1681, he was captured, and at Edinburgh tried and sentenced, and 27 July was beheaded.

Car'hart, Henry Smith, American scientist: b. Coeymans, N. Y., 27 March 1844. He was graduated at Wesleyan University in 1869, and since then has taught physics and chemistry. Since 1886 he has been professor of physics at the University of Michigan. He has written 'Primary Batteries'; 'University Physics'; 'Electrical Measurements'; and other books.

Carheil, Étienne de, ä-tē-ĕn dĕ kä-rä-ē, French Jesuit missionary in North America: d. after 1721. He labored for more than half a century among the Canadian Hurons and Iroquois, and was long stationed at Michilimachinac.

Ca'ria, in ancient geography, the country forming the southwest corner of Asia Minor,

bounded on the north by Lydia or Mæonia, from which it was separated by the Mæander; on the east by Phrygia, on the southeast by Lycia, and on the south and west by the Mediterranean. Some confusion, however, exists in regard to its boundaries. Part of it was settled by Greek colonies of Ionians and Dorians, who dispossessed the original inhabitants. It was included in the dominions of Crœsus, king of Lydia, and on his overthrow by Cyrus was transferred to the Persian monarchy, under whose protection a dynasty of Carian princes was established. Halicarnassus was the residence of these sovereigns, among whom were the two celebrated queens, the first and second Artemisia. The progress of the Roman conquests ultimately extinguished the independence of Caria, and about 129 B.C. it was incorporated in the Roman province of Asia.

Cariaco, kä-rē-ä'kō, Venezuela, a seaport in the state of Bermudez, situated to the east of the Gulf of Cariaco, near the mouth of a river of the same name, adjoining a large plain, covered with plantations. Its trade is chiefly in cotton and sugar. The Gulf of Cariaco is 38 miles long, from 5 to 10 broad, from 80 to 100 fathoms deep, surrounded by lofty mountains. Pop. 7,000.

Cariacou, kär'ĭ ä koo, the name given to American deer of the genus Cariacus, found in all parts of North America up to lat. 43° N. It is smaller than the common stag, and its color varies with the seasons from reddish-brown to slaty-blue.

Cariama, sä-rē-ä'ma, a bird (Cariama cristata), a native of Brazil and Paraguay, where its loud scream is a familiar sound on the campos, and where it is domesticated and trained to guard fowls. With an allied Argentine bird (Chunga burmeisteri) it constitutes a family (Cariamidæ) of great zoological interest, combining as it does characters of the bustards, caracara eagles, and cranes, with each of which it has been at times associated.

Carib, kär'ĭb, a native American race which attained its highest development in the West Indies. Originating in the valley of the Orinoco, this race spread along the coasts, northward and southward, to a great distance, and especially from island to island of the Lesser and Greater Antilles and the Bahamas. At the time of the discovery of America its language was spoken, with dialectic variations, from the coast of Florida to lower Brazil,— wherever large canoes could carry the swarming, warlike tribes. The Caribs were the Vikings of South America. The race name survives in "Caribbean" Sea, "Caribbee" Islands, the word "cannibal," etc.; the race itself is still well represented at various points in South America. In the West Indies, however, the large native population disappeared rapidly after the Spanish conquest, Caribs and other tribes of the same stock (Arawaks, Lucayos, Boriqueños, etc.) either succumbing under the new conditions or losing their distinctive characteristics by blending with Europeans and Africans. Surviving groups of West Indian Caribs may be studied to-day in the island of Dominica. A few remained in Martinique and St. Vincent up to the time of the volcanic eruptions in 1902. Great Britain deported 5,000

CARIBBEAN SEA

Caribs from St. Vincent to the island of Ruatan in the Gulf of Honduras in 1796; thence they migrated to the Central American coast, where their numerous descendants have become a not inconsiderable element in the population of the mainland. In the 'Proceedings of the American Association for the Advancement of Science' (1902, Vol. LI.), Mr. J. Walter Fewkes of the Bureau of American Ethnology calls attention to the different characteristics which the Caribs displayed in different circumstances and localities. Thus the natives in the Bahamas, Cuba, Haiti, and Porto Rico were mild, agricultural people who had lost in vigor, while gaining a rudimentary knowledge of the arts of peace, by their sedentary life. On the other hand, constant incursions from the home of the race (the Orinoco region in Venezuela) kept alive the savage customs and ferocious spirit of the Caribs of the Lesser Antilles. Such incursions took place even after the date of the Spanish settlements. The houses of the more peaceful Carib communities did not differ greatly from those of the peasantry in the same regions at the present time. In lieu of clothing, Carib men and girls covered their bodies, as well as their faces, with paint, to protect them from the bites of insects and the heat of the sun. A woven cloth of palm fibre, called *nagua*,— a breech-cloth with long ends,— was worn by the chiefs and the married women. For purposes of decoration, and to distinguish members of one family or community from those of another, designs of animals and plants were painted on the body. Their social organization closely resembled that of the North American Indians, the unit of organization being the clan, ruled by a *cacique* (chief). Combinations were sometimes formed by a number of caciques for mutual defense, and extensive territories were subjected to the control of the more ambitious leaders. Among the insignia of the cacique's rank were the gold disk called *guarim*, worn on his breast, and a stone amulet tied to his forehead. His numerous wives were practically slaves. *Ex officio*, he was a member of the priesthood. Columbus at first received the impression that the Caribs lacked spiritual insight; longer sojourn among them, however, convinced him that they worshipped many supernatural beings whom they represented by idols, called *zemis;* they had temples for this purpose, in which rude idols were set up to be consulted as oracles by the priests. It is probable that belief in a future life, although not universally held, as some authorities assert, was generally taught by the priests; and it is quite certain that the latter possessed great influence, being physicians to the people as well as ministers to the *zemis*.

Like other savage races of the region from which they came, the Caribs were anthropophagi; yet the evil prominence given to them through the coining of the word *cannibal* (a Latinized form of *Carib*) is not wholly merited. The discoverers, finding a great number of human skulls in the Carib houses, jumped to the conclusion that each skull was the trophy of some revolting feast. In point of fact, the Caribs, being ancestor-worshippers, preserved these relics in honor of defunct members of their family.

MARRION WILCOX,
Authority on Latin-America.

Caribbean (kăr-ĭ-bē'ạn) Sea, a part of the Atlantic Ocean occupying a basin 750,000 square miles in area, bounded by South and Central America, and the Greater and Lesser Antilles. Its perimeter is wholly mountainous. Mountain folds (continued in submarine ridges from the Greater Antilles to Honduras) mark its limits on the north and south; but the volcanic chain of the Lesser Antilles rises on the east, and the volcanoes of Central America in the remote past formed a wall separating it from the Pacific on the west. Separating it from the Atlantic are steep submarine ridges, of which the Lesser Antilles are the summits. A portion of the broad equatorial stream, which flows from east to west, from the coast of Africa to that of Brazil, enters the Caribbean between the islands at the southern end of the Antillean chain: the waters of this sea, therefore, move from east to west and northwest, and seek an exit through the Yucatan Channel. But the latter is too small to allow an outflow equal to the inflow into the Caribbean; so that, after the trades have forced the equatorial water into the Caribbean basin, it must remain there a considerable length of time, thus becoming superheated, before it passes into the Gulf of Mexico, where, owing to similar differences between the rate of inflow and outflow, the water becomes still more superheated before passing through the Florida Straits as the Gulf Stream. The main westerly current in the Caribbean, after passing through the Banks Strait, between the Mosquito Reef and Jamaica, is joined by the current of the Windward Channel. The trade-winds, blowing with a steady velocity across the Caribbean region, from east to west, make the surface of this sea much rougher than that of the Gulf of Mexico; they mitigate the tropical heat at all points where their influence is felt; and the moisture they bring from the Atlantic is precipitated in the form of abundant rains against the eastern slopes of the mountains, both on the islands and the mainland. Hence the distinction between "windward" and "leeward" regions, insisted upon especially in the West Indies. The Gulf of Mexico, sheltered behind the Antilles and Yucatan, is practically a "leeward" expanse; but the summer climate of Texas and the great plains is somewhat modified by Caribbean trade-winds.

Recent studies of the Caribbean basin have disclosed its interesting submarine topography — "a configuration which, if it could be seen, would be as picturesque in relief as the Alps or Himalayas. Nowhere can such contrasts of relief be found within short distances. Some deeps vie in profundity with the altitudes of the near-by Andes. . . . Some of the depressions, like the Bartlett Deep, are narrow troughs, only a few miles in width, but hundreds of miles in length, three miles in depth, and bordered by steep precipices. . . . There are long ridges beneath the waters, which, if elevated, would stand up like islands of to-day. . . . Again, vast areas are underlain by shallow banks . . . often approaching the surface of the water, like that extending from Jamaica to Honduras. . . . The greater islands and the mainlands are bordered in places by submerged shelves." (From 'Cuba and Porto Rico': see authorities below.) All the islands are, then, to be regarded, from a physiographic point of view, as the "tops of a varied configuration which has its greatest relief beneath the sea⁹; and some of these submarine valleys and mountains have yielded a surprising number of animal forms previously unknown. Dredgings in depths of over 2,000 fathoms have brought to light new species of crustacea, and forms resembling the fossils of past geological epochs are taken alive in those profound marine valleys. Many phosphorescent creatures are found; in certain places "dense forests of pentacrini undulate on the bottom like aquatic plants"; on the submerged banks and in the shallows, coral polyps and mollusks are employed as actively now as ever, in extracting the lime carried in solution by the sea-water, to build its shells and corals which are so large a part of the rock-making material in all this region, from Yucatan to Porto Rico. The most important marine highways for Caribbean commerce are those on the north: the Windward, Anegada, and Mona passages, and the Yucatan Channel. (For the origin of the name, see CARIBS.) Consult: Agassiz, 'The Gulf Stream' (in annual report Smithsonian Inst. to July 1891, Washington 1893); Hill, of United States Geological Survey, 'Cuba and Porto Rico' (1898).

MARRION WILCOX,
Authority on Latin-America.

Caribbee, kă-rĭ-bē', or **St. Lucia Bark,** a bark sometimes substituted for cinchona (q.v.), though not containing its characteristic alkaloid. It is procured from the *Exostemma Caribæum,* a tree growing in the West Indies. This bark is in convex fragments, covered with a yellow epidermis, and has a very bitter taste and very faint smell.

Caribbee (kăr'ĭ bē) **Islands,** a name commonly given to that portion of the chain of Lesser Antilles between the Virgin and South American groups. See ANTILLES.

Caribe, any of a group of small, robust, voracious fishes, often of singular form, and allied in structure to salmon, which abound in South American tropical rivers. They have numerous teeth, well fitted to biting out pieces of flesh, and instantly seize upon any disabled or soft-bodied creature in the water, and devour it or worry it. Hook-and-line fishing is almost useless where these little bandits are numerous, as they rob the hooks of bait, or tear to pieces anything caught before it can be lifted out of their reach. They will even attack and badly wound human bathers. One of the best known and most dreaded is the piraya of the Amazon, which is said to come in crowds wherever blood is shed in the water. These fishes constitute the subfamily *Serrasalmoninæ,* of the family *Characinidæ,* and are intermediate between the cyprinoids and the salmonoids. A distinguishing characteristic is the fact that the abdomen is serrated with sharp spines.

Caribou, kă-rĭ-boo', the name of two species of reindeer found in Canada. One of these, *Rangifer grœnlandicus,* known as the barren ground caribou, inhabits the barren country in the north of British North America, extending also into Greenland. In color it is reddish-brown above and white below in summer, but the winter coat is whiter and denser. It migrates northward in summer, but on the approach of winter it travels south to the forest country. The other species, the woodland caribou (*R. caribou*), is larger, but has smaller and less

branched horns. It inhabits the wooded country to the south of the places frequented by the above species. It is of a general dun-gray color, and the height at the shoulder is about three and a half feet. It is rather shy, and its fleetness enables it readily to distance those in pursuit. Its food consists mainly of lichens, but other vegetable products are also eaten.

Caribou, Maine, town in Aroostook County, 200 miles north of Bangor, on the Canadian P. R.R. It has two banks, a State fish hatchery, court-house, numerous churches and public schools. Its principal products are lumber, starch and potatoes. About 40 per cent of the population is French. Pop. (1900) 4,758.

Car'ica (from Caria, a district of Asia Minor, whence it was supposed to have come), a genus of plants, the typical one of the order of Papayads (*Papayaceæ*). It contains about 10 species, all natives of tropical America. They are small trees without branches, and with large, variously lobed leaves, resembling those of some kinds of palm. They exude an acrid, milky juice when wounded. The most remarkable species is the *C. papaya,* the Papaw-tree, a small tree, seldom above 20 feet high, with a stem about a foot in diameter, tapering gradually to the top, where it is about four or five inches. The fruit is of a dingy orange-yellow color, oblong, about 10 inches long by three or four broad. The ripe fruit is made into sauce or preserved in sugar, and the juice of the unripe fruit is used to remove freckles. The leaves are employed as a substitute for soap. *C. digitata,* a tree which grows in Brazil, where it is called chamburu, is regarded almost with superstitious awe as a deadly poison. For the North American species, see PAPAW.

Caricature and Caricaturists. The two great modern cartoonists have been Sir John Tenniel and Thomas Nast, the former being to all Europe what the latter was to all America, and in connection with these two can be said all that need be said of caricaturists of our time. True, Nast was practically alone in his field, and he did not work as long as did Tenniel, still, to judge him at his best, though the period was comparatively short, he stood high as a picture-maker of that class. Nast was as brave as his subject, Tweed, was crooked, and the two furnished the best series of caricatures by far that have ever been seen in this, or, it might be said, in any other country. Nast, however, was not the draughtsman that Tenniel was, but what he lacked in artistic finish, he made up in power and force of expression.

Since the day of Tenniel and Nast, caricaturing seems to have fallen into less virile hands. Tenniel and Nast each drew a caricature once a week, while now caricaturists draw seven or eight in that time. Formerly the best caricaturists were employed on the weekly papers, while now the better class are employed on the great dailies. But the times have brought this about, not necessarily the caricaturists. Workingmen have no time to read, and a picture which may tell all at a glance means more to them than the ablest editorial that the combined editors of the country could write. A picture can be understood by all, whereas we have many languages and we speak but few, and read fewer. Words we forget, but pictures stay, filed away in our minds, and we refer to them on a moment's notice. Every day, as the pace quickens, and the press for time increases, we find our time for reading diminishes, thus the biograph excels the finest description ever written of the same thing.

We sometimes see so-called comic art, which is not comic, and called caricatures which are not true caricatures. A man who draws a picture of a man with a broad grin and winking with one eye, or cross-eyed, or perhaps a man standing with one foot on his other toe, is not necessarily a caricaturist any more than is the man who puts big feet and big noses on every person he draws. A young caricaturist who had submitted a picture to a critic for his judgment and had received a severe lecture on the bad drawing it displayed, made an attempt to hide behind the fact that it was a caricature, and therefore shouldn't be considered as the critic was considering it. Whereupon he replied: "No, never try to hide behind that. Remember one thing: that poor drawing is not caricature, and another, that all the bad artists in the country are not caricaturists. On the contrary, those who exaggerate the salient features must draw them even better, as more attention is called to a big nose or large ears if they are made conspicuously large, than would be the case otherwise."

But there is something else that a successful caricaturist must possess. That one thing, whatever it may be called, is of more importance than the art of drawing properly, and is a certain force of character, or of individuality which at once suggests strength of purpose and power. It can convey the feeling of sadness, of brute force, or of excruciating mirth, yet many very fine draughtsmen who are styled caricaturists, never draw with that spirit predominant, and without it their productions are not true caricatures.

Thus, in trying to be caricaturists, such men are robbed of the chance of being serious illustrators, in which work they might succeed; and they never succeed as caricaturists.

There are three kinds of good caricatures: First, the strong, powerful, almost brutal; second, the humorous, the one instantly compelling laughter; and last, but not the least in effect, the pathetic; a picture capable of causing men to weep. The most effective are the powerful and the pathetic. The humorous is indeed attractive, if not overdone, but you soon forget its meaning. It can attack any and all things, from the weather to the President, without offense. But the most effective caricature is one that the subject of which would rather you would not print. Probably none can be made more powerful than the pathetic when it is timed and tempered just right, as its appeal to the sympathy is the surest way to the emotions. No caricaturist ever drew a caricature that would cause people to shed tears on seeing it, unless the artist shed tears when he drew it, any more than one could draw an angry political boss unless at the time of drawing one wore the same angry and hateful expression on one's own face. So with the humorist. One must wear a broad smile when he draws a man laughing, unless one is drawing him from life; and unless one is smiling when drawing smiling people, the subjects will seem to look and laugh only in mechanical fashion.

If the caricaturist is strong enough in his line to be called one, the first person he wins is himself. Once he has settled in his own mind that he is working for a just cause, it will be noticed at once that his work improves, and if he continues to study and put his heart and soul into it, others will be converted and he will acquire a following. If a cartoonist in his politics keeps side by side with his pictures he will be much more of a caricaturist than one who will work on a Democratic paper one day and the next on the Republican side. A young man in starting out should study and choose for himself and in that way he will find that he can lend more power and force to his work. It would be hard to imagine Thomas Nast being in private life a sympathizer with Tweed. The difficulty with caricaturists is that they are sometimes like the politician after the election, when he says: "No wonder the other side won; 'they bought us.'" What interest could one take outside of the mechanical reproduction if one knew that the caricaturist who had one year drawn powerful caricatures for one party would turn around the next year and work for the opposition. The power of a caricature becomes power only when the reader of the picture is convinced that that which is represented in the picture really did happen, and that cannot be done by a caricaturist if one day he is with the poor, and the next day with the rich; or in the same relation with any case that comes up.

The late John J. Ingalls said that the caricature did harm that good might follow. Caricatures, to be effective, should be founded on fragments of truth, though you are permitted to dig below the frost line. Without truth at the bottom they are powerless, and with truth at the bottom they are powerful and everlasting. Though Tweed, the man, is dead, Tweed, in the caricature, still lives, a prisoner in stripes, with ball and chain to his leg. A good caricature may be called an exaggeration of the truth. In these times there are great opportunities for the cartoonist. The billionaire will have to deal kindly and justly with his fellowmen, or else he will be more of a target than ever before, but the honest man need never fear a caricature; on the contrary, he can laugh and go about his business, and if he is attacked, the attacks will react in his favor. But they cannot be recommended as the steady diet for a dishonest person, since whether he has conscience or not, if they don't bring him to justice they will give him many a sleepless night.

Bibliography.— Flögel, 'Geschichte des Grotesk-Komischen' (1778); Champfleury, 'Histoire général de la caricature' (1865–80); Wright, 'History of Caricature and Grotesque' (1875); Parton, 'Caricature and Other Comic Arts' (1877); Grand Cartaret, 'Les moeurs et la caricature en Allemagne, en Aubriche et en Suisse' (1885); Everitt, 'English Caricaturists of the 19th Century' (1886).

HOMER DAVENPORT,
New York World.

Caries, kăr′ĭ-ēz, a form of local death in bone, due to a variety of agents. Caries is usually distinguished from necrosis, another type of local death in bone, by the slower disintegration of the bone affected by the carious process. Necrosis usually results in the death of large pieces of bone, with the formation of sequestra.

Caries is a gradual disintegration without sequestration. Caries is the result of inflammation of the softer tissues in the bone spaces, and is due usually to some definite form of irritant. It may be that of a gas, such as chlorine, or phosphorus, the latter causing in match-workers a form of caries of the jaw; but bacteria of tuberculosis and syphilis are the most frequent causes. Tuberculous caries is the most frequent form of the disease. See HIP JOINT DISEASE; TUBERCULOSIS OF BONE. For caries of the teeth, see TEETH.

Carigara, kä-rē-gä′rạ, Philippines, a town of the province of Leyte, situated on the north coast of the island, 22 miles west of Tacloban. It has a harbor formed by a bight extending 11 miles inland, carries on a considerable coast trade, and is an important hemp port. Pop. 14,000.

Carignano, kä-rēn-yä′nō, Italy, a city in the province of Turin, 11 miles south of the latter on the left bank of the Po. It is surrounded by old walls, and has a handsome square ornamented with arcades, some fine churches, some silk-spinning mills, and sugar-refineries. From this town is named a branch of the house of Savoy. Pop. 7,000.

Carillon, kä-rē-yŏn, a kind of chime, played either by hand or clockwork on a number of bells, forming a complete series or scale of tones or semi-tones, like those of the organ or harpsichord.

Carimata, kä-rē-mä′tạ, or Karimata, a name applied to the strait between Borneo and Billiton; also to a cluster of a hundred islets and reefs (area, 57 square miles; pop. 500) in that strait; and lastly, to the principal member of the group, whose highest point reaches 2,600 feet.

Carina′tæ, the name given by Merrem to one of the primary divisions of birds, variously ranked as an order (Huxley), a subclass (most modern ornithologists) an intermediate division (Gadow), or split up and distributed (Stejneger). The sternum is provided with a median keel or carina for the attachment of the chief muscles of flight. In a few flightless members, as the dodo, the keel has become abortive, and a few birds not generally recognized as belonging to the Carinatæ have keeled sterna, but are distinguished by other characters, such as the possession of a lizard-like tail, or a dromæognathous palate. The vast majority of living birds are carinate.

Carini, kä-rē′nē, Italy, a city in the island of Sicily, 11 miles northwest of Palermo. It is beautifully situated four miles from the sea, in a fertile region. It has a Gothic castle of the 14th century. Fishing is the chief occupation. The district produces much corn and wine. Pop. about 14,000.

Carin′thia (Ger. KÄRNTHEN), a duchy or province of Austria, between lat. 46° 24′ and 47° 7′ N., and lon. 12° 35′ and 15° 10′ E., bounded on the north by Salzburg and Styria, on the east by Styria, on the south by Carniola, and on the west by Italy and Tyrol; area, 3,986 square miles. It is extremely mountainous, generally sterile, and one of the most thinly populated provinces of Austria. The arable land does not exceed 290,000 acres, but there are some fertile valleys, and a considerable extent

of rich pasture land. It has several rivers and lakes. Of the former the principal is the Drave. All of them abound with fish. The country does not yield corn enough for the consumption of the inhabitants, who import the deficiency from Hungary. The cereals most extensively cultivated are rye and oats. Some wine is produced in Lower Carinthia, but it is of inferior quality. Cattle, sheep, and horses are raised in considerable numbers, but the mines of Carinthia are the main sources of its wealth. The chief of these are lead, iron, and calamine. Various kinds of gems are met with. Its operative industry is chiefly confined to the working of its metallic ores, though there are also manufactories of woolens, cottons, silk stuffs, etc., most of which are in Klagenfurt, the capital. The principal towns are Klagenfurt and Villach. Carinthia formed part of the empire of Charlemagne, and afterward belonged to the dukes of Friuli. It subsequently passed through various hands, and finally became an appendage of the Austrian crown in 1321. In 1809 it was annexed to the empire of Napoleon, but was restored to Austria in 1814. Nearly all the inhabitants are Roman Catholics. Pop. (1900) 367,344.

Cari′nus, Marcus Aurelius, Roman emperor: d. 285 A.D. He was the elder of the two sons of the Roman emperor Carus, who conjointly succeeded to the throne on the death of their father, 284 A.D. His brother was supposed to have been murdered on his return from the East, and Carinus, ruling alone, became one of the most profligate and cruel of the Roman emperors. The soldiers having rebelled, and proclaimed Diocletian emperor, Carinus collected the troops that were in Italy and marched into Mœsia to meet Diocletian, and quell the revolt. A decisive battle was fought near Margus, in which Carinus gained the victory, but in the moment of triumph he was slain by one of his own officers, whom the vices of the emperor had outraged.

Caripe, kä-rē′pä, Venezuela, a town situated in a valley on the northern part of the province of Bermudez. It was formerly the headquarters of the Capuchins, and contains the ruins of their church cloister. In the vicinity are the large caves, described by Humboldt, in which lives the bird known as guacharo, a kind of nighthawk. Pop. about 4,000.

Carisbrooke, kăr′ĭs-brúk, England, a village in Hampshire, pleasantly situated at the foot of a hill, near the centre of the Isle of Wight, and overlooked by the ruins of its ancient castle, where Charles I. was imprisoned 13 months, previous to his trial and execution. The castle and grounds cover 20 acres. The parish church of St. Mary is a venerable structure, with a fine tower containing a chime of bells. It was formerly attached to a Benedictine priory founded under William the Conqueror, but the priory no longer exists. In 1859 a Roman villa was discovered at Carisbrooke, and the place seems to have been a fortress at the time of the Roman occupation. Pop. about 9,000.

Carissimi, Giacomo, jä′kō-mō kä-rēs′sē-mē, Italian composer: b. Marino, 1604; d. Rome, 12 Jan. 1674. He became musical director of the church of St. Apollinaris in Rome in 1628, and continued in that position until his death. He wrote many oratorios, cantatas, and notets, and has been praised for his characteristic expression of feeling, and his easy, flowing style. He deserves most honor for the improvement of the recitative, having given it a more expressive and natural language, and he greatly developed the sacred cantata. His oratorio 'Jonah' has been revived in recent times. It anticipates in the descriptive passages some of the effects since elaborated by the modern classical composers, and it is altogether distinguished by freedom, boldness, and striking antiphonal imitations.

Carl, William C., American organist: b. Bloomfield, N. J., 2 March 1865. He is a member of the American Guild of Organists, a director of the Guilmant Organ School, New York, and organist of the First Presbyterian Church there. He has published 'Several Songs and Organ Arrangements' (1892); 'Masterpieces for the Organ' (1898); 'Thirty Postludes for the Organ' (1900).

Carlén, kär-län', Emilia Smith Flygare, Swedish novelist: b. Strömstad, 8 Aug. 1807; d. Stockholm, 5 Feb. 1892. In 1838 she published her first novel, 'Waldemar Klein,' and among the best of her subsequent works are the 'Professor' (1840); 'A Year' (1846); 'The Brother's Bet'; and 'The Guardian' (1851). Several of her novels have been translated into English. In 1827 she married a physician named Flygare, and in 1841, after the death of her first husband, she married J. G. Carlén (q.v.), a lawyer and poet. In 1878 she published a volume of 'Reminiscences of Swedish Literary Life.' She had clear insight into the conditions of human life, especially of life in the middle class, and she describes it with admirable fidelity.

Carlén, Johan Gabriel, yō'hän gä'brē ĕl, Swedish poet and romancer: b. Westgotland, Sweden, 9 July 1814; d. Stockholm, 6 July 1875. He was the second husband of Emilia Carlén (q.v.), and was the author of 'Romanser Svenska Volklifet' ('Romances of Swedish Life') (1840); etc.

Carleton, kärl'tŏn, Guy, first Lord Dorchester, British General and Colonial Governor: b. Ireland 3 Sept. 1724; d. Maidenhead, England, 10 Nov. 1808. He served under General Amherst at the second siege of Louisbourg 1758, and under Wolfe in 1759 at Quebec, where he was wounded. In 1762, he greatly distinguished himself in the British attack on Havana. Sent out as Lieutenant Governor of Quebec in 1766, he remained closely identified with Canada for well-nigh forty years. He inspired the Quebec Act (1774); when the Revolutionary War broke out he was commander of the British army in Canada, defended Quebec with great skill, and, reinforced by a British squadron in May 1776, forced Benedict Arnold's army to retire. In 1782 he became commander-in-chief of the British army in North America and during his command peace was finally concluded. Again appointed Governor of Quebec in 1786 he was soon rewarded with a peerage as Baron Dorchester. He helped to frame the Constitutional Act of 1791, which divided Canada into two provinces. He remained at Quebec until 1796, and died in England in 1808, aged eighty-four. By defeating Arnold's attack on Canada, Carleton really saved British North America to Great Britain. He was a stern but humane officer, and

was especially loved by the newly conquered French whom he ruled in Canada.
GEORGE M. WRONG,
Professor of History University of Toronto.

Carleton, Henry Guy, American journalist and dramatist: b. Fort Union, New Mexico, 21 June 1855. He pursued journalism in New Orleans and New York, and has written several plays, including 'Memnon, a Tragedy'; 'Victor Durand' (presented 1884); and 'The Pembertons' (presented 1890).

Carleton, James Henry, American soldier: b. Maine, 1814; d. San Antonio, Texas, 7 Jan. 1873. In February 1839 he took part in the "Aroostook r," relative to the northeast boundary of the United States, and later was commissioned second lieutenant in the 1st United States Dragoons. In 1846 he took part in Kearny's expedition to the Rocky Mountains, served on Gen. Wood's staff in the Mexican war, receiving the brevet rank of major for gallantry at Buena Vista; and later was chiefly employed in exploring expeditions and against hostile Indians. In 1861 he was ordered to southern California, raised the famous "California column," and marched across the Yuma and Gila deserts to Mesilla on the Rio Grande. As commander of the Department of New Mexico he was active in a number of severe engagements. For his services he was brevetted major-general, 13 March 1865; became lieutenant-colonel of the 4th Cavalry, 31 July 1866; and was promoted colonel of the 2d Cavalry, June 1868, and ordered with his regiment to Texas. He wrote 'The Battle of Buena Vista' (1848).

Carleton, Will, American poet: b. Hudson, Mich., 21 Oct. 1845. He is best known in literature by his ballads of home life, many of them having gained great popularity. His books include 'Poems' (1871); 'Farm Legends' (1875); 'City Ballads' (1888); 'City Legends' (1889); 'City Festivals'; 'Rhymes of Our Planet'; 'The Old Infant, and Similar Stories'; 'Young Folks' Centennial Rhymes.'

Carleton, William, Irish novelist: b. Prillisk, County of Tyrone, 1794; d. Dublin, 30 Jan. 1869. Son of a peasant, he had to endure all the miseries of a poor Irishman's lot. His education commenced at a hedge-school, and terminated with two years' training in an academy at Glasslough. Thence he went to Dublin, with about three shillings in his pocket, and after a little began to support himself by private teaching. He also began writing f r the 'Christian Examiner,' and in 1830 published his 'Traits and Stories of the Irish Peasantry.' Popular tastes and critical judgment were both satisfied by the novelty of contents and freshness of style. A second series followed in 1833, and was as universally welcomed. Among later works of his are 'Fardorougha, the Miser' (1839); 'The Misfortunes of Barney Branagan' (1841); 'Valentine M'Clutchy' (1845); 'The Black Prophet' (1847); 'The Tithe Proctor' (1849); 'Willy Reilly' (1855); and 'The Evil Eye' (1860). Ireland has found in Carleton a faithful and fearless exponent of her thoughts and feelings; but outsiders cannot help thinking him somewhat too much of a partisan. He enjoyed a government allowance of £200 per annum several years before his death.

Carleton Place, Canada, town of Lanark County, Ontario; on a navigable tributary of the Ottawa called the Mississippi River, at the foot of Mississippi Lake, and on the Canadian Pacific Ry.; 28 miles southwest of Ottawa, 46 miles northwest of Brockville. It has a fine water power, large lumber and shingle mills, and woolen and iron manufactories; schools, churches, banks, and weekly newspapers; water and sewerage systems; and is lighted by gas and electricity. The neighborhood is a favorite camping ground for summer pleasure parties. Pop. (1901) 4,059.

Carli, Giovanni Rinaldo, jō-vän′nē rē-näl′-dō kär lē, COUNT, Italian writer: b. Capo d'Istria, 11 April 1720; d. 22 Feb. 1795. He was of an ancient, noble family, and early manifested an inclination for the study of the Middle Ages, with which he connected the study of belles-lettres and of poetry. In his 24th year the senate of Venice made him professor of astronomy and naval science. He published his works (1784–94) in 15 volumes, under the title 'Opere del Sig. Commendatore D. Gian Rinaldo, Conte Carli, Presidente,' etc., but this edition does not include his 'Delle Monete' (1754–60); and 'Delle Antichità Italiche' (1788–91).

Car′lin, Thomas, American politician: b. Kentucky, 1790; d. 2 Feb. 1852. He removed to Illinois in 1813, and gradually accumulated wealth, and became known and respected among the scattered population about him. He was elected governor in 1838, and retained that office for four years, during a period of unusual and violent political excitement. Illinois, having engaged largely in internal improvements, suffered severely from the commercial revulsion which was then paralyzing the whole country. She was much in debt, and had within her borders no specie, and no available means of payment. The discussion of the slavery question, too, was then furious, and had just led to the tragic death of E. P. Lovejoy. At the same time the Mormons took up their position at Nauvoo, and politicians were beginning those movements for partisan ends which seemed likely to throw the State into anarchy, and which ended ere long in the violent death of the Mormon leader. That Gov. Carlin, amid such a condition of affairs, was three times re-elected to the chief magistracy, affords a sure indication both of his popularity and his force of character.

Carline Thistle. See THISTLE.

Car′linville, Ill., a city and county-seat of Macoupin County, 60 miles southwest of Springfield; on the Chicago & Alton, and other railroads. It has a prosperous local trade and manufactures of bricks and tiles, agricultural implements, etc. There are coal-mines in the vicinity. It is the seat of Blackburn University, a Presbyterian institution. Its court-house is considered one of the finest public buildings in the State. Pop. (1900) 3,502.

Carlisle, kär-līl′, **Charles Arthur,** American business man: b. Chillicothe, Ohio, May 4. 1864. He received a public school education, and early in life began work on the Marietta & Cincinnati Ry. as messenger boy. From 1884–86 he was connected with the 'Ohio State Journal;' and in the latter year returned to railroad work in the freight department of the 'Nickel Plate' road; in 1890 he was made purchasing agent of the 'Burke System' of railroads; later became director of the Studebaker Brothers Manufacturing Company at South Bend, Ind., and in 1904 was elected president of the American Trust Company of South Bend. He is vice-president of the National Association of Manufacturers; is a member of the American Academy of Political and Social Science, and of the American Institute of Civics, and is prominent in charitable work and public affairs in his home city.

Carlisle, George William Frederic Howard, 7th earl, b. 18 April 1802; d. 4 Dec. 1864. He became earl 7 Oct. 1848, previous to which, as Lord Morpeth, he had traveled extensively in the United States. He was a long time attaché to the British embassy at St. Petersburg. In the reformed House of Commons he represented the West Riding of Yorkshire, and under the Melbourne ministry was secretary of state for Ireland. In 1841 he was defeated in the West Riding by his Conservative opponents. In 1846, under the administration of Lord John Russell, he was appointed commissioner of woods and forests, and chancellor of the duchy of Lancaster. He was the first of the Whig noblemen of the official class to give in his adhesion to the views of the Anti-Corn Law League. In 1856 he delivered before the Mechanics' Institute at Leeds two lectures, since published, on the life and writings of Pope, and on the United States. Previous to the Crimean war, he made a tour in the east of Europe, and published his 'Diary in Turkish and Greek Waters.' On the accession of Lord Palmerston in 1855, he was nominated lord lieutenant of Ireland, which office he held till the resignation of the Palmerston ministry in 1858. A work by him entitled 'The Second Vision of Daniel' was published in 1858.

Carlisle, John Griffin, American statesman: b. Kenton County, Ky., 5 Sept. 1835. He received a common-school education, studied law, and was admitted to the bar in 1858. He served several terms in the lower house of the State legislature. During the Civil War he actively opposed secession, and in 1866 and 1869 was a member of the State senate. He was lieutenant-governor of Kentucky, 1871–5; was elected to Congress, 1876, and five times re-elected. His ability soon made him one of the Democratic leaders. In the 48th, 49th, and 50th congresses he was chosen speaker. In 1890 he was elected United States senator, but resigned in March 1893, to accept the portfolio of secretary of the treasury in President Cleveland's Cabinet. At the close of his term he settled in New York to practise law.

Carlisle, Pa., borough and county-seat of Cumberland County, on the Cumberland V., and the Gettysburg & H. R.R.'s; 18 miles west of Harrisburg. It is the farming and manufacturing trade centre of Cumberland County, and is the site of Dickinson College, founded 1783, Metzger Female College, and the United States Indian Training School. It has a national bank, large manufacturing establishments, Hamilton Library, Todd Hospital, and an assessed property valuation of $3,000,000. It was the headquarters of Washington during the Whisky Rebellion in 1794, and was bombarded by the Confederates in 1863. Pop. (1900) 9,626.

Carlisle Indian School. See UNITED STATES INDIAN TRAINING AND INDUSTRIAL SCHOOL.

Carl'ists, a Spanish political faction which advocates the claims of Carlos of Bourbon and his descendants to the Spanish throne. In 1833 the Carlists, whose chief strength lay in the Basque provinces, and who, because of their Catholic traditions and tendencies, were secretly favored by the Pope and the eastern powers, raised the standard of revolt. They had the advantage until 1836, when Espartero inflicted on them a terrific defeat at Luchana. In August 1839 their commander, Maroto, treacherously made peace, and the remaining Carlists soon fled to France. In 1873 the grandson of the first pretender raised another revolt in the Basque provinces of Navarre and Biscay, but after several sharp conflicts the rebels were hemmed in along the north coast, and in 1876 the pretender and his chief supporters fled into France.

Carll, John Franklin, American geologist: b. Long Island, N. Y., 7 May 1828. He became identified with coal oil development early in life, and has perfected many oil-pumping devices. Since 1874 he has been connected with the Pennsylvania Geological Survey.

Carlone, kär-lō'nä, the name of an Italian family of distinguished artists, who flourished chiefly in the 17th and 18th centuries. The most celebrated of them are: 1. TADDEO, a native of Lombardy, who excelled in sculpture, and was employed, along with his brother Joseph, by the courts of England, Spain, and Mantua; d. 1613. 2. GIOVANNI, eldest son of Taddeo: b. Genoa, 1590; d. 1630. He made great progress in painting under the tuition of his father and Peter Sorri, and, having afterward studied under Passignano, distinguished himself particularly by his frescoes, in which the freedom and spirit of his design, the depth of his expression, grandeur of his conception, and the richness of his coloring are particularly admired. 3. GIOVANNI BATTISTA, brother of the former: b. Genoa, 1598; d. 1680. He was also a scholar of Passignano, and painted with his brother, whose style he followed so exactly that it is difficult to distinguish their pictures. He ultimately entered the service of the Duke of Savoy. He excelled particularly in frescoes, which are so soft, fresh, and uniform that they resemble oil paintings. 4. ANDREA, son of Giovanni Battista: b. 1627; d. 1697. He rose to great eminence as a painter. He took chiefly for his models Titian, Veronese, and Tintoretto, and founded a school of painting in Perugia.

Carlos de Bourbon, DON MARIA ISIDOR, mä-rē'ä ēs'ẹ-dôr, second son of Charles IV. of Spain and brother of Ferdinand VII.: b. 29 March 1788; d. Trieste, 10 March 1855. In 1808 he was compelled by Napoleon along with his brother, who had now succeeded to the throne, to renounce all claims to the succession, and was detained with Ferdinand in captivity at Valençay in France till 1814. In 1816 he married Maria Francisca d'Assis, daughter of John VI. of Portugal, his brother the king of Spain having at the same time espoused another daughter of

John as his second wife. This last marriage, like Ferdinand's first, having turned out unproductive of issue, a prospect opened to Don Carlos of succeeding to the crown, which almost assumed the shape of absolute certainty when a third marriage contracted by Ferdinand proved equally unsuccessful with the two former in producing an heir to the Spanish monarchy. On the death of Ferdinand's third wife in 1829 he again married, and, by a pragmatic sanction, the contingency of a female heir was provided for by the repeal of the Salic law, which excluded such from the throne. On 10 Oct. 1830, Maria Isabella, afterward queen of Spain, was born. In 1832 Don Carlos' party succeeded by taking advantage of the king's imbecile condition to obtain a repeal of the pragmatic sanction: but this advantage was only temporary, as Ferdinand disowned his act on recovering the use of his reason. The following year Don Carlos was exiled with his wife to Portugal; and having refused to return from thence to be present at the taking of the oath of allegiance to the young queen, he was commanded by Ferdinand to retire to the Papal States. On 29 Sept. 1833 Ferdinand VII. died, and a few days afterward his consort the queen-regent repeated the order to his brother to quit the country. The latter, however, now announced himself as legitimate king of Spain, and was recognized as such by a considerable party who excited a civil war in his favor, and thenceforward were designated by the title of Carlists. After a course of hostilities extending over several years with varying success, he found himself obliged in 1839 to take shelter in France. In the meantime he and his descendants had been formally excluded from the succession by a vote of the Cortes in 1836. On arriving in France the castle of Bourges was assigned him as a residence, and he was also detained a prisoner there for a considerable time owing to his refusal to make the renunciations demanded of him. In 1845 he resigned his claims in favor of his eldest son, and in 1847 was permitted to take up his abode in Trieste, where he died.

Carlos, Don, dŏn kär'lōs, Infant of Spain, son of Philip II. and Maria of Portugal: b. Valladolid, 8 July 1545; d. 1568. He was sickly, and one of his legs was shorter than the other. The extreme indulgence with which he was educated by Joan, sister of the king, confirmed his violent, obstinate, and vindictive disposition. In 1560 Philip caused him to be acknowledged heir of the throne by the estates assembled at Toledo, and in 1562 he sent him to the University of Alcala de Henares in hopes that the study of the sciences would soften his turbulent character. Contemporary historians differ in the description of the prince. According to some he had a thirst for glory, an elevated courage, pride, and a love of power. According to others he was fond of whatever was strange and uncommon; an accident or opposition irritated him to frenzy; address and submission softened him. He is also represented as a favorer of the insurgents in the Netherlands, and in particular as an enemy of the Inquisition; yet he possessed neither knowledge nor principles, nor even sufficient understanding to be capable of liberal views. With him all was passionate excitement, which resistance converted into fury. Llorente has corrected the accounts of the character and fate of this prince from authentic sources in his work on the Spanish Inquisition (q.v.). According to him Don Carlos was arrogant, brutal, ignorant, and ill-educated. This much is certain, that at the Congress of Cateau Cambrésis (1559) the marriage of Don Carlos with Elizabeth, daughter of Henry II. of France, was proposed; but Philip, being left a widower by the death of Mary of England, took the place of his son. Don Carlos is said to have loved Elizabeth, and to have never forgiven his father for having deprived him of her. Llorente proves, however, that Don Carlos never had fallen in love with the queen, and that she was never too intimate with him. In 1563 Philip, who had no other heir than Don Carlos, considering him unfit for the throne, sent for his nephews, the archdukes Rodolph and Ernestus, to secure to them the succession to his dominions. Don Carlos, who lived in continual misunderstanding with his father, resolved in 1565 to leave Spain, and was on the point of embarking when Ruy Gomez de Silva, a confidant both of Philip and Carlos, dissuaded him from his resolution. In 1567, when the rebellion in the Low Countries disquieted Philip, Don Carlos wrote to several grandees of the kingdom that he had the intention of going to Germany. He disclosed his plan to his uncle, Don John of Austria, who told Philip what Don Carlos had confided to him. It is believed that he was touched by the sufferings of the people of the Netherlands. Philip himself seemed to believe that his son intended to go to the Netherlands. The infant had often shown a vehement desire to participate in the government. But Philip, jealous of his own authority, treated his son coolly and with reserve, while he gave his confidence to the Duke of Alva, to Ruy Gomez de Silva, Don Juan of Austria, and Spinola. Don Carlos conceived an invincible aversion to them. The architect of the Escurial, Louis de Foix, narrates the following story relating to Don Carlos, which has been preserved to us by De Thou. The prince had always under his pillow two naked swords, two loaded pistols, and at the side of his bed several guns, and a chest full of other firearms. He was often heard to complain that his father had deprived him of his bride. On Christmas evening he confessed to a priest that he had resolved to murder a man. The priest, therefore, refused him absolution. The prior of the monastery of Atocha artfully drew from him expressions from which it could be inferred that he meditated an attempt upon his own father. The story was then communicated to the king, who exclaimed, "I am the man whom my son intends to murder; but I shall take measures to prevent it." Thus Philip, impelled by hatred or fear, by policy or superstition, resolved on the destruction of his only son, in whom he saw only a criminal, unworthy of the crown. On the night of 18 Jan. 1568 while Don Carlos was buried in a deep sleep, Count Lerma entered his chamber and removed his arms. Then appeared the king, preceded by Ruy Gomez de Silva, the Duke of Feria, the grand prior of the order of St. John, brother of the Duke of Alva, and several officers of the guard, and state councilors. Don Carlos still slept. They awoke him: he beheld the king his father, and exclaimed, "I am a dead man." Then, addressing Philip, he said,

"Does your majesty wish to kill me? I am not mad, but reduced to despair by my sufferings." He conjured with tears those who were present to put him to death. "I am not come," answered the king, "to put you to death, but to punish you as a father, and to bring you back to your duty." He then commanded him to rise, deprived him of his domestics, ordered a box of papers under his bed to be seized, and committed him to the care of the Duke of Feria and six noblemen, enjoining them not to permit him to write nor to speak with any one. These guards clothed Don Carlos in a mourning dress, took from his chamber the tapestry, the furniture, and even his bed. Don Carlos, full of rage and despair, caused a large fire to be kindled, under pretext of the extreme cold of the winter, and threw himself suddenly into the flames. It was with difficulty that he was rescued. He attempted by turns to finish his life by thirst, by hunger, by eating to excess. After Philip had endeavored to justify his measures to the Pope and the principal sovereigns of Europe, and had also given notice to the superior clergy, the courts of justice, and the cities of his empire, of what had passed, he referred the case of the prince, not to the Inquisition, but to the council of state, under the direction of Cardinal Espinosa, who was state councilor, grand inquisitor, and president of the junta of Castile. This court is said, after a minute examination and hearing many witnesses, to have condemned him to death. Other accounts, however, state that he died of a malignant fever before any judgment was passed, after having taken the sacrament with much devotion, and having asked his father's pardon, 24 July 1568. The melancholy fate of Don Carlos has served as a subject for several tragedies — those of Schiller, Alfieri, Otway, and Campistron.

Carlos I., King of Portugal since 19 Oct. 1889. He was born on 28 Sept. 1863, son of King Luiz I. and Queen Maria Pia who was the daughter of King Victor Emmanuel II. of Italy; and he is a descendant of King John IV., sometimes called "The Restorer" — that Dom João, Duke of Bragança, who was proclaimed king when the revolution of 1640 wrested (with English aid) Portugal from Spain. In 1905, when the present head of the Bragança family visited King Edward VII., the historical friendship of Portugal and England was clearly in evidence. Carlos married (22 May 1886) Princess Marie Amelia, daughter of Philippe d'Orleans, Comte de Paris. Their sons are: Prince Louis Philippe, heir apparent, born 1887, and Prince Manuel, born 1889.

Carlota, kär-lō'ta, Philippines, (1) a town of Negros Occidental, situated in the western part of the island of Negros, 20 miles south of Bacolod. Pop. 12,004. (2) A town in the eastern part of the island of Negros (Negros Oriental), where the insular government owns a plantation of 2,000 acres. Pop. 6,386.

Carlot'ta (MARIE CARLOTTA AMELIE), empress of Mexico: b. near Brussels, 7 June 1840. She was the daughter of Leopold I., king of Belgium, and married Maximilian, Archduke of Austria, 27 June 1857. In 1864 she went with her husband to Mexico and remained there till 1866, when the dissatisfaction against the empire forced her husband to send her to ask help from France. She could obtain no assistance from Napoleon III. and went to Rome to appeal to the Pope. Before negotiations there were completed, her health gave way under the strain, and after the end of the empire and the execution of her husband she became totally insane. She was taken to the Château de Bouchoute, near Brussels, Belgium, where she lives, an incurable invalid.

Carlovin'gians, the second dynasty of the French or Frankish kings, which supplanted the Merovingians, deriving the name from Charles Martel or his grandson Charlemagne (that is, Karl or Charles the Great). Its origin is usually traced to Arnulph, a bishop of Metz, who died in 631. Charles Martel became mayor of the palace in 714 to the Merovingian *roi fainéant* Childeric, and in this office was succeeded by his son Pepin le Bref, who in 752 deposed the merely nominal king and himself assumed that title. He was succeeded by Charlemagne and his brother Carloman (768-771). Charlemagne became sole king in 771, and extended greatly the dominions of the family. In 800 Leo III. crowned him emperor of the west. On his death in 814 he was succeeded by his son Louis le Débonnaire. He divided his empire among his sons, and at his death, in 840, his son Charles the Bald became king of France. He died in 877, and was succeeded by a number of feeble princes. The dynasty came to an end with Louis V., who died in 987. The house of Capet followed it.

Carlovitz, or **Carlowitz.** See KARLOWITZ.

Carlow, kär-low, Ireland, an inland county in the province of Leinster, surrounded by Kildare, Wicklow, Wexford, Kilkenny, and Queen's County. It is generally level or undulating except in the southeastern parts. The chief rivers are the Slaney and Barrow. From the remarkable fertility of its soil it is altogether an agricultural county, producing a great deal of butter, corn, flour, and other agricultural produce for exportation. Agriculture is here carried on with as much skill and knowledge of recent improvements as anywhere in Ireland, and there is less poverty than in most parts. Area 353 square miles. Pop. (1901) 37,723.

Carlow, Ireland, a town of the county of Carlow, on the Barrow, 34 miles southwest of Dublin, with which it is connected by railway and canal. It has two principal streets intersecting at right angles. A bridge of five arches leads over the Barrow to the suburban village of Graigue, in Queen's County. The principal public buildings are the Roman Catholic cathedral and college, three convents, barracks, a lunatic asylum, a court-house, town-hall, union workhouse, an infirmary, and a fever hospital. It is lighted by electricity, and has an excellent watersupply. Carlow is the principal mart for the agricultural produce of the surrounding country, and carries on an extensive trade in corn, meal, butter, etc. On rising ground to the south stand the ruins of the ancient castle of Carlow, still presenting a very imposing appearance. Pop. (1901) 7,200.

Carlsbad, kärls'bät, Bohemia, a town on the Tepl, near its influx to the Eger, 116 miles west by north of Prague. It is widely celebrated for its hot mineral springs, and is frequented in summer by visitors of the most aristocratic character from all parts of Europe. In the season, April to October, the visitors number

Vol. 3—50.

from 25,000 to 30,000. Set in most lovely scenery, the town is well built, and offers good accommodation for its guests. The temperature of the hot springs varies from 117° to 167° F. The principal spring, the Sprudel, has a very large volume, and is forced up to a height of three feet from the ground. Altogether, the daily flow of the springs of Carlsbad is estimated at 2,000,000 gallons. The principal ingredient in the water is sulphate of soda. The whole town of Carlsbad appears to stand on a vast caldron of boiling water, which is kept from bursting only by the safety-valves the springs provide. Ascribing its foundation to the Emperor Charles IV. (1347), Carlsbad was made a free town by Joseph I. Pop. (1903) about 15,000.

Carlsbad, Congress of, a conference of ministers representing Austria, Prussia, and many small German states, which met at Carlsbad in August 1819 to discuss the democratic tendencies then manifesting themselves in Germany. Its members recommended to their governments and to the German Diet, the famous 'Carlsbad Decrees,' which were adopted by the Diet, 20 Sept. 1819. Among the most important of the decrees were those recommending severe press censorship, the establishment at Mainz of a central commission for the investigation of political intrigues, the suppression of the secret student organization, the Burschenshaft, and government inspection of the universities.

Carlsburg, kärls'boorg, or **Karlsburg,** Austro-Hungary, a town (ancient Apulum) on the right bank of the Maros, 33 miles northwest of Hermannstadt. It consists of an upper and a lower town, situated on opposite sides of the river, and communicating by a long bridge. It is defended by a citadel, and has a cathedral with a number of ancient monuments, a mint where the gold and silver obtained in Transylvania are purified and coined, an observatory with a good collection of instruments, an excellent library, a theological college, a gymnasium, normal school, arsenal, and barracks. Pop. 8,000.

Carlscrona, kärls'krö-nạ, or **Karlskrona** ("Charles' Crown"), Sweden, a seaport at the southern extremity of the peninsula, on the Baltic, capital of the län or province of Blekinge or Carlscrona. It stands on several rocky islets connected with one another and with the mainland by bridges, has broad, clean, but somewhat steep streets, with houses mostly built of wood. The harbor is safe and spacious, the entrance protected by forts. It was founded by Charles XII. in 1680. As the chief Swedish naval station the town largely depends on the trade thereby occasioned, but it has also a considerable export trade in timber, tar, potash, tallow, etc. Pop. (1900) 23,955.

Carlsen, Emil, American artist: b. Denmark, 1848. He came to the United States in 1872 and studied art in Boston. Since 1891 he has lived in New York and has exhibited frequently there. His especial field is still life painting, but he is also favorably known as a landscape artist.

Carlshamn, kärls'häm ("Charles' Haven"), Sweden, a seaport town, 27 miles west of Carlscrona, in a beautiful valley at the mouth of the Mie-A. It is regularly built, and its square market-place, planted on all sides with trees, has a fine appearance. It has an elegant town-house, a good harbor, and an active trade. Timber and articles of timber constitute the chief exports. The manufactures are sail-cloth, sacking, tobacco, leather, etc.; and there is also some ship-building. Pop. (1890) 7,191.

Carlson, kärl'sŏn, **Fredrik Ferdinand,** Swedish historian: b. Upland, 13 June 1811; d. Stockholm, 18 March 1887. He was prominent in public matters for many years, being minister of ecclesiastical affairs, 1863–70, and again, 1875–8. He wrote, among other works, a 'History of Sweden' (1855–87), which ranks high because of its exhaustive accuracy and literary merit.

Carlsruhe, kärls'roo-ŭ, or **Karlsruhe** ("Charles' Rest"), Germany, the capital of the grand-duchy of Baden. It was laid out in 1715, and is one of the most regularly built towns in Europe. The castle of the grand-duke stands in the centre of the city, and from this point a number of streets radiate fan fashion, at regular distances from each other. Other streets intersect these in parallel circles. The roads leading to the city correspond to this regular disposition, which, as is apt to be the case in strictly regular cities, often leaves upon the traveler the impression of monotony rather than that of agreeable order. The city is ornamented with several beautiful public buildings, including the palace, in front of which is a bronze statue of the founder of the city, the margrave, Charles William, the parliament house, town hall, etc. The court library contains 150,000 volumes; there are also here several valuable museums and cabinets, a botanic garden, several institutions for the promotion of literature and the fine arts, and sundry industrial establishments, such as a foundry and electro-plating work, an engine factory, carriage works, etc. Pop. (1900) 97,164.

Carlstad, kärl städ, Sweden, a town on the capital of the län of the same name, on an island in Lake Wener formed by the two mouths of the Klar, and connected with the mainland by a bridge across either stream. It is beautifully situated, regularly built, is the seat of a bishop, and has a cathedral, gymnasium, town-house, etc., and some trade in copper, timber, iron, and grain. Pop. (1900) 11,869.

Carlstadt, Andreas Rudolf, än'drä äs roo dŏlf kärl'stät, **Bodenstein,** German theologian: b. Carlstadt, Franconia, 1480; d. Basel, Switzerland, 25 Dec. 1541. He is celebrated in the history of the Reformation for his fanaticism as well as his misfortunes. He was appointed professor of theology at Wittenberg in 1513. His learning enabled him to render great support to Luther in his first steps for the introduction of a reformation. In 1520 he was included in the bull which condemned Luther; and his spirited appeal from the Pope to a general council, of which he gave the first example, as well as his opinion, openly expressed, in favor of the marriage of the priesthood, which soon gained ground, was among the many proofs which he gave of his zeal for the Reformation. While Luther was at Wartburg Carlstadt's zeal urged him to acts of violence. He even instigated the people and students to the destruction of the altars and the images of the saints, greatly to the displeasure of Luther, who lost

the friendship of Carlstadt by his opposition to his excesses. In 1524 he publicly declared himself the opponent of Luther, and the Elector Frederick banished him from the country in September 1524. Carlstadt upon this commenced the controversy respecting the sacrament, denying, in opposition to Luther, the bodily presence of Christ in the sacramental elements, and recognizing in the rite a token of remembrance simply. This controversy was carried on with the bitterest animosity; and Zwinglius having declared himself in favor of Carlstadt's doctrine, a dispute ensued between the Swiss and Wittenberg theologians, which ended in the separation of the Calvinists and Lutherans. Carlstadt in the meantime, being suspected, not without reason, of having taken part in the revolt of the peasants in Franconia, was obliged to wander through Germany, and being ultimately reduced to extreme distress, sought relief of Luther, who procured him an asylum at Kenberg, on condition that he should refrain from the expression of his opinions. Here he lived nearly three years. His restless mind, however, soon led him to break his promise, by the publication of some writings in 1528; and he even went so far as to plot against Luther's person. To escape from the consequences of his conduct he repaired to Switzerland at the end of the same year, where he was appointed vicar of Altstadt, in the valley of the Rhine; in 1530, deacon at Zürich; and in 1534, vicar and professor of theology at Basel.

Carlstadt, Austria, a town in Croatia, 34 miles southwest of Agram, agreeably situated in a perfectly level and richly cultivated plain near the junction of the Kulpa, Korana, and Dobra, which are here navigable. It consists of the town proper and the citadel, together with the suburb of Dubovacz. It is the seat of a Greek bishopric, is tolerably well built, and has an important trade. Pop. (1890) 5,559.

Carl'ton, Charles, Anglo-American educator: b. Eythorne, Kent, England, 21 Aug. 1821; d. Bonham, Texas, 13 Feb. 1902. He removed to Toronto, Ontario, spent several years as a seaman and subsequently while working on a farm at Fredonia, N. Y., studied for the ministry, and was graduated from Bethany College, W. Va., in 1849. He was successively pastor in Georgetown, Ky.; Lexington, Mo.; Little Rock and Van Buren, Ark., and in 1867 removed to Bonham which continued his home for the rest of his life. There he established a co-educational school called Bonham Seminary, which in 1882 changed its name to Carlton College and became an institution for women solely. He was a prominent leader in the Christian denomination in Texas.

Carlyle, kär-līl', **Alexander,** Scottish clergyman: b. Prestonpans, 26 Jan. 1722; d. Inveresk, 25 Aug. 1805. He was educated at the universities of Edinburgh and Glasgow, and afterward studied at the University of Leyden. Having been licensed as a preacher, in 1747 he was presented to the parish of Inveresk, in Mid Lothian, where he continued to the end of his life. He was one of the leaders of the Moderate party in the Scottish Church, the party which, during the latter half of the 18th century, ruled with such predominating sway, and included the names of Robertson, Blair, and Home among its members. As an eloquent debater and skilful ecclesiastical leader in the General Assembly he had no rival. He strenuously resisted all attempts to give additional influence to the popular element in ecclesiastical matters. He left behind him a well-known autobiography, which, though commenced in his 79th year, is a singularly interesting production, both from the vigor and sprightliness of its style, and the pictures which it presents of Scottish society in the 18th century. After remaining long in manuscript it was published in 1860, under the editorship of John Hill Burton.

Carlyle, Jane Baillie Welsh, Scottish letter writer; b. Haddington, Scotland, 14 July 1801; d. London, 21 April 1866. She was the daughter of John Welsh, a Haddington surgeon, and was married to Thomas Carlyle (q.v.) 17 Oct. 1826. Her letters, edited by her husband, were published in 1883.

Carlyle, Joseph Dacre, English orientalist: b. Carlisle, 1759; d. Newcastle-upon-Tyne. 12 April 1804. He was graduated from Cambridge, became Chancellor of Carlisle in 1793, Professor of Arabic at Cambridge in 1795, and was subsequently appointed to the Turkish embassy. He published 'Specimens of Arabic Poetry' (1796); 'Poems' (1805), and a translation of an Arabic history of Egypt. His Arabic Bible was published in 1811.

Carlyle, Thomas, Scotch essayist, historian, and miscellaneous writer: b. Ecclefechan, near Annandale, in Dumfriesshire, Scotland, 4 Dec. 1795; d. London, 4 Feb. 1881. Carlyle's ancestors were said to have come to Annandale from Carlisle, England. in the time of David II., but at the author's birth the immediate family was living in very narrow circumstances at Ecclefechan, where the grandfather Thomas was village carpenter and his five sons masons. The second of these, James, a man of "largest natural adornment," assertive, choleric, honest, and pious. with an uncommon gift of forcible expression, married as his second wife Margaret Aitken, a woman of affectionate nature and piety of mind. By her he had four sons and five daughters, of whom the eldest was Thomas. The third son. John Carlyle (q.v.). became distinguished as the translator of Dante. Thomas, like the other children, was brought up with much affectionate care. His parents intended him for the church and gave him all the education in their power. He early learned his letters and soon became a voracious reader. At 10 he was sent to the grammar school at Annan, where. as a moody, sensitive child, he was much bullied by the other boys, and probably suffered acutely. At the age of 13 he was ready to enter Edinburgh University, which he attended from 1809 to 1814. without, however, taking a degree. His individuality did not readily allow itself to be molded to the academic routine. Finding himself unable, because of religious doubts, to enter the ministry. he went to Annan Academy as tutor in mathematics, in 1814. Later he taught at Kirkcaldy, where he made the acquaintance of Edward Irving (q.v.), one of his warmest friends. Irving's friendship was of great value to Carlyle, and his library enabled the latter to gratify his love of reading and to mitigate the distaste which he felt for teaching. In October 1818 the work became so repellent that he resigned from his school. saying that "it were better to perish than to continue school-

mastering." Then he went to Edinburgh to try to earn his living.

The next three years were perhaps the most trying of his life. He was tormented to an uncommon degree by his lifelong enemy, dyspepsia, and as a result was greatly depressed in spirit. Uncertain what career to follow, trying his hand at many vocations and different studies, miserably poor, finding his only employment for a time in writing hack articles, he was "mentally and physically adrift" in the sense that is described in his "Everlasting No" of 'Sartor Resartus.' Toward the middle of 1821, however, he seems, by much resolution and energy of will, to have shaken off much of the depression, to have attained the position of the "Everlasting Yea." The men who at this time most influenced him were the Germans, particularly Goethe, the mystic Richter, and the philosopher Fichte. German literature was now his most absorbing study, and later this study bore fruit in his 'Life of Schiller' (1823-4), his translation of Goethe's 'Wilhelm Meister' (1824), and in several essays. These books mark his formal entrance into literature. Up to the time of their publication Carlyle's published writing had been a series of articles for Sir David Brewster's Encyclopedia, a translation of Legendre's 'Geometry,' to which he prefixed an 'Essay on Proportion,' and miscellaneous hack work. The 'Life of Schiller' and the translation of 'Wilhelm Meister' met with favorable reviews, and the translation is usually regarded as one of the best of all renderings into English. While he was at work on these books, he was (1822-4) tutor in a well-to-do family, the Bullers, from whom he received £200 a year for not disagreeable work. In spite of the kindness of his patrons, he managed, as was usual with him during life, to find much fault with his surroundings and to utter complaints with very little fairness or reserve. A trip (1824) to London and Paris broke the monotony of his existence, and gave him many new impressions and opinions in what was a critical period of his growth. Returning to Scotland in 1825 he established himself at Hoddam Hill, a farm near the Solway, where he farmed and wrote. On 17 Oct. 1826, Carlyle, after a somewhat prolonged, vacillating. and rather stormy wooing, succeeded in marrying Jane Baillie Welsh, a woman in many ways as remarkable as himself and distinguished as a descendant of John Knox. The humors and distempers of their married life have become proverbial, and are to be found most fully recorded in Froude's biography. Both seem to have been extremely and unintelligently self-willed and so vain as to be wholly lacking in reticence about their domestic life. For two years they lived at Scotsbrig near Edinburgh, where they had the advantage of intelligent society of the capital, and where Carlyle supported himself by writing for the reviews. In the *Edinburgh Review*, under the editorship of his friend Jeffrey (q.v.), he published. in 1827, his well-known essay on 'Richter' and 'The State of German Literature,' an article which led to the famous correspondence with Goethe. For several years, the *Edinburgh* and other reviews were his only medium of publication. He essayed a novel but failed, and was disappointed in his attempts to secure the chair in moral philosophy at Saint Andrews and a professorship in London University.

CARLYLE

In May 1828 the Carlyles removed to a lonely farm, Craigenputtoch, overlooking the Solway. Here he wrote his 'Essay on Burns,' one of his most sympathetic pieces of criticism (*Edinburgh Review*, 1828), several other essays of much importance, as 'Voltaire,' 'Novalis,' and his 'Sartor Resartus,' the book for which he is perhaps most famous. Refused by several publishers, 'Sartor Resartus' first saw light in *Fraser's Magazine*, between December 1833 and August 1834, where it excited such a storm of protest that no separate English edition appeared till 1838. Meanwhile (1836) it first appeared in book form in America, where it was especially commended by Emerson. This most characteristic book of Carlyle purports to be a review by an English editor of a treatise by a learned German professor, Herr Teufelsdröckh, with whose life and opinions it deals. The book is written around the famous Philosophy of Clothes, designed by Swift (q.v.), and is in the main symbolical of Carlyle's creed at this time—that as clothes express the taste of the wearer, so life in all its forms may be regarded as the vesture of the mind. The idea is not a very original one, but is expressed with such oddity of phrase and image that it appears as profound as forcible. The most interesting feature is the account of the moral and spiritual attire of Teufelsdröckh, who is Carlyle himself. It is the querulous, stormy tale of early suffering, lack of sympathy from fellowmen, disappointment alike in the business of the head and the affairs of the heart, despondency and despair over the great question why man is in the universe, doubt and wavering, and final acceptance of the facts of existence with the hope of solution through stern endeavor. The book might be called a prose epic of the inner life, and it is wholly egoistic and anthropocentric.

In 1834, the Carlyles removed to London, where they settled in Cheyne Row, Chelsea, and here were their headquarters for the remainder of their lives. Soon after the change he began his 'French Revolution,' which was completed in 1837 and which gave him much more reputation than he had heretofore enjoyed. During the same period he wrote the 'Diamond Necklace' and the articles on 'Mirabeau' and 'Sir Walter Scott,' the honorarium from which was of great benefit in his impecunious state. The success of the history enabled him, in the four following years, to gain audience for four series of lectures, 'German Literature,' the 'History of European Literature,' 'Revolutions,' and the more characteristic 'Heroes and Hero-Worship.' Published in book form in 1841, this series remains to-day one of the most widely read of Carlyle's works and is perhaps the clearest expression of his philosophy of history. "As I take it," he says, "Universal history, the history of what man has accomplished in this world, is at bottom the history of the great men who have worked there." The moral animus of the book is expressed farther on in the same introduction: "We cannot look, however imperfectly, upon a great man, without gaining something by him. He is the living light-fountain which it is good and pleasant to be near." Again, speaking of the Hero as a man of letters, he tells us the purpose of all his own writing: "The writer of a book, is he not a preacher, preaching not to this parish or that, on this day or that, but to all men in all times and places."

The book may conveniently mark an important time in Carlyle's life. The pamphlet on 'Chartism' of 1840 had enunciated a doctrine, of a political sort, that "Might is right,"—"one of the few strings," says Nichol, "on which, with all the variations of a political Paganini, he played through life." About this time, in short, his ideas of history, of morals, of politics, of his own mission, seem to have crystallized. Furthermore, his circumstances had definitively bettered. His name was well-known, and he was able to refuse a chair of history at Edinburgh University and later another at Saint Andrews. In 1842, the death of Mrs. Carlyle's mother threw an income of at least £200 in the hands of the Carlyles and relieved them of fear of penury.

From this time on Carlyle's work falls mainly into two main classes: (1) the lives of great individuals and (2) pamphlets of a quasi-political sort, powerful lashings of modern institutions. The most important of the latter, 'Past and Present,' written in seven weeks, appeared in 1843. Herein Carlyle commits a common and characteristic fallacy in comparing a charming picture of monastic England with some of the worst things of modern life, to the obvious disadvantage of the latter and, by extension and implication, to modern civilization as a whole. Nevertheless, the book makes a strong appeal to our humanity, and is perhaps the best example of Carlyle's many protests against modern barbarism. It is said to have been productive of good in factory legislation. Meanwhile he was engaged on an important work of the first class spoken of,—'Cromwell,' which, after three years' preparation, appeared in 1845. Carlyle, with characteristic thoroughness, spent a large part of the summers of 1842 and 1843 in visiting the battlefields of the Civil War. It is significant that the "great man" was now, with Carlyle, not necessarily a man of letters, as in his works previous to the 'French Revolution,' but a man of political prowess as well, and this tendency to exalt the man of might reached its climax in the 'History of Frederick II.' The years between 'Cromwell' and the beginning of 'Frederick' are marked by his notable 'Latter-Day Pamphlets' (1849), one of the most denunciatory of his books, and his 'Life of John Stirling' (1851), a dear friend who had died six years before and who, like Edward King and Arthur Hallam, is chiefly remembered through the work of a greater man. After a trip in the fall of 1851, with the Brownings, to France, where he met the chief literary celebrities of the time—and passed unfavorable comment on them as on all affairs French—he settled down to the planning of the 'History of Frederick II.' On the preparation for this work and the composition of it he was engaged for the next 13 years. His study was indefatigable and he made two trips to Germany, in 1852 and 1858, to study the battlefields of Frederick. In 1850 the first two volumes were published with great success, the third in 1862, the fourth in 1864, and the fifth and sixth in 1865. During the composition he had done practically no side work: a somewhat unintelligent dialogue, 'Ilias Americana in Nuce,' on the American War, and his 'Prinzenraub' are the only pieces.

The compilation of 'Frederick' marks the climax of Carlyle's life. It won for him recognition in England as the foremost of prose writers,

THOMAS CARLYLE.

and in Germany, too, his fame was naturally great. Even the Scotch decided to honor a prophet of their own country: he was elected Lord Rector of Edinburgh University, and in the spring of 1866 delivered the inaugural address, on the 'Reading of Books.' While on his trip he received news of the death of Mrs. Carlyle, which, in spite of their disagreements, was a severe blow to him and may be said to mark the beginning of his decline. He was over 70 years of age and the labor of 'Frederick' had left him worn and weary. Thereafter he wrote only three books of comparative importance, 'Shooting Niagara—and After,' of the type of 'Past and Present,' the 'Early Kings of Norway,' of the hero type, and 'Reminiscences of Jane Carlyle and of Jeffrey and Edward Irving,' written in the months following the death of his wife, but not published until after his death. His last public utterance, according to Froude, was a letter which he wrote, in May 1877, to the *Times*, protesting against the moral support which England was giving to Turkey in the war with Russia. His life at this time is described as one surrounded by honors and supported by a few staunch friends, but as one of growing weariness and desire to be at rest, until, after two years of physical feebleness, he died quietly in his 86th year.

Carlyle's character and place in literature have, since his death, as during his life, been subjects of much comment and of comment of the most diverse sorts. He has been extolled on the one hand as the greatest of prophets, the most eloquent of sages; and condemned, on the other, as the noisiest of egoists. It is therefore impossible to fix with any approximation his value as a character or as a man of letters, in the sense that Milton, Addison, Gray, and others may be tolerably well characterized. His severest critics, like Mr. Robertson, are undoubtedly right when they accuse him of inconsistency and irrationality and when they point out in his character certain elements of brutality and narrow egoism, and yet the fact remains that he has been the awakening force of many men and that there is a feeling abroad that he is one of the great names in English prose. Perhaps the most sensible of these opposing views may best be summed up in Huxley's words (letter to Lord Stanley, 9 March 1881): "Few men can have dissented more strongly from his way of looking at things than I; but I should not yield to the most devoted of his followers in gratitude for the bracing, wholesome influence of his writings when, as a very young man, I was essaying without rudder or compass to strike out a course for myself."

In view of such diverse opinions, all of which contain truth, it seems necessary merely to protest against those extremist views which have just been referred to. Whether one regards him as the wisest of men or the noisiest of hypocrites is, after all, a question of temper or of what one regards as valuable in the universe, and usually has value only as the expression of personal opinion. Carlyle's influence, like that of Dr. Johnson, is the personal influence of a powerful and upright man rather than that of a philosopher or a discoverer of new truth. His personal qualities as expressed in his writings— his integrity, his earnestness, his independence, his sincerity, his hatred of sham, cant, and affectation, his vigor—are what count in his hold on people. As a system, his work, as his critics justly remark, is unscientific and untrue. His work, so voluminous and, on the face of it, consisting of translations, literary, biographical, historical essays and books, tracts of the times, and satires, comes down to the glorification of a galaxy of interesting and, in different ways, powerful individuals: Schiller, Goethe, Cromwell, Frederick, himself (in 'Sartor Resartus'), and others, and to the doctrine that their power is good. There is, of course, no means of testing the general truth of such views. They are really personal. He is, therefore, to be regarded as a seer, a prophet, a preacher, who feels deeply a, rather than *the*, meaning of life, and exhorts his readers to feel rightly and live rightly, to "do the duty which lies next them," to "work and despair not." These things he said with an impressiveness equalled by few men and to a very large body of listeners.

Bibliography.—Of the numerous editions of Carlyle's writings the best, aside from his correspondence, is probably the Ashburton Edition, in 17 vols. The 'Early Letters of Thomas Carlyle,' the 'Correspondence between Goethe and Thomas Carlyle,' and the 'Correspondence of Thomas Carlyle and Ralph Waldo Emerson,' edited by C. E. Norton are the best editions of his letters. Froude's 'Thomas Carlyle,' in 4 vols. (1882-4), is the great biography, and is, incidentally, the most censured biography of recent times, because of the frankness with which it discloses the domestic life of the Carlyles. Excellent short lives are those of John Nichol, in the 'English Men of Letters Series,' Richard Garnett, in the 'Great Writers Series' (to which there is added a very full bibliography), and Sir Leslie Stephen, in the *Dictionary of National Biography*. The critical essays of Matthew Arnold ('Emerson' in 'Discourses in America'), Augustine Birrell ('Obiter Dicta'), J. R. Lowell ('Prose Works,' vol. ii.), John Morley ('Miscellanies,' vol. i.), J. M. Robertson ('Modern Humanists'), the severest of Carlyle's critics, and Stephen ('Hours in a Library,' vol. iii.), may be cited as representing different views among the most eminent of modern critics. Consult also Froude's 'Letters and Memorials of Jane Welsh Carlyle.'

WILLIAM T. BREWSTER,
Professor of English, Columbia University.

Carmack, Edward Ward, American politician: b. near Castilian Springs, Sumner County, Tenn., 5 Nov. 1858. He studied law and after admission to the bar practised his profession at Columbia, Tenn. He was member of the State legislature in 1884; was on the editorial staff of the 'Nashville American' (1886-8), and subsequently became editor-in-chief; and in 1892 became editor of the 'Memphis Commercial.' He served two terms in Congress as Democratic representative from the 10th Tennessee district 1897-1901, and in the year last named was appointed to the United States Senate.

Carmagnola, Francesco, frän-chĕs'kō kär-män-yō'la. Italian *condottiere;* b. Carmagnola, about 1390; d. Venice, 3 May 1432. His real name was Bussone, but he adopted as his own the name of his birthplace. The son of a peasant, he was a herdsman in his youth; but enlisting in the service of the Duke of Milan (Filippo Maria

Visconti), he rapidly rose in rank, and aided his master in regaining a great part of Lombardy, and in extending his possessions. The Duke, however, became suspicious of his loyalty, confiscated his property, cast his wife and children into prison, and banished him; upon which Carmagnola entered the service of the republic of Venice, from which he received the appointment of generalissimo. He wrested Brescia from the Duke of Milan, and entirely routed his army at the battle of Macalo in 1427. After the battle he released his prisoners, which was frequently done at that time by *condottieri,* but incurring the suspicions of the Venetian senate for doing so, and his subsequent military operations not proving successful, he was recalled to Venice, under the pretext that his advice was needed for affairs of state, placed under arrest, accused of treason, put to the torture and beheaded.

Carmagnole, kär-män-yōl, a name applied in the early times of the French republic (1792-3) to a song which was accompanied by a dance. The song contained 13 couplets and the following refrain:

" Dansons la carmagnole
Vive le son, vive le son
Dansons la carmagnole,
Vive le son du canon."

The appellation originated, probably, from the name given to a peculiar form of vest worn by the confederates of Marseilles, who came to Paris in August 1792, to co-operate with the revolutionaries of the capital. The author and composer of the song are unknown. It is notable simply for its historical associations; not for the intrinsic merits of words or music. The song and dance were first used at the time of the indignation of the people on account of the veto allowed to the king on the resolves of the National Assembly. The Carmagnole was commonly sung and danced at popular festivals, executions, and eruptions of popular discontent. Afterward the name was also applied to the national guards, who wore a dress of a peculiar cut, and to the enthusiastic supporters of the Revolution. Several members of the National Convention — Barère, for instance — by way of jest, gave this name to their communications to the assembly.

Car'man, Elbert S., American editor: b. Hempstead, N. Y., 1836; d. New York, 28 Feb. 1900. He was graduated at Brown University in 1858, began contributing to the 'Turf, Field, and Farm' and similar publications early in life, and became owner and editor of the 'Rural New Yorker' in 1876. In connection with the last publication he established a farm at River Edge, N. J., where he gave much of his time to testing new plants, vines, and seeds, and also to originating new varieties of vegetables, fruits, and grains.

Carman, Ezra Ayers, American military officer: b. Metuchen, N. J., 27 Feb. 1834. He was graduated at the Western Military Institute, Kentucky, in 1855, and was assistant professor of mathematics in the University of Nashville in 1855-6. He served through the Civil War in the Army of the Potomac and the Army of the Cumberland; and attained the rank of brigadier-general of volunteers. He was comptroller of Jersey City in 1871-5; clerk in the United States Department of Agriculture in 1877-85; and a member of the Antietam Battlefield Board.

Carman, William Bliss, Canadian poet and journalist: b. Fredericton, N. B., 15 April 1861. He was educated at the universities of New Brunswick, Edinburgh, and Harvard, and has since done much journalistic work for New York and Boston papers. His verse has been widely read and his successive volumes include: 'Low Tide on Grand Pré' (1893); 'A Sea Mark' (1895); 'Behind the Arras' (1895); 'Ballads of Lost Haven' (1897); 'By the Aurelian Wall' (1897); 'Songs from Vagabondia,' joint author with R. Hovey (1894); 'More Songs from Vagabondia' (with Hovey) (1896); 'Last Songs from Vagabondia' (with Hovey) (1900); 'A Winter Holiday.' In 1903 he became editor of 'The Literary World.'

Carmarthen, kär-mär'thĕn, or **Caermarthen** (Welsh, *Caer Fyrddyn*), South Wales, a seaport town, capital of Carmarthenshire, 9 miles from Carmarthen Bay, Bristol Channel, and 14 miles northwest of Llanelly, on the right bank of the Towy. The principal buildings are the county hall, St. Peter's church, and St. David's church. Besides the established churches there are numerous places of worship belonging to other denominations. Of public and private schools the most prominent are the South Wales Training College, Sir Thomas Powell's Free Grammar School, Queen Elizabeth's Grammar School, etc. There are also two infirmaries and a literary and scientific institution. There are some tin and lead works, cloth manufactories, and iron foundries, and the salmon fishery is extensive. Pop. (1901) 9,935.

Carmarthenshire, or **Caermarthenshire,** South Wales, a maritime county, and the largest of all the Welsh counties; extreme length, 53 miles; breadth, 35 miles; area, 594,405 acres. It is mountainous generally, but not so rugged as some other Welsh counties. Some of the vales are beautiful, particularly that of Towy, which is 30 miles in length. The principal river, the Tywi or Towy, rises in Cardiganshire. This river and the Tave are the only navigable streams in the county. The valleys are fertile, and numerous herds of small black cattle are raised on the hills. The mineral products of the county are iron, lead, coal, and limestone. There are few manufactures. Pop. (1901) 135,325.

Carmaux, kär-mō, France, a city in the department of Tarn, nine miles northeast of Albi by rail. It is one of the great coal-mining centres of France, the annual output of coal sometimes reaching as much as 600,000 tons. Serious strikes and riots took place here in 1892.

Car'mel, a mountain ridge in Palestine, constituting part of Lebanon, on the southern frontier of Galilee, in the pashalic of Acca. It consists of several rich, woody heights, separated by fertile and habitable valleys within a circuit of about 28 miles, and terminates at the mouth of the Kishon in a lovely plain, which forms the southern coast of the Gulf of Ptolemais or Acca, on the Mediterranean. Upon different parts of this mountain there are ruins of churches and monasteries from the time of the Christian kingdom of Jerusalem, and the cave which, according to tradition, was inhabited by the prophet Elijah.

Car'melites, one of the four mendicant orders of the Roman Catholic Church; its full title is Friars of Our Lady of Mount Carmel. The order has, traditionally, a very ancient origin, but as a religious order approved by the Roman Catholic Church is contemporary with the Dominican and Franciscan orders. According to the legends the Carmelites trace the origin of their order back to the early days of the kingdom of Israel, the time of the prophets Elijah (Elias) and Elisha (Elisæus). Elias, in his early manhood, says the legend, retired for religious contemplation to Mount Carmel, and there, taught by an angel, gathered to himself a number of men of like disposition, and instituted a society of contemplatives for worship of the true God and the attainment of spiritual perfection. Among the disciples attracted to this school of religion were the youths who afterward were the minor prophets Jonah, Micah, and Obadiah; and at a later period the renowned philosopher of Magna Græcia, Pythagoras, was numbered among the inquirers after the true religion and the science of divine things in this great school of the prophets: Pythagoras' instructor was the prophet Daniel. Elijah's wife instituted an order of female recluses. As pointing to the existence on Mount Carmel of some such institution as the legend postulates, reference is made to 1 Kings xviii. 19 and following; 2 Kings ii. 25; and 2 Kings iv. 25.

The world outside the precincts of those religious communities appears to have been entirely ignorant of this ancient institution till early in the 13th century, when Phocas, a Greek monk of Patmos, brought to the Latin patriarch of Constantinople intelligence of the existence in olden time of a great monastic or eremitic establishment on Mount Carmel, of which traces still remained. The site of the ancient ruins was occupied by a venerable monk from Calabria and 10 companion monks; and for these Phocas petitioned the patriarch to formulate or to approve a rule of monastic or eremitical life. This was done, and afterward the rule was approved by Pope Honorius III. in 1224. The connection of this order with the ancient school of the prophets, even if the traditional story be accepted, seems to lack proof. All that we are told which could give color to the claim that the new eremites are in the line of succession from the eminent school of prophets is, that in a vision Elias gave orders to the monk from Calabria to found a religious establishment on the ancient site. The community was expelled by the Saracens from its seat on Mount Carmel and took refuge in the west. One of the earliest houses of the Carmelite order in the west was founded at Alnwick in England; and about the same time, near the middle of the 13th century, St. Louis, the king, founded at Paris the first Carmelite house in France — the Carmes, of terrible celebrity in the great Revolution. Pope Innocent IV. modified the rule of the order and assimilated it to the Dominican and Franciscan rule. One of the traditions represents Jesus and his mother as initiates of the ancient order; and Saint Simon Stock, sixth general of the order, an Englishman, received from the hands of the Virgin the scapulary of Mount Carmel with the assurance that whoso should die wearing that scapulary would surely not be damned. A relaxation of the primitive severity of the rule was permitted by Eugenius IV. in 1431, and

this led to a scission of the order into two suborders, the Conventuals or Calced (wearing shoes) and the Observants or Discalced (shoeless or barefooted). Pope Benedict XIII. in 1725 permitted the order to add to the statues in Saint Peter's Church of founders of religious orders, one to their founder, which was erected with the inscription: "Universus Ordo Carmelitarum Fundatori suo Sancto Eliæ prophetæ erexit" ("The whole order of the Carmelites erected this statue to their founder, Saint Elias, the prophet"). The order of Carmelite nuns dates from the middle of the 15th century. In 1562 the great mystic Saint Teresa, who was a Carmelite nun, in virtue of a papal brief established a separate branch of the sisterhood, under a very severe rule: these are the Barefoot Carmelite Nuns. She then undertook to restore in the original order of Carmelite Friars the ancient severity of discipline, and succeeded; the result is the order or suborder of the Barefoot or Discalced Carmelites. The Carmelite order, in its several forms, has establishments all over the world. The headquarters of the order in America are at Niagara Falls.

Car'men, a novel by Prosper Mérimée, published in 1847. Don José Lizzarrabengoa, Navarrese and corporal in a cavalry regiment, meets at Seville a gypsy known as Carmen. While taking her to prison for a murderous assault on another woman, he connives at her escape, and is reduced to the ranks. Jealous, he kills his lieutenant, and joins a band of smugglers. In a duel he kills Garcia, her *rom* or husband, and becomes her *rom* in turn. He offers to forget everything if she will go with him to America. She refuses, for the sake of another lover, as he believes, and he threatens to kill her. She answers that it is so ordained, but that "free Carmen has been, and free she will always be." Don José kills her, buries her body in the woods, rides to Cordova, and delivers himself to the authorities. The romance is best known in its operatic version, the adaptation having been made by Meilhac and Halévy.

Carmen Seculare. See HORACE.

Carmen Sylva, pen name of ELIZABETH, queen of Rumania (q.v.).

Carmi, Ill., a city and county-seat of White County, 150 miles southeast of Springfield, on the Little Wabash River. It is the centre of an agricultural region and exports fruit, grain, flour, tile, and lumber. It has flouring and saw mills, brick works, machine shops, etc. Pop. (1900) 2,939.

Carmichael, kär'mĭ-kal, **Frederic Falkiner,** Irish clergyman and author: b. 1831. He was educated privately, and entering the Anglican ministry in 1857 held several church preferments in Dublin, becoming a canon of Christ Church Cathedral, Dublin, 1886. He has published: 'Jesus Christ, the Way, the Truth, the Life'; 'Donellan Lectures' (1876); 'The Responsibilities of God.'

Carmichael, Montgomery, English civil servant: b. Birkenhead, England, 17 May 1857. He was educated at Bonn and Munich and entered the English consular service in 1890. In 1892 he was appointed vice-consul at Leghorn, and he has been vice-consul for West Tuscany from 1896. He is a regular contributor to the 'Saturday Review,' and has published 'Sketches and Stories, Grave and Gay' (1896); 'In Tuscany,' a delightfully sympathetic description of Tuscan life (1901); 'The Lady Poverty' (1901); 'Life of John William Walshe,' a strongly conceived piece of imaginary biography (1902).

Car'minatives, remedies that cause a warm, pleasant sensation in the stomach and act as stimulants to the muscles, causing peristalsis, thus relieving flatus; and that increase the flow of the gastric and intestinal secretions. Most of the drugs containing volatile oils are carminatives; as, the mint family, parsley, anise, fennel, caraway, cardamom, ginger, cinnamon, cloves, etc. See Volatile Oils.

Car'mine, the most splendid of all the red colors, is made from the cochineal insect, or *Coccus cacti.* The finest is that which is thrown down from an aqueous infusion by chloride of tin. This, after depositing, is collected and dried. The operations require the greatest care, for the brilliancy of the color is affected by the weather, light, and temperature. The color produced by alum has a darker tint, and constitutes lake. Carmine, or carminic acid, is also the name given by chemists to the coloring matter of cochineal. The acid is a purplish body, extremely soluble in water and in alcohol. It forms salts with the heavy metals, and it yields various products when acted on by chlorine, nitric acid, and other re-agents. Carmine is used to some extent in dyeing, in water-color painting, to color artificial flowers, confectionery, etc.

Carmo'na (ancient Carmo), a town in Spain, 20 miles from Seville, on a height overlooking a large plain covered with olive-trees. It is well built, containing many handsome mansions belonging to the nobility, who, though usually resident in Seville, spend part of the year here. The principal square is well planted, and, among other edifices, possesses a handsome Gothic church with a lofty spire. Another conspicuous object is a Moorish castle, flanked with massive towers, and there are two old Roman gates. The manufactures are chiefly woolen hats, leather, and earthenware. Recent important excavations on the site of the ancient necropolis, to the west of the modern town, have brought to light a large number of tombs and funeral triclinia in almost perfect preservation. Considerable portions of the Moorish wall and Alcazar still remain. Pop. (1903) 18,000.

Carmontel, kär-môn-tĕl, or **Carmontelle,** Louis Carrogis, loo-ē kär-rō-zhē, French poet: b. Paris, 15 Aug. 1717; d. there, 26 Dec. 1806. He is best known by his 'Proverbes Dramatiques' (10 vols.). These are without much connection in themselves, being, in fact, only a series of dramatic scenes, but are well adapted for private theatres. The fertility of Carmontel was as extraordinary as his ease in writing. He is said to have left, besides his printed works and his pieces for the theatre, more than a hundred volumes of manuscripts.

Carnac, kär-nạk, France, a village in the department of Morbihan, on a height near the coast, 15 miles southeast of Lorient, and remarkable for the so-called Druidical monuments in its vicinity. These consist of more than 1,100 rude blocks of gray granite, some of which are upward of 18 feet high, standing on end in the midst of a wide heath. They are in the form of unpolished obelisks, with the vertex reversed, and are arranged in 11 lines, forming 10 avenues, with a curved row at one end. There are many gaps in the lines; almost every house and wall in the vicinity is seemingly built from this artificial quarry. They are evidently of very ancient date, but their origin is unknown. Pop. (1891) 2,901. See Lukis, 'Chambered Barrows and Other Historic Monuments in Morbihan' (1875); Miln, 'Excavations at Carnac' (1877-81).

Carnahuba. See Carnauba.

Car'nall, Rudolph von, German mining engineer: b. Glatz, 1804; d. 1874. He began the study of mining in Berlin in 1823, was connected with the mining industry in Upper Silesia and rose to be superintendent of mines and director of the general mining office in Breslau. He took part in founding the German Geological Society, lectured at the University of Berlin on the science of mining engineering, and rendered important service to the development of German mining.

Car'nallite, a hydrous chloride of potassium and magnesium, found at Stassfurt, Prussia, and of great commercial importance as being one of the minerals from which come the world's supply of potash salts. See Potassium.

Carnarvon, Henry Howard Molyneux (4th Earl of), English statesman: b. London, 24 June 1831; d. 28 June 1890. He succeeded his father in the earldom in 1849, and was secretary of state for the colonies, June 1866 to March 1867. During his secretaryship he devised a scheme for the federation of the British North American Colonies, subsequently approved by Parliament. He was again colonial secretary, 1874-8, and lord-lieutenant of Ireland, 1885-6. He published 'The Druses of Mount Lebanon' (1860).

Carnarvon, or **Caernarvon,** Wales, a seaport town and parliamentary borough, on the southeast side of the Menai Strait, and capital of the county, 209 miles northwest of London. The ancient walls thrown around it by Edward I., and flanked by round towers, are still fairly entire. The magnificent castle or palace of Edward I., and in which Edward II. was born, stands at the west end of the town, almost overhanging the sea, and is externally entire. Including its court-yards, etc., it covers about two acres of ground. There are extensive ironworks in the town, which supply machinery for steamers, etc. Pop. (1901) 9,760.

Carnar'vonshire, or **Caernarvonshire,** Wales, a maritime county having Carnarvon Bay on the west; Denbigh on the east; the island of Anglesea and the Irish Sea on the north; and Cardigan Bay on the south. Its extreme length, southwest to northeast, is about 52 miles; extreme breadth, 20 miles, although the greater portion of it does not exceed seven or eight miles on an average; area, 369,477 acres. This county is traversed throughout its whole length by lofty mountains, including the Snowdon range, whose highest peak is 3,557 feet above the sea. There are other summits varying from 1,500 feet to more than 3,000 feet. Dairy farming, and cattle, horse, and sheep breeding are the principal occupations of the farmer. The cattle and sheep are of a small breed. Lead and copper ores are found in the mountains south, and there are slate quarries at Bethesda.

CARNATION

Llanberis, and Nantlle, which have been extensively and profitably worked. Pop. (1901) 126,835.

Carnatic, kär-năt'ĭc, former province of British India, on the east coast of the peninsula. Its limits were ill defined, but it is commonly thought to have extended from Cape Comorin to lat. 16° N., and from the coast line to an average of about 80 miles inland. It was formerly included in the dominions of the nabob of Arcot, and the contentions arising from a disputed succession first brought the French and English into collision, and ended by the subjugation of the Carnatic under the British influence, which was completely effected in 1801. The Carnatic as one of the wealthy provinces has been the cause of endless native warfare and bloodshed, by which, whoever was victor, the unhappy cultivator suffered in the end; as each successive ruler, feeling his tenure uncertain, cared only to make revenue while the power lasted, an example which was but too closely imitated by his unscrupulous ministers and officials. The Carnatic is now included within the administration of the presidency of Madras.

Carnation, a half-hardy perennial herb (*Dianthus caryophyllus*) of the natural order *Caryophyllaceæ*, a native of southern Europe. It has more or less erect stems with enlarged joints, linear opposite leaves covered with a bloom, and solitary, variously colored terminal perfumed flowers, which naturally appear during summer, but which are produced artificially by certain varieties throughout the year. The plant has been in cultivation for its flowers for more than 2,000 years, but not until the early years of the 16th century did its flowers become greatly differentiated from their original flesh tint, which suggested the popular name (Latin *carnatio*). So numerous became the varieties that systems of classification were adopted. The popular European system of to-day is: (1) "Selfs," flowers of one color; (2) flakes, flowers with yellow or white ground and striped with either rose, scarlet, or purple; (3) "bizarres," resembling flakes except that they are striped with more than one color; (4) "picotees," with white or yellow petals margined with red, etc. The summer-blooming carnations which suggested this classification are little grown in America, but are very popular in Europe. They seem to demand a moist, cool climate. The group most cultivated in America and known as perpetual-flowering tree, or monthly carnations, originated in France about 1840 as the result of crossing and selection. The first of these varieties imported into America is said to have arrived in 1868, since when the growing of carnations under glass as a crop has developed. The extent of the industry is very great and is steadily growing. According to the census report of 1900 the value of the carnation crop in 1899 was about $4,000,000, produced in about 9,000 American commercial greenhouses.

Propagation of the monthly carnations is usually effected by means of cuttings of young stems. When well rooted they are potted in good soil and kept until late spring, when they are transplanted to the open ground or to the benches where they are to blossom. A winter temperature ranging between 50 and 55° at night and preferably only 10° higher during the day, is desirable. At the end of the winter they are thrown away.

The most common insect pests of the carnation are the red spider and the green aphis. The red spider thrives best in dry atmosphere, and is most easily controlled by syringing with water and evaporating (not burning) sulphur in the greenhouse once a week for about five weeks, when the insects become troublesome. The green fly or green aphis seems to thrive under any ordinary conditions. It is usually fought with tobacco fumes or various extracts of tobacco. Three fungous diseases are often troublesome: Rust (*Uromyces caryophyllinus*), spot, or blight (*Septoria dianthi*), and anthracnose (*Volutella sp*). These are largely prevented by judicious management, and when they occur may be controlled by destroying diseased plants and by spraying with Bordeaux mixture (see FUNGICIDE). Rust appears on the stems and leaves as blisters which break and expose brown spores. Spot consists of brown dots with black centres where the spores are borne. Anthracnose is characterized by grayish-brown spots. (Bailey, 'Cyclopædia of American Horticulture,' New York 1900-1902). Thirty-seven acres of land are devoted to the raising of carnations at a nursery in Los Angeles, California. Nine greenhouses, each 200 feet long and 15 feet wide, together holding 35 tons of glass, are used to raise the young plants.

Carna'tion (Latin, *caro, carnis*, "flesh"), in the fine arts, the coloring of the skin of the human body. The use of carnation requires very attentive study and great skill in the artist. It varies with the sex of the individual, with the classes and countries to which the subjects belong, with the passions, the state of the health, etc. The cheeks are, in a healthy subject, of a lively red; the breast, neck, and upper part of the arms of a soft white; the belly yellowish. At the extremities the color becomes colder, and at the joints assumes a violet tint, on account of the transparency of the skin. All these shades require to be softly blended. Two faults in carnation are chiefly to be avoided,— hardness, the fault of the masters of the 15th century, and too great weakness. Guido Reni not infrequently painted his flesh so that it appeared almost bloodless. The French school has gone farthest in this respect. The flesh of the followers of this school often looks like porcelain or wax. Titian and Rubens are unrivaled in carnation.

Carnauba, kär-nä-oo'bạ, the Brazilian name of the palm, *Copernica cerifera*, which has its leaves coated with waxy scales (whence the name wax-palm), yielding a useful wax by boiling. The fruit and pith are eaten, the leaves are variously employed, and the wood is used in building.

Carne'ades, Greek philosopher: b. Cyrene, Africa, 213 B.C.; d. 123 B.C. He studied first under Diogenes the Stoic, but subsequently attended the lectures of Egesinus, who explained the doctrines of Arcesilaus; and succeeding his master in the chair of the academy, he restored its reputation by softening the prevailing pyrrhonism and admitting practical probabilities. The doctrine of Carneades specifically was, that "as the senses, the understanding, and the imagination frequently deceive us, they cannot be the infallible judges of truth, but that from the impression made by the senses we infer appearanecs of truth, which, with respect to the conduct of life, are a sufficient guide." He was a strenuous opposer of Chrysippus, and attacked with great vigor the system of theology of the Stoics. He was an advocate of free-will against the fate of the same sect, and urged just the same difficulties in reconciling divine prescience with the freedom of human actions as have divided some contending sects of Christianity. One of the most distinguished events of his life was his being joined in an embassy to Rome wth Diogenes the Stoic and Critolaus the Peripatetic, in order to gain the mitigation of a fine levied by the Roman senate on the Athenians. This extraordinary embassy was successful, and Carneades so captivated the people by his eloquence, one day delivering a harangue in praise of justice, and on the next proving it to be an odious institution, that Cato the censor, fearful of its effect on the Roman youth, persuaded the senate to send the philosophers back to their schools without delay. In his latter years Carneades became totally blind; he died in his 90th year, continually complaining of the shortness of life, and lamenting that the same nature which composed the human frame could dissolve it.

Carnegie, Andrew, American iron-master, manufacturer and philanthropist: b. Dunfermline, Scotland, 25 Nov. 1837. None even of the mighty makers of their own fortunes began closer to absolute zero; certainly none who have owed success not to fortunate speculations, but to steady labor, sagacity, and self-culture, the natural working of the highest powers on opportunities open to all and less to him than to most. His father owned a small hand-loom business, which was closed in 1848 by the competition of steam. He then emigrated to the United States and settled in Allegheny City, Pa. The 10-year-old child here became a bobbin-boy at 20 cents a day; his alertness in a few months brought him transference to an engine-room, his penmanship and arithmetic a chance to do clerical work. Next a telegraph messenger boy at Pittsburg (with a mother and younger brother to support from his slender wages), he promptly mastered telegraphy, was soon given a place as operator, and won himself extra earnings and experience in composition as a newspaper telegraph reporter. Superior fitness brought him the post of telegraphic train-despatcher to the Pennsylvania R.R.; then of secretary to its general superintendent, Col. Scott; and in 1860, when his chief became vice-president, Mr. Carnegie was made superintendent of the Western Division. Meantime his business fortune had opened with the tentative adoption by the road, through his agency, of the Woodruff sleeping-car system, in which he shrewdly embarked some borrowed money; his expert knowledge made it investment, not speculation; and his dividends went partially into oil lands around Oil City, selected with equal judgment. At the outbreak of the war, Col. Scott was made assistant secretary of war, and gave Mr. Carnegie charge of the eastern military railroads and telegraph lines, and of this department there was no complaint or scandal, and no breakdown except of Mr. Carnegie's health from overwork. He was also the third man wounded on the Union side, while removing obstructions from the Washington tracks.

Already a small capitalist, in 1862 the Pennsylvania road's experiments in replacing wooden with iron bridges led him to forecast the future monopoly of the latter, and organize the Keystone Bridge Works, which built the first iron bridge across the Ohio. To increase their profit by furnishing their own iron, he entered the field which has made him one of the industrial sovereigns of all time. The first step was the erection of the Union Iron Mills, furnaces and rolling mills; the last, after inspection of the Bessemer process in England, to establish it in this country in 1868. The story since is one of swift aggregation of plant on plant, till they have dominated their class, and become one of the chief industrial factors of the entire business world in this its greatest age. By 1888 he had acquired a controlling interest in his foremost rival, the Homestead Steel Works, and in seven other immense establishments centred around Pittsburg; in 1899 he consolidated all these into one giant structure, the Carnegie Steel Company; and in 1901 he retired from business life, transferring his company at a valuation of $500,000,000 to be merged into one still vaster, the United States Steel Corporation, formed by J. Pierpont Morgan. His United States residence is in New York; his summer establishment at Skibo Castle, in the extreme north of Scotland.

Such supreme success, fairly won in a struggle with the world, is of course the result of a supreme individual genius not to be taught or explained; but as the amount of work any one man can do unassisted is a trifle, the chief instrumentality is always the faculty of organization. Mr. Carnegie himself once said that the organization *was* the business; that if striped at a blow of all his material property and business connections, but left his organization, in four years he would have re-established himself. But the organization is simply the men who work it, with their capacity of selecting capable subordinates, and understanding public needs and the means of supplying them; and this leaves the faculty of creating and sustaining it no nearer solution than before. In the last analysis it means a nicely accurate judgment of *men*, resulting from an intuitive gift informed and tested by long experience; and as men are not pawns, it implies the power of persuading them into and keeping them in alliance as well.

Always a generous and helpful man, he had definitely begun, a few years before his retirement, a new existence consecrated to public service, and to which he will owe enduring remembrance. Another generation would have forgotten the mere business man, however great; for after all it would have had steel from some source, if perhaps less cheaply; but it could not have had from lesser men, and would not have had from any, the splendid, judicious, and permanently useful gifts with which he has endowed it, and which no change of social ideals can render obsolete or harmful. No one has ever so royally returned to the public what he had (to its own benefit) drawn from the public. This is his own expressed conviction of duty; that "surplus wealth is a sacred trust to be administered for the highest good of the people," and that sometime "the man who dies possessed of millions free and ready to be distributed, will die disgraced." But he is equally

ANDREW CARNEGIE.

SKIBO CASTLE, MR. CARNEGIE'S HOME IN SCOTLAND.

emphatic in declaring that indiscriminate giving is mostly sheer mischief, and that no person and no community can be permanently helped except by their own co-operation. Therefore, every gift of his to a community is conditioned on the latter supporting it; and all those to institutions are thought out, and so bestowed that they forward the work without impairing the springs of public interest, or the ties to the public, which must after all be their permanent stay. These gifts are mostly not to charities in the current sense, relief of material distresses, for which the spirit of human brotherhood should be adequate; but for that mental and spiritual cultivation which should raise communities out of the lowest plane of social evils. An apparent exception, which, however, is not charity but justice and business sense, is the endowment of $4,000,000 given for an annuity fund to the workers at Homestead. The remainder of his benefactions may be divided broadly into institutions for research and the discovery of fertile new ideas; those for teaching the best of ideas and their practical applicances already known; and those for storing the results of knowledge and creation and distributing them to the public — in a word, universities, colleges, and technical schools, and libraries. Even the organs he has presented to several hundred churches may be classed in this category; as he genially observed, he is willing to indorse unreservedly all the utterances of the organs, but not of the preachers. The total amount of his benefactions to date is upward of $70,000,000, of which some $55,000,000 has been given in the United States, and with much more ultimately assured. The greatest single foundation will be the Carnegie Institute at Pittsburg, an enormous technological school, with library, art gallery, and every imaginable accessory,— the people's college of what he thinks the coming type,— which has received $10,000,000 already and is promised $25,000,000 in all. Next is the Carnegie Institution (q.v.) at Washington, to promote original research and enable original workers to use their whole time for study, experiment, and creation; perhaps his most valuable benefaction ultimately, since new ideas are at once the scarcest and the most valuable items of the world's income, and the work of one great man outweighs that of 10 generations of small ones. Of the others, perhaps the most useful, considering the work, and the chief, is the gift of $600,000 to the Tuskegee Normal and Industrial Institute in Alabama, conditioned on the trustees using enough of its income annually to free Booker T. Washington, its head, from money cares and the need of "drumming" support for his college. Sixty-five libraries in New York have received $5,200,-000; one in St. Louis $1,000,000, and two in Detroit and San Francisco $750,000 each; libraries at Homestead, Braddock, and Duquesne $1,000,000; and the universities in Scotland $10,000,000. In 1905 he established the Carnegie Foundation of $10,000,000, the income from which provides retiring pensions for teachers in non-sectarian colleges, universities, and technical schools in the United States, Canada and Newfoundland.

Mr. Carnegie has also won fame as an author. His first works, 'Notes of a Trip Around the World' (1879) and 'Our Coaching Trip' (1882) were printed first for private circulation, but published in consequence of the

great pressure for private copies. 'An American Four-in-Hand in Britain' (1883) and 'Round the World' (1884) followed; but his greatest success was attained with 'Triumphant Democracy' (1886), which sold 40,000 copies within two years. 'The Gospel of Wealth' (1900); 'The Empire of Business' (1902) and 'James Watt' (1905) have maintained his reputatiou as a clear, forcible, and interesting writer.

Carnegie Institution, an educational body incorporated 4 Jan. 1902, in Washington, D. C., by John Hay, secretary of State; Edwin D. White, justice of the supreme court; Daniel C. Gilman, ex-president of Johns Hopkins University; Charles D. Walcott, superintendent of United States Geological Survey; Dr. John S. Billings, director of the New York Public Library; and Carroll D. Wright, United States commissioner of labor. The aims of the university as expressed by the founder are: (1) To increase the efficiency of the universities and other institutions of learning throughout the country by utilizing and adding to their existing facilities, and by aiding teachers in the various institutions for the experimental and other work in these institutions as far as may be advisable; (2) to discover the exceptional man in every department of study, whenever and wherever found to enable him by financial aid to make the work for which he seems especially designed his life work; (3) to promote original research, paying great attention thereto as being one of the chief purposes of this institution; (4) to increase the facilities for higher education; (5) to enable such students as may find Washington the best point for their special studies to avail themselves of such advantages as may be open to them in the museums, libraries, laboratories, observatory, meteorological, piscicultural, and forestry schools and kindred institutions of the several departments of the government; (6) to insure the prompt publication and distribution of the results of scientific investigation, a field considered to be highly important.

The board of trustees elected by the corporators of the institution was as follows: The President of the United States (ex-officio), the president of the United States Senate, the speaker of the House of Representatives, the secretary of the Smithsonian Institution, the president of the National Academy of Sciences, and Grover Cleveland (New Jersey), John S. Billings (New York), William N. Frew (Pennsylvania), Lyman J. Gage (Illinois), Daniel C. Gilman (Maryland), John Hay (District of Columbia), Abram S. Hewitt (New Jersey), Henry L. Higginson (Massachusetts), Henry Hitchcock (Missouri), Charles L. Hutchinson (Illinois), William Lindsay (Kentucky), Seth Low (New York), Wayne McVeagh (Pennsylvania), D. O. Mills (California), S. Weir Mitchell (Pennsylvania), W. W. Morrow (California), Elihu Root (New York), John C. Spooner (Wisconsin), Andrew D. White (New York), Edward D. White (Louisiana), Charles D. Walcott (District of Columbia), and Carroll D. Wright (District of Columbia).

The trustees on 29 Jan. 1902, received from Mr. Carnegie the deed of gift of $10,000,000, and elected Daniel C. Gilman president. In 1905 R. S. Woodward succeeded him.

Carne'ia, a national festival of the ancient Spartans celebrated in honor of Apollo, and in the Spartan month Carneios. The festival lasted nine days, during which the Spartans were not allowed to enter upon a hostile campaign.

Carnelian, a beautiful, translucent chalcedony (q.v.), usually of rich brownish-red color, though sometimes brown or more rarely yellow. Some of the finest Greek and Roman intaglios and seal rings are of carnelian or sard, which is a brownish-red or dark-brown carnelian. Sardonyx (q.v.) or sard with a white top, is cut into beautiful cameos. Fine carnelians come from Nova Scotia, Brazil, Uruguay, Arabia, and India. Cambay, in Hindustan, is a noted market for the Indian stones. The native jewelers, like the lapidaries of Idar (see AGATE), intensify the colors by baking the stones in the sun for several weeks and then in ovens.

Carneri, Bartholomäus von, bär-tō-lō mä'oos fōn kär-nä'rē, Austrian poet and politician: b. Trent 1821. His volume of poems 'Plough and Sword' was greatly admired. He has published 'Foundation of Ethic' (1881); 'Der Moderne Mensch' (1900); etc.

Car'nifax Ferry, W. Va., place at which occurred a battle of the Civil War, 10 Sept 1861. On 23 August Gen. John B. Floyd, who had marched from Lewisburg, crossed to the north side of Gauley River at Carnifax Ferry with five regiments of Virginia infantry, 100 cavalry, and five guns, aggregating about 2,600 men. The 7th Ohio had been guarding the ferry, but had been recalled to within six miles of Gauley Bridge, and then ordered to return to Cross Lanes, two miles from Floyd's position, which it reached in the night of the 25th. Early on the morning of the 26th Floyd advanced, surprised the regiment while at breakfast, and routed it, killing and wounding 45 and capturing 96. About 200 men escaped to Gauley Bridge and about 400 were collected and led by Major Casement to Charleston on the Kanawha. Floyd's intention in crossing the Gauley was to force the retreat of Gen. J. D. Cox from Gauley Bridge down the Kanawha Valley, whither he proposed to follow him and make a raid of 50 miles into Ohio, but Gen. H. A. Wise, who commanded one of his two brigades, had refused to obey his order to cross the Gauley, upon which Floyd abandoned his idea of invading Ohio, and intrenched his position in a bend of the Gauley, both flanks resting on the precipices rising abruptly from the river. The presence of Floyd north of the Gauley gave Gen. Rosecrans some uneasiness, and turned his attention from the Cheat Mountain region where he had been confronting Gen. R. E. Lee. Leaving Gen. J. J. Reynolds to oppose Lee, he drew troops from posts in the rear and assembled at Bulltown seven and a half regiments of Ohio infantry, two batteries of artillery and three companies of cavalry, which were formed into three brigades, commanded by Gen. H. W. Benham, and Colonels E. P. Scammon and R. L. McCook. On 9 September he marched from Bulltown, crossed Big Birch Mountain, drove the 36th Virginia and a company of cavalry from Summersville, on the morning of the 10th, and followed to Cross Lanes, which he reached at 2 P.M., and heard that Floyd was intrenched about two miles distant. Benham, commanding the leading brigade, was ordered to advance cautiously and feel Floyd closely, but not to engage him until the entire column came up,

unless he saw a good opening. Benham drove in Floyd's pickets, and believing that he was in full retreat, pushed rashly forward in the face of a severe artillery fire, becoming closely engaged and making some spirited charges upon Floyd's works, which were repulsed. He then called for help. Rosecrans hastened up the brigades of Scammon and McCook, and going to the front, was surprised that the reconnoissance ordered had developed into a severe and badly conducted engagement. It was too late to withdraw without giving the appearance of defeat; other efforts were made, in which Scammon and McCook participated; but it was growing dark, the men were exhausted after their march of 17 miles, and Rosecrans withdrew, intending to renew the fight in the morning. During the night Floyd recrossed the Gauley, destroyed the foot-bridge behind him, sunk the ferry-boat and, with Wise, retreated to Sewell Mountain. The Union troops, fully exposed and not well handled, had 17 killed and 141 wounded. The Confederates, well protected by log-works, had none killed and 21 wounded. Consult Official Records, Vol. V.

E. A. CARMAN.

Carnio'la (German, KRAIN), a province of Austria, with an area of 3,856 English square miles. It is covered with lofty mountains, some of which are about 10,000 feet high, and, generally speaking, is one of the most unfertile regions of the empire. Some districts, however, produce considerable quantities of wheat, barley, wine, and, in the south, fruits of various kinds, and excellent flax. There are some iron, lead, and quicksilver mines, the latter exceedingly rich. It abounds in clays and valuable stones, and in coal and marble. There are considerable manufactures of iron, fine linen, lace, woolen cloth, flannel, worsted stockings, leather, wooden articles, etc. Its chief exports are steelwares, quicksilver, hats, linens, glasswares, wax, wine, flour, etc.; principal imports — salt, oil, fruit, coffee, sugar, tobacco, cloths, cattle, etc. Carniola was made a duchy in the 12th century, under the dominion of the Counts of Tyrol, who became extinct in 1335, and were succeeded by the Earls of Goerz. After the treaty of Vienna, in 1809, it was ceded to France, and incorporated in the kingdom of Illyria. In 1814 it came again into the possession of Austria. Capital, Laibach. Pop. (1900) 508,348.

Car'nival. The same views which led men to propitiate the higher invisible powers by gifts, sacrifices, and purifications, also introduced fasts, abstinence from pleasure, and penauces. By fast is meant an abstinence from the usual means of nourishment, in order to mortify the appetites, and thereby to propitiate the Deity. In every nation of importance customs of this kind are found. Their historical origin is in the religious customs of the East, where the priests were originally the physicians of the people, and prescribed these fasts as a part of the regimen necessary in this warm region, as well as from religious views. Fasts are observed to this day in the East. The religions of the Persians and the Hindus, those of the Mohammedans, and of the worshippers of the Lama, insist much on fasts. Few traces of them are found in the religion of the ancient people of the North. The earliest Christians fasted on the vigils (q.v.).

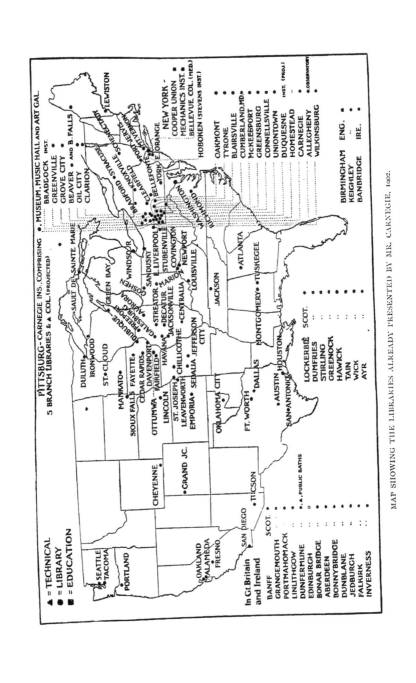

MAP SHOWING THE LIBRARIES ALREADY PRESENTED BY MR. CARNEGIE, 1902.

The fasts on the *jejunia quatuor tempestatum*, which continued for three days every quarter of the year, were penances, as was that of the period of 40 days (before Easter, or rather before Good Friday, *Quadrigesimæ*), which was called, by way of excellence, the fast, and which commemorated the 40 days' fast of Jesus in the wilderness. With regard to the origin of Christian fasts, opinions differ. The most common is, that Telesphorus, bishop of Rome, in the middle of the second century, first instituted the 40 days' fast as a rule of the Church. By Pope Gregory the Great, about 600, Ash Wednesday was made the beginning of the fast, and the day before was called fast eve, because in the night of this day, at twelve o'clock, the fast began. This fast was preceded by a feast of three days, very obnoxious to the strict zealots. "Christians," it is said, "on these days deliver themselves up to voluntary madness, put on masks, exchange sexes, clothe themselves like spectres, give themselves up to Bacchus and Venus, and consider all pleasure allowable." This is the origin of the present carnival, or *Fasching*, as it is called in the south of Germany, and which continues in that country from Twelfth Day to Ash Wednesday. The name carnival is derived from the Latin *caro, carnis*, flesh, and *vale*, farewell (according to Ducange, from the Latin denomination of the feasts in the Middle Ages, *carnis levamen*, solace of the flesh), because at that time people took leave of flesh. Previously to the commencement of their long abstinence, men devoted themselves to enjoyment, particularly during the last three days of the carnival. The carnival is nothing but the Saturnalia of the Christian Romans, who could not forget their pagan festivals. At least it greatly resembles the Saturnalia which were celebrated annually in December, with all kinds of mirth, pleasure, and freedom, in honor of Saturn, and the golden age when he governed the world, and to preserve the remembrance of the liberty and equality of man in the youth of the world. In Rome, the carnival brought to view, in a lively manner, the old Saturnalia in a new form. During the last days of the carnival, and particularly during the day which preceded the long fast, mummeries, plays, tricks, and freedom of every kind, abounded. From Italy, the modern Saturnalia passed to the other Christian countries of Europe. The wealthiest class commenced their amusements 8 or 10 days before Ash Wednesday, the middle classes 2 or 3 days, the poor only observed one day (the *Fastnacht* of the Germans). In the amusements of this period the dramatic poetry of Germany had its origin, after the cities had attained a flourishing condition. Its first traces appeared in the 13th century. The mummeries of the carnival produced the idea of adopting some character, and carrying it through. To please the multitude, and make the laugh more certain, the manners of common life were caricatured. These exhibitions afterward became more cultivated and developed. On fast eve persons in disguise sometimes went from one house to another, to make sport with their friends and acquaintances. A merry society of this kind formed a plan to represent some scene in their disguises, and hold a regular conversation at one of these mummeries. The unknown players received praises, entertainments, or presents. Encouraged by this success, the company grew stronger, their fables and speeches became longer by degrees, until they attained to regular representations of human life. It was in Nüremberg, renowned for its wares and its wit, that the first fast eve's play was produced, coarse and frolicsome, to suit the taste of the citizens. The earliest of these pieces that have come down to us date from 1450–70; they have a near relationship to the masques of the English and the farces of the French, as have the spiritual fast eve's plays, religious burlesques, to the Mysteries and Moralities. In Italy the carnival is now celebrated with the greatest show and spirit at Rome. It lasts for the 10 days preceding Ash Wednesday, certain observances taking place on certain days. Some days, for instance, are devoted to the throwing of comfits, or of small plaster pellets that take their place, these being flung from the balconies of the houses upon the persons in the streets — especially in the Corso — who retaliate in the same way, and in order that they may do this many of them are mounted upon lofty cars or other vehicles, all being masked. On other days the finest equipages move along in procession, and flowers instead of comfits are thrown. Races of riderless horses in the Corso are another prominent feature of carnival time. After sunset on Shrove Tuesday everybody carries a lighted taper (these being known as *moccoletti*), and each tries to extinguish as many others as he can while keeping his own alight. Venice, Turin, Milan, Naples, Florence, etc., also celebrate the carnival with more or less ceremony, and the same can be said of various towns of the south of France, Nice in particular. The carnival at Rome has been excellently described by Goethe. In Germany the carnival is celebrated with brilliancy only in the Catholic cities of the Rhine valley, Mayence, Bonn, but above all Cologne. In Protestant countries, generally, the feast is not observed to any extent.

Carniv′ora, broadly, those animals which prey upon other animals; but in a restricted sense, that order of mammals to which the cat, dog, bear, and seal belong. The head is small in proportion to the bulk of the body, and the skin is well covered with hair. The limbs, four in number, are fully developed, and are adapted either for walking or swimming. Two sets of teeth, deciduous or milk and permanent, are always developed in succession, and in both sets incisors, canines, and molars, are distinguishable. The order is divided into two groups, the *Fissipedia,* which include such animals as the lion, wolf, bear, etc., whose life is terrestrial: and the *Pinnipedia,* or those which are specially adapted for aquatic life.

1. *Fissipedia.*— All the carnivores of this division, except the sea-otter (*Enhydra*), have six incisor teeth in each jaw, the canine teeth are prominent, and one of the molar series in each jaw is usually compressed laterally, so as to present a cutting edge. The toes are furnished with claws, and the anterior limbs are used for seizing and holding prey as well as for walking. The skull is contracted behind the orbits, so as to give an hour-glass form when seen from above. The hollow formed by this constriction on each side of the head is bridged over by the wide zygomatic arch, and thus gives room for the powerful muscles of mastication. The lower jaw is articulated to the skull, so that it can only be moved up and down. The incisor

and canine teeth are represented by the formula $i\frac{3-3}{3-3}$, $c\frac{1-1}{1-1}$. The teeth behind the canines increase in size from before backwards, and vary from $\frac{4-4}{3-3}$ in the cat, to $\frac{8-8}{8-8}$ in the South African otocyon, the total number of teeth of all kinds ranging from 30 to 48. The posterior teeth are divided into premolars and molars; the last of the premolar series in the upper, and the first of the molar series in the lower jaw presenting the lateral compression and trenchant margin which earns for them the name of sectorial or carnassial teeth. Behind the carnassial the molars have tuberculated crowns. The stomach is simple and undivided, and, as a general rule, is more rounded in the flesh-eating genera. The limbs terminate in digits, which are never fewer than four, and are furnished with sharp claws, which in the *Felidæ* are retractile within sheaths of the integument on the dorsal surface of the toes. In walking, the extremities of the toes are applied to the ground, as in the "digitigrade" cat and dog; or the whole sole of the foot is put down, as in the "plantigrade" bear. The six families included under the fissipede carnivores are: (1) *Felidæ:* lion, tiger, leopard, cat, etc. These present the highest type of the carnivorous structure. The claws are retractile. (2) *Canidæ:* wolf, dog, jackal, fox, etc. The claws are not retractile, and the gape is longer. The toes in this and the previous family are five on the anterior and four on the posterior extremities; (3) *Hyænidæ:* hyæna, aardwolf, etc. The hyænas have the anterior limbs longer than the posterior, and both terminate in four toes. The skull and dentition approximate to those of the Felidæ; (4) *Viverridæ.* The supple elongated bodies of these animals are intermediate between those of the cats and the martens. Some, as the civet, gennet, zibet, have the claws retractile; in others, as the ichneumon and rasse, they are not retractile. Those mentioned are digitigrade, but the suricate of central Africa is plantigrade. In this family glands are found under the tail, the secretions of which have powerful odors. The diet of this family is not purely animal. (5) *Mustelidæ.* The members of this family have elongated bodies with short limbs, terminating usually in five-toed feet with retractile or non-retractile claws. The marten, weasel, polecat, ermine, glutton, or wolverene, constitute one sub-family of exclusively terrestrial life. The badgers, the skunks, and the like, constitute another division. (6) *Ursidæ.* In this family the carnassial tooth is no longer trenchant, but tuberculated. All are plantigrade, but the habits and aspect vary considerably, and include, besides the bears, the raccoons, panda, and several lesser forms. The raccoon and its allies are sometimes made a family with the name *Procyonidæ.*

2. *Pinnipedia.*— The aquatic carnivores comprise three families, represented by the walrus or sea-horse, the eared seals, and the common seals. They are related to the preceding families through the otters and the bears, and agree in having the extremities modified into swimming organs or flippers, and the teeth more uniform in character. See SEALS; WALRUS.

Carnivora, Fossil. The evolution of the *Carnivora* through the Tertiary Period is shown by numerous fossil species. These indicate that the modern carnivores are descended from a group of primitive *Carnivora* (see CREODONTA) of the early Eocene, and have gradually diverged from a single stock, of which the *Viverridæ*, or civets, are the nearest living representatives. From these the dogs branched out in one direction, the mustelines, hyænas, and cats in others, while the bears and raccoons are offshoots of primitive dogs. Many intermediate stages are known, between dogs and bears (as *Amphicyon*, *Hyænarctos*), dogs and raccoons (*Phlaocyon*), mustelines and civets (*Plesictis*, etc.), civets and hyænas (*Ictitherium*). No true *Carnivora* are found fossil in South America until the end of the Tertiary, and (with a single exception) none exist now in Australia. In both continents their place was supplied by carnivorous marsupials (see MARSUPIALIA), which branched out into groups more or less paralleling the true *Carnivora* of the northern hemisphere. See also BEARS; CATS; DOGS; FOSSIL.

Carnivorous Plants, plants of various genera which subsist partly upon insects and other small animals which they entrap in various ways. The apparatus in each case is a modified leaf or part of a leaf, and in some cases the modifications are so curious, so well adapted to the use to which they are put, and so perfect in action, that the plants seem almost intelligent. The object sought by these plants seems to be to supply themselves with nitrogenous food, which is generally in meagre supply where they usually live — undrained swamps. Probably, too, such plants as do not live in these habitats formerly did, but have not yet lost the use of the apparatus. A case of this kind is exhibited by the genus *Utricularia* (see BLADDERWORT). In this genus various species provided with active bladders, which act like eel-traps, live submerged in ponds; other species, also possessing active but less perfect and useful traps, live in the marshy soil of swamps. Still others live on dry ground, but these have usually abortive traps. The conclusion is that as the ponds became swamps, and the swamps were converted into dry land, the supply of nitrogenous food increased, and hence the traps became aborted, because they were no longer needed.

Probably the most nearly intelligent of these carnivorous plants is the Venus' fly-trap (*Dionæa*), found in the southeastern United States. The trap consists of two pieces hinged together. On the margins are bristles, and in the interior a few sensitive hairs, which, when touched, act like a trigger, and the apparatus closes. Should an insect cause this action the bristles will prevent its escape and the trap will remain closed until its digestion is complete, when the trap will open, cast out the indigestible portions, and be ready for another victim. If the trap fails to catch its prey, or if it be sprung by something it cannot utilize, it will open again in a short time. In the sundew (*Drosera*) the leaves are provided with glandular hairs which close over the insect that alights upon the leaf, and a glistening sticky substance holds it fast until its digestible parts are absorbed by the plant.

In the pitcher-plants (*Sarracenia, Nepenthes*, etc.), the pitcher consists of a tube either with or without a lid or hood. Around the mouth there is usually a sugary secretion which acts as a lure. The insect that alights cannot escape

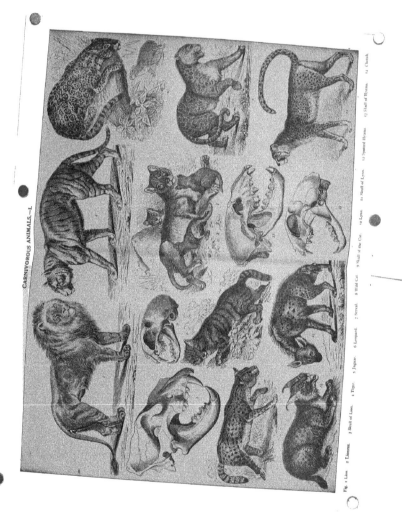

CARNIVOROUS ANIMALS.—I.

Fig. 1 Lion.   2 Lioness.   3 Skull of Lion.   4 Tiger.   5 Jaguar.   6 Leopard.   7 Serval.   8 Wild Cat.   9 Skull of the Cat.   10 Lynx.   11 Skull of Lynx.   12 Spotted Hyæna.   13 Skull of Hyæna.   14 Cheetah.

Fig. 1 Aard Wolf. 2 Hunting Dog, or Hyena-Dog. 3 Wolf. 4 Skull of Wolf. 5 Dhole, or Kholsun. 6 Jackal. 7 Brazilian Fox. 8 Common Fox. 9 Fennec.
10 Civet. 11 Genet. 12 Zibet. 13 Ichneumon. 14 Raccoon. 15 Marten. 16 Skull of Marten. 17 Weasel. 18 Polecat. 19 Otter. 20 Skull of Otter.

because the tube is lined with hairs that force him downward to the bottom of the tube, which is usually partly filled with water. Some other genera m which the carnivorous habit is developed are *Darlingtonia, Aldrovandra,* and *Pinguicula.* Consult: Darwin, 'Insectivorous Plants.'

Carnochan, kär'nō-kăn, **John Murray,** American surgeon, famous for his bold and skilful operations: b. Savannah, Ga., 4 July 1817; d. New York, 28 Oct. 1887. He studied at Edinburgh and at various European universities; and began his practice in New York in 1847. In 1851 he became professor of surgery at the New York Medical College, and surgeon-in-chief to the State Immigrant Hospital. At one time he cured neuralgia by excising the whole trunk of the second branch of the fifth pair of nerves. In 1852 he tied the femoral artery to cure exaggerated nutrition. He also tied the primitive carotid artery on both sides, to cure elephantiasis of the neck. In 1853 he exsected the entire radius, in 1854 the entire ulna. He published a treatise on 'Congenital Dislocations,' and a translation of Rokitausky's 'Pathological Anatomy.'

Carnot, Lazare Hippolyte, lä-zär ē-pō-lēt kär-nō, French statesman, second son of the preceding: b. St. Omer, 6 April 1801; d. 16 March 1888. He was of liberal opinions, became a disciple of St. Simon, and wrote the 'Exposition générale de la doctrine Saint Simonienne,' the authorship of which was, with his consent, ascribed to Bazard. But as soon as St. Simonism assumed the form of a religious creed, Carnot parted with his friends, and became a journalist, and the chief editor of the 'Revue encyclopédique.' He was also entrusted with the publication of Grégoire's and Barère's 'Mémoires.' He was elected to the chamber of deputies in 1839, and re-elected in 1842 and 1846. After the revolution of February 1848, he was minister of public instruction until 5 July, and improved, as such, the condition of the teachers, rendered the normal schools free, and established free lectures. In 1848 he was elected to the constituant, and 10 March 1850, to the legislative assembly. After the *coup d'état* of December 1851, he left France; during his absence, he was elected a member of the *corps législatif,* but refused to take the oath. He was re-elected in 1857, but again refused to serve. He published the memoirs of his father (1860-4).

Carnot, Lazare Nicolas Marguerite, lä zär nĭk-ō-lä mär-gä-rēt, French soldier and statesman: b. Nolay, Burgundy, 1753; d. Magdeburg, 2 Aug. 1823. From his youth he exhibited an uncommon talent for the mathematical and military sciences, entered the corps of engineers, and rose in office by the favor of the Prince of Condé. He published, afterward, 'Mathematical Essays,' which caused him to be elected a member of several learned societies. His eulogy on Vauban received the prize of the Academy of Dijon. In 1791 he was appointed deputy to the constituent assembly, but at first took part only in military affairs. On his proposal the officers of the nobility were removed from the army, and others substituted from the citizens. He also proposed that implicit obedience should only be demanded of the soldier in presence of the enemy, at other times he should have all the privileges and rights of the citizen; a strange proposal to come from a military chief. As a member of the convention he voted for the death of Louis. In the following March he was sent to the army of the north, where he put himself at the head and repulsed the enemy. On his return to the convention he was made a member of the Committee of Public Safety. The influence of Carnot in the military operations now began to be more deeply felt. In possession of all the plans deposited in the archives of Louis XIV., he organized and directed the French armies; and his direction undoubtedly contributed very much to their success. After the fall of Robespierre he was often accused, but always acquitted, because his duty had been to take care of the defense of the country, and he could not be made answerable for the cruel decrees of Robespierre, in which Carnot's name, as he was a member of the committee, was of course to be found. At the establishment of the directory in 1795 Carnot was chosen a member, and for some time maintained an important influence. Barras at length succeeded him in the department of war, and was ever after his enemy. His plan for the overthrow of Barras was unsuccessful, and with some others he was sentenced to transportation on the 18th Fructidor (Sept. 4) 1797. He fled to Germany and published a defense, which was eagerly read in Paris, and by the exposure of the conduct of his former colleagues hastened their overthrow on the 30th Prairial (June 18) 1799. After the 18th Brumaire Carnot was recalled, and appointed *inspecteur aux revues,* and two months later, in April 1800, minister of war. He soon after retired into the bosom of his family, but was called to the tribunate, 9 March 1802. He often opposed the views of the government, voted against the consulship for life, and his was the only voice raised against the proposal for the imperial dignity. He remained, however, a member of the tribunate till it was abolished, passed the next seven years of his life in retirement, and published several valuable military works. In 1814 Napoleon gave him the chief command at Antwerp. He connected a vigorous defense with a careful regard for the interest of the city, which, by the command of Louis XVIII., he afterward surrendered to the British General Graham. He still retained his titles and his honors, but as a firm republican he could never expect the favor of the court; particularly as, in his memorial to the king, he openly and severely censured the measures of government, in consequence of which he was passed over in the new organization of the Academy of Sciences. When Napoleon was once more at the helm of state in 1815, he made Carnot count and peer of the empire, and pressed upon him the ministry of the interior. Carnot discharged the difficult duties of this office with his usual integrity. After the emperor's second fall he was made a member of the provisory government of France, and was afterward the only one of the members of it comprehended in the ordinance of 24 July. He retired to Cerney, where he employed his pen on political subjects: then to Warsaw with his family; and finally to Magdeburg. Among Carnot's writings the most valuable are his 'Essai sur les Machines'; 'Réflexions sur la Métaphysique du Calcul infinitésimal'; 'Sur la Géometrie de Position'; 'De la Défense des Places fortes'; 'Exposé de la Conduite politique de Carnot, depuis le 1 Juill. 1814.' In Magdeburg Carnot published 'Mémoire sur la Fortification primitive,' and a volume of poems. He was rigid in his love of virtue, a scholar, a general, and an inflexible republican. He was universally esteemed, both in France and in foreign lands, and was honored by all parties.

Carnot, Marie François Sadi, mä-rē fräṅ-swä sä-dē, French president, grandson of Carnot (q.v.): b. Limoges, 11 Aug. 1837; d. Lyons, 24 June 1894. He was educated at the École Polytechnique and became a civil engineer. In 1871 M. Gambetta appointed him prefeet of the Seine-Inférieure, and intrusted him with the duty of seeing to the defenses of his department, a task which he fulfilled with great ability. M. Brisson gave him the portfolio of public works in his cabinet of 1885, and in the following year he became minister of finance, retaining this post under Brisson's successor, De Freycinet. In 1887 he was elected president of the French republic in succession to M. Jules Grévy, but before his term of office had expired he was assassinated at Lyons by an Italian anarchist named Caserio.

Carnot, Nicolas Léonard Sadi, nǐk-ō-lä lä-ō-när sä-dē, French physicist: b. Paris 1 June 1796; d. there, 24 Aug. 1832. He was educated at the polytechnic school; in 1814 he entered the engineer corps, where he served until 1828, becoming captain in 1824. In 1824 he published his book, 'Reflexions sur la Puissance Notrice du Feu,' in which he laid down the principle that the efficiency of a thermodynamic engine is proportional to the amount of heat transferred from the source of heat to the condenser; and that heat passes only from a warmer to a colder body. This is called the second law of thermodynamics and is known also as Carnot's principle.

Carnotite, a mineral first described in 1899, and now one of the most important ores of uranium. It is a hydrous vanadate of uranium and potassium, its formula being, perhaps, $K_2O. 2U_2O_5. V_2O_4. 3H_2O$. Radium has been shown to be present in it and radiographs may be made from the crude mineral. It seems likely that it will become an important ore of radium. It is a canary-yellow crystalline powder, usually occurring disseminated through sandstone, but sometimes in earthy masses of considerable richness. Its chief locality is in Montrose County, Colo., but it has recently been reported from Utah.

Carnutes, kär-nū'tēz, or **Carnuti,** ti, an ancient tribe living in central Gaul. At war with Cæsar in 52 B.C.

Caro, kä'rō, Annibale, Italian author: b. Citta Nuova, 1507; d. 1566. In 1543 he was appointed secretary to Pietro Ludovico Farnese, Duke of Parma and Piacenza, who entrusted him with several missions to Charles V. After the assassination of the Duke his own life was in considerable danger. He took refuge in Parma, and was treated in a friendly manner by the new Duke Octavio Farnese, whose two brothers, the cardinals, Ranuccio and Alexander, took him successively into their service. With the latter he remained from 1548 to his death in 1566, and received from him several ecclesiastical preferments. Caro devoted himself chiefly to the study of numismatics and the Tuscan language,

and his pure and elegant style in verse and prose soon became generally admired. His translation of the Æneid in blank verse is excellent. After his death appeared a translation by him of Longus, and of Aristotle's 'Rhetoric'; also 'Rime' (1569), and 'Lettere familiari' (1572-5), the former of which are admired for the elegance of the verse, and the latter as models of beautiful Italian prose.

Caro, Elme Marie, ĕlm mä rē kä-ro, French philosopher: b. Poitiers, 4 March 1826; d. 13 July 1887. He was a lecturer at the École Normale of Paris in 1857, professor at the Sorbonne 1867, and a member of the French Academy in 1876. He was one of the popular lecturers of his day and his lectures in defense of the Christian religion were largely attended, being especially popular with women. He published 'L' Idée de Dieu et ses nouveaux Critiques'; 'La Philosophie de Goethe'; 'La Materialisme et la Science'; 'Études Morales sur le Temps présent'; 'Nelanges et Portraits.'

Caro, Jakob, yä kŏb kä'ro, German historian: b. Gnesen, 2 Feb. 1836. He was educated at Berlin and Leipsic, traveled in Galicia and southern Russia, and in 1863 became lecturer at the University of Jena and later professor; in 1868 he was professor at Breslau. He has written 'Das Interregnum Polens 1856' (1861); 'Liber Cancellariæ Stanislai Ciolek' (1871-4); 'Lessing und Swift, Studien uber Nathan den Weisen' (1869); 'Aus der Kanzlei Kaiser Siegsmunds' (1879); 'Das Bundniss zu Canterbury' (1880); 'Beata und Halszka, eine Polnisch-Russische Geschichte aus dem 16. Jahrhundert.' (1880); and a continuation of Röpell's 'Geschichte Polens.'

Caro, Miguel Antonio, mē-gĕl' än-tō'nē-ō, Colombian prose-writer and poet: b. Bogotá, Colombia, 10 Nov. 1843. He has been an editor and contributor to periodicals. His principal works are 'Poems' (1866); 'Hours of Love,' a prose work; and a translation into Spanish verse of Virgil's complete works (3 vols. 1873-5). He is a correspondent of the Royal Spanish Academy, and in 1886 was national librarian in the Colombian Congress.

Carob, kär'ŏb, or Algaro'ba-bean (*Ceratonia siliqua*), a leguminous plant of the suborder *Cæsalpineæ*, growing wild in all the countries bordering the Mediterranean, and more especially in the Levant. It has a dark-green foliage, and produces pods in which the seeds are embedded in nutritious pulp, of the taste and consistence of manna. The names "locust" and "St. John's bread" have been given to the legumes of this plant, from an idea that they were the food eaten, along with wild honey, by the Baptist in the wilderness. The legumes are sometimes imported into this country as food for horses, this being their principal use in the south of Europe and the north of Africa, where the plant is cultivated. Singers are said to chew the seeds for improving the voice.

Caröe, kä'rō, William Douglas, English architect of Danish parentage: b. Liverpool, 1857. He was educated at Trinity College, Cambridge, and studied architecture with the eminent architect, John L. Pearson. He is architect to Southwell Cathedral and to the Diocesan societies of Lichfield and Derbyshire, as well as to the dean and chapter of Canter-

CAROL — CAROLINA

bury. Among his principal works are the archbishop's palace at Canterbury, bishop's palace at Bristol; St. David's Church at Exeter; Wycombe Abbey School; and the Jubilee Monument to Queen Victoria at Mentone, France. He has also restored many buildings of historic interest.

Carol, a song of praise sung at Christmas or Easter. It originally meant a song accompanied with dancing, in which sense it is frequently used by the old poets. It appears to have been danced by many performers, by taking hands, forming a ring, and singing as they went round. It has been said that the oldest carol was that sung by the heavenly host when the birth of the Saviour was announced to the shepherds on the plains of Bethlehem. It is probable that the practice of singing carols at Christmas-tide arose in imitation of this, as the majority of the carols declared the good tidings of great joy; and the title of Noels, nowells, or novelles, applied to carols, would seem to bear out this idea. Carol singing is of great antiquity among Christian communities, as the carol by Aurelius Prudentius, of the 4th century, will show.

Carolan, kär'ō lăn, **Turlogh,** Irish musical genius: b. near Nobber, County of Westmeath, about 1670; d. 1738. Having lost his sight when a child, he studied the harp, and in after life not only maintained himself thereby, but even became famous.

Carolanos, kä-rō-lä'nōs, a heathen tribe of the Philippines, living in the mountain lands of the island of Negros, especially the Cordillera of Canyan. They are of Malayan stock and may be identical with the Buquitnon, though that cannot be determined. Practically nothing is known of them.

Caroli, Pietro Francesco, pē ä trō frän-chěs'kō kä'rō lē, Italian painter: b. Turin 1638; d. 1716. He studied painting at Venice, Florence, and Rome, and was professor in the Academy of Rome at his death. He is celebrated for his careful execution and beautiful coloring, and excelled particularly in perspective, of his skill of which he has left excellent specimens in his drawings of the interior of some of the Roman churches.

Carolina, kä-rō-lē'nạ. This name is generally given to a famous law of the German Empire, of the year 1532, under Charles V., which he himself called an ordinance of criminal procedure (*Peinliche Gerichtsordnung*). From him it was at a later period called *Constitutio criminalis Carolina,* or shortly *Carolina.* The arbitrary administration of justice, the disorder and cruelty which had become customary in the courts of Germany, where many a process was begun and ended with torture, and persons were sentenced even to death without regular process, gave occasion to this law. From the beginning of the peace of the land the necessity of such a law was felt throughout the country; but it was difficult in this, as in all other cases, to make the different members of the empire agree on one general measure. The Baron Johann von Schwarzenberg was chiefly instrumental in introducing this ordinance. He became minister of state of the Prince-bishop of Bamberg, and succeeded in procuring an ordinance of criminal procedure for Bamberg to be
Vol. 3—31.

drawn up and published in 1507. The same was also adopted in 1510 by the margrave of Brandenburg and Franconia; and at last a law of criminal procedure for the empire at large was passed by the diet at Ratisbon, in 1532. The Carolina contains 219 articles, which regulate the standing and oaths of judges, the character of witnesses, the penalties of different crimes, and the circumstances in which torture at that time common in criminal jurisprudence should be applied. Several German princes, as the elector of Saxony, the elector of Brandenburg, and of the palatinate, protested against it, in order to protect the laws of their states and their own privileges against the legislative power of the emperor; but at last the Carolina was established in almost every part of the empire. From the connection of Switzerland with Germany, and the fact that several Swiss towns were imperial cities, German laws frequently passed into Switzerland, and the Carolina became the law by which even the Swiss troops in the service of the kings of France were governed until the French Revolution.

Caroli'na Allspice. See CALYCANTHUS.

Carolina, Original Constitution of. For many years after the subversion of the old English order by political and religious insubordination, 1642–60, the dominant idea of the conservatives was to prevent its recurrence, as with the conservatives after the French Revolution; and their chief dread was of republicans and dissenters. It is an almost grotesque incident of this reaction, that by far its narrowest embodiment came from a liberal philosopher and an unbelieving incendiary politician,—John Locke and Lord Shaftesbury (Anthony Ashley Cooper). A group of eight noblemen, headed by the famous Lord Clarendon, and including Shaftesbury, were granted on 24 March 1663, a tract called the province of Carolina, after Charles II.; as extended 30 June 1665, it included the present North and South Carolina and Georgia, and in theory stretched west to the Pacific. "To avoid erecting a numerous democracy," in their own words, they had Locke, who was Shaftesbury's secretary, draw up (whether on his own lines or Shaftesbury's is a moot point) a form of government called the "Fundamental Constitutions," which is a classic for impractical absurdity even among Utopias. The mass of the people (not alone, be it remembered, the future immigrants, but a considerable population already living there in pure democracy) were to be hereditary "leet-men," or serfs of the soil. Next above them was a sort of upper middle-class commons called "lords of the manor," who could let out 10-acre tenant farms. Over both (as the charter gave the proprietors the right to create titles of nobility other than English ones) were a fantastic self-perpetuating colonial *noblesse,* of "landgraves" and "caciques." Crowning the whole were the proprietors; the eldest was "palatine" or viceroy, the others were admiral, chamberlain, high constable, chief justice, chancellor, high steward, and treasurer. The "leet-men" held three fifths of the land; the nobility and "lords of the manor" one fifth, not to be alienated after 1700; the proprietors the remaining fifth. The province was divided checkerboard fashion into squares, first of counties; then each county into eight "signeries" for the proprietors, eight "baronies" for the nobility (each signory and barony to contain 12,000 acres, perpetually annexed to the title), and four "precincts," and each precinct into four "colonies" for the serfs. There was a Parliament; but the commons were carefully kept. powerless by giving them only 14 members out of 50, making only freeholders of 500 acres eligible to seats, and electing them for life; with the further proviso that landgraves could sit in either house at will, and vote on the same measures in both. All initiative was in a supreme executive council, which prepared and submitted all legislation to Parliament; and the proprietors had a veto on all. Each proprietor had a superior court at which he presided in person or by proxy; each nobleman held a court-leet for his barony, and there were precinct courts. The laws were worthy of this closet constitution. The English Church was established and supported by public taxation, in a province inhabited largely by Quakers, and the rest by Scotch Presbyterians, Huguenots, Lutherans, etc. No one could live or hold property in or be a freeman of the province who did not acknowledge God, and that he is to be publicly worshipped. Every person above 17 not a member of some church, or who did not subscribe the "Fundamental Constitutions" and promise in writing to defend and maintain them, should be an outlaw. There was a severe censorship of the press, of ceremonies, of fashions, and of sports, in the hands of the nobility. Paid lawyers were prohibited; thus compelling the commons to put themselves under a relation of "clientage," in Roman fashion, to the nobility to avoid ruin. All commentaries on the constitution or laws were forbidden. This constitution was to replace one under which the people were ruled by a council of 12, chosen half by the proprietors and half by the Assembly; that Assembly consisting of 12 elected freeholders, so that the people had 18 out of 25 votes; with entire freedom of religion, civil marriage, security for five years from suit on cause arising outside of the country (for protection of emigrant debtors), exemption from taxation for the first year, and no political or social superiors anywhere. That is, free Englishmen in virtual democracy were to become at a blow the serfs and villeins of the time of the Norman Conquest. The proprietors bound themselves by solemn compact to maintain this incredibly foolish instrument as unalterable forever, and evidently expected men to emigrate to a savage wilderness on such terms. Five successive forms of this constitution were promulgated before its entire abandonment in 1693, each in turn proclaimed permanent and unalterable; and the result, especially in Albemarle County (afterward North Carolina), was simple anarchy. The people set them utterly at naught; and while the former system had been legally abolished, it continued in force by sufferance. Resistance to law as a first principle of life became ingrained in them; and the character of the colony was long and deeply injured by the quarter-century of attempt to force its people, new and old, into this iron mold of extreme feudalism. For further history, see NORTH CAROLINA; SOUTH CAROLINA.

Carolina-pink, Maryland Pinkroot, or **Worm-grass,** names given to the *Spigelia marilandica*, a plant of the order *Loganiaceæ*, bearing scarlet flowers, and having a root used as a vermifuge. It occurs in rich woods, and ex-

tends from New Jersey, west, north, and south, to Wisconsin and Texas.

Carolina Ridge, in geology, the name given to an elevation of the bottom of the Atlantic Ocean off North Carolina, that occurred in Miocene time. It deflected the Gulf Stream and caused a great change in climate along the Atlantic coast. See MIOCENE; TERTIARY.

Car'oline Amelia Elizabeth, Queen of England, wife of George IV., king of Great Britain and Hanover, second daughter of Duke Charles William Ferdinand of Brunswick: b. 17 May 1768; d. London, 6 Aug. 1821. She was married to the Prince of Wales, afterward George IV., in 1795. After the birth of her daughter, Charlotte Augusta (7 Jan. 1796), her husband abandoned her, declaring that no one could force his inclinations. This was the beginning of the disgraceful dispute between the two parties, which lasted till the death of Caroline, and exposed her honor to repeated accusations from her husband. The Princess of Wales lived retired from the court, at a country-seat at Blackheath, till 1808. In 1813 the contest was renewed between the two parties, the Princess of Wales complaining, as a mother, of the difficulties opposed to her seeing her daughter. In 1814 the princess obtained permission to go to Brunswick, and afterward to make the tour of Italy and Greece, in which the Italian Bergami was her confidant and attendant. Many infamous reports were afterward circulated, relating to the connection between the Princess and Bergami. When the Prince of Wales ascended the throne, 29 Jan. 1820, he offered her an income of £50,000 sterling, on condition that she should renounce the title of Queen of England, and every title appertaining to that dignity, and should not again return to England. She refused the proposal, returned to England, 5 June, and the next day entered London amid public demonstrations of welcome. She was now tried for adultery, but not convicted, and in this trial Brougham acted as the queen's attorney-general. Though banished from the court, the queen still lived at Brandenburg House, maintaining a style suitable to her rank. She was refused admission to Westminster Abbey on the occasion of the coronation of her husband, on 19 July 1821, and published a protest in the newspapers. Her tomb at Brunswick has a very short inscription, in which she is called the unhappy queen of England.

Caroline Matilda, Queen of Denmark, daughter of Frederick Louis, Prince of Wales: b. 1751; d. Celle, Hanover, 10 May 1775. She was married in 1766 to King Christian VII. of Denmark. She became the object of court intrigues caused by the jealousy of the grandmother and stepmother of her husband. These led to the execution for treason of Counts Struensee and Brandt, who were of the queen's party, and to the imprisonment of the queen herself, who was liberated through the interference of her brother, George III. of England. Her last hours are described in a small work, 'Die letzen Stunden der Königin von Danemark.'

Caroline, The, an American steamboat used in 1837 by the American sympathizers with the Canadian insurgents under William Lyon Mackenzie (q.v.). The latter, after years of agitation, had gathered a band of insurgents in December, and attempted to seize Toronto, capture the lieutenant-governor and his cabinet, and proclaim a republic. He was defeated, and fled to Navy Island on the British side of the Niagara River. Some hundreds of American sympathizers joined him, and he set up a "provisional government," issued paper money, and offered bounties for volunteers and a reward for the apprehension of the lieutenant-governor. On 29 December an American steamer, the Caroline, crossed over to his camp from Schlosser on the American side, laden with reinforcements, provisions, and munitions; and returning, lay at Schlosser that night full of men presumably ready for a similar trip the next day. The Canadians, incensed at this outrageous violation of neutrality, sent over an armed party in boats to enforce it. They boarded the Caroline, hustled the passengers and crew ashore, killing one man (Amos Durfee) on shore in the fray, towed the vessel out into the stream, set it on fire, and sent it over Niagara. A great uproar ensued. President Van Buren issued a proclamation ordering the neutrality laws to be respected, and, calling out the militia under Winfield Scott, he then demanded reparation from the British government. The latter naturally showed no great alacrity in responding. Shortly afterward, one Alexander McLeod came over to the American side, boasting that he was one of the boarding party and had killed one of the Caroline's men with his own hand. He was arrested, indicted by the grand jury for the murder of Durfee, and imprisoned to await his trial. Fox, the English minister, demanded his release; the secretary of state (Forsyth of Georgia) replied that he was in the hands of justice in New York State, and must await its course; Lord Palmerston thereupon assumed for the English government full responsibility for the assault on the Caroline, and again demanded his release. But Fox in his letter curiously added that the government had every reason to believe that McLeod was not one of the boarding party; in which case, of course, he was either a mendacious braggart or a common murderer, and the matter of the Caroline was irrelevant. Webster, then secretary of state, replied, ignoring this point, that if the case were in a Federal court the President would order a *nolle prosequi* entered; but it being in a State court, he could only await its action, and if it did not discharge McLeod, the case should go up to the United States supreme court. In the July term of 1838 a writ of *habeas corpus* was sued for in the New York supreme court, but refused. McLeod was acquitted, however, and the whole affair dropped.

Caroline Books, or Libri Carolini, a theological work in four books, prepared under the direction of Charlemagne (Carolus Magnus), in connection with the disputed question of image worship that seriously agitated the Church during the reign of that monarch. The second synod of Nicæa had given its approval to the use of images, agreeing in this point with the views of the Eastern Church. Owing to a misunderstanding of the Nicæan canons through a bad translation, which seemed to make the Eastern synod declare that the worship due to God alone, *latria*, should be paid to images, the 'Libri Carolini' severely reviewed the doctrine. The condemnation of image worship as formulated in the Caroline Books does not, however, bear upon the inferior honor, *dulia*, paid to the saints and their images, or that given to the Virgin, *hyperdulia*.

Caroline Islands, a large archipelago in the North Pacific Ocean, between lat. 3° and 12° N., and lon. 132° and 163° 6′ E., and between the Philippines and the Marshall isles. Area, about 560 square miles. It contains many groups, embracing in all about 500 islands and islets. Many of them are mere coral reefs, little elevated above the ocean. The most westerly group is the Paloas, or Pelew Islands, which contain seven large and many small ones, all of coralline formation. The next group, Yap or Gouap, lies northeast of the last. In its chief island, which is mountainous, precious metals have been found. The other principal groups are Lutke, Mortlock, Siniavin, Enderby, and Hogoleu. The most easterly island is Ulalan. The most important vegetable productions are palms, bread-fruit trees, and bananas. The inhabitants, numbering about 35,000, though mainly Micronesians, include various races, and have made very different degrees of progress in civilization. In the central groups they are of a handsome physical type, active and industrious, and have some commerce. On the east generally, and on the west, with the exception of the Pelew Islands, the inhabitants, though apparently of the same stock, are far less advanced. The islands were discovered in 1527 by the Portuguese, who gave them the name of Sequeira. In 1686 they were annexed and renamed in honor of Charles II. by the Spaniards, who soon changed the name to New Philippines. After several futile missionary attempts in the 18th century, Spain took little active interest in the group until August 1885, when the German flag was raised over Yap. A serious dispute followed this act, and the question being submitted to the Pope as arbitrator, he decided in favor of Spain, reserving special trade privileges to Germany. In 1887 disturbances broke out at Ponapé, in which the governor, who had arrested one of the American Protestant missionaries, was killed by the natives; but the rising was soon suppressed. In February 1899 Germany purchased from Spain for about $3,300,000 the Caroline and Pelew islands, and all of the Ladrones, but Guam, which had been ceded to the United States in the treaty of peace that ended the Spanish-American war.

Carolingians. See CARLOVINGIANS.

Carolus-Duran, Auguste Émile, ā-mĕl kä-rō-lüs-dü-räṅ, French portrait painter: b. Lille, 4 July 1837. His name was originally Charles Auguste Émile Durand. He was a pupil of Suchon, and received the medal of honor at the Salon of 1819. Ten years later he was created commander of the Legion of Honor. He is a brilliant colorist, and as a painter of women has long been a favorite. Many American artists have studied under him in Paris. Among characteristic works of his are 'La Prière du Soir' (1863); 'The Lady with the Glove': and portraits of Émile Girardin; Queen Maria Pia, of Portugal; Countess of Warwick; and Duchess of Marlborough.

Carolus, a gold coin struck in the reign of Charles I., and originally 20 shillings in value, afterward 23 shillings. The name was given also to various other coins.

Carora, kä-rō'rä, Venezuela, a city of the state of Lara, situated 95 miles south of Coro on a tributary of the Tocuyo River. It was founded by the Spaniards in 1572. It has a considerable trade in gums, rubber, and cochineal, and the raising of cattle mules is one of the chief industries. Pop. 8,000.

Carotid Artery, either of the two great arteries which convey the blood from the aorta to the head and the brain. In the article on the aorta (q.v.) the origin of the carotid arteries is described,— that from the right side springing from the innominate artery to supply most of the right side of the head; that on the left side arising directly from the aorta to supply all of the structures of the left side of the head. Apart from these slight variations in their origin on the two sides, the carotid arteries and their branches are practically duplicated in the two halves of the head. Thus the main branches, the common carotids, soon branch into two, the external and internal carotids. This division takes place about at the level of the thyroid cartilage. The external carotid supplies the upper part of the front and side of the neck, the tongue, larynx, pharynx, face, the pterygoid regions, the upper part of the back of the neck, the scalp, and the major portions of the brain membranes. The internal carotid soon enters the skull and supplies the greater part of the brain tissue, the orbital structures (the eye, etc.), and portions of the brain membranes. The branches of homologous arteries of the two sides anastomose somewhat, although many of the arteries of the brain are terminal arteries and do not anastomose. Occlusion of one of these vessels in the brain usually results in permanent injury. In deep cuts of the throat these arteries may be involved, but they he very deep as a rule and are not often severed. (Morris, 'Anatomy'; Gray, 'Anatomy.')

Car'otin (Lat. *carota*, "a carrot"), the coloring-matter of the carrot. Its formula is doubtful, for although carotin appears, from such analyses as have been made, to be a simple hydrocarbon, no other strongly colored hydrocarbon is known, and hence the probability is that oxygen is also an essential constituent. It may be extracted from the chopped carrot by the action of carbon disulphide, in which (as also in benzene) it is very soluble. It crystallizes in small, red plates, which are insoluble in water and in alcohol. A similar compound, called "hydrocarotin," is also known.

Carotto (kä-rō'tō) **Family.** 1. GIAN FRANCESCO, jän frän-chěs'kō, Italian painter: b. Verona, 1470; d. there, 1546. He studied under Liberale at Verona and under Andrea Montegna at Mantua. His earlier productions are in imitation of the style of Montegna; but at a later period the study of the works of Leonardo da Vinci and Raphael produced a decided change. Carotto is not distinguished by the grandeur of his conceptions, but excels in character and expression, and in the softness and the warmth of coloring. Verona contains most of his works. Among these is the 'History of Tobias,' a series of pictures in the church of Saint Eufemia. 2. GIOVANNI, jō-vän'nĕ, Italian painter: d. 1555. He was the brother of Gian, and his pupil. He was chiefly an architectural painter and is celebrated for his copies of ancient ruins. He is also said to have given instruction to Paul Veronese.

Carouge, Switzerland, a town of the canton of Geneva, on the left bank of the Arve, opposite Geneva, with which it is connected by a bridge. It has machine-works, foundries, dyeworks, and manufactures of watches. It was ceded to Switzerland in 1816, until which time it had been the capital of the Sardinian province of Carouge, which was suppressed in 1837. Pop. (1902) 7,500.

Carp, a name applied to many fishes belonging to the *Cyprinidæ*. The members of this family inhabit fresh waters, and are extremely numerous in genera, species, and individuals. It is estimated that there are more than 1,000 species. One group of the family, found in North America, includes fishes known as suckers, buffalo-fishes, redhorses, and mullets, while another group contains the minnows, dace, fatheads, chubs, etc. They are all soft-finned fishes, with a stout, serrated spine, which stands in front of both the dorsal and the anal fins. There are no teeth in the mouth, but they are developed in the pharyngeal bones; that is, in the throat. The flesh is not of the best quality, and is full of fine bones. The name carp is especially applied to one fish — *Cyprinus carpio*. This was introduced into North America from Europe by the United States Fish Commission, but it came originally from Asia. It inhabits our streams and lakes, where it is increasing rapidly in numbers. It reaches a length of two feet and may attain a weight of 40 pounds. It is a scaly, compressed, robust fish, with well-developed barbels and dorsal fin, and a short anal, and is of a brownish hue. Owing to its hardiness, its durability under extreme temperatures, the facility with which it may be raised because of its adaptability to sluggish ponds and swampy lakes, it might form an important element in the fish food-supply of the North American interior, since farmers can raise it easily in their mill-ponds. It feeds upon vegetable fare, larvæ, insects, etc., and during the winter month's hibernates, at which time it requires no food. The eggs, also, are very hardy, and number several hundred thousands to each individual. They adhere to aquatic grasses and weeds.

The carp is usually covered with large scales; but one variety of it, the "mirror carp," has only a few large scattered scales; while another species, the "leather carp," is wholly without scales. (Consult the publications of the United States Fish Commission.)

Carp-sucker, a common and little-valued fresh-water fish of the genus *Carpiodes*, related to the buffalo-fishes and suckers. It is found throughout the central part of the United States, takes its name from its carp-like form, averages about two feet in length, and is a dull green above, grading into silver beneath.

Carpaccio, Vittore, vě tō rä kär-pä'chō, Italian artist: b. Istria, about 1450; d. 1525. He was one of the most celebrated masters of the old Venetian school, and was the rival of Bellini and the last Vivarino. All that is known of his life is that he belonged to Venice, of which he has reproduced in the back-ground of his pictures the streets and monuments. His distinguishing characteristics are natural expression, vivid conception, correct arrangement, and great variety of figures and costumes. He also excelled as an architectural and landscape painter. His favorite employment was the dramatic representation of sacred subjects, several of which he has illustrated by a series of paintings. Of these the most celebrated are the histories of St. Ursula and St. Stephen. The former, consisting of nine pictures, is now in the Academy at Venice, and has been engraved; the latter, in five pictures, is in Paris, Milan, and Berlin. The 'Madonna and Child Enthroned,' supposed to be an earlier production, is in the National Gallery, London. BENEDETTO, CARPACIO, a son or grandson of the above, flourished about the middle of the 16th century, and is known for a fine painting of the 'Coronation of the Virgin' in the church of Capo d'Istria.

Carpani, Giuseppe, joo sĕp'pĕ kär-pä'nē, Italian dramatist and writer on music: b. Villalbese, near Milan, 28 Jan. 1752; d. Vienna, 22 Jan. 1825. Having prepared for the profession of the law, he afterward devoted himself to litcrary pursuits, and produced a great number of plays and operas partly translations and partly original. In 1792 he was editor of the 'Gazzetta di Milano,' and wrote violent articles against the French Revolution. He was obliged to leave the city after the invasion of the French, and went to Vienna, where he was appointed censor and director of the theatre. In 1809 he accompanied the Archduke John in the expedition against Napoleon. Under the title of 'Haydine,' he published a series of curious and interesting letters on the life and works of his friend Haydn, the composer. These letters, published in a French translation as an original work by L. A. C. Bombet, or, as other biographers state, by Beyle (known under the *nom de plume* of Stendhal), gave rise to a great literary controversy, in which Carpani vindicated his authorship most successfully.

Carpa'thian Mountains, a range of mountains in central Europe, forming for the greater part of their extent a natural boundary of Hungary, in the shape of a semicircular belt of nearly 800 miles in length, extending from Orsova on the Servian frontier, to Presburg. Its breadth is considerable, reaching a maximum of 240 to 250 miles, between the Banat and Transylvania. The Carpathian chain may be divided into two great sections, the East and the West Carpathians, the former curving from the mouth of the Nera to the source of the Theiss, and forming the boundary between Austria and Rumania; the latter proceeding from the sources of the Theiss and the Pruth, and terminating on the banks of the Danube west of Presburg, and forming the boundary between Hungary and Galicia. To the western Carpathians belongs the remarkable group of the Tatra, in which is situated the culminating summit of the whole system, the Gerlsdorf Peak, 8,737 feet. Several other peaks exceed 8,000 feet. The loftiest summit of the eastern Carpathians reaches an elevation of 8,318 feet. The most remarkable and frequented passes are those of Teregova, leading from Orsova to Temeswar; of Vulkar, forming the valley in which the Schyl flows; and of the Rothenthurm, in a gorge formed by the Aluta at the foot of Mount Szurul. The outer bend of the Carpathians is much steeper than that which descends toward the valleys of Transylvania and Hungary. The

only important rivers which actually rise in the chain are the Vistula, the Dniester, and the Theiss. The formation of the Carpathians took place mostly in the Tertiary period, and was practically completed at the end of the Miocene. The eastern part of the Carpathian chain, from Orsova to the source of the Burcza, near Kronstadt, is entirely composed of primitive rocks. These are succeeded by grauwacke, which extends to the sources of the Theiss, and is only interrupted by a primitive group between the pass of Borgo and the source of the Viso. A great chain of trachyte appears on the frontiers of the Bukowina, and stretches to the point where the Aluta begins to flow southwest. To the west of this chain, on approaching the plains, an extensive tract of sandstone belonging to the coal formation begins to appear, and covers the greater part of Transylvania. Tertiary formations surround the vast plains of Hungary, which consist of a rich alluvium, and must once have been the bed of a lake. Basalt frequently occurs, but no distinct traces of extinct volcanoes have been found. The Carpathian range is rich in minerals, including gold, silver, quicksilver, copper, and iron. Salt occurs in beds, which have sometimes a thickness of 600 or 700 feet, and are apparently inexhaustible. On the plateaus corn and fruit are grown to the height of 1,500 feet; higher up the mountain steeps are covered with forests of pine, some of them as high as 5,500 feet. About 6,000 feet seems to be the vegetable limit. Above it a few lichens may be found, but in general nothing is seen but bare, steep rocks, many of them in the form of conical peaks.

Carpathos, kär'pa thŏs, an island in the Ægean Sea, now called Skarpanto. It is now under Turkish rule; in ancient times it belonged to Rhodes.

Carpeaux, Jean Baptiste, zhŏn băp'tēst kär-pō, French sculptor: b. Valenciennes, France, 14 May 1827; d. Courbevoie, near Paris, 12 Oct. 1875. He studied at the School of Architecture in Valenciennes, and later went to Paris, becoming a pupil of Rude and of Duret. In 1854 he obtained the Prix de Rome. His bronze 'Neapolitan Boy' attracted notice; and 'Ugolino and His Four Sons' (1863), also in bronze, though it defied the canons of sculpture, made him famous. He settled in Paris in 1862. His masterpiece, a marble group, 'The Dance,' in the façade of the New Opera in Paris, fully showed his dramatic power and the exuberance of his imagination; but it provoked much hostile criticism as involving an attempt to stretch beyond their natural province the limits of plastic art. The most notable of his later works is the great fountain in the Luxembourg Gardens.

Car'pel, the leaf forming the pistil. Several carpels may enter into the composition of one pistil.

Carpenta'ria, Gulf of, a large gulf indenting the northern coast of Australia, named for its discoverer, Pieter Carpenter. Cape York Peninsula, the northern extremity of Queensland, is on the east, and Arnhem Land on the west. It contains a number of islands, among them Groote Eylandt, Sir Edward Pellew Islands, and Wellesley Islands. Its maximum width is about 400 miles, and its length 460 miles. The land around is generally low.

Carpenter, Charles Carroll, American naval officer : b. Greenfield, Mass., 27 Feb. 1834 ; d. 1 April 1899. He was promoted commodore 15 May 1893, and rear-admiral 11 Nov. 1894 ; was commander-in-chief of the United States Asiatic squadron from 27 Aug. 1894, till 9 Nov. 1895 ; and was retired on reaching the age-limit, 28 Feb. 1896. During the summer of 1895 he rendered invaluable service in China in protecting American missionaries and in co-operating with United States Minister Charles Denby and the British and Chinese authorities to preserve peace, particularly after the Kucheng massacre.

Carpenter, Cyrus C., American soldier and politician : b. Susquehanna County, Pa., 1829 ; d. Fort Dodge, Iowa, 29 May 1898. Having been left at the age of 10 years a penniless orphan, he was apprenticed to a tailor, in the meantime gaining a limited education in the district school. In 1854 he went to Fort Dodge, Iowa, as a government surveyor ; then became successively principal of the first school established in Fort Dodge, government land agent, and in 1858 a member of the state legislature. Upon the outbreak of the Civil War he entered the army in the commissary department, serving for two years on the staff of General Dodge and for one year with General Logan, and was mustered out after having attained the rank of lieutenant-colonel. He was twice elected register of the State Land Office, in 1866 and 1868, and in 1872 was elected governor of the State, holding that office for four years.

Carpenter, Edmund Janes, American journalist : b. North Attleboro, Mass., 16 Oct. 1845. He was for many years on the editorial staffs of Providence, New Haven and Boston papers, and has published 'A Woman of Shawmut: a Romance of Massachusetts Bay Colony, 1640' (1892) ; 'America in Hawaii' (1898).

Carpenter, Edward, English socialistic writer : b. Brighton, England, 29 Aug. 1844. He was educated at Trinity Hall, Cambridge, and was for some time Fellow and lecturer there, as well as curate under the noted F. D. Maurice. In 1874 he gave up his fellowship and left the ministry, and until 1881 lectured on science and music in university extension work. He has since devoted his time to literary work, market gardening, and socialist propaganda. In 1884 he visited the United States in order to meet Walt Whitman. He has published 'Towards Democracy'; 'Love's Coming of Age'; 'Angels' Wings'; 'Adam's Peak to Elephanta'; Iolaus : an Anthology of Friendship.'

Carpenter, Esther Bernon, American prose-writer : b. Wakefield, R. I., 1848 ; d. 1883. She contributed to magazines ; published 'The Huguenot Influence in Rhode Island'; and 'South Country Neighbors' (1887).

Carpenter, Francis Bicknell, American painter : b. Homer, N. Y., 6 Aug. 1830 ; d. New York, 23 May 1900. He studied with Sanford Thayer at Syracuse, N. Y. (1844), and in 1852 became an associate of the National Academy. Among his works are a portrait of President Fillmore, in the City Hall, New York; a portrait of President Lincoln, in the capitol at Albany, N. Y.; and the 'Emancipation Proclamation' (1864), in the capitol at Washington. While executing the last-named painting he was closely associated with President Lincoln, and his observations during this period are em-

bodied in his book entitled 'Six Months in the White House with Abraham Lincoln.'

Carpenter, Frank George, American journalist : b. Mansfield, Ohio, 8 May 1855. He has been connected with various newspapers, and has made several important newspaper tours. He has published a series of geographical • readers; 'Through Asia with the Children' (1898); 'Through North America with the Children' (1891) ; 'South America : Social, Industrial and Political' (1900).

Carpenter, George M., American jurist : b. on the island of Rhode Island, Narragansett Bay, R. I., 1844 ; d. Katwyk, Holland, 31 July 1896. After graduating from Brown University in 1864 he became a newspaper reporter, serving for several years on the staff of the 'Press' and of the 'Journal' of Providence. He later became court stenographer ; studied law in his leisure moments ; and after admission to the bar, entered into partnership in Providence with a former preceptor. When the laws of the State were to be revised in 1889 he was selected as one of the commission to perform that important duty, and upon the completion of that work was elected a judge of the State Supreme Court. When President Arthur created a vacancy in the United States District Court of Rhode Island by sending Judge Colt to the Circuit Court, he appointed Carpenter to the position thus left vacant, and as a judge in this court many important cases were tried before him, the most important of which was the government suit against the American Bell Telephone Company for annulment of the Berliner patent.

Carpenter, George Rice, American literary critic : b. off the coast of Labrador, 25 Oct. 1863. He was graduated from Harvard University in 1886, and subsequently studied in Paris and Berlin. He was instructor at Harvard, 1888–90, professor of English in the Massachusetts Institute of Technology, 1890–3, and professor of rhetoric at Columbia University from 1893. He has written a 'Life of John Greenleaf Whittier' (1902) ; 'Elements of Rhetoric and Composition'; 'Life of H. W. Longfellow'; 'Principles of English Grammar.'

Carpenter, Gilbert Saltonstall, American military officer : b. Medina, Ohio, 17 April 1836. He was graduated at Western Reserve College in 1859 ; was admitted to the bar in 1861, and immediately afterward entered the Union army with the 19th Ohio Volunteer Infantry. Soon afterward he was transferred to the 18th United States Infantry, with which he served through the Civil War, in which he received the brevet of captain for gallantry in the battle of Stone River. Subsequently he rendered service in various Indian campaigns ; was commissioned a brigadier-general of volunteers in the war with Spain in 1898 ; and became colonel of the 18th United States Infantry, 20 June 1899. His volunteer appointment was made in recognition of his gallantry at El Caney, Cuba. He retired in January 1900.

Carpenter, Henry Bernard, Irish Unitarian clergyman : b. Dublin, Ireland, 22 April 1840 ; d. Sorrento, Maine, 17 July 1890. He was a brother of William Boyd Carpenter, bishop of Ripon, and was educated at Oxford University. He was for a time chaplain to the Earl of Belmore. He subsequently became a Unitarian, and coming to the United States in 1874 was pastor of the Hollis Street Church in Boston, 1878-87. He published 'Liber Amoris,' a volume of verse, and after his death a collection of his poems was edited by J. J. Roche (q.v). He was a brilliant speaker and very popular as such.

Carpenter, Joseph Estlin, English Unitarian scholar: b. Ripley, Sussex, 5 Oct. 1844. He was educated at University College, London, and Manchester New College (now at Oxford). He was minister of Oakfield Road Church, Clifton, 1866-9, and of Mill Hill Chapel, Leeds, 1869-75, and is now vice-principal of Manchester New College, and Case lecturer on comparative religion there. He is one of the very foremost living authorities as a Sanskrit scholar and biblical critic, and besides editing Ewald's 'History of Israel' (Vols. III.-V.), and translating Tiele's 'Outlines of the History of Religion,' is the author of 'Life and Work of Mary Carpenter' (1879); 'Life in Palestine'; and 'The First Three Gospels: Their Origin and Relations' (1890). With Rhys Davids he has edited the 'Sumaïrgala Vilasini' (1886) ; and the 'Digha Nikaya' (1889). With Harford-Battersby he has also edited the Hexateuch according to the revised version.

Carpenter, Lant, English Unitarian clergyman : b. Kidderminster, 2 Sept. 1780 ; d. at sea, 5 April 1840. Designed for the ministry, he was sent in 1797 to the Northampton Academy. That school being temporarily discontinued, young Carpenter was placed at Glasgow College, where, however, he did not continue the length of time necessary to take his degree. Leaving college in 1801, he spent some time in teaching, and as librarian of the Athenæum, Liverpool. At Liverpool, Carpenter's views were so clearly in sympathy with those of the Unitarian denomination generally, that he received several invitations to the pastoral charge of Unitarian congregations, and a call to a professorship in their college at York. In 1805 he accepted a call to Exeter, where he continued for 12 years. In 1806 the University of Glasgow gave him the degree of LL.D., although he had applied only for the degree of M.A. From Exeter he removed to the pastoral charge of the Unitarian congregation at Bristol (1817), where he continued until his death, which occurred by falling from a vessel between Naples and Leghorn, while on a tour for his health. Dr. Carpenter's piety was of an eminently practical turn. The instruction of children was an object of constant interest. Amid all his pastoral and literary labors he always found time and energies to devote to juvenile instruction, and, even against the prejudices of his congregations, established Sunday-schools among the children of Exeter and Bristol. In his pastoral charges at Exeter and Bristol, he was active in co-operation with others in the establishment of libraries, schools, savings banks, and institutions for general improvement and welfare. His published works are mainly theológical and doctrinal, in support of the Unitarian sentiments he had early espoused. Among his more important works are 'An Introduction to the Geography of the New Testament'; 'Unitarianism the Doctrine of the Gospel'; 'Examination of the Charges Against Unitarianism'; 'Harmony of the Gospels'; and a volume of sermons. Mild in controversy, faithful in humane labors, and practically devoted to the improvement of society,

Dr. Carpenter was greatly respected even by those who were his most staunch antagonists in theology.

Carpenter, Louis George, American engineer : b. Orion, Mich., 28 March 1861. He was graduated at Michigan Agricultural College in 1869, and after serving there as instructor in mathematics and engineering took post-graduate courses at the University of Michigan and Johns Hopkins University. In 1888 he became professor of engineering at the Colorado Agricultural College and meteorologist and irrigation engineer at the Agricultural Experiment Station, and organized the first course in irrigation engineering given in any American college. He founded the American Society of Irrigation Engineers in 1891. He has published Government Reports, 'Artesian Wells in Colorado' (1890); 'Irrigation Progress in Colorado' (1891).

Carpenter, Louis H., American military officer : b. Glassboro, N. J., 11 Feb. 1839. He entered the 6th United States Cavalry, and served in the Army of the Potomac through numerous engagements. He was an aide-de-camp to Gen. Sheridan ; was commissioned colonel of volunteers in 1865, subsequently served in various Indian campaigns, became colonel of the 5th United States Cavalry in 1897, brigadier-general of volunteers in 1898, and brigadier-general, U. S. A., 18 Oct. 1899, for services in the Spanish-American war, and particularly as commander of the Department of Porto Principe, Cuba. He was retired 19 Oct. 1899.

Carpenter, Margaret Sarah, English painter : b. Salisbury, England, in 1793 ; d. London, 13 Nov. 1872. Her first studies in art were obtained from the collection of Lord Radnor at Longford Castle, and later she competed for several years for the prizes offered by the Society of Arts, several times successfully, and once being awarded the gold medal for the study of a boy's head. In 1814 she went to London where she secured for herself a wide reputation as a portrait painter ; in that year her exhibits of a portrait of Lord Folkestone at the Royal Academy and the pictures 'Fortune-Teller' and 'Peasant Boy' at the British Institution at once gained for her great popularity and marked the beginnings of her rapid rise. In 1866 upon the death of her husband, W. H. Carpenter, keeper of the prints and drawings in the British Museum, she was granted by the Queen an annual pension of £100. Between the years 1816-1866 she exhibited 147 pictures at the Royal Academy, 50 at the British Institution and 19 at the Society of British Artists. Chief among her pictures are: 'Lord Kilcoursie and Lady Sarah de Crespigny' (1812); 'Lord Folkestone' (1814); 'Mr. Barring' (1815) ; 'Sir Henry Bunbury' (1822); 'Lady Eastnor' (1825); 'Lord de Tabley' (1829); 'Justice Coleridge' (1830) ; 'Lady Denbigh' (1831) ; 'Mrs. Herries' (1832) ; 'Lady King, daughter of Lord Byron' (1835) ; 'Archbishop Sumner' (1852) ; etc. In the National Portrait gallery are also three portraits from her brush — those of Richard Parkes Bonington, the painter: John Gibson, the sculptor ; and Patrick F. Tytler, the historian. In the South Kensington Museum are three pictures : 'Devotion' (1822) ; 'The Sisters' (1840) ; and 'An Old Woman Spinning.'

Carpenter, Mary, English philanthropist : b. Exeter, 3 April 1807 ; d. Bristol, 15 June 1877.

She was the eldest daughter of Lant Carpenter (q.v.). Her special work was for the neglected children of the poor and young criminals. She established a number of schools and reformatories, including the Red Lodge, a girls' school at Bristol, of which she was superintendent. She visited India in 1866, 1868, 1869, and 1875; and came to the United States and Canada in 1873, where she spoke on prison reform. She wrote 'Reformatory Schools for the Children of the Perishing and Dangerous Classes' (1851); 'Juvenile Delinquents' (1853); 'Our Convicts' (1864); and 'Six Months in India.' See J. E. Carpenter, 'Life of Mary Carpenter' (1879).

Carpenter, Matthew Hale, American legislator; b. Moretown, Vt., 22 Dec. 1824; d. Washington, D. C., 24 Feb. 1881. He studied at West Point, 1843-4; was admitted to the bar in 1845, and afterward studied under Rufus Choate. He removed in 1848 to Wisconsin, where he acquired a great reputation as a lawyer and orator. He was sent to the United States Senate from Wisconsin in 1869 and in 1879.

Carpenter, Rolla Clinton, American engineer: b. Orion, Mich., 26 June 1852. He was educated at the Michigan Agricultural College, the University of Michigan, and Cornell University; was professor in the Michigan Agricultural College, 1878-90, and later became professor of experimental engineering in Cornell. He has written 'Experimental Engineering'; 'Heating and Ventilation'; and numerous papers on engineering topics.

Carpenter, Stephen Cutter, American journalist: b. England; d. about 1820. He came to the United States in 1803, and settled in Charleston, S. C., where he founded and published with John Bristed the 'Monthly Register Magazine and Review of the United States.' Later he was editor of the 'Mirror of Taste and Dramatic Censor,' in which appeared some clever sketches of American actors. His works include: 'Memoirs of Jefferson, Containing a Concise History of the United States from the Acknowledgment of Their Independence, with a View of the Rise and Progress of French Influence and French Principles in that Country' (1809); 'Select American Speeches, Forensic and Parliamentary, with Prefatory Remarks, a Sequel to Dr. Chapman's Select Speeches' (1815); and under the pen-name of "DONALD CAMPBELL," 'Overland Journey to India' (2d ed. 1809-10), and 'Letter on the Present Times.'

Carpenter, William, American author: b. England, 1830; d. Baltimore, Md., 1 Sept. 1896. He was by trade a printer and had worked for various publishing houses in London, but in 1879 he went to the United States, settled in Baltimore, and began to teach stenography. He first brought himself into public notice by the publication of his theories concerning the shape of the earth in a poem, 'The Earth not a Globe, by Common Sense' (1864). He then attempted to explain and defend his theories both by science and religion in numerous prose works, among which were: 'Sir Isaac Newton's Theoretical Astronomy examined and refuted by Common Sense'; 'Water not Convex: the Earth not a Globe'; 'Bosh and Bunkum: Religious Arguments why the Earth is not Round'; 'Proctor's Planet Earth', in answer to Proctor's 'Lessons in Elementary Astronomy.' Among his other

works may be mentioned: 'Something about Spiritualism: a Reply to Professor Airy's Ipswich Lectures to Workingmen'; 'Mr. Lockyer's Logic'; 'The Delusion of the Day'; etc. He also published two magazines, 'Carpenter's Folly' (1887), of which only a few numbers were issued, and 'Shorthand' (1893-4).

Carpenter, William, English editor and author: b. Saint James, Westminster, 1797; d. Colebrooke Row, Islington, 21 April 1874. Being the son of a poor tradesman he was put to work early in life and obtained no education, but entering the service of a bookseller he soon learned to speak fluently several ancient and modern languages, and took great interest in the study of biblical subjects. He wrote several works on religious subjects and was connected in an editorial capacity with a number of periodicals. With William Greenfield he edited the 'Scripture Biblica' which was later known as 'Critica Biblica' (4 vols., 1824-7); in rapid succession he became editor of 'Shipping Gazette' (1836); 'Era' (1838); 'Railway Observer' (1843); 'Lloyd's Weekly News' (1844); 'Court Journal' (1848); 'Sunday Times' and 'Bedfordshire Independent' (1854). He issued a publication 'Political Letters' (1830-1), which he claimed was not liable to the stamp duty on newspapers, but at his trial in 1831 was convicted and imprisoned for some time. Carpenter wrote many treatises on the subject of political reformation and from 1851-3 was honorary secretary to the Chancery Reform Association. Among these works are: 'The Elector's Manual' (1832); The Political Text-book' (1833); 'Peerage for the People' (1841); 'The Corporation of London as it is and as it should be' (1847). Of his other publications the most noteworthy are: 'Sancta Biblica' (1825); 'Calendarium Palestinæ, exhibiting the Principal Events in Scripture History' (1825); 'Old English and Hebrew Proverbs explained and illustrated' (1826); 'Scripture Natural History' (1828); 'Anecdotes of the French Revolution of 1830' (1830); 'Life and Times of John Milton' (1836); 'The Biblical Companion' (1836); 'Relief for the Unemployed: Emigration and Colonization Considered' (1841); 'Clarke's Christian Inheritance' (5th ed. 1843); 'A Comprehensive Dictionary of English Synonyms' (6th ed. 1865); 'An Introduction to the Reading and Study of the English Bible' (3 vols., 1867-8); etc.

Carpenter, William Benjamin, English physiologist and naturalist: b. Exeter, 29 Oct. 1813; d. 19 Nov. 1885. He was the eldest son of Lant Carpenter (q.v.); was educated in his father's school at Bristol, and in 1833 entered University College, London, as a medical student. Two years later he went to Edinburgh University, where he graduated as M.D. in 1839; and in that year he produced his first important work, 'The Principles of General and Comparative Physiology.' In 1844 he was elected a Fellow of the Royal Society and also obtained the Fullerian professorship of physiology at the Royal Institution. From 1847 till 1852 he was editor of the 'British and Foreign Medico-Chirurgical Review,' and in 1856 he was appointed registrar of the University of London, a post which he resigned in 1879. He wrote several well-known works on physiology, one of which has been already referred to. Others are: 'Principles of Mental Physiology' (4th ed. 1876); and 'Principles of Human

Physiology' (1846, new edition by H. Power 1881). Still other works of his are: 'Introduction to the Study of the Foraminifera' (1862); 'The Microscope and Its Revelations' (1868, 6th ed. 1881); 'The Physiology of Temperance and Total Abstinence' (1853); besides many papers in scientific journals. He took a leading part in the expeditions sent out by government in 1868–70 for deep-sea exploration in the North Atlantic, and was chosen president of the British Association at Brighton in 1872.

Carpenter, William Henry, American philologist: b. Utica, N. Y., 15 July 1853. He received a university education in the United States and Europe, became instructor in rhetoric and lecturer on North European literature in Cornell University in 1883, instructor of German and Scandinavian languages in Columbia University, adjunct professor of Germanic languages and literature in the same institution in 1890, and subsequently professor of Germanic philology there. He has published several works in the line of his specialty.

Carpenter-bee, a species of bee (*Xylocopa virginica*) which burrows into dead tree-trunks, lumber, and even into woodwork of buildings. It is a large, black-bodied bee, as big as the biggest bumblebee. Its burrow is about half an inch in diameter, runs horizontally across the grain of the wood for a short distance, then forms a tunnel at right angles to this entrance, running sometimes 12 to 18 inches. When the tunnels are complete, the cells are made and supplied with pollen. The cells are about seven eighths of an inch long, and are separated from each other by partitions made of sawdust glued together. When the eggs, which are laid one in each cell, are hatched, the larvæ feed on the pollen-deposit until they are ready to bore their way out. The carpenter-bee will use the same burrow again and again, and its home is sometimes utilized by other species of bees.

Car'penters' Hall, Philadelphia, on the south side of Chestnut Street between Third and Fourth. It was built shortly after 1770 (as an assembly house and club) for the carpenters' guild of that city, and probably for civic uses if desired. In 1774 it became famous as the chosen meeting-place of several conventions for the liberation of the colonies. The first was on 15 July, when the committee of correspondence of the colony appointed a session of committees from each county, as "the most effective means toward a union." Later, on 5 September, the first Continental Congress met in its "plain but spacious rooms" on the lower floor, although the State house had been offered them. Behind its closed doors were prepared the papers which Chatham said ranked with the greatest of the world. The second Congress also began its sessions there, 10 May 1775.

Carpentras, kär-pän-trä, France, a town of the department of Vaucluse, situated 14 miles northeast of Avignon. In Roman times it was known as Carpentoracte, was a place of importance, and possessed many handsome edifices, of which a few traces are left. The principal structures are an aqueduct, which crossed the valley of the Auzon by 48 arches; a Roman triumphal arch, a Gothic cathedral, and the library. Carpentras has a considerable local trade, and weekly markets, which are among the most important in southern France. It was formerly the seat of a bishopric, and Pope Clement V. had his residence there in 1313.

Carpentry, the art of combining pieces of timber to support a weight or sustain pressure. The work of the carpenter is intended to give stability to a structure; that of the joiner is applied to finishing and decoration. The scientific principles of carpentry are founded on the doctrines of the composition and resolution of mechanical forces, and a knowledge of these doctrines, either theoretical or practical, is indispensable to the skilled carpenter. To go into the principles of the art would be merely to explain a particular application of these mechanical forces, which would be beyond the scope and limits of this work. An explanation of the terms employed in carpentry may, however, be useful to the general reader. The term "frame" is applied to any assemblage of pieces of timber firmly connected together. The points of meeting of the pieces of timber in a frame are called "joints." "Lengthening" a beam is uniting pieces of timber into one length by joining their extremities. When neatness is not required this is done by "fishing." In this mode the ends of the beams are abutted together, and a piece of timber placed on each side and secured by bolts passed through the whole. Sometimes the parts are indented together, and pieces termed "keys" are notched into the beams and side pieces. When it is desirable to maintain the same depth and width throughout the beam "scarfing" is employed. This is cutting from each beam a part of the thickness of the timber, of the length of the intended joint, and on opposite sides, so that the pieces may be jointed together, and bolted or hooped. In bolting scarfs, side plates of iron are used to protect the wood. When greater strength is required than can be produced by a single beam, "building" and "trussing" beams are resorted to. Building beams is combining two or more beams in depth so as to have the effect of one. In trussing the beam is cut in two in the direction of its length, and supported with cross-beams, as in roofing. "Mortise" and "tenon" is a mode of jointing timber. An excavation called a mortise is made in one piece, and a projecting tongue to fit it, called a tenon, in the other. The tenon is confined in the mortise by a pin penetrating it laterally through the side of the mortised beam, or by an external strap of iron passing round the mortised beam and rivetted in the one terminating in the tenon. The timber frame-work of floors is called "naked flooring." It is of three kinds — single, double, and framed. Single flooring consists of a series of joists stretching across the whole void from wall to wall, without an intermediate support. The flooring boards are laid on the top of these, and the ceiling of the lower story fixed to the under side. Double flooring consists in laying binding joists across the floor about six feet apart, crossed above by bridging joists, and also crossed below by the ceiling joists. Framed flooring is provided with girders or beams in addition to the binding, bridging, and ceiling joists. To prevent the transmission of sound, a double ceiling of lath and plaster is sometimes used, but generally pugging is inserted between the roof and the ceiling. "Cornice bracketing" consists in rough wooden profiles of the room cornices, which are afterward lathed round and plastered. Partitions, when not required to bear weight, are formed by laying along the floor a piece of timber called a "sill," together with a corresponding piece along the ceiling joists, the space within being filled with vertical pieces called "quarters," to which the lath is nailed. When the partition has weight to support, it has to be trussed with posts and braces. The timbers which support the steps of a wooden staircase are termed the "carriage." They consist of two pieces of timber inclined to the "rake," or projection of the steps, and termed "rough strings," which may rest upon a piece of timber projected horizontally from the upper wall, called a "pitching" or "apron" piece, which also supports the joists of the landing or "half pace." The "roof" is the framework by which the covering of a building is supported. It may consist of a series of pieces of timber with their one ends resting on the opposite walls, and their other ends meeting in a point, which are called "rafters." When loaded with the weight of the covering, this framework would be apt to thrust out the roof; a third piece is consequently added, which, like a string, connects the lower extremities of the rafters and prevents them from spreading. This is called a "tie," and the whole frame a "couple." When the tie is of such a length that it is apt to droop in the middle, or "sag," by its own weight, a fourth piece is added to unite it directly with the apex of the rafters; this is called the "king-post." If the rafters, too, are liable to sag, cross pieces called "struts" are introduced, uniting their centres with the centre of the tie. Instead of the king-posts and struts, the centre of each rafter may be joined to the tie by a piece falling perpendicularly on the latter, and to each other by a piece running across parallel to and above the tie, forming a parallelogram with the perpendiculars and the section of the tie enclosed by them. The suspending pieces are called "queen-posts," and the horizontal one a "collar-beam." The whole frame, constructed in either way, is called a truss. The trussed frames are placed at intervals of about 18 feet apart, and support horizontal pieces called "purlins," which run the whole length of the roof and support the common rafters with their covering.

The principal instruments used in carpentry are saws, as the circular-, band-, and tenonsaws; planes, as the jack-plane, smoothing-plane, molding-plane, etc.; chisels, gouges, brad-awls, gimlets, descriptions of which will be found in their places.

Carpet (Lat. *carpere*, to "pluck" or "card," as wool), a thick woolen fabric used for covering floors. The word originally meant (in old French) a coarse cloth in which packages were wrapped for packing upon the backs of men and animals. As man advanced in civilization and desire for comfort, he began to use his packing *carpite* as a wrap for himself and to cover his feet and limbs at night. From that he began to use it to protect his sandaled feet from cold stone floors. Then the material was made finer and gradually embellished with colors and designs. The art progressed most rapidly in the cold mountain districts of western Asia — Persia, Turkey, Syria. The people of these regions had time, patience, and a love for things

beautiful. They produced wonderful results with wool, camel's hair, or goat's hair, combined with a flaxen warp. All their work was (and still is) done most laboriously by hand on looms of the crudest sort. These fabrics of the better sort are almost indestructible with ordinary wear. Carpets are still in use in some of the palaces of Persia which have been constantly used since the end of the 16th century.

When woven floor-coverings were first used by man is hard to tell. Fragments of what might be such are found in Egyptian excavations, indicating a possible use of them as early as 3000 B.C. That the skins of animals and rush mats were used by prehistoric man as protection from the cold stone of the cave dwelling is certain. Cyrus the Great had wonderful carpets when he placed Persia at the forefront of nations. Alexander found them in use in his victorious march through Asia to India.

The art of carpet-making in its best sense still remains with the Orient. No Occidental possesses the matchless patience properly to weave by hand the marvelous creations of the Far East. Some of the Indian carpets approach the fineness of those of Persia. The jute and cotton rugs of Japan, and the grass mattings of China, are samples of this art in poorer material.

In the United States there are samples of native workmanship which compare well with the productions of the East. The work of the Navajo Indian in particular is very quaint and perfect. His rugs or blankets, colored with native pigments and laboriously woven by hand, will wear for many years. Cortez found the palaces of Montezuma covered with grand rugs, many of them made of the skins of humming-birds sewn together.

Carpet Industry in America. Like most American industries the manufacture of carpets had its beginnings in the Old World.

Probably the first carpetings made on a large scale were made in an establishment founded by Henry IV., King of France, at the Louvre in 1607. This establishment was followed in 1627 by one called the "Savonnerie" at Chaillot, the building having previously been used as a soap factory, and by one at Beauvais, established in 1664 by Colbert, minister of Louis XIV. Many of the weavers employed in these factories were Protestants and the revocation of the Edict of Nantes in 1685 caused a tremendous emigration of these people to other countries, more particularly to England, Holland, and Flanders. Thus in England in 1735 we find that in the town of Kidderminster the manufacture of ingrain carpetings had been established, and although carpet-making had been attempted as far back as the reign of Edward III. at Bristol, it did not gain a permanent foothold in the country until after the immigrations from France. In 1745 the Earl of Pembroke established a factory at Wilton in which he employed only French weavers, and this was followed in 1750 by an establishment founded at Fulham by a Capuchin friar for the manufacture of Savonnerie carpetings, but this was a failure.

The manufacture of Brussels carpet was introduced into England from Flanders, where it undoubtedly originated, by John Broom, who put the first loom into operation in 1749. This loom, though the secret of its operation was carefully guarded, was copied and within a short time there were a number of similar looms in operation and so successful were the makers of this kind of carpet that Kidderminster rapidly became the centre of trade for this class of goods.

With the opening up of trade with the colonies, the carpet manufacturers of the old world began to look westward for new markets and along with the early settlers came men who had learned the art of weaving and were seeking new fields in which their energies might have full sway.

Of the early carpet dealers in this country the first records are meagre, but in Parker's ʿNew York Gazette,ʾ issue of 30 June 1760, an advertisement appeared reading as follows: "J. Alexander and Company have removed their store to Mr. Kayne's house on Smith Street, where Mr. Proctor, watch-maker, lately lived, where they sell check handkerchiefs, linens of different kinds, lawns and minonets, Scot's carpets, broad and narrow cloths, shoes of different kinds, undershirts, hats, stockings, with several other goods; Eine Scot's barley and herrings. Also a choice parcel of Old Madeira in pipes." Thus we see that carpets were sold in this country as early as the middle of the 18th century, but the manufacture did not commence until many years after the introduction.

The history of carpet-making in America may be divided into two periods: the first covering the times when all carpets were made on hand looms, and extending up to the year 1841, when the perfected power loom was introduced; the second period extending from 1841, when Erastus B. Bigelow of Boston, Mass., brought forth his perfected power loom and completely revolutionized the methods of carpet-making, up to the present time.

The earliest records show that W. P. Sprague was the pioneer in the weaving of carpets and in 1791 opened a factory in Philadelphia for the manufacture of Axminster carpeting. It was the importation of this style of carpet that first suggested the principle of the protective tariff duty. At the time Alexander Hamilton, as secretary of the treasury, transmitted a message to the House of Representatives in which he recommended that a duty of 2½ per cent be laid on all imported carpets "to which the nature of the articles suggests no objection, and which may at the same time furnish a motive the more to the fabrication of them at home, toward which some beginnings have been made." This factory was followed in 1804 by one at Worcester, Mass., owned by Peter and Ebenezer Stowell, in which were six looms invented and constructed by themselves.

The manufacture of ingrain carpets in this country was begun early in the 19th century, the first ingrain mill probably being that established in 1810 by George M. Conradt, a native of Würtemberg, Germany, at Frederick City, Md. There carpets were made on a hand loom on a drum having rows of pegs similar to the cylinder of a music box, by which the harness was worked. In 1821 a factory was established in New York by John and Nicholas Haight, with J. W. Mitchell, a Scotchman, who had come from Kilmarnock, the centre of the ingrain trade in Scotland, as superintendent. In 1825 Alexander Wright, who was the superin-

tendent of a factory at Medway, Mass., owned by Henry Burdette, attempted to learn the processes of the Jacquard system, but was unable to gain any knowledge of them because the secrets were so jealously guarded that he was not even permitted to enter the mill. He thereupon went to Scotland, and after purchasing the best hand looms on the market and securing mechanics to operate them, returned and started the manufacture of carpets on a scale which for those times was very extensive. The factory was in 1828 sold complete to the Lowell Manufacturing Company, the machinery and looms being transferred to their new mill in Lowell upon its completion. Alexander Wright was the first superintendent of this mill, and together with Claude Wilson, one of the mechanics whom he had brought with him from Scotland, devised many improvements in the Jacquard loom, making it simple in construction, eliminating the more complex parts in the machinery, and making the operation more easy and certain. Of course these looms did not reach a state of perfection till many years afterward, and the machinery was so expensive, the operation so tedious, and the skill required so great, in the making, that it was thought that the demand for carpets would not justify such an outlay, but through perseverance and the gradual introduction of improved methods the efforts put forth by the Lowell company were amply repaid and the founders lived to see the establishment become one of the largest carpet factories in the country.

In 1840 the carpet industry was started in New York by Robert Beattie, followed in 1841 by E. S. Higgins and Company, who engaged in the manufacture of ingrain carpetings. In 1844 Alexander Smith started a factory at West Farms, N. Y. In 1845 John Bromley commenced to manufacture in Philadelphia and was practically the pioneer in what has grown to be the largest manufacturing centre of the country; where more yards of carpet of all grades are made than in any other city in the world, and where some of the finest factories in the world are located.

At this time the manufacture of carpet in this country was only engaged in on rather limited lines; in Massachusetts there were seven factories in operation; in Connecticut there were four; in New York, eight; in New Jersey, four; Maryland had one; and in Pennsylvania there were five, all of which were in or near Philadelphia. Of the total number of looms then in operation, 1,500, probably not more than 1,250 were used for ingrains, the others being used for the manufacture of Brussels, damasks, Venetians, or rugs. The largest mills then were: The Lowell company, operating 150 looms; W. H. McKnight, Saxonville, Mass., 150 looms; Orrin Thompson, Thompsonville and Tariffville, Conn., 250 looms; and W. H. Chatham, Philadelphia, 160 looms, while numbered among them were the first plants of such concerns as the Hartford Carpet Company, Robert Beattie and Sons, E. S. Higgins Carpet Company, and McCallum and McCallum.

It was in 1841 that the second period in the history began. Erastus B. Bigelow (q.v.), a young medical student in Boston, 20 years of age, in 1839 became interested in the weaving of coach-lace and started in to improve on the machinery by which this class of goods was made, with the result that inside of two years he had brought forth an invention by the use of which the cost of the manufacture of these goods, which had been 22 cents a yard, was reduced to 3 cents. The same year he introduced a power loom for weaving ingrain carpets, raising the product of 8 yards a day possible on the hand loom to 10 or 12 yards, and later, after making several improvements, extending this total to 25 or 27 yards a day. He also invented and patented the power loom for weaving Jacquard Brussels, Wilton, and tapestry carpets. He was, however, unable to interest any of the manufacturers in his inventions and finally started a plant of his own at Clinton, Mass., and which was later organized as the Bigelow Carpet Company, now one of our greatest and most progressive companies. The exclusive right to use his process of manufacture in England was at once purchased by the Crossleys of England and A. & E. S. Higgins of New York and the Roxbury Carpet Company of Massachusetts acquired the use in the United States of his loom for tapestry and velvet during the term of the patent.

To John Johnson of Halifax, England, belongs the credit of first manufacturing tapestry Brussels and velvet carpetings in this country. He began operations at Newark, N. J., in a mill with 25 looms, but this later was moved to Troy, N. Y., and in 1855 was purchased by the Roxbury Carpet Company and moved to Roxbury, Mass. The product of these looms originally was 5 yards per day; in 1856 it had advanced to 16 yards under the management of the Roxbury company, and now the average output per loom ranges from 60 to 65 yards, mainly possible through the introduction of the Bigelow inventions.

In 1856 Halcyon Skinner, a mechanic in the employ of Alexander Smith at his West Farms factory, began his investigations into the construction of a power loom with the intention of making one himself of superior capabilities, and the result of his labors was that about a year later his patent was brought forth, but owing to the destruction of the mill by fire it was not until 1864 that his loom was put into operation in the new factory which Smith had built at Yonkers, N. Y. In January 1877 Skinner invented his power loom for the manufacture of Moquette carpetings and later several important improvements were made on this not only by him but by his sons, Charles and A. L. Skinner. This increased the output of 1½ yards a day, the result of the labors of two men and a boy, to about 11 yards a day, and this has gradually been increased till the output now reaches about 15,000,000 yards a year, made in 1,000 power looms and employing over 5,000 people.

Of the more recent inventions the most interesting is perhaps that of James Dunlap of Philadelphia, who patented a process of printing tapestry carpeting in the cloth, a marked improvement over all other previous methods because of the fact that the coloring matter was pressed down into the roots of the pile and extended entirely through the fabric.

The following figures, taken from the government census of 1900, give some idea of the

magnitude to which this industry has grown since its inception in this country:

Number of establishments	133
Capital	$44,449,299
Salaried officials, clerks, etc.	687
Salaries	$881,398
Wage-earners, average number	28,411
Wages	$11,121,383
Cost of materials used	$27,228,719
Value of production	$48,192,351
Total number of looms operating	10,754
Total number yards of carpets made	75,531,827

The carpet industry is principally carried on in the States of Pennsylvania, New York, Massachusetts, and New Jersey. The operations in Pennsylvania are mainly conducted in Philadelphia and its suburbs, the factories located there employing about three-eighths of the capital invested and producing about one half of the total output. Of the 4,693 ingrain looms in operation, 3,737 were in Pennsylvania, and there were 537 of the 1,831 tapestry Brussels and tapestry velvet looms located there, and 1,220, or more than one half, of the Smyrna looms. New Jersey following with 794, and New York with 295 looms. There were in New York 1,057 of the tapestry looms in operation and in Massachusetts 217. Massachusetts had 752 of the 1,812 Brussels, Wilton, and similar looms, followed by New York with 542, and Pennsylvania with 267.

Of the 10,754 looms in operation 9,706 were operated by power and 1,048 by hand. There were used for the manufacture of ingrains 4,693 looms; for Venetians, 80; tapestry Brussels, 1,094; tapestry velvet, 737; body Brussels, 544; Wilton, 507; Axminster, 611; Moquette, 150; and rugs, 2,338.

In the number of yards of carpet produced there has also been a tremendous growth. The value of carpets other than rag produced in 1850 was $5,401,234, using materials costing $3,075,592. In 1900 the value of the production of the mills had increased to $48,192,351, and the cost of the materials used to $27,228,719. While it is true that the value of the goods produced in 1900 is only slightly in excess of that produced in 1890, the total number of yards produced, yard wide, and three quarter, all counted in, in 1900 exceeded the production of 1890 by 760,917 yards. In the manufacture of rugs there has also been a large increase, the total output in 1890, exclusive of Smyrna carpets, being 1,565,303 yards, valued at $2,628,781, while in 1900 it had increased to 8,984,194 yards valued at $5,948,898, an increase in valuation of $3,320,117.

On the artistic side the improvement has been equally great. Many inventions for the weaving of designs have been brought forth which have to a marked degree added to the variety and beauty of the designs of the coverings now on our floors, and even the humblest citizen is enabled to have on his floor fabrics both attractive and artistic.

Carpet-baggers, Carpet-bag Governments. The admission of the southern negroes to the franchise after the war involved their organization and leadership, and their representation in State and national offices by intelligent whites. As no southern whites of character would undertake what they regarded as a crusade against civilization, the task fell to northern Republicans. Those who undertook it were of all grades of personal integrity and honesty of purpose, from sincere old-fashioned abolitionists to mere scalawag adventurers; but they had one characteristic in common: the lack of property interests in the South to make its injury theirs. Hence the name, implying that their only possessions there were in their carpet-bags. The name was at first given only to those whose one motive for residence there was election to office from thence; and the purpose of many was voiced in the utterance of one high official, that when he could no longer hold office from there he would no longer live there. But the régime of monstrous plunder and social and industrial ruin which the system brought on, the levying of fraudulent taxes, and the piling up of huge State debts for the future, soon effaced all distinctions. All Northerners who upheld the system or tried to protect the negroes' voting rights were confounded under the name; all State governments in any way protected from overthrow by United States troops were "carpet-bag" governments; and finally the entire years of Reconstruction, and that attempt itself, are compendiously known as the "Carpet-Bag Régime."

Carpet-beetle, a small beetle (*Anthrenus scrophulariæ*), often wrongly called "buffalo-bug." In the grub or larval state, it is injurious to carpets and similar fabrics. It is an active, brown, hairy larva, the size of a grain of wheat, which works in a hidden manner from the under surface, sometimes making irregular holes, but more frequently following the floor-cracks and cutting long slits in a carpet. This insect was brought from Europe about 1874, and is abundant in the New England States and westward to Kansas. The adult insect is a minute, broad-oval beetle, about three six-teenths of an inch long, with a red stripe down the middle of the back. When disturbed it folds up its limbs and feigns death. As a general thing the beetles begin to appear in the autumn, and continue to issue, in heated houses, throughout the winter and following spring. Soon after issuing they pair, and the females lay their eggs in convenient spots. The eggs hatch in a few days, and the larvæ develop rapidly. Their development is retarded by cold weather or by lack of food, and they may remain alive for an indefinite period. When, under normal conditions, the larva reaches full growth, the yellowish pupa is formed within the last larval skin, from which the beetle emerges later. The beetles are day-fliers, and when not engaged in egg-laying are attracted to the light. They fly to the windows, and may often be found upon the sills or panes. The carpet beetle is very difficult to exterminate, and the best preventative is the use of movable rugs on hard-wood floors. Suspected carpets should be taken up, beaten, sprayed out of doors with benzine, and then be well aired. Before relaying the carpet, tarred roofing-paper should be laid upon the floor.

Another similar pest is the black carpet-beetle (*Attagenus piceus*), whose larva is readily distinguished from the buffalo-bug by its cylindrical shape and lighter color. It is not so fond of working in cracks and cutting long slits in carpets, and in general is not so dangerous a species as the other. It sometimes produces in feather-beds a peculiar felting of the ticking. It has also been known to infest flour-mills, and is to a certain extent a feeder upon cereal products. Two years are required for its development from egg to beetle. Consult Howard and Marlatt, 'Household Insects' (U. S. Department of Agriculture, Washington, 1896).

Carpet Sweepers. — Carpet sweepers of a crude pattern were made in England hundreds of years ago, but not until 1876 was this device seriously considered as a time-saving, labor-saving household article. Several attempts had been made in this country as early as 1856 to produce a satisfactory carpet sweeper, but all fell short of the requirement. To Mr. M. R. Bissell is due the credit of producing the first carpet sweeper that did its work properly and satisfied the user, and over 9,000,000 Bissell carpet sweepers are now in use throughout the world.

It is justly claimed for the carpet sweeper that it is at once the modern sanitary device for sweeping carpets and rugs, that it performs the work in one quarter the time the corn broom requires, and with 95 per cent less effort; that it raises no dust, thus protecting the furniture, draperies, brie-à-brac, etc.; that it confines all the dangerous germs within the pan receptacles, after which the contents can be burned or buried, thus promoting health and cleanliness at the same time.

The carpet sweeper has been constantly improved until today it is a thing of beauty as well as utility, and its use is recommended by the leading physicians of the world. As dust is admittedly a carrier of disease, it is clearly apparent that the sweeper is invaluable as a health-promoting appliance in the home, confining as it does all the dust and dangerous germs, to say nothing of its labor-saving, time-saving qualities.

Carpi, kär'pē, Italy, a town in the province of Modena and nine miles north of the city of Modena. It is the seat of a bishopric, and began to Bologna. It is surrounded by walls, defended by a citadel, and has a cathedral, a seminary, and manufactures of straw hats and spun silk. The neighborhood produces rice, wheat, hemp, and flax. Pop. about 6,000.

Carpio, Bernardo del. See BERNARDO DEL CARPIO.

Carpio, Manuel, mä'noo ĕl kär'pē-ō, Mexican poet and politician: b. Casamaloapan, 1 March 1791; d. 11 Feb. 1860. He studied medicine and became professor of physiology in the University of Mexico, and entering political life he became a leader of the Conservatives. In 1825 and 1848 he was deputy, in 1851 senator, and in 1853 councilor of state. Several editions of his 'Poesias' have been published, the latest in 1883.

Car'pophore, a stalk bearing the pistil, and raising it above the whorl of the stamens, as in *Passiflora*. Also applied to the stalk between the achenes of *Umbelliferæ*.

Carpus, in anatomy, the bones between the forearm and hand, the wrist in man, or corresponding part in other animals. See HAND.

Carpzov, kärp'tsŏf, the name of a German family which has furnished several eminent jurists and theologians. The founder of the family was Simon Carpzov, burgomaster of Brandenburg, in the middle of the 16th century. He had two sons: Joachim, who at his death at Glückstadt in Holstein, in 1628, was commander-in-chief of the Danish army; and Benedict, b. 1565; d. 1624. He was appointed professor of law at Wittenberg in 1595, became chancellor of the Dowager-electress Sophia at Kolditz, but afterward returned to Wittenberg. A second Benedict, son of the former, b. Wittenberg 1595; d. 1666; became assessor of the supreme court and professor of law at Leipsic in 1645, then councilor of the court of appeal and member of the privy-council at Dresden. He was one of the most eminent jurists of his day, and is the author of several valuable legal works; but is justly censured for the severity and cruelty of his proceedings. He is said to have signed the death-warrants of not fewer than 20,000 persons. JOHANN BENEDICT CARPZOV, his brother (b. Rochlitz, 1607; d. 1657); became professor of theology at Leipsic, and is famed as the author of the 'Systema Theologicum' (1653). He left five sons, one of whom, JOHANN BENEDICT (b. 1639; d. 1669), became professor of theology and pastor of St. Thomas' church at Leipsic, distinguished himself by his knowledge of Hebrew language and literature, and translated several rabbinical works. Another member of the family, JOHANN GOTTLIEB CARPZOV, born at Dresden in 1679, became professor of Oriental languages at Leipsic, and died as superintendent at Lübeck in 1767. He was one of the most eminent theologians of his time, and wrote, among other treatises, 'Critica Sacra Veteris Testamenti' (1728); 'Introductio in Libros Canonicos Veteris Testamenti.'

Carquinez, kär-kē'nĕs, or **Karquenas,** a strait between Contra Costa and Salano counties, California; its greatest width is two miles and its length seven miles; it is navigable, and connects the bays of San Pablo and Suisin.

Carr, Dabney, American colonial politician; d. May 1773. He was a member of the house of burgesses of Virginia, and moved and eloquently supported a resolution to appoint a committee of grievances and correspondence, in consequence of British encroachments. His resolution was adopted, 3 March 1773. He married a sister of Jefferson, by whom he is described as a man of sound judgment and inflexible purpose, mingled with amiability, and of a fanciful eloquence.

Carr, Eugene Asa, American army officer: b. Concord, N. Y., 20 March 1830. He was graduated at the United States Military Academy in 1850, and joined the Mounted Rifles. He accompanied the Sioux Expedition in 1855, and was active in suppressing the insurrections on the Kansas border in 1856. In 1860 he was engaged in a campaign against the Comanche Indians. He was in active service throughout the Civil War, commanding the 4th Division of the Army of the Southwest, and subsequently acting as commander of the same army. He commanded a division in the Vicksburg campaign in 1863, and led the assault on the works of that city, 18 May. In December 1863 he was assigned to the Army of Arkansas. At the close of the war he was promoted to brigadier-general, U. S. A., and brevetted major-general of volunteers. In 1868-9 he was engaged against the Sioux and Cheyenne Indians, and afterward took part in other expeditions against hostile Indians. He fought in 13 engagements with Indians, was four times wounded in action, and received a congressional medal of honor and the thanks of the legislatures of Nebraska, Colorado, and New Mexico. He was retired in 1893.

Carr, Frank Osmond, English composer: b. near Bradford, England, 23 April 1858. He was educated at Cambridge University from which he received the degree of doctor of music in 1891. He has furnished the music to the opera librettos of 'Faddimir,' 'Joan of Arc,' and 'Out of Town,' by Arthur Reed Ropes (q.v.), and also that for W. H. Gilbert's opera, 'His Excellency.'

Carr, Henry Lascelles, English journalist: b. Knottingly, Yorkshire, 1841; d. 5 Oct. 1902. He was educated for the Anglican priesthood at St. Aidan's Theological College, Birkenhead, but after qualifying for orders decided upon a literary career. After being for some time on the staff of the Liverpool *Daily Post,* he removed to Cardiff, where he was successively sub-editor, manager, editor and part proprietor of the *Western Mail.* He retired in 1901. He published 'Yankee Land and the Yankees'; 'Letters from the United States of America.'

Carr, Joseph Bradford, American military officer: b. Albany, N. Y., 16 Aug. 1828; d. Troy, N. Y., 24 Feb. 1895. He joined the militia in 1849, and rose to the rank of colonel. In 1861 he was appointed colonel of the 28th New York Volunteers, and led them at the battle of Big Bethel and in McClellan's Peninsular campaign. He took part in the battles of Chancellorsville and Gettysburg, and for his bravery throughout the war he was brevetted a major-general of volunteers. After the war he became prominent in Republican politics in New York State, and was elected secretary of state in 1879, 1881, and 1883. In 1885 he was an unsuccessful candidate for lieutenant-governor.

Carr, Joseph William Comyns, English art critic and dramatist: b. 1849. He was educated at London University and was admitted a barrister of the Inner Temple in 1869. He has been English editor of 'L'Art' and art critic of the 'Pall Mall Gazette.' He has published 'Drawings by the Old Masters' (1877); 'The Abbey Church of Saint Albans' (1878); 'Examples of Contemporary Art' (1878); 'Essays on Art'; 'Papers on Art'; 'A Fireside Hamlet'; 'The United Pair'; 'The Naturalist'; 'The Friar'; 'Forgiveness'; 'King Arthur.'

Carr, Lucien, American archæologist: b. Lincoln County, Missouri, 1829. He received a collegiate education and from 1876 to 1894 was assistant curator in the Peabody Museum. He has written 'Mounds of the Mississippi Valley' (1883); 'Missouri, a Bone of Contention' (1888); 'Prehistoric Remains of Kentucky' (with N. S. Shaler).

Carr, or **Ker, Robert,** VISCOUNT ROCHESTER, EARL OF SOMERSET, a British politician: b. Scotland; d. July 1645. He followed James I. to England when that monarch became Elizabeth's successor. James chose him as his chief favorite and adviser, knighted him, gave him a seat in the House of Lords, and assisted him in his schemes for a marriage with Lady Essex. The latter after procuring a divorce was married to the earl, and in 1615 the couple were tried for the murder of Sir Thomas Overbury. They were condemned to death but pardoned.

Carr, SIR Robert, British commissioner in New England: b. Northumberland; d. Bristol, England, 1 June 1667. He was appointed to that office by Charles II. in 1664, in conjunction with Nicolls, Cartwright, and Maverick. In 1664, Nicolls and Carr captured New Amsterdam from the Dutch, calling it New York, in honor of the king's brother, the Duke of York, afterward James II. Carr forced the Swedes and Dutch on the Delaware into a capitulation. He returned to Boston in 1665, and, in conjunction with his coadjutors, assumed the principal powers of government.

Carracci, or **Caracci,** Agostino, ä-gōs-tē'-nō kär-rä'chē, Italian artist: b. Bologna 1558; d. Parma 1602. One of a family of artists who founded the Bolognese or Eclectic school of painting. He was a brother of Annibale Carracci, and distantly related to Lodovico Carracci, under whose guidance he studied art. He attained great mastery in engraving, and engraved more pieces than he painted, in order, it is said, to please his brother Annibale, who became envious of his fame after one of Agostino's pictures had obtained a prize in preference to one of his own, and another excellent picture — 'The Last Communion of St. Jerome' — had gained his brother universal admiration. In 1600 Agostino accompanied Annibale to Rome, and assisted him in painting the Farnesian Gallery. As many persons said that the engraver worked better than the painter, Annibale removed his brother, under the pretext that his style, though elegant, was not grand enough. Agostino went then to the court of the Duke of Parma, and painted there a picture representing the heavenly, the earthly, and the venal love. There was only one figure wanting when, exhausted by labor and mortification, he died. He wrote a treatise on perspective and architecture. As an engraver he deserves great praise, and often corrected the imperfect outlines of his originals.

Carracci, Annibale, än-nē-bä'lé, Italian painter: b. Bologna, 1560; d. Rome, 1609. He worked first with his father, who was a tailor. By the advice of Lodovico Carracci he learned drawing, and made the most astonishing progress, copying first the pieces of Correggio, Titian, and Paul Veronese, and painting, like them, small pictures, before he undertook large ones. In the academy founded by the Carracci he taught the rules of arrangement and distribution of figures. He is one of the greatest imitators of Correggio. His 'St. Roque Distributing Alms,' now in Dresden, was the first painting which gave him reputation. His 'Genius of Glory' is likewise celebrated. In the Farnesian Gallery at Rome, which he, aided by his brother Agostino, painted (1600–4), there breathes an antique elegance and all the grace of Raphael. You find there imitations of Tibaldi (who painted at Bologna about 1550 with Nicolo del Abate), of Michael Angelo (the style, indeed, somewhat softened), and the excellencies of the Venetian and Lombard schools. Outside of Bologna he is acknowledged as the greatest of the Carracci. In that city, however, Lodovico is more admired. Agostino, perhaps, had more invention, and Lodovico more talent for teaching; but Annibale had a loftier spirit, and his style is more eloquent and noble. He was buried at the side of Raphael in the Pantheon. His best picture is that of 'The Three Maries,' now at Castle Howard, in Yorkshire, England.

Carracci, Lodovico, lō-dō-vē'kō, Italian painter: b. Bologna, 1555; d. 1619. He was the eldest of the three Carracci, and is regarded as the chief founder of their school. He was the son of a butcher, and appeared at first to be more fit for grinding colors than for transferring them to canvas. But his slowness did not arise from deficiency of talent, but from zeal for excellence. He detested all that was called ideal, and studied only nature, which he imitated with great care. At Florence he studied under Andrea del Sarto, and enjoyed the instruction of Passignano. He went to Parma for the purpose of studying Correggio, who was then imitated by almost all the Florentine painters. At Bologna he endeavored to gain popularity for his new principles among the young artists, and united himself with his relatives, Agostino and Annibale Carracci, whom he sent in 1580 to Parma and Venice. In 1589 they established an academy for painters at Bologna, called the Academia degli Incamminati (from *incamminare*, to put in the way), which they directed jointly till 1600, the year of the departure of Agostino and Annibale for Rome. From that time till his death Lodovico was sole director. The academy was so successful that similar institutions in Bologna had to be closed. Among his most famous pupils were Domenichino and Guido Reni. His first principle was, that the study of nature must be united with the imitation of the best masters. He soon gave an example of this principle in his 'Prophecy of John the Baptist,' in the monastery of the Carthusians, imitating in single figures the style of Raphael, Titian, and Tintoretto. The finest works of Lodovico are in Bologna, especially in the picture gallery or *Pinacoteca*, and among them are 'The Annunciation'; 'The Transfiguration'; and 'St. George and the Dragon.' He excelled in architectural views and in drawing, and in general was very thorough in all the branches of his art. He also executed several fine engravings.

Carrageen, kär'rạ gēn, **Carragheen,** or **Irish Moss,** a name applied to several species of marine algæ found abundantly near Waterford, Ireland, at a place called Carragheen, from which the name is derived. It abounds also on the rocks in other localities in Great Britain and Ireland, and is found on the east coast of North America. The species from which the carrageen of commerce is chiefly derived is a seaweed called *Chondrus crispus*. The frond is thick, cartilaginous, somewhat fan-shaped, and repeatedly forked; color, various shades of purple or green. It is gathered from the rocks, washed, bleached in the sun, and dried, and is then the Irish moss of commerce. In hot water it swells up, and on boiling it dissolves. The results of the analysis of Irish moss are somewhat discordant; but the main constituent is a mucilage, which differs from gums, starches, and jellies by not giving their characteristic reactions. It is nutritious, and is substituted for animal jelly and starches in the preparation of soup, jellies, creams, and similar dishes. It is of value in pulmonary troubles, and is also used by painters and others in the preparation of size. It is sometimes confounded with Iceland moss, which is a lichen. See ICE-LAND Moss.

Carrara, kär-rä'rä. Italy, a city in the province of Massa-e-Carrara, Tuscany, on the Lavensa, near the Mediterranean, and 60 miles west-northwest of Florence. An academy of sculpture is established here, and several artists have their residence, attracted by the convenience of obtaining marble almost cost-free. Carrara has some fine churches, an academy of the fine arts, a statue of Garibaldi, and is surrounded by marble hills, which have made it celebrated. Most of the inhabitants are employed in, or in connection with, the quarries. Pop. 42,000. See CARRARA MARBLE.

Carrara (kär-rä′rä) **Marble** (so called from the city of Carrara), the variety of marble generally employed by statuaries. It is a white crystalline limestone, sometimes with black or purplish veins, and occurs in deposits of enormous extent — veritable "marble mountains." Carrara marble, which was formerly supposed to be a primitive limestone, is now considered an altered sub-carboniferous limestone. The plutonic action to which it has been subjected, has served to obliterate the traces of fossils. The mountains containing the marble are situated a few miles from the sea, and reach the height of over 5,000 feet. Although the quarries have been worked for 2,000 years, having furnished the material for the Pantheon at Rome, the supply is still practically inexhaustible. Those quarries supplying the pure white marble used for statuary are the most valuable. The so-called "Carrara district," embracing the communes of Carrara, Massa, Pietrasanta, Seravezza, Stazrema, and Arni, is the centre of the marble industry. Carrara and Massa are the two most important, the former having a population in the city itself of 21,000 people, with an additional 21,000 in the mountain villages surrounding it and forming part of the commune. These villages are inhabited almost entirely by the quarrymen and laboring class. The commune of Massa has a population of about 24,000. Broadly speaking, the entire male population of these two communities is actively engaged in some branch of the marble industry. There were in 1901 in the district 611 quarries in active operation, of which 345 are at Carrara, 50 at Massa, and the rest distributed among the places named above. In addition to these, there are perhaps double this number which have been opened and afterward abandoned as being unproductive, or in which, for various reasons, active work has for the time being ceased. Under the sanction of ancient laws, the mountains where the quarries are found are the property and under the direct control of the municipality of the district in which they are located. Applications for leases are made to the syndic of the town, and within a reasonable time, after survey, etc., the concession is granted. The concession is permanent, the only conditions being that the grantee should formally renew it every 30 years, pay the annual rent, and work the property. The rent is merely nominal. Failure to pay it for two successive years or to develop the property in the same length of time renders the concession void. Quarries thus leased may be sold or transferred, or left as an inheritance by the grantee at any time, without formal permission from the grantor. Until 1890 most of the output of the quarries was transported to the local mills, and to the Marina for shipping, by ox-teams. But now the quarry railroad, completed in 1890, greatly facilitates this transportation. From Carrara it makes the difficult ascent of the mountains, through many tunnels and over high viaducts, to a point some 1,500 feet above the sea-level. Tremendous obstacles were overcome in the construction of these 15 miles of railroad, the completion of which cost about $4,000,000. Although largely patronized by the quarry owners, it has not as yet entirely supplanted the former method of hauling by ox-team.

Carraray, Philippines, a small island about 30 miles long and 6 miles wide. It has coal deposits. The population is sparse and wholly uncivilized, subsisting by trade with the neighboring islands of Samar and Luzon.

Carré, Michel, mē-shĕl kä-rā, French dramatist: b. Paris, 1819; d. Argenteuil, near Paris, 27 June 1872. He first published a volume of poems, 'Folles rimes'; then turned to the drama and wrote 'La Jeunesse de Luther' (1843) and 'Scaramouche et Pascariel.' He then worked in collaboration with other authors, especially with Jules Barbier. With him he wrote many dramas, vaudevilles, and opera librettos, several of which met with much success; among his other works are 'Van Dyck a Londres' (with Narrey, 1848); 'Jobin et Nanette' (with Battu, 1849); and 'Le Tourbillon' (with Deslandes, 1866).

Carrel, Nicolas Armand, nĭk-ō-lä är-män kä-rĕl, French writer and republican leader: b. Rouen, 8 May 1800; d. 24 July 1836. He was educated at the military school of St. Cyr. He entered enthusiastically into several of the secret political societies which were numerous in France after the restoration of the Bourbons. In 1819, when lieutenant of the garrisons of Belfort and Neubreisach, he became implicated in a conspiracy, and though his conduct escaped investigation he was removed with his regiment to Marseilles. He resigned his commission to take an active part in the politics of his time. Finally settled in Paris, he zealously prosecuted his historical and political studies, and became intimate with Thiers, Mignet, and Augustin Thierry, particularly the last. He published a 'History of the Counter Revolution in England,' and in 1830 united with Thiers and Mignet in editing the *National,* which soon rose to be the leading opposition newspaper. After the revolution his colleagues joined the government, and he was left with the chief direction of the paper, which still continued in opposition. In 1832 the *National* became openly republican. Carrel was mortally wounded in a duel with Émile de Girardin. He has been called the Bayard of republican journalism.

Carreño, Teresa, tä-rā′sä kä-rā′ñō, Venezuelan pianist: b. Caracas, 22 Dec. 1853. She was educated by her father and by Julius Heheni; in 1862 she appeared as a concert player in New York and attracted the interest of Gottschalk, who gave her some instruction especially in regard to playing his own compositions. She has traveled widely in America, and given many concerts; she not only has a high rank as a pianist, but also has won success as a concert singer, and has published a number of musical compositions. Her first husband was Sauret, the violinist, from whom she was divorced; she has also married and divorced Tagliapietra, the singer, and Eugene d'Albert, the pianist.

CARRENO DE MIRANDA — CARRIAGE

Carreño de Miranda, Juan, hoo-än kär-rä'ñō dä mē-rän'dä, Spanish painter: b. Avilés, Asturias, 25 March 1614; d. Madrid, 1685. He was a pupil of Bartolomé Roman and Pedro de Las Cuevas in Madrid, and became court painter. He painted many portraits and excelled in religious subjects. As a colorist the Spaniards rank him with Titian and Van-dyke. His principal paintings are a 'Magdalen in the Desert,' at Madrid; a 'Holy Family,' at Toledo; and a 'Baptism of our Saviour,' at Alcala de Henares.

Carrer, Luigi, loo-ē'jē kär'rĕr, Italian poet: b. Venice, 1801; d. 23 Dec. 1850. He was professor of philosophy at Padua, from 1830 to 1833, when he went to Venice, where he con-ducted a literary journal for nine years, during which time he was also appointed by the muni-cipal council professor in the school of arts and sciences, and director of the museum. Here he published several works, the most popular of which is 'L'Anello di Sette Gemme,' a poetic description of the history and customs of Venice.

Carrera, kär-rä'rä, the name of three brothers distinguished as Chilean revolution-ists — José Miguel, Juan José, and Luis. The chief of them, José Miguel, was born at San-tiago, 15 Oct. 1785; d. 5 Sept. 1821. They were the sons of a rich landholder in Santiago, Don Ignacio Carrera. One of them served in Europe until 1811, and attained the rank of lieutenant-colonel and commandant of a Spanish regiment of hussars. The three brothers took an active part in the revolution from its commencement, and in November 1811 obtained the effective control of the revolutionary government. José Miguel Carrera was elected first president of Chile. In 1813 he was deposed and succeeded by O'Higgins. The brothers Juan José and Luis, were apprehended in 1817 near Mendoza, on a political charge, and having been first in-duced to attempt an escape, were brought to trial and executed 18 March 1818. José Miguel raised a body of troops to revenge their death, and a conspiracy was formed in his favor; but it was detected and suppressed, and he himself being defeated and taken prisoner, was executed on the same spot as his brothers.

Carrera, Rafael, Guatemalan revolution-ist: b. Guatemala, 1814; d. there, 14 April 1865. He was of mixed Indian and negro blood. In 1837 he placed himself at the head of a band of insurgent mountaineers. Enlisting the sympa-thies of the Indian population, the rebellion spread. Carrera was in turns courted and ca-ressed by members of the opposite factions which divided the government. In February 1838, he occupied the city of Guatemala with 6,000 In-dians, and succeeded in restraining his follow-ers from anticipated pillage and massacre. Hav-ing secured his victory, he became dictator in 1840, and from 1844 to 1848 was president of Guatemala; was re-elected in 1852, and made president for life in 1854. He recalled the Jesuits, who in 1767 were banished, and in 1863 he engaged in war with Salvador. After cap-turing San Salvador, the capital, he deposed President Barrios and appointed Dueñas in his stead.

Carrera, Valentino, väl ĕn tē nō kär-rä'rä, Italian dramatic poet: b. Turin, 19 Dec. 1834. He is one of the most original dramatists of

Italy, especially in comedy. Among his many comedies, vaudevilles, etc., the play which won for him a wide reputation was 'La Quaderna di Nanni' (1870), a perfect picture of Floren-tine life.

Carrere, John Merven, American archi-tect: b. Rio de Janeiro, Brazil, 9 Nov. 1858. He was of American parentage and his education was obtained in Switzerland. He graduated from the École des Beaux Arts, Paris, in 1882, and since 1884 has been a partner in the firm of Carrere & Hastings, New York. The firm designed the Ponce de Leon and Alcazar hotels at Saint Augustine, Florida, and are the archi-tects of the New York Public Library.

Carrhæ, kär'rē, the name of the site of an ancient city in northwestern Mesopotamia, sup-posed to have been the biblical Haran. It is famous in history for the disastrous defeat of Crassus, 53 B.C.

Carriacou, kär-rē-ạ-koo', the largest of the Grenadine islands, in the British West In-dies, seven miles long and from two to four broad. It is well cultivated, and produces good crops of cotton. The town and harbor of Hills-borough are on its west side.

Carriage, a general term for vehicles of all sorts, especially wheeled vehicles; in a nar-rower sense confined to those vehicles that carry persons only, for pleasure or business. The carriage is as old as the wheel. The first man who cut two slices from a tree-trunk and mounted them on an axle was the builder of the first carriage. The early Egyptians and Assyrians knew how to make wheels, as evi-denced by carvings on their monuments. Some of these show a wheel made with tire and spokes, a construction indicating considerable mechanical knowledge.

Wheels held in place by wooden pins in the axle, a pole to which the horses were attached, and a rude box open at the rear, constituted the early chariots. These and the primitive carts were always two-wheeled. Four-wheeled carriages came into use with the for-mation of comparatively smooth roads, being ill adapted to rough and unkept highways. The earliest vehicles were made almost wholly of wood, pinned together, the holes being often burned in, and the parts tied with thongs. The Romans made use of the two-wheeled *carruca* (from which word "carriage" is derived), but although chariots of war and carts for trans-portation were comparatively common from early times, the carriage proper, for convey-ing persons, was in very slight use before the 16th century.

As late as 1550 there were only three coaches in all Paris, and the stage coach did not make its appearance in England until 1555. When the coach and covered carriage first came into use they were considered fit only for women and children, men scorning to seek such protection from the weather as is afforded by a covered vehicle. By the opening of the 17th century the coach had become popular, and not only crowned heads, but titled families, com-mouly employed them, emblazoned with their arms and decorated to the highest degree. Some of the most beautiful and elegant handi-work of that period was expended in the orna-mentation of coaches. Elaborate painting, upholstery, and joiner-work combined to produce the most sumptuous of vehicles. No such extreme effort at display has characterized carriages of later generations.

About 1625 the hackney coach came into existence in London, and the hired cab soon became an established institution. The increase of post-roads and general improvement in highways caused a gradual increase in private carriages and wheeled vehicles of all sorts during the 17th and 18th centuries. The bodies of these early carriages and coaches were suspended by leather straps, and depended on these, in combination with the springiness of the timber employed, to reduce the shocks and iolts to the occupants. That they were jolty enough to afford considerable exercise can be testified to by those who have taken up the modern sport of coaching in imitation of the old-time tally-ho coach. About 1700, steel springs were introduced, but they did not make very rapid headway. The C spring was a radical improvement, but gave way to the elliptic spring, which was invented in 1804 and remains in use to the present day. The rubber-tired wheel was borrowed from the bicycle about 1875, and still further added to the comfort of carriage riders, while the pneumatic tire of more recent date affords the latest refinement of comfort.

The various wheeled vehicles that may be grouped under the name "carriage" embrace a wide nomenclature, the best known being here grouped:

Auto-carriage, an automobile carriage. See AUTOMOBILE.

Barouche, a four-wheeled, falling top carriage, with low body, two inside seats facing, and an outer driver's seat.

Berlin, a four-wheeled covered carriage having a rear seat behind the body.

Britzska, or *Breet,* a four-wheeled Russian carriage with falling top and a rear seat uncovered.

Brougham, a four-wheeled covered carriage with outer driver's seat, and the fore body cut under so as to turn short. The *miniature brougham* seats only two.

Buckboard, a very simple form of carriage, in which a springboard or boards take the place of the springs, the seat being placed in the centre of the springboard.

Buggy, a light carriage with either two or four wheels, and with or without a top.

Cab (short for *cabriolet,* but of more general meaning), a carriage licensed to carry passengers for hire, usually closed, with an outer driver's seat.

Cabriolet, a two-wheeled (later four-wheeled), two-seated, covered carriage with falling top.

Calash, or *Calèche,* a two-wheeled carriage with a falling or folding top, a seat for two passengers, and a narrow seat on the dashboard for the driver; much used in Canada. The top itself is also called a calash.

Car, (1) a railway carriage; (2) a carriage of unusual magnificence, as for use in a procession; (3) a van; (4) one of various special forms of vehicle, as the Irish jaunting-car.

Cariole, a small, light, open carriage, somewhat resembling the calash.

Carryall, a four-wheeled covered carriage, light and commodious, having two or more seats.

Cart, (1) a two-wheeled, light, topless pleasure vehicle; (2) a heavy two-wheeled springless vehicle, with a strong box, for carrying rough material.

Chaise, originally a two-wheeled, one-horse vehicle with a top, the body being hung on straps; later, a light, topless, four-wheeled carriage of varying construction.

Chariot, the early two-wheeled war-carriage; also a light 18th-century coach, with one inner seat and a driver's seat.

Coach, a four-wheeled covered carriage of large size, having two or more inner seats and one or more outside — a tally-ho; also, a two-seated four-wheeled cab, or large hack.

Coupé, a four-wheeled carriage, low-bodied, with an outer driver's seat.

Curricle, a simple form of two-wheeled two-horse carriage.

Dog-cart, a light pleasure cart with back-to-back seats, the rear seat covering a box to carry a dog or dogs.

Drag, a form of coach or tally-ho, sometimes uncovered.

Drosky, a long-bodied, four-wheeled Russian carriage. In its primitive form the body is a plank on which the passengers ride astride; also, in some European cities, a public hack.

Fiacre, the French name for a public cab.

Gig, a very light, small-bodied, two-wheeled, one-horse vehicle, with seat for one.

Hack, a hackney coach; loosely, any cab.

Hackney Coach, a four-wheeled coach kept for hire.

Hanson, or *Hansom Cab,* a two-wheeled, low-bodied, one-horse, covered carriage, having a single seat, closed in with front doors, and seat for the driver behind.

Jaunting-Car, a light two-wheeled, sometimes four-wheeled, vehicle having a perch in front for the driver, and longitudinal seats extended over the wheels, and a well between them for baggage.

Landau, a coach-like vehicle having a top, the forward part of which is removable and the rear part folding.

Landaulet, a one-seated landau.

Omnibus, a four-wheeled covered carriage with long body, seats running longitudinally, a rear door with steps; often with seats on the roof.

Phaeton, a light pleasure carriage of varying construction, usually low-bodied.

Rockaway, a four-wheeled pleasure carriage with two seats and permanent top.

Sociable, a four-wheeled topless pleasure carriage, with facing seats.

Stage, a four-wheeled carriage of large size, with several seats inside and on top, for long journeys; called also stage coach; loosely, an omnibus.

Sulky, a two-wheeled carriage, of skeleton construction, with a seat for one directly on the shafts.

Surrey, a light four-wheeled box carriage with two seats, and often side-bars.

Tally-ho, a four-in-hand coach.

T Cart, a pleasure cart having a T-shaped body.

Trap, a pleasure carriage; a term used very loosely.

Van, a very large covered wagon for conveying bulky articles, as furniture.

Victoria, a four-wheeled carriage with falling top, a seat in the body for two, and an elevated driver's seat cut under.

Wagon, a heavy four-wheeled vehicle, usually with rectangular box, for carrying goods, sometimes with removable seats, and often with removable top.

Wagonette, a light wagon for pleasure riding, with longitudinal seats facing each other, and entered by steps and a door in the rear.

To these might be added many more compound names, as top-buggy, box-buggy, post-chaise, etc. It is difficult sometimes to draw the line of distinction absolutely between many of the forms of carriages here named. Even the very common names of "coach" and "cab" overlap in use, that which one would call a cab in one part of the country being known as a coach in some other section.

The important parts common to the typical form of carriage are as follows: Body, seat, top, hood, dashboard, apron, step, springs, running-gear, perch, forward gear, clip, fifth-wheel, tongue, shafts, swingletree, doubletree, axle, wheel, hub, spoke, felloe, tire. The body of a carriage is commonly made of selected hard wood, ash, oak, hickory, etc., being preferred. It is put together with iron braces, screws, mortises, and tenons, and glue. The top, if permanent, is supported on selected wood uprights, or, if falling, is framed of iron or steel rods that fold up and open into a braced position. Leather, canvas, and leatherette are used as coverings. The gear, axles, shafts, poles, etc., are commonly of wood, selected with special reference to straight grain and consequent strength. The parts are largely reinforced with metal at all points where special strength or resistance to friction is essential. The tendency is to increase the use of metal to replace wood, and many carriages are made with steel axles and side-bars.

The fifth-wheel is the circular device in which the forward axle turns, and is made of iron or steel. The axles have metal boxes, which in the old style are lubricated with axle-grease, but in many modern vehicles roller-bearings are being substituted, that run with very little or no lubrication. The regulation wooden carriage-wheel has spokes let into the hub and felloes, the whole being held together by the pressure of an iron tire. Instead of making a wheel in the form of a flat disk, the practice is to make it dishing; that is, with the spokes inclining slightly away from the body of the carriage. The reason for this is that a vehicle wheel that is one of a pair receives the most strain when the vehicle is on an incline tipped to one side. In this position of severest strain the spokes of the wheel on the lower side nearest the ground, bear the weight, and when dished are inclined to the best position to receive the load.

This dishing of the wheel produces a necessity for placing the axle box slightly out of alignment. A dished wheel running on a straight axle tends to bear against the end nut, and work off the axle. By drawing the axle skein slightly inward at the forward side this tendency is overcome, and the wheel runs true. The wire wheel, or bicycle wheel, as it is commonly called, is made on a different principle, and dishing of the spokes and drawing of the axle are unnecessary. In these wheels the hub

may be regarded as suspended from the tire, and the wire spokes are so spread that they receive the strains due to an inclined roadway to as good advantage as would the spokes of a dished wooden wheel.

Previous to 1850 most carriages were built by wheelwrights, assisted by blacksmiths, and the wheelwright's shop was to be found beside the blacksmith's shop in nearly every village. The development of carriage manufactories has changed all this, and the occupation of the country wheelwright is almost gone, a few remaining who do simply a general repairing business. The carriage factories buy their lumber and hardware and supplies in large quantities, and use up the raw material in a more economical manner than could the wheelwright. But their greatest advantage is the use of special machinery. In tirework alone there are four special machines employed, the tire-bender, tire-setter, tire-upsetter, and tire-shrinker. Special lathes have been designed for turning out spokes, axles, hubs, etc., and there are hub-borers and templates, and all the conveniences equivalent to those used in the construction of general machinery. Amesbury, Mass., is a centre of carriage manufacture, but there are factories scattered through various parts of the United States.

The term "railway carriage" was commonly employed in the early days of railroads, and is still in use in Great Britain, where "coach" is, however, the technical word, but in the United States it has given way almost wholly to the shorter and more distinguishing "car" (q.v.). The most recent development in carriages is the auto-carriage, or automobile (q.v.).

For further information as to carriages and carriage-building, see Richardson, 'Practical Carriage Building' and 'The Blacksmith and Wheelwright.'

Carriages of Machines.— The term "carriage" is also applied to any traveling or moving part of a machine that serves to carry or transport something, usually back and forth. In this sense carriage is to be distinguished from "conveyor," which is applied to more or less similar devices for transporting something that is picked up at one point and dropped or discarded at another. Examples of machine-carriages are the lathe-carriage, being that part of the lathe that travels back and forth, carrying the cutting tool; the carriage of a planer or shaper, performing a similar office; and the typewriter carriage, being the moving part that supports the sheet of paper and the platen.

C. H. COCHRANE.

Carriage and Wagon Industry. Probably one of the most salient features in the progress of the world and one which has added greatly to the sum-total of human happiness, has been transportation by means of vehicles. The attempt to discover the birth-place of the industry and the study of the advancement in the art of construction are of great interest not only for the history itself, but for the fact that in it are bound the true history of the advancement of the world; the histories of peoples, long forgot, who have contributed largely to the comfort and ease which we now enjoy. The historical records of which we are possessed prove that mankind has utilized wheels as a means of transportation from the earliest periods. The float was undoubtedly the first means of constructive transportation and from this we find the inventive genius of man devising all manner of conveyances for use on land. First came the sledge and this gradually developed into a more perfect mode of conveyance, mounted on rollers, until we have the axle and the wheel. The roller made from a tree trunk with the centre shaped down so as to make a rotating axle was the most primitive form of wheel. The next move came in shape of the substitution of two shorter sections of tree trunk attached to a rotating axle; then came the stationary axle on which the wheels revolved. Carts drawn by men and by oxen and innumerable chariots may be seen on the great sculptured stones now in the British Museum, taken from the ruins of the city of Nimrod near Ninevah. The body is framed up with posts and a top rail and the basket is made of handsome wicker-work; the wheels are about 42 inches in height, well proportioned, have six spokes, and over them is an arched guard to prevent anything from coming into contact with them. On another slab, the king's chariot, with an elegant canopy overhead, and carrying also the charioteer and an arms-bearer, is shown. The next noteworthy advancement was in the cart wheel, which was similar in shape to that now in use in the inland districts of Mexico. The Assyrian Empire, though founded prior to that of the Egyptians, did nothing whatever to advance the methods in construction, and it was left to the Egyptian to originate and develop the more perfect chariot, which for centuries afterward was the sole means of land transportation and which was connected with all great undertakings. In Biblical, mythological and all ancient history, chariots form an interesting and important part. In Biblical history the chariot is frequently referred to; the strength of a nation was determined by the number of chariots in its army. Pharaoh gave much time and thought to the improvement and use of the chariot, with such effect that he was enabled to overtake the children of Israel in their flight, although his whole army was eventually engulfed in the Red Sea. In the New Testament we find the word "carriage" referred to as baggage. "After those days we took up our carriages and went up to Jerusalem." During these years the chariot developed and finally wagons for use on the farm made their appearance, some having two and others four wheels. To the Etrurians must be given the credit for first putting into use the canopy. Solomon tells in one of his songs of a beautiful stagecoach, which he built for his "Beloved," of cedarwood, having a canopy of wonderful beauty and richness, supported by pillars of gold. According to Herodotus (450 B.C.), the Scythians built and had in daily use two-wheeled carts with a platform and basket and thatched with the reeds among which these people lived, and when not in use those baskets were taken off the carts and used as tents. The Greeks and Romans had of course made use of the horse in drawing their chariots, and in the story of the Trojan War, Achilles is described as dragging the body of Hector, lashed to his chariot, around the walls of Troy.

There was little of luxury in any of the vehicles of ancient days; the chariot with all its splendor of decoration was a comfortless thing without springs; even the triumphal and funeral cars of early history were springless; their demand and use for other than warlike or agricultural purposes was limited; but as the world progressed so did the vehicle, and though the improvement was slow, it was nevertheless sure. The *Arcera* was developed and first used in Rome as an ambulance; then followed the *Lectica* and the *Basterna*, similar to the *Palanquins* of India to-day, superbly decorated and upholstered in finest silk, with cushions stuffed with rose leaves. Following this came the *Carpentum*, decidedly a ladies' vehicle, which became very popular and was named in honor of Carmenta, the mother of Evander, the leader of the Arcadian Colony into Latium. Then followed the *Carruca*, from which our modern name of "carriage" undoubtedly comes. This was a gorgeous affair, mounted originally upon one wheel after the fashion of a modern wheelbarrow, but later on two and then four wheels. The Romans considered it a great honor to ride in a *Carruca* and those vehicles were often highly decorated in gold, silver and ivory. As the *Carruca* became the popular vehicle for pleasure use, the *Chariot* for warlike purposes, so did the *Benna* come into general use as the popular vehicle for agricultural purposes. Julius Cæsar (55 B.C.) brought back with him from his triumphant visit to Britain, a chariot that surpassed for destructiveness and convenience any then known, indicating that other nations were making progress in the manufacture of vehicles even beyond the confines of Rome.

During the "Imperial Reign of Terror" under the brutal ruler, Nero, we find but slight improvement in construction, although vehicles were extensively used. The practice of letting out vehicles for hire is of quite respectable, not to say hoary age, for Suetonius, a noted Roman biographer and historian, mentions the custom as very general in his day, 150 A.D., and in his writings refers to these hired vehicles under the name of *Rheda*, the *Rheda Meritoria*, and the *Vehiculæ Meritoria*, both the latter on the order of a hackney coach open and closed.

When the world awakened from its apparent long sleep of the Middle Ages, during which the art of vehicle construction, like all other arts, sank into oblivion, manufacturing was revived and from this awakening, about 1400 A.D., very marked improvements are found. Emperors and kings vied with each other in the effort to outshine and outclass one another, and through this rivalry we note substantial advancement. In 1550 it is said that there were but three coaches in Paris, and within the next century we find the feudal lords throughout continental Europe supplying themselves with the most extravagant and luxurious of equipages, some costing more than $10,000 each. The artist's skill was employed, poets sang beautiful songs in their praise, and the epidemic spread, creating an eager desire in all to outrival their neighbors. Legislators became alarmed and a bill was introduced into the British Parliament seeking "to restrain the excessive use of coaches." Taylor, the poet, complained as follows:

Carroaches, coaches, jades and Flanders mares,
Do rob us of our shares, our wares, our fares;
Against the ground we stand and knock our heels,
Whilst all our profit runs away on wheels.

Stow, in his survey of London, gives credit to Gulliam Booner, a Dutchman, who in 1564

CARRIAGE AND WAGON INDUSTRY

became the Queen's coachman, as being the first to bring coaches into England. In 1582 the French king presented to Queen Elizabeth an exceedingly marvelous "coache" with four of the fairest white "moiles." This wonderful state coach, with its highly ornamented and canopied body, was without springs. It was a sort of triumphal car for state parades. Her usual mode of locomotion was by water or on horseback. Captain Bailey introduced Hackney coaches into England in 1625, and by his wideawake advertising methods, made them the talk of all London.

Carriages without wheels were in use as late as the 17th century and were known as litters and were supported upon the backs of horses by means of shafts attached before and behind the litter. Carriages or wheels propelled otherwise than by horses, are to be found in Japan, known as the *Jinrikisha*, and are drawn by a man running between the shafts. The modern vehicle has assumed almost limitless shapes and forms, and ages of progress lie between the gorgeous chariots and state cars of the ancient Romans and the modern buggy. From the old time stage coach we have progressed to the drag or tally-ho; we no longer have the postchaise or the curricle; but many of the olden types are still to be seen, of course with many changes and improvements, of which the American buggy probably represents the acme of development of the carriage-maker's art. Many of these types have been imported from abroad, among them the English brougham, named for Lord Brougham; the landau, taking its title from the German town where it originated; and a few specimens of the Irish jaunting-car, which were so popular in their native land. In 1834, the hansom cab was patented by Mr. Hanson, and this originally was a square body hung in the centre of a square frame, with two wheels 7 feet 6 inches in diameter and of the same height as the vehicle. The hackney coach was purely an English product, but to-day we see its lineal descendant in the American hack.

It was not, however, until after the middle of the 17th century that the manufacture of carriages gained much impetus, but from that time we find the brains and ingenuity of the American constantly making changes and improvements and, while the progress was slow but steady, the industry took a wonderful place in the history and development of our nation. All vehicles prior to 1750 were absolutely springless as previously stated; the running gears were very imperfect; the leather thorough-brace, which preceded the steel spring and which gave the first relief from the jolting of the old deadaxle carriage, was the first step in advancement in this line. The body of the carriage was suspended on these thorough-braces which were stretched from upright iron jacks at each end of the running part, and gave the carriage a long swinging motion, which, even though extremely uncomfortable, was far superior to the jolt caused by the springless vehicle. Next came the spring jack, made of steel plates, and which later was given a sweeping curve, and from which our more modern C spring evolved. The elliptic spring came into use about 100 years ago, and at about the same time the Collings axle was invented.

The post-chaise began to be used as a general means of travel in the beginning of the 18th century. It was a rambling affair, the body hung very high on leather straps, the wheels far apart and the postilions rode the "near" horses. This was improved upon until we see the stately chariot with its richly draped coachman's seat, but which, however, was not used except at state functions or at royal receptions. Before the Revolution, very little manufacturing was done in this country, the main business being repairing. The aristocracy of those times living in the large cities imported their coaches, carriages and phaetons from England and France, and of course the manufacturing end of the business languished through lack of customers. The number of repair shops grew as the number of vehicles increased and in all the large cities these establishments thrived, employing, for the most part, the skilled workmen who came from England, Ireland, and Scotland.

The Revolution had left its mark upon the land, and during the times of poverty and distress which followed, there was little use made of vehicles of any kind except among the wealthier class, and it was fortunate for the mechanics and tradesmen that this class found the means of transportation inadequate and insufficient to cope with the amount of travel made necessary by the foundation of the new republic. The next development was the chaise set upon two wheels, and it became very popular and came into greater demand as the prosperity of the country grew. It was known as the shay and became the subject of the well-known poem by Oliver Wendell Holmes, entitled 'The One-Horse Shay.' At the beginning these chaises were built without dashers, had high wheels and the tops were stationary. This style of vehicle grew to be very popular and for some years there were no changes made in construction.

In the early part of the 18th century the stagecoach was introduced into England and in 1745 the first line was established between London and Edinburgh, a distance of 400 miles, and it was stated "that a two-end glass coach machine, hung on steel springs, exceeding light and easy, would go through in 10 days in summer and 12 in winter, the passengers lying over during the Sabbath at one of the villages on the route." They were introduced into the United States some years later and it is a mistaken idea that the stagecoach was unknown in America prior to 1810, for William Brant, attorney for Gen. Hancock, states that in 1776 when Hancock married Dorothy Quincy, he took her by stagecoach to Philadelphia on his wedding journey. The roads at this time were little better than bridle-paths and in them were many ruts or quagmires, making travel uncertain, slow, and uncomfortable. In 1770 President Quincy of Harvard College wrote as follows of a stage journey between Boston and New York: "The carriages were old and shackling and much of the harness made of ropes. One pair of horses carried us 18 miles. We generally reached our resting place for the night, if no accident intervened, at 10 o'clock, and after a frugal supper, went to bed, with a notice that we should be called at 3 o'clock next morning, which generally proved to be half past two, and then, whether it snowed or rained, the traveller must rise and make ready by the help

CARRIAGE AND WAGON INDUSTRY

of a horn lantern and a farthing candle, and proceed on his way over bad roads, sometimes getting out to help the coachman lift the coach out of a quagmire or rut, and arriving at New York after a week's travel, wondering at the ease, as well as the expedition, with which our journey was effected." In 1791, there were only 1,905 miles of post-roads in the United States and in these roads were many bottomless sloughs, and corduroy bridges which consisted of logs laid crosswise over swamps sometimes for long distances, but with the improvement of the roads and the advancement of civilization we find the industry of vehicle construction developing and spreading in America. Military roads and post-roads were built by the government across the mountains of Virginia, connecting the East with the valley of Ohio; through the forests of Maine to the town of Houlton on the New Brunswick frontier, and also in other parts of the country. Stage lines were established on these roads and thrived; much capital was invested; the busi-' ness rapidly grew, and the returns from the investments proved enormous. Factories began to spring up here and there. The great Canestoga wagon, with its broad wheels, and canvas-covered body, and drawn by six or eight horses, came into use in New York, New Jersey, and Pennsylvania, for the transportation of freight and passengers. Troy, N. Y., became famous for its coaches and wherever used they were sure of patronage; Salem and Worcester, Mass., loomed up as manufacturing centres, but the most famous was undoubtedly the Concord coach, originally made in Concord, N. H., by the house of Abbot, Downing & Company, who later in 1815, moved to Salem, Mass.

The War of 1812 further helped the industry in that it threw us upon our own resources and started the emigrant and pioneer toward the great unknown West. This necessitated the emigrant wagon or prairie-schooner as it was called, and after that the lighter farm wagon. Stylish carriages and fine coaches began to come into demand in all the large cities. Boston, New Haven, Bridgeport, Newark, all had flourishing shops, and New York, Philadelphia, Baltimore and Wilmington were rapidly coming to the front. A considerable trade with the planters in the West Indies grew up, the vehicles being exchanged for the products of the plantations. These vehicles, which were two wheeled, and had very long shafts, were known as volantes. The wheels were placed in the rear, thus throwing a large portion of the weight on the horse's back, and besides this, the postilion rode the horse, giving him a double load.

As the emigration toward the West became greater and greater, the establishment of permanent factories and repair shops became necessary and the volume of business began to assume considerable proportions. One of the first to enter this new field was John Studebaker, who in 1835 settled at Ashland, Ohio, and there opened a small shop, though it remained however for his five sons to lay the foundation of the business at South Bend, Ind., operating under the name of Studebaker Brothers Manufacturing Company (q.v.), and who are now the largest wagon and carriage manufacturers in the world. It is a far cry from a village blacksmith shop with its solitary forge and one an-

vil to the marvelously equipped factories now operating, and when one considers the vast output (the Studebakers turn out over 100,000 vehicles per year) he wonders where the markets are and where the purchasers are to be found. In the early part of the 19th century, the business was carried on by what was known as the "dicker" system. Money was seldom used in the transactions; the wood-workers, blacksmiths, etc., taking parts in exchange or as they said, "swapped," and the final settlement was made in the finished carriage. This involved less chance of being in debt, and according to the old operators, was much safer than the cash payments. But the country rapidly outgrew this system, and well organized and well equipped shops took their places and it seems as though we have almost reached the limit in quick and cheap methods of production, but undoubtedly the inventive genius of the American will continue to assert itself along this line and, instead of retrograding, we shall advance and always keep abreast of the times.

The greater portion of vehicles now built is made by the thousand and the making of the different parts in large quantities has to a great extent lessened the labor and cost of production; hence the cheapness in the price of vehicles at the present time. Of course there are many different grades of vehicles made in this country and, while in some instances the price is a fair indication of the quality of stock employed in the making, yet the tendency of the times is that the best grade of workmanship and material obtainable shall be put in all styles of vehicles, regardless of price, and the manufacturer who disregards this tendency may sometime regret it. There is no reason why the downward rush of the selling price, which has been made possible only by the decline in the cost of production, should lower the quality or grade of the article produced; nor is this true of the large manufacturer in this country, who, realizing that the average American, having neither the time nor the ability to make a close examination of the construction, and would not if he had, is perfectly willing to pay well for a good article, who, I say, is bound by this trust put in him to give to the public the finest grade of work which the highest skill and care of the best designers and mechanics can produce. The most noteworthy feature in vehicle construction at the beginning of the 20th century is the rapidly increasing use of rubber tires. These tires first came into use about 1890, but were used mainly for trotting sulkies or runabouts and were not adaptable for the majority of pleasure vehicles for some time. The tires were then made solid and universally approved and broader tires were later adopted, especially in wagons to carry heavy loads, owing to the strong movement for good roads throughout the United States.

In 1872 the "Carriage Builders National Association" was founded by the leading manufacturers of the country. Realizing the necessity of having skilled workmen for the trade, a fund was raised to establish a school in New York city, where carriage drafting and construction was to be taught. This was a great success and has contributed largely to the advanced methods now in use in all our modern factories.

Some idea of the vast amount of business

done in the United States and the remarkable advancement in the last 20 years in all branches of the industry is given in the following tables: which only 129 acres is embraced in the town proper, the remainder belonging to the territory of the county. The Bay of Carrickfergus

COMPARATIVE SUMMARY FOR YEARS 1880, 1890, 1900.

Year	Number of Establishments	Capital	Salaried Officers, Clerks, etc.		Wage-Earners		Miscellaneous Expenses	Cost of Materials Used	Value of Product Including Custom Work and Repairing
			Number	Salaries	Average Number	Wages			
1880	3,841	$ 37,973,493	....	....	45,394	$18,988,615	....	$30,597,086	$ 64,951,617
1890	8,614	104,210,602	9,194	$7,533,221	64,259	32,665,301	$6,022,972	49,889,173	114,551,907
1900	7,632	118,187,838	4,302	4,073,932	65,240	28,814,911	6,261,469	56,676,073	121,537,276
CARRIAGE AND WAGON MATERIAL.									
1880	412	$ 7,034,718	....	....	7,502	$2,733,004	....	$4,781,095	$10,114,352
1890	539	13,028,161	932	$ 842,194	9,996	4,366,233	$ 821,743	7,387,904	16,262,293
1900	588	19,083,775	1,023	1,002,199	15,387	5,987,267	1,202,666	13,048,608	25,027,123
MAKING TOTAL IN ALL BRANCHES OF									
1880	4,253	$ 45,008,211	....	....	52,896	$21,721,619	....	$35,378,181	$ 76,065,969
1890	9,153	117,238,763	10,126	$8,375,415	74,255	37,031,534	$6,844,715	57,277,077	130,814,200
1900	8,220	137,273,613	5,325	5,076,131	77,927	34,802,178	7,464,135	69,724,681	146,564,399

From the foregoing tables it will be noted that there was a rapid growth in number of establishments doing business as well as in employees and wages paid, during the 10 years from 1880 to 1890, but a decline from 1890 to 1900; while at the same time the output in 1900 was far in excess of that of 1890, and during the 20 years from 1880 to 1900 nearly doubled. The marvelous methods of consolidation and concentration worked out during these years and the introduction of labor-saving machinery are partly responsible for the great increase of output as compared to the number of factories in operation, and the rapid growth in the population has tended to cheapen the labor, hence the decrease in cost of production in comparison to the value of the finished product. It will also be noticed that the increase in the cost of materials used from 1890 to 1900 in comparison to the increase in value is all out of proportion, proving, as has been before stated, that the public require the finest material construction for practically the same purchasing price. The sharp competition among the builders and dealers has also helped to keep down the value of products. The business will, however, if prosperity and wisdom rule, continue to grow as fast as the increased capacity of the purchasing class can consume the increased output; new markets are rapidly opening and there is no reason why the future of the carriage and wagon industry should not prove as bright as has the past.*　　　　　J. M. STUDEBAKER.

Carrickfergus, kăr-rĭk-fèr'gŭs, Ireland, a seaport town in the county of Antrim, 10 miles by rail northeast of Belfast. It is a municipal borough, and also a county of itself, called the county of the town of Carrickfergus. It comprizes an area of about 25 square miles, of

*In the making of this article, "The Evolution of the Vehicle," by Col. Charles Arthur Carlisle, junior member of the Studebaker Brothers Manufacturing Company, and the files and data in hand by the "Scientific American," were used as a basis.

is a small indentation on the north side of Belfast Lough. It is memorable in history as the landing-place of King William III., who disembarked on its shore at the quay of the town of Carrickfergus, on 14 June 1690. The castle stands upon a rock projecting into the bay, and is still maintained as a fortress, having a number of guns on the walls and a small garrison. The public buildings besides the Episcopal, Roman Catholic, and other churches, are a townhall, court-house, market-house, etc. Pop. (1891) 8,923.

Carrier, Common. See COMMON CARRIER.

Carrier, Jean Baptiste, zhŏn băp-tēst kär-rē-â, French Jacobin: b. Yolet, near Aurillac, 1756; d. Paris 16 Dec. 1794. At the beginning of the Revolution he was an obscure attorney, but in 1792 was chosen a member of the convention. He aided in the establishment of the revolutionary tribunal, 10 March 1793, and exhibited the wildest rage for persecution. He voted for the death of Louis XVI., demanded the arrest of the Duke of Orleans, 6 April 1793, and contributed greatly to the outbreak of 31 May. On 8 Oct. 1793, he was sent to Nantes with a commission to suppress the civil war and finally put down the Vendeans. Multitudes, informally and precipitately condemned, were executed daily; but Carrier resolved to destroy the prisoners by numbers at a time and without a trial. He first caused 94 priests to be conveyed to a boat with a perforated bottom, under pretence of transporting them, but in reality with a view of having them drowned by night. This artifice was repeated a number of times, and the victims were of every age and of both sexes. These wholesale murders by drowning were called noyades. It has been estimated that 15,000 individuals perished in this manner. The banks of the Loire were strewed with the dead, and the water was so polluted that drinking it was prohibited. Out of terror people refrained for a time from drawing public attention to these atrocities, but at last the truth began to become known, and Carrier was recalled. Shortly after the fall of Robespierre he was arrested and brought before the revolutionary tribunal, which condemned him to death, and he was guillotined accordingly.

Carriera, Rosalba, Italian painter: b. Venice 1675; d. 1757. She is chiefly known by her portraits in crayon. In 1705 she became a member of the Academy of St. Luke in Rome, and in 1720 of the Academy of Bologna. She visited Paris in 1720 and painted portraits of King Louis XV. and members of the court. She was elected a member of the French Academy and in 1721 returned to Venice. She was a great worker and toward the end of her life became blind from overwork.

Carrière, Moritz, German author: b. Griedel, Hesse, 5 March 1817; d. Munich 19 Jan. 1895. He studied philosophy at Giessen, Göttingen, Berlin, and in Italy. In 1849 he became professor of philosophy at Giessen and after 1853 held that position at Munich. He was a defender of Christianity, opposed Ultramontanism, and was of the liberal school. He also took high rank as an art critic. Among his published works are: 'Der Kölner Dom als freie deutsche Kirche' (1843); 'Abälard und Heloise' (1844); 'Die Religion in ihrem Begriff' (1841); 'Die philosophische Weltanschauung der Reformationszeit' (1847); 'Das Charakterbild Cromwells' (1851); 'Die Kunst im Zusammenhang der Kulturentwickelung und die Ideale der Menschheit' (1863–71); 'Geschmack und Gewissen' (1882).

Carrier-Belleuse, Albert Ernest, äl-bär ĕr-nä kä-rĕ-ä-bĕl-lĕrz, French sculptor: b. Anizy-le-Château 12 June 1824; d. Paris 3 June 1887. He was a pupil of David d'Angers, and while studying was compelled to earn his living by making models for the manufacturers of bronzes. Toward the close of his life he was director of the porcelain works at Sèvres. His works include marble sculptures and terra-cotta busts; among them are 'Angelica'; 'Madonna and Child' (in the Church of St. Vincent de Paul in Paris); 'Sleeping Hebe'; 'Forsaken Psyche'; and a number of busts of remarkable truthfulness to life.

Carrier-pigeon. See HOMING PIGEON.

Carrier Shell, or **Mason Shell,** a gastropod mollusk of the genus *Phorus,* which covers its shell with grains of sand, shell, coral, etc. These bits are fastened by an exudation from the mantle, and are apparently protective in their purpose.

Carrières, Louis de, French theologian of the Roman Catholic Church: b. Cluvilé 1662; d. Paris 11 June 1717. In 1689 joined the Congregation of the Oratory and became well known as a theologian. At the request of Bousset he published a 'Commentaire Littéral' (24 vols. 1701–16), reprinted Paris 1872.

Car'rington, Edward, American soldier: b. Charlotte County, Va., 11 Feb. 1749; d. 28 Oct. 1810. He was lieutenant-colonel of Gen. Harrison's artillery regiment, quartermaster-general under Gen. Greene, a delegate to the Continental Congress, and foreman of the jury in Aaron Burr's trial for treason.

Carrington, Henry Beebee, American lawyer, soldier and historian: b. Wallingford, Conn.,

2 March 1824. He graduated at Yale in 1845; taught at Tarrytown, N. Y., 1846 and at Yale Law School 1847; began the practice of law in Columbus, Ohio, in 1848, and took an active part in the anti-slavery movement. In the convention which met in 1854 to organize the Republican party, Carrington was a member of the committee appointed to correspond with persons in the different States with a view of making the movement national. In 1857 he was Adjutant-General on the staff of Gov. Chase and organized the State militia in preparation for war. In 1861 he was appointed colonel of the 18th United States infantry, served through the Civil War, and afterward was in service on the plains; was wounded in war with Sioux Indians and retired in 1870; he became professor of military science and tactics in Wabash College, Ind., a position which he held till 1873. He has written: 'Russia as a Nation'; 'American Classics'; 'Ad-sa-ra-ka, Land of Massacre'; 'Battles of the American Revolution'; 'Washington the Soldier,' and other works.

Carrington, Paul, American statesman: b. Charlotte County, Va., 24 Feb. 1733; d. 22 June 1818. He was graduated at the College of William and Mary. During the Revolution he was a member of various conventions and of the Committee of Safety; opposed the Stamp-Act resolutions of Patrick Henry; became a member of the court of appeals, and in the Virginia convention voted for the adoption of the Federal Constitution.

Carrington, Richard, English astronomer: b. Chelsea, 26 May 1826; d. November 1875. Carrington entered Trinity College, Cambridge, in 1844, to prepare for the Church, but his scientific tendencies being awakened by the lectures of Prof. Challis he turned his attention to astronomy. He held the post of observer at the University of Durham from 1849 to 1852. He was elected a Fellow of the Royal Society (7 June 1860). His work 'Observations on the Spots on the Sun' (1863) furnished data that materially affected the study of solar physics.

Carrion-crow, any of several large carrion-eating birds. The only true carrion-crow (*Corvus corone*) is found in England. It is larger than a crow, of black plumage, and with feathered neck. It is seldom seen in flocks, and lives upon carrion, small mammals, eggs, and birds. In the southern United States the name is locally given to the black vulture (*Catharista atrata*), but closely related to the turkey-buzzard (q.v.), but smaller, and resembling it in habits and public service as a scavenger. Its bluish and spotted eggs number from one to three and are placed in a nest built under logs and bushes.

Carrion-flowers, certain species of the genus *Stapelia* (natural order *Asclepiadaceæ*), so called because of their putrid odor. In the United States the name is also given to the *Smilax herbacea,* a liliaceous plant.

Carroll, Charles, "of Carrollton," American patriot: b. Annapolis, Md., 20 Sept. 1737; d. Baltimore, 14 Nov. 1832. He attended several schools abroad; studied law in Paris and London, where he became a member of the Inner Temple; returned to his native country in 1764; was elected to the Continental Congress in 1775, and with the other members

WILD CARROT.

signed the Declaration of Independence, on 2 August of the following year. To make certain his identity, he added "of Carrollton" to his signature, thus distinguishing himself from another by using the name of his family mansion. After many more years of important public service to the State of Maryland and to the new republic, in 1804 he withdrew to private life at Carrollton, which was his patrimonial estate, and where as his life advanced he became an object of universal veneration. He survived by six years all the other signers of the Declaration.

Carroll, Henry King, American clergyman and editor: b. Dennisville, N. J., 15 Nov. 1848. He was on the staff of 'Hearth and Home' (Methodist), and from 1876 to 1898 was religious and political editor of the *Independent*. He has written 'The Religious Forces of the United States'; and many reviews, reports, and miscellaneous papers. He supervised the compilation of religious statistics for the 11th census, and in 1898 was appointed to prepare a report on the internal conditions of Porto Rico. In 1900 he became a secretary of the Methodist Episcopal Church Missionary Society.

Car'roll, Howard, American journalist: b. Albany, N. Y., 1854. He began newspaper work in New York as reporter for the *Times*, of which he subsequently became special Washington correspondent. He has since held several responsible business positions and is the author of 'A Mississippi Incident'; 'Twelve Americans: Their Lives and Times.'

Car'roll, John, American prelate: b. Upper Marlborough, Md., 8 Jan. 1735; d. Georgetown, D. C., 3 Dec. 1815. He was a cousin of Charles Carroll of Carrollton, and first Roman Catholic bishop in the United States. At the age of 13 he was sent to Belgium to be educated. He was professor (1759-71) at St. Omer's and Liège, then, becoming a Jesuit, was made prefect of the Jesuit College at Bruges. On the suppression of the Jesuits in 1774, he returned to the United States. In 1784, at the suggestion of Franklin, he was appointed superior of the Roman Catholic clergy in the United States; was made bishop in 1789; and in 1808 was created archbishop of the archdiocese of Baltimore. Georgetown College was founded by Bishop Carroll in 1791.

Carroll, John Joseph, American Roman Catholic clergyman: b. Enniscrone County, Sligo, Ireland, 24 June 1856. He came to the United States in infancy, was educated in St. Michael's College, Toronto, Ontario, and at St. Joseph's Theological Seminary in Troy, N. Y. He became assistant priest in the Cathedral of the Holy Name, Chicago, in 1880, and subsequently rector of St. Thomas' Church there. He is a Gælic scholar of prominence and has written 'Notes and Observations on the Aryan Race and Tongue' (1894); 'Prehistoric Ocenpatiou of Ireland by the Gælic Aryans.'

Carroll, Lewis. See DODGSON, CHARLES LUTWIDGE.

Carron Oil, a mixture of equal parts of linseed oil and lime water, much used as a dressing for burns. It has no particular advantages over other simpler and neater dressings, notably vaseline, or oxide of zinc ointment. Its name is derived from its use in the Carron Foundry, Scotland.

Carronade', an iron gun introduced in 1779 by the director of the Carron Foundry, in Scotland, from which it took its name, said to have been invented in 1752 by Gen. Melville, and first used in the American Revolutionary War. They were of large calibre, and lighter than common cannon: but they admitted of only a small charge of powder and had a very confined range. See ORDNANCE.

Carrot, a biennial plant (*Daucus carota*) of the natural order *Umbelliferæ*. It is a native of Europe, introduced into America, and is known as a troublesome weed upon poor land especially in the eastern United States. It is more favorably known by its cultivated varieties which are said to have been derived originally from Holland prior to the 16th century, since when it has become deservedly popular in all temperate climates. Certain large-rooted varieties are raised for stock feeding. The most popular culinary varieties are small, rapidly growing plants of diversely formed roots. Since they are most used as a flavoring in soups, stews, and other dishes which have not become specially popular in America, they are less cultivated here than in Europe, where these dishes are commonly made. The plants succeed best in a warm, friable, rich soil, well supplied with moisture, free from stones, weeds, etc., and in the best physical condition. The seed may be sown in drills one half foot apart as soon as the ground has become warm, since they are slow to germinate and since the seedlings are very tiny. A few radish seeds of an early maturing variety are usually planted with them to break the soil and indicate the positions of the rows, so that cultivation may be commenced early. The radishes are pulled when they reach edible size and the carrots given clean cultivation, the plants being thinned to stand two or three inches apart. When they reach edible size they are bunched and marketed. The larger growing kinds are planted in rows 24 to 30 inches apart and the plants thinned to 3 or 4 inches. When mature they are stored in pits or root cellars. Few diseases attack the carrot, and the few harmful insects are usually controlled by their parasites. The average percentage composition of carrots is: Water 88.6; nitrogen-free extract, 7.6; carbohydrate, 1.3; protein. 1.1; fat, a trace; ash, about 1 per cent. They resemble other root and tuber vegetables in their succulence and nutritive value. They are greatly relished by stock, especially horses, but are usually replaced in American rations by cheaper foods.

Car'rotin. See CAROTIN.

Carrousel, kä-roo-sĕl', formerly an exhibition of various knightly exercises, as riding at the ring, throwing the spear, etc., which were celebrated at the courts of princes on festival occasions with great pomp and splendor. They are very ancient, but are first mentioned in history in 842, on occasion of the meeting held by Charles the Bold and Louis the German. They were superseded by tournaments, but when these had fallen were again revived. Their introduction or revival in France took place after tournaments had fallen out of fashion in consequence of the accident which ended in the death of Henry II. Similar fêtes had already long existed among the Moors, Spaniards, and Italians. These exhibitions were common during the continuance of the old French monarchy. The Place du Carrousel in Paris was so called from one of these fêtes given there in 1662, in honor of Mademoiselle de la Vallière. The greatest extravagancies were enacted at these displays. Recitations accompanied them, some verse in outrageous taste, and full of absurd allegorical personages, being usually recited in honor of the heroine of the fête, although genuine dramatic performances were sometimes given by professional actors. In the United States the name carrousel is applied to a merry-go-round, a machine with a revolving circular platform and fixed wooden horses, etc., upon which both children and grown people ride for amusement.

Carruth', Frances Weston, American writer: b. Newton, Mass., 12 July 1867. Since 1896 she has lived in New York, engaged in literary work. Her published volumes include: 'Those Dale Girls'; 'The Way of Belinda.'

Carruth, Fred Hayden, American journalist: b. Lake City, Minn., 1862. He was on the editorial staff of the New York *Tribune* 1888–92, and has been more recently editor of the humorous department of 'Harper's Magazine.' He has published 'The Adventures of Jones' (1895); 'The Voyage of the Rattletrap' (1896); 'Mr. Milo Bush and Other Worthies' (1899).

Carruth, William Herbert, American scholar: b. Ossawattomie, Kan., 5 April 1859. He was educated in the University of Kansas, and at Harvard, and has been professor of German in the former institution from 1887. He has published 'Schiller's Wallenstein with Introduction and Notes' (1894): and other German texts similarly edited.

Carruthers, kăr-roo'thĕrz, **William A.,** American novelist: b. Virginia, about 1800; d. Savannah, Ga., about 1850. He was professionally a physician, but wrote a number of spirited romances founded on incidents in American history. His best work is 'The Cavaliers of Virginia, or the Recluse of Jamestown, an Historical Romance of the Old Dominion' (1832). He is the author also of 'The Knights of the Horse-Shoe' (1845).

Carrying-trade, a phrase used in political economy, and also in commercial transactions. It usually refers to the commerce of different countries with each other, and is most frequently applied to carriage by sea. In a purely commercial sense the carrying-trade is simply the carriage of commodities from one place or country to another, irrespective of the mode of conveyance. In political economy the term is used in a special and restricted sense. In considering the entire commerce of a country it may be found that a part of that commerce is not directly with any one foreign country, but consists in supplying facilities for the conveyance of goods from one foreign country to another. The ships of the United States, for example, may be employed in carrying goods between India and China. This is called a carrying-trade. The carrying-trade does not consist merely in the occasional charter of vessels to foreign merchants for a foreign voyage. Though this may be included in it, its regular organization implies more than this. A ship-owner, instead of lending his vessels incidentally to foreign merchants, may build or purchase them expressly for the purpose of conveying goods between different foreign ports at his own risk, and may even invest capital in merchandise to be so conveyed. It is to this abnormal development of commerce that the term carrying-trade in its restricted sense is applied. It is an investment of capital common in the case of commercial communities which have acquired great surplus wealth, or from the limited range of their territory, have few home investments. From the earliest time, the principal commercial communities, especially the great trading cities of antiquity, and those of the Middle Ages which have formed communities in themselves, have embarked largely in this kind of commerce.

Carryl, Charles Edward, American broker and author: b. New York, 30 Dec. 1841. He has been a member of the New York Stock Exchange from 1874 and has published 'Davy and the Goblin,' a very popular juvenile in the manner of 'Alice in Wonderland' (1884); 'The Admiral's Caravan' (1891).

Carryl, Guy Wetmore, American humorous writer: b. New York, 4 March 1873; d. New York 1 April 1904. He was a son of C. E. Carryl (q.v.), and the author of 'Fables for the Frivolous' (1898); 'Mother Goose for Grown-Ups' (1900); etc.

Carson, Christopher, popularly known as KIT CARSON, American mountaineer, trapper, and guide: b. Madison County, Ky., 24 Dec. 1809; d. Fort Lynn, Col., 23 May 1868. While yet an infant his family emigrated to what is now Howard County, Mo. At 15 years of age he was apprenticed to a saddler, with whom he continued two years, when he joined a hunting expedition. The next eight years of his life were passed as a trapper, which pursuit he relinquished on receiving the appointment of a hunter to Bent's fort, where he continued for eight years more. At the expiration of this time, he chanced to meet Fremont, by whom he was engaged as guide in his subsequent explorations. In 1847 Carson was sent to Washington as bearer of despatches, and received an appointment as lieutenant in the rifle corps of the United States army. In 1853 he drove 6,500 sheep to California, a difficult but successful undertaking, and on his return to Taos was appointed Indian agent in New Mexico. He served in the Federal army during the Civil War, attaining the rank of brevet brigadier-general.

Carson, Hampton Lawrence, American publicist: b. Philadelphia, Pa., 21 Feb. 1852. He was graduated at the University of Pennsylvania in 1871, and became a lawyer, rising speedily to prominence by speeches and addresses on topics of the time. He has written: 'History of the Supreme Court of the United States'; 'The Law of Criminal Conspiracies as Found in American Cases'; 'History of the One Hundredth Anniversary of the Promulgation of the Constitution of the United States'; and is a lecturer on law at the University of Pennsylvania.

Car'son City, Nev., a city, capital of the State and county-seat of Ormsby County; on the Virginia & Truckee R.R., 32 miles southeast of Reno. The city is in a mining and agricultural district, and is the location of a branch mint, a Federal building, State capitol, State prison, an orphans' home, and an Indian school. The business is mainly connected with mining, agriculture, and lumbering. Here are railroad and machine shops, etc. Carson City is only 12 miles from Lake Tahoe, and, on account of its beautiful scenery at the base of the Sierra Nevada, is a popular summer resort. Pop. (1900) 2,100.

Carson River, a river of Nevada, rising in the Sierra Nevada and flowing northeast for about 150 miles. It then divides, and the main branch flows into Carson Lake, a small lake with no apparent outlet. The other branch flows in the opposite direction, and is lost in Carson Sink.

Carstairs, William, Scottish clergyman of political eminence: b. Cathcart, near Glasgow, 1649; d. 1715. He pursued his studies at the universities of Edinburgh and Utrecht. He returned to Scotland with the view of entering the ministry, but after receiving a license to preach resolved to return to Holland. As he was to pass through London, he was employed by Argyle and his party to treat with the English exclusionists and became privy to the Rye-house plot. On the discovery of that conspiracy he was apprehended. After a rigorous confinement in irons he was subjected to the torture, and endured this trial with great firmness; but being afterward deluded with the hopes of a full pardon, and assured that his answers should never be made evidence against any one, he submitted to make a judicial declaration. Being released he returned to Holland, and was received by the Prince of Orange as a sufferer in his cause. The prince made him one of his own chaplains, and procured his election to the office of minister of the English congregation at Leyden. He accompanied the prince in his expedition, and always remained about his person, both at home and abroad. During this reign he was the chief agent between the Church of Scotland and the court, and was very instrumental in the establishment of Presbyterianism, to which William was averse. On the death of William he was no longer employed on public business; but Anne retained him as her chaplain-royal, and made him principal of the University of Edinburgh. When the union of the two kingdoms was agitated he took a decided part in its favor. The memory of Carstairs is for the most part revered by his countrymen as that of an enlightened patriot; and few men of active power and influence have steered between parties more ably and beneficially.

Carstens, Asmus Jakob, Danish painter: b. St. Jürgen, near Schleswig, 10 May 1754; d. 26 May 1798. He was a miller's son, but received a superior education from his mother. He had a youthful passion for painting, but after his mother's death was placed in a mercantile house. After quitting his master, he went to Copenhagen, where he struggled on for seven years, supporting himself by portrait painting, at the same time working at a large historical picture on the 'Death of Æschylus.' He went to Italy after finishing this work, then lived at Lübeck for five years, toiling on in obscurity, when he was introduced by the poet Overbeck to a wealthy patron, by whose aid he went to Berlin, where the merit of his 'Fall of the Angels,' a colossal picture, containing over 200 figures, gained him a professorship in the Academy of Fine Arts. Two years' labor in Berlin enabled him to accomplish his cherished wish to go to Rome, and study the works of Michael Angelo and Raphael. His best works were designs in aquarelle, and painting in fresco; he rarely painted in oil. His cartoons at Weimar have been engraved by Müller. Homer, Pindar, Aristophanes, and Dante supplied him with his best subjects; and among the painters who endeavored to infuse a classic spirit into the fine arts of the 18th century, he holds a prominent position. His works are distinguished by correctness of form and outline, gracefulness of attitude, and loftiness and vigor of expression; but they frequently exhibit a certain harshness, arising from too close imitation. He was often defective in anatomy and perspective, and having begun late to paint in oil, was unacquainted with the secrets of coloring.

Cart, a carriage with two wheels, fitted to be drawn by one horse or other animal, and used in husbandry or commerce for carrying many sorts of goods. There are various descriptions of carts used in agriculture, and for many kinds of agricultural work the cart is preferable to the wagon. The ordinary cart for heavy goods has no springs, but there are many carts provided with springs.

Cartagena, kär ta jē'nä, Colombia, capital of the department of Bolivar, founded Jan. 21, 1533, by Pedro de Heredia. Early in the 17th century it ranked next below Mexico among the cities of the Western world, and was called "Queen of the Indies." At that time its inhabitants numbered about 20,000, of whom 3,000 were Spaniards; it was strongly fortified, and one of the main entrepôts of commerce between the hemispheres — a distinction due, in part, to its proximity to the Isthmian route, but even more to the excellence of its harbor, which is one of the best on the northern coast of South America. As the principal stronghold of Spanish America, it was repeatedly attacked: by a French fleet in 1544; by the English under Drake in 1585; again by the French in 1697; and by the English under Vernon in 1741. The town remained Spanish until 1815, when Bolivar took it; but the same year it was surrendered to the royalists, after a memorably heroic defense; and finally it was taken by Republican forces 25 Sept. 1821. Its population at present is little more than one half the number accredited to it three centuries ago. Cartagena is situated in lat. 10° 25' 48" N., lon. 75° 34' W.

Cartagena, Spain, a city and fortified seaport and naval arsenal in the province of Murcia, and 31 miles south-southeast of the city Murcia. Its harbor is one of the largest and safest in the Mediterranean. The city, located at the northern end of the harbor, is surrounded by a lofty wall, flanked with bastions. The principal buildings are the cathedral, dating from the 13th century, now converted into a simple parish church; the old castle, supposed to date from the foundation of the city by the Carthaginians; the barracks, arsenal, presidio or convict establishment, the military hospital, Hospital de Caridad, the artillery park, the observatory, the convents of St. Augustine and Monjas, and several other convents and churches. Great improvements have been made recently in the accommodation for shipping by the construction of moles, wharves, breakwaters, and a floating dock. Lead smelting is largely carried on; and there are also in the neighborhood rich mines of excellent iron, which are connected with the harbor by means of a tramway about eight miles in length. Esparto grass, compressed by hydraulic power, is largely shipped; other exports are iron ore, lead and lead ore, copper ore, zinc ore, fruits, etc. Cartagena (ancient Carthago Nova) was founded by the Carthaginians under Hasdrubal about 228 B.C. It was taken by Scipio Africanus 210 B.C., and afterward became a Roman colony. In 425 A.D. the Vandals largely destroyed it; and in 711, after having been in possession of the Visigoths, it was again destroyed by the Saracens. When Spain possessed her colonies, and was in a flourishing condition, Cartagena was one of her most important naval stations, and carried on a very extensive commerce. In 1873 a body of communists obtained possession of the city and fortifications, but they were compelled to surrender in the following year. Pop., 100,000.

Cartago, kär-tä'gō, Colombia, a town in the valley of the Cauca, on the Viega, a tributary of that river. Its trade is principally in dried beef, pigs, fruits, coffee, cacao, and tobacco. The sugarcane thrives well here. Cartago is the entrepôt for the trade of Santa-Fe-de-Bogotà. The climate is hot, but dry and healthy. Pop. about 8,000.

Cartago, Costa Rica, a city, formerly capital of Costa Rica, on the right bank of a river of its own name, 14 miles east-southeast of San José. It was once a place of considerable commercial importance, and had a population of about 37,000. It was so ruined by an earthquake 2 Sept. 1841, that only 100 houses and a church were left standing. It had already been superseded both as a capital and a seat of commerce by San José. The railroad from San José to Limon passes through it. Near the town are the springs of Aguacaliente, and also Mount Cartago or Irazu, an active volcano, rising 11,480 feet above the sea-level. Pop. about 3,500.

Carte, Thomas, English historian: b. Clifton-upon-Dunsmoor, Warwickshire, April 1686; d. near Abingdon, 2 April 1754. He was educated at University College, Oxford, and Cambridge. His first publication was entitled 'The Irish Massacre Set in a Clear Light, etc.,' in which he defended Charles I. from the common charge of secretly instigating the rebellion and massacre in Ireland in 1641. During the rebellion of 1715, a warrant was issued for his apprehension, which he eluded by concealment; and later when it was supposed that he was concerned in a conspiracy, and a reward of £1,000 was offered for his capture, he escaped to France. Here he collected material for an English edition of the 'History of Thuanus' (de Thou). At length Queen Caroline procured leave for his return to England. His important work, the 'Life of James, Duke of Ormonde,' was published in 1735-6, and gained him great reputation, especially with the Tory party. In 1744 he was arrested on a suspicion of being employed by the Pretender,

but was discharged. He published three volumes of his 'History of England' between 1747 and 1752, the fourth, which brought down the history to 1654, not appearing until after his death. The character of this work is deservedly high for research. Hume and other historians have been indebted to it, but the prejudices of the author are everywhere conspicuous.

Carte-blanche, kärt-blänch, a blank sheet of paper to be filled up with such conditions as the person to whom it is given may think proper; hence absolute freedom of action.

Carte de Visite, kärt dĕ vē-zēt, literally a visiting card, a photographic likeness executed on a card somewhat larger than a visiting card, and usually inserted in a photographic album. Cartes de visite were introduced by Disdéri in 1854.

Cartel', an agreement for the delivery of prisoners or deserters; also, a written challenge to a duel. A cartel-ship is a ship commissioned in time of war to exchange prisoners; also to carry proposals between hostile powers.

Car'ter, Elizabeth, English poet and linguist: b. Deal, 16 Dec. 1717; d. London, 19 Feb. 1806. She was the daughter of Dr. Nicholas Carter, a clergyman of Kent, and was educated by her father, soon becoming mistress of Latin, Greek, French, and German; to which she afterward added Italian, Spanish, Portuguese, Hebrew, and Arabic. She was for 50 years the friend of Dr. Johnson. Several of her poetical attempts appeared in the 'Gentleman's Magazine' before she attained her 17th year, and these procured her much celebrity. In 1739 she translated the critique of Crousaz on 'Pope's Essay on Man,' and in the same year gave a translation of Algarotti's explanation of the Newtonian philosophy. She published a translation of 'Epictetus,' in 1758.

Carter, Franklin, American educator: b. Waterbury, Conn., 30 Sept. 1837. He was graduated at Williams College in 1862, was professor of Latin there in 1865-72, and of German at Yale in 1872-81, and became president of Williams College 1882, resigning in 1901. He wrote a 'Life of Mark Hopkins' and a translation of Goethe's 'Iphigenia in Tauris.'

Carter, Sir Frederic Bowker Terrington, Canadian jurist: b. Saint John's, Newfoundland, 12 Feb. 1819; d. Saint John's 28 Feb. 1900. He was called to the Newfoundland bar in 1842, served in the Newfoundland assembly from 1855 to 1878, and two years later became chief justice of Newfoundland. He was knighted in 1878.

Carter, George R., American politician: b. Honolulu, Hawaii, 1866; was educated at Phillips Andover College and Yale University. In 1891 he was appointed Hawaiian consul at Seattle, Wash. He returned to Honolulu in 1896 and was governor of Hawaii by appointment of President Roosevelt 1903-7.

Carter, Henry. See LESLIE, FRANK.

Carter, James Coolidge, American lawyer: b. Lancaster, Mass., 14 Oct. 1827; d. New York 14 Feb. 1905. He was educated at Harvard, and his admission to the bar took place in New York in 1853. He was counsel for the city of New York in the famous case of the people against William Tweed, and in 1875 was appointed a member of the commission to devise a system of municipal rule for the cities of the State of New York. He published: 'The Proposed Codification of Our Common Law' (1884); 'The Provinces of the Written and the Unwritten Law' (1889); 'The Ideal and Actual Law' (1890).

Carter, James Madison Gore, American author: b. Johnson County, Ill., 15 April 1843. He was educated at the State Normal University. St. John's College, and Northwestern University Medical School. He served in an Illinois regiment during the Civil War, being captured and taken to Libby Prison. Among his works are: 'Outlines of Medical Botany of the United States'; 'Catarrhal Diseases of the Respiratory Organs'; and 'Diseases of the Stomach'; and various monographs on medical topics.

Carter, Louise Leslie, American actress. Her stage career began 10 Nov. 1890, when she appeared in the 'Ugly Duckling' in New York. Her other roles have been the Quakeress in 'Miss Helyett'; Maryland Calvert in 'The Heart of Maryland'; Zaza in 'Zaza'; Madame Du Barry in 'Du Barry'; and Adrea in 'Adrea.' She was married to William L. Payne 13 July 1906. See Strang, 'Famous Actresses.'

Carter, Samuel Powhatan, American naval and military officer: b. Elizabethtown, Tenn., 6 Aug. 1819; d. Washington, D. C., 26 May 1891. He became a midshipman in 1840, fought in the Mexican war in coast attack, and in 1856 took part in the capture of the barrier forts, Canton, China. In 1861 he was detailed to go to Tennessee, where he started the Tennessee brigade. All through the Civil War he was of great service to the government, and for his gallantry was brevetted major-general of volunteers. In 1882 he was promoted rear-admiral on the retired list.

Carter, Thomas Henry, American politician: b. Scioto County, Ohio, 30 Oct. 1854. He was bred to farming, but later became a lawyer, removing to Montana in 1882. He was Montana's first representative in Congress (1891), United States senator from that State from 1895 to 1901, chairman of the National Republican Committee in 1892-6, and was appointed in 1900 United States commissioner to the St. Louis Exposition.

Carter, William H., American military officer and author: b. Nashville, Tenn. In 1868 he entered the United States Military Academy. Successively promoted, he became in 1898 lieutenant-colonel and assistant adjutant-general, and brigadier-general 15 July 1902. He served on the frontier from 1873-07; from 1897-1902 he was connected with the War Department; till August 1903 in the Army War College; to 3 Dec. 1903 assistant chief of staff; and since 23 Feb. 1904 Commanding Department of the Visayas, Philippine Islands. He wrote: 'Horses, Saddles, and Bridles'; 'Historical Sketch 6th United States Cavalry'; and 'From Yorktown to Santiago.'

Carteret, Antoine Alfred Desire, Swiss statesman and fabulist: b. Geneva 2 April 1813; d. there 31 Jan. 1889. His political career was long and brilliant; and in literature he made a name with pleasing 'Fables' (1873), and a novel, 'Two Friends' (1872), descriptive of Genevese customs.

Carteret, kär'te rĕt, SIR George, English provincial proprietor: b. St. Ouen, Jersey, be-

tween 1609-17; d. 14 Jan. 1679. He had a distinguished career in the British navy, was an active supporter of the royalist cause, was made lieutenant-governor of the island of Jersey and vice-admiral. He manifested an interest in colonization and received a royal grant, "in perpetual inheritance," of certain lands in America "to be called New Jersey," the name being taken from the island of which he had been governor. In 1651 he surrendered to the commonwealth and served for a time in the French navy, returning to England at the restoration. He was made treasurer of the navy in 1661 and suspended in 1669 for mismanagement of funds. In 1664 he was made joint proprietor with Lord Berkeley of the province of New Jersey under a grant from the Duke of York, and in 1676, when the province was divided, East Jersey fell to his share. He was one of the first proprietors of Carolina.

Carteret, John, EARL GRANVILLE, British statesman: b. 22 April 1690; d. Bath, 2 Jan. 1763. He received his education at Westminster School and Christ Church College, Oxford. From Oxford he proceeded to London, plunged into the political and social excitements of the period, made the acquaintance of Swift, and in 1710 married Lady Frances Worsley. Entering the House of Lords on 25 May 1711, as second Baron Carteret, he espoused the side of the Whigs, then led by Stanhope and Sunderland, and in 1714 made his first speech in the House of Lords in support of the Protestant Succession. On the accession of George I. Carteret became a lord of the bedchamber. In 1719 he was appointed by Stanhope, ambassador extraordinary to Sweden, and succeeded in arranging two treaties of peace, the first between Sweden, Hanover, and Prussia, and the second between Denmark and Sweden. In 1721 he was appointed to one of the two foreign secretaryships, that for the "Southern Department" of Europe, and as such, attended, in 1723, the congress of Cambria, which attempted the settlement of differences between Germany and Spain, and accompanied George I. to Berlin. In 1724 Carteret was appointed lord-lieutenant of Ireland. Though he came into collision with Swift over the Drapier prosecution, the two ultimately became warm friends. Between 1730 and 1742 Carteret took the lead in the House of Lords of the party opposed to Sir Robert Walpole. When this opposition succeeded in overthrowing Walpole, Carteret became the real head of the administration, but was driven from power by the Pelhams in 1744. In the same year he became Earl Granville on the death of his mother, who had been created Countess Granville in her own right.

Carteret, Philip, English provincial governor: d. 1682. He was appointed governor of the province of New Jersey by the proprietors, Berkeley and George Carteret, and was given power to grant land to settlers. He reached New Jersey in 1665, bringing with him about 30 settlers, and settled at Elizabethtown. He avoided trouble with the Indians by adopting the wise policy of buying the land from them or requiring the colonists to do so. In 1672 he went to England for a time, but returned in 1674, and during his absence New Jersey was in the possession of the Dutch for a year, 1673-4. In 1676 when the division of the province into East and West Jersey was completed he became governor of East Jersey, holding the position till his death.

Cartesianism, the philosophy of René Descartes (q.v.) and his school, among whom may be reckoned Geulinex, Malebranche Arnauld, Nicole, and even many who stood outside the circle of professional philosophers like Bousset and Fénélon. Spinoza and Leibnitz have much in common with Descartes in standpoint and method, but the divergencies of their systems from his are too great to justify us in classifying them as Cartesians. Among the many noteworthy points in Descartes' system we may mention the deliberate determination to doubt everything that could intelligibly be called in question. This was not scepticism, but a principle of method that he employed to enable him to reach something absolutely certain. This basal fact he found in the famous proposition, "I think, therefore I am" (*Cogito ergo sum, je pense donc je suis*). No doubt could shake the certainty the ego possesses of its own existence. Moreover, Descartes finds in consciousness certain ideas that are not due to experience and not the product of the imagination. These ideas he pronounces connate, original possessions of the mind. Among them the chief is that of the conception of God as an infinite idea, Descartes argues, proves the actual existence of God as its cause, for no finite being can be the author of the idea of infinity. Having thus established the existence of God, Descartes maintains that the veracity of God warrants us in believing that whatever we perceive through the medium of clear and distinct ideas must be true. Adopting the traditional notion of substance he holds that besides the infinite substance, God, there are two finite created substances, namely, matter or extended substance, and mind or thinking substance. These have no attributes in common, and are absolutely opposed to each other. Thus his philosophy is a Dualism (q.v.). In the human organism these two substances are united. The soul has its seat in the pineal gland, and at this point receives influences from the body, and in turn controls and governs the direction of bodily movements. Descartes' account of the physical world is given in terms of the mechanical theory, the principles of which he was one of the earliest thinkers to formulate clearly. All bodies are extended, figured, substances, without any internal properties or differences. Everything that takes place in the physical world consists in the movement of an extended body. Thus the sciences of physical nature can be comprehended in a mathematical physics which has for its data, the size, shape, velocity (amount of motion) and direction of the various bodies of which the physical world is composed. God at the beginning created bodies with a fixed quantity of motion and rest; and since God is unchanging, this amount is subject to no increase or diminution. From this statement, which is couched in scholastic language, has come, through a closer analysis of conceptions, the modern principle of the conservation of energy. Descartes' view of the relation of body and mind was not satisfactory even to the members of his own school, and led to the doctrine of Occasionalism and with Spinoza to a

thorough-going Parallelism (q.v.). He also left to his successors the further elaboration of the problem regarding the relation of the one infinite substance, God, to the two created substances. In the 'Passions de l'âme' he made an important contribution to the psychology of the emotions, deriving all forms of emotional experience from the six primary emotions, wonder, love, hate, desire, joy, and grief.

Consult: Descartes' 'Discourse on Method'; 'Meditations on the First Philosophy,' and 'Principles of Philosophy,' in Veitch's or Torrey's translation; see also Kuno Fischer, 'Descartes and His School,' English translation by J. Gordy; Norman Smith, 'Studies in the Cartesian Philosophy'; J. P. Mahaffy, 'Descartes' (in 'Blackwood Philosophical Classics'), article 'Cartesianism' in the 'Encyclopedia Britannica'; any standard history of philosophy *in loco*.

J. E. CREIGHTON,
Professor of Philosophy, Cornell University.

Car'thage (conjectural native name, the Phoenician *Kereth-hadeshoth*, new city, from which the Greek *Karchēdon*, and the Roman *Carthago* are supposed to have been derived), the most famous city of Africa in antiquity, capital of a rich and powerful commercial republic. It was situated on the north coast, not far from the modern Tunis. According to tradition, Dido, fleeing from Tyre, came to this country, where the inhabitants agreed to give her as much land as could be compassed by an ox-hide. Dido cut the hide into small thongs, with which she enclosed a large piece of land. Carthage was founded, according to Aristotle, 287 years later than Utica. Becker supposes it to have been a joint colony or factory, in the Anglo-Indian sense, of Tyre and Utica. The actual date of its foundation is much contested. The date commonly given is 878 B.C. The history of Carthage is usually divided into three periods. The first is the epoch of its gradual rise; the second that of the struggles with other states occasioned by its extended power; the third that of its decline and fall. These epochs interlock each other, and it is only as a matter of convenience that we can interpose exact dividing dates between them. The first epoch has been extended as far as to 410 B.C.; the second limited to the period chiefly distinguished by wars with Greece, 401–265; the third is the period occupied with the Roman wars, and ending with the fall of Carthage.

Carthage appears early to have been independent of Tyre. There existed, however, a close relationship between them, due to affinity of race and religion. This appears from various incidents in their history, as when the Tyrians refused to follow Cambyses in a contemplated attack on Carthage, and when Alexander, having attacked Tyre, the women and children were sent to Carthage. There is no evidence that the government of Carthage was ever monarchical. She appears soon to have acquired an ascendency over the earlier Tyrian colonies, Utica, Tunis, Hippo, Leptis, and Hadrumetum. This was probably gained without any effort as the result of her material prosperity. The rise of Carthage, then, may be attributed to the superiority of her site for commercial purposes, and the enterprise of her inhabitants. Her relations with the native populations, as is evident from her subsequent history, would always be those of a superior with inferior races. Some of them were directly subject to Carthage, others contributed to her strength by recruiting her armies, although frequently in hostility with her. She established colonies for commercial purposes along the whole northern coast of Africa, west of Cyrenaica, and these colonies enabled her to maintain and extend her influence over the native tribes. These colonies, together with most of the earlier Phœnician colonies subject to her, possessed little strength in themselves, and easily fell a prey to an invader; hence they were in the end a source of weakness, although it is not easy to see how her prosperity could have been attained without them. It is only after the north of Africa has thus been placed at her command that Carthage appears formally on the stage of history. One of her earliest recorded contests is that with Cyrene, when the boundary between the two states was fixed, to the advantage of Carthage, at the bottom of the Greater Syrtis, the Carthaginian envoys, according to the traditional story, consenting to be buried on the spot. The immediate wants of the city were provided for by the cultivation of the surrounding territory, which alone was directly dependent on her.

Commerce naturally led Carthage to conquest. The advantages, both for the promotion and protection of her trade, of possessing islands in the Mediterranean, led to her first enterprises. Expeditions to Sicily and Sardinia appear to have been undertaken before the middle of the 6th century. The war was carried on in the latter half of this century by Mago, and his sons Hasdrubal and Hamilcar. At the same time a war arose with the Africans on account of the refusal of the Carthaginians to continue the payment of a ground-rent for their city. In this the Carthaginians were unsuccessful, but at a subsequent period they achieved their object. Sardinia was their first conquest. They guarded it with the utmost jealousy. The Romans, by the first treaty 509 B.C., were allowed to touch at it; but this permission was withdrawn in the second. It was the entrepôt of their trade with Europe, and lessened their dependence on their own territory for corn. They founded its capital, Caralis, now Cagliari. They soon after occupied Corsica, where they united with the Tyrrhenians, its previous possessors, against the Greeks. Sicily was already occupied by Greek and Phœnician colonies. The latter, on the decline of Tyre, seem to have fallen under the dominion of Carthage, which gave her a footing on the island. The Greeks were still the more powerful party, and the Carthaginians occupied themselves in promoting dissensions among their cities. When the Greeks were occupied with the Persian invasion, they organized a great expedition to take possession of the island, in which they landed 300,000 men, contributed by all their dependencies. Among these Sardinians, Corsicans, and Ligurians, the latter from the gulfs of Lyons and Genoa, are enumerated. They were totally defeated by Gelon, tyrant of Syracuse, and their leader slain, in the battle of Himera, 480 B.C. The Balearic, and many smaller islands in the Mediterranean, had already been occupied by the Carthaginians. Spain had also been colonized by them with peaceable commercial settlements. No other great enterprise took place in the first period of her history.

The war with the Greeks in Sicily was renewed in 409. Hannibal, the son of Gisco, landed an army at Lilybæum, in the spring of that year, and reduced Selinus and Himera. In a subsequent expedition Agrigentum was subdued. A pestilence seconded the efforts of Dionysius and saved Syracuse, 396 B.C. A treaty put an end to the war in 392. The struggle between the Greeks and the Carthaginians continued with varying success throughout the remainder of this period. Its most remarkable event was the invasion of Africa by Agathocles, 310 B.C. Defeated in Sicily by the Carthaginians, to avert the total ruin of his affairs, he raised an army and passed over to Africa. The most extraordinary success awaited him, showing at once the weakness of the hold which Carthage had of her external possessions on the continent, and the danger she constantly encountered from factions and dissensions within the city itself. Agathocles was the precursor of Scipio. After the death of Agathocles the Carthaginians renewed their enterprise in Sicily, and had nearly completed its conquest when the Greeks called in the aid of Pyrrhus, who for a time arrested their progress 277-5 B.C. Notwithstanding numerous and disastrous defeats in their contests with the Greeks, the Carthaginians seemed, after the departure of Pyrrhus, to have the conquest of Sicily at length within their power. A dissension with the Mamertines, their former allies, called in the Romans, and with their invasion, 264 B.C., the third period of Carthaginian history begins.

The first Punic war, in which Rome and Carthage contended for the dominion of Sicily, was prolonged for 23 years, 264 to 241 B.C., and ended, through the exhaustion of the resources of Carthage, in her expulsion from the island. The second Punic war, conducted on the side of the Carthaginians by the genius of Hannibal, lasted 17 years, 218 to 201 B.C., and after just missing the overthrow of Rome, ended in the complete humiliation of Carthage. The policy of Rome, at the end of this war, in placing Carthage, disarmed, at the mercy of her African enemies, and raising her a powerful opponent in Masinissa, occasioned the third Punic war, in which Rome was the aggressor. It lasted only three years, but served to throw a halo of glory round the fall of Carthage, in whose total ruin it ended. This war, begun 150 B.C., ended, in 146 B.C., in the destruction of the last vestige of its power.

The repeated and not always unsuccessful struggles of Carthage with her African neighbors, in the very midst of her schemes of foreign conquest, indicate the marvelous tension to which a power inherently so weak was wrought in those great enterprises which virtually grasped at the supremacy of the world. In this matter the experience of Carthage was not unparalleled by that of Rome; but the great difference between them was that the former was surrounded by alien tribes, the latter by races kindred in language and manners, with whom, after conquest, she could easily unite. The invasion and conquest of Spain, begun by Hamilcar and carried on by Hasdrubal and Hannibal, and which led to the second Punic war, can only be mentioned in passing.

Carthage perished leaving no historians to tell her tale: hence many interesting circumstances in her history can never be known, and what is preserved has the color of partial and often hostile authority. The constitution of Carthage has occupied much of the attention of scholars, but still remains in many points obscure. The name of king occurs in the Greek accounts of it, and the first Carthaginian general who is recorded to have invaded Sicily and Sardinia is called Malchus, the Phœnician for king, but the monarchical constitution, as commonly understood, never appears to have existed in it. The officers called kings by the Greeks were two in number, the heads of an oligarchical republic, commonly called suffetes, the original name being considered identical with the Hebrew *shofetim*, judges. These officers were always chosen from the principal families, and were elected annually. It is not known if they could be re-elected. There was a Senate of 300, and the citizens were divided into classes similar to the Roman tribes, curiæ, and gentes. There was a smaller body of 30 chosen from the Senate, sometimes another smaller council of 10. Various other officers are mentioned, but the particulars regarding them are often obscure, and sometimes contradictory.

After the destruction of Carthage, her territory became the Roman province of Africa. A curse was pronounced upon the site of the city, and any attempt to rebuild it prohibited. The attempt was, however, made 24 years after her fall, by Caius Gracchus, one of the leading men of Rome. The same plan was entertained by Julius Cæsar, and it was accomplished by Augustus. The new city became the seat of the proconsul of Old Africa in place of Utica, and continued to flourish till the Vandal invasion. It became distinguished in the annals of the Christian Church. Cyprian was its bishop, and Tertullian is supposed to have been a native of it. It was taken and destroyed by the Arabs, under Hassan, in 647.

The religion of the ancient Carthaginians was essentially that of their Phœnician ancestors. They worshipped Moloch or Baal, to whom they offered human sacrifices; Hercules, the patron deity of Tyre and her colonies; Astarte, and other deities, which were identified with the heavenly bodies, but propitiated by cruel or lascivious rites. Their religion was considerably modified by their intercourse with the Greeks. After their defeat by Gelon he made it a condition of peace with them that they should abandon human sacrifices. Some of their deities were identified with those of the Greeks, and they adopted others of that people, and no doubt received also some of their ideas regarding them. Consult Arnold's and Mommsen's histories of Rome; R. B. Smith 'Carthage and the Carthaginians'; A. Church, 'Carthage, or the Empire of Africa'; N. Davis, 'Carthage and Her Remains.'

Carthage, Mo., city and county-seat of Jasper County, in the southwestern part of the State; on Spring River, and on the St. Louis & San F., Missouri Pac., Iron M.,' and Carthage and Western Railways, 150 miles south of Kansas City. It is the centre of a fertile farming and fruit-raising region, and in the vicinity are rich mines of zinc and lead and extensive quarries of marble and building stone. The city exports large shipments of stone, marble, grain, flour, strawberries and other fruits, poultry, live stock, and hides. It has six large quarries, zinc and stone works, stove, bed-spring, furniture, and canning factories, flour and woolen mills, and machine shops. There are four banks with $400,000 capital and an annual business of $2,000,000; and daily and weekly newspapers. Carthage has a county court-house (cost $100,-000), a public library, good public schools, a business college, a piano school, and is the seat of Carthage Collegiate Institute. The following churches are represented: Presbyterian, Cumberland Presbyterian, Congregationalist, Baptist, Methodist (North and South), Episcopal, Christian, Roman Catholic, Dunkard, and Adventist. The site of the city was first settled in 1833 by Henry Piercy. On 28 March 1842 it was made the county-seat and named Carthage. The town was practically destroyed in the Civil War (see CARTHAGE, BATTLE OF) and has been almost entirely rebuilt since 1866. The government is vested in a mayor and ten councilmen elected for a term of two years. Pop. (1900) 9,416.

W. J. SEWALL,
Editor 'Carthage Press.'

Carthage, Battle of. On 17 June 1861, Gen. Nathaniel Lyon, U. S. A., drove the Confederates from Boonville, Mo., and Claiborne F. Jackson, the disloyal governor of Missouri, ordered a concentration of the State troops, who adhered to him, in the southwestern part of the State, to unite with the Arkansas troops, under the command of Gen. Ben. McCulloch. Anticipating McCulloch's movement into Missouri, Lyon ordered Gen. T. W. Sweeny, with three Union regiments, a small detachment of regulars, and some artillery, from St. Louis to Springfield. These were pushed forward by rail to Rolla and thence by road, and 28 June Col. Franz Sigel, with the 3d Missouri, arrived at Sarcoxie, southwest of Springfield, and 15 miles southeast of Carthage, Jasper County. Here Sigel learned that Gen. Sterling Price, with about 800 Missourians, was near Neosho, 22 miles south, and that Jackson, with other State troops, was to the north, 15 or 20 miles beyond Lamar, marching south. He concluded to move first on Price to disperse him, and then turn north on Jackson, his object being to prevent a junction of the two forces, and to open communication with Lyon, who was marching south from Booneville; but when he started after Price, on the morning of the 29th, he heard that he had retreated to join McCulloch, upon which he turned his thoughts toward Jackson, but continued his march to Neosho, where he was joined a few days later by Col. Salomon, with the 5th (Union) Missouri. Capt. Conrad's company of the 3d was left to hold Neosho, and on the 4th of July Sigel, with the two regiments and two batteries of four guns each, marched to Spring River, a short distance southeast of Carthage, where he heard that Jackson, with over 4,000 men, was but nine miles in his front in the direction of Lamar. On the morning of the 5th, with about 1,000 men and eight guns, he advanced slowly, his train three miles in the rear, driving back the enemy's mounted skirmishers, and about nine miles beyond Carthage came upon Jackson's troops in line of battle on elevated ground, four divisions under command of Gens. James S. Raines, John B. Clark, M. M. Parsons, and W. Y. Slack, numbering nearly 5,000 men, 1,200 of whom were unarmed. About

1,800 were mounted men, armed with shotguns, and judiciously posted on the flanks of the infantry. Jackson had eight guns. After some skirmishing Sigel, at 10 o'clock, brought up seven guns and opened fire, which was promptly returned, but not effectively, for, being in want of proper ammunition, the Confederate guns were charged with pieces of chain, iron spikes, broken iron, and round stones or pebbles. After a desultory artillery fire of three hours the Confederate horsemen advanced from both flanks and making a wide circuit, to avoid Sigel's artillery, began to close in on him and threaten his train, whereupon, disposing four guns in rear and two on either flank he fell back, harassed at every step, until he reached Carthage, where he made a stand. But, as the enemy was still pressing hard on him, working on both flanks and threatening the road to Springfield, he again fell back, skirmishing all the way, some two or three miles beyond Carthage, where pursuit ended, and Sigel marched to Sarcoxie, and thence by way of Mount Vernon to Springfield, where Lyon joined him on the 13th. The Union loss was 13 killed and 31 wounded, to which must be added the loss of Conrad's company of 94 men surprised and captured at Neosho, on the 5th, by Churchill's Arkansas regiment of McCulloch's command. The Confederate loss was about 30 killed and 125 wounded. The day after the engagement Jackson marched from Carthage and met McCulloch and Price coming to join him. Consult: Official Records, Vol. III.; Century 'Battles and Leaders of the Civil War' (Vol. I.). E. A. CARMAN.

Carthage, New. See CARTAGENA.

Carthage'na. See CARTAGENA.

Carthu'sians, an order of monks in the Roman Catholic Church, founded in 1084 by Bruno (St. Bruno), a priest of the diocese of Rheims and principal of the theological school there. What specially prompted Bruno to retire from the world was the openly confessed contempt of his bishop for piety and religion. It was a saying of this bishop that while it was a fine thing to be archbishop of Rheims, it was too bad that he had to sing masses. Bruno, with a little band of his friends, who were of the same mind with him, sought solitude in the diocese of Grenoble, and settled in a wilderness near that city called the *Cartusium*. It was a region of terrible aspect, with naked and precipitous rocks surrounded by sterile hills; and the poet Gray, in the five Latin Alcaic stanzas which in 1741 he wrote in the album of the monastery of Cartusium or La Grande Chartreuse, notes the austere features of the locality in terms which recall the picture drawn of it by Bruno's contemporaries, the *invias rupes*, the *fera juga*, the *clivos praeruptos*, the *nemorum noctem* (impassable cliffs, rugged mountains, precipitous heights, gloomy forests). His institute was the most rigorous of all the monastic orders, and the Carthusians might boast — were they given to boasting — that theirs is the only monastic order that never has had to undergo reformation to bring it back to its first rigor. Bruno gave his community a rule of life which was not committed to writing; it prescribed perpetual silence, abstinence from flesh-meats, habitual wearing of the cilicium or horsehair shirt, and the like austerities. But he retained withal his love of

letters, and communicated to his brethren a taste for science and learning. Besides the customary religious exercises of all monastic institutes, his monks were required to occupy a part of the time in manual labor and the other part in the work of transcribing the ancient authors and the more important public documents and records of the time. Before long there was founded in the wilderness of the *Cartusium* a collateral branch for women recluses, under substantially the same rule.

A written rule was given to the Carthusians by Guigo, fifth prior of the Cartusium — the head of a Carthusian institute is always prior, not abbot — in 1129. It forbids the practice of austerities not prescribed by the founder and establishes in perpetuity the provisions of Bruno's rule. Guigo wrote a 'Manual for Monks' in which he names reading, meditation, prayer, and contemplation as the means of reaching the perfection of the Christian and religious life. The original establishment, the Cartusium, or La Grande Chartreuse, contributed to the mother house of the order continuously, the troublous time of the Revolution excepted, down to the year 1903, when under the law for regulation or suppression of monastic houses in France, the religious community was dispossessed and turned out of the home in which it had lived during more than 800 years. The latest rule of the order of Carthusians dates from 1581. In many respects it is not as rigorous as the rule given by Bruno and Guigo. The use of linen is still forbidden, the abstinence from flesh-meats is still enforced, as is also the rule of silence. The Carthusian "house" is still an assembly of detached small houses or cells comprised within an enclosure, with a patch of ground around each little house. The general of the Carthusians resides — rather till the expulsion of the inmates did reside — at La Grande Chartreuse, not at Rome, as do the generals of most of the religious orders.

Cartier, SIR George Etienne, Canadian statesman: b. St. Antoine, Verchères County, Quebec, 6 Sept. 1814; d. London, 21 May 1873. He claimed descent from the family to which Jacques Cartier belonged; was among the followers of Papineau in the rebellion of 1837, distinguishing himself for his courage, but ultimately was obliged to take refuge in the United States. Returning when amnesty was decreed, he resumed the practise of law and attained to some eminence in his profession. He entered the Canadian Parliament as a Conservative in 1848, became a Cabinet Minister in 1855, and from that time till his death was closely associated with the English-speaking Conservative leader, Sir John A. Macdonald (q.v.). Cartier was Prime Minister 1858-62. When Canadian Federation was set on foot he took a prominent part in the negotiations, and it was under his leadership, aided by the church, that French-speaking Canada was reconciled to the Federal system. He carried on the negotiations with the Hudson Bay Co. which resulted in the surrender to Canada of the company's rights in the Northwest, and it was he who carried through the Canadian Parliament the bill creating the Province of Manitoba. This bill embodied elaborate safe-guards for Roman Catholic separate schools, but its provisions were swept away in the well-known later agitation for a uniform school system in Manitoba. Perhaps Cartier's principal domestic achievement was the enactment in 1864 of the Civil Code for what is now the Province of Quebec. In 1868 he was created a Baronet, to reward his services in establishing the new Dominion. He carried through the Canadian House of Commons in 1872 the first charter of the Canadian Pacific Railway. When Sir John Macdonald's government fell in 1873 Cartier was involved in the discredit to his chief, springing from what is known in Canadian history as the Pacific scandal. Sir John Macdonald relied greatly upon Cartier's influence with the French Canadians, which, however, had declined before his death.

GEORGE M. WRONG,
Professor of History, University of Toronto.

Cartier, Jacques, French navigator: b. St. Malo, 31 Dec. 1491; d. 1557. After gaining some experience in fishing-fleets off the Labrador coast, he commanded an expedition to North America in 1534, entering the Strait of Belle Isle, and took possession of the mainland of Canada in the name of Francis I. The next year he sailed up the St. Lawrence as far as the present Montreal. In 1541 he went out as captain-general in command of a first detachment of ships to prepare the way for Roberval, who had been named viceroy. Finding, however, that his chief did not arrive, after he had waited some time, he returned to St. Malo. The natives usually received him well, but when about to return from his second voyage he treacherously kidnapped Donnaconna, one of the chiefs, and some others, in order to show them in his native country. His book, 'Discours du Voyage fait par le Capitaine Jacques Cartier aux Terres neufves de Canada,' was published in 1598.

Cartilage, one of the primary tissues of animal structures, of the connective-tissue class, characterized by its peculiar basement substance. The most abundant form of cartilage is the hyaline variety, but there are also fibrous and fibro-elastic cartilages. Hyaline cartilage, particularly abundant on the ends of the bones, is whitish and translucent, firm and elastic. The cells are imbedded in an abundant homogeneous basement substance which is made up largely of chondrin. Fibrous cartilage is less abundant, and its basement substance is fibrillated. It is found about the intervertebral cartilage masses, about the joints, and around the tendons of some of the larger muscles. The fibro-elastic form is found only in certain structures,— the epiglottis, the larynx, the Eustachian tube, and in the external ear. Cartilage tissues protect the ends of the long bones by reason of their firm elasticity. They provide strong, firm, and yet movable structures where bone, by reason of its rigidity, would not be serviceable, as in the epiglottis, larynx, etc.

Carton, Florent. See DANCOURT.

Carton, Sydney, the hero in Dickens' 'Tale of Two Cities.'

Cartoon (It. *cartone,* from Lat. *charta,* paper), a term having various significations. In painting, it denotes a sketch on thick paper, pasteboard, or other material, used as a model for a large picture, especially in fresco, oil, tapestry, and sometimes in glass and mosaic. In fresco painting, cartoons are particularly useful, because in this a quick process is necessary, and

a fault cannot easily be corrected. In applying cartoons, the artist commonly traces them through, covering the back of the design with black-lead or red chalk; then, laying the picture on the wall or other matter, he passes lightly over each stroke of the design with a point, which leaves an impression of the color on the plate or wall; or the outlines of the figures are pricked with a needle, and then, the cartoon being placed against the wall, a bag of coal-dust is drawn over the holes, in order to transfer the outlines to the wall. In fresco painting, the figures were formerly cut out and fixed firmly on the moist plaster. The painter then traced their contour with a pencil of wood or iron, so that the outlines of the figures appeared on the fresh plaster, with a slight but distinct impression, when the cartoon was taken away. In the manufacture of a certain kind of tapestry the figures are still cut out, and laid behind or under the woof, by which the artist directs his operations. In this case the cartoons must be colored. In very modern times the term is commonly applied to pictures caricaturing notable characters or events of the moment. See CARICATURE AND CARICATURISTS.

The most famous cartoons in existence are those executed by Raphael for the celebrated tapestries of the Vatican, which were made at Arras, and hence called Arazzi. Two sets of these tapestries were ordered by Leo. X., one for the Vatican and the other for presentation to King Henry VIII. The second set, or fragments of it, are still in existence on the Continent. The cartoons lay for a time neglected at Arras, and have repeatedly fallen into neglect again, so that out of 25, the original number, only seven remain, and these have had to be restored. They were purchased at the advice of Rubens by Charles I. about 1630. On the sale of his effects they were purchased by the order of Cromwell for the nation, but again fell into neglect in the time of Charles II. William III. had them restored, and built a gallery for them at Hampton Court, where they remained, until in 1865 they were lent to the South Kensington Museum. The subjects of the seven are: (1) Paul Preaching at Athens; (2) The Death of Ananias; (3) Elymas the Sorcerer Struck with Blindness; (4) Christ's Charge to Peter; (5) The Sacrifice at Lystra; (6) Peter and John Healing the Cripple at the Beautiful Gate of the Temple; (7) The Miraculous Draught of Fishes. The cartoons have been repeatedly engraved, among others by Dorigny, Holloway, and Gribelin. They have also been extensively made known by photographs.

The cartoon of the School of Athens, carried to Paris by the French, and a fragment of the Battle of Maxentius and Constantine, are preserved in the Ambrosian Gallery at Milan. There are, likewise, cartoons by Giulio Romano in the Sala Borgia, by Domenichino and other Italian masters, who caused their pictures to be executed, in a great degree, by their scholars, after these cartoons. The value set upon cartoons by the old Italian masters may be seen by Giovanni Armenini's 'Precetti dello Pittura' (1687). In later times large paintings, particularly in fresco, were not executed so frequently. The artists also labored with less care, and formed their great works more from small sketches. In modern times some German artists have prepared accurate cartoons. Among them is Cornelius, whose cartoons for his fresco paintings in Munich have acquired much celebrity. He prepared, too, a cartoon for the fresco picture representing 'Joseph Interpreting the Dream.' Overbeck and Julius Schnorr may also be mentioned for their cartoons.

Cartouche, Louis Dominique, loo-ē dŏm-ĭ-nēk kär-toosh, French robber: b. Paris, about 1693; d. Châtelet, France, 28 Nov. 1721. He was the leader of a noted company of robbers, and being captured was broken alive on the wheel in 1721. His life has formed the subject of a modern French drama, and was formerly represented on the English stage.

Cartouche, or **Cartouch** (French *cartouche*). (1) A wooden case about three inches thick at bottom, and girt round with marline, holding 200, 300, or 400 musket-balls, with 8 or 10 iron balls weighing one pound each, to be fired from a mortar, gun, or howitzer for the defense of a pass, retrenchment, etc. Such missiles have been superseded. In French military language cartouche signifies the entire charge of a firearm. (2) In architecture, sculpture, etc., an ornament representing a scroll of paper, being usually in the form of a table, or flat member, with wavings, whereon is some inscription or device. (3) The name given by the French literati to that oval ring or border which includes, in the Egyptian hieroglyphics, the names of persons of high distinction. (4) In heraldry a name given to a sort of oval shield, much used by the Popes and secular princes in Italy, and others, both clergy and laity, for painting or engraving their arms on.

Cartridge, a case of paper, parchment, metal, or flannel suited to the bore of firearms, and holding the exact charge, including, in the case of small arms, both powder and bullet (or shot). In loading with the old style of cartridge for muzzle-loading rifles, the paper over the powder was bitten or twisted off and the powder poured in, the bullet being then inserted and rammed home. The cartridges used for breech-loading rifles contain the powder in a case of solid brass, and have the percussion-cap by which they are ignited fixed in the base. Such cases can be refilled and used a number of times in succession. Cartridges for shot-guns are similar to those for rifles, but are usually of less solid construction, being commonly of strong paper with a base of metal. Those for large guns are usually made of flannel and contain only the powder. Blank-cartridge is a cartridge without ball or shot. Cartridges for blasting are filled with dynamite or other explosive.

Cartridge-paper, a thick paper originally made for the manufacture of cartridges, but extensively used in the arts, its rough surface giving it an advantage for drawing upon, as a wall paper, and for other purposes.

Cartwright, Edmund, English inventor: b. Marnham, Nottinghamshire, 24 April 1743; d. Hastings, Sussex, 30 Oct. 1823. He was educated at University College, Oxford, and having taken orders in the Church, obtained first the living of Brampton, near Chesterfield, and afterward that of Goadby-Marwood, in Leicestershire. It was, however, only after he had reached 40 years of age that his attention was first turned to the subject on which his claim to remembrance is founded. In the summer of 1784 he

began to investigate the subject of mechanical weaving, and experiment regarding improvements. His efforts were crowned with success, and in April of the following year he brought his first power-loom into action. It was not, in fact, in respect of economy of labor, any advance upon the ordinary hand-loom; but the idea which subsequent improvements have carried so far in advance of hand-loom weaving was there. The introduction of Cartwright's loom was opposed both by manufacturers and workmen; and the first mill erected for them, containing 500 looms, was burned down. His attention once turned in the direction of mechanical improvement, he continued to make progress in discovery. He not only perfected his power-loom, but took out 10 patents for different inventions, among which was one for combing wool. He expended much of his means in these investigations, and in 1809 he received as an acknowledgment of their value a grant from Parliament of £10,000, which relieved him from straitened circumstances, although, it is said, it did not cover his expenditure. He also received premiums for various improvements from the Society of Arts and the board of agriculture.

Cartwright, John, English reformer, brother of Edmund Cartwright (q.v.): b. Marnham, Nottinghamshire, 17 Sept. 1740; d. London, 23 Sept. 1824. He entered the navy in 1758, and became a first lieutenant in 1766. In 1774 his attention was turned to politics. In his 'Letters on American Independence' (Independence of America considered as supremely useful and glorious to Great Britain), written in this year, he advocated a union between the colonies and the mother state, under separate legislatures, and argued this great question on the foundation of natural, inherent right; maintaining "that the liberty of man is not derived from charters, but from God, and that it is original in every one." In 1775 he was appointed major of the Nottinghamshire militia, and after several ineffectual attempts on the part of government to remove him from that post, his dismission was finally accomplished in 1792, in consequence of an act of Parliament. In the American war Lord Howe was desirous of having him with him in America; but Major Cartwright, although always eager for promotion in the navy, refused the proposal, alleging that he could not fight in a cause which he disapproved. From this time he devoted himself to the favorite objects of annual parliaments and universal suffrage. He was the author of a Declaration of Rights, distributed by the Society for Constitutional Information. The French revolution was warmly welcomed by Cartwright. In the trials of Tooke, Hardy, Thelwall, and other reformers, Cartwright was present as a witness, and displayed much firmness and fearlessness. By his writings, public addresses, etc., he continued to promote the work of reform and constitutional liberty; and as late as 1820 was tried for conspiracy and sedition, for advising the inhabitants of Birmingham, which had then no parliamentary representative, to send what he called their "legislatorial attorney" to the house; but he escaped with a fine of £100. Major Cartwright was not a political reformer only. The plan of making the slave-trade piracy is said to have been first developed in his 'Letters on the Slave-Trade.' A statue has been erected in London to his memory.

Cartwright, Peter, American Methodist clergyman: b. Virginia, 1 Sept. 1785; d. near Pleasant Plains, Ill., 25 Sept. 1872. He was ordained in Kentucky in 1806, and in 1823 removed to Illinois, where he labored for nearly half a century. He also sat in the State legislature there, and in 1846 was defeated by Abraham Lincoln in an election for congressman. Admired for his eloquence and strong common sense, he was also loved for his quaint eccentricity of manner, and possessed great influence in his own denomination.

Cartwright, SIR Richard John, Canadian statesman: b. Kingston, Ont., 4 Dec. 1835. He was educated at Trinity College, Dublin, and entered Canadian politics as a Conservative, but on account of a disagreement with Sir John A. Macdonald joined the Liberal party. He has served in the Canadian Parliament almost continually since 1863. He was minister of finance from 1873 until 1878, when his opposition to the policy of protection caused his downfall. He is an able speaker and an authority on finance. In 1897 he was a member of a Canadian commercial commission to the United States. He was knighted in 1879.

Cartwright, Thomas, English Puritan divine: b. Hertfordshire, 1535; d. Warwick, 27 Dec. 1603. He suffered imprisonment and exile more than once for his nonconformist opinions. He was a learned man, and at one time professor of divinity at Cambridge. His chief books are: 'A Second Admonition to the Parliament' (the first one having been published in 1572); 'A Confutation of the Rhemist's Translation'; 'Harmonia Evangelica'; and a criticism of Hooker's 'Ecclesiastical Polity.'

Carucate, kär'ü kāt, in mediæval times, as much land as one team could plow in the year. The size varied according to the nature of the soil and practice of husbandry in different districts.

Carupano, kä-roo'pä-nō, Venezuela, a seaport of the State of Bermudez, on the north coast of the peninsula of Paria, with a lighthouse and good roadstead. The surrounding district is fertile, and has mines of copper, sulphur, silver, lead, and lignite. The city exports cocoa, coffee, fish, etc., and has various manufactures. Pop. about 10,000.

Carus, kä-rùs, **Julius Victor,** German zoologist: b. Leipsic, 25 Aug. 1823. After studying at Leipsic, Würzburg, and Freiburg, he became at the age of 26 keeper of the Oxford museum of comparative anatomy. In 1853, two years after his return to his native city, he was appointed professor of comparative anatomy and director of the Zoological Institute there. Among his numerous writings are: 'System der Tierischen Morphologie' (1853); 'Handbuch der Zoologie'; and 'Geschichte der Zoologie.' He has translated most of Darwin's works into German.

Carus, Karl Gustav, goo'stäf, German physician and physiologist: b. Leipsic, 3 Jan. 1789; d. Dresden, 28 July 1869. He became professor of midwifery at the Medical Academy, and then royal physician, being subsequently a privy-councilor. He published a great number of writings covering a wide field of science, including medicine, physiology, anatomy, psychology, physics, painting, besides

memoirs of his life. Among these are 'System der Physiologie' (1838-40); 'Lebenserinnerungen und Denkwürdigkeiten' (1865-6); 'Lehrbuch der Zootomie' (1818); 'Über den Blutkreislauf der Insekten' (1827); 'Psyche' (1851).

Carus, kär'ŭs, **Marcus Aurelius,** Roman emperor: b. Nerona, Dalmatia, about 222 A.D.; d. near Ctesiphon, Mesopotamia, 283. His father was an African, and his mother a noble Roman lady. He was proclaimed emperor by the legions, on the assassination of Probus, 282. He caused justice to be executed upon the assassins. He gained a signal victory over the Sarmatians, and prosecuted the war against the Persians. Undertaking the campaign in midwinter, and making a rapid march through Thrace and Asia Minor, he ravaged Mesopotamia, made himself master of Seleucia, and carried his arms beyond the Tigris.

Carus, Paul, American philosophical writer: b. Ilsenburg, Germany, 18 July 1852. He was educated in the universities of Strassburg and Tübingen, and has been a resident of Chicago for several years, where he is editor of 'The Open Court' and 'The Monist.' He has published: 'The Ethical Problem'; 'Fundamental Problems'; 'The Soul of Man'; 'Primer of Philosophy'; 'Truth in Fiction'; 'Monism and Meliorism'; 'The Religion of Science'; 'The Philosophy of the Tool'; 'Our Need of Philosophy'; 'Science: a Religious Revelation'; 'The Gospel of Buddha'; 'Kanna'; 'Nirvana'; 'Homilies of Science'; 'Chinese Philosophy'; 'The Idea of a God'; 'Buddhism and Its Christian Critics'; 'The Dawn of a New Era'; 'Kant and Spencer'; 'The Nature of the State'; 'The History of the Devil'; 'Whence and Whither'; 'Eros and Psyche.'

Carus-Wilson, Charles Ashley, Canadian scientist: b. Eastry, England. He was graduated at Cambridge (1887) and became a civil engineer. Since 1890 he has been professor of engineering science at McGill University. He has written 'Electro-Dynamics,' and many monographs on his science.

Carutti di Cantogno, Domenico, dō-mä'-nē-kō kä-rüt'tē dē kän-tōn'yō, BARON, Italian historian and publicist: b. Cumiana, near Turin, 26 Nov. 1821. As a young man he took to romance writing, but was speedily absorbed in politics and rose to great distinction. When he resumed the pen, it was to compile such solid works as 'History of the Reign of Victor Amadeus II.' (1856) and 'History of the Reign of Charles Emanuel III.' (1859), which are interesting and scholarly.

Carvajal, kär-vä-häl', **Gas'par de,** Spanish missionary: b. Spain, early in the 16th century; d. Lima, Peru, 1584. He entered the Dominican order and went to Peru in 1533. In 1538 he accompanied the expedition of Gonzalo Pizarro to the countries east of the Quito as chaplain. He was appointed sub-prior of the convent of San Rosario at Lima; after the pacification of Peru he was sent to the mission of Tucuman and after working among the Indians there was made vicar-national of the province of Tucuman. With the aid of the Dominicans, whom he brought into the country, he established several Indian towns and Spanish colonies.

Carvajal, Tomas José Gonzales, tō'mä hō'sä gŏn thä'lĕs, Spanish statesman and author: b. Seville, 21 Dec. 1753; d. 9 Nov. 1834. He was appointed in 1795 governor of the new colonies in Sierra Morena and Andalusia, and protested against the French invasion of Spain in 1808. From 1809 to 1811 he served as commissary in the Spanish army against Bonaparte; in 1813 became minister of finance; relinquished these offices to assume the directorship of the royal university of Isidro, where he became involved in difficulties by establishing a professorship of constitutional law. He was arrested and detained in prison from 1815 to 1820, when the revolution reinstated him at San Isidro. A counter revolution brought his opponents into power, and he was exiled from 1823 to 1827. However, at the time of his death he was member of the supreme council of war, of the military department of the Spanish and Indian boards, and a grandee of Spain. He learned Hebrew at the age of 57 in order to translate the Psalms. This translation has gained for him a high reputation for poetical power.

Carvalho, José da Silva, hō'sä dä sĕl vä kär-väl'yō, Portuguese statesman: b. Beira 1782; d. 3 Feb. 1845. He was a member of the regency and appointed minister of justice until 1823, when, on the downfall of the constitutional government, of which he was a foremost champion, he was obliged to resort to flight to England, where he remained until 1826, when he returned to Lisbon, but Don Miguel's success again compelled him to leave. Eventually he was named a member of the council of guardianship instituted by Don Pedro for the young queen, Donna Maria, and succeeded in negotiating the first English loan for Portugal. Having accompanied Don Pedro to the Azores, he filled, on his return to Portugal, important offices, and became finance minister in 1832. In 1835 he retired with the Palmella administration, and was presently obliged to retire to England, where he remained until 1838, when a general amnesty was proclaimed.

Carvalho, Paez de Andrade, Manuel de, pä-ĕth' dä än-drä'dä mä'noo-ĕl dä kär-väl'yō Brazilian politician: b. about 1797; d. Rio de Janeiro, 18 June 1855. Elected temporary president of Pernambuco in December 1823, he led a revolt the next year against Pedro I., the emperor, and on 2 July 1824, announced a republic entitled 'Confederacao do Equador.' On the suppression of the revolt in October, Carvalho fled to England, but subsequently returned to Brazil and was a senator from 1835.

Carvel-built, a term applied to a ship or boat, the planks of which are all flush and not overlapping, as in clinker-built boats.

Car'ver, John, first governor of the Plymouth colony: b. England, about 1575; d. Plymouth, Mass, April 1621. He joined the Leyden colony of English exiles about 1608, and as their agent assisted in securing a charter from the Virginia Company and in selecting and equipping the Mayflower. He was elected governor, probably 11 Nov. 1620, after the Mayflower reached Provincetown, showed great ability and judgment in governing the infant colony after the landing at Plymouth, and established by a treaty with the Indians peaceful relations that remained for many years undisturbed. He was re-elected in March 1621, but died a few days afterward. His chair and sword are still preserved as Pilgrim relics.

Carver, Jonathan, American traveler: b. Stillwater, N. Y. (the universal ascription to Connecticut is an error), 1732; d. London, 1780. He embraced a military career, and in the French war of 1756 commanded a company of provincials, in the expedition across the lakes against Canada. When peace was concluded in 1763, Carver undertook to explore the vast territory which Great Britain had gained. His object was to acquire a knowledge of the manners, customs, languages, soil, and natural productions of the nations and region beyond the Mississippi, and to ascertain the breadth of the continent by penetrating to the Pacific over its widest part, between lat. 43° and 46° N. He accordingly set out from Boston in 1766, and having reached Michilimackinac, the remotest English post, applied to Mr. Rogers, the governor, for an assortment of goods as presents for the Indians dwelling in the parts through which his course was to be directed. Receiving a portion of the supply which he desired, and a promise that the residue should be sent to him at the Falls of St. Anthony, he continued his journey. But not obtaining the goods at the appointed place, in consequence of their having been disposed of elsewhere by those to whom the governor had intrusted them, he found it necessary to return to La Prairie du Chien. He then, in the beginning of the year 1767, directed his steps northward, with a view of finding a communication from the heads of the Mississippi into Lake Superior, in order to meet, at the grand portage on the northwest side of that lake, the traders that usually came about this season from Michilimackinac, from whom he intended to purchase goods, and then to pursue his journey. He reached Lake Superior in good time; but unfortunately the traders whom he met there could not furnish him with any goods, as they had barely enough for their own purposes, and, in consequence, he was obliged to return to the place whence he first departed, which he did in October 1768, after remaining some months on the north and east borders of Lake Superior, and exploring the bays and rivers that empty themselves into that body of water. He soon after repaired to England with the view of publishing his journal and charts, and of obtaining reimbursement for the expenses which he had incurred. Having undergone a long examination before the lords commissioners of trade and plantations, he received permission to publish his papers; but when they were nearly ready for the press an order was issued from the council-board, requiring him to deliver immediately into the plantation office all his charts and journals. He was, consequently, obliged to repurchase them at a great expense from the bookseller to whom he had disposed of them — a loss for which he received no indemnification, but was forced to be satisfied with that obtained for his other expenses. He had fortunately kept copies of his papers, and he published them 10 years afterward in Boston, while in the situation of a clerk of a lottery. He died in want of the common necessaries of life in 1780, aged 48 years. His works are: 'Travels Through the Interior Parts of North America' (1778); 'Treatise on the Culture of the Tobacco Plant' (1779).

Carving, as a branch of sculpture, the art of cutting a hard material by means of a sharp instrument: but there are extended uses of the term, as shown below.

The term is generally employed for work which is strictly decorative as distinguished from grand sculpture; thus the wrought stone leafage, scroll work and even animal forms in a Gothic porch are *carving* in common parlance, and so are the human figures of the porch if they are conventional or stiff, as often happens in mediæval work. In a Roman temple or a neo-classic edifice the leafage of Corinthian capitals or of any panel or string-course would be called *carving*, while the statues and even the reliefs of human subjects would be spoken of as sculpture (q.v.). Small pieces, even of human subjects, such as decorative statuettes and groups, are spoken of as carving, and these may be wrought in wood, ivory, bone, marble, and other stones, and even in hard and semi-precious stones, such as agate and jade. The carvings of the Chinese and Japanese are especially in demand in western lands, because of their picturesque beauty. When they are of wood they are often painted, gilded or lacquered with a rich polychromatic effect.

Throughout the middle ages of Europe, ivory statuettes, backs of mirrors, and purely ornamental objects were treated in the same way, the carving being helped out by color and gold with extraordinary results.

Carving, when done in very hard material, such as rock crystal and jade, requires much use of the drill, in which case the meaning of the term must be extended to include the result produced by a rapidly revolving pin with emery powder or the like. One of the most ingenious and useful purposes to which carving has been converted in more modern times is that of engraving wood-cuts or blocks for printing. (See Wood-Engraving.) Carving has been applied to almost innumerable uses in manufactures as well as in art. Some of these applications have given way to the art of engraving in metal and other processes, but new ones are continually arising. The first carving-machine was invented about 1800, and many others have since been patented.

Cary, Alice, American poet: b. near Cincinnati, Ohio, 26 April 1820; d. New York, 12 Feb. 1871. When quite young she began writing sketches and poems for the press, and in 1852 she, with her sister, Phœbe (q.v.), removed to New York, where they lived during the rest of their lives. In 1850 the sisters published a volume entitled 'Poems by Alice and Phœbe Cary.' Alice soon after published 'Clovernook, or Recollections of Our Neighborhood in the West' (1851-3); 'Lyra, and Other Poems' (1853); 'Hagar, a Story of To-day' (1852); 'Married, not Mated,' a novel (1856); 'Lyrics and Hymns'; 'The Bishop's Son'; 'The Lover's Diary' (1867); and 'Snow Berries: A Book for Young Folks' (1869). The verse of the Cary sisters still retains a hold upon the affections of readers and not a few lines of theirs have become familiarized by frequent quotation. While living in New York they attracted about them a circle of literary people, and for 15 years their Sunday evening receptions were a feature in the literary life of the city.

Cary, Annie Louise, American singer: b. Wayne, Maine, 22 Oct. 1842. She studied in Milan, made her operatic début in Copenhagen in 1868, had a successful European career for three years, and returned in 1870 to the United States, where she won great popularity and remained, with the exception of one brilliant European tour, until 1882, when she married Charles M. Raymond, and retired from the stage while her voice was still unimpaired. Since then she has sung only in private or for charity.

Cary, Archibald, American statesman: b. Virginia, about 1730; d. Chesterfield, Va., September 1786. He early became a member of the House of Burgesses, and in 1764 served on the committee which reported the address to the king, lords, and commons, on the principles of taxation; and in 1770 was one of the signers of the "Mercantile Association," which pledged its members to use no British fabrics thereafter, the design being to resist by practical measures the encroachments of the government. In 1773 he was one of the celebrated committee of correspondence by which the colonies were united into one great league against Parliament. When the State government was organized he was returned to the Senate, where he presided with great dignity and efficiency. At this time occurred the incident with which his name is most generally connected. The scheme of a dictatorship had been broached, and without his knowledge or consent Patrick Henry was spoken of for the post. In the midst of the general agitation Cary met Henry's half-brother in the lobby of the assembly, and said to him: "Sir, I am told that your brother wishes to be dictator. Tell him from me, that the day of his appointment shall be the day of his death, for he shall find my dagger in his heart before the sunset of that day." The project was speedily abandoned. He was a good representative of the former race of Virginia planters, delighting in agricultural pursuits, in blooded horses, and improved breeds of cattle, which he imported from England, and attended to with great care.

Cary, Edward, American journalist: b. Albany, N. Y., 5 June 1840. He has long been connected with the editorial staff of the New York *Times*. His principal published work is a 'Life of George William Curtis' (1894).

Cary, Elisabeth Luther, American writer: b. Brooklyn, N. Y., 1867. She is a daughter of Edward Cary (q.v.), and has published translations from the French of 'Sarcey and Melchior Vogue.' Her own works include 'Alfred Tennyson: His Homes, His Friends, and His Work'. (1898); 'Robert Browning; Poet and Man' (1899); 'The Rossettis: Dante, Gabriel, and Christina' (1900).

Cary, George Lowell, American Unitarian theologian: b. Medway, Mass., 10 May 1830. He was graduated at Harvard College in 1852; and was a professor at Antioch College, 1856-62. Since 1862 he has been professor of New Testament literature in Meadville Theological Seminary, Pennsylvania, of which he is also president. He has published 'Introduction to the Greek of the New Testament' (1878); 'The Synoptic Gospels' (1900).

Cary, Henry Francis, English translator of Dante: b. Gibraltar, Spain, 6 Dec. 1772; d. London, 14 Aug. 1844. In 1790 he entered Christ Church, Oxford, and he took orders in

1796. In 1796 he was presented to the vicarage of Abbot's Bromley, Staffordshire, and in 1800 he removed to Kingsbury, in Warwickshire, another living to which he had been presented. His studies while at college had embraced a wide range of Italian, French, and English literature, and in 1805 he gave proof of his Italian scholarship, as well as of his poetic powers, by the publication of the 'Inferno' of Dante in English blank-verse, accompanied by the Italian text. The entire translation of the 'Divina Commedia' was accomplished in 1812, and the work was now published complete, but it lay unnoticed for several years, till Samuel Taylor Coleridge drew attention to its merits. It has since been recognized as a standard English work. Cary subsequently translated the 'Birds' of Aristophanes (1824), and the 'Odes' of Pindar, and wrote a continuation of Johnson's 'Lives of the English Poets,' and a series of 'Lives of Early French Poets.' He was for some time curate of the Savoy, London, and in 1826 was appointed assistant-keeper of printed books in the British Museum, which office he resigned in consequence of his being passed by on the appointment of Mr. Panizzi in 1837 to the office of keeper of the printed books. The government in 1841 granted him a pension of £200 a year as a recognition of his literary abilities, and he devoted himself henceforth to the annotation of a new edition of his translation of ·Dante, and to editing editions of the English poets Pope, Cowper, Milton, Young, etc. He was buried in Westminster Abbey.

Cary, Lott, American negro slave: b. Virginia, 1780; d. 1828. He educated himself, became a Baptist minister, purchased the freedom of himself and his two children for $850, and joined the colony sent in 1822 to Liberia, where he performed inestimable services in behalf of the new republic. He was acting as agent with full power when he was accidentally killed while making cartridges for defense against the slave traders.

Cary, Lucius. See FALKLAND.

Cary, Phœbe, American poet and prose-writer, sister of Alice Cary (q.v.): b. Cincinnati, Ohio, 4 Sept. 1824; d. Newport, R. I., 31 July 1871. She contributed numerous sketches to various periodicals; and with her sister published several books, among which are 'Poems and Parodies' (1854); and 'Poems of Faith, Hope, and Love.' She will be longest remembered as the author of the popular hymn beginning, 'One Sweetly Solemn Thought.'

Cary, Samuel Fenton, American politician: b. Cincinnati, Ohio, 18 Feb. 1814. He represented Ohio in Congress in 1867–9; was the only Republican representative to vote against the impeachment of President Johnson; and was an unsuccessful candidate for Vice-President in 1876, on the Independent, or so-called "Greenback" ticket headed by Peter Cooper.

Cary Rebellion, in North Carolina, an outcome of the religious and political disturbances set going by the constitution of Locke and Shaftesbury, whose laws and discriminations survived itself. (See CAROLINA, ORIGINAL CONSTITUTION OF.) One of these, requiring an oath to support the constitution and laws, debarred the Quakers (who were among the most influential of the early settlers, and by no means

inclined to submit peaceably to oppression) from voting or holding office, or being witnesses in criminal suits. The establishment of and taxation for the Church of England was a common grievance to all the colony, nearly all its population being dissenters; and there were other obnoxious ordinances. At this time Albemarle County (North Carolina) had its separate deputy-governor, appointed by the governor of the entire colony; and in 1704 Sir Nathaniel Johnson so appointed Robert Daniel, a churchman, and "landgrave" or hereditary noble and councilor. He tried to enforce the laws; and one John Porter, an influential Quaker, shortly went to England to complain of him and of vexatious legislation against his sect. One of the proprietors, John Archdale (q.v.), ex-governor, was himself a Quaker, and induced the other proprietors to remove Daniel; and Johnson appointed Thomas Cary, a Carolina merchant, said to have been Archdale's son-in-law, in his place. Cary, however, felt bound to enforce the laws, and again the Quakers complained. Cary was removed (the accepted account says he was in ill odor with the proprietors for having been short in his accounts as collector of revenue for them); and this time the appointment of a deputy for Albemarle was taken from the governor, and a new proprietary council formed, with Porter and several other Quakers on it. On Porter's return to America in 1707, he convened the council, which elected William Glover, a churchman, president. Glover insisted on enforcement of the laws as before, and Porter's party turned against him, declared his election illegal, struck a bargain with Cary, and elected him president in Glover's place. Glover and his section refused to recognize the validity of the new election, and held their meetings in one room of the executive mansion, while Cary and his councilors met in the other. Daniel, as a landgrave, was *ipso facto* a councilor, and sat alternately in both. Each party issued writs for election to the Assembly, and it seems to have been held without formal recognition of either; but Cary's party held the majority. In 1710 Edward Hyde, a relative of Clarendon's, was appointed deputy-governor by the proprietors, and came out in August 1710 to assume office. His commission was to be taken from Tynte, who had succeeded Johnson; but Tynte had died, and Hyde had only his letters from the proprietors to show. The Cary party, however, was glad to acknowledge him so long as it held the power and he confirmed it; but the next Assembly was held by its enemies, Hyde apparently aided it in enforcing the laws in favor of the Church, and Cary's party promptly refused to acknowledge his authority and made open war on him. Cary attacked Edenton with two armed vessels, but was repulsed, and Hyde called on Gov. Spotswood of Virginia for help. Spotswood admitted that the revolters were "dangerous incendiaries," but said the country was almost inaccessible, and he had only militia; but finally sent some of his marines from the guard-ships at Hampton Roads. Cary, with his chief men, Levy, Truitt, etc., thereupon went to Virginia, apparently for temporary refuge, declaring that they would go to England and appeal to the proprietors. Spotswood took them at their word, and sent them, seemingly against their will, to England; and they disappear from history. That they were discharged, however, is apparent from a circular letter of Lord Dartmouth to the colonies, at this juncture, to send no more prisoners to England for trial without proof of their guilt. At home, the burgesses refused to provide for the defense of the colony unless they could have share in the government and what they held to be their rights; and the result was a fearful desolation in a war which soon broke out with the Tuscaroras.

Ca'rya, a genus of American plants belonging to the order *Juglandaceæ. C. alba* is the common hickory. The seeds of *C. amara,* with oil of chamomile, are useful in colic. See HICKORY.

Caryatides, or **Caryatids,** kăr-ĭ-ăt'ĭ-dĕz, in architecture, a name used to designate female figures made to support a roof, cornice, etc., instead of columns. The goddess Artemis (Diana), who had a temple in Caryæ, a Peloponnesian city, was for this reason called *Karyatis.* In honor of her, virgins danced in a festive procession during an annual feast, which suggested to architects the idea of adopting the images of virgins to serve as columns. Thus Lessing and others explain the name and form of the caryatides. Another explanation of their origin is the following: The inhabitants of Caryæ allied themselves with the Persians in their war with the Greeks. The Greeks, on the successful termination of that struggle, exterminated the mâles of Caryæ, and reduced all the women to slavery. As a mark of infamy, and to perpetuate the memory of the transaction, the architects of the time made statues representing these women in the servile office of supporting entablatures. There are fine examples in the Erectheum at Athens and British Museum.

Caryocar, kă-rĭ'ō-kär, a genus of plants belonging to the natural order *Ternstræmiaceæ,* consisting of lofty trees, natives of tropical America, which produce good timber. They have evergreen, ternate or pinnate leaves, and flowers in racemes. *C. nuciferum,* a species abundant in British Guiana, yields the kidney-shaped souari-nuts, or butternuts. Other species are *C. glabrum* and *C. amygdaliferum.*

Caryophyllaceæ, kăr-ĭ-ō-fĭ-lā'sẹ-ē, an order of plants, of which the pink, named by botanists in early times *Caryophyllus,* and more recently *Dianthus,* may be considered as the type. The plants of this order are readily distinguished by their opposite undivided leaves, without stipules, the tumid articulations of the stems, and the disposal of the seeds upon a free central placenta, surrounded by several carpellary leaves. Several species are cultivated by florists; a few are used in medicine, and the *Saponaria officinalis* and *Lychnis diurna* yield a mucilage resembling soap. The Clove-pink (*Dianthus caryophyllus*) is the origin of all the cultivated varieties of carnations, picotees, bizarres, flakes, etc. There are about 60 genera and 1,100 species.

Caryop'sis, the small peculiar, one-seeded, dry indehiscent fruit of the grasses, as wheat, barley, etc.

Caryo'ta, a genus of palms, with doubly pinnate leaves, the best-known species of which (*C. urens*) is a native of most of tropical Asia; it supplies an inferior kind of sago, and from its juice is made toddy or palm-wine. The leaf-stalks yield kittul fibre, which is used in making baskets, brooms, etc.

Ca'rysfort Reef, a coral reef near the southern extremity of Florida, on which is erected a lighthouse of the first order, 112 feet high.

Casa, Giovanni della, jō-văn'nē dĕl'lạ kä'-zä, Italian writer: b. Mugello, near Florence, 1503; d. Rome, 14 Nov. 1566. He studied in Bologna, Florence, and Rome, and entered as an ecclesiastic into the service of the two cardinals Alessandro Farnese, the first of whom, in 1534, ascended the papal chair, under the name of Paul III. He rose through various offices in the Church, including the archbishopric of Benevento, till Paul IV. made him his private secretary. His most celebrated work is 'Galateo, ovvero de' Costumi' (1560), a manual of good-breeding, to which another book, 'Degli Uffizj communi tra gli Amici Superiori e Inferiori,' forms a supplement. This last is a translation of his Latin treatise, 'De Officiis Inter Potentiore et Tenuiores Amicos.' The best and most complete edition of his works appeared at Venice (1752).

Casa Braccio, bräch'ō, Italian romance, by Francis Marion Crawford, published 1896. The first half of the novel is much the better.

Casa Grande, kä'zạ grän'dã, the ruins of a prehistoric building in Arizona, near the Gila River, within 20 miles of the Casa Grande station. Built of adobe with walls, in some places five feet thick at the base, narrowing toward the top, it is the best-preserved structure of a type which was probably widely distributed. The space enclosed by the walls now standing measures about 43 by 59 feet; and the walls, which are high, show that there were three, and perhaps four, stories. There are three central rooms and two end rooms. A large area surrounding this building is covered with mounds and débris of other buildings, indicating that there was originally a considerable settlement on the site. It was built by a Pueblo or allied race, and the evidence is in favor of the theory that they were the ancestors of the Pima Indians who now inhabit the region. In 1889 Congress made an appropriation for the preservation and repair of the Casa Grande, and the whole area has been made government property. During the removal of the débris a number of specimens of pottery and stone implements have been found. The ruins were seen by Coronado's expedition and mentioned by Cataneda; they were carefully described by Father Menge, who, with Father Pinto, visited them in 1694 and 1697. John R. Bartlett was the first to give a detailed description of them in modern times in his 'Personal Narrative of Explorations and Incidents in Texas, New Mexico, California, Sonora, and Chihuahua' (1849). The best and most recent accounts are found in the publications of the Bureau of American Ethnology (13th and 15th annual reports).

Casabianca, Louis, loo ē kä-zä-bē-än-kä, French naval officer: b. Bastia, Corsica, about 1755; d. 1 Aug. 1798. He sat in the National Convention of 1792; and in 1798 was captain of the flagship L'Orient in the expedition to Egypt. He was mortally wounded at the battle of the Nile, 1 Aug. 1798; the ship caught fire; his 10-year-old son would not leave him, and both were killed by the exploding of the ship. The story of their death is the subject of Mrs. Hemans' well-known poem.

Casal, or Cazal, Manuel Ayres de, mä'noo-él ï'rĕz dä kä-säl', Portuguese geographer: b. in the last half of the 18th century; d. Lisbon about 1850. Having received an excellent education, he took holy orders, but afterward devoted himself to the exploration of Brazil. He has been styled the father of Brazilian geography, and his principal work, entitled 'Corografia Brasilica' (1817), elicited the admiration of Humboldt and of other competent judges.

Casale, or Casale de Monferrato, kä sä lä mŏn-fĕr-rä'tō, Italy, a city in the province of Alessandria, on the right bank of the Po, 18 miles north-northwest of Alessandria. The citadel, founded by Duke Vicenzo in 1590, was one of the strongest in Italy, but its ramparts have been converted into promenades, and its defenses are now insignificant. In 1640 the Spaniards were defeated here by the Duc d'Harcourt, and the possession of the town was repeatedly contested by the Austrians and French during the wars of Napoleon. Casale was the capital of the ancient Montferrat. It is the seat of a bishop and of a district court of justice, and has a cathedral which is said to have been founded in the 8th century. Its church of San Domenico, containing a tomb in memory of the Princess Palæologi, is remarkable for the elegance of its design, and several fine works of art are found in other of its churches. Among the prominent articles of trade are silk, and sirup manufactured from the roots of a species of reed. Pop. about 32,000.

Casale Pusterlengo, kä-sä'lä pŭs-tĕr-lĕn'-gō, Italy, a town in the province of Milan, southeast of Lodi, beautifully situated in a fine plain between the Po and the Adda. It has a trade in Parmesan cheese. In 1796 the Austrians were attacked here by the French, and driven back to Lodi. Pop. 6,304.

Casalmaggiore, kä-säl-mäd-jō rē, Italy, a town in the province of Cremona, and 22 miles southeast of the city of Cremona (with which there is railway connection), on the left bank of the Po. There are a cathedral and other churches, theatre, etc. The manufactures include pottery and glass-ware; and there is a trade in wine, grain, hemp, and cheese. In 1448 the Venetians were defeated here by Francesco Sforza. Pop. 15,648.

Casamicciola, kä-sä-mē'chō-lä, Italy, a favorite watering-place on the island of Ischia, beautifully situated in a valley on the north side of Monte Epomeo, with hot springs (158° F.), baths, hotels, etc. The season extends from June to September. By the earthquake of 28 July 1883, the place was almost entirely destroyed.

Casanare, kä-zä-nä're, a river of the Republic of Colombia, which flows through a region called by the same name, and after an easterly course of 180 miles empties into the Meta.

Casanova, Francesco, frän-chĕs'kō kä-sä-nō'vä, Italian painter: b. London 1730; d. Brühl, near Vienna, 1805. He went to Venice with his parents, was in Paris in 1751, but after a brief stay went to Dresden, where he remained from 1752 to 1756. Here he studied and copied the paintings of Wouverman. He acquired renown as a painter of battle pieces, and

was admitted to the Academy of Fine Arts in 1763. Catherine II. of Russia employed him to paint her victories over the Turks. He settled in Vienna in 1785, and the gallery there contains several of his paintings.

Casanova de Seingalt, Giovanni Jacopo, jō-vän'nē yä'kō pō kä-sä-nō'vä dĕ săn-gäl, Italian adventurer: b. Venice 1725; d. Dux, Bohemia, 4 June 1798. He was the son of an actor and actress; he studied law at Padua, but gave this up to study for the priesthood. He was expelled from the Seminary of St. Cypsian for a scandalous intrigue, and was also imprisoned for a short time. The influence of his mother procured him a place in the establishment of Cardinal Aquaviva, but he did not retain it long; and after visiting Rome, Naples, Corfu, and Constantinople, in the characters of diplomatist, preacher, abbot, lawyer, and charlatan, he was imprisoned at Venice in 1755, but escaped owing to his wonderful keenness and skill. In his travels throughout Europe he formed associations with many distinguished characters, Louis XV., Rousseau, Voltaire, Suvaroff, Frederick the Great, and Catherine II. His most celebrated work is his 'Memoirs' (1828–38), in which he relates with a cynical freedom the whole of his extraordinary adventures, and presents a picture of society without conventional disguise. Among his dupes were Mme. de Pompadour, Frederick the Great, and even that other prince of charlatans, Cagliostro. Besides his 'Memoirs,' Casanova was the author of several works of history or imagination in French and Italian, which show the versatility of his genius. The most remarkable are 'Recit de sa Captivite' (1788), and a translation in verse of the Iliad.

Casas, Bartolomé de las, bär-tō'lō-mä dä läs kä'säs, Spanish prelate: b. Seville 1474; d. Madrid July 1566. In his 19th year he accompanied his father, who sailed with Columbus, to the West Indies. Five years afterward he returned to Spain, and pursuing his studies he entered the priesthood. He accompanied Columbus in his second voyage to Hispaniola (Haiti), and on the conquest of Cuba settled there, and distinguished himself by his humane conduct toward the oppressed natives. He set at liberty the Indians who had fallen to his share in the division; and so much was he interested for them, that in 1516 he went to Spain to lay a statement of their case before King Ferdinand, whose death at that time prevented any measures for their benefit. The regent, Cardinal Ximenes, however, appointed a commission to examine circumstances on the spot, and to determine accordingly. Las Casas to accompany them, with the title of Protector of the Indians. The commissioners found that it was impossible to liberate the Indians, and therefore endeavored to secure their humane treatment; but Las Casas, still dissatisfied, remonstrated so warmly that he was obliged to take refuge in a convent from the rage of the planters. He again returned to Europe; and on the accession of Charles V., in consequence of his representations, the council appointed a chief judge to re-examine the points of controversy between the partisans of Indian liberty and the colonists. Las Casas, in his zeal for the Indians, became the author (or the encourager at least) of the slave-trade, by proposing to purchase negroes from the Portuguese in Africa to supply the planters with laborers, of the want of whom they complained; and this was unfortunately put into execution. He next applied for a grant of an unoccupied tract, in order to try his own plan with a new colony. This he at length obtained, and with 200 persons, whom he persuaded to accompany him, landed at Porto Rico in 1521, but found that an expedition was advancing to ravage this very tract, and convey its inhabitants to Hispaniola as slaves. He endeavored in vain to prevent the threatened danger, and with the few who still adhered to him returned to Hispaniola to solicit succor. During his absence the natives attacked the colonists with such success that in a short time not a Spaniard remained in that part of South America. Las Casas, in despair at the failure of his project, retired to the Dominican convent at St. Domingo, and assumed the habit of the order. Notwithstanding his retirement his zeal in the cause of the Indians did not abate; and being sent on à mission to Spain by a chapter of his order at Chiapas in 1542, he pleaded their cause with his pristine warmth, and composed his famous treatise 'Brevisima Relacion de la Destruccion de las Indias,' in which he exposed the cruelties practised by the Spaniards. His unremitting perseverance at length obtained a new set of laws and regulations, by which the natives were greatly relieved. In 1544 he returned to America as bishop of Chiapas, but left it three years later, and resigned his bishopric in 1550. Besides the treatise above named he wrote 'Historia de las Indias.' This was first printed in 1875-6. It is one of the most notable of books, not only in its contents,— as a history of Spanish discoveries from 1492 to 1520, and a contemporary Spanish Catholic criticism as well as story of Columbus,— but in the circumstances which prevented its publication for more than 300 years, and which still leave it inaccessible except to readers of Spanish. See Llorente, '(Œuvres de las Casas' (1822) ; Quintana, 'Vidas de Espagñoles Celebres' ; Helps, 'Life of Las Casas and Spanish Conquest' (1868) ; Fabie, 'Vida y Escritas de Las Casas' (1879) ; Sabin, 'Works of Las Casas' (1870).

Casas Grandes, kä'säs grän'däs (Span. "great houses"), a town in Chihuahua, Mexico, on the Casas Grandes or San Miguel River, 35 miles south of Llanos, and 125 miles southwest of El Paso, remarkable for a number of ruins, apparently relics of an aboriginal race. These ruins are found about half a mile from the small Mexican village, partly on the declivity of a small hill, and partly on the plain at its foot. They consist chiefly of the remains of a large edifice of the pueblo type, built entirely of a substance resembling adobe, mud mixed with grass and straw and formed into blocks 22 inches thick and about three feet long. The portions which must have been constructed of wood have entirely crumbled away. The outer walls are almost all prostrate, except at the corners, and were probably only one story high; the inner walls are better preserved, varying in height from 5 to 50 feet, and being in some cases five feet thick at the base. The portions remaining erect seem to indicate an original height of from three to six stories. The doorways have the tapering form noticed in the ancient structures of Central America and Yucatan, and over them

are circular openings in the partition walls. The stairways were probably of wood, and placed on the outside. Clavigero, in his 'History of Mexico,' tells us that the building, according to popular tradition, was erected by the Mexicans in their peregrination, and that it consisted "of three floors, with a terrace above them, and without any entrance to the lower floor. The door for entrance to the building is on the second floor, so that a scaling ladder is necessary." The main features of the edifice seem to have been three large structures connected by ranges of corridors or low apartments, and enclosing several courtyards of various dimensions. The extent from north to south must have been 800 feet, and from east to west about 250 feet. A range of narrow rooms lighted by circular openings near the top, and having pens or enclosures three or four feet high in one corner, supposed to be granaries, extends along one of the main walls. Many of the apartments are very large, and some of the enclosures are too vast ever to have been covered by a roof. About 200 feet west of the main building are three mounds of loose stones and 200 feet west of these are the remains of a building, one story high and 150 feet square, consisting of a number of apartments ranged around a square court. The inhabitants of this communal structure seem to have disappeared long before the Spaniards noticed the ruins in the latter part of the 17th century. Throughout the northern part of Mexico the name Casas Grandes is applied to deserted buildings of a similar type.

For some distance south the plain is covered with tracts of ancient buildings, and for 20 leagues along the Casas Grandes and Llanos rivers are found artificial mounds from which have been dug up stone axes, corn-grinders, and various articles of pottery, such as pipes, jars, pitchers, etc., of a texture far superior to that made by the Mexicans of the present day, and generally ornamented with angular figures of blue, red, brown, and black, on a red or white ground. The best specimens command a high price in Chihuahua and neighboring towns. On the summit of a mountain, about 10 miles from the ruins above described, are the remains of an ancient stone fortress, attributed to the same people who built the Casas Grandes, and probably intended as a lookout. See PUEBLOS.

Casati, Gaetano, gä-ä-tä'nō kä sä'tē, Italian explorer in Africa: b. Monza, Italy, 1830; d. Como 7 March 1902. He entered the army of Piedmont at 21, and resigning in 1879 went to Africa, commissioned by the Società d' Esplorazione Commerciale d' Africa. He joined his countryman, Gessi Pasha, in the Bahr-el-Gazelle valley, but the schemes of the Mahdi in 1883 shut him up in the Niam-Niam region with Emin Pasha. At the request of the latter he consented to act as "President" in King Kabba Rega's country, but after being at first well treated by that monarch he was later condemned to death. Escaping with great difficulty to the Albert Nyanza Lake, and losing all his notes and manuscripts, he was finally rescued by Emin Pasha in 1888. The expedition of Stanley came a little later to the relief of both. On his return to Italy Casati published a volume descriptive of his adventures, entitled 'Dieci anni in Equatoria.'

Casaubon, Isaac, ē-zäk kä-zō-bòṅ, Swiss classical scholar : b. Geneva 1559 ; d. London about July 1614. In his ninth year he spoke Latin fluently. In his 19th year he entered the university at Geneva, where he studied Greek, theology, the Oriental languages, etc., and in 1582 succeeded Portus as professor of the Greek language. In 1586 he married the daughter of the famous printer Henry Stephens. In 1596 he accepted a professorship of Greek and belles-lettres at Montpellier, but held it only two years. In 1600 Henry IV. invited him to Paris. His Protestantism, the jealousy of other scholars, and perhaps his rather unyielding character, were the occasion of many unpleasant occurrences, for which, however, he was indemnified by the office of royal librarian. After the death of Henry IV. in 1610 he went to England on the invitation of the Archbishop of Canterbury, where he was received with distinction, was presented with a prebend in Canterbury Cathedral, and had a pension conferred on him by James I., with whom he was a great favorite. He was buried in Westminster Abbey. Casaubon was a liberal theologian, a man of extensive learning, a good translator, and an excellent critic. As a critic, he commented on Diogenes, Laertius, Aristotle, Theophrastus, Suetonius, Persius, Polybius, Theocritus, Strabo, Dionysius of Halicarnassus, Athenæus, Pliny the Younger, etc. Nearly all the ancient classics are indebted to his valuable researches. His profound dissertation on the satirical poetry of the Greeks and the satire of the Romans ('De Satyrica Græca Poësi et Romanorum Satira') deserves particular praise. His theological writings are of less value. His diary, which had been preserved by his son, Meric, was published in 1850 under the title of 'Ephemerides.' A 'Life of Casaubon' was written by Mark Pattison (1875).

Casaubon, Meric, son of the preceding, Swiss classical scholar in England: b. Geneva 14 Aug. 1599; d. Oxford 14 July 1671. He went to school at Sedan, and in 1611 followed his father to England, and studied at Eton and Christ Church, Oxford. He held successively several livings in the Church, when the revolution, which brought Charles I. to the scaffold, deprived him of his income. Still he rejected the proposal of Cromwell to write the history of his time, as also the invitation of Queen Christina to live in Sweden. On the return of the Stuarts he was rewarded for his loyalty by restoration to his offices in the Church, which he held till his death. Besides various works in Latin, he wrote several in English on theological and other subjects. He also wrote some critical works on the classics, a treatise, 'De Verborum Usu' (1647) ; etc.

Cashin. See KASBIN.

Casca, Publius Servilius, Roman statesman: d. 42 B.C. He assisted in the assassination of Julius Cæsar in 44 B.C., and, according to Plutarch, he struck the first blow, in the back of the neck.

Cascade Range, a range of mountains in North America, parallel to and about 120 miles from the Pacific Coast, extending from the Sierra Nevada in California northward through Oregon and Washington into British Columbia. The highest peaks are Mount Rainier in Washington, 14,526 feet, and Mount Shasta in California, 14,440 feet. The name is derived from the cascades formed by the Columbia River in breaking through the range.

Cascape'diac River, Great, a river of Canada, in the province of Quebec, flowing southeast into Chaleur Bay. Its length is 130 miles.

Cascapediac River, Little, a river of Canada, in the province of Quebec, east of the Great Cascapediac, and with an almost parallel but shorter course.

Cascara Sagrada, the bark of a northwestern tree (Rhamnus Purshiana, or California buckthorn), of the natural order Rhamnaceæ. The composition of cascara is extremely complex, but its main action is due to the volatile oils, the anthracene resins, at least three, the amaroids, and the tannin. It stimulates peristalsis, increases the intestinal juices, and has marked effects on general excretion. It is an excellent laxative, and one of the very best cathartics for habitual and chronic constipation. It is best used in the form of a fluid extract. Because of its valuable properties, many patent drugs with similarly sounding names have been foisted on the public. These mostly contain other and more powerful and pernicious cathartics. See BUCKTHORN.

Carcarilla, the bark of a tree (Croton eleuteria), of the family Euphorbiaceæ. This is a shrub of the Bahamas and now yields most of the cascarilla of commerce, although in former years other species were used. It contains tannic acid, volatile oils, cascarillin, a glycoside, and some resin. In medicine it is used as an aromatic bitter in combination with other remedies for constipation, indigestion, and loss of appetite.

Cas'co Bay, a bay on the southwest coast of Maine. It is about 20 miles wide and so deep as to constitute one of the best harbors of the world, for all kinds of vessels. It contains many islands.

Case, Augustus Ludlow, American naval officer: b. Newburg, N. Y., 3 Feb. 1813; d. Washington, D. C., 17 Feb. 1893. He entered the navy as a midshipman in 1828. In the Mexican war he took part in the capture of Vera Cruz and Tobasco, and during the Civil War served as fleet captain of the North Atlantic blockading squadron. He took part in the capture of Forts Hatteras and Clark, and cut out the blockade-runner Kate, under the fire of the forts at New Inlet, N. C. He was a lighthouse inspector in 1867; chief of bureau of ordnance, 1869; commander of the European squadron in 1873; and was retired in 1875.

Case, Leonard, American philanthropist: b. Cleveland 27 June 1820; d. 6 Jan. 1880. He graduated at Yale College in 1842, and continued to pursue literary and scientific studies, contributing to the best magazines. Inheriting from his father a large estate in the city of Cleveland, he deeded a certain part of it for the founding and maintenance of an educational institution, which was incorporated after his death as the Case School of Applied Science (q.v.).

Case, Thomas, English philosophical scholar. He was educated at Rugby, and Balliol College, Oxford, and has been Wsynflete professor of moral and metaphysical philosophy at

Oxford from 1889. He has published 'Materials for History of Athenian Democracy from Solon to Pericles' (1874); 'Realism in Morals' (1877); 'Physical Realism' (1888); 'St. Mary's Clusters' (1893).

Case, in grammar, a form, modification, or inflection of a noun or pronoun, indicating or corresponding to its relationship to some other word or words in a phrase or sentence, as, John (nominative case) speaks; John's (possessive) dog barks; John beats his dog (objective). In adjectives, case is merely sympathetic, the adjective agreeing in case with the noun which it qualifies. In English, nouns undergo only one inflection representing a different case from the nominative or general form of the noun; all other cases are represented either by prepositions or by the position of the noun in the sentence, the nominative case usually preceding the verb, the objective or accusative following it. The single inflected case in English is the possessive or genitive (John's). English pronouns have three cases — nominative, genitive, and accusative, as *he, his, him*. The last often serves as a dative. Adjectives undergo no modifications in English. In Sanskrit there are eight cases — nominative, accusative, instrumental, dative, genitive, ablative, locative, and vocative. In Latin there are six cases — nominative, genitive, dative, accusative, vocative, ablative. In Greek there are five, the ablative not being used. In both Latin and Greek there are traces of a locative case. In French, Italian, Spanish, and Portuguese, the nouns have no case-inflections. In German both nouns and adjectives are inflected for case. There are four cases in German — nominative, genitive, dative, accusative.

In law, the word has various meanings. An "action upon the case" is one in which damages are sued for, for some cause of complaint where the injury done is not direct, as in trespass, but consequential. A "case stated" is a statement prepared by one court for the decision of a point of law by a superior court. A "special case" is a written statement of facts agreed on by two or more litigants in an action, in order that a court may decide their legal effect.

In letter-press printing, a case is a receptacle for types, generally made of wood, 34 inches long, 15 inches wide, and 1¼ inches deep, and divided into compartments or "boxes," each of which contains types of one class or letter. A pair of cases consists of an upper and a lower case; the upper one has 98 boxes, and contains the capitals, small capitals, and some other signs that are only occasionally required in composition; the lower one has 54 boxes, and holds the letters of the small characters, figures, spaces, and most of the points. Thus the small characters are habitually spoken of by printers as "lower-case" letters, and the capitals, etc., as "upper-case" letters. The places assigned to the several letters of the alphabet in the boxes of the case are not precisely the same in all printing-offices, but the differences are few. The different sizes of the boxes in the lower case depend upon the comparative frequency with which the several letters occur in the composition, and the position in the case allotted to each letter is such as to afford the greatest facility in composing. The letter *e*, which is the most run upon in the English language, has a box much larger than any of the other compart-

ments, and is placed directly in front of the compositor. In the upper case the boxes are of uniform size, and the letters are placed in nearly alphabetical order, the comparatively rare occurrence of capitals rendering it less important which letter is nearest the compositor's hand. Cases are mounted in a slanting position upon a frame of convenient height.

Cases are named from their use or construction, as "Italic case," a two-third case for holding Italic type; "two-third case," a single case in which two thirds of the space is equivalent to the ordinary lower case, and the remaining third is occupied by the capitals, etc.; "job case," a single case suited to holding a small job font of type; "rule case," a case for holding brass rule; "sort-case," a case for containing "sorts." The manufacture of cases has received a serious setback since the introduction of type-composing machines. See PRINTING.

Case-hardening, the process of converting the surface of certain kinds of malleable-iron goods into steel, thereby making them harder, less liable to rust, and capable of taking on a better polish. Fire-irons, gun-locks, keys, and other articles of limited size, are very commonly so treated, but the process is sometimes applied to large objects, such as iron railway-bars. The articles are first formed, and heated to redness with powdered charcoal or cast-iron, the malleable iron taking carbon from either of these to form a skin of steel upon it; the heated objects are then cooled in cold water, or in oil when they are of a delicate nature. Yellow prussiate or potash or parings of leather have also been a good deal used for coating iron articles with steel by heating them together. Some chemists consider that in this case nitrogen combines with the iron and effects the hardening. The coating of steel is very thin, seldom exceeding one sixteenth of an inch. A Swedish ironmaster has found that a very excellent case-hardening is obtained by treating iron or steel objects with a mixture of animal matter, such as rasped leather or horn, and arsenious acid dissolved in hydrochloric acid, and heating as usual.

Case School of Applied Science, The, at Cleveland, Ohio, founded by Leonard Case (q.v.) of that city. In 1877 a deed of trust was executed setting apart certain real estate for the support of the institution, the deed to take effect upon his death, which occurred in 1880. The Case School was incorporated 29 March 1880. Instruction began in 1881, with a class of 16 students, the school being carried on from that time until the summer of 1885 in the old Case homestead. A commodious building having been erected for the use of the school, it was occupied at the beginning of the term in September 1885. A year later the building with all that it contained was destroyed by fire. It was promptly rebuilt and occupied in 1888. Since that time several additional buildings for laboratory and shop exercises have been erected, with superior apparatus and appliances, and museums are in the course of development. The Case School of Applied Science offers eight regular courses of instruction, each requiring four years. They are civil engineering, mechanical engineering, electrical engineering, mining engineering, physics, chemistry, architecture, and general science. There are 126 professors and instructors and 353 students. The degree of bachelor of science is granted to all who complete one of the regular courses. That of master of science may be conferred upon graduates who have devoted at least one year exclusively to graduate study. Professional degrees, namely, civil engineer, mechanical engineer, electrical engineer, and engineer of mines may also be conferred after one year of graduate study or after professional work in positions of responsibility, for three years after graduation. The property left by Mr. Case as an endowment for the support of the school is valued at about $2,000,000, and the amount invested in buildings and equipment is about $350,000. The school derives its support in part also from tuition fees. Its government rests with a corporation consisting of 20 men, from whom six, known as trustees, are selected.

Case-shot, a projectile formed by putting a quantity of bullets into a cylindrical tin box called a "canister," that just fits the bore of the gun. In case of necessity, the canister is filled with broken pieces of iron, nails, stones, etc. The case is closed at both ends by a disk of wood or iron. Shot of this sort is thrown from cannons and howitzers, and is very injurious to the enemy, because the balls contained in the canister spread, diverging in proportion to the distance. The balls vary in weight, according to the character of the ordnance, from one or two pounds to half an ounce each. The range within which case-shot are used sometimes extends to 500, but seldom exceeds 200 to 300 yards. It is also called "canister-shot." The shrapnel-shell, in its present cylindrical shape, may be considered a variety of case-shot. See ORDNANCE.

Case-worm. See CADDIS-FLY.

Casein, kā'sē-ĭn (Lat. *caseus,* "cheese") a substance resembling albumen in its general properties, and obtained from milk. The older chemists gave the name "casein" both to the precipitated substance that is now known by that name, and to the corresponding substance as it exists in solution in the milk; but it is usual at the present time to distinguish the latter as "caseinogen." Caseinogen is the principal nitrogenous constituent of milk, and is precipitated as a curdy mass when acetic acid or a mineral acid is added to milk that has been previously diluted by the addition of its own bulk of water. If the caseinogen so prepared is made into a paste and then treated with a small quantity of rennet, the mass sets at once into a solid clot, consisting of true casein; but Hammarstein has shown that if the caseinogen is first washed entirely free from calcium phosphate, rennet is without action upon it. The precise function of the calcium phosphate is obscure, and the same may be said of the chemical relations of the proteids in general. If rennet is added to fresh milk a bulky deposit of casein comes down immediately; but to obtain the casein in pure form, the oily matters in the milk should be first removed by the action of a centrifugal separator, and the casein, after precipitation, should be compressed so as to expel as much of the whey as possible. Caseinogen is not precipitated by heat, nor does it (like fibrinogen) coagulate spontaneously. The coagulation observed when milk is boiled is due to the albumen present, and not to the casein; and that which occurs upon standing may be due

either to the generation of lactic acid through the fermentation of the lactose present, or to the rennet-like action of the ptomaines liberated by micro-organisms that happen to fall into the milk from the air. According to the analyses of Chittenden and Painter, the elementary percentage composition of casein is as follows: Carbon, 53.30; hydrogen, 7.07; nitrogen, 15.91; sulphur, 0.82; phosphorus, 0.87; oxygen, 22.03. Casein is insoluble in water, but dissolves easily in alkaline solutions. It also dissolves in very weak hydrochloric acid, from which it is again precipitated upon the addition of the same reagent in more concentrated form. When freshly prepared it is soluble in a strong solution of borax, and in this form it is used as an adhesive under the name "casein glue." A compound of casein with lime is also used in the arts for "animalizing" cotton cloth, so that the fibres will retain colors that otherwise would not adhere to them. See PROTEID.

Casemates (Sp. *casa,* "a house," and *matare,* "to kill"), in fortification, vaults which are proof against bombs, and which may be constructed under a parapet and provided with embrasures or ports through which guns are fired. They may serve, at the same time, as a place for keeping the heavy ordnance and various stores, and in case of necessity as habitations for the garrison or shelter for sick or wounded.

Caserta, kä-zär'tä, Italy, the capital of the province of Caserta, 17 miles northeast of Naples. It is the seat of a bishop, and contains many fine buildings. The principal edifice is a palace, one of the finest in Europe, a large and richly decorated structure commenced in 1752 by Charles III. of Spain, and situated among gardens adorned with numerous ancient and modern statues. The principal manufactures are silk goods, carpets, linen, etc. The district produces excellent fruit and wine. About two and a half miles to the northeast is Caserta Vecchia (Old Caserta), the new town being distinguished as Caserta Nuova. Pop. 33,000.

Caserta (formerly TERRA DI LAVORO), a province of Italy, north of Naples, along the Mediterranean Sea. Its chief industries are agriculture and cattle raising; there are also some flourishing manufactures. Area, 2,033 square miles. Pop. 749,414.

Casey, Silas, American army officer: b. East Greenwich, R. I., 12 July 1807; d. Brooklyn 22 Jan. 1882. He was graduated from the United States Military Academy at West Point in 1826; served in the Mexican war, being present at the battles of Contreras, Churubusco, Molino del Rey, and the siege of Chapultepec. When the Civil War broke out he was given charge of organizing the volunteers near Washington; later served in the Army of the Potomac, and won much distinction at Fair Oaks; was president of the board to examine candidates for officers of colored troops in 1863-5; brevetted major-general, U. S. A., 13 March 1865; and retired in 1868. His publications include 'System of Infantry Tactics' (1862); and 'Infantry Tactics for Colored Troops.' (1863).

Casey, Thomas Lincoln, American military engineer: b. Sackett's Harbor, N. Y., 10 May 1831; d. Washington, D. C., 26 March 1896. He graduated from West Point in 1852, and entered the engineer corps of the army. During the Civil War he was superintending engineer of defenses on the coast of Maine, and on special duty with the North Atlantic squadron in the first expedition against Fort Fisher. In 1865 he was brevetted colonel for gallant services during the war. In 1868 he was put in charge of one of the departments in the chief engineer's office at Washington; in 1873 was sent abroad for professional service; and in 1877 was placed in charge of the construction of the state, war, and navy building, and of the Washington aqueduct, and also of the Department of Public Buildings and Grounds. Later he built the White House conservatory and the Army Medical Museum, completed the Washington monument, and took charge of the construction of the Congressional Library. He was president of the board of engineers for fortifications at New York in 1886–8; was promoted chief of engineers and brigadier-general in 1888; and was elected to the National Academy of Sciences in 1890.

Cash Register, an automatic mechanism for registering money accounts. It is probably the most antique and, yet in its improved form, the most modern appliance known to commerce. The ancients, more than 6000 years ago, used a registering device, termed an Abacus, for the purpose of indicating visibly to the seller and buyer the amount purchased. The cash register is an absolute necessity. By infallible mechanism it provides not only a correct registration of all the cash received, but at the same time, with the aid of a miniature printing press, it records or prints the details of each and every transaction that occurs, upon a printed strip or tape, thus keeping the proprietor in constant touch with each and every detail of his business, and offering him at a glance, a thousand times a day, if necessary, without the slightest trouble or inconvenience, a diagram of the progress of each department in his store, as well as the industry of each clerk. The push of the industrious one can be noted and appreciated. It furnishes a chart that enables the business man to direct and control his affairs as the pilot controls the movements of his vessel by the compass before him. The miniature printing press attached to the modern cash register also cuts off and issues a printed check or bill, which is handed by the clerk to the customer for payment to the cashier, thus saving a great amount of time and unnecessary labor in writing. The use of the modern cash register is indispensable to the business man, because it furnishes him with a labor-saving device of unerring accuracy for the most sensitive and vital part of his business, "his cash and credit." The prime object of a cash register is to protect and secure a correct accounting of all the cash received or paid out, and where a credit business is done, to so systematize the accounts as to insure a correct record of the same. The good qualities of the modern cash register consist in boldly proclaiming or indicating each and every transaction, and correctly recording or transmitting the indication to the adding and printing mechanism, so that the customer, clerks and proprietor may depend upon a correct accounting of each and every detail of the business.

Cash Register Industry. The cash register industry originated in the United States,

which now exports each month large invoices of costly and improved registers to every civilized country. No such mechanisms have ever been imported into the United States; and indeed none are in general commercial use in Europe which were not manufactured in this country.

The simplest of such devices are what are known to the trade as Autographies; they are a box with, maybe, a cash drawer, a spring to open the same, a bell to be rung by the opening of the drawer, a roll of paper to be written on and then pass out of sight, for reference and preservation. Many of these autographies, for petty convenience, are manufactured; they require little notice, as they do not differ in principle from a pencil and slate.

The improved cash registers which have created an industry are in extensive use in retail stores, for the purpose of preserving a record of the sales made. Their primary object is to afford a convenient means of making a record, and to insure the accuracy of it, so that the proprietor may know at the end of each day the exact amount of the day's sales, and that each has been accurately and honestly registered. The essentials of such a mechanism have been stated to be: (1) a series of operating keys representing different amounts of money; (2) a registering mechanism upon which the values of the operated keys are added and preserved; (3) an indicating mechanism by which, when any key is operated, an indicating tablet representing the value of such key is exposed to view; (4) an alarm which is sounded by the operation of each key, to call attention to the exposed indication; and usually, (5) a money drawer which is automatically unlocked and thrown open at the operation of any one of the keys. The indicating mechanism gives utility to the machine by compelling the clerk to operate the proper key when he registers each sale. It is the protective element of the machine. Cash registers of the most improved type are not only widely used in stores, but, it is claimed, are " needed and can be sold wherever cash is handled."

The cash register industry has been wholly created within the last twenty years. Certain inventions, contributing some essentials of a successful register, had been known before at home and abroad; but in 1883, these were only models on paper, and no cash register had then been devised which was in commercial use in this or any other country. Prior to this date, however, the National Manufacturing Company at Dayton, Ohio,— a name since changed to National Cash Register Company — was making these machines under the Ritty & Birch patents, which were afterward upheld by the Supreme Court of the United States. They covered an improved device for holding and releasing the indicators.

None of the prior patented devices had either gone into use, or were fitted for practical use; so that in a commercial sense, Ritty & Birch were not only pioneers as to the extent of their improvement, but the actual creators of the first practical cash registers as a whole. The Ritty & Birch invention " brought success to what prior inventions had essayed and in some part accomplished."

The advantage thus obtained was followed

by great business enterprise and the liberal encouragement of further invention; the National Company now owns 537 Letters Patent of the United States and 394 foreign patents; and in its five invention departments at its factory, employs a corps of inventors, who are followed by forty skilled mechanics doing experimental work.

This company maintains branch factories at Berlin, Germany, and Toronto, Canada; but its main factories are at Dayton, Ohio. Here they occupy nine buildings, covering 892,144 square feet of floor space, and 140 acres of ground. In convenience and attractiveness, and for light, heat, ventilation and all sanitary things, these structures are designed to be models of any use for factory purposes. They have an output of about 5,000 machines per month; mostly of the newer and costlier kinds; about one-third of which are exported to foreign countries. These exported cash registers are adapted to the various currencies of England, Germany, Austria, Hungary, France and Belgium, Norway and Sweden, Holland, Spain, Cuba and Mexico and all Spanish-speaking countries, Brazil and Portugal, India, also Russia. Registers are sold for use in Japan and China, but not yet in the currency of those countries.

Among the more important improvements which inventors have worked out into practical advantage on a cash register may be named:

1. The totalizing counter, which adds all the registrations into one total.

2. The tape-printer, which prints the amount of each registration.

3. The check-printer, which prints, cuts off and throws out a check giving the figures of each registration, with the initials of the clerk making the sale.

4. The throw-out counter, which made it possible to print the amounts of all transactions on the detail tape and check which is issued, but prevents any amount, other than cash transactions, being so added into the totalizing counter.

5. A variation of the foregoing, which adapted it to print, instead of a check, an itemized bill, such as is used in the larger stores and offices.

6. The multiple-counter, which provides a separate adding mechanism for each person who operates the machine.

7. The multiple-drawer feature, or a series of cash drawers attached to one machine, giving the equivalent of many machines in one. This feature may be attached to the different types of registers, and gives the advantage of a separate machine for each individual, so that separate records are made not only of the transactions of each, but mistakes of any one of the different number of clerks using it, are readily identified.

8. Distant indication, which is a means for electrically indicating at a distance; namely, in the proprietor's office, home, or front show window, the sales made as registered on the machine.

Among newer improvements of cash registers are: (1) the application of electricity as a motive power, giving great rapidity of operation and saving of manual work; and (2) the application of cash registering mechanisms to conform to the special requirements of systems of express companies, telegraph companies, banking offices, department stores post-offices,

railroad offices, wholesale houses, telephone stations and government departments.

Firms who have, in the United States, made and sold cash registers are, or have been, Hopkins & Robinson, at Louisville; The Boston Cash Register and Indicator Co.; the Bensingers, at Chicago; the Sun, at Greenfield, Ohio; the Hallwood, at Columbus; the Kruse Co.; the Union, at Trenton, N. J.; the Globe and the Osborne, at Detroit; The Ideal, of New Jersey; the Chicago Cash Register Co.

Most of these manufacturers are out of active business, but they sold nearly all registers which remain in use in this country that are not Nationals. A cash register has this peculiarity about it, not common to other manufactured things,— the user often does not want it to work rightly; hence, to have value at all, it requires very high workmanship and perfection of part; and any device not so built, has not, thus far, been a commercial success. A good cash register must be one that cannot be beaten. To "beat" a register is to apparently operate it without proper indication and addition in registration. It must be built so as not only to operate accurately, but so that it cannot be prevented from working properly.

The National factory at Dayton employs 3,500 working men and women. About 40,000 persons annually visit this factory. A general interest, which this seems to indicate, and certain unique and perhaps original features in the factory methods of the National Cash Register Company, may justify a few words in explanation of them:

"There is no factory superintendent, but in place of such an official a chairman and a factory committee which holds daily or frequent sessions. This chairman after conference and advice from the committee, directs all departments in the making force. In and over each of all the departments, are subordinate committees, with a chairman who has like authority; and these all work in co-operation."

Nearly all important orders received by employes are first discussed and revised by these committees. In all the selling force, this system, "combining the methods of a military organization and a democracy into a somewhat novel co-operation," are in fixed and successful use. Liberal expenditures by the National Company and co-operative organization of employes for their "welfare work" seem to have won a deserved repute, at least are successfully carried out.

For officers and many of the men and women employes, attractive lunches are provided, for which a moderate charge is made, not intended to be the whole cost; training schools for employes, their children and others in the neighborhood; calisthenics, a dancing school, a boys' garden, rest rooms with a trained nurse and free baths on the company's time, libraries, and a cooking school are some of the interesting features annexed at the company's cost, to the factory work.

In connection with, and as a part of its system of co-operation, the company has paid out in the last five years, for prizes for suggestions alone, $10,152.68. During the year 1903, 5,078 suggestions were submitted in writing by the factory and office employes, of which number 1,536 were adopted, after having been first passed to a special committee for careful examination and report. The company claims these "welfare" expenditures pay in the good will proffered, and in the good will and better work they produce.

A. A. THOMAS,
Secretary National Cash Register Co.

Cashan or **Kashan** or **Kashin,** a town of Persia in the province of Irak-Ajemee, noted for its production of shawls, silk stuffs, and other goods. It is one of the most flourishing towns in Persia, and has a royal palace, numerous mosques, colleges, bazaars and baths. The inhabitants are noted for their industry, and besides shawls and silk stuffs already mentioned, they manufacture copper goods, gold and silver articles, brocade and cottons. They also have an active trade in agricultural produce, and carry on commerce with all parts of the Orient and with Europe by way of Ispahan. The silk stuffs produced at Cashan are held in high esteem, and are worn largely by the Shah and his entourage. Foreigners from the West who have visited the place have found the inhabitants, who belong chiefly to the Shiite sect of Mohammedans, more enlightened and liberal in their treatment of strangers than most Orientals. Many of the merchants are very wealthy, but are compelled by the oppressive exactions of public officials to hide their riches as much as possible from view. The interior of the homes of some of them, which present a neglected aspect on the outside, are said to be palatial in splendor. The province of Irak-Ajemee, in which Cashan is situated, has nearly the same boundaries as the country known to the ancients as Great Media, or Media Proper. It is the most productive portion of Persia, fertile and with a flourishing trade. Cashan has a population of about 15,000. See PERSIA.

Cash'el, Ireland, a town in Tipperary County, about 49 miles northeast of Cork; noted as containing the most interesting ruins in Ireland. These consist of a Gothic cathedral founded in 1169; a stone-roofed chapel, built in 1127; Hore Abbey, founded in 1260; the palace of the Munster kings; and a round tower, 90 feet in height and 56 feet in circumference. They are built on the Rock of Cashel, forming the summit of the slope which the town occupies. Here was held the great synod, in 1172, when the Irish priests first acknowledged the authority of the English Church and state. Cashel is a Roman Catholic archdiocese.

Cashew' (a corruption of *acajou,* the French form of the native Brazilian name *acajaiba*), a tree (*Anacardium occidentale*) of the order *Anacardiaceæ,* common in the West Indies. It has alternate, obtuse, ovate leaves, and bears bunches of red, scented flowers. The juice of the stem is used as a varnish; and an aromatic drug is prepared by decoction and maceration of several parts of the tree, afterward consolidated by evaporation. The nut is small, kidney-shaped, ash-gray, and is seated on the end of a large fleshy receptacle. The shell consists of three layers, the outer and inner of which are hard and dry, but the intermediate layer contains a quantity of black, extremely acrid, caustic oil, which is destroyed by roasting the nuts before eating them. The oil is applied to floors in India to protect them from the attacks of white ants. A wine is made from the fleshy receptacle; and a gum with properties similar to those of gum arabic is obtained from the plant.

Cashgar, or **Kashgar,** the capital city of eastern Turkestan, in the province of Sin-Kiang or Kashgaria. It is situated on the Kizil-Daria or Kashgar River, in a position of strategic importance, 100 miles northwest of Yarkand, and comprises an old and a new town. The latter was built in 1838, is strongly garrisoned, and contains the palace of the Chinese governor. There are considerable manufactures of cotton, gold and silver cloths, carpets, etc., and an extensive trade, its position at the junction of several great routes making it the emporium of much of the commerce of central Asia. It was the capital of an independent kingdom till conquered by the Chinese during the 18th century. In 1865 it revolted but was again subdued in 1876-7. Pop. about 62,000.

Cashibo, kä shē'bō, or **Cachibo,** a savage tribe living near the Ucayale River, a tributary of the Amazon, in eastern Peru.

Cashier, To, in a military sense to dismiss from the service by annuling or withdrawing an officer's commission. It is not an official term in the United States, and is commonly construed among military men as having a more disgraceful significance than "dismissal," although there is no analogy or precedent in the use of the word by leading English authors to support this construction. Macaulay uses the term in the sense of simple dismissal or annulment of commission. Nevertheless in ordinary military parlance it means dismissal in disgrace, and its use in any other sense is regarded as unjustified.

Cash'mere, or **Kashmir,** a principality in the northwest of Hindustan, subject to a Maharajah belonging to the Sikh race, but under British protection and supervision. It is composed of various provinces or districts, of which Cashmere proper is the most famous and interesting. It is situated in the southwestern portion of the state, and largely consists of an elevated valley intersected by the Jhelum. Besides Cashmere proper, the state embraces the territory of Jamoo, Balti or Iskardo, and Ladakh and Gilghit. The whole principality thus formed is estimated to cover about 80,900 square miles, and its population in 1901 was 3,000,000. It extends from about lat. 32° to 37° N. and from about lon. 73° to 80° E. The territory of Jamoo, which forms the most populous portion of the principality, lies to the north of the Punjab, between the spurs of the Himalaya Mountains leading up to Cashmere and enclosed by the upper courses of the Chenab and Ravee. Its chief town is of the same name. Balti, also called Little Tibet, is an elevated region on the Upper Indus, to the north of Cashmere proper, lying to the southwest of the Karakorum Mountains, and having for its capital Iskardo or Skardo. Ladakh, also called Middle Tibet, lies to the southeast of Balti, between the Himalaya and Karakorum Mountains, and is also traversed by the Indus. Its passes form some of the most important media of communication for central Asia. Its capital is Leh on the Indus. Gilghit is a district on the northwest of Balti. Cashmere and Jamoo is the official title of the

CASHMERE GOAT

whole. The principal river is the Indus, which traverses the state from southeast to northwest, and then takes a sharp turn to the southwest. The upper course of the Chenab is also in the state. Cashmere proper is a valley surrounded by gigantic mountains, belonging to the Himalayas, and traversed by the river Jhelum (formerly Hydaspes). The whole area of the enclosed region is about 4,500 square miles, and of the bottom of the valley about 2,000 square miles. From three sides only seven passes lead to this region; to the east the Himalaya presents an insurmountable barrier of snow. The splendor and sublimity of the diadem of snow-capped mountains, the beauty and richness of the hills which form the ascent to the higher peaks, it is impossible to describe. The elevated situation of the valley, and the mountains of snow which surround it, render the climate temperate; and it is, on the whole, pleasant and healthy. This region, about 5,200 feet above the sea, is watered by numerous streams, and is blessed with an abundance of the finest productions. The Asiatics therefore call it the paradise of India, the flower-garden, and the garden of eternal spring, and such names. The hills are covered with forests and Alpine pastures; at the foot of these are fields of corn; along the sides of the rivers rice is planted; rich orchards extend over the foremost ranges of hills; mulberry-trees are cultivated in abundance for the support of the silk-worms, and are entwined with vines, from whose grapes wine very similar to Madeira is prepared. The fruits of warm climates do not ripen here. The valley is famous for its flowers, with which all the gardens and meadows abound. Violets, roses, narcissuses, and innumerable European flowers, besides many that are not known in Europe, grow wild. The roses and jasmine yield the finest aromatic oils, which form an article of export. Two thirds of the inhabitants are Mohammedans, the remainder Hindus. The capital, Cashmere, is situated on the Jhelum. It is a dirty, ill-built town, extending on both sides of the river for about two miles, with few noteworthy buildings. Jamoo is the winter capital. Besides agricultural and pastoral pursuits the inhabitants carry on certain manufactures, especially woolens and artistic metal work. The manufacture of the celebrated Cashmere shawls is not so extensive as it once was, since manufactories have been established at Amritsir, in the Punjab, and elsewhere, which compete successfully with those of Cashmere. The genuine Cashmere shawls, however, are said to be of a better quality, owing to the fact that they are made of wool from the wild goat and other wild animals, this wool being, properly speaking, a soft down with which all the animals of this region are clad during the winter season. The shawls are woven in stripes, which are afterward very skilfully sewed together. Cashmere has had a varied history during the different periods distinguished as pro-Buddhistic, Buddhistic, Hindu, and Mohammedan. Buddhism, when driven from Hindustan, found a refuge in Cashmere. Mohammedanism was introduced in the 14th century. In 1586 the country was conquered by Akbar, and became part of the Mogul empire. In 1752 it was subjugated by the Afghans, under whom it remained till 1819, when it was conquered by the Sikhs. In 1846 the Sikh governor, Gholah Singh, made a separate treaty with the British, by which he acknowledged their supremacy, and agreed to lend them assistance when required. Accordingly he sent a contingent to act with the British forces against Delhi in 1857. A small annual tribute is paid to the British, partly consisting of Cashmere shawls. Under the supervision of the Indian authorities and the British resident at the court of Cashmere, great improvements in the internal condition of the state have recently been effected. The revenue system has been remodeled, and a new land revenue settlement has been completed. According to a recent blue book "An impulse has in consequence been given to agricultural pursuits, cultivation has increased, and local industries in silk culture, vineyards, wine factories, hop gardens, and orchards are being developed. . . . The posts and telegraphs in Cashmere have been taken over by the government of India, with the result of an increase in efficiency and of a saving in expense to the Cashmere state. The Cashmere troops have improved, and have shown their value in active service. Large expenditure has been incurred on public works, particularly on the improvement of the Jhelum and Gilghit roads, and on the construction in the capital, Srinagar, of water-works." A railway belonging to the Indian system now enters the country. The inhabitants are a fine race physically, tall, strong, and well built, with regular features. About two thirds of them are Mohammedans, the remainder mostly Hindus. Earthquakes frequently occur, and one that took place in 1885 caused the loss of thousands of lives.

Cashmere Goat (*Capra hircus,* var. *laniger*), a variety of the common goat remarkable for its fine downy fleece, said to be found in perfection only in Tibet, but also found elsewhere, as in Ladakh or Middle Tibet, now a province of the principality of Cashmere. It is found both in a wild state and as a domestic animal; the former is said to yield the best wool or down. The favorite food of these animals is said to be buds, aromatic plants, rue, and heath. The people of Tibet give the goats at least once a week some salt. If they are transferred from their cold mountainous abode into a warm country, the wool deteriorates. It grows very slowly in the warm part of the year, and more vigorously as the cold season approaches. The colder the region the heavier is the animal's fleece. Proper food and careful tending increase the fineness of the wool. Yearlings, as in the case with the merino sheep, afford the finest wool. A full-grown goat yields not more than eight ounces. The goats which pasture in the highest vales of Tibet have a bright ochre color. In lower grounds the color becomes of a yellowish-white, and still farther downwards, entirely white. The goats of Tibet and Cashmere have the fine curled wool close to the skin, just as the under hair of our common goat lies below the coarse upper hair. The wool is shorn in the spring, shortly before the warm season — the time when the animal in its natural state seeks thorns and hedges in order to free itself from the burden of its warm covering. A large shawl of the finest quality requires five pounds of the wool; *one of the inferior quality from three to four pounds. The flesh of the Cashmere goat tastes as well as that of the common one, and its milk is as rich if it is well tended.

Casiguran Bay, kä-sē-goo'rän, an inlet on the east coast of the province of Principe, Luzon, Philippine Islands, reached through Casiguran Sound. The sound is about nine miles long from Cape Ildefonso to a narrow passage affording access to the bay. The bay itself is about three quarters of a mile long and two and a half miles wide. Its depth is some 16 to 26 fathoms.

Casimir, käs ĭ mēr, properly Kazimierz ("foünder of peace"), was the name of many Polish princes and kings. I. CASIMIR I., b. 1015; d. 1058. During his minority he was under the regency of his mother and was driven from the kingdom with her. In 1041 his power was re-established, and through his efforts the predominance of Christianity was decided in Poland. 2. CASIMIR III., b. 1309; d. 5 Nov. 1370, called Casimir the Great, who succeeded his father, Vladislav Loketek, as king of Poland in 1333, was the most distinguished of this name. He added Little Russia and Red Russia to his dominions, and repelled the Tartars, who then threatened Poland. He founded the University of Cracow (1364), as well as several schools and hospitals, and showed great anxiety for the advancement of the arts and of learning in his kingdom. In 1347 he caused a new code of laws to be compiled, and protected the peasants, on which account he was called the peasants' king. He had a Jewish mistress who procured for her nation those liberties which they enjoy in Poland to the present day. With him the line of the Piasti, which had ruled in Poland for nearly 530 years, became extinct.

Casimir-Perier, Jean Paul Pierre, President of the French republic: b. Paris 8 Nov. 1847; d. there 11 March 1907. He served in the Franco-Prussian war, and received the decoration of the Legion of Honor for bravery. In 1876 he was elected to the Chamber of Deputies; in 1890 vice-president of the chamber, and in 1893, president. He resigned to become premier, which office he held till the assassination of President Carnot, when he was chosen his successor on the first ballot (June 1894). He resigned the office of president, January 1895, and was succeeded by Félix Faure.

Casino, kà sē'nō, or Monte Casino, a celebrated Benedictine abbey in Italy, in the Neapolitan province of Caserta, near the small town of South Germano, and about 45 miles from the city of Naples, founded by St. Benedict of Norcia in 529. It is situated on a mountain, from which it derives its name, near the ruins of the ancient Casinum, and is approached by a well paved and winding road. The abbey, after having suffered repeated reverses, finally became considerable for its privileges and its wealth, and in the 11th and 12th centuries was the seat of science, particularly of medicine, the celebrated school of Salerno having been founded by the monks of Monte Casino. The church is very magnificent, although overloaded with ornament, and contains the tomb of the founder. The monastery has served as a place of refuge to several sovereigns and pontiffs, and was formerly much visited by pilgrims and travelers, who were entertained free of expense. It is still visited by travelers or tourists, but it is no longer a conventual institution, being now devoted to education. The railway from Rome now passes near it.

Casino, a name generally given to a kind of club-house or place of amusement, containing rooms for dancing, playing at billiards, etc. The word is originally Italian, being a diminutive of the Italian word *casa*, signifying a house; and was at first applied to small houses which the nobles of Florence, Venice, and other Italian cities often possessed at a distance from their ordinary residences, and which were devoted to purposes of social enjoyment.

Casiri, kä-sē'rē, Michael, Orientalist and Syro-Maronite clergyman: b. Tripoli, Syria, 1710; d. Madrid 1791. He studied in the College of St. Peter and St. Marcellino; and in 1734 entered the clerical profession. The following year he accompanied the learned Assemanni to Syria, where he was going, at the command of the Pope, to attend the synod of the Maronites, and in 1738 gave, at Rome, an exact account of the religous tenets of the Maronites. He afterward taught in his monastery the Arabic, Syrian, and Chaldee languages, theology and philosophy; and in the year 1748 was invited to Madrid, where he was appointed to an office in the royal library. In 1749 he devoted his attention, by the king's orders, to the library of the Escurial, of which he subsequently became the superintendent. Here he collected the materials for his celebrated work, 'Bibliotheca Arabico-Hispana,' which enumerates in 1851 articles the manuscripts of the Escurial Library, perhaps the richest in Europe in Arabic manuscripts. This work, though not entirely free from errors, contains very important information and valuable extracts, and is indispensable to every Orientalist.

Caskets, The, a group of rocks in the English Channel, seven miles from Alderney. They have often been fatal to vessels, and, in 1119, Prince William, son of Henry I., and his suite, perished here. In 1744 the Victory ship of war, of 110 guns, also was shipwrecked upon them. On the highest there is a lighthouse.

Cas'ler, John Overton, American soldier: b. Frederick County, Va., 1 Dec. 1838. He served in the Confederate army during the Civil War and was a prisoner of war from February to May 1865. He lived in Texas 1877–89, and has since been a resident of Oklahoma City, where he is justice of the peace. He is the commander of the Oklahoma division of United Confederate Veterans, and has published 'Four Years in the Stonewall Brigade' (1893); 'Lilian Stuart, the Heroine of the Rappahannock' (1889).

Casoria, kä-sō-rē'ä, Italy, a town in the province of Naples (Napoli), six miles northeast of Naples. It has four fine churches, and is the residence of a district judge. Silk is produced in the neighborhood. Pietro Martino, the painter, was born here. Pop. about 10,000.

Caspari, käs-pä're, Karl Paul, German Church historian: b. Dessau 8 Feb. 1814; d. 11 April 1892. He became professor of theology at Christiania in 1857. His Arabic grammar is in high repute, and his contributions to the study of the Old Testament include works on Obadiah, Isaiah, Micah, and Daniel. Besides his 'Anecdotes of Ecclesiastical History' he published at Christiania 'The Origin of the Story of the Baptismal Symbol, and the Rule of Faith,' extensions of which appeared in 1875 and 1879.

Caspe, käs'pä, Spain, a town in the province of Zaragoza, 12 miles north-northeast of Alcañiz, left bank of the Guadalupe, near its confluence with the Ebro, on several small hills and in the intervening valleys. It has paved streets, one principal and nine smaller squares, a handsome Gothic collegiate and two other churches, several chapels, three schools, a town-hall and prison in a suppressed convent, an hospital, and several public fountains. Manufactures — wine, oil, and soap. Some trade is also carried on in grain and cattle. Pop. 8,427.

Cas'pian Gates, a name given to the Russian fortress Dariel, situated in a narrow defile of the Caucasus, on the Terek, 80 miles north of Tiflis.

Caspian Sea, a large lake or inland sea between Europe and Asia, now nearly surrounded by Russian territory but having Persia on the south; 730 miles in length from north to south, and from 130 to ·270 in breadth; area about 170,000 square miles; the largest isolated sheet of water on the globe. The water is less salt than that of the ocean, of a bitter taste, and of an ochre color, without ebb or flow. In some places it is exceedingly deep, yet it abounds in shallows, so as to prevent the navigation of ships which draw more than 9 or 10 feet of water. The level of the Caspian Sea is considerably lower than that of the ocean. Among the rivers which flow into it are the Volga, Ural, Terek, and Kur. In ancient times the Oxus (Amoo Daria) also flowed into it. It has no outlet. The fisheries here, which are very valuable, occupy and train many seamen. Sturgeons and sterlets are caught in great quantities, and there are also salmon-trout, perch, *Silurus glanis,* two kinds of carp, and porpoises; seals abound in the upper coasts, and tortoises between the mouths of the Volga and the Ural. In the northern region the first fishing season, called the caviar season, occurs between March and May, when the Volga, Ural, etc., are getting cleared of ice. The second season is in July, when the sturgeon descend the rivers; and the third or open-sea fishing goes on from September to November. The only ports at all worthy the name on or near the Caspian are Astrakhan, Baku, Derbend, and Astrabad (in Persia). The navigation is at all times difficult and often perilous. Steam packets are now established on this sea. The Russians have also a fleet of war vessels in the Caspian, and a new naval station has been established at Krasnovodsk, on the east side of the sea. By means of river and canal there is water communication between the Caspian and the Black Sea, Baltic, and White Sea.

Cass, Lewis, American statesman, diplomatist, and soldier: b. Exeter, N. H., 9 Oct. 1782; d. Detroit, Mich., 17 June 1866. In 1800 he removed to Marietta, Ohio, where he entered on the study of the law. He was admitted to the bar in December 1802, and soon after established himself at Zanesville, where he gradually acquired practice. In 1806 he was elected to the Ohio legislature. He served in the first year of the second war with England and in 1813 was appointed governor of Michigan Ter-

ritory, holding office till July 1831. Michigan at this time had no territorial legislature, and the business of selecting laws for it from the codes of the States devolved on Governor Cass and the territorial judges. Governor Cass was also *ex officio* superintendent of Indian affairs for the territory, which then included what now constitutes the two States of Michigan and Wisconsin, and this remained for several years the most important part of his duties. Of all this extensive territory, it was only a little tract bordering on Lake Erie and the Detroit River to which the Indian title had yet been extinguished. Within the bounds of his Indian superintendency, ultimately made to embrace all the tribes northwest of the Ohio, there were reckoned to be 40,000 Indians, mustering at least 9,000 warriors. The recent hostilities, and the distrust and suspicions of the Indians, occasioned by the constant calls upon them for additional cessions of land, rendered this office one of great delicacy and difficulty. But Governor Cass, while steadily carrying out the policy of acquisition, succeeded also in maintaining the respect, and even in securing the affection of the Indians. In 1817 he obtained, in conjunction with Governor McArthur, a cession of most of the remaining Indian lands within the state of Ohio, with adjoining tracts in Indiana and Michigan, to the extent of 4,000,000 acres in the whole. This cession removed the Indian barrier hitherto intervening between the settlements of Ohio and those of Michigan. In 1819 he met the Chippewas at Saginaw, and obtained a cession of lands in the peninsula of Michigan to the extent of 6,000,000 acres. As yet the northwestern regions were very imperfectly known. At the suggestion of Governor Cass, an expedition, in which he himself bore a conspicuous part, and of which an account has been published by Schoolcraft, was set on foot in 1820, for exploring the northern shore of Lake Superior, and the course of the upper Mississippi. The next year, by a long, circuitous river navigation, he visited Chicago, then nothing but a military post, with a wide wilderness all about it, and there made a treaty with the Chippewas, Ottawas, and Potawatamies, by which a large additional tract was obtained, completing the extinction of the Indian title to the peninsula of Michigan south of Grand river. In 1828 he made two treaties, one at Green Bay, the other at St. Joseph's, by which many millions of acres were ceded to the United States. Up to his resignation of the office of governor of Michigan, in July, 1831, he had concluded 19 treaties with the Indians, by which cessions had been acquired in Ohio, Indiana, Illinois, Michigan, and Wisconsin, to an amount equal to nearly or quite a fourth part of the entire area of those states. When President Jackson reconstructed his cabinet in August, 1831, Cass was appointed Secretary of War. The policy of the removal of the Indians, especially the southern tribes, to districts west of the Mississippi, had been warmly espoused by Gen. Jackson. The defense of this policy, which had elicited much criticism and a warm opposition, was ably entered upon by Secretary Cass in his first annual report. In 1836 he was appointed minister to France, a post which he held till 1842. He was on excellent terms with Louis Philippe, of whose character he gave a very friendly and favorable account in his 'King, Court, and Government of France,' published in 1840, originally as an article in the 'Democratic Review.' By far the most remarkable incident of his diplomatic career occurred just at its close, in his attack on the quintuple treaty for the suppression of the slave trade. He was United States Senator (1845–8), and having opposed the Wilmot Proviso, became the Democratic candidate for President in 1848, but was defeated. He returned to the Senate in 1849, and was secretary of state (1857–60), resigning because President Buchanan would not consent to strengthen the garrison at Fort Sumter. He wrote: 'History, Traditions, and Languages of the Indians' 1823; 'France, Its King, Court, and Government.' See 'Lives' by Schoolcraft (1848); Smith (1856); McLaughlin (1891).

Cassagnac, Adolphe Bernard Granier de, ăd-ŏlf bär-när grä-nē-ã dĕ käs sän yăc, French journalist and politician: b. 1806; d. 31. Jan. 1880. He began his career at Paris as contributor of literary criticisms to the *Journal des Débats*, and soon made himself known, and latterly notorious, as editor of various papers, the *Globe*, the *Pouvoir*, the *Pays*, etc., and as being involved in many controversies and duels. He published various books, chiefly historical. Among the principal are: 'Portraits Littéraires'; 'Histoire des Causes de la Révolution Française'; 'Histoire des Girondins'; 'L'Empereur et la Démocratie Moderne.'

Cassagnac, Paul-Adolphe Marie Prosper (pōl ăd-ŏlf mä-rē prŏs pär) **Granier de,** son of Adolphe; had a career and a reputation not dissimilar to those of his father. He was born 2 Dec. 1842; d. at Saint Loir-et-cher, 4 Nov. 1904. He was taken prisoner at Sedan in 1871, and underwent eight months' confinement in Silesia. His violent advocacy of Bonapartism led him into innumerable duels, and he was on several occasions summoned for libelous articles in the *Pays* and other newspapers. He was also a vigorous supporter of Gen. Boulanger. After 1884 he edited a journal known as *L'Autorité*. He wrote a 'Histoire de la Troisiène République' (1875); 'Empire et Royanti.'

Cassan'der, king of Macedon, son of Antipater: b. about 354 B.C.; d. 297 B.C. He disputed the sovereignty of Macedon with Polysperchon, whom Antipater had appointed regent at his death in 319 B.C. Allying himself with Ptolemy and Antigonus, he conquered Athens; captured Olympias, the mother of Alexander the Great, and put her to death; and connected himself with the royal family by marrying Thessalonica, half-sister to Alexander. He joined, in 315 B.C., the coalition against the growing power of Antigonus; murdered the rightful heir to the throne, Alexander Ægus, and his mother Roxana; and took the title of king in 306 B.C., which was confirmed to him by the decisive battle of Ipsus in 301 B.C.

Cassan'dra, also called **Alexandra,** daughter of Priam and Hecuba, and twin-sister of Helenus. Both children, according to tradition, were playing in the vestibule of the temple of the Thymbræan Apollo, not far from Ilium; and having stayed there too late to be carried home, a couch of laurel twigs was prepared for them in the temple. When the nurses went to them the next morning they found two serpents at the side of the children, which,

instead of injuring them, harmlessly licked their ears. This miracle produced a still greater one: the hearing of the children was rendered so acute that they could distinguish the voices of the gods. Cassandra subsequently spent much of her time in the temple of Apollo, who, becoming enamored of her charms, disclosed to her all the secrets of the prophetic art, and in return demanded her love. But Cassandra, when her curiosity was satisfied, refused the dishonorable reward. Apollo, incensed at this, solemnly decreed that her prophecies should never find belief. She frequently and continually foretold the destruction of Troy, and warned her countrymen in vain against the deceitful horse. When Troy was conquered, and Cassandra, with the other maidens, fled to the temple of Minerva, Ajax, son of Oïleus, tore her from the altar, deflowered the virgin in the sacred place, and dragged her away to the other female slaves, with her hands tied. On the division of the booty she fell to Agamemnon, who carried her as his slave and mistress to Mycenæ. Clytæmnestra murdered them both. Agamemnon had twins by her — Teledamus and Pelops, who were put to death by Ægisthus. The ancients regarded this rape of Cassandra as a most infamous atrocity. It has often afforded a subject to poets and sculptors. The Locrians, the countrymen of Ajax, were afflicted on this account for many years with storms, and their country was desolated with the plague.

Cassandra, the most westerly of the three tongues of the Chalcidic peninsula, between the gulfs of Salonica and Cassandra. Its ancient name was Pallene. The Gulf of Cassandra was anciently Toronaicus Sinus.

Cassano d'Adda, käs-sä'nō däd'dä, Italy, a town in the province of Milan, and 16 miles north-northeast of the town of Milan, pleasantly situated on a hill on the right bank of the Adda. It is very old, and built mostly of bricks. A bridge of 800 paces connects it with the opposite bank of the river. There are numerous silk-mills. Its military position on the right bank of the Adda has caused it to be the scene of several battles. Here Ezzelino da Romano, the leader of the Ghibellines in Italy, in the time of the Emperor Frederick II., was defeated in 1259; here also Prince Eugene was defeated in 1705, by the Duke de Vendôme, and the French under Moreau, by Suwarow in 1799. Pop. of commune about 10,000.

Cassareep, käs'şa-rēp, **Cassireepe,** or **Cassiripe,** the concentrated juice of the roots of the common or bitter cassava (*Manihot utilissima*), flavored by aromatics, and deprived of its poisonous properties by boiling. It is used to give a relish to soups and other dishes, and forms the basis of the West Indian "pepperpot." It is a powerful antiseptic, and is very useful in keeping meat fresh in a tropical climate.

Cassas, Louis François, loo-ē frän-swä käs-sä, French landscape-painter and architeet: b. Azay-lc-Ferron, 1756; d. 1827. He went to Italy when very young, and carried with him a collection of views from nature, which he afterward enlarged by others taken in Sicily, Istria, and Dalmatia. He next accompanied the Count of Choiseul Gouffier, ambassador to Constantinople, compared the topography of Troy with the accounts given of it by the ancients, took drawings of the remains and the surrounding country, and traveled through Asia Minor, Syria, Palestine, and part of Egypt. On his return he was appointed inspector and professor of design at the Gobelins in Paris. The models which he had made of the most celebrated architectural works of different countries were purchased by Napoleon, who rewarded him with a pension, and caused them to be placed in the Parisian School of Arts. From the materials collected in his travels have been compiled 'Voyage Pittoresque de la Syrie, de la Phénicie, de la Palestine, et de la Basse Égypte' (1799), and 'Voyage Historique et Pittoresque de l'Istrie et de la Dalmatie' (1802, with sixty-nine copper plates). The original drawings for both works were admirable oil paintings, and they were deposited in the Bibliothèque Royale. Cassas was invested with several orders of knighthood.

Cassation, a term used in the courts on the Continent of Europe. It is derived from the Middle Ages, and signifies the annulling of any act or decision if the forms prescribed by law have been neglected, or if anything is contained in it contrary to law.

Cassation, Court of (Cour de Cassation), one of the most important institutions of modern France, which gives to the whole jurisdiction of that country coherency and uniformity without endangering the necessary independence of the courts. It was established by the first National Assembly, and has been preserved, in every essential respect, under all the changes of the Revolution and Restoration. It has been maintained even in those districts which, by their union with France became subjected to French laws, but by the Peace of Paris again became part of the Prussian monarchy. In France, as early as the reign of Louis IX. (1226–70), petitions were presented to the king by appellants from the decisions of the courts. In later times appeals to the parliaments, as the highest courts of the kingdom, came into use, and their decisions were not liable to be set aside by the ordinary forms of law. Yet the parties were allowed to dispute even these decisions if they were founded upon errors of fact or violated undisputed principles of law; and by an ordinance of 1302 it was provided that the parties should be allowed royal letters for the defense of their rights against the decisions of the supreme courts (lettres de grâce de dire contre les arrêts), which should be issued from the chancery (by the chancellor of France). The case was then sent back to the parliament for further investigation, but was examined and decided in the presence of the king himself, or of a special commissioner. An abuse, however, crept in of transferring these cases to the royal council, where they were decided by officers called maîtres des requêtes. These letters received the name of lettres de proposition d'erreur, and during the civil commotions at the end of the 14th century began to be more frequently presented to the council, which, as soon as one party complained of the partiality of the parliaments, transferred the case to its own bar, and obstructed the course of justice by lettres d'état suspensions of the process, on the pretext of the absence of one of the parties in the service of the king). Under the Chancellor Poyet (1538–42), this abuse reached its highest pitch: but the Chancellors Olivier (1545–51), and

Hôpital (1560–8), the two great reformers of French jurisprudence, limited the use of these lettres till, by the Ordinance of Blois (1576), all the provisions against the decisions of the parliaments were reduced to these three: — the proposition d'erreur, for an error of fact; requête civile, to restore the parties to their former condition on account of the fraud of one of the parties or the mistakes of the attorney; and cassation (petition for abrogation), for violation of forms or settled principles of law. By the famous Order of Procedure of 1667 the first of these provisions was abolished, but the province of the requête civile and cassation was enlarged and more precisely defined. The former was always brought before the court itself and decided there, the latter before the council. For this purpose, in the conseil privé, or conseil des parties, a particular committee was formed, consisting of the chancellor, the four secretaries of state (ministers of the departments), the council of state, and all the maîtres des requêtes (in 1789, 78 in number). The decisions of this committee were too much influenced by the will of the king and the ministers, and by various other circumstances, so that they did not enjoy great respect, though they often exposed acts of great injustice on the part of the parliament and other high courts. It was therefore abolished in the first National Assembly, and its place supplied by an independent court — the tribunal de cassation (decrees of 27 Nov. and 1 Dec. 1790), which was retained in all the constitutions and received under the imperial government (1804) the name cour de cassation, which it still retains. It consisted, according to the organization of 1800, of 48 members, chosen from the senate, on the nomination of the consuls, who elected their own president from among themselves. The appointment of president was afterward vested in the emperor. In the Charte Constitutionelle of 1814 the number of members of the court de cassation was fixed at 49, at which it still remains. The members are appointed for life by the president of the republic, and consist of a first president, three presidents of sections, and 45 councilors, besides certain honorary members. The minister of justice, or keeper of the seals (garde des sceaux) has the right of presiding on certain occasions. This court never decides on the main question at issue, but on the competency of the other courts and on the petitions to have their decisions reviewed or annulled, and assigns the question to another court if a decision is to be set aside for an evident violation of the forms or the principles of the law. For this purpose it is divided into three sections or chambers: — the chambre des requêtes, which decides on the admissibility of the petitions in civil cases; the chambre de cassation civile; and the chambre de cassation criminelle. After a decision has been reversed, if a second court decides the same case in the same way, and an appeal is entered again, the court of cassation must either request an authentic explanation of the law from the government, or at least all the three sections must unite, to pronounce a second reversal or cassation; and if a third decision is the same as the preceding, the court before which the case is again brought must submit to the doctrine of the court of cassation on the point of law in dispute. This system, which dates from 2 April 1837, gives great authority to this court in matters of jurisprudence. According to the law in force before 1837, the court before which a case was brought for decision a third time was not required to adopt the views of the court of cassation, but after the third decision there was no further appeal. The government, however, in that case gave an authentic interpretation of the law if there was any occasion for so doing. Until the end of 1852 there was a similar court of cassation for the Prussian province of the Rhine, but in 1853 its jurisdiction was transferred to the supreme Prussian tribunal sitting at Berlin. The sentences of the court of cassation are not only recorded in the journals of the courts, the decisions of which are reversed, but published likewise in an official bulletin, by which consistency and uniformity are preserved. The tribunal of cassation has enjoyed from its commencement the respect and confidence of France, and has numbered among its members several of the most distinguished lawyers; as the President Henrion de Fansey, the councilors, Chabot, Merlin, and Carnot.

Cassatt', Alexander Johnston, American railway president: b. Pittsburg, Pa., 8 Dec. 1839; d. Philadelphia, Pa., 28 Dec. 1906. He was educated in the University of Heidelberg, and the Rensselaer Institute, Troy, N. Y., in 1859 was employed as civil engineer in surveying a railroad route in Georgia. He entered the service of the Pennsylvania Railroad as rodman in 1861, became general superintendent of the Pennsylvania system and general manager of the lines east of Pittsburg, 1871-4; third vice-president, 1874; and first vice-president, 1880. He resigned this last-named post in 1882, but was elected a director in 1883, and in June 1899 was elected president of the Pennsylvania system. He was president of seven companies, and a director in 23, including transportation, banks, and trust companies.

Cassatt, Mary, American artist b. Pittsburg, Pa., about 1855. In 1875 she went to Europe to study art, and lived for some years in Spain, where she gave particular attention to the works of Velasquez. Removing to Paris, she was influenced by the work of Manet and Legas, and exhibited in the Impressionist Exposition about 1880. In 1898 she exhibited some of her works in New York city. Returning to Europe, she established a studio in Paris, where she has since lived. She has gained considerable fame as an etcher, ranking among the first of the modern artists in this medium.

Cassava, kăs-sä'vạ, **Manioc,** măn'ĭ-ŏk, or **Mandioc,** a South American shrub (*Manihot utilissima*) belonging to the natural order *Euphorbiaceæ*, sub-order *Crotoneæ*. There are two forms, popularly known as bitter and sweet, both of which are widely cultivated in tropical America for their fleshy, cylindrical, starchy roots, which form a large part of the food of the natives, and from which tapioca is made. They have also been introduced into other warm countries, especially Africa, and have quickly gained important positions as food crops.

The plant, which attains a height and breadth of four feet or more, is rather bushy, since its numerous knotty, brittle, pithy stems have many palmate leaves. The flowers, which appear in midsummer, are green or yellowish and inconspicuous, and are succeeded by wing-angled capsules. The best results are obtained on light, sandy, well-drained soils. The land is prepared as for corn, but instead of planting seed, stem cuttings are covered by the plow, and when the plants appear they are cultivated with the same implements used in corn-growing. In about seven months the white soft roots, which occasionally weigh 30 pounds, and are sometimes three feet long and three inches thick, are dug by hand, washed, grated, or ground to pulp. The juice, or poisonous part, is carefully pressed out, and when boiled, becomes the delicious sauce called cassar, much esteemed by epicures. The flour that remains after pressure is formed into thin, round cakes, and baked. To a European accustomed to eat bread, these, though sweetish and not unpalatable, have an insipid taste. If placed in close vessels, and preserved from the attacks of insects, cassava bread may be kept for several months without injury.

Poisoning by the bitter cassava is due to the presence of minute quantities of hydrocyanic acid. This is a very common ingredient of many fruits and seeds, but usually is modified as the fruit ripens. The general process of manufacture of cassava destroys or drives off the free hydrocyanic acid. The symptoms of this poison are very acute. Death is very sudden from paralysis of the heart and respiratory centres. Non-fatal poisoning is accompanied with great prostration, nausea, vomiting, and collapse. There are no efficient antidotes.

The natives of South America throw a number of cakes of cassava together to heat, after which they soak them in water, which causes a rapid fermentation to take place; and from the liquor thus obtained they make a very sharp and disagreeable, but intoxicating beverage, which will not keep longer than 24 hours without spoiling.

From the pure flour of cassava is formed the substance called tapioca, which is frequently used for jelly, puddings, and other culinary purposes. This is separated from the fibrous parts of the roots by taking a small quantity of the pulp after the juice is extracted and working it in the hand till a thick, white cream appears on the surface. This, being scraped off and washed in water, gradually subsides to the bottom. After the water is poured off the remaining moisture is dissipated by a slow fire, the substance being constantly stirred, until at length it forms into grains about the size of sago. These become hard by keeping, and are the purest and most wholesome part of the cassava. The roots of the sweet cassava are also used as stock-food and to make glucose and starch. Florida is the only State in which sweet cassava has attracted much attention, but it seems to be not very profitable there on account of the high price of labor and fertilizers.

Cassegrainian Telescope, a form of the reflecting-telescope in which the great speculum is perforated like the Gregorian, but the rays converging from the surface of the mirror are reflected back by a small convex mirror in the axis of the telescope, and come to a focus at a point near the aperture in the speculum, where they form an inverted image, which is viewed by the eyepiece screwed into the tube behind the speculum.

Cassel, käs'sĕl, or **Kassel,** formerly the residence of the Elector of Hesse-Cassel, and now the chief town in the Prussian province of Hessen-Nassau, lies on the Fulda, 91 miles north-northeast of Frankfort-on-the-Main. It is divided into the Altstadt, or Old Town; the Ober Neustadt, or Upper New Town; the Unter Neustadt, or Lower New Town; and the new West Quarter; all but the third being on the left bank of the river. Cassel has several fine squares, or open areas, on the principal of which, the Friedrichsplatz, stands the electoral palace, an indifferent structure; and next to it the museum, a handsome building, containing a library of 170,000 volumes, and many valuable MSS. At one end of this area is a handsome triumphal arch and war monument overlooking the Fulda valley, in which is the Karlsaue, finely laid out, and forming a favorite promenade. On this side of the city are also the building for the courts and government offices, the Bellevue palace containing the academy of arts, and the handsome picture-gallery containing some fine examples of the old masters, especially the Flemish and Dutch. The other more noticeable public areas are the Königsplatz, in the form of a circle; the Friedrich-Wilhelmsplatz, with an ornamental fountain; the Ständeplatz, a broad tree-planted avenue, etc. The most noteworthy church is the Protestant church of St. Martin, with a nave of the 14th and a choir of the 15th century. An observatory is likewise situated here. Cassel has iron-foundries and machine-shops, works for railway-carriages, mathematical instruments, pianos, gloves, jute works, etc. In the vicinity is Wilhelmshöhe, the ex-elector's summer palace, the temporary residence of Napoleon III. after Sedan. Pop. (1901) about 107,000.

Cas'sia, a genus of leguminous plants, of the tribe *Cæsalpineæ,* inhabiting the tropical parts of the world, consisting of trees, shrubs, or herbs, the leaflets of several species of which constitute the well-known drug called senna. That imported from Alexandria is obtained from *C. acutifolia* and *C. obovata. C. fistula* is found wild in India. Its legumes contain a quantity of thick pulp, which is a mild laxative and cathartic, and enters into the composition of the confection of cassia and the confection of senna. It belongs to the sugar class of laxatives, its properties being due for the most part to the water-attracting properties of sugar while in the intestinal canal. The leaves and flowers are also purgative. The bark and roots of several of the Indian species are much used in medicine. "Cassia bark" is a common name for the bark of an entirely different plant, *Cinnamomum cassia,* belonging to the laurel family. It is much imported into Europe, mostly from China, and is also called *Cassia lignea.* Its flavor somewhat resembles that of cinnamon, and as it is cheaper it is often substituted for it, but more particularly for the preparation of what is called oil of cinnamon. The cassia of the Bible was probably cassia bark. Cassia buds, which are similar in flavor, are the unripened fruits of this tree.

Cassia'nus, otherwise called JOANNES MASSILIENSIS and JOANNES EREMITA, early theological writer and zealous advocate of the monastic system, b. about 360, probably in Scythia. It is certain, however, that he traveled extensively in the East, spent a few years in Bethlehem, traveled to Egypt and seems to have visited the hermits in the desert. He was deeply attached to Saint Chrysostom and when the latter, through the intrigues of his opponents, was removed from the episcopal chair, Cassianus was sent with Germanus to Rome to present a memorial from the clergy who adhered to Chrysostom. Here he became personally acquainted with Pelagius. About 415 he went to Marseilles, where he continued a course of restless activity as a presbyter till his death, which took place some time between 430 and 450. He founded two monasteries on the principles laid down by him in his works 'De Institutis Cœnobirum' and 'Collationes Patrum Sceticorum' (that is, 'Conferences of the Monks in the Desert of Sketis'). The views advanced in these works, and still more the strong leaning which he showed to the dogmas of Pelagius, involved him in a controversy with Augustine. He ultimately modified his opinions so far as to adopt the system to which theologians have given the name of Semi-pelagianism, holding that man, since the fall, is not absolutely incapable of good, but, on the contrary, both derives from nature the seeds of virtue, and is able of himself to commence their primary development, though he requires the aid of divine grace to bring them to maturity. These views found great favor with the monks of France, and long maintained their ground in opposition to the efforts of Augustine and his friend Prosper of Aquitania. The best edition of the works of Cassianus is that of Frankfort (1722, fol.).

Cas'sin, John, American ornithologist: b. near Chester, Pa., 6 Sept. 1813; d. Philadelphia 10 Jan. 1869. He resided in Philadelphia from 1834, and excepting a few years partially given to mercantile pursuits, devoted himself to the study of ornithology. He contributed descriptions of new species and synoptical reviews of various families to the 'Proceedings' and the 'Journal' of the Philadelphia academy of natural science; and his more elaborate publications are 'Birds of California and Texas,' containing descriptions and colored engravings of 50 species not given by Audubon; 'Mammalogy and Ornithology of the Wikes Exploring Expedition'; 'Ornithology of the Japan Expedition'; 'Ornithology of Gilliss's Astronomical Expedition to Chile'; and the chapters on rapacious and wading birds in the 'Ornithology of the Pacific Railroad Explorations and Surveys.' His works are the result of careful research, and are especially valuable for their descriptions and classification of many birds not given in the previous works of Wilson and Audubon. According to Cones he was the only American ornithologist as familiar with the birds of the Old World as with those of America.

Cassini, Giovanni Domenico, jŏ vän'nē dō-mĕ'nē-cō käs-sē'nē, Italian astronomer: b. Perinaldo, near Nice, 8 June 1625; d. Paris 14 Sept. 1712. He studied at Genoa with the Jesuits. Chance turned his attention to astronomy, in which he made such rapid progress that in 1650 the senate of Bologna bestowed on him the first professorship of astronomy at the university. A meridian had been drawn by Ignatio Dante (1575) in the church of St. Petronia in that city. In 1653 Cassini conceived the idea of extending and correcting it. In two years he completed this difficult task, the first-fruits of which were more correct tables of the sun, a more precise determination of its parallax, and an excellent table of refractions. By an observation at Città della Piave he discovered the shadows cast by the satellites of Jupiter on the disk of that planet when they are between it and the sun. By means of these he corrected /his theory of the motion of the satellites; he also determined the period of Jupiter's revolution. In 1668 he published his 'Ephemerides of the Satellites of Jupiter.' In 1673 he settled in France. He discovered four new satellites of Saturn and the zodiacal light, proved that the axis of the moon is not perpendicular to the plane of the ecliptic, and showed the causes of her libration. The laws of this motion are one of his finest discoveries. He also wrote observations on the Indian calendar. The meridian commenced by Picard and Lahire was continued by Cassini in 1700 to the extreme limits of Roussillon, and when measured 100 years later showed a difference of only 21 toises (about 134 feet). He lost his sight some years before his death. His 'Opera Astronomica' was published at Rome in 1666.

Cassini, Jacques, zhäk, French astronomer: b. Paris 18 Feb. 1677; d. Thury, department of Oisi, 16 April 1756. He was the son of Giovanni Domenico and succeeded him in his post at the Paris observatory. In 1694 he was admitted into the Academy of Sciences. His labors to determine the figure of the earth are well known. The first measurement of 1718 made the degrees of the meridian shorter toward the north than toward the south, whence it was concluded that the earth was an oblong spheroid. Cassini continued the measurement, and maintained this opinion in his work 'De la Grandeur et de la Figure de la Terre.' In order to settle the question the Academy was commissioned in 1733 to measure the whole length of France from Brest to Strasburg. Cassini directed this undertaking, but was led into some errors by the defective instruments of former observers. The astronomical tables which he compiled were published at Paris in 1740. He wrote a great work on the inclinations of the orbits of Saturn's satellites and ring. In addition to his astronomical works, he wrote several essays on subjects in natural philosophy, etc.

Cassini, Jacques Dominique, zhäk dṓ-mē-něk, Count de, French astronomer: b. Paris 30 June 1748; d. Paris (?) 18 Oct. 1845. He was the son of Cassini de Thury and succeeded his father in 1784 as director of the Paris observatory. He was a member of the Academy, and a statesman of ability as well as a mathematician. In 1789 he completed the topographical work which was begun by his father. The 'Atlas National' was a reduction of it on a scale of one third. Cassini was arrested by order of the revolutionary tribunal. He escaped with life, but lost the copper-plates of the 'Carte de France,' which had cost 500,000 francs. Napoleon made him a count of the empire.

Cassini de Thury, de tü-rē, César François, sä-zär frän-swä, French astronomer: b. Paris 17 June 1714; d. 4 Sept. 1784; son of Jacques Cassini. He was a member of the Academy from his 22d year, and director of the observatory in 1756. He undertook a geometrical survey of the whole of France. When the support of the government was withdrawn in 1756, Cassini formed a society for advancing the requisite sums, which were to be repaid by the sale of the maps constructed from the survey. The work was almost entirely finished when he died.

Cassinian, or Cassian Oval, a special cartesian oval. It is the locus of a point the product of whose distances from two fixed points is constant. It varies in shape as the constant product and the distance between the fixed points are differently chosen, and may break up into two separate, but symmetrical figures. Another special form is that of Bernouilli's lemniscate.

Cassino, a game at cards usually played by four persons (although more can enter the game), two on each side. In it the ten of diamonds, technically called big cassino, counts two; and little cassino, the two of spades, counts one. The points possible to be scored in one deal (exclusive of sweeps) number 9. They are: Big cassino, 2; little cassino, 1; cards, 1; spades, 1; each ace, 1 = 4. A sweep is counted when a player takes up all the cards on the table. The object sought in the game (besides the points already enumerated) is to arrange the cards on the board in combination so that the sum of the spots on the cards thus combined may equal those on one card in the hand of the player, who has the right to take as many cards from the board as he can thus combine; or he may capture any card from the board the counterpart of which he has in hand.

Cassiodo'rus, Flavius Magnus Aurelius, Roman historian and statesman, who lived from about 468 to 568. He entered the service of the Ostrogoth king of Italy, Odoacer, at the age of about 20 years and under him and his successor Theodoric was treasurer of the kingdom and councilor, administering his office with extraordinary prudence in a most difficult time. As statesman, scholar, and historian he kept alive the lamp of the Græco-Roman learning after the overwhelming of the ancient civilization by the barbarians. After a term of 50 years in public station he withdrew to a monastic institution founded by himself in his native province Bruttium and there spent the remaining 30 years of his useful life, imbuing his monks with a love of the ancient learning and employing them in copying the ancient texts of profane no less than of religious writings. He may be regarded as the father of the monastic *Scriptorium* to which modern learning is indebted for great part of what has come down to us of the ancient literature and of the history of the west in those troublous times. He composed manuals of rhetoric and grammar which were used as text-books in the schools of the Middle Ages till the revival of the ancient learning, and which inspired men with a longing for the ancient knowledge. Of great service also were his works 'De Artibus ac Disciplinis Liberalium Litterarum' (of the liberal arts and courses of study), and his 'De Institutione Divinarum Litterarum' (instruction in scriptural knowledge); but above all his 12 books of 'Epistolæ Variæ' (various letters), containing decrees of the Ostrogothic kings, upon which is based the whole history of Italy under the rule of those barbarian potentates: this collection was first printed at Augsburg 1533. With one Epiphanius he made a compendious Latin version, entitled 'Tripartita Historia' (tripartite history) of the history of the Church as written by the three Greek historians, Socrates, Sozomen, and Theodoret, and continued Socrates' history to the year 518. An edition of his complete works was printed at Rouen in 1679 and at Venice in 1729. His 'Life' was written by the eminent Benedictine, Sainte Marthe, and published in Paris in 1694.

Cassiopeia, kăs-ĭ-ō-pē'yạ, in Greek mythology, daughter of Arabus and wife of Cepheus, to whom she bore Andromeda. She dared to compare her daughter's beauty to that of the Nereids, who, enraged thereat, besought Poseidon for vengeance. The god, in compliance with the request of the water-nymphs, laid waste the dominions of Cepheus by means of a deluge and a dreadful sea-monster.

In astronomy Cassiopeia is a conspicuous constellation in the northern hemisphere, situated next to Cepheus. In 1572 a new and brilliant star appeared in it, which, however, after a short time, gradually diminished, and at last disappeared entirely. The five brightest stars in the constellation of Cassiopeia are arranged in the form of a straggling W, which is easily recognized.

Cassiquiari, käs-sē-kē-ä'rē, or Cassiquiare, a deep rapid river of South America, in Venezuela, branching off from the Orinoco, and forming a water-way by which that river has navigable communication with the Rio Negro. It leaves the Orinoco in lat. 3° 10′ N.; lon. 66° 20′ W., about 20 miles west of Esmeralda, and, after a southwest course of 128 miles, falls into the Rio Negro near San Carlos, in lat. 2° 5′ N.; lon. 67° 40′ W. It is estimated to carry off about a third of the water of the Orinoco, being 100 yards broad where it leaves that river, and about 600 yards at its junction with the Rio Negro. By means of this river, the Rio Negro, the Amazon and its tributaries, it is practicable to sail from the interior of Brazil to the mouth of the Orinoco.

Cassiterides, käs-sĭ-tĕr'ĭ-dēz, a name derived from the Greek *kassiteros*, tin, and anciently applied, but with no uniformity or precision, to the tin district of Cornwall, to the Scilly Isles, or to small islands off the northwest coast of Spain.

Cassit'erite, native dioxide of tin, SnO_2, crystallizing in the tetragonal system, and also occurring uniform and in rolled grains. The crystals are usually brown or black, brittle with an uneven fracture, and with a specific gravity of from 6.8 to 7.1, and a hardness of from 6 to 7. Ordinary massive or crystallized cassiterite is often called "tinstone," especially in England; "wood tin" is a botryoidal form, "stream tin" is the mineral in small rolled pebbles found in the streams or placer deposits and is formed by the disintegration of stanniferous rocks. Cassiterite is the most important ore of tin. It occurs in Cornwall (England), Saxony, Bohemia, Galicia, Greenland, Sweden, and in Australia, the Malay Peninsula, Banca, Bolivia, and Mexico. In the

United States it is found in small amounts in various States, and it has been mined to some extent in Virginia and in South Dakota. A promising deposit has recently been reported from San Bernardino County, Cal., where mining operations have been carried on for some time with apparent success.

Cassius, kăsh'ŭs, Andreas, Dutch physician who flourished during the 17th century. He graduated at Leyden in 1632, was physician to the Duke of Holstein and Bishop of Lübeck, and died at Hamburg in 1673. His name is best known in connection with a purple color obtained from gold, which was briefly described in a treatise published by his son in 1685.

Cassius Longi'nus, Gaius, the friend of Brutus, was the quæstor of Crassus, and preserved the few troops of that general who escaped from the bloody battle with the Parthians. With these he defended Syria against the Parthians till the arrival of Bibulus. In the famous civil war that broke out between Pompey and Cæsar he espoused the cause of the former, and, as commander of his naval forces, rendered him important services. When Cæsar, after the victory of Pharsalia, was in pursuit of Pompey, he advanced with a few vessels, while crossing the Hellespont, against a fleet of 70 sail commanded by Cassius, and called upon him to surrender. The latter, astonished by his daring courage, surrendered at his summons. Cæsar pardoned him, and afterward bestowed various honors on him; but Cassius, who had always cherished feelings of bitter hatred toward Cæsar, joined in the conspiracy against him, and, with the aid of several fellow-conspirators, assassinated him, 44 B.C. He then together with Brutus, raised an army to maintain the cause of their faction. They were met by Octavianus and Antony, who professed themselves the avengers of Cæsar, at Philippi. The wing which Cassius commanded being defeated, he imagined that all was lost, and killed himself, 42 B.C. See BRUTUS; CÆSAR.

Cassius, Purple of. See PURPLE OF CASSIUS.

Cassivellaunus, kăs-ĭ-vĕ-lô'nŭs (in Shakespeare's 'Cymbeline,' CASSIBELAN), a noble and warlike British chief of the Catuvellauni, who, when Cæsar invaded Britain in 54 B.C., held sway over several tribes living to the north of the Thames, and led the resistance to the advance of the Roman general. Having advanced to the Thames, Cæsar found the Britons under Cassivellaunus posted on the north bank of the river prepared to dispute his passage. He crossed, however, without much difficulty, but the British charioteers persistently harassed his line of march. The Trinobantes, a tribe of Essex and Middlesex, soon sent in their submission to Cæsar, and as their example was followed by others, Cassivellaunus found himself unable to oppose resistance to the Romans. His stronghold, which contained many cattle, was captured by Cæsar; and an attempt made to storm Cæsar's naval camp proving unsuccessful, Cassivellaunus sued for peace, gave hostages, and promised an annual tribute.

Cassock, a name formerly applied to a long loose gown worn over the other garments, in which sense the word is found in Shakespeare. It is now applied to a long, close-fitting garment worn by priests and clerics and in Catholic countries forming the ordinary dress of the priest. Priests wear a black cassock; bishops and other prelates, purple: cardinals, red; and the Pope, white.

Cas'sowary, a corruption of a Malayan name for birds of the family *Casuariidæ* belonging to the *Ratitæ*, their affinities being greatest with the emu. The shortness of their wings totally unfits them for flight. As in others of this group, the pectoral or wing muscles are comparatively slight and weak, while those of their posterior limbs are very robust and powerful. The wings of the ostrich are of some assistance to it in running, but those of the cassowary are too short to be of service in this way, and with the exception of the ends of the five stiff quills are completely hidden beneath the plumage. The cassowaries have three toes, all provided with nails, of which the inner one is much elongated.

The cassowaries constitute a single genus (*Casuarius*) all the species of which have a long compressed bill, a cancellated bony crest or helmet on the head, and stiff barbless quills on the wings. Several species are known, and of these one of the most familiar is the helmeted cassowary of Ceram (*C. galeatus*), which has the head surmounted by an osseous prominence covered with a sort of horny helmet; the skin of the head and superior part of the neck is naked, of a deep-blue and fiery-red tint, with pendent caruncles or wattles. The naked rigid quills on the wings are used as weapons of defense, but the cassowary is rather timorous and shy. It is about 5½ feet long from the tip of the bill to the extremity of the longest claw. The head and neck together measure 18 inches; the largest toe, including the claw, is 5 inches; and the claw of the inner toe is 3½ inches long.

All the feathers of the cassowary, which have a peculiar structure, are of the same kind, contour feathers serving only for covering, and externally are all of one color. In this genus the aftershaft is as long as the shaft and both are filamentous. The double feathers are of unequal length, some on the rump being 12 or 14 inches long, while others are only 3. The stem or shaft is flat, shining, black, and knotted below, having a beard arising from each knot. The helmet is black in front and yellow behind. The eye is of a bright yellow, and more than an inch in diameter.

The anatomy of the cassowary differs very materially from that of the ostrich, which it resembles so much in general appearance. The intestines are short, and the cæcum small; there is no stomach intermediate to the crop and gizzard, and the cloaca is not larger in proportion than that of other birds. It feeds on fruits, eggs of birds, etc., and inhabits the forest districts.

As might be inferred from its structure, the cassowary is a swift runner, and its mode of progression, being unaided by wings, is as peculiar as it is efficient. In running, the cassowary appears to strike out powerfully with one leg, so as to project its body violently forward with a bounding motion, far surpassing the speed of a horse. It also kicks violently when, in a state of captivity, it is provoked to anger, and can inflict a very severe blow. The eggs of the galeated cassowary are green, and are neither so round nor so large as those of the ostrich. The shell is marked by numerous little deep-green tubercles. The largest of their eggs measure about 15 inches in circumference. Eight species, with a number of local races, are known, distributed with New Guinea as a centre to this and surrounding islands and the adjacent parks of Australia. See also EMU; OS-TRICH.

Consult Rothschild, 'Transactions of the Zoological Society,' London, 1901; Mosenthal & Harting, 'Ostriches and Ostrich-Farming.'

Cassowary-tree. See CASUARINA.

Cast, in the fine arts, is an impression taken by means of wax or plaster of Paris from a statue, bust, bas-relief, or any other model, animate or inanimate. In taking a cast from a living person's face, it is necessary, first, to anoint the eyebrows and eyelashes, and any hairs about the cheeks and temples, with a little sweet-oil; then to insert two tubes (oiled also) of pasteboard into the nostrils, so that breathing may be performed through them; a handkerchief is then to be tied loosely over the face, and the head sloped backward in an elbow chair or sofa. Powdered and calcined plaster of Paris is then mixed with spring water to the consistence of cream, and poured in between the face and handkerchief to the depth of half an inch. On becoming fixed or hard, it is removed and left to dry. When dried thoroughly it is well soaked with linseed-oil, and an impression may then be taken from it, in plaster of Paris or soft clay; the hollow cast being first split longitudinally down the nose, so that the object cast may be more easily removed.

It ought to be observed that all models should be divided into several pieces or joints; thus, in that covering any round body, one side must be covered first with the plaster, and the sides pared with a knife, and smeared with clay and water, then the remaining part of the object covered with plaster, and a joint will thus be formed between the two parts; for, wherever the mixture of clay and water has been applied with a hair brush, the cast will not adhere, and therefore will be easily separated with the blunt edge of a knife. It is usual also to make small pits or depressions of the size of small buttons, on the edges of the joints of molds, so that they may lock together well when added, and thus fit closely.

Plaster casts are varnished by a mixture of soap and white wax in boiling water. A quarter of an ounce of soap is dissolved in a pint of water, and an equal quantity of wax afterward incorporated. The cast is dipped in this liquid, and after drying a week is polished by rubbing with soft linen. The surface produced in this manner approaches to the polish of marble. When plaster casts are to be exposed to the weather, their durability is greatly increased by saturating them with linseed-oil, with which wax or rosin may be combined. When intended to resemble bronze, a soap is used made of linseed-oil and soda, colored by the sulphates of copper and iron. Walls and ceilings are rendered waterproof in the same way.

Cast, or **Casting-line,** a gut line used in angling, from two to four yards in length, having artificial flies attached to it at intervals of about two feet. For trout fishing the line is generally made of braided waterproof silk, and a leader of silkworm gut attached to the end of the line.

Cast Iron, Malleable. Malleable cast iron is a grade of metal which has a special composition, such that when annealed for a continued period of time, it becomes malleable, can be bent and twisted, and otherwise approaches a steel in character.

The castings, when taken from the sand of the foundry, are very hard and brittle. The fracture is dead white (the ordinary iron casting appearing gray to black when freshly broken).

The tensile strength of a good malleable casting should run between 42,000 and 48,000 pounds per square inch, though for ordinary purposes, 35,000 pounds is quite good enough. Castings have been made running up to 63,000 pounds per square inch, but these would be too stiff for general use, being better adapted to railroad work. The elongation of a malleable casting runs between 2.5 to 5 per cent measured in two inches. The transverse strength measured by a bar placed on supports 12 inches apart, and load applied at the centre, should be from 3,000 to 5,000 pounds for high quality material, and at least 2,500 for the ordinary product. The resilience of a malleable casting may be taken as eight times as high as a gray-iron one. Hence the great advantage of using malleable castings to resist shock. In fact where the shocks are light and often repeated, this casting will stand up better than a steel one.

The malleablization of cast iron has been known since the early part of the 18th century. The first record we have is by Réamur in 1722. He states that a hard casting, by being imbedded in ore and kept at a high temperature for a number of days, changed its structure, and became soft and malleable. The process as then practised is still in vogue, and all attempts to hasten or otherwise modify it have not given continuously good results.

The fundamental principle upon which the whole process rests is the conversion of the combined carbon in a white casting of a suitable composition to an amorphous form of carbon, which remains in the casting as a mechanical mixture. It is not crystalline like graphite, but in other respects behaves like it, and is determined chemically in the same manner.

To understand this, let us consider the two great divisions of cast iron — the Gray and the White. In the former we have nearly all the carbon present in a mechanical admixture, as graphite flakes situate between the crystals of the iron proper, and if less than 0.20 per cent., the casting is dead soft. If the combined carbon is as high as 0.80 per cent., the rest of about 3.00 per cent. being in the form of graphite, the casting will be a hard one. Now in the case of the white irons, the carbon is nearly all combined, and almost no graphite in mechanical admixture is present. Hence an exceedingly hard material is the result. It is the object of the malleablizing process to convert this chemically combined carbon in a white iron, or in a hard gray one for that matter, to an amorphous form, to which the name "temper carbon" has been given (from "temperguss," German for malleable casting). Any graphite present in the original casting is not changed, but with long-continued heat gives an opportunity for the entrance of oxygen, with ruinous results to the casting. Hence the short annealing of gray castings to benefit them, while the white casting can be annealed for six days, and then re-annealed again, without seriously hurting its strength.

There are two tendencies in the malleable casting industry, which result in different grades of metal. In Europe, from whence the process came, and where the irons used are not as pure, the annealing process is carried out longer than here, and hence much of the carbon present is removed from the casting by oxidizing it out. The result is a very ductile casting, but with a gray to white fracture (the fracture of a steel however, not of a hard white iron). The castings, moreover, are nearly all very light. In this country, with better irons, we have shortened the anneal to just get the conversion of the carbon, without attempting to burn it out by prolonged annealing, and hence we have a black heart in the casting. This is especially noticeable as we make very heavy work, comparatively speaking. Sections of one inch are common, and even heavier work is done, but with the use of chills in casting them, so that the carbon be surely all combined, and the casting dead white before the annealing is begun. Otherwise, if more than a slight mottling is present in the fracture, the casting is sure to come out "rotten" in strength (as it is called) when leaving the anneal. The temperature of the bath of molten metal has an important bearing on this, for with a very hot metal, heavy sections can be cast and still have their fracture white, while the same castings would be gray were the bath of melted metal colder.

The contraction of a white casting, as made for malleable purposes is 3/16″ to 5/16″ per foot, but in annealing one half of this is taken up by expansion, and hence the ordinary gray iron shrinkage is allowed for in making the patterns. For special work, however, it will pay to watch the action of the metal in the sand mold, and due allowances should be made in the pattern for abnormal contractions on the part of the casting, so that the dimensions of the annealed casting may come out all right.

As the metal when ready to pour may not always be at the desired temperature, let us take the temperature changes during the pour, going up steadily), it is best to pour the thin castings first, provided the iron be hot enough for this, then the medium weight castings, and finally the thick ones. By this time the metal will be very hot and the danger from excessive mottling avoided. If the iron is very hot in the first place it is still best to pour the lightest work first, then the heaviest, leaving the medium work for the last. Great care should be exercised to see that paterns are so proportioned that no shrinkage occurs in the interior of the metal. This is certain to take place at abrupt changes of section, at sharp angles, and in heavy parts. Hence all sharp junctions on patterns should have fillets, and where great changes of section cannot be avoided, chills should be placed against the work. This will send the shrinkage into the interior of the casting where it will not matter so much.

In general three things affect the state of a

hard casting which will allow it to anneal properly or not. First the chemical composition of the metal itself. Second the thickness of the sections of the casting, and third the pouring temperature. The last two items have been gone over above. It remains to give specifications for the first. The most powerful agent affecting the state of the carbon present in a casting is the silicon. As it is necessary to have a casting white in fracture as it leaves the sand, the silicon must be very low. Then with the proper pouring temperature, and when poured into sections suitable for the composition employed, the results will be good. Naturally this will principally depend upon the thickness of the work made, as this cannot be changed, and then upon the heat of the iron, which can be regulated by careful melting. The thinner the castings, the higher the silicon the mixture can stand. Thus for pipe fittings, the silicon may run up to 1.00 per cent. in the casting. For couplers, and other heavy railroad castings the silicon has to run down as low as .45 per cent in order to get the best results. When charcoal irons were used exclusively (these standing more punishment in melting than the coke irons of the present day), the silicon oftentimes ran as low as 0.28 per cent. in a casting and still this was first-rate. The general average, however, for all around medium and fairly heavy work is 0.65 per cent. silicon in the casting, which means about 0.85 per cent. to 0.90 per cent. in the mi ture. 0.45 per cent. may be considered the lowest range for heavy castings, and 1.00 per cent. the highest, for the lightest of castings.

The phosphorus should not exceed 0.225 per cent., the manganese not over 0.30, the sulphur as low as possible, preferably not over 0.05 in the casting, though in Europe, where the long anneal counteracts this evil, the sulphur goes very high, sometimes even up to 0.30 per cent.

The lower the total carbon, down to 2.75 below which trouble arises, the stronger will be the casting. Hence steel scrap is added to make the metal low in its carbon content. This is a much better plan than to refine the iron in the process to get the carbon low. In general it is best to simply melt a mixture, and then get it out of the furnace as quickly as possible, in order to get it away from oxidizing influences as quickly as may be. Five to 10 per cent. of steel may be added, also malleable scrap, if necessary. In a 10-ton heat the best proportion of the mixture is five tons of pig iron, one ton malleable scrap, 500 pounds steel scrap, and the balance the sprues of the previous work. The practical effect of these steel and other additions are about as follows: 100 pounds wrought iron scrap equal 250 pounds steel, equal 2,000 pounds malleable scrap. Mixtures thus arranged come out about the same in strength, all other things being equal.

Charcoal iron is now being used only where the source of supply is close, and its cost is but 50c. to a dollar over the best "Coke Malleable" or "Bessemer Malleable," as coke irons made specially for the malleable foundry are called (the last named being a Bessemer iron with the phosphorus a little higher than is allowed for steel). It is best to use these classes of "malleable" as pig irons, for they are made with an extra amount of coke, and are much less oxidized than the irons blown under high pressure and very hot blast.

The mixtures used in the malleable foundry are as follows: Where the cupola is used for malleable castings in addition to making pots for annealing, the regular mixture as used for the air furnace or open hearth furnace must be reduced slightly in silicon, as the cupola burns out less of this element. Hence about 0.25 per cent. is to be added to the amount of silicon required in the casting. In the case of the furnaces, about 0.30 per cent. to 0.35 per cent. must be added. For pots it is advisable to use good pig irons, and to utilize salamanders and the large scrap pieces that are unsafe to put into the furnace. The silicon in the pots as cast should be about 0.60 per cent., and hence about 0.85 per cent. should go into the cupola.

The mixtures for air furnace and the open hearth furnace are about the same. Possible the air furnace should have a little more silicon, as it is under the influence of the gases from co bustion longer. There is also necessary an occasional use of ferrosilicon, especially in the open hearth, as through accident, the metal may be badly burnt and the addition of ferrosilicon brings about the proper composition, though the metal should not be put into castings, but cast into pigs, to be fed subsequently into the regular mixtures in small quantities at a time. About 250 to 500 pounds ferrosilicon is usually all that is necessary for this purpose. The actual amount can be calculated at the time from the supposed loss of silicon in th bath.

Malleable castings are made in the cupola, the air furnace, the open hearth furnace, and in the crucible. The last named process is now only practiced in Europe, being too expensive in this country, though turning out a most excellent product. The cupola process makes the poorest castings, as the metal is in contact with the fuel in this method. Hence the absorption of sulphur, and oxidizing influences which are partly avoided in other processes. The peculiar constitution of the metal as cast makes it necessary to anneal it at a temperature some 200 to 300 degrees F. higher than ordinary air-furnace iron, which means a greater expense for wear and tear on the ovens and annealing pots. This class of castings is therefore only used for the cheaper grades of malleable castings, such as pipe fittings, and hardware castings, where great strength is not essential, and enough ductility is had to satisfy the demands made on the work. The selling price is also about half a cent a pound less than the high grade metal.

The bulk of the malleable castings made in this country come from the air furnace. This is an excellent melting process, can be manipulated easily, is not too expensive, and will probably continue to be the method used in most of our malleable works. The air furnace, as used for malleable purposes is somewhat different than that used for making rolls and gun castings. It is illustrated herewith.

The entire roof can be taken off in sections, called "bungs," so that the sand bottom can be made, and the charge put in. Where more

CAST IRON

than one heat is made without remaking the bottom, only a few bungs are lifted away after the first heat and the furnace is charged quickly, so as to keep it hot as long as possible. Firing is done at one end, and the charge when ready

work and burning or partly fusing it together. The layers are about one inch thick, and are repeated until the proper shape is made. It takes from four to five hours to melt a 10-ton heat after this is charged, depending upon the

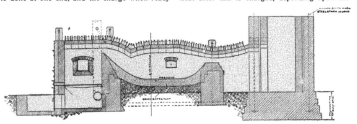

Fig. 1—Longitudinal Section of Air Furnace for Malleable Castings.

is tapped at one side, or both if two spouts are provided. It is very important to get a heat out

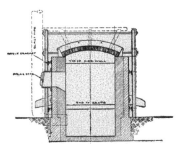

Fig. 2—Section Through Fire-Box of Air Furnace for Malleable Castings.

quickly, as the metal is continuously oxidizing while in the furnace, after it has reached the proper composition. A ten-ton heat, when poured into small castings often takes three quarters of an hour to tap, and hence the first iron and the very last may be two different things. Hence the dividing up of the work to get the class of metal best suited to the castings to be made. The amount of coal used to melt iron in a well constructed air furnace is four pounds iron to one pound coal. In the case of the cupola, while- ordinary gray iron practice requires one pound coal to every eight pounds iron, in malleable work, it takes one pound coke to only four pounds iron, or just the same as good air furnace practise. It is but just to say, however, that in many foundries of the country, the air furnaces are so poorly constructed that oftentimes one pound coal melts only two pounds iron.

Bottom is made placing layers of fire sand, that is sand with about 98 per cent. silica, and very free from fluxing impurities, on the brick-

quality of the bituminous coal used, and the construction of the furnace. From six to eight heats can be made on the same bottom, with but little repairing, but the usual run is from two to four. In order to know when the heat is ready, a test plug, so called, is cast. This plug is about of a diameter equal to the heaviest section of the castings to be made. It is about eight inches long, and the mold for it is made by simply pushing the pattern into the sand in a box. The metal is taken from the bath by a small ladle dipped into it as deeply as possible. After pouring, as soon as the iron is set, the plug is grasped with a tongs, is dipped into water to cool it, and then broken across. The fracture is observed, and if properly crystalline, and with but little or no mottling, the heat is ready to tap. If there is too much mottling, that is too much graphite left, the process is continued to burn out more silicon, and also get the metal hotter, and another test plug taken. Experience will tell just how long a heat still has to run until ready to tap. After the iron has melted, the slag is skimmed off, and this gives a good chance for refining action, with means the burning out of silicon. The test plug is always taken after skimming, which is often done for the second time. When the heat is tapped, the men take it off in hand ladles, and pour the molds, throwing the iron into them as quickly as possible so that the necessarily small gates do not prevent the metal from filling the molds by chilling and resulting in "short pours."

The open hearth process (See STEEL — CRUCIBLE PROCESS) is by far the best one in general use, but is confined to those works where great quantities are made year in and year out. Thus there are several works where about 80 tons of castings are made daily, and in which the use of the open hearth is a paying proposition, especially as the same furnace can be used for making acid steel heats in place of malleable cast iron, as desired. The fuel consumption for the open hearth corresponds to one pound coal for six pounds iron melted; showing a considerable economy over all other methods. The use of a gas producer system, however, where

CAST IRON

natural gas is not available, makes the installation an elaborate one, and not desirable where the proper class of help is not available.

In the case of the open hearth, the furnace is always hot, and hence a heat is finished about an hour sooner than in the air furnace. The iron gets hotter, and can be taken out in five ton ladles to be distributed afterwards and as the metal is not as long in contact with the gases as in the air furnace process, it is of better quality. The most economical size of furnace is the 20 ton, with the crane ladle to take off the metal in large quantities, so that tapping is not so long continued a matter as in the air furnace. The latest patented invention to assist in this is the application of two or more spouts to the furnace, so that metal may be taken out at different levels. In this way the surface of the bath, which is punished most by the gases, may be taken off first. Then while this is being poured off, the next part of the heat, now the top, is again taken off, and finally if three spouts are used, the bottom may be

the oven. In this way they will not be cracked before going into the annealing ovens. The modern tendency is to introduce the sand blast for cleaning, as this removes every particle of sand from the hard castings. Where the iron has been allowed to get too low in silicon, or "high" as it is called, in contradistinction to "low" iron, where the silicon is too high, and the metal mottled or even gray; the sand is apt to burn on so hard that the tumbling all day does not remove it all. Here the sand blast is excellent.

From the sorting room the castings go to the annealing room, or rather to a part of it in which the packing is done. To anneal the hard castings they are placed into so-called "saggers" or annealing pots. These are simple box like shells, with no bottom, about one inch thick, and say 18″x24″x15″ high. Three or four of these are placed over each other, and on a "stool" high enough to allow a free circulation of the gases under it. The castings are carefully placed in these pots and packed with "scale" in

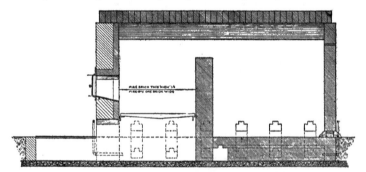

Fig. 3—Longitudinal Section Through Fire-Box of Annealing Oven for Malleable Castings.

taken out as long as half an hour afterwards without any deterioration or change in the metal.

From the foundry the castings, after shaking out the molds, go to the hard tumbling room, where they are freed from the adhering sand. This is done by means of tumbling barrels into which the castings, and a supply of "stars" made of the same hard iron, are placed. Where castings are liable to crack by this tumbling about, sticks of wood are introduced, so that as they strike them, no damage is done. Where delicate castings are made, these are pickled in dilute sulphuric or in hydrofluoric acid.

After cleaning the hard castings, they are carefully sorted out, the cracked or otherwise defective pieces thrown out, to go back into the furnace again, and the good ones are sent into the annealing room. Where castings are made which crack as soon as they cool, on account of their shape, such as the hand wheels or freight cars for braking purposes, these while still red hot in the sand, are taken into small ovens where they are kept quite hot for a time, and are then allowed to cool very slowly with

such a way that when red hot, the whole may not settle and warp the work. This scale is puddle scale, hammer scale, or even iron ore. For that matter, as the process is more of a conversion of the combined carbon into the "temper carbon" the castings can be packed in fire clay or sand and good results obtained. But the puddle scale seems to give the best results, with greatest cheapness. The flakes that fall from the annealing pots, these lasting only for 7 to 14 heats, can be crushed and make the finest kind of packing material, being pure oxide of iron, and no further scale than the initial lot need be purchased.

The pots, properly filled, are covered with a "mud" made of the sand rolled off the hard castings mixed with water. The joints of the pots are also carefully daubed up with this mud; the pots are introduced into the oven either run in by a special carriage in the old style ovens, or lowered in from the crane in the new ovens, the tops of which can be removed. The ovens are now fired and within 36 to 48 hours, the full temperature of 1,350 degrees F. in the coldest portion of the coldest pot is reached. This temperature is kept up preferably 60 hours, and the oven then allowed to cool slowly before the pots are withdrawn. The ovens are so constructed that they are heated inside and under the whole bottom, so that a difference of not more than 100 degrees F. throughout the portion filled with work may exist.

that all work from that heat can be traced and its quality known. The test bar has the further advantage of showing up the condition of the furnace, poor working on the part of which is immediately detected by a white rim on the casting.

The production of malleable castings in this country runs up to the enormous figure of 650,-

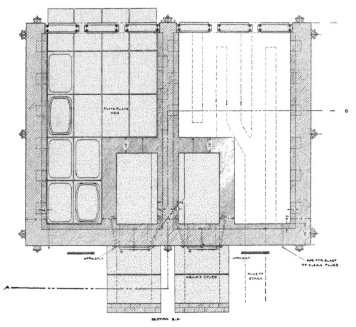

Fig. 4—Plan of Annealing Oven for Malleable Castings.

After the pots are taken out, they are dumped, the castings taken from the scale, and the former sent to the soft tumbling room. Here they are packed with small pieces of annealed mallable castings, or with wood and leather, such as old shoes, etc., so that the adhering scale is removed, and a fine coat of graphite is given them. They come out shining black, and can be shipped direct, or else coated with asphalt, as required. Sometimes the castings must be straightened, which should always be done cold, either by drop hammer or hydraulic press. Test plugs are usually cast on the important work, so that breaking these off on inspection, the quality of the metal in the particular casting is revealed at a glance. Test bars for physical test should also be taken off with the first and last portion of every heat, so

000 tons annually. In Europe about 50,000 tons are made in the same time. Most of the large companies now make steel castings in addition, as malleable cast iron though most excellent for shock, is not strong enough to stand under the terrific strains that are now put on the structures where this work is used. Thus the 100,000 lb. cars now require steel couplers, as the malleable ones tear apart, yet the latter will stand all the bumping that comes along, while steel will not. The principal use for malleable castings is for railroad work. Next comes agricultural machinery. After that a great variety of work, such as pipe fittings, hardware, machine parts, pistols, tools, etc. The demand is constantly growing, and while steel was supposed to be driving it out, this has not turned out to be so, but for every casting that must be made,

the proper material is sure to find its way in, and will eventually stay ther.

RICHARD MOLDENKE,
Specialist on Metallurgy of Cast Iron and Expert in Malleable Castings.

Cast Steel, blister steel which has been broken up, fused in a crucible, cast into ingots, and rolled. The process of making cast steel was invented by Banjamin Huntsman, of Attercliff, near Sheffield, in 1770. See STEEL — OPEN HEARTH MANUFACTURE; STEEL — THE BESSEMER PROCESS; STEEL — ELECTRICAL PROCESSES OF MANUFACTURE; STEEL — MANUFACTURE OF CRUCIBLE; STEEL — SPECIAL OR ALLOY STEELS.

Castagno, Andrea del, än-drä'ä děl käs-tän'yō, Italian painter: b. Castagno, Tuscany, about the end of the 14th or beginning of the 15th century; d. 1480. Being early deprived of his parents, who were extremely poor, he was employed by his uncle to tend cattle in the fields, and in that situation, by his surprising and untutored essays in the art, attracted the notice of Bernardetto de Medici, who placed him under the tuition of one of the best masters Florence then afforded. At first he painted only in distemper and fresco, and was in high repute when Florence was visited by Domenico Veneziano, who had learned from Antonello da Messina the new method of painting in oil and varnish, till then unknown in Tuscany. The splendor of this mode of coloring was much admired, and by a pretended friendship for Domenico, Castagno obtained his secret; but not satisfied with this he desired to be the sole possessor, and determined to murder his friend and benefactor. This he effected without any suspicion, and continued to practise his ill-acquired art with great success. The real author of this atrocious act was never discovered until Andrea made a full confession of his guilt shortly before his death. The best of his remaining works are at Florence, in the church of St. Lucia de Magnuoli, and in the monastery Degli Angeli. The latter contains a crucifixion by him painted on a wall.

Castaigne, André, än-drä käs-tän, French artist: b. Angoulême 1861. He studied at the Suisse Academy and at the École des Beaux Arts in Paris; he exhibited at the Paris Salon in 1884 and several times in later years. Among his pictures are 'Dante and Beatrice'; 'The Deluge'; 'Portrait of Vicomte de Dampierre'; and 'After the Combat' (in the Peabody Gallery at Baltimore). In 1890 he came to the United States and remained here until 1895. He was director of an art school in Baltimore and in 1891 began the illustrating work by which he is best known to the American public. His first work of this character was 'The Forty Niners' Ball' in the 'Century Magazine' for May 1891; since then he has illustrated for several of the leading magazines; his designs include the pictures of the Texas cowboys in 'Scribner's Magazine' and the World's Fair drawings and illustrations for 'Polly' in the 'Century.' On his return to France he became instructor in the Colarossi Academy and opened a studio in Paris. See 'The Critic' Vol. XXIII., 57; 'The Bookbuyer' XII., 506.

Casta'lia, a celebrated fountain in Greece, the sacred spring of the Delphic oracle, at which all the pilgrims to Apollo's shrine were obliged to purify themselves. It issues from a fissure between two peaked cliffs, which form the summit of a semicircular range of rocks, anciently called the Phædriades. These immediately adjoin Mount Parnassus, and rise to the height of 2,000 feet. The Castalian spring was said to impart poetic inspiration to those who drank of it, but it was only latterly by the Roman poets that it was invested with this tribute. It is now called the Fountain of St. John, from a small chapel dedicated to St. John which stands near its source.

Castalides, käs-täl'ĭ-dēz, the Muses, so called from the fountain Castalia, at the foot of Parnassus.

Castalio, Sébastien, sä-bäs-tē-ôn käs-täl-yō, French theologian: b. Dauphiny 1515; d. Basel 20 Dec. 1563. His original name was Châteillon. Through the influence of Calvin he was made professor of classical literature at Geneva. Having quarreled with the reformer, who caused his banishment in 1544, he repaired to Basel, where he taught the Greek language; but as his stipend did not suffice to support his numerous family, he was compelled to employ part of his time in agricultural labors. He made a Latin translation of the Bible, the best edition of which is in folio, Basel, 1573. He defended the right of free discussion in a collection of maxims compiled from various sources.

Casta'nea, a trade name for the Brazilnut and the genuine name for the chestnut (qq.v.).

Cas'tanets, small wooden rattles, made in the shape of two bowls or cups, fitted together and tied by a string, and then fastened to the thumbs. The fingers being rapidly struck upon them, a tremulous sound is produced, which marks exactly the measure of the dance. Something similar to this was the *krotalon* of the ancients, who also made use of small cymbals in their dances and festivals in honor of Bacchus. It is probable, however, that they had their origin in the East, and were brought by the Moors into Spain. Here, too, they received their name *castañuelas*, from being commonly made of the wood of the chestnut (*castaño*), or from their color. They are still in use in Spain, and here and there in the south of France. The charm of variety has also procured for them a place in ballets and operas.

Castanheda, Fernao Lopez de, fĕr-nä'o lō'-thĕs'kō Hä-vē-är' dä käs-tän-yä'dä, Portuguese historian: b. Santarem about 1500; d. Coimbra 23 March 1559. His father having been appointed to an important post in India, he was taken thither in youth, and was thus led to make the careful and unremitting researches embodied in the 'History of the Discovery and Conquest of India by the Portuguese' (1551–61), a work upon which Camoens drew largely in the course of his epic activity.

Castaños, Don Francisco Xavier de, frän-thĕs'kō Hä-vē-är' dä käs-tä'ñōs, Duke of Baylen, Spanish military officer: b. Madrid 22 April 1756; d. Madrid 24 Sept. 1852. Educated in military science in Germany, on the invasion of the country by Napoleon, he received the command of a division of the Spanish army, and in July 1808 compelled 18,000 French, under Gen. Dupont de l'Etang, to surrender at Baylen, but was in turn defeated by

Lannes in November of the same year at Tudela.
Under Wellington he served as general of the
4th Spanish *corps d'armée*, and took part in
the battles of Albuera, Salamanca, and Vittoria.
In 1815 he was placed at the head of the Spanish army for the invasion of France, which was
rendered unnecessary by the victory at Waterloo. In 1825 he was called to the State Council,
where he became a decided opponent of the
Carlist party.

Caste, a social class whose burdens and
privileges are hereditary. The word is from.the
Portuguese *casta,* race, and was applied by the
Portuguese, who became familiar with Hindustan, to the classes in India whose occupations,
privileges, and duties are hereditary. This term
is sometimes applied to the hereditary classes
in Europe; and we speak of the spirit or the
prerogatives and usurpations of a caste, to express particularly that peculiar constitution of
society which makes distinction dependent on
the accidents of birth or fortune. The division
into castes, where it appears in its most typical
form, comes to us from a period to which
the light of history does not extend; hence its
origin cannot be clearly traced: but it is highly
probable that wherever it exists it was originally
grounded on a difference of descent and in
modes of living, and that the separate castes
were originally separate races of people. This
institution has been found among many nations.
According to the accounts collected by Clavigero, some traces of it were apparent among the
Peruvians and Mexicans; but it prevails principally in the East, where it has existed from
the earliest times, and has become blended with
the political condition of the people. The division into castes was entirely interwoven in the
whole fabric of civil society, in ancient Egypt
and India. In Egypt this division was perfected
as a political institution in the flourishing period
of the Pharoahs; and the lines of separation
which had been drawn in earlier times by a
difference of descent and different modes of
living were then rendered still more distinct.
The number of castes in that country is variously
stated by Herodotus, Plato, Diodorus, and Strabo. The institution of caste, however, is best
known to us as it exists in Hindustan, where
it is well known to have existed since perhaps
1,500 or 2,000 years before the Christian era.
The great Indian castes are four in number,
namely, the Brahmans or sacerdotal class; the
Kshatriyas or military class; the Vaisyas or
mercantile class; and the Sudras or servile class.
The three castes first named are regarded as
being altogether of a higher character than the
fourth, rejoicing in the peculiar religious distinction of being "twice-born" as contrasted
with the "once-born" Sudras. This distinction
is undoubtedly ethnical in its origin, the twice-
born castes being descendants of the Aryan
invaders and conquerors of the country, while
the once-born are the representatives of the conquered. Caste, however, is a much more complicated thing than would be supposed from this
brief statement, since the principle of caste classification according to employment as well as to
race has long prevailed, and from early times
there has been an intricate mingling of castes.
The Brahmans are the sacerdotal caste, but, according to Sir W. W. Hunter ('The Indian Empire,' 2d edition, 1893), "Even among the Brahmans, whose pride of race and continuity of
VOL. 3 — 55

tradition should render them the firmest ethnical
unit among the Indian castes, classification by
employment and by geographical situation, plays
a very important part; and the Brahmans, so
far from being a compact unit, are made up of
several hundred castes, who cannot inter-marry
nor eat food cooked by each other. . . . In
many parts of India, Brahmans may be found
earning their livelihood as porters, shepherds,
cultivators, potters, and fishermen, side by side
with others who would rather starve, and see
their wives and little ones die of hunger, than
demean themselves to manual labor, or allow
food prepared by a man of inferior caste to
pass their lips." Altogether some 1,886 separate Brahmanical tribes have been enumerated.
and the Kshatriyas or Rajputs now number 590
tribes in different parts of India. "In many
outlying provinces we see non-Aryan chiefs and
warlike tribes turn into Aryan Rájputs before
our eyes. Well-known legends have been handed down of large bodies of aliens being incorporated from time to time even into the Brahman caste." While there has been a tendency in
the different provinces for every separate employment to develop into a distinct caste, there
are also instances of castes changing their employment and raising themselves in the social
scale. Thus the Vaisyas, who were anciently
that Aryan caste upon whom the tillage of the
soil fell, have become the merchants and bankers of India, leaving to the Sudras and mixed
castes the labor of cultivation. "Each caste is
to some extent a trade-guild, a mutual assurance society, and a religious sect. As a trade
union it insists on the proper training of the
youth of its craft, regulates the wages of its
members, deals with trade delinquents, supplies
courts of arbitration, and promotes good fellowship by social gatherings. . . . The caste
or guild exercises a surveillance over each of its
members, from the close of childhood until
death. If a man behaves well he will rise to an
honored place in his caste; and the desire for
such local distinctions exercises an important
influence in the life of a Hindu. But the caste
has its punishments as well as its rewards. The
fine usually takes the form of a compulsory feast
to the male members of the caste. This is the
ordinary means of purification or of making
amends for breaches of the caste code." A person who has become an "out-caste," or lost his
caste position and privileges, may generally recover them in this way.

Castel Nuovo, käs'tĕl nwŏ'vŏ, or **Novo,**
Austria, a town and commune of Dalmatia, in
the circle of Cattaro. It stands near the entrance
to the Gulf of Cattaro, and is surrounded by
walls which have suffered much from repeated
sieges and earthquakes. It contains two
churches, a Roman Catholic and a Greek; a
lazaretto, and custom-house. The chief manufacture is in articles of brass. The country
around is beautiful and fertile. The population
of the town is small, but that of the commune
is about 10,000, most of whom belong to the
Greek Church.

Castel Vetrano, käs'tĕl vä-trä'nō, Sicily, a
town in the province and 27 miles southeast of
Trapani, on a rocky hill. It lies in a fertile
district, is regularly built, has several churches,
grammar school, with municipal museum, etc.
The white wine produced in the neighborhood

is esteemed the best in Sicily. Articles of coral and alabaster are manufactured here. Pop. (estimated) 25,000.

Castelar, käs tä lär, Emilio, Spanish statesman: b. Cadiz 8 Sept. 1832; d. Murcia 25 May 1899. He studied at Madrid, and in 1856 became professor of history and philosophy in the university there. He began early to write on letters and politics in the newspapers and magazines, and in 1864 started *La Democracia (The Democrat)*, in the pages of which he inveighed fiercely against the government. After the abortive rising of 1866 he was condemned to death, but contrived to escape to Paris, returning when the revolution of 1868 began. All his ardor and eloquence could not hinder the crowning of King Amadeus, though it helped to bring about his downfall in 1873. In September of that year the Cortes made Castelár dictator, but the orator proved somewhat ineffectual in action, and found himself unable to crush either the "red demagogy of Socialism on the one hand, or the white demagogy of Carlism" on the other. In the beginning of 1874 a hostile vote in the Cortes obliged him to resign, and soon after the *pronunciamiento* in favor of Alfonso XII. drove him across the frontier. He returned to Spain in 1876, and was returned to the Cortes, where, till his retirement in 1893, he often spoke with all his old eloquence. His chief writings are: 'Civilization' (2d ed. 1865); 'Questions, Political and Social' (3 vols. 1870); 'Parliamentary Discussion' (3 vols. 1871); 'History of the Republican Movement in Europe' (2 vols. 1874); 'The Oriental Question' (1876).

Castelein, Matthiis de, mä-tē'ïs dĕ käs'tē-lïn, Dutch poet: b. Pamele (Oudenarde) 1485; d. 1550. He was the acknowledged lawgiver and pattern of all the Dutch rhetoricians of his time, in his 'Art of Rhetoric.' He composed many plays, two of them were published; one of these is the 'Story of Pyramus and Thisbe.' He wrote also 'Ballads' and a volume of 'Various Lays,' in melodious verse.

Castellamare, käs-tĕl-lä-mä'rĕ, or Castel-lammare, Italy, a seaport town on the Gulf of Naples, 17 miles southeast of the city, at the beginning of the peninsula of Sorrento, and 10 miles northeast of that town. It extends for a mile along the shore at the base and on the slope of a spur of Monte Sant' Angelo (4,735 feet high), a mountain which commands a splendid prospect. From its pleasant surroundings, it is a favorite summer resort of the Neapolitans, as well as tourists, and has several good hotels, one of them formerly a royal residence. The harbor is protected by a mole, and there is an arsenal with a dockyard. The town owes its name to a castle built by the Emperor Frederick II. in the 13th century. Castellamare occupies the site of the ancient Stabiæ, overwhelmed, with Herculaneum and Pompeii, by an eruption of Vesuvius, 79 A.D.; and it was here that the elder Pliny met his death by approaching too near the mountain while it was in a state of eruption. The modern town was afterward built from the ruins of Stabiæ. Pop. about 33,000.

Cas'tellan, or Chatelain, properly the owner or commander of a castle. In Flanders and France the title went with the possession of certain districts, and in Normandy and Bur-

gundy châtelains ranked next after bailiffs, with both civil and military authority. In Germany the châtelains were imperial officers with military and civil jurisdiction in fortified places.

Castellane, Esprit Victor Elizabeth Boniface, és-prĕ vĕk-tōr ä-lē-zä-bĕt bŏn-ĭ-fäs, COUNT OF, French marshal: b. Lyons 1788; d. 1862. He entered the army in 1804, and took part in most of Napoleon's campaigns. After the restoration he became colonel of the Hussars of the Royal Guard. He fought in Spain (1823), and at the siege of Antwerp (1832), and as lieutenant-general commanded the Army of the Pyrenees. In the February revolution (1848), he lost his command, and in consequence went over to Louis Napoleon. In 1850 he became commander at Lyons, and in 1852 marshal and senator. His 'Memoirs,' published in 1896, though crude in style, are valuable for their mass of minute detail.

Castelli, Benedetto, bä nä dĕt'tō käs-tĕl'lē, a pupil of Galileo: b. Brescia 1577; d. 1644. He was a monk and became abbot of a Benedictine monastery of the congregation of Monte Cassino. He afterward became a professor of mathematics, and taught with distinguished success both at the University of Pisa and at the Collegio della Sapienza at Rome. Torricelli was his pupil. He distinguished himself in hydraulics, and rendered important services to Urban VIII. in his projects for the regulation of Italian rivers. He may be regarded as the founder of that branch of hydraulics which relates to the velocity of running water, though his fundamental principle, that the velocity is proportional to the height of the reservoir, is inaccurate, and was demonstrated to be so by Torricelli, who showed that the velocity is proportioned, not to the height, but to the square root of the height. In his investigations as to the measurement of time Castelli made use of the pendulum. His principal work, entitled 'Della Misura dell' Acque Correnti,' published at Rome in 1628, was translated into French in 1664.

Castelli, Ignaz Franz, Austrian dramatist: b. Vienna 6 May 1781; d. there 5 Feb. 1862. He was educated for the law, but following his inclination for the drama, gained access to the orchestras of theatres aṣ a player of the violin. His circumstances compelling him to look out for some means of support, he accepted various subordinate offices, but using his leisure in composing patriotic songs for the Austrian army, he was brought into favorable notice. His songs having given umbrage to Napoleon, he fled to Hungary. In 1815 he accompanied Count Cavriani as secretary to Paris, and afterward he served in the same capacity with Baron Münch von Bellinghausen in Upper Italy. In 1840 he retired with a pension and the office of state librarian. The author of many poems, popular songs, and miscellaneous writings, he was at various times connected with the press of Vienna, but is best known by his voluminous productions for the stage. Over 100 plays, partly adapted from the French, partly original, are attributed to him. In 1848, more than 100,000 copies of his political pamphlets in favor of the Revolution found eager purchasers.

Castellio, käs-tĕl-lĭ-ō, Sebastianus, French theologian and humanist, translator of the Bible into pure and classic Latin: he was a native of

Dauphiny: b. 1515; d. Basel 1563, in exile and in extreme poverty. His family name was Châteillon, which he latinized after the fashion of that time into Castellio. At the invitation of Calvin he settled at Geneva, where he became professor of the ancient classic literatures, but because of differences regarding questions of religious belief he was deposed from the professorship and banished from Geneva. His Latin version of the Bible retained little or nothing of the profoundly Hebrew character of the scriptural writings, and was justly censured by Calvin and the Calvinists. Theodore Beza, to offset this "work of Satan," as he called it, made a Latin translation of the Bible himself, striving to retain the Oriental flavor of the original in every respect. Castellio also wrote a book in defense of the right to hold and publish views deemed by Church and state to be heretical; this, too, evoked a reply from Beza. Castellio wrote also a tractate on 'Predestination Opposed to the Views of Calvin'; it was published after the author's death by Faustus Socinus in 1578.

Castello, käs-tĕl'lō, Gabriel Lancelot, Italian antiquary: b. Palermo 1727; d. 1794. He was descended from a noble family, and was placed under a private tutor with a view to study botany, chemistry, etc.; but accidentally meeting with some old coins which had been dug up by a plowman, he was seized with a great desire to decipher them, and from that time devoted himself to antiquarian pursuits. He formed a splendid collection of the remains of antiquity found in Sicily, and his museum was always open to foreigners as well as to natives. On his death-bed he bequeathed a large quantity of books, etc., to the public library of Palermo. At his death he was honorary member of the Royal Society and of the Academy at Paris. He published several works.

Castello-Branco, Camillo, kä-mĕl'lō kästĕl'lō brän'kō, Portuguese novelist and poet: b. Lisbon 16 March 1826; d. 6 June 1890. He is the most popular of the modern romancists of Portugal, and at the same time the most national in tone, spirit, and form. Realism characterizes his numerous novels (over 100), the best known being: 'Love of Perdition' (1862); 'The Marquis of Torres Novas'; 'Brilliants from Brazil.' All of them are genuine pictures of Portuguese life. Among his poetic compositions, the collection published under the title, 'A Book' (1854), holds the first place.

Castellon, Francisco, frän-chĕs'kō käs-tĕl-yōn', Nicaraguan revolutionist: b. about 1815; d. 2 Sept. 1855. He was the leader in a revolt at Leon in 1853, which was unsuccessful, and fled to Honduras, whence he returned in June of the next year. It was by his invitation that the filibustering expedition under William Walker went from the United States in 1854.

Castellon de la Plana, dä lä plä'nä, Spain, capital of the province of Castellon, 40 miles north-northeast of Valencia. It stands in a large and fertile plain, watered by the Mijares, from which an ample supply of water is brought into the town by an aqueduct supposed to have been constructed by Jayme I. of Aragon, who, in 1233, wrested Castellon from the Moors. It is well built, and has considerable manufactures of sailcloth, and woolen and hempen fabrics, ropes, paper, soap, etc., and some trade in hemp, grain, and fruit. The painters Ribalta, father

and son, were born here. Pop. of town 31,272; of province, 304,477.

Castelnau, käs-tĕl-now, Francis (COMTE), French traveler: b. London 1812; d. Melbourne, Victoria, 4 Feb. 1880. He traveled extensively in Canada, the United States, and Mexico, and under the protection of the French government undertook an exploration of South America in 1843, accompanied by D'Osery, a botanist; Weddell, a botanist; and Deville, a taxidermist. After his return to France, in 1847, Count Castelnau published 'Expedition dans les parties centrales de l'Amerique du Sud' (1850–1), a work in six volumes, of which one was by M. Weddell. Castelnau afterward traveled in Arabia, and was successively consul at Bahia, the Cape of Good Hope, and Singapore, and at the time of his death was consul-general at Melbourne.

Castelnaudary, käs-tĕl-nō-dä-rē, France, a town in the department of Aude, on a height above the Canal du Midi, 22 miles westnorthwest of Carcassonne. It was built by the Visigoths on the site of a rich town which had been destroyed, and was named Castellum Novum Arianorum, from which its present name is corrupted. It rises in the form of an amphitheatre, and was anciently the capital of a district, and strongly fortified. It was the scene of much barbarity by the inquisitors in 1237, was almost totally destroyed by Edward the Black Prince in 1355, and is famous for the battle fought beneath its walls in 1632 between the troops of Louis XIII. and those of Gaston of Orleans, which resulted in favor of Louis chiefly in consequence of the inactivity of the Duke of Orleans. The Duke of Montmorency was wounded in this battle and taken prisoner, and afterward executed at Toulouse by order of the king, Louis XIII. It is indifferently built, but has manufactures of coarse cloth, several distilleries and tanneries, and one of the largest grain and flour markets in the south of France. Pop. about 10,000.

Castelnovo, Leo di, lä'ō dē käs-tĕl-nō'vō. See PULLE, LEOPOLDO, COUNT.

Castelnuovo, Enrico, ĕn-rē'cō käs-tĕl nwō vō, Italian novelist: b. Florence 1839. His stories have attained great popularity; among them: 'Prof. Romualdo' (1878); 'Two Conventions' (1885); 'Reminiscences and Fancies' (1886). He is one of the acknowledged Italian masters of the "novel of the inner life" (romano intimo).

Castelvecchio, Riccardo, rē-cär'dō käs tĕl vĕk'ē-ō. See PULLE, GIULIO, COUNT.

Casti, Giambatista, jäm-bä-tēs'tä käs'tē, Italian poet: b. Prato, in the vicinity of Florence, 1721; d. 7 Feb. 1803. He studied at Montefiascone, became professor there, was appointed a canon, and made a journey to France. Receiving an invitation from the Prince of Rosenberg, who became acquainted with him in Florence, he went to Vienna, and was presented to Joseph II., who knew how to appreciate the genius of the poet, and delighted in his conversation. Casti took advantage of every opportunity of visiting other courts, and joined several embassies without office or title. Catherine II. received him in the most flattering manner. He visited also the court of Berlin, and several other German courts. After his return to Vienna, Prince Rosenberg, the director of the Imperial Theatre, caused him to be appointed *poeta Cesareo* on the death of Metastasio. After the death of Joseph II. Casti requested his dismission, and retired to Florence, where he wrote many of his works. In 1783 he went to Paris. His 'Novelle Galanti' were republished at Paris 1804, under the title 'Novelle di Giamb. Casti,' in three volumes. They are 48 in number. Almost all are of a licentious character, but written in a lively, original, and graceful style. The same may be said of his didactic-satirical poem, 'Gli Animali Parlanti, Poema Epico di Giamb. Casti' (Milan 1802, 5 vols.). There are translations of it in French, German, and English. Casti's 'Rime Anacreontiche' are pleasing, and his comic operas, 'La Grotta di Trofonio' and 'Il Re Teodoro in Venezia,' etc., are full of wit and originality.

Castiglione, Baldassare, bäl-däs-sä'rä käs-tēl-yō'nä, Italian writer: b. Casatico, in the territory of Mantua, 1478; d. 8 Feb. 1529. He studied at Milan, and entered into the services of the Duke Ludovico Sforza, and afterward of the Duke of Urbino, of whose elegant and splendid court he soon became an ornament. By him he was sent as an envoy to Henry VII. of England, and afterward in the same capacity to Louis XII., at Milan. In 1513 Castiglione appeared as ambassador at the court of Leo X., where he became intimate with the most distinguished literati and artists. In 1521 he obtained for the new Duke of Urbino, Federigo, the command of the Papal troops, and in 1524 was employed by Pope Clement VII. to conduct his negotiations with Charles V. When Rome was plundered by the Constable of Bourbon in 1527 he was accused of negligence, and his health was undermined by chagrin. He refused to accept the rich bishopric of Avila, which was offered to him by the emperor, until the Pope should be reconciled with Charles. Among his works, the 'Libro del Cortegiano' is the most celebrated. It teaches the art of succeeding at court. His few Italian and Latin poems are elegant. His letters are valuable contributions to political and literary history.

Castiglione, Carlo Ottavio, COUNT, Italian scholar: b. Milan 1784; d. Genoa 10 April 1849. His *magnum opus*, published in 1826, is a work in which he seeks to ascertain the origin and the history of the towns in Barbary whose names are found on Arabic coins. Out of Italy, however, he is best known by his edition of some fragments of the Mœso-Gothic translation of the Bible by Ulfilas, which had been discovered in 1817 by Cardinal Mai among the palimpsests of the Ambrosian Library.

Castiglione, Giovanni Benedetto, jō vän nē bä-nä-dět'tō, Italian painter: b. Genoa 1616; d. 1670. He was a pupil of Paggi, Ferrari, and Antony van Dyck, studied at Rome, Florence, Parma, and Venice, and formed his style on the best masters. He is particularly celebrated as a painter of animals, and in these subjects, as well as his other paintings, is remarkable for softness, elegance, and beauty. Of his larger pieces, the most celebrated are the 'Creation of the Beasts,' 'Their Entrance with Noah into the Ark,' and 'Jacob's Return with His Family and Servants, His Flocks, and Herds'—all in the Brignol Palace. He also

distinguished himself as an engraver, and from his skill in the production of light and shade has been called the second Rembrandt.

Castiglione Del Stiviere, děl stěv-yä'rä, Italy, a small city in the province of Mantua, 17 miles southeast of the town of Brescia, 22 miles northwest of Mantua. It is well built, surrounded by walls, defended by an ancient castle, and contains a large square adorned with a central fountain, three churches, and a town hall. A well-attended annual fair is held in June. The French obtained here a decisive victory over the Austrians on 5 Aug. 1796, which gave to Marshal Augereau his title of Duc de Castiglione.

Castile, New. See NEW CASTILE.

Castilho, Antonio Feliciano, än-to'nē-ō fä-lě-chē-ä'nō käs-tēl'yō, Portuguese poet: b. Lisbon 26 Jan. 1800; d. 18 June 1875. Though almost blind, he studied jurisprudence at Coimbra. His first poetical composition, 'Letters of Echo and Narcissus,' published while he was a student, won him great celebrity. He excelled in pastorals; and to this class belong his 'Spring' and 'Love and Melancholy, or the Latest Heloïse.' He had a deep sympathy with nature, and was a master of elegiac verse.

Castilla, käs-tēl'yä, **Ramon,** Peruvian soldier and politician: b. Tarapaca 30 Aug. 1796; d. there 30 May 1867. He served in the Spanish cavalry until 1821, when Gen. San Martin proclaimed Peruvian independence. Castilla, then a lieutenant, joined the liberating army, in which he distinguished himself. He was elected president of Peru in 1845. At the expiration of his term of office, in 1851, he was succeeded by Gen. José Rufino Echénique, but usurped the power in 1855, and was, by a majority of 70,374 votes, re-elected to the presidency in August 1858. After being succeeded by San Roman in 1862, Castilla lived in retirement till his appointment to the presidency of the senate in 1865.

Castillejo, käs-tēl-yä'hō, **Christoval de,** Spanish poet, the last representative of the ancient Spanish poetry: b. Cindad Rodrigo about 1494; d. Vienna 12 June 1556. He opposed the introduction of Italian styles into the poetry of Spain, and justified his opposition by demonstrating in his own work the competence of the traditional styles of Spain for the expression of all moods and all sentiments. His satiric vein, especially in the 'Dialogue on the Condition of Women' and the 'Sermon on Loves,' offended both clergy and laity.

Castilloa Elastica, a lofty forest-tree, belonging to the Bread-fruits (*Artocarpeæ*). Some specimens have near the ground a circumference of from 10 to 12 feet. The tree is native to southern Mexico and the Central American countries, and supplies the Central American rubber of commerce. This rubber, instead of being molded, as is Para rubber, made into sheets (hence called sheet-rubber), and hung up to dry. *Castilloa elastica* has been found to be cultivable in India and Ceylon.

Castillon, käs-tē-yōn, France, a town in the department of Gironde, on the right bank of the Dordogne, 33 miles east of Bordeaux by rail. Beneath its walls, on 13 June 1453, the English met with a signal defeat, their leader, Earl Talbot of Shrewsbury, and his son, being slain. Part of the battle is described in the fourth act of Shakespeare's 'King Henry VI., Part I.'

Castine, Vincent, văṅ-sŏṅ käs-tĕn, BARON DE, French soldier: b. Oleron 1650; d. 1722. He went to Canada in 1665, established a mercantile house at Penobscot (now the town and port of entry of Castine, Me.), in 1687, and married the daughter of the Penobscot chief. In 1696 he captured Pemaquid, at the head of 200 Indians. He assisted in the defense of Fort Royal, in 1706, and was there wounded the following year. His son, who succeeded him in command of the Penobscots, was made prisoner and taken to Boston in 1721.

Casting, the running of melted metal into a mold, so as to produce an object in metal having the shape of the mold. Iron-casting or iron-founding is carried on by three methods, the first called "open sand-casting," the second, "sand-casting between flasks," and the third, "loam-casting." In most of these an exact pattern, usually of wood, is employed by the founder. The floor of every foundry is composed, for several feet deep, of a loamy sand, in which deep pits may be sunk to bury large molds. This floor must be kept exceedingly dry, and free from any wet or moisture, otherwise the melted matter, converting the watery particles into vapor, would blow up the building and destroy the workmen. In the place where the mold is to be made, a layer of sand is lightly sprinkled through a sieve on the floor, and the wooden pattern pressed firmly down into it, level with the surface. The sand is then to be shoveled up all around, level with the top of the pattern, and rammed down with a tool. A moist sponge is then used for slightly wetting the sand all round the edges of the pattern, to make its particles adhere together. The next operation is lifting the pattern out of the sand by one or more screws, screwed into the wood. If the pattern is small, this can be easily done by one or more men; but in very large works it is effected by a crane. The workman then uses a pair of bellows for blowing away any small pieces of sand which may have fallen into the mold, and then sifts some finely powdered charcoal over its surface. It is now ready for filling with metal. In small works this is done by ladles and in large by small channels made in the sand, leading from the mold to the mouth of the furnace. When the mold is filled, the hot metal is covered with sand to keep the air from it while it is cooling.

Sand-casting between flasks is used for more complex articles than the former; such, for instance, as if they were cut into two or more pieces (provided the cutting planes were parallel to each other), each separate piece might be cast in open sand. The flasks are iron frames furnished with four handles, by which they may be lifted, and having iron points fitting into holes prepared in the other flask for joining them accurately together. The under flask being placed upon a board, filled with sand, and the sand rammed tight into it, the workman then takes the pattern and presses one half of it into the sand, and smooths the sand up to the sides of it with a trowel; he then sets the empty flask over the other, adjusting its points to the holes, and after sprinkling some sand which has been burned (to free it from moisture) over the sand in the under flask, he fills the upper one with sand, and rams it down; he next, with a piece of wood, put through the sand in the upper

flask, makes a hole to pour the metal through. The upper flask, with the sand in it, is then raised off by men by the handles, or in large works by a crane, and the pattern lifted out. The flask is then put on again, and heavy weights laid upon it to keep it down ready for casting. It must be observed that at every uppermost point of large molds a small hole must be bored through the sand in the upper flask, to allow the rarefied air to escape out of the mold when melted metal is poured in. To save expense it is now customary to make flasks of any size that may be wanted, out of rectangular iron plates, which are fitted together by means of screws and bolts. This obviates the necessity of keeping a large store of flasks of different sizes, and enables the caster to adapt the form of the flask to that of the model for which it is intended.

Loam-casting is used for bulky, hollow articles, such as cylinders, large pipes, caldrons, boilers, etc., and is conducted in this manner: If, for instance, a large cylinder is to be cast, a mold has first to be made as follows: To a beam in the roof of the foundry is affixed a perpendicular spindle, with three or four holes through it to fix an iron arm in, at different heights, by means of a nut. This arm has two bars placed at such a distance as to be capable of receiving a wooden plank, which can be firmly secured to them by means of two clamps. The operation is then begun by laying an iron ring upon the ground, and adjusting it so as to be concentric to the spindle. A cylinder of brickbats, or clay and wet loam (instead of mortar), is then built upon it, some inches less in diameter than the intended cylinder, for which this is to form a core; the brickbats are then firmly bound together with iron hoops, annealed wire, etc., and a fire is lighted within the erection to dry it. When the loam used between the bricks is dry, a coating of loam is spread over the whole, and is perfectly smoothed by causing the edge of the perpendicular board to revolve round it. This coat makes it of the proper size for the inside of the cylinder to be cast, and is called the core of the mold. Another cylinder is built, plastered, and smoothed in the same way (except that no hoops are used), whose diameter is the same as the outside of the cylinder to be cast. When this is finished it is covered with a coating of charcoal, ground up with water like paint, laid on with a brush, and a thin coating of loam is laid on; this is bound round with hoops, and to these four hooks are fixed to lift it by; a thick coat of loam and hair is then laid over it. When all these are dry a man gets down into the cylinder, and with a small pick pulls down all the bricks in the inside cylinder, and then with a trowel cuts away all the loam, leaving the inside of the external cylinder (which is called the mold) quite smooth. This is effected by the coating of powdered charcoal, which prevents the two coats of loam from adhering. A deep pit is now dug in some convenient part of the foundry, into which the core is let down by a crane. The core being placed in the pit, the mold is let down after it by the same means; and when they are adjusted, the sand is thrown and rammed round about half the height; a flat cover of dried loam is then put on the top of the mold and core, and round pieces of wood are put in the holes which had before been made in the cover for pouring the metal in. The burying of the mold is then completed. When it is all leveled, the sticks which keep open the holes for the metal are carefully withdrawn, and small channels made from the furnace to allow the melted iron to find its way to the mold. When the form is more complicated, as in pearlike shapes, etc., where a man cannot be introduced to pick out the bricks, the mold must be sawn in two perpendicularly with a fine saw to get it off. It is then put together again round the core, and the crack plastered up with loam.

Casting Away of Mrs. Lecks and Mrs. Aleshine, The, a story by Frank R. Stockton. This chronicle sets forth the curious experiences of Mrs. Lecks and Mrs. Aleshine; two middle-aged widows, from a little New England village, who, having "means," decide to see the world and pay a visit to the son of one of them, who has gone into business in Japan. On the steamer crossing the Pacific they meet a young Mr. Craig, who tells the story. The two ladies and Mr. Craig are cast away in most preposterous circumstances, on a lonely isle in mid-ocean. Many of the scenes, like the escape from drowning of the two widows, are of the very essence of true humor, of a grotesque form; and the story-teller's invention never once flags. The tale presents, intentionally of course, neither evolution nor climax, but only a succession of the oddest incidents. It is a good example of Stockton's unique method of story-telling — the matter extremely absurd and the manner extremely grave, the narrative becoming more and more matter-of-fact and minutely realistic, as the events themselves grow more and more incredible.

Castle, Edmund, English Orientalist: b. 1606; d. about 1685. His life was spent mainly in the compilation of his 'Lexicon Heptaglotton Hebraicum, Chaldaicum, Syriacum, Samaritanum, Æthiopicum, Arabicum et Persicum' (1669), the Syriac division of which is still considered valuable, and he also aided Walton in the preparation of his 'Polyglot.'

Castle, Egerton, English author: b. 12 March 1858. He was educated at Glasgow University and Cambridge. After a brief military career he turned to literature and journalism, and has written: 'Schools and Masters of Fence' (1884); 'Bibliotheca Dimicatoria' (1891); 'Consequences' (1891); 'La Bella and Others' (1892); 'English Book Plates' (1892); 'Saviolo,' a play (1893); 'The Light of Scarthey' (1895); 'The Jerningham Letters' (1896); 'The Pride of Jennico' (1898); and 'Young April' (1899); 'Desperate Remedies,' a play; 'The Bath Comedy' (1899); 'Marshfield the Observer'; 'The Secret Orchard' (1900); 'The House of Romance' (1902); 'The Rose of the World' (1905). The last named novel, with 'The Pride of Jennico' and 'The Bath Comedy,' were written jointly by Mr. Castle and his wife, Agnes Castle.

Castle, a word derived from the Latin *castellum*, a diminutive of *castrum*, a fortress or stronghold. The word *castellum* was frequently applied by the Romans as a military term to denote a redoubt. The word has come to be used as the designation of those strongholds which, in feudal times, served at once as residences and as places of defense for the nobles, and which continued to exist until the invention

of gunpowder changed the whole system of fortification. The royal residences among the Franks resembled in some points both the Roman villa and the Roman camp, and those of the Frankish nobles differed little from those of the kings, except in point of simplicity. Strictly speaking, only the grand feudatories had the right to erect fortified castles, and then only after receiving the royal consent; but the grand feudatories very early began to take it upon themselves to grant the privilege of erecting castles to their vassals, and these again to those of a still lower grade. In this way large numbers of castles began to spring up at an early period in France, Germany, England, and elsewhere.

The castles of the Norman Conquest in England were probably the first stone buildings erected there. The great square keep of Rochester Castle is probably of this period; it is about 70 feet square, with projecting corner turrets, and as it now stands is 100 feet high, but the battlements have been altered and its original character lost. A heavy wall divides the huge structure into two nearly equal parts, and within this wall a well is arranged which communicates with all three stories; the outer walls are 12 feet thick at the base and the masonry is very perfect. Little is known of the ancient disposition of the minor buildings. There is no doubt that a high and battlemented wall enclosed a court or perhaps two courts, an inner and an outer bail, as they are called; that the keep was enclosed by the inner bail, but always so near the wall that a postern could communicate with the outer moat, and that within the enclosing wall, often built up against its interior face, were stables and storerooms, and also lodgings for the garrison, which last, however, might be temporary structures. This wall was always surrounded by a deep and broad moat, which might be filled with water in a low country, or, when dry, served merely to increase the effective height of the walls and to disarrange the approach of the besiegers. There was always a chapel, but in Rochester Castle this is built against the southeast corner of the keep and opens from its principal floor. In such an early castle the keep is the only very strong place, as a vigorous attack would breach or scale the outer wall very soon.

The castles of the 12th and 13th centuries were far more elaborate, and their tendency was toward separate posts, each defensible by itself. Every tower could be shut up and defended, its little garrison resisting even after the neighboring works had been captured or rendered indefensible.· This arrangement had the disadvantage that a very bold and sudden attack might capture the strongest parts of the castle, even the keep itself, before assistance could come to it. The typical castle of the 12th century is the famed Chateau Gaillard in Normandy, and of the 13th century the famous castle at Coucy, near Laon in northern France; and in the British Isles, Kidwelly in Wales, which remains in a perfectly traceable condition. The perfect castle was not developed until the time when gunpowder was about to make it useless. Thus the Chateau of Pierrefonds, north of Paris, and near Compiègne, was built about 1400, and in this the faults of the earlier castles were avoided. The walls are everywhere of nearly equal height, the galleries of defense are continuous so that the soldiers of the garrison may run easily the whole length of the walls, and these galleries are two or even three deep, allowing the defenders to throw a prodigious rain of projectiles upon any attacking party. These galleries, built of stone, replace the temporary wooden galleries, always put up on the walls of earlier castles when an attack was anticipated. It is to be noted that the attack and defense in mediæval fortifications was vertical; the higher the wall the more formidable was the blow delivered by a falling ball of stone, or a timber or iron bar; while the projectiles from crossbows and military engines would certainly lose nothing, and the garrison in this way was removed far above the assailant, who must come close under the walls to attack. This attack, then, consisted, in the case of a well defended place, chiefly in breaching or undermining the walls. Escalade was only possible where the garrison was weak or in poor condition or surprised.

Castles often had outer works, thus the barbican or barbacan is strictly a defense built outside of the principal gate, yand intended to keep the enemy away from it for a certain length of time. When a castle was near a river an outwork would be built on the other bank, covering the bridge leading to the castle. When the site was high, with steep approaches, a covered way might be built to protect the whole of the path leading up to the castle, and the foot of this would have an outwork or strong post capable of some defense.

The introduction of fire-arms and especially of cannon heavy enough to breach the walls, compelled a change in the old castles, which were often ruined as consistent pieces of mediæval fortification by having their towers cut down to accommodate artillery of defense. A round stone tower 200 feet high would be cut down to a kind of bastion 30 feet high, with a parapet and embrasures for cannon around its platform. Even this was only temporary, for it was soon found that the effect of artillery fire was irresistible by stone walls, and these were abandoned for the sloping rampart of earth introduced in the 16th century. See FORTIFICATIONS.

The term castle was applied to the sea-coast forts which defended our modern sea-ports previous to 1870, and of which some still remain. It was held that the stone wall, 8 or 10 feet thick, carefully built of granite blocks, with the embrasures covered by wrought iron plates and allowing of a great accumulation of guns within a small space, were proof against the attack of a fleet; and this because the fire from the decks of ships cannot be so exact as to produce a breach. It was assumed that the enemy would not be able to make a landing near with effective guns. Thus, at the entrance to Savannah, Fort Pulaski was a "sea-coast castle" of that type, but it was breached in a few hours by the rifled guns landed on Tybee Island.

In modern English nomenclature, a name compounded with castle (such as Castle Howard, Berkeley Castle, and the like) is used for habitable buildings which may have been erected on the site or immediate grounds of an ancient building of defense or within its old walls; but this is a mere whim in the selection of an arbitrary name. On the other hand, Windsor Castle, the favorite residence of Queen Victoria, has retained much of its mediæval defensive character, but the rooms inhabited by the royal family are of the reign of George IV., and the only part of the ancient work which remains in full use is the great chapel dedicated to St. George, a famous and beautiful building completed in the time of Henry VII.

RUSSELL STURGIS.

Castle Garden, the former immigrant depot in New York, at the point of Manhattan Island, in Battery Park. In the early days of the city the place was a small, fortified island a few feet from the mainland: later it became a public hall for assemblies and concerts. Here Jenny Lind made her American début. Many years ago the island was incorporated with the general area of the Battery by filling the intervening space with earth and rock; new buildings were erected, and the place was devoted to the purpose of landing steerage immigrants. In 1890 it ceased to be used as an immigrant depot, and was turned over to the Park Commissioners of the city of New York. The old fort is now used as a public aquarium.

Castle of Otran'to, The, by Horace Walpole. This story, with its natural personages actuated by supernatural agencies, is the prototype of that extraordinary series of romantic fictions which began with Anne Radcliffe, and was superseded only by the Waverley novels. The reader's interest is aroused with the first page of the romance, and never flags. Conrad, son of Manfred, Prince of Otranto, about to marry Isabella, daughter of the Marquis of Vicenza, is found in the castle court, dashed to pieces under an enormous helmet. Now deprived of an heir, Manfred declares to Isabella his intention of marrying her himself; when, to his horror, his grandfather's portrait descends from the wall, and signs to Manfred to follow him. Isabella meanwhile, by the assistance of a peasant, Theodore, escapes to Friar Jerome. For this intervention, Manfred, now returned from his tête-à-tête with his grandfather's phantom, leads the youth into the court to be executed, when he is found to be Jerome's son, and is spared. At this moment a herald appears demanding of Manfred, in the name of Prince Frederick, his daughter Isabella, and the resignation of the principality of Otranto usurped from Frederick; who follows the proclamation, is admitted to the castle and informed of Manfred's desire to marry Isabella, when word comes that she has escaped from Jerome's protection. A series of ludicrous portents hastens the dénouement: drops of blood flow from the nose of the statue of Alphonso, the prince from whose heirs the dukedom has been wrested; unrelated arms and legs appear in various parts of the castle; and finally, in the midst of the rocking of earth, and the rattling of "more than mortal armor," the walls of the castle are thrown down, the inmates having presumably escaped. From the ruins the statue of Alphonso, raised to gigantic proportions, cries, "Behold in Theodore the true heir of Alphouso." Isabella, having been rescued at the critical moment, is of course married to Theodore.

This wildly romantic tale, published in 1764, was enthusiastically received by the public; who, as Mr. Leslie Stephen so well says, "rejoiced to be reminded that men once lived in castles, believed in the Devil, and did not take snuff or wear powdered wigs.»

Castle Peak, in Mono County, California, lying to the north of Mono Lake in lat. 38° 10′ N. It rises to about 13,000 feet above the sea.

Castle Rackrent, by Maria Edgeworth. This, as the author announces, is «an Hibernian tale taken from facts and from the manners of the Irish squire before the year 1782.» The memoirs of the Rackrent family are recounted by Thady Quirk, an old steward, who has been from childhood devotedly attached to the house of Rackrent. The old retainer's descriptions of the several masters under whom he has served, vividly portray various types of the «fine old Irish gentleman.» Sir Walter Scott has acknowledged that his original idea, when he began his career as a novelist, was to be to Scotland what Miss Edgeworth was to Ireland.

Cas′tlebar, Ireland, the capital of County Mayo. It is on the Castlebar River, 10 miles northeast of Westport; has infantry and cavalry barracks, and some linen manufactures. In 1641 occurred here the massacre of the English Parliamentary army in the Irish rebellion; in 1789 Castlebar was held for a fortnight by the French general, Humbert; and in 1846–7 it suffered greatly from famine. Pop. about 4,000.

Cas′tleford, England, a thriving manufacturing town in the West Riding of Yorkshire, on the Aire, here crossed by a bridge, 10 miles southeast from Leeds. The public buildings include the church of All Saints, several denominational chapels, schools, a market-hall, mechanics' institute, etc. There are numerous collieries in the neighborhood; and the town has extensive manufactures of glass bottles, earthernware, and chemicals. Pop. (1901) 17,382.

Cas′tlemaine, Australia, a municipal town in the colony of Victoria, in the county of Talbot, at the junction of Barker and Forest creeks, 78 miles northwest of Melbourne, on the Melbourne & Echuca R. R., with branch communication by Maryborough with Ballarat. The town is pleasantly situated and well laid out, and the buildings, both public and private, are of a superior character. The principal public buildings are the town-hall, the hospital, the supreme court, and the mechanics' institute. Castlemaine owes its importance to the mining industry carried on in its neighborhood. Pop. (1901) 6,082.

Cas′tlemon, Harry. See Fosdick, Charles Austin.

Castlereagh, kăs′ĕl rā, Robert Stuart, Viscount, English statesman: b. 18 June 1769; d. 12 Aug. 1822. He was educated at Armagh, and at St. John's College, Cambridge. He turned Tory in 1795, and next year became keeper of the privy seal; but he continued a steadfast supporter of Catholic emancipation. Still, he believed that emancipation with an independent Irish parliament would mean simply a transference of tyranny from the Protestant oligarchy to a Catholic democracy; hence, as chief secretary from 1797, he bent his whole energies to forwarding Pitt's measure of union. Transferred by the union from Dublin to Westminster, he accepted office in the Addington ministry (1802) as president of the board of control; but the true second era in his career was

as war minister under Pitt from July 1805 to January 1806, and again under Portland from April 1807 to September 1809. His real greatness begins with March 1812, when, as foreign secretary under Lord Liverpool, he became the soul of the coalition against Napoleon, which, during the momentous campaigns of 1813–4, was kept together by him, and by him alone. He represented England at the congresses of Chatillon and Vienna in 1814–5, at the Treaty of Paris in 1815, at the Congress of Aix-la-Chapelle in 1818; and he was preparing to start for a congress at Verona, when, in a fit of insanity, he committed suicide with a pen-knife at Foots Cray, his Kentish seat.

Castlereagh, Ireland, a barony in the County of Down. The castle stands on the summit of a Danish rath, and was once the seat of an O'Neil. It is now the property of the Marquis of Downshire. The barony gives the title of viscount to the Marquis of Londonderry.

Cas′tleton, England, a village in the County of Derby, situated at the bottom of a rugged eminence, on which stands the ancient castle called Peak Castle, erected by William Peveril, natural son of the Conquerer. The houses are chiefly of stone. It contains the parish church, a fine specimen of the early pointed style; two Methodist chapels, and a free grammar-school. The inhabitants are mostly employed in mining; but many derive a subsistence from the manufacture of ornamental articles from spar. It is the scene of Scott's novel, 'Peveril of The Peak.'

Cas′tletown, Great Britain, a seaport and former capital of the Isle of Man, on Castletown Bay, 11 miles southwest of Douglas. Castle Rushen, now a prison, occupies the site of a Danish fortress of the 10th century, which was almost wholly demolished by Robert Bruce in 1313. The grounds of Rushen Abbey (11th century), near the station, are now market gardens. Near by is the small building where the House of Keys assembled for about 170 years. Brewing, tanning, and lime-burning are carried on. Near Castletown is King William's College, an Elizabethan pile, rebuilt after the fire of 1844.

Cas′tor and Pollux (the latter called by the Greeks Polydeuces), the sons of Tyndareus, king of Lacedæmon and Leda, or, according to some, of Zeus and Leda. The fable runs that Leda brought forth two eggs, one of which contained Pollux and Helen, the other Castor and Clytemnestra. Pollux and Helen, being the offspring of Zeus, were immortal; but Castor and Clytemnestra were begotten by Tyndareus, and mortal. Homer's account is that both Castor and Pollux were the sons of Tyndareus, and that Helen was the daughter of Zeus. The two brothers were inseparable companions, equally brave and spirited, and attached to each other with the fondest affection. Castor was particularly skilled in the art of breaking horses, and Pollux in boxing and wrestling. They were among the heroes of the Argonautic expedition, in which they acquired divine honors; for a terrible tempest having arisen on the voyage, and all with loud voices calling on the gods to save them, there suddenly appeared over the heads of Castor and Pollux two star-like meteors, and the tempest subsided. From this time they were the patron deities of mariners, and received the name of Dioscuri ("sons of Zeus"); and from them the name of Castor and Pollux was given to the fires that are often seen on the masts of vessels in storms, and which are electrical phenomena. After their return they released their sister Helen from the confinement in which Theseus had for some time held her. They were also among the heroes of the Calydonian hunt. They wooed the daughters of Leucippus, Phœbe and Hilaeira or Elaeira, and carried them off and married them. Having become involved in a quarrel with Idas and Lynceus, the sons of Aphareus, Castor killed Lynceus, and was slain by Idas. Pollux revenged his brother's death by killing Idas, but full of grief for the loss of Castor, he besought Zeus either to take away his life or grant that his brother might share his immortality. Zeus listened to his request, and Pollux and his brother alternately resided one day on earth and the other in the heavenly abodes of the gods. It is doubtful whether the ancients understood them as being together or separate in their alternate passage between the upper and the lower worlds. The former opinion seems to be the oldest; the latter to have gained ground subsequently. Temples and altars were consecrated to them. In great perils, especially in battles, the ancients believed that they frequently appeared to mortals as two youths on white steeds, in shining garments, with meteors over their heads; and then they were chiefly called Dioscuri. They were also represented side by side, either riding or standing, each holding a horse by the rein, with spears in their hands and stars on their heads. In the heavens the Dioscuri appear as one of the 12 constellations of the zodiac, with the name of Gemini (the Twins).

Castor, or Castor'eum, an odorous substance obtained from two glandular sacs connected with the sexual organs in both sexes of the beaver. In past years it was utilized for medical purposes, especially as a remedy in diseases of the uterus, and in the case of catalepsy, hysteria, and other spasmodic diseases. What little now reaches market is used as an ingredient of perfumes, but most of it is kept by northern trappers as a scent for baiting their traps, and is known as barkstone.

Castor Oil (*Oleum ricini*), the fixed oil expressed from the seeds of *Ricinus communis*, of the family *Euphorbiaceæ*. The oil is obtained from the seeds by various processes. The seeds are sometimes boiled and the oil skimmed from the water, or the oil may be taken up by solvents, such as alcohol, ether, etc. In the large manufacturing pharmacy houses in the United States the seeds are first warmed slightly and then passed between rollers, or other forms of pressure apparatus. The oil is collected and decanted, or mixed with boiling water and purified. The average yield of high-grade oil is from 40 to 50 per cent in weight. Care must be exercised in the amount of heating of the seeds, else a very active and acrid toxalbumin, ricin, which is present in the seed coat, is added to the oil. This tends to render the oil very griping in its action. Unscrupulous manufacturers have been known to add small quantities of ricin to adulterated oil. Seconds. or sorts, are inferior qualities of oil.

When fresh and pure castor oil should be a clear, colorless, viscid oil, with a faint, mild odor, a bland and unpleasant taste. Its specific gravity should be .950-970 at 60° F. It should be soluble in equal parts of alcohol; in all proportions of absolute alcohol, or in glacial acetic acid, and tested to exclude other mixed oils, is soluble at 60° F. in three times its volume of a mixture of 19 parts of alcohol and one part ot water. This test will detect an admixture of over five per cent of other oils. Castor oil congeals at —18° F. The chemical structure shows castor oil to be composed almost entirely of ricinoleic acid. This is broken up in the intestines by saponification, and sets free the active agent of the drug's action. Castor oil is a reliable cathartic. It empties the bowel completely, largely by its stimulating intestinal peristalsis, and is probably the best cathartic for children with overloaded intestines. In intestinal fermentation and putrefaction accompanied by diarrhœa, it is excellent. It causes a number of loose, not very watery movements, attended with mild griping. There is a tendency to constipation following its use; hence, it is not of service in habitual constipation. As it is extremely disagreeable for many, its taste may be disguised by orange peel, or best in some aromatic frothy or carbonated mixture, as in some coffee, soda water, or sarsaparilla soda water. From a teaspoonful to a tablespoonful is the usual dose.

Castor-oil Plant, Castor-bean, or Palma Christi, a tropical herb (*Ricinus communis*) of the natural order *Euphorbiaceæ*, a native of Africa and Asia, whence it has become distributed in warm countries throughout the world. In cool climates it is a half-hardy annual, but in frostless regions it is a perennial, often becoming a small tree. Its large palmate leaves. sometimes more than two feet in diameter, and its green or red stems, which in the central United States may attain a height of 12 feet, and in the tropics 30 or 40 feet, are very striking in flower borders and clumps of shrubbery. The unisexual flowers are borne in terminal racemes, and the female ones are succeeded by three-celled spiny capsules which explode when the seed is ripe, throwing the seed to a considerable distance. The seeds have long been employed for making castor oil, which is used for lubricating, for making sticky fly-paper, and in medicine. About half the demand of the American market is met by the crops grown in Kansas, Missouri, Oklahoma, and adjacent territory, but since the introduction of petroleum products the oil has a smaller use as a lubricant than formerly, and since the importation of various palm oils its use in soap-making has declined. It is also less popular as a medicine than it used to be. The crop is not considered a paying one. Castor-oil pomace (the oil cake after the oil has been extracted) is a highly valuable nitrogeneous fertilizer.

Castor'idæ. See BEAVER.

Castoroi'des, a gigantic, extinct, beaver-like rodent of the Pleistocene epoch in North America. It was as large as a black bear, and inhabited the cold, swampy, evergreen forests of the north, its remains being found chiefly in peat-bogs along with bones of the mastodon.

Castrameta'tion, the art of tracing out and disposing to advantage the several parts of a camp on the ground. See CAMP.

Castration, the removal of the testicles or ovaries of animals. Castration is usually performed to limit reproduction, to change the character of the working animal, making him more docile and easier to train, or to improve the quality of meat for eating, as in capons. In human beings castration is a surgical procedure and is usually performed for the relief of some irremediable or malignant disease. Thus in tuberculosis and cancer of the testicles, and in malignant or painful disease of the ovaries, the operation is justifiable. There has been a large amount of needless removal of the ovaries in women. The after results are often more annoying than the original disease.

The change produced in men by emasculation is highly remarkable, and assimilates their constitution in some respects to that of females. The elasticity of the fibres and muscles is weakened, and the cellular membrane becomes charged with a much larger quantity of fat; the growth of the beard is prevented; the upper part of the windpipe contracts considerably, and the castrate acquires the physiognomy and voice of a female. On the moral character it likewise appears to have some influence by weakcuing the intellectual faculties and rendering the subject unfeeling, morose, faint-hearted, and on the whole incapable of performing those deeds which require a high, magnanimous disposition. The most numerous class of castrates are those who are made such by the removal of the testicles. Another class are not deprived of the parts of generation, but have them ingeniously injured in such a manner as to leave them the faculty of copulating, but deprive them of the power of begetting. Juvenal mentions these as the particular favorites of the licentious Roman ladies. To the third class belong those who are entirely deprived of their genital members. They are used in preference, by the Turks, as keepers of their women. The castrates of all three classes are called eunuchs. Those of the third class, to distinguish them from the two others, are frequently termed entire eunuchs. The word eunuch is Greek, and signifies "guard" or "keeper of the bed." The castration of adults produces some change in the disposition, but little in the bodily constitution. Even the power of engendering continues for a short time. According to the accounts of ancient historians, the Lydians, celebrated for effeminacy, castrated women. The latter are said to have used these beings as guards of their wives and daughters. With females the operation produces a completely opposite effect to that which it has on men. The sexual appetite ceases, a beard appears on the chin and upper lip, the breasts vanish, the voice becomes harsh, etc. Boerhaave and Pott relate modern instances of this kind. Among the evils which religious fanaticism has at all times produced, castration is conspicuous. The emperors Constantine and Justinian were obliged to use their utmost power to oppose this religious frenzy, and could put a stop to it only by punishing it like murder. The Valerians, a religious sect whose minds had been distracted by the example of Origen, not only considered this mutilation of themselves a duty which religion imposed on them, but believed themselves bound to perform the same, by fair means or foul, on all those who came into their power. In Italy the castration of boys, in order to form them for

soprano singers, was in use for a long time. Clement XIV. prohibited this abuse, which, notwithstanding, did not cease till comparatively recent times, and in some Italian towns was not only suffered but exercised with such shameful openness that the practitioners gave public notice of their profession. In modern times severe laws were enacted against castration, and the custom is probably now extinct. Beings thus mutilated were common on the European stage. It is remarkable that so odious and unnatural an operation should produce the fine natural an operation should produce the fine tones of the singer, which all had to acknowledge notwithstanding the disagreeable effect of the association.

Castrén, käs-trän', Matthias Alexander, Finnish philologist: b. Tervola 2 Dec. 1813; d. Helsingfors 7 May 1852. While attending, as a young man, the University of Helsingfors he conceived the project of tracing out the various detached branches of the Finnish races and languages, and presenting their ethnological and philological phenomena in one general view. Following out this idea he undertook in 1838 a pedestrian excursion through Finnish Lapland, and another in 1840 through the district of Karelia, with the view of studying the primitive language of that country, and enabling himself to translate therefrom into Swedish the great Finnish epic of the 'Kalevala.' This last work was accomplished by him after his return. He soon, however, resumed his travels, and for several years continued to prosecute his researches among the nations of the Arctic regions, both in Europe and Asia, including the Norwegian and Russian Lapps, and the Samoyeds of Siberia and the coasts of the White Sea. Naturally of a weakly constitution, and in a failing state of health, he was frequently obliged in addition to submit in the course of his journeys to the most extreme privations. Having returned home from his last journey to the Samoyeds, he was appointed in 1851 professor of the Finnish and old Scandinavian languages in the University of Helsingfors, but died before he had been able to add much more to his work — a martyr to the cause of science. Among his writings are: his translation of the 'Kalevala'; 'Elementa Grammatices Syrjænæ'; 'Elementa Grammatices Tscheremissæ'; and 'De Affixis Personalibus Linguarum Altaicarum'; besides travels and other works published after his death.

Castres, kästr, France, a town (ancient CASTRUM ALBIENSUM) in the department of Tarn, 23 miles south-southeast of Albi, on the Agout, which divides it into two parts — Castres Proper, north side, and Villegoudon, south side of the river. The public buildings include the hôtel de ville, formerly the episcopal palace, which contains a public library, and has a garden laid out on the plan of the Tuileries; three churches, one of them Protestant; two hospitals, a theatre, cavalry barracks, etc. The manufactures consist of fine cloths, coarse cloth for the troops, flannels, blankets, and other woolen goods, linen, glue, and black soap. There are also bleaching-grounds, dyeworks, tanneries, paper-mills, forges, and brass-foundries. Trade is also carried in in silk, cotton, liqueurs, and confectionery. Castres has a communal college and two seminaries. The town arose round an abbey of the Benedictines (which is said to have been founded in the 9th century), and was already in the 12th century a place of importance. During the religious wars of the 16th century Castres was the scene of many conflicts. Louis XIII., to whom the town surrendered in 1629, ordered its fortifications to be razed to the ground. Pop. about 20,000.

Castries, Charles Eugène Gabriel de la Croix, shärl ė-zhän gä-brë-ėl dė la krwä käs-trė, MARQUIS OF, French soldier: b. 1727; d. 1801. He entered the army, fought at Dettingen and in lower Alsace, became lieutenant of Languedoc and governor of Montpellier and Cette, and under Marshal Saxe commanded the army in Flanders, where he covered the sieges of Menin, Ypres, and Courtray, and ended the campaign with the battle of Courtray. He afterward fought at Fontenoy, Raocoux, and Laufeld. During the Seven Years' war he added greatly to his fame, was made lieutenant-general, and was dangerously wounded in the battle of Rossbach. In 1783 he was marshal of France, and emigrating in 1791 found an asylum with the Duke of Brunswick. He subsequently commanded the army of the French princes in Champagne, and countersigned the manifesto issued by Monsieur in 1793. In 1797 he formed, in conjunction with St. Priest, the so-called cabinet of Louis XVIII. at Blankenburg.

Castriota, käs-trė-ō'tä, George. See SCANDERBEG.

Castro, käs'trō, Augustin, Mexican poet: b. Cordova, Vera Cruz, 24 Jan. 1728; d. Bologna, Italy, 1790. He became a Jesuit priest and a teacher of philosophy, and was a skilful translator of classical authors. Among his original works in poetry are: 'Hernán Cortez' and 'Charts,' a guide for young poetic genius. His versions of Sappho, Euripides, Horace, Seneca, Milton, and Fénelon have received high praise from scholars.

Castro, Cipriano, Venezuelan military leader: b. Capacho, Venezuela, near the frontier of Colombia, about 1855. His parents were Spanish mestizos of the peasant class. He attended school in Capacho. While still a very young man he took an active part in politics in Capacho, as a Liberal. His first military exploit consisted in scoring a moderate success in the so-called "Battle of Capacho" (1886) against Morales, the local representative of the Lopez government. He remained a leader of the Liberal party in his state until 1892. In that year began Crespo's rebellion against Andueza. Castro, supporting Andueza's cause, was victorious in the battle of 15 May 1892, in Táriba; defeating Morales who now was under Crespo's command. In Caracas, however, the insurgents triumphed. Crespo entered the capital 6 Oct. 1892. Castro remained in control of Táchira and Merida, but before the end of the year withdrew across the Colombian frontier and bought a farm near Cúcuta on the Colombian side of Santander. For the next six or seven years he was a farmer and cattle-raiser. Invited by Crespo to take office as head of the custom-house at Puerto Cabello, he declined this offer, but promised Crespo not to join his enemies or attack his government. Andrade was Crespo's successor. Castro went to Caracas and called on the new president. Accounts of this visit differ. Castro's partisans assert that he

again refused the tender of an office under the government; according to another version he was insulted, and left the Yellow House vowing vengeance. When he returned to his home some political friends and relations of Andrade's who lived in Cúcuta procured from the Colombian government an order for his arrest. For about two months he was in hiding; then he invaded Venezuela with only 60 men (23 joining him, in three days he collected a force of 1,500. The first skirmish was in the country between San Cristóbal and Rubio. In Las Pilas the commander of the government's frontier troops fell. At Zumbador about 2,000 men led by Morales were defeated. Castro laid siege to San Cristóbal, where Peñalosa was strongly entrenched. About 6,000 men under Fernandez were sent against him from Caracas. An indecisive engagement occurred. Then Castro left Fernandez in the rear, and marched toward the capital, defeating several government forces on the way. Andrade having fled the country, Castro entered the capital, opened the prison in which Hernandez had been confined for many months, and declared himself "jefe supremo"— neither president nor dictator, but "supreme military leader." The constituent assembly made him provisional president of Venezuela, 30 March 1901, and on 20 February 1902 he was elected president for the term of six years. Hernandez promptly revolted, and was put back into prison. Celestino Peraza was the next rebel; and after Peraza came Matos, who intrigued to gain the support of foreign governments. He resigned the presidency temporarily on 9 April 1906. See VENEZUELA.

Castro, Guillen de, Spanish dramatist: b. Valencia 1569; d. Madrid 28 July 1631. He was at one time commander of a Neapolitan fortress. In his later years he lived in Madrid, and was on intimate terms with Lope de Vega. Castro's memory has been chiefly preserved by his authorship of 'Las Mocedades del Cid,' to the first part of which Corneille was indebted for the plot and many of the beauties of his celebrated tragedy. The other plays of Castro are badly constructed, and chiefly distinguished for their intensely national spirit.

Castro, Ines de, ē nēs dä, Spanish lady: d. 1355. She was descended from the royal line of Castile. After the death of Constantia, wife of Pedro, son of Alfonso IV., king of Portugal, in 1345, Ines was secretly married by Pedro, whose mistress she had already been. As he steadily rejected all propositions for a new marriage, his secret was suspected, and the envious rivals of Ines were fearful that her brothers and family would gain a complete ascendency over the future king. At length Alfonso resolved to put Ines to death. The first time that Pedro left Ines, the king hastened to Coimbra, where she was living in the convent of St. Clara with her children. The arrival of Alfonso filled the unhappy lady with terror. She threw herself with her children at the king's feet, and begged for mercy. Alfonso was softened, but afterward gave his counselors permission to commit the murder, and it was executed that very hour. Ines expired under the daggers of her enemies. She was buried in the convent where she was murdered. Pedro took arms against his father, but soon became reconciled to him

Two years later Alfonso died; the assassins had already left the kingdom and taken refuge with Pedro the Cruel of Castile. An exchange of fugitives was carried out. Of the three murderers of Ines, one escaped, but the other two were tortured in the presence of the young king Pedro at Santarem in 1360. Their hearts were torn out, their bodies burned, and their ashes scattered to the winds. Two years later, it is said, King Pedro at Catacneda declared on oath that after the death of Constantia he had obtained the consent of the Pope to his union with Ines, and had married her. The archbishop and Lobato confirmed the assertions of the king; and the Papal document to which the king referred was publicly exhibited. The king caused the body of Ines to be disinterred, and placed on a throne, adorned with the diadem and royal robes, and required all the nobility of the kingdom to approach and kiss the hem of her garment, rendering her when dead that homage which she had not received in her life. The body was interred at Alcobaça, where a splendid monument of white marble was erected, on which was placed her statue, with a royal crown on her head. The history of the unhappy Ines has furnished many poets of different nations with materials for tragedies, and the Portuguese muse has immortalized her through the lips of Camoens, in whose celebrated 'Lusiad' the history of her love is one of the finest episodes.

Castro, Joao de, zhō-own' dä, Portuguese navigator: b. Lisbon 7 Feb. 1500; d. 6 June 1548. In 1538 he accompanied the viceroy Garcia de Neronha, his uncle, to India, as commander of a vessel, and in 1540 was in the expedition that explored the Red Sea, of which he made charts and scientific descriptions. His profound knowledge of mathematics and languages made these works of great value. They were published under the title of 'The Log-book of Don John de Castro, on the Voyage which the Portuguese made to the Red Sea.' After his return he was made commander of a fleet to rid the European seas of pirates; was appointed governor of India in 1545, in which office he defeated the great army of the Moors, under Adhel Khan, and completely subjugated Malacea. In 1547 he was commissioned viceroy of India, but died shortly afterward.

Castro, Jose Maria, hō-sä' mä rē'ä, Costa Rican statesman: b. San Jose 1 Sept. 1818. He was educated at the University of Leon; Nicaragua, and held positions under the government of Costa Rica. In 1846 he was vice-president and in 1847 was elected president. After Costa Rica withdrew from the Central American states, he resigned the presidency, but held diplomatic positions. From 1866 to the rise of the Jimenez government (1868) he was again president.

Castro Urdiales, a seaport town of Spain, on the Bay of Biscay, in the province of Santander. It was sacked by the French in 1811, but has since been neatly rebuilt. A ruined convent of the templars is in the vicinity. It has a safe harbor, and extensive fisheries. Pop. (1900) about 13,000.

Castro-Del-Rio, a town in Spain, Andalusia, 16 miles southeast of Cordova, on a slope above the Guadajoz. The more ancient portion is surrounded by a dilapidated wall, flanked

with towers, and entered by one gate, which was defended by an Arab castle, now also ruinous. The modern portion is outside the walls, and extends along the foot of the hill on its north side. The most of the streets are wide and regular, lined with well-built houses and handsome public edifices. The church is large and handsome, and there are also several convents, two colleges, primary schools, hospitals, and manufactures of linen, woolen, and earthenware. Pop. (1887) 11,290.

Castrogiovanni, or **Castro Giovanni** (anc. ENNA), a city of Sicily, in the district of Caltanisetta, on a plateau in the centre of the island, 4,000 feet above the sea. The climate is healthy, the soil fertile, and water abundant. The old feudal fortress of Enna is the chief edifice. It contains also a cathedral. It was the fabled birthplace of Ceres, and the site of her most famous temple. About five miles distant is the lake of Pergusa, where Proserpine, according to the poets, was carried off by Pluto. During the first servile war the insurgent slaves made Enna their headquarters. It was captured by the Saracens in the 9th and by the Normans in the 11th century. Pop. 19,800.

Cas'trum Dolor'is, a Latin term signifying castle of grief, has a different meaning from *catafalco.* The latter is used to denote an elevated tomb, containing the coffin of a distinguished person, together with the tapers around, ornaments, armorial bearings, inscriptions, etc., placed in the midst of a church or hall. The *castrum doloris* is the whole room in which the *catafalco* is elevated, with all the decorations. The sarcophagus, usually empty, is exposed for show upon an elevation covered with black cloth, under a canopy surrounded with candelabra. Upon the coffin is laid some mark of the rank of the deceased, as his epaulette or sword, and, when the deceased was a sovereign or a member of a ruling family, princely insignia are placed on surrounding seats. The French call the *castrum doloris, chapelle ardente,* sometimes also *chambre ardente;* but the latter has also a separate meaning.

Castuera, käs-too-ä'rä, Spain, a town in the province of Badajoz, near the right bank of the Guadalefra. Most of its streets are straight, clean, and well paved. It has two squares, lined with substantial houses; the principal one contains the town-hall, prisons, and spacious modern parish church. The inhabitants are engaged in weaving, making earthenware, tiles, bricks, shoes. Trade is carried on in cattle, wool, wine, grain, and oil. Pop. 7,133.

Casualty Insurance. See INSURANCE, CASUALTY.

Casuarina, käs-ū-a-rī'na, or **Botany-bay Oak,** the single genus of the natural order of *Casuarinaceæ,* or cassowary-trees. There are about 30 species, natives chiefly of Australia. They are jointed leafless trees or shrubs, nearly related to the birches, having their male one-stamened flowers in whorled catkins, and their fruits in indurated cones. Some of them produce timber called beefwood, from its color. *C. quadrivalvis* is called the she-oak, *C. equisetifolia,* the swamp-oak.

Cas'uistry, the science or art of determining cases of conscience and the moral character of human acts; so called from *casus conscien-*

tiæ, a case of conscience. Wherever the question rises, Is such an act allowable by moral law? there is a case of conscience and matter of casuistry, and in deciding the question for himself, as everyone habitually does, everyone is a casuist. But in current usage a casuist is one who, skilled in the prescriptions of the divine moral law and its interpretation whether by lawgivers, moralists, or theologians, studies either suppositions or actual cases of conscience and judges whether a given act, or even a given thought is consistent with or in violation of moral law — for, unlike the civil lawgiver or the ministers of civil law, the casuist must determine the moral character of thoughts no less, or rather more, than of acts. The professional casuist is inevitable in the system of the Catholic Church, where the minister of religion, in his capacity of *confessarius* or confessor must be the counselor and director of penitents and resolve for them questions of guilt or innocence, questions touching the obligation to restitution, for example of goods, or reparation of damage to a neighbor's reputation by slander; granting or withholding absolution according to the merits. For the minister of the sacrament of penance acts under Jesus Christ's commission, whose sins ye shall forgive, whose sins ye shall retain, shall be forgiven or retained; and to execute that commission the minister of the sacrament must decide for himself and the penitent the moral character of the acts. The science or art of casuistry has doubtless been carried to extraordinary lengths; but though the questions which it treats are such as touch individually and most intimately daily and hourly the many millions of souls who resort to the confessional, the works of writers on casuistry, though voluminous, would count as a scant armful compared with only one part of the works contained in a law library — those which record the decisions of the civil courts. It is true also and inevitable that casuistry like law lore is often employed as a means of escaping from legal penalty or of quieting the sense of guilt. As there are lawyers who for a fee will defend any cause however defenseless morally, even to the extent of working injustice — loss of property, loss of reputation to the party opposite — so there are casuists who by their overinclining to an indulgent interpretation of the divine moral law, release or cut the nerve of moral responsibility, administer an opiate to conscience.

Probabilism is the name given to the doctrine which declares to be lawful *in foro conscientiæ* an act the moral correctness of which is affirmed by any theologian of weight (*doctor gravis*); or, as defined by Liguori, a probable opinion is one which rests on a solid foundation (*fundamento gravi*) both of reason and of authority, so that it is able to move the assent (*flectere assensum*) of a prudent man, though with fear regarding the opposite. But a writer in a great encyclopædia, who regards probabilism as "the most remarkable doctrine they (the casuists) promulgated — a doctrine which it is hard to believe that any one ever ventured to assert" teaches that "according to probabilism" "any opinion which has been expressed by a 'grave doctor' may be looked upon as possessing a fair amount of probability, and may, therefore, be safely followed, even

though one's conscience may insist upon the opposite course": the last clause is gratuitous and has no warrant in the teachings of Catholic moralists, who unanimously hold that an act done in defiance of conscience, even be it a plainly erroneous conscience, is a sin.

Viewed in the abstract, the rule of the probabilists is not an unreasonable one: it is acted upon daily by whoever, doubting his own judgment, asks counsel of others whom he regards as trustworthy advisers, even though they be not grave doctors (*graves doctores*). It is admitted that some of the probabilists, even the greatest of them, as Escobar, Suarez, Busembaum, did not always guard the doctrine against misconstruction, and gave occasion for views of moral obligation which were too lax: but the ecclesiastical censure has fallen upon such erroneous teachings, without discrediting for Catholic moralists the principle of probabilism. Let any other school of moral teaching set to itself the same task which confronts the moral theologian of the Catholic Church, that is, to define with precision the moral character of every act, every thought, every imagination that has relation to the moral law, and it will be seen whether probabilism must not have a place in its system.

Ca'sus Bel'li, the material grounds which justify (or are alleged by one of the parties concerned to justify) a declaration of war (q.v.). The *casus belli* is not seldom a very trifling one, and does not necessarily indicate the real *causa belli* or cause of the war.

Cas'well, Richard, American lawyer: b. Maryland 3 Aug. 1729; d. 20 Nov. 1789. He removed to North Carolina in 1746; was president of the Provincial Congress which framed the State Constitution (1776), and first governor of the State, three times re-elected; was also a delegate to the convention which framed the Federal Constitution in 1787.

Cat (*Felis domesticus*), a well-known domesticated quadruped of the order *Carnivora*, the same name being also given to allied forms of the same order. Some have thought that the domestic breed owed its origin to the wild cat; but there are considerable differences between them, the latter being larger, and having a shorter and thicker tail, which also does not taper. The domestic cat belongs to a genus — that which contains the lion and tiger — better armed for the destruction of animal life than any other quadruped. Its short and powerful jaws, trenchant teeth, cunning disposition, combined with nocturnal habits (for which its eyesight is naturally adapted) and much patience in pursuit, give it great advantages over its prey. It is characterized by six incisor teeth above and below; two canine teeth in each jaw, powerful and formed for tearing; molar or cheek teeth, four in the upper jaw and three m the lower, thin, pointed, and wedge-shaped, formed for cutting. The head is large, round, and wide; the eyes have the pupil often oblong; the tongue has strong horny papillæ, directed backward. The feet are formed for walking; the toes are five in number on the fore feet, and four on the hind feet, armed with strong, sharp, and hooked claws, retracted when the animal walks. The intestines are very short, as in all animals living almost exclusively on animal food. The cat in a degree partakes of all the attributes of its race. Its food in a state of domestication is necessarily very various, but always of flesh or fish if it can be obtained. Instances of its catching the latter are known, though usually the cat is extremely averse to wetting itself. It is a very cleanly animal, avoiding any sort of filth, and preserving its fur in a very neat condition. Its fur is easily injured by water on account of the want of oil in it, and it can be rendered highly electric by friction. The cat goes with young for 63 days, and brings forth usually from three to six at a litter, which remain blind for nine days. It is usually regarded as less intelligent than the dog, but this is by no means certain. It has a singular power of finding its way home when taken to a distance and covered up by the way. The wild cat (*Felis catus*) is still found in various parts of Europe and western Asia, chiefly in forest regions, making its lair in hollow trees or clefts of rocks. It is a very fierce animal. There are a number of other animals, of similar size and habits, known as cats, such as the fishing-cat (*F. viverrina*) of Bengal and eastern Asia, the leopard cat (*F. bengalensis*) of northern India and southeastern Asia, the marbled cat (*F. marmoräta* of the same region, the rusty-spotted cat (*F: robiginösa*), a small Indian species, etc. For varieties of the domestic cat see CAT, THE DOMESTIC.

Cat, Domestic, The. There is little doubt that the influence of the domestic cat upon American civilization has received less consideration than it deserves, for a great deal of the advance in agriculture, as well as of the spreading out over the vast woodlands and prairies of America, has been made possible by this much abused and misunderstood animal. For places suddenly thrown open to settlement the cat is often one of the first things sought, is one of the first of the necessary household gods, and goes in with the cooking-stove and the dish-pan. The reason for this is, that on our great prairies mice are found in countless thousands. The settler, not being near a town, buys his goods by the wagon-load, and, being able to go to the base of supplies only once or twice a year, stores his food in barrels and sacks, enough, perhaps, for six months ahead. This opportunity is not lost by the mice, which, swarming indoors out of the prairie grass, find ideal conditions; abundance of food, warmth, shelter, and comfort. If the simple eating of the food ended the trouble, it would not be so bad, but field-mice, imbued as they are with the instinct of storing everything, have a knack of mixing different things together — the rice with the coffee, sugar with both, etc., until there is a *potpourri* that no one can separate, and cooking is made impossible.

After such happening the settler speedily seeks a cat, and the prices paid would astonish those who think cats merely a nuisance. How much food cats have saved, how much property they have guarded from destruction, what plagues of vermin they have kept in check, from the time this country was first settled, it is impossible to compute. But for their sleepless vigilance the large cities would quickly be overrun with rats and mice. How indispensable their service is may be seen in the condition of farms in the British Isles, rendered useless by rats and mice, because the cat, as well as the

hawk and the owl, is suppressed to make way for the game preserve, to afford the pleasure of shooting for a few weeks, or perhaps, only a few days in the year.

The cat, then, is a necessary adjunct to our civilization, a factor and an institution to dislodge which would imperil our status as a nation; and until a substitute can be found the cat is an economic necessity in our daily life that cannot be done away with without upsetting the balance of nature greatly to our disadvantage. This fact is recognized by the government, which appropriates money every year for the maintenance of cats in the post-offices and other public buildings of the larger cities, in order to keep down the vermin that would gnaw holes in mail-sacks and destroy public records and other property. It is recognized in the national printing-office of France, where vast quantities of paper are stored, and where an army of cats is retained to keep the mice in check. In Vienna it is regarded as a part of good municipal government to take care of the cats. The United States government has systematized its cat service in public institutions, and in Pittsburg a certain strain has been bred to live in cold-storage houses, and is developing characteristics peculiar to this kind of life. In warehouses, corn-cribs, barns, mills, and wherever grain or food is stored, cats must be kept.

Having shown, to a limited extent, the necessity of keeping cats, we will now turn to the advance made in their care and selection; for the arousing of interest which has come from the scientific breeding of cats for exhibition purposes is destined to lift the family to its proper place in public economy, where the breeding and keeping of them can be properly regulated, their health cared for, the diseased put out of the way, and the family, as a whole, elevated to the position to which its beauty and usefulness entitle it. To be effective, they must be taken care of, for well-fed cats are the best mousers.

The origin of the domestic cat is shrouded in mystery, and to the Egyptians we have to turn for such of its early history as is reliable. The Egyptians being an agricultural people, and the raising of wheat their main industry, they quickly grasped the fact of the usefulness of the cat; and the earliest ones were probably obtained by taming kittens of the native species (*Felis caligata*), and to these we most likely owe the greater part of our short-haired cats. Possibly when the Aryans made their pilgrimage from Asia they brought specimens of the short-haired, domestic cats from India, for there are, at the present day in India, domestic cats that are not likely to have any Egyptian blood in their veins. Whatever the origin of the domestic cat, it is probable that in comparison to the date of the domestication of the horse, dog, ox, etc., the advent of the cat to our firesides is comparatively recent. Though cats appear on tombs, or as illustrations, as far back as 1600 B.C., this date may be said to be comparatively recent if we consider the question in relation to the probable date of the domestication of the dog. The Egyptians loved their cats, understood their usefulness, and ended by worshipping them as sacred animals, and giving them a careful burial, for the mummies of cats, beautifully wrapped in expensive fabrics, are constantly coming to light when excavations

EUROPEAN WILDCAT (*Felis Catus*)

are made in and around some of the buried cities of Egypt. The Greeks and Romans, about whom we have a clearer knowledge, and whose times seem to come nearer our own, appear not to have paid much attention to cats, and they have left us nothing in their literature, inscriptions, or paintings that leads us to any knowledge of the history of the domestic cat. There seems to be no record that the cat became domesticated in France or in England before the 9th century, but at that time it was considered of great value and was a regular object of trade.

American interest in the cat is often said to have originated within the last eight years, that is, since the advent of exhibitions and the taking up of the cat cult by the public. This impression is not borne out by facts, for we have exhibitors who have intimately studied cats, have bred and raised them, and have cared for them for over 50 years, and cat-shows were held in Maine between 1860 and 1870, even before the great exhibition instituted in London by the well-known animal painter, Harrison Weir, in the year 1871. But cat-shows in America were not known outside of Maine until one was held in the Madison Square Garden, New York, in 1895. The exhibitions in England have gone on from Mr. Weir's first show up to the present time, so that the marking epochs in modern cat history may be dated from the Crystal Palace show in 1871, and the New York show in April 1895. From these shows has arisen what may be described as a cult, or in some ways an industry. Numbers of individuals, principally women, have taken up the cat as a partial means of livelihood, selling those they rear by exhibiting them to the public, the outcome of which has been the production of different colors, strains, and families. Clubs have arisen for the care and maintenance of exhibitions; registers and stud-books have been started; and the importation of cats of known pedigree is duly recognized by our government as one of the many things to be considered and provided for in a tariff schedule.

The varieties or breeds recognized in shows are the Persian, Siamese, Abyssinian, and ordinary domestic short-haired cats. The Persian and Angora may be said to be the same cat, though distinctions were drawn in old days; but these were very indefinite, and at the present time we draw up rules and regulations for two large groups, the Long-haired Cats and the Short-haired Cats, and these are judged by points and classified by color distinctions. Angora is a small place, and comparatively few cats could have come from there, but many have come from other parts of Asia. Taking the long-haired division first, because commercially it is the most prominent, the judge requires that the cat shall be short in body with a short tail and short legs, the latter shorter in front than behind. The chest should be wide, the loin square and firm, the bones of the legs well developed, and the frame sturdy. The head that corresponds with this formation and is required, is a broad, round head with short, wide nose, eyes large and round, and set well apart. The ears, a most important feature, should be as small as possible and placed on the side of the head, the base of the ear being narrow, not gaping wide open, with a tuft of hair at the apex. This standard is more or

less based upon original imported specimens from Asia; and if studied it will be found that the probable ancestor of our domestic long-hairs, *Felis manul*, or the wild long-haired cat of the interior of Asia, is built on these lines. The colors most valuable and most approved are the light silvers, smokes, blues (or slate color) white, black, orange, cream, and tortoise-shells; and the tabbies of different colors are also favorites. The tabby-cat is a cat that has a light ground-color and is spotted, barred or striped with darker color, and the word "tabby" has no reference to the sex of the animal. The name "tabbie" is derived from Atab, a street in Bagdad celebrated for its manufacture of watered or moiré silks, which in England were called *atabi* or "taffety." The most usual colors in tabby-cats are yellow, marked with orange or red, making what are called orange tabbies; yellow brown, marked with black, making the brown tabbies; gray, marked with darker stripes, giving us the gray tabbies; and pale silver, marked with black or a sort of dark blue verging on black, from which we have the silver tabbies. The great feature required in tabby-cats is that the ground-color should afford as distinct a contrast to the stripes, bars, or spots, as possible; the colors should be vivid and the marks very plain. There are spotted tabbies, and in these the spots must be round, clear, and distinct; but we seldom see a good one of this variety unless it came from India, the home of the best spotted tabbies. The solid-colored cats are the whites, blues, blacks, and smokes; although recently the silvers, creams, and oranges have in a few instances almost attained perfection in being without marks or foreign color. The tortoise-shell cats are black, red, and yellow; when accompanied by white, the patches are more clear and distinct, and this feature is what is aimed at. Tortoise-shell males are almost unknown, and orange females are very scarce.

The eyes of a cat are an important feature, and should be large, round, and pleasant in expression. Although color of eye is a great feature, many judges prefer large, well-placed, pleasant eyes to those that are more correct in color but badly placed, or are small and mean in expression, or give the cat a sour look. The color of eyes required may be briefly summed up as blue (as deep as possible) for a white cat; emerald-green for light silver, or chinchillas, as they have been called; and yellow to orange, as deep as possible, for all other varieties. The color and beauty of the cat's eyes vary according to the state of health, the light, and the time of day, and judges have to be careful in this matter. The body-colors can be defined as white, as pure as possible; black, deep and glossy; blue or slate, sound and pure from root to tip of hair, showing no light shadings or light under-color; smoke, a deep plumcolor, silver undercoat; ruff, and stomach, cream, light fawn or cream color; whether marked or unmarked, should be as rich and strong as possible. The tortoise-shells marked with clear distinct patches, clean-cut and free from each other. The fur of the long-haired cats should be fine, long, silky, and glossy; wooliness is deprecated, but is more inclined to appear in certain colors, such as orange and cream; and blacks may have a rather coarser texture of coat if they make it up in color. But in whites, silvers, blues, smokes, and in brown tabbies there can be no excuse found for anything but exquisite quality.

In the short-haired division we must consider our old fireside friend first, and coloration in this variety is much the same as in the long-hairs, though we do not often find smokes or so many silvers, and the blue-eyed whites have probably been bred from the long-haired cats. But as to color, color of eyes, and classification, the rules specified for long-hairs fit the short-hairs except that the tabby-cats are more distinctly marked and more brilliant, as the colors are not clouded or mixed by the length of the hair. White cats with blue eyes are generally deaf, but not always. The short-haired cat is rather different in formation to the long-haired cat, the face is more angular, or rather the nose may come to a finer point, though its cheeks should be well developed. The eyes are differently placed, yet should be full and large, the ears larger, closer together, more toward the top of the head, wider at the base, and more pointed at the apex. The body should be moderately long, slender, and elegant. The great thing to avoid in all cats is coarseness, and size alone is not a recommendation.

The Siamese is a distinct variety which comes from the palace of the king of Siam or from a few families of nobles. These cats are conceded to be the most intelligent and companionable of all cats, but having been much inbred, are not easily reared and do not increase very fast. The climate of California suits the Siamese cat, and the variety is found there in fair numbers and doing well. The points valued in this cat are a rather small and flat head, a small and elegant body of a light fawn or biscuit color, with chocolate-colored legs, mask, and tail. The more decided the contrast — that is, the lighter the body color and the darker the points — the better. The Siamese are much appreciated as show-cats. Chocolate-colored cats of this variety are found and are valuable. The fur most approved is very fine and glossy, resembling beaver. The eyes are blue, the color as rich as possible.

The Manx cat makes a distinct species in our exhibitions, and is classed by itself. Besides the absence of tail, which is the distinguishing feature of this cat, a different formation of body is required; namely, that the fore legs should be short and the rump rise as abruptly as possible, making the hind legs longer than the fore legs, so that the cat seems to jump forward like a rabbit, and is sometimes called a rabbit-cat. The head should be neat, round, and rather small, and the cat itself small, short, and compact. The Manx cat may be of any of the recognized colors. There is a distinction between this variety and our other domestic cats. Gambier Bolton who studied the question, and traveled to collect specimens for the British Zoological Society, coincides with the naturalist Kempfer, and recognizes a strong likeness in these cats to those of the islands in the East, the Malay peninsula, Japan, China, and lands contiguous. All the cats in those parts, even the Siamese, seem to have peculiar formations of the tail, whether cut short, forked, kinked, or otherwise. These cats are smaller; there are differences in the call or language, ways, and character, that have been observed by these students. The origin of the Manx cat is now attributed to the arrival of these cats on the Isle of Man from ships belonging to the Spanish Armada that were wrecked there. These cats were most probably previously brought from Japan or other parts of eastern Asia, for cats now brought from Japan are exactly like our Manx. A cat with his tail cut off, showing a stump, does not constitute a Manx cat for the student.

Other cats found in show-rooms are the Abyssinians, but they do not make much headway and have not yet arrived in America. The males are generally darker than the females, and the color of these cats should be a deep brown ticked with black, somewhat resembling the back of a wild rabbit, with a distinct black band running down the back to the tip of the tail. The inner sides of the legs and belly are more of an orange tint than the body, and are marked in some cases with a few dark patches. The eyes are deep yellow, tinged with green; nose dark-red, edged with black; ears rather small, dark-brown, with black edges and tips; and the pads of the feet are black. Attempts have been made to copy this cat, and it has been attempted to exhibit, as such, slightly marked ordinary short-haired cats, but they are not the genuine breed. The absence of tabby-markings is the point most sought and prized, and if kept pure the characteristics of these cats are peculiar. The Abyssinian cat has never been very numerous at exhibitions, perhaps because it is a short-haired cat, though short-haired cats, when good exhibition specimens, bring large prices. Cats marked with white have not found much favor in British exhibitions, but have always been popular at American shows, and Madame Ronner, the great French painter of cats, usually depicts her cats — that is, the dark ones — with some white patches. If cats are marked with white, they are preferred with four white paws and a white face; that is, the white starting in a sharp point between the eyes, spreading out onto the lips, making a triangle with the apex on the forehead, and continuing thence down the chest, but not spreading to the shoulders or going round the neck or over the back. Any marking, in an "any other class," that is regular and even, and forms anything like a regular pattern, should be recognized and encouraged by a judge; besides which, any effort made to bring out a new variety or color must be taken note of and encouraged. There is now a tendency to encourage Dutch marked cats, which means black patches on the cheeks, a white blaze up the face, joining a broad, white belt which goes completely round the cat halfway between the ears and tail. Of the cats indigenous to the American continent, which might be suitable for domestication, few have been tried in a domestic way, and the species that inhabit this country are not many. I have seen the wild cat or gray lynx, at shows, behaving in the most exemplary manner. Having been brought up from infancy by children, and perfectly tame, it was more at ease in a large show-room, and not nearly as nervous as the ordinary show-feline. So that if it were not for the size of the creature, its possibilities as a domestic animal were certainly good; but unfortunately our time does not seem to be destined to take in hand or give us any fresh species of domesticated animal; what we have are handed

CATS.

1. Manx.
2. Brown Tabby.
3. Smoke Persian.

4. Silver Tabby.
5. White Persian.
6. Shaded Silver.

down through the ages. In this particular we are not original, for we destroy more often than we create, and we seem to have no time for trying to subdue or lead into bondage any new varieties of mammals. The puma, cougar, or mountain lion ranges over the whole of North and South America, but is too large for domestic purposes; yet it has never been aggressive against man, and, if history is to be thoroughly credited, was quite the reverse with early settlers till driven to exile and filled with fear by man himself. The ocelot is one of our most beautiful varieties, and varies somewhat in color, with sometimes a gray body-color, but more often yellow. It is clearly marked with dark color in spots, bars, and splotches, and is very handsome, but larger and more powerful than the domestic cat. These cats have been taken when young, and reared; and although comparatively tame and sociable till about a year old, they then become savage and impossible and have to be caged or killed.

A very pretty cat that has been exhibited in America is the margay from Central and South America, where it inhabits the woods. I have handled this cat at a show and found it very tame and with a passion for being caressed. The margay is light red or orange, beautifully and regularly spotted with small black spots, the ears small, round, and pointing forward, whitish-gray at the backs, edged with black. It is a small cat, very handsome and refined, and if the effort could be made to obtain some more of the species these cats would be a very valuable addition to our varieties and to our home circles. Geoffroy's cat is another small spotted cat, of which a few have been introduced into England, but it is too early to state what the future increase may be. The pampas cat is another feline not amenable to domestic life.

As a rule our best white cats with blue eyes come from India and some of the best are brought from Tibet. In crossing the Himalayan Mountains with these cats carriers slit their noses to enable them to breathe with greater ease the rarified atmosphere of the high altitudes. Cats with slit noses are much valued. As to cats coming from this place or that, such as Persia, Angora, etc., a good deal of proof is required before any particular claim can be accepted. I have failed to find any long-haired cats at Teheran, the capital of Persia, and Angora, as I have said, is but a small place. We probably obtained many of our long-haired cats from around the Persian Gulf, and more from India, many of which come down from the interior of Asia with the Arab horse-traders. Cats vary in their adaptability to changes of climate, and no doubt to this factor we owe what we have and what breeds we can retain and perpetuate. The Siamese soon succumbs to dampness, but the long-haired cats, in some cases, took to the climate of Maine early in the century, when brought from the East. They bred extensively, and increased and became an article of commerce to the large cities, long before these cities held shows. These cats went by the name of Angoras, and in fact the ordinary nomenclature of the country defines all long-haired cats as Angoras. The Maine cats were often carelessly bred, and when shows commenced and competition came they had to give way to the more finely bred English cats, but in other cases they held their own and the

blood has been perpetuated. The Maine cats are found in all colors, and some are very big and strong, but these have been probably crossed with short-haired cats, and a great deal of hybridizing has been done even in England. There is a Russian long-haired cat, but it has not gained much favor, being solitary in its habits, unsociable in character, coarse in body and fur, and dingy in color. A few have been brought from Persia, but they had the faculty of attaching themselves more to other cats than to their owners. They are originally the same cat as the Asiatic,— that is, the Persian or Angora; and the first long-haired cats must have been brought over by sailors and travelers from the East. All long-haired cats seem to have a common origin in Pallas' cat (*Felis manul*).

Another cat that has created a great deal of interest is the Maltese. This cat is hard to account for, but should be blue or slate in color and greatly resembles what in Great Britain is called the Russian or Archangel cat, specimens of which have often been brought from Russia; but lately quite an influx of blue cats has come from Iceland. Whether cold winters are calculated to develop blue cats I do not know, but it is sufficiently evident that northern climates have produced most cats of that color. Blue cats are not numerous in Great Britain, although they are becoming more so by introduction. Here in America we have plenty scattered all over the States, but how they gained their name of Maltese I have never been able to discover, for there is no blue cat indigenous to the island of Malta. Probably the cats were brought there in early times from the same source whence the English now obtain theirs, and, the color being peculiar, these cats were selected, or by superior hardiness they may have selected themselves. However, many people who are not cat-exhibitors or who do not know much about cats scientifically keep their short-haired blue "Maltese" and are proud of them. The Chartreuse monks had blue long-haired cats many years ago.

Some writers have told us that long-haired cats are less affectionate than short-haired cats. This is a mistake, although long-haired cats, on the average, are more intense, more nervous, more highly strung, more pugilistic, and have more pluck and daring than the short-haired cats. The cat has great intelligence; in fact, is one of the most intelligent if not the most intelligent of the domestic animals, and it is this fact that precludes the possibility of teaching the average cat tricks. For the cat sees through the manœuvre, and refuses to be made a fool of. In respect to memory they are phenomenal and far exceed the average dog in this quality. Their powers of conversation are well developed, accompanied by delicate inflexions of the voice that need to be known to be understood. Dupont de Nemours says: "The cat has also the advantage of a language in which the same vowels as those pronounced by the dog exist, with six consonants in addition, m, n, g, h, v, and f." It requires study to get to know cats, and Rouvière, the actor, said that no one could really understand a cat unless he himself became one. A cat, of all the domestic animals, has retained the greatest part of its wild nature and traits, and the easiest way to get at a cat is by kindness and by trying to learn cat ways.

A cat never gives in to coercion. Liberty is the last thing it will resign; and often it will not resign that except in exchange for death. The cat should be used as the emblem of liberty.

It is a mistake to suppose that a cat cares only for places, for it is only the innate conservatism of the animal that gives this impression. Regularity is the keynote of its existence and what it does one day it likes to do the next; and certainly to places where it has been reared and has lived it shows great attachment. But on the contrary there are cats that would settle down anywhere, that have crossed and recrossed the Atlantic Ocean, and have lived quietly in any locality their owners chose. A cat is one of the finest mothers on earth.

The fortunes of the cat are now more or less regulated by clubs and associations, and there are homes, hospitals, and refuges in many places and in many lands. The principal clubs are the National Cat Club founded in 1887, with headquarters in London; the Scottish Cat Club, founded in 1894; the Cat Club, London, founded in 1898; the Northern Counties Cat Club, the Silver and Smoke Persian Cat Society, the Siamese Club, and the Orange, Cream, Fawn, and Tortoise-shell, founded in 1900; the Black and White Club, the Blue Persian Society, the Chinchilla Cat Club, the Short-haired Cat Club, the Midland Counties Cat Club, the British Cat Club, and the Manx Cat Club, founded in 1901. All the above are in Great Britain, but many have members in America. In the United States there are the Beresford Cat Club, founded in 1899, with headquarters in Chicago; the Atlantic Cat Club, with headquarters in New York; the Chicago Cat Club, the Louisville Cat Club, the Pacific Cat Club, the Orange and Cream Society, with headquarters in Chicago, the Washington, D. C., Cat Club, the Detroit Club, etc. All these have been founded since 1899; so we can see that the advances made of late years have been sudden and rapid; and they will continue to grow; for shows are held in many of the principal cities and are yearly fixtures. The Chicago shows have brought together the largest number of cats, 259, at the show held in the Coliseum in January 1902. Prices for cats increase; and whereas $25 was considered a good price five or six years ago, some of the best have been recently sold for $250 each, and many at $75 and $100. The largest price of which we have record as having actually been paid in cash for a cat is $300, which was the price Lady Decies paid Mrs. Greenwood for Lord Southampton; although I expect to see this exceeded in time to come, for competition enhances values, and the best specimens and most perfect will bring high prices from those who want them. All this will tend to draw attention to the cat and better the race and its general conditions.

Cats have had their artists: the Egyptians, the Japanese, the Chinese, Salvator Rosa, Gottfried Mind ("The Raphael of Cats"), Burbank (a master little known), Cornelius Wisscher, the Dutch artist, whose "Tom" cat has become typical, J. J. Grandville, Harrison Weir, Louis Wain, Madame Ronner, and Adam.

Members of the English royal family breed and exhibit cats at the regular exhibitions of the present day. The Duchess of Connaught, the sister-in-law of the King, was the organizer of the National Cat Club, one of the associations which maintains a thoroughly reliable stud-book for cats; Queen Alexandra herself is one of the active members of the Ladies' Kennel Club, and both Princess Christian and her daughter, Princess Victoria of Schleswig-Holstein, have taken many first prizes with their valuable feline pets.

A Few Hints to Breeders.—Do not try to keep too many; a good cat well reared will bring more money than 8 or 10 badly nurtured, undersized kittens. Cats are not gregarious, and when crowded together become diseased and mangy, and prematurely die. One litter of really good cats will give more pleasure and profit to the owner than five or six litters of poor ones.

Liberty is necessary to the health alike of the present and of the coming generations, and these latter should never be out of our minds when mating.

Meat is the main diet of all the *carnivora* to which order domestic cats belong. The best diet for cats is composed largely of meat, for which their teeth are adapted. Without meat they will not long remain healthy. They vary in their tastes, and what is fancied by one is not always preferred by another. Fish they are fond of, but as a rule house-cats should not be given much raw fish. Cats kept in confinement should have grass, vegetables, and changes of diet provided for them. Grass is a necessity.

Epidemics that sweep through different countries and continents at stated periods decimate the cat family, and it is well to be prepared for such occasions by having none but the healthiest and best of animals. Distemper, the greatest of cat scourges, is best treated by nursing, care, and cleanliness. Fleas convey embryonic worms which infest cats, and should be rigorously kept down. They breed in cracks in the floor, in bedding, and in the ground, and war waged upon their haunts will be work well laid out.

Do not use nauseating drugs for ailing cats, but choose the mildest remedies that will effect a cure. Do not be prejudiced against a course of treatment till you have tried it well; and remember that supposed cures suddenly made are not always effectual. Cats, when ill, require sympathy as much as human beings, and more so than any other animal, in order to battle successfully with disease, for they have a tendency to be very pessimistic and sorry for themselves, and to recover or fail quickly. They suffer mostly from distemper, worms, eczema, bronchitis, pneumonia, and liver diseases, and occasionally from catarrhal fever. If you are acquainted with a good homœopathic physician, and have any idea of what ails your cat, consult him and abide by his advice.

Do not breed from your queens too young, although many good kittens have been raised from queens not a year old, if strong and healthy. Male cats will not mate as early in life as the queens, and are seldom of much use till a year old. Do not cross long-haired cats with short-haired cats, for you spoil the type of both. Siamese cats will breed with other cats, but the progeny are never good for the show-room; and the Siamese being a distinct breed, does not amalgamate with any of the other varieties. The Manx cat is better kept pure, or

CATS.

1. White Persian.
2. Light Silver.
3. Cream Persian.

4. Siamese.
5. Silver Persian.
6. Short Hair Tortoise Shell.

the type degenerates and the result is not satisfactory.

Remember, when trying to rear good cats, that what is at the mouth and the care bestowed upon the young and growing animals cover 50 or even 75 per cent of essential requirements. The best blood in the world will not bring prize-winners or nice pets if they are badly reared. The crucial period takes in the first six months; when the young cat is well grown, and at seven months of age is through teething, you will have an animal that may live 20 years or more. Healthy cats are more long-lived than dogs, and authentic records tell of not a few over 20 years of age, and of some even 30.

Kittens should not be taken away from their mothers before they are at least eight weeks old; and if three months old, it will be still better. Care should be exercised in the diet of kittens at an early age. Sudden changes or sudden chills will bring on gastritis. Milk, unless pure, is more dangerous than meat, which in a raw state may be given scraped or minced at a very early age. Milk is better when mixed with Robinson's prepared barley according to the directions on the box, unless you can obtain warm milk from a cow that has not been too long in milk. The most dangerous diet for highly bred kittens is cold skimmed milk of an uncertain age.

To destroy a cat, or put it out of its misery when too sick to recover, administer a few drops of chloral, place the cat, if possible, in a tight box, and when the cat is fast asleep drop into the box a sponge saturated with two or three ounces of chloroform.

Bibliography.—Woodruffe Hill, 'Diseases of the Cat'; Mrs. Cashel Hoey, 'The Cat, Past and Present'; Agnes Repplier, 'The Fireside Sphinx'; C. H. Ross, 'Book of Cats'; Frances Simpson, 'The Book of the Cat'; Harrison Weir, 'Our Cats'; H. M. Winslow, 'Concerning Cats'; and the following periodicals: 'Our Cats' (Manchester, Eng.); 'The Cat Journal' (Palmyra, N. Y.); 'Fur and Feather' (London); and the 'Ladies' Field.'

E. N. BARKER.

Cat-bird, one of two kinds of birds. (1) In North America a familiar songster (*Galeoscoptes carolinensis*), so called because of its mewing call-note, which is strikingly similar to the plaint of a kitten in distress. This, however, is not its only note, its wild and melodious warbling in the morning and the evening being also typical of the musical thrush family to which it belongs. It is about nine inches long, and of a dark slate color, with a black cap, and a reddish patch under the tail. It is migratory only in the northern States, spends its winters in the South, and frequents bushy pastures and gardens, being one of the few species which follow the course of agriculture, and being rarely found far from the habitations of the farmer. It is of great service to the agriculturist in devouring wasps, grubs, worms, and insects, which, with fruits and berries of all kinds, especially of sumach, sweet gum and poke, constitute its food. It has a brilliant and varied song, in which it seems to mimic the notes of other birds; when in a domestic state it will imitate strains of instrumental music. The nest, generally built in bramble thickets,

is large, and constructed of twigs and briers mixed with leaves, weeds, and grass, lined with dark fibrous roots arranged in a circular manner. Its eggs, from four to six in number, are of a greenish-blue color, without spots. Its attachment to its young is remarkable, and it will often feed and raise the young of other birds. It migrates during the night. It frequently attacks the common blacksnake, which, in the absence of the bird, rifles its nest. (2) In Australia, one of the bower-birds (*Ailurœdus crassirostris*), so named because of its cat-like call.

Cat-boat, a boat having one mast stepped just abaft the bow and carrying a sail laced to a boom and gaff, resembling a schooner's mainsail. In general cat-boats are very broad in beam, averaging 1:3. They are usually equipped with a centre-board, which, with the extreme forward position of the mast, enables them to point high into the wind, and makes them remarkably quick in stays. They are principally employed as pleasure craft on the coasts and inland navigable waters of the United States, and are consequently of shallow draft.

Cat Island, one of the Bahama Islands, about 46 miles in length from north to south, and three to seven miles in its mean breadth. Pop. 3,000. This island was long identified with the Guanahani of Columbus, the first portion of land belonging to the New World on which he landed, 12 Oct. 1492. It is now thought by most that not this island but Watling Island, lying a little to the southeast, is the true Guanahani, the first landfall of Columbus.

Cat-owl, any of several widely distributed large owls, so called because of their feline habits and cat-like face. The best known American cat-owl is the barrel owl (*Syrnium nebulosum*), one of the largest birds of its kind, large specimens reaching 24 inches in length. It has no ear-tufts, and the general color is whitish, everywhere transversely barred with deep umber brown, except on the abdomen, where the stripes run lengthwise. It is a lover of the woods, where its coughing cry resounds afar in the darkness, and where it breeds in hollows or among the branches of trees.

It is not migratory, and often nests very early in the spring. This owl has the reputation of being especially destructive of poultry, but in truth it lives mainly on mice, of which it devours vast numbers each season, and hence is the benefactor rather than the marauder of the farm. Consult Fisher, 'Hawks and Owls of the United States.'

Cat-shark, any of various members of the *Scylliorhinidœ,* a group of true sharks which are characterized by having two dorsal fins, the anterior of which is placed over or behind the ventrals, and by having the tail not bent upward. Some of these are called also "roussettes." The name cat-shark is also applied to the leopard-shark (*Triakis semifasciatus*).

Cat-snake, a small opisthoglyph (see OPISTHOGLYPHA) serpent (*Tarbophis vivax*) of Asia Minor and southeastern Europe. Its color is dull; it is sluggish in movement; and reaches a length of three feet. It has long, recurved teeth in the lower jaw which serve to hold its prey (mainly lizards) until they are overcome by the snake's grooved poison-fangs. It is distinguished by being the only venomous snake of the opisthoglyph type in Europe.

Catabangenes. See CATUBANGANES.

Catacaos, kä-tä-kä'ōs, Peru, a city centrally situated in the maritime department of Piura, and on the Piura River. It is about 70 miles east of Piura, the capital of the department. Pop. 25,000.

Catachre'sis, a term used in rhetoric with a somewhat vague signification. It denotes any trope or figure of speech that is considered to be too violent. Thus any trope, whether a metaphor, an instance of metonymy, or any other, may become a catachresis if it is stretched too far. For example, the scriptural phrase "the blood of the grape" is often quoted as a case of catachresis, because it is thought too violent a metaphor to use "blood" for the blood-red juice of the grape.

Cat'aclysm, in geology, a physical catastrophe of great extent, supposed to have occurred at different periods, and to have been the efficient cause of various phenomena observed in the surface configuration of localities. The belief in cataclysmic movements as geological agents has largely given place to that in the working of ordinary agencies over long periods of time.

Cat'acombs, subterranean caves or vaults used as burial-places. All nations have been accustomed to some outward manifestation of regard for the dead, such as funeral solemnities, the consecration of grounds for sepulture, the erection of monuments, etc. Some nations, as the Egyptians, constructed pyramids and labyrinths to contain the remains of the departed. Others, as the Phœnicians and after them the Greeks, hollowed out the rocks for tombs, surrounding their towns with vast magazines, containing the bones of their fathers. Asia Minor, the coast of Africa, and Cyrenais, afford instances of these singular and gigantic works. The discovery of these monuments has always excited the curiosity of travelers and the attention of artists. The latter have applied themselves to learn from them the character of architecture and painting at different periods; and though they have often found only coarse representations, the productions of art in its infancy or decline, they have occasionally met with types of perfection. Many monuments of this description have been preserved to our days, and still contain traces of the painting and architecture with which they were decorated. There are catacombs existing in Syria, Persia, and among the most ancient Oriental nations. But the revolutions in these countries, and the changes which they have occasioned, have deprived us of the documents which would have given us exact information regarding them.

The description of the catacombs in Upper Egypt gives us an idea of those whose existence is still unknown to us. They contain the history of the country, and the customs and manners of the people, painted or sculptured in many monuments of the most admirable preservation. The subterranean caves of these countries, like almost all of the kind, have their origin in quarries. From the depths of the mountains which contain them, stone was taken, which served for the building of the neighboring towns, and also of the great edifices and pyramids which ornament the land. They are dug in a mountain situated in the neighborhood of the Nile, and furnished the Romans with materials for the construction of buildings in their colonial establishments. The excavations in these mountains are found throughout a space of 15 to 20 leagues, and form subterraneous caverns which appear to be the work of art; but there is neither order nor symmetry in them. They contain vast and obscure apartments, low and irregular vaults, supported in different parts with piles left purposely by the workmen. Some holes, of about six feet in length and two feet wide, give rise to the conjecture that they were destined for sepulchres. Cells of very small dimensions, formed in the hollows of these obscure caverns, prove them to have been the abode of recluses.

In Sicily and Asia Minor a prodigious number of grottoes and excavations have been discovered containing sepulchres. Some appear to have served as retreats to the victims of despotism. The greater part are the work of the waters which traverse the mountains of these regions, as for instance the great cave of Noto, which passes for one of the wonders of Sicily. This cave, the height, length, and breadth of which are equal, has been formed by the Cassibili River, which runs at the bottom, and traverses it for the length of 100 fathoms. In the interior of this cave are a number of houses and tombs. At Gela, on the south coasts, there are abodes for the living and sepulchres for the dead, cut in the rocks; at Agrigentum subterraneous caves, labyrinths, and tombs, arranged with great order and symmetry. There are also caverns in the environs of Syracuse which may be ranked with the principal monuments of this description, from their extent and depth, their architectural ornaments, and from some historical recollections attached to them. The catacombs in the tufa mountains of Capo di Monte, near Naples, consist of subterraneous galleries, halls, rooms, basilicas, and rotundas, which extend to the distance of two Italian miles. Throughout there are seen niches for coffins (*loculi*) and bones. A description of them was given by Celano in 1643. They probably owe their origin to the quarries which afforded tufa for the walls of the cities Palæopolis and Neapolis, and afterward served as sepulchres for the Christian congregations.

The most numerous and extensive catacombs are those in the immediate neighborhood of Rome, at San Sebastiano, San Lorenzo, etc., the earliest of which of certain date belongs to the year 111 A.D. They are composed of interminable subterraneous galleries, extending underneath the town itself as well as the neighboring country, and are said to contain not less than 6,000,000 tombs. The name of catacombs, according to St. Gregory, was at first applied to designate exclusively the cave in which the bodies of St. Peter and St. Paul were buried, and it was only at a later period that it came to be given to all the subterraneous passages which were used as public burying-places. It is now regarded as certain that in times of persecution the early Christians frequently took refuge in the catacombs, in order to celebrate there in secret the ceremonies of their religion; but it is not less certain that the catacombs served also as places of burial to the early Christians, and that in spite of the contrary opinion which prevailed for two centuries, and even down to our day, the catacombs were not for the most part abandoned quarries, but were excavated by the Christians themselves. It is found that originally the cemeteries of Rome were made up of separate tombs, which rich Christians constructed for themselves and their brethren, and which they held as private property under the protection of the law. But in course of time this was changed. At the end of the 2d century there existed certain cemeteries not the property of individuals but of the Church. Such was that which Pope Zephyrinus (202–19) intrusted to the superintendence of Calixtus, and which took its name from that bishop. Some years later, under Pope Fabian (236–51), there were already several such common burying-places belonging to the Christian congregations, and their number went on increasing till the time of Constantine, when the catacombs ceased to be used as burying-places. From the time of Constantine down to the 8th century they continued to be used as places of worship by the Christians, but during the siege of Rome by the Lombards they were in part destroyed, and soon became entirely inaccessible, so that they were forgotten. The first excavations in them were made by Antonio Bosio between 1560 and 1600. The results of these excavations were published in his 'Roma Sotterranea' (Rome, 1632), which was translated into Latin by P. Aringhi (Rome 1657). Among the more modern works on the subject may be mentioned: Rochette's 'Tableau des Catacombes de Rome' (Paris 1837); Perret's 'Les Catacombes de Rome' (Paris 1851–6); and 'La Roma Sotterranea Cristiana' by De Rossi (Rome 1864–77), containing the results of very careful investigations made by the author, who is justly regarded as the foremost student, in fact, father of this branch of archæology.

The catacombs of Paris, situated on the left bank of the Seine, are almost equally celebrated. The name itself, which has been given to this labyrinth of caverns and galleries from its resemblance to the asylums and places of refuge of the persecuted Christians under Naples and Rome, informs us of the purpose to which it has been applied since 1786. These galleries were originally the quarries from which materials were excavated for constructing the edifices of the capital. The weight of the super-incumbent houses rendered it necessary to prop them; and when the cemeteries of the demolished churches and the burying-grounds were cleared in 1786, the government resolved to deposit the bones in these quarries, which were consecrated for that purpose. The first cemetery that was suppressed was the Cimetière des Innocents, and the bones from it were deposited beneath what is now Petit-Montrouge. The ossuary now extends much farther. The relics of 10 or more generations were here united in the repose of the grave. Many times as great as the living tide that rolls over this spot is its subterraneous population. By the light of wax tapers, a person may descend about 70 feet to a world of silence, over which the Parisian police keep watch as strictly as over

the world of noise and confusion above. He will then enter a gallery where only two can go abreast. A black streak on the stones of the walls points out the way, which, from the great number of by-passages, it would be difficult for the visitor to retrace without this aid or without guides.

Among the curiosities here is a plan of the harbor of Mahon, which an ingenious soldier faithfully copied from memory, in the material of the quarries. Entering the hall, one is ushered into the realms of death by the inscription which once stood over the entrance to the churchyard of St. Sulpice: "Has ultra metas requiescunt beatam spem exspectantes" ("Beyond these bounds rest those awaiting the hope of bliss fulfilled"). Narrow passages between walls of skeletons; chambers in which monuments, altars, candelabra, constructed of human bones, with festoons of skulls and thigh-bones, interspersed occasionally with inscriptions, not always the most happily selected, from ancient and modern authors, excite the gloomy impression which is always produced, even in the most light-minded, by the sight of the dissolution of the human frame. Wearied of these horrible embellishments, the visitor enters a simple chapel, without bones, and containing an altar of granite. The inscription "D. M. II et III Septembr. MDCCXCII." recalls to memory the victims of the September massacres, whose remains are here united. On leaving these rooms, consecrated to death, where, however, the air is always preserved pure by means of air-holes, the visitor may pass to a geological cabinet, formed by Héricart de Thury, the director of the Carrières sous Paris. Specimens of the minerals furnished by the regions traversed, and a collection of diseased bones, in a contiguous hall, scientifically arranged, are the last curiosities which these excavations offer. More than 600 yards to the east of the road to Orleans the visitor finally returns to the light of day. Strangers may visit the catacombs in company with the government officials at the periodical visits. An account of these subterranean passages is that which was published by M. Dunkel in 1885.

The Etruscan tombs were not, strictly speaking, catacombs, yet as subterranean places of sepulture they may appropriately be referred to. They were usually hewn out of cliffs on the sides of a hill and were variously arranged, sometimes tier above tier and sometimes on a level. There was a central chamber with smaller ones opening from it. In the latter there were stone benches to receive the bodies of the dead.

Catacoustics, kăt-ạ-koos'tĭks or -kows'tĭks, the science which treats of reflected sounds, or that part of acoustics which considers the properties of echoes.

Catafalque, kăt'ạ fălk, an ornamental structure, in the form of a scaffolding or stage, for temporary use at ceremonious funerals. It is placed over the coffin containing a body lying in state, as in a church or other public edifice, and is sometimes used as a hearse, or set, as the representation of a tomb, over a grave.

Cat'alan, a native of Catalonia, or northeastern Spain, or the language of Catalonia, which holds a position similar to the provençal, having been early cultivated, and boasting a considerable literature. It was established as a literary language by the close of the 13th century, and is still to some extent used as such in its own region.

Cat'alan, a blast furnace for reducing ores, extensively used in the north of Spain, particularly in the province of Catalonia. It consists of a four-sided cavity or hearth, which is always placed within a building and separated from the main wall thereof by a thinner interior wall, which in part constitutes one side of the furnace. The blast-pipe comes through the wall, and enters the fire through a twyer which slants downward. The bottom is formed of a refractory stone, which is renewable. The furnace has no chimneys. The blast is produced by means of a fall of water, usually from 22 to 27 feet high, through a rectangular tube, into a rectangular cistern below, to whose upper part the blast-pipe is connected, the water escaping through a pipe below. This apparatus is exterior to the building, and is said to afford a continuous blast of great regularity; the air, when it passes into the furnace, is, however, impregnated with moisture.

Catalan Grand Company, The, a name of a troop of adventurers raised by Roger di Flor about the beginning of the 14th century. Roger first gave his services to Frederick, king of Sicily, in his war with Robert, Duke of Calabria, but when peace was concluded between the two princes, being at a loss how to maintain his soldiers, he proposed to lead them to the East to contend against the Turks, who were then desolating the eastern empire. Andronicus, then emperor of the East, gladly accepted the offered assistance of Roger, and submitted to all the conditions which he imposed. Roger set sail from Messina, Sicily, in 1303, with 26 vessels partly equipped at his own expense. The number of the troops embarked with him is said to have amounted to about 8,000 men of different nations, Sicilians, Catalans, Aragonese, etc. The Catalans, either because they were, the most numerous or for some other reason, gave their name to the whole company. On his arrival at Constantinople Roger was received with great rejoicings, and was elevated to the dignity of grand duke. A bloody affray between the Genoese and the Catalans marked the first period of the stay of these adventurers in Constantinople. Andronicus hastened to get them to cross over into Asia. This they did in the spring of 1304, and in the same year they defeated the Turks completely. In 1305 he took Ancyra, and forced the Turks to raise the siege of Philadelphia, but he was not so successful in his attempt to take Magnesia. After a long and ineffective siege he recrossed into Europe in 1306, bringing along with him his Catalans, who left behind them everywhere traces of their plunder and violence. When they had reached Europe they took up their quarters at Gallipoli. But Andronicus, who was by this time very anxious to be rid of his formidable allies, now received Roger with great coldness, and even obliged him to give up his title of grand duke in favor of Berengarius. The sudden departure of Berengarius, however, and the simultaneous incursions of the Turks into Asia Minor, compelled Andronicus again to appeal to Roger and his Catalans for

assistance. Roger was raised to the dignity of Cæsar to appease him for the slights that had been put on him. But this only caused him to be regarded with more jealousy by the Greeks, and especially by Michael, the son of Andronicus, who was associated with his father in the empire. The result was that before he could start once more for Asia he was assassinated (1306 or 1307). The Catalans now turned their arms against the Byzantines, in order to avenge the death of their leader, and defeated them in several battles. They then passed into Greece and entered the service of the Duke of Athens, but no long time afterward they turned against him and defeated him in the battle of Cephissus (1311). They now became masters of Attica, where they maintained themselves for four years, when they were finally defeated by Philes near Bizyn (1315).

Catalanganes, kä-tä-län-gäns', a Malay people of Mongoloid type, living in the flood plain of the Catalangan River (province of Isabela, Luzon). They are heathen and peaceable, and speak the same language as the Irayas.

Catalani, Alfredo, äl-frä'dō kä-tä-lä'nē, Italian composer: b. Lucca 19 July 1854; d. Milan 7 Aug. 1893. He was graduated at the Paris Conservatory and settled in Milan, where he achieved fame with brilliant operas, especially 'Dejanice,' 'Lorely,' and 'La Wally.'

Catalani, Angel'ica, Italian singer: b. Sinigaglia, most probably in 1782, although several other years are given; d. Paris 13 June 1849. As early as her 7th year her magnificent voice had become the subject of general remark, but it was not till the age of 14 that she received any instruction in the higher departments of the musical art. At 16 she was compelled by family misfortunes to turn her talents to account, and made her first appearance on the stage at Venice. She afterward filled the grand soprano parts at the operas of Milan, Florence, Rome, and Naples, and in 1799 accepted an engagement at the opera of Lisbon, where she continued for five years. She then visited successively Madrid, Paris, London, and the principal towns of Great Britain, in all of which her success and profits were immense. In 1814 she returned to Paris to take the management of the Italian opera there, but sustained thereby severe pecuniary losses from the injudicious interference of her husband, de Valabrégue. formerly a captain in the French army. On Napoleon's return in 1815 she was obliged to resign the direction of the opera, but resumed it again on the second restoration. In 1818 she again resigned the direction of the opera, and from that year till 1828 made repeated professional tours through the Continent and Great Britain. In 1830 she retired from public life to a villa in the neighborhood of Florence, and here she resided with her family and gave instruction to girls who manifested indications of local talent, one condition being required from them that they should adopt the name of Catalini. She was a woman of majestic appearance, and her voice displayed a wonderful degree of power, flexibility, and compass. She rather, however, astonished and overpowered an audience than touched or subdued their hearts by her marvelous execution.

Catalau'nian Plain, the wide plain around Châlons-sur-Marne, in France, famous as the field where Aëtius, the Roman general, and Theodoric, king of the West Goths, gained a complete victory over Attila and the Huns, 451 A.D.

Cataldo, kä-täl'dō, St., Italy, a town in the province of Caltanissetta, five m¹les west-south-west of the town of Caltanissetta. The sulphur works in the environs produce annually about 1,875 long tons. Pop. 12,800.

Cat'alepsy, a peculiar motor phenomenon, not a disease, that is found in a number of nervous disorders. It consists of a persistent muscular attitude of some part of the body, and may or may not be attended by unconsciousness. Thus a person may place the right arm or leg, or another may so place the limb, in a peculiar, or awkward, or in fact any position. This position is maintained by the patient for a very long time, usually a time much longer than a normal individual could maintain it. 'Almost any muscle group may be involved. The patients may squat on the floor, or stand on one leg for hours, or hold both arms in the air almost all day. There seems to be some form of muscle anæsthesia and the position of the limb seems to be unknown and unfelt by the patient. This symptom is very frequent in cases of true hysteria, and it is also found in a number of other affections that cluster about hysteria. Thus it is present in somnambulism, in hypnosis, in a peculiar mental state known as catatonia, and in stuporous melancholia,— all of which have much in common, being affections superimposed on the hysterical nervous organization, a type of make-up of a character, whose main features are assuming a definite recognition by students of the functions of the nervous system. See Janet, 'Mental State of Hystericals'; Raymond, 'Obsessions et Psychasthenies'; Starr, 'Text-Book of Nervous Diseases.' See HYSTERIA.

Cataloguing. See LIBRARY.

Catalo'nia, Spain, an old province (ancient TARRACONENSIS), bounded north by France, east by the Mediterranean, south by Valencia, and west by Aragon; area, 12,480 square miles. The country in general is mountainous, but intersected with fertile valleys, while the mountains themselves are covered with valuable woods and fruit-trees, as the slopes are plentifully supplied with water by an artificial system of irrigation. The main river of Catalonia is the Ebro; there are also the Segre, Ter, Llobregat, and many smaller rivers. Corn, wine, oil, flax, hemp, legumes, and almost every kind of fruit. are abundant. There are also quarries of marble of all colors, of crystal and alabaster; mines of lead, tin, iron, alum, vitriol, and salt, and formerly of gold and silver. On the coast is a coral-fishery. Catalonia is naturally much less fertile than either of the Castiles; but it surpasses every other province in Spain in the industry and intelligence of its inhabitants, and the improvements which have been effected in manufactures, agriculture, and commerce. It comprises the modern provinces of Tarragona, Gerona, Lerida, and Barcelona. The principal towns are Barcelona, Tortosa, Tarragona, Gerona, Manresa, and Lerida. Pop. 1,980,000.

Catal'pa, a genus of deciduous trees of the natural order *Bignoniaceæ*. There are about eight species, all natives of the northern hemisphere, four being hardy in cool temperate climates. They are all ornamental because of their large, bright-green leaves and conspicuous panicles of large, two-lipped, bell-shaped, white or yellowish flowers followed by long pods which persist until spring. Several of the species are highly esteemed for their timber, which is especially valued as fence-posts and railway-ties because of their durability when in contact with the soil. For this reason they are frequently planted, especially *C. speciosa*, which is one of the hardiest. They are easily propagated by seeds sown in spring or by ripewood cuttings, and they succeed well upon moist loams from New England southward. A leaf-spot disease, *Phyllosticta catalpæ*, which sometimes attacks the foliage, may be controlled with anv standard fungicide (q.v.).

Catalyt'ic Action, Catalysis, or **Catalysm.** When chemical decomposition is brought about in any compound, and its ingredients are made to enter into new combinations in consequence of the introduction of another body, which does not itself form a part of any of these combinations, nor lose either of its constituents, but acts in some manner not understood, apparently by its mere presence or contact, to excite this chemical action, the force is called by Berzelius catalytic. A small quantity of yeast thus acts to cause a mixture of sugar and water to ferment, and form the new combinations of carbonic acid and alcohol; the addition of $\frac{1}{1000}$ part of oxalic acid to boiling syrup of sugar, causes it to become fluid as water, and refuse to crystallize. Liebig objected to this introduction of a new theoretical force, which does not actually explain the phenomenon by giving it a name, but tends to satisfy the understanding with a plausible explanation, and thus hinder further research.

Catamaran, kăt'a-ma̧-răn, a sort of raft used in the East Indies, Brazil, and elsewhere. Those of the island of Ceylon, Madras, and other parts of the Indian coast, are formed of three logs. The timber preferred for their construction is the dup-wood or *cherne-maram*, the pine-varnish tree. Their length is from 20 to 25 feet, and breadth 2½ to 3½ feet. The logs of which they are constructed are secured together by means of three spreaders and cross lashings through small holes. The centre log is much the largest, and is pointed at the fore end. These floats are navigated with great skill by one or two men in a kneeling posture. They think nothing of passing through the surf which lashes the beach at Madras, and at other parts of these coasts, when even the boats of the country could not live upon the waves, and they are also propelled out to the shipping at anchor when boats of the best construction would be swamped. In the monsoons, when a sail can be got on them, a small outrigger is placed at the end of two poles as a balance, with a bamboo mast and yard, and a mat or cotton-cloth sail.

Catamarca, kä-tä-mär'cä, Argentine Republic, a province, bounded north by Salta, east by Tucuman and Santiago del Estero, south by Cordova and Rioja, and west by Rioja and Chile; area, about 47,530 square miles. The.

surface is very mountainous in parts, except the southern, where it stretches out into a large plain. The loftiest and best known of the mountains is the Sierra de Aconquija, which stretches from south to north, and attains in its culminating point near its southern extremity a height of more than 16,000 feet. The Santa Maria, flowing north to the Huachipas, is the only river of any importance, but as every valley has its mountain stream, the whole province is well watered. The soil is fertile, producing large crops of maize and wheat, and supporting large numbers of live stock, especially goats. The vine is also cultivated, and yields wine and spirits which bear a high name in the surrounding countries. The principal exports are beasts of burden, horned cattle, and hides and goat-skins, raw or tanned. The principal mineral is iron, but gold, silver, and lead are also found. The capital is Catamarca. Pop. 99,000, chiefly of Indian extraction, with a considerable mixture of Spaniards.

Catamarca, Argentine Republic, the capital of the province of Catamarca, situated in a valley 82 miles northeast of Rioja. It is connected by rail with Rioja and all the chief towns of the republic, and is the trade centre of a fertile district. It was founded about 1680, and has a fine church and a college. Pop. 7,500.

Catamount, a short form of the phrase «cat of the mountain,» frequently found in the older books about America, and still occasionally used as a name for the lynx of the eastern United States, and sometimes for the puma, or «panther,» once common in New England. The term is so indefinite that it is well that it has fallen into disuse.

Catanduanes, kä-tän-dwä′nĕz, Philippines, an island lying northeast of the province of Albay, Luzon; its length is 44 miles north and south; width, 29 miles at the southern end; area, 704 square miles. The mountain system consists of three ranges that radiate from Mount Catilamong near the centre of the island; the rest of the surface is irregular, covered with low hills. The most important rivers are the Ocó and the Bató or Cabugao; there are also a number of smaller rivers, and the island is well watered. The soil is fertile, and rice, cotton, corn, and hemp are raised; indigo and cocoanuts are exported. The natives find gold, both dust and nuggets, in the gravel beds of many of the rivers. The largest town is Birac (pop. 5,832). The island does not form a province of itself, but is a constituent part of the province of Albay, and is included in the military department of Luzon. Pop. 33,300.

Cata′nia (ancient CATANA), Italy, a city of Sicily, in the province of Catania, on the borders of the valley of Noto, the see of a bishop, the suffragan of Monreal; 47 miles south-southwest of Messina, 85 east-southeast of Palermo. It is situated on a gulf of the Mediterranean, at the foot of Mount Ætna. This city has been repeatedly visited by violent earthquakes, and partially laid in ruins by lava from eruptions of Mount Ætna. The most disastrous eruption was that of 1669, by which many of the antiquities of Catania were overwhelmed, and the worst earthquake was that of 1693, when 18,000 people were destroyed. Although again greatly injured by the earthquake of 1783, Catania is now re-

viving with great splendor, and has much more the features of a metropolis than Palermo. The principal streets are wide and well paved with lava. Most of the edifices have an air of magnificence unknown in other parts of the island, and the town has a title to rank among the elegant cities of Europe. An obelisk of red granite, placed on the back of an antique elephant of touchstone, stands in the centre of the great square, which is formed by the town hall, seminary, and cathedral. The cathedral, a fine building, was founded in 1091 by Count Roger, but required to be mostly rebuilt after the earthquake of 1693. It is dedicated to St. Agatha, the patroness of the city. The suppressed Benedietine monastery of St. Nicholas, comprising a church (with splendid organ), library, museum, and other extensive buildings, was long celebrated for wealth and splendor. The university was founded about 1445. The ruins of the amphitheatre, which was more extensive than the Coliseum at Rome, are still to be seen, as also the remains of the theatre, baths, aqueducts, sepulchral chambers, hippodrome, and several temples. The industries include the manufacture of silk and cotton goods, and the mining of sulphur. The harbor was formerly a good one, but by the eruption of 1669 its entrance was almost entirely choked up, and it is only in recent times that it has been improved, a considerable amount of money having been spent on it. The trade of Catania is of some importance, the principal export being sulphur, next to which come oranges and lemons, almonds and other fruits, and wine. Cereals, textiles, and other manufactures are the chief imports. The exports have an average annual value of about $5,000,000. A circular railway runs from Catania round the base of Mount Ætna. Pop. 147,000.

Catanzaro, kä-tän-zä′rō (ancient CATACIUM), Italy, a city and capital of the southern province of the same name, on a height, eight miles from the Gulf of Squillace. It suffered severely from the great earthquake of 1783, but is still a place of some importance, defended by a citadel, and containing a cathedral and various other churches, an academy of sciences, one of the four great civil courts of the kingdom, a lyceum, and three hospitals. The manufactures consist chiefly of silk and velvet, and there is some trade in wheat, wine, oil, etc. Pop. about 30,000.

Cataphoresis, kăt-a-fōr-ē-sĭs, a method of introducing remedies into the body by means of electricity. While certain substances can be made to penetrate the skin by means of electrical currents, the general cataphoretic method has not found favor with conservative and careful observers.

Cataphrac′ti, a group of fishes known also as «mailed-cheeked,» characterized by having a bridge-like bone running from below the eye to the gill covers. The group includes the rock-fishes, scorpion-fishes, sculpins, sea-poachers, lump-suckers, and sea-snails. Most of these live in the sea, but in North America there are several species of sculpins which dwell in fresh-water streams and lakes, and are known as mullets. The names *Loricati* and *Pareiopliteæ* are also applied to this group. Consult: Jordan and Evermann, 'Fishes of North and Middle America.'